Features

Visit us on the Web at
http://www.census.gov/statab/www/

ACKNOWLEDGMENTS

Ian R. O'Brien was responsible for the technical supervision and coordination of this volume under the direction of **Lars B. Johanson**, Chief, Statistical Compendia Branch. Assisting in the research and analytical phases of assigned sections and in the development aspects of new tables were **Richard P. Kersey**, **Jean F. Mullin**, **Michael Sellner**, and **Sean R. Wilburn**. **Catherine Lavender** provided primary editorial assistance. Other editorial assistance was rendered by **April C. Harris**, **Connie Nadzadi**, **LaKeisha Powell**, and **Virginia Zamaitis**.

Maps were designed and produced by **Connie Beard** and **Jessica Dobrowolski** of the Cartographic Products Management Branch within the Geography Division.

Monique D. Lindsay, **Theodora Forgione**, **Linda Chen**, and **Donald Meyd** of the Administrative and Customer Services Division, **Francis Grailand Hall**, Chief, provided publications and printing management, graphics design and composition, and editorial review for print and electronic media. General direction and production management were provided by **Claudette E. Bennett**, Assistant Division Chief, and **Wanda Cevis**, Chief, Publications Services Branch.

The cooperation of many contributors to this volume is gratefully acknowledged. The source note below each table credits the various government and private sector agencies that have collaborated in furnishing the information for the *Statistical Abstract*.

Statistical Abstract
of the United States: 2010

Issued October 2009

U.S. Department of Commerce
Gary Locke,
Secretary

Dennis F. Hightower,
Deputy Secretary

Economics and Statistics
Administration
Rebecca M. Blank,
Under Secretary for Economic Affairs

U.S. CENSUS BUREAU
Robert M. Groves,
Director

SUGGESTED CITATION

U.S. Census Bureau,
Statistical Abstract of the
United States: 2010
(129th Edition)
Washington, DC,
2009

ECONOMICS
AND STATISTICS
ADMINISTRATION

**Economics
and Statistics
Administration**

Rebecca M. Blank,
Under Secretary
for Economic Affairs

U.S. CENSUS BUREAU

Robert M. Groves,
Director

Thomas L. Mesenbourg,
Deputy Director and
Chief Operating Officer

Ted A. Johnson,
Associate Director for Administration
and Chief Financial Officer

Francis Grailand Hall,
Chief, Administrative
and Customer Services Division

U.S. GOVERNMENT PRINTING OFFICE OFFICIAL EDITION NOTICE

This is the Official U.S. Government edition of this publication and is
herein identified to certify its authenticity. The Superintendent of
Documents of the U.S. Government Printing Office requests that any
reprinted edition clearly be labeled as a copy of the authentic work.
Use of the 0-16 ISBN prefix is for U.S. Government Printing Office
Official Editions only.

ISBN: 978-0-16-083885-9

NATIONAL BIBLIOGRAPHY OF U.S. GOVERNMENT PUBLICATIONS

Statistical Abstract of the United States : 2010.—129 ed.
  Includes index.
  ISBN 978-0-16-083885-9
  ISSN 0081-4741
1. United States—Statistics. I. United States. Census Bureau.

HA 202.S8 2009
317.3

Library of Congress Card No. 0418089

http://purl.access.gpo.gov/GPO/LPS2878

For sale by the Superintendent of Documents, U.S. Government Printing Office
Internet: bookstore.gpo.gov   Phone: toll free (866) 512-1800;   DC area (202) 512-1800
Fax: (202) 512-2104   Mail: Stop SSOP, Washington, DC 20402-0001

ISBN 978-0-16-083885-9

Preface

The *Statistical Abstract of the United States,* published since 1878, is the standard summary of statistics on the social, political, and economic organization of the United States. It is designed to serve as a convenient volume for statistical reference and as a guide to other statistical publications and sources. The latter function is served by the introductory text to each section, the source note appearing below each table, and Appendix I, which comprises the Guide to Sources of Statistics, the Guide to State Statistical Abstracts, and the Guide to Foreign Statistical Abstracts.

This volume includes a selection of data from many statistical sources, both government and private. Publications cited as sources usually contain additional statistical detail and more comprehensive discussions of definitions and concepts. Data not available in publications issued by the contributing agency but obtained from the Internet or unpublished records are identified in the source notes. More information on the subjects covered in the tables so noted may generally be obtained from the source.

Except as indicated, figures are for the United States as presently constituted. Although emphasis in the *Statistical Abstract* is primarily given to national data, many tables present data for regions and individual states and a smaller number for metropolitan areas and cities. Appendix II, Metropolitan and Micropolitan Statistical Areas: Concepts, Components, and Population, presents explanatory text, a complete current listing and population data for metropolitan and micropolitan areas defined as of December 2006. Statistics for the Commonwealth of Puerto Rico and for island areas of the United States are included in many state tables and are supplemented by information in Section 29. Additional information for states, cities, counties, metropolitan areas, and other small units,

as well as more historical data are available in various supplements to the *Abstract* (see inside back cover).

Statistics in this edition are generally for the most recent year or period available by summer 2009. Each year over 1,400 tables and charts are reviewed and evaluated; new tables and charts of current interest are added, continuing series are updated, and less timely data are condensed or eliminated. Text notes and appendices are revised as appropriate. In addition, three special features—*Historical Statistics, State Rankings,* and *USA Statistics in Brief*—can be found on our Web site: <http://www.census.gov /compendia/statab/>.

Changes in this edition—This year we have introduced 53 new tables covering a wide range of subject areas. These include a presentation of new data from the 2007 Census of Agriculture and the first wave of new data from the 2007 Economic Census, as well as, several new tables with new data from the Federal Reserve Board's Survey of Consumer Finances. Among other areas for which we have introduced new material are induction of labor, parent participation in school-related activities, federal aid to state and local governments, type of work flexibility provided to employees, residential energy consumption, public drinking water systems, and suicide rates by sex and country. For a complete list of new tables, see section titled "New Tables," p. xi.

Section 18, Natural Resources has been renamed Forestry, Fishing, and Mining, in order to make this section more accessible to the user.

Statistical Abstract on other media— The *Abstract* is available on the Internet and on CD-ROM. Both versions contain the same material as the book, except for a few copyrighted tables for which we did not receive permission to release in these

V

formats. Our Internet site <http://www .census.gov/compendia/statab/> contains this 2010 edition plus earlier editions in Adobe Acrobat .pdf format. Spreadsheet files for each table in the book are also available on the Web site and CD-ROM (free distribution of single copies on request). In many cases, the spreadsheet files show more years and/or subject/geographical detail.

Statistics for states and metropolitan areas—Extensive data for states and metropolitan areas of the United States can be found in the *State and Metropolitan Area Data Book: 2010.* This publication minus some data items, as well as selected rankings of the states and metropolitan areas, is available on our Internet site at <http: //www.census.gov/compendia/smadb>.

Statistics for counties and cities— Extensive data for counties can be found in the *County and City Data Book: 2007.* It features 175 data items covering everything from age and agriculture to retail trade and water use for all states and counties with U.S. totals for comparison. Also included are approximately 80 data items for cities with populations of 25,000 or more. Six tables present nearly 80 additional data items from the 2005 American Community Survey for 242 incorporated places with populations of 100,000 or more.

This publication is available on our Internet site at <http://www.census.gov /compendia/ccdb> (tentative). For a database with over 6,000 county items, go to USA Counties at <http://censtats .census.gov/usa/usa.shtml>.

Limitations of the data—The contents of this volume were taken from many sources. All data from censuses and surveys or from administrative records are subject to error arising from a number of factors: Sampling variability (for statistics based on samples), reporting errors in the data for individual units, incomplete coverage, nonresponse, imputations, and processing error. (See also Appendix III, p. 899.) The Census Bureau cannot accept the responsibility for the accuracy or limitations of the data presented here, other than those for which it collects. The responsibility for selection of the material and for proper presentation, however, rests with the Census Bureau.

For additional information on data presented—Please consult the source publications available in local libraries, on the Internet, or write to the agency indicated in the source notes. Write to the U.S. Census Bureau only if it is cited as the source.

Suggestions and comments—Users of the Statistical Abstract and its supplements (see inside back cover) are urged to make their data needs known for consideration in planning future editions. Suggestions and comments for improving coverage and presentation of data should be sent to the Director, U.S. Census Bureau, Washington, DC 20233; or e-mail us at <ACSD.US.Data@census.gov>, or visit <ask.census.gov> for further information on the Abstract.

Contents

[Numbers following subjects are page numbers]

U.S. Census Bureau, Statistical Abstract of the United States: 2010

U.S. Census Bureau, Statistical Abstract of the United States: 2010

New Tables

xi

Guide to Tabular Presentation

Example of Table Structure

Table 525. **Seizure Statistics for Intellectual Property Rights (IPR) by Commodity and Trading Partner: 2007 and 2008**

[In thousands of dollars (196,754 represents $196,754,000, except as indicated). Customs and Border Protection (CBP) is dedicated to protecting against the importation of goods which infringe/violate Intellectual Property Rights (IPR) by devoting substantial resources toward identifying and seizing shipments of infringing articles]

Commodity	2007	2008	Trading partner	2007	2008
Number of IPR seizures	13,657	14,992			
Total domestic value of IPR seizures [1]	196,754	272,729	China	158,083	221,662
Footwear.	77,781	102,317	India	855	16,258
Wearing apparel	27,006	25,120	Hong Kong	12,729	13,434
Handbags/wallets/backpacks.	14,214	29,609	Taiwan.	3,454	2,632
Computers/hardware	9,337	7,590	Korea, South	903	1,028
Pharmaceuticals	11,138	28,107	Dominican Republic	23	942
Consumer electronics [2]	16,042	22,998	Pakistan.	2,531	780
Sunglasses	3,952	7,919	Vietnam	484	748
Computers/Technology Components.	9,337	7,590	United Arab Emirates	373	659
Media [3]	7,884	5,967	Indonesia	97	649
All others.	27,616	29,942	All other countries	17,223	13,938

[1] Domestic value is the cost of the seized goods, plus the costs of shipping and importing the goods into the U.S. and an amount for profit. [2] Consumer electronics includes cell phones and accessories, radios, power strips, electrical tools and appliances. [3] Includes motion pictures on tape, laser disc, and DVD; interactive and computer software on CD-ROM, and floppy discs; and music on CD or tape.
Source: U.S. Department of Homeland Security, Customs and Border Protection, "Import, Commercial Enforcement, Intellectual Property Rights, Seizure Statistics"; <http://www.cbp.gov/xp/cgov/trade/priority_trade/ipr/seizure/>.

Headnotes immediately below table titles provide information important for correct interpretation or evaluation of the table as a whole or for a major segment of it.

Footnotes below the bottom rule of tables give information relating to specific items or figures within the table.

Unit indicators show the *specified quantities* in which data items are presented. They are used for two primary reasons. Sometimes data are not available in absolute form and are estimates (as in the case of many surveys). In other cases we round the numbers in order to save space to show more data, as in the case above.

EXAMPLES OF UNIT INDICATOR INTERPRETATION FROM TABLE

Year	Item	Unit Indicator	Number shown	Multiplier
2007	Total domestic value of IPR seizures .	$ Thousands	196,754	1,000

To Determine the Figure it is Necessary to Multiply the Number Shown by the Unit Indicator:

Value of seizures by Customs and Border Protection − 196,754 x $1,000 = $196,754,000 ($197 million)

When a table presents data with more than one unit indicator, they are found in the headnotes and column headings (Tables 2 and 26), spanner (Table 39), stub (Table 25), or unit column (Table 153). When the data in a table are shown in the same unit indicator, it is shown in boldface as the first part of the headnote (Table 2). If no unit indicator is shown, data presented are in absolute form (Table 1).

Vertical rules are used to separate independent sections of a table (Table 1), or in tables where the stub is continued into one or more additional columns (Table 2).

Averages—An average is a single number or value that is often used to represent the "typical value" of a group of numbers. It is regarded as a measure of "location" or "central tendency" of a group of numbers.

The *arithmetic mean* is the type of average used most frequently. It is derived by summing the individual item values of a particular group and dividing the total by the number of items. The arithmetic mean is often referred to as simply the "mean" or "average."

The *median* of a group of numbers is the middle number or value when each item in the group is arranged according to size (lowest to highest or visa versa); it generally has the same number of items above it as well as below it. If there is an even number of items in the group, the median is taken to be the average of the two middle numbers.

Per capita (or per person) quantities—a per capita figure represents an average computed for every person in a specified group (or population). It is derived by taking the total for an item (such as income, taxes, or retail sales) and dividing it by the number of persons in the specified population.

Index numbers—An index number is the measure of difference or change, usually expressed as a percent, relating one quantity (the variable) of a specified kind to another quantity of the same kind. Index numbers are widely used to express changes in prices over periods of time, but may also be used to express differences between related subjects for a single point in time.

To compute a price index, a base year or period is selected. The base year price (of the commodity or service) is then designated as the base or reference price to which the prices for other years or periods are related. Many price indexes use the year 1982 as the base year; in tables this is shown as "1982 = 100." A method of expressing the price relationship is: The price of a set of one or more items for a related year (e.g. 1990) **divided by** the price of the same set of items for the base year (e.g. 1982). The result multiplied by 100 provides the index number. When 100 is subtracted from the index number, the result equals the percent change in price from the base year.

Average annual percent change—Unless otherwise stated in the *Abstract* (as in Section 1, Population), average annual percent change is computed by use of a *compound interest formula*. This formula assumes that the rate of change is constant throughout a specified compounding period (1 year for average annual rates of change). The formula is similar to that used to compute the balance of a savings account that receives compound interest. According to this formula, at the end of a compounding period the amount of accrued change (e.g., school enrollment or bank interest) is added to the amount that existed at the beginning of the period. As a result, over time (e.g., with each year or quarter), the same rate of change is applied to a larger and larger figure.

The *exponential formula*, which is based on continuous compounding, is often used to measure population change. It is preferred by population experts, because they view population and population-related subjects as changing without interruption, ever ongoing. Both exponential and compound interest formulas assume a constant rate of change. The former, however, applies the amount of change continuously to the base rather

than at the end of each compounding period. When the average annual rates are small (e.g., less than 5 percent) both formulas give virtually the same results. For an explanation of these two formulas as they relate to population, see U.S. Census Bureau, *The Methods and Materials of Demography,* Vol. 2, 3d printing (rev.), 1975, pp. 372–381.

Current and constant dollars—Statistics in some tables in a number of sections are expressed in both current and constant dollars (see, e.g., Table 659 in Section 13, Income, Expenditures, Poverty, and Wealth). Current dollar figures reflect actual prices or costs prevailing during the specified year(s). Constant dollar figures are estimates representing an effort to remove the effects of price changes from statistical series reported in dollar terms. In general, constant dollar series are derived by dividing current dollar estimates by the appropriate price index for the appropriate period (e.g., the Consumer Price Index). The result is a series as it would presumably exist if prices were the same throughout, as in the base year—in other words, as if the dollar had constant purchasing power. Any changes in this constant dollar series would reflect only changes in real volume of output, income, expenditures, or other measure.

Explanation of Symbols

The following symbols, used in the tables throughout this book, are explained in condensed form in footnotes to the tables where they appear:

– Represents zero or rounds to less than half the unit of measurement shown.

B Base figure too small to meet statistical standards for reliability of a derived figure.

D Figure withheld to avoid disclosure pertaining to a specific organization or individual.

NA Data not enumerated, tabulated, or otherwise available separately.

S Figure does not meet publication standards for reasons other than that covered by symbol B, above.

X Figure not applicable because column heading and stub line make entry impossible, absurd, or meaningless.

Z Entry would amount to less than half the unit of measurement shown.

In many tables, details will not add to the totals shown because of rounding.

Telephone & Internet Contacts

To help *Abstract* users find more data and information about statistical publications, we are issuing this list of contacts for federal agencies with major statistical programs. The intent is to give a single, first-contact point-of-entry for users of statistics. These agencies will provide general information on their statistical programs and publications, as well as specific information on how to order their publications. We are also including the Internet (World Wide Web) addresses for many of these agencies. These URLs were current in July 2009.

Executive Office of the President

Office of Management and Budget
Administrator
Office of Information and Regulatory
  Affairs
Office of Management and Budget
725 17th Street, NW
Washington, DC 20503
Information: 202-395-3080
Internet address:
  http://www.whitehouse.gov/omb

Department of Agriculture

Economic Research Service
Information Center
U.S. Department of Agriculture
1800 M Street, NW
Washington, DC 20036-5831
Information and Publications:
  202-694-5050
Internet address:
  http://www.ers.usda.gov/

National Agricultural Statistics Service
National Agricultural Statistics Service
USDA-NASS
1400 Independence Ave., SW
Washington, DC 20250
Information hotline: 1-800-727-9540
Internet address:
  http://www.nass.usda.gov/

Department of Commerce

U.S. Census Bureau
Customer Services Branch
U.S. Census Bureau
4600 Silver Hill Road
Washington, DC 20233
Information and Publications:
  1-800-923-8282
Internet address:
  http://www.census.gov/

Bureau of Economic Analysis
Bureau of Economic Analysis
1441 L Street, NW
Washington, DC 20230
Information and Publications:
  202-606-9900
Internet address: http://www.bea.gov/

Department of Commerce—Con.

International Trade Administration
International Trade Administration
1401 Constitution Ave., NW
Washington, DC 20230
Information: 1-800-872-8723
Internet address: http://trade.gov/

*National Oceanic and Atmospheric
  Administration*
National Oceanic and Atmospheric
  Administration Central Library
U.S. Department of Commerce
1315 East-West Highway
SSMC3, 2nd Floor
Silver Spring, MD 20910
Library: 301-713-2600 x.124
Internet address:
  http://www.lib.noaa.gov/

Department of Defense

Department of Defense
Office of Public Communication
1400 Defense Pentagon
Washington, DC 20301-1400
Information: 703-428-0711
Internet address:
  http://www.defenselink.mil

Department of Education

National Library of Education
U.S. Department of Education
400 Maryland Avenue, SW
Washington, DC 20202
Education Information and Statistics:
  1-800-872-5327
Education Publications: 1-877-433-7827
Internet address: http://www.ed.gov/

Department of Energy

Energy Information Administration
National Energy Information Center
Energy Information Administration
1000 Independence Ave., SW
Washington, DC 20585
Information and Publications:
  202-586-8800
Internet address:
  http://www.eia.doe.gov/

Department of Health and Human Services

Health Resources and Services Administration

HRSA Information Center
P.O. Box 2910
Merrifield, VA 22116
Information Center: 1-888-275-4772
Internet address: http://www.hrsa.gov/

Substance Abuse and Mental Health Services Administration

Substance Abuse and Mental Health Services Administration
1 Choke Cherry Road
Rockville, MD 20857
Information: 240-276-2130
Publications: 1-877-726-4727
Internet address:
http://www.samhsa.gov/

Centers for Disease Control and Prevention

Public Inquiries/MASO
1600 Clifton Road
Atlanta, GA 30333
Public Inquiries: 1-800-311-3435
Internet address: http://www.cdc.gov/

Centers for Medicare and Medicaid Services (CMS)

U.S. Department of Health and Human Services
7500 Security Boulevard
Baltimore, MD 21244
Information: 1-877-267-2323
Internet address:
http://www.cms.hhs.gov/

National Center for Health Statistics

National Center for Health Statistics
3311 Toledo Road
Hyattsville, MD 20782
Information: 1-800-232-4636
Internet address:
http://www.cdc.gov/nchs

Department of Homeland Security

Office of Public Affairs
245 Murray Lane, SW
Washington, DC 20528
Information and Publications:
202-282-8010
Internet address: http://www.dhs.gov

Department of Housing and Urban Development

Office of the Assistant Secretary for Community Planning and Development
451 7th St., SW
Washington, DC 20410
Information: 202-708-1112
Publications: 1-800-767-7468
Internet address: http://www.hud.gov/

Department of the Interior

U.S. Geological Survey

USGS National Center
12201 Sunrise Valley Drive
Reston, VA 20192
Information and Publications:
1-888-275-8747
Internet address for minerals:
http://minerals.usgs.gov/
Internet address for other materials:http://ask.usgs.gov/

Department of Justice

Bureau of Justice Statistics

Statistics Division
810 7th Street, NW
Washington, DC 20531
Information and Publications:
1-800-851-3420
Internet address:
http://www.ojp.usdoj.gov/bjs/

National Criminal Justice Reference Service

P.O. Box 6000
Rockville, MD 20849-6000
Publications: 1-800-851-3420
Internet address: http://www.ncjrs.gov/

Federal Bureau of Investigation

Federal Bureau of Investigations
J. Edgar Hoover Building
935 Pennsylvania Avenue, NW
Washington, DC 20535-0001
Information: 202-324-3000
Internet address: http://www.fbi.gov/

Department of Labor

Bureau of Labor Statistics

Office of Publications and Special Studies Services
Bureau of Labor Statistics
Postal Square Building
2 Mass. Ave., NE
Washington, DC 20212-0001
Information and Publications:
202-691-5200
Internet address: http://www.bls.gov/

Employment and Training Administration

U.S. Department of Labor
Francis Perkins Building
200 Constitution Ave., NW
Washington, DC 20210
Information and Publications:
1-877-872-5627
Internet address: http://www.doleta.gov/

U.S. Census Bureau, Statistical Abstract of the United States: 2010

Department of Transportation

Federal Aviation Administration
800 Independence Ave., SW
Washington, DC 20591
Information and Publications:
1-866-835-5322
Internet address: http://www.faa.gov/

Bureau of Transportation Statistics
1200 New Jersey Avenue, SE
Washington, DC 20590
Products and Statistical Information:
1-800-853-1351
Internet address: http://www.bts.gov/

Federal Highway Administration
Office of Public Affairs
U.S. Department of Transportation
1200 New Jersey Avenue, SE
Washington, DC 20590
Information: 202-366-0660
Internet address:
http://www.fhwa.dot.gov/

National Highway Traffic Safety Administration
Office of Public & Consumer Affairs
1200 New Jersey Avenue, SE
West Building
Washington, DC 20590
Information and Publications:
1-888-327-4236
Internet address:
http://www.nhtsa.dot.gov/

Department of the Treasury

Internal Revenue Service
Statistics of Income Division
Internal Revenue Service
P. O. Box 2608
Washington, DC 20013-2608
Information and Publications:
202-874-0410
Internet address:
http://www.irs.gov/taxstats/

Department of Veterans Affairs

Department of Veterans Affairs
Office of Public Affairs
810 Vermont Ave., NW
Washington, DC 20420
Information: 202-273-6000
Internet address: http://www.va.gov/

Independent Agencies

Administrative Office of the U.S. Courts
Office of Public Affairs
1 Columbus Circle, NE
Washington, DC 20544
Information: 202-502-2600
Internet address:
http://www.uscourts.gov/

Board of Governors of the Federal Reserve System
Division of Research and Statistics
Federal Reserve System
20th & Constitution Avenue, NW
Washington, DC 20551
Information: 202-452-3000
Publications: 202-452-3245
Internet address:
http://www.federalreserve.gov/

Environmental Protection Agency
Environmental Protection Agency
Ariel Rios Building
1200 Pennsylvania Ave., NW
Washington, DC 20460
Publications: 1-800-490-9198
Internet address: http://www.epa.gov/

National Science Foundation
Office of Legislation and Public Affairs
National Science Foundation
4201 Wilson Boulevard
Arlington, Virginia 22230
Information: 703-292-5111
Publications: 703-292-7827
Internet address: http://www.nsf.gov/

Securities and Exchange Commission
Office of Public Affairs
Securities and Exchange Commission
100 F Street, NE
Washington, DC 20549
Information: 202-942-8088
Publications: 202-551-4040
Internet address: http://www.sec.gov/

Social Security Administration
Social Security Administration
Office of Public Inquiries
6401 Security Boulevard
Baltimore, MD 21235
Information and Publications:
1-800-772-1213
Internet address:
http://www.socialsecurity.gov

Section 1

Population

This section presents statistics on the growth, distribution, and characteristics of the U.S. population. The principal source of these data is the U.S. Census Bureau, which conducts a decennial census of population, a monthly population survey, a program of population estimates and projections, and a number of other periodic surveys.

Decennial censuses—The U.S. Constitution provides for a census of the population every 10 years, primarily to establish a basis for apportionment of members of the House of Representatives among the states. For over a century after the first census in 1790, the census organization was a temporary one, created only for each decennial census. In 1902, the Census Bureau was established as a permanent federal agency, responsible for enumerating the population and also for compiling statistics on other population and housing characteristics.

Historically, the enumeration of the population has been a complete (100 percent) count. That is, an attempt is made to account for every person, for each person's residence, and for other characteristics (sex, age, family relationships, etc.). Since the 1940 census, in addition to the complete count information, some data have been obtained from representative samples of the population. In the 1990 and 2000 censuses, variable sampling rates were employed. For most of the country, 1 in every 6 households (about 17 percent) received the long form or sample questionnaire; in governmental units estimated to have fewer than 2,500 inhabitants, every other household (50 percent) received the sample questionnaire to enhance the reliability of sample data for small areas. Exact agreement is not to be expected between sample data and the 100-percent count. Sample data may be used with confidence where large numbers are involved and assumed to indicate trends and relationships where small numbers are involved.

Current Population Survey (CPS)—This is a monthly nationwide survey of a scientifically selected sample representing the noninstitutionalized civilian population. The sample is located in 824 areas with coverage in every state and the District of Columbia and is subject to sampling error. At the present time, about 60,000 occupied households are eligible for interview every month; of these, about 8 percent are, for various reasons, unavailable for interview.

While the primary purpose of the CPS is to obtain monthly statistics on the labor force, it also serves as a vehicle for inquiries on other subjects. Using CPS data, the Census Bureau issues a series of publications under the general title of *Current Population Reports*.

Estimates of population characteristics based on the CPS will not agree with the counts from the census because the CPS and the census use different procedures for collecting and processing the data for racial groups, the Hispanic population, and other topics. Caution should also be used when comparing estimates for various years because of the periodic introduction of changes into the CPS. Beginning in January 1994, a number of changes were introduced into the CPS that effect all data comparisons with prior years. These changes included the results of a major redesign of the survey questionnaire and collection methodology and the introduction of 1990 census population controls, adjusted for the estimated undercount. Beginning with the 2001 CPS Annual Demographic Supplement, the independent estimates used as control totals for the CPS are based on civilian population benchmarks consistent with Census 2000. In March 2002, the sample size of the Annual Demographic Supplement was increased to approximately 78,000. In 2003 the name of the March supplement was changed to Annual Social and Economic Supplement. These changes in population controls had relatively little

U.S. Census Bureau, Statistical Abstract of the United States: 2010

impact on derived measures such as means, medians, and percent distribution, but did have a significant impact on levels.

American Community Survey (ACS)—This is a nationwide survey to obtain data about demographic, social, economic, and housing information of people, households, and housing units. The survey collects the same type of information that has been collected every 10 years from the long-form questionnaire of the census, which the American Community Survey will replace. Beginning 2006, the estimates include the household population and the population living in institutions, college dormitories, and other group quarters.

Population estimates and projections—Estimates of the United States population are derived by updating the resident population enumerated in Census 2000 with information on the components of population change: births, deaths, and net international migration. The April 1, 2000, population used in these estimates reflects modifications to the Census 2000 population as documented in the Count Question Resolution program.

Registered births and deaths are estimated from data supplied by the National Center for Health Statistics. The net international migration component consists of four parts: (1) the net international migration of the foreign born, (2) the net migration of natives to and from the United States, (3) the net migration between the United States and Puerto Rico, and (4) the net overseas movement of the Armed Forces population. Data from the ACS are used to estimate the annual net migration of the foreign-born population. Estimates of the net migration of natives and net migration between Puerto Rico and the United States prior to 2005 are derived from the Demographic Analysis and Population Estimates (DAPE) project (see Population Division Working Paper Series, No. 63 and No. 64). Estimates for net migration between Puerto Rico and the U.S. for 2005 and later years are derived from the ACS and the Puerto Rico Community Survey. Estimates of the net overseas movement of the Armed Forces are derived from data collected by the Defense Manpower Data Center.

Estimates for state and county areas are based on the same components of change data and sources as the national estimates with the addition of net internal migration. Estimates of net internal migration are derived from federal income tax returns from the Internal Revenue Service, group quarters data from the Federal-State Cooperative Program, and Medicare data from the Centers for Medicare and Medicaid Services.

The population by age for April 1, 1990, reflects modifications to the 1990 census data counts. The review of detailed 1990 information indicated that respondents tended to report age as of the date of completion of the questionnaire, not as of April 1, 1990. In addition, there may have been a tendency for respondents to round up their age if they were close to having a birthday. A detailed explanation of the age modification procedure appears in 1990 Census of Population and Housing, Data Paper Listing CPH-L74.

Population estimates and projections are available on the Census Bureau Internet site <http://www.census.gov>. These estimates and projections are consistent with official decennial census figures with no adjustment for estimated net census coverage. However, the categories for these estimates and projections by race have been modified and are not comparable to the census race categories (see section below under "Race"). For details on methodology, see the sources cited below the individual tables.

Immigration—Immigration (migration *to* a country) is one component of international migration; the other component is emigration (migration *from* a country). In its simplest form, international migration is defined as any movement across a national border. In the United States, federal statistics on international migration are produced primarily by the U.S. Census Bureau and the Office of Immigration Statistics of the U.S. Department of Homeland Security (DHS).

The Census Bureau collects data used to estimate international migration through its decennial censuses and numerous surveys of the U.S. population.

The Office of Immigration Statistics publishes immigration data in annual flow reports and the *Yearbook of Immigration*

2   Population

Statistics. Data for these publications are collected from several administrative data sources including the DS-230 Application for Immigrant Visa and Alien Registration (U.S. Department of State) for new arrivals, and the I-485 Application to Register Permanent Residence or Adjust Status (U.S. Citizenship and Immigration Services—USCIS) for persons adjusting immigrant status.

An immigrant, or legal permanent resident, is a foreign national who has been granted lawful permanent residence in the United States. New arrivals are foreign nationals living abroad who apply for an immigrant visa at a consular office of the Department of State, while individuals adjusting status are already living in the United States and file an application for adjustment of status to lawful permanent residence with USCIS. Individuals adjusting status include refugees, asylees, and various classes of nonimmigrants. A refugee is an alien outside the United States who is unable or unwilling to return to his or her country of origin because of persecution or a well-founded fear of persecution. Asylees must meet the same criteria as refugees, but are located in the United States or at a port of entry. After 1 year of residence, refugees and asylees are eligible to adjust to legal permanent resident status. Nonimmigrants are foreign nationals granted temporary entry into the United States. The major activities for which nonimmigrant admission is authorized include temporary visits for business or pleasure, academic or vocational study, temporary employment, and to act as a representative of a foreign government or international organization. DHS collects information on the characteristics of a proportion of nonimmigrant admissions, those recorded on the I-94 Arrival/Departure Record.

U.S. immigration law gives preferential immigration status to persons with a close family relationship with a U.S. citizen or legal permanent resident, persons with needed job skills, persons who qualify as refugees or asylees, and persons who are from countries with relatively low levels of immigration to the United States. Immigration to the United States can be divided into two general categories: (1) classes of admission subject to the annual worldwide limitation and (2) classes of admission exempt from worldwide limitations. Numerical limits are imposed on visas issued and not on admissions. In 2008, the annual limit for preference visas subject to limitation was 388,704, which included a family-sponsored preference limit of 226,000 and an employment-based preference limit of 162,704. Classes of admission exempt from the worldwide limitation include immediate relatives of U.S. citizens, refugees and asylees adjusting to permanent residence, and other various classes of special immigrants.

Metropolitan and micropolitan areas—The U.S. Office of Management and Budget (OMB) defines metropolitan and micropolitan statistical areas according to published standards that are applied to Census Bureau data. The general concept of a metropolitan or micropolitan statistical area is that of a core area containing a substantial population nucleus, together with adjacent communities having a high degree of economic and social integration with that core. Currently defined metropolitan and micropolitan statistical areas are based on application of 2000 standards to 2000 decennial census data as updated by application of those standards to more recent Census Bureau population estimates. The term "metropolitan area" (MA) was adopted in 1990 and referred collectively to metropolitan statistical areas (MSAs), consolidated metropolitan statistical areas (CMSAs), and primary metropolitan statistical areas (PMSAs). The term "core-based statistical area" (CBSA) became effective in 2003 and refers collectively to metropolitan and micropolitan statistical areas. For descriptive details and a list of titles and components of metropolitan and micropolitan statistical areas, see Appendix II.

Urban and rural—For Census 2000, the Census Bureau classified as urban all territory, population, and housing units located within urbanized areas (UAs) and urban clusters (UCs). A UA consists of densely settled territory that contains 50,000 or more people, while a UC consists of densely settled territory with at least 2,500 people but fewer than 50,000 people. From the 1950 census through

U.S. Census Bureau, *Statistical Abstract of the United States: 2010*

the 1990 census, the urban population consisted of all people living in UAs and most places outside of UAs with a census population of 2,500 or more.

UAs and UCs encompass territory that generally consists of:

- A cluster of one or more block groups or census blocks each of which has a population density of at least 1,000 people per square mile at the time.

- Surrounding block groups and census blocks each of which has a population density of at least 500 people per square mile at the time.

- Less densely settled blocks that form enclaves or indentations, or are used to connect discontiguous areas with qualifying densities.

They also may include an airport located adjacent to qualifying densely settled area if it has an annual enplanement (aircraft boarding) of at least 10,000 people.

"Rural" for Census 2000 consists of all territory, population, and housing units located outside of UAs and UCs. Prior to Census 2000, rural consisted of all territory, population, and housing outside of UAs and outside of other places designated as "urban." For Census 2000, many more geographic entities, including metropolitan areas, counties, and places, contain both urban and rural territory, population, and housing units.

Residence—In determining residence, the Census Bureau counts each person as an inhabitant of a usual place of residence (i.e., the place where one lives and sleeps most of the time). While this place is not necessarily a person's legal residence or voting residence, the use of these different bases of classification would produce the same results in the vast majority of cases.

Race—For the 1990 census, the Census Bureau collected and published racial statistics as outlined in Statistical Policy Directive No. 15 issued by the OMB. This directive provided standards on ethnic and racial categories for statistical reporting to be used by all federal agencies. According to the directive, the basic racial categories were American Indian or Alaska Native, Asian or Pacific Islander, Black, and White. (The directive identified

Hispanic origin as an ethnicity.) The question on race for Census 2000 was different from the one for the 1990 census in several ways. Most significantly, respondents were given the option of selecting one or more race categories to indicate their racial identities. Because of these changes, the Census 2000 data on race are not directly comparable with data from the 1990 census or earlier censuses. Caution must be used when interpreting changes in the racial composition of the United States population over time. Census 2000 adheres to the federal standards for collecting and presenting data on race and ethnicity as established by the OMB in October 1997. Starting with Census 2000, the OMB requires federal agencies to use a minimum of five race categories: White, Black or African American, American Indian or Alaska Native, Asian, and Native Hawaiian or Other Pacific Islander. Additionally, to collect data on individuals of mixed race parentage, respondents were allowed to select one or more races. For respondents unable to identify with any of these five race categories, the OMB approved and included a sixth category—"Some other race" on the Census 2000 questionnaire. The Census 2000 question on race included 15 separate response categories and three areas where respondents could write in a more specific race group. The response categories and write-in answers can be combined to create the five minimum OMB race categories plus "Some other race." People who responded to the question on race by indicating only one race are referred to as the *race alone* population, or the group that reported only one race category. Six categories make up this population: White alone, Black or African American alone, American Indian and Alaska Native alone, Asian alone, Native Hawaiian and Other Pacific Islander alone, and Some other race alone. Individuals who chose more than one of the six race categories are referred to as the *Two or More Races* population, or as the group that reported more than one race. Additionally, respondents who reported one race together with those who reported the same race plus one or more other races are combined to create the *race alone or in combination* categories. For example, the *White alone or in combination group* consists of those respondents who reported only White or who reported White combined with one or more other race groups, such as "White and Black or African American," or "White and Asian and American Indian and Alaska Native." Another way to think of the group who reported White alone or in combination is as the total number of people who identified entirely or partially as White. This group is also described as people who reported White, whether or not they reported any other race.

The *alone or in combination* categories are tallies of *responses* rather than *respondents*. That is, the alone or in combination categories are not mutually exclusive. Individuals who reported two races were counted in two separate and distinct alone or in combination race categories, while those who reported three races were counted in three categories, and so on. Consequently, the sum of all alone or in combination categories equals the number of races reported, which exceeds the total population.

The concept of race, as used by the Census Bureau, reflects self-identification by people according to the race or races with which they most closely identify. These categories are sociopolitical constructs and should not be interpreted as being scientific or anthropological in nature. Furthermore, the race categories include both racial and national-origin groups. Additionally, data are available for the American Indian and Alaska Native tribes. A detailed explanation of race can be found at <http://www.census.gov/prod /cen2000/doc/sf1.pdf>.

Data for the population by race for April 1, 2000, (shown in Tables 6, 9, and 10) are modified counts and are not comparable to Census 2000 race categories. These numbers were computed using Census 2000 data by race that had been modified to be consistent with the 1997 OMB's "Revisions to the Standards for the Classification of Federal Data on Race and Ethnicity," (Federal Register Notice, Vol. 62, No 210, October 1997). A detailed explanation of the race modification procedure appears on the Census Web page <http://www.census.gov/popest /archives/files/MRSF-01-US1.html>.

In the CPS and other household sample surveys in which data are obtained through personal interview, respondents are asked to classify their race as: (1) White; (2) Black, African American, or Negro; (3) American Indian or Alaska Native; (4) Asian; (5) Native Hawaiian or Other Pacific Islander. Beginning January 2003, respondents were allowed to report more than one race to indicate their mixed racial heritage.

Hispanic population—The Census Bureau collected data on the Hispanic-origin population in the 2000 census by using a self-identification question. Persons of Spanish/Hispanic/Latino origin are those who classified themselves in one of the specific Hispanic origin categories listed on the questionnaire—Mexican, Puerto Rican, Cuban, as well as those who indicated that they were of Other Spanish/ Hispanic/Latino origin (persons whose origins are from Spain, the Spanish-speaking countries of Central or South America, or the Dominican Republic).

In the CPS, information on Hispanic persons is gathered by using a self-identification question. The respondents are first asked whether or not they are of Hispanic, Spanish, or Latino origin and based on their response are further classified into the following categories: Mexican or Mexican American or Chicano; Puerto Rican; Cuban; Central or South American; or Other Hispanic, Spanish, or Latino origin group.

Traditional and current data collection and classification treat race and Hispanic origin as two separate and distinct concepts in accordance with guidelines from the OMB. Race and Hispanic origin are two separate concepts in the federal statistical system. People who are Hispanic may be any race and people in each race group may be either Hispanic or Not Hispanic. Also, each person has two attributes, their race (or races) and whether or not they are Hispanic. The overlap of race and Hispanic origin is the main comparability issue. For example, Black Hispanics (Hispanic Blacks) are included in both the number of Blacks and in the number of Hispanics. For further information, see Census Web page <http://www.census .gov/population/www/socdemo /compraceho.html>.

Foreign-born and native populations—The Census Bureau separates the U.S. resident population into two groups based on whether or not a person was a U.S. citizen or U.S. national at the time of birth. Anyone born in the United States, Puerto Rico, or a U.S. Island Area (such as Guam) or born abroad to a U.S. citizen parent is a U.S. citizen at the time of birth and consequently included in the *native population*. The term *foreign-born population* refers to anyone who is not a U.S. citizen or U.S. national at birth. This includes naturalized U.S. citizens, legal permanent resident aliens (immigrants), temporary migrants (such as foreign students), humanitarian migrants (such as refugees), and people illegally present in the United States. The Census Bureau provides a variety of demographic, social, economic, geographic, and housing information on the foreign-born population in the United States at <http://www.census .gov/population/www/socdemo/foreign/>.

Mobility status—The U.S. population is classified according to mobility status on the basis of a comparison between the place of residence of each individual at the time of the survey or census and the place of residence at a specified earlier date. Nonmovers are all persons who were living in the same house or apartment at the end of the period as at the beginning of the period. Movers are all persons who were living in a different house or apartment at the end of the period than at the beginning of the period. Movers are further classified as to whether they were living in the same or different county, state, region, or were movers from abroad. Movers from abroad include all persons whose place of residence was outside the United States (including Puerto Rico, other U.S. Island Area, or a foreign country) at the beginning of the period.

Living arrangements—Living arrangements refer to residency in households or in group quarters. A "household" comprises all persons who occupy a "housing unit," that is, a house, an apartment or other group of rooms, or a single room that constitutes "separate living quarters." A household includes the related family members and all the unrelated persons, if any, such as lodgers, foster children, or employees who share the housing unit. A

person living alone or a group of unrelated persons sharing the same housing unit is also counted as a household. See text, Section 20, Construction and Housing, for definition of housing unit.

All persons not living in housing units are classified as living in group quarters. These individuals may be institutionalized, e.g., under care or custody in juvenile facilities, jails, correctional centers, hospitals, or nursing homes; or they may be residents in noninstitutional group quarters such as college dormitories, group homes, or military barracks.

Householder—The householder is the person in whose name the home is owned or rented. If a home is owned or rented jointly by a married couple, either the husband or the wife may be listed first.

Family—The term family refers to a group of two or more persons related by birth, marriage, or adoption and residing together in a household. A family includes among its members the householder.

Subfamily—A subfamily consists of a married couple and their children, if any, or one parent with one or more never-married children under 18 years old living in a household. Subfamilies are divided into "related" and "unrelated" subfamilies. A related subfamily is related to, but does not include, the householder or the spouse of the householder. Members of a related subfamily are also members of the family with whom they live. The number of related subfamilies, therefore, is not included in the count of families. An unrelated subfamily may include persons such as guests, lodgers, or resident employees and their spouses and/or children; none of whom is related to the householder.

Married couple—A married couple is defined as a husband and wife living together in the same household, with or without children and other relatives.

Statistical reliability—For a discussion of statistical collection and estimation, sampling procedures, and measures of statistical reliability applicable to Census Bureau data, see Appendix III.

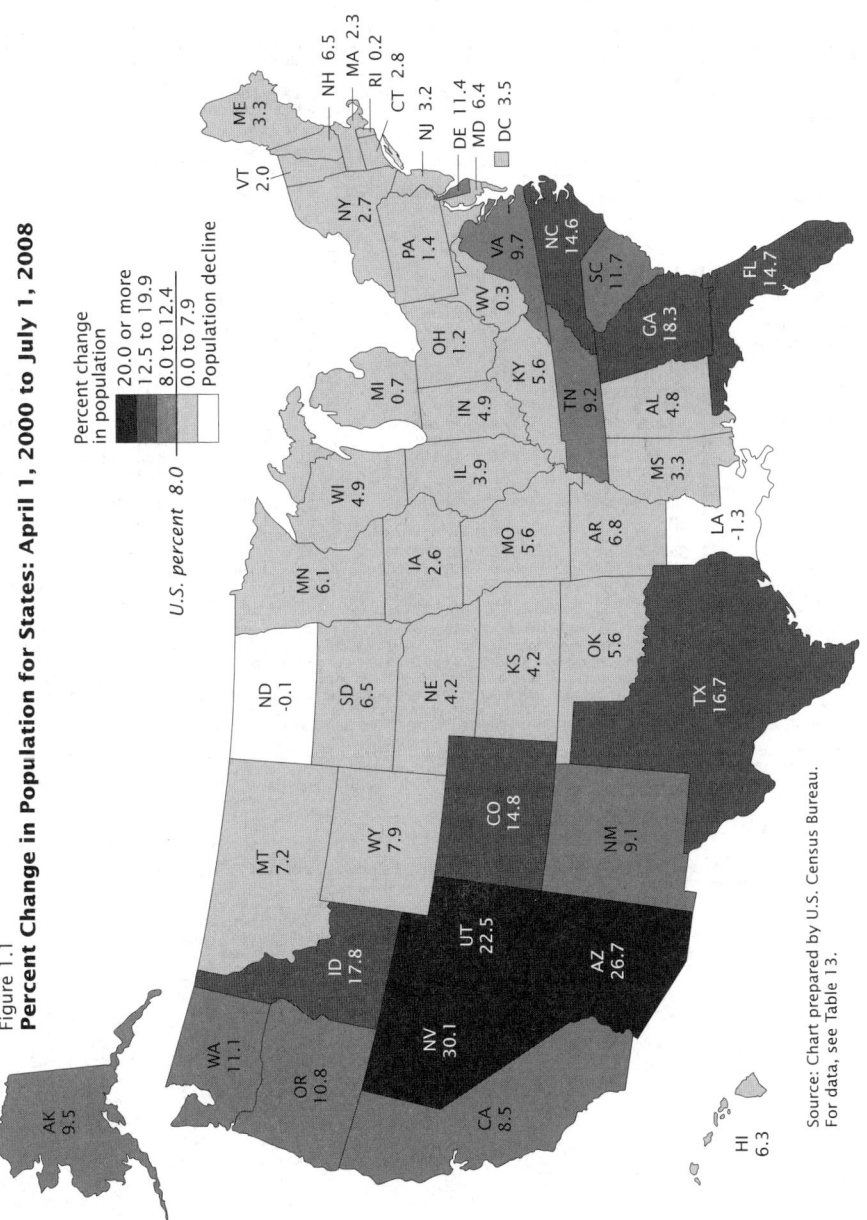

Figure 1.1
Percent Change in Population for States: April 1, 2000 to July 1, 2008

Percent change
in population

- 20.0 or more
- 12.5 to 19.9
- 8.0 to 12.4
- 0.0 to 7.9
- Population decline

U.S. percent 8.0

AK 9.5
WA 11.1
OR 10.8
CA 8.5
NV 30.1
ID 17.8
MT 7.2
WY 7.9
UT 22.5
CO 14.8
AZ 26.7
NM 9.1
ND -0.1
SD 6.5
NE 4.2
KS 4.2
OK 5.6
TX 16.7
MN 6.1
IA 2.6
MO 5.6
AR 6.8
LA -1.3
WI 4.9
IL 3.9
MI 0.7
IN 4.9
OH 1.2
KY 5.6
TN 9.2
MS 3.3
AL 4.8
GA 18.3
FL 14.7
SC 11.7
NC 14.6
VA 9.7
WV 0.3
PA 1.4
NY 2.7
VT 2.0
ME 3.3
NH 6.5
MA 2.3
RI 0.2
CT 2.8
NJ 3.2
DE 11.4
MD 6.4
DC 3.5
HI 6.3

Source: Chart prepared by U.S. Census Bureau.
For data, see Table 13.

Population   7

Table 1. **Population and Area: 1790 to 2000**

[Area figures represent area on indicated date including in some cases considerable areas not then organized or settled, and not covered by the census. Area data include Alaska beginning in 1870 and Hawaii beginning in 1900. Total area figures for 1790 to 1970 have been recalculated on the basis of the remeasurement of states and counties for the 1980 census, but not on the basis of the 1990 census. The land and water area figures for past censuses have not been adjusted and are not strictly comparable with the total area data for comparable dates because the land areas were derived from different base data, and these values are known to have changed with the construction of reservoirs, draining of lakes, etc. Density figures are based on land area measurements as reported in earlier censuses]

Census date	Resident population				Area (square miles)		
	Number	Per square mile of land area	Increase over preceding census		Total	Land	Water [1]
			Number	Percent			
1790 (Aug. 2).......	3,929,214	4.5	(X)	(X)	891,364	864,746	24,065
1800 (Aug. 4).......	5,308,483	6.1	1,379,269	35.1	891,364	864,746	24,065
1810 (Aug. 6).......	7,239,881	4.3	1,931,398	36.4	1,722,685	1,681,828	34,175
1820 (Aug. 7).......	9,638,453	5.5	2,398,572	33.1	1,792,552	1,749,462	38,544
1830 (June 1)	12,866,020	7.4	3,227,567	33.5	1,792,552	1,749,462	38,544
1840 (June 1)	17,069,453	9.8	4,203,433	32.7	1,792,552	1,749,462	38,544
1850 (June 1)	23,191,876	7.9	6,122,423	35.9	2,991,655	2,940,042	52,705
1860 (June 1)	31,443,321	10.6	8,251,445	35.6	3,021,295	2,969,640	52,747
1870 (June 1)	[2]39,818,449	[2]11.2	8,375,128	26.6	3,612,299	3,540,705	68,082
1880 (June 1)	50,189,209	14.2	10,370,760	26.0	3,612,299	3,540,705	68,082
1890 (June 1)	62,979,766	17.8	12,790,557	25.5	3,612,299	3,540,705	68,082
1900 (June 1)	76,212,168	21.5	13,232,402	21.0	3,618,770	3,547,314	67,901
1910 (Apr. 15)	92,228,496	26.0	16,016,328	21.0	3,618,770	3,547,045	68,170
1920 (Jan. 1).......	106,021,537	29.9	13,793,041	15.0	3,618,770	3,546,931	68,284
1930 (Apr. 1)......	123,202,624	34.7	17,181,087	16.2	3,618,770	3,554,608	60,607
1940 (Apr. 1)......	132,164,569	37.2	8,961,945	7.3	3,618,770	3,554,608	60,607
1950 (Apr. 1)......	151,325,798	42.6	19,161,229	14.5	3,618,770	3,552,206	63,005
1960 (Apr. 1)......	179,323,175	50.6	27,997,377	18.5	3,618,770	3,540,911	74,212
1970 (Apr. 1)......	203,302,031	57.5	23,978,856	13.4	3,618,770	3,536,855	78,444
1980 (Apr. 1)......	[3]226,542,199	64.0	23,240,168	11.4	3,618,770	3,539,289	79,481
1990 (Apr. 1)......	[4]248,718,302	70.3	22,176,103	9.8	[5]3,717,796	3,536,278	[5]181,518
2000 (Apr. 1)......	[6]281,424,603	79.6	32,706,301	13.1	3,794,083	3,537,438	256,645

X Not applicable. [1] Data for 1790 to 1980 cover inland water only. Data for 1990 comprise Great Lakes, inland, and coastal water. Data for 2000 comprise Great Lakes, inland, territorial, and coastal water. [2] Revised to include adjustments for underenumeration in southern states; unrevised number is 38,558,371 (10.9 per square mile). [3] Total population count has been revised since the 1980 census publications. Numbers by age, race, Hispanic origin, and sex have not been corrected. [4] The April 1, 1990, census count includes count question resolution corrections processed through December 1997, and does not include adjustments for census coverage errors. [5] Data reflect corrections made after publication of the results. [6] Reflects modifications to the Census 2000 population as documented in the Count Question Resolution program.

Source: U.S. Census Bureau, 2000 Census of Population and Housing, *Population and Housing Counts*, Series PHC-3-1, United States Summary; *Notes and Errata, 2000* SF/01-ER ; <http://www.census.gov/prod/cen2000/notes/errata.pdf>; *Areas of the United States: 1940*; Area data for 1990: unpublished data from TIGER ; and Davis, Warren; personal correspondence; U.S. Census Bureau, 23 June 2006.

Table 2. **Population: 1960 to 2008**

[**In thousands, except percent (180,671 represents 180,671,000). Estimates as of July 1**. Civilian population excludes Armed Forces. For basis of estimates, see text, this section]

Year	Resident population, including Armed Forces overseas		Resident population	Civilian population
	Population	Percent change [1]		
1960	180,671	1.60	179,979	178,140
1965	194,303	1.26	193,526	191,605
1966	196,560	1.16	195,576	193,420
1967	198,712	1.09	197,457	195,264
1968	200,706	1.00	199,399	197,113
1969	202,677	0.98	201,385	199,145
1970	205,052	1.17	203,984	201,895
1971	207,661	1.27	206,827	204,866
1972	209,896	1.08	209,284	207,511
1973	211,909	0.96	211,357	209,600
1974	213,854	0.92	213,342	211,636
1975	215,973	0.99	215,465	213,789
1976	218,035	0.95	217,563	215,894
1977	220,239	1.01	219,760	218,106
1978	222,585	1.06	222,095	220,467
1979	225,055	1.11	224,567	222,969
1980	227,726	1.19	227,225	225,621
1981	229,966	0.98	229,466	227,818
1982	232,188	0.97	231,664	229,995
1983	234,307	0.91	233,792	232,097
1984	236,348	0.87	235,825	234,110
1985	238,466	0.90	237,924	236,219
1986	240,651	0.92	240,133	238,412
1987	242,804	0.89	242,289	240,550
1988	245,021	0.91	244,499	242,817
1989	247,342	0.95	246,819	245,131
1990	250,132	1.13	249,623	247,983
1991	253,493	1.34	252,981	251,370
1992	256,894	1.34	256,514	254,929
1993	260,255	1.31	259,919	258,446
1994	263,436	1.22	263,126	261,714
1995	266,557	1.18	266,278	264,927
1996	269,667	1.17	269,394	268,108
1997	272,912	1.20	272,647	271,394
1998	276,115	1.17	275,854	274,633
1999	279,295	1.15	279,040	277,841
2000	282,385	1.11	282,172	280,927
2001	285,267	1.02	285,040	283,804
2002	288,028	0.97	287,727	286,460
2003	290,704	0.93	290,211	288,991
2004	293,310	0.90	292,892	291,631
2005	295,994	0.92	295,561	294,370
2006	298,766	0.94	298,363	297,183
2007	301,714	0.99	301,290	300,135
2008	304,483	0.92	304,060	302,887

[1] Percent change from immediate preceding year.

Source: U.S. Census Bureau, 1960 to 1979: *Current Population Reports* P25-802 and P25-917; 1980 to 1989: "Monthly Estimates of the United States Population: April 1, 1980, to July 1, 1999, with Short-Term Projections to November 1, 2000" (published 2 January 2001); <http://www.census.gov/popest/archives/1990s/nat-total.txt>; 1990 to 1999: "national intercensal estimates (1990–2000)" (published 13 August 2004); <http://www.census.gov/popest/archives/EST90INTERCENSAL/US-EST90INT-datasets.html>; 2000 to 2008: "Monthly Population Estimates for the United States: April 1, 2000 to December 1, 2008 (NA-EST2008-01)" (released December 22, 2008); <http://www.census.gov/popest/national/tables/NA-EST2008-01.xls>.

8   Population

Table 3. Resident Population Projections: 2009 to 2050

[**307,212 represents 307,212,000. As of July 1**. Projections are based on assumptions about future births, deaths, and net international migration. More information on methodology and assumptions is available at <http://www.census.gov/population/www/projections/methodstatement.html>]

Year	Number (1,000)	Percent change [1]	Year	Number (1,000)	Percent change [1]	Year	Number (1,000)	Percent change [1]
2009	307,212	1.0	2023	351,018	0.9	2037	395,961	0.8
2010	310,233	1.0	2024	354,235	0.9	2038	399,184	0.8
2011	313,232	1.0	2025	357,452	0.9	2039	402,415	0.8
2012	316,266	1.0	2026	360,667	0.9	2040	405,655	0.8
2013	319,330	1.0	2027	363,880	0.9	2041	408,906	0.8
2014	322,423	1.0	2028	367,090	0.9	2042	412,170	0.8
2015	325,540	1.0	2029	370,298	0.9	2043	415,448	0.8
2016	328,678	1.0	2030	373,504	0.9	2044	418,743	0.8
2017	331,833	1.0	2031	376,708	0.9	2045	422,059	0.8
2018	335,005	1.0	2032	379,912	0.9	2046	425,395	0.8
2019	338,190	1.0	2033	383,117	0.8	2047	428,756	0.8
2020	341,387	0.9	2034	386,323	0.8	2048	432,143	0.8
2021	344,592	0.9	2035	389,531	0.8	2049	435,560	0.8
2022	347,803	0.9	2036	392,743	0.8	2050	439,010	0.8

[1] Percent change from immediate preceding year. 2009, change from 2008.

Source: U.S. Census Bureau, "2008 National Population Projections" (released August 2008); <http://www.census.gov/population/www/projections/2008projections.html>.

Table 4. Components of Population Change: 2000 to 2008

[**In thousands (281,425 represents 281,425,000), except as indicated**. Resident population]

Period	Population as of beginning of period	Net increase [1]		Births	Deaths	Net international migration [3]	Population as of end of period
		Total	Percent [2]				
April 1, 2000 to July 1, 2000 [4] . . .	281,425	747	0.3	989	561	319	282,172
July 1, 2000 to July 1, 2001	282,172	2,868	1.0	4,047	2,419	1,200	285,040
July 1, 2001 to July 1, 2002	285,040	2,687	0.9	4,007	2,430	1,078	287,727
July 1, 2002 to July 1, 2003	287,727	2,484	0.9	4,053	2,423	822	290,211
July 1, 2003 to July 1, 2004	290,211	2,681	0.9	4,113	2,450	986	292,892
July 1, 2004 to July 1, 2005	292,892	2,668	0.9	4,121	2,433	948	295,561
July 1, 2005 to July 1, 2006	295,561	2,802	0.9	4,178	2,418	1,006	298,363
July 1, 2006 to July 1, 2007	298,363	2,927	1.0	4,289	2,421	866	301,290
July 1, 2007 to July 1, 2008	301,290	2,769	0.9	4,329	2,448	889	304,060

[1] Includes a residual which represents the change in population that cannot be attributed to any specific demographic component. [2] Percent of population at beginning of period. [3] Includes: (a) the net international migration of the foreign born, (b) the net migration between the United States and Puerto Rico, (c) the net migration of natives to and from the United States, and (d) the net overseas movement of the Armed Forces population. [4] The April 1, 2000, Population Estimates base reflects changes to the Census 2000 population from the Count Question Resolution program.

Source: U.S. Census Bureau, "Population, Population change and estimated components of population change: April 1, 2000 to July 1, 2008" (released December 22, 2008); <http://www.census.gov/popest/national/files/NST-EST2008-alldata.txt>.

Table 5. Components of Population Change by Race and Hispanic Origin: 2000 to 2008

[**In thousands (22,635 represents 22,635,000,000)**. Resident population. Covers period April 1, 2000, to July 1, 2008. The April 1, 2000, Population Estimates base reflects changes to the Census 2000 population from the Count Question Resolution program]

Race and Hispanic origin	Net increase [1]	Natural increase	Births	Deaths	Net international migration [2]
Total	**22,635**	**14,124**	**34,126**	**20,002**	**8,115**
One race.	21,366	12,959	32,834	19,875	8,017
White	14,533	8,723	25,740	17,017	5,492
Black or African American	3,354	2,701	5,120	2,419	603
American Indian and Alaska Native. . .	420	353	450	97	63
Asian	2,960	1,113	1,445	332	1,829
Native Hawaiian and Other Pacific Islander	100	69	79	10	30
Two or more races	1,269	1,165	1,292	127	98
Race alone or in combination: [3]					
White	15,677	9,789	26,912	17,123	5,564
Black or African American	4,022	3,333	5,786	2,454	636
American Indian and Alaska Native. . .	637	550	718	168	81
Asian	3,474	1,563	1,934	370	1,890
Native Hawaiian and Other Pacific Islander	206	159	185	25	45
Hispanic [4]	11,637	7,258	8,159	901	4,318
White alone, not Hispanic.	3,914	2,249	18,422	16,173	1,405

[1] See footnote 1, Table 4. [2] See footnote 3, Table 4. [3] In combination with one or more other races. The sum of the five race groups adds to more than the total population because individuals may report more than one race. [4] Persons of Hispanic origin may be any race.

Source: U.S. Census Bureau, "Cumulative Estimates of the Components of Resident Population Change by Race and Hispanic Origin for the United States: April 1, 2000 to July 1, 2008 (NC-EST2008-05)" (released May 14, 2009); <http://www.census.gov/popest/national/asrh/NC-EST2008/NC-EST2008-05.xls>.

Population 9

Table 6. Resident Population by Sex, Race, and Hispanic-Origin Status: 2000 to 2008

[281,425 represents 281,425,000. As of July, except as noted. Data shown are modified race counts; see text, this section]

Characteristic	Number (1,000)					Percent change, 2000 to 2008
	2000 [1] (April 1)	2005	2006	2007	2008	
BOTH SEXES						
Total	**281,425**	**295,561**	**298,363**	**301,290**	**304,060**	**8.0**
One race	277,527	290,891	293,533	296,292	298,893	7.7
White	228,107	237,204	238,999	240,882	242,639	6.4
Black or African American.	35,705	37,732	38,160	38,622	39,059	9.4
American Indian and Alaska Native	2,664	2,918	2,972	3,028	3,083	15.8
Asian	10,589	12,512	12,865	13,211	13,549	28.0
Native Hawaiian and Other Pacific Islander	463	525	538	550	562	21.5
Two or more races	3,898	4,669	4,830	4,998	5,167	32.6
Race alone or in combination: [2]						
White	231,436	241,228	243,168	245,203	247,113	6.8
Black or African American.	37,105	39,534	40,047	40,599	41,127	10.8
American Indian and Alaska Native	4,225	4,613	4,694	4,779	4,862	15.1
Asian	12,007	14,244	14,662	15,075	15,480	28.9
Native Hawaiian and Other Pacific Islander	907	1,035	1,061	1,087	1,112	22.7
Not Hispanic	246,118	253,032	254,378	255,818	257,116	4.5
One race.	242,712	248,987	250,201	251,504	252,664	4.1
White	195,577	198,037	198,518	199,060	199,491	2.0
Black or African American	34,314	36,068	36,422	36,809	37,172	8.3
American Indian and Alaska Native.	2,097	2,240	2,269	2,299	2,329	11.0
Asian	10,357	12,232	12,574	12,910	13,238	27.8
Native Hawaiian and Other Pacific Islander . . .	367	410	418	426	435	18.4
Two or more races	3,406	4,045	4,177	4,314	4,452	30.7
Race alone or in combination: [2]						
White	198,477	201,514	202,114	202,780	203,336	2.4
Black or African American	35,499	37,591	38,015	38,477	38,916	9.6
American Indian and Alaska Native.	3,456	3,686	3,732	3,781	3,828	10.8
Asian	11,632	13,781	14,179	14,572	14,957	28.6
Native Hawaiian and Other Pacific Islander . . .	752	845	863	881	899	19.6
Hispanic [3]	35,306	42,529	43,985	45,472	46,944	33.0
One race.	34,815	41,904	43,332	44,788	46,228	32.8
White	32,530	39,166	40,480	41,822	43,148	32.6
Black or African American	1,391	1,664	1,738	1,813	1,887	35.6
American Indian and Alaska Native.	566	679	703	729	754	33.2
Asian	232	280	290	301	311	33.9
Native Hawaiian and Other Pacific Islander . . .	95	116	120	124	128	33.7
Two or more races	491	624	654	684	715	45.6
Race alone or in combination: [2]						
White	32,959	39,714	41,054	42,423	43,777	32.8
Black or African American	1,606	1,943	2,032	2,122	2,211	37.7
American Indian and Alaska Native.	770	927	962	998	1,034	34.4
Asian	375	463	483	503	523	39.6
Native Hawaiian and Other Pacific Islander . . .	155	190	198	205	213	37.4
MALE						
Total	**138,056**	**145,465**	**146,946**	**148,466**	**149,925**	**8.6**
One race	136,146	143,163	144,563	145,997	147,370	8.2
White	112,478	117,397	118,374	119,375	120,326	7.0
Black or African American.	16,972	17,973	18,189	18,418	18,640	9.8
American Indian and Alaska Native	1,333	1,461	1,488	1,517	1,545	15.9
Asian	5,128	6,065	6,238	6,408	6,574	28.2
Native Hawaiian and Other Pacific Islander	235	267	273	279	286	21.5
Two or more races	1,910	2,302	2,384	2,469	2,555	33.7
Race alone or in combination: [2]						
White	114,116	119,387	120,438	121,516	122,545	7.4
Black or African American.	17,644	18,849	19,109	19,384	19,651	11.4
American Indian and Alaska Native	2,088	2,284	2,325	2,368	2,410	15.4
Asian	5,834	6,931	7,137	7,341	7,541	29.2
Native Hawaiian and Other Pacific Islander	456	520	534	547	560	22.7
Not Hispanic	119,894	123,514	124,235	124,981	125,670	4.8
Hispanic [3]	18,162	21,951	22,712	23,485	24,254	33.5
FEMALE						
Total	**143,368**	**150,096**	**151,417**	**152,824**	**154,135**	**7.5**
One race	141,381	147,728	148,970	150,295	151,523	7.2
White	115,628	119,806	120,625	121,506	122,313	5.8
Black or African American.	18,733	19,759	19,971	20,203	20,419	9.0
American Indian and Alaska Native	1,331	1,458	1,484	1,512	1,539	15.6
Asian	5,461	6,447	6,626	6,803	6,975	27.7
Native Hawaiian and Other Pacific Islander	227	258	264	270	276	21.6
Two or more races	1,987	2,368	2,447	2,529	2,612	31.4
Race alone or in combination: [2]						
White	117,321	121,841	122,730	123,686	124,568	6.2
Black or African American.	19,461	20,685	20,939	21,215	21,476	10.4
American Indian and Alaska Native	2,137	2,329	2,369	2,411	2,452	14.7
Asian	6,173	7,313	7,525	7,734	7,940	28.6
Native Hawaiian and Other Pacific Islander	451	514	527	540	553	22.6
Not Hispanic	126,224	129,518	130,143	130,837	131,446	4.1
Hispanic [3]	17,144	20,578	21,273	21,987	22,689	32.3

[1] See footnote 3, Table 7.   [2] In combination with one or more other races. The sum of the five race groups adds to more than the total population because individuals may report more than one race.   [3] Persons of Hispanic origin may be any race.

Source: U.S. Census Bureau, "Annual Estimates of the Population by Sex, Race, and Hispanic Origin for the United States: April 1, 2000 to July 1, 2008 (NC-EST2008-03)" (released May 14, 2009); <http://www.census.gov/popest/national/asrh /NC-EST2008/NC-EST2008-03.xls>.

Table 7. Resident Population by Sex and Age: 1980 to 2008

[In thousands, except as indicated (226,546 represents 226,546,000). 1980, 1990, and 2000 data are enumerated population as of April 1; data for other years are estimated population as of July 1. Excludes Armed Forces overseas. For definition of median, see Guide to Tabular Presentation]

Age group	1980 [1] Total	Male	Female	1990 [2] Total	Male	Female	2000 [3] Total	Male	Female	2002, total	2003, total	2004, total	2005, total	2006, total	2007, total	2008 Total	Male	Female
Total	226,546	110,053	116,493	248,791	121,284	127,507	281,425	136,056	143,368	287,727	290,211	292,892	295,561	298,363	301,290	304,060	149,925	154,135
Under 5 years	16,348	8,362	7,986	18,765	9,603	9,162	19,176	9,811	9,365	19,534	19,770	20,059	20,301	20,436	20,730	21,006	10,748	10,258
5 to 9 years	16,700	8,539	8,161	18,042	9,236	8,806	20,550	10,523	10,026	19,965	19,738	19,580	19,506	19,655	19,837	20,065	10,259	9,806
10 to 14 years	18,242	9,316	8,926	17,067	8,742	8,325	20,528	10,520	10,008	21,098	21,178	21,099	20,823	20,562	20,292	20,055	10,262	9,792
15 to 19 years	21,168	10,755	10,413	17,893	9,178	8,714	20,219	10,391	9,828	20,346	20,446	20,677	20,994	21,246	21,446	21,514	11,027	10,487
20 to 24 years	21,319	10,663	10,655	19,143	9,749	9,394	18,963	9,688	9,275	20,266	20,591	20,814	20,888	20,931	20,962	21,059	10,845	10,214
25 to 29 years	19,521	9,705	9,816	21,336	10,708	10,629	19,382	9,799	9,583	18,861	19,000	19,391	19,869	20,488	20,956	21,334	10,941	10,393
30 to 34 years	17,561	8,677	8,884	21,838	10,866	10,973	20,511	10,322	10,189	20,777	20,634	20,356	19,948	19,532	19,445	19,598	9,959	9,639
35 to 39 years	13,965	6,862	7,104	19,851	9,837	10,014	22,707	11,319	11,388	21,814	21,348	20,974	20,913	21,072	21,123	20,994	10,569	10,425
40 to 44 years	11,669	5,708	5,961	17,593	8,679	8,914	22,442	11,130	11,313	22,932	22,950	23,004	22,801	22,409	21,959	21,507	10,746	10,762
45 to 49 years	11,090	5,388	5,702	13,747	6,741	7,006	20,093	9,890	10,203	21,267	21,745	22,093	22,451	22,755	22,855	22,880	11,314	11,566
50 to 54 years	11,710	5,621	6,089	11,315	5,494	5,821	17,586	8,608	8,978	18,693	19,031	19,481	19,981	20,455	21,016	21,492	10,539	10,954
55 to 59 years	11,615	5,482	6,133	10,489	5,009	5,480	13,469	6,509	6,961	15,082	15,718	16,479	17,340	18,207	18,244	18,583	9,015	9,569
60 to 64 years	10,088	4,670	5,418	10,627	4,947	5,679	10,806	5,137	5,669	11,500	12,108	12,583	12,993	13,351	14,481	15,103	7,236	7,867
65 to 74 years	15,581	6,757	8,824	18,048	7,908	10,140	18,391	8,303	10,088	18,283	18,349	18,472	18,640	18,915	19,370	20,123	9,265	10,858
75 to 84 years	7,729	2,867	4,862	10,014	3,745	6,268	12,361	4,879	7,482	12,761	12,887	12,981	13,056	13,068	13,057	13,025	5,336	7,689
85 years and over	2,240	682	1,559	3,022	841	2,181	4,240	1,227	3,013	4,547	4,716	4,849	5,057	5,281	5,515	5,722	1,864	3,858
5 to 13 years	31,159	15,923	15,237	31,839	16,301	15,538	37,026	18,964	18,062	36,953	36,725	36,311	36,026	35,970	35,940	36,005	18,414	17,590
14 to 17 years	16,247	8,298	7,950	13,345	6,860	6,485	16,093	8,285	7,808	16,344	16,484	16,797	17,051	17,188	17,189	16,931	8,671	8,260
18 to 24 years	30,022	15,054	14,969	26,961	13,744	13,217	27,141	13,873	13,268	28,379	28,744	29,063	29,134	29,236	29,407	29,757	15,309	14,449
18 years and over	162,791	77,473	85,321	184,841	88,519	96,322	209,130	100,996	108,133	214,896	217,232	219,726	222,182	224,769	227,431	230,118	112,091	118,027
55 years and over	47,253	20,458	26,796	52,200	22,450	29,748	59,267	26,055	33,212	62,173	63,779	65,363	67,086	68,822	70,668	72,556	32,715	39,840
65 years and over	25,550	10,306	15,245	31,084	12,494	18,589	34,992	14,410	20,582	35,591	35,952	36,301	36,752	37,264	37,942	38,870	16,465	22,405
75 years and over	9,969	3,549	6,421	13,036	4,586	8,449	16,601	6,106	10,495	17,308	17,603	17,830	18,112	18,349	18,573	18,747	7,200	11,547
Median age (years)	30.0	28.8	31.3	32.8	31.6	34.0	35.3	34.0	36.5	35.7	35.9	36.1	36.3	36.5	36.7	36.8	35.5	38.1

[1] Total population count has been revised since the 1980 census publications. Numbers by age and sex have not been corrected.   [2] The data shown have been modified from the official 1990 census counts. See text of this section for explanation. The April 1, 1990, estimates base (248,790,925) includes count resolution corrections processed through August 1997. It generally does not include adjustments for census coverage errors. However, it includes adjustments estimated for the 1995 Test Census in various localities in California, New Jersey, and Louisiana; and the 1998 census dress rehearsals in California and Wisconsin. These adjustments amounted to a total of 81,052 persons.   [3] The April 1, 2000, population estimates base reflects changes to the Census 2000 population from the Count Question Resolution program.

Source: U.S. Census Bureau, Current Population Reports, P25-1095; "Table US-EST90INT-04—Intercensal Estimates of the United States Resident Population by Age Groups and Sex, 1990–2000: Selected Months" (published 13 September 2002); <http://www.census.gov/popest/archives/EST90INTERCENSAL/US-EST90INT-04.html>; and "Annual Estimates of the Population by Sex and Five-Year Age Groups for the United States: April 1, 2000 to July 1, 2008 (NC-EST2008-01)" (released May 14, 2009); <http://www.census.gov/popest/national/asrh/NC-EST2008-01.xls>.

Table 8. Resident Population Projections by Sex and Age: 2010 to 2050

[In thousands, except as indicated (310,233 represents 310,233,000). As of July 1. Projections are based on assumptions about future births, deaths, and net international migration. More information on methodology and assumptions is available at <http://www.census.gov/population/www/projections/methodstatement.html>. For definition of median, see Guide to Tabular Presentation]

Age	2010 Total	2010 Male	2010 Female	2015 Total	2015 Male	2015 Female	2020	2025	2030	2035	2040	2045	2050	Pct. dist. 2010	Pct. dist. 2015	Pct. dist. 2020	Pct. dist. 2025	Pct. dist. 2050
Total	310,233	152,753	157,479	325,540	160,424	165,116	341,387	357,452	373,504	389,531	405,655	422,059	439,010	100.0	100.0	100.0	100.0	100.0
Under 5 years	21,100	10,779	10,320	22,076	11,278	10,798	22,846	23,484	24,161	25,056	26,117	27,171	28,148	6.8	6.8	6.7	6.6	6.4
5 to 9 years	20,886	10,654	10,232	21,707	11,074	10,633	22,732	23,548	24,232	24,953	25,893	26,998	28,096	6.7	6.7	6.7	6.6	6.4
10 to 14 years	20,395	10,421	9,975	21,658	11,049	10,609	22,571	23,677	24,567	25,319	26,105	27,108	28,274	6.6	6.7	6.6	6.6	6.4
15 to 19 years	21,770	11,159	10,611	21,209	10,844	10,365	22,554	23,545	24,723	25,408	26,501	27,272	28,422	7.0	6.5	6.6	6.6	6.5
20 to 24 years	21,779	11,100	10,680	22,342	11,378	10,963	21,799	23,168	24,191	24,855	26,408	27,354	28,171	7.0	6.9	6.4	6.5	6.4
25 to 29 years	21,418	10,873	10,545	22,440	11,353	11,048	22,949	22,417	23,804	24,647	26,102	27,138	28,126	6.9	6.9	6.7	6.3	6.4
30 to 34 years	20,400	10,308	10,092	22,099	11,182	10,917	23,112	23,699	23,216	23,848	25,745	27,040	28,039	6.6	6.8	6.8	6.6	6.3
35 to 39 years	20,267	10,191	10,076	20,841	10,506	10,335	22,586	23,645	23,279	24,061	25,321	26,462	27,799	6.5	6.4	6.6	6.6	6.3
40 to 44 years	21,010	10,509	10,500	20,460	10,247	10,214	21,078	22,851	23,944	24,612	24,224	25,726	26,897	6.8	6.3	6.2	6.4	6.2
45 to 49 years	22,596	11,165	11,430	21,001	10,447	10,553	20,502	21,154	24,279	24,884	24,759	24,411	25,933	7.3	6.5	6.2	5.9	6.1
50 to 54 years	22,109	10,827	11,282	22,367	10,977	11,390	20,852	20,404	21,087	22,884	24,025	24,750	24,621	7.1	6.9	6.0	5.7	5.9
55 to 59 years	19,517	9,450	10,067	21,682	10,524	11,158	21,994	20,575	20,186	20,903	22,703	23,867	24,445	6.3	6.7	6.4	5.8	5.6
60 to 64 years	16,758	8,024	8,733	18,861	9,023	9,838	21,009	21,377	20,080	19,760	20,513	22,305	23,490	5.4	5.8	6.2	6.0	5.4
65 to 69 years	12,261	5,747	6,514	15,812	7,449	8,364	17,861	19,957	20,381	19,230	18,989	19,776	21,543	4.0	4.9	5.2	5.6	4.9
70 to 74 years	9,202	4,191	5,011	11,155	5,109	6,046	14,452	16,399	18,404	18,879	17,906	17,754	18,570	3.0	3.4	4.2	4.6	4.2
75 to 79 years	7,282	3,159	4,123	7,901	3,480	4,421	9,656	12,598	14,390	16,249	16,771	16,016	15,964	2.3	2.4	2.8	3.5	3.6
80 to 84 years	5,733	2,302	3,431	5,676	2,342	3,334	6,239	7,715	10,173	11,735	13,375	13,925	13,429	1.8	1.7	1.8	2.2	3.1
85 to 89 years	3,650	1,297	2,353	3,786	1,409	2,376	3,817	4,278	5,383	7,215	8,450	9,767	10,303	1.2	1.2	1.1	1.2	2.3
90 to 94 years	1,570	473	1,097	1,856	591	1,265	1,976	2,047	2,360	3,044	4,180	5,007	5,909	0.5	0.6	0.6	0.6	1.3
95 to 99 years	452	108	344	546	142	404	669	739	795	952	1,270	1,803	2,229	0.1	0.2	0.2	0.2	0.5
100 years and over	79	15	65	105	21	84	135	175	208	239	298	409	601	(Z)	(Z)	(Z)	(Z)	0.1
5 to 13 years	37,123	18,945	18,178	39,011	19,900	19,111	40,792	42,490	43,858	45,170	46,743	48,664	50,697	12.0	12.0	11.9	11.9	11.5
14 to 17 years	16,994	8,713	8,281	17,019	8,699	8,320	18,048	18,892	19,796	20,496	21,126	21,834	22,728	5.5	5.2	5.3	5.3	5.2
18 to 24 years	30,713	15,675	15,037	30,885	15,746	15,139	30,817	32,555	34,059	35,695	37,038	38,234	39,538	9.9	9.5	9.0	9.1	9.0
16 years and over	243,639	118,739	124,900	255,864	124,858	131,006	268,722	282,014	295,595	309,084	322,265	335,328	348,811	78.5	78.6	78.7	78.9	79.5
18 years and over	235,016	114,316	120,700	247,434	120,547	126,887	259,702	272,585	285,688	298,809	311,669	324,389	337,437	75.8	76.0	76.1	76.3	76.9
16 to 64 years	203,410	101,447	101,963	209,027	104,316	104,711	213,917	218,107	223,503	231,540	241,027	250,872	260,264	65.6	64.2	62.7	61.0	59.3
55 years and over	76,504	34,766	41,737	87,381	40,090	47,291	97,807	105,860	112,358	118,206	124,455	130,628	136,658	24.7	26.8	28.6	29.6	31.1
65 years and over	40,229	17,292	22,937	46,837	20,542	26,295	54,804	63,907	72,092	77,543	81,238	84,456	88,547	13.0	14.4	16.1	17.9	20.2
75 years and over	18,766	7,354	11,412	19,870	7,985	11,885	22,492	27,551	33,308	39,435	44,343	46,926	48,434	6.0	6.1	6.6	7.7	11.0
85 years and over	5,751	1,893	3,859	6,292	2,163	4,130	6,597	7,239	8,745	11,450	14,198	16,985	19,041	1.9	1.9	1.9	2.0	4.3
Median age (years)	36.9	35.5	38.2	37.1	35.9	38.4	37.7	38.2	38.7	39.0	38.9	38.9	39.0	(X)	(X)	(X)	(X)	(X)

X Not applicable.   Z Less than 0.05 percent.

Source: U.S. Census Bureau, "2008 National Population Projections," released August 2008; <http://www.census.gov/population/www/projections/2008projections.html>.

Table 9. Resident Population by Race, Hispanic Origin, and Age: 2000 and 2008

[In thousands (281,425 represents 281,425,000); except as indicated. 2000, as of April and 2008, as of July. For definition of median, see Guide to Tabular Presentation]

Age group	Total 2000[1]	Total 2008	White alone 2000[1]	White alone 2008	Black or African American alone 2000[1]	Black or African American alone 2008	American Indian, Alaska Native alone 2000[1]	American Indian, Alaska Native alone 2008	Asian alone 2000[1]	Asian alone 2008	Native Hawaiian, Other Pacific Islander alone 2000[1]	Native Hawaiian, Other Pacific Islander alone 2008	Two or more races 2000[1]	Two or more races 2008	Hispanic origin[2] 2000[1]	Hispanic origin[2] 2008	Not Hispanic White alone 2000[1]	Not Hispanic White alone 2008
Total	281,425	304,060	228,107	242,639	35,705	39,059	2,664	3,083	10,589	13,549	463	562	3,898	5,167	35,306	46,944	195,577	199,491
Under 5 years	19,176	21,006	14,657	15,771	2,925	3,150	233	286	708	931	41	51	613	817	3,718	5,288	11,288	11,065
5 to 9 years	20,550	20,065	15,688	15,287	3,320	2,939	258	247	716	845	44	45	524	701	3,624	4,464	12,392	11,222
10 to 14 years . . .	20,528	20,055	15,843	15,294	3,221	3,072	264	241	715	819	42	44	443	583	3,163	3,989	12,961	11,660
15 to 19 years . . .	20,219	21,514	15,745	16,417	3,024	3,445	251	273	776	827	44	46	380	506	3,172	3,850	12,836	12,903
20 to 24 years . . .	18,963	21,059	14,826	16,313	2,729	3,147	218	267	848	862	46	46	297	425	3,409	3,663	11,681	12,949
25 to 29 years . . .	19,382	21,334	15,217	16,570	2,645	3,038	204	252	1,019	1,055	42	50	254	368	3,385	4,141	12,077	12,740
30 to 34 years . . .	20,511	19,598	16,349	16,213	2,710	2,629	202	214	980	1,212	39	47	231	283	3,125	3,730	13,451	11,456
35 to 39 years . . .	22,707	20,994	18,372	16,448	2,910	2,741	217	209	937	1,292	38	43	233	283	2,825	3,279	15,753	12,981
40 to 44 years . . .	22,442	21,507	18,346	17,129	2,772	2,780	202	208	870	1,118	33	40	219	260	2,304	2,795	16,213	14,085
45 to 49 years . . .	20,093	22,880	16,615	18,556	2,330	2,821	169	212	770	1,021	27	38	183	232	1,775	2,187	14,973	15,964
50 to 54 years . . .	17,586	21,492	14,794	17,640	1,846	2,512	135	187	641	916	21	31	149	206	1,361	1,650	13,530	15,615
55 to 59 years . . .	13,469	18,583	11,479	15,436	1,332	2,027	95	151	443	779	15	25	106	166	960	1,204	10,582	13,907
60 to 64 years . . .	10,806	16,806	9,214	12,827	1,082	1,442	70	112	350	577	11	18	78	127	750	853	8,511	11,706
65 to 69 years . . .	9,534	11,349	8,238	9,696	895	1,055	52	77	279	419	8	13	61	88	599	653	7,675	8,899
70 to 74 years . . .	8,858	8,774	7,799	7,510	742	815	38	55	224	321	6	9	49	63	477	496	7,348	6,899
75 to 79 years . . .	7,416	7,275	6,634	6,338	557	603	27	40	159	242	4	7	36	46	327	346	6,325	5,871
80 to 84 years . . .	4,945	5,750	4,466	5,090	350	430	15	27	90	167	2	4	22	32	180	194	4,296	4,763
85 to 89 years . . .	2,790	3,572	2,525	3,191	200	250	8	15	43	94	1	2	12	19	98	82	2,432	3,007
90 to 94 years . . .	1,113	1,575	1,007	1,410	82	110	3	7	15	38	1	1	4	9	39	30	970	1,333
95 to 99 years . . .	287	483	254	424	27	41	1	3	4	11	–	–	1	3	11	7	243	396
100 years and over . .	50	92	41	78	7	10	–	1	1	2	–	–	–	1	3	2	39	71
5 to 13 years	37,026	36,005	28,381	27,452	5,923	5,358	471	438	1,288	1,501	78	80	885	1,175	6,186	7,661	22,754	20,475
14 to 17 years . . .	16,093	16,931	12,523	12,891	2,426	2,714	205	212	590	655	33	37	315	421	2,438	3,143	10,290	10,024
18 to 24 years . . .	27,141	29,757	21,197	22,968	3,944	4,531	315	378	1,178	1,197	64	64	444	619	4,744	5,162	16,827	18,235
16 years and over . .	217,151	238,734	178,790	193,094	25,633	29,220	1,857	2,257	8,304	10,790	328	413	2,237	2,960	24,204	32,412	156,352	163,073
18 years and over . .	209,130	230,118	172,546	186,525	24,431	27,836	1,755	2,147	8,003	10,462	311	394	2,084	2,754	22,964	30,851	151,245	157,928
16 to 64 years . . .	182,159	199,864	147,826	159,356	22,773	25,905	1,713	2,032	7,488	9,495	305	376	2,051	2,699	22,471	29,751	127,023	131,835
55 years and over . .	59,267	72,556	51,656	62,001	5,274	6,784	310	487	1,608	2,650	48	80	371	553	3,444	5,515	48,422	56,851
65 years and over . .	34,992	38,870	30,964	33,738	2,860	3,315	144	225	815	1,295	23	37	186	261	1,734	2,661	29,329	31,238
75 years and over . .	16,601	18,747	14,927	16,531	1,223	1,445	55	92	312	554	8	15	77	110	657	1,156	14,306	15,441
85 years and over . .	4,240	5,722	3,827	5,103	316	411	13	26	63	146	2	4	18	32	151	313	3,685	4,807
Median age (years) . . .	35.3	36.8	36.6	38.2	30.0	31.4	27.7	29.5	32.5	35.8	26.8	29.8	19.8	19.7	25.8	27.7	38.6	41.1

– Represents or rounds to zero.   [1] April 1, 2000, population estimates base reflects changes to the Census 2000 population from the Count Question Resolution program.   [2] Persons of Hispanic origin may be any race.

Source: U.S. Census Bureau, "Annual Estimates of the Population by Race, Hispanic Origin, Sex and Age for the United States: April 1, 2000 to July 1, 2008 (NC-EST2008-04)" (released May 14, 2009); <http://www.census.gov/popest/national/asrh/NC-EST2008-asrh.html>.

Table 10. Resident Population by Race, Hispanic Origin, and Single Years of Age: 2008

[In thousands, except as indicated (304,060 represents 304,060,000). **As of July 1.** For derivation of estimates, see text, this section]

Age	Total	Race White alone	Black or African American alone	American Indian, Alaska Native alone	Asian alone	Native Hawaiian and Other Pacific Islander alone	Two or more races	Hispanic origin [1]	Not-Hispanic White alone
Total........	**304,060**	**242,639**	**39,059**	**3,083**	**13,549**	**562**	**5,167**	**46,944**	**199,491**
Under 5 years old. . .	21,006	15,771	3,150	286	931	51	817	5,288	11,065
Under 1 year old. .	4,313	3,220	660	61	189	10	173	1,108	2,237
1 year old	4,276	3,187	660	60	189	10	169	1,109	2,204
2 years old	4,171	3,130	627	57	185	10	163	1,060	2,191
3 years old	4,122	3,104	610	55	185	10	157	1,023	2,196
4 years old	4,124	3,130	593	53	183	10	154	988	2,238
5 to 9 years old	20,065	15,287	2,939	247	845	45	701	4,464	11,222
5 years old	4,076	3,105	581	52	181	10	149	959	2,231
6 years old	4,044	3,081	588	50	173	9	144	934	2,226
7 years old	4,100	3,118	604	50	175	9	143	919	2,281
8 years old	3,945	3,008	585	48	159	9	135	848	2,239
9 years old	3,900	2,976	581	47	157	9	130	804	2,246
10 to 14 years old . .	20,055	15,294	3,072	241	819	44	583	3,989	11,660
10 years old	3,908	2,978	589	47	161	9	125	798	2,253
11 years old	3,934	3,002	593	47	164	9	119	796	2,278
12 years old	4,016	3,070	605	48	167	9	117	802	2,339
13 years old	4,081	3,114	632	49	164	9	113	802	2,383
14 years old	4,115	3,130	653	50	163	9	109	792	2,407
15 to 19 years old . .	21,514	16,417	3,445	273	827	46	506	3,850	12,903
15 years old	4,200	3,192	677	52	164	9	106	790	2,471
16 years old	4,272	3,255	686	55	164	9	104	785	2,538
17 years old	4,344	3,315	698	55	164	9	102	776	2,607
18 years old	4,426	3,382	711	56	167	9	100	771	2,678
19 years old	4,272	3,274	673	55	168	9	94	728	2,609
20 to 24 years old . .	21,059	16,313	3,147	267	862	46	425	3,663	12,949
20 years old	4,217	3,248	650	54	166	9	90	725	2,585
21 years old	4,186	3,238	633	53	165	9	87	720	2,579
22 years old	4,222	3,273	629	53	172	9	85	726	2,607
23 years old	4,251	3,304	625	53	176	9	83	740	2,624
24 years old	4,183	3,249	610	53	182	9	80	753	2,555
25 to 29 years old . .	21,334	16,570	3,038	252	1,055	50	368	4,141	12,740
25 years old	4,259	3,313	614	54	191	9	79	792	2,581
26 years old	4,293	3,337	614	51	203	10	77	824	2,574
27 years old	4,337	3,371	615	51	215	10	75	838	2,596
28 years old	4,325	3,355	617	50	222	11	71	858	2,561
29 years old	4,119	3,194	578	46	224	10	66	828	2,428
30 to 34 years old . .	19,598	15,213	2,629	214	1,212	47	283	4,041	11,456
30 years old	4,005	3,116	547	45	225	10	62	826	2,350
31 years old	3,949	3,068	536	44	233	10	59	821	2,306
32 years old	3,849	2,985	514	42	242	10	56	812	2,230
33 years old	3,956	3,069	524	42	256	9	55	808	2,317
34 years old	3,840	2,975	507	41	256	9	52	774	2,254
35 to 39 years old . .	20,994	16,448	2,741	209	1,292	43	260	3,730	12,981
35 years old	3,931	3,038	527	41	263	9	52	770	2,322
36 years old	4,118	3,204	546	42	264	9	53	760	2,497
37 years old	4,344	3,410	569	43	259	9	54	752	2,711
38 years old	4,423	3,485	572	43	261	9	53	752	2,787
39 years old	4,179	3,309	528	40	244	8	49	696	2,663
40 to 44 years old . .	21,507	17,129	2,780	208	1,118	40	233	3,279	14,085
40 years old	4,101	3,243	530	40	234	8	46	681	2,610
41 years old	4,109	3,271	528	40	218	8	45	654	2,664
42 years old	4,222	3,353	554	41	219	8	46	653	2,747
43 years old	4,506	3,594	588	43	225	8	48	658	2,982
44 years old	4,570	3,668	580	44	222	8	48	632	3,082
45 to 49 years old . .	22,880	18,556	2,821	212	1,021	38	232	2,795	15,964
45 years old	4,551	3,665	569	43	219	8	47	600	3,109
46 years old	4,561	3,699	562	43	203	8	47	580	3,161
47 years old	4,603	3,747	561	42	199	7	46	555	3,233
48 years old	4,680	3,791	583	43	208	8	47	558 ·	3,273
49 years old	4,484	3,655	545	40	192	7	45	503	3,189

See footnote at end of table.

U.S. Census Bureau, Statistical Abstract of the United States: 2010

Table 10. **Resident Population by Race, Hispanic Origin, and Single Years of Age: 2008**—Con.

[In thousands, except as indicated (304,060 represents 304,060,000). As of July 1. For derivation of estimates, see text, this section]

Age	Total	Race						Hispanic origin [1]	Not-Hispanic White alone
		White alone	Black or African American alone	American Indian, Alaska Native alone	Asian alone	Native Hawaiian and Other Pacific Islander alone	Two or more races		
50 to 54 years old ..	21,492	17,640	2,512	187	916	31	206	2,187	15,615
50 years old.....	4,484	3,667	533	40	193	7	44	478	3,224
51 years old.....	4,426	3,628	525	39	186	6	43	460	3,202
52 years old.....	4,249	3,484	497	37	183	6	41	435	3,081
53 years old.....	4,262	3,500	495	37	184	6	40	426	3,106
54 years old.....	4,071	3,361	461	35	171	6	38	388	3,002
55 to 59 years old ..	18,583	15,436	2,027	151	779	25	166	1,650	13,907
55 years old.....	3,930	3,259	432	33	165	5	36	364	2,922
56 years old.....	3,792	3,153	412	31	157	5	34	340	2,838
57 years old.....	3,686	3,060	407	30	151	5	33	328	2,756
58 years old.....	3,664	3,030	407	30	160	5	32	326	2,729
59 years old.....	3,511	2,935	369	27	145	5	30	293	2,663
60 to 64 years old ..	15,103	12,827	1,442	112	577	18	127	1,204	11,706
60 years old.....	3,472	2,929	346	26	137	4	30	279	2,670
61 years old.....	3,638	3,124	327	26	127	4	30	265	2,877
62 years old.....	2,694	2,274	263	20	109	4	23	233	2,058
63 years old.....	2,677	2,264	262	20	105	3	22	221	2,057
64 years old.....	2,622	2,236	244	19	98	3	21	205	2,045
65 to 69 years old ..	11,349	9,696	1,055	77	419	13	88	853	8,899
65 years old.....	2,702	2,327	242	18	91	3	21	194	2,146
66 years old.....	2,367	2,024	217	16	88	3	18	176	1,859
67 years old.....	2,183	1,859	206	15	83	3	17	166	1,703
68 years old.....	2,109	1,787	207	15	82	3	16	164	1,633
69 years old.....	1,988	1,700	184	13	74	2	15	152	1,558
70 to 74 years old ..	8,774	7,510	815	55	321	9	63	653	6,899
70 years old.....	1,934	1,653	180	13	72	2	14	145	1,518
71 years old.....	1,801	1,540	167	12	67	2	13	136	1,413
72 years old.....	1,748	1,495	164	11	64	2	12	130	1,373
73 years old.....	1,732	1,484	161	11	62	2	12	129	1,363
74 years old.....	1,559	1,338	143	9	56	2	11	114	1,231
75 to 79 years old ..	7,275	6,338	603	40	242	7	46	496	5,871
75 years old.....	1,540	1,326	138	9	55	2	10	107	1,225
76 years old.....	1,496	1,300	126	8	50	1	10	103	1,203
77 years old.....	1,454	1,274	115	8	48	1	9	99	1,180
78 years old.....	1,451	1,266	119	8	48	1	9	99	1,173
79 years old.....	1,334	1,172	104	7	42	1	8	88	1,089
80 to 84 years old ..	5,750	5,090	430	27	167	4	32	346	4,763
80 years old.....	1,298	1,145	99	6	40	1	8	82	1,067
81 years old.....	1,226	1,084	93	6	36	1	7	74	1,014
82 years old.....	1,138	1,006	86	5	33	1	6	69	941
83 years old.....	1,091	967	81	5	31	1	6	64	907
84 years old.....	996	887	71	4	27	1	5	57	833
85 to 89 years old ..	3,572	3,191	250	15	94	2	19	194	3,007
90 to 94 years old ..	1,575	1,410	110	7	38	1	9	82	1,333
95 to 99 years old ..	483	424	41	3	11	–	3	30	396
100 years old and over...........	92	78	10	1	2	–	1	7	71
Median age (years)..	36.8	38.2	31.4	29.5	35.8	29.8	19.7	27.7	41.1

– Represents or rounds to zero.   [1] Persons of Hispanic origin may be any race.

Source: U.S. Census Bureau, "Monthly Resident Population Estimates by Age, Sex, Race and Hispanic Origin for the United States: April 1, 2000 to July 1, 2008" (released May 14, 2009); <http://www.census.gov/popest/national/asrh/2008-nat-res.html>.

Table 11. Resident Population Projections by Race, Hispanic-Origin Status, and Age: 2010 and 2015

[In thousands (310,233 represents 310,233,000), except as indicated. As of July 1. Projections are based on assumptions about future births, deaths, and net international migration. More information on methodology and assumptions is available at <http://www.census.gov/population/www/projections/methodstatement.html>. For definition of median, see Guide to Tabular Presentation]

Age group	Total		White alone		Black alone		American Indian and Alaska Native alone		Asian alone		Native Hawaiian, Other Pacific Islander alone		Two or more races		Hispanic origin [1]		White alone, not of Hispanic origin	
	2010	2015	2010	2015	2010	2015	2010	2015	2010	2015	2010	2015	2010	2015	2010	2015	2010	2015
Total	310,233	325,540	246,630	256,306	39,909	42,137	3,188	3,472	14,415	16,527	592	662	5,499	6,435	49,726	57,711	200,853	203,208
Under 5 years	21,100	22,076	15,944	16,563	3,034	3,191	286	311	943	1,004	53	56	840	951	5,053	5,622	11,375	11,487
5 to 9 years	20,886	21,707	15,888	16,412	3,011	3,084	264	292	927	1,018	49	55	746	845	4,888	5,452	11,448	11,465
10 to 14 years	20,395	21,658	15,560	16,467	3,021	3,080	244	271	894	1,034	45	52	631	754	4,513	5,401	11,440	11,540
15 to 19 years	21,770	21,209	16,570	16,143	3,410	3,096	268	252	932	1,030	48	48	541	639	4,473	5,040	12,472	11,524
20 to 24 years	21,779	22,342	16,731	16,976	3,330	3,449	275	273	938	1,047	47	50	459	546	4,010	4,873	13,049	12,499
25 to 29 years	21,418	22,440	16,544	17,125	3,107	3,374	261	279	1,063	1,106	48	49	395	467	3,887	4,311	12,959	13,160
30 to 34 years	20,400	22,099	15,711	16,915	2,845	3,158	228	264	1,245	1,305	52	52	319	405	4,039	4,166	11,974	13,068
35 to 39 years	20,267	20,841	15,674	15,946	2,691	2,872	210	230	1,376	1,413	47	54	269	325	3,868	4,236	12,078	12,023
40 to 44 years	21,010	20,460	16,610	15,763	2,713	2,690	205	211	1,199	1,476	42	48	241	272	3,431	3,979	13,423	12,062
45 to 49 years	22,596	21,001	18,202	16,561	2,838	2,679	216	204	1,064	1,272	40	43	236	242	3,002	3,491	15,415	13,316
50 to 54 years	22,109	22,367	18,049	17,691	2,650	2,765	200	214	957	1,115	34	40	219	234	2,425	3,036	15,800	15,177
55 to 59 years	19,517	21,682	16,134	17,561	2,170	2,545	165	196	840	1,001	27	34	181	216	1,862	2,450	14,409	15,417
60 to 64 years	16,758	18,861	14,087	15,582	1,671	2,042	130	160	704	875	21	27	145	176	1,417	1,867	12,769	13,849
65 to 69 years	12,261	15,812	10,446	13,285	1,130	1,528	87	123	483	717	15	21	99	138	974	1,387	9,534	11,994
70 to 74 years	9,202	11,155	7,867	9,511	845	990	61	80	350	469	10	14	69	91	710	920	7,201	8,650
75 to 79 years	7,282	7,901	6,331	6,780	619	690	41	53	236	310	7	9	48	60	514	637	5,848	6,183
80 to 84 years	5,733	5,676	5,093	4,957	427	458	26	32	151	186	4	5	33	38	354	424	4,759	4,558
85 to 89 years	3,650	3,786	3,290	3,374	247	271	14	17	78	99	2	3	19	22	195	257	3,106	3,131
90 to 94 years	1,570	1,866	1,423	1,674	106	125	5	7	27	39	1	1	8	10	78	117	1,350	1,564
95 to 99 years	452	546	407	492	35	40	1	2	7	9	–	–	2	3	26	35	383	459
100 years and over	79	105	69	92	8	10	–	–	1	1	–	–	1	1	6	9	63	83
5 to 13 years	37,123	39,011	28,273	29,577	5,412	5,529	459	511	1,636	1,844	85	97	1,259	1,454	8,501	9,786	20,536	20,678
14 to 17 years	16,994	17,019	12,941	12,937	2,619	2,478	205	204	741	818	38	39	450	543	3,585	4,112	9,648	9,175
18 to 24 years	30,713	30,885	23,536	23,483	4,741	4,703	387	374	1,315	1,468	66	70	668	787	5,788	6,869	18,225	17,173
16 years and over	243,639	255,864	196,026	203,643	30,201	32,171	2,343	2,547	11,466	13,267	435	489	3,168	3,747	34,372	40,202	164,202	166,441
18 years and over	235,016	247,434	189,473	197,229	28,844	30,940	2,237	2,446	11,095	12,861	416	470	2,950	3,487	32,576	38,192	159,295	161,868
16 to 64 years	203,410	209,027	161,100	163,478	26,783	28,059	2,108	2,232	10,132	11,437	397	436	2,890	3,384	31,515	36,416	131,959	129,819
55 years and over	76,504	87,381	65,147	73,437	7,258	8,698	531	671	2,877	3,706	87	114	604	755	6,136	8,104	59,421	65,888
65 years and over	40,229	46,837	34,926	40,164	3,418	4,111	235	314	1,333	1,831	39	53	278	363	2,858	3,786	32,243	36,623
75 years and over	18,766	19,870	16,613	17,368	1,442	1,594	87	111	500	645	14	18	110	133	1,173	1,479	15,509	15,978
85 years and over	5,751	6,292	5,189	5,632	397	445	20	26	113	149	3	4	29	36	305	418	4,902	5,238
Median age (yrs.)	36.9	37.1	38.4	38.6	31.7	32.8	29.9	31.1	36.0	37.5	30.5	32.0	19.9	20.2	27.5	27.8	41.3	42.1

– Represents or rounds to zero. [1] Persons of Hispanic origin may be any race.

Source: U.S. Census Bureau, "2008 National Population Projections," released August 2008; <http://www.census.gov/population/www/projections/2008projections.html>.

U.S. Census Bureau, Statistical Abstract of the United States: 2010

Figure 1.2
Center of Population: 1790 to 2000

[Prior to 1960, excludes Alaska and Hawaii. The median center is located at the intersection of two median lines, a north-south line constructed so that half of the nation's population lives east and half lives west of it, and an east-west line selected so that half of the nation's population lives north and half lives south of it. The mean center of population is that point at which an imaginary, flat, weightless, and rigid map of the United States would balance if weights of identical value were placed on it so that each weight represented the location of one person on the date of the census]

Year	Median center		Mean center		
	Latitude-N	Longitude	Latitude-N	Longitude-W	Approximate location
1790 (August 2)	(NA)	(NA)	39 16 30	76 11 12	In Kent County, MD, 23 miles E of Baltimore MD
1850 (June 1)..	(NA)	(NA)	38 59 00	81 19 00	In Wirt County, WV, 23 miles SE of Parkersburg, WV[1]
1900 (June 1)..	40 03 32	84 49 01	39 09 36	85 48 54	In Bartholomew County, IN, 6 miles SE of Columbus, IN
1950 (April 1)..	40 00 12	84 56 51	38 50 21	88 09 33	In Richland County, IL, 8 miles NNW of Olney, IL
1960 (April 1)..	39 56 25	85 16 60	38 35 58	89 12 35	In Clinton County, IL, 6.5 miles NW of Centralia, IL
1970 (April 1) .	39 47 43	85 31 43	38 27 47	89 42 22	In St. Clair County, IL, 5.3 miles ESE of Mascoutah, IL
1980 (April 1)..	39 18 60	86 08 15	38 08 13	90 34 26	In Jefferson County, MO, .25 mile W of DeSoto, MO
1990 (April 1)..	38 57 55	86 31 53	37 52 20	91 12 55	In Crawford County, MO, 10 miles SE of Steelville, MO
2000 (April 1)..	38 45 23	86 55 51	37 41 49	91 48 34	In Phelps County, MO, 3 miles E of Edgar Springs, MO

NA Not available.   [1]West Virginia was set off from Virginia, Dec. 31, 1862, and admitted as a state, June 19, 1863.

U.S. Census Bureau, Statistical Abstract of the United States: 2010

Table 12. **Resident Population—States: 1980 to 2008**

[In thousands (226,546 represents 226,546,000). 1980, 1990, and 2000 data as of April 1, data for other years as of July 1. Insofar as possible, population shown for all years is that of present area of state. See Appendix III]

State	1980 [1]	1990, estimates base [2]	2000, estimates base [3]	2003	2004	2005	2006	2007	2008
United States	226,546	248,791	281,425	290,211	292,892	295,561	298,363	301,290	304,060
Alabama.	3,894	4,040	4,447	4,487	4,507	4,537	4,588	4,627	4,662
Alaska	402	550	627	650	661	669	676	681	686
Arizona.	2,718	3,665	5,131	5,586	5,750	5,961	6,178	6,353	6,500
Arkansas	2,286	2,351	2,673	2,718	2,740	2,769	2,804	2,831	2,855
California	23,668	29,811	33,872	35,307	35,630	35,885	36,121	36,378	36,757
Colorado.	2,890	3,294	4,302	4,548	4,600	4,663	4,751	4,843	4,939
Connecticut.	3,108	3,287	3,406	3,468	3,475	3,479	3,488	3,490	3,501
Delaware	594	666	784	814	826	839	850	862	873
District of Columbia	638	607	572	577	580	582	585	588	592
Florida	9,746	12,938	15,983	16,937	17,314	17,702	18,019	18,200	18,328
Georgia	5,463	6,478	8,187	8,733	8,911	9,094	9,319	9,523	9,686
Hawaii	965	1,108	1,212	1,238	1,252	1,264	1,275	1,277	1,288
Idaho	944	1,007	1,294	1,363	1,390	1,424	1,461	1,496	1,524
Illinois	11,427	11,431	12,420	12,611	12,666	12,704	12,760	12,826	12,902
Indiana.	5,490	5,544	6,081	6,179	6,211	6,249	6,294	6,336	6,377
Iowa	2,914	2,777	2,926	2,933	2,943	2,952	2,967	2,983	3,003
Kansas.	2,364	2,478	2,689	2,722	2,731	2,742	2,756	2,777	2,802
Kentucky	3,661	3,687	4,042	4,111	4,136	4,166	4,199	4,236	4,269
Louisiana	4,206	4,222	4,469	4,474	4,488	4,496	4,244	4,373	4,411
Maine.	1,125	1,228	1,275	1,303	1,308	1,311	1,313	1,315	1,316
Maryland	4,217	4,781	5,297	5,495	5,539	5,576	5,602	5,619	5,634
Massachusetts.	5,737	6,016	6,349	6,441	6,437	6,434	6,443	6,468	6,498
Michigan.	9,262	9,295	9,938	10,066	10,090	10,093	10,084	10,050	10,003
Minnesota.	4,076	4,376	4,919	5,047	5,078	5,105	5,143	5,182	5,220
Mississippi	2,521	2,575	2,845	2,867	2,885	2,898	2,897	2,921	2,939
Missouri	4,917	5,117	5,597	5,705	5,743	5,785	5,833	5,878	5,912
Montana	787	799	902	917	926	935	945	957	967
Nebraska	1,570	1,578	1,711	1,733	1,741	1,751	1,760	1,769	1,783
Nevada	800	1,202	1,998	2,234	2,324	2,402	2,484	2,554	2,600
New Hampshire	921	1,109	1,236	1,281	1,292	1,301	1,309	1,312	1,316
New Jersey.	7,365	7,748	8,414	8,590	8,621	8,635	8,640	8,653	8,683
New Mexico	1,303	1,515	1,819	1,868	1,889	1,913	1,938	1,964	1,984
New York	17,558	17,991	18,977	19,231	19,301	19,336	19,367	19,429	19,490
North Carolina	5,882	6,632	8,047	8,410	8,523	8,661	8,845	9,042	9,222
North Dakota	653	639	642	633	636	635	636	638	641
Ohio	10,798	10,847	11,353	11,430	11,445	11,451	11,458	11,478	11,486
Oklahoma.	3,025	3,146	3,451	3,496	3,512	3,530	3,568	3,608	3,642
Oregon.	2,633	2,842	3,421	3,552	3,576	3,622	3,681	3,736	3,790
Pennsylvania.	11,864	11,883	12,281	12,318	12,336	12,352	12,388	12,420	12,448
Rhode Island.	947	1,003	1,048	1,071	1,071	1,064	1,059	1,053	1,051
South Carolina.	3,122	3,486	4,012	4,143	4,197	4,249	4,325	4,405	4,480
South Dakota	691	696	755	766	774	779	787	796	804
Tennessee	4,591	4,877	5,689	5,850	5,907	5,983	6,068	6,149	6,215
Texas	14,229	16,986	20,852	22,062	22,425	22,811	23,368	23,843	24,327
Utah	1,461	1,723	2,233	2,380	2,440	2,501	2,585	2,669	2,736
Vermont	511	563	609	617	618	619	620	621	621
Virginia.	5,347	6,189	7,079	7,363	7,455	7,547	7,628	7,699	7,769
Washington.	4,132	4,867	5,894	6,110	6,180	6,255	6,361	6,450	6,549
West Virginia.	1,950	1,793	1,808	1,802	1,803	1,804	1,807	1,810	1,814
Wisconsin.	4,706	4,892	5,364	5,474	5,509	5,539	5,569	5,599	5,628
Wyoming	470	454	494	499	503	506	513	523	533

[1] See footnote 3, Table 1. [2] The April 1, 1990, census counts include corrections processed through August 1997, results of special censuses and test censuses, and do not include adjustments for census coverage errors. [3] Reflects modifications to the Census 2000 population as documented in the Count Question Resolution program and geographic program revisions.

Source: U.S. Census Bureau, Current Population Reports, P25-1106; "Table CO-EST2001-12-00—Time Series of Intercensal State Populaton Estimates: April 1, 1990 to April 1, 2000" (published 11 April 2002); <http://www.census.gov/popest/archives /2000s/vintage2001/CO-EST2001-12/CO-EST2001-12-00.html>; and "Table 1: Annual Estimates of the Resident Population for the United States, Regions, States, and Puerto Rico: April 1, 2000 to July 1, 2008 (NST-EST2008-01)" (published 22 December 2008); <http://www.census.gov/popest/states/NST-ann-est.html>.

18   Population

Table 13. **State Population—Rank, Percent Change, and Population Density: 1980 to 2008**

[**As of April 1, except 2008, as of July 1.** Insofar as possible, population shown for all years is that of present area of state. Minus sign (–) indicates decrease. See Appendix III]

State	Rank				Percent change			Population per square mile of land area [1]		
	1980	1990	2000	2008	1980-1990	1990-2000	2000-2008	1990	2000	2008
United States.	(X)	(X)	(X)	(X)	9.8	13.1	8.0	70.3	79.6	86.0
Alabama	22	22	23	23	3.8	10.1	4.8	79.6	87.6	91.9
Alaska	50	49	48	47	36.9	14.0	9.5	1.0	1.1	1.2
Arizona	29	24	20	14	34.8	40.0	26.7	32.3	45.2	57.2
Arkansas	33	33	33	32	2.8	13.7	6.8	45.1	51.3	54.8
California	1	1	1	1	26.0	13.6	8.5	191.1	217.2	235.7
Colorado	28	26	24	22	14.0	30.6	14.8	31.8	41.5	47.6
Connecticut	25	27	29	29	5.8	3.6	2.8	678.5	702.9	722.7
Delaware	47	46	45	45	12.1	17.6	11.4	341.0	401.1	446.9
District of Columbia . . .	(X)	(X)	(X)	(X)	–4.9	–5.7	3.5	9,884.4	9,316.4	9,639.0
Florida	7	4	4	4	32.7	23.5	14.7	239.9	296.4	339.9
Georgia	13	11	10	9	18.6	26.4	18.3	111.9	141.4	167.3
Hawaii	39	41	42	42	14.9	9.3	6.3	172.6	188.6	200.6
Idaho	41	42	39	39	6.7	28.5	17.8	12.2	15.6	18.4
Illinois	5	6	5	5	(Z)	8.6	3.9	205.6	223.4	232.1
Indiana	12	14	14	16	1.0	9.7	4.9	154.6	169.5	177.8
Iowa	27	30	30	30	–4.7	5.4	2.6	49.7	52.4	53.7
Kansas	32	32	32	33	4.8	8.5	4.2	30.3	32.9	34.2
Kentucky	23	23	25	26	0.7	9.6	5.6	92.8	101.7	107.5
Louisiana	19	21	22	25	0.4	5.9	–1.3	96.9	102.6	101.3
Maine	38	38	40	40	9.2	3.8	3.3	39.8	41.3	42.7
Maryland	18	19	19	19	13.4	10.8	6.4	489.1	541.9	576.4
Massachusetts	11	13	13	15	4.9	5.5	2.3	767.4	809.8	828.8
Michigan	8	8	8	8	0.4	6.9	0.7	163.6	175.0	176.1
Minnesota	21	20	21	21	7.4	12.4	6.1	55.0	61.8	65.6
Mississippi	31	31	31	31	2.2	10.5	3.3	54.9	60.6	62.6
Missouri	15	15	17	18	4.1	9.3	5.6	74.3	81.2	85.8
Montana	44	44	44	44	1.6	12.9	7.2	5.5	6.2	6.6
Nebraska	35	36	38	38	0.5	8.4	4.2	20.5	22.3	23.2
Nevada	43	39	35	35	50.1	66.3	30.1	10.9	18.2	23.7
New Hampshire	42	40	41	41	20.5	11.4	6.5	123.7	137.8	146.7
New Jersey	9	9	9	11	5.2	8.6	3.2	1,044.5	1,134.4	1,170.6
New Mexico	37	37	36	36	16.3	20.1	9.1	12.5	15.0	16.4
New York	2	2	3	3	2.5	5.5	2.7	381.0	401.9	412.8
North Carolina	10	10	11	10	12.8	21.4	14.6	136.2	165.2	189.3
North Dakota	46	47	47	48	–2.1	0.5	–0.1	9.3	9.3	9.3
Ohio	6	7	7	7	0.5	4.7	1.2	264.9	277.3	280.5
Oklahoma	26	28	27	28	4.0	9.7	5.6	45.8	50.3	53.0
Oregon	30	29	28	27	7.9	20.4	10.8	29.6	35.6	39.5
Pennsylvania	4	5	6	6	0.2	3.4	1.4	265.1	274.0	277.8
Rhode Island	40	43	43	43	5.9	4.5	0.2	960.3	1,003.2	1,005.6
South Carolina	24	25	26	24	11.7	15.1	11.7	115.8	133.2	148.8
South Dakota	45	45	46	46	0.8	8.5	6.5	9.2	9.9	10.6
Tennessee	17	17	16	17	6.2	16.7	9.2	118.3	138.0	150.8
Texas	3	3	2	2	19.4	22.8	16.7	64.9	79.6	92.9
Utah	36	35	34	34	17.9	29.6	22.5	21.0	27.2	33.3
Vermont	48	48	49	49	10.0	8.2	2.0	60.8	65.8	67.2
Virginia	14	12	12	12	15.8	14.4	9.7	156.3	178.8	196.2
Washington	20	18	15	13	17.8	21.1	11.1	73.1	88.6	98.4
West Virginia	34	34	37	37	–8.0	0.8	0.3	74.5	75.1	75.4
Wisconsin	16	16	18	20	4.0	9.6	4.9	90.1	98.8	103.6
Wyoming	49	50	50	50	–3.4	8.9	7.9	4.7	5.1	5.5

X Not applicable.   Z Less than 0.05 percent.   [1] Persons per square mile were calculated on the basis of land area data from the 2000 census.

Source: U.S. Census Bureau, Current Population Reports, P25-1106; "ST-99-3 State Population Estimates: Annual Time Series, July 1, 1990 to July 1, 1999" (published 29 December 1999); <http://www.census.gov/population/estimates/state/st-99 -3.txt>; "Table CO-EST2001-12-00—Time Series of Intercensal State Population Estimates: April1, 1990 to April1, 2000" (released April 11, 2002); <http://www.census.gov/popest/archives/2000s/vintage2001/CO-EST2001-12/CO-EST2001-12-00.html>; and "Table 2: Cumulative Estimates of Resident Population Change for the United States, Regions, States, and Puerto Rico and Region and State Rankings: April 1, 2000 to July 1, 2008 (NST-EST2008-02)" (released December 22, 2008); <http://www.census.gov/popest/states /NST-pop-chg.html>.

U.S. Census Bureau, Statistical Abstract of the United States: 2010

Table 14. State Resident Population—Projections: 2010 to 2030

[As of July 1. **4,596 represents 4,596,000.** These state projections were produced in correspondence with the U.S. interim projections released in March 2004. Projections in this table were developed for each of the 50 states and the District of Columbia by age and sex for the years 2000 to 2030, based on Census 2000 results. These projections differ from forecasts in that they represent the results of the mathematical projection model given that current state-specific trends in fertility, mortality, domestic migration, and net international migration continue. The projections to 2008 have been superseded by population estimates which are shown in Table 12. Minus sign (−) indicates decrease]

State	Number (1,000)					Change, 2000–2030		Rank	
	2010	2015	2020	2025	2030	Number (1,000)	Percent	Total population, 2030	Percent change, 2000–2030
Alabama	4,596	4,663	4,729	4,800	4,874	427	9.6	24	35
Alaska	694	733	774	821	868	241	38.4	46	12
Arizona	6,637	7,495	8,456	9,532	10,712	5,582	108.8	10	2
Arkansas	2,875	2,969	3,060	3,151	3,240	567	21.2	32	21
California	38,067	40,123	42,207	44,305	46,445	12,573	37.1	1	13
Colorado	4,832	5,049	5,279	5,523	5,792	1,491	34.7	22	14
Connecticut	3,577	3,635	3,676	3,691	3,689	283	8.3	30	38
Delaware	884	927	963	991	1,013	229	29.2	45	18
District of Columbia . . .	530	506	481	455	433	−139	−24.2	(X)	(X)
Florida	19,252	21,204	23,407	25,912	28,686	12,703	79.5	3	3
Georgia	9,589	10,231	10,844	11,439	12,018	3,831	46.8	8	8
Hawaii	1,341	1,386	1,412	1,439	1,466	255	21.0	41	22
Idaho	1,517	1,630	1,741	1,853	1,970	676	52.2	37	6
Illinois	12,917	13,097	13,237	13,341	13,433	1,014	8.2	5	39
Indiana	6,392	6,518	6,627	6,721	6,810	730	12.0	18	31
Iowa	3,010	3,026	3,020	2,993	2,955	29	1.0	34	48
Kansas	2,805	2,853	2,891	2,919	2,940	252	9.4	35	36
Kentucky	4,265	4,351	4,424	4,490	4,555	513	12.7	27	30
Louisiana	4,613	4,674	4,719	4,762	4,803	334	7.5	26	41
Maine	1,357	1,389	1,409	1,414	1,411	136	10.7	42	32
Maryland	5,905	6,208	6,498	6,763	7,022	1,726	32.6	16	16
Massachusetts	6,649	6,759	6,856	6,939	7,012	663	10.4	17	33
Michigan	10,429	10,599	10,696	10,714	10,694	756	7.6	11	40
Minnesota	5,421	5,668	5,901	6,109	6,306	1,387	28.2	20	20
Mississippi	2,971	3,014	3,045	3,069	3,092	248	8.7	33	37
Missouri	5,922	6,070	6,200	6,315	6,430	835	14.9	19	27
Montana	969	999	1,023	1,037	1,045	143	15.8	44	25
Nebraska	1,769	1,789	1,803	1,813	1,820	109	6.4	38	42
Nevada	2,691	3,058	3,452	3,863	4,282	2,284	114.3	28	1
New Hampshire	1,386	1,457	1,525	1,586	1,646	411	33.2	40	15
New Jersey	9,018	9,256	9,462	9,637	9,802	1,388	16.5	13	24
New Mexico	1,980	2,042	2,084	2,107	2,100	281	15.4	36	26
New York	19,444	19,547	19,577	19,540	19,477	501	2.6	4	46
North Carolina	9,346	10,011	10,709	11,449	12,228	4,178	51.9	7	7
North Dakota	637	635	630	621	607	−36	−5.5	49	50
Ohio	11,576	11,635	11,644	11,606	11,551	197	1.7	9	47
Oklahoma	3,592	3,662	3,736	3,821	3,913	463	13.4	29	29
Oregon	3,791	4,013	4,260	4,536	4,834	1,413	41.3	25	10
Pennsylvania	12,584	12,711	12,787	12,802	12,768	487	4.0	6	45
Rhode Island	1,117	1,140	1,154	1,158	1,153	105	10.0	43	34
South Carolina	4,447	4,642	4,823	4,990	5,149	1,137	28.3	23	19
South Dakota	786	797	802	802	800	46	6.0	47	43
Tennessee	6,231	6,502	6,781	7,073	7,381	1,691	29.7	15	17
Texas	24,649	26,586	28,635	30,865	33,318	12,466	59.8	2	4
Utah	2,595	2,783	2,990	3,226	3,485	1,252	56.1	31	5
Vermont	653	673	691	703	712	103	16.9	48	23
Virginia	8,010	8,467	8,917	9,364	9,825	2,747	38.8	12	11
Washington	6,542	6,951	7,432	7,996	8,625	2,731	46.3	14	9
West Virginia	1,829	1,823	1,801	1,766	1,720	−88	−4.9	39	49
Wisconsin	5,727	5,883	6,005	6,088	6,151	787	14.7	21	28
Wyoming	520	528	531	529	523	29	5.9	50	44

X Not applicable.

Source: U.S. Census Bureau, "Table A1: Interim Projections of the Total Population for the United States and States: April 1, 2000 to July 1, 2030"; published 21 April 2005; <http://www.census.gov/population/www/projections/projectionsagesex.html>.

20   Population

Table 15. **State Resident Population—Components of Change: 2000 to 2008**

[**Covers period April 1, 2000, to July 1, 2008**. Minus sign (–) indicates net decrease or net outflow]

State	Numeric population change [1]	Births	Deaths	Natural increase (births minus deaths)	Net migration Total	Net migration Inter-national [2]	Net migration Domestic
United States	22,635,122	34,126,003	20,001,837	14,124,166	8,114,516	8,114,516	(X)
Alabama.	214,545	502,457	381,403	121,054	104,991	31,180	73,811
Alaska	59,362	86,062	25,068	60,994	–5,469	4,418	–9,887
Arizona.	1,369,573	777,821	358,950	418,871	934,622	216,347	718,275
Arkansas	182,004	321,462	228,239	93,223	96,503	27,399	69,104
California	2,885,016	4,498,700	1,949,619	2,549,081	446,991	1,825,697	–1,378,706
Colorado.	637,441	572,317	238,415	333,902	311,974	142,990	168,984
Connecticut.	95,648	349,142	240,639	108,503	5,127	102,954	–97,827
Delaware	89,497	94,756	58,098	36,658	56,652	14,270	42,382
District of Columbia	19,780	65,262	45,978	19,284	–19,173	26,071	–45,244
Florida	2,345,527	1,807,546	1,402,089	405,457	1,973,423	694,850	1,278,573
Georgia	1,498,932	1,152,539	547,410	605,129	785,691	243,788	541,903
Hawaii	76,660	149,871	73,124	76,747	5,035	31,317	–26,282
Idaho	229,861	185,668	84,458	101,210	131,362	17,780	113,582
Illinois	481,903	1,505,709	860,742	644,967	–159,182	425,893	–585,075
Indiana.	296,270	721,567	457,005	264,562	53,231	70,998	–17,767
Iowa	76,174	322,292	226,042	96,250	–13,010	36,665	–49,675
Kansas.	113,318	330,717	199,889	130,828	–21,213	46,742	–67,955
Kentucky	226,961	461,118	330,473	130,645	105,235	31,392	73,843
Louisiana	–58,172	529,099	343,559	185,540	–302,162	23,233	–325,395
Maine.	41,534	115,128	102,476	12,652	34,624	5,371	29,253
Maryland	337,081	618,156	361,871	256,285	51,063	137,096	–86,033
Massachusetts.	148,854	654,936	455,424	199,512	–84,830	212,930	–297,760
Michigan.	64,930	1,076,193	709,627	366,566	–315,621	157,174	–472,795
Minnesota.	300,901	581,309	310,702	270,607	48,311	90,111	–41,800
Mississippi	93,952	359,230	232,926	126,304	–17,028	10,717	–27,745
Missouri	314,927	647,107	447,939	199,168	90,674	52,563	38,111
Montana.	65,250	96,154	68,168	27,986	38,505	2,178	36,327
Nebraska	72,166	214,642	124,319	90,323	–11,435	27,560	–38,995
Nevada	601,910	291,976	146,164	145,812	463,706	85,475	378,231
New Hampshire	80,024	121,931	82,247	39,684	46,235	14,241	31,994
New Jersey.	268,301	933,185	589,220	343,965	–53,930	384,687	–438,617
New Mexico	165,315	235,551	120,968	114,583	59,499	34,375	25,124
New York	513,481	2,072,765	1,269,085	803,680	–698,895	876,969	–1,575,864
North Carolina	1,175,914	1,015,065	602,159	412,906	783,382	192,099	591,283
North Dakota.	–714	67,788	47,328	20,460	–17,787	3,323	–21,110
Ohio	132,750	1,245,352	891,908	353,444	–249,542	96,251	–345,793
Oklahoma.	191,721	429,240	290,192	139,048	63,268	42,897	20,371
Oregon.	368,623	386,610	250,696	135,914	251,213	92,394	158,819
Pennsylvania	167,227	1,202,038	1,058,648	143,390	77,383	133,564	–56,181
Rhode Island.	2,469	103,887	79,787	24,100	–16,268	24,945	–41,213
South Carolina.	467,991	474,308	316,327	157,981	317,782	41,786	275,996
South Dakota.	49,357	93,397	56,494	36,903	9,694	4,592	5,102
Tennessee	525,618	666,266	467,760	198,506	306,693	61,962	244,731
Texas.	3,475,163	3,165,880	1,280,933	1,884,947	1,563,694	851,909	711,785
Utah	503,220	424,054	108,785	315,269	110,952	63,855	47,097
Vermont	12,444	53,705	41,778	11,927	3,546	5,081	–1,535
Virginia.	690,064	850,119	474,104	376,015	321,605	162,200	159,405
Washington.	655,081	682,387	376,362	306,025	365,045	166,335	198,710
West Virginia.	6,123	171,606	172,121	–515	15,428	4,344	11,084
Wisconsin.	264,259	584,322	380,478	203,844	49,575	59,423	–9,848
Wyoming	38,886	57,611	33,641	23,970	17,347	2,125	15,222

X Not applicable. [1] Total population change includes a residual. This residual represents the change in population that cannot be attributed to any specific demographic component. [2] Net international migration includes the international migration of both native and foreign-born populations. Specifically, it includes: (a) the net international migration of the foreign born, (b) the net migration between the United States and Puerto Rico, (c) the emigration of natives from the United States, and (d) the net overseas movement of the Armed Forces population.

Source: U.S. Census Bureau, "Cumulative Estimates of the Components of Resident Population Change for the United States, Regions, States, and Puerto Rico: April 1, 2000 to July 1, 2008 (NST-EST2008-04)" (released December 22, 2008); <http://www.census.gov/popest/states/tables/NST-EST2008-04.xls>.

Table 16. Resident Population by Age and State: 2008

[In thousands, except percent (304,060 represents 304,060,000). As of July. Includes Armed Forces stationed in area]

State	Total	Under 5 years	5 to 17 years	18 to 24 years	25 to 34 years	35 to 44 years	45 to 54 years	55 to 64 years	65 to 74 years	75 to 84 years	85 years and over	Percent 65 years and over
U.S.	304,060	21,006	52,936	29,757	40,932	42,501	44,372	33,686	20,123	13,025	5,722	12.8
AL	4,662	311	811	451	608	623	674	542	345	212	85	13.8
AK	686	52	128	74	104	95	108	75	31	14	5	7.3
AZ	6,500	516	1,191	602	933	871	846	678	445	295	123	13.3
AR	2,855	202	500	264	382	373	396	331	215	134	59	14.3
CA	36,757	2,705	6,660	3,854	5,255	5,350	5,152	3,667	2,127	1,375	612	11.2
CO	4,939	358	849	466	745	720	743	547	279	165	67	10.4
CT	3,501	212	601	325	405	512	561	408	237	162	79	13.7
DE	873	59	147	84	109	121	128	102	64	41	16	13.9
DC	592	36	76	76	109	85	77	63	37	23	11	11.9
FL	18,328	1,141	2,864	1,607	2,295	2,487	2,609	2,138	1,536	1,130	521	17.4
GA	9,686	741	1,808	920	1,385	1,462	1,379	1,010	553	305	122	10.1
HI	1,288	87	198	125	182	174	180	152	90	69	32	14.8
ID	1,524	122	291	148	213	193	208	167	98	59	26	12.0
IL	12,902	894	2,285	1,311	1,788	1,809	1,873	1,366	812	524	239	12.2
IN	6,377	443	1,142	606	854	871	938	709	423	272	119	12.8
IA	3,003	201	511	306	369	381	444	344	214	152	79	14.8
KS	2,802	203	498	293	368	360	408	306	180	125	62	13.1
KY	4,269	285	723	381	587	593	632	502	308	184	75	13.3
LA	4,411	311	797	471	594	568	639	489	289	179	72	12.3
ME	1,316	71	203	113	149	182	220	178	103	67	29	15.1
MD	5,634	372	969	543	731	825	875	639	366	222	92	12.1
MA	6,498	384	1,043	666	832	951	1,003	748	429	299	143	13.4
MI	10,003	626	1,765	974	1,245	1,383	1,537	1,169	680	437	187	13.0
MN	5,220	358	896	507	696	720	812	580	330	213	107	12.5
MS	2,939	221	546	306	385	379	410	320	198	122	52	12.7
MO	5,912	399	1,022	560	783	787	882	673	416	267	122	13.6
MT	967	61	159	95	120	116	152	126	72	45	20	14.2
NE	1,783	132	315	187	232	225	257	195	117	83	41	13.5
NV	2,600	199	469	212	388	382	362	292	171	94	32	11.4
NH	1,316	75	218	119	151	194	223	165	89	56	24	12.9
NJ	8,683	557	1,490	769	1,067	1,312	1,359	976	585	390	175	13.3
NM	1,984	148	354	203	268	250	278	224	137	87	36	13.1
NY	19,490	1,208	3,200	1,999	2,560	2,795	2,911	2,209	1,332	878	398	13.4
NC	9,222	653	1,591	883	1,235	1,341	1,325	1,055	618	373	148	12.4
ND	641	42	101	83	81	74	94	72	44	33	18	14.7
OH	11,486	744	1,987	1,082	1,463	1,556	1,751	1,333	807	535	229	13.7
OK	3,642	267	639	370	498	459	512	407	259	162	70	13.5
OR	3,790	243	624	338	534	510	560	476	262	166	76	13.3
PA	12,448	737	2,025	1,204	1,465	1,693	1,926	1,488	922	679	310	15.4
RI	1,051	61	168	115	130	148	161	121	70	52	26	14.1
SC	4,480	303	763	438	582	611	641	545	327	193	77	13.3
SD	804	59	140	83	101	96	117	93	56	40	21	14.4
TN	6,215	416	1,062	551	845	875	912	735	449	265	106	13.2
TX	24,327	2,027	4,698	2,455	3,578	3,439	3,299	2,357	1,332	807	333	10.2
UT	2,736	269	581	330	446	326	313	225	132	82	33	9.0
VT	621	33	96	62	71	85	104	85	46	28	12	14.0
VA	7,769	523	1,301	768	1,064	1,139	1,157	876	514	305	122	12.1
WA	6,549	433	1,108	610	926	925	990	772	416	253	115	12.0
WV	1,814	105	281	158	231	240	274	241	150	97	39	15.7
WI	5,628	362	952	554	719	768	875	647	379	254	117	13.3
WY	533	38	90	54	72	65	83	65	35	21	9	12.3

Source: U.S. Census Bureau, "Annual Estimates of the Resident Population by Sex and Age for States and for Puerto Rico: April 1, 2000 to July 1, 2008" (released May 14, 2009); <http://www.census.gov/popest/states/asrh/SC-EST2008-02.html>.

Table 17. **Age Dependency Ratios by State: 2000 and 2008**

[2000, as of April; 2008 as of July]

State	Age dependency ratio [1]		Child dependency ratio [2]		Old-age dependency ratio [3]	
	2000	2008	2000	2008	2000	2008
United States	**61.6**	**59.0**	**41.5**	**38.7**	**20.1**	**20.3**
Alabama	62.1	60.8	40.9	38.7	21.1	22.1
Alaska	56.5	50.5	47.6	39.4	8.9	11.0
Arizona	65.7	65.4	44.2	43.4	21.6	21.9
Arkansas	65.1	63.6	42.0	40.2	23.1	23.3
California	61.1	57.9	44.0	40.2	17.1	17.7
Colorado	54.5	53.3	39.5	37.5	14.9	15.9
Connecticut	62.7	58.4	40.2	36.7	22.5	21.6
Delaware	60.8	60.1	39.9	37.8	20.9	22.3
District of Columbia	47.8	44.6	29.7	27.4	18.1	17.3
Florida	67.7	64.6	38.3	36.0	29.5	28.6
Georgia	56.5	57.3	41.5	41.4	15.0	15.9
Hawaii	60.4	58.5	39.2	35.1	21.3	23.4
Idaho	66.1	64.0	47.4	44.4	18.7	19.6
Illinois	61.8	58.4	42.3	39.0	19.5	19.3
Indiana	62.0	60.3	41.9	39.8	20.1	20.5
Iowa	66.6	62.7	41.8	38.6	24.8	24.1
Kansas	66.0	61.5	44.0	40.4	22.0	21.1
Kentucky	59.0	58.4	39.1	37.4	19.9	21.0
Louisiana	63.6	59.7	44.6	40.1	18.9	19.6
Maine	61.3	56.3	38.1	32.6	23.2	23.6
Maryland	58.5	55.9	40.6	37.1	17.9	18.8
Massachusetts	59.2	54.7	37.6	34.0	21.6	20.7
Michigan	62.3	58.6	42.4	37.9	19.9	20.7
Minnesota	61.9	57.5	42.4	37.8	19.6	19.6
Mississippi	64.8	63.2	44.9	42.6	19.9	20.6
Missouri	64.0	60.4	41.8	38.6	22.1	21.9
Montana	63.7	58.7	41.7	36.1	21.9	22.5
Nebraska	66.3	62.8	43.8	40.8	22.6	22.0
Nevada	57.7	59.0	40.4	40.8	17.3	18.1
New Hampshire	58.8	54.4	39.8	34.4	19.0	19.9
New Jersey	61.4	58.3	40.0	37.3	21.4	21.0
New Mexico	65.0	62.4	46.3	41.1	19.3	21.3
New York	60.3	56.2	39.6	35.3	20.7	20.9
North Carolina	57.4	57.9	38.4	38.4	19.0	19.5
North Dakota	66.0	58.7	41.6	35.4	24.4	23.3
Ohio	63.2	59.9	41.5	38.0	21.7	21.9
Oklahoma	64.1	62.2	42.4	40.3	21.7	21.8
Oregon	60.1	56.7	39.6	35.9	20.5	20.8
Pennsylvania	65.1	60.1	39.3	35.5	25.8	24.6
Rhode Island	61.8	55.8	38.2	33.9	23.5	21.9
South Carolina	59.4	59.0	40.1	37.8	19.3	21.2
South Dakota	70.0	64.2	45.6	40.5	24.4	23.7
Tennessee	58.6	58.7	39.0	37.8	19.6	20.9
Texas	61.7	60.8	45.7	44.5	16.1	16.3
Utah	68.6	66.8	54.3	51.8	14.4	15.0
Vermont	58.6	53.1	38.4	31.8	20.2	21.4
Virginia	55.6	55.2	38.2	36.4	17.4	18.8
Washington	58.5	55.0	40.7	36.5	17.8	18.6
West Virginia	60.2	58.7	35.6	33.8	24.5	24.9
Wisconsin	62.9	57.9	41.6	36.9	21.3	21.1
Wyoming	60.7	57.3	41.9	37.9	18.8	19.4

[1] The age dependency ratio is derived by dividing the combined under-18 and 65-and-over populations by the 18-to-64 population and multiplying by 100. [2] The child dependency ratio is derived by dividing the population under 18 by the 18-to-64 population and multiplying by 100. [3] The old-age dependency ratio is derived by dividing the population 65 and over by the 18-to-64 population and multiplying by 100.

Source: U.S. Census Bureau, Table GCT-T6-R "Age Dependency Ratio of the Total Population"; Table GCT-T7-R "Child Dependency Ratio of the Total Population"; and Table GCT-T8-R "Old-Age Dependency Ratio of the Total Population"; using American FactFinder; <http://factfinder.census.gov/>.

Population 23

Table 18. **Resident Population by Age and State—Projections: 2010 and 2015**

[As of July 1. 1,092 represents 1,092,000. These projections were produced in correspondence with the U.S. interim projections released in March 2004. Projections in this table were developed for each of the 50 states and the District of Columbia by age and sex for the years 2000 to 2030, based on Census 2000 results. These projections differ from forecasts in that they represent the results of the mathematical projection model given that current state-specific trends in fertility, mortality, domestic migration, and net international migration continue. The projections to 2008 have been superseded by population estimates which are shown in Table 16]

State	Population (1,000)										Percent of population, 2015	
	Under 18 years old		18 to 44 years old		45 to 64 years old		65 to 74 years old		75 years old and over		Under 18 years old	65 years old and over
	2010	2015	2010	2015	2010	2015	2010	2015	2010	2015		
AL.	1,092	1,089	1,605	1,575	1,251	1,259	354	427	295	312	23.4	15.9
AK.	184	199	270	280	184	178	35	49	21	26	27.2	10.2
AZ.	1,688	1,892	2,349	2,529	1,678	1,892	516	711	406	470	25.2	15.8
AR.	703	721	996	998	765	782	227	274	185	194	24.3	15.8
CA.	9,497	9,820	14,787	15,240	9,391	9,835	2,333	2,972	2,060	2,256	24.5	13.0
CO	1,189	1,256	1,863	1,886	1,263	1,280	282	369	235	258	24.9	12.4
CT.	814	807	1,257	1,251	990	1,001	253	308	262	270	22.2	15.9
DE.	202	210	309	305	249	264	68	87	57	61	22.6	16.0
DC	114	112	237	225	118	108	32	34	29	27	22.1	12.2
FL.	4,086	4,455	6,315	6,614	5,431	6,002	1,773	2,345	1,646	1,789	21.0	19.5
GA	2,502	2,679	3,724	3,822	2,382	2,543	564	723	417	464	26.2	11.6
HI	316	330	477	479	357	350	101	131	90	96	23.8	16.3
ID	400	427	554	583	381	400	99	129	82	91	26.2	13.5
IL	3,197	3,215	4,842	4,798	3,277	3,307	826	979	774	799	24.5	13.6
IN	1,596	1,614	2,328	2,333	1,656	1,664	425	508	386	398	24.8	13.9
IA	711	707	1,049	1,031	800	794	217	259	233	236	23.4	16.3
KS.	699	708	1,004	1,001	727	724	185	225	190	194	24.8	14.7
KY.	1,002	1,007	1,540	1,526	1,165	1,181	309	376	249	262	23.1	14.6
LA.	1,172	1,176	1,665	1,642	1,194	1,192	313	379	270	285	25.2	14.2
ME	269	269	462	455	413	415	110	142	102	108	19.3	18.0
MD	1,406	1,487	2,212	2,283	1,568	1,601	386	478	332	359	23.9	13.5
MA	1,484	1,474	2,440	2,402	1,817	1,857	454	567	454	458	21.8	15.2
MI	2,487	2,479	3,822	3,799	2,785	2,814	699	852	635	654	23.4	14.2
MN	1,290	1,349	2,027	2,069	1,433	1,475	343	429	327	346	23.8	13.7
MS	759	753	1,052	1,028	781	801	209	254	170	179	25.0	14.4
MO	1,411	1,436	2,111	2,123	1,578	1,589	432	518	390	404	23.7	15.2
MT	212	216	324	326	287	284	77	100	68	74	21.6	17.4
NE.	446	454	619	608	460	455	119	145	125	126	25.4	15.2
NV.	665	752	961	1,033	735	851	199	264	131	158	24.6	13.8
NH	304	313	494	508	408	418	97	129	82	88	21.5	14.9
NJ.	2,088	2,104	3,252	3,239	2,446	2,528	632	760	600	625	22.7	15.0
NM	479	485	669	654	553	560	153	201	126	142	23.7	16.8
NY.	4,421	4,353	7,227	7,077	5,144	5,173	1,346	1,589	1,306	1,354	22.3	15.1
NC	2,269	2,438	3,471	3,586	2,445	2,611	641	810	520	565	24.4	13.7
ND	142	139	223	219	174	169	46	56	51	51	21.8	17.0
OH	2,744	2,723	4,123	4,054	3,121	3,093	816	980	771	786	23.4	15.2
OK	895	915	1,264	1,260	938	933	266	316	229	238	25.0	15.1
OR	863	916	1,412	1,470	1,022	1,036	263	348	231	242	22.8	14.7
PA.	2,748	2,741	4,385	4,334	3,496	3,487	960	1,159	997	990	21.6	16.9
RI	249	248	410	412	300	304	76	94	82	81	21.8	15.4
SC.	1,036	1,061	1,579	1,581	1,226	1,271	343	439	263	290	22.9	15.7
SD.	194	196	269	264	209	209	55	67	60	61	24.6	16.1
TN.	1,479	1,539	2,249	2,275	1,673	1,720	461	570	368	399	23.7	14.9
TX.	6,785	7,376	9,417	9,848	5,859	6,248	1,426	1,826	1,162	1,287	27.7	11.7
UT.	819	872	1,021	1,073	520	556	127	162	108	119	31.3	10.1
VT.	132	132	232	235	195	193	50	67	43	46	19.6	16.9
VA.	1,880	1,982	2,997	3,085	2,139	2,207	554	703	441	490	23.4	14.1
WA	1,488	1,561	2,481	2,591	1,777	1,833	429	567	367	399	22.5	13.9
WV	382	373	618	595	536	525	156	190	136	140	20.4	18.1
WI	1,319	1,343	2,076	2,067	1,561	1,591	392	487	380	395	22.8	15.0
WY	116	115	177	174	154	150	40	52	33	37	21.9	16.8

Source: U.S. Census Bureau, "File 2. Annual projections by 5-year and selected age groups by sex"; published 21 April 2005; <http://www.census.gov/population/www/projections/projectionsagesex.html>.

Table 19. **Resident Population by Race, Hispanic Origin, and State: 2008**

[In thousands (304,060 represents 304,060,000). **As of July**. Persons of Hispanic origin may be any race. Due to the complexities associated with the production of detailed characteristics' estimates at the state level, the values of the estimates at lower levels of geography may not necessarily sum to estimates at higher levels of geography]

State	Total population	One race — White alone	Black or African American alone	American Indian/ Alaska Native alone	Asian alone	Native Hawaiian and Other Pacific Islander alone	Two or more races	Hispanic origin	Non-Hispanic White alone
U.S.....	**304,060**	**242,639**	**39,059**	**3,083**	**13,549**	**562**	**5,167**	**46,944**	**199,491**
AL........	4,662	3,311	1,230	25	45	2	50	135	3,191
AK.......	686	485	29	105	31	4	32	42	451
AZ........	6,500	5,623	270	316	162	13	116	1,956	3,796
AR........	2,855	2,307	450	24	31	3	41	160	2,160
CA........	36,757	28,170	2,451	444	4,582	157	952	13,457	15,538
CO........	4,939	4,432	211	60	131	7	97	997	3,507
CT........	3,501	2,951	362	13	121	3	51	419	2,584
DE........	873	648	183	4	25	1	12	59	597
DC........	592	237	322	2	20	1	10	51	196
FL........	18,328	14,628	2,916	91	416	18	259	3,845	11,059
GA........	9,686	6,333	2,908	36	277	8	124	777	5,629
HI	1,288	382	40	8	506	117	236	112	321
ID	1,524	1,442	14	23	17	2	25	156	1,297
IL.........	12,902	10,209	1,920	45	559	9	159	1,967	8,348
IN	6,377	5,612	578	20	87	3	77	332	5,305
IA	3,003	2,828	81	13	47	2	33	126	2,711
KS........	2,802	2,486	172	29	62	2	51	255	2,250
KY........	4,269	3,838	329	11	42	2	46	102	3,748
LA........	4,411	2,860	1,410	28	64	2	47	148	2,731
ME........	1,316	1,269	14	8	12	(Z)	14	17	1,254
MD........	5,634	3,572	1,658	20	286	4	93	376	3,252
MA........	6,498	5,601	456	20	321	6	94	557	5,147
MI	10,003	8,121	1,425	62	237	4	155	414	7,751
MN........	5,220	4,649	239	65	185	3	80	217	4,458
MS........	2,939	1,781	1,093	15	24	1	26	66	1,724
MO	5,912	5,027	679	30	86	5	85	190	4,856
MT........	967	875	7	62	6	1	17	29	851
NE........	1,783	1,630	80	19	30	1	23	140	1,500
NV........	2,600	2,103	211	39	161	14	72	669	1,486
NH........	1,316	1,256	16	4	25	1	14	35	1,225
NJ	8,683	6,602	1,256	30	664	8	123	1,419	5,354
NM........	1,984	1,667	59	192	28	3	36	891	828
NY........	19,490	14,310	3,363	111	1,369	21	317	3,250	11,697
NC........	9,222	6,819	1,992	116	177	7	112	685	6,198
ND........	641	586	7	36	5	(Z)	7	13	575
OH........	11,486	9,736	1,382	29	181	4	153	302	9,474
OK........	3,642	2,846	290	291	63	4	148	279	2,600
OR........	3,790	3,416	76	54	138	11	94	416	3,033
PA	12,448	10,634	1,343	27	304	6	134	594	10,134
RI	1,051	930	67	7	29	1	17	122	828
SC........	4,480	3,080	1,276	19	55	3	48	184	2,921
SD........	804	709	9	68	6	(Z)	11	21	692
TN........	6,215	4,995	1,043	21	83	3	70	231	4,791
TX	24,327	20,046	2,898	185	841	31	326	8,870	11,526
UT........	2,736	2,543	35	38	54	21	46	329	2,236
VT........	621	599	5	2	7	(Z)	7	9	591
VA........	7,769	5,674	1,546	29	378	7	135	531	5,201
WA	6,549	5,520	245	113	438	32	201	644	4,944
WV	1,814	1,715	65	4	12	1	18	21	1,696
WI	5,628	5,047	342	56	115	2	67	286	4,787
WY	533	500	7	14	4	1	8	41	463

Z Less than 500.

Source: U.S. Census Bureau, "Annual State Resident Population Estimates for 6 Race Groups (5 Race Alone Groups and One Group with Two or more Race Groups) by Age, Sex, and Hispanic Origin: April 1, 2000 to July 1, 2008" (released May 14, 2009); <http://www.census.gov/popest/states/asrh/files/SC-EST2008-alldata6-ALL.csv>.

Population   25

Table 20. Large Metropolitan Statistical Areas—Population: 1990 to 2008

[1990 and 2000, as of April 1; beginning 2005 as of July 1 (658 represents 658,000). Covers metropolitan statistical areas with 250,000 and over population in 2008, as defined by the U.S. Office of Management and Budget as of November 2007. All geographic boundaries for 2000 to 2008 population estimates are defined as of January 1, 2008. For definitions and components of all metropolitan and micropolitan areas, see Appendix II. Minus sign (–) indicates decrease]

Metropolitan statistical area	Number (1,000)					Percent change		
	1990	2000, estimates base [1]	2005	2007	2008	1990 to 2000 [2]	2000 to 2008 [1]	Rank, 2008
Akron, OH	658	695	700	699	699	5.7	0.5	72
Albany-Schenectady-Troy, NY	810	826	846	852	854	2.0	3.4	57
Albuquerque, NM	599	730	797	833	846	21.7	15.9	59
Allentown-Bethlehem-Easton, PA-NJ	687	740	785	802	808	7.8	9.2	62
Anchorage, AK	266	320	351	360	365	20.1	14.1	137
Ann Arbor, MI	283	323	344	348	347	14.1	7.6	143
Asheville, NC	308	369	391	404	408	19.9	10.6	118
Atlanta-Sandy Springs-Marietta, GA	3,069	4,248	4,946	5,261	5,376	38.4	26.6	8
Atlantic City-Hammonton, NJ	224	253	268	270	271	12.6	7.2	165
Augusta-Richmond County, GA-SC	436	500	517	528	534	14.7	6.9	95
Austin-Round Rock, TX	846	1,250	1,465	1,593	1,653	47.7	32.2	36
Bakersfield, CA	545	662	749	787	800	21.4	21.0	63
Baltimore-Towson, MD	2,382	2,553	2,647	2,664	2,667	7.2	4.5	20
Baton Rouge, LA	624	706	729	769	774	13.2	9.7	67
Beaumont-Port Arthur, TX	361	385	380	376	378	6.6	–1.8	132
Birmingham-Hoover, AL	957	1,051	1,088	1,109	1,118	10.0	6.3	48
Boise City-Nampa, ID	320	465	544	587	600	45.4	29.0	85
Boston-Cambridge-Quincy, MA-NH	4,134	4,392	4,455	4,492	4,523	6.2	3.0	10
Boulder, CO [3]	209	270	282	289	293	29.1	8.7	157
Bradenton-Sarasota-Venice, FL	489	590	668	685	688	20.5	16.6	74
Bridgeport-Stamford-Norwalk, CT	828	883	892	891	895	6.6	1.4	56
Brownsville-Harlingen, TX	260	335	371	385	393	28.9	17.2	128
Buffalo-Niagara Falls, NY	1,189	1,170	1,140	1,127	1,124	–1.6	–3.9	47
Canton-Massillon, OH	394	407	408	408	408	3.3	0.2	120
Cape Coral-Fort Myers, FL	335	441	541	588	593	31.6	34.5	86
Cedar Rapids, IA	211	237	247	252	255	12.6	7.7	175
Charleston, WV	308	310	304	304	304	0.6	–1.8	152
Charleston-North Charleston-Summerville, SC	507	549	601	630	645	8.3	17.4	80
Charlotte-Gastonia-Concord, NC-SC	1,025	1,331	1,518	1,646	1,702	29.8	27.9	34
Chattanooga, TN-GA	433	477	502	514	518	10.0	8.8	98
Chicago-Naperville-Joliet, IL-IN-WI	8,182	9,099	9,391	9,497	9,570	11.2	5.2	3
Cincinnati-Middletown, OH-KY-IN	1,845	2,010	2,101	2,144	2,155	8.9	7.2	24
Clarksville, TN-KY	189	232	252	262	261	22.6	12.6	170
Cleveland-Elyria-Mentor, OH	2,102	2,148	2,116	2,095	2,088	2.2	–2.8	26
Colorado Springs, CO	409	537	589	608	618	31.3	14.9	83
Columbia, SC	549	647	691	716	728	17.9	12.5	69
Columbus, GA-AL	266	282	288	287	288	5.7	2.1	160
Columbus, OH	1,405	1,613	1,712	1,753	1,773	14.8	9.9	32
Corpus Christi, TX	368	403	411	413	415	9.7	3.0	115
Dallas-Fort Worth-Arlington, TX	3,989	5,162	5,818	6,153	6,300	29.4	22.1	4
Davenport-Moline-Rock Island, IA-IL	368	376	373	376	378	2.1	0.4	133
Dayton, OH	844	848	843	839	837	0.5	–1.4	61
Deltona-Daytona Beach-Ormond Beach, FL	371	443	486	500	498	19.6	12.3	102
Denver-Aurora, CO [3]	1,667	2,179	2,358	2,453	2,507	30.7	15.0	21
Des Moines-West Des Moines, IA	416	481	524	546	556	15.6	15.5	90
Detroit-Warren-Livonia, MI	4,249	4,453	4,496	4,458	4,425	4.8	–0.6	11
Duluth, MN-WI	269	275	274	274	275	2.3	–0.3	164
Durham, NC	345	424	458	478	490	23.7	15.6	103
El Paso, TX	592	680	710	730	742	14.9	9.2	68
Erie, PA	276	281	279	279	279	1.9	–0.6	163
Eugene-Springfield, OR	283	323	335	343	347	14.2	7.3	145
Evansville, IN-KY	325	343	348	350	350	5.5	2.2	142
Fayetteville, NC	298	337	345	351	356	13.1	5.8	140
Fayetteville-Springdale-Rogers, AR-MO	239	347	408	435	444	44.9	27.9	110
Flint, MI	430	436	439	434	429	1.3	–1.7	111
Fort Collins-Loveland, CO	186	251	276	287	293	35.1	16.4	158
Fort Smith, AR-OK	234	273	282	289	291	16.7	6.5	159
Fort Wayne, IN	354	390	402	409	411	10.1	5.4	117
Fresno, CA	667	799	871	895	909	19.8	13.7	54

See footnotes at end of table.

U.S. Census Bureau, Statistical Abstract of the United States: 2010

Table 20. **Large Metropolitan Statistical Areas—Population: 1990 to 2008**—Con.

[1990 and 2000, as of April 1; beginning 2005 as of July 1 (658 represents 658,000). Covers metropolitan statistical areas with 250,000 and over population in 2008, as defined by the U.S. Office of Management and Budget as of November 2007. All geographic boundaries for 2000 to 2008 population estimates are defined as of January 1, 2008. For definitions and components of all metropolitan and micropolitan areas, see Appendix II. Minus sign (−) indicates decrease]

Metropolitan statistical area	Number (1,000)					Percent change		Rank, 2008
	1990	2000, estimates base [1]	2005	2007	2008	1990 to 2000 [2]	2000 to 2008 [1]	
Gainesville, FL	191	232	248	256	259	21.5	11.3	173
Grand Rapids-Wyoming, MI	646	740	768	775	777	14.6	4.9	66
Green Bay, WI	244	282	296	301	303	16.0	7.2	153
Greensboro-High Point, NC	540	643	673	696	706	19.1	9.7	71
Greenville-Mauldin-Easley, SC	472	560	589	613	625	18.6	11.6	82
Hagerstown-Martinsburg, MD-WV	193	223	250	261	264	15.6	18.4	169
Harrisburg-Carlisle, PA	474	509	520	528	531	7.3	4.3	97
Hartford-West Hartford-East Hartford, CT	1,124	1,149	1,179	1,186	1,191	2.2	3.6	45
Hickory-Lenoir-Morganton, NC	292	342	354	360	363	16.9	6.2	138
Holland-Grand Haven, MI	188	238	254	258	260	26.9	9.3	171
Honolulu, HI	836	876	900	901	905	4.8	3.3	55
Houston-Sugar Land-Baytown, TX	3,767	4,715	5,303	5,598	5,728	25.2	21.5	6
Huntington-Ashland, WV-KY-OH	288	289	284	284	284	0.2	−1.5	161
Huntsville, AL	293	343	369	386	396	16.8	15.5	127
Indianapolis-Carmel, IN	1,294	1,525	1,643	1,693	1,715	17.8	12.5	33
Jackson, MS	447	497	521	534	537	11.2	8.1	93
Jacksonville, FL	925	1,123	1,248	1,298	1,313	21.4	17.0	40
Kalamazoo-Portage, MI	293	315	320	322	324	7.3	2.8	148
Kansas City, MO-KS	1,637	1,836	1,937	1,981	2,002	12.2	9.0	29
Killeen-Temple-Fort Hood, TX	269	331	354	371	379	23.0	14.6	131
Kingsport-Bristol-Bristol, TN-VA	276	298	300	303	305	8.3	2.1	151
Knoxville, TN	535	616	658	681	691	15.2	12.2	73
Lafayette, LA	209	239	247	256	259	14.5	8.4	172
Lakeland-Winter Haven, FL	405	484	538	573	581	19.4	20.0	87
Lancaster, PA	423	471	489	498	502	11.3	6.7	101
Lansing-East Lansing, MI	433	448	456	455	454	3.5	1.4	107
Las Vegas-Paradise, NV	741	1,376	1,703	1,828	1,866	85.6	35.6	30
Lexington-Fayette, KY	348	408	432	446	453	17.2	11.0	108
Lincoln, NE	229	267	285	291	295	16.5	10.8	155
Little Rock-North Little Rock-Conway, AR	535	611	645	666	675	14.1	10.6	76
Los Angeles-Long Beach-Santa Ana, CA	11,274	12,366	12,815	12,785	12,873	9.7	4.1	2
Louisville/Jefferson County, KY-IN	1,056	1,162	1,207	1,232	1,245	10.0	7.1	42
Lubbock, TX	230	250	263	268	271	8.6	8.4	166
Madison, WI	432	502	540	554	562	16.1	11.9	89
Manchester-Nashua, NH	336	381	398	401	402	13.4	5.6	126
McAllen-Edinburg-Mission, TX	384	569	667	705	727	48.5	27.6	70
Memphis, TN-MS-AR	1,067	1,205	1,253	1,279	1,286	12.9	6.7	41
Miami-Fort Lauderdale-Pompano Beach, FL	4,056	5,008	5,375	5,392	5,415	23.5	8.1	7
Milwaukee-Waukesha-West Allis, WI	1,432	1,501	1,534	1,543	1,549	4.8	3.2	39
Minneapolis-St. Paul-Bloomington, MN-WI	2,539	2,969	3,132	3,198	3,230	16.9	8.8	16
Mobile, AL	379	400	398	404	406	5.6	1.6	122
Modesto, CA	371	447	500	509	511	20.6	14.2	100
Montgomery, AL	305	347	356	366	366	13.6	5.6	135
Myrtle Beach-North Myrtle Beach-Conway, SC	144	197	228	250	257	36.5	30.9	174
Naples-Marco Island, FL	152	251	305	314	315	65.3	25.4	150
Nashville-Davidson—Murfreesboro—Franklin, TN	1,048	1,312	1,449	1,520	1,551	25.1	18.2	38
New Haven-Milford, CT	804	824	840	844	846	2.5	2.7	58
New Orleans-Metairie-Kenner, LA	1,264	1,317	1,312	1,109	1,134	4.1	−13.9	46
New York-Northern New Jersey-Long Island, NY-NJ-PA	16,846	18,323	18,812	18,923	19,007	8.8	3.7	1
Norwich-New London, CT	255	259	265	264	265	1.6	2.1	168
Ocala, FL	195	259	301	324	330	32.9	27.3	147
Ogden-Clearfield, UT	352	443	491	518	531	25.8	20.1	96
Oklahoma City, OK	971	1,095	1,154	1,189	1,206	12.8	10.1	44
Omaha-Council Bluffs, NE-IA	686	767	810	828	838	11.8	9.2	60
Orlando-Kissimmee, FL	1,225	1,645	1,936	2,029	2,055	34.3	24.9	27
Oxnard-Thousand Oaks-Ventura, CA	669	753	789	792	798	12.6	5.9	64
Palm Bay-Melbourne-Titusville, FL	399	476	526	535	537	19.4	12.7	94
Pensacola-Ferry Pass-Brent, FL	344	412	445	451	453	19.7	9.9	109
Peoria, IL	359	367	367	371	372	2.3	1.5	134
Philadelphia-Camden-Wilmington, PA-NJ-DE-MD	5,436	5,687	5,787	5,823	5,838	4.6	2.7	5
Phoenix-Mesa-Scottsdale, AZ	2,238	3,252	3,873	4,166	4,282	45.3	31.7	12
Pittsburgh, PA	2,468	2,431	2,372	2,354	2,351	−1.5	−3.3	22

See footnotes at end of table.

Population 27

Table 20. **Large Metropolitan Statistical Areas—Population: 1990 to 2008**—Con.

[1990 and 2000, as of April 1; beginning 2005 as of July 1 (658 represents 658,000). Covers metropolitan statistical areas with 250,000 and over population in 2008, as defined by the U.S. Office of Management and Budget as of November 2007. All geographic boundaries for 2000 to 2008 population estimates are defined as of January 1, 2008. For definitions and components of all metropolitan and micropolitan areas, see Appendix II. Minus sign (–) indicates decrease]

Metropolitan statistical area	Number (1,000)				Percent change		
	1990	2000, estimates base [1]	2005	2007	2008	1990 to 2000 [2]	2000 to 2008 [1]	Rank, 2008
Portland-South Portland-Biddeford, ME	441	488	511	512	514	10.5	5.4	99
Portland-Vancouver-Beaverton, OR-WA	1,524	1,928	2,087	2,166	2,207	26.5	14.5	23
Port St. Lucie, FL.	251	319	376	399	404	27.2	26.4	124
Poughkeepsie-Newburgh-Middletown, NY . . .	567	622	662	669	673	9.6	8.2	77
Providence-New Bedford-Fall River, RI-MA. . .	1,510	1,583	1,610	1,598	1,597	4.8	0.9	37
Provo-Orem, UT	269	377	464	523	541	39.9	43.5	92
Raleigh-Cary, NC.	544	797	953	1,044	1,089	46.5	36.6	50
Reading, PA	337	374	393	401	404	11.0	8.0	125
Reno-Sparks, NV.	257	343	394	409	415	33.3	21.0	116
Richmond, VA.	949	1,097	1,173	1,211	1,226	15.6	11.7	43
Riverside-San Bernardino-Ontario, CA.	2,589	3,255	3,872	4,067	4,116	25.7	26.5	14
Roanoke, VA.	269	288	292	296	298	7.4	3.4	154
Rochester, NY.	1,002	1,038	1,035	1,032	1,034	3.5	–0.4	51
Rockford, IL	284	320	339	351	354	12.9	10.7	141
Sacramento—Arden-Arcade—Roseville, CA . .	1,481	1,797	2,032	2,082	2,110	21.3	17.4	25
St. Louis, MO-IL [4]	2,581	2,699	2,773	2,805	2,817	4.6	4.4	18
Salem, OR	278	347	372	385	392	24.9	12.8	129
Salinas, CA	356	402	407	405	408	13.0	1.6	119
Salt Lake City, UT	768	969	1,046	1,095	1,116	26.1	15.2	49
San Antonio, TX	1,408	1,712	1,879	1,985	2,031	21.6	18.7	28
San Diego-Carlsbad-San Marcos, CA	2,498	2,814	2,932	2,960	3,001	12.6	6.7	17
San Francisco-Oakland-Fremont, CA.	3,684	4,124	4,158	4,216	4,275	11.9	3.7	13
San Jose-Sunnyvale-Santa Clara, CA	1,534	1,736	1,743	1,786	1,819	13.1	4.8	31
San Luis Obispo-Paso Robles, CA	217	247	258	262	265	13.6	7.5	167
Santa Barbara-Santa Maria-Goleta, CA	370	399	402	402	405	8.0	1.5	123
Santa Cruz-Watsonville, CA.	230	256	250	251	253	11.3	–1.0	176
Santa Rosa-Petaluma, CA.	388	459	462	462	467	18.1	1.8	105
Savannah, GA	258	293	314	329	334	13.6	14.0	146
Scranton—Wilkes-Barre, PA	575	561	548	549	549	–2.6	–2.0	91
Seattle-Tacoma-Bellevue, WA	2,559	3,044	3,197	3,298	3,345	18.9	9.9	15
Shreveport-Bossier City, LA	360	376	381	388	390	4.5	3.6	130
South Bend-Mishawaka, IN-MI	297	317	315	316	317	6.8	0.1	149
Spartanburg, SC	227	254	265	275	281	11.9	10.6	162
Spokane, WA	361	418	440	456	463	15.7	10.7	106
Springfield, MA	673	680	686	687	688	1.0	1.1	75
Springfield, MO	299	368	400	420	426	23.3	15.7	113
Stockton, CA	481	564	656	668	672	17.3	19.3	78
Syracuse, NY	660	650	646	644	644	–1.5	–1.0	81
Tallahassee, FL.	259	320	342	353	357	23.6	11.5	139
Tampa-St. Petersburg-Clearwater, FL	2,068	2,396	2,637	2,715	2,734	15.9	14.1	19
Toledo, OH	654	659	654	651	649	0.8	–1.5	79
Trenton-Ewing, NJ	326	351	362	364	365	7.7	4.0	136
Tucson, AZ.	667	844	948	997	1,012	26.5	19.9	52
Tulsa, OK.	761	860	881	904	916	12.9	6.6	53
Utica-Rome, NY	317	300	295	294	294	–5.3	–2.0	156
Vallejo-Fairfield, CA	339	395	407	407	408	16.2	3.3	121
Virginia Beach-Norfolk-Newport News, VA-NC.	1,451	1,577	1,649	1,660	1,658	8.7	5.2	35
Visalia-Porterville, CA	312	368	405	419	426	18.0	15.8	112
Washington-Arlington-Alexandria, DC-VA-MD-WV	4,122	4,796	5,222	5,302	5,358	16.3	11.7	9
Wichita, KS.	511	571	584	595	604	11.7	5.7	84
Wilmington, NC	200	275	316	339	347	37.2	26.4	144
Winston-Salem, NC	361	422	446	462	468	16.7	10.9	104
Worcester, MA	710	750	778	782	784	5.8	4.5	65
York-Hanover, PA	340	382	406	420	425	12.4	11.2	114
Youngstown-Warren-Boardman, OH-PA	614	603	581	571	566	–1.7	–6.1	88

[1] The April 1, 2000, estimates base reflects changes to the Census 2000 population resulting from legal boundary updates as of January 1 of the estimates year, other geographic program changes, and Count Question Resolution actions. [2] Based on 2000 Census numbers as tabulated. [3] Broomfield County, CO, was formed from parts of Adams, Boulder, Jefferson, and Weld Counties, CO, on November 15, 2001, and is coextensive with Broomfield city. For purposes of defining and presenting data for metropolitan statistical areas, Broomfield city is treated as if it were a county at the time of the 1990 and 2000 censuses. [4] The portion of Sullivan city in Crawford County, Missouri, is legally part of the St. Louis, MO-IL MSA. Data shown here do not include this area.

Source: U.S. Census Bureau, "Table 1—Annual Estimates of the Population of Metropolitan and Micropolitan Statistical Areas: April 1, 2000 to July 1, 2008 (CBSA-EST2008-01)" (published 19 March 2009); <http://www.census.gov/popest/metro /CBSA-est2008-annual.html>.

Table 21. **50 Largest Metropolitan Statistical Areas in 2008—Components of Population Change: 2000 to 2008**

[Covers period April 1, 2000, to July 1, 2008 (1,128 represents 1,128,000). Covers metropolitan statistical areas as defined by the U.S. Office of Management and Budget as of November 2007. All geographic boundaries for 2000 to 2008 population estimates are defined as of January 1, 2008. For definitions and components of all metropolitan and micropolitan areas, see Appendix II. Minus sign (–) indicates decrease or outmigration]

Metropolitan statistical area	Total change [1]	Natural increase (Number (1,000))			Net migration			Percent change
		Total	Births	Deaths	Total	International	Domestic migration	
Atlanta-Sandy Springs-Marietta, GA	1,128	405	640	235	599	189	410	26.6
Austin-Round Rock, TX	403	139	196	57	270	62	208	32.2
Baltimore-Towson, MD	114	92	285	194	–3	33	–35	4.5
Birmingham-Hoover, AL	66	33	124	91	33	9	23	6.3
Boston-Cambridge-Quincy, MA-NH	131	173	464	292	–85	172	–256	3.0
Buffalo-Niagara Falls, NY	–46	6	105	100	–46	10	–56	–3.9
Charlotte-Gastonia-Concord, NC-SC	371	109	196	87	268	44	224	27.9
Chicago-Naperville-Joliet, IL-IN-WI	471	593	1,165	572	–120	401	–521	5.2
Cincinnati-Middletown, OH-KY-IN	145	98	245	146	–1	18	–19	7.2
Cleveland-Elyria-Mentor, OH	–60	45	220	175	–104	26	–130	–2.8
Columbus, OH	160	108	213	106	57	31	26	9.9
Dallas-Fort Worth-Arlington, TX	1,138	543	817	274	574	304	269	22.1
Denver-Aurora, CO [2]	327	194	309	115	137	97	41	15.0
Detroit-Warren-Livonia, MI	–27	169	487	318	–238	95	–332	–0.6
Hartford-West Hartford-East Hartford, CT	42	31	113	83	17	28	–11	3.6
Houston-Sugar Land-Baytown, TX	1,013	488	740	252	468	277	191	21.5
Indianapolis-Carmel, IN	190	104	208	104	86	22	64	12.5
Jacksonville, FL	190	60	145	85	135	12	123	17.0
Kansas City, MO-KS	166	115	240	126	54	30	24	9.0
Las Vegas-Paradise, NV	490	117	216	99	380	68	312	35.6
Los Angeles-Long Beach-Santa Ana, CA	507	983	1,621	637	–420	847	–1,267	4.1
Louisville/Jefferson County, KY-IN	82	43	134	91	41	12	29	7.1
Memphis, TN-MS-AR	81	74	162	88	11	13	–2	6.7
Miami-Fort Lauderdale-Pompano Beach, FL	407	178	573	395	217	439	–223	8.1
Milwaukee-Waukesha-West Allis, WI	49	72	178	106	–50	25	–74	3.2
Minneapolis-St. Paul-Bloomington, MN-WI	261	221	378	156	53	75	–23	8.8
Nashville-Davidson—Murfreesboro—Franklin, TN	239	80	172	92	139	26	112	18.2
New Orleans-Metairie-Kenner, LA	–182	43	139	96	–298	11	–309	–13.9
New York-Northern New Jersey-Long Island, NY-NJ-PA	683	955	2,120	1,166	–687	1,145	–1,833	3.7
Oklahoma City, OK	111	64	146	82	52	21	32	10.1
Orlando-Kissimmee, FL	410	103	219	116	312	75	237	24.9
Philadelphia-Camden-Wilmington, PA-NJ-DE-MD	151	185	626	441	–12	100	–112	2.7
Phoenix-Mesa-Scottsdale, AZ	1,030	319	532	213	717	175	542	31.7
Pittsburgh, PA	–80	–26	205	232	–42	16	–58	–3.3
Portland-Vancouver-Beaverton, OR-WA	280	116	238	122	175	71	103	14.5
Providence-New Bedford-Fall River, RI-MA	14	37	158	122	–16	31	–47	0.9
Raleigh-Cary, NC	292	81	123	42	207	35	172	36.6
Richmond, VA	129	47	128	81	87	13	74	11.7
Riverside-San Bernardino-Ontario, CA	861	301	512	211	573	100	472	26.5
Sacramento—Arden-Arcade—Roseville, CA	313	117	236	119	204	66	138	17.4
St. Louis, MO-IL [3]	118	96	303	207	–14	28	–41	4.4
Salt Lake City, UT	147	122	168	46	8	41	–33	15.2
San Antonio, TX	320	141	251	110	187	31	156	18.7
San Diego-Carlsbad-San Marcos, CA	187	213	376	163	–10	104	–114	6.7
San Francisco-Oakland-Fremont, CA	151	220	462	241	–93	260	–353	3.7
San Jose-Sunnyvale-Santa Clara, CA	83	154	229	75	–65	169	–234	4.8
Seattle-Tacoma-Bellevue, WA	301	172	347	175	130	108	21	9.9
Tampa-St. Petersburg-Clearwater, FL	338	20	257	237	328	62	266	14.1
Virginia Beach-Norfolk-Newport News, VA-NC	81	96	197	101	–10	–1	–9	5.2
Washington-Arlington-Alexandria, DC-VA-MD-WV	562	387	637	250	138	256	–118	11.7

[1] Total population change includes residual. This residual represents the change in population that cannot be attributed to any specific demographic component of change. See "State & County terms & definitions" at <http://www.census.gov/popest/topics/terms/states.html>. [2] Broomfield County, CO, was formed from parts of Adams, Boulder, Jefferson, and Weld Counties, CO, on November 15, 2001, and is coextensive with Broomfield city. For purposes of defining and presenting data for metropolitan statistical areas, Broomfield city is treated as if it were a county at the time of the 2000 census. [3] The portion of Sullivan city in Crawford County, Missouri, is legally part of the St. Louis, MO-IL MSA. Data shown here do not include this area.

Source: U.S. Census Bureau, "Table 10—Cumulative Estimates of the Components of Population Change for Metropolitan and Micropolitan Statistical Areas: April 1, 2000 to July 1, 2008 (CBSA-EST2008-10)" (published 19 March 2009); <http://www.census.gov/population/www/estimates/CBSA-est2008-comp-chg.html>.

Table 22. Metropolitan Statistical Areas With More Than 750,000 Persons in 2008—Population by Age: 2008

[In thousands (854 represents 854,000). As of July 1. Covers metropolitan statistical areas as defined by the U.S. Office of Management and Budget as of November 2007. All geographic boundaries are defined as of January 1, 2008. For definitions and components of all metropolitan and micropolitan areas, see Appendix II]

Metropolitan statistical area	Number (1,000)						Percent under 18 years	Percent 65 years and over
	Total	Under 18 years	18 to 44 years	45 to 64 years	65 to 74 years	75 years and over		
Albany-Schenectady-Troy, NY	854	181	324	233	57	59	21.2	13.6
Albuquerque, NM	846	211	316	216	54	49	25.0	12.2
Allentown-Bethlehem-Easton, PA-NJ	808	183	285	221	57	64	22.6	14.9
Atlanta-Sandy Springs-Marietta, GA	5,376	1,443	2,132	1,353	266	182	26.8	8.3
Austin-Round Rock, TX	1,653	430	728	369	70	55	26.0	7.6
Bakersfield, CA	800	239	328	162	39	33	29.8	9.0
Baltimore-Towson, MD	2,667	630	986	722	174	155	23.6	12.3
Baton Rouge, LA	774	197	308	190	44	36	25.5	10.3
Birmingham-Hoover, AL	1,118	272	403	298	77	68	24.3	12.9
Boston-Cambridge-Quincy, MA-NH	4,523	999	1,721	1,228	292	283	22.1	12.7
Bridgeport-Stamford-Norwalk, CT	895	223	301	252	61	58	24.9	13.2
Buffalo-Niagara Falls, NY	1,124	241	396	312	83	92	21.5	15.5
Charlotte-Gastonia-Concord, NC-SC	1,702	446	663	432	91	70	26.2	9.5
Chicago-Naperville-Joliet, IL-IN-WI	9,570	2,451	3,648	2,414	565	493	25.6	11.1
Cincinnati-Middletown, OH-KY-IN	2,155	539	788	569	136	123	25.0	12.0
Cleveland-Elyria-Mentor, OH	2,088	490	701	592	153	153	23.5	14.7
Columbus, OH	1,773	451	701	439	100	82	25.4	10.2
Dallas-Fort Worth-Arlington, TX	6,300	1,755	2,537	1,482	304	221	27.9	8.3
Dayton, OH	837	193	295	226	64	58	23.1	14.6
Denver-Aurora, CO	2,507	637	967	661	135	107	25.4	9.6
Detroit-Warren-Livonia, MI	4,425	1,090	1,551	1,235	285	264	24.6	12.4
Fresno, CA	909	271	359	190	46	44	29.8	9.9
Grand Rapids-Wyoming, MI	777	204	292	196	44	41	26.2	10.9
Hartford-West Hartford-East Hartford, CT	1,191	267	427	331	82	84	22.4	13.9
Honolulu, HI	905	199	341	226	64	75	22.0	15.4
Houston-Sugar Land-Baytown, TX	5,728	1,616	2,243	1,395	277	197	28.2	8.3
Indianapolis-Carmel, IN	1,715	457	640	434	99	85	26.6	10.7
Jacksonville, FL	1,313	322	481	358	88	64	24.5	11.6
Kansas City, MO-KS	2,002	515	727	530	122	108	25.7	11.5
Las Vegas-Paradise, NV	1,866	493	723	453	116	81	26.4	10.6
Los Angeles-Long Beach-Santa Ana, CA	12,873	3,315	5,067	3,093	736	662	25.8	10.9
Louisville/Jefferson County, KY-IN	1,245	301	443	343	84	74	24.1	12.7
Memphis, TN-MS-AR	1,286	350	467	335	75	59	27.2	10.4
Miami-Fort Lauderdale-Pompano Beach, FL	5,415	1,204	1,885	1,423	420	483	22.2	16.7
Milwaukee-Waukesha-West Allis, WI	1,549	387	545	425	98	94	24.9	12.4
Minneapolis-St. Paul-Bloomington, MN-WI	3,230	812	1,222	869	177	150	25.1	10.1
Nashville-Davidson—Murfreesboro—Franklin, TN	1,551	383	596	407	93	72	24.7	10.6
New Haven-Milford, CT	846	195	309	225	56	61	23.1	13.8
New Orleans-Metairie-Kenner, LA	1,134	267	403	324	75	65	23.5	12.3
New York-Northern New Jersey-Long Island, NY-NJ-PA	19,007	4,434	7,100	4,991	1,279	1,202	23.3	13.1
Oklahoma City, OK	1,206	304	459	301	77	66	25.2	11.8
Omaha-Council Bluffs, NE-IA	838	224	313	209	49	43	26.7	11.0
Orlando-Kissimmee, FL	2,055	488	778	515	144	129	23.8	13.3
Oxnard-Thousand Oaks-Ventura, CA	798	207	292	208	49	42	25.9	11.4
Philadelphia-Camden-Wilmington, PA-NJ-DE-MD	5,838	1,395	2,101	1,574	389	380	23.9	13.2
Phoenix-Mesa-Scottsdale, AZ	4,282	1,169	1,643	977	258	235	27.3	11.5
Pittsburgh, PA	2,351	482	780	685	187	217	20.5	17.2
Portland-Vancouver-Beaverton, OR-WA	2,207	533	836	604	129	106	24.1	10.6
Providence-New Bedford-Fall River, RI-MA	1,597	351	595	428	106	116	22.0	13.9
Raleigh-Cary, NC	1,089	285	443	272	52	37	26.2	8.1
Richmond, VA	1,226	289	466	326	77	68	23.6	11.8
Riverside-San Bernardino-Ontario, CA	4,116	1,174	1,679	851	208	204	28.5	10.0
Rochester, NY	1,034	230	377	286	71	70	22.2	13.6
Sacramento-Arden-Arcade-Roseville, CA	2,110	520	830	510	128	122	24.6	11.8
St. Louis, MO-IL [1]	2,817	678	1,005	768	188	178	24.1	13.0
Salt Lake City, UT	1,116	330	443	246	53	42	29.6	8.6
San Antonio, TX	2,031	561	780	470	115	105	27.6	10.8
San Diego-Carlsbad-San Marcos, CA	3,001	744	1,218	702	164	173	24.8	11.2
San Francisco-Oakland-Fremont, CA	4,275	924	1,629	1,183	278	261	21.6	12.6
San Jose-Sunnyvale-Santa Clara, CA	1,819	443	714	464	109	89	24.4	10.9
Seattle-Tacoma-Bellevue, WA	3,345	770	1,286	935	192	161	23.0	10.6
Tampa-St. Petersburg-Clearwater, FL	2,734	592	930	733	226	252	21.7	17.5
Tucson, AZ	1,012	239	366	253	75	79	23.6	15.2
Tulsa, OK	916	235	328	239	61	53	25.6	12.5
Virginia Beach-Norfolk-Newport News, VA-NC	1,658	412	647	409	102	88	24.8	11.4
Washington-Arlington-Alexandria, DC-VA-MD-WV	5,358	1,300	2,079	1,440	311	228	24.3	10.1
Worcester, MA	784	185	290	213	47	49	23.6	12.3

[1] The portion of Sullivan city in Crawford County, Missouri, is legally part of the St. Louis, MO-IL MSA. Data shown here do not include this area.

Source: U.S. Census Bureau, USA Counties; <http://censtats.census.gov/usa/usa.shtml> (accessed 23 July 2009).

[In thousands (854 represents 854,000). As of July 1. Covers metropolitan statistical areas as defined by the U.S. Office of Management and Budget as of November 2007. All geographic boundaries are defined as of January 1, 2008. For definitions and components of all metropolitan and micropolitan areas, see Appendix II]

Metropolitan statistical area	Total persons	White alone	Black or African American alone	American Indian and Alaska Native alone	Asian alone	Native Hawaiian and Other Pacific Islander alone	Two or more races	Hispanic origin [1]
Albany-Schenectady-Troy, NY	854	748	65	2	25	(Z)	13	29
Albuquerque, NM	846	726	31	52	17	2	18	377
Allentown-Bethlehem-Easton, PA-NJ	808	739	38	2	20	1	9	91
Atlanta-Sandy Springs-Marietta, GA	5,376	3,353	1,696	21	225	5	77	520
Austin-Round Rock, TX	1,653	1,407	130	12	75	2	27	498
Bakersfield, CA	800	684	52	14	32	2	17	377
Baltimore-Towson, MD	2,667	1,744	769	9	103	2	41	89
Baton Rouge, LA	774	478	275	2	12	(Z)	7	20
Birmingham-Hoover, AL	1,118	778	313	4	12	1	10	36
Boston-Cambridge-Quincy, MA-NH	4,523	3,819	352	13	271	4	64	367
Bridgeport-Stamford-Norwalk, CT	895	745	96	3	39	1	11	138
Buffalo-Niagara Falls, NY	1,124	945	138	9	19	(Z)	14	39
Charlotte-Gastonia-Concord, NC-SC	1,702	1,227	398	9	46	1	21	152
Chicago-Naperville-Joliet, IL-IN-WI	9,570	7,181	1,715	37	510	8	118	1,904
Cincinnati-Middletown, OH-KY-IN	2,155	1,826	262	5	37	1	25	42
Cleveland-Elyria-Mentor, OH	2,088	1,605	413	5	38	1	26	90
Columbus, OH	1,773	1,431	251	5	56	1	29	54
Dallas-Fort Worth-Arlington, TX	6,300	4,938	907	48	302	10	95	1,731
Dayton, OH	837	686	122	2	13	(Z)	13	15
Denver-Aurora, CO	2,507	2,195	145	27	86	4	50	562
Detroit-Warren-Livonia, MI	4,425	3,185	1,018	16	142	2	63	166
Fresno, CA	909	738	53	18	79	2	19	443
Grand Rapids-Wyoming, MI	777	685	61	4	13	1	12	64
Hartford-West Hartford-East Hartford, CT	1,191	997	133	4	39	1	17	134
Honolulu, HI	905	232	36	5	404	77	151	71
Houston-Sugar Land-Baytown, TX	5,728	4,296	982	36	331	7	76	1,945
Indianapolis-Carmel, IN	1,715	1,403	252	5	32	1	23	84
Jacksonville, FL	1,313	952	294	5	39	1	22	78
Kansas City, MO-KS	2,002	1,670	244	11	41	3	33	145
Las Vegas-Paradise, NV	1,866	1,449	194	20	136	12	55	531
Los Angeles-Long Beach-Santa Ana, CA	12,873	9,671	991	125	1,788	45	254	5,719
Louisville/Jefferson County, KY-IN	1,245	1,039	169	4	16	1	15	36
Memphis, TN-MS-AR	1,286	660	585	4	23	1	13	51
Miami-Fort Lauderdale-Pompano Beach, FL	5,415	4,072	1,124	26	120	7	66	2,143
Milwaukee-Waukesha-West Allis, WI	1,549	1,221	253	10	41	1	22	132
Minneapolis-St. Paul-Bloomington, MN-WI	3,230	2,766	215	27	161	2	59	155
Nashville-Davidson—Murfreesboro—Franklin, TN	1,551	1,251	241	6	32	1	20	86
New Haven-Milford, CT	846	690	110	3	29	1	13	113
New Orleans-Metairie-Kenner, LA	1,134	699	385	6	30	1	14	71
New York-Northern New Jersey-Long Island, NY-NJ-PA	19,007	13,097	3,691	96	1,795	24	305	4,112
Oklahoma City, OK	1,206	953	132	47	36	1	36	117
Omaha-Council Bluffs, NE-IA	838	736	66	5	17	1	13	64
Orlando-Kissimmee, FL	2,055	1,600	330	10	76	3	35	473
Oxnard-Thousand Oaks-Ventura, CA	798	697	17	10	53	2	19	303
Philadelphia-Camden-Wilmington, PA-NJ-DE-MD	5,838	4,256	1,225	16	258	4	79	394
Phoenix-Mesa-Scottsdale, AZ	4,282	3,755	209	108	124	10	77	1,322
Pittsburgh, PA	2,351	2,089	196	4	36	1	25	27
Portland-Vancouver-Beaverton, OR-WA	2,207	1,931	68	22	120	8	58	231
Providence-New Bedford-Fall River, RI-MA	1,597	1,436	87	9	39	2	25	150
Raleigh-Cary, NC	1,089	807	219	6	41	1	15	99
Richmond, VA	1,226	802	369	6	32	1	17	49
Riverside-San Bernardino-Ontario, CA	4,116	3,375	330	59	236	15	101	1,879
Rochester, NY	1,034	873	119	3	23	(Z)	16	54
Sacramento-Arden-Arcade-Roseville, CA	2,110	1,595	160	25	234	14	81	399
St. Louis, MO-IL [2]	2,817	2,205	514	8	53	1	35	63
Salt Lake City, UT	1,116	1,016	20	12	32	15	21	177
San Antonio, TX	2,031	1,797	139	21	39	3	32	1,080
San Diego-Carlsbad-San Marcos, CA	3,001	2,387	166	31	309	16	92	927
San Francisco-Oakland-Fremont, CA	4,275	2,737	384	29	947	31	146	873
San Jose-Sunnyvale-Santa Clara, CA	1,819	1,145	52	15	552	6	48	487
Seattle-Tacoma-Bellevue, WA	3,345	2,617	191	41	353	22	121	255
Tampa-St. Petersburg-Clearwater, FL	2,734	2,281	322	13	73	3	41	400
Tucson, AZ	1,012	891	38	36	26	2	19	335
Tulsa, OK	916	712	84	67	14	1	39	69
Virginia Beach-Norfolk-Newport News, VA-NC	1,658	1,031	530	8	51	2	36	72
Washington-Arlington-Alexandria, DC-VA-MD-WV	5,358	3,341	1,417	22	462	6	110	660
Worcester, MA	784	713	30	2	28	1	10	65

Z Less than 500. [1] Persons of Hispanic origin may be any race. [2] The portion of Sullivan city in Crawford County, Missouri, is legally part of the St. Louis, MO-IL MSA. Data shown here do not include this area.

Source: U.S. Census Bureau, USA Counties; <http://censtats.census.gov/usa/usa.shtml> (accessed 23 July 2009).

Population   31

Table 24. **Population by Core Based Statistical Area (CBSA) Status and State: 2008**

[2000, as of April 1; 2008 as of July 1 (304,060 represents 304,060,000). Covers core-based statistical areas (metropolitan and micropolitan statistical areas) as defined by the U.S. Office of Management and Budget as of November 2007. All geographic boundaries for 2000 to 2008 population estimates are defined as of January 1, 2008. For definitions and components of all metropolitan and micropolitan areas, see Appendix II. Minus sign (–) indicates decrease]

State	Total popula-tion, 2008 (1,000)	Inside Core-Based Statistical Area (metropolitan or micropolitan statistical area), 2008				Outside CBSA, 2008		Percent change, 2000–2008 [1]		
		Total		Metro-politan (1,000)	Micro-politan (1,000)	Number (1,000)	Percent	Metro-politan	Micro-politan	Outside CBSAs
		Number (1,000)	Percent							
U.S. . . .	**304,060**	**284,820**	**93.7**	**254,190**	**30,630**	**19,240**	**6.3**	**9.2**	**4.0**	**0.2**
AL	4,662	4,180	89.7	3,327	853	481	10.3	6.2	5.2	–4.2
AK	686	520	75.7	463	57	166	24.3	15.0	–2.6	0.4
AZ	6,500	6,410	98.6	6,029	381	90	1.4	28.4	9.9	1.3
AR	2,855	2,276	79.7	1,708	569	579	20.3	12.6	0.5	–2.0
CA	36,757	36,499	99.3	35,924	575	258	0.7	8.6	4.0	6.0
CO	4,939	4,534	91.8	4,260	274	405	8.2	15.8	12.2	6.5
CT	3,501	3,501	100.0	3,196	305	–	–	2.6	4.7	–
DE	873	873	100.0	685	188	–	–	9.3	20.1	–
DC	592	592	100.0	592	–	–	–	3.5	–	–
FL	18,328	17,921	97.8	17,247	674	408	2.2	14.8	12.9	12.3
GA	9,686	8,844	91.3	7,885	959	842	8.7	20.8	8.4	8.5
HI	1,288	1,288	100.0	905	383	–	–	3.3	14.3	–20.4
ID	1,524	1,326	87.0	1,000	325	198	13.0	23.9	10.0	3.8
IL	12,902	12,297	95.3	11,235	1,062	605	4.7	4.9	–1.8	–3.1
IN	6,377	6,014	94.3	4,989	1,025	362	5.7	6.5	–0.3	–0.9
IA	3,003	2,207	73.5	1,692	515	795	26.5	8.2	–2.1	–4.9
KS	2,802	2,398	85.6	1,786	612	405	14.4	8.6	1.4	–8.2
KY	4,269	3,253	76.2	2,451	802	1,016	23.8	7.8	5.0	1.0
LA	4,411	4,106	93.1	3,277	829	305	6.9	–1.9	1.6	–2.5
ME	1,316	931	70.7	770	162	385	29.3	4.5	3.1	0.9
MD	5,634	5,551	98.5	5,332	219	83	1.5	6.2	11.1	5.3
MA	6,498	6,471	99.6	6,471	–	27	0.4	2.3	–	9.1
MI	10,003	9,232	92.3	8,157	1,074	772	7.7	0.7	1.9	–1.7
MN	5,220	4,573	87.6	3,814	759	648	12.4	7.9	3.8	–0.9
MS	2,939	2,295	78.1	1,295	1,000	643	21.9	8.4	–0.1	–0.8
MO	5,912	5,121	86.6	4,346	775	790	13.4	6.7	5.0	0.5
MT	967	641	66.3	341	300	326	33.7	8.3	15.6	–0.4
NE	1,783	1,441	80.8	1,040	401	342	19.2	10.3	1.3	–8.2
NV	2,600	2,552	98.1	2,335	216	49	1.9	31.9	20.5	1.3
NH	1,316	1,268	96.4	821	447	47	3.6	6.6	6.0	8.6
NJ	8,683	8,683	100.0	8,683	–	–	–	3.2	–	–
NM	1,984	1,908	96.1	1,314	594	77	3.9	14.5	0.8	–6.9
NY	19,490	19,064	97.8	17,946	1,118	426	2.2	3.0	–1.1	–0.9
NC	9,222	8,497	92.1	6,486	2,011	725	7.9	18.3	7.6	4.4
ND	641	455	70.9	311	143	187	29.1	9.7	–4.8	–10.1
OH	11,486	10,979	95.6	9,269	1,710	507	4.4	1.4	0.1	0.6
OK	3,642	3,085	84.7	2,325	760	557	15.3	7.8	3.6	–0.5
OR	3,790	3,650	96.3	2,952	699	140	3.7	12.8	5.3	–0.2
PA	12,448	12,068	96.9	10,468	1,600	381	3.1	1.4	1.3	–0.4
RI	1,051	1,051	100.0	1,051	–	–	–	0.2	–	–
SC	4,480	4,210	94.0	3,419	790	270	6.0	13.9	7.8	–2.5
SD	804	587	73.0	370	218	217	27.0	18.3	1.4	–4.7
TN	6,215	5,585	89.9	4,556	1,029	629	10.1	10.5	7.5	3.3
TX	24,327	22,950	94.3	21,344	1,605	1,377	5.7	18.9	4.1	0.9
UT	2,736	2,602	95.1	2,438	164	134	4.9	23.8	19.4	6.7
VT	621	459	73.9	208	251	162	26.1	4.8	–	1.8
VA	7,769	6,939	89.3	6,662	277	830	10.7	10.9	6.1	2.5
WA	6,549	6,323	96.5	5,744	579	227	3.5	11.5	10.3	4.9
WV	1,814	1,369	75.4	1,007	362	446	24.6	2.4	–0.8	–3.2
WI	5,628	4,859	86.3	4,103	756	769	13.7	6.0	2.8	1.3
WY	533	383	71.8	161	222	150	28.2	8.5	9.0	5.7

– Represents or rounds to zero.   [1] The April 1, 2000 estimates base reflects changes to the Census 2000 population resulting from legal boundary updates as of January 1 of the estimates year, other geographic program changes, and the Count Question Resolution program.

Source: U.S. Census Bureau, "Metropolitan and Micropolitan Statistical Area Estimates Population and Population Change by CBSA Status" (published 19 March 2009); <http://www.census.gov/popest/metro/CBSA-est2008-CBSAstatus.html> and unpublished data.

Table 25. Population in Coastal Counties: 1980 to 2008

[Population as of April 1, except as indicated (3,537 represents 3,537,000). Areas as defined by U.S. National Oceanic and Atmospheric Administration, 1992. Covers 673 counties and equivalent areas with at least 15 percent of their land area either in a coastal watershed (drainage area) or in a coastal cataloging unit (a coastal area between watersheds). See Appendix III]

Year		Counties in coastal regions					Balance of United States
	Total	Total	Atlantic	Gulf of Mexico	Great Lakes	Pacific	
Land area, 2000 (1,000 sq. mi.)	3,537	889	148	115	115	511	2,649
POPULATION							
1980 (mil.)........................	226.5	119.8	53.7	13.1	26.0	27.0	106.7
1990 (mil.)........................	248.7	133.4	59.0	15.2	25.9	33.2	115.3
2000 (mil.)........................	281.4	148.3	65.2	18.0	27.3	37.8	133.1
2008 (July 1) (mil.)	304.1	157.5	69.2	20.1	27.4	40.8	146.6
1980 (percent).....................	100	53	24	6	11	12	47
1990 (percent).....................	100	54	24	6	10	13	46
2000 (percent).....................	100	53	23	6	10	13	47
2008 (July 1) (percent)	100	52	23	7	9	13	48

Source: U.S. Census Bureau, 1980 Census of Population, Vol. 1, Chapter A (PC80-1-A-1), *U.S. Summary*; 1990 Census of Population and Housing (CPH1); and unpublished data.

Table 26. States with Coastal Counties—Population, Housing Units, Establishments, and Employees by Coastal Region and State: 2000 to 2008

[281,425 represents 281,425,000. Population and housing as of July 1, except 2000 as of April 1. See headnote, Table 25. Minus sign (–) indicates decrease]

Coastal region and state	Population					Housing units			Private nonfarm [3]	
	2000 [1] (1,000)	2008				Number			Estab-lish-ments, 2007 (1,000)	Employ-ees, 2007 (1,000)
		Num-ber (1,000)	Percent of state total	Percent change, 2000-2008	Per square mile, 2008 [2]	2000 [1] (1,000)	2008 (1,000)	Percent change, 2000-2008		
United States, total ..	281,425	304,060	(X)	8.0	86	115,904	129,065	11.4	7,705	120,604
Interior U.S.	133,103	146,564	(X)	10.1	55	55,918	63,365	13.3	3,609	58,155
Coastal counties, total ..	148,322	157,495	(X)	6.2	177	59,986	65,700	9.5	4,096	62,450
Atlantic................	65,198	69,188	(X)	6.1	468	26,821	29,268	9.1	1,902	28,313
Maine	1,184	1,228	93.3	3.7	61	599	647	7.9	40	474
New Hampshire	1,007	1,078	81.9	7.1	256	432	474	9.8	32	450
Massachusetts	6,125	6,271	96.5	2.4	949	2,531	2,640	4.3	171	2,981
Rhode Island	1,048	1,051	100.0	0.2	1,006	440	452	2.7	30	438
Connecticut	3,406	3,501	100.0	2.8	723	1,386	1,443	4.1	93	1,530
New York	13,573	14,149	72.6	4.2	1,825	5,285	5,511	4.3	396	5,510
New Jersey	8,312	8,573	98.7	3.1	1,214	3,269	3,472	6.2	240	3,576
Pennsylvania	5,750	5,940	47.7	3.3	863	2,334	2,457	5.3	146	2,588
Delaware..............	784	873	100.0	11.4	447	343	393	14.5	25	396
Maryland..............	4,865	5,161	91.6	6.1	681	1,970	2,133	8.3	129	2,039
District of Columbia......	572	592	100.0	3.5	9,639	275	285	3.8	21	455
Virginia	4,794	5,269	67.8	9.9	379	1,912	2,178	13.9	137	2,242
North Carolina	1,985	2,134	23.1	7.5	109	905	1,045	15.6	49	654
South Carolina	1,653	1,869	41.7	13.0	123	750	906	20.8	48	643
Georgia..............	822	902	9.3	9.8	75	346	395	14.4	21	280
Florida	9,320	10,598	57.8	13.7	566	4,043	4,836	19.6	321	4,056
Gulf of Mexico	18,003	20,148	(X)	11.9	176	7,718	8,985	16.4	470	7,021
Florida	6,249	7,262	39.6	16.2	231	3,074	3,754	22.1	191	2,387
Georgia..............	95	100	1.0	5.4	62	40	45	10.8	2	30
Alabama	712	747	16.0	4.9	86	319	366	14.8	18	260
Mississippi............	588	599	20.4	1.9	88	246	261	6.1	13	183
Louisiana	3,510	3,449	78.2	-1.7	134	1,439	1,445	0.4	83	1,296
Texas	6,850	7,991	32.8	16.7	199	2,599	3,115	19.8	163	2,864
Great Lakes	27,325	27,358	(X)	0.1	237	11,405	12,069	5.8	666	11,188
New York	3,650	3,579	18.4	-1.9	167	1,586	1,629	2.7	83	1,375
Pennsylvania	281	279	2.2	-0.6	348	114	118	3.6	7	119
Ohio	4,418	4,330	37.7	-2.0	410	1,869	1,955	4.6	109	1,875
Michigan	8,859	8,927	89.2	0.8	175	3,782	4,049	7.1	212	3,303
Indiana	1,378	1,427	22.4	3.5	351	556	608	9.3	33	590
Illinois...............	6,021	6,007	46.6	-0.2	4,312	2,322	2,439	5.0	152	2,680
Wisconsin	2,469	2,561	45.5	3.7	166	1,055	1,141	8.2	62	1,145
Minnesota	248	247	4.7	-0.6	23	121	129	6.6	8	101
Pacific	37,796	40,802	(X)	8.0	80	14,042	15,379	9.5	1,058	15,928
Washington	4,587	5,107	78.0	11.3	207	1,919	2,197	14.5	148	2,042
Oregon	1,808	1,952	51.5	8.0	93	794	868	9.3	61	819
California.............	29,660	31,881	86.7	7.5	410	10,650	11,564	8.6	798	12,349
Alaska	530	574	83.6	8.4	2	219	237	7.9	17	210
Hawaii	1,212	1,288	100.0	6.3	201	461	513	11.4	33	507

X Not applicable.   [1] Reflects modifications to the Census 2000 population as documented in the Count Question Resolution program and geographic program revisions.   [2] Calculated on the basis of land area data from the 2000 census.   [3] Covers establishments with payroll. Excludes most government employees, railroad employees, self-employed persons. Employees are for the week including March 12.

Source: U.S. Census Bureau, USA Counties; <http://censtats.census.gov/usa/usa.shtml> (accessed 13 August 2009); and "County Business Patterns"; <http://www.census.gov/econ/cbp/index.html>.

Table 27. **Incorporated Places With 175,000 or More Inhabitants in 2008—Population: 1990 to 2008**

[In thousands, except as indicated (223 represents 223,000). As of April 1, except beginning 2005 as of July 1. Beginning with 2000 estimates base, data refer to boundaries in effect on January 1, 2008; 1990 and 2000 census data, boundaries in effect on January 1, 2000. Minus sign (–) indicates decrease. See Appendix III]

Incorporated place	Number (1,000)					Percent change		Rank, 2008
	1990	2000, estimates base [1]	2005	2007	2008	1990 to 2000 [2]	2000 to 2008 [1]	
Akron, OH	223	217	210	208	208	–2.7	–4.4	97
Albuquerque, NM	387	449	496	515	522	15.9	16.2	34
Amarillo, TX	158	174	182	186	187	10.0	7.8	119
Anaheim, CA	267	329	330	331	335	23.0	2.0	55
Anchorage, AK	226	260	276	278	279	15.0	7.3	67
Arlington, TX [3]	262	333	361	369	374	27.1	12.4	50
Arlington, VA [3]	171	189	200	204	210	10.9	10.8	96
Atlanta, GA	394	418	483	520	538	5.8	28.7	33
Augusta-Richmond County, GA [4] . . .	186	195	192	192	194	4.8	–0.5	113
Aurora, CO	222	276	296	310	319	24.6	15.4	58
Austin, TX	497	659	700	739	758	32.1	15.0	15
Bakersfield, CA	188	244	293	314	321	31.4	31.8	57
Baltimore, MD	736	651	640	640	637	–11.5	–2.2	20
Baton Rouge, LA	223	229	222	227	224	2.2	–2.2	84
Birmingham, AL	266	242	232	230	229	–8.7	–5.6	83
Boise City, ID	142	195	200	203	205	30.8	5.3	100
Boston, MA	575	589	597	608	609	2.5	3.4	22
Brownsville, TX	114	142	165	172	175	22.6	23.2	129
Buffalo, NY	328	293	278	272	271	–10.8	–7.4	69
Chandler, AZ	91	177	231	244	247	94.7	39.5	76
Charlotte, NC	428	567	631	669	687	26.4	21.3	18
Chesapeake, VA	152	199	216	219	220	31.1	10.5	88
Chicago, IL	2,783	2,896	2,837	2,833	2,853	4.1	–1.5	3
Chula Vista, CA	135	174	211	216	219	28.3	26.4	89
Cincinnati, OH	365	331	331	333	333	–9.1	0.6	56
Cleveland, OH	506	477	449	438	434	–5.5	–9.2	41
Colorado Springs, CO	282	361	371	376	380	28.0	5.3	48
Columbus, GA	[4]179	186	188	187	187	[4]4.0	0.4	120
Columbus, OH	639	713	737	747	755	11.3	5.9	16
Corpus Christi, TX	258	277	282	285	286	7.4	3.2	64
Dallas, TX	1,007	1,189	1,246	1,266	1,280	18.1	7.7	8
Denver, CO	468	554	563	583	599	18.6	8.1	24
Des Moines, IA	193	199	194	195	197	2.8	–1.0	112
Detroit, MI	1,028	951	921	917	912	–7.5	–4.1	11
Durham, NC	149	188	206	217	223	25.5	18.9	85
El Paso, TX	516	564	589	603	613	9.3	8.7	21
Fontana, CA	88	142	175	183	185	46.7	30.4	122
Fort Lauderdale, FL	150	171	183	183	183	1.6	7.3	124
Fort Wayne, IN	206	252	247	251	252	–0.1	–	73
Fort Worth, TX	449	541	621	679	703	19.1	29.9	17
Fremont, CA	173	203	199	200	203	17.3	–0.3	102
Fresno, CA	355	430	458	468	476	20.3	10.8	35
Garland, TX	181	216	213	217	219	19.3	1.3	90
Gilbert, AZ	30	115	182	206	216	265.6	88.7	94
Glendale, AZ	151	220	243	250	252	45.0	14.5	74
Glendale, CA	180	195	198	196	197	8.3	1.1	111
Grand Rapids, MI	189	198	194	193	193	4.7	–2.2	114
Greensboro, NC	192	228	237	246	251	16.9	9.8	75
Henderson, NV	65	175	231	248	252	169.4	43.8	71
Hialeah, FL	188	226	218	211	211	20.5	–7.0	95
Honolulu, HI [3]	376	372	375	374	375	–1.2	0.8	49
Houston, TX	1,697	1,974	2,076	2,209	2,242	15.1	13.6	4
Huntington Beach, CA	181	190	193	192	193	4.7	1.6	115
Huntsville, AL	161	160	166	171	177	–1.7	10.5	127
Indianapolis, IN [4]	732	782	788	795	798	6.9	2.1	14
Irvine, CA	111	144	186	200	208	28.4	44.0	98
Irving, TX	155	192	190	198	201	23.5	5.1	107
Jacksonville, FL	635	736	786	804	808	15.8	9.8	13
Jersey City, NJ	229	240	238	240	241	4.8	0.4	78
Kansas City, MO	435	442	443	450	452	1.5	2.3	39
Knoxville, TN	174	175	180	184	185	–0.1	5.4	123
Laredo, TX	126	178	206	216	222	40.1	24.6	86
Las Vegas, NV	259	480	543	556	558	84.7	16.3	28
Lexington-Fayette, KY	225	261	272	278	282	15.6	8.3	65
Lincoln, NE	193	227	242	248	252	17.0	11.0	72
Little Rock, AR	177	183	186	188	190	3.4	3.4	118
Long Beach, CA	430	462	470	463	464	7.4	0.5	37
Los Angeles, CA	3,486	3,695	3,810	3,807	3,834	6.0	3.8	2
Louisville/Jefferson County, KY [4] . . .	[5]269	551	557	557	557	[5]–4.7	1.1	30
Lubbock, TX	187	200	213	218	220	6.9	10.4	87
Madison, WI	191	209	224	229	232	9.0	10.7	81
Memphis, TN	664	691	676	673	670	–2.1	–3.0	19

See footnotes at end of table.

Table 27. **Incorporated Places With 175,000 or More Inhabitants in 2008—Population: 1990 to 2008**—Con.

[In thousands, except as indicated (223 represents 223,000). **As of April 1, except beginning 2005 as of July 1**. Beginning with 2000 estimates base, data refer to boundaries in effect on January 1, 2008; 1990 and 2000 census data, boundaries in effect on January 1, 2000. Minus sign (−) indicates decrease. See Appendix III]

Incorporated place	Number (1,000)					Percent change		Rank, 2008
	1990	2000, estimates base [1]	2005	2007	2008	1990 to 2000 [2]	2000 to 2008 [1]	
Memphis, TN	664	691	676	673	670	−2.1	−3.0	19
Mesa, AZ	291	398	450	460	464	36.2	16.4	38
Miami, FL	359	362	382	407	413	0.8	14.0	43
Milwaukee, WI	629	597	602	603	604	−5.1	1.3	23
Minneapolis, MN	368	383	376	380	383	3.9	–	47
Mobile, AL	198	199	190	191	191	0.3	−4.1	116
Modesto, CA	166	189	205	203	203	13.5	7.5	101
Montgomery, AL	191	202	200	204	203	5.6	0.5	103
Moreno Valley, CA	119	142	176	187	191	19.9	34.1	117
Nashville-Davidson, TN [4]	488	546	580	591	596	11.7	9.3	26
New Orleans, LA	497	485	455	288	312	−2.5	−35.7	59
New York, NY	7,323	8,009	8,214	8,310	8,364	9.4	4.4	1
Newark, NJ	275	273	277	279	279	−0.6	2.4	68
Newport News, VA	171	181	182	181	180	5.1	−0.6	126
Norfolk, VA	261	234	237	236	234	−10.3	−0.1	80
North Las Vegas, NV	48	116	176	211	217	140.8	88.0	92
Oakland, CA	372	399	393	399	404	7.4	1.2	44
Oklahoma City, OK	445	506	532	545	552	13.8	9.0	31
Omaha, NE	373	400	423	433	439	4.6	9.7	40
Orlando, FL	166	193	215	229	231	12.0	19.7	82
Oxnard, CA	142	171	182	184	186	19.6	8.8	121
Philadelphia, PA	1,586	1,518	1,457	1,449	1,447	−4.3	−4.6	6
Phoenix, AZ	989	1,322	1,465	1,535	1,568	33.6	18.6	5
Pittsburgh, PA	370	335	316	312	310	−9.6	−7.3	60
Plano, TX	128	222	251	260	267	73.5	20.3	70
Portland, OR	486	529	535	548	558	8.9	5.4	29
Raleigh, NC	221	288	348	378	393	24.9	36.1	45
Reno, NV	139	183	206	214	217	29.8	18.4	93
Richmond, VA	203	198	198	200	202	−2.4	2.0	105
Riverside, CA	227	256	287	292	295	12.6	15.5	61
Rochester, NY	230	220	210	207	207	−4.4	−5.9	99
Sacramento, CA	370	407	450	458	464	10.0	13.9	36
Salt Lake City, UT	160	182	177	179	182	13.6	–	125
San Antonio, TX	998	1,160	1,260	1,326	1,351	14.7	16.5	7
San Bernardino, CA	171	188	190	198	199	8.3	5.4	109
San Diego, CA	1,111	1,223	1,255	1,261	1,279	10.1	4.6	9
San Francisco, CA	724	777	777	799	809	7.3	4.2	12
San Jose, CA	783	896	907	931	948	14.2	5.9	10
Santa Ana, CA	294	338	338	337	339	14.8	0.3	54
Scottsdale, AZ	130	203	227	233	235	55.8	16.2	79
Seattle, WA	516	563	573	589	599	9.1	6.2	25
Shreveport, LA	199	201	198	199	200	0.6	−0.5	108
Spokane, WA	178	197	198	201	202	9.8	2.7	104
St. Louis, MO	397	348	353	356	354	−12.2	1.8	52
St. Paul, MN	272	287	277	278	280	5.5	−2.5	66
St. Petersburg, FL	240	249	248	246	245	3.3	−1.4	77
Stockton, CA	212	243	283	286	287	15.0	18.1	63
Tacoma, WA	177	194	194	195	197	9.1	1.9	110
Tampa, FL	280	303	326	335	341	8.4	12.3	53
Tempe, AZ	142	159	166	172	176	11.7	10.7	128
Toledo, OH	333	314	301	296	293	−5.8	−6.6	62
Tucson, AZ	418	487	524	537	542	16.4	11.2	32
Tulsa, OK	367	393	381	384	386	7.0	−1.9	46
Virginia Beach, VA	393	425	438	435	434	8.2	2.0	42
Washington, DC	607	572	582	588	592	−5.7	3.5	27
Wichita, KS	311	352	354	361	366	10.7	4.0	51
Winston-Salem, NC	168	201	208	215	218	10.6	8.0	91
Worcester, MA	170	173	175	175	175	1.8	1.4	130
Yonkers, NY	188	196	198	198	202	4.2	2.9	106

– Represents or rounds to zero. [1] Based on the April 1, 2000, population estimates base which reflects changes to the Census 2000 population from the Count Question Resolution program and geographic program revisions. [2] Based on 2000 Census numbers as tabulated. [3] The population shown is for the census designated place (CDP). [4] Represents the portion of a consolidated city that is not within one or more separately incorporated places. [5] Data are for the incorporated place of Louisville city before consolidation of the city and county governments.

Source: U.S. Census Bureau, 2000 Census of Population and Housing, *Population and Housing Unit Counts* PHC-3; and "Annual Estimates of the Resident Population for Incorporated Places Over 100,000, Ranked by July 1, 2008 Population: April 1, 2000 to July 1, 2008 (SUB-EST2008-01)" (released July 1, 2009); <http://www.census.gov/popest/cities/tables /SUB-EST2008-01.xls>.

Population 35

Table 28. **Incorporated Places by Population Size: 1990 to 2008**

[152.9 represents 152,900,000. See Appendix III]

Population size	Number of incorporated places				Population (mil.)				Percent of total			
	1990	2000	2005	2008	1990	2000 [1]	2005	2008	1990	2000 [1]	2005	2008
Total	19,262	19,496	19,496	19,496	152.9	177.1	184.7	190.0	100.0	100.0	100.0	100.0
1,000,000 or more....	8	9	9	9	20.0	23.0	23.6	24.2	13.0	13.0	12.8	12.7
500,000 to 999,999 ...	15	21	23	25	10.1	13.5	15.0	16.5	6.6	7.6	8.1	8.7
250,000 to 499,999 ...	41	38	38	41	14.2	13.7	13.7	14.1	9.3	7.8	7.4	7.4
100,000 to 249,999 ...	131	176	184	198	19.1	26.1	27.9	29.4	12.5	14.7	15.1	15.5
50,000 to 99,999	309	374	413	424	21.2	25.7	28.6	29.1	13.9	14.5	15.5	15.3
25,000 to 49,999	567	657	679	686	20.0	23.0	23.6	23.9	13.0	13.0	12.8	12.6
10,000 to 24,999	1,290	1,466	1,502	1,521	20.3	23.1	23.6	24.1	13.3	13.0	12.8	12.7
Under 10,000	16,901	16,755	16,648	16,592	28.2	29.0	28.7	28.7	18.4	16.3	15.5	15.1

[1] The April 1, 2000, population estimates base reflects modifications to the Census 2000 population as documented in the Count Question Resolution program.

Source: U.S. Census Bureau, *1990 Census of Population and Housing, Population and Housing Unit Counts* (CPH-2-1); and "Annual Estimates of the Resident Population for Incorporated Places: April 1, 2000 to July 1, 2008 (SUB-EST2008-04-XX)" (released July 1, 2009); <http://www.census.gov/popest/cities/SUB-EST2008-4.html>.

Table 29. **Urban and Rural Population by State: 1990 and 2000**

[222,361 represents 222,361,000. As of April 1. Resident population. For urban definitions, see text, this section]

State	Urban population				Rural popula- tion, 2000 (1,000)	State	Urban population				Rural popula- tion, 2000 (1,000)
	1990		2000, current definition				1990		2000, current definition		
	Former defini- tion (per- cent)	Current defini- tion (per- cent)	Number (1,000)	Percent			Former defini- tion (per- cent)	Current defini- tion (per- cent)	Number (1,000)	Percent	
U.S., total ..	75.2	78.0	222,361	79.0	59,061	MS.	47.1	49.1	1,387	48.8	1,457
						MO	68.7	69.6	3,883	69.4	1,712
						MT.	52.5	56.4	488	54.1	414
AL	60.4	56.8	2,466	55.4	1,981	NE	66.1	67.2	1,194	69.8	518
AK	67.5	61.0	411	65.6	216	NV	88.3	87.4	1,829	91.5	170
AZ	87.5	86.5	4,524	88.2	607	NH.	51.0	57.2	732	59.3	503
AR	53.5	52.0	1,404	52.5	1,269	NJ	89.4	93.5	7,939	94.4	475
CA	92.6	93.7	31,990	94.4	1,882	NM	73.0	75.0	1,364	75.0	456
CO	82.4	83.8	3,633	84.5	668	NY	84.3	87.4	16,603	87.5	2,374
CT	79.1	87.0	2,988	87.7	418	NC	50.4	57.8	4,849	60.2	3,200
DE	73.0	79.2	628	80.1	156	ND	53.3	53.4	359	55.9	283
DC	100.0	100.0	572	100.0	–						
FL	84.8	88.0	14,270	89.3	1,712	OH.	74.1	77.5	8,782	77.4	2,571
						OK.	67.7	65.2	2,255	65.3	1,196
GA	63.2	68.7	5,864	71.6	2,322	OR.	70.5	74.9	2,694	78.7	727
HI	89.0	90.5	1,108	91.5	103	PA	68.9	76.8	9,464	77.1	2,817
ID	57.4	62.2	859	66.4	434	RI	86.0	89.9	953	90.9	95
IL	84.6	86.4	10,910	87.8	1,510	SC	54.6	61.5	2,427	60.5	1,585
IN	64.9	69.1	4,304	70.8	1,776	SD	50.0	50.3	391	51.9	363
IA	60.6	59.4	1,787	61.1	1,139	TN	60.9	62.7	3,620	63.6	2,069
KS	69.1	69.5	1,921	71.4	768	TX	80.3	81.2	17,204	82.5	3,648
KY	51.8	55.9	2,254	55.8	1,788	UT	87.0	86.8	1,970	88.2	263
LA	68.1	72.9	3,246	72.6	1,223						
ME.	44.6	42.6	513	40.2	762	VT	32.2	40.2	232	38.2	376
						VA	69.4	71.5	5,170	73.0	1,909
MD	81.3	85.0	4,559	86.1	738	WA	76.4	79.9	4,831	82.0	1,063
MA	84.3	90.5	5,801	91.4	548	WV	36.1	46.9	833	46.1	976
MI	70.5	75.2	7,419	74.7	2,519	WI	65.7	67.3	3,664	68.3	1,700
MN	69.9	69.0	3,490	70.9	1,429	WY	65.0	67.1	321	65.1	172

– Represents zero.

Source: U.S. Census Bureau, 2000 Census of Population and Housing, *Population and Housing Unit Counts* PHC-3.

Table 30. Mobility Status of the Population by Selected Characteristics: 1981 to 2008

[As of March (221,641 represents 221,641,000). For persons 1 year old and over. Based on comparison of place of residence in immediate prior year and year shown. Excludes members of the Armed Forces except those living off post or with their families on post. Based on Current Population Survey, Annual Social and Economic Supplement. See text, this section and Appendix III. For composition of regions, see map, inside front cover]

Mobility period and characteristic	Total (1,000)	Non-movers	Movers (different house in United States)		Different county			Movers from abroad
			Total	Same county	Total	Same state	Different state	
1981	221,641	83	17	10	6	3	3	1
1991	244,884	83	16	10	6	3	3	1
2001	275,611	86	14	8	6	3	3	1
2008, total	294,851	88	12	8	4	2	2	–
1 to 4 years old	16,648	83	17	12	5	3	2	–
5 to 9 years old	20,018	87	13	9	4	2	2	–
10 to 14 years old	20,038	90	10	7	3	1	1	–
15 to 19 years old	21,314	89	11	7	3	2	1	–
20 to 24 years old	20,529	73	27	18	9	5	3	1
25 to 29 years old	21,057	75	24	16	8	5	3	1
30 to 44 years old	61,221	87	13	8	4	2	2	–
45 to 64 years old	77,237	94	6	4	2	1	1	–
65 to 74 years old	19,588	96	4	2	2	1	1	–
75 to 84 years old	12,912	97	3	2	1	1	1	–
85 years old and over	4,289	96	3	2	1	1	1	–
Northeast	53,348	92	8	5	2	1	1	–
Midwest	64,498	89	11	7	3	2	1	–
South	108,125	87	13	9	5	3	2	–
West	68,880	87	13	9	4	2	2	1
Persons 16 years old and over	233,885	88	11	7	4	2	2	–
Civilian labor force	153,091	87	12	8	4	2	2	–
Employed	144,791	88	12	8	4	2	2	–
Unemployed	8,301	79	21	14	6	3	3	1
Armed Forces	890	67	29	12	17	3	13	4
Not in labor force	79,903	91	9	6	3	2	1	–
Employed civilians, 16 years old and over	144,791	88	12	8	4	2	2	–
Management, business, and financial	21,558	90	9	6	4	2	2	–
Professional	30,634	88	11	7	5	3	2	–
Service	24,023	85	14	10	4	2	1	–
Sales	16,339	87	12	8	4	2	2	–
Office and administrative support	19,528	88	12	9	3	2	1	–
Farming, fishing, and forestry	972	83	16	11	5	3	2	1
Construction and extraction	8,587	85	14	11	4	2	1	–
Installation, maintenance, and repair	5,037	89	11	7	4	2	1	–
Production	9,180	89	11	7	3	2	1	–
Transportation and material moving	8,932	86	14	10	4	2	2	–
Tenure:								
Owner occupied units	208,212	95	5	3	2	1	1	–
Renter occupied units	86,639	72	27	19	8	5	3	1

– Represents or rounds to zero.

Source: U.S. Census Bureau, "Geographical Mobility: 2007 to 2008, Detailed Tables"; <http://www.census.gov/population/www/socdemo/migrate.html>.

Table 31. Movers by Type of Move and Reason for Moving: 2008

[As of March (35,167 represents 35,167,000). For persons 1 year old and over. Based on comparison of place of residence in 2007 and 2008. Excludes members of the Armed Forces except those living off post or with their families on post. Based on Current Population Survey, Annual Social and Economic Supplement. See text, this section and Appendix III]

Reason for move	All movers	Intra-county	Inter-county	From abroad	Reason for move	All movers	Intra-county	Inter-county	From abroad
Total (1,000)	35,167	23,013	11,009	1,145	Housing-related reasons	40.1	50.9	21.1	4.7
PERCENT DISTRIBUTION					Wanted to own home/not rent	5.8	7.1	3.5	0.3
Total	100.0	100.0	100.0	100.0	New/better house/apartment	13.8	18.3	5.7	1.2
Family-related reasons	30.5	30.9	30.3	25.3	Better neighborhood/less crime	5.1	6.0	3.5	1.6
Change in marital status	5.7	5.7	5.7	3.7	Cheaper housing	8.2	9.9	5.3	0.8
To establish own household	10.5	12.5	6.6	6.3	Other housing	7.2	9.6	3.0	0.9
Other family reasons	14.4	12.6	18.0	15.5	Other reasons	8.5	5.9	12.5	21.2
Work-related reasons	20.9	12.3	36.0	48.7	Attend/leave college	2.5	1.2	4.4	10.3
New job/job transfer	8.4	2.2	20.0	21.3	Change of climate	0.6	0.3	1.3	0.3
To look for work/lost job	2.3	1.1	3.4	13.8	Health reasons	1.3	1.1	1.9	0.4
Closer to work/easier commute	6.2	6.3	6.3	3.5	Natural disaster	0.2	0.1	0.3	–
Retired	0.4	0.3	0.6	0.3	Other reason	3.9	3.3	4.6	10.1
Other job-related reason	3.7	2.4	5.7	9.8					

– Represents or rounds to zero.

Source: U.S. Census Bureau, "Geographical Mobility: 2007 to 2008, Detailed Tables"; <http://www.census.gov/population/www/socdemo/migrate.html>.

Population 37

Table 32. **Mobility Status of Households by Household Income: 2008**

[As of March (116,819 represents 116,819,000). Covers householders 15 years old and over. Based on comparison of place of residence in 2007 and 2008. Excludes members of the Armed Forces except those living off post or with their families on post. Based on Current Population Survey, Annual Social and Economic Supplement. See text, this section and Appendix III]

Household income in 2007	Total (1,000)	Non-movers	Percent distribution Movers (different house in United States) Total	Same county	Different county Total	Same state	Different state	Movers from abroad
Householders, 15 years and over. . .	116,819	88	11	8	4	2	2	–
Less than $5,000	3,416	76	22	15	7	4	2	2
$5,000 to $9,999.	5,042	84	16	12	4	2	2	–
$10,000 to $14,999	7,051	86	14	10	4	2	2	–
$15,000 to $24,999	13,532	86	14	10	4	3	2	–
$25,000 to $34,999	12,532	85	14	10	4	3	2	–
$35,000 to $49,999	16,526	87	13	9	4	2	2	–
$50,000 to $69,999	17,579	89	11	7	4	2	2	–
$70,000 to $99,999	17,541	91	9	5	3	2	1	–
$100,000 and over	23,599	94	6	4	3	1	1	–

– Represents or rounds to zero.

Source: U.S. Census Bureau, "Geographical Mobility: 2007 to 2008, Detailed Tables"; <http://www.census.gov/population/www/socdemo/migrate.html>.

Table 33. **Mobility Status of Resident Population by State: 2007**

[In percent, except as indicated (297,545 represents 297,545,000,000). Based on comparison of place of residence in 2006 and 2007. The American Community Survey universe includes the household population and the population living in institutions, college dormitories, and other group quarters. Based on a sample and subject to sampling variability. See text, this section and Appendix III]

State	Population 1 year old and over [1] (1,000)	Same house in 2006	Different house in United States in 2006 Same county	Different county	State	Population 1 year old and over [1] (1,000)	Same house in 2006	Different house in United States in 2006 Same county	Different county
U.S.. .	297,545	84.0	9.4	5.9					
					MO	5,800	83.1	9.1	7.5
AL	4,567	83.3	9.8	6.4	MT	946	82.9	10.0	6.8
AK	673	78.7	11.6	8.4	NE	1,749	82.5	10.4	6.6
AZ	6,242	79.9	13.2	5.9	NV	2,526	79.4	13.9	6.0
AR	2,795	81.2	11.3	7.1	NH	1,303	85.5	7.9	6.3
CA	36,025	84.5	10.2	4.5					
					NJ	8,575	89.1	6.1	4.2
CO	4,793	80.5	9.8	9.1	NM	1,942	84.0	9.2	6.4
CT	3,461	87.5	7.8	4.2	NY	19,065	88.2	7.1	4.0
DE	855	85.0	8.7	5.7	NC	8,935	82.3	9.6	7.5
DC	580	80.6	10.0	8.2	ND	631	83.0	9.3	7.0
FL	18,024	83.2	10.0	6.0					
					OH	11,320	84.6	9.9	5.1
GA	9,409	81.8	8.8	8.8	OK	3,567	80.0	11.8	7.7
HI	1,266	84.1	9.8	4.8	OR	3,703	81.1	11.1	7.3
ID	1,476	80.6	10.8	7.9	PA	12,286	87.2	7.5	4.9
IL	12,681	85.7	9.0	4.8	RI	1,046	86.6	8.1	4.7
IN	6,258	83.5	10.0	6.1					
					SC	4,352	84.0	8.3	7.2
IA	2,949	83.7	9.3	6.7	SD	784	83.8	8.6	7.4
KS	2,736	81.8	10.6	7.1	TN	6,074	83.4	10.2	6.1
KY	4,185	83.8	9.1	6.7	TX	23,512	80.7	11.6	6.9
LA	4,237	84.1	8.8	6.7	UT	2,595	81.0	11.1	7.1
ME	1,301	85.9	8.0	5.8					
					VT	615	85.5	7.7	6.4
MD	5,542	86.0	7.2	6.1	VA	7,612	83.6	6.6	9.0
MA	6,380	86.5	7.9	4.8	WA	6,382	81.4	11.2	6.4
MI	9,945	85.6	9.0	5.0	WV	1,795	86.9	7.1	5.8
MN	5,126	85.7	7.5	6.3	WI	5,532	84.7	9.6	5.4
MS	2,876	83.7	9.3	6.7	WY	516	79.5	11.8	8.2

[1] Includes persons moving from abroad, not shown separately.

Source: U.S. Census Bureau, 2007 American Community Survey, B07003 "Residence 1 Year Ago by Sex," using American FactFinder; <http://factfinder.census.gov/> (23 September 2008).

Table 34. **Persons 65 Years Old and Over—Characteristics by Sex: 1990 to 2008**

[As of March, except as noted (29.6 represents 29,600,000). Covers civilian noninstitutional population. Excludes members of Armed Forces except those living off post or with their families on post. Data for 1990 are based on 1980 census population controls; 2000 data based on 1990 census population controls; beginning 2005, data based on 2000 census population controls and an expanded sample of households. Based on Current Population Survey; see text, this section and Appendix III]

Characteristic	Total				Male				Female			
	1990	2000	2005	2008	1990	2000	2005	2008	1990	2000	2005	2008
Total (million)	29.6	32.6	35.2	36.8	12.3	13.9	15.1	15.8	17.2	18.7	20.0	21.0
PERCENT DISTRIBUTION												
Marital status:												
Never married	4.6	3.9	4.1	4.1	4.2	4.2	4.4	4.2	4.9	3.6	3.9	4.0
Married.	56.1	57.2	57.7	57.0	76.5	75.2	74.9	74.5	41.4	43.8	44.7	43.9
Spouse present	54.1	54.6	54.8	54.6	74.2	72.6	71.7	71.9	39.7	41.3	42.0	41.7
Spouse absent	2.0	2.6	2.9	2.4	2.3	2.6	3.2	2.6	1.7	2.5	2.7	2.3
Widowed.	34.2	32.1	30.3	29.8	14.2	14.4	13.7	13.8	48.6	45.3	42.9	41.9
Divorced.	5.0	6.7	7.9	9.1	5.0	6.1	7.0	7.5	5.1	7.2	8.5	10.2
Educational attainment:												
Less than ninth grade	28.5	16.7	13.4	11.2	30.0	17.8	13.2	11.3	27.5	15.9	13.5	11.1
Completed 9th to 12th grade, but												
no high school diploma	[1]16.1	13.8	12.7	11.4	[1]15.7	12.7	11.9	10.8	[1]16.4	14.7	13.3	11.8
High school graduate	[2]32.9	35.9	36.3	36.9	[2]29.0	30.4	31.6	32.0	[2]35.6	39.9	39.9	40.5
Some college or associate's degree. .	[3]10.9	18.0	18.7	20.1	[3]10.8	17.8	18.4	19.2	[3]11.0	18.2	19.0	20.8
Bachelor's or advanced degree.	[4]11.6	15.6	18.9	20.5	[4]14.5	21.4	24.9	26.7	[4]9.5	11.4	14.3	15.8
Labor force participation: [5]												
Employed	11.5	12.4	14.5	16.1	15.9	16.9	19.1	20.5	8.4	9.1	11.1	12.7
Unemployed	0.4	0.4	0.5	0.7	0.5	0.6	0.7	1.0	0.3	0.3	0.4	0.5
Not in labor force	88.1	87.2	84.9	83.2	83.6	82.5	80.2	78.5	91.3	90.6	88.5	86.7
Percent below poverty level [6].	11.4	9.7	9.8	9.7	7.8	6.9	7.0	6.6	13.9	11.8	11.9	12.0

[1] Represents those who completed 1 to 3 years of high school.   [2] Represents those who completed 4 years of high school.
[3] Represents those who completed 1 to 3 years of college.   [4] Represents those who completed 4 years of college or more.
[5] Annual averages of monthly figures. Source: U.S. Bureau of Labor Statistics, *Employment and Earnings*, January issues. See footnote 2, Table 574.   [6] Poverty status based on income in preceding year.

Source: Except as noted, U.S. Census Bureau, *Current Population Reports*, P20-546, and earlier reports; "Educational Attainment"; <http://www.census.gov/population/www/socdemo/educ-attn.html>; "Families and Living Arrangements"; <http://www.census.gov/population/www/socdemo/hh-fam.html>; and "Detailed Poverty Tabulations from the CPS"; <http://www.census.gov/hhes/www/poverty/detailedpovtabs.html>.

Table 35. **Persons 65 Years Old and Over—Living Arrangements and Disability Status: 2007**

[In thousands (37,841 represents 37,841,000), except as indicated. The American Community Survey universe includes the household population and the population living in institutions, college dormitories, and other group quarters. Based on a sample and subject to sampling variability; see text, this section and Appendix III]

Relationship by household type	Number	Percent distribu- tion	Type of disability	Total	65 to 74 years old	75 years old and over
Total	37,841	100.0	**Persons with a disability. . . . . . .**	**14,735**	**5,674**	**9,061**
In households	35,981	95.1				
In family households	24,716	65.3	With a sensory disability.	5,893	1,847	4,046
Householder.	12,257	32.4	With a physical disability.	11,285	4,394	6,891
Spouse	8,826	23.3	With a mental disability.	4,467	1,426	3,041
Parent	2,117	5.6	With a self-care disability	3,772	1,134	2,638
Other relatives	1,362	3.6	With a go-outside-home disability	6,354	1,731	4,623
Nonrelatives	154	0.4				
In nonfamily households.	11,265	29.8				
Householder.	10,778	28.5				
Living alone	10,265	27.1				
Not living alone	513	1.4				
Nonrelatives	486	1.3				
In group quarters	1,859	4.9				

Source: U.S. Census Bureau, 2007 American Community Survey; B09017. Relationship by Household Type (Including Living Alone) for the Population 65 Years and Over; B18002. Sex by Age by Disability Status for the Civilian Noninstitutionalized Population 5 Years and Over; B18003. Sex by Age by Sensory Disability for the Civilian Noninstitutionalized Population 5 Years and Over; B18004. Sex by Age by Physical Disability for the Civilian Noninstitutionalized Population 5 Years and Over; B18005. Sex by Age by Mental Disability for the Civilian Noninstitutionalized Population 5 Years and Over; B18006. Sex by Age by Self-Care Disability for the Civilian Noninstitutionalized Population 5 Years and Over; B18007. Sex by Age by Go-Outside-Home Disability for the Civilian Noninstitutionalized Population 16 Years and Over; using American FactFinder; <http://factfinder.census.gov/> (accessed 15 October 2008).

Table 36. **Selected Characteristics of Racial Groups and Hispanic Population: 2007**

[In thousands (197,892 represents 197,892,000), except as indicated. The American Community Survey universe includes the household population and the population living in institutions, college dormitories, and other group quarters. Based on a sample and subject to sampling variability; see text of this section and Appendix III. For definition of median, see Guide to Tabular Presentation]

Characteristic	Total population	White alone	Black or African American alone	American Indian and Alaska Native alone	Asian alone
EDUCATIONAL ATTAINMENT					
Persons 25 years old and over, total	197,892	152,051	22,172	1,426	9,046
Less than 9th grade	12,575	7,626	1,251	132	741
9th to 12th grade, no diploma	18,098	12,181	3,152	208	547
High school graduate (includes equivalency).	59,658	46,127	7,613	476	1,604
Some college, no degree	38,522	30,333	4,709	316	1,066
Associate's degree.	14,705	11,603	1,620	113	614
Bachelor's degree	34,364	27,847	2,534	119	2,696
Graduate degree	19,969	16,333	1,293	62	1,777
Percent high school graduate or higher	84.5	87.0	80.1	76.2	85.8
Percent bachelor's degree or higher	27.5	29.1	17.3	12.7	49.5
OCCUPATION					
Employed civilian population, 16 years old and over, total	142,588	109,123	15,248	931	6,542
Management, professional, and related occupations	49,291	39,900	4,094	236	3,069
Management, business, and financial operations occupations	20,012	16,592	1,483	90	1,036
Professional and related occupations	29,279	23,309	2,611	146	2,033
Service occupations	23,883	16,364	3,675	209	1,029
Sales and office occupations	36,471	28,302	4,053	213	1,506
Farming, fishing, and forestry occupations	996	725	40	15	12
Construction, extraction, and maintenance occupations	13,796	10,876	928	126	244
Construction and extraction occupations	8,869	6,872	549	90	112
Installation, maintenance, and repair occupations	4,926	4,004	379	36	132
Production, transportation, and material moving occupations	18,151	12,957	2,458	133	682
Production occupations	9,374	6,744	1,079	65	468
Transportation and material moving occupations.	8,777	6,212	1,380	68	214
FAMILY INCOME IN THE PAST 12 MONTHS					
Total families	75,119	57,921	8,464	537	3,118
Less than $10,000	3,350	1,872	952	56	105
$10,000 to $19,999	5,562	3,538	1,147	74	195
$20,000 to $29,999	6,885	4,779	1,120	71	215
$30,000 to $39,999	7,244	5,315	988	66	226
$40,000 to $49,999	7,040	5,369	826	52	227
$50,000 to $59,999	6,626	5,197	698	43	223
$60,000 to $74,999	8,815	7,090	807	52	329
$75,000 to $99,999	10,918	8,947	881	56	466
$100,000 to $124,999.	7,034	5,875	484	30	361
$125,000 to $149,999.	3,966	3,323	249	18	236
$150,000 to $199,999.	3,858	3,259	193	12	277
$200,000 or more	3,822	3,357	119	9	260
Median family income in the past 12 months (dol.). . .	61,173	65,652	40,259	40,310	77,046
POVERTY STATUS IN THE PAST 12 MONTHS [2]					
Persons below poverty level	38,052	22,284	8,807	576	1,376
Percent below poverty level	13.0	10.2	24.7	25.3	10.6
Families below poverty level	7,162	4,076	1,801	115	250
Percent below poverty level	9.5	7.0	21.3	21.4	8.0
HOUSING TENURE					
Total householders	112,378	87,486	13,248	787	4,183
Owner-occupied	75,515	63,190	6,155	437	2,537
Renter-occupied	36,863	24,296	7,093	350	1,645

See footnotes at end of table.

Table 36. **Selected Characteristics of Racial Groups and Hispanic Population: 2007**—Con.

[See headnote, page 40]

Characteristic	Native Hawaiian and Other Pacific Islander alone	Some other race alone	Two or more races	Hispanic origin[1]	White alone, not Hispanic
EDUCATIONAL ATTAINMENT					
Persons 25 years old and over, total	**254**	**10,361**	**2,582**	**24,823**	**138,468**
Less than 9th grade	16	2,656	153	5,924	4,498
9th to 12th grade, no diploma	24	1,724	263	3,861	10,176
High school graduate (includes equivalency).	101	3,022	715	7,004	42,383
Some college, no degree	55	1,417	627	3,606	28,343
Associate's degree.	21	511	223	1,315	10,863
Bachelor's degree	27	747	394	2,151	26,524
Graduate degree	11	285	208	963	15,681
Percent high school graduate or higher	84.2	57.7	83.9	60.6	89.4
Percent bachelor's degree or higher	14.7	10.0	23.3	12.5	30.5
OCCUPATION					
Employed civilian population, 16 years old and over, total	**210**	**8,424**	**2,110**	**19,740**	**98,515**
Management, professional, and related occupations	46	1,296	649	3,496	37,859
Management, business and financial operations occupations	19	544	249	1,475	15,723
Professional and related occupations	27	752	400	2,021	22,136
Service occupations	48	2,115	444	4,796	13,854
Sales and office occupations	62	1,761	576	4,241	25,999
Farming, fishing, and forestry occupations	2	192	11	474	456
Construction, extraction, and maintenance occupations	22	1,415	186	3,185	9,180
Construction and extraction occupations	15	1,116	115	2,483	5,555
Installation, maintenance, and repair occupations	6	299	71	702	3,625
Production, transportation, and material moving occupations	31	1,645	245	3,549	11,167
Production occupations	12	889	117	1,911	5,781
Transportation and material moving occupations	19	756	128	1,638	5,386
FAMILY INCOME IN THE PAST 12 MONTHS					
Total families	**94**	**4,003**	**982**	**9,585**	**52,678**
Less than $10,000	5	293	67	649	1,548
$10,000 to $19,999	8	507	94	1,230	2,858
$20,000 to $29,999	8	591	101	1,393	4,022
$30,000 to $39,999	11	536	102	1,261	4,633
$40,000 to $49,999	7	462	97	1,065	4,801
$50,000 to $59,999	9	373	82	859	4,742
$60,000 to $74,999	12	418	107	987	6,555
$75,000 to $99,999	15	418	135	995	8,406
$100,000 to $124,999.	8	199	77	522	5,570
$125,000 to $149,999.	5	93	42	258	3,168
$150,000 to $199,999.	4	71	42	212	3,127
$200,000 or more	2	41	34	153	3,250
Median family income in the past 12 months (dol.). . .	58,990	41,323	53,152	42,074	68,083
POVERTY STATUS IN THE PAST 12 MONTHS [2]					
Persons below poverty level	66	3,890	1,054	9,219	17,404
Percent below poverty level	15.7	21.2	16.8	20.7	9.0
Families below poverty level	13	770	137	1,773	3,140
Percent below poverty level	13.7	19.2	14.0	18.5	6.0
HOUSING TENURE					
Total householders	**122**	**5,029**	**1,523**	**12,311**	**80,690**
Owner-occupied	56	2,309	831	6,142	59,577
Renter-occupied	66	2,721	692	6,170	21,113

[1] Persons of Hispanic origin may be any race.   [2] For explanation of poverty level, see text, Section 13.

Source: U.S. Census Bureau, 2007 American Community Survey; B15002. Sex by Educational Attainment for the Population 25 Years and Over, B24010. Sex by Occupation for the Employed Civilian Population 16 Years and Over, B19101. Family Income in the Past 12 Months (In 2007 Inflation-Adjusted Dollars), B19113. Median Family Income in the Past 12 Months (In 2007 Inflation-Adjusted Dollars), B17001. Poverty Status in the Past 12 Months by Sex by Age, B17010. Poverty Status in the Past 12 Months of Families by Family Type by Presence of Related Children Under 18 Years by Age of Related Children, B25003. Tenure; using American FactFinder; <http://factfinder.census.gov/>.

Population   41

Table 37. American Indian and Alaska Native Population by Tribe: 2000

[As of April. This table shows data for American Indian and Alaska Native tribes alone or in combination of tribes or races. Respondents who identified themselves as American Indian or Alaska Native were asked to report their enrolled or principal tribe. Therefore, data shown here reflect the written tribal entries reported on the questionnaire. Some of the entries (for example, Iroquois, Sioux, Colorado River, and Flathead) represent nations or reservations. The information on tribe is based on self-identification and includes federally or state-recognized tribes, as well as bands and clans]

American Indian and Alaska Native tribe	Number	American Indian and Alaska Native tribe	Number
Total persons [1]	4,119,301	Osage.	15,897
Apache	96,833	Ottawa	10,677
Blackfeet	85,750	Paiute	13,532
Cherokee.	729,533	Pima.	11,493
Cheyenne	18,204	Potawatomi	25,595
Chickasaw	38,351	Pueblo	74,085
Chippewa	149,669	Puget Sound Salish.	14,631
Choctaw	158,774	Seminole	27,431
Colville	9,393	Shoshone	12,026
Comanche	19,376	Sioux	153,360
Cree	7,734	Tohono O'odham.	20,087
Creek	71,310	United Houma Nation.	8,713
Crow.	13,394	Ute.	10,385
Delaware	16,341	Yakama.	10,851
Iroquois	80,822	Yaqui	22,412
Kiowa	12,242	Yuman	8,976
Latin American Indian	180,940	Alaskan Athabascan	18,838
Lumbee	57,868	Aleut.	10,548
Menominee	9,840	Eskimo	54,761
Navajo	298,197	Tlingit-Haida.	22,365

[1] Includes other tribes not shown separately.

Source: U.S. Census Bureau, *The American Indian and Alaska Native Population: 2000*, Census 2000 Brief (C2KBR/01-15), February 2002.

Table 38. Population Living on Selected Reservations, Trust Lands, and Alaska Native Areas: 2000

[As of April. OTSA = Oklahoma Tribal Statistical Area; SDAISA = State Designated American Indian Statistical Area; ANRC = Alaska Native Regional Corporation]

Reservation, Trust Land, or Alaska Native Area	Total population	American Indian and Alaska Native population alone	American Indian and Alaska Native population alone or in combination with one or more races
Navajo Nation Reservation and Off-Reservation Trust Land, AZ—NM—UT.	180,462	173,987	175,228
Cherokee OTSA, OK	462,327	76,041	104,482
Creek OTSA, OK	704,565	51,296	77,253
Lumbee SDAISA, NC	474,100	58,238	62,327
Choctaw OTSA, OK	224,472	29,521	39,984
Cook Inlet ANRC, AK	364,205	24,923	35,972
Chickasaw OTSA, OK.	277,416	22,946	32,372
Calista ANRC, AK.	23,032	19,617	20,353
United Houma Nation SDAISA, LA	839,880	11,019	15,305
Sealaska ANRC, AK	71,507	11,320	15,059
Pine Ridge Reservation and Off-Reservation Trust Land, SD—NE	15,521	14,304	14,484
Doyon ANRC, AK.	97,190	11,182	14,128
Kiowa-Comanche-Apache-Fort Sill Apache OTSA, OK	193,260	9,675	13,045
Fort Apache Reservation, AZ	12,429	11,702	11,854
Citizen Potawatomi Nation-Absentee Shawnee OTSA, OK.	106,624	6,733	10,617
Gila River Reservation, AZ.	11,257	10,353	10,578
Cheyenne-Arapaho OTSA, OK	157,869	7,402	10,310
Tohono O'odham Reservation and Off-Reservation Trust Land, AZ	10,787	9,718	9,794
Osage Reservation, OK.	44,437	6,410	9,209
Rosebud Reservation and Off-Reservation Trust Land, SD	10,469	9,040	9,165
San Carlos Reservation, AZ.	9,385	8,921	9,065
Blackfeet Reservation and Off-Reservation Trust Land, MT	10,100	8,507	8,684
Yakama Reservation and Off-Reservation Trust Land, WA.	31,799	7,411	8,193
Turtle Mountain Reservation and Off-Reservation Trust Land, MT—ND—SD	8,331	8,009	8,043
Flathead Reservation, MT	26,172	6,999	7,883
Zuni Reservation and Off-Reservation Trust Land, NM—AZ	7,758	7,426	7,466
Bering Straits ANRC, AK	9,196	6,915	7,274
Sac and Fox OTSA, OK	55,690	5,334	7,232
Eastern Cherokee Reservation, NC.	8,092	6,665	6,898
Wind River Reservation and Off-Reservation Trust Land, WY.	23,250	6,544	6,864
Hopi Reservation and Off-Reservation Trust Land, AZ.	6,946	6,573	6,633
Fort Peck Reservation and Off-Reservation Trust Land, MT	10,321	6,391	6,577
Cheyenne River Reservation and Off-Reservation Trust Land, SD.	8,470	6,249	6,346
NANA ANRC, AK	7,208	5,944	6,181
Standing Rock Reservation, SD—ND.	8,250	5,964	6,054
Bristol Bay ANRC, AK.	7,892	5,336	5,749
Arctic Slope ANRC, AK.	7,385	5,050	5,453
Crow Reservation and Off-Reservation Trust Land, MT	6,894	5,165	5,275
Red Lake Reservation, MN	5,162	5,071	5,087

Source: U.S. Census Bureau, 2000 Census of Population and Housing, *Profiles of General Demographic Characteristics*. See also <http://factfinder.census.gov/home/aian/index.html>.

42   Population

Table 39. **Social and Economic Characteristics of the Hispanic Population: 2008**

[As of March, except labor force status, annual average (46,026 represents 46,026,000). Excludes members of the Armed Forces except those living off post or with their families on post. Based on Current Population Survey; see text, this section and Appendix III]

Characteristic	Number (1,000)					Percent distribution				
	His-panic, total [1]	Mexi-can	Puerto Rican	Cuban	Cen-tral, South Ameri-can	His-panic, total [1]	Mexi-can	Puerto Rican	Cuban	Central, South Ameri-can
Total persons.	**46,026**	**30,272**	**4,030**	**1,612**	**7,578**	**100.0**	**100.0**	**100.0**	**100.0**	**100.0**
Under 5 years old	5,014	3,669	355	91	639	10.9	12.1	8.8	5.7	8.4
5 to 14 years old	8,322	5,902	710	182	1,092	18.1	19.5	17.6	11.3	14.4
15 to 44 years old	22,456	14,856	1,910	659	3,931	48.9	49.1	47.4	40.8	51.9
45 to 64 years old	7,679	4,510	771	392	1,480	16.7	14.9	19.2	24.3	19.5
65 years old and over	2,555	1,336	285	288	436	5.6	4.4	7.1	17.9	5.8
EDUCATIONAL ATTAINMENT										
Persons 25 years old and over	**25,274**	**15,736**	**2,264**	**1,153**	**4,689**	**100.0**	**100.0**	**100.0**	**100.0**	**100.0**
High school graduate or more	15,737	8,689	1,729	922	3,241	62.3	55.2	76.4	80.0	69.1
Bachelor's degree or more	3,367	1,436	352	324	951	13.3	9.1	15.5	28.1	20.3
LABOR FORCE STATUS [2]										
Civilians 16 years old and over	**32,141**	**20,474**	**2,854**	**1,422**	**(NA)**	**100.0**	**100.0**	**100.0**	**100.0**	**100.0**
Civilian labor force	22,024	14,009	1,822	897	(NA)	68.5	68.4	63.8	63.1	(NA)
Employed	20,346	12,931	1,634	841	(NA)	63.3	63.2	57.3	59.1	(NA)
Unemployed	1,678	1,078	188	57	(NA)	5.2	5.3	6.6	4.0	(NA)
Unemployment rate [3]	7.6	7.7	10.3	6.3	(NA)	(X)	(X)	(X)	(X)	(X)
Male	7.6	7.5	11.6	7.0	(NA)	(X)	(X)	(X)	(X)	(X)
Female	7.7	8.1	8.9	5.3	(NA)	(X)	(X)	(X)	(X)	(X)
Not in labor force	10,116	6,465	1,032	525	(NA)	31.5	31.6	36.2	36.9	(NA)
HOUSEHOLDS										
Total	**13,339**	**8,149**	**1,395**	**610**	**2,413**	**100.0**	**100.0**	**100.0**	**100.0**	**100.0**
Family households	10,394	6,620	967	427	1,881	77.9	81.2	69.3	70.0	78.0
Married-couple families [4]	6,888	4,563	514	307	1,173	51.6	56.0	36.8	50.3	48.6
Male householder, no spouse present	983	651	70	35	195	7.4	8.0	5.0	5.7	8.1
Female householder, no spouse present	2,522	1,406	384	85	513	18.9	17.3	27.5	13.9	21.3
Nonfamily households	2,945	1,529	428	183	532	22.1	18.8	30.7	30.0	22.0
Male householder	1,654	915	226	91	296	12.4	11.2	16.2	14.9	12.3
Female householder.	1,291	614	202	92	236	9.7	7.5	14.5	15.1	9.8
Size:										
One person	2,203	1,105	358	147	376	16.5	13.6	25.7	24.1	15.6
Two people	3,033	1,698	347	233	537	22.7	20.8	24.9	38.2	22.3
Three people	2,529	1,424	284	119	569	19.0	17.5	20.4	19.5	23.6
Four people	2,678	1,760	227	73	516	20.1	21.6	16.3	12.0	21.4
Five people	1,712	1,246	114	27	264	12.8	15.3	8.2	4.4	10.9
Six people	727	554	36	5	111	5.5	6.8	2.6	0.8	4.6
Seven people or more	457	363	30	6	41	3.4	4.5	2.2	1.0	1.7
FAMILY INCOME IN 2007										
Total families [5]	**10,397**	**6,624**	**967**	**427**	**1,838**	**100.0**	**100.0**	**100.0**	**100.0**	**100.0**
Less than $5,000	394	252	58	11	64	3.8	3.8	6.0	2.5	3.5
$5,000 to $14,999	976	591	128	41	160	9.4	8.9	13.2	9.7	8.8
$15,000 to $24,999	1,585	1,114	123	58	239	15.3	16.8	12.7	13.6	13.0
$25,000 to $34,999	1,518	1,054	100	52	253	14.6	15.9	10.4	12.1	13.7
$35,000 to $49,999	1,743	1,137	166	66	305	16.8	17.2	17.2	15.5	16.6
$50,000 to $74,999	1,977	1,204	161	81	405	19.0	18.2	16.6	19.0	22.0
$75,000 and over	2,202	1,272	231	118	411	21.2	19.2	23.9	27.5	22.4
POVERTY STATUS IN 2007										
Families below poverty level [6]	2,045	1,389	221	58	294	19.7	21.0	22.8	13.6	16.0
Persons below poverty level [6]	9,890	6,927	1,000	235	1,266	21.5	22.9	24.8	14.6	16.8
HOUSEHOLD TENURE										
Total occupied units.	**13,339**	**8,150**	**1,395**	**611**	**2,345**	**100.0**	**100.0**	**100.0**	**100.0**	**100.0**
Owner occupied	6,552	4,188	544	379	947	49.1	51.4	39.0	62.0	40.4
Renter occupied [7]	6,787	3,961	852	232	1,398	50.9	48.6	61.0	38.0	59.6

NA Not available.   X Not applicable.   [1] Includes other Hispanic groups not shown separately.   [2] Source: U.S. Bureau of Labor Statistics, "Employment and Earnings Online," January 2009; <http://stats.bls.gov/opub/ee/home.htm>.   [3] Total unemployment as percent of civilian labor force.   [4] In married-couple families, Hispanic origin refers to the householder.   [5] Includes families in group quarters.   [6] For explanation of poverty level, see text, Section 13.   [7] Includes no cash rent.

Source: Except as noted, U.S. Census Bureau, "Educational Attainment"; <http://www.census.gov/population/www/socdemo/educ-attn.html>; "Families and Living Arrangements"; <http://www.census.gov/population/www/socdemo/hh-fam.html>; "Detailed Income Tabulations from the CPS; <http://www.census.gov/hhes/www/income/dinctabs.html>; "Detailed Poverty Tabulations from the CPS"; <http://www.census.gov/hhes/www/poverty/detailedpovtabs.html>, and unpublished data.

Population   43

Table 40. Native and Foreign-Born Population by State: 2007

[263,561 represents 263,561,000. The American Community Survey universe includes the household population and the population living in institutions, college dormitories, and other group quarters. Based on a sample and subject to sampling variability; see text of this section and Appendix III. See headnote, Table 44]

State	Native popu-lation (1,000)	Foreign-born population Number (1,000)	Percent of total popu-lation	Percent entered 2000 or later	State	Native popu-lation (1,000)	Foreign-born population Number (1,000)	Percent of total popu-lation	Percent entered 2000 or later
U.S., total . .	**263,561**	**38,060**	**12.6**	**27.7**					
					MO	5,670	208	3.5	36.7
AL	4,491	137	3.0	44.1	MT	942	16	1.7	25.2
AK	635	49	7.2	27.6	NE	1,676	99	5.6	35.4
AZ	5,347	992	15.6	33.7	NV	2,068	498	19.4	28.7
AR	2,716	118	4.2	36.6	NH	1,248	68	5.1	29.0
CA	26,529	10,024	27.4	22.2					
					NJ	6,955	1,731	19.9	25.7
CO	4,376	485	10.0	32.7	NM	1,787	183	9.3	27.0
CT	3,053	450	12.8	27.0	NY	15,092	4,206	21.8	23.6
DE	799	66	7.6	35.5	NC	8,431	630	7.0	40.2
DC	514	74	12.6	34.4	ND	624	16	2.4	48.1
FL	14,810	3,441	18.9	29.0					
					OH	11,047	419	3.7	32.2
GA	8,676	868	9.1	36.5	OK	3,435	182	5.0	37.7
HI	1,062	221	17.3	21.8	OR	3,380	368	9.8	27.2
ID	1,415	84	5.6	28.3	PA	11,768	665	5.4	30.7
IL	11,084	1,769	13.8	26.0	RI	923	135	12.7	24.4
IN	6,081	264	4.2	36.1					
					SC	4,218	190	4.3	38.4
IA	2,871	117	3.9	37.8	SD	782	15	1.8	35.3
KS	2,609	167	6.0	38.6	TN	5,907	250	4.1	40.8
KY	4,134	108	2.5	45.9	TX	20,075	3,829	16.0	28.6
LA	4,150	143	3.3	35.7	UT	2,430	216	8.2	38.0
ME	1,273	44	3.4	26.5					
					VT	600	21	3.4	21.6
MD	4,924	695	12.4	32.7	VA	6,918	794	10.3	33.8
MA	5,536	914	14.2	30.0	WA	5,673	795	12.3	30.9
MI	9,462	609	6.1	30.6	WV	1,789	23	1.3	30.4
MN	4,853	345	6.6	36.9	WI	5,349	252	4.5	34.2
MS	2,869	49	1.7	44.1	WY	506	16	3.1	35.8

Source: U.S. Census Bureau, 2007 American Community Survey; C05002. Place of Birth by Citizenship Status; and C05005. Year of Entry by Citizenship Status; using American FactFinder; <http://factfinder.census.gov/>; (accessed 24 September 2008).

Table 41. Nativity and Place of Birth of Resident Population—25 Largest Cities: 2007

[750 represents 750,000. The American Community Survey universe includes the household population and the population living in institutions, college dormitories, and other group quarters. Based on a sample and subject to sampling variability; see text of this section and Appendix III. See headnote, Table 44]

City	Total population (1,000)	Native population Total (1,000)	Born in United States (1,000)	Born outside United States (1,000)	Foreign-born population Total Number (1,000)	Percent of total population	Entered 2000 or later Number (1,000)	Percent of foreign-born population
Austin, TX.	750	604	595	9	145	19.4	60	41.3
Baltimore, MD	637	600	595	5	37	5.8	16	41.9
Boston, MA	613	438	422	15	175	28.6	59	33.9
Charlotte, NC	675	587	581	6	88	13.1	39	44.1
Chicago, IL	2,738	2,147	2,097	51	591	21.6	154	26.1
Columbus, OH	733	665	659	6	68	9.3	32	47.8
Dallas, TX.	1,240	914	906	8	326	26.3	105	32.1
Denver, CO.	588	478	473	6	110	18.7	39	35.1
Detroit, MI.	808	765	760	4	44	5.4	15	33.8
El Paso, TX.	605	450	440	10	155	25.6	34	22.1
Fort Worth, TX.	651	528	522	6	123	18.8	39	31.7
Houston, TX	2,047	1,478	1,458	20	569	27.8	185	32.5
Indianapolis, IN [1]	793	735	730	5	58	7.3	27	45.9
Jacksonville, FL.	809	741	725	16	68	8.4	21	30.2
Los Angeles, CA	3,806	2,289	2,259	30	1,517	39.9	339	22.3
Memphis, TN.	637	602	598	4	35	5.5	17	49.5
Nashville-Davidson, TN [1].	593	532	526	6	62	10.4	26	42.7
New York, NY	8,275	5,227	4,915	311	3,048	36.8	722	23.7
Philadelphia, PA.	1,450	1,288	1,240	49	161	11.1	54	33.3
Phoenix, AZ	1,514	1,125	1,113	12	389	25.7	147	37.9
San Antonio, TX.	1,284	1,112	1,090	22	173	13.4	47	27.0
San Diego, CA.	1,277	954	935	19	323	25.3	81	24.9
San Francisco, CA	765	495	482	13	270	35.3	55	20.4
San Jose, CA	922	555	544	11	368	39.8	87	23.7
Washington, DC.	588	514	508	6	74	12.6	26	34.4

[1] Represents the portion of a consolidated city that is not within one or more separately incorporated places.

Source: U.S. Census Bureau, 2007 American Community Survey; C05002. Place of Birth by Citizenship Status; and C05005. Year of Entry by Citizenship Status; using American FactFinder; <http://factfinder.census.gov/>; (accessed 24 September 2008).

44   Population

Table 42. **Native and Foreign-Born Populations by Selected Characteristics: 2008**

[In thousands (299,106 represents 299,106,000). As of March. The foreign-born population includes anyone who is not a U.S. citizen at birth. This includes legal permanent residents (immigrants), temporary migrants (such as students), humanitarian migrants (such as refugees), and persons illegally present in the United States. Based on Current Population Survey, Annual Social and Economic Supplement which includes the civilian noninstitutional population plus Armed Forces living off post or with their families on post; see text, this section, and Appendix III]

Characteristic	Total population	Native population	Foreign-born population			
			Total	Natural-ized citizen	Not U.S. citizen	Year of entry: 2000 to March 2008
Total.	**299,106**	**261,842**	**37,264**	**15,050**	**22,214**	**10,932**
Under 5 years old.	20,902	20,599	302	69	233	302
5 to 14 years old	40,056	38,275	1,781	301	1,480	1,318
15 to 24 years old.	41,843	37,612	4,231	881	3,350	2,345
25 to 34 years old.	40,146	32,160	7,986	1,904	6,082	3,467
35 to 44 years old.	42,132	33,969	8,163	3,018	5,145	1,834
45 to 54 years old.	43,935	37,550	6,385	3,274	3,111	874
55 to 64 years old.	33,302	29,279	4,023	2,490	1,533	431
65 to 74 years old.	19,588	17,083	2,504	1,716	788	237
75 to 84 years old.	12,912	11,462	1,450	1,056	394	101
85 years old and over	4,289	3,853	437	339	98	22
Median age (years).	36.6	35.7	40.1	49.0	34.9	29.0
Male.	146,856	128,179	18,677	6,900	11,777	5,781
Female.	152,250	133,663	18,587	8,150	10,437	5,151
MARITAL STATUS						
Persons 15 years old and over	**238,148**	**202,967**	**35,181**	**14,680**	**20,501**	**9,310**
Married.	123,721	102,096	21,624	9,691	11,933	5,109
Widowed.	14,315	12,572	1,743	1,152	591	163
Divorced.	23,362	21,253	2,109	1,118	991	257
Separated.	5,184	4,096	1,088	390	698	236
Never married	71,565	62,950	8,616	2,328	6,288	3,545
EDUCATIONAL ATTAINMENT						
Persons 25 years old and over	**196,305**	**165,356**	**30,944**	**13,798**	**17,151**	**6,966**
Not high school graduate	26,340	16,851	9,489	2,694	6,795	2,217
High school graduate/some college	112,177	99,537	12,641	6,337	6,304	2,483
Bachelor's degree.	37,559	32,154	5,406	2,966	2,440	1,353
Advanced degree.	20,228	16,816	3,413	1,801	1,612	912
EARNINGS IN 2007 [1]						
Persons 15 years old and over with earnings.	**108,597**	**91,313**	**17,284**	**7,389**	**9,896**	**4,173**
Under $15,000.	6,736	4,991	1,745	420	1,324	626
$15,000 to $24,999.	17,733	13,470	4,263	1,199	3,064	1,334
$25,000 to $34,999.	20,146	16,871	3,275	1,283	1,992	794
$35,000 to $49,999.	23,785	20,772	3,013	1,547	1,466	552
$50,000 to $74,999.	21,933	19,393	2,540	1,475	1,065	442
$75,000 and over.	18,264	15,816	2,448	1,464	984	424
Median earnings (dollars) [2].	40,320	41,133	31,763	41,358	26,701	25,804
HOUSEHOLD SIZE [3]						
Total households.	**116,783**	**101,104**	**15,680**	**7,469**	**8,211**	**3,310**
One person.	32,167	29,161	3,005	1,653	1,352	573
Two persons	38,737	34,910	3,826	2,090	1,736	784
Three persons	18,522	15,588	2,934	1,312	1,622	778
Four persons.	15,865	12,914	2,951	1,276	1,675	655
Five persons	7,332	5,663	1,668	663	1,005	286
Six persons.	2,694	1,889	805	288	517	143
Seven persons or more.	1,467	978	489	186	303	91
INCOME IN 2007 [3]						
Total family households.	**77,873**	**66,015**	**11,858**	**5,570**	**6,288**	**2,405**
Under $15,000.	5,549	4,454	1,096	349	747	372
$15,000 to $24,999.	6,772	5,264	1,508	520	988	371
$25,000 to $34,999.	7,367	5,852	1,515	549	965	338
$35,000 to $49,999.	10,680	8,993	1,687	756	931	311
$50,000 to $74,999.	15,634	13,388	2,246	1,119	1,128	420
$75,000 and over.	31,871	28,064	3,805	2,277	1,530	593
Median income (dollars) [2]	62,359	65,021	50,867	61,591	41,292	40,686
POVERTY STATUS IN 2007 [4]						
Persons below poverty level	**37,276**	**31,126**	**6,150**	**1,426**	**4,724**	**2,662**
Persons at or above poverty level	261,423	230,330	31,093	13,624	17,469	8,255
HOUSEHOLD TENURE [3]						
Total households.	116,783	101,104	15,680	7,469	8,211	3,310
Owner-occupied unit	79,331	71,056	8,275	5,100	3,175	780
Renter-occupied unit [5].	37,454	30,048	7,406	2,370	5,036	2,530

[1] Covers only year-round full-time workers. [2] For definition of median, see Guide to Tabular Presentation. [3] Based on citizenship of householder. [4] Persons for whom poverty status is determined. Excludes unrelated individuals under 15 years old. [5] Includes occupiers who paid no cash rent.

Source: U.S. Census Bureau, unpublished data.

Population 45

Table 43. Foreign-Born Population—Selected Characteristics by Region of Origin: 2008

[In thousands (37,264 represents 37,264,000). As of March. The term foreign-born refers to anyone who is not a U.S. citizen at birth. This includes naturalized U.S. citizens, legal permanent residents (immigrants), temporary migrants (such as foreign students), humanitarian migrants (such as refugees), and persons illegally present in the United States. Based on Current Population Survey, Annual Social and Economic Supplement; see text, this section and Appendix III]

Characteristic	Total foreign-born	Europe	Asia	Latin America Total	Carib-bean	Central America[1]	South America	Other areas
Total	**37,264**	**4,644**	**9,978**	**20,034**	**3,406**	**14,278**	**2,350**	**2,602**
Under 5 years old	302	26	100	138	16	108	13	39
5 to 14 years old	1,781	148	467	1,006	140	752	113	160
15 to 24 years old	4,231	362	910	2,656	344	2,065	247	304
25 to 34 years old	7,986	601	1,968	4,910	516	3,844	549	503
35 to 44 years old	8,163	742	2,175	4,688	711	3,496	480	558
45 to 54 years old	6,385	829	1,834	3,264	645	2,188	431	458
55 to 64 years old	4,023	649	1,310	1,798	489	1,018	292	265
65 to 74 years old	2,504	595	743	979	310	533	136	188
75 to 84 years old	1,450	506	384	470	191	213	67	91
85 years old and over	437	187	87	126	43	62	20	37
EDUCATIONAL ATTAINMENT								
Persons 25 years old and over	**30,944**	**4,108**	**8,501**	**16,235**	**2,905**	**11,353**	**1,977**	**2,100**
Less than ninth grade	6,009	454	635	4,795	343	4,312	139	125
9th to 12th grade (no diploma).	3,481	189	424	2,768	331	2,321	117	99
High school graduate.	7,922	1,146	1,728	4,546	980	2,891	675	502
Some college or associate's degree	4,714	778	1,258	2,153	600	1,129	423	526
Bachelor's degree	5,406	881	2,640	1,375	459	493	424	509
Advanced degree	3,413	661	1,816	598	192	207	199	339
High school graduate or more	21,454	3,465	7,442	8,672	2,231	4,720	1,721	1,876
Bachelor's degree or more	8,818	1,541	4,456	1,973	650	700	623	848
INCOME IN 2007								
Total family households	**11,858**	**1,453**	**3,150**	**6,440**	**1,170**	**4,570**	**700**	**814**
Under $15,000	1,096	83	205	736	176	505	55	71
$15,000 to $24,999	1,508	144	247	1,054	137	852	65	63
$25,000 to $34,999	1,515	132	226	1,069	157	842	71	87
$35,000 to $49,999	1,687	160	333	1,113	189	840	84	81
$50,000 to $74,999	2,246	258	573	1,246	194	869	183	169
$75,000 and over	3,805	675	1,567	1,221	317	662	242	342
Median income (dol.)[2]	50,867	70,667	74,249	39,062	42,604	36,037	58,851	62,192
POVERTY STATUS IN 2007[3]								
Persons below poverty level	6,150	428	1,070	4,257	663	3,334	261	395
Persons at or above poverty level	31,093	4,219	8,904	15,758	2,743	10,925	2,090	2,213

[1] Includes Mexico.   [2] For definition of median, see Guide to Tabular Presentation.   [3] Persons for whom poverty status is determined. Excludes unrelated individuals under 15 years old.

Source: U.S. Census Bureau, unpublished data.

Table 44. Foreign-Born Population by Citizenship Status and Place of Birth: 2007

[In thousands, except percent (38,060 represents 38,060,000). The term foreign-born refers to anyone who is not a U.S. citizen at birth. This includes naturalized U.S. citizens, legal permanent residents (immigrants), temporary migrants (such as foreign students), humanitarian migrants (such as refugees), and persons illegally present in the United States. The American Community Survey universe includes the household population and the population living in institutions, college dormitories, and other group quarters. Based on a sample and subject to sampling variability; see text, this section and Appendix III]

Region	Foreign-born population, total	Naturalized citizen	Not U.S. citizen Number	Percent of foreign-born
Total [1]	**38,060**	**16,182**	**21,878**	**57**
Latin America	20,410	6,311	14,099	69
Caribbean	3,387	1,838	1,549	46
Central America	14,450	3,386	11,065	77
Mexico	11,739	2,561	9,177	78
Other Central America	2,712	824	1,888	70
South America	2,572	1,087	1,485	58
Asia	10,185	5,830	4,355	43
Europe	4,990	3,010	1,980	40
Africa.	1,419	(NA)	(NA)	(NA)
Northern America.	839	(NA)	(NA)	(NA)
Oceania	217	(NA)	(NA)	(NA)

NA Not available.   [1] Includes persons born at sea.

Source: U.S. Census Bureau, 2007 American Community Survey; B05002. Place of Birth by Citizenship Status; C05006. Place of Birth for the Foreign-Born Population; and B05007. Place of Birth by Year of Entry by Citizenship Status for The Foreign-Born Population, using American FactFinder; <http://factfinder.census.gov> (accessed 29 September 2008).

Table 45. Persons Obtaining Legal Permanent Resident Status: 1901 to 2008

[8,795 represents 8,795,000. **For fiscal years ending in year shown**; see text, Section 8. Rates based on Census Bureau estimates as of July 1 for resident population through 1929 and for total population thereafter (excluding Alaska and Hawaii prior to 1959)]

Period	Number (1,000)	Rate [1]	Year	Number (1,000)	Rate [1]
1901 to 1910	8,795	10.4	1990	1,536	6.1
1911 to 1920	5,736	5.7	1995	720	2.7
1921 to 1930	4,107	3.5	2000	841	3.0
1931 to 1940	528	0.4	2001	1,059	3.7
1941 to 1950	1,035	0.7	2002	1,059	3.7
1951 to 1960	2,515	1.5	2003	704	2.4
1961 to 1970	3,322	1.7	2004	958	3.3
1971 to 1980	4,399	2.0	2005	1,122	3.8
1981 to 1990	7,256	3.0	2006	1,266	4.2
1991 to 2000	9,081	3.4	2007	1,052	3.5
2001 to 2008	8,328	3.5	2008	1,107	3.6

[1] Annual rate per 1,000 U.S. population. Rate computed by dividing sum of annual immigration totals by sum of annual U.S. population totals for same number of years.

Source: U.S. Department of Homeland Security, Office of Immigration Statistics, *2008 Yearbook of Immigration Statistics.* See also <http://www.dhs.gov/ximgtn/statistics/publications/yearbook.shtm>.

Table 46. Refugee Arrivals and Individuals Granted Asylum by Country of Nationality: 2005 to 2008

[For year ending September 30. Data shown provide information on the number of persons admitted to the United States as refugees or granted asylum in the United States in the year shown. In cases with no country of nationality refers to country of last residence. For definitions of refugee and asylee, see text, this section. Based on data from the Bureau of Population, Refugees, and Migration of the U.S. Department of State and the Executive Office for Immigration Review of the U.S. Department of Justice]

Country of nationality	Refugee arrivals			Country of nationality	Asylees		
	2005	2007	2008		2005	2007	2008
Total	53,738	48,218	60,108	Total	25,188	25,124	22,930
Burma	1,447	13,896	18,139	China	5,228	6,359	5,459
Iraq	198	1,608	13,823	Colombia	3,363	2,177	1,646
Bhutan	–	–	5,320	Haiti	2,938	1,648	1,237
Iran	1,856	5,481	5,270	Venezuela	1,104	1,152	1,057
Cuba	6,360	2,922	4,177	Iraq	286	671	1,002
Burundi	214	4,545	2,889	Ethiopia	728	843	899
Somalia	10,405	6,969	2,523	Indonesia	470	776	580
Vietnam	2,009	1,500	1,112	Russia	484	496	574
Ukraine	2,889	1,605	1,022	Guatemala	386	680	552
Liberia . . . . . . , . .	4,289	1,606	992	Nepal . . . . , . .	312	413	497
Other countries [1] . . .	24,071	8,086	4,841	Other countries [1]	9,889	9,909	9,427

– Represents zero.   [1] Includes unknown.

Source: U.S. Department of Homeland Security, Office of Immigration Statistics, Annual Flow Report, *Refugees and Asylees: 2008,* June 2009. See also <http://www.dhs.gov/xlibrary/assets/statistics/publications/oisrfafr2008.pdf>.

Table 47. Estimated Unauthorized Immigrants by Selected States and Countries of Birth: 2000 and 2008

[In thousands (8,460 represents 8,460,000). As of January. Unauthorized immigrants refers to foreign-born persons who entered the United States without inspection or who were admitted temporarily and stayed past the date they were required to leave. Unauthorized aliens who have applied for but have not yet received approval to lawfully remain in the United States are considered to be unauthorized. These estimates were calculated using a "residual method," whereby estimates of the legally resident foreign-born population were subtracted from the total foreign-born population in order to derive the unauthorized immigrant population. All of these component populations were resident in the United States on January 1, 2008, and entered during the 1980–2007 period. Persons who entered the United States prior to 1980 were assumed to be legally resident. Estimates of the legally resident foreign-born were based primarily on administrative data of the Department of Homeland Security, while estimates of the total foreign-born population were obtained from the American Community Survey of the U.S. Census Bureau. Estimates for 2000 are based on the same methodology, assumptions, and definitions with the exception that data from Census 2000 were used to estimate the foreign-born population in 2000 that entered the United States from January 1, 1980 through December 31, 1999]

State of residence	2000	2008	Country of birth	2000	2008
United States, total	8,460	11,600	Total	8,460	11,600
California	2,510	2,850	Mexico	4,680	7,030
Texas	1,090	1,680	El Salvador	430	570
Florida	800	840	Guatemala	290	430
New York	540	640	Philippines	200	300
Arizona	330	560	Honduras	160	300
Illinois	440	550	Korea	180	240
Georgia	220	460	China	190	220
New Jersey	350	400	Brazil	100	180
North Carolina	260	380	Ecuador	110	170
Nevada	170	280	India	120	160
Other states	1,760	2,950	Other countries	2,000	2,000

Source: U.S. Department of Homeland Security, Office of Immigration Statistics, "Estimates of the Unauthorized Immigrant Population Residing in the United States: January 2008" (published February 2009); <http://www.dhs.gov/xlibrary/assets/statistics/publications/oisillpe2008.pdf>.

Population   47

Table 48. **Persons Obtaining Legal Permanent Resident Status by Class of Admission: 2000 to 2008**

[For years ending September 30. For definition of immigrants, see text, this section]

Class of admission	2000	2004	2005	2006	2007	2008
Total	841,002	957,883	1,122,257	1,266,129	1,052,415	1,107,126
New arrivals.	407,279	373,962	383,955	446,881	431,368	466,558
Adjustments.	433,723	583,921	738,302	819,248	621,047	640,568
Family-sponsored preferences.	235,092	214,355	212,970	222,229	194,900	227,761
Unmarried sons/daughters of U.S. citizens and their children	27,635	26,380	24,729	25,432	22,858	26,173
Spouses, unmarried sons/daughters of alien residents and their children	124,540	93,609	100,139	112,051	86,151	103,456
Married sons/daughters of U.S. citizens [1]	22,804	28,695	22,953	21,491	20,611	29,273
Brothers or sisters of U.S. citizens [1]	60,113	65,671	65,149	63,255	65,280	68,859
Employment-based preferences	106,642	155,330	246,877	159,081	162,176	166,511
Priority workers [1]	27,566	31,291	64,731	36,960	26,697	36,678
Professionals with advanced degrees or aliens of exceptional ability [1]	20,255	32,534	42,597	21,911	44,162	70,046
Skilled workers, professionals, unskilled workers [1]	49,589	85,969	129,070	89,922	85,030	48,903
Special immigrants [1]	9,014	5,407	10,133	9,539	5,481	9,524
Employment creation (investors) [1]	218	129	346	749	806	1,360
Immediate relatives of U.S. citizens	346,350	417,815	436,115	580,348	494,920	488,483
Spouses	196,405	252,193	259,144	339,843	274,358	265,671
Children [2]	82,638	88,088	94,858	120,064	103,828	101,342
Parents	67,307	77,534	82,113	120,441	116,734	121,470
Refugees	56,091	61,013	112,676	99,609	54,942	90,030
Asylees.	6,837	10,217	30,286	116,845	81,183	76,362
Diversity [3]	50,920	50,084	46,234	44,471	42,127	41,761
Cancellation of removal	12,154	32,702	20,785	29,516	14,927	11,128
Parolees	3,162	7,121	7,715	4,569	1,999	1,172
Nicaraguan Adjustment and Central American Relief Act (NACARA)	20,364	2,292	1,155	661	340	296
Haitian Refugee Immigration Fairness Act (HRIFA) . . .	435	2,451	2,820	3,375	2,448	1,580
Other	2,955	4,503	4,624	5,425	2,453	2,042

[1] Includes spouses and children. [2] Includes orphans. [3] Includes categories of immigrants admitted under three laws intended to diversify immigration: P.L. 99-603, P.L. 100-658, and P.L. 101-649.

Source: U.S. Department of Homeland Security, Office of Immigration Statistics, *2008 Yearbook of Immigration Statistics.* See also <http://www.dhs.gov/ximgtn/statistics/publications/yearbook.shtm>.

Table 49. **Persons Obtaining Legal Permanent Resident Status by Selected Country of Birth and Selected Characteristics: 2008**

[For year ending September 30]

Age, marital status, class of admission	Total [1]	Mexico	China	India	Philip-pines	Cuba	Vietnam	Colom-bia	Haiti
Total	1,107,126	189,989	80,271	63,352	54,030	49,500	31,497	30,213	26,007
Under 18 years old	220,173	39,701	12,593	8,613	11,913	7,361	7,339	5,676	7,390
18 to 24 years old	144,735	29,472	8,024	5,061	6,052	5,848	4,410	3,874	4,018
25 to 34 years old	261,548	42,065	14,213	20,067	9,478	10,243	5,807	6,458	5,301
35 to 44 years old	216,968	32,084	21,363	12,873	9,046	13,031	6,117	6,182	4,318
45 to 54 years old	123,716	17,213	11,731	6,921	6,411	6,490	4,480	4,821	2,313
55 to 64 years old	79,375	14,958	6,079	5,641	6,373	3,966	2,267	2,179	1,336
65 years old and over	60,604	14,494	6,268	4,176	4,755	2,561	1,077	1,023	1,331
Unknown	7	2	–	–	2	–	–	–	–
Single	410,938	65,111	22,597	14,139	20,857	21,004	12,248	10,774	16,744
Married	637,807	115,946	54,052	46,442	29,986	21,127	17,630	17,693	8,466
Other	53,633	8,201	3,462	2,595	3,073	7,008	1,571	1,585	621
Unknown	4,748	731	160	176	114	361	48	161	176
Family-sponsored preferences. . . .	227,761	66,693	16,403	15,042	13,799	2,562	16,016	3,633	9,675
Employment-based preferences . . .	166,511	8,767	15,329	25,577	9,193	12	420	3,208	117
Immediate relatives of U.S. citizens	488,483	111,703	26,515	19,116	30,662	3,183	12,330	15,074	8,958
Diversity programs.	41,761	11	25	65	8	224	3	9	–
Refugee and asylee adjustments . .	166,392	416	21,891	3,423	304	43,455	2,404	8,194	5,620
Other	16,218	2,399	108	129	64	64	324	95	1,637

– Represents zero.   [1] Includes other countries not shown separately.

Source: U.S. Department of Homeland Security, Office of Immigration Statistics, unpublished data.

Table 50. Persons Obtaining Legal Permanent Resident Status by Country of Birth: 1981 to 2008

[In thousands (7,256.0 represents 7,256,000). For years ending Sept. 30. Persons by country prior to 1996 are unrevised]

Country of birth	1981–1990, total	1991–2000, total	2001–2007, total	2008	Country of birth	1981–1990, total	1991–2000, total	2001–2007, total	2008
All countries [1]	7,256.0	9,080.5	7,220.5	1,107.1	Philippines	495.3	505.3	415.0	54.0
Europe [1]	705.6	1,309.1	1,043.1	119.1	Syria	20.6	26.1	18.2	2.6
Albania	(NA)	26.2	34.9	5.8	Taiwan [5]	(6)	106.3	64.1	9.1
Armenia	(X)	[2]26.6	19.9	3.6	Thailand	64.4	48.4	41.8	6.6
Belarus	(X)	[2]28.9	18.9	2.4	Turkey	20.9	26.3	27.4	4.2
Bosnia and Herzegovina	(X)	[2]38.8	85.1	1.5	Vietnam	401.4	420.8	214.8	31.5
Bulgaria	(NA)	23.1	30.5	3.0	Africa [1]	192.3	382.5	526.1	105.9
France	23.1	27.4	26.4	4.9	Egypt	31.4	46.7	46.6	8.7
Germany	70.1	67.6	56.1	7.1	Ethiopia	27.2	49.3	67.1	12.9
Ireland	32.8	58.9	10.9	1.5	Ghana	14.9	35.6	41.5	8.2
Italy	32.9	22.5	18.5	2.5	Nigeria	35.3	67.2	70.1	12.5
Poland	97.4	169.5	92.1	8.4	Somalia	(NA)	20.1	35.5	10.7
Portugal	40.0	22.7	8.4	0.8	Oceania	(NA)	47.9	42.0	5.3
Romania	38.9	57.5	39.8	4.9	North America [1]	3,125.0	3,910.1	2,500.0	393.3
Russia	(X)	[2]127.8	113.1	11.7	Canada	119.2	137.2	123.6	15.1
Serbia and Montenegro [3,4]	19.2	25.8	37.6	3.3	Mexico	1,653.3	2,250.5	1,199.2	190.0
Soviet Union [3]	84.0	103.8	21.3	5.3	Cuba	159.2	178.7	196.4	49.5
Ukraine	(X)	[2]141.0	118.8	10.8	Dominican Republic	251.8	340.8	194.0	31.9
United Kingdom	142.1	135.6	110.6	14.3	Haiti	140.2	181.7	140.9	26.0
Uzbekistan	(X)	[2]22.9	19.4	6.4	Jamaica	213.8	173.4	120.6	18.5
Asia [1]	2,817.4	2,890.2	2,473.1	383.6	Trinidad and Tobago	39.5	63.2	44.1	5.9
Bangladesh	15.2	66.0	63.5	11.8	El Salvador	214.6	217.3	194.5	19.7
Cambodia	116.6	18.5	25.1	3.7	Guatemala	87.9	103.0	121.8	16.2
China [5]	[6]388.8	424.4	447.3	80.3	Honduras	49.5	66.7	46.0	6.5
Hong Kong	63.0	74.0	32.4	3.4	Nicaragua	44.1	94.6	49.6	3.6
India	261.9	383.0	472.6	63.4	Panama	29.0	24.0	12.3	1.7
Iran	154.8	112.5	79.3	13.9	South America [1]	455.9	539.3	617.4	98.6
Iraq	19.6	40.7	28.3	4.8	Argentina	25.7	24.3	34.9	5.4
Israel	36.3	31.9	30.7	5.9	Brazil	23.7	52.2	84.6	12.2
Japan [7]	43.2	61.4	55.3	6.8	Colombia	124.4	130.8	170.8	30.2
Jordan [7]	32.6	39.7	26.6	3.9	Ecuador	56.0	76.3	77.3	11.7
Korea	338.8	171.1	146.8	26.7	Guyana	95.4	73.8	56.0	6.8
Laos	145.6	43.5	11.4	2.2	Peru	64.4	105.6	99.3	15.2
Lebanon	41.6	43.4	27.9	4.3	Venezuela	17.9	29.9	53.3	10.5
Pakistan	61.3	124.5	97.4	19.7					

NA Not available. X Not applicable. [1] Includes countries not shown separately. [2] Covers years 1992–2000. [3] Prior to 1992, data include independent republics; beginning in 1992, data are for unknown republic only. [4] Yugoslavia (unknown republic) prior to February 7, 2003. [5] See footnote 4, Table 1296. [6] Data for Taiwan included with China. [7] Prior to 2003, includes Palestine; beginning in 2003, Palestine included in Unknown.

Source: U.S. Department of Homeland Security, Office of Immigration Statistics, *2008 Yearbook of Immigration Statistics.* See also <http://www.dhs.gov/ximgtn/statistics/publications/yearbook.shtm>.

Table 51. Refugees and Asylees Obtaining Legal Permanent Resident Status by Country of Birth: 1991 to 2008

[For years ending September 30]

Country of birth	1991–2000, total	2001–2007, total	2008	Country of birth	1991–2000, total	2001–2007, total	2008
Total [1]	1,016,820	845,314	166,392	Iran	24,251	27,511	3,465
Europe [1]	425,047	262,770	18,801	Iraq	22,488	15,566	1,420
Albania	3,250	7,845	1,465	Laos	37,203	4,721	1,218
Armenia	1,794	8,953	1,701	Pakistan	1,649	6,025	999
Azerbaijan	[2]10,566	5,079	532	Thailand	22,716	11,180	2,122
Belarus	[2]21,592	7,685	711	Vietnam	206,530	31,019	2,404
Bosnia and Herzegovina	[2]37,251	80,890	772	Africa [1]	51,469	136,587	38,303
Croatia	1,786	9,292	106	Ethiopia [6]	17,829	20,768	4,086
Moldova	[2]10,150	8,612	721	Kenya	1,438	7,648	2,610
Poland	7,451	328	33	Liberia	3,836	15,386	5,240
Romania	15,682	1,076	147	Sierra Leone	272	7,154	1,584
Russia	[2]54,488	26,678	3,114	Somalia	16,737	32,585	10,141
Serbia and Montenegro [3,4]	6,242	23,320	969	Sudan	5,174	17,458	2,693
Soviet Union [3]	117,783	5,660	382	Oceania	291	1,146	116
Ukraine	[2]96,974	50,682	2,690	North America [1]	183,251	197,763	51,726
Uzbekistan	[2]17,991	8,262	3,416	Cuba	142,571	168,771	43,455
Asia [1]	350,702	206,783	44,538	Guatemala	2,029	4,802	951
Afghanistan	9,711	10,972	1,092	Haiti	9,354	15,985	5,620
Burma	721	7,039	2,199	Nicaragua	22,468	1,578	169
Cambodia	6,358	1,260	209	South America [1]	5,840	38,981	12,643
China [5]	7,577	56,312	21,891	Colombia	1,129	25,384	8,194
India	2,538	17,035	3,423	Peru	2,500	5,036	812
				Venezuela	1,390	4,763	2,497

[1] Includes other countries and unknown not shown separately. [2] Covers years 1992–2000. [3] Prior to 1992, data include independent republics; beginning in 1992, data are for unknown republic only. [4] Yugoslavia (unknown republic) prior to February 7, 2003. [5] See footnote 4, Table 1296. [6] Prior to 1993, data include Eritrea.

Source: U.S. Department of Homeland Security, Office of Immigration Statistics, *2008 Yearbook of Immigration Statistics.* See also <http://www.dhs.gov/ximgtn/statistics/publications/yearbook.shtm>.

Population 49

Table 52. Population by Selected Ancestry Group and Region: 2007

[In thousands (301,261 represents 301,261,000). Covers single and multiple ancestries. Ancestry refers to a person's ethnic origin or descent, roots, or heritage; or the place of birth of the person, the person's parents, or ancestors before their arrival in the United States. The American Community Survey universe includes the household population and the population living in institutions, college dormitories, and other group quarters. Based on a sample and subject to sampling variability; see text, this section and Appendix III. For composition of regions, see map, inside front cover]

Ancestry group	Total (1,000)	North-east	Mid-west	South	West	Ancestry group	Total (1,000)	North-east	Mid-west	South	West
		Percent distribution by region						Percent distribution by region			
Total population[1]	301,621	18	22	36	23	Iranian	414	13	8	24	54
Afghan	84	17	4	24	56	Irish	36,496	26	24	32	18
Albanian	175	58	24	13	5	Israeli	151	42	8	23	27
American	19,381	11	21	55	13	Italian	17,844	45	17	21	16
Arab[1]	1,546	26	24	27	23	Latvian	86	29	27	18	25
Egyptian	195	39	12	23	26	Lithuanian	746	39	29	18	14
Iraqi	62	7	48	17	28	Northern European	229	14	17	22	47
Jordanian	64	21	20	32	27	Norwegian	4,656	6	49	12	33
Lebanese	489	25	26	29	20	Pennsylvania German	370	55	25	12	7
Moroccan	76	36	14	33	18	Polish	9,976	33	37	18	12
Palestinian	92	18	23	33	27	Portuguese	1,472	45	3	12	39
Syrian	151	37	17	25	21	Romanian	475	25	27	21	26
Arab	266	19	33	26	22	Russian	3,153	37	17	21	25
Armenian	446	22	10	9	59	Scandinavian	623	7	31	18	44
Assyrian/Chaldean/Syriac	84	3	59	6	32	Scotch-Irish	5,314	15	18	45	22
Australian	98	20	19	25	37	Scottish	6,019	17	20	37	26
Austrian	778	33	22	23	23	Serbian	173	20	45	18	18
Basque	65	4	3	13	80	Slavic	145	29	27	23	21
Belgian	380	11	54	16	19	Slovak	814	44	34	14	8
Brazilian	346	49	5	32	14	Slovene	169	14	58	13	14
British	1,308	16	17	39	28	Sub-Saharan African[1]	2,702	22	17	45	16
Bulgarian	96	18	31	26	25	Cape Verdean	84	87	2	7	4
Cajun	112	3	5	85	7	Ethiopian	160	8	18	41	32
Canadian	712	28	17	27	28	Ghanaian	85	46	11	33	10
Croatian	421	25	40	14	21	Nigerian	224	23	16	47	13
Czech	1,625	12	46	26	16	Somalian	90	9	45	15	30
Czechoslovakian	322	22	33	26	20	African	1,729	18	17	50	14
Danish	1,449	8	33	14	46	Swedish	4,340	13	39	16	32
Dutch	5,071	16	35	27	22	Swiss	1,019	16	35	19	31
Eastern European	391	45	12	21	21	Turkish	171	40	10	32	19
English	28,177	17	21	37	25	Ukrainian	971	41	20	18	22
European	2,998	13	20	32	34	Welsh	1,921	20	23	30	27
Finnish	678	12	47	13	28	West Indian[1,2]	2,479	48	3	44	5
French (except Basque)	9,616	25	24	32	20	British West Indian	99	66	2	28	4
French Canadian	2,184	41	21	23	15	Haitian	814	41	2	54	2
German	50,754	16	39	26	19	Jamaican	905	50	4	43	4
Greek	1,380	34	23	23	20	Trinidadian and Tobagonian	186	64	2	31	4
Guyanese	194	75	2	21	2	West Indian	278	63	4	27	5
Hungarian	1,565	32	31	20	17	Yugoslavian	359	21	30	21	28

[1] Includes other groups not shown separately. [2] Excludes Hispanic-origin groups.

Source: U.S. Census Bureau, 2007 American Community Survey; B04006. People Reporting Ancestry; using American FactFinder; <http://factfinder.census.gov/> (accessed 29 September 2008).

Table 53. Languages Spoken at Home by Language: 2007

[280,950 represents 280,950,000. The American Community Survey universe includes the household population and the population living in institutions, college dormitories, and other group quarters. Based on a sample and subject to sampling variability; see text of this section and Appendix III]

Language	Number (1,000)	Language	Number (1,000)
Total population 5 years old and over	280,950	Other Indic languages	616
Speak only English	225,506	Other Indo-European languages	421
Spanish or Spanish Creole	34,547	Chinese	2,465
French (incl. Patois, Cajun)	1,356	Japanese	459
French Creole	629	Korean	1,062
Italian	799	Mon-Khmer, Cambodian	185
Portuguese or Portuguese Creole	687	Hmong	181
German	1,104	Thai	144
Yiddish	159	Laotian	149
Other West Germanic languages	270	Vietnamese	1,207
Scandinavian languages	135	Other Asian languages	625
Greek	330	Tagalog	1,480
Russian	851	Other Pacific Island languages	359
Polish	638	Navajo	171
Serbo-Croatian	277	Other Native North American languages	201
Other Slavic languages	312	Hungarian	91
Armenian	222	Arabic	767
Persian	350	Hebrew	214
Gujarathi	287	African languages	700
Hindi	533	Other and unspecified languages	117
Urdu	345		

Source: U.S. Census Bureau, 2007 American Community Survey; B16001. Language Spoken at Home by Ability to Speak English for the Population 5 Years and Over; using American FactFinder; <http://factfinder.census.gov/> (accessed: 29 September 2008).

50   Population

Table 54. **Language Spoken at Home by State: 2007**

[280,950 represents 280,950,000. The American Community Survey universe includes the household population and the population living in institutions, college dormitories, and other group quarters. Based on a sample and subject to sampling variability; see text, this section and Appendix III]

State	Population 5 years and over (1,000)	English only (1,000)	Language other than English		State	Population 5 years and over (1,000)	English only (1,000)	Language other than English	
			Number (1,000)	Percent of population 5 years and over				Number (1,000)	Percent of population 5 years and over
U.S.	280,950	225,506	55,444	19.7	MO	5,485	5,168	317	5.8
AL......	4,319	4,135	184	4.3	MT......	899	862	37	4.1
AK......	633	532	101	15.9	NE......	1,646	1,498	148	9.0
AZ......	5,840	4,177	1,663	28.5	NV......	2,372	1,721	650	27.4
AR......	2,638	2,470	168	6.4	NH......	1,241	1,143	98	7.9
CA......	33,891	19,450	14,442	42.6	NJ......	8,130	5,868	2,262	27.8
CO......	4,512	3,756	756	16.7	NM......	1,829	1,176	653	35.7
CT......	3,290	2,651	640	19.4	NY......	18,098	12,868	5,229	28.9
DE......	806	709	97	12.0	NC......	8,429	7,615	815	9.7
DC......	552	472	80	14.5	ND.....	599	564	35	5.9
FL......	17,105	12,639	4,466	26.1	OH......	10,727	10,081	646	6.0
GA......	8,818	7,762	1,057	12.0	OK......	3,357	3,081	276	8.2
HI	1,196	890	305	25.5	OR......	3,511	3,006	505	14.4
ID	1,383	1,247	136	9.8	PA	11,703	10,596	1,107	9.5
IL......	11,962	9,359	2,603	21.8	RI	996	789	207	20.8
IN	5,904	5,466	437	7.4	SC......	4,114	3,873	241	5.9
IA	2,791	2,607	184	6.6	SD.....	740	694	46	6.3
KS......	2,581	2,325	256	9.9	TN.....	5,751	5,415	336	5.8
KY......	3,963	3,799	164	4.1	TX......	21,925	14,487	7,438	33.9
LA......	3,997	3,669	328	8.2	UT......	2,393	2,061	332	13.9
ME......	1,247	1,155	92	7.4	VT......	589	559	30	5.1
MD......	5,244	4,468	775	14.8	VA......	7,202	6,246	956	13.3
MA......	6,072	4,843	1,229	20.2	WA.....	6,046	5,034	1,012	16.7
MI	9,436	8,585	851	9.0	WV	1,708	1,669	39	2.3
MN......	4,844	4,380	465	9.6	WI	5,246	4,817	429	8.2
MS......	2,706	2,614	92	3.4	WY	487	457	30	6.2

Source: U.S. Census Bureau, 2007 American Community Survey; C16005. Nativity by Language Spoken at Home by Ability to Speak English for the Population 5 Years and Over; using American FactFinder; <http://factfinder.census.gov/> (accessed 30 September 2008).

Table 55. **Language Spoken at Home—25 Largest Cities: 2007**

[690 represents 690,000. The American Community Survey universe includes the household population and the population living in institutions, college dormitories, and other group quarters. Based on a sample and subject to sampling variability; see text this section and Appendix III]

City	Population 5 years and over (1,000)	English only (1,000)	Language other than English, total[1]				Spanish (1,000)	Other Indo-European languages (1,000)	Asian and Pacific Island languages (1,000)
			Number (1,000)	Percent of population 5 years and over	Speak English less than "very well" (1,000)				
Austin, TX	690	445	245	35.6	107	191	22	26
Baltimore, MD.	591	540	51	8.7	18	22	14	10
Boston, MA	579	368	211	36.5	105	89	73	39
Charlotte, NC.........	617	515	102	16.5	53	57	19	20
Chicago, IL	2,534	1,619	915	36.1	443	632	166	82
Columbus, OH	675	599	76	11.2	34	23	23	15
Dallas, TX	1,129	635	495	43.8	283	446	20	21
Denver, CO	537	372	165	30.7	87	129	16	11
Detroit, MI	750	677	73	9.7	39	49	11	3
El Paso, TX	548	144	404	73.7	153	392	5	6
Fort Worth, TX	590	399	191	32.3	95	165	9	13
Houston, TX..........	1,870	1,040	830	44.4	468	687	50	72
Indianapolis, IN [2]......	727	651	75	10.3	38	50	12	7
Jacksonville, FL	746	658	87	11.7	35	39	24	18
Los Angeles, CA.......	3,531	1,434	2,097	59.4	1,070	1,544	232	275
Memphis, TN	586	538	47	8.1	28	30	7	8
Nashville-Davidson, TN [2] .	550	473	77	14.0	34	40	14	13
New York, NY.........	7,708	4,010	3,698	48.0	1,824	1,865	1,061	584
Philadelphia, PA	1,343	1,077	265	19.7	121	125	70	57
Phoenix, AZ	1,374	820	554	40.3	288	469	40	22
San Antonio, TX	1,178	628	550	46.7	160	512	20	14
San Diego, CA	1,185	743	443	37.3	204	262	44	127
San Francisco, CA	725	400	325	44.8	177	85	44	191
San Jose, CA.........	854	373	481	56.4	241	217	53	204
Washington, DC	552	472	80	14.5	25	41	22	8

[1] Includes other language groups not shown separately.   [2] Represents the portion of a consolidated city that is not within one or more separately incorporated places.

Source: U.S. Census Bureau, 2007 American Community Survey; C16005. Nativity by Language Spoken at Home by Ability to Speak English for the Population 5 Years and Over; using American FactFinder; <http://factfinder.census.gov/> (accessed 30 September 2008).

Population 51

Table 56. **Marital Status of the Population by Sex, Race, and Hispanic Origin: 1990 to 2008**

[In millions, except percent (181.8 represents 181,800,000). As of March. Persons 18 years old and over. Excludes members of Armed Forces except those living off post or with their families on post. Beginning 2005, population controls based on Census 2000 and an expanded sample of households. Based on Current Population Survey, see text of this section, and Appendix III]

Marital status, race, and Hispanic origin	Total				Male				Female			
	1990	2000	2005	2008	1990	2000	2005	2008	1990	2000	2005	2008
Total [1]	181.8	201.8	217.2	224.5	86.9	96.9	104.8	108.8	95.0	104.9	112.3	115.8
Never married	40.4	48.2	53.9	58.3	22.4	26.1	29.6	32.0	17.9	22.1	24.3	26.3
Married [2]	112.6	120.1	127.4	128.7	55.8	59.6	63.3	64.1	56.7	60.4	64.0	64.5
Widowed.................	13.8	13.7	13.8	14.3	2.3	2.6	2.7	2.9	11.5	11.1	11.1	11.4
Divorced	15.1	19.8	22.1	23.3	6.3	8.5	9.2	9.8	8.8	11.3	12.9	13.6
Percent of total	100.0	100.0	100.0	100.0	100.0	100.0	100.0	100.0	100.0	100.0	100.0	100.0
Never married	22.2	23.9	24.8	25.9	25.8	27.0	28.2	29.4	18.9	21.1	21.6	22.7
Married [2]	61.9	59.5	58.6	57.3	64.3	61.5	60.4	58.9	59.7	57.6	56.9	55.7
Widowed.................	7.6	6.8	6.4	6.4	2.7	2.7	2.6	2.7	12.1	10.5	9.9	9.8
Divorced	8.3	9.8	10.2	10.4	7.2	8.8	8.8	9.0	9.3	10.8	11.5	11.7
White, total [3]	155.5	168.1	177.5	182.6	74.8	81.6	86.6	89.5	80.6	86.6	90.9	93.1
Never married	31.6	36.0	39.7	42.8	18.0	20.3	22.6	24.4	13.6	15.7	17.0	18.5
Married [2]	99.5	104.1	108.3	108.8	49.5	51.8	54.0	54.5	49.9	52.2	54.2	54.3
Widowed.................	11.7	11.5	11.5	11.9	1.9	2.2	2.3	2.4	9.8	9.3	9.2	9.4
Divorced	12.6	16.5	18.1	19.1	5.4	7.2	7.6	8.2	7.3	9.3	10.4	10.9
Percent of total	100.0	100.0	100.0	100.0	100.0	100.0	100.0	100.0	100.0	100.0	100.0	100.0
Never married	20.3	21.4	22.3	23.5	24.1	24.9	26.1	27.2	16.9	18.1	18.7	19.8
Married [2]	64.0	62.0	61.0	59.6	66.2	63.5	62.4	60.9	61.9	60.3	59.7	58.3
Widowed.................	7.5	6.8	6.5	6.5	2.6	2.7	2.6	2.7	12.2	10.8	10.2	10.1
Divorced	8.1	9.8	10.2	10.5	7.2	8.8	8.8	9.1	9.0	10.7	11.5	11.7
Black, total [3]	20.3	24.0	25.2	26.4	9.1	10.7	11.2	11.8	11.2	13.3	13.9	14.6
Never married	7.1	9.5	10.2	10.9	3.5	4.3	4.7	5.1	3.6	5.1	5.5	5.8
Married [2]	9.3	10.1	10.3	10.6	4.5	5.0	5.0	5.2	4.8	5.1	5.2	5.4
Widowed.................	1.7	1.7	1.7	1.7	0.3	0.3	0.3	0.3	1.4	1.4	1.4	1.4
Divorced	2.1	2.8	2.9	3.2	0.8	1.1	1.1	1.2	1.3	1.7	1.8	2.0
Percent of total	100.0	100.0	100.0	100.0	100.0	100.0	100.0	100.0	100.0	100.0	100.0	100.0
Never married	35.1	39.4	40.6	41.3	38.4	40.2	42.0	42.9	32.5	38.3	39.5	39.7
Married [2]	45.8	42.1	41.0	40.1	49.2	46.7	45.5	44.2	43.0	38.0	37.4	37.0
Widowed.................	8.5	7.0	6.6	6.5	3.7	2.8	2.7	2.8	12.4	10.5	10.0	9.6
Divorced	10.6	11.5	11.7	12.1	8.8	10.3	9.8	10.1	12.0	12.8	13.3	13.7
Asian, total [3]	(NA)	(NA)	9.4	10.3	(NA)	(NA)	4.5	4.8	(NA)	(NA)	4.9	5.4
Never married	(NA)	(NA)	2.3	2.6	(NA)	(NA)	1.3	1.5	(NA)	(NA)	1.0	1.2
Married [2]	(NA)	(NA)	6.2	6.7	(NA)	(NA)	2.9	3.1	(NA)	(NA)	3.3	3.5
Widowed.................	(NA)	(NA)	0.4	0.5	(NA)	(NA)	0.1	0.1	(NA)	(NA)	0.3	0.4
Divorced	(NA)	(NA)	0.5	0.4	(NA)	(NA)	0.2	0.1	(NA)	(NA)	0.3	0.3
Percent of total	100.0	100.0	100.0	100.0	100.0	100.0	100.0	100.0	100.0	100.0	100.0	100.0
Never married	(NA)	(NA)	24.8	25.8	(NA)	(NA)	29.7	30.9	(NA)	(NA)	20.3	21.2
Married [2]	(NA)	(NA)	65.6	65.1	(NA)	(NA)	64.7	64.7	(NA)	(NA)	66.5	65.4
Widowed.................	(NA)	(NA)	4.3	4.9	(NA)	(NA)	1.3	1.6	(NA)	(NA)	6.7	7.7
Divorced	(NA)	(NA)	5.3	4.3	(NA)	(NA)	4.1	2.8	(NA)	(NA)	6.4	5.6
Hispanic, total [4]	13.6	21.1	27.5	30.3	6.7	10.4	14.1	15.6	6.8	10.7	13.4	14.6
Never married	3.7	5.9	8.6	9.7	2.2	3.4	5.2	5.8	1.5	2.5	3.4	3.9
Married [2]	8.4	12.7	15.6	17.2	4.1	6.2	7.8	8.7	4.3	6.5	7.8	8.5
Widowed.................	0.5	0.9	1.0	1.1	0.1	0.2	0.2	0.2	0.4	0.7	0.8	0.8
Divorced	1.0	1.6	2.2	2.3	0.4	0.7	0.9	0.9	0.6	1.0	1.3	1.4
Percent of total	100.0	100.0	100.0	100.0	100.0	100.0	100.0	100.0	100.0	100.0	100.0	100.0
Never married	27.2	28.0	31.3	32.0	32.1	32.3	36.7	37.2	22.5	23.4	25.6	26.7
Married [2]	61.7	60.2	57.0	56.8	60.9	59.7	55.6	55.8	62.4	60.7	58.7	58.2
Widowed.................	4.0	4.2	3.7	3.6	1.5	1.6	1.5	1.3	6.5	6.5	6.1	5.5
Divorced	7.0	7.6	7.9	7.6	5.5	6.4	6.3	5.8	8.5	9.3	9.7	9.6
Non-Hispanic White, total [3,4]	(NA)	(NA)	151.9	154.5	(NA)	(NA)	73.4	74.9	(NA)	(NA)	78.5	79.6
Never married	(NA)	(NA)	31.8	34.0	(NA)	(NA)	17.8	19.1	(NA)	(NA)	13.9	14.9
Married [2]	(NA)	(NA)	93.5	92.7	(NA)	(NA)	46.6	46.3	(NA)	(NA)	47.0	46.3
Widowed.................	(NA)	(NA)	10.6	10.9	(NA)	(NA)	2.1	2.2	(NA)	(NA)	8.5	8.6
Divorced	(NA)	(NA)	16.0	16.9	(NA)	(NA)	6.8	7.3	(NA)	(NA)	9.2	9.6
Percent of total	100.0	100.0	100.0	100.0	100.0	100.0	100.0	100.0	100.0	100.0	100.0	100.0
Never married	(NA)	(NA)	20.9	22.0	(NA)	(NA)	24.3	25.5	(NA)	(NA)	17.7	18.8
Married [2]	(NA)	(NA)	61.5	60.0	(NA)	(NA)	63.5	61.8	(NA)	(NA)	59.7	58.2
Widowed.................	(NA)	(NA)	6.9	7.1	(NA)	(NA)	2.8	3.0	(NA)	(NA)	10.8	10.8
Divorced	(NA)	(NA)	10.6	10.9	(NA)	(NA)	9.3	9.7	(NA)	(NA)	11.7	12.1

NA Not available.   [1] Includes persons of other races not shown separately.   [2] Includes persons who are married with spouse present, married with spouse absent, and separated.   [3] Beginning 2005, data represent persons who selected this race group only and exclude persons reporting more than one race. The CPS in 1990 and 2000 only allowed respondents to report one race group. See also comments on race in the text for this section.   [4] Hispanic persons may be any race.

Source: U.S. Census Bureau, Current Population Reports, P20-537 and earlier reports; and "Families and Living Arrangements"; <http://www.census.gov/population/www/socdemo/hh-fam.html>.

Table 57. Marital Status of the Population by Sex and Age: 2008

[As of March (108,783 represents 108,783,000). Excludes members of Armed Forces except those living off post or with their families on post. Population controls based on Census 2000 and an expanded sample of households. Based on Current Population Survey, see text, this section, and Appendix III]

Sex and age	Number of persons (1,000)					Percent distribution				
	Total	Never married	Married [1]	Wid-owed	Divorced	Total	Never married	Married [1]	Wid-owed	Divorced
Male	**108,783**	**31,969**	**64,129**	**2,912**	**9,772**	**100.0**	**29.4**	**58.9**	**2.7**	**9.0**
18 to 19 years old	3,998	3,907	90	–	1	100.0	97.7	2.3	–	–
20 to 24 years old	10,380	9,064	1,229	9	78	100.0	87.3	11.8	0.1	0.8
25 to 29 years old	10,711	6,299	4,078	15	318	100.0	58.8	38.1	0.1	3.0
30 to 34 years old	9,471	3,270	5,581	17	603	100.0	34.5	58.9	0.2	6.4
35 to 39 years old	10,283	2,387	6,938	24	935	100.0	23.2	67.5	0.2	9.1
40 to 44 years old	10,585	2,088	7,180	54	1,264	100.0	19.7	67.8	0.5	11.9
45 to 54 years old	21,530	3,087	15,079	228	3,136	100.0	14.3	70.0	1.1	14.6
55 to 64 years old	16,072	1,213	12,211	398	2,250	100.0	7.5	76.0	2.5	14.0
65 to 74 years old	8,973	399	7,104	619	851	100.0	4.4	79.2	6.9	9.5
75 years old and over . . .	6,781	255	4,640	1,549	338	100.0	3.8	68.4	22.8	5.0
Female	**115,766**	**26,299**	**64,521**	**11,395**	**13,551**	**100.0**	**22.7**	**55.7**	**9.8**	**11.7**
18 to 19 years old	3,856	3,658	181	3	14	100.0	94.9	4.7	0.1	0.4
20 to 24 years old	10,127	7,990	1,978	20	139	100.0	78.9	19.5	0.2	1.4
25 to 29 years old	10,326	4,695	5,106	47	479	100.0	45.5	49.4	0.5	4.6
30 to 34 years old	9,596	2,504	6,255	57	780	100.0	26.1	65.2	0.6	8.1
35 to 39 years old	10,438	1,675	7,476	94	1,193	100.0	16.0	71.6	0.9	11.4
40 to 44 years old	10,806	1,462	7,538	165	1,640	100.0	13.5	69.8	1.5	15.2
45 to 54 years old	22,389	2,298	15,415	745	3,930	100.0	10.3	68.9	3.3	17.5
55 to 64 years old	17,215	1,181	11,346	1,464	3,225	100.0	6.9	65.9	8.5	18.7
65 to 74 years old	10,602	444	6,023	2,662	1,472	100.0	4.2	56.8	25.1	13.9
75 years old and over . . .	10,411	392	3,205	6,137	678	100.0	3.8	30.8	58.9	6.5

– Represents or rounds to zero.   [1] Includes persons who are married with spouse present, married with spouse absent, and separated.

Source: U.S. Census Bureau, "America's Families and Living Arrangements: 2008, Table A1. Marital Status of People 15 Years and Over, by Age, Sex, Personal Earnings, Race, and Hispanic Origin, 2008"; published January 2009; <http://www.census.gov/population/www/socdemo/hh-fam/cps2008.html>.

Table 58. Living Arrangements of Persons 15 Years Old and Over by Selected Characteristics: 2008

[In thousands (237,993 represents 237,993,000). As of March. See headnote, Table 57]

Living arrangement	Total	15 to 19 years old	20 to 24 years old	25 to 34 years old	35 to 44 years old	45 to 54 years old	55 to 64 years old	65 to 74 years old	75 years old and over
Total [1]	**237,993**	**21,297**	**20,507**	**40,105**	**42,112**	**43,919**	**33,287**	**19,575**	**17,192**
Alone	32,167	143	1,507	3,931	3,800	5,579	5,995	4,542	6,671
With spouse.	120,258	195	2,748	19,198	26,980	28,573	22,474	12,592	7,497
With other persons	85,568	20,959	16,252	16,976	11,332	9,767	4,818	2,441	3,024
White [2]	192,842	16,274	16,011	31,374	33,457	35,906	28,003	16,649	15,168
Alone	25,939	95	1,128	2,932	2,859	4,372	4,878	3,725	5,952
With spouse.	102,956	162	2,384	16,243	22,496	24,204	19,526	11,145	6,796
With other persons	63,947	16,017	12,499	12,199	8,102	7,330	3,599	1,779	2,420
Black [2]	28,493	3,340	2,913	5,271	5,249	5,198	3,372	1,832	1,317
Alone	4,618	44	280	659	678	907	877	626	545
With spouse.	8,813	20	171	1,304	2,194	2,395	1,593	753	384
With other persons	15,062	3,276	2,462	3,308	2,377	1,896	902	453	388
Asian [2]	10,776	810	866	2,266	2,363	1,900	1,305	752	512
Alone	916	1	54	237	151	134	121	108	110
With spouse.	6,163	4	82	1,175	1,704	1,468	990	498	241
With other persons	3,697	805	730	856	508	298	194	146	161
Hispanic origin [3]	32,677	3,798	3,616	8,134	6,900	4,885	2,789	1,530	1,025
Alone	2,203	14	128	388	352	420	370	285	245
With spouse.	15,002	85	763	3,994	4,190	2,919	1,721	897	432
With other persons	15,472	3,699	2,725	3,752	2,358	1,546	698	348	348
Non-Hispanic White [2, 3] .	162,522	12,805	12,726	23,824	27,032	31,319	25,397	15,212	14,207
Alone	23,923	83	1,017	2,584	2,533	3,993	4,534	3,457	5,722
With spouse.	88,816	83	1,680	12,491	18,556	21,426	17,901	10,293	6,384
With other persons	49,783	12,639	10,029	8,749	5,943	5,900	2,962	1,462	2,101

[1] Includes other races and non-Hispanic groups not shown separately.   [2] See footnote 3, Table 56.   [3] Persons of Hispanic origin may be any race.

Source: U.S. Census Bureau, "America's Families and Living Arrangements: 2008, Table A2. Family Status and Household Relationship of People 15 Years and Over, by Marital Status, Age, Sex, Race, and Hispanic Origin: 2008"; published January 2009; <http://www.census.gov/population/www/socdemo/hh-fam/cps2008.html> and unpublished data.

Population   53

Table 59. **Households, Families, Subfamilies, and Married Couples: 1980 to 2008**

[In thousands, except as indicated (80,776 represents 80,776,000). As of March. Excludes members of Armed Forces except those living off post or with their families on post. Beginning 2005, population controls based on Census 2000 and an expanded sample of households. Based on Current Population Survey, see text, this section and Appendix III. Minus sign (–) indicates decrease]

Type of unit	1980	1990	2000	2005	2006	2007	2008	Percent change 1980– 1990	1990– 2000	2000– 2008
Households	80,776	93,347	104,705	113,343	114,384	116,011	116,783	16	12	12
Persons per household.	2.76	2.63	2.62	2.57	2.57	2.56	2.56	(X)	(X)	(X)
White [1]	70,766	80,163	87,671	92,880	93,588	94,705	95,112	13	9	8
Black [1]	8,586	10,486	12,849	13,809	14,002	14,354	14,551	22	23	13
Hispanic [2]	3,684	5,933	9,319	12,178	12,519	12,973	13,339	61	57	43
Family households	59,550	66,090	72,025	76,858	77,402	78,425	77,873	11	9	8
Married couple	49,112	52,317	55,311	57,975	58,179	58,945	58,370	7	6	6
Male householder [3]	1,733	2,884	4,028	4,901	5,130	5,063	5,100	66	40	27
Female householder [3]	8,705	10,890	12,687	13,981	14,093	14,416	14,404	25	17	14
Nonfamily households	21,226	27,257	32,680	36,485	36,982	37,587	38,910	28	20	19
Male householder	8,807	11,606	14,641	16,543	16,753	17,338	17,872	32	26	22
Female householder	12,419	15,651	18,039	19,942	20,230	20,249	21,038	26	15	17
One person	18,296	22,999	26,724	30,137	30,453	31,132	32,167	26	16	20
Families.	59,550	66,090	72,025	76,858	77,402	78,425	77,873	11	9	8
Persons per family.	3.29	3.17	3.17	3.13	3.13	3.13	3.15	(X)	(X)	(X)
With own children [4].	31,022	32,289	34,605	36,211	36,466	36,757	35,709	4	7	3
Without own children [4].	28,528	33,801	37,420	40,647	40,936	41,668	42,164	18	11	13
Married couple	49,112	52,317	55,311	57,975	58,179	58,945	58,370	7	6	6
With own children [4]	24,961	24,537	25,248	25,919	25,982	26,158	25,173	–2	3	(Z)
Without own children [4]	24,151	27,780	30,062	32,056	32,197	32,787	33,197	15	8	10
Male householder [3]	1,733	2,884	4,028	4,901	5,130	5,063	5,100	66	40	27
With own children [4]	616	1,153	1,786	2,021	2,095	2,015	2,162	87	55	21
Without own children [4]	1,117	1,731	2,242	2,880	3,035	3,049	2,937	55	30	31
Female householder [3]	8,705	10,890	12,687	13,981	14,093	14,416	14,404	25	17	14
With own children [4]	5,445	6,599	7,571	8,270	8,389	8,585	8,374	21	15	11
Without own children [4]	3,261	4,290	5,116	5,711	5,703	5,832	6,030	32	19	18
Unrelated subfamilies	360	534	571	515	504	567	526	48	7	9
Married couple	20	68	37	62	36	89	95	(B)	(B)	(B)
Male reference persons [3] . . .	36	45	57	61	59	52	63	(B)	(B)	(B)
Female reference persons [3] . . .	304	421	477	392	409	429	368	39	13	–23
Related subfamilies	1,150	2,403	2,984	3,427	3,265	3,829	3,855	109	24	29
Married couple	582	871	1,149	1,336	1,312	1,645	1,664	50	32	45
Father-child [3].	54	153	201	387	347	331	335	(B)	31	67
Mother-child [3].	512	1,378	1,634	1,704	1,606	1,852	1,855	169	19	14
Married couples	49,714	53,256	56,497	59,373	59,528	60,676	60,129	7	6	6
With own household	49,112	52,317	55,311	57,975	58,179	58,945	58,370	7	6	6
Without own household	602	939	1,186	1,398	1,348	1,731	1,759	56	26	48
Percent without	1.2	1.8	2.1	2.4	2.3	2.9	2.9	(X)	(X)	(X)

B Not shown; base less than 75,000.   X Not applicable.   Z Less than 0.5 percent.   [1] Beginning with the 2003 Current Population Survey (CPS), respondents could choose more than one race. Beginning 2005, data shown represent persons who selected this race group only and exclude persons reporting more than one race. The CPS prior to 2003 only allowed respondents to report one race group. See also comments on race in the text for this section.   [2] Persons of Hispanic origin may be any race.   [3] No spouse present.   [4] Under 18 years old.

Source: U.S. Census Bureau, "Families and Living Arrangements"; <http://www.census.gov/population/www/socdemo/hh-fam.html>.

Table 60. **Married Couples by Race and Hispanic Origin of Spouses: 1980 to 2008**

[In thousands (49,714 represents 49,714,000). As of March. Persons 15 years old and over. Persons of Hispanic origin may be of any race. Based on Current Population Survey; see headnote, Table 59 and Appendix III]

Race and origin of spouses	1980	1990	2000	2008
Married couples, total [1].	49,714	53,256	56,497	60,129
Interracial married couples, total	651	964	1,464	2,340
White [2]/Black [2]	167	211	363	481
Black husband/White wife	122	150	268	317
White husband/Black wife	45	61	95	164
White [2]/other race [3]	450	720	1,051	1,737
Black [2]/other race [3]	34	33	50	122
HISPANIC ORIGIN				
Hispanic/Hispanic	1,906	3,085	4,739	6,390
Hispanic/other origin (not Hispanic).	891	1,193	1,743	2,222
All other couples (not of Hispanic origin)	46,917	48,979	50,015	51,517

[1] Includes other married couples not shown separately.   [2] See footnote 1, Table 59.   [3] "Other race" is any race other than White or Black, such as American Indian, Japanese, Chinese, etc. This total excludes combinations of other races by other races.

Source: U.S. Census Bureau, Table MS-3. Interracial Married Couples: 1980 to 2002 (published 15 September 2004); <http://www.census.gov/population/www/socdemo/hh-fam.html>; and unpublished data.

54 Population

Table 61. **Households and Persons Per Household by Type of Household: 1990 to 2008**

[As of March (93,347 represents 93,347,000). See headnote, Table 59]

Type of household	Households						Persons per household		
	Number (1,000)			Percent distribution					
	1990	2000	2008	1990	2000	2008	1990	2000	2008
Total households	**93,347**	**104,705**	**116,783**	**100**	**100**	**100**	**2.63**	**2.62**	**2.56**
Family households	66,090	72,025	77,873	71	69	67	3.22	3.24	3.22
Married couple family	52,317	55,311	58,370	56	53	50	3.25	3.26	3.22
Male householder, no spouse present	2,884	4,028	5,100	3	4	4	3.04	3.16	3.21
Female householder, no spouse present. . .	10,890	12,687	14,404	12	12	12	3.10	3.17	3.21
Nonfamily households.	27,257	32,680	38,910	29	31	33	1.22	1.25	1.25
Living alone	22,999	26,724	32,167	25	26	27	1.00	1.00	1.00
Male householder.	11,606	14,641	17,872	12	14	15	1.33	1.34	1.34
Living alone	9,049	11,181	13,870	10	11	12	1.00	1.00	1.00
Female householder	15,651	18,039	21,038	17	17	18	1.14	1.17	1.17
Living alone	13,950	15,543	18,297	15	15	16	1.00	1.00	1.00

Source: U.S. Census Bureau, Current Population Reports, P20-537, and earlier reports; and "Families and Living Arrangements"; <http://www.census.gov/population/www/socdemo/hh-fam.html>.

Table 62. **Households by Age of Householder and Size of Household: 1990 to 2008**

[In millions (93.3 represents 93,300,000). As of March. Based on Current Population Survey; see headnote, Table 59]

Age of householder and size of household	1990	2000	2005	2008					
				Total [1]	White [2]	Black [2]	Asian [2]	His-panic [3]	Non-Hispanic White [3]
Total.	**93.3**	**104.7**	**113.3**	**116.8**	**95.1**	**14.5**	**4.5**	**13.3**	**82.8**
Age of householder:									
15 to 24 years old	5.1	5.9	6.7	6.5	5.0	1.1	0.2	1.2	3.9
25 to 29 years old	9.4	8.5	9.2	9.4	7.4	1.3	0.4	1.6	5.9
30 to 34 years old	11.0	10.1	10.1	9.8	7.5	1.4	0.6	1.8	5.9
35 to 44 years old	20.6	24.0	23.2	22.4	17.7	3.1	1.1	3.1	14.5
45 to 54 years old	14.5	20.9	23.4	24.5	19.9	3.2	0.9	2.5	17.6
55 to 64 years old	12.5	13.6	17.5	19.9	16.6	2.3	0.6	1.5	15.2
65 to 74 years old	11.7	11.3	11.5	12.2	10.4	1.3	0.3	0.8	9.6
75 years old and over . . .	8.4	10.4	11.6	11.8	10.5	0.9	0.2	0.6	10.0
One person	23.0	26.7	30.1	32.2	25.9	4.6	0.9	2.2	23.9
Male	9.0	11.2	12.8	13.9	11.2	1.9	0.4	1.1	10.1
Female	14.0	15.5	17.3	18.3	14.7	2.7	0.5	1.1	13.8
Two persons	30.1	34.7	37.4	38.7	32.7	4.1	1.2	3.0	29.9
Three persons	16.1	17.2	18.3	18.5	14.6	2.5	0.9	2.5	12.4
Four persons	14.5	15.3	16.4	15.9	12.8	1.9	0.8	2.7	10.3
Five persons	6.2	7.0	7.2	7.3	5.9	0.8	0.3	1.7	4.3
Six persons	2.1	2.4	2.5	2.7	2.1	0.4	0.1	0.7	1.4
Seven or more. . . .	1.3	1.4	1.4	1.5	1.0	0.2	0.1	0.4	0.6

[1] Includes other races, not shown separately. [2] Beginning with the 2003 Current Population Survey (CPS), respondents could choose more than one race. 2008 data represent persons who selected this race group only and exclude persons reporting more than one race. The CPS in prior years only allowed respondents to report one race group. See also comments on race in the text for this section. [3] Hispanic persons may be any race.

Source: U.S. Census Bureau, Current Population Reports, P20-537, and earlier reports; and "Families and Living Arrangements"; <http://www.census.gov/population/www/socdemo/hh-fam.html>.

Table 63. **Unmarried-Partner Households by Region and Sex of Partners: 2007**

[The American Community Survey universe includes the household population and the population living in institutions, college dormitories, and other group quarters. For composition of regions, see inside front cover. Based on a sample and subject to sampling variability; see text, this section and Appendix III]

Item	Total	Northeast	Midwest	South	West
Total households	**112,378**	**20,594**	**25,778**	**41,381**	**24,625**
Unmarried-partner households	6,209	1,173	1,432	2,077	1,527
Male householder and male partner	396	74	77	139	105
Male householder and female partner.	2,834	527	666	947	693
Female householder and female partner	358	76	70	117	94
Female householder and male partner	2,622	496	619	873	634
All other households	106,169	19,421	24,346	39,305	23,098

Source: U.S. Census Bureau, 2007 American Community Survey; B11009. Unmarried-Partner Households and Household Type by Sex of Partner; using American FactFinder; <http://factfinder.census.gov/> (accessed 29 September 2008).

Table 64. Families by Number of Own Children Under 18 Years Old: 2000 to 2008

[As of March (72,025 represents 72,025,000). Based on Current Population Survey; see headnote, Table 67]

Race, Hispanic origin, and year	Number of families (1,000) Total	No children	One child	Two children	Three or more children	Percent distribution Total	No children	One child	Two children	Three or more children
ALL FAMILIES [1]										
2000	72,025	37,420	14,311	13,215	7,080	100	52	20	18	10
2005	76,858	40,647	15,069	13,741	7,400	100	53	20	18	10
2008, total	77,873	42,164	15,160	13,158	7,391	100	54	19	17	9
Married couple	58,370	33,197	9,733	9,886	5,555	100	57	17	17	9
Male householder [2]	5,100	2,937	1,323	597	242	100	58	26	12	5
Female householder [2]	14,404	6,030	4,104	2,675	1,594	100	42	28	19	11
WHITE FAMILIES [3]										
2000	60,251	32,144	11,496	10,918	5,693	100	53	19	18	9
2005	63,079	34,255	11,872	11,127	5,825	100	54	19	18	9
2008, total	63,566	35,378	11,784	10,650	5,754	100	56	19	17	9
Married couple	50,247	29,082	8,051	8,421	4,693	100	58	16	17	9
Male householder [2]	3,892	2,166	1,077	478	171	100	56	28	12	4
Female householder [2]	9,427	4,129	2,655	1,752	891	100	44	28	19	9
BLACK FAMILIES [3]										
2000	8,664	3,882	2,101	1,624	1,058	100	45	24	19	12
2005	8,902	4,077	2,059	1,641	1,125	100	46	23	18	13
2008, total	9,256	4,327	2,216	1,562	1,152	100	47	24	17	12
Married couple	4,322	2,332	819	690	481	100	54	19	16	11
Male householder [2]	796	496	166	87	48	100	62	21	11	6
Female householder [2]	4,138	1,499	1,231	784	622	100	36	30	19	15
ASIAN FAMILIES [3]										
2005	3,142	1,535	730	646	230	100	49	23	21	7
2008, total	3,299	1,648	753	649	248	100	50	23	20	8
Married couple	2,647	1,234	623	572	218	100	46	24	22	8
Male householder [2]	221	170	27	15	9	100	77	12	7	4
Female householder [2]	431	245	103	62	21	100	57	24	14	5
HISPANIC FAMILIES [4]										
2000	7,561	2,747	1,791	1,693	1,330	100	36	24	22	18
2005	9,521	3,528	2,130	2,163	1,699	100	37	22	23	18
2008, total	10,394	3,962	2,350	2,316	1,766	100	38	23	22	17
Married couple	6,888	2,464	1,478	1,656	1,291	100	36	21	24	19
Male householder [2]	983	619	187	114	63	100	63	19	12	6
Female householder [2]	2,522	880	684	546	412	100	35	27	22	16
NON-HISPANIC WHITE FAMILIES [3, 4]										
2005	54,257	30,965	9,924	9,151	4,217	100	57	18	17	8
2008, total	53,902	31,680	9,649	8,478	4,095	100	59	18	16	8
Married couple	43,739	26,741	6,692	6,845	3,461	100	61	15	16	8
Male householder [2]	2,991	1,598	911	369	112	100	53	30	12	4
Female householder [2]	7,171	3,341	2,046	1,263	520	100	47	29	18	7

[1] Includes other races and non-Hispanic groups not shown separately. [2] No spouse present. [3] Beginning with the 2003 Current Population Survey (CPS), respondents could choose more than one race. Beginning 2005, data represent persons who selected this race group only and exclude persons reporting more than one race. The CPS prior to 2003 only allowed respondents to report one race group. See also comments on race in the text for this section. [4] Hispanic persons may be any race.

Source: U.S. Census Bureau, Current Population Reports, P20-537 and earlier reports; and "Families and Living Arrangements"; <http://www.census.gov/population/www/socdemo/hh-fam.html> and unpublished data.

Table 65. Family Households With Own Children Under Age 18 by Type of Family, 2000 and 2008, and by Age of Householder, 2008

[As of March (34,605 represents 34,605,000). See headnote, Table 67]

Age of householder	Family households with children Number (1,000)	Percent of all family households	Married couple households with children Number (1,000)	Percent of all married couple households	Male householder with children [1] Number (1,000)	Percent of all male householder families [1]	Female householder with children [1] Number (1,000)	Percent of all female householder families [1]
2000, total	34,605	48	25,248	46	1,786	44	7,571	60
2008, total	35,709	46	25,173	43	2,162	42	8,374	58
15 to 24 years old	1,779	53	711	58	174	21	894	68
25 to 34 years old	9,842	74	6,455	72	633	53	2,753	90
35 to 44 years old	14,195	80	10,453	74	736	69	3,007	85
45 to 54 years old	8,306	46	6,340	46	495	47	1,471	48
55 to 64 years old	1,316	10	1,034	9	90	17	191	12
65 years old and over	272	2	179	2	35	7	58	3

[1] No spouse present.

Source: U.S. Census Bureau, Current Population Reports, P20-537 and earlier reports; and "America's Families and Living Arrangements: 2008"; published January 2009; <http://www.census.gov/population/www/socdemo/hh-fam/cps2008.html>.

Table 66. Families by Type, Race, and Hispanic Origin: 2008

[In thousands (77,873 represents 77,873,000). As of March. Excludes members of Armed Forces except those living off post or with their families on post. Population controls based on Census 2000 and an expanded sample of households. Based on Current Population Survey, see text of this section and Appendix III]

Characteristic	All families	Married couple families — All races [1]	White [2]	Black [2]	Asian [2]	Hispanic [3]	Non-Hispanic White [2,3]	Female family householder [4] — All races [1]	White [2]	Black [2]	Asian [2]	Hispanic [3]	Non-Hispanic White [2,3]	Male family householder, [4] all races
All families	**77,873**	**58,370**	**50,247**	**4,322**	**2,647**	**6,888**	**43,739**	**14,404**	**9,427**	**4,138**	**431**	**2,522**	**7,171**	**5,100**
Age of householder:														
Under 25 years old	3,359	1,224	1,060	89	23	331	749	1,318	794	433	45	314	515	817
25 to 34 years old	13,253	8,993	7,663	611	491	1,794	5,984	3,065	1,794	1,063	87	631	1,245	1,196
35 to 44 years old	17,601	12,989	10,887	1,083	733	1,989	8,996	3,551	2,286	1,053	107	706	1,658	1,061
45 to 54 years old	17,949	13,842	11,757	1,174	662	1,391	10,436	3,043	2,098	792	90	452	1,687	1,064
55 to 64 years old	13,218	11,144	9,706	803	442	781	8,976	1,562	1,052	424	54	241	832	513
65 to 74 years old	7,503	6,365	5,672	382	206	401	5,290	940	671	218	26	110	570	197
75 years old and over	4,990	3,813	3,503	181	90	202	3,309	925	731	155	22	69	665	252
Without own children under 18	42,164	33,197	29,082	2,332	1,234	2,464	26,741	6,030	4,129	1,499	245	880	3,341	2,937
With own children under 18	35,709	25,173	21,165	1,990	1,414	4,425	16,998	8,374	5,298	2,639	186	1,642	3,830	2,162
One own child under 18	15,160	9,733	8,051	819	623	1,478	6,692	4,104	2,655	1,231	103	684	2,046	1,323
Two own children under 18	13,158	9,886	8,421	690	572	1,656	6,845	2,675	1,752	784	62	546	1,263	597
Three or more own children under 18	7,391	5,555	4,693	481	218	1,291	3,461	1,594	891	622	21	412	520	242
Average per family with own children under 18	1.86	1.92	1.94	2.01	1.67	2.06	1.90	1.77	1.72	1.91	1.55	1.93	1.62	1.53
Age of own children:														
Of any age	46,995	31,696	26,582	2,565	1,809	5,189	21,691	12,206	8,016	3,574	293	2,156	6,085	3,093
Under 25 years old	41,647	29,221	24,572	2,330	1,635	4,875	19,976	9,837	6,251	3,074	226	1,869	4,588	2,589
Under 12 years old	26,125	18,722	15,744	1,442	1,066	3,549	12,399	5,933	3,670	1,932	129	1,237	2,577	1,470
Under 6 years old	15,733	11,510	9,714	839	649	2,312	7,542	3,312	1,941	1,179	79	733	1,289	912
Under 3 years old	9,192	6,867	5,851	473	366	1,341	4,583	1,769	1,035	637	39	391	689	556
Under 1 year old	3,401	2,602	2,257	171	117	475	1,806	582	363	193	3	140	238	217
Members 65 and older:														
Without members 65 and older	61,852	45,909	39,218	3,578	2,165	6,022	33,529	11,783	7,532	3,584	319	2,216	5,556	4,160
With members 65 and older	16,021	12,461	11,029	744	482	867	10,210	2,621	1,895	554	112	306	1,615	940
Marital status of householder:														
Married, spouse present	58,370	58,370	50,247	4,322	2,647	6,888	43,739	(X)	(X)	(X)	(X)	(X)	(X)	(X)
Married, spouse absent	2,721	(X)	(X)	(X)	(X)	(X)	(X)	2,079	1,350	584	91	567	853	642
Separated	1,932	(X)	(X)	(X)	(X)	(X)	(X)	1,546	1,003	468	40	416	634	386
Other	789	(X)	(X)	(X)	(X)	(X)	(X)	533	347	116	51	151	219	256
Widowed	2,718	(X)	(X)	(X)	(X)	(X)	(X)	2,269	1,686	468	69	245	1,457	449
Divorced	6,575	(X)	(X)	(X)	(X)	(X)	(X)	4,968	3,788	929	122	662	3,179	1,607
Never married	7,489	(X)	(X)	(X)	(X)	(X)	(X)	5,087	2,604	2,157	150	1,047	1,682	2,401

X Not applicable.   [1] Includes other races and non-Hispanic groups not shown separately.   [2] Beginning with the 2003 Current Population Survey (CPS), respondents could choose more than one race. Data represent persons who selected this race group only and exclude persons reporting more than one race. See also comments on race in the text for this section.   [3] Persons of Hispanic origin may be any race.   [4] No spouse present.

Source: U.S. Census Bureau, "America's Families and Living Arrangements: 2008"; published January 2009; <http://www.census.gov/population/www/socdemo/hh-fam/cps2008.html> and unpublished data.

Table 67. Family Groups With Children Under 18 Years Old by Race and Hispanic Origin: 1990 to 2008

[In thousands. As of March (34,670 represents 34,670,000). Family groups comprise family households, related subfamilies, and unrelated subfamilies. Excludes members of Armed Forces except those living off post or with their families on post. Beginning 2005, population controls based on Census 2000 and an expanded sample of households. Based on Current Population Survey, see text of this section, and Appendix III]

Race and Hispanic origin of householder or reference person	Number (1,000)					Percent distribution		
	1990	2000	2005	2007	2008	1990	2000	2008
All races, total [1]........	34,670	37,496	39,317	39,983	38,938	100	100	100
Two-parent family groups [2]........	24,921	25,771	26,482	28,276	27,344	72	69	70
One-parent family groups.........	9,749	11,725	12,835	11,707	11,594	28	31	30
Maintained by mother...........	8,398	9,681	10,366	9,965	9,753	24	26	25
Maintained by father...........	1,351	2,044	2,469	1,742	1,841	4	5	4
White, total [3]........	28,294	30,079	30,960	31,357	30,451	100	100	100
Two-parent family groups [2]........	21,905	22,241	22,319	23,646	22,857	77	74	75
One-parent family groups.........	6,389	7,838	8,641	7,711	7,594	23	26	25
Maintained by mother...........	5,310	6,216	6,747	6,359	6,138	19	21	20
Maintained by father...........	1,079	1,622	1,894	1,353	1,456	4	5	5
Black, total [3]........	5,087	5,530	5,495	5,761	5,603	100	100	100
Two-parent family groups [2]........	2,006	2,135	2,065	2,404	2,256	39	39	40
One-parent family groups.........	3,081	3,396	3,430	3,357	3,347	61	61	59
Maintained by mother...........	2,860	3,060	3,037	3,067	3,080	56	55	55
Maintained by father...........	221	335	393	289	267	4	6	5
Asian, total [3]........	(NA)	1,469	1,757	1,794	1,789	100	100	100
Two-parent family groups [2]........	(NA)	1,184	1,472	1,568	1,513	(NA)	81	84
One-parent family groups.........	(NA)	285	285	226	276	(NA)	19	15
Maintained by mother...........	(NA)	236	222	185	225	(NA)	16	12
Maintained by father...........	(NA)	49	63	42	51	(NA)	3	3
Hispanic, total [4]........	3,429	5,503	6,752	7,193	7,213	100	100	100
Two-parent family groups [2]........	2,289	3,625	4,346	4,984	5,072	67	66	70
One-parent family groups.........	1,140	1,877	2,406	2,209	2,141	33	34	30
Maintained by mother...........	1,003	1,565	1,964	1,987	1,903	29	28	26
Maintained by father...........	138	313	442	221	238	4	6	3
Non-Hispanic White, total [3,4]...	(NA)	24,847	24,730	24,697	23,765	100	100	100
Two-parent family groups [2]........	(NA)	18,750	18,253	18,956	18,099	(NA)	75	76
One-parent family groups.........	(NA)	6,096	6,476	5,741	5,666	(NA)	25	24
Maintained by mother...........	(NA)	4,766	4,984	4,585	4,423	(NA)	19	18
Maintained by father...........	(NA)	1,331	1,492	1,155	1,243	(NA)	5	5

NA Not available.   [1] Includes other races and non-Hispanic groups not shown separately.   [2] Beginning 2007, includes children living both with married and unmarried parents.   [3] Beginning with the 2003 Current Population Survey (CPS), respondents could choose more than one race. Beginning 2005, data represent persons who selected this race group only and exclude persons reporting more than one race. The CPS prior to 2003 allowed respondents to report only one race group. See also comments on race in the text for this section.   [4] Hispanic persons may be any race.

Source: U.S. Census Bureau, Current Population Reports, P20-537, and earlier reports; and "Families and Living Arrangements"; <http://www.census.gov/population/www/socdemo/hh-fam.html>.

Table 68. Parents and Children in Stay-At-Home Parent Family Groups: 1995 to 2008

[In thousands (22,973 represents 22,973,000). Family groups with children include those families that maintain their own household (family households with own children); those that live in the home of a relative (related subfamilies); and those that live in the home of a nonrelative (unrelated subfamilies). Stay-at-home parent groups are married-couple family groups with children under 15 where one parent is in the labor force all of the previous year and their spouse is out of the labor force for the entire year with the reason 'taking care of home and family.' Only married couples with children under 15 are included. Based on Current Population Survey; see Appendix III]

Year	Married-couple family groups with children under 15 years old			Children under 15 years old in married-couple family groups		
	Total	With stay-at-home mothers	With stay-at-home fathers	Total in married-couple family groups	With stay-at-home mothers	With stay-at-home fathers
1995	22,973	4,440	64	41,008	9,106	125
1996	22,808	4,633	49	40,739	9,693	115
1997	22,779	4,617	71	40,798	9,788	140
1998	22,881	4,555	90	41,038	9,432	196
1999	22,754	4,731	71	41,003	9,796	143
2000	22,953	4,785	93	41,860	10,087	180
2001	22,922	4,934	81	41,862	10,194	148
2002	23,339	5,206	106	41,802	10,573	189
2003	23,209	5,388	98	41,654	11,028	175
2004	23,160	5,571	147	41,409	11,205	268
2005	23,305	5,584	142	41,111	11,224	247
2006	23,232	5,646	159	41,259	11,372	283
2007	23,507	5,563	165	41,558	11,193	303
2008	22,445	5,327	140	41,037	11,132	234

Source: U.S. Census Bureau, Table SHP-1. Parents and Children in Stay-At-Home Parent Family Groups: 1994 to Present; published January 2009; <http://www.census.gov/population/www/socdemo/hh-fam.html>.

Table 69. Children Under 18 Years Old by Presence of Parents: 2000 to 2008

[As of **March (72,012 represents 72,012,000)**. Excludes persons under 18 years old who maintained households or family groups. Based on Current Population Survey; see headnote, Table 67]

Race Hispanic origin, and year	Number (1,000)	Both parents [1]	Percent living with—						
			Mother only					Father only	Neither parent
			Total	Divorced	Married, spouse absent	Never married	Widowed		
ALL RACES [2]									
2000	72,012	69.1	22.4	7.9	4.5	9.2	1.0	4.2	4.2
2005	73,494	67.3	23.4	7.9	4.6	10.1	0.8	4.8	4.5
2007	73,746	70.7	22.6	7.7	4.7	9.4	0.8	3.2	3.5
2008	74,107	69.9	22.8	7.5	4.6	9.8	0.9	3.5	3.8
WHITE [3]									
2000	56,455	75.3	17.3	(NA)	(NA)	(NA)	(NA)	4.3	3.1
2005	56,234	73.5	18.4	7.9	4.0	5.8	0.7	4.7	3.4
2007	56,223	76.8	17.3	7.6	3.8	5.2	0.6	3.2	2.7
2008	56,482	76.0	17.5	7.5	3.9	5.3	0.7	3.6	2.9
BLACK [3]									
2000	11,412	37.6	49.0	(NA)	(NA)	(NA)	(NA)	4.2	9.2
2005	11,293	35.0	50.2	8.7	8.1	32.0	1.3	5.0	9.8
2007	11,310	39.5	50.2	8.5	9.3	31.0	1.4	3.6	6.8
2008	11,342	37.5	51.1	8.6	8.2	32.7	1.6	3.3	8.1
ASIAN [3]									
2005	2,843	83.6	10.2	4.0	2.3	2.7	1.3	3.6	2.5
2007	2,953	87.2	9.0	1.8	3.5	2.9	0.7	1.6	2.1
2008	2,980	85.1	10.2	2.7	3.5	3.2	0.9	2.3	2.4
HISPANIC [4]									
2000	11,613	65.1	25.1	(NA)	(NA)	(NA)	(NA)	4.4	5.4
2005	14,241	64.7	25.4	6.1	7.1	11.4	0.8	4.8	5.2
2007	15,113	69.9	24.5	6.4	7.0	10.4	0.7	2.1	3.6
2008	15,642	69.7	24.1	5.8	7.0	10.5	0.7	2.3	3.9
NON-HISPANIC WHITE [3, 4]									
2005	43,106	75.9	16.4	8.5	3.1	4.2	0.7	4.8	2.9
2007	42,261	78.6	15.3	8.1	2.8	3.7	0.6	3.6	2.5
2008	42,052	77.8	15.5	8.1	3.0	3.7	0.7	4.1	2.6

NA Not available. [1] Beginning in 2007, includes children living both with married and unmarried parents. [2] Includes other races and non-Hispanic groups not shown separately. [3] Beginning with the 2003 Current Population Survey (CPS), respondents could choose more than one race. Beginning 2005, data represent persons who selected this race group only and exclude persons reporting more than one race. The CPS prior to 2003 allowed respondents to report only one race group. See also comments on race in the text for this section. [4] Hispanic persons may be any race.

Source: U.S. Census Bureau, "Families and Living Arrangements"; <http://www.census.gov/population/www/socdemo /hh-fam.html>.

Table 70. Grandparents Living With Grandchildren by Race and Sex: 2007

[**6,210 represents 6,210,000**. Covers both grandparents living in own home with grandchildren present and grandparents living in grandchildren's home. The American Community Survey universe includes the household population and the population living in institutions, college dormitories, and other group quarters. Based on a sample and subject to sampling variability; see text, this section and Appendix III]

Race, Hispanic origin, and sex	Grandparents living with grandchildren, total	Grandparents responsible for grandchildren		
		Total	30 to 59 years old	60 years old and over
Grandparents living with own grandchildren under 18 years old (1,000)	6,210	2,514	1,681	833
PERCENT DISTRIBUTION				
Total	100.0	100.0	100.0	100.0
White alone	59.5	60.6	60.1	61.6
Black or African American alone	19.3	24.1	24.1	23.9
American Indian and Alaska Native alone	1.4	1.9	1.9	1.9
Asian alone	7.6	3.3	2.3	5.3
Native Hawaiian and Other Pacific Islander alone	0.3	0.3	0.3	0.3
Some other race alone	10.3	8.2	9.5	5.6
Two or more races	1.5	1.7	1.8	1.4
Hispanic origin [1]	23.2	19.0	21.1	14.8
White alone, not Hispanic	47.2	50.4	49.1	52.9
Male	35.4	37.1	35.2	40.9
Female	64.6	62.9	64.8	59.1

[1] Persons of Hispanic origin may be any race.

Source: U.S. Census Bureau, American Community Survey 2007, Subject Table S1002; using American FactFinder; <http://factfinder.census.gov/>; (accessed 29 September 2008).

Population   59

Table 71. Nonfamily Households by Sex and Age of Householder: 2008

[In thousands (17,872 represents 17,872,000). As of March. See headnote, Table 72]

Item	Male householder					Female householder				
	Total	15 to 24 yrs. old	25 to 44 yrs. old	45 to 64 yrs. old	65 yrs. old and over	Total	15 to 24 yrs. old	25 to 44 yrs. old	45 to 64 yrs. old	65 yrs. old and over
Total	17,872	1,668	6,678	6,406	3,119	21,038	1,526	4,140	6,871	8,500
One person (living alone) . .	13,870	845	4,681	5,427	2,914	18,297	805	3,050	6,147	8,296
Nonrelatives present	4,002	823	1,996	980	203	2,742	721	1,092	724	203
Never married.	9,030	1,601	4,779	2,202	447	6,729	1,460	2,950	1,753	565
Married [1]	1,652	35	616	723	278	1,190	35	318	547	291
Widowed	1,916	7	45	361	1,503	7,381	10	98	1,127	6,146
Divorced	5,275	25	1,238	3,121	891	5,738	21	774	3,444	1,500

[1] No spouse present.

Source: U.S. Census Bureau, "America's Families and Living Arrangements: 2008" (published January 2009); <http://www.census.gov/population/www/socdemo/hh-fam/cps2008.html>.

Table 72. Persons Living Alone by Sex and Age: 1990 to 2008

[As of March (22,999 represents 22,999,000). Excludes members of Armed Forces except those living off post or with their families on post. Beginning 2005, population controls based on Census 2000 and an expanded sample of households. Based on Current Population Survey, see text, this section and Appendix III]

Sex and age	Number of persons (1,000)						Percent distribution				
				2007					2007		
	1990	2000	2005	Total	Male	Female	1990	2000	Total	Male	Female
Total	22,999	26,724	30,137	32,167	13,870	18,297	100	100	100	100	100
15 to 24 years old	1,210	1,144	1,521	1,650	845	805	5	4	5	6	4
25 to 34 years old	3,972	3,848	3,836	3,931	2,361	1,570	17	14	12	17	9
35 to 44 years old	3,138	4,109	3,988	3,800	2,320	1,480	14	15	12	17	8
45 to 64 years old	5,502	7,842	10,180	11,574	5,427	6,147	24	29	36	39	34
65 to 74 years old	4,350	4,091	4,222	4,542	1,459	3,083	19	15	14	11	17
75 years old and over . . .	4,825	5,692	6,391	6,671	1,457	5,213	21	21	21	11	28

Source: U.S. Census Bureau, "Families and Living Arrangements"; <http://www.census.gov/population/www/socdemo/hh-fam.html>.

Table 73. Group Quarters Population by Type of Group Quarter and Selected Characteristics: 2007

[In percent, except as indicated (8,121 represents 8,121,000). The American Community Survey universe includes the household population and the population living in institutions, college dormitories, and other group quarters. Based on a sample and subject to sampling variability; see text, this section and Appendix III]

Characteristic	Total group quarters popu-lation [1]	Adult cor-rec-tional facili-ties	Nurs-ing facili-ties/ skilled nurs-ing facili-ties	Col-lege/ uni-ver-sity hous-ing	Characteristic	Total group quarters popu-lation [1]	Adult cor-rec-tional facili-ties	Nurs-ing facili-ties/ skilled nurs-ing facili-ties	Col-lege/ uni-ver-sity hous-ing
Total population (1,000) .	8,121	2,100	1,788	2,287	One race (1,000)	7,917	2,026	1,777	2,225
PERCENT DISTRIBUTION					PERCENT DISTRIBUTION				
Male	58.8	90.6	31.7	46.2	White	68.6	46.8	84.0	77.1
Female	41.2	9.4	68.3	53.8	Black or African American .	22.2	41.2	12.8	12.6
Under 15 years old	1.1	(X)	(X)	(X)	American Indian and Alaska Native	1.2	2.0	0.4	0.6
15 to 17 years old	2.0	0.5	(X)	1.4	Asian	3.1	0.9	1.2	7.1
18 to 24 years old	37.8	19.0	0.1	96.2	Native Hawaiian and Other				
25 to 34 years old	11.9	32.4	0.6	1.9	Pacific Islander	0.1	0.2	–	0.2
35 to 44 years old	10.9	27.4	1.8	0.2	Some other race	4.8	9.0	1.5	2.4
45 to 54 years old	8.4	15.5	3.9	0.2	Two or more races (1,000) . .	205	74	12	61
55 to 64 years old	4.9	4.2	7.6	0.1					
65 to 74 years old	4.2	0.8	12.9	–	Hispanic origin [2]	10.6	18.9	4.5	5.9
75 to 84 years old	7.9	0.2	30.0	(X)	Not Hispanic	89.4	81.1	95.5	94.1
85 years old and over	10.8	–	43.1	(X)	White alone, Not Hispanic	62.0	36.6	80.7	72.1

– Represents zero. X Not applicable. [1] Includes other types of group quarters not shown separately. [2] Persons of Hispanic origin may be any race.

Source: U.S. Census Bureau, 2007 American Community Survey; S2601A. Characteristics of the Group Quarters Population; and S2601B. Characteristics of the Group Quarters Population by Group Quarters Type; using American FactFinder; <http://factfinder.census.gov/> (accessed 29 September 2008).

Table 74. **Population in Group Quarters by State: 2000 to 2008**

[In thousands (7,780 represents 7,780,000). 2000, as of April; beginning 2005, as of July. For definition of group quarters, see text, this section]

State	2000 [1]	2005	2008	State	2000 [1]	2005	2008	State	2000 [1]	2005	2008
U.S.	**7,780**	**8,105**	**8,247**	KS......	82	82	82	ND......	24	26	27
				KY......	115	115	115	OH......	299	305	315
AL......	115	118	120	LA......	136	133	123	OK......	112	111	115
AK......	19	23	21	ME......	35	37	38	OR......	77	82	82
AZ......	110	113	119					PA......	433	456	470
AR......	74	78	81	MD......	134	139	143	RI	39	38	38
CA......	820	845	866	MA......	221	236	244				
				MI	250	257	258				
CO......	103	108	109	MN......	136	142	144	SC......	135	141	146
CT......	108	113	113	MS......	95	97	100	SD......	28	30	31
DE......	25	24	24					TN......	148	152	152
DC......	36	35	35	MO	164	169	169	TX......	561	595	597
FL	389	412	426	MT......	25	26	27	UT......	40	44	44
				NE......	51	52	53				
GA......	234	265	270	NV......	34	33	33				
HI	36	38	34	NH......	36	38	39	VT......	21	21	22
ID	31	34	35					VA......	231	243	250
IL......	322	337	345	NJ......	195	195	196	WA	136	140	144
IN	178	184	189	NM......	36	42	42	WV	43	46	46
				NY......	581	603	609	WI	156	162	163
IA	104	104	106	NC......	254	271	282	WY	14	14	15

[1] The April 1, 2000, Population Estimates base reflects changes to the Census 2000 population from the Count Question Resolution program and geographic program revisions.

Source: U.S. Census Bureau, "Annual Resident Population Estimates, Estimated Components of Resident Population Change, and Rates of the Components of Resident Population Change for States and Counties: April 1, 2000 to July 1, 2008" (released March 19, 2009); <http://www.census.gov/popest/counties/files/CO-EST2008-ALLDATA.csv>.

Table 75. **Self-Described Religious Identification of Adult Population: 1990 to 2008**

[In thousands (175,440 represents 175,440,000). The methodology of the American Religious Identification Survey (ARIS) 2008 replicated that used in previous surveys. The three surveys are based on random-digit-dialing telephone surveys of residential households in the continental U.S.A (48 states): 54,461 interviews in 2008, 50,281 in 2001, and 113,723 in 1990. Respondents were asked to describe themselves in terms of religion with an open-ended question. Interviewers did not prompt or offer a suggested list of potential answers. Moreover, the self-description of respondents was not based on whether established religious bodies, institutions, churches, mosques or synagogues considered them to be members. Quite the contrary, the surveys sought to determine whether the respondents themselves regarded themselves as adherents of a religious community. Subjective rather than objective standards of religious identification were tapped by the surveys]

Religious group	1990	2001	2008	Religious group	1990	2001	2008
Adult population, total [1] ...	**175,440**	**207,983**	**228,182**	Church of the Brethren	206	358	231
				Nondenominational [3]	194	2,489	8,032
Total Christian [2]	151,225	159,514	173,402	Disciples of Christ	144	492	263
Catholic...................	46,004	50,873	57,199	Reformed/Dutch Reform	161	289	206
Baptist...................	33,964	33,820	36,148	Apostolic/New Apostolic	117	254	970
Protestant-no denomination				Quaker	67	217	130
supplied	17,214	4,647	5,187	Christian Reform	40	79	381
Methodist/Wesleyan	14,174	14,039	11,366	Foursquare Gospel	28	70	116
Lutheran	9,110	9,580	8,674				
Christian-no denomination				Total other religions [2]	5,853	7,740	8,796
supplied.................	8,073	14,190	16,834	Jewish.................	3,137	2,837	2,680
Presbyterian..............	4,985	5,596	4,723	Muslim.................	527	1,104	1,349
Pentecostal/Charismatic	3,116	4,407	5,416	Buddhist	404	1,082	1,189
Episcopalian/Anglican.........	3,043	3,451	2,405	Hindu	227	766	582
Mormon/Latter-Day Saints......	2,487	2,697	3,158	Unitarian/Universalist	502	629	586
Churches of Christ..........	1,769	2,593	1,921	Native American	47	103	186
Jehovah's Witness..........	1,381	1,331	1,914	Wiccan	8	134	342
Seventh-Day Adventist	668	724	938	Pagan	(NA)	140	340
Assemblies of God..........	617	1,105	810	Spiritualist	(NA)	116	426
Holiness/Holy	610	569	352	Other unclassified	837	386	735
Congregational/United Church							
of Christ................	438	1,378	736	No religion specified, total [2] ...	14,331	29,481	34,169
Church of the Nazarene	549	544	358	Atheist.................	[4]	902	1,621
Church of God	590	943	663	Agnostic.................	[4]1,186	991	1,985
Orthodox (Eastern)	502	645	824	No religion	13,116	27,486	30,427
Evangelical/Born Again........	546	1,088	2,154				
Mennonite	235	346	438				
Christian Science............	214	194	339	Refused to reply to question. . .	4,031	11,246	11,815

NA Not available.   [1] Refers to the total number of adults in all fifty states. All other figures are based on projections from surveys conducted in the continental United States (48 states).   [2] Includes other groups not shown separately.   [3] Because of the subjective nature of replies to open-ended questions, these categories are the most unstable as they do not refer to clearly identifiable denominations as much as underlying feelings about religion. Thus they may be the most subject to fluctuation over time.   [4] Atheist included in Agnostic.

Source: 1990 data, Barry A. Kosmin and Seymour P. Lachman, "One Nation Under God: Religion in Contemporary American Society," 1993; 2001 data, Barry A. Kosmin and Ariela Keysar, *Religion in A Free Market: Religious and Non-Religious Americans, Who, What, Why, Where*; Institute for the Study of Secularism in Society and Culture, Trinity College, Hartford, CT. See also <http://www.trincoll.edu/Academics/AcademicResources/values/ISSSC/archive.htm> and <www.AmericanReligionSurvey-ARIS.org> (copyright).

Population   61

Table 76. Religious Bodies—Selected Data

[**Membership data: 2,500 represents 2,500,000.** Includes the self-reported membership of religious bodies with 750,000 or more as reported to the *Yearbook of American and Canadian Churches.* Groups may be excluded if they do not supply information. The data are not standardized so comparisons between groups are difficult. The definition of "church member" is determined by the religious body]

Religious body	Year reported	Churches reported	Membership (1,000)
African Methodist Episcopal Church.	1999	4,174	2,500
African Methodist Episcopal Zion Church	2007	3,337	1,400
American Baptist Churches in the USA	2007	5,558	1,358
Assemblies of God.	2007	12,362	2,863
Baptist Bible Fellowship International.	1997	4,500	1,200
Catholic Church.	2007	18,479	67,117
Christian Churches and Churches of Christ.	1988	5,579	1,072
Christian Methodist Episcopal Church	2006	3,500	850
Church of God in Christ.	1991	15,300	5,500
Church of God (Cleveland, Tennessee)	2007	6,588	1,054
Church of Jesus Christ of Latter-day Saints.	2007	13,201	5,873
Churches of Christ.	2006	13,000	1,639
Episcopal Church.	2007	7,055	2,117
Evangelical Lutheran Church in America.	2007	10,448	4,710
Greek Orthodox Archdiocese of America	2006	560	1,500
Jehovah's Witnesses	2007	12,487	1,092
Lutheran Church—Missouri Synod.	2007	6,167	2,383
National Baptist Convention of America Inc.	2000	(NA)	3,500
National Baptist Convention, U.S.A., Inc.	2004	9,000	5,000
National Missionary Baptist Convention of America.	1992	(NA)	2,500
Orthodox Church in America.	2004	737	1,064
Pentecostal Assemblies of the World, Inc.	2006	1,750	1,500
Presbyterian Church (U.S.A.).	2007	10,820	2,941
Progressive National Baptist Convention, Inc.	1995	2,000	2,500
Seventh Day Adventist Church	2007	4,833	1,000
Southern Baptist Convention	2007	44,696	16,267
United Church of Christ.	2007	5,377	1,145
United Methodist Church.	2006	34,398	7,932

NA Not available.

Source: National Council of Churches USA, New York, NY, *2009 Yearbook of American & Canadian Churches*, annual (copyright). For more church-related information, visit <http://www.ncccusa.org>, or call 888-870-3325.

Table 77. Christian Church Adherents, 2000, and Jewish Population, 2008—States

[**133,377 represents 133,377,000.** Christian church adherents were defined as "all members, including full members, their children and the estimated number of other regular participants who are not considered as communicant, confirmed or full members." The Jewish population includes Jews who define themselves as Jewish by religion as well as those who define themselves as Jewish in cultural terms. Data on Jewish population are based primarily on a compilation of individual estimates made by local Jewish federations. Additionally, most large communities have completed Jewish demographic surveys from which the Jewish population can be determined]

State	Christian adherents 2000		Jewish population 2008		State	Christian adherents 2000		Jewish population 2008	
	Number (1,000)	Percent of population [1]	Number (1,000)	Percent of population [1]		Number (1,000)	Percent of population [1]	Number (1,000)	Percent of population [1]
U.S.	133,377	47.4	6,489	2.2	MO	2,813	50.3	59	1.0
AL.	2,418	54.4	9	0.2	MT.	401	44.4	1	0.1
AK.	210	33.6	6	0.9	NE.	995	58.2	7	0.4
AZ.	1,946	37.9	106	1.7	NV.	604	30.2	70	2.7
AR.	1,516	56.7	2	0.1	NH.	571	46.2	10	0.8
CA.	14,328	42.3	1,200	3.3	NJ	4,262	50.7	479	5.5
CO.	1,604	37.3	90	1.9	NM.	1,041	57.2	11	0.6
CT.	1,828	53.7	113	3.2	NY.	9,569	50.4	1,618	8.4
DE.	299	38.2	15	1.7	NC.	3,598	44.7	28	0.3
DC.	331	57.8	28	4.8	ND.	468	72.9	(Z)	0.1
FL.	5,904	36.9	655	3.6	OH.	4,912	43.3	149	1.3
GA.	3,528	43.1	128	1.3	OK.	2,079	60.3	5	0.1
HI	431	35.6	8	0.6	OR.	1,029	30.1	32	0.8
ID	624	48.3	1	0.1	PA.	6,751	55.0	287	2.3
IL.	6,457	52.0	279	2.2	RI	646	61.7	19	1.8
IN	2,578	42.4	17	0.3	SC.	1,874	46.7	11	0.3
IA	1,698	58.0	6	0.2	SD.	510	67.6	(Z)	(Z)
KS.	1,307	48.6	18	0.7	TN	2,867	50.4	19	0.3
KY.	2,141	53.0	11	0.3	TX	11,316	54.3	130	0.5
LA	2,599	58.2	10	0.2	UT.	1,659	74.3	4	0.2
ME.	450	35.3	14	1.1	VT.	230	37.8	5	0.9
MD.	2,012	38.0	241	4.3	VA.	2,807	39.7	98	1.3
MA.	3,725	58.7	278	4.3	WA	1,872	31.8	43	0.7
MI	3,970	39.9	87	0.9	WV	646	35.7	2	0.1
MN.	2,974	60.5	47	0.9	WI	3,198	59.6	28	0.5
MS.	1,549	54.5	2	0.1	WY	229	46.4	1	0.2

Z Fewer than 500 or .05 percent. [1] Based on U.S. Census Bureau data for resident population enumerated as of April 1, 2000, and estimated as of July 1, 2008.

Source: Christian church adherents—Dale E. Jones, Sherri Doty, Clifford Grammich, James E. Horsch, Richard Houseal, John P. Marcum, Kenneth M. Sanchagrin, and Richard H. Taylor, *Religious Congregations and Membership in the United States: 2000*, 2002 (copyright); Glenmary Research Center, Nashville, TN; <www.glenmary.org/grc>; Jewish population—American Jewish Committee, New York, NY, *American Jewish Year Book* (copyright).

Births, Deaths, Marriages, and Divorces

This section presents vital statistics data on births, deaths, abortions, fetal deaths, fertility, life expectancy, marriages, and divorces. Vital statistics are compiled for the country as a whole by the National Center for Health Statistics (NCHS) and published in its annual report, *Vital Statistics of the United States,* in certain reports of the *Vital and Health Statistics* series, *National Vital Statistics Reports and Health, United States.* Reports in this field are also issued by the various state bureaus of vital statistics. Data on fertility and selected characteristics of women who had a child in the last year, and on marital status and marital history are compiled by the U.S. Census Bureau from its Current Population Survey (CPS; see text, Section 1) and published in *Current Population Reports,* P20 Series. Data on abortions are published by the Alan Guttmacher Institute, New York, NY, in selected issues of *Perspectives on Sexual and Reproductive Health* online at <www.guttmacher.org/sections /abortion.php>.

Registration of vital events—The registration of births, deaths, fetal deaths, and other vital events in the United States is primarily a state and local function. There are 57 vital registration jurisdictions in the U.S.: the fifty states, five territories (Puerto Rico, etc.) District of Columbia, and New York City. Each of the 57 jurisdictions has a direct statistical reporting relationship with NCHS. Vital events occurring to U.S. residents outside the United States are not included in the data.

Births and deaths—The live-birth, death, and fetal-death statistics prepared by NCHS are based on vital records filed in the registration offices of all states, New York City, and the District of Columbia. The annual collection of death statistics on a national basis began in 1900 with a national death-registration area of ten states and the District of Columbia; a similar annual collection of birth statistics for a national birth-registration area began in 1915, also with ten reporting

states and the District of Columbia. Since 1933, the birth- and death-registration areas have comprised the entire United States, including Alaska (beginning 1959) and Hawaii (beginning 1960). National statistics on fetal deaths were first compiled for 1918 and annually since 1922.

Prior to 1951, birth statistics came from a complete count of records received in the Public Health Service (now received in NCHS). From 1951 through 1971, they were based on a 50-percent sample of all registered births (except for a complete count in 1955 and a 20- to 50-percent sample in 1967). Beginning in 1972, they have been based on a complete count for states participating in the Vital Statistics Cooperative Program (VSCP) (for details, see the technical appendix in *Vital Statistics of the United States*) and on a 50-percent sample of all other areas. Beginning in 1986, all reporting areas participated in the VSCP. Mortality data have been based on a complete count of records for each area (except for a 50-percent sample in 1972). Beginning in 1970, births to and deaths of nonresident aliens of the United States and U.S. citizens outside the United States have been excluded from the data. Fetal deaths and deaths among Armed Forces abroad are excluded. Data based on samples are subject to sampling error; for details, see annual issues of *Vital Statistics of the United States.*

Mortality statistics by cause of death are compiled in accordance with World Health Organization regulations according to the *International Classification of Diseases* (ICD). The ICD is revised approximately every 10 years. The tenth revision of the ICD was employed beginning in 1999. Deaths for prior years were classified according to the revision of the ICD in use at the time. Each revision of the ICD introduces a number of discontinuities in mortality statistics; for a discussion of those between the ninth and tenth revisions of the ICD, see *National Vital Statistics*

Reports, Vol. 56, Nos. 2 and 10. Preliminary mortality data are based on a percentage of death records weighted up to the total number of deaths reported for the given year; for a discussion of preliminary data, see *National Vital Statistics Reports*, Vol. 56, No. 16. Information on tests of statistical significance, differences between death rates, and standard errors can also be found in the reports mentioned above.

Some of the tables present age-adjusted death rates in addition to crude death rates. Age-adjusted death rates shown in this section were prepared using the direct method, in which age-specific death rates for a population of interest are applied to a standard population distributed by age. Age adjustment eliminates the differences in observed rates between points in time or among compared population groups that result from age differences in population composition.

Fertility and life expectancy—The total fertility rate, defined as the number of births that 1,000 women would have in their lifetime if, at each year of age, they experienced the birth rates occurring in the specified year, is compiled and published by NCHS. Other data relating to social and medical factors that affect fertility rates, such as contraceptive use and birth expectations, are collected and made available by both NCHS and the Census Bureau. NCHS figures are based on information in birth and fetal death certificates and on the periodic National Surveys of Family Growth; Census Bureau data are based on decennial censuses and the CPS.

Data on life expectancy, the average remaining lifetime in years for persons who attain a given age, are computed and published by NCHS. For details, see *National Vital Statistics Reports*, Vol. 57, No. 14 and <http://www.cdc.gov/nchs/fastats/lifexpec.htm>.

Marriage and divorce—In 1957 and 1958 respectively, the National Office of Vital Statistics established marriage- and divorce-registration areas. Beginning in 1957, the marriage-registration area comprised 30 states, plus Alaska, Hawaii, Puerto Rico, and the Virgin Islands; it currently includes 42 states and the District of Columbia. The divorce-registration area, starting in 1958 with 14 states, Alaska, Hawaii, and the Virgin Islands, currently includes a total of 31 states and the Virgin Islands. Procedures for estimating the number of marriages and divorces in the registration states are discussed in *Vital Statistics of the United States*, Vol. III—Marriage and Divorce. Total counts of events for registration and nonregistration states are gathered by collecting already summarized data on marriages and divorces reported by state offices of vital statistics and by county offices of registration. The collection and publication of detailed marriage and divorce statistics was suspended beginning in January 1996. For additional information, contact the National Center for Health Statistics online at <http://www.cdc.gov/nchs/datawh/datasite/frnotice.htm>.

Vital statistics rates—Except as noted, vital statistics rates computed by NCHS are based on decennial census population figures as of April 1 for 1960, 1970, 1980, 1990, and 2000; and on midyear population figures for other years, as estimated by the Census Bureau (see text, Section 1).

Race—Data by race for births, deaths, marriages, and divorces from NCHS are based on information contained in the certificates of registration. The Census Bureau's Current Population Survey obtains information on race by asking respondents to classify their race as (1) White, (2) Black, (3) American Indian or Alaska Native, (4) Native Hawaiian or Other Pacific Islander, and (5) Asian.

Beginning with the 1989 data year, NCHS is tabulating its birth data primarily by race of the mother. In 1988 and prior years, births were tabulated by race of the child, which was determined from the race of the parents as entered on the birth certificate.

Trend data by race shown in this section are by race of mother beginning with the 1980 data. Hispanic origin of the mother is reported and tabulated independently of race. Thus, persons of Hispanic origin may be any race. The majority of women of Hispanic origin are reported as White.

Statistical reliability—For a discussion of statistical collection, estimation, and sampling procedures and measures of reliability applicable to data from NCHS and the Census Bureau, see Appendix III.

Table 78. Live Births, Deaths, Marriages, and Divorces: 1960 to 2007

[4,258 represents 4,258,000. Beginning 1970, excludes births to, and deaths of nonresidents of the United States. See Appendix III]

Year	Number — Births (1,000)	Deaths Total (1,000)	Deaths Infant [1] (1,000)	Marriages [2] (1,000)	Divorces [3] (1,000)	Rate per 1,000 population — Births	Deaths Total	Deaths Infant [1]	Marriages [2]	Divorces [3]
1960	4,258	1,712	111	1,523	393	23.7	9.5	26.0	8.5	2.2
1970	3,731	1,921	75	2,159	708	18.4	9.5	20.0	10.6	3.5
1971	3,556	1,928	68	2,190	773	17.2	9.3	19.1	10.6	3.7
1972	3,258	1,964	60	2,282	845	15.6	9.4	18.5	10.9	4.0
1973	3,137	1,973	56	2,284	915	14.8	9.3	17.7	10.8	4.3
1974	3,160	1,934	53	2,230	977	14.8	9.1	16.7	10.5	4.6
1975	3,144	1,893	51	2,153	1,036	14.6	8.8	16.1	10.0	4.8
1976	3,168	1,909	48	2,155	1,083	14.6	8.8	15.2	9.9	5.0
1977	3,327	1,900	47	2,178	1,091	15.1	8.6	14.1	9.9	5.0
1978	3,333	1,928	46	2,282	1,130	15.0	8.7	13.8	10.3	5.1
1979	3,494	1,914	46	2,331	1,181	15.6	8.5	13.1	10.4	5.3
1980	3,612	1,990	46	2,390	1,189	15.9	8.8	12.6	10.6	5.2
1981	3,629	1,978	43	2,422	1,213	15.8	8.6	11.9	10.6	5.3
1982	3,681	1,975	42	2,456	1,170	15.9	8.5	11.5	10.6	5.1
1983	3,639	2,019	41	2,446	1,158	15.6	8.6	11.2	10.5	5.0
1984	3,669	2,039	40	2,477	1,169	15.6	8.6	10.8	10.5	5.0
1985	3,761	2,086	40	2,413	1,190	15.8	8.8	10.6	10.1	5.0
1986	3,757	2,105	39	2,407	1,178	15.6	8.8	10.4	10.0	4.9
1987	3,809	2,123	38	2,403	1,166	15.7	8.8	10.1	9.9	4.8
1988	3,910	2,168	39	2,396	1,167	16.0	8.9	10.0	9.8	4.8
1989	4,041	2,150	40	2,403	1,157	16.4	8.7	9.8	9.7	4.7
1990	4,158	2,148	38	2,443	1,182	16.7	8.6	9.2	9.8	4.7
1991	4,111	2,170	37	2,371	1,187	16.2	8.6	8.9	9.4	4.7
1992	4,065	2,176	35	2,362	1,215	15.8	8.5	8.5	9.3	4.8
1993	4,000	2,269	33	2,334	1,187	15.4	8.8	8.4	9.0	4.6
1994	3,953	2,279	31	2,362	1,191	15.0	8.8	8.0	9.1	4.6
1995	3,900	2,312	30	2,336	1,169	14.6	8.7	7.6	8.9	4.4
1996	3,891	2,315	28	2,344	1,150	14.4	8.6	7.3	8.8	4.3
1997	3,881	2,314	28	2,384	1,163	14.2	8.5	7.2	8.9	4.3
1998 [4] . . .	3,942	2,337	28	2,244	1,135	14.3	8.5	7.2	8.4	4.2
1999 [4] . .	3,959	2,391	28	2,358	(NA)	14.2	8.6	7.1	8.6	4.1
2000 [4] . .	4,059	2,403	28	2,329	(NA)	14.4	8.5	6.9	8.3	4.1
2001 [4] . .	4,026	2,416	28	2,345	(NA)	14.1	8.5	6.8	8.2	4.0
2002 [5] . .	4,022	2,443	28	2,254	(NA)	13.9	8.5	7.0	7.8	3.9
2003 [5] . .	4,090	2,448	28	2,245	(NA)	14.1	8.4	6.9	7.7	3.8
2004 [5] . .	4,112	2,398	28	2,279	(NA)	14.0	8.2	6.8	7.8	3.7
2005 [5] . .	4,138	2,448	28	[6]2,249	(NA)	14.0	8.3	6.9	[6]7.6	[6]3.6
2006 [5] . .	4,266	2,426	29	[6,8]2,160	(NA)	14.2	8.1	6.7	[6,8]7.4	[6]3.7
2007 [5,7]. .	4,317	2,424	29	[6]2,205	(NA)	14.3	8.0	6.6	[6]7.3	[6]3.6

NA Not available. [1] Infants under 1 year, excluding fetal deaths; rates per 1,000 registered live births. [2] Includes estimates for some states through 1965 and also for 1976 and 1977, and marriage licenses for some states for all years except 1973 and 1975. Beginning 1978, includes nonlicensed marriages in California. [3] Includes reported annulments and some estimated state figures for all years. [4] Divorce rate excludes data for California, Colorado, Indiana, and Louisiana; population for this rate also excludes these states. [5] Divorce rate excludes data for California, Georgia, Hawaii, Indiana, Louisiana, and Minnesota in 2005 and 2006; California, Georgia, Hawaii, Indiana, and Louisiana in 2004; California, Hawaii, Indiana, Louisiana, and Oklahoma in 2003; and California, Indiana, and Oklahoma in 2002. Populations for these rates also exclude these states. [6] Provisional data. Includes nonresidents. [7] Preliminary data. For births and deaths. [8] Excludes Louisiana.

Source: U.S. National Center for Health Statistics, *Vital Statistics of the United States*, and *National Vital Statistics Reports (NVSR)*; <http://www.cdc.gov/nchs/nvss.htm>.

Table 79. Live Births, Birth Rates, and Fertility Rates by Hispanic-Origin: 2000 to 2007

[4,059 represents 4,059,000. Represents registered births. Excludes births to nonresidents of the United States. Data are based on Hispanic origin and race of mother. Persons of Hispanic origin may be any race. See Appendix III]

Hispanic-origin status and race of mother	Number of births (1,000) 2000	2005	2006	2007, prel.	Birth rate per 1,000 population 2000	2005	2006	2007, prel.	Fertility rate [1] 2000	2005	2006	2007, prel.
Total [2]	4,059	4,138	4,266	4,317	14.4	14.0	14.2	14.3	65.9	66.7	68.5	69.5
Hispanic origin	816	986	1,039	1,062	23.1	23.1	23.4	23.3	95.9	99.4	101.5	102.1
Mexican.	582	693	718	(NA)	25.0	24.7	24.8	(NA)	105.1	107.7	109.0	(NA)
Puerto Rican.	58	63	67	(NA)	18.1	17.2	17.6	(NA)	73.5	72.1	74.0	(NA)
Cuban	13	16	17	(NA)	9.7	10.2	10.4	(NA)	49.3	50.4	49.3	(NA)
Central and South American [3]	113	151	165	(NA)	21.8	22.8	23.9	(NA)	85.1	93.2	98.6	(NA)
Other and unknown Hispanic.	49	62	72	(NA)	[3]	[3]	[3]	(NA)	[3]	[3]	[3]	(NA)
Non-Hispanic [4]	3,200	3,123	3,196	(NA)	13.2	12.4	12.6	(NA)	61.1	60.4	62.0	(NA)
White	2,363	2,280	2,309	2,312	12.2	11.5	11.6	11.5	58.5	58.3	59.5	60.1
Black.	604	584	617	627	17.3	15.7	16.5	16.4	71.4	67.2	70.6	71.6

NA Not available. [1] Live births per 1,000 women age 15 to 44 years in specified group. [2] Includes all races and Hispanic origin status not stated. [3] Rates for the Central and South American population include other and unknown Hispanic. [4] Includes other races not shown separately.

Source: U.S. National Center for Health Statistics, *National Vital Statistics Reports (NVSR)*, *Births: Final Data for 2006*, Vol. 57, No. 7, January 7, 2009 and *Births: Preliminary Data for 2007*, Vol. 57, No. 12, March 18, 2009.

Births, Deaths, Marriages, and Divorces 65

Table 80. Births and Birth Rates by Race, Sex, and Age: 1980 to 2007

[Births in thousands (3,612 represents 3,612,000). Births by race of mother. Excludes births to nonresidents of the United States. For population bases used to derive these data, see text this section, and Appendix III]

Item	1980	1990	1995	2000	2001	2002	2003	2004	2005	2006	2007, prel.
Live births [1]	3,612	4,158	3,900	4,059	4,026	4,022	4,090	4,112	4,138	4,266	4,317
White.	2,936	3,290	3,099	3,194	3,178	3,175	3,226	3,223	3,229	3,310	(NA)
Black	568	684	603	623	606	594	600	616	633	666	(NA)
American Indian, Eskimo, Aleut.	29	39	37	42	42	42	43	44	45	47	49
Asian or Pacific Islander	74	142	160	201	200	211	221	229	231	241	255
Male	1,853	2,129	1,996	2,077	2,058	2,058	2,094	2,105	2,119	2,184	(NA)
Female.	1,760	2,029	1,903	1,982	1,968	1,964	1,996	2,007	2,019	2,081	(NA)
Males per 100 females (sex ratio)	105	105	105	105	105	105	105	105	105	105	(NA)
Age of mother:											
Under 20 years old	562	533	512	478	454	433	421	422	421	442	451
20 to 24 years old.	1,226	1,094	966	1,018	1,022	1,022	1,032	1,034	1,040	1,081	1,083
25 to 29 years old.	1,108	1,277	1,064	1,088	1,058	1,060	1,086	1,104	1,132	1,182	1,209
30 to 34 years old.	550	886	905	929	943	951	976	966	951	950	962
35 to 39 years old.	141	318	384	452	452	454	468	476	483	499	500
40 to 44 years old.	(NA)	(NA)	(NA)	90	93	96	101	104	105	106	105
45 to 49 years old.	(NA)	(NA)	(NA)	4	5	5	6	6	6	7	7
Mean age of mother at first birth (years) .	22.7	24.2	24.5	24.9	25.0	25.1	25.2	25.2	25.2	25.0	(NA)
Birth rate per 1,000 population	**15.9**	**16.7**	**14.6**	**14.4**	**14.1**	**13.9**	**14.1**	**14.0**	**14.0**	**14.2**	**14.3**
White.	15.1	15.8	14.1	13.9	13.7	13.5	13.6	13.5	13.4	13.7	(NA)
Black	21.3	22.4	17.8	17.0	16.3	15.7	15.7	16.0	16.2	16.8	(NA)
American Indian, Eskimo, Aleut.	20.7	18.9	15.3	14.0	13.7	13.8	13.8	14.0	14.2	14.9	15.2
Asian or Pacific Islander	19.9	19.0	16.7	17.1	16.4	16.5	16.8	16.8	16.5	16.6	17.2
Age of mother:											
10 to 14 years old.	1.1	1.4	1.3	0.9	0.8	0.7	0.6	0.7	0.7	0.6	0.6
15 to 19 years old.	53.0	59.9	56.0	47.7	45.3	43.0	41.6	41.1	40.4	41.9	42.5
20 to 24 years old.	115.1	116.5	107.5	109.7	106.2	103.6	102.6	101.7	102.2	105.9	106.4
25 to 29 years old.	112.9	120.2	108.8	113.5	113.4	113.6	115.6	115.5	115.5	116.7	117.5
30 to 34 years old.	61.9	80.8	81.1	91.2	91.9	91.5	95.1	95.3	95.8	97.7	99.9
35 to 39 years old.	19.8	31.7	34.0	39.7	40.6	41.4	43.8	45.4	46.3	47.3	47.5
40 to 44 years old. [2]	3.9	5.5	6.6	8.0	8.1	8.3	8.7	8.9	9.1	9.4	9.5
45 to 49 years old [2].	0.2	0.2	0.3	0.5	0.5	0.5	0.5	0.5	0.6	0.6	0.6
Fertility rate per 1,000 women [3]	**68.4**	**70.9**	**64.6**	**65.9**	**65.3**	**64.8**	**66.1**	**66.3**	**66.7**	**68.5**	**69.5**
White.	65.6	68.3	63.6	65.3	65.0	64.8	66.1	66.1	66.3	68.0	(NA)
Black	84.9	84.8	71.0	70.0	67.6	65.8	66.3	67.6	69.0	72.1	(NA)
American Indian, Eskimo, Aleut.	82.7	76.2	63.0	58.7	58.1	58.0	58.4	58.9	59.9	63.1	64.7
Asian or Pacific Islander	73.2	69.6	62.6	65.8	64.2	64.1	66.3	67.1	66.6	67.5	71.4

NA Not available.   [1] Includes other races not shown separately.   [2] Beginning 2000, rates computed by relating births to women aged 45 to 54 years old to women 45 to 49 years old.   [3] Number of live births per 1,000 women, 15 to 44 years old in specified group.

Source: U.S. National Center for Health Statistics, National Vital Statistics Reports (NVSR), *Births: Final Data for 2006*, Vol. 57, No. 7, January 7, 2009; and *Births: Preliminary Data for 2007*, Vol. 57, No. 12, March 18, 2009; and earlier reports.

Table 81. Births and Birth Rates by Plurality of Birth and Race and Hispanic Origin of Mother: 1990 to 2006

[Persons of Hispanic origin may be of any race. See headnote, Table 79. See Appendix III]

Birth order	1990 [1]	2000	2003	2004	2005	2006
All births, total number [2]	**4,158,212**	**4,058,814**	**4,089,950**	**4,112,052**	**4,138,349**	**4,265,555**
Twin births	93,865	118,916	128,665	132,219	133,122	137,085
Triplet and higher order multiple births	3,028	7,325	7,663	7,275	6,694	6,540
Multiple birth rate [3]	23.3	31.1	33.3	33.9	33.8	33.7
Twin birth rate [4]	22.6	29.3	31.5	32.2	32.2	32.1
Triplet and higher order multiple birth rate [5]	72.8	180.5	187.4	176.9	161.8	153.3
Non-Hispanic White births, total number . . .	**2,626,500**	**2,362,968**	**2,321,904**	**2,296,683**	**2,279,768**	**2,308,640**
Twin births	60,210	76,018	81,691	83,346	82,223	83,108
Triplet and higher order multiple births	2,358	5,821	5,922	5,590	4,966	4,805
Multiple birth rate [3]	23.8	34.6	37.7	38.7	38.2	38.1
Twin birth rate [4]	22.9	32.2	35.2	36.3	36.1	36.0
Non-Hispanic Black births, total number . . .	**661,701**	**604,346**	**576,033**	**578,772**	**583,759**	**617,247**
Twin births	17,646	20,173	20,010	20,605	21,254	22,702
Triplet and higher order multiple births	306	506	631	577	616	580
Multiple birth rate [3]	27.1	34.2	35.8	36.6	37.5	37.7
Twin birth rate [4]	26.7	33.4	34.7	35.6	36.4	36.8
Hispanic births, total number	**595,073**	**815,868**	**912,329**	**946,349**	**985,505**	**1,039,077**
Twin births	10,713	16,470	19,472	20,351	21,723	22,698
Triplet and higher order multiple births	235	659	784	723	761	787
Multiple birth rate [3]	18.4	21.0	22.2	22.3	22.8	22.6
Twin birth rate [4]	18.0	20.2	21.3	21.5	22.0	21.8

[1] Data by Hispanic-origin status exclude data for New Hampshire and Oklahoma, which did not report Hispanic origin.   [2] Includes other races not shown separately.   [3] Number of live births in all multiple deliveries per 1,000 live births.   [4] Number of live births in twin deliveries per 1,000 live births.   [5] Number of live births in triplet and other higher-order deliveries per 100,000 live births.

Source: U.S. National Center for Health Statistics, National Vital Statistics Report (NVSR), *Births: Final Data for 2006*, Vol. 57, No. 7, January 7, 2009.

Table 82. **Live Births by State and Island Areas: 2007**

[Number of births, except rate. By place of residence. Registered births. Excludes births to nonresidents of the United States. By race and Hispanic origin of mother. Preliminary data for 2007 are based on 98.7% of births for that year. For 47 of the 50 states and the District of Columbia, over 99 percent of births are included; for Louisiana, over 90 percent are included. The percent completeness for two states, Georgia and Michigan were 86.4 and 80.2, respectively. See Appendix III]

State and island area	All races [1]	Non-Hispanic white	Non-Hispanic black	Asian or Pacific Islander	American Indian, Eskimo, Aleut	His-panic [2]	Birth rate [3]	Fertility rate [4]
United States	4,317,119	2,312,473	627,230	254,734	49,284	1,061,970	14.3	69.5
Alabama.	64,749	38,464	19,740	942	189	5,391	14.0	68.7
Alaska	11,101	6,291	409	835	2,836	825	16.2	77.5
Arizona.	102,992	42,521	3,914	3,597	6,700	46,373	16.2	81.1
Arkansas	41,377	27,720	8,080	721	261	4,515	14.6	73.1
California	566,352	155,930	31,777	74,292	3,626	296,942	15.5	72.5
Colorado.	70,805	41,853	3,122	2,493	755	22,221	14.6	69.8
Connecticut.	41,663	24,897	5,183	2,441	238	8,832	11.9	59.5
Delaware	12,171	6,494	3,215	530	16	1,912	14.1	68.4
District of Columbia	8,862	2,227	4,936	259	2	1,450	15.1	60.0
Florida	239,143	107,843	51,835	7,988	805	70,833	13.1	68.4
Georgia	152,021	70,735	49,278	5,696	437	24,319	15.9	73.7
Hawaii	19,137	4,557	426	12,958	77	3,007	14.9	76.0
Idaho	25,019	20,190	139	416	451	3,870	16.7	83.4
Illinois	180,856	95,508	31,655	9,212	262	44,151	14.1	67.4
Indiana.	89,847	68,907	10,229	1,693	118	8,805	14.2	69.7
Iowa	40,885	34,521	1,804	1,021	315	3,355	13.7	70.1
Kansas.	42,004	30,512	3,059	1,367	376	6,689	15.1	75.6
Kentucky	59,370	49,842	5,418	1,018	114	3,092	14.0	68.6
Louisiana	66,260	36,172	25,343	1,160	476	3,188	15.4	73.3
Maine.	14,120	13,186	325	223	125	209	10.7	55.6
Maryland	78,096	36,128	26,198	5,484	151	10,608	13.9	65.6
Massachusetts.	77,962	53,274	7,262	6,013	185	10,900	12.1	57.4
Michigan.	125,394	85,528	22,343	4,337	765	8,441	12.4	61.5
Minnesota.	73,745	53,856	6,615	5,412	1,673	5,939	14.2	69.7
Mississippi	46,501	23,068	20,894	475	309	1,708	15.9	76.9
Missouri	81,928	62,211	12,610	1,978	435	4,667	13.9	68.8
Montana.	12,444	9,623	62	145	1,599	372	13.0	68.6
Nebraska	26,923	20,008	1,794	754	618	4,068	15.2	76.2
Nevada	41,202	16,959	3,615	3,544	576	16,144	16.1	79.6
Now Hampshire	14,169	12,620	203	540	54	593	10.8	53.8
New Jersey.	116,060	56,139	17,863	11,944	188	30,027	13.4	66.1
New Mexico	30,555	8,662	522	1,330	3,835	17,007	15.5	76.4
New York	253,458	125,632	42,738	24,084	629	60,134	13.1	62.1
North Carolina	131,016	72,416	30,635	3,988	1,772	22,113	14.5	69.6
North Dakota.	8,840	7,277	129	110	1,012	278	13.8	69.8
Ohio	150,882	115,583	24,222	3,291	320	6,611	13.2	65.5
Oklahoma.	55,078	35,334	4,914	1,259	6,517	7,173	15.2	76.0
Oregon.	49,352	34,256	1,145	2,712	955	10,133	13.2	66.1
Pennsylvania.	150,731	107,818	21,281	6,260	407	13,793	12.1	61.9
Rhode Island.	12,375	5,999	1,045	536	159	2,588	11.7	55.8
South Carolina.	62,891	34,411	20,489	1,159	274	6,215	14.3	69.9
South Dakota	12,259	9,351	212	149	2,158	471	15.4	80.0
Tennessee	86,707	58,588	17,768	2,003	387	8,383	14.1	68.8
Texas.	407,640	140,272	46,397	16,032	1,064	204,498	17.1	80.1
Utah	55,131	42,844	539	1,761	768	9,042	20.8	94.4
Vermont	6,513	6,178	95	91	14	78	10.5	53.2
Virginia.	108,874	62,155	23,842	8,021	176	14,966	14.1	67.0
Washington.	88,958	56,299	3,812	9,303	2,492	16,881	13.8	66.9
West Virginia.	21,992	20,700	778	181	23	253	12.1	63.1
Wisconsin.	72,796	54,549	7,240	2,895	1,255	6,934	13.0	65.0
Wyoming	7,893	6,361	79	79	333	969	15.1	77.7
Puerto Rico	46,636	1,381	115	(NA)	(NA)	45,123	11.8	55.2
Virgin Islands	1,674	125	1,139	–	82	270	15.2	74.0
Guam	(NA)	(NA)	(NA)	(NA)	(NA)	(NA)	(NA)	(NA)
American Samoa	1,288	(NA)	(NA)	1,288	–	(NA)	20.1	90.5
Northern Marianas . . .	1,345	(NA)	(NA)	1,327	–	(NA)	15.9	38.8

– Represents or rounds to zero.   NA Not available.   [1] Includes persons of other groups not shown separately.   [2] Persons of Hispanic origin may be any race.   [3] Per 1,000 estimated population.   [4] Number of births per 1,000 women age 15 to 44 years.

Source: U.S. National Center for Health Statistics, National Vital Statistics Reports (NVSR), *Births: Preliminary Data for 2007*, Vol. 57, No. 12, March 18, 2009.

Births, Deaths, Marriages, and Divorces   67

Table 83. Total Fertility Rate by Race and Hispanic Origin: 1980 to 2007

[Based on race of mother. Excludes births to nonresidents of United States. The *total fertility rate* is the number of births that 1,000 women would have in their lifetime if, at each year of age, they experienced the birth rates occurring in the specified year. A total fertility rate of 2,110 represents "replacement level" fertility for the total population under current mortality conditions (assuming no net immigration). See Appendix III]

Race and Hispanic origin	1980	1990	2000	2003	2004	2005	2006	2007 [1]
Total [2]	1,840	2,081	2,056	2,043	2,046	2,054	2,101	2,123
White	1,773	2,003	2,051	2,061	2,055	2,056	2,096	(NA)
Black	2,177	2,480	2,129	1,999	2,033	2,071	2,155	(NA)
American Indian, Eskimo, Aleut. . .	2,165	2,185	1,773	1,732	1,735	1,750	1,829	1,861
Asian or Pacific Islander	1,954	2,003	1,892	1,873	1,898	1,889	1,919	2,043
Hispanic [3]	(NA)	2,960	2,730	2,786	2,825	2,885	2,960	2,992

NA Not available.   [1] Preliminary data.   [2] For 1980 and 1990, includes births to races not shown separately. Beginning 2000, unknown race of mother is imputed.   [3] Persons of Hispanic origin may be any race.

Source: U.S. National Center for Health Statistics, National Vital Statistics Report (NVSR), *Births: Final Data for 2006*, Vol. 57, No. 7, January 7, 2009 and *Births: Preliminary Data for 2007*, Vol. 57, No. 12, March 18, 2009.

Table 84. Teenagers—Births and Birth Rates by Age, Race, and Hispanic Origin: 1990 to 2007

[Birth rates per 1,000 women in specified group, see text, this section. Based on race and Hispanic origin of mother]

Age, race, and Hispanic origin	Number of births					Birth rate				
	1990	2000	2005	2006	2007 [1]	1990	2000	2005	2006	2007 [1]
All races, 15 to 19 years	[2]521,826	468,990	414,593	435,436	445,045	59.9	47.7	40.5	41.9	42.5
15 to 17 years old	183,327	157,209	133,191	138,943	140,640	37.5	26.9	21.4	22.0	22.2
18 and 19 years old	338,499	311,781	281,402	296,493	304,405	88.6	78.1	69.9	73.0	73.9
White	354,482	333,013	295,265	308,344	(NA)	50.8	43.2	37.0	38.2	(NA)
Black	151,613	118,954	103,905	111,019	(NA)	112.8	77.4	61.9	64.6	(NA)
American Indian, Eskimo, Aleut	(NA)	8,055	7,807	8,261	8,925	81.1	58.3	52.7	55.0	59.0
Asian or Pacific Islander . . .	(NA)	8,968	7,616	7,812	8,022	26.4	20.5	17.0	17.0	17.3
Hispanic [3]	(NA)	129,469	136,906	145,669	148,453	100.3	87.3	81.7	83.0	81.7
Non-Hispanic White	(NA)	204,056	165,005	169,729	173,104	42.5	32.6	25.9	26.6	27.2
Non-Hispanic Black	(NA)	116,019	96,813	103,725	106,224	116.2	79.2	60.9	63.7	64.3

NA Not available.   [1] Preliminary data.   [2] Includes races other than White and Black not shown separately.   [3] Persons of Hispanic origin may be any race.

Source: U.S. National Center for Health Statistics, National Vital Statistics Reports (NVSR), *Births: Final Data for 2006*, Vol. 57, No. 7, January 7, 2009 and *Births: Preliminary Data for 2007*, Vol. 57, No. 12, March 18, 2009.

Table 85. Births to Unmarried Women by Race, Hispanic Origin, and Age of Mother: 1990 to 2006

[1,165 represents 1,165,000. Excludes births to nonresidents of United States. Persons of Hispanic origin may be any race. Marital status is inferred from a comparison of the child's and parents' surnames on the birth certificate for those states that do not report on marital status. No estimates included for misstatements on birth records or failures to register births. Based on race and Hispanic origin of mother. See also Appendix III]

Race and age of mother	Number (1,000)					Percent distribution					Birth rate [1]			
	1990	1995	2000	2005	2006	1990	1995	2000	2006		1990	1995	2000	2006
Total live births [2] . . .	1,165	1,254	1,347	1,527	1,642	100.0	100.0	100.0	100.0		43.8	44.3	44.1	50.6
White	670	785	866	1,023	1,104	57.5	62.6	64.3	67.2		32.9	37.0	38.2	46.1
Black	455	421	427	439	468	39.1	33.6	31.7	28.5		90.5	74.5	70.5	71.5
American Indian, Eskimo, Aleut	(NA)	(NA)	(NA)	28	31	(NA)	(NA)	(NA)	1.9		(NA)	(NA)	(NA)	(NA)
Asian or Pacific Islander.	(NA)	(NA)	(NA)	37	40	(NA)	(NA)	(NA)	2.4		(NA)	(NA)	20.9	25.9
Hispanic	[3]219	278	348	473	518	[3]18.8	22.1	25.8	31.6		[3]89.6	88.8	87.3	106.1
Non-Hispanic White. . . .	[3]443	504	522	578	615	[3]38.0	40.2	38.7	37.4		[3]24.4	28.1	28.0	32.0
Non-Hispanic Black. . . .	(NA)	(NA)	415	408	436	(NA)	(NA)	30.8	26.6		(NA)	(NA)	(NA)	(NA)
Under 15 years	11	11	8	7	6	0.9	0.9	0.6	0.4		(NA)	(NA)	(NA)	(NA)
15 to 19 years	350	376	369	345	367	30.0	30.0	27.4	22.3		42.5	43.8	39.0	36.2
20 to 24 years	404	432	504	585	626	34.7	34.5	37.4	38.1		65.1	68.7	72.2	79.5
25 to 29 years	230	229	255	332	366	19.7	18.2	18.9	22.3		56.0	54.3	58.5	74.9
30 to 34 years	118	133	130	162	174	10.1	10.6	9.7	10.6		37.6	38.9	39.3	54.8
35 to 39 years	44	60	65	76	82	3.8	4.8	4.8	5.0		17.3	19.3	19.7	26.8
40 years and over.	9	13	16	21	22	0.7	1.0	1.2	1.3		3.6	4.7	5.0	[4]6.5

NA Not available.   [1] Rate per 1,000 unmarried women (never-married, widowed, and divorced) estimated as of July 1. Total rate and rates by race/Hispanic origin cover women 15 to 44 years old. Rate for unmarried women 40 years and over relate births to women 40 years and over to unmarried women 40 to 44 years old.   [2] Includes races other than White and Black not shown separately.   [3] Excludes data for New Hampshire and Oklahoma, which did not report Hispanic origin.   [4] Birth rates computed by relating births to unmarried mothers aged 40 years and over to unmarried women aged 40–44 years.

Source: U.S. National Center for Health Statistics, National Vital Statistics Reports (NVSR), *Births: Final Data for 2006*, Vol. 57, No. 7, January 7, 2009 and earlier reports.

Table 86. **Births to Teens and Unmarried Mothers and Births With Low Birth Weight by Race and Hispanic Origin: 1990 to 2007**

[Represents registered births. Excludes births to nonresidents of the United States. Data are based on race and Hispanic origin of mother. See Appendix III]

Race and Hispanic origin	1990	1995	2000	2004	2005	2006	2007, prel.
Percent of births to teenage mothers	12.8	13.1	11.8	10.3	10.2	10.4	10.5
White	10.9	11.5	10.6	9.3	9.3	9.4	(NA)
Black	23.1	23.1	19.7	17.1	16.9	17.0	(NA)
American Indian, Eskimo, Aleut	19.5	21.4	19.7	17.9	17.7	17.6	18.4
Asian or Pacific Islander	5.7	5.6	4.5	3.4	3.3	3.3	3.2
Hispanic origin [1]	16.8	17.9	16.2	14.3	14.1	14.3	14.2
Non-Hispanic	(NA)	(NA)	10.7	9.1	8.9	9.1	(NA)
White	(NA)	(NA)	8.7	7.4	7.3	7.4	7.5
Black	(NA)	(NA)	19.8	17.3	17.0	17.2	17.3
Percent of births to unmarried mothers	26.6	32.2	33.2	35.8	36.9	38.5	39.7
White	16.9	25.3	27.1	30.5	31.7	33.3	(NA)
Black	66.7	69.9	68.5	68.8	69.3	70.2	(NA)
American Indian, Eskimo, Aleut	53.6	57.2	58.4	62.3	63.5	64.6	65.2
Asian or Pacific Islander	13.2	16.3	14.8	15.5	16.2	16.5	16.9
Hispanic origin [1]	36.7	40.8	42.7	46.4	48.0	49.9	51.3
Non-Hispanic	(NA)	(NA)	30.8	32.5	33.4	34.8	(NA)
White	(NA)	(NA)	22.1	24.5	25.3	26.6	27.8
Black	(NA)	(NA)	68.7	69.3	69.9	70.7	71.6
Percent of births with low birth weight [2]	7.0	7.3	7.6	8.1	8.2	8.3	8.2
White	5.7	6.2	6.5	7.1	7.2	7.2	(NA)
Black	13.3	13.1	13.0	13.4	13.6	13.6	(NA)
American Indian, Eskimo, Aleut	6.1	6.6	6.8	7.5	7.4	7.5	7.5
Asian or Pacific Islander	(NA)	6.9	7.3	7.9	8.0	8.1	8.1
Hispanic origin [1]	6.1	6.3	6.4	6.8	6.9	7.0	6.9
Non-Hispanic	(NA)	(NA)	7.9	8.5	8.6	8.7	(NA)
White	(NA)	(NA)	6.6	7.2	7.3	7.3	7.2
Black	(NA)	(NA)	13.1	13.7	14.0	14.0	13.8

NA Not available. [1] Persons of Hispanic origin may be any race. [2] Births less than 2,500 grams (5 lb., 8 oz.).

Source: U.S. National Center for Health Statistics, National Vital Statistics Reports (NVSR), *Births: Final Data for 2006*, Vol. 57, No. 7, January 7, 2009, and *Births: Preliminary Data for 2007*, Vol. 57, No. 12, March 18, 2009.

Table 87. **Births by Race, Hispanic Origin, and Method of Delivery: 1990 to 2006**

[In thousands (4,111 represents 4,111,000), except rate. 1990 excludes data for Oklahoma, which did not report method of delivery on the birth certificate. Persons of Hispanic origin may be any race. See Appendix III]

Method of delivery	1990	2000	2005	2006 Total [1]	2006 Hispanic	2006 Non-Hispanic White	2006 Non-Hispanic Black
Births, total	4,111	4,059	4,138	4,266	1,039	2,309	617
Vaginal	3,111	3,108	2,874	2,930	729	1,581	411
Caesarean deliveries	914	924	1,249	1,321	308	719	204
Not stated	85	27	16	15	2	9	2
Caesarean delivery rate [2]	22.7	22.9	30.3	31.1	29.7	31.3	33.1

NA Not available. [1] Includes other races not shown separately. [2] Caesarean rates are the number of caesarean deliveries per 100 total deliveries.

Source: U.S. National Center for Health Statistics, National Vital Statistics Reports (NVSR), *Births: Final Data for 2006*, Vol. 57, No. 7, January 7, 2009 and earlier reports.

Table 88. **Rates of Induction of Labor by Gestational Age: 1990 to 2006**

[In percent. Data are for singleton births]

Gestational age	1990 [1]	1995	2000	2001	2002	2003	2004	2005	2006
All gestations	9.6	16.2	20.2	20.8	21.1	21.1	21.7	22.8	23.1
Under 37 weeks (preterm)	6.9	11.6	14.8	14.7	14.7	14.5	15.1	15.6	15.6
Under 32 weeks	5.0	7.8	9.2	8.9	8.8	8.6	8.7	8.9	8.9
32–33 weeks	6.4	10.6	13.3	12.8	12.8	12.8	13.0	13.4	13.5
34–36 weeks	7.5	12.6	16.2	16.2	16.2	16.0	16.7	17.3	17.3
37 weeks and over (term)	9.9	16.7	20.8	21.6	21.8	21.9	22.5	23.7	(NA)
37–39 weeks	7.9	14.3	18.9	19.6	19.8	19.8	20.6	21.7	22.0
40–41 weeks	10.7	18.5	22.9	24.1	24.6	24.8	25.3	26.8	27.4
42 weeks and over	14.9	21.3	24.4	24.4	24.3	24.3	25.4	26.2	26.8

NA Not available. [1] Oklahoma did not report induction of labor.

Source: U.S. National Center for Health Statistics, National Vital Statistics Reports (NVSR), *Births: Final Data for 2006*, Vol. 57, No. 7, January 7, 2009 and unpublished data.

Births, Deaths, Marriages, and Divorces   69

Table 89. **Births to Teenage Mothers and Unmarried Women and Births With Low Birth Weight—States and Island Areas: 2000 to 2007**

[Represents registered births. Excludes births to nonresidents of the United States. Based on 100 percent of births in all states and the District of Columbia. 2007 data are preliminary and based on a substantial proportion of vital records for that year. See Table 82 and Appendix III]

State and Island area	Births to teenage mothers, percent of total [1]		Births to unmarried women, percent of total		Percent of births with low birth weight [2]		State and Island area	Births to teenage mothers, percent of total [1]		Births to unmarried women, percent of total		Percent of births with low birth weight [2]	
	2000	2007	2000	2007	2000	2007		2000	2007	2000	2007	2000	2007
U.S.	**11.8**	**10.5**	**33.2**	**39.7**	**7.6**	**8.2**	NV	12.7	10.8	36.4	42.0	7.2	8.2
AL	15.7	13.6	34.3	38.4	9.7	10.4	NH	6.8	6.6	24.7	31.4	6.3	6.3
AK	11.8	10.1	33.0	37.2	5.6	5.7	NJ	7.1	6.4	28.9	34.4	7.7	8.5
AZ	14.3	12.7	39.3	45.2	7.0	7.1	NM	17.4	15.7	45.6	51.8	8.0	8.8
AR	17.3	14.6	35.7	43.4	8.6	9.1	NY	8.2	7.0	36.6	40.7	7.7	8.2
CA	10.6	9.5	32.7	38.9	6.2	6.9	NC	13.0	11.7	33.3	41.2	8.8	9.2
CO	11.7	9.7	25.0	25.4	8.4	9.0	ND	9.2	8.0	28.3	32.6	6.4	6.3
CT	7.8	6.9	29.3	35.1	7.4	8.1	OH	12.1	11.0	34.6	42.2	7.9	8.7
DE	12.3	10.4	37.9	46.9	8.6	9.3	OK	15.9	13.9	34.3	41.3	7.5	8.2
DC	14.2	12.1	60.3	58.5	11.9	11.1	OR	11.3	8.9	30.1	35.1	5.6	6.1
FL	12.6	10.9	38.2	46.1	8.0	8.7	PA	9.9	9.3	32.7	39.7	7.7	8.4
GA	13.9	12.2	37.0	43.3	8.6	9.1	RI	10.2	9.7	35.5	44.0	7.2	8.0
HI	10.3	8.5	32.2	36.9	7.5	8.0	SC	15.3	13.4	39.8	46.6	9.7	10.1
ID	11.6	9.1	21.6	25.5	6.7	6.5	SD	11.6	9.8	33.5	38.4	6.2	7.0
IL	11.4	10.1	34.5	40.1	7.9	8.5	TN	14.7	13.2	34.5	42.8	9.2	9.4
IN	12.5	11.2	34.7	42.4	7.4	8.5	TX	15.3	13.5	30.5	40.7	7.4	8.4
IA	10.0	8.7	28.0	34.3	6.1	6.8	UT	8.9	6.9	17.3	19.6	6.6	6.7
KS	12.0	10.3	29.0	36.5	6.9	6.0	VT	8.0	7.6	28.1	36.6	6.1	6.2
KY	14.1	12.9	31.0	39.3	8.2	9.3	VA	9.9	8.6	29.9	35.2	7.9	8.6
LA	17.0	13.7	45.6	50.9	10.3	11.0	WA	10.2	8.4	28.2	33.2	5.6	6.3
ME	9.4	8.4	31.0	39.1	6.0	6.3	WV	15.9	12.5	31.7	40.3	8.3	9.5
MD	9.9	8.9	34.6	40.9	8.6	9.1	WI	10.2	8.7	29.3	35.4	6.5	7.0
MA	6.6	6.4	26.5	33.4	7.1	7.9	WY	13.5	11.8	28.8	34.7	8.3	9.1
MI	10.5	10.1	33.3	39.4	7.9	8.2							
MN	8.3	7.1	25.8	32.7	6.1	6.7	PR	(NA)	18.3	49.7	59.3	10.8	12.4
MS	18.8	17.1	46.0	53.7	10.7	12.3	VI	(NA)	12.8	66.7	71.5	9.1	12.3
MO	13.1	11.4	34.6	40.5	7.6	7.8	GU	(NA)	(NA)	54.8	(NA)	7.6	(NA)
MT	11.6	9.7	30.8	35.9	6.2	7.2	AS	(NA)	7.4	35.5	33.0	2.7	3.3
NE	10.2	8.6	27.2	33.4	6.8	7.0	MP	(NA)	8.5	(NA)	46.1	8.9	7.0

NA Not available. [1] Defined as mothers who are 19 years of age or younger. [2] Less than 2,500 grams (5 pounds-8 ounces).

Source: U.S. National Center for Health Statistics, National Vital Statistics Reports (NVSR), *Births: Preliminary Data for 2007*, Vol. 57, No. 12, March 18, 2009.

Table 90. **Infants Who Were Breastfed by Maternal Age and Race-Ethnicity: 1999 to 2006**

[In percent. Covers period from 1999 through 2006. Breastfeeding was defined as ever having been breastfed or received breast milk. Based on data from National Health and Nutrition Examination Surveys (NHANES)]

Race and ethnicity	Under 20 years old	20 to 29 years old	30 years old and older
Total	43	65	75
Non-Hispanic white	40	65	77
Non-Hispanic black	30	44	56
Mexican American	66	75	76

Source: U.S. National Center for Health Statistics, Breastfeeding in the United States Findings from the National Health and Nutrition Examination Surveys: 1999–2006, NCHS Data Brief, No. 5, April 2008. See also <http://www.cdc.gov/nchs/data/databriefs/db05.htm>.

Table 91. **Women Who Had a Child in the Last Year by Age: 1990 to 2008**

[3,913 represents 3,913,000. As of June. See headnote, Table 92]

Age of mother	Women who had a child in last year (1,000)			Total births per 1,000 women			First births per 1,000 women		
	1990	2000	2008	1990	2000	2008	1990	2000	2008
Total	3,913	3,934	3,960	67.0	64.6	64.2	26.4	26.7	25.3
15 to 29 years old	2,568	2,432	2,372	90.8	85.9	76.7	43.2	43.1	37.4
15 to 19 years old . .	338	586	371	39.8	59.7	35.6	30.1	38.7	23.1
20 to 24 years old . .	1,038	850	864	113.4	91.8	85.1	51.8	47.1	46.8
25 to 29 years old . .	1,192	996	1,138	112.1	107.9	109.8	46.2	43.7	42.7
30 to 44 years old	1,346	1,502	1,587	44.7	46.1	51.6	10.6	12.5	13.1
30 to 34 years old . .	892	871	874	80.4	87.9	90.9	21.9	27.5	27.6
35 to 39 years old . .	377	506	550	37.3	45.1	52.9	6.5	9.6	9.5
40 to 44 years old . .	77	125	163	8.6	10.9	15.2	1.2	2.3	3.5

Source: U.S. Census Bureau, *Current Population Reports*, P20-543RV and unpublished data.

Table 92. **Women Who Had a Child in the Last Year by Selected Characteristics: 1990 to 2008**

[58,381 represents 58,381,000. As of June. Covers civilian noninstitutional population. Since the number of women who had a birth during the 12-month period was tabulated and not the actual numbers of births, some small underestimation of fertility for this period may exist due to the omission of: (1) Multiple births, (2) Two or more live births spaced within the 12-month period (the woman is counted only once), (3) Women who had births in the period and who did not survive to the survey date, (4) Women who were in institutions and therefore not in the survey universe. These births would not have been recorded in the vital registration system. These losses may be somewhat offset by the inclusion in the CPS of births to immigrants whose children were not born in the United States and births to nonresident women. Based on Current Population Survey (CPS); see Appendix III]

| Characteristic | Total women (1,000) | Percent childless | Women who had a child in the last year | | | |
| | | | Total births | | First births | |
			Number (1,000)	Per 1,000 women	Number (1,000)	Per 1,000 women
1990	58,381	41.6	3,913	67.0	1,540	26.4
2000 . . . . ¹.	60,873	42.8	3,934	64.6	1,626	26.7
2008, total ¹.	**61,692**	**45.7**	**3,960**	**64.2**	**1,560**	**25.3**
15 to 19 years old.	10,405	93.7	371	35.6	240	23.1
20 to 24 years old.	10,156	70.6	864	85.1	475	46.8
25 to 29 years old.	10,362	46.2	1,138	109.8	443	42.7
30 to 34 years old.	9,618	26.8	874	90.9	265	27.6
35 to 39 years old.	10,403	19.4	550	52.9	99	9.5
40 to 44 years old.	10,748	17.8	163	15.2	37	3.5
White alone	47,616	46.4	3,034	63.7	1,183	24.8
White alone, non-Hispanic.	37,846	48.5	2,276	60.1	925	24.4
Black alone	8,940	41.4	613	68.5	258	28.9
Asian alone	3,276	46.1	188	57.4	80	24.5
Hispanic ¹	10,586	38.1	819	77.4	277	26.1
Married, husband present.	26,271	18.1	2,445	93.1	895	34.1
Married, husband absent ²	2,515	22.7	189	75.0	53	21.1
Widowed or divorced.	4,480	21.0	147	32.9	44	9.9
Never married	28,426	77.2	1,179	41.5	568	20.0
Educational attainment:						
Not a high school graduate	12,882	62.5	703	54.6	248	19.2
High school, 4 years	15,010	33.5	1,067	71.1	427	28.4
Some college, no degree	12,953	48.7	789	60.9	309	23.8
Associate's degree	5,115	31.7	306	59.9	89	17.5
Bachelor's degree	11,094	47.8	694	62.6	287	25.9
Graduate or professional degree	4,638	40.6	400	86.3	200	43.2
Labor force status:						
In labor force	42,809	44.6	2,261	52.8	1,015	23.7
Employed	39,641	44.0	2,051	51.7	910	23.0
Unemployed	3,168	52.0	210	66.2	104	33.0
Not in labor force.	18,883	48.3	1,699	90.0	545	28.9
Family income:						
Under $10,000	3,422	41.2	298	87.2	122	35.5
$10,000 to $19,999	4,500	39.4	356	79.1	140	31.2
$20,000 to $24,999	2,586	44.3	190	73.3	70	27.1
$25,000 to $29,999	2,927	43.0	230	78.6	93	31.7
$30,000 to $34,999	2,966	42.9	228	76.7	57	19.1
$35,000 to $49,999	7,473	46.8	454	60.8	195	26.0
$50,000 to $74,999	10,134	47.0	594	58.6	229	22.6
$75,000 and over	17,203	47.9	1,020	59.3	404	23.5

¹ Includes women of other races and women with family income not reported, not shown separately.   ² Persons of Hispanic origin may be any race.   ² Includes separated women.

Source: U.S. Census Bureau, *Current Population Reports*, P20-543RV and unpublished data.

Table 93. **Women Who Had a Child in the Last Year by Age and Labor Force Status: 1990 to 2008**

[3,913 represents 3,913,000. See headnote, Table 92. See Appendix III]

| Year | Total, 15 to 44 years old | | | 15 to 29 years old | | | 30 to 44 years old | | |
| | Number (1,000) | In the labor force | | Number (1,000) | In the labor force | | Number (1,000) | In the labor force | |
		Number (1,000)	Percent		Number (1,000)	Percent		Number (1,000)	Percent
1990	3,913	2,068	53	2,568	1,275	50	1,346	793	59
1995	3,696	2,034	55	2,252	1,150	51	1,444	884	61
2000	3,934	2,170	55	2,432	1,304	54	1,502	866	58
2004	3,746	2,045	55	2,205	(NA)	(NA)	1,542	(NA)	59
2006	3,974	2,221	56	2,399	1,273	53	1,576	948	60
2008	3,960	2,261	57	2,372	1,299	55	1,587	962	61

NA Not available.

Source: U.S. Census Bureau, *Current Population Reports*, P20-555; earlier reports and unpublished data.

Births, Deaths, Marriages, and Divorces   71

Table 94. Persons Who Have Ever Had Sexual Contact by Selected Characteristics: 2002

[In percent except as indicated (61,147 represents 61,147,000). Based on the National Survey of Family Growth, see Appendix III]

Characteristic	Number (1,000)	Number of opposite-sex partners in lifetime							Any same-sex sexual contact [2]
		Any	One	Two	3 to 6	7 to 14	15 or more	Median number [1]	
Males, 15 to 44 years old [3] ...	61,147	90.3	12.8	8.1	27.5	19.3	22.6	5.4	6.0
15 to 19 years old	10,208	61.6	23.0	9.2	20.7	6.2	2.5	1.9	4.5
20 to 24 years old	9,883	91.1	15.9	11.7	33.5	14.1	15.9	3.8	5.5
25 to 44 years old	41,056	97.3	9.6	7.0	27.8	23.7	29.2	6.7	6.5
25 to 29 years old............	9,226	95.2	10.0	8.8	29.4	23.2	23.8	5.9	5.7
30 to 34 years old............	10,138	97.2	10.7	6.9	28.5	21.9	29.2	6.4	(NA)
35 to 39 years old............	10,557	98.2	8.9	7.0	28.0	25.5	28.8	6.9	(NA)
40 to 44 years old............	11,135	98.2	8.8	5.4	25.6	24.2	34.2	8.2	(NA)
White only, non-Hispanic	38,738	90.3	13.4	8.3	27.1	19.2	22.3	5.3	(NA)
Black only, non-Hispanic	6,940	91.8	5.8	5.9	24.1	22.2	33.8	8.3	(NA)
Hispanic or Latino origin	10,188	91.8	13.7	8.6	32.8	18.6	18.1	4.5	(NA)
Currently married	25,808	100.0	15.4	8.5	30.5	22.3	23.3	5.2	3.4
Currently cohabiting	5,653	100.0	4.7	6.4	34.1	26.6	28.3	6.6	5.3
Never married, not cohabiting......	25,412	76.8	13.9	8.7	24.0	13.8	16.4	4.3	8.6
Formerly married, not cohabiting....	4,274	100.0	0.7	3.6	22.5	24.6	48.6	11.9	7.1
Females, 15 to 44 years old [3] .	61,561	91.4	22.5	10.8	32.6	16.3	9.2	3.3	11.2
15 to 19 years old	9,834	62.2	27.2	9.0	19.1	5.0	1.9	1.4	10.6
20 to 24 years old	9,840	91.1	24.6	13.0	32.2	14.4	6.9	2.8	14.2
25 to 44 years old	41,887	98.4	20.9	10.7	36.0	19.4	11.4	3.8	10.7
25 to 29 years old............	9,249	97.5	22.5	11.7	31.3	20.1	11.9	3.5	14.1
30 to 34 years old............	10,272	98.0	20.5	9.4	38.8	18.0	11.3	3.8	(NA)
35 to 39 years old............	10,853	98.9	20.2	11.2	35.8	20.5	11.2	3.9	(NA)
40 to 44 years old............	11,512	98.6	20.4	10.5	37.4	19.1	11.2	3.8	(NA)
White only, non-Hispanic	39,498	92.1	21.0	10.6	32.1	18.2	10.2	3.6	(NA)
Black only, non-Hispanic	8,250	92.4	12.4	8.4	44.8	18.0	8.8	4.1	(NA)
Hispanic or Latino origin	9,107	89.5	34.6	14.9	27.2	8.2	4.6	1.7	(NA)
Currently married	28,327	100.0	30.8	12.2	34.0	15.6	7.4	2.7	7.2
Currently cohabiting	5,570	100.0	13.7	12.2	39.2	20.4	14.5	4.3	17.6
Never married, not cohabiting......	21,568	75.4	18.3	9.4	27.7	12.8	7.2	3.1	13.5
Formerly married, not cohabiting....	6,096	100.0	6.5	8.1	37.8	28.5	19.1	5.6	16.3

NA Not available. [1] Excludes those who have never had sexual intercourse with a person of the opposite sex. For definition of median, see Guide to Tabular Presentation. [2] Same-sex sexual contact was measured using significantly different questions for males and females. [3] Includes persons of other or multiple races and origin groups, not shown separately.

Source: U.S. National Center for Health Statistics, *Advance Data*, No. 362; "Sexual Behavior and Selected Health Measures: Men and Women 15–44 Years of Age, United States, 2002," September 15, 2005, and unpublished data.

Table 95. Males and Females Who Have Had Sexual Contact in Last 12 Months by Number and Sex of Partners: 2002

[In percent except as indicated (61,147 represents 61,147,000). Based on the National Survey of Family Growth, see Appendix III]

Sex and age	Number (1,000)	Percent distribution							Number of partners not ascertained
		Total	No partners in last 12 months	One partner		Two or more partners			
				Same sex [1]	Oppo-site sex	Same sex only [1]	Oppo-site sex only	Both same and opposite sex [1]	
Males 15 to 44 years old	61,147	100.0	14.8	0.7	62.2	0.9	17.6	1.0	2.6
15 to 19 years old	10,208	100.0	45.1	0.8	29.7	(S)	21.8	0.9	1.4
20 to 24 years old	9,883	100.0	14.2	0.4	48.8	0.9	30.9	1.5	3.2
25 to 44 years old	41,056	100.0	7.4	0.7	73.6	1.1	13.4	1.0	2.8
25 to 29 years old............	9,226	100.0	10.0	0.5	66.6	0.9	18.4	1.1	2.5
30 to 34 years old............	10,138	100.0	5.6	0.9	74.3	1.0	14.5	1.3	2.4
35 to 39 years old............	10,557	100.0	7.1	0.9	76.5	1.2	11.4	0.5	2.5
40 to 44 years old............	11,135	100.0	7.0	0.7	75.9	1.3	10.1	1.0	3.8
Females 15 to 44 years old ...	61,561	100.0	13.9	1.1	66.8	0.2	12.7	3.1	2.2
15 to 19 years old	9,834	100.0	42.9	1.7	30.5	(S)	16.8	5.8	2.1
20 to 24 years old	9,840	100.0	12.5	0.4	58.9	0.2	21.1	4.8	1.9
25 to 44 years old	41,887	100.0	7.4	1.1	77.2	0.2	9.8	2.0	2.2
25 to 29 years old............	9,249	100.0	6.1	0.5	74.1	0.4	14.1	2.8	2.0
30 to 34 years old............	10,272	100.0	7.1	0.5	78.5	(S)	9.7	2.1	1.9
35 to 39 years old............	10,853	100.0	7.3	1.8	76.8	(S)	9.4	2.5	2.0
40 to 44 years old............	11,512	100.0	9.0	1.4	78.8	(S)	6.7	0.9	3.0

S Does not meet standards for reliability or precision. [1] Same-sex sexual contact was measured using significantly different questions for males and females.

Source: U.S. National Center for Health Statistics, *Advance Data*, No. 362; "Sexual *Advance Data*", No. 362; "Sexual Behavior and Selected Health Measures: Men and Women 15–44 Years of Age, United States, 2002," September 15, 2005, and unpublished data.

Table 96. Select Family Planning and Medical Service Use by Women, 15 to 44 Years of Age: 2002

[61,561 represents 61,561,000. Based on the National Survey of Family Growth, see Appendix III. For women who received at least one family planning or medical service in the 12 months prior to the interview]

		Percent using—							
		Family planning services			Medical services				
Characteristic	Number (1,000)	At least one family planning service	Birth control method	Birth control checkup or test	At least one medical service	Preg-nancy test	Pap smear	Pelvic exam	Counseling/test/treatment for STD [1]
All women [2]	61,561	41.7	33.9	23.6	69.1	19.7	64.4	59.7	12.6
15 to 19 years old	9,834	39.9	31.1	22.0	40.6	18.3	34.6	27.0	15.2
15 to 17 years old	5,819	31.8	22.2	15.8	28.0	11.4	23.2	17.9	11.1
18 to 19 years old	4,016	51.6	43.9	31.0	58.9	28.2	51.2	40.2	21.1
20 to 24 years old	9,840	63.3	54.0	35.7	75.7	31.5	69.7	60.6	22.3
25 to 29 years old	9,249	55.4	46.3	30.2	75.9	30.2	70.7	66.0	16.6
30 to 34 years old	10,272	47.0	39.1	27.2	78.1	22.2	72.7	69.7	12.2
35 to 39 years old	10,853	30.5	23.9	18.6	71.5	13.6	68.3	65.9	6.9
40 to 44 years old	11,512	19.5	14.0	10.8	71.8	5.9	69.4	67.0	4.4
Currently married...........	28,327	39.5	31.5	21.3	77.2	21.1	73.1	69.8	8.1
Currently cohabiting	5,570	50.4	43.2	30.2	77.2	31.0	72.2	64.7	20.3
Never married, not cohabiting	21,568	44.4	36.4	25.4	55.8	16.5	50.7	43.9	15.9
Formerly married, not cohabiting. . .	6,096	34.5	28.0	22.0	71.0	14.1	66.0	64.0	14.4
White only, Non-Hispanic	39,498	43.1	36.4	25.4	70.1	17.3	66.1	63.2	11.8
Black only, Non-Hispanic........	8,250	39.4	30.6	21.8	74.4	23.7	69.1	58.1	15.7
Hispanic [3]	9,107	39.7	28.9	20.6	63.4	24.3	57.1	48.5	12.5

[1] STD stands for sexually transmitted disease.   [2] Includes other races not shown separately.   [3] Persons of Hispanic origin may be any race.

Source: U.S. National Center for Health Statistics, *Advance Data*, Number 350, "Use of Contraception and Use of Family Planning Services in the United States: 1982–2002," December 10, 2004.

Table 97. Current Contraceptive Use by Women by Race and Marital Status: 2002

[In percent, except total (61,561 represents 61,561,000). Based on the National Survey of Family Growth; see Appendix III]

		Race/ethnicity			Marital status		
Contraceptive status and method	All women [1, 2]	White only, Non-Hispanic	Black only, Non-Hispanic	Hispanic [3]	Never married, not cohabiting	Cur-rently married	Formerly married, not cohabiting
All women (1,000)	61,561	39,498	8,250	9,107	21,568	28,327	6,096
PERCENT DISTRIBUTION							
Using contraception (contraceptors) [4]..............	61.9	64.6	57.6	59.0	44.0	72.9	64.4
Female sterilization	16.7	15.4	22.6	19.9	4.4	21.7	35.3
Male sterilization.............	5.7	7.6	1.3	2.6	0.4	11.2	2.2
Pill	18.9	22.2	13.1	13.0	21.8	17.2	12.3
Implant, Lunelle ™	0.8	0.5	0.6	1.8	0.4	1.0	0.5
3-month injectable (Depo-Provera ™)..........	3.3	2.7	5.4	4.3	4.2	2.2	1.7
Intrauterine device (IUD)	1.3	1.0	0.8	3.2	0.2	1.9	1.9
Diaphragm.	0.2	0.2	0.1	–	0.2	0.2	–
Condom	11.1	10.7	11.4	10.9	10.3	12.0	8.0
Periodic abstinence— calendar rhythm	0.7	0.8	0.3	0.6	0.2	1.3	0.3
Periodic abstinence— natural family planning	0.2	0.3	0.1	0.3	–	0.4	–
Withdrawal.	2.5	2.6	1.5	2.2	1.6	3.0	1.3
Other methods [5].............	0.6	0.7	0.5	0.3	0.2	0.7	0.9
Not using contraception	38.1	35.4	42.4	41.0	56.0	27.1	35.6
Surgically sterile-female (noncontraceptive).............	1.5	1.6	1.6	0.9	0.4	2.1	3.0
Nonsurgically sterile-female or male [6]........................	1.6	1.7	1.4	1.7	1.0	2.0	2.5
Pregnant or postpartum	5.3	4.7	5.7	6.9	2.3	7.5	2.2
Seeking pregnancy	4.2	4.0	4.3	5.2	0.8	6.9	2.0
Other nonuse.................	25.5	23.6	29.5	26.4	51.4	8.6	26.0
Never had intercourse or no intercourse in 3 months before interview.	18.1	17.0	19.0	18.7	42.9	2.3	17.7
Had intercourse in 3 months before interview.	7.4	6.5	10.4	7.7	8.5	6.3	8.2
All other nonusers	–	0.1	0.1	–	–	–	0.1

– Represents or rounds to zero.   [1] Includes other races not shown separately.   [2] Includes women who are currently cohabiting not shown separately.   [3] Persons of Hispanic origin may be any race.   [4] Percents may not add to the total who were using contraception because more than one method could have been used in the month of interview.   [5] Includes implants, injectables, morning-after pill, suppository, Today ™ sponge, and less frequently used methods.   [6] Persons sterile from illness, accident, or congenital conditions.

Source: U.S. National Center for Health Statistics, *Advance Data*, Number 350, "Use of Contraception and Use of Family Planning Services in the United States: 1982–2002," December 10, 2004.

Births, Deaths, Marriages, and Divorces   73

Table 98. Outcomes of Assisted Reproductive Technology (ART) Procedures: 2000 to 2006

[In 1996, Centers for Disease Control (CDC) initiated data collection regarding (ART) procedures performed in the United States, as mandated by the Fertility Clinic Success Rate and Certification Act. ARTs include those infertility treatments in which both eggs and sperm are handled in the laboratory for the purpose of establishing a pregnancy (i.e. in vitro fertilization and related procedures)]

Year	Procedures started [1]	Number of pregnancies	Live birth deliveries [2]	Live born infants
2000	99,629	30,557	25,228	35,025
2001	107,587	35,726	29,344	40,687
2002	115,392	40,046	33,141	45,751
2003	122,872	43,503	35,785	48,756
2004	127,977	44,774	36,760	49,458
2005	134,260	47,651	38,910	52,041
2006	138,198	50,571	41,343	54,656

[1] Excludes procedures for which new treatments were being evaluated. [2] A live-birth delivery is defined as the delivery of one or more live born infants.

Source: U.S. Centers for Disease Control and Prevention, Morbidity and Mortality Weekly Report (MMWR) Surveillance Summary Reports, *Assisted Reproductive Technology Surveillance - United States, 2006* ; Vol. 58, No. SS-5, June 12, 2009. See also <http://www.cdc.gov/mmwr/preview/mmwrhtml/ss5805a1.htm>.

Table 99. Abortions—Number and Rate by Race: 1990 to 2005

[58,700 represents 58,700,000]

Year	All races Women 15 to 44 years old (1,000)	Abortions Number (1,000)	Abortions Rate per 1,000 women	White Women 15 to 44 years old (1,000)	Abortions Number (1,000)	Abortions Rate per 1,000 women [1]	Black Women 15 to 44 years old (1,000)	Abortions Number (1,000)	Abortions Rate per 1,000 women [1]	Other Women 15 to 44 years old (1,000)	Abortions Number (1,000)	Abortions Rate per 1,000 women [1]
1990 [2]	58,700	1,609	27.4	48,224	1,039	21.5	7,905	505	63.9	2,571	65	25.1
1991	59,305	1,557	26.2	48,560	982	20.2	8,053	507	62.9	2,692	68	26.2
1992	59,417	1,529	25.7	48,435	943	19.5	8,170	517	63.3	2,812	69	24.4
1993 [2]	59,712	1,495	25.0	48,497	908	18.7	8,282	517	62.4	2,933	70	23.9
1994 [2]	60,020	1,423	23.7	48,592	856	17.6	8,390	492	58.6	3,039	76	23.7
1995	60,368	1,359	22.5	48,719	817	16.8	8,496	462	54.4	3,153	80	25.3
1996	60,704	1,360	22.4	48,837	797	16.3	8,592	483	56.2	3,275	81	24.6
1997 [2]	61,041	1,335	21.9	48,942	777	15.9	8,694	479	55.1	3,405	79	23.1
1998 [2]	61,326	1,319	21.5	49,012	762	15.5	8,785	476	54.2	3,528	81	23.1
1999	61,475	1,315	21.4	48,974	743	15.2	8,851	485	54.8	3,650	87	24.0
2000	61,631	1,313	21.3	48,936	733	15.0	8,907	488	54.8	3,788	92	24.4
2001 [2]	61,673	1,291	20.9	48,868	717	14.7	8,962	476	53.1	3,843	99	25.7
2002 [2]	62,044	1,269	20.5	48,998	706	14.4	9,026	468	51.8	4,020	96	23.8
2003 [2]	61,911	1,250	20.2	48,782	695	14.2	9,054	458	50.6	4,075	97	23.8
2004	62,033	1,222	19.7	48,758	674	13.8	9,116	453	49.7	4,160	95	22.9
2005	62,074	1,206	19.4	48,678	662	13.6	9,177	452	49.3	4,219	92	21.9

[1] Aged 15–44. [2] Total numbers of abortions in 1990, 1993, 1994, 1997, 1998 and 2001–2003 have been estimated by interpolation.

Source: R.K. Jones, M.R.S. Zolna, S.K. Henshaw, and L.B. Finer, "Abortion in the United States: *Incidence and Access to Services, 2005,*" Perspectives on Sexual and Reproductive Health, 40(1):6-16, and unpublished data from Guttmacher Institute.

74   Births, Deaths, Marriages, and Divorces

Table 100. **Abortions by Selected Characteristics: 1990 to 2005**

[1,609 represents 1,609,000. Number of abortions from surveys conducted by source; characteristics from the U.S. Centers for Disease Control's (CDC) annual abortion surveillance summaries, with adjustments for changes in states reporting data to the CDC each year]

Characteristic	Number (1,000)			Percent distribution			Abortion rate per 1,000 women [1]		
	1990	2000	2005	1990	2000	2005	1990	2000	2005
Total abortions	1,609	1,313	1,206	100.0	100.0	100.0	27.4	21.3	19.4
Age of woman:									
Less than 15 years old [1]	13	9	7	0.8	0.7	0.6	7.9	4.4	3.2
15 to 19 years old	351	235	196	21.8	17.9	16.2	40.6	24.0	19.1
20 to 24 years old	532	430	396	33.1	32.7	32.8	56.7	45.9	38.9
25 to 29 years old	360	303	287	22.4	23.0	23.7	34.0	31.8	29.2
30 to 34 years old	216	190	179	13.4	14.5	14.8	19.7	18.6	18.0
35 to 39 years old	108	110	104	6.7	8.4	8.7	10.7	9.7	10.0
40 years old and over [2]	29	37	38	1.8	2.8	3.2	3.2	3.2	3.3
Race and ethnicity of woman:									
White.	1,039	733	662	64.6	55.8	54.9	21.5	15.0	13.6
Black.	505	488	452	31.4	37.2	37.5	63.9	54.8	49.3
Other.	65	92	92	4.0	7.0	7.6	25.1	24.4	21.9
Hispanic.	195	261	263	12.1	19.8	21.8	35.1	30.3	26.5
Non-Hispanic White	852	479	415	52.9	36.5	34.4	19.7	11.7	10.5
Marital status of woman: [3]									
Married	341	246	208	21.0	19.0	17.2	10.6	7.9	6.9
Unmarried	1,268	1,067	999	79.0	81.0	82.8	47.7	34.9	31.0
Number of prior live births:									
None	780	533	491	49.0	41.0	41.0	32.0	20.2	(NA)
One.	396	361	321	25.0	28.0	27.0	36.9	32.5	(NA)
Two.	280	260	241	17.0	20.0	20.0	20.5	18.9	(NA)
Three	102	104	100	6.0	8.0	8.0	15.6	14.8	(NA)
Four or more.	50	56	53	3.0	4.0	4.0	14.7	16.5	(NA)
Number of prior induced abortions:									
None	891	699	644	55.0	53.0	53.0	(NA)	(NA)	(NA)
One.	443	355	321	28.0	27.0	27.0	(NA)	(NA)	(NA)
Two or more	275	259	241	17.0	20.0	20.0	(NA)	(NA)	(NA)
Weeks of gestation:									
Less than 9 weeks	825	749	728	51.3	57.1	60.4	(NA)	(NA)	(NA)
9 to 10 weeks	416	269	217	25.8	20.5	18.0	(NA)	(NA)	(NA)
11 to 12 weeks	195	138	118	12.1	10.5	9.8	(NA)	(NA)	(NA)
13 weeks or more	173	156	142	10.8	11.9	11.8	(NA)	(NA)	(NA)

NA Not available.　[1] Denominator of rate is women aged 14.　[2] Denominator of rate is women aged 40-44.　[3] Separated women are included with married.

Source: R.K. Jones, M.R.S. Zolna, S.K. Henshaw, and L.B. Finer, *"Abortion in the United States: Incidence and Access to Services, 2005,"* Perspectives on Sexual and Reproductive Health, 2008, 40(1):6-16; S.K. Henshaw and K. Kost, *Trends in the Characteristics of Women Obtaining Abortions, 1974-2004,* New York: Guttmacher Institute, 2008; and unpublished data from the Guttmacher Institute.

Table 101. **Abortions—Number and Rate by State of Occurrence, 2000 and 2005, and Residence, 2005**

[Number of abortions by state of occurrence from surveys of hospitals, clinics, and physicians identified as providers of abortion services conducted by the Guttmacher Institute. The Guttmacher Institute reallocates abortions to the woman's state of residence for survey years. Abortion rates are computed per 1,000 women 15 to 44 years of age on July 1 of specified year]

State	Occurrence				Residence, 2005		State	Occurrence				Residence, 2005	
	Number		Rate [1]		Num-ber	Rate [1]		Number		Rate [1]		Num-ber	Rate [1]
	2000	2005	2000	2005				2000	2005	2000	2005		
U.S..	1,312,990	1,206,200	21.3	19.4	1,198,960	19.3	MO ..	7,920	8,400	6.6	7.0	14,900	12.5
AL . . .	13,830	11,340	14.2	12.1	10,840	11.5	MT. . .	2,510	2,150	13.5	11.9	2,020	11.2
AK . . .	1,660	1,880	11.7	13.2	2,130	14.9	NE. . .	4,250	3,220	11.6	9.1	2,990	8.4
AZ . . .	17,940	19,480	16.5	16.1	19,710	16.3	NV. . .	13,740	13,530	32.4	27.7	12,990	26.6
AR . . .	5,540	4,710	10.8	9.3	5,200	9.3	NH. . .	3,010	3,170	11.2	11.8	3,060	11.4
CA . . .	236,060	208,430	31.2	26.9	206,260	26.6	NJ . . .	65,780	61,150	36.3	34.5	60,330	34.0
CO. . .	15,530	16,120	16.0	16.2	14,720	14.8	NM. . .	5,760	6,220	14.7	15.7	6,690	16.9
CT . . .	15,240	16,780	21.1	23.8	17,340	24.6	NY. . .	164,630	155,960	39.1	37.7	152,340	36.9
DE. . .	5,440	5,150	31.3	29.2	4,140	23.5	NC. . .	37,610	34,500	21.1	18.9	29,730	16.3
DC. . .	9,800	7,230	68.2	50.8	6,390	44.2	ND. . .	1,340	1,230	9.9	9.6	890	7.0
FL . . .	103,050	92,300	32.0	26.7	85,360	24.7	OH. . .	40,230	35,060	16.5	14.9	33,140	14.1
GA. . .	32,140	33,180	16.9	16.6	32,040	16.0	OK. . .	7,390	6,950	10.1	9.7	7,420	10.3
HI . . .	5,630	5,350	22.2	21.3	5,330	21.2	OR. . .	17,010	13,200	23.6	18.1	11,900	16.3
ID . . .	1,950	1,810	7.0	6.2	2,540	8.7	PA . . .	36,570	34,150	14.3	13.9	38,110	15.5
IL . . .	63,690	50,970	23.2	18.9	48,420	18.0	RI . . .	5,600	5,290	24.1	23.3	4,680	20.6
IN . . .	12,490	11,150	9.4	8.6	13,180	10.2	SC. . .	8,210	7,080	9.3	8.0	13,320	15.0
IA . . .	5,970	6,370	9.8	10.9	6,130	10.5	SD. . .	870	790	5.5	5.1	980	6.4
KS. . .	12,270	10,410	21.4	18.6	5,620	10.0	TN . . .	19,010	18,140	15.2	14.5	15,520	12.4
KY. . .	4,700	3,870	5.3	4.9	6,060	7.0	TX . . .	89,160	85,760	18.8	17.4	84,560	17.1
LA . . .	13,100	11,400	13.0	11.8	10,330	10.7	UT. . .	3,510	3,630	6.7	6.4	3,610	6.4
ME. . .	2,650	2,770	9.9	10.7	2,840	10.9	VT. . .	1,660	1,490	12.7	11.9	1,810	14.5
MD. . .	34,560	37,590	29.0	31.3	35,250	29.3	VA . . .	28,780	26,520	18.1	16.4	30,590	18.9
MA. . .	30,410	27,270	21.4	19.8	27,800	20.2	WA . . .	26,200	23,260	20.3	17.8	23,680	18.1
MI . . .	46,470	40,600	21.6	19.5	39,930	19.2	WV . . .	2,540	2,360	6.8	6.7	2,700	7.7
MN. . .	14,610	13,910	13.5	13.1	13,370	12.6	WI . . .	11,130	9,800	9.6	8.6	10,920	9.6
MS. . .	3,780	3,090	6.0	5.0	7,930	12.9	WY ..	100	70	1.0	0.7	1,220	12.2

[1] Rate per 1,000 women, 15 to 44 years old.

Source: R.K. Jones et al., *Abortion in the United States: Incidence and Access to Services, 2005,* Perspectives on Sexual and Reproductive Health 40:6, 2008, and unpublished data. See also <http://www.guttmacher.org/>.

Births, Deaths, Marriages, and Divorces　75

Table 102. **Expectation of Life at Birth, 1970 to 2006, and Projections, 2010 to 2020**

[**In years.** Excludes deaths of nonresidents of the United States. See Appendix III]

Year	Total			White			Black		
	Total	Male	Female	Total	Male	Female	Total	Male	Female
1970	70.8	67.1	74.7	71.7	68.0	75.6	64.1	60.0	68.3
1975	72.6	68.8	76.6	73.4	69.5	77.3	66.8	62.4	71.3
1980	73.7	70.0	77.4	74.4	70.7	78.1	68.1	63.8	72.5
1981	74.1	70.4	77.8	74.8	71.1	78.4	68.9	64.5	73.2
1982	74.5	70.8	78.1	75.1	71.5	78.7	69.4	65.1	73.6
1983	74.6	71.0	78.1	75.2	71.6	78.7	69.4	65.2	73.5
1984	74.7	71.1	78.2	75.3	71.8	78.7	69.5	65.3	73.6
1985	74.7	71.1	78.2	75.3	71.8	78.7	69.3	65.0	73.4
1986	74.7	71.2	78.2	75.4	71.9	78.8	69.1	64.8	73.4
1987	74.9	71.4	78.3	75.6	72.1	78.9	69.1	64.7	73.4
1988	74.9	71.4	78.3	75.6	72.2	78.9	68.9	64.4	73.2
1989	75.1	71.7	78.5	75.9	72.5	79.2	68.8	64.3	73.3
1990	75.4	71.8	78.8	76.1	72.7	79.4	69.1	64.5	73.6
1991	75.5	72.0	78.9	76.3	72.9	79.6	69.3	64.6	73.8
1992	75.8	72.3	79.1	76.5	73.2	79.8	69.6	65.0	73.9
1993	75.5	72.2	78.8	76.3	73.1	79.5	69.2	64.6	73.7
1994	75.7	72.4	79.0	76.5	73.3	79.6	69.5	64.9	73.9
1995	75.8	72.5	78.9	76.5	73.4	79.6	69.6	65.2	73.9
1996	76.1	73.1	79.1	76.8	73.9	79.7	70.2	66.1	74.2
1997	76.5	73.6	79.4	77.2	74.3	79.9	71.1	67.2	74.7
1998	76.7	73.8	79.5	77.3	74.5	80.0	71.3	67.6	74.8
1999	76.7	73.9	79.4	77.3	74.6	79.9	71.4	67.8	74.7
2000 [1]	76.8	74.1	79.3	77.3	74.7	79.9	71.8	68.2	75.1
2001 [1]	76.9	74.2	79.4	77.4	74.8	79.9	72.0	68.4	75.2
2002 [1]	76.9	74.3	79.5	77.4	74.9	79.9	72.1	68.6	75.4
2003 [1, 2]	77.1	74.5	79.6	77.6	75.0	80.0	72.3	68.8	75.6
2004 [1, 2]	77.5	74.9	79.9	77.9	75.4	80.4	72.8	69.3	76.0
2005 [1, 2]	77.4	74.9	79.9	77.9	75.4	80.4	72.8	69.3	76.1
2006 [1, 2]	77.7	75.1	80.2	78.2	75.7	80.6	73.2	69.7	76.5
Projections: [3]									
2010	78.3	75.7	80.8	78.9	76.5	81.3	73.8	70.2	77.2
2015	78.9	76.4	81.4	79.5	77.1	81.8	75.0	71.4	78.2
2020	79.5	77.1	81.9	80.0	77.7	82.4	76.1	72.6	79.2

[1] Life expectancies for 2000–2006 were calculated using a revised methodology and may differ from those previously published. [2] Multiple-race data were reported by 25 states and the District of Columbia in 2006, by 21 states and the District of Columbia in 2005, by 15 states in 2004, and by 7 states in 2003. The multiple-race data for these reporting areas were bridged to the single-race categories of the 1977 OMB standards for comparability with other reporting areas. [3] Based on middle mortality assumptions; for details, see source. Source: U.S. Census Bureau, 2008 National Population Projections, released August, 2008. See <http://www.census.gov/population/www/projections/2008projections.html>.

Source: Except as noted, U.S. National Center for Health Statistics, National Vital Statistics Reports (NVSR), *Deaths: Final Data for 2006*, Vol. 57, No. 14, April 17, 2009.

Table 103. **Average Number of Years of Life Remaining by Sex and Age: 1989 to 2006**

[Excludes deaths of nonresidents of the United States. See Appendix III]

Age (years)	Total			Male			Female		
	1989–1991	1999–2001	2006	1989–1991	1999–2001	2006	1989–1991	1999–2001	2006
0	75.4	76.8	77.7	71.8	74.1	75.1	78.8	79.5	80.2
1	75.1	76.4	77.2	71.6	73.7	74.7	78.5	79.0	79.7
5	71.2	72.5	73.3	67.7	69.8	70.8	74.6	75.0	75.8
10	66.3	67.5	68.4	62.8	64.8	65.8	69.7	70.1	70.8
15	61.4	62.6	63.4	57.9	59.9	60.9	64.7	65.2	65.9
20	56.6	57.8	58.6	53.3	55.2	56.1	59.9	60.3	61.0
25	51.9	53.1	53.9	48.7	50.5	51.5	55.0	55.4	56.1
30	47.2	48.3	49.2	44.1	45.9	46.9	50.2	50.6	51.3
35	42.6	43.5	44.4	39.6	41.2	42.2	45.4	45.7	46.4
40	38.0	38.9	39.7	35.1	36.6	37.6	40.7	41.0	41.7
45	33.4	34.3	35.2	30.7	32.1	33.1	36.0	36.3	37.0
50	29.0	29.9	30.7	26.4	27.8	28.8	31.4	31.7	32.5
55	24.8	25.6	26.5	22.3	23.6	24.7	27.1	27.3	28.0
60	20.9	21.5	22.4	18.5	19.7	20.7	22.9	23.1	23.8
65	17.3	17.8	18.5	15.1	16.1	17.0	19.0	19.1	19.7
70	14.0	14.3	14.9	12.1	12.8	13.6	15.4	15.4	15.9
75	11.0	11.1	11.6	9.4	9.9	10.5	12.1	12.0	12.3
80	8.4	8.4	8.7	7.1	7.4	7.8	9.1	9.1	9.3
85	6.2	6.2	6.4	5.3	5.5	5.7	6.7	6.6	6.8
90	4.5	4.5	4.6	3.9	4.0	4.1	4.7	4.7	4.8
95	3.3	3.2	3.2	2.9	2.8	2.9	3.4	3.3	3.3
100	2.5	2.3	2.3	2.3	2.0	2.0	2.5	2.3	2.3

Source: U.S. National Center for Health Statistics, National Vital Statistics Reports (NVSR), *U.S. Decennial Life Tables for 1999–2001, United States Life Tables*, Vol. 57, No. 1, August 5, 2008 and unpublished data.

76 Births, Deaths, Marriages, and Divorces

Table 104. Selected Life Table Values: 1979 to 2006

[See Appendix III]

Age and sex	Total[1]								White								Black							
	1979–1981[2]	1990	1995	2000	2003	2004	2005[3]	2006[3]	1979–1981[2]	1990	1995	2000	2003	2004	2005[3]	2006[3]	1979–1981[2]	1990	1995	2000	2003	2004	2005[3]	2006[3]
EXPECTATION OF LIFE IN YEARS																								
At birth: Male	70.1	71.8	72.5	74.3	74.7	75.2	74.9	75.1	70.8	72.7	73.4	74.9	75.3	75.7	75.4	75.7	64.1	64.5	65.2	68.3	68.9	69.5	69.3	69.7
Female	77.6	78.8	78.9	79.7	80.0	80.4	79.9	80.2	78.2	79.4	79.6	80.1	80.4	80.8	80.4	80.6	72.9	73.6	73.9	75.2	75.9	76.3	76.1	76.5
Age 20: Male	51.9	53.3	53.8	55.3	55.8	56.2	55.9	56.1	52.5	54.0	54.5	55.8	56.2	56.6	56.3	56.6	46.4	46.7	47.3	50.0	50.6	51.2	51.0	51.3
Female	59.0	59.8	59.9	60.5	60.8	61.2	60.7	61.0	59.4	60.3	60.3	60.9	61.1	61.5	61.0	61.3	54.9	54.9	55.5	56.6	57.2	57.7	57.4	57.8
Age 40: Male	33.6	35.1	35.6	36.7	37.2	37.6	37.3	37.6	34.0	35.6	36.1	37.1	37.6	37.9	37.7	37.9	29.5	30.1	30.6	32.3	32.9	33.4	33.2	33.5
Female	39.8	40.6	40.7	41.2	41.5	41.9	41.4	41.7	40.2	41.0	41.0	41.7	41.8	42.1	41.7	41.9	36.3	36.8	37.0	37.8	38.4	38.8	38.5	38.9
Age 50: Male	25.0	26.4	27.0	27.9	28.5	28.8	28.5	28.8	25.3	26.7	27.3	28.2	28.7	29.1	28.8	29.0	22.0	22.5	23.1	24.2	24.7	25.1	24.9	25.2
Female	30.7	31.3	31.4	32.0	32.3	32.7	32.2	32.5	31.0	31.7	31.7	32.2	32.5	32.9	32.4	32.6	27.8	28.2	28.5	29.1	29.8	30.1	29.8	30.2
Age 65: Male	14.2	15.1	15.6	16.2	16.8	17.1	16.8	17.0	14.3	15.2	15.7	16.3	16.8	17.2	16.9	17.1	13.3	13.2	13.7	14.2	14.8	15.2	14.9	15.1
Female	18.4	18.9	18.9	19.3	19.7	20.0	19.5	19.7	18.6	19.1	19.0	19.4	19.7	20.0	19.5	19.8	17.1	17.2	17.2	17.7	18.3	18.6	18.2	18.6
EXPECTED DEATHS PER 1,000 ALIVE AT SPECIFIED AGE[4]																								
At birth: Male	13.9	10.3	8.3	7.5	7.6	7.5	7.6	7.3	12.3	9.7	7.0	6.2	6.4	6.2	6.3	6.1	23.0	19.7	16.2	15.6	15.6	15.3	15.2	14.5
Female	11.2	8.2	6.8	6.2	6.1	6.1	6.2	6.1	9.7	7.6	5.6	5.1	5.1	5.1	5.1	5.0	19.3	16.3	13.8	12.7	12.4	12.4	12.3	12.2
Age 20: Male	1.8	1.6	(NA)	1.3	1.3	1.3	1.3	1.3	1.8	1.4	(NA)	1.2	1.2	1.2	1.2	1.2	2.2	2.0	(NA)	2.0	1.9	1.8	1.9	1.8
Female	0.6	0.5	(NA)	0.5	0.5	0.5	0.5	0.5	0.6	0.5	(NA)	0.4	0.5	0.4	0.4	0.4	0.7	0.7	(NA)	0.6	0.6	0.6	0.5	0.5
Age 40: Male	3.0	3.1	(NA)	2.6	2.6	2.4	2.3	2.3	2.6	2.7	(NA)	2.4	2.3	2.3	2.3	2.2	6.9	7.1	(NA)	4.6	4.3	3.9	3.6	3.6
Female	1.6	1.4	(NA)	1.5	1.5	1.5	1.4	1.4	1.4	1.2	(NA)	1.3	1.4	1.3	1.3	1.3	3.2	3.1	(NA)	2.8	2.7	2.6	2.4	2.4
Age 50: Male	7.8	6.2	(NA)	5.7	5.7	5.6	5.2	5.2	7.1	5.6	(NA)	5.2	5.2	5.2	4.9	4.8	14.9	12.8	(NA)	11.2	10.5	10.1	8.7	8.5
Female	4.2	3.5	(NA)	3.3	3.3	3.2	3.1	3.1	3.8	3.2	(NA)	2.9	2.9	2.9	2.8	2.9	7.7	6.6	(NA)	6.2	6.1	5.9	5.5	5.3
Age 65: Male	28.2	22.9	(NA)	20.0	18.5	17.8	13.9	13.7	27.4	23.0	(NA)	19.2	17.8	17.1	13.6	13.4	38.5	36.8	(NA)	29.6	29.1	28.4	18.7	18.6
Female	14.3	13.5	(NA)	12.7	11.9	11.5	10.0	10.0	13.6	12.8	(NA)	12.2	11.4	11.0	9.6	9.4	21.6	21.4	(NA)	18.2	17.7	16.9	13.3	13.0
NUMBER SURVIVING TO SPECIFIED AGE PER 1,000 BORN ALIVE																								
Age 20: Male	973	979	981	984	985	985	984	985	975	981	981	986	986	987	987	985	961	963	967	973	974	974	973	975
Female	982	986	987	989	989	989	989	990	984	988	987	990	991	991	991	990	972	976	978	981	982	982	982	983
Age 40: Male	933	938	940	953	954	955	954	955	940	946	940	958	958	959	958	959	885	880	885	918	918	925	922	925
Female	965	971	971	975	975	976	975	976	969	975	971	978	978	978	977	978	941	944	944	955	958	958	958	960
Age 50: Male	890	899	899	917	918	921	918	920	901	912	899	925	925	927	924	920	801	801	803	855	864	869	865	872
Female	941	950	950	954	954	954	953	954	947	957	950	960	959	959	957	954	896	904	902	915	919	921	920	924
Age 65: Male	706	741	750	779	787	792	784	791	724	760	750	794	800	805	797	791	551	571	581	640	659	668	658	674
Female	835	851	855	863	867	870	866	871	848	864	855	874	877	879	874	880	733	751	758	780	786	792	788	799

NA Not available. [1] Includes other races not shown separately. [2] Decennial life tables are based on population data from a decennial census and reported deaths of the 3-year period surrounding the census year; the census year is the middle year. The annual tables are based on deaths in a single year, and except for census years, on postcensal population estimates. [3] Life expectancies for 2005–2006 were calculated using a revised methodology and may differ from those previously published. [4] See footnote 2, Table 105.

Source: U.S. National Center for Health Statistics, National Vital Statistics Reports (NVSR), "U.S. Decennial Life Tables for 1979–1981"; <http://www.cdc.gov/nchs/products/life_tables.htm#1979_1981>. U.S. Life Tables, 2004, Vol. 56, No. 9, December 28, 2007; Deaths: Final Data for 2006, Vol. 57, No. 14, 17 April 2009.

Table 105. **Expectation of Life and Expected Deaths by Race, Sex, and Age: 2006**

[Life expectancies were calculated using a revised methodology and may differ from those previously published. The methodology uses vital statistics death rates for ages under 66 and modeled probabilities of death for ages 66 to 100 based on blended vital statistics and Medicare probabilities of dying]

Age (years)	Expectation of life in years					Expected deaths per 1,000 alive at specified age [2]				
	Total [1]	White		Black		Total [1]	White		Black	
		Male	Female	Male	Female		Male	Female	Male	Female
At birth	77.7	75.7	80.6	69.7	76.5	6.71	6.12	5.01	14.48	12.23
1	77.2	75.1	80.0	69.7	76.5	0.44	0.40	0.39	0.76	0.60
2	76.3	74.2	79.0	68.7	75.5	0.30	0.29	0.23	0.46	0.48
3	75.3	73.2	78.0	67.8	74.6	0.21	0.22	0.17	0.37	0.24
4	74.3	72.2	77.1	66.8	73.6	0.18	0.18	0.15	0.27	0.24
5	73.3	71.2	76.1	65.8	72.6	0.17	0.17	0.13	0.27	0.21
6	72.3	70.2	75.1	54.8	71.6	0.15	0.16	0.12	0.26	0.18
7	71.3	69.2	74.1	63.9	70.6	0.14	0.15	0.11	0.24	0.16
8	70.4	68.2	73.1	62.9	69.6	0.12	0.13	0.10	0.20	0.14
9	69.4	67.3	72.1	61.9	68.6	0.10	0.10	0.09	0.15	0.13
10	68.4	66.3	71.1	60.9	67.7	0.09	0.08	0.08	0.10	0.14
11	67.4	65.3	70.1	59.9	66.7	0.09	0.08	0.08	0.10	0.15
12	66.4	64.3	69.1	58.9	65.7	0.12	0.13	0.10	0.17	0.17
13	65.4	63.3	68.1	57.9	54.7	0.20	0.24	0.15	0.34	0.20
14	64.4	62.3	67.1	56.9	63.7	0.31	0.39	0.21	0.58	0.23
15	63.4	61.3	66.1	56.0	62.7	0.43	0.54	0.27	0.84	0.27
16	62.4	60.4	65.2	55.0	61.7	0.55	0.69	0.33	1.09	0.32
17	61.5	59.4	54.2	54.1	60.8	0.65	0.84	0.38	1.31	0.36
18	60.5	58.4	63.2	53.1	59.8	0.74	0.98	0.41	1.50	0.42
19	59.6	57.5	62.2	52.2	58.8	0.82	1.10	0.43	1.67	0.47
20	58.6	56.6	61.3	51.3	57.8	0.89	1.23	0.44	1.84	0.54
21	57.7	55.6	60.3	50.4	56.9	0.97	1.35	0.45	2.01	0.60
22	56.7	54.7	59.3	49.5	55.9	1.02	1.43	0.46	2.15	0.67
23	55.8	53.8	58.3	48.6	54.9	1.03	1.44	0.47	2.23	0.71
24	54.8	52.9	57.4	47.7	54.0	1.02	1.40	0.48	2.26	0.75
25	53.9	51.9	56.4	46.8	53.0	1.00	1.35	0.49	2.28	0.79
26	53.0	51.0	55.4	46.0	52.1	0.99	1.31	0.50	2.30	0.83
27	52.0	50.1	54.5	45.1	51.1	0.98	1.27	0.51	2.31	0.87
28	51.1	49.1	53.5	44.2	50.1	0.98	1.26	0.53	2.34	0.92
29	50.1	48.2	52.5	43.3	49.2	1.00	1.27	0.55	2.38	0.98
30	49.2	47.3	51.5	42.4	48.2	1.02	1.29	0.57	2.43	1.04
31	48.2	46.3	50.6	41.5	47.3	1.05	1.31	0.60	2.47	1.12
32	47.3	45.4	49.6	40.6	46.3	1.09	1.34	0.64	2.58	1.21
33	46.3	44.5	48.6	39.7	45.4	1.13	1.37	0.69	2.59	1.30
34	45.4	43.5	47.7	38.8	44.5	1.18	1.42	0.74	2.66	1.40
35	44.4	42.6	46.7	37.9	43.5	1.24	1.48	0.80	2.75	1.51
36	43.5	41.6	45.7	37.0	42.6	1.32	1.55	0.86	2.86	1.63
37	42.5	40.7	44.8	36.1	41.7	1.41	1.66	0.94	2.99	1.78
38	41.6	39.8	43.8	35.3	40.7	1.53	1.80	1.04	3.16	1.96
39	40.7	38.9	42.9	34.4	39.8	1.68	1.97	1.15	3.36	2.17
40	39.7	37.9	41.9	33.5	38.9	1.84	2.15	1.27	3.58	2.37
41	38.8	37.0	41.0	32.6	38.0	2.00	2.34	1.39	3.83	2.59
42	37.9	36.1	40.0	31.8	37.1	2.18	2.55	1.52	4.12	2.82
43	37.0	35.2	39.1	30.9	36.2	2.38	2.77	1.66	4.48	3.08
44	36.1	34.3	38.2	30.1	35.3	2.59	3.01	1.81	4.89	3.36
45	35.2	33.4	37.2	29.2	34.5	2.81	3.26	1.98	5.31	3.66
46	34.3	32.5	36.3	28.4	33.6	3.03	3.52	2.14	5.76	3.95
47	33.4	31.6	35.4	27.6	32.7	3.27	3.80	2.31	6.28	4.26
48	32.5	30.8	34.5	26.8	31.9	3.53	4.11	2.48	6.92	4.57
49	31.6	29.9	33.6	26.0	31.0	3.82	4.45	2.65	7.65	4.90
50	30.7	29.0	32.6	25.2	30.2	4.13	4.83	2.85	8.47	5.25
51	29.9	28.2	31.7	24.4	29.4	4.46	5.22	3.06	9.32	5.63
52	29.0	27.4	30.8	23.7	28.5	4.80	5.62	3.30	10.10	6.01
53	28.2	26.5	29.9	23.0	27.7	5.13	6.01	3.57	10.76	6.39
54	27.3	25.7	29.1	22.3	26.9	5.46	6.37	3.84	11.29	6.76
55	26.5	24.9	28.2	21.6	26.1	5.79	6.73	4.13	11.80	7.14
56	25.6	24.1	27.3	20.9	25.3	6.14	7.11	4.44	12.34	7.54
57	24.8	23.2	26.4	20.2	24.5	6.52	7.54	4.78	12.88	7.96
58	24.0	22.4	25.6	19.5	23.8	6.98	8.05	5.20	13.48	8.43
59	23.2	21.6	24.7	18.8	23.0	7.52	8.67	5.69	14.16	8.96
60	22.4	20.9	23.8	18.2	22.2	8.17	9.40	6.29	14.97	9.58
61	21.6	20.9	23.0	17.5	21.5	8.90	10.22	6.96	15.88	10.30
62	20.8	20.1	22.2	16.9	20.7	9.65	11.07	7.64	16.79	11.06
63	20.0	19.3	21.4	16.3	20.0	10.35	11.86	8.25	17.55	11.78
64	19.2	18.6	20.6	15.7	19.3	10.99	12.59	8.80	18.12	12.41
65	18.5	17.1	19.8	15.1	18.6	11.65	13.36	9.40	18.57	13.01
70	14.9	13.6	15.9	12.3	15.1	16.01	18.25	13.65	22.05	16.72
75	11.6	10.5	12.3	9.8	12.0	23.15	25.77	21.02	25.72	22.66
80	8.7	7.8	9.3	7.7	9.3	30.69	32.57	30.17	26.22	28.04
85	6.4	5.7	6.7	5.9	7.1	34.73	34.06	37.36	22.77	30.41
90	4.6	4.0	4.7	4.5	5.3	30.44	26.27	36.07	15.76	26.97
95	3.2	2.8	3.3	3.5	3.9	17.84	12.62	23.12	7.97	17.71
100	2.3	2.0	2.2	2.6	2.8	17.37	8.04	23.73	9.12	28.48

[1] Includes other races not shown separately.   [2] Based on the proportion of the cohort who are alive at the beginning of the indicated age who will die before reaching the age shown plus 1. For example, out of every 1,000 people alive and exactly 50 years old at the beginning of the period, between 4 and 5 (4.13) will die before reaching their 51st birthdays.

Source: U.S. National Center for Health Statistics, unpublished data.

78   Births, Deaths, Marriage, and Divorces

Table 106. **Deaths and Death Rates by Sex, Race, and Hispanic Origin: 1980 to 2006**

[1,990 represents 1,990,000. Rates are per 1,000 population for specified groups. Excludes deaths of nonresidents of the United States and fetal deaths. For explanation of age adjustment, see text, this section. The standard population for age adjustment is the projected year 2000 population of the United States. See Appendix III. Data for Hispanic origin and specified races other than White and Black should be interpreted with caution because of inconsistencies between reporting Hispanic origin and race on death certificates and censuses and surveys]

Sex, race, and Hispanic origin	1980	1990	1995	1999	2000	2001	2002	2003	2004	2005	2006
Deaths [1] **(1,000)**	1,990	2,148	2,312	2,391	2,403	2,416	2,443	2,448	2,398	2,448	2,426
Male [1] (1,000)	1,075	1,113	1,173	1,175	1,178	1,183	1,199	1,202	1,182	1,208	1,202
Female [1] (1,000).	915	1,035	1,139	1,216	1,226	1,233	1,244	1,246	1,216	1,240	1,224
White (1,000)	1,739	1,853	1,987	2,061	2,071	2,080	2,103	2,104	2,057	2,098	2,078
Male (1,000).	934	951	997	1,005	1,007	1,011	1,025	1,026	1,007	1,028	1,022
Female (1,000).	805	902	990	1,056	1,064	1,068	1,077	1,078	1,049	1,070	1,055
Black (1,000)	233	265	286	285	286	288	290	291	287	293	290
Male (1,000).	130	145	154	146	145	146	147	148	146	149	149
Female (1,000).	103	120	132	139	141	142	143	143	141	144	141
Asian or Pacific Islander (1,000)	11	21	28	34	35	37	38	40	41	43	45
Male (1,000).	7	12	16	18	19	20	20	21	21	23	23
Female (1,000).	4	9	12	15	16	17	18	19	19	20	21
American Indian, Eskimo, Aleut (1,000).	7	8	10	11	11	12	12	13	13	14	14
Male (1,000).	4	5	6	6	6	6	7	7	7	8	8
Female (1,000).	3	3	4	5	5	6	6	6	6	6	6
Hispanic origin [2] (1,000)	(NA)	(NA)	(NA)	104	107	113	117	122	122	131	133
Male (1,000).	(NA)	(NA)	(NA)	58	60	63	66	68	69	74	74
Female (1,000)	(NA)	(NA)	(NA)	46	47	50	51	54	54	57	59
Non-Hispanic, White (1,000) . .	(NA)	(NA)	(NA)	1,953	1,960	1,963	1,982	1,979	1,933	1,967	1,945
Male (1,000).	(NA)	(NA)	(NA)	945	945	946	958	956	938	954	948
Female (1,000)	(NA)	(NA)	(NA)	1,008	1,015	1,017	1,024	1,023	995	1,013	997
Death rates [1]	8.8	8.6	8.7	8.6	8.5	8.5	8.5	8.4	8.2	8.3	8.1
Male [1].	9.8	9.2	9.0	8.6	8.5	8.5	8.5	8.4	8.2	8.3	8.1
Female [1]	7.9	8.1	8.4	8.5	8.6	8.5	8.5	8.4	8.2	8.2	8.1
White	8.9	8.9	9.0	9.0	9.0	9.0	9.0	8.9	8.6	8.7	8.6
Male	9.8	9.3	9.3	9.1	8.9	8.8	8.8	8.8	8.5	8.6	8.5
Female . .".	8.1	8.5	8.9	9.2	9.1	9.1	9.1	9.0	8.7	8.8	8.6
Black	8.8	8.7	8.5	7.9	7.8	7.7	7.7	7.6	7.4	7.5	7.3
Male	10.3	10.1	9.8	8.8	8.3	8.2	8.2	8.1	7.9	8.0	7.9
Female	7.3	7.5	7.6	7.6	7.3	7.3	7.2	7.2	7.0	7.0	6.8
Asian or Pacific Islander.	3.0	2.8	2.9	3.0	3.0	3.0	3.0	3.0	3.0	3.1	3.1
Male	3.8	3.3	3.4	3.3	3.3	3.4	3.3	3.3	3.2	3.3	3.3
Female	2.2	2.3	2.5	2.6	2.6	2.7	2.7	2.8	2.7	2.8	2.9
American Indian, Eskimo, Aleut.	4.9	4.0	4.1	4.0	3.8	3.9	4.0	4.2	4.2	4.4	4.4
Male	6.0	4.8	4.6	4.3	4.2	4.2	4.4	4.6	4.5	4.8	4.8
Female	3.8	3.3	3.6	3.7	3.5	3.6	3.7	3.9	3.8	4.0	4.0
Hispanic origin [2]	(NA)	(NA)	(NA)	3.1	3.0	3.1	3.0	3.1	3.0	3.1	3.0
Male	(NA)	4.1	(NA)	3.7	3.3	3.3	3.3	3.3	3.2	3.3	3.2
Female	(NA)	2.9	(NA)	2.9	2.7	2.8	2.7	2.8	2.7	2.8	2.7
Non-Hispanic, White	(NA)	(NA)	(NA)	9.9	9.9	9.9	10.0	9.9	9.7	9.8	9.7
Male	(NA)	9.9	(NA)	9.8	9.8	9.8	9.8	9.8	9.6	9.7	9.6
Female	(NA)	9.0	(NA)	10.0	10.1	10.1	10.1	10.1	9.8	9.9	9.7
Age-adjusted death rates [1]	10.4	9.4	9.2	8.8	8.7	8.5	8.5	8.3	8.0	8.0	7.8
Male [1]	13.5	12.0	11.5	10.7	10.5	10.3	10.1	9.9	9.6	9.5	9.2
Female [1]	8.2	7.5	7.5	7.3	7.3	7.2	7.2	7.1	6.8	6.8	6.6
White	10.1	9.1	8.9	8.5	8.5	8.4	8.3	8.2	7.9	7.9	7.6
Male	13.2	11.7	11.1	10.4	10.3	10.1	9.9	9.7	9.4	9.3	9.1
Female	8.0	7.3	7.3	7.2	7.2	7.1	7.0	6.9	6.7	8.5	6.5
Black	13.1	12.5	12.2	11.4	11.4	11.2	11.0	10.8	10.7	10.3	9.8
Male	17.0	16.4	15.8	14.3	14.0	13.8	13.4	13.2	12.7	12.5	12.2
Female	10.3	9.8	9.7	9.3	9.3	9.1	9.0	8.9	8.6	8.5	8.1
Asian or Pacific Islander.	5.9	5.8	6.2	5.2	5.1	4.9	4.7	4.7	4.4	4.4	4.3
Male	7.9	7.2	7.9	6.4	6.2	6.0	5.8	5.6	5.3	5.3	5.2
Female	4.3	4.7	4.9	4.3	4.2	4.1	4.0	3.9	3.8	3.7	3.6
American Indian, Eskimo, Aleut.	8.7	7.2	7.2	7.8	7.1	6.9	6.8	6.9	6.5	6.6	6.4
Male	11.1	9.2	8.6	9.3	8.4	8.0	7.9	8.0	7.6	7.8	7.4
Female	6.6	5.6	5.9	6.7	6.0	5.9	5.8	5.9	5.6	5.7	5.6
Hispanic origin [2]	(NA)	(NA)	(NA)	6.8	6.7	6.6	6.3	6.2	5.9	5.9	5.6
Male	(NA)	8.9	(NA)	8.3	8.2	8.0	7.7	7.5	7.1	7.2	6.8
Female	(NA)	5.4	(NA)	5.6	5.5	5.4	5.2	5.2	4.9	4.9	4.7
Non-Hispanic, White	(NA)	(NA)	(NA)	8.6	8.6	8.4	8.4	8.3	8.0	8.0	7.8
Male	(NA)	11.7	(NA)	10.5	10.4	10.1	10.0	9.8	9.5	9.5	9.2
Female	(NA)	7.3	(NA)	7.2	7.2	7.1	7.1	7.0	6.8	6.8	6.6

NA Not available.   [1] Includes other races, not shown separately.   [2] Persons of Hispanic origin may be any race.

Source: U.S. National Center for Health Statistics, National Vital Statistics Reports (NVSR), Deaths: Final Data for 2006, Vol. 57, No. 14, 17 April 2009.

Births, Deaths, Marriages, and Divorces   79

Table 107. Death Rates by Age, Sex, and Race: 1950 to 2006

[Rates per 100,000 population]

Characteristic	All ages [1]	Under 1 year	1–4 years	5–14 years	15–24 years	25–34 years	35–44 years	45–54 years	55–64 years	65–74 years	75–84 years	85 years and over
MALE												
1950	1,106	3,728	152	71	168	217	429	1,067	2,395	4,931	10,426	21,636
1960	1,105	3,059	120	56	152	188	373	992	2,310	4,914	10,178	21,186
1970	1,090	2,410	93	51	189	215	403	959	2,283	4,874	10,010	17,822
1980	977	1,429	73	37	172	196	299	767	1,815	4,105	8,817	18,801
1990	918	1,083	52	29	147	204	310	610	1,553	3,492	7,889	18,057
2000	853	807	36	21	115	139	255	543	1,231	2,980	6,973	17,501
2003	840	777	35	20	117	141	255	552	1,166	2,772	6,642	15,794
2004	818	754	32	19	115	140	244	544	1,129	2,645	6,394	15,031
2005	827	762	33	19	118	143	243	548	1,131	2,612	6,350	14,889
2006	815	756	31	18	119	147	239	541	1,110	2,516	6,178	14,309
White:												
1990	931	896	46	26	131	176	268	549	1,467	3,398	7,845	18,268
2000	888	668	33	20	106	124	234	497	1,163	2,906	6,933	17,716
2005	865	640	31	17	110	131	229	509	1,068	2,553	6,343	15,157
2006	852	633	28	16	112	135	224	505	1,051	2,456	6,182	14,577
Black:												
1990	1,008	2,112	86	41	252	431	700	1,261	2,618	4,946	9,130	16,955
2000	834	1,568	55	28	181	261	453	1,018	2,080	4,254	8,486	16,791
2005	799	1,437	47	27	172	254	396	949	1,954	3,747	7,667	13,810
2006	787	1,407	47	25	171	254	392	922	1,892	3,669	7,393	13,206
Asian or Pacific Islander [2]:												
1990	334	605	45	21	76	80	131	287	789	2,041	5,009	12,446
2000	333	529	23	13	55	55	105	250	642	1,661	4,328	12,125
2005	334	465	21	14	57	56	94	242	545	1,404	3,759	9,839
2006	331	470	18	11	62	54	89	233	551	1,329	3,606	9,525
American Indian, Eskimo, Aleut [2]:												
1990	476	1,057	77	33	220	256	365	620	1,211	2,462	5,389	11,244
2000	416	700	45	20	136	179	295	520	1,090	2,478	5,351	10,726
2005	482	882	72	23	145	206	337	589	1,124	2,254	4,373	8,419
2006	477	1,058	58	17	156	194	339	592	1,030	2,147	4,198	7,540
FEMALE												
1950	824	2,855	127	49	89	143	290	642	1,405	3,333	8,400	19,195
1960	809	2,321	98	37	61	107	229	527	1,196	2,872	7,633	19,008
1970	808	1,864	75	32	68	102	231	517	1,099	2,580	6,678	15,518
1980	785	1,142	55	24	58	76	159	413	934	2,145	5,440	14,747
1990	812	856	41	19	49	74	138	343	879	1,991	4,883	14,274
2000	855	663	29	15	43	64	143	313	772	1,921	4,815	14,719
2003	843	619	28	14	44	65	149	318	733	1,823	4,676	14,063
2004	815	613	27	14	44	64	144	314	707	1,761	4,522	13,280
2005	825	619	25	14	43	64	144	320	699	1,736	4,520	13,298
2006	806	622	26	13	43	64	142	318	687	1,678	4,388	12,759
White:												
1990	847	690	36	18	46	62	117	309	823	1,924	4,839	14,401
2000	912	551	26	14	41	55	126	281	731	1,868	4,785	14,891
2005	883	515	23	13	42	58	130	291	664	1,700	4,519	13,498
2006	864	517	24	12	42	59	129	292	655	1,646	4,395	12,966
Black:												
1990	748	1,736	68	28	69	160	299	639	1,453	2,866	5,688	13,310
2000	733	1,280	45	20	58	122	272	588	1,227	2,690	5,697	13,941
2005	704	1,180	37	19	51	110	250	568	1,104	2,342	5,264	12,790
2006	684	1,195	39	17	51	107	245	548	1,076	2,240	5,029	12,197
Asian or Pacific Islander [2]:												
1990	234	518	32	13	29	38	70	183	483	1,089	3,128	10,254
2000	262	434	20	12	22	28	66	156	391	996	2,882	9,052
2005	283	395	18	12	26	29	58	143	353	906	2,530	7,793
2006	286	357	21	10	25	29	57	145	333	898	2,526	7,560
American Indian, Eskimo, Aleut [2]:												
1990	330	689	38	26	69	102	156	381	806	1,679	3,073	8,201
2000	346	492	40	18	59	85	172	285	772	1,900	3,850	9,118
2005	399	753	46	17	68	91	194	366	699	1,781	3,603	7,065
2006	400	690	51	17	64	92	205	342	687	1,657	3,746	6,634

[1] Figures for age not stated are included in "All ages" but not distributed among age groups.   [2] The death rates for specified races other than White and Black should be interpreted with caution because of inconsistencies between reporting race on death certificates and censuses and surveys.

Source: U.S. National Center for Health Statistics, *Health, United States, 2008.* See also <http://cdc.gov/nchs/hus.htm>.

U.S. Census Bureau, Statistical Abstract of the United States: 2010

Table 108. Age-Adjusted Death Rates by Sex, Race, and Hispanic Origin: 1960 to 2006

[Age-adjusted rates per 100,000 population; see headnote, Table 106. Populations enumerated as of April 1 for census years and estimated as of July 1 for all other years. Beginning 1970, excludes deaths of nonresidents of the United States. Data for Hispanic-origin and specified races other than White and Black should be interpreted with caution because of inconsistencies reporting race on death certificates and on censuses and surveys. See Appendix III]

Sex, race, and Hispanic origin	1960	1970	1980	1990	2000	2002	2003	2004	2005	2006
ALL RACES [1]										
Total	1,339	1,223	1,039	939	869	845	833	801	799	777
Male	1,609	1,542	1,348	1,203	1,054	1,014	994	956	951	925
Female	1,105	971	818	751	731	715	706	679	678	658
WHITE										
Total	1,311	1,193	1,013	910	850	829	817	786	785	764
Male	1,586	1,514	1,318	1,166	1,029	993	974	937	933	908
Female	1,074	944	796	729	715	701	693	667	667	648
BLACK										
Total	1,578	1,518	1,315	1,250	1,121	1,083	1,066	1,027	1,017	982
Male	1,811	1,874	1,698	1,645	1,404	1,341	1,319	1,269	1,253	1,216
Female	1,370	1,229	1,033	975	928	902	886	855	846	813
ASIAN OR PACIFIC ISLANDER										
Total	(NA)	(NA)	590	582	506	474	466	444	440	429
Male	(NA)	(NA)	787	716	624	578	563	535	534	516
Female	(NA)	(NA)	426	469	417	396	393	376	369	363
AMERICAN INDIAN, ESKIMO, ALEUT										
Total	(NA)	(NA)	867	716	709	677	685	650	663	642
Male	(NA)	(NA)	1,112	916	842	794	797	758	775	740
Female	(NA)	(NA)	662	562	605	581	592	558	568	556
HISPANIC ORIGIN [2]										
Total	(NA)	(NA)	(NA)	(NA)	666	629	621	587	591	564
Male	(NA)	(NA)	(NA)	886	818	767	748	707	717	676
Female	(NA)	(NA)	(NA)	537	546	518	516	486	485	469
NON-HISPANIC, WHITE										
Total	(NA)	(NA)	(NA)	(NA)	856	838	826	797	797	777
Male	(NA)	(NA)	(NA)	1,171	1,035	1,002	984	949	945	923
Female	(NA)	(NA)	(NA)	735	722	710	702	678	678	660

NA Not available.   [1] For 1960 to 1990 includes deaths among races not shown separately.   [2] Persons of Hispanic origin may be any race.

Source: U.S. National Center for Health Statistics, National Vital Statistics Reports (NVSR), *Deaths: Final Data for 2006*, Vol. 57, No. 14, April 17, 2009.

Table 109. Death Rates by Hispanic-Origin Status, Sex, and Age: 2000 to 2006

[Rates per 100,000 population. Rates are based on populations enumerated as of April 1 for census years and estimated as of July 1 for all other years. Excludes deaths of nonresidents of the United States. Data for Hispanic-origin should be interpreted with caution because of inconsistencies between reporting Hispanic origin and race on death certificates and censuses and surveys]

Age	Hispanic male			Hispanic female			Non-Hispanic White male			Non-Hispanic White female		
	2000	2005	2006	2000	2005	2006	2000	2005	2006	2000	2005	2006
Age-adjusted [1]	818	717	676	546	485	469	1,035	945	923	722	678	660
Crude[2]	331	334	324	275	278	275	979	971	962	1,007	993	975
Under 1 year	637	670	641	554	555	538	659	626	622	531	497	504
1 to 4 years	32	33	29	28	25	24	32	30	27	24	22	23
5 to 14 years	18	15	16	13	12	12	20	17	16	14	13	12
15 to 24 years	108	120	121	32	37	35	104	106	108	43	42	43
25 to 34 years	120	116	113	43	41	43	123	134	141	57	62	63
35 to 44 years	211	182	177	101	91	87	234	236	233	128	137	136
45 to 54 years	439	417	404	224	216	215	498	517	515	285	299	300
55 to 64 years	966	876	844	548	494	487	1,171	1,080	1,064	742	677	668
65 to 74 years	2,288	2,029	1,911	1,423	1,292	1,223	2,931	2,585	2,490	1,891	1,730	1,677
75 to 84 years	5,395	4,857	4,493	3,625	3,366	3,223	6,978	6,420	6,278	4,819	4,580	4,461
85 years and over	13,086	10,141	9,436	11,203	9,068	8,804	17,853	15,401	14,841	14,972	13,683	13,151

[1] See headnote, Table 106.   [2] The total number of deaths in a given time period divided by the total resident population as of July 1.

Source: U.S. National Center for Health Statistics, National Vital Statistics Reports (NVSR), *Deaths: Final Data for 2006*, Vol. 57, No. 14, April 17, 2009.

Births, Deaths, Marriages, and Divorces   81

Table 110. **Deaths and Death Rates by State and Island Areas: 1990 to 2007**

[**2,148 represents 2,148,000.** By state of residence. Except as noted, excludes deaths of nonresidents of the United States. Caution should be used in comparing death rates by state; rates are affected by the population composition of the area. For explanation of age adjustment, see text, this section. See also Appendix III]

State and Island Area	Number of deaths (1,000)						Death rate per 1,000 population [2]						Age-adjusted death rate, 2007 [1]
	1990	1995	2000	2005	2006	2007 [1]	1990	1995	2000	2005	2006	2007 [1]	
United States ...	2,148	2,312	2,403	2,448	2,426	2,424	8.6	8.7	8.5	8.3	8.1	8.0	7.6
Alabama.........	39	42	45	47	47	47	9.7	10.0	10.1	10.3	10.2	10.1	9.3
Alaska	2	3	3	3	3	3	4.0	4.2	4.6	4.8	5.0	5.1	7.6
Arizona.........	29	35	41	46	46	46	7.9	8.4	7.9	7.7	7.5	7.2	6.8
Arkansas	25	27	28	28	28	28	10.5	10.8	10.6	10.1	9.9	9.9	8.8
California	214	224	230	237	237	234	7.2	7.1	6.8	6.6	6.5	6.4	6.7
Colorado........	22	25	27	30	30	30	6.6	6.7	6.3	6.4	6.2	6.2	7.0
Connecticut......	28	29	30	29	29	29	8.4	9.0	8.8	8.4	8.3	8.2	6.9
Delaware	6	6	7	7	7	7	8.7	8.8	8.8	8.9	8.4	8.5	7.7
District of Columbia .	7	7	6	5	5	5	12.0	12.4	10.5	10.0	9.2	8.8	8.7
Florida	134	153	164	171	170	168	10.4	10.8	10.3	9.6	9.4	9.2	6.9
Georgia	52	58	64	67	68	68	8.0	8.1	7.8	7.4	7.2	7.2	8.4
Hawaii	7	8	8	9	9	9	6.1	6.4	6.8	7.2	7.3	7.4	6.1
Idaho	7	9	10	11	11	11	7.4	7.3	7.4	7.4	7.2	7.2	7.3
Illinois	103	108	107	104	102	100	9.0	9.2	8.6	8.1	8.0	7.8	7.6
Indiana.........	50	53	55	56	56	54	8.9	9.2	9.1	8.9	8.8	8.5	8.1
Iowa	27	28	28	28	27	27	9.7	9.9	9.6	9.4	9.2	9.1	7.2
Kansas	22	24	25	25	25	24	9.0	9.3	9.2	9.0	8.9	8.8	7.8
Kentucky	35	37	40	40	40	40	9.5	9.6	9.8	9.6	9.5	9.5	9.0
Louisiana	38	40	41	44	40	40	8.9	9.1	9.2	9.8	9.3	9.3	9.2
Maine..........	11	12	12	13	12	12	9.0	9.5	9.7	9.7	9.3	9.5	7.7
Maryland	38	42	44	44	44	44	8.0	8.3	8.3	7.8	7.8	7.8	7.8
Massachusetts.....	53	55	57	54	53	53	8.8	9.1	8.9	8.4	8.3	8.2	7.1
Michigan........	79	84	87	87	86	87	8.5	8.8	8.7	8.6	8.5	8.6	8.1
Minnesota.......	35	38	38	38	37	37	7.9	8.1	7.7	7.3	7.2	7.2	6.6
Mississippi	25	27	29	29	29	28	9.8	10.0	10.1	10.0	9.8	9.7	9.4
Missouri	50	54	55	55	55	54	9.8	10.2	9.8	9.4	9.4	9.2	8.3
Montana........	7	8	8	9	8	9	8.6	8.8	9.0	9.1	9.0	9.0	7.7
Nebraska	15	15	15	15	15	15	9.4	9.3	8.8	8.5	8.4	8.6	7.4
Nevada	9	13	15	19	19	19	7.8	8.2	7.6	7.9	7.6	7.3	8.0
New Hampshire....	8	9	10	10	10	10	7.7	8.0	7.8	7.8	7.7	7.8	7.3
New Jersey.......	70	74	75	72	70	70	9.1	9.3	8.9	8.3	8.1	8.0	7.2
New Mexico	11	13	13	15	15	15	7.0	7.4	7.4	7.8	7.8	7.8	7.5
New York	169	168	158	152	149	148	9.4	9.3	8.3	7.9	7.7	7.7	6.9
North Carolina.....	57	65	72	75	75	76	8.6	9.0	8.9	8.6	8.4	8.4	8.3
North Dakota......	6	6	6	6	6	6	8.9	9.3	9.1	9.0	9.2	8.7	6.8
Ohio	99	106	108	109	107	107	9.1	9.5	9.5	9.5	9.3	9.3	8.3
Oklahoma........	30	33	35	36	35	36	9.7	10.0	10.2	10.2	9.9	10.0	9.2
Oregon.........	25	28	30	31	31	31	8.8	9.0	8.6	8.5	8.5	8.4	7.5
Pennsylvania......	122	128	131	130	126	125	10.3	10.6	10.7	10.4	10.1	10.1	7.9
Rhode Island......	10	10	10	10	10	10	9.5	9.8	9.6	9.3	9.1	9.2	7.5
South Carolina.....	30	34	37	39	39	39	8.5	9.1	9.2	9.1	9.0	9.0	8.5
South Dakota	6	7	7	7	7	7	9.1	9.5	9.3	9.1	9.1	8.6	6.9
Tennessee	46	51	55	57	57	57	9.5	9.8	9.7	9.6	9.4	9.3	8.9
Texas	125	138	150	156	157	161	7.4	7.4	7.2	6.8	6.7	6.7	7.8
Utah	9	11	12	13	14	14	5.3	5.6	5.5	5.4	5.4	5.3	6.9
Vermont	5	5	5	5	5	5	8.2	8.5	8.4	8.1	8.1	8.3	7.3
Virginia.........	48	53	56	58	58	58	7.8	8.0	8.0	7.6	7.5	7.5	7.7
Washington......	37	41	44	46	46	47	7.6	7.5	7.5	7.3	7.2	7.3	7.2
West Virginia......	19	20	21	21	21	21	10.8	11.1	11.7	11.4	11.4	11.6	9.5
Wisconsin........	43	45	46	47	46	46	8.7	8.8	8.7	8.4	8.3	8.3	7.3
Wyoming	3	4	4	4	4	4	7.1	7.7	7.9	8.0	8.4	8.2	8.0
Puerto Rico	26	30	28	30	28	29	7.3	8.1	7.2	7.5	7.2	7.4	7.2
Virgin Islands	(Z)	1	1	1	1	1	4.6	5.8	5.3	6.1	5.7	6.4	6.5
Guam..........	1	1	1	1	1	1	3.9	4.1	4.2	4.0	4.0	4.5	6.2
American Samoa .	(NA)	(NA)	(Z)	(Z)	(Z)	(Z)	(NA)	(NA)	3.3	4.4	4.6	3.9	13.1
Northern Marianas	(NA)	(NA)	(Z)	(Z)	(Z)	(Z)	(NA)	(NA)	1.9	2.3	2.1	1.7	10.0

NA Not available. Z Less than 500. [1] Preliminary data. U.S. totals include only events occuring within the 50 states and the District of Columbia. [2] Rates based on enumerated resident population as of April 1 for 1990 and 2000; estimated resident population as of July 1 for all other years.

Source: U.S. National Center for Health Statistics, National Vital Statistics Reports (NVSR), *Deaths: Final Data for 2006,* Vol. 57, No. 14, April 17, 2009; *Deaths: Preliminary Data for 2007,* Vol. 58, No. 1, August 19, 2009; and earlier reports.

Table 111. **Fetal and Infant Deaths: 1990 to 2005**

[See Appendix III]

Year	Fetal deaths			Infant deaths		Fetal mortality rate [1]			Perinatal mortality rate	
	Total [2]	20 to 27 weeks [3]	28 weeks or more [3]	Less than 7 days	Less than 28 days	Total [1]	20 to 27 weeks [3]	28 weeks or more [3]	Defin- ition I [4]	Defin- ition II [5]
1990 ...	31,386	13,427	17,959	19,439	23,591	7.49	3.22	4.30	8.95	13.12
1995 ...	27,294	13,043	14,251	15,483	19,186	6.95	3.33	3.64	7.60	11.84
1996 ...	27,069	12,990	14,079	14,947	18,556	6.91	3.33	3.60	7.43	11.64
1997 ...	26,486	12,800	13,686	14,827	18,507	6.78	3.29	3.51	7.32	11.51
1998 ...	26,702	13,229	13,473	15,061	18,915	6.73	3.35	3.41	7.21	11.50
1999 ...	26,884	13,457	13,427	14,874	18,700	6.74	3.39	3.38	7.12	11.44
2000 ...	27,003	13,497	13,506	14,893	18,733	6.61	3.31	3.32	6.97	11.19
2001 ...	26,373	13,122	13,251	14,622	18,275	6.51	3.25	3.28	6.90	11.02
2002 ...	25,943	13,072	12,871	15,020	18,791	6.41	3.24	3.19	6.91	11.05
2003 ...	25,653	13,168	12,485	15,152	18,935	6.23	3.21	3.04	6.74	10.83
2004 ...	25,655	12,894	12,761	14,836	18,602	6.20	3.13	3.09	6.69	10.70
2005 ...	25,894	13,327	12,567	15,013	18,782	6.22	3.21	3.03	6.64	10.73

[1] Fetal deaths with stated or presumed gestation of 20 weeks or more. [2] Not stated gestational age proportionally distributed. [3] Rate per 1,000 live births and fetal deaths in specified group. [4] Infant deaths of less than 7 days with stated or presumed period of gestation of 28 weeks or more, per 1,000 live births and fetal deaths. [5] Infant deaths of less than 28 days and fetal deaths with stated or presumed period of gestation of 20 weeks or more per 1,000 live births and fetal deaths.

Source: U.S. National Center for Health Statistics, National Vital Statistics Reports (NVSR), *Fetal and Perinatal Mortality, U.S., 2005*, Vol. 57. No. 8, January 28, 2009.

Table 112. **Infant, Neonatal, and Maternal Mortality Rates by Race: 1980 to 2005**

[**Deaths per 1,000 live births, except as noted.** Data based on death certificates, fetal death records, and birth certificates. Excludes deaths of nonresidents of U.S. See also Appendix III]

Race and year	Infant mortality [1]	Neonatal mortality [1]		Post- neonatal mortality [1]	Fetal mortality rate [2]	Late fetal mortality rate [3]	Perinatal mortality rate [4]	Maternal mortality rate [5]
		Under 28 days	Under 7 days					
ALL RACES								
1980	12.6	8.5	7.1	4.1	9.1	6.2	13.2	9.2
1990	9.2	5.8	4.8	3.4	7.5	4.3	9.1	8.2
1995	7.6	4.9	4.0	2.7	7.0	3.6	7.6	7.1
2000	6.9	4.6	3.7	2.3	6.6	3.3	7.0	9.8
2001	6.8	4.5	3.6	2.3	6.5	3.3	6.9	9.9
2002	7.0	4.7	3.7	2.3	6.4	3.2	6.9	8.9
2003	6.9	4.6	3.7	2.2	6.2	3.0	6.7	[6]12.1
2004	6.8	4.5	3.6	2.3	6.2	3.1	6.7	[6]13.1
2005	6.9	4.5	3.6	2.3	6.2	3.0	6.6	[6]15.1
WHITE [7]								
1980	10.9	7.4	6.1	3.5	8.1	5.7	11.8	6.7
1990	7.6	4.8	3.9	2.8	6.4	3.8	7.7	5.4
1995	6.3	4.1	3.3	2.2	5.9	3.3	6.5	4.2
2000	5.7	3.8	3.0	1.9	5.6	2.9	5.9	7.5
2001	5.7	3.8	3.0	1.9	5.5	2.9	5.9	7.2
2002	5.8	3.9	3.1	1.9	5.5	2.8	5.9	[6]6.0
2003	5.7	3.9	3.1	1.8	5.2	2.7	5.8	[6]8.7
2004	5.7	3.8	3.0	1.9	5.3	(NA)	(NA)	[6]9.3
2005	5.7	3.8	3.0	1.9	5.3	(NA)	(NA)	[6]11.1
BLACK [7]								
1980	22.2	14.6	12.3	7.6	14.7	9.1	21.3	21.5
1990	18.0	11.6	9.7	6.4	13.3	6.7	16.4	22.4
1995	15.1	9.8	8.2	5.3	12.7	5.7	13.8	22.1
2000	14.1	9.4	7.6	4.7	12.4	5.4	13.0	22.0
2001	14.0	9.2	7.6	4.8	12.1	5.3	12.8	24.7
2002	14.4	9.5	7.8	4.8	11.9	5.2	12.8	24.9
2003	14.0	9.4	7.5	4.6	12.0	5.1	12.4	[6]30.5
2004	13.8	9.1	7.3	4.7	11.5	(NA)	(NA)	[6]34.7
2005	13.7	9.1	7.3	4.7	11.4	(NA)	(NA)	[6]36.5

NA Not available. [1] Infant (under 1 year of age), neonatal (under 28 days), early neonatal (under 7 days), and postneonatal (28 days–11 months). [2] Number of fetal deaths of 20 weeks or more gestation per 1,000 live births plus fetal deaths. [3] Number of fetal deaths of 28 weeks or more gestation (late fetal deaths) per 1,000 live births plus late fetal deaths. [4] Number of late fetal deaths plus infant deaths within 7 days of birth per 1,000 live births plus late fetal deaths. [5] Per 100,000 live births from deliveries and complications of pregnancy, childbirth, and the puerperium. Beginning 2000, deaths are classified according to the tenth revision of the *International Classification of Diseases;* earlier years classified according to the revision in use at the time; see text, this section. [6] Increase partially reflects the use of a separate item on the death certificate on pregnancy status by an increasing number of states. [7] Infant deaths are tabulated by race of decedent; fetal deaths and live births are tabulated by race of mother.

Source: U.S. National Center for Health Statistics, *Health, United States, 2008.* See also <http://cdc.gov/nchs/hus.htm>.

Table 113. Infant Mortality Rates by Race—States: 1980 to 2006

[**Deaths per 1,000 live births, by place of residence.** Represents deaths of infants under 1 year old, exclusive of fetal deaths. Excludes deaths of nonresidents of the United States. See headnote, Table 112, and Appendix III]

State	Total [1]				White				Black			
	1980	1990	2000	2006	1980	1990	2000	2006	1980	1990	2000	2006
United States	12.6	9.2	6.9	6.7	10.9	7.6	5.7	5.6	22.2	18.0	14.1	13.3
Alabama.	15.1	10.8	9.4	9.0	11.6	8.1	6.6	6.7	21.6	16.0	15.4	14.2
Alaska	12.3	10.5	6.8	6.9	9.4	7.6	5.8	4.5	19.5	(B)	(B)	(B)
Arizona.	12.4	8.8	6.7	6.4	11.8	7.8	6.2	6.0	18.4	20.6	17.6	16.9
Arkansas	12.7	9.2	8.4	8.5	10.3	8.4	7.0	6.9	20.0	13.9	13.7	15.7
California	11.1	7.9	5.4	5.0	10.6	7.0	5.1	4.8	18.0	16.8	12.9	12.1
Colorado.	10.1	8.8	6.2	5.7	9.8	7.8	5.6	5.5	19.1	19.4	19.5	12.4
Connecticut.	11.2	7.9	6.6	6.2	10.2	6.3	5.6	4.9	19.1	17.6	14.4	14.8
Delaware	13.9	10.1	9.2	8.3	9.8	9.7	7.9	6.2	27.9	20.1	14.8	14.3
District of Columbia	25.0	20.7	12.0	11.3	17.8	(B)	(B)	(B)	26.7	24.6	16.1	14.5
Florida	14.6	9.6	7.0	7.3	11.8	6.7	5.4	5.9	22.8	16.8	12.6	11.9
Georgia	14.5	12.4	8.5	8.1	10.8	7.4	5.9	5.8	21.0	18.3	13.9	12.9
Hawaii	10.3	6.7	8.1	5.6	11.6	6.1	6.5	(B)	(B)	(B)	(B)	(B)
Idaho.	10.7	8.7	7.5	6.8	10.7	8.6	7.5	6.7	(NA)	(B)	(B)	(B)
Illinois	14.8	10.7	8.5	7.3	11.7	7.9	6.6	6.0	26.3	22.4	17.1	13.7
Indiana.	11.9	9.6	7.8	8.0	10.5	7.9	6.9	6.7	23.4	17.4	15.8	18.7
Iowa	11.8	8.1	6.5	5.1	11.5	7.9	6.0	4.9	27.2	21.9	21.1	(B)
Kansas.	10.4	8.4	6.8	7.1	9.5	8.0	6.4	6.1	20.6	17.7	12.2	19.3
Kentucky	12.9	8.5	7.2	7.5	12.0	8.2	6.7	6.8	22.0	14.3	12.7	15.0
Louisiana	14.3	11.1	9.0	9.9	10.5	8.1	5.9	6.2	20.6	16.7	13.3	15.8
Maine.	9.2	6.2	4.9	6.3	9.4	6.7	4.8	6.2	(B)	(B)	(B)	(B)
Maryland	14.0	9.5	7.6	8.0	11.6	6.8	4.8	6.0	20.4	17.1	13.2	11.8
Massachusetts.	10.5	7.0	4.6	4.8	10.1	6.1	4.0	4.6	16.8	11.9	9.9	8.0
Michigan.	12.8	10.7	8.2	7.4	10.6	7.4	6.0	5.8	24.2	21.6	18.2	14.9
Minnesota.	10.0	7.3	5.6	5.2	9.6	6.7	4.8	4.7	20.0	23.7	14.6	8.3
Mississippi	17.0	12.1	10.7	10.6	11.1	7.4	6.8	7.1	23.7	16.2	15.3	14.6
Missouri	12.4	9.4	7.2	7.4	11.1	7.9	5.9	6.1	20.7	18.2	14.7	14.9
Montana.	12.4	9.0	6.1	5.8	11.8	6.0	5.5	5.0	(NA)	(B)	(B)	(B)
Nebraska	11.5	8.3	7.3	5.6	10.7	6.9	6.4	5.2	25.2	18.9	20.3	10.6
Nevada	10.7	8.4	6.5	6.4	10.0	8.2	6.0	5.8	20.6	14.2	12.7	15.7
New Hampshire	9.9	7.1	5.7	6.1	9.9	6.0	5.5	5.7	22.5	(B)	(B)	(B)
New Jersey	12.5	9.0	6.3	5.5	10.3	6.4	5.0	4.4	21.9	18.4	13.6	11.5
New Mexico	11.5	9.0	6.6	5.8	11.3	7.6	6.3	5.7	23.1	(B)	(B)	(B)
New York	12.5	9.6	6.4	5.6	10.8	7.4	5.4	4.9	20.0	18.1	10.9	9.2
North Carolina	14.5	10.6	8.6	8.1	12.1	8.0	6.3	6.0	20.0	16.5	15.7	15.1
North Dakota.	12.1	8.0	8.1	5.8	11.7	7.2	7.5	4.9	27.5	(B)	(B)	(B)
Ohio	12.8	9.8	7.6	7.8	11.2	7.8	6.3	6.1	23.0	19.5	15.4	16.9
Oklahoma.	12.7	9.2	8.5	8.0	12.1	9.1	7.9	6.8	21.8	14.3	16.9	15.4
Oregon.	12.2	8.3	5.6	5.5	12.2	7.0	5.5	5.3	15.9	(B)	(B)	(B)
Pennsylvania	13.2	9.6	7.1	7.6	11.9	7.4	5.8	6.2	23.1	20.5	15.7	15.2
Rhode Island.	11.0	8.1	6.3	6.1	10.9	7.0	5.9	5.7	(B)	(B)	(B)	(B)
South Carolina.	15.6	11.7	8.7	8.4	10.8	8.1	5.4	5.7	22.9	17.3	14.8	13.8
South Dakota	10.9	10.1	5.5	6.9	9.0	8.0	4.3	5.3	(NA)	(B)	(B)	(B)
Tennessee	13.5	10.3	9.1	8.7	11.9	7.3	6.8	6.8	19.3	17.9	18.0	16.0
Texas.	12.2	8.1	5.7	6.2	11.2	6.7	5.1	5.5	18.8	14.7	11.4	12.0
Utah	10.4	7.5	5.2	5.1	10.5	6.0	5.1	5.1	27.3	(B)	(B)	(B)
Vermont	10.7	6.4	6.0	5.5	10.7	5.9	6.1	5.6	(B)	(B)	(B)	(B)
Virginia.	13.6	10.2	6.9	7.1	11.9	7.4	5.4	5.4	19.8	19.5	12.4	13.3
Washington	11.8	7.8	5.2	4.7	11.5	7.3	4.9	4.4	16.4	20.6	9.4	7.4
West Virginia	11.8	9.9	7.6	7.4	11.4	8.1	7.4	6.7	21.5	(B)	(B)	28.6
Wisconsin	10.3	8.2	6.6	6.4	9.7	7.7	5.5	5.0	18.5	19.0	17.2	18.3
Wyoming	9.8	8.6	6.7	7.0	9.3	7.5	6.5	6.6	25.9	(B)	(B)	(B)
Puerto Rico	(NA)	(NA)	9.7	8.8	(NA)	(NA)	10.2	9.5	(NA)	(NA)	(B)	(B)
Virgin Islands	(NA)	(NA)	13.4	(B)	(NA)	(NA)	(B)	(B)	(B)	(B)	(B)	(B)
Guam	(NA)	(NA)	5.8	13.3	(NA)	(NA)	(B)	(B)	(B)	(B)	(B)	(B)
American Samoa . . .	(NA)	(NA)	(B)	(B)	(B)	(B)	(B)	(B)	(B)	(B)	(B)	(B)
Northern Marianas . . .	(NA)	(NA)	(B)	(B)	(B)	(B)	(B)	(B)	(B)	(B)	(B)	(B)

B Base figure too small to meet statistical standards for reliability.   NA Not available.   [1] Includes other races, not shown separately.

Source: U.S. National Center for Health Statistics, National Vital Statistics Reports (NVSR), *Deaths: Final Data for 2006*, Vol. 57, No. 14, April 17, 2009 and earlier reports.

Table 114. Age-Adjusted Death Rates by Major Causes: 1960 to 2006

[**Rates per 100,000 population**; see headnote, Table 106. Beginning 1999, deaths classified according to tenth revision of International Classification of Diseases; for earlier years, causes of death were classified according to the revisions then in use. Changes in classification of causes of death due to these revisions may result in discontinuities in cause-of-death trends. See Appendix III]

Year	Diseases of heart	Malignant neo-plasms (cancer)	Cere-bro-vascular diseases	Chronic lower respi-ratory diseases	Acci-dents[1]	Diabetes mellitus	Influenza and pneu-monia	Nephritis, nephrotic syndrome, and nephrosis	Septi-cemia	Intentional self-harm (suicide)
1960	559.0	193.9	177.9	12.5	63.1	22.5	53.7	10.6	1.2	12.5
1961	545.3	193.4	173.1	12.6	60.6	22.1	43.4	10.0	1.2	12.2
1962	556.9	193.3	174.0	14.2	62.9	22.6	47.1	9.6	1.3	12.8
1963	563.4	194.7	173.9	16.5	64.0	23.1	55.6	9.2	1.5	13.0
1964	543.3	193.6	167.0	16.3	64.1	22.5	45.4	8.9	1.5	12.7
1965	542.5	195.6	166.4	18.3	65.8	22.9	46.8	8.3	1.5	13.0
1966	541.2	196.5	165.8	19.2	67.6	23.6	47.9	7.9	1.6	12.7
1967	524.7	197.3	159.3	19.2	66.2	23.4	42.2	7.3	1.6	12.5
1968	531.0	198.8	162.5	20.7	65.5	25.3	52.8	6.1	1.7	12.4
1969	516.8	198.5	155.4	20.9	64.9	25.1	47.9	6.0	1.7	12.7
1970	492.7	198.6	147.7	21.3	62.2	24.3	41.7	5.5	2.0	13.1
1971	492.9	199.3	147.6	21.8	60.3	23.9	38.4	5.2	2.2	13.1
1972	490.2	200.3	147.3	22.8	60.2	23.7	41.3	5.2	2.4	13.3
1973	482.0	200.0	145.2	23.6	59.3	23.0	41.2	5.0	2.6	13.1
1974	458.8	201.5	136.8	23.2	52.7	22.1	35.5	4.7	3.0	13.2
1975	431.2	200.1	123.5	23.7	50.8	20.3	34.9	4.7	3.1	13.6
1976	426.9	202.5	117.4	24.9	48.7	19.5	38.8	4.9	3.5	13.2
1977	413.7	203.5	110.4	24.7	48.8	18.2	31.0	4.8	3.8	13.7
1978	409.9	204.9	103.7	26.3	48.9	18.3	34.5	4.8	4.2	12.9
1979	401.6	204.0	97.1	25.5	46.5	17.5	26.1	8.6	4.3	12.6
1980	412.1	207.9	96.4	28.3	46.4	18.1	31.4	9.1	5.0	12.2
1981	397.0	206.4	89.5	29.0	43.4	17.6	30.0	9.1	5.4	12.3
1982	389.0	208.3	84.2	29.1	40.1	17.2	26.5	9.4	5.9	12.5
1983	388.9	209.1	81.2	31.6	39.1	17.6	29.8	9.6	6.7	12.4
1984	378.8	210.8	78.7	32.4	38.8	17.2	30.6	10.0	7.4	12.6
1985	375.0	211.3	76.6	34.5	38.5	17.4	34.5	10.4	8.3	12.5
1986	365.1	211.5	73.1	34.8	38.6	17.2	34.8	10.4	9.0	13.0
1987	355.9	211.7	71.6	35.0	38.2	17.4	33.8	10.4	9.3	12.8
1988	352.5	212.5	70.6	36.5	38.9	18.0	37.3	10.4	9.7	12.5
1989	332.0	214.2	66.9	36.6	37.7	20.5	35.9	9.6	8.8	12.3
1990	321.8	216.0	65.3	37.2	36.3	20.7	36.8	9.3	8.6	12.5
1991	312.5	215.2	62.9	37.9	34.7	20.7	34.7	9.3	8.6	12.3
1992	304.0	213.5	61.5	37.7	33.2	20.7	32.8	9.4	8.4	12.0
1993	308.1	213.5	62.7	40.7	34.2	21.9	35.0	9.7	8.6	12.1
1994	297.5	211.7	62.6	40.3	34.2	22.6	33.6	9.4	8.3	11.9
1995	293.4	209.9	63.1	40.1	34.4	23.2	33.4	9.5	8.4	11.8
1996	285.7	206.7	62.5	40.6	34.5	23.8	32.9	9.6	8.4	11.5
1997	277.7	203.4	61.1	41.1	34.2	23.7	33.3	9.8	8.6	11.2
1998	267.4	202.1	62.8	43.8	35.6	24.2	24.2	9.8	8.9	11.1
1999	266.5	200.8	61.6	45.4	35.3	25.0	23.5	13.0	11.3	10.5
2000	257.6	199.6	60.9	44.2	34.9	25.0	23.7	13.5	11.3	10.4
2001	247.8	196.0	57.9	43.7	35.7	25.3	22.0	14.0	11.4	10.7
2002	240.8	193.5	56.2	43.5	36.9	25.4	22.6	14.2	11.7	10.9
2003	232.3	190.1	53.5	43.3	37.3	25.3	22.0	14.4	11.6	10.8
2004	217.0	185.8	50.0	41.1	37.7	24.5	19.8	14.2	11.2	10.9
2005	211.1	183.8	46.6	43.2	39.1	24.6	20.3	14.3	11.2	10.9
2006	200.2	180.7	43.6	40.5	39.8	23.3	17.8	14.5	11.0	10.9

[1] Unintentional injuries.

Source: U.S. National Center for Health Statistics, *Health, United States, 2008.* See also <http://www.cdc.gov/nchs/hus.htm>; National Vital Statistics Reports (NVSR), *Deaths: Final Data for 2006,* Vol. 57, No. 14, April 17, 2009; and unpublished data.

Table 115. Deaths and Death Rates by Selected Causes: 2005 and 2006

[**Rates per 100,000 population.** Figures are weighted data rounded to the nearest individual, so categories may not add to total or subtotal. Excludes deaths of nonresidents of the United States. Deaths classified according to tenth revision of International Classification of Diseases. See also Appendix III]

Cause of death	2005 Number	2005 Rate	2005 Age-adjusted rate [1]	2006 Number	2006 Rate	2006 Age-adjusted rate [1]
All causes [2]	2,448,017	825.9	798.8	2,426,264	810.4	776.5
Major cardiovascular diseases [2].	856,030	288.8	277.3	823,746	275.1	261.2
Diseases of heart.	652,091	220.0	211.1	631,636	211.0	200.2
Acute rheumatic fever and chronic rheumatic heart disease	3,365	1.1	1.1	3,257	1.1	1.1
Hypertensive heart disease	29,282	9.9	9.4	29,788	9.9	9.4
Hypertensive heart and renal disease.	3,172	1.1	1.0	2,918	1.0	0.9
Ischemic heart disease	445,687	150.4	144.4	425,425	142.1	134.9
Acute myocardial infarction	151,004	50.9	49.1	141,462	47.2	45.0
Other heart diseases.	170,585	57.6	55.2	170,248	56.9	53.9
Heart failure	58,933	19.9	18.9	60,337	20.2	18.9
Essential (primary) hypertension and hypertensive renal disease.	24,902	8.4	8.0	23,855	8.0	7.5
Cerebrovascular diseases	143,579	48.4	46.6	137,119	45.8	43.6
Atherosclerosis	11,841	4.0	3.8	8,652	2.9	2.7
Malignant neoplasms [2].	559,312	188.7	183.8	559,888	187.0	180.7
Malignant neoplasms of lip, oral cavity, and pharynx. . .	7,773	2.6	2.5	7,720	2.6	2.5
Malignant neoplasms of esophagus.	13,499	4.6	4.4	13,686	4.6	4.4
Malignant neoplasms of stomach	11,514	3.9	3.8	11,345	3.8	3.7
Malignant neoplasms of colon, rectum, and anus.	53,252	18.0	17.5	53,549	17.9	17.2
Malignant neoplasms of liver and intrahepatic bile ducts	16,076	5.4	5.2	16,525	5.5	5.3
Malignant neoplasms of pancreas	32,760	11.1	10.8	33,454	11.2	10.8
Malignant neoplasms of trachea, bronchus, and lung . .	159,292	53.7	52.6	158,664	53.0	51.5
Malignant melanoma of skin.	8,345	2.8	2.7	8,441	2.8	2.7
Malignant neoplasm of breast	41,491	14.0	13.5	41,210	13.8	13.2
Malignant neoplasm of ovary	14,787	5.0	4.8	14,857	5.0	4.8
Malignant neoplasm of prostate	28,905	9.8	9.5	28,372	9.5	9.2
Malignant neoplasms of kidney and renal pelvis	12,517	4.2	4.1	12,379	4.1	4.0
Malignant neoplasm of bladder	13,253	4.5	4.3	13,474	4.5	4.3
Malignant neoplasms of meninges, brain, and other parts of central nervous system	13,152	4.4	4.3	12,886	4.3	4.2
Malignant neoplasms of lymphoid, hematopoietic, and related tissue [2]	55,028	18.6	18.2	55,045	18.4	17.9
Non-Hodgkins' lymphoma.	20,873	7.0	6.9	20,594	6.9	6.7
Leukemia	21,623	7.3	7.1	21,944	7.3	7.1
Accidents (unintentional injuries)	117,809	39.7	39.1	121,599	40.6	39.8
Transport accidents [2]	48,441	16.3	16.2	48,412	16.2	16.0
Motor vehicle accidents	45,343	15.3	15.2	45,316	15.1	15.0
Nontransport accidents [2]	69,368	23.4	22.9	73,187	24.4	23.8
Falls.	19,656	6.6	6.4	20,823	7.0	6.6
Accidental drowning and submersion	3,582	1.2	1.2	3,579	1.2	1.2
Accidental exposure to smoke, fire, and flames	3,197	1.1	1.1	3,109	1.0	1.0
Accidental poisoning and exposure to noxious substances	23,618	8.0	7.9	27,531	9.2	9.1
Chronic lower respiratory diseases [2].	130,933	44.2	43.2	124,583	41.6	40.5
Emphysema	14,002	4.7	4.6	12,551	4.2	4.1
Asthma	3,884	1.3	1.3	3,613	1.2	1.2
Other chronic lower respiratory diseases [2]	112,181	37.8	37.0	107,609	36.0	34.9
Influenza and pneumonia [2]	63,001	21.3	20.3	56,326	18.8	17.8
Pneumonia.	61,189	20.6	19.7	55,477	18.5	17.5
Septicemia.	34,136	11.5	11.2	34,234	11.4	11.0
Human immunodeficiency virus (HIV) disease	12,543	4.2	4.2	12,113	4.0	4.0
Anemias	4,624	1.6	1.5	3,996	1.3	1.3
Diabetes mellitus.	75,119	25.3	24.6	72,449	24.2	23.3
Parkinson's disease.	19,544	6.6	6.4	19,566	6.5	6.3
Alzheimer's disease.	71,599	24.2	22.9	72,432	24.2	22.6
Chronic liver disease and cirrhosis	27,530	9.3	9.0	27,555	9.2	8.8
Alcoholic liver disease.	12,928	4.4	4.2	13,050	4.4	4.1
Cholelithiasis and other disorders of gallbladder	3,072	1.0	1.0	3,114	1.0	1.0
Nephritis, nephrotic syndrome, and nephrosis [2]	43,901	14.8	14.3	45,344	15.1	14.5
Renal failure	42,868	14.5	14.0	43,344	14.5	13.9
Intentional self-harm (suicide)	32,637	11.0	10.9	33,300	11.1	10.9
Intentional self-harm (suicide) by discharge of firearms	17,002	5.7	5.7	16,883	5.6	5.5
Intentional self-harm (suicide) by other and unspecified means and their sequelae	15,635	5.3	5.2	16,417	5.5	5.4
Assault (homicide).	18,124	6.1	6.1	18,573	6.2	6.2
Events of undetermined intent	4,742	1.6	1.6	5,131	1.7	1.7
Injury by firearms [3]	30,694	10.4	10.2	30,896	10.3	10.2
Drug-induced deaths [3]	33,541	11.3	11.3	38,396	12.8	12.7
Alcohol-induced deaths [3]	21,634	7.3	7.0	22,073	7.4	7.0
Injury at work [4].	5,113	2.2	2.1	5,298	2.2	2.2
Enterocolitis due to Clostridium difficile	(NA)	(NA)	(NA)	6,225	2.1	2.0

[1] See headnote, Table 108. [2] Includes other causes not shown separately. [3] Included in selected categories. [4] Injury at work described in "Technical Notes" in source.

Source: U.S. National Center for Health Statistics, National Vital Statistics Reports (NVSR), *Deaths: Final Data for 2006*, Vol. 57, No. 14, April 17, 2009.

86   Births, Deaths, Marriages, and Divorces

Table 116. Deaths by Age and Selected Causes: 2006

[Deaths are classified according to the Tenth Revision of the International Classification of Diseases. See Appendix III]

Cause of death	All ages[1]	Under 1 year	1 to 4 years	5 to 14 years	15 to 24 years	25 to 34 years	35 to 44 years	45 to 54 years	55 to 64 years	65 to 74 years	75 to 84 years	85 years and over
All causes[2]	2,426,264	28,527	4,631	6,149	34,887	42,952	83,043	185,031	281,401	390,093	667,338	701,992
Septicemia	34,234	269	88	84	139	291	870	2,260	4,032	6,064	10,745	9,392
Human immunodeficiency virus (HIV) disease	12,113	7	1	15	206	1,182	4,010	4,377	1,722	475	107	11
Malignant neoplasms[2]	559,888	76	377	907	1,644	3,656	13,917	50,334	101,454	137,554	164,889	85,072
Malignant neoplasm of esophagus	13,686	–	–	–	3	29	279	1,524	3,289	3,691	3,515	1,355
Malignant neoplasms of colon, rectum, and anus	53,549	–	1	1	42	323	1,330	4,499	8,626	11,709	16,024	10,992
Malignant neoplasms of liver and intrahepatic bile ducts	16,525	2	15	16	31	87	361	2,406	3,842	3,830	4,161	1,774
Malignant neoplasm of pancreas	33,454	–	–	1	5	49	506	2,730	6,298	8,473	10,260	5,130
Malignant neoplasms of trachea, bronchus, and lung	158,664	1	1	5	27	155	2,023	12,608	31,317	47,882	48,732	15,915
Malignant neoplasm of breast	41,210	–	–	2	13	368	2,352	6,115	8,871	7,961	9,346	6,182
Malignant neoplasm of ovary	14,857	–	–	3	23	79	401	1,666	3,048	3,573	4,061	2,001
Malignant neoplasm of prostate	28,372	–	–	–	–	–	40	405	2,273	5,603	11,157	8,887
Malignant neoplasm of bladder	13,474	–	–	–	1	18	104	528	1,568	2,810	4,874	3,571
Malignant neoplasm of lymphoid, hematopoietic and related tissue[2]	55,045	32	132	298	662	828	1,536	3,696	7,695	12,335	17,974	9,856
Non-Hodgkins lymphoma	20,594	1	7	36	131	219	515	1,417	2,886	4,543	7,007	3,831
Leukemia	21,944	31	124	256	465	460	715	1,398	2,823	4,735	6,863	4,074
In situ neoplasms, benign neoplasms, and neoplasms of uncertain or unknown behavior	14,122	65	60	76	100	143	316	794	1,315	2,369	4,750	4,134
Diabetes mellitus	72,449	6	7	28	165	673	2,094	5,692	11,432	15,483	21,763	15,105
Parkinson's disease	19,566	–	1	–	2	4	15	66	397	2,310	9,101	7,669
Alzheimer's disease	72,432	1	–	–	–	2	12	104	655	3,812	22,915	44,933
Major cardiovascular diseases[2]	823,746	508	218	363	1,376	4,099	15,420	47,037	80,714	119,102	240,862	314,006
Diseases of heart[2]	631,636	346	161	253	1,076	3,307	12,339	38,095	65,477	92,752	180,451	237,339
Hypertensive heart disease	29,788	1	–	2	52	288	1,358	3,586	4,130	3,660	6,232	10,277
Ischemic heart diseases	425,425	22	7	13	138	1,054	6,699	24,990	46,706	66,685	125,225	153,855
Acute myocardial infarction	141,462	11	5	6	60	422	2,676	9,746	18,373	24,795	41,624	43,739
Other heart diseases	170,248	320	154	231	873	1,903	4,135	9,164	14,030	21,240	47,065	71,126
Heart failure	60,337	19	9	12	37	86	332	1,225	2,801	5,960	17,309	32,544
Cerebrovascular diseases	137,119	142	54	95	210	527	2,221	6,341	10,518	18,223	43,719	55,068
Influenza and pneumonia	56,326	263	125	71	184	335	841	2,007	3,154	6,061	16,668	26,617
Chronic lower respiratory diseases	124,583	30	43	68	151	255	892	3,924	12,375	28,236	47,406	31,203
Pneumonitis due to solids and liquids[2]	16,887	11	9	13	30	78	166	437	855	1,750	5,284	8,254
Chronic liver disease and cirrhosis	27,555	5	3	–	26	316	2,551	7,712	7,217	4,917	3,778	1,026
Nephritis, nephrotic syndrome, and nephrosis[2]	45,344	162	14	18	99	276	785	2,245	4,368	7,453	14,536	15,388
Renal failure	43,344	154	10	12	89	250	745	2,151	4,207	7,171	13,915	14,640
Certain conditions originating in the perinatal period[2]	14,444	14,321	65	24	14	4	–	–	–	–	–	–
Accidents (unintentional injuries)[2]	121,599	1,147	1,610	2,258	16,229	14,954	17,534	19,675	11,446	8,420	13,708	14,561
Motor vehicle accidents	45,316	140	588	1,339	11,015	7,348	6,677	6,615	4,518	2,916	2,906	1,240
Falls	20,823	23	38	42	242	318	628	1,290	1,592	2,392	6,227	8,031
Accidental poisoning and exposure to noxious substances	27,531	16	27	69	2,936	5,267	7,542	8,234	2,415	483	340	202
Intentional self-harm (suicide)	33,300	(X)	(X)	227	4,189	4,985	6,591	7,426	4,583	2,384	2,075	840
By discharge of firearms	16,883	(X)	(X)	63	1,978	2,150	2,821	3,481	2,562	1,689	1,562	577
By other and unspecified means and their sequelae[2]	16,417	(X)	(X)	164	2,211	2,835	3,770	3,945	2,021	695	513	263
Assault (homicide)	18,573	336	366	390	5,717	4,725	3,020	2,209	1,012	398	279	102

– Represents zero. X Not applicable. [1] Includes persons with age not stated, not shown separately. [2] Includes other causes, not shown separately.

Source: U.S. National Center for Health Statistics, National Vital Statistics Reports (NVSR), *Deaths: Final Data for 2006*, Vol. 57, No. 14, April 17, 2009.

Table 117. **Deaths and Death Rates by Leading Causes of Death and Age: 2006**

[**Rates per 100,000 population in specified group**. Data are based on the tenth revision of the International Classification of Diseases (ICD). See Appendix III]

Age and cause of death	Number	Rate	Age and cause of death	Number	Rate
ALL AGES [1]			Accidents (unintentional injuries)	17,534	40.2
All causes [2]	**2,426,264**	**810.4**	Malignant neoplasms	13,917	31.9
Diseases of heart.	631,636	211.0	Diseases of heart.	12,339	28.3
Malignant neoplasms	559,888	187.0	Intentional self-harm (suicide).	6,591	15.1
Cerebrovascular diseases	137,119	45.8	Human immunodeficiency virus (HIV)		
Chronic lower respiratory diseases . . .	124,583	41.6	disease.	4,010	9.2
Accidents (unintentional injuries)	121,599	40.6	Assault (homicide)	3,020	6.9
Diabetes mellitus	72,449	24.2	Chronic liver disease and cirrhosis . . .	2,551	5.8
Alzheimer's disease	72,432	24.2	Cerebrovascular diseases	2,221	5.1
Influenza and pneumonia.	56,326	18.8	Diabetes mellitus	2,094	4.8
Nephritis, nephrotic syndrome, and			Septicemia	870	2.0
nephrosis	45,344	15.1	**45 TO 54 YEARS**		
Septicemia	34,234	11.4	**All causes** [2]	**185,031**	**427.5**
1 TO 4 YEARS			Malignant neoplasms	50,334	116.3
			Diseases of heart.	38,095	88.0
All causes [2]	**4,631**	**28.4**	Accidents (unintentional injuries)	19,675	45.5
Accidents (unintentional injuries)	1,610	9.9	Chronic liver disease and cirrhosis . . .	7,712	17.8
Congenital malformations,			Intentional self-harm (suicide).	7,426	17.2
deformations, and chromosomal			Cerebrovascular diseases	6,341	14.7
abnormalities.	515	3.2	Diabetes mellitus	5,692	13.2
Malignant neoplasms	377	2.3	Human immunodeficiency virus (HIV)		
Assault (homicide)	366	2.2	disease.	4,377	10.1
Diseases of heart.	161	1.0	Chronic lower respiratory diseases . . .	3,924	9.1
Influenza and pneumonia.	125	0.8	Viral hepatitis.	2,911	6.7
Septicemia	88	0.5	**55 TO 64 YEARS**		
Certain conditions originating in the					
perinatal period	65	0.4	**All causes** [2]	**281,401**	**890.9**
In situ neoplasms [3]	60	0.4	Malignant neoplasms	101,454	321.2
Cerebrovascular diseases	54	0.3	Diseases of heart.	65,477	207.3
			Chronic lower respiratory diseases . . .	12,375	39.2
5 TO 14 YEARS			Accidents (unintentional injuries)	11,446	36.2
All causes [2]	**6,149**	**15.2**	Diabetes mellitus	11,432	36.2
Accidents (unintentional injuries)	2,258	5.6	Cerebrovascular diseases	10,518	33.3
Malignant neoplasms	907	2.2	Chronic liver disease and cirrhosis . . .	7,217	22.8
Assault (homicide)	390	1.0	Intentional self-harm (suicide).	4,583	14.5
Congenital malformations,			Nephritis, nephrotic syndrome and		
deformations, and chromosomal			nephrosis	4,368	13.8
abnormalities.	344	0.9	Septicemia	4,032	12.8
Diseases of heart.	253	0.6			
Intentional self-harm (suicide).	219	0.5	**65 TO 74 YEARS**		
Chronic lower respiratory diseases . . .	115	0.3	**All causes** [2]	**390,093**	**2,062.1**
Cerebrovascular diseases	95	0.2	Malignant neoplasms	137,554	727.2
Septicemia . . . . [2].	84	0.2	Diseases of heart.	92,752	490.3
In situ neoplasms [2].	76	0.2	Chronic lower respiratory diseases . . .	28,236	149.3
			Cerebrovascular diseases	18,223	96.3
15 TO 24 YEARS			Diabetes mellitus	15,483	81.8
All causes [2]	**34,887**	**82.2**	Accidents (unintentional injuries)	8,420	44.5
Accidents (unintentional injuries)	16,229	38.2	Nephritis, nephrotic syndrome, and		
Assault (homicide)	5,717	13.5	nephrosis	7,453	39.4
Intentional self-harm (suicide).	4,189	9.9	Septicemia	6,064	32.1
Malignant neoplasms	1,644	3.9	Influenza and pneumonia.	6,061	32.0
Diseases of heart.	1,076	2.5	Chronic liver disease and cirrhosis . . .	4,917	26.0
Congenital malformations,					
deformations, and chromosomal			**75 TO 84 YEARS**		
abnormalities.	460	1.1	**All causes** [2]	**667,338**	**5,115.0**
Cerebrovascular diseases	210	0.5	Diseases of heart.	180,451	1,383.1
Human immunodeficiency virus (HIV)			Malignant neoplasms	164,889	1,263.8
disease.	206	0.5	Chronic lower respiratory diseases . . .	47,406	363.4
Influenza and pneumonia.	184	0.4	Cerebrovascular diseases	43,719	335.1
Pregnancy, childbirth and the			Alzheimers disease.	22,915	175.6
puerperium	179	0.4	Diabetes mellitus	21,763	166.8
			Influenza and pneumonia.	16,668	127.8
25 TO 34 YEARS			Nephritis, nephrotic syndrome, and		
All causes [2]	**42,952**	**106.3**	nephrosis	14,536	111.4
Accidents (unintentional injuries)	14,954	37.0	Accidents (unintentional injuries)	13,708	105.1
Intentional self-harm (suicide).	4,985	12.3	Septicemia	10,745	82.4
Assault (homicide)	4,725	11.7			
Malignant neoplasms	3,656	9.0	**85 YEARS AND OVER**		
Diseases of heart.	3,307	8.2	**All causes** [2]	**701,992**	**13,253.1**
Human immunodeficiency virus (HIV)			Diseases of heart.	237,339	4,480.8
disease.	1,182	2.9	Malignant neoplasms	85,072	1,606.1
Diabetes mellitus	673	1.7	Cerebrovascular diseases	55,068	1,039.6
Cerebrovascular diseases	527	1.3	Alzheimers disease.	44,933	848.3
Congenital malformations,			Chronic lower respiratory diseases . . .	31,203	589.1
deformations, and chromosomal			Influenza and pneumonia.	26,617	502.5
abnormalities.	437	1.1	Nephritis, nephrotic syndrome and		
Influenza and pneumonia.	335	0.8	nephrosis	15,388	290.5
			Diabetes mellitus	15,105	285.2
35 TO 44 YEARS			Accidents (unintentional injuries)	14,561	274.9
All causes [2]	**83,043**	**190.2**	Septicemia	9,392	177.3

[1] Includes deaths under 1 year of age.   [2] Includes other causes not shown separately.   [3] Includes benign neoplasms and neoplasms of uncertain or unknown behavior.

Source: U.S. National Center for Health Statistics, National Vital Statistics Reports (NVSR) *Deaths: Final Data for 2006*, Vol. 57, No. 14, April 24, 2009.

Table 118. Age-Adjusted Death Rates for Major Causes of Death—States and Island Areas: 2006

[Age adjusted rates per 100,000 resident population estimated as of July 1. By place of residence. Excludes nonresidents of the United States. Causes of death classified according to tenth revisions of International Classification of Diseases. See text, this section for explanation of age adjustment. See Appendix III]

State and island areas	Total	Diseases of heart	Malig-nant neo-plasms (cancer)	Cerebro-vascular diseases	Chronic lower respira-tory diseases	Accidents Total	Accidents Motor vehicle acci-dents	Diabetes mellitus	Alzhei-mer's dis-ease	Influ-enza and pneu-monia	Nephritis, nephrotic syndrome and nephrosis
U.S.	776.5	200.2	180.7	43.6	40.5	39.8	15.0	23.3	22.6	17.8	14.5
AL.	952.4	253.3	197.7	55.3	46.7	53.8	26.6	29.3	30.3	18.6	22.2
AK.	775.9	167.2	177.4	47.2	37.2	51.9	13.1	25.6	24.7	13.5	12.6
AZ.	724.1	164.2	155.7	34.5	43.7	53.8	21.4	19.0	31.4	18.1	8.8
AR.	888.9	233.0	196.0	58.8	47.4	49.1	25.9	26.9	23.9	23.9	19.3
CA.	700.2	192.5	162.3	44.9	39.1	31.6	12.2	22.1	24.1	21.8	8.0
CO	716.8	151.6	157.7	38.9	49.3	42.1	12.3	16.6	27.7	15.4	12.1
CT.	714.8	177.3	177.8	36.3	35.5	34.6	10.1	19.2	16.2	18.5	13.7
DE.	784.0	201.2	191.4	41.7	37.5	37.9	16.4	20.5	20.4	15.1	16.5
DC	892.9	260.0	198.7	36.9	21.5	38.1	6.8	30.6	18.3	12.6	11.1
FL.	711.3	175.1	172.0	35.3	35.9	46.0	18.9	21.7	17.0	9.7	10.5
GA	858.8	213.2	180.4	51.3	45.1	43.8	18.9	20.6	25.7	19.7	21.7
HI	629.6	147.2	147.6	43.2	19.4	31.7	11.9	18.1	12.2	16.2	11.8
ID	747.4	168.5	163.2	51.8	46.6	47.0	20.4	23.0	28.1	15.8	9.2
IL	781.1	204.4	187.2	45.3	36.9	34.3	10.9	21.6	20.6	20.1	19.2
IN	847.6	217.2	197.7	49.0	50.8	38.7	15.0	25.8	25.2	17.0	20.8
IA	730.3	184.7	179.6	42.9	45.3	35.4	14.6	21.9	26.3	18.8	5.7
KS.	794.7	183.6	180.5	46.5	49.9	41.5	17.4	24.7	24.3	19.4	18.8
KY.	915.2	235.5	211.2	50.3	55.0	57.5	22.0	25.9	26.7	21.3	21.0
LA.	930.1	232.3	203.5	51.5	39.6	56.6	23.7	35.5	30.5	19.6	25.2
ME	775.0	174.0	193.8	41.3	49.3	40.6	14.3	21.4	29.0	16.6	15.7
MD	793.0	205.6	186.8	43.6	34.3	26.1	12.9	22.4	17.1	19.9	14.1
MA	719.7	169.5	186.7	37.6	34.5	32.0	7.3	15.4	19.4	22.5	18.5
MI	813.7	227.0	191.0	44.7	42.9	34.9	11.5	26.8	21.7	15.8	15.8
MN	672.8	133.9	171.2	39.4	33.3	35.2	11.6	21.4	22.2	10.8	12.8
MS	961.2	270.9	209.2	53.4	46.7	63.8	33.3	23.8	25.0	20.8	22.5
MO	848.3	224.4	196.2	49.5	47.3	49.7	18.8	23.4	24.1	19.3	17.1
MT	781.4	168.4	170.6	41.3	53.6	55.8	27.3	23.0	19.6	15.0	11.9
NE.	735.3	165.0	176.9	43.8	44.2	35.9	14.8	22.1	22.6	15.8	12.2
NV.	843.7	226.7	183.2	39.6	49.0	44.5	17.9	12.8	14.7	19.8	22.0
NH	724.9	178.3	182.6	35.5	44.4	33.7	9.5	21.2	26.5	15.1	11.6
NJ.	736.6	200.9	182.3	35.8	30.3	28.7	8.8	25.9	16.5	13.5	17.1
NM	775.5	172.6	158.3	37.6	45.5	67.1	24.1	30.5	17.7	18.0	13.2
NY.	701.2	233.1	169.0	29.8	30.1	25.9	8.1	18.3	9.1	22.5	11.0
NC	843.6	195.3	192.8	52.4	45.9	47.0	19.2	24.9	26.4	19.6	18.9
ND	726.9	181.5	183.2	49.3	34.5	39.5	17.9	26.3	33.6	15.1	6.5
OH	840.8	216.1	198.0	45.1	47.9	40.2	11.7	29.6	27.0	15.0	13.8
OK	920.4	251.1	194.8	53.4	57.1	56.3	21.8	30.3	23.5	22.7	15.4
OR	770.5	160.0	181.3	47.9	45.7	40.5	13.5	28.2	29.0	12.5	8.7
PA.	800.8	207.1	190.8	43.4	35.4	39.4	12.8	22.2	18.9	16.1	19.0
RI	747.4	200.8	181.7	31.2	38.2	36.4	7.8	16.2	20.3	19.5	12.9
SC.	864.6	200.2	193.2	51.6	43.2	53.2	24.1	25.0	31.5	16.4	18.9
SD.	740.5	177.0	171.9	42.9	39.7	53.0	24.2	27.1	29.8	16.5	6.2
TN.	908.3	233.3	204.7	54.9	47.8	54.2	22.8	27.1	34.6	24.9	12.4
TX.	783.9	197.4	174.5	48.3	39.9	41.0	16.8	26.1	25.9	17.3	15.3
UT.	706.3	156.3	136.4	36.4	31.9	30.9	13.9	26.1	21.4	18.2	11.1
VT.	721.7	175.5	171.8	37.8	46.3	45.2	14.1	24.9	26.2	10.8	7.4
VA.	781.0	190.8	183.9	48.8	37.4	35.7	12.5	21.8	22.3	17.9	19.2
WA	722.5	165.8	174.2	42.9	43.1	41.1	11.4	24.4	38.3	12.7	6.6
WV	941.3	236.9	205.9	47.6	56.6	62.2	23.1	33.1	21.8	20.6	20.8
WI	746.6	181.1	181.2	44.6	38.8	42.7	13.5	19.7	24.2	15.7	15.4
WY	822.8	189.4	175.4	45.3	67.0	58.9	29.7	23.7	21.8	22.6	11.2
PR [1]. . . .	724.6	146.7	121.1	40.7	27.2	29.6	12.3	65.3	34.0	24.9	24.2
VI [1]	648.7	175.7	108.2	43.0	(S)	29.1	(S)	42.5	(S)	(S)	(S)
GU [1]. . . .	615.5	196.7	110.0	72.1	(S)	26.5	(S)	27.3	(S)	(S)	(S)
AS [1]. . . .	1,312.0	304.9	169.1	(S)	(S)	(S)	(S)	162.7	(S)	(S)	(S)
MP [1]. . . .	997.6	72.2	288.5	(S)	(S)	(S)	(S)	(S)	(S)	(S)	(S)

S Figure does not meet standards of reliability or precision.   [1] Age-adjusted death rates for Puerto Rico, Virgin Islands, Guam, American Samoa, and Northern Marianas are calculated using different age groups in the weighting procedure; see source "Technical Notes."

Source: U.S. National Center for Health Statistics, National Vital Statistics Reports (NVSR), *Deaths: Final Data for 2006*, Vol. 57, No. 14, April 17, 2009.

Births, Deaths, Marriages, and Divorces 89

Table 119. **Death Rates From Heart Disease by Selected Characteristics: 1980 to 2006**

[Rates per 100,000 population. See headnote, Tables 106 and 114. See Appendix III]

Characteristic	1980	1990	2000	2001	2002	2003	2004	2005	2006
Total, age adjusted	**412.1**	**321.8**	**257.6**	**247.8**	**240.8**	**232.3**	**217.0**	**211.1**	**200.2**
Total, crude [1]	336.0	289.5	252.6	245.8	241.7	235.6	222.2	220.0	211.0
Under 1 year	22.8	20.1	13.0	11.9	12.4	11.0	10.3	8.7	8.4
1 to 4 years	2.6	1.9	1.2	1.5	1.1	1.2	1.2	0.9	1.0
5 to 14 years	0.9	0.9	0.7	0.7	0.6	0.6	0.6	0.6	0.6
15 to 24 years	2.9	2.5	2.6	2.5	2.5	2.7	2.5	2.7	2.5
25 to 34 years	8.3	7.6	7.4	8.0	7.9	8.2	7.9	8.1	8.2
35 to 44 years	44.6	31.4	29.2	29.6	30.5	30.7	29.3	28.9	28.3
45 to 54 years	180.2	120.5	94.2	92.9	93.7	92.5	90.2	89.7	88.0
55 to 64 years	494.1	367.3	261.2	246.9	241.5	233.2	218.8	214.8	207.3
65 to 74 years	1,218.6	894.3	665.6	635.1	615.9	585.0	541.6	518.9	490.3
75 to 84 years	2,993.1	2,295.7	1,780.3	1,725.7	1,677.2	1,611.1	1,506.3	1,460.8	1,383.1
85 years and over.	7,777.1	6,739.9	5,926.1	5,664.2	5,446.8	5,278.4	4,895.9	4,778.4	4,480.8
Male, age adjusted	**538.9**	**412.4**	**320.0**	**305.4**	**297.4**	**286.6**	**267.9**	**260.9**	**248.5**
White	539.6	409.2	316.7	301.8	294.1	282.9	264.6	258.0	245.2
Black	561.4	485.4	392.5	384.5	371.0	364.3	342.1	329.8	320.6
American Indian, Alaska Native	320.5	264.1	222.2	200.7	201.2	203.2	182.7	173.2	170.2
Asian, Pacific Islander	286.9	220.7	185.5	169.8	169.8	158.3	146.5	141.1	136.3
Hispanic origin [2]	(NA)	270.0	238.2	232.6	219.8	206.8	193.9	192.4	175.2
Non-Hispanic, White [2]	(NA)	413.6	319.9	304.8	297.7	286.9	268.7	262.2	250.0
Male, crude	**368.6**	**297.6**	**249.8**	**242.5**	**240.7**	**235.0**	**222.8**	**221.1**	**214.0**
Under 1 year	25.5	21.9	13.3	11.8	12.9	12.1	10.9	9.4	8.8
1 to 4 years	2.8	1.9	1.4	1.5	1.1	1.1	1.1	1.0	1.1
5 to 14 years	1.0	0.9	0.8	0.7	0.7	0.7	0.6	0.6	0.7
15 to 24 years	3.7	3.1	3.2	3.2	3.3	3.4	3.2	3.6	3.3
25 to 34 years	11.4	10.3	9.6	10.3	10.5	10.5	10.5	10.8	11.2
35 to 44 years	68.7	48.1	41.4	41.7	43.1	42.8	40.9	40.7	39.5
45 to 54 years	282.6	183.0	140.2	136.6	138.4	136.2	132.3	131.5	128.9
55 to 64 years	746.8	537.3	371.7	349.8	343.4 ·	331.7	312.8	306.9	296.8
65 to 74 years	1,728.0	1,250.0	898.3	851.3	827.1	785.3	723.8	692.3	660.5
75 to 84 years	3,834.3	2,968.2	2,248.1	2,177.3	2,110.1	2,030.3	1,893.6	1,829.4	1,743.5
85 years and over.	8,752.7	7,418.4	6,430.0	6,040.5	5,823.5	5,621.5	5,239.3	5,143.4	4,819.9
Female, age adjusted	**320.8**	**257.0**	**210.9**	**203.9**	**197.2**	**190.3**	**177.3**	**172.3**	**162.2**
White	315.9	250.9	205.6	198.7	192.1	185.4	172.9	168.2	158.6
Black	378.6	327.5	277.6	269.8	263.2	253.8	236.5	228.3	212.5
American Indian, Alaska Native	175.4	153.1	143.6	127.0	123.6	127.5	119.9	115.9	113.2
Asian, Pacific Islander	132.3	149.2	115.7	112.9	108.1	104.2	96.1	91.9	87.3
Hispanic origin [2]	(NA)	177.2	163.7	161.0	149.7	145.8	130.0	129.1	118.9
Non-Hispanic, White [2]	(NA)	252.6	206.8	200.0	193.7	187.1	175.1	170.3	160.9
Female, crude	**305.1**	**281.8**	**255.3**	**249.0**	**242.7**	**236.2**	**221.6**	**218.9**	**208.0**
Under 1 year	20.0	18.3	12.5	12.0	11.8	9.8	9.7	8.0	7.9
1 to 4 years	2.5	1.9	1.0	1.4	1.0	1.3	1.2	0.9	0.9
5 to 14 years	0.9	0.8	0.5	0.7	0.6	0.5	0.6	0.6	0.6
15 to 24 years	2.1	1.8	2.1	1.8	1.7	2.1	1.7	1.7	1.8
25 to 34 years	5.3	5.0	5.2	5.6	5.2	5.7	5.2	5.3	5.1
35 to 44 years	21.4	15.1	17.2	17.6	18.0	18.6	17.7	17.1	17.0
45 to 54 years	84.5	61.0	49.8	50.7	50.6	50.2	49.6	49.2	48.5
55 to 64 years	272.1	215.7	159.3	151.8	147.2	141.9	131.5	129.1	124.1
65 to 74 years	828.6	616.8	474.0	455.9	440.1	417.5	388.6	372.7	346.3
75 to 84 years	2,497.0	1,893.8	1,475.1	1,428.9	1,389.7	1,331.1	1,245.6	1,210.5	1,136.7
85 years and over.	7,350.5	6,478.1	5,720.9	5,506.8	5,283.3	5,126.7	4,741.5	4,610.8	4,322.1

NA Not available.   [1] The total numbers of deaths in a given time period divided by the total resident population as of July 1.   [2] Persons of Hispanic origin may be any race. Prior to 1997 excludes data from States lacking an Hispanic-origin item on their death certificates. See text, this section.

Source: U.S. National Center for Health Statistics, *Health, United States, 2008.* See also <http://cdc.gov/nchs/hus.htm>.

Table 120. **Death Rates From Cerebrovascular Diseases by Sex and Age: 1990 to 2006**

[Rates per 100,000 population. See headnote, Tables 106 and 114. See Appendix III]

Age	Total				Male				Female			
	1990	2000	2005	2006	1990	2000	2005	2006	1990	2000	2005	2006
All ages, age adjusted . .	**65.3**	**60.9**	**46.6**	**43.6**	**68.5**	**62.4**	**46.9**	**43.9**	**62.6**	**59.1**	**45.6**	**42.6**
All ages, crude [1]	57.8	59.6	48.4	45.8	46.7	46.9	38.8	37.0	68.4	71.8	57.8	54.4
Under 1 year	3.8	3.3	3.1	3.4	4.4	3.8	3.5	3.9	3.1	2.7	2.6	2.9
1 to 4 years.	0.3	0.3	0.4	0.3	0.3	(B)	0.5	0.3	0.3	0.4	0.3	0.4
5 to 14 years.	0.2	0.2	0.2	0.2	0.2	0.2	0.3	0.3	0.2	0.2	0.2	0.2
15 to 24 years	0.6	0.5	0.5	0.5	0.7	0.5	0.4	0.5	0.6	0.5	0.5	0.5
25 to 34 years	2.2	1.5	1.4	1.3	2.1	1.5	1.5	1.4	2.2	1.5	1.2	1.2
35 to 44 years	6.4	5.8	5.2	5.1	6.8	5.8	5.2	5.3	6.1	5.7	5.1	4.8
45 to 54 years	18.7	16.0	15.0	14.7	20.5	17.5	16.5	16.4	17.0	14.5	13.6	13.0
55 to 64 years	47.9	41.0	33.0	33.3	54.3	47.2	38.5	38.7	42.2	35.3	27.9	28.2
65 to 74 years	144.2	128.6	101.1	96.3	166.6	145.0	113.6	108.0	126.7	115.1	90.5	86.5
75 to 84 years	498.0	461.3	359.0	335.1	551.1	490.8	372.9	345.5	466.2	442.1	349.5	328.0
85 years and over	1,628.9	1,589.2	1,141.8	1,039.6	1,528.5	1,484.3	1,023.3	932.4	1,667.6	1,632.0	1,196.1	1,089.8

B Base figure too small to meet statistical standards for reliability.   [1] The total numbers of deaths in a given time period divided by the total resident population as of July 1.

Source: U.S. National Center for Health Statistics, *Health, United States, 2008.* See also <http://cdc.gov/nchs/hus.htm>.

Table 121. Death Rates From Malignant Neoplasms by Selected Characteristics: 1990 to 2006

[Rates per 100,000 population. Beginning 2000, cause of death is coded according to ICD-10; for explanation, see text, this section. For explanation of age adjustment, see headnote, Table 106. See Appendix III]

Characteristic	1990	2000	2002	2003	2004	2005	2006
Total, age adjusted	**216.0**	**199.6**	**193.5**	**190.1**	**185.8**	**183.8**	**180.7**
Total, crude [1]	**203.2**	**196.5**	**193.2**	**191.5**	**188.6**	**188.7**	**187.0**
Under 1 year	2.3	2.4	1.8	1.9	1.8	1.8	1.8
1 to 4 years.	3.5	2.7	2.6	2.5	2.5	2.3	2.3
5 to 14 years.	3.1	2.5	2.6	2.6	2.5	2.5	2.2
15 to 24 years	4.9	4.4	4.3	4.0	4.1	4.1	3.9
25 to 34 years	12.6	9.8	9.7	9.4	9.1	9.0	9.0
35 to 44 years	43.3	36.6	35.8	35.0	33.4	33.2	31.9
45 to 54 years	158.9	127.5	123.8	122.2	119.0	118.6	116.3
55 to 64 years	449.6	366.7	351.1	343.0	333.4	326.9	321.1
65 to 74 years	872.3	816.3	792.1	770.3	755.1	742.7	727.2
75 to 84 years	1,348.5	1,335.6	1,311.9	1,302.5	1,280.4	1,274.8	1,263.8
85 years old and over	1,752.9	1,819.4	1,723.9	1,698.2	1,653.3	1,637.7	1,606.1
AGE-ADJUSTED RATES							
Male	280.4	248.9	238.9	233.3	227.7	225.1	220.1
Female.	175.7	167.6	163.1	160.9	157.4	155.6	153.6
White male	272.2	243.9	235.2	230.1	224.4	222.3	217.9
Black male	397.9	340.3	319.6	308.8	301.2	293.7	284.9
American Indian, Alaska Native male	145.8	155.8	141.9	139.9	147.1	147.6	(NA)
Asian, Pacific Islander male	172.5	150.8	137.9	137.2	136.3	133.0	(NA)
Hispanic male, [2]	174.7	171.7	161.4	156.5	151.2	152.7	143.4
Non-Hispanic, White male [2]	276.7	247.7	239.6	234.6	229.2	227.3	223.4
White female.	174.0	166.9	162.4	160.2	157.0	155.2	153.6
Black female	205.9	193.8	190.3	187.7	182.5	179.6	176.1
American Indian, Alaska Native female. . . .	106.9	108.3	112.9	105.6	108.6	105.9	(NA)
Asian, Pacific Islander female.	103.0	100.7	95.9	96.7	92.0	94.5	(NA)
Hispanic female, [2]	111.9	110.8	106.1	105.9	101.4	102.0	100.4
Non-Hispanic, White female [2]	177.5	170.0	165.9	163.8	160.9	159.1	157.6
DEATH RATES FOR MALIGNANT NEOPLASM OF BREASTS FOR FEMALES							
All ages, age adjusted	33.3	29.4	27.6	26.6	24.4	24.1	23.5
All ages, crude [1]	34.0	31.3	29.7	28.9	27.5	27.3	26.9
Under 25 years	(B)	(B)	(B)	(B)	(B)	(B)	(B)
25 to 34 years	2.9	2.6	2.5	2.2	2.0	1.8	1.8
35 to 44 years	17.8	14.1	13.4	12.0	11.3	11.3	10.8
45 to 54 years	45.4	38.3	35.3	32.9	29.3	28.7	27.6
55 to 64 years	78.6	66.8	61.6	59.2	55.8	54.5	53.7
65 to 74 years	111.7	98.3	92.4	88.9	81.6	79.2	76.9
75 to 84 years	146.3	137.6	129.3	128.9	119.5	119.2	119.2
85 years old and over	196.8	201.7	193.4	200.8	178.6	177.9	169.9
DEATH RATES FOR MALIGNANT NEOPLASM OF TRACHEA, BRONCHUS, AND LUNG							
All ages, age adjusted	37.1	41.3	41.6	41.3	40.9	40.5	40.0
All ages, crude [1]	39.4	45.4	46.0	46.1	45.9	45.9	45.7
Under 25 years	(Z)	(Z)	(Z)	(Z)	(Z)	(Z)	(Z)
25 to 34 years	0.5	0.5	0.4	0.4	0.3	0.3	0.4
35 to 44 years	5.2	5.3	5.8	5.1	5.2	5.1	4.5
45 to 54 years	34.5	25.0	24.3	24.4	24.2	24.5	24.6
55 to 64 years	105.0	93.3	88.8	87.1	83.9	80.7	78.2
65 to 74 years	177.6	206.9	207.7	204.8	205.0	199.6	197.0
75 to 84 years	190.1	265.6	277.8	279.4	277.0	280.9	280.3
85 years old and over	138.1	212.8	217.0	221.0	221.3	226.2	226.9

B Base figure too small to meet statistical standards for reliability of a derived figure.   NA Not available.   Z Less than 0.05.   [1] The total number of deaths in a given time period divided by the total resident population as of July 1.   [2] Excludes data from states lacking an Hispanic-origin item on their death certificates. See text, this section.

Source: U.S. National Center for Health Statistics, *Health, United States, 2008.* See also <http://www.cdc.gov/nchs/hus.htm>.

Births, Deaths, Marriages, and Divorces   91

Table 122. **Death Rates From Suicide by Selected Characteristics: 1990 to 2006**

[Rates per 100,000 population. Beginning 2000, cause of death is coded according to ICD-10; for explanation, see text, this section. For explanation of age adjustment, see headnote, Table 106. See Appendix III]

Characteristic	1990	2000	2002	2003	2004	2005	2006
All ages, age adjusted	12.5	10.4	10.9	10.8	10.9	10.9	10.9
All ages, crude [1]	12.4	10.4	11.0	10.8	11.0	11.0	11.1
Under 1 year.	(X)	(X)	(X)	(X)	(X)	(X)	(X)
1 to 4 years.	(X)	(X)	(X)	(X)	(X)	(X)	(X)
5 to 14 years.	0.8	0.7	0.6	0.6	0.7	0.7	0.5
15 to 24 years	13.2	10.2	9.9	9.7	10.3	10.0	9.9
25 to 34 years	15.2	12.0	12.6	12.7	12.7	12.4	12.3
35 to 44 years	15.3	14.5	15.3	14.9	15.0	14.9	15.1
45 to 54 years	14.8	14.4	15.7	15.9	16.6	16.5	17.2
55 to 64 years	16.0	12.1	13.6	13.8	13.8	13.9	14.5
65 to 74 years	17.9	12.5	13.5	12.7	12.3	12.6	12.6
75 to 84 years	24.9	17.6	17.7	16.4	16.3	16.9	15.9
85 years and over	22.2	19.6	18.0	16.9	16.4	16.9	15.9
AGE ADJUSTED							
Male	21.5	17.7	18.4	18.0	18.0	18.0	18.0
Female.	4.8	4.0	4.2	4.2	4.5	4.4	4.5
White male	22.8	19.1	20.0	19.6	19.6	19.6	19.6
Black male	12.8	10.0	9.8	9.2	9.6	9.2	9.4
American Indian, Alaska Native male	20.1	16.0	16.4	16.6	18.7	18.9	18.3
Asian, Pacific Islander male	9.6	8.6	8.0	8.5	8.4	7.3	7.9
Hispanic male [2]	13.7	10.3	9.9	9.7	9.8	9.4	8.8
Non-Hispanic, White male [2]	23.5	20.2	21.4	21.0	21.0	21.2	21.4
White female.	5.2	4.3	4.7	4.6	5.0	4.9	5.1
Black female	2.4	1.8	1.6	1.9	1.8	1.9	1.4
American Indian, Alaska Native female. . . .	3.6	3.8	4.1	3.5	5.9	4.6	5.1
Asian, Pacific Islander female.	4.1	2.8	3.0	3.1	3.5	3.3	3.4
Hispanic female [2].	2.3	1.7	1.8	1.7	2.0	1.8	1.8
Non-Hispanic, White female [2]	5.4	4.7	5.1	5.0	5.4	5.3	5.6

X Not applicable. [1] The total number of deaths in a given time period divided by the total resident population as of July 1. [2] Data for 1990 exclude data from states lacking an Hispanic-origin item on their death certificates. Persons of Hispanic origin may be any race.

Source: U.S. National Center for Health Statistics, *Health, United States, 2008.* See also <http://www.cdc.gov/nchs/hus.htm>.

Table 123. **Death Rates From Human Immunodeficiency Virus (HIV) Disease by Selected Characteristics: 1990 to 2006**

[Rates per 100,000 population. Beginning 2000, cause of death is coded according to ICD 10; for explanation, see text this section. For explanation of age adjustment, see headnote, Table 106. See Appendix III]

Characteristic	1990	2000	2002	2003	2004	2005	2006
All ages, age adjusted	10.2	5.2	4.9	4.7	4.5	4.2	4.0
All ages, crude [1]	10.1	5.1	4.9	4.7	4.4	4.2	4.0
Under 1 year.	2.7	(B)	(B)	(B)	(B)	(B)	(B)
1 to 4 years.	0.8	(B)	(B)	(B)	(B)	(B)	(B)
5 to 14 years.	0.2	0.1	0.1	0.1	0.1	(B)	(B)
15 to 24 years	1.5	0.5	0.4	0.4	0.5	0.4	0.5
25 to 34 years	19.7	6.1	4.6	4.0	3.7	3.3	2.9
35 to 44 years	27.4	13.1	12.7	12.0	10.9	9.9	9.2
45 to 54 years	15.2	11.0	11.2	10.9	10.6	10.6	10.1
55 to 64 years	6.2	5.1	5.1	5.4	5.4	5.3	5.5
65 to 74 years	2.0	2.2	2.2	2.4	2.4	2.3	2.5
75 to 84 years	0.7	0.7	0.8	0.7	0.8	0.8	0.8
85 years and over	(B)	(B)	(B)	(B)	(B)	(B)	(B)
AGE ADJUSTED							
Male	18.5	7.9	7.4	7.1	6.6	6.2	5.9
Female.	2.2	2.5	2.5	2.4	2.4	2.3	2.2
White male	15.7	4.6	4.3	4.2	3.8	3.6	3.4
Black male	46.3	35.1	33.3	31.3	29.2	28.2	26.3
American Indian, Alaska Native male	3.3	3.5	3.4	3.5	4.3	4.0	3.3
Asian or Pacific Islander male.	4.3	1.2	1.5	1.1	1.2	1.0	1.1
Hispanic male [2]	28.8	10.6	9.1	9.2	8.2	7.5	7.0
Non-Hispanic, White male [2]	14.1	3.8	3.5	3.4	3.1	3.0	2.8
White female.	1.1	1.0	0.9	0.9	0.9	0.8	0.7
Black female	10.1	13.2	13.4	12.8	13.0	12.0	12.2
American Indian, Alaska Native female. . . .	(B)	1.0	(B)	1.5	1.5	1.5	1.5
Asian or Pacific Islander female	(B)	0.2	(B)	(B)	(B)	(B)	(B)
Hispanic female [2].	3.8	2.9	2.6	2.7	2.4	1.9	1.9
Non-Hispanic, White female [2].	0.7	0.7	0.6	0.6	0.6	0.6	0.6

B Base figure too small to meet statistical standards for reliability of a derived figure. [1] The total number of deaths in a given time period divided by the total resident population as of July 1. [2] Data for 1990 exclude data from states lacking an Hispanic-origin item on their death certificates. Persons of Hispanic origin may be any race.

Source: U.S. National Center for Health Statistics, National Vital Statistics Reports (NVSR), *Health, United States, 2008.* See also <http://cdc.gov/nchs/hus.htm>.

Table 124. **Deaths—Life Years Lost and Mortality Costs by Age, Sex, and Cause: 2005**

[2,448 represents 2,448,000. **Life years lost:** Number of years person would have lived in absence of death. **Mortality cost:** value of lifetime earnings lost by persons who die prematurely]

Characteristic	Number of deaths (1,000)	Life years lost [1] Total (1,000)	Per death	Mortality cost [2] Total (mil. dol.)	Per death (dol.)
2005, total [3]	**2,448**	**41,556**	**17.0**	**565,966**	**231,218**
Under 5 years old............	33	2,569	77.4	35,697	1,075,355
5 to 14 years old	7	463	70.1	8,622	1,306,014
15 to 24 years old	34	2,034	59.4	54,679	1,597,211
25 to 44 years old	127	5,594	44.2	169,003	1,333,778
45 to 64 years old	398	12,519	31.4	248,645	624,032
65 years old and over.........	1,849	18,377	9.9	49,320	26,680
Heart disease	652	8,720	13.4	92,744	142,234
Cancer....................	559	10,612	19.0	141,596	253,165
Cerebrovascular diseases	144	1,689	11.8	14,355	99,982
Accidents and adverse effects ...	118	3,952	33.6	96,465	819,222
Other.....................	975	16,583	17.0	220,806	226,449
Male.................	**1,207**	**21,999**	**18.2**	**410,432**	**339,909**
Under 5 years old............	19	1,411	75.1	22,263	1,185,278
5 to 14 years old	4	262	67.9	5,536	1,436,712
15 to 24 years old	26	1,481	58.1	43,272	1,696,356
25 to 44 years old	83	3,544	42.9	123,548	1,495,879
45 to 64 years old	280	7,273	26.0	179,456	641,142
65 years old and over.........	797	8,029	10.1	36,357	45,626
Heart disease	323	4,704	14.6	72,785	225,470
Cancer....................	290	5,696	19.6	99,673	343,205
Cerebrovascular diseases	57	639	11.3	9,145	161,629
Accidents and adverse effects ...	76	2,678	35.1	75,916	994,631
Other.....................	461	8,282	18.0	152,913	331,457
Female............	**1,240**	**19,557**	**15.8**	**155,534**	**125,402**
Under 5 years old............	14	1,158	80.3	13,434	932,103
5 to 14 years old	3	202	73.3	3,087	1,122,828
15 to 24 years old	9	553	63.3	11,407	1,307,343
25 to 44 years old	44	2,051	46.5	45,455	1,030,314
45 to 64 years old	119	5,246	44.3	69,188	583,633
65 years old and over.........	1,052	10,348	9.8	12,963	12,325
Heart disease	329	4,016	12.2	19,959	60,622
Cancer....................	269	4,916	18.3	41,924	155,916
Cerebrovascular diseases	87	1,050	12.1	5,210	59,886
Accidents and adverse effects ...	41	1,273	30.7	20,549	496,038
Other.....................	514	8,301	16.2	67,893	132,154

[1] Based on life expectancy at year of death.   [2] Cost estimates based on the person's age, sex, life expectancy at the time of death, labor force participation rates, annual earnings, value of homemaking services, and a 3 percent discount rate by which to convert to present worth the potential aggregate earnings lost over the years.   [3] Total excludes 255 deaths for which age is unknown.

Source: Wendy Max and Yanling Shi, Institute for Health & Aging, University of California San Francisco, CA., unpublished data.

Table 125. **Percent Reaching Stated Anniversary by Sex and Years of Marriage: 2004**

[In percent except number of marriages. Data are for first marriages only]

Sex and year of marriage	Number of marriages (1,000s)	Anniversary [1] 5th	10th	15th	20th	25th	30th	35th	40th
Men									
1955 to 1959...............	**3,884**	**96.4**	**88.3**	**80.3**	**73.8**	**70.4**	**67.3**	**64.7**	**61.4**
1960 to 1964 [2]...............	4,602	95.1	85.0	75.2	69.7	65.0	62.4	59.7	52.5
1965 to 1969 [2]...............	6,161	90.5	76.9	67.4	62.3	58.6	55.5	48.2	(X)
1970 to 1974 [2]...............	7,075	88.5	74.4	64.6	58.1	53.8	46.2	(X)	(X)
1975 to 1979 [2]...............	7,001	88.1	73.0	65.2	59.6	49.5	(X)	(X)	(X)
1980 to 1984 [2]...............	7,625	88.7	73.7	65.3	53.8	(X)	(X)	(X)	(X)
1985 to 1989 [2]...............	7,838	89.3	76.4	60.6	(X)	(X)	(X)	(X)	(X)
1990 to 1994 [2]...............	8,070	89.4	70.0	(X)	(X)	(X)	(X)	(X)	(X)
Women									
1955 to 1959...............	**4,890**	**94.0**	**86.8**	**79.4**	**72.4**	**67.2**	**63.5**	**58.9**	**54.7**
1960 to 1964 [2]...............	5,548	92.8	82.3	72.7	66.5	60.4	56.1	52.7	44.9
1965 to 1969 [2]...............	7,023	89.5	74.9	65.7	60.0	55.1	51.3	43.8	(X)
1970 to 1974 [2]...............	8,139	87.1	71.6	61.4	55.4	50.6	42.1	(X)	(X)
1975 to 1979 [2]...............	7,714	85.3	70.0	61.4	55.7	46.4	(X)	(X)	(X)
1980 to 1984 [2]...............	8,058	86.5	70.7	63.1	52.4	(X)	(X)	(X)	(X)
1985 to 1989 [2]...............	8,064	85.7	73.0	56.9	(X)	(X)	(X)	(X)	(X)
1990 to 1994 [2]...............	8,546	87.2	69.2	(X)	(X)	(X)	(X)	(X)	(X)

X Not applicable.   [1] People reaching stated anniversary.   [2] Approximately 10 percent of the cohort has not reached the stated anniversary by the end of the latest specified time period. Because of this, estimates for this group for the highest anniversary are low.

Source: U.S. Census Bureau, Survey of Income and Program Participation (SIPP) Reports, "Number, Timing and Duration of Marriages and Divorces: 2004"; <http://www.census.gov/population/www/socdemo/marr-div/2004detailedtables.html>.

Births, Deaths, Marriages, and Divorces   93

Table 126. Marriages and Divorces—Number and Rate by State: 1990 to 2007

[**2,443.5 represents 2,443,500.** By place of occurence. See Appendix III]

State	Marriages [1]						Divorces [3]					
	Number (1,000)			Rate per 1,000 population [2]			Number (1,000)			Rate per 1,000 population [2]		
	1990	2000	2007	1990	2000	2007	1990	2000	2007	1990	2000	2007
U.S. [4]	2,443.5	2,329.0	2,204.6	9.8	8.3	7.3	1,182.0	(NA)	(NA)	4.7	4.1	3.6
Alabama	43.1	45.0	42.4	10.6	10.3	9.2	25.3	23.5	19.8	6.1	5.4	4.3
Alaska	5.7	5.6	5.8	10.2	8.9	8.4	2.9	2.7	3.0	5.5	4.4	4.3
Arizona [5]	36.8	38.7	39.5	10.0	7.9	6.2	25.1	21.6	24.5	6.9	4.4	3.9
Arkansas.	36.0	41.1	33.7	15.3	16.0	11.9	16.8	17.9	16.8	6.9	6.9	5.9
California.	237.1	196.9	225.8	7.9	5.9	6.2	128.0	(NA)	(NA)	4.3	(NA)	(NA)
Colorado.	32.4	35.6	29.2	9.8	8.6	6.0	18.4	(NA)	21.2	5.5	(NA)	4.4
Connecticut	26.0	19.4	17.3	7.9	5.9	4.9	10.3	6.5	10.7	3.2	2.0	3.1
Delaware.	5.6	5.1	4.7	8.4	6.7	5.5	3.0	3.2	3.9	4.4	4.2	4.5
District of Columbia.	5.0	2.8	2.1	8.2	5.4	3.6	2.7	1.5	1.0	4.5	3.0	1.6
Florida	141.8	141.9	157.6	10.9	9.3	8.6	81.7	81.9	86.4	6.3	5.3	4.7
Georgia	66.8	56.0	64.0	10.3	7.1	6.7	35.7	30.7	(NA)	5.5	3.9	(NA)
Hawaii	18.3	25.0	27.3	16.4	21.2	21.3	5.2	4.6	(NA)	4.6	3.9	(NA)
Idaho	14.1	14.0	15.4	13.9	11.0	10.3	6.6	6.9	7.4	6.5	5.4	4.9
Illinois.	100.6	85.5	75.3	8.8	7.0	5.9	44.3	39.1	32.8	3.8	3.2	2.6
Indiana	53.2	34.5	51.2	9.6	5.8	8.1	(NA)	(NA)	(NA)	(NA)	(NA)	(NA)
Iowa.	24.9	20.3	20.1	9.0	7.0	6.7	11.1	9.4	7.8	3.9	3.3	2.6
Kansas	22.7	22.2	18.6	9.2	8.3	6.7	12.6	10.6	9.2	5.0	4.0	3.3
Kentucky.	49.8	39.7	33.6	13.5	10.0	7.9	21.8	21.6	19.7	5.8	5.4	4.6
Louisiana	40.4	40.5	32.8	9.6	9.3	7.6	(NA)	(NA)	(NA)	(NA)	(NA)	(NA)
Maine	11.9	10.5	10.1	9.7	8.3	7.7	5.3	5.8	5.9	4.3	4.6	4.5
Maryland.	46.3	40.0	35.5	9.7	7.7	6.3	16.1	17.0	17.4	3.4	3.3	3.1
Massachusetts . . .	47.7	37.0	38.4	7.9	6.0	6.0	16.8	18.6	14.5	2.8	3.0	2.2
Michigan	76.1	66.4	59.1	8.2	6.7	5.9	40.2	39.4	35.5	4.3	4.0	3.5
Minnesota	33.7	33.4	29.8	7.7	6.9	5.7	15.4	14.8	(NA)	3.5	3.1	(NA)
Mississippi.	24.3	19.7	15.7	9.4	7.1	5.4	14.4	14.4	14.2	5.5	5.2	4.9
Missouri	49.1	43.7	39.4	9.6	7.9	6.7	26.4	26.5	22.4	5.1	4.8	3.8
Montana	6.9	6.6	7.1	8.6	7.4	7.4	4.1	2.1	3.6	5.1	2.4	3.7
Nebraska	12.6	13.0	12.4	8.0	7.8	7.0	6.5	6.4	5.5	4.0	3.8	3.1
Nevada.	120.6	144.3	126.4	99.0	76.7	49.3	13.3	18.1	16.6	11.4	9.6	6.5
New Hampshire . .	10.5	11.6	9.4	9.5	9.5	7.1	5.3	7.1	5.1	4.7	5.8	3.9
New Jersey	58.7	50.4	45.4	7.6	6.1	5.2	23.6	25.6	25.7	3.0	3.1	3.0
New Mexico [5] . . .	13.3	14.5	11.2	8.8	8.3	5.7	7.7	9.2	8.4	4.9	5.3	4.3
New York [5]	154.8	162.0	130.6	8.6	8.9	6.8	57.9	62.8	55.9	3.2	3.4	2.9
North Carolina . . .	51.9	65.6	68.1	7.8	8.5	7.5	34.0	36.9	37.4	5.1	4.8	4.1
North Dakota	4.8	4.6	4.2	7.5	7.3	6.6	2.3	2.0	1.5	3.6	3.2	2.4
Ohio.	98.1	88.5	70.9	9.0	7.9	6.2	51.0	49.3	37.9	4.7	4.4	3.3
Oklahoma	33.2	15.6	26.2	10.6	4.6	7.3	24.9	12.4	18.8	7.7	3.7	5.2
Oregon	25.3	26.0	29.4	8.9	7.8	7.8	15.9	16.7	14.8	5.5	5.0	4.0
Pennsylvania	84.9	73.2	71.1	7.1	6.1	5.7	40.1	37.9	35.3	3.3	3.2	2.8
Rhode Island	8.1	8.0	6.8	8.1	8.0	6.4	3.8	3.1	3.0	3.7	3.1	2.8
South Carolina . . .	55.8	42.7	31.4	15.9	10.9	7.1	16.1	14.4	14.4	4.5	3.7	3.3
South Dakota	7.7	7.1	6.2	11.1	9.6	7.7	2.6	2.7	2.4	3.7	3.6	3.1
Tennessee.	68.0	88.2	65.6	13.9	15.9	10.6	32.3	33.8	29.9	6.5	6.1	4.9
Texas	178.6	196.4	179.9	10.5	9.6	7.5	94.0	85.2	79.5	5.5	4.2	3.3
Utah.	19.4	24.1	22.6	11.2	11.1	8.6	8.8	9.7	8.9	5.1	4.5	3.4
Vermont	6.1	6.1	5.3	10.9	10.2	8.6	2.6	5.1	2.4	4.5	8.6	3.8
Virginia	71.0	62.4	58.0	11.4	9.0	7.5	27.3	30.2	29.5	4.4	4.3	3.8
Washington	46.6	40.9	41.8	9.5	7.0	6.5	28.8	27.2	28.9	5.9	4.7	4.5
West Virginia	13.0	15.7	13.0	7.2	8.7	7.2	9.7	9.3	9.0	5.3	5.2	5.0
Wisconsin	38.9	36.1	32.2	7.9	6.8	5.8	17.8	17.6	16.1	3.6	3.3	2.9
Wyoming.	4.9	4.9	4.8	10.7	10.3	9.3	3.1	2.8	2.9	6.6	5.9	5.5

NA Not available. [1] Data are counts of marriages performed, except as noted. [2] Based on total population residing in area; population enumerated as of April 1 for 1990 and 2000; estimated as of July 1 for all other years. [3] Includes annulments. [4] U.S. total for the number of divorces is an estimate which includes states not reporting. Beginning 2000, divorce rates based solely on the combined counts and populations for reporting states and the District of Columbia. The collection of detailed data of marriages and divorces was suspended in January 1996. [5] Some figures for marriages are marriage licenses issued.

Source: U.S. National Center for Health Statistics, National Vital Statistics Reports (NVSR), *Births, Marriages, Divorces, and Deaths: Provisional Data for 2007*, Vol. 56, No. 21, July 14, 2008 and prior reports.

Health and Nutrition

This section presents statistics on health expenditures and insurance coverage, including Medicare and Medicaid, medical personnel, hospitals, nursing homes and other care facilities, injuries, diseases, disability status, nutritional intake of the population, and food consumption. Summary statistics showing recent trends on health care and discussions of selected health issues are published annually by the U.S. National Center for Health Statistics (NCHS) in *Health, United States*. Data on national health expenditures, medical costs, and insurance coverage are compiled by the U.S. Centers for Medicare & Medicaid Services (CMS) and appear on the CMS Web site at <http://www.cms .hhs.gov/NationalHealthExpendData/> and in the annual *Medicare and Medicaid Statistical Supplement* to the *Health Care Financing Review*. Statistics on health insurance are also collected by NCHS and are published in Series 10 of *Vital and Health Statistics*. NCHS also conducts periodic surveys of nutrient levels in the population, including estimates of food and nutrient intake, overweight and obesity, hypercholesterolemia, hypertension, and clinical signs of malnutrition. Data are published in Series 10 and 11 of *Vital and Health Statistics*. Statistics on hospitals are published annually by the Health Forum, L.L.C.; an American Hospital Association (AHA) company, in AHA Hospital Statistics. The primary source for data on nutrition and on annual per capita consumption of food is *Diet Quality and Food Consumption*, issued by the U.S. Department of Agriculture. Data are available on the Web site at <http://www.ers.usda .gov/Briefing/DietQuality>.

National health expenditures—CMS compiles estimates of national health expenditures (NHE) to measure spending for health care in the United States. The NHE accounts are structured to show spending by type of expenditure (i.e., hospital care, physician and clinical care, dental care, and other professional care;

home health care; retail sales of prescription drugs; other medical nondurables; vision products and other medical durables; nursing home care and other personal health expenditures; plus other health expenditures such as public health activities, administration, and the net cost of private health insurance; plus medical sector investment, the sum of noncommercial medical research and capital formation in medical sector structures and equipment; and by source of funding (e.g., private health insurance, out-of-pocket payments, and a range of public programs including Medicare, Medicaid, and those operated by the U.S. Department of Veterans Affairs (VA)).

Data used to estimate health expenditures come from existing sources, which are tabulated for other purposes. The type of expenditure estimates rely upon statistics produced by such groups as the AHA, the Census Bureau, and the U.S. Department of Health and Human Services (HHS). Source of funding estimates are constructed using administrative and statistical records from the Medicare and Medicaid programs, the U.S. Department of Defense and VA medical programs, the Social Security Administration, Census Bureau's *Governmental Finances*, state and local governments, other HHS agencies, and other nongovernment sources.

Medicare, Medicaid, and CHIP—Since July 1966, the federal Medicare program has provided two coordinated plans for nearly all people age 65 and over: (1) a hospital insurance plan, which covers hospital and related services and (2) a voluntary supplementary medical insurance plan, financed partially by monthly premiums paid by participants, which partly covers physicians' and related medical services. Such insurance also applies, since July 1973, to disabled beneficiaries of any age after 24 months of entitlement to cash benefits under the social security or railroad retirement programs and to persons with end stage renal disease.

On January 1, 2006, Medicare began to provide coverage for prescription drugs as mandated by the Medicare Prescription Drug, Improvement, and Modernization Act of 2003 (MMA). This benefit is available on a voluntary basis to everyone with Medicare, and beneficiaries pay a monthly premium to enroll in one of Medicare's prescription drug plans.

Medicaid is a health insurance program for certain low-income people. These include: certain low-income families with children; people on supplemental security income; certain low-income pregnant women and children; and people who have very high medical bills. There are special rules for those who live in nursing homes and for disabled children living at home. Medicaid is funded and administered through a state/federal partnership. Although there are broad federal requirements for Medicaid, states have a wide degree of flexibility to design their program. The Children's Health Insurance Program Reauthorization Act of 2009 (CHIPRA or Public Law 111-3) reauthorized the Children's Health Insurance Program (CHIP). The program went into effect on April 1, 2009. CHIP replaces the State Children's Health Insurance Program (SCHIP). It will preserve coverage for the millions of children who rely on CHIP today and provides the resources for states to reach millions of additional uninsured children. CHIP was designed as a federal/state partnership, similar to Medicaid, with the goal of expanding health insurance to children whose families earn too much money to be eligible for Medicaid, but not enough money to purchase private insurance.

Health resources—Hospital statistics based on data from AHA's yearly survey are published annually in *AHA Hospital Statistics* and cover all hospitals accepted for registration by the Association. To be accepted for registration, a hospital must meet certain requirements relating to number of beds, construction, equipment, medical and nursing staff, patient care, clinical records, surgical and obstetrical facilities, diagnostic and treatment facilities, laboratory services, etc. Data obtained from NCHS cover all U.S. hospitals that meet certain criteria for inclusion. The criteria are published in *Vital and Health Statistics* reports, Series 13.

Statistics on the demographic characteristics of persons employed in the health occupations are compiled by the U.S. Bureau of Labor Statistics and reported in *Employment and Earnings* (monthly) (see Table 603, Section 12, Labor Force, Employment, and Earnings). Data based on surveys of health personnel and utilization of health facilities providing long-term care, ambulatory care, emergency room care, and hospital care are presented in NCHS Series 13, "National Health Statistics Reports (NHSR)." Statistics on patient visits to health care providers, as reported in health interviews, appear in NCHS Series 10, *National Health Interview Survey Data.*

The CMS's *Health Care Financing Review* and its annual *Medicare and Medicaid Statistical Supplement* present data for hospitals and nursing homes as well as extended care facilities and home health agencies. These data are based on records of the Medicare program and differ from those of other sources because they are limited to facilities meeting federal eligibility standards for participation in Medicare.

Disability and illness—General health statistics, including morbidity, disability, injuries, preventive care, and findings from physiological testing are collected by NCHS in its National Health Interview Survey and its National Health and Nutrition Examination Surveys and appear in *Vital and Health Statistics,* Series 10 and 11, respectively. Annual incidence data on notifiable diseases are compiled by the Public Health Service (PHS) at its Centers for Disease Control and Prevention in Atlanta, Georgia, and are published as a supplement to its *Morbidity and Mortality Weekly Report (MMWR).* The list of diseases is revised annually and includes those which, by mutual agreement of the states and PHS, are communicable diseases of national importance.

Statistical reliability—For discussion of statistical collection, estimation, and sampling procedures and measures of reliability applicable to data from NCHS and CMS, see Appendix III.

Table 127. National Health Expenditures—Summary, 1960 to 2007, and Projections, 2008 to 2018

[In billions of dollars (28 represents $28,000,000,000). Excludes Puerto Rico and Island Areas]

Year	Total expenditures [1]	Private expenditures Total [2]	Out-of-pocket	Insurance	Public expenditures Total	Federal	State and local	Health services and supplies Total [3]	Hospital care	Physician and clinical services	Prescription drugs	Nursing home care
1960	28	21	13	6	7	3	4	25	9	5	3	1
1961	29	22	13	6	7	3	4	26	10	6	3	1
1962	32	24	14	7	8	4	4	29	11	6	3	1
1963	35	26	15	8	9	4	5	31	12	7	3	1
1964	39	29	17	9	10	4	5	34	13	8	3	1
1965	42	32	18	10	10	5	6	37	14	8	4	1
1966	46	32	18	10	14	8	6	41	16	9	4	2
1967	52	33	18	10	19	12	7	47	18	10	4	2
1968	59	37	21	12	22	14	8	53	21	11	5	3
1969	66	41	23	13	25	16	9	59	24	12	5	3
1970	75	47	25	15	28	18	10	67	28	14	5	4
1971	83	51	26	18	32	21	12	74	31	16	6	5
1972	93	57	29	21	36	23	13	83	34	17	6	5
1973	103	63	32	23	40	25	15	93	38	19	7	6
1974	117	69	34	26	48	30	17	106	45	22	7	7
1975	133	77	37	30	56	36	20	121	52	25	8	8
1976	152	89	41	37	63	43	20	139	60	28	9	10
1977	173	102	45	45	71	47	23	159	67	33	9	12
1978	195	114	48	52	80	54	26	179	76	35	10	14
1979	220	129	53	60	91	61	30	203	87	41	11	16
1980	254	148	59	69	106	72	35	234	101	47	12	19
1981	294	172	66	81	123	83	40	271	118	55	13	21
1982	331	195	72	94	136	92	44	305	134	61	15	23
1983	365	216	79	105	150	103	47	336	145	68	17	26
1984	402	239	87	119	163	113	50	372	155	77	20	29
1985	440	263	96	131	177	123	54	409	165	90	22	32
1986	472	278	104	136	194	133	61	440	177	100	24	34
1987	513	301	109	149	212	144	68	478	190	112	27	36
1988	574	344	119	175	230	155	75	535	207	127	31	40
1989	639	383	125	205	256	174	82	596	227	142	35	46
1990	714	427	136	234	287	194	93	667	252	158	40	53
1991	782	456	140	255	325	223	102	731	277	175	44	58
1992	849	485	143	275	364	253	111	794	300	190	48	62
1993	913	512	145	296	400	279	121	853	317	201	51	65
1994	962	526	143	308	436	304	132	900	330	210	54	68
1995	1,017	552	146	325	465	327	138	953	341	221	61	74
1996	1,069	580	152	343	488	348	140	1,003	352	229	69	80
1997	1,125	614	162	359	511	365	146	1,054	365	241	78	84
1998	1,191	663	175	385	528	372	156	1,112	376	256	89	90
1999	1,265	710	184	418	555	390	165	1,180	395	270	105	91
2000	1,353	756	193	455	597	418	179	1,264	417	289	121	95
2001	1,469	807	200	498	662	464	198	1,376	451	313	138	102
2002	1,602	881	211	551	722	509	213	1,498	488	338	158	106
2003	1,735	956	225	604	779	552	227	1,623	527	367	174	110
2004	1,855	1,015	235	646	840	600	240	1,733	567	394	189	115
2005	1,981	1,082	247	690	899	640	259	1,850	607	422	200	121
2006	2,113	1,140	255	731	973	708	265	1,976	649	450	217	125
2007	2,241	1,206	269	775	1,036	754	281	2,098	697	479	227	131
2008, proj.	2,379	1,270	279	817	1,109	811	298	2,227	747	509	235	137
2009, proj.	2,509	1,319	283	854	1,190	873	317	2,350	789	539	245	144
2010, proj.	2,624	1,374	291	892	1,251	912	338	2,458	830	552	256	151
2011, proj.	2,770	1,438	302	934	1,332	972	360	2,596	877	577	272	159
2012, proj.	2,931	1,507	314	979	1,424	1,040	384	2,746	932	604	289	168
2013, proj.	3,111	1,584	327	1,029	1,527	1,118	410	2,916	993	636	308	177
2014, proj.	3,313	1,673	345	1,087	1,640	1,202	438	3,107	1,056	675	330	188
2015, proj.	3,541	1,773	363	1,152	1,768	1,298	470	3,322	1,125	719	356	200
2016, proj.	3,790	1,881	383	1,222	1,909	1,404	505	3,556	1,201	766	385	212
2017, proj.	4,062	1,997	404	1,297	2,064	1,521	543	3,811	1,285	815	418	226
2018, proj.	4,353	2,120	427	1,376	2,233	1,649	584	4,086	1,374	865	454	241

[1] Includes medical research and medical facilities construction not shown separately. [2] Includes other private expenditures not shown separately. [3] Includes other objects of expenditure not shown separately.

Source: U.S. Centers for Medicare & Medicaid Services, Office of the Actuary, "National Health Statistics Group"; <http://www.cms.hhs.gov/NationalHealthExpendData/>.

Health and Nutrition   97

Table 128. National Health Expenditures by Type: 1990 to 2007

[In billions of dollars (714.1 represents $714,100,000,000), except percent. Excludes Puerto Rico and Island Areas]

Type of expenditure	1990	2000	2002	2003	2004	2005	2006	2007
Total	**714.1**	**1,353.2**	**1,602.3**	**1,734.9**	**1,854.8**	**1,980.6**	**2,112.7**	**2,241.2**
Annual percent change [1]	11.8	7.0	9.0	8.3	6.9	6.8	6.7	6.1
Percent of gross domestic product	12.3	13.8	15.3	15.8	15.9	15.9	16.0	16.2
Private expenditures	**427.4**	**756.4**	**880.7**	**956.0**	**1,014.9**	**1,081.6**	**1,139.7**	**1,205.5**
Health services and supplies	401.0	705.4	821.8	893.3	947.0	1,007.4	1,061.6	1,123.9
Out-of-pocket payments	136.2	192.6	211.2	224.6	234.9	247.0	255.0	268.6
Insurance premiums [2]	233.7	454.7	551.1	603.7	645.9	690.0	731.3	775.0
Other	31.1	58.0	59.5	65.0	66.3	70.4	75.3	80.4
Medical research	1.0	2.5	3.1	3.3	3.4	3.7	4.0	4.3
Medical structures and equipment [3]	25.4	48.5	55.9	59.3	64.5	70.5	74.1	77.3
Public expenditures	**286.8**	**596.8**	**721.6**	**779.0**	**839.9**	**899.0**	**973.0**	**1,035.7**
Percent federal of public	67.6	70.0	70.5	70.9	71.4	71.2	72.7	72.8
Health services and supplies	265.8	559.0	676.5	729.8	786.1	843.0	914.5	974.2
Medicare [4]	109.5	224.4	264.8	282.7	311.2	339.4	402.3	431.2
Public assistance medical payments [5] . .	78.7	207.4	259.0	282.2	303.4	325.3	324.6	344.7
Temporary disability insurance [6]	0.1	0.1	0.1	0.1	0.1	0.1	0.1	0.1
Workers' compensation (medical) [6]	17.4	25.4	30.0	31.8	32.4	32.3	32.3	32.4
Defense Dept. hospital, medical	10.4	13.7	18.7	21.8	24.5	26.1	29.2	31.7
Maternal, child health programs	1.7	2.7	2.7	2.7	2.6	2.6	2.7	2.7
Public health activities	20.0	43.4	52.1	53.7	54.0	56.6	60.3	64.1
Veterans' hospital, medical care.	10.8	18.9	22.6	26.3	27.7	29.6	31.5	33.8
Medical vocational rehabilitation.	0.3	0.4	0.5	0.5	0.5	0.5	0.5	0.5
State and local hospitals [7]	13.2	13.7	15.5	16.8	17.9	18.8	19.2	20.6
Other [8]	3.8	9.0	10.7	11.2	11.7	11.8	11.9	12.4
Medical research	11.7	23.1	29.5	32.2	35.4	36.6	37.4	38.1
Medical structures and equipment [3]	9.2	14.7	15.6	17.0	18.4	19.4	21.1	23.4

[1] Change from immediate prior year. [2] Covers insurance benefits and amount retained by insurance companies for expenses, additions to reserves, and profits (net cost of insurance). [3] Represents expenditures for total medical sector acquisitions of structures and equipment including structures that house medical professionals' offices. [4] Represents expenditures for benefits and administrative cost from federal hospital and medical insurance trust funds under old-age, survivors, disability, and health insurance programs; see text this section. [5] Payments made directly to suppliers of medical care (primarily Medicaid). [6] Includes medical benefits paid under public law by private insurance carriers, state governments, and self-insurers. [7] Expenditures not offset by other revenues. [8] Covers expenditures for Substance Abuse and Mental Health Services Administration, Indian Health Service; school health and other programs.

Source: U.S. Centers for Medicare & Medicaid Services, Office of the Actuary, "National Health Expenditure Group." See also <http://www.cms.hhs.gov/NationalHealthExpendData/>.

Table 129. National Health Expenditures by Object, 1990 to 2007, and Projections, 2008

[In billions of dollars (714.0 represents $714,000,000,000). Excludes Puerto Rico and outlying areas]

Object of expenditure	1990	2000	2002	2003	2004	2005	2006	2007	2008, proj.
Total	**714.0**	**1,353.2**	**1,602.3**	**1,734.9**	**1,854.8**	**1,980.6**	**2,112.7**	**2,241.2**	**2,378.6**
Spent by—									
Consumers	369.8	647.4	762.3	828.3	880.8	937.0	986.3	1,043.5	1,096.1
Out-of-pocket	136.1	192.6	211.2	224.6	234.9	247.0	255.0	268.6	278.8
Private insurance.	233.7	454.7	551.1	603.7	645.9	690.0	731.3	775.0	817.4
Public	286.7	596.8	721.6	779.0	839.9	899.0	973.0	1,035.7	1,108.6
Other [1]	57.5	109.0	118.4	127.6	134.2	144.6	153.4	162.0	173.8
Spent for—									
Health services and supplies.	666.7	1,264.4	1,498.3	1,623.1	1,733.1	1,850.4	1,976.1	2,098.1	2,226.6
Personal health care expenses	607.5	1,139.2	1,340.3	1,447.5	1,550.2	1,655.1	1,765.5	1,878.3	1,992.6
Hospital care.	251.6	416.9	488.4	527.4	566.8	607.5	649.3	696.5	746.5
Physician and clinical services	157.5	288.6	337.9	366.7	393.6	422.2	449.7	478.8	508.5
Dental services	31.5	62.0	73.3	76.9	81.5	86.4	90.5	95.2	99.9
Other professional services [2]	18.2	39.1	45.6	49.0	52.9	56.0	58.7	62.0	65.8
Home health care.	12.6	30.5	34.2	38.0	42.7	48.1	53.0	59.0	64.4
Prescription drugs	40.3	120.6	157.6	174.2	188.8	199.7	216.8	227.5	235.4
Other nondurable medical products .	22.5	29.8	30.4	32.1	32.7	34.0	35.3	37.4	39.0
Durable medical equipment [3]	11.2	19.4	20.8	22.4	22.8	23.8	24.2	24.5	25.2
Nursing home care	52.6	95.3	105.7	110.5	115.2	120.6	125.4	131.3	137.4
Other personal health care.	9.6	37.1	46.3	50.4	53.3	56.9	62.5	66.2	70.5
Public administration and net cost of private health insurance [4]	39.2	81.8	105.8	121.9	128.8	138.7	150.4	155.7	165.6
Public health activities	20.0	43.4	52.1	53.7	54.0	56.6	60.2	64.1	68.3
Medical research [5]	12.7	25.6	32.5	35.5	38.8	40.2	41.3	42.4	43.6
Medical structures and equipment [6].	34.7	63.2	71.5	76.3	83.0	90.0	95.2	100.7	108.4

[1] Includes nonpatient revenues, privately funded construction, and industrial inplant. [2] Includes services of registered and practical nurses in private duty, podiatrists, optometrists, physical therapists, clinical psychologists, chiropractors, naturopaths, and Christian Science practitioners. [3] Includes expenditures for eyeglasses, hearing aids, orthopedic appliances, artificial limbs, crutches, wheelchairs, etc. [4] Includes administrative expenses of federally financed health programs. [5] Research and development expenditures of drug companies and other manufacturers and providers of medical equipment and supplies are excluded from research expenditures, but are included in the expenditure class in which the product falls. [6] Represents expenditures for total medical sector acquisitions of structures and equipment including structures that house medical professionals' offices.

Source: U.S. Centers for Medicare & Medicaid Services, Office of the Actuary, "National Health Statistics Group"; <http://www.cms.hhs.gov/NationalHealthExpendData/>.

98 Health and Nutrition

Table 130. Health Services and Supplies—Per Capita Consumer Expenditures by Object: 1990 to 2007

[In dollars, except percent. Based on U.S. Census Bureau estimates of total U.S. population as of July 1, excluding Armed Forces and federal employees abroad and civilian population of outlying areas. Excludes research, structures and equipment]

Object of expenditure	1990	2000	2002	2003	2004	2005	2006	2007
Total, national	**2,627**	**4,475**	**5,199**	**5,583**	**5,904**	**6,247**	**6,606**	**6,947**
Annual percent change [1]	10.6	6.1	7.8	7.4	5.8	5.8	5.7	5.2
Hospital care	991	1,475	1,695	1,814	1,931	2,051	2,171	2,306
Physician and clinical services	621	1,022	1,173	1,261	1,341	1,426	1,503	1,585
Dental services.	124	219	255	264	278	292	302	315
Other professional services [2]	72	138	158	169	180	189	196	205
Home health care	50	108	119	131	145	162	177	195
Prescription drugs	159	427	547	599	643	674	725	753
Other nondurable medical products	88	105	106	110	111	115	118	124
Durable medical equipment [2]	44	69	72	77	78	80	81	81
Nursing home care	207	337	367	380	392	407	419	435
Other personal health care	38	131	161	173	181	192	209	219
Public administration and net cost of private health insurance	155	290	367	419	439	468	503	516
Public health activities	79	154	181	185	184	191	201	212
Total, private consumer [3]	**1,457**	**2,291**	**2,645**	**2,849**	**3,001**	**3,164**	**3,297**	**3,455**
Hospital care	430	558	651	706	755	794	861	927
Physician and clinical services	384	598	688	740	787	845	896	947
Dental services.	120	209	239	248	261	274	284	295
Other professional services [2]	49	88	97	105	113	117	122	128
Home health care	20	44	35	36	37	38	38	38
Prescription drugs	130	329	411	439	464	488	478	486
Other nondurable medical products	86	100	100	104	105	108	110	116
Durable medical equipment [2]	36	53	52	54	55	57	56	56
Nursing home care	87	129	133	135	135	136	140	149
Net cost of private health insurance	115	184	239	283	291	307	312	313

[1] Change from immediate prior year.   [2] See footnotes for corresponding objects in Table 129.   [3] Represents out-of-pocket payments and private health insurance.

Source: U. S. Centers for Medicare and Medicaid Services, Office of the Actuary, "National Health Statistics Group"; <http://www.cms.hhs.gov/NationalHealthExpendData/>.

Table 131. Public Expenditures for Health Services and Supplies: 2007

[In millions of dollars (974,186 represents $974,186,000,000). Excludes Puerto Rico and Island Areas. Excludes research, structures, and equipment]

Type of selected service	Total [1]	Federal	State and local	Medicare [2] (OAS-DHI)	Workers' compen-sation [3]	Public assist-ance [4]	Defense Dept. [5]	Veterans
Total [1]	**974,186**	**712,914**	**261,272**	**431,225**	**32,424**	**344,655**	**31,662**	**33,817**
Hospital care	384,327	307,772	76,555	196,242	6,220	124,664	15,953	22,485
Physician and clinical services	161,349	133,527	27,822	96,104	12,721	36,119	6,234	3,571
Prescription drugs	80,807	66,503	14,303	47,019	3,092	23,066	4,817	2,617
Nursing home care	81,618	57,042	24,576	23,222	–	55,134	–	3,262
Public administration and net cost of private health insurance	59,530	40,231	19,299	21,582	7,738	26,643	3,088	183
Public health activities	64,093	9,670	54,423	–	–	–	–	–

– Represents zero.   [1] Includes other items not shown separately.   [2] Covers hospital and medical insurance payments and administrative costs under Old-Age, Survivors, Disability, and Health Insurance program (OASDHI).   [3] Medical benefits.   [4] Covers Medicaid and other medical public assistance. Excludes funds paid into Medicare trust fund by states to cover premiums for public assistance recipients and medically indigent persons.   [5] Includes care for retirees and military dependents.

Source: U. S. Centers for Medicare and Medicaid Services, Office of the Actuary, "National Health Statistics Group"; <http://www.cms.hhs.gov/NationalHealthExpendData/>.

Table 132. Personal Health Care—Third Party Payments and Private Consumer Expenditures, 1990 to 2007, and Projections, 2008

[In billions of dollars (607.5 represents $607,500,000,000), except percent. See headnote, Table 133]

Item	1990	2000	2002	2003	2004	2005	2006	2007	2008, proj.
Personal health care expenditures	607.5	1,139.6	1,340.8	1,445.9	1,547.7	1,653.7	1,762.0	1,878.3	1,992.6
Third party payments, total	**471.4**	**946.7**	**1,129.3**	**1,221.0**	**1,312.8**	**1,406.6**	**1,505.5**	**1,609.7**	**1,713.9**
Percent of personal health care	77.6	83.1	84.2	84.4	84.8	85.1	85.4	85.7	86.0
Private insurance payments	204.6	403.1	482.4	521.2	560.2	598.6	634.6	680.3	719.6
Public expenditures	236.2	486.7	588.7	636.2	687.7	739.0	798.2	850.6	910.8
Other [1]	30.5	57.0	58.3	63.6	64.9	69.0	72.7	78.8	83.5
Private consumer expenditures [2]	**340.7**	**596.0**	**693.8**	**746.1**	**795.1**	**845.7**	**891.1**	**948.9**	**998.4**
Percent met by private insurance	60.1	67.6	69.5	69.9	70.5	70.8	71.2	71.7	72.1
Hospital care	109.1	159.7	187.7	204.8	221.3	235.1	256.2	280.0	300.6
Percent met by private insurance	89.6	91.4	91.7	91.6	91.6	91.6	91.6	91.7	91.8
Physician and clinical services	97.5	168.9	198.3	215.2	231.1	250.3	265.8	286.1	303.9
Percent met by private insurance	69.0	80.9	82.2	82.6	82.7	82.7	82.6	82.7	82.8
Prescription drugs	33.0	93.0	118.4	127.7	136.3	144.5	142.7	146.6	147.2
Percent met by private insurance	32.2	64.0	65.9	65.4	66.1	66.2	66.6	67.6	67.6

[1] Includes nonpatient revenues and industrial inplant health services.   [2] Includes expenditures not shown separately. Represents out-of-pocket payments and private health insurance benefits. Excludes net cost of insurance.

Source: U. S. Centers for Medicare and Medicaid Services, Office of the Actuary, "National Health Statistics Group"; <http://www.cms.hhs.gov/NationalHealthExpendData/>.

Health and Nutrition   99

Table 133. **Personal Health Care Expenditures by Object and Source of Payment: 2007**

[In millions of dollars (1,878,275 represents $1,878,275,000,000). Excludes Puerto Rico and Island Areas. Covers all expenditures for health services and supplies, except net cost of insurance and administration, public health activities, and administration for government and philanthropic agencies for fund-raising activities]

Object of expenditure	Total	Private payments					Public	Third party pay-ments [2]
		Total	Consumer					
			Total	Out-of-pocket pay-ments	Private health insur-ance	Other [1]		
Total	1,878,275	1,027,711	948,898	268,568	680,330	78,814	850,564	1,609,708
Hospital care	696,539	312,212	280,025	23,172	256,853	32,187	384,327	673,367
Physician and clinical services	478,768	317,419	286,113	49,618	236,495	31,306	161,349	429,150
Dental services	95,171	89,116	89,046	42,106	46,940	70	6,055	53,065
Other professional services [3]	62,001	41,673	38,509	15,884	22,625	3,163	20,328	46,116
Home health care	59,031	12,634	11,505	5,951	5,553	1,129	46,397	53,079
Prescription drugs	227,453	146,647	146,647	47,567	99,079	–	80,807	179,886
Other nondurable medical products ...	37,357	35,017	35,017	35,017	–	–	2,341	2,341
Durable medical equipment [3]	24,450	16,940	16,940	13,951	2,989	–	7,510	10,499
Nursing home care	131,338	49,720	45,096	35,302	9,795	4,624	81,618	96,037
Other personal health care	66,167	6,334	–	–	–	6,334	59,833	66,167

– Represents zero.   [1] Includes nonpatient revenues and industrial inplant.   [2] Covers private health insurance, other private payments (excluding out-of-pocket payments), and government.   [3] See footnotes for corresponding objects on Table 129.

Source: U.S. Centers for Medicare and Medicaid Services, Office of the Actuary "National Health Statistics Group"; <http://www.cms.hhs.gov/NationalHealthExpendData/>.

Table 134. **Hospital Care, Physician and Clinical Service, Nursing Home Care, and Prescription Drug Expenditures by Source of Payment: 1990 to 2007**

[In billions of dollars (251.6 represents $251,600,000,000). Excludes Puerto Rico and island areas]

Source of payment	1990	2000	2002	2003	2004	2005	2006	2007
Hospital care, total	251.6	416.9	488.4	527.4	566.8	607.5	649.3	696.5
Out-of-pocket payments	11.3	13.6	15.6	17.2	18.7	19.8	21.4	23.2
Third-party payments	240.3	403.2	472.8	510.1	548.1	587.7	627.9	673.4
Private health insurance	97.8	144.0	172.1	188.0	202.8	215.4	236.1	256.9
Other private funds	10.4	21.9	21.6	24.8	25.3	27.3	29.9	32.2
Public	132.0	237.3	279.1	297.4	320.0	345.0	362.0	384.3
Federal	101.7	191.9	225.9	241.3	260.0	277.9	291.0	307.8
State and local	30.3	45.4	53.2	56.1	60.0	67.1	71.0	76.6
Medicare [1]	67.8	124.4	145.3	153.2	165.5	179.5	187.6	196.2
Medicaid [2]	26.7	71.1	84.4	90.3	96.8	105.1	110.2	120.0
Physician and clinical services, total	157.6	288.6	337.9	366.7	393.6	422.2	449.7	478.8
Out-of-pocket payments	30.2	32.2	35.3	37.5	40.0	43.3	46.4	49.6
Third-party payments	127.3	256.4	302.6	329.2	353.6	379.0	403.3	429.2
Private health insurance	67.3	136.7	163.1	177.7	191.1	207.1	221.5	236.5
Other private funds	11.3	22.2	24.3	26.0	26.2	27.6	29.2	31.3
Public	48.7	97.6	115.2	125.5	136.3	144.2	152.5	161.3
Federal	38.0	78.9	93.7	102.6	112.0	118.7	126.2	133.5
State and local	10.7	18.6	21.6	22.9	24.3	25.6	26.3	27.8
Medicare [1]	29.4	58.2	67.4	73.5	80.9	86.4	91.9	96.1
Medicaid [2]	7.0	19.1	23.8	25.4	27.8	29.7	31.1	33.2
Nursing home care, total	52.6	95.3	105.7	110.5	115.2	120.6	125.4	131.3
Out-of-pocket payments	19.0	28.7	29.7	30.5	30.9	31.5	32.7	35.3
Third-party payments	33.6	66.6	76.0	79.9	84.2	89.1	92.6	96.0
Private health insurance	2.9	7.9	8.7	8.7	8.7	8.8	9.3	9.8
Other private funds	3.8	4.5	4.0	4.2	4.3	4.4	4.6	4.6
Public	26.9	54.1	63.3	67.1	71.3	75.9	78.8	81.6
Federal	16.3	36.4	44.4	46.0	49.1	51.9	54.3	57.0
State and local	10.6	17.8	18.9	21.1	22.2	24.0	24.5	24.6
Medicare [1]	1.7	10.1	13.9	14.7	16.9	19.1	21.1	23.2
Medicaid [2]	24.1	42.0	47.1	49.7	51.5	53.7	54.5	54.8
Prescription drugs, total	40.3	120.6	157.6	174.2	188.8	199.7	216.8	227.5
Out-of-pocket payments	22.4	33.4	40.4	44.1	46.2	48.7	46.7	47.6
Third-party payments	17.9	87.2	117.3	130.1	142.6	151.0	170.1	179.9
Private health insurance	10.6	59.5	77.9	83.4	90.0	95.8	96.2	99.1
Other private funds	–	–	–	–	–	–	–	–
Public	7.3	27.7	39.3	46.6	52.6	55.2	73.9	80.8
Federal	3.2	15.9	23.1	27.8	31.4	32.7	58.7	66.5
State and local	4.0	11.8	16.2	18.9	21.2	22.5	15.1	14.3
Medicare [1]	0.2	2.1	2.5	2.5	3.4	4.0	39.5	47.0
Medicaid [2]	5.1	20.2	27.8	32.5	36.3	37.2	19.1	18.8

– Represents zero.   [1] Medicare expenditures come from federal funds.   [2] Medicaid expenditures come from federal, state, and local funds.

Source: U.S. Centers for Medicare and Medicaid Services, Office of the Actuary, "National Health Statistics Group"; <http://www.cms.hhs.gov/NationalHealthExpendData/>.

100   Health and Nutrition

Table 135. **Consumer Price Indexes of Medical Care Prices: 1980 to 2008**

[1982–1984 = 100. Indexes are annual averages of monthly data based on components of consumer price index for all urban consumers; for explanation, see text, Section 14 and Appendix III]

Year	Medical care, total	Medical care services				Medical care commodities		Annual percent change [3]		
		Total [1]	Professional services			Hospital and related services		Medical care, total	Medical care services	Medical care commodities
			Total [1]	Physi-cians	Dental		Total [2]	Prescrip-tion drugs and medical supplies		
1980. . . .	74.9	74.8	77.9	76.5	78.9	69.2	75.4	72.5	11.0	11.3	9.3
1985. . . .	113.5	113.2	113.5	113.3	114.2	116.1	115.2	120.1	6.3	6.1	7.2
1990. . . .	162.8	162.7	156.1	160.8	155.8	178.0	163.4	181.7	9.0	9.3	8.4
1995. . . .	220.5	224.2	201.0	208.8	206.8	257.8	204.5	235.0	4.5	5.1	1.9
2000. . . .	260.8	266.0	237.7	244.7	258.5	317.3	238.1	285.4	4.1	4.3	3.2
2002. . . .	285.6	292.9	253.9	260.6	281.0	367.8	256.4	316.5	4.7	5.1	3.6
2003. . . .	297.1	306.0	261.2	267.7	292.5	394.8	262.8	326.3	4.0	4.5	2.5
2004. . . .	310.1	321.3	271.5	278.3	306.9	417.9	269.3	337.1	4.4	5.0	2.5
2005. . . .	323.2	336.7	281.7	287.5	324.0	439.9	276.0	349.0	4.2	4.8	2.5
2006. . . .	336.2	350.6	289.3	291.9	340.9	468.1	285.9	363.9	4.0	4.1	3.6
2007. . . .	351.1	369.3	300.8	303.2	358.4	498.9	290.0	369.2	4.4	5.3	1.4
2008. . . .	364.1	384.9	311.0	311.3	376.9	534.0	296.0	378.3	3.7	4.2	2.1

[1] Includes other services not shown separately. [2] Includes other commodities not shown separately. [3] Percent change from the immediate prior year.

Source: Bureau of Labor Statistics, *CPI Detailed Report Tables*; <http://www.bls.gov/cpi/cpi_dr.htm>. See also *Monthly Labor Review* at <http://www.bls.gov/opub/mlr/welcome.htm>.

Table 136. **Average Annual Expenditures Per Consumer Unit for Health Care: 2005 to 2007**

[In dollars, except percent. See text, Section 13 and headnote, Table 664. For composition of regions, see map, inside front cover]

Item	Health care, total		Health insurance	Medical services	Drugs and medical supplies [1]	Percent distribution		
	Amount	Percent of total expen-ditures				Health insurance	Medical services	Drugs and medical supplies [1]
2005	2,664	5.7	1,361	677	626	51.1	25.4	23.5
2006	2,766	5.7	1,465	670	631	53.0	24.2	22.8
2007	2,853	5.7	1,545	709	599	54.2	24.9	21.0
Age of reference person:								
Under 25 years old	800	2.7	397	267	137	49.6	33.4	17.1
25 to 34 years old	1,740	3.7	918	556	267	52.8	32.0	15.3
35 to 44 years old	2,315	3.9	1,269	651	396	54.8	28.1	17.1
45 to 54 years old	2,792	4.8	1,386	772	633	49.6	27.7	22.7
55 to 64 years old	3,476	6.5	1,751	883	842	50.4	25.4	24.2
65 to 74 years old	4,967	11.8	2,821	1,027	1,119	56.8	20.7	22.5
75 years old and over	4,275	14.1	2,716	651	909	63.5	15.2	21.3
Race of reference person:								
White and other	3,011	5.8	1,619	756	637	53.8	25.1	21.2
Black	1,689	4.7	1,001	370	319	59.3	21.9	18.9
Origin of reference person:								
Hispanic	1,486	3.6	744	468	275	50.1	31.5	18.5
Non-Hispanic	3,035	6.0	1,652	742	641	54.4	24.4	21.1
Region of residence:								
Northeast.	2,645	5.1	1,535	576	535	58.0	21.8	20.2
Midwest.	3,097	6.5	1,632	811	655	52.7	26.2	21.1
South	2,800	6.2	1,539	639	622	55.0	22.8	22.2
West.	2,860	5.1	1,475	829	556	51.6	29.0	19.4
Size of consumer unit:								
One person	1,790	6.1	994	403	394	55.5	22.5	22.0
Two or more persons	3,302	5.7	1,778	839	685	53.8	25.4	20.7
Two persons	3,709	7.0	2,005	872	833	54.1	23.5	22.5
Three persons	2,876	5.0	1,564	697	616	54.4	24.2	21.4
Four persons	3,147	4.7	1,684	935	529	53.5	29.7	16.8
Five persons or more	2,840	4.4	1,498	819	523	52.7	28.8	18.4
Income before taxes:								
Quintiles of income:								
Lowest 20 percent	1,474	7.2	895	232	347	60.7	15.7	23.5
Second 20 percent	2,448	7.9	1,397	522	529	57.1	21.3	21.6
Third 20 percent	2,826	6.7	1,538	661	627	54.4	23.4	22.2
Fourth 20 percent	3,268	5.7	1,771	848	650	54.2	25.9	19.9
Highest 20 percent	4,244	4.4	2,122	1,283	838	50.0	30.2	19.7
Education:								
Less than a high school graduate . .	2,003	6.6	1,136	391	476	56.7	19.5	23.8
High school graduate	2,594	6.6	1,502	533	558	57.9	20.5	21.5
High school graduate with some college	2,654	5.8	1,381	735	537	52.0	27.7	20.2
Associate's degree	2,998	5.7	1,643	706	648	54.8	23.5	21.6
Bachelor's degree	3,362	5.1	1,777	907	679	52.9	27.0	20.2
Master's, professional, doctoral degree	4,105	5.2	2,096	1,202	807	51.1	29.3	19.7

[1] Includes prescription and nonprescription drugs.

Source: U.S. Bureau of Labor Statistics, *Consumer Expenditure Survey*, annual; <http://www.bls.gov/cex/>.

Health and Nutrition 101

Table 137. **Medicare Disbursements by Type of Beneficiary: 1990 to 2008**

[In millions of dollars (109,709 represents $109,709,000,000). For years ending Sept. 30. Distribution of benefits by type is estimated and subject to change. See headnote, Table 142]

Selected type of beneficiary	1990	1995	2000	2004	2005	2006	2007	2008 [1]
Total disbursements	109,709	180,096	219,276	301,488	336,876	380,457	434,829	455,076
HI, Part A disbursements [2]	66,687	114,883	130,284	166,998	184,142	184,901	202,827	230,240
Benefits	65,722	113,394	125,992	163,764	181,934	185,100	203,990	226,275
Aged	58,503	100,107	110,261	140,704	155,925	157,273	172,748	184,267
Disabled	7,218	13,288	15,731	23,060	26,009	27,827	31,242	33,524
SMI, Part B disbursements [2]	43,022	65,213	88,992	134,274	151,537	161,647	179,651	177,709
Benefits	41,498	63,490	88,875	131,357	147,449	154,381	172,698	174,805
Aged	36,837	54,830	76,340	109,890	122,905	127,848	142,839	151,298
Disabled	4,661	8,660	12,535	21,467	24,544	26,534	29,859	31,991
SMI, Part D disbursements [2]	(X)	(X)	(X)	216	1,198	33,909	52,351	47,126
Benefits	(X)	(X)	(X)		73	33,506	51,336	46,734
Transitional assistance benefit payments. . .	(X)	(X)	(X)	216	1,125	229	10	–

– Represents or rounds to zero.   X Not applicable.   [1] A transfer of expenditures between Parts A and B took place during 2008 that corrected for accounting errors that happened during FY2005–2007. The transfer is reflected in the "Benefits" data and is the sum of "Aged," Benefits and the Transfer." For Table 142, the total for Parts A and B is the sum of the "Providers and the Transfer." The Part A "Benefits" total increased by $8,484,000,000 while Part B "Benefits" total decreased by the same amount. [2] Other types not shown separately.

Source: U.S. Centers for Medicare and Medicaid Services, Trustees Report and Trust Funds, and unpublished data. See also <http://www.cms.hhs.gov/ReportsTrustFunds/>.

Table 138. **Children's Health Insurance Program (CHIP)—Enrollment and Expenditures by State: 2000 and 2008**

[(3,357.4 represents 3,357,400) For year ending September 30. This program provides health benefits coverage to children living in families whose incomes exceed the eligibility limits for Medicaid. Although it is generally targeted to families with incomes at or below 200 percent of the federal poverty level, each state may set its own income eligibility limits, within certain guidelines. States have three options: they may expand their Medicaid programs, develop a separate child health program that functions independently of Medicaid, or do a combination of both]

State	Enrollment [1] (1,000)		Expenditures [2] (mil. dol.)		State	Enrollment [1] (1,000)		Expenditures [2] (mil. dol.)	
	2000	2008	2000	2008		2000	2008	2000	2008
U.S. . . .	**3,357.4**	**7,368.5**	**1,928.8**	**6,896.6**	MO	72.8	136.1	41.2	79.6
AL	37.6	110.8	31.9	108.8	MT	8.3	22.7	4.3	24.9
AK	13.4	18.7	18.1	14.4	NE	11.4	48.8	6.1	35.6
AZ	59.6	112.1	29.4	119.4	NV	15.9	38.6	9.0	28.8
AR	1.9	93.4	1.5	113.2	NH	4.3	12.2	1.6	11.2
CA	484.4	1,692.1	187.3	1,259.3	NJ	89.0	151.8	46.9	323.1
CO	34.9	99.6	13.9	82.5	NM	8.0	14.9	3.4	124.3
CT	19.9	22.3	12.8	26.3	NY	769.5	517.3	401.0	326.9
DE	4.5	11.2	1.5	9.7	NC	103.6	251.7	65.5	193.7
DC	2.3	8.7	5.8	10.1	ND	2.6	7.6	1.8	13.5
FL	227.5	354.4	125.7	272.3	OH	118.3	251.3	53.1	227.5
GA	120.6	311.2	48.7	225.0	OK	57.7	117.5	51.3	99.4
HI	(Z)	28.8	0.4	17.6	OR	37.1	73.7	12.5	66.3
ID	12.4	43.5	7.5	35.4	PA	119.7	256.6	70.7	204.5
IL	62.5	356.5	32.7	292.9	RI	11.5	26.0	10.4	59.1
IN	44.4	125.0	53.7	102.4	SC	60.4	73.6	46.6	57.8
IA	20.0	50.4	15.5	55.3	SD	5.9	15.3	3.1	15.6
KS	26.3	51.2	12.8	47.9	TN	14.9	63.6	41.7	77.5
KY	55.6	67.7	60.0	90.3	TX	131.1	731.9	41.4	698.0
LA	50.0	147.9	25.3	159.2	UT	25.3	51.1	12.8	50.3
ME	22.7	30.9	11.4	33.4	VT	4.1	6.5	1.4	5.7
MD	93.1	132.9	92.2	156.2	VA	37.7	155.3	18.6	131.3
MA	113.0	201.0	44.2	259.3	WA	2.6	16.8	0.6	43.4
MI	55.4	67.8	36.2	172.9	WV	21.7	37.6	9.7	36.8
MN	(Z)	5.6	(Z)	71.4	WI	47.1	52.9	21.4	75.3
MS	12.2	84.4	21.1	142.9	WY	2.5	9.0	1.0	8.7

[2] Z Less than 50 or $50,000.   [1] Number of children ever enrolled during the year in Children's Health Insurance Program. [2] Expenditures for which states are entitled to federal reimbursement under Title XXI and which reconciles any advance of Title XXI federal funds made on the basis of estimates.

Source: U.S. Centers for Medicare & Medicaid Services, *The Children's Health Insurance Program (CHIP), Annual Enrollment Report* and the Statement of Expenditures for the CHIP Program (CMS-21). See also <http://www.cms.hhs.gov/NationalCHIPPolicy/> and <http://www.cms.hhs.gov/medicaid/mbes/default.asp>.

Table 139. **Medicare Enrollees: 1990 to 2008**

[In millions (34.3 represents 34,300,000). As of July 1. Includes Puerto Rico and island areas and enrollees in foreign countries and unknown place of residence. SMI is Supplemental Medical Insurance. See headnote, Table 142]

Item	1990	1995	2000	2004	2005	2006	2007	2008
Total	34.3	37.6	39.7	41.9	42.6	43.4	44.3	45.2
Aged	31.0	33.2	34.3	35.4	35.8	36.3	37.0	37.8
Disabled	3.3	4.4	5.4	6.5	6.8	7.1	7.3	7.4
Hospital insurance, Part A	33.7	37.2	39.3	41.5	42.2	43.1	43.9	44.9
Aged	30.5	32.7	33.8	35.0	35.4	36.0	36.6	37.5
Disabled	3.3	4.4	5.4	6.5	6.8	7.1	7.3	7.4
SMI, Part B	32.6	35.6	37.3	39.1	39.8	40.4	41.1	41.7
Aged	29.6	31.7	32.6	33.5	33.8	34.1	34.6	35.2
Disabled	2.9	3.9	4.8	5.7	6.0	6.2	6.4	6.6
SMI, Part D	(X)	(X)	(X)	1.2	1.8	30.5	31.2	32.3
Medicare Advantage [1]	1.3	2.7	6.2	4.7	5.8	7.3	8.7	10.0

X Not applicable.   [1] Prior to 2004, Medicare Advantage was referred to as Medicare + Choice.

Source: U.S. Centers for Medicare and Medicaid Services, Office of the Actuary, CMS Statistics Medicare Enrollment, "National Trends." See <http://www.cms.hhs.gov/MedicareEnrpts/>.

Table 140. **Medicare—Enrollment by State and Other Areas: 2000 to 2007**

[In thousands (39,620 represents 39,620,000). Hospital (HI) and/or supplementary medical insurance (SMI) enrollment as of July 1]

State and area	2000	2005	2006	2007	State and area	2000	2005	2006	2007
All areas [1]	39,620	42,395	43,314	44,263	MT	137	146	150	156
U.S.	38,762	41,003	42,020	43,259	NE	254	259	263	268
AL	685	740	766	789	NV	240	294	304	318
AK	42	51	54	57	NH	170	185	191	204
AZ	675	777	805	841	NJ	1,203	1,215	1,236	1,257
AR	439	464	480	496	NM	234	261	273	285
CA	3,901	4,158	4,241	4,369	NY	2,715	2,758	2,796	2,841
CO	467	513	533	558	NC	1,133	1,255	1,300	1,359
CT	515	520	527	537	ND	103	103	104	105
DE	112	125	130	136	OH	1,701	1,731	1,766	1,805
DC	75	72	73	74	OK	508	531	549	565
FL	2,804	3,008	3,064	3,133	OR	489	532	547	567
GA	916	1,016	1,063	1,111	PA	2,095	2,108	2,144	2,184
HI	165	180	184	189	RI	172	171	173	175
ID	165	188	196	207	SC	568	637	664	697
IL	1,635	1,674	1,702	1,741	SD	119	123	126	129
IN	852	893	915	941	TN	829	903	938	975
IA	477	484	491	500	TX	2,265	2,491	2,598	2,708
KS	390	397	403	412	UT	206	231	242	254
KY	623	668	689	711	VT	89	95	98	102
LA	602	630	616	639	VA	893	981	1,011	1,045
ME	216	233	238	247	WA	736	807	837	873
MD	645	687	704	723	WV	338	351	359	367
MA	961	961	976	997	WI	783	818	835	854
MI	1,403	1,468	1,502	1,541	WY	65	70	72	74
MN	654	691	708	729	Outlying areas [2] . . .	537	622	633	(NA)
MS	419	449	459	469	Pending state designations [3] . . .	321	769	660	(NA)
MO	861	901	922	946					

NA Not available.   [1] Includes Outlying Areas and Pending State Designation.   [2] Includes American Samoa, Federated States of Micronesia, Guam Marshall Islands, Northern Marianas, Puerto Rico, Virgin Islands, and Wake Island.   [3] Include foreign countries and unknown places of residence.

Source: U.S. Centers for Medicare and Medicaid Services, Medicare Enrollment Reports. See also <http://www.cms.hhs.gov/MedicareEnrpts/>.

Table 141. **Medicaid—Selected Characteristics of Persons Covered: 2007**

[In thousands, except percent (39,327 represents 39,327,000). Represents number of persons as of March of following year who were enrolled at any time in year shown. Excludes unrelated individuals under age 15. Persons did not have to receive medical care paid for by Medicaid in order to be counted. See headnote, Table 555]

Poverty status	Total [1]	White alone [2]	Black alone [3]	Asian alone [4]	Hispanic [5]	Under 18 years old	18–44 years old	45–64 years old	65 years old and over
Persons covered, total . . .	39,327	27,046	8,910	1,520	10,298	20,673	9,827	5,565	3,263
Below poverty level	16,247	10,031	4,909	508	4,484	9,105	4,080	2,223	840
Above poverty level	23,080	17,015	4,001	1,012	5,814	11,568	5,747	3,342	2,423
Percent of population covered	13.2	11.3	23.7	11.5	22.4	27.9	8.9	7.2	8.9
Below poverty level	43.6	39.9	53.1	37.7	45.3	68.3	29.6	33.7	23.6
Above poverty level	8.8	8.0	14.1	8.5	16.1	19.1	5.9	4.7	7.3

[1] Includes other races not shown separately.   [2] White alone refers to people who reported White and did not report any other race category.   [3] Black alone refers to people who reported Black and did not report any other race category.   [4] Asian alone refers to people who reported Asian and did not report any other race category.   [5] Persons of Hispanic origin may be of any race.

Source: U.S. Census Bureau, Current Population Reports, *Income, Poverty, and Health Insurance Coverage in the United States: 2007*, P60-235 (issued August 2008); and "Table HI02. Health Insurance Coverage Status and Type of Coverage by Selected Characteristics for People in the Poverty Universe: 2007"; and "Table HI03. Health Insurance Coverage Status and Type of Coverage by Selected Characteristics for Poor People in the Poverty Universe: 2007." See <http://www.census.gov/hhes /www/hlthins/hlthin07.html>.

Health and Nutrition   103

Table 142. **Medicare Benefits by Type of Provider: 1990 to 2008**

[In millions of dollars (65,721 represents $65,721,000,000). For years ending Sept. 30. Distribution of benefits by type is estimated and subject to change. The Medicare program has two components: Hospital Insurance (HI) or Medicare Part A and Supplementary Medical Insurance (SMI) consisting of Medicare Part B and Part D. See text in this section for details. **See footnote 1, Table 137, for 2008 data changes**]

Type of provider	1990	1995	2000	2004	2005	2006	2007	2008
Hospital insurance benefits (Part A), total	**65,721**	**113,395**	**125,992**	**163,764**	**181,934**	**185,100**	**203,990**	**226,275**
Inpatient hospital	57,012	81,095	86,561	114,375	122,656	122,101	125,918	128,754
Skilled nursing facility	2,761	8,684	10,269	16,673	18,712	19,658	22,161	23,919
Home health agency	3,295	15,715	4,880	5,213	5,885	5,864	6,233	6,570
Hospice	318	1,854	2,818	6,572	7,679	8,811	10,448	11,399
Managed care	2,335	6,047	21,463	20,932	27,001	28,667	39,230	47,150
Supplementary medical insurance benefits (Part B), total.	**41,498**	**63,490**	**88,876**	**131,357**	**147,449**	**154,381**	**172,698**	**174,805**
Physician fee schedule	(NA)	31,110	35,958	52,224	57,211	57,923	58,832	59,762
Durable medical equipment	(NA)	3,576	4,577	7,687	7,894	8,266	8,138	8,534
Carrier lab [1]	(NA)	2,819	2,194	3,206	3,521	3,678	4,049	4,172
Other carrier [2]	(NA)	4,513	7,154	13,794	15,195	15,253	15,695	16,395
Hospital [3]	(NA)	8,448	8,516	16,931	18,970	20,042	22,725	23,054
Home health	(NA)	223	4,281	5,577	6,750	7,442	9,056	9,956
Intermediary lab [4]	(NA)	1,437	1,748	2,670	2,821	2,813	3,048	2,976
Other intermediary [5]	(NA)	5,110	6,099	10,459	11,353	11,751	13,430	13,236
Managed care	(NA)	6,253	18,348	18,809	23,735	27,213	37,724	45,203
Supplementary medical insurance benefits (Part D), total [6]	**(X)**	**(X)**	**(X)**	**216**	**1,198**	**33,735**	**51,346**	**46,734**

NA Not available. X Not applicable. [1] Lab services paid under the lab fee schedule performed in a physician's office lab or an independent lab. [2] Includes free-standing ambulatory surgical center's facility costs, ambulance, and supplies. [3] Includes the hospital facility costs for Medicare Part B services which are predominantly in the outpatient department. The physician reimbursement associated with these services is included on the "Physician Fee Schedule" line. [4] Lab fee services paid under the lab fee schedule performed in a hospital outpatient department. [5] Includes ESRD (End Stage Renal Disease) free-standing dialysis facility payments and payments to rural health clinics, outpatient rehabilitation facilities, psychiatric hospitals, and federally qualified health centers. [6] Starting with 2006, Part D provides subsidized access to drug insurance coverage on a voluntary basis for all beneficiaries and premium and cost-sharing subsidies for low-income enrollees. Benefits prior to 2006 were for transitional assistance to beneficiaries with low income.

Source: U.S. Centers for Medicare and Medicaid Services, unpublished data. See <http://www.cms.hhs.gov/ReportsTrustFunds/>.

Table 143. **Medicare Insurance Trust Funds: 1990 to 2008**

[In billions of dollars (126.3 represents $126,300,000,000) SMI is Supplemental Medical Insurance. See headnote, Table 142]

Type of trust fund	1990	1995	2000	2003	2004	2005	2006	2007	2008
TOTAL MEDICARE									
Total income	126.3	175.3	257.1	291.6	317.7	357.5	437.0	462.1	480.8
Total expenditures.	111.0	184.2	221.8	280.8	308.9	336.4	408.3	431.7	468.1
Assets, end of year	114.4	143.4	221.5	280.0	288.8	309.8	338.5	368.9	381.6
HOSPITAL INSURANCE (Part A)									
Net contribution income [1]	72.1	103.3	154.5	159.2	167.2	182.6	194.2	205.3	213.4
Interest received [2]	8.5	10.8	11.7	15.8	16.0	16.1	16.4	17.5	16.4
Benefit payments [3]	66.2	116.4	126.8	154.3	167.6	180.0	189.0	200.2	232.3
Assets, end of year	98.9	130.3	177.5	256.0	269.3	285.8	305.4	326.0	321.3
SMI (Part B)									
Net premium income	11.3	19.7	20.6	27.4	31.4	37.5	42.9	46.8	50.2
Transfers from general revenue.	33.0	39.0	65.9	86.4	100.4	118.1	132.7	139.6	146.8
Interest received [2]	1.6	1.6	3.5	2.0	1.5	1.4	1.8	2.2	3.6
Benefit payments [3]	42.5	65.0	88.9	123.8	135.0	149.2	165.9	176.4	180.3
Assets, end of year	15.5	13.1	44.0	24.0	19.4	24.0	32.3	42.1	59.4
SMI (Part D)									
Net premium income	(X)	(X)	(X)	(X)	–	–	3.5	4.0	5.0
Transfers from general revenue [4]	(X)	(X)	(X)	(X)	0.4	1.1	39.1	38.7	37.3
Interest received	(X)	(X)	(X)	(X)	–	–	–	–	–
Benefit payments [4]	(X)	(X)	(X)	(X)	0.4	1.1	47.0	48.8	49.0
Assets, end of year	(X)	(X)	(X)	(X)	–	–	0.8	0.8	0.9

– Represents zero. X Not applicable. [1] Includes income from taxation of benefits beginning in 1994. Includes premiums from aged ineligibles enrolled in Hospital Insurance (HI). [2] Includes recoveries of amounts reimbursed from the trust fund. [3] Beginning 1998, monies transferred to the SMI trust fund for home health agency costs, as provided for by P.L. 105-33, are included in HI benefit payments but excluded from SMI benefit payments. [4] These amounts for 2004 and 2005 include amounts transferred for transitional assistance for Part D of Medicare.

Source: U.S. Centers for Medicare and Medicaid Services, Annual Report of the Board of Trustees of the Federal Hospital Insurance Trust Fund and Annual Report of the Board of Trustees of the Federal Supplementary Medical Insurance Trust Fund. See also <http://www.cms.hhs.gov/ReportsTrustFunds/>.

Table 144. Medicaid—Beneficiaries and Payments: 2000 to 2006

[For year ending September 30 (42,887 represents 42,887,000)]

Basis of eligibility and type of service	Beneficiaries (1,000) [1]				Payments (mil. dol.)			
	2000	2004	2005 [2]	2006 [3]	2000	2004	2005 [2]	2006 [3]
Total	42,887	55,002	57,643	57,757	168,443	257,748	275,569	269,858
Age 65 and over	3,730	4,318	4,396	4,375	44,560	59,541	63,358	58,186
Blind/Disabled	6,890	7,933	8,210	8,335	72,772	111,614	119,647	116,907
Children	19,018	25,613	26,337	26,784	23,490	39,194	42,012	45,022
Adults	8,671	12,225	12,529	12,605	17,671	30,522	32,385	33,043
Foster Care Children.	761	846	875	919	3,309	5,011	5,337	5,714
Unknown	3,817	4,048	5,267	4,703	6,639	11,668	12,547	10,619
BCCA WOMEN [4]	(NA)	19	29	37	(NA)	199	283	367
Capitated care [5].	21,292	29,528	33,496	35,046	25,026	42,601	46,421	50,153
Clinic services	7,678	11,102	11,913	11,858	6,138	8,336	8,986	8,736
Dental services	5,922	9,037	9,328	9,514	1,413	2,867	3,045	3,123
Home health services	1,007	1,146	1,195	1,191	3,133	4,566	5,361	5,917
ICF/MR services [6]	119	114	109	107	9,376	11,193	11,730	11,854
Inpatient hospital services	4,913	5,425	5,488	6,268	24,131	34,914	35,347	36,466
Lab and X-ray services	11,439	15,875	16,020	16,202	1,292	2,695	2,927	2,988
Mental health facility services [7] . . .	100	117	120	138	1,769	2,326	2,333	2,392
Nursing facility services.	1,706	1,709	1,712	1,722	34,528	42,008	44,675	45,674
Other care [8]	9,022	12,387	12,347	12,249	14,755	24,951	26,624	29,186
Outpatient hospital services	13,170	15,888	16,314	16,015	7,082	10,261	10,228	10,454
Other practitioner services	4,758	5,933	5,904	5,881	664	951	1,182	1,148
PCCM services [9]	5,649	8,548	8,750	8,722	177	500	235	253
Prescribed drugs	20,325	27,549	28,385	27,310	19,898	39,476	42,830	28,243
Physician services	18,965	23,612	24,204	23,265	6,809	10,061	11,278	10,581
Personal support services [10]	4,559	6,254	6,809	6,847	11,629	18,494	20,729	21,624
Sterilizations	137	174	179	177	128	207	212	194
Unknown	74	81	73	68	496	1,344	1,428	873

NA Not available. [1] Beneficiaries data do not add due to number of beneficiaries that are reported in more than one category. [2] 2005 beneficiary data is not available for Maine; 2004 data is reported. [3] 2006 beneficiary data is not available for Maine; 2004 data is reported. 2006 beneficiary data is not available for Nevada; 2005 data is reported. [4] Women-Breast and Cervical Cancer Assistance. [5] HMO payments and prepaid health plans. [6] Intermediate care facilities for mentally retarded. [7] Inpatient mental health-aged and inpatient mental health-under 21. [8] Includes beneficiaries of, and payments for, other care not shown separately. [9] Primary Care Case Management Services. [10] Includes personal care services, rehabilitative services, physical occupational targeted case management services, speech therapies, hospice services, nurse midwife services, nurse practitioner services, private duty nursing services, and religious nonmedical health care institutions.

Source: U.S. Centers for Medicare and Medicaid Services, Medicaid Program Statistics, Medicaid Statistical Information System; <http://www.cms.hhs.gov/MedicaidDataSourcesGenInfo/02_MSISDATA.asp#TopOfPage>.

Table 145. Medicaid—Summary by State: 2000 and 2006

[(42,887 represents 42,887,000). For year ending September 30. See headnote, Table 144]

State	Beneficiaries [1] (1,000)		Payments [2] (mil. dol.)		State	Beneficiaries [1] (1,000)		Payments [2] (mil. dol.)	
	2000	2006	2000	2006		2000	2006	2000	2006
U.S.	42,887	57,757	168,443	269,858	MO	890	1,136	3,274	4,771
AL	619	845	2,393	3,897	MT	104	115	422	639
AK	96	121	473	954	NE	229	248	960	1,451
AZ	681	1,019	2,112	3,153	NV [4]	138	257	516	1,090
AR	489	753	1,543	2,778	NH	97	126	651	855
CA	7,918	10,427	17,105	29,010	NJ	822	1,004	4,714	7,512
CO	381	625	1,809	2,679	NM	376	516	1,249	2,333
CT	420	518	2,839	3,986	NY	3,420	5,194	26,148	40,235
DE	115	171	529	947	NC	1,214	1,631	4,834	8,121
DC	139	159	793	1,385	ND	63	74	358	510
FL	2,373	3,123	7,433	12,569	OH	1,305	2,021	7,115	11,834
GA	1,369	1,818	3,624	6,042	OK	507	726	1,604	2,934
HI	194	227	600	989	OR	558	516	1,714	2,274
ID	131	217	594	1,057	PA	1,492	2,089	6,366	11,406
IL	1,519	2,195	7,807	9,963	RI	179	212	1,070	1,647
IN	706	999	2,977	5,011	SC	689	862	2,765	4,013
IA	314	431	1,477	2,524	SD	102	131	402	606
KS	263	343	1,227	1,996	TN	1,568	1,591	3,491	5,955
KY	764	900	2,921	4,135	TX	2,633	3,910	9,277	13,764
LA	761	1,149	2,632	3,978	UT	225	288	960	1,521
ME [3]	194	294	1,310	2,366	VT	139	150	480	813
MD	626	759	3,003	5,219	VA	627	821	2,479	4,173
MA	1,060	1,167	5,413	8,661	WA	896	1,128	2,435	5,230
MI	1,352	1,872	4,881	7,139	WV	342	373	1,394	2,226
MN	558	718	3,280	5,505	WI	577	973	2,968	4,451
MS	605	745	1,808	3,144	WY	46	69	215	412

[1] Persons who had payments made on their behalf at any time during the fiscal year. [2] Payments are for fiscal year and reflect federal and state contribution payments. Data exclude disproportionate share hospital payments. Disproportionate share hospitals receive higher medicaid reimbursement than other hospitals because they treat a disproportionate share of Medicaid patients. [3] 2005 and 2006 beneficiary data are not available for Maine: 2004 data are reported. [4] 2006 beneficiary data are not available for Nevada: 2005 data are reported.

Source: U.S. Centers for Medicare and Medicaid Services, Medicaid, Program Statistics, Medicaid Statistical Information System.

Health and Nutrition 105

Table 146. Medicaid Managed Care Enrollment by State and Other Areas: 1995 to 2008

[For year ending June 30. (33,373 represents 33,373,000)]

State and other areas	Total enroll-ment [1] (1,000)	Managed care enrollment [2] Num-ber (1,000)	Managed care enrollment [2] Per-cent of total	State and other areas	Total enroll-ment [1] (1,000)	Managed care enrollment [2] Num-ber (1,000)	Managed care enrollment [2] Per-cent of total	State and other areas	Total enroll-ment [1] (1,000)	Managed care enrollment [2] Num-ber (1,000)	Managed care enrollment [2] Per-cent of total
1995	33,373	9,800	29.4	HI	211	167	79.1	NC	1,354	905	66.9
2000	33,690	18,786	55.8	ID	187	156	83.4	ND	54	31	58.3
2003	42,741	24,406	58.4	IL	2,107	1,168	55.4	OH	1,784	1,275	71.5
2004	44,356	26,914	60.7	IN	882	630	71.4	OK	583	511	87.6
2005	45,392	28,576	63.0	IA	363	296	81.6	OR	418	381	91.2
2006	45,653	29,830	65.3	KS	279	234	83.8	PA	1,833	1,487	81.1
2007	45,962	29,463	64.1	KY	732	665	90.8	RI	178	110	61.9
				LA	1,007	692	68.7	RI			
2008, total	47,143	33,428	70.2	ME	259	163	63.1	SC	689	647	93.8
				MD	711	516	72.7	SD	102	101	98.8
U.S.	46,080	32,443	71.6	MA	1,115	697	60.3	TN	1,207	1,207	100.0
AL	765	504	66.0	MI	1,547	1,363	88.1	TX	3,041	2,116	69.6
AK	97	-	-	MN	617	385	62.4	UT	208	178	85.7
AZ	1,049	949	90.5	MS	670	485	72.4	VT	141	129	91.0
AR	622	500	80.4	MO	833	811	97.3	VA	754	472	62.7
CA	6,607	3,409	51.6	MT	83	30	36.0	WA	961	858	89.3
CO	430	414	96.4	NE	202	172	84.8	WV	311	139	44.6
CT	435	284	65.3	NV	189	157	82.9	WI	907	474	52.3
DE	153	115	63.7	NH	113	88	77.6	WY	61	-	-
DC	146	93	63.3	NJ	915	660	72.1	PR	1,016	985	96.9
FL	2,276	1,442	63.3	NM	473	293	62.0	VI	7	-	-
GA	1,271	1,168	91.9	NY	4,147	2,714	65.4				

- Represents zero. [1] The unduplicated Medicaid enrollment figures include individuals in state health care reform programs that expand eligibility beyond traditional Medicaid eligibility standards. [2] The unduplicated managed care enrollment figures include enrollees receiving comprehensive and limited benefits.

Source: U.S. Centers for Medicare and Medicaid Services, "2008 Medicaid Managed Care Enrollment Report." See <http://www.cms.hhs.gov/MedicaidDataSourcesGenInfo/04_MdManCrEnrllRep.asp>.

Table 147. Health Maintenance Organizations (HMOs): 1990 to 2007

[As of January 1 (33.0 represents 33,000,000). An HMO is a prepaid health plan delivering comprehensive care to members through designated providers, having a fixed periodic payment for health care services, and requiring members to be in a plan for a specified period of time (usually 1 year). A group HMO delivers health services through a physician group that is controlled by the HMO unit or contracts with one or more independent group practices to provide health services. An individual practice association (IPA) HMO contracts directly with physicians in independent practice, and/or contracts with one or more associations of physicians in independent practice, and/or contracts with one or more multispecialty group practices. Data are based on a census of HMOs]

Model type	Number of plans 1990	2000	2004 [2]	2005 [4]	2006 [3 4]	2007 [3 4]	Enrollment [1] (mil.) 1990	2000	2004 [2]	2005 [4]	2006 [3 4]	2007 [3 4]
Total	572	568	412	420	548	531	33.0	80.9	68.8	69.2	73.9	73.9
IPA	360	278	176	171	191	174	13.7	33.4	24.6	23.5	22.4	23.3
Group [5]	212	102	96	98	122	116	19.3	15.2	15.3	16.4	20.7	19.7
Mixed	(NA)	188	140	141	134	103	(NA)	32.3	28.9	29.0	25.5	21.4

NA Not available. [1] 1990–1995 exclude enrollees participating in open-ended plans; beginning 1999, includes open-ended enrollment. [2] Starting with 2004 data, Puerto Rico and Guam included in the total. [3] 2006 and 2007 data include "HMO Medicaid only plans." [4] 2005–2007 totals include plans that did not provide enough information to be classified as a model type. [5] 2006 and 2007 data includes data for "Network, Staff and Group" types categorized under the "Group" model type.

Source: HealthLeaders-InterStudy, Nashville, TN, The Competitive Edge, copyright). See also <http://www.interstudypublications.com/>.

Table 148. Persons Enrolled in Health Maintenance Organizations (HMOs) by State: 2006 and 2007

[As of January 1 (64,494 represents 64,494,000). Data are based on a census of health maintenance organizations]

State	Number 2007 (1,000)	Percent of population 2006	2007	State	Number 2007 (1,000)	Percent of population 2006	2007	State	Number 2007 (1,000)	Percent of population 2006	2007
US	64,494	23.8	21.5	KS	362	14.8	13.1	ND	1	0.4	0.2
				KY	271	6.2	6.4	OH	2,080	23.2	18.1
AL	120	3.1	2.6	LA	282	9.5	6.6	OK	227	7.0	6.3
AK	-	-	-	ME	366	36.6	27.7	OR	875	24.8	23.6
AZ	1,522	34.2	24.7	MD	1,428	29.1	25.4	PA	3,214	26.9	25.8
AR	85	3.5	3.0	MA	2,265	44.2	35.2	RI	220	25.0	20.6
CA	15,992	49.2	43.9	MI	2,796	26.6	27.7	SC	295	7.4	6.8
CO	1,004	25.9	21.1	MN	704	23.4	13.6	SD	66	7.5	8.4
CT	1,053	31.3	30.1	MS	3	0.8	0.1	TN	1,510	25.8	25.0
DE	153	15.5	18.0	MO	1,050	18.6	18.0	TX	2,364	12.1	10.1
DC	332	55.4	57.0	MT	48	7.3	5.1	UT	719	26.1	28.2
FL	3,584	24.5	19.8	NE	97	7.9	5.5	VT	95	24.5	15.3
GA	2,157	15.4	23.0	NV	541	24.7	21.7	VA	1,341	19.5	17.5
HI	601	46.8	46.7	NH	216	21.5	16.4	WA	1,186	18.3	18.5
ID	64	2.9	4.4	NJ	1,884	24.4	21.6	WV	197	8.9	10.8
IL	1,626	15.2	12.7	NM	374	23.7	19.1	WI	1,224	26.3	22.0
IN	1,441	25.7	22.8	NY	5,784	27.5	30.0	WY	13	2.0	2.6
IA	238	11.5	8.0	NC	423	9.8	4.8				

- Represents zero.

Source: HealthLeaders-InterStudy, Nashville, TN, The Competitive Edge, copyright). See also <http://www.interstudypublications.com/>.

Table 149. **Health Insurance Coverage Status by Selected Characteristics: 2006 and 2007**

[(296,824 represents 296,824,000). Persons as of following year for coverage in the year shown. Government health insurance includes Medicare, Medicaid, and military plans. Based on Current Population Survey, Annual Social and Economic Supplement (ASES). As of March. See text, Section 1 and Appendix III]

Characteristic	Number (1,000)							Percent			
		Covered by private or government health insurance						Not covered by health insurance	Covered by private or government health insurance			Not covered by health insurance
			Private		Government					Private		
	Total persons	Total [1]	Total	Group health [2]	Medi-care	Medi-caid			Total [1]	Private	Medi-caid	
2006 [3]	296,824	249,829	201,690	177,152	40,343	38,281	46,995	84.2	67.9	12.9	15.8
2007	299,106	253,449	201,991	177,446	41,375	39,554	45,657	84.7	67.5	13.2	15.3
Age:											
Under 18 years	74,403	66,254	47,750	44,252	518	20,899	8,149	89.0	64.2	28.1	11.0
Under 6 years	24,944	22,326	14,793	13,971	235	8,364	2,618	89.5	59.3	33.5	10.5
6 to 11 years	23,820	21,355	15,567	14,621	138	6,604	2,465	89.7	65.4	27.7	10.3
12 to 17 years	25,639	22,573	17,391	15,661	145	5,932	3,066	88.0	67.8	23.1	12.0
18 to 24 years	28,398	20,407	17,074	13,747	180	3,563	7,991	71.9	60.1	12.5	28.1
25 to 34 years	40,146	29,817	26,430	24,505	501	3,237	10,329	74.3	65.8	8.1	25.7
35 to 44 years	42,132	34,415	31,067	29,009	924	3,027	7,717	81.7	73.7	7.2	18.3
45 to 54 years	43,935	37,161	33,350	30,805	1,795	3,103	6,774	84.6	75.9	7.1	15.4
55 to 64 years	33,302	29,291	25,114	22,569	3,179	2,462	4,011	88.0	75.4	7.4	12.0
65 years and over	36,790	36,103	21,206	12,558	34,278	3,263	686	98.1	57.6	8.9	1.9
Sex: Male	146,855	122,309	99,180	88,077	17,943	17,976	24,546	83.3	67.5	12.2	16.7
Female	152,250	131,140	102,811	89,369	23,431	21,578	21,111	86.1	67.5	14.2	13.9
Race: White alone [4]	239,399	205,099	167,905	146,398	35,117	27,172	34,300	85.7	70.1	11.4	14.3
Black alone [4]	37,775	30,403	20,169	18,525	4,303	8,986	7,372	80.5	53.4	23.8	19.5
Asian alone [4]	13,268	11,034	9,067	8,107	1,195	1,528	2,234	83.2	68.3	11.5	16.8
Hispanic origin [5]	46,026	31,256	20,194	18,551	2,887	10,348	14,770	67.9	43.9	22.5	32.1
Household income:											
Less than $25,000	55,267	41,728	16,650	10,325	15,822	18,976	13,539	75.5	30.1	34.3	24.5
$25,000–$49,999	68,915	54,400	39,742	33,099	12,567	11,436	14,515	78.9	57.7	16.6	21.1
$50,000–$74,999	58,355	49,867	43,967	39,782	5,779	4,730	8,488	85.5	75.3	8.1	14.5
$75,000 or more	116,568	107,453	101,633	94,240	7,207	4,412	9,115	92.2	87.2	3.8	7.8
Persons below poverty	37,276	25,741	7,893	5,076	5,106	16,247	11,535	69.1	21.2	43.6	30.9

[1] Includes other government insurance not shown separately. Persons with coverage counted only once in total, even though they may have been covered by more than one type of policy.   [2] Related to employment of self or other family members.   [3] The estimates are revised from the originally published data.   [4] Refers to people who reported specified race and did not report any other race category.   [5] Persons of Hispanic origin may be any race.

Source: U.S. Census Bureau, Current Population Reports; Income, Poverty, and Health Insurance Coverage in the United States: 2007, P60-235; issued August 2008. Table HI01 Health Insurance Data, Health Insurance Coverage Status and Type of Coverage by Selected Characteristics: 2007. Table HI02. Health Insurance Coverage Status and Type of Coverage by Selected Characteristics for People in the Poverty Universe: 2007; <http://www.census.gov/hhes/www/hlthins/hlthin07.html>.

Table 150. **Persons With and Without Health Insurance Coverage by State: 2007**

[253,449 represents 253,499,000. Based on the Current Population Survey, Annual Social and Economic Supplement (ASES). As of March. See text, Section 1 and Appendix III]

State	Total persons covered (1,000)	Total persons not covered		Children not covered		State	Total persons covered (1,000)	Total persons not covered		Children not covered	
		Number (1,000)	Percent of total	Number (1,000)	Percent of total			Number (1,000)	Percent of total	Number (1,000)	Percent of total
U.S. [1]	253,449	45,657	15.3	8,149	11.0	MO	5,062	729	12.6	150	10.4
AL	4,021	549	12.0	82	7.3	MT	793	146	15.6	28	12.6
AK	552	123	18.2	21	11.4	NE	1,522	232	13.2	45	10.0
AZ	5,204	1,164	18.3	234	13.8	NV	2,126	441	17.2	94	14.3
AR	2,354	451	16.1	44	6.2	NH	1,177	137	10.5	19	6.5
CA	29,682	6,613	18.2	1,013	10.7	NJ	7,208	1,348	15.8	270	12.9
CO	4,077	801	16.4	157	13.0	NM	1,509	437	22.5	77	15.5
CT	3,150	326	9.4	43	5.2	NY	16,543	2,519	13.2	395	8.9
DE	766	96	11.2	16	7.5	NC	7,673	1,510	16.4	272	12.1
DC	526	55	9.5	7	6.2	ND	553	61	10.0	11	7.9
FL	14,426	3,648	20.2	785	19.2	OH	9,979	1,322	11.7	239	8.6
GA	7,831	1,662	17.5	289	11.5	OK	2,920	631	17.8	116	12.6
HI	1,172	96	7.5	14	4.8	OR	3,130	632	16.8	92	10.6
ID	1,292	209	13.9	46	11.0	PA	11,138	1,176	9.5	207	7.4
IL	10,988	1,700	13.4	210	6.6	RI	931	113	10.8	21	8.8
IN	5,546	717	11.4	83	5.2	SC	3,664	721	16.4	152	14.2
IA	2,695	275	9.3	34	4.8	SD	708	80	10.1	16	8.0
KS	2,376	345	12.7	54	7.7	TN	5,268	883	14.4	135	9.1
KY	3,637	570	13.6	82	8.0	TX	17,742	5,962	25.2	1,435	21.4
LA	3,421	776	18.5	137	12.5	UT	2,317	340	12.8	87	10.4
ME	1,197	115	8.8	14	5.1	VT	545	69	11.2	12	9.4
MD	4,804	762	13.7	146	10.5	VA	6,548	1,135	14.8	187	10.2
MA	6,000	340	5.4	43	3.0	WA	5,773	737	11.3	106	6.8
MI	8,776	1,151	11.6	149	6.2	WV	1,541	254	14.1	18	4.6
MN	4,758	433	8.3	80	6.4	WI	5,023	451	8.2	77	5.8
MS	2,358	545	18.8	94	12.1	WY	447	70	13.6	12	9.6

[1] The estimates are revised from the originally published data.

Source: U.S. Census Bureau, Current Population Reports; Income, Poverty, and Health Insurance Coverage in the United States: 2007, P60-235 (issued August 2008). Table HI05. Health Insurance Coverage Status and Type of Coverage by State for All People: 2007. See also <http://www.census.gov/hhes/www/hlthins/hlthin07.html>.

Health and Nutrition 107

Table 151. **People Without Health Insurance for the Entire Year by Selected Characteristics: 2006 and 2007**

[In thousands, except as noted (296,824 represents 296,824,000). Based on the Current Population Survey; Annual Social and Economic Supplement (ASEC); see text, Section 1 and Appendix III]

Characteristic	2006			2007		
		Uninsured persons			Uninsured persons	
	Total persons	Number	Percent distribution	Total persons	Number	Percent distribution
Total [1,2]	296,824	46,995	100.0	299,106	45,657	100.0
Under 18 years	74,101	8,661	18.4	74,403	8,149	17.8
18 to 24 years	28,405	8,323	17.7	28,398	7,991	17.5
25 to 34 years	39,868	10,713	22.8	40,146	10,329	22.6
35 to 44 years	42,762	8,018	17.1	42,132	7,717	16.9
45 to 64 years	75,652	10,737	22.8	77,237	10,785	23.6
65 years and over	36,035	541	1.2	36,790	686	1.5
Male	145,689	25,531	54.3	146,855	24,546	53.8
Female.	151,135	21,464	45.7	152,250	21,111	46.2
White alone [3]	237,892	35,486	75.5	239,399	34,300	75.1
White alone or in combination . .	242,592	36,248	77.1	244,145	34,977	76.6
Black alone [3].	37,369	7,652	16.3	37,775	7,372	16.1
Black alone or in combination . .	39,083	7,921	16.9	39,683	7,624	16.7
Asian alone [3].	13,194	2,045	4.4	13,268	2,234	4.9
Asian alone or in combination . .	14,348	2,160	4.6	14,444	2,321	5.1
Hispanic	44,854	15,296	32.5	46,026	14,770	32.3
White alone, not Hispanic.	196,252	21,162	45.0	196,768	20,548	45.0

[1] Includes other races not shown separately. [2] The estimates are revised from the originally published data. [3] Refers to people who reported specified race and did not report any other race category. [4] Persons of Hispanic origin may be of any race.

Source: U.S. Census Bureau, Current Population Reports, Income, Poverty, and Health Insurance Coverage in the United States: 2007, P60-235. *Health Insurance Coverage Status and Type of Coverage by Selected Characteristics: 2007*. See also <http://www.census.gov/hhes/www/hlthins/hlthin07.html/>.

Table 152. **Percent of Workers Participating in Health Care Benefit Programs and Percent of Participants Required to Contribute: 2008**

[Based on National Compensation Survey, a sample survey of 12,872 private industry establishments of all sizes, representing over 107 million workers; see Appendix III. See also Table 640. The data below marks the first release of data on employee benefits under new industry and occupational classifications]

Characteristic	Percent of workers participating—				Single coverage medical plan		Family coverage medical plan	
	Medical care	Dental care	Vision care	Outpatient prescription drug coverage	Employee contributions required (percent)	Average monthly contribution [1] (dol.)	Employee contributions required (percent)	Average monthly contribution [1] (dol.)
Total	53	37	22	51	77	87.69	87	330.99
Worker characteristics:								
Management, professional, and related	68	51	30	65	79	85.76	90	330.88
Management, business, and financial	77	57	31	74	80	82.79	91	316.15
Professional and related.	64	48	30	61	78	87.54	90	339.50
Service	29	20	14	28	82	96.00	91	350.84
Sales and office	51	35	19	49	80	89.62	91	352.05
Sales and related	42	28	16	40	82	94.37	91	347.95
Office and administrative support	57	40	21	55	79	87.13	91	354.13
Natural resources, con- struction, and mainte- nance	62	37	26	59	63	91.34	75	329.44
Production, transportation, and material moving	61	40	24	58	74	80.93	83	288.01
Production	67	45	26	64	75	81.03	83	278.45
Transportation, and material moving.	55	34	21	52	73	80.80	83	300.50
Full-time [2]	65	45	27	62	77	86.74	87	328.83
Part-time [2]	14	11	7	14	78	101.39	88	363.44
Union [3]	79	62	47	76	49	67.89	57	227.74
Nonunion	50	34	19	48	82	89.88	93	342.18
Average hourly wage [4]								
Less than $7.85	13	NA	NA	12	89	90.30	94	341.07
$7.85 to under $10.13	28	17	10	26	83	97.35	92	355.70
$10.13 to under $15.00 . . .	55	36	20	52	81	89.06	92	342.56
$15.00 to under $23.25 . . .	67	44	25	64	74	85.68	87	327.74
$23.25 to under $34.79 . . .	72	54	35	69	70	86.08	80	319.12
$34.79 or greater	75	60	35	73	78	84.22	87	313.18

[1] The average is presented for all covered workers and excludes workers without the plan provision. Averages are for plans stating a flat monthly cost. [2] Employees are classified as working either a full-time or part-time schedule based on the definition used by each establishment. [3] Union workers are those whose wages are determined through collective bargaining. [4] The National Compensation Survey—Benefits program presents wage data in percentiles rather than dollar amounts; see "Technical Note" in source.

Source: U.S. Bureau of Labor Statistics, *National Compensation Survey: Employee Benefits in Private Industry in the United States, March, 2008* (issued August 2008). See also <http://www.bls.gov/ncs/ebs/publications.htm>.

108   Health and Nutrition

Table 153. **Retail Prescription Drug Sales: 1995 to 2008**

[2,125 represents 2,125,000,000]

Sales outlet	Unit	1995	2000	2002	2003	2004	2005	2006	2007	2008
Number of prescriptions	Mil..	2,125	2,865	3,139	3,215	3,274	3,279	3,420	3,515	3,536
Traditional chain	Mil..	908	1,335	1,463	1,483	1,500	1,518	1,605	1,660	1,684
Independent	Mil..	672	698	719	736	738	714	732	745	732
Mass merchant.	Mil..	238	293	339	345	353	359	375	390	400
Supermarkets	Mil..	221	394	444	462	470	465	476	478	481
Mail order	Mil..	86	146	174	189	214	223	232	242	238
Percent distribution of brand/generic mix:										
Brand drugs.	Percent.	59.8	57.6	57.9	55.0	54.1	50.6	46.8	41.8	35.5
Generic drugs	Percent.	40.2	42.4	42.1	45.0	47.5	51.3	53.2	58.2	64.5
Retail sales	Bil. dol.	72.2	145.6	182.7	204.2	220.1	232.0	250.6	259.4	253.6
Traditional chain	bil. dol.	27.8	59.1	73.3	82.6	87.5	91.8	100.6	104.8	104.1
Independent	bil. dol.	22.0	33.4	38.0	41.2	43.3	44.6	46.2	47.2	43.8
Mass merchant.	bil. dol.	7.7	13.5	18.0	20.0	21.5	22.5	24.3	25.7	24.8
Supermarkets	bil. dol.	7.4	17.4	23.1	25.2	26.9	27.6	28.9	28.5	25.8
Mail order	bil. dol.	7.4	22.1	30.2	35.0	40.8	45.5	50.5	53.1	55.1
Average prices [1]										
All prescriptions	Dollars	30.01	45.79	55.37	59.52	62.64	63.87	66.97	69.91	71.69
Brand drugs.	Dollars	40.22	65.29	77.49	85.57	91.80	97.65	107.48	119.51	121.18
Generic drugs	Dollars	14.84	19.33	24.89	27.69	28.23	29.21	31.39	34.34	35.22
Average prescription cost [1] . .	Dollars	(NA)	(NA)	(NA)	(NA)	(NA)	(NA)	66.97	69.91	(NA)
Manufacturer receives	Dollars	(NA)	(NA)	(NA)	(NA)	(NA)	(NA)	51.97	54.30	(NA)
Wholesaler receives	Dollars	(NA)	(NA)	(NA)	(NA)	(NA)	(NA)	2.07	2.44	(NA)
Retailer receives.	Dollars	(NA)	(NA)	(NA)	(NA)	(NA)	(NA)	12.93	13.17	(NA)

NA Not available.   [1] Excludes mail order.

Source: National Association of Chain Drug Stores, Alexandria, VA, *NACDS Foundation Chain Pharmacy Industry Profile, 2008* (copyright); <http://www.nacds.org>.

Table 154. **Annual Receipts/Revenue for Health Care Industries: 2000 to 2007**

[In millions of dollars (1,033,029 represents $1,033,029,000,000). Based on the North American Industry Classification System, 2002 (NAICS); see text, Section 15. All firms in NAICS 6211, 6212, 6213, and 6215 are defined as taxable. Estimates for the nonemployer portion are derived from administrative records data provided by other federal agencies. These data are available only at the total revenue level. See Appendix III]

Selected kind of business	2002 NAICS code	Total, all firms			Taxable employer firms		
		2000	2005	2007	2000	2005	2007
Health care and social assistance	62	1,033,029	1,478,399	1,664,547	500,932	730,440	835,940
Ambulatory health care services [1]	621	419,402	610,806	692,854	376,095	549,489	624,879
Offices of physicians	6211	213,806	310,780	346,043	213,806	310,780	346,043
Offices of dentists	6212	60,931	83,636	93,645	60,931	83,636	93,645
Offices of other health practitioners	6213	32,037	45,095	50,380	32,037	45,095	50,380
Offices of chiropractors.	62131	7,570	9,876	10,833	7,570	9,876	10,833
Offices of optometrists	62132	7,639	9,793	11,037	7,639	9,793	11,037
Offices of mental health practitioners.	62133	3,516	4,066	4,567	3,516	4,066	4,567
Offices of PT/OT/speech therapy & audiology [2]	62134	8,486	14,195	16,052	8,486	14,195	16,052
Outpatient care centers	6214	(S)	69,464	82,133	(S)	31,487	40,677
Medical & diagnostic laboratories.	6215	23,450	34,690	38,558	23,450	34,690	38,558
Home health care services	6216	26,841	43,969	53,664	16,879	29,736	37,714
Other ambulatory health care services	6219	15,565	23,172	28,431	9,421	14,065	17,862
Hospitals [1]	622	423,889	611,522	687,135	42,908	71,315	83,644
General medical & surgical hospitals	6221	397,526	573,007	642,670	36,926	58,568	68,110
Psychiatric & substance abuse hospitals	6222	13,422	13,914	16,041	2,189	2,317	3,215
Other specialty hospitals	6223	12,941	24,601	28,424	3,793	10,430	12,319
Nursing and residential care facilities [1]	623	112,706	145,578	160,037	66,245	85,294	95,295
Nursing care facilities.	6231	67,238	83,515	90,677	49,816	61,240	67,881
Residential mental retardation/health facilities	6232	16,718	22,932	25,543	4,726	6,693	7,698
Residential mental retardation facilities	62321	11,570	15,607	17,709	3,297	4,638	5,345
Community care facilities for the elderly	6233	22,104	30,612	34,676	10,812	16,070	18,220
Continuing care retirement communities. . . .	623311	12,948	17,609	20,121	3,576	5,677	6,662
Homes for the elderly	623312	9,156	13,003	14,555	7,236	10,393	11,558
Other residential care facilities.	6239	6,646	8,519	9,141	891	1,291	1,496
Social assistance [1]	624	77,032	110,493	124,521	15,684	24,342	32,122
Individual and family services	6241	37,311	52,806	61,558	3,824	7,395	10,252
Community food and housing, and emergency and other relief services..	6242	12,281	18,935	18,579	46	(S)	(S)
Vocational rehabilitation services	6243	9,458	13,921	13,425	1,593	2,655	2,715
Child day care services	6244	17,982	24,831	30,959	10,221	14,170	18,977

S Figure does not meet publication standards.   [1] Includes other kinds of business not shown separately.   [2] Offices of physical, occupational, and speech therapists, and audiologists.

Source: U.S. Census Bureau, *"Service Annual Survey"* (published March 2008); <http://www.census.gov/services>.

Health and Nutrition 109

Table 155. Receipts for Selected Health Care Industries by Source of Revenue: 2002 and 2007

[In millions of dollars (248,824 represents $248,824,000,000). Based on the 2002 North American Industry Classification System (NAICS), see text, Section 15. Based on a sample of taxable employer firms only and does not include nonemployer revenue. See Appendix III]

Source of revenue	Offices of physicians (NAICS 6211)		Offices of dentists (NAICS 6212)		Hospitals (NAICS 622)		Nursing and residential care facilities (NAICS 623)	
	2002	2007	2002	2007	2002	2007	2002	2007
Total	248,824	346,043	71,103	93,645	500,113	687,135	127,114	160,037
Medicare	59,756	74,032	(S)	789	161,306	177,200	16,332	25,997
Medicaid.	17,923	18,321	2,462	3,690	59,385	69,408	51,629	59,285
Other government [1]	2,479	4,687	(S)	454	26,174	34,139	9,973	11,332
Worker's compensation	8,416	7,219	(S)	86	5,478	6,658	(S)	(S)
Private insurance	121,246	173,245	36,618	42,593	185,985	286,764	7,124	7,423
Patient (out-of-pocket). . . . .;. . . .	26,022	35,333	30,744	42,575	26,108	31,251	[2]31,432	[2]37,849
Other patient care sources, n.e.c [3] . . .	8,679	19,162	(S)	2,861	11,829	22,412	3,321	6,518
Nonpatient care revenue	4,304	(S)	(S)	(S)	23,848	(S)	(S)	(S)

S Figure does not meet publication standards. [1] Veterans, National Institute of Health, Indian Affairs, etc. [2] Represents payment from patients and their families plus patients' assigned social security benefits. [3] n.e.c. represents not elsewhere classified.

Source: U.S. Census Bureau, *Service Annual Survey, 2007*; <http://www.census.gov/econ/www/servmenu.html>.

Table 156. Employment in the Health Service Industries: 1990 to 2008

[In thousands (9,296 represents 9,296,000). See headnote, Table 612. Based on the North American Industry Classification System 2007 code; see text, Section 15. For more information on the NAICS changes, please see <http://stats.bls.gov/ces/cesnaics07.htm>]

Industry	2007 NAICS code [1]	1990	2000	2003	2004	2005	2006	2007	2008
Health care and social assistance [1]	62	9,296	12,718	13,893	14,190	14,536	14,925	15,380	15,819
Ambulatory health care services [1]	621	2,842	4,320	4,786	4,952	5,114	5,286	5,474	5,661
Offices of physicians	6211	1,278	1,840	2,003	2,048	2,094	2,148	2,202	2,266
Offices of dentists	6212	513	688	744	760	774	784	808	819
Offices of other health practitioners	6213	276	438	503	527	549	571	600	629
Medical and diagnostic laboratories	6215	129	162	182	190	198	202	211	219
Home health care services	6216	288	633	733	777	821	866	914	958
Hospitals [1]	622	3,513	3,954	4,245	4,285	4,345	4,423	4,515	4,641
General medical and surgical hospitals	6221	3,305	3,745	4,005	4,042	4,096	4,167	4,242	4,351
Psychiatric and substance abuse hospitals . .	6222	113	86	92	92	93	98	99	102
Other hospitals	6223	95	123	148	151	156	162	174	189
Nursing and residential care facilities [1]	623	1,856	2,583	2,786	2,818	2,855	2,893	2,958	3,008
Nursing care facilities.	6231	1,170	1,514	1,580	1,577	1,577	1,581	1,603	1,614

[1] Includes other industries not shown separately.

Source: U.S. Bureau of Labor Statistics, *Employment and Earnings*, March issues. See also <http://stats.bls.gov/ces/home.htm>.

Table 157. Osteopathic Physicians: 2001 to 2009

Osteopathic physicians are fully qualified physicians licensed to practice medicine and to perform surgery. Osteopathic medicine has a strong emphasis on the interrelationship of the body's nerves, muscles, bones and organs. Doctors of osteopathic medicine, or D.O.s, apply the philosophy of treating the whole person to the prevention, diagnosis and treatment of illness, disease and injury]

Characteristics	2001	2005	2009	Characteristics	2001	2005	2009
Characteristics	2001	2005	2009	Unknown	28	318	208
Total number of DOs	46,990	56,512	67,167	Self-identified practice specialty [1].	31,996	38,442	46,031
Sex				Family and general practice. . . .	14,102	17,800	18,792
Female	10,875	15,147	20,808	General internal Medicine	2,592	3,107	4,596
Male	36,115	41,365	46,359	General pediatrics/adolescent			
Age				medicine	958	1,176	1,716
Less than 35 years old	9,866	12,983	15,246	Obstetrics and gynecology . . .	1,219	1,465	1,986
35 to 44 years old	14,798	16,179	19,212	Pediatric specialties	320	348	532
45 to 54 years old	12,754	13,845	15,985	Osteopathic specialties [2]	414	464	805
55 to 64 years old	4,706	7,998	10,327	Other specialties	12,001	13,431	17,396
65 years old and over	4,838	5,189	6,189	Unknown	390	651	208

[1] DOs are assumed to be in active practice if they are under age 65 and have not informed the AOA that they have retired or are inactive. DOs are assumed to be in postdoctoral training (internship, residency or fellowship) if they are within 4 years of graduation or if the AOA has received information that they are in a postdoctoral program. [2] Osteopathic self-identified practice specialties include OMT (osteopathic manipulative treatment) and OMM (osteopathic manipulative medicine). OMT is the therapeutic application of manually guided forces by an osteopathic physician to improve physiologic function and/or support homeostasis that has been altered by somatic dysfunction. OMM is the application of osteopathic philosophy, structural diagnosis, and use of OMT in the patient's diagnosis and management.

American Osteopathic Association, Chicago, IL.; *AOA Annual Statistics*. See <http://www.osteopathic.org/index.cfm?PageID=aoaannualrprt>.

Table 158. **Physicians by Sex and Specialty: 1980 to 2007**

[In thousands (467.7 represents 467,700). As of Dec. 31, except 1990 as of Jan. 1, and as noted. Includes Puerto Rico and Island Areas]

Activity	1980 Total	1980 Office-based	1990 Total	1990 Office-based	2000 Total	2000 Office-based	2007 Total	2007 Office-based
Doctors of medicine, total [1]	467.7	272.0	615.4	361.0	813.8	490.4	941.3	562.9
Place of medical education:								
U.S. medical graduates	370.0	226.2	483.7	286.2	616.8	376.5	697.8	424.0
International medical graduates [2]	97.7	45.8	131.8	74.8	197.0	113.9	243.5	138.9
Sex: Male	413.4	251.4	511.2	311.7	618.2	382.3	674.3	407.1
Female	54.3	20.6	104.2	49.2	195.5	108.1	267.0	155.8
Allergy/immunology.	1.5	1.4	3.4	2.5	4.0	3.1	4.3	3.3
Anesthesiology	16.0	11.3	26.0	17.8	35.7	27.6	41.7	31.6
Cardiovascular diseases	9.8	6.7	15.9	10.7	21.0	16.3	22.6	17.5
Child psychiatry	3.3	2.0	4.3	2.6	6.2	4.3	7.3	5.3
Dermatology	5.7	4.4	7.6	6.0	9.7	8.0	10.9	9.0
Diagnostic radiology	7.0	4.2	15.4	9.8	21.1	14.6	24.9	17.3
Emergency medicine.	5.7	3.4	14.2	8.4	23.1	14.5	30.8	20.0
Family practice	27.5	18.4	47.6	37.5	71.6	54.2	84.2	67.3
Gastroenterology	4.0	2.7	7.5	5.2	10.6	8.5	12.5	10.0
General practice.	32.5	29.6	22.8	20.5	15.2	13.0	10.3	8.7
General surgery.	34.0	22.4	38.4	24.5	36.7	24.5	37.7	25.6
Internal medicine	71.5	40.6	98.3	58.0	134.5	89.7	158.0	108.6
Neurological surgery	3.3	2.5	4.4	3.1	5.0	3.7	5.4	4.0
Neurology	5.7	3.3	9.2	5.6	12.3	8.6	14.8	10.5
Obstetrics and gynecology	26.3	19.5	33.7	25.5	40.2	31.7	42.6	34.4
Ophthalmology	13.0	10.6	16.1	13.1	18.1	15.6	18.2	15.9
Orthopedic surgery	14.0	10.7	19.1	14.2	22.3	17.4	24.5	19.3
Otolaryngology	6.6	5.3	8.1	6.4	9.4	7.6	10.1	8.2
Pathology	13.6	6.1	16.6	7.5	18.8	10.6	19.8	11.6
Pediatrics	29.5	18.2	41.9	27.1	63.9	43.2	76.3	53.3
Physical med./rehab.	2.1	1.0	4.1	2.2	6.5	4.3	8.3	5.9
Plastic surgery.	3.0	2.4	4.6	3.8	6.2	5.3	7.2	6.1
Psychiatry	27.5	16.0	35.2	20.1	39.5	25.0	41.6	27.5
Pulmonary diseases	3.7	2.0	6.1	3.7	8.7	5.9	10.5	7.5
Radiology	11.7	7.8	8.5	6.1	8.7	6.7	9.0	6.9
Urological surgery	7.7	6.2	9.4	7.4	10.3	8.5	10.5	8.8
Unspecified.	12.3	5.0	8.1	1.6	8.3	3.8	7.9	3.9
Not classified.	20.6	(X)	12.7	(X)	45.1	(X)	52.7	(X)
Other categories [3]	32.1	(X)	55.4	(X)	75.2	(X)	112.0	(X)

X Not applicable.   [1] Includes other categories not shown.   [2] International medical graduates received their medical education in schools outside the United States and Canada.   [3] Includes inactive and address unknown.

Source: Except as noted, American Medical Association, Chicago, IL, *Physician Characteristics and Distribution in the U.S.,* annual (copyright).

Table 159. **Active Physicians and Nurses by State: 2007**

[As of December 31. Excludes doctors of osteopathy, physicians with addresses unknown, and inactive status. Includes all physicians not classified according to activity status. As of May. Nurses data comes from the Bureau of Labor Statistics]

State	Physicians Total	Physicians Rate [1]	Nurses Total	Nurses Rate [1]	State	Physicians Total	Physicians Rate [1]	Nurses Total	Nurses Rate [1]
United States. .	816,727	271	2,468,340	819	Missouri	14,462	246	56,290	958
Alabama.	10,094	218	42,180	912	Montana.	2,110	221	7,160	748
Alaska.	1,556	228	5,150	756	Nebraska	4,342	245	17,870	1,010
Arizona.	13,321	210	34,580	544	Nevada	4,796	188	14,670	574
Arkansas	5,758	203	21,920	774	New Hampshire	3,607	275	12,730	970
California	97,743	269	233,200	641	New Jersey.	27,373	316	78,510	907
Colorado.	12,576	260	36,850	761	New Mexico	4,785	244	11,400	580
Connecticut.	13,135	376	34,690	994	New York	76,925	396	166,990	859
Delaware	2,163	251	8,420	977	North Carolina.	22,987	254	80,090	886
District of Columbia .	4,745	807	8,110	1,380	North Dakota.	1,559	244	7,000	1,097
Florida	45,110	248	148,180	814	Ohio	30,615	267	114,920	1,001
Georgia	20,708	217	62,230	653	Oklahoma	6,260	173	25,700	712
Hawaii	4,049	317	9,620	753	Oregon.	10,253	274	29,700	795
Idaho	2,526	169	9,600	642	Pennsylvania.	37,924	305	126,370	1,017
Illinois	35,932	280	104,130	812	Rhode Island.	3,955	376	10,600	1,007
Indiana.	13,745	217	54,770	864	South Carolina.	10,122	230	35,040	795
Iowa	5,647	189	29,550	990	South Dakota	1,743	219	9,670	1,215
Kansas.	6,181	223	24,070	867	Tennessee	16,206	264	54,960	894
Kentucky	9,843	232	39,120	923	Texas.	51,080	214	157,870	662
Louisiana	11,487	263	39,090	894	Utah	5,553	208	16,670	625
Maine.	3,662	278	13,850	1,053	Vermont	2,320	374	5,660	912
Maryland	23,680	421	48,840	869	Virginia	21,132	274	57,740	750
Massachusetts.	30,335	469	78,280	1,210	Washington	17,413	270	49,910	774
Michigan	25,146	250	84,480	841	West Virginia	4,201	232	16,970	938
Minnesota.	15,194	293	52,690	1,017	Wisconsin	14,507	259	50,690	905
Mississippi	5,196	178	25,350	868	Wyoming	965	184	4,250	812

[1] Per 100,000 resident population. Based on U.S. Census Bureau estimates as of July 1.

Source: Physicians: American Medical Association, Chicago, IL, *Physician Characteristics and Distribution in the U.S.,* annual (copyright); Nurses: Bureau of Labor Statistics, Occupational Employment Statistics, Occupational Employment and Wages; *May 2007 Wage and Employment Statistics*; <http://www.bls.gov/oes/home.htm#data>.

Health and Nutrition   111

Table 160. Percent Distribution of Number of Visits to Health Care Professionals by Selected Characteristics: 2000 and 2007

[Covers ambulatory visits to doctor's offices and emergency departments, and home health care visits during a 12-month period. Based on the redesigned National Health Interview Survey, a sample survey of the civilian noninstitutionalized population]

Characteristic	None 2000	None 2007	1–3 visits 2000	1–3 visits 2007	4–9 visits 2000	4–9 visits 2007	10 or more visits 2000	10 or more visits 2007
All persons [1, 2] SEX [2]	16.7	16.4	45.4	47.2	24.6	23.6	13.3	12.8
Male	21.7	21.3	45.9	47.3	22.3	20.9	10.1	10.5
Female AGE	11.9	11.5	44.8	47.1	27.0	26.3	16.3	15.1
Under 18 years old	12.3	10.3	53.8	57.0	26.2	25.5	7.6	7.2
18 to 44 years old	23.5	24.1	45.2	46.3	19.1	18.4	12.2	11.2
45 to 64 years old	15.0	14.9	43.4	45.3	25.7	23.9	15.9	15.9
65 to 74 years old	9.0	8.4	34.5	35.4	34.5	36.0	22.1	20.3
75 years old and over RACE [2, 3]	5.8	5.5	29.3	30.6	39.3	36.4	25.6	27.5
Race alone:								
White	16.1	16.2	45.1	46.8	25.2	24.0	13.6	13.0
Black or African American	17.2	15.5	46.7	48.4	23.4	23.4	12.6	12.7
American Indian or Alaska Native	21.3	21.5	43.0	43.1	20.0	21.5	15.7	13.9
Asian	20.3	22.0	49.2	48.9	20.8	19.9	9.7	9.2
Two or more races HISPANIC ORIGIN AND RACE [2, 3, 4]	12.1	13.0	41.7	45.4	28.2	24.1	18.0	17.5
Hispanic or Latino	26.8	25.2	41.8	44.6	19.8	20.3	11.6	9.9
Mexican	31.0	28.0	40.8	42.9	17.8	19.5	10.3	9.6
Not Hispanic or Latino	15.2	14.7	45.9	47.7	25.3	24.2	13.6	13.4
White, non-Hispanic	14.5	14.1	45.4	47.4	25.9	24.8	14.1	13.7
Black, non-Hispanic	17.1	15.1	46.8	48.6	23.5	23.5	12.6	12.8

[1] Includes other categories not shown separately.   [2] Estimates are age adjusted to the year 2000 standard using six age groups: Under 18 years, 18–44 years, 45–54 years, 55–64 years, 65–74 years, and 75 years and over.   [3] Estimates by race and Hispanic origin are tabulated using the 1997 standards for federal data on race and ethnicity. Estimates for specific race groups are shown when they meet requirements for statistical reliability and confidentiality. The categories "White only," "Black or African American only," "American Indian and Alaska Native (AI/AN) only," and "Asian only" include persons who reported only one racial group; and the category "2 or more races" includes persons who reported more than one of the five racial groups in the 1997 Standards or one of the five racial groups and "Some other race."   [4] Persons of Hispanic or Latino origin may be of any race or combination of races.

Source: U.S. National Center for Health Statistics, *Health, United States, 2009*. See <www.cdc.gov/nchs/hus.htm>.

Table 161. Adults 18 Years and Over Who Used Complementary and Alternative Medicine (CAM) in the Past Twelve Months by Selected Type of Therapy: 2002 and 2007

[The denominators for statistics shown exclude persons with unknown CAM information. Estimates were age adjusted to the year 2000 U.S. standard population using four age groups: 18 to 24 years, 25 to 44 years, 45 to 64 years, and 65 years and over]

Therapy	2002 Number (1,000)	2002 Percent	2007 Number (1,000)	2007 Percent
Alternative medical systems:				
Acupuncture	2,136	1.1	3,141	1.4
Homeopathic treatment	3,433	1.7	3,909	1.8
Biologically based therapies:				
Nonvitamin, nonmineral, natural products [1]	38,183	18.9	38,797	17.7
Diet-based therapies [2, 3]	7,099	3.5	7,893	3.6
Vegetarian diet	3,184	1.6	3,351	1.5
Atkins diet	3,417	1.7	2,673	1.2
South Beach	(X)	(X)	2,334	1.1
Megavitamin therapy	5,739	2.8	(X)	(X)
Manipulative and body-based therapies:				
Chiropractic care [4]	15,226	7.5	(X)	(X)
Chiropractic or Osteopathic manipulation [4]	(X)	(X)	18,740	8.6
Massage	10,052	5.0	18,068	8.3
Movement therapies	(X)	(X)	3,146	1.5
Pilates	(X)	(X)	3,015	1.4
Mind-body therapies:				
Meditation	15,336	7.6	20,541	9.4
Guided imagery	4,194	2.1	4,866	2.2
Progressive relaxation	6,185	3.0	6,454	2.9
Deep breathing exercises	23,457	11.6	27,794	12.7
Yoga	10,386	5.1	13,172	6.1
Tai chi	2,565	1.3	2,267	1.0

X Not applicable.   [1] While questions were asked about nonvitamin, nonmineral, natural products in both 2002 and 2007, the data are not comparable due primarily to question order and the specific nonvitamin, nonmineral, natural product covered.   [2] The totals of the numbers and percents of the categories listed under "Diet-based therapies" are greater than the number and percent of their respective category heading because respondents could choose more than one of the categories.   [3] While questions were asked about Diet-based therapies in both 2002 and 2007, the data are not comparable because respondents were asked about the South Beach Diet in 2007, but not in 2002.   [4] While questions were asked about chiropractic therapy in both 2002 and 2007, the data are not comparable because respondents were asked about chiropractic care in 2002 and chiropractic or osteopathic manipulation in 2007.

Source: U.S. National Center for Health Statistics, National Health Statistics Reports, Number 12, December 10, 2008; <http://www.cdc.gov/nchs/data/nhsr/nhsr012.pdf>.

Table 162. **Ambulatory Care Visits to Physicians' Offices and Hospital Outpatient and Emergency Departments: 2007**

[(1,200.0 represents 1,200,000,000). Based on the annual National Ambulatory Medical Care Survey and National Hospital Ambulatory Medical Care Survey and subject to sampling error; see source for details]

Characteristic	Number of visits (mil.)				Visits per 100 persons			
	Total	Physi-cian offices	Outpa-tient dept.	Emer-gency dept.	Total	Physi-cian offices	Outpa-tient dept.	Emer-gency dept.
Total	**1,200.0**	**994.3**	**88.9**	**116.8**	**405.0**	**335.6**	**30.0**	**39.4**
Age:								
Under 15 years old	205.8	167.5	16.0	22.3	338.2	275.3	26.3	36.7
15 to 24 years old	111.2	81.6	10.6	19.0	267.9	196.6	25.6	45.7
25 to 44 years old	259.3	203.2	22.7	33.5	317.5	248.8	27.8	41.0
45 to 64 years old	334.1	283.9	25.7	24.5	439.3	373.3	33.8	32.2
65 to 74 years old	142.5	127.8	7.8	6.9	745.9	668.9	40.9	36.2
75 years old and over	147.2	130.4	6.1	10.6	858.7	761.0	35.7	62.0
Sex:								
Male	500.8	413.8	33.4	53.6	345.3	285.3	23.0	37.0
Female	699.2	580.5	55.5	63.2	462.3	383.8	36.7	41.8
Race: [2]								
White	966.2	818.2	62.8	85.2	406.9	344.6	26.5	35.9
Black/African American.	168.0	118.3	21.8	27.9	449.9	316.8	58.4	74.6
Asian	44.9	40.6	2.1	2.1	337.4	305.4	15.9	16.0
Native Hawaiian/Other Pacific Islander.	4.3	3.6	[1]0.3	0.3	807.0	686.4	[1]61.4	59.2
American Indian/Alaska Native.	12.5	10.9	[1]0.6	[1]1.0	433.1	377.0	[1]20.4	[1]35.7
More than one race reported	4.2	2.7	[1]1.2	0.3	86.7	55.1	[1]25.7	5.9
Expected sources of payment: [3]								
Private insurance	722.0	640.9	35.5	45.6	(X)	(X)	(X)	(X)
Medicare	274.9	239.1	15.7	20.1	(X)	(X)	(X)	(X)
Medicaid/CHIP [4]	181.2	122.4	29.5	29.4	(X)	(X)	(X)	(X)
Worker's compensation	15.2	12.5	0.9	1.8	(X)	(X)	(X)	(X)
No insurance: [5]	74.9	48.7	8.3	17.9	(X)	(X)	(X)	(X)
Self pay	68.2	45.6	5.6	17.0	(X)	(X)	(X)	(X)
No charge	7.5	3.5	[1]2.8	1.2	(X)	(X)	(X)	(X)
Other	34.9	27.6	4.6	2.8	(X)	(X)	(X)	(X)
Unknown	54.3	39.9	3.9	10.5	(X)	(X)	(X)	(X)

X Not applicable. [1] Figures do not meet standard of reliability or precision. [2] Race data were missing for 28.7 percent of ambulatory care visits, including 31.5 percent of visits to physician offices, 15.8 percent of visits to hospital outpatient departments, and 14.9 percent of visits to emergency departments. Missing data were imputed, and readers are advised to treat the resulting estimates with caution. More information is available at the website below. [3] Starting with 2006 data, more than one source of payment could be reported per visit. Prior years showed primary source only. [4] CHIP is Children's Health Insurance Program. [5] "No insurance" is defined as having only "self-pay" or "no charge/charity" as payment sources.

Source: U.S. National Center for Health Statistics, National Health Statistics Reports, forthcoming; <http://www.cdc.gov/nchs/ahcd.htm>.

Table 163. **Visits to Office-Based Physicians and Hospital Outpatient Departments by Diagnosis: 2002 and 2007**

[393.2 represents 393,200,000). See headnote, Table 162]

Leading diagnosis [1]	Number (mil.)		Rate per 1,000 persons [2]		Leading diagnosis [1]	Number (mil.)		Rate per 1,000 persons [2]	
	2002	2007	2002	2007		2002	2007	2002	2007
Male, all ages	**393.2**	**447.2**	**2,848**	**3,083**	**Female, all ages**	**580.1**	**636.0**	**4,001**	**4,205**
Under 15 years old [3]	**92.3**	**97.2**	**2,979**	**3,122**	**Under 15 years old** [3]	**85.8**	**86.3**	**2,901**	**2,904**
Routine infant or child health check	19.6	20.4	632	654	Routine infant or child health check	18.1	20.1	613	675
Acute upper respiratory infections [4]	8.3	9.3	268	298	Acute upper respiratory infections [4]	7.6	8.6	256	288
Otitis media and Eusta-chian tube disorders	7.0	6.4	226	207	Otitis media and Eusta-chian tube disorders	6.8	5.1	231	173
Asthma	2.8	4.7	90	150	Acute pharyngitis	3.4	3.0	116	101
15 to 44 years old [3]	**100.4**	**105.4**	**1,654**	**1,715**	**15 to 44 years old** [3]	**194.8**	**212.6**	**3,160**	**3,445**
General medical examina-tion	4.8	4.5	80	74	Normal pregnancy	19.7	19.5	320	316
Spinal disorders.	3.3	4.3	54	69	Gynecological examination. .	7.7	8.6	126	140
Acute respiratory infec-tions [4]	3.6	3.9	59	63	Complications of preg-the puerperium.	4.8	7.1	79	116
Essential hypertension . . .	2.4	3.9	39	54	General medical examina-tion	6.2	6.2	100	100
45 to 64 years old [3]	**106.3**	**127.4**	**3,313**	**3,447**	**45 to 64 years old** [3]	**157.3**	**182.2**	**4,611**	**4,660**
Essential hypertension . . .	10.2	9.4	318	256	Essential hypertension . . .	11.4	9.7	335	249
Diabetes mellitus	5.7	6.4	179	173	Spinal disorders.	4.3	7.2	127	184
Spinal disorders.	4.1	5.5	128	150	Rheumatism, excluding back.	4.5	6.5	132	166
Arthropathies and related disorders.	3.9	4.9	121	132	Malignant neoplasms	3.4	5.5	101	140
65 years old and over [3] . . .	**94.3**	**117.2**	**6,578**	**7,549**	**65 years old and over** [3] . . .	**142.1**	**154.9**	**7,238**	**7,478**
Malignant neoplasms	5.5	8.4	382	540	Essential hypertension . . .	16.9	12.7	860	614
Essential hypertension . . .	8.0	7.7	557	498	Malignant neoplasms	4.5	7.5	230	360
Diabetes mellitus	6.3	5.7	440	369	Diabetes mellitus	6.3	6.2	321	298
Ischemic heart disease . . .	4.8	5.4	336	349					

[1] Based on the International Classification of Diseases, 9th Revision, clinical modification, (ICD-9-CM). [2] Based on U.S. Census Bureau estimated civilian population as of July 1. [3] Includes other first-listed diagnoses, not shown separately. [4] Excluding pharyngitis.

Source: U.S. National Center for Health Statistics, National Health Statistics Reports, forthcoming; <http://www.cdc.gov/nchs/ahcd.htm>.

Health and Nutrition 113

Table 164. Visits to Hospital Emergency Departments by Diagnosis: 2007

[53,632 represents 53,632,000. See headnote, Table 162]

Leading diagnosis [1]	Number (1,000)	Rate per 1,000 persons [2]	Leading diagnosis [1]	Number (1,000)	Rate per 1,000 persons [2]
MALE			**FEMALE**		
All ages	**53,632**	**372**	**All ages**	**63,170**	**421**
Under 15 years old [3]	**12,233**	**394**	**Under 15 years old [3]**	**10,072**	**340**
Acute upper respiratory infections [4]	1,249	40	Acute respiratory infections [4]	929	31
Otitis media and Eustachian tube disorders	944	30	Otitis media and Eustachian tube disorders	614	21
Open wound of head	651	21	Unspecified viral and chlamydial infections	503	17
Contusion with intact skin surface	583	19	Contusion with intact skin surface	451	15
Pyrexia of unknown origin	541	17	Pyrexia of unknown origin	433	15
15 to 44 years old [3]	**22,685**	**368**	**15 to 44 years old [3]**	**29,780**	**481**
Open wound, excluding head	1,259	20	Abdominal pain	1,947	31
Contusions with intact skin surfaces	1,050	17	Complications of pregnancy, childbirth and the puerperium	1,784	29
Sprains and strains, excluding ankle and back	744	13	Contusions with intact skin surfaces	1,074	17
Chest pain	724	12	Chest pain	882	14
Cellulitis and abscess	716	12	Sprains and strains of neck and back	880	14
45 to 64 years old [3]	**11,715**	**324**	**45 to 64 years old [3]**	**12,776**	**334**
Chest pain	697	19	Chest pain	690	18
Open wound, excluding head	557	15	Abdominal pain	650	17
Spinal disorders	416	12	Spinal disorders	482	13
Cellulitis and abscess	402	11	Contusion with intact skin surface	429	11
Contusion with intact skin surface	375	10	Arthropathies and related disorders	357	9
65 years old and over [3]	**6,999**	**460**	**65 years old and over [3]**	**10,541**	**517**
Heart disease, excluding ischemic	461	30	Chest pain	576	28
Chest pain	422	28	Contusion with intact skin surface	548	27
Pneumonia	225	15	Heart disease, excluding ischemic	520	25
Cellulitis and abscess	206	14	Urinary tract infection site not specified	391	19
Open wound, excluding head	197	13	Abdominal pain	322	16

[1] Based on the International Classification of Diseases, 9th Revision, Clinical Modification (ICD-9-CM). [2] Based on U.S. Census Bureau estimated civilian noninstitutional population as of July 1. [3] Includes other first-listed diagnosis, not shown separately. [4] Excluding pharyngitis.

Source: U.S. National Center for Health Statistics, *National Health Statistics Reports*, forthcoming. See <http://www.cdc.gov/nchs/ahcd.htm>.

Table 165. Procedures for Inpatients Discharged From Short-Stay Hospitals: 1990 to 2006

[(23,051 represents 23,051,000). Procedure categories are based on the International Classification of Diseases, 9th Revision, Clinical Modification. See headnote, Table 170]

Sex and type of procedure	Number of procedures (1,000)				Rate per 1,000 population[1]			
	1990	1995	2000	2006	1990	1995	2000	2006
Surgical procedures, total [2]	**23,051**	**22,530**	**23,244**	**28,036**	**92.4**	**86.2**	**83.6**	**94.0**
Coronary artery bypass graft [3]	392	573	519	444	1.6	2.2	1.9	1.5
Cesarean section	945	785	855	1,295	3.8	3.0	3.1	4.3
Repair of current obstetric laceration	795	964	1,136	1,308	3.2	3.7	4.1	4.4
Cardiac catheterization	995	1,068	1,221	1,115	4.0	4.1	4.4	3.7
Reduction of fracture [4]	609	577	628	672	2.4	2.2	2.3	2.3
Male, total [2]	**8,538**	**8,388**	**8,689**	**11,199**	**70.6**	**65.9**	**63.9**	**76.4**
Reduction of fracture [4]	312	292	285	326	2.6	2.3	2.1	2.2
Cardiac catheterization	620	660	732	666	5.1	5.2	5.4	4.5
Coronary artery bypass graft [3]	286	423	371	320	2.4	3.3	2.7	2.2
Female, total [2]	**14,513**	**14,142**	**14,556**	**16,837**	**113.0**	**105.3**	**102.4**	**111.0**
Cesarean section	945	785	855	1,295	7.4	5.8	6.0	8.5
Repair of current obstetric laceration	795	964	1,136	1,308	6.2	7.2	8.0	8.6
Hysterectomy	591	583	633	569	4.6	4.3	4.5	3.8
Diagnostic and other nonsurgical procedures [5]	**17,455**	**17,278**	**16,737**	**17,927**	**70.0**	**66.1**	**60.2**	**60.1**
Angiocardiography and arteriography [6]	1,735	1,834	2,005	1,698	7.0	7.0	7.2	5.7
Respiratory therapy	1,164	1,127	991	1,088	4.7	4.3	3.6	3.6
Manual assisted delivery	750	866	898	1,207	3.0	3.3	3.2	4.0
Diagnostic ultrasound	1,608	1,181	886	888	6.4	4.5	3.2	3.0
Fetal electrocardiogram and fetal monitoring	1,377	935	750	797	5.6	3.6	2.7	2.7
Male, total [5]	**7,378**	**7,261**	**6,965**	**7,283**	**61.0**	**57.1**	**51.2**	**49.7**
Angiocardiography and arteriography [6]	1,051	1,076	1,157	938	8.7	8.5	8.5	6.4
Respiratory therapy	586	572	507	561	4.9	4.5	3.7	3.8
Computerized Axial Tomographic scan	736	473	345	366	6.1	3.7	2.5	2.5
Female, total [5]	**10,077**	**10,016**	**9,772**	**10,645**	**78.5**	**74.6**	**68.8**	**70.2**
Manual assisted delivery	750	866	898	1,207	5.9	6.5	6.3	8.0
Fetal EKG and fetal monitoring	1,377	935	750	797	10.8	7.0	5.5	5.3
Respiratory therapy	578	555	484	527	4.5	4.1	3.4	3.5
Diagnostic ultrasound	941	682	501	477	7.3	5.1	3.5	3.1

[1] Based on Census Bureau estimated civilian population as of July 1. Population estimates based on the 1990 census were used to calculate rates for 1990 through 2000. Population estimates based on the 2000 census were used to calculate rates for 2001 through 2006. [2] Includes other types of surgical procedures not shown separately. [3] It is possible for a discharge to have more than one of these recorded. [4] Excluding skull, nose, and jaw. [5] Includes other nonsurgical procedures not shown separately. [6] Using contrast material.

Source: U.S. National Center for Health Statistics, *Vital and Health Statistics*, Series 13 and unpublished data; <http://www.cdc.gov/nchs/products/pubs/pubd/series/ser.htm>.

114   Health and Nutrition

Table 166. Hospitals—Summary Characteristics: 1990 to 2007

[For beds, (1,213 represents 1,213,000). Covers hospitals accepted for registration by the American Hospital Association; see text, this section. Short-term hospitals have an average patient stay of less than 30 days; long-term, an average stay of longer duration. Special hospitals include obstetrics and gynecology; eye, ear, nose, and throat; rehabilitation, orthopedic, chronic, and other special hospitals except psychiatric, tuberculosis, alcoholism, and chemical dependency hospitals]

Item	1990	1995	2000	2002	2003	2004	2005	2006	2007
Number:									
All hospitals	6,649	6,291	5,810	5,794	5,764	5,759	5,756	5,747	5,708
With 100 beds or more	3,620	3,376	3,102	3,032	3,007	2,972	2,942	2,928	2,901
Nonfederal [1]	6,312	5,992	5,565	5,554	5,525	5,520	5,530	5,526	5,495
Community hospitals [2]	5,384	5,194	4,915	4,927	4,895	4,919	4,936	4,927	4,897
Nongovernmental nonprofit	3,191	3,092	3,003	3,025	2,984	2,967	2,958	2,919	2,913
For profit	749	752	749	766	790	835	868	889	873
State and local government	1,444	1,350	1,163	1,136	1,121	1,117	1,110	1,119	1,111
Long-term general and special	131	112	131	124	126	108	115	127	135
Psychiatric	757	657	496	477	477	466	456	462	444
Tuberculosis	4	3	4	4	4	4	4	3	2
Federal	337	299	245	240	239	239	226	221	213
Beds (1,000): [3]									
All hospitals	1,213	1,081	984	976	965	956	947	947	945
Rate per 1,000 population [4]	4.9	4.1	3.5	3.4	3.3	3.3	3.2	3.2	3.1
Beds per hospital	182	172	169	168	167	166	165	164	166
Nonfederal [1]	1,113	1,004	931	926	917	908	901	901	899
Community hospitals [2]	927	873	824	821	813	808	802	802	801
Rate per 1,000 population [4]	3.7	3.3	2.9	2.8	2.8	2.8	2.7	2.7	2.7
Nongovernmental nonprofit	657	610	583	582	575	567	561	559	554
For profit	102	106	110	108	110	112	114	115	116
State and local government	169	157	131	130	120	127	128	128	131
Long-term general and special	25	19	18	18	18	15	15	16	17
Psychiatric	158	110	87	85	85	86	82	84	79
Tuberculosis	(Z)	(Z)	(Z)	(Z)	(Z)	(Z)	(Z)	(Z)	(Z)
Federal	98	78	53	50	47	58	46	46	46
Average daily census (1,000): [5]									
All hospitals	844	710	650	662	657	658	656	653	645
Community hospitals [2]	619	548	526	540	539	541	540	538	533
Nongovernmental nonprofit	455	393	382	391	389	388	388	384	380
For profit	54	55	61	64	65	68	68	67	66
State and local government	111	100	83	84	84	84	85	86	87
Expenses (bil. dol.): [6]									
All hospitals	234.9	320.3	395.4	462.2	498.1	533.8	570.5	607.3	638.5
Nonfederal [1]	219.6	300.0	371.5	432.5	467.2	499.0	533.7	560.8	599.7
Community hospitals [2]	203.7	285.6	356.6	416.6	450.1	481.2	515.7	551.8	581.0
Nongovernmental nonprofit	150.7	209.6	267.1	312.7	337.7	359.4	386.0	412.8	435.5
For profit	18.8	26.7	35.0	40.1	44.0	48.9	51.8	54.9	55.8
State and local government	34.2	49.3	54.5	63.8	68.4	72.8	77.9	83.9	89.8
Long-term general and special	2.7	2.2	2.8	3.6	3.6	3.6	3.6	4.0	3.9
Psychiatric	12.9	11.7	11.9	12.1	13.1	13.8	13.9	15.0	14.5
Tuberculosis	0.1	0.4	(Z)	(Z)	(Z)	(Z)	(Z)	(Z)	(Z)
Federal	15.2	20.2	23.9	29.7	30.9	34.8	36.8	37.5	38.8
Personnel (1,000): [7]									
All hospitals	4,063	4,273	4,454	4,610	4,650	4,695	4,790	4,907	5,024
Nonfederal [1]	3,760	3,971	4,157	4,312	4,350	4,379	4,479	4,569	4,699
Community hospitals [2]	3,420	3,714	3,911	4,069	4,108	4,147	4,260	4,343	4,465
Nongovernmental nonprofit	2,533	2,702	2,919	3,039	3,058	3,076	3,154	3,207	3,286
For profit	273	343	378	380	391	405	421	423	432
State and local government	614	670	614	651	658	665	681	713	747
Long-term general and special	55	38	41	46	45	42	38	43	44
Psychiatric	280	215	200	193	194	185	182	193	187
Tuberculosis	1	1	1	1	1	1	1	1	1
Federal	303	301	297	299	300	315	311	338	325
Outpatient visits (mil.)	368.2	483.2	592.7	640.5	648.6	662.1	673.7	690.4	693.5
Emergency	92.8	99.9	106.9	114.2	115.1	116.9	118.9	122.6	124.7

Z Less than 500 beds or $50 million.   [1] Includes hospital units of institutions.   [2] Short-term (average length of stay less than 30 days) general and special (e.g., obstetrics and gynecology; eye, ear, nose and throat; rehabilitation, etc. except psychiatric, tuberculosis, alcoholism, and chemical dependency). Excludes hospital units of institutions.   [3] Number of beds at end of reporting period.   [4] Based on Census Bureau estimated resident population as of July 1. 1990 and 2000 based on enumerated resident population as of April 1. Estimates reflect revisions based on the 2000 census of population.   [5] The average number of people served on an inpatient basis on a single day during the reporting period.   [6] Excludes new construction.   [7] Includes full-time equivalents of part-time personnel.

Source: Health Forum, An American Hospital Association Company, Chicago, IL, *AHA Hospital Statistics 2009 Edition,* and prior years (copyright); <http://www.ahadata.com/>.

Table 167. **Average Cost to Community Hospitals Per Patient: 1990 to 2007**

[In dollars, except percent. Covers nonfederal short-term general or special hospitals (excluding psychiatric or tuberculosis hospitals and hospital units of institutions). Total cost per patient based on total hospital expenses (payroll, employee benefits, professional fees, supplies, etc.). Data have been adjusted for outpatient visits]

Type of expense and hospital	1990	1995	2000	2001	2002	2003	2004	2005	2006	2007
Average cost per day, total......	687	968	1,149	1,217	1,290	1,379	1,450	1,522	1,612	1,690
Annual percent change [1].......	7.8	4.0	4.2	5.9	6.0	6.9	5.1	5.0	5.9	4.8
Nongovernmental nonprofit	692	994	1,182	1,255	1,329	1,429	1,501	1,585	1,686	1,772
For profit...................	752	947	1,057	1,121	1,181	1,264	1,362	1,412	1,472	1,519
State and local government	635	878	1,064	1,114	1,188	1,238	1,291	1,329	1,400	1,460
Average cost per stay, total	4,947	6,216	6,649	6,980	7,346	7,796	8,166	8,793	8,970	9,342
Nongovernmental nonprofit	5,001	6,279	6,717	7,052	7,458	7,905	8,266	8,670	9,190	9,574
For profit...................	4,727	5,425	5,642	5,972	6,161	6,590	7,139	7,351	7,422	7,740
State and local government	4,838	6,445	7,106	7,400	7,773	8,205	8,473	8,793	9,147	9,446

[1] Change from immediate prior year.

Source: Health Forum, An American Hospital Association Company, Chicago, IL, *AHA Hospital Statistics 2009 Edition*, and prior years (copyright); <http://www.ahadata.com/>.

Table 168. **Community Hospitals—States: 2000 and 2007**

[In thousands, (823.6 represents 823,600). For definition of community hospitals see footnote 2, Table 166]

State	Number of hospitals		Beds (1,000)		Patients admitted (1,000)		Average daily census [1] (1,000)		Outpatient visits (mil.)		Average cost per day (dol.)	
	2000	2007	2000	2007	2000	2007	2000	2007	2000	2007	2000	2007
United States ...	4,915	4,897	823.6	800.9	33,089	35,346	525.7	533.3	521.4	603.3	1,149	1,690
Alabama.........	108	109	16.4	15.7	680	696	9.8	9.7	8.0	8.2	980	1,332
Alaska..........	18	22	1.4	1.6	47	57	0.8	0.9	1.3	1.8	1,495	2,104
Arizona.........	61	66	10.9	12.2	539	675	6.8	8.4	5.3	7.3	1,311	2,039
Arkansas	83	84	9.8	9.5	368	366	5.7	5.2	4.4	5.2	908	1,353
California	389	355	72.7	69.3	3,315	3,276	47.8	47.0	44.9	45.9	1,438	2,165
Colorado.........	69	75	9.4	9.7	397	426	5.4	6.6	6.7	7.8	1,280	1,998
Connecticut.......	35	34	7.7	7.5	349	397	5.8	5.8	6.7	7.6	1,373	1,988
Delaware	5	6	1.8	2.3	83	107	1.4	1.8	1.5	1.8	1,311	1,778
District of Columbia .	11	10	3.3	3.4	129	136	2.5	2.5	1.3	2.4	1,512	2,381
Florida	202	200	51.2	51.6	2,119	2,388	31.0	33.9	21.8	23.5	1,161	1,652
Georgia	151	147	23.9	25.5	863	964	15.0	17.2	11.2	13.8	978	1,279
Hawaii	21	23	3.1	2.9	100	111	2.3	2.1	2.5	1.9	1,088	1,556
Idaho...........	42	39	3.5	3.3	123	134	1.8	1.8	2.2	2.9	1,003	1,643
Illinois	196	190	37.3	34.6	1,531	1,606	22.4	22.2	25.1	30.7	1,278	1,799
Indiana..........	109	114	19.2	17.0	700	691	10.8	9.6	14.1	16.7	1,132	1,849
Iowa	115	117	11.8	10.5	360	368	6.8	6.2	9.2	10.6	740	1,132
Kansas	129	128	10.8	10.1	310	325	5.7	5.5	5.3	6.4	837	1,093
Kentucky	105	104	14.8	14.4	582	612	9.1	8.7	8.7	9.5	929	1,390
Louisiana	123	129	17.5	15.5	654	631	9.8	9.4	10.0	10.4	1,075	1,417
Maine..........	37	37	3.7	3.5	147	152	2.4	2.3	3.2	4.7	1,148	1,729
Maryland	49	49	11.2	11.7	587	698	8.2	8.9	6.0	7.3	1,315	2,113
Massachusetts.....	80	78	16.6	16.5	740	842	11.7	12.0	16.7	19.6	1,467	2,113
Michigan.........	146	143	26.1	25.4	1,106	1,204	16.9	17.2	24.9	27.9	1,211	1,642
Minnesota........	135	131	16.7	15.8	571	635	11.2	10.8	7.3	9.9	932	1,500
Mississippi	95	95	13.6	12.7	425	418	8.0	7.3	3.7	4.4	719	1,179
Missouri.........	119	117	20.1	18.5	773	833	11.7	11.8	14.8	17.0	1,185	1,768
Montana.........	52	52	4.3	4.0	99	107	2.9	2.6	2.6	3.0	579	975
Nebraska........	85	85	8.2	7.5	209	215	4.8	4.4	3.4	4.2	743	1,250
Nevada	22	33	3.8	5.1	199	244	2.7	3.5	2.2	2.7	1,285	1,875
New Hampshire....	28	28	2.9	2.8	111	122	1.7	1.8	2.8	4.1	1,201	1,854
New Jersey.......	80	73	25.3	21.5	1,074	1,084	17.3	15.4	16.3	17.1	1,299	2,014
New Mexico	35	35	3.5	3.7	174	170	2.0	2.0	3.1	4.1	1,388	1,900
New York	215	202	66.4	62.4	2,416	2,541	52.1	50.3	46.4	53.1	1,118	1,673
North Carolina.....	113	113	23.1	23.2	971	1,028	16.0	16.6	12.4	14.8	1,061	1,433
North Dakota......	42	41	3.9	3.5	89	89	2.3	2.1	1.7	1.8	747	958
Ohio...........	163	171	33.8	32.9	1,404	1,542	20.6	21.2	26.9	33.1	1,198	1,833
Oklahoma........	108	113	11.1	10.9	429	454	6.2	6.5	4.7	5.3	1,031	1,424
Oregon..........	59	58	6.6	6.8	330	347	3.9	4.2	7.3	8.2	1,461	2,336
Pennsylvania......	207	187	42.3	39.7	1,796	1,880	28.8	28.1	31.8	36.8	1,080	1,626
Rhode Island......	11	11	2.4	2.4	119	129	1.7	1.8	2.1	2.6	1,313	1,923
South Carolina.....	63	67	11.5	12.0	495	519	8.0	8.2	7.8	6.0	1,101	1,557
South Dakota......	48	51	4.3	4.2	99	100	2.8	2.8	1.7	1.8	476	869
Tennessee	121	133	20.6	21.7	737	970	11.5	14.7	10.3	11.8	1,078	1,396
Texas...........	403	409	55.9	58.1	2,367	2,468	33.1	35.1	29.4	32.5	1,274	1,806
Utah	42	41	4.3	4.6	194	224	2.4	2.7	4.5	5.0	1,375	1,959
Vermont.........	14	14	1.7	1.4	52	50	1.1	0.9	1.2	2.8	888	1,434
Virginia.........	88	87	16.9	16.9	727	787	11.4	11.9	9.5	12.9	1,057	1,622
Washington.......	84	87	11.1	11.3	505	574	6.6	7.1	9.6	11.2	1,511	2,332
West Virginia......	57	56	8.0	7.5	288	287	4.8	4.6	5.2	6.5	844	1,176
Wisconsin........	118	124	15.3	14.0	558	613	9.1	8.7	10.9	13.1	1,055	1,682
Wyoming	24	24	1.9	2.0	48	53	1.1	1.2	0.9	1.0	677	887

[1] The average number of people served on an inpatient basis on a single day during the reporting period.

Source: Health Forum, An American Hospital Association Company, Chicago, IL, *AHA Hospital Statistics 2009 Edition*, and prior years (copyright).

Table 169. **Hospital Use Rates by Type of Hospital: 1990 to 2007**

Type of hospital	1990	1995	2000	2003	2004	2005	2006	2007
Community hospitals: [1]								
Admissions per 1,000 population [2]	125	116	117	120	119	119	118	117
Admissions per bed	34	35	40	43	43	44	44	43
Average length of stay (days) [3]	7.2	6.5	5.8	5.7	5.6	5.6	5.5	5.5
Outpatient visits per admission	9.7	13.4	15.8	16.2	16.3	16.5	16.9	17.1
Outpatient visits per 1,000 population [2]	1,207	1,556	1,852	1,937	1,946	1,976	2,002	2,000
Surgical operations (million [4])	21.9	23.2	26.1	27.1	27.4	27.5	28.1	28.1
Number per admission	0.7	0.7	0.8	0.8	0.8	0.8	0.7	0.8
Nonfederal psychiatric:								
Admissions per 1,000 population [2]	2.9	2.7	2.4	2.6	2.7	2.5	2.3	2.3
Days in hospital per 1,000 population [2]	190	122	93	91	88	89	82	82

[1] Short term (average length of stay less than 30 days) general and special (e.g., obstetrics and gynecology; eye, ear, nose and throat; rehabilitation, etc. except psychiatric, tuberculosis, alcoholism and chemical dependency). Excludes hospital units of institutions. [2] Based on U.S. Census Bureau estimated resident population as of July 1. Estimates reflect revisions based on the 2000 census of population. 1990 and 2000 based on enumerated resident population as of April 1. [3] Number of inpatient days divided by number of admissions. [4] 21.9 represents 21,900,000.

Source: Health Forum, An American Hospital Association Company, Chicago, IL, *AHA Hospital Statistics 2009 Edition* and prior years (copyright); <http://www.healthforum.com/>.

Table 170. **Hospital Utilization Rates by Sex: 1990 to 2006**

[(30,788 represents 30,788,000). Represents estimates of inpatients discharged from noninstitutional, short-stay hospitals, exclusive of federal hospitals. Excludes newborn infants. Based on sample data collected from the National Hospital Discharge Survey, a sample survey of hospital records of patients discharged in year shown; subject to sampling variability]

Item and sex	1990	1995	2000	2001	2002	2003	2004	2005	2006
Patients discharged (1,000).	30,788	30,722	31,706	32,653	33,727	34,738	34,864	34,667	34,854
Patients discharged per 1,000 persons,									
total [1]	122	116	114	115	118	120	119	117	117
Male	100	94	92	93	95	98	97	96	95
Female	143	136	135	137	139	141	141	138	138
Days of care per 1,000 persons, total [1] . .	784	620	560	562	572	578	574	562	558
Male	694	551	491	490	506	507	505	498	495
Female	869	686	627	631	635	646	641	624	619
Average stay (days).	6.4	5.4	4.9	4.9	4.9	4.8	4.8	4.8	4.8
Male	6.9	5.8	5.3	5.3	5.3	5.2	5.2	5.2	5.2
Female	6.1	5.0	4.6	4.6	4.6	4.6	4.5	4.5	4.5

[1] Rates are computed using Census Bureau estimates of the civilian population as of July 1. Rates for 1990 and 1995 were based on population estimates adjusted for the net underenumeration in the 1990 census. Rates for 2000 and later were calculated using 2000-based postcensal estimates.

Source: U.S. National Center for Health Statistics, *Vital and Health Statistics,* Series 13 and unpublished data; <http://www.cdc.gov/nchs/products/series.htm>.

Table 171. **Hospital Utilization Measures for HIV Patients: 1990 to 2006**

[HIV represents human immunodeficiency virus. See headnote, Table 170]

Measure of utilization	Unit	1990	1995	2000	2004	2005	2006
Number of patients discharged	1,000. . . .	146	249	173	204	185	223
Male.	1,000. . . .	114	183	115	132	113	145
Female	1,000. . . .	32	66	58	73	72	78
Rate of patient discharges [1]	Rate	5.8	9.4	6.2	7.0	6.3	7.5
Number of days of care.	1,000. . . .	2,188	2,326	1,257	1,477	1,244	1,418
Male.	1,000. . . .	1,777	1,649	895	876	751	907
Female	1,000. . . .	411	677	362	601	493	511
Rate of days of care [1]	Rate	86.9	87.6	45.2	50.5	42.2	47.6
Average length of stay	Days	14.9	9.3	7.3	7.2	6.7	6.3
Male.	Days	15.5	9.0	7.8	6.7	6.7	6.2
Female	Days	12.9	10.3	6.3	8.3	6.8	6.5

[1] Per 10,000 population. Based on Census Bureau estimated civilian population as of July 1. Populations for 1990 and 1995 were adjusted for the net underenumeration in the 1990 census. Populations for 2000 and later were 2000-based postcensal estimates.

Source: National Center for Health Statistics, *Vital and Health Statistics,* Series 13 and unpublished data; <http://www.cdc.gov/nchs/products/series.htm>.

U.S. Census Bureau, Statistical Abstract of the United States: 2010

Table 172. Hospital Discharges and Days of Care: 2002 and 2006

[(33,727 represents 33,727,000). See headnote, Table 170. For composition of regions, see map, inside front cover]

Age, race, and region	Discharges Number (1,000)		Discharges Per 1,000 persons [1]		Days of care per 1,000 persons [1]		Average stay (days)	
	2002	2006	2002	2006	2002	2006	2002	2006
Total [2]	33,727	34,854	118	117	572	558	4.9	4.8
Age:								
Under 1 year old.	810	751	201	182	1,134	1,162	5.6	6.4
1 to 4 years old	713	682	46	42	159	141	3.5	3.4
5 to 14 years old	1,016	865	25	21	109	97	4.4	4.5
15 to 24 years old.	3,083	3,132	77	75	266	264	3.5	3.5
25 to 34 years old.	3,897	4,045	99	101	328	346	3.3	3.4
35 to 44 years old.	3,757	3,623	84	84	368	358	4.4	4.3
45 to 64 years old.	7,723	8,686	116	116	575	579	5.0	5.0
65 to 74 years old.	4,642	4,793	254	253	1,412	1,317	5.6	5.2
75 years old and over	8,085	8,278	467	451	2,795	2,541	6.0	5.6
Race:								
White	20,806	20,907	90	88	436	414	4.9	4.7
Black	3,995	4,241	109	111	584	621	5.3	5.6
Asian/Pacific Islander.	538	619	45	45	243	244	5.4	5.4
American Indian/Eskimo/ Aleut.	173	103	63	36	330	151	5.2	4.2
Region:								
Northeast	6,990	7,277	129	133	727	703	5.6	5.3
Midwest	7,503	7,951	115	120	512	508	4.4	4.2
South	12,994	13,140	127	121	618	595	4.9	4.9
West.	6,239	6,486	96	94	430	432	4.5	4.6

[1] Rates were calculated using U.S. Census Bureau 2000-based postcensal estimates of the civilian population as of July 1.
[2] Includes other races not shown separately.

Source: U.S. National Center for Health Statistics, Vital and Health Statistics, Series 13 and unpublished data; <http://www.cdc.gov/nchs/products/series.htm>.

Table 173. Hospital Discharges and Days of Care by Selected Diagnosis: 2006

[(13,990 represents 13,990,000). Represents estimates of inpatients discharged from noninstitutional, short-stay hospitals, exclusive of federal hospitals. Excludes newborn infants. Diagnostic categories are based on the International Classification of Diseases, Ninth Revision, Clinical Modification. See headnote, Table 170]

Sex, age, and selected first-listed diagnosis [1]	Discharges Number (1,000)	Per 1,000 persons [2]	Average stay (days)	Sex, age, and selected first-listed diagnosis [1]	Discharges Number (1,000)	Per 1,000 persons [2]	Average stay (days)
Male				**Female**			
All ages [4]	13,990	95.5	5.2	All ages, [4]	20,864	137.5	4.5
Under 18 years [4]	1,515	40.2	4.9	Under 18 years [4].	1,389	38.6	4.5
Injury	167	4.4	[5]3.9	Injury	82	2.3	[5]3.9
Pneumonia	101	2.7	[5]3.3	Pneumonia	79	2.2	3.5
Asthma	[5]99	[5]2.6	[5]2.1	Acute bronchitis and bronchiolitis	[5]69	[5]1.91	[5]2.9
18–44 years [4]	2,701	47.7	5.0	18–44 years [4]	7,492	134.4	3.2
Injury	398	7.0	4.8	Childbirth	3,980	71.4	2.6
Serious mental illness (psychoses) [6]	336	5.9	8.2	Serious mental illness (psychoses) [6]	370	6.6	7.1
Alcohol and drug [7].	186	3.3	[5]4.4	Injury	176	3.2	3.7
Heart disease.	173	3.1	3.7	Uterine fibroids	103	1.8	2.4
45–64 years [4]	4,287	117.6	5.1	45–64 years [4]	4,399	114.7	4.9
Heart disease.	803	22.0	3.7	Heart disease.	481	12.6	4.2
Injury	252	6.9	6.6	Serious mental illness (psychoses) [6]	243	6.3	8.9
Cancer, all	222	6.1	6.6	Cancer, all	217	5.7	5.8
Serious mental illness (psychoses) [6]	179	4.9	8.8	Osteoarthritis	191	5.0	3.8
65–74 years [5]	2,241	258.4	5.1	65–74 years [4]	2,552	249.1	5.3
Heart disease.	519	59.8	4.3	Heart disease	406	39.7	4.7
Cancer, all	151	17.4	6.7	Osteoarthritis	169	16.5	3.7
Stroke.	105	12.1	4.7	Cancer, all	160	15.6	6.9
Pneumonia	101	11.6	5.1	Pneumonia	112	10.9	5.8
75–84 years [4]	2,236	422.0	5.7	75–84 years [4]	3,016	389.3	5.6
Heart disease.	496	93.7	4.8	Heart disease	570	73.5	4.9
Pneumonia	141	26.6	5.4	Injury	222	28.6	5.4
Cancer, all	114	21.5	8.0	Pneumonia	140	18.1	5.8
Stroke.	113	21.4	4.5	Stroke	134	17.2	4.8
85 years and over [4] . . .	1,010	598.4	5.4	85 years and over [4] . . .	2,015	558.4	5.7
Heart disease.	209	123.9	4.7	Heart disease	424	117.4	4.8
Pneumonia	82	48.7	5.6	Injury	203	56.3	5.4
Injury	71	41.9	5.2	Pneumonia	134	37.2	5.9

[1] The first-listed diagnosis is the one specified as the principal diagnosis or the first diagnosis listed on the face sheet or discharge summary of the medical record. It is usually the main cause of the hospitalization. The number of first-listed diagnoses is the same as the number of discharges. [2] Crude estimates. [3] Estimates are age adjusted to the year 2000 standard population using six age groups: under 18 years, 18–44 years, 45–54 years, 55–64 years, 65–74 years, and 75 years and over. [4] Includes discharges with first-listed diagnoses not shown in table. [5] Estimates are considered unreliable. [6] These estimates are for nonfederal short-stay hospitals only and do not include serious mental illness discharges. [7] Includes abuse, dependence, and withdrawal. These estimates are for nonfederal short-stay hospitals only and do not include alcohol and drug discharges from other types of facilities or programs such as the Department of Veterans Affairs or day treatment programs.

Source: Centers for Disease Control and Prevention, National Center for Health Statistics, National Hospital Discharge Survey; <http://www.cdc.gov/nchs/products/series.htm>.

118   Health and Nutrition

Table 174. Selected Cosmetic Plastic Surgical Procedures: 2002 to 2008

[In thousands (6,889.5 represents 6,889,500). As of December 31. The final data are projected to reflect nationwide statistics and are based on a survey of doctors who have been certified by the American Board of Medical Specialties recognized boards, including but not limited to the American Board of Plastic Surgery. Data for the procedures include but are not limited to those performed by American Society for Aesthetic Plastic Surgery (ASAPS) members. ASAPS members are plastic surgeons certified by the American Board of Plastic Surgery who specialize in cosmetic surgery and nonsurgical procedures in the United States. Procedures are ranked by total number for latest year shown]

Procedure	2002	2003	2004	2005	2006	2007	2008
Total all procedures	6,889.5	8,252.0	11,855.0	11,428.8	11,456.8	11,701.0	10,258.6
Total surgical procedures.	1,620.7	1,819.5	2,120.0	2,131.0	1,922.8	2,079.0	1,766.7
Breast augmentation.	249.6	280.4	334.1	364.6	383.9	399.4	355.7
Lipoplasty (Liposuction).	372.8	384.6	478.3	455.5	403.7	456.8	341.1
Blepharoplasty (eyelid surgery).	229.1	267.6	290.3	231.5	210.0	240.8	195.1
Rhinoplasty (nose reshaping)	157.0	172.4	166.2	200.9	141.9	151.8	152.4
Abdominoplasty (tummy tuck).	83.0	117.7	151.0	169.3	172.5	185.3	147.4
Total nonsurgical procedures	5,268.8	6,432.5	9,735.0	9,297.7	9,534.0	9,622.0	8,491.9
Botox injection.	1,658.7	2,272.1	2,837.3	3,294.8	3,181.6	2,775.2	2,464.1
Laser hair removal	736.5	923.2	1,411.9	1,566.9	1,475.3	1,412.7	1,281.0
Hyaluronic acid [1]	(X)	116.2	882.5	1,194.2	1,593.6	1,448.7	1,262.8
Chemical peel	495.4	722.2	1110.4	556.2	558.4	575.1	591.8
Laser skin resurfacing.	72.5	127.5	589.7	475.7	576.5	509.9	570.9
Total female procedures	6,081.9	7,177.9	10,681.4	10,443.8	10,516.7	10,602.5	9,394.8
Total surgical procedures.	1,407.7	1,559.4	1,887.3	1,918.1	1,730.5	1,877.1	1,600.7
Breast augmentation.	249.6	280.4	334.1	364.6	383.9	399.4	355.7
Lipoplasty (Liposuction).	316.5	323.0	416.6	402.9	350.4	398.8	309.7
Blepharoplasty (eyelid surgery).	192.8	216.8	249.3	198.1	182.4	208.2	166.4
Abdominoplasty (tummy tuck).	79.7	112.7	145.3	164.1	164.8	180.5	143.0
Breast reduction.	125.6	147.2	144.4	160.5	145.3	153.1	139.9
Total nonsurgical procedures	4,674.2	5,618.6	8,794.1	8,525.7	8,786.2	8,725.4	7,794.1
Botox injection. . , ...	1,424.9	1,963.0	2,525.4	2,990.7	2,881.1	2,445.7	2,239.0
Hyaluronic acid [1]	(X)	104.7	838.9	1,149.2	1,519.9	1,364.5	1,200.4
Laser hair removal	588.5	695.2	1,215.1	1,334.7	1,308.7	1,227.0	1,101.3
Chemical peel	453.5	640.1	977.3	533.0	530.1	536.0	554.5
Laser skin resurfacing.	68.2	116.5	520.3	432.6	528.1	479.8	532.0
Microdermabrasion [2].	936.2	774.3	999.1	939.5	922.0	743.7	517.3
IPL laser treatment [3].	(X)	(X)	(X)	(X)	(X)	584.5	479.9
Sclerotherapy (Spider veins).	291.1	431.3	479.2	548.0	541.3	467.8	417.5
Total male procedures	807.7	1,074.1	1,173.6	984.9	940.0	1,098.6	863.7
Total surgical procedures.	213.1	260.1	232.7	212.9	192.3	202.0	166.0
Lipoplasty (Liposuction).	56.3	61.6	61.6	52.5	53.3	58.0	31.5
Rhinoplasty (nose reshaping)	39.0	53.4	39.0	45.9	33.1	31.7	30.2
Blepharoplasty (eyelid surgery).	36.3	50.8	41.1	33.4	27.6	32.6	28.7
Gynecomastia (male breast reduction)	16.6	22.0	19.6	17.7	23.7	20.3	19.1
Hair transplantation.	17.3	14.9	19.5	11.2	11.2	16.5	18.1
Facelift.	11.1	13.6	11.8	13.0	14.1	12.4	13.4
Total nonsurgical procedures	594.6	814.0	932.6	772.0	747.7	896.6	697.8
Botox injection.	233.8	309.1	311.9	304.1	300.5	329.5	225.1
Laser hair removal	147.9	228.0	196.8	232.2	166.6	185.7	179.7
Hyaluronic acid [1]	(X)	11.5	43.6	45.0	73.6	84.2	62.4
IPL laser treatment [3].	(X)	(X)	(X)	(X)	(X)	63.2	46.9
Microdermabrasion [2].	96.2	84.0	99.2	84.4	71.1	85.9	39.8
Laser skin resurfacing.	4.2	11.0	69.4	43.1	48.5	30.1	38.9

X Not applicable.   [1] In 2003, the FDA has approved hyaluronan injections for filling soft tissue defects such as facial wrinkles.   [2] Procedure for reducing fine lines, "crow's feet," age spots, and acne scars.   [3] IPL is intense pulse light. One of the procedures available for facial rejuvenation.

Source: The American Society for Aesthetic Plastic Surgery, Statistics, annual (copyright). See <http://www.surgery.org/media/statistics>.

Table 175. Organ Transplants and Grafts: 1990 to 2008

[As of end of year. Based on reports of procurement programs and transplant centers in the United States, except as noted]

Procedure	Number of procedures						Number of centers		Number of people waiting, 2008	1-year patient survival rates, 2007 (percent)
	1990	1995	2000	2005	2007	2008	1990	2008		
Transplant: [1]										
Heart	2,095	2,342	2,172	2,125	2,210	2,163	148	126	2,805	88.7
Heart-lung	52	69	47	35	30	27	79	51	84	89.7
Lung.	203	869	955	1,406	1,469	1,478	70	66	1,899	80.8
Liver.	2,631	3,818	4,816	6,443	6,493	6,318	85	127	15,766	88.1
Kidney	9,358	10,957	13,258	16,481	16,624	16,517	232	242	79,882	95.4
Kidney-pancreas. .	459	915	910	903	862	837	(NA)	(NA)	2,215	95.5
Pancreas.	60	103	420	541	469	436	84	143	1,494	92.3
Intestine	1	21	29	178	198	185	(NA)	45	216	73.7
Multi-organ [1] . . .	71	124	213	518	(NA)	(NA)	(NA)	(NA)	(NA)	(NA)
Cornea grafts [2,3] . . .	40,631	44,652	50,197	48,298	50,122	(NA)	[3]107	[3](NA)	(NA)	(NA)

NA Not available.   [1] Kidney-pancreas and heart-lung transplants are each counted as one procedure. All other multiorgan transplants, excluding kidney-pancreas and heart-lung, are included in the multiorgan row. Based on the Organ Procurement and Transplant Network (OPTN) as of May 30, 2009. The data have been supplied by UNOS under contract with HHS. This work was supported in part by Health Resources and Services Administration contract 231-00-0015. The authors alone are responsible for the reporting and interpretation of these data. Data subject to change based on future data submission or correction.   [2] 1990–1992, number of procedures and eye banks include Canada. From 1995 on, the data is for the U.S. only.   [3] Eye bank.

Source: U.S. Department of Health and Human Services, Health Resources and Services Administration, Office of Special Programs, Division of Transplantation, Rockville, MD; United Network for Organ Sharing (UNOS), Richmond, VA; University Renal Research and Education Association; Eye Bank Association of America, Washington, DC; and unpublished data. See also <http://www.optn.org/>.

Health and Nutrition   119

Table 176. **Cancer—Estimated New Cases, 2009, and Survival Rates: 1990–1992 to 1999–2005**

[1,479 represents 1,479,000. The 5-year relative survival rate, which is derived by adjusting the observed survival rate for expected mortality, represents the likelihood that a person will not die from causes directly related to their cancer within 5 years. Survival data shown are based on those patients diagnosed while residents of an area listed below during the time periods shown. Data are based on information collected as part of the National Cancer Institute's Surveillance, Epidemiology and End Results (SEER) program, a collection of 9 population-based registries in five states (Connecticut, Hawaii, Iowa, New Mexico, Utah) and four metropolitian areas (Atlanta, Detroit, San Francisco-Oakland, and Seattle-Puget Sound)]

Site	Estimated new cases,[1] 2009 (1,000) Total	Male	Female	5-year relative survival rates (percent) White 1990– 1992	1993– 1995	1996– 1998	1999– 2005	Black 1990– 1992	1993– 1995	1996– 1998	1999– 2005
All sites[2]	1,479	766	713	62.4	63.4	65.6	69.1	48.2	52.9	55.5	59.4
Lung	219	116	103	14.5	15.1	15.4	16.6	10.8	13.0	12.7	12.9
Breast[3]	194	2	192	86.7	88.0	89.6	91.3	71.8	72.8	76.5	78.9
Colon and rectum	147	76	71	63.2	61.5	64.1	68.0	53.8	52.9	55.2	57.0
Colon	106	52	54	64.0	61.4	63.8	67.4	54.2	52.3	54.7	55.6
Rectum	41	24	17	61.3	61.7	64.7	69.4	52.2	54.8	56.5	61.0
Prostate	192	192	(X)	95.3	96.2	98.0	99.9	85.5	91.5	94.2	97.9
Bladder	71	53	18	81.9	82.2	80.7	82.6	64.7	61.7	62.3	67.8
Corpus uteri	42	(X)	42	87.2	86.5	86.9	87.2	57.0	61.7	64.1	63.1
Non-Hodgkin's lymphoma[4]	66	36	30	52.9	54.5	61.0	70.1	42.0	42.0	54.4	59.9
Oral cavity and pharynx	36	25	10	58.7	60.9	61.1	64.4	33.3	38.2	36.3	46.1
Leukemia[4]	45	26	19	48.0	49.5	50.8	54.8	37.4	42.3	39.1	46.3
Melanoma of skin	69	39	30	89.6	89.7	91.1	92.9	60.3	66.8	74.9	77.7
Pancreas	42	21	21	4.7	4.2	4.4	5.7	3.7	3.7	3.6	5.3
Kidney	58	35	22	62.1	63.1	63.4	69.4	57.7	58.6	67.3	65.9
Stomach	21	13	8	19.3	20.6	21.0	25.3	23.8	19.8	23.8	26.1
Ovary	22	(X)	22	42.4	42.7	45.1	45.5	37.8	43.3	41.3	37.2
Cervix uteri[5]	11	(X)	11	71.9	74.7	74.6	73.1	58.8	64.0	65.3	64.8

X Not applicable.   [1] Estimates provided by American Cancer Society, <www.cancer.org>, are based on rates from the National Cancer Institute's SEER program.   [2] Includes other sites not shown separately.   [3] Survival rates for female only.   [4] All types combined.   [5] Invasive cancer only.

Source: U.S. National Institutes of Health, National Cancer Institute; <http://seer.cancer.gov/csr/1975_2006/>.

Table 177. **Cancer—Estimated New Cases and Deaths by State: 2009**

[In thousands (1,479.4 represents 1,479,400). Excludes basal and squamous cell skin cancers and in situ carcinomas except urinary bladder]

State	New cases[1] Total[2]	Female breast	Lung & bron-chus	Deaths Total[2]	Female breast	Lung & bron-chus	State	New cases[1] Total[2]	Female breast	Lung & bron-chus	Deaths Total[2]	Female breast	Lung & bron-chus
U.S...	1,479.4	192.4	219.4	562.3	40.2	159.4	MO	30.1	3.9	5.6	12.6	0.9	4.1
							MT	5.3	0.6	0.7	2.0	0.1	0.6
AL	24.1	3.0	4.0	9.9	0.7	3.1	NE	8.8	1.2	1.2	3.4	0.2	0.9
AK	2.5	0.4	0.4	0.8	0.1	0.2	NV	12.0	1.4	1.9	4.6	0.3	1.3
AZ	27.6	3.5	4.0	10.3	0.7	2.8	NH	7.6	1.0	1.1	2.6	0.2	0.8
AR	14.8	1.8	2.6	6.2	0.4	2.2							
CA	152.2	21.7	17.9	54.6	4.0	12.8	NJ	47.9	6.4	6.3	16.5	1.5	4.2
							NM	8.8	1.1	1.0	3.3	0.2	0.7
CO	20.3	2.8	2.2	6.7	0.5	1.7	NY	101.6	13.5	13.6	34.2	2.6	8.8
CT	20.7	2.8	2.7	7.0	0.5	1.8	NC	42.3	5.5	6.7	18.6	1.3	5.6
DE	4.7	0.6	0.8	1.9	0.1	0.6	ND	3.2	0.4	0.4	1.3	0.1	0.4
DC	2.6	0.3	0.4	1.0	0.1	0.2							
FL	102.2	12.7	17.8	41.3	2.7	12.2	OH	62.4	7.3	10.7	24.4	1.8	7.3
							OK	18.1	2.3	3.2	7.4	0.5	2.4
GA	39.1	5.4	6.2	15.0	1.1	4.7	OR	19.2	2.7	2.6	7.4	0.5	2.1
HI	6.4	0.9	0.7	2.3	0.1	0.6	PA	74.2	9.4	10.5	28.7	2.1	8.1
ID	6.8	0.8	0.8	2.5	0.2	0.6	RI	6.3	0.8	0.9	2.2	0.1	0.6
IL	61.0	7.6	9.2	23.2	1.8	6.5							
IN	31.3	3.7	5.4	12.8	0.9	4.0	SC	22.1	2.8	3.7	9.1	0.6	2.9
IA	16.7	2.1	2.6	6.4	0.4	1.8	SD	4.1	0.5	0.6	1.6	0.1	0.5
KS	13.1	1.8	2.1	5.3	0.4	1.6	TN	32.6	4.0	5.4	13.3	0.9	4.5
KY	24.1	2.8	4.7	9.4	0.6	3.4	TX	98.2	13.1	14.2	36.0	2.6	9.8
LA	22.2	2.7	3.7	8.8	0.7	2.7	UT	8.9	1.1	0.6	2.8	0.3	0.5
ME	9.0	1.1	1.4	3.2	0.2	1.0							
							VT	3.6	0.5	0.5	1.2	0.1	0.4
MD	26.7	3.7	4.1	10.3	0.8	2.9	VA	34.2	4.9	5.3	13.9	1.1	4.3
MA	36.1	4.8	5.1	13.1	0.9	3.6	WA	32.3	4.5	4.1	11.2	0.8	3.1
MI	53.6	6.5	8.2	20.5	1.4	5.8	WV	10.2	1.2	2.0	4.5	0.3	1.5
MN	23.7	3.3	3.3	9.0	0.6	2.4	WI	27.6	3.5	4.0	11.2	0.8	2.9
MS	14.2	1.8	2.3	6.1	0.4	2.0	WY	2.5	0.3	0.3	1.0	0.1	0.3

[1] Estimates are offered as a rough guide and should be interpreted with caution.   [2] Includes other types of cancer not shown separately.

Source: American Cancer Society, Inc., Atlanta, Georgia, Cancer Facts and Figures—2009 (copyright); <http://www.cancer.org /docroot/STT/stt_0.asp>.

120   Health and Nutrition

Table 178. Selected Notifiable Diseases—Cases Reported: 1980 to 2007

[190.9 represents 190,900. As of June 30, 2008. Figures should be interpreted with caution. Although reporting of some of these diseases is incomplete, the figures are of value in indicating trends of disease incidence. Includes cases imported from outside the United States]

Disease	1980	1990	1995	2000	2003	2004	2005	2006	2007
AIDS [1]	(2)	41,595	71,547	40,758	44,232	44,108	41,120	(NA)	37,503
Botulism [3]	89	92	97	138	129	133	135	165	144
Brucellosis (undulant fever)	183	85	98	87	104	114	120	121	131
Chickenpox (Varicella) [4] (1,000)	190.9	173.1	120.6	27.4	20.9	32.9	32.2	48.4	40.1
Coccidoidomycosis	(2)	(2)	(2)	2,867	4,870	6,449	6,542	8,917	8,121
Cryptosporidiosis	(2)	(2)	(NA)	3,128	3,506	3,577	5,659	6,071	11,170
Domestic arboviral diseases [5]									
West Nile: neuroinvasive	(2)	(2)	(2)	(2)	2,866	1,142	1,309	1,495	1,227
nonneuroinvasive	(2)	(2)	(2)	(2)	(2)	(2)	1,691	2,774	2403
Enterohemorrhagic Escherichia coli O157:H7	(2)	(2)	2,139	4,528	2,671	2,544	2,621	(2)	(2)
Giardiasis	(2)	(2)	(2)	(2)	19,709	20,636	19,733	18,953	19,417
Haemophilus influenza	(2)	(2)	1,180	1,398	2,013	2,085	2,304	2,436	2,541
Hansen disease (Leprosy) [6]	223	198	144	91	95	105	87	66	101
Hepatitis: A (infectious) (1,000)	29.1	31.4	31.6	13.4	7.7	5.7	4.5	3.6	3.0
B (serum) (1,000)	19.0	21.1	10.8	8.0	7.5	6.2	5.1	4.7	4.5
C/Non-A, non-B	(2)	2,600	4,576	3,197	1,102	720	652	766	845
Legionellosis	(2)	1,370	1,241	1,127	2,232	2,093	2,301	2,834	2,716
Lyme disease	(2)	(2)	11,700	17,730	21,273	19,804	23,305	19,931	27,444
Malaria	2,062	1,292	1,419	1,560	1,402	1,458	1,494	1,474	1,408
Meningococcal infections	2,840	2,451	3,243	2,256	1,756	1,361	1,245	1,194	1,077
Mumps (1,000)	8.6	5.3	0.9	0.3	0.2	0.3	0.3	6.6	0.8
Pertussis [7] (1,000)	1.7	4.6	5.1	7.9	11.6	25.8	25.6	15.6	10.5
Psittacosis	124	113	64	17	12	12	16	21	12
Rabies, animal	6,421	4,826	7,811	6,934	6,846	6,345	5,915	5,534	5,862
Rocky Mountain spotted fever	1,163	651	590	495	1,091	1,713	1,936	2,288	2,221
Rubella [8]	3,904	1,125	128	176	7	10	11	11	12
Salmonellosis [9] (1,000)	33.7	48.6	46.0	39.6	43.7	42.2	45.3	45.8	48.0
Shigellosis [10] (1,000)	19.0	27.1	32.1	22.9	23.6	14.6	16.2	15.5	19.8
Streptococcal disease, invasive, Group A	(2)	(2)	(2)	3,144	5,872	4,395	4,715	5,407	5,294
Streptococcus pneumoniae, invasive:									
Drug-resistant	(2)	(2)	(2)	4,533	2,356	2,590	2,996	3,308	3,329
Age less than 5 years	(2)	(2)	(2)	(2)	845	1,162	1,495	1,861	563
Tetanus	95	64	41	35	20	34	27	41	28
Toxic-shock syndrome	(2)	322	191	135	133	95	90	101	92
Trichinosis	131	129	29	16	6	5	16	15	5
Tuberculosis [11] (1,000)	27.7	25.7	22.9	16.4	14.9	14.5	14.1	13.8	13.3
Typhoid fever	510	552	369	377	356	322	324	353	434
Sexually tranomitted diseases.									
Chlamydia (1,000)	(2)	(2)	478	702	877	929	976	1,031	1,108
Gonorrhea (1,000)	1,004	690	393	359	335	330	340	358	356
Syphilis (1,000)	69	134	69	32	34	33	33	37	41

– Represents zero. [1] Acquired immunodeficiency syndrome was not a notifiable disease until 1984. Figures are shown for years in which cases were reported to the CDC. Beginning 1995, based on revised classification system and expanded surveillance case definition. 2006 data are not available, see source for details. [2] Disease was not notifiable. [3] Includes foodborne, infant, wound, and unspecified cases. [4] Chickenpox was taken off the nationally notifiable list in 1991 but many states continue to report. [5] The national surveillance case definitions for the arboviral diseases was revised in 2005, and nonneuroinvasive arboviral diseases were added to the list of nationally notifiable infectious diseases. [6] Data on chronic hepatitis B and hepatitis C virus infection (past or present) are not included because they are undergoing data quality review. [7] Whooping cough. [8] German measles. Excludes congenital syndrome. [9] Excludes typhoid fever. [10] Bacillary dysentery. [11] Newly reported active cases.

Source: *Summary of Notifiable Diseases, United States, 2007, Morbidity and Mortality Weekly Report*, Vol. 56, No. 53, July 9, 2009; <http://www.cdc.gov/mmwr/PDF/wk/mm5653.pdf>.

Table 179. AIDS, Chlamydia, and Lyme Diease, 2007, Cases Reported by State

State	AIDS	Chlamydia	Lyme diease	State	AIDS	Chlamydia	Lyme diease	State	AIDS	Chlamydia	Lyme diease
U.S.	37,503	1,108,374	27,444	KS	132	8,180	8	ND	8	1,789	12
				KY	292	8,798	6	OH	703	47,434	33
AL	391	25,153	13	LA	879	19,362	2	OK	264	12,529	1
AK	32	4,911	10	ME	46	2,541	529	OR	239	9,849	26
AZ	585	24,866	2	MD	1,394	23,150	2,576	PA	1,750	42,469	3,994
AR	196	9,954	8	MA	612	16,145	2,988	RI	66	3,177	177
CA	4,952	141,928	75	MI	628	37,353	51	SC	742	26,431	31
CO	355	17,186	–	MN	197	13,413	1,238	SD	15	2,620	–
CT	528	11,454	3,058	MS	352	21,686	1	TN	658	26,866	50
DE	171	3,479	715	MO	542	23,308	10	TX	2,964	85,786	87
DC	871	6,029	116	MT	25	2,748	4	UT	68	5,721	7
FL	3,961	57,575	30	NE	80	5,132	9	VT	6	1,057	138
GA	1,877	42,913	11	NV	335	9,514	15	VA	634	24,579	959
HI	78	5,659	(1)	NH	51	2,055	896	WA	427	18,784	12
ID	23	3,722	9	NJ	1,164	21,536	3,134	WV	76	3,168	84
IL	1,348	55,470	149	NM	113	9,460	5	WI	199	19,555	1,814
IN	329	20,712	55	NY	4,810	80,717	4,165	WY	13	1,197	7
IA	76	8,643	123	NC	1,024	30,611	53				

– Represents zero. [1] Not notifiable.

Source: *Summary of Notifiable Diseases, United States, 2007, Morbidity and Mortality Weekly Report*, Vol. 56, No. 53, July 9, 2009; <http://www.cdc.gov/mmwr/PDF/wk/mm5653.pdf>.

Health and Nutrition 121

Table 180. **Reported AIDS Cases for Adults and Adolescents by Transmission Category and Sex: 2007**

[Provisional. For cases reported in the year shown. Includes Puerto Rico, Virgin Islands, Guam, and U.S. Pacific Islands. Acquired immunodeficiency syndrome (AIDS) is a specific group of diseases or conditions which are indicative of severe immunosuppression related to infection with the human immunodeficiency virus (HIV). Data are subject to retrospective changes and may differ from those data in Table 178. For information on HIV death rates, go to Table 123]

Transmission category	2007			Cumulative through 2007[1]		
	Total	Male	Female	Total	Male	Female
Persons 13 years old and over, total	38,297	28,320	9,977	1,021,242	820,037	201,205
Male-to-male sexual contact	14,383	14,383	(X)	445,645	445,645	(X)
Injection drug use	4,736	3,103	1,633	235,842	166,251	69,591
Male-to-male sexual contact and						
injection drug use	1,514	1,514	(X)	67,797	67,797	(X)
Hemophilia/coagulation disorder	46	37	9	5,567	5,212	355
High-risk heterosexual contact.	7,504	2,791	4,713	142,852	52,623	90,229
Sex with injection drug user.	985	281	704	38,766	11,941	26,825
Sex with bisexual male.	233	(X)	233	5,415	(X)	5,415
Sex with person with hemophilia	14	4	10	603	90	513
Sex with HIV-infected person, transfusion recipient . .	56	31	25	1,403	584	819
Sex with HIV-infected person,						
risk factor not specified.	6,216	2,475	3,741	96,665	40,008	56,657
Receipt of blood transfusion, blood						
components, or tissue.	109	50	59	9,315	5,181	4,134
Other/risk not reported or identified	10,005	6,442	3,563	114,224	77,328	36,896

X Not applicable.   [1] Includes persons with a diagnosis of AIDS, reported from the beginning of the epidemic through 2007. Cumulative total includes persons with characteristics unknown.

Source: U.S. Centers for Disease Control and Prevention, Atlanta, GA, *HIV/AIDS Surveillance Report, 2007*, Volume 19; <http://www.cdc.gov/hiv/topics/surveillance/resources/reports/2007report/default.htm> (revised 19 February 2009).

Table 181. **Estimated Numbers of Persons Living With Acquired Immunodeficiency Syndrome (AIDS) by Year, Age, and Selected Characteristics: 2000 to 2007**

[Provisional. These numbers do not represent reported case counts. Rather, these numbers are point estimates, which result from adjustments of reported case counts. The reported case counts are adjusted for reporting delays and for redistribution of cases in persons initially reported without an identified risk factor. The estimates do not include adjustment for incomplete reporting. Data for years 2004 to 2006 have been revised. See the Commentary section in the report]

Age and characteristic	2000	2004	2005	2006	2007
Total [1, 2]	320,177	404,438	424,871	446,098	468,578
AGE AS OF END OF YEAR					
Less than 13 years old	2,843	1,722	1,428	1,142	889
13 and 14 years old	513	785	770	725	659
15 to 24 years old	4,944	6,638	7,300	7,817	8,507
25 to 34 years old	54,473	45,138	43,442	42,784	43,014
35 to 44 years old	143,920	156,570	156,271	154,096	150,059
45 to 54 years old	85,445	130,515	143,090	156,328	170,008
55 to 64 years old	22,089	41,381	48,544	56,504	65,494
65 years old and over	5,950	10,450	12,232	14,386	17,005
RACE/ETHNICITY					
White, not Hispanic.	119,420	141,348	146,995	153,118	159,338
Black, not Hispanic.	132,090	170,224	179,369	188,740	199,124
Asian/Pacific Islander	2,612	3,372	3,679	4,006	4,398
American Indian/Alaska Native	1,099	1,449	1,543	1,612	1,700
Hispanic [3].	63,894	72,662	77,016	81,635	86,244
TRANSMISSION CATEGORY MALE ADULT/ADOLESCENT					
Males 13 years old and over, total	248,726	301,547	316,029	331,269	347,284
Male-to-male sexual contact.	142,069	180,944	191,228	202,134	213,510
Injection drug use.	57,778	60,165	61,164	62,283	63,636
Male-to-male sexual contact and injection drug use . . .	22,603	26,833	27,487	28,081	28,691
High-risk heterosexual contact	22,568	30,537	32,979	35,489	38,067
Other [4]	3,708	3,068	3,172	3,282	3,380
FEMALE ADULT/ADOLESCENT					
Females 13 years old and over, total	67,601	87,835	93,214	98,695	104,560
Injection drug use.	26,656	31,192	31,980	32,717	33,531
Heterosexual contact	39,121	54,792	59,277	63,910	68,798
Other [4]	1,824	1,851	1,958	2,068	2,231
CHILD (LESS THAN 13 YEARS OLD AT DIAGNOSIS)					
Total	3,848	3,818	3,835	3,820	3,792
Perinatal	3,706	3,615	3,631	3,618	3,592
Other [5]	142	202	204	203	200

[1] Includes persons of unknown or multiple race and of unknown sex. Because column totals were calculated independently of the values for the subpopulations, the values in each column may not sum to the column total.   [2] Persons who reported multiple racial categories or whose race was unknown are included in the total numbers.   [3] Hispanics/Latinos can be of any race.   [4] Includes hemophilia, blood transfusion, perinatal exposure and risk not reported or not identified.   [5] Includes hemophilia, blood transfusion, and risk not reported or not identified.

Source: U.S. Centers for Disease Control and Prevention, Atlanta, GA, *HIV/AIDS Surveillance Report, 2007*, Volume 19; <http://www.cdc.gov/hiv/topics/surveillance/resources/reports/2007report/default.htm> (revised 19 February 2009).

Table 182. **Learning Disability or Attention Deficit Hyperactivity Disorder for Children 3–17 Years of Age by Selected Characteristics: 2007**

[In thousands, except percent (61,518 represents 61,518,000). Learning Disability is based on the question, "Has a representative from a school or a health professional ever told you that (child's name) has a learning disability?" Attention Deficit Hyperactivity Disorder is based on the question, "Has a doctor or health professional ever told you that (child's name) had Attention Hyperactivity Disorder or Attention Deficit Disorder?"]

Selected characteristic	Total	Ever told had—			
		Learning disability		Attention deficit hyperactivity disorder	
		Number [1]	Percent [2]	Number [1]	Percent [2]
Total [3]	61,518	4,624	7.5	4,452	7.2
SEX [4]					
Male	31,575	3,034	9.7	3,161	10.0
Female.	29,943	1,590	5.3	1,291	4.3
AGE					
3 to 4 years old	8,369	179	2.1	[6]170	[6]2.0
5 to 11 years old	27,932	1,867	6.7	1,644	5.9
12 to 17 years old	25,216	2,577	10.2	2,637	10.5
RACE					
Race Alone [4, 5]	59,576	4,464	7.5	4,200	7.0
White	46,548	3,519	7.5	3,354	7.2
Black or African American.	9,553	740	7.7	718	7.4
American Indian or Alaska Native.	948	[6]115	[6]11.3	[6]71	[6]7.7
Asian	2,402	[6]90	3.7	[6]57	[6]2.5
Native Hawaiian or Other Pacific Islander.	126	–	–	–	–
Two or more races [4, 7]	1,942	[6]160	8.6	251	13.3
Black or African American and White . . .	715	(B)	[6]9.0	[6]89	[6]13.2
American Indian or Alaska Native and White	469	[6]75	[6]15.6	[6]92	[6]18.8
HISPANIC ORIGIN AND RACE: [4, 8]					
Hispanic or Latino	12,323	817	6.7	495	4.1
Mexican or Mexican American.	8,472	590	7.1	334	4.0
Not Hispanic or Latino.	49,195	3,807	7.7	3,957	8.0
White, single race	35,442	2,823	7.9	2,948	8.2
Black or African American, single race . .	9,111	716	7.8	703	7.6

– Represents zero.   B Base figure too small to meet statistical standards for reliability of a derived figure.   [1] Unknowns for the columns are not included in the frequencies, but they are included in the "Total" column.   [2] Unknowns for the column variables are not included in the denominators when calculating percentages.   [3] Includes other races not shown separately.   [4] Percents are age-adjusted to the 2000 projected U.S. standard population using age groups 3–4 years, 5–11 years, and 12–17 years.   [5] Refers to persons who indicated only a single race group.   [6] Figures do not meet standard of reliability or precision.   [7] Refers to all persons who indicated more than one race group.   [8] Persons of Hispanic or Latino origin may be any race or combination of races.

Source: National Center for Health Statistics, *Vital and Health Statistics*, Series 10, Number 239, Summary Health Statistics for U.S. Children: National Health Interview Survey, 2007; <http://www.cdc.gov/nchs/data/series/sr_10/sr10_239.pdf>.

Table 183. **Children and Youth With Disabilities Served by Selected Programs: 1995 to 2007**

[In thousands (5,078.8 represents 5,078,800). As of Fall. For children and youth children and youth ages 6 to 21 served under the Individuals with Disabilities Education Act (IDEA) Part B. Includes outlying areas]

Disability	1995	2000	2002	2003	2004	2005	2006	2007
Total	5,078.8	5,773.9	5,959.1	6,045.4	6,116.4	6,113.5	6,085.6	6,007.8
Specific learning disabilities	2,601.8	2,881.6	2,878.6	2,867.1	2,839.3	2,782.8	2,711.8	2,620.2
Speech or language impairments. . .	1,026.9	1,093.4	1,110.9	1,128.1	1,149.6	1,156.9	1,162.1	1,154.2
Mental retardation.	585.6	613.4	591.7	582.6	567.6	546.0	523.5	498.2
Emotional disturbance	439.2	474.3	482.0	484.5	484.5	472.5	458.8	440.2
Multiple disabilities	94.5	122.9	130.8	132.7	133.4	134.0	133.8	132.6
Hearing impairments	68.0	70.8	72.0	72.0	72.6	72.4	72.8	72.2
Orthopedic impairments	63.2	73.0	74.0	68.2	65.4	63.1	62.0	60.5
Other health impairments	134.2	294.0	393.0	452.7	512.2	561.6	600.4	631.2
Visual impairments	25.5	26.0	26.1	25.9	26.1	26.0	26.5	26.4
Autism	29.1	79.6	118.8	141.1	166.5	193.8	224.6	258.3
Deaf-blind	1.4	1.3	1.6	1.7	1.7	1.6	1.4	1.4
Traumatic brain injury	9.6	14.9	21.5	22.5	23.3	23.5	23.8	23.9
Developmental delay [1]	(X)	28.6	58.3	66.3	74.4	79.1	84.0	88.6

X Not applicable.   [1] States had the option of reporting children ages 3 to 9 under developmental delay beginning 1997.

Source: U.S. Department of Education, Office of Special Education. See <http://www.ideadata.org/index.html>.

U.S. Census Bureau, *Statistical Abstract of the United States: 2010*

Table 184. **Children Under 18 Years of Age Receiving Special Education or Early Intervention Services: 2007**

[In thousands, except percent (73,727 represents 73,727,000). Receiving special education or early intervention services is based on the question, "Do any of the following (family members under 18 years of age) receive special education or early intervention services?"]

Selected characteristic	Total	Persons under 18 years who were receiving special education early intervention services	
		Number [1]	Percent [2]
Total [3]	73,727	4,601	6.3
SEX [4]			
Male	37,685	3,072	8.1
Female..	36,042	1,529	4.2
AGE			
Under 12 years old..............................	48,526	2,638	5.4
12 to 17 years old	25,200	1,963	7.8
RACE			
Race Alone [4, 5]	71,411	4,437	6.2
White	55,721	3,529	6.3
Black or African American......................	11,473	745	6.5
American Indian or Alaska Native................	1,083	[6]98	9.1
Asian	2,998	64	2.1
Native Hawaiian or Other Pacific Islander	136	–	–
Two or more races [4, 7]	2,316	164	7.2
HISPANIC ORIGIN AND RACE:[4, 8]			
Hispanic or Latino	15,349	684	4.5
Mexican or Mexican American...................	10,721	431	4.0
Not Hispanic or Latino..........................	58,378	3,917	6.7
White, single race.............................	41,781	2,921	7.0
Black or African American, single race	10,937	717	6.5

– Represents zero. [1] Unknowns for the columns are not included in the frequencies, but they are included in the "Total" column. [2] Unknowns for the column variables are not included in the denominators when calculating percentages. [3] Includes other races not shown separately. [4] Percents are age-adjusted to the 2000 projected U.S. standard population using two age groups 0–11 years, and 12–17 years. [5] Refers to persons who indicated only a single race group. [6] Figures do not meet standard of reliability or precision. [7] Refers to all persons who indicated more than one race group. [8] Persons of Hispanic or Latino origin may be any race or combination of races.

Source: National Center for Health Statistics, Vital and Health Statistics, Series 10, Number 238, Summary Health Statistics for the U.S. Population: National Health Interview Survey, 2007; <http://www.cdc.gov/nchs/data/series/sr_10/sr10_238.pdf>.

Table 185. **Disabilities Tallied by Age Group and by State: 2007**

[In thousands (41,199 represents 41,199,000). Based on data from American Community Survey (ACS). See text, Section 1 and Appendix III]

State	Total	5 to 15 years [1]	16 to 64 years [2]	65 years and over [3]	State	Total	5 to 15 years [1]	16 to 64 years [2]	65 years and over [3]
U.S.	41,199	2,758	23,706	14,735	MO	918	61	542	315
AL......	877	51	529	298	MT......	144	8	83	53
AK......	90	6	62	22	NE......	219	17	124	79
AZ......	819	53	454	313	NV......	294	16	176	102
AR......	548	37	323	188	NH......	166	13	97	56
CA.....	4,267	252	2,433	1,582	NJ......	955	64	507	384
CO.....	538	31	332	175	NM......	299	16	170	113
CT.....	411	27	226	159	NY......	2,518	161	1,403	954
DE.....	115	8	65	42	NC......	1,367	91	818	458
DC.....	77	6	46	25	ND......	78	5	39	34
FL......	2,613	139	1,317	1,157	OH.....	1,699	128	995	576
GA.....	1,235	82	748	405	OK.....	621	37	372	212
HI	156	7	80	69	OR.....	570	37	334	200
ID	194	15	113	66	PA.....	1,855	127	1,039	688
IL.......	1,502	106	828	567	RI	155	11	92	52
IN	899	67	530	303	SC.....	679	36	404	239
IA	397	30	221	147	SD.....	101	6	56	39
KS.....	368	28	207	133	TN.....	1,050	67	636	347
KY.....	824	56	514	254	TX.....	3,031	247	1,752	1,032
LA.....	713	53	424	236	UT.....	278	26	165	88
ME.....	240	16	144	79	VT.....	94	7	56	30
MD.....	672	51	386	235	VA.....	950	64	544	343
MA.....	834	61	479	294	WA	940	65	575	299
MI	1,512	118	893	501	WV	399	19	250	130
MN.....	592	41	341	210	WI	701	51	403	247
MS.....	552	33	337	182	WY	74	5	44	24

[1] Persons aged 5–15 were classified as having a disability if they reported any one of the four conditions: sensory, physical, mental, or self-care disability. [2] Persons aged 16–64 were classified as having a disability if they reported any one of the six conditions; sensory, physical, mental, self-care disability, go-outside-home or employment disability. [3] Persons 65 years and over were classified as having a disability if they reported any one of the five conditions; sensory, physical, mental, self-care disability, or go-outside-home disability.

Source: U.S. Census Bureau, "American Factfinder, 2007 American Community Survey, Summary Table, Sex by Age by Disability Status for the Civilian Noninstitutionalized Population 5 Years and Over"; <http://www.factfinder.census.gov/>.

124   Health and Nutrition

Table 186. **Children Immunized Against Specified Diseases: 1995 to 2007**

[In percent. Covers civilian noninstitutionalized population ages 19 months to 35 months. Based on estimates from the National Immunization Survey. The health care providers of the children are contacted to verify and/or complete vaccination information. Results are based on race/ethnic status of the child]

Vaccination	1995, total	2000, total	2007 [1] Total	White, non-Hispanic	Black, non-Hispanic	His-panic [2]	American Indian/ Alaska Native [3]	Asian [3]
Diphtheria-tetanus-pertussis (DTP) diphtheria-tetanus:								
3+ doses	95.0	94.0	95.5	95.5	93.9	96.1	97.3	96.4
4+ doses	79.0	82.0	84.5	85.3	82.3	83.8	86.4	87.5
Polio: 3+ doses.	88.0	90.0	92.6	92.6	91.1	93.0	94.8	95.0
Measles, mumps, rubella vaccine.	90.0	91.0	92.3	92.1	91.5	92.6	96.2	93.9
Hib: 3+ doses [4].	92.0	93.0	92.6	92.9	90.8	93.5	95.0	91.0
Hepatitis B: 3+ doses.	68.0	90.0	92.7	92.5	91.2	93.6	96.7	93.8
Varicella [5]	(NA)	68.0	90.0	89.2	89.8	90.6	94.9	93.7
PCV: 3+ doses [6].	(X)	(X)	90.0	89.8	89.5	91.0	94.0	86.8
4+ DTP/3+ polio/1+ MMR [7].	76.0	78.0	82.8	83.3	81.0	82.4	85.6	85.5
4+ DTP/3+ polio/1+ MMR/3+ Hib	74.0	76.0	81.8	82.6	79.5	81.5	85.3	81.9
4+ DTP/3+ polio/1+ MCV/3+ Hib/3+ HepB [8]	55.1	72.8	77.4	77.5	75.3	78.0	82.7	79.4

NA Not available. X Not Applicable. [1] Children in the Q1²007–Q4²007 National Immunization Survey were born between January 2004 and June 2006. [2] Children of Hispanic ethnicity may be any race. [3] Non-Hispanic. [4] Haemophilus influenzae type B. [5] Data collection for varicella (chicken pox) began in July 1996. [6] PCV = Pneumococcal conjugate vaccine. [7] MMR = Measles, mumps, and rubella. [8] Children are considered immunized with this series.

Source: U.S. Centers for Disease Control and Prevention, Atlanta, GA, National Immunization Program, Data and Statistics, *Immunization Coverage in the U.S.;* <http://www.cdc.gov/vaccines/stats-surv/imz-coverage.htm#nis>.

Table 187. **Asthma Incidence Among Children Under 18 Years of Age by Selected Characteristics: 2007**

[In thousands, except percent (73,728 represents 73,728,000). Based on the National Health Interview Survey, a sample survey of the civilian noninstitutionalized population; see Appendix III]

Selected characteristic	Total	Ever told had asthma Number [1]	Ever told had asthma Percent [2]	Still have asthma Number [1]	Still have asthma Percent [2]
Total [3]	**73,728**	**9,605**	**13.1**	**6,703**	**9.1**
SEX [4]					
Male	37,686	5,550	14.8	3,660	9.8
Female.	36,042	4,055	11.3	3,043	8.5
AGE					
0 to 4 years old	20,579	1,636	8.0	1,395	6.8
5 to 11 years old	27,932	3,702	13.3	2,445	8.8
12 to 17 years old	25,216	4,267	17.0	2,862	11.4
RACE					
Race Alone [4, 5]	71,316	9,091	12.8	6,339	8.9
White	55,646	6,278	11.3	4,263	7.7
Black or African American.	11,429	2,253	19.8	1,769	[6]15.6
American Indian or Alaska Native.	1,169	[6]154	14.5	[6]90	[6]8.4
Asian	2,937	362	12.4	217	7.5
Native Hawaiian or Other Pacific Islander.	134	(B)	[6]25.1	–	–
Two or more races [4, 7]	2,412	514	22.6	364	15.9
HISPANIC ORIGIN AND RACE: [4, 8]					
Hispanic or Latino	15,350	1,937	12.9	1,422	9.4
Mexican or Mexican American.	10,572	1,267	12.4	896	8.7
Not Hispanic or Latino.	58,378	7,668	13.1	5,280	9.0
White, single race	41,811	4,591	10.8	3,030	7.1
Black or African American, single race	10,862	2,133	19.8	1,659	15.4

– Represents zero. B Figure too small to meet statistical standards for reliability of a derived figure. [1] Unknowns for the columns are not included in the frequencies, but they are included in the "Total" column. [2] Unknowns for the column variables are not included in the denominators when calculating percentages. [3] Includes other races not shown separately. [4] Estimates are age-adjusted to the 2000 projected U.S. standard population using age groups 0–4 years, 5–11 years, and 12–17 years. [5] Refers to persons who indicated only a single race group. [6] Figures do not meet standard of reliability or precision. [7] Refers to all persons who indicated more than one race group. [8] Persons of Hispanic or Latino origin may be of any race or combination of races.

Source: National Center for Health Statistics, *Vital and Health Statistics, Series 10, Number 239, Summary Health Statistics for U.S. Children: National Health Interview Survey, 2007;* <http://www.cdc.gov/nchs/data/series/sr_10/sr10_239.pdf>.

Health and Nutrition 125

Table 188. **Persons With Limitation of Activity Caused by Chronic Conditions: 2000 to 2007**

[In percent. Limitation of activity is assessed by asking respondents a series of questions about limitations in their ability to perform activities usual for their age group because of a physical, mental, or emotional problem. Based on the National Health Interview Survey, a sample survey of the civilian noninstitutionalized population; see Appendix III]

Characteristic	2000	2005	2006	2007	Characteristic	2000	2005	2006	2007
Total [1,2]	**11.7**	**11.7**	**11.6**	**12.0**	Male [2]	11.7	11.7	11.6	11.9
Under 18 years old. . . .	6.0	7.0	7.3	7.2	Female [2]	11.5	11.6	11.5	11.9
18 to 44 years old	5.8	5.7	5.5	6.0					
45 to 54 years old	12.4	11.9	12.5	12.7	White, non-Hispanic [2] . . .	11.5	11.8	11.8	12.1
55 to 64 years old	19.7	19.9	20.0	19.6	Black, non-Hispanic [2] . . .	14.3	14.2	14.1	15.6
65 to 74 years old	26.1	25.2	24.8	26.5	Hispanic [2,3]	10.3	10.5	10.0	10.2
75 years and over old . .	45.1	43.5	41.6	43.3	Mexican	10.4	11.4	9.8	9.6

[1] Includes all other races not shown separately. [2] Estimates for all persons are age adjusted to the year 2000 standard using six age groups: Under 18 years, 18–44 years, 45–54 years, 55–64 years, 65–74 years, and 75 years and over. [3] Persons of Hispanic origin may be any race.

Source: U.S. National Center for Health Statistics, *Health, United States, annual*; <http://www.cdc.gov/nchs/hus.htm>.

Table 189. **Persons 65 Years Old and Over With Limitation of Activity Caused by Chronic Conditions: 2000 to 2007**

[In percent. Covers noninstitutionalized persons 65 years old and over. To determine activities of daily living (ADL) limitations respondents were asked "Because of a physical, mental, or emotional problem, does (this person) need the help of other persons with personal care needs, such as eating, bathing, dressing, or getting around inside this home?" Instrumental activities of daily living (IADL) were determined by asking respondents "Because of a physical, mental, or emotional problem, does (this person) need the help of other persons in handling routine needs, such as everyday household chores, doing necessary business, shopping, or getting around for other purposes?" See also headnote, Table 188]

Characteristic	Percent with ADL limitation				Percent with IADL limitation			
	2000	2005	2006	2007	2000	2005	2006	2007
Total [1,2]	**6.3**	**6.2**	**5.8**	**6.7**	**12.7**	**12.0**	**11.2**	**12.4**
Male [2]	5.1	4.6	4.6	4.8	9.2	8.1	7.9	8.5
Female [2]	7.0	7.2	6.6	7.9	15.1	14.8	13.6	15.1
65 to 74 years old	3.3	3.2	3.2	3.2	6.6	6.4	5.6	6.2
75 years old and over	9.5	9.4	8.6	10.4	19.3	18.3	17.3	19.1
White, non-Hispanic.	5.7	5.4	5.2	6.0	12.1	11.2	10.2	11.4
Black, non-Hispanic [2,3].	10.1	10.1	11.1	11.3	19.1	17.7	19.7	19.9
Hispanic or Latino [2,3]	8.6	10.7	7.7	9.0	13.4	16.9	12.8	14.8
Mexican.	9.4	12.0	7.6	7.3	16.3	19.6	12.2	13.8

[1] Includes other races not shown separately. [2] Estimates are age adjusted to the year 2000 standard using two age groups: 65–74 years and 75 years and over. [3] Persons of Hispanic origin may be of any race.

Source: U.S. National Center for Health Statistics, *Health, United States, annual*; http://www.cdc.gov/nchs/hus.htm.

Table 190. **Nursing Homes—Selected Characteristics: 2004**

[Beds: 1,730 represents 1,730,000. Covers licensed and/or certified nursing homes in the conterminous United States that had three or more beds. Based on the 2004 National Nursing Home Survey, a two-stage survey sample of nursing homes and their residents. Subject to sampling variability]

Characteristic	Nursing homes	Beds			Current residents		Full-time equivalent employees [2]	
		Number (1,000)	Per nursing home	Number (1,000)	Occupancy rate [1]	Number (1,000)	Rate per 100 beds
Total	**16,100**	**1,730**	**107.6**	**1,492**	**86.3**	**1,053**	**60.9**
Ownership:							
Proprietary.	9,900	1,074	108.6	918	85.5	615	57.2
Voluntary nonprofit.	5,000	504	101.6	440	87.4	326	64.6
Government and other	1,200	152	123.6	134	87.9	113	74.1
Certification: [3]							
Medicare and medicaid certified	14,100	1,600	113.5	1,380	86.2	972	60.8
Medicare only.	[4]700	[4]33	[4]50.6	28	85.0	20	59.7
Medicaid only	1,100	76	69.0	68	89.1	41	53.7
Bed size:							
Fewer than 50 beds.	2,200	76	33.8	62	82.1	43	56.6
50-99 beds.	6,000	455	75.7	423	92.9	254	55.8
100-199 beds	6,800	903	132.0	789	87.3	563	62.4
200 beds or more	1,000	296	298.2	219	73.9	193	65.3
Region:							
Northeast.	2,800	382	136.0	331	86.8	263	68.9
Midwest.	5,300	527	99.4	448	85.1	286	54.2
South	5,400	586	108.2	502	85.6	353	60.3
West	2,600	236	92.1	211	89.5	151	64.1
Affiliation:							
Chain	8,700	939	107.9	812	86.5	540	57.4
Independent	7,400	791	107.2	680	86.0	514	65.0

[1] Number of residents divided by number of available beds multiplied by 100. [2] Includes only those employees providing direct health-related services to residents. Includes nurses, nurses' aides, orderlies, dental hygienists, physical therapists, speech pathologists and/or audiologists, dieticians or nutritionists, podiatrists, and social workers. [3] Estimates for nursing homes that are "not certified" are not shown because the sample size was less than 30 and figures are unreliable. [4] Figure does not meet standards of reliability or precision.

Source: U.S. National Center for Health Statistics, National Nursing Home Survey. See also <http://www.cdc.gov /nchs/nnhs.htm>.

126   Health and Nutrition

Table 191. **Persons 18 Years and Over With Selected Diseases and Conditions by Selected Characteristics: 2007**
[In thousands (223,181 represents 223,181,000). Based on National Health Interview Survey, a sample survey of the civilian noninstitutionalized population; see Appendix III]

Selected characteristic	Total persons	Persons with selected diseases and conditions					
		Diabetes[1,2]	Ulcers[1]	Kidney disease[3,4]	Liver disease[3]	Arthritis diagnosis[5]	Chronic joint symptoms[5]
Total[6].....................	223,181	17,273	14,501	3,343	2,649	46,429	53,945
SEX							
Male......................	107,750	8,391	6,591	1,482	1,200	18,584	23,574
Female....................	115,431	8,882	7,910	1,861	1,449	27,845	30,371
AGE							
18 to 44 years old..............	110,890	2,432	4,616	759	749	7,810	14,776
45 to 64 years old..............	76,136	8,093	5,641	1,226	1,374	21,428	24,820
65 to 74 years old..............	19,258	3,840	2,119	593	368	8,322	7,140
75 years old and over	16,897	2,908	2,125	766	158	8,870	7,210
RACE							
Race alone[7]...................	220,175	17,014	14,280	3,231	2,562	45,726	52,982
White....................	180,815	12,936	12,567	2,547	2,181	39,515	45,344
Black or African American...........	26,366	2,857	1,226	576	243	4,801	5,580
American Indian or Alaska Native.......	2,222	325	[8]162	(B)	(B)	522	611
Asian	10,437	823	300	[8]74	97	846	1,407
Native Hawaiian or other Pacific Islander....	335	(B)	(B)	–	–	(B)	(B)
Two or more races[9]...............	3,006	259	221	[8]112	[8]87	703	963
HISPANIC ORIGIN AND RACE[10]							
Hispanic or Latino	29,857	2,316	1,190	429	388	3,410	4,645
Mexican or Mexican American.........	18,309	1,422	688	282	220	1,742	2,584

– Represents zero. B Figure too small to meet statistical standards for reliability of a derived figure. [1] Respondents were asked if they had ever been told by a health professional that they had an ulcer or diabetes. A person may be represented in more than one column. [2] Excludes borderline diabetes. [3] Respondents were asked if they had been told in the last 12 months by a health professional that they had weak or failing kidneys or any kind of liver condition. [4] Excludes kidney stones, bladder infections, or incontinence. [5] Respondents were asked if they had ever been told by a health professional that they had some form of arthritis, rheumatoid arthritis, gout, lupus or fibromyalgia. Respondents with joint symptoms (excluding back and neck) that began more than 3 months prior to interview; were classified as having chronic joint symptoms. [6] Total includes other races not shown separately. [7] Refers to persons who indicated only a single race group. [8] Figures do not meet standard of reliability or precision. [9] Refers to all persons who indicated more than one race group. [10] Persons of Hispanic or Latino origin may be of any race or combination of races.

Source: U.S. National Center for Health Statistics, *Vital and Health Statistics*, Series 10, Number 240, *Summary Health Statistics for U.S. Adults: National Health Interview Survey, 2007*; <http://www.cdc.gov/nchs/data/series/sr_10/sr10_240.pdf>.

Table 192. **Persons 18 Years of Age and Over With Selected Circulatory Diseases by Selected Characteristics: 2007**
[In thousands (223,181 represents 223,181,000). In separate questions, respondents were asked if they had ever been told by a doctor or other health professional that they had: hypertension (or high blood pressure); coronary heart disease, angina (or angina pectoris); heart attack (or myocardial infarction); any other heart condition or disease not already mentioned; or a stroke. A person may be represented in more than one column. Based on National Health Interview Survey, a sample survey of the civilian noninstitutionalized population; see Appendix III]

Characteristic	Total persons	Selected circulatory diseases			
		Heart disease		Hypertension[3]	Stroke
		All types[1]	Coronary[2]		
Total[4].....................	223,181	25,095	13,674	52,920	5,426
SEX					
Male	107,750	12,790	8,099	24,959	2,293
Female....................	115,431	12,305	5,575	27,961	3,133
AGE					
18 to 44 years old	110,890	4,591	1,041	9,094	285
45 to 64 years old	76,136	9,266	5,091	24,383	2,156
65 to 74 years old	19,258	5,199	3,571	9,763	1,205
75 years old and over...............	16,897	6,040	3,971	9,679	1,780
RACE					
Race alone[5]...................	220,175	24,638	13,434	52,229	5,334
White	180,815	21,439	11,666	42,217	4,211
Black or African American............	26,366	2,384	1,321	7,681	829
American Indian or Alaska Native........	2,222	201	[6]78	474	(B)
Asian	10,437	607	370	1,758	199
Native Hawaiian or Other Pacific Islander........	335	(B)	–	[6]98	–
Two or more races[7]	3,006	457	240	691	91
HISPANIC ORIGIN AND RACE[8]					
Hispanic or Latino	29,857	1,969	1,136	4,537	489
Mexican or Mexican American.........	18,309	947	597	2,381	249

– Represents zero. B Figure too small to meet statistical standards for reliability of a derived figure. [1] Heart disease includes coronary heart disease, angina pectoris, heart attack, or any other heart condition or disease. [2] Coronary heart disease includes coronary heart disease, angina pectoris, or heart attack. [3] Persons had to have been told on two or more different visits that they had hypertension, or high blood pressure, to be classified as hypertensive. [4] Includes other races not shown separately. [5] Refers to persons who indicated only a single race group. [6] Figures do not meet standard of reliability or precision. [7] Refers to all persons who indicated more than one race group. [8] Persons of Hispanic or Latino origin may be any race or combination of races.

Source: U.S. National Center for Health Statistics, *Vital and Health Statistics*, Series 10, Number 240, *Summary Health Statistics for U.S. Adults: National Health Interview Survey, 2007*; <http://www.cdc.gov/nchs/data/series/sr_10/sr10_240.pdf>.

Health and Nutrition   127

Table 193. Selected Respiratory Diseases Among Persons 18 Years of Age and Over by Selected Characteristics: 2007

[In thousands (223,181 represents 223,181,000). Respondents were asked in two separate questions if they had ever been told by a doctor or other health professional that they had emphysema or asthma. Respondents who had been told they had asthma were asked if they still had asthma. Respondents were asked in three separate questions if they had been told by a doctor or other health professional in the past 12 months that they had hay fever, sinusitis, or bronchitis. Based on the National Health Interview Survey, a sample survey of the civilian noninstitutionalized population; see Appendix III]

Selected characteristic	Total persons	Emphy- sema	Asthma Ever	Asthma Still	Hay fever	Sinusitis	Chronic bronchitis
Total [2]............	223,181	3,736	24,402	16,177	16,882	25,953	7,604
SEX							
Male...........	107,750	2,018	10,383	5,825	7,120	9,748	2,559
Female...........	115,431	1,718	14,020	10,351	9,763	16,205	5,045
AGE							
18 to 44 years old.........	110,890	226	12,996	7,996	7,420	10,261	2,515
45 to 64 years old.........	76,136	1,765	7,895	5,476	7,210	11,154	3,226
65 to 74 years old.........	19,258	861	2,030	1,591	1,302	2,589	1,050
75 years old and over.........	16,897	884	1,481	1,113	950	1,949	813
RACE							
Race alone: [3]	220,175	3,612	23,824	15,781	16,589	25,555	7,367
White.........	180,815	3,341	19,997	13,229	14,265	21,990	6,356
Black or African American.........	26,366	210	2,699	2,025	1,489	2,872	825
American Indian or Alaska Native.........	2,222	(B)	[4]241	[4]146	[4]159	186	[4]58
Asian.........	10,437	[4]21	842	357	675	502	121
Native Hawaiian or other Pacific Islander.........	335	–	(B)	(B)	–	(B)	(B)
Two or more races [5].........	3,006	[4]124	579	396	293	398	237
HISPANIC ORIGIN AND RACE [6]							
Hispanic or Latino.........	29,857	262	2,687	1,664	1,471	2,053	503
Mexican or Mexican American.........	18,309	97	1,331	784	862	1,161	206
Not Hispanic or Latino.........	193,324	3,474	21,715	14,512	15,411	23,900	7,101
White, single race.........	153,359	3,093	17,615	11,743	12,933	20,080	5,914
Black or African American, single race.....	25,574	199	2,585	1,963	1,447	2,817	805

– Represents zero. B Figure too small to meet statistical standards for reliability of a derived figure. [1] A person may be represented in more than one column. [2] Total includes other races not shown separately. [3] Refers to persons who indicated only a single race group. [4] Figure does not meet standard of reliability or precision. [5] Refers to all persons who indicated more than one race group. [6] Persons of Hispanic or Latino origin may be any race or combination of races.
Source: U.S. National Center for Health Statistics, *Vital and Health Statistics, Series 10, Number 240, Summary Health Statistics for U.S. Adult: National Health Interview Survey, 2007*; <http://www.cdc.gov/nchs/data/series/sr_10/sr10_240.pdf>.

Table 194. Persons 18 Years of Age and Over With Migraines and Pains in the Neck, Lower Back, Face, or Jaw by Selected Characteristics: 2007

[In thousands (223,181 represents 223,181,000). Based on National Health Interview Survey, a sample survey of the civilian noninstitutionalized populaion, Appendix III]

Selected characteristic	Total persons	Migraines or severe headaches [2]	Pain in neck [3]	Pains in lower back [3]	Pains in face or jaw [3]
Total [4]............	223,181	27,364	29,019	57,070	9,062
SEX					
Male...........	107,750	7,956	11,665	25,334	2,581
Female...........	115,431	19,409	17,354	31,736	6,481
AGE					
18 to 44 years old.........	110,890	16,427	11,833	24,555	4,649
45 to 64 years old.........	76,136	9,277	12,073	21,860	3,455
65 to 74 years old.........	19,258	1,075	2,833	5,650	607
75 years and over.........	16,897	585	2,280	5,005	350
RACE					
Race alone [5]	220,175	26,792	28,485	56,016	8,825
White.........	180,815	22,241	24,727	47,523	7,532
Black or African American.........	26,366	3,010	2,473	6,006	814
American Indian or Alaska Native.........	2,222	463	336	543	[6]192
Asian.........	10,437	1,049	897	1,799	264
Native Hawaiian or other Pacific Islander....	335	(B)	(B)	[6]146	(B)
Two or more races [7].........	3,006	572	534	1,053	237
HISPANIC ORIGIN AND RACE [8]					
Hispanic or Latino.........	29,857	3,462	3,321	6,851	970
Mexican or Mexican American.........	18,309	1,928	1,925	3,955	516
Not Hispanic or Latino.........	193,324	23,902	25,698	50,218	8,092
White, single race.........	153,359	19,132	21,729	41,463	6,711
Black or African American, single race.....	25,574	2,933	2,408	5,666	759

B Figure to small to meet statistical standards for reliability of a derived figure. [1] A person may be represented in more than one column. [2] Respondents were asked, "During the past 3 months, did you have a severe headache or migraine?" Respondents were instructed to report pain that had lasted a whole day or more and, conversely, not to report fleeting or minor aches or pains. [3] Respondents were asked, "During the past 3 months, did you have a neck pain; or low back pain; or facial ache or pain in the jaw muscles or the joint in front of the ear?" Respondents were instructed to report pain that had lasted a whole day or more and, conversely, not to report fleeting or minor aches or pains. [4] Total includes other races not shown separately. [5] Refers to persons who indicated only a single race group. [6] Figure does not meet standard of reliability or precision. [7] Refers to all persons who indicated more than one race group. [8] Persons of Hispanic or Latino origin may be any race or combination of races.
Source: U.S. National Center for Health Statistics, *Vital and Health Statistics, Series 10, Number 240, Summary Health Statistics for U.S. Adults: National Health Interview Survey, 2007*; <http://www.cdc.gov/nchs/data/series/sr_10/sr10_240.pdf>

128 Health and Nutrition

Table 195. Injury and Poisoning Episodes and Conditions by Age and Sex: 2007

[**34,347 represents 34,347,000.** Covers all medically attended injuries and poisonings occurring during the 5-week period prior to the survey interview. Age adjustment is used to adjust for differences in the age distribution of populations being compared. There may be more than one condition per episode. Based on the National Health Interview Survey, a sample survey of the civilian noninstitutionalized population; see Appendix III]

External cause and nature of injury	Total	Total, age-adjusted [1]	Under 12 years old	12 to 21 years old	22 to 44 years old	45 to 64 years old	65 years old and over	Male, total	Female, total
			Both sexes						
EPISODES									
Number (1,000)............	34,347	(X)	4,468	7,191	11,173	6,861	4,655	18,422	15,925
Annual rate per 1,000 population, total [2]................	115.7	116.6	92.1	172.1	118.5	90.1	128.7	126.7	105.1
Fall	43.4	43.9	51.1	54.0	32.5	28.2	80.7	41.6	45.0
Struck by or against a person or an object...	15.7	15.9	10.7	33.9	18.7	[4]9.1	[4]7.1	19.8	11.7
Transportation [3]..........	12.7	12.6	[4]2.4	14.3	16.1	14.9	[4]11.2	12.3	13.1
Overexertion	12.7	12.8	[4]0.3	21.6	17.2	10.6	[4]11.6	12.7	12.7
Cutting, piercing instruments.	10.3	10.3	[4]8.8	[4]12.8	12.6	[4]8.9	[4]6.3	14.3	6.4
Poisoning [5]	[4]1.6	[4]1.5	[4]3.2	[4]3.1	[4]0.4	[4]1.8	–	[4]1.2	[4]1.9
CONDITIONS									
Annual rate per 1,000 population, total [2]................	154.4	154.8	115.6	196.4	156.8	140.0	181.7	157.9	151.0
Sprains/strains.............	45.0	44.7	[4]11.3	60.3	52.6	48.9	44.2	42.9	47.0
Open wounds	20.7	20.9	28.7	20.1	19.6	15.8	23.5	29.0	12.6
Fractures	21.6	21.7	20.0	44.6	16.5	15.4	23.1	24.4	18.9
Contusions	25.6	25.7	17.2	22.0	22.8	24.2	51.6	17.7	33.3

– Represents zero.   X Not applicable.   [1] Data were age-adjusted using the 2000 standard population using age groups: under 12 years, 12–21 years, 22–44 years, 45–64 years, and 65 years and over.   [2] Includes other items not shown separately.   [3] Includes the categories "Motor vehicle traffic"; "Pedal cycle, other"; "Pedestrian, other"; and "Transport, other."   [4] Figure does not meet standard of reliability or precision.   [5] Poisoning episodes are assumed to have a single condition resulting from the episode.

Source: U.S. National Center for Health Statistics, *Vital and Health Statistics, unpublished data.*

Table 196. Injuries Associated With Selected Consumer Products: 2007

[Estimates calculated from a representative sample of hospitals with emergency treatment departments in the United States. Data are estimates of the number of emergency-room treated cases nationwide associated with various products. Product involvement does not necessarily mean the product caused the accident. Products were selected from the U.S. Consumer Product Safety Commission's National Electronic Injury Surveillance System (NEISS)]

Product	Number	Product	Number
Home workshop equipment:		Stairs or steps	1,161,945
Saws (hand or power)	87,725	Other doors [2]	304,556
Hammers......................	35,037	Home entertainment equipment:	
Household packaging and containers:		Televisions....................	59,844
Household containers and packaging	205,324	Personal use items:	
Bottles and jars.................	72,485	Footwear......................	155,224
Housewares:		Wheelchairs...................	118,901
Knives.......................	429,368	Crutches, canes, walkers	91,849
Tableware and flatware.............	99,010	Yard and garden equipment:	
Drinking glasses	74,004	Lawn mowers..................	78,773
Home furnishing		Sports and recreation equipment:	
Beds........................	532,061	Bicycles......................	515,871
Chairs......................	318,994	Skateboards...................	143,682
Tables [1]......................	309,252	Trampolines	107,345
Household cabinets, racks, and shelves ..	269,617	Playground climbing equipment	77,845
Bathtubs and showers	238,847	Swings or swing sets	59,144
Home structures, construction:			
Floors or flooring materials	1,166,310		

[1] Excludes baby-changing and television tables or stands.   [2] Excludes glass doors and garage doors.

Source: National Safety Council, Itasca, IL, *Injury Facts, annual* (copyright); <http://www.nsc.org/lrs/statstop.aspx>.

Table 197. Costs of Unintentional Injuries: 2007

[**684.4 represents $684,400,000,000.** Covers costs of deaths or disabling injuries together with vehicle accidents and fires]

Cost	Amount (bil. dol.)					Percent distribution				
	Total [1]	Motor vehicle	Work	Home	Other	Total [1]	Motor vehicle	Work	Home	Other
Total	684.4	257.7	175.3	164.7	108.3	100.0	100.0	100.0	100.0	100.0
Wage and productivity losses [2]	344.4	88.5	84.1	104.4	71.1	50.3	34.3	48.0	63.4	65.7
Medical expense	134.0	38.5	35.3	38.1	24.3	19.6	14.9	20.1	23.1	22.4
Administrative expenses [3]	129.2	86.1	40.4	8.3	8.1	18.9	33.4	23.0	5.0	7.5
Motor vehicle damage	42.6	42.6	1.7	(NA)	(NA)	6.2	16.5	1.0	(NA)	(NA)
Employer uninsured cost [4]	19.5	2.0	10.4	4.8	2.6	2.8	0.8	5.9	2.9	2.4
Fire loss	14.7	(NA)	3.4	9.1	2.2	2.1	(NA)	1.9	5.5	2.0

NA Not available.   [1] Excludes duplication between work and motor vehicle; $21.6 billion in 2007.   [2] Actual loss of wages and household production, and the present value of future earnings lost.   [3] Home and other costs may include costs of administering medical treatment claims for some motor-vehicle injuries filed through health insurance plans.   [4] Estimate of the uninsured costs incurred by employers, representing the money value of time lost by noninjured workers.

Source: National Safety Council, Itasca, IL, *Injury Facts, annual* (copyright); <http://www.nsc.org/lrs/statstop.aspx>.

Health and Nutrition   129

Table 198. Use of Mammography for Women 40 Years Old and Over by Patient Characteristics: 1990 to 2005

[Percent of women having a mammogram within the past 2 years. Covers civilian noninstitutional population. Based on National Health Interview Survey; see Appendix III]

Characteristic	1990	2000 [1]	2005 [2]	Characteristic	1990	2000 [1]	2005 [2]
Total [3]	51.4	70.4	66.8	Years of school completed:			
40 to 49 years old	55.1	64.3	63.5	No high school diploma or GED .	36.4	57.7	52.8
50 years old and over.	49.7	73.6	68.4	High school diploma or GED . . .	52.7	69.7	64.9
50 to 64 years old	56.0	78.7	71.8	Some college or more	62.8	76.2	72.7
65 years old and over	43.4	67.9	63.8				
White, non-Hispanic.	52.7	72.2	68.4	Poverty status: [5]			
Black, non-Hispanic.	46.0	67.9	65.2	Below poverty	28.7	54.8	48.5
Hispanic origin [4]	45.2	61.2	58.8	At or above poverty	54.8	72.1	68.8

[1] Adjusted data—data for 2000 have been reweighted using the 2000 census population controls. [2] Data for 2005 are weighted using the 2000 Census Population controls. [3] Includes other races not shown separately and unknown education level and poverty status. [4] Persons of Hispanic origin may be of any race or combination of races. [5] For explanation of poverty level, see text, Section 13.

Source: U.S. National Center for Health Statistics, *Health, United States Annual*, annual. See also <http://www.cdc.gov/nchs/hus.htm>.

Table 199. Current Cigarette Smoking: 1990 to 2007

[In percent. Prior to 1992, a current smoker is a person who has smoked at least 100 cigarettes and who now smokes. Beginning 1995, definition includes persons who smoke only "some days." Excludes unknown smoking status. Based on National Health Interview Survey; for details, see Appendix III]

Sex, age, and race	1990 [1]	2000	2005	2007	Sex, age, and race	1990 [1]	2000	2005	2007
Total smokers, age-adjusted [2]	25.3	23.1	20.8	19.7	Black, total	32.5	26.2	26.5	24.6
					18 to 24 years	21.3	[4]20.9	21.6	21.4
					25 to 34 years	33.8	23.2	29.8	32.3
Male.	28.0	25.2	23.4	22.0	35 to 44 years	42.0	30.7	23.3	17.4
Female	22.9	21.1	18.3	17.5	45 to 64 years	36.7	32.2	32.4	28.3
White male.	27.6	25.4	23.3	22.2	65 years and over . .	21.5	14.2	16.8	14.3
Black male.	32.8	25.7	25.9	23.4	Female, total	22.8	20.9	18.1	17.4
White female	23.5	22.0	19.1	18.5	18 to 24 years.	22.5	24.9	20.7	19.1
Black female	20.8	20.7	17.1	15.6	25 to 34 years.	28.2	22.3	21.5	19.6
					35 to 44 years.	24.8	26.2	21.3	19.6
Total smokers [3] . . .	25.5	23.2	20.9	19.8	45 to 64 years.	24.8	21.7	18.8	19.5
					65 years and over	11.5	9.3	8.3	7.6
Male, total	28.4	25.6	23.9	22.3	White, total	23.4	21.4	18.7	18.1
18 to 24 years.	26.6	28.1	28.0	25.4	18 to 24 years	25.4	28.5	22.6	21.6
25 to 34 years.	31.6	28.9	27.7	28.8	25 to 34 years	28.5	24.9	23.1	21.4
35 to 44 years.	34.5	30.2	26.0	23.2	35 to 44 years	25.0	26.6	22.2	20.7
45 to 64 years.	29.3	26.4	25.2	22.6	45 to 64 years	25.4	21.4	18.9	19.6
65 years and over . . .	14.6	10.2	8.9	9.3	65 years and over . .	11.5	9.1	8.4	8.0
White, total	28.0	25.7	23.6	22.3	Black, total	21.2	20.8	17.3	15.9
18 to 24 years	27.4	30.4	29.7	26.5	18 to 24 years	[4]10.0	[4]14.2	14.2	[4]8.7
25 to 34 years	31.6	29.7	27.7	29.0	25 to 34 years	29.1	15.5	16.9	14.9
35 to 44 years	33.5	30.6	26.3	24.4	35 to 44 years	25.5	30.2	19.0	17.7
45 to 64 years	28.7	25.8	24.5	22.1	45 to 64 years	22.6	25.6	21.0	22.6
65 years and over . .	13.7	9.8	7.9	8.9	65 years and over . .	11.1	10.2	10.0	6.4

[1] Data prior to 1997 are not strictly comparable with data for later years due to the 1997 questionnaire redesign. [2] Data are age adjusted to the year 2000 standard using five age groups: 18–24 years, 25–34 years, 35–44 years, 45–64 years, 65 years and over. [3] Crude, not age adjusted. [4] Figure does not meet standard of reliability or precision.

Source: U.S. National Center for Health Statistics, *Health, United States*, 2009. See also <http://www.cdc.gov/nchs/hus.htm>.

Table 200. Current Cigarette Smoking by Sex and State: 2007

[In percent. Current cigarette smoking is defined as persons 18 years and older who reported having smoked 100 or more cigarettes during their lifetime and who currently smoke every day or some days. Based on the Behavioral Risk Factor Surveillance System, a telephone survey of health behaviors of the civilian, noninstitutionalized U.S. population, 18 years old and over; for details, see source]

State	Total	Male	Female	State	Total	Male	Female	State	Total	Male	Female
U.S. [1] . .	19.8	21.3	18.4	KS	17.9	18.7	17.1	ND	21.0	22.2	19.8
				KY	28.3	28.8	27.8	OH	23.1	24.2	22.1
AL	22.5	25.7	19.7	LA	22.6	26.4	19.1	OK	25.8	28.0	23.8
AK	22.2	24.6	19.7	ME	20.1	21.0	19.3	OR	16.9	18.9	14.9
AZ	19.8	23.4	16.3	MD	17.1	18.4	16.0	PA	20.9	20.7	21.1
AR	22.4	24.8	20.2	MA	16.4	17.4	15.5	RI	17.0	17.8	16.3
CA	14.3	18.1	10.6	MI	21.2	23.5	19.0	SC	21.9	25.3	18.8
CO	18.7	19.7	17.7	MN	16.5	18.3	14.7	SD	19.8	20.1	19.5
CT	15.5	16.6	14.5	MS	24.0	27.8	20.5	TN	24.3	25.7	22.9
DE	19.0	17.6	20.3	MO	24.6	26.0	23.3	TX	19.4	22.0	16.9
DC	17.3	19.1	15.7	MT	19.5	19.8	19.3	UT	11.7	15.5	8.0
FL	19.3	21.3	17.5	NE	19.9	23.2	16.8	VT	17.6	19.5	15.9
GA	19.3	21.2	17.5	NV	21.5	23.4	19.6	VA	18.6	20.3	16.9
HI	17.0	19.8	14.3	NH	19.4	20.2	18.6	WA	16.8	18.0	15.7
ID	19.2	20.9	17.4	NJ	17.2	19.4	15.2	WV	27.0	28.6	25.5
IL	20.2	22.1	18.4	NM	20.8	23.6	18.1	WI	19.6	19.6	19.5
IN	24.1	25.9	22.4	NY	18.9	21.6	16.5	WY	22.1	22.8	21.4
IA	19.8	21.4	18.3	NC	22.9	25.3	20.7				

[1] Represents median value among the states and DC. For definition of median, see Guide to Tabular Presentations.

Source: U.S. Centers for Disease Control and Prevention, Atlanta, GA, *Morbidity and Mortality Weekly Report*, Vol. 58, No. 09, (released 13 March 2009); <http://www.cdc.gov/mmwr>.

Table 201. Substance Abuse Treatment Facilities and Clients: 1995 to 2007

[As of October 2 (1995); as of October 1 (1997–2000), as of March 29 (2002), and as of March 31 (2003–2006), and March 30, 2007. Based on the Uniform Facility Data Set (UFDS)/National Survey of Substance Abuse Treatment Services (N-SSATS) survey, a census of all known facilities that provide substance abuse treatment in the United States and associated jurisdictions. Selected missing data for responding facilities were imputed]

Primary focus	Number	Primary focus	Number	Type of care and type of problem	Number of clients
FACILITIES		CLIENTS		2007, total [1,4]	1,135,425
1995	10,746	1995	1,009,127	Outpatient rehabilitation . . .	1,004,208
1998	13,455	1998	1,038,378	Outpatient detoxification. . .	12,705
2000	13,428	2000	1,000,896	24-hour rehabilitation.	104,657
2002	13,720	2002	1,136,287	24-hour detoxification	13,855
2003	13,623	2003	1,092,546		
2004	13,454	2004	1,072,251	2007, total [1,4]	1,133,436
2005	13,371	2005	1,081,049	Drug only	412,400
2006	13,771	2006	1,130,881	Alcohol only...........	211,094
2007, total [4]	13,648	2007, total [4]	1,135,425	Both alcohol & drug......	509,919
Substance abuse treatment services	8,360	Substance abuse treatment services	768,047	Total with a drug problem [2]	922,342
Mental health services. . .	949	Mental health services. . .	47,803	Total with an alcohol problem [3]	721,018
General health care	189	General health care	12,747		
Both substance abuse and mental health.....	3,957	Both substance abuse and mental health.....	297,907		
Other..............	193	Other..............	8,921		

[1] Excludes clients at facilities that did not provide data on type of substance abuse problem treated.   [2] The sum of clients with a drug problem and clients with both diagnoses.   [3] The sum of clients with an alcohol problem and clients with both diagnoses.   [4] Data for 2007 is based on preliminary data and is subject to change.

Source: U.S. Substance Abuse and Mental Health Services Administration, Uniform Facility Data Set (UFDS): Annual surveys for 1995–1999, and Office of Applied Studies, Substance Abuse and Mental Health Services Administration, National Survey of Substance Abuse Treatment Services (N-SSATS), 2000–2007. See <http://oas.samhsa.gov/oasftp.cfm#Data>.

Table 202. Drug Use by Type of Drug and Age Group: 2002 and 2007

[In percent. Data comes from the National Survey on Drug Use and Health (NSDUH). Current users are those who used drugs at least once within month prior to this study. Based on a representative sample of the U.S. population age 12 and older, including persons living in households and in some group quarters such as dormitories and homeless shelters. Estimates are based on computer-assisted interviews of about 68,000 respondents. Subject to sampling variability; see source]

Age and type of drug	Ever used		Current user		Age and type of drug	Ever used		Current user	
	2002	2007	2002	2007		2002	2007	2002	2007
12 YEARS OLD AND OVER					10 TO 25 YEARS OLD				
Any illicit drug [1]...........	46.0	46.1	8.3	8.0	Any illicit drug [1]...........	59.8	57.4	20.2	19.7
Marijuana and hashish	40.4	40.6	6.2	5.8	Marijuana and hashish	53.8	50.8	17.3	16.4
Cocaine..............	14.4	14.5	0.9	0.8	Cocaine..............	15.4	15.0	2.0	1.7
Crack..............	3.6	3.5	0.2	0.2	Hallucinogens	24.2	19.2	1.9	1.5
Heroin.............	1.6	1.5	0.1	0.1	Inhalants	15.7	11.3	0.5	0.4
Hallucinogens	14.6	13.8	0.5	0.4	Any psychotherapeutic [2,3]..	28.3	29.9	5.5	6.0
LSD..............	10.4	9.1	0.0	0.1	Alcohol	86.7	85.2	60.5	61.2
Ecstasy	4.3	5.0	0.3	0.2	"Binge" alcohol use [4]	(NA)	(NA)	40.9	41.8
Inhalants	9.7	9.1	0.3	0.2	Cigarettes	71.2	64.7	40.8	36.2
Any psychotherapeutic [2,3]..	20.4	20.3	2.7	2.8	Smokeless tobacco	23.7	20.1	4.8	5.3
Pain relievers.........	12.6	13.3	1.9	2.1	Cigars................	45.6	42.3	11.0	11.8
Tranquilizers	8.2	8.2	0.8	0.7					
Stimulants [3]........	10.0	8.7	0.6	0.4	26 TO 34 YEARS OLD				
Methamphetamine [3].	6.5	5.3	0.3	0.2	Any illicit drug [1]...........	58.3	56.6	10.5	10.9
Sedatives	4.2	3.4	0.2	0.1	Marijuana and hashish	52.2	50.3	7.7	7.9
Alcohol	83.1	82.3	51.0	51.1	Cocaine..............	17.6	16.6	1.2	1.4
"Binge" alcohol use [4]	(NA)	(NA)	22.9	23.3	Hallucinogens	20.6	22.0	0.5	0.7
Cigarettes	69.1	65.3	26.0	24.2	Inhalants	14.1	14.0	0.1	0.2
Smokeless tobacco	19.9	18.2	3.3	3.2	Any psychotherapeutic [2,3]..	25.7	27.2	3.7	3.5
Cigars................	37.4	35.7	5.4	5.4					
Pipe tobacco	17.0	14.3	0.8	0.8	35 YEARS OLD AND OVER				
					Any illicit drug [1]...........	42.7	44.6	4.6	4.6
12 TO 17 YEARS OLD					Marijuana and hashish	38.0	40.2	3.1	3.0
Any illicit drug [1]...........	30.9	26.2	11.6	9.5	Cocaine..............	15.4	15.9	0.6	0.6
Marijuana and hashish	20.6	16.2	8.2	6.7	Hallucinogens	12.6	12.5	0.1	0.1
Cocaine..............	2.7	2.1	0.6	0.4	Inhalants	7.2	7.4	0.1	0.1
Hallucinogens	5.7	3.5	1.0	0.7	Any psychotherapeutic [2,3]..	18.5	18.2	1.6	1.9
Inhalants	10.5	9.6	1.2	1.2					
Any psychotherapeutic [2,3]..	13.7	11.7	4.0	3.3	26 YEARS OLD AND OVER				
Alcohol	43.4	39.4	17.6	15.9	Alcohol	88.0	87.5	53.9	54.1
"Binge" alcohol use [4]	(NA)	(NA)	10.7	9.7	"Binge" alcohol use [4]	(NA)	(NA)	21.4	21.9
Cigarettes	33.3	23.7	13.0	9.8	Cigarettes	73.7	70.9	25.2	24.1
Smokeless tobacco	8.0	7.7	2.0	2.4	Smokeless tobacco	20.9	19.3	3.2	3.0
Cigars................	7.6	13.0	4.5	4.2	Cigars................	39.0	37.5	4.6	4.4

NA Not available.   [1] Illicit drugs include marijuana/hashish, cocaine (including crack), heroin, hallucinogens, inhalants, or prescription-type psychotherapeutics used nonmedically.   [2] Nonmedical use of prescription-type psychotherapeutics includes the nonmedical use of pain relievers, tranquilizers, stimulants, or sedatives and does not include over-the-counter drugs.   [3] Includes data from new methamphetamine items added in 2006 and 2007. Previous estimates have been adjusted to be comparable with new data and differ from those in reports prior to the 2007 data year.   [4] Binge alcohol use is defined as drinking five or more drinks on the same occasion (i.e., at the same time or within a couple of hours of each other) on at least 1 day in the past 30 days.

Source: U.S. Substance Abuse and Mental Health Services Administration, National Survey on Drug Use and Health, 2002 and 2007; <http://oas.samhsa.gov/nhsda.htm>.

Health and Nutrition 131

Table 203. **Estimated Use of Selected Drugs by State: 2006 to 2007**

[20,107 represents 20,107,000. Data in this table cover a 2 year period. Data is based on the National Survey on Drug Use and Health (NSDUH). Current users are those persons 12 years old and over who used drugs at least once within month prior to this study. Based on national sample of respondents (see also headnote, Table 202). The state estimates were produced by combining the prevalence rate based on the state sample data and the prevalence rate based on a national regression model applied to local-area county and census block group/tract-level estimates from the state (i.e., a survey-weighted hierarchical Bayes estimation approach). The parameters of the regression model are estimated from the entire national sample. For comparison purposes, the data shown here display estimates for all 50 states and the District of Columbia utilizing the modeled estimates for all 51 areas]

State	Estimated current users (1,000)					Current users as percent of population				
	Any illicit drug [1]	Mari- juana	Any illicit drug other than mari- juana [1]	Ciga- rettes	Binge alcohol [2]	Any illicit drug [1]	Mari- juana	Any illicit drug other than mari- juana [1]	Ciga- rettes	Binge alcohol [2]
U.S.	20,107	14,631	9,442	60,807	57,181	8.1	5.9	3.8	24.6	23.2
AL.	266	172	148	1,090	714	7.0	4.5	3.9	28.6	18.8
AK.	57	43	21	131	121	10.7	8.1	3.9	24.6	22.7
AZ.	459	269	279	1,265	1,159	9.1	5.3	5.5	25.0	22.9
AR.	198	135	113	688	516	8.6	5.8	4.9	29.8	22.3
CA.	2,708	1,949	1,188	5,885	6,412	9.1	6.6	4.0	19.8	21.6
CO	431	324	179	960	1,029	11.0	8.2	4.6	24.4	26.2
CT.	231	182	94	612	734	7.9	6.2	3.2	21.0	25.1
DE.	61	44	27	175	165	8.6	6.3	3.8	24.7	23.2
DC	60	49	24	128	143	12.1	9.8	4.8	25.8	28.6
FL.	1,168	835	588	3,734	3,506	7.7	5.5	3.9	24.6	23.1
GA	570	433	251	1,866	1,604	7.5	5.7	3.3	24.6	21.1
HI	78	56	29	215	240	7.5	5.3	2.8	20.6	22.9
ID	88	64	40	255	236	7.4	5.4	3.4	21.4	19.8
IL	772	574	348	2,693	2,757	7.3	5.4	3.3	25.6	26.2
IN	437	312	210	1,452	1,160	8.4	6.0	4.1	28.0	22.3
IA	129	95	64	622	681	5.2	3.8	2.6	25.1	27.5
KS.	166	126	84	581	572	7.4	5.6	3.7	25.8	25.4
KY.	281	202	137	1,058	742	8.1	5.8	3.9	30.4	21.3
LA	284	187	164	944	847	8.2	5.4	4.7	27.1	24.4
ME	108	94	37	304	261	9.6	8.3	3.3	26.9	23.1
MD	326	235	161	1,032	977	7.0	5.1	3.5	22.3	21.1
MA	531	427	222	1,159	1,448	9.8	7.9	4.1	21.4	26.7
MI	765	589	323	2,161	2,110	9.1	7.0	3.9	25.8	25.2
MN	357	312	139	1,091	1,235	8.3	7.3	3.2	25.4	28.8
MS	167	108	88	620	440	7.1	4.6	3.7	26.4	18.7
MO	386	267	200	1,410	1,173	8.0	5.5	4.2	29.2	24.3
MT	82	69	31	190	214	10.3	8.7	3.9	23.9	26.9
NE.	98	73	47	368	351	6.7	5.1	3.2	25.4	24.3
NV.	186	125	85	555	499	9.0	6.1	4.1	26.9	24.2
NH	110	92	39	259	286	9.8	8.2	3.5	23.2	25.6
NJ.	469	337	217	1,588	1,656	6.5	4.7	3.0	21.9	22.9
NM	153	112	63	376	333	9.6	7.0	3.9	23.5	20.9
NY.	1,467	1,117	582	3,619	3,769	9.1	6.9	3.6	22.4	23.3
NC	522	385	262	1,885	1,491	7.2	5.3	3.6	25.8	20.4
ND	33	26	14	134	169	6.2	5.0	2.6	25.3	32.0
OH	746	576	328	2,751	2,409	7.9	6.1	3.5	28.9	25.3
OK	247	151	134	893	618	8.5	5.2	4.6	30.6	21.2
OR	317	237	132	712	678	10.2	7.6	4.2	22.8	21.7
PA.	729	530	324	2,620	2,456	7.0	5.1	3.1	25.1	23.5
RI	112	92	49	227	250	12.5	10.3	5.5	25.3	27.9
SC	235	173	114	1,051	782	6.6	4.8	3.2	29.4	21.9
SD.	43	34	16	166	182	6.7	5.3	2.6	25.9	28.3
TN.	444	288	262	1,535	967	8.8	5.7	5.2	30.5	19.2
TX.	1,249	799	744	4,682	4,279	6.7	4.3	4.0	24.9	22.8
UT.	130	85	69	353	315	6.4	4.2	3.4	17.5	15.6
VT.	61	54	22	125	137	11.5	10.0	4.1	23.4	25.6
VA.	513	411	227	1,506	1,413	8.2	6.6	3.6	24.1	22.6
WA	544	397	243	1,169	1,199	10.2	7.4	4.6	21.9	22.5
WV	113	81	64	479	289	7.4	5.3	4.2	31.1	18.8
WI	383	273	196	1,306	1,341	8.2	5.9	4.2	28.1	28.8
WY	37	30	17	126	116	8.7	6.9	3.9	29.4	26.9

[1] Illicit drugs include marijuana/hashish, cocaine (including crack), heroin, hallucinogens, inhalants, or prescription-type psychotherapeutics used nonmedically. Illicit drugs other than marijuana include cocaine (including crack), heroin, hallucinogens, inhalants, or prescription-type psychotherapeutics used nonmedically. [2] Binge alcohol use is defined as drinking five or more drinks on the same occasion (i.e., at the same time or within a couple of hours of each other) on at least 1 day in the past 30 days.

Source: U.S. Substance Abuse and Mental Health Services Administration, *National Survey on Drug Use and Health, 2006 and 2007*; <http://www.oas.samhsa.gov/nhsda.htm>.

132   Health and Nutrition

Table 204. **Cumulative Percent Distribution of Population by Height and Sex: 2003 to 2006**

[Data are based on National Health and Nutrition Examination Survey (NHANES), a sample of the civilian noninstitutional population. For this survey, the respondent participates in an interview and a physical examination. For persons 20 years old and over. Height was measured without shoes. Based on sample and subject to sampling variability; see source]

Height	Males						Females					
	20–29 years	30–39 years	40–49 years	50–59 years	60–69 years	70–79 years	20–29 years	30–39 years	40–49 years	50–59 years	60–69 years	70–79 years
Percent under—												
4'10"	–	–	–	–	–	–	1.1	[1]0.9	(B)	2.0	1.7	[1]2.6
4'11"	–	–	–	–	–	(B)	2.2	2.1	[1]2.0	3.1	3.0	5.9
5'	–	(B)	–	–	(B)	(B)	5.5	5.2	6.3	8.2	6.1	13.5
5'1"	(B)	(B)	(B)	(B)	(B)	(B)	10.6	12.1	11.7	13.6	14.3	23.1
5'2"	(B)	(B)	[1]0.3	(B)	(B)	(B)	18.5	19.6	19.6	20.8	23.9	37.3
5'3"	[1]1.2	2.6	[1]1.2	(B)	[1]2.0	[1]1.1	32.1	30.4	31.1	36.6	40.9	55.4
5'4"	2.8	4.8	2.8	[1]2.7	4.1	5.3	47.4	45.2	46.3	53.6	54.1	68.7
5'5"	6.0	8.7	3.7	4.9	8.3	12.5	60.7	61.4	63.1	65.4	70.3	82.2
5'6"	10.8	13.6	8.5	10.8	14.0	20.2	74.2	74.1	75.6	79.1	82.7	90.0
5'7"	16.7	20.3	15.4	19.6	21.9	28.8	85.6	83.4	85.3	90.1	90.5	96.1
5'8"	25.8	30.8	24.9	30.6	36.4	42.4	94.0	91.3	91.5	95.8	96.0	99.0
5'9"	37.8	42.7	38.8	43.5	48.6	54.1	97.2	96.1	95.7	98.9	96.9	99.7
5'10"	49.7	57.7	54.3	56.2	61.7	71.1	98.8	98.6	98.4	99.5	98.2	100.0
5'11"	62.4	71.1	65.9	71.3	72.0	84.0	99.6	99.6	99.8	99.7	99.7	100.0
6'	73.5	80.7	78.0	80.7	84.9	89.0	99.8	99.9	100.0	99.9	99.7	100.0
6'1"	85.0	88.5	88.1	87.6	91.5	94.0	99.8	99.9	100.0	100.0	100.0	100.0
6'2"	91.4	92.1	94.6	93.2	95.3	97.1	100.0	100.0	100.0	100.0	100.0	100.0
6'3"	95.5	95.9	97.6	96.8	98.3	98.6	100.0	100.0	100.0	100.0	100.0	100.0
6'4"	98.7	97.7	99.3	98.8	99.3	99.5	100.0	100.0	100.0	100.0	100.0	100.0
6'5"	99.0	99.0	99.4	99.2	100.0	100.0	100.0	100.0	100.0	100.0	100.0	100.0
6'6"	99.8	99.7	99.9	99.8	100.0	100.0	100.0	100.0	100.0	100.0	100.0	100.0

– Represents zero.   B Base figure too small to meet statistical standards of reliability of a derived figure.   [1] Figure does not meet standard of reliability or precision.

Source: U.S. National Center for Health Statistics and unpublished data; <http://www.cdc.gov/nchs/nhanes.htm>.

Table 205. **Cumulative Percent Distribution of Population by Weight and Sex: 2003 to 2006**

[See headnote, Table 204. Data are based on National Health and Nutrition Examination Survey (NHANES). Weight was measured without shoes. Pregnant females were excluded from the analyses. Based on sample and subject to sampling variability; see source]

Weight	Males						Females					
	20–29 years	30–39 years	40–49 years	50–59 years	60–69 years	70–79 years	20–29 years	30–39 years	40–49 years	50–59 years	60–69 years	70–79 years
Percent under—												
100 lbs	(B)	(B)	–	–	(B)	(B)	2.6	(B)	(B)	(B)	(B)	(B)
110 lbs	(B)	(B)	(B)	–	(B)	(B)	7.2	2.4	[1]1.9	[1]2.9	[1]3.3	4.9
120 lbs	[1]1.5	(B)	(B)	(B)	(B)	(B)	18.9	14.8	8.9	9.1	7.1	12.4
130 lbs	4.5	[1]1.4	[1]1.5	3.1	[1]2.2	3.2	32.3	22.7	15.6	17.8	15.1	22.2
140 lbs	10.1	6.0	3.1	4.6	4.6	7.9	46.6	35.7	26.5	25.9	24.5	34.3
150 lbs	16.5	11.5	6.2	9.0	8.0	13.5	55.0	45.2	39.7	35.7	34.8	47.3
160 lbs	28.2	20.9	12.3	15.2	13.3	22.0	63.1	55.1	49.6	47.0	46.1	59.7
170 lbs	39.6	31.0	20.1	24.9	22.7	32.0	71.8	62.7	58.1	58.4	57.4	69.5
180 lbs	52.4	41.3	30.3	37.0	30.9	44.4	77.9	71.9	65.4	65.7	66.6	79.8
190 lbs	62.8	50.8	42.3	46.3	43.2	54.2	82.1	77.6	70.4	72.0	74.8	86.9
200 lbs	70.4	60.6	52.5	55.8	52.6	65.5	86.5	81.0	77.2	77.6	80.1	88.7
210 lbs	76.5	68.6	63.3	64.8	64.8	75.3	88.3	85.8	82.1	82.0	85.1	92.5
220 lbs	80.8	76.7	72.3	73.2	73.5	85.5	90.5	88.5	84.5	85.5	88.8	94.8
230 lbs	84.9	84.8	77.7	79.7	80.0	89.5	93.2	90.8	88.5	88.4	91.7	96.7
240 lbs	88.6	89.2	83.9	85.7	86.2	91.7	94.8	93.1	90.7	91.3	93.4	97.9
250 lbs	92.0	91.6	88.8	89.9	90.9	93.5	95.3	94.6	93.5	93.2	95.3	98.7
260 lbs	93.9	93.9	92.5	91.2	93.7	95.6	96.3	96.0	95.1	95.1	97.2	99.2
270 lbs	95.3	94.9	93.8	93.5	96.0	97.6	97.2	97.2	95.8	96.3	98.2	99.4
280 lbs	96.2	95.6	95.8	95.7	97.0	98.0	98.4	97.9	97.2	97.3	98.6	99.4
290 lbs	96.6	96.2	96.2	97.2	98.1	99.0	98.7	98.3	98.1	97.6	98.6	99.5
300 lbs	96.8	97.2	97.1	98.5	98.2	99.4	98.8	98.6	98.4	98.4	98.9	99.6
320 lbs	98.0	98.5	98.5	99.3	99.0	99.8	99.7	99.1	99.2	98.9	99.4	100.0
340 lbs	98.7	99.1	99.1	99.6	99.5	100.0	99.7	99.6	99.6	99.3	99.4	100.0
360 lbs	99.3	99.2	99.5	99.8	99.7	100.0	99.9	99.8	100.0	99.7	99.6	100.0
380 lbs	99.5	99.6	99.6	100.0	100.0	100.0	99.9	99.9	100.0	99.7	99.6	100.0
400 lbs	99.6	99.8	99.9	100.0	100.0	100.0	99.9	99.9	100.0	100.0	100.0	100.0
420 lbs	99.6	99.8	99.9	100.0	100.0	100.0	99.9	100.0	100.0	100.0	100.0	100.0
440 lbs	99.8	99.9	99.9	100.0	100.0	100.0	100.0	100.0	100.0	100.0	100.0	100.0

– Represents zero.   B Base figure too small to meet statistical standards of reliability of a derived figure.   [1] Figure does not meet standard of reliability or precision.

Source: U.S. National Center for Health Statistics and unpublished data; <http://www.cdc.gov/nchs/nhanes.htm>.

Health and Nutrition   133

Table 206. Age-Adjusted Percent Distributions of Body Mass Index (BMI) Among Persons 18 Years Old and Over by Selected Characteristics: 2003 to 2006

[See headnote, Table 203. Body Mass Index (BMI) is a measure that adjusts body weight for height. It is calculated as weight in kilograms divided by height in meters squared. For both men and women, underweight is indicated by a BMI under 18.5; healthy weight is indicated by a BMI greater than or equal to 18.5 and less than 25.0; overweight is greater than or equal to 25.0 and less than 30.0; obesity is indicated by a BMI greater than or equal to 30.0. BMI is calculated from the measurement of the participants' weight and height during the examination. Based on the National Health and Nutrition Examination Survey (NHANES)]

Selected characteristic	Under-weight	Healthy weight	Above healthy weight		
			Total	Overweight	Obese
Total [1] (age-adjusted)	1.9	32.5	65.6	32.9	32.6
Total [1] (crude)	1.9	32.1	66.0	33.1	33.0
Age: [2]					
18 to 44 years old	2.6	37.4	60.0	29.7	30.3
45 to 64 years old	1.1	25.5	73.4	35.0	38.4
65 to 74 years old	[3]0.9	25.1	73.9	39.1	34.8
75 years old and over	1.7	34.5	63.9	39.7	24.1
Sex:					
Male	1.5	27.9	70.6	39.1	31.5
Female	2.3	37.2	60.5	26.9	33.7
Race/ethnicity and sex:					
Not Hispanic or Latino:					
White, male	1.6	27.9	70.5	38.8	31.6
White, female	2.6	40.2	57.2	26.1	31.1
Black alone or African American, male.	1.7	28.8	69.5	35.1	34.4
Black alone or African American, female	[3]1.2	20.3	78.4	26.0	52.4
Mexican or Mexican American, male	[3]0.5	26.4	73.1	45.0	28.1
Mexican or Mexican American, female	(B)	26.4	72.3	31.3	41.0
Education: [4]					
Less than a high school diploma	1.5	29.4	69.1	33.8	35.3
High school diploma or GED	1.3	26.9	71.8	34.1	37.7
Some college, bachelor's degree, or higher . . .	1.4	31.7	66.9	34.9	32.0

B Base figure too small to meet statistical standards for reliability of a derived figure.   [1] Total includes other race/ethnicities not shown separately and persons with unknown race/ethnicity.   [2] Estimates for age groups are not age adjusted.   [3] Figure does not meet standard of reliability or precision.   [4] Education is shown only for persons 25 years old and over.

Source: U.S. National Center for Health Statistics, unpublished data; <http://www.cdc.gov/nchs/nhanes.htm>.

Table 207. Age-Adjusted Percentage of Persons Engaging in Physical Activity and Fitness by Selected Characteristics: 2006

[In percent. Covers persons 18 years old and over. Based on the National Health Interview Survey, a sample survey of the civilian noninstitutionalized population. Leisure-time physical activity is assessed by asking respondents a series of questions about participation in moderate and vigorous-intensity physical activities. To assess muscle-strengthening activities, respondents were asked about leisure-time physical activities specifically designed to strengthen their muscles]

Characteristic	No leisure-time physical activity [1]	Regular Physical activity-moderate or vigorous [2]	Muscular strength and endur-ance [3]	Characteristic	No leisure-time physical activity [1]	Regular Physical activity-moderate or vigorous [2]	Muscular strength and endur-ance [3]
Total	39.2	30.9	19.4	Two or more races. . .	34.7	29.9	25.7
SEX				HISPANIC ORIGIN AND RACE			
Male	38.1	33.1	22.0	Hispanic or Latino.	53.0	22.6	13.1
Female	40.1	28.9	17.0	Not Hispanic or Latino . .	37.0	32.3	20.5
AGE [4]				White, non-Hispanic. .	48.2	33.7	18.0
18 to 24 years old . . .	34.4	38.1	26.5	Black, non-Hispanic. .	35.1	24.8	21.1
25 to 44 years old . . .	34.7	33.4	22.5	Education level (persons aged			
45 to 64 years old . . .	39.4	29.5	17.3	25 years years and over):			
65 to 74 years old . . .	47.6	26.2	12.1	Less than 9th grade. .	66.6	15.0	5.3
75 years old and over	59.3	17.3	9.4	Grades 9 thru 11	59.5	17.3	7.2
RACE				High School graduate.	47.2	23.5	13.3
Race alone				Some college or AA degree	34.7	31.7	20.7
White	38.0	31.8	19.7	College graduate or above	23.1	43.4	28.6
Black or African American.	48.1	24.9	17.8				
American Indian or Alaska Native	33.6	29.0	16.5				
Asian or Pacific Islander	(NA)	(NA)	(NA)				

[1] Persons with no moderate- or vigorous-intensity activity for at least 10 minutes at a time.   [2] Regular physical activity is moderate-intensity physical activity at least 5 times a week for 30 minutes/time or vigorous-intensity physical activity for at least 3 times/week for 20 minutes/time.   [3] Persons who participated in muscle strengthening activities at least 2 times/week.   [4] Age data are not age-adjusted.

Source: U.S. National Center for Chronic Disease Prevention and Health Promotion, "Nutrition and Physical Activity" and unpublished data; <http://wonder.cdc.gov/data2010/>.

Table 208. High School Students Engaged in Physical Activity by Sex: 2007

[In percent. For students in grades 9 to 12. Based on the Youth Risk Behavior Survey, a school-based survey and subject to sampling error; for details see source]

Characteristic	Met currently recommended levels of physical activity [1]	Did not meet currently recommended levels of physical activity [2]	Enrolled in physical education class — Total [3]	Enrolled in physical education class — Attended daily	Played on at least one sports team [4]	Injured while exercising or playing sports [5]	Used computers 3 or more hours/day [6]	Watched 3 or more hours/day of TV [7]
All students	34.7	24.9	53.6	30.3	56.3	21.9	24.9	35.4
Male	43.7	18.0	57.7	33.2	62.1	24.1	29.1	37.5
Grade 9.	44.4	17.1	68.3	39.7	63.4	26.0	30.5	42.0
Grade 10.	45.1	16.3	62.3	35.7	64.7	24.5	30.0	38.1
Grade 11	45.2	18.0	51.4	27.9	63.0	23.8	29.5	35.4
Grade 12.	38.7	21.5	44.6	27.5	56.2	20.9	25.6	32.8
Female	25.6	31.8	49.4	27.3	50.4	19.3	20.6	33.2
Grade 9.	31.5	26.1	65.1	40.4	54.7	21.7	24.9	37.2
Grade 10.	24.4	31.7	51.2	26.1	50.8	20.8	22.6	35.9
Grade 11	24.6	34.3	38.8	19.8	52.5	18.2	17.9	29.6
Grade 12.	20.6	36.2	38.5	20.2	41.9	14.8	14.8	28.9

[1] Were physically active doing any kind of physical activity that increased their heart rate and made them breathe hard some of the time for a total of at least 60 minutes/day for at least 5 or more days during the 7 days before the survey. [2] Did not participate 60 or more minutes of any kind of physical activity that increased their heart rate and made them breathe hard some of the time on at least 1 day during the 7 days before the survey. [3] On one or more days in an average week when they were in school. [4] Run by their school or community groups during the 12 months before the survey. [5] Students who saw a doctor or nurse for an injury that happened while exercising or playing sports. [6] For activity that was not school related. [7] On an average school day.

Source: U.S. Centers for Disease Control and Prevention, Atlanta, GA, Youth Risk Behavior Surveillance—United States, 2007, *Morbidity and Mortality Weekly Report*, Vol. 57, No. SS-4, June 6, 2008. See <http://www.cdc.gov/mmwr/preview/mmwrhtml /ss5704a1.htm>.

Table 209. Households and Persons Having Problems With Access to Food: 2003 to 2007

[**112,214 represents 112,214,000.** Food-secure means that a household had access at all times to enough food for an active healthy life for all household members, with no need for recourse to socially unacceptable food sources or extraordinary coping behaviors to meet their basic food needs. Food-insecure households had limited or uncertain ability to acquire acceptable foods in socially acceptable ways. Households with very low food security (a subset of food-insecure households) were those in which food intake of one or more household members was reduced and normal eating patterns disrupted due to inadequate resources for food. The severity of food insecurity in households is measured through a series of questions about experiences and behaviors known to characterize households that are having difficulty meeting basic food needs. These experiences and behaviors generally occur in an ordered sequence as the severity of food insecurity increases. As resources become more constrained, adults in typical households first worry about having enough food, then they stretch household resources and juggle other necessities, then decrease the quality and variety of household members' diets, then decrease the frequency and quantity of adults' food intake, and finally decrease the frequency and quantity of children's food intake. All questions refer to the previous 12 months and include a qualifying phrase reminding respondents to report only those occurrences that resulted from inadequate financial resources. Restrictions to food intake due to dieting or busy schedules are excluded. The omission of homeless persons may be a cause of underreporting. Data are from the Food Security Supplement to the Current Population Survey (CPS); for details about the CPS, see text, Section 1, Population, and Appendix III]

Household food security level	Number (1,000) 2003	2004	2005	2006	2007	Percent distribution 2003	2004	2005	2006	2007
Households, total	112,214	112,967	114,437	115,609	117,100	100.0	100.0	100.0	100.0	100.0
Food-secure	99,631	99,473	101,851	102,961	104,089	88.8	88.1	89.0	89.1	88.9
Food-insecure	12,583	13,494	12,586	12,648	13,011	11.2	11.9	11.0	10.9	11.1
With low food security [1]	8,663	9,045	8,158	8,031	8,262	7.7	8.0	7.1	6.9	7.0
With very low food security [2]	3,920	4,449	4,428	4,617	4,749	3.5	3.9	3.9	4.0	4.1
With very low food security among children [3]	207	274	270	221	323	0.5	0.7	0.7	0.6	0.8
Adult members.	213,441	215,564	217,897	220,423	223,467	100.0	100.0	100.0	100.0	100.0
In food-secure households . . .	190,451	191,236	195,172	197,536	199,672	89.2	88.7	89.6	89.6	89.4
In food-insecure households	22,990	24,328	22,725	22,887	23,795	10.8	11.3	10.4	10.4	10.6
With low food security	16,358	16,946	15,146	15,193	15,602	7.7	7.9	7.0	6.9	7.0
With very low food security [2]	6,632	7,382	7,579	7,694	8,193	3.1	3.4	3.5	3.5	3.7
Child members.	72,969	73,039	73,604	73,587	73,575	100.0	100.0	100.0	100.0	100.0
In food-secure households	59,704	59,171	61,201	60,959	61,140	81.8	81.0	83.1	82.8	83.1
In food-insecure households	13,265	13,868	12,403	12,628	12,435	18.2	19.0	16.9	17.2	16.9
With very low food security among children [3]	420	545	606	430	691	0.6	0.7	0.8	0.6	0.9

[1] Prior to 2006, USDA described these households as food insecure without hunger. [2] Food intake of one or more members in these households was reduced and normal eating patterns disrupted at some time during the year because of the household's food insecurity. Prior to 2006, USDA described these households as food insecure with hunger. [3] Percentages omit households with no children. The food security survey measures food security status at the household level. Not all children residing in food-insecure households were directly affected by the households food insecurity. Similarly, not all children in households classified as having very low food security among children were subject to the reductions in food intake and disruptions in eating patterns that characterize this condition. Young children, in particular, are often protected from effects of the households food insecurity.

Source: U.S. Dept. of Agriculture, Economic Research Service, *Household Food Security in the United States, 2007, Economic Research Report Number 66*; November 2008; <http://www.ers.usda.gov/publications/err66/>.

Health and Nutrition 135

Table 210. **Per Capita Consumption of Selected Beverages by Type:
1980 to 2007**

[In gallons. See headnote, Table 212. Per capita consumption uses U.S. resident population, July 1, for all beverages except coffee, tea, and fruit juices which use U.S. total population (Resident plus Armed Forces overseas), July 1]

Commodity	1980	1990	1995	2000	2003	2004	2005	2006	2007
Nonalcoholic	105.5	134.6	138.0	150.9	151.2	153.0	153.1	154.2	153.1
Milk (plain and flavored).	27.6	25.7	23.9	22.5	21.6	21.3	21.0	21.0	20.7
Whole	17.0	10.5	8.6	8.1	7.6	7.3	7.0	6.7	6.4
Reduced-fat, light, and skim	10.5	15.2	15.3	14.4	14.0	14.0	14.1	14.2	14.3
Tea	7.3	6.9	7.9	7.8	7.5	8.0	8.0	8.4	8.4
Coffee.	26.7	26.8	20.2	26.3	24.3	24.7	24.3	24.4	24.6
Bottled water	2.7	8.8	11.6	16.7	21.6	23.2	25.5	27.7	29.1
Carbonated soft drinks.	33.6	47.1	50.6	53.2	52.6	52.5	51.7	50.6	48.8
Diet.	(NA)	14.0	13.8	13.8	15.1	15.4	15.3	15.2	14.9
Regular	(NA)	33.1	36.8	39.4	37.5	37.0	36.3	35.4	33.9
Fruit juices.	7.6	6.9	8.0	9.0	8.6	8.7	8.3	8.2	8.2
Fruit drinks, cocktails, and ades. . . .	(NA)	12.3	15.0	14.8	14.5	14.3	13.9	13.5	12.9
Canned iced tea	(NA)	0.1	0.7	(NA)	(NA)	(NA)	(NA)	(NA)	(NA)
Vegetable juices	(NA)	(NA)	(NA)	0.5	0.5	0.5	0.5	0.5	0.5
Alcoholic.	28.3	27.5	24.7	25.0	25.2	25.3	25.2	25.5	25.7
Beer.	24.3	23.9	21.8	21.7	21.6	21.7	21.5	21.7	21.8
Wine [1]	2.1	2.0	1.7	2.0	2.2	2.3	2.3	2.4	2.5
Distilled spirits	2.0	1.5	1.2	1.3	1.3	1.4	1.4	1.4	1.4

NA Not available.   [1] Beginning 1983, includes wine coolers.

Source: U.S. Department of Agriculture, Economic Research Service, *Food Consumption, Prices, and Expenditures,
1970–1997*; Food Consumption (Per Capita) Data System; <http://www.ers.usda.gov/data/foodconsumption/>.

Table 211. **Nutrition—Nutrients in Foods Available for Civilian Consumption
Per Capita Per Day: 1970 to 2006**

[Computed by the Center for Nutrition Policy and Promotion (CNPP). Based on Economic Research Service (ERS) estimates of per capita quantities of food available for consumption from "Food Consumption, Prices, and, Expenditures", on imputed consumption data for foods no longer reported by ERS, and on CNPP estimates of quantities of produce from home gardens. Food supply estimates do not reflect loss of food or nutrients from further marketing or home processing. Enrichment and fortification levels of iron, zinc, thiamin, riboflavin, niacin, folate, vitamin A, vitamin B_6, vitamin B_{12}, and Vitamin C are included]

Nutrient	Unit	1970–79	1980–89	1990–99	2000	2006
Food energy	Kilocalories.	3,200	3,400	3,600	3,900	3,900
Carbohydrate.	Grams	395	421	478	495	474
Fiber	Grams	20	22	24	24	25
Protein	Grams	96	100	108	111	111
Total fat [1]	Grams	143	151	150	169	178
Saturated.	Grams	49	50	48	52	54
Monounsaturated	Grams	57	61	64	75	77
Polyunsaturated	Grams	27	30	31	35	39
Cholesterol	Milligrams.	430	420	400	410	420
Vitamin A	Micrograms RAE [2] . . .	1,050	1,050	1,100	1,090	940
Carotene.	Micrograms.	560	600	710	690	690
Vitamin E	Milligrams a-TE [3] . . .	14	16	17	20	21
Vitamin C	Milligrams.	109	115	118	121	106
Thiamin.	Milligrams.	2	3	3	3	3
Riboflavin	Milligrams.	3	3	3	3	3
Niacin.	Milligrams.	25	29	31	32	32
Vitamin B_6.	Milligrams.	2	2	2	2	2
Folate [4].	Micrograms DFE [5] . . .	341	383	504	902	874
Vitamin B_{12}	Micrograms.	9	8	8	8	8
Calcium	Milligrams.	930	930	980	980	960
Phosphorus	Milligrams.	1,540	1,590	1,690	1,720	1,700
Magnesium	Milligrams.	340	360	390	400	400
Iron	Milligrams.	17	20	23	23	23
Zinc	Milligrams.	13	14	15	15	16
Copper	Milligrams.	2	2	2	2	2
Potassium	Milligrams.	3,510	3,550	3,720	3,780	3,620
Sodium [6].	Milligrams.	1,210	1,210	1,240	1,230	1,150
Selenium.	Micrograms.	133	143	163	179	181

[1] Includes other types of fat not shown separately.   [2] Retinol activity equivalents.   [3] Alpha-Tocopherol equivalents.
[4] Reflects new terminology from Institute of Medicine's Dietary Reference Intakes reports.   [5] Dietary Folate Equivalents (DFE).
[6] Does not include amount from processed foods; underestimates actual availability.

Source: U.S. Dept. of Agriculture, Center for Nutrition Policy and Promotion, *Nutrient Content of the U.S. Food Supply,
1909–2006*. Data also published by Economic Research Service in *Food Consumption, Prices, and Expenditures*, annual. See
<http://www.cnpp.usda.gov/>.

Table 212. **Per Capita Consumption of Major Food Commodities: 1980 to 2007**

[**In pounds, retail weight, except as indicated.** Consumption represents the residual after exports, nonfood use and ending stocks are subtracted from the sum of beginning stocks, domestic production, and imports. Based on Census Bureau estimated resident population]

Commodity	Unit	1980	1990	1995	2000	2005	2006	2007
Red meat, total (boneless, trimmed weight) [1, 2] . .	Pounds . .	126.4	112.2	113.6	113.7	110.3	110.0	110.6
Beef.	Pounds . .	72.1	63.9	63.5	64.5	62.5	62.8	62.2
Veal	Pounds . .	1.3	0.9	0.8	0.5	0.4	0.4	0.3
Lamb and mutton	Pounds . .	1.0	1.0	0.9	0.8	0.8	0.8	0.8
Pork. . . . . [2] . . .	Pounds . .	52.1	46.4	48.4	47.8	46.6	46.0	47.3
Poultry (boneless, trimmed weight) [2]	Pounds . .	40.8	56.2	62.1	67.9	73.7	74.3	73.7
Chicken	Pounds . .	32.7	42.4	48.2	54.2	60.6	60.9	59.9
Turkey	Pounds . .	8.1	13.8	13.9	13.7	13.2	13.3	13.8
Fish and shellfish (boneless, trimmed weight) . . .	Pounds . .	12.4	14.9	14.8	15.2	16.2	16.5	16.3
Eggs	Number . .	271	234	232	251	255	257	249
Shell.	Number . .	236	186	172	178	172	175	170
Processed. . . . . . . [3]	Number . .	35	48	60	73	83	81	79
Dairy products, total [3]	Pounds . .	543.1	568.0	576.2	592.2	597.7	606.0	606.1
Fluid milk products [4]	Gallons . .	27.9	26.2	24.6	23.2	22.2	22.2	22.0
Beverage milks	Gallons . .	27.6	25.7	23.9	22.5	21.0	21.0	20.7
Plain whole milk.	Gallons . .	16.5	10.2	8.3	7.7	6.7	6.5	6.1
Plain reduced-fat milk (2%)	Gallons . .	6.3	9.1	8.0	7.1	6.9	6.9	6.9
Reduced fat milk (1%) and skim milk	Gallons . .	3.1	4.9	6.1	6.1	5.6	5.7	5.7
Flavored whole milk	Gallons . .	0.6	0.3	0.3	0.4	0.3	0.3	0.3
Flavored milks other than whole	Gallons . .	0.6	0.8	0.8	1.0	1.4	1.4	1.4
Buttermilk	Gallons . .	0.5	0.4	0.3	0.3	0.2	0.2	0.2
Yogurt (excl. frozen).	1/2 pints. .	4.6	7.8	11.4	12.0	19.1	20.4	21.3
Fluid cream products [5]	1/2 pints. .	10.5	14.3	15.6	18.3	24.1	24.2	24.7
Cream [6]	1/2 pints. .	6.3	8.7	9.4	11.6	14.9	15.4	15.7
Sour cream and dips	1/2 pints. .	3.4	4.7	5.4	6.1	8.3	7.9	8.2
Condensed and evaporated milks	Pounds . .	7.0	7.9	6.8	5.8	5.9	6.4	7.6
Whole milk.	Pounds . .	3.8	3.1	2.3	2.0	2.2	2.2	2.0
Skim milk.	Pounds . .	3.3	4.8	4.5	3.8	3.7	4.2	5.6
Cheese [7]	Pounds . .	17.5	24.6	26.9	29.8	31.6	32.5	32.7
American [8]	Pounds . .	9.6	11.1	11.7	12.7	12.7	13.1	12.8
Cheddar	Pounds . .	6.8	9.0	9.0	9.7	10.3	10.4	10.0
Italian [8]	Pounds . .	4.4	9.0	10.3	12.1	13.3	13.7	14.1
Mozzarella	Pounds . .	3.0	6.9	8.0	9.3	10.2	10.5	10.9
Other [8]	Pounds . .	3.3	4.3	5.0	4.8	5.6	5.8	5.8
Swiss.	Pounds . .	1.3	1.4	1.1	1.0	1.3	1.3	1.3
Cream and Neufchatel	Pounds . .	0.9	1.6	2.2	2.3	2.4	2.5	2.6
Cottage cheese, total.	Pounds . .	4.5	3.4	2.7	2.6	2.7	2.6	2.6
Lowfat	Pounds . .	0.8	1.2	1.2	1.3	1.4	1.4	1.4
Frozen dairy products	Pounds . .	26.4	28.5	29.0	28.0	25.0	26.0	25.2
Ice cream.	Pounds . .	17.5	15.8	15.5	16.7	14.6	14.7	14.0
Lowfat ice cream.	Pounds . .	7.1	7.7	7.4	7.3	6.7	6.9	7.0
Sherbet	Pounds . .	1.2	1.2	1.3	1.2	1.2	1.2	1.3
Frozen yogurt	Pounds . .	(NA)	2.8	3.4	2.0	1.3	1.3	1.2
Fats and oils:								
Total, fat content only	Pounds . .	56.9	62.3	64.2	81.7	85.5	84.6	84.9
Butter (product weight)	Pounds . .	4.5	4.4	4.4	4.5	4.5	4.7	4.7
Margarine (product weight)	Pounds . .	11.3	10.9	9.1	8.2	4.0	4.6	4.5
Lard (direct use)	Pounds . .	2.3	0.9	0.4	0.8	1.6	1.7	1.6
Edible beef tallow (direct use)	Pounds . .	1.1	0.6	2.7	4.0	3.8	3.9	2.9
Shortening	Pounds . .	18.2	22.2	22.2	31.5	29.0	24.9	21.0
Salad and cooking oils	Pounds . .	21.2	25.2	26.5	33.7	42.8	44.6	50.2
Other edible fats and oils	Pounds . .	1.5	1.2	1.6	1.5	1.6	2.1	1.7
Flour and cereal products [9]	Pounds . .	144.9	181.0	188.7	199.2	192.1	194.0	196.9
Wheat flour	Pounds . .	116.9	135.9	140.0	146.3	134.2	135.6	138.1
Rice, milled	Pounds . .	9.5	15.8	17.1	18.9	20.8	20.7	20.5
Corn products	Pounds . .	12.9	21.4	24.9	28.4	31.4	31.9	32.4
Oat products	Pounds . .	3.9	6.5	5.5	4.4	4.6	4.6	4.7
Caloric sweeteners, total [10]	Pounds . .	120.2	132.4	144.1	148.8	142.3	139.1	136.3
Sugar, refined cane and beet	Pounds . .	83.6	64.4	64.9	65.5	63.2	62.4	62.0
Corn sweeteners [11]	Pounds . .	35.3	66.8	77.9	81.8	77.7	75.1	72.9
High-fructose corn syrup.	Pounds . .	19.0	49.6	57.6	62.6	59.2	58.3	56.2
Other:								
Cocoa beans	Pounds . .	3.4	5.4	4.5	5.9	6.5	6.4	6.0
Coffee (green beans).	Pounds . .	10.3	10.3	7.9	10.3	9.5	9.5	9.6
Peanuts (shelled)	Pounds . .	5.1	6.1	5.7	5.9	6.7	6.5	6.3
Tree nuts (shelled)	Pounds . .	1.8	2.5	1.9	2.6	2.7	3.3	3.3

NA Not available.   [1] Excludes edible offals.   [2] Excludes shipments to Puerto Rico and the other U.S. possessions.   [3] Milk-equivalent, milk-fat basis. Includes butter.   [4] Fluid milk figures are aggregates of commercial sales and milk produced and consumed on farms.   [5] Includes eggnog not shown separately.   [6] Heavy cream, light cream, and half-and-half.   [7] Excludes full-skim American, cottage, pot, and baker's cheese.   [8] Includes other cheeses not shown separately.   [9] Includes rye flour and barley products not shown separately. Excludes quantities used in alcoholic beverages.   [10] Dry weight. Includes edible syrups (maple, molasses, etc.) and honey not shown separately.   [11] Includes glucose and dextrose not shown separately.

Source: U.S. Department of Agriculture, Economic Research Service, *Food Consumption, Prices, and Expenditures, Food Availability (Per Capita) Data System*; <http://www.ers.usda.gov/data/foodconsumption/>.

Health and Nutrition 137

Table 213. **Per Capita Utilization of Selected Commercially Produced Fruits and Vegetables: 1980 to 2007**

[In pounds, farm weight. Domestic food use of fresh fruits and vegetables reflects the fresh-market share of commodity production plus imports and minus exports]

Commodity	1980	1990	1995	2000	2003	2004	2005	2006	2007
Fruits and vegetables, total [1]	**603.6**	**642.5**	**682.3**	**708.9**	**701.8**	**700.4**	**687.8**	**675.3**	**680.0**
Fruits, total	265.0	256.8	274.6	285.6	279.7	278.6	270.8	269.5	263.0
Fresh fruits	106.2	116.6	123.1	128.5	128.3	128.1	126.3	129.4	126.2
Noncitrus	80.5	95.6	99.6	105.0	104.4	105.4	104.6	107.8	108.1
Apples	19.4	19.8	18.9	17.5	16.9	18.9	16.7	17.9	16.4
Bananas	20.8	24.3	27.1	28.4	26.2	25.8	25.2	25.1	26.0
Cantaloupes	5.8	9.2	9.0	11.1	10.8	10.0	9.8	9.6	9.9
Grapes	4.0	7.9	7.5	7.4	7.7	7.8	8.6	7.6	8.0
Peaches and nectarines	7.1	5.5	5.3	5.3	5.2	5.1	4.8	4.6	4.5
Pears	2.6	3.3	3.4	3.4	3.1	3.0	2.9	3.2	3.1
Pineapples	1.5	2.0	1.9	3.2	4.4	4.4	4.4	5.2	5.0
Plums and prunes	1.5	1.5	0.9	1.2	1.2	1.1	1.1	1.0	1.0
Strawberries	2.0	3.2	4.1	4.9	5.3	5.5	5.8	6.1	6.4
Watermelons	10.7	13.3	15.2	13.8	13.5	13.0	14.0	15.9	16.3
Other [2]	5.1	5.4	6.3	8.7	10.1	10.8	10.7	11.6	11.5
Fresh citrus	26.1	21.4	23.8	23.5	23.9	22.7	21.7	21.6	18.1
Oranges	14.3	12.4	11.8	11.7	11.9	10.8	11.4	10.2	7.5
Grapefruit	7.3	4.4	6.0	5.1	4.1	4.1	2.7	2.3	2.8
Other [3]	4.5	4.6	6.0	6.7	7.9	7.8	7.6	9.0	7.8
Processed fruits	158.8	140.2	151.4	157.1	151.4	150.5	144.5	140.2	136.9
Frozen fruits [4]	3.3	4.3	5.2	4.2	5.1	4.4	5.1	4.5	4.4
Dried fruits [5]	11.2	12.1	12.6	10.4	9.9	9.3	10.1	10.2	9.6
Canned fruits [6]	24.5	20.9	17.3	17.5	17.2	16.9	16.5	15.4	15.9
Fruit juices [7]	119.0	102.7	116.0	124.6	118.9	119.5	112.4	109.2	106.1
Vegetables, total	338.6	385.7	407.7	423.4	422.1	421.8	416.9	405.8	417.0
Fresh vegetables	151.6	170.5	181.3	199.2	200.2	201.5	198.3	196.2	202.2
Asparagus (all uses)	0.3	0.6	0.6	1.0	1.0	1.1	1.1	1.1	1.1
Broccoli	1.4	3.4	4.3	5.9	5.5	5.6	5.6	6.2	6.0
Cabbage	8.0	8.3	8.1	8.9	7.6	8.3	8.1	8.2	8.6
Carrots	6.2	8.3	11.2	9.2	8.8	8.8	8.8	8.8	9.0
Cauliflower	1.1	2.2	1.6	1.7	1.6	1.6	1.5	1.7	1.7
Celery (all uses)	7.4	7.2	6.9	6.3	6.3	6.2	5.9	6.1	6.4
Corn	6.5	6.7	7.8	9.0	9.5	9.2	8.9	8.7	9.1
Cucumbers	3.9	4.7	5.6	6.4	6.2	6.5	6.3	6.4	6.3
Head lettuce	25.6	27.7	22.2	23.5	22.2	21.3	21.1	20.2	20.3
Mushrooms	1.2	2.0	2.0	2.6	2.6	2.6	2.6	2.6	2.6
Onions	11.4	15.1	17.8	18.9	19.5	21.7	21.1	19.9	21.7
Snap beans	1.3	1.1	1.6	2.0	2.0	1.9	1.8	2.1	2.2
Bell peppers (all uses)	2.9	4.5	6.2	7.0	6.9	7.0	7.1	7.0	6.8
Potatoes	51.1	46.7	49.2	47.1	46.9	45.9	42.5	37.3	39.2
Sweet potatoes (all uses)	4.4	4.4	4.2	4.2	4.7	4.6	4.5	4.6	5.2
Tomatoes	12.8	15.5	16.8	19.0	19.5	20.0	20.2	20.0	20.3
Other fresh vegetables [8]	6.0	11.8	14.7	26.7	29.4	29.2	31.0	35.5	35.6
Processed vegetables	187.0	215.2	226.4	224.1	221.9	220.3	218.7	209.6	214.7
Selected vegetables for freezing [9]	51.5	66.8	78.8	79.3	78.9	79.0	76.4	74.5	76.0
Selected vegetables for canning [10]	102.5	110.3	108.2	103.2	101.1	102.8	105.1	94.7	97.2
Vegetables for dehydrating [11]	10.5	14.6	14.5	17.3	17.3	15.3	13.9	14.1	14.1
Potatoes for chips	16.5	16.4	16.4	15.9	17.3	16.6	16.2	18.8	18.7
Pulses [12]	5.9	7.2	8.4	8.5	7.3	6.7	7.0	7.5	8.7

[1] Excludes wine grapes.   [2] Apricots, avocados, cherries, cranberries, kiwifruit, mangoes, papayas, and honeydew melons.   [3] Lemons, limes, tangerines, and tangelos.   [4] Apples, apricots, blackberries, blueberries, boysenberries, cherries, loganberries, peaches, plums, prunes, raspberries, and strawberries.   [5] Apples, apricots, dates, figs, peaches, pears, prunes, and raisins.   [6] Apples, apricots, cherries, olives, peaches, pears, pineapples, plums, and prunes.   [7] Apple, cranberry, grape, grapefruit, lemon, lime, orange, pineapple, and prunes.   [8] Artichokes, brussels sprouts, eggplant, escarole, endive, garlic, romaine, leaf lettuce, radishes, spinach, and squash. Beginning 2000, includes collard greens, kale, mustard greens, okra, pumpkin, and turnip greens.   [9] Asparagus, snap beans, lima beans, broccoli, carrots, cauliflower, sweet corn, green peas, potatoes, spinach, and miscellaneous vegetables.   [10] Asparagus, snap beans, beets, cabbage, carrots, chili peppers, sweet corn, cucumbers for pickling, green peas, lima beans, mushrooms, spinach, and tomatoes.   [11] Onions and potatoes.   [12] Dry peas, lentils, and dry edible beans.

Source: U.S. Department of Agriculture, Economic Research Service, *Food Consumption, Prices, and Expenditures, Food Availability (Per Capita) Data System;* <http://www.ers.usda.gov/data/foodconsumption/>.

Section 4
Education

This section presents data primarily concerning formal education as a whole, at various levels, and for public and private schools. Data shown relate to the school-age population and school enrollment, educational attainment, education personnel, and financial aspects of education. In addition, data are shown for charter schools, security measures used in schools, computer usage in schools, and adult education. The chief sources are the decennial census of population and the Current Population Survey (CPS), both conducted by the U.S. Census Bureau (see text, Section 1, Population); annual, biennial, and other periodic surveys conducted by the National Center for Education Statistics (NCES), a part of the U.S. Department of Education; and surveys conducted by the National Education Association.

The censuses of population have included data on school enrollment since 1840 and on educational attainment since 1940. The CPS has reported on school enrollment annually since 1945 and on educational attainment periodically since 1947.

The NCES is continuing the pattern of statistical studies and surveys conducted by the U.S. Office of Education since 1870. The annual *Digest of Education Statistics* provides summary data on pupils, staff, finances, including government expenditures, and organization at the elementary, secondary, and higher education levels. It is also a primary source for detailed information on federal funds for education, projections of enrollment, graduates, and teachers. *The Condition of Education,* issued annually, presents a summary of information on education of particular interest to policymakers. NCES also conducts special studies periodically.

The census of governments, conducted by the Census Bureau every 5 years (for the years ending in "2" and "7"), provides data on school district finances and state and local government expenditures for education. Reports published by the Bureau of Labor Statistics contain data relating civilian labor force experience to educational attainment (see also Tables 579, 606, and 614 in Section 12, Labor Force, Employment, and Earnings).

Types and sources of data—The statistics in this section are of two general types. One type, exemplified by data from the Census Bureau, is based on direct interviews with individuals to obtain information about their own and their family members' education. Data of this type relate to school enrollment and level of education attained, classified by age, sex, and other characteristics of the population. The school enrollment statistics reflect attendance or enrollment in any regular school within a given period; educational attainment statistics reflect the highest grade completed by an individual, or beginning 1992, the highest diploma or degree received.

Beginning in 2001, the CPS used Census 2000 population controls. From 1994 to 2000, the CPS used 1990 census population controls plus adjustment for undercount. Also the survey changed from paper to computer-assisted technology. For years 1981 through 1993, 1980 census population controls were used; 1971 through 1980, 1970 census population controls had been used. These changes had little impact on summary measures (e.g., medians) and proportional measures (e.g., enrollment rates); however, use of the controls may have significant impact on absolute numbers.

The second type, generally exemplified by data from the NCES and the National Education Association, is based on reports from administrators of educational institutions and of state and local agencies having jurisdiction over education. Data of this type relate to enrollment, attendance, staff, and finances for the nation, individual states, and local areas.

U.S. Census Bureau, Statistical Abstract of the United States: 2010

Unlike the NCES, the Census Bureau does not regularly include specialized vocational, trade, business, or correspondence schools in its surveys. The NCES includes nursery schools and kindergartens that are part of regular grade schools in their enrollment figures. The Census Bureau includes all nursery schools and kindergartens. At the higher education level, the statistics of both agencies are concerned with institutions granting degrees or offering work acceptable for degree-credit, such as junior colleges.

School attendance—All states require that children attend school. While state laws vary as to the ages and circumstances of compulsory attendance, generally they require that formal schooling begin by age 6 and continue to age 16.

Schools—The NCES defines a school as "a division of the school system consisting of students composing one or more grade groups or other identifiable groups, organized as one unit with one or more teachers to give instruction of a defined type, and housed in a school plant of one or more buildings. More than one school may be housed in one school plant, as is the case when the elementary and secondary programs are housed in the same school plant."

Regular schools are those which advance a person toward a diploma or degree. They include public and private nursery schools, kindergartens, graded schools, colleges, universities, and professional schools.

Public schools are schools controlled and supported by local, state, or federal governmental agencies; private schools are those controlled and supported mainly by religious organizations or by private persons or organizations.

The Census Bureau defines *elementary* schools as including grades 1 through 8; *high* schools as including grades 9 through 12; and *colleges* as including junior or community colleges, regular 4-year colleges, and universities and graduate or professional schools. Statistics reported by the NCES and the National Education Association by type of organization, such as elementary level and secondary level, may not be strictly comparable with those from the Census Bureau because the grades included at the two levels vary, depending on the level assigned to the middle or junior high school by the local school systems.

School year—Except as otherwise indicated in the tables, data refer to the school year which, for elementary and secondary schools, generally begins in September of the preceding year and ends in June of the year stated. For the most part, statistics concerning school finances are for a 12-month period, usually July 1 to June 30. Enrollment data generally refer to a specific point in time, such as fall, as indicated in the tables.

Statistical reliability—For a discussion of statistical collection, estimation, and sampling procedures and measures of statistical reliability applicable to the Census Bureau and the NCES data, see Appendix III.

U.S. Census Bureau, Statistical Abstract of the United States: 2010

Figure 4.1
Elementary and Secondary Enrollment by Grade Level: 2000 to 2017

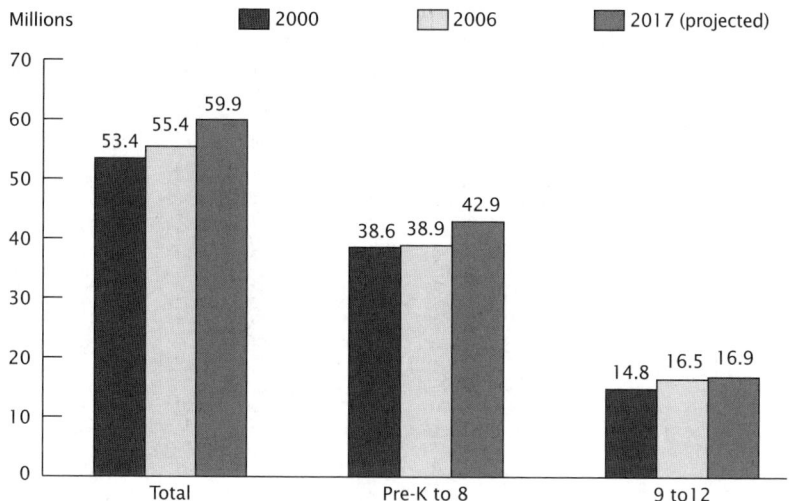

Source: Chart prepared by U.S. Census Bureau. For data, see Table 214.

Figure 4.2
Bachelor's Degrees Earned by Field: 1990 to 2007

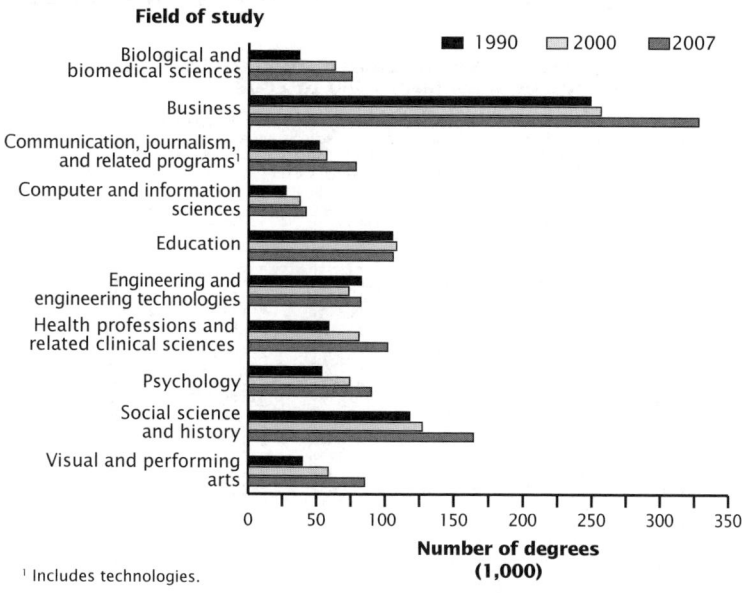

¹ Includes technologies.

Source: Chart prepared by U.S. Census Bureau. For data, see Table 291.

U.S. Census Bureau, Statistical Abstract of the United States: 2010

Table 214. **School Enrollment: 1980 to 2018**

[In thousands (58,306 represents 58,306,000). As of fall]

Year	All levels			Pre-K through grade 8		Grades 9 through 12		College [1]	
	Total	Public	Private	Public	Private	Public	Private	Public	Private
1980	58,306	50,335	7,971	27,647	3,992	13,231	1,339	9,457	2,640
1985	57,226	48,901	8,325	27,034	4,195	12,388	1,362	9,479	2,768
1988	58,485	50,349	8,136	28,501	4,036	11,687	1,206	10,161	2,894
1989	59,279	51,120	8,159	29,152	4,035	11,390	1,163	10,578	2,961
1990	60,269	52,061	8,208	29,878	4,084	11,338	1,150	10,845	2,974
1991	62,087	53,357	8,730	30,506	4,518	11,541	1,163	11,310	3,049
1992	62,987	54,208	8,779	31,088	4,528	11,735	1,148	11,385	3,102
1993	63,438	54,654	8,784	31,504	4,536	11,961	1,132	11,189	3,116
1994	64,177	55,245	8,932	31,898	4,624	12,213	1,162	11,134	3,145
1995	65,020	55,933	9,087	32,341	4,721	12,500	1,197	11,092	3,169
1996	65,912	56,733	9,180	32,764	4,720	12,847	1,213	11,121	3,247
1997	66,573	57,323	9,250	33,073	4,726	13,054	1,218	11,196	3,306
1998	67,034	57,677	9,357	33,346	4,748	13,193	1,240	11,138	3,369
1999	67,667	58,166	9,501	33,488	4,765	13,369	1,254	11,309	3,482
2000	68,685	58,956	9,729	33,688	4,878	13,515	1,292	11,753	3,560
2001	69,920	59,905	10,014	33,938	4,993	13,734	1,326	12,233	3,695
2002	71,015	60,935	10,080	34,116	4,886	14,067	1,334	12,752	3,860
2003	71,540	61,397	10,143	34,202	4,761	14,338	1,338	12,857	4,043
2004	72,154	61,775	10,379	34,178	4,731	14,617	1,356	12,980	4,292
2005	72,674	62,135	10,539	34,205	4,699	14,909	1,374	13,022	4,466
2006 . . . .,. . .	73,155	62,479	10,676	34,221	4,708	15,078	1,389	13,180	4,579
2007, proj. [2] . . .	73,827	62,961	10,867	34,383	4,720	15,087	1,389	13,491	4,757
2008, proj.	74,437	63,527	10,910	34,667	4,739	14,955	1,377	13,904	4,794
2009, proj.	74,942	63,924	11,018	34,973	4,754	14,815	1,363	14,137	4,900
2010, proj.	75,289	64,233	11,056	35,335	4,783	14,698	1,347	14,200	4,926
2011, proj.	75,781	64,661	11,120	35,732	4,818	14,617	1,329	14,312	4,974
2012, proj.	76,407	65,202	11,205	36,126	4,859	14,641	1,319	14,435	5,027
2013, proj.	77,162	65,844	11,318	36,523	4,910	14,716	1,303	14,605	5,105
2014, proj.	77,958	66,527	11,431	36,903	4,967	14,866	1,294	14,758	5,170
2015, proj.	78,756	67,220	11,536	37,160	5,006	15,186	1,307	14,874	5,223
2016, proj.	79,515	67,873	11,641	37,496	5,051	15,396	1,318	14,981	5,273
2017, proj.	80,303	68,542	11,761	37,838	5,096	15,588	1,335	15,116	5,331
2018, proj.	81,047	69,175	11,873	38,179	5,139	15,754	1,355	15,241	5,379

[1] Data beginning 1996 based on new classification system. See footnote 1, Table 269.   [2] Pre-K through 12 are projections; college data are actual.

Source: U.S. National Center for Education Statistics, *Digest of Education Statistics*, annual, and *Projections of Education Statistics*, annual.

Table 215. **School Expenditures by Type of Control and Level of Instruction in Constant (2007 to 2008) Dollars: 1980 to 2008**

[In millions of dollars (436,517 represents $436,517,000,000). For school years ending in year shown. Data shown reflect historical revisions. Total expenditures for public elementary and secondary schools include current expenditures, interest on school debt and capital outlay. Data deflated by the Consumer Price Index, all urban consumers, on a school- year basis (supplied by the National Center for Education Statistics). See also Appendix III. Based on survey of state education agencies; see source for details]

Year		Elementary and secondary schools			Colleges and universities [2]		
	Total	Total	Public	Private [1]	Total	Public	Private
1980	436,517	281,316	261,682	19,634	155,200	102,991	52,209
1985	479,085	299,038	274,219	24,820	180,046	116,722	63,324
1989	582,126	365,748	337,100	28,648	216,378	137,905	78,471
1990	609,931	385,423	354,745	30,678	224,508	143,003	81,505
1991	624,938	393,995	362,694	31,301	230,943	146,958	83,985
1992	640,190	400,946	369,238	31,707	239,245	151,410	87,834
1993	653,278	407,934	375,702	32,232	245,444	155,325	90,119
1994	667,694	416,705	384,129	32,577	250,988	158,266	92,723
1995	683,165	425,633	392,697	32,936	257,531	162,519	95,012
1996	696,798	435,800	402,366	33,434	260,998	163,777	97,221
1997	717,876	451,560	417,189	34,371	266,316	167,832	98,485
1998	746,684	473,315	437,582	35,733	273,370	173,881	99,489
1999	776,920	494,882	457,827	37,055	282,038	180,819	101,219
2000	811,989	515,886	477,495	38,391	296,103	190,485	105,618
2001	852,431	537,818	496,709	41,109	314,613	205,963	108,650
2002	894,347	560,840	517,238	43,602	333,506	217,932	115,574
2003	924,996	572,891	528,832	44,059	352,105	229,044	123,061
2004	944,560	584,217	539,508	44,709	360,343	233,291	127,052
2005	967,210	597,219	551,718	45,501	369,991	238,321	131,671
2006 [1, 3]	984,841	608,679	562,507	46,172	376,162	241,021	135,141
2007 [1]	1,007,000	624,000	577,000	48,000	383,000	246,000	136,000
2008 [1]	1,017,000	631,000	583,000	48,000	386,000	250,000	136,000

[1] Estimated.   [2] Data beginning 1996 based on new classification system. See footnote 1, Table 269.   [3] Detail may not add to total due to rounding.

Source: U.S. National Center for Education Statistics, *Digest of Education Statistics*, annual.

Table 216. **School Enrollment, Faculty, Graduates, and Finances—Projections: 2008 to 2014**

[As of fall, except as indicated (55,380 represents 55,380,000)]

Item	Unit	2008	2009	2010	2011	2012	2013	2014
ELEMENTARY AND SECONDARY SCHOOLS								
School enrollment, total	1,000 . . .	55,380	55,500	55,632	55,850	56,144	56,545	57,012
Pre-kindergarten through grade 8 . . .	1,000 . . .	38,929	39,179	39,457	39,799	40,193	40,592	41,005
Grades 9 through 12	1,000 . . .	16,451	16,322	16,175	16,051	15,951	15,952	16,006
Public	1,000 . . .	49,470	49,623	49,788	50,034	50,349	50,767	51,239
Pre-kindergarten through grade 8 . .	1,000 . . .	34,383	34,667	34,973	35,335	35,732	36,126	36,523
Grades 9 through 12	1,000 . . .	15,087	14,955	14,815	14,698	14,617	14,641	14,716
Private	1,000 . . .	5,910	5,878	5,845	5,817	5,795	5,778	5,773
Pre-kindergarten through grade 8 . .	1,000 . . .	4,546	4,512	4,484	4,464	4,461	4,466	4,483
Grades 9 through 12	1,000 . . .	1,364	1,366	1,361	1,353	1,335	1,312	1,290
Classroom teachers, total FTE [1]	1,000 . . .	3,665	3,689	3,705	3,725	3,763	3,812	3,867
Public	1,000 . . .	3,205	3,233	3,249	3,271	3,310	3,358	3,410
Private	1,000 . . .	456	456	456	454	453	454	457
High school graduates, total [2]	1,000 . . .	3,322	3,329	3,295	3,273	3,225	3,211	3,193
Public	1,000 . . .	3,011	3,019	2,983	2,962	2,912	2,905	2,889
Public schools: [2]								
Average daily attendance (ADA)	1,000 . . .	46,127	46,270	46,424	46,653	46,947	47,337	47,777
Current dollars: [3]								
Current school expenditure	Bil. dol. . .	482	489	493	496	507	521	536
Per pupil in fall enrollment	Dollar . . .	10,457	10,575	10,614	10,634	10,799	10,996	11,218
Constant (2006–2007) dollars: [3, 4]								
Current school expenditure	Bil. dol. . .	475	500	515	520	540	566	(NA)
Per pupil in fall enrollment	Dollar . . .	10,324	10,846	11,141	11,208	11,574	12,060	(NA)
HIGHER EDUCATION								
Enrollment, total.	1,000 . . .	18,248	18,699	19,037	19,126	19,286	19,462	19,710
Male	1,000 . . .	7,816	8,071	8,210	8,252	8,288	8,319	8,359
Full-time.	1,000 . . .	5,029	5,161	5,292	5,322	5,341	5,355	5,383
Part-time	1,000 . . .	2,786	2,910	2,918	2,930	2,946	2,964	2,976
Female	1,000 . . .	10,432	10,628	10,827	10,874	10,998	11,143	11,351
Full-time.	1,000 . . .	6,240	6,335	6,541	6,577	6,663	6,756	6,907
Part-time	1,000 . . .	4,192	4,292	4,286	4,297	4,335	4,387	4,444
Public	1,000 . . .	13,491	13,904	14,137	14,200	14,312	14,435	14,605
Four-year institutions	1,000 . . .	7,167	7,314	7,470	7,512	7,581	7,652	7,755
Two-year institutions	1,000 . . .	6,324	6,591	6,667	6,688	6,731	6,783	6,850
Private	1,000 . . .	4,757	4,794	4,900	4,926	4,974	5,027	5,105
Four-year institutions	1,000 . . .	4,464	4,485	4,583	4,608	4,654	4,705	4,778
Two-year institutions	1,000 . . .	294	309	317	318	320	322	327
Undergraduate	1,000 . . .	15,604	16,005	16,304	16,384	16,510	16,633	16,811
Graduate	1,000 . . .	2,294	2,339	2,369	2,376	2,405	2,450	2,509
First-time professional	1,000 . . .	351	355	364	366	371	379	390
Full-time equivalent.	1,000 . . .	13,783	14,087	14,424	14,498	14,624	14,756	14,959
Public	1,000 . . .	9,740	10,022	10,250	10,301	10,384	10,471	10,606
2-year	1,000 . . .	5,994	6,124	6,278	6,317	6,376	6,434	6,523
4-year	1,000 . . .	3,745	3,898	3,972	3,984	4,008	4,037	4,083
Private.	1,000 . . .	4,043	4,064	4,174	4,198	4,239	4,284	4,353
2-year	1,000 . . .	3,775	3,782	3,884	3,907	3,947	3,990	4,054
4-year	1,000 . . .	268	282	290	291	292	295	299
Degrees conferred, total [2]	1,000 . . .	3,081	3,133	3,220	3,265	3,330	3,368	3,420
Associate's	1,000 . . .	738	745	762	771	784	791	802
Bachelor's	1,000 . . .	1,570	1,599	1,648	1,669	1,706	1,719	1,737
Master's	1,000 . . .	620	631	648	659	670	684	702
Doctoral	1,000 . . .	62	64	67	70	72	75	77
First-professional	1,000 . . .	91	93	95	97	98	99	101

NA Not available.   [1] Full-time equivalent.   [2] For school year ending in June the following year.   [3] Limited financial projections are shown due to the uncertain behavior of inflation over the long term.   [4] Based on the Consumer Price Index (CPI) for all urban consumers, U.S. Bureau of Labor Statistics. CPI adjusted to a school year basis by NCES.

Source: U.S. National Center for Education Statistics, *Projections of Education Statistics to 2018*, NCES 2009-062. See also <http://www.nces.ed.gov/surveys/AnnualReports/>.

Education   143

Table 217. **Federal Funds for Education and Related Programs: 2005 to 2008**

[In millions of dollars (146,207.0 represents $146,207,000,000), except percent. For fiscal years ending in September. Figures represent on-budget funds]

Level, agency, and program	2005	2007	2008[1]
Total, all programs	**146,207.0**	**147,527.7**	**(NA)**
Percent of federal budget outlays	5.9	5.4	(NA)
Elementary/secondary education programs	**68,957.7**	**70,604.2**	**72,839.2**
Department of Education[2]	37,477.6	37,562.1	38,900.3
Grants for the disadvantaged	14,635.6	14,486.9	15,036.3
School improvement programs	7,918.1	7,083.7	7,447.9
Indian education	121.9	118.0	116.7
Special education	10,940.3	11,777.3	11,771.7
Vocational and adult education	1,967.1	1,955.8	2,125.6
Education reform—Goals 2000	−35.0	(X)	(X)
Department of Agriculture	12,577.3	14,246.0	15,207.9
Child nutrition programs	11,901.9	13,082.0	3 14,401.9
Agricultural Marketing Service—commodities	399.3	878.0	542.0
Department of Defense[2]	1,786.3	1,772.3	1,817.0
Overseas dependents schools	1,060.9	1,062.4	1,031.4
Section VI schools[4]	410.2	385.0	432.7
Department of Health and Human Services	8,003.3	7,901.7	7,922.7
Head Start	6,842.3	6,888.0	6,878.0
Social security student benefits	1,161.0	1,013.7	1,044.7
Department of Homeland Security[5]	0.5	0.5	0.6
Department of the Interior[2]	938.5	728.1	763.7
Mineral Leasing Act and other funds	140.0	123.1	128.1
Indian Education	797.5	604.0	634.7
Department of Justice	554.5	719.6	730.0
Inmate programs	554.5	713.6	724.0
Department of Labor	5,654.0	5,226.0	5,018.0
Job Corps	1,521.0	1,605.0	1,490.0
Department of Veterans Affairs	1,815.0	2,300.6	2,330.0
Vocational rehab for disabled veterans	1,815.0	2,300.6	2,330.0
Other agencies and programs	153.2	147.4	149.0
Higher education programs[2]	**38,587.3**	**37,465.3**	**37,968.6**
Department of Education[2]	31,420.0	30,052.0	30,267.1
Student financial assistance	15,209.5	15,355.7	17,474.4
Federal Family Education Loans[6]	10,777.5	6,033.3	3,941.5
Department of Agriculture	62.0	64.4	66.7
Department of Commerce	(NA)	(NA)	(NA)
Department of Defense	1,858.3	1,846.9	1,946.4
Tuition assistance for military personnel	608.1	607.5	603.6
Service academies	300.8	354.5	330.2
Senior ROTC	537.5	434.7	549.6
Professional development education	411.9	450.1	463.0

Level, agency, and program	2005	2007	2008[1]
Department of Health and Human Services[2]	1,433.5	1,159.3	1,176.0
Health professions training programs	581.7	302.1	318.2
National Health Service Corps scholarships[8]	45.0	40.0	40.0
National Institutes of Health training grants[8]	756.0	761.0	756.0
Department of Homeland Security[5]	36.4	48.9	52.1
Department of the Interior	249.2	176.7	187.0
Shared revenues, Mineral Leasing Act and other receipts—estimated education share	146.2	52.4	59.2
Indian programs	103.0	124.3	127.8
Department of State	424.0	473.0	498.0
Department of Transportation	73.0	74.0	76.0
Department of Veterans Affairs[2]	2,478.6	2,955.8	3,061.2
Post-Vietnam veterans	1.1	0.9	0.8
All-volunteer-force educational assistance	2,071.0	2,227.5	2,321.5
Other agencies and programs[2]	552.2	614.4	638.1
National Endowment for the Humanities	29.3	40.4	41.0
National Science Foundation	490.0	527.0	535.0
Other education programs[2]	**6,908.5**	**7,214.9**	**7,877.8**
Department of Education[2]	3,538.9	3,756.4	4,222.9
Administration	548.8	539.4	565.4
Rehabilitative services and handicapped research	2,973.3	3,177.0	3,603.6
Department of Agriculture	468.6	515.0	516.3
Department of Health and Human Services	313.0	307.0	329.0
Department of Homeland Security[5]	278.2	307.1	354.1
Department of Justice	26.1	28.1	29.5
Department of State	109.3	114.1	115.0
Other agencies and programs[2]	2,174.3	2,187.0	2,310.7
Agency for International Development	574.0	629.2	640.0
Library of Congress	430.0	463.0	360.0
National Endowment for the Arts	2.5	2.9	3.2
National Endowment for the Humanities	88.0	80.6	81.0
Research programs at universities and related institutions[2]	**31,753.5**	**32,243.3**	**(NA)**
Department of Agriculture	709.7	584.3	(NA)
Department of Defense	2,675.9	2,447.6	(NA)
Department of Energy	4,339.9	4,649.5	(NA)
Department of Health and Human Services	16,358.0	16,337.0	(NA)
National Aeronautics and Space Administration	2,763.1	3,033.5	(NA)
National Science Foundation	3,503.2	3,841.5	(NA)

NA Not available.   X Not applicable.   [1] Estimated except U.S. Department of Education, which are actual budget reports.   [2] Includes other programs and agencies, not shown separately.   [3] Purchased under Section 32 of the Act of August 1935 for use in child nutrition programs.   [4] Program provides for the education of dependents of federal employees residing on federal property where free public education is unavailable in the nearby community.   [5] The U.S. Department of Homeland Security was created on January 24, 2003, under public law (107-296).   [6] Includes Federal Direct Loans.   [7] Instructional costs only including academics, audiovisual, academic computer center, faculty training, military training, physical education, and libraries.   [8] Includes alcohol, drug abuse, and mental health training programs.

Source: U.S. National Center for Education Statistics, *Digest of Education Statistics*, annual.

Table 218. School Enrollment by Age: 1970 to 2007

[As of October (60,357 represents 60,357,000). Covers civilian noninstitutional population enrolled in nursery school and above. Based on Current Population Survey, see text, Section 1, and Appendix III]

Age	1970	1980	1985	1990	1995	2000	2004	2005	2006	2007
ENROLLMENT (1,000)										
Total, 3 to 34 years old. . . .	60,357	57,348	58,013	60,588	66,939	69,560	72,418	72,768	72,270	72,970
3 and 4 years old	1,461	2,280	2,801	3,292	4,042	4,097	4,552	4,383	4,534	4,491
5 and 6 years old	7,000	5,853	6,697	7,207	7,901	7,648	7,561	7,486	7,628	7,792
7 to 13 years old	28,943	23,751	22,849	25,016	27,003	28,296	28,006	27,936	27,504	27,532
14 and 15 years old	7,869	7,282	7,362	6,555	7,651	7,885	8,327	8,375	8,252	8,137
16 and 17 years old	6,927	7,129	6,654	6,098	6,997	7,341	8,086	8,472	8,203	8,205
18 and 19 years old	3,322	3,788	3,716	4,044	4,274	4,926	4,961	5,109	5,306	5,566
20 and 21 years old	1,949	2,515	2,708	2,852	3,025	3,314	3,904	4,069	3,839	3,916
22 to 24 years old.	1,410	1,931	2,068	2,231	2,545	2,731	3,221	3,254	3,256	3,375
25 to 29 years old.	1,011	1,714	1,942	2,013	2,216	2,030	2,479	2,340	2,373	2,577
30 to 34 years old.	466	1,105	1,218	1,281	1,284	1,292	1,321	1,344	1,376	1,379
35 years old and over	(NA)	1,290	1,766	2,439	2,830	2,653	3,042	3,013	2,927	2,997
ENROLLMENT RATE										
Total, 3 to 34 years old. . . .	56.4	49.7	48.3	50.2	53.7	55.8	56.2	56.5	56.0	56.1
3 and 4 years old	20.5	36.7	38.9	44.4	48.7	52.1	54.0	53.6	55.7	54.5
5 and 6 years old	89.5	95.7	96.1	96.5	96.0	95.6	95.4	95.4	94.6	94.7
7 to 13 years old	99.2	99.3	99.2	99.6	98.9	98.2	98.4	98.6	98.3	98.4
14 and 15 years old	98.1	98.2	98.1	99.0	98.9	98.7	98.5	98.0	98.3	98.7
16 and 17 years old	90.0	89.0	91.7	92.5	93.6	92.8	94.5	95.1	94.6	94.3
18 and 19 years old	47.7	46.4	51.6	57.3	59.4	61.2	64.4	67.6	65.5	66.8
20 and 21 years old	31.9	31.0	35.3	39.7	44.9	44.1	48.9	48.7	47.5	48.4
22 to 24 years old.	14.9	16.3	16.9	21.0	23.2	24.6	26.3	27.3	26.7	27.3
25 to 29 years old.	7.5	9.3	9.2	9.7	11.6	11.4	13.0	11.9	11.7	12.4
30 to 34 years old.	4.2	6.4	6.1	5.8	6.0	6.7	6.6	6.9	7.2	7.2
35 years old and over	(NA)	1.4	1.6	2.1	2.2	1.9	2.0	2.0	1.9	1.9

NA Not available.

Source: U.S. Census Bureau, Current Population Reports, PPL-148; earlier PPL and P-20 reports; and data published on the Internet; <http://www.census.gov/population/www/socdemo/school.html>.

Table 219. School Enrollment by Race, Hispanic Origin, and Age: 1980 to 2007

[(54,257 represents 54,257,000). See headnote, Table 218]

Age	White [1]			Black [1]			Hispanic origin [2]		
	2000	2005	2007	2000	2005	2007	2000	2005	2007
ENROLLMENT (1,000)									
Total, 3 to 34 years old. . . .	54,257	55,715	55,731	11,115	10,885	10,962	9,928	12,502	13,358
3 and 4 years old	3,091	3,380	3,406	725	655	693	518	773	923
5 and 6 years old	5,959	5,707	5,934	1,219	1,144	1,208	1,390	1,532	1,746
7 to 13 years old	22,061	21,310	21,014	4,675	4,317	4,136	4,373	5,394	5,569
14 and 15 years old	6,176	6,429	6,238	1,260	1,321	1,262	1,093	1,431	1,520
16 and 17 years old	5,845	6,520	6,270	1,106	1,281	1,283	959	1,357	1,320
18 and 19 years old	3,924	4,006	4,325	716	707	792	617	681	870
20 and 21 years old	2,688	3,262	3,145	416	430	459	311	447	468
22 to 24 years old.	2,101	2,411	2,542	393	475	479	309	419	415
25 to 29 years old.	1,473	1,740	1,869	353	307	421	198	310	348
30 to 34 years old.	939	950	988	252	248	229	160	158	179
35 years old and over	2,087	2,299	2,289	387	499	513	235	307	349
ENROLLMENT RATE									
Total, 3 to 34 years old. . . .	55.1	55.9	55.5	59.0	58.4	58.4	51.3	50.9	51.7
3 and 4 years old	50.2	54.2	54.1	59.9	52.2	58.5	35.9	43.0	48.2
5 and 6 years old	95.3	95.3	94.8	96.3	95.9	94.0	94.3	93.8	94.3
7 to 13 years old	98.2	98.6	98.4	98.0	98.6	98.0	97.5	97.6	97.9
14 and 15 years old	98.4	98.3	98.7	99.6	95.8	99.0	96.2	97.3	98.4
16 and 17 years old	92.8	95.4	94.6	91.4	93.1	93.4	87.0	92.6	90.6
18 and 19 years old	61.3	68.0	67.1	57.2	62.8	61.7	49.5	54.3	57.2
20 and 21 years old	44.9	49.3	50.1	36.6	37.6	38.7	26.1	30.0	32.3
22 to 24 years old.	23.7	26.0	26.3	24.2	28.0	28.0	18.2	19.5	18.8
25 to 29 years old.	10.4	11.3	11.5	14.3	11.7	15.0	7.4	7.8	8.3
30 to 34 years old.	6.0	6.2	6.6	9.6	10.0	9.4	5.6	4.2	4.5
35 years old and over	1.8	1.8	1.8	2.6	3.1	3.0	2.0	2.0	2.1

[1] Starting 2005, data are for persons who selected this race group only. See footnote 2, Table 224.   [2] Persons of Hispanic origin may be any race.

Source: U.S. Census Bureau, Current Population Reports, PPL-148; earlier PPL and P-20 reports; and data published on the Internet; <http://www.census.gov/population/www/socdemo/school.html>.

Table 220. **Enrollment in Public and Private Schools: 1970 to 2007**

[In millions (52.2 represents 52,200,000), except percent. As of October. For civilian noninstitutional population. For **1970 to 1985**, persons 3 to 34 years old; **beginning 1990**, for 3 years old and over. For enrollment 35 years old and over, see Table 218]

Year	Public						Private					
	Total	Nur-sery	Kinder-garten	Ele-mentary	High school	College	Total	Nur-sery	Kinder-garten	Ele-mentary	High school	College
1970	52.2	0.3	2.6	30.0	13.5	5.7	8.1	0.8	0.5	3.9	1.2	1.7
1975	52.8	0.6	2.9	27.2	14.5	7.7	8.2	1.2	0.5	3.3	1.2	2.0
1980	(NA)	0.6	2.7	24.4	(NA)	(NA)	(NA)	1.4	0.5	3.1	(NA)	(NA)
1985	49.0	0.9	3.2	23.8	12.8	8.4	9.0	1.6	0.6	3.1	1.2	2.5
1990 [1]	53.8	1.2	3.3	26.6	11.9	10.7	9.2	2.2	0.6	2.7	0.9	2.9
1991	54.5	1.1	3.5	26.6	12.2	11.1	9.4	1.8	0.6	3.0	1.0	3.0
1992	55.0	1.1	3.5	27.1	12.3	11.1	9.4	1.8	0.6	3.1	1.0	3.0
1993	56.0	1.2	3.5	27.7	12.6	10.9	9.4	1.8	0.7	2.9	1.0	3.0
1994	58.6	1.9	3.3	28.1	13.5	11.7	10.7	2.3	0.6	3.4	1.1	3.3
1995	58.7	2.0	3.2	28.4	13.7	11.4	11.1	2.4	0.7	3.4	1.2	3.3
1996	59.5	1.9	3.4	28.1	14.1	12.0	10.8	2.3	0.7	3.4	1.2	3.2
1997	61.6	2.3	3.3	29.3	14.6	12.1	10.5	2.2	0.7	3.1	1.2	3.3
1998	60.8	2.3	3.1	29.1	14.3	12.0	11.3	2.3	0.7	3.4	1.2	3.6
1999	60.8	2.3	3.2	29.2	14.4	11.7	11.4	2.3	0.7	3.6	1.3	3.5
2000	61.2	2.2	3.2	29.4	14.4	12.0	11.0	2.2	0.7	3.5	1.3	3.3
2001	62.4	2.2	3.1	29.8	14.8	12.4	10.8	2.1	0.6	3.4	1.2	3.5
2002	62.8	2.2	3.0	29.7	15.1	12.8	11.3	2.2	0.6	3.5	1.3	3.7
2003	63.8	2.6	3.1	29.2	15.8	13.1	11.1	2.4	0.6	3.4	1.3	3.5
2004	64.3	2.5	3.4	29.2	15.5	13.7	11.3	2.3	0.6	3.4	1.3	3.7
2005	64.2	2.5	3.3	29.0	15.8	13.4	11.5	2.1	0.6	3.4	1.4	4.0
2006	64.1	2.5	3.6	29.0	15.6	13.5	11.1	2.2	0.5	3.1	1.5	3.8
2007	65.1	2.6	3.7	29.1	15.8	14.1	10.8	2.1	0.5	3.1	1.3	3.9
Percent White:												
1970.	84.5	59.5	84.4	83.1	85.6	90.7	93.4	91.1	88.2	94.1	96.1	92.8
1980.	(NA)	68.2	80.7	80.9	(NA)	(NA)	(NA)	89.0	87.0	90.7	(NA)	(NA)
1990.	79.8	71.7	78.3	78.9	79.2	84.1	87.4	89.6	83.2	88.2	89.4	85.0
2000 [2]	77.0	69.4	77.3	76.7	78.0	78.0	83.5	84.9	82.8	85.9	84.6	79.8
2004 [2]	75.2	68.5	75.2	75.0	75.4	76.7	82.4	82.7	82.1	85.1	88.0	77.8
2005 [2]	75.7	71.3	78.0	75.2	76.0	76.7	81.4	83.6	79.0	83.0	83.6	78.4
2006 [2]	75.6	72.1	76.0	75.7	74.9	76.8	80.9	83.4	78.4	81.9	83.1	78.0
2007 [2]	75.4	73.2	77.6	75.3	75.2	77.1	80.4	80.9	81.3	82.1	86.1	76.6

NA Not available. [1] Beginning 1990, based on a revised edit and tabulation package. [2] Beginning 2004, for persons who selected this race group only. See footnote 2, Table 224.

Source: U.S. Census Bureau, Current Population Reports, PPL-148; earlier PPL and P-20 reports; and data published on the Internet; <http://www.census.gov/population/www/socdemo/school.html>.

Table 221. **School Enrollment by Sex and Level: 1970 to 2007**

[In millions (60.4 represents 60,400,000). As of October. For the civilian noninstitutional population. **Prior to 1980**, persons 3 to 34 years old; **beginning 1980**, 3 years old and over. Elementary includes kindergarten and grades 1–8; high school, grades 9–12; and college, 2-year and 4-year colleges, universities, and graduate and professional schools. Data for college represent degree-credit enrollment. See headnote, Table 218]

Year	All levels [1]			Elementary			High school			College		
	Total	Male	Female	Total	Male	Female	Total	Male	Female	Total	Male	Female
1970	60.4	31.4	28.9	37.1	19.0	18.1	14.7	7.4	7.3	7.4	4.4	3.0
1980	58.6	29.6	29.1	30.6	15.8	14.9	14.6	7.3	7.3	11.4	5.4	6.0
1985	59.8	30.0	29.7	30.7	15.7	15.0	14.1	7.2	6.9	12.5	5.9	6.6
1989 [2]	61.5	30.8	30.7	32.5	16.7	15.8	12.9	6.6	6.3	13.2	6.0	7.2
1990	63.0	31.5	31.5	33.2	17.1	16.0	12.8	6.5	6.4	13.6	6.2	7.4
1991	63.9	32.1	31.8	33.8	17.3	16.4	13.1	6.8	6.4	14.1	6.4	7.6
1992	64.6	32.2	32.3	34.3	17.7	16.6	13.3	6.8	6.5	14.0	6.2	7.8
1993	65.4	32.9	32.5	34.8	17.9	16.9	13.6	7.0	6.6	13.9	6.3	7.6
1994	69.3	34.6	34.6	35.4	18.2	17.2	14.6	7.4	7.2	15.0	6.8	8.2
1995	69.8	35.0	34.8	35.7	18.3	17.4	15.0	7.7	7.3	14.7	6.7	8.0
1996	70.3	35.1	35.2	35.5	18.3	17.3	15.3	7.9	7.4	15.2	6.8	8.4
1997	72.0	35.9	36.2	36.3	18.7	17.6	15.8	8.0	7.7	15.4	6.8	8.6
1998	72.1	36.0	36.1	36.4	18.7	17.7	15.6	7.9	7.6	15.5	6.9	8.6
1999	72.4	36.3	36.1	36.7	18.8	17.9	15.9	8.2	7.7	15.2	7.0	8.2
2000	72.2	36.8	36.4	36.7	18.9	17.9	15.8	8.1	7.7	15.3	6.7	8.6
2001	73.1	36.3	36.9	36.9	19.0	17.9	16.1	8.2	7.8	15.9	6.9	9.0
2002	74.0	36.8	37.3	36.7	18.9	17.8	16.4	8.3	8.0	16.5	7.2	9.3
2003	74.9	37.3	37.6	36.3	18.7	17.6	17.1	8.6	8.4	16.6	7.3	9.3
2004	75.5	37.4	38.0	36.5	19.0	17.6	16.8	8.4	8.4	17.4	7.6	9.8
2005	75.8	37.4	38.4	36.4	18.6	17.7	17.4	8.9	8.5	17.5	7.5	9.9
2006	75.2	37.2	38.0	36.1	18.5	17.6	17.1	8.8	8.4	17.2	7.5	9.7
2007	76.0	37.6	38.4	36.3	18.6	17.7	17.1	8.8	8.3	18.0	7.8	10.1

[1] Includes nursery schools, not shown separately. [2] Data beginning 1989, based on a revised edit and tabulation package.

Source: U.S. Census Bureau, Current Population Reports, PPL-148; earlier PPL and P-20 reports; and data published on the Internet; <http://www.census.gov/population/www/socdemo/school.html>.

Table 222. School Enrollment by Control and Level: 1980 to 2008

[In thousands (58,305 represents 58,305,000). **As of fall.** Data below college level are for regular day schools and exclude subcollegiate departments of colleges, federal schools, and home-schooled children. College data include degree-credit and nondegree-credit enrollment. Based on survey of state education agencies; see source for details. For more projections, see Tables 214 and 216]

Control of school and level	1980	1990	1995	2000	2003	2004	2005	2006	2007, proj.	2008, proj.
Total	58,305	60,269	65,020	68,685	71,551	72,154	72,674	73,153	73,958	74,079
Public.	50,335	52,061	55,933	58,956	61,399	61,776	62,135	62,479	63,135	63,387
Private	7,971	8,208	9,087	9,729	10,152	10,379	[1]10,539	10,674	10,823	10,692
Pre-kindergarten through 8 . .	31,639	33,962	37,062	38,566	38,990	38,934	38,929	38,932	39,271	39,585
Public	27,647	29,878	32,341	33,688	34,202	34,179	34,205	34,221	34,589	34,903
Private	3,992	4,084	4,721	4,878	4,788	4,756	[1]4,723	4,711	4,681	4,681
Grades 9 through 12	14,570	12,488	13,697	14,807	15,649	15,948	16,258	16,462	16,439	16,294
Public	13,231	11,338	12,500	13,515	14,338	14,617	14,908	15,078	15,055	14,922
Private	1,339	1,150	1,197	1,292	1,311	1,331	[1]1,350	1,384	1,385	1,372
College [2].	12,097	13,819	14,261	15,312	16,911	17,272	17,487	17,759	18,248	[3]18,200
Public	9,457	10,845	11,092	11,753	12,859	12,980	13,022	13,180	13,491	[3]13,562
Private	2,640	2,974	3,169	3,560	4,053	4,292	4,466	4,579	4,757	[3]4,638
Not-for-profit	2,528	2,760	2,929	3,109	3,341	3,412	3,455	3,513	(NA)	(NA)
For profit	112	214	240	450	712	880	1,011	1,066	(NA)	(NA)

NA Not available. [1] Estimated. [2] Data beginning 2000, reflects new classification system. See footnote 1, Table 269. [3] Data are actual.

Source: U.S. National Center for Education Statistics, *Digest of Education Statistics*, annual, and *Projections of Education Statistics*, annual.

Table 223. Students Who Are Foreign Born or Who Have Foreign-Born Parents: 2007

[In thousands (49,251 represents 49,251,000), except percent. **As of October.** Covers civilian noninstitutional population enrolled in elementary school and above. Based on Current Population Survey, see text, Section 1 and Appendix III]

Characteristic	All students	Students with at least one foreign-born parent					
		Total		Foreign-born student		Native student	
		Number	Percent	Number	Percent	Number	Percent
ELEMENTARY AND HIGH SCHOOL							
Total [1].	**49,251**	**11,523**	**23.4**	**2,640**	**5.4**	**8,883**	**18.0**
White [2].	37,417	8,024	21.4	1,816	4.9	6,207	16.6
White, non-Hispanic.	28,476	2,049	7.2	437	1.5	1,612	5.7
Black [2].	7,668	1,122	14.6	289	3.8	833	10.9
Asian [2, 3]	2,059	1,911	92.8	501	24.3	1,409	68.4
Hispanic [4]	9,640	6,281	65.2	1,446	15.0	4,835	50.2
COLLEGE, 1 TO 4 YEARS							
Total [1].	**14,364**	**3,130**	**21.8**	**1,350**	**9.4**	**1,780**	**12.4**
White [2].	11,128	1,886	16.9	771	6.9	1,115	10.0
White, non-Hispanic.	9,388	793	8.4	332	3.5	461	4.9
Black [2].	2,061	434	21.1	253	12.3	181	8.8
Asian [2, 3]	730	684	93.7	299	41.0	386	52.9
Hispanic [4]	1,922	1,196	62.2	475	24.7	721	37.5
GRADUATE SCHOOL							
Total [1].	**3,591**	**927**	**25.8**	**589**	**16.4**	**338**	**9.4**
White [2].	2,707	441	16.3	246	9.1	195	7.2
White, non-Hispanic.	2,479	328	13.2	198	8.0	131	5.3
Black [2].	440	104	23.6	67	15.2	37	8.4
Asian [2, 3]	372	354	95.2	260	69.9	93	25.0
Hispanic [4]	250	124	49.6	48	19.2	75	30.0

[1] Includes other races not shown separately. [2] For persons who selected this race group only. See footnote 2, Table 224. [3] Data are for Asians only; excludes Pacific Islanders. [4] Persons of Hispanic origin may be any race.

Source: U.S. Census Bureau, Current Population Survey, unpublished data; <http://www.census.gov/population/www/socdemo/school.html>.

U.S. Census Bureau, Statistical Abstract of the United States: 2010

Table 224. **Educational Attainment by Race and Hispanic Origin: 1970 to 2008**

[In percent. For persons 25 years old and over. 1970 and 1980 as of April 1 and based on sample data from the censuses of population. **Other years as of March** and based on the Current Population Survey; see text, Section 1 and Appendix III. See Table 225 for data by sex]

Year	Total [1]	White [2]	Black [2]	Asian and Pacific Islander [2]	Hispanic [3] Total [4]	Mexican	Puerto Rican	Cuban
HIGH SCHOOL GRADUATE OR MORE [5]								
1970	52.3	54.5	31.4	62.2	32.1	24.2	23.4	43.9
1980	66.5	68.8	51.2	74.8	44.0	37.6	40.1	55.3
1990	77.6	79.1	66.2	80.4	50.8	44.1	55.5	63.5
1995	81.7	83.0	73.8	(NA)	53.4	46.5	61.3	64.7
2000	84.1	84.9	78.5	85.7	57.0	51.0	64.3	73.0
2004	85.2	85.8	80.6	[6]86.8	58.4	51.9	71.8	72.1
2005	85.2	85.8	81.1	87.6	58.5	52.2	72.4	73.3
2006	85.5	86.1	80.7	87.4	59.3	53.1	72.3	74.9
2007	85.7	86.2	82.3	87.8	60.3	53.9	73.5	79.8
2008	86.6	87.1	83.0	88.7	62.3	55.2	76.4	80.0
COLLEGE GRADUATE OR MORE [5]								
1970	10.7	11.3	4.4	20.4	4.5	2.5	2.2	11.1
1980	16.2	17.1	8.4	32.9	7.6	4.9	5.6	16.2
1990	21.3	22.0	11.3	39.9	9.2	5.4	9.7	20.2
1995	23.0	24.0	13.2	(NA)	9.3	6.5	10.7	19.4
2000	25.6	26.1	16.5	43.9	10.6	6.9	13.0	23.0
2004	27.7	28.2	17.6	[6]49.4	12.1	7.9	14.0	24.0
2005	27.7	28.1	17.6	50.2	12.0	8.2	13.8	24.6
2006	28.0	28.4	18.5	49.7	12.4	8.5	15.1	24.4
2007	28.7	29.1	18.5	52.1	12.7	9.0	16.4	27.2
2008	29.4	29.8	19.6	52.6	13.3	9.1	15.5	28.1

NA Not available.   [1] Includes other races not shown separately.   [2] Beginning 2004, for persons who selected this race group only. The 2003 Current Population Survey (CPS) allowed respondents to choose more than one race. Beginning 2003, data represent persons who selected this race group only and exclude persons reporting more than one race. The CPS in prior years only allowed respondents to report one race group. See also comments on race in the text for Section 1.   [3] Persons of Hispanic origin may be any race.   [4] Includes persons of other Hispanic origin not shown separately.   [5] Through 1990, completed 4 years of high school or more and 4 years of college or more.   [6] Starting in 2004, data are for Asians only, excludes Pacific Islanders.

Source: U.S. Census Bureau, U.S. Census of Population, 1960, 1970, and 1980, Vol. 1; and Current Population Reports, P20-550, and earlier reports; and data published on the Internet; <http://www.census.gov/population/www/socdemo /educ-attn.html>.

Table 225. **Educational Attainment by Race, Hispanic Origin, and Sex: 1970 to 2008**

[In percent. See Table 224 for headnote and totals for both sexes]

Year	All races [1] Male	Female	White [2] Male	Female	Black [2] Male	Female	Asian and Pacific Islander [2] Male	Female	Hispanic [3] Male	Female
HIGH SCHOOL GRADUATE OR MORE [4]										
1970	51.9	52.8	54.0	55.0	30.1	32.5	61.3	63.1	37.9	34.2
1980	67.3	65.8	69.6	68.1	50.8	51.5	78.8	71.4	45.4	42.7
1990	77.7	77.5	79.1	79.0	65.8	66.5	84.0	77.2	50.3	51.3
1995	81.7	81.6	83.0	83.0	73.4	74.1	(NA)	(NA)	52.9	53.8
2000	84.2	84.0	84.8	85.0	78.7	78.3	88.2	83.4	56.6	57.5
2004	84.8	85.4	85.3	86.3	80.4	80.8	[5]88.7	[5]85.0	57.3	59.5
2005	84.9	85.5	85.2	86.2	81.0	81.2	90.4	85.2	57.9	59.1
2006	85.0	85.9	85.5	86.7	80.1	81.2	89.6	85.5	58.5	60.1
2007	85.0	86.4	85.3	87.1	81.9	82.6	89.8	85.9	58.2	62.5
2008	85.9	87.2	86.3	87.8	81.8	84.0	90.8	86.9	60.9	63.7
COLLEGE GRADUATE OR MORE [4]										
1970	13.5	8.1	14.4	8.4	4.2	4.6	23.5	17.3	7.8	4.3
1980	20.1	12.8	21.3	13.3	8.4	8.3	39.8	27.0	9.4	6.0
1990	24.4	18.4	25.3	19.0	11.9	10.8	44.9	35.4	9.8	8.7
1995	26.0	20.2	27.2	21.0	13.6	12.9	(NA)	(NA)	10.1	8.4
2000	27.8	23.6	28.5	23.9	16.3	16.7	47.6	40.7	10.7	10.6
2004	29.4	26.1	30.0	26.4	16.6	18.5	[5]53.7	[5]45.6	11.8	12.3
2005	28.9	26.5	29.4	26.8	16.0	18.8	54.0	46.8	11.8	12.1
2006	29.2	26.9	29.7	27.1	17.2	19.0	52.5	47.1	11.9	12.9
2007	29.5	28.0	29.9	28.3	18.0	19.0	55.2	49.3	11.8	13.7
2008	30.1	28.8	30.5	29.1	18.7	20.4	55.8	49.8	12.6	14.1

NA Not available.   [1] Includes other races not shown separately.   [2] Beginning 2004, for persons who selected this race group only. See footnote 2, Table 224.   [3] Persons of Hispanic origin may be any race.   [4] Through 1990, completed 4 years of high school or more and 4 years of college or more.   [5] Starting in 2004, data are for Asians only, excludes Pacific Islanders.

Source: U.S. Census Bureau, U.S. Census of Population, 1970 and 1980, Vol. 1; and Current Population Reports, P20-550, and earlier reports; and data published on the Internet; <http://www.census.gov/population/www/socdemo/educ-attn.html>.

Table 226. **Educational Attainment by Selected Characteristics: 2008**

[For persons 25 years old and over (196,305 represents 196,305,000). As of March. Based on the Current Population Survey; see text, Section 1 and Appendix III. For composition of regions, see map, inside front cover]

Characteristic	Population (1,000)	Percent of population—highest level					
		Not a high school graduate	High school graduate	Some college, but no degree	Associate's degree [1]	Bachelor's degree	Advanced degree
Total persons	196,305	13.4	31.2	17.2	8.8	19.1	10.3
Age:							
25 to 34 years old	40,146	11.9	28.1	18.4	9.3	23.5	8.8
35 to 44 years old	42,132	11.4	28.6	17.1	9.9	21.8	11.2
45 to 54 years old	43,935	10.8	32.0	17.5	10.2	19.2	10.4
55 to 64 years old	33,302	11.2	30.7	18.1	8.9	18.3	12.8
65 to 74 years old	19,588	19.0	35.7	15.9	6.0	13.4	10.0
75 years old or over.	17,202	26.7	38.1	14.1	4.1	10.3	6.7
Sex:							
Male	94,470	14.1	31.2	16.7	7.9	19.1	11.0
Female	101,835	12.8	31.1	17.7	9.6	19.2	9.7
Race:							
White [2]	160,658	12.9	31.3	17.2	8.9	19.3	10.4
Black [2]	22,251	17.0	35.1	19.5	8.8	13.6	6.1
Other	13,396	13.8	23.0	13.9	7.5	25.8	16.1
Hispanic origin:							
Hispanic	25,274	37.7	29.6	13.3	6.1	9.4	4.0
Non-Hispanic	171,031	9.8	31.4	17.8	9.1	20.6	11.2
Region:							
Northeast.	36,328	11.9	33.9	12.8	8.2	20.5	12.8
Midwest.	42,886	10.2	34.2	18.3	9.5	18.5	9.3
South	71,802	15.3	31.5	17.2	8.4	18.0	9.6
West.	45,289	14.6	25.6	19.8	9.1	20.5	10.4
Marital status:							
Never married.	33,696	14.2	30.3	17.4	7.8	20.9	9.4
Married, spouse present	117,364	11.1	29.9	16.5	9.1	21.1	12.1
Married, spouse absent [3] . . .	3,101	28.2	28.4	14.6	6.9	13.2	8.7
Separated	4,761	23.4	34.3	18.7	7.2	12.4	4.0
Widowed	14,276	26.9	39.1	14.9	5.5	9.0	4.5
Divorced	23,107	11.4	33.7	21.8	10.7	14.9	7.5
Civilian labor force status:							
Employed	125,843	8.6	28.5	17.7	10.1	22.6	12.5
Unemployed.	5,831	20.1	37.2	17.8	8.1	12.2	4.5
Not in the labor force . . . . . ,	64,630	22.1	36.8	10.2	6.3	13.0	6.6

[1] Includes vocational degrees.   [2] For persons who selected this race group only. See footnote 2, Table 224.   [3] Excludes those separated.

Source: U.S. Census Bureau, Current Population Survey; <http://www.census.gov/population/www/socdemo/educ-attn.html>.

Table 227. **Mean Earnings by Highest Degree Earned: 2007**

[In dollars. For persons 18 years old and over with earnings. Persons as of March the following year. Based on Current Population Survey; see text, Section 1 and Appendix III. For definition of mean, see Guide to Tabular Presentation]

Characteristic	Total persons	Mean earnings by level of highest degree (dol.)							
		Not a high school graduate	High school graduate only	Some college, no degree	Asso- ciate's	Bache- lor's	Master's	Profes- sional	Doctorate
All persons [1]	42,064	21,484	31,286	33,009	39,746	57,181	70,186	120,978	95,565
Age:									
25 to 34 years old	37,352	21,678	28,982	31,843	36,741	48,256	55,401	81,458	74,489
35 to 44 years old	48,851	24,383	36,060	41,542	42,489	63,124	75,739	134,240	94,631
45 to 54 years old	51,058	25,801	36,562	44,201	45,145	68,131	81,419	127,818	110,410
55 to 64 years old	49,214	24,842	34,161	40,838	42,344	61,862	71,063	138,844	102,956
65 years old and over. . .	36,497	24,703	25,678	31,938	32,021	48,245	51,519	93,672	73,417
Sex:									
Male	50,110	24,985	36,839	39,375	47,190	70,898	86,966	142,282	108,941
Female	32,899	15,315	24,234	26,527	33,276	43,127	54,772	83,031	69,251
White [2]	43,139	22,289	32,223	33,465	40,373	58,652	71,321	122,885	97,254
Male	51,781	25,886	38,214	40,508	48,444	73,477	89,678	144,371	110,480
Female	32,899	15,278	24,276	26,007	33,223	42,846	54,532	82,758	69,778
Black [2]	33,333	17,439	27,179	31,318	36,445	46,502	56,398	94,049	96,092
Male	35,668	19,705	29,640	32,236	38,921	53,029	63,801	(B)	(B)
Female	31,317	14,869	24,724	30,599	34,774	41,560	51,695	(B)	(B)
Hispanic [3]	29,910	21,303	27,604	29,384	35,348	44,696	68,040	84,512	(B)
Male	33,040	23,923	30,932	33,643	42,140	50,805	81,069	95,907	(B)
Female	25,262	15,574	22,283	24,884	29,279	38,584	54,263	(B)	(B)

B Base figure too small to meet statistical standards for reliability of a derived figure.   [1] Includes other races not shown separately.   [2] For persons who selected this race group only. See footnote 2, Table 224.   [3] Persons of Hispanic origin may be any race.

Source: U.S. Census Bureau, Current Population Survey; <http://www.census.gov/population/www/socdemo/educ-attn.html>.

Education   149

Table 228. **Educational Attainment by State: 1990 to 2007**

[In percent. 1990 and 2000 as of April. 2007, represents annual averages for calendar year. For persons 25 years old and over. Based on the 1990 and 2000 Census of Population and the American Community Survey, which includes the household population and the population living in institutions, college dormitories, and other group quarters. See text, Section 1 and Appendix III]

State	1990 High school graduate or more	1990 Bachelor's degree or more	1990 Advanced degree or more	2000 High school graduate or more	2000 Bachelor's degree or more	2000 Advanced degree or more	2007 High school graduate or more	2007 Bachelor's degree or more	2007 Advanced degree or more
United States . . .	75.2	20.3	7.2	80.4	24.4	8.9	84.5	27.5	10.1
Alabama	66.9	15.7	5.5	75.3	19.0	6.9	80.4	21.4	8.0
Alaska.	86.6	23.0	8.0	88.3	24.7	8.6	90.5	26.0	9.9
Arizona	78.7	20.3	7.0	81.0	23.5	8.4	83.5	25.3	9.2
Arkansas	66.3	13.3	4.5	75.3	16.7	5.7	81.1	19.3	6.5
California	76.2	23.4	8.1	76.8	26.6	9.5	80.2	29.5	10.5
Colorado	84.4	27.0	9.0	86.9	32.7	11.1	88.9	35.0	12.5
Connecticut	79.2	27.2	11.0	84.0	31.4	13.3	88.0	34.7	15.4
Delaware	77.5	21.4	7.7	82.6	25.0	9.4	87.4	26.1	10.4
District of Columbia . . .	73.1	33.3	17.2	77.8	39.1	21.0	85.7	47.5	26.0
Florida.	74.4	18.3	6.3	79.9	22.3	8.1	84.9	25.8	8.9
Georgia	70.9	19.3	6.4	78.6	24.3	8.3	82.9	27.1	9.5
Hawaii	80.1	22.9	7.1	84.6	26.2	8.4	89.4	29.2	9.9
Idaho	79.7	17.7	5.3	84.7	21.7	6.8	88.4	24.5	7.6
Illinois	76.2	21.0	7.5	81.4	26.1	9.5	85.7	29.5	11.0
Indiana	75.6	15.6	6.4	82.1	19.4	7.2	85.8	22.1	7.9
Iowa	80.1	16.9	5.2	86.1	21.2	6.5	89.6	24.3	7.5
Kansas	81.3	21.1	7.0	86.0	25.8	8.7	89.1	28.8	9.8
Kentucky	64.6	13.6	5.5	74.1	17.1	6.9	80.1	20.0	8.0
Louisiana	68.3	16.1	5.6	74.8	18.7	6.5	79.9	20.4	6.6
Maine	78.8	18.8	6.1	85.4	22.9	7.9	89.4	26.7	9.2
Maryland	78.4	26.5	10.9	83.8	31.4	13.4	87.4	35.2	15.7
Massachusetts	80.0	27.2	10.6	84.8	33.2	13.7	88.4	37.9	16.0
Michigan	76.8	17.4	6.4	83.4	21.8	8.1	87.4	24.7	9.5
Minnesota	82.4	21.8	6.3	87.9	27.4	8.3	91.0	31.0	10.0
Mississippi	64.3	14.7	5.1	72.9	16.9	5.8	78.5	18.9	6.4
Missouri.	73.9	17.8	6.1	81.3	21.6	7.6	85.6	24.5	8.9
Montana	81.0	19.8	5.7	87.2	24.4	7.2	90.0	27.0	8.6
Nebraska	81.8	18.9	5.9	86.6	23.7	7.3	89.6	27.5	8.8
Nevada	78.8	15.3	5.2	80.7	18.2	6.1	83.7	21.8	7.5
New Hampshire	82.2	24.4	7.9	87.4	28.7	10.0	90.5	32.5	11.5
New Jersey	76.7	24.9	8.8	82.1	29.8	11.0	87.0	33.9	12.7
New Mexico	75.1	20.4	8.3	78.9	23.5	9.8	82.3	24.8	10.2
New York.	74.8	23.1	9.9	79.1	27.4	11.8	84.1	31.7	13.5
North Carolina	70.0	17.4	5.4	78.1	22.5	7.2	83.0	25.6	8.6
North Dakota	76.7	18.1	4.5	83.9	22.0	5.5	89.0	25.7	6.4
Ohio	75.7	17.0	5.9	83.0	21.1	7.4	87.1	24.1	8.8
Oklahoma	74.6	17.8	6.0	80.6	20.3	6.8	84.8	22.8	7.6
Oregon	81.5	20.6	7.0	85.1	25.1	8.7	88.0	28.3	10.3
Pennsylvania	74.7	17.9	6.6	81.9	22.4	8.4	86.8	25.8	9.9
Rhode Island	72.0	21.3	7.8	78.0	25.6	9.7	83.0	29.8	11.8
South Carolina	68.3	16.6	5.4	76.3	20.4	6.9	82.1	23.5	8.2
South Dakota	77.1	17.2	4.9	84.6	21.5	6.0	88.2	25.0	7.0
Tennessee	67.1	16.0	5.4	75.9	19.6	6.8	81.4	21.8	7.6
Texas	72.1	20.3	6.5	75.7	23.2	7.6	79.1	25.2	8.2
Utah	85.1	22.3	6.8	87.7	26.1	8.3	90.2	28.7	9.1
Vermont	80.8	24.3	8.9	86.4	29.4	11.1	90.3	33.6	12.9
Virginia	75.2	24.5	9.1	81.5	29.5	11.6	85.9	33.6	13.7
Washington	83.8	22.9	7.0	87.1	27.7	9.3	89.3	30.3	10.8
West Virginia	66.0	12.3	4.8	75.2	14.8	5.9	81.2	17.3	6.6
Wisconsin	78.6	17.7	5.6	85.1	22.4	7.2	89.0	25.4	8.5
Wyoming	83.0	18.8	5.7	87.9	21.9	7.0	91.2	23.4	7.7

Source: U.S. Census Bureau, 1990 Census of Population, CPH-L-96; 2000 Census of Population, P37, "Sex by Educational Attainment for the Population 25 Years and Over"; using American FactFinder; 2007 American Community Survey, R1501. "Percent of Persons 25 Years and Over Who Have Completed High School," R1502. "Percent of Persons 25 Years and Over Who Have Completed a Bachelor's Degree," and R1503. "Percent of Persons 25 Years and Over Who Have Completed an Advanced Degree"; using American FactFinder.

Table 229. **Children With Parental Involvement in Home Literacy Activities: 1993 to 2007**

[In percent, except number of children (8,579 represents 8,579,000). For children 3 to 5 years old not yet enrolled in kindergarten who participated in activities with a family member. Based on the School Readiness Early Childhood Program Participation Surveys of the National Household Education Surveys Program; see source and Appendix III. See also Table 230]

Characteristic	Children (1,000)		Read to [1]		Told a story [1]		Taught letters, words, or numbers [1]		Visited a library [2]	
	1993	2007	1993	2007	1993	2005	1993	2005	1993	2007
Total	8,579	8,686	78	83	43	54	58	77	38	36
Age:										
3 years old	3,889	3,755	79	84	46	54	57	75	34	36
4 years old	3,713	3,738	78	83	41	53	58	77	41	35
5 years old	976	1,193	76	83	36	55	58	80	38	39
Race/ethnicity:										
White, non-Hispanic	5,902	4,664	85	91	44	53	58	76	42	41
Black, non-Hispanic	1,271	1,312	66	78	39	54	63	81	29	25
Hispanic [3]	1,026	1,899	58	68	38	50	54	74	26	27
Other	381	812	73	87	50	64	59	82	43	46
Mother's home language: [4]										
English	7,805	7,244	81	88	44	55	58	78	39	38
Not English	603	1,312	42	57	36	45	52	69	26	24
Mother's highest education: [4]										
Less than high school	1,036	808	60	56	37	39	56	70	22	20
High school	3,268	2,048	76	74	41	51	56	78	31	29
Vocational ed or some college . . .	2,624	2,658	83	86	45	57	60	79	44	33
College degree	912	1,849	90	95	48	56	56	75	55	43
Graduate/professional training or degree	569	1,194	90	95	50	64	60	76	59	53

[1] Three or more times in the past week.   [2] At least once in the past month.   [3] Persons of Hispanic origin may be any race.
[4] Excludes children with no mother in the household and no female guardian.

Source: U.S. National Center for Education Statistics, Statistical Brief, NCES 2000-026, November 1999; the Early Childhood Program Participation Survey, National Household Education Surveys Program, 2005, unpublished data; and the School Readiness Survey, 2007, unpublished data; <http://nces.ed.gov/nhes>.

Table 230. **Children's School Readiness Skills: 1993 to 2007**

[In percent. For children 3 to 5 years old not yet enrolled in kindergarten. Based on the School Readiness Surveys of the National Household Education Survey Program; see source for details. See also Table 229]

Characteristic	Recognizes all letters		Counts to 20 or higher		Writes name		Reads or pretends to read storybooks		Has 3 to 4 skills	
	1993	2007	1993	2007	1993	2007	1993	2005	1993	2005
Total	21	32	52	63	50	60	72	70	35	42
Age:										
3 years old	11	17	37	47	22	34	66	67	15	24
4 years old	28	38	62	73	70	76	75	73	49	55
5 years old	36	59	78	84	84	88	81	72	65	66
Sex:										
Male	19	31	49	61	47	56	68	70	32	40
Female	23	33	56	65	53	63	76	71	39	45
Race/ethnicity:										
White, non-Hispanic	23	36	56	69	52	64	76	75	39	47
Black, non-Hispanic	18	37	53	69	45	58	63	67	31	44
Hispanic [1]	10	15	32	41	42	49	59	55	22	26
Other	22	39	49	69	52	61	70	79	36	48
Mother's employment status: [2]										
Employed	23	34	57	66	52	63	75	72	39	46
Unemployed	17	14	41	42	46	41	67	61	29	32
Not in the labor force	18	31	49	60	47	58	68	69	32	39
Family type:										
Two parents	22	33	54	64	51	62	74	72	37	44
None or one parent	18	27	49	57	47	52	65	65	31	36
Poverty status: [3]										
Above threshold	24	35	57	67	53	64	74	75	40	47
Below threshold	12	21	41	48	41	46	64	54	23	26

[1] Persons of Hispanic origin may be any race.   [2] Excludes children with no mother in the household and no female guardian.   [3] Children are considered poor if they lived in households with incomes below the poverty threshold, which is a dollar amount determined by the federal government to meet the household's need, given its size and composition.

Source: U.S. Department of Education, U.S. National Center for Education Statistics, *Home Literacy Activities and Signs of Children's Emerging Literacy*, 1993, NCES 2000-026, November 1999; the Early Childhood Program Participation Survey, National Household Education Surveys Program (NHES), 2005, unpublished data; and the NHES School Readiness Survey, 2007, unpublished data; <http://nces.ed.gov/nhes>.

Education 151

Table 231. **Children Who Speak a Language Other Than English at Home by Region: 2007**

[In thousands (10,918 represents 10,918,000), except percent. For children 5 to 17 years old. For more on languages spoken at home, see Tables 54-55. Based on the American Community Survey; see text Section 1, and Appendix III]

Characteristic	U.S.	Northeast	Midwest	South	West
Children who speak another language at home	10,918	1,853	1,339	3,443	4,284
Percent of children 5 to 17 years old	20.5	20.3	11.4	17.6	33.6
Speak Spanish	7,872	1,005	804	2,735	3,328
Speak English "very well"	5,804	801	578	1,969	2,457
Speak English less than "very well"	2,068	204	226	766	872
Speak other Indo-European languages	1,479	525	288	374	291
Speak English "very well"	1,189	420	225	303	241
Speak English less than "very well"	289	105	63	71	50
Speak Asian and Pacific Island languages	1,173	226	156	250	542
Speak English "very well"	853	165	112	183	393
Speak English less than "very well"	320	60	44	68	148
Speak other languages	394	97	92	83	122
Speak English "very well"	323	77	74	68	104
Speak English less than "very well"	71	20	17	15	19
Have difficulty speaking English [1]	2,748	389	350	920	1,089
Language spoken at home in linguistically isolated [2] households	3,046	456	345	990	1,255
Speak only English	156	35	20	52	50
Speak Spanish	2,263	247	226	794	995
Speak other Indo-European languages	230	82	42	59	47
Speak Asian and Pacific Island languages	335	73	40	70	152
Speak other languages	62	18	17	14	12

[1] Children ages 5 to 17 who speak English less than "very well." [2] A household in which no person age 14 or over speaks English at least "very well."

Source: U.S. Census Bureau, 2007 American Community Survey; Table B16003 "Age by Language Spoken at Home for the Population 5 Years and Over" and Table C16004 "Age By Language Spoken at Home For the Population 5 Years and Over in Linguistically Isolated Households," using American Factfinder; <http://factfinder.census.gov/> (accessed 29 September 2008).

Table 232. **Preprimary School Enrollment—Summary: 1970 to 2007**

[As of October. Civilian noninstitutional population (10,949 represents 10,949,000). Includes public and nonpublic nursery school and kindergarten programs. Excludes 5-year-olds enrolled in elementary school. Based on Current Population Survey. See text, Section 1 and Appendix III]

Item	1970	1980	1985	1990	1995	2000	2005	2006	2007
NUMBER OF CHILDREN (1,000)									
Population, 3 to 5 years old	10,949	9,284	10,733	11,207	12,518	11,858	12,134	12,187	12,325
Total enrolled [1]	4,104	4,878	5,865	6,659	7,739	7,592	7,801	8,009	8,056
Nursery	1,094	1,981	2,477	3,378	4,331	4,326	4,529	4,636	4,569
Public	332	628	846	1,202	1,950	2,146	2,409	2,481	2,532
Private	762	1,353	1,631	2,177	2,381	2,180	2,120	2,156	2,037
Kindergarten	3,010	2,897	3,388	3,281	3,408	3,266	3,272	3,373	3,487
Public	2,498	2,438	2,847	2,767	2,799	2,701	2,804	2,960	3,087
Private	511	459	541	513	608	565	468	413	400
White [2]	3,443	3,994	4,757	5,389	6,144	5,861	6,025	6,145	6,191
Black [2]	586	725	919	964	1,236	1,265	1,148	1,225	1,213
Hispanic [3]	(NA)	370	496	642	1,040	1,155	1,494	1,624	1,751
3 years old	454	857	1,035	1,205	1,489	1,540	1,715	1,716	1,717
4 years old	1,007	1,423	1,765	2,086	2,553	2,556	2,668	2,817	2,774
5 years old	2,643	2,598	3,065	3,367	3,697	3,496	3,418	3,476	3,565
ENROLLMENT RATE									
Total enrolled [1]	37.5	52.5	54.6	59.4	61.8	64.0	64.3	65.7	65.4
White [2]	37.8	52.7	54.7	59.7	63.0	63.2	65.1	66.0	68.7
Black [2]	34.9	51.8	55.8	57.8	58.9	68.5	62.0	66.7	69.7
Hispanic [3]	(NA)	43.3	43.3	49.0	51.1	52.6	56.1	59.8	63.0
3 years old	12.9	27.3	28.8	32.6	35.9	39.2	41.3	42.4	41.5
4 years old	27.8	46.3	49.1	56.0	61.6	64.9	66.2	68.8	67.8
5 years old	69.3	84.7	86.5	88.8	87.5	87.6	86.4	85.8	87.1

NA Not available. [1] Includes races not shown separately. [2] Beginning 2003, for persons who selected this race group only. See footnote 2, Table 224. [3] Persons of Hispanic origin may be any race. The method of identifying Hispanic children was changed in 1980 from allocation based on status of mother to status reported for each child. The number of Hispanic children using the new method is larger.

Source: U.S. Census Bureau, Current Population Reports, PPL-148, and earlier PPL and P-20 reports; and data published on the Internet; <http://www.census.gov/population/www/socdemo/school.html>.

Table 233. **Public Charter and Traditional Schools—Selected Characteristics: 2006 to 2007**

[43,575 represents 43,575,000. A public charter school is a public school that, in accordance with an enabling state statute, has been granted a charter exempting it from selected state and local rules and regulations]

Characteristic	All schools Tradi-tional	All schools Public charter	Elementary Tradi-tional	Elementary Public charter	Secondary Tradi-tional	Secondary Public charter	Combined Tradi-tional	Combined Public charter
Number of schools	79,339	3,970	56,571	2,133	18,775	1,081	3,993	756
Enrollment (1,000).	43,575	1,157	27,976	611	14,429	236	1,170	310
PERCENT DISTRIBUTION OF STUDENTS								
Race/ethnicity.	100.0	100.0	100.0	100.0	100.0	100.0	100.0	100.0
White, non-Hispanic	54.6	38.7	52.8	34.5	58.0	35.7	54.7	49.1
Black, non-Hispanic	16.5	30.8	16.6	35.2	16.0	28.2	20.7	24.2
Hispanic [1]	21.6	23.7	23.2	23.6	18.8	29.1	18.1	19.7
Asian/Pacific Islander	4.9	3.6	4.8	3.9	5.1	3.5	2.8	3.3
American Indian/Alaska Native	1.1	1.3	1.1	1.0	1.1	2.0	2.1	1.3
Other.	1.3	2.0	1.5	1.9	1.0	1.6	1.6	2.5
PERCENT DISTRIBUTION OF SCHOOLS								
Size of enrollment	100.0	100.0	100.0	100.0	100.0	100.0	100.0	100.0
Less than 300 students.	28.3	66.7	23.5	63.4	33.8	79.2	69.3	57.9
300 to 599 students	39.4	23.1	47.4	26.1	20.3	15.7	16.8	25.3
600 to 999 students	21.9	7.2	24.4	8.9	17.2	2.7	8.3	8.6
1,000 students or more	10.5	3.1	4.7	1.6	28.7	2.4	5.6	8.2
Percent minority enrollment.	100.0	100.0	100.0	100.0	100.0	100.0	100.0	100.0
Less than 10.0	26.2	11.6	24.9	10.2	31.0	11.6	21.2	15.5
10.0 to 24.9	18.4	17.0	18.7	16.2	18.3	15.7	15.1	21.0
25.0 to 49.9	18.9	17.0	19.1	15.8	18.3	17.1	20.0	20.2
50.0 to 74.9	13.5	12.8	13.4	11.5	13.1	15.9	17.0	11.8
75.0 or more	23.0	41.7	24.0	46.4	19.3	39.7	26.7	31.5
Percent of students eligible for free or reduced-price lunch [2]	100.0	100.0	100.0	100.0	100.0	100.0	100.0	100.0
Less than 15.0	18.3	23.3	17.5	19.8	21.1	24.9	17.3	30.8
15.0 to 29.9	17.0	11.8	15.4	12.3	22.8	12.3	12.3	9.7
30.0 to 49.9	23.0	15.7	21.8	15.6	27.0	17.4	21.5	13.6
50.0 to 74.9	23.6	21.9	24.6	20.9	19.6	24.1	28.2	21.7
75.0 or more	18.1	27.3	20.8	31.4	9.6	21.2	20.7	24.2

[1] Persons of Hispanic origin may be any race.   [2] Excludes data for schools not providing information on eligibility for free or reduced-price lunch.

Source: U.S. National Center for Education Statistics, Common Core of Data, "Public Elementary/Secondary School Universe Survey," 2006–07, unpublished data.

Table 234. **Public Elementary and Secondary Schools by Type and Size of School: 2006 to 2007**

[Enrollment in thousands (49,066 represents 49,066,000). Data reported by schools, rather than school districts. Based on the Common Core of Data Survey; see source for details]

Enrollment size of school	Number of schools Total	Number of schools Elemen-tary [2]	Number of schools Second-ary [3]	Number of schools Com-bined [4]	Number of schools Other [5]	Enrollment [1] Total	Enrollment [1] Elemen-tary [2]	Enrollment [1] Second-ary [3]	Enrollment [1] Com-bined [4]	Enrollment [1] Other [5]
Total	98,793	68,990	23,436	5,984	383	49,066	31,273	16,068	1,673	51
PERCENT										
Total	100.00	100.00	100.00	100.00	100.00	100.00	100.00	100.00	100.00	100.00
Under 100 students.	10.71	5.92	18.00	36.67	60.16	0.94	0.63	1.10	4.88	16.36
100 to 199 students	9.60	8.40	11.10	17.81	17.89	2.75	2.68	2.27	7.97	18.99
200 to 299 students	11.53	12.59	8.62	11.05	6.78	5.58	6.73	3.02	8.41	12.25
300 to 399 students	13.75	16.22	8.07	7.40	7.59	9.24	12.01	3.96	7.91	19.24
400 to 499 students	13.44	16.53	6.07	6.86	3.52	11.57	15.66	3.83	9.45	11.30
500 to 599 students	10.98	13.30	5.78	4.62	1.63	11.53	15.37	4.45	7.79	6.29
600 to 699 students	8.20	9.63	5.21	3.52	0.27	10.17	13.14	4.75	7.03	1.22
700 to 799 students	5.60	6.40	4.04	2.45	0.81	8.01	10.08	4.24	5.63	4.23
800 to 999 students	6.62	6.74	7.09	3.46	0.27	11.27	12.59	8.94	9.42	1.72
1,000 to 1,499 students . . .	5.67	3.80	11.68	3.61	1.08	13.01	9.32	20.16	13.45	8.39
1,500 to 1,999 students . . .	2.10	0.38	7.32	1.34	–	6.93	1.35	17.78	7.14	–
2,000 to 2,999 students . . .	1.48	0.08	5.74	0.84	–	6.71	0.38	19.11	6.08	–
3,000 or more students . . .	0.34	0.01	1.29	0.39	–	2.29	0.04	6.41	4.83	–
Average enrollment [1]	521	473	711	325	138	521	473	711	325	138

– Represents zero.   [1] Exclude data for schools not reporting enrollment.   [2] Includes schools beginning with grade 6 or below and with no grade higher than 8.   [3] Includes schools with no grade lower than 7.   [4] Includes schools beginning with grade 6 or below and ending with grade 9 or above.   [5] Includes special education, alternative, and other schools not classified by grade span.

Source: U.S. National Center for Education Statistics, *Digest of Education Statistics,* annual.

Education   153

Table 235. Public Elementary and Secondary Schools—Summary: 1980 to 2007

[For school year ending in year shown, except as indicated (48,041 represents 48,041,000). Data are estimates]

Item	Unit	1980	1985	1990	1995	2000	2006	2007
School districts, total	Number. . . .	16,044	15,812	15,552	14,947	15,403	15,732	15,501
ENROLLMENT								
Population 5–17 years old [1]	1,000.	48,041	44,787	44,949	48,855	52,811	53,132	53,216
Percent of resident population.	Percent	21.4	19.0	18.2	18.6	18.8	18.0	17.8
Fall enrollment [2].	1,000.	41,778	39,354	40,527	43,898	46,577	48,724	48,785
Percent of population								
5–17 years old	Percent	87.0	87.9	90.2	89.9	88.2	91.7	91.7
Elementary [3]	1,000.	24,397	23,830	26,253	28,148	29,243	29,732	29,733
Secondary [4].	1,000.	17,381	15,524	14,274	15,750	17,334	18,993	19,051
Average daily attendance (ADA)	1,000.	38,411	36,530	37,573	40,792	43,313	45,465	45,704
High school graduates	1,000.	2,762	2,424	2,327	2,282	2,544	2,843	2,900
INSTRUCTIONAL STAFF								
Total [5]	**1,000. . . . . .**	**2,521**	**2,473**	**2,685**	**2,919**	**3,273**	**3,559**	**3,613**
Classroom teachers	1,000.	2,211	2,175	2,362	2,565	2,891	3,116	3,158
Average salaries:								
Instructional staff.	Dollar	16,715	24,666	32,638	38,349	43,837	50,606	52,508
Classroom teachers.	Dollar	15,970	23,600	31,367	36,675	41,807	48,804	50,758
REVENUES								
Revenue receipts	Mil. dol.	97,635	141,013	208,656	273,255	369,754	506,971	532,123
Federal	Mil. dol.	9,020	9,533	13,184	18,764	26,346	45,819	46,835
State	Mil. dol.	47,929	69,107	100,787	129,958	183,986	238,041	251,053
Local	Mil. dol.	40,686	62,373	94,685	124,533	159,421	223,111	234,235
EXPENDITURES								
Total	**Mil. dol. . . . .**	**96,105**	**139,382**	**209,698**	**276,584**	**374,782**	**521,800**	**549,516**
Current expenditures								
(day schools)	Mil. dol.	85,661	127,230	186,583	242,995	320,954	443,641	466,612
Other current expenditures [6]	Mil. dol.	1,859	2,109	3,341	5,564	6,618	9,032	9,467
Capital outlay	Mil. dol.	6,504	7,529	16,012	21,646	37,552	52,741	56,373
Interest on school debt	Mil. dol.	2,081	2,514	3,762	6,379	9,659	16,385	17,064
In current dollars:								
Revenue receipts per pupil								
enrolled.	Dollar	2,337	3,583	5,149	6,225	7,939	10,405	10,908
Current expenditures per pupil								
enrolled.	Dollar	2,050	3,233	4,604	5,535	6,891	9,105	9,565
In constant (2007) dollars: [7]								
Revenue receipts per pupil								
enrolled.	Dollar	5,713	6,972	8,140	8,529	9,598	10,792	10,908
Current expenditures per pupil								
enrolled.	Dollar	5,012	6,291	7,279	7,585	8,331	9,444	9,565

[1] Estimated resident population as of July 1 of the previous year, except 1980, 1990, and 2000 population enumerated as of April 1. Estimates reflect revisions based on the 2000 Census of Population. [2] Fall enrollment of the previous year. [3] Kindergarten through grade 6. [4] Grades 7 through 12. [5] Full-time equivalent. [6] Current expenses for summer schools, adult education, post-high school vocational education, personnel retraining, etc., when operated by local school districts and not part of regular public elementary and secondary day-school program. [7] Compiled by U.S. Census Bureau. Deflated by the Consumer Price Index, all urban consumers (for school year July through June) supplied by U.S. National Center for Education Statistics.

Source: Except as noted, National Education Association, Washington, DC, Estimates of School Statistics Database (copyright).

Table 236. Public Elementary and Secondary School Enrollment by Grade: 1980 to 2006

[In thousands (40,877 represents 40,877,000). As of fall of year. Based on survey of state education agencies; see source for details]

Grade	1980	1985	1990	1995	1999	2000	2001	2002	2003	2004	2005	2006
Pupils enrolled [1]	40,877	39,422	41,217	44,840	46,857	47,204	47,672	48,183	48,540	48,795	49,113	49,299
Pre-kindergarten to 8 [1]	27,647	27,034	29,878	32,341	33,488	33,688	33,938	34,116	34,202	34,178	34,205	34,221
Pre-K and Kindergarten . . .	2,689	3,192	3,610	4,173	4,148	4,158	4,244	4,349	4,453	4,534	4,656	4,706
First	2,894	3,239	3,499	3,671	3,684	3,636	3,614	3,594	3,613	3,663	3,691	3,750
Second	2,800	2,941	3,327	3,507	3,656	3,634	3,593	3,565	3,544	3,560	3,606	3,640
Third	2,893	2,895	3,297	3,445	3,691	3,676	3,653	3,623	3,611	3,580	3,586	3,627
Fourth	3,107	2,771	3,248	3,431	3,686	3,711	3,695	3,669	3,619	3,612	3,578	3,585
Fifth	3,130	2,776	3,197	3,438	3,604	3,707	3,727	3,711	3,685	3,635	3,633	3,601
Sixth	3,038	2,789	3,110	3,395	3,564	3,663	3,769	3,788	3,772	3,735	3,670	3,660
Seventh	3,085	2,938	3,067	3,422	3,541	3,629	3,720	3,821	3,841	3,818	3,777	3,715
Eighth	3,086	2,982	2,979	3,356	3,497	3,538	3,616	3,700	3,709	3,809	3,825	3,765
Grades 9 to 12 [1]	13,231	12,388	11,338	12,500	13,369	13,515	13,734	14,067	14,338	14,617	14,909	15,078
Ninth	3,377	3,439	3,169	3,704	3,935	3,963	4,012	4,105	4,190	4,281	4,287	4,260
Tenth	3,368	3,230	2,896	3,237	3,415	3,491	3,528	3,584	3,675	3,750	3,866	3,881
Eleventh	3,195	2,866	2,612	2,826	3,034	3,083	3,174	3,229	3,277	3,369	3,455	3,551
Twelfth	2,925	2,550	2,381	2,487	2,782	2,803	2,863	2,990	3,046	3,094	3,180	3,276

[1] Includes unclassified students not shown separately.

Source: U.S. National Center for Education Statistics, Digest of Education Statistics, annual.

154 Education

Table 237. **Public Elementary and Secondary Schools and Enrollment—States: 2006 to 2007**

[**For schools with membership (49,066 represents 49,066,000).** Based on the Common Core of Data Program; see source for details]

State	Total number of schools with member- ship	Total number of students (1,000)	Regular — Number of schools	Regular — Percent of students	Special education[1] — Number of schools	Special education[1] — Percent of students	Vocational education[2] — Number of schools	Vocational education[2] — Percent of students	Alternative education[3] — Number of schools	Alternative education[3] — Percent of students
Total.........	94,164	49,066	87,619	98.2	1,457	0.4	334	0.4	4,754	1.1
Alabama.........	1,383	743	1,344	99.5	17	0.2	2	(Z)	20	0.2
Alaska..........	499	133	451	90.5	1	(Z)	–	–	47	9.5
Arizona.........	1,906	1,065	1,831	98.2	8	0.1	5	0.5	62	1.2
Arkansas	1,084	476	1,074	99.7	–	–	1	0.1	9	0.3
California	9,659	6,275	8,471	97.2	121	0.4	–	–	1,067	2.4
Colorado........	1,736	793	1,639	98.2	8	0.1	5	0.1	84	1.7
Connecticut.......	1,110	575	1,021	97.1	34	0.6	17	1.7	38	0.5
Delaware	204	122	178	92.7	13	1.3	6	5.1	7	1.0
District of Columbia	216	73	189	92.0	12	2.1	5	2.5	10	3.4
Florida	3,645	2,672	3,079	97.8	126	0.5	24	0.1	416	1.5
Georgia	2,159	1,629	2,126	99.6	8	0.1	–	–	25	0.3
Hawaii	284	181	281	99.9	2	0.1	–	–	1	0.1
Idaho..........	683	267	609	98.1	3	(Z)	–	–	71	1.8
Illinois	4,235	2,118	4,035	99.2	85	0.3	–	–	115	0.5
Indiana.........	1,898	1,044	1,872	99.7	6	(Z)	–	–	20	0.2
Iowa	1,504	482	1,423	98.9	10	0.2	–	–	71	0.9
Kansas.........	1,396	460	1,392	100.0	4	(Z)	–	–	–	–
Kentucky	1,366	647	1,209	98.8	10	0.1	–	–	147	1.1
Louisiana	1,407	676	1,254	96.7	39	0.2	–	–	114	3.1
Maine..........	643	194	641	100.0	2	(Z)	–	–	–	–
Maryland	1,408	852	1,311	97.8	42	0.6	10	1.0	45	0.6
Massachusetts.....	1,875	969	1,845	97.2	–	–	30	2.8	–	–
Michigan........	3,904	1,714	3,456	96.6	162	1.3	16	0.1	270	2.0
Minnesota.......	2,244	841	1,636	96.2	256	1.6	1	(Z)	351	2.2
Mississippi	904	495	904	100.0	–	–	–	–	–	–
Missouri	2,270	920	2,241	99.6	3	(Z)	7	0.2	19	0.1
Montana........	830	144	825	99.9	2	(Z)	–	–	3	0.1
Nebraska	1,096	288	1,084	99.7	12	0.3	–	–	–	–
Nevada	573	423	543	98.7	–	–	1	0.4	29	0.9
New Hampshire....	482	204	482	100.0	–	–	–	–	–	–
New Jersey.......	2,470	1,387	2,339	97.6	77	0.7	54	1.7	–	–
New Mexico......	825	327	795	98.7	4	0.2	–	–	26	1.1
New York	4,692	2,808	4,408	96.6	151	1.6	30	1.4	103	0.4
North Carolina....	2,382	1,444	2,277	99.3	21	0.2	4	(Z)	80	0.5
North Dakota......	494	97	494	100.0	–	–	–	–	–	–
Ohio	3,850	1,832	3,807	99.7	33	0.2	9	0.1	1	(Z)
Oklahoma........	1,792	639	1,783	99.8	4	(Z)	–	–	5	0.2
Oregon.........	1,268	555	1,230	99.0	2	(Z)	–	–	36	0.9
Pennsylvania......	3,235	1,846	3,150	96.9	–	–	85	3.1	–	–
Rhode Island......	322	150	303	97.0	3	0.1	4	1.2	12	1.6
South Carolina.....	1,115	703	1,115	100.0	–	–	–	–	–	–
South Dakota	687	121	687	100.0	–	–	–	–	–	–
Tennessee	1,671	978	1,625	99.3	12	0.1	9	0.3	25	0.2
Texas..........	8,099	4,598	7,143	98.3	–	–	–	–	956	1.7
Utah	955	524	806	98.0	53	0.8	2	(Z)	94	1.1
Vermont	315	93	314	100.0	–	–	–	–	1	(Z)
Virginia.........	1,858	1,220	1,845	99.8	3	(Z)	–	–	10	0.2
Washington.......	2,226	1,027	1,872	96.3	92	0.4	2	(Z)	260	3.3
West Virginia......	729	281	700	99.6	7	0.1	3	(Z)	19	0.3
Wisconsin........	2,209	877	2,137	99.4	4	(Z)	2	(Z)	66	0.5
Wyoming	367	85	343	98.5	5	0.1	–	–	19	1.5

– Represents zero.   Z Less than 0.05 percent.   [1] Focuses on special education with materials and instructional approaches adapted to meet the students' needs.   [2] Focuses on vocational, technical, or career education and provides education and training in at least one semi-skilled or technical occupation.   [3] Addresses the needs of students that typically cannot be met in the regular school setting and provides nontraditional education.

Source: U.S. National Center for Education Statistics, Common Core of Data, "Public Elementary/Secondary School Universe Survey," 2006–07, Version 1b.

Education   155

Table 238. **Selected Statistics for the Largest Public School Districts: 2005 to 2006**

[For the 50 largest districts by enrollment size. Based on reports from state education agencies in the spring 2006. Data from the Common Core Data Program; see source for details. School district boundaries are not necessarily the same as city or county boundaries]

School district	City	County	Number of students [1]	Number of full-time equivalent (FTE) teachers	Number of 2004–05 completers [2]	Number of schools
New York City Public Schools, NY	New York	New York	1,014,058	70,889	41,322	1,408
Los Angeles Unified, CA	Los Angeles	Los Angeles	727,319	34,961	29,741	808
Puerto Rico Department of Education, PR. . .	San Juan	San Juan	563,490	42,036	30,371	1,523
City of Chicago, IL	Chicago	Cook	420,982	27,039	16,866	633
Dade County, FL	Miami	Miami-Dade	362,070	20,606	18,702	394
Clark County, NV	Las Vegas	Clark	294,131	14,862	10,314	314
Broward County, FL	Fort Lauderdale	Broward	271,630	15,717	14,436	285
Houston Independent School District, TX . . .	Houston	Harris	210,292	12,082	8,476	312
Hillsborough County, FL.	Tampa	Hillsborough	193,757	10,924	9,614	261
Philadelphia City School District, PA.	Philadelphia	Philadelphia	184,560	10,060	10,819	270
Hawaii Department of Education, HI.	Honolulu	Honolulu	182,818	11,226	11,014	285
Orange County, FL	Orlando	Orange	175,609	10,737	9,434	211
Palm Beach County, FL.	West Palm Beach	Palm Beach	174,935	10,084	9,523	236
Fairfax County, VA	Falls Church	Fairfax	163,753	13,090	11,570	207
Dallas Independent School District, TX	Dallas	Dallas	161,244	10,324	6,832	255
Gwinnett County, GA.	Lawrenceville	Gwinnett	144,598	9,801	7,045	122
Montgomery County, MD	Rockville	Montgomery	139,398	9,371	9,351	199
Prince George's County Public Schools, MD .	Upper Marlboro	Prince George's	133,325	8,395	7,947	205
Detroit City, MI	Detroit	Wayne	133,255	7,187	5,673	235
San Diego Unified, CA.	San Diego	San Diego	132,482	7,332	6,653	219
Duval County, FL	Jacksonville	Duval	126,662	7,526	6,276	182
Charlotte-Mecklenburg, NC.	Charlotte	Mecklenburg	124,005	8,616	5,836	142
Wake County, NC	Raleigh	Wake	120,996	8,179	6,659	138
Memphis City School District, TN.	Memphis	Shelby	120,275	7,085	5,946	194
Pinellas County, FL.	Largo	Pinellas	112,174	6,799	5,949	173
Baltimore County, MD	Baltimore	Baltimore	107,043	7,388	7,238	168
Cobb County, GA	Marietta	Cobb	106,724	7,065	6,354	110
DeKalb County, GA.	Decatur	De Kalb	102,310	6,858	5,199	148
Jefferson County, KY.	Louisville	Jefferson	98,537	5,780	5,194	172
Albuquerque, NM	Albuquerque	Bernalillo	94,022	6,139	4,650	169
Long Beach Unified, CA.	Long Beach	Los Angeles	93,589	4,298	4,956	90
Milwaukee, WI	Milwaukee	Milwaukee	92,395	5,420	3,915	235
Polk County, FL	Bartow	Polk	89,443	6,046	4,380	153
Baltimore City, MD	Baltimore	Baltimore City	87,643	5,666	4,145	197
Jefferson County, CO	Golden	Jefferson	86,332	4,785	5,651	162
Cypress-Fairbanks Independent School District, TX	Houston	Harris	86,256	5,521	4,622	75
Austin Independent School District, TX	Austin	Travis	81,155	5,630	3,746	124
Fulton County, GA	Atlanta	Fulton	81,100	5,634	4,291	95
Fort Worth Independent School District, TX . .	Fort Worth	Tarrant	80,336	4,794	3,608	147
Fresno Unified, CA	Fresno	Fresno	79,046	3,737	4,022	106
Northside Independent School District, TX. . .	San Antonio	Bexar	78,711	4,867	4,238	95
Jordan, UT	Sandy	Salt Lake	77,110	3,120	4,922	92
Lee County School District, FL	Fort Myers	Lee	75,634	4,322	3,728	101
Brevard County, FL.	Viera	Brevard	75,233	4,489	4,493	117
Mesa Unified District, AZ	Mesa	Maricopa	74,626	3,805	4,391	89
Virginia Beach City Public Schools, VA	Virginia Beach	Va. Beach City	74,303	5,647	4,778	88
Anne Arundel County, MD	Annapolis	Anne Arundel	73,565	4,754	4,861	121
Nashville-Davidson, TN	Nashville	Davidson	72,713	4,951	3,390	132
Denver County, CO.	Denver	Denver	72,312	3,974	2,849	148
Guilford County Schools, NC	Greensboro	Guilford	68,951	4,621	4,087	111

[1] Number of students receiving educational services from the school district. [2] Includes high school diploma recipients and other completers (e.g., certificates of attendance) but does not include high school equivalents (GEDs).

Source: U.S. Department of Education, National Center for Education Statistics, Common Core of Data (CCD), "Local Education Agency Universe Survey," 2005–06, Version 1a.

Table 239. **Public Elementary and Secondary School Enrollment by State: 1990 to 2006**

[In thousands (29,878 represents 29,878,000), except rate. As of fall. Includes unclassified students. Based on survey of state education agencies; see source for details]

State	Enrollment								Enrollment rate [2]		
	Prekindergarten through grade 8 [1]				Grades 9 through 12 [1]						
	1990	2000	2005	2006	1990	2000	2005	2006, est.	1990	2000	2006
United States. . . .	**29,878**	**33,688**	**34,205**	**34,221**	**11,338**	**13,515**	**14,908**	**15,078**	**91.2**	**88.8**	**92.7**
Alabama	527	539	529	529	195	201	212	215	93.2	89.5	91.3
Alaska	85	94	91	90	29	39	42	42	97.4	93.4	99.4
Arizona	479	641	740	758	161	237	355	307	93.3	88.6	93.1
Arkansas	314	318	336	337	123	132	138	140	95.8	90.2	95.5
California	3,615	4,408	4,466	4,410	1,336	1,733	1,971	1,997	92.6	90.7	94.9
Colorado	420	517	550	559	154	208	230	235	94.6	89.7	95.8
Connecticut	347	406	400	398	122	156	175	177	90.2	90.9	93.7
Delaware	73	81	85	85	27	34	36	37	87.2	80.0	83.6
District of Columbia	61	54	56	52	19	15	21	20	100.6	83.8	92.0
Florida	1,370	1,760	1,873	1,867	492	675	802	805	92.6	89.9	92.2
Georgia	849	1,060	1,145	1,167	303	385	453	463	93.7	91.4	92.8
Hawaii	123	132	127	126	49	52	55	55	87.4	85.2	89.2
Idaho	160	170	183	187	61	75	79	80	96.9	90.1	94.4
Illinois	1,310	1,474	1,480	1,478	512	575	631	641	86.9	86.5	91.6
Indiana	676	703	724	730	279	286	311	316	90.4	85.9	91.2
Iowa	345	334	326	326	139	161	157	157	92.1	90.9	93.4
Kansas	320	323	321	326	117	147	147	143	92.5	89.7	93.9
Kentucky	459	471	487	487	177	194	192	196	90.5	91.3	94.3
Louisiana	586	547	482	492	199	197	172	184	88.1	82.5	87.0
Maine	155	146	133	132	60	61	62	62	96.5	89.8	91.4
Maryland	527	609	589	579	188	244	271	273	89.1	85.0	85.5
Massachusetts	604	703	675	671	230	273	297	298	88.8	88.3	91.0
Michigan	1,145	1,222	1,191	1,163	440	498	551	552	90.3	89.4	93.2
Minnesota	546	578	558	558	211	277	281	282	91.3	89.1	92.2
Mississippi	372	364	358	356	131	134	137	139	91.3	87.3	90.0
Missouri	588	645	635	634	228	268	203	288	86.5	86.3	88.9
Montana	111	105	98	97	42	50	48	47	94.1	88.5	89.7
Nebraska	198	195	195	196	76	91	92	92	88.7	85.9	90.9
Nevada	150	251	296	303	51	90	116	121	98.6	92.3	94.0
New Hampshire	126	147	139	136	46	61	67	67	89.1	88.9	90.1
New Jersey	784	968	971	964	306	346	425	425	85.9	86.2	91.5
New Mexico	208	225	230	230	94	95	97	98	94.4	84.9	92.3
New York	1,828	2,029	1,909	1,888	770	853	906	922	86.6	83.6	85.4
North Carolina	783	945	1,003	1,027	304	348	413	417	94.8	90.7	93.8
North Dakota	85	72	66	64	33	37	33	32	92.6	90.2	92.7
Ohio	1,258	1,294	1,261	1,253	514	541	578	583	88.0	86.1	90.2
Oklahoma	425	445	457	460	154	178	178	179	95.1	95.1	100.6
Oregon	340	379	380	381	132	167	173	182	90.6	87.5	90.7
Pennsylvania	1,172	1,258	1,228	1,220	496	556	603	651	83.5	82.8	90.1
Rhode Island	102	114	104	102	37	44	50	50	87.5	85.4	86.7
South Carolina	452	493	498	497	170	184	204	206	93.9	90.8	92.8
South Dakota	95	88	84	83	34	41	38	38	89.9	84.9	85.8
Tennessee	598	668	677	692	226	241	277	286	93.5	88.7	92.6
Texas	2,511	2,943	3,268	3,320	872	1,117	1,257	1,280	98.4	95.0	101.3
Utah	325	333	358	371	122	148	151	152	97.8	94.2	95.3
Vermont	71	70	65	64	25	32	32	32	94.3	89.9	94.3
Virginia	728	816	841	842	270	329	372	379	94.2	89.6	93.6
Washington	613	694	699	695	227	310	333	332	94.1	89.6	92.4
West Virginia	224	201	197	198	98	85	84	84	95.7	95.6	99.7
Wisconsin	566	595	584	585	232	285	291	292	86.1	85.6	93.4
Wyoming	71	60	57	58	27	30	27	27	97.7	92.0	96.4

[1] Includes unclassified. [2] Percent of persons 5–17 years old. Based on enumerated resident population as of April 1, 1990 and estimated resident population as of July 1 for 2000 and 2006.

Source: U.S. National Center for Education Statistics, *Digest of Education Statistics*, annual.

Table 240. **Public Schools Reporting Incidents of Crime by Incident Type and Selected School Characteristic: 2005 to 2006**

[For school year. Includes incidents that happen in school buildings, on school grounds, on school buses, and at places that hold school-sponsored events or activities. Based on sample; see source for details]

School characteristic	Total number of schools	Percent of schools with—				Rate per 1,000 students			
		Violent incidents [1]	Serious violent incidents [2]	Theft [3]	Other incidents [4]	Violent incidents [1]	Serious violent incidents [2]	Theft [3]	Other incidents [4]
All public schools	83,200	78	17	46	68	31.2	1.2	5.1	9.6
Level: [5]									
Primary.	48,600	67	11	28	55	25.2	0.9	1.6	4.7
Middle.	15,500	94	25	69	88	51.6	1.9	7.8	11.9
High school	11,700	95	32	86	94	25.7	1.4	8.7	15.7
Combined	7,400	84	17	55	75	29.2	1.1	7.0	12.8
Enrollment size:									
Less than 300	20,800	64	11	30	53	34.5	2.8	(S)	12.3
300 to 499.	23,800	77	12	37	63	34.0	0.7	3.3	6.7
500 to 999.	29,300	82	19	52	74	30.9	1.1	4.5	7.7
1,000 or more	9,300	96	37	86	95	28.6	1.3	7.2	13.4
Percent minority enrollment: [6]									
Less than 5 percent	16,600	72	13	43	62	26.9	0.9	4.8	8.6
5 to 20 percent.	20,600	74	16	43	63	22.9	0.9	5.2	9.3
20 to 50 percent.	18,600	80	17	48	71	28.4	1.4	5.5	9.6
50 percent or more	25,600	83	22	48	72	39.9	1.5	4.8	10.1

S Figure does not meet publication standards. [1] Violent incidents include rape, sexual battery other than rape, physical attack or fight with or without a weapon, threat of physical attack with or without a weapon, and robbery with or without a weapon. [2] Serious violent incidents include rape, sexual battery other than rape, physical attack or fight with a weapon, threat of physical attack with a weapon, and robbery with or without a weapon. [3] Theft or larceny (taking things worth over $10 without personal confrontation). Includes pocket picking, stealing purse or backpack (if left unattended or no force was used to take from owner), theft from motor vehicles, etc. [4] Other incidents include possession of a firearm or explosive device, possession of knife or sharp object, distribution of illegal drugs, possession or use of alcohol or illegal drugs, and vandalism. [5] Primary schools are defined as schools in which the lowest grade is not higher than grade 3 and the highest grade is not higher than grade 8. Middle schools are defined as schools in which the lowest grade is not lower than grade 4 and the highest grade is not higher than grade 9. High schools are defined as schools in which the lowest grade is not lower than grade 9 and the highest grade is not higher than grade 12. Combined schools include all other combination of grades, including K–12 schools. [6] These estimates exclude data from Tennessee because schools in this state did not report estimates of student race.

Source: U.S. National Center for Education Statistics, *Crime, Violence, Discipline, and Safety in U.S. Public Schools 2005–06,* NCES 2007-361, September 2007.

Table 241. **Percent of Public Schools Reporting Selected Types of Disciplinary Problems Occurring at School by Selected School Characteristics: 2005 to 2006**

[In percent. For school year. "At school" includes activities that happen in school buildings, on school grounds, on school buses, and at places that hold school-sponsored events or activities. Based on sample; see source for details]

School characteristic	Happens daily or at least once a day						Happens at all	
	Student racial tensions	Student bullying	Student sexual harassment of other students [1]	Student verbal abuse of teachers	Wide-spread disorder in class-rooms	Student acts of disrespect for teachers	Undesirable gang activities [2]	Undesirable cult or extremist group activities [3]
All public schools	2.8	24.5	3.5	9.5	2.3	18.3	16.8	3.6
Level: [4]								
Primary.	1.5	20.6	1.6	6.1	[5]0.8	12.1	7.6	[5]1.1
Middle.	6.0	43.0	8.6	16.0	5.2	30.5	31.5	5.0
High school	5.0	22.3	6.2	17.3	4.8	30.4	38.7	11.0
Combined	(S)	14.5	(S)	[5]5.6	(S)	14.3	12.4	[5]5.8
Enrollment size:								
Less than 300	(S)	19.4	[5]2.3	5.9	[5]1.5	12.1	7.5	[5]2.4
300 to 499.	2.5	21.9	2.4	8.3	[5]1.6	14.2	9.4	[5]2.3
500 to 999.	3.2	28.5	4.1	9.5	2.7	20.7	18.9	2.9
1,000 or more	6.4	29.9	7.4	20.4	4.9	34.8	50.9	12.1
Percent minority enrollment: [6]								
Less than 5 percent	[5]0.6	20.5	2.2	2.7	[5]0.8	11.0	2.5	[5]1.1
5 to 20 percent.	1.9	23.4	4.3	6.1	0.8	12.9	7.8	2.9
20 to 50 percent.	5.1	23.3	3.1	12.0	2.1	21.4	19.6	5.9
50 percent or more	3.4	28.9	3.6	15.3	4.8	25.2	31.6	3.8

S Figure does not meet publication standards. [1] Sexual harassment includes "unsolicited, offensive behavior that inappropriately asserts sexuality over another person. This behavior may be verbal or nonverbal." [2] Gang includes an "ongoing loosely organized association of three or more persons, whether formal or informal, that has a common name, signs, symbols, or colors, whose members engage, either individually or collectively, in violent or other forms of illegal behavior." [3] Cult or extremist group includes "a group that espouses radical beliefs and practices, which may include a religious component, that are widely seen as threatening the basic values and cultural norms of society at large." [4] Primary schools are defined as schools in which the lowest grade is not higher than grade 3 and the highest grade is not higher than grade 8. Middle schools are defined as schools in which the lowest grade level is not lower than grade 4 and the highest grade is not higher than grade 9. High school are defined as schools in which the lowest grade is not lower than grade 9 and the highest grade is not higher than grade 12. Combined schools include all other combinations of grades, including K–12 schools. [5] Interpret data with caution. [6] These estimates exclude data from Tennessee because schools in this state did not report estimates of student race.

Source: U.S. National Center for Education Statistics, *Crime, Violence, Discipline, and Safety in U.S. Public Schools 2005–06,* NCES 2007-361, September 2007.

Table 242. Students Who Reported Carrying a Weapon: 1999 to 2007

[In percent. For students in grades 9 to 12. Percentages are based on students who reported carrying a weapon at least one day during the previous thirty days. Weapons are such things as guns, knives, and clubs. Based on the Youth Risk Behavior Surveillance System. See source for details. See also <http://www.cdc.gov/HealthyYouth/yrbs/index.htm>]

Student Characteristic	Anywhere					On school property				
	1999	2001	2003	2005	2007	1999	2001	2003	2005	2007
Total...................	17.3	17.4	17.1	18.5	18.0	6.9	6.4	6.1	6.5	5.9
Sex:										
Male....................	28.6	29.3	26.9	29.8	28.5	11.0	10.2	8.9	10.2	9.0
Female..................	6.0	6.2	6.7	7.1	7.5	2.8	2.9	3.1	2.6	2.7
Race/ethnicity:										
White, non-Hispanic	16.4	17.9	16.7	18.7	18.2	6.4	6.1	5.5	6.1	5.3
Black, non-Hispanic............	17.2	15.2	17.3	16.4	17.2	5.0	6.3	6.9	5.1	6.0
Hispanic [1]	18.7	16.5	16.5	19.0	18.5	7.9	6.4	6.0	8.2	7.3
Asian, non-Hispanic...........	13.0	10.6	11.6	7.0	7.8	6.5	7.2	[2]6.6	[2]2.8	4.1
American Indian, non-Hispanic	21.8	31.2	29.3	25.6	20.6	[2]11.6	16.4	12.9	7.7	7.7
Pacific Islander, non-Hispanic	25.3	17.4	[2]16.3	[2]20.0	25.5	9.3	[2]10.0	[2]4.9	[2]15.4	[2]9.5
More than one race............	22.2	25.2	29.8	26.7	19.0	11.4	13.2	[2]13.3	11.9	5.0
Grade:										
9th........................	17.6	19.8	18.0	19.9	20.1	7.2	6.7	5.3	6.4	6.0
10th.......................	18.7	16.7	15.9	19.4	18.8	6.6	6.7	6.0	6.9	5.8
11th.......................	16.1	16.8	18.2	17.1	16.7	7.0	6.1	6.6	5.9	5.5
12th.......................	15.9	15.1	15.5	16.9	15.5	6.2	6.1	6.4	6.7	6.0

[1] Persons of Hispanic origin may be any race. [2] Data should be interpreted with caution.

Source: U.S. Department of Education, National Center for Education Statistics and U.S. Department of Justice, Bureau of Justice Statistics, *Indicators of School Crime and Safety: 2008*, April 2009, NCES 2009-022. See also <http://nces.ed.gov/pubsearch/pubsinfo.asp?pubid=2009022>.

Table 243. Parent Participation in School-Related Activities by Selected School, Student, and Family Characteristics: 2007

[In percent, except as noted (51,600 represents 51,600,000). For school year ending in 2007. Covers parents with children in kindergarten through grade 12. Homeschooled students are excluded]

Characteristic	Number of students in grades K through 12 (1,000)	Participation in school activities by parent or other household member				
		Attended a general school or PTO/PTA [1] meeting	Attended a regularly scheduled parent-teacher conference	Attended a school or class event	Volunteered or served on school committee	Participated in school fundraising
Total....................	51,600	89	78	74	46	65
School type: [2]						
Public, assigned	37,168	89	76	72	42	63
Public, chosen	7,951	88	81	74	45	62
Private, religious	4,560	96	86	86	73	85
Private, nonreligious	1,438	97	90	86	68	72
School size: [2]						
Under 301.......................	7,644	90	87	80	59	73
300–600	16,094	91	86	79	54	71
600–1,000	13,685	90	80	74	45	65
1,000 or more....................	13,847	87	62	66	32	55
Students sex:						
Male............................	26,875	89	79	71	45	65
Female..........................	24,725	90	77	78	48	66
Students race/ethnicity:						
White, non-Hispanic....................	29,832	91	78	80	54	72
Black, non-Hispanic....................	7,837	87	77	65	35	58
Hispanic [3]	9,767	87	80	65	32	51
Asian or Pacific Islander, non-Hispanic	1,566	90	80	72	46	62
Other, non-Hispanic...................	2,598	90	74	76	47	62
Students grade level: [4]						
K–2nd grade	11,516	93	90	78	63	72
3rd–5th grade.....................	11,519	94	92	83	57	71
6th–8th grade.....................	12,058	91	76	72	38	63
9th–12th grade	16,503	83	61	68	34	57
Parents highest education level:						
Less than high school	3,504	75	70	48	20	34
High school graduate or equivalent.........	11,070	84	74	65	33	55
Vocational/technical or some college........	14,844	89	77	72	42	67
Bachelors degree	11,353	94	81	83	56	72
Graduate or professional school..........	10,829	95	82	87	64	77
Parents language at home:						
Both/only parent(s) speak(s) English........	45,219	90	78	77	49	69
One of two parents speaks English.........	1,022	82	75	63	42	54
No parent speaks English..............	5,359	84	82	57	22	38

[1] Parent Teacher Organization (PTO) or Parent Teacher Association (PTA) meeting. [2] Variables for school characteristics (school type and school size) have a certain number of missing cases due to school nonreport; therefore, the number of students across the categories for each school variable does not sum to the total number of students. [3] Persons of Hispanic origin may be any race. [4] Students whose parents reported the students grade equivalent as ungraded were excluded from the analyses of grade level.

Source: U.S. Department of Education, National Center for Education Statistics, Parent and Family Involvement in Education Survey of the National Household Education Surveys Program (NHES), 2007.

Education   159

Table 244. School Enrollment Below Postsecondary—Summary by Sex, Race, and Hispanic Origin: 2007

[In thousands (58,011 represents 58,011,000), except percent and rate. As of October. Covers civilian noninstitutional population enrolled in nursery school through high school. Based on Current Population Survey, see text, Section 1 and Appendix III]

Characteristic	Total			Race and Hispanic origin				
				White [2]				
	Number [1]	Male	Female	Total	Non-Hispanic	Black [2]	Asian [2]	Hispanic [3]
All students	**58,011**	**29,743**	**28,268**	**44,185**	**33,467**	**8,974**	**2,367**	**11,535**
Nursery.	4,628	2,335	2,293	3,545	2,711	700	171	905
Full day	2,174	1,084	1,090	1,548	1,151	442	91	421
Part day.	2,454	1,251	1,203	1,998	1,560	259	80	484
Kindergarten	4,132	2,181	1,951	3,223	2,279	605	137	990
Elementary	32,169	16,456	15,713	24,431	18,306	4,926	1,421	6,582
High school	17,082	8,771	8,311	12,986	10,171	2,743	638	3,058
Students in public schools	51,082	26,299	24,783	38,471	28,357	8,232	2,110	10,866
Nursery	2,570	1,297	1,273	1,880	1,225	485	77	711
Full day	1,234	641	593	854	536	288	38	336
Part day	1,336	656	680	1,025	689	197	40	375
Kindergarten.	3,656	1,944	1,711	2,836	1,929	548	112	954
Elementary.	29,052	14,926	14,125	21,869	15,998	4,572	1,305	6,299
High school	15,804	8,131	7,673	11,886	9,204	2,627	616	2,902
Population 15 to 17 years old	12,321	6,308	6,013	9,443	7,528	1,927	439	2,060
Percent below modal grade [4] . .	30.0	33.7	26.2	28.3	26.8	39.2	24.2	34.0
Students, 10th to 12th grade	11,584	5,879	5,705	8,927	7,274	1,781	404	1,785
Annual dropout rate.	3.3	3.5	3.1	2.8	2.1	4.3	7.5	5.5
Population 18 to 24 years old	28,778	14,515	14,263	22,392	17,669	4,182	1,165	5,175
Percent dropouts	10.2	11.6	8.8	10.0	10.0	10.2	7.4	25.3
Percent high school graduates .	83.9	81.5	86.4	84.5	89.0	81.8	86.7	67.4
Percent enrolled in college	38.8	35.6	42.1	39.2	42.6	33.4	56.4	26.6

[1] Includes other races not shown separately. [2] For persons who selected this race group only. See footnote 2, Table 224. [3] Persons of Hispanic origin may be any race. [4] The modal grade is the grade most common for a given age.

Source: U.S. Census Bureau, Current Population Survey, unpublished data; <http://www.census.gov/population/www/socdemo/school.html>.

Table 245. Elementary and Secondary Schools—Teachers, Enrollment, and Pupil-Teacher Ratio: 1970 to 2007

[In thousands (2,292 represents 2,292,000), except ratios. As of fall. Data are for full-time equivalent teachers. Based on surveys of state education agencies and private schools; see source for details]

Year	Teachers			Enrollment			Pupil-teacher ratio		
	Total	Public	Private	Total	Public	Private	Total	Public	Private
1970	2,292	2,059	233	51,257	45,894	5,363	22.4	22.3	23.0
1975	2,453	2,198	255	49,819	44,819	5,000	20.3	20.4	19.6
1980	2,485	2,184	301	46,208	40,877	5,331	18.6	18.7	17.7
1983	2,476	2,139	337	44,967	39,252	5,715	18.2	18.4	17.0
1984	2,508	2,168	340	44,908	39,208	5,700	17.9	18.1	16.8
1985	2,549	2,206	343	44,979	39,422	5,557	17.6	17.9	16.2
1986	2,592	2,244	348	45,205	39,753	5,452	17.4	17.7	15.7
1987	2,631	2,279	352	45,487	40,008	5,479	17.3	17.6	15.6
1988	2,668	2,323	345	45,430	40,189	5,242	17.0	17.3	15.2
1989	2,713	2,357	356	45,741	40,543	5,198	17.0	17.2	15.7
1990	2,759	2,398	361	46,451	41,217	5,234	17.0	17.2	15.6
1991	2,797	2,432	365	47,728	42,047	5,681	17.1	17.3	15.6
1992	2,827	2,459	368	48,500	42,823	5,677	17.2	17.4	15.4
1993 [1]	2,874	2,504	370	49,133	43,465	5,668	17.1	17.4	15.3
1994 [1]	2,925	2,552	373	49,898	44,111	5,787	17.1	17.3	15.5
1995	2,974	2,598	376	50,759	44,840	5,918	17.1	17.3	15.7
1996 [1]	3,051	2,667	384	51,544	45,611	5,933	16.9	17.1	15.5
1997 [1]	3,138	2,746	391	52,071	46,127	5,944	16.6	16.8	15.2
1998 [1]	3,230	2,830	400	52,525	46,539	5,988	16.3	16.4	15.0
1999	3,319	2,911	408	52,876	46,857	6,018	15.9	16.1	14.7
2000 [1]	3,366	2,941	424	53,373	47,204	6,169	15.9	16.0	14.5
2001 [1]	3,440	3,000	441	53,992	47,672	6,320	15.7	15.9	14.3
2002 [1]	3,476	3,034	442	54,403	48,183	6,220	15.7	15.9	14.1
2003 [1]	3,490	3,049	441	54,639	48,540	6,099	15.7	15.9	13.8
2004 [1]	3,536	3,091	445	54,882	48,795	6,087	15.5	15.8	13.7
2005 [1]	3,593	3,143	450	55,187	49,113	6,073	15.4	15.6	13.5
2006 [1]	3,637	3,180	457	55,396	49,299	6,097	15.2	15.5	13.4
2007 [2]	3,665	3,205	460	55,579	49,470	6,110	15.2	15.4	13.3

[1] Private school numbers are estimated based on data from the Private School Universe Survey. [2] Projection.

Source: U.S. National Center for Education Statistics, *Digest of Education Statistics*, annual and *Projections of Educational Statistics*.

Table 246. Public Elementary and Secondary School Teachers—Selected Characteristics: 2004 to 2005

[For school year (449 represents 449,000). Based on the 2004–2005 Teacher Follow-up Survey, a component of the School and Staffing Survey, and subject to sampling error; for details, see also <http://nces.ed.gov/surveys/sass/>. Excludes prekindergarten teachers]

Characteristic	Unit	Age				Sex		Race/ethnicity		
		Under 30 years old	30–39 years old	40–49 years old	Over 50 years old	Male	Fe-male	White [1]	Black [1]	His-panic [2]
Total teachers [3]	1,000 ...	449	769	750	976	723	2,220	2,502	216	124
Highest degree held:										
Bachelor's	Percent..	80.9	57.1	44.9	37.6	2.4	0.7	49.7	53.7	67.9
Master's	Percent..	17.7	38.8	48.8	49.4	51.8	50.9	43.2	38.7	22.1
Education specialist	Percent..	0.6	3.4	5.5	9.6	38.8	42.6	5.5	5.8	7.6
Doctorate	Percent..	(X)	0.3	0.5	1.3	6.5	5.3	0.6	1.2	0.2
Full-time teaching experience:										
Less than 3 years	Percent..	26.2	4.3	2.5	0.8	5.5	6.2	5.7	6.5	9.8
3 to 9 years	Percent..	73.3	56.7	19.3	8.8	35.9	33.1	31.9	47.3	40.0
10 to 20 years	Percent..	0.5	39.0	47.5	25.4	26.7	32.1	31.6	20.3	37.8
20 years or more	Percent..	(X)	(X)	30.7	65.0	31.9	28.6	30.9	26.0	12.4
Full-time teachers	1,000 ...	411	706	687	902	687	2,018	2,284	207	120
Earned income	Dollars..	37,510	43,288	48,392	54,577	50,823	46,328	47,710	45,981	45,941
Salary	Dollars..	37,093	42,607	47,662	53,590	49,207	45,865	46,864	45,672	45,646

X Not applicable.   [1] Non-Hispanic.   [2] People of Hispanic origin may be any race.   [3] Includes teachers with no degrees and associate's degrees not shown separately.

Source: U.S. National Center for Education Statistics, "Teacher Followup Survey, 2004–05," unpublished data.

Table 247. Public Elementary and Secondary Schools—Number and Average Salary of Classroom Teachers, 1990 to 2007, and by State, 2007

[Estimates for school year ending in June of year shown (2,362 represents 2,362,000). Schools classified by type of organization rather than by grade-group; elementary includes kindergarten]

Year and state	Teachers [1] (1,000)			Avg. salary ($1,000)			Year and state	Teachers [1] (1,000)			Avg. salary ($1,000)		
	Total	Ele-men-tary	Sec-ond-ary	All teach-ers	Ele-men-tary	Sec-ond-ary		Total	Ele-men-tary	Sec-ond-ary	All teach-ers	Ele-men-tary	Sec-ond-ary
1990	2,362	1,390	972	31.4	30.8	32.0	MD	59.3	34.4	24.9	56.9	56.7	57.2
1995	2,565	1,517	1,048	36.7	36.1	37.5	MA	73.2	29.2	44.0	58.3	58.3	58.3
1999	2,818	1,669	1,149	40.5	40.2	41.2	MI	96.7	53.6	43.1	55.5	55.5	55.5
2000	2,891	1,696	1,195	41.8	41.3	42.5	MN	52.8	26.8	26.0	49.7	49.7	49.7
2001	2,947	1,735	1,213	43.4	42.9	44.1	MS	33.5	19.8	13.7	40.2	39.6	40.9
2002	2,992	1,751	1,240	44.7	44.2	45.3	MO	67.6	34.5	33.1	41.8	41.8	41.7
2003	3,020	1,769	1,251	45.7	45.4	46.1	MT	10.5	7.0	3.6	41.2	41.2	41.2
2004	3,042	1,782	1,260	46.5	46.2	47.0	NE	21.3	13.6	7.7	42.0	42.0	42.0
2005	3,072	1,799	1,273	47.5	47.1	47.7	NV	22.1	12.9	9.2	45.2	45.2	45.2
2006	3,116	1,821	1,295	48.8	48.4	49.0	NH	15.8	10.9	4.9	46.5	46.5	46.5
2007, U.S.	3,158	1,886	1,272	50.8	50.7	50.8	NJ	112.3	74.5	37.8	59.6	58.7	61.2
AL	50.0	28.5	21.5	43.4	43.1	43.8	NM	21.7	14.8	6.9	42.8	42.6	43.1
AK	8.0	5.3	2.7	54.7	54.7	54.7	NY	207.7	102.9	104.8	59.6	59.6	59.6
AZ	52.7	37.5	15.3	44.7	43.5	47.7	NC	95.5	71.8	23.7	46.1	46.1	46.1
AR	34.1	16.6	17.5	44.2	44.2	44.2	ND	7.6	5.1	2.4	38.8	39.1	38.1
CA	304.2	222.9	81.3	63.6	63.6	63.6	OH	119.3	81.2	38.0	51.9	51.9	51.9
CO	47.0	24.0	23.0	45.8	45.5	46.1	OK	42.2	21.2	21.0	42.4	41.6	43.2
CT	42.5	29.0	13.5	60.8	60.8	60.8	OR	29.3	18.9	10.4	50.9	50.7	51.3
DE	8.0	4.0	4.1	54.7	54.9	54.5	PA	123.2	60.1	63.0	55.0	55.0	55.0
DC	5.5	3.6	1.9	59.0	59.0	59.0	RI	14.9	9.3	5.6	56.0	56.0	56.0
FL	167.8	85.2	82.6	45.3	45.3	45.3	SC	48.2	33.6	14.7	43.9	42.2	43.0
GA	112.9	68.4	44.5	49.9	49.4	50.7	SD	9.0	6.3	2.7	35.4	35.5	35.2
HI	11.5	6.1	5.3	51.9	51.9	51.9	TN	61.9	43.6	18.3	43.8	43.2	44.7
ID	14.8	7.7	7.1	42.8	42.8	42.8	TX	311.7	159.9	151.8	44.9	44.5	45.4
IL	131.9	89.8	42.2	58.2	55.8	64.1	UT	23.0	12.4	10.6	41.2	41.2	41.2
IN	61.2	32.8	28.4	47.8	49.1	47.7	VT	9.0	4.6	4.4	45.3	45.3	45.3
IA	35.4	23.3	12.1	43.1	43.3	42.8	VA	102.1	59.8	42.3	45.5	45.3	45.9
KS	34.4	16.9	17.4	43.4	43.4	43.4	WA	54.0	29.5	24.4	47.9	47.9	47.8
KY	42.0	29.8	12.2	43.6	43.4	44.2	WV	19.9	14.2	5.7	40.5	40.4	41.0
LA	46.4	32.7	13.7	42.8	42.8	42.8	WI	59.3	40.6	18.7	47.9	48.0	47.7
ME	16.6	11.2	5.5	42.1	42.1	42.1	WY	6.5	3.3	3.2	50.7	50.4	51.0

[1] Full-time equivalent.

Source: National Education Association, Washington, DC, Estimates of School Statistics Database (copyright).

Education 161

Table 248. Teacher Stayers, Movers, and Leavers by Sector: 1988 to 1989 and 2004 to 2005

[2,386.5 represents 2,386,500. Data compare the teaching status of teacher between one school year and the prior year. Stayers are teachers who were teaching in the same school in both years. Movers are teachers who were still teaching in the current school year but in a different school. Leavers are teachers who left the teaching profession. Based on the School and Staffing Survey; see source for details]

Characteristic	Public				Private			
	Total [1]	Stayers	Movers	Leavers	Total [1]	Stayers	Movers	Leavers
NUMBER (1,000)								
1988–89	2,386.5	2,065.8	188.4	132.3	311.9	242.5	29.7	39.7
2004–05	3,214.9	2,684.2	261.1	269.6	465.3	374.6	27.6	63.1
PERCENT DISTRIBUTION								
Total, 2004-05	100.0	83.5	8.1	8.4	100.0	80.5	5.9	13.6
Age:								
Less than 30 years old	100.0	76.3	14.7	9.0	100.0	68.1	11.8	20.1
30 to 39 years old	100.0	84.2	9.0	6.8	100.0	80.6	5.2	14.2
40 to 49 years old	100.0	87.6	7.1	5.3	100.0	84.3	5.0	10.7
50 years old or more	100.0	83.7	4.5	11.8	100.0	84.7	3.8	[2]11.5
Sex:								
Male	100.0	83.9	8.3	7.7	100.0	80.5	5.2	14.2
Female	100.0	83.4	8.1	8.6	100.0	80.5	6.1	13.4
Race/ethnicity:								
White, non-Hispanic	100.0	83.9	7.9	8.2	100.0	81.3	5.7	13.0
Black, non-Hispanic	100.0	79.3	9.7	11.0	100.0	67.8	9.2	[2]23.0
Hispanic, single or more than one race	100.0	80.6	10.1	9.3	100.0	70.3	7.6	22.1
Asian, Native Hawaiian, or Other Pacific Islander, non-Hispanic	100.0	81.8	7.9	[2]10.3	100.0	89.7	2.7	7.6
American Indian/Alaska Native, non-Hispanic	100.0	93.1	5.0	1.9	100.0	65.5	[2]18.5	[2]16.0
More than one race, non-Hispanic . . .	100.0	88.1	6.6	[2]5.3	100.0	65.8	[2]13.4	[2]20.8
Full-time teaching experience:								
No full-time teaching experience	100.0	63.3	17.1	19.6	100.0	73.6	4.0	22.3
1 to 3 years' experience	100.0	77.1	14.8	8.1	100.0	71.0	10.1	18.9
4 to 9 years' experience	100.0	82.7	9.4	7.9	100.0	77.2	6.7	16.1
10 to 19 years' experience	100.0	88.2	6.3	5.5	100.0	88.3	3.8	7.8
20 years or more experience	100.0	84.9	3.9	11.2	100.0	89.7	3.3	7.0
Main assignment field:								
Early childhood/general elementary . . .	100.0	84.5	7.4	8.1	100.0	81.1	6.8	12.2
Special education	100.0	78.9	11.1	10.0	100.0	72.2	[2]7.4	20.4
Arts/music	100.0	84.7	9.3	6.0	100.0	77.6	4.4	18.0
English/language arts	100.0	83.2	9.0	7.8	100.0	81.1	5.6	13.3
Mathematics	100.0	84.6	8.6	6.8	100.0	83.8	5.4	10.7
Natural sciences	100.0	88.5	5.6	5.9	100.0	84.0	5.9	10.1
Social sciences	100.0	85.6	6.0	8.4	100.0	81.8	4.8	13.4
Other	100.0	81.3	8.0	10.7	100.0	79.2	5.3	15.5

[1] Total teachers prior school year.   [2] Interpret data with caution. The standard error for this estimate is equal to 50 percent.

Source: U.S. National Center for Education Statistics, *Teacher Attrition and Mobility: Results for the 2004–05 Teacher Follow-up Survey* NCES 2007-307, January 2007.

Table 249. Public and Private School Teachers Who Moved to a Different School or Left Teaching by Reason: 2004 to 2005

[In percent. Movers are teachers who were still teaching in the current school year but had moved to a different school after the 2003–04 school year. Leavers are teachers who left the teaching profession after the 2003–04 school year. Based on the School and Staffing Survey; see source for details]

Reason for moving	Movers		Reason for leaving	Leavers	
	Public	Private		Public	Private
New school is closer to home	26.2	22.8	Changed residence	11.2	17.4
Better safety and benefits	16.5	46.4	Pregnancy or child rearing	18.7	24.6
Higher job security	19.1	33.4	Health	11.8	13.2
Opportunity for a better teaching assignment . .	38.1	33.1	Retirement	31.4	10.2
Dissatisfaction with workplace conditions at previous school	32.7	21.4	School staffing action [1]	14.6	17.7
Dissatisfaction with support from administrators at previous school	37.2	27.0	Better salary or benefits	14.2	21.8
Dissatisfaction with changes in job description or responsibilities	18.3	17.5	To pursue a position other than that of a K–12 teacher	25.3	29.5
Laid off or involuntarily transferred	18.7	19.2	To take courses to improve career opportunities within the field of education .	8.9	9.8
Did not have enough autonomy over classroom at previous school	10.4	7.6	To take courses to improve career opportunities outside the field of education.	5.3	7.3
Dissatisfaction with opportunities for professional development at previous school .	12.8	19.7	Dissatisfied with teaching as a career	14.6	10.8
Other dissatisfaction with previous school	31.2	29.7	Dissatisfied with previous school or teaching assignment	16.0	18.1
			Other family or personal reasons	20.4	30.6

[1] For example reduction in force, lay-off, school closing, school reorganization, reassignment.

Source: U.S. National Center for Education Statistics, *Teacher Attrition and Mobility: Results for the 2004–05 Teacher Follow-up Survey*, NCES 2007-307, January 2007.

162   Education

Table 250. **Average Salary and Wages Paid in Public School Systems: 1985 to 2008**

[In dollars. For school year ending in year shown. Data reported by a stratified sample of school systems enrolling 300 or more pupils. Data represent unweighted means of average salaries paid school personnel reported by each school system]

Position	1985	1990	1995	2000	2004	2005	2006	2007	2008
ANNUAL SALARY									
Central-office administrators:									
Superintendent (contract salary). . . .	56,954	75,425	90,198	112,158	125,609	128,770	134,436	141,191	148,387
Deputy/assoc. superintendent	52,877	69,623	81,266	97,251	113,790	116,186	122,078	128,307	134,245
Assistant superintendent.	48,003	62,698	75,236	88,913	100,808	103,212	106,492	111,963	116,833
Administrators for—									
Finance and business.	40,344	52,354	61,323	73,499	82,269	83,678	86,390	91,718	96,490
Instructional services	43,452	56,359	66,767	79,023	84,866	88,950	91,094	95,025	99,748
Public relations/information	35,287	44,926	53,263	60,655	70,291	70,502	72,378	77,121	80,534
Staff personnel services	44,182	56,344	65,819	76,608	86,333	86,966	90,097	94,761	98,190
Technology	(X)	(X)	(X)	(X)	76,139	76,308	78,249	81,809	86,085
Subject area supervisors.	34,422	45,929	54,534	63,103	67,098	68,714	71,984	75,982	78,309
School building administrators:									
Principals:									
Elementary	36,452	48,431	58,589	69,407	75,144	76,182	79,496	82,414	85,907
Junior high/middle	39,650	52,163	62,311	73,877	80,060	81,514	84,685	87,866	91,334
Senior high	42,094	55,722	66,596	79,839	86,160	86,938	90,260	92,965	97,486
Assistant principals:									
Elementary	30,496	40,916	48,491	56,419	62,213	63,140	65,770	67,735	71,192
Junior high/middle	33,793	44,570	52,942	60,842	66,360	67,600	70,268	73,020	76,053
Senior high	35,491	46,486	55,556	64,811	70,495	71,401	73,622	75,121	79,391
Classroom teachers	23,587	31,278	37,264	42,213	45,646	45,884	48,160	49,294	51,329
Auxiliary professional personnel:									
Counselors.	27,593	35,979	42,486	48,195	52,303	52,500	53,744	55,930	57,618
Librarians.	24,981	33,469	40,418	46,732	50,403	50,720	53,331	54,881	56,933
School nurses.	19,944	26,090	31,066	35,540	40,201	40,520	41,746	43,277	46,025
Secretarial/clerical personnel:									
Central office:									
Secretaries	15,343	20,238	23,935	28,405	31,830	32,716	34,132	35,629	36,657
Accounting/payroll clerks	15,421	20,088	24,042	28,498	32,632	33,217	34,812	35,991	37,732
Typists/data entry clerks	12,481	16,125	18,674	22,853	25,318	26,214	26,899	28,940	30,072
School building level:									
Secretaries	12,504	16,184	19,170	22,630	24,964	25,381	26,396	27,398	28,810
Library clerks.	9,911	12,152	14,381	16,509	18,427	18,443	19,125	19,806	21,004
HOURLY WAGE RATE									
Other support personnel:									
Teacher aides:									
Instructional	5.89	7.43	8.77	10.00	11.22	11.35	11.77	12.32	12.86
Noninstructional.	5.60	7.08	8.29	9.77	11.08	11.23	11.75	12.19	12.70
Custodians	6.90	8.54	10.05	11.35	12.47	12.61	13.20	13.78	14.19
Cafeteria workers	5.42	6.77	7.89	9.02	10.18	10.33	10.70	11.16	11.60
Bus drivers.	7.27	9.21	10.69	12.48	13.79	14.18	14.81	15.48	16.56

X Not applicable.

Source: Educational Research Service, Arlington, VA, *National Survey of Salaries and Wages in Public Schools,* annual. (All rights reserved. Copyright.)

Table 251. **Public School Employment: 1990 and 2006**

[In thousands (3,181 represents 3,181,000). Covers all public elementary-secondary school districts with 100 or more full-time employees]

Occupation	1990					2006 [1]				
	Total	Male	Female	White [2]	Black [2]	Total	Male	Female	White [2]	Black [2]
All occupations	3,181	914	2,267	2,502	463	4,615	1,179	3,436	3,476	606
Officials, administrators	43	28	15	37	4	64	30	34	51	7
Principals and assistant										
principals.	90	56	34	70	13	125	57	68	91	22
Classroom teachers [3]	1,746	468	1,278	1,469	192	2,534	611	1,923	2,070	239
Elementary schools	875	128	747	722	103	1,272	170	1,102	1,031	111
Secondary schools	662	304	358	570	66	957	379	578	791	91
Other professional staff	227	58	170	187	30	383	76	308	305	47
Teachers' aides [4]	324	54	270	208	69	483	60	423	313	92
Clerical, secretarial staff.	226	5	221	181	24	300	10	290	214	35
Service workers [5]	524	245	279	348	129	726	335	391	431	164

[1] Excludes HI state.   [2] Excludes individuals of Hispanic origin.   [3] Includes other classroom teachers not shown separately.   [4] Includes technicians.   [5] Includes craftworkers and laborers.

Source: U.S. Equal Employment Opportunity Commission, *Elementary-Secondary Staff Information (EEO-5),* biennial.

Education 163

Table 252. Public Elementary and Secondary School Finances by Enrollment-Size Group: 2005 to 2006

[In millions of dollars (521,116 represents $521,116,000,000). Data are based on annual survey. For details, see source. See also Appendix III]

Item	All school systems	School systems with enrollment of—						
		50,000 or more	25,000 to 49,999	15,000 to 24,999	7,500 to 14,999	5,000 to 7,499	3,000 to 4,999	Under 3,000
TOTAL AMOUNT								
General revenue	521,116	108,839	64,508	48,670	72,956	47,420	60,765	117,958
From federal sources	47,101	11,601	6,174	4,181	5,973	3,299	4,403	11,470
Through state	43,529	10,964	5,837	3,943	5,455	3,046	4,124	10,159
Child nutrition programs	8,913	2,242	1,265	934	1,211	693	904	1,665
Direct	3,572	637	336	238	518	253	278	1,312
From state sources [1]	242,785	48,544	31,212	25,025	34,957	20,926	26,590	55,532
General formula assistance	163,966	29,831	21,158	17,510	24,352	14,299	18,046	38,771
Compensatory programs	5,873	1,137	1,490	675	818	570	459	725
Special education	15,248	3,794	1,640	1,193	1,886	1,235	1,691	3,807
From local sources	231,230	48,694	27,122	19,464	32,027	23,196	29,773	50,955
Taxes	153,671	25,109	17,845	13,456	22,804	16,800	21,404	36,254
Contributions from parent government	39,189	16,726	3,923	2,391	4,181	3,193	4,079	4,696
From other local governments	5,297	567	772	331	479	433	714	2,000
Current charges	13,737	2,171	1,601	1,292	2,037	1,272	1,648	3,717
School lunch	6,769	977	798	700	1,066	711	904	1,613
Other	19,337	4,121	2,982	1,994	2,525	1,498	1,927	4,289
General expenditure	526,649	111,992	65,993	50,060	73,612	47,654	59,912	117,426
Current spending	451,488	93,831	54,925	42,076	63,200	41,350	52,377	103,729
By function: Instruction	271,843	58,082	33,008	25,368	38,253	25,156	31,655	60,321
Support services	156,003	30,680	18,981	14,346	21,672	14,218	18,143	37,964
Other current spending	23,642	5,069	2,936	2,362	3,274	1,976	2,580	5,444
By object:								
Total salaries and wages	272,654	56,693	34,055	26,216	38,832	25,197	31,637	60,025
Total employee benefits	88,151	17,981	10,059	8,355	12,760	8,384	10,597	20,015
Other	90,683	19,158	10,811	7,505	11,608	7,769	10,144	23,688
Capital outlay	58,809	14,736	8,919	6,548	7,967	4,690	5,648	10,301
Interest on debt	13,752	3,124	1,995	1,352	1,959	1,221	1,573	2,529
Payments to other governments	2,600	301	154	85	486	393	313	867
Debt outstanding	322,725	73,690	42,808	32,278	45,929	29,413	38,048	60,559
Long-term	312,753	69,555	42,282	31,759	44,723	28,769	37,080	58,586
Short-term	9,972	4,135	526	519	1,206	644	968	1,974
Long-term debt issued	52,171	12,900	7,024	6,045	7,307	4,792	5,500	8,604
Long-term debt retired	27,194	4,511	3,245	2,506	4,267	2,879	3,600	6,187
PER PUPIL AMOUNTS								
Fall enrollment (1,000)	48,381	9,957	6,456	5,043	7,059	4,369	5,542	9,956
General revenue	10,771	10,931	9,992	9,650	10,335	10,855	10,965	11,848
From federal sources	974	1,165	956	829	846	755	794	1,152
From state sources [1]	5,018	4,876	4,835	4,962	4,952	4,790	4,798	5,578
General formula assistance	3,389	2,996	3,277	3,472	3,450	3,273	3,257	3,894
Special education	315	381	254	237	267	283	305	382
From local sources [1]	4,779	4,891	4,201	3,859	4,537	5,310	5,373	5,118
Taxes	3,176	2,522	2,764	2,668	3,231	3,845	3,863	3,642
Contributions from parent government	810	1,680	608	474	592	731	736	472
Current charges	284	218	248	256	289	291	297	373
School lunch	140	98	124	139	151	163	163	162
General expenditure [1]	10,692	11,003	10,044	9,769	10,263	10,724	10,631	11,592
Current spending	9,138	9,179	8,329	8,186	8,788	9,281	9,271	10,217
By function: Instruction	5,543	5,726	5,041	4,987	5,360	5,667	5,631	5,994
Support services	3,225	3,081	2,940	2,845	3,070	3,254	3,274	3,813
By object:								
Total salaries and wages	5,636	5,694	5,275	5,198	5,501	5,768	5,709	6,029
Total employee benefits	1,822	1,806	1,558	1,657	1,808	1,919	1,912	2,010
Capital outlay	1,216	1,480	1,382	1,298	1,129	1,074	1,019	1,035
Interest on debt	284	314	309	268	278	279	284	254
Debt outstanding	6,671	7,401	6,631	6,400	6,506	6,733	6,866	6,083
Long-term	6,464	6,986	6,550	6,297	6,336	6,585	6,691	5,885

[1] Includes other sources not shown separately.

Source: U.S. Census Bureau, Public Education Finances, 2006, April 2008; <http://www.census.gov/govs/school>.

Table 253. **Public Elementary and Secondary Estimated Finances, 1980 to 2007, and by State, 2007**

[In millions of dollars (101,724 represents $101,724,000,000), except as noted. For school years ending in June of year shown]

Year and state	Receipts							Expenditures			
		Revenue receipts							Current expenditures		
			Source							Ele-mentary and second-ary day schools	Average per pupil in ADA [4]	
	Total	Total	Federal	State	Local	Non-revenue receipts [1]	Total [2]	Per capita [3] (dol.)		Amount (dol.)	Rank
1980	101,724	97,635	9,020	47,929	40,686	4,089	96,105	428	85,661	2,230	(X)
1985	146,976	141,013	9,533	69,107	62,373	5,963	139,382	591	127,230	3,483	(X)
1990	218,126	208,656	13,184	100,787	94,685	9,469	209,698	850	186,583	4,966	(X)
1995	288,501	273,255	18,764	129,958	124,533	15,246	276,584	1,051	242,995	5,957	(X)
2000	390,861	369,754	26,346	183,986	159,421	21,106	374,782	1,343	320,954	7,410	(X)
2001	426,200	397,255	28,300	198,802	170,152	28,946	404,271	1,437	344,033	7,870	(X)
2002	449,039	416,891	32,213	206,112	178,565	32,148	427,577	1,500	363,551	8,210	(X)
2003	472,531	436,056	36,176	214,210	185,670	36,475	451,674	1,570	386,028	8,662	(X)
2004	488,959	455,013	40,629	215,480	198,904	33,946	469,623	1,618	400,931	8,930	(X)
2005	519,291	477,371	42,908	225,142	209,321	41,921	496,199	1,694	422,346	9,367	(X)
2006	550,995	506,971	45,819	238,041	223,111	44,024	521,800	1,765	443,641	9,758	(X)
2007, total. . . .	**581,648**	**532,123**	**46,835**	**251,053**	**234,235**	**49,524**	**549,516**	**1,842**	**466,612**	**10,209**	**(X)**
Alabama	8,466	7,988	708	4,071	3,210	478	7,095	1,546	6,214	8,661	40
Alaska	1,513	1,346	169	855	322	167	1,486	2,197	1,381	11,900	12
Arizona.	8,437	8,431	672	4,369	3,390	6	7,173	1,161	5,888	6,067	49
Arkansas.	4,564	4,308	484	2,422	1,402	255	4,515	1,610	4,050	10,398	20
California.	80,298	70,452	7,915	41,494	21,043	9,846	72,011	1,994	57,335	9,441	31
Colorado.	8,463	7,428	560	3,165	3,702	1,036	8,516	1,792	7,063	9,592	30
Connecticut	8,343	8,331	530	3,217	4,584	13	8,339	2,391	7,462	13,370	6
Delaware.	1,894	1,676	156	1,072	448	218	1,898	2,232	1,536	13,283	7
District of Columbia	882	882	112	–	770	–	1,228	2,098	980	18,260	(X)
Florida	31,734	28,390	2,534	11,134	14,723	3,344	30,136	1,672	22,723	8,991	36
Georgia	20,226	17,876	1,510	7,942	8,424	2,350	17,273	1,854	15,015	9,953	26
Hawaii	3,018	2,986	257	2,681	48	32	2,299	1,803	1,999	12,084	10
Idaho	2,330	2,024	205	1,360	459	306	2,250	1,540	1,912	7,618	46
Illinois	24,426	21,566	1,858	5,926	13,782	2,860	24,071	1,887	22,038	11,489	15
Indiana	10,620	10,063	805	5,354	3,903	557	11,516	1,830	9,497	9,875	27
Iowa	5,182	4,812	316	2,229	2,266	371	4,578	1,543	3,931	8,680	39
Kansas	5,399	5,017	346	2,891	1,779	382	5,272	1,913	4,221	10,174	23
Kentucky	5,315	5,290	689	2,655	1,947	25	6,149	1,464	5,588	9,413	32
Louisiana	8,087	7,143	1,234	3,043	2,866	944	7,004	1,650	6,039	9,655	29
Maine	2,584	2,425	243	967	1,215	159	2,584	1,968	2,362	12,994	8
Maryland.	11,409	11,337	771	4,517	6,050	72	10,974	1,959	9,621	11,881	13
Massachusetts . . .	14,227	14,226	763	6,688	6,775	1	13,864	2,152	12,492	13,710	5
Michigan	19,934	19,574	1,576	11,484	6,514	359	19,245	1,908	17,705	11,376	16
Minnesota	10,684	9,429	705	6,911	1,813	1,255	10,623	2,065	8,405	10,809	19
Mississippi.	4,034	3,933	602	2,120	1,211	101	3,803	1,313	3,393	7,189	47
Missouri	10,416	9,242	868	3,004	5,370	1,174	8,540	1,464	7,340	8,857	38
Montana	1,400	1,372	169	655	549	28	1,306	1,381	1,254	10,119	25
Nebraska	2,607	2,585	209	965	1,411	21	2,703	1,536	2,402	9,087	33
Nevada	4,647	3,104	230	1,005	1,869	1,543	3,912	1,575	2,969	7,060	48
New Hampshire . .	2,554	2,401	154	994	1,253	153	2,438	1,863	2,222	11,879	14
New Jersey	21,173	21,167	697	7,747	12,722	6	21,096	2,442	20,377	14,824	3
New Mexico.	3,519	3,329	474	2,374	481	190	3,442	1,776	2,979	10,138	24
New York	43,312	43,033	3,123	19,646	20,264	279	44,833	2,315	39,914	15,263	2
North Carolina . . .	12,506	11,423	1,183	7,390	2,850	1,083	12,877	1,456	11,368	8,634	41
North Dakota	975	965	134	323	507	10	962	1,511	783	8,991	37
Ohio.	20,748	16,837	1,302	7,066	8,469	3,911	18,865	1,646	16,178	9,809	28
Oklahoma	5,600	5,218	649	2,680	1,889	382	5,212	1,461	4,733	7,939	44
Oregon	7,000	5,734	547	2,906	2,281	1,267	5,588	1,518	5,105	10,275	21
Pennsylvania	24,169	23,984	1,762	8,675	13,547	185	24,068	1,943	20,296	11,971	11
Rhode Island	1,636	1,636	52	592	991	–	1,952	1,843	1,867	12,095	9
South Carolina . . .	8,967	7,077	699	3,083	3,295	1,890	7,586	1,754	5,884	9,008	35
South Dakota. . . .	1,217	1,139	177	374	587	78	1,094	1,389	977	8,126	43
Tennessee.	7,783	7,444	824	3,409	3,211	340	7,403	1,220	6,904	7,772	45
Texas	51,399	43,459	4,505	16,487	22,466	7,940	45,363	1,941	36,277	8,445	42
Utah.	3,965	3,470	381	1,857	1,233	495	3,377	1,306	2,697	6,060	50
Vermont	1,420	1,397	107	1,212	78	23	1,381	2,227	1,239	15,940	1
Virginia	15,275	14,313	928	5,921	7,464	963	15,110	1,981	12,300	10,874	18
Washington	11,365	10,273	870	6,384	3,019	1,092	11,397	1,792	8,738	9,085	34
West Virginia	3,314	3,042	382	1,816	845	272	3,288	1,820	2,833	10,236	22
Wisconsin	11,122	10,069	578	5,198	4,294	1,053	10,431	1,873	8,999	11,064	17
Wyoming	1,490	1,478	111	722	644	12	1,390	2,712	1,131	14,277	4

– Represents or rounds to zero. X Not applicable. [1] Amount received by local education agencies from the sales of bonds and real property and equipment, loans, and proceeds from insurance adjustments. [2] Includes interest on school debt and other current expenditures not shown separately. [3] Based on U.S. Census Bureau estimated resident population, as of July 1, the previous year, except 1990 and 2000 population enumerated as of April 1. [4] Average daily attendance.

Source: National Education Association, Washington, DC, Estimates of School Statistics Database (copyright).

Education 165

Table 254. **Computers for Student Instruction in Elementary and Secondary Schools: 2005 to 2006**

[54,848 represents 54,848,000. Market Data Retrieval collects student use computer information in elementary and secondary schools nationwide through a comprehensive annual technology survey that utilizes mail, telephone, and Internet data methods]

Level	Total schools	Total enroll- ment (1,000)	Number of com- puters [1] (1,000)	Stu- dents per com- puter	Schools with a wireless network (percent)	Schools with distance learning programs for stu- dents (per- cent) [2]	Schools with lap- top com- puters (per- cent) [3]	Schools with high speed Internet access (per- cent) [4]	Schools with video- stream- ing (percent)
U.S. total..........	114,749	54,848	14,165	3.9	54.2	19.1	59.7	84.3	43.4
Public schools, total	91,977	49,567	12,914	3.8	54.4	20.3	60.0	85.7	45.0
Elementary	53,245	23,805	5,612	4.2	49.1	11.2	55.4	85.0	41.3
Middle/junior high	14,310	9,376	2,503	3.7	61.6	15.6	66.2	85.8	53.2
Senior high	17,282	14,028	4,067	3.4	64.0	43.8	67.9	87.5	50.4
K to 12/other	7,140	2,358	733	3.2	54.7	43.2	61.7	85.9	41.0
Catholic schools, total.....	7,673	2,481	554	4.5	51.0	7.1	60.3	74.0	29.7
Elementary	6,326	1,797	358	5.0	46.5	3.8	57.9	71.6	27.3
Secondary..........	1,179	621	179	3.5	67.7	20.8	70.0	83.8	38.8
K to 12/other	168	63	17	3.8	73.1	7.7	65.4	73.1	38.5
Other private schools, total..	15,099	2,800	697	4.0	52.1	6.5	50.1	66.4	24.1
Elementary	7,426	1,171	283	4.1	52.9	2.0	51.4	67.6	26.5
Secondary..........	1,274	265	77	3.4	67.5	18.1	54.2	68.7	24.1
K to 12/other	6,399	1,363	338	4.0	47.1	9.5	47.4	64.2	20.8

[1] Includes estimates for schools not reporting number of computers. [2] Distance learning programs as determined by respondents. [3] For student instruction. [4] Statistics based on responses to those indicating type of Internet connection. High speed includes Internet connection types: T1, T3, and cable modem.

Source: Market Data Retrieval, Shelton, CT, unpublished data (copyright).

Table 255. **Private Schools: 2007 to 2008**

[4,997 represents 4,997,000. Based on the Private School Survey, conducted every 2 years; see source for details. For composition of regions, see map, inside front cover]

Characteristic	Schools				Students (1,000)				Teachers (1,000) [1]			
	Num- ber	Ele- mentary	Sec- ond- ary	Com- bined	Total	Ele- mentary	Sec- ond- ary	Com- bined	Total	Ele- mentary	Sec- ond- ary	Com- bined
Total........	28,218	16,348	2,932	8,938	4,997	2,438	827	1,732	442	193	69	180
School type:												
Catholic	7,401	5,966	1,093	342	2,154	1,452	595	107	146	94	42	9
Parochial	3,363	3,126	161	76	873	786	63	24	56	50	5	2
Diocesan......	3,064	2,470	501	93	905	598	281	26	61	39	19	2
Private	973	370	431	172	377	68	252	57	30	6	18	5
Other religious	13,955	7,166	836	5,952	1,909	695	128	1,087	180	64	13	103
Conservative Christian	4,907	1,692	176	3,040	770	196	26	548	68	17	2	49
Affiliated	2,539	1,602	238	699	449	202	43	204	45	20	5	20
Unaffiliated. . . .	6,508	3,873	422	2,213	690	298	58	334	67	27	6	34
Nonsectarian.....	6,863	3,216	1,003	2,645	934	291	104	539	116	35	14	67
Regular.......	2,879	1,447	377	1,055	632	168	68	396	73	19	9	46
Special emphasis.....	2,457	1,545	371	541	195	109	23	63	24	14	3	7
Special education.....	1,527	224	254	1,049	106	13	13	80	19	2	2	14
Program emphasis:												
Regular elem/sec . .	22,905	14,040	2,151	6,714	4,589	2,282	775	1,532	388	173	63	152
Montessori	1,345	1,179	(B)	160	87	72	(B)	14	11	9	(B)	1
Special program emphasis	863	476	99	288	119	51	14	54	14	6	2	6
Special education. .	1,738	271	272	1,196	117	15	14	88	21	3	2	16
Vocational/tech	(B)	(B)	(B)	(B)	(B)	(B)	(B)	(B)	(B)	(B)	(B)	(B)
Alternative.	1,210	256	401	554	76	11	23	42	8	1	2	5
Early childhood . . .	152	126	(X)	(B)	7	6	(X)	(B)	1	(Z)	(B)	(B)
Size:												
Less than 50	8,944	5,048	842	3,053	228	131	19	78	35	17	4	14
50 to 149	8,421	5,053	655	2,714	777	477	62	238	88	49	8	31
150 to 299	5,964	4,087	458	1,420	1,269	863	100	306	105	64	10	31
300 to 499	2,800	1,629	383	788	1,078	626	149	303	85	42	13	29
500 to 749	1,237	456	289	491	746	269	177	300	58	16	13	28
750 or more	853	75	304	473	900	72	320	508	71	5	21	46
Region:												
Northeast	6,531	3,776	965	1,790	1,202	594	277	332	115	48	25	42
Midwest	7,070	4,979	649	1,442	1,176	731	223	222	92	53	17	22
South........	8,902	4,247	643	4,012	1,653	613	165	875	156	54	14	88
West	5,716	3,346	675	1,695	966	501	162	304	80	38	13	29

B Does not meet standard of reliability or precision. X Not applicable. Z Less than 500. [1] Full-time equivalents.

Source: U.S. National Center for Education Statistics, Private School Universe Survey, 2007–2008; <http://nces.ed.gov/surveys/pss/>.

Table 256. Percentage of Students Participating in After-School Activities by School Activity and Student Characteristics: 2005

[Estimates include all students in kindergarten through eighth grade, not older than 15 years, not homeschooled, participating in weekly after-school activity. Students could participate in multiple activities and are not limited to students who have activities for supervision, therefore percentages may sum to more than 100. Includes participation in school-based or center-based after-school programs and participation in after-school activities that were not part of school- or center-based programs]

Characteristic	Number of students (1,000)	After-school activities						
		Sports	Religious activities or instruction	Arts (e.g., music, dance, painting)	Scouts	Volunteer work or community service	Academic activities (e.g., tutoring, math lab)	Clubs (e.g., year-book, debate club)
Total...................	14,282	73	46	42	22	19	16	13
GRADE								
K to 2...................	3,932	72	41	42	26	7	8	5
3 to 5...................	5,125	73	45	43	29	16	17	12
6 to 8...................	5,225	74	51	42	13	32	21	20
SEX								
Male...................	7,150	81	44	30	21	17	17	11
Female.................	7,131	65	48	55	23	21	15	15
RACE/ETHNICITY								
White, non-Hispanic.............	9,927	75	47	44	25	20	14	14
Black, non-Hispanic.............	1,549	59	53	33	14	19	29	9
Hispanic [1].................	1,627	77	40	36	14	15	16	10
Asian or Pacific Islander, non-Hispanic...	334	67	29	53	15	16	29	20
Other race, non-Hispanic [2]..........	844	66	45	53	25	21	15	12
HOUSEHOLD INCOME								
$25,000 or less.................	1,819	63	49	35	16	16	19	10
$25,001 to $50,000..............	2,794	62	49	37	21	21	18	13
$50,001 to $75,000..............	3,450	74	47	41	26	17	15	12
$75,001 to $100,000.............	2,327	77	45	45	26	21	16	15
$100,001 or more................	3,892	82	43	49	21	19	14	14

[1] Persons of Hispanic origin may be any race. [2] "Other race, non-Hispanic" includes children who were multiracial and not of Hispanic ethnicity, or who were American Indian or Alaska Native, or were not Hispanic, White, Black, Asian, or Pacific Islander.

Source: U.S. National Center for Education Statistics, After-School Programs and Activities Survey of the 2006 National Household Education Surveys Program (ASPA-NHES: 2005); <http://nces.ed.gov/pubs2006/afterschool/tables/table_13.asp?referrer=report>.

Table 257. Percentage of Students Participating in Weekly Nonparental After-School Care Arrangements by Activities, Arrangement Type, and Student Characteristics: 2005

[Estimates include all students in kindergarten through eighth grade, not older than 15 years, not homeschooled, participating in at least one weekly after-school care arrangement. Students could participate in multiple activities and are not limited to students who have activities for supervision, therefore percentages may sum to more than 100]

Characteristic	Number of students (1,000)	After-school activities						
		Homework, educational activities, reading, writing	Computers	Arts (perform or study music, crafts, drama)	Chores, work	Outdoor play, sports	Indoor play	Television, videos, video games, listen to music
Total...................	16,005	77	18	24	9	43	30	42
ARRANGEMENT TYPE [1]								
Relative...................	5,274	81	14	12	9	37	26	61
Nonrelative.................	1,962	71	2	16	5	52	42	37
School- or center-based.............	7,065	70	17	38	2	46	32	11
Self-care...................	4,267	76	20	10	19	26	13	22
GRADE								
K to 2...................	4,839	68	14	32	4	49	43	39
3 to 5...................	5,364	83	18	25	7	48	33	37
6 to 8...................	5,802	80	21	18	14	35	17	50
SEX								
Male...................	8,599	75	17	19	8	50	31	45
Female.................	7,406	80	18	31	10	36	29	39
RACE/ETHNICITY								
White, non-Hispanic.............	8,130	73	17	25	8	46	32	42
Black, non-Hispanic.............	3,324	86	21	20	10	40	28	42
Hispanic [2].................	3,060	81	16	25	8	43	31	43
Asian or Pacific Islander, non-Hispanic....	404	80	24	35	4	40	21	30
Other race, non-Hispanic [3]..........	1,087	76	14	31	9	40	30	45
HOUSEHOLD INCOME								
$25,000 or less.................	4,246	79	20	21	9	41	29	47
$25,001 to $50,000..............	4,100	77	17	25	11	44	30	46
$50,001 to $75,000..............	3,246	76	17	23	8	44	32	38
$75,001 to $100,000.............	2,023	77	17	27	7	41	31	39
$100,001 or more................	2,389	76	17	28	6	47	31	35

[1] Includes students who participate in more than one arrangement type. [2] Persons of Hispanic origin may be any race. [3] "Other race, non-Hispanic" includes children who were multiracial and not of Hispanic ethnicity, or who were American Indian or Alaska Native, or were not Hispanic, White, Black, Asian, or Pacific Islander.

Source: U.S. National Center for Education Statistics, After-School Programs and Activities Survey of the 2006 National Household Education Surveys Program (ASPA-NHES: 2005) <http://nces.ed.gov/pubs2006/afterschool/tables/table_9.asp?referrer=report>.

Education 167

Table 258. SAT Scores and Characteristics of College-Bound Seniors: 1970 to 2008

[For school year ending in year shown. Data are for the SAT I: Reasoning Tests. SAT I: Reasoning Test replaced the SAT in March 1994. Scores between the two tests have been equated to the same 200-800 scale and are thus comparable. Scores for 1995 and prior years have been recentered and revised]

Type of test and characteristic	Unit	1970	1980	1985	1990	1995	2000	2005	2006	2007	2008
AVERAGE TEST SCORES [1]											
Critical reading, total [2]	Point.	537	502	509	500	504	505	508	503	502	502
Male	Point.	536	506	514	505	505	507	513	505	504	504
Female.	Point.	538	498	503	496	502	504	505	502	502	500
Math, total [2].	Point.	512	492	500	501	506	514	520	518	515	515
Male	Point.	531	515	522	521	525	533	538	536	533	533
Female.	Point.	493	473	480	483	490	498	504	502	499	500
Writing	Point.	(X)	(X)	(X)	(X)	(X)	(X)	(X)	497	494	494
Male	Point.	(X)	(X)	(X)	(X)	(X)	(X)	(X)	491	489	488
Female.	Point.	(X)	(X)	(X)	(X)	(X)	(X)	(X)	502	500	501
PARTICIPANTS											
Total [3].	1,000	(NA)	922	977	1,026	1,068	1,260	1,476	1,466	1,495	1,519
Male	Percent. . .	(NA)	48.2	48.3	47.8	46.4	46.2	46.5	46.4	46.4	46.4
White	Percent . . .	(NA)	82.1	81.0	73.0	69.2	66.4	62.3	62.1	60.8	59.8
Black	Percent . . .	(NA)	9.1	7.5	10.0	10.7	11.2	11.6	11.3	11.7	12.1
Obtaining scores [1] of—											
600 or above:											
Critical reading	Percent . . .	(NA)	(NA)	(NA)	20.3	21.9	21.1	22.5	21.4	21.2	21.0
Math	Percent . . .	(NA)	(NA)	(NA)	20.4	23.4	24.2	26.5	25.8	24.5	25.0
Writing.	Percent . . .	(X)	(X)	(X)	(X)	(X)	(X)	(X)	18.9	18.4	18.3
Below 400:											
Critical reading	Percent . . .	(NA)	(NA)	(NA)	17.3	16.4	15.9	15.5	16.6	16.5	17.0
Math	Percent . . .	(NA)	(NA)	(NA)	15.8	16.0	14.7	13.8	14.3	14.8	15.0
Writing.	Percent . . .	(X)	(X)	(X)	(X)	(X)	(X)	(X)	17.8	18.4	18.5

NA Not available.   X Not applicable.   [1] Minimum score, 200; maximum score, 800.   [2] 1970 estimates based on total number of persons taking SAT. For 2008, based on 1,518,859 test takers.   [3] 922 represents 922,000.

Source: The College Board, *College-Bound Seniors 2008*. Copyright 1967 to 2008; <http://www.collegeboard.com>. Reproduced with permission.

Table 259. ACT Program Scores and Characteristics of College-Bound Students: 1970 to 2008

[For academic year ending in year shown. Except as indicated, test scores and characteristics of college-bound students. Through 1980, data based on 10 percent sample; thereafter, based on all ACT tested graduating seniors]

Type of test and characteristic	Unit	1970	1980	1985	1990 [1]	1995 [1]	2000 [1]	2005 [1]	2006 [1]	2007 [1]	2008 [1]
TEST SCORES [2]											
Composite	Point . . .	19.9	18.5	18.6	20.6	20.8	21.0	20.9	21.1	21.2	21.1
Male.	Point . . .	20.3	19.3	19.4	21.0	21.0	21.2	21.1	21.2	21.2	21.2
Female	Point . . .	19.4	17.9	17.9	20.3	20.7	20.9	20.9	21.0	21.0	21.0
English.	Point . . .	18.5	17.9	18.1	20.5	20.2	20.5	20.4	20.6	20.7	20.6
Male.	Point . . .	17.6	17.3	17.6	20.1	19.8	20.0	20.0	20.1	20.2	20.1
Female	Point . . .	19.4	18.3	18.6	20.9	20.6	20.9	20.8	21.0	21.0	21.0
Math	Point . . .	20.0	17.4	17.2	19.9	20.2	20.7	20.7	20.8	21.0	21.0
Male.	Point . . .	21.1	18.9	18.6	20.7	20.9	21.4	21.3	21.5	21.6	21.6
Female	Point . . .	18.8	16.2	16.0	19.3	19.7	20.2	20.2	20.3	20.4	20.4
Reading [3]	Point . . .	19.7	17.2	17.4	(NA)	21.3	21.4	21.3	21.4	21.5	21.4
Male.	Point . . .	20.3	18.2	18.3	(NA)	21.1	21.2	21.0	21.1	21.2	21.2
Female	Point . . .	19.0	16.4	16.6	(NA)	21.4	21.5	21.5	21.6	21.6	21.5
Science reasoning [4]	Point . . .	20.8	21.1	21.2	(NA)	21.0	21.0	20.9	20.9	21.0	20.8
Male.	Point . . .	21.6	22.4	22.6	(NA)	21.6	21.6	21.4	21.2	21.4	21.3
Female	Point . . .	20.0	20.0	20.0	(NA)	20.5	20.6	20.5	21.0	20.5	20.4
PARTICIPANTS [5]											
Total [6].	1,000. . .	788	822	739	817	945	1,065	1,186	1,206	1,301	1,422
Male	Percent .	52	45	46	46	44	43	44	44	45	45
White	Percent .	(NA)	83	82	73	69	72	66	63	60	63
Black	Percent .	4	8	8	9	9	10	12	12	12	13
Obtaining composite scores of—[7]											
27 or above	Percent .	14	13	14	12	13	14	14	14	15	16
18 or below	Percent .	21	33	32	35	34	32	34	33	32	33

NA Not available.   [1] Beginning 1990, not comparable with previous years because a new version of the ACT was introduced. Estimated average composite scores for prior years: 1989, 20.6; 1988, 1987, and 1986, 20.8.   [2] Minimum score, 1; maximum score, 36.   [3] Prior to 1990, social studies; data not comparable with previous years.   [4] Prior to 1990, natural sciences; data not comparable with previous years.   [5] Beginning 1985, data are for seniors who graduated in year shown and had taken the ACT in their junior or senior years. Data by race are for those responding to the race question.   [6] 788 represents 788,000.   [7] Prior to 1990, 26 or above and 15 or below.

Source: ACT, Inc., Iowa City, IA, *High School Profile Report*, annual.

168   Education

Table 260. **Proficiency Levels on Selected NAEP Tests for Students in Public Schools by State: 2007**

[Represents percent of public school students scoring at or above basic and proficient levels. Basic denotes mastery of the knowledge and skills that are fundamental for proficient work at a given grade level. Proficient represents solid academic performance. Students reaching this level demonstrated competency over challenging subject matter. For more detail, see <http://www.nagb.org/pubs/pubs.html>. Based on the National Assessment of Educational Progress (NAEP) tests which are administered to a representative sample of students in public schools, private schools, and Department of Defense schools. Data shown here are for public school students only]

State	Grade 4 Math		Grade 8 Math		Grade 4 Reading		Grade 8 Reading	
	At or above basic	At or above proficient	At or above basic	At or above proficient	At or above basic	At or above proficient	At or above basic	At or above proficient
U.S. average.......	81	39	70	31	66	32	73	29
Alabama............	70	26	55	18	62	29	62	21
Alaska.............	79	38	73	32	62	29	71	27
Arizona............	74	31	66	26	56	24	65	24
Arkansas..........	81	37	65	24	64	29	70	25
California	70	30	59	24	53	23	62	21
Colorado...........	82	41	75	37	70	36	79	35
Connecticut........	84	45	73	35	73	41	77	37
Delaware..........	87	40	74	31	73	34	77	31
District of Columbia	49	14	34	8	39	14	48	12
Florida	86	40	68	27	70	34	71	28
Georgia	79	32	64	25	66	28	70	26
Hawaii	77	33	59	21	59	26	62	20
Idaho..............	85	40	75	34	70	35	78	32
Illinois............	79	36	70	31	65	32	75	30
Indiana............	89	46	76	35	68	33	76	31
Iowa	87	43	77	35	74	36	80	36
Kansas............	89	51	81	40	72	36	81	35
Kentucky	79	31	69	27	68	33	73	28
Louisiana	73	24	64	19	52	20	64	19
Maine..............	85	42	78	34	73	36	83	37
Maryland	80	40	74	37	69	36	76	33
Massachusetts.......	93	58	85	51	81	49	84	43
Michigan...........	80	37	66	29	66	32	72	28
Minnesota..........	87	51	81	43	73	37	80	37
Mississippi	70	21	54	14	51	19	60	17
Missouri	82	38	72	30	67	32	75	31
Montana...........	88	44	79	38	75	39	85	39
Nebraska	80	38	74	35	71	35	79	35
Nevada	74	30	60	23	57	24	63	22
New Hampshire	91	52	78	38	76	41	82	37
New Jersey.........	90	52	77	40	77	43	81	39
New Mexico	70	24	57	17	58	24	62	17
New York	85	43	70	30	69	36	75	32
North Carolina.......	85	41	73	34	64	29	71	28
North Dakota........	91	46	86	41	75	35	84	32
Ohio	87	46	76	35	73	36	79	36
Oklahoma..........	82	33	66	21	65	27	72	26
Oregon............	79	35	73	35	62	28	77	34
Pennsylvania........	85	47	77	38	73	40	79	36
Rhode Island........	80	34	65	28	65	31	69	27
South Carolina.......	80	36	71	32	59	26	69	25
South Dakota	86	41	81	39	71	34	83	37
Tennessee	76	29	64	23	61	27	71	26
Texas..............	87	40	78	35	66	30	73	28
Utah	83	39	72	32	69	34	75	30
Vermont............	89	49	81	41	74	41	84	42
Virginia............	87	42	77	37	74	38	79	34
Washington..........	84	44	75	36	70	36	77	34
West Virginia........	81	33	61	19	63	28	68	23
Wisconsin..........	85	47	76	37	70	36	76	33
Wyoming	88	44	80	36	73	36	80	33

Source: U.S. Department of Education, National Center for Education Statistics, National Assessment of Educational Progress (NAEP), 2007 Mathematics and Reading Assessments; <http://nces.ed.gov/nationsreportcard/> (accessed 15 March 2008).

Education 169

Table 261. Public High School Graduates by State: 1980 to 2007

[In thousands (2,747.7 represents 2,747,700). For school year ending in year shown]

State	1980	1990	2000	2007, proj.	State	1980	1990	2000	2007, proj.
United States ...	2,747.7	2,320.3	2,553.8	2,950.5	Missouri............	62.3	49.0	52.8	59.7
Alabama	45.2	40.5	37.8	38.1	Montana	12.1	9.4	10.9	10.1
Alaska............	5.2	5.4	6.6	7.9	Nebraska..........	22.4	17.7	20.1	19.9
Arizona	28.6	32.1	38.3	69.1	Nevada	8.5	9.5	14.6	17.5
Arkansas..........	29.1	26.5	27.3	27.9	New Hampshire	11.7	10.8	11.8	14.2
California..........	249.2	236.3	309.9	375.9					
Colorado	36.8	33.0	38.9	46.9	New Jersey	94.6	69.8	74.4	95.6
Connecticut	37.7	27.9	31.6	37.5	New Mexico........	18.4	14.9	18.0	17.4
Delaware..........	7.6	5.6	6.1	7.1	New York..........	204.1	143.3	141.7	158.9
District of Columbia [1]..	5.0	3.6	2.7	3.4	North Carolina	70.9	64.8	62.1	81.1
Florida............	87.3	88.9	106.7	150.3	North Dakota	9.9	7.7	8.6	7.2
Georgia...........	61.6	56.6	62.6	76.6	Ohio	144.2	114.5	111.7	119.7
Hawaii............	11.5	10.3	10.4	10.7	Oklahoma	39.3	35.6	37.6	36.9
Idaho.............	13.2	12.0	16.2	16.4	Oregon	29.9	25.5	30.2	32.0
Illinois............	135.6	108.1	111.8	130.1	Pennsylvania	146.5	110.5	114.0	129.9
Indiana	73.1	60.0	57.0	61.1	Rhode Island	10.9	7.8	8.5	10.2
Iowa	43.4	31.8	33.9	35.5	South Carolina	38.7	32.5	31.6	38.1
Kansas	30.9	25.4	29.1	29.6	South Dakota	10.7	7.7	9.3	8.2
Kentucky..........	41.2	38.0	36.8	38.9	Tennessee.........	49.8	46.1	41.6	50.8
Louisiana..........	46.3	36.1	38.4	31.7	Texas	171.4	172.5	212.9	255.8
Maine	15.4	13.8	12.2	13.4	Utah	20.0	21.2	32.5	31.5
Maryland	54.3	41.6	47.8	57.1	Vermont	6.7	6.1	6.7	7.1
Massachusetts	73.8	55.9	53.0	62.5	Virginia	66.6	60.6	65.6	78.7
Michigan	124.3	93.8	97.7	106.8	Washington	50.4	45.9	57.6	65.1
Minnesota	64.9	49.1	57.4	59.6	West Virginia	23.4	21.9	19.4	17.3
Mississippi	27.6	25.2	24.2	24.5	Wisconsin	69.3	52.0	58.5	64.1
					Wyoming..........	6.1	5.8	6.5	5.4

[1] Beginning in 1990, graduates from adult programs are excluded.

Source: U.S. National Center for Education Statistics, *Digest of Education Statistics*, annual.

Table 262. High School Dropouts by Race and Hispanic Origin: 1980 to 2007

[In percent. As of October]

Item	1980	1985	1990 [1]	1995	2000	2001	2002	2003	2004	2005	2006	2007
EVENT DROPOUTS [2]												
Total [3]	6.0	5.2	4.5	5.4	4.5	4.7	3.3	3.8	4.4	3.6	3.5	3.3
White [4]...........	5.6	4.8	3.9	5.1	4.3	4.6	3.0	3.7	4.2	3.1	3.5	2.8
Male.............	6.4	4.9	4.1	5.4	4.7	5.3	3.0	3.9	4.9	3.4	3.9	2.8
Female...........	4.9	4.7	3.8	4.8	4.0	3.8	3.0	3.4	3.5	2.7	3.1	2.7
Black [4]...........	8.3	7.7	7.7	6.1	5.6	5.7	4.4	4.5	5.2	6.9	3.7	4.3
Male.............	8.0	8.3	6.9	7.9	7.6	6.1	5.1	4.1	4.8	7.5	3.2	4.9
Female...........	8.5	7.2	8.6	4.4	3.8	5.4	3.8	4.9	5.7	6.2	4.3	3.6
Hispanic [5].........	11.5	9.7	7.7	11.6	6.8	8.1	5.3	6.5	8.0	4.7	6.4	5.5
Male.............	16.9	9.3	7.6	10.9	7.1	7.6	6.2	7.7	11.5	5.6	6.3	5.5
Female...........	6.9	9.8	7.7	12.5	6.5	8.7	4.4	5.4	4.6	3.9	6.6	5.6
STATUS DROPOUTS [6]												
Total [3]	15.6	13.9	14.4	13.9	12.4	13.0	12.3	11.8	12.1	11.3	11.0	10.2
White [4]...........	14.4	13.5	14.1	13.6	12.2	13.4	12.2	11.6	11.9	11.3	10.8	10.0
Male.............	15.7	14.7	15.4	14.3	13.5	15.3	13.7	13.3	13.7	13.2	12.4	11.7
Female...........	13.2	12.3	12.8	13.0	10.9	11.4	10.6	9.8	10.0	9.4	9.2	8.3
Black [4]...........	23.5	17.6	16.4	14.4	15.3	13.8	14.6	14.2	15.1	12.9	13.0	10.2
Male.............	26.0	18.8	18.6	14.2	17.4	16.9	16.9	16.7	17.9	14.8	11.2	10.0
Female...........	21.5	16.6	14.5	14.6	13.5	11.0	12.5	12.0	12.7	11.2	14.7	10.3
Hispanic [5].........	40.3	31.5	37.7	34.7	32.3	31.7	30.1	28.4	28.0	27.3	26.2	25.3
Male.............	42.6	35.8	40.3	34.2	36.8	37.1	33.8	31.7	33.5	32.1	31.0	29.2
Female...........	38.1	27.0	35.0	35.4	27.3	25.5	25.6	24.7	21.7	21.8	21.0	21.1

[1] Beginning 1990, reflects new editing procedures for cases with missing data on school enrollment.   [2] Percent of students who drop out in a single year without completing high school. For grades 10 to 12.   [3] Includes other races, not shown separately.   [4] Beginning 2003, for persons who selected this race group only. See footnote 2, Table 224.   [5] Persons of Hispanic origin may be any race.   [6] Percent of the population who have not completed high school and are not enrolled, regardless of when they dropped out. For persons 18 to 24 years old.

Source: U.S. Census Bureau, Current Population Reports, PPL-148; and earlier PPL and P-20 reports; and data published on the Internet; <http://www.census.gov/population/www/socdemo/school.html>.

Table 263. High School Dropouts by Age, Race, and Hispanic Origin: 1980 to 2007

[As of October (5,212 represents 5,212,000). **For persons 14 to 24 years old.** See Table 265 for definition of dropouts]

Age and race	Number of dropouts (1,000)					Percent of population				
	1980	1990	1995	2000	2007	1980	1990	1995	2000	2007
Total dropouts [1, 2] . . .	**5,212**	**3,854**	**3,963**	**3,883**	**3,384**	**12.0**	**10.1**	**9.9**	**9.1**	**7.4**
16 to 17 years.	709	418	406	460	448	8.8	6.3	5.4	5.8	2.6
18 to 21 years.	2,578	1,921	1,980	2,005	1,499	15.8	13.4	14.2	12.9	9.1
22 to 24 years.	1,798	1,458	1,491	1,310	1,438	15.2	13.8	13.6	11.8	11.6
White [2, 3]	4,169	3,127	3,098	3,065	2,578	11.3	10.1	9.7	9.1	7.3
16 to 17 years.	619	334	314	366	330	9.2	6.4	5.4	5.8	2.5
18 to 21 years.	2,032	1,516	1,530	1,558	1,103	14.7	13.1	13.8	12.6	8.7
22 to 24 years.	1,416	1,235	1,181	1,040	1,145	14.0	14.0	13.4	11.7	11.8
Black [2, 3]	934	611	605	705	495	16.0	10.9	10.0	10.9	7.2
16 to 17 years.	80	73	70	84	70	6.9	6.9	5.8	7.0	2.6
18 to 21 years.	486	345	328	383	257	23.0	16.0	15.8	16.0	10.4
22 to 24 years.	346	185	194	232	168	24.0	13.5	12.5	14.3	9.8
Hispanic [2, 4]	919	1,122	1,355	1,499	1,446	29.5	26.8	24.7	23.5	17.6
16 to 17 years.	92	89	94	121	136	16.6	12.9	10.7	11.0	4.5
18 to 21 years.	470	502	652	733	613	40.3	32.9	29.9	30.0	20.6
22 to 24 years.	323	523	598	602	697	40.6	42.8	37.4	35.5	31.6

[1] Includes other groups not shown separately. [2] Includes persons 14 to 15 years not shown separately. [3] For 2007, for persons who selected this race group only. See footnote 2, Table 224. [4] Persons of Hispanic origin may be of any race.
Source: U.S. Census Bureau, *Current Population Reports*, PPL-148; and earlier PPL and P-20 reports; and data published on the Internet; <http://www.census.gov/population/www/socdemo/school.html>.

Table 264. Enrollment Status by Race, Hispanic Origin, and Sex: 2000 and 2007

[As of October (15,553 represents 15,553,000). For persons 18 to 21 years old. For the civilian noninstitutional population. Based on the Current Population Survey; see text, Section 1 and Appendix III]

Characteristic	Total persons 18 to 21 years old (1,000)		Percent distribution							
			Enrolled in high school		High school graduates				Not high school graduates	
					Total		In college			
	2000	2007	2000	2007	2000	2007	2000	2007	2000	2007
Total [1]	**15,553**	**16,422**	**9.4**	**9.6**	**77.6**	**81.1**	**43.5**	**47.9**	**12.9**	**9.1**
White [2]	12,383	12,725	8.9	9.0	78.5	82.1	44.4	49.5	12.6	8.7
Black [2]	2,389	2,472	12.6	13.0	71.3	76.5	34.7	37.5	10.0	10.4
Hispanic [3]	2,439	2,972	12.5	11.8	57.2	67.0	25.3	32.7	30.0	20.6
Male [1]	7,814	8,329	11.0	11.2	74.7	78.5	38.9	43.6	14.3	10.0
White [2]	6,313	6,434	10.6	10.8	75.7	79.2	39.8	44.6	13.7	9.7
Black [2]	1,096	1,238	14.9	14.2	66.0	75.6	27.4	35.5	19.1	9.9
Hispanic [3]	1,269	1,550	14.4	13.4	51.8	63.1	21.9	25.8	33.7	22.8
Female [1]	7,739	8,093	7.9	8.0	80.6	83.7	48.1	52.4	11.5	8.3
White [2]	6,070	6,291	7.1	7.1	81.3	85.1	49.3	54.5	11.4	7.6
Black [2]	1,293	1,233	10.7	11.7	75.9	77.1	40.9	39.6	13.5	10.9
Hispanic [3]	1,169	1,421	10.6	10.1	63.1	71.2	28.9	40.2	26.1	18.3

[1] Includes other races not shown separately. [2] For 2007, for persons who selected this race group only. See footnote 2, Table 224. [3] Persons of Hispanic origin may be any race.
Source: U.S. Census Bureau, Current Population Reports, PPL-148; and earlier PPL and P-20 reports; and data published on the Internet; <http://www.census.gov/population/www/socdemo/school.html>.

Table 265. Employment Status of High School Graduates and Dropouts Not Enrolled in School by Sex and Race: 1980 to 2008

[In thousands (11,622 represents 11,622,000), except percent. As of October. For civilian noninstitutional population 16 to 24 years old. Based on Current Population Survey; see text, Section 1 and Appendix III]

Employment status, sex, and race	Graduates [1]				Dropouts [3]			
	1980	1990	2000 [2]	2008 [2]	1980	1990	2000 [2]	2008 [2]
Civilian population	**11,622**	**8,370**	**7,351**	**7,321**	**5,254**	**3,800**	**3,776**	**3,010**
In labor force	9,795	7,107	6,195	5,761	3,549	2,506	2,612	1,901
Percent of population	84.3	84.9	84.3	78.7	67.5	66.0	69.2	63.1
Employed	8,567	6,279	5,632	4,856	2,651	1,993	2,150	1,410
Percent of labor force	87.5	88.3	90.9	84.3	74.7	79.5	82.3	74.2
Unemployed	1,228	828	563	905	898	513	463	491
Unemployment rate, total [4]	12.5	11.7	9.1	15.7	25.3	20.5	17.7	25.8
Male	13.5	11.1	9.3	17.6	23.5	18.8	16.3	26.3
Female	11.5	12.3	8.8	12.8	28.7	23.5	20.3	25.0
White [5]	10.8	9.0	7.2	13.7	21.6	17.0	15.0	22.9
Black [5]	26.1	26.0	18.1	23.5	43.9	43.3	33.2	40.1
Not in labor force	1,827	1,262	1,156	1,560	1,705	1,294	1,163	1,109
Percent of population	15.7	15.1	15.7	21.3	32.5	34.0	30.8	36.8

NA Not available. [1] For persons not enrolled in college who have completed 4 years of high school only. [2] Data not strictly comparable with data for earlier years. See text, this section, and February 2000 and 2008 issues of *Employment and Earnings*. [3] For persons not in regular school and who have not completed the 12th grade nor received a general equivalency degree. [4] Includes other races not shown separately. [5] For 2008, for persons who selected this race group only. See footnote 2, Table 224.
Source: U.S. Bureau of Labor Statistics; *News*, USDL 09-0454, 28 April 2009; and unpublished data. See <http://www.bls.gov/news.release/hsgec.toc.htm>.

Table 266. General Educational Development (GED) Credentials Issued: 1980 to 2006

[GEDs issued in thousands (479 represents 479,000). For the 50 states and DC]

Year	GEDs issued	Percent distribution by age of test taker				
		19 years old or under	20 to 24 years old	25 to 29 years old	30 to 34 years old	35 years old and over
1980	479	37	27	13	8	15
1985	413	32	26	15	10	16
1990	410	36	25	13	10	15
1995	504	38	25	13	9	15
2000	487	45	25	11	7	13
2001	648	41	26	11	8	14
2002	330	49	25	10	6	11
2003	387	47	26	10	7	11
2004	406	46	26	11	6	10
2005	424	45	26	12	7	11
2006	464	46	25	12	6	11

Source: U.S. National Center for Education Statistics, *Digest of Education Statistics*, annual.

Table 267. College Enrollment of Recent High School Completers: 1970 to 2007

[2,758 represents 2,758,000. For persons 16 to 24 years old who graduated from high school in the preceding 12 months. Includes persons receiving GEDs. Based on surveys and subject to sampling error; data will not agree with data in other tables]

Year	Number of high school completers (1,000)						Percent enrolled in college [5]					
	Total [1]	Male	Female	White [2]	Black [2, 3]	His-panic [3, 4]	Total [1]	Male	Female	White [2]	Black [2, 3]	His-panic [3, 4]
1970 . . .	2,758	1,343	1,415	2,461	(NA)	(NA)	51.7	55.2	48.5	52.0	(NA)	(NA)
1975 . . .	3,185	1,513	1,672	2,701	302	132	50.7	52.6	49.0	51.1	41.7	58.0
1980 . . .	3,088	1,498	1,589	2,554	350	130	49.3	46.7	51.8	49.8	42.7	52.3
1985 . . .	2,668	1,287	1,381	2,104	332	141	57.7	58.6	56.8	60.1	42.2	51.0
1990 . . .	2,362	1,173	1,189	1,819	331	121	60.1	58.0	62.2	63.0	46.8	42.7
1995 . . .	2,599	1,238	1,361	1,861	349	288	61.9	62.6	61.3	64.3	51.2	53.7
1998 . . .	2,810	1,452	1,358	1,980	386	314	65.6	62.4	69.1	68.5	61.9	47.4
1999 . . .	2,897	1,474	1,423	1,978	436	329	62.9	61.4	64.4	66.3	58.9	42.3
2000 . . .	2,756	1,251	1,505	1,938	393	300	63.3	59.9	66.2	65.7	54.9	52.9
2001 . . .	2,549	1,277	1,273	1,834	381	241	61.8	60.1	63.5	64.3	55.0	51.7
2002 . . .	2,796	1,412	1,384	1,903	382	344	65.2	62.1	68.4	69.1	59.4	53.6
2003 . . .	2,677	1,306	1,372	1,832	327	314	63.9	61.2	66.5	66.2	57.5	58.6
2004 . . .	2,752	1,327	1,425	1,854	398	286	66.7	61.4	71.5	68.8	62.5	61.8
2005 . . .	2,675	1,262	1,414	1,799	345	390	68.6	66.5	70.4	73.2	55.7	54.0
2006 . . .	2,692	1,328	1,363	1,805	318	382	66.0	65.8	66.1	68.5	55.5	57.9
2007 . . .	2,955	1,511	1,444	2,043	416	355	67.2	66.1	68.3	69.5	55.7	64.0

NA Not available. [1] Includes other races not shown separately. [2] Beginning 2003, for persons of this race group only. See footnote 2, Table 224. [3] Due to small sample size, data are subject to relatively large sampling errors. [4] Persons of Hispanic origin may be any race. [5] As of October.

Source: U.S. National Center for Education Statistics, *Digest of Education Statistics*, annual.

Table 268. College Enrollment by Sex and Attendance Status: 2004 to 2008

[As of fall. In thousands (17,272 represents 17,272,000). Includes enrollment at branch campuses, some additional (primarily 2-year) colleges and excludes a few institutions that did not award degrees. Includes enrollment at institutions that were eligible to participate in Title IV federal financial aid programs. Includes unclassified students. (Students taking courses for credit, but are not candidates for degrees.)]

Sex and age	2004		2005		2006		2007		2008, proj.	
	Total	Part-time	Total	Part-time	Total	Part-time	Total	Part-time	Total	Part-time
Total	17,272	6,662	17,487	6,690	17,759	6,802	18,248	6,979	18,200	6,937
Male	7,387	2,648	7,456	2,653	7,575	2,696	7,816	2,787	7,822	2,767
14 to 17 years old	78	15	78	41	82	16	75	17	82	18
18 to 19 years old	1,551	239	1,592	235	1,705	297	1,805	273	1,799	313
20 to 21 years old	1,743	358	1,778	318	1,673	341	1,633	288	1,705	347
22 to 24 years old	1,380	419	1,355	405	1,470	466	1,551	544	1,512	478
25 to 29 years old	1,045	536	978	539	1,051	488	1,020	435	1,117	518
30 to 34 years old	518	317	545	306	557	325	659	430	572	333
35 years old and over. . .	1,073	764	1,130	809	1,037	762	1,074	799	1,035	761
Female	9,885	4,014	10,032	4,038	10,184	4,106	10,432	4,192	10,378	4,170
14 to 17 years old	122	19	121	27	149	48	104	9	109	42
18 to 19 years old	2,027	311	2,018	338	2,064	318	2,173	327	2,154	336
20 to 21 years old	1,908	382	2,000	430	1,975	363	2,129	452	2,018	369
22 to 24 years old	1,657	543	1,717	571	1,724	634	1,811	685	1,777	649
25 to 29 years old	1,341	720	1,406	709	1,350	696	1,502	824	1,413	733
30 to 34 years old	812	523	809	499	852	480	770	449	862	488
35 years old and over. . .	2,018	1,516	1,960	1,464	2,070	1,567	1,943	1,446	2,044	1,552

Source: U.S. National Center for Education Statistics, *Digest of Education Statistics*, annual.

Table 269. Higher Education—Institutions and Enrollment 1980 to 2007

[As of fall **(686 represents 686,000)**. Covers universities, colleges, professional schools, junior and teachers' colleges, both publicly and privately controlled, regular session. Includes estimates for institutions not reporting. See also Appendix III]

Item	Unit	1980	1990	2000	2003	2004	2005	2006	2007
ALL INSTITUTIONS									
Number of institutions [1]	Number . .	**3,231**	**3,559**	**4,182**	**4,236**	**4,216**	**4,276**	**4,314**	**4,352**
4-year.	Number. . .	1,957	2,141	2,450	2,530	2,533	2,582	2,629	2,675
2-year.	Number. . .	1,274	1,418	1,732	1,706	1,683	1,694	1,685	1,677
Instructional staff—									
(lecturer or above) [2]	1,000	**686**	**817**	**(NA)**	**1,175**	**(NA)**	**1,290**	**(NA)**	**(NA)**
Percent full-time	Percent. . .	66	61	(NA)	54	(NA)	52	(NA)	(NA)
Total enrollment [3, 4]	1,000	**12,097**	**13,819**	**15,312**	**16,900**	**17,272**	**17,487**	**17,759**	**18,248**
Male.	1,000	5,874	6,284	6,722	7,256	7,387	7,456	7,575	7,816
Female	1,000	6,223	7,535	8,591	9,645	9,885	10,032	10,184	10,432
4-year institutions	1,000	7,571	8,579	9,364	10,408	10,726	10,999	11,240	11,630
2-year institutions	1,000	4,526	5,240	5,948	6,493	6,546	6,488	6,519	6,618
Full-time	1,000	7,098	7,821	9,010	10,312	10,610	10,797	10,957	11,270
Part-time	1,000	4,999	5,998	6,303	6,589	6,662	6,690	6,802	6,978
Public.	1,000	9,457	10,845	11,753	12,857	12,980	13,022	13,180	13,491
Private	1,000	2,640	2,974	3,560	4,043	4,292	4,466	4,579	4,757
Not-for-profit.	1,000	2,528	2,760	3,109	3,341	3,412	3,455	3,513	3,571
For profit	1,000	112	213	450	703	880	1,011	1,066	1,186
Undergraduate [4].	1,000	10,475	11,959	13,155	14,474	14,781	14,964	15,184	15,604
Men	1,000	5,000	5,380	5,778	6,224	6,340	6,409	6,513	6,728
Women	1,000	5,475	6,579	7,377	8,250	8,441	8,555	8,671	8,876
First-time freshmen	1,000	2,588	2,257	2,428	2,605	2,630	2,657	2,707	(NA)
First professional	1,000	278	273	307	329	335	337	343	351
Men	1,000	199	167	164	166	168	170	174	178
Women	1,000	78	107	143	163	166	167	170	173
Graduate [4].	1,000	1,343	1,586	1,850	2,098	2,157	2,186	2,231	2,294
Men	1,000	675	737	780	865	879	877	887	910
Women	1,000	670	849	1,071	1,233	1,278	1,309	1,344	1,383
2-YEAR INSTITUTIONS									
Number of institutions [1, 5]	Number . .	**1,274**	**1,418**	**1,732**	**1,706**	**1,683**	**1,694**	**1,605**	**1,677**
Public .	Number. . .	945	972	1,076	1,086	1,061	1,053	1,045	1,032
Private	Number. . .	329	446	656	620	622	641	640	645
Instructional staff—									
(lecturer or above) [2]	1,000	**192**	**(NA)**	**(NA)**	**359**	**(NA)**	**373**	**(NA)**	**(NA)**
Enrollment [3, 4]	1,000	**4,526**	**5,240**	**5,948**	**6,494**	**6,546**	**6,488**	**6,519**	**6,618**
Public	1,000	4,329	4,996	5,697	6,209	6,244	6,184	6,225	6,324
Private	1,000	198	244	251	285	302	304	293	294
Male.	1,000	2,047	2,233	2,559	2,690	2,698	2,680	2,705	(NA)
Female	1,000	2,479	3,007	3,390	3,804	3,848	3,808	3,814	(NA)
4-YEAR INSTITUTIONS									
Number of institutions [1, 5]	Number . .	**1,957**	**2,141**	**2,450**	**2,530**	**2,533**	**2,582**	**2,629**	**2,675**
Public.	Number. . .	552	595	622	634	639	640	643	653
Private	Number. . .	1,405	1,546	1,828	1,896	1,894	1,942	1,986	2,022
Instructional staff—									
(lecturer or above) [2]	1,000	**494**	**(NA)**	**(NA)**	**814**	**(NA)**	**917**	**(NA)**	**(NA)**
Enrollment [3, 4]	1,000	**7,571**	**8,579**	**9,364**	**10,417**	**10,726**	**10,999**	**11,240**	**11,630**
Public	1,000	5,129	5,848	6,055	6,649	6,737	6,838	6,955	7,167
Private	1,000	2,442	2,730	3,308	3,768	3,990	4,162	4,285	4,464
Male.	1,000	3,827	4,051	4,163	4,570	4,690	4,776	4,870	(NA)
Female	1,000	3,743	4,527	5,201	5,847	6,037	6,224	6,370	(NA)

NA Not available.   [1] Number of institutions includes count of branch campuses. Due to revised survey procedures, data beginning 1990 are not comparable with previous years. Beginning 1996 (2000 for this table), data reflect a new classification of institutions; this classification includes some additional, primarily 2-year, colleges and excludes a few institutions that did not award degrees. Includes institutions that were eligible to participate in Title IV federal financial aid programs.   [2] Due to revised survey methods, data beginning 1990 not comparable with previous years.   [3] Branch campuses counted according to actual status, e.g., 2-year branch in 2-year category.   [4] Includes unclassified students. (Students taking courses for credit, but are not candidates for degrees.)   [5] Includes schools accredited by the National Association of Trade and Technical Schools.

Source: U.S. National Center for Education Statistics, *Digest of Education Statistics*, annual; and unpublished data.

Education 173

Table 270. **College Enrollment by Selected Characteristics: 1990 to 2007**

[In thousands (13,818.6 represents 13,818,600). **As of fall**. Nonresident alien students are not distributed among racial/ethnic groups]

Characteristic	1990	2000 [1]	2003 [1]	2004 [1]	2005 [1]	2006 [1]	2007 [1]
Total	13,818.6	15,312.3	16,900.5	17,272.0	17,487.5	17,758.9	18,248.1
Male	6,283.9	6,721.8	7,255.6	7,387.3	7,455.9	7,574.8	7,815.9
Female.	7,534.7	8,590.5	9,644.9	9,884.8	10,031.6	10,184.1	10,432.2
Public.	10,844.7	11,752.8	12,857.1	12,980.1	13,021.8	13,180.1	13,490.8
Private	2,973.9	3,559.5	4,043.4	4,291.9	4,465.6	4,578.7	4,757.3
2-year	5,240.1	5,948.4	6,492.9	6,545.9	6,488.1	6,518.5	6,617.9
4-year	8,578.6	9,363.9	10,407.6	10,726.2	10,999.4	11,240.3	11,630.2
Undergraduate.	11,959.2	13,155.4	14,473.9	14,780.6	14,964.0	15,184.3	15,603.8
Graduate	1,586.2	1,850.3	2,097.5	2,156.9	2,186.5	2,231.1	2,293.6
First professional	273.4	306.6	329.1	334.5	337.0	343.4	350.8
White [2]	10,722.5	10,462.1	11,275.4	11,422.8	11,495.4	11,572.4	11,756.2
Male	4,861.0	4,634.6	4,927.9	4,988.0	5,007.2	5,046.2	5,146.1
Female.	5,861.5	5,827.5	6,347.5	6,434.8	6,488.2	6,526.2	6,610.1
Public.	8,385.4	7,963.4	8,531.4	8,546.3	8,518.2	8,540.5	8,640.3
Private	2,337.0	2,498.7	2,744.1	2,876.5	2,977.3	3,032.0	3,116.0
2-year	3,954.3	3,804.1	4,076.7	4,063.8	3,998.6	3,969.1	3,975.2
4-year	6,768.1	6,658.0	7,198.7	7,359.0	7,496.9	7,603.4	7,781.0
Undergraduate.	9,272.6	8,983.5	9,662.5	9,771.3	9,828.6	9,885.4	10,046.6
Graduate	1,228.4	1,258.5	1,378.6	1,413.3	1,428.7	1,445.3	1,465.0
First professional	221.5	220.1	234.3	238.2	238.1	241.7	244.7
Black [2]	1,247.0	1,730.3	2,068.9	2,164.7	2,214.6	2,279.6	2,383.4
Male	484.7	635.3	730.6	758.4	774.1	795.4	838.1
Female.	762.3	1,095.0	1,338.2	1,406.3	1,440.4	1,484.2	1,545.3
Public.	976.4	1,319.2	1,533.5	1,574.6	1,580.4	1,612.6	1,667.6
Private	270.6	411.1	535.3	590.1	634.2	667.0	715.7
2-year	524.3	734.9	879.9	905.8	901.1	917.9	941.7
4-year	722.8	995.4	1,189.0	1,258.9	1,313.4	1,361.7	1,441.7
Undergraduate.	1,147.2	1,548.9	1,838.2	1,918.5	1,955.4	2,005.7	2,092.6
Graduate	83.9	157.9	204.9	220.4	233.2	247.2	263.5
First professional	15.9	23.5	25.8	25.9	26.0	26.8	27.3
Hispanic	782.4	1,461.8	1,716.0	1,809.6	1,882.0	1,964.3	2,076.2
Male	353.9	627.1	709.1	745.1	774.6	810.0	861.6
Female.	428.5	834.7	1,006.9	1,064.5	1,107.3	1,154.3	1,214.5
Public.	671.4	1,229.3	1,414.6	1,477.4	1,525.6	1,594.3	1,685.4
Private	111.0	232.5	301.4	332.2	356.4	370.1	390.7
2-year	424.2	843.9	932.6	972.4	981.5	1,014.3	1,067.4
4-year	358.2	617.9	783.4	837.2	900.5	950.0	1,008.7
Undergraduate.	724.6	1,351.0	1,579.6	1,666.9	1,733.6	1,810.1	1,915.9
Graduate	47.2	95.4	119.5	125.8	130.7	135.8	140.9
First professional	10.7	15.4	16.9	17.0	17.7	18.4	19.3
American Indian/ Alaska Native	102.8	151.2	172.7	176.1	176.3	181.1	190.0
Male	43.1	61.4	67.1	68.6	68.4	71.2	74.4
Female.	59.7	89.7	105.6	107.5	107.9	110.0	115.6
Public.	90.4	127.3	144.3	144.4	143.0	145.9	153.3
Private	12.4	23.9	28.3	31.8	33.3	35.2	36.7
2-year	54.9	74.7	82.2	82.2	80.7	100.0	108.6
4-year	47.9	76.5	90.4	93.9	95.6	81.1	81.4
Undergraduate.	95.5	138.5	157.8	160.3	160.4	164.2	171.3
Graduate	6.2	10.3	12.5	13.4	13.4	14.5	16.1
First professional	1.1	2.3	2.3	2.4	2.5	2.5	2.6
Asian/ Pacific Islander	572.4	978.2	1,075.7	1,108.7	1,134.4	1,165.5	1,217.9
Male	294.9	465.9	498.1	511.6	522.0	536.0	562.5
Female.	277.5	512.3	577.6	597.1	612.4	629.5	655.4
Public.	461.0	770.5	845.2	866.1	881.9	903.8	942.5
Private	111.5	207.7	230.5	242.6	252.4	261.7	275.4
2-year	215.2	401.9	425.3	430.7	434.4	442.8	456.4
4-year	357.2	576.3	650.4	678.0	700.0	722.7	761.5
Undergraduate.	500.5	845.5	922.7	949.9	971.4	997.9	1,042.1
Graduate	53.2	95.8	111.7	115.9	118.4	121.9	127.8
First professional	18.7	36.8	41.3	42.9	44.6	45.7	48.0
Nonresident alien . . .	391.5	528.7	591.8	590.2	584.8	595.9	624.5
Male	246.3	297.3	322.7	315.6	309.5	316.1	333.2
Female.	145.2	231.4	269.2	274.6	275.3	279.8	291.2
Public.	260.0	343.1	388.0	371.4	372.8	383.1	401.7
Private	131.4	185.6	203.9	218.8	212.0	212.8	222.8
2-year	67.1	89.0	96.2	90.9	91.8	93.4	95.8
4-year	324.3	439.7	495.6	499.2	493.1	502.5	528.7
Undergraduate.	218.7	288.0	313.0	313.8	314.7	321.0	335.3
Graduate	167.3	232.3	270.4	268.1	262.1	266.4	280.3
First professional	5.4	8.4	8.4	8.2	8.1	8.4	8.8

[1] Data beginning 2000 reflect a new classification of institutions; see footnote 1, Table 269.   [2] Non-Hispanic.

Source: U.S. National Center for Education Statistics, *Digest of Education Statistics*, annual.

174   Education

Table 271. **Degree-Granting Institutions, Number and Enrollment by State: 2006**

[**17,759 represents 17,759,000**. Number of institutions beginning in academic year. Opening fall enrollment of resident and extension students attending full-time or part-time. Excludes students taking courses for credit by mail, radio, or TV, and students in branches of U.S. institutions operated in foreign countries. See Appendix III]

State	Number of institutions [1]	Enrollment (1,000)							Minority enrollment			Nonresident alien
		Total	Male	Female	Public	Private	Full-time	White [2]	Total [3]	Black [2]	Hispanic	
United States..	**4,352**	**17,759**	**7,575**	**10,184**	**13,180**	**4,579**	**10,957**	**11,572**	**5,591**	**2,280**	**1,964**	**596**
Alabama	68	258	107	152	231	28	171	168	84	75	4	6
Alaska.	7	30	12	18	29	1	13	21	8	1	1	1
Arizona	76	567	228	339	331	236	364	360	186	55	91	21
Arkansas	49	147	59	88	131	16	95	110	35	28	3	3
California	416	2,435	1,076	1,358	2,048	387	1,240	1,035	1,325	188	655	75
Colorado	80	308	135	174	232	76	189	232	71	18	36	5
Connecticut	46	177	74	103	112	64	113	127	43	19	15	7
Delaware	10	51	20	31	38	13	33	36	14	10	2	1
District of Columbia	16	110	44	66	6	104	64	51	51	39	5	7
Florida.	184	886	366	520	652	234	505	497	361	159	167	28
Georgia	135	435	176	259	346	89	290	260	163	133	12	13
Hawaii	22	67	28	39	50	17	40	17	44	1	2	6
Idaho	14	78	34	43	59	19	53	69	7	1	4	2
Illinois	177	831	357	473	553	278	486	539	267	118	98	25
Indiana	106	368	163	205	272	96	256	303	52	32	11	13
Iowa	65	239	101	137	151	88	152	204	27	13	8	7
Kansas	60	193	86	107	171	23	115	156	29	12	9	8
Kentucky	71	249	106	142	204	45	153	215	29	22	3	5
Louisiana	84	224	90	134	193	32	163	141	78	65	6	6
Maine	30	66	27	40	48	18	41	61	4	1	1	1
Maryland	57	319	131	189	261	59	173	182	124	89	13	14
Massachusetts . . .	122	452	191	260	192	259	311	325	100	36	29	27
Michigan	105	634	271	363	512	123	369	480	132	87	18	23
Minnesota	112	376	157	219	244	132	234	307	58	29	8	10
Mississippi	42	151	58	93	137	15	116	87	63	59	1	1
Missouri.	128	377	159	218	218	159	229	296	71	47	11	10
Montana	23	48	22	26	43	5	35	40	6	(Z)	1	1
Nebraska.	42	125	56	69	94	30	82	107	14	6	5	3
Nevada	23	112	49	63	102	10	52	70	40	9	17	2
New Hampshire . .	28	71	29	41	42	29	48	63	6	1	2	2
New Jersey	60	386	168	218	308	77	234	228	142	55	53	16
New Mexico	42	132	55	77	122	10	69	56	73	4	55	3
New York.	307	1,160	489	671	636	525	822	695	392	161	133	74
North Carolina . . .	130	496	198	297	406	90	313	331	154	122	14	11
North Dakota	22	50	24	26	43	7	37	43	5	1	1	1
Ohio	207	620	267	353	453	167	424	498	104	76	13	17
Oklahoma	59	206	89	117	178	28	133	145	52	19	8	9
Oregon	60	198	87	111	160	38	121	160	32	5	11	6
Pennsylvania	263	707	306	401	388	319	510	554	129	74	23	24
Rhode Island	14	82	36	46	40	41	60	64	14	5	6	3
South Carolina . . .	66	212	83	130	176	36	144	143	66	59	4	3
South Dakota	24	49	21	28	38	11	32	43	5	1	(Z)	1
Tennessee	105	291	119	171	205	85	209	215	69	57	5	6
Texas	214	1,253	540	713	1,094	159	696	638	567	156	339	48
Utah	36	202	102	100	148	54	121	175	22	3	10	5
Vermont	25	41	19	23	24	17	30	37	3	1	1	1
Virginia	112	456	193	263	358	98	278	308	137	90	18	12
Washington	76	348	151	197	297	51	215	262	76	15	21	10
West Virginia	44	101	44	57	87	14	75	90	8	5	1	2
Wisconsin	73	340	147	193	272	68	217	291	42	18	10	7
Wyoming	10	35	16	19	33	2	19	31	3	(Z)	1	1
U.S. military [4] . .	5	12	10	2	12	(X)	12	10	2	1	1	(Z)

X Not applicable.   Z Fewer than 500.   [1] Branch campuses counted as separate institutions.   [2] Non-Hispanic.
[3] Includes other races not shown separately.   [4] Service schools.

Source: U.S. National Center for Education Statistics, *Digest of Education Statistics*, annual.

Education 175

Table 272. **College Enrollment by Sex, Age, Race, and Hispanic Origin: 1980 to 2007**

[In thousands (11,387 represents 11,387,000). As of October for the civilian noninstitutional population, 14 years old and over. Based on the Current Population Survey; see text, Section 1 and Appendix III]

Characteristic	1980	1990 [1]	1995	2000	2001	2002	2003	2004	2005	2006	2007
Total [2]	11,387	13,621	14,715	15,314	15,873	16,497	16,638	17,383	17,472	17,020	17,770
Male [3]	5,430	6,192	6,703	6,682	6,875	7,240	7,318	7,575	7,539	7,427	7,749
18 to 24 years	3,604	3,922	4,089	4,342	4,437	4,629	4,697	4,866	4,972	4,874	5,156
25 to 34 years	1,325	1,412	1,561	1,361	1,476	1,460	1,590	1,604	1,486	1,571	1,625
35 years old and over ..	405	772	985	918	908	1,071	970	1,033	1,019	982	968
Female [3]	5,957	7,429	8,013	8,631	8,998	9,258	9,319	9,808	9,933	9,593	10,021
18 to 24 years	3,625	4,042	4,452	5,109	5,192	5,404	5,667	5,742	5,859	5,712	6,004
25 to 34 years	1,378	1,749	1,788	1,846	1,946	1,941	1,904	2,091	2,115	2,087	2,212
35 years old and over ..	802	1,546	1,684	1,589	1,776	1,797	1,660	1,850	1,838	1,793	1,804
White [3,4]	9,925	11,488	12,021	11,999	12,208	12,781	12,870	13,381	13,467	13,112	13,693
18 to 24 years	6,334	6,635	7,011	7,566	7,548	7,921	8,150	8,354	8,499	8,298	8,780
25 to 34 years	2,328	2,698	2,686	2,339	2,469	2,515	2,545	2,748	2,647	2,725	2,769
35 years old and over ..	1,051	2,023	2,208	1,978	2,103	2,236	2,075	2,143	2,206	2,090	2,144
Male	4,804	5,235	5,535	5,311	5,383	5,719	5,714	5,944	5,844	5,772	5,989
Female	5,121	6,253	6,486	6,689	6,826	7,062	7,155	7,438	7,624	7,340	7,705
Black [3,4]	1,163	1,393	1,772	2,164	2,230	2,278	2,144	2,301	2,297	2,304	2,473
18 to 24 years	688	894	988	1,216	1,206	1,227	1,225	1,238	1,229	1,321	1,395
25 to 34 years	289	258	426	567	562	542	503	522	520	502	629
35 years old and over ..	156	207	334	361	429	454	388	502	448	480	449
Male	476	587	710	815	781	802	798	776	864	886	1,006
Female	686	807	1,062	1,349	1,449	1,476	1,346	1,525	1,435	1,418	1,468
Hispanic origin [3,5]	443	748	1,207	1,426	1,700	1,656	1,714	1,975	1,942	1,914	2,131
18 to 24 years	315	435	745	899	1,035	979	1,115	1,223	1,216	1,182	1,375
25 to 34 years	118	168	250	309	392	414	380	460	438	461	487
35 years old and over ..	(NA)	130	193	195	260	249	207	271	257	271	269
Male	222	364	568	619	731	705	703	852	804	789	864
Female	221	384	639	807	969	951	1,011	1,123	1,139	1,125	1,267

NA Not available.   [1] Beginning 1990, based on a revised edit and tabulation package.   [2] Includes other races not shown separately.   [3] Includes persons 14 to 17 years old not shown separately.   [4] Beginning 2003, persons who selected this race group only. See footnote 2, Table 224.   [5] Persons of Hispanic origin may be any race.

Source: U.S. Census Bureau, *Current Population Reports*, PPL-148; and earlier PPL and P-20 reports. See <http://www.census.gov/population/www/socdemo/school.html>.

Table 273. **Foreign (Nonimmigrant) Student Enrollment in College: 1980 to 2008**

[In thousands (286 represents 286,000). For fall of the previous year]

Region of origin	1980	1990	1995	1997	1998	1999	2000	2001	2002	2003	2004	2005	2006	2007	2008
All regions ...	286	387	453	458	481	491	515	548	583	586	573	565	565	583	624
Africa	36	25	21	22	23	26	30	34	38	40	38	36	36	36	36
Nigeria	16	4	2	2	2	3	4	4	4	6	6	6	6	6	6
Asia [1,2]	165	245	292	291	308	308	315	339	363	367	356	356	346	367	405
China [3]	1	33	39	43	47	51	54	60	63	65	62	63	63	68	81
Taiwan [3]	18	31	36	30	31	31	29	29	29	28	26	26	28	29	29
Hong Kong	10	11	13	11	10	9	8	8	8	8	7	7	8	8	8
India..........	9	26	34	31	34	37	42	55	67	75	80	80	77	84	95
Indonesia	2	9	12	12	13	12	11	12	12	10	9	8	8	7	8
Iran	51	7	3	2	2	2	2	2	2	2	2	2	2	3	3
Japan..........	12	30	45	46	47	46	47	46	47	46	41	42	39	35	34
Malaysia	4	14	14	15	15	12	9	8	7	7	6	6	6	5	5
Saudi Arabia ...	10	4	4	4	5	5	5	5	6	4	4	3	3	8	10
South Korea	5	22	34	37	43	39	41	46	49	52	52	53	59	62	69
Thailand	7	7	11	13	15	12	11	11	12	10	9	9	9	9	9
Europe [4]	23	46	65	68	72	74	78	81	82	78	74	72	85	83	84
Latin America [1,5] ...	42	48	47	50	51	55	62	64	68	69	66	68	65	65	64
Mexico	6	7	9	9	10	10	11	11	13	13	13	13	14	14	15
Venezuela	10	3	4	5	5	5	5	5	6	5	6	5	5	4	4
North America	16	19	23	24	23	23	24	26	27	27	28	29	29	29	29
Canada........	15	18	23	23	22	23	24	25	27	27	27	28	28	28	29
Oceania	4	4	4	4	4	4	5	5	5	5	5	4	5	4	5

[1] Includes countries not shown separately.   [2] Beginning 2006, excludes Cyprus and Turkey.   [3] With the establishment of diplomatic relations with China on January 1, 1979, the U.S. government recognized the People's Republic of China as the sole legal government of China and acknowledged the Chinese position that there is only one China and that Taiwan is part of China.   [4] Beginning 2006, includes Cyprus and Turkey.   [5] Includes Mexico, Central America, Caribbean, and South America.

Source: Institute of International Education, New York, NY, *Open Doors Report on International Educational Exchange*, annual (copyright).

U.S. Census Bureau, *Statistical Abstract of the United States: 2010*

Table 274. College Enrollment—Summary by Sex, Race, and Hispanic Origin: 2007

[In thousands (17,956 represents 17,956,000), except percent. As of October. Covers civilian noninstitutional population 15 years old and over enrolled in colleges and graduate schools. Based on Current Population Survey. See text, Section 1 and Appendix III]

Characteristic	Total			Race and Hispanic origin				
				White [2]				
	Number [1]	Male	Female	Total	Non-Hispanic	Black [2]	Asian [2]	Hispanic [3]
Total enrollment	17,956	7,826	10,130	13,835	11,867	2,501	1,103	2,172
15 to 17 years old	186	76	109	141	104	27	10	41
18 to 19 years old	4,075	1,903	2,172	3,242	2,739	492	201	559
20 to 21 years old	3,794	1,729	2,065	3,053	2,677	436	204	412
22 to 24 years old	3,292	1,524	1,768	2,485	2,117	468	252	404
25 to 29 years old	2,496	1,029	1,466	1,817	1,509	400	206	332
30 to 34 years old	1,342	596	746	952	816	229	123	155
35 years old and over	2,772	968	1,804	2,144	1,904	449	105	269
Type of school:								
2-year	4,814	2,060	2,753	3,709	2,970	735	211	812
15 to 19 years old	1,496	703	793	1,228	984	172	61	263
20 to 24 years old	1,630	728	902	1,215	983	265	88	257
25 years old and over. . .	1,687	629	1,058	1,266	1,003	297	62	291
4-year	9,551	4,344	5,206	7,419	6,418	1,326	520	1,111
15 to 19 years old	2,740	1,264	1,476	2,138	1,841	344	148	337
20 to 24 years old	4,615	2,196	2,419	3,679	3,211	552	272	508
25 years old and over. . .	2,195	884	1,312	1,601	1,367	430	100	266
Graduate school	3,591	1,420	2,171	2,707	2,479	440	373	250
15 to 24 years old	864	341	524	661	618	90	99	51
25 to 34 years old	1,560	663	897	1,158	1,032	171	209	132
35 years old and over. . .	1,166	417	749	888	828	179	65	67
Public	14,072	6,166	7,906	10,856	9,137	1,968	841	1,888
2-year	4,417	1,863	2,555	3,405	2,712	661	202	753
4-year	7,393	3,434	3,959	5,712	4,855	1,038	415	955
Graduate	2,261	869	1,392	1,739	1,570	269	224	179
Percent of students:								
Employed full-time.	18.4	16.8	20.0	18.5	18.6	20.6	14.9	17.7
Employed part-time	24.1	22.6	25.4	26.0	27.6	15.8	18.9	19.6

[1] Includes other races not shown separately. [2] For persons who selected this race group only. See footnote 2, Table 224. [3] Persons of Hispanic origin may be any race.

Source: U.S. Census Bureau, unpublished data. See <http://www.census.gov/population/www/socdemo/school.html>.

Table 275. Higher Education Enrollments in Languages Other Than English: 1970 to 2006

[As of fall (1,111.5 represents 1,111,500). For credit enrollment]

Enrollment	1970	1980	1983	1986	1990	1995	1998	2002	2006
Registrations [1] (1,000)	1,111.5	924.8	966.0	1,003.2	1,184.1	1,138.8	1,193.8	1,397.3	1,577.8
By selected language (1,000):									
Spanish	389.2	379.4	386.2	411.3	533.9	606.3	656.6	746.3	823.0
French	359.3	248.4	270.1	275.3	272.5	205.4	199.1	202.0	206.4
German	202.6	126.9	128.2	121.0	133.3	96.3	89.0	91.1	94.3
Italian	34.2	34.8	38.7	40.9	49.7	43.8	49.3	63.9	78.4
American Sign Language	(X)	(X)	(X)	(X)	1.6	4.3	11.4	60.8	78.8
Japanese	6.6	11.5	16.1	23.5	45.7	44.7	43.1	52.2	66.6
Chinese	6.2	11.4	13.2	16.9	19.5	26.5	28.5	34.2	51.6
Latin.	27.6	25.0	24.2	25.0	28.2	25.9	26.1	29.8	32.2
Russian	36.2	24.0	30.4	34.0	44.6	24.7	23.8	23.9	24.8
Hebrew.	16.6	19.4	18.2	15.6	13.0	13.1	15.8	22.8	23.8
Ancient Greek	16.7	22.1	19.4	17.6	16.4	16.3	16.4	20.4	22.8
Arabic.	1.3	3.5	3.4	3.4	3.5	4.4	5.5	10.6	24.0
Portuguese	5.1	4.9	4.4	5.1	6.2	6.5	6.9	8.4	10.3
Korean	0.1	0.4	0.7	0.9	2.3	3.3	4.5	5.2	7.1
Index (1965 = 100).	107.3	89.3	93.2	96.8	114.3	109.9	115.2	134.9	152.3

X Not applicable. [1] Includes other languages not shown separately.

Source: Furman, Nelly, David Goldberg, and Natalia Lusin. Enrollments in Languages Other Than English in United States Institutions of Higher Education, Fall 2006. Modern Language Association, 13 November 2007 (copyright). For 1968 to 2002, consult prior Association of Departments of Foreign Languages (ADFL) Bulletins.

Education 177

Table 276. College Freshmen—Summary Characteristics: 1980 to 2008

[In percent, except as indicated (24.5 represents $24,500). As of fall for first-time full-time freshmen in 4-year colleges and universities. Based on sample survey and subject to sampling error; see source]

Characteristic	1980	1985	1990	1995	2000	2005	2006	2007	2008
Sex: Male	48.8	48.9	46.9	45.6	45.2	45.0	45.1	45.2	45.4
Female	51.2	51.1	53.1	54.4	54.8	55.0	54.9	54.8	54.6
Applied to more than three colleges	31.5	35.4	42.9	44.4	50.5	55.4	56.5	56.5	60.1
Average grade in high school:									
A– to A+	26.6	28.7	29.4	36.1	42.9	46.6	46.0	45.9	47.2
B– to B+	58.2	57.1	57.0	54.2	50.5	48.0	49.4	49.0	48.0
C to C+	14.9	14.0	13.4	9.6	6.5	5.4	4.6	5.0	4.7
D	0.2	0.2	0.2	0.1	0.1	0.1	0.1	0.1	0.1
Political orientation:									
Liberal	21.0	22.4	24.6	22.9	24.8	27.1	28.4	29.3	31.0
Middle of the road	57.0	53.1	51.7	51.3	51.9	45.0	43.3	43.4	43.3
Conservative	19.0	21.3	20.6	21.8	18.9	22.6	23.9	23.1	20.7
Probable field of study:									
Arts and humanities	10.5	10.1	10.5	11.2	12.1	12.8	13.1	12.8	13.5
Biological sciences	4.5	4.5	4.9	8.3	6.6	7.6	8.3	8.6	9.3
Business	21.2	24.6	21.1	15.4	16.7	17.4	17.9	17.7	16.8
Education	8.4	6.9	10.3	10.1	11.0	9.9	9.5	9.2	8.2
Engineering	11.2	11.0	9.7	8.1	8.7	8.3	8.0	7.5	9.4
Physical science	3.2	3.2	2.8	3.1	2.6	3.1	3.1	3.2	3.2
Social science	8.2	9.4	11.0	9.9	10.0	10.7	11.2	11.1	11.5
Professional	15.5	13.1	13.0	16.5	11.6	14.6	13.0	14.5	13.8
Technical	3.1	2.4	1.1	1.2	2.1	1.2	1.1	1.0	1.0
Data processing/computer programming	1.7	1.7	0.7	0.8	1.5	0.5	0.5	0.6	0.5
Other [1]	14.0	15.1	15.8	16.0	17.9	14.1	14.2	14.2	13.2
Communications	2.4	2.8	2.9	1.8	2.7	2.0	2.2	1.8	1.8
Computer science	2.6	2.4	1.7	2.2	3.7	1.1	1.1	1.1	1.0
Personal objectives—very important or essential:									
Being very well off financially	62.5	69.2	72.3	72.8	73.4	74.5	73.4	74.4	76.8
Developing a meaningful philosophy of life	62.5	46.9	45.9	45.4	42.4	45.0	46.3	49.2	51.4
Keeping up to date with political affairs	45.2	(NA)	46.6	32.3	28.1	36.4	37.2	37.2	39.5
Median family income ($1,000)	24.5	37.3	46.6	54.8	64.4	73.2	76.2	77.9	77.5

NA Not available.   [1] Includes other fields not shown separately.

Source: The Higher Education Research Institute, University of California, Los Angeles, CA, *The American Freshman: National Norms,* annual.

Table 277. Residence and Migration of College Freshmen by State: 2006

[As of Fall. Includes first-time postsecondary students who had graduated from high school in the previous 12 months and were enrolled at public and private not-for-profit 4-year degree-granting institutions that participated in Title IV federal financial aid programs. Excludes respondents for whom state residence and/or migration are unknown. Also excludes U.S. Service Academies (Air Force Academy, Coast Guard Academy, Merchant Marine Academy, Military Academy, and Naval Academy)]

State	Total freshmen enrollment in institutions located in the state	Percentage of all enrolled freshmen who are enrolled in their home state	Percentage of freshmen state residents who are attending in-state [1]	State	Total freshmen enrollment in institutions located in the state	Percentage of all enrolled freshmen who are enrolled in their home state	Percentage of freshmen state residents who are attending in-state [1]
U.S.	1,326,915	73.3	74.6	MO	26,915	71.1	77.4
AL	21,739	68.3	86.7	MT	5,276	67.4	74.6
AK	2,178	89.3	58.7	NE	10,637	75.8	79.2
AZ	17,521	65.5	79.6	NV	6,494	85.0	75.3
AR	14,073	74.6	87.6	NH	8,808	37.6	41.8
CA	107,247	89.1	83.5	NJ	23,684	84.8	40.1
CO	22,361	74.1	73.8	NM	6,729	83.7	72.5
CT	17,760	53.2	41.2	NY	101,299	72.6	72.9
DE	5,100	37.7	51.7	NC	44,324	72.0	87.8
DC	8,776	7.2	28.5	ND	5,496	51.2	73.1
FL	60,223	80.0	83.4	OH	61,401	81.5	81.3
GA	37,652	78.8	77.3	OK	17,339	75.5	86.9
HI	3,201	65.4	44.9	OR	12,709	65.3	69.6
ID	7,156	61.7	73.6	PA	81,766	65.7	78.5
IL	48,271	79.9	64.5	RI	11,510	25.8	54.2
IN	42,857	70.2	86.9	SC	20,413	68.7	85.9
IA	17,922	60.9	79.8	SD	5,470	66.8	74.6
KS	13,691	76.0	79.1	TN	26,822	73.4	80.3
KY	20,936	75.4	86.5	TX	79,356	91.8	83.2
LA	22,520	85.2	89.4	UT	13,928	63.8	89.9
ME	7,371	61.1	57.9	VT	5,905	28.0	41.8
MD	19,171	64.6	46.4	VA	36,672	69.9	73.1
MA	47,947	49.9	58.8	WA	19,000	77.2	69.4
MI	48,470	86.7	86.5	WV	11,078	61.1	87.6
MN	25,155	72.0	62.8	WI	31,979	73.9	77.1
MS	8,808	66.6	82.0	WY	1,495	60.1	54.9

[1] Students residing in a particular state when admitted to an institution anywhere, either in their home state or another state.

Source: U.S. Department of Education, National Center for Education Statistics, Fall 2006 Integrated Postsecondary Education Data System (IPEDS), Spring 2007.

Table 278. Average Total Price of Attendance of Undergraduate Education: 2007 to 2008

[In dollars. Excludes students attending more than one institution. Price of attendance includes tuition and fees, books and supplies, room and board, transportation, and personal and other expenses allowed for federal cost of attendance budgets. Based on the 2007–2008 National Postsecondary Student-Aid Study; see source for details. Includes Puerto Rico. See also Appendix III]

| | | Type of institution | | | | | |
| Student characteristic | All institu- tions [1] | Public 2-year | Public 4-year | | Private not-for-profit 4-year | | Private for-profit |
			Non- doctorate	Doctor- ate	Non- doctorate	Doctor- ate	
Total	**14,006**	**7,033**	**12,657**	**16,615**	**25,194**	**31,628**	**20,636**
Age: [2]							
18 years or younger.	17,065	12,630	16,664	19,888	32,586	38,311	19,868
19 to 23 years	16,059	6,830	10,128	12,513	17,861	22,540	20,376
24 to 29 years	11,551	8,035	11,188	13,833	17,823	21,294	20,275
30 to 39 years	10,994	3,854	5,739	7,319	8,446	10,419	21,305
40 years or older.	9,269	8,268	14,912	18,501	31,809	37,581	21,265
Sex:							
Male.	13,957	7,406	13,778	17,661	30,099	35,206	21,765
Female	14,044	6,856	10,701	13,005	17,458	20,772	20,133
Race:							
One race:							
White.	14,446	6,546	9,690	12,452	15,561	17,839	20,888
Black or African American	13,235	5,992	9,062	10,623	14,722	14,452	20,141
Asian.	15,122	7,121	12,668	16,486	25,512	31,163	22,203
American Indian/Alaska Native	12,150	7,013	13,170	16,707	26,717	32,236	25,013
Native Hawaiian or other Pacific Islander . . .	12,904	6,974	12,824	15,891	21,412	26,817	23,122
Other race	12,788	6,990	10,511	15,513	19,548	27,808	24,076
More than one race	15,077	7,313	13,285	18,271	29,162	36,973	23,245
Hispanic or Latino [3]	12,419	6,920	12,644	16,757	24,765	32,182	19,753
Attendance pattern:							
Full-time, full-year.	22,368	7,330	10,436	15,078	27,614	(S)	28,638
Full-time, part-year.	12,227	6,718	12,988	16,878	18,659	40,521	16,653
Part-time, full-year.	10,655	6,759	10,879	15,650	16,534	(S)	19,259
Part-time, part-year	5,231	7,495	13,028	17,256	28,172	34,460	11,810

S Data do not meet publication standards. [1] Includes public less-than-2-year and private not-for-profit less-than-4-year. [2] As of 31 December 2007. [3] Persons of Hispanic origin may be any race.

Source: U.S. National Center for Education Statistics, "Student Financial Aid Estimates for 2007–08," NCES 2009-166 (published 14 April 2009); <http://nces.ed.gov/surveys/npsas/>.

Table 279. Higher Education Price Indexes: 2002 to 2008

[1983 = 100. For years ending June 30. The Higher Education Price Index (HEPI), calculated for the July–June academic fiscal year, reflects prices paid by colleges and universities for the following eight cost factors: faculty salaries, administrative salaries, clerical and service employees, fringe benefits, miscellaneous services, supplies and materials, and utilities. Minus sign (–) indicates decrease]

| Item and year | Index, total | Personnel compensation | | | | | Contracted services, supplies, and equipment | | |
		Faculty salaries	Adminis- trative salaries	Clerical salaries	Service employee salaries	Fringe benefits	Miscella- neous services	Supplies and materials	Utilities
INDEXES									
2002	212.7	222.7	236.4	205.4	189.6	277.1	205.8	128.2	118.1
2003	223.5	229.4	255.7	211.1	193.9	292.3	209.5	132.2	157.6
2004	231.7	234.2	263.3	217.1	197.6	312.8	216.4	135.6	176.4
2005	240.8	240.7	274.0	223.4	201.4	327.2	222.7	145.5	200.2
2006	253.1	248.2	287.7	229.5	205.5	343.7	228.8	158.1	255.7
2007	260.3	257.6	299.2	237.7	213.6	360.8	238.3	165.3	220.6
2008	273.2	268.1	314.0	245.0	220.4	380.7	246.5	180.0	252.0
ANNUAL PERCENT CHANGE [1]									
2002	3.0	3.8	3.1	3.9	3.8	5.9	3.0	–1.7	–16.0
2003	5.1	3.0	8.2	2.8	2.3	5.5	1.8	3.1	33.5
2004	3.7	2.1	3.0	2.8	1.9	7.0	3.3	2.6	11.9
2005	3.9	2.8	4.1	2.9	1.9	4.6	2.9	7.3	13.5
2006	5.1	3.1	5.0	2.7	2.0	5.0	2.7	8.7	27.7
2007	2.8	3.8	4.0	3.6	4.0	5.0	4.2	4.5	–13.7
2008	5.0	4.1	5.0	3.1	3.2	5.5	3.4	8.9	14.2

[1] Percent change from the immediate prior year.

Source: The Commonfund Institute, Wilton, CT, (copyright); <http://www.commonfund.org>.

Table 280. Federal Student Financial Assistance: 1995 to 2009

[For award years July 1 of year shown to the following June 30 (35,477 represents $35,477,000,000). Funds utilized exclude operating costs, etc., and represent funds given to students]

Type of assistance	1995	2000	2005	2006	2007	2008, est.	2009, est.
FUNDS UTILIZED (mil. dol.)							
Total.	35,477	44,007	72,634	77,191	82,817	90,706	94,286
Federal Pell Grants	5,472	7,956	12,693	12,817	14,381	16,428	18,180
Academic Competitiveness Grants	(X)	(X)	(X)	340	350	440	490
SMART[1] Grants	(X)	(X)	(X)	310	230	260	270
Federal Supplemental Educational Opportunity Grant	764	907	1,084	1,080	1,068	959	(X)
Federal Work-Study	764	939	1,050	1,042	1,063	1,171	1,171
Federal Perkins Loan	1,029	1,144	1,593	1,618	1,383	1,103	(X)
Federal Direct Student Loan (FDSL)	8,296	10,348	12,930	12,677	13,022	14,103	14,867
Federal Family Education Loans (FFEL)	19,152	22,712	43,284	47,307	51,320	56,242	59,308
NUMBER OF AWARDS (1,000)							
Total.	13,667	15,043	21,317	22,304	23,036	23,858	22,947
Federal Pell Grants	3,612	3,899	5,167	5,165	5,428	5,578	5,764
Academic Competitiveness Grants	(X)	(X)	(X)	400	456	559	643
SMART[1] Grants	(X)	(X)	(X)	80	72	79	85
Federal Supplemental Educational Opportunity Grant	1,083	1,175	1,419	1,417	1,450	1,255	(X)
Federal Work-Study	702	713	710	694	697	792	792
Federal Perkins Loan	688	639	727	725	650	503	(X)
Federal Direct Student Loan (FDSL)	2,339	2,739	2,971	2,841	2,764	2,857	2,961
Federal Family Education Loans (FFEL)	5,243	5,878	10,323	10,982	11,519	12,235	12,702
AVERAGE AWARD (dol.)							
Total.	2,596	2,925	3,407	3,461	3,595	3,802	4,109
Federal Pell Grants	1,515	2,041	2,456	2,482	2,650	2,945	3,154
Academic Competitiveness Grants/SMART[2] Grants . .	(X)	(X)	(X)	850	768	787	762
SMART[1] Grants	(X)	(X)	(X)	3,875	3,194	3,291	3,176
Federal Supplemental Educational Opportunity Grant	705	772	764	762	736	764	(X)
Federal Work-Study	1,088	1,318	1,478	1,500	1,524	1,478	1,478
Federal Perkins Loan	1,496	1,790	2,190	2,231	2,125	2,190	(X)
Federal Direct Student Loan (FDSL)	3,547	3,778	4,352	4,462	4,711	4,936	5,021
Federal Family Education Loans (FFEL)	3,653	3,864	4,193	4,308	3,941	4,597	4,669
COHORT DEFAULT RATE [2]							
Federal Perkins Loan	12.6	9.9	8.1	7.8	8.3	(NA)	(NA)

NA Not available.   X Not applicable.   [1] National Science and Mathematics Access to Retain Talent.   [2] As of June 30. Represents the percent of borrowers entering repayment status in year shown who defaulted in the following year.
Source: U.S. Dept. of Education, Office of Postsecondary Education, unpublished data.

Table 281. State and Local Financial Support for Higher Education by State: 2005 to 2008

[For 2007–2008 fiscal year, except as indicated (10,475.1 represents 10,475,100). Data for the 50 states]

State	2007–2008 FTE enrollment [1] (1,000)	2007–2008 Educational appropriations per FTE [2] (dol.)	Appropriations for higher ed. as a percent of state and local tax revenue 2005–2006 [3]	State	2007–2008 FTE enrollment [1] (1,000)	2007–2008 Educational appropriations per FTE [2] (dol.)	Appropriations for higher ed. as a percent of state and local tax revenue 2005–2006 [3]
Total ...	10,475.1	7,059	6.0	MO	179.4	6,032	5.2
				MT	35.6	4,940	5.7
AL	186.3	7,586	11.0	NE	75.5	7,622	8.3
AK	18.7	14,601	6.9	NV	63.3	9,102	6.2
AZ	223.9	7,614	5.4	NH	34.1	3,541	2.6
AR	107.4	6,481	8.6	NJ	238.0	7,960	4.3
CA	1,731.8	7,177	6.3	NM	85.2	9,598	12.0
CO	161.3	4,213	3.7	NY	526.5	8,871	4.1
CT	77.1	10,762	4.2	NC	357.6	8,949	10.2
DE	31.6	7,226	6.0	ND	35.8	5,579	9.1
FL	537.9	6,483	5.2	OH	391.7	4,998	5.0
GA	310.8	8,198	8.5	OK	131.2	7,164	7.9
HI	35.5	13,150	7.4	OR	129.3	5,647	5.0
ID	44.0	8,685	8.1	PA	339.0	5,886	4.2
IL	391.4	7,585	5.1	RI	30.1	6,089	4.2
IN	229.3	5,430	6.2	SC	144.7	6,585	8.5
IA	115.0	6,372	7.6	SD	29.6	5,018	7.5
KS	129.7	6,125	7.4	TN	169.9	7,371	7.8
KY	142.4	7,643	8.9	TX	804.9	6,962	7.5
LA	165.8	7,748	8.2	UT	102.4	7,116	8.3
ME	35.5	6,804	4.2	VT	20.0	3,167	3.0
MD	206.2	7,646	4.9	VA	281.9	5,805	5.3
MA	144.6	8,705	4.0	WA	221.3	7,086	6.1
MI	388.7	5,778	5.6	WV	73.5	5,892	7.1
MN	200.2	6,248	6.1	WI	219.0	6,810	5.1
MS	117.6	6,534	9.4	WY	23.1	15,151	9.4

[1] Full-time equivalent. Includes degree enrollment and enrollment in public postsecondary programs resulting in a certificate or other formal recognition. Includes summer sessions. Excludes medical enrollments.   [2] State and local appropriations for general operating expenses of public postsecondary education. Includes state-funded financial aid to students attending in-state public institutions. Excludes sums for research, agricultural extension, and teaching hospitals and medical schools.   [3] Includes state and local appropriations for public and independent postsecondary education (including sums for research, agricultural extension, and teaching hospitals and medical schools).
Source: State Higher Education Executive Officers, Boulder, CO (copyright); <http://www.sheeo.org>.

180   Education

Table 282. Institutions of Higher Education—Charges: 1985 to 2008

[In dollars. Estimated. **For the entire academic year ending in year shown.** Figures are average charges per full-time equivalent student. Room and board are based on full-time students]

Academic control and year	Tuition and required fees [1]				Board rates [2]				Dormitory charges			
	All institutions	2-yr. colleges	4-yr. colleges	Other 4-yr. schools	All institutions	2-yr. colleges	4-yr. colleges	Other 4-yr. schools	All institutions	2-yr. colleges	4-yr. colleges	Other 4-yr. schools
Public:												
1985	971	584	1,386	1,117	1,241	1,302	1,276	1,201	1,196	921	1,237	1,200
1990	1,356	756	2,035	1,608	1,635	1,581	1,728	1,561	1,513	962	1,561	1,554
1995	2,057	1,192	2,977	2,499	1,949	1,712	2,108	1,866	1,959	1,232	1,992	2,044
2000	2,506	1,338	3,768	3,091	2,364	1,834	2,628	2,239	2,440	1,549	2,516	2,521
2003	2,903	1,483	4,686	3,668	2,669	2,164	2,895	2,580	2,930	1,954	3,023	3,032
2004	3,319	1,702	5,363	4,141	2,823	2,233	3,084	2,724	3,107	2,086	3,232	3,198
2005	3,629	1,849	5,939	4,512	2,931	2,353	3,222	2,809	3,304	2,174	3,427	3,413
2006	3,874	1,935	6,399	4,765	3,035	2,306	3,372	2,899	3,545	2,251	3,654	3,672
2007	4,102	2,018	6,842	5,020	3,191	2,390	3,498	3,083	3,757	2,407	3,875	3,881
2008, prel.	4,307	2,063	7,171	5,291	3,329	2,408	3,669	3,217	3,941	2,495	4,076	4,069
Private:												
1985	5,315	3,485	6,843	5,135	1,462	1,294	1,647	1,405	1,426	1,424	1,753	1,309
1990	8,147	5,196	10,348	7,778	1,948	1,811	2,339	1,823	1,923	1,663	2,411	1,774
1995	11,111	6,914	14,537	10,653	2,509	2,023	3,035	2,362	2,587	2,233	3,469	2,347
2000	14,081	8,235	19,307	13,361	2,882	2,922	3,157	2,790	3,224	2,808	4,070	2,976
2003	16,383	10,651	22,716	15,416	3,206	3,870	3,602	3,071	3,752	3,232	4,724	3,478
2004	17,327	11,546	24,128	16,298	3,364	4,432	3,778	3,222	3,945	3,581	4,979	3,647
2005	18,154	12,122	25,643	17,050	3,485	3,728	3,855	3,370	4,171	4,243	5,263	3,854
2006	18,862	12,450	26,954	17,702	3,647	4,726	4,039	3,517	4,380	3,994	5,517	4,063
2007	20,048	12,708	28,580	18,848	3,785	3,429	4,166	3,672	4,606	4,613	5,691	4,302
2008, prel.	21,113	13,172	30,260	19,798	3,994	4,089	4,373	3,877	4,808	4,812	6,007	4,467

[1] For in-state students. [2] Beginning 1990, rates reflect 20 meals per week, rather than meals served 7 days a week.

Source: U.S. National Center for Education Statistics, *Digest of Education Statistics,* annual.

Table 283. Voluntary Financial Support of Higher Education: 1990 to 2008

[For school years ending in years shown (**9,800 represents $9,800,000,000**). Voluntary support, as defined in Gift Reporting Standards, excludes income from endowment and other invested funds as well as all support received from federal, state, and local governments and their agencies and contract research]

Item	Unit	1990	1995	2000	2004	2005	2006	2007	2008
Estimated support, total	Mil. dol.	9,800	12,750	23,200	24,400	25,600	28,000	29,750	31,600
Individuals	Mil. dol.	4,770	6,540	12,220	11,000	12,100	14,100	13,920	14,820
Alumni	Mil. dol.	2,540	3,600	6,800	6,700	7,100	8,400	8,270	8,700
Business corporations	Mil. dol.	2,170	2,560	4,150	4,400	4,400	4,600	4,800	4,900
Foundations	Mil. dol.	1,920	2,460	5,080	6,200	7,000	7,100	8,500	9,100
Fundraising consortia and other organizations	Mil. dol.	700	940	1,380	1,550	1,730	1,825	2,150	2,400
Religious organizations	Mil. dol.	240	250	370	350	370	375	380	380
Current operations	Mil. dol.	5,440	7,230	11,270	13,600	14,200	15,000	16,100	17,070
Capital purposes	Mil. dol.	4,360	5,520	11,930	10,800	11,400	13,000	13,650	14,530
Support per student	Dollars	724	893	1,568	1,444	1,482	1,614	1,684	1,760
In 2008 dollars	Dollars	1,192	1,261	1,961	1,646	1,634	1,710	1,748	1,760
Expenditures, higher education	Bil. dol.	134.7	183.0	236.8	316.8	335.0	356.0	373.0	394.8
Expenditures per student	Dollars	9,946	12,814	16,008	18,743	19,396	20,358	21,107	21,987
In 2008 dollars	Dollars	16,384	18,103	20,015	21,362	21,382	21,742	21,917	21,987
Institutions reporting support	Number	1,056	1,086	945	971	997	1,014	1,023	1,052
Total support reported	Mil. dol.	8,214	10,992	19,419	19,630	20,953	23,475	25,247	27,323
Private 4-year institutions	Mil. dol.	5,072	6,500	11,047	10,695	11,011	12,857	13,675	14,296
Public 4-year institutions	Mil. dol.	3,056	4,382	8,254	8,802	9,780	10,421	11,321	12,766
2-year colleges	Mil. dol.	85	110	117	133	163	197	251	261

Source: Council for Aid to Education, New York, NY, *Voluntary Support of Education,* annual.

Table 284. Average Salaries for College Faculty Members: 2007 to 2009

[In thousands of dollars (**71.4 represents $71,400**). **For academic year ending in year shown.** Figures are for 9 months teaching for full-time faculty members in 2-year and 4-year institutions with ranks. Fringe benefits averaged in 2007, $19,746 in public institutions and $23,040 in private institutions; in 2008, $20,178 in public institutions and $24,193 in private institutions; and in 2009, $21,691 in public institutions and $25,374 in private institutions]

Type of control and academic rank	2007	2008	2009	Type of control and academic rank	2007	2008	2009
Public: All ranks	71.4	73.2	77.0	Private: [1] All ranks	84.2	88.2	92.3
Professor	95.6	98.3	104.5	Professor	116.2	122.2	128.3
Associate professor	69.2	72.2	75.2	Associate professor	75.7	79.2	82.9
Assistant professor	58.5	60.8	63.4	Assistant professor	62.9	65.8	69.0
Instructor	41.8	43.4	44.7	Instructor	45.6	49.9	51.6

[1] Excludes church-related colleges and universities.

Source: American Association of University Professors, Washington, DC, *AAUP Annual Report on the Economic Status of the Profession.*

Education 181

Table 285. Employees in Higher Education Institutions by Sex and Occupation: 1995 to 2007

[In thousands (2,662.1 represents 2,662,100). As of fall. Based on complete census taken every other year; see source]

Year and status	Total	Professional staff									Nonprofessional staff, total
		Total	Executive, administrative, and managerial		Faculty [1]		Research/ instruction assistants		Other		
			Male	Female	Male	Female	Male	Female	Male	Female	
1995, total	2,662.1	1,744.9	82.1	65.3	562.9	368.8	124.0	91.9	177.2	272.7	917.2
Full-time	1,801.4	1,066.5	79.2	61.8	360.2	190.7	–	–	151.5	223.2	734.9
Part-time	860.7	678.4	2.9	3.6	202.7	178.1	124.0	91.9	25.6	49.5	182.3
2005, total [2] . . .	3,379.1	2,459.9	95.2	101.1	714.5	576.0	167.5	149.6	262.8	393.2	919.2
Full-time	2,179.9	1,432.1	92.9	97.2	401.5	274.1	–	–	231.4	335.0	747.8
Part-time	1,199.2	1,027.8	2.4	3.9	312.9	301.9	167.5	149.6	31.4	58.2	171.4
2007, total	3,561.4	2,629.4	102.3	115.3	743.8	627.6	173.1	155.9	282.9	428.6	932.0
Full-time	2,281.2	1,526.8	99.6	110.7	409.1	294.3	–	–	248.5	364.6	754.4
Part-time	1,280.2	1,102.6	2.7	4.6	334.7	333.2	173.1	155.9	34.4	64.0	177.6

– Represents zero.   [1] Instruction and research.   [2] Beginning 2005, data reflect the new classification of institutions. See footnote 1, Table 269.

Source: U.S. National Center for Education Statistics, *Digest of Education Statistics*, annual.

Table 286. Faculty in Institutions of Higher Education: 1980 to 2007

[In thousands (686 represents 686,000), except percent. As of fall. Based on complete census taken every other year; see source]

Year	Total	Employment status		Control		Level			Percent		
		Full-time	Part-time	Public	Private	4-Year	2-Year or less	Part-time	Public	2-Year or less
1980 [1]	686	450	236	495	191	494	192	34	72	28
1985 [1]	715	459	256	503	212	504	211	36	70	30
1991 [2]	826	536	291	581	245	591	235	35	70	28
1995	932	551	381	657	275	647	285	41	70	31
1997 [3]	990	569	421	695	295	683	307	43	70	31
1999 [3]	1,028	591	437	713	315	714	314	43	69	31
2001 [3]	1,113	618	495	771	342	764	349	44	69	31
2003 [3]	1,174	630	544	792	382	814	359	46	67	31
2005 [3]	1,290	676	615	841	449	917	373	48	65	29
2007 [3]	1,371	703	668	877	494	991	381	49	64	28

[1] Estimated on the basis of enrollment.   [2] Data beginning 1991 not comparable to prior years.   [3] Beginning 1997, data reflect the new classification of institutions. See footnote 1, Table 269.

Source: U.S. National Center for Education Statistics, *Digest of Education Statistics*, annual.

Table 287. Salary Offers to Candidates for Degrees: 2005 to 2008

[In dollars. Data are average beginning salaries based on offers made by business, industrial, government, nonprofit, and educational employers to graduating students. Data from representative colleges throughout the United States]

Field of study	Bachelor's			Master's [1]			Doctoral		
	2005	2007	2008	2005	2007	2008	2005	2007	2008
Accounting.	42,940	46,292	48,020	45,992	49,723	50,124	(NA)	(NA)	(NA)
Business administration/ management [2]	39,480	43,256	46,171	[3]50,513	[3]55,222	61,353	[3]66,500	[3]90,625	[3]91,734
Marketing.	36,409	39,269	41,506	[3]47,000	(NA)	[3]43,300	(NA)	(NA)	(NA)
Engineering:									
Civil.	43,774	48,998	51,780	48,619	51,297	56,300	[3]59,216	[3]62,275	[3]60,981
Chemical	53,639	59,218	63,773	62,845	[3]66,542	[3]66,338	[3]73,317	[3]76,688	82,419
Computer.	52,242	55,920	60,280	58,631	[3]67,304	[3]75,712	[3]69,625	[3]95,250	[3]96,235
Electrical	51,773	55,333	57,603	64,781	[3]68,247	72,814	[3]75,066	[3]77,860	85,045
Mechanical.	50,175	54,057	57,024	60,223	63,209	65,121	69,757	[3]70,928	72,068
Nuclear [4]	[3]51,225	[3]55,966	58,531	[3]59,059	[3]62,848	[3]62,109	(NA)	(NA)	(NA)
Petroleum.	62,236	[3]59,408	75,621	[3]65,000	[3]57,000	[3]87,000	(NA)	(NA)	(NA)
Engineering technology. .	45,790	50,808	53,511	(NA)	(NA)	(NA)	(NA)	(NA)	(NA)
Chemistry	38,635	41,820	43,951	(NA)	(NA)	[3]54,093	55,874	[3]61,822	66,985
Mathematics.	43,304	46,547	49,759	[3]34,500	[3]54,688	[3]68,400	[3]55,047	[3]56,727	[3]68,095
Physics	[3]44,700	[3]43,886	49,616	[3]62,500	[3]67,406	(NA)	[3]54,897	[3]50,725	[3]54,827
Humanities.	31,565	31,345	[3]40,702	[3]35,212	[3]39,808	[3]39,099	[3]43,728	[3]44,199	[3]41,400
Social sciences [5].	31,621	33,881	39,476	[3]40,575	[3]42,930	[3]52,605	[3]46,838	[3]49,225	[3]56,509
Computer science	50,664	53,051	61,110	64,840	65,463	73,826	[3]84,025	[3]79,086	[3]87,216

NA Not available.   [1] Candidates with 1 year or less of full-time nonmilitary employment.   [2] For master's degree, offers are after nontechnical undergraduate degree.   [3] Fewer than 50 offers reported.   [4] Includes engineering physics.   [5] Excludes economics.

Source: National Association of Colleges and Employers, Bethlehem, PA (copyright). Reprinted with permission from Fall 2005, 2007, and 2008 Salary Survey. All rights reserved.

Table 288. Earned Degrees Conferred by Level and Sex: 1960 to 2007

[In thousands (477 represents 477,000), except percent. Based on survey; see Appendix III]

Year ending	All degrees Total	All degrees Percent male	Associate's Male	Associate's Female	Bachelor's Male	Bachelor's Female	Master's Male	Master's Female	First professional Male	First professional Female	Doctoral Male	Doctoral Female
1960 [1]	477	65.8	(NA)	(NA)	254	138	51	24	(NA)	(NA)	9	1
1970	1,271	59.2	117	89	451	341	126	83	33	2	26	4
1975	1,666	56.0	191	169	505	418	162	131	49	7	27	7
1980	1,731	51.1	184	217	474	456	151	147	53	17	23	10
1985	1,828	49.3	203	252	483	497	143	143	50	25	22	11
1990	1,940	46.6	191	264	492	560	154	171	44	27	24	14
1991	2,025	45.8	199	283	504	590	156	181	44	28	25	15
1992	2,108	45.6	207	297	521	616	162	191	45	29	26	15
1993	2,167	45.5	212	303	533	632	169	200	45	30	26	16
1994	2,206	45.1	215	315	532	637	176	211	45	31	27	17
1995 [2]	2,218	44.9	218	321	526	634	179	219	45	31	27	18
1996 [2]	2,248	44.2	220	336	522	642	179	227	45	32	27	18
1997 [2]	2,288	43.6	224	347	521	652	181	238	46	33	27	19
1998 [2]	2,298	43.2	218	341	520	664	184	246	45	34	27	19
1999 [2]	2,323	42.7	218	342	519	682	186	254	44	34	25	19
2000 [2]	2,385	42.6	225	340	530	708	192	265	44	36	25	20
2001 [2]	2,416	42.4	232	347	532	712	194	274	43	37	25	20
2002 [2]	2,494	42.2	238	357	550	742	199	283	43	38	24	20
2003 [2]	2,621	42.1	253	380	573	775	211	301	42	39	24	22
2004 [2]	2,755	41.8	260	405	595	804	230	329	42	41	25	23
2005 [2]	2,850	41.6	268	429	613	826	234	341	44	43	27	26
2006 [2]	2,936	41.3	270	443	631	855	238	356	44	44	29	27
2007 [2]	3,007	41.2	275	453	650	875	238	366	45	45	30	30

NA Not available. [1] First-professional degrees are included with bachelor's degrees. [2] Beginning 1996, data reflect the new classification of institutions. See footnote 1, Table 269.

Source: U.S. National Center for Education Statistics, *Digest of Education Statistics*, annual.

Table 289. Degrees Earned by Level and Race/Ethnicity: 1990 to 2007

[For school year ending in year shown. Based on survey; see Appendix III]

Level of degree and race/ethnicity	Total 1990	Total 2000 [1]	Total 2005 [1]	Total 2006 [1]	Total 2007 [1]	Percent distribution 1990	Percent distribution 2000 [1]	Percent distribution 2007 [1]
Associate's degrees, total	455,102	564,933	696,660	713,066	728,114	100.0	100.0	100.0
White, non-Hispanic	376,816	408,772	475,513	485,297	491,572	82.8	72.4	67.5
Black, non-Hispanic	34,326	60,221	86,402	89,784	91,529	7.5	10.7	12.6
Hispanic	21,504	51,573	78,557	80,854	85,410	4.7	9.1	11.7
Asian or Pacific Islander	13,066	27,782	33,669	35,201	37,266	2.9	4.9	5.1
American Indian/Alaska Native	3,430	6,497	8,435	8,552	8,583	0.8	1.2	1.2
Nonresident alien	5,960	10,088	14,084	13,378	13,754	1.3	1.8	1.9
Bachelor's degrees, total	1,051,344	1,237,875	1,439,264	1,485,242	1,524,092	100.0	100.0	100.0
White, non-Hispanic	887,129	929,106	1,049,141	1,075,561	1,099,850	84.4	75.1	72.2
Black, non-Hispanic	61,046	108,013	136,122	142,420	146,653	5.8	8.7	9.6
Hispanic	32,829	75,059	101,124	107,588	114,936	3.1	6.1	7.5
Asian or Pacific Islander	39,230	77,912	97,209	102,376	105,297	3.7	6.3	6.9
American Indian/Alaska Native	4,390	8,719	10,307	10,940	11,455	0.4	0.7	0.8
Nonresident alien	26,698	39,066	45,361	46,357	45,901	2.5	3.2	3.0
Master's degrees, total	324,301	457,056	574,618	594,065	604,607	100.0	100.0	100.0
White, non-Hispanic	254,299	320,485	379,350	393,357	399,267	78.4	70.1	66.0
Black, non-Hispanic	15,336	35,874	54,482	58,976	62,574	4.7	7.8	10.3
Hispanic	7,892	19,253	31,485	32,438	34,822	2.4	4.2	5.8
Asian or Pacific Islander	10,439	23,218	32,783	34,029	36,134	3.2	5.1	6.0
American Indian/Alaska Native	1,090	2,246	3,295	3,504	3,575	0.3	0.5	0.6
Nonresident alien	35,245	55,980	73,223	71,761	68,235	10.9	12.2	11.3
Doctoral degrees, total	38,371	44,808	52,631	56,067	60,616	100.0	100.0	100.0
White, non-Hispanic	26,221	27,843	30,261	31,601	34,071	68.3	62.1	56.2
Black, non-Hispanic	1,149	2,246	3,056	3,122	3,727	3.0	5.0	6.1
Hispanic	780	1,305	1,824	1,882	2,034	2.0	2.9	3.4
Asian or Pacific Islander	1,225	2,420	2,911	3,257	3,541	3.2	5.4	5.8
American Indian/Alaska Native	98	160	237	230	249	0.3	0.4	0.4
Nonresident alien	8,898	10,834	14,342	15,975	16,994	23.2	24.2	28.0
First-professional degrees, total	70,988	80,057	87,289	87,655	90,064	100.0	100.0	100.0
White, non-Hispanic	60,487	59,637	63,429	63,590	64,546	85.2	74.5	71.7
Black, non-Hispanic	3,409	5,555	6,313	6,223	6,474	4.8	6.9	7.2
Hispanic	2,425	3,865	4,445	4,446	4,700	3.4	4.8	5.2
Asian or Pacific Islander	3,362	8,584	10,501	10,645	11,686	4.7	10.7	13.0
American Indian/Alaska Native	257	564	564	710	681	0.4	0.7	0.8
Nonresident alien	1,048	1,852	2,037	2,041	1,977	1.5	2.3	2.2

[1] Beginning 2000, data reflect the new classification of institutions. See footnote 1, Table 269.

Source: U.S. National Center for Education Statistics, *Digest of Education Statistics*, annual.

Education 183

Table 290. **Degrees and Awards Earned Below Bachelor's by Field: 2007**

[Covers associate's degrees and other awards based on postsecondary curriculums of less than 4 years in institutions of higher education. Based on survey; see Appendix III]

Field of study	Less than 1-year awards		1- to less than 4-year awards		Associate's degrees	
	Total	Women	Total	Women	Total	Women
Total [1]	248,941	136,934	189,005	117,136	728,114	452,927
Agriculture and natural resources, total.	3,376	881	1,626	596	5,838	2,212
Architecture and related services.	164	69	178	111	517	286
Area, ethnic, cultural, and gender studies	379	278	121	85	164	111
Biological and biomedical sciences	111	79	29	18	2,060	1,384
Business, management, and marketing.	32,981	22,373	15,589	11,753	99,998	67,002
Communications and communications technologies.	1,223	496	1,214	430	5,704	2,519
Computer and information sciences	8,403	3,025	4,856	1,786	27,712	7,253
Construction trades.	8,946	491	7,266	291	3,895	199
Education	2,949	2,642	1,830	1,678	13,021	11,248
Engineering and engineering technologies.	7,786	1,283	6,533	892	31,335	4,345
English language and literature/letters	995	630	266	165	1,249	871
Family and consumer sciences	10,739	9,053	3,521	2,851	9,124	8,791
Foreign languages and literatures	799	579	463	416	1,207	1,012
Health professions and related sciences	92,276	74,365	86,344	75,273	145,436	124,222
Nursing.	4,327	3,896	29,529	26,612	1,509	1,380
Legal professions and studies.	1,558	1,350	2,266	1,969	10,391	9,345
Liberal arts and sciences, general studies, and humanities.	318	236	4,271	2,500	250,030	156,319
Library science.	163	153	52	43	84	76
Mathematics	40	17	7	3	827	279
Mechanics and repairers	17,103	1,203	21,177	828	15,432	712
Military technologies	74	9	5	–	781	140
Multi/interdisciplinary studies.	525	294	873	593	15,838	9,260
Parks, recreation, leisure, and fitness studies. . . .	347	173	182	110	1,251	502
Personal and culinary services	6,922	5,260	9,564	7,927	16,103	7,686
Philosophy and religion	11	3	74	25	375	260
Physical sciences and science technologies	291	145	303	167	3,404	1,456
Precision production trades	6,019	353	4,985	233	1,973	124
Psychology	138	122	25	24	2,213	1,696
Public administration and social services.	845	684	549	441	4,338	3,742
Security and protective services	20,893	5,204	5,265	1,338	28,208	12,727
Social sciences and history	352	159	200	97	7,080	4,586
Theology and religious vocations	139	86	445	215	608	295
Transportation and material moving	16,659	1,924	2,102	80	1,674	232
Visual and performing arts	5,417	3,315	6,824	4,198	20,244	12,035

– Represents zero. [1] Includes other fields of study not shown separately.

Source: U.S. National Center for Education Statistics, *Digest of Education Statistics*, annual.

Table 291. **Bachelor's Degrees Earned by Field: 1980 to 2007**

[The new Classification of Instructional Programs was introduced in 2002–03. Data for previous years has been reclassified where necessary to conform to the new classifications. Based on survey; see Appendix III]

Field of study	1980	1990	2000	2005	2006	2007
Total [1]	929,417	1,051,344	1,237,875	1,439,264	1,485,242	1,524,092
Agriculture and natural resources	22,802	12,900	24,238	23,002	23,053	23,133
Architecture and related services	9,132	9,364	8,462	9,237	9,515	9,717
Area, ethnic, cultural, and gender studies.	2,840	4,447	6,212	7,569	7,879	8,194
Biological and biomedical sciences	46,190	37,204	63,005	64,611	69,178	75,151
Business	186,264	248,568	256,070	311,574	318,042	327,531
Communication, journalism, and related programs [2] . .	28,616	51,572	57,058	75,238	76,936	78,420
Computer and information sciences.	11,154	27,347	37,788	54,111	47,480	42,170
Education	118,038	105,112	108,034	105,451	107,238	105,641
Engineering and engineering technologies	69,387	82,480	73,419	79,743	81,610	82,072
English language and literature/letters	32,187	46,803	50,106	54,379	55,096	55,122
Family and consumer sciences/human sciences	18,411	13,514	16,321	20,074	20,775	21,400
Foreign languages, literatures, and linguistics	12,480	13,133	15,886	18,386	19,410	20,275
Health professions and related clinical sciences	63,848	58,983	80,863	80,685	91,973	101,810
Legal professions and studies	683	1,632	1,969	3,161	3,302	3,596
Liberal arts and sciences, general studies, and humanities	23,196	27,985	36,104	43,751	44,898	44,255
Mathematics and statistics.	11,378	14,276	11,418	14,351	14,770	14,954
Multi/interdisciplinary studies	11,457	16,557	28,561	30,243	32,012	33,792
Parks, recreation, leisure, and fitness studies	5,753	4,582	17,571	22,888	25,490	27,430
Philosophy and religious studies.	7,069	7,034	8,535	11,584	11,985	11,969
Physical sciences and science technologies	23,407	16,056	18,331	18,905	20,318	21,073
Psychology.	42,093	53,952	74,194	85,614	88,134	90,039
Public administration and social services	16,644	13,908	20,185	21,769	21,986	23,147
Security and protective services	15,015	15,112	24,877	30,723	35,319	39,206
Social sciences and history	103,662	118,083	127,101	156,892	161,485	164,183
Theology and religious vocations	6,170	5,185	6,789	9,284	8,548	8,696
Transportation and materials moving	213	2,387	3,395	4,904	5,349	5,657
Visual and performing arts.	40,892	39,934	58,791	80,954	83,297	85,186

[1] Includes other fields of study not shown separately. [2] Includes technologies.

Source: U.S. National Center for Education Statistics, *Digest of Education Statistics*, annual and unpublished data.

184 Education

Table 292. **Master's and Doctoral Degrees Earned by Field: 1980 to 2007**

[The new Classification of Instructional Programs was introduced in 2002–03. Data for previous years has been reclassified where necessary to conform to the new classifications. Based on survey; see Appendix III]

Field of study	1980	1990	2000	2005	2006	2007
MASTER'S DEGREES						
Total [1]	**298,081**	**324,301**	**457,056**	**574,618**	**594,065**	**604,607**
Agriculture and natural resources	3,976	3,382	4,360	4,746	4,640	4,623
Architecture and related services.	3,139	3,499	4,268	5,674	5,743	5,951
Area, ethnic, cultural, and gender studies	852	1,191	1,544	1,755	2,080	1,699
Biological and biomedical sciences	6,322	4,906	6,781	8,199	8,681	8,747
Business	55,008	76,676	111,532	142,617	146,406	150,211
Communication, journalism, and related programs [2] .	3,082	4,353	5,525	7,195	7,745	7,272
Computer and information sciences.	3,647	9,677	14,990	18,416	17,055	16,232
Education	101,819	84,890	123,045	167,490	174,620	176,572
Engineering and engineering technologies	16,765	25,294	26,726	35,133	33,530	32,162
English language and literature/letters	6,026	6,317	7,022	8,468	8,845	8,742
Family and consumer sciences/human sciences . . .	2,690	1,679	1,882	1,827	1,983	2,080
Foreign languages, literatures, and linguistics	3,067	3,018	3,037	3,407	3,539	3,443
Health professions and related clinical sciences. . . .	15,374	20,406	42,593	46,703	51,380	54,531
Legal professions and studies	1,817	1,888	3,750	4,170	4,453	4,486
Liberal arts and sciences, general studies, and humanities	2,646	1,999	3,256	3,680	3,702	3,634
Library science	5,374	4,341	4,577	6,213	6,448	6,767
Mathematics and statistics	2,860	3,624	3,208	4,477	4,730	4,884
Multi/interdisciplinary studies	2,494	3,182	3,487	4,252	4,491	4,762
Parks, recreation, leisure, and fitness studies	647	529	2,322	3,740	3,992	4,110
Philosophy and religious studies	1,204	1,327	1,376	1,647	1,739	1,716
Physical sciences and science technologies	5,167	5,410	4,810	5,678	5,922	5,839
Psychology	9,938	10,730	15,740	18,830	19,770	21,037
Public administration and social services	17,560	17,399	25,594	29,552	30,510	31,131
Security and protective services	1,805	1,151	2,609	3,991	4,277	4,906
Social sciences and history	12,176	11,634	14,066	16,952	17,369	17,665
Theology and religious vocations.	3,872	4,941	5,534	5,815	6,092	6,446
Visual and performing arts	8,708	8,481	10,918	13,183	13,530	13,767
DOCTORAL DEGREES						
Total [1]	**32,615**	**38,371**	**44,808**	**52,631**	**56,067**	**60,616**
Agriculture and natural resources	991	1,295	1,168	1,173	1,194	1,272
Architecture and related services.	79	103	129	179	201	178
Area, ethnic, cultural, and gender studies	151	125	205	189	226	233
Biological and biomedical sciences	3,527	3,837	5,180	5,578	5,775	6,354
Business	767	1,093	1,194	1,498	1,711	2,029
Communication, journalism, and related programs [2] .	193	272	357	468	464	480
Computer and information sciences.	240	627	779	1,119	1,416	1,595
Education	7,314	6,503	6,409	7,681	7,584	8,261
Engineering and engineering technologies	2,546	5,030	5,421	6,601	7471	8,123
English language and literature/letters	1,196	986	1,470	1,212	1,254	1,178
Family and consumer sciences/human sciences . . .	192	273	327	331	340	337
Foreign languages, literatures, and linguistics	857	816	1,086	1,027	1,074	1,059
Health professions and related clinical sciences. . . .	821	1,449	2,053	5,868	7,128	8,355
Legal professions and studies	40	111	74	98	129	143
Liberal arts and sciences, general studies, and humanities	192	63	83	109	84	77
Mathematics and statistics	724	917	1,075	1,176	1,293	1,351
Multi/interdisciplinary studies	318	442	792	983	987	1,093
Parks, recreation, leisure, and fitness studies	21	35	134	207	194	218
Philosophy and religious studies	374	445	598	586	578	637
Physical sciences and science technologies	3,044	4,116	3,963	4,114	4,489	4,846
Psychology	3,395	3,811	4,731	5,106	4,921	5,153
Public administration and social services	342	508	537	673	704	726
Security and protective services	18	38	52	94	80	85
Social sciences and history	3,230	3,010	4,095	3,819	3,914	3,844
Theology and religious vocations.	1,315	1,317	1,630	1,422	1,429	1,573
Visual and performing arts	655	849	1,127	1,278	1,383	1,364

[1] Includes other fields of study not shown separately.   [2] Includes technologies.

Source: U.S. National Center for Education Statistics, *Digest of Education Statistics,* annual and unpublished data.

Education 185

Table 293. **First Professional Degrees Earned in Selected Professions: 1970 to 2007**

[First professional degrees include degrees which require at least 6 years of college work for completion (including at least 2 years of preprofessional training). Based on survey; see Appendix III]

Type of degree and sex of recipient	1970	1980	1985	1990	1995	2000	2004	2005	2006	2007
Medicine (M.D.):										
Institutions conferring degrees.....	86	112	120	124	119	118	118	120	119	120
Degrees conferred, total..........	8,314	14,902	16,041	15,075	15,537	15,286	15,442	15,461	15,455	15,730
Percent to women	8.4	23.4	30.4	34.2	38.8	42.7	46.4	47.3	48.9	49.2
Dentistry (D.D.S. or D.M.D.):										
Institutions conferring degrees.....	48	58	59	57	53	54	53	53	54	55
Degrees conferred, total..........	3,718	5,258	5,339	4,100	3,897	4,250	4,335	4,454	4,389	4,596
Percent to women	0.9	13.3	20.7	30.9	36.4	40.1	41.6	43.8	44.5	44.6
Law (LL.B. or J.D.):										
Institutions conferring degrees.....	145	179	181	182	183	190	195	198	197	200
Degrees conferred, total..........	14,916	35,647	37,491	36,485	39,349	38,152	40,209	43,423	43,440	43,486
Percent to women	5.4	30.2	38.5	42.2	42.6	45.9	49.4	48.7	48.0	47.6
Theological (B.D., M.Div., M.H.L.):										
Institutions conferring degrees.....	(NA)	(NA)	(NA)	(NA)	192	198	200	(NA)	(NA)	(NA)
Degrees conferred, total..........	5,298	7,115	7,221	5,851	5,978	6,129	5,332	5,533	5,666	5,990
Percent to women	2.3	13.8	18.5	24.8	25.7	29.2	34.2	35.6	33.6	33.2

NA Not available.

Source: U.S. National Center for Education Statistics, *Digest of Education Statistics*, annual.

Table 294. **Participation in Adult Education: 2004 to 2005**

[In thousands (211,607 represents 211,607,000), except percent. For the civilian noninstitutional population 16 years old. Adult education includes enrollment in formal education activities in the previous 12 months. Excludes participants in only postsecondary degree, certificate, or diploma programs as full-time students. Based on the Adult Education Survey of the National Household Education Survey Program and subject to sampling error; see source and Appendix III for details. For more data on adult education, see Table 624]

Characteristic	Adult population (1,000)	Number taking adult education courses[1] (1,000)	Percent of total[1]	Type of course (percent)		
				College or university degree program	Work-related course	Personal interest course
Total, 2005.	**211,607**	**93,939**	**44**	**4**	**27**	**21**
Age:						
16 to 30 years old.	48,544	25,040	52	8	25	23
31 to 40 years old.	40,009	20,839	52	6	34	23
41 to 50 years old.	45,662	21,983	48	3	36	20
51 to 65 years old.	46,211	18,767	41	2	28	20
66 years old and over	31,181	7,310	23	–	5	19
Sex:						
Male.	101,596	41,724	41	4	24	18
Female	110,011	52,216	47	4	29	24
Race/ethnicity:						
White, Non-Hispanic	146,614	66,909	46	4	29	22
Black, Non-Hispanic	23,467	10,878	46	4	27	24
Hispanic[2]	26,101	9,824	38	4	17	15
Other	15,426	6,328	41	5	24	22
Educational attainment:						
Less than high school	31,017	6,851	22	–	4	11
High school diploma or GED.	64,334	20,955	33	2	17	16
Some college.	58,545	30,070	51	6	31	25
Bachelor's degree or higher	57,711	36,063	62	7	46	29
Marital status:						
Married	132,008	58,748	45	3	29	21
Living with partner, unmarried	12,498	4,879	39	4	26	16
Separated/divorced/widowed.	30,170	10,874	36	2	20	19
Never married	36,930	19,439	53	8	23	26
Employment/occupation:						
Employed	152,450	78,879	52	5	36	22
Professional or managerial	48,647	34,138	70	8	56	29
Services, sales, or support	65,289	31,609	48	5	31	22
Trades.	38,514	13,132	34	2	19	13
Unemployed or not in labor force in past 12 months	59,157	15,060	25	1	4	20
Household income:						
$20,000 or less	34,670	9,552	28	2	11	16
$20,001 to $35,000	35,839	12,866	36	2	18	17
$35,001 to $50,000	33,376	14,122	42	2	23	22
$50,001 to $75,000	47,114	22,494	48	5	33	21
$75,001 or more.	60,607	34,904	58	5	39	27
Children under 10 in household:						
Yes	57,560	26,746	46	5	29	20
No	154,047	67,193	44	4	26	22

– Represents or rounds to zero.   [1] Includes English as a second language, basic education skills, vocational or technical diploma programs, and apprenticeship programs each with a total participation rate of about 1 percent.   [2] Persons of Hispanic origin may be any race.

Source: U.S. Department of Education, National Center for Education Statistics, Adult Education Survey of the National Household Education Surveys Program 2005, unpublished data.

186   Education

Law Enforcement, Courts, and Prisons

This section presents data on crimes committed, victims of crimes, arrests, and data related to criminal violations and the criminal justice system. The major sources of these data are the Bureau of Justice Statistics (BJS), the Federal Bureau of Investigation (FBI), and the Administrative Office of the U.S. Courts. BJS issues many reports—see our Guide to Sources for a complete listing. The Federal Bureau of Investigation's major annual reports are *Crime in the United States, Law Enforcement Officers Killed and Assaulted*, annual, and *Hate Crimes*, annual, which present data on reported crimes as gathered from state and local law enforcement agencies.

Legal jurisdiction and law enforcement—Law enforcement is, for the most part, a function of state and local officers and agencies. The U.S. Constitution reserves general police powers to the states. By act of Congress, federal offenses include only offenses against the U.S. government and against or by its employees while engaged in their official duties and offenses which involve the crossing of state lines or an interference with interstate commerce. Excluding the military, there are 52 separate criminal law jurisdictions in the United States: one in each of the 50 states, one in the District of Columbia, and the federal jurisdiction. Each of these has its own criminal law and procedure and its own law enforcement agencies. While the systems of law enforcement are quite similar among the states, there are often substantial differences in the penalties for like offenses.

Law enforcement can be divided into three parts: Investigation of crimes and arrests of persons suspected of committing them; prosecution of those charged with crime; and the punishment or treatment of persons convicted of crime.

Crime—The U.S. Department of Justice administers two statistical programs to measure the magnitude, nature, and impact of crime in the nation: the Uniform Crime Reporting (UCR) Program and the National Crime Victimization Survey (NCVS). Each of these programs produces valuable information about aspects of the nation's crime problem. Because the UCR and NCVS programs are conducted for different purposes, use different methods, and focus on somewhat different aspects of crime, the information they produce together provides a more comprehensive panorama of the nation's crime problem than either could produce alone.

Uniform Crime Reports (UCR)—The FBI's UCR Program, which began in 1929, collects information on the following crimes reported to law enforcement authorities—Part 1 offenses (detail data reported): murder and nonnegligent manslaughter, forcible rape, robbery, aggravated assault, burglary, larceny-theft, motor vehicle theft, and arson. For Part 2 offenses, law enforcement agencies report only arrest data for 21 additional crime categories. For UCR definitions of criminal offenses (including those listed), please go to: <www.fbi.gov/ucr/cius2006/about/offense_definitions.html>.

The UCR Program compiles data from monthly law enforcement reports or individual crime incident records transmitted directly to the FBI or to centralized state agencies that then report to the FBI. The Program thoroughly examines each report it receives for reasonableness, accuracy, and deviations that may indicate errors. Large variations in crime levels may indicate modified records procedures, incomplete reporting, or changes in a jurisdiction's boundaries. To identify any unusual fluctuations in an agency's crime counts, the Program compares monthly reports to previous submissions of the agency and with those for similar agencies.

The UCR Program presents crime counts for the nation as a whole, as well as for regions, states, counties, cities, towns, tribal law enforcement, and colleges and

U.S. Census Bureau, Statistical Abstract of the United States: 2010

universities. This permits studies among neighboring jurisdictions and among those with similar populations and other common characteristics.

The UCR Program annually publishes its findings in a preliminary release in the spring of the following calendar year, followed by a detailed annual report, *Crime in the United States*, issued in the fall. In addition to crime counts and trends, this report includes data on crimes cleared, persons arrested (age, sex, and race), law enforcement personnel (including the number of sworn officers killed or assaulted), and the characteristics of homicides (including age, sex, and race of victims and offenders; victim-offender relationships; weapons used; and circumstances surrounding the homicides). Other periodic reports are also available from the UCR Program.

National Crime Victimization Survey (NCVS)—The 2006 national crime victimization estimates are not comparable to previous years because of changes in methodology. The methodological changes included: a new sample, a change in the method of handling first-time interviews with households, and a change in the method of interviewing. For more information on methodology, go to <http://www.ojp.usdoj.gov/bjs/abstract/cv06.htm>.

A second perspective on crime is provided by this survey of the Bureau of Justice Statistics (BJS). The NCVS is an annual data collection (interviews of persons age 12 or older), conducted by the U.S. Census Bureau for the BJS. As an ongoing survey of households, the NCVS measures crimes of violence and theft both reported and not reported to police. It produces national rates and levels of personal and property victimization. No attempt is made to validate the information against police records or any other source.

The NCVS measures rape/sexual assault, robbery, assault, pocket-picking, purse snatching, burglary, and motor vehicle theft. The NCVS includes crimes reported to the police, as well as those not reported.

Murder and kidnapping are not covered. The so-called victimless crimes, such as drunkenness, drug abuse, and prostitution, also are excluded, as are crimes for which it is difficult to identify knowledgeable respondents or to locate data records.

Crimes of which the victim may not be aware also cannot be measured effectively. Buying stolen property may fall into this category, as may some instances of embezzlement. Attempted crimes of many types probably are under recorded for this reason. Events in which the victim has shown a willingness to participate in illegal activity also are excluded.

In any encounter involving a personal crime, more than one criminal act can be committed against an individual. For example, a rape may be associated with a robbery, or a household offense, such as a burglary, can escalate into something more serious in the event of a personal confrontation. In classifying the survey-measured crimes, each criminal incident has been counted only once—by the most serious act that took place during the incident and ranked in accordance with the seriousness classification system used by the FBI. The order of seriousness for crimes against persons is as follows: rape, robbery, assault, and larceny. Personal crimes take precedence over household offenses.

A *victimization,* basic measure of the occurrence of crime, is a specific criminal act as it affects a single victim. The number of victimizations is determined by the number of victims of such acts. Victimization counts serve as key elements in computing rates of victimization. For crimes against persons, the rates are based on the total number of individuals age 12 and over or on a portion of that population sharing a particular characteristic or set of traits. As general indicators of the danger of having been victimized during the reference period, the rates are not sufficiently refined to represent true measures of risk for specific individuals or households.

An *incident* is a specific criminal act involving one or more victims; therefore the number of incidents of personal crimes is lower than that of victimizations.

Courts—Statistics on criminal offenses and the outcome of prosecutions are incomplete for the country as a whole, although data are available for many states individually.

Since 1982, through its National Judicial Reporting Program, the BJS has surveyed a nationally representative sample of 300 counties every 2 years and collected detailed information on demographic characteristics of felons, conviction offenses, type of sentences, sentence lengths, and time from arrest to conviction and sentencing.

The bulk of civil and criminal litigation in the country is commenced and determined in the various state courts. Only when the U.S. Constitution and acts of Congress specifically confer jurisdiction upon the federal courts may civil or criminal litigation be heard and decided by them. Generally, the federal courts have jurisdiction over the following types of cases: suits or proceedings by or against the United States; civil actions between private parties arising under the Constitution, laws, or treaties of the United States; civil actions between private litigants who are citizens of different states; civil cases involving admiralty, maritime, or private jurisdiction; and all matters in bankruptcy.

There are several types of courts with varying degrees of legal jurisdiction. These jurisdictions include original, appellate, general, and limited or special. A court of original jurisdiction is one having the authority initially to try a case and pass judgment on the law and the facts; a court of appellate jurisdiction is one with the legal authority to review cases and hear appeals; a court of general jurisdiction is a trial court of unlimited original jurisdiction in civil and/or criminal cases, also called a "major trial court"; a court of limited or special jurisdiction is a trial court with legal authority over only a particular class of cases, such as probate, juvenile, or traffic cases.

The 94 federal courts of original jurisdiction are known as the U.S. district courts. One or more of these courts is established in every state and one each in the

District of Columbia, Puerto Rico, the Virgin Islands, the Northern Mariana Islands, and Guam. Appeals from the district courts are taken to intermediate appellate courts of which there are 13, known as U.S. courts of appeals and the United States Court of Appeals for the Federal Circuit. The Supreme Court of the United States is the final and highest appellate court in the federal system of courts.

Juvenile offenders—For statistical purposes, the FBI and most states classify as juvenile offenders persons under the age of 18 years who have committed a crime or crimes.

Delinquency cases are all cases of youths referred to a juvenile court for violation of a law or ordinance or for seriously "antisocial" conduct. Several types of facilities are available for those adjudicated delinquents, ranging from the short-term physically unrestricted environment to the long-term very restrictive atmosphere.

Prisoners and jail inmates—BJS started to collect annual data in 1979 on prisoners in federal and state prisons and reformatories. Adults convicted of criminal activity may be given a prison or jail sentence. A *prison* is a confinement facility having custodial authority over adults sentenced to confinement of more than 1 year. A *jail* is a facility, usually operated by a local law enforcement agency, holding persons detained pending adjudication and/or persons committed after adjudication to 1 year or less.

Data on inmates in local jails were collected by the BJS for the first time in 1970. Since then, BJS has conducted censuses of facilities and inmates every 5 to 6 years. In 1984, BJS initiated an annual survey of jails conducted in noncensus years.

Statistical reliability—For discussion of statistical collection, estimation and sampling procedures, and measures of statistical reliability pertaining to the National Crime Victimization Survey and Uniform Crime Reporting Program, see Appendix III.

U.S. Census Bureau, Statistical Abstract of the United States: 2010

Table 295. **Crimes and Crime Rates by Type of Offense: 1980 to 2007**

[(1,345 represents 1,345,000). Data include offenses actually reported to law enforcement and also offense estimations for nonreporting and partially reporting agencies within each state. Rates are based on Census Bureau estimated resident population as of **July 1; 1980, 1990, and 2000, enumerated as of April 1.** See source for details. For definitions of types of crimes, go to <http://www.fbi.gov/ucr/cius2007/about/offense_definitions.html/>]

Item and year	Violent crime					Property crime			
	Total	Murder [1]	Forcible rape	Robbery	Aggra-vated assault	Total	Burglary	Larceny/theft	Motor vehicle theft
Number of offenses (1,000):									
1980	1,345	23	83	566	673	12,064	3,795	7,137	1,132
1985	1,328	19	88	498	723	11,103	3,073	6,926	1,103
1990	1,820	23	103	639	1,055	12,655	3,074	7,946	1,636
1993	1,926	25	106	660	1,136	12,219	2,835	7,821	1,563
1994	1,858	23	102	619	1,113	12,132	2,713	7,880	1,539
1995	1,799	22	97	581	1,099	12,064	2,594	7,998	1,472
1996	1,689	20	96	536	1,037	11,805	2,506	7,905	1,394
1997	1,636	18	96	499	1,023	11,558	2,461	7,744	1,354
1998	1,534	17	93	447	977	10,952	2,333	7,376	1,243
1999	1,426	16	89	409	912	10,208	2,101	6,956	1,152
2000 [2]	1,425	16	90	408	912	10,183	2,051	6,972	1,160
2001 [2]	1,439	16	91	424	909	10,437	2,117	7,092	1,228
2002	1,424	16	95	421	891	10,455	2,151	7,057	1,247
2003	1,384	17	94	414	859	10,443	2,155	7,027	1,261
2004	1,360	16	95	401	847	10,319	2,144	6,937	1,238
2005 [3]	1,391	17	94	417	862	10,175	2,155	6,783	1,236
2006 [3]	1,418	17	93	447	861	9,984	2,184	6,607	1,193
2007	1,408	17	90	445	856	9,843	2,179	6,569	1,096
Rate per 100,000 population:									
1980	597	10	37	251	299	5,353	1,684	3,167	502
1985	558	8	37	209	304	4,666	1,292	2,911	464
1990	730	9	41	256	423	5,073	1,232	3,185	656
1993	747	10	41	256	441	4,740	1,100	3,034	606
1994	714	9	39	238	428	4,660	1,042	3,027	591
1995	685	8	37	221	418	4,591	987	3,043	560
1996	637	7	36	202	391	4,451	945	2,980	526
1997	611	7	36	186	382	4,316	919	2,892	506
1998	568	6	35	166	361	4,053	863	2,730	460
1999	523	6	33	150	334	3,744	770	2,551	423
2000 [2]	507	6	32	145	324	3,618	729	2,477	412
2001 [2]	505	6	32	149	319	3,658	742	2,486	431
2002	494	6	33	146	310	3,631	747	2,451	433
2003	476	6	32	143	295	3,591	741	2,417	434
2004	463	6	32	137	289	3,514	730	2,362	422
2005 [3]	469	6	32	141	291	3,432	727	2,288	417
2006 [3]	474	6	31	149	288	3,335	729	2,207	398
2007	467	6	30	148	284	3,264	723	2,178	363

[1] Includes nonnegligent manslaughter. [2] The murder and nonnegligent homicides that occurred as a result of the events of September 11, 2001, were not included in this table. [3] The 2006 data have been revised.

Source: U.S. Department of Justice, Federal Bureau of Investigation, "Crime in the United States"; <http://www.fbi.gov/ucr/cius2007/index.html>.

Table 296. **Crimes and Crime Rates by Type and Area: 2007**

[In thousands (1,408 represents 1,408,000), except rate. Rate per 100,000 population; based on Census Bureau estimated resident population as of **July 1.** See headnote, Table 295. For definitions of types of crimes, go to <http://www.fbi.gov/ucr/cius2007/about/offense_definitions.html/>

Type of crime	United States		Metropolitan statistical areas [1]		Cities outside metropolitan areas		Nonmetropolitan counties	
	Total	Rate	Total	Rate	Total	Rate	Total	Rate
Violent crime	1,408	467	1,265	504	79	395	64	209
Murder and nonnegligent manslaughter	17	6	15	6	1	4	1	3
Forcible rape	90	30	75	30	8	38	8	25
Robbery	445	148	428	170	12	62	5	16
Aggravated assault	856	284	747	298	58	291	50	165
Property crime	9,843	3,264	8,577	3,417	758	3,774	509	1,668
Burglary	2,179	723	1,859	740	157	783	163	536
Larceny-theft	6,569	2,178	5,698	2,270	565	2,815	305	1,000
Motor vehicle theft	1,096	363	1,020	406	35	176	40	132

[1] For definition, see Appendix II.

Source: U.S. Department of Justice, Federal Bureau of Investigation, "Crime in the United States"; <http://www.fbi.gov/ucr/cius2007/index.html/>.

Table 297. **Crime Rates by State, 2006 and 2007, and by Type, 2007**

[**Rates per 100,000 population.** Data include offenses actually reported to law enforcement and also offense estimations for nonreporting and partially reporting agencies within each state. Based on Census Bureau estimated resident population as of **July 1.** For definitions of types of crimes, go to <http://www.fbi.gov/ucr/cius2007/about/offense_definitions.html/>]

State	Violent crime						Property crime				
	2006, total [1]	2007					2006, total	2007			
		Total	Mur-der [2]	Forc-ible rape	Rob-bery	Aggra-vated assault		Total	Bur-glary	Lar-ceny/ theft	Motor vehicle theft
United States.....	474	467	5.6	30	148	284	3,335	3,264	723	2,178	363
Alabama..........	425	448	8.9	33	160	246	3,936	3,972	980	2,685	308
Alaska...........	688	661	6.4	77	85	492	3,605	3,380	539	2,487	354
Arizona..........	501	483	7.4	29	152	294	4,628	4,414	912	2,738	763
Arkansas.........	552	529	6.7	45	107	371	3,968	3,953	1,131	2,574	247
California.........	533	523	6.2	25	193	299	3,171	3,033	648	1,784	600
Colorado.........	392	348	3.1	41	71	233	3,451	3,006	591	2,069	345
Connecticut	281	256	3.0	19	103	131	2,504	2,400	433	1,705	262
Delaware..........	682	689	4.3	39	197	449	3,418	3,370	733	2,369	268
District of Columbia [3].......	1,508	1,414	30.8	33	724	627	4,654	4,914	667	2,955	1,292
Florida...........	712	723	6.6	34	209	473	3,986	4,089	996	2,689	404
Georgia..........	471	493	7.5	23	182	281	3,889	3,901	950	2,505	446
Hawaii...........	281	273	1.7	25	86	160	4,230	4,225	709	2,993	523
Idaho	247	239	3.3	39	16	182	2,419	2,247	465	1,633	149
Illinois [4, 5]	542	533	5.9	32	180	316	3,020	2,936	588	2,085	264
Indiana	315	334	5.6	28	124	176	3,502	3,397	739	2,349	308
Iowa	284	295	1.2	30	44	219	2,803	2,616	567	1,885	164
Kansas	425	453	3.9	44	73	332	3,750	3,679	730	2,640	309
Kentucky	263	295	4.8	33	96	162	2,545	2,518	653	1,661	205
Louisiana.........	698	730	14.2	32	142	541	3,994	4,076	1,039	2,684	354
Maine	116	118	1.6	30	27	60	2,519	2,429	507	1,826	96
Maryland	679	642	9.8	21	236	375	3,481	3,432	660	2,266	505
Massachusetts	447	432	2.9	25	109	295	2,391	2,392	553	1,606	232
Michigan .,.......	562	536	6.7	46	133	351	3,213	3,066	749	1,898	419
Minnesota [5]........	318	289	2.2	36	92	159	3,080	3,037	571	2,225	241
Mississippi........	299	291	7.1	36	98	150	3,209	3,201	958	1,990	253
Missouri..........	546	505	6.5	29	122	347	3,827	3,738	739	2,595	405
Montana..........	254	288	1.5	30	20	236	2,688	2,765	316	2,266	183
Nebraska..........	282	302	3.8	30	62	207	3,341	3,161	510	2,359	293
Nevada...........	742	751	7.5	43	270	430	4,089	3,778	968	1,939	871
New Hampshire	139	137	1.1	25	33	78	1,874	1,892	379	1,414	99
New Jersey	352	329	4.4	12	145	168	2,292	2,213	432	1,529	253
New Mexico........	643	664	8.2	52	118	486	3,937	3,726	964	2,308	454
New York..........	435	414	4.2	15	161	234	2,053	1,979	336	1,497	145
North Carolina	476	466	6.5	26	150	284	4,121	4,087	1,201	2,578	309
North Dakota	128	142	1.9	32	11	97	2,000	1,890	338	1,408	143
Ohio.............	350	343	4.5	39	159	141	3,679	3,455	859	2,302	295
Oklahoma	497	500	6.1	43	93	357	3,604	3,526	943	2,211	372
Oregon	280	288	1.9	34	76	176	3,672	3,526	609	2,529	388
Pennsylvania	439	417	5.8	28	157	226	2,444	2,361	451	1,698	213
Rhode Island	228	227	1.8	24	71	130	2,587	2,623	495	1,823	305
South Carolina	766	788	8.0	40	144	597	4,242	4,272	1,026	2,860	386
South Dakota	171	169	2.1	39	14	114	1,620	1,652	299	1,261	92
Tennessee.........	760	753	6.4	35	179	533	4,128	4,089	1,002	2,734	352
Texas	516	511	5.9	35	162	307	4,082	4,121	955	2,773	393
Utah	224	235	2.2	34	54	145	3,516	3,500	588	2,580	333
Vermont	137	124	1.9	20	13	90	2,305	2,323	500	1,720	103
Virginia	282	270	5.3	23	99	143	2,478	2,466	411	1,873	182
Washington	346	333	2.7	41	94	196	4,480	4,031	815	2,634	582
West Virginia	280	275	3.5	20	47	204	2,622	2,525	597	1,736	193
Wisconsin	284	291	3.3	22	98	168	2,818	2,838	497	2,101	240
Wyoming..........	240	239	3.1	31	16	190	2,981	2,866	449	2,265	152

[1] 2006 data have been revised. [2] Includes nonnegligent manslaughter. [3] Includes offenses reported by the Zoological Police and the Metro Transit Police. [4] Limited data for 2006 and 2007 were available for Illinois. [5] The data collection methodology for the offense of forcible rape used by the Illinois and the Minnesota state Uniform Crime Reporting (UCR) Programs (with the exception of Rockford, Illinois, and Minneapolis and St. Paul, Minnesota) does not comply with national UCR guidelines. Consequently, their state figures for forcible rape (with the exception of Rockford, Illinois, and Minneapolis and St. Paul, Minnesota) have been estimated for inclusion in this table.

Source: U.S. Department of Justice, Federal Bureau of Investigation, "Crime in the United States"; <http://www.fbi.gov/ucr/cius2007/index.html/>.

U.S. Census Bureau, Statistical Abstract of the United States: 2010

Table 298. Crime Rates by Type—Selected Large Cities: 2007

[Offenses known to law enforcement per 100,000 population. Based on U.S. Census Bureau estimated resident population. For definitions of types of crimes, go to <http://www.fbi.gov/ucr/cius2007/about/offense_definitions.htm/>

City ranked by population size, 2007 [1]	Violent crime					Property crime			
	Total	Murder	Forcible rape	Robbery	Aggravated assault	Total	Burglary	Larceny-theft	Motor vehicle theft
New York, NY	614	6.0	10.6	265	332	1,819	254	1,403	161
Los Angeles, CA	718	10.2	25.9	348	334	2,621	507	1,506	608
Chicago, IL	(²)	15.7	(²)	546	617	4,472	876	2,937	659
Houston, TX	1,132	16.2	32.0	529	555	5,684	1,339	3,449	897
Phoenix, AZ	724	13.8	33.0	321	356	5,826	1,246	3,227	1,353
Philadelphia, PA	1,475	27.3	66.6	715	667	4,305	803	2,728	774
Las Vegas MPD, NV	1,017	8.9	53.9	392	563	4,392	1,141	2,025	1,226
San Antonio, TX	556	9.3	48.2	186	313	6,390	1,272	4,607	511
San Diego, CA	502	4.7	23.5	166	308	3,502	609	1,845	1,049
Dallas, TX	1,069	16.1	41.2	583	429	6,776	1,814	3,849	1,113
San Jose, CA	402	3.5	23.2	114	261	2,575	476	1,412	686
Honolulu, HI	288	2.1	24.9	104	157	4,106	638	2,923	545
Detroit, MI	2,289	45.8	39.6	764	1,440	6,772	2,064	2,430	2,278
Jacksonville, FL	1,022	15.4	31.2	391	584	5,696	1,394	3,698	604
Indianapolis, IN	1,234	14.3	63.3	507	649	6,308	1,679	3,666	963
Columbus, OH	852	10.7	89.8	523	228	6,996	1,952	4,198	846
San Francisco, CA	874	13.6	17.0	514	330	4,696	692	3,199	804
Charlotte-Mecklenburg PD, NC	986	10.4	38.5	435	502	6,993	1,766	4,407	821
Austin, TX	540	4.2	45.8	203	287	6,341	1,120	4,808	413
Fort Worth, TX	667	8.6	49.9	242	367	5,469	1,343	3,726	400
Memphis, TN	1,951	19.1	67.5	728	1,136	8,062	2,183	4,953	926
Baltimore, MD	1,631	45.2	23.4	624	939	4,796	1,182	2,682	932
Louisville Metro, KY	679	11.4	31.1	306	331	4,734	1,216	3,008	510
El Paso, TX	418	2.8	41.9	77	297	3,201	349	2,361	492
Boston, MA	1,155	11.0	44.4	379	721	4,153	644	2,932	578
Washington, DC	1,347	30.8	32.6	677	606	4,712	666	2,801	1,245
Seattle, WA	627	4.1	15.4	260	347	5,804	1,023	3,793	988
Denver, CO	619	8.2	51.6	182	377	3,908	993	2,022	893
Milwaukee, WI	1,403	18.3	41.2	616	728	6,667	1,083	4,232	1,352
Nashville, TN	1,509	12.9	51.4	446	999	5,577	1,083	4,029	465
Oklahoma City, OK	851	10.7	60.1	258	522	5,892	1,496	3,546	850
Portland, OR	688	4.1	52.0	240	392	5,870	899	4,084	886
Tucson, AZ	784	9.4	52.9	274	448	(³)	915	(³)	1,293
Albuquerque, NM	990	9.2	59.8	280	641	5,709	1,096	3,631	982
Atlanta, GA	1,624	25.9	29.8	719	849	7,286	1,781	4,093	1,412
Long Beach, CA	723	8.9	29.1	318	367	2,738	613	1,522	603
Fresno, CA	644	11.0	21.0	234	379	4,441	825	2,764	852
Sacramento, CA	1,113	9.6	42.1	436	626	5,298	1,177	2,802	1,319
Mesa, AZ	489	4.8	38.5	136	310	4,388	643	3,094	651
Cleveland, OH	1,465	20.5	85.0	914	445	6,142	2,057	2,542	1,542
Virginia Beach, VA	250	3.7	20.2	127	99	2,989	495	2,359	134
Omaha, NE	597	9.7	43.8	189	354	4,784	775	3,213	796
Miami, FL	1,492	19.0	13.9	618	840	5,163	1,177	3,042	945
Oakland, CA	1,918	30.3	75.4	875	937	5,968	1,196	2,258	2,514
Tulsa, OK	1,193	14.4	78.4	268	832	6,303	1,794	3,545	964
Colorado Springs, CO	531	7.2	76.2	141	306	4,425	850	3,178	397
Arlington, TX	696	3.5	41.9	199	451	5,665	1,195	4,029	441
Minneapolis, MN	1,503	12.7	121.8	679	690	6,072	1,660	3,556	856
Raleigh, NC	571	6.3	27.0	227	311	3,476	803	2,390	283
Wichita, KS	945	11.4	75.1	155	703	5,793	1,216	3,981	596
St. Louis, MO	2,198	39.6	73.2	793	1,292	9,736	2,093	5,839	1,804
Santa Ana, CA	572	6.8	19.1	229	317	2,292	298	1,377	617
Tampa, FL	1,060	8.3	23.7	357	671	4,974	1,252	3,081	642
Anaheim, CA	425	5.1	28.6	173	218	2,625	545	1,699	381
Cincinnati, OH	1,079	19.0	94.2	590	376	6,177	1,865	3,710	601
Bakersfield, CA	615	4.7	12.9	197	400	5,038	1,110	3,091	837
Pittsburgh, PA	1,107	16.7	41.3	511	538	4,463	1,095	2,876	493
Aurora, CO	548	4.6	62.1	190	292	3,833	754	2,519	559
Riverside, CA	632	4.0	30.4	229	369	3,727	744	2,366	617
Stockton, CA	1,419	9.8	35.3	543	830	6,285	1,364	3,965	956
Toledo, OH	1,228	4.4	50.9	413	759	6,689	1,998	4,058	633
Corpus Christi, TX	826	5.9	83.1	174	564	6,540	1,189	5,063	288
Anchorage, AK	846	7.7	90.4	159	589	3,909	512	2,955	442
Newark, NJ	853	37.1	21.4	393	401	3,806	683	1,565	1,558
Buffalo, NY	1,275	19.7	59.9	560	635	5,893	1,603	3,461	829
Lexington, KY	656	5.9	40.7	202	408	3,427	775	2,428	224
St. Paul, MN	857	5.2	63.7	286	502	4,093	992	2,336	764
Plano, TX	260	0.8	19.6	62	178	3,069	533	2,374	162
Mobile, AL [4]	451	15.0	9.1	295	131	5,569	1,438	3,688	443
New Orleans, LA	1,564	94.7	52.1	523	894	7,063	2,284	3,333	1,446

[1] Kansas City, Missouri did not report twelve months of data. Conquently, the data are not included in this table.   [2] The data collection methodology for the offense of forcible rape used by the Illinois and Minnesota state programs (with the exception of Rockford, Illinois, and Minneapolis and St Paul, Minnesota) does not comply with national UCR Program guidelines. Consequently, their figures for forcible rape and violent crime (of which forcible rape is a part) are not published in this table.   [3] It was determined that the agency did not follow national Uniform Crime Reporting (UCR) Program guidelines for reporting an offense. Consequently, this figure is not included in this table.   [4] The population for the city of Mobile, Alabama, includes 61,856 inhabitants from the jurisdiction of the Mobile County Sheriff's Department.

Source: U.S. Department of Justice, Federal Bureau of Investigation, "Crime in the United States"; <http://www.fbi.gov/ucr/cius2007/data/table08.html/>.

Table 299. **Murder Victims—Circumstances and Weapons Used or Cause of Death: 2000 to 2007**

[The Uniform Crime Reporting (UCR) Program defines murder and nonnegligent manslaughter as the willful (nonnegligent) killing of one human being by another. The classification of this offense is based solely on police investigation as opposed to the determination of a court, medical examiner, coroner, jury, other judicial body. For more information on murder, go to <http://www.fbi.gov/ucr/cius2007/offenses/violentcrime/murderhomicide.html/>]

Characteristic	2000	2005	2006	2007	Characteristic	2000	2005	2006	2007
Murders, total. . . .	**13,230**	**14,965**	**15,087**	**14,831**	Juvenile gang killings .	653	756	864	676
CIRCUMSTANCES [1]					Institutional killings. . .	10	12	22	11
Felonies, total	2,229	2,189	2,472	2,184	Sniper attack	8	2	2	1
Rape.	58	45	32	31	Other - not specified .	1,901	1,938	2,187	2,186
Robbery	1,077	930	1,053	924	Unknown.	4,070	5,635	5,230	5,475
Burglary.	76	91	80	86					
Larceny-theft	23	12	16	11	TYPE OF WEAPON OR				
Motor vehicle theft. . .	25	32	16	20	CAUSE OF DEATH [2]				
Arson	81	39	27	58	Total firearms	8,661	10,158	10,225	10,086
Prostitution and					Handguns	6,778	7,565	7,836	7,361
commercialized vice.	6	13	8	11	Rifles	411	445	438	450
Other sex offenses . .	10	9	18	9	Shotguns	485	522	490	455
Narcotic drug laws. . .	589	597	806	583	Other not specified or				
Gambling.	12	2	4	4	type unknown	53	138	107	115
Other - not specified .	272	419	412	447	Firearms, type not				
Suspected felony type . .	60	45	57	67	stated	934	1,488	1,354	1,705
Other than felony type					Knives or cutting				
total	6,871	7,096	7,328	7,105	instruments [3]	1,782	1,920	1,830	1,796
Romantic triangle . . .	122	118	104	105	Blunt objects [3]	617	608	618	647
Child killed by					Personal weapons [4] . . .	927	905	841	854
babysitter.	30	26	27	34	Poison	8	9	12	10
Brawl due to influence					Explosives.	9	2	1	1
of alcohol.	188	123	106	117	Fire	134	125	117	130
Brawl due to influence					Narcotics.	20	46	48	49
of narcotics.	99	97	53	61	Drowning.	15	20	12	12
Argument over money					Strangulation	166	118	137	134
or property	206	210	198	192	Asphyxiation.	92	96	106	108
Other arguments. . . .	3,589	3,718	3,644	3,645	All other [5]	799	958	1,140	1,004
Gangland killings. . . .	65	96	121	77					

[1] Murder total includes other types of circumstances not shown separately. [2] Murder total includes other types of weapons or causes of deaths not shown separately. [3] Refers to club, hammer, etc. [4] Hands, fists, feet, etc. [5] Includes poison, drowning, explosives, narcotics, and unknown.

Source: U.S. Department of Justice, Federal Bureau of Investigation, "Crime in the United States"; <http://www.fbi.gov/ucr /cius2007/index.html>.

Table 300. **Murder Victims by Age, Sex, and Race: 2007**

[See headnote, Table 299]

Age	Total	Sex			Race			
		Male	Female	Unknown	White	Black	Other	Unknown
Murders, total	**14,831**	**11,618**	**3,177**	**36**	**6,948**	**7,316**	**345**	**222**
Percent of total	100	78.3	21.4	0.2	46.8	49.3	2.3	1.5
Under 18 years old [1]	1,554	1,070	482	2	752	740	40	22
18 years old and over [1]	13,013	10,367	2,641	5	6,089	6,482	301	141
Infant (under 1 year old)	210	116	93	1	139	57	9	5
1 to 4 years old	322	162	159	1	169	142	6	5
5 to 8 years old	88	47	41	–	55	28	4	1
9 to 12 years old	75	39	36	–	39	30	4	2
13 to 16 years old	487	380	107	–	206	265	9	7
17 to 19 years old	1,443	1,272	171	–	538	867	23	15
20 to 24 years old	2,733	2,355	374	4	1,091	1,555	58	29
25 to 29 years old	2,215	1,871	344	–	871	1,284	36	24
30 to 34 years old	1,651	1,366	285	–	735	860	40	16
35 to 39 years old	1,243	949	293	1	575	622	32	14
40 to 44 years old	1,127	787	340	–	596	476	36	19
45 to 49 years old	960	689	271	–	544	381	25	10
50 to 54 years old	698	522	176	–	422	261	11	4
55 to 59 years old	451	338	113	–	268	164	16	3
60 to 64 years old	292	202	90	–	196	80	13	3
65 to 69 years old	181	123	58	–	111	57	11	2
70 to 74 years old	130	84	46	–	96	30	3	1
75 years old and over	261	135	126	–	190	63	5	3
Age unknown	264	181	54	29	107	94	4	59

– Represents zero. [1] Does not include unknown ages.

Source: U.S. Department of Justice, Federal Bureau of Investigation,"Crime in the United States"; <http://www.fbi.gov/ucr /cius2007/index.html>.

U.S. Census Bureau, Statistical Abstract of the United States: 2010

Table 301. **Homicide Trends: 1980 to 2005**

[Not all agencies which report offense information to the FBI also submit supplemental data on homicides. To account for the total number of homicide victims, the data were weighted to match national and state estimates prepared by the FBI; hence, detail may not equal total. For more information on the methodology, go to <http://www.ojp.usdoj.gov/bjs/homicide/homtrnd.htm#contents>]

Year	Number of victims						Rate [1]					
	Total	Male	Female	White	Black	Other	Total	Male	Female	White	Black	Other
1980	23,040	17,788	5,232	12,275	9,767	327	10.2	16.2	4.5	6.3	37.7	5.7
1985	18,976	14,079	4,880	10,590	7,891	399	8.0	12.2	4.0	5.2	27.6	5.5
1990	23,438	18,304	5,115	11,279	11,488	400	9.4	15.0	4.0	5.4	37.6	4.2
1993	24,526	18,937	5,550	11,278	12,435	601	9.5	15.0	4.2	5.3	38.7	5.5
1994	23,326	18,294	5,007	10,773	11,856	526	9.0	14.4	3.8	5.0	36.4	4.6
1995	21,606	16,552	5,022	10,376	10,444	581	8.2	12.9	3.7	4.8	31.6	4.9
1996	19,645	15,153	4,469	9,483	9,476	512	7.4	11.7	3.3	4.3	28.3	4.1
1997	18,208	14,057	4,125	8,620	8,842	524	6.8	10.7	3.0	3.9	26.0	4.1
1998	16,974	12,753	4,139	8,389	7,931	393	6.3	9.7	3.0	3.8	23.0	2.9
1999	15,522	11,704	3,800	7,777	7,139	458	5.7	8.8	2.7	3.5	20.5	3.3
2000	15,586	11,818	3,733	7,560	7,425	399	5.5	8.6	2.6	3.3	20.5	2.7
2001	16,037	12,232	3,775	7,884	7,522	424	5.6	8.8	2.6	3.4	20.4	2.8
2002	16,204	12,410	3,764	7,784	7,758	437	5.6	8.8	2.6	3.3	20.8	2.7
2003	16,582	12,804	3,693	7,932	7,893	468	5.7	9.0	2.5	3.4	20.9	2.8
2004	16,137	12,556	3,543	7,944	7,562	417	5.5	8.7	2.4	3.3	19.7	2.4
2005	16,692	13,122	3,545	8,017	7,999	437	5.5	9.0	2.3	3.3	20.6	2.5

[1] Rate is per 100,000 inhabitants.

Source: U.S. Department of Justice, Office of Justice Programs, Bureau of Justice Statistics, *Homicide Trends in the United States, 1976–2005*; http://www.ojp.usdoj.gov/bjs/homicide/homtrnd.htm#contents>.

Table 302. **Homicide Victims by Race and Sex: 1980 to 2006**

[**Rates per 100,000 resident population in specified group.** Excludes deaths to nonresidents of United States. Effective with data for 1999, causes of death are classified by The Tenth Revision International Classification of Diseases (ICD-10), replacing the Ninth Revision (ICD-9)used for 1979–98 data. In ICD-9, the category Homicide also inludes death as a result of legal intervention. ICD-10 has two separate categories for these two causes of death. Some caution should be used in comparing data between 1998 and 1999. See text, Section 2]

Year	Homicide victims					Homicide rate [2]				
	Total [1]	White		Black		Total [1]	White		Black	
		Male	Female	Male	Female		Male	Female	Male	Female
1980	24,278	10,381	3,177	8,385	1,898	10.7	10.9	3.2	66.6	13.5
1985	19,893	8,122	3,041	6,616	1,666	8.3	8.2	2.9	48.4	11.0
1990	24,932	9,147	3,006	9,981	2,163	10.0	9.0	2.8	69.2	13.5
1994	24,926	9,055	2,921	10,083	2,124	9.6	8.5	2.6	65.1	12.4
1995	22,895	8,336	3,028	8,847	1,936	8.7	7.8	2.7	56.3	11.1
1996	20,971	7,570	2,747	8,183	1,800	7.9	7.0	2.5	51.5	10.2
1997	19,846	7,343	2,570	7,601	1,652	7.4	6.7	2.3	47.1	9.3
1998	18,272	6,707	2,534	6,873	1,547	6.8	6.1	2.2	42.1	8.6
1999	16,889	6,162	2,466	6,214	1,434	6.2	5.6	2.2	37.5	7.8
2000	16,765	5,925	2,414	6,482	1,385	6.1	5.3	2.1	38.6	7.5
2001	20,308	8,254	3,074	6,780	1,446	7.1	7.2	2.6	38.3	7.4
2002	17,638	6,282	2,403	6,896	1,391	6.1	5.4	2.0	38.4	7.0
2003	17,732	6,337	2,372	7,083	1,309	6.1	5.4	2.0	38.9	6.6
2004	17,357	6,302	2,341	6,839	1,296	5.9	5.3	1.9	37.1	6.4
2005	18,124	6,457	2,313	7,412	1,257	6.1	5.4	1.9	39.7	6.2
2006	18,573	6,514	2,346	7,677	1,355	6.2	5.4	1.9	40.6	6.6

[1] Includes races not shown separately. [2] Rate based on enumerated population figures as of April 1 for 1980, 1990, and 2000; estimated resident population as of July 1 for other years.

Source: U.S. National Center for Health Statistics, *Vital Statistics of the United States*, annual; *National Vital Statistics Reports (NVSR)* (formerly *Monthly Vital Statistics Report)*; and unpublished data.

Table 303. **Forcible Rape—Number and Rate: 1980 to 2007**

[For definition of rape, go to<http://www.fbi.gov/ucr/cius2007/about/offense_definitions.html>

Item	1980	1990	1995	2000	2002	2003	2004	2005	2006	2007
NUMBER										
Total	82,990	102,560	97,460	90,186	95,235	93,883	95,089	94,347	92,757	90,427
By force	63,599	86,541	85,249	81,111	86,655	85,837	87,147	86,597	85,266	83,333
Attempt	19,391	16,019	12,211	9,075	8,580	8,046	7,942	7,750	7,491	7,094
RATE										
Per 100,000 population	36.8	41.1	37.1	32.0	33.1	32.3	32.4	31.8	31.0	30.0
Per 100,000 females	71.6	80.5	72.5	62.7	65.0	63.5	63.8	62.5	60.9	59.1

Source: U.S. Department of Justice, Federal Bureau of Investigation, "Violent Crime, Forcible Rape;" <http://www.fbi.gov/ucr/cius2007/offenses/violent_crime/forcible_rape.html>.

Table 304. **Criminal Victimizations and Victimization Rates: 1995 to 2007**

[(39,926 represents 39,926,000). Based on National Crime Victimization Survey; see text, this section and Appendix III. The 2006 estimates should not be compared to 2007 or to estimates for 2005 and earlier years, due to changes in methodology. For more information on these changes, go to <http://www.ojp.usdoj.gov/bjs/pub/pdf/cv07.pdf>. For definitions of crimes, go to <http://www.ojp .usdoj.gov/bjs/abstract/cvus/definitions.htm>]

Type of crime	Number of victimizations (1,000)				Victimization rates [1]			
	1995	2000	2005	2007	1995	2000	2005	2007
All crimes, total	**39,926**	**25,893**	**23,441**	**22,880**	**(X)**	**(X)**	**(X)**	**(X)**
Personal crimes [2]	**10,436**	**6,597**	**5,401**	**5,371**	**46.2**	**29.1**	**22.1**	**21.5**
Crimes of violence	10,022	6,323	5,174	5,177	44.5	27.9	21.2	20.7
Completed violence	2,960	2,044	1,659	1,579	12.9	9.0	6.8	6.3
Attempted/threatened violence . . .	7,061	4,279	3,515	3,598	31.6	18.9	14.4	14.4
Rape/sexual assault	363	261	192	248	1.6	1.2	0.8	1.0
Rape/attempted rape	252	147	130	141	1.1	0.6	0.5	0.6
Rape	153	92	69	70	0.7	0.4	0.3	0.3
Attempted rape	99	55	61	71	0.4	0.2	0.2	0.3
Sexual assault	112	114	62	108	0.5	0.5	0.3	0.4
Robbery	1,171	732	625	597	5.3	3.2	2.6	2.4
Completed/property taken	753	520	415	444	3.5	2.3	1.7	1.8
With injury.	224	160	143	170	1.0	0.7	0.6	0.7
Without injury	529	360	272	274	2.4	1.6	1.1	1.1
Attempted to take property	418	212	210	153	1.8	0.9	0.9	0.6
With injury.	84	66	64	43	0.4	0.3	0.3	0.2
Without injury	335	146	145	110	1.4	0.6	0.6	0.4
Assault	8,487	5,330	4,357	4,331	37.6	23.5	17.8	17.3
Aggravated.	2,050	1,293	1,052	859	8.8	5.7	4.3	3.4
With injury.	533	346	331	221	2.4	1.5	1.4	0.9
Threatened with weapon	1,517	946	722	638	6.4	4.2	3.0	2.5
Simple.	6,437	4,038	3,305	3,473	28.9	17.8	13.5	13.9
With minor injury	1,426	989	795	758	6.0	4.4	3.3	3.0
Without injury	5,012	3,048	2,510	2,715	22.9	13.4	10.3	10.8
Personal theft [3]	414	274	227	194	1.7	1.2	0.9	0.8
Property crimes	**29,490**	**19,297**	**18,040**	**17,508**	**279.5**	**178.1**	**154.0**	**146.5**
Household burglary.	5,004	3,444	3,456	3,215	47.4	31.8	29.5	26.9
Completed.	4,232	2,909	2,900	2,563	40.0	26.9	24.8	21.4
Attempted forcible entry	773	534	556	652	7.4	4.9	4.7	5.5
Motor vehicle theft	1,717	937	978	980	16.2	8.6	8.4	8.2
Completed.	1,163	642	775	796	10.8	5.9	6.6	6.7
Attempted	554	295	203	184	5.5	2.7	1.7	1.5
Theft	22,769	14,916	13,606	13,314	215.9	137.7	116.2	111.4
Completed [4].	21,857	14,300	13,116	12,777	207.6	132.0	112.0	106.9
Attempted	911	616	489	537	8.4	5.7	4.2	4.5

X Not applicable.   [1] Per 1,000 persons age 12 or older for "Personal crime"; per 1,000 households for "Property crime." [2] The victimization survey cannot measure murder because of the inability to question the victim.   [3] Includes pocket picking, purse snatching, and attempted purse snatching.   [4] Includes thefts in which the amount taken was not ascertained.

Source: U.S. Department of Justice, Office of Justice Programs, Bureau of Justice Statistics, National Crime Victimization Survey, *Criminal Victimization*, annual, and series NCJ-224390, December 2008. See also <http://www.ojp.usdoj.gov/bjs /abstract/cv07.htm>.

Table 305. **Victimization Rates by Type of Crime and Characteristics of the Victim: 2007**

[Rate per 1,000 persons age 12 years or older. Total population for age 12 or older was 250,344,870. Based on National Crime Victimization Survey. See headnote, Table 304]

Characteristic of the victim	All crimes	Crimes of violence						Personal theft [1]
		Total	Rape/ sexual assault	Robbery	Assault			
					Total	Aggra- vated	Simple	
Total	**21.5**	**20.7**	**1.0**	**2.4**	**17.3**	**3.4**	**13.9**	**0.8**
Male	23.4	22.5	[2]0.1	3.4	19.1	4.5	14.5	0.9
Female.	19.6	18.9	1.8	1.4	15.6	2.4	13.2	0.7
12 to 15 years old	44.2	43.4	[2]1.0	4.2	38.2	2.8	35.5	[2]0.8
16 to 19 years old	51.7	50.1	2.4	6.4	41.4	7.2	34.2	[2]1.6
20 to 24 years old	36.3	35.2	2.9	3.5	28.7	7.5	21.2	[2]1.1
25 to 34 years old	25.8	24.7	1.2	3.4	20.1	4.8	15.3	1.1
35 to 49 years old	18.3	17.7	1.0	1.4	15.3	3.2	12.1	[2]0.6
50 to 64 years old	11.9	11.6	[2]0.3	1.7	9.5	2.3	7.2	[2]0.3
65 years old and over. . .	3.3	2.5	[2]0.1	[2]0.6	1.8	[2]0.3	1.5	[2]0.8
White.	20.5	19.9	1.0	1.9	17.0	3.2	13.9	0.6
Black	26.1	24.3	[2]0.5	4.9	18.8	4.4	14.4	1.9
Other [3]	12.5	11.4	[2]1.2	[2]1.8	8.3	2.7	5.7	[2]1.1
Hispanic	19.6	18.6	[2]0.3	3.9	14.5	3.0	11.4	[2]1.0
Non-Hispanic.	21.8	21.0	1.1	2.2	17.8	3.5	14.3	0.7
Household income:								
Less than $7,500	52.7	50.7	[2]2.5	[2]4.1	44.1	5.4	38.7	[2]2.0
$7,500–$14,999	40.9	39.0	[2]1.5	6.7	30.7	6.6	24.0	[2]1.9
$15,000–$24,999	27.2	25.9	[2]1.5	3.3	21.1	3.5	17.6	[2]1.3
$25,000–$34,999	28.1	27.5	[2]0.5	2.7	24.3	4.6	19.7	[2]0.6
$35,000–$49,999	22.1	21.7	1.5	3.0	17.2	3.5	13.6	[2]0.4
$50,000–$74,999	20.3	19.8	[2]0.5	1.1	18.3	3.3	14.9	[2]0.5
$75,000 or more.	14.8	14.1	[2]0.4	1.3	18.3	3.3	14.9	0.6

[1] Includes pocket picking, completed purse snatching, and attempted purse snatching.   [2] Based on 10 or fewer sample cases.   [3] Includes American Indians, Alaska Natives, Asians, Native Hawaiians, and other Pacific Islanders.

Source: U.S. Department of Justice, Office of Justice Programs, Bureau of Justice Statistics, National Crime Victimization Survey, *Criminal Victimization,* annual, and series NCJ-224390, December 2008; <http://www.ojp.usdoj.gov/bjs/abstract/cv07.htm>.

Law Enforcement, Courts, and Prisons   195

Table 306. Victim-Offender Relationship in Crimes of Violence by Characteristics of the Criminal Incident: 2007

[In percent. Covers only crimes of violence. Total population age 12 or older was 250,344,870. Based on National Crime Victimization Survey; see text, this section and Appendix III. The 2006 estimates should not be compared to 2007 or to estimates for 2005 and earlier years, due to changes in methodology. See headnote, Table 304]

Selected characteristics of incident	Total	Rape/ sexual assault	Robbery	Assault		
				Total	Aggra-vated [1]	Simple
Total	**100**	**100**	**100**	**100**	**100**	**100**
Victim/offender relationship: [2]						
Relatives.	10.7	13.5	7.1	11.0	10.9	11.1
Well-known	23.4	28.9	8.4	25.2	17.3	27.1
Casual acquaintance	14.0	15.5	3.6	15.4	12.7	16.0
Stranger	40.0	31.2	65.7	36.9	48.0	34.2
Time of day: [4]						
6 a.m. to 6 p.m.	55.2	35.0	39.4	58.6	45.6	61.6
6 p.m. to midnight.	29.7	40.6	43.8	27.1	39.8	24.1
Midnight to 6 a.m.	11.1	21.9	11.9	10.3	12.6	9.8
Location of crime:						
At or near victim's home or lodging	35.6	48.9	30.5	35.6	40.9	34.3
Friend's/relative's/neighbor's home.	6.7	15.3	[3]2.8	6.7	10.1	6.0
Commercial places	11.4	[3]4.3	6.5	11.9	9.0	12.5
Parking lots/garages	6.6	[3]2.2	14.8	5.8	8.2	5.2
School	15.1	[3]6.3	6.7	16.9	4.5	19.8
Streets other than near victim's home. . .	15.7	[3]10.0	32.2	13.8	18.5	12.7
Other [5]	8.7	[3]3.1	6.4	9.4	9.0	9.5
Victim's activity: [6]						
At work or traveling to or from work	17.0	[3]6.4	18.2	(NA)	17.4	17.4
School	15.4	[3]8.1	[3]11.1	(NA)	4.0	19.3
Activities at home	25.7	29.3	14.8	(NA)	32.4	25.7
Shopping/errands	4.8	[3]6.7	7.1	(NA)	[3]4.1	4.4
Leisure activities away from home	22.5	26.6	23.5	(NA)	25.9	21.2
Traveling.	8.1	[3]9.2	17.1	(NA)	12.3	5.4
Other [7]	6.3	[3]13.7	7.7	(NA)	[3]3.9	6.1
Distance from victim's home: [8]						
Inside home or lodging	19.0	41.1	12.9	18.5	20.9	17.9
Near victim's home	17.8	[3]10.5	19.2	18.1	19.7	17.7
1 mile or less	17.6	[3]8.5	25.6	17.1	18.0	16.8
5 miles or less	22.0	[3]11.8	20.9	22.8	19.4	23.6
50 miles or less	19.3	23.7	15.4	19.6	17.0	20.2
More than 50 miles	3.3	[3]4.5	[3]5.2	3.0	4.5	2.7
Weapons:						
No weapons present	71.8	91.4	40.8	74.9	5.4	91.1
Weapons present	20.4	[3]5.6	47.0	17.6	92.5	(X)

NA Not available.   X Not applicable.   [1] An aggravated assault is any assault in which an offender possesses or uses a weapon or inflicts serious injury.   [2] Excludes "don't know" relationships.   [3] Based on 10 or fewer sample cases.   [4] Excludes "not known and not available" time of day.   [5] Includes areas on public transportation or inside station, in apartment yard, park, field, playground, or other areas.   [6] Excludes "don't know" and "not available" victim activity.   [7] Includes sleeping.   [8] Excludes "don't know" and "not available" distance from victim's home.

Source: U.S. Department of Justice, Office of Justice Programs, Bureau of Justice Statistics, National Crime Victimization Survey, Criminal Victimization, annual and Series NCJ-224390, December 2008. See also <http://www.ojp.usdoj.gov/bjs /abstract/cv07.htm>.

Table 307. Violence by Intimate Partners by Sex, 1995 to 2007, and by Type of Crime, 2007

[Violence includes rape and sexual assault, robbery, aggravated assault, simple assault and homicide. Intimates are defined as spouses, ex-spouses, current boy/girlfriends, and ex-boy/girlfriends. Based on the National Crime Victimization Survey; see text, this section and Appendix III. Table data have been revised]

Year and type of crime	All persons		Female victims		Male victims	
	Number	Rate per 1,000 [1]	Number	Rate per 1,000 [1]	Number	Rate per 1,000 [1]
1995	975,510	4.5	858,100	7.7	117,410	1.1
2000	670,900	3.0	560,230	4.8	110,670	1.0
2002	588,020	2.5	498,210	4.2	89,810	0.8
2003	540,700	2.3	444,140	3.6	96,560	0.8
2004	612,650	2.5	474,250	3.8	138,400	1.2
2005	493,110	2.0	385,850	3.1	107,260	0.9
2006 [2]	779,040	3.2	617,190	4.9	161,840	1.3
2007, total	**646,790**	**2.6**	**564,430**	**4.4**	**82,360**	**0.7**
Rape or sexual assault	55,110	0.2	55,110	0.4	(B)	(B)
Robbery	43,270	0.2	37,320	0.3	5,960	–
Aggravated assault.	85,010	0.3	69,010	0.5	16,000	0.1
Simple assault.	446,510	1.8	399,370	3.1	47,140	0.4
Homicide	1,531	0.5	1,185	0.8	346	0.2

– Rounds to zero.   B Base figure too small to meet statistical standards for reliability of derived figure.   [1] Rates are for the number of victimizations per 1,000 persons aged 12 or older. Except for Homicide, the number of victimizations is per 1000,000 persons aged 12 or older.   [2] Due to changes in methodology, the 2006 national crime victimization rates are not comparable to previous years or to 2007; and cannot be used for yearly trend comparisons. However, the overall patterns of victimization at the national level can be examined. See Criminal Victimization, 2007, at <http://www.ojp.usdoj.gov/bjs /abstract/cv07.htm>.

Source: U.S. Department of Justice, Office of Justice Programs, Bureau of Justice Statistics, National Crime Victimization Survey, Intimate Partner Violence in the United States, Series NCJ-210675, December 2007 and Crime Victimization, annual, Series NCJ-224390; <http://www.ojp.usdoj.gov/bjs/intimate/ipv.htm>.

U.S. Census Bureau, Statistical Abstract of the United States: 2010

Table 308. **Stalking and Harassment Victimization in the United States: 2006**

[Survey based on a total population 246,500,200, age 18 or older. The survey defines stalking as a course of conduct directed at a specific person that would cause a reasonable person to feel fear. The survey characterizes individuals as victims of harassment who experience the behaviors associated with stalking but neither reported feeling fear as a result of such conduct nor experienced actions that would cause a reasonable person to feel fear]

Characteristic [1]	Number			Rate per 1,000 persons		
	All	Stalking	Harass-ment	All	Stalking	Harass-ment
All victims.	**5,857,030**	**3,424,100**	**2,432,930**	**23.8**	**13.9**	**9.9**
Gender						
Male.	2,032,460	892,340	1,140,120	16.9	7.4	9.5
Female	3,824,570	2,531,770	1,292,800	30.3	20.0	10.2
Age						
18 to 19 years old.	379,610	238,990	140,620	47.2	29.7	17.5
20 to 24 years old.	929,710	576,870	352,840	45.7	28.4	17.3
25 to 34 years old.	1,198,195	805,260	392,930	30.1	20.2	9.9
35 to 49 years old.	1,971,290	1,139,320	831,970	29.9	17.3	12.6
50 to 64 years old.	1,046,650	534,870	511,780	20.4	10.4	10.0
65 years old and over	331,580	128,790	202,790	9.3	3.6	5.7
Race						
White	4,835,270	2,860,810	1,974,460	24.1	14.2	9.8
Black	678,230	363,280	314,950	22.7	12.2	10.5
American Indian/Alaska Native	55,890	[2]33,150	[2]22,740	33.0	[2]19.6	[2]13.4
Asian/Pacific Islander.	151,670	79,790	71,890	13.4	7.0	6.4
More than one race [3]	135,960	87,080	48,880	49.3	31.6	17.7
Hispanic origin						
Hispanic	487,320	312,490	174,830	16.5	10.6	5.9
Non-Hispanic	5,308,010	3,089,570	2,218,440	24.7	14.4	10.3
Marital status						
Never married	2,143,400	1,321,870	821,530	26.9	16.6	10.3
Married.	2,078,830	1,071,630	1,007,200	16.8	8.7	8.1
Divorced or separated	1,363,540	895,620	467,920	51.8	34.0	17.8
Widowed.	229,450	107,730	121,720	16.0	7.5	8.5
Household income						
Less than $7,500	395,740	266,800	128,940	47.0	31.7	15.3
$7,500 to $14,999.	583,840	399,620	184,210	40.1	27.4	12.6
$15,000 to $24,999.	724,270	474,220	250,050	32.3	21.1	11.1
$25,000 to $34,999.	625,680	362,180	263,500	27.4	15.8	11.5
$35,000 to $49,999.	765,580	480,750	284,830	25.2	15.8	9.4
$50,000 to $74,999.	877,660	476,420	401,230	23.1	12.6	10.6
$75,000 or more.	1,063,860	542,730	521,130	18.8	9.6	9.2

[1] Table excludes missing data.   [2] Based on 10 or fewer sample cases.   [3] Includes all persons of any race, including persons who identify two or more races.

Source: U.S. Department of Justice, Office of Justice Programs, Bureau of Justice Statistics, National Crime Victimization Survey, The Supplemental Victimization Survey; Stalking Victimization in the United States, Series NCJ-224527, January 2009. See also <http://www.ojp.usdoj.gov/bjs/abstract/svus.htm>.

Table 309. **Fraud and Identity Theft—Consumer Complaints by State: 2008**

[**Rate per 100,000 population. As of December 31.** Based on Census Bureau population estimate. Federal Trade Commission (FTC) has developed and maintained a complaint data base called the Consumer Sentinel. This database collects information about consumer fraud and identity theft from the FTC and over 115 other organizations and makes the information available to law enforcement. See appendices in the annual report for list of contributing organizations]

Consumer state	Fraud complaints		Identity theft victims		Consumer state	Fraud complaints		Identity theft victims	
	Number	Rate	Number	Rate		Number	Rate	Number	Rate
U.S. [1]	806,146	265.1	302,757	99.6	MT.	2,410	249.1	450	46.5
AL.	11,417	244.9	4,342	93.1	NE.	4,353	244.1	1,055	59.2
AK.	2,253	328.3	490	71.4	NV.	8,953	344.3	3,275	126.0
AZ.	20,610	317.1	9,683	149.0	NH.	3,985	302.9	759	57.7
AR.	5,492	192.3	2,068	72.4	NJ.	24,830	286.0	8,181	94.2
CA.	106,623	290.1	51,140	139.1	NM.	4,807	242.2	2,081	104.9
CO.	17,755	359.5	4,983	100.9	NY.	44,996	230.9	22,647	116.2
CT.	8,552	244.3	3,031	86.6	NC.	23,128	250.8	7,609	82.5
DE.	2,630	301.2	759	86.9	ND.	1,041	162.3	229	35.7
DC.	2,685	453.7	979	165.4	OH.	29,506	256.9	8,237	71.7
FL.	57,472	313.6	24,440	133.3	OK.	8,099	222.4	2,696	74.0
GA.	27,470	283.6	10,748	111.0	OR.	12,584	332.0	2,937	77.5
HI	3,689	286.4	711	55.2	PA.	30,711	246.7	10,723	86.1
ID	3,970	260.5	867	56.9	RI	2,417	230.0	824	78.4
IL.	30,578	237.0	13,726	106.4	SC.	10,556	235.6	3,292	73.5
IN	15,159	237.7	4,589	72.0	SD.	1,333	165.8	272	33.8
IA	5,895	196.3	1,347	44.9	TN.	15,893	255.7	4,982	80.2
KS.	7,101	253.4	2,005	71.6	TX.	60,633	249.2	31,708	130.3
KY.	8,173	191.4	2,396	56.1	UT.	7,345	268.4	1,775	64.9
LA.	8,978	203.5	3,819	86.6	VT.	1,535	247.1	296	47.6
ME.	3,138	238.4	623	47.3	VA.	24,695	317.9	6,349	81.7
MD.	19,585	347.6	5,412	96.1	WA.	21,730	331.8	5,855	89.4
MA.	15,515	238.8	5,408	83.2	WV	3,709	204.4	866	47.7
MI	22,805	228.0	8,363	83.6	WI	13,142	233.5	3,152	56.0
MN.	13,259	254.0	3,528	67.6	WY	1,397	262.3	250	46.9
MS.	4,498	153.1	2,367	80.5					
MO	17,056	288.5	4,433	75.0					

[1] Data represents only fraud and other complaints reported by state consumers. Identity theft reported by state victims.

Source: U.S. Federal Trade Commission, Consumer Sentinel Network Databook, *Consumer Fraud and Identity Theft complaint data, January–December 2008* (issued February 2009); <http://www.ftc.gov/sentinel/reports.shtml>.

Law Enforcement, Courts, and Prisons   197

Table 310. **Robbery and Property Crimes by Type and Selected Characteristics: 1990 to 2007**

[(639 represents 639,000.) For definitions of types of crimes, see <http://www.fbi.gov/ucr/cius2007/about/offense_definitions.html>]

Characteristic of offenses	Number of offenses (1,000)				Rate per 100,000 population				Average value lost (dol.)	
	1990	2000	2005	2007	1990	2000	2005	2007	2005	2007
Robbery, total [1]	**639**	**408**	**417**	**445**	**256.3**	**144.9**	**140.7**	**147.6**	**1,239**	**1321**
Type of crime:										
Street or highway	359	188	184	195	144.2	66.7	62.1	64.6	1,020	1,113
Commercial house.........	73	57	60	62	29.5	20.1	20.1	20.6	1,662	1,499
Gas station	18	12	12	12	7.1	4.1	4.0	3.9	1,104	1,097
Convenience store........	39	26	24	25	15.6	9.3	8.0	8.3	677	800
Residence	62	50	59	68	25.1	17.7	20.0	22.4	1,332	1,516
Bank.................	9	9	9	9	3.8	3.1	3.0	3.1	4,113	4,201
Weapon used:										
Firearm	234	161	175	158	94.1	57.0	59.0	61.9	(NA)	(NA)
Knife or cutting instrument. . . .	76	36	37	31	30.7	12.8	12.5	12.0	(NA)	(NA)
Other dangerous weapon	61	53	39	33	24.5	18.9	13.2	13.1	(NA)	(NA)
Strongarm	268	159	166	147	107.7	56.4	56.0	57.7	(NA)	(NA)
Burglary, total	**3,074**	**2,050**	**2,154**	**2,179**	**1,232.2**	**728.4**	**726.7**	**722.5**	**1,771**	**1,991**
Forcible entry.............	2,150	1,297	1,310	1,161	864.5	460.7	440.0	454.5	(NA)	(NA)
Unlawful entry	678	615	701	616	272.8	218.7	237.5	241.1	(NA)	(NA)
Attempted forcible entry	245	138	133	123	98.7	49.0	45.2	48.2	(NA)	(NA)
Residence................	2,033	1,335	1,417	1,479	817.4	474.3	477.9	490.3	1,813	1,991
Nonresidence.......... 2	1,041	715	738	700	418.5	254.1	248.8	232.2	1,687	1,989
Occurred during the night [2]	1,135	699	708	715	456.4	248.3	238.9	237.2	(NA)	(NA)
Occurred during the day [2]	1,151	836	890	966	462.8	297.2	328.8	320.2	(NA)	(NA)
Larceny-theft, total	**7,946**	**6,972**	**6,783**	**6,569**	**3,185.1**	**2,477.3**	**2,286.3**	**2,177.8**	**857**	**886**
Pocket picking	81	36	29	27	32.4	12.7	9.8	9.1	346	728
Purse snatching	82	37	42	38	32.8	13.2	14.2	12.6	404	402
Shoplifting	1,291	959	940	979	519.1	340.7	317.0	324.6	184	205
From motor vehicles	1,744	1,754	1,752	1,707	701.3	623.3	590.6	565.9	704	722
Motor vehicle accessories	1,185	677	693	599	476.3	240.6	233.6	198.6	482	554
Bicycles	443	312	249	224	178.2	110.9	83.9	74.4	267	273
From buildings	1,118	914	852	789	449.4	324.6	287.3	261.6	1,738	1,263
From coin-operated machines. . . .	63	46	41	31	25.4	16.2	13.8	10.3	232	363
Other	1,940	2,232	2,184	2,174	780.0	793.0	736.1	720.6	1,137	1,357
Motor vehicles, total [3]	**1,636**	**1,160**	**1,236**	**1,096**	**655.8**	**412.2**	**417.4**	**363.3**	**6,204**	**6,755**
Automobiles...............	1,304	877	907	715	524.3	311.5	304.5	279.9	(NA)	(NA)
Trucks and buses	238	209	219	176	95.5	74.1	76.2	68.9	(NA)	(NA)

NA Not available.   [1] Includes other crimes not shown separately.   [2] Unknown data not included.   [3] Includes other types of motor vehicles not shown separately.

Source: U.S. Department of Justice, Federal Bureau of Investigation, "Offenses Known to Law Enforcement"; <http://www.fbi.gov/ucr/cius2007/offenses/index.html>.

Table 311. **Property Victimization Rates by Selected Household Characteristics: 2007**

[(17,508 represents 17,508,000. Total number of households was 119,503,530. Based on National Crime Victimization Survey (NCVS); see text, this section and Appendix III. The 2006 estimates should not be compared to 2007 or to estimates for 2005 and earlier years, due to changes in methodology. See headnote, Table 304]

Characteristic	Number of victimizations (1,000)				Victimization rate per 1,000 households			
	Total	Burglary	Motor vehicle theft	Theft	Total	Burglary	Motor vehicle theft	Theft
Total	**17,508**	**3,215**	**980**	**13,314**	**146.5**	**26.9**	**8.2**	**111.4**
Race:								
White	13,823	2,444	687	10,692	141.9	25.1	7.1	109.7
Black	2,558	560	213	1,785	170.0	37.2	14.2	118.6
Other	738	130	44	564	129.2	22.8	7.7	98.7
Ethnicity:								
Hispanic	2,550	412	213	1,925	190.5	30.8	15.9	143.8
Non-Hispanic	14,947	2,803	767	11,378	141.2	26.5	7.2	107.5
Household income:								
Less than $7,500	934	252	49	633	213.1	57.6	11.1	144.4
$7,500 to $14,999	1,360	346	73	942	201.3	51.2	10.8	139.4
$15,000 to $24,999	1,595	320	105	1,169	167.0	33.5	11.0	122.4
$25,000 to $34,999	1,559	254	96	1,209	154.6	25.2	9.5	119.8
$35,000 to $49,999	2,010	376	101	1,532	151.2	28.3	7.6	115.2
$50,000 to $74,999	2,155	326	118	1,711	144.3	21.8	7.9	114.6
$75,000 or more........	3,348	393	163	2,792	146.3	17.2	7.1	122.0

Source: U.S. Department of Justice, Office of Justice Programs, Bureau of Justice Statistics, National Crime Victimization Survey, Criminal Victimization, annual; and Series NCJ-224390, December 2008. See also <http://www.ojp.usdoj.gov/bjs/abstract/cv07.htm>.

Table 312. **Hate Crimes—Number of Incidents, Offenses, Victims, and Known Offenders by Bias Motivation: 2000 to 2007**

[The FBI collected statistics on hate crimes from 13,241 law enforcement agencies representing over 260 million inhabitants in 2007. Hate crime offenses cover incidents motivated by race, religion, sexual orientation, ethnicity/national origin, and disability]

Bias motivation	Incidents reported	Offenses	Victims [1]	Known offenders [2]
2000, total	8,213	9,619	10,117	7,690
2005, total	7,163	8,380	8,804	6,804
2006, total	7,722	9,080	9,652	7,330
2007, Total.	**7,624**	**9,006**	**9,535**	**6,965**
Race, total.	**3,870**	**4,724**	**4,956**	**3,707**
Anti-White	749	871	908	828
Anti-Black	2,658	3,275	3,434	2,509
Anti-American Indian/Alaska native.	61	75	76	63
Anti-Asian/Pacific Islander	188	219	234	165
Anti-multiracial group.	214	284	304	142
Ethnicity/national origin, total	**1,007**	**1,256**	**1,347**	**1,155**
Anti-Hispanic	595	775	830	758
Anti-other ethnicity/national origin.	412	481	517	397
Religion, total.	**1,400**	**1,477**	**1,628**	**576**
Anti-Jewish	969	1,010	1,127	320
Anti-Catholic	61	65	70	31
Anti-Protestant	57	59	67	22
Anti-Islamic	115	133	142	104
Anti-other religious group	130	140	148	62
Anti-multi-religious group	62	64	66	32
Anti-atheism/agnosticism/etc.	6	6	8	5
Sexual orientation, total	**1,265**	**1,460**	**1,512**	**1,454**
Anti-male homosexual	772	864	890	923
Anti-female homosexual.	145	184	197	147
Anti-homosexual.	304	362	375	349
Anti-heterosexual	22	27	27	19
Anti-bisexual	22	23	23	16
Disability, total	**79**	**82**	**84**	**70**
Anti-physical	20	20	20	27
Anti-mental	59	62	64	43
Multiple bias [3]	**3**	**7**	**8**	**3**

[1] The term "victim" may refer to a person, business, institution, or a society as a whole. [2] The term "known offender" does not imply that the identity of the suspect is known, but only that an attribute of the suspect has been identified which distinguishes him/her from an unknown offender. [3] In a "multiple-bias incident" two conditions must be met: more than one offense type must occur in the incident and at least two offense types must be motivated by different biases.

Source: U.S. Department of Justice, Federal Bureau of Investigation, Uniform Crime Reports, "About Hate Crime Statistics, 2007"; <http://www.fbi.gov/ucr/hc2007/>.

Table 313. **Hate Crimes Reported by State: 2007**

[(260,230 represents 260,230,000). See headnote, Table 312]

State	Number of participating agencies	Population covered (1,000)	Agencies submitting incidents	Incidents reported	State	Number of participating agencies	Population covered (1,000)	Agencies submitting incidents	Incidents reported
United States [1]	**13,241**	**260,230**	**2,025**	**7,624**					
Alabama	156	2,388	5	6	Montana	96	944	11	21
Alaska	1	284	1	8	Nebraska	162	1,267	9	44
Arizona	78	5,755	26	161	Nevada	32	2,527	6	63
Arkansas	265	2,765	27	33	New Hampshire	143	1,022	25	43
California	727	36,553	276	1,400	New Jersey	512	8,685	207	748
Colorado	213	4,733	48	156	New Mexico	48	1,174	4	14
Connecticut	101	3,502	53	127	New York	273	15,336	29	493
Delaware	53	854	14	49	North Carolina	369	7,422	33	75
District of Columbia	2	588	2	41	North Dakota	77	579	10	14
Florida	490	18,152	73	166	Ohio	534	8,699	76	312
Georgia	18	681	3	13	Oklahoma	293	3,617	26	30
Idaho	108	1,498	16	38	Oregon	239	3,744	40	170
Illinois	60	4,946	45	167	Pennsylvania	1,173	12,075	24	83
Indiana	127	2,900	13	40	Rhode Island	47	1,058	7	47
Iowa	226	2,952	16	27	South Carolina	480	4,408	55	127
Kansas	348	2,138	45	110	South Dakota	105	672	9	37
Kentucky	324	3,841	23	48	Tennessee	461	6,156	58	239
Louisiana	103	2,515	14	31	Texas	999	23,879	60	242
Maine	149	1,317	30	72	Utah	117	2,620	28	55
Maryland	156	5,618	25	150	Vermont	80	611	11	21
Massachusetts	337	6,272	85	353	Virginia	408	7,710	83	323
Michigan	593	9,932	185	627	Washington	244	6,437	54	195
Minnesota	321	5,197	47	157	West Virginia	338	1,687	21	44
Mississippi	58	705	–	–	Wisconsin	374	5,599	21	69
Missouri	561	5,700	39	114	Wyoming	62	516	7	21

– Represents zero. [1] No data available for Hawaii.

Source: U.S. Department of Justice, Federal Bureau of Investigation, Uniform Crime Reports, "About Hate Crime Statistics, 2007"; <http://www.fbi.gov/ucr/hc2007/>.

Law Enforcement, Courts, and Prisons 199

Table 314. **Persons Arrested by Charge and Selected Characteristics: 2007**

[In thousands (10,698.3 represents 10,698,300). Represents arrests (not charges) reported by approximately 11,936 agencies with a total 2007 population of almost 226 million as estimated by FBI. Age and sex data are mandatory, while race data are optional and not always reported with arrest data; hence, two different total number of arrests. See source for details. For definitions of crimes, go to <http://www.fbi.gov/ucr/cius2007/about/offense_definitions.html>]

Offense	Total arrests	Male	Female	Total arrests	White	Black	American Indian or Alaska Native	Asian or Pacific Islander
Total [1]	10,698.3	8,111.0	2,587.3	10,656.7	7,426.3	3,003.1	143.0	84.4
Serious crimes:								
Murder and nonnegligent manslaughter	10.1	9.1	1.0	10.1	4.8	5.1	0.1	0.1
Forcible rape	17.1	16.9	0.2	17.1	11.0	5.7	0.2	0.2
Robbery	96.7	85.5	11.2	96.6	40.6	54.8	0.6	0.6
Aggravated assault	327.1	257.6	69.6	326.3	208.8	110.0	4.4	3.2
Burglary.......................	228.8	195.6	33.3	228.3	156.4	68.1	2.2	1.7
Larceny/theft	897.6	538.9	358.7	894.2	610.6	261.7	11.9	10.0
Motor vehicle theft...............	89.0	73.2	15.8	88.8	55.2	31.8	1.0	0.8
Arson	11.5	9.6	1.8	11.4	8.5	2.7	0.1	0.1
Other assaults	984.0	735.6	248.4	980.5	642.0	316.2	14.0	8.3
Nonserious crimes:								
Forgery and counterfeiting	78.0	48.2	29.8	77.8	54.1	22.5	0.4	0.7
Fraud	185.2	103.6	81.6	184.4	127.4	54.6	1.4	1.1
Embezzlement	17.0	8.3	8.8	17.0	10.8	5.8	0.1	0.2
Stolen property—buying, receiving, possessing.....................	92.2	73.4	18.8	91.9	57.9	32.6	0.7	0.8
Vandalism	221.0	183.5	37.5	220.1	166.2	48.6	3.3	1.9
Weapons; carrying, possessing, etc.....	142.7	131.7	11.1	142.4	82.3	57.7	1.1	1.3
Prostitution and commercialized vice.....	59.4	18.9	40.5	59.3	34.2	23.3	0.6	1.3
Sex offenses (except forcible rape and prostitution)	62.8	57.2	5.5	62.6	46.0	15.4	0.6	0.6
Drug abuse violations..............	1,386.4	1,125.1	261.3	1,382.8	880.7	485.1	8.9	8.1
Gambling......................	9.2	8.3	0.8	9.1	2.2	6.8	–	0.1
Offenses against family and children.....	88.9	66.4	22.5	88.4	60.1	26.1	1.7	0.5
Driving under the influence	1,056.0	836.7	219.3	1,050.8	929.5	97.5	14.3	9.6
Liquor laws....................	478.7	345.7	133.0	474.7	406.2	49.4	14.4	4.6
Drunkenness	451.1	378.9	72.2	449.1	375.4	62.3	8.9	2.5
Disorderly conduct................	540.3	398.2	142.1	537.8	342.2	183.8	8.4	3.5
Vagrancy......................	25.6	19.9	5.7	25.6	15.5	9.5	0.5	0.1
Suspicion......................	1.6	1.3	0.3	1.6	0.9	0.6	–	–
Curfew and loitering law violations	109.8	76.0	33.8	109.6	70.0	37.5	1.0	1.1
Runaways	82.5	36.2	46.3	82.2	57.0	22.4	1.7	1.2
All other offenses (except traffic)	2,948.0	2,271.4	676.6	2,936.2	1,969.9	905.7	40.5	20.2

– Rounds to zero. [1] These data represent the number of persons arrested; however, some persons may be arrested more than once during a year. Therefore, the statistics in this table could, in some cases, represent multiple arrests of the same person.

Source: U.S. Department of Justice, Federal Bureau of Investigation, "Crime in the United States, Arrests" (released September 2008); <http://www.fbi.gov/ucr/cius2007/arrests/index.html>.

Table 315. **Juvenile Arrests for Selected Offenses: 1980 to 2007**

[169,439 represents 169,439,000. Juveniles are persons under 18 years of age]

Offense	1980	1990	1995	2000	2002	2003	2004	2005	2006	2007
Number of contributing agencies	8,178	10,765	10,037	9,904	10,946	11,368	11,437	11,778	11,250	11,936
Population covered (1,000) ...	169,439	204,543	206,762	204,965	220,157	219,562	222,147	230,176	216,687	225,519
NUMBER										
Violent crime, total	77,220	97,103	123,131	78,450	71,059	69,060	68,247	73,377	73,991	73,427
Murder................	1,475	2,661	2,812	1,027	1,014	960	829	968	956	1,011
Forcible rape...........	3,668	4,971	4,556	3,402	3,553	3,195	3,186	3,088	2,519	2,633
Robbery	38,529	34,944	47,240	24,206	19,491	18,950	19,000	22,356	26,092	26,324
Aggravated assault.......	33,548	54,527	68,523	49,815	47,001	45,955	45,232	46,965	44,424	43,459
Weapon law violations	21,203	33,123	46,506	28,514	26,786	29,512	30,530	34,468	34,700	33,187
Drug abuse, total [1]........	86,685	66,300	149,236	146,594	133,557	134,746	135,056	137,809	143,639	147,382
Sale and manufacturing....	13,004	24,575	34,077	26,432	22,086	21,987	21,136	21,607	20,975	21,046
Heroin/cocaine	1,318	17,511	19,187	11,000	8,832	7,848	7,852	7,863	7,855	7,257
Marijuana	8,876	4,372	10,682	11,792	9,962	10,463	9,743	9,845	9,575	10,412
Synthetic narcotics	465	346	701	945	974	1,043	1,119	1,071	1,156	1,134
Dangerous nonnarcotic drugs	2,345	2,346	3,507	2,695	2,318	2,633	2,422	2,828	2,389	2,243
Possession............	73,681	41,725	115,159	120,432	111,471	112,759	113,920	116,202	113,905	118,318
Heroin/cocaine	2,614	15,194	21,253	12,586	10,669	9,932	10,805	11,131	11,146	9,593
Marijuana	64,465	20,940	82,015	95,962	85,769	87,909	87,717	88,909	88,249	94,851
Synthetic narcotics	1,524	1,155	2,047	2,052	2,805	2,872	3,279	3,235	3,108	3,069
Dangerous nonnarcotic drugs	5,078	4,436	9,844	9,832	11,928	12,046	12,119	12,927	11,402	10,805

[1] For 2006 and 2007, the totals provided for sale/manufacturing and possession are based on law enforcement agencies supplying 12 months complete drug breakdown information to the Uniform Crime Reporting Program; therefore; the totals may not match those shown for drug abuse.

Source: U.S. Department of Justice, Federal Bureau of Investigation, "Crime in the United States, Arrests" (released September 2008). See <http://www.fbi.gov/ucr/cius2007/arrests/index.html>.

Table 316. **Suspects Arrested for Federal Offenses and Booked by U.S. Marshal Service (USMS) by Offense: 1995 to 2005**

[Persons suspected of violating federal law may be arrested by any one of the many federal agencies empowered to make arrests, or by state or local authorities. Regardless of which agency makes the arrest, federal suspects are typically transferred to the custody of the U.S. Marshals Service for booking, processing, and detention. See Methodology for a listing of detailed offense categories within each major offense category]

Most serious offense	1995	1996	1997	1998[2]	1999[1,2]	2000[2]	2001[2]	2002[2]	2003	2004	2005
All offenses[3]	83,324	85,195	91,747	104,119	109,340	115,589	118,896	124,074	131,064	140,755	140,200
Violent offenses[4]	3,873	4,519	4,801	4,989	4,254	4,250	4,843	4,723	4,484	4,587	4,243
Property offenses	16,245	16,191	16,288	16,786	16,569	16,842	16,824	17,268	17,258	15,609	14,899
Fraudulent[5]	12,804	12,729	12,912	13,219	13,116	13,432	13,397	13,976	14,169	12,709	12,365
Other[6]	3,441	3,462	3,376	3,567	3,453	3,410	3,427	3,292	3,089	2,900	2,534
Drug offenses	23,768	24,682	26,843	30,012	31,867	32,630	33,589	33,730	34,217	32,980	33,061
Public-order offenses	10,336	9,578	9,324	9,234	9,841	10,063	9,156	8,772	8,591	8,618	8,989
Regulatory	697	656	749	775	752	621	687	524	425	335	299
Other	9,639	8,922	8,575	8,459	9,089	9,442	8,469	8,248	8,166	8,283	8,690
Weapon offenses[7]	3,724	3,131	3,235	3,539	4,268	5,203	6,007	7,488	9,416	9,936	9,560
Immigration offenses[7]	10,600	12,026	14,994	20,942	22,849	25,205	24,794	25,270	27,620	39,135	38,041
Supervision violations	13,498	13,304	13,995	15,157	15,603	17,133	18,978	21,777	23,605	23,399	24,250
Material witness	1,143	1,617	2,169	3,398	4,016	4,203	3,679	3,918	4,615	5,385	6,078
Unknown or indeterminable offenses	137	147	163	62	73	60	1,026	1,128	1,258	1,106	1,079

[1] Starting in 1999 and through the current year of data, nonviolent sex offenses were reclassified from violent offenses to public-order offenses.   [2] Data for 1998 through 2002 are not directly comparable to 2003 through 2005 because of changes in the data processing methodology. See note 2 on page 24, chapter 1 of the 2004 Compendium of Federal Justice Statistics.   [3] Includes suspects whose offense category could not be determined.   [4] In this table violent offenses may include nonnegligent manslaughter.   [5] Fradulent property excludes tax fraud.   [6] Excludes fraudulent property and includes destruction of property and trespassing.   [7] Beginning in 2001, weapon and immigration offenses became major offense categories. Previously, theses offenses were classified within Public-order offenses.

Source: U.S. Department of Justice, Office of Justice Programs, Bureau of Justice Statistics, Federal Justice Statistics, 2005, Series NCJ 220383, September 2008; http://www.ojp.usdoj.gov/bjs/abstract/fjs05.htm.

Table 317. **Suspects in Criminal Matters Investigated by U.S. Attorneys by Offense: 1995 to 2005**

[The most serious offense investigated is based on the criminal lead charge as determined by the assistant U.S. attorney responsible for the criminal matter]

Most serious offense	1995	1996	1997	1998	1999[1]	2000	2001	2002	2003	2004	2005
All offenses[2]	102,220	97,776	110,034	115,692	117,994	123,559	121,818	124,335	130,078	141,212	143,640
Violent offenses[3]	5,720	6,570	7,354	7,527	5,768	6,036	6,225	6,392	5,688	5,714	5,485
Property offenses	31,759	28,962	29,916	30,125	28,011	28,423	28,608	27,321	27,375	24,956	25,570
Fraudulent[4]	27,836	25,245	25,854	26,328	24,200	24,679	25,275	24,019	24,261	22,182	23,052
Other[5]	3,923	3,717	4,062	3,797	3,811	3,744	3,333	3,302	3,114	2,774	2,518
Drug offenses	31,686	30,227	34,027	36,355	37,313	38,959	37,944	38,150	37,416	37,501	40,038
Public-order offenses	19,036	18,918	22,857	21,244	22,816	24,180	23,980	23,472	23,717	21,277	21,583
Regulatory	5,371	5,154	5,423	6,541	6,332	5,737	5,411	4,738	5,366	4,959	5,037
Other	13,665	13,764	17,434	14,703	16,484	18,443	18,569	18,734	18,351	16,318	16,546
Weapon offenses[6]	5,376	4,462	4,870	4,907	6,982	8,589	8,989	11,200	14,022	14,398	13,689
Immigration offenses[6]	7,256	7,122	9,366	14,114	15,539	16,495	15,378	16,699	20,341	35,858	36,559
Unknown or indeterminable offenses	1,387	1,515	1,644	1,420	1,565	877	694	1,101	1,519	1,508	716

[1] Starting in 1999 and through the current year of data, nonviolent sex offenses were reclassified from violent offenses to public-order offenses.   [2] Includes suspects whose offense category could not be determined. See Methodology for a listing of detailed offense categories within each major offense category.   [3] In this table, violent offenses may include nonnegligent manslaughter.   [4] Fradulent property excludes tax fraud.   [5] Excludes fraudulent property and includes destruction of property and trespassing.   [6] Beginning in 2001, weapon and immigration offenses became major offense categories. Previously, theses offenses were classified within public-order offenses.

Source: U.S. Department of Justice, Office of Justice Programs, Bureau of Justice Statistics, Federal Justice Statistics, 2005, Series NCJ 220383, September 2008; <http://www.ojp.usdoj.gov/bjs/abstract/fjs05.htm>.

Law Enforcement, Courts, and Prisons 201

Table 318. **Drug Arrest Rates for Drug Abuse Violations, 1990 to 2007, and by Region, 2007**

[Rate per 100,000 inhabitants. Based on Census Bureau estimated resident population as of July 1, except 1990 and 2000, enumerated as of April 1. For composition of regions, see map, inside front cover]

Offense	1990	2000	2005	2007 Total	North-east	Mid-west	South	West
Drug arrest rate, total	435.3	587.1	600.9	585.9	507.1	426.2	655.0	675.7
Sale and/or manufacture	139.0	122.7	109.9	102.7	114.3	78.1	112.3	101.6
Heroin or cocaine [1]	93.7	60.8	47.8	46.3	72.1	26.3	51.8	36.9
Marijuana	26.4	34.2	29.6	30.9	28.8	32.9	30.1	31.9
Synthetic or manufactured drugs	2.7	6.4	8.6	8.8	5.5	4.8	17.1	4.6
Other dangerous nonnarcotic drugs. . .	16.2	21.3	23.9	16.7	8.0	14.1	13.3	28.2
Possession	296.3	464.4	490.9	483.2	392.7	348.1	542.7	574.1
Heroin or cocaine [1]	144.4	138.7	131.5	126.0	113.2	62.7	149.6	153.6
Marijuana	104.9	244.4	228.9	246.5	224.3	226.4	313.8	200.0
Synthetic or manufactured drugs	6.6	12.0	21.0	19.4	11.6	13.6	28.2	18.8
Other dangerous nonnarcotic drugs. . .	40.4	69.4	109.6	91.2	43.7	45.4	51.0	201.7

[1] Includes other derivatives such as morphine, heroin, and codeine.

Source: U.S. Department of Justice, Federal Bureau of Investigation, "Crime in the United States"; <http://www.fbi.gov/ucr/07cius /arrests/index.html>, and unpublished data.

Table 319. **Federal Drug Arrests and Seizures by Type of Drug: 1990 to 2008**

[For fiscal years ending in year shown]

Drug	1990	1995	2000	2003	2004	2005	2006	2007	2008
Number of Arrests, total [1,2]	22,085	23,701	36,844	26,003	26,835	28,064	27,155	27,179	24,954
Heroin.	2,057	2,548	3,622	2,521	2,485	2,449	2,314	2,151	2,505
Cocaine.	12,399	12,036	16,373	11,381	11,961	13,005	13,026	12,735	11,805
Marijuana.	5,155	6,231	8,573	6,031	6,309	6,109	5,977	6,797	6,048
Methamphetamine.	2,474	2,886	8,276	6,070	6,080	6,501	5,838	5,496	4,596
Seizure in (pounds), total [3]	720,947	1,544,588	2,871,109	2,965,601	3,048,722	2,816,695	2,643,634	3,680,313	3,505,091
Cocaine.	235,890	233,989	248,859	245,413	336,078	391,934	329,772	362,216	199,463
Heroin.	1,704	2,971	3,341	5,803	4,088	3,898	4,124	5,683	3,729
Marijuana.	483,353	1,305,702	2,611,802	2,705,821	2,700,362	2,410,131	2,300,553	3,304,154	3,293,736
Methamphetamine.	(NA)	1,926	7,107	8,564	8,194	10,732	9,185	8,260	8,163

NA Not available. [1] Arrests are for Drug Enforcement Administration only. [2] Includes other drug-related arrests not shown. [3] Reflects the combined drug seizure effort of the Drug Enforcement Administration, the Federal Bureau of Investigation, the U.S. Customs Services, and beginning October 1995, the U.S. Border Patrol within the jurisdiction of the United States as well as maritime seizures by the U.S. Coast Guard. Based on reports to the federal-wide Drug Seizure System, which eliminates duplicate reporting of a seizure involving more than one federal agency. [4] Includes other drug seizures not shown.

Source: U.S. Drug Enforcement Administration, Stats and Facts, and unpublished data from federal-wide Drug Seizure System (15 May 2008). See also <http://www.usdoj.gov.dea/statistics.html>.

Table 320. **Background Checks for Firearm Transfers: 1994 to 2007**

[In thousands (87,180 represents 87,180,000), except rates]

Inquiries and rejections	Total 1994-2007 [1]	Interim period 1994-1998 [2]	Permanent Brady [3] 1998 [4]	2000	2002	2003	2004	2005	2006	2007
Applications and denials:										
Applications received.	87,180	12,740	893	8,621	7,699	7,831	8,084	8,278	8,612	8,658
Applications denied	1,631	312	20	204	153	126	126	132	134	136
Denied (Percent)	1.9	2.4	2.2	2.4	2.0	1.6	1.6	1.6	1.6	1.6
Selected reasons for rejection:										
Felony indictment/conviction. .	493	44	(NA)	147	88	53	53	57	52	49
Other.	403	18	(NA)	57	65	73	73	75	83	87
Felony denials per 1,000 applications	(NA)	(NA)	(NA)	17.0	11.4	6.8	6.6	6.9	6.0	5.7

NA Not available. [1] Number of applications and estimates of denials for firearm transfers or permits since the inception of the Brady Act, 1994–2007. [2] Background checks on applicants were conducted by state and local agencies, mainly on handgun transfers. See "Presale Handgun Checks, the Brady Interim Period, 1994–98" (NCJ 175034). [3] The period beginning November 30, 1998 is the effective date for the Brady Handgun Violence Prevention Act, P.L. 103-159, 1993. The National Instant Criminal Background Check System (NICS) began operations. Checks on handgun and long gun transfers are conducted by the Federal Bureau of Investigation (FBI), and by state and local agencies. Totals combine Firearm Inquiry Statistics (FIST) estimates for state and local agencies with transactions and denials reported by the FBI. [4] For the period of November 30 to December 31, 1998. Counts are from the NICS operations report and may include multiple transactions for the same application.

Source: U.S. Department of Justice, Office of Justice Programs, Bureau of Justice Statistics, Background Checks for Firearm Transfers, 2007, Series NCJ 223197, July 2008; <http://www.ojp.usdoj.gov/bjs/pub/html/bcft/2007/bcft07st.htm>.

202   Law Enforcement, Courts, and Prisons

Table 321. **Law Enforcement Officers Killed and Assaulted: 1990 to 2007**

[Contains statistics on felonious and accidental deaths of duly sworn local, state, tribal, and federal law enforcement officers. For composition of regions, see map, inside front cover]

Item	1990	1995	2000	2002	2003	2004	2005	2006	2007
OFFICERS KILLED									
Total killed	132	133	134	131	133	139	122	114	140
Northeast	13	16	13	10	13	18	12	12	13
Midwest	20	19	32	22	20	25	23	20	20
South.	68	63	67	64	66	66	58	48	77
West	23	32	19	28	31	24	24	31	28
Puerto Rico.	8	2	3	7	3	5	5	3	2
Island areas, foreign									
countries	–	1	–	–	–	1	–	–	–
Total feloniously killed	65	74	51	56	52	57	55	48	57
Firearms	56	63	47	51	45	54	50	46	55
Handgun	47	44	33	38	34	36	42	36	38
Rifle	8	14	10	10	10	13	3	8	8
Shotgun.	1	5	4	3	1	5	5	2	8
Blunt instrument	–	–	–	–	1	–	–	–	–
Bomb	–	8	–	–	–	–	–	–	–
Knife/cutting instrument . . .	3	1	1	1	–	1	–	–	–
Personal weapons [1]	2	–	–	–	–	–	–	–	–
Vehicle	1	2	3	4	6	2	5	2	2
Other	3	–	–	–	–	–	–	–	–
Total accidentally killed	67	59	83	75	81	82	67	66	83
OFFICERS ASSAULTED									
Population covered (1,000) [2] .	197,426	191,759	204,599	219,425	225,770	226,273	222,874	227,361	231,764
Number of—									
Reporting agencies	9,343	8,503	8,940	10,164	10,539	10,589	10,119	10,596	10,856
Officers employed	410,131	428,379	452,531	491,009	501,738	501,462	489,393	504,147	517,875
Total assaulted	72,091	57,762	58,398	59,526	58,600	59,692	57,820	59,396	59,201
Firearm	3,651	2,354	1,749	1,927	1,879	2,114	2,157	2,290	2,176
Knife/cutting instrument	1,647	1,356	1,015	1,061	1,084	1,123	1,059	1,055	1,023
Other dangerous weapon . . .	7,423	6,414	8,132	8,526	8,180	8,645	8,379	8,611	8,507
Personal weapons [1]	59,370	47,638	47,502	48,012	47,457	47,810	46,225	47,440	47,495

– Represents zero. [1] Includes hands, fists, feet, etc. [2] Represents the number of persons covered by agencies shown.

Source: U.S. Department of Justice, Federal Bureau of Investigation, "Law Enforcement Officers Killed and Assaulted, 2007"; <http://www.fbi.gov/ucr/killed/2007/index.html/>.

Table 322. U.S. Supreme Court—Cases Filed and Disposition: 1980 to 2007

[Statutory term of court begins first Monday in **October**]

Action	1980	1990	1995	2000	2003	2004	2005	2006	2007
Total cases on docket	5,144	6,316	7,565	8,965	8,882	8,588	9,608	10,256	9,602
Appellate cases on docket	2,749	2,351	2,456	2,305	2,058	2,041	2,025	2,069	1,969
From prior term	527	365	361	351	336	300	354	346	355
Docketed during present term	2,222	1,986	2,095	1,954	1,722	1,741	1,671	1,723	1,614
Cases acted upon	2,324	2,042	2,130	2,024	1,798	1,727	1,703	1,736	1,666
Granted review	167	114	92	85	74	69	63	62	85
Denied, dismissed, or withdrawn	1,999	1,802	1,945	1,842	1,641	1,529	1,554	1,611	1,529
Summarily decided	90	81	62	63	37	89	46	39	30
Cases not acted upon	425	309	326	281	260	314	322	333	303
Pauper cases on docket	2,371	3,951	5,098	6,651	6,818	6,543	7,575	8,181	7,628
Cases acted upon [1]	2,027	3,436	4,514	5,736	6,036	5,815	6,533	7,186	6,753
Granted review	17	27	13	14	13	11	15	15	10
Denied, dismissed, or withdrawn	1,968	3,369	4,439	5,658	6,005	5,061	6,459	6,925	6,562
Summarily decided	32	28	55	61	13	737	58	239	175
Cases not acted upon	344	515	584	915	782	728	1,042	995	875
Original cases on docket	24	14	11	9	6	4	8	6	5
Cases disposed of during term	7	3	5	2	2	–	4	1	1
Total cases available									
for argument	264	201	145	138	140	128	122	108	125
Cases disposed of	162	131	93	89	93	87	87	80	78
Cases argued	154	125	90	86	91	87	88	78	75
Cases dismissed or remanded									
without argument	8	6	3	3	2	–	1	2	3
Cases remaining	102	70	52	49	47	41	31	28	47
Cases decided by signed opinion	144	121	87	83	89	85	82	74	72
Cases decided by per curiam opinion.	8	4	3	4	2	2	5	4	2
Number of signed opinions.	123	112	75	77	73	74	69	67	67

– Represents zero. [1] Includes cases granted review and carried over to next term, not shown separately.

Source: Office of the Clerk, Supreme Court of the United States, unpublished data.

Law Enforcement, Courts, and Prisons   203

Table 323. **U.S. District Courts—Civil Cases Commenced and Pending: 2000 to 2008**

[For years ending June 30]

Type of case	Cases commenced				Cases pending			
	2000	2005	2007	2008	2000	2005	2007	2008
Cases total [1]	**263,049**	**282,758**	**272,067**	**256,354**	**249,692**	**267,270**	**267,774**	**286,193**
Contract actions [1]	54,494	28,590	34,071	34,818	38,262	26,712	30,631	30,696
Recovery of overpayments [2]	25,636	3,380	3,053	3,491	12,107	1,953	1,708	1,686
Real property actions	6,481	4,541	4,456	5,607	4,249	4,512	4,321	4,525
Tort actions	40,877	75,273	77,257	59,588	63,116	76,821	83,046	105,763
Personal injury	36,867	52,215	73,004	55,777	59,232	72,716	78,464	101,181
Personal injury product liability [1]	15,349	35,615	51,557	39,664	31,772	46,575	52,346	74,440
Asbestos	7,893	1,628	15,422	23,726	4,949	1,073	14,525	35,857
Other personal injury	21,518	16,600	21,447	16,113	27,460	26,141	26,118	26,741
Personal property damage	4,010	23,058	4,253	3,811	3,884	4,105	4,582	4,582
Actions under statutes [1]	161,187	171,922	156,152	156,277	144,053	157,357	149,622	145,077
Civil rights [1]	41,226	36,724	31,975	31,632	44,259	40,596	36,469	34,652
Employment	21,404	17,998	13,608	13,036	24,456	21,344	16,863	15,452
Bankruptcy suits	3,378	3,428	3,182	2,630	2,555	2,650	2,533	1,793
Commerce (ICC rates, etc.)	1,007	492	317	373	444	395	276	217
Environmental matters	894	726	763	900	1,355	1,193	1,045	1,219
Prisoner petitions	57,706	62,698	53,222	55,374	43,560	47,870	47,172	46,229
Forfeiture and penalty	2,246	2,214	2,221	2,324	1,772	2,156	2,245	2,237
Labor laws	14,229	18,643	18,630	16,685	11,267	15,725	15,111	15,171
Protected property rights [3]	8,745	11,809	11,132	9,636	7,858	10,507	9,827	9,019
Securities commodities and exchanges	2,500	2,371	1,369	1,669	3,578	5,192	4,030	3,621
Social security laws	14,365	16,066	12,964	13,329	13,667	15,420	13,214	13,181
Tax suits	938	1,348	1,485	1,448	1,068	1,222	1,376	1,366
Freedom of information	335	426	325	294	380	378	380	365

[1] Includes other types not shown separately. [2] Includes enforcement of judgments in student loan cases, and overpayments of veterans benefits. [3] Includes copyright, patent, and trademark rights.

Source: Administrative Office of the U.S. Courts, *Statistical Tables for the Federal Judiciary,* annual. See also <http://www.uscourts.gov/>.

Table 324. **U.S. District Courts—Offenders Convicted and Sentenced to Prison and Length of Sentence: 2000 and 2005**

Selected most serious offense of conviction	Offenders convicted [1]		Offenders sentenced to prison [1, 2]		Mean length of sentence for incarceration (months) [3]	
	2000	2005	2000	2005	2000	2005
Total	**68,156**	**78,042**	**50,451**	**61,151**	**56.7**	**61.1**
Violent offenses [4]	2,557	2,500	2,360	2,329	86.5	100.8
Murder [5]	283	137	249	132	94.2	136.8
Assault	253	489	188	411	33.0	49.5
Robbery	1579	1388	1,532	1,349	93.0	101.6
Property offenses	12,454	11,259	7,462	6,609	24.2	26.8
Fraudulent	10,396	9,837	6,272	5,823	22.5	25.8
Embezzlement	917	548	506	272	14.8	16.5
Fraud [6]	8,177	8,322	5,008	4,938	23.5	26.2
Forgery	86	64	41	29	19.1	15.1
Counterfeiting	1,216	903	717	584	20.8	27.4
Other [4]	2,058	1,422	1,190	786	33.2	34.1
Larceny [7]	1,394	970	689	427	27.3	21
Arson	158	171	134	143	71.8	79.6
Transportation of stolen property	272	159	200	123	33.4	36.1
Drug offenses [4]	24,206	25,576	22,352	23,665	75.5	85.8
Public-order offenses [4]	4,585	5,823	2,989	4,219	45.8	53.8
Regulatory	1,376	754	647	346	28.4	33.1
Other [8]	3,209	5,069	2,342	3,873	46.5	55.7
Tax law violations [8]	655	509	355	327	18.5	23.4
Escape	487	940	447	641	19.2	21.5
Racketeering and extortion	951	1,637	778	1,367	81.5	73.8
Nonviolent sex offenses [9]	475	1,157	429	1,090	47.1	68.5
Obscene material [9]	28	11	7	8	(B)	(B)
Weapon offenses [10]	4,196	8,834	3,834	8,183	91.4	83.1
Immigration offenses [10]	11,125	16,872	10,073	14,922	29.5	25.7
Misdemeanors [11]	8,961	7,178	1,356	1,224	10.4	5.4

B Base figures too small to meet statistical standards for reliability of a derived figure. [1] Total may not equal the sum of individual sanctions. [2] All sentences to incarceration, including split, mixed, life and indeterminate sentences. [3] Excludes sentences of life, death, and indeterminate sentences. [4] Includes offenses not shown separately. [5] Includes nonnegligent manslaughter. [6] Excludes tax fraud. [7] Excludes transportation of stolen property. [8] Includes tax fraud. [9] Denotes the mail or transport thereof. [10] Beginning in 2001, "Weapon and Immigration" offenses became major offense categories. Previously, these offenses were classified within "Public-order offenses". [11] Includes misdemeanors, petty offenses, unknown offense levels, and drug possession.

Source: U.S. Department of Justice, Office of Justice Programs, Bureau of Justice Statistics, *Federal Justice Statistics, 2005;* Series NCJ 220383, September 2008; <http://www.ojp.usdoj.gov/bjs/abstract/fjs05.htm>.

204   Law Enforcement, Courts, and Prisons

Table 325. **Criminal Appeals Filed by Offense: 1995 to 2005**

[Appeals were classified into the offense category that represents the offense of conviction. Offenses represent the statutory offense charged against a defendant in a criminal appeal]

Most serious offense of conviction	1995	1996	1997	1998	1999 [1]	2000	2001	2002	2003	2004	2005
All offenses [2]	**10,162**	**10,889**	**10,521**	**10,535**	**10,251**	**9,162**	**11,281**	**11,569**	**11,968**	**12,517**	**14,644**
Violent offenses [3]	700	685	739	742	559	490	591	606	601	673	748
Property offenses	1,767	2,093	1,972	1,947	1,739	1,482	1,681	1,726	1,842	1,873	2,104
Fraudulent [4]	1,323	1,581	1,519	1,439	1,338	1,164	1,299	1,389	1,478	1,524	1,673
Other [5]	444	512	453	508	401	318	382	337	364	349	431
Drug offenses	4,499	5,099	4,750	4,845	4,513	3,843	4,529	4,689	4,565	4,678	5,778
Public-order offenses	886	985	1,050	878	954	827	1,024	876	894	955	1,025
Regulatory	220	196	224	178	162	150	144	128	137	142	159
Other	666	789	826	700	792	677	880	642	757	813	866
Weapon offenses [6] . [6]	1,034	1,183	1,135	982	1,070	872	1,266	1,386	1,681	2,024	2,242
Immigration offenses [6]	277	353	417	693	934	1,179	1,654	1,679	1,821	1,856	2,373
Unknown or indeterminable offenses	999	491	458	448	482	469	536	607	564	458	374

[1] Starting in 1999 and through the current data year, nonviolent sex offenses were reclassified from "Violent offenses" to "Public-order offenses." [2] Include suspects whose offense category could not be determined. See Methodology for a listing of detailed offense categories within each major offense category. [3] In this table, "Violent offenses" may include nonnegligent manslaughter. [4] Fraudulent property excludes tax fraud. [5] Excludes fraudulent property and includes destruction of property and trespassing. [6] Beginning in 2001, "Weapon" and "Immigration" offenses became major offense categories. Previously, these offenses were classified within "Public-order offenses."

Source: U.S. Department of Justice, Office of Justice Programs, Bureau of Justice Statistics, *Federal Justice Trends,* 2005. Series NCJ 220383, September 2008. See also <http://www.ojp.usdoj.gov/bjs/abstract/fjs05.htm>.

Table 326. **Authorized Intercepts of Communication—Summary: 1980 to 2008**

[**As of December 31.** Data for jurisdictions with statutes authorizing or approving interception of wire or oral communication]

Item	1980	1990	1995	2000	2003	2004	2005	2006	2007	2008
Jurisdictions: [1]										
With wiretap statutes	28	40	41	45	47	47	47	47	47	47
Reporting interceptions	22	25	19	26	24	20	23	24	25	23
Intercept applications authorized	564	872	1,156	1,266	1,442	1,710	1,773	1,839	2,208	1,891
Intercept installations [2]	524	812	1,024	1,139	1,367	1,633	1,694	1,714	2,119	1,809
Federal	79	321	527	472	576	723	624	461	454	384
State	445	491	497	667	791	910	1,070	1,253	1,005	1,425
Intercepted communications, average [3]	1,058	1,487	2,028	1,769	3,004	3,017	2,835	2,685	3,106	2,707
Incriminating average [3]	315	321	459	402	993	619	629	547	920	514
Persons arrested [4]	1,871	2,057	2,577	3,411	3,674	4,506	4,674	4,376	4,830	4,133
Convictions [4]	259	420	494	736	844	634	776	711	984	810
Major offense specified:										
Gambling	199	116	95	49	49	90	42	56	55	54
Drugs	282	520	732	894	1,104	1,308	1,433	1,473	1,792	1,593
Homicide and assault	13	21	30	72	80	48	82	119	132	92
Racketeering	(NA)	(NA)	98	76	96	138	94	90	98	58

NA Not available [1] Jurisdictions include federal government, 44 states and the Virgin Islands, and District of Columbia. [2] Based on the number of orders for which intercept devices were installed as reported by the prosecuting official. [3] Average per authorized installation. [4] Based on information received from intercepts installed in year shown; additional arrests/convictions will occur in subsequent years but are not shown here.

Source: Administrative Office of the U.S. Courts, *Report on Applications for Orders Authorizing or Approving the Interception of Wire, Oral or Electronic Communications* (Wiretap Report), annual. See also <http://www.uscourts.gov/wiretap08/contents.html>.

Table 327. **Federal Prosecutions of Public Corruption: 1990 to 2007**

[**As of Dec. 31.** Prosecution of persons who have corrupted public office in violation of Federal Criminal Statutes]

Prosecution Status	1990			2000			2005			2007		
	Charged	Con-victed	Await-ing trial	Charged	Con-victed	Await-ing trial	Charged	Con-victed	Await-ing trial	Charged	Con-victed	Await-ing trial
Total [1]	1,176	1,084	300	1,000	938	327	1,163	1,027	451	1,141	1,014	487
Federal officials	615	583	103	441	422	92	445	390	118	426	405	116
State officials	96	79	28	92	91	37	96	94	51	128	85	65
Local officials	257	225	98	211	183	89	309	232	148	284	275	127
Others involved	208	197	71	256	242	109	313	311	134	303	249	179

[1] Includes individuals who are neither public officials nor employees, but were involved with public officials or employees in violating the law, not shown separately.

Source: U.S. Department of Justice, Criminal Division, *Report to Congress on the Activities and Operations of the Public Integrity Section,* <http://www.usdoj.gov/criminal/pin/>.

U.S. Census Bureau, Statistical Abstract of the United States: 2010

Table 328. **Delinquency Cases Disposed by Juvenile Courts by Reason for Referral: 1990 to 2005**

[In thousands (1,346 represents 1,346,000), except rate. A delinquency offense is an act committed by a juvenile for which an adult could be prosecuted in a criminal court. Disposition of a case involves taking a definite action such as waiving the case to criminal court, dismissing the case, placing the youth on probation, placing the youth in a facility for delinquents, or such actions as fines, restitution, and community service]

Reason for referral	1990	1995	1997	1998	1999	2000	2001	2002	2003	2004	2005
All delinquency offenses ..	**1,346**	**1,807**	**1,870**	**1,799**	**1,720**	**1,702**	**1,688**	**1,676**	**1,674**	**1,688**	**1,682**
Case rate [1]............	52.5	63.0	63.4	60.3	56.9	55.4	54.3	53.4	53.1	53.5	53.2
Person offenses [2]...........	257	398	413	404	396	391	402	401	408	416	428
Criminal homicide.........	2	3	2	2	2	2	2	2	1	1	1
Forcible rape............	4	6	5	5	4	4	5	4	5	4	4
Robbery	28	42	36	30	26	22	22	21	22	21	26
Aggravated assault.........	52	73	61	57	51	51	48	46	47	47	49
Property offenses [2]...........	786	906	861	786	709	678	641	637	624	616	591
Burglary	145	148	147	135	117	111	107	106	104	99	96
Larceny-theft	349	432	406	360	326	314	293	292	284	283	262
Motor vehicle theft	71	54	52	45	39	37	38	38	38	35	33
Arson	7	11	9	9	9	9	9	9	9	9	8
Drug law violations...........	71	162	189	188	188	196	203	192	191	196	194
Public order offenses [2]........	232	341	408	420	426	438	442	445	452	462	470
Obstruction of justice........	89	137	192	212	209	215	217	214	217	216	225
Disorderly conduct	56	91	92	89	96	100	104	114	116	125	128
Weapons offenses	31	47	45	43	40	37	37	35	37	41	44
Liquor law violations	17	18	16	19	20	25	25	26	26	26	25
Nonviolent sex offenses.....	11	10	12	12	13	14	15	15	14	14	14

[1] Number of cases disposed per 1,000 youth (ages 10 to 17) at risk of referral to juvenile court.   [2] Total include other offenses not shown.

Source: National Center for Juvenile Justice, Pittsburgh, PA, *Juvenile Court Statistics,* annual. See also <http://www.ojjdp.ncjrs.org /ojstatbb/index.html>.

Table 329. **Delinquency Cases and Case Rates by Sex and Race: 1995 to 2005**

[See headnote, Table 328]

Sex, race, and offense	Number of cases disposed			Case rate [1]		
	1995	2000	2005	1995	2000	2005
Male, total	**1,401,800**	**1,271,100**	**1,221,600**	**95.1**	**80.6**	**75.5**
Person......................	299,600	281,600	301,000	20.3	17.9	18.6
Property....................	701,000	506,200	429,600	47.6	32.1	26.5
Drugs......................	138,500	162,600	155,200	9.4	10.3	9.6
Public order.................	262,600	320,600	335,900	17.8	20.3	20.8
Female, total	**405,500**	**431,200**	**460,300**	**29.0**	**28.8**	**29.9**
Person......................	98,800	109,300	126,600	7.1	7.3	8.2
Property....................	204,800	172,100	160,900	14.7	11.5	10.4
Drugs......................	23,600	33,000	39,000	1.7	2.2	2.5
Public order.................	78,400	116,900	133,700	5.6	7.8	8.7
White, total	**1,215,300**	**1,164,800**	**1,080,600**	**53.2**	**48.2**	**44.0**
Person......................	236,300	243,700	243,100	10.3	10.1	9.9
Property....................	647,300	474,800	397,500	28.3	19.7	16.2
Drugs......................	107,000	146,800	142,900	4.7	6.1	5.8
Public order.................	224,700	299,500	297,100	9.8	12.4	12.1
Black, total	**541,400**	**489,000**	**556,000**	**124.3**	**101.1**	**107.8**
Person......................	152,000	137,000	174,800	34.9	28.3	33.9
Property....................	230,100	179,800	174,300	52.8	37.2	33.8
Drugs......................	52,300	44,500	46,300	12.0	9.2	9.0
Public order.................	107,100	127,700	160,700	24.6	26.4	31.2
Other races, total...........	**568,900**	**514,700**	**578,500**	**33.8**	**27.8**	**24.5**
Person......................	157,200	142,400	179,700	6.8	5.8	5.3
Property....................	245,300	192,000	183,100	19.1	13.6	10.1
Drugs......................	53,800	47,000	49,200	1.9	2.5	2.7
Public order.................	112,600	133,300	166,600	6.2	5.9	6.4

[1] Cases per 1,000 youth (ages 10 to 17) at risk.

Source: National Center for Juvenile Justice, Pittsburgh, PA, *Juvenile Court Statistics,* annual. See also <http://www.ojjdp.ncjrs.org /ojstatbb/index.html>.

U.S. Census Bureau, Statistical Abstract of the United States: 2010

Table 330. **Child Abuse and Neglect Cases Substantiated and Indicated—Victim Characteristics: 2000 to 2007**

[Based on reports alleging child abuse and neglect that were referred for investigation by the respective child protective services agency in each state. The reporting period may be either calendar or fiscal year. The majority of States provided duplicated counts. Also, varying number of states reported the various characteristics presented below. A substantiated case represents a type of investigation disposition that determines that there is sufficient evidence under state law to conclude that maltreatment occurred or that the child is at risk of maltreatment. An indicated case represents a type of disposition that concludes that there was a reason to suspect maltreatment had occurred]

Item	2000		2005 [1]		2006 [1]		2007	
	Number	Percent	Number	Percent	Number	Percent	Number	Percent
TYPES OF SUBSTANTIATED MALTREATMENT [2]								
Victims, total	864,837	116.5	900,143	114.0	885,258	114.1	753,351	114.3
Neglect.	517,118	59.8	573,581	63.7	567,850	64.1	530,770	70.5
Physical abuse	167,713	19.4	153,166	17.0	142,147	16.1	122,019	16.2
Sexual abuse	87,770	10.2	84,452	9.4	78,166	8.8	70,793	9.4
Emotional maltreatment.	66,965	7.7	66,054	7.3	58,563	6.6	52,712	7.0
Medical neglect	25,498	3.0	17,637	2.0	19,542	2.2	16,523	2.2
Other and unknown	146,184	16.9	139,063	15.4	144,108	16.3	68,059	9.0
SEX OF VICTIM [3, 4]								
Victims, total	864,837	100.0	900,143	100.0	885,258	100.0	753,351	100.0
Male	413,744	47.8	425,739	47.3	427,001	48.2	362,964	48.2
Female.	446,230	51.6	455,992	50.7	455,548	51.5	388,090	51.5
AGE OF VICTIM [3, 4]								
Victims, total	864,837	100.0	901,143	100.0	885,258	100.0	753,351	100.0
1 year and younger	133,094	15.4	155,674	17.3	160,785	18.2	144,137	19.1
2 to 5 years old	205,790	23.8	222,246	24.7	221,902	25.1	188,381	25.0
6 to 9 years old	212,186	24.5	192,962	21.4	194,239	21.9	165,119	21.9
10 to 13 years old	176,071	20.4	171,005	19.0	164,064	18.5	133,513	17.7
14 to 17 years old	126,207	14.6	138,846	15.4	140,797	15.9	116,759	15.5
18 years old and over	992	0.1	469	0.1	535	0.1	407	0.1

[1] Data have been revised. [2] A child may be a victim of more than one maltreatment. Therefore, the total for this item adds up to more than 100 percent. [3] The increase in unknown age, sex, and race in 2005 is due to some states reporting summary data without breakdown of corresponding fields. [4] Unknown data not shown.

Source: U.S. Department of Health and Human Services, Administration for Children and Families, Statistics and Research, Child Maltreatment 2007, annual. See also <http://www.acf.hhs.gov/programs/cb/pubs/cm07/index.htm>.

Table 331. **Child Abuse and Neglect Cases Reported and Investigated by State: 2007**

[See headnote, Table 330]

State and outlying area	Population under 18 years old	Number of reports [1]	Number of children subject of an investigation [2]	Number of child victims [3]	State and outlying area	Population under 18 years old	Number of reports [1]	Number of children subject of an investigation [2]	Number of child victims [3]
Total . .	74,904,677	1,860,259	3,359,284	753,351	MT.	219,498	8,699	14,477	1,886
					NE.	446,145	11,290	26,709	4,108
AL	1,123,537	18,710	27,531	9,247	NV.	660,002	16,342	34,039	5,417
AK	182,218	4,906	8,222	3,138	NH.	298,186	6,834	9,958	912
AZ	1,669,866	33,188	76,400	4,025	NJ	2,063,789	44,606	68,985	7,543
AR	700,537	27,846	57,986	9,847					
CA	9,383,924	232,297	441,467	88,319	NM.	500,276	14,853	23,776	6,065
CO.	1,192,679	31,520	49,764	10,588	NY.	4,413,414	155,509	259,687	83,502
CT	820,216	26,479	39,755	9,875	NC.	2,217,680	66,814	133,230	25,976
DE.	205,646	5,693	13,546	2,116	ND.	142,809	3,586	6,272	1,288
DC.	113,720	4,506	11,166	2,757	OH.	2,751,874	77,436	119,591	38,484
FL	4,043,560	154,951	343,836	53,484	OK.	899,507	35,870	64,287	13,173
GA	2,531,609	48,965	115,348	35,729	OR.	862,908	26,381	42,198	11,552
					PA	2,786,719	23,513	23,513	4,177
HI	285,694	2,527	4,643	2,075	RI	233,115	7,710	11,808	3,857
ID	407,712	7,089	11,022	1,582	SC	1,059,917	18,337	41,579	12,762
IL	3,199,159	68,101	150,102	31,058					
IN	1,586,518	41,900	65,034	18,380	SD	196,890	3,627	6,869	1,485
IA	711,403	23,093	35,875	14,051	TN	1,471,486	62,183	101,435	16,059
KS	696,082	16,912	25,412	2,272	TX	6,623,366	166,584	283,355	71,111
KY	1,003,973	48,600	77,221	18,778	UT	816,822	20,386	32,134	13,611
LA	1,079,560	19,293	30,801	9,468	VT	131,353	2,564	3,222	872
ME.	279,467	6,710	11,009	4,118	VA	1,826,179	30,196	61,342	6,413
MD.	1,358,797	(NA)	(NA)	(NA)	WA	1,536,368	35,262	52,386	6,984
					WV	387,381	21,962	49,357	7,109
MA.	1,432,856	39,801	80,752	37,690	WI	1,321,279	26,978	39,671	7,856
MI	2,446,856	(NA)	(NA)	(NA)	WY	125,365	2,442	4,959	772
MN.	1,260,282	18,993	27,557	6,847					
MS.	768,704	17,871	27,563	7,002	PR	1,002,944	15,709	32,810	10,696
MO	1,424,830	54,635	79,623	7,235					

NA Not available. [1] The number of investigations includes assessments. The number of investigations is based on the total number of investigations that received a disposition in 2007. [2] The number of "Children Subject of an Investigation" is based on the total number of children who were included in an investigation or assessment. [3] Victims are defined as children subject of a substantiated, indicated, or alternative response-victim maltreatment.

Source: U.S. Department of Health and Human Services, Administration for Children and Families, Statistics and Research, Child Maltreatment 2007, annual. See also <http://www.acf.hhs.gov/programs/cb/pubs/cm07/index.htm>.

Law Enforcement, Courts, and Prisons **207**

Table 332. Felony Convictions in State Courts: 2000 to 2004

[In 2004, an estimated 1,145,438 persons were convicted of a felony (federal and state courts). Of that number, 1,078,920 were convicted in state courts, the vast majority (95%) of whom pleaded guilty. At the time of sentencing, about 3 out of 4 felons sentenced (77%) were sentenced for a single felony]

Most serious conviction	Felony convictions in state courts					
	2000		2002		2004	
	Number	Percent	Number	Percent	Number	Percent
All offenses	924,700	100.0	1,051,000	100.0	1,078,920	100.0
Violent offenses	173,200	18.7	197,030	18.8	194,570	18.0
Murder [1]	8,600	0.9	8,990	0.9	8,400	0.8
Rape/Sexual assault	31,500	3.4	35,500	3.4	33,190	3.1
Robbery	36,800	4.0	38,430	3.7	38,850	3.6
Aggravated assault	79,400	8.6	95,600	9.1	94,380	8.7
Other violent [2]	17,000	1.8	18,510	1.8	19,750	1.8
Property offenses	262,000	28.3	325,200	30.9	310,680	28.8
Burglary	79,300	8.6	100,640	9.6	93,870	8.7
Larceny [3]	100,000	10.8	124,320	11.8	119,340	11.1
Fraud/forgery [4]	82,700	8.9	100,240	9.5	97,470	9.0
Drug offenses	319,700	34.6	340,330	32.4	362,850	33.6
Possession	116,300	12.6	127,530	12.1	161,090	14.9
Trafficking	203,400	22.0	212,810	20.2	201,760	18.7
Weapon offenses	28,200	3.1	32,470	3.1	33,010	3.1
Other offenses [5]	141,600	15.3	155,970	14.8	177,810	16.5

[1] A small number of cases were classified as nonnegligent manslaughter when it was unclear if the conviction offense was murder or nonnegligent manslaughter.   [2] Includes offenses such as negligent manslaughter and kidnaping.   [3] When vehicle theft could not be distinguished from other theft, the case was coded as "other theft." This results in a conservative estimate of vehicle thefts.   [4] Includes embezzlement.   [5] Composed of nonviolent offenses such as receiving stolen property and vandalism.

Source: U.S. Department of Justice, Office of Justice Programs, Bureau of Justice Statistics, *Criminal Sentencing Statistics,* Series NCJ 215646, July 2007; <http://www.ojp.usdoj.gov/bjs/sent.htm>.

Table 333. Employment by State and Local Law Enforcement Agencies by Type of Agency and Employee: 2004

[As of September 30.]

Type of agency	Number of agencies	Number of employees					
		Full-time			Part-time		
		Total	Sworn	Civilian	Total	Sworn	Civilian
Total [1]	17,876	1,076,897	731,903	344,994	105,252	45,982	59,270
Local police..........	12,766	573,152	446,974	126,178	62,693	28,712	33,981
Sheriffs' offices	3,067	326,531	175,018	151,513	27,004	11,784	15,220
Primary State	49	89,265	58,190	31,075	708	31	677
Special jurisdiction	1,481	85,126	49,398	35,728	14,342	5,063	9,279
Constable/marshal	513	2,823	2,323	500	505	392	113

[1] Excludes agencies with less than one full-time officer or the equivalent in part-time officers.

Source: U.S. Bureau of Justice Statistics, *Census of State and Local Law Enforcement Agencies, 2004,* Series NCJ 212749, June 2007. See also <http://www.ojp.usdoj.gov/bjs/abstract/csllea04.htm>.

Table 334. State and Local Government Expenditures Per Capita by Criminal Justice Function and State: 2006

[In dollars. See Table 453 for more details]

State	Total justice system	Police protection	Judicial and legal	Corrections	State	Total justice system	Police protection	Judicial and legal	Corrections
Total.........	597	264	123	210	Missouri	417	202	77	138
Alabama	420	201	78	141	Montana	519	201	132	185
Alaska	894	318	263	313	Nebraska	436	190	81	166
Arizona.........	643	275	137	232	Nevada..........	757	357	177	223
Arkansas........	443	180	78	186	New Hampshire ...	422	209	87	126
California........	871	355	214	301	New Jersey	728	347	159	221
Colorado........	562	252	99	210	New Mexico......	636	262	129	245
Connecticut	604	259	168	177	New York	828	393	170	265
Delaware........	795	335	173	287	North Carolina	452	216	62	174
District of Columbia.	1,325	848	124	353	North Dakota	376	166	94	116
Florida	669	328	117	224	Ohio............	551	235	142	174
Georgia	519	210	95	214	Oklahoma	443	188	79	177
Hawaii	550	218	192	140	Oregon.........	604	254	100	250
Idaho..........	468	189	101	178	Pennsylvania	548	204	118	225
Illinois..........	523	294	94	136	Rhode Island	596	270	143	183
Indiana.........	380	165	67	148	South Carolina....	396	197	55	143
Iowa...........	409	192	97	121	South Dakota.....	423	167	78	178
Kansas.........	472	230	105	137	Tennessee.......	432	199	86	147
Kentucky........	399	157	92	150	Texas..........	483	208	85	189
Louisiana	631	275	121	235	Utah...........	498	211	114	173
Maine..........	385	168	76	140	Vermont	475	219	93	163
Maryland........	667	286	120	261	Virginia.........	542	227	95	219
Massachusetts....	577	260	140	177	Washington......	535	208	105	222
Michigan........	571	231	114	227	West Virginia	378	131	107	141
Minnesota.......	513	251	118	143	Wisconsin	586	257	99	229
Mississippi.......	391	194	68	130	Wyoming........	837	323	163	351

Source: U.S. Department of Justice, Office of Justice Programs, Bureau of Justice Statistics, *Expenditures and Employment Statistics,* Series NCJ 224394. See also <http://www.ojp.usdoj.gov/bjs/eande.htm>.

Table 335. **Prisoners Under Jurisdiction of Federal or State Correctional Authorities—Summary by State: 1990 to 2007**

[For years ending December 31. To have jurisdiction over a prisoner, a state or the federal system must have legal authority over the prisoner]

State	1990	2000	2005	2006	2007	State	1990	2000	2005	2006	2007
U.S. [1] .	773,919	1,391,261	1,527,929	1,570,691	1,598,316	MS.	8,375	20,241	20,515	21,068	22,431
Federal. .	65,526	145,416	187,618	193,046	199,618	MO	14,943	27,543	30,823	30,167	29,857
State . . .	708,393	1,245,845	1,340,311	1,377,645	1,398,698	MT	1,425	3,105	3,532	3,563	3,462
						NE [5]	2,403	3,895	4,455	4,407	4,505
AL [2]	15,665	26,332	27,888	28,241	29,412	NV [6]	5,322	10,063	11,782	12,901	13,400
AK [2]	2,622	4,173	4,812	5,069	5,167	NH	1,342	2,257	2,530	2,805	2,943
AZ [3]	14,261	26,510	33,565	35,801	37,746	NJ	21,128	29,784	27,359	27,371	26,827
AR.	7,322	11,915	13,541	13,729	14,314	NM.	3,187	5,342	6,571	6,639	6,466
CA.	97,309	163,001	170,676	175,512	174,282	NY	54,895	70,199	62,743	63,315	62,623
CO [2]	7,671	16,833	21,456	22,481	22,841	NC.	18,411	31,266	36,365	37,460	37,970
CT [2]	10,500	18,355	19,442	20,566	20,924	ND.	483	1,076	1,385	1,363	1,416
DE [2]	3,471	6,921	6,966	7,186	7,276	OH.	31,822	45,833	45,854	49,166	50,731
DC [4, 5] . .	9,947	7,456	(NA)	(NA)	(NA)	OK.	12,285	23,181	26,676	26,243	25,849
FL	44,387	71,319	89,768	92,969	98,219	OR.	6,492	10,580	13,411	13,707	13,948
GA [3]	22,411	44,232	48,749	52,792	54,256	PA	22,290	36,847	42,380	44,397	45,969
HI [2]	2,533	5,053	6,146	5,967	5,978	RI [2]	2,392	3,286	3,654	3,996	4,018
ID	1,961	5,535	6,818	7,124	7,319	SC.	17,319	21,778	23,160	23,616	24,239
IL.	27,516	45,281	44,919	45,106	45,215	SD.	1,341	2,616	3,463	3,359	3,311
IN [2]	12,736	20,125	24,455	26,091	27,132	TN	10,388	22,166	26,369	25,745	26,267
IA [3]	3,967	7,955	8,737	8,838	8,732	TX	50,042	166,719	169,003	172,116	171,790
KS	5,775	8,344	9,068	8,816	8,696	UT [2]	2,496	5,637	6,382	6,433	6,509
KY	9,023	14,919	19,662	20,000	22,457	VT [2]	1,049	1,697	2,078	2,215	2,145
LA	18,599	35,207	36,083	37,012	37,540	VA	17,593	30,168	35,344	36,688	38,069
ME [6] . . .	1,523	1,679	2,023	2,120	2,222	WA	7,995	14,915	17,382	17,561	17,772
MD.	17,848	23,538	22,737	22,945	23,433	WV	1,565	3,856	5,312	5,733	6,056
MA.	8,345	10,722	10,701	11,032	11,436	WI	7,465	20,754	22,697	23,415	23,743
MI	34,267	47,718	49,546	51,577	50,233	WY	1,110	1,680	2,047	2,114	2,084
MN.	3,176	6,238	9,281	9,108	9,468						

NA Not available. [1] U.S. total includes federal prisoners not distributed by state. This total includes all inmates held in public and private adult correctional facilities. [2] Data include both total jail and prison population. Prisons and jails form one integrated system. [3] Numbers are for custody rather than jurisdiction counts. [4] The transfer of responsibility for sentenced felons from the District of Columbia to the federal system was completed by the year end 2001. [5] The District of Columbia inmates sentenced to more than 1 year are now under the responsibility of the Bureau of Prisons. [6] Estimates only. Data for 2007 were not available at the time of publication.

Source: U.S. Department of Justice, Office of Justice Programs, Bureau of Justice Statistics, *Prisoners in 2007,* Series NCJ 224280 and earlier reports. See also <http://www.ojp.usdoj.gov/bjs/abstract/p07.htm/>.

Table 336. **Adults on Probation or Parole, Incarcerated in Jail or Prison: 1980 to 2007**

[As of December 31, except jail counts as of June 30]

Year	Total [1]	Supervision rate per 100,000 adults	Community supervision		Incarceration		Male [2]	Female [2]
			Probation	Parole	Jail	Prison		
1980.	1,840,400	1.1	1,118,097	220,438	182,288	319,598	(NA)	(NA)
1985.	3,011,500	1.7	1,968,712	300,203	254,986	487,593	2,606,000	405,500
1990.	4,350,343	2.3	2,670,234	531,407	405,320	743,382	3,746,300	601,700
1992.	4,762,600	2.5	2,811,611	658,601	441,781	850,566	4,050,300	712,300
1993.	4,944,000	2.6	2,903,061	676,100	455,500	909,381	4,215,800	728,200
1994.	5,141,300	2.7	2,981,022	690,371	479,800	990,147	4,377,400	763,900
1995.	5,342,900	2.8	3,077,861	679,421	507,044	1,078,542	4,513,000	822,100
1996.	5,482,700	2.8	3,164,996	679,733	510,400	1,127,528	4,629,900	852,800
1997.	5,725,800	2.9	3,296,513	694,787	557,974	1,176,564	4,825,300	900,500
1998.	6,126,100	3.1	3,670,441	696,385	584,372	1,224,469	(NA)	(NA)
1999.	6,331,400	3.1	3,779,922	714,457	596,485	1,287,172	(NA)	(NA)
2000 [3].	6,445,100	3.1	3,826,209	723,898	621,149	1,316,333	5,376,300	1,068,800
2001 [3]	6,581,700	3.1	3,931,731	732,333	631,240	1,330,007	5,468,900	1,112,800
2002 [3]	6,758,800	3.1	4,024,067	750,934	665,475	1,367,547	5,579,500	1,179,300
2003 [3, 4]	6,924,500	3.2	4,120,012	769,925	691,301	1,390,279	5,724,200	1,200,300
2004 [3]	6,995,100	3.2	4,143,792	771,852	713,990	1,421,345	5,767,300	1,227,800
2005 [3]	7,051,900	3.1	4,166,757	780,616	747,529	1,448,344	5,823,200	1,228,700
2006 [5]	7,181,500	3.2	4,215,361	799,058	766,010	1,492,973	5,885,300	1,296,000
2007 [6, 7]	7,328,200	3.2	4,293,163	824,365	780,581	1,512,576	6,027,500	1,300,200

NA Not available. [1] Totals may not add due to individuals having multiple correctional statuses. [2] Estimated. [3] The jail population includes juveniles held as adults. [4] Due to changes in reporting, total probation and parole counts include estimated counts for Massachusetts, Pennsylvania, and Washington. [5] Illinois did not provide prison or parole data for 2006, therefore, all prison and parole data for Illinois were estimated. [6] Illinois and Nevada did not provide prison data for 2007; therefore, all prison data for these states were estimated. [7] Oklahoma did not provide probation or parole data for 2007, therefore, all probation and parole data were estimated.

Source: U.S. Department of Justice, Office of Justice Programs, Bureau of Justice Statistics (BJS), Prisoners Inmates at Midyear 2008—Statistical Tables; Jail Inmates at Midyear 2008—Statistical Tables; Probation and Parole in the United States, 2007—Statistical Tables; *Prisoners in 2007; Probation and Parole in the United States, 2007;* and *Prisoners in 2006.* See also <http://www.ojp.usdoj.gov/bjs/correct.htm>.

Law Enforcement, Courts, and Prisons 209

Table 337. Jail Inmates by Sex, Race, and Hispanic Origin: 1990 to 2008

[As of June 30. Data based on the Annual Survey of Jails, a sample survey and subject to sampling variability]

Characteristic	1990	1995	2000	2004	2005	2006	2007	2008
Total inmates [1, 2] . .	405,320	507,044	621,149	713,990	747,529	765,819	780,174	785,556
Incarceration rate								
per 100,000 residents. .	163	193	220	243	252	256	259	259
Rated capacity [3, 4] . . .	389,171	545,763	677,787	755,603	789,001	794,984	810,543	828,413
Adult	403,019	499,300	613,534	706,907	740,770	759,717	773,341	777,852
Male.	365,821	448,000	543,120	619,908	646,807	661,164	673,346	678,677
Female.	37,198	51,300	70,414	86,999	93,963	98,552	99,995	99,175
Juveniles [5]	2,301	7,800	7,615	7,083	6,759	6,102	6,833	7,703
White, non-Hispanic	169,600	203,300	260,500	317,400	331,000	336,500	338,200	333,300
Black, non-Hispanic	172,300	220,600	256,300	275,400	290,500	295,900	301,700	308,000
Hispanic/Latino	58,100	74,400	94,100	108,300	111,900	119,200	125,500	128,500
Other [6].	5,400	8,800	10,200	12,900	13,000	13,500	13,900	14,000

[1] Total does not include offenders who were supervised outside of jail facilities. [2] Race/Hispanic origin data do not include the two or more race data. [3] Beginning 1995, rated capacity subject to sampling error. [4] Rated capacity is the number of beds or inmates assigned by a rating official to facilities within each jurisdiction. [5] Juveniles are persons held under the age of 18. Includes juveniles who were tried or awaiting trial as adults. [6] Excludes persons of Hispanic or Latino origin. Includes American Indians, Alaska Natives, Asians, and Pacific Islanders.

Source: U.S. Department of Justice, Office of Justice Programs, Bureau of Justice Statistics, Jail Inmates at Midyear, Series NCJ 2221945 and NCJ 225709 annual. See also <http://www.ojp.usdoj.gov/bjs/jails.htm>.

Table 338. Prisoners Under Federal or State Jurisdiction by Sex: 1980 to 2007

[Prisoners, as of December 31. Includes all persons under jurisdiction of federal and state authorities rather than those in the custody of such authorities. Represents inmates sentenced to maximum term of more than a year]

Year	Total [1]	Rate [2]	State	Male	Female	Year	Total [1]	Rate [2]	State	Male	Female
1980. . .	315,974	139	295,363	303,643	12,331	1997. . .	1,195,498	445	1,100,511	1,121,663	73,835
1985. . .	480,568	202	447,873	459,223	21,345	1998. . .	1,245,402	461	1,141,720	1,167,802	77,600
1988. . .	603,732	247	560,994	573,587	30,145	1999. . .	1,304,074	476	1,189,799	1,221,611	82,463
1989. . .	680,907	276	633,739	643,643	37,264	2000. . .	1,331,278	[3]470	1,204,323	1,246,234	85,044
1990. . .	739,980	297	689,577	699,416	40,564	2001. . .	1,345,217	470	1,208,708	1,260,033	85,184
1991. . .	789,610	313	732,914	745,808	43,802	2002. . .	1,380,516	476	1,237,476	1,291,450	89,066
1992. . .	846,277	332	780,571	799,776	46,501	2003. . .	1,408,361	482	1,256,442	1,315,790	92,571
1993. . .	932,074	359	857,675	878,037	54,037	2004. . .	1,433,728	486	1,274,591	1,337,730	95,998
1994. . .	1,016,691	389	936,896	956,566	60,125	2005. . .	1,462,866	491	1,296,693	1,364,178	98,688
1995. . .	1,085,022	411	1,001,359	1,021,059	63,963	2006. . .	1,504,660	501	1,331,127	1,401,317	103,343
1996. . .	1,137,722	427	1,048,907	1,068,123	69,599	2007. . .	1,532,817	506	1,353,613	1,427,282	105,535

[1] Includes prisoners under the legal authority of state or federal correctional officials. [2] Rate per 100,000 estimated population. Based on U.S. Census Bureau estimated resident population. [3] Decrease in incarceration rate from 1999 to 2000 due to use of new Census numbers.

Source: U.S. Department of Justice, Office of Justice Programs, Bureau of Justice Statistics, Prisoners in 2007, Series NCJ 224280, annual. See also <http://www.ojp.usdoj.gov/bjs/abstract/p07.htm>.

Table 339. Prisoners Under Sentence of Death by Characteristic: 1980 to 2007

[As of December 31. Excludes prisoners under sentence of death who remained within local correctional systems pending exhaustion of appellate process or who had not been committed to prison]

Characteristic	1980	1990	1995	1999	2000	2001	2002	2003	2004	2005	2006	2007
Total [1, 2]	688	2,346	3,064	3,540	3,601	3,577	3,562	3,377	3,320	3,245	3,233	3,220
White.	418	1,368	1,732	1,960	1,989	1,968	1,939	1,882	1,856	1,802	1,806	1,804
Black and other	270	978	1,332	1,580	1,612	1,609	1,623	1,495	1,464	1,443	1,427	1,416
Under 20 years old.	11	8	20	16	11	4	4	1	1	–	–	1
20 to 24 years old	173	168	264	251	237	192	153	133	95	61	51	42
25 to 34 years old	334	1,110	1,068	1,108	1,103	1,099	1,058	965	896	816	735	680
35 to 54 years old	186	1,006	1,583	1,958	2,019	2,043	2,069	1,969	1,977	2,012	2,043	2,060
55 years old and over.	10	64	119	194	223	243	273	306	345	365	399	437
Years of school completed:												
7 years or less	68	178	191	201	214	212	215	213	207	192	186	183
8 years	74	186	195	221	233	236	234	227	221	206	195	189
9 to 11 years	204	775	979	1,142	1,157	1,145	1,130	1,073	1,053	1,030	1,015	989
12 years	162	729	995	1,157	1,184	1,183	1,173	1,108	1,091	1,105	1,098	1,089
More than 12 years.	43	209	272	307	315	304	294	270	262	256	248	248
Unknown.	163	279	422	499	490	501	511	483	480	465	486	522
Marital status:												
Never married	268	998	1,412	1,689	1,749	1,763	1,746	1,641	1,622	1,586	1,577	1,558
Married	229	632	718	731	739	716	709	684	658	649	626	635
Divorced [3]	217	726	924	1,107	1,105	1,102	1,102	1,049	1,034	1,019	1,025	1,027
Time elapsed since sentencing:												
Less than 12 months	185	231	287	259	208	151	147	137	117	122	105	110
12 to 47 months	389	753	784	800	786	734	609	495	421	399	382	352
48 to 71 months	102	438	423	499	507	476	468	451	388	299	262	262
72 months and over	38	934	1,560	1,969	2,092	2,220	2,333	2,291	2,388	2,434	2,479	2,496
Legal status at arrest:												
Not under sentence	384	1,345	1,764	2,088	2,202	2,189	2,165	2,048	2,026	1,979	1,952	1,963
Parole or probation [4]	115	578	866	886	921	918	909	845	809	792	778	760
Prison or escaped.	45	128	110	125	126	135	141	137	145	144	142	143
Unknown.	170	305	314	428	344	339	342	344	334	339	356	354

– Represents zero. [1] Revisions to the total number of prisoners were not carried to the characteristics except for race. [2] Includes races not shown separately. [3] Includes persons married but separated, widows, widowers, and unknown. [4] Includes prisoners on mandatory conditional release, work release, other leave, AWOL or bail. Covers 28 prisoners in 1990; 33 in 1995; 26 in 1998; 21 in 1999 and 2000; 17 in 2001, 2002, and 2003; 15 in 2004; and 14 in 2005, 2006, and 2007.

Source: U.S. Department of Justice, Office of Justice Programs, Bureau of Justice Statistics, Capital Punishment, Series NCJ 224528, annual. See also <http://www.ojp.usdoj.gov/bjs/cp.htm#publications>.

210 Law Enforcement, Courts, and Prisons

Table 340. **Prisoners Executed Under Civil Authority by Sex and Race: 1930 to 2008**

[Excludes executions by military authorities]

Year or period	Total [1]	Male	Female	White	Black	Executed for murder Total [1]	Executed for murder White	Executed for murder Black
All years, 1930–2008 ..	4,995	4,952	43	2,479	2,459	4,470	2,392	2,023
1960 to 1967.	191	190	1	98	93	155	87	68
1968 to 1976.	–	–	–	–	–	–	–	–
1977 to 2008.	1,136	1,125	11	728	393	1,136	728	393
1985	18	18	–	11	7	18	11	7
1990	23	23	–	16	7	23	16	7
1995	56	56	–	33	22	56	33	22
1996	45	45	–	31	14	45	31	14
1997	74	74	–	45	27	74	45	27
1998	68	66	2	48	18	68	48	18
1999	98	98	–	61	33	98	61	33
2000	85	83	2	49	35	85	49	35
2001	66	63	3	48	17	66	48	17
2002	71	69	2	53	18	71	53	18
2003	65	65	–	44	20	65	44	20
2004	59	59	–	39	19	59	39	19
2005	60	59	1	41	19	60	41	19
2006	53	53	–	32	21	53	32	21
2007	42	42	–	28	14	42	28	14
2008	37	37	–	20	17	37	20	17

– Represents zero. [1] Includes races other than White or Black.

Source: Through 1978, U.S. Law Enforcement Assistance Administration; thereafter, U.S. Department of Justice, Office of Justice Programs, Bureau of Justice Statistics, *Capital Punishment*, annual. See also <http://www.ojp.usdoj.gov/bjs /abstract/cp07.htm>.

Table 341. **Prisoners Executed Under Civil Authority by State: 1977 to 2008**

[Alaska, District of Columbia, Hawaii, Iowa, Maine, Massachusetts, Michigan, Minnesota, New Jersey, North Dakota, Rhode Island, Vermont, West Virginia, and Wisconsin are jurisdictions without a death penalty]

State	1977 to 2008	2005	2006	2007	2008	State	1977 to 2008	2005	2006	2007	2008	State	1977 to 2008	2005	2006	2007	2008
U.S..	1,136	60	53	42	37	IL	12	–	–	–	–	OH . . .	28	4	5	2	2
						IN	19	5	1	2	–	OK . . .	88	4	4	3	2
AL . . .	38	4	1	3	–	KY . . .	3	–	–	–	1	OR . . .	2	–	–	–	–
AZ . . .	23	–	–	1	–	LA . . .	27	–	–	–	–	PA . . .	3	–	–	–	–
AR . . .	27	1	–	–	–	MD . . .	5	1	–	–	–	SC . . .	40	3	1	1	3
CA . . .	13	2	1	–	–	MS . . .	10	1	1	–	2	SD . . .	1	–	–	1	–
CO . . .	1	–	–	–	–	MO . . .	66	5	–	–	–	TN . . .	4	–	1	2	–
CT . . .	1	1	–	–	–	MT . . .	3	–	1	–	–	TX . . .	423	19	24	26	18
DE . . .	14	1	–	–	–	NE . . .	3	–	–	–	–	UT . . .	6	–	–	–	–
FL. . . .	66	1	4	–	2	NV . . .	12	–	1	–	–	VA . . .	102	–	4	–	4
GA . . .	43	3	–	1	3	NM . . .	1	–	–	–	–	WA . . .	4	–	–	–	–
ID	1	–	–	–	–	NC . . .	43	5	4	–	–	WY . . .	1	–	–	–	–

– Represents zero.

Source: Through 1978, U.S. Law Enforcement Assistance Administration; thereafter, U.S. Department of Justice, Office of Justice Programs, Bureau of Justice Statistics, *Capital Punishment*, 2007, Series NCJ 224528, annual. See also <http://www.ojp .usdoj.gov/bjs/cp.htm>.

Table 342. **Fire Losses—Total and Per Capita: 1980 to 2007**

[5,579 represents $5,579,000,000. Includes allowance for uninsured and unreported losses but excludes losses to government property and forests. Represents incurred losses]

Year	Total (mil. dol.)	Per capita [1] (dol.)	Year	Total (mil. dol.)	Per capita [1] (dol.)	Year	Total (mil. dol.)	Per capita [1] (dol.)
1980	5,579	24.56	1992	13,588	53.28	2000	13,457	[3]47.69
1985	7,753	32.70	1993	11,331	43.96	2001 [2]	17,118	[3]60.04
1986	8,488	35.21	1994	12,778	49.08	2002	17,586	[3]61.09
1987	8,504	34.96	1995	11,887	45.23	2003	21,129	[3]72.75
1988	9,626	39.11	1996	12,544	47.29	2004	17,344	[3]59.16
1989	9,514	38.33	1997	12,940	48.32	2005	20,427	[3]69.03
1990	9,495	38.07	1998	11,510	45.59	2006	[3]20,340	[3]68.08
1991	11,302	44.82	1999	12,428	45.58	2007	22,680	[3]74.95

[1] Based on U.S. Census Bureau estimated resident population as of July 1. Enumerated population as of April 1 for 1980, 1990, and 2000. [2] Does not include insured fire losses related to terrorism. [3] Data have been revised.

Source: Insurance Information Institute, New York, NY. The III Insurance Fact Book, annual; and Financial Services Fact Book, annual (copyright). Data from ISO and Highline Data LLC. See also <http://www.iii.org>.

Law Enforcement, Courts, and Prisons 211

Table 343. **The U.S. Fire Service: Departments and Personnel: 1990 to 2007**

[(In thousands 1,025.7 represents 1,025,700.) A fire department is a public or private organization that provides fire prevention, fire suppression, and associated emergency and non-emergency services to a jurisdiction such as a county, municipality, or organized fire district. For 2007, there are an estimated 30,185 fire departments in the United States. These fire departments have an estimated 51,950 fire stations, 68,050 pumpers, 6,750 aerial apparatus and 74,350 other suppression vehicles. A fire department responds to a fire every 20 seconds]

Item	1990	1995	2000	2002	2003	2004	2005	2006	2007
Fire departments									
Total	30,391	31,197	30,339	30,310	30,542	30,400	30,300	30,635	30,185
All career.	1,949	1,831	2,178	2,044	2,018	1,917	2,087	2,321	2,263
Mostly career.	1,338	1,660	1,667	1,480	1,582	1,242	1,766	1,731	1,765
Mostly volunteer	4,000	4,581	4,523	4,886	5,271	4,084	4,902	5,134	4,989
All volunteer.	23,104	23,125	21,971	21,900	21,671	23,157	21,575	21,449	21,168
Fire Department personnel									
(1,000)	1,025.7	1,098.9	1,064.2	1,108.3	1,096.9	1,100.8	1,136.7	1,140.9	1,148.8
Career [1]	253.0	260.9	286.8	291.7	296.9	305.2	313.3	317.0	323.4
Volunteer [2]	772.7	838.0	777.4	816.6	800.1	795.6	823.7	824.0	825.5

[1] Career firefighters include full-time uniform firefighters regardless of assignment (i.e., suppression, administrative, prevention/inspection, etc.). Career firefighters do not include firefighters who work for the state or federal government or in private fire brigades.   [2] Volunteer firefighters include any active part-time (call or volunteer) firefighters.

Source: National Fire Protection Association, Quincy, MA, Annual Fire Department Profile Report, an unpublished NFPA annual report.

Table 344. **Fires—Number and Loss by Type and Property Use: 2004 to 2007**

[1,550 represents 1,550,000 and property loss of 9,794 represents $9,794,000,000. Based on annual sample survey of fire departments. No adjustments were made for unreported fires and losses]

Type and property use	Number (1,000)				Direct property loss (mil. dol.) [1]			
	2004	2005	2006	2007	2004	2005	2006	2007
Fires, total.	1,550	1,602	1,642	1,557	9,794	10,672	11,307	14,639
Structure	526	511	524	531	8,314	9,193	9,636	10,638
Outside of structure [2]	69	78	82	85	108	93	262	707
Brush and rubbish	514	594	627	561	–	–	–	–
Vehicle.	297	290	278	257	1,304	1,318	1,319	1,411
Other	144	129	131	123	68	68	90	[3]1,883
Structure by property use:								
Public assembly	13	13	13	15	316	320	444	498
Educational	7	6	6	6	68	67	105	100
Institutional	6	8	8	7	25	40	42	41
Stores and offices.	24	23	20	21	586	687	691	642
Residential.	411	396	413	414	5,948	6,875	6,990	7,546
1-2 family units [4]	302	287	304	300	4,948	5,781	5,936	6,225
Apartments.	94	94	92	99	885	948	896	1,164
Other residential [5]	15	15	17	15	115	146	158	157
Storage [5].	32	30	29	31	748	590	650	670
Industry, utility, defense [6] . .	12	12	12	12	423	376	573	779
Special structures	21	23	23	25	200	238	141	362

– Represents zero.   [1] Direct property damage figures do not include indirect losses, like business interruption, and adjustments for inflation.   [2] Includes outside storage, crops, timber, etc.   [3] Includes California Fire Storm with an estimated $1.8 billion in property loss.   [4] Includes mobile homes.   [5] Includes hotels and motels, college dormitories, boarding houses, etc.   [6] Data underreported as some incidents were handled by private fire brigades or fixed suppression systems which do not report.

Source: National Fire Protection Association, Quincy, MA, "2007 U.S. Fire Loss," NFPA Journal, September 2008, and prior issues (copyright 2008). See also <http://www.nfpa.org/categoryList.asp?categoryID=15&URL=Research%20&%20Reports>.

Table 345. **Fires and Property Loss for Incendiary and Suspicious Fires and Civilian Fire Deaths and Injuries by Selected Property Type: 2004 to 2007**

[526 represents 526,000. Based on sample survey of fire departments]

Characteristic	2004	2005	2006	2007	Characteristic	2004	2005	2006	2007
NUMBER (1,000)					Residential property.	3,225	3,055	2,620	2,895
Structure fires, total . .	526	511	524	531	One- and two-family dwellings	2,680	2,575	2,155	2,350
Structure fires that were intentionally set	37	32	31	32	Apartments.	510	460	425	515
					Vehicles	550	520	490	385
PROPERTY LOSS [1] (mil. dol.)					CIVILIAN FIRE INJURIES				
Structure fires, total . .	8,314	9,193	9,636	10,638	Injuries, total [2]	17,785	17,925	16,400	17,675
Structure fires that were intentionally set	714	664	775	773	Residential property.	14,175	13,825	12,925	14,000
					One- and two-family dwellings	10,500	10,300	8,800	9,650
CIVILIAN FIRE DEATHS					Apartments.	3,200	3,000	3,700	3,950
Deaths, total [2]	3,900	3,675	3,245	3,430	Vehicles	1,500	1,650	1,200	1,675

[1] Direct property loss only.   [2] Includes other not shown separately.

Source: National Fire Protection Association, Quincy, MA, "2007 U.S. Fire Loss," NFPA Journal, September 2008, and prior issues (copyright 2008). See also <http://www.nfpa.org/categoryList.asp?categoryID=15&URL=Research%20&%20Reports>.

212   Law Enforcement, Courts, and Prisons

Geography and Environment

This section presents a variety of information on the physical environment of the United States, starting with basic area measurement data and ending with climatic data for selected weather stations around the country. The subjects covered between those points are mostly concerned with environmental trends but include related subjects such as land use, water consumption, air pollutant emissions, toxic releases, oil spills, hazardous waste sites, municipal waste and recycling, threatened and endangered wildlife, and the environmental industry.

The information in this section is selected from a wide range of federal agencies that compile the data for various administrative or regulatory purposes, such as the Environmental Protection Agency (EPA), U.S. Geological Survey (USGS), National Oceanic and Atmospheric Administration (NOAA), Natural Resources Conservation Service (NRCS), and National Atlas® of the United States. New information on the Great Lakes profile and lengths of shorelines, and wildfires by number and by acreage, may be found in Tables 347, 348 and 376.

Area—For the 2000 census and 2008, area measurements were calculated by computer based on the information contained in a single, consistent geographic database, the Topologically Integrated Geographic Encoding & Referencing system (TIGER®) database. The 2008 area measurements may be found in Table 346.

Geography—The USGS conducts investigations, surveys, and research in the fields of geography, geology, topography, geographic information systems, mineralogy, hydrology, and geothermal energy resources as well as natural hazards. The USGS provides United States cartographic data through the Earth Sciences Information Center, water resources data through the *Water Resources of the United States* at <http://water.usgs.gov/pubs/>.

In a joint project with the U.S. Census Bureau, during the 1980s, the USGS provided the basic information on geographic features for input into a national geographic and cartographic database prepared by the Census Bureau, called TIGER® database. Since then, using a variety of sources, the Census Bureau has updated these features and their related attributes (names, descriptions, etc.) and inserted current information on the boundaries, names, and codes of legal and statistical geographic entities. The 2008 area measures, land and water, including their classifications, reflect base feature updates made in the Master Address File (MAF)/TIGER database through May 1, 2008. The boundaries of the states and equivalent areas are as of January 1, 2008. Maps prepared by the Census Bureau using the TIGER® database show the names and boundaries of entities and are available on a current basis.

An inventory of the nation's land resources by type of use/cover was conducted by the National Resources Inventory Conservation Services (NRCS) every 5 years beginning in 1977 through 1997. Beginning with the release of the 2001 estimates, this program shifted to become an annual release of land use data. The most recent survey results, which were published for the year 2003, covered all nonfederal land for the contiguous 48 states.

Environment—The principal federal agency responsible for pollution abatement and control activities is the Environmental Protection Agency (EPA). It is responsible for establishing and monitoring national air quality standards, water quality activities, solid and hazardous waste disposal, and control of toxic substances. Many of these series now appear in the Envirofacts portion of the EPA Web site at <http://www.epa.gov/enviro/>.

The Clean Air Act, which was last amended in 1990, requires the EPA to set National Ambient Air Quality Standards

Geography and Environment   213

(NAAQS) (40 CFR part 50) for pollutants considered harmful to public health and the environment. The Clean Air Act established two types of national air quality standards. **Primary standards** set limits to protect public health, including the health of "sensitive" populations such as asthmatics, children, and the elderly. **Secondary standards** set limits to protect public welfare, including protection against decreased visibility, damage to animals, crops vegetation, and buildings. See <http://www.epa.gov/air/criteria.html>. The EPA Office of Air Quality Planning and Standards (OAQPS) has set National Ambient Air Quality Standards for six principal pollutants, which are called "criteria" pollutants. These pollutants are: Carbon Monoxide, Lead, Nitrogen Dioxide, Particulate Matter ($PM_{2.5}$ and $_{10}$), Ozone, and Sulfur Dioxide. NAAQS are periodically reviewed and revised to include any additional or new health or welfare data. Table 361 gives some of the health-related standards for the six air pollutants having NAAQS. Data gathered from state networks are periodically submitted to EPA's National Aerometric Information Retrieval System (AIRS) for summarization in annual reports on the nationwide status and trends in air quality. For details, see "Air Trends" on the EPA Web site at <http://www.epa.gov/airtrends/index.html>.

The Toxics Release Inventory (TRI), published by the EPA, is a valuable source of information on approximately 650 chemicals that are being used, manufactured, treated, transported, or released into the environment. Sections 313 of the Emergency Planning and Community Right-to-Know Act (EPCRA) and 6607 of the Pollution Prevention Act (PPA), mandate that a publicly-accessible toxic chemical database be developed and maintained by EPA. This database, known as the TRI, contains information concerning waste management activities and the release of toxic chemicals by facilities that manufacture, process, or otherwise use said materials. Data on the release of these chemicals are collected from about 22,000 facilities and facilities added in 1998 that have the equivalent of 10 or more full-time employees and meet the established thresholds for manufacturing, processing, or "other use" of listed chemicals. Facilities must report their releases and other waste management quantities. Since 1994 federal facilities have been required to report their data regardless of industry classification. In May 1997, EPA added seven new industry sectors that reported to the TRI for the first time in July 1999 for the 1998 reporting year. More current information on this program can be found at <http://www.epa.gov/tri/index.htm>.

Climate—NOAA, through the National Weather Service and the National Environmental Satellite, Data, and Information Service, is responsible for climate data. NOAA maintains about 11,600 weather stations, of which over 3,000 produce autographic precipitation records, about 600 take hourly readings of a series of weather elements, and the remainder record data once a day. These data are reported monthly in the Climatological Data and Storm Data, published monthly and annually in the Local Climatological Data (published by location for major cities).

The normal climatological temperatures, precipitation, and degree days listed in this publication are derived for comparative purposes and are averages for the 30-year period, 1971–2000. For stations that did not have continuous records for the entire 30 years from the same instrument site, the normals have been adjusted to provide representative values for the current location. The information in all other tables is based on data from the beginning of the record at that location through 2007.

U.S. Census Bureau, Statistical Abstract of the United States: 2010

Table 346. Land and Water Area of States and Other Entities: 2008

[One square mile = 2.59 square kilometers. Table data have been revised. The area measurements were derived from the Census Bureau's Master Address File/ Topologically Integrated Geographic Encoding and Referencing (MAF/TIGER) geographic database. The boundaries of the states and equivalent areas are as of January 1, 2008. The land and water areas, including their classifications, reflect base feature updates made in the MAF/TIGER database through May 1, 2008. These updates show increases in total water area and decreases in land area for nearly every state. For more details, see <http://www.census.gov/geo/www/tiger /tgrshp2008/tgrshp2008.html>]

State and other areas	Total area Sq. mi.	Total area Sq. km.	Land area Sq. mi.	Land area Sq. km.	Water area Total Sq. mi.	Water area Total Sq. km.	Inland (sq. mi.)	Coastal (sq. mi.)	Great Lakes (sq. mi.)	Territorial (sq. mi.)
Total	3,805,142	9,855,318	3,535,846	9,157,841	269,296	697,477	86,478	43,201	59,959	76,392
United States. .	3,795,951	9,831,513	3,531,822	9,147,420	264,129	684,094	86,409	43,185	59,959	74,575
Alabama	52,420	135,768	50,644	131,168	1,776	4,600	1,057	518	(X)	201
Alaska	664,988	1,722,319	570,665	1,478,022	94,323	244,297	20,028	28,162	(X)	46,133
Arizona	113,990	295,235	113,595	294,211	396	1,026	396	–	(X)	–
Arkansas	53,178	137,732	52,030	134,758	1,149	2,976	1,149	–	(X)	–
California.	163,694	423,967	155,766	403,434	7,928	20,534	2,842	222	(X)	4,864
Colorado	104,094	269,604	103,641	268,430	454	1,176	454	–	(X)	–
Connecticut	5,544	14,358	4,840	12,536	703	1,821	164	539	(X)	–
Delaware.	2,489	6,445	1,949	5,048	539	1,396	74	372	(X)	93
District of Columbia.	68	177	61	158	7	18	7	–	(X)	–
Florida	65,758	170,312	53,603	138,832	12,154	31,479	5,373	1,128	(X)	5,653
Georgia.	59,425	153,911	57,501	148,928	1,924	4,983	1,420	49	(X)	455
Hawaii	10,926	28,300	6,428	16,649	4,499	11,652	40	–	(X)	4,459
Idaho	83,568	216,442	82,643	214,045	926	2,398	926	–	(X)	–
Illinois.	57,916	150,002	55,518	143,792	2,398	6,211	836	–	1,562	–
Indiana	36,417	94,321	35,823	92,782	594	1,538	361	–	233	–
Iowa	56,273	145,746	55,858	144,672	415	1,075	415	–	(X)	–
Kansas	82,278	213,101	81,762	211,764	516	1,336	516	–	(X)	–
Kentucky.	40,411	104,665	39,492	102,284	919	2,380	919	–	(X)	–
Louisiana	51,988	134,649	43,199	111,885	8,789	22,764	4,433	1,951	(X)	2,405
Maine	35,384	91,644	30,841	79,878	4,543	11,766	2,282	613	(X)	1,647
Maryland	12,406	32,131	9,705	25,136	2,700	6,993	736	1,854	(X)	111
Massachusetts . . .	10,554	27,336	7,801	20,205	2,754	7,133	461	977	(X)	1,316
Michigan	96,713	250,486	56,528	146,408	40,185	104,079	2,164	–	38,021	–
Minnesota	86,935	225,163	79,607	206,182	7,328	18,980	4,782	–	2,546	–
Mississippi.	48,432	125,438	46,920	121,523	1,512	3,916	772	591	(X)	149
Missouri	69,702	180,529	68,716	177,974	987	2,556	987	–	(X)	–
Montana	147,039	380,831	145,541	376,951	1,498	3,880	1,498	–	(X)	–
Nebraska	77,349	200,334	76,825	198,977	524	1,357	524	–	(X)	–
Nevada.	110,572	286,382	109,780	284,330	792	2,051	792	–	(X)	–
New Hampshire . .	9,348	24,210	8,952	23,186	396	1,026	328	–	(X)	68
New Jersey	8,723	22,592	7,354	19,047	1,369	3,546	458	402	(X)	509
New Mexico.	121,590	314,919	121,297	314,159	293	759	293	–	(X)	–
New York	54,555	141,298	47,126	122,056	7,429	19,241	1,979	977	3,990	482
North Carolina . . .	53,819	139,391	48,619	125,923	5,200	13,468	4,044	–	(X)	1,157
North Dakota	70,698	183,109	69,001	178,713	1,697	4,395	1,697	–	(X)	–
Ohio.	44,825	116,097	40,858	105,822	3,967	10,275	467	–	3,500	–
Oklahoma	69,899	181,038	68,603	177,682	1,296	3,357	1,296	–	(X)	–
Oregon	98,379	254,801	95,985	248,601	2,394	6,200	1,063	74	(X)	1,256
Pennsylvania	46,055	119,281	44,739	115,874	1,316	3,408	567	–	749	–
Rhode Island	1,545	4,001	1,034	2,678	511	1,323	187	9	(X)	315
South Carolina . . .	32,021	82,934	30,070	77,881	1,951	5,053	1,044	74	(X)	832
South Dakota. . . .	77,116	199,730	75,811	196,350	1,305	3,380	1,305	–	(X)	–
Tennessee.	42,144	109,154	41,235	106,799	910	2,357	910	–	(X)	–
Texas	268,597	695,666	261,226	676,575	7,371	19,091	5,607	406	(X)	1,358
Utah	84,897	219,883	82,191	212,875	2,706	7,009	2,706	–	(X)	–
Vermont	9,616	24,906	9,217	23,872	400	1,036	400	–	(X)	–
Virginia	42,775	110,787	39,493	102,287	3,282	8,500	1,106	1,729	(X)	447
Washington	71,298	184,661	66,449	172,103	4,849	12,559	1,646	2,537	(X)	666
West Virginia	24,230	62,755	24,038	62,258	192	497	192	–	(X)	–
Wisconsin	65,496	169,636	54,154	140,259	11,342	29,376	1,984	–	9,358	–
Wyoming.	97,812	253,334	97,088	251,458	724	1,875	724	–	(X)	–
Puerto Rico.	5,325	13,791	3,424	8,868	1,901	4,924	68	16	(X)	1,817
Island Areas:	3,866	10,013	600	1,554	3,266	8,459	(NA)	(NA)	(X)	(NA)
American Samoa .	583	1,510	77	199	506	1,311	(NA)	(NA)	(X)	(NA)
Guam	571	1,479	210	544	361	935	(NA)	(NA)	(X)	(NA)
No. Mariana Islands	1,975	5,115	179	464	1,796	4,652	(NA)	(NA)	(X)	(NA)
Virgin Islands of the U.S.	738	1,911	134	347	604	1,564	(NA)	(NA)	(X)	(NA)
U.S. minor outlying islands [1]	16	41	16	41	–	–	(NA)	(NA)	(X)	(NA)

– Represents or rounds to zero.   NA Not available.   X Not applicable.   [1] Baker, Howland, and Jarvis Islands; Johnston Atoll, Kingman Reef, Midway Islands, Navassa Island, Palmyra Atoll, and Wake Island.

Source: U.S. Census Bureau, unpublished data from the Census TIGER "R" database.

Geography and Environment   215

Table 347. **Great Lakes Profile**

[The Great Lakes contain the largest supply of freshwater in the world, holding about 18% of the worlds total freshwater and about 90% of the United States total freshwater. The Lakes are a series of five interconnecting large lakes, one small lake, four connecting channels, and the St. Lawrence Seaway. Combined, the lakes cover an area of over 94,000 square miles (245,000 square kilometers) and contain over 5,400 cubic miles (23,000 cubic kilometers) of water]

Characteristics	Unit	Lake Superior	Lake Michigan	Lake Huron	Lake Erie	Lake Ontario
Length	Miles	350	307	206	241	193
Breadth	Miles	160	118	183	57	53
Depth						
Average	Feet	489	279	159	62	283
Maximum	Feet	1,333	923	750	210	802
Volume.	Cubic miles. .	2,935	1,180	849	116	393
Water Surface Area [1]	Square miles.	31,700	22,300	23,000	9,910	7,340
Retention/Replacement Time [2] . . .	Years.	191	99	22	2.6	6

[1] Includes both U.S. and Canada surface area.   [2] The amount of time it takes for lakes to get rid of pollutants.

Source: Department of Commerce, National Oceanic and Atmospheric Administration, Great Lakes Environmental Research Laboratory, "About Our Great Lakes," June 2004; <http://www.glerl.noaa.gov/pr/ourlakes/intro.html>.

Table 348. **Great Lakes Length of Shoreline in Separate Basin**

[In statute miles]

Shorelines	Total	Canada	U.S.	MI	MN	WI	IL	IN	OH	PA	NY
Total.	10,368	5,127	5,241	3,288	189	820	63	45	312	51	473
Lake Superior.	2,980	1,549	1,431	917	189	325	–	–	–	–	–
St. Marys River.	297	206	91	91	–	–	–	–	–	–	–
Lake Michigan	1,661	–	1,661	1,058	–	495	63	45	–	–	–
Lake Huron	3,350	2,416	934	934	–	–	–	–	–	–	–
St Clair River	128	47	81	81	–	–	–	–	–	–	–
Lake St. Clair.	160	71	89	89	–	–	–	–	–	–	–
Detroit River.	107	43	64	64	–	–	–	–	–	–	–
Lake Erie.	860	366	494	54	–	–	–	–	312	51	77
Niagara River.	99	34	65	–	–	–	–	–	–	–	65
Lake Ontario	726	395	331	–	–	–	–	–	–	–	331

– Represents zero.

Source: State of Michigan, Department of Environment Quality, "Great Lakes, Shorelines of the Great Lakes"; <http://www.michigan.gov/deq /0,1607,7-135-3313_3677-15959—,00.html>.

Table 349. **Largest Lakes in the United States**

[The list of lakes include manmade lakes and those that are only partially within the United States. For more information on the National Atlas of the United States, see <http://nationalatlas.gov/partners.html/>]

Lake	Location	Area in Sq. miles	Lake	Location	Area in Sq. miles
Lake Superior	MI-MN-WI-Ontario	31,700	Lake Pontchartrain . .	Louisiana	631
Lake Huron.	MI-Ontario	23,000	Lake Sakakawea [1] . .	North Dakota	520
Lake Michigan	IL-IN-MI-WI.	22,300	Lake Champlain	NY-VT-Quebec	490
Lake Erie	MI-NY-OH-PA-Ontario. . . .	9,910	Becharof Lake	Alaska	453
Lake Ontario	NY-Ontario	7,340	Lake St. Clair	MI-Ontario	430
Great Salt Lake	Utah	2,117	Red Lake	Minnesota	427
Lake of the Woods . .	MN-Manitoba-Ontario	1,485	Selawik Lake.	Alaska	404
Iliamna Lake	Alaska	1,014	Fort Peck Lake [1] . . .	Montana	393
Lake Oahe [1]	ND-SD.	685	Salton Sea	California	347
Lake Okeechobee . .	Florida.	662	Rainy Lake	MN-Ontario.	345

[1] Manmade lakes.

Source: U.S. Geological Survey, 2003, and National Oceanic and Atmospheric Administration, Great Lakes, 2002; The National Atlas of the United States of America; Lakes; <http://nationalatlas.gov/articles/mapping/a_general.html>.

Table 350. U.S.–Canada and U.S.–Mexico Border Lengths

[For 2007, there were more than 63 million passenger trips between the United States and Canada each year, and more than 217 million between the United States and Mexico. See Table 1234 for more passenger trip detail. Only those States with international borders are included in the table below. For more information on the National Atlas of the United States, see also <http://nationalatlas.gov/partners.html>

State	Length of international border (statute miles) [1]	State	Length of international border (statute miles) [1]
United States–Canada total	**5,525**	Ohio	146
Alaska	1,585	Pennsylvania	42
Idaho	45	Vermont	90
Maine	611	Washington	427
Michigan	721		
Minnesota	547	**United States–Mexico total**	**1,933**
Montana	545	Arizona	373
New Hampshire	58	California	140
New York	445	New Mexico	180
North Dakota	310	Texas	1,241

[1] Statute mile equals one mile.

Source: U.S. Geological Survey, "The National Atlas of the United States, *Borders*"; <http://nationalatlas.gov/articles/mapping/a_general.html>.

Table 351. Coastline and Shoreline of the United States by State

[In statute miles. Each statute mile equals one mile. The term **coastline** is used to describe the general outline of the seacoast. For the table below, United States coastline measurements were made from small-scale maps, and the coastline was generalized. The coastlines of large sounds and bays were included. Measurements were made in 1948. **Shoreline** is the term used to describe a more detailed measure of the seacoast. The tidal shoreline figures in the table below were obtained in 1939–1940 from the largest-scale charts and maps then available. Shoreline of the outer coast, offshore islands, sounds, and bays were included, as well as the tidal portion of rivers and creeks. Only states with a coastline or shoreline are included in the following table. For more information on the National Atlas of the United States, see also <http://nationalatlas.gov/partners.html>]

State	General coastline	Tidal shoreline	State	General coastline	Tidal shoreline
United States	**12,383**	**88,633**	Mississippi	44	359
Alabama	53	607	New Hampshire	13	131
Alaska	6,640	33,904	New Jersey	130	1,792
California	840	3,427	New York	127	1,850
Connecticut	–	618	North Carolina	301	3,375
Delaware	28	381	Oregon	296	1,410
Florida	1,350	8,426	Pennsylvania	–	89
Georgia	100	2,344	Rhode Island	40	384
Hawaii	750	1,052	South Carolina	187	2,876
Louisiana	397	7,721	Texas	367	3,359
Maine	228	3,478	Virginia	112	3,315
Maryland	31	3,190	Washington	157	3,026
Massachusetts	192	1,519			

– Represents zero.

Source: National Oceanic Atmospheric Administration, 1975; The National Atlas of the United States, *Coastline and Shoreline*; <http://nationalatlas.gov/articles/mapping/a_general.html>.

Table 352. Flows of Largest U.S. Rivers—Length, Discharge, and Drainage Area

River	Location of mouth	Source stream (name and location)	Length (miles) [1]	Average discharge at mouth (1,000 cubic ft. per second)	Drainage area (1,000 sq. mi.)
Missouri	Missouri	Red Rock Creek, MT	2,540	76.2	[2]529
Mississippi	Louisiana	Mississippi River, MN	[3]2,340	[4]593	[2, 5]1,150
Yukon	Alaska	McNeil River, Canada	1,980	225	[2]328
St. Lawrence	Canada	North River, MN	1,900	348	[2]396
Rio Grande	Mexico-Texas	Rio Grande, CO	1,900	([7])	336
Arkansas	Arkansas	East Fork Arkansas River, CO	1,460	41	161
Colorado . . [6]	Mexico	Colorado River, CO	1,450	([7])	246
Atchafalaya [6]	Louisiana	Tierra Blanca Creek, NM	1,420	58	95.1
Ohio	Illinois-Kentucky	Allegheny River, PA	1,310	281	203
Red [6]	Louisiana	Tierra Blanca Creek, NM	1,290	56	93.2
Brazos	Texas	Blackwater Draw, NM	1,280	([7])	45.6
Columbia	Oregon-Washington . . .	Columbia River, Canada	1,240	265	[2]258
Snake	Washington	Snake River, WY	1,040	56.9	108
Platte	Nebraska	Grizzly Creek, CO	990	([7])	84.9
Pecos	Texas	Pecos River, NM	926	([7])	44.3
Canadian	Oklahoma	Canadian River, CO	906	([7])	46.9
Tennessee	Kentucky	Courthouse Creek, NC	886	68	40.9

[1] From source to mouth. [2] Drainage area includes both the United States and Canada. [3] The length from the source of the Missouri River to the Mississippi River and thence to the Gulf of Mexico is about 3,710 miles. [4] Includes about 167,000 cubic ft. per second diverted from the Mississippi into the Atchafalaya River but excludes the flow of the Red River. [5] Excludes the drainage areas of the Red and Atchafalaya Rivers. [6] In east-central Louisiana, the Red River flows into the Atchafalaya River, a distributary of the Mississippi River. Data on average discharge, length, and drainage area include the Red River, but exclude all water diverted into the Atchafalaya from the Mississippi River. [7] Less than 15,000 cubic feet per second.

Source: U.S. Geological Survey, *"Largest Rivers in the United States"*;<http://pubs.usgs.gov/of/1987/ofr87-242/> (revised May, 1990).

Geography and Environment 217

Table 353. Extreme and Mean Elevations by State and Other Areas

[One foot = .305 meter. There are 2,130 square miles of the United States below sea level (Death Valley is the lowest point). There are 20,230 square miles above 10,000 feet (Mount McKinley is the highest point in the United States). (–) Minus sign indicates below sea level]

State and other areas	Highest point Name	Elevation Feet	Elevation Meters	Lowest point Name	Elevation Feet	Elevation Meters	Approximate mean elevation Feet	Approximate mean elevation Meters
U.S..	Mt. McKinley (AK)	20,320	6,198	Death Valley (CA). . . .	−282	−86	2,500	763
AL	Cheaha Mountain	2,407	734	Gulf of Mexico	(1)	(1)	500	153
AK	Mount McKinley	20,320	6,198	Pacific Ocean.	(1)	(1)	1,900	580
AZ	Humphreys Peak.	12,633	3,853	Colorado River	70	21	4,100	1,251
AR	Magazine Mountain	2,753	840	Ouachita River	55	17	650	198
CA	Mount Whitney	14,494	4,419	Death Valley.	−282	−86	2,900	885
CO	Mt. Elbert.	14,433	4,402	Arikaree River.	3,315	1,011	6,800	2,074
CT	Mt. Frissell on south slope . .	2,380	726	Long Island Sound . . .	(1)	(1)	500	153
DE	Ebright Road [2]	448	137	Atlantic Ocean	(1)	(1)	60	18
DC	Tenleytown at Reno Reservoir.	410	125	Potomac River	1	(Z)	150	46
FL	Britton Hill	345	105	Atlantic Ocean	(1)	(1)	100	31
GA	Brasstown Bald.	4,784	1,459	Atlantic Ocean	(1)	(1)	600	183
HI	Pu'u Wekiu, Mauna Kea. . . .	13,796	4,208	Pacific Ocean.	(1)	(1)	3,030	924
ID	Borah Peak	12,662	3,862	Snake River	710	217	5,000	1,525
IL	Charles Mound	1,235	377	Mississippi River	279	85	600	183
IN	Hoosier Hill	1,257	383	Ohio River	320	98	700	214
IA	Hawkeye Point	1,670	509	Mississippi River. . . .	480	146	1,100	336
KS	Mount Sunflower.	4,039	1,232	Verdigris River	679	207	2,000	610
KY	Black Mountain.	4,145	1,264	Mississippi River	257	78	750	229
LA	Driskill Mountain	535	163	New Orleans	−8	−2	100	31
ME.	Mount Katahdin	5,268	1,607	Atlantic Ocean	(1)	(1)	600	183
MD.	Hoye Crest.	3,360	1,025	Atlantic Ocean	(1)	(1)	350	107
MA.	Mount Greylock.	3,491	1,065	Atlantic Ocean	(1)	(1)	500	153
MI	Mount Arvon.	1,979	604	Lake Erie.	571	174	900	275
MN.	Eagle Mountain.	2,301	702	Lake Superior.	601	183	1,200	366
MS	Woodall Mountain	806	246	Gulf of Mexico	(1)	(1)	300	92
MO	Taum Sauk Mountain	1,772	540	St. Francis River	230	70	800	244
MT	Granite Peak	12,799	3,904	Kootenai River	1,800	549	3,400	1,037
NE	Panorama Point	5,424	1,654	Missouri River.	840	256	2,600	793
NV	Boundary Peak.	13,140	4,007	Colorado River	479	146	5,500	1,678
NH	Mount Washington.	6,288	1,918	Atlantic Ocean	(1)	(1)	1,000	305
NJ	High Point	1,803	550	Atlantic Ocean	(1)	(1)	250	76
NM.	Wheeler Peak.	13,161	4,014	Red Bluff Reservoir . . .	2,842	867	5,700	1,739
NY	Mount Marcy	5,344	1,630	Atlantic Ocean	(1)	(1)	1,000	305
NC	Mount Mitchell	6,684	2,039	Atlantic Ocean	(1)	(1)	700	214
ND	White Butte	3,506	1,069	Red River of the North.	750	229	1,900	580
OH	Campbell Hill	1,550	473	Ohio River	455	139	850	259
OK	Black Mesa	4,973	1,517	Little River	289	88	1,300	397
OR	Mount Hood	11,239	3,428	Pacific Ocean.	(1)	(1)	3,300	1,007
PA	Mount Davis	3,213	980	Delaware River	(1)	(1)	1,100	336
RI	Jerimoth Hill.	812	248	Atlantic Ocean	(1)	(1)	200	61
SC	Sassafras Mountain	3,560	1,086	Atlantic Ocean	(1)	(1)	350	107
SD	Harney Peak	7,242	2,209	Big Stone Lake.	966	295	2,200	671
TN	Clingmans Dome.	6,643	2,026	Mississippi River	178	54	900	275
TX	Guadalupe Peak	8,749	2,668	Gulf of Mexico	(1)	(1)	1,700	519
UT	Kings Peak	13,528	4,126	Beaverdam Wash	2,000	610	6,100	1,861
VT	Mount Mansfield	4,393	1,340	Lake Champlain	95	29	1,000	305
VA	Mount Rogers.	5,729	1,747	Atlantic Ocean	(1)	(1)	950	290
WA.	Mount Rainier.	14,411	4,395	Pacific Ocean.	(1)	(1)	1,700	519
WV	Spruce Knob	4,863	1,483	Potomac River	240	73	1,500	458
WI	Timms Hill	1,951	595	Lake Michigan	579	177	1,050	320
WY	Gannett Peak.	13,804	4,210	Belle Fourche River. . .	3,099	945	6,700	2,044
Puerto Rico.	Cerro de Punta.	4,390	1,339	Atlantic Ocean	(1)	(1)	1,800	549
American Samoa . .	Lata Mountain	3,160	964	Pacific Ocean.	(1)	(1)	1,300	397
Guam	Mount Lamlam	1,332	406	Pacific Ocean.	(1)	(1)	330	101
U.S. Virgin Islands .	Crown Mountain	1,556	475	Atlantic Ocean	(1)	(1)	750	229

Z Less than 0.5 meter. [1] Sea level. [2] At DE-PA state line.

Source: U.S. Geological Survey, for highest and lowest points, "Elevations and Distances in the United States"; <http://egsc.usgs.gov/isb/pubs/booklets/elvadist/elvadist.html>; (released 29 April 2005). For mean elevations see, *Elevations and Distances in the United States,* 1983 edition.

218 Geography and Environment

Table 354. **Land Cover/Use by Type: 1982 to 2003**

[In millions of acres (1,937.7 represents 1,937,700,000), except percent. Excludes Alaska, Hawaii, and District of Columbia. For inventory-specific glossary of key terms, see <http://www.nrcs.usda.gov/technical/NRI/glossaries.html>]

Year	Total surface area	Nonfederal rural land								Fed-eral land
		Rural land, total [1]	Crop-land	Pasture land	Range-land	Forest land	Other rural land	Devel-oped land	Water areas	
Land										
1982	1,937.7	1,417.2	420.4	131.4	414.5	402.6	48.3	72.8	48.6	399.1
1992	1,937.6	1,400.2	381.2	125.1	406.6	404.0	49.3	86.5	49.4	401.5
2002	1,937.7	1,378.1	368.4	117.3	405.3	404.9	50.6	107.3	50.4	401.9
2003	1,937.7	1,377.3	367.9	117.0	405.1	405.6	50.2	108.1	50.4	401.9
Percent of total land										
1982	100.0	73.1	21.7	6.8	21.4	20.8	2.5	3.8	2.5	20.6
1992	100.0	72.3	19.7	6.5	21.0	20.9	2.5	4.5	2.5	20.7
2002	100.0	71.1	19.0	6.1	20.9	20.9	2.6	5.5	2.6	20.7
2003	100.0	71.1	19.0	6.0	20.9	20.9	2.6	5.6	2.6	20.7

[1] Includes Conservation Reserve Program land not shown separately.

Source: U.S. Department of Agriculture, Natural Resources and Conservation Service, *2003 Annual National Resources Inventory.* See also <http://www.nrcs.usda.gov/technical/NRI>.

Table 355. **Wetlands on Nonfederal Land and Water Areas by Land Cover/Use and Farm Production Region: 2003**

[In thousands of acres (110,760 represents 110,760,000). Represents palustrine and estuarine wetlands; see source]

Farm production region [1]	Total	Crop-land [2]	Forest land	Range-land	Other rural land	Developed land	Water area
Wetlands, total	110,760	16,730	65,440	7,740	15,800	1,590	3,460
Lake states	22,460	2,710	15,480	–	3,880	160	230
Southeast	22,360	940	16,010	970	3,460	420	560
Delta states	17,950	3,240	11,020	270	2,730	190	500
Northeast	14,150	1,250	10,890	–	1,550	240	220
Northern plains	7,640	3,020	210	2,870	1,090	80	370
Appalachian	7,460	400	6,080	–	570	110	300
Southern plains	5,590	970	2,350	970	520	230	550
Mountain	4,780	1,570	220	2,010	820	30	130
Corn belt	4,690	1,330	2,440	–	380	100	440
Pacific	3,680	1,300	740	650	800	30	160

– Represents or rounds to zero.   [1] Ten regions established by USDA, Economic Research Service, that group states according to differences in soils, slope of land, climate, distance to market, and storage and marketing facilities.   [2] Includes pastureland and Conservation Reserve Program (CRP) lands.

Source: U.S. Department of Agriculture, Natural Resources Conservation Service, 2003 Annual National Resources Inventory. See also <http://www.nrcs.usda.gov/technical/NRI/>.

Table 356. **Land Cover/Use by State: 2003**

[In thousands of acres (1,937,664 represents 1,937,664,000), except percent. Excludes Alaska, District of Columbia, Hawaii, and Island Areas]

State	Total surface area	Selected nonfederal rural land, percent of total			State	Total surface area	Selected nonfederal rural land, percent of total		
		Crop-land	Range-land	Forest land			Crop-land	Range-land	Forest land
United States . . .	1,937,664	19.0	20.9	20.9	Nebraska.	49,510	39.5	46.6	1.6
Alabama	33,424	7.5	0.2	64.4	Nevada	70,763	0.9	11.7	0.4
Arizona	72,964	1.3	44.2	5.7	New Hampshire . . .	5,941	2.1	–	65.6
Arkansas	34,037	22.1	0.1	44.1	New Jersey	5,216	10.1	–	30.8
California	101,510	9.3	17.5	13.7	New Mexico	77,823	2.0	51.3	7.0
Colorado	66,625	12.5	37.2	4.9	New York	31,361	17.1	–	56.1
Connecticut	3,195	5.4	–	53.4	North Carolina	33,709	16.4	–	45.9
Delaware	1,534	29.8	–	22.2	North Dakota	45,251	53.6	24.5	1.0
Florida	37,534	7.7	7.2	33.9	Ohio	26,445	42.5	–	27.3
Georgia	37,741	11.0	–	58.0	Oklahoma	44,738	20.1	31.6	16.5
Idaho	53,488	10.2	12.0	7.5	Oregon	62,161	6.0	15.1	20.5
Illinois	36,059	66.5	–	11.0	Pennsylvania	28,995	17.7	–	53.9
Indiana	23,158	57.5	–	16.5	Rhode Island	813	2.5	–	45.9
Iowa	36,017	70.8	–	6.4	South Carolina	19,939	11.9	–	56.0
Kansas	52,661	50.3	30.1	2.9	South Dakota	49,358	34.6	44.7	1.0
Kentucky	25,863	21.2	–	40.6	Tennessee	26,974	17.6	–	44.3
Louisiana	31,377	17.3	0.9	42.5	Texas	171,052	14.9	56.2	6.2
Maine	20,966	1.8	–	84.0	Utah	54,339	3.1	19.6	3.5
Maryland	7,870	19.3	–	30.1	Vermont	6,154	9.5	–	67.1
Massachusetts	5,339	4.7	–	49.9	Virginia	27,087	10.6	–	48.7
Michigan	37,349	21.7	–	44.7	Washington	44,035	14.7	13.3	28.9
Minnesota	54,010	39.1	–	30.3	West Virginia	15,508	5.3	–	68.1
Mississippi	30,527	16.3	–	54.9	Wisconsin	35,920	28.7	–	40.4
Missouri.	44,614	30.7	0.2	28.1	Wyoming	62,603	3.5	44.0	1.5
Montana	94,110	15.4	39.0	5.7					

–Represents zero.

Source: U.S. Department of Agriculture, Natural Resources and Conservation Service, Summary Report, 2003 Annual National Resources Inventory. See also <http://www.nrcs.usda.gov/technical/NRI/>.

Geography and Environment   219

Table 357. U.S. Wetland Resources and Deepwater Habitats by Type: 1998 to 2004

[In thousands of acres (148,618.8 represents 148,618,800). Wetlands and deepwater habitats are defined separately because the term wetland does not include permanent water bodies. Deepwater habitats are permanently flooded land lying below the deepwater boundary of wetlands. Deepwater habitats include environments where surface water is permanent and often deep, so that water, rather than air, is the principal medium within which the dominant organisms live, whether or not they are attached to the substrate. As in wetlands, the dominant plants are hydrophytes; however, the substrates are considered nonsoil because the water is too deep to support emergent vegetation. In general terms, wetlands are lands where saturation with water is the dominant factor determining the nature of soil development and the types of plant and animal communities living in the soil and on its surface. The single feature that most wetlands share is soil or substrate that is at least periodically saturated with or covered by water. Wetlands are lands transitional between terrestrial and aquatic systems where the water table is usually at or near the surface or the land is covered by shallow water. For more information on wetlands, see the "Classification of Wetlands and Deepwater Habitats of the United States" at <http://www.fws.gov/wetlands/_documents/gNSDI/ClassificationWetlandsDeepwaterHabitatsUS.pdf/>]

Wetland or deepwater category	Estimated area, 1998	Estimated area, 2004	Change, 1998 to 2004
All wetlands and deepwater habitats, total	**148,618.8**	**149,058.5**	**439.7**
All deepwater habitats, total	41,046.6	41,304.5	247.9
Lacustrine [1]	16,610.5	16,773.4	162.9
Riverine [2]	6,765.5	6,813.3	47.7
Estuarine Subtidal [3]	17,680.5	17,717.8	37.3
All wetlands, total	107,562.3	107,754.0	191.8
Intertidal wetlands [4]	5,328.7	5,300.3	−28.4
Marine intertidal	130.4	128.6	−1.9
Estuarine intertidal nonvegetated	594.1	600.0	5.9
Estuarine intertidal vegetated	4,604.2	4,571.7	−32.4
Freshwater wetlands	102,233.6	102,453.8	220.2
Freshwater nonvegetated	5,918.7	6,633.9	715.3
Freshwater vegetated	96,414.9	95,819.8	−495.1
Freshwater emergent [5]	26,289.6	26,147.0	−142.6
Freshwater forested [6]	51,483.1	52,031.4	548.2
Freshwater shrub [7]	18,542.2	17,641.4	−900.8

[1] The lacustrine system includes deepwater habitats with all of the following characteristics: (1) situated in a topographic depression or a dammed river channel; (2) lacking trees, shrubs, persistent emergents, emergent mosses or lichens with greater than 30 percent coverage; (3) total area exceeds 20 acres (8 hectares).   [2] The riverine system includes deepwater habitats contained within a channel, with the exception of habitats with water containing ocean derived salts in excess of 0.5 parts per thousand.   [3] The estuarine system consists of deepwater tidal habitats and adjacent tidal wetlands that are usually semi-enclosed by land but have open, partly obstructed, or sporadic access to the open ocean, and in which ocean water is at least occasionally diluted by freshwater runoff from the land. Subtidal is where the substrate is continuously submerged by marine or estuarine waters.   [4] Intertidal is where the substrate is exposed and flooded by tides. Intertidal includes the splash zone of coastal waters.   [5] Emergent wetlands are characterized by erect, rooted, herbaceous hydrophytes, excluding mosses and lichens. This vegetation is present for most of the growing season in most years. These wetlands are usually dominated by perennial plants.   [6] Forested wetlands are characterized by woody vegetation that is 20 feet tall or taller.   [7] Shrub wetlands include areas dominated by woody vegetation less than 20 feet tall. The species include true shrubs, young trees, and trees or shrubs that are small or stunted because of environmental conditions.

Source: U.S. Fish and Wildlife Service, *Status and Trends of Wetlands in the Conterminous United States, 1998 to 2004,* December 2005. See also <http://www.fws.gov/wetlands/_documents/gSandt/NationalReports/statustrendswetlandsconterminousUS1998to2004 .pdf>.

Table 358. U.S. Water Withdrawals Per Day by End Use: 1940 to 2000

[(140 represents 140,000,000,000). Includes the District of Columbia, Puerto Rico and U.S. Virgin Islands. Withdrawal signifies water physically withdrawn from a source. Includes fresh and saline water; excludes water used for hydroelectric power]

Year	Total (bil. gal.)	Per capita [1] (gal.)	Irrigation (bil. gal.)	Public supply (bil. gal.) [2]	Rural (bil. gal.) [3]	Industrial and misc. [4] (bil. gal.)	Steam electric utilities (bil. gal.)
1940	140	1,027	71	10	3.1	29	23
1950	180	1,185	89	14	3.6	37	40
1955	240	1,454	110	17	3.6	39	72
1960	270	1,500	110	.21	3.6	38	100
1965	310	1,602	120	24	4.0	46	130
1970	370	1,815	130	27	4.5	47	170
1975	420	1,972	140	29	4.9	45	200
1980	440	1,953	150	34	5.6	45	210
1985	399	1,650	137	38	7.8	31	187
1990	408	1,620	137	41	7.9	30	195
1995	402	1,500	134	40	8.9	29	190
2000	408	1,430	137	43	9.2	23	196

[1] Based on U.S. Census Bureau resident population as of July 1.   [2] Includes commercial water withdrawals.   [3] Rural farm and nonfarm household and garden use, and water for farm stock and dairies.   [4] For 1940 to 1960, includes manufacturing and mineral industries, rural commercial industries, air-conditioning, resorts, hotels, motels, military, other state and federal agencies, and miscellaneous; thereafter, includes manufacturing, mining and mineral processing, ordnance, construction, and miscellaneous.

Source: 1940–1960, U.S. Bureau of Domestic Business Development, based principally on committee prints, *Water Resources Activities in the United States,* for the Senate Committee on National Water Resources, U.S. Senate, thereafter, U.S. Geological Survey, *Estimated Use of Water in the United States in 2000,* circular 1268. See also <http://pubs.usgs.gov/circ /2004/circ1268/> (released 12 March 2004).

Table 359. **Oil Spills in U.S. Water—Number and Volume: 2000 to 2008**

[These summary statistics are based on reported discharges of oil and petroleum based products into U.S. navigable waters, including territorial waters (extending 3 to 12 miles from the coastline), tributaries, the contiguous zone, onto shoreline, or into other waters that threaten the marine environment. Spills associated with Hurricanes Katrina and Rita have been excluded]

Spill characteristic	Number of spills				Spill volume (gallons)			
	2000	2005	2007	2008	2000	2005	2007	2008
Total	8,354	4,073	4,032	3,586	1,431,370	2,364,169	654,143	759,689
Size of spill (gallons):								
1 to 100	8,058	3,857	3,827	3,429	39,355	33,041	30,539	25,098
101 to 1,000	219	166	168	130	78,779	62,357	58,639	51,733
1,001 to 3,000	37	26	18	11	67,529	46,019	36,380	20,170
3,001 to 5,000	12	9	8	7	45,512	36,803	32,609	26,596
5,001 to 10,000	16	7	6	3	112,415	58,453	45,800	21,800
10,001 to 50,000	6	5	2	3	108,400	106,870	52,122	61,000
50,001 to 100,000	4	1	2	2	266,380	84,000	104,053	82,274
100,001 to 1,000,000	2	1	1	2	713,000	110,000	294,000	471,018
1,000,000 and over	–	1	–	–	–	1,826,626	–	–
Source:								
Tankship	111	40	42	35	608,176	2,975	4,056	1,337
Tankbarge	229	130	118	110	133,540	2,006,774	4,537	286,654
All other vessels	5,220	1,789	1,930	1,622	291,927	115,906	175,667	261,799
Facilities	1,054	996	1,063	1,023	311,604	92,399	138,223	163,999
Pipelines	25	20	25	18	17,021	111,253	294,874	14,494
All other nonvessels	566	264	333	312	45,136	13,422	26,144	22,510
Unknown	1,149	834	521	466	23,966	21,440	10,642	8,896

– Represents zero.

Source: U.S. Coast Guard, *Pollution Incidents In and Around U.S. Waters, A Spill/Release Compendium: 1969–2004*, 2004–2008: U.S. Coast Guard Marine Information for Safety and Law Enforcement (MISLE) System based on an April 2009 data extraction. Data are unpublished. See also <http://homeport.uscg.mil./mycg/portal/ep/home.do>.

Table 360. **Hazardous Waste Generated, Shipped, and Received by State and Other Area: 2007**

[In thousands of tons (46,693.3 represents 46,693,300). Covers hazardous waste regulated under the Resource Conservation and Recovery Act (RCRA)of 1976 as amended. For exclusions of data from the 2007 National Biennial RCRA Hardous Waste Report, see the section of the report titled "The Data Presented in This National Biennial Report"]

State and other area	Generated	Shipped	Received	State and other area	Generated	Shipped	Received
Total	46,693.3	7,165.4	7,199.2	Nebraska	38.7	39.9	32.4
				Nevada	10.0	14.5	112.7
United States	46,629.9	7,119.3	7,196.5	New Hampshire	5.4	5.4	–
				New Jersey	596.1	596.8	220.8
Alabama	416.9	206.1	136.9	New Mexico	944.6	6.2	4.8
Alaska	2.5	2.1	0.1	New York	1,267.6	274.6	201.0
Arizona	56.7	54.1	46.5	North Carolina	96.0	102.7	18.6
Arkansas	495.8	324.4	358.5	North Dakota	538.6	1.2	0.3
California	608.7	643.1	491.0	Ohio	1,608.2	713.9	804.0
Colorado	54.9	40.0	34.4	Oklahoma	134.4	42.3	69.2
Connecticut	32.5	40.3	42.2	Oregon	75.0	64.2	65.1
Delaware	19.7	19.4	0.1	Pennsylvania	388.8	295.7	460.9
District of Columbia	0.8	0.8	–	Rhode Island	4.6	9.4	6.4
Florida	152.7	55.8	23.7	South Carolina	151.4	189.2	187.8
Georgia	102.6	53.2	5.7	South Dakota	0.8	0.9	0.1
Hawaii	1.2	1.2	0.2	Tennessee	1,079.1	56.9	31.0
Idaho	5.6	8.1	456.6	Texas	13,272.3	810.7	493.9
Illinois	1,122.9	235.9	420.4	Utah	82.8	88.6	134.8
Indiana	958.0	404.8	510.0	Vermont	3.0	2.5	0.3
Iowa	49.0	48.8	0.4	Virginia	94.9	83.8	18.0
Kansas	292.7	121.0	221.2	Washington	147.2	65.7	40.8
Kentucky	139.9	167.6	75.1	West Virginia	76.6	49.5	13.5
Louisiana	15,892.6	474.1	352.3	Wisconsin	310.3	155.6	55.4
Maine	5.3	5.1	0.6	Wyoming	4.0	4.0	–
Maryland	43.6	46.8	43.2				
Massachusetts	248.3	60.9	94.3				
Michigan	2,397.4	277.1	430.3	Guam	0.1	0.1	0.6
Minnesota	101.7	57.4	249.7	Navajo Nation	0.4	0.4	–
Mississippi	2,239.7	21.5	55.7	Puerto Rico	60.0	42.8	2.7
Missouri	228.1	66.4	175.7	Trust Territories	–	–	–
Montana	29.5	9.4	–	Virgin Islands	3.2	3.1	–

– Represents or rounds to zero.

Source: U.S. Environmental Protection Agency, *The National Biennial RCRA Hardous Waste Report (Based on 2007 Data)*, series EPA530-R-03-007. See also <http://www.epa.gov/epawaste/inforesources/data/biennialreport/index.htm>.

Geography and Environment 221

Table 361. National Ambient Air Pollutant Concentrations by Type of Pollutant: 2001 to 2007

[Data represent annual composite averages of pollutant based on daily 24-hour averages of monitoring stations, except carbon monoxide which is based on the second-highest, nonoverlapping, 8-hour average; ozone, the fourth-highest maximum 8-hour value; and lead, the maximum quarterly average of ambient lead levels. Based on data from the Air Quality System. $\mu g/m^3$ = micrograms of pollutant per cubic meter of air; ppm = parts per million]

Pollutant	Unit	Monitoring stations, number	Air quality standard [1]	2001	2002	2003	2004	2005	2006	2007
Carbon monoxide	ppm	322	[2]9	3.3	2.9	2.7	2.5	2.3	2.2	2.0
Ozone	ppm	1,013	[3]0.075	0.081	0.085	0.080	0.074	0.079	0.077	0.077
Sulfur dioxide	ppm	406	[4]0.03	0.0046	0.0043	0.0043	0.0041	0.0041	0.0037	0.0035
Particulates (PM-10)	$\mu g/m^3$	734	[5]150	86.5	86.8	84.4	69.6	65.2	75.6	68.5
Fine particulates (PM2.5) annual average	$\mu g/m^3$	725	[6]15	13.2	12.7	12.3	11.9	12.9	11.6	11.9
Fine particulates (PM2.5) daily average	$\mu g/m^3$	725	[7]35	34.1	32.9	30.8	30.5	33.5	28.7	30.9
Nitrogen dioxide	ppm	313	[8]0.053	0.015	0.015	0.014	0.013	0.013	0.013	0.012
Lead	$\mu g/m^3$	103	[9]0.15	0.35	0.17	0.17	0.21	0.16	0.14	0.155

[1] Refers to the primary National Ambient Air Quality Standard. [2] Based on 8-hour standard of 9 ppm. [3] Based on annual standard of 0.03 ppm. [4] Based on 8-hour standard of 0.075 ppm. On March 12, 2008, EPA revised the level of the primary and secondary 8-hour ozone standards to 0.075 ppm. [5] Based on 24-hour (daily) standard of 150 mg/m^3. The particulates (PM-10) standard replaced the previous standard for total suspended particulates in 1987. In 2006, EPA revoked the annual PM-10 standard. [6] Based on annual standard of 15 mg/m^3. The PM-2.5 national monitoring network was deployed in 1999. National trend data prior to that time is not available. [7] Based on daily standard of 35 mg/m^3. The PM-2.5 national monitoring network was deployed in 1999. National trend data prior to that time is not available. [8] Based on annual standard of 0.053 ppm. [9] Based on 3-month standard of 1.5 $\mu g/m^3$.

Source: U.S. Environmental Protection Agency, *Latest Findings on National Air Quality—Status and Trends through 2007*; released November 2008; <http://www.epa.gov/air/airtrends/2008/index.html>.

Table 362. Selected National Air Pollutant Emissions: 1970 to 2007

[In thousands of tons (4,320 represents 4,320,000), except as indicated. Particular Matter (PM-10 is equal to or less than ten microns in diameter; PM-2.5 is equal to or less than 2.5 microns effective diameter. The methodology used to estimate emission data for 1970 thru 1984 and for 1985 thru the current year is different. Beginning with 1985, the methodology for more recent years is described in the document available at <http://www.epa.gov/ttn/chief/net/2005inventory.html>]

Year	Ammonia	Carbon monoxide	Nitrogen oxide	PM-10	PM-10 [1]	PM-2.5	PM-2.5 [1]	Sulfur dioxide	Volatile organic compounds
1970	(NA)	204,042	26,882	13,022	13,022	(NA)	(NA)	31,218	34,659
1980	(NA)	185,408	27,080	7,013	7,013	(NA)	(NA)	25,926	31,107
1990	4,320	154,188	25,527	27,753	27,753	7,560	7,560	23,077	24,108
1995	4,659	126,778	24,955	25,820	25,820	6,929	6,929	18,619	22,042
2000	4,907	114,465	22,599	23,748	22,962	7,287	6,503	16,348	17,511
2003	4,136	106,244	20,327	21,313	18,426	5,564	3,095	14,756	20,769
2004	4,138	101,433	19,521	21,298	18,420	5,551	3,089	14,737	20,373
2005	4,143	96,619	18,711	21,285	18,416	5,536	3,082	14,714	19,976
2006	4,135	92,128	17,694	19,326	16,406	5,491	2,998	13,513	19,159
2007	4,131	88,254	17,025	17,374	14,455	5,450	2,958	12,925	18,423

NA Not available. [1] Without condensables.

Source: U.S. Environmental Protection Agency, *National Emissions Inventory (NEI) Air Pollution Emissions Trends Data, 1970–2002;* <http://www.epa.gov/ttn/chief/trends/index.html#tables>; *Air and Radiation; Air Trends;* <http://www.epa.gov/airtrends/index.html>.

Table 363. Selected Air Pollutant Emissions by Pollutant and Source: 2007

[In thousands of tons, except as indicated (4,131 represents 4,131,000). See headnote, Table 362]

Source	Ammonia	Carbon monoxide	Nitrogen oxide	PM-10	PM-2.5	Sulfur dioxide	Volatile organic compounds
Total emissions	4,131	88,254	17,025	17,374	5,450	12,925	18,423
Fuel combustion, stationary sources	65	5,304	6,000	1,359	1,034	11,255	1,626
Electric utilities	32	689	3,331	565	442	8,973	49
Industrial	16	1,253	1,941	329	172	1,705	141
Other fuel combustion	17	3,362	728	465	420	577	1,436
Industrial processes	215	3,828	1,034	1,459	745	1,057	7,262
Chemical and allied product manufacturing	23	284	70	40	30	258	238
Metals processing	3	986	69	79	52	213	46
Petroleum and related industries	3	356	346	23	17	232	580
Other	159	489	413	963	349	323	414
Solvent utilization	–	2	7	8	7	–	4,249
Storage and transport	1	118	19	58	22	5	1,354
Waste disposal and recycling	26	1,593	110	288	268	26	381
Highway vehicles	307	41,610	5,563	172	114	91	3,602
Off highway [1]	3	18,762	4,164	297	276	396	2,650
Miscellaneous [2]	3,541	18,750	264	14,087	3,281	126	3283

– Rounds to zero. [1] Includes emissions from farm tractors and other farm machinery, construction equipment, industrial machinery, recreational marine vessels, and small general utility engines such as lawn mowers. [2] Includes emissions such as from forest fires and other kinds of burning, various agricultural activities, fugitive dust from paved and unpaved roads, and other construction and mining activities, and natural sources.

Source: U.S. Environmental Protection Agency, *National Emissions Inventory (NEI) Air Pollution Emissions Trends Data; 1970–2002;* <http://www.epa.gov/ttn/chief/trends/index.html#tables>; *Air and Radiation; Air Trends;* <http://www.epa.gov/airtrends/index.html>.

Table 364. **Emissions of Greenhouse Gases by Type and Source: 1990 to 2007**

[In millions of metric tons (6,241.8 represents 6,241,800,000). Metric ton = 2,200 lbs. Emission estimates were mandated by Congress through Section 1605(a)of the Energy Policy Act of 1992 (Title XVI). Data shown below, by type and source, are measured in terms of their carbon dioxide equivalent]

Type and source	1990	2000	2003	2004	2005	2006	2007 [1]
CARBON DIOXIDE EQUIVALENT							
Total emissions	6,241.8	7,075.0	7,098.8	7,230.1	7,256.9	7,179.7	7,282.4
Carbon dioxide, total	5,021.4	5,892.6	5,938.7	6,023.9	6,032.3	5,945.8	6,021.8
From energy use by sector							
Residential	961.7	1,181.6	1,224.6	1,220.7	1,254.9	1,197.9	1,249.5
Commercial	787.5	1,015.2	1,027.1	1,042.3	1,060.2	1,043.0	1,087.4
Industrial	1,686.9	1,786.4	1,719.1	1,744.2	1,672.3	1,652.4	1,639.7
Transportation . . . . ₂	1,582.6	1,872.6	1,897.2	1,958.9	1,988.0	2,013.4	2,014.4
Adjustments to energy [2]	-82.4	-60.9	-28.3	-44.3	-46.5	-66.8	-74.2
Adjusted energy subtotal	4,936.3	5,794.8	5,839.7	5,921.9	5,928.9	5,839.9	5,916.7
Other sources	85.1	97.8	98.9	102.0	103.4	105.9	105.1
Methane	782.1	685.7	676.5	679.7	679.4	686.9	699.9
Energy sources	299.5	280.2	276.7	281.3	277.8	280.8	287.0
Agricultural sources	199.0	206.8	207.6	207.5	210.4	212.7	214.5
Waste management	280.6	195.5	189.3	188.0	188.6	190.8	195.7
Industrial processes	2.9	3.2	2.9	3.0	2.7	2.7	2.6
Nitrous oxide	336.0	344.6	334.6	361.5	370.8	375.7	383.9
Agricultural sources	251.2	254.1	250.1	275.4	281.2	285.5	292.4
Energy use	51.1	67.9	64.8	66.3	69.4	69.9	71.1
Industrial processes	28.8	16.7	13.7	13.7	14.0	14.0	14.0
Waste management	4.9	5.9	6.0	6.1	6.2	6.3	6.4
High-GWP gases [3]	102.4	152.1	149.0	165.0	174.5	171.3	176.9

[1] 2007 preliminary data. [2] Carbon dioxide (CO2) emissions from U.S. Territories are added to the U.S. total, and CO2 emissions from fuels used for international transport (both ocean-going vessels and airplanes), are subtracted to derive total U.S. greenhouse as emissions. [3] High-global warming potential gases: hyrdofluorocarbons (HFCs), perfluorocarbons (PFCs), and sulfur hexafluoride (SF6).

Source: U.S. Energy Information Administration, *Greenhouse Gas Emissions in the United States, 2007*, Series DOE/EIA-0573 (2007), annual. See also <http://www.eia.doe.gov/oiaf/1605/ggrpt/index.html>.

Table 365. **Municipal Solid Waste Generation, Materials Recovery, Combustion With Energy Recovery, and Discards: 1980 to 2007**

[In millions of tons (151.6 represents 151,600,000), except as indicated. Covers post-consumer residential and commercial solid wastes which comprise the major portion of typical municipal collections. Excludes mining, agricultural and industrial processing, demolition and construction wastes, sewage sludge, and junked autos and obsolete equipment wastes. Based on material-flows estimating procedure and wet weight as generated]

Item and material	1980	1990	2000	2004	2005	2006	2007
Waste generated	151.6	205.2	239.1	249.8	250.4	254.2	254.1
Per person per day (lb.)	3.7	4.5	4.7	4.7	4.6	4.7	4.6
Total materials recovery	14.5	33.2	69.4	78.0	79.4	82.2	85.0
Per person per day (lb.)	0.4	0.7	1.4	1.5	1.5	1.5	1.5
Combustion with energy recovery	2.7	29.7	33.7	31.5	31.6	31.9	31.9
Per person per day (lb.)	0.1	0.7	0.7	0.6	0.6	0.6	0.6
Discards to landfill, other disposal	134.4	142.3	136.0	140.3	139.4	140.1	137.2
Per person per day (lb.)	3.2	3.1	2.6	2.6	2.6	2.6	2.5
PERCENT DISTRIBUTION OF GENERATION							
Percent of total generation	71.8	71.4	74.5	74.0	73.7	73.6	73.2
Paper and paperboard	36.4	35.4	36.7	34.6	33.9	33.6	32.7
Glass	10.0	6.4	5.3	5.2	5.3	5.3	5.3
Metals	10.2	8.1	7.9	8.0	8.0	8.1	8.2
Plastics	4.5	8.3	10.7	11.8	11.7	11.7	12.1
Rubber and leather	2.8	2.8	2.8	2.9	2.9	2.9	2.9
Textiles	1.7	2.8	3.9	4.4	4.5	4.7	4.7
Wood	4.6	6.0	5.5	5.6	5.6	5.5	5.6
Other	1.7	1.6	1.7	1.7	1.7	1.7	1.7
Total other waste	28.2	28.6	25.5	26.0	26.3	26.4	26.8
Food scraps	8.6	10.1	11.2	11.8	12.1	12.2	12.5
Yard trimmings	18.1	17.1	12.8	12.7	12.8	12.7	12.8
Miscellaneous organic wastes	1.5	1.4	1.5	1.5	1.5	1.5	1.5

Source: Franklin Associates, a Division of ERG, Prairie Village, KS, *Municipal Solid Waste in the United States: 2007 Facts and Figures*. Prepared for the U.S. Environmental Protection Agency. See also <http://www.epa.gov/osw/nonhaz/municipal /msw99.htm>.

Geography and Environment   223

Table 366. **Generation and Recovery of Selected Materials in Municipal Solid Waste: 1980 to 2007**

[In millions of tons (151.6 represents 151,600,000), except as indicated. Covers post-consumer residential and commercial solid wastes which comprise the major portion of typical municipal collections. Excludes mining, agricultural and industrial processing, construction and demolition wastes, sewage sludge, and junked autos and obsolete equipment wastes. Based on material-flows and construction estimating procedure and wet weight as generated]

Item and material	1980	1990	2000	2004	2005	2006	2007
Waste generated, total [1]	151.6	205.2	239.0	249.8	250.4	254.2	254.1
Paper and paperboard	55.2	72.7	87.7	86.5	84.8	83.4	83.0
Glass.	15.1	13.1	12.8	12.9	13.3	13.5	13.6
Metals: Ferrous.	12.6	12.6	14.1	15.0	15.0	15.5	15.6
Aluminum.	1.7	2.8	3.2	3.3	3.3	3.4	3.4
Other nonferrous	1.2	1.1	1.6	1.7	1.7	1.8	1.8
Plastics	6.8	17.1	25.5	29.5	29.2	29.8	30.7
Food scraps	13.0	20.8	26.8	29.4	30.2	31.0	31.7
Yard trimmings	27.5	35.0	30.5	31.8	32.1	32.4	32.6
Materials recovered, total [1]	14.5	33.2	69.3	78.0	79.4	82.2	85.0
Paper and paperboard	11.7	20.2	37.6	40.7	42.0	43.9	45.2
Glass.	0.8	2.6	2.9	2.7	2.8	2.9	3.2
Metals: Ferrous.	0.4	2.2	4.7	5.2	5.0	5.3	5.3
Aluminum.	0.3	1.0	0.9	0.7	0.7	0.7	0.7
Other nonferrous	0.5	0.7	1.1	1.2	1.2	1.2	1.2
Plastics	0.2	0.4	1.5	1.7	1.8	2.1	2.1
Food scraps	(Z)	(Z)	0.7	0.7	0.7	0.7	0.8
Yard trimmings.	(Z)	4.2	15.8	19.9	19.9	20.1	20.9
Percent of generation recovered, total [1]	9.6	16.2	29.0	31.2	31.7	32.3	33.4
Paper and paperboard	21.3	27.8	42.8	47.1	49.5	51.4	54.5
Glass.	5.0	20.1	22.6	21.2	21.0	21.3	23.7
Metals: Ferrous.	2.9	17.6	33.2	34.4	33.6	33.9	33.8
Aluminum.	17.9	35.9	26.9	21.6	20.7	20.3	21.8
Other nonferrous	46.6	66.4	66.3	69.6	69.0	69.3	69.3
Plastics	0.3	2.2	5.8	5.8	6.0	6.9	6.8
Food scraps	(Z)	(Z)	2.5	2.2	2.3	2.2	2.6
Yard trimmings.	(Z)	12.0	51.7	62.4	61.9	62.0	64.1

Z Less than 5,000 tons or .05 percent. [1] Includes products not shown separately.

Source: Franklin Associates, a Division of ERG, Prairie Village, KS, *Municipal Municipal Solid Waste in the United States: 2007 Facts and Figures*. Prepared for the U.S. Environmental Protection Agency. See also <http://www.epa.gov/osw/nonhaz/municipal /msw99.htm>.

Table 367. **Municipal Solid Waste—Generation, Recovery, and Discards by Selected Type of Product: 2007**

[See headnote, Table 366]

Type of product	Generation (1,000 tons)	Recovery — Products recovered (1,000 tons)	Recovery — Percent of generation	Discards (1,000 tons)
Paper and paperboard products [1]	83,010	45,240	54.5	37,760
Nondurable goods.	43,060	20,320	47.2	22,740
Newsprint.	7,840	6,160	78.6	1,680
Groundwood inserts	3,140	2,380	75.8	760
Magazines	2,550	1,010	39.6	1,540
Office-type papers	6,000	4,310	71.8	1,690
Standard mail	5,910	2,380	40.3	3,530
Other commercial printing	6,260	3,590	57.3	2,670
Containers and packaging	39,940	24,920	62.4	15,020
Corrugated boxes	31,230	22,990	73.6	8,240
Folding cartons	5,530	1,510	27.3	4,020
Glass products [1]	13,580	3,220	23.7	10,360
Containers and packaging	11,470	3,220	28.1	8,250
Beer and soft drink bottles	7,710	2,660	34.5	5,050
Wine and liquor bottles.	1,670	250	15.0	1,420
Food and other bottles and jars	2,090	310	14.8	1,780
Metal products [1]	20,750	7,230	34.8	13,520
Ferrous	15,640	5,280	33.8	10,360
Aluminum.	3,350	730	21.8	2,620
Other nonferrous	1,760	1,220	69.3	540
Plastics [1]	30,730	2,090	6.8	28,640
Plastics in durable goods	10,420	500	4.8	9,920
Plastics in nondurable goods	6,680	(Z)	(Z)	6,680
Plastics in containers and packaging . . .	13,630	1,590	11.7	12,040
Rubber and leather [1]	7,480	1,100	14.7	6,380
Rubber in tires	3,160	1,100	34.8	2,060

Z Less than 5,000 tons or .05 percent. [1] Includes products not shown separately.

Source: Franklin Associates, a Division of ERG, Prairie Village, KS, *Municipal Solid Waste in the United States: 2007 Facts and Figures*. Prepared for the U.S. Environmental Protection Agency. See also <http://www.epa.gov/osw/nonhaz/municipal /msw99.htm>.

224   Geography and Environment

Table 368. **Toxic Chemical Releases and Transfers by Media: 2002 to 2007**

[In millions of pounds (4,747.2 represents 4,747,200,000), except as indicated. Based on reports filed as required by Section 313 of the Emergency Planning and Community Right-to-Know Act (EPCRA, or Title III of the Superfund Amendments and Reauthorization Act of 1986), Public Law 99-499. The Pollution Prevention Act (PPA) of 1990 mandates collection of data on toxic chemicals that are treated on-site, recycled, and combusted for energy recovery. Owners and operators of facilities that are classified within North American Industrial Classification Code groups 31 through 33, 2121, 2122, 2211, 4246, 4247 and 562; have 10 or more full-time employees, and that manufacture, process, or otherwise use any listed toxic chemical in quantities greater than the established threshold in the course of a calendar year are covered and required to report. Includes all Persistent, Bioaccumulative, Toxic (PBT) chemicals and vanadium and vanadium compounds. Data for all the years have been revised]

Media	2002	2003	2004	2005	2006	2007
Total facilities reporting.	25,108	24,533	24,317	23,965	23,300	21,966
Total on- and off-site disposal or other releases.	4,747.2	4,446.4	4,245.7	4,356.0	4,309.3	4,086.2
On-site releases	4,261.6	3,960.5	3,730.8	3,821.5	3,773.0	3,538.0
Air emissions.	1,614.4	1,584.9	1,542.4	1,513.3	1,409.4	1,311.6
Surface water discharges	243.4	230.7	247.7	251.9	245.2	232.0
Underground injection class I	206.5	207.2	210.3	211.5	199.8	187.6
Underground injection class II-V	20.5	22.0	27.7	20.2	20.1	21.5
RCRA subtitle C landfills [1]	156.0	199.8	155.5	158.5	155.3	153.4
Other landfills	267.2	265.0	257.1	255.9	251.1	249.2
Land treatment/application farming	24.3	18.2	21.5	23.7	26.8	21.7
Surface impoundments	771.6	822.6	726.4	789.7	829.9	775.8
Other land disposal	957.8	610.2	542.1	596.9	635.4	585.2
Off-site releases	485.6	485.9	514.9	534.5	536.3	548.2
Total transfers offsite for further waste management	3,928.9	3,697.0	3,986.0	3,923.8	3,959.4	3,818.4
Tranfers to recycling	2,021.5	1,903.0	2,066.1	2,075.7	2,155.1	2,105.1
Transfers to energy recovery.	739.9	650.0	649.9	608.4	554.9	522.7
Transfers to treatment	264.1	279.1	326.8	337.3	329.3	280.0
Transfers to POTWs [2]	304.0	269.8	259.4	263.4	258.3	243.1
Transfers to POTWs metal and metal compounds [2].	2.0	1.9	1.7	1.8	1.8	1.9
Other off-site transfers	0.9	0.9	71.5	0.4	0.2	0.2
Transfers off-site for disposal or other releases	596.6	592.2	610.7	636.9	659.8	665.4
Total production-related waste managed	26,000.4	25,056.5	25,830.9	24,811.5	24,529.3	24,195.8
Recycled on-site	7,652.5	7,143.3	7,140.4	6,721.1	6,816.5	6,819.9
Recycled off-site	2,015.8	1,905.1	2,066.7	2,080.5	2,154.2	2,084.5
Energy recovery on-site	2,789.1	2,641.6	2,609.6	2,448.1	2,692.3	2,331.1
Energy recovery off-site	740.6	649.8	649.2	608.2	554.2	520.7
Treated on-site	7,355.7	7,616.2	8,445.0	7,908.8	7,290.0	7,678.9
Treated off-site	552.7	518.9	565.9	575.3	552.9	498.8
Quantity disposed or otherwise release of on- and off-site	4,894.1	4,581.7	4,354.2	4,469.5	4,464.9	4,261.8
Non-production-related waste managed	18.2	25.3	19.2	24.3	18.2	14.4

[1] RCRA = Resource Conservation and Recovery Act. [2] POTW (Publicly Owned Treatment Work) is a wastewater treatment facility that is owned by a state or municipality.

Source: U.S. Environmental Protection Agency, Toxic Release Inventory (TRI) Program, *2007 TRI Public Data Release eReport*. See <http://www.epa.gov/tri/tridata/tri07/index.htm> (released 19 March 2009).

Table 369. **Toxic Chemical Releases by Industry: 2007**

[In millions of pounds (4,086.2 represents 4,086,200,000), except as indicated. See headnote, Table 368]

Industry	2002 NAICS [1] code	Total on- and off-site releases	On-site release Total	On-site release Air emissions	Other surface impound- ments	Off-site releases/ transfers to disposal [2]
Total [3]	(X)	4,086.2	3,538.0	1,311.6	771.1	548.2
Coal mining	2121	13.4	13.4	0.5	0.1	(Z)
Metal mining.	2122	1,154.8	1,152.4	3.3	598.6	2.4
Electric utilities	2211	1,008.4	926.4	637.6	127.3	82.0
Food/beverages/tobacco.	311/312	150.7	140.7	47.2	0.2	9.9
Textiles	313/314	3.3	2.6	2.2	0.2	0.7
Apparel	315	(Z)	(Z)	(Z)	–	(Z)
Leather	316	1.3	0.4	0.3	–	0.9
Wood products	321	18.9	18.0	17.7	(Z)	0.9
Paper	322	197.8	190.7	151.1	3.8	7.2
Printing and publishing.	323/51	13.0	12.7	12.6	–	0.3
Petroleum	324	72.6	66.4	41.6	(Z)	6.3
Chemicals	325	479.4	429.8	179.2	12.8	49.6
Plastics and rubber	326	50.6	43.0	42.3	(Z)	7.6
Stone/clay/glass	327	27.2	24.3	21.5	0.1	2.9
Cement	32731	10.8	10.6	8.5	0.1	0.2
Primary metals	331	487.4	194.6	45.0	25.7	292.8
Fabricated metals	332	56.3	29.9	27.8	(Z)	26.4
Machinery	333	8.7	4.8	4.7	–	3.9
Computers/electronic products. . . .	334	7.5	5.2	2.1	–	2.4
Electrical equipment.	335	7.6	3.5	3.4	(Z)	4.1
Transportation equipment	336	52.9	43.1	42.1	(Z)	9.8
Furniture	337	10.3	10.2	10.2	–	0.1
Miscellaneous Manufacturing.	339	7.2	3.8	3.8	–	3.4
Chemical wholesalers	4246	2.0	2.0	2.0	–	0.1
Petroleum bulk terminals	4247	2.6	2.3	2.3	(Z)	0.3
Hazardous waste	562	210.0	177.1	0.5	0.6	32.9
No codes [3].	(X)	31.4	30.1	2.2	1.6	1.2

– Represents zero.   X Not applicable.   Z less than 50,000.   [1] North American Industry Classification System, see text, Section 12.   [2] Includes off-site disposal to underground injection for Class I wells, Class II to V wells, other surface impoundments, land releases, and other releases, not shown separately.   [3] Includes industries with no specific industry identified.

Source: U.S. Environmental Protection Agency, *2007 TRI Public Data Release eReport*. See also <http://www.epa.gov/tri/tridata/tri07/index.htm> (released 19 March 2009).

Geography and Environment   225

Table 370. Toxic Chemical Releases by State and Outlying Area: 2007

[In millions of pounds (4,086.2 represents 4,086,200,000). Based on reports filed as required by Section 313 of the EPCRA. See headnote, Table 368]

State and outlying area	Total on-and off-site releases	On-site release Total [1]	On-site release Air emissions	On-site release Other surface impoundments	Off-site releases/transfers to disposal	State and outlying area	Total on-and off-site releases	On-site release Total [1]	On-site release Air emissions	On-site release Other surface impoundments	Off-site releases/transfers to disposal
Total .	4,086.2	3,538.0	1,311.6	771.1	548.2	NH	4.0	3.9	3.8	(Z)	0.1
U.S. total .	4,080.0	3,532.2	1,306.2	771.1	547.9	NJ	20.6	17.1	9.0	–	3.5
AL	113.5	89.7	47.2	15.8	23.8	NM	18.3	18.1	1.0	1.5	0.2
AK	584.7	584.4	1.4	253.2	0.3	NY	34.9	27.9	14.2	3.0	7.0
AZ	88.0	86.3	4.0	14.9	1.8	NC	122.1	104.7	82.3	6.7	17.4
AR	43.8	33.9	16.2	2.3	10.0	ND	22.1	13.7	4.5	5.0	8.4
CA	54.0	46.3	15.3	(Z)	7.7	OH	274.4	220.8	115.1	12.5	53.6
CO	24.4	19.1	2.9	3.9	5.4	OK	34.1	27.1	15.3	0.7	7.0
CT	4.1	3.0	2.6	(Z)	1.1	OR	22.4	20.6	9.8	(Z)	1.8
DE	17.4	10.3	6.9	(Z)	7.1	PA	163.1	100.1	79.4	0.7	63.0
DC	(Z)	(Z)	(Z)	(Z)	(Z)	RI.....	0.5	0.2	0.2	–	0.3
FL	120.5	113.3	61.4	14.8	7.1	SC	67.1	57.4	46.9	2.4	9.7
GA	117.2	114.2	83.3	16.6	3.0	SD	7.8	7.4	1.9	(Z)	0.3
HI.....	3.0	2.9	2.3	–	0.2	TN	120.6	107.9	53.7	31.4	12.6
ID.....	68.4	67.4	4.2	13.1	1.0	TX	222.6	195.5	71.5	4.3	27.0
IL.....	114.3	90.9	40.7	7.2	23.4	UT	169.1	166.7	9.3	91.0	2.4
IN.....	229.0	125.1	63.2	11.1	103.9	VT	0.3	0.2	(Z)	–	0.1
IA.....	43.4	33.2	24.1	2.7	10.2	VA	67.9	63.3	40.2	1.6	4.6
KS	26.2	20.5	11.6	1.7	5.7	WA	28.4	26.1	8.9	12.6	2.3
KY	98.2	86.3	61.8	7.4	11.9	WV	85.7	68.9	53.3	2.6	16.8
LA	130.4	122.7	51.9	3.5	7.8	WI	46.3	26.7	19.9	0.0	19.6
ME	11.1	9.4	5.0		1.7	WY	15.5	14.4	2.2	1.1	1.1
MD	50.5	46.3	41.0	(Z)	4.3						
MA	6.5	4.5	4.2	0.2	2.0	American Samoa ..	(Z)	(Z)	(Z)	–	–
MI	96.2	66.7	49.4	6.5	29.6	Guam....	0.3	0.2	0.1	(Z)	(Z)
MN	28.1	25.2	11.3	2.5	2.8	Northern Marianas .	(Z)	(Z)	(Z)	(Z)	(Z)
MS	59.5	57.3	22.3	10.8	2.3	Puerto Rico	5.2	4.8	4.8	–	0.3
MO	96.8	92.6	18.3	55.8	4.3	U.S. Virgin Islands ..	0.8	0.7	0.5	–	(Z)
MT	48.3	46.5	3.9	13.4	1.8						
NE	32.9	26.4	5.8	(Z)	6.5						
NV	221.5	219.0	1.4	136.5	2.5						

– Represents zero. Z Less than 50,000. [1] Includes other types of release not shown separately.
Source: U.S. Environmental Protection Agency, Toxic Release Inventory (TRI) Program, *2007 TRI Public Data Release Report* (released 19 March 2009). See <http://www.epa.gov/tri/tridata/tri07/index.htm>.

Table 371. Hazardous Waste Sites on the National Priority List by State and Outlying Area: 2008

[As of December 31. Includes both proposed and final sites listed on the National Priorities List for the Superfund program as authorized by the Comprehensive Environmental Response, Compensation, and Liability Act (CERCLA) of 1980 and the Superfund Amendments and Reauthorization Act (SARA) of 1986. For information on CERCLA and SARA, see also <http://www.epa.gov/superfund/action/law/cercla.htm>]

State and outlying area	Total sites	Rank	Percent distribution	Federal	Non-Federal	State and outlying area	Total sites	Rank	Percent distribution	Federal	Non-Federal
Total	1,318	(X)	(X)	163	1,155	Nebraska	13	32	1.0	1	12
United States ...	1,301	(X)	(X)	161	1,140	Nevada	1	49	0.1	–	1
Alabama.........	15	26	1.2	3	12	New Hampshire....	21	19	1.7	1	20
Alaska.........	5	45	0.4	5	–	New Jersey.......	116	1	9.3	8	108
Arizona.........	9	39	0.7	2	7	New Mexico	14	29	1.1	1	13
Arkansas	9	40	0.7	–	9	New York	86	4	6.9	4	82
California	97	2	7.8	24	73	North Carolina	32	13	2.6	2	30
Colorado.........	20	20	1.6	3	17	North Dakota......	–	50	0.0	–	–
Connecticut.......	15	24	1.2	1	14	Ohio	40	10	3.2	5	35
Delaware........	14	27	1.1	1	13	Oklahoma........	9	42	0.7	1	8
District of Columbia .	1	(X)	0.1	1	–	Oregon.........	12	36	1.0	2	10
Florida	52	6	4.2	6	46	Pennsylvania......	96	3	7.7	6	90
Georgia	16	23	1.3	2	14	Rhode Island......	12	37	1.0	2	10
Hawaii	3	46	0.2	2	1	South Carolina.....	26	17	2.1	2	24
Idaho	9	41	0.7	2	7	South Dakota	2	47	0.2	1	1
Illinois	49	7	3.9	5	44	Tennessee	14	30	1.1	4	10
Indiana.........	31	14	2.5	–	31	Texas..........	49	8	3.9	4	45
Iowa	12	33	1.0	1	11	Utah	19	22	1.5	4	15
Kansas.........	12	34	1.0	1	11	Vermont.........	11	38	0.9	–	11
Kentucky........	14	28	1.1	1	13	Virginia.........	30	15	2.4	11	19
Louisiana........	13	31	1.0	1	12	Washington.......	48	9	3.8	13	35
Maine..........	12	35	1.0	3	9	West Virginia......	9	43	0.7	2	7
Maryland	19	21	1.5	10	9	Wisconsin........	38	11	3.0	–	38
Massachusetts.....	32	12	2.6	6	26	Wyoming	2	48	0.2	1	1
Michigan........	67	5	5.4	1	66						
Minnesota.......	25	18	2.0	2	23	Guam	2	(X)	(X)	1	1
Mississippi	6	44	0.5	–	6	Puerto Rico	13	(X)	(X)	1	12
Missouri	29	16	2.3	3	26	Virgin Islands	2	(X)	(X)	–	2
Montana	15	25	1.2	–	15						

– Represents zero. X Not applicable.
Source: U.S. Environmental Protection Agency, *Supplementary Materials: CERCLIS3/WasteLan Database* (published 6 July 2009). See also <http://www.epa.gov/osw/inforesources/data/biennialreport/>.

226 Geography and Environment

Table 372. Environmental Industry—Revenues and Employment by Industry Segment: 2000 to 2008

[218.7 represents $218,700,000,000. Covers approximately 30,000 private and public companies engaged in revenue-generating environmental activities]

Industry segment	Revenue (bil. dol.)				Employment			
	2000	2005	2007	2008	2000	2005	2007	2008
Industry total.	218.7	265.6	295.1	315.7	1,410,500	1,595,100	1,718,000	1,871,800
Analytical services [1]	1.8	1.8	1.9	1.9	20,200	20,000	20,000	21,100
Wastewater treatment works [2]	28.7	35.6	39.2	40.8	118,800	141,100	153,200	164,200
Solid waste management [3]	39.4	47.8	52.7	55.3	221,400	256,500	278,200	300,200
Hazardous waste management [4].	8.2	8.7	9.1	9.2	44,800	45,000	45,600	45,900
Remediation/industrial services.	10.1	11.0	12.1	12.7	100,200	96,600	103,100	111,100
Consulting and engineering	17.4	22.4	25.4	27.1	184,000	220,800	246,400	270,400
Water equipment and chemicals	19.8	24.8	27.6	28.7	130,500	153,000	166,100	179,800
Instrument manufacturing	3.8	4.8	5.5	5.9	30,200	35,500	39,200	43,300
Air pollution control equipment [5]	19.0	18.8	18.3	18.0	129,600	123,400	118,900	113,900
Waste management equipment [6].	10.0	10.1	10.8	11.2	75,500	72,900	75,400	78,500
Process and prevention technology . . .	1.2	1.5	1.8	1.9	29,000	28,100	30,700	34,300
Water utilities [7]	29.9	35.1	38.0	39.3	130,000	145,200	154,200	163,300
Resource recovery [8]	16.0	21.0	25.1	32.0	127,000	156,600	171,900	204,900
Clean energy systems and power [9] . . .	13.4	22.3	27.7	31.7	69,300	100,400	115,100	140,900

[1] Covers environmental laboratory testing and services. [2] Mostly revenues collected by municipal entities for sewage or wastewater plants. [3] Covers such activities as collection, transportation, transfer stations, disposal, landfill ownership and management for solid waste and recyclables. [4] Transportation and disposal of hazardous, medical, and nuclear waste. [5] Includes stationary and mobile sources. [6] Includes vehicles, containers, liners, processing, and remediation equipment. [7] Revenues generated from the sale of water, majority in public sector. [8] Revenues generated from the sale of recovered metals, paper, plastic, etc. [9] Revenues generated from the sale of equipment & systems and electricity.

Source: Environmental Business International, Inc., San Diego, CA, *Environmental Business Journal*, monthly (copyright). See also <http://www.ebiusa.com/>.

Table 373. Threatened and Endangered Wildlife and Plant Species: 2009

[As of April. Endangered species: One in danger of becoming extinct throughout all or a significant part of its natural range. Threatened species: One likely to become endangered in the foreseeable future]

Item	Mam- mals	Birds	Rep- tiles	Amphib- ians	Fishes	Snails	Clams	Crusta- ceans	Insects	Arach- nids	Plants
Total listings	358	275	119	34	151	36	72	22	61	12	749
Endangered species, total . . .	325	254	79	22	85	25	64	19	51	12	601
United States	69	75	13	14	74	24	62	19	47	12	600
Foreign	256	179	66	8	11	1	2	–	4	–	1
Threatened species, total . . .	33	21	40	12	66	11	8	3	10	–	148
United States	13	15	24	11	65	11	8	3	10	–	146
Foreign	20	6	16	1	1	–	–	–	–	–	2

– Represents zero.

Source: U.S. Fish and Wildlife Service, *Endangered Species Bulletin*, bimonthly. See also <http://ecos.fws.gov/tess_public/Boxscore.do/> (accessed 19 May 2009).

Table 374. Tornadoes, Floods, Tropical Storms, and Lightning: 1995 to 2007

Weather type	1995	1999	2000	2001	2002	2003	2004	2005	2006	2007
Tornadoes: [1]										
Number.	1,235	1,343	1,071	1,216	941	1,376	1,819	1,264	1,103	1,098
Lives lost.	30	94	41	40	55	54	35	38	67	81
Injuries	650	1,842	882	743	968	1,087	396	537	990	659
Property loss (mil. dol.) . .	411	1,990	424	630	801	1,263	537	422	752	1,408
Floods and flash floods:										
Lives lost.	80	68	38	48	49	85	82	43	76	70
Injuries	57	301	47	277	88	65	128	38	23	51
Property loss (mil. dol.) . .	1,251	1,421	1,255	1,220	655	2,541	1,696	1,538	3,768	1,278
North Atlantic tropical storms and hurricanes [2].	19	12	15	15	12	21	16	27	10	15
Direct deaths on U.S. mainland	17	19	–	24	51	14	34	1,016	–	1
Property loss in U.S. (bil.dol.)	5.9	4.2	8.1	5.2	1.1	1.9	18.9	93.0	2.4	38.8
Lightning:										
Deaths	85	46	51	44	51	44	32	38	48	45
Injuries	433	243	364	371	256	237	280	309	246	138

– Represents zero. [1] Source: U.S. National Weather Service, <http://www.spc.noaa.gov/climo/torn/monthlytornstats.html>. A violent, rotating column of air descending from a cumulonimbus cloud in the form of a tubular- or funnel-shaped cloud, usually characterized by movements along a narrow path and wind speeds from 100 to over 300 miles per hour. Also known as a "twister" or "waterspout." [2] Source: National Hurricane Center (NHC), Coral Gables, FL, unpublished data. For data on individual hurricanes, see the NHC Web site at <http://www.nhc.noaa.gov/>.

Source: Except as noted, U.S. National Oceanic and Atmospheric Administration (NOAA), National Weather Service (NWS), *Office of Climate, Water, and Weather Services, Natural Hazard Statistics*, monthly. See also NOAA Web site at <http://www.nws.noaa.gov/om/hazstats.shtml>.

Geography and Environment   227

Table 375. Major U.S. Weather Disasters: 2005 to 2008

[2.0 represents $2,000,000,000. Covers only weather-related disasters costing $1 billion or more]

Event	Description	Time period	Estimated cost[1] (bil. dol.)	Deaths
2008 Widespread drought	Severe drought and heat caused agricultural losses in areas of the south and west. Record low lake levels also occurred in areas of the southeast. Includes states of CA, GA, NC, SC, TN, and TX.	Entire year 2008	Over $2.0 bil	–
Hurricane Ike	Category 2 hurricane makes landfall in Texas as the largest (in size) Atlantic hurricane on record, causing wind and considerable surge in coastal areas and significant flooding damage in AR, IL, IN, KY, LA, MO, OH, PA, and TX.	Sept. 2008	Over 27.0	82
Hurricane Gustav	Category 2 hurricane makes landfall in Louisiana causing significant wind, storm surge, and flood damage in AL, AR, LA, and MS.	Sept. 2008	5.0	43
Hurricane Dolly	Category 2 hurricane makes landfall in southern Texas causing considerable wind and flood damage in TX and NM.	July 2008	Over 1.2	3
U.S. wildfires	Drought conditions across numerous western, central, and southeastern states (15) caused thousands of wildfires that burned national acreage exceeding 5.2 million acres (mainly in the west).	Summer–Fall 2008	Over 2.0	16
Midwest flood	Heavy rainfall and flooding caused significant agricultural loss and property damage in seven states with Iowa being hardest hit with widespread rainfall totals ranging from 4 to 6 inches.	June 2008	Over 15.0	–
Midwest/Mid-Atlantic storms	An outbreak of tornadoes and thunderstorms over the states of IA, IL, IN, KS, NE, MD, MI, MN, MO, OK, VA, WI, WV.	June 2008	Over 1.1	18
Midwest/Ohio Valley storms	Outbreak of tornadoes over the midwest/Ohio Valley region (IL, IN, IA KS, MN, NE, OK, WY, and CO).	May 2008	Over 2.4	13
Southeast/Midwest tornadoes	Series of tornadoes and severe thunderstorms across the southeast and midwest states (AL, AR, IN, KY,MS, OH, TN, TX) with 87 tornadoes confirmed.	Feb. 2008	Over 1.0	57
Great Plains and Eastern Drought	Severe drought with periods of extreme heat resulting in major reductions in crop yields, along with very low stream flows and lake levels.	Entire year 2007	5.0	(²)
Western Wildfires	Continued drought conditions and high winds over much of the western U.S. resulting in numerous wildfires.	Summer–Fall 2007	Over 1.0	12
Spring Freeze	Widespread severe freeze over much of the east and midwest causing losses in fruit crops, field crops, and in the ornamental industry.	Apr. 2007	2.0	–
Severe storms and tornadoes	Flooding, hail, tornadoes, and severe thunderstorms across numerous eastern and southern states.	Apr. 2007	1.5	9
Freeze	Widespread agricultural freeze over a good portion of California destroying numerous agricultural crops.	Jan. 2007	1.4	1
Widespread drought	Rather severe drought affecting crops in states especially during the spring-summer, centered over the Great Plains region, with other areas affected across portions of the south and far west.	Spring–Summer 2006	Over 6.0	(²)
Severe storms and tornadoes	Outbreak of tornadoes over portions of the midwest and south during a week-long period.	March 2006	Over 1.0	10+
Numerous wildfires	Wildfires mainly over the western half of the country, due to dry weather and high wind, burning nearly 10 million acres (new record for period since 1960).	Entire year 2006	Over 1.0	28+
Hurricane Wilma	Category 3 hurricane makes landfall in southwest Florida, causing considerable damage from major flooding and strong winds in southeast Florida.	Oct. 2005	Over 16.0	35
Hurricane Rita	Category 3 hurricane makes landfall on the Texas-Lousiana border coastal region, causing wind and surge damage along the coast and flood damage in FL, MS, LA, AR, and TX.	Sept. 2005	Over 16.0	119
Hurricane Katrina	Category 3 hurricane makes landfall as a Category 1 near Miami, FL, and on the LA, MS coast, causing massive damage in addition to flood and wind in AL, FL, TN, KY, OH, and GA.	Aug. 2005	Over 125.0	1,300+
Hurricane Dennis	Category 3 hurricane makes landfall in western Florida causing wind and surge damage, also causing wind and flood damage to GA, MS, and TN.	July 2005	Over 2.0	12+
Midwest drought	Midwest drought caused crop losses in AR, IL, IN, MO, OH, and WI.	Spring–Summer 2005	Over 1.0	–

– Represents zero.   [1] Represents actual dollar costs at the time of event and is not adjusted for inflation.   [2] Some deaths reported due to heat but not beyond typical annual averages.

Source: U.S. National Oceanic and Atmospheric Administration, National Climatic Data Center, "Billion Dollar U.S. Weather Disasters, 1980–2008" (released 1 January 2009). See also <http://www.ncdc.noaa.gov/oa/reports/billionz.htmls>.

228   Geography and Environment

Table 376. Wildland Fires, Number and Acres: 1970 to 2008

[3,279 represents 3,279,000. There are three distinct types of wildland fires: wildfire, wildland fire use, and prescribed fire. Wildland fire is any nonstructure fire that occurs in the wildland]

Year	Total [1] Fires (number)	Total [1] Acres (1,000)	Year	Total [1] Fires (number)	Total [1] Acres (1,000)	State	Top states ranked by wildland acres burned — Wildland [1] Fires (number)	Wildland [1] Acres (1,000)	Prescribed [2] Fires (number)	Prescribed [2] Acres (1,000)
1970...	121,736	3,279	1999	92,487	5,626	TX	16,713	1,570,586	35	15,315
1975...	134,872	1,791	2000	92,250	7,393	CA	5,812	1,339,839	827	87,416
1980...	234,892	5,261	2001	84,079	3,571	NM	1,207	487,652	106	71,930
1985...	82,591	2,896	2002	73,457	7,185	OK	5,572	196,563	23	8,426
1990...	66,481	4,622	2003	63,629	3,961	MT	1,424	166,842	299	36,820
1994...	79,107	4,074	[3]2004	65,461	8,098	FL	2,939	156,102	432	402,967
1995...	82,234	1,841	2005	66,753	8,689	WA	1,303	147,264	83	6,292
1996...	96,363	6,066	2006	96,385	9,874	CO	1,133	141,966	184	43,048
1997...	66,196	2,857	2007	85,705	9,328	OR	1,766	136,572	781	112,450
1998...	81,043	1,330	2008	78,979	5,292	ID	997	116,796	511	57,365

[1] Data are for wildland fires only. The data do not include wildland fire use and prescribed fires.   [2] Prescribed fire is any fire which are ignited by management action under certain predetermined conditions to meet specific objectives related to to hazardous fuels or habitat improvement.   [3] 2004 fires and acres do not include state lands for North Carolina.
Source   National Interagency Coordination Center, "Wildland Fires and Acres (1960–2008)"; <http://www.nifc.gov/fire_info/fires_acres.htm> (accessed 23 February 2009).

Table 377. Highest and Lowest Temperatures by State Through 2003

State	Highest temperatures — Station	Tempera- ture (F)	Date	Lowest temperatures — Station	Tempera- ture (F)	Date
U.S. ...	Greenland Ranch, CA. .	134	Jul. 10, 1913	Prospect Creek, AK . . .	-80	Jan. 23, 1971
AL	Centerville	112	Sep. 5, 1925	New Market	-27	Jan. 30, 1966
AK	Fort Yukon	100	[1]Jun. 27, 1915	Prospect Creek Camp . .	-80	Jan. 23, 1971
AZ	Lake Havasu City	128	Jun. 29, 1994	Hawley Lake	-40	Jan. 7, 1971
AR	Ozark	120	Aug. 10, 1936	Pond.	-29	Feb. 13, 1905
CA	Greenland Ranch	134	Jul. 10, 1913	Boca	-45	Jan. 20, 1937
CO....	Bennett	118	Jul. 11, 1888	Maybell	-61	Feb. 1, 1985
CT	Danbury	106	Jul. 15, 1995	Coventry	-32	[2]Jan. 22, 1961
DE	Milleboro	110	Jul. 21, 1930	Millsboro	-17	Jan. 17, 1893
FL	Monticello	109	Jun. 29, 1931	Tallahassee	-2	Feb. 13, 1899
GA....	Greenville	112	Aug. 20, 1983	CCC Camp F-16.	-17	[1]Jan. 27, 1940
HI.....	Pahala	100	Apr. 27, 1931	Mauna Kea Obs. 111.2. .	12	May 17, 1979
ID.....	Orofino	118	Jul. 28, 1934	Island Park Dam	-60	Jan. 18, 1943
IL......	East St. Louis.	117	Jul. 14, 1954	Congerville.	-36	Jan. 5, 1999
IN......	Collegeville	116	Jul. 14, 1936	New Whiteland	-36	Jan. 19, 1994
IA......	Keokuk	118	Jul. 20, 1934	Elkader	-47	[2]Feb. 3, 1996
KS.....	Alton (near)	121	[2]Jul. 24, 1936	Lebanon	-40	Feb. 13, 1905
KY.....	Greensburg	114	Jul. 28, 1930	Shelbyville	-37	Jan. 19, 1994
LA.....	Plain Dealing	114	Aug. 10, 1936	Minden	-16	Feb. 13, 1899
ME.....	North Bridgton	105	[2]Jul. 10, 1911	Van Buren	-48	Jan. 19, 1925
MD.....	Cumberland & Frederick.	109	[2]Jul. 10, 1936	Oakland	-40	Jan. 13, 1912
MA.....	New Bedford & Chester .	107	Aug. 2, 1975	Chester	-35	Jan. 12, 1981
MI.....	Mio.	112	Jul. 13, 1936	Vanderbilt	-51	Feb. 9, 1934
MN.....	Moorhead	114	[2]Jul. 6, 1936	Tower	-60	Feb. 2, 1996
MS.....	Holly Springs	115	Jul. 29, 1930	Corinth	-19	Jan. 30, 1966
MO.....	Warsaw & Union	118	[2]Jul. 14, 1954	Warsaw	-40	Feb. 13, 1905
MT.....	Medicine Lake	117	Jul. 5, 1937	Rogers Pass	-70	Jan. 20, 1954
NE.....	Minden	118	[2]Jul. 24, 1936	Oshkosh	-47	[2]Dec. 22, 1989
NV.....	Laughlin	125	[2]Jun. 29, 1994	San Jacinto	-50	Jan. 8, 1937
NH.....	Nashua	106	Jul. 4, 1911	Mt. Washington.	-47	Jan. 29, 1934
NJ.....	Runyon	110	Jul. 10, 1936	River Vale	-34	Jan. 5, 1904
NM.....	Waste Isolat Pilot Plt . . .	122	Jun. 27, 1994	Gavilan	-50	Feb. 1, 1951
NY.....	Troy	108	Jul. 22, 1926	Old Forge	-52	[2]Feb. 18, 1979
NC.....	Fayetteville.	110	Aug. 21, 1983	Mt. Mitchell	-34	Jan. 21, 1985
ND.....	Steele	121	[2]Jul. 6, 1936	Parshall.	-60	Feb. 15, 1936
OH.....	Gallipolis (near).	113	[2]Jul. 21, 1934	Milligan	-39	Feb. 10, 1899
OK.....	Tipton	120	[2]Jun. 27, 1994	Watts	-27	[2]Jan. 18, 1930
OR.....	Pendleton	119	[2]Aug. 10, 1898	Seneca	-54	[2]Feb. 10, 1933
PA	Phoenixville	111	[2]Jul. 10, 1936	Smethport	-42	[1]Jan. 5, 1904
RI.....	Providence.	104	Aug. 2, 1975	Greene	-25	Feb. 5, 1996
SC.....	Camden	111	[2]Jun. 28, 1954	Caesars Head	-19	Jan. 21, 1985
SD.....	Gannvalley.	120	Jul. 5, 1936	McIntosh	-58	Feb. 17, 1936
TN.....	Perryville	113	[2]Aug. 9, 1930	Mountain City	-32	Dec. 30, 1917
TX	Monahans	120	[2]Jun. 28, 1994	Seminole	-23	[2]Feb. 8, 1933
UT	Saint George	117	Jul. 5, 1985	Peter's Sink	-69	Feb. 1, 1985
VT	Vernon	105	Jul. 4, 1911	Bloomfield	-50	Dec. 30, 1933
VA	Balcony Falls	110	Jul. 15, 1954	Mtn. Lake Bio. Stn.	-30	Jan. 22, 1985
WA....	Ice Harbor Dam	118	[2]Aug. 5, 1961	Mazama & Winthrop . . .	-48	Dec. 30, 1968
WV....	Martinsburg	112	[2]Jul. 10, 1936	Lewisburg	-37	Dec. 30, 1917
WI	Wisconsin Dells	114	Jul. 13, 1936	Couderay.	-55	Feb. 4, 1996
WY.....	Basin	115	Aug. 8, 1983	Riverside R.S.	-66	Feb. 9, 1933

[1] Estimated.   [2] Also on earlier dates at the same or other places.

Source: U.S. National Oceanic and Atmospheric Administration, National Environmental Satellite, Data, and Information Services (NESDIS), National Climatic Data Center (NCDC), Temperature Extremes and Drought. See <http://www.ncdc.noaa.gov/oa/climate/severeweather/temperatures.html>.

Geography and Environment   229

Table 378. Normal Daily Mean, Maximum, and Minimum Temperatures— Selected Cities

[**In Fahrenheit degrees.** Airport data except as noted. Based on standard 30-year period, 1971 through 2000]

State	Station	Daily mean temperature			Daily maximum temperature			Daily minimum temperature		
		Jan.	July	Annual average	Jan.	July	Annual average	Jan.	July	Annual average
AL	Mobile	50.1	81.5	66.8	60.7	91.2	77.4	39.5	71.8	56.2
AK	Juneau	25.7	56.8	41.5	30.6	64.3	47.6	20.7	49.2	35.3
AZ	Phoenix	54.2	92.8	72.9	65.0	104.2	84.5	43.4	81.4	61.1
AR	Little Rock	40.1	82.4	62.1	49.5	92.8	72.7	30.8	72.0	51.5
CA	Los Angeles	57.1	69.3	63.3	65.6	75.3	70.6	48.6	63.3	56.1
	Sacramento	46.3	75.4	61.1	53.8	92.4	73.7	38.8	58.3	48.4
	San Diego	57.8	70.9	64.4	65.8	75.8	70.8	49.7	65.9	58.1
	San Francisco	49.4	62.8	57.3	55.9	71.1	65.1	42.9	54.5	49.6
CO	Denver	29.2	73.4	50.1	43.2	88.0	64.2	15.2	58.7	35.8
CT	Hartford	25.7	73.7	50.2	34.1	84.9	60.5	17.2	62.4	40.0
DE	Wilmington	31.5	76.6	54.4	39.3	86.0	63.6	23.7	67.3	45.1
DC	Washington	34.9	79.2	57.5	42.5	88.3	66.4	27.3	70.1	48.6
FL	Jacksonville	53.1	81.6	68.0	64.2	90.8	78.4	41.9	72.4	57.6
	Miami	68.1	83.7	76.7	76.5	90.9	84.2	59.6	76.5	69.1
GA	Atlanta	42.7	80.0	62.2	51.9	89.4	72.0	33.5	70.6	52.3
HI	Honolulu	73.0	80.8	77.5	80.4	87.8	84.7	65.7	73.8	70.2
ID	Boise	30.2	74.7	52.0	36.7	89.2	62.6	23.6	60.3	41.3
IL	Chicago	22.0	73.3	49.1	29.6	83.5	58.3	14.3	63.2	39.8
	Peoria	22.5	75.1	50.8	30.7	85.7	60.7	14.3	64.6	40.9
IN	Indianapolis	26.5	75.4	52.5	34.5	85.6	62.3	18.5	65.2	42.7
IA	Des Moines	20.4	76.1	50.0	29.1	86.0	59.8	11.7	66.1	40.2
KS	Wichita	30.2	81.0	56.4	40.1	92.9	67.4	20.3	69.1	45.2
KY	Louisville	33.0	78.4	57.0	41.0	87.0	66.0	24.9	69.8	47.9
LA	New Orleans	52.6	82.7	68.8	61.8	91.1	78.0	43.4	74.2	59.6
ME	Portland	21.7	68.7	45.8	30.9	78.8	55.2	12.5	58.6	36.3
MD	Baltimore	32.3	76.5	54.6	41.2	87.2	65.1	23.5	65.8	44.2
MA	Boston	29.3	73.9	51.6	36.5	82.2	59.3	22.1	65.5	43.9
MI	Detroit	24.5	73.5	49.8	31.1	83.4	58.4	17.8	63.6	41.0
	Sault Ste. Marie	13.2	63.9	40.1	21.5	75.7	49.6	4.9	52.0	30.5
MN	Duluth	8.4	65.5	39.1	17.9	76.3	48.7	-1.2	54.6	29.3
	Minneapolis-St. Paul. . . .	13.1	73.2	45.4	21.9	83.3	54.7	4.3	63.0	35.9
MS	Jackson	45.0	81.4	64.1	55.1	91.4	75.0	35.0	71.4	53.2
MO	Kansas City	26.9	78.5	54.2	36.0	88.8	64.3	17.8	68.2	44.0
	St. Louis	29.6	80.2	56.3	37.9	89.8	65.7	21.2	70.6	46.9
MT	Great Falls	21.7	66.2	43.8	32.1	82.0	56.4	11.3	50.4	31.1
NE	Omaha	21.7	76.7	50.7	31.7	87.4	61.5	11.6	65.9	39.8
NV	Reno	33.6	71.3	51.3	45.5	91.2	67.4	21.8	51.4	35.2
NH	Concord	20.1	70.0	45.9	30.6	82.9	57.7	9.7	57.1	34.1
NJ	Atlantic City	32.1	75.3	53.5	41.4	85.1	63.6	22.8	65.4	43.3
NM	Albuquerque	35.7	78.5	56.8	47.6	92.3	70.4	23.8	64.7	43.2
NY	Albany	22.2	71.1	47.6	31.1	82.2	57.6	13.3	60.0	37.5
	Buffalo	24.5	70.8	48.0	31.1	79.6	55.9	17.8	62.1	39.9
	New York [1]	32.1	76.5	54.6	38.0	84.2	61.7	26.2	68.8	47.5
NC	Charlotte	41.7	80.3	61.4	51.3	90.1	71.7	32.1	70.6	51.0
	Raleigh	39.7	78.8	59.6	49.8	89.1	70.6	29.6	68.5	48.6
ND	Bismarck	10.2	70.4	42.3	21.1	84.5	54.5	-0.6	56.4	30.1
OH	Cincinnati	29.7	76.3	54.2	38.0	86.4	64.0	21.3	66.1	44.3
	Cleveland	25.7	71.9	49.7	32.6	81.4	58.1	18.8	62.3	41.2
	Columbus	28.3	75.1	52.9	36.2	85.3	62.6	20.3	64.9	43.2
OK	Oklahoma City	36.7	82.0	60.1	47.1	93.1	71.1	26.2	70.8	49.2
OR	Portland	39.9	68.1	53.5	45.6	79.3	62.1	34.2	56.9	44.8
PA	Philadelphia	32.3	77.6	55.3	39.0	85.5	63.2	25.5	69.7	47.4
	Pittsburgh	27.5	72.6	51.0	35.1	82.7	60.4	19.9	62.4	41.5
RI	Providence	28.7	73.3	51.1	37.1	82.6	60.2	20.3	64.1	42.0
SC	Columbia	44.6	82.0	63.6	55.1	92.1	74.8	34.0	71.8	52.5
SD	Sioux Falls	14.0	73.0	45.1	25.2	85.6	57.2	2.9	60.3	33.0
TN	Memphis	39.9	82.5	62.4	48.6	92.1	72.1	31.3	72.9	52.5
	Nashville	36.8	79.1	58.9	45.6	88.7	69.0	27.9	69.5	48.8
TX	Dallas-Fort Worth	44.1	85.0	65.5	54.1	95.4	75.8	34.0	74.6	55.1
	El Paso	45.1	83.3	64.7	57.2	94.5	77.1	32.9	72.0	52.1
	Houston	51.8	83.6	68.8	62.3	93.6	79.4	41.2	73.5	58.2
UT	Salt Lake City	29.2	77.0	52.0	37.0	90.6	62.9	21.3	63.4	41.2
VT	Burlington	18.0	70.6	45.2	26.7	81.4	54.5	9.3	59.8	35.8
VA	Norfolk	40.1	79.1	59.6	47.8	86.8	67.8	32.3	71.4	51.4
	Richmond	36.4	77.9	57.6	45.3	87.5	67.8	27.6	68.3	47.4
WA	Seattle-Tacoma	40.9	65.3	52.3	45.8	75.3	59.8	35.9	55.3	44.8
	Spokane	27.3	68.6	47.3	32.8	82.5	57.4	21.7	54.6	37.2
WV	Charleston	33.4	73.9	54.5	42.6	84.9	65.4	24.2	62.9	43.5
WI	Milwaukee	20.7	72.0	47.5	28.0	81.1	55.9	13.4	62.9	39.2
WY	Cheyenne	25.9	67.7	45.0	37.1	81.9	57.6	14.8	53.4	32.3
PR	San Juan	76.6	82.2	79.9	82.4	87.4	85.5	70.8	76.9	74.2

[1] City office data.

Source: U.S. National Oceanic and Atmospheric Administration, National Environmental Satellite, Data, and Information Services (NESDIS), National Climatic Data Center (NCDC), Temperature Extremes and Drought. Weather/Climate events. See also <http://www.ncdc.noaa.gov/oa/climate/online/ccd/nrmmax.txt>; and <http://www.ncdc.noaa.gov/oa/climate/online/ccd/nrmmin.txt>; and <http://www.ncdc.noaa.gov/oa/climate/online/ccd/nrmavg.txt>.

230 Geography and Environment

Table 379. **Highest Temperature of Record—Selected Cities**

[**In Fahrenheit degrees.** Airport data, except as noted. For period of record through 2007]

State	Station	Length of record (years)	Jan.	Feb.	Mar.	Apr.	May	June	July	Aug.	Sept.	Oct.	Nov.	Dec.	Annual [1]
AL	Mobile	66	84	82	90	94	100	102	104	105	99	93	87	81	105
AK	Juneau	63	57	57	61	74	82	86	90	84	73	61	56	54	90
AZ	Phoenix	70	88	92	100	105	113	122	121	116	118	107	95	88	122
AR	Little Rock	66	83	85	91	95	98	105	112	109	106	97	86	80	112
CA	Los Angeles	72	91	92	95	102	97	104	97	98	110	106	101	94	110
	Sacramento	57	70	76	88	95	105	115	114	110	108	104	87	72	115
	San Diego	67	88	90	93	98	96	101	99	98	111	107	97	88	111
	San Francisco	80	72	78	85	92	97	106	105	100	103	99	85	75	106
CO	Denver	65	73	77	84	90	96	104	105	101	97	89	80	75	105
CT	Hartford	53	72	73	89	96	99	100	102	102	99	91	81	76	102
DE	Wilmington	60	75	78	86	94	96	100	102	101	100	91	85	75	102
DC	Washington	66	79	82	89	95	99	101	104	105	101	94	86	79	105
FL	Jacksonville	66	85	88	91	95	100	103	105	102	100	96	88	84	105
	Miami	65	88	89	93	96	96	98	98	98	97	95	91	87	98
GA	Atlanta	59	79	80	89	93	95	101	105	104	98	95	84	79	105
HI	Honolulu	38	88	88	88	91	93	92	94	93	95	94	93	89	95
ID	Boise	68	63	71	81	92	99	109	111	110	102	94	78	65	111
IL	Chicago	49	65	72	88	91	93	104	104	101	99	91	78	71	104
	Peoria	68	70	72	86	92	94	105	104	103	100	93	81	71	105
IN	Indianapolis	68	71	76	85	89	93	102	104	102	100	91	81	74	104
IA	Des Moines	68	67	73	91	93	98	103	105	108	101	95	81	69	108
KS	Wichita	55	75	87	89	96	100	110	113	110	108	97	86	83	113
KY	Louisville	60	77	77	86	91	95	102	106	105	104	93	84	76	106
LA	New Orleans	61	83	85	89	92	96	100	101	102	101	94	87	84	102
ME	Portland	67	67	64	88	85	94	98	99	103	95	88	74	71	103
MD	Baltimore	57	75	79	89	94	98	101	104	105	100	94	83	77	105
MA	Boston	56	69	70	89	94	95	100	102	102	100	90	79	76	102
MI	Detroit	49	62	70	81	89	93	104	102	100	98	91	77	69	104
	Sault Ste. Marie	67	45	49	75	85	89	93	97	98	95	81	67	62	98
MN	Duluth	66	52	55	78	88	90	94	97	97	95	86	71	55	97
	Minneapolis-St. Paul	69	58	61	83	95	97	102	105	102	98	90	77	68	105
MS	Jackson	44	83	85	89	94	99	105	106	107	104	95	88	84	107
MO	Kansas City	35	71	78	86	93	95	105	107	109	106	95	82	74	109
	St. Louis	50	76	85	89	93	94	102	107	107	104	94	85	76	107
MT	Great Falls	70	67	70	78	89	93	101	105	106	98	91	76	69	106
NE	Omaha	71	69	78	89	97	99	105	114	110	104	96	83	72	114
NV	Reno	66	71	75	83	89	97	103	108	105	101	91	77	70	108
NH	Concord	66	69	67	89	95	97	98	102	101	98	90	80	73	102
NJ	Atlantic City	64	78	75	87	94	99	106	104	103	99	90	84	77	106
NM	Albuquerque	68	69	76	85	89	98	107	105	101	100	91	77	72	107
NY	Albany	61	71	68	89	92	94	99	100	99	100	89	82	71	100
	Buffalo	64	72	71	81	94	91	96	97	99	98	87	80	74	99
	New York [2]	139	72	75	86	96	99	101	106	104	102	94	84	75	106
NC	Charlotte	68	79	81	90	93	100	103	103	104	104	98	85	80	104
	Raleigh	63	80	84	92	95	97	104	105	105	104	98	88	81	105
ND	Bismarck	68	63	69	81	93	98	111	112	109	105	95	79	65	112
OH	Cincinnati	46	69	75	84	89	93	102	103	102	98	91	81	75	103
	Cleveland	66	73	74	83	88	92	104	103	102	101	90	82	77	104
	Columbus	68	74	75	85	89	94	102	100	101	100	91	80	76	102
OK	Oklahoma City	54	80	92	93	100	104	105	110	110	108	96	87	86	110
OR	Portland	67	66	71	80	90	100	102	107	107	105	92	73	65	107
PA	Philadelphia	66	74	74	87	95	97	100	104	101	100	96	81	73	104
	Pittsburgh	55	72	76	82	89	91	98	103	100	97	87	82	74	103
RI	Providence	54	69	72	85	98	95	97	102	104	100	86	78	77	104
SC	Columbia	60	84	84	91	94	101	107	107	107	101	101	90	83	107
SD	Sioux Falls	62	66	70	87	94	100	110	108	108	104	94	81	63	110
TN	Memphis	66	79	81	86	94	99	104	108	107	103	95	86	81	108
	Nashville	68	78	84	86	91	97	106	107	106	105	94	84	79	107
TX	Dallas-Fort Worth	54	88	95	96	101	103	113	110	109	111	102	89	89	113
	El Paso	68	80	83	89	98	105	114	112	108	104	96	87	80	114
	Houston	38	84	91	91	95	99	103	104	107	109	96	89	85	109
UT	Salt Lake City	79	63	69	78	89	99	104	107	106	100	89	75	69	107
VT	Burlington	64	66	62	84	91	93	100	100	101	98	85	75	67	101
VA	Norfolk	59	80	82	88	97	100	101	103	104	99	95	86	80	104
	Richmond	78	81	83	93	96	100	104	105	104	103	99	86	81	105
WA	Seattle-Tacoma	63	64	70	78	85	93	96	100	99	98	89	74	64	100
	Spokane	60	59	63	71	90	96	101	103	108	98	86	67	56	108
WV	Charleston	60	79	79	89	94	93	98	104	104	102	93	85	80	104
WI	Milwaukee	67	62	68	82	91	93	101	103	103	98	89	77	68	103
WY	Cheyenne	72	66	71	74	83	91	100	100	96	95	83	75	69	100
PR	San Juan	53	92	96	96	97	96	97	95	97	97	98	96	94	98

- Represents zero.   [1] Represents the highest observed temperature in any month.   [2] City office data.

Source: U.S. National Oceanic and Atmospheric Administration, *Comparative Climatic Data,* annual; <http://www.ncdc.noaa.gov/oa/climate/online/ccd/hghtmp.txt>.

Geography and Environment   231

Table 380. **Lowest Temperature of Record—Selected Cities**

[**In Fahrenheit degrees.** Airport data, except as noted. For period of record through 2007]

State	Station	Length of record (years)	Jan.	Feb.	Mar.	Apr.	May	June	July	Aug.	Sept.	Oct.	Nov.	Dec.	Annual [1]
AL	Mobile	66	3	11	21	32	43	49	60	59	42	30	22	8	3
AK	Juneau	63	-22	-22	-15	6	25	31	36	27	23	11	-5	-21	-22
AZ	Phoenix	70	17	22	25	32	40	50	61	60	47	34	25	22	17
AR	Little Rock	66	-4	-5	11	28	40	46	54	52	37	29	17	-1	-5
CA	Los Angeles	72	23	32	34	39	43	48	49	51	47	16	34	32	16
	Sacramento	57	21	23	26	31	36	41	48	49	42	36	26	18	18
	San Diego	67	29	36	39	41	48	51	55	57	51	43	38	34	29
	San Francisco	80	24	25	30	31	36	41	43	42	38	34	25	20	20
CO	Denver	65	-25	-30	-11	-2	22	30	43	41	17	3	-8	-25	-30
CT	Hartford	53	-26	-21	-6	9	28	35	44	36	30	17	1	-14	-26
DE	Wilmington	60	-14	-6	2	18	30	41	48	43	36	24	14	-7	-14
DC	Washington	66	-5	4	11	24	34	47	54	49	39	29	16	1	-5
FL	Jacksonville	66	7	19	23	31	45	47	61	59	48	36	21	11	7
	Miami	65	30	32	32	46	53	60	69	68	68	51	39	30	30
GA	Atlanta	59	-8	5	10	26	37	46	53	55	36	28	3	–	-8
HI	Honolulu	38	53	53	55	57	60	65	66	67	66	61	57	54	53
ID	Boise	68	-17	-15	6	19	22	31	35	34	23	11	-3	-25	-25
IL	Chicago	49	-27	-19	-8	7	24	36	40	41	28	17	1	-25	-27
	Peoria	68	-25	-19	-10	14	25	39	47	41	26	19	-2	-23	-25
IN	Indianapolis	68	-27	-21	-7	16	28	37	44	41	28	17	-2	-23	-27
IA	Des Moines	68	-24	-26	-22	9	30	38	47	40	26	14	-4	-22	-26
KS	Wichita	55	-12	-21	-2	15	31	43	51	48	31	18	1	-16	-21
KY	Louisville	60	-22	-19	-1	22	31	42	50	46	33	23	-1	-15	-22
LA	New Orleans	61	14	16	25	32	41	50	60	60	42	35	24	11	11
ME	Portland	67	-26	-39	-21	8	23	33	40	33	23	15	3	-21	-39
MD	Baltimore	57	-7	-3	6	20	32	40	50	45	35	25	13	–	-7
MA	Boston	56	-12	-4	5	16	34	45	50	47	38	28	15	-7	-12
MI	Detroit	49	-21	-15	-4	10	25	36	41	38	29	17	9	-10	-21
	Sault Ste. Marie	67	-36	-35	-24	-2	18	26	36	29	25	16	-10	-31	-36
MN	Duluth	66	-39	-39	-29	-5	17	27	35	32	22	8	-23	-34	-39
	Minneapolis–St. Paul	69	-34	-32	-32	2	18	34	43	39	26	13	-17	-29	-34
MS	Jackson	44	2	10	15	27	38	47	51	54	35	26	17	4	2
MO	Kansas City	35	-17	-19	-10	12	30	42	51	43	31	17	1	-23	-23
	St. Louis	50	-18	-12	-5	22	31	43	51	47	36	23	1	-16	-18
MT	Great Falls	70	-37	-35	-29	-6	15	31	36	30	16	-11	-25	-43	-43
NE	Omaha	71	-23	-21	-16	5	27	38	44	43	25	13	-9	-23	-23
NV	Reno	66	-16	-16	-2	13	18	21	33	24	20	8	1	-16	-16
NH	Concord	66	-33	-37	-16	8	21	30	35	29	21	10	-5	-22	-37
NJ	Atlantic City	64	-10	-11	4	12	25	37	42	40	32	20	10	-7	-11
NM	Albuquerque	68	-17	-5	8	19	16	40	52	50	37	21	-7	-7	-17
NY	Albany	61	-28	-21	-21	10	26	36	40	34	24	16	5	-22	-28
	Buffalo	64	-16	-20	-7	12	26	35	43	38	32	20	9	-10	-20
	New York [2]	139	-6	-15	3	12	32	44	52	50	39	28	5	-13	-15
NC	Charlotte	68	-5	5	4	21	32	45	53	50	39	24	11	2	-5
	Raleigh	63	-9	–	11	23	31	38	48	46	37	19	11	4	-9
ND	Bismarck	68	-44	-43	-31	-12	15	30	35	33	11	-10	-30	-43	-44
OH	Cincinnati	46	-25	-11	-11	15	27	39	47	43	31	16	1	-20	-25
	Cleveland	66	-20	-15	-5	10	25	31	41	38	32	19	3	-15	-20
	Columbus	68	-22	-13	-6	14	25	35	43	39	31	20	5	-17	-22
OK	Oklahoma City	54	-4	-3	3	20	37	47	53	51	36	16	11	-8	-8
OR	Portland	67	-2	-3	19	29	29	39	43	44	34	26	13	6	-3
PA	Philadelphia	66	-7	-4	7	19	28	44	51	44	35	25	15	1	-7
	Pittsburgh	55	-22	-12	-1	14	26	34	42	39	31	16	-1	-12	-22
RI	Providence	54	-13	-7	1	14	29	41	48	40	33	20	6	-10	-13
SC	Columbia	60	-1	5	4	26	34	44	54	53	40	23	12	4	-1
SD	Sioux Falls	62	-36	-31	-23	5	17	33	38	34	22	9	-17	-28	-36
TN	Memphis	66	-4	-11	12	28	38	48	52	48	36	25	9	-13	-13
	Nashville	68	-17	-13	2	23	34	42	51	47	36	26	-1	-10	-17
TX	Dallas–Fort Worth	54	4	7	15	29	41	51	59	56	43	29	20	-1	-1
	El Paso	68	-8	8	14	23	31	46	57	56	41	25	1	5	-8
	Houston	38	12	3	22	31	44	52	62	60	48	29	19	7	3
UT	Salt Lake City	79	-22	-30	2	14	25	35	40	37	27	16	-14	-21	-30
VT	Burlington	64	-30	-30	-20	2	24	33	39	35	25	15	-2	-26	-30
VA	Norfolk	59	-3	8	18	28	36	45	54	49	45	27	20	7	-3
	Richmond	78	-12	-10	11	23	31	40	51	46	35	21	10	-1	-12
WA	Seattle–Tacoma	63	–	11	29	28	34	38	43	44	35	28	6	6	–
	Spokane	60	-22	-24	-7	17	24	33	37	35	22	7	-21	-25	-25
WV	Charleston	60	-16	-12	–	19	26	33	46	41	34	17	6	-12	-16
WI	Milwaukee	67	-26	-26	-10	12	21	33	40	44	28	18	-5	-20	-26
WY	Cheyenne	72	-29	-34	-21	-8	16	25	38	36	8	-1	-16	-28	-34
PR	San Juan	53	61	62	60	64	66	69	69	70	69	46	66	59	46

– Represents zero.   [1] Represents the lowest observed temperature in any month.   [2] City office data.

Source: U.S. National Oceanic and Atmospheric Administration, *Comparative Climatic Data*, annual. See also <http://www.ncdc.noaa.gov/oa/climate/online/ccd/lowtmp.txt>.

Table 381. Normal Monthly and Annual Precipitation—Selected Cities

[In inches. Airport data, except as noted. The table data are the 30-year average values computed from the data recorded during the period 1971–2000]

State	Station	Jan.	Feb.	Mar.	Apr.	May	June	July	Aug.	Sept.	Oct.	Nov.	Dec.	Annual
AL	Mobile	5.75	5.10	7.20	5.06	6.10	5.01	6.54	6.20	6.01	3.25	5.41	4.66	66.29
AK	Juneau	4.81	4.02	3.51	2.96	3.48	3.36	4.14	5.37	7.54	8.30	5.43	5.41	58.33
AZ	Phoenix	0.83	0.77	1.07	0.25	0.16	0.09	0.99	0.94	0.75	0.79	0.73	0.92	8.29
AR	Little Rock	3.61	3.33	4.88	5.47	5.05	3.95	3.31	2.93	3.71	4.25	5.73	4.71	50.93
CA	Los Angeles	2.98	3.11	2.40	0.63	0.24	0.08	0.03	0.14	0.26	0.36	1.13	1.79	13.15
	Sacramento	3.84	3.54	2.80	1.02	0.53	0.20	0.05	0.06	0.36	0.89	2.19	2.45	17.93
	San Diego	2.28	2.04	2.26	0.75	0.20	0.09	0.03	0.09	0.21	0.44	1.07	1.31	10.77
	San Francisco	4.45	4.01	3.26	1.17	0.38	0.11	0.03	0.07	0.20	1.04	2.49	2.89	20.11
CO	Denver	0.51	0.49	1.28	1.93	2.32	1.56	2.16	1.82	1.14	0.99	0.98	0.63	15.81
CT	Hartford	3.84	2.96	3.88	3.86	4.39	3.85	3.67	3.98	4.13	3.94	4.06	3.60	46.16
DE	Wilmington	3.43	2.81	3.97	3.39	4.15	3.59	4.28	3.51	4.01	3.08	3.19	3.40	42.81
DC	Washington	3.21	2.63	3.60	2.77	3.82	3.13	3.66	3.44	3.79	3.22	3.03	3.05	39.35
FL	Jacksonville	3.69	3.15	3.93	3.14	3.48	5.37	5.97	6.87	7.90	3.86	2.34	2.64	52.34
	Miami	1.88	2.07	2.56	3.36	5.52	8.54	5.79	8.63	8.38	6.19	3.43	2.18	58.53
GA	Atlanta	5.02	4.68	5.38	3.62	3.95	3.63	5.12	3.67	4.09	3.11	4.10	3.82	50.20
HI	Honolulu	2.73	2.35	1.89	1.11	0.78	0.43	0.50	0.46	0.74	2.18	2.26	2.85	18.29
ID	Boise	1.39	1.14	1.41	1.27	1.27	0.74	0.39	0.30	0.76	0.76	1.38	1.38	12.19
IL	Chicago	1.75	1.63	2.65	3.68	3.38	3.63	3.51	4.62	3.27	2.71	3.01	2.43	36.27
	Peoria	1.50	1.67	2.83	3.56	4.17	3.84	4.02	3.16	3.12	2.76	2.99	2.40	36.03
IN	Indianapolis	2.48	2.41	3.44	3.61	4.35	4.13	4.42	3.82	2.88	2.76	3.61	3.03	40.95
IA	Des Moines	1.03	1.19	2.21	3.58	4.25	4.57	4.18	4.51	3.15	2.62	2.10	1.33	34.72
KS	Wichita	0.84	1.02	2.71	2.57	4.16	4.25	3.31	2.94	2.96	2.45	1.82	1.35	30.38
KY	Louisville	3.28	3.25	4.41	3.91	4.88	3.76	4.30	3.41	3.05	2.79	3.80	3.69	44.54
LA	New Orleans	5.87	5.47	5.24	5.02	4.62	6.83	6.20	6.15	5.55	3.05	5.09	5.07	64.16
ME	Portland	4.09	3.14	4.14	4.26	3.82	3.28	3.32	3.05	3.37	4.40	4.72	4.24	45.83
MD	Baltimore	3.47	3.02	3.93	3.00	3.89	3.43	3.85	3.74	3.98	3.16	3.12	3.35	41.94
MA	Boston	3.92	3.30	3.85	3.60	3.24	3.22	3.06	3.37	3.47	3.79	3.98	3.73	42.53
MI	Detroit	1.91	1.88	2.52	3.05	3.05	3.55	3.16	3.10	3.27	2.23	2.66	2.51	32.89
	Sault Ste. Marie	2.64	1.60	2.41	2.57	2.50	3.00	3.14	3.47	3.71	3.32	3.40	2.91	34.67
MN	Duluth	1.12	0.83	1.69	2.09	2.95	4.25	4.20	4.22	4.13	2.46	2.12	0.94	31.00
	Minneapolis-St. Paul	1.04	0.79	1.86	2.31	3.24	4.34	4.04	4.05	2.69	2.11	1.94	1.00	29.41
MS	Jackson	5.67	4.50	5.74	5.98	4.86	3.82	4.69	3.66	3.23	3.42	5.04	5.34	55.95
MO	Kansas City	1.15	1.31	2.44	3.38	5.39	4.44	4.42	3.54	4.64	3.33	2.30	1.64	37.98
	St. Louis	2.14	2.28	3.60	3.69	4.11	3.76	3.90	2.98	2.96	2.76	3.71	2.86	38.75
MT	Great Falls	0.68	0.51	1.01	1.40	2.53	2.24	1.45	1.65	1.23	0.93	0.59	0.67	14.89
NE	Omaha	0.77	0.80	2.13	2.94	4.44	3.95	3.86	3.21	3.17	2.21	1.82	0.92	30.22
NV	Reno	1.06	1.06	0.86	0.35	0.62	0.47	0.24	0.27	0.45	0.42	0.80	0.88	7.48
NH	Concord	2.97	2.36	3.04	3.07	3.33	3.10	3.37	3.21	3.16	3.46	3.57	2.90	37.60
NJ	Atlantic City	3.60	2.85	4.06	3.45	3.38	2.66	3.86	4.32	3.14	2.86	3.26	3.15	40.59
NM	Albuquerque	0.49	0.44	0.61	0.50	0.60	0.65	1.27	1.73	1.07	1.00	0.62	0.49	9.47
NY	Albany	2.71	2.27	3.17	3.25	3.67	3.74	3.50	3.68	3.31	3.23	3.31	2.76	38.60
	Buffalo	3.16	2.42	2.99	3.04	3.35	3.82	3.14	3.87	3.84	3.19	3.92	3.80	40.54
	New York [1]	4.13	3.15	4.37	4.28	4.69	3.84	4.62	4.22	4.23	3.85	4.36	3.95	49.69
NC	Charlotte	4.00	3.55	4.39	2.95	3.66	3.42	3.79	3.72	3.83	3.66	3.36	3.18	43.51
	Raleigh	4.02	3.47	4.03	2.80	3.79	3.42	4.29	3.78	4.26	3.18	2.97	3.04	43.05
ND	Bismarck	0.45	0.51	0.85	1.46	2.22	2.59	2.58	2.15	1.61	1.28	0.70	0.44	16.84
OH	Cincinnati	2.92	2.75	3.90	3.96	4.59	4.42	3.75	3.79	2.82	2.96	3.46	3.28	42.60
	Cleveland	2.48	2.29	2.94	3.37	3.50	3.89	3.52	3.69	3.77	2.73	3.38	3.14	38.71
	Columbus	2.53	2.20	2.89	3.25	3.88	4.07	4.61	3.72	2.92	2.31	3.19	2.93	38.52
OK	Oklahoma City	1.28	1.56	2.90	3.00	5.44	4.63	2.94	2.48	3.98	3.64	2.11	1.89	35.85
OR	Portland	5.07	4.18	3.71	2.64	2.38	1.59	0.72	0.93	1.65	2.88	5.61	5.71	37.07
PA	Philadelphia	3.52	2.74	3.81	3.49	3.88	3.29	4.39	3.82	3.88	2.75	3.16	3.31	42.05
	Pittsburgh	2.70	2.37	3.17	3.01	3.80	4.12	3.96	3.38	3.21	2.25	3.02	2.86	37.85
RI	Providence	4.37	3.45	4.43	4.16	3.66	3.38	3.17	3.90	3.70	3.69	4.40	4.14	46.45
SC	Columbia	4.66	3.84	4.59	2.98	3.17	4.99	5.54	5.41	3.94	2.89	2.88	3.38	48.27
SD	Sioux Falls	0.51	0.51	1.81	2.65	3.39	3.49	2.93	3.01	2.58	1.93	1.36	0.52	24.69
TN	Memphis	4.24	4.31	5.58	5.79	5.15	4.30	4.22	3.00	3.31	3.31	5.76	5.68	54.65
	Nashville	3.97	3.69	4.87	3.93	5.07	4.08	3.77	3.28	3.59	2.87	4.45	4.54	48.11
TX	Dallas-Fort Worth	1.90	2.37	3.06	3.20	5.15	3.23	2.12	2.03	2.42	4.11	2.57	2.57	34.73
	El Paso	0.45	0.39	0.26	0.23	0.38	0.87	1.49	1.75	1.61	0.81	0.42	0.77	9.43
	Houston	3.68	2.98	3.36	3.60	5.15	5.35	3.18	3.83	4.33	4.50	4.19	3.69	47.84
UT	Salt Lake City	1.37	1.33	1.91	2.02	2.09	0.77	0.72	0.76	1.33	1.57	1.40	1.23	16.50
VT	Burlington	2.22	1.67	2.32	2.88	3.32	3.43	3.97	4.01	3.83	3.12	3.06	2.22	36.05
VA	Norfolk	3.93	3.34	4.08	3.38	3.74	3.77	5.17	4.79	4.06	3.47	2.98	3.03	45.74
	Richmond	3.55	2.98	4.09	3.18	3.95	3.54	4.67	4.18	3.98	3.60	3.06	3.12	43.91
WA	Seattle-Tacoma	5.13	4.18	3.75	2.59	1.77	1.49	0.79	1.02	1.63	3.19	5.90	5.62	37.07
	Spokane	1.82	1.51	1.53	1.28	1.60	1.18	0.76	0.68	0.76	1.06	2.24	2.25	16.67
WV	Charleston	3.25	3.19	3.90	3.25	4.30	4.09	4.86	4.11	3.45	2.67	3.66	3.32	44.05
WI	Milwaukee	1.85	1.65	2.59	3.78	3.06	3.56	3.58	4.03	3.30	2.49	2.70	2.22	34.81
WY	Cheyenne	0.45	0.44	1.05	1.55	2.48	2.12	2.26	1.82	1.43	0.75	0.64	0.46	15.45
PR	San Juan	3.02	2.30	2.14	3.71	5.29	3.52	4.16	5.22	5.60	5.06	6.17	4.57	50.76

[1] City office data.

Source: U.S. National Oceanic and Atmospheric Administration, Comparative Climatic Data, annual. See also <http:www.ncdc.noaa.gov/oa/climate/online/ccd/nrmpcp.txt>.

Geography and Environment 233

Table 382. **Mean Number of Days With Precipitation of 0.01 Inch or More—Selected Cities**

[0.01 is the smallest amount of precipitation numerically recorded, and includes the liquid water equivalent of frozen precipitation. Airport data, except as noted. For period of record through 2007]

State	Station	Length of record (years)	Jan.	Feb.	Mar.	Apr.	May	June	July	Aug.	Sept.	Oct.	Nov.	Dec.	Annual
AL	Mobile	66	10	9	10	7	8	11	15	13	9	6	7	9	114
AK	Juneau	63	18	16	18	16	16	15	17	17	21	23	19	21	217
AZ	Phoenix	68	3	4	3	1	–	–	4	4	2	2	2	3	28
AR	Little Rock	65	9	8	10	9	10	8	8	6	7	7	8	9	99
CA	Los Angeles	72	6	6	5	3	1	–	–	1	1	2	3	5	33
	Sacramento	68	10	8	8	5	2	1	1	1	1	3	7	9	56
	San Diego	67	6	6	6	4	1	–	1	–	1	2	4	6	37
	San Francisco	80	11	10	9	6	2	1	1	1	1	3	7	10	62
CO	Denver	65	5	5	8	8	10	8	9	8	6	5	5	5	82
CT	Hartford	53	11	10	11	11	12	11	9	9	9	8	10	11	122
DE	Wilmington	60	10	9	10	10	11	10	9	8	8	7	9	9	110
DC	Washington	66	10	8	10	9	11	9	9	8	7	7	8	9	105
FL	Jacksonville	66	8	7	8	6	7	12	14	14	13	8	6	7	110
	Miami	65	6	6	6	6	10	15	16	17	17	14	8	6	127
GA	Atlanta	73	11	10	11	8	9	10	11	9	7	6	8	10	110
HI	Honolulu	58	9	8	8	8	6	5	7	5	6	8	9	9	88
ID	Boise	68	11	9	9	8	7	5	2	2	3	5	10	11	82
IL	Chicago	49	10	9	12	12	11	10	9	9	8	9	10	10	119
	Peoria	68	9	8	10	11	11	9	8	8	8	8	9	9	108
IN	Indianapolis	68	11	10	12	12	12	10	9	8	7	8	10	11	120
IA	Des Moines	68	7	7	9	10	11	10	9	9	8	7	7	7	101
KS	Wichita	54	5	5	7	7	10	9	7	7	7	6	5	5	80
KY	Louisville	60	11	10	12	11	11	10	10	8	7	7	10	11	118
LA	New Orleans	59	9	8	8	6	7	11	14	13	9	6	7	9	107
ME	Portland	67	11	9	11	11	12	11	9	9	8	9	11	11	122
MD	Baltimore	57	10	8	10	10	11	9	9	9	7	7	8	9	107
MA	Boston	56	11	10	11	11	11	10	9	9	8	9	10	11	120
MI	Detroit	49	13	10	12	12	11	10	9	9	9	9	11	13	128
	Sault Ste. Marie	66	18	14	12	11	11	11	10	10	13	14	17	19	160
MN	Duluth	66	11	9	10	10	12	12	11	11	11	9	10	11	127
	Minneapolis-St. Paul	69	8	7	9	10	11	11	9	9	9	8	8	9	108
MS	Jackson	44	10	9	9	8	9	8	10	9	7	6	8	9	102
MO	Kansas City	35	7	7	9	10	11	10	8	8	8	7	7	6	98
	St. Louis	50	8	8	10	11	11	9	8	8	7	8	9	9	106
MT	Great Falls	70	8	7	9	9	11	12	7	7	7	6	6	7	96
NE	Omaha	71	6	6	8	9	11	10	9	9	8	6	5	6	93
NV	Reno	65	6	6	6	4	4	3	2	2	2	4	6	6	47
NH	Concord	66	10	9	11	11	12	11	10	9	9	9	11	10	122
NJ	Atlantic City	64	10	9	10	11	10	8	9	8	7	7	9	9	107
NM	Albuquerque	68	3	4	4	3	4	3	8	9	5	4	3	4	54
NY	Albany	61	12	10	12	12	13	11	10	10	9	9	11	12	131
	Buffalo	64	19	16	15	14	12	10	10	10	11	11	15	19	162
	New York [1]	138	11	9	11	10	11	10	10	9	8	8	9	10	116
NC	Charlotte	68	10	9	10	8	9	9	11	9	7	6	7	9	104
	Raleigh	63	10	9	10	9	10	9	11	10	7	7	8	9	109
ND	Bismarck	68	7	6	8	7	10	11	9	8	7	5	6	7	91
OH	Cincinnati	60	12	11	12	12	11	10	10	9	7	8	10	12	124
	Cleveland	66	16	14	15	14	13	10	10	9	9	11	14	16	151
	Columbus	68	13	11	13	13	13	11	10	9	8	8	11	12	132
OK	Oklahoma City	68	5	6	7	7	9	8	6	6	7	6	5	5	77
OR	Portland	67	18	15	17	14	12	9	3	4	7	12	18	18	147
PA	Philadelphia	67	10	9	10	10	11	10	9	8	8	7	9	10	112
	Pittsburgh	55	16	13	15	13	12	11	10	9	9	10	12	15	145
RI	Providence	54	11	9	11	11	11	10	8	9	8	8	10	11	117
SC	Columbia	60	10	9	9	7	8	9	11	10	7	6	7	9	103
SD	Sioux Falls	62	6	6	8	9	10	11	9	8	8	6	6	6	93
TN	Memphis	57	10	9	10	9	9	8	8	7	7	6	8	9	100
	Nashville	66	11	10	11	10	10	9	10	8	7	7	9	10	112
TX	Dallas-Fort Worth	54	7	6	7	7	8	6	4	4	6	6	6	6	73
	El Paso	68	3	3	2	1	2	3	7	7	5	4	2	3	42
	Houston	38	10	8	9	6	8	9	9	9	8	7	8	9	100
UT	Salt Lake City	79	10	8	9	9	8	5	4	5	5	6	8	9	86
VT	Burlington	64	14	11	12	12	13	12	12	12	11	11	14	14	148
VA	Norfolk	59	10	9	10	10	10	9	11	10	8	7	8	9	111
	Richmond	70	10	9	10	9	10	9	11	9	8	7	8	9	109
WA	Seattle–Tacoma	63	18	15	16	13	10	9	5	5	8	13	17	18	147
	Spokane	60	14	11	11	9	9	7	4	4	5	7	12	14	107
WV	Charleston	60	15	13	14	13	13	11	12	10	9	9	11	13	143
WI	Milwaukee	67	11	9	11	12	11	10	9	9	8	9	10	10	119
WY	Cheyenne	72	5	6	9	9	11	10	10	10	7	5	7	5	93
PR	San Juan	52	17	13	12	13	15	15	19	18	17	17	18	19	193

– Represents zero. [1] City office data.

Source: U.S. National Oceanic and Atmospheric Administration, *Comparative Climatic Data*, annual. See also <http://www.ncdc.noaa.gov/oa/climate/online/ccd/prge01.txt>.

U.S. Census Bureau, Statistical Abstract of the United States: 2010

Table 383. **Snow, Hail, Ice Pellets, and Sleet—Selected Cities**

[In inches. Airport data, except as noted. For period of record through 2007. **T denotes trace.** Stations may show snowfall (hail) during the warm months]

State	Station	Length of record (years)	Jan.	Feb.	Mar.	Apr.	May	June	July	Aug.	Sept.	Oct.	Nov.	Dec.	Annual
AL	Mobile	65	0.1	0.1	0.1	T	T	–	T	–	–	–	T	0.1	0.4
AK	Juneau	63	25.9	18.3	15.3	3.3	T	T	–	–	T	1.0	12.4	21.2	96.9
AZ	Phoenix	62	T	–	T	T	T	–	–	–	–	T	–	T	–
AR	Little Rock	56	2.4	1.5	0.5	T	T	T	–	–	–	T	0.2	0.6	5.2
CA	Los Angeles	62	T	T	T	–	–	–	–	–	–	–	–	T	–
	Sacramento	50	T	T	T	–	T	–	–	–	–	–	–	T	–
	San Diego	60	T	–	T	T	–	–	–	–	–	–	T	–	–
	San Francisco	69	–	T	T	–	–	–	–	–	–	–	–	–	–
CO	Denver	63	8.1	7.4	12.3	8.7	1.6	–	T	T	1.6	3.8	8.9	7.9	60.3
CT	Hartford	50	13.3	12.5	10.1	1.5	–	T	–	–	–	0.1	2.1	10.7	50.3
DE	Wilmington	57	6.8	6.7	3.2	0.2	T	T	T	–	–	0.1	0.9	3.4	21.4
DC	Washington	64	5.4	5.6	2.3	2.3	T	T	T	T	–	–	0.8	3.0	17.2
FL	Jacksonville	60	T	–	–	T	–	T	T	–	–	–	–	–	–
	Miami	59	–	–	–	–	–	–	–	–	–	–	–	–	–
GA	Atlanta	68	1.0	0.5	0.4	T	–	–	T	–	–	T	T	0.2	2.1
HI	Honolulu	52	–	–	–	–	–	–	–	–	–	–	–	–	–
ID	Boise	68	6.3	3.6	1.7	0.6	0.1	T	T	T	T	0.1	2.3	5.6	20.4
IL	Chicago	48	11.2	7.9	6.6	1.6	0.1	T	T	T	T	0.4	2.1	8.3	38.0
	Peoria	64	6.5	5.1	4.2	0.8	T	T	T	–	T	0.1	2.1	6.3	25.0
IN	Indianapolis	76	6.9	5.7	3.5	0.5	T	T	–	T	–	0.2	1.9	5.5	23.9
IA	Des Moines	64	8.3	7.3	6.1	1.9	T	T	T	–	T	0.3	3.1	6.6	33.3
KS	Wichita	54	4.0	4.1	2.7	0.2	T	T	T	T	T	–	1.4	3.6	15.9
KY	Louisville	60	5.1	4.2	3.1	0.1	T	T	T	T	–	0.1	1.0	2.5	16.2
LA	New Orleans	51	T	0.1	T	T	T	–	–	–	–	–	T	0.1	0.2
ME	Portland	67	19.0	16.4	13.3	3.1	0.2	–	T	–	T	0.2	3.3	14.9	70.0
MD	Baltimore	57	6.2	7.2	3.6	0.1	T	T	T	–	–	T	1.0	3.3	21.5
MA	Boston	70	12.8	12.0	8.2	0.9	–	T	T	T	–	T	1.3	8.0	43.2
MI	Detroit	49	10.9	9.1	6.8	1.9	T	–	–	–	T	0.2	2.5	10.0	41.4
	Sault Ste. Marie	60	29.2	18.6	14.4	5.9	0.5	T	T	T	0.1	2.4	15.6	30.7	117.0
MN	Duluth	64	17.9	12.4	14.0	6.8	0.7	T	T	T	0.1	1.6	12.6	15.6	81.3
	Minneapolis-St. Paul	65	10.5	8.1	10.6	2.8	0.1	T	T	T		0.5	7.6	9.5	49.7
MS	Jackson	38	0.5	0.2	0.2	T	–	–	–	T	–	T		0.1	1.0
MO	Kansas City	73	5.4	4.4	3.4	0.8	T	T	T	T		0.1	1.3	4.5	19.8
	St. Louis	71	5.3	4.5	3.7	0.5	T	T	T	–	–	T	1.4	4.1	19.4
MT	Great Falls	70	9.2	8.6	10.7	7.0	1.9	0.3	T	0.1	1.5	3.5	7.6	8.0	58.3
NE	Omaha	72	7.6	6.9	6.3	1.1	0.1	T	T	T		0.3	2.6	5.7	30.5
NV	Reno	58	6.0	5.2	4.3	1.2	0.8	–	–	–	–	0.3	2.5	4.6	25.0
NH	Concord	66	17.8	14.1	11.5	2.8	0.1	T	–	T		0.1	3.8	14.3	64.0
NJ	Atlantic City	58	5.0	5.6	2.5	0.3	T	T	T	–	–	T	0.4	2.4	16.3
NM	Albuquerque	68	2.5	2.1	1.8	0.6	T	T	T	–	T	0.1	1.2	3.0	11.3
NY	Albany	61	17.0	13.6	11.7	2.8	0.1	T	T	–	T	0.2	4.0	14.7	63.8
	Buffalo	64	24.3	17.9	12.4	3.2	0.2	T	T	T	T	0.7	11.0	24.0	93.7
	New York[1]	139	7.7	8.7	5.1	0.9	T	–	T	–	–	T	0.9	5.6	28.9
NC	Charlotte	68	2.2	1.8	1.2	T	T	T	T	–	–	T	0.1	0.5	5.8
	Raleigh	63	2.8	2.6	1.3	T	T	T	T	–	–	–	0.1	0.8	7.6
ND	Bismarck	68	7.7	6.9	8.4	4.0	0.9	T	T	T	0.2	1.9	6.7	7.0	43.8
OH	Cincinnati	60	7.2	5.6	4.1	0.5	–	T	T	T	–	0.3	2.0	3.8	23.5
	Cleveland	66	14.3	12.5	10.8	2.9	0.1	T	T	–	T	0.6	5.0	12.7	58.6
	Columbus	60	8.8	6.2	4.5	1.0	T	T	T	T	–	0.1	2.2	5.4	28.1
OK	Oklahoma City	68	3.2	2.4	1.5	T	T	T	T	T	T		0.6	1.9	9.6
OR	Portland	55	3.2	1.1	0.4	T	–	T	–	T	–		0.4	1.4	6.5
PA	Philadelphia	65	6.1	7.1	3.4	0.3	T	T	–	–	T		0.7	3.4	21.1
	Pittsburgh	55	11.9	9.3	8.3	1.8	0.1	T	T	T		0.4	3.4	8.4	43.5
RI	Providence	54	9.7	9.9	7.4	0.7	0.2	–	–	–	–	0.1	1.3	7.1	36.5
SC	Columbia	59	0.6	0.8	0.2	T	T	–	T	T	–	–	T	0.3	1.9
SD	Sioux Falls	62	6.9	8.0	9.3	3.1	T	T	T	T		0.9	6.0	7.0	41.0
TN	Memphis	50	2.2	1.4	0.8	T	T	T	–	–	T		0.1	0.6	5.1
	Nashville	61	3.7	3.0	1.5	–	–	T	–	T	–	–	0.4	1.4	10.0
TX	Dallas-Fort Worth	49	1.1	1.0	0.2	T	T	–	–	–	T		0.1	0.2	2.6
	El Paso	58	1.3	0.8	0.4	0.3	T	T	T	–	T	–	1.0	1.6	5.3
	Houston	73	0.2	0.2	T	T	T	–	–	–	–	–	T	T	0.4
UT	Salt Lake City	79	13.4	9.9	9.0	4.9	0.6	T	T	T	0.1	1.3	6.8	12.1	58.1
VT	Burlington	64	19.4	16.6	13.9	4.2	0.2	–	T	T		0.2	6.6	18.7	79.0
VA	Norfolk	57	3.0	2.9	1.0	–	T	T	–	T	–	–	–	1.0	7.9
	Richmond	68	5.0	3.8	2.4	0.1	T	–	T	–	–	T	0.4	2.0	13.8
WA	Seattle-Tacoma	52	4.9	1.6	1.3	0.1	T	T	–	–	–	T	1.1	2.4	11.4
	Spokane	60	15.1	7.4	3.8	0.6	0.1	T	–	–	T	0.4	6.3	14.1	48.0
WV	Charleston	53	10.7	8.6	5.3	0.9	–	T	T	T	T	0.2	2.4	5.2	33.5
WI	Milwaukee	67	13.9	9.4	8.2	2.0	0.1	T	T	T		0.2	3.0	10.7	47.0
WY	Cheyenne	72	6.1	6.5	11.8	9.2	3.4	0.2	T	T	1.1	3.9	7.2	6.7	56.1
PR	San Juan	52	–	–	–	–	–	–	T	–	–	–	–	–	–

– Represents zero. [1] City office data.

Source: U.S. National Oceanic and Atmospheric Administration, *Comparative Climatic Data*, annual. See also <http://www.ncdc.noaa.gov/oa/climate/online/ccd/avgsnf.txt>.

U.S. Census Bureau, Statistical Abstract of the United States: 2010

Table 384. Cloudiness, Average Wind Speed, Heating and Cooling Degree Days, and Average Relative Humidity—Selected Cities

[Airport data, except as noted. For period of record through 2006, except heating and cooling normals for period 1971–2000. M = morning. A = afternoon]

State	Station	Cloudiness—average percentage of days [1] — Length of record (yr.)	Annual	Average wind speed (m.p.h.) — Length of record (yr.)	Annual	Jan.	July	Heating degree days	Cooling degree days	Average relative humidity (percent) — Length of record (yr.)	Annual M	Annual A	Jan. M	Jan. A	July M	July A
AL	Mobile	47	72.1	58	8.8	10.1	6.9	1,667	2,548	44	87	64	82	66	89	67
AK	Juneau	47	87.9	61	8.2	8.0	7.5	8,574	–	40	80	70	78	75	79	67
AZ	Phoenix	57	42.3	61	6.2	5.3	7.1	1,040	4,355	46	49	23	63	31	42	19
AR	Little Rock	35	67.5	64	7.7	8.4	6.7	3,084	2,086	42	82	62	79	65	85	61
CA	Los Angeles	60	59.8	58	7.5	6.7	7.9	1,286	682	47	79	66	71	61	86	68
	Sacramento	49	48.5	56	7.8	6.9	8.9	2,666	1,248	20	83	46	91	70	76	29
	San Diego	55	60.0	66	7.0	6.0	7.5	1,063	866	46	77	63	72	58	82	67
	San Francisco	68	56.2	79	10.6	7.2	13.6	2,862	142	47	84	63	86	68	86	60
CO	Denver	61	68.5	50	8.7	8.7	8.3	6,128	695	38	67	40	63	48	67	33
CT	Hartford	41	77.5	52	8.4	8.9	7.3	6,104	759	47	77	53	72	57	78	51
DE	Wilmington	47	73.4	58	9.0	9.8	7.8	4,887	1,125	59	78	55	75	60	79	54
DC	Washington	48	73.8	58	9.4	10.0	8.3	3,999	1,560	46	75	54	70	55	76	53
FL	Jacksonville	47	74.2	57	7.8	8.1	7.0	1,353	2,636	70	89	56	87	57	88	58
	Miami	46	79.7	57	9.2	9.5	7.9	155	4,383	42	83	61	84	59	82	63
GA	Atlanta	61	69.9	68	9.1	10.4	7.7	2,827	1,810	46	82	56	78	58	87	59
HI	Honolulu	47	75.3	57	11.3	9.4	13.1	–	4,561	37	72	56	80	61	67	51
ID	Boise	56	67.1	67	8.7	7.9	8.4	5,809	769	67	69	43	80	70	53	21
IL	Chicago	37	77.0	48	10.3	11.6	8.4	6,493	835	48	80	64	77	70	81	61
	Peoria	52	73.9	63	9.8	10.9	7.8	6,095	998	47	82	66	79	72	85	65
IN	Indianapolis	64	76.0	58	9.6	10.9	7.5	5,521	1,042	47	84	62	81	70	86	59
IA	Des Moines	46	71.3	57	10.7	11.4	8.9	6,432	1,052	45	80	65	76	70	82	63
KS	Wichita	39	64.9	53	12.2	11.9	11.3	4,765	1,658	53	79	60	78	66	78	55
KY	Louisville	47	74.6	59	8.3	9.5	6.8	4,352	1,443	46	81	58	77	64	84	57
LA	New Orleans	47	72.3	58	8.2	9.3	6.1	1,417	2,776	58	87	67	84	69	90	69
ME	Portland	54	72.3	66	8.7	9.0	7.6	7,325	347	66	79	59	75	60	80	59
MD	Baltimore	45	71.2	56	8.8	9.3	7.6	4,634	1,220	53	78	54	72	57	80	53
MA	Boston	60	73.2	49	12.4	13.7	11.0	5,630	777	42	73	58	68	58	73	57
MI	Detroit	37	79.5	48	10.2	11.8	8.5	6,449	727	48	81	60	80	69	81	54
	Sault Ste. Marie	54	81.9	65	9.2	9.6	7.8	9,230	145	65	85	66	80	73	88	61
MN	Duluth	47	79.0	57	11.0	11.6	9.4	9,742	189	45	81	68	77	72	85	64
	Minneapolis-St. Paul	57	74.0	68	10.5	10.5	9.4	7,882	699	47	78	64	75	69	79	60
MS	Jackson	30	69.6	43	6.9	8.2	5.2	2,368	2,290	43	89	64	85	69	92	66
MO	Kansas City	23	67.1	34	10.6	11.1	9.2	5,249	1,325	34	80	66	76	68	83	66
	St. Louis	47	72.4	57	9.6	10.6	8.0	4,757	1,561	46	81	64	80	69	82	61
MT	Great Falls	57	78.4	65	12.5	14.8	10.0	7,675	326	45	68	45	66	61	67	30
NE	Omaha	49	69.6	70	10.5	10.9	8.8	6,312	1,095	42	81	65	78	69	83	64
NV	Reno	53	56.7	64	6.6	5.6	7.2	5,601	493	43	68	31	79	50	58	18
NH	Concord	54	75.3	64	6.7	7.2	5.7	7,485	442	41	81	53	76	58	83	51
NJ	Atlantic City	37	74.2	48	9.8	10.7	8.3	5,113	935	42	81	56	78	58	82	57
NM	Albuquerque	56	54.2	67	8.9	8.0	8.9	4,281	1,290	46	58	29	67	38	58	27
NY	Albany	57	81.1	68	8.9	9.8	7.5	6,861	544	41	80	58	77	63	80	55
	Buffalo	52	85.2	67	11.8	13.9	10.2	6,693	548	46	80	63	79	72	78	55
	New York [2]	42	70.8	69	9.3	10.6	7.6	4,744	1,160	72	72	56	68	59	75	55
NC	Charlotte	49	70.2	57	7.4	7.8	6.6	3,208	1,644	46	82	53	77	55	86	56
	Raleigh	47	69.7	57	7.6	8.2	6.7	3,465	1,521	42	85	54	79	54	88	57
ND	Bismarck	56	74.5	67	10.2	10.0	9.2	8,809	471	47	80	62	76	71	83	55
OH	Cincinnati	44	77.8	59	9.0	10.4	7.2	5,200	1,053	44	82	60	79	68	85	57
	Cleveland	54	81.9	65	10.5	12.2	8.6	6,097	712	46	80	62	78	70	81	57
	Columbus	46	80.3	57	8.3	9.8	6.5	5,546	925	47	81	59	77	67	83	55
OK	Oklahoma City	44	61.9	58	12.2	12.5	10.9	3,663	1,907	41	79	61	77	63	79	57
OR	Portland	47	81.3	58	7.9	9.9	7.6	4,366	398	66	85	59	85	75	81	44
PA	Philadelphia	55	74.5	66	9.5	10.3	8.2	4,759	1,235	47	76	54	73	59	78	53
	Pittsburgh	43	83.8	54	9.0	10.4	7.3	5,829	726	46	80	58	77	66	83	54
RI	Providence	42	73.2	53	10.4	10.9	9.4	5,754	714	43	75	55	71	56	77	56
SC	Columbia	48	68.5	58	6.8	7.2	6.3	2,595	2,063	40	86	51	82	53	88	53
SD	Sioux Falls	50	71.2	58	11.0	10.9	9.8	7,746	757	43	82	66	78	71	83	61
TN	Memphis	43	67.7	58	8.8	10.0	7.5	3,033	2,190	67	80	60	77	65	83	61
	Nashville	54	72.0	65	8.0	9.1	6.5	3,658	1,656	41	82	63	78	67	87	63
TX	Dallas-Fort Worth	42	63.0	53	10.7	11.0	9.8	2,370	2,571	43	80	61	78	64	77	55
	El Paso	53	47.1	64	8.8	8.3	8.3	2,604	2,165	46	56	27	64	33	60	29
	Houston	26	75.3	37	7.6	8.1	6.6	1,525	2,893	37	89	67	84	69	91	65
UT	Salt Lake City	69	65.8	77	8.8	7.5	9.5	5,607	1,089	46	67	43	79	69	51	21
VT	Burlington	52	84.1	63	9.0	9.7	8.0	7,665	489	41	77	59	73	64	78	53
VA	Norfolk	47	71.0	58	10.5	11.4	8.9	3,342	1,630	58	78	58	74	59	81	59
	Richmond	50	72.7	58	7.7	8.1	6.9	3,878	1,466	72	83	53	79	56	84	56
WA	Seattle-Tacoma	51	84.2	58	8.8	9.5	8.1	4,797	173	47	84	62	82	74	82	49
	Spokane	48	76.4	59	8.9	8.7	8.6	6,820	394	47	78	52	86	79	64	27
WV	Charleston	47	82.2	59	5.8	6.9	4.8	5,427	1,064	59	84	57	78	63	90	59
WI	Milwaukee	55	75.3	66	11.5	12.6	9.7	7,096	616	46	79	67	76	70	81	65
WY	Cheyenne	60	71.0	49	12.9	15.1	10.4	7,289	280	47	65	44	57	50	69	37
PR	San Juan	40	80.0	51	8.3	8.3	9.6	–	5,426	51	79	65	82	64	79	67

– Represents zero.   [1] Percent of days that are either partly cloudy or cloudy.   [2] Airport data for sunshine.

Source: U.S. National Oceanic and Atmospheric Administration, *Comparative Climatic Data*, annual. See also <http://www.ncdc.noaa.gov/oa/climate/online/ccd/clpcdy.txt>; <http://www.ncdc.noaa.gov/oa/climate/online/ccd/wndspd.txt>; <http://www.ncdc.noaa.gov/oa/climate/online/ccd/nrmhdd.txt>; <http://www.ncdc.noaa.gov/oa/climate/online/ccd/nrmcdd.txt>; and <http://www.ncdc.noaa.gov/oa/climate/online/ccd/relhum.txt>.

Section 7
Elections

This section relates primarily to presidential, congressional, and gubernatorial elections. Also presented are summary tables on congressional legislation; state legislatures; Black, Hispanic, and female officeholders; population of voting age; voter participation; and campaign finances.

Official statistics on federal elections, collected by the Clerk of the House, are published biennially in *Statistics of the Presidential and Congressional Election* and *Statistics of the Congressional Election.* Federal and state elections data appear also in *America Votes,* a biennial volume published by CQ Press (a division of Congressional Quarterly, Inc.), Washington, DC. Federal elections data also appear in the U.S. Congress, *Congressional Directory,* and in official state documents. Data on reported registration and voting for social and economic groups are obtained by the U.S. Census Bureau as part of the Current Population Survey (CPS) and are published in Current Population Reports, Series P20 (see text, Section 1).

Almost all federal, state, and local governmental units in the United States conduct elections for political offices and other purposes. The conduct of elections is regulated by state laws or, in some cities and counties, by local charter. An exception is that the U.S. Constitution prescribes the basis of representation in Congress and the manner of electing the president and grants to Congress the right to regulate the times, places, and manner of electing federal officers. Amendments to the Constitution have prescribed national criteria for voting eligibility. The 15th Amendment, adopted in 1870, gave all citizens the right to vote regardless of race, color, or previous condition of servitude. The 19th Amendment, adopted in 1919, further extended the right to vote to all citizens regardless of sex. The payment of poll taxes as a prerequisite to voting in federal elections was banned by the 24th Amendment in

1964. In 1971, as a result of the 26th Amendment, eligibility to vote in national elections was extended to all citizens, 18 years old and over.

Presidential election—The Constitution specifies how the president and vice president are selected. Each state elects, by popular vote, a group of electors equal in number to its total of members of Congress. The 23d Amendment, adopted in 1961, grants the District of Columbia three presidential electors, a number equal to that of the least populous state. Subsequent to the election, the electors meet in their respective states to vote for president and vice president. Usually, each elector votes for the candidate receiving the most popular votes in his or her state. A majority vote of all electors is necessary to elect the president and vice president. If no candidate receives a majority, the House of Representatives, with each state having one vote, is empowered to elect the president and vice president, again, with a majority of votes required.

The 22nd Amendment to the Constitution, adopted in 1951, limits presidential tenure to two elective terms of 4 years each or to one elective term for any person who, upon succession to the presidency, has held the office or acted as President for more than 2 years.

Congressional election—The Constitution provides that representatives be apportioned among the states according to their population, that a census of population be taken every 10 years as a basis for apportionment, and that each state have at least one representative. At the time of each apportionment, Congress decides what the total number of representatives will be. Since 1912, the total has been 435, except during 1960 to 1962 when it increased to 437, adding one representative each for Alaska and Hawaii. The total reverted to 435 after

U.S. Census Bureau, Statistical Abstract of the United States: 2010

reapportionment following the 1960 census. Members are elected for 2-year terms, all terms covering the same period. The District of Columbia, American Samoa, Guam, and the Virgin Islands each elect one nonvoting delegate, and Puerto Rico elects a nonvoting resident commissioner.

The Senate is composed of 100 members, two from each state, who are elected to serve for a term of 6 years. One-third of the Senate is elected every 2 years. Senators were originally chosen by the state legislatures. The 17th Amendment to the Constitution, adopted in 1913, prescribed that senators be elected by popular vote.

Voter eligibility and participation— The Census Bureau publishes estimates of the population of voting age and the percent casting votes in each state for presidential and congressional election years. These voting-age estimates include a number of persons who meet the age requirement but are not eligible to vote, (e.g. aliens and some institutionalized persons). In addition, since 1964, voter participation and voter characteristics data have been collected during November of election years as part of the CPS. These survey data include noncitizens in the voting age population estimates, but exclude members of the Armed Forces and the institutional population.

Statistical reliability—For a discussion of statistical collection and estimation, sampling procedures, and measures of statistical reliability applicable to Census Bureau data, see Appendix III.

Figure 7.1
Vote Cast for President by Major Political Party: 2000 to 2008

[1]Candidates with 1 million or more votes: 2000—Green, Ralph Nader.

Source: Chart prepared by U.S. Census Bureau. For data, see Tables 385 and 386.

Table 385. **Vote Cast for President by Major Political Party: 1952 to 2008**

[In thousands (61,552 represents 61,552,000), except percent and electoral vote. Prior to 1960, excludes Alaska and Hawaii; prior to 1964, excludes DC. Vote cast for major party candidates includes the votes of minor parties cast for those candidates]

Year	Candidates for President		Vote cast for President						
	Democratic	Republican	Total popular vote [1] (1,000)	Democratic			Republican		
				Popular vote		Electoral vote	Popular vote		Electoral vote
				Number (1,000)	Per-cent		Number (1,000)	Per-cent	
1952....	Stevenson	Eisenhower ...	61,552	27,315	44.4	89	33,779	54.9	442
1956....	Stevenson	Eisenhower ...	62,027	26,739	43.1	73	35,581	57.4	457
1960....	Kennedy	Nixon	68,836	34,227	49.7	303	34,108	49.5	219
1964....	Johnson	Goldwater	70,098	42,825	61.1	486	27,147	38.7	52
1968....	Humphrey	Nixon	73,027	30,989	42.4	191	31,710	43.4	301
1972....	McGovern	Nixon	77,625	28,902	37.2	17	46,740	60.2	520
1976....	Carter.......	Ford	81,603	40,826	50.0	297	39,148	48.0	240
1980....	Carter.......	Reagan......	86,497	35,481	41.0	49	43,643	50.5	489
1984....	Mondale	Reagan......	92,655	37,450	40.4	13	54,167	58.5	525
1988....	Dukakis	Bush........	91,587	41,717	45.5	111	48,643	53.1	426
1992....	Clinton	Bush........	104,600	44,858	42.9	370	38,799	37.1	168
1996....	Clinton	Dole	96,390	47,402	49.2	379	39,198	40.7	159
2000....	Gore........	Bush........	105,594	50,996	48.3	266	50,465	47.8	271
2004....	Kerry........	Bush........	122,349	58,895	48.1	251	61,873	50.6	286
2008....	Obama	McCain	131,407	69,498	52.9	365	59,948	45.6	173

[1] Include votes for minor party candidates, independents, unpledged electors, and scattered write-in votes.

Source: U.S. House of Representatives, Office of the Clerk, *Statistics of the Presidential and Congressional Election*, biennial (published 10 July 2009). See also <http://clerk.house.gov/member_info/election.html>.

Table 386. **Vote Cast for Leading Minority Party Candidates for President: 1952 to 2008**

[In thousands (135 represents 135,000). See headnote, Table 385. Data do not include write-ins, scatterings, or votes for candidates who ran on party tickets not shown]

Year	Candidate	Party	Popular vote (1,000)	Candidate	Party	Popular vote (1,000)
1952 ..	Vincent Hallinan....	Progressive	135	Stuart Hamblen	Prohibition.........	73
1956 [1] .	T. Coleman Andrews.	States' Rights.......	91	Eric Hass	Socialist Labor......	41
1960 ..	Eric Hass	Socialist Labor......	46	Rutherford Decker ..	Prohibition.........	46
1964 ...	Eric Hass	Socialist Labor	43	Clifton DeBerry	Socialist Workers	22
1968 ..	George Wallace....	American Independent.	9,446	Henning Blomen ...	Socialist Labor......	52
1972 [1] .	John Schmitz......	American..........	993	Benjamin Spock....	People's	9
1976 ..	Eugene McCarthy ..	Independent	680	Roger McBride.....	Libertarian.........	172
1980 ..	John Anderson	Independent	5,251	Ed Clark..........	Libertarian.........	920
1984 ..	David Bergland	Libertarian.........	227	Lyndon H. LaRouche.	Independent	79
1988 ..	Ron Paul	Libertarian.........	410	Lenora B. Fulani ...	New Alliance	129
1992 ..	H. Ross Perot	Independent	19,722	Andre Marrou	Libertarian.........	281
1996 ..	H. Ross Perot	Reform	7,137	Ralph Nader	Green............	527
2000 ..	Ralph Nader	Green............	2,530	Pat Buchanan	Reform	324
2004 ..	Ralph Nader	Independent	156	Michael Badnarik ...	Libertarian.........	369
2008 ..	Ralph Nader	Independent	739	Bob Barr..........	Libertarian.........	515

[1] Data include write-ins, scatterings, and/or votes for candidates who ran on party tickets not shown.

Source: U.S. House of Representatives, Office of the Clerk, *Statistics of the Presidential and Congressional Election*, biennial (published 10 July 2009). See also <http://clerk.house.gov/member_info/election.html>.

Table 387. **Democratic and Republican Percentages of Two-Party Presidential Vote by Selected Characteristics of Voters: 2004 and 2008**

[In percent. Covers citizens of voting age living in private housing units in the contiguous United States. Percentages for Democratic Presidential vote are computed by subtracting the percentage Republican vote from 100 percent; third-party or independent votes are not included as valid data. Data are from the National Election Studies and are based on a sample and subject to sampling variability; for details, see source]

Characteristic	2004		2008		Characteristic	2004		2008	
	Demo-cratic	Repub-lican	Demo-cratic	Repub-lican		Demo-cratic	Repub-lican	Demo-cratic	Repub-lican
Total [1]......	50	50	55	45	Black	90	10	99	1
Year of birth:					Education:				
1975 or later....	66	34	65	35	Less than high				
1959 to 1974....	45	55	56	44	school	69	31	72	28
1943 to 1958 ...	44	56	54	46	High school				
1927 to 1942 ...	51	49	41	59	diploma/				
1911 to 1926 ...	52	48	52	48	equivalent	46	54	57	43
1895 to 1910 ...	–	–	–	–	Some college,				
Sex:					no degree	47	53	53	47
Male	46	54	52	48	College	50	50	51	49
Female	53	47	57	43	Union household ..	64	36	60	40
Race:					Nonunion house-				
White	42	58	44	56	hold	46	54	54	46

– Represents zero.   [1] Includes other characteristics, not shown separately.

Source: American National Election Studies; <http://www.electionstudies.org/>.

Elections   239

Table 388. **Electoral Vote Cast for President by Major Political Party—States: 1968 to 2008**

[D = Democratic, R = Republican. For composition of regions, see map, inside front cover]

State	1968 [1]	1972 [2]	1976 [3]	1980	1984	1988 [4]	1992	1996	2000 [5]	2004 [6]	2008
Democratic ...	191	17	297	49	13	111	370	379	266	251	365
Republican ...	301	520	240	489	525	426	168	159	271	286	173
Northeast:											
Democratic	102	14	86	4	–	53	106	106	102	101	101
Republican	24	108	36	118	113	60	–	–	4	–	–
Midwest:											
Democratic	31	–	58	10	10	29	100	100	68	57	97
Republican	118	145	87	135	127	108	29	29	61	66	27
South:											
Democratic	45	3	149	31	3	8	68	80	15	16	71
Republican	77	165	20	138	174	168	116	104	168	173	118
West:											
Democratic	13	–	4	4	–	21	96	93	81	77	96
Republican	82	102	97	98	111	90	23	26	38	47	28
AL.............	([1])	R-9	D-9	R-9	R-9	R-9	R-9	R-9	R-9	R-9	R-9
AK.............	R-3	R-3	R-3	R-3	R-3	R-3	R-3	R-3	R-3	R-3	R-3
AZ.............	R-5	R-6	R-6	R-6	R-7	R-7	R-8	D-8	R-8	R-10	R-10
AR.............	([1])	R-6	D-6	R-6	R-6	R-6	D-6	D-6	R-6	R-6	R-6
CA.............	R-40	R-45	R-45	R-45	R-47	R-47	D-54	D-54	D-54	D-55	D-55
CO.............	R-6	R-7	R-7	R-7	R-8	R-8	R-8	R-8	R-8	R-9	D-9
CT.............	D-8	R-8	R-8	R-8	R-8	R-8	D-8	D-8	D-8	D-7	D-7
DE.............	R-3	R-3	D-3	R-3	R-3	R-3	D-3	D-3	D-3	D-3	D-3
DC.............	D-3	D-3	D-3	D-3	D-3	D-3	D-3	D-3	[5]D-2	D-3	D-3
FL.............	R-14	R-17	D-17	R-17	R-21	R-21	R-25	D-25	R-25	R-27	D-27
GA	([1])	R-12	D-12	D-12	R-12	R-12	D-13	R-13	R-13	R-15	R-15
HI	D-4	R-4	D-4	D-4	D-4	D-4	D-4	D-4	D-4	D-4	D-4
ID	R-4	R-4	R-4	R-4	R-4	R-4	R-4	R-4	R-4	R-4	R-4
IL	R-26	R-26	R-26	R-26	R-24	R-24	D-22	D-22	D-22	D-21	D-21
IN	R-13	R-13	R-13	R-13	R-12	R-12	R-12	R-12	R-12	R-11	D-11
IA	R-9	R-8	R-8	R-8	R-8	D-8	D-7	D-7	D-7	R-7	D-7
KS	R-7	R-7	R-7	R-7	R-7	R-7	R-6	R-6	R-6	R-6	R-6
KY.............	R-9	R-9	D-9	R-9	R-9	R-9	D-8	D-8	R-8	R-8	R-8
LA	([1])	R-10	D-10	R-10	R-10	R-10	D-9	D-9	R-9	R-9	R-9
ME	D-4	R-4	R-4	R-4	R-4	R-4	D-4	D-4	D-4	D-4	D-4
MD	D-10	R-10	D-10	D-10	R-10	R-10	D-10	D-10	D-10	D-10	D-10
MA	D-14	D-14	D-14	R-14	R-13	D-13	D-12	D-12	D-12	D-12	D-12
MI	D-21	R-21	R-21	R-21	R-20	D-20	D-18	D-18	D-18	D-17	D-17
MN	D-10	R-10	D-10	D-10	D-10	D-10	D-10	D-10	D-10	[6]D-9	D-10
MS	([1])	R-7	D-7	R-7	R-7	R-7	R-7	R-7	R-7	R-6	R-6
MO	R-12	R-12	D-12	R-12	R-11	R-11	D-11	D-11	R-11	R-11	R-11
MT	R-4	R-4	R-4	R-4	R-4	R-4	D-3	R-3	R-3	R-3	R-3
NE.............	R-5	R-5	R-5	R-5	R-5	R-5	R-5	R-5	R-5	R-5	[7]R-4
NV.............	R-3	R-3	R-3	R-3	R-4	R-4	D-4	D-4	R-4	R-5	D-5
NH	R-4	R-4	R-4	R-4	R-4	R-4	D-4	D-4	R-4	D-4	D-4
NJ.............	R-17	R-17	R-17	R-17	R-16	R-16	D-15	D-15	D-15	D-15	D-15
NM	R-4	R-4	R-4	R-4	R-5	R-5	D-5	D-5	D-5	R-5	D-5
NY.............	D-43	R-41	D-41	R-41	R-36	D-36	D-33	D-33	D-33	D-31	D-31
NC.............	[1]R-12	R-13	D-13	R-13	R-13	R-13	R-14	R-14	R-14	R-15	D-15
ND	R-4	R-3	R-3	R-3	R-3	R-3	R-3	R-3	R-3	R-3	R-3
OH	R-26	R-25	D-25	R-25	R-23	R-23	D-21	D-21	R-21	R-20	D-20
OK	R-8	R-8	R-8	R-8	R-8	R-8	R-8	R-8	R-8	R-7	R-7
OR	R-6	R-6	R-6	R-6	R-7	D-7	D-7	D-7	D-7	D-7	D-7
PA.............	D-29	R-27	D-27	R-27	R-25	R-25	D-23	D-23	D-23	D-21	D-21
RI	D-4	R-4	D-4	D-4	R-4	D-4	D-4	D-4	D-4	D-4	D-4
SC.............	R-8	R-8	D-8	R-8	R-8	R-8	R-8	R-8	R-8	R-8	R-8
SD.............	R-4	R-4	R-4	R-4	R-3	R-3	R-3	R-3	R-3	R-3	R-3
TN.............	R-11	R-10	D-10	R-10	R-11	R-11	D-11	D-11	R-11	R-11	R-11
TX.............	D-25	R-26	D-26	R-26	R-29	R-29	R-32	R-32	R-32	R-34	R-34
UT.............	R-4	R-4	R-4	R-4	R-5	R-5	R-5	R-5	R-5	R-5	R-5
VT.............	R-3	R-3	R-3	R-3	R-3	R-3	D-3	D-3	D-3	D-3	D-3
VA.............	R-12	[2]R-11	R-12	R-12	R-12	R-12	R-13	R-13	R-13	R-13	D-13
WA.............	D-9	R-9	[3]R-8	R-9	R-10	D-10	D-11	D-11	D-11	D-11	D-11
WV.............	D-7	R-6	D-6	D-6	R-6	[4]D-5	D-5	D-5	R-5	R-5	R-5
WI.............	R-12	R-11	D-11	R-11	R-11	D-11	D-11	D-11	D-11	D-10	D-10
WY.............	R-3	R-3	R-3	R-3	R-3	R-3	R-3	R-3	R-3	R-3	R-3

– Represents zero. [1] Excludes 46 electoral votes cast for American Independent George C. Wallace as follows: AL 10, AR 6, GA 12, LA 10, MS 7, and NC 1. [2] Excludes one electoral vote cast for Libertarian John Hospers in Virginia. [3] Excludes one electoral vote cast for Ronald Reagan in Washington. [4] Excludes one electoral vote cast for Lloyd Bentsen for President in West Virginia. [5] Excludes one electoral vote left blank by a Democratic elector in the District of Columbia. [6] Excludes one electoral vote cast for Democratic vice presidential nominee John Edwards in Minnesota. [7] Excludes one electoral vote for Barack Obama in Nebraska.

Source: U.S. House of Representatives, Office of the Clerk, *Statistics of the Presidential and Congressional Election*, biennial (published 10 July 2009). See also <http://clerk.house.gov/member_info/election.html>.

Table 389. **Popular Vote Cast for President by Political Party—States:**
2004 and 2008

[In thousands (122,349 represents 122,349,000), except percent]

State	2004					2008				
				Percent of total vote					Percent of total vote	
	Total [1]	Democratic party	Republican party	Democratic party	Republican party	Total [1]	Democratic party	Republican party	Democratic party	Republican party
United States. .	**122,349**	**58,895**	**61,873**	**48.1**	**50.6**	**131,407**	**69,498**	**59,948**	**52.9**	**45.6**
Alabama.	1,883	694	1,176	36.8	62.5	2,100	813	1,267	38.7	60.3
Alaska	313	111	191	35.5	61.1	326	124	194	37.9	59.4
Arizona.	2,013	894	1,104	44.4	54.9	2,293	1,035	1,230	45.1	53.6
Arkansas	1,055	470	573	44.5	54.3	1,087	422	638	38.9	58.7
California	12,421	6,745	5,510	54.3	44.4	13,562	8,274	5,012	61.0	37.0
Colorado.	2,130	1,002	1,101	47.0	51.7	2,401	1,289	1,074	53.7	44.7
Connecticut.	1,579	857	694	54.3	43.9	1,647	998	629	60.6	38.2
Delaware	375	200	172	53.3	45.8	412	255	152	61.9	36.9
District of Columbia .	228	203	21	89.2	9.3	266	246	17	92.5	6.5
Florida	7,610	3,584	3,965	47.1	52.1	8,391	4,282	4,046	51.0	48.2
Georgia	3,302	1,366	1,914	41.4	58.0	3,924	1,844	2,049	47.0	52.2
Hawaii	429	232	194	54.0	45.3	456	326	121	71.5	26.4
Idaho	598	181	409	30.3	68.4	655	236	403	36.1	61.5
Illinois	5,274	2,892	2,346	54.8	44.5	5,522	3,419	2,031	61.9	36.8
Indiana.	2,468	969	1,479	39.3	59.9	2,751	1,374	1,346	49.9	48.9
Iowa	1,507	742	752	49.2	49.9	1,537	829	682	53.9	44.4
Kansas.	1,188	435	736	36.6	62.0	1,236	515	700	41.7	56.6
Kentucky	1,796	713	1,069	39.7	59.5	1,827	752	1,048	41.2	57.4
Louisiana	1,943	820	1,102	42.2	56.7	1,961	783	1,148	39.9	58.6
Maine.	741	397	330	53.6	44.6	731	422	295	57.7	40.4
Maryland	2,384	1,334	1,025	56.0	43.0	2,632	1,629	960	61.9	36.5
Massachusetts.	2,927	1,804	1,071	61.6	36.6	3,103	1,904	1,109	61.4	35.7
Michigan.	4,839	2,479	2,314	51.2	47.8	5,002	2,873	2,049	57.4	41.0
Minnesota.	2,828	1,445	1,347	51.1	47.6	2,910	1,573	1,275	54.1	43.8
Mississippi	1,140	458	673	40.2	59.0	1,290	555	725	43.0	56.2
Missouri	2,731	1,259	1,456	46.1	53.3	2,925	1,442	1,446	49.3	49.4
Montana.	450	174	266	38.6	59.1	490	232	243	47.3	49.5
Nebraska	778	254	513	32.7	65.9	801	333	453	41.6	56.5
Nevada	830	397	419	47.9	50.5	968	534	413	55.1	42.7
New Hampshire	678	341	331	50.2	48.8	711	385	317	54.1	44.5
New Jersey.	3,612	1,911	1,670	52.9	46.2	3,868	2,215	1,613	57.3	41.7
New Mexico	756	371	377	49.0	49.8	830	472	347	56.9	41.8
New York	7,448	4,181	2,807	56.1	37.7	7,722	4,805	2,753	62.2	35.6
North Carolina	3,501	1,526	1,961	43.6	56.0	4,298	2,143	2,128	49.8	49.5
North Dakota.	313	111	197	35.5	62.9	317	141	169	44.6	53.3
Ohio	5,628	2,741	2,860	48.7	50.8	5,708	2,940	2,678	51.5	46.9
Oklahoma.	1,464	504	960	34.4	65.6	1,463	502	960	34.4	65.6
Oregon.	1,837	943	867	51.3	47.2	1,828	1,037	738	56.7	40.4
Pennsylvania	5,770	2,938	2,794	50.9	48.4	6,013	3,276	2,656	54.5	44.2
Rhode Island.	437	260	169	59.4	38.7	472	297	165	62.9	35.1
South Carolina.	1,618	662	938	40.9	58.0	1,921	862	1,035	44.9	53.9
South Dakota	388	149	233	38.4	59.9	382	171	203	44.7	53.2
Tennessee	2,437	1,036	1,384	42.5	56.8	2,600	1,087	1,479	41.8	56.9
Texas.	7,411	2,833	4,527	38.2	61.1	8,078	3,529	4,479	43.7	55.5
Utah	928	241	664	26.0	71.5	952	328	596	34.4	62.6
Vermont	312	184	121	58.9	38.8	325	219	99	67.5	30.4
Virginia.	3,195	1,455	1,717	45.5	53.7	3,723	1,960	1,725	52.6	46.3
Washington.	2,859	1,510	1,305	52.8	45.6	3,037	1,751	1,229	57.7	40.5
West Virginia.	756	327	424	43.2	56.1	713	304	397	42.6	55.7
Wisconsin	2,997	1,490	1,478	49.7	49.3	2,983	1,677	1,262	56.2	42.3
Wyoming	244	71	168	29.0	68.7	255	83	165	32.5	64.7

[1] Includes other parties.

Source: U.S. House of Representatives, Office of the Clerk, *Statistics of the Presidential and Congressional Election*, biennial (published 10 July 2009). See also <http://clerk.house.gov/member_info/election.html>.

Table 390. **Vote Cast for U.S. Senators, 2006 and 2008, and Incumbent Senators, 2009—States**

[**1,527** represents 1,527,000. D = Democrat, R = Republican, I = Independent]

State	2006 Total (1,000) [2]	2006 Percent for leading party	2008 Total (1,000) [2]	2008 Percent for leading party	Incumbent senators and year term expires [1] Name, party, and year	Incumbent senators and year term expires [1] Name, party, and year
Alabama	(X)	(X)	2,060	R-63.4	Jeffrey Sessions (R) 2015	Richard Shelby (R) 2011
Alaska	(X)	(X)	318	D-47.8	Lisa Murkowski (R) 2011	Mark Begich (D) 2015
Arizona	1,527	R-53.3	(X)	(X)	Jon Kyl (R) 2013	John McCain (R) 2011
Arkansas	(X)	(X)	1,012	D-79.5	Blanche Lincoln (D) 2011	Mark Pryor (D) 2015
California	8,541	D-59.4	(X)	(X)	Barbara Boxer (D) 2011	Dianne Feinstein (D) 2013
Colorado	(X)	(X)	2,332	D-52.8	Mark Udall (D) 2015	Michael F. Bennett (D) 2011
Connecticut	1,135	D-39.7	(X)	(X)	Christopher Dodd (D) 2011	Joseph Lieberman (I) 2013
Delaware	243	D-70.2	398	D-64.7	Edward E. Kaufman (D) 2015	Thomas Carper (D) 2013
Florida	4,794	D-60.3	(X)	(X)	Mel Martinez (R) 2011	Bill Nelson (D) 2013
Georgia	(X)	(X)	2,266	R-54.2	Saxby Chambliss (R) 2015	Johnny Isakson (R) 2011
Hawaii	343	D-61.3	(X)	(X)	Daniel Akaka (D) 2013	Daniel Inouye (D) 2011
Idaho	(X)	(X)	645	R-57.7	James E. Risch (R) 2015	Michael Crapo (R) 2011
Illinois	(X)	(X)	5,330	D-67.8	Richard Durbin (D) 2015	Roland Burris (D) 2011
Indiana	1,341	R-87.4	(X)	(X)	Evan Bayh (D) 2011	Richard Lugar (R) 2013
Iowa	(X)	(X)	1,503	D-62.7	Chuck Grassley (R) 2011	Tom Harkin (D) 2015
Kansas	(X)	(X)	1,211	R-60.1	Sam Brownback (R) 2011	Pat Roberts (R) 2015
Kentucky	(X)	(X)	1,801	R-53.0	Jim Bunning (R) 2011	Mitch McConnell (R) 2015
Louisiana [3]	(X)	(X)	1,897	D-52.1	Mary Landrieu (D) 2015	David Vitter (R) 2011
Maine	545	R-74.4	724	R-61.3	Susan Collins (R) 2015	Olympia Snowe (R) 2013
Maryland	1,781	D-54.2	(X)	(X)	Barbara Mikulski (D) 2011	Benjamin Cardin (D) 2013
Massachusetts . . .	2,244	D-66.9	3,103	D-63.6	Edward Kennedy (D) 2013	John Kerry (D) 2015
Michigan	3,780	D-56.9	4,849	D-62.7	Carl Levin (D) 2015	Debbie Stabenow (D) 2013
Minnesota	2,203	D-58.1	2,888	D-42.0	Al Franken (D) 2015	Amy Klobuchar (D) 2013
Mississippi	611	R-63.6	1,247	R-61.4	Thad Cochran (R) 2015	Roger Wicker (R) 2013
Missouri	2,128	D-49.6	(X)	(X)	Christopher Bond (R) 2011	Claire McCaskill (D) 2013
Montana	407	D-49.2	478	D-72.9	Max Baucus (D) 2015	John Tester (D) 2013
Nebraska	592	D-63.9	793	R-57.5	Mike Johanns (R) 2015	Ben Nelson (D) 2013
Nevada	583	R-55.4	(X)	(X)	John Ensign (R) 2013	Harry Reid (D) 2011
New Hampshire . . .	(X)	(X)	695	D-51.6	Judd Gregg (R) 2011	Jeanne Shaheen (D) 2015
New Jersey	102	D-57.2	3,482	D-56.0	Robert Menendez (D) 2013	Frank Lautenberg (D) 2015
New Mexico	559	D-70.6	824	D-61.3	Jeff Bingaman (D) 2013	Tom Udall (D) 2015
New York	4,701	D-57.4	(X)	(X)	Kirsten Gillibrand (D) 2013	Charles Schumer (D) 2011
North Carolina	(X)	(X)	4,272	D-52.7	Richard Burr (R) 2011	Kay R. Hagan (D) 2015
North Dakota	218	D-68.8	(X)	(X)	Kent Conrad (D) 2013	Byron Dorgan (D) 2011
Ohio	4,019	D-56.2	(X)	(X)	Sherrod Brown (D) 2013	George Voinovich (R) 2011
Oklahoma	(X)	(X)	1,347	R-56.7	Tom Coburn (R) 2011	James Inhofe (R) 2015
Oregon	(X)	(X)	1,768	D-48.9	Jeff Merkley (D) 2015	Ron Wyden (D) 2011
Pennsylvania	4,081	D-58.6	(X)	(X)	Robert Casey Jr. (D) 2013	Arlen Specter (D) 2011
Rhode Island	385	D-53.5	439	D-73.1	Sheldon Whitehouse (D) 2013	Jack Reed (D) 2015
South Carolina . . .	(X)	(X)	1,871	R-57.5	Jim DeMint (R) 2011	Lindsey Graham (R) 2015
South Dakota	(X)	(X)	381	D-62.5	Tim Johnson (D) 2015	John Thune (R) 2011
Tennessee	1,834	R-50.7	2,425	R-65.1	Lamar Alexander (R) 2015	Bob Corker (R) 2013
Texas	4,315	R-61.7	7,912	R-54.8	John Cornyn (R) 2015	Kay Hutchinson (R) 2013
Utah	571	R-62.4	(X)	(X)	Robert Bennett (R) 2011	Orrin Hatch (R) 2013
Vermont	262	R-32.4	(X)	(X)	Bernard Sanders (I) 2013	Patrick Leahy (D) 2011
Virginia	2,370	D-49.6	3,643	D-65.0	Jim Webb (D) 2013	Mark Warner (D) 2015
Washington	2,084	D-56.9	(X)	(X)	Maria Cantwell (D) 2013	Patty Murray (D) 2011
West Virginia	207	D-77.0	702	D-63.7	Robert Byrd (D) 2013	John Rockefeller (D) 2015
Wisconsin	2,138	D-67.3	(X)	(X)	Russell Feingold (D) 2011	Herb Kohl (D) 2013
Wyoming	196	R-68.9	250	D-75.6	Michael Enzi (R) 2015	John Barrasso (R) 2013

X Not applicable.   [1] As of 3 August 2009.   [2] Includes vote cast for minor parties.   [3] Louisiana holds an open-primary election with candidates from all parties running on the same ballot. Any candidate who receives a majority is elected.

Source: U.S. House of Representatives, Office of the Clerk, *Statistics of the Presidential and Congressional Election*, biennial (published 10 July 2009). See also <http://clerk.house.gov/member_info/electionInfo/index.html>.

Table 391. **Vote Cast for U.S. Representatives by Major Political Party—States: 2004 to 2008**

[In thousands (113,192 represents 113,192,000), except percent. R = Republican, D = Democrat, and I = Independent. In each state, totals represent the sum of votes cast in each Congressional District or votes cast for Representative-at-Large in states where only one member is elected. In all years there are numerous districts within the state where either the Republican or Democratic party had no candidate. In some states the Republican and Democratic vote includes votes cast for the party candidate by endorsing parties]

State	2004				2006				2008			
	Total [1]	Demo-cratic	Repub-lican	Percent for leading party	Total [1]	Demo-cratic	Repub-lican	Percent for leading party	Total [1]	Demo-cratic	Repub-lican	Percent for leading party
U.S.	113,192	52,745	55,713	R-49.2	80,976	42,082	35,675	D-52.0	122,586	64,888	51,953	D-52.9
AL	1,793	708	1,080	R-60.2	1,140	502	628	R-55.0	1,855	718	1,121	R-60.4
AK	300	67	213	R-71.1	235	94	133	R-56.6	317	143	159	R-50.1
AZ [2]	1,871	598	1,128	R-60.3	1,493	627	771	R-51.7	2,156	1,055	1,022	D-49.0
AR [2]	791	426	358	D-53.9	763	457	306	D-59.8	787	415	215	D-52.8
CA	11,624	6,224	5,031	D-53.5	8,296	4,720	3,314	D-56.9	12,322	7,381	4,516	D-59.9
CO	2,039	995	992	D-48.8	1,539	833	624	D-54.1	2,284	1,260	991	D-55.2
CT	1,429	786	630	D-55.0	1,075	649	420	D-60.4	1,527	909	505	D-59.5
DE [2]	356	106	246	R-69.1	252	98	144	R-57.2	385	146	235	R-61.1
FL [2]	5,627	2,212	3,319	R-59.0	3,852	1,600	2,183	R-56.7	7,421	3,435	3,792	R-51.1
GA	2,961	1,141	1,820	R-61.5	2,070	932	1,138	R-55.0	3,655	1,858	1,797	D-50.8
HI	417	262	148	D-62.9	338	220	118	D-65.0	456	320	83	D-70.2
ID	572	171	401	R-70.1	445	177	248	R-55.7	638	260	377	R-59.2
IL	4,989	2,675	2,272	D-53.6	3,453	1,986	1,423	D-57.5	5,248	3,176	1,961	D-60.5
IN	2,416	999	1,382	R-57.2	1,667	812	832	R-49.9	2,677	1,389	1,241	D-51.9
IA	1,458	625	823	R-56.4	1,033	493	522	R-50.6	1,482	759	698	D-51.3
KS	1,156	387	724	R-62.6	845	369	459	R-54.3	1,208	470	690	R-57.1
KY [2]	1,635	602	1,017	R-62.2	1,254	602	612	R-48.8	1,750	761	955	R-54.6
LA [2]	1,259	478	780	R-62.0	916	309	580	R-63.0	1,046	398	594	R-56.8
ME	710	418	283	D-58.9	536	351	163	D-65.4	710	432	278	D-60.8
MD	2,254	1,311	896	D-58.2	1,701	1,099	547	D-64.6	2,498	1,677	763	D-67.2
MA	2,927	2,060	435	D-70.4	2,244	1,632	199	D-72.7	3,103	2,246	318	D-72.4
MI	4,631	2,242	2,289	R-49.4	3,646	1,923	1,625	D-52.7	4,811	2,517	2,114	D-52.3
MN	2,722	1,400	1,236	D-51.4	2,179	1,153	925	D-52.9	2,803	1,612	1,069	D-57.5
MS	1,116	335	659	R-59.0	601	260	304	R-50.7	1,265	732	527	D-57.9
MO	2,667	1,193	1,430	R-53.6	2,097	992	1,049	R-50.0	2,821	1,413	1,313	D-50.1
MT	444	146	286	R-64.4	406	159	239	R-58.9	481	156	308	R-64.1
NE	765	231	515	R-67.3	596	262	334	R-56.1	775	265	511	R-65.8
NV	791	334	421	R-53.2	575	288	260	D-50.1	908	457	384	D-50.4
NH	652	244	396	R-60.8	403	209	190	D-52.0	675	365	295	D-54.1
NJ........	3,285	1,721	1,515	D-52.4	2,137	1,208	903	D-56.5	3,438	1,912	1,462	D-55.6
NM	743	385	358	D-51.8	561	313	248	D-55.8	815	457	321	D-56.1
NY	7,448	3,457	2,209	D-46.4	4,687	2,538	1,160	D-54.1	7,722	4,006	1,800	D-51.9
NC	3,413	1,670	1,743	R-51.1	1,941	1,027	914	D-52.9	4,215	2,294	1,902	D-54.4
ND	311	185	126	D-59.6	218	143	70	D-65.7	314	195	119	D-62.0
OH	5,184	2,515	2,650	R-51.1	3,961	2,082	1,870	D-52.6	5,374	2,752	2,491	D-51.2
OK	1,375	389	875	R-63.7	905	373	518	R-57.2	1,337	504	803	R-60.0
OR	1,772	952	762	D-53.7	1,357	766	557	D-56.4	1,683	1,036	436	D-61.6
PA	5,151	2,478	2,565	R-49.8	4,013	2,229	1,732	D-55.5	5,788	3,209	2,521	D-55.4
RI........	402	279	113	D-69.5	373	265	42	D-71.0	438	304	119	D-69.3
SC	1,439	486	913	R-63.5	1,086	473	600	R-55.2	1,874	920	940	R-50.1
SD	389	208	179	D-53.4	334	230	98	D-69.1	379	256	123	D-67.6
TN	2,219	1,032	1,161	R-52.3	1,715	861	800	D-50.2	2,302	1,196	978	D-51.9
TX	6,959	2,714	4,013	R-57.7	4,141	1,831	2,094	R-50.6	7,529	2,979	4,204	R-55.8
UT	909	362	520	R-57.3	570	244	292	R-51.3	937	394	504	R-53.8
VT	305	22	74	I-67.5	263	140	117	D-53.2	298	248	(X)	D-83.2
VA	3,004	1,023	1,817	R-60.5	2,297	947	1,223	R-53.2	3,495	1,853	1,591	D-53.0
WA	2,730	1,609	1,095	D-58.9	2,054	1,244	798	D-60.6	2,914	1,725	1,189	D-59.2
WV	722	415	303	D-57.6	455	264	191	D-58.0	646	432	213	D-66.9
WI........	2,822	1,369	1,381	R-48.9	2,063	1,003	1,040	R-50.4	2,775	1,384	1,275	D-49.9
WY	239	100	132	R-55.2	196	92	93	R-47.6	250	107	131	R-52.6

X Not applicable.   [1] Includes votes cast for minor parties.   [2] State law does not require tabulation of votes for unopposed candidates.

Source: U.S. House of Representatives, Office of the Clerk, *Statistics of the Presidential and Congressional Election*, biennial (published 10 July 2009). See also <http://clerk.house.gov/member_info/electionInfo/index.html>.

Elections   243

Table 392. **Vote Cast for U.S. Representatives by Major Political Party— Congressional Districts: 2008**

[In some states the Democratic and Republican vote includes votes cast for the party candidate by endorsing parties]

State and district	Democratic candidate Name	Percent of total	Republican candidate Name	Percent of total
AL	(X).......	(X)	(X).......	(X)
1st...	(1).......	(1)	Bonner.....	98.27
2d ...	Bright.....	50.23	Love	49.61
3d ...	Segall	45.84	Rogers.....	54.03
4th...	Sparks.....	25.11	Aderholt....	74.76
5th...	Griffith	51.52	Parker.....	47.94
6th...	(1).......	(1)	Bachus.....	97.79
7th...	Davis......	98.63	(1).......	(1)
AK	Berkowitz ...	44.97	Young	50.14
AZ	(X).......	(X)	(X).......	(X)
1st...	Kirkpatrick...	55.88	Hay	39.43
2d ...	Thrasher....	37.16	Franks	59.44
3d ...	Lord......	42.07	Shadegg....	54.08
4th...	Pastor	72.11	Karg	21.25
5th...	Mitchell.....	53.16	Schweikert ..	43.57
6th...	Schneider...	34.55	Flake......	62.42
7th...	Grijalva....	63.26	Sweeney ...	32.79
8th...	Giffords	54.72	Bee	42.82
AR	(X).......	(X)	(X).......	(X)
1st...	Berry	(2)	(1).......	(1)
2d ...	Snyder.....	76.54	(1).......	(1)
3d ...	(1).......	(1)	Boozman ...	78.53
4th...	Ross	86.17	(1).......	(1)
CA	(X).......	(X)	(X).......	(X)
1st...	Thompson ..	68.10	Starkewolf...	23.36
2d ...	Morris	42.11	Herger	57.89
3d ...	Durston	43.93	Lungren	49.49
4th...	Brown	49.76	McClintock ..	50.24
5th...	Matsui	74.27	Smith......	20.80
6th...	Woolsey	71.69	Halliwell	24.06
7th...	Miller......	72.82	Petersen....	21.79
8th...	Pelosi......	71.87	Walsh	9.68
9th...	Lee	86.06	Hargrave ...	9.70
10th..	Tauscher ...	65.12	Gerber	31.13
11th..	McNerney...	55.27	Andal......	44.72
12th..	Speier	75.11	Conlon	18.46
13th..	Stark	76.43	Chui.......	23.57
14th..	Eshoo	69.77	Santana	22.22
15th..	Honda	71.66	Cordi	23.26
16th..	Lofgren	71.34	Winston	24.06
17th..	Farr.......	73.88	Taylor......	25.82
18th..	Cardoza	100.00	(1).......	(1)
19th..	(1).......	(1)	Radanovich..	98.43
20th..	Costa......	74.33	Lopez	25.67
21st..	Johnson	31.61	Nunes	68.39
22d ..	(1).......	(1)	McCarthy ...	100.00
23d ..	Capps	68.07	Kokkonen ...	31.93
24th..	Jorgensen...	41.85	Gallegly	58.15
25th..	Conaway ...	42.27	McKeon	57.73
26th..	Warner.....	40.44	Dreier......	52.64
27th..	Sherman ...	68.51	Singh......	24.83
28th..	Berman	99.89	(1).......	(1)
29th..	Schiff......	68.91	Hahn	26.74
30th..	Waxman	100.00	(1).......	(1)
31st..	Becerra	100.00	(1).......	(1)
32d ..	Solis	99.99	(1).......	(1)
33d ..	Watson.....	87.57	Crowley II ...	12.43
34th..	Roybal-Allard.	77.09	Balding.....	22.91
35th..	Waters	82.58	Hayes	13.24
36th..	Harman	68.64	Gibson.....	31.36
37th..	Richardson..	74.94	(1).......	(1)
38th..	Napolitano ..	81.73	(1).......	(1)
39th..	Sanchez....	69.67	Lenning	30.33
40th..	Avalos	37.45	Royce	62.55
41st..	Prince	38.35	Lewis......	61.65
42d ..	Chau	39.84	Miller......	60.16
43d ..	Baca	69.14	Roberts	30.86
44th..	Hedrick.....	48.81	Calvert.....	51.19
45th..	Bornstein ...	41.71	Mack	58.29
46th..	Cook	43.08	Rohrabacher.	52.52
47th..	Sanchez....	69.49	Avila	25.43
48th..	Young	40.67	Campbell ...	55.61
49th..	Hamilton....	37.45	Issa.......	58.30
50th..	Leibham	45.18	Bilbray.....	50.24
51st..	Filner......	72.75	Joy	24.21
52d ..	Lumpkin	38.95	Hunter	56.37
53d ..	Davis......	68.49	Crimmins	27.45
CO	(X).......	(X)	(X).......	(X)
1st...	DeGette	71.94	Lilly	23.78
2d ...	Polis	62.60	Starin......	33.86
3d ...	Salazar.....	61.61	Wolf.......	38.39
4th...	Markey.....	56.20	Musgrave ...	43.80
5th...	Bidlack.....	37.04	Lamborn....	60.03
6th...	Eng.......	39.33	Coffman	60.67
7th...	Perlmutter...	63.48	Lerew......	36.52
CT	(X).......	(X)	(X).......	(X)
1st...	Larson	65.81	Visconti	26.01
2d ...	Courtney ...	61.60	Sullivan	32.37
3d ...	DeLauro....	68.86	Itshaky.....	19.70
4th...	Himes	48.37	Shays	47.56
5th...	Murphy.....	53.25	Cappiello ...	38.96
DE	Hartley-Nagle.....	37.99	Castle	61.08
FL	(X).......	(X)	(X).......	(X)
1st...	Bryan......	29.82	Miller......	70.18
2d ...	Boyd	61.88	Mulligan	38.08
3d ...	Brown	(2)	(1).......	(1)
4th...	McGovern...	34.75	Crenshaw ...	65.25
5th...	Russell.....	38.85	Brown-Waite .	61.15
6th...	Cunha	39.11	Stearns	60.89
7th...	Armitage....	38.00	Mica	62.00
8th...	Grayson....	52.01	Keller......	47.99
9th...	Mitchell.....	36.27	Bilirakis	62.17
10th..	Hackworth...	39.32	Young	60.68
11th..	Castor	71.66	Adams, Jr. ..	28.34
12th..	Tudor......	42.54	Putnam	57.46
13th..	Jennings....	37.49	Buchanan ..	55.54
14th..	Neeld......	24.77	Mack	59.44
15th..	Blythe	41.99	Posey	53.10
16th..	Mahoney ...	39.91	Rooney	60.09
17th..	Meek......	(2)	(1).......	(1)
18th..	Taddeo.....	42.13	Ros-Lehtinen.	57.87
19th..	Wexler.....	66.16	Lynch......	27.24
20th..	Schultz.....	77.48	(1).......	(1)
21st..	Martinez....	42.10	Diaz-Balart ..	57.90
22d ..	Klein	54.68	West	45.32
23d ..	Hastings....	82.18	Thorpe, Jr. ..	17.80
24th..	Kosmas	57.20	Feeney.....	41.11
25th..	Garcia	46.95	Diaz-Balart ..	53.05
GA	(X).......	(X)	(X).......	(X)
1st...	Gillespie	33.47	Kingston....	66.53
2d ...	Bishop, Jr. ..	68.95	Ferrell	31.05
3d ...	Camp.......	34.30	Westmoreland......	65.69
4th...	Johnson, Jr. .	99.91	(1).......	(1)
5th...	Lewis......	99.95	(1).......	(1)
6th...	Jones......	31.52	Price	68.48
7th...	Heckman ...	37.97	Linder	62.03
8th...	Marshall	57.24	Goddard....	42.76
9th...	Scott	24.49	Deal.......	75.51
10th..	Saxon	39.27	Broun......	60.73
11th..	Gammon ...	31.81	Gingrey	68.19
12th..	Barrow.....	66.00	Stone......	34.00
13th..	Scott	69.04	Honeycutt ..	30.96
HI	(X).......	(X)	(X).......	(X)
1st...	Abercrombie .	70.60	Tataii	17.45
2d ...	Hirono	69.75	Evans	18.70
ID	(X).......	(X)	(X).......	(X)
1st...	Minnick.....	50.61	Sali	49.39
2d ...	Holmes.....	28.90	Simpson....	70.89

See footnotes at end of table.

244   Elections

Table 392. **Vote Cast for U.S. Representatives by Major PoliticalParty— Congressional Districts: 2008**—Con.

[See headnote, p. 244]

State and district	Democratic candidate Name	Percent of total	Republican candidate Name	Percent of total	State and district	Democratic candidate Name	Percent of total	Republican candidate Name	Percent of total
IL.....	(X)........	(X)	(X)......	(X)	5th...	Tsongas....	74.72	[1]......	[1]
1st...	Rush......	85.87	Members...	14.13	6th...	Tierney.....	66.79	Baker.....	28.00
2d...	Jackson, Jr...	89.41	Williams...	10.59				Cunning-	
3d...	Lipinski.....	73.28	Hawkins...	21.37	7th...	Markey.....	70.48	ham.....	22.57
			Cunning-		8th...	Capuano....	76.03	[1]......	[1]
4th...	Gutierrez....	80.60	ham.....	11.48	9th...	Lynch......	76.29	[1]	[1]
5th...	Emanuel....	73.94	Hanson....	22.04	10th...	Delahunt....	75.02	[1]......	[1]
6th...	Morgenthaler.	42.43	Roskam...	57.57	MI.....	(X)........	(X)	(X)......	(X)
7th...	Davis......	85.02	Miller.....	14.98	1st...	Stupak.....	65.04	Casperson..	32.74
8th...	Bean......	60.72	Greenberg..	39.28	2d...	Johnson.....	34.81	Hoekstra...	62.36
9th...	Schakowsky..	74.66	Younan....	21.99	3d...	Sanchez....	35.37	Ehlers.....	61.11
10th...	Seals......	47.44	Kirk......	52.56	4th...	Concannon..	35.68	Camp.....	61.94
11th...	Halvorson...	58.40	Ozinga....	34.48	5th...	Kildee.....	70.36	Sawicki....	26.96
12th...	Costello.....	71.40	Richardson,Jr.	24.95	6th...	Cooney.....	38.56	Upton.....	58.86
13th...	Harper......	43.65	Biggert....	53.55	7th...	Schauer....	48.78	Walberg...	46.47
14th...	Foster......	57.75	Oberweis...	42.25	8th...	Alexander...	40.23	Rogers....	56.53
15th...	Cox	35.81	Johnson....	64.19	9th...	Peters......	52.08	Knollenberg.	42.63
16th...	Abboud.....	36.08	Manzullo...	60.87	10th...	Denison.....	31.17	Miller.....	66.30
17th...	Hare......	99.77	[1]	[1]	11th...	Larkin......	45.37	McCotter...	51.41
18th...	Callahan....	37.94	Schock....	58.88	12th...	Levin......	72.07	Copple....	23.87
19th...	Davis......	33.38	Shimkus...	64.46	13th...	Kilpatrick....	74.13	Gubics....	19.08
IN.....	(X)........	(X)	(X)......	(X)	14th...	Conyers, Jr...	92.40	[1]......	[1]
1st...	Visclosky...	70.90	Leyva.....	27.18	15th...	Dingell.....	70.70	Lynch.....	24.95
2d...	Donnelly....	67.09	Puckett....	30.23	MN....	(X)........	(X)	(X)......	(X)
3d...	Montagano...	39.70	Souder....	55.04	1st...	Walz......	62.50	Davis.....	32.93
4th...	Ackerson....	40.13	Buyer.....	59.87	2d...	Sarvi......	42.55	Kline.....	57.29
5th...	Ruley......	34.45	Burton....	65.55	3d...	Madia......	40.85	Paulsen...	48.48
6th...	Welsh......	33.38	Pence.....	63.95	4th...	McCollum...	68.44	Matthews..	31.31
7th...	Carson.....	65.08	Campo....	34.92	5th...	Ellison......	70.88	White.....	22.00
8th...	Ellsworth....	64.74	Goode....	35.26	6th...	Tinklenberg..	43.43	Bachmann..	46.41
9th...	Hill......	57.77	Sodrel.....	38.41	7th...	Peterson....	72.20	Menze....	27.67
IA.....	(X)........	(X)	(X)......	(X)	8th...	Oberstar....	67.69	Cummins...	32.15
1st...	Braley......	64.61	Hartsuch...	35.39	MS....	(X)........	(X)	(X)......	(X)
			Miller-		1st...	Childers.....	54.47	Davis.....	43.88
2d...	Loebsack....	57.24	Meeks....	38.80	2d...	Thompson...	69.05	Cook.....	30.95
3d...	Boswell....	56.40	Schmett...	42.13	3d...	Gill......	37.46	Harper....	62.54
4th...	Greenwald..	39.43	Latham....	60.57	4th...	Taylor......	74.54	McCay III..	25.46
5th...	Hubler......	37.38	King......	59.84	MO....	(X)........	(X)	(X)......	(X)
KS....	(X)........	(X)	(X)......	(X)	1st...	Clay......	86.86	[1]......	[1]
1st...	Bordonaro...	13.27	Moran....	81.88	2d...	Haas......	35.41	Akin.....	62.28
2d...	Boyda.....	46.21	Jenkins...	50.61	3d...	Carnahan...	66.37	Sander....	30.41
3d...	Moore......	56.44	Jordan....	39.66	4th...	Skelton....	65.91	Parnell....	34.09
4th...	Betts, Jr...	32.38	Tiahrt....	63.41	5th...	Cleaver.....	64.37	Turk.....	35.63
KY....	(X)........	(X)	(X)......	(X)	6th...	Barnes.....	36.86	Graves....	59.43
1st...	Ryan......	35.65	Whitfield...	64.35	7th...	Monroe.....	28.16	Blunt.....	67.76
2d...	Boswell.....	47.43	Guthrie....	52.57	8th...	Allen......	26.16	Emerson...	71.44
3d...	Yarmuth....	59.37	Northup...	40.63				Luetke-	
4th...	Kelley.....	36.97	Davis.....	63.03	9th...	Baker	47.49	meyer....	49.99
5th...	[1]........	[1]	Rogers.....	84.11	MT....	Driscoll.....	32.42	Rehberg...	64.14
6th...	Chandler....	64.66	Larson....	35.34	NE....	(X)........	(X)	(X)......	(X)
LA [3]....	(X)........	(X)	(X)......	(X)	1st...	Yashirin....	29.64	Fortenberry..	70.36
1st...	Harlan......	34.32	Scalise....	65.68	2d...	Esch......	48.07	Terry.....	51.93
2d [4]..	Jefferson....	46.83	Cao......	49.54	3d...	Stoddard....	23.13	Smith.....	76.87
3d...	Melancon....	[2]	[1]	[1]	NV....	(X)........	(X)	(X)......	(X)
4th [4]	Carmouche..	47.69	Fleming....	48.07	1st...	Berkley.....	67.65	Wegner....	28.32
5th...	[1]........	[1]	Alexander..	[2]	2d...	Derby......	41.44	Heller.....	51.82
6th...	Cazayoux, Jr..	40.29	Cassidy....	48.12	3d...	Titus......	47.43	Porter.....	42.29
7th...	Cravins, Jr...	34.33	Boustany,Jr..	61.88	NH....	(X)........	(X)	(X)......	(X)
ME....	(X)........	(X)	(X)......	(X)	1st...	Shea-Porter..	51.76	Bradley....	45.86
1st...	Pingree.....	54.90	Summers...	45.10	2d...	Hodes......	56.44	Horn......	41.42
2d...	Michaud....	67.44	Frary.....	32.56	NJ....	(X)........	(X)	(X)......	(X)
MD....	(X)........	(X)	(X)......	(X)	1st...	Andrews....	72.40	Glading....	25.95
1st...	Kratovil, Jr...	49.12	Harris.....	48.33	2d...	Kurkowski...	39.09	LoBiondo..	59.06
	Ruppers-				3d...	Adler.......	52.08	Myers.....	47.92
2d...	berger.....	71.86	Matthews..	28.14	4th...	Zeitz......	32.63	Smith.....	66.21
3d...	Sarbanes....	69.66	Harris.....	30.08	5th...	Shulman....	42.40	Garrett....	55.87
4th...	Edwards....	85.83	James....	12.85	6th...	Pallone, Jr...	66.95	McLeod...	31.61
5th...	Hoyer......	73.65	Bailey.....	23.97	7th...	Stender.....	42.22	Lance.....	50.22
6th...	Dougherty...	38.79	Bartlett....	57.76	8th...	Pascrell, Jr...	71.11	Straten....	28.17
7th...	Cummings...	79.50	Hargadon..	18.58	9th...	Rothman....	67.53	Micco.....	31.04
8th...	Hollen......	75.07	Hudson....	21.68	10th...	Payne......	98.92	[1]	[1]
MA....	(X)........	(X)	(X)......	(X)				Frelinghuy-	
1st...	Olver......	69.67	Bech.....	25.86	11th...	Wyka......	37.01	sen.....	61.84
2d...	Neal......	76.39	[1]	[1]	12th...	Holt......	63.12	Bateman...	35.32
3d...	McGovern...	75.04	[1]	[1]	13th...	Sires......	75.36	Turula....	21.74
4th...	Frank	64.30	Sholley....	23.94					

See footnotes at end of table.

U.S. Census Bureau, Statistical Abstract of the United States: 2010

Table 392. **Vote Cast for U.S. Representatives by Major Political Party—Congressional Districts: 2008**—Con.

[See headnote, p. 244]

State and district	Democratic candidate Name	Percent of total	Republican candidate Name	Percent of total	State and district	Democratic candidate Name	Percent of total	Republican candidate Name	Percent of total
NM....	(X).......	(X)	(X).......	(X)	3d...	Blumenauer.	74.54	Lopez.....	20.84
1st...	Heinrich....	55.65	White.....	44.35	4th...	DeFazio....	82.34	(¹)........	(¹)
2d...	Teague....	55.96	Tinsley.....	44.04	5th...	Schrader...	54.25	Erickson....	38.33
3d...	Lujan......	56.74	East.......	30.47	PA....	(X).......	(X)	(X).......	(X)
NY....	(X).......	(X)	(X).......	(X)	1st...	Brady......	90.76	Muhammad..	9.24
1st...	Bishop.....	43.52	Zeldin.....	30.72	2d...	Fattah.....	88.93	Lang......	11.07
2d...	Israel......	48.71	Stalzer.....	23.77	3d...	Dahlkemper..	51.25	English.....	48.75
3d...	Long......	29.18	King......	46.62	4th...	Altmire.....	55.86	Hart......	44.14
4th...	McCarthy...	50.82	Martins....	28.27	5th...	McCracken..	41.04	Thompson..	56.72
5th...	Ackerman...	51.43	Berney.....	20.92	6th...	Roggio.....	47.90	Gerlach....	52.10
6th...	Meeks.....	67.12	(¹)........	(¹)	7th...	Sestak.....	59.59	Williams....	40.41
7th...	Crowley....	60.29	Britt, Jr.....	10.25	8th...	Murphy.....	56.77	Manion.....	41.63
8th...	Nadler.....	60.08	Lin......	14.57	9th...	Barr.......	36.08	Shuster....	63.92
9th...	Weiner.....	52.25	(¹)........	(¹)	10th..	Carney.....	56.33	Hackett....	43.67
10th..	Towns.....	67.80	Grupico....	3.59	11th..	Kanjorski...	51.63	Barletta....	48.37
11th..	Clarke.....	68.50	Carr......	5.04	12th..	Murtha.....	57.85	Russell.....	42.15
12th..	Velazquez...	63.56	Romaguera..	6.86	13th..	Schwartz...	62.79	Kats.......	34.53
13th..	McMahon...	47.89	Straniere....	27.78	14th..	Doyle......	91.26	(¹)........	(¹)
14th..	Maloney....	64.25	Heim......	15.80	15th..	Bennett....	41.43	Dent......	58.57
15th..	Rangel.....	69.49	Daniels.....	6.39	16th..	Slater.....	39.39	Pitts.......	55.82
16th..	Serrano....	72.75	Mohamed....	2.33	17th..	Holden.....	63.68	Gilhooley...	36.32
17th..	Engel.....	61.40	Goodman...	14.77	18th..	O'Donnell...	35.93	Murphy.....	64.07
18th..	Lowey.....	55.41	Russell.....	24.25	19th..	Avillo, Jr...	33.35	Platts......	66.65
19th..	Hall.......	44.05	Lalor......	32.39	RI....	(X).......	(X)	(X).......	(X)
20th..	Gillibrand...	53.48	Treadwell...	29.86	1st...	Kennedy....	68.52	Scott......	24.22
21st..	Tonko......	51.24	Buhrmaster..	27.34	2d...	Langevin...	70.02	Zaccaria....	29.81
22d..	Hinchey....	50.75	Phillips.....	26.39	SC....	(X).......	(X)	(X).......	(X)
23d..	Oot......	26.81	McHugh....	46.23	1st...	Ketner.....	47.89	Brown, Jr...	51.93
24th..	Arcuri......	43.01	Hanna.....	36.64	2d...	Miller......	46.18	Wilson.....	53.74
25th..	Maffei......	46.03	Sweetland..	33.10	3d...	Dyer......	35.23	Barrett.....	64.69
26th..	Kryzan.....	33.91	Lee.......	38.62	4th...	Corden.....	36.91	Inglis......	60.09
27th..	Higgins.....	57.65	Humiston....	17.18	5th...	Spratt, Jr...	61.64	Spencer....	36.99
28th..	Slaughter...	57.16	Crimmen....	15.45	6th...	Clyburn....	67.48	Harrelson...	32.47
29th..	Massa.....	42.80	Kuhl, Jr.....	37.79	SD....	Sandlin.....	67.56	Lien.......	32.44
NC....	(X).......	(X)	(X).......	(X)	TN....	(X).......	(X)	(X).......	(X)
1st...	Butterfield..	70.28	Stephens...	29.72	1st...	Russell.....	24.54	Roe.......	71.82
2d...	Etheridge...	66.93	Mansell....	31.27	2d...	Scott......	21.89	Duncan, Jr..	78.11
3d...	Weber.....	34.10	Jones......	65.90	3d...	Vandagriff...	27.40	Wamp.....	69.37
4th...	Price......	63.32	Lawson.....	36.68	4th...	Davis......	58.76	Lankford....	37.81
5th...	Carter......	41.63	Foxx......	58.37	5th...	Cooper.....	65.84	Donovan....	31.01
6th...	Bratton.....	33.00	Coble......	67.00	6th...	Gordon.....	74.42	(¹)........	(¹)
7th...	McIntyre....	68.84	Breazeale...	31.16	7th...	Morris.....	31.42	Blackburn...	68.58
8th...	Kissell.....	55.38	Hayes.....	44.62	8th...	Tanner.....	99.97	(¹)........	(¹)
9th...	Taylor......	35.89	Myrick.....	62.37	9th...	Cohen.....	87.85	(¹)........	(¹)
10th..	Johnson....	42.45	McHenry....	57.55	TX....	(X).......	(X)	(X).......	(X)
11th..	Shuler.....	61.96	Mumpower..	35.83	1st...	(¹)........	(¹)	Gohmert....	87.58
12th..	Watt.......	71.56	Cobb, Jr....	28.44	2d...	(¹)........	(¹)	Poe.......	88.92
13th..	Miller......	65.93	Webster....	34.07	3d...	Daley......	38.03	Johnson....	59.75
ND....	Pomeroy....	61.97	Sand......	38.03	4th...	Melancon...	29.28	Hall......	68.80
OH....	(X).......	(X)	(X).......	(X)	5th...	(¹)........	(¹)	Hensarling..	83.59
1st...	Driehaus....	52.47	Chabot.....	47.48	6th...	Otto.......	35.61	Barton.....	62.02
2d...	Wulsin.....	37.46	Schmidt....	44.83	7th...	Skelly.....	42.36	Culberson...	55.90
3d...	Mitakides...	36.68	Turner.....	63.32	8th...	Hargett.....	24.79	Brady......	72.56
4th...	Carroll.....	34.83	Jordan.....	65.17	9th...	Green......	93.65	(¹)........	(¹)
5th...	Mays......	35.91	Latta......	64.09	10th..	Doherty....	43.15	McCaul.....	53.89
6th...	Wilson.....	62.28	Stobbs.....	32.84	11th..	(¹)........	(¹)	Conaway....	88.33
7th...	Neuhardt...	41.78	Austria.....	58.22	12th..	Smith.....	30.60	Granger....	67.59
8th...	Von Stein...	32.10	Boehner....	67.90	13th..	Waun......	22.35	Thornberry..	77.65
9th...	Kaptur.....	74.37	Leavitt.....	25.63	14th..	(¹)........	(¹)	Paul.......	100.00
10th..	Kucinich....	57.02	Trakas.....	39.13	15th..	Hinojosa....	65.71	Zamora....	31.95
11th..	Fudge.....	85.22	Pekarek....	14.71	16th..	Reyes.....	82.14	(¹)........	(¹)
12th..	Robinson...	42.24	Tiberi......	54.79	17th..	Edwards....	52.98	Curnock....	45.50
13th..	Sutton.....	64.70	Foster.....	35.29	18th..	Jackson-Lee.	77.32	Faulk......	20.34
14th..	O'Neill.....	38.74	LaTourette..	58.32	19th..	Fullingim....	24.95	Neugebauer.	72.44
15th..	Kilroy.....	45.94	Stivers.....	41.90	20th..	Gonzalez...	71.90	Litoff......	25.18
16th..	Boccieri...	55.36	Schuring....	44.64	21st..	(¹)........	(¹)	Smith......	80.00
17th..	Ryan......	78.15	Grassell....	21.85	22d..	Lampson....	45.36	Olson......	52.43
18th..	Space.....	59.87	Dailey.....	40.13	23d..	Rodriguez...	55.76	Larson.....	41.92
OK....	(X).......	(X)	(X).......	(X)	24th..	Love......	41.07	Marchant...	55.98
1st...	Oliver......	33.83	Sullivan....	66.17	25th..	Doggett....	65.83	Morovich....	30.45
2d...	Boren......	70.47	Wickson....	29.53	26th..	Leach.....	36.43	Burgess....	60.17
3d...	Robbins....	23.57	Lucas......	69.72	27th..	Ortiz......	57.95	Vaden.....	38.38
4th...	Cummings..	29.21	Cole......	66.02	28th..	Cuellar.....	68.71	Fish......	29.22
5th...	Perry......	34.11	Fallin......	65.89	29th..	Green......	74.65	Story......	23.89
OR....	(X).......	(X)	(X).......	(X)	30th..	Johnson....	82.48	Wood......	15.87
1st...	Wu.......	71.50	(¹)........	(¹)	31st..	Ruiz.......	36.58	Carter.....	60.27
2d...	Lemas.....	25.75	Walden....	69.50	32d..	Roberson...	40.57	Sessions...	57.25

See footnotes at end of table.

246 Elections

Table 392. Vote Cast for U.S. Representatives by Major Political Party—Congressional Districts: 2008—Con.

[See headnote, p. 244]

State and district	Democratic candidate Name	Percent of total	Republican candidate Name	Percent of total	State and district	Democratic candidate Name	Percent of total	Republican candidate Name	Percent of total
UT	(X)........	(X)	(X)........	(X)	4th...	Fearing.....	36.91	Hastings....	63.09
1st...	Bowen.....	30.47	Bishop.....	64.85	5th...	Mays......	34.72	Rodgers....	65.28
2d...	Matheson...	63.35	Dew.......	34.47	6th...	Dicks......	66.86	Cloud......	33.14
3d...	Spencer....	28.28	Chaffetz....	65.61	7th...	McDermott..	83.65	Beren......	16.35
VT	Welch.....	83.25	(¹)........	(¹)	8th...	Burner.....	47.22	Reichert....	52.78
VA	(X)........	(X)	(X)........	(X)	9th...	Smith......	65.45	Postma....	34.55
1st...	Day, Jr.....	41.75	Wittman....	56.58	WV	(X)........	(X)	(X)........	(X)
2d...	Nye III.....	52.40	Drake......	47.46	1st...	Mollohan....	99.93	(¹)........	(¹)
3d...	Scott......	97.02	(¹)........	(¹)	2d...	Barth......	42.92	Capito.....	57.07
4th...	Miller.....	40.37	Forbes.....	59.51	3d...	Rahall II....	66.92	Gearheart...	33.08
5th...	Perriello....	50.09	Goode, Jr...	49.86	WI	(X)........	(X)	(X)........	(X)
6th...	Rasoul.....	36.61	Goodlatte...	61.57	1st...	Krupp......	34.69	Ryan......	63.97
7th...	Hartke.....	37.10	Cantor.....	62.72	2d...	Baldwin....	69.33	Theron.....	30.56
8th...	Moran.....	67.94	Ellmore.....	29.68	3d...	Kind.......	63.19	Stark......	34.44
9th...	Boucher....	97.07	(¹)........	(¹)	4th...	Moore.....	87.63	(¹)........	(¹)
10th..	Feder......	38.83	Wolf.......	58.80				Sensenbren-	
11th..	Connolly....	54.69	Fimian.....	43.05	5th...	(¹)........	(¹)	ner, Jr.	79.58
WA	(X)........	(X)	(X)........	(X)	6th...	Kittelson....	36.21	Petri.......	63.71
1st...	Inslee.....	67.76	Ishmael....	32.24	7th...	Obey......	60.79	Mielke.....	39.14
2d...	Larsen.....	62.39	Bart.......	37.61	8th...	Kagen.....	54.00	Gard......	45.90
3d...	Baird......	64.01	Delavar....	35.99	WY	Trauner....	42.78	Lummis....	52.59

X Not applicable. ¹ No candidate. ² According to state law, it is not required to tabulate votes for unopposed candidates. ³ Louisiana holds an open-primary election with candidates from all parties running on the same ballot. Any candidate who receives a majority is elected; if no candidate receives 50 percent, there is a run-off election in November between the top two finishers. ⁴ Reflects votes cast in the run-off election held on 6 December 2008.

Source: U.S. House of Representatives, Office of the Clerk, *Statistics of the Presidential and Congressional Election*, biennial (published 10 July 2009). See also <http://clerk.house.gov/member_info/election.html>.

Table 393. Composition of Congress by Political Party: 1975 to 2009

[D = Democratic, R = Republican. As of beginning of first session of each Congress. Data reflect immediate result of elections. Vacancies and third party candidates are noted]

Year	Party and president	Congress	House Majority party	House Minority party	House Other	Senate Majority party	Senate Minority party	Senate Other
1975 [1]	R (Ford)	94th	D-291	R-144	–	D-61	R-37	2
1977 [2]	D (Carter)	95th	D-292	R-143	–	D-61	R-38	1
1979 [2]	D (Carter)	96th	D-277	R-158	–	D-58	R-41	1
1981 [2]	R (Reagan)	97th	D-242	R-192	1	R-53	D-46	1
1983	R (Reagan)	98th	D-269	R-166	–	R-54	D-46	–
1985	R (Reagan)	99th	D-253	R-182	–	R-53	D-47	–
1987	R (Reagan)	100th	D-258	R-177	–	R-55	D-45	–
1989	R (Bush)	101st	D-260	R-175	–	D-55	R-45	–
1991 [3]	R (Bush)	102d	D-267	R-167	1	D-56	R-44	–
1993 [3]	D (Clinton)	103d	D-258	R-176	1	D-57	R-43	–
1995 [3]	D (Clinton)	104th	R-230	D-204	1	R-52	D-48	–
1997 [4]	D (Clinton)	105th	R-226	D-207	2	R-55	D-45	–
1999 [3]	D (Clinton)	106th	R-223	D-211	1	R-55	D-45	–
2001 [4, 6]	R (Bush)	107th	R-221	D-212	2	D-50	R-50	–
2003 [5, 6]	R (Bush)	108th	R-229	D-204	1	R-51	D-48	1
2005 [5]	R (Bush)	109th	R-232	D-202	1	R-55	D-44	1
2007 [7]	R (Bush)	110th	D-233	R-202	–	D-49	R-49	2
2009 [7, 8, 9]	D (Obama)	111th	D-256	R-178	–	D-55	R-41	2

– Represents zero. ¹ Senate had one Independent and one Conservative-Republican. ² Senate had one Independent. ³ House had one Independent-Socialist. ⁴ House had one Independent-Socialist and one Independent. ⁵ House and Senate each had one vacancy. ⁶ House had one vacancy. ⁷ Senate had two Independents. ⁸ House had one vacancy. ⁹ Senate had 2 vacancies.

Source: U.S. House of Representatives, Office of the Clerk, *Official List of Members*, annual. See also <http://clerk.house.gov /member_info/olm_111.pdf>.

Elections 247

Table 394. Composition of Congress by Political Party Affiliation—States: 2003 to 2009

[Figures are for the beginning of the first session. Dem. = Democratic; Rep. = Republican]

State	Representatives								Senators							
	108th Cong.,[1] 2003		109th Cong.,[1,2,3] 2005		110th Cong., 2007		111th Cong.,[4] 2009		108th Cong.,[5] 2003		109th Cong.,[3,5] 2005		110th Cong.,[6] 2007		111th Cong.,[6] 2009	
	Dem.	Rep.	Dem.	Rep.	Dem.	Rep.	Dem.	Rep.	Dem.	Rep.	Dem.	Rep.	Dem.	Rep.	Dem.	Rep.
U.S. ...	205	229	202	231	233	202	254	178	48	51	44	55	49	49	58	40
AL......	2	5	2	5	2	5	3	4	–	2	–	2	–	2	–	2
AK......	–	1	–	1	–	1	–	1	–	2	–	2	–	2	1	1
AZ......	2	6	2	6	4	4	5	3	–	2	–	2	–	2	–	2
AR......	3	1	3	1	3	1	3	1	2	–	2	–	2	–	2	–
CA......	33	20	33	20	34	19	33	19	2	–	2	–	2	–	2	–
CO	2	5	3	4	4	3	5	2	–	2	1	1	1	1	2	–
CT......	2	3	2	3	4	1	5	–	2	–	2	–	1	–	1	–
DE......	–	1	–	1	–	1	–	1	2	–	2	–	2	–	2	–
FL......	7	18	7	18	9	16	10	15	2	–	1	1	1	1	1	1
GA	5	8	6	7	6	7	6	7	1	1	–	2	–	2	–	2
HI	2	–	2	–	2	–	2	–	2	–	2	–	2	–	2	–
ID	–	2	–	2	–	2	1	1	–	2	–	2	–	2	–	2
IL	9	10	10	9	10	9	11	7	1	1	2	–	2	–	2	–
IN	3	6	2	7	5	4	5	4	1	1	1	1	1	1	1	1
IA	1	4	1	4	3	2	3	2	1	1	1	1	1	1	1	1
KS......	1	3	1	3	2	2	1	3	–	2	–	2	–	2	–	2
KY......	1	5	1	5	2	4	2	4	–	2	–	2	–	2	–	2
LA......	3	4	2	5	2	5	1	6	2	–	1	1	1	1	1	1
ME......	2	–	2	–	2	–	2	–	–	2	–	2	–	2	–	2
MD	6	2	6	2	6	2	7	1	2	–	2	–	2	–	2	–
MA	10	–	10	–	10	–	10	–	2	–	2	–	2	–	2	–
MI......	6	9	6	9	6	9	8	7	2	–	2	–	2	–	2	–
MN	4	4	4	4	5	3	5	3	1	1	1	1	1	1	2	–
MS	2	2	2	2	2	2	3	1	–	2	–	2	–	2	–	2
MO	4	5	4	5	4	5	4	5	–	2	–	2	1	1	1	1
MT	–	1	–	1	–	1	–	1	1	1	1	1	2	–	2	–
NE......	–	3	–	3	–	3	–	3	1	1	1	1	1	1	1	1
NV......	1	2	1	2	1	2	2	1	1	1	1	1	1	1	1	1
NH......	–	2	–	2	2	–	2	–	–	2	–	2	–	2	1	1
NJ......	7	6	7	6	7	6	8	5	2	–	2	–	2	–	2	–
NM	1	2	1	2	1	2	3	–	1	1	1	1	1	1	2	–
NY......	19	10	20	9	23	6	25	3	2	–	2	–	2	–	2	–
NC	6	7	6	7	7	6	8	5	1	1	–	2	–	2	1	1
ND	1	–	1	–	1	–	1	–	2	–	2	–	2	–	2	–
OH	6	12	6	11	7	11	10	8	–	2	–	2	1	1	1	1
OK	1	4	1	4	1	4	1	4	–	2	–	2	–	2	–	2
OR	4	1	4	1	4	1	4	1	1	1	1	1	1	1	2	–
PA......	7	12	7	12	11	8	12	7	–	2	–	2	1	1	2	–
RI......	2	–	2	–	2	–	2	–	1	1	1	1	2	–	2	–
SC......	2	4	2	4	2	4	2	4	1	1	–	2	–	2	–	2
SD......	–	1	1	–	1	–	1	–	2	–	1	1	1	1	1	1
TN......	5	4	5	4	5	4	5	4	–	2	–	2	–	2	–	2
TX......	17	15	11	21	13	19	12	20	–	2	–	2	–	2	–	2
UT......	1	2	1	2	1	2	1	2	–	2	–	2	–	2	–	2
VT......	–	–	–	–	1	–	1	–	1	–	1	–	1	–	1	–
VA......	3	8	3	8	3	8	6	5	–	2	–	2	1	1	2	–
WA	6	3	6	3	6	3	6	3	2	–	2	–	2	–	2	–
WV......	2	1	2	1	2	1	2	1	2	–	2	–	2	–	2	–
WI......	4	4	4	4	5	3	5	3	2	–	2	–	2	–	2	–
WY	–	1	–	1	–	1	–	1	–	2	–	2	–	2	–	2

– Represents zero.   [1] Vermont had one Independent-Socialist representative.   [2] Ohio had one vacancy due to the resignation of Rob Portman, 29 April 2005.   [3] As of June 28, 2005.   [4] Three vacancies—one in California due to the resignation of Hilda L. Solis, 24 February 2009; one in Illinois due to the resignation of Rahm Emanuel, 6 January 2009; and one in New York due to the resignation of Kirsten E. Gillibrand, 26 January 2009.   [5] Vermont had one Independent senator.   [6] Vermont and Connecticut both had one Independent senator.

Source: U.S. House of Representatives, Office of the Clerk, *Official List of Members,* annual. See also <http://clerk.house.gov/member_info/olm_111.pdf>.

Table 395. **Members of Congress—Selected Characteristics: 1993 to 2007**

[As of beginning of first session of each Congress, (January 3), except as noted. Figures for Representatives exclude vacancies]

Members of Congress and year	Male	Female	Black [1]	API [2]	His- panic [3]	Age [4] (in years) Under 40	40 to 49	50 to 59	60 to 69	70 and over	Seniority [5,6] Less than 2 yrs.	2 to 9 yrs.	10 to 19 yrs.	20 to 29 yrs.	30 yrs. or more
REPRESENTATIVES															
103d Cong., 1993 [7] . . .	388	47	[8]38	7	17	47	151	128	89	15	118	141	132	32	12
104th Cong., 1995. . . .	388	47	[9]40	7	17	53	155	135	79	13	92	188	110	36	9
106th Cong., 1999. . . .	379	56	[9]39	6	19	23	116	173	87	35	41	236	104	46	7
107th Cong., 2001. . . .	376	59	[9]39	7	19	14	97	167	117	35	44	155	158	63	14
108th Cong., 2003. . . .	376	59	[9]39	5	22	19	86	174	121	32	54	178	140	48	13
109th Cong., 2005. . . .	369	65	[9]42	4	23	22	96	175	113	28	37	173	158	48	18
110th Cong., 2007. . . .	361	74	[9]42	4	23	20	91	172	118	34	62	159	160	37	17
SENATORS															
103d Cong., 1993 [7] . . .	93	7	1	2	–	1	16	48	22	12	15	30	39	11	5
104th Cong., 1995. . . .	92	8	1	2	–	1	14	41	27	17	12	38	30	15	5
106th Cong., 1999. . . .	91	9	–	2	–	–	14	38	35	13	8	39	33	14	6
107th Cong., 2001. . . .	87	13	–	2	–	–	8	39	33	18	11	34	30	14	9
108th Cong., 2003. . . .	86	14	–	2	–	1	12	29	34	24	9	42	29	13	7
109th Cong., 2005. . . .	86	14	1	2	2	–	17	29	33	21	9	41	29	14	7
110th Cong., 2007. . . .	84	16	1	2	3	–	11	31	34	24	12	42	24	13	9

– Represents zero. [1] Source: Joint Center for Political and Economic Studies, Washington, DC, *Black Elected Officials: Statistical Summary,* annual (copyright). [2] Asian and Pacific Islanders. Source: Prior to 2005, Library of Congress, Congressional Research Service, "Asian Pacific Americans in the United States Congress," Report 94-767 GOV; starting 2005, U.S. House of Representatives, "House Press Gallery," <http://www.house.gov/daily/> (as of 8 May 2008) and U.S. Senate, "Minorities in the Senate," <http://www.senate.gov/artandhistory/history/common/briefing/minority_senators.htm> (as of 8 May 2008). [3] Source: National Association of Latino Elected and Appointed Officials, Washington, DC, *National Roster of Hispanic Elected Officials,* annual. [4] Some members do not provide date of birth. [5] Represents consecutive years of service. [6] Some members do not provide years of service. [7] Includes members elected to fill vacant seats through 14 June 1993. [8] Includes District of Columbia delegate but not Virgin Islands delegate. [9] Includes District of Columbia and Virgin Islands delegate.
Source: Except as noted, compiled by U.S. Census Bureau from data published in *Congressional Directory,* biennial. See also <http://www.gpoaccess.gov/cdirectory/browse.html>.

Table 396. **U.S. Congress—Measures Introduced and Enacted and Time in Session: 1991 to 2008**

[Excludes simple and concurrent resolutions]

Item	102d Cong., 1991–92	103d Cong., 1993–94	104th Cong., 1995–96	105th Cong., 1997–98	106th Cong., 1999–00	107th Cong., 2001–02	108th Cong., 2003–04	109th Cong., 2005–06	110th Cong., 2007–08
Measures introduced	6,775	8,544	6,808	7,732	9,158	9,130	8,625	10,703	11,228
Bills	6,212	7,883	6,545	7,532	8,968	8,953	8,468	10,560	11,081
Joint resolutions	563	661	263	200	190	177	157	143	147
Measures enacted	609	473	337	404	604	337	504	590	416
Public [1]	589	465	333	394	580	331	498	589	416
Private [2]	20	8	4	10	24	6	6	1	–
HOUSE OF REPRESENTATIVES									
Number of days	280	265	290	251	272	265	243	241	282
Number of hours	1,796	1,887	2,445	2,001	2,179	1,694	1,894	1,917	2,368
Number of hours per day. . .	6.4	7.1	8.4	8.0	8.0	6.4	7.8	8.0	8.4
SENATE									
Number of days	287	291	343	296	303	322	300	297	374
Number of hours	2,292	2,514	2,876	2,188	2,200	2,279	2,486	2,250	2,365
Number of hours per day. . .	8.0	8.6	8.4	7.4	7.3	7.1	8.3	7.6	6.3

– Represents zero. [1] Laws on public matters that apply to all persons. [2] Laws designed to provide legal relief to specified persons or entities adversely affected by laws of general applicability.
Source: U.S. Congress, *Congressional Record* and *Daily Calendar,* selected issues. See also <http://www.senate.gov/pagelayout/reference/two_column_table/Resumes.htm>.

Table 397. **Congressional Bills Vetoed: 1961 to 2009**

Period	President	Total vetoes	Regular vetoes	Pocket vetoes	Vetoes sustained	Bills passed over veto
1961–63.	John F. Kennedy.	21	12	9	21	–
1963–69.	Lyndon B. Johnson	30	16	14	30	–
1969–74.	Richard M. Nixon	43	26	17	36	7
1974–77.	Gerald R. Ford	66	48	18	54	12
1977–81.	Jimmy Carter	31	13	18	29	2
1981–89.	Ronald W. Reagan	78	39	39	69	9
1989–93.	George Bush	44	29	15	43	1
1993–2001	William J. Clinton	37	36	1	34	2
2001–2009	George W. Bush	10	10	–	7	3
2009 [1]	Barack Obama	–	–	–	–	–

– Represents zero. [1] For the period 20 January 2009 through 16 April 2009.

Source: U.S. Congress, Senate Library, *Presidential Vetoes ... 1789–1968*; U.S. Congress, *Calendars of the U.S. House of Representatives and History of Legislation,* annual. See also <http://clerk.house.gov/art_history/house_history/vetoes.html>.

Elections   249

Table 398. **Number of Governors by Political Party Affiliation: 1975 to 2009**

[Reflects figures after inaugurations for each year]

Year	Demo-cratic	Repub-lican	Indepen-dent/other	Year	Demo-cratic	Repub-lican	Indepen-dent/other	Year	Demo-cratic	Repub-lican	Indepen-dent/other
1975	36	13	1	1998	17	32	1	2004	22	28	–
1980	31	19	–	1999	17	31	1	2005	22	28	–
1985	34	16	–	2000	18	30	2	2006	22	28	–
1990	29	21	–	2001	19	29	2	2007	28	22	–
1995	19	30	1	2002	22	27	1	2008	28	22	–
1997	17	32	1	2003	23	27	–	2009	28	22	–

– Represents zero.

Source: National Governors Association, Washington, DC, 1970–87 and 1991–2008, *Directory of Governors of the American States, Commonwealths & Territories*, annual; and 1988–90, *Directory of Governors*, annual (copyright).

Table 399. **Vote Cast for and Governor Elected by State: 2006 to 2008**

[In thousands (1,250 represents 1,250,000), except percent. D = Democratic, R = Republican]

State	2006 Total vote [1]	2006 Republican	2006 Democrat	2006 Percent leading party	2008 Total vote [1]	2008 Republican	2008 Democrat	2008 Percent leading party	Current governor [2]
AL.	1,250	718	520	R-57.4	(X)	(X)	(X)	(X)	Bob Riley
AK.	238	115	97	R-48.1	(X)	(X)	(X)	(X)	[3]Sean Parnell
AZ.	1,534	544	960	D-62.6	(X)	(X)	(X)	(X)	Jan Brewer
AR.	774	315	430	D-55.5	(X)	(X)	(X)	(X)	Mike Beebe
CA.	8,679	4,850	3,377	R-55.9	(X)	(X)	(X)	(X)	Arnold Schwarzenegger
CO	1,558	626	888	D-57.0	(X)	(X)	(X)	(X)	Bill Ritter
CT.	1,123	710	398	R-63.2	(X)	(X)	(X)	(X)	M. Jodi Rell
DE.	(X)	(X)	(X)	(X)	395	127	267	D-67.5	Jack Markell
FL.	4,829	2,520	2,178	R-52.2	(X)	(X)	(X)	(X)	Charlie Crist
GA	2,122	1,230	811	R-57.9	(X)	(X)	(X)	(X)	Sonny Perdue
HI	349	215	122	R-61.7	(X)	(X)	(X)	(X)	Linda Lingle
ID	489	276	199	R-52.7	(X)	(X)	(X)	(X)	C. L. "Butch" Otter
IL	3,586	1,369	1,736	D-48.4	(X)	(X)	(X)	(X)	Pat Quinn
IN	(X)	(X)	(X)	(X)	2,704	1,564	1,082	R-57.8	Mitch Daniels
IA	1,059	467	569	D-53.7	(X)	(X)	(X)	(X)	Chet Culver
KS.	850	344	492	D-57.9	(X)	(X)	(X)	(X)	[4]Mark Parkinson
KY [5]	1,055	436	620	D-58.7	(X)	(X)	(X)	(X)	Steven Beshear
LA [5]	1,298	699	398	R-54.0	(X)	(X)	(X)	(X)	Bobby Jindal
ME	551	166	210	D-38.1	(X)	(X)	(X)	(X)	John Baldacci
MD	1,717	825	942	D-52.7	(X)	(X)	(X)	(X)	Martin O'Malley
MA	2,244	784	1,235	D-55.0	(X)	(X)	(X)	(X)	Deval Patrick
MI.	3,801	1,608	2,143	D-56.3	(X)	(X)	(X)	(X)	Jennifer M. Granholm
MN	2,218	1,029	1,007	R-46.4	(X)	(X)	(X)	(X)	Tim Pawlenty
MS [5]	744	431	313	R-57.9	(X)	(X)	(X)	(X)	Haley Barbour
MO	(X)	(X)	(X)	(X)	2,878	1,136	1,681	D-58.4	Jeremiah Nixon
MT	(X)	(X)	(X)	(X)	487	158	319	D-65.5	Brian Schweitzer
NE.	593	436	145	R-73.3	(X)	(X)	(X)	(X)	Dave Heineman
NV.	582	279	256	R-47.9	(X)	(X)	(X)	(X)	Jim Gibbons
NH	404	105	298	D-74.0	683	189	479	D-70.2	John Lynch
NJ [6].	2,290	985	1,225	D-53.5	(X)	(X)	(X)	(X)	Jon Corzine
NM	559	174	385	D-68.8	(X)	(X)	(X)	(X)	Bill Richardson
NY.	4,698	1,106	2,741	D-58.3	(X)	(X)	(X)	(X)	[7]David Paterson
NC	(X)	(X)	(X)	(X)	4,269	2,001	2,146	D-50.3	Bev Perdue
ND	(X)	(X)	(X)	(X)	316	235	74	R-74.4	John Hoeven
OH	4,184	1,471	2,428	D-58.0	(X)	(X)	(X)	(X)	Ted Strickland
OK	926	310	616	R-66.5	(X)	(X)	(X)	(X)	Brad Henry
OR	1,400	534	579	D-41.3	(X)	(X)	(X)	(X)	Ted Kulongoski
PA.	4,093	1,622	2,471	D-60.4	(X)	(X)	(X)	(X)	Edward Rendell
RI	388	197	190	R-51.0	(X)	(X)	(X)	(X)	Don Carcieri
SC.	1,092	602	489	R-55.1	(X)	(X)	(X)	(X)	Mark Sanford
SD.	356	207	121	R-61.7	(X)	(X)	(X)	(X)	Mike Rounds
TN.	1,819	541	1,247	D-68.6	(X)	(X)	(X)	(X)	Phil Bredesen
TX.	4,399	1,717	1,310	R-39.0	(X)	(X)	(X)	(X)	Rick Perry
UT.	(X)	(X)	(X)	(X)	907	701	175	R-77.9	[8]Gary Herbert
VT.	263	148	108	R-56.3	319	170	70	R-53.4	Jim Douglas
VA [6].	1,984	912	1,026	D-52.0	(X)	(X)	(X)	(X)	Tim Kaine
WA	(X)	(X)	(X)	(X)	3,003	1,404	1,599	D-53.2	Chris Gregoire
WV	(X)	(X)	(X)	(X)	706	182	493	D-69.8	Joe Manchin III
WI	2,162	979	1,139	D-52.7	(X)	(X)	(X)	(X)	Jim Doyle
WY	194	58	136	D-69.8	(X)	(X)	(X)	(X)	Dave Freudenthal

X Not applicable. [1] Includes minor party and scattered votes. [2] As of 22 September 2009. Source: National Governors Association, Washington, DC. See <http://www.nga.org>. [3] Data are for Sarah Palin, who served from 4 December 2006 until her resignation 26 July 2009. [4]Data are for Kathleen Sebelius, who served from 2006 until her resignation on 28 April 2009. [5] Voting year 2007. [6] Voting year 2005. [7] Data are for Eliot Spitzer, who served from January 2007 until his resignation 17 March 2008. [8]Data are for Jon Huntsman, who served from 2005 until his resignation on 7 August 2009.

Source: Except as noted, The Council of State Governments, Lexington, KY, *The Book of States 2009*, annual (copyright).

250 Elections

Table 400. Political Party Control of State Legislatures by Party: 1985 to 2009

[As of beginning of year. Nebraska has a nonpartisan legislature]

Year	Legislatures under— Democratic control	Legislatures under— Split control or tie	Legislatures under— Republican control	Year	Legislatures under— Democratic control	Legislatures under— Split control or tie	Legislatures under— Republican control	Year	Legislatures under— Democratic control	Legislatures under— Split control or tie	Legislatures under— Republican control
1985	27	11	11	1995	18	12	19	2003	16	12	21
1987	28	12	9	1996	16	15	18	2004	17	11	21
1989 [1]	28	13	8	1997	20	11	18	2005	19	10	20
1990	29	11	9	1999	20	12	17	2006	19	10	20
1992	29	14	6	2000	16	15	18	2007	22	12	15
1993	25	16	8	2001	16	15	18	2008	23	14	12
1994	24	17	8	2002	17	15	17	2009	27	14	8

[1] A party change during the year by a Democratic representative broke the tie in the Indiana House of Representatives, giving the Republicans control of both chambers.

Source: National Conference of State Legislatures, Denver, CO, State Legislatures, periodic.

Table 401. Composition of State Legislatures by Political Party Affiliation: 2008 and 2009

[Data as of March and reflect February election results in year shown, except as noted. Figures reflect immediate results of elections, including holdover members in state houses which do not have all of their members running for reelection. Dem. = Democrat, Rep. = Republican, Vac. = Vacancies. In general, Lower House refers to body consisting of state representatives; Upper House, of state senators]

State	Lower House 2008 Dem.	Rep.	Other	Vac.	Lower House 2009 Dem.	Rep.	Other	Vac.	Upper House 2008 Dem.	Rep.	Other	Vac.	Upper House 2009 Dem.	Rep.	Other	Vac.
U.S.	2,985	2,403	17	7	3,041	2,346	18	6	1,020	898	3	1	1,021	890	2	9
AL [1]	62	43	–	–	62	43	–	–	23	12	–	–	19	13	–	3
AK [2]	17	23	–	–	18	22	–	–	9	11	–	–	10	10	–	–
AZ [3]	27	33	–	–	24	36	–	–	13	17	–	–	12	18	–	–
AR [2]	75	25	–	–	71	28	1	–	27	8	–	–	27	8	–	–
CA [2]	47	32	–	1	51	29	–	–	25	15	–	–	25	14	–	1
CO [2]	40	25	–	–	38	27	–	–	20	15	–	–	21	14	–	–
CT [3]	107	44	–	–	114	36	–	1	24	12	–	–	24	12	–	–
DE [2]	19	22	–	–	24	17	–	–	13	8	–	–	16	5	–	–
FL [2]	42	78	–	–	44	76	–	–	14	26	–	–	14	26	–	–
GA [3]	73	107	–	–	73	107	–	–	22	34	–	–	22	34	–	–
HI [2]	44	7	–	–	45	6	–	–	21	4	–	–	23	2	–	–
ID [3]	19	51	–	–	18	52	–	–	7	28	–	–	7	28	–	–
IL [4]	67	51	–	–	70	48	–	–	37	22	–	–	37	22	–	–
IN [2]	51	49	–	–	52	48	–	–	17	33	–	–	17	33	–	–
IA [2]	53	47	–	–	56	44	–	–	30	20	–	–	32	18	–	–
KS [2]	47	78	–	–	49	76	–	–	10	30	–	–	9	31	–	–
KY [2]	64	36	–	–	65	35	–	–	15	22	1	–	15	21	1	1
LA [1]	60	43	1	1	51	50	3	1	25	14	–	–	22	15	–	2
ME [3]	90	59	2	–	95	55	1	–	18	17	–	–	20	15	–	–
MD [1]	104	37	–	–	104	36	1	–	33	14	–	–	33	14	–	–
MA [3]	140	19	–	1	142	16	1	1	35	5	–	–	35	5	–	–
MI [2]	58	52	–	–	67	43	–	–	17	21	–	–	16	21	–	1
MN [2]	85	48	1	–	87	47	–	–	45	22	–	–	46	21	–	–
MS [1]	75	47	–	–	74	48	–	–	27	25	–	–	27	25	–	–
MO [2]	71	92	–	–	74	89	–	–	14	20	–	–	11	23	–	–
MT [2]	49	50	–	–	50	50	–	–	26	24	–	–	23	27	–	–
NE [5]	(5)	(5)	(5)	(5)	(5)	(5)	(5)	(5)	(5)	(5)	(5)	(5)	(5)	(5)	(5)	(5)
NV [3]	27	15	–	–	28	14	–	–	10	11	–	–	12	9	–	–
NH [3]	237	158	1	4	224	175	–	1	14	10	–	–	14	10	–	–
NJ [2]	48	32	–	–	48	32	–	–	23	17	–	–	23	16	–	–
NM [2]	42	28	–	–	45	25	–	–	24	18	–	–	27	15	–	–
NY [3]	108	42	–	–	108	41	1	–	29	33	–	–	32	30	–	–
NC [3]	68	52	–	–	68	52	–	–	31	19	–	–	30	20	–	–
ND [1]	33	61	–	–	36	58	–	–	21	26	–	–	21	26	–	–
OH [2]	46	53	–	–	53	46	–	–	12	21	–	–	12	21	–	–
OK [2]	44	57	–	–	40	61	–	–	24	24	–	–	22	26	–	–
OR [2]	31	29	–	–	36	24	–	–	18	10	1	1	18	12	–	–
PA [2]	102	101	–	–	104	99	–	–	21	29	–	–	21	29	–	–
RI [3]	61	13	1	–	69	6	–	–	33	5	–	–	33	4	1	–
SC [2]	51	73	–	–	52	71	–	1	19	27	–	–	19	27	–	–
SD [3]	20	50	–	–	24	46	–	–	15	20	–	–	14	21	–	–
TN [2]	53	46	–	–	49	50	–	–	16	16	1	–	14	19	–	–
TX [2]	71	79	–	–	74	76	–	–	11	20	–	–	12	19	–	–
UT [2]	20	55	–	–	22	53	–	–	8	21	–	–	8	21	–	–
VT [3]	93	49	8	–	95	48	7	–	23	7	–	–	23	7	–	–
VA [2]	44	54	2	–	45	53	2	–	21	19	–	–	21	19	–	–
WA [2]	63	35	–	–	61	36	–	1	32	17	–	–	31	18	–	–
WV [2]	72	28	–	–	71	29	–	–	23	11	–	–	26	8	–	–
WI [2]	47	52	–	–	52	46	1	–	18	15	–	–	18	15	–	–
WY [2]	17	43	–	–	19	41	–	–	7	23	–	–	7	23	–	–

– Represents zero.   [1] Members of both houses serve 4-year terms.   [2] Upper House members serve 4-year terms and Lower House members serve 2-year terms.   [3] Members of both houses serve 2-year terms.   [4] Illinois—4 and 2-year term depending on district.   [5] Nebraska—4-year term and only state to have a nonpartisan legislature.

Source: The Council of State Governments, Lexington, KY, The Book of States 2009, annual (copyright).

Elections   251

Table 402. Women Holding State Public Offices by Office and State: 2008

[As of January. For data on women in U.S. Congress, see Table 395]

State	Total	State-wide elective executive office [1]	State legislature Total	State legislature Percent [2]	State	Total	State-wide elective executive office [1]	State legislature Total	State legislature Percent [2]
U.S.	1,824	73	1,751	24	MO	43	3	40	20
					MT	38	1	37	25
AL	23	5	18	13	NE	10	1	9	(3)
AK	14	1	13	22	NV	22	3	19	30
AZ	34	3	31	34	NH	150	–	150	35
AR	29	1	28	21	NJ	35	–	35	29
CA	34	1	33	28	NM	37	3	34	30
CO	38	2	36	36	NY	50	–	50	24
CT	57	4	53	28	NC	49	4	45	26
DE	20	1	19	31	ND	26	2	24	17
FL	38	1	37	23	OH	26	2	24	18
GA	50	3	47	20	OK	22	3	19	13
HI	26	1	25	33	OR	30	1	29	32
ID	26	1	25	24	PA	38	1	37	15
IL	49	1	48	27	RI	23	1	22	19
IN	30	2	28	19	SC	15	–	15	9
IA	35	1	34	23	SD	18	–	18	17
KS	51	3	48	29	TN	23	–	23	17
KY	19	1	18	13	TX	36	2	34	19
LA	22	–	22	15	UT	20	–	20	19
ME	58	–	58	31	VT	70	1	69	38
MD	59	–	59	31	VA	23	–	23	16
MA	51	1	50	25	WA	54	2	52	35
MI	31	2	29	20	WV	20	1	19	14
MN	73	3	70	35	WI	32	3	29	22
MS	25	–	25	14	WY	22	1	21	23

– Represents zero.   [1] Excludes women elected to the judiciary, women appointed to state cabinet-level positions, women elected to executive posts by the legislature, and elected members of university Board of Trustees or Board of Education.   [2] Calculated by U.S. Census Bureau based on total (male and female) state legislature (both upper and lower houses) data from Table 401.   [3] Nebraska—4-year term and only state to have a nonpartisan legislature.

Source: Center for the American Woman and Politics, Eagleton Institute of Politics, Rutgers University, New Brunswick, NJ, information releases (copyright).

Table 403. Percent of Women in National Parliaments by Country: 2009

[Compiled on the basis of information provided by National Parliaments as of May 31 2009]

Country	Lower or single House Election year	Lower or single House Percent women	Upper House or Senate Election year	Upper House or Senate Percent women	Country	Lower or single House Election year	Lower or single House Percent women	Upper House or Senate Election year	Upper House or Senate Percent women
Afghanistan	2005	27.7	2005	21.6	Kazakhstan	2007	15.9	2008	4.3
Argentina	2007	40.0	2007	38.9	Korea, South	2008	13.7	(X)	(X)
Australia	2007	26.7	2007	35.5	Mexico	2006	23.2	2006	18.0
Austria	2008	27.9	(1)	24.6	Namibia	2004	26.9	2004	26.9
Belarus	2008	31.8	2008	33.9	Netherlands	2006	41.3	2007	34.7
Belgium	2007	35.3	2007	38.0	Nicaragua	2006	18.5	(X)	(X)
Bosnia and Herzegovina. . .	2006	11.9	2007	13.3	Pakistan	2008	22.5	2009	17.0
Cambodia	2008	16.3	2006	14.8	Philippines	2007	20.5	2007	17.4
Canada	2008	22.1	(1)	34.4	Poland	2007	20.2	2007	8.0
Chile	2005	15.0	2005	5.3	Russia..............	2007	14.0	(1)	4.7
China [2]	2008	21.3	(X)	(X)	Rwanda.............	2008	56.3	2003	34.6
Czech Republic.	2006	15.5	2008	17.3	Saudi Arabia	2009	–	(X)	(X)
Dominican Republic......	2006	19.7	2006	3.1	Slovenia	2008	13.3	2007	2.5
Ethiopia.............	2005	21.9	2005	18.8	South Africa [4]	2009	43.5	2009	29.6
France	2007	18.2	2008	21.9	Spain	2008	36.3	2008	30.0
Gabon...............	2009	16.7	2009	17.6	Sudan..............	2005	18.1	2005	6.0
Germany	2005	32.2	(1)	21.7	Switzerland	2007	28.5	2007	21.7
Guinea [3]	(3)	(3)	(X)	(X)	Thailand	2007	11.7	2008	16.0
Iran	2008	2.8	(X)	(X)	United Kingdom	2005	19.5	(1)	19.7
Iraq	2005	25.5	(X)	(X)	United States [5]	2008	16.8	2008	15.3
Ireland	2007	13.3	2007	21.7	Uruguay	2004	12.1	2004	12.9
Italy	2008	21.3	2008	18.0	Uzbekistan...........	2004	17.5	2005	15.0
Japan	2005	9.4	2007	18.2	Zimbabwe	2008	15.2	2008	24.7

– Represents zero.   X Not applicable.   [1] Term of the chamber is not fixed (i.e., renewals do not take place on the same date, but rather when individual mandates expire).   [2] With the establishment of diplomatic relations with China on January 1, 1979, the U.S. government recognized the People's Republic of China as the sole legal government of China and acknowledged the Chinese position that there is only one China and that Taiwan is part of China.   [3] The parliament was dissolved following the December 2008 coup.   [4] The Upper House figures on the distribution of seats do not include the 36 special rotating delegates appointed on an ad hoc basis, and all percentages given are therefore calculated on the basis of the 55 permanent seats.   [5] Percent of voting members.

Source: Inter-Parliamentary Union, Geneva, Switzerland, "Women in National Parliaments"; <http://www.ipu.org/wmn-e /classif.htm> (released 31 May 2009).

252   Elections

Table 404. **Black Elected Officials by Office, 1970 to 2002, and State, 2002**

[**As of January 2002,** no Black elected officials had been identified in Montana or South Dakota]

State	Total	U.S. and state legisla- tures[1]	City and county offices[2]	Law enforce- ment[3]	Educa- tion[4]	State	Total	U.S. and state legisla- tures[1]	City and county offices[2]	Law enforce- ment[3]	Educa- tion[4]
1970 (Feb.) ..	1,469	179	715	213	362	MD........	192	40	101	41	10
1980 (July)...	4,890	326	2,832	526	1,206	MA........	79	6	60	2	11
1990 (Jan.) ..	7,335	436	4,485	769	1,645	MI........	353	24	153	62	114
1995 (Jan.) ..	8,385	604	4,954	987	1,840	MN........	20	2	4	10	4
1999 (Jan.) ..	8,896	618	5,354	997	1,927	MS........	950	46	646	121	137
2000 (Jan.) ..	9,001	621	5,420	1,037	1,923	MO........	206	19	145	17	25
2001 (Jan.) ..	9,061	633	5,456	1,044	1,928	NE........	9	1	5	–	3
						NV........	13	5	4	2	2
2002 (Jan.) ..	**9,430**	**636**	**5,753**	**1,081**	**1,960**	NH........	5	5	–	–	–
AL........	757	36	569	56	96	NJ........	269	18	162	–	89
AK........	2	1	1	–	–	NM........	4	1	–	2	1
AZ........	13	1	1	6	5	NY........	328	34	90	84	120
AR........	535	15	374	17	129	NC........	523	28	369	31	95
CA........	234	10	78	76	70	ND........	1	–	1	–	–
CO........	17	4	5	8	–	OH........	305	21	197	35	52
CT........	69	14	46	3	6	OK........	115	6	85	4	20
DE........	29	4	18	–	7	OR........	5	3	1	1	–
DC........	174	[5]2	169	–	3	PA........	215	19	85	75	36
FL........	275	25	180	43	27	RI........	8	7	1	–	–
GA........	640	53	413	48	126	SC........	547	32	345	12	158
HI........	1	1	–	–	–	TN........	195	18	118	28	31
ID........	1	–	1	–	–	TX........	466	19	306	47	94
IL........	619	28	327	59	205	UT........	5	1	3	1	–
IN........	94	13	54	13	14	VT........	1	1	–	–	–
IA........	12	1	8	1	2	VA........	248	16	132	16	84
KS........	16	7	4	3	2	WA........	24	2	9	11	2
KY........	62	5	45	6	6	WV........	19	2	13	3	1
LA........	739	32	408	132	167	WI........	33	8	15	5	5
ME........	2	–	1	–	–	WY........	1	–	1	–	–

– Represents zero.   [1] Includes elected state administrators.   [2] County commissioners and councilmen, mayors, vice mayors, aldermen, regional officials, and other.   [3] Judges, magistrates, constables, marshals, sheriffs, justices of the peace, and other.   [4] Members of state education agencies, college boards, school boards, and other.   [5] Includes one shadow senator (an elected official who lobbied Congress on D.C. issues, but is not sworn in at the federal level and has no voting privileges).

Source: Joint Center for Political and Economic Studies, Washington, DC, *Black Elected Officials: A Statistical Summary,* annual (copyright) and <http://www.jointcenter.org/publications_recent_publications/black_elected_officials>.

Table 405. **Hispanic Public Elected Officials by Office, 1985 to 2008, and State, 2008**

[**As of January of year shown.** For states not shown, no Hispanic public officials had been identified]

State	Total	State execu- tives and legisla- tors[1]	County and muni- cipal officials	Judicial and law enforce- ment	Educa- tion and school boards	State	Total	State execu- tives and legisla- tors[1]	County and muni- cipal officials	Judicial and law enforce- ment	Educa- tion and school boards
1985 ...	3,147	129	1,316	517	1,185	MD	11	4	6	–	1
1990 ...	4,004	144	1,819	583	1,458	MA	20	4	9	–	7
2000 ...	5,019	217	1,852	447	2,503	MI.....	14	3	2	4	5
2001 ...	5,205	223	1,846	454	2,682	MN	5	3	1	1	–
2002 ...	4,303	227	1,960	532	1,603	MO	2	1	1	–	–
2003 ...	4,432	231	1,958	549	1,694	MT	3	1	–	2	–
2004 ...	4,651	253	2,059	638	1,723	NE	3	1	1	–	1
2005 ...	4,853	266	2,149	678	1,760	NV	12	6	2	–	3
2006 ...	4,932	244	2,151	693	1,835	NH	4	3	1	–	–
2007 ...	4,954	270	2,152	685	1,847	NJ.....	117	10	61	–	46
						NM	654	49	338	105	162
2008 ...	**5,240**	**283**	**2,266**	**738**	**1,952**	NY	61	19	27	13	2
AK	1	–	1	–	–	NC	4	2	2	–	–
AZ	362	19	135	53	155	ND	1	–	1	–	–
CA	1,127	35	416	42	634	OH	6	–	5	–	1
CO	152	9	104	8	31	OK	2	–	–	–	2
CT	28	6	18	–	4	OR	12	2	5	5	–
DE	2	1	1	–	–	PA	9	1	5	–	1
FL.....	150	21	87	35	7	RI.....	7	3	4	–	–
GA	6	3	1	2	–	SC	1	1	–	–	–
HI.....	2	1	1	–	–	TN	3	1	2	–	–
ID.....	2	2	–	–	–	TX	2,245	44	918	441	842
IL.....	111	13	60	8	30	UT	8	3	3	2	–
IN.....	17	1	11	3	2	VA	3	1	1	–	1
IA.....	1	–	1	–	–	WA	35	4	19	–	13
KS	10	4	6	–	–	WI.....	9	1	3	4	1
KY	2	–	1	–	1	WY	5	2	3	–	–
LA	10	–	3	4	–						

– Represents zero.   [1] Includes U.S. Senators and Representatives, not shown separately.

Source: National Association of Latino Elected and Appointed Officials (NALEO) Educational Fund, Washington, DC, *National Directory of Latino Elected Officials,* annual.

Elections   253

Table 406. Voting-Age Population—Reported Registration and Voting by Selected Characteristics: 1996 to 2008

[193.7 represents 193,700,000. As of November. Covers civilian noninstitutional population 18 years old and over. Includes aliens. Figures are based on Current Population Survey (see text, Section 1 and Appendix III) and differ from those in Table 408 based on population estimates and official vote counts]

Characteristic	Voting-age population (mil.)							Percent reporting they registered							Percent reporting they voted						
								Presidential election years				Congressional election years			Presidential election years				Congressional election years		
	1996	1998	2000	2002	2004	2006	2008	1996	2000	2004	2008	1998	2002	2006	1996	2000	2004	2008	1998	2002	2006
Total [1]	**193.7**	**198.2**	**202.6**	**210.4**	**215.7**	**220.6**	**225.5**	**65.9**	**63.9**	**65.9**	**64.9**	**62.1**	**60.9**	**61.6**	**54.2**	**54.7**	**58.3**	**58.2**	**41.9**	**42.3**	**43.6**
18 to 20 years old	10.8	11.4	11.9	11.7	11.5	11.6	11.7	45.6	40.5	50.7	49.3	32.1	32.6	37.0	31.2	28.4	41.0	41.0	13.5	15.1	17.1
21 to 24 years old	13.9	14.1	14.9	15.6	16.4	16.2	16.6	51.2	49.3	52.1	56.0	35.0	42.5	44.9	33.4	35.4	42.5	46.6	19.2	18.7	21.9
25 to 34 years old	40.1	38.6	37.3	38.5	39.0	39.4	40.2	56.9	54.7	55.6	56.5	52.4	50.2	50.3	43.1	43.7	46.9	48.5	28.0	27.1	28.3
35 to 44 years old	43.3	44.5	44.5	43.1	42.6	41.5	41.5	66.5	63.8	64.2	61.4	62.4	60.0	59.3	54.9	55.0	56.9	55.2	40.7	40.2	40.1
45 to 64 years old	53.7	57.4	61.4	66.9	71.0	75.0	78.1	73.5	71.2	72.7	70.4	71.1	69.4	69.6	64.4	64.1	66.6	65.0	53.6	53.1	54.3
65 years old and over	31.9	32.3	32.8	33.9	34.7	35.8	37.5	77.0	76.1	76.9	75.0	75.4	75.8	75.4	67.0	67.6	68.9	68.1	59.5	61.0	60.5
Male [2]	92.6	95.2	97.1	100.9	103.8	106.5	109.0	64.4	62.2	64.0	62.6	60.6	58.9	59.5	52.8	53.1	56.3	55.7	41.4	41.4	42.4
Female	101.0	103.0	105.5	109.5	111.9	114.1	116.5	67.3	65.6	67.6	67.0	63.5	62.8	63.5	55.5	56.2	60.1	60.4	42.4	43.0	44.7
White [2]	162.8	165.8	168.7	174.1	176.6	179.9	183.2	67.7	65.6	67.9	66.6	63.9	63.1	64.0	56.0	56.4	60.3	59.6	43.3	44.1	45.8
Black [2]	22.5	23.3	24.1	24.4	24.9	25.7	26.5	63.5	63.6	64.4	65.5	60.2	58.8	57.4	50.6	53.5	56.3	60.8	39.6	39.7	38.6
Asian [2,3]	(NA)	(NA)	8.0	9.6	9.3	9.9	10.5	(NA)	30.7	34.9	37.3	(NA)	30.7	32.9	(NA)	25.4	29.8	32.1	(NA)	19.4	21.8
Hispanic [4]	18.4	20.3	21.6	25.2	27.1	29.0	30.9	35.7	34.9	34.3	37.6	33.7	32.6	32.1	26.7	27.5	28.0	31.6	20.0	18.9	19.3
Region: [5]																					
Northeast	38.3	38.5	38.9	41.1	41.0	41.2	41.5	64.7	63.7	65.3	63.7	60.8	60.8	60.3	54.5	55.2	58.6	57.4	41.2	41.4	42.8
Midwest	45.2	45.9	46.4	48.8	48.4	49.0	49.4	71.6	70.2	72.8	70.6	68.2	66.5	68.3	59.3	60.9	65.0	63.4	47.3	47.1	50.7
South	68.1	70.1	70.7	74.2	77.2	80.0	80.4	65.9	64.5	65.5	65.5	62.7	61.6	62.0	52.2	53.5	56.4	57.7	38.6	41.6	40.3
West	42.1	43.7	45.5	46.3	49.1	50.4	52.2	60.8	56.9	60.1	59.4	56.0	54.0	55.4	51.8	49.9	54.4	54.6	42.3	39.0	42.4
School years completed:																					
8 years or less	14.1	13.3	12.9	12.3	12.6	12.1	11.1	40.7	36.1	32.5	30.1	40.2	32.4	29.5	28.1	26.8	23.6	23.4	24.6	19.4	17.1
High school:																					
Less than high school graduate [6]	21.0	21.0	20.1	20.9	20.7	20.2	19.1	47.9	45.9	45.8	43.2	43.4	41.6	39.6	33.8	33.6	34.6	33.7	25.0	23.3	22.8
High school graduate or GED [6]	65.2	65.6	66.3	68.9	68.5	70.0	70.4	62.2	60.1	61.5	59.5	58.6	57.1	57.5	49.1	49.4	52.4	50.9	37.1	37.1	37.6
College:																					
Some college or associate's degree	50.9	52.9	55.3	57.3	58.9	60.2	63.8	72.9	70.0	73.7	72.0	68.3	66.7	68.3	60.5	60.3	66.1	65.0	46.2	45.8	47.3
Bachelor's or advanced degree	42.5	45.4	48.0	51.0	54.9	58.2	61.1	80.4	77.3	78.1	76.8	75.1	74.4	73.9	73.0	72.0	74.2	73.3	57.2	58.5	59.5
Employed	125.6	130.5	133.4	134.9	138.8	143.3	143.2	67.0	64.7	67.1	66.4	62.6	61.7	62.7	55.2	55.5	60.0	60.1	41.2	42.1	43.9
Unemployed	6.4	5.2	4.9	7.7	7.3	6.2	9.5	52.5	46.1	56.3	57.2	48.5	48.1	48.5	37.2	35.1	46.4	48.8	28.4	27.2	28.0
Not in labor force	61.6	62.5	64.2	67.8	69.6	70.5	72.8	65.1	63.8	64.4	62.9	62.1	60.9	60.7	54.1	54.5	56.2	55.5	44.5	44.2	44.3

NA Not available. [1] Includes other races not shown separately. [2] Beginning with the 2003 Current Population Survey (CPS), respondents could choose more than one race. 2004 and 2006 data represent persons who selected this race group only and exclude persons reporting more than one race. The CPS in prior years only allowed respondents to report one race group. See also comments on race in the text for Section 1. [3] Prior to 2004, this category was "Asian and Pacific Islanders," therefore rates are not comparable with prior years. [4] Hispanic persons may be any race. [5] For composition of regions, see map, inside cover. [6] The General Educational Development (GED) Test measures how well a non-high school graduate has mastered the skills and general knowledge that are acquired in a 4-year high school education. Successfully passing the exam is a credential generally considered to be equivalent to a high school diploma.

Source: U.S. Census Bureau, Current Population Reports, P20-557, and earlier reports; "Voting and Registration in the Election of November 2008" (published 20 July 2009); <http://www.census.gov/population/www/socdemo/voting.html>; and unpublished data.

Table 407. Reported Registration and Voting by State: 2008

[225,499 represents 225,499,000. As of November. See headnote, Table 406]

State	Voting-age population (1,000)	Percent of voting-age population Registered	Percent of voting-age population Voted	State	Voting-age population (1,000)	Percent of voting-age population Registered	Percent of voting-age population Voted
U.S.....	225,499	64.9	58.2	MO	4,430	72.8	64.2
AL	3,497	69.7	60.8	MT.	731	70.6	64.7
AK	488	70.8	62.4	NE	1,308	71.8	64.5
AZ	4,688	61.3	53.3	NV	1,946	59.0	52.8
AR	2,108	62.5	51.8	NH	1,015	74.5	69.8
CA	26,993	55.1	51.2	NJ	6,489	62.0	56.0
CO	3,694	66.0	62.5	NM	1,473	63.6	57.4
CT	2,651	66.4	60.8	NY	14,665	57.7	51.5
DE	648	69.1	63.0	NC	6,845	71.6	63.8
DC	469	69.0	65.3	ND	484	82.3	66.3
FL	14,069	62.4	56.5	OH	8,499	71.9	64.5
GA	7,018	65.9	59.6	OK	2,667	67.4	56.5
HI	977	53.5	46.8	OR	2,904	67.5	62.6
ID	1,095	66.0	58.8	PA	9,449	68.3	60.8
IL	9,521	64.6	57.1	RI	804	70.6	63.0
IN	4,686	66.3	58.8	SC	3,313	72.0	63.4
IA	2,244	72.6	66.9	SD	590	74.9	66.1
KS	2,037	65.9	59.8	TN	4,692	62.3	53.6
KY	3,179	71.1	61.4	TX	17,295	58.5	48.8
LA	3,161	75.7	68.0	UT	1,859	56.8	50.5
ME.	1,020	78.5	70.2	VT	487	70.9	63.2
MD	4,218	67.0	61.9	VA	5,720	69.1	63.8
MA	4,962	66.4	61.3	WA	4,912	67.2	62.6
MI	7,487	73.9	65.0	WV	1,395	65.7	53.1
MN	3,898	75.2	70.8	WI	4,212	73.5	68.5
MS.	2,109	75.3	68.2	WY	397	67.9	62.9

Source: U.S. Census Bureau, *Current Population Reports*, P20-557, and earlier reports; "Voting and Registration in the Election of November 2008" (published 20 July 2009); <http://www.census.gov/population/www/socdemo/voting.html>; and unpublished data.

Table 408. Participation in Elections for President and U.S. Representatives: 1932 to 2008

[75,768 represents 75,768,000. As of November, except as noted. Estimated resident population 21 years old and over, 1932–70, except as noted, and 18 years old and over thereafter; includes Armed Forces stationed in the U.S. Prior to 1958, excludes Alaska and prior to 1960, excludes Hawaii. District of Columbia is included in votes cast for President beginning 1964]

Year	Resident popu-lation (incl. aliens) of voting age (1,000)	Votes cast For Presi-dent (1,000)	Votes cast Per-cent of voting-age popu-lation	Votes cast For U.S. Repre-senta-tives (1,000)	Votes cast Per-cent of voting-age popu-lation	Year	Resident popu-lation (incl. aliens) of voting age (1,000)	Votes cast For Presi-dent (1,000)	Votes cast Per-cent of voting-age popu-lation	Votes cast For U.S. Repre-senta-tives (1,000)	Votes cast Per-cent of voting-age popu-lation
1932	75,768	39,817	52.6	(NA)	(NA)	1972	140,777	77,625	55.1	71,188	50.6
1934	77,997	(X)	(X)	32,804	42.1	1974	146,338	(X)	(X)	52,313	35.7
1936	80,174	45,647	56.9	(NA)	(NA)	1976	152,308	81,603	53.6	74,259	48.8
1938	82,354	(X)	(X)	(NA)	(NA)	1978	158,369	(X)	(X)	54,584	34.5
1940	84,728	49,815	58.8	(NA)	(NA)	1980	163,945	86,497	52.8	77,874	47.5
1942	86,465	(X)	(X)	28,074	32.5	1982	169,643	(X)	(X)	63,881	37.7
1944	85,654	48,026	56.1	45,110	52.7	1984	173,995	92,655	53.3	82,422	47.4
1946	92,659	(X)	(X)	34,410	37.1	1986	177,922	(X)	(X)	59,758	33.6
1948	95,573	48,834	51.1	46,220	48.4	1988	181,956	91,587	50.3	81,682	44.9
1950	98,134	(X)	(X)	40,430	41.2	1990	185,812	(X)	(X)	62,355	33.6
1952	99,929	61,552	61.6	57,571	57.6	1992	189,493	104,600	55.2	97,198	51.3
1954	102,075	(X)	(X)	42,583	41.7	1994	193,010	(X)	(X)	70,494	36.5
1956	104,515	62,027	59.3	58,886	56.3	1996	196,789	96,390	49.0	90,233	45.9
1958	106,447	(X)	(X)	45,719	43.0	1998	201,270	(X)	(X)	66,605	33.1
1960	109,672	68,836	62.8	64,124	58.5	2000	[2]209,816	105,594	50.3	98,800	47.1
1962	112,952	(X)	(X)	51,242	45.4	2002	[2]214,896	(X)	(X)	74,707	34.7
1964	114,090	70,098	61.4	65,879	57.7	2004	[2]219,726	122,349	55.6	113,192	51.5
1966	116,638	(X)	(X)	52,902	45.4	2006	[2]224,769	(X)	(X)	80,976	36.0
1968	120,285	73,027	60.7	66,109	55.0	2008	[2]230,118	131,407	57.1	122,586	53.3
1970	124,498	(X)	(X)	54,259	43.6						

NA Not available. X Not applicable. [1] Population 18 and over in Georgia, 1944–70, and in Kentucky, 1956–70; 20 and over in Alaska and 20 and over in Hawaii, 1960–70. Source: Through 1990, U.S. Census Bureau, "Table 4. Participation in Elections for President and U.S. Representatives: 1930 to 1992;" <http://www.census.gov/population/socdemo/voting/p25-1117 /tab03-04.pdf> (released May 1994). For 1992–1998, "Estimates and Projections of the Voting-Age Population, 1992 to 2000, and Percent Casting Votes for President, by State: November 1992 and 1996" (published 31 July 2000); <http://www.census.gov /population/socdemo/voting/proj00/tab03.txt>. Starting 2000, "Annual Estimates of the Resident Population by Sex and Selected Age Groups for the United States: April 1, 2000 to July 1, 2008," (NC-EST2008-02); <http://www.census.gov/popest/national/asrh /NC-EST2008/NC-EST2008-02.xls/> (released 14 May 2009). [2] As of July 1.

Source: Except as noted, U.S. House of Representatives, Office of the Clerk, Statistics of the Presidential and Congressional Election, biennial (published 10 July 2009). See also <http://clerk.house.gov/member_info/electionInfo/index.html>.

Table 409. **Resident Population of Voting Age and Percent Casting Votes—States: 2000 to 2008**

[209,816 represents 209,816,000. Estimated population, 18 years old and over. Includes Armed Forces stationed in each state, aliens, and institutional population]

| State | Voting-age population (1,000) [1] | | | | Percent casting votes for— | | | | | |
| | | | | | Presidential electors | | | U.S. Representatives | | |
	2000	2004	2006	2008	2000	2004	2008	2000	2006	2008
U.S. ...	**209,816**	**219,726**	**224,769**	**230,118**	**50.3**	**55.7**	**57.1**	**47.1**	**36.0**	**53.3**
AL.......	3,330	3,400	3,471	3,540	50.0	55.4	59.3	43.2	32.9	52.4
AK.......	437	475	492	506	65.3	65.8	64.4	62.8	47.7	62.6
AZ.......	3,792	4,232	4,548	4,793	40.4	47.6	47.9	38.7	32.8	45.0
AR.......	1,998	2,060	2,110	2,153	46.1	51.2	50.5	31.7	36.2	36.6
CA......	24,734	26,197	26,726	27,392	44.3	47.4	49.5	42.2	31.0	45.0
CO	3,221	3,454	3,580	3,732	54.1	61.7	64.3	50.4	43.0	61.2
CT......	2,570	2,636	2,662	2,689	56.8	59.9	61.2	51.1	40.4	56.8
DE......	591	626	647	667	55.4	59.9	61.8	52.9	38.9	57.8
DC	457	464	472	480	44.2	49.0	55.4	(X)	(X)	(X)
FL.......	12,392	13,428	14,001	14,324	48.1	56.7	58.6	40.4	27.5	51.8
GA	6,052	6,557	6,853	7,137	42.7	50.4	55.0	39.9	30.2	51.2
HI	917	960	988	1,003	40.1	44.7	45.5	37.1	34.2	45.5
ID	929	1,010	1,063	1,111	54.0	59.3	59.0	53.0	41.9	57.4
IL	9,193	9,448	9,566	9,722	51.6	55.8	56.8	47.8	36.1	54.0
IN	4,517	4,639	4,713	4,792	48.7	53.2	57.4	47.7	35.4	55.9
IA	2,195	2,231	2,256	2,290	61.6	67.5	67.1	58.1	45.8	64.7
KS.......	1,979	2,032	2,062	2,102	54.2	58.4	58.8	52.3	41.0	57.5
KY.......	3,054	3,144	3,198	3,261	50.6	57.1	56.0	47.0	39.2	53.7
LA.......	3,252	3,318	3,179	3,303	54.3	58.6	59.4	37.0	28.8	31.7
ME	976	1,017	1,030	1,042	66.8	72.8	70.2	65.4	52.0	68.2
MD	3,954	4,160	4,235	4,293	51.2	57.3	61.3	48.7	40.2	58.2
MA	4,861	4,961	4,997	5,071	56.2	59.0	61.2	56.2	44.9	61.2
MI	7,360	7,554	7,606	7,613	57.5	64.1	65.7	55.3	47.9	63.2
MN	3,645	3,811	3,884	3,966	66.9	74.2	73.4	64.9	56.1	70.7
MS	2,074	2,122	2,137	2,172	47.9	53.7	59.4	47.6	28.1	58.2
MO	4,178	4,326	4,411	4,490	56.5	63.1	65.1	55.7	47.6	62.8
MT	673	706	726	747	61.0	63.8	65.6	61.0	55.9	64.4
NE.......	1,263	1,297	1,315	1,336	55.2	60.0	60.0	54.1	45.3	58.0
NV.......	1,502	1,729	1,845	1,932	40.6	48.0	50.1	39.1	31.2	47.0
NH	930	985	1,006	1,022	61.2	68.9	69.5	59.8	40.0	66.0
NJ.......	6,343	6,514	6,562	6,635	50.2	55.4	58.3	47.1	32.6	51.8
NM	1,313	1,393	1,482	1,482	45.6	54.3	56.0	44.7	39.0	55.0
NY.......	14,314	14,715	14,872	15,082	48.6	50.6	51.2	48.5	31.5	51.2
NC	6,112	6,447	6,692	6,979	47.7	54.3	61.6	45.5	29.0	60.4
ND	481	489	493	498	59.9	63.9	63.5	59.4	44.2	63.0
OH	8,478	8,631	8,687	8,756	55.5	65.2	65.2	54.1	45.6	61.4
OK	2,562	2,633	2,678	2,736	48.2	55.6	53.5	42.4	33.8	48.9
OR	2,583	2,731	2,824	2,922	59.4	67.3	62.5	55.7	48.1	57.6
PA.......	9,367	9,495	9,584	9,686	52.4	60.8	62.1	48.6	41.9	59.8
RI	803	826	823	822	51.0	52.9	57.4	47.9	45.3	53.3
SC.......	3,013	3,171	3,280	3,414	45.9	51.0	56.3	43.9	33.1	54.9
SD.......	553	577	591	606	57.2	67.2	63.0	56.9	56.4	62.6
TN.......	4,304	4,481	4,609	4,736	48.2	54.4	54.9	43.1	37.2	48.6
TX.......	15,042	16,195	16,888	17,601	42.6	45.8	45.9	39.8	24.5	42.8
UT.......	1,523	1,682	1,785	1,887	50.6	55.2	50.5	49.8	31.9	49.7
VT.......	462	480	487	492	63.6	65.1	66.0	61.3	54.0	60.6
VA.......	5,364	5,656	5,811	5,946	51.1	56.5	62.6	45.2	39.5	58.8
WA	4,395	4,665	4,835	5,008	56.6	61.3	60.6	54.2	42.5	58.2
WV	1,406	1,414	1,419	1,428	46.1	53.5	50.0	41.2	32.1	45.2
WI	4,005	4,170	4,243	4,314	64.9	71.9	69.2	62.6	48.6	64.3
WY	365	380	389	404	58.5	64.1	63.1	58.1	50.4	61.7

X Not applicable.   [1] As of July 1. Source: U.S. Census Bureau, "Annual Estimates of the Resident Population by Sex and Age for States: April 1, 2000, to July 1, 2008," (SC-EST2008-02); <http://www.census.gov/popest/states/asrh/SC-EST2008-02 .html> (released 14 May 2009).

Source: Except as noted, U.S. House of Representatives, Office of the Clerk, *Statistics of the Presidential and Congressional Election,* biennial (published 10 July 2009). See also <http://clerk.house.gov/member_info/electionInfo/index.html>.

256   Elections

Table 410. **Political Action Committees—Number by Committee Type: 1980 to 2009**

[As of December 31, except 2009 as of May 22]

Committee type	1980	1990	1995	2000	2005	2006	2007	2008	2009
Total....................	2,551	4,172	4,016	3,907	4,210	4,183	4,234	4,611	4,481
Corporate	1,206	1,795	1,674	1,545	1,622	1,582	1,601	1,598	1,574
Labor.....................	297	346	334	317	290	273	273	272	275
Trade/membership/health........	576	774	815	860	925	937	925	995	1,104
Nonconnected	374	1,062	1,020	1,026	1,233	1,254	1,300	1,594	1,390
Cooperative.................	42	59	44	41	37	37	38	49	43
Corporation without stock........	56	136	129	118	103	100	97	103	95

Source: U.S. Federal Election Commission, press release of May 2009.

Table 411. **Political Action Committees—Financial Activity Summary by Committee Type: 2003 to 2008**

[In millions of dollars (915.7 represents $915,700,000). Covers financial activity during 2-year calendar period indicated]

Committee type	Receipts			Disbursements [1]			Contributions to candidates		
	2003–04	2005–06	2007–08	2003–04	2005–06	2007–08	2003–04	2005–06	2007–08
Total	915.7	477.4	1,212.4	842.9	394.1	1,180.0	310.5	141.1	412.8
Corporate	239.0	131.2	313.4	221.6	116.3	298.6	115.6	56.5	158.3
Labor.................	191.7	100.3	262.1	182.9	73.1	265.0	52.1	21.1	62.7
Trade/membership/health...	181.8	95.4	372.7	170.1	74.6	364.6	83.2	38.0	66.6
Nonconnected	289.4	141.6	241.0	255.2	122.6	229.5	52.5	22.0	112.9
Cooperative	4.2	2.7	10.3	3.9	1.9	9.9	2.9	1.4	6.9
Corporation without stock. ..	9.6	6.1	13.0	9.2	5.7	12.4	4.2	2.1	5.5

[1] Comprises contributions to candidates, independent expenditures, and other disbursements.

Source: U.S. Federal Election Commission, *FEC Reports on Financial Activity, Final Report, Party and Non-party Political Committees*, biennial.

Table 412. **Presidential Campaign Finances—Federal Funds for General Election: 1996 to 2008**

[In millions of dollars (152.6 represents $152,600,000). Based on FEC certifications, audit reports, and Dept. of Treasury reports]

1996		2000		2004		2008	
Candidate	Amount	Candidate	Amount	Candidate	Amount	Candidate	Amount
Total	152.6	Total	147.7	Total	150.1	Total	84.2
Clinton.......	61.8	Bush........	67.6	Bush........	74.6	Obama	–
Dole.........	61.8	Gore........	67.6	Kerry........	74.6	McCain	84.1
Perot........	29.0	Buchanan	12.6	Nader	0.9	Nader	0.1

– Represents zero.

Source: U.S. Federal Election Commission, periodic press releases.

Table 413. **Presidential Campaign Finances—Primary Campaign Receipts and Disbursements: 1999 to 2008**

[In millions of dollars (351.6 represents $351,600,000). Covers campaign finance activity during 2-year calendar period indicated. Covers candidates who received federal matching funds or who had significant financial activity]

Item	Total [1]			Democratic			Republican		
	1999–00	2003–04	2007–08 [2, 3]	1999–00	2003–04	2007–08 [2]	1999–00	2003–04	2007–08 [3]
Receipts, total [4]	351.6	673.9	1,346.6	96.6	401.8	950.1	236.7	269.6	392.6
Individual contributions....	238.2	611.4	1,325.6	66.7	351.0	932.6	159.1	258.9	390.0
Federal matching funds ...	61.6	28.0	21.0	29.3	27.2	17.5	26.5	–	2.6
Disbursements	343.5	661.1	1,414.6	92.2	389.7	1,043.9	233.2	268.9	450.2

– Represents zero. [1] Includes other parties, not shown separately. [2] Obama activity includes both Primary and General election funds because he used a single committee for both elections. Dodd received $1,961,742 in matching funds; however his committee reported the receipt of $1,447,568. Gravel received an additional $115,966 in matching funds in early 2009. [3] Tancredo received an additional $83,775 in matching funds in early 2009. [4] Includes other types of receipts, not shown separately.

Source: U.S. Federal Election Commission, *FEC Reports on Financial Activity, Final Report, Presidential Pre-Nomination Campaigns*, quadrennial.

U.S. Census Bureau, Statistical Abstract of the United States: 2010

Table 414. **Congressional Campaign Finances—Receipts and Disbursements: 2003 to 2008**

[**708.5 represents $708,500,000**. Covers all campaign finance activity during 2-year calendar period indicated for primary, general, run-off, and special elections. Data have been adjusted to eliminate transfers between all committees within a campaign. For further information on legal limits of contributions, see Federal Election Campaign Act of 1971, as amended]

Item	House of Representatives						Senate					
	Amount (mil. dol.)			Percent distribution			Amount (mil. dol.)			Percent distribution		
	2003–04	2005–06	2007–08	2003–04	2005–06	2007–08	2003–04	2005–06	2007–08	2003–04	2005–06	2007–08
Total receipts [1]	708.5	875.4	1,005.2	100	100	100	497.6	564.6	434.1	100	100	100
Individual contributions	396.7	478.9	538.8	56	55	54	324.1	383.2	267.0	65	68	62
Other committees	225.4	279.8	300.4	32	32	30	63.7	68.9	78.2	13	12	18
Candidate loans	47.4	56.1	77.6	7	6	8	39.8	47.0	24.2	8	8	6
Candidate contributions	7.8	14.7	32.4	1	2	3	38.2	37.5	5.7	8	7	1
Democrats	307.4	417.5	561.0	43	48	56	250.6	291.8	237.3	50	52	55
Republicans	399.2	453.6	440.8	56	52	44	246.1	245.8	196.1	49	44	45
Others	1.9	4.2	3.4	(Z)	(Z)	(Z)	0.9	26.9	0.7	(Z)	5	(Z)
Incumbents	452.6	532.6	581.7	64	61	58	171.7	278.4	234.1	35	49	54
Challengers₂	118.2	188.7	252.2	17	22	25	79.5	186.6	135.0	16	33	31
Open seats [2]	137.8	154.1	171.3	19	18	17	246.4	99.6	65.1	50	18	15
Total disbursements . . .	660.3	854.8	929.9	100	100	100	496.4	562.9	449.4	100	100	100
Democrats	288.5	395.5	491.0	44	46	53	254.6	288.6	229.6	51	51	51
Republicans	370.0	455.2	435.6	56	53	47	241.0	249.3	202.0	49	44	45
Others	1.8	4.1	3.3	(Z)	(Z)	(Z)	0.8	25.0	17.9	(Z)	4	4
Incumbents	410.1	519.2	527.6	62	61	57	171.7	274.3	251.2	35	49	56
Challengers₂	116.6	185.6	246.7	18	22	27	76.6	187.1	132.9	15	33	30
Open seats [2]	133.6	150.0	155.6	20	18	17	248.1	101.5	65.4	50	18	15

Z Less than $50,000 or 0.5 percent.   [1] Includes other types of receipts, not shown separately.   [2] Elections in which an incumbent did not seek reelection.

Source: U.S. Federal Election Commission, *FEC Reports on Financial Activity, Final Report, U.S. Senate and House Campaigns,* biennial.

Table 415. **Contributions to Congressional Campaigns by Political Action Committees (PAC) by Type of Committee: 1997 to 2008**

[In millions of dollars (**158.7 represents $158,700,000**). Covers amounts given to candidates in primary, general, run-off, and special elections during the 2-year calendar period indicated. For number of political action committees, see Table 410]

Type of committee	Total [1]	Democrats	Republicans	Incumbents	Challengers	Open seats [2]
HOUSE OF REPRESENTATIVES						
1997–98	158.7	77.6	80.9	124.0	14.9	19.8
1999–00	193.4	98.2	94.7	150.5	19.9	23.0
2001–02	206.9	102.6	104.2	161.0	13.8	32.1
2003–04	225.4	98.6	126.6	187.3	15.6	22.5
2005–06	279.8	125.0	154.8	232.0	24.4	23.5
2007–08, total [3]	300.4	184.3	116.1	245.7	35.8	18.9
Corporate	108.0	56.7	51.3	99.4	5.0	3.6
Trade association [4]	85.6	47.6	38.0	73.6	7.2	4.8
Labor	53.4	49.7	3.7	37.5	11.3	4.6
Nonconnected [5]	43.9	25.1	18.8	27.0	11.6	5.4
SENATE						
1997–98	48.1	20.7	27.3	34.3	6.6	7.2
1999–00	51.9	18.7	33.2	33.5	7.1	11.3
2001–02	59.2	25.4	33.8	37.0	14.2	8.1
2003–04	63.7	28.4	35.3	39.3	5.6	18.8
2005–06	68.9	28.6	37.5	50.0	9.9	8.7
2007–08, total [3]	78.2	33.5	44.3	56.6	12.8	9.0
Corporate	32.4	11.2	21.2	26.8	2.5	3.1
Trade association [4]	19.4	7.2	12.2	14.9	2.5	2.0
Labor	7.0	6.5	0.5	2.8	2.9	1.2
Nonconnected [5]	17.5	7.8	9.7	10.7	4.4	2.5

[1] Includes other parties, not shown separately.   [2] Elections in which an incumbent did not seek reelection.   [3] Includes other types of political action committees not shown separately.   [4] Includes membership organizations and health organizations.   [5] Represents "ideological" groups as well as other issue groups not necessarily ideological in nature.

Source: U.S. Federal Election Commission, *FEC Reports on Financial Activity, Party and Non-Party Political Committees, Final Report,* biennial.

Section 8
State and Local Government Finances and Employment

This section presents data on revenues, expenditures, debt, and employment of state and local governments. Nationwide statistics relating to state and local governments, their numbers, finances, and employment are compiled primarily by the U.S. Census Bureau through a program of censuses and surveys. Every fifth year (for years ending in "2" and "7"), the Census Bureau conducts a census of governments involving collection of data for all governmental units in the United States. In addition, the Census Bureau conducts annual surveys which cover all the state governments and a sample of local governments.

Annually, the Census Bureau releases information on the Internet which presents financial data for the federal government, nationwide totals for state and local governments, and state-local data by states. Also released annually is a series on state, city, county, and school finances and on state and local public employment. There is also a series of quarterly data releases covering tax revenue and finances of major public employee retirement systems.

Basic information for Census Bureau statistics on governments is obtained by mail canvass from state and local officials; however, financial data for each of the state governments and for many of the large local governments are compiled from their official records and reports by Census Bureau personnel. In over two-thirds of the states, all or part of local government financial data are obtained through central collection arrangements with state governments. Financial data on the federal government are primarily based on the *Budget* published by the Office of Management and Budget (see text, Section 9, Federal Government Finances and Employment).

Governmental units—The governmental structure of the United States includes, in addition to the federal government and

the states, thousands of local governments—counties, municipalities, townships, school districts, and many "special districts." In 2007, 89,527 local governments were identified by the census of governments (see Tables 410–412). As defined by the census, governmental units include all agencies or bodies having an organized existence, governmental character, and substantial autonomy. While most of these governments can impose taxes, many of the special districts—such as independent public housing authorities and numerous local irrigation, power, and other types of districts—are financed from rentals, charges for services, benefit assessments, grants from other governments, and other nontax sources. The count of governments excludes semi-autonomous agencies through which states, cities, and counties sometimes provide for certain functions—for example, "dependent" school systems, state institutions of higher education, and certain other "authorities" and special agencies which are under the administrative or fiscal control of an established governmental unit.

Finances—The financial statistics relate to government fiscal years ending June 30 or at some date within the 12 previous months. The following governments are exceptions and are included as though they were part of the June 30 group; ending September 30, the state governments of Alabama and Michigan, the District of Columbia, and Alabama school districts; and ending August 31, the state governments of Nebraska, Texas, and Chicago school districts. New York State ends its fiscal year on March 31. The federal government ended the fiscal year June 30 until 1976 when its fiscal year, by an act of Congress, was revised to extend from Oct. 1 to Sept. 30. A 3-month quarter (July 1 to Sept. 30, 1976) bridged the transition.

Nationwide government finance statistics have been classified and presented in

U.S. Census Bureau, Statistical Abstract of the United States: 2010

terms of uniform concepts and categories, rather than according to the highly diverse terminology, organization, and fund structure utilized by individual governments.

Statistics on governmental finances distinguish among general government, utilities, liquor stores, and insurance trusts. *General government* comprises all activities except utilities, liquor stores, and insurance trusts. Utilities include government water supply, electric light and power, gas supply, and transit systems. Liquor stores are operated by 17 states and by local governments in 6 states. Insurance trusts relate to employee retirement, unemployment compensation, and other social insurance systems administered by the federal, state, and local governments.

Data for cities or counties relate only to municipal or county and their dependent agencies and do not include amounts for other local governments in the same geographic location. Therefore, expenditure figures for "education" do not include spending by the separate school districts which administer public schools within most municipal or county areas. Variations in the assignment of governmental responsibility for public assistance, health, hospitals, public housing, and other functions to a lesser degree also have an important effect upon reported amounts of city or county expenditure, revenue, and debt.

Employment and payrolls—These data are based mainly on mail canvassing of state and local governments. Payroll includes all salaries, wages, and individual fee payments for the month specified, and employment relates to all persons on governmental payrolls during a pay period of the month covered—including paid officials, temporary help, and (unless otherwise specified) part-time as well as full-time personnel. Effective with the 1997 Census of Governments, the reference period for measuring government employment was changed from October of the calendar year to March of the calendar year. As a result, there was no annual survey of government employment covering the October 1996 period. The prior reference month of October was used from 1958 to 1995. Figures shown for individual governments cover major dependent agencies such as institutions of higher education, as well as the basic central departments and agencies of the government.

Statistical reliability—For a discussion of statistical collection and estimation, sampling procedures, and measures of statistical reliability applicable to Census Bureau data, see Appendix III.

U.S. Census Bureau, Statistical Abstract of the United States: 2010

Table 416. **Number of Governmental Units by Type: 1962 to 2007**

Type of government	1962	1967	1972	1977	1982	1987	1992	1997	2002	2007
Total units	91,237	81,299	78,269	79,913	81,831	83,237	85,006	87,504	87,576	89,527
U.S. government	1	1	1	1	1	1	1	1	1	1
State government.	50	50	50	50	50	50	50	50	50	50
Local governments	91,186	81,248	78,218	79,862	81,780	83,186	84,955	87,453	87,525	89,476
County	3,043	3,049	3,044	3,042	3,041	3,042	3,043	3,043	3,034	3,033
Municipal.	18,000	18,048	18,517	18,862	19,076	19,200	19,279	19,372	19,429	19,492
Township and town . . .	17,142	17,105	16,991	16,822	16,734	16,691	16,656	16,629	16,504	16,519
School district.	34,678	21,782	15,781	15,174	14,851	14,721	14,422	13,726	13,506	13,051
Special district	18,323	21,264	23,885	25,962	28,078	29,532	31,555	34,683	35,052	37,381

Source: U.S. Census Bureau, *Census of Governments, Volume 1, Number 1, Government Organization,* Series GC07(1)-1), quinquennial; <http://www.census.gov/govs/www/cog2007.html>.

Table 417. **Number of Local Governments by Type—States: 2007**

[Governments in existence in January. Limited to governments actually in existence. Excludes, therefore, a few counties and numerous townships and "incorporated places" existing as areas for which statistics can be presented as to population and other subjects, but lacking any separate organized county, township, or municipal government. See Appendix III]

State	All governmental units [1]	County	Municipal	Township [1]	School district	Special district [2] Total [3]	Natural resources	Fire protection	Housing [4]
United States. . .	89,476	3,033	19,492	16,519	13,051	37,381	7,227	5,873	3,463
Alabama	1,185	67	458	–	131	529	69	11	150
Alaska	177	14	148	–	15	–	–	14	–
Arizona.	645	15	90	–	239	301	78	150	–
Arkansas.	1,548	75	502	–	247	724	250	81	119
California.	4,344	57	478	–	1,044	2,765	473	353	70
Colorado.	2,416	62	270	–	180	1,904	180	252	89
Connecticut	649	–	30	149	17	453	1	72	114
Delaware.	338	3	57	–	19	259	238	–	3
District of Columbia.	2	–	1	–	1	–	–	–	–
Florida.	1,623	66	411	–	95	1,051	125	61	94
Georgia	1,439	154	535	–	180	570	38	2	191
Hawaii	19	3	1	–	15	14	–	–	–
Idaho	1,240	44	200	–	116	880	174	150	10
Illinois.	6,994	102	1,299	1,432	912	3,249	1,026	841	113
Indiana	3,231	91	567	1,008	293	1,272	139	1	65
Iowa.	1,954	99	947	–	380	528	247	66	23
Kansas.	3,931	104	627	1,353	316	1,531	258	1	197
Kentucky.	1,346	118	419	–	175	634	126	156	13
Louisiana	526	60	303	–	68	95	8	3	–
Maine.	850	16	22	466	98	248	15	–	34
Maryland.	256	23	157	–	76	38	–	20	–
Massachusetts	861	5	45	306	82	423	16	16	252
Michigan	2,893	83	533	1,242	579	456	79	25	–
Minnesota	3,526	87	854	1,788	341	456	144	–	162
Mississippi.	1,000	82	296	–	164	458	249	33	55
Missouri	3,723	114	952	312	536	1,809	329	357	124
Montana	1,273	54	129	–	332	758	132	220	13
Nebraska	2,659	93	530	454	288	1,294	83	417	168
Nevada.	198	16	19	–	17	146	33	18	5
New Hampshire . . .	545	10	13	221	164	137	10	16	21
New Jersey	1,383	21	324	242	549	247	15	196	–
New Mexico.	863	33	101	–	96	633	576	–	6
New York	3,403	57	618	929	680	1,119	3	891	–
North Carolina	963	100	548	–	–	315	145	–	94
North Dakota	2,699	53	357	1,320	198	771	78	281	35
Ohio.	3,702	88	938	1,308	668	700	106	85	77
Oklahoma	1,880	77	594	–	567	642	100	30	137
Oregon	1,546	36	242	–	234	1,034	204	271	21
Pennsylvania	4,871	66	1,016	1,546	515	1,728	5	–	90
Rhode Island	134	–	8	31	4	91	4	37	25
South Carolina	698	46	268	–	85	299	48	83	43
South Dakota.	1,983	66	309	916	166	526	103	84	49
Tennessee.	928	92	347	–	14	475	109	1	96
Texas	4,835	254	1,209	–	1,081	2,291	442	139	387
Utah.	599	29	242	–	40	288	82	18	17
Vermont	733	14	45	237	293	144	14	16	10
Virginia	511	95	229	–	1	186	47	–	–
Washington	1,845	39	281	–	296	1,229	178	375	43
West Virginia	663	55	232	–	55	321	14	–	37
Wisconsin	3,120	72	592	1,259	441	756	251	–	177
Wyoming.	726	23	99	–	55	549	131	64	–

– Represents zero. [1] Includes "town" governments in the six New England States and in Minnesota, New York, and Wisconsin. [2] Single function districts. [3] Includes other special districts not shown separately. [4] Includes community development

Source: U.S. Census Bureau, *Census of Governments,* Vol. 1, No. 1, Government Organization, Series GC07(1)-1), quinquennial; <http://harvester.census.gov/gid/gid07/options.html>.

Table 418. **State and Local Government Current Receipts and Expenditures in the National Income and Product Accounts: 1990 to 2008**

[In billions of dollars (737.8 represents $737,800,000,000). For explanation of national income, see text, Section 13. Minus sign (−) indicates net loss]

Item	1990	1995	2000	2003	2004	2005	2006	2007	2008
Current receipts	**737.8**	**990.2**	**1,319.5**	**1,494.2**	**1,594.3**	**1,714.4**	**1,811.4**	**1,902.8**	**1,935.1**
Current tax receipts	519.1	672.1	893.2	979.4	1,061.2	1,162.3	1,242.2	1,304.1	1,318.6
Personal current taxes	122.6	158.1	236.6	226.6	249.0	277.1	303.3	325.4	333.4
Income taxes	109.6	141.7	217.3	204.5	225.0	252.1	277.0	298.3	305.9
Other	13.0	16.4	19.4	22.2	23.9	25.1	26.3	27.1	27.4
Taxes on production and imports . . .	374.1	482.4	621.1	717.5	769.2	829.0	878.2	917.8	937.6
Sales taxes	184.3	242.7	316.6	347.7	370.0	399.1	421.5	436.3	436.3
Property taxes	161.5	202.6	254.6	307.9	327.5	347.5	369.6	390.9	404.6
Other	28.3	37.0	49.9	61.9	71.7	82.4	87.1	90.3	96.7
Taxes on corporate income.	22.5	31.7	35.5	35.3	43.0	56.3	60.7	60.9	47.6
Contributions for government social insurance	10.0	13.6	11.0	19.8	23.6	24.2	23.1	22.8	23.7
Income receipts on assets	68.4	68.4	92.2	72.9	75.4	85.9	94.7	100.3	103.7
Interest receipts	64.1	62.9	84.0	62.9	64.3	73.4	80.6	84.6	87.7
Dividends	0.2	1.0	1.9	2.2	2.4	2.5	2.7	2.8	3.0
Rents and royalties	4.2	4.5	6.3	7.9	8.7	10.0	11.4	12.8	13.1
Current transfer receipts	133.5	224.1	315.4	422.7	437.2	450.3	456.5	481.3	496.7
Federal grants-in-aid	111.4	184.1	247.3	338.5	349.1	360.9	358.0	376.3	388.3
From business (net)	7.1	13.5	28.8	33.5	32.2	31.7	38.3	40.9	42.0
From persons.	14.9	26.5	39.2	50.6	56.0	57.6	60.2	64.1	66.5
Current surplus of government enterprises	6.7	12.0	7.7	−0.6	−3.0	−8.3	−5.0	−5.7	−7.6
Current expenditures	**730.5**	**978.2**	**1,269.5**	**1,514.5**	**1,592.8**	**1,684.9**	**1,765.3**	**1,892.4**	**2,015.2**
Consumption expenditures.	544.6	696.1	917.8	1,073.8	1,120.3	1,191.2	1,269.6	1,355.9	1,454.4
Government social benefit payments to persons	127.7	217.6	271.7	353.0	383.8	403.5	401.0	430.8	455.8
Interest payments.	57.9	64.2	79.5	87.7	88.4	89.9	94.3	98.5	102.0
Subsidies	0.4	0.3	0.5	0.1	0.4	0.4	0.4	7.1	3.0
Net state and local government saving.	**7.2**	**12.0**	**50.0**	**−20.4**	**1.5**	**29.5**	**46.2**	**10.4**	**−80.1**
Social insurance funds	2.0	4.0	2.0	3.8	7.1	7.6	6.5	5.5	5.6
Other	5.3	8.0	47.9	−24.1	−5.6	21.9	39.7	4.9	−85.6

Source: U.S. Bureau of Economic Analysis, *Survey of Current Business,* April 2009. See also <http://www.bea.gov /national/nipaweb/SelectTable.asp?selected=N>.

Table 419. **Federal Grants-in-Aid to State and Local Governments: 1990 to 2009**

[135,325 represents $135,325,000,000, except as indicated. For year ending Sept. 30. Minus sign (−) indicates decrease]

Year	Current dollars							Constant (2000) dollars	
			Grants to individuals		Grants as percent of—				
	Total grants (mil. dol.)	Annual percent change [1]	Total (mil. dol.)	Percent of total grants	State/ local govt. expendi- tures [2]	Federal outlays	Gross domestic product	Total grants (bil. dol.)	Annual percent change [1]
1990	135,325	11.0	77,264	57.1	25.2	10.8	2.4	172.1	6.3
1994	210,596	8.8	134,153	63.7	30.9	14.4	3.0	238.1	6.3
1995	224,991	6.8	144,427	64.2	31.5	14.8	3.1	247.9	4.1
1996	227,811	1.3	146,493	64.3	30.8	14.6	3.0	245.5	−1.0
1997	234,160	2.8	148,236	63.3	30.2	14.6	2.9	247.7	0.9
1998	246,128	5.1	160,305	65.1	30.3	14.9	2.9	257.3	3.9
1999	267,886	8.5	172,384	64.5	31.2	15.7	2.9	275.6	7.1
2000	285,874	6.6	182,592	64.1	27.4	16.0	2.9	285.9	3.7
2001	318,542	11.4	203,920	64.0	28.3	17.1	3.2	310.7	8.7
2002	352,895	10.8	227,373	64.4	29.4	17.5	3.4	338.4	8.9
2003	388,542	10.1	246,570	63.5	31.0	18.0	3.6	363.3	7.4
2004	407,512	4.9	262,177	64.3	31.3	17.8	3.5	370.4	2.0
2005	428,018	5.0	273,898	64.0	31.1	17.3	3.5	373.6	0.9
2006	434,099	1.4	272,585	62.8	29.7	16.3	3.3	364.0	−2.6
2007	443,797	2.2	284,362	64.1	28.3	16.3	3.3	361.3	−0.7
2008	461,317	3.9	300,820	65.2	26.9	15.5	3.2	357.3	−1.1
2009, est. . . .	567,823	23.1	371,671	65.5	(NA)	14.2	4.0	440.4	23.3

NA Not available. [1] Average annual percent change from prior year shown. For explanation, see Guide to Tabular Presentation. For 1990, change from 1989. [2] Expenditures from own sources as defined in the national income and product accounts.

Source: U.S. Office of Management and Budget, *Budget of the United States, Historical Tables,* annual; <http://www.whitehouse.gov /omb/budget>.

U.S. Census Bureau, Statistical Abstract of the United States: 2010

Table 420. **Total Outlays for Grants to State and Local Governments—Selected Agencies and Programs: 1990 to 2009**

[In millions of dollars (135,325 represents $135,325,000,000). For year ending Sept 30. Includes trust funds]

Selected programs	1990	2000	2004	2005	2006	2007	2008	2009 est.
Total outlays for grants	135,325	285,874	407,512	428,018	434,099	443,797	461,317	567,823
Energy	461	433	608	636	651	667	524	1,455
Natural resources and environment	3,745	4,595	6,009	5,858	6,062	6,060	5,902	6,240
Environmental Protection Agency [1]	2,874	3,490	4,018	3,734	3,966	4,016	3,854	3,858
Agriculture	1,285	724	995	933	749	803	862	1,016
Transportation	19,174	32,222	41,298	43,368	46,681	47,945	51,216	62,735
Grants for airports [1]	1,220	1,624	2,958	3,530	3,841	3,874	3,808	3,498
Federal-aid highways [2]	13,854	24,711	29,791	30,915	32,703	33,222	35,429	37,887
Urban mass transportation [1]	3,728	5,262	–	–	–	8,984	9,847	13,156
Community and regional development	4,965	8,665	12,604	20,167	21,285	20,653	19,221	21,801
Rural community advance program.	139	479	797	814	773	760	5	(NA)
Community development fund	2,818	4,955	5,388	4,985	5,012	10,867	8,935	8,010
Homeland Security	1,184	2,439	5,490	13,541	14,731	8,267	8,630	10,597
State and local programs	(NA)	(NA)	1,535	2,116	2,601	2,385	2,870	3,331
Firefighter assistance grants	(NA)	(NA)	508	1,185	228	499	(NA)	(NA)
Operations, planning, and support	11	192	387	132	(NA)	(NA)	(NA)	(NA)
Mitigation grants	(NA)	13	23	39	34	32	33	(NA)
Disaster relief	1,173	2,234	3,037	10,069	11,868	5,351	5,724	7,263
Education, training, employment, social services [3]	21,780	36,672	54,201	57,247	60,512	58,077	58,904	69,627
Education for the disadvantaged [3]	4,437	8,511	12,417	14,539	14,604	14,409	14,799	15,720
School improvement programs [3]	1,080	2,394	6,542	6,569	5,589	5,299	5,208	5,087
Special education	1,485	4,696	9,465	10,661	11,582	11,585	12,078	11,452
Social services-block grant	2,749	1,827	1,752	1,822	1,848	1,956	1,843	1,909
Children and family services programs	2,618	5,843	8,326	8,490	8,492	8,496	8,633	10,563
Training and employment services	3,042	2,957	3,883	3,372	4,566	3,006	3,052	4,072
Health	43,890	124,843	189,883	197,848	197,347	208,311	218,025	281,244
Substance abuse, and mental health services [3]	1,241	1,931	2,241	3,203	3,183	3,179	2,847	2,877
Grants to states for Medicaid [3]	41,103	117,921	176,231	181,720	180,625	190,624	201,426	262,389
State children's health insurance fund [3]	(NA)	1,220	4,607	5,129	5,451	6,000	6,900	8,466
Income security	36,768	68,653	85,983	90,885	89,816	90,971	96,102	108,942
SNAP (formerly Food Stamp Program) [3]	2,130	3,508	4,204	4,385	4,608	4,602	4,935	5,238
Child nutrition programs [3]	4,871	9,060	11,035	11,726	12,263	12,871	13,761	15,381
Temporary assistance for needy families [3] . . .	(NA)	15,464	17,725	17,357	16,897	16,876	17,532	18,623
Veterans benefits and services [3]	134	434	493	552	625	639	695	807
Administration of justice	574	5,263	5,084	4,784	4,961	4,603	4,201	6,378

NA Not available.   [1] Grants include trust funds.   [2] Trust funds.   [3] Includes grants for payments to individuals.

Source: U.S. Office of Management and Budget, *Budget of the United States Government, Historical Tables*, annual; <http://www.whitehouse.gov/omb>.

Table 421. **Federal Aid to State and Local Governments—Selected Programs by State: 2000 to 2007**

[In millions of dollars (219,943 represents $219,943,000,000). For fiscal year ending September 30]

State	2000	2005	2006	2007	State	2000	2005	2006	2007
U.S.	291,943	403,660	428,154	439,794	MO	5,671	7,407	7,374	7,955
AL	4,570	6,306	6,565	6,869	MT	1,439	2,021	1,755	1,835
AK	2,260	2,671	2,425	2,431	NE	1,682	2,256	2,240	2,328
AZ	4,501	7,965	8,190	8,672	NV	1,244	2,213	2,792	2,320
AR	2,657	4,179	4,335	4,474	NH	1,116	1,483	1,579	1,626
CA	33,158	46,029	46,033	49,976	NJ	8,212	10,479	11,117	11,929
CO	3,273	4,538	4,751	4,900	NM	2,774	4,097	4,070	4,347
CT	3,771	4,539	5,017	4,963	NY	30,038	43,438	41,863	43,297
DE	818	1,142	1,194	1,225	NC	7,911	11,568	11,455	12,448
DC	2,963	3,450	1,935	2,137	ND	1,155	1,394	1,274	1,281
FL	11,676	19,046	19,115	20,033	OH	10,560	13,726	14,275	15,731
GA	7,192	8,914	9,278	10,465	OK	3,587	4,935	5,092	5,516
HI	1,221	1,731	1,858	1,971	OR	3,597	4,808	4,821	5,003
ID	1,229	1,814	1,829	2,031	PA	12,765	18,103	17,963	18,981
IL	11,271	14,616	14,689	16,141	RI	1,526	1,937	2,007	2,105
IN	5,142	6,483	6,990	7,258	SC	4,017	5,326	5,851	5,863
IA	2,639	3,594	3,651	3,688	SD	1,131	1,336	1,422	1,280
KS	2,315	2,872	3,242	3,415	TN	6,160	9,083	8,169	9,031
KY	4,720	5,779	5,828	6,370	TX	17,350	25,622	29,327	28,104
LA	5,248	7,148	9,014	13,278	UT	1,910	2,633	2,774	2,845
ME	1,850	2,623	2,455	2,546	VT	900	1,213	1,294	1,546
MD	5,538	6,800	7,006	7,372	VA	4,615	6,330	6,997	7,173
MA	7,500	9,989	10,438	11,224	WA	5,707	7,681	7,375	8,050
MI	9,486	12,113	11,645	12,822	WV	2,542	3,482	3,353	3,571
MN	4,599	5,878	6,441	7,001	WI	4,504	6,563	6,240	6,719
MS	3,420	5,168	7,183	8,239	WY	1,014	2,243	1,998	1,898

Source: U.S. Census Bureau, *Federal Aid to States For Fiscal Year 2007* (published September 2008). See also <http://www.census.gov/prod/2008pubs/fas-07.pdf>.

U.S. Census Bureau, *Statistical Abstract of the United States: 2010*

Table 422. Federal Aid to State and Local Governments—Selected Programs by State: 2007

[In millions of dollars (439,794 represents $439,794,000,000). For fiscal year ending September 30. Negative amounts (–) are refunds (from the recipients) of advances from a prior year, or represent reductions in the amount of funds originally obligated to the recipients for the particular program or program category during the fiscal year]

State and island areas	Federal aid, total [1]	Department of Agriculture — Food and Nutrition Service — Total	Child nutrition programs	Supplemental Nutrition Assistance Program (SNAP)	Special supplemental food program (WIC)	Other	Department of Education — Total	Office of Elementary and Secondary Education — Special education programs	No child left behind act	Title 1 programs	Other
United States, total .	439,794	25,492	12,765	4,601	5,309	2,817	35,142	9,789	4,572	10,859	9,923
Alabama	6,869	435	240	44	98	53	579	176	84	194	125
Alaska	2,431	122	37	10	22	53	132	–	3	–	129
Arizona	8,672	506	279	53	113	61	861	176	94	254	338
Arkansas	4,474	301	162	23	59	57	376	117	60	124	75
California	49,976	3,153	1,590	511	824	228	4,905	1,123	647	1,726	1,409
Colorado	4,900	257	125	30	56	45	533	146	71	129	188
Connecticut	4,963	176	95	28	–	53	355	134	51	97	73
Delaware	1,225	69	36	10	–	23	124	32	24	32	37
District of Columbia	2,137	63	29	16	–	17	142	18	24	48	53
Florida	20,033	1,118	709	70	279	60	2,070	603	208	671	588
Georgia	10,465	882	545	74	195	67	95	2	6	–	87
Hawaii	1,971	118	47	16	30	26	250	46	30	53	121
Idaho	2,031	142	59	12	21	50	191	55	33	44	58
Illinois	16,141	850	487	108	186	68	1,608	496	217	534	361
Indiana	7,258	406	239	42	82	42	611	244	75	195	97
Iowa	3,688	230	113	20	–	96	321	114	41	60	106
Kansas	3,415	226	128	18	40	40	129	11	6	–	112
Kentucky	6,370	411	218	41	91	61	148	9	5	3	131
Louisiana	13,278	472	274	53	87	58	40	1	4	–	35
Maine	2,546	90	44	10	16	20	177	56	29	46	45
Maryland	7,372	319	167	43	74	34	658	235	73	176	173
Massachusetts	11,224	349	196	53	–	99	693	249	83	195	167
Michigan	12,822	661	322	109	141	88	1,238	396	180	466	196
Minnesota	7,001	392	191	63	80	57	513	209	73	109	123
Mississippi	8,239	389	215	30	69	75	546	121	78	166	182
Missouri	7,955	416	234	50	77	55	103	2	11	–	90
Montana	1,835	107	36	13	13	46	205	40	32	41	92
Nebraska	2,328	154	81	17	26	31	245	75	36	49	84
Nevada	2,320	132	73	17	28	14	245	62	32	76	75
New Hampshire	1,626	56	24	7	11	14	161	53	31	30	47
New Jersey	11,929	469	255	88	–	126	1,014	364	125	283	242
New Mexico	4,347	214	134	6	42	32	381	88	91	163	-
New York	43,297	1,558	828	281	355	93	3,156	729	472	1,284	671
North Carolina	12,448	754	425	82	160	87	1,043	337	118	287	301
North Dakota	1,281	73	28	10	11	24	154	29	26	32	67
Ohio	15,731	755	385	132	168	70	84	3	11	–	70
Oklahoma	5,516	400	211	54	80	55	608	159	76	141	233
Oregon	5,003	432	133	59	61	179	481	142	59	134	145
Pennsylvania	18,981	773	377	154	149	94	1,365	509	188	465	204
Rhode Island	2,105	73	36	10	–	26	19	3	–	–	16
South Carolina	5,863	360	220	21	78	39	582	188	72	179	143
South Dakota	1,280	92	37	12	14	29	73	1	2	–	70
Tennessee	9,031	524	290	61	118	55	724	235	96	199	193
Texas	28,104	2,209	1,409	176	489	134	3,460	948	435	1,167	910
Utah	2,845	174	92	23	33	26	284	87	33	46	117
Vermont	1,546	73	19	19	13	23	124	28	27	30	40
Virginia	7,173	402	184	82	89	48	866	278	95	214	279
Washington	8,050	450	205	55	105	85	654	218	87	173	176
West Virginia	3,571	189	85	17	31	56	272	79	43	98	52
Wisconsin	6,719	352	176	50	69	58	663	209	74	156	225
Wyoming	1,898	50	18	6	8	18	133	29	27	29	48
Island areas:											
American Samoa	135	25	11	5	7	2	28	5	1	–	22
Micronesia	98	–	–	–	–	–	6	4	–	–	1
Guam	308	22	8	3	7	4	44	15	1	–	28
Marshall Islands	90	–	–	–	–	–	5	3	–	–	3
Northern Marianas . . .	89	17	7	10	–	1	16	5	–	–	11
Palau	25	–	–	–	–	–	3	1	–	–	2
Puerto Rico	5,405	2,015	181	1,585	200	49	640	89	121	337	94
Virgin Islands	233	32	14	7	–	10	6	–	–	–	5
Undistributed amounts . .	1,128	5	–	–	–	5	–	–	–	–	–

See footnotes at end of table.

U.S. Census Bureau, Statistical Abstract of the United States: 2010

Table 422. Federal Aid to State and Local Governments—Selected Programs by State: 2007—Con.

[See headnote, page 264]

State and island areas	FEMA total [3]	Department of Housing and Urban Development						Department of Labor			
		Total	Community development block grants	Public housing programs				State unemployment insurance and employment Total	Workforce invest- ment	Other
				Low rent hous- ing assis- tance	Hous- ing certi- ficate pro- gram	Capital pro- gram	Other	Total	Work- force service		
United States, total .	4,548	47,971	10,899	24,888	2,715	3,338	6,132	8,291	3,863	3,141	1,288
Alabama	68	626	82	372	18	70	84	103	49	37	17
Alaska	20	195	21	41	3	3	127	56	29	19	8
Arizona	7	424	74	162	14	9	165	111	43	47	20
Arkansas	18	277	34	174	17	24	28	76	37	27	12
California	232	4,985	591	3,347	235	100	713	1,015	472	415	129
Colorado	13	460	42	310	35	18	56	113	53	44	15
Connecticut	15	798	56	514	85	35	108	106	62	29	15
Delaware	6	118	9	64	21	4	20	33	13	8	12
District of Columbia. . . .	–	–643	44	–1,029	29	181	91	20	14	2	4
Florida	586	1,736	228	1,071	63	70	305	256	115	106	35
Georgia	31	1,146	117	634	27	109	260	196	104	79	13
Hawaii	3	185	19	114	6	19	26	39	17	10	11
Idaho	1	84	17	38	13	1	15	41	25	10	6
Illinois.	32	2,358	186	1,373	194	303	303	389	184	158	47
Indiana	9	597	79	388	18	32	81	181	87	64	30
Iowa.	30	257	51	156	9	7	34	78	36	20	22
Kansas	287	204	34	126	9	14	21	79	28	42	9
Kentucky.	14	501	58	319	12	45	68	126	57	48	22
Louisiana	1,227	5,112	4,519	429	25	67	71	124	36	77	11
Maine.	15	232	27	134	35	6	31	48	23	13	13
Maryland.	13	97	88	606	60	83	93	191	72	34	85
Massachusetts	15	2,049	136	1,423	249	72	168	162	86	58	18
Michigan	6	1,110	156	558	173	45	179	468	222	174	73
Minnesota	19	668	73	366	99	33	97	130	74	31	26
Mississippi.	524	1,938	1,645	210	15	24	43	129	31	90	8
Missouri	122	647	82	415	22	39	90	146	59	68	20
Montana	3	123	18	53	3	3	46	33	15	8	10
Nebraska	71	156	21	91	5	15	25	34	21	8	5
Nevada.	4	201	34	121	8	9	28	50	30	12	8
New Hampshire	31	181	20	110	18	7	26	27	16	7	4
New Jersey	17	1,700	126	1,098	215	78	182	213	131	61	21
New Mexico.	21	184	25	101	8	8	42	55	20	20	15
New York	301	5,613	643	3,768	215	465	521	491	240	199	52
North Carolina	42	881	79	565	26	64	146	311	168	90	52
North Dakota	8	96	11	52	1	3	28	21	13	6	2
Ohio.	29	1,832	196	1,173	98	111	255	333	144	156	33
Oklahoma	71	391	46	183	15	21	126	77	35	28	14
Oregon.	23	367	43	198	29	12	84	149	66	58	26
Pennsylvania	80	1,914	236	1,059	160	176	283	353	188	115	50
Rhode Island	–	304	21	193	33	15	43	38	23	11	4
South Carolina	12	430	51	258	16	28	77	160	72	70	18
South Dakota	9	118	19	45	12	2	42	25	13	8	4
Tennessee.	18	665	58	396	32	75	104	160	72	69	19
Texas	180	2,067	320	1,272	90	147	239	482	181	258	43
Utah.	7	132	26	79	5	3	19	61	36	15	10
Vermont	2	97	11	55	14	3	15	191	78	6	106
Virginia	41	922	79	522	82	107	133	68	11	40	16
Washington	23	679	87	399	8	31	154	222	99	77	46
West Virginia	3	223	49	130	11	10	23	145	92	38	15
Wisconsin	4	515	73	254	77	15	95	69	28	18	22
Wyoming.	3	40	9	20	2	1	8	20	11	5	4
Island areas:											
American Samoa. . . .	1	4	3	–	–	–	1	–	–	–	–
Micronesia	4	–	–	–	–	–	–	–	–	–	–
Guam	7	41	3	32	–	2	3	3	–	2	–
Marshall Islands	–	–	–	–	–	–	–	–	–	–	–
Northern Marianas. . .	4	5	1	4	–	–	1	1	–	–	–
Palau	–	–	–	–	–	–	–	–	–	–	–
Puerto Rico	26	799	120	395	46	178	60	80	30	44	6
Virgin Islands	1	55	4	39	2	7	3	6	4	1	1
Undistributed amounts. .	190	205	1	–91	–	331	–	–	–	–	–

See footnotes at end of table.

State and Local Government Finances and Employment 265

Table 422. Federal Aid to State and Local Governments—Selected Programs by State: 2007—Con.

[See headnote, page 264]

State and island areas	Department of Health and Human Services						Department of Transportation				Other federal aid [4]
	Total	Administration for Children and Families			Centers for Medicare and Medicaid services	Other	Total	Highway trust fund	Federal Transit Administration	Other	
		Children & family services (Head Start)	Foster care and adoption assistance	Temporary assistance for needy families							
United States, total ..	252,150	8,477	6,537	16,917	195,305	24,914	47,955	33,694	9,286	4,975	18,244
Alabama............	3,803	137	39	112	3,108	407	927	768	64	96	328
Alaska.............	806	48	22	52	566	117	730	410	53	267	370
Arizona............	5,758	186	127	263	4,725	457	712	436	209	67	294
Arkansas...........	2,835	88	44	68	2,403	231	468	377	22	69	124
California	29,910	1,048	1,576	3,996	20,501	2,788	4,411	2,660	1,290	462	1,364
Colorado...........	2,363	193	82	117	1,619	352	767	486	185	96	394
Connecticut.........	2,963	67	119	262	2,216	300	431	336	63	32	121
Delaware	676	17	8	28	543	80	131	101	13	16	68
District of Columbia	1,466	49	34	106	1,029	249	487	132	309	46	603
Florida	11,025	333	220	591	8,501	1,380	2,713	2,123	341	249	529
Georgia	6,264	204	105	471	4,847	638	1,510	1,296	124	90	341
Hawaii	995	36	36	113	685	124	234	115	47	71	146
Idaho.............	1,046	42	12	28	831	133	383	347	13	23	143
Illinois	8,584	335	294	583	6,385	988	1,894	1,144	546	204	427
Indiana............	4,433	128	127	198	3,594	387	794	660	70	64	227
Iowa	2,203	71	59	149	1,691	232	429	347	43	39	141
Kansas............	1,800	70	55	86	1,423	167	588	514	27	47	102
Kentucky	4,061	135	77	177	3,368	304	825	678	54	94	283
Louisiana	5,139	180	61	206	4,176	515	820	661	75	84	345
Maine.............	1,656	41	23	77	1,399	116	216	171	21	24	112
Maryland	3,995	115	163	236	3,011	471	936	601	181	153	1,356
Massachusetts........	6,895	150	119	481	5,584	561	783	465	275	43	278
Michigan...........	7,621	302	180	746	5,618	775	1,343	1,084	154	105	375
Minnesota..........	4,238	116	73	276	3,325	448	788	587	110	91	252
Mississippi	3,456	187	18	110	2,790	351	1,026	921	17	88	232
Missouri	5,190	161	94	220	4,269	445	1,044	832	96	116	287
Montana...........	772	46	19	41	553	111	397	331	13	53	195
Nebraska	1,252	51	25	49	978	149	302	241	20	41	114
Nevada	1,035	26	37	53	754	165	409	300	52	58	243
New Hampshire.......	823	23	18	48	634	101	243	179	13	51	104
New Jersey.........	6,547	158	123	417	5,116	734	1,686	917	676	93	283
New Mexico	2,335	78	36	70	1,958	193	391	316	31	44	767
New York	28,057	609	508	2,057	22,970	1,913	3,336	1,555	1,647	135	784
North Carolina.......	7,990	275	116	348	6,569	682	1,144	899	168	77	283
North Dakota........	524	37	15	27	360	85	272	231	14	27	134
Ohio	10,798	311	379	1,045	8,161	901	1,494	1,164	183	147	406
Oklahoma..........	3,120	131	71	135	2,456	327	596	507	43	46	252
Oregon............	2,600	113	86	155	1,960	286	651	400	205	45	300
Pennsylvania........	11,953	293	420	677	9,291	1,270	1,978	1,398	475	105	566
Rhode Island........	1,290	33	24	107	1,019	106	291	228	30	33	92
South Carolina.......	3,489	110	41	94	2,927	317	633	565	36	32	197
South Dakota	607	46	9	24	437	92	257	214	12	31	98
Tennessee	5,546	161	71	175	4,670	469	902	730	57	115	493
Texas.............	16,329	634	275	531	13,186	1,703	2,563	1,887	450	227	814
Utah	1,436	58	26	72	1,095	184	459	282	128	50	291
Vermont	786	23	18	48	627	69	194	163	16	15	80
Virginia............	3,603	133	101	152	2,740	477	942	693	122	126	329
Washington.........	4,411	173	127	338	3,236	537	1,195	745	319	131	416
West Virginia........	2,075	61	50	85	1,680	199	476	388	22	66	189
Wisconsin	4,056	131	107	321	3,081	417	788	641	94	54	272
Wyoming	367	22	4	30	259	53	253	218	9	26	1,032
Island areas:											
American Samoa	22	5	–	–	9	8	11	1	–	10	44
Micronesia.........	4	–	–	–	–	4	–	–	–	–	85
Guam............	43	6	–	3	15	20	36	6	2	28	112
Marshall Islands	1	–	–	–	–	1	–	–	–	–	83
Northern Marianas ...	7	1	–	–	5	2	20	1	–	19	19
Palau	4	2	–	–	–	2	–	–	–	–	18
Puerto Rico	1,035	271	67	57	348	292	148	78	50	20	662
Virgin Islands	42	13	–	3	7	19	17	11	1	5	76
Undistributed amounts ..	14	5	–	–	–	9	481	150	–	330	234

– Represents or rounds to zero.   [1] Total includes programs not shown separately.   [2] For Puerto Rico, amount shown is for nutritional assistance grant program, all other amounts are grant payments for food stamp administration.   [3] FEMA = Federal Emergency Management Agency. FEMA is part of the U.S. Department of Homeland Security.   [4] Represents aid for other programs not shown.

Source: U.S. Census Bureau, Federal Aid to States for Fiscal Year 2007 (published September 2008). See also <http://www.census.gov/prod/2008pubs/fas-07.pdf>.

266   State and Local Government Finances and Employment

Table 423. **State and Local Governments—Summary of Finances: 1990 to 2006**

[In millions of dollars (1,032,115 represents $1,032,115,000,000) except as indicated. For fiscal year ending in year shown; see text, this section. Local government amounts are estimates subject to sampling variation; see Appendix III and source. Minus sign (-) indicates net loss]

Item	1990	2000	2003	2004	2005	2006
Revenue [1]	1,032,115	1,942,328	2,047,337	2,435,084	2,528,912	2,736,542
From Federal government	136,802	291,950	389,264	425,683	438,432	452,233
Public welfare	59,961	148,549	199,789	217,176	225,691	225,605
Highways	14,368	24,414	30,052	30,692	33,672	34,559
Education	23,233	45,873	61,901	71,010	74,136	79,397
Health and hospitals	5,904	15,611	21,491	23,316	22,725	23,819
Housing and community development	9,655	17,690	24,713	26,560	28,018	29,121
Other and unallocable	23,683	39,812	51,317	56,929	54,191	59,732
From state and local sources	895,313	1,650,379	1,658,073	2,009,401	2,090,761	2,186,018
General, net intergovernmental	712,700	1,249,373	1,373,948	1,464,058	1,588,462	1,733,785
Taxes	501,619	872,351	938,972	1,010,277	1,099,200	1,195,254
Property	155,613	249,178	296,683	318,242	335,981	359,109
Sales and gross receipts	177,885	309,290	337,787	360,629	384,383	412,114
Individual income	105,640	211,661	199,407	215,215	242,273	268,599
Corporation net income	23,566	36,059	31,369	33,716	43,138	52,931
Other	38,915	66,164	73,726	82,475	93,425	102,500
Charges and miscellaneous	211,081	377,022	434,976	453,781	489,262	538,531
Utility and liquor stores	58,642	89,546	108,388	114,054	119,843	131,642
Water supply system	17,674	30,515	34,736	36,087	37,377	40,274
Electric power system	29,268	42,436	53,938	55,980	59,157	65,387
Gas supply system	5,216	8,049	8,985	9,783	10,382	8,724
Transit system	3,043	3,954	5,391	6,506	6,937	10,881
Liquor stores	3,441	4,592	5,338	5,338	5,990	6,377
Insurance trust revenue [2]	123,970	311,460	175,737	431,289	382,456	418,881
Employee retirement	94,268	273,881	120,157	365,265	316,576	352,521
Unemployment compensation	18,441	23,366	35,335	38,362	35,243	36,989
Direct expenditure	972,695	1,742,914	2,159,772	2,260,330	2,368,692	2,500,583
By function:						
Direct general expenditure [2]	831,573	1,502,768	1,817,513	1,903,194	2,012,422	2,121,946
Education [2]	288,148	521,612	621,335	655,361	689,057	727,967
Elementary and secondary	202,009	365,181	428,503	452,055	473,406	500,528
Higher education	73,418	134,352	164,187	173,086	182,146	191,758
Highways	61,057	101,336	117,696	118,179	124,602	135,412
Public welfare	107,287	233,350	306,463	335,257	362,932	370,325
Health	24,223	51,366	61,703	63,125	66,971	71,110
Hospitals	50,412	75,976	93,175	96,551	103,404	110,455
Police protection	30,577	56,798	67,361	69,707	74,727	79,000
Fire protection	13,186	23,102	27,854	28,330	31,439	34,167
Natural resources	12,330	20,235	22,808	23,299	25,057	25,482
Sanitation and sewerage	28,453	45,261	51,723	55,908	58,069	61,900
Housing and community development	15,479	26,590	35,275	37,221	39,969	41,980
Parks and recreation	14,326	25,038	31,765	30,467	31,941	34,769
Financial administration	16,217	29,300	34,911	36,163	36,519	37,441
Interest on general debt [3]	49,739	69,814	77,277	81,723	81,119	85,660
Utility and liquor stores [3]	77,801	114,916	148,996	159,732	160,682	174,679
Water supply system	22,101	35,789	43,260	44,806	45,799	47,752
Electric power system	30,997	39,719	54,355	59,299	58,612	66,308
Gas supply system	2,989	3,724	5,300	6,717	7,075	9,064
Transit system	18,788	31,883	41,678	44,237	44,310	46,327
Liquor stores	2,926	3,801	4,402	4,673	4,885	5,228
Insurance trust expenditure [2]	63,321	125,230	193,263	197,405	195,588	203,958
Employee retirement	38,355	95,679	127,197	137,537	145,796	156,180
Unemployment compensation	16,499	18,648	51,547	43,278	29,849	28,097
Current operation	700,131	1,288,746	1,579,290	1,662,510	1,764,453	1,863,003
Capital outlay	123,102	217,063	263,198	269,976	277,200	295,368
Construction	89,144	161,694	203,035	209,395	216,254	229,529
Equipment, land, and existing structures	33,958	55,369	60,162	60,581	60,947	65,839
Assistance and subsidies	27,227	31,375	35,080	36,922	39,469	41,035
Interest on debt (general and utility)	58,914	80,499	88,940	93,518	91,981	97,198
Insurance benefits and repayments	63,321	125,230	193,263	197,405	195,588	203,958
Expenditure for salaries and wages [4]	340,654	548,796	647,211	666,041	693,146	721,255
Debt outstanding, year end	858,006	1,451,815	1,812,667	1,951,661	2,086	2,201
Long-term	838,700	1,427,524	1,772,197	1,913,286	2,054,838	2,167,684
Short-term	19,306	24,291	40,470	38,374	30,759	33,208
Long-term debt:						
Issued	108,468	184,831	345,784	346,813	321,960	339,333
Retired	64,831	121,897	215,218	241,111	223,862	227,682

[1] Aggregates exclude duplicative transactions between state and local governments; see source. [2] Includes amounts not shown separately. [3] Interest on utility debt included in "utility and liquor stores expenditure." For total interest on debt, see "Interest on debt (general and utility)." [4] Included in items above.

Source: U.S. Census Bureau Federal, State and Local Governments, *State and Local Government Finances*, Series GF, No. 3 thereafter (published July 2008); <http://www.census.gov/govs/estimate/historicaldata2006.html>.

Table 424. **State and Local Governments—Revenue and Expenditures by Function: 2005 and 2006**

[In millions of dollars (2,529,193 represents $2,529,193,000,000) For fiscal year ending in year shown; see text, this section. Local government amounts are estimates subject to sampling variation; see Appendix III and source]

Item	2005 State and local	2005 State	2005 Local	2006 State and local	2006 State	2006 Local
Revenue [1]	**2,529,193**	**1,641,957**	**1,308,507**	**2,736,542**	**1,773,208**	**1,406,440**
Intergovernmental revenue [1]	438,432	407,860	451,844	452,233	419,143	476,196
Total revenue from own sources [1]	2,090,761	1,234,097	856,663	2,186,018	1,385,376	1,243,748
General revenue from own sources.	1,588,462	878,854	709,608	1,733,785	966,233	767,552
Taxes [2].	1,099,200	650,612	448,588	1,195,254	710,864	484,390
Property	335,981	11,342	324,639	359,109	11,794	347,315
Individual income	242,273	221,597	20,676	268,599	245,883	22,717
Corporation income	43,138	38,691	4,447	52,931	47,466	5,465
Sales and gross receipts	384,383	312,584	71,798	412,114	332,972	79,142
General sales	262,981	212,921	50,060	282,179	226,712	55,467
Selective sales [2]	121,402	99,663	21,739	129,936	106,260	23,675
Motor fuel	35,767	34,567	1,200	36,972	35,702	1,270
Alcoholic beverages	5,125	4,706	419	5,369	4,925	444
Tobacco products	13,337	12,917	420	14,975	14,499	476
Public utilities.	22,390	10,909	11,480	23,669	11,426	12,243
Motor vehicle and operators' license.	21,713	20,270	1,443	20,520	19,015	1,505
Death and gift.	5,422	5,340	82	4,875	4,745	130
Charges and miscellaneous [2]	489,262	228,242	261,020	538,531	255,369	283,162
Current charges [2]	309,826	124,186	185,639	334,841	137,401	197,440
Education [2].	90,153	69,010	21,143	96,898	74,306	22,592
School lunch sales	6,500	22	6,479	6,745	22	6,723
Higher education	76,683	68,010	8,673	82,127	73,195	8,932
Natural resources	3,369	2,349	1,021	3,548	2,449	1,099
Hospitals	79,092	29,378	49,714	83,658	31,718	51,939
Sewerage.	31,610	39	31,571	33,804	49	33,754
Solid waste management	12,931	473	12,458	13,633	476	13,157
Parks and recreation	8,024	1,360	6,663	8,659	1,462	7,197
Housing and community development	4,846	573	4,273	5,075	622	4,452
Airports	14,391	1,042	13,350	15,471	1,152	14,320
Sea and inland port facilities	3,394	987	2,407	3,699	1,066	2,633
Highways	9,845	6,028	3,817	16,302	10,326	5,976
Interest earnings.	59,011	31,917	27,094	71,495	38,207	33,288
Special assessments	6,323	752	5,571	7,094	779	6,316
Sale of property	2,837	1,060	1,777	3,941	1,115	2,826
Utility and liquor store revenue	119,843	19,746	100,097	125,265	15,816	109,449
Insurance trust revenue	382,456	335,498	46,958	418,881	366,586	52,296
Expenditure [1]	**2,373,408**	**1,471,936**	**1,313,908**	**2,507,086**	**1,551,555**	**1,390,867**
Intergovernmental expenditure [1].	4,617	403,488	13,565	6,504	428,925	12,915
Direct expenditure [1].	2,368,791	1,068,449	1,300,342	2,500,583	1,122,631	1,377,952
General expenditure [2].	2,012,594	874,491	1,138,103	2,121,946	918,205	1,203,740
Education [2]	689,057	191,553	497,504	727,967	202,474	525,493
Elementary and secondary education	473,406	5,614	467,792	500,528	6,025	494,503
Higher education	182,146	152,434	29,712	191,758	160,769	30,990
Public welfare	362,932	318,144	44,788	370,325	324,714	45,611
Hospitals.	103,476	42,676	60,801	110,455	44,320	66,135
Health	66,971	31,452	35,519	71,110	32,994	38,115
Highways	124,604	76,575	48,028	135,412	84,289	51,123
Police protection.	74,727	10,011	64,716	79,066	10,838	68,228
Fire protection	31,439	–	31,439	34,167	–	34,167
Corrections	59,156	38,321	20,835	62,667	40,413	22,254
Natural resources	25,057	17,094	7,963	25,482	18,146	7,336
Sewerage	36,600	1,109	35,491	39,220	1,266	37,955
Solid waste management.	21,469	3,184	18,285	22,679	3,254	19,425
Housing and community development	39,969	4,982	34,987	41,980	5,153	36,827
Governmental administration	108,874	47,710	61,163	111,335	46,814	64,521
Parks and recreation	31,941	4,482	27,459	34,769	4,876	29,893
Interest on general debt.	81,119	34,315	46,804	85,660	37,808	47,852
Utility.	155,797	21,824	133,973	169,451	24,904	144,547
Liquor store expenditure	4,885	4,082	803	5,228	4,338	890
Insurance trust expenditure	195,516	168,052	27,463	203,958	175,183	28,775
By character and object:						
Current operation.	1,764,526	739,988	1,024,538	1,863,023	774,651	1,088,372
Capital outlay	277,299	94,181	183,119	295,368	101,432	193,936
Construction	216,268	77,039	139,229	229,529	83,858	145,672
Equipment, land, and existing structure	61,032	17,142	43,890	65,839	17,575	48,264
Assistance and subsidies	39,469	30,181	9,287	41,035	31,644	9,391
Interest on debt (general and utility)	91,981	36,047	55,935	97,198	39,720	57,478
Insurance benefits and repayments	195,516	168,052	27,463	203,958	175,183	28,775
Expenditure for salaries and wages [3]	*693,146*	*194,447*	*498,699*	*721,255*	*203,164*	*518,091*

– Represents or rounds to zero.   [1] Aggregates exclude duplicative transactions between levels of government; see source.
[2] Includes amounts not shown separately.   [3] Included in items shown above.

Source: U.S. Census Bureau, Federal, State, and Local Governments, Finance, *State and Local Government Finances: 2005-06* (published July 2008); <http://www.census.gov/govs/www/estimate06.html>.

Table 425. **State and Local Governments—Capital Outlays: 1990 to 2006**

[In millions of dollars (123,102 represents $123,102,000,000), except percent. For fiscal year ending in year shown; see text, this section. Local government amounts are subject to sampling variation; see Appendix III and source. Minus sign (−) indicates net loss]

Level and function	1990	2000	2001	2002	2003	2004	2005	2006
State & local governments: Total.	123,102	217,063	233,258	257,071	263,198	269,976	277,299	295,368
Annual percent change [1]	9.0	9.4	7.5	10.2	2.4	2.6	2.7	6.5
By function:								
Education [2]	25,997	60,968	65,116	71,680	70,813	74,597	77,779	82,505
Elementary and secondary	18,057	45,150	48,404	53,294	51,118	52,977	54,509	59,256
Higher education.	7,441	15,257	15,911	17,652	19,044	21,121	22,782	22,798
Highways	33,867	56,439	60,108	66,017	65,523	65,964	69,644	76,371
Health and hospitals	3,848	5,502	5,630	6,126	7,158	7,241	7,711	8,538
Natural resources	2,545	4,347	4,908	4,247	4,244	4,657	4,543	4,473
Housing [3]	3,997	6,184	5,888	6,939	7,660	7,578	7,880	8,130
Air transportation	3,434	6,717	8,420	8,551	9,066	9,731	9,326	9,064
Water transportation [4]	924	1,618	4,306	1,691	3,721	1,798	1,598	1,850
Sewerage	8,356	10,093	9,224	11,574	12,467	14,068	14,171	15,336
Parks and recreation	3,877	6,916	8,540	9,093	9,224	7,866	8,151	9,267
Utilities	16,601	24,847	24,553	30,241	34,538	37,432	34,879	36,795
Water	6,873	10,542	10,742	11,831	13,536	13,651	14,402	14,356
Electric	3,976	4,177	4,812	6,538	6,438	7,173	6,055	7,793
Gas	310	400	453	358	422	582	544	520
Transit.	5,443	9,728	8,545	11,514	14,142	16,026	13,879	14,126
Other	19,657	33,431	36,566	40,912	38,784	39,044	41,618	43,039
State governments: Total	45,524	76,233	81,881	89,767	91,943	90,950	94,181	101,432
Annual percent change [1]	5.6	11.3	7.4	9.6	2.4	−1.1	3.6	7.7
By function:								
Education [2]	7,253	14,077	14,936	16,589	17,727	19,632	20,632	20,623
Highways	24,850	41,651	44,761	49,119	48,719	48,566	51,578	57,025
Health and hospitals	1,531	2,228	2,390	2,241	2,930	2,763	3,278	3,469
Natural resources	1,593	2,758	3,105	2,766	2,788	2,957	2,670	2,588
Housing [3]	119	860	600	582	774	222	338	196
Air transportation	339	561	667	525	846	795	615	519
Water transportation [4]	202	310	362	346	410	388	367	493
Sewerage	333	403	393	405	405	881	486	650
Parks and recreation	601	1,044	1,185	1,483	1,098	945	931	1,146
Utilities	2,605	4,232	3,641	5,145	7,084	5,211	4,319	5,907
Other	6,098	8,108	9,840	10,567	9,163	8,589	8,967	8,817
Local governments: Total	77,578	140,830	151,377	167,304	171,255	179,026	183,119	193,936
Annual percent change [1]	4.5	8.4	7.5	10.5	2.4	4.5	2.3	5.9
By function:								
Education [2]	18,744	46,890	50,180	55,091	53,087	54,965	57,147	61,882
Elementary and secondary	17,669	44,629	47,808	52,804	50,475	52,261	54,068	58,677
Higher education.	1,076	2,261	2,072	2,286	2,612	2,704	3,079	3,205
Highways	9,017	14,789	15,347	16,898	16,804	17,398	18,066	19,346
Health and hospitals	2,316	3,274	3,239	3,886	4,228	4,478	4,433	5,069
Natural resources	952	1,589	1,803	1,481	1,456	1,699	1,873	1,885
Housing [3]	3,878	5,324	5,288	6,358	6,886	7,356	7,542	7,934
Air transportation	3,095	6,156	7,753	8,026	8,221	8,936	8,712	8,545
Water transportation [4]	722	1,308	3,944	1,345	3,310	1,410	1,231	1,357
Sewerage	8,023	9,690	8,831	11,169	12,062	13,186	13,685	14,687
Parks and recreation	3,276	5,872	7,355	7,611	8,126	6,921	7,221	8,122
Utilities	13,996	20,615	20,912	25,096	27,455	32,221	30,560	30,888
Other	13,559	25,323	26,726	30,345	29,621	30,454	32,650	34,222

[1] Change from immediate/prior year except 1990, change from 1989. [2] Includes other education not shown separately.
[3] Includes community development. [4] Includes terminals.

Source: U.S. Census Bureau, Federal, State, and Local Governments, Finance, *State and Local Government Finances: 2004–05* (published July 2008) and unpublished data. See also <http://www.census.gov/govs/www/estimate06.html>.

Table 426. **State and Local Governments—Expenditures for Public Works: 2000 to 2006**

[In millions of dollars (230,569 represents $230,569,000,000), except percent. Public works include expenditures for current operations and capital outlays on highways, airports, water transport and terminals, sewerage, solid waste management, water supply, and mass transit systems. Represents direct expenditures excluding intergovernmental grants]

Item	Total	Highways	Airport transpor- tation	Water transport and terminals	Sewer- age	Solid waste manage- ment	Water supply	Mass transit
2000, Total.	230,569	101,336	13,160	3,141	28,052	17,208	35,789	31,883
State	74,974	61,942	1,106	863	955	2,347	354	7,407
Local	155,595	39,394	12,054	2,277	27,098	14,861	35,435	24,476
Capital expenditures (percent) . . .	41.9	55.7	51.0	51.5	36.0	8.9	29.5	30.5
2005, Total.	294,695	124,604	17,962	3,951	36,600	21,469	45,799	44,310
State	92,823	76,575	1,406	1,156	1,109	3,184	319	9,074
Local	201,872	48,028	16,556	2,795	35,491	18,285	45,480	35,237
Capital expenditures (percent) . . .	42.4	55.9	51.9	40.4	38.7	9.3	31.4	31.3
2006, Total.	314,069	135,412	18,393	4,286	39,220	22,679	47,752	46,327
State	101,839	84,289	1,432	1,327	1,266	3,254	337	9,934
Local	212,230	51,123	16,961	2,958	37,955	19,425	47,415	36,393
Capital expenditures (percent) . . .	42.4	56.4	49.3	43.2	39.1	9.3	30.1	30.5

Source: U.S. Census Bureau, Federal, State, and Local Governments,Finance, *State and Local Government Finances: 2005–06* (published July 2008) and unpublished data. See also <http://www.census.gov/govs/www/estimate06.html>.

Table 427. **State and Local Governments—Indebtedness: 1990 to 2006**

[In billions of dollars (858.0 represents $858,000,000,000). For fiscal year ending in year shown; see text, this section. Local government amounts are estimates subject to sampling variation; see Appendix III and source]

Item	Debt outstanding — Total	Cash and security holdings	Long-term — Total	Long-term — Public debt for private sources	Long-term — All other	Short-term	Long-term — Net long-term[1]	Long-term — Debt issued	Long-term — Debt retired
1990: Total	858.0	1,490.8	838.7	294.1	544.6	19.3	474.4	108.5	64.8
State	318.3	963.3	315.5	154.4	161.1	2.8	125.5	43.5	22.9
Local	539.8	527.5	523.2	139.7	383.5	16.5	348.9	65.0	42.0
1994: Total	1,074.7	1,888.5	1,048.0	301.6	746.4	26.7	672.8	207.8	166.6
State	411.0	1,247.7	406.1	170.2	235.9	4.9	200.8	78.5	61.3
Local	663.7	640.9	641.9	131.5	510.5	21.8	472.0	129.3	105.3
1995: Total	1,115.4	2,058.5	1,088.3	300.6	787.7	27.0	697.3	129.3	95.1
State	427.2	1,393.9	421.1	176.8	244.4	6.1	205.3	52.6	37.5
Local	688.1	664.6	667.2	123.9	543.3	20.9	491.9	76.8	57.6
1996: Total	1,169.7	2,261.7	1,145.7	312.6	833.0	24.0	751.6	141.1	106.5
State	452.4	1,562.9	446.5	186.4	260.2	5.8	220.3	60.2	42.4
Local	717.3	698.8	699.1	126.3	572.8	18.2	531.3	80.9	64.1
1997: Total	1,224.5	2,546.9	1,207.9	329.0	878.9	16.6	797.7	151.3	109.3
State	456.7	1,785.1	454.5	193.7	260.8	2.1	222.6	54.4	41.1
Local	767.9	761.8	753.4	135.3	618.1	14.5	575.1	96.8	68.2
1998: Total	1,283.6	2,890.2	1,266.3	335.8	930.5	17.3	842.6	204.4	144.6
State	483.1	2,058.6	480.9	202.3	278.7	2.2	237.2	83.4	58.1
Local	800.4	831.6	785.4	133.6	651.8	15.1	605.4	120.9	86.5
1999: Total	1,369.3	3,168.5	1,351.4	351.1	1,000.3	17.8	907.3	229.4	153.1
State	510.5	2,265.9	507.8	213.9	293.9	2.7	249.4	83.2	55.6
Local	858.8	902.5	843.6	137.2	706.4	15.2	657.9	146.2	97.5
2000: Total	1,451.8	3,503.7	1,427.5	372.6	1,054.9	24.3	959.6	184.8	121.9
State	547.9	2,518.9	541.5	227.3	314.2	6.4	266.9	75.0	44.4
Local	903.9	984.8	886.0	145.3	740.7	17.9	692.7	109.8	77.5
2001: Total	1,554.0	3,592.1	1,531.9	395.1	1,136.8	22.1	1,038.6	199.6	130.6
State	576.5	2,537.7	572.8	238.2	334.7	3.7	287.4	81.3	50.7
Local	977.5	1,054.3	959.1	157.0	802.1	18.5	751.2	118.3	79.9
2002: Total	1,681.4	3,650.7	1,638.1	417.7	1,220.5	43.2	1,121.0	262.7	161.9
State	636.8	2,555.4	618.2	258.5	359.6	18.6	311.8	104.2	64.9
Local	1,044.6	1,095.3	1,020.0	159.2	860.8	24.6	809.2	158.5	97.0
2003: Total	1,812.7	3,696.1	1,772.2	431.4	1,340.8	40.5	1,242.7	345.8	215.2
State	697.9	2,594.2	681.8	267.3	414.5	16.1	366.2	148.8	85.9
Local	1,114.7	1,101.9	1,090.4	164.1	926.3	24.3	876.5	196.9	129.3
2004: Total	1,951.7	4,120.1	1,913.3	448.4	1,464.9	38.4	1,349.6	346.8	241.1
State	754.2	2,930.1	740.4	268.4	472.0	13.7	412.2	158.4	107.1
Local	1,197.5	1,189.9	1,172.9	180.0	992.9	24.6	937.4	188.5	134.0
2005: Total	2,085.6	4,439.4	2,054.8	480.6	1,574.2	30.8	1,441.1	322.0	231.8
State	813.8	3,156.4	808.3	296.1	512.2	5.6	444.7	131.5	101.8
Local	1,271.8	1,283.0	1,246.5	184.5	1,062.0	25.2	996.4	190.5	130.0
2006: Total	2,200.9	4,807.1	2,167.7	505.1	1,662.6	33.2	1,519.5	339.3	227.7
State	870.9	3,436.4	860.3	315.9	544.4	10.6	473.4	147.0	95.0
Local	1,330.0	1,370.7	1,307.4	189.1	1,118.2	22.6	1,046.0	192.4	132.7

[1] Net long-term debt outstanding is the amount of long-term debt held by a government for which no funds have been set aside for its repayment.

Source: U.S. Census Bureau, 1990, *Government Finances,* Series GF, No. 5, annual; thereafter, Federal, State, and Local Governments, Finance, *State and Local Government Finances: 2005–06* and unpublished data. See also <http://www.census.gov/govs/www/estimate06.html>.

Table 428. **New Security Issues, State and Local Governments: 1990 to 2008**

[In billions of dollars (122.9 represents 122,900,000,000). Data sources for discontinued Statistical Supplement to the Federal Reserve Bulletin]

Type of issue, issuer, or use	1990	1995	2000	2002	2003	2004	2005	2006	2007	2008
All issues, new and refunding [1]	122.9	145.7	180.4	363.9	384.3	357.9	409.6	389.5	426.2	385.7
By type of issue:										
General obligation	39.5	57.0	64.5	145.3	144.1	130.5	145.8	115.1	130.5	112.0
Revenue	83.3	88.7	115.9	214.8	238.0	227.4	263.8	274.4	295.7	273.7
By type of issuer:										
State	15.0	14.7	19.9	33.9	49.8	47.4	31.6	28.3	35.0	31.7
Special district of statutory authority [2]	75.9	93.5	121.2	259.1	253.5	234.2	298.6	293.4	315.3	282.0
Municipality, county, or township	32.0	37.5	39.3	67.1	79.0	76.3	79.4	67.9	75.9	71.9
Issues for new capital.	97.9	102.4	154.3	242.9	264.7	228.4	223.8	262.5	275.3	213.0
By use of proceeds:										
Education	17.1	24.0	38.7	57.9	70.4	65.4	71.0	70.3	70.9	56.8
Transportation	11.8	11.9	19.7	22.1	23.8	20.5	25.4	30.2	27.9	26.0
Utilities and conservation.	10.0	9.6	11.9	33.4	10.3	9.2	9.9	7.8	11.4	12.2
Industrial aid	6.6	6.6	7.1	7.2	22.3	19.1	18.6	35.0	38.1	24.3
Other purposes	31.7	30.8	47.3	73.0	97.7	80.4	60.6	72.7	82.9	62.0

[1] Par amounts of long-term issues based on date of sale.   [2] Includes school districts.

Source: Board of Governors of the Federal Reserve System. Statistical Supplement to the Federal Reserve Bulletin, monthly. Based on data from Securities Data Company; <http://www.federalreserve.gov/econresdata/releases/govsecure/govsecure20090131.htm>.

270   State and Local Government Finances and Employment

Table 429. State and Local Governments—Total Revenue and Expenditures by State: 2000 to 2006

[In millions of dollars (1,942,328 represents $1,942,328,000,000), except as indicated. For fiscal year ending in year shown; see text, this section. These data cannot be used to compute the deficit or surplus for any single government, as these are estimates for all state and local governments within a state area. For further information, see the 2006 Government Finance and Employment Classification Manual at <http://www.census.gov/govs/classification/class06.html>]

State	Revenue				Expenditures			
	2000	2004	2005	2006	2000	2004	2005	2006
United States. . .	1,942,328	2,435,084	2,529,193	2,736,542	1,746,943	2,265,051	2,373,408	2,507,086
Alabama	25,726	32,065	33,377	35,697	25,319	31,268	33,241	35,276
Alaska	10,525	11,038	11,404	13,247	8,628	10,019	10,027	10,788
Arizona.	27,778	38,388	41,103	45,324	27,293	36,072	39,300	42,763
Arkansas.	13,833	18,027	18,866	20,798	12,245	16,323	17,224	18,503
California.	270,380	358,673	381,910	404,541	236,645	328,029	344,704	365,041
Colorado.	29,603	38,744	38,915	41,158	26,173	34,395	35,063	37,107
Connecticut	25,828	29,295	30,490	33,554	24,011	28,837	29,649	31,502
Delaware.	6,224	7,102	7,637	8,467	5,153	6,922	7,595	8,292
District of Columbia.	6,383	8,829	9,919	11,075	6,527	8,493	8,787	10,091
Florida	92,402	129,687	135,562	151,624	84,301	115,547	130,858	140,638
Georgia	49,310	57,902	60,297	65,307	43,517	58,435	58,905	63,053
Hawaii	8,488	9,983	11,000	11,999	8,254	9,870	10,534	11,018
Idaho	7,590	9,754	10,004	10,850	6,404	8,426	8,915	9,330
Illinois.	80,695	100,247	99,826	108,037	74,727	95,421	97,745	100,995
Indiana	32,716	40,977	44,261	51,062	31,250	39,333	42,048	44,033
Iowa.	17,220	22,545	23,204	24,840	17,275	20,634	21,486	23,102
Kansas	16,235	18,550	19,990	21,602	14,419	18,361	18,948	20,295
Kentucky.	25,200	26,834	28,044	31,152	21,473	26,871	26,963	29,514
Louisiana	27,109	34,107	35,858	39,729	25,018	31,089	32,578	35,314
Maine	8,554	11,131	11,383	11,700	7,652	10,031	10,207	10,713
Maryland.	33,949	44,288	45,075	48,367	30,598	38,540	41,373	44,280
Massachusetts	46,103	60,795	62,109	66,603	44,362	58,208	59,312	61,910
Michigan	70,112	80,185	81,055	88,461	61,506	77,621	75,980	77,016
Minnesota	38,785	42,956	45,465	48,830	35,424	42,144	42,936	44,820
Mississippi.	16,672	20,670	21,113	24,015	15,379	19,450	20,041	22,109
Missouri	31,635	40,033	41,340	44,201	27,953	35,571	37,186	39,551
Montana	5,643	7,088	7,438	8,019	4,983	6,198	6,412	6,948
Nebraska	11,650	15,479	15,905	17,006	10,031	14,075	14,332	15,320
Nevada.	11,885	16,888	18,953	20,363	11,230	16,182	17,405	18,818
New Hampshire . . .	6,948	8,703	8,911	9,380	6,222	8,346	8,679	9,030
New Jersey	62,331	75,083	79,126	85,517	54,590	72,660	79,845	82,928
New Mexico.	13,073	14,918	16,656	18,452	11,195	14,068	15,596	16,404
New York	188,907	224,429	234,681	266,263	171,858	219,325	226,951	240,996
North Carolina	50,542	63,458	64,813	67,479	46,135	56,543	60,747	64,330
North Dakota	4,495	6,524	5,239	5,772	4,041	4,486	4,794	4,926
Ohio.	80,074	105,382	102,498	107,494	68,418	89,598	91,959	97,514
Oklahoma	18,760	23,954	24,552	26,811	15,962	20,879	22,005	23,967
Oregon	28,644	33,734	32,406	36,149	24,086	28,215	29,084	30,549
Pennsylvania	80,546	102,238	103,692	109,300	75,624	94,598	101,484	104,228
Rhode Island	7,427	9,665	9,731	10,271	6,432	8,937	9,226	9,667
South Carolina	23,467	30,547	33,278	34,676	23,436	30,451	33,011	34,234
South Dakota	4,277	5,593	5,857	6,062	3,760	4,612	4,973	5,210
Tennessee.	33,625	42,125	44,863	47,256	32,010	41,760	42,708	44,399
Texas	120,666	153,761	162,748	176,919	109,634	144,880	151,927	160,532
Utah	14,954	18,917	19,183	20,781	13,044	16,707	17,269	18,527
Vermont	4,019	5,266	5,393	5,732	3,766	4,812	5,179	5,390
Virginia	44,175	54,162	56,658	61,647	38,092	47,801	51,529	55,853
Washington	46,372	54,738	57,510	63,055	41,794	54,317	55,800	56,588
West Virginia	10,760	14,117	14,576	14,044	9,990	12,201	12,120	12,387
Wisconsin	43,003	48,698	48,235	47,967	34,559	42,410	43,146	45,316
Wyoming	7,030	6,816	7,084	7,885	3,743	5,080	5,619	5,972

Source: U.S. Census Bureau, Annual Survey of State & Local Government Finances, 2000–2006; <http://www.census.gov/govs/www/estimate.html/>.

State and Local Government Finances and Employment 271

Table 430. State and Local Governments—Revenue by State: 2006

[In millions of dollars (2,736,542 represents $2,736,542,000,000). For fiscal year ending in year shown; see text, this section]

State	Total revenue	General revenue from own sources			Select Taxes					
		Total	Intergovernmental from federal government	General revenue from own sources	Total[1]	Property	Sales and gross receipts	Individual income	Corporation income	Other taxes
United States . .	2,736,542	2,186,018	452,233	1,733,785	1,195,254	359,109	412,114	268,599	52,931	81,981
Alabama	35,697	29,586	7,692	21,894	12,768	1,927	6,130	2,876	559	1,020
Alaska.	13,247	11,023	2,406	8,617	3,665	969	436	–	822	1,371
Arizona	45,324	36,483	8,818	27,665	19,940	5,524	9,347	3,253	890	733
Arkansas	20,798	17,203	4,529	12,674	8,747	1,320	4,642	2,013	369	273
California	404,541	293,049	56,402	236,647	163,749	37,225	52,019	51,220	10,316	10,381
Colorado	41,158	32,631	5,333	27,298	17,224	5,269	6,216	4,259	458	791
Connecticut	33,554	28,944	4,596	24,348	19,872	7,566	4,971	5,778	635	696
Delaware	8,467	7,217	1,241	5,976	3,618	531	441	1,077	296	1,241
District of Columbia . .	11,075	9,171	3,060	6,111	4,545	1,214	1,257	1,232	220	595
Florida.	151,624	123,635	23,674	99,961	66,695	23,045	32,344	–	2,406	7,694
Georgia	65,307	55,807	11,405	44,402	31,025	8,946	12,031	8,040	891	836
Hawaii.	11,999	10,467	2,010	8,457	6,199	983	3,168	1,551	148	139
Idaho	10,850	8,856	1,963	6,894	4,503	1,239	1,497	1,223	198	223
Illinois	108,037	87,470	15,946	71,524	52,144	19,555	17,893	8,635	2,400	2,053
Indiana	51,062	45,838	7,493	38,345	22,950	8,408	7,660	4,995	1,044	617
Iowa	24,840	20,641	4,511	16,130	10,256	3,392	3,342	2,483	285	343
Kansas	21,602	18,334	3,484	14,850	10,452	3,274	3,817	2,402	381	398
Kentucky	31,152	26,315	6,746	19,569	13,558	2,421	5,081	3,922	1,113	817
Louisiana.	39,729	33,543	10,038	23,505	15,724	2,470	8,766	2,501	506	1,347
Maine	11,700	10,540	2,692	7,847	5,806	2,211	1,670	1,369	188	273
Maryland	48,367	41,832	7,882	33,950	25,789	5,962	6,223	9,847	847	2,464
Massachusetts	66,603	52,249	9,740	42,509	30,636	10,829	6,092	10,483	1,859	1,076
Michigan	88,461	68,243	13,967	54,277	36,017	13,525	11,863	6,699	1,886	1,138
Minnesota	48,830	39,380	7,209	32,171	22,491	5,341	7,439	6,863	1,072	1,252
Mississippi.	24,015	20,217	7,379	12,838	8,180	2,076	3,990	1,255	317	420
Missouri.	44,201	35,510	8,619	26,891	18,312	4,985	7,074	4,821	364	773
Montana	8,019	6,729	2,031	4,698	3,020	1,059	518	769	154	375
Nebraska.	17,006	12,919	2,618	10,301	6,875	2,234	2,189	1,545	262	522
Nevada	20,363	16,578	2,392	14,185	9,764	2,509	5,747	–	–	1,346
New Hampshire	9,380	8,092	1,652	6,440	4,517	2,780	708	81	543	317
New Jersey	85,517	73,388	11,746	61,642	47,308	20,549	10,608	10,507	2,508	2,694
New Mexico	18,452	15,372	4,090	11,282	6,974	954	3,208	1,124	377	1,124
New York	266,263	209,641	43,914	165,727	123,661	36,438	31,601	38,612	9,046	7,076
North Carolina	67,479	57,199	13,239	43,960	30,013	6,985	10,320	9,467	1,308	1,324
North Dakota	5,772	4,943	1,299	3,644	2,368	634	836	276	120	432
Ohio	107,494	81,005	18,051	62,954	43,247	12,596	12,980	13,766	1,136	1,849
Oklahoma	26,811	22,449	5,409	17,040	11,257	1,802	4,232	2,756	304	1,600
Oregon	36,149	25,579	5,418	20,161	12,403	3,685	1,079	5,537	489	1,133
Pennsylvania	109,300	87,489	18,114	69,375	49,063	14,214	14,267	12,326	2,117	5,309
Rhode Island	10,271	8,538	2,179	6,359	4,680	1,888	1,405	1,019	170	141
South Carolina	34,676	28,877	6,769	22,107	12,444	3,960	4,487	2,727	297	795
South Dakota	6,062	4,836	1,383	3,453	2,241	767	1,216	–	62	135
Tennessee	47,256	36,046	8,663	27,383	17,240	4,126	10,094	193	928	1,482
Texas	176,919	144,881	31,080	113,801	75,732	32,486	34,104	–	–	7,467
Utah	20,781	16,793	3,518	13,275	8,283	1,877	3,315	2,277	348	362
Vermont	5,732	5,112	1,355	3,757	2,753	1,148	811	542	86	106
Virginia	61,647	51,280	7,135	44,145	30,059	9,233	8,091	9,073	863	2,291
Washington	63,055	46,024	8,785	37,238	25,169	6,911	15,413	–	–	2,406
West Virginia	14,044	12,672	3,390	9,283	5,882	1,059	2,246	1,298	533	659
Wisconsin	47,967	38,370	7,125	31,245	22,300	8,024	6,283	5,907	808	942
Wyoming	7,885	7,027	2,045	4,982	3,136	985	947	–	–	1,127

See footnotes at end of table.

272 State and Local Government Finances and Employment

Table 430. State and Local Governments—Revenue by State: 2006—Con.

[See headnote page 272]

State	General revenue from own sources								Utility and liquor stores	Insurance trust revenue
	Current charges and miscellaneous revenue									
		Current charges				Miscellaneous revenue				
	Total	Total [1]	Education	Hospitals	Sewerage	Total [1]	Interest earnings	Special assessments		
United States ..	**538,531**	**334,841**	**96,898**	**83,658**	**33,804**	**203,690**	**71,495**	**7,094**	**125,265**	**418,881**
Alabama	9,126	6,735	1,927	3,548	352	2,391	904	24	2,284	3,649
Alaska.	4,952	964	178	91	68	3,988	1,352	8	284	1,936
Arizona	7,724	4,418	1,683	515	533	3,306	1,169	76	3,754	5,088
Arkansas	3,927	2,679	986	894	205	1,248	485	29	791	2,805
California	72,898	47,740	8,539	11,795	4,654	25,158	9,142	1,316	23,929	87,563
Colorado	10,074	6,308	2,372	1,230	612	3,767	1,394	433	2,016	6,511
Connecticut	4,476	2,446	972	396	232	2,030	780	29	641	3,969
Delaware	2,357	1,154	454	14	153	1,203	246	349	311	939
District of Columbia . .	1,565	574	30	–	177	992	221	1	793	1,112
Florida.	33,266	20,942	3,621	4,953	2,184	12,324	3,627	1,196	7,505	20,484
Georgia	13,377	8,995	2,261	3,291	825	4,382	1,377	46	3,966	5,534
Hawaii.	2,258	1,497	262	414	186	761	246	23	226	1,305
Idaho	2,391	1,730	404	637	145	661	229	36	185	1,711
Illinois	19,379	12,147	3,946	1,276	942	7,232	2,735	361	3,205	17,361
Indiana	15,395	11,261	2,998	2,429	832	4,133	1,301	44	1,892	3,332
Iowa	5,873	4,235	1,516	1,730	293	1,638	663	33	820	3,216
Kansas	4,398	2,806	1,228	622	270	1,592	627	82	1,023	2,245
Kentucky	6,010	3,688	1,358	1,119	334	2,322	877	35	1,321	3,517
Louisiana.	7,781	4,796	1,087	2,281	306	2,985	1,202	47	1,231	4,955
Maine	2,042	1,118	407	74	140	924	277	14	95	1,066
Maryland	8,161	5,122	2,336	144	790	3,039	990	75	696	5,630
Massachusetts	11,873	5,814	2,060	494	832	6,059	2,595	441	2,943	11,411
Michigan	18,260	12,062	4,786	2,864	1,401	6,198	2,008	199	2,101	17,399
Minnesota	9,680	6,196	2,224	1,217	566	3,485	1,187	346	1,644	7,563
Mississippi	4,658	3,635	979	2,062	174	1,023	299	10	659	2,918
Missouri.	8,580	5,393	2,132	1,552	534	3,186	1,409	44	1,482	7,209
Montana	1,678	937	455	47	70	742	281	61	94	1,136
Nebraska.	3,426	1,905	729	543	136	1,521	414	61	2,825	1,263
Nevada	4,421	2,594	547	547	368	1,827	590	139	1,029	2,757
New Hampshire	1,923	1,061	523	6	91	862	436	1	88	783
New Jersey	14,334	8,419	2,871	846	1,201	5,915	1,814	17	1,678	10,451
New Mexico	4,307	1,664	526	493	130	2,644	844	34	464	2,617
New York.	42,067	22,612	3,978	5,732	1,672	19,454	5,316	132	12,112	44,511
North Carolina	13,947	10,138	2,718	3,730	1,379	3,809	1,691	34	3,187	6,622
North Dakota	1,276	768	401	4	38	508	249	57	104	725
Ohio	19,707	12,513	5,235	2,719	1,593	7,194	2,598	226	2,243	23,592
Oklahoma	5,783	3,696	1,625	843	231	2,087	576	19	1,351	3,011
Oregon	7,758	4,903	1,361	998	666	2,855	833	109	1,321	8,904
Pennsylvania	20,312	12,356	4,329	1,875	1,830	7,956	3,819	88	2,665	17,888
Rhode Island	1,679	761	374	4	84	918	392	7	186	1,548
South Carolina	9,663	7,180	1,807	3,736	378	2,483	720	88	2,851	2,948
South Dakota	1,212	561	260	34	51	651	290	12	210	996
Tennessee	10,143	5,871	1,664	2,131	525	4,272	1,043	83	7,744	3,466
Texas	38,068	22,055	7,015	6,496	2,408	16,013	6,479	162	9,089	22,950
Utah	4,992	3,467	1,210	851	235	1,525	607	32	1,612	2,205
Vermont	1,004	589	404	–	46	415	174	4	180	400
Virginia	14,086	9,185	2,944	2,246	919	4,901	1,647	151	1,619	8,276
Washington	12,070	8,619	2,222	2,232	1,208	3,450	1,239	126	5,139	11,388
West Virginia	3,400	1,681	680	237	180	1,719	418	31	175	1,130
Wisconsin	8,945	5,787	2,107	978	583	3,158	1,228	114	1,364	8,234
Wyoming	1,846	1,066	166	684	44	781	455	8	139	655

– Represents or rounds to zero.   [1] Includes items not shown separately.

Source: U.S. Census Bureau; Federal, State and Local Governments, *State Government Finances;* <http://www.census.gov/govs/www/estimate06.html> (accessed May 2008).

State and Local Government Finances and Employment   273

Table 431. **State and Local Governments—Expenditures and Debt by State: 2006**

[In millions of dollars (2,507,086 represents $2,507,806,000,000), except as indicated. For fiscal year ending in year shown; see text, this section]

State	Total expendi- ture [1]	General expenditure								
		Total	Direct general expenditures							
			Total	Educa- tion	Public welfare	Health	Hospi- tals	High- ways	Police protec- tion	Correc- tions
United States..	2,507,086	2,128,449	2,121,946	727,967	370,325	71,110	110,455	135,412	79,066	62,667
Alabama	35,276	30,755	30,721	10,910	5,150	1,392	3,762	1,929	924	646
Alaska.	10,788	9,364	9,359	2,456	1,397	213	134	1,304	215	212
Arizona	42,763	35,764	35,747	11,800	6,060	1,511	882	2,466	1,692	1,428
Arkansas	18,503	16,599	16,585	6,383	3,444	383	868	1,132	505	521
California	365,041	297,136	293,473	92,371	44,667	11,524	14,715	15,446	13,095	10,914
Colorado	37,107	30,813	30,780	10,938	3,507	941	1,537	2,069	1,203	1,001
Connecticut	31,502	27,529	27,484	9,929	4,636	657	1,215	1,277	905	618
Delaware	8,292	7,466	7,459	2,646	1,242	340	61	620	286	245
District of Columbia	10,091	8,004	8,004	1,478	1,841	508	161	96	493	206
Florida.	140,638	122,730	122,624	35,345	17,951	3,874	6,138	8,911	5,928	4,048
Georgia.	63,053	54,250	54,210	21,292	8,493	1,848	3,712	2,719	1,962	2,000
Hawaii.	11,018	9,850	9,846	2,913	1,444	517	408	445	279	179
Idaho	9,330	8,433	8,426	2,875	1,466	214	654	740	276	261
Illinois	100,995	84,256	84,195	29,445	13,444	2,578	2,353	5,370	3,761	1,732
Indiana	44,033	39,927	39,894	14,882	6,460	741	3,052	2,394	1,039	934
Iowa	23,102	20,722	20,605	7,779	3,530	444	1,914	1,862	570	359
Kansas	20,295	18,054	18,044	6,737	2,847	408	722	1,788	635	376
Kentucky	29,514	25,335	25,319	8,701	5,681	643	1,173	1,876	662	629
Louisiana.	35,314	30,506	30,475	9,131	4,561	715	3,122	2,107	1,167	999
Maine	10,713	9,989	9,966	2,999	2,497	496	121	798	221	183
Maryland	44,280	39,416	39,382	14,392	6,510	1,493	453	2,431	1,605	1,461
Massachusetts . . .	61,910	52,691	52,418	17,029	11,449	847	1,332	2,252	1,673	1,141
Michigan	77,016	66,619	66,534	26,336	9,891	4,163	2,990	3,621	2,333	2,289
Minnesota	44,820	38,798	38,762	13,055	9,175	932	1,567	3,055	1,294	739
Mississippi.	22,109	19,262	19,250	6,430	3,752	364	2,332	1,723	561	377
Missouri.	39,551	34,606	34,539	11,934	5,998	1,394	2,280	2,757	1,179	805
Montana	6,948	6,228	6,226	2,161	860	361	91	697	191	176
Nebraska.	15,320	11,726	11,688	4,348	2,003	409	599	1,098	334	293
Nevada.	18,818	16,105	16,099	5,129	1,792	306	763	1,465	889	556
New Hampshire . .	9,030	8,155	8,147	3,137	1,472	125	55	620	274	165
New Jersey	82,928	71,230	71,180	27,787	12,439	1,165	1,750	3,566	3,010	1,919
New Mexico	16,404	14,874	14,866	5,216	2,866	392	833	1,194	509	476
New York.	240,996	195,357	194,728	57,190	43,176	5,195	13,187	8,707	7,585	5,104
North Carolina . . .	64,330	55,997	55,905	19,964	9,838	3,102	4,359	3,343	1,916	1,547
North Dakota	4,926	4,517	4,515	1,665	729	79	23	573	106	74
Ohio	97,514	82,137	82,045	28,758	16,646	3,986	3,291	4,639	2,689	1,994
Oklahoma	23,967	20,898	20,832	8,029	4,070	579	837	1,508	672	632
Oregon	30,549	25,343	25,324	8,338	3,877	894	1,352	1,798	938	922
Pennsylvania	104,228	89,634	89,373	31,435	20,252	3,772	2,253	6,742	2,535	2,796
Rhode Island	9,667	8,286	8,247	2,710	2,150	162	115	395	286	195
South Carolina . . .	34,234	29,085	29,057	10,565	4,775	973	3,734	1,697	854	620
South Dakota	5,210	4,674	4,665	1,539	749	122	86	668	132	141
Tennessee.	44,399	34,479	34,386	10,900	7,593	1,438	2,667	2,186	1,210	896
Texas	160,532	138,391	138,254	56,039	20,357	2,463	8,269	11,021	4,876	4,430
Utah	18,527	15,620	15,611	5,937	2,356	466	702	1,098	557	446
Vermont	5,390	4,920	4,913	2,029	1,123	140	5	380	136	101
Virginia	55,853	50,438	50,390	19,243	7,270	1,674	2,627	2,943	1,737	1,756
Washington	56,588	45,221	45,175	15,350	6,706	2,101	3,129	2,945	1,328	1,413
West Virginia	12,387	11,454	11,435	4,280	2,348	313	288	1,102	237	254
Wisconsin	45,316	39,440	39,413	14,337	7,203	1,513	1,122	3,264	1,434	1,276
Wyoming	5,972	5,371	5,369	1,693	586	239	660	578	165	180

See footnotes at end of table.

U.S. Census Bureau, Statistical Abstract of the United States: 2010

[See headnote, page 274]

State	General expenditure								Utility and liquor store expenditures	Insurance trust expenditures	Debt outstanding
	Direct general expenditure										
	Natural resources	Parks and recreation	Housing and community development	Sewerage	Solid waste management	Governmental administration	Interest on general debt	Other direct general expenditures			
United States . .	**25,482**	**34,769**	**41,980**	**39,220**	**22,679**	**111,335**	**85,660**	**195,134**	**174,679**	**203,958**	**2,200,892**
Alabama.	311	468	444	575	287	1,155	807	1,898	2,357	2,164	22,310
Alaska.	277	89	227	81	67	667	388	1,800	407	1,017	9,449
Arizona.	576	1,246	398	753	359	2,168	1,308	2,866	4,449	2,550	34,655
Arkansas	230	190	182	231	197	874	433	1,060	805	1,099	11,815
California	5,555	5,278	8,990	5,307	3,716	19,416	11,637	30,206	33,244	34,660	299,534
Colorado.	470	1,055	679	705	93	1,913	1,736	2,869	2,800	3,493	39,932
Connecticut.	94	261	651	309	382	1,512	1,372	3,303	961	3,012	32,228
Delaware	91	96	120	172	84	609	241	670	365	461	6,087
District of Columbia	–	332	560	237	266	455	320	875	1,959	128	8,020
Florida	3,306	2,451	1,634	2,368	2,397	7,278	4,267	17,333	8,851	9,056	119,674
Georgia	464	885	919	1,160	782	2,776	1,134	3,654	4,947	3,856	42,086
Hawaii	123	229	173	201	184	598	555	1,584	345	823	9,504
Idaho	229	114	49	151	101	518	194	706	275	622	4,442
Illinois	466	2,705	2,046	1,222	562	4,071	4,748	8,410	5,917	10,821	110,788
Indiana.	355	480	822	1,046	261	1,797	1,441	3,893	2,004	2,102	34,347
Iowa	274	340	181	273	165	891	534	1,583	1,016	1,363	13,806
Kansas.	251	242	237	299	130	959	832	1,583	1,086	1,155	19,907
Kentucky	443	272	345	309	257	1,245	1,260	1,914	1,489	2,690	32,480
Louisiana	624	519	527	470	318	1,626	1,234	3,477	1,461	3,347	24,733
Maine.	176	67	223	137	118	471	328	1,188	102	623	7,473
Maryland	491	1,068	964	734	543	2,257	1,437	3,323	1,538	3,327	30,673
Massachusetts. . . .	285	371	1,509	1,041	414	2,315	3,711	6,355	4,270	4,949	86,940
Michigan.	460	804	964	1,587	478	3,194	2,597	4,370	3,257	7,139	70,825
Minnesota.	527	862	798	540	323	1,971	1,616	2,510	2,135	3,887	36,618
Mississippi	251	167	228	192	139	756	464	1,546	1,288	1,560	11,161
Missouri	358	573	597	632	123	1,413	1,547	2,726	1,871	3,074	33,957
Montana	238	79	107	79	64	423	206	666	161	559	5,787
Nebraska	241	205	166	120	74	514	244	1,137	3,097	497	9,336
Nevada	155	635	223	219	36	1,221	704	1,780	1,649	1,064	20,581
New Hampshire . . .	79	86	175	104	116	420	451	783	458	417	9,952
New Jersey	488	1,013	1,048	1,137	1,101	3,263	2,751	8,426	3,298	8,401	79,281
New Mexico	283	291	186	130	135	835	464	1,143	410	1,121	10,707
New York	549	2,120	4,461	3,401	2,499	8,683	8,923	21,683	23,499	22,140	241,407
North Carolina	584	803	819	1,334	663	2,147	1,428	3,924	4,528	3,806	43,938
North Dakota.	196	93	53	33	39	230	169	618	124	284	3,486
Ohio	418	911	1,870	2,280	513	5,014	3,073	4,927	3,434	11,943	63,658
Oklahoma.	220	318	182	343	174	1,116	703	1,300	1,312	1,757	15,244
Oregon.	424	458	500	641	143	1,652	1,053	2,369	1,798	3,408	26,919
Pennsylvania.	641	867	1,872	1,674	668	4,697	4,309	4,936	5,292	9,302	106,042
Rhode Island.	44	60	212	118	106	504	343	648	293	1,088	8,945
South Carolina. . . .	233	313	371	337	304	1,639	1,039	1,556	2,802	2,347	32,159
South Dakota	140	106	93	63	34	273	170	442	234	302	4,560
Tennessee	269	488	516	598	356	1,587	1,007	2,423	7,941	1,980	27,931
Texas.	1,257	1,666	1,924	2,470	1,043	5,348	6,040	10,274	11,527	10,615	165,572
Utah	216	380	264	321	146	1,250	446	1,040	1,952	955	15,327
Vermont	92	36	110	59	36	226	172	318	256	214	3,854
Virginia	250	973	977	950	660	2,660	1,854	4,137	2,361	3,054	46,388
Washington.	714	832	796	982	564	1,933	1,838	4,372	6,784	4,584	56,655
West Virginia.	160	135	125	220	64	821	358	806	376	557	8,937
Wisconsin.	697	625	441	816	353	1,655	1,693	3,126	1,681	4,196	38,834
Wyoming	211	110	16	61	45	320	78	592	211	390	1,947

– Represents or rounds to zero.   [1] Includes items not shown separately.

Source: U.S. Census Bureau; Federal, State, and Local Governments, *State and Local Government Finances;* <http://www.census.gov/govs/estimate06.html> (accessed May 2008).

Table 432. State Resources, Expenditures, and Balances: 2007 and 2008

[In millions of dollars (1,438,071 represents $1,438,071,000,000). For fiscal year ending in year shown; see text; this section. **General funds** exclude special funds earmarked for particular purposes, such as highway trust funds and federal funds; they support most on-going broad-based state services and are available for appropriation to support any governmental activity. Minus sign (–) indicates net loss]

State	Expenditures by fund source				State general fund					
	Total, 2007	Total[2] 2008[1]	General fund 2008[1]	Federal fund 2008[1]	Resources[3,4] 2007	2008[1]	Expenditures[4] 2007	2008[1]	Balance[5] 2007	2008[1]
United States ..	1,438,071	1,555,690	688,595	421,161	641,899	658,728	652,272	688,595	–10,373	–29,867
Alabama	36,419	43,423	16,535	12,377	7,489	7,863	36,419	43,423	–28,930	–35,560
Alaska	11,546	12,504	5,080	2,862	5,101	6,420	11,546	12,504	–6,445	–6,084
Arizona	27,441	28,637	10,059	10,083	9,553	9,587	27,441	28,637	–17,888	–19,050
Arkansas	16,113	19,188	4,346	6,219	5,440	5,529	16,113	19,188	–10,673	–13,659
California	182,903	203,697	103,542	58,669	95,413	101,190	182,903	203,697	–87,490	[6]–102,507
Colorado	16,712	17,993	7,240	3,987	7,539	7,726	16,712	17,993	–9,173	–10,267
Connecticut	22,798	23,445	16,340	1,684	15,743	16,320	22,798	23,445	–7,055	–7,125
Delaware	7,948	8,071	3,281	1,169	3,290	3,366	7,948	8,071	–4,658	[6]–4,705
Florida.........	66,112	70,360	28,063	19,615	26,404	24,469	66,112	70,360	–39,708	–45,892
Georgia	37,374	38,679	18,565	10,012	18,840	19,365	37,374	38,679	–18,534	[6]–19,314
Hawaii	10,653	12,659	5,360	1,947	5,142	5,287	10,653	12,659	–5,511	–7,372
Idaho..........	5,456	6,429	2,844	2,138	2,811	2,862	5,456	6,429	–2,645	–3,567
Illinois	46,215	47,823	22,165	12,091	23,937	24,716	46,215	47,823	–22,278	–23,107
Indiana	22,797	24,089	12,730	7,818	12,626	12,931	22,797	24,089	–10,171	–11,158
Iowa	15,069	16,365	5,859	4,467	5,646	6,062	15,069	16,365	–9,423	–10,303
Kansas	11,969	13,097	6,112	3,582	5,794	5,926	11,969	13,097	–6,175	–7,171
Kentucky	22,280	25,570	9,444	7,690	8,574	8,664	22,280	25,570	–13,706	–16,906
Louisiana	29,473	40,453	9,713	19,836	9,680	9,997	29,473	40,453	–19,793	–30,456
Maine	7,196	7,518	3,110	2,501	3,020	3,040	7,196	7,518	–4,176	–4,478
Maryland	29,469	30,808	14,462	6,673	12,940	13,614	29,469	30,808	–16,529	–17,194
Massachusetts ...	41,776	41,190	27,278	2,388	19,736	20,888	41,776	41,190	–22,040	[6]–20,302
Michigan	42,570	43,839	9,898	14,040	8,318	9,164	42,570	43,839	–34,252	–34,675
Minnesota	27,102	28,934	17,864	6,394	15,908	15,851	27,102	28,934	–11,194	[6]–13,083
Mississippi	15,302	16,727	4,163	8,598	4,790	4,837	15,302	16,727	–10,513	–11,890
Missouri........	21,030	22,980	8,449	6,361	7,717	7,957	21,030	22,980	–13,313	–15,023
Montana	4,703	5,645	1,972	1,768	1,838	1,773	4,703	5,645	–2,865	–3,872
Nebraska	8,162	9,574	3,491	2,804	3,408	3,407	8,162	9,574	–4,754	–6,167
Nevada	8,197	7,742	3,195	1,503	3,145	3,053	8,197	7,742	–5,052	–4,689
New Hampshire. . .	4,540	4,665	1,480	1,420	2,291	2,346	4,540	4,665	–2,249	–2,319
New Jersey	45,393	49,089	32,638	9,609	31,202	31,485	45,393	49,089	–14,191	–17,604
New Mexico	14,464	14,241	6,016	4,588	5,828	6,019	14,464	14,241	–8,636	[6]–8,222
New York	112,764	116,056	53,385	34,680	53,842	55,829	112,764	116,056	–58,922	[6]–60,227
North Carolina...	39,670	47,245	20,376	17,316	18,712	18,832	39,670	47,245	–20,958	–28,413
North Dakota	3,369	3,602	1,202	1,180	1,224	1,335	3,369	3,602	–2,145	–2,267
Ohio	53,168	54,861	24,623	8,832	25,931	26,659	53,168	54,861	–27,237	–28,202
Oklahoma	19,327	20,888	7,000	5,593	5,983	5,969	19,327	20,888	–13,345	–14,919
Oregon	20,294	23,396	7,223	5,087	6,430	5,947	20,294	23,396	–13,864	–17,449
Pennsylvania	56,922	59,863	27,206	18,474	27,449	28,188	56,922	59,863	–29,473	–31,675
Rhode Island	6,732	7,299	3,370	2,040	3,231	3,436	6,732	7,299	–3,501	–3,863
South Carolina ...	19,989	21,278	7,406	7,345	6,659	6,510	19,989	21,278	–13,330	[6]–14,768
South Dakota	3,059	3,398	1,147	1,367	1,092	1,177	3,059	3,398	–1,967	–2,221
Tennessee	24,760	27,295	12,196	9,637	10,195	10,553	24,760	27,295	–14,565	–16,742
Texas	81,023	89,650	43,595	26,330	38,338	38,209	81,023	89,650	–42,685	–51,441
Utah	9,985	12,578	5,784	2,471	5,308	5,294	9,985	12,578	–4,677	–7,284
Vermont........	5,148	5,221	1,229	1,281	1,151	1,190	5,148	5,221	–3,997	–4,031
Virginia	34,833	35,313	16,523	6,336	15,566	15,751	34,833	35,313	–19,267	–19,562
Washington	29,943	32,345	14,601	6,799	14,180	14,331	29,943	32,345	–15,763	–18,014
West Virginia	18,542	18,920	3,857	3,489	3,753	3,819	18,542	18,920	–14,789	–15,101
Wisconsin.......	34,256	36,091	13,446	7,536	12,618	12,868	34,256	36,091	–21,638	–23,223
Wyoming	5,105	4,957	3,132	475	1,073	1,118	5,105	4,957	–4,032	–3,839

[1] Estimated. [2] Includes bonds and other state funds not shown separately. [3] Includes funds budgeted, adjustments, and balances from previous year. [4] May or may not include budget stabilization fund transfers, depending on state accounting practices. [5] Resources less expenditures. [6] Ending balance includes the balance in a budget stabilization fund.

Source: National Association of State Budget Officers, Washington, DC, *2007 State Expenditure Report*, and *State General Fund* from NASBO, *Fiscal Survey of the States*, Fall 2008, semiannual (copyright). See also <http://www.nasbo.org/publications.php>.

Table 433. Bond Ratings for State Governments by State: 2008

[**As of fourth quarter.** Key to investment grade ratings are in declining order of quality. The ratings from AA to CCC may be modified by the addition of a (+) or (−) sign to show relative standing within the major rating categories. S&P: AAA, AA, A, BBB, BB, B, CCC, CC, C; Moody's: Aaa, Aa, A, Baa, Ba, B, Caa, Ca, C; Numerical modifiers 1, 2, and 3 are added to letter-rating. Fitch: AAA, AA, A, BBB, BB, B, CCC, CC, C]

State	Standard & Poor's	Moody's	Fitch	State	Standard & Poor's	Moody's	Fitch
Alabama	AA	Aa2	AAA	Montana	AA	Aa2	AA
Alaska	AA+	Aa2	AA	Nebraska	¹AA+ (ICR)	(²)	(NA)
Arizona	¹AA (ICR)	Aa3	(NA)	Nevada	AA+	Aa1	AA+
Arkansas	AA	Aa2	(NA)	New Hampshire	AA	Aa2	AA
California	A+	A1	A+	New Jersey	AA	Aa3	AA−
Colorado	¹AA (ICR)	(²)	(NA)	New Mexico	AA+	Aa1	(NA)
Connecticut	AA	Aa3	AA	New York	AA	Aa3	AA−
Delaware	AAA	Aaa	AAA	North Carolina	AAA	Aaa	AAA
Florida	AAA	Aa1	AA+	North Dakota	¹AA (ICR)	Aa2	(NA)
Georgia	AAA	Aaa	AAA	Ohio	AA+	Aa1	AA+
Hawaii	AA	Aa2	AA	Oklahoma	AA+	Aa3	AA
Idaho	¹AA (ICR)	Aa2	(NA)	Oregon	AA	Aa2	AA
Illinois	AA	Aa3	AA−	Pennsylvania	AA	Aa2	AA
Indiana	¹AAA (ICR)	Aa1	(NA)	Rhode Island	AA	Aa3	AA−
Iowa	¹AAA (ICR)	Aa1	AA+	South Carolina	AA+	Aaa	AAA
Kansas	¹AA+ (ICR)	Aa1	(NA)	South Dakota	¹AA (ICR)	(²)	(NA)
Kentucky	¹AA− (ICR)	Aa2	(NA)	Tennessee	AA+	Aa1	AA+
Louisiana	A+	A1	A+	Texas	AA	Aa1	AA+
Maine	AA	Aa3	AA	Utah	AAA	Aaa	AAA
Maryland	AAA	Aaa	AAA	Vermont	AA+	Aaa	AA+
Massachusetts	AA	Aa2	AA	Virginia	AAA	Aaa	AAA
Michigan	AA−	Aa3	AA−	Washington	AA+	Aa1	AA
Minnesota	AAA	Aa1	AAA	West Virginia	AA	Aa3	AA−
Mississippi	AA	Aa3	AA	Wisconsin	AA	Aa3	AA−
Missouri	AAA	Aaa	AAA	Wyoming	¹AA+ (ICR)	(²)	(NA)

NA Not available.   ¹ Standard and Poor's Issue Credit Rating (ICR) is a current opinion of an obliger with respect to a specific financial obligation, a specific class of financial obligations, or a specific financial program.   ² Not rated.

Source: Standard & Poor's, New York, NY (copyright), <http://www2.standardandpoors.com/portal/site/sp/en/us/page .home/home/0,0,0,0,0,0,0,0,0,0,0,0,0,0,0,0.html/>; Moody's Investors Service, New York, NY (copyright), <http://www.moodys.com /cust/defaultalt.asp>; Fitch Ratings, New York, NY (copyright), <http://www.fitchratings.com/>.

Table 434. Bond Ratings for City Governments by Largest Cities: 2007

[**As of fourth quarter.** See headnote in Table 427]

Cities ranked by 2000 population	Standard & Poor's	Moody's	Fitch	Cities ranked by 2000 population	Standard & Poor's	Moody's	Fitch
New York, NY	AA	Aa3	AA−	Oakland, CA	AA−	A1	A+
Los Angeles, CA	AA	Aa2	AA	Mesa, AZ	AA	A1	(NA)
Chicago, IL	AA−	Aa3	AA	Tulsa, OK	AA	Aa2	(NA)
Houston, TX	AA	Aa3	AA−	Omaha, NE	AAA	Aa1	(NA)
Philadelphia, PA	BBB	Baa1	BBB+	Minneapolis, MN	AAA	Aa1	AAA
Phoenix, AZ	AAA	Aa1	(NA)	Honolulu, HI	AA	Aa2	AA
San Diego, CA	A	A2	A+	Miami, FL	A+	A2	A
Dallas, TX	AA+	Aa1	(NA)	Colorado Springs, CO	AA	Aa3	(NA)
San Antonio, TX	AAA	Aa1	AA+	St. Louis, MO	A+	A2	A
Detroit, MI	BBB	Baa3	BBB	Wichita, KS	AA+	Aa2	(NA)
San Jose, CA	AAA	Aa1	AA+	Santa Ana, CA	(¹)	(²)	(NA)
Indianapolis, IN	AAA	Aa1	(NA)	Pittsburgh, PA	BBB	Baa1	BBB
San Francisco, CA	AA	Aa2	AA−	Arlington, TX	AA+	Aa1	(NA)
Jacksonville, FL	AA	Aa2	AA	Cincinnati, OH	AA+	Aa1	(NA)
Columbus, OH	AAA	Aaa	AAA	Anaheim, CA	AA	Aa2	(NA)
Austin, TX	AAA	Aa1	(NA)	Toledo, OH	A+	A3	(NA)
Baltimore, MD	AA−	Aa3	A+	Tampa, FL	(¹)	Aa2	(NA)
Memphis, TN	AA	A1	A+	Buffalo, NY	BBB+	Baa2	(NA)
Milwaukee, WI	AA	Aa2	AA+	St. Paul, MN	AAA	Aa2	(NA)
Boston, MA	AA+	Aa1	AA	Corpus Christi, TX	AA−	A1	AA−
Washington, DC	A+	A1	A+	Aurora, CO	AA	Aa2	(NA)
El Paso, TX	AA	Aa3	AA−	Raleigh, NC	AAA	Aaa	AAA
Seattle, WA	AAA	Aaa	AAA	Newark, NJ	AA	Baa2	(NA)
Denver, CO	AAA	Aa1	AA+	Lexington–Fayette, KY	(¹)	Aa2	(NA)
Nashville–Davidson, TN	AA	Aa2	AA	Anchorage, AK	AA	Aa3	AA
Charlotte, NC	AAA	Aaa	AAA	Louisville, KY	(¹)	Aa2	(NA)
Fort Worth, TX	AA−	Aa2	AA	Riverside, CA	AA−	(²)	AA
Portland, OR	(¹)	Aaa	(NA)	St Petersburg, FL	(¹)	A1	(NA)
Oklahoma City, OK	AA+	Aa1	(NA)	Bakersfield, CA	(¹)	(²)	(NA)
Tucson, AZ	AA	Aa3	AA	Stockton CA	³A (ICR)	A2	(NA)
New Orleans, LA	BB	Baa3	BBB−	Birmingham, AL	AA	Aa3	AA−
Las Vegas, NV	AA	Aa2	AA	Jersey City, NJ	NR	Baa2	BBB
Cleveland, OH	A (Lease)	A2	A+	Norfolk, VA	AA	A1	AA
Long Beach, CA	AA−	Aa3	(NA)	Baton Rouge, LA	(¹)	(²)	(NA)
Albuquerque, NM	AAA	Aa2	AA	Hialeah, FL	(¹)	(²)	(NA)
Kansas City, MO	AA	Aa3	AAA	Lincoln, NE	AAA	Aaa	(NA)
Fresno, CA	AA	A1	AA−	Greensboro, NC	AAA	Aaa	AAA
Virginia Beach, VA	AAA	Aa1	AA+	Plano, TX	AAA	Aaa	AAA
Atlanta, GA	AA−	Aa3	(NA)	Rochester, NY	A	A2	(NA)
Sacramento, CA	AA	Aa2	(NA)				

NA Not available.   ¹ Not reviewed.   ² Issuer Rating/No General Obligation.   ³ Standard and Poor's Issue Credit Rating (ICR) is a current opinion of an obliger with respect to a specific financial obligation, a specific class of financial obligations, or a specific financial program.

Source: Standard & Poor's, New York, NY (copyright), <http://www2.standardandpoors.com/portal/site/sp/en/us/page .home/home/0,0,0,0,0,0,0,0,0,0,0,0,0,0,0,0.html/>; Moody's Investors Service, New York, NY (copyright), <http://www.moodys.com /cust/defaultalt.asp>; Fitch Ratings, New York, NY (copyright), <http://www.fitchratings.com/>.

State and Local Government Finances and Employment   277

Table 435. **Estimated State and Local Taxes Paid by a Family of Three for Largest City in Selected States: 2007**

[Data based on average family of three (two wage earners and one school-age child) owning their own home and living in a city where taxes apply. Comprises state and local sales, income, auto, and real estate taxes. For definition of median, see Guide to Tabular Presentation]

City	Total taxes paid by gross family income level (dollars)					Total taxes paid as percent of income				
	$25,000	$50,000	$75,000	$100,000	$150,000	$25,000	$50,000	$75,000	$100,000	$150,000
Albuquerque, NM . . .	2,958	4,577	6,758	9,248	13,707	11.8	9.2	9.0	9.2	9.1
Atlanta, GA	3,346	4,854	7,452	10,117	15,402	13.4	9.7	9.9	10.1	10.3
Baltimore, MD	2,638	7,105	10,070	13,410	20,196	10.6	14.2	13.4	13.4	13.5
Boston, MA.	2,647	3,892	5,950	8,117	12,228	10.6	7.8	7.9	8.1	8.2
Charlotte, NC	3,327	5,004	7,679	10,586	15,761	13.3	10.0	10.2	10.6	10.5
Chicago, IL	3,398	3,547	5,144	6,930	9,592	13.6	7.1	6.9	6.9	6.4
Columbus, OH.	3,384	5,589	8,039	10,971	16,977	13.5	11.2	10.7	11.0	11.3
Denver, CO.	2,975	3,561	5,570	7,703	11,107	11.9	7.1	7.4	7.7	7.4
Detroit, MI.	3,173	6,180	9,223	12,894	19,281	12.7	12.4	12.3	12.9	12.9
Honolulu, HI	3,318	3,239	5,352	7,719	11,939	13.3	6.5	7.1	7.7	8.0
Houston, TX	2,758	4,398	5,640	7,206	10,174	11.0	8.8	7.5	7.2	6.8
Indianapolis, IN	3,370	6,133	8,658	11,463	17,677	13.5	12.3	11.5	11.5	11.8
Jacksonville, FL. . . .	2,707	3,026	3,936	5,175	7,637	10.8	6.1	5.2	5.2	5.1
Kansas City, MO . . .	3,464	5,104	7,588	10,126	14,954	13.9	10.2	10.1	10.1	10.0
Las Vegas, NV	2,625	2,957	3,809	4,800	6,595	10.5	5.9	5.1	4.8	4.4
Los Angeles, CA . . .	2,711	3,197	5,378	8,049	13,945	10.8	6.4	7.2	8.0	9.3
Memphis, TN.	2,993	4,406	5,560	7,033	9,718	12.0	8.8	7.4	7.0	6.5
Milwaukee, WI.	2,638	5,921	8,597	11,642	17,652	10.6	11.8	11.5	11.6	11.8
Minneapolis, MN . . .	2,672	4,188	6,832	9,432	14,572	10.7	8.4	9.1	9.4	9.7
New Orleans, LA . . .	3,157	3,810	6,080	8,667	12,924	12.6	7.6	8.1	8.7	8.6
New York City, NY . .	2,753	4,259	7,382	10,725	17,521	11.0	8.5	9.8	10.7	11.7
Oklahoma City, OK. .	3,337	4,845	7,040	9,554	13,916	13.3	9.7	9.4	9.6	9.3
Omaha, NE.	2,780	5,359	7,817	10,903	16,828	11.1	10.7	10.4	10.9	11.3
Philadelphia, PA. . . .	4,233	8,629	11,606	14,884	21,955	16.9	17.3	15.5	14.9	14.6
Phoenix, AZ	3,161	3,403	5,079	7,150	10,356	12.6	6.8	6.8	7.2	6.9
Portland, OR.	2,891	4,174	6,278	8,853	14,191	11.6	8.3	8.4	8.9	9.5
Seattle, WA.	2,860	2,836	3,715	4,867	6,353	11.4	5.7	5.0	4.9	4.2
Virginia Beach, VA . .	2,859	4,103	6,229	8,496	12,490	11.4	8.2	8.3	8.5	8.3
Washington, DC. . . .	2,768	3,590	5,617	8,258	13,050	11.1	7.2	7.5	8.3	8.7
Wichita, KS.	2,996	4,497	6,997	9,942	14,774	12.0	9.0	9.3	9.9	9.8
Average [1]. . . .	2,964	4,423	6,529	8,920	13,467	11.9	8.8	8.7	8.9	9.0
Median [1]	2,860	4,398	6,355	8,906	13,916	11.4	8.8	8.5	8.9	9.3

[1] Based on selected cities and District of Columbia. For complete list of cities, see Table 436.

Source: Government of the District of Columbia, Office of the Chief Financial Officer, "Tax Rates and Revenues, Tax Burden Comparisons, Nationwide Comparison," annual (published August 2008); <http://www.cfo.dc.gov/cfo/>.

Table 436. **Residential Property Tax Rates for Largest City in Each State: 2007**

[The real property tax is a function of housing values, real estate tax rates, assessment levels, homeowner exemptions and credits. Effective rate is the amount each jurisdiction considers based upon assessment level used. Assessment level is ratio of assessed value to assumed market value. Nominal rates represent the "announced" rates levied by the jurisdiction]

City	Effective tax rate per $100		Assessment level (percent)	Nominal rate per $100	City	Effective tax rate per $100		Assessment level (percent)	Nominal rate per $100
	Rank	Rate				Rank	Rate		
Bridgeport, CT.	1	2.89	70.0	4.13	Louisville, KY	28	1.24	100.0	1.24
Indianapolis, IN	2	2.75	100.0	2.75	Charlotte, NC	29	1.22	93.8	1.30
Philadelphia, PA	3	2.64	32.0	8.26	Oklahoma City, OK . .	30	1.21	11.0	10.98
Houston, TX	4	2.53	100.0	2.53	Manchester, NH.	31	1.20	100.0	1.20
Baltimore MD	5	2.44	100.0	2.44	Boise, ID	32	1.18	92.8	1.27
Providence, RI	6	2.28	100.0	2.28	Kansas City, MO	33	1.16	19.0	6.13
Milwaukee, WI.	7	2.26	100.0	2.26	Minneapolis, MN	34	1.15	93.9	1.23
Des Moines, IA	8	2.09	45.6	4.59	Salt Lake City, UT . . .	35	1.20	100.0	1.15
Detroit, MI	9	2.03	31.0	6.56	Las Vegas, NV	36	1.14	35.0	3.27
Fargo, ND	10	2.03	4.4	45.90	Los Angeles, CA	37	1.10	100.0	1.10
Omaha, NE	11	1.99	97.0	2.05	Boston, MA	38	1.10	100.0	1.10
Memphis, TN	12	1.74	23.3	7.47	Portland, OR.	39	1.07	49.2	2.17
Jackson, MS.	13	1.72	10.0	17.16	Columbia, SC	40	0.98	4.0	24.60
Columbus, OH	14	1.69	35.0	4.84	Phoenix, AZ	41	0.97	10.0	9.67
Burlington, VT.	15	1.69	100.0	1.69	Virginia Beach, VA . . .	42	0.89	100.0	0.89
Atlanta, GA.	16	1.67	40.0	4.18	Washington, DC	43	0.88	100.0	0.88
Newark, NJ.	17	1.60	64.4	2.49	Seattle, WA	44	0.86	86.8	1.00
Jacksonville, FL.	18	1.57	93.8	1.67	Charleston, WV.	45	0.86	60.0	1.44
Portland, ME.	19	1.55	95.0	1.63	Chicago, IL.	46	0.70	10.0	6.98
Wilmington, DE	20	1.53	47.2	3.24	Birmingham, AL.	47	0.70	10.0	6.95
Albuquerque, NM. . . .	20	1.46	30.0	4.86	Cheyenne, WY	48	0.67	9.5	7.10
Anchorage, AK	22	1.45	100.0	1.45	New York City, NY . . .	49	0.62	3.9	16.03
Billings, MT.	23	1.42	67.0	2.12	Denver, CO	50	0.56	8.0	7.06
Little Rock, AR	24	1.41	20.0	7.05	Honolulu, HI	51	0.33	100.0	0.33
Sioux Falls, SD	25	1.40	85.0	1.65	Unweighted average .	(X)	1.44	59.0	5.61
New Orleans, LA	26	1.39	10.0	13.85	Median	(X)	1.39	(X)	(X)
Wichita, KS.	27	1.35	11.5	11.77					

X Not applicable.

Source: Government of the District of Columbia, Office of the Chief Financial Officer, Tax Rates and Revenues, "Tax Burden Comparisons, Nationwide Comparison," annual; <http://www.cfo.dc.gov/cfo/>.

U.S. Census Bureau, Statistical Abstract of the United States: 2010

Table 437. Gross Revenue From Parimutuel and Amusement Taxes and Lotteries by State: 2004 to 2006

[In millions of dollars (50,758.5 represents $50,758,500,000). For fiscal years; see text, this section]

State	2004, total gross revenue	2005, total gross revenue	Total gross revenue	Amusement taxes [1]	Parimutuel taxes	Total [2]	Prizes	Administration	Proceeds available from ticket sales
						2006 Lottery revenue — Apportionment of funds			
United States. .	50,758.5	72,695.9	78,521.2	5,541.5	304.4	72,675.3	53,542.5	2,208.8	16,924.0
Alabama.	3.3	3.2	3.3	0.1	3.2	–	–	–	–
Alaska	2.4	2.5	2.4	2.4	(X)	–	–	–	–
Arizona.	343.3	372.1	438.7	0.6	0.5	437.5	259.1	37.8	140.6
Arkansas	4.6	4.8	5.5	(X)	5.5	–	–	–	–
California	2,810.6	3,139.6	3,371.3	(X)	38.0	3,333.3	1,932.7	151.8	1,248.8
Colorado.	510.8	513.9	533.1	105.6	3.4	424.1	274.0	29.7	120.4
Connecticut.	1,355.3	1,307.4	1,383.2	457.8	9.1	916.3	587.4	38.4	290.5
Delaware	379.6	6,842.4	7,144.4	(X)	0.2	7,144.2	6,778.5	48.4	317.3
Florida	2,928.5	3,307.1	3,739.9	(X)	28.1	3,711.8	2,340.9	146.4	1,224.5
Georgia	2,376.3	2,546.6	2,751.9	(X)	(X)	2,751.9	1,815.6	120.2	816.2
Hawaii	(X)	(X)	(X)	(X)	(X)	–	–	–	–
Idaho	101.4	105.3	122.5	(X)	1.0	121.4	76.7	10.4	34.4
Illinois	2,370.4	2,521.8	2,656.7	826.8	10.5	1,819.3	1,158.2	55.4	605.7
Indiana.	1,439.4	1,486.5	1,569.9	805.5	4.7	759.6	493.1	48.1	218.4
Iowa	412.0	419.4	486.6	252.6	2.3	231.7	122.3	29.2	80.2
Kansas.	215.7	198.4	216.0	0.6	3.0	212.4	131.0	23.0	58.4
Kentucky	695.8	676.7	710.5	0.2	14.6	695.6	444.9	43.7	207.0
Louisiana	855.6	848.0	970.5	603.9	53.0	313.6	168.2	27.5	117.9
Maine.	193.5	199.1	227.9	10.7	3.7	213.4	144.2	16.1	53.1
Maryland	1,408.9	1,401.1	1,470.9	10.7	2.0	1,458.2	904.1	53.9	500.2
Massachusetts.	4,386.5	4,222.7	4,208.9	4.3	4.2	4,200.4	3,234.5	83.3	882.5
Michigan.	1,952.7	2,035.1	2,191.4	155.5	9.9	2,026.0	1,298.5	64.2	663.3
Minnesota.	403.2	420.8	453.1	51.3	1.5	400.2	282.0	22.4	95.9
Mississippi	167.3	223.1	145.7	145.7	(X)	–	–	–	–
Missouri	1,049.5	1,064.5	1,201.2	344.1	(X)	857.1	572.8	34.3	250.1
Montana.	85.2	85.1	94.9	57.3	–	37.6	20.7	7.2	9.7
Nebraska	99.0	100.4	112.1	5.8	0.3	106.0	63.7	12.6	29.7
Nevada	861.5	934.6	1,045.8	1,045.8	(X)	–	–	–	–
New Hampshire	232.2	220.6	252.1	0.7	2.9	248.6	152.4	16.7	79.5
New Jersey.	2,533.7	2,623.2	2,774.6	502.3	(X)	2,272.3	1,345.7	88.7	837.9
New Mexico	178.2	177.5	201.7	56.7	0.4	144.7	92.2	18.9	36.8
New York	5,528.5	5,873.5	6,321.7	1.0	28.9	6,291.8	3,853.3	261.2	2,177.3
North Carolina	11.5	11.2	225.2	11.8	(X)	213.5	133.1	16.1	64.3
North Dakota.	12.7	28.2	31.1	9.4	0.5	21.3	11.0	3.4	6.8
Ohio	2,170.6	2,039.9	2,091.7	(X)	10.6	2,081.1	1,311.1	95.1	674.8
Oklahoma	8.2	6.2	195.3	1.8	1.7	191.9	109.7	13.2	69.1
Oregon.	1,612.5	1,735.3	2,216.4	0.1	3.1	2,213.2	1,571.6	65.2	576.3
Pennsylvania	2,189.5	2,453.4	2,838.2	0.5	25.6	2,812.1	1,804.9	63.6	943.6
Rhode Island.	1,314.0	1,460.8	1,542.7	(X)	3.5	1,539.2	1,208.3	8.4	322.5
South Carolina.	922.7	925.6	1,100.2	36.6	(X)	1,063.5	702.3	43.1	318.1
South Dakota.	141.6	564.1	580.6	7.1	0.3	573.2	447.6	7.7	117.9
Tennessee	(X)	789.4	930.9	(X)	(X)	930.9	620.8	51.7	258.4
Texas.	3,522.8	3,511.1	3,619.8	25.7	11.0	3,583.1	2,310.6	184.6	1,087.9
Utah	(X)	(X)	(X)	(X)	(X)	–	–	–	–
Vermont	87.0	87.2	98.7	(X)	(X)	98.7	66.5	9.6	22.6
Virginia.	1,262.4	1,258.4	1,289.2	0.1	(X)	1,289.1	773.6	64.9	450.7
Washington.	483.3	431.3	449.5	0.1	1.9	447.5	291.8	33.7	122.0
West Virginia.	683.3	13,094.2	14,027.7	(X)	13.6	14,014.1	13,342.2	30.0	641.9
Wisconsin.	451.2	422.4	475.4	0.3	1.2	473.9	293.9	29.1	150.9
Wyoming	0.2	0.4	0.2	(X)	0.2	–	–	–	–

– Represents or rounds to zero.   X Not applicable.   [1] Represents nonlicense taxes.   [2] Excludes commissions.

Source: U.S. Census Bureau, Federal, State and Local Governments, State Government Finances, Lottery, and unpublished data; <http://www.census.gov/govs/state/06lottery.html>.

Table 438. Lottery Sales—Type of Game and Use of Proceeds: 1990 to 2008

[In millions of dollars (20,017 represents $20,017,000,000). For fiscal years]

Game	1990	1995	2000	2004	2005	2006	2007	2008
Total ticket sales.	20,017	31,931	37,201	47,697	47,364	51,595	52,414	53,360
Instant [1]	5,204	11,511	15,459	23,011	25,946	28,342	29,736	30,471
Three-digit [2]	4,572	5,737	5,341	5,389	5,428	5,456	5,586	5,544
Four-digit [2]	1,302	1,941	2,711	3,195	3,300	3,400	3,499	3,605
Lotto [3]	8,563	10,594	9,160	10,472	9,707	11,015	10,014	10,292
Other [4]	376	2,148	4,530	5,630	2,983	3,382	3,579	3,448
State proceeds (net income) [5]	7,703	11,100	11,404	15,094	15,779	17,220	17,627	17,877

[1] Player scratches a latex section on ticket which reveals instantly whether ticket is a winner.   [2] Players choose and bet on three or four digits, depending on game, with various payoffs for different straight order or mixed combination bets.   [3] Players typically select six digits out of a large field of numbers. Varying prizes are offered for matching three through six numbers drawn by lottery.   [4] Includes break-open tickets, spiel, keno, video lottery, etc.   [5] Sales minus prizes and expenses equal net government income.

Source: TLF Publications, Inc., Boyds, MD, 2008 World Lottery Almanac (copyright); <http://www.lafleurs.com/>.

State and Local Government Finances and Employment   279

Table 439. **State Governments—Summary of Finances: 1990 to 2006**

[In millions of dollars (673,119 represents $673,119,000,000), For fiscal year ending in year shown; see text, this section]

Item	1990	2000	2001	2002	2003	2004	2005	2006
Borrowing and revenue	673,119	1,336,798	1,257,148	1,205,999	1,430,303	1,727,347	1,757,221	1,906,455
Borrowing.	40,948	75,968	76,843	108,170	134,644	140,682	115,264	133,247
Total Revenue	632,172	1,260,829	1,180,305	1,097,829	1,295,659	1,586,665	1,641,957	1,773,208
General revenue.	517,429	984,783	1,049,298	1,062,305	1,112,349	1,194,056	1,286,714	1,385,376
Taxes	300,489	539,655	559,679	535,241	548,991	590,414	650,612	710,864
Sales and gross receipts	147,069	252,147	258,018	262,361	273,811	293,326	312,584	332,972
General.	99,702	174,461	179,319	179,665	184,597	197,949	212,921	226,712
Motor fuels	19,379	29,968	31,026	31,968	32,269	33,762	34,567	35,702
Alcoholic beverages	3,191	4,104	4,167	4,249	4,399	4,593	4,706	4,925
Tobacco products	5,541	8,391	8,644	8,902	11,482	12,303	12,917	14,499
Other	19,256	35,222	34,863	37,576	41,065	44,718	47,474	51,134
Licenses.	18,842	32,598	32,866	35,391	35,863	39,679	42,584	45,241
Motor vehicles	9,848	15,099	15,141	15,641	16,009	17,336	18,221	19,015
Corporations in general	3,099	6,460	6,384	5,842	6,129	6,339	7,148	7,579
Other	5,895	11,039	11,341	13,908	13,725	16,004	17,216	18,648
Individual income	96,076	194,573	208,079	185,697	181,933	196,255	221,597	245,883
Corporation net income	21,751	32,522	31,687	25,123	28,384	30,229	38,691	47,466
Property	5,848	10,996	10,430	9,702	10,471	10,714	11,342	11,794
Other.	10,902	16,819	18,597	16,967	18,529	20,211	23,813	27,509
Charges and miscellaneous.	90,612	170,747	183,998	191,641	201,741	209,029	228,242	255,369
Intergovernmental revenue	126,329	274,382	305,621	335,423	361,617	394,613	407,860	419,143
From federal government.	118,353	259,114	288,309	317,581	343,308	374,694	386,283	397,597
Public welfare	59,397	147,150	165,800	181,517	196,954	214,528	222,909	222,916
Education	21,271	42,086	45,760	51,103	56,362	64,913	68,275	73,493
Highways	13,931	23,790	27,894	29,641	29,481	29,606	32,677	33,536
Health and hospitals	5,475	14,223	16,426	17,875	19,559	20,377	20,443	21,144
Other	18,279	31,865	32,428	37,445	40,951	45,270	41,980	46,508
From local governments	7,976	15,268	17,312	17,842	18,309	19,919	21,576	21,546
Utility revenue	3,305	4,513	6,930	11,935	12,518	12,955	14,627	15,816
Liquor store revenue . . , ...	2,907	3,895	4,092	4,288	4,518	4,866	5,118	5,430
Insurance trust revenue [1]	108,530	267,639	119,985	19,301	166,274	374,788	335,498	366,586
Employee retirement	78,898	230,166	79,527	-25,244	110,839	308,896	269,617	300,350
Unemployment compensation . . .	18,370	23,260	23,221	26,960	35,191	38,230	35,243	36,864
Expenditure and debt redemption	**592,213**	**1,125,828**	**1,235,568**	**1,334,969**	**1,426,715**	**1,497,114**	**1,555,611**	**1,627,579**
Total Expenditure	572,318	1,084,097	1,186,108	1,280,290	1,359,048	1,406,175	1,471,936	1,551,555
General expenditure	508,284	964,723	1,045,296	1,109,227	1,163,968	1,209,436	1,277,979	1,347,130
Education.	184,935	346,465	374,444	389,390	411,094	429,341	454,364	481,877
Public welfare	104,971	238,890	262,346	287,016	314,407	339,409	370,219	378,605
Health	20,029	42,066	43,732	50,293	50,221	49,559	48,957	51,121
Hospitals	22,637	32,578	34,538	37,393	38,395	40,426	43,103	44,800
Highways.	44,249	74,415	78,786	84,198	85,726	86,166	91,063	99,559
Police protection	5,166	9,788	10,145	10,706	11,144	10,766	11,426	12,233
Corrections.	17,266	35,129	38,165	38,918	39,188	39,314	40,592	42,720
Natural resources	9,909	15,967	17,309	17,821	18,577	18,652	18,850	20,034
Housing and community development	2,856	4,726	5,009	5,989	8,112	7,191	7,708	7,918
Other and unallocable	96,267	164,698	180,823	187,504	187,106	188,613	191,697	208,302
Utility expenditure	7,131	10,723	18,632	20,279	22,405	21,676	21,824	24,904
Liquor store expenditure	2,452	3,195	3,347	3,498	3,697	3,924	4,082	4,338
Insurance trust expenditure [1]	54,452	105,456	118,833	147,286	168,979	171,139	168,052	175,183
Employee retirement	29,562	75,971	83,770	91,971	103,049	111,376	118,333	127,493
Unemployment compensation . . .	16,423	18,583	22,920	42,017	51,411	43,174	29,776	28,009
By character and object:								
Intergovernmental expenditure	175,028	327,070	350,327	364,789	382,197	389,706	403,488	428,925
Direct expenditure.	397,291	757,027	835,782	915,501	976,852	1,016,469	1,068,449	1,122,631
Current operation	258,046	523,114	580,374	620,763	656,989	691,652	739,988	774,651
Capital outlay	45,524	76,233	81,881	89,919	91,943	90,950	94,181	101,432
Construction	34,803	59,681	64,668	71,035	72,374	73,372	77,039	83,858
Land and existing structure . . .	3,471	4,681	4,643	5,305	6,945	6,576	6,259	6,135
Equipment	7,250	11,871	12,570	13,579	12,623	11,002	10,883	11,440
Assistance and subsidies	16,902	22,136	23,496	24,313	25,901	28,104	30,181	31,644
Interest on debt.	22,367	30,089	31,198	33,220	33,040	34,624	36,047	39,720
Insurance benefits [2]	54,452	105,456	118,833	147,286	168,979	171,139	168,052	175,183
Debt redemption	19,895	41,730	49,460	54,678	67,666	90,939	83,675	76,024
Debt outstanding, year end. . . .	**318,254**	**547,876**	**576,494**	**642,202**	**697,929**	**754,150**	**813,846**	**870,939**
Long-term [3].	315,490	541,497	572,831	623,558	681,796	740,414	808,293	860,310
Full-faith and credit	74,972	138,525	147,130	159,502	179,372	209,385	(NA)	(NA)
Nonguaranteed.	240,518	402,972	425,701	464,056	502,424	531,030	(NA)	(NA)
Short-term.	2,764	6,379	3,663	18,644	16,133	13,736	5,553	10,629
Net long-term [4]	125,524	266,870	287,450	317,829	366,207	412,194	444,685	473,447
Full-faith and credit only	63,481	128,384	137,341	149,580	170,137	200,295	(NA)	(NA)

NA Not available.   [1] Includes other items not shown seperately.   [2] Includes repayments.   [3] As of fiscal year 2005, the Census Bureau no longer collects government debt information by the character of long-term debt. For further information, see the 2006 Government Finance and Employment Classification Manual at <http://www.census.gov/govs/classification/class06.html>.   [4] Less cash and investment assets specifically held for redemption of long-term debt.

Source: U.S. Census Bureau, 2006 Survey of State Government Finances, 2006. See also <http://www.census.gov/govs/www/state.html>.

U.S. Census Bureau, Statistical Abstract of the United States: 2010

Table 440. State Governments—Revenue by State: 2006

[In millions of dollars (1,773,208 represents $1,773,208,000,000), except as noted. For fiscal year ending in year shown; See text, this section. Includes local shares of state imposed taxes]

State	Total revenue[1,2]	General revenue Total	Intergovernmental Total	Intergovernmental From federal government	Own sources Total	Total taxes	Current charges	Miscellaneous general revenue	Utility and liquor store revenue	Insurance trust revenue
United States. . .	1,773,208	1,385,376	419,143	397,597	966,233	710,864	137,401	117,968	21,246	366,586
Alabama	23,671	20,306	7,588	6,977	12,718	8,530	2,832	1,357	178	3,187
Alaska	10,845	8,920	2,156	2,152	6,764	2,484	519	3,760	16	1,909
Arizona.	28,011	23,155	8,094	7,607	15,061	11,890	1,420	1,752	26	4,830
Arkansas.	16,481	13,701	4,288	4,267	9,413	7,016	1,697	700	–	2,780
California.	263,765	188,444	53,685	48,287	134,759	111,347	13,329	10,083	5,504	69,817
Colorado.	23,467	17,493	4,726	4,657	12,767	8,522	2,404	1,841	–	5,973
Connecticut	22,897	19,460	4,177	4,161	15,283	12,132	1,573	1,578	27	3,410
Delaware.	6,840	5,955	1,219	1,177	4,736	2,861	808	1,067	12	874
Florida	83,745	66,561	20,004	19,709	46,558	37,202	4,734	4,622	22	17,162
Georgia	37,594	32,353	10,609	10,336	21,743	17,034	2,790	1,919	–	5,241
Hawaii	9,857	8,552	1,834	1,833	6,718	4,919	1,142	657	–	1,305
Idaho	7,786	5,979	1,836	1,823	4,143	3,143	532	468	97	1,710
Illinois.	62,729	49,271	13,387	12,849	35,884	28,129	3,885	3,870	–	13,457
Indiana	32,855	29,604	7,270	7,059	22,333	13,626	6,861	1,846	–	3,251
Iowa.	16,809	13,434	4,296	4,089	9,138	6,119	2,017	1,002	164	3,211
Kansas.	13,615	11,449	3,315	3,229	8,134	6,275	1,135	723	–	2,167
Kentucky.	23,543	20,061	6,375	6,354	13,686	9,953	2,335	1,398	–	3,481
Louisiana	27,680	22,926	9,079	9,026	13,846	9,651	2,361	1,834	4	4,750
Maine	8,639	7,574	2,580	2,573	4,993	3,599	650	745	–	1,066
Maryland.	31,005	26,270	6,968	6,738	19,303	14,625	2,642	2,036	109	4,625
Massachusetts	45,499	36,522	8,801	8,431	27,721	19,395	3,265	5,060	168	8,809
Michigan	62,087	46,001	12,552	12,329	33,450	23,715	5,896	3,839	718	15,368
Minnesota	34,773	27,691	6,661	6,661	21,030	17,331	2,214	1,485	–	7,082
Mississippi.	17,744	14,604	6,973	6,855	7,631	5,990	1,174	467	221	2,918
Missouri	28,760	22,373	7,936	7,773	14,436	10,180	2,167	2,089	–	6,388
Montana	6,130	4,935	1,826	1,819	3,110	2,126	477	506	59	1,136
Nebraska	9,103	8,045	2,472	2,417	5,573	3,961	770	842	–	1,058
Nevada.	12,342	9,461	1,980	1,827	7,481	6,153	632	696	124	2,757
New Hampshire . . .	6,373	5,186	1,718	1,522	3,469	2,081	689	699	418	769
New Jersey	57,610	46,446	11,378	10,828	35,067	26,266	4,682	4,119	734	10,430
New Mexico.	14,734	12,117	3,855	3,750	8,262	5,111	911	2,240	–	2,617
New York	166,078	123,561	45,773	39,698	77,789	57,403	8,052	12,334	7,231	35,286
North Carolina	45,474	38,884	12,906	12,183	25,978	20,603	3,286	2,089	–	6,590
North Dakota	4,370	3,667	1,213	1,188	2,454	1,622	533	299	–	702
Ohio.	75,304	51,249	16,525	16,120	34,724	24,536	6,211	3,977	654	23,402
Oklahoma	19,651	16,226	5,150	5,045	11,116	7,817	1,814	1,485	468	2,917
Oregon	25,743	16,495	4,640	4,611	11,855	7,590	2,431	1,834	346	8,901
Pennsylvania	73,134	55,419	15,327	15,100	40,092	29,051	6,426	4,615	1,258	16,457
Rhode Island	7,670	6,194	2,148	2,028	4,046	2,742	511	793	30	1,446
South Carolina	23,720	19,436	6,867	6,463	12,568	7,760	3,305	1,503	1,339	2,945
South Dakota.	4,182	3,220	1,251	1,236	1,968	1,189	246	534	–	963
Tennessee.	26,316	23,644	8,202	8,024	15,442	10,650	1,794	2,998	–	2,672
Texas	103,964	83,471	28,709	27,814	54,762	36,592	8,614	9,556	–	20,493
Utah.	14,166	11,789	3,236	3,157	8,553	5,462	2,201	891	171	2,205
Vermont	4,881	4,459	1,288	1,288	3,171	2,407	439	325	40	382
Virginia	40,273	32,619	6,673	6,196	25,946	17,192	5,441	3,313	473	7,181
Washington	40,832	29,284	7,729	7,438	21,555	16,411	3,280	1,864	505	11,043
West Virginia	11,435	10,262	3,224	3,157	7,038	4,558	1,101	1,379	66	1,106
Wisconsin	33,411	25,708	6,633	6,488	19,075	13,795	3,023	2,257	–	7,703
Wyoming.	5,617	4,897	2,009	1,958	2,888	2,122	149	617	64	655

– Represents or rounds to zero. [1] Includes amounts for categories not shown separately. [2] Duplicate intergovernmental transactions are excluded.

Source: U.S. Census Bureau, *Federal, State, and Local Governments, Finance, Survey of State Government Finances*, 2006. See also <http://www.census.gov/govs/www/state.html>.

State and Local Government Finances and Employment   281

Table 441. State Government Tax Collections by State: 2007

[In millions of dollars (750,282 represents $750,282,000,000)]

State	All taxes	Total prop-erty tax	Sales and gross receipts taxes								
			General sales and gross receipts		Selective sales taxes						
			Total	receipts	Total [1]	Alco-holic bever-ages	Insur-ance premi-ums	Motor fuels	Public Utilities	Tobacco prod-ucts	Other
United States [2]	750,282	12,157	345,828	236,333	109,495	5,157	15,345	36,524	10,986	15,262	19,996
Alabama	8,868	274	4,390	2,278	2,112	159	277	568	745	151	210
Alaska	3,443	66	220	–	220	35	55	39	4	70	13
Arizona	12,397	429	7,339	5,684	1,655	63	441	769	23	358	–
Arkansas	7,392	633	3,855	2,904	950	47	139	462	–	148	146
California	114,737	2,304	40,434	32,669	7,764	334	2,178	3,433	601	1,079	103
Colorado	9,206	–	3,450	2,219	1,231	34	182	662	10	228	–
Connecticut	12,848	–	4,964	3,030	1,933	40	234	440	173	254	318
Delaware	2,906	–	459	–	459	15	110	117	48	88	81
Florida	35,738	41	27,535	21,749	5,786	654	786	2,306	1,044	454	515
Georgia	18,637	79	8,210	6,382	1,829	160	343	1,083	–	243	–
Hawaii	5,094	–	3,228	2,558	670	46	99	90	124	86	226
Idaho	3,537	–	1,669	1,278	391	7	86	232	2	55	7
Illinois	29,517	60	14,310	7,817	6,493	156	309	1,454	1,834	639	1,272
Indiana	14,098	5	7,752	5,424	2,329	40	191	881	12	361	10
Iowa	6,470	–	2,768	1,787	981	14	105	447	–	135	–
Kansas	6,893	73	3,057	2,242	815	101	130	431	1	121	28
Kentucky	9,895	494	4,590	2,818	1,773	102	148	571	53	178	716
Louisiana	10,860	39	5,374	3,481	1,892	54	402	617	19	103	32
Maine	3,582	37	1,691	1,055	636	20	85	231	24	159	92
Maryland	15,094	595	5,812	3,448	2,364	29	385	754	133	278	776
Massachusetts	20,664	–	5,996	4,076	1,920	72	397	676	–	438	329
Michigan	23,849	2,323	11,602	7,983	3,619	136	224	1,034	21	1,132	903
Minnesota	17,780	675	7,302	4,471	2,831	72	318	644	–	448	1,298
Mississippi	6,395	48	4,098	3,156	943	42	192	449	10	56	9
Missouri	10,705	26	4,814	3,273	1,542	31	295	737	–	109	30
Montana	2,320	202	530	–	530	26	63	211	41	91	38
Nebraska	4,071	2	1,953	1,484	468	26	37	321	3	72	5
Nevada	6,305	184	5,126	3,213	1,913	40	259	328	11	138	48
New Hampshire	2,172	385	735	–	735	13	87	129	73	139	291
New Jersey	29,107	4	11,942	8,346	3,597	102	445	565	982	785	258
New Mexico	5,205	57	2,483	1,844	639	30	104	245	16	46	138
New York	63,162	–	19,506	10,880	8,626	194	1,172	516	774	982	4,959
North Carolina	22,613	–	8,866	5,202	3,664	246	487	1,609	372	241	692
North Dakota	1,783	2	809	484	324	6	30	139	35	24	80
Ohio	24,811	34	11,223	7,781	3,442	92	450	1,720	172	997	–
Oklahoma	8,904	–	2,938	1,964	974	80	197	397	30	231	28
Oregon	7,743	22	783	–	783	14	56	417	22	271	–
Pennsylvania	30,838	64	14,483	8,662	5,821	265	694	2,143	1,299	1,018	122
Rhode Island	2,766	1	1,357	876	481	11	57	132	102	120	56
South Carolina	8,689	9	4,577	3,234	1,344	147	123	533	40	32	430
South Dakota	1,256	–	1,019	711	307	13	59	123	1	47	55
Tennessee	11,345	–	8,355	6,764	1,592	112	375	860	8	136	102
Texas	40,315	–	31,811	20,435	11,377	736	1,292	3,075	995	1,331	3,910
Utah	5,889	–	2,625	1,954	671	36	124	382	30	62	37
Vermont	2,559	889	845	334	511	19	55	87	10	64	274
Virginia	18,972	21	6,000	3,539	2,461	168	385	919	140	172	678
Washington	17,693	1,689	13,852	10,861	2,991	253	392	1,129	444	445	326
West Virginia	4,654	4	2,228	1,130	1,098	9	111	349	153	111	347
Wisconsin	14,483	120	6,037	4,159	1,878	52	157	996	351	314	8
Wyoming	2,025	266	826	698	128	3	24	72	3	25	1

See footnotes at end of table.

282 State and Local Government Finances and Employment

Table 441. **State Government Tax Collections by State: 2007**—Con.

[See headnote, page 282]

State	License taxes				Income taxes			Other taxes		
	Total [1]	Selected license taxes							Selected other taxes	
		Cor-pora-tion	Motor vehicle oper-ators	Occu-pancy and business, n.e.c. [3]	Total	Indi-vidual	Cor-pora-tion net	Total [1]	Death and gift	Sever-ance
United States [2] . . .	46,883	8,308	2,131	13,390	319,286	265,907	53,379	26,128	4,901	10,729
Alabama	477	99	16	125	3,525	3,020	506	202	1	144
Alaska.	127	1	–	30	814	–	814	2,216	–	2,216
Arizona	403	11	27	99	4,182	3,196	986	44	–	44
Arkansas	298	23	15	92	2,531	2,168	363	74	–	22
California	7,502	64	228	4,346	64,476	53,318	11,158	22	6	15
Colorado	343	9	10	35	5,275	4,795	479	137	1	137
Connecticut	362	18	38	87	7,160	6,335	825	362	178	–
Delaware	1,006	624	3	241	1,328	1,025	302	113	1	–
Florida.	1,875	196	173	239	2,443	–	2,443	3,845	43	46
Georgia	497	61	44	133	9,817	8,799	1,017	34	1	–
Hawaii.	156	1	–	30	1,661	1,560	101	48	–	–
Idaho	264	2	7	56	1,595	1,406	188	9	–	7
Illinois	2,441	201	68	645	12,345	9,408	2,936	360	260	–
Indiana	587	7	229	39	5,603	4,616	987	151	150	1
Iowa	615	36	7	92	2,992	2,667	325	95	78	–
Kansas	303	56	20	25	3,272	2,745	527	188	56	132
Kentucky	459	77	17	111	4,030	3,042	988	322	44	275
Louisiana.	566	315	12	95	3,967	3,214	753	915	11	904
Maine	227	7	11	92	1,542	1,358	184	84	55	–
Maryland	722	74	26	146	7,461	6,679	782	504	224	–
Massachusetts	676	25	82	162	13,507	11,400	2,107	485	250	–
Michigan	1,375	20	51	152	8,229	6,443	1,786	320	1	82
Minnesota	973	7	48	297	8,415	7,231	1,184	415	108	35
Mississippi	396	126	31	80	1,771	1,402	369	82	–	82
Missouri.	630	77	17	166	5,225	4,835	391	8	–	–
Montana	308	3	9	85	1,012	833	179	268	1	265
Nebraska	207	7	9	63	1,864	1,651	213	45	27	2
Nevada	802	72	16	434	–	–	–	193	1	62
New Hampshire	207	4	13	84	703	107	596	142	–	–
New Jersey	1,513	320	40	587	14,416	11,540	2,877	1,232	587	–
New Mexico	238	3	5	27	1,575	1,150	425	853	–	844
New York.	1,328	72	157	149	39,996	34,580	5,416	2,332	1,053	–
North Carolina	1,338	399	127	162	12,154	10,589	1,566	254	178	2
North Dakota	128	–	4	51	453	317	136	391	–	391
Ohio	2,139	402	82	837	11,334	10,032	1,303	80	72	8
Oklahoma	953	50	14	203	3,975	3,414	561	1,038	67	942
Oregon	833	11	32	275	6,002	5,596	406	104	80	13
Pennsylvania	2,847	777	58	723	12,099	9,813	2,287	1,344	737	–
Rhode Island	94	4	1	33	1,265	1,086	179	49	36	–
South Carolina	471	67	52	142	3,551	3,239	312	80	2	–
South Dakota	156	3	2	75	77	–	77	5	1	5
Tennessee	1,260	635	45	259	1,344	223	1,120	386	111	2
Texas	5,736	3,215	117	763	–	–	–	2,768	5	2,763
Utah	202	5	22	37	2,960	2,561	399	102	–	102
Vermont	117	5	5	27	665	581	83	44	18	–
Virginia	674	57	46	161	11,520	10,239	1,281	758	153	2
Washington	882	24	61	233	–	–	–	1,270	183	49
West Virginia	182	9	1	42	1,900	1,361	539	341	–	328
Wisconsin	861	17	31	303	7,257	6,334	923	208	121	5
Wyoming	126	10	2	19	–	–	–	806	3	804

– Represents zero or rounds to zero.   [1] Includes other items not shown separately.   [2] Details will not add to the totals shown because of rounding.   [3] n.e.c. means not elsewhere classified.

Source: U.S. Census Bureau, Federal, State, and Local Governments, *Tax collections, State government tax collections*, annual. See also <http://www.census.gov/govs/www/statetax07.html> (accessed May 2009).

State and Local Government Finances and Employment   283

Table 442. **State Governments—Expenditures and Debt by State: 2006**

[**In millions of dollars** (1,551,555 represents $1,551,555,000,000), **except as indicated.** For fiscal year ending in year shown; see text, this section]

State	Total expendi- ture [1]	General expenditure								
		Total	Inter- govern- mental	Direct expenditures						
				Total [1]	Educa- tion	Public welfare	Health	Hospi- tals	High- ways	Police protec- tion
United States ...	1,551,555	1,347,130	428,925	918,205	202,474	324,714	32,994	44,320	84,289	10,838
Alabama.........	22,261	20,010	5,000	15,010	4,358	5,093	951	1,114	1,129	140
Alaska	8,599	7,528	1,217	6,311	965	1,393	156	30	1,131	66
Arizona..........	25,731	23,284	8,607	14,678	3,067	5,797	1,284	62	1,359	214
Arkansas	14,370	13,303	3,866	9,437	2,252	3,426	344	666	792	103
California	225,317	191,607	88,317	103,290	20,169	30,053	2,153	5,564	9,222	1,302
Colorado.........	20,151	16,966	5,621	11,344	3,438	2,936	653	355	960	107
Connecticut.......	20,675	17,772	3,428	14,343	2,621	4,526	531	1,215	801	198
Delaware	6,520	6,019	1,130	4,890	1,068	1,241	313	61	491	99
Florida	76,142	67,862	19,345	48,517	6,885	16,922	2,988	602	5,836	465
Georgia	34,945	31,300	9,753	21,547	5,865	8,351	804	699	1,423	227
Hawaii	8,914	8,090	158	7,932	2,913	1,423	474	408	268	11
Idaho	6,353	5,660	1,606	4,054	901	1,432	134	45	480	43
Illinois	55,768	48,052	13,946	34,105	6,732	12,921	1,954	927	2,947	390
Indiana..........	26,959	24,956	8,082	16,874	5,107	5,855	501	262	1,588	199
Iowa	14,942	13,470	3,882	9,588	2,479	3,427	101	920	1,021	81
Kansas..........	12,553	11,440	3,596	7,844	2,005	2,791	163	122	1,086	95
Kentucky	21,992	19,335	4,384	14,951	3,517	5,636	422	859	1,498	162
Louisiana	24,221	21,027	5,654	15,373	3,168	4,505	557	1,549	1,508	217
Maine...........	7,855	7,232	1,217	6,014	883	2,461	473	54	539	64
Maryland	28,966	25,722	6,916	18,805	3,800	6,362	1,163	453	1,612	324
Massachusetts.....	39,880	36,037	6,815	29,222	5,377	11,384	737	453	1,533	402
Michigan.........	53,087	46,793	19,408	27,386	8,313	9,099	650	2,038	1,516	291
Minnesota........	30,989	27,449	10,868	16,581	4,157	7,626	383	293	1,209	227
Mississippi	16,293	14,554	4,827	9,728	1,886	3,716	264	766	1,155	89
Missouri	24,335	21,701	5,386	16,314	2,917	5,902	1,026	1,155	1,708	190
Montana.........	5,195	4,584	1,088	3,496	777	823	275	41	561	32
Nebraska	7,702	7,358	1,721	5,637	1,379	1,933	350	220	644	60
Nevada	10,342	9,153	3,667	5,486	1,320	1,534	174	208	656	94
New Hampshire....	5,988	5,212	1,385	3,827	850	1,284	100	55	418	44
New Jersey.......	54,073	43,350	11,060	32,289	7,013	11,470	763	1,570	2,368	505
New Mexico	13,399	12,278	3,745	8,533	1,896	2,782	351	686	888	116
New York	142,853	115,454	45,616	69,838	9,394	33,259	1,636	4,348	3,850	718
North Carolina.....	41,108	37,180	11,261	25,919	7,271	8,457	1,176	1,261	2,834	445
North Dakota......	3,633	3,360	736	2,625	720	688	46	23	396	21
Ohio	64,929	52,720	17,131	35,589	8,392	14,027	1,415	1,951	2,424	240
Oklahoma........	16,882	14,767	3,857	10,910	3,018	4,036	441	172	913	145
Oregon..........	20,071	16,565	4,948	11,617	2,440	3,613	278	1,088	1,000	190
Pennsylvania......	64,917	55,566	13,650	41,915	8,932	16,936	743	2,125	5,290	658
Rhode Island......	6,956	5,872	999	4,874	801	2,137	152	115	302	55
South Carolina.....	23,431	19,785	4,699	15,086	3,793	4,756	842	1,216	1,400	169
South Dakota	3,465	3,175	634	2,542	481	735	99	53	469	29
Tennessee	23,968	22,413	5,910	16,502	3,507	7,436	1,136	416	1,501	144
Texas...........	85,514	75,896	19,265	56,631	14,431	20,015	825	2,488	7,851	564
Utah	12,045	10,966	2,384	8,582	2,647	2,270	293	672	756	138
Vermont	4,648	4,379	1,358	3,021	784	1,121	132	5	226	74
Virginia..........	34,776	31,831	10,019	21,812	5,987	5,945	528	2,407	2,248	285
Washington.......	33,915	29,056	7,821	21,235	5,806	6,621	1,253	1,529	1,728	201
West Virginia......	9,791	9,200	2,078	7,122	1,677	2,343	249	81	1,021	54
Wisconsin........	30,125	26,277	9,561	16,716	3,944	5,642	393	918	1,308	112
Wyoming	4,011	3,564	1,301	2,263	372	573	168	2	424	37

See footnotes at end of table.

Table 442. State Governments—Expenditures and Debt by State: 2006—Con.

[See headnote, page 284]

State	General expenditure—Con. — Direct expenditures—Con. — Corrections	Parks and recreation	Housing and community development	Sewerage	Solid waste management	Governmental administration	Interest on general debt	Other	Expenditures — Utility and liquor store	Insurance trust	Cash and security holdings	Debt outstanding, total
United States. .	40,413	4,876	5,153	1,266	3,254	46,814	37,808	78,992	29,242	175,183	3,436,442	870,939
Alabama	444	38	8	–	7	491	248	990	199	2,051	38,674	6,373
Alaska	210	10	111	–	–	491	302	1,446	78	993	51,918	6,260
Arizona	826	211	75	–	30	579	405	769	29	2,418	43,894	8,410
Arkansas	395	88	16	–	24	542	157	631	–	1,068	23,867	4,534
California	6,467	354	186	140	1,260	7,884	5,285	13,250	5,878	27,832	501,604	109,417
Colorado	689	77	86	2	21	654	657	710	22	3,164	56,137	13,267
Connecticut	618	36	134	–	175	1,011	1,075	1,403	276	2,627	37,484	24,036
Delaware	245	62	54	–	68	473	173	541	75	425	11,566	4,204
Florida	2,441	153	81	–	248	2,600	1,134	8,162	79	8,201	171,406	29,312
Georgia	1,332	177	174	5	101	645	448	1,295	43	3,602	69,541	10,493
Hawaii	179	72	93	1	–	385	432	1,273	–	823	18,319	5,792
Idaho	191	29	11	–	–	272	123	392	73	621	14,652	2,455
Illinois	1,140	116	192	17	111	1,079	2,360	3,218	–	7,716	125,478	53,655
Indiana	600	54	226	10	15	584	758	1,116	39	1,964	55,492	17,322
Iowa	237	21	22	3	4	484	261	528	111	1,361	32,858	6,598
Kansas	269	25	58	–	5	434	285	506	–	1,114	16,656	5,744
Kentucky	438	129	129	19	80	761	431	870	–	2,657	39,183	9,775
Louisiana	499	236	38	–	9	638	663	1,785	4	3,190	48,820	11,735
Maine	127	12	119	2	10	267	229	777	–	623	15,830	5,000
Maryland	1,158	140	228	78	–	1,149	781	1,556	607	2,637	54,926	16,403
Massachusetts . . .	878	178	351	300	45	1,496	3,132	2,955	230	3,613	90,093	65,310
Michigan	1,685	80	483	–	9	1,073	1,069	1,078	525	5,769	100,105	28,986
Minnesota	380	146	63	–	37	849	426	787	98	3,441	59,234	7,435
Mississippi	283	36	11	–	–	238	212	1,071	179	1,560	29,150	4,870
Missouri	602	41	153	–	28	494	929	1,169	–	2,635	71,433	17,669
Montana	143	14	43	1	2	265	156	362	52	559	14,438	4,354
Nebraska	199	29	1	–	–	183	80	559	–	344	11,973	1,844
Nevada	261	24	10	–	18	334	181	672	125	1,064	27,086	4,050
New Hampshire . .	113	13	88	3	11	191	344	314	366	410	11,859	7,433
New Jersey	1,336	442	228	21	151	1,708	1,518	3,197	2,335	8,389	96,997	47,801
New Mexico	291	57	64	–	4	460	311	625	–	1,121	41,328	6,316
New York	2,591	478	386	25	204	4,559	3,565	4,823	12,776	14,623	304,642	105,306
North Carolina . . .	1,148	163	147	1	34	937	563	1,484	145	3,783	85,842	17,749
North Dakota	56	16	21	–	–	126	104	409	–	273	9,913	1,770
Ohio	1,451	88	272	474	27	1,881	1,292	1,656	418	11,791	183,221	24,713
Oklahoma	541	91	13	1	12	441	499	586	403	1,712	32,294	8,138
Oregon	542	72	114	–	35	875	479	892	179	3,327	68,956	11,007
Pennsylvania	1,515	212	27	1	65	2,164	1,416	1,833	1,257	8,094	126,111	32,121
Rhode Island	172	15	38	33	62	537	276	358	129	955	14,627	6,964
South Carolina . . .	436	84	119	–	4	885	521	862	1,302	2,344	38,785	13,737
South Dakota	106	26	38	–	–	151	114	241	–	290	11,480	3,146
Tennessee	509	125	30	16	35	640	194	813	6	1,549	34,211	3,821
Texas	3,044	78	35	3	160	1,451	1,019	4,668	14	9,604	241,172	24,501
Utah	301	38	56	7	12	744	239	410	123	955	24,781	5,931
Vermont	101	16	7	–	10	145	146	191	61	208	6,101	2,982
Virginia	1,079	99	129	75	43	847	747	1,394	452	2,493	73,475	17,611
Washington	953	62	80	–	52	618	836	1,499	423	4,435	83,988	18,329
West Virginia	214	52	15	29	12	542	225	609	70	522	11,098	5,406
Wisconsin	852	26	23	–	11	603	962	1,923	3	3,845	88,479	19,866
Wyoming	126	35	7	–	2	134	44	337	58	390	15,269	983

– Represents or rounds to zero.   [1] Includes items not shown separately.

Source: U.S. Census Bureau; Federal, State, and Local Governments, Finance, "State Government Finances, 2006"; <http://www.census.gov/govs/www/state06.html> (published April 2009).

State and Local Government Finances and Employment 285

Table 443. **Local Governments—Revenue by State: 2006**

[In millions of dollars (1,406,440 represents $1,406,440,000,000), except as noted. For fiscal year ending in year shown; see text, this section]

State	Total revenue [1]	General revenue								
		Total	Inter-govern-mental revenue	General revenue from own sources						
				Total	Taxes					
					Total	Property	Sales and gross receipt	Indi-vidual income	Corpora-tion income	Other taxes
United States....	1,406,440	1,243,748	476,196	767,552	484,390	347,315	79,142	22,717	5,465	28,246
Alabama	17,746	15,000	5,825	9,176	4,239	1,677	1,896	110	–	522
Alaska.	3,414	3,116	1,263	1,853	1,180	915	227	–	–	24
Arizona	25,864	21,878	9,275	12,603	8,051	5,129	2,408	–	–	511
Arkansas	8,125	7,310	4,049	3,261	1,731	745	952	–	–	34
California	229,633	193,462	91,574	101,888	52,402	34,964	12,077	–	–	5,361
Colorado	22,677	20,124	5,593	14,531	8,701	5,269	2,963	–	–	440
Connecticut	14,768	13,594	4,530	9,065	7,740	7,566	–	–	–	174
Delaware	2,825	2,461	1,221	1,240	758	531	9	58	–	160
District of Columbia . .	11,075	9,171	3,060	6,111	4,545	1,214	1,257	1,232	220	595
Florida	86,833	76,028	22,624	53,403	29,494	22,857	4,759	–	–	1,862
Georgia	37,829	33,571	10,912	22,659	13,992	8,870	4,586	–	–	535
Hawaii.	2,379	2,152	412	1,740	1,281	983	157	–	–	39
Idaho	4,684	4,498	1,746	2,751	1,360	1,239	34	–	–	82
Illinois	60,794	53,684	18,045	35,639	24,016	19,491	3,717	–	–	664
Indiana	26,507	24,534	8,522	16,012	9,325	8,400	86	613	–	175
Iowa	11,834	11,009	4,017	6,992	4,138	3,392	610	69	–	50
Kansas	11,546	10,445	3,729	6,716	4,177	3,209	883	1	–	73
Kentucky	11,688	10,332	4,449	5,883	3,605	1,915	425	1,003	112	147
Louisiana	17,658	16,226	6,567	9,659	6,073	2,424	3,447	–	–	198
Maine	4,334	4,239	1,385	2,854	2,207	2,169	2	–	–	24
Maryland	23,483	21,682	7,035	14,647	11,164	5,385	500	3,696	–	1,583
Massachusetts	30,969	25,592	10,804	14,788	11,240	10,829	154	–	–	257
Michigan	43,377	39,245	18,418	20,827	12,302	11,285	256	473	–	289
Minnesota	24,244	21,876	10,735	11,141	5,159	4,706	213	–	–	237
Mississippi	10,455	9,796	4,589	5,207	2,191	2,031	68	–	–	91
Missouri.	21,012	18,709	6,253	12,455	8,132	4,959	2,405	330	20	403
Montana	2,899	2,805	1,216	1,588	893	864	4	–	–	25
Nebraska.	9,693	6,663	1,936	4,727	2,913	2,232	330	–	–	321
Nevada	12,335	11,430	4,725	6,704	3,611	2,346	754	–	–	511
New Hampshire	4,511	4,410	1,439	2,971	2,436	2,396	–	–	–	40
New Jersey	39,887	38,923	12,349	26,574	21,041	20,546	115	–	–	381
New Mexico	7,173	6,710	3,690	3,020	1,864	899	820	–	–	137
New York.	149,274	135,169	47,230	87,939	66,258	36,438	12,389	7,799	5,028	4,485
North Carolina	34,366	30,676	12,694	17,982	9,410	6,985	1,953	–	–	443
North Dakota	2,094	1,967	777	1,190	746	633	97	–	–	16
Ohio	49,861	47,428	19,198	28,230	18,711	12,562	1,635	3,907	34	446
Oklahoma	10,900	9,922	3,998	5,924	3,440	1,802	1,518	–	–	118
Oregon	15,362	14,039	5,733	8,305	4,813	3,661	306	121	51	672
Pennsylvania	53,851	49,755	20,473	29,283	20,012	14,154	488	3,304	–	2,066
Rhode Island	3,800	3,542	1,229	2,313	1,938	1,886	6	–	–	45
South Carolina	15,489	13,974	4,435	9,539	4,684	3,950	287	–	–	426
South Dakota	2,464	2,200	716	1,485	1,052	767	248	–	–	20
Tennessee	26,365	17,827	5,886	11,941	6,590	4,126	2,075	–	–	237
Texas	94,335	82,790	23,752	59,038	39,140	32,486	5,778	–	–	568
Utah	9,159	7,548	2,826	4,722	2,822	1,877	781	–	–	164
Vermont	2,162	1,964	1,378	586	346	324	10	–	–	13
Virginia	31,350	28,636	10,437	18,199	12,867	9,213	2,364	–	–	1,138
Washington	31,173	25,689	10,006	15,683	8,758	5,281	2,506	–	–	939
West Virginia	4,570	4,371	2,127	2,245	1,324	1,055	58	–	–	211
Wisconsin	24,165	22,270	10,100	12,170	8,505	7,910	328	–	–	267
Wyoming	3,448	3,309	1,214	2,094	1,014	767	199	–	–	27

See footnotes at end of table.

U.S. Census Bureau, *Statistical Abstract of the United States: 2010*

Table 443. **Local Governments—Revenue by State: 2006**—Con.

[See headnote, page 286]

State	Current charges & miscel-laneous general revenue	Current charges Total [1]	Educa-tion	Hospi-tal	Sewer-age	Miscellaneous general revenue Total [1]	Interest earn-ings	Special assess-ment	Utility rev-enue	Liquor store rev-enue	Insur-ance trust revenue
United States ...	283,162	197,440	22,592	51,939	33,754	85,722	33,288	6,316	109,449	947	52,296
Alabama.........	4,937	3,903	331	2,562	352	1,034	438	24	2,284	–	461
Alaska	672	444	29	90	68	228	134	8	268	3	27
Arizona.........	4,553	2,998	494	515	533	1,554	673	76	3,727	–	258
Arkansas	1,529	982	148	218	205	547	251	29	791	–	24
California	49,486	34,411	2,425	7,565	4,654	15,075	5,643	1,308	18,425	–	17,746
Colorado........	5,829	3,903	393	972	612	1,926	605	433	2,016	–	537
Connecticut......	1,325	872	121	–	232	452	163	29	614	–	559
Delaware	483	347	17	–	153	136	51	15	299	–	65
District of Columbia .	1,565	574	30	–	177	992	221	1	793	–	1,112
Florida	23,910	16,208	1,786	4,624	2,184	7,702	2,397	1,196	7,483	–	3,322
Georgia	8,667	6,205	528	2,906	825	2,462	1,149	46	3,966	–	292
Hawaii	459	355	–	–	186	104	61	21	226	–	–
Idaho	1,391	1,198	85	612	145	194	65	36	185	–	1
Illinois	11,624	8,262	1,186	842	942	3,362	1,254	361	3,205	–	3,904
Indiana.........	6,687	4,400	374	2,423	832	2,287	473	44	1,892	–	81
Iowa	2,854	2,218	469	963	292	636	242	33	819	–	6
Kansas.........	2,539	1,671	359	556	270	868	410	82	1,023	–	79
Kentucky	2,277	1,353	119	297	334	924	515	35	1,321	–	35
Louisiana	3,586	2,435	55	1,283	306	1,151	514	47	1,228	–	205
Maine..........	647	468	46	70	140	179	66	14	95	–	–
Maryland	3,484	2,480	614	–	790	1,003	316	75	587	210	1,005
Massachusetts.....	3,547	2,548	301	487	832	999	277	33	2,775	–	2,603
Michigan........	8,524	6,165	1,076	870	1,401	2,359	819	199	2,101	–	2,031
Minnesota.......	5,982	3,982	437	1,053	566	2,000	735	346	1,644	243	481
Mississippi	3,016	2,460	349	1,607	174	556	171	10	659	–	–
Missouri	4,324	3,226	652	1,012	534	1,097	514	44	1,482	–	822
Montana........	695	460	66	42	70	235	71	61	94	–	–
Nebraska	1,814	1,135	205	390	136	679	215	61	2,825	–	205
Nevada	3,094	1,962	123	530	368	1,132	301	135	905	–	–
New Hampshire....	535	371	53	–	91	164	67	1	88	–	14
New Jersey......	5,533	3,737	1,008	122	1,187	1,796	493	17	943	–	21
New Mexico	1,156	753	100	111	130	403	153	34	464	–	–
New York	21,681	14,561	1,328	3,099	1,672	7,120	2,244	132	4,881	–	9,224
North Carolina....	8,572	6,852	535	2,995	1,379	1,720	712	34	3,187	470	32
North Dakota.....	444	235	45	–	38	209	61	57	104	–	23
Ohio	9,519	6,302	1,097	1,080	1,590	3,217	1,643	226	2,243	–	190
Oklahoma.......	2,484	1,882	299	665	231	602	213	19	883	–	94
Oregon.........	3,493	2,472	453	262	666	1,021	397	109	1,320	–	3
Pennsylvania.....	9,271	5,930	839	49	1,830	3,341	2,038	88	2,665	–	1,430
Rhode Island.....	374	250	35	1	82	125	34	7	156	–	102
South Carolina....	4,855	3,875	238	2,540	378	980	371	88	1,512	–	3
South Dakota	433	316	62	34	51	117	51	12	210	21	33
Tennessee	5,351	4,078	396	2,072	525	1,274	626	83	7,744	–	795
Texas..........	19,898	13,441	1,920	3,834	2,397	6,457	3,362	162	9,089	–	2,456
Utah	1,900	1,266	78	29	235	634	221	31	1,612	–	–
Vermont	239	150	24	–	46	90	21	4	187	–	18
Virginia	5,332	3,744	359	229	919	1,588	649	151	1,619	–	1,095
Washington.......	6,925	5,339	327	1,411	1,208	1,586	595	126	5,139	–	345
West Virginia......	920	580	35	166	162	340	158	31	175	–	24
Wisconsin.......	3,665	2,764	483	69	583	901	359	92	1,364	–	531
Wyoming	1,080	917	62	683	44	164	79	8	139	–	–

– Represents or rounds to zero.   [1] Includes items not shown separately.

Source: U.S. Census Bureau; Federal, State, and Local Governments, "State Government Finances"; <http://www.census.gov/govs/www/estimate06.html> (published April 2009).

Table 444. **Local Governments—Expenditures and Debt by State: 2006**

[In millions of dollars (1,390,867 represents $1,390,867,000,000), except as indicated. For fiscal year ending in year shown; see text, this section]

State	Total expenditures [1]	General expenditures							
		Total [1]	Direct expenditures						
			Total [1]	Education	Public welfare	Health	Hospitals	Highways	Police protection
United States ...	1,390,867	1,216,655	1,203,740	525,493	45,611	38,115	66,135	51,123	68,228
Alabama.........	17,995	15,724	15,711	6,552	57	442	2,648	800	784
Alaska..........	3,402	3,048	3,048	1,491	4	57	104	173	149
Arizona.........	25,984	21,432	21,070	8,733	263	227	820	1,108	1,479
Arkansas	7,993	7,156	7,148	4,131	18	39	202	340	403
California	224,607	190,413	190,183	72,202	14,614	9,370	9,151	6,223	11,793
Colorado........	22,557	19,449	19,436	7,501	572	288	1,182	1,109	1,096
Connecticut......	14,213	13,143	13,141	7,308	110	126	–	476	707
Delaware	2,898	2,571	2,570	1,578	–	27	–	128	187
District of Columbia .	10,091	8,004	8,004	1,478	1,841	508	161	96	493
Florida	83,994	74,366	74,107	28,460	1,029	887	5,536	3,074	5,462
Georgia	37,933	32,774	32,663	15,427	142	1,043	3,013	1,296	1,734
Hawaii	2,258	1,913	1,913	–	21	43	–	177	267
Idaho..........	4,580	4,376	4,373	1,974	34	81	609	260	233
Illinois	59,133	50,110	50,089	22,713	523	624	1,426	2,423	3,370
Indiana.........	25,135	23,032	23,020	9,774	605	240	2,790	806	839
Iowa	12,016	11,108	11,017	5,300	103	344	994	841	489
Kansas.........	11,345	10,218	10,201	4,732	55	245	600	702	540
Kentucky	11,891	10,369	10,368	5,183	45	222	313	379	500
Louisiana	16,729	15,115	15,103	5,963	56	158	1,574	598	950
Maine..........	4,055	3,953	3,952	2,116	36	23	67	259	158
Maryland	22,470	20,850	20,576	10,592	148	330	–	819	1,280
Massachusetts.....	29,379	24,003	23,196	11,652	65	110	878	719	1,271
Michigan........	43,341	39,239	39,148	18,023	792	3,513	952	2,105	2,042
Minnesota.......	24,800	22,317	22,181	8,899	1,549	549	1,274	1,846	1,067
Mississippi	10,632	9,523	9,522	4,544	36	100	1,566	567	472
Missouri	20,536	18,226	18,225	9,017	95	367	1,125	1,049	989
Montana........	2,841	2,731	2,730	1,383	37	86	50	136	158
Nebraska	9,305	6,056	6,051	2,969	70	60	379	454	274
Nevada	12,164	10,639	10,613	3,809	259	133	555	809	795
New Hampshire....	4,488	4,388	4,319	2,287	188	25	–	203	230
New Jersey......	40,194	39,219	38,891	20,774	969	402	180	1,198	2,505
New Mexico	6,754	6,344	6,333	3,320	83	40	147	305	392
New York	150,453	132,213	124,889	47,796	9,917	3,559	8,839	4,857	6,867
North Carolina....	35,066	30,661	29,986	12,693	1,381	1,926	3,097	509	1,472
North Dakota......	2,036	1,901	1,890	946	41	33	–	177	85
Ohio...........	50,164	46,996	46,456	20,366	2,619	2,571	1,340	2,216	2,449
Oklahoma........	10,876	9,922	9,922	5,011	34	139	665	595	527
Oregon.........	15,422	13,722	13,707	5,899	264	617	264	798	748
Pennsylvania......	52,704	47,461	47,457	22,503	3,316	3,029	129	1,452	1,877
Rhode Island......	3,671	3,374	3,374	1,909	13	10	–	94	231
South Carolina.....	15,504	14,000	13,971	6,772	20	131	2,517	296	686
South Dakota	2,370	2,124	2,124	1,058	14	23	33	199	103
Tennessee	26,251	17,885	17,884	7,393	157	301	2,251	686	1,067
Texas..........	95,471	82,947	81,623	41,608	342	1,638	5,781	3,169	4,312
Utah	8,867	7,038	7,030	3,291	85	173	30	343	419
Vermont	2,094	1,893	1,892	1,245	1	9	–	154	62
Virginia.........	31,055	28,585	28,578	13,255	1,325	1,146	220	695	1,452
Washington......	30,477	23,968	23,940	9,545	85	848	1,600	1,216	1,128
West Virginia......	4,660	4,319	4,313	2,604	5	64	207	81	183
Wisconsin........	24,759	22,730	22,697	10,393	1,561	1,119	204	1,956	1,322
Wyoming	3,259	3,106	3,106	1,321	12	71	658	154	128

See footnotes at end of table.

U.S. Census Bureau, Statistical Abstract of the United States: 2010

Table 444. **Local Governments—Expenditures and Debt by State: 2006**—Con.

[See headnote, page 288]

State	General expenditures—Con.										
	Direct expenditures—Con.										
	Corrections	Sewerage	Solid waste	Parks and recreation	Housing and community development	Governmental administration	Interest on general debt	Other	Utility expenditures	Insurance trust expenditures	Debt outstanding
United States..	22,254	37,955	19,425	29,893	36,827	64,521	47,852	116,141	144,547	28,775	1,329,953
Alabama	202	575	280	430	436	664	558	908	2,158	113	15,937
Alaska.	2	81	67	78	116	176	86	355	327	24	3,189
Arizona	602	753	328	1,035	324	1,588	903	2,097	4,420	132	26,245
Arkansas	127	231	172	102	166	332	276	429	805	32	7,281
California	4,447	5,167	2,455	4,923	8,804	11,532	6,352	16,956	27,366	6,828	190,118
Colorado	311	703	72	979	593	1,259	1,079	2,159	2,779	330	26,664
Connecticut	–	309	208	225	517	501	297	1,900	685	385	8,192
Delaware	–	172	15	34	66	136	68	129	290	36	1,883
District of Columbia	206	237	266	332	560	455	320	875	1,959	128	8,020
Florida.	1,607	2,368	2,149	2,298	1,553	4,678	3,132	9,171	8,773	855	90,362
Georgia.	668	1,155	681	708	746	2,131	686	2,359	4,904	254	31,593
Hawaii.	–	200	184	157	81	212	123	311	345	–	3,712
Idaho	70	151	101	84	38	245	71	313	203	2	1,987
Illinois	592	1,206	451	2,589	1,854	2,992	2,388	5,192	5,917	3,105	57,133
Indiana	334	1,036	247	426	596	1,213	684	2,777	1,966	138	17,024
Iowa	122	270	161	319	159	407	273	1,055	905	2	7,207
Kansas	108	299	125	217	179	526	547	1,077	1,086	42	14,163
Kentucky	191	290	177	143	216	484	829	1,043	1,489	33	22,705
Louisiana	499	470	309	283	489	988	571	1,691	1,457	157	12,997
Maine	56	135	108	56	105	203	100	411	102	–	2,473
Maryland	303	657	543	928	736	1,107	656	1,767	746	690	14,271
Massachusetts . . .	263	741	369	193	1,159	819	579	3,400	4,040	1,335	21,630
Michigan	604	1,587	469	723	481	2,121	1,528	3,292	2,732	1,370	41,840
Minnesota	359	540	285	717	736	1,122	1,190	1,732	1,739	445	29,183
Mississippi	94	192	139	130	217	518	252	475	1,108	–	6,291
Missouri.	203	632	96	532	445	919	617	1,557	1,871	439	16,289
Montana	32	78	62	66	64	159	49	305	110	–	1,433
Nebraska.	94	120	74	176	166	330	164	578	3,097	152	7,491
Nevada	294	219	18	611	213	887	523	1,108	1,524	–	16,531
New Hampshire . .	52	101	105	74	87	229	107	469	92	7	2,519
New Jersey	583	1,116	949	571	820	1,555	1,233	5,228	963	12	31,480
New Mexico	185	130	130	234	122	375	153	518	410	–	4,391
New York.	2,513	3,376	2,294	1,641	4,075	4,125	5,358	16,860	10,723	7,517	136,101
North Carolina . . .	399	1,333	629	640	673	1,211	866	2,440	3,994	23	26,188
North Dakota	18	33	39	78	32	104	66	209	124	11	1,716
Ohio	544	1,805	486	823	1,598	3,134	1,781	3,271	3,016	151	38,945
Oklahoma	91	342	163	227	169	675	204	713	909	45	7,106
Oregon	379	641	108	386	386	776	575	1,477	1,619	81	15,912
Pennsylvania	1,281	1,674	603	656	1,845	2,533	2,892	3,103	4,035	1,208	73,920
Rhode Island	23	84	44	45	173	146	67	290	165	133	1,981
South Carolina . . .	184	337	300	229	252	753	519	695	1,500	4	18,422
South Dakota	35	63	34	80	55	123	56	201	218	12	1,414
Tennessee	387	582	321	364	486	946	813	1,610	7,935	431	24,109
Texas	1,386	2,467	883	1,588	1,889	3,896	5,022	5,606	11,513	1,011	141,070
Utah	145	314	134	342	208	506	207	630	1,829	–	9,395
Vermont	–	59	26	19	42	81	27	127	195	6	872
Virginia	677	875	617	874	848	1,814	1,107	2,743	1,908	562	28,777
Washington	460	982	512	770	716	1,316	1,002	2,873	6,361	148	38,326
West Virginia	40	191	52	83	110	279	133	197	306	35	3,531
Wisconsin	425	816	342	599	418	1,052	730	1,203	1,678	352	18,967
Wyoming	54	61	43	75	9	186	34	255	153	–	965

– Represents or rounds to zero. [1] Includes other items not shown seperately.

Source: U.S. Census Bureau, Federal, State and Local Governments, "State Government Finances"; <http://www.census.gov/govs/www/estimate06.html> (published April 2009).

State and Local Government Finances and Employment 289

Table 445. City Governments—Revenue for Largest Cities: 2006

[In millions of dollars (83,520 represents $83,520,000,000). For fiscal years ending in year shown; see text this section. Cities ranked by estimated resident population as of July 1. Data reflect inclusion of fiscal activity of dependent school systems where applicable. Regarding intercity comparisons, see text this section. See Appendix III]

Cities ranked by 2006 population	Total revenue [1]	General revenue — Total	Intergovernmental — Total	From federal government	From state/ local government	From local government	General revenue from own sources — Total	Taxes — Total [1]	Taxes — Property	Sales and gross receipts — Total	General sales	Public utilities	Current charges — Total [1]	Parks and recreation	Sewerage	Miscellaneous — Total [1]	Interest earnings	Utility revenue [3]	Insurance trust revenue
New York, NY [2]	83,520	70,823	25,957	3,722	22,045	191	44,866	35,104	12,754	5,953	4,439	516	6,380	63	1,151	3,382	1,153	3,472	9,224
Los Angeles, CA	14,199	7,863	952	282	670	–	6,911	3,233	1,090	1,362	552	673	2,413	105	599	1,264	461	3,143	3,193
Chicago, IL	8,812	7,257	1,325	449	876	–	5,933	2,179	429	1,454	275	555	2,872	–	144	881	248	347	1,207
Houston, TX	4,449	3,119	550	195	328	27	2,569	1,492	781	664	423	187	808	26	330	269	153	341	989
Phoenix, AZ	3,377	2,903	1,115	581	488	46	1,788	1,023	261	692	537	84	581	26	232	184	137	288	186
Philadelphia, PA [2]	7,345	5,809	2,478	653	1,712	113	3,332	2,450	394	200	125	–	698	1	240	184	105	1,007	529
San Antonio, TX	3,283	1,469	191	54	120	17	1,278	612	292	173	–	45	431	24	280	234	110	1,573	242
San Diego, CA	3,266	2,100	410	175	216	20	1,690	744	488	198	–	89	694	63	396	252	144	332	833
Dallas, TX	3,027	2,277	165	123	36	6	2,112	857	313	106	–	112	861	35	240	394	100	207	543
San Jose, CA	1,924	1,498	217	50	141	27	1,281	660	285	114	–	62	440	15	185	181	29	20	406
Honolulu, HI [2]	1,483	1,337	197	117	79	1	1,140	807	591	371	213	61	284	23	241	50	47	146	–
Detroit, MI	3,184	2,132	694	97	543	54	1,439	867	309	47	–	106	452	4	351	119	48	314	739
Jacksonville, FL [2]	3,292	1,829	323	72	251	–	1,506	745	365	371	327	1	383	16	158	379	94	1,187	276
Indianapolis, IN	3,749	3,014	646	86	550	10	2,367	1,638	923	213	–	91	506	26	74	224	178	687	48
San Francisco, CA [2]	7,955	5,647	2,155	87	1,664	404	3,492	2,047	1,486	598	–	–	1,045	11	172	400	26	426	1,882
Columbus, OH	1,227	1,058	198	82	103	13	860	560	40	186	124	30	228	23	166	72	26	169	–
Austin, TX	2,272	1,037	108	54	30	24	929	457	124	20	–	4	378	11	–	94	93	1,032	203
Louisville/Jefferson, KY [2]	1,090	975	170	73	89	8	805	515	301	186	–	5	150	11	102	140	86	115	–
Memphis, TN	3,777	1,882	1,149	63	557	529	733	449	236	55	–	32	153	5	120	134	32	1,587	308
Ft. Worth, TX	1,132	712	56	–	56	–	656	417	286	144	99	56	154	10	149	85	48	184	237
Baltimore, MD [2]	3,339	2,922	1,504	262	1,205	38	1,418	1,023	558	141	102	32	261	3	199	134	50	109	308
Charlotte City, NC	1,613	1,507	350	76	114	161	1,157	366	178	87	–	124	558	–	71	233	20	80	26
El Paso, TX	822	627	92	74	17	–	535	339	255	39	–	214	134	3	–	62	48	81	115
Boston, MA	3,626	3,103	1,368	100	1,264	3	1,735	1,333	1,255	141	–	26	193	42	288	209	23	112	411
Seattle, WA	2,481	1,424	144	41	100	3	1,279	784	237	307	146	54	387	26	178	108	72	882	176
Washington, DC [2]	9,248	8,674	2,589	2,589	–	–	6,085	4,545	1,214	1,257	817	15	574	4	109	966	205	96	369
Milwaukee, WI	1,392	931	450	69	306	67	481	250	237	55	–	31	185	45	70	48	15	59	402
Denver, CO [2]	2,472	2,121	237	17	219	2	1,884	849	720	534	460	49	810	11	78	225	99	166	185
Las Vegas, NV	883	883	387	8	272	107	496	250	45	–	–	28	183	9	82	63	33	–	–
Nashville-Davidson, TN [2]	3,237	1,955	446	56	438	–	1,509	1,101	54	271	271	19	236	12	84	172	33	1,008	275
Oklahoma City, OK	1,069	950	96	54	39	2	854	451	54	319	319	38	268	24	205	135	15	78	41
Portland, OR	1,053	961	181	79	71	56	780	419	102	196	196	–	294	21	38	67	6	91	–
Tucson, AZ	953	756	213	28	170	15	492	305	186	219	219	–	149	15	98	37	43	126	72
Albuquerque, NM	1,146	1,047	320	118	259	33	727	414	199	110	110	–	239	31	148	74	43	98	1
Atlanta, GA	1,696	1,517	323	119	114	90	1,194	354	165	219	110	38	650	–	–	190	155	146	34

– Represents or rounds to zero.   [1] Includes revenue sources not shown separately.   [2] Represents, in effect, city-county consolidated government.   [3] Includes water, electric, and transit.

Source: U.S. Census Bureau, Federal, State, and Local Governments, "Government Finances, 2006." See also <http://www.census.gov/govs/> (published April 2009).

Table 446. City Governments—Expenditures and Debt for Largest Cities: 2006

[In millions of dollars (82,454 represents $82,454,000,000). For fiscal year ending in year shown; see headnote, Table 445]

Cities ranked by 2006 population	Total expenditures	Total direct expenditures	General expenditures — Total [1]	Education	Housing and community development	Public welfare	Health and hospitals	Police protection	Fire protection	Corrections	Highways	Parks and recreation	Sewerage	Solid waste management	Governmental administration [2]	Interest on general debt	Utility expenditures [3]	Insurance trust expenditures	Debt outstanding
New York, NY [4]	82,454	77,456	66,237	17,472	3,710	9,811	8,976	3,971	1,519	1,314	1,526	559	2,161	1,100	1,178	3,205	8,699	7,517	85,234
Los Angeles, CA	12,315	12,315	7,252	1	275	—	202	1,659	589	—	561	332	498	238	842	410	3,675	1,388	15,723
Chicago, IL	7,622	7,544	6,033	—	257	135	178	1,175	390	20	454	77	101	183	153	756	316	1,272	15,862
Houston, TX	3,982	3,953	3,295	—	255	—	98	571	381	13	139	129	384	67	139	357	307	380	11,403
Phoenix, AZ	3,362	3,349	2,592	—	100	—	—	367	187	350	127	577	198	99	114	251	672	97	7,373
Philadelphia, PA [4]	6,745	6,660	5,077	—	234	555	1,292	510	172	—	71	94	189	98	332	114	1,054	614	5,825
San Antonio, TX	3,626	3,617	1,546	—	35	43	44	242	161	9	112	157	248	57	88	81	2,010	70	6,055
San Diego, CA	2,431	2,418	1,803	—	339	—	27	336	160	8	82	142	290	52	80	70	413	215	2,795
Dallas, TX	2,713	2,704	2,194	—	41	7	15	268	143	—	121	124	196	67	192	229	276	242	8,557
San Jose, CA [4]	1,894	1,866	1,703	—	186	7	26	227	116	—	95	138	144	79	157	204	36	156	4,368
Honolulu, HI [4]	1,473	1,473	1,228	35	46	—	66	180	82	62	107	100	159	137	98	100	246	—	3,155
Detroit, MI	3,349	3,248	2,168	—	98	16	84	447	192	75	146	79	402	107	157	147	627	554	7,515
Jacksonville, FL [4]	3,474	3,343	1,847	—	33	47	619	206	96	170	200	77	198	86	97	217	1,447	180	11,022
Indianapolis, IN	3,412	3,398	2,592	102	268	91	1,246	188	70	10	110	149	301	40	173	193	741	79	4,125
San Francisco, CA [4]	6,908	6,908	5,305	—	148	605	—	317	211	41	143	200	155	—	714	406	1,008	595	8,738
Columbus, OH	1,152	1,144	1,012	—	8	—	124	212	144	—	94	60	193	34	72	93	140	—	1,703
Austin, TX	2,304	2,304	1,159	—	35	10	75	176	88	—	83	96	137	43	58	80	1,036	110	3,887
Louisville/Jefferson, KY [4]	925	924	868	—	39	17	11	130	47	—	15	38	33	18	31	102	57	—	2,550
Memphis, TN	3,508	3,479	1,815	1,029	36	—	15	180	132	—	65	58	76	43	45	62	1,502	191	2,747
Ft. Worth, TX [4]	1,047	1,047	766	—	21	—	147	161	81	—	85	391	147	35	128	26	197	83	1,231
Baltimore, MD [4]	3,289	3,212	2,930	950	86	2	5	348	134	106	192	52	253	69	27	58	101	259	2,287
Charlotte City, NC	1,448	1,436	1,019	—	42	—	16	151	77	13	96	25	44	40	55	44	413	16	2,665
El Paso, TX	725	725	476	—	22	—	184	81	52	206	35	34	215	13	67	25	187	61	1,005
Boston, MA	3,341	3,038	2,813	999	82	150	14	279	160	75	51	195	175	58	434	57	171	357	1,459
Seattle, WA	2,424	2,311	1,400	—	45	36	669	190	135	39	113	332	237	114	37	52	932	93	3,465
Washington, DC	8,543	8,291	8,256	1,478	560	1,846	32	493	176	52	96	4	66	266	37	320	169	118	7,824
Milwaukee, WI	1,302	1,274	1,026	—	123	—	55	218	99	—	132	216	79	76	132	37	72	203	1,199
Denver, CO [4]	2,415	2,357	2,110	679	103	98	3	165	87	—	86	80	40	—	117	289	199	106	5,845
Las Vegas, NV	747	600	745	—	18	—	168	158	105	—	90	72	109	5	105	16	—	—	352
Nashville-Davidson, TN [4]	3,270	3,269	2,046	950	9	—	—	137	101	49	91	83	146	21	137	148	1,084	140	3,837
Oklahoma City, OK	1,115	1,115	960	—	54	9	—	137	111	36	162	89	192	31	52	30	138	17	1,049
Portland, OR	1,210	1,210	1,059	—	43	—	—	134	79	—	70	71	29	3	36	85	71	80	2,524
Tucson, AZ	874	874	694	—	32	19	—	122	56	—	55	107	185	36	31	46	146	35	1,090
Albuquerque, NM	843	843	760	—	5	—	—	152	66	—	43	103	29	45	61	37	83	—	777
Atlanta, GA	2,025	1,979	1,552	—		—			66				185	45		87	407	65	6,425

— Represents or rounds to zero. [1] Includes expenditure sources not shown separately. [2] Excludes public buildings. [3] Includes water, electric, and transit. [4] Represents, in effect, city-county consolidated government.

Source: U.S. Census Bureau, Federal, State and Local Governments, "Government Finances, 2006." See also <http://www.census.gov/govs/estimate06.html> (published April 2009).

State and Local Government Finances and Employment 291

Table 447. County Governments—Revenue for Largest Counties: 2006

[In millions of dollars (21,586 represents $21,586,000,000). For fiscal year ending in year shown; see text, this section. See Appendix III]

Counties ranked by 2006 population	Total revenue[1]	General revenue Total	Intergovernmental Total[1]	From federal gov. Total[1]	From federal gov. Housing[2]	From state gov. Total[1]	From state gov. Public welfare	From state gov. Health and hospitals	From local government	General revenue from own sources Total	Taxes Total[1]	Taxes Property	Sales and gross receipts Total	Sales and gross receipts General sales	Current charges Total[1]	Current charges Parks and recreation	Current charges Sewerage[3]	Current charges Hospitals	Misc. general revenue Total[1]	Misc. general revenue Interest earnings
Los Angeles, CA	21,586	17,015	9,177	386	4	8,556	4,815	1,311	235	7,838	3,285	3,009	127	42	3,802	95	83	2,220	751	235
Cook, IL	3,378	2,851	606	41	–	564	287	–	1	2,245	1,536	810	702	358	577	47	–	333	132	49
Harris, TX	3,165	3,165	647	91	23	471	174	216	85	2,518	1,318	1,232	56	–	815	3	–	256	385	245
Maricopa, AZ	2,015	2,015	952	55	–	869	167	27	28	1,062	781	604	144	144	80	4	–	–	202	128
Orange, CA	4,439	3,464	1,926	51	9	1,800	650	172	75	1,538	626	536	46	43	622	42	114	–	289	181
San Diego, CA	5,117	4,027	2,880	167	8	2,447	986	473	266	1,147	686	585	27	18	259	3	24	–	201	110
Dade, FL	6,528	6,263	1,353	896	120	413	–	55	44	4,910	1,871	1,283	480	119	2,477	36	508	1,084	562	289
Dallas, TX	1,662	1,623	254	9	–	233	150	19	12	1,369	649	597	12	–	608	–	–	545	111	29
Riverside, CA	3,399	3,399	1,898	61	13	1,683	904	208	154	1,502	666	534	43	35	581	7	71	184	255	99
San Bernardino, CA	3,919	3,290	2,043	134	18	1,826	918	240	83	1,247	383	326	25	17	680	7	73	331	183	62
Wayne, MI	1,991	1,848	1,117	122	8	862	14	522	134	731	448	423	16	–	229	7	75	10	54	19
King, WA	2,239	2,108	520	135	16	266	–	178	119	1,588	1,005	446	534	431	499	4	333	–	84	51
Broward, FL	2,326	2,270	466	119	10	203	–	6	144	1,804	927	780	124	–	676	16	172	475	201	111
Clark, NV	4,446	3,980	1,051	87	6	792	38	23	173	2,928	1,333	577	484	113	1,082	66	96	688	513	83
Santa Clara, CA	3,497	3,497	1,717	37	–	1,603	971	180	78	1,779	800	605	143	140	872	4	3	146	107	37
Tarrant, TX	1,150	1,150	273	51	24	219	–	189	4	877	515	478	15	–	203	–	–	389	158	124
Bexar, TX	1,113	1,113	203	6	–	188	101	44	9	909	396	363	27	–	421	–	–	–	93	70
Suffolk, NY	2,744	2,592	580	29	7	538	275	153	13	2,012	1,701	556	1,119	1,114	174	10	24	–	137	50
Alameda, CA	3,198	2,696	1,468	31	3	1,399	737	311	38	1,228	480	399	26	15	609	–	–	341	139	66
Sacramento, CA	3,235	2,559	1,563	46	–	1,457	811	202	60	997	428	275	89	63	373	13	83	–	195	65
Nassau, NY	3,347	3,347	1,444	73	21	696	397	136	–	1,903	906	906	965	953	431	23	2	247	244	39
Cuyahoga, OH	2,170	2,170	964	20	19	940	503	260	4	1,206	565	336	184	169	383	–	–	341	258	198
Palm Beach, FL	1,873	1,823	239	102	9	136	–	–	1	1,584	967	685	154	–	421	13	199	–	196	37
Allegheny, PA	1,486	1,419	1,026	63	47	961	282	467	2	393	302	262	38	23	64	4	–	–	27	6
Oakland, MI	1,162	1,051	574	201	6	218	6	61	155	477	350	326	9	–	85	9	18	4	42	15
Hillsborough, FL	1,836	1,663	259	75	32	183	45	–	1	1,404	901	605	274	199	395	2	78	–	108	44
Hennepin, MN	1,843	1,843	854	50	8	785	353	169	19	989	478	459	–	–	388	1	70	284	123	30
Franklin, OH	1,158	1,156	459	14	4	419	193	128	26	696	459	334	85	85	97	4	3	–	140	124
Orange, FL	1,753	1,704	285	85	–	199	5	–	–	1,420	506	342	104	–	322	47	146	–	156	95
Contra Costa, CA	2,506	2,071	899	113	102	705	391	113	81	1,173	406	326	24	10	670	45	24	404	96	33
Fairfax, VA	5,137	4,343	1,024	122	68	874	146	76	28	3,319	2,673	2,117	326	155	426	1	232	–	220	127
St Louis, MO	727	683	71	15	11	54	1	5	–	612	512	152	347	312	78	7	4	–	21	6
Salt Lake, UT	683	532	76	17	–	51	–	–	–	456	346	203	112	79	70	1	–	–	21	5
Fulton, GA	532	1,000	102	15	11	70	32	14	9	898	733	522	178	164	71	7	12	–	40	37
Westchester, NY	1,162	2,459	508	29	23	484	245	116	10	1,951	1,041	607	426	407	838	31	30	563	94	46

– Represents or rounds to zero.   [1] Includes revenue sources not shown separately.   [2] Includes community development.   [3] Includes fee for sewerage and solid waste management.

Source: U.S. Census Bureau, "Survey of State & Local Government Finances"; <http://www.census.gov/govs/www/estimate06.html>.

Table 448. County Governments—Expenditures and Debt for Largest Counties: 2006

[In millions of dollars (18,720 represents $18,720,000,000). For fiscal year ending in year shown; see text, this section and Appendix III]

Counties ranked by 2006 population	Total expenditures [1]	Total direct expenditures	General expenditures														Interest on general debt	Utility expenditures [2]	Employee retirement expenditures	Debt outstanding
			Total [1]	Education	Housing and community development	Public welfare	Health	Hospitals	Police protection	Correction	Highways	Parks and recreation	Natural resources	Sewerage and solid waste management	Governmental administration				
Los Angeles, CA	18,720	18,439	16,859	890	5	4,515	1,925	2,454	1,213	1,128	273	248	424	66	1,572	63	1,798	2,713	3
Cook, IL	3,048	3,036	2,665	–	10	8	41	916	85	350	119	118	–	–	620	–	383	3,246	3
Harris, TX	3,207	3,207	3,207	–	12	43	208	888	364	70	266	24	142	6	329	–	–	8,538	8
Maricopa, AZ	1,813	1,517	1,813	34	13	376	81	–	69	354	138	8	90	100	391	–	–	1,880	2
Orange, CA	3,482	3,428	3,217	244	14	764	328	–	282	263	54	20	67	29	433	–	265	2,856	3
San Diego, CA	4,205	3,843	3,879	425	102	989	518	–	207	297	175	278	20	502	523	–	326	1,845	2
Dade, FL	6,931	6,921	6,344	–	295	7	71	1,380	425	229	153	3	47	–	273	587	13	10,985	10
Dallas, TX	1,547	1,547	1,533	4	32	660	42	1,010	32	99	43	10	–	66	131	–	–	423	1
Riverside, CA	3,156	2,994	3,156	367	78	799	325	271	265	177	162	18	66	71	277	–	204	1,298	2
San Bernardino, CA	3,335	3,187	3,131	379	9	153	219	376	242	203	74	67	56	67	247	–	111	1,912	1
Wayne, MI	1,828	1,771	1,717	–	8	2	474	49	35	250	124	53	46	413	330	441	–	643	3
King, WA	2,226	2,180	1,785	–	30	46	344	1	121	127	112	127	19	149	246	147	–	3,167	3
Broward, FL	2,215	2,160	2,068	–	15	187	99	495	353	190	43	319	11	42	183	526	–	3,225	5
Clark, NV	4,013	3,953	3,487	214	22	624	60	905	467	136	483	31	4	3	268	–	–	5,865	2
Santa Clara, CA	3,350	3,274	3,350	–	9	7	365	446	105	258	102	2	–	–	336	–	–	910	1
Tarrant, TX	1,034	1,034	1,034	–	23	43	95	578	34	98	35	43	1	–	136	–	–	1,981	2
Bexar, TX	1,029	1,004	1,029	–	1	504	52	–	42	73	11	1	–	79	89	–	–	933	1
Suffolk, NY	2,750	2,454	2,568	161	7	557	337	394	431	124	42	34	32	–	116	182	216	1,797	3
Alameda, CA	2,563	2,559	2,303	39	6	741	319	87	87	271	27	61	36	94	281	44	183	1,327	3
Sacramento, CA	2,804	2,741	2,603	154	10	573	430	380	224	233	133	92	–	111	240	18	–	2,167	3
Nassau, NY	3,633	3,243	3,631	181	23	438	298	576	688	215	127	62	2	13	189	2	–	3,532	2
Cuyahoga, OH	2,131	2,112	2,131	–	57	72	327	–	26	94	54	9	7	169	260	–	–	3,338	1
Palm Beach, FL	1,777	1,690	1,686	–	63	351	50	–	216	102	112	78	37	–	193	91	60	1,818	2
Allegheny, PA	1,477	1,385	1,416	–	9	7	461	–	32	76	29	3	–	98	106	–	36	613	1
Oakland, MI	988	964	926	32	32	89	266	8	52	132	123	20	30	75	131	27	–	339	2
Hillsborough, FL	1,911	1,781	1,718	10	23	458	134	480	165	83	109	36	55	52	222	193	–	2,174	2
Hennepin, MN	1,856	1,847	1,849	–	7	289	288	–	85	58	108	–	–	6	112	7	–	544	3
Franklin, OH	1,164	1,126	1,160	–	30	79	320	–	30	153	47	–	–	232	162	3	–	2,178	1
Orange, FL	1,689	1,652	1,675	–	106	379	42	437	142	116	159	–	20	23	128	14	198	3,074	4
Contra Costa, CA	2,253	2,198	2,054	127	162	227	189	–	89	37	100	–	28	259	155	1	198	1,106	1
Fairfax, VA	4,831	4,759	4,328	2,195	10	24	178	–	196	20	37	144	–	4	174	197	306	3,701	1
St Louis, MO	725	495	696	–	–	46	47	–	77	63	83	30	5	14	66	4	–	410	–
Salt Lake, UT	519	519	519	–	–	62	26	78	32	83	25	78	–	62	92	–	25	197	1
Fulton, GA	1,111	909	952	–	8	–	35	591	65	134	26	4	1	92	259	100	59	749	–
Westchester, NY	2,629	2,311	2,586	95	–	455	277	–	41	–	43	56	–	146	107	44	–	1,594	1

– Represents or rounds to zero. [1] Includes expenditure categories not shown separately. [2] Includes water, gas, electric, and transit.

Source: U.S. Census Bureau, Federal, State and Local Governments, "State & Local Government Finances"; <http://www.census.gov/govs/www/estimate06.html>.

State and Local Government Finances and Employment   293

Table 449. Governmental Employment and Payrolls: 1982 to 2007

[Employees in thousands (15,841 represents 15,841,000), payroll in millions of dollars (23,173 represents $23,173,000,000). Data are for the month of October through 1992. Beginning with the 1997 survey, data are for the month of March. Covers both full-time and part-time employees. Local government data are estimates subject to sampling variation; see Appendix III and source]

Type of government	1982	1987	1992	1997	2000	2002	2004	2005	2006	2007
EMPLOYEES (1,000)										
Total	15,841	17,212	18,745	19,540	20,876	21,039	21,494	21,725	22,048	22,118
Federal (civilian)[1]	2,848	3,091	3,047	2,807	2,899	2,690	2,733	2,720	2,721	2,730
State and local	12,993	14,121	15,698	16,733	17,976	18,349	18,759	19,004	19,327	19,387
Percent of total	82	82	84	86	86	87	87	87	88	88
State	3,744	4,116	4,595	4,733	4,877	5,072	5,041	5,078	5,128	5,202
Local	9,249	10,005	11,103	12,000	13,099	13,277	13,719	13,926	14,199	14,186
Counties	1,824	1,963	2,253	2,425	(NA)	2,729	(NA)	(NA)	(NA)	(NA)
Municipalities	2,397	2,493	2,665	2,755	(NA)	2,972	(NA)	(NA)	(NA)	(NA)
School districts	4,194	4,627	5,134	5,675	(NA)	6,367	(NA)	(NA)	(NA)	(NA)
Townships	356	393	424	455	(NA)	488	(NA)	(NA)	(NA)	(NA)
Special districts	478	529	627	691	(NA)	721	(NA)	(NA)	(NA)	(NA)
PAYROLLS (mil. dol.)										
Total	23,173	32,669	43,120	49,156	58,166	63,923	68,759	71,599	74,638	78,586
Federal (civilian)[1]	5,959	7,924	9,937	9,744	11,485	11,599	12,844	13,475	13,896	14,427
State and local	17,214	24,745	33,183	39,412	46,681	52,323	55,914	58,123	60,741	64,160
Percent of total	74	76	77	80	80	82	81	81	81	82
State	5,022	7,263	9,828	11,413	13,279	14,838	15,477	16,062	16,769	17,792
Local	12,192	17,482	23,355	27,999	33,402	37,486	40,437	42,062	43,972	46,368
Counties	2,287	3,270	4,698	5,750	(NA)	7,902	(NA)	(NA)	(NA)	(NA)
Municipalities	3,428	4,770	6,207	7,146	(NA)	9,714	(NA)	(NA)	(NA)	(NA)
School districts	5,442	7,961	10,394	12,579	(NA)	16,720	(NA)	(NA)	(NA)	(NA)
Townships	370	522	685	869	(NA)	1,124	(NA)	(NA)	(NA)	(NA)
Special districts	665	959	1,370	1,654	(NA)	2,026	(NA)	(NA)	(NA)	(NA)

NA Not available.   [1] Includes employees outside the United States.

Source: U.S. Census Bureau, Federal, State, and Local Governments, "Government Employment and Payroll"; <http://www.census.gov/govs/apes/index.html>.

Table 450. All Governments—Employment and Payroll by Function: 2007

[Employees in thousands (22,116 represents 22,116,000); payroll in millions of dollars (78,583 represents $78,583,000,000). See headnote, Table 449]

Function	Employees (1,000)					Payrolls (mil. dol.)				
	Total	Federal (civilian)[1]	State and local			Total	Federal (civilian)[1]	State and local		
			Total	State	Local			Total	State	Local
Total	22,116	2,730	19,386	5,200	14,186	78,583	14,427	64,156	17,789	46,368
National defense[2]	699	699	(X)	(X)	(X)	2,992	2,992	(X)	(X)	(X)
Postal Service	768	768	(X)	(X)	(X)	3,529	3,529	(X)	(X)	(X)
Space research and technology	19	19	(X)	(X)	(X)	156	156	(X)	(X)	(X)
Elem. and secondary education	7,875	(X)	7,875	64	7,812	24,494	(X)	24,494	229	24,265
Higher education	2,940	(X)	2,940	2,375	565	8,228	(X)	8,228	6,821	1,408
Other education	110	10	99	99	(X)	435	66	369	369	(X)
Health	614	141	473	190	283	2,580	919	1,661	714	947
Hospitals	1,251	173	1,078	444	634	5,020	1,036	3,985	1,666	2,318
Public welfare	551	8	543	240	303	1,861	60	1,801	813	988
Social insurance administration	145	64	82	81	(X)	680	367	313	310	(X)
Police protection	1,164	166	997	109	889	5,347	943	4,404	513	3,892
Fire protection	417	(X)	417	(X)	417	1,749	(X)	1,749	(X)	1,749
Correction	779	37	743	475	268	2,999	188	2,810	1,808	1,002
Streets & highways	560	3	558	241	316	2,075	20	2,054	959	1,095
Air transportation	95	46	50	3	46	603	391	212	17	195
Water transport/terminals	18	4	13	5	8	73	13	60	22	38
Solid waste management	119	(X)	119	2	117	383	(X)	383	10	373
Sewerage	135	(X)	135	2	133	526	(X)	526	10	516
Parks & recreation	432	24	408	40	367	941	117	824	110	714
Natural resources	391	187	204	159	45	1,775	1,072	703	562	141
Housing & community development	136	15	121	–	121	526	102	425	–	425
Water supply	178	–	178	1	177	676	–	676	4	672
Electric power	80	–	80	4	76	426	–	426	24	403
Gas supply	13	–	13	–	13	47	–	47	–	47
Transit	244	(X)	244	34	211	1,088	–	1,088	176	912
Libraries	193	4	189	1	188	419	26	392	2	390
State liquor stores	9	(X)	9	9	(X)	22	(X)	22	22	(X)
Financial administration	541	109	432	177	254	2,249	669	1,580	692	888
Other government administration	448	24	424	62	362	1,278	147	1,131	236	894
Judicial and legal	509	61	448	178	271	2,332	434	1,898	823	1,074
Other & unallocable	685	168	517	206	311	3,076	1,179	1,897	876	1,021

– Represents or rounds to zero.   X Not applicable.   [1] Includes employees outside the United States.   [2] Includes international relations.

Source: U.S. Census Bureau, Federal, State, and Local Governments, "Government Employment and Payroll"; <http://www.census.gov/govs/apes/index.html>.

Table 451. **State and Local Government—Employer Costs per Hour Worked: 2009**

[In dollars. As of March. Based on a sample; see source for details. Collection of severance pay and supplemental unemployment plans, which comprised "other benefits" and was published in all tables, was discontinued beginning with the March 2006 estimates. For additional data, see Table 638]

Occupation and industry	Total compensation	Wages and salaries	Benefit cost					
			Total	Paid leave	Supplemental pay	Insurance	Retirement and savings	Legally required benefits
Total workers..................	**39.51**	**25.97**	**13.53**	**3.24**	**0.34**	**4.48**	**3.14**	**2.33**
Occupational group:								
Management, professional, and related ...	48.32	32.83	15.49	3.81	0.26	4.96	3.77	2.70
Professional and related...........	47.62	32.45	15.17	3.59	0.24	4.96	3.76	2.62
Teachers [1]	54.37	37.89	16.48	3.69	0.14	5.47	4.32	2.86
Primary, secondary, and special education school teachers..........	52.41	37.13	15.29	2.47	0.15	5.77	4.21	2.68
Sales and office..................	26.94	16.63	10.32	2.43	0.20	4.06	1.94	1.69
Office and administrative support......	27.13	16.70	10.44	2.46	0.20	4.12	1.97	1.69
Service.......................	28.86	17.49	11.37	2.58	0.56	3.63	2.73	1.87
Industry group:								
Education and health services	41.88	28.33	13.55	3.14	0.21	4.68	3.19	2.32
Educational services	42.28	28.77	13.50	3.05	0.15	4.76	3.24	2.30
Elementary and secondary schools...	41.60	28.66	12.94	2.26	0.15	4.95	3.34	2.24
Junior colleges, colleges, and universities	44.83	29.34	15.48	5.69	0.14	4.16	2.97	2.53
Health care and social assistance	39.16	25.31	13.85	3.81	0.60	4.13	2.84	2.47
Hospitals...................	35.64	22.88	12.77	3.40	0.73	4.30	2.02	2.31
Public administration	36.71	22.69	14.01	3.52	0.57	4.25	3.31	2.37

[1] Includes postsecondary teachers; primary, secondary, and special education teachers; and other teachers and instructors.

Source: U.S. Bureau of Labor Statistics, *National Compensation Survey, Benefits, Archives, 2009 National Survey Compensation Publications List, Employer Costs for Employee Compensation News Release,* March 2009; <http://www.bls.gov/ncs/ncspubs.htm> (published March 2009).

Table 452. **State and Local Government—Full-Time Employment and Salary by Sex and Race/Ethnic Group: 1980 to 2005**

[As of June 30. (2,350 represents 2,350,000). Excludes school systems and educational institutions. Based on reports from state governments (42 in 1980; 47 in 1983; 49 in 1981 and 1984 through 1987; and 50 in 1989 through 1991) and a sample of county, municipal, township, and special district jurisdictions employing 15 or more nonelected, nonappointed full-time employees. Beginning 1993, only for State and Local Governments with 100 or more employees. For definition of median, see Guide to Tabular Presentation]

Year and occupation	Employment (1,000)						Median annual salary ($1,000)					
				Minority						Minority		
	Male	Female	White [1]	Total [2]	Black [1]	Hispanic [3]	Male	Female	White [1]	Total [2]	Black [1]	Hispanic [3]
1980	2,350	1,637	3,146	842	619	163	15.2	11.4	13.8	11.8	11.5	12.3
1981	2,740	1,925	3,591	1,074	780	205	17.7	13.1	16.1	13.5	13.3	14.7
1983	2,674	1,818	3,423	1,069	768	219	20.1	15.3	18.5	15.9	15.6	17.3
1984	2,700	1,880	3,458	1,121	799	233	21.4	16.2	19.6	17.4	16.5	18.4
1985	2,789	1,952	3,563	1,179	835	248	22.3	17.3	20.6	18.4	17.5	19.2
1986	2,797	1,982	3,549	1,230	865	259	23.4	18.1	21.5	19.6	18.7	20.2
1987	2,818	2,031	3,600	1,249	872	268	24.2	18.9	22.4	20.9	19.3	21.1
1989	3,030	2,227	3,863	1,394	961	308	26.1	20.6	24.1	22.1	20.7	22.7
1990	3,071	2,302	3,918	1,456	994	327	27.3	21.8	25.2	23.3	22.0	23.8
1991	3,110	2,349	3,965	1,494	1,011	340	28.4	22.7	26.4	23.8	22.7	24.5
1993	2,820	2,204	3,588	1,436	948	341	30.6	24.3	28.5	25.9	24.2	26.8
1995	2,960	2,355	3,781	1,534	993	379	33.5	27.0	31.4	26.3	26.8	28.6
1997	2,898	2,307	3,676	1,529	973	392	34.6	27.9	32.2	30.2	27.4	29.5
1999	2,939	2,393	3,723	1,609	1,012	417	37.0	29.9	34.8	31.1	29.6	31.2
2001	3,080	2,554	3,888	1,746	1,077	471	39.8	32.1	37.5	34.0	31.5	33.8
2003	3,134	2,610	3,919	1,826	1,097	508	42.2	34.7	40.0	35.9	33.6	36.6
2005, total	**3,185**	**2,644**	**3,973**	**1,856**	**1,100**	**532**	**44.1**	**36.4**	**41.5**	**37.7**	**35.3**	**38.9**
Officials/administrators.......	223	137	290	70	42	18	68.6	61.3	66.0	65.1	63.0	65.2
Professionals......	650	839	1,067	422	234	100	54.4	47.0	50.5	48.9	44.8	49.0
Technicians.......	272	203	335	140	74	43	44.1	36.0	41.0	38.0	35.6	39.1
Protective service...	959	220	832	347	208	115	45.3	36.6	44.4	42.2	38.5	47.4
Paraprofessionals....	101	286	223	164	112	38	32.7	29.8	31.5	29.2	27.6	31.7
Admin. support	126	796	596	326	186	106	32.3	30.4	30.5	31.0	30.1	31.4
Skilled craft.......	412	23	315	120	68	39	39.7	32.9	39.3	40.0	37.3	41.3
Service/maintenance.	442	138	314	266	177	73	32.3	24.9	31.1	30.0	29.2	30.8

[1] Non-Hispanic.   [2] Includes other minority groups not shown separately.   [3] Persons of Hispanic origin may be of any race.

Source: U.S. Equal Employment Opportunity Commission, Employment Statistics, Job Patterns for Minorities and Women in State and Local Government (EEO-4) and earlies editions; <http://www.eeoc.gov/stats/employment.html>.

State and Local Government Finances and Employment   295

Table 453. **State and Local Government Full-Time Equivalent Employment by Selected Function and State: 2007**

[In thousands (1,740.2 represents 1,740,200). For March. Local government amounts are estimates subject to sampling variation; see Appendix III and source]

State	Total [1]		Education Elementary and secondary		Education Higher education		Public welfare		Health		Hospitals	
	State	Local	State	Local	State	Local	State	Local	State	Local	State	Local
United States..	1,740.2	7,087.7	52.1	6,762.3	1,596.7	325.5	235.3	283.5	183.3	251.5	417.1	572.3
Alabama	41.1	102.8	–	102.8	37.9	–	4.5	1.3	5.8	5.5	11.7	26.2
Alaska.	8.7	16.5	3.1	16.3	5.3	0.1	1.8	0.2	0.7	0.4	0.2	0.7
Arizona	31.7	134.4	–	122.2	28.3	12.2	5.9	2.3	2.5	2.9	0.7	5.5
Arkansas	24.8	71.8	–	71.6	23.3	0.1	3.7	0.1	5.3	0.4	5.7	1.7
California	147.4	770.7	–	700.4	143.2	70.2	3.7	68.1	11.8	44.3	39.8	67.8
Colorado	37.3	105.1	–	103.9	36.0	1.2	2.1	5.9	1.2	3.9	5.3	9.4
Connecticut	20.8	90.1	–	90.1	17.9	–	2.5	1.7	1.9	1.3	9.4	–
Delaware	8.1	15.6	–	15.6	7.7	–	1.6	–	2.2	0.3	1.9	–
District of Columbia	–	12.0	(X)	11.2	(X)	0.9	(X)	1.6	(X)	1.6	(X)	1.6
Florida.	59.9	361.3	–	335.4	56.6	25.9	9.4	7.2	23.9	8.2	3.8	48.4
Georgia	54.5	240.6	–	240.6	51.2	–	9.2	1.9	5.3	10.6	7.1	19.9
Hawaii.	35.6	–	26.6	–	8.9	–	0.9	0.1	2.5	0.2	4.3	–
Idaho	8.5	34.1	–	32.6	8.0	1.5	1.7	0.1	1.1	1.1	0.8	6.3
Illinois	56.1	304.5	–	282.3	54.0	22.2	9.8	6.6	2.6	7.9	10.5	12.8
Indiana	56.0	143.1	–	143.1	54.8	–	4.6	1.2	1.9	3.5	2.6	26.1
Iowa	26.3	81.4	–	74.5	25.2	6.9	3.1	1.2	0.4	2.3	7.4	11.0
Kansas	20.6	90.3	–	82.6	19.9	7.8	2.5	0.8	1.2	3.2	3.2	8.1
Kentucky	35.7	116.4	–	116.4	33.0	0.0	6.7	0.6	2.2	5.1	4.9	4.2
Louisiana	32.1	98.3	1.2	98.3	27.4	–	5.2	0.9	3.7	1.6	13.9	18.3
Maine	7.4	37.8	0.1	37.8	7.1	–	3.2	0.4	1.3	0.3	0.6	0.7
Maryland	28.6	132.5	–	122.0	26.3	10.4	6.8	3.6	6.9	4.7	4.9	–
Massachusetts . . .	31.4	151.1	0.1	151.0	30.2	0.1	6.9	2.2	7.5	2.9	7.6	3.9
Michigan	72.8	223.3	0.9	209.6	70.5	13.7	10.2	2.8	2.1	9.0	17.9	10.8
Minnesota	40.0	118.8	–	118.8	36.2	–	3.0	10.2	2.3	4.0	5.2	10.2
Mississippi	20.6	80.2	–	73.7	19.1	6.5	2.4	0.3	2.9	0.2	12.2	19.2
Missouri.	30.2	148.9	–	142.1	28.5	6.7	7.9	2.8	3.2	3.6	11.6	11.7
Montana	7.4	23.0	–	22.6	7.0	0.3	1.6	0.5	0.9	0.8	0.6	0.8
Nebraska.	12.9	47.3	–	44.5	12.4	2.8	2.6	0.8	0.7	0.7	4.1	4.5
Nevada	10.7	42.6	–	42.6	10.6	–	1.6	0.9	1.3	0.9	1.4	4.9
New Hampshire . .	6.9	36.3	–	36.3	6.6	–	1.5	2.7	1.0	0.2	0.8	–
New Jersey	54.1	221.4	19.5	210.6	31.3	10.9	9.3	12.0	4.4	4.5	18.5	2.5
New Mexico	20.4	52.0	–	48.5	19.2	3.5	1.9	1.1	2.4	0.5	10.4	1.0
New York.	55.5	514.1	–	489.8	50.9	24.3	6.5	48.4	9.7	19.2	45.4	52.9
North Carolina . . .	56.9	237.3	–	217.6	53.9	19.7	2.1	15.5	5.0	15.9	17.4	37.2
North Dakota	8.2	14.8	–	14.8	8.0	–	0.5	0.9	1.2	0.6	1.0	–
Ohio	71.9	254.2	–	248.8	69.3	5.4	3.0	24.8	3.7	17.5	15.5	11.8
Oklahoma	31.1	92.2	–	91.8	29.1	0.4	6.6	0.2	5.9	1.4	2.8	9.8
Oregon	20.5	77.1	–	68.9	19.7	8.1	6.7	0.9	1.5	4.3	5.4	2.5
Pennsylvania	61.2	267.7	–	258.3	56.7	9.4	12.0	21.0	1.8	5.2	11.9	0.7
Rhode Island	6.7	21.5	0.6	21.5	5.6	–	1.6	0.1	1.2	0.1	1.1	–
South Carolina . . .	31.2	104.3	–	104.3	28.6	–	4.3	0.3	6.2	2.3	7.5	21.2
South Dakota	5.6	19.6	–	19.2	5.2	0.5	1.1	0.2	0.7	0.3	1.0	0.4
Tennessee	35.0	128.2	–	128.2	32.8	–	8.2	2.1	4.0	4.3	7.6	21.6
Texas	115.5	690.7	–	650.6	110.6	40.1	23.3	3.7	12.6	24.1	34.0	49.3
Utah	24.6	50.2	–	50.2	23.4	–	3.1	0.7	2.0	1.3	7.0	0.4
Vermont	5.3	19.8	–	19.8	4.7	–	1.3	–	0.8	–	0.2	–
Virginia	54.9	198.6	–	197.2	52.0	1.4	2.4	8.5	5.5	6.1	15.0	2.3
Washington	55.1	101.3	–	101.3	53.0	–	9.4	1.7	5.3	4.0	9.9	14.5
West Virginia	13.8	43.0	–	43.0	12.4	–	3.3	–	0.8	1.2	1.6	2.5
Wisconsin	35.1	129.5	–	119.6	34.0	10.0	1.4	12.4	1.6	6.3	3.4	1.3
Wyoming	3.8	19.8	–	17.5	3.6	2.3	0.7	0.1	0.7	0.4	0.8	5.8

See footnote at end of table.

U.S. Census Bureau, Statistical Abstract of the United States: 2010

Table 453. **State and Local Government Full-Time Equivalent Employment by Selected Function and State: 2007**—Con.

[**In thousands (236.8 represents 236,800). For March.** Local government amounts are estimates subject to sampling variation; see Appendix III and source]

State	Highways		Police protection		Fire protection		Corrections		Parks and recreation		Government administration	
	State	Local	State	Local	State	Local	State	Local	State	Local	State	Local
United States . .	**236.8**	**301.1**	**106.6**	**826.6**	**(X)**	**336.7**	**470.5**	**260.2**	**34.8**	**237.0**	**402.1**	**698.5**
Alabama	4.6	7.1	1.6	12.0	(X)	5.6	5.0	3.2	0.6	3.8	6.8	8.0
Alaska.	3.1	0.6	0.4	1.3	(X)	0.8	1.8	0.1	0.1	0.6	3.2	1.9
Arizona	2.7	5.0	2.0	18.8	(X)	8.2	9.0	6.0	0.4	6.0	6.6	19.0
Arkansas	3.5	3.6	1.2	6.8	(X)	2.7	5.1	2.2	0.7	1.1	4.2	5.8
California	20.8	22.2	13.3	92.3	(X)	35.1	55.7	33.3	3.4	37.0	30.8	99.5
Colorado	3.1	6.0	1.2	12.8	(X)	5.8	6.8	3.8	0.3	6.8	6.5	11.4
Connecticut	3.0	3.5	2.1	8.6	(X)	4.5	7.6	–	0.2	2.0	9.0	4.5
Delaware	1.6	2.1	1.0	3.5	(X)	0.0	2.9	–	0.3	0.2	2.9	1.7
District of Columbia	(X)	0.6	(X)	4.0	(X)	1.9	(X)	0.9	(X)	1.0	(X)	3.4
Florida.	7.3	16.0	4.4	61.0	(X)	28.0	29.1	17.0	1.4	20.1	29.9	45.4
Georgia.	5.9	8.5	2.0	25.6	(X)	12.4	19.8	9.7	2.6	6.1	9.2	23.1
	0.8	0.8	–	3.7	(X)	1.9	2.4	–	0.2	1.9	3.9	2.3
Idaho	1.6	1.8	0.5	3.5	(X)	1.3	1.9	1.3	0.2	0.8	2.1	3.9
Illinois	6.4	11.9	4.0	44.8	(X)	16.9	12.1	10.0	0.6	17.6	10.5	31.4
Indiana	4.4	6.0	1.9	15.2	(X)	7.4	7.3	6.0	0.2	3.4	4.9	17.2
Iowa	2.4	5.9	1.0	6.3	(X)	2.0	3.2	1.4	0.1	2.0	4.1	6.0
Kansas	3.5	5.1	1.1	8.0	(X)	3.3	3.6	2.9	0.6	2.5	4.8	7.3
Kentucky	4.6	3.1	2.4	7.8	(X)	4.0	4.1	3.6	1.5	2.0	9.3	5.7
Louisiana.	4.9	5.0	1.7	14.8	(X)	5.6	7.2	5.3	1.0	3.8	6.2	11.7
Maine	2.4	1.7	0.5	2.6	(X)	1.8	1.3	0.7	0.2	0.7	2.7	2.8
Maryland	4.7	5.0	2.4	16.6	(X)	6.9	12.2	3.4	0.4	6.8	10.0	9.6
Massachusetts . . .	3.7	6.0	6.4	17.7	(X)	12.9	6.0	2.8	0.5	2.3	15.7	8.7
Michigan	3.0	9.3	2.7	20.0	(X)	7.9	17.0	5.5	0.3	4.4	7.6	25.4
Minnesota	4.4	7.4	1.0	10.7	(X)	2.5	4.1	5.5	0.6	4.4	7.1	13.0
Mississippi	3.2	4.8	1.2	7.6	(X)	3.3	3.5	1.9	0.4	1.2	2.3	6.8
Missouri.	6.6	6.9	2.3	15.9	(X)	6.8	12.4	3.2	0.6	4.5	7.8	12.2
Montana	2.2	1.3	0.4	2.1	(X)	0.7	1.2	0.7	0.1	0.4	2.3	2.5
Nebraska.	2.2	2.9	0.8	4.1	(X)	1.3	2.9	1.4	0.3	1.0	1.8	4.4
Nevada	1.7	1.3	0.8	6.9	(X)	2.8	3.8	2.8	0.2	3.7	3.4	6.6
New Hampshire . .	1.8	1.7	0.4	3.3	(X)	1.9	1.4	0.7	0.2	0.5	2.3	2.2
New Jersey	7.2	10.8	4.6	31.8	(X)	8.7	10.2	7.0	2.2	6.1	22.4	20.7
New Mexico	2.6	1.9	0.7	5.5	(X)	2.3	4.0	2.5	0.9	2.2	5.3	4.3
New York.	12.8	28.5	6.4	83.9	(X)	24.4	34.4	25.4	2.6	12.3	37.6	39.7
North Carolina . . .	11.1	4.0	3.8	22.2	(X)	8.2	21.4	4.7	1.2	5.7	11.7	13.2
North Dakota	1.1	1.1	0.2	1.3	(X)	0.3	0.7	0.3	0.1	0.8	1.5	1.3
Ohio	7.2	13.2	2.7	30.0	(X)	16.8	16.7	8.9	0.6	8.8	11.9	34.5
Oklahoma	3.0	5.9	1.9	9.4	(X)	4.2	5.8	1.3	1.0	1.9	5.4	6.9
Oregon	3.7	4.0	1.3	7.7	(X)	3.7	5.1	3.4	0.5	3.2	8.5	7.6
Pennsylvania	13.4	10.7	6.4	26.6	(X)	6.2	17.3	13.0	1.4	3.6	14.5	33.0
Rhode Island	0.8	0.9	0.3	3.2	(X)	2.3	1.7	–	0.1	0.8	2.8	1.7
South Carolina . . .	4.8	2.6	2.1	11.0	(X)	4.8	7.8	2.8	0.6	3.1	4.8	9.5
South Dakota	1.0	1.4	0.3	1.5	(X)	0.4	0.9	0.6	0.1	0.5	1.4	1.8
Tennessee	4.4	6.9	2.0	16.7	(X)	7.3	7.2	6.4	1.2	3.1	6.8	13.4
Texas	16.0	21.2	4.2	60.4	(X)	23.8	45.1	28.1	1.1	14.6	17.7	48.9
Utah	1.6	1.6	0.8	5.2	(X)	2.2	3.3	2.0	0.3	2.8	4.5	5.2
Vermont	1.1	1.1	0.6	0.9	(X)	0.4	1.2	–	0.1	0.1	2.0	1.2
Virginia	9.0	4.7	3.2	18.7	(X)	10.0	14.5	8.9	1.1	8.4	8.6	17.6
Washington	7.5	7.3	2.1	12.5	(X)	8.3	8.9	4.9	0.7	5.6	6.3	16.9
West Virginia	5.0	0.9	1.0	2.9	(X)	1.0	3.3	0.2	0.6	0.9	3.6	4.1
Wisconsin	1.5	8.7	0.9	15.0	(X)	4.9	9.9	3.8	0.2	3.0	5.6	11.8
Wyoming	1.8	0.9	0.3	1.8	(X)	0.4	1.0	0.6	0.1	0.7	1.3	1.9

– Represents or rounds to zero.   X Not applicable.   [1] Includes other categories not shown separately.

Source: U.S. Census Bureau, Federal, State, and Local Government, "Government Employment and Payroll"; <http://www.census.gov/govs/apes/index.html> (published May 2009).

State and Local Government Finances and Employment   297

Table 454. State and Local Government Employment and Average Monthly Earnings by State: 2000 to 2007

[4,083 represents 4,083,000. As of March. Full-time equivalent employment is a derived statistic that provides an estimate of a government's total full-time employment by converting part-time employees to a full-time amount]

State	Full-time equivalent employment (1,000)						Average monthly earnings [2] (dol.)					
	State			Local [1]			State			Local [1]		
	2000	2006	2007	2000	2006	2007	2000	2006	2007	2000	2006	2007
United States . . .	4,083	4,251	4,307	10,995	11,885	12,147	3,374	4,098	4,276	3,169	3,807	3,945
Alabama	80	85	89	182	187	196	2,841	3,681	3,785	2,431	2,903	3,017
Alaska	23	25	26	25	27	27	3,842	4,398	4,565	3,818	4,193	4,442
Arizona	65	67	68	182	218	232	3,055	3,788	4,004	2,942	3,835	4,074
Arkansas	49	58	59	96	104	106	2,842	3,138	3,301	2,175	2,724	2,779
California	355	394	387	1,322	1,425	1,448	4,451	5,497	5,684	4,062	5,065	5,392
Colorado	66	67	68	164	188	195	3,779	4,693	4,722	3,076	3,806	3,858
Connecticut	66	62	62	111	126	126	3,909	5,063	5,187	3,856	4,542	4,545
Delaware	24	26	26	21	24	25	3,222	3,946	4,117	3,163	4,147	3,875
District of Columbia . . .	(X)	(X)	(X)	45	47	47	(X)	(X)	(X)	3,923	4,992	5,174
Florida	185	191	189	580	676	702	3,149	3,519	3,734	2,865	3,608	3,801
Georgia	120	124	126	334	381	393	2,899	3,492	3,590	2,677	3,217	3,261
Hawaii	55	55	57	14	15	14	2,926	3,845	3,981	3,352	4,253	4,464
Idaho	23	22	22	51	57	58	3,022	3,579	3,976	2,478	2,930	3,088
Illinois	128	132	125	493	503	520	3,441	4,438	4,802	3,307	3,991	4,075
Indiana	83	90	90	232	243	250	2,990	3,632	3,752	2,711	3,326	3,322
Iowa	55	53	53	121	133	129	3,656	4,744	4,927	2,727	3,134	3,328
Kansas	43	44	45	128	141	143	3,071	3,580	3,753	2,491	3,001	3,149
Kentucky	74	79	80	149	165	167	3,051	3,529	3,609	2,339	2,789	2,786
Louisiana	95	83	85	185	192	180	2,807	3,516	3,663	2,278	2,772	2,896
Maine	21	22	23	51	56	54	2,983	3,676	3,838	2,609	3,071	3,209
Maryland	91	90	90	182	201	210	3,312	4,294	4,371	3,535	4,399	4,595
Massachusetts	96	91	96	232	241	239	3,683	4,586	4,758	3,403	4,171	4,380
Michigan	142	135	145	351	352	349	3,934	4,452	4,672	3,518	4,012	4,173
Minnesota	73	77	78	206	196	203	3,892	4,762	4,808	3,255	3,986	4,043
Mississippi	56	55	56	133	134	133	2,752	3,197	3,283	2,121	2,744	2,745
Missouri	91	90	90	208	230	238	2,678	3,137	3,213	2,678	3,060	3,158
Montana	18	19	20	34	35	36	2,931	3,496	3,797	2,546	2,912	3,052
Nebraska	30	33	32	78	85	81	2,514	3,345	3,522	2,779	3,383	3,506
Nevada	22	26	29	61	77	82	3,444	4,202	4,657	3,817	4,504	4,675
New Hampshire	19	19	20	46	51	53	3,079	3,899	4,048	2,830	3,317	3,521
New Jersey	133	157	156	316	355	357	4,075	5,048	5,375	3,967	4,703	4,914
New Mexico	48	51	52	70	77	81	2,811	3,300	3,577	2,494	2,938	2,946
New York	251	249	253	924	941	979	3,859	4,860	4,908	3,961	4,641	4,736
North Carolina	123	139	143	328	372	399	3,012	3,614	3,722	2,708	3,151	3,319
North Dakota	16	18	18	23	23	24	2,826	3,368	3,409	2,778	3,450	3,537
Ohio	136	137	143	459	480	470	3,369	4,053	4,459	3,118	3,633	3,745
Oklahoma	64	67	70	134	147	146	2,821	3,355	3,594	2,280	2,720	2,849
Oregon	53	57	60	124	124	131	3,269	3,832	4,055	3,332	3,917	4,019
Pennsylvania	150	161	160	388	407	434	3,436	3,905	4,138	3,296	3,924	3,885
Rhode Island	20	21	20	36	31	33	3,772	4,700	4,795	3,550	4,499	4,471
South Carolina	79	76	76	155	172	178	2,741	3,312	3,376	2,474	3,063	3,069
South Dakota	13	14	14	28	31	30	2,777	3,342	3,538	2,359	2,896	2,903
Tennessee	81	83	85	218	241	240	2,786	3,337	3,515	2,631	3,105	3,189
Texas	269	282	290	909	1,033	1,054	3,095	3,641	3,868	2,643	3,126	3,277
Utah	49	50	51	73	79	81	2,880	3,631	3,963	2,836	3,326	3,576
Vermont	14	15	15	23	26	25	3,153	4,053	4,193	2,534	3,071	3,384
Virginia	119	123	125	269	308	317	3,229	3,836	4,054	2,928	3,537	3,687
Washington	112	117	120	193	216	220	3,551	4,206	4,405	3,835	4,619	4,783
West Virginia	32	37	38	61	60	63	2,694	3,092	3,210	2,517	2,792	2,932
Wisconsin	64	68	69	220	220	213	3,710	4,465	4,617	3,210	3,841	3,876
Wyoming	11	13	13	29	33	35	2,589	3,481	3,613	2,660	3,279	3,598

X Not applicable.   [1] Estimates subject to sampling variation; see Appendix III and source.   [2] For full-time employees.

Source: U.S. Census Bureau, *2007 Annual Survey of Government Employment*, "U.S. Summary Table" (published May 2008); <http://www.census.gov/govs/apes/index.html>.

Table 455. **City Government Employment and Payroll—Largest Cities: 2000 to 2007**

[In thousands, (458.1 represents 458,100), except as noted. As of March. See footnote 4, Table 445, for those areas representing city-county consolidated governments. See headnote, Table 454 for full-time equivalent employment definition]

Cities ranked by 2007 population [1]	Total employment (1,000)			Full-time equivalent employment		Payroll (mil. dol.)			Average monthly earnings for full-time employees (dol.)	
	2000	2005	2007	2000	2007	2000	2005	2007	2000	2007
New York, NY	458.1	443.4	448.5	429.3	422.5	1,708.8	1,958.4	2,067.8	4,150	5,044
Los Angeles, CA	49.4	53.5	57.0	48.4	55.8	230.1	303.6	358.4	4,793	6,484
Chicago, IL.	41.3	42.6	40.0	40.7	39.5	171.3	171.3	172.5	4,239	4,395
Houston, TX	25.2	21.9	21.7	24.9	21.5	75.2	73.6	80.3	3,037	3,753
Phoenix, AZ	13.0	14.3	16.1	12.7	16.0	50.3	67.1	113.0	4,024	7,278
Philadelphia, PA.	31.1	31.4	31.1	30.0	30.2	109.2	127.4	139.0	3,637	4,618
San Antonio, TX.	16.9	17.3	16.6	15.7	15.8	48.0	61.8	59.0	3,160	3,818
San Diego, CA.	12.3	11.7	11.6	11.4	10.7	46.9	57.7	57.6	4,201	5,517
Dallas, TX.	15.6	14.8	15.2	15.2	14.9	50.4	61.7	68.5	3,332	4,663
San Jose, CA	7.6	9.4	7.4	6.9	6.6	36.3	52.4	47.5	5,569	7,593
Detroit, MI.	40.7	37.4	13.9	36.1	13.7	132.1	142.9	53.9	3,693	3,953
Honolulu, HI	9.8	9.7	9.3	9.1	8.6	30.9	36.7	38.6	3,435	4,575
Jacksonville, FL.	10.1	11.4	10.5	9.7	10.3	35.6	45.6	43.2	3,815	4,248
Indianapolis, IN	12.4	17.1	17.2	12.0	15.9	36.7	53.9	57.8	3,115	3,617
San Francisco, CA	27.7	29.2	29.5	27.7	28.0	141.6	191.3	196.6	5,112	7,253
Columbus, OH.	9.1	8.4	8.7	8.8	8.4	30.1	35.1	38.8	3,478	4,688
Austin, TX.	10.6	12.4	12.3	10.1	11.9	31.2	47.8	54.2	3,128	4,583
Louisville, KY.	4.6	8.4	8.1	4.3	7.8	11.8	25.9	28.1	2,844	3,707
Ft. Worth, TX.	6.1	6.4	6.1	5.7	5.8	18.9	24.1	25.1	3,394	4,470
Memphis, TN.	28.2	28.9	28.5	26.9	25.7	80.3	90.4	95.2	3,024	3,796
Charlotte, NC	5.2	6.0	6.5	5.1	6.3	17.1	23.4	26.6	3,408	4,265
Baltimore, MD	30.8	27.2	29.3	29.2	27.6	95.3	102.5	121.0	3,361	4,463
El Paso, TX.	5.9	5.7	5.9	5.8	5.7	15.6	16.4	18.3	2,701	3,225
Milwaukee, WI	7.9	8.0	6.9	7.7	6.7	28.5	31.9	29.2	3,706	4,387
Boston, MA.	23.3	22.4	21.3	22.0	20.3	80.2	97.0	100.6	3,734	5,019
Seattle, WA.	11.4	12.8	11.8	10.3	10.9	48.3	57.1	60.3	4,726	5,773
Nashville, TN.	20.6	22.2	23.2	19.6	21.7	62.3	76.3	85.3	3,235	4,010
Denver, CO.	14.5	12.4	13.3	13.7	12.6	47.3	53.0	61.1	3,534	4,953
Washington, DC.	37.7	37.6	38.4	36.5	36.8	139.4	164.6	185.2	3,863	5,150
Las Vegas, NV	2.6	3.0	3.2	2.5	3.0	11.2	16.6	19.3	4,681	6,548
Portland, OR	6.2	6.2	6.7	5.4	5.8	23.4	27.5	31.6	4,416	5,624
Oklahoma City, OK.	5.1	4.9	4.7	4.8	4.4	16.0	19.5	20.8	3,457	4,790
Tucson, AZ	7.1	6.8	6.3	5.8	5.8	16.0	24.1	26.2	2,787	4,697
Atlanta, GA	8.8	8.0	10.0	8.6	9.6	25.6	29.1	36.2	2,974	3,795
Albuquerque, NM	7.1	6.9	8.0	6.6	7.6	18.3	21.5	18.5	2,868	2,523
Fresno, CA	3.2	4.0	4.9	3.1	4.3	12.7	17.5	20.3	4,073	4,857
Long Beach, CA	6.1	6.0	5.8	5.7	5.4	25.7	27.6	29.9	4,855	5,816
Sacramento, CA.	4.4	5.1	5.6	4.0	4.8	17.0	23.3	31.5	4,400	7,208
Mesa, AZ	3.5	4.3	4.7	3.3	4.5	13.4	19.8	23.2	4,072	5,270
Kansas, MO	6.8	6.6	6.7	6.6	6.7	21.3	25.1	27.2	3,246	4,114
Cleveland, OH.	10.1	7.9	7.8	9.4	7.6	27.8	30.1	31.5	2,989	4,133
Virginia Beach, VA	19.7	21.8	19.7	17.4	18.0	43.4	55.5	61.8	2,679	3,715
Omaha, NE.	3.4	3.0	3.1	2.9	2.8	10.6	12.7	13.5	3,874	4,974
Miami, FL.	3.8	3.7	4.3	3.6	4.2	15.1	17.3	21.9	4,276	5,381
Oakland, CA	4.2	5.5	5.2	4.2	5.2	24.8	41.0	35.1	5,861	6,825
Tulsa, OK	4.5	4.3	4.4	4.5	4.3	13.7	14.9	16.9	3,126	3,930
Minneapolis, MN	6.3	5.9	6.0	5.8	5.5	21.3	24.0	25.4	3,866	4,747
Colorado Springs, CO.	7.4	7.7	7.7	6.9	7.1	25.3	31.2	33.4	3,747	4,738
Raleigh, NC	3.2	3.8	4.1	2.9	3.6	8.9	11.8	13.5	3,114	3,978
Arlington, TX	3.0	2.7	2.7	2.4	2.4	7.1	9.6	10.7	3,090	4,733
Wichita, KS.	3.6	4.0	3.9	3.1	3.2	9.3	11.3	12.0	3,072	3,772
St. Louis, MO	8.0	6.9	6.7	7.6	6.5	24.1	23.7	24.8	3,176	3,806
Santa Ana, CA.	2.5	2.5	1.9	2.2	1.7	10.1	13.4	12.1	5,606	7,597
Tampa, FL	4.3	4.7	4.8	4.2	4.8	14.1	18.1	20.3	3,370	4,341
Anaheim, CA.	3.2	3.5	3.8	2.5	2.7	11.5	15.7	16.8	5,267	7,403
Cincinnati, OH	6.5	6.3	6.4	6.4	5.8	21.3	26.1	24.4	3,504	4,481
Bakersfield, CA	1.3	1.3	1.6	1.2	1.5	5.3	6.8	8.2	4,469	5,439
Aurora, CO	2.5	2.7	2.8	2.5	2.8	9.0	12.0	13.4	3,682	4,823
Pittsburgh, PA	4.4	3.6	3.2	4.3	3.2	15.3	15.3	14.8	3,593	4,665
Toledo, OH	2.8	2.9	2.9	2.8	2.9	10.0	12.6	13.2	3,628	4,611
Riverside, CA	2.1	2.4	2.6	1.9	2.3	8.0	11.3	13.5	4,625	6,160
Stockton, CA.	2.3	2.2	2.2	1.9	1.8	7.1	9.4	10.3	4,054	5,938
Corpus Christi, TX	3.5	3.1	3.2	3.3	3.1	8.6	10.1	10.6	2,675	3,486
Newark, NJ	5.5	6.9	4.2	5.2	3.7	22.3	30.6	16.7	4,371	4,678
Anchorage, AK	10.1	10.9	10.9	9.0	9.8	34.6	41.7	44.8	3,973	4,731
Lexington, KY	4.0	4.3	4.8	3.6	4.2	10.2	13.1	14.8	2,910	3,784
St. Paul, MN	4.2	3.2	3.2	3.2	3.0	13.3	13.5	14.6	4,189	5,143
Buffalo, NY	11.4	11.9	12.6	10.5	11.5	43.4	47.8	48.0	4,457	4,275
Plano, TX	2.0	2.4	2.4	1.8	2.2	6.4	9.0	10.7	3,702	5,155
Glendale, AZ	1.5	2.2	1.9	1.4	1.9	4.7	8.6	9.2	3,275	4,834
Lincoln, NE	2.7	3.0	2.9	2.5	2.7	8.2	11.2	11.6	3,382	4,436
St. Petersburg, FL	3.2	3.9	4.2	3.0	4.1	9.9	12.9	16.0	3,366	4,119
Chandler, AZ	1.4	1.7	1.8	1.2	1.6	3.9	7.0	8.7	3,204	5,397

[1] 2007 based on estimated resident population as of July 1.

Source: U.S. Census Bureau, Federal, State, and Local Governments, *2007 Annual Survey of Government Employment* (published March 2009); <http://www.census.gov/govs/apes/index.html>.

State and Local Government Finances and Employment **299**

Table 456. **County Government Employment and Payroll—Largest Counties: 2000 to 2007**

[In thousands, (98.8 represents 98,800). As of March. See text, this section. See headnote, Table 454, for full-time equivalent employment definition]

Counties ranked by 2007 population [1]	Total employment (1,000)			Full-time equivalent employment		Payroll (mil. dol.)			Average monthly earnings for full-time employees (dol.)	
	2000	2005	2007	2000	2007	2000	2005	2007	2000	2007
Los Angeles, CA	98.8	99.5	105.7	94.2	102.2	396.7	475.0	551.4	4,274	5,460
Cook, IL	28.9	27.8	25.7	28.9	25.7	99.3	126.3	122.7	3,445	4,780
Harris, TX	19.8	21.7	23.7	19.4	22.6	59.5	77.4	94.0	3,063	4,133
Maricopa, AZ	15.3	16.4	14.2	15.0	13.8	43.7	54.9	62.5	2,934	4,551
Orange, CA	24.3	25.0	22.1	22.5	21.2	81.4	104.9	100.4	3,623	4,674
San Diego, CA	19.5	19.7	23.7	18.2	22.3	66.3	83.9	109.1	3,651	4,906
Dade, FL	36.0	43.8	47.8	35.1	46.7	130.3	190.8	238.7	3,817	5,256
Dallas, TX	12.5	15.2	16.1	12.0	15.2	36.4	54.5	62.9	3,055	4,147
Riverside, CA	16.6	20.1	21.2	15.4	20.5	54.2	90.6	105.6	3,534	5,156
San Bernardino, CA	20.6	19.9	20.8	18.8	19.5	67.6	84.0	95.8	3,664	4,991
Wayne, MI	6.7	5.8	5.6	6.7	5.5	25.8	25.1	25.2	3,914	4,630
King, WA	15.8	14.5	14.6	14.2	14.0	52.1	64.6	72.7	3,812	5,372
Clark, NV	16.6	19.1	20.9	15.2	18.8	60.3	88.4	106.1	4,169	5,693
Broward, FL	11.0	12.9	13.8	10.8	13.4	37.0	48.4	60.9	3,437	4,600
Santa Clara, CA	14.9	18.0	19.1	14.3	18.1	65.3	100.4	118.0	4,655	6,600
Tarrant, TX	6.9	9.4	10.5	6.8	10.3	19.0	34.4	38.8	2,811	3,784
Bexar, TX	9.5	10.1	10.5	9.1	10.2	23.6	27.9	34.0	2,619	3,345
Alameda, CA	12.1	11.3	11.8	11.1	11.3	51.1	60.9	72.2	4,619	6,440
Suffolk, NY	12.9	14.2	15.7	11.3	14.2	51.9	68.2	79.8	4,686	5,686
Sacramento, CA	13.3	14.9	14.3	12.6	13.8	50.3	71.0	70.7	4,094	5,158
Nassau, NY	18.9	16.8	21.6	16.9	19.2	71.3	76.6	108.2	4,295	5,837
Cuyahoga, OH.	16.1	15.7	16.0	16.1	15.4	49.2	57.1	62.7	3,065	3,969
Palm Beach, FL.	8.6	10.5	11.4	8.5	11.0	27.0	40.4	57.3	3,200	5,332
Allegheny, PA	7.0	6.8	7.3	6.8	6.9	17.6	20.2	22.0	2,605	3,217
Oakland, MI	4.5	4.6	4.7	4.3	4.4	15.6	18.9	19.9	3,697	4,555
Hillsborough, FL.	16.2	13.9	12.3	12.2	10.6	34.4	39.1	45.9	2,993	4,437
Hennepin, MN	13.0	11.4	11.2	11.0	10.3	41.5	49.3	47.8	3,815	4,676
Franklin, OH	6.6	6.7	6.6	6.5	6.3	19.2	21.7	22.7	2,962	3,632
Orange, FL	9.9	10.5	11.3	9.3	10.2	28.0	35.7	43.4	3,092	4,244
Contra Costa, CA	10.7	10.0	10.4	9.5	9.1	44.7	41.6	47.6	4,779	5,240
Fairfax, VA	35.3	44.7	43.9	32.3	39.0	117.5	165.4	190.0	3,746	4,923
St. Louis, MO	4.2	3.9	5.8	4.1	4.3	12.9	14.0	15.1	3,215	3,853
Fulton, GA	7.9	7.6	4.0	7.7	3.9	25.0	29.2	14.9	3,356	3,873
Travis, TX	3.5	4.6	8.2	3.5	7.9	10.6	15.7	33.5	3,057	4,408
Pima, AZ	8.0	7.2	4.8	7.2	4.7	20.0	22.5	17.9	2,859	3,796
Westchester, NY	6.9	7.3	8.1	6.3	7.5	26.6	29.8	27.7	4,240	3,855
Milwaukee, WI	8.5	9.3	11.0	8.1	10.2	26.5	35.7	35.4	3,314	3,434
Montgomery, MD	37.4	40.6	7.7	28.8	7.1	123.1	175.3	24.9	4,619	3,502
Du Page, IL	3.9	3.6	42.2	3.6	35.1	11.8	14.1	198.0	3,360	6,013
Pinellas, FL.	6.2	6.6	3.7	6.1	3.5	18.5	25.7	15.6	3,039	4,488
Erie, NY	10.9	11.3	7.1	9.8	6.9	33.4	37.4	30.4	3,578	4,375
Shelby, TN	13.1	14.2	11.4	12.4	10.1	35.1	45.4	40.8	2,842	4,138
Fresno, CA	8.6	9.2	15.1	8.2	14.5	26.0	32.9	51.1	3,293	3,546
Bergen, NJ	5.8	5.7	9.2	4.1	8.5	13.0	23.7	32.8	3,178	3,846
Mecklenburg, NC	23.8	27.1	5.7	21.1	4.9	58.2	82.1	23.6	2,834	5,040
Hamilton, OH.	5.9	6.1	29.7	5.7	26.9	15.3	20.5	100.2	2,679	3,851
Wake, NC.	17.8	21.0	6.1	15.8	5.9	44.7	65.3	21.5	2,876	3,626
Macomb, MI	3.0	3.2	23.8	2.8	22.7	8.9	12.0	78.3	3,333	3,461
Prince Georges, MD	29.4	32.2	3.3	26.3	3.1	90.8	112.1	12.9	3,564	4,347
Ventura, CA	8.6	8.6	34.1	8.3	30.6	31.5	43.2	127.3	3,829	4,428
Kern, CA	9.2	10.3	9.0	8.6	8.6	30.3	40.7	50.8	3,504	6,026
Baltimore, MD	23.3	27.5	11.9	20.7	10.7	63.8	92.9	44.2	3,227	4,148
Middlesex, NJ	4.5	4.3	29.0	4.0	24.7	14.4	16.6	105.6	3,881	4,448
Gwinnett, GA.	3.8	4.5	5.0	3.5	4.4	11.4	16.7	19.6	3,243	4,747
Montgomery, PA.	3.5	4.1	5.1	3.4	4.8	9.2	12.4	19.0	2,783	3,993
Essex, NJ.	5.6	5.0	4.2	5.0	4.0	19.3	21.0	12.0	4,048	3,029
Pierce, WA	3.4	3.6	5.4	3.2	4.8	13.0	16.6	23.7	4,216	5,083
Dekalb, GA	6.5	7.1	3.8	6.2	3.7	19.5	25.1	19.2	3,170	5,310
El Paso, TX.	4.0	4.7	7.5	4.0	7.2	10.4	15.3	27.2	2,685	3,795
Collin, TX	1.1	1.4	4.8	1.1	4.7	2.8	5.0	17.2	2,557	3,772
Monroe, NY.	7.0	6.9	1.7	5.9	1.7	20.4	22.8	6.6	3,430	3,846
Hidalgo, TX.	1.9	2.2	6.7	1.9	5.9	4.0	5.6	24.5	2,174	4,266
Lake, IL	3.2	3.3	2.7	2.9	2.7	9.6	13.0	6.9	3,277	2,527
San Mateo, CA	6.2	7.2	3.4	5.8	3.2	24.6	35.5	14.3	4,415	4,553
Multnomah, OR	6.0	5.0	7.8	5.2	7.3	15.0	16.6	39.1	3,050	6,059
Oklahoma City, OK.	2.6	2.3	4.9	2.3	4.5	4.4	5.7	20.6	1,860	4,634
Cobb, GA.	3.9	4.7	2.4	3.8	2.3	11.9	16.2	5.9	3,353	2,663
Snohomish, WA.	2.4	3.2	5.0	2.4	4.5	9.3	13.5	18.5	3,906	4,201
San Joaquin, CA	7.4	7.7	2.3	6.8	2.2	22.6	30.4	9.0	3,509	4,128
Jackson, MO.	2.1	1.9	8.1	2.0	7.1	5.0	5.8	34.3	2,519	4,841
Jefferson, AL.	4.8	4.5	2.1	4.7	2.0	14.7	16.9	6.4	3,122	3,208
Norfolk, MA.	0.6	0.5	4.4	0.5	4.3	1.6	2.0	17.4	2,977	4,035

[1] 2007 based on estimated resident population as of July 1.

Source: U.S. Census Bureau, Federal, State, and Local Governments, *Annual Survey of Government Employment* (published March 2009); <http://www.census.gov/govs/apes/index.html>.

Federal Government Finances and Employment

This section presents statistics relating to the financial structure and the civilian employment of the federal government. The fiscal data cover taxes, other receipts, outlays, and debt. The principal sources of fiscal data are the *Budget of the United States Government* and related documents, published annually by the Office of Management and Budget (OMB), and the U.S. Department of the Treasury's *United States Government Annual Report* and its *Appendix*. Detailed data on tax returns and collections are published annually by the Internal Revenue Service. The personnel data relate to staffing and payrolls. They are published by the Office of Personnel Management and the Bureau of Labor Statistics. Data on federally owned land and real property are collected by the General Services Administration and presented in its annual "Federal Real Property Report."

Budget concept—Under the unified budget concept, all federal monies are included in one comprehensive budget. These monies comprise both federal funds and trust funds. Federal funds are derived mainly from taxes and borrowing and are not restricted by law to any specific government purpose. Trust funds, such as the Unemployment Trust Fund, collect certain taxes and other receipts for use in carrying out specific purposes or programs in accordance with the terms of the trust agreement or statute. Fund balances include both cash balances with the Treasury and investments in U.S. securities. Part of the balance is obligated, part unobligated. Prior to 1985, the budget totals, under provisions of law, excluded some federal activities—including the Federal Financing Bank, the Postal Service, the Synthetic Fuels Corporation, and the lending activities of the Rural Electrification Administration. The Balanced Budget and Emergency Deficit Control Act of 1985 (P.L.99-177) repealed the off-budget status of these entities and placed social security (federal old-age and survivors insurance and the federal disability insurance trust funds) off-budget. Though social security is now off-budget and, by law, excluded from coverage of the congressional budget resolutions, it continues to be a federal program.

Receipts arising from the government's sovereign powers are reported as governmental receipts; all other receipts; i.e., from business-type or market-oriented activities, are offset against outlays. Outlays are reported on a checks-issued (net) basis (i.e., outlays are recorded at the time the checks to pay bills are issued).

Debt concept—For most of U.S. history, the total debt consisted of debt borrowed by the Treasury (i.e., public debt). The present debt series includes both public debt and agency debt. The *gross federal debt* includes money borrowed by the Treasury and by various federal agencies; it is the broadest generally used measure of the federal debt. *Total public debt* is covered by a statutory debt limitation and includes only borrowing by the Treasury.

Treasury receipts and outlays—All receipts of the government, with a few exceptions, are deposited to the credit of the U.S. Treasury regardless of ultimate disposition. Under the Constitution, no money may be withdrawn from the Treasury unless appropriated by the Congress.

The day-to-day cash operations of the federal government clearing through the accounts of the U.S. Treasury are reported in the *Daily Treasury Statement*. Extensive detail on the public debt is published in the *Monthly Statement of the Public Debt of the United States*.

Budget receipts such as taxes, customs duties, and miscellaneous receipts, which are collected by government agencies, and outlays represented by checks issued and cash payments made by disbursing officers as well as government agencies are reported in the *Daily Treasury Statement of Receipts and Outlays of the United States Government* and in the Treasury's *United States Government Annual Report* and its *Appendix*. These deposits in and payments from accounts maintained by government agencies are on the same basis as the unified budget.

The quarterly *Treasury Bulletin* contains data on fiscal operations and related Treasury activities, including financial statements of government corporations and other business-type activities.

Income tax returns and tax collections—Tax data are compiled by the Internal Revenue Service of the Treasury Department. The annual *Internal Revenue Service Data Book* gives a detailed account of tax collections by kind of tax. The agency's annual *Statistics of Income* reports present detailed data from individual income tax returns and corporation income tax returns. The quarterly *Statistics of Income Bulletin* presents data on such diverse subjects as tax-exempt organizations, unincorporated businesses, fiduciary income tax and estate tax returns, sales of capital assets by individuals, international income and taxes reported by corporations and individuals, and estate tax wealth.

Employment and payrolls—The Office of Personnel Management collects employment and payroll data from all departments and agencies of the federal government, except the Central Intelligence Agency, the National Security Agency, and the Defense Intelligence Agency. Employment figures represent the number of persons who occupied civilian positions at the end of the report month shown and who are paid for personal services rendered for the federal government, regardless of the nature of appointment or method of payment. Federal payrolls include all payments for personal services rendered during the report month and payments for accumulated annual leave of employees who separate from the service. Since most federal employees are paid on a biweekly basis, the calendar month earnings are partially estimated on the basis of the number of work days in each month where payroll periods overlap.

Federal employment and payroll figures are published by the Office of Personnel Management in its *Federal Civilian Workforce Statistics—Employment and Trends*. It also publishes biennial employment data for minority groups, data on occupations of white- and blue-collar workers, and data on employment by geographic area; reports on salary and wage distribution of federal employees are published annually. General schedule is primarily white-collar; wage system primarily blue-collar. Data on federal employment are also issued by the Bureau of Labor Statistics in its *Monthly Labor Review* and in Employment and Earnings and by the U.S. Census Bureau in its annual publication *Public Employment*.

U.S. Census Bureau, Statistical Abstract of the United States: 2010

Figure 9.1
Federal Budget Summary: 1990 to 2009

Receipts, outlays, and surplus or deficit
Trillions of constant (2000) dollars

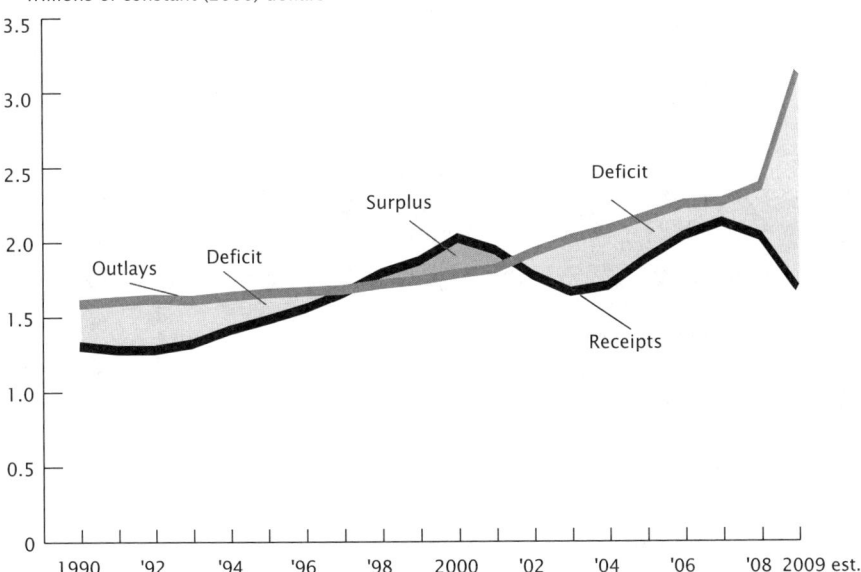

Outlays and federal debt as a percent of gross domestic product (GDP)

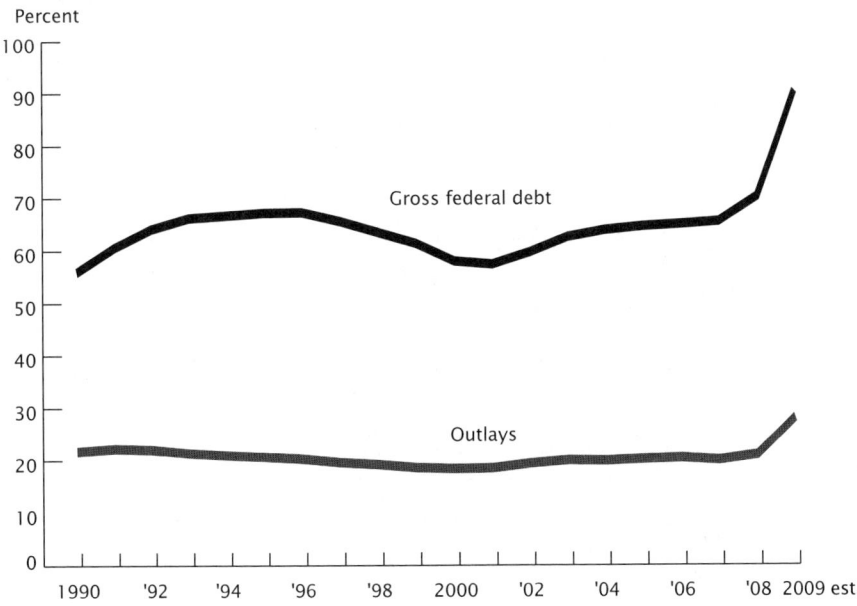

Source: Charts prepared by U.S. Census Bureau. For data, see Tables 457 & 458.

Federal Government Finances and Employment   303

Table 457. Federal Budget—Receipts and Outlays: 1960 to 2009

[92.5 represents $92,500,000,000). For fiscal years ending in year shown; see text, Section 8. See also headnote, Table 459]

Fiscal year	In current dollars (bil. dol)			In constant (2000) dollars (bil. dol)			As percentage of GDP [1]		
	Receipts	Outlays	Surplus or deficit (−)	Receipts	Outlays	Surplus or deficit (−)	Receipts	Outlays	Surplus or deficit (−)
1960........	92.5	92.2	0.3	528.5	526.8	1.7	17.8	17.8	0.1
1970........	192.8	195.6	−2.8	815.9	828.0	−12.0	19.0	19.3	−0.3
1980........	517.1	590.9	−73.8	1,028.3	1,175.1	−146.8	19.0	21.7	−2.7
1985........	734.1	946.4	−212.3	1,082.6	1,395.7	−313.1	17.7	22.8	−5.1
1990........	1,032.1	1,253.1	−221.0	1,309.4	1,589.9	−280.4	18.0	21.8	−3.9
1991........	1,055.1	1,324.3	−269.2	1,282.6	1,609.9	−327.3	17.8	22.3	−4.5
1992........	1,091.3	1,381.6	−290.3	1,282.7	1,623.9	−341.2	17.5	22.1	−4.7
1993........	1,154.5	1,409.5	−255.1	1,323.2	1,615.5	−292.3	17.5	21.4	−3.9
1994........	1,258.7	1,461.9	−203.2	1,414.0	1,642.2	−228.2	18.1	21.0	−2.9
1995........	1,351.9	1,515.9	−164.0	1,482.4	1,662.2	−179.8	18.5	20.7	−2.2
1996........	1,453.2	1,560.6	−107.4	1,557.9	1,673.0	−115.2	18.9	20.3	−1.4
1997........	1,579.4	1,601.3	−21.9	1,661.2	1,684.2	−23.0	19.3	19.6	−0.3
1998........	1,722.0	1,652.7	69.3	1,793.1	1,721.0	72.1	20.0	19.2	0.8
1999........	1,827.6	1,702.0	125.6	1,874.9	1,746.0	128.9	20.0	18.6	1.4
2000........	2,025.5	1,789.2	236.2	2,025.5	1,789.2	236.2	20.9	18.4	2.4
2001........	1,991.4	1,863.2	128.2	1,945.9	1,820.6	125.3	19.8	18.5	1.3
2002........	1,853.4	2,011.2	−157.8	1,777.8	1,929.2	−151.3	17.9	19.4	−1.5
2003........	1,782.5	2,160.1	−377.6	1,665.5	2,018.2	−352.8	16.5	20.0	−3.5
2004........	1,880.3	2,293.0	−412.7	1,707.2	2,081.9	−374.7	16.3	19.9	−3.6
2005........	2,153.9	2,472.2	−318.3	1,886.5	2,165.4	−278.8	17.6	20.2	−2.6
2006........	2,407.3	2,655.4	−248.2	2,038.5	2,248.7	−210.2	18.5	20.4	−1.9
2007........	2,568.2	2,728.9	−160.7	2,125.8	2,258.9	−133.0	18.8	20.0	−1.2
2008........	2,524.3	2,982.9	−458.6	2,006.0	2,370.4	−364.4	17.7	21.0	−3.2
2009 estimate...	2,156.7	3,997.8	−1,841.2	1,686.9	3,127.0	−1,440.1	15.1	28.1	−12.9

[1] Gross domestic product; see text, Section 13.

Source: U.S. Office of Management and Budget, *Budget of the United States Government, Historical Tables,* annual. See also <http://www.whitehouse.gov/omb/budget/>.

Table 458. Federal Budget Debt: 1960 to 2009

[290.5 represents $290,500,000,000. As of the end of the fiscal year. See text, Section 8]

Fiscal year	Total (bil. dol.)					As percentage of GDP [1]				
	Gross federal debt	Federal govern- ment accounts	Held by the public			Gross Federal debt	Federal govern- ment accounts	Held by the public		
			Total	Federal Reserve System	Other			Total	Federal Reserve System	Other
1960........	290.5	53.7	236.8	26.5	210.3	56.0	10.3	45.6	5.1	40.5
1970........	380.9	97.7	283.2	57.7	225.5	37.6	9.6	28.0	5.7	22.3
1980........	909.0	197.1	711.9	120.8	591.1	33.4	7.2	26.1	4.4	21.7
1985........	1,817.4	310.2	1,507.3	169.8	1,337.5	43.8	7.5	36.3	4.1	32.2
1990........	3,206.3	794.7	2,411.6	234.4	2,177.1	55.9	13.9	42.0	4.1	37.9
1991........	3,598.2	909.2	2,689.0	258.6	2,430.4	60.6	15.3	45.3	4.4	41.0
1992........	4,001.8	1,002.1	2,999.7	296.4	2,703.3	64.1	16.1	48.1	4.8	43.3
1993........	4,351.0	1,102.6	3,248.4	325.7	2,922.7	66.1	16.8	49.4	5.0	44.4
1994........	4,643.3	1,210.2	3,433.1	355.2	3,077.9	66.7	17.4	49.3	5.1	44.2
1995........	4,920.6	1,316.2	3,604.4	374.1	3,230.3	67.2	18.0	49.2	5.1	44.1
1996........	5,181.5	1,447.4	3,734.1	390.9	3,343.1	67.3	18.8	48.5	5.1	43.4
1997........	5,369.2	1,596.9	3,772.3	424.5	3,347.8	65.6	19.5	46.1	5.2	40.9
1998........	5,478.2	1,757.1	3,721.1	458.2	3,262.9	63.5	20.4	43.1	5.3	37.8
1999........	5,605.5	1,973.2	3,632.4	496.6	3,135.7	61.4	21.6	39.8	5.4	34.4
2000........	5,628.7	2,218.9	3,409.8	511.4	2,898.4	58.0	22.9	35.1	5.3	29.9
2001........	5,769.9	2,450.3	3,319.6	534.1	2,785.5	57.4	24.4	33.0	5.3	27.7
2002........	6,198.4	2,658.0	3,540.4	604.2	2,936.2	59.7	25.6	34.1	5.8	28.3
2003........	6,760.0	2,846.6	3,913.4	656.1	3,257.3	62.6	26.3	36.2	6.1	30.2
2004........	7,354.7	3,059.1	4,295.5	700.3	3,595.2	63.9	26.6	37.3	6.1	31.3
2005........	7,905.3	3,313.1	4,592.2	736.4	3,855.9	64.6	27.1	37.5	6.0	31.5
2006........	8,451.4	3,622.4	4,829.0	768.9	4,060.0	65.0	27.8	37.1	5.9	31.2
2007........	8,950.7	3,915.6	5,035.1	779.6	4,255.5	65.6	28.7	36.9	5.7	31.2
2008........	9,985.8	4,183.0	5,802.7	491.1	5,311.6	70.2	29.4	40.8	3.5	37.3
2009 estimate...	12,867.5	4,336.1	8,531.4	(NA)	(NA)	90.4	30.4	59.9	(NA)	(NA)

NA not available.   [1] Gross domestic product; see text, Section 13.

Source: U.S. Office of Management and Budget, *Budget of the United States Government, Historical Tables,* annual. See also <http://www.whitehouse.gov/omb/budget/>.

304   Federal Government Finances and Employment

Table 459. **Federal Budget Outlays by Type: 1990 to 2009**

[1,253.1 represents $1,253,100,000,000. For years ending September 30. Given the inherent imprecision in deflating outlays, the data shown in constant dollars present a reasonable perspective—not precision. The deflators and the categories that are deflated are as comparable over time as feasible. Minus sign (–) indicates offset]

Type	Unit	1990	2000	2005	2006	2007	2008	2009, est.
Current dollar outlays	Bil. dol...	1,253.1	1,789.2	2,472.2	2,655.4	2,728.9	2,982.9	3,997.8
National defense [1]	Bil. dol. . .	299.3	294.4	495.3	521.8	551.3	616.1	690.3
Nondefense, total	Bil. dol. . .	953.8	1,494.8	1,976.9	2,133.6	2,177.7	2,366.8	3,307.5
Payments for individuals	Bil. dol. . .	585.7	1,054.5	1,490.0	1,591.8	1,689.3	1,824.6	2,090.3
Direct payments [2]	Bil. dol. . .	507.0	867.7	1,211.9	1,315.0	1,400.9	1,519.9	1,711.8
Grants to state and local governments .	Bil. dol. . .	78.7	186.8	278.1	276.8	288.4	304.7	378.5
All other payments	Bil. dol. . .	56.4	99.1	149.9	157.3	155.4	156.6	189.3
Net interest [2]	Bil. dol. . .	184.3	222.9	184.0	226.6	237.1	252.8	142.7
All other [2]	Bil. dol. . .	164.0	160.9	218.2	226.2	178.1	219.0	976.9
Undistributed offsetting receipts [2]	Bil. dol. . .	–36.6	–42.6	–65.2	–68.3	–82.2	–86.2	–91.7
Constant (2000) dollar outlays	Bil. dol...	1,589.9	1,789.2	2,165.4	2,248.7	2,258.9	2,370.4	3,127.0
National defense [1]	Bil. dol. . .	382.7	294.4	407.4	411.9	422.1	461.3	511.9
Nondefense, total	Bil. dol. . .	1,207.0	1,494.8	1,758.0	1,836.8	1,836.8	1,909.0	2615.1
Payments for individuals	Bil. dol. . .	732.5	1,054.5	1,338.4	1,386.7	1,439.7	1,483.7	1,715.2
Direct payments [2]	Bil. dol. . .	634.0	867.7	1,088.8	1,145.7	1,194.3	1,236.3	1,405.1
Grants to state and local governments .	Bil. dol. . .	98.4	186.8	249.6	240.9	245.4	247.4	310.1
All other grants	Bil. dol. . .	73.3	99.1	124.3	123.5	116.3	110.3	131.1
Net interest [2]	Bil. dol. . .	226.9	222.9	163.3	194.5	198.1	206.2	114.8
All other [2]	Bil. dol. . .	228.0	160.9	184.8	185.2	144.2	171.9	720.0
Undistributed offsetting receipts [2]	Bil. dol. . .	–53.5	–42.6	–52.7	–53.0	–61.6	–63.1	–66.1
Outlays as percent of GDP [3]	Percent. .	21.8	18.4	20.2	20.4	20.0	21.0	28.1
National defense [1]	Percent. .	5.2	3.0	4.0	4.0	4.0	4.3	4.8
Nondefense, total	Percent. .	16.6	15.4	16.2	16.4	16.0	16.6	23.2
Payments for individuals	Percent. .	10.2	10.9	12.2	12.2	12.4	12.8	14.7
Direct payments [2]	Percent. .	8.8	8.9	9.9	10.1	10.3	10.7	12.0
Grants to state and local governments. . .	Percent. .	1.4	1.9	2.3	2.1	2.1	2.1	2.7
All other grants	Percent. .	1.0	1.0	1.2	1.2	1.1	1.1	1.3
Net interest [2]	Percent. .	3.2	2.3	1.5	1.7	1.7	1.8	1.0
All other [2]	Percent. .	2.9	1.7	1.8	1.7	1.3	1.5	6.9
Undistributed offsetting receipts [2]	Percent. .	–0.6	–0.4	–0.5	–0.5	–0.6	–0.6	–0.6

[1] Includes a small amount of grants to state and local governments and direct payments for individuals. [2] Includes some off–budget amounts; most of the off–budget amounts are direct payments for individuals (social security benefits). [3] Gross domestic product; see text, Section 13.

Source: U.S. Office of Management and Budget, *Budget of the United States Government, Historical Tables*, annual. See also <http://www.whitehouse.gov/omb/budget/>.

Table 460. **Federal Budget Outlays by Agency: 1990 to 2009**

[In billions of dollars (1,253.1 represents $1,253,100,000,000). For years ending September 30]

Department or other unit	1990	2000	2005	2006	2007	2008	2009, est.
Outlays, total [1]	1,253.1	1,789.2	2,472.2	2,655.4	2,728.9	2,982.9	3,997.8
Legislative Branch.	2.2	2.9	4.0	4.1	4.3	4.4	4.9
The Judiciary Branch	1.6	4.1	5.5	5.8	6.0	6.3	6.8
Agriculture	45.9	75.1	85.3	93.5	84.4	90.8	116.2
Commerce	3.7	7.8	6.1	6.4	6.5	7.7	11.8
Defense—Military	289.7	281.1	474.4	499.4	528.6	594.7	665.0
Education	23.0	33.5	72.9	93.4	66.4	66.0	49.7
Energy	12.1	15.0	21.3	19.6	20.1	21.4	29.3
Health and Human Services	175.5	382.3	581.5	614.3	672.0	700.5	817.8
Homeland Security	7.2	13.2	38.7	69.1	39.2	40.7	49.2
Housing and Urban Development.	20.2	30.8	42.5	42.4	45.6	49.1	65.1
Interior	5.8	8.0	9.3	9.1	10.5	9.9	11.5
Justice	5.9	16.8	22.4	23.3	23.3	26.5	29.0
Labor	26.1	31.9	46.9	43.1	47.5	58.8	121.9
State.	4.8	6.7	12.7	13.0	13.7	17.5	22.4
Transportation	25.6	41.6	56.6	60.1	61.7	64.9	79.7
Treasury	253.9	390.5	410.2	464.7	490.6	548.8	1,032.4
Veterans Affairs.	29.0	47.1	69.8	69.8	72.8	84.8	96.5
Corps of Engineers	3.3	4.2	4.7	6.9	3.9	5.1	12.6
Other Defense—Civil Programs	21.7	32.9	43.5	44.4	47.1	45.8	48.5
Environmental Protection Agency	5.1	7.2	7.9	8.3	8.3	7.9	8.4
Executive Office of the President	0.2	0.3	7.7	5.4	3.0	1.2	0.8
International Assistance Programs	10.1	12.1	15.0	13.9	12.8	11.4	13.6
National Aeronautics and Space Administration. . .	12.4	13.4	15.6	15.1	15.9	17.8	19.6
National Science Foundation	1.8	3.5	5.4	5.5	5.5	5.8	6.7
Office of Personnel Management	31.9	48.7	59.5	62.4	58.4	64.4	68.5
Social Security Administration (on-budget)	17.3	45.1	54.6	53.3	54.9	58.6	78.6
Social Security Administration (off-budget)	245.0	396.2	506.8	532.5	566.8	599.2	646.4
Undistributed offsetting receipts	–98.9	–173.0	–226.2	–237.5	–260.2	–277.8	–277.5

[1] Includes other agencies, not shown separately.

Source: U.S. Office of Management and Budget, *Budget of the United States Government, Historical Tables*, annual. See also <http://www.whitehouse.gov/omb/budget/>.

Federal Government Finances and Employment   305

Table 461. **Federal Outlays by Detailed Function: 1990 to 2009**

[In billions of dollars (1,253.1 represents $1,253,100,000,000). For years ending September 30. Minus sign (–) indicates decrease.]

Superfunction and function	1990	2000	2004	2005	2006	2007	2008	2009, est.
Total outlays	1,253.1	1,789.2	2,293.0	2,472.2	2,655.4	2,728.9	2,982.9	3,997.8
National defense [1]	299.3	294.4	455.8	495.3	521.8	551.3	616.1	690.3
Department of Defense-Military	289.7	281.1	436.5	474.1	499.3	528.6	594.7	665.0
Military personnel	75.6	76.0	113.6	127.5	127.5	127.5	138.9	146.8
Operation and maintenance	88.3	105.8	174.0	188.1	203.8	216.6	244.8	271.8
Procurement	81.0	51.7	76.2	82.3	89.8	99.6	117.4	142.7
Research, development, test, and evaluation	37.5	37.6	60.8	65.7	68.6	73.1	75.1	78.2
Military construction	5.1	5.1	6.3	5.3	6.2	7.9	11.6	20.0
Atomic energy defense activities	9.0	12.1	16.6	18.0	17.5	17.1	17.1	18.5
International affairs [1]	13.8	17.2	26.9	34.6	29.5	28.5	28.9	34.7
International development and humanitarian assistance	5.5	6.5	13.8	17.7	16.7	15.5	14.1	18.3
International security assistance	8.7	6.4	8.4	7.9	7.8	8.0	9.5	10.0
Conduct of foreign affairs	3.1	4.7	7.9	9.1	8.6	8.4	10.4	12.8
General science, space, and technology	14.4	18.6	23.1	23.6	23.6	25.6	27.8	31.2
General science and basic research	2.8	6.2	8.4	8.9	9.1	10.3	10.6	12.3
Space flight, research, and supporting activities	11.6	12.4	14.6	14.8	14.5	15.3	17.2	18.8
Energy	3.3	–0.8	–0.2	0.4	0.8	–0.9	0.6	8.8
Energy supply	2.0	–1.8	–1.6	–0.9	0.2	–2.0	–0.4	3.3
Natural resources and environment [1]	17.1	25.0	30.7	28.0	33.1	31.8	31.9	42.2
Water resources	4.4	5.1	5.6	5.7	8.0	5.1	6.1	13.8
Conservation and land management	4.0	6.8	9.8	6.2	7.8	9.6	8.7	10.6
Recreational resources	1.4	2.6	3.0	3.0	3.1	3.0	3.3	3.4
Pollution control and abatement	5.2	7.4	8.5	8.1	8.6	8.4	8.1	8.7
Agriculture	11.8	36.5	15.4	26.6	26.0	17.7	18.4	20.4
Farm income stabilization	9.7	33.4	11.2	22.0	21.4	13.1	13.8	15.8
Agricultural research and services	2.1	3.0	4.3	4.5	4.6	4.6	4.6	4.6
Commerce and housing credit [1]	67.6	3.2	5.3	7.6	6.2	0.5	27.9	758.2
Mortgage credit	3.8	–3.3	2.7	–0.9	–0.6	–5.0	0.0	109.6
Postal service	2.1	2.1	–4.1	–1.2	–1.0	–3.2	–3.1	–1.5
Deposit insurance	57.9	–3.1	–2.0	–1.4	–1.1	–1.5	18.8	120.3
Transportation [1]	29.5	46.9	64.6	67.9	70.2	72.9	77.6	94.3
Ground transportation	19.0	31.7	40.7	42.3	45.2	46.8	50.0	62.4
Air transportation	7.2	10.6	16.7	18.8	18.0	18.1	19.4	21.8
Water transportation	3.2	4.4	6.9	6.4	6.7	7.7	8.1	9.5
Community and regional development [1]	8.5	10.6	15.8	26.3	54.5	29.6	24.0	28.0
Community development	3.5	5.5	6.2	5.9	5.8	11.8	10.2	10.4
Disaster relief and insurance	2.1	2.6	7.3	17.7	46.1	15.2	11.2	13.8
Education, training, employment, and social services [1]	37.2	53.8	88.0	97.6	118.6	91.7	91.3	79.3
Elementary, secondary, and vocational education	9.9	20.6	34.4	38.3	39.7	38.4	38.9	45.6
Higher education	11.1	10.1	25.3	31.4	50.5	24.6	23.6	–0.2
Research and general education aids	1.6	2.6	3.0	3.1	3.1	3.2	3.2	3.6
Training and employment	5.6	6.8	7.9	6.9	7.2	7.1	7.2	8.9
Social services	8.1	12.6	15.9	16.3	16.5	16.7	16.8	19.7
Health	57.7	154.5	240.1	250.6	252.8	266.4	280.6	353.4
Health care services	47.6	136.2	210.1	219.6	220.8	233.9	247.8	315.8
Health research and training	8.6	16.0	27.1	28.1	28.8	29.3	29.9	33.7
Consumer and occupational health and safety	1.5	2.3	2.9	2.9	3.1	3.2	3.0	3.9
Medicare	98.1	197.1	269.4	298.6	329.9	375.4	390.8	430.8
Income security [1]	148.7	253.7	333.1	345.8	352.5	366.0	431.3	519.3
General retirement and disability insurance (excluding social security)	5.1	5.2	6.6	7.0	4.6	7.8	8.9	8.0
Federal employee retirement and disability	52.0	77.2	88.7	93.4	98.3	103.9	109.0	115.9
Unemployment compensation	18.9	23.0	45.0	35.4	33.8	35.1	45.3	106.5
Housing assistance	15.9	28.9	36.8	37.9	38.3	39.7	40.6	53.3
Food and nutrition assistance	24.0	32.5	46.0	50.8	53.9	54.5	60.7	80.1
Social security	248.6	409.4	495.5	523.3	548.5	586.2	617.0	680.5
Veterans benefits and services [1]	29.1	47.1	59.8	70.2	69.8	72.8	84.7	96.7
Income security for veterans	15.3	24.9	30.8	35.8	35.8	35.7	41.3	46.5
Veterans education, training, and rehabilitation	0.2	1.3	2.6	2.8	2.6	2.7	2.7	4.5
Hospital and medical care for veterans	12.1	19.5	26.9	28.8	29.9	32.3	37.0	41.3
Veterans housing	0.5	0.4	–2.0	0.9	–1.2	–0.9	–0.4	–0.4
Administration of justice	10.2	28.5	45.6	40.0	41.0	41.2	47.1	53.3
Federal law enforcement activities	4.8	12.1	19.1	19.9	20.0	19.6	24.6	28.2
Federal litigative and judicial activities	3.6	7.8	9.7	9.6	10.1	11.0	11.8	12.2
Federal correctional activities	1.3	3.7	5.5	5.9	6.2	6.3	6.9	7.0
Criminal justice assistance	0.5	4.9	11.3	4.6	4.8	4.3	3.9	6.0
General government	10.5	13.0	22.3	17.0	18.2	17.4	20.3	21.9
Net interest [1]	184.3	222.9	160.2	184.0	226.6	237.1	252.8	142.7
Interest on Treasury debt securities (gross)	264.7	361.9	321.7	352.3	405.9	430.0	451.1	392.3
Interest received by on-budget trust funds	–46.3	–69.3	–67.8	–69.2	–71.6	–72.0	–77.8	–68.0
Interest received by off-budget trust funds	–16.0	–59.8	–86.2	–91.8	–97.7	–106.0	–113.7	–117.8
Allowances	–	–	–	–	–	–	–	3.6
Undistributed offsetting receipts	–36.6	–42.6	–58.5	–65.2	–68.3	–82.2	–86.2	–91.7

– Represents or rounds to zero.   [1] Includes functions not shown separately.

Source: U.S. Office of Management and Budget, *Budget of the United States Government, Historical Tables,* annual. See also <http://www.whitehouse.gov/omb/budget/>.

U.S. Census Bureau, Statistical Abstract of the United States: 2010

Table 462. **Outlays for Payments for Individuals by Category and Major Program: 1990 to 2009**

[In billions of dollars (585.7 represents 585,700,000,000). For fiscal years ending September 30]

Category and program	1990	2000	2004	2005	2006	2007	2008	2009, est.
Total, payments for individuals.	585.7	1,054.5	1,397.8	1,490.7	1,592.7	1,690.3	1,825.7	2,091.3
Social security and railroad retirement.	250.5	410.5	496.4	523.4	554.5	586.7	617.4	678.4
Social security:								
Old age and survivors insurance	221.9	351.4	414.8	434.0	457.7	483.3	506.6	559.3
Disability insurance	24.4	54.4	76.5	84.2	91.2	97.5	104.7	114.9
Railroad retirement (excl. social security)	4.1	4.6	5.2	5.3	5.6	5.8	6.1	4.2
Federal employees retirement and insurance.	64.1	100.3	117.4	126.7	132.1	137.8	148.0	159.3
Military retirement	21.5	32.8	37.0	39.0	41.1	43.5	45.8	48.7
Civil service retirement	31.0	45.1	52.1	54.7	57.8	60.9	63.5	67.1
Veterans service-connected compensation	10.7	20.8	26.3	30.9	31.0	31.1	36.3	41.0
Other.	0.8	1.7	2.0	2.2	2.2	2.4	2.5	2.6
Unemployment assistance	17.4	21.1	43.1	33.1	31.9	33.2	43.4	104.3
Medical care.	164.3	362.7	515.4	562.5	606.0	682.5	715.1	827.3
Medicare:								
Hospital insurance	65.9	127.9	164.1	182.8	183.9	205.0	223.8	242.5
Supplementary medical insurance	41.5	87.2	131.8	151.0	191.7	230.1	231.1	255.4
State children's health insurance	−	1.2	4.6	5.1	5.5	6.0	6.9	8.6
Medicaid	41.1	117.9	176.2	181.7	180.6	190.6	201.4	262.4
Indian health.	1.1	2.4	3.1	3.1	3.3	3.3	3.3	4.0
Hospital and medical care for veterans.	12.0	19.3	21.6	23.1	24.4	30.5	31.1	34.0
Health resources and services	1.4	3.9	5.5	5.9	6.1	5.9	6.3	6.1
Substance abuse and mental health services	1.2	2.5	3.1	3.2	3.2	3.2	3.1	3.4
Health care tax credit	−	−	0.1	0.1	0.1	0.1	0.1	0.2
Uniformed Services retiree health care fund	−	−	5.2	6.3	7.1	7.6	7.9	8.7
Other.	(Z)	0.3	0.1	0.2	0.2	0.2	0.2	2.1
Assistance to students	11.2	10.9	25.7	32.1	51.7	31.0	31.1	30.7
Veterans education benefits	0.8	1.6	2.4	3.2	3.3	3.4	3.6	5.1
Student assistance, Department of Education and other	10.4	9.2	23.3	28.9	48.4	27.5	27.5	25.6
Housing assistance	15.9	24.1	30.8	31.8	32.1	33.0	33.4	45.4
Food and nutrition assistance	23.9	32.4	45.9	50.7	53.8	54.3	60.5	79.9
Food stamp program (including Puerto Rico)	15.9	18.3	28.6	32.6	34.6	34.9	39.3	56.1
Child nutrition and special milk programs	5.0	9.2	11.2	11.9	12.4	13.0	13.9	15.6
Supplemental feeding programs (WIC [1] and CSFP [2])	2.1	4.0	4.9	5.0	5.1	5.3	6.2	7.0
Commodity donations and other	0.8	0.9	1.2	1.2	1.7	1.1	1.1	1.3
Public assistance and related programs. . . .	34.9	88.3	111.5	123.3	125.1	126.3	168.6	157.2
Supplemental security income program	11.5	29.5	31.2	35.3	34.3	32.8	38.0	41.2
Family support payments to states and TANF [3].	12.2	18.4	21.5	21.3	20.9	21.1	21.8	23.1
Low income home energy assistance . . .	1.3	1.5	1.9	2.1	2.6	2.5	2.7	4.3
Earned income tax credit.	4.4	26.1	33.1	34.6	36.2	38.3	40.6	41.5
Legal services.	0.3	0.3	0.3	0.3	0.3	0.3	0.3	0.4
Payments to states for daycare assistance	−	3.3	4.8	4.9	5.3	5.1	5.0	5.8
Veterans non-service-connected pensions.	3.6	3.0	3.3	3.7	3.5	3.4	3.8	4.0
Payments to states for foster care/adoption assistance	1.6	5.5	6.3	6.4	6.4	6.6	6.8	7.1
Payment where child credit exceeds tax liability.	−	0.8	8.9	14.6	15.5	16.2	34.0	23.2
Other public assistance.	−	−	−	(Z)	0.1	0.1	15.6	5.3
All other payments for individuals	3.5	4.3	11.5	7.1	5.6	5.6	8.1	8.7
Coal miners and black lung benefits	1.5	1.0	0.8	0.7	0.7	0.6	0.6	3.1
Veterans insurance and burial benefits. . .	1.4	1.4	1.4	1.4	1.4	1.3	1.4	1.4
D.C. employee retirement	−	0.4	0.5	2.2	0.5	0.5	0.5	0.5
Aging services programs	−	0.9	1.3	1.4	1.4	1.4	1.4	1.5
Energy employees compensation fund. . .	−	−	0.3	0.6	0.9	1.0	1.1	1.0
September 11th victim compensation. . . .	−	−	6.3	(Z)	(Z)	−	−	−
Refugee assistance and other	0.6	0.6	0.9	0.8	0.8	0.8	3.2	1.2

− Represents zero.   Z Less than $50,000,000.   [1] WIC means Women, Infants, and Children.   [2] CSFP means Commodity Supplemental Food Program.   [3] TANF means Temporary Assistance for Needy Families.

Source: U.S. Office of Management and Budget, *Budget of the United States Government, Historical Tables*, annual. See also <http://www.whitehouse.gov/omb/budget/>.

Federal Government Finances and Employment   307

Table 463. **Federal Budget Receipts by Source: 1990 to 2009**

[In billions of dollars (1,032.1 represents $1,032,100,000,000). For years ending September 30. Receipts reflect collections. Covers both federal funds and trust funds; see text, this section]

Source	1990	2000	2004	2005	2006	2007	2008	2009, est.
Total federal receipts	1,032.1	2,025.5	1,880.3	2,153.9	2,407.3	2,568.2	2,524.3	2,156.7
Individual income taxes.	466.9	1,004.5	809.0	927.2	1,043.9	1,163.5	1,145.7	953.0
Corporation income taxes	93.5	207.3	189.4	278.3	353.9	370.2	304.3	146.8
Social insurance and retirement receipts . . .	380.0	652.9	733.4	794.1	837.8	869.6	900.2	899.2
Excise taxes.	35.3	68.9	69.9	73.1	74.0	65.1	67.3	66.3
Other.	56.3	92.0	78.7	81.1	97.6	99.8	106.7	91.4
Social insurance and retirement receipts	**380.0**	**652.9**	**733.4**	**794.1**	**837.8**	**869.6**	**900.2**	**899.2**
Employment and general retirement	353.9	620.5	689.4	747.7	790.0	824.3	856.5	850.7
Old-age and survivors insurance (off-budget)	255.0	411.7	457.1	493.6	520.1	542.9	562.5	559.8
Disability insurance (off-budget)	26.6	68.9	77.6	83.8	88.3	92.2	95.5	95.0
Hospital insurance	68.6	135.5	150.6	166.1	177.4	184.9	194.0	191.5
Railroad retirement/pension fund.	2.3	2.7	2.3	2.3	2.3	2.3	2.4	2.4
Unemployment insurance funds	21.6	27.6	39.5	42.0	43.4	41.1	39.5	44.0
Other retirement	4.5	4.8	4.6	4.5	4.4	4.3	4.2	4.5
Federal employees retirement-employee share	4.4	4.7	4.5	4.4	4.3	4.2	4.1	4.4
Excise taxes, total	**35.3**	**68.9**	**69.9**	**73.1**	**74.0**	**65.1**	**67.3**	**66.3**
Federal funds [1]	15.6	22.7	24.6	22.5	22.5	11.1	15.7	16.1
Alcohol	5.7	8.1	8.1	8.1	8.5	8.6	9.3	9.1
Tobacco	4.1	7.2	7.9	7.9	7.7	7.6	7.6	12.7
Telephone	3.0	5.7	6.0	6.0	4.9	−2.1	1.0	1.0
Transportation fuels	−	0.8	1.4	−0.8	−2.4	−3.3	−5.1	−6.0
Trust funds [1]	19.8	46.2	45.3	50.5	51.5	54.0	51.6	50.1
Highway	13.9	35.0	34.7	37.9	38.5	39.4	36.4	36.0
Airport and airway	3.7	9.7	9.2	10.3	10.4	11.5	12.0	11.3
Black lung disability	0.7	0.5	0.6	0.6	0.6	0.6	0.7	0.4
Inland waterway	0.1	0.1	0.1	0.1	0.1	0.1	0.1	0.1
Oil spill liability	0.1	0.2	−	−	0.1	0.5	0.3	0.5
Aquatic resources	0.2	0.3	0.4	0.4	0.5	0.6	0.6	0.6
Tobacco assessments	−	−	−	0.9	0.9	0.9	1.1	1.0
Vaccine injury compensation.	0.2	0.1	0.1	0.1	0.2	0.2	0.3	0.2

− Represents zero.   [1] Includes other funds, not shown separately.

Source: U.S. Office of Management and Budget, *Budget of the United States Government, Historical Tables,* annual. See also <http://www.whitehouse.gov/omb/budget/>.

Table 464. **Federal Trust Fund Income, Outlays, and Balances: 2008 to 2010**

[In billions of dollars (12.5 represents $12,500,000,000). For years ending September 30. Receipts deposited. Outlays on a checks–issued basis less refunds collected. Balances: That which have not been spent. See text, this section, for discussion of the budget concept and trust funds]

Description	Income			Outlays			Balances [1]		
	2008	2009, est.	2010, est.	2008	2009, est.	2010, est.	2008	2009, est.	2010, est.
Airport and airway trust fund.	12.5	11.7	12.1	12.9	11.9	12.9	9.7	9.5	8.8
Federal civilian employees' retirement funds	90.9	95.7	98.2	63.7	67.2	69.9	728.9	757.3	785.6
Federal employees' health benefits fund. . .	35.3	37.6	40.6	35.6	37.7	40.5	15.5	15.4	15.6
Foreign military sales trust fund	21.8	24.0	21.6	17.2	19.6	21.6	14.2	18.5	18.6
Highway trust fund	44.5	36.4	37.8	43.1	47.8	40.2	16.8	5.4	3.0
Medicare:									
Hospital insurance (HI) trust fund.	234.8	234.3	239.9	226.8	245.8	254.9	318.9	307.4	292.4
Supplemental medical insurance trust fund	249.6	264.0	278.2	238.0	258.6	279.9	59.1	64.5	62.8
Military retirement fund	80.8	75.0	102.4	45.8	48.7	49.7	250.9	277.2	330.0
Railroad retirement trust funds	3.0	2.9	9.8	10.4	10.9	11.1	23.3	15.3	14.0
Social security: Old–age, survivors and disability insurance trust funds	802.8	807.8	839.9	617.2	667.4	701.7	2,366.4	2,506.9	2,645.0
Unemployment trust funds	43.9	60.0	67.5	46.7	103.8	89.2	73.5	29.8	23.6
Veterans' life insurance trust funds	1.2	1.1	1.0	1.6	1.7	1.6	11.5	10.9	10.3
Other trust funds	26.2	33.4	27.9	22.1	26.3	25.1	64.4	71.5	74.4

[1] Balances available on a cash basis (rather than an authorization basis) at the end of the year. Balances are primarily invested in federal debt securities.

Source: U.S. Office of Management and Budget, *Budget of the United States Government, Analytical Perspectives,* annual. See also <http://www.whitehouse.gov/omb/budget/>.

Table 465. **Tax Expenditures Estimates Relating to Individual and Corporate Income Taxes by Selected Function: 2008 to 2011**

[In millions of dollars (11,190 represents $11,190,000,000). For years ending September 30. Tax expenditures are defined as revenue losses attributable to provisions of the federal tax laws which allow a special exclusion, exemption, or deduction from gross income or which provide a special credit, a preferential rate of tax, or a deferral of liability. Minus sign (–) indicates decrease]

Function and provision	2008	2009	2010	2011
National Defense:				
Exclusion of benefits and allowances to armed forces personnel	11,190	11,710	10,210	10,550
International affairs:				
Exclusion of income earned abroad by U.S. citizens	5,070	5,320	5,590	5,870
Deferral of income from controlled foreign corporations (normal tax method)	31,580	30,960	32,720	33,870
Deferred taxes for financial firms on certain income earned overseas	5,570	5,460	5,770	5,980
General science, space, and technology:				
Expensing of research and experimentation expenditures (normal tax method)	5,180	3,820	3,500	4,560
Credit for increasing research activities	7,440	8,010	5,880	3,850
Energy:				
Alternative fuel production credit.	590	70	80	10
Commerce and housing:				
Financial institutions and insurance:				
Exclusion of interest on life insurance savings.	21,190	22,790	24,450	26,770
Housing:				
Deductibility of mortgage interest on owner-occupied homes	88,500	97,280	107,980	119,750
Deductibility of state and local property tax on owner-occupied homes.	29,130	20,850	14,980	24,550
Capital gains exclusion on home sales.	30,090	27,980	30,460	39,530
Exclusion of net imputed rental income	1,720	5,850	2,200	2,230
Exception from passive loss rules for $25,000 of rental loss.	8,430	8,840	9,160	9,580
Credit for low-income housing investments	3,210	3,750	4,340	4,920
Accelerated depreciation on rental housing (normal tax method).	9,690	10,150	10,770	13,620
Commerce:				
Capital gains (except agriculture, timber, iron ore, and coal).	24,240	23,640	28,920	24,840
Step-up basis of capital gains at death.	21,590	19,530	20,830	25,210
Accelerated depreciation of machinery and equipment (normal tax method)	55,890	–11,140	–3,820	–1,190
Expensing of certain small investments (normal tax method)	930	90	910	–3,400
Graduated corporation income tax rate (normal tax method)	2,460	2,460	2,880	3,090
Deduction for U.S. production activities	10,660	10,820	14,140	16,890
Transportation:				
Exclusion of reimbursed employee parking expenses.	2,920	3,000	3,120	3,270
Education, training, employment, and social services:				
Education:				
HOPE tax credit.	3,770	3,800	3,890	4,650
Lifetime Learning tax credit	2,470	2,460	2,510	2,980
Exclusion of interest on bonds for private nonprofit educational facilities.	860	1,870	1,960	2,110
Parental personal exemption for students age 19 years or over	4,690	2,670	1,660	2,680
Deductibility of charitable contributions (education).	4,330	4,880	5,270	5,670
Training, employment, and social services:				
Child credit.	28,420	27,250	27,032	20,250
Credit for child and dependent care expenses.	3,020	3,670	2,070	1,920
Deductibility of charitable contributions, other than education and health	38,200	43,370	46,980	50,550
Health:				
Exclusion of employer contributions for medical insurance premiums [1]	131,080	142,010	155,050	169,190
Self-employed medical insurance premiums.	5,080	5,470	6,020	6,680
Deductibility of medical expenses.	9,320	9,660	10,760	12,540
Exclusion of interest on hospital construction bonds.	1,350	2,940	3,070	3,310
Deductibility of charitable contributions (health).	4,310	4,890	5,300	5,700
Income security:				
Exclusion of workers compensation benefits.	5,830	5,920	6,010	6,110
Net exclusion of pension contributions and earnings:				
Employer plans	46,120	45,670	44,370	42,420
401(k) plans	47,000	50,000	53,000	66,000
Individual Retirement Accounts.	11,700	12,700	13,500	14,800
Keogh plans	12,000	13,000	14,000	15,000
Exclusion of other employee benefits:				
Premiums on group term life insurance	2,230	2,250	2,320	2,460
Earned income tax credit.	5,380	5,740	6,130	6,390
Social security:				
Exclusion of social security benefits:				
Social security benefits for retired workers	19,700	20,610	19,330	20,420
Social security benefits for disabled.	5,420	5,770	5,840	6,230
Social security benefits for dependents and survivors	3,570	3,610	3,280	3,350
Veterans' benefits and services:				
Exclusion of veterans' death benefits and disability compensation	3,870	3,950	4,140	4,480
General purpose fiscal assistance:				
Exclusion of interest on public purpose state and local bonds	11,110	24,610	25,730	27,820
Deductibility of nonbusiness state and local taxes other than on				
owner-occupied homes.	49,140	36,270	30,290	48,750
Addendum: Aid to state and local governments:				
Deductibility of:				
Property taxes on owner-occupied homes	29,130	20,850	14,980	24,550
Nonbusiness state and local taxes other than on owner-occupied homes	49,140	36,270	30,290	48,750
Exclusion of interest on State and local bonds for:				
Public purposes.	11,110	24,610	25,730	27,820
Private nonprofit educational facilities.	860	1,870	1,960	2,110
Hospital construction.	1,350	2,940	3,070	3,310

[1] Includes medical care.

Source: U.S. Office of Management and Budget, *Budget of the United States Government, Analytical Perspectives,* annual. See also <http://www.whitehouse.gov/omb/budget/>.

Federal Government Finances and Employment 309

Table 466. **U.S. Savings Bonds: 1990 to 2008**

[In billions of dollars (122.5 represents $122,500,000,000), except percent. As of September 30]

Item	1990	1995	2000	2001	2002	2003	2004	2005	2006	2007	2008
Amounts outstanding, total [1]	122.5	181.5	177.7	179.5	185.5	192.6	194.1	189.9	189.2	181.5	177.8
Sales	7.8	7.2	5.6	8.0	12.5	13.2	10.3	6.5	8.5	3.6	3.6
Accrued discounts	8.0	9.5	6.9	8.4	7.7	7.3	6.9	6.7	7.5	7.2	7.1
Redemptions [2]	7.5	11.8	14.5	13.8	12.5	12.2	14.6	13.8	16.0	10.8	10.7
Percent of total outstanding. . .	6.1	6.5	8.2	7.7	6.7	6.3	7.5	7.3	8.5	6.0	6.0

[1] Interest-bearing debt only for amounts at end of year.   [2] Matured and unmatured bonds.

Source: U.S. Department of the Treasury, Bureau of Public Debt; <http://www.treasurydirect.gov/govt/reports/pd/pd_sbntables_downloadable_files.htm> (accessed January 2009).

Table 467. **Federal Funds—Summary Distribution by State: 2007**

[In millions of dollars (2,556,213 represents $2,556,213,000,000), except as indicated. For year ending Sept. 30. Data for grants, salaries and wages, and direct payments to individuals are on an expenditures basis; procurement data are on an obligation basis]

State and Island area	Federal funds		Agency		Object category			
	Total	Per capita [1] (dol.)	Defense	Non-defense	Direct payments	Procure-ment	Grants	Salaries and wages
United States [2]	**2,556,213**	**8,195**	**430,466**	**2,125,748**	**1,367,400**	**440,377**	**495,842**	**252,594**
Alabama.	47,889	9,571	11,474	36,416	26,085	10,596	7,734	3,474
Alaska	9,378	13,654	3,309	6,069	1,994	2,340	2,996	2,048
Arizona.	48,012	7,519	11,756	36,256	23,932	10,519	9,368	4,193
Arkansas	22,454	7,655	1,799	20,655	14,336	1,236	5,108	1,773
California	260,422	7,006	47,433	212,989	132,777	45,720	57,636	24,289
Colorado.	34,828	7,222	7,487	27,341	16,840	6,740	6,149	5,098
Connecticut.	32,378	8,756	9,299	23,079	15,502	9,306	5,715	1,855
Delaware	6,234	6,862	716	5,518	3,853	410	1,387	584
District of Columbia	43,475	68,938	5,636	37,839	5,131	14,722	5,881	17,742
Florida	147,091	7,905	20,255	126,835	98,123	15,757	21,411	11,800
Georgia	71,079	6,910	15,160	55,919	35,082	14,197	12,391	9,407
Hawaii	14,062	10,555	5,467	8,595	5,664	2,328	2,452	3,617
Idaho	10,946	6,797	787	10,159	5,500	2,154	2,226	1,066
Illinois	88,669	6,443	7,656	81,013	54,244	8,969	17,925	7,531
Indiana.	47,254	6,939	7,074	40,180	28,956	6,687	8,833	2,779
Iowa	21,649	7,344	1,623	20,026	14,080	1,929	4,239	1,401
Kansas.	22,737	7,809	3,901	18,835	12,780	3,375	3,754	2,827
Kentucky	35,927	8,945	5,527	30,399	20,229	4,752	6,890	4,057
Louisiana	43,036	16,357	4,474	38,562	20,897	4,577	14,617	2,945
Maine.	11,850	8,350	2,134	9,715	6,369	1,655	2,807	1,019
Maryland	70,617	12,256	14,911	55,706	28,743	21,103	9,302	11,469
Massachusetts.	61,028	8,944	11,272	49,756	30,691	11,949	14,391	3,996
Michigan.	71,652	6,665	6,352	65,299	45,911	7,765	13,848	4,127
Minnesota.	40,075	6,189	2,694	37,382	26,393	3,112	7,875	2,695
Mississippi	30,616	14,574	6,438	24,178	14,447	6,555	7,408	2,207
Missouri	55,564	8,952	12,536	43,028	28,771	12,342	9,505	4,946
Montana.	8,497	8,464	673	7,824	4,669	570	2,228	1,031
Nebraska	13,986	7,895	1,605	12,381	8,786	1,040	2,724	1,436
Nevada	15,474	5,859	2,055	13,419	8,753	2,133	2,980	1,608
New Hampshire	9,764	6,763	1,724	8,040	5,318	1,887	1,813	745
New Jersey.	63,972	7,070	8,345	55,627	38,277	8,541	12,326	4,828
New Mexico	22,418	10,784	2,578	19,840	8,362	6,773	4,991	2,291
New York	157,789	7,932	10,265	147,525	87,285	11,738	48,136	10,630
North Carolina	65,863	6,992	10,169	55,694	37,762	5,133	14,169	8,799
North Dakota.	6,766	9,903	1,000	5,766	3,713	688	1,449	915
Ohio	105,214	7,044	8,920	96,293	72,696	8,984	17,475	6,058
Oklahoma.	30,686	8,130	4,928	25,759	17,668	2,853	6,326	3,838
Oregon.	25,242	6,391	1,863	23,379	15,506	1,830	5,794	2,113
Pennsylvania.	117,151	8,324	13,872	103,279	74,492	14,483	20,856	7,321
Rhode Island.	9,077	8,255	1,055	8,022	5,158	658	2,384	876
South Carolina.	37,056	7,813	7,317	29,739	20,129	6,647	6,465	3,815
South Dakota	8,280	10,135	741	7,540	5,294	630	1,516	841
Tennessee	51,456	8,329	4,754	46,702	28,945	9,562	9,888	3,062
Texas.	171,766	7,119	42,146	129,620	84,864	39,276	29,458	18,168
Utah	17,158	6,090	4,304	12,854	7,394	3,957	3,397	2,411
Vermont	5,579	8,496	950	4,629	2,696	932	1,490	461
Virginia.	110,105	13,489	48,323	61,782	38,247	45,391	9,195	17,272
Washington	52,455	7,602	10,605	41,850	26,601	9,219	9,693	6,942
West Virginia.	17,067	8,966	675	16,391	10,401	1,355	3,730	1,581
Wisconsin	38,177	6,197	4,121	34,056	23,969	4,445	7,543	2,220
Wyoming	5,355	10,082	549	4,806	2,251	504	2,000	600

[1] Based on U.S. Census Bureau estimated resident population as of July 1.   [2] Includes Island areas, not shown separately.

Source: U.S. Census Bureau, *Consolidated Federal Funds Report, 2007* (issued September 2008). See also <http://www.census.gov/govs/www/cffr/index.html>.

310   Federal Government Finances and Employment

Table 468. **Internal Revenue Gross Collections by Type of Tax: 2004 to 2008**

[2,019 represents $2,019,000,000,000. For years ending September 30. See text, this section, for information on taxes]

Type of tax	Gross collection (bil. dol.)					Percent of total				
	2004	2005	2006	2007	2008	2004	2005	2006	2007	2008
United States, total	2,019	2,269	2,519	2,692	2,745	100.0	100.0	100.0	100.0	100.0
Individual income taxes	990	1,108	1,236	1,366	1,426	49.1	48.8	49.1	50.8	52.0
Withheld by employers.	747	787	849	929	971	37.0	34.7	33.7	34.5	35.4
Employment taxes	717	771	815	850	883	35.5	34.0	32.4	31.6	32.2
Old-age and disability insurance . . .	706	760	803	838	871	35.0	33.5	31.9	31.1	31.7
Unemployment insurance	7	7	8	7	7	0.3	0.3	0.3	0.3	0.3
Railroad retirement	4	5	5	5	5	0.2	0.2	0.2	0.2	0.2
Corporation income taxes	231	307	381	396	354	11.4	13.5	15.1	14.7	12.9
Estate and gift taxes	26	26	29	27	30	1.3	1.1	1.1	1.0	1.1
Excise taxes	55	57	58	53	52	2.7	2.5	2.3	2.0	1.9

Source: U.S. Internal Revenue Service, *IRS Data Book,* annual (Publication 55B). See also <http://www.irs.gov/taxstats/article /0,,id=102174,00.html>.

Table 469. **Individual Income Tax Returns Filed—Examination Coverage: 1995 to 2008**

[114,683 represents 114,683,000. See the annual *IRS Data Book,* (Publication 55B), for a detailed explanation]

Year	Returns filed [1] (1,000)	Returns examined			Total recommended additional tax [3] ($1,000)	Average recommended additional tax per return (dollars)[3]
		Total [2] (1,000)	Percent coverage			
1995	114,683	1,919	1.7		7,756,954	4,041
1996	116,060	1,942	1.7		7,600,191	3,915
1997	118,363	1,519	1.3		8,363,918	5,505
1998	120,342	1,193	1.0		6,095,698	5,110
1999	122,547	1,100	0.9		4,458,474	4,052
2000	124,887	618	0.5		3,388,905	5,486
2001	127,097	732	0.6		3,301,860	4,512
2002	129,445	744	0.6		3,636,486	4,889
2003	130,341	849	0.7		4,559,902	5,369
2004	130,134	997	0.8		6,201,693	6,220
2005	130,577	1,199	0.0		13,355,007	11,138
2006	132,276	1,284	1.0		13,045,221	10,160
2007	134,543	1,385	1.0		15,705,155	11,343
2008	137,850	1,392	1.0		12,462,770	8,956

[1] Returns generally filed in previous calendar year.   [2] Includes taxpayer examinations by correspondence.   [3] For 1995 to 1997, amount includes associated penalties.

Source: U.S. Internal Revenue Service, *IRS Data Book,* annual (Publication 55B). See also <http://www.irs.gov/taxstats/article /0,,id=102174,00.html>.

Table 470. **Federal Individual Income Tax Returns—Adjusted Gross Income, Taxable Income, and Total Income Tax: 2005 and 2006**

[134,373 represents 134,373,000. For tax years. Based on a sample of returns, see source and Appendix III]

Item	2005		2006		Percent change in amount, 2005–06
	Number of returns (1,000)	Amount (mil. dol.)	Number of returns (1,000)	Amount (mil. dol.)	
Adjusted gross income (less deficit)	134,373	7,422,496	138,395	8,030,843	8.2
Exemptions [1]	269,043	839,904	275,257	891,912	6.2
Taxable income	104,331	5,137,166	106,667	5,579,145	8.6
Total income tax	90,593	934,836	92,741	1,023,920	9.5
Alternative minimum tax	4,005	17,421	3,967	21,565	23.8

[1] The number of returns columns represent the number of exemptions.

Source: U.S. Internal Revenue Service, *Statistics of Income Bulletin,* Fall issues.

Table 471. **Federal Individual Income Tax Returns—Adjusted Gross Income (AGI) by Selected Source of Income and Income Class: 2006**

[In millions of dollars (8,030,843 represents $8,030,843,000,000), except as indicated. For the tax year. Minus sign (–) indicates net loss was greater than net income. Based on sample; see Appendix III]

Item	Total [1]	Under $10,000	$10,000 to $19,999	$20,000 to $29,999	$30,000 to $39,999	$40,000 to $49,999	$50,000 to $99,999	$100,000 and over
Number of all returns (1,000)	138,395	26,096	22,649	18,662	14,152	10,687	29,995	16,153
Adjusted gross income [2]	8,030,843	27,801	337,396	463,115	492,158	478,796	2,119,228	4,112,350
Salaries and wages	5,469,370	113,482	255,089	381,074	408,124	389,321	1,670,502	2,251,778
Interest received	222,707	10,859	9,581	9,081	8,491	8,360	40,330	136,006
Dividends in AGI	199,359	4,954	4,582	4,449	4,174	5,242	27,885	148,074
Business, profession, net profit less loss	281,527	5,303	25,527	17,752	14,711	13,569	56,207	148,458
Sales of property, [3] net gain less loss	783,664	8,477	2,814	3,406	4,190	5,141	37,815	721,820
Pensions and annuities in AGI. . .	450,454	9,983	33,216	36,006	36,200	36,783	161,497	136,770
Rents and royalties, net income less loss [4]	466,088	–41,327	–129	588	1,435	1,485	20,514	483,522

[1] Includes a small number of returns with no adjusted gross income.   [2] Includes other sources, not shown separately.
[3] Includes sales of capital assets and other property; net gain less loss.   [4] Excludes rental passive losses disallowed in the computation of AGI; net income less loss.

Source: U.S. Internal Revenue Service, *Statistics of Income Bulletin*, Fall issues.

Table 472. **Federal Individual Income Tax Returns—Total and Selected Sources of Adjusted Gross Income: 2005 and 2006**

[134,373 represents 134,373,000. For tax years. Based on a sample of returns, see source and Appendix III. Minus sign (–) indicates decrease]

Item	2005 Number of returns (1,000)	2005 Amount (mil. dol.)	2006 Number of returns (1,000)	2006 Amount (mil. dol.)	Change in amount, 2005–06 Net change (mil. dol.)	Change in amount, 2005–06 Percent change
Adjusted gross income (less deficit) [1]	134,373	7,422,496	138,395	8,030,843	608,347	8.2
Salaries and wages	114,071	5,155,407	116,379	5,469,370	313,963	6.1
Taxable interest	59,249	162,433	62,401	222,707	60,275	37.1
Ordinary dividends	31,175	166,482	31,620	199,359	32,877	19.7
Qualified dividends	25,854	118,980	26,584	137,196	18,215	15.3
Business or profession net income (less loss) . .	21,057	269,701	21,656	281,527	11,826	4.4
Net capital gain	26,196	668,015	26,668	779,462	111,447	16.7
Capital gain distributions [2]	13,393	35,581	14,511	59,417	23,836	67.0
Sales of property other than capital assets, net gain (less loss)	1,777	3,663	1,779	4,202	539	14.7
Sales of property other than capital assets, net gain	901	12,843	895	14,021	1,177	9.2
Taxable social security benefits	12,661	124,829	13,749	144,404	19,575	15.7
Total rental and royalty net income (less net loss) [3]	9,949	28,237	9,988	23,427	–4,810	–17.0
Partnership and S corporation net income (less loss)	7,531	402,327	7,619	425,477	23,151	5.8
Estate and trust net income (less loss)	529	16,484	596	17,183	699	4.2
Farm net income (less loss)	1,981	–12,169	1,958	–15,331	–3,163	–26.0
Farm net income	611	8,484	552	7,684	–800	–9.4
Unemployment compensation	7,888	27,857	7,378	26,524	–1,334	–4.8
Taxable pensions and annuities	23,247	420,145	24,098	450,454	30,310	7.2
Taxable Individual Retirement Account distributions	9,387	112,277	9,965	124,706	12,428	11.1
Other net income (less loss) [4]	(NA)	26,863	(NA)	29,938	3,075	11.4
Gambling earnings	1,809	24,884	1,871	27,902	3,018	12.1

NA Not available.   [1] Includes sources of income not shown separately.   [2] Includes both Schedule D and non-Schedule D capital gain distributions.   [3] Includes farm rental net income (less loss).   [4] Other net income (less loss) represents data reported on Form 1040, line 21, except net operating loss, the foreign-earned income exclusion, and gambling earnings.

Source: U.S. Internal Revenue Service, *Statistics of Income Bulletin*, Fall issues.

U.S. Census Bureau, Statistical Abstract of the United States: 2010

Table 473. **Federal Individual Income Tax Returns—Net Capital Gains and Capital Gain Distributions From Mutual Funds: 1988 to 2006**

[14,309 represents 14,309,000. For tax years. Based on a sample of returns, see source and Appendix III. Minus sign (–) indicates decrease]

Tax year	Net capital gain (less loss)				Capital gain distributions [2]			
	Number of returns (1,000)	Current dollars (mil. dol.)	Constant (1982–1984) dollars [1]		Number of returns (1,000)	Current dollars (mil. dol.)	Constant (1982–1984) dollars [1]	
			Amount (mil. dol.)	Percent change			Amount (mil. dol.)	Percent change
1988	14,309	153,768	129,981	(X)	4,274	3,879	3,279	(X)
1989	15,060	145,631	117,444	–9.6	5,191	5,483	4,422	34.9
1990	14,288	114,231	87,400	–25.6	5,069	3,905	2,988	–32.4
1991	15,009	102,776	75,460	–13.7	5,796	4,665	3,425	14.6
1992	16,491	118,230	84,269	11.7	5,917	7,426	5,293	54.5
1993	18,409	144,172	99,773	18.4	9,998	11,995	8,301	56.8
1994	18,823	142,288	96,011	–3.8	9,803	11,322	7,640	–8.0
1995	19,963	170,415	111,821	16.5	10,744	14,391	9,443	23.6
1996	22,065	251,817	160,495	43.5	12,778	24,722	15,757	66.9
1997	24,240	356,083	221,859	38.2	14,969	45,132	28,120	78.5
1998	25,690	446,084	273,671	23.4	16,070	46,147	28,311	0.7
1999	27,701	542,758	325,785	19.0	17,012	59,473	35,698	26.1
2000	29,521	630,542	366,169	12.4	17,546	79,079	45,923	28.6
2001	25,956	326,527	184,375	–49.6	12,216	13,609	7,685	–83.3
2002	24,189	238,789	132,734	–28.0	7,567	5,343	2,970	–61.4
2003	22,985	294,354	159,975	20.5	7,265	4,695	2,552	–14.1
2004	25,267	473,662	250,747	56.7	10,733	15,336	8,119	218.1
2005	26,196	668,015	342,046	36.4	13,393	35,581	18,219	124.4
2006	26,668	779,462	386,638	13.0	14,511	59,417	29,473	61.8

X Not applicable. [1] Constant dollars were calculated using the U.S. Bureau of Labor Statistics consumer price index for urban consumers (CPI-U, 1982–84 = 100). See Table 709. [2] Capital gain distributions are included in net capital gain (less loss). For 1988–1996, and 1999 and later years, capital gain distributions from mutual funds are the sum of the amounts reported on the Form 1040 and Schedule D. For 1997 and 1998, capital gain distributions were reported entirely on the Schedule D.

Source: U.S. Internal Revenue Service, *Statistics of Income Bulletin,* Fall issues.

Table 474. **Alternative Minimum Tax: 1986 to 2006**

[609 represents 609,000. For tax years. Based on a sample of returns, see source and Appendix III]

Tax year	Highest statutory alternative minimum tax rate (percent)	Alternative minimum tax		Tax year	Highest statutory alternative minimum tax rate (percent)	Alternative minimum tax	
		Number of returns (1,000)	Amount (mil. dol.)			Number of returns (1,000)	Amount (mil. dol.)
1986	20	609	6,713				
1987	21	140	1,675	1997	28	618	4,005
1988	21	114	1,028	1998	[1]28	853	5,015
1989	21	117	831	1999	[1]28	1,018	6,478
1990	21	132	830	2000	[1]28	1,304	9,601
1991	24	244	1,213	2001	[1]28	1,120	6,757
1992	24	287	1,357	2002	[1]28	1,911	6,854
1993	28	335	2,053	2003	[1]28	2,358	9,470
1994	28	369	2,212	2004	[1]28	3,096	13,029
1995	28	414	2,291	2005	[1]28	4,005	17,421
1996	28	478	2,813	2006	[1]28	3,967	21,565

[1] Top rate on most long-term capital gains was 20 percent; beginning 2003, the rate was 15 percent.

Source: U.S. Internal Revenue Service, *Statistics of Income Bulletin,* Fall 2008, volume 28, no. 2. See also <http://www.irs.gov/taxstats/index.html>.

Federal Government Finances and Employment 313

Table 475. **Federal Individual Income Tax Returns— Sources of Net Losses Included in Adjusted Gross Income: 2004 to 2006**

[5,194 represents 5,194,000. For tax years. Based on a sample of returns, see source and Appendix III]

Item	2004 Number of returns (1,000)	2004 Amount (mil. dol.)	2005 Number of returns (1,000)	2005 Amount (mil. dol.)	2006 Number of returns (1,000)	2006 Amount (mil. dol.)
Total net losses.	(NA)	303,458	(NA)	319,587	(NA)	343,271
Business or profession net loss.	5,194	43,007	5,308	45,016	5,447	48,738
Net capital loss [1]	11,513	25,492	10,023	22,137	8,642	18,752
Net loss, sales of property other than capital assets.	892	7,971	877	9,180	884	9,819
Total rental and royalty net loss.	[2]4,380	38,466	4,554	43,988	4,658	49,927
Partnership and S corporation net loss. . . .	2,498	82,697	2,539	89,694	2,597	102,747
Estate and trust net loss	36	1,436	36	1,654	45	1,942
Farm net loss	1,416	20,610	1,371	20,653	1,406	23,015
Net operating loss [3]	830	75,012	863	79,452	917	80,796
Other net loss [4]	359	8,768	346	7,811	347	7,535

NA Not available.   [1] Includes only the portion of capital losses allowable in the calculation of adjusted gross income. Only $3,000 of net capital loss per return ($1,500 for married filing separately) are allowed to be included in negative total income. Any excess is carried forward to future years.   [2] Includes farm rental net loss.   [3] Net operating loss is a carryover of the loss from a business when taxable income from a prior year was less than zero.   [4] Other net loss represents losses reported on Form 1040, line 21, except net operating loss and the foreign-earned income exclusion.

Source: U.S. Internal Revenue Service, *Statistics of Income Bulletin,* Fall issues.

Table 476. **Federal Individual Income Tax Returns—Number, Income Tax, and Average Tax by Size of Adjusted Gross Income: 2000 and 2006**

[129,374 represents 129,374,000. Based on sample of returns; see Appendix III]

Size of adjusted gross income	Number of returns (1,000) 2000	Number of returns (1,000) 2006	Adjusted gross income (AGI) (bil. dol.) 2000	Adjusted gross income (AGI) (bil. dol.) 2006	Income tax total [1] (bil. dol.) 2000	Income tax total [1] (bil. dol.) 2006	Tax as percent of AGI (for taxable returns only) 2000	Tax as percent of AGI (for taxable returns only) 2006	Average tax (for taxable returns only) (dol.) 2000	Average tax (for taxable returns only) (dol.) 2006
Total	129,374	138,395	6,365	8,031	981	1,024	16	14	10,129	11,041
Less than $1,000 [2].	2,966	4,378	−58	−90	−	−	(NA)	(NA)	648	3,893
$1,000 to $2,999	5,385	4,822	11	10	−	−	7	3	134	61
$3,000 to $4,999	5,599	5,108	22	20	−	−	4	5	179	176
$5,000 to $6,999	5,183	4,780	31	−	1	−	5	2	297	110
$7,000 to $8,999	4,972	4,776	40	38	1	−	4	3	331	253
$9,000 to $10,999	5,089	4,458	51	45	1	−	5	2	470	245
$11,000 to $12,999. . . .	4,859	4,869	58	58	2	1	6	3	704	371
$13,000 to $14,999	4,810	4,614	67	65	3	1	6	4	883	540
$15,000 to $16,999	4,785	4,516	76	72	3	2	7	4	1,052	709
$17,000 to $18,999	4,633	4,343	83	78	4	2	7	5	1,279	881
$19,000 to $21,999	6,502	6,055	133	124	7	4	8	5	1,565	1,073
$22,000 to $24,999	5,735	5,936	135	139	8	5	8	6	1,815	1,382
$25,000 to $29,999	8,369	8,750	229	240	16	10	8	7	2,248	1,800
$30,000 to $39,999	13,548	14,152	471	492	40	27	9	7	3,094	2,446
$40,000 to $49,999	10,412	10,687	466	479	46	33	10	8	4,462	3,485
$50,000 to $74,999	17,076	18,855	1,045	1,158	116	94	11	9	6,824	5,300
$75,000 to $99,999	8,597	11,140	738	961	100	90	14	10	11,631	8,198
$100,000 to $199,999. . .	8,083	12,088	1,066	1,606	184	209	17	13	22,783	17,388
$200,000 to $499,999. . .	2,136	3,121	614	895	146	177	24	20	68,628	56,831
$500,000 to $999,999 . .	396	589	269	400	76	94	28	24	192,092	160,215
$1,000,000 or more	240	354	817	1,211	226	273	28	23	945,172	772,805

− Represents or rounds to zero.   NA Not available.   [1] Consists of income tax after credits (including alternative minimum tax).   [2] In addition to low income taxpayers, this size class (and others) includes taxpayers with "tax preferences," not reflected in adjusted gross income or taxable income which are subject to the "alternative minimum tax" (included in total income tax).

Source: U.S. Internal Revenue Service, *Statistics of Income Bulletin,* quarterly and Fall issues.

314   Federal Government Finances and Employment

Table 477. Federal Individual Income Tax Returns— Selected Itemized Deductions and the Standard Deduction: 2005 and 2006

[47,755 represents 47,755,000. For tax years. Based on a sample of returns, see source and Appendix III. Minus sign (–) indicates decrease]

Item	2005 Number of returns [1] (1,000)	2005 Amount (mil. dol.)	2006 Number of returns [1] (1,000)	2006 Amount (mil. dol.)	Percent change, 2005–06 Number of returns [1]	Percent change, 2005–06 Amount
Total itemized deductions before limitation	**47,755**	**1,167,135**	**49,124**	**1,264,390**	**2.9**	**8.3**
Medical and dental expenses after 7.5 percent AGI limitation	9,917	67,354	10,209	70,704	2.9	5.0
Taxes paid [2]	47,353	400,390	48,661	432,774	2.8	8.1
State and local income taxes	34,570	227,581	35,666	246,382	3.2	8.3
State and local general sales taxes	11,423	17,271	11,249	18,924	–1.5	9.6
Interest paid [3]	39,016	405,718	40,285	470,475	3.3	16.0
Home mortgage interest.	38,575	383,733	39,831	443,152	3.3	15.5
Charitable contributions [4].	41,381	183,391	41,438	186,647	0.1	1.8
Other than cash contributions	25,371	48,057	24,748	52,631	–2.5	9.5
Casualty and theft losses.	814	14,984	206	5,136	–74.7	–65.7
Miscellaneous deductions after 2-percent AGI limitation. .	12,407	76,183	12,314	76,666	–0.8	0.6
Total unlimited miscellaneous deductions	1,522	19,114	1,606	21,988	5.5	15.0
Itemized deductions in excess of limitation	6,323	45,324	6,789	35,152	7.4	–22.4
Total itemized deductions after limitation	**47,755**	**1,121,811**	**49,124**	**1,229,237**	**2.9**	**9.6**
Total standard deduction	**84,841**	**580,748**	**86,584**	**607,464**	**2.1**	**4.6**
Total deductions (after itemized deduction limitation)	**132,597**	**1,702,559**	**135,707**	**1,836,701**	**2.3**	**7.9**

[1] Returns with no adjusted gross income are excluded from the deduction counts. For this reason, the sum of the number of returns with total itemized deductions and the number of returns with total standard deduction is less than the total number of returns for all filers. [2] Includes real estate taxes, personal property taxes, and other taxes not shown separately. [3] Includes investment interest and deductible mortgage "points" not shown separately. [4] For more information, see Table 572.

Source: U.S. Internal Revenue Service, *Statistics of Income Bulletin,* Fall issues.

Table 478. Federal Individual Income Tax Returns—Statutory Adjustments: 2005 and 2006

[33,591 represents 33,591,000. For tax years. Based on a sample of returns, see source and Appendix III]

Item	2005 Number of returns (1,000)	2005 Amount (mil. dol.)	2006 Number of returns (1,000)	2006 Amount (mil. dol.)	Percent change in amount, 2005–06
Total statutory adjustments	**33,591**	**109,397**	**33,981**	**113,845**	**4.1**
Payments to an Individual Retirement Account	3,256	12,003	3,231	12,534	4.4
Educator expenses deduction.	3,504	878	3,167	806	–8.2
Moving expenses adjustment	1,134	3,077	1,083	3,159	2.7
Student loan interest deduction.	8,073	5,053	8,541	6,157	21.9
Tuition and fees deduction.	4,696	10,847	4,016	9,621	–11.3
Self-employment tax deduction	16,695	22,734	17,075	23,925	5.2
Self-employment health insurance deduction	3,901	19,646	3,804	20,303	3.3
Payments to a self-employed retirement (Keogh) plan. . .	1,257	21,268	1,228	22,012	3.5
Forfeited interest penalty	806	266	1,164	430	61.7
Alimony paid	588	8,954	585	9,116	1.8
Other adjustment [1]	(NA)	1,515	(NA)	1,245	–17.8

NA Not available. [1] Includes foreign housing adjustment, Medical Savings Accounts deduction, jury duty pay deduction, and other adjustments for 2005 and 2006.

Source: U.S. Internal Revenue Service, *Statistics of Income Bulletin,* Fall issues.

Federal Government Finances and Employment 315

Table 479. **Federal Individual Income Tax Returns—Itemized Deductions and Statutory Adjustments by Size of Adjusted Gross Income: 2006**

[49,124 represents 49,124,000. Based on a sample of returns; see Appendix III]

Item	Unit	Total	Adjusted gross income class Under $10,000	$10,000 to $19,999	$20,000 to $29,999	$30,000 to $39,999	$40,000 to $49,999	$50,000 to $99,999	$100,000 and over
Returns with itemized deductions:									
Number of returns [1, 2]	1,000 ..	49,124	923	2,306	3,358	4,363	4,546	19,117	14,510
Amount [1, 2]	Mil. dol..	1,229,237	13,933	34,215	48,571	65,218	71,839	371,502	623,958
Medical and dental expenses: [3]									
Returns	1,000 ..	10,209	575	1,358	1,404	1,379	1,196	3,386	911
Amount	Mil. dol..	70,704	4,159	10,265	8,853	7,864	7,405	21,815	10,343
Taxes paid:									
Returns [2]	1,000 ..	48,661	874	2,213	3,265	4,278	4,495	19,044	14,492
Amount, total	Mil. dol..	432,774	2,622	5,854	9,396	14,401	17,812	110,712	271,978
State and local income taxes: [4]									
Returns	1,000 ..	46,916	758	1,977	3,045	4,045	4,313	18,508	14,269
Amount	Mil. dol..	265,306	584	1,436	3,205	5,776	8,101	57,223	188,980
Real estate taxes:									
Returns	1,000 ..	42,584	672	1,686	2,477	3,433	3,676	17,047	13,594
Amount	Mil. dol..	156,384	1,901	4,105	5,693	7,918	8,953	49,485	78,330
Interest paid:									
Returns	1,000 ..	40,285	602	1,464	2,337	3,330	3,572	16,392	12,587
Amount	Mil. dol..	470,475	5,695	12,662	19,519	28,025	30,769	162,274	211,530
Home mortgage interest:									
Returns	1,000 ..	39,831	593	1,447	2,317	3,314	3,550	16,290	12,321
Amount	Mil. dol..	443,152	5,655	12,550	19,301	27,781	30,367	160,577	186,920
Charitable contributions:									
Returns	1,000 ..	41,438	541	1,545	2,411	3,315	3,607	16,497	13,523
Amount	Mil. dol..	186,647	633	2,608	4,680	6,826	7,947	44,221	119,731
Unreimbursed employee business expenses:									
Returns	1,000 ..	15,985	86	367	932	1,452	1,599	7,174	4,376
Amount	Mil. dol..	75,601	340	1,620	4,617	7,050	7,419	30,937	23,619
Returns with statutory adjustments:									
Number of returns [2]	1,000 ..	33,981	4,318	4,160	3,423	3,121	2,868	9,430	6,660
Amount of adjustments	Mil. dol..	113,845	6,137	5,916	6,260	6,107	6,545	25,556	57,325
Payments to IRAs: [4]									
Returns	1,000 ..	3,231	98	214	359	363	400	1,098	698
Amount	Mil. dol..	12,534	301	551	1,027	1,141	1,435	4,350	3,728
Deduction for self-employment tax:									
Returns	1,000 ..	17,075	3,202	2,869	1,627	1,301	1,138	3,681	3,256
Amount	Mil. dol..	23,925	1,376	2,202	1,691	1,448	1,357	5,496	10,355
Self-employment health insurance:									
Returns	1,000 ..	3,804	360	363	349	302	273	894	1,263
Amount	Mil. dol..	20,303	1,299	1,297	1,383	1,260	1,149	4,516	9,398
Payments to Keogh plans:									
Returns	1,000 ..	1,228	22	22	24	40	44	260	817
Amount	Mil. dol..	22,012	100	83	107	251	303	2,386	18,782

[1] After limitations. [2] Includes other deductions and adjustments, not shown separately. [3] Before limitation. [4] State and local taxes include income taxes and sales taxes.

Source: U.S. Internal Revenue Service, *Statistics of Income Bulletin*, Fall issues.

Table 480. **Federal Individual Income Tax Returns—Selected Tax Credits: 2004 to 2006**

[41,694 represents 41,694,000. For tax years. Based on a sample of returns, see source and Appendix III]

Item	2004 Number of returns (1,000)	2004 Amount (mil. dol.)	2005 Number of returns (1,000)	2005 Amount (mil. dol.)	2006 Number of returns (1,000)	2006 Amount (mil. dol.)
Total tax credits [1]	41,694	52,367	42,246	55,316	46,092	58,939
Child care credit	6,317	3,338	6,501	3,462	6,467	3,487
Earned income credit [2]	2,975	768	2,896	745	2,960	797
Foreign tax credit	4,700	6,758	5,398	9,362	6,418	10,958
General business credit	249	635	251	878	387	1,302
Minimum tax credit	275	902	290	1,081	359	1,032
Child tax credit [3]	25,989	32,300	25,951	32,048	25,742	31,742
Education credits	7,181	6,017	7,057	6,120	7,725	7,022
Retirement savings contribution credit	5,289	1,012	5,294	945	5,192	894

[1] Includes credits not shown separately. [2] Represents portion of earned income credit used to offset income tax before credits. [3] Excludes refundable portion.

Source: U.S. Internal Revenue Service, *Statistics of Income Bulletin*, Fall issues.

Table 481. **Federal Individual Income Tax Returns by State: 2006**

[139,231 represents 139,231,000. For tax year. Data will not agree with data in other tables due to differing survey methodology used to derive state data]

State	Total number of returns (1,000)	Adjusted gross income (mil. dol.)			Itemized deductions (mil. dol.)				Income tax (mil. dol.)
		Total [1]	Salaries and wages	Net capital gain	Total	State and local income tax	Real estate taxes	Mortgage interest paid	
U.S.	**139,231**	**7,945,456**	**5,469,458**	**724,512**	**1,244,098**	**251,465**	**158,951**	**480,952**	**1,023,645**
AL	2,029	96,624	67,707	6,748	12,745	2,159	568	4,524	10,979
AK	341	17,947	12,671	1,013	1,751	24	282	898	2,263
AZ	2,597	147,978	97,962	15,215	24,264	3,664	1,821	11,251	17,983
AR	1,185	50,652	36,183	2,801	6,291	1,442	300	1,929	5,433
CA	15,988	1,035,152	699,105	107,773	219,123	50,632	22,911	98,655	137,232
CO	2,229	138,876	92,919	15,693	22,525	4,184	1,758	10,948	18,063
CT	1,714	141,719	94,294	15,783	22,749	6,087	4,059	7,891	23,162
DE	412	24,150	16,767	1,808	3,644	834	267	1,535	3,009
DC	288	21,406	13,628	2,712	3,906	1,207	245	1,363	3,305
FL	8,656	510,337	300,721	75,264	72,045	2,403	10,689	30,219	71,125
GA	4,076	216,332	154,940	17,890	37,407	7,499	3,372	14,350	25,885
HI	638	33,031	22,287	3,122	5,307	1,193	280	2,542	3,769
ID	641	31,709	20,846	3,747	5,047	1,099	438	1,933	3,488
IL	5,980	362,236	250,723	32,967	51,576	7,380	9,724	21,571	48,970
IN	2,969	142,501	104,505	7,823	17,773	3,764	1,762	6,558	15,909
IA	1,378	66,193	47,218	3,606	8,409	1,947	927	2,628	7,106
KS	1,289	66,433	46,822	4,149	8,785	2,093	961	2,701	7,871
KY	1,823	82,559	59,556	4,780	11,233	2,980	864	3,830	8,773
LA	1,895	91,888	63,359	6,575	11,780	1,870	492	4,159	11,429
ME	634	29,467	20,258	2,265	4,313	1,108	585	1,484	3,090
MD	2,717	181,096	129,330	12,970	36,834	9,849	3,681	15,307	23,281
MA	3,144	222,928	150,330	23,993	35,042	8,857	5,248	13,196	31,884
MI	4,655	233,373	168,174	11,806	35,403	5,971	5,527	14,051	26,793
MN	2,560	145,576	104,315	9,788	24,542	6,154	2,683	9,741	17,874
MS	1,234	49,860	36,163	2,951	7,032	1,035	346	1,901	5,083
MO	2,721	131,089	93,076	8,060	18,089	3,902	1,783	6,514	15,084
MT	466	20,405	12,819	2,171	2,902	625	280	1,024	2,163
NE	833	41,039	29,065	2,953	5,593	1,270	764	1,665	4,654
NV	1,211	77,212	47,479	11,878	13,518	449	1,054	6,562	10,428
NH	661	40,176	28,635	3,634	5,395	430	1,314	2,355	5,177
NJ	4,230	302,073	218,419	20,872	54,577	12,736	12,142	18,217	43,578
NM	887	39,283	26,969	2,781	4,804	880	347	2,007	4,434
NY	8,964	604,209	398,947	70,037	105,093	35,122	15,949	27,988	89,772
NC	4,006	203,103	143,551	14,625	33,252	8,431	2,734	11,732	22,977
ND	315	14,229	9,780	914	1,235	176	173	360	1,576
OH	5,521	266,210	193,758	14,147	37,979	10,865	5,425	13,310	30,242
OK	1,544	74,932	50,314	5,965	9,834	2,280	641	2,832	9,030
OR	1,695	88,483	58,569	7,927	16,691	4,606	1,757	6,455	9,928
PA	6,041	320,782	225,758	22,494	42,476	9,361	6,977	14,483	39,844
RI	517	28,128	19,919	2,141	4,557	1,049	763	1,719	3,466
SC	1,949	91,821	63,229	7,284	14,242	3,045	1,109	5,152	9,923
SD	378	17,668	11,237	1,776	1,529	49	179	538	2,140
TN	2,742	134,041	96,066	10,491	14,726	421	1,331	6,021	16,329
TX	10,090	562,875	395,476	51,366	59,775	1,120	11,073	21,654	76,431
UT	1,075	57,463	39,908	5,109	10,651	2,052	703	3,759	6,254
VT	319	15,780	10,476	1,656	2,080	473	404	725	1,762
VA	3,619	230,255	163,227	17,918	38,575	8,166	4,344	17,315	29,555
WA	3,018	186,216	124,815	19,527	26,379	645	3,559	13,200	24,114
WV	770	31,973	23,496	1,183	2,807	749	152	987	3,251
WI	2,738	141,048	100,837	9,799	21,736	5,491	3,727	7,182	16,408
WY	258	17,059	9,385	2,969	1,540	97	101	590	2,536
Other [2]	1,593	67,881	63,463	11,591	4,532	1,543	374	1,441	8,829

[1] Includes other items, not shown separately. [2] Includes returns filed from Army Post Office and Fleet Post Office addresses by members of the armed forces stationed overseas; returns by other U.S. citizens abroad; and returns filed by residents of Puerto Rico with income from sources outside of Puerto Rico or with income earned as U.S. government employees.

Source: U.S. Internal Revenue Service, *Statistics of Income Bulletin,* Spring issues.

Federal Government Finances and Employment 317

Table 482. Federal Individual Income Tax—Tax Liability and Effective and Marginal Tax Rates for Selected Income Groups: 2000 to 2008

[Refers to income after exclusions but before deductions for itemized or standard deductions and for personal exemptions. Tax liability is after reductions for tax credits. As a result of the tax credits, tax liability can be negative, which means that the taxpayer receives a payment from the government. The effective rate represents tax liability, which may be negative as a result of the tax credits, divided by stated income. The marginal tax rate is the percentage of the first additional dollar of income which would be paid in income tax. Tax credits which increase with income can result in negative marginal tax rates. Computations assume itemized deductions (in excess of floors) of 18 percent of adjusted gross income or the standard deduction, whichever is greater. All income is assumed to be from wages and salaries. Does not include social security and Medicare taxes imposed on most wages and salaries]

Adjusted gross income	2000	2004	2005	2006	2007	2008[1]
TAX LIABILITY (dol.)						
Single person, no dependents:						
$5,000	[2]-353	[2]-383	[2]-383	[2]-383	[2]-383	[1,2]-683
$10,000	[2]391	[2]91	[2]46	[2]-7	[2]-73	[1,2]-415
$20,000	1,920	1,450	1,405	1,355	1,296	[1]656
$30,000	3,270	2,868	2,845	2,818	2,789	[1]2156
$40,000	4,988	4,163	4,075	4,048	4,019	[1]3394
$50,000	7,284	6,213	6,115	5,983	5,824	[1]5119
$75,000	13,024	11,338	11,240	11,108	10,949	[1]10244
$100,000	19,233	16,719	16,571	16,368	16,119	15969
Married couple, two dependents, with one spouse working:						
$5,000	[2]-2,000	[2]-2,000	[2]-2,000	[2]-2,000	[2]-2,000	[1,2]-3,200
$10,000	[2]-3,888	[2]-4,000	[2]-4,000	[2]-4,000	[2]-4,000	[1,2]-5425
$20,000	[2,3]-2,349	[2,4]-4,643	[2,4]-4,986	[2,4]-5,169	[2,4]-5,404	[1,2,4]-7,484
$30,000	[2,3]475	[2,3,4]-2,359	[2,3,4]-2,810	[2,3,4]-3,108	[2,3,4]-3,490	[1,2,3,4]-5,143
$40,000	[3]2,218	[3,4]-30	[3,4]-150	[3,4]-280	[3,4]-428	[1,3,4]-2,637
$50,000	[3]3,470	[3]1,470	[3]1,350	[3]1,200	[3]1,073	[1,3]-838
$75,000	[3]7,384	[3]4,650	[3]4,575	[3]4,490	[3]4,403	[1,3]2,523
$100,000	[3]13,124	[3]8,875	[3]8,630	[3]8,315	[3]7,948	[1,3]5,888
EFFECTIVE RATE (percent)						
Single person, no dependents:						
$5,000	[2]-7.1	[2]-7.7	[2]-7.7	[2]-7.7	[2]-7.7	[1,2]-13.7
$10,000	[2]3.9	[2]0.9	[2]0.5	[2]-0.1	[2]-0.7	[1,2]-4.2
$20,000	9.6	7.3	7	6.8	6.5	[2]3.3
$30,000	10.9	9.6	9.5	9.4	9.3	[2]7.2
$40,000	12.5	10.4	10.2	10.1	10.1	[2]8.5
$50,000	14.6	12.4	12.2	12.0	11.6	[2]10.2
$75,000	17.4	15.1	15	14.8	14.6	[2]13.7
$100,000	19.2	16.7	16.6	16.4	16.1	16.0
Married couple, two dependents, with one spouse working:						
$5,000	[2]-40.0	[2]-40.0	[2]-40.0	[2]-40.0	[2]-40.0	[1,2]-64.0
$10,000	[2]-38.9	[2]-40.0	[2]-40.0	[2]-39.3	[2]-40.0	[1,2]-54.3
$20,000	[2,3]-11.7	[2,4]-23.2	[2,4]-24.9	[2,4]-21.2	[2,4]-27.0	[1,2,4]-37.4
$30,000	[2,3]1.6	[2,3,4]-7.9	[2,3,4]-9.4	[2,3,4]-4.3	[2,3,4]-11.6	[1,2,3,4]-17.1
$40,000	[3]5.5	[3,4]-0.1	[3,4]-0.4	[3,4]1.6	[3,4]-1.1	[1,3,4]-6.6
$50,000	[3]6.9	[3]2.9	[3]2.7	[3]4.2	[3]2.1	[1,3]-1.7
$75,000	[3]9.8	[3]6.2	[3]6.1	[3]6.9	[3]5.9	[1,3]3.4
$100,000	[3]13.1	[3]8.9	[3]8.6	[3]10.4	[3]7.9	[1,3]5.9
MARGINAL TAX RATE (percent)						
Single person, no dependents:						
$5,000	–	[2]-7.7	[2]-7.7	[2]-7.7	[2]-7.7	[2]-7.7
$10,000	[2]22.7	[2]17.7	[2]17.7	[2]17.7	[2]17.7	[2]17.7
$20,000	15.0	15.0	15.0	15.0	15.0	15.0
$30,000	15.0	15.0	15.0	15.0	15.0	15.0
$40,000	28.0	25.0	15.0	15.0	15.0	15.0
$50,000	28.0	25.0	25.0	25.0	25.0	25.0
$75,000	28.0	25.0	25.0	25.0	25.0	25.0
$100,000	31.0	28.0	28.0	28.0	28.0	25.0
Married couple, two dependents, with one spouse working:						
$5,000	[2]-40.0	[2]-40.0	[2]-40.0	[2]-40.0	[2]-40.0	[2]-40.0
$10,000	–	[2]-40.0	[2]-40.0	[2]-40.0	[2]-40.0	[2]-55.0
$20,000	[2,3]21.1	[2,4]6.1	[2,4]6.1	[2,4]6.1	[2,4]6.1	[2,4]6.1
$30,000	[2]36.1	[2,3,4]31.1	[2,3,4]31.1	[2,3,4]31.1	[2,3,4]31.1	[2,3,4]31.1
$40,000	15.0	[3,4]15.0	[3,4]15.0	[3,4]15.0	[3,4]15.0	[3,4]31.1
$50,000	15.0	15.0	15.0	15.0	15.0	15.0
$75,000	28.0	15.0	15.0	15.0	15.0	15.0
$100,000	28.0	25.0	25.0	25.0	25.0	25.0

– Represents zero. [1] Includes effect of the Recovery Rebate paid in 2008 under the Economic Stimulus Act of 2008 (P.L. 110-185). [2] Includes effect from the refundable earned income credit. [3] Includes effect from the child tax credit. [4] Includes effect from the additional (refundable) child tax credit.

Source: U.S. Department of the Treasury, Office of Tax Analysis, unpublished data.

318   Federal Government Finances and Employment

Table 483. **Federal Individual Income Tax—Current Income Equivalent to 2000 Constant Income for Selected Income Groups: 2000 to 2008**

[Constant 2000 incomes calculated by using the U.S. Bureau of Labor Statistics Consumer Price Index for Urban Consumers (CPI-U); see Table 709, section 14. See also headnote, Table 482]

Adjusted gross income Constant 2000 dollars	2000	2004	2005	2006	2007	2008[1]
REAL INCOME EQUIVALENT (dol.)						
$5,000	5,000	5,480	5,670	5,850	6,020	6,250
$10,000	10,000	10,970	11,340	11,710	12,040	12,500
$20,000	20,000	21,940	22,680	23,410	24,080	25,010
$30,000	30,000	32,910	34,020	35,120	36,120	37,510
$40,000	40,000	43,880	45,370	46,830	48,160	50,010
$50,000	50,000	54,850	56,710	58,540	60,200	62,520
$75,000	75,000	82,270	85,060	87,800	90,310	93,770
$100,000	100,000	109,700	113,410	117,070	120,410	125,030
TAX LIABILITY (dol.)						
Single person, no dependents:						
$5,000	[2]-353	[2]-390	[2]-399	[2]-412	[2]-428	[1,2]-738
$10,000	[2]391	[2]262	[2]283	[2]295	[2]287	[1,2]-29
$20,000	1,920	1,741	1,807	1,867	1,908	[1]1,408
$30,000	3,270	3,225	3,339	3,447	3,542	[1]3,087
$40,000	4,988	4,958	5,166	5,333	5,447	[1]5,121
$50,000	7,284	7,207	7,491	7,733	7,915	[1]7,685
$75,000	13,024	12,828	13,302	13,732	14,087	[1]14,692
$100,000	19,233	18,946	19,649	20,287	20,805	[1]21,705
Married couple, 2 dependents with one spouse working:						
$5,000	[2]-2,000	[2]-2,192	[2]-2,268	[2]-2,340	[2]-2,408	[1,2]-3,700
$10,000	[2]-3,888	[2,4]-4,333	[2,4]-4,451	[2,4]-4,598	[2]-4,760	[1,2,4]-6,624
$20,000	[2,3]-2,349	[2,4]-4,525	[2,4]-4,823	[2,4]-4,963	[2,4]-5,157	[1,2,3,4]-6,693
$30,000	[2,3]475	[2,3,4]-1,456	[2,3,4]-1,561	[2,3,4]-1,518	[2,3,4]-1,589	[1,2,3,4]-3,410
$40,000	[3]2,218	[3]552	[3]656	[3]745	[3,4]797	[1,3]-836
$50,000	[3]3,470	[3]2,172	[3]2,325	[3]2,465	[3]2,582	[1,3]987
$75,000	[3]7,384	[3]5,544	[3]5,812	[3]6,064	[3]6,286	[1,3]4,831
$100,000	[3]13,124	[3]10,864	[3]11,579	[3]12,214	[3]12,682	[1,3]11,819
EFFECTIVE TAX RATE (percent)						
Single person, no dependents:						
$5,000	[2]-7.1	[2]-7.1	[2]-7.0	[2]-7.0	[2]-7.1	[1,2]-11.8
$10,000	[2]3.9	[2]2.4	[2]2.5	[2]2.5	[2]2.4	[1,2]-0.2
$20,000	9.6	7.9	8.0	8.0	7.9	[1]5.6
$30,000	10.9	9.8	9.8	9.8	9.8	[1]8.2
$40,000	12.5	11.3	11.4	11.4	11.3	[1]10.2
$50,000	14.6	13.1	13.2	13.2	13.1	[1]12.3
$75,000	17.4	15.6	15.6	15.6	15.6	[1]15.7
$100,000	19.2	17.3	17.3	17.3	17.3	[1]17.4
Married couple, 2 dependents with one spouse working:						
$5,000	[2]-40.0	[2]-40.0	[2]-40.0	[2]-40.0	[2]-40.0	[1,2]-59.2
$10,000	[2]-38.9	[2,4]-39.5	[2,4]-39.3	[2,4]-39.3	[2]-39.5	[1,2,4]-53.0
$20,000	[2,3]-11.7	[2,4]-20.6	[2,4]-21.3	[2,4]-21.2	[2,4]-21.4	[1,2,3,4]-26.8
$30,000	[2,3]1.6	[2,3,4]-4.4	[2,3,4]-4.6	[2,3,4]-4.2	[2,3,4]-4.4	[1,2,3,4]-9.1
$40,000	[3]5.5	[3]1.3	[3]1.4	[3]1.6	[3,4]1.7	[1,3]-1.7
$50,000	[3]6.9	[3]4.0	[3]4.1	[3]4.2	[3]4.3	[1,3]1.7
$75,000	[3]9.8	[3]6.7	[3]6.8	[3]6.9	[3]7.0	[1,3]5.2
$100,000	[3]13.1	[3]9.9	[3]10.2	[3]10.4	[3]10.5	[1,3]9.5
MARGINAL TAX RATE (percent)						
Single person, no dependents:						
$5,000	–					
$10,000	[2]22.7	[2]17.7	[2]17.7	[2]17.7	[2]17.7	[2]7.7
$20,000	15.0	15.0	15.0	15.0	15.0	15.0
$30,000	15.0	15.0	15.0	15.0	15.0	15.0
$40,000	28.0	25.0	25.0	25.0	25.0	25.0
$50,000	28.0	25.0	25.0	25.0	25.0	25.0
$75,000	28.0	25.0	25.0	25.0	25.0	25.0
$100,000	31.0	28.0	28.0	28.0	28.0	28.0
Married couple, 2 dependents with one spouse working:						
$5,000	[2]-40.0	[2]-40.0	[2]-40.0	[2]-40.0	[2]-40.0	[2]-40.0
$10,000		[4]-15.0	[4]-15.0	[4]-15.0	[4]-15.0	[4]-15.0
$20,000	[2,3]21.1	[2,4]6.1	[2,4]6.1	[2,4]6.1	[2,4]6.1	[2,3,4]31.1
$30,000	[2]36.1	[2,3,4]31.1	[2,3,4]31.1	[2,3,4]31.1	[2,3,4]31.1	[2,3,4]31.1
$40,000	15.0	15.0	15.0	15.0	15.0	15.0
$50,000	15.0	15.0	15.0	15.0	15.0	15.0
$75,000	28.0	15.0	15.0	15.0	15.0	15.0
$100,000	28.0	25.0	[3]30.1	[3]30.1	[3]30.1	[3]30.1

– Represents zero.   [1] Includes effect of the Recovery Rebate paid in 2008 under the Economic Stimulus Act of 2008 (P.L. 110-185).   [2] Includes effect from the refundable earned income credit.   [3] Includes effect from the child tax credit.   [4] Includes effect from the additional (refundable) child tax credit.

Source: U.S. Department of the Treasury, Office of Tax Analysis, unpublished data.

Table 484. **Federal Civilian Employment and Annual Payroll by Branch: 1970 to 2008**

[2,997 represents 2,997,000. For fiscal year ending in year shown. See text, Section 8. Includes employees in U.S. territories and foreign countries. Data represent employees in active-duty status, including intermittent employees. Annual employment figures are averages of monthly figures. Excludes Central Intelligence Agency, National Security Agency, and, as of November 1984, the Defense Intelligence Agency; and as of October 1996, the National Imagery and Mapping Agency]

Year	Total (1,000)	Percent of U.S. employed [1]	Executive (1,000) Total	Executive (1,000) Defense	Legis-lative (1,000)	Judicial (1,000)	Executive Total	Executive Total	Executive Defense	Legisla-tive	Judicial
1970 . . .	[2]2,997	3.81	2,961	1,263	29	7	27,322	26,894	11,264	338	89
1980 . . .	[2]2,987	3.01	2,933	971	40	14	58,012	56,841	18,795	883	288
1985 . . .	3,001	2.80	2,944	1,080	39	18	80,599	78,992	28,330	1,098	509
1990 . . .	[2]3,233	2.72	3,173	1,060	38	23	99,138	97,022	31,990	1,329	787
1995 . . .	2,943	2.36	2,880	852	34	28	118,304	115,328	31,753	1,598	1,379
2000 . . .	[2]2,879	2.10	2,816	681	31	32	130,832	127,472	29,607	1,619	1,741
2002 . . .	2,699	1.98	2,635	671	31	34	136,611	132,893	28,845	1,781	1,938
2003 . . .	2,743	1.99	2,677	669	31	34	143,380	139,506	29,029	1,908	1,966
2004 . . .	2,714	1.95	2,649	668	30	34	148,037	144,134	29,128	1,977	1,927
2005 . . .	2,709	1.91	2,645	671	30	34	152,222	148,275	29,331	2,048	1,900
2006 . . .	2,700	1.87	2,636	676	30	34	160,570	156,543	29,580	2,109	1,918
2007 . . .	2,695	1.85	2,632	674	30	33	161,394	157,010	29,025	2,119	2,265
2008 . . .	2,730	1.88	2,666	682	30	34	167,166	162,675	29,749	2,162	2,328

[1] Civilian employed only. See Table 574, Section 12.   [2] Includes temporary census workers.

Source: U.S. Office of Personnel Management, *Federal Civilian Workforce Statistics—Employment and Trends*, bimonthly; and unpublished data. See also <http://www.opm.gov/feddata>.

Table 485. **Full-Time Federal Civilian Employment—Employees and Average Pay by Pay System: 2000 to 2008**

[As of March 31 (1,671 represents 1,671,000). Excludes employees of Congress and federal courts, maritime seamen of U.S. Department of Commerce, and small number for whom rates were not reported. See text, this section, for explanation of general schedule and wage system]

Pay system	Employees (1,000) 2000	Employees (1,000) 2006	Employees (1,000) 2007	Employees (1,000) 2008	Average annual pay (dol.) 2000	Average annual pay (dol.) 2006	Average annual pay (dol.) 2007	Average annual pay (dol.) 2008
Total, excluding postal. . .	1,671	1,740	1,845	1,885	50,429	65,253	65,825	69,061
General Schedule	1,216	1,243	1,330	1,265	49,428	64,305	65,856	68,674
Wage system	205	185	200	200	37,082	45,522	46,317	47,652
Other	250	312	315	420	66,248	80,756	78,134	80,444
Postal pay system [1]	788	696	685	663	37,627	46,807	48,752	50,294

[1] Source: Career employees—U.S. Postal Service, *Annual Report of the Postmaster General*. See also <http://www.usps.com/financials/cspo/welcome.htm>; Average pay—U.S. Postal Service, *Comprehensive Statement of Postal Operations*, annual.

Source: Except as noted, U.S. Office of Personnel Management, "Pay Structure of the Federal Civil Service," annual (publication discontinued) and unpublished data; <http://www.opm.gov/feddata/>.

Table 486. **Paid Civilian Employment in the Federal Government by State: 2000 and 2007**

[As of December 31. In thousands (2,766 represents 2,766,000). Excludes Central Intelligence Agency, Defense Intelligence Agency, seasonal and on-call employees, and National Security Agency]

State	2000	2007	State	2000	2007	State	2000	2007
U.S. [1]	2,766	1,812	KY	30	22	OH.	84	46
AL	48	37	LA	33	21	OK.	43	35
AK	14	12	ME.	13	10	OR.	29	20
AZ	43	37	MD.	130	113	PA	107	66
AR	20	14	MA.	53	27	RI	10	6
CA	248	153	MI	58	27	SC.	26	20
CO.	51	37	MN.	34	17	SD.	9	8
CT.	21	8	MS.	24	19	TN	50	26
DE.	5	3	MO	54	35	TX	162	124
DC.	181	145	MT.	11	10	UT	30	28
FL	113	80	NE	15	9	VT	6	4
GA.	89	71	NV	13	10	VA	145	133
HI	23	22	NH.	8	4	WA	62	50
ID	11	9	NJ	62	29	WV	18	17
IL.	94	48	NM.	25	24	WI	30	14
IN	37	22	NY	134	67	WY	6	5
IA	18	9	NC	57	38			
KS	25	15	ND	8	6			

[1] Includes employees outside the United States and in states not specified, not shown separately.

Source: U.S. Office of Personnel Management, "Employment by Geographic Area," biennial (publication discontinued) and unpublished data; <http://www.opm.gov/feddata/>.

Table 487. Federal Civilian Employment by Branch and Agency: 1990 to 2008

[For years ending September 30. **Annual averages of monthly figures.** Excludes Central Intelligence Agency, National Security Agency; the Defense Intelligence Agency; and, as of October 1996, the National Imagery and Mapping Agency]

Agency	1990	2000	2005	2006	2007	2008
Total, all agencies	**3,128,267**	**2,708,101**	**2,708,753**	**2,700,007**	**2,694,929**	**2,730,040**
Legislative Branch	37,495	31,157	30,303	30,067	29,573	29,919
Judicial Branch	23,605	32,186	33,690	33,834	32,921	33,682
Executive Branch	3,067,167	2,644,758	2,644,764	2,636,106	2,632,435	2,666,440
Executive Office of the President	1,731	1,658	1,736	1,709	1,719	1,717
Executive Departments	2,065,542	1,592,200	1,689,914	1,689,351	1,696,893	1,740,979
State	25,288	27,983	33,808	33,968	34,657	35,779
Treasury	158,655	143,508	114,194	112,000	111,577	111,335
Defense	1,034,152	676,268	670,790	676,452	673,722	682,142
Justice	83,932	125,970	105,102	106,159	106,946	107,970
Interior	77,679	73,818	73,599	71,593	70,256	70,515
Agriculture	122,594	104,466	104,989	101,887	99,629	98,720
Commerce [1]	69,920	47,652	38,927	40,335	40,163	41,339
Labor . . . . [2] . .	17,727	16,040	15,599	15,434	15,855	16,269
Health & Human Services [2]	123,959	62,605	60,944	60,756	61,217	62,344
Housing & Urban Development	13,596	10,319	10,086	9,814	9,718	9,599
Transportation [3]	67,364	63,598	55,975	53,573	53,536	54,676
Energy	17,731	15,692	15,050	14,838	14,696	14,857
Education	4,771	4,734	4,429	4,257	4,146	4,210
Veterans Affairs	248,174	219,547	236,363	236,938	245,537	265,390
Homeland Security [3]	(X)	(X)	149,977	151,771	155,397	165,839
Independent agencies [4]	999,894	1,050,900	953113 [4]	945,046	933,833	923,744
Board of Governors Federal Reserve System . .	1,525	2,372	1,851	1,869	1,874	1,873
Environmental Protection Agency	17,123	18,036	17,964	18,166	19,153	18,127
Equal Employment Opportunity Commission . . .	2,880	2,780	2,421	2,285	2,191	2,209
Federal Communications Commission	1,778	1,965	1,936	1,857	1,827	1,809
Federal Deposit Insurance Corporation	17,641	6,958	4,998	4,583	4,573	4,726
Federal Trade Commission	988	1,019	1,046	1,027	1,094	1,131
General Services Administration	20,277	14,334	12,685	12,460	12,099	11,929
National Archives & Records Administration . . .	3,120	2,702	3,048	3,051	2,973	3,068
National Aeronautics & Space Administration . .	24,872	18,819	19,105	18,448	19,378	18,531
National Labor Relations Board	2,263	2,054	1,822	1,832	1,772	1,670
National Science Foundation	1,318	1,247	1,325	1,325	1,356	1,383
Nuclear Regulatory Commission	3,353	2,858	3,230	3,297	3,609	3,833
Office of Personnel Management	6,636	3,780	4,333	4,954	5,291	5,375
Peace Corps	1,178	1,065	1,064	1,075	1,077	1,035
Railroad Retirement Board	1,772	1,176	1,010	1,004	990	977
Securities & Exchange Commission	2,302	2,955	3,933	3,760	3,534	3,562
Small Business Administration	5,128	4,150	4,288	6,148	4,234	3,813
Smithsonian Institution	5,092	5,065	4,981	4,953	5,008	4,929
Social Security Administration [2]	(X)	64,471	65,861	64,004	62,769	62,337
Tennessee Valley Authority	28,392	13,145	12,721	12,624	12,293	11,727
U.S. Information Agency	8,555	2,436	2,212	2,144	2,046	2,052
U.S. International Development Cooperation Agency	4,698	2,552	2,644	2,723	2,761	2,515
U.S. Postal Service	816,886	860,726	767,972	760,039	753,254	744,405

X Not applicable.   [1] Includes enumerators for the 1990 and 2000 census.   [2] Social Security Administration was separated from the Department of Health and Human Services effective April 1995.   [3] See text, Section 10, concerning the development of the Department of Homeland Security.   [4] Includes agencies with fewer than 1,000 employees in 2005, not shown separately.

Source: U.S. Office of Personnel Management, *Federal Civilian Workforce Statistics—Employment and Trends*, bimonthly. See also <http://www.opm.gov/feddata/>.

Table 488. Federal Employees—Summary Characteristics: 1990 to 2006

[As of September 30. **In percent, except as indicated.** For civilian employees, excluding U.S. Postal Service employees]

Characteristic	1990	1995	2000	2001	2002	2003	2004	2005	2006
Average age (years) [1]	42.3	44.3	46.3	46.5	46.5	46.7	46.8	46.9	46.9
Average length of service (years)	13.4	15.5	17.1	17.1	16.8	16.8	16.6	16.4	16.3
Retirement eligible: [2]									
Civil Service Retirement System	8	10	17	19	23	27	30	33	37
Federal Employees Retirement System . . .	3	5	11	10	11	12	13	13	13
Bachelor's degree or higher	35	39	41	41	41	41	42	43	43
Sex: Male	57	56	55	55	55	55	56	56	56
Female	43	44	45	45	45	45	44	44	44
Race and national origin:									
Total minorities	27.4	28.9	30.4	30.6	30.8	31.1	31.4	31.7	32.1
Black	16.7	16.8	17.1	17.1	17.0	17.0	17.0	17.0	17.2
Hispanic	5.4	5.9	6.6	6.7	6.9	7.1	7.3	7.4	7.5
Asian/Pacific Islander	3.5	4.2	4.5	4.6	4.7	4.8	5.0	5.1	5.1
American Indian/Alaska Native	1.8	2.0	2.2	2.2	2.2	2.1	2.1	2.1	2.1
Disabled	7.0	7.0	7.0	7.0	7.0	7.0	7.0	7.0	7.0
Veterans preference	30.0	26.0	24.0	24.0	23.0	22.0	22.0	22.0	22.0
Vietnam era veterans	17.0	17.0	14.0	13.0	13.0	13.0	12.0	11.0	10.0
Retired military	4.9	4.2	3.9	4.2	4.4	4.6	4.9	5.4	5.7
Retired officers	0.5	0.5	0.5	0.6	0.7	0.8	0.9	1.0	1.1

[1] For full-time permanent employees.   [2] Represents full-time permanent employees under the Civil Service Retirement System (excluding hires since January 1984), and the Federal Employees Retirement System (since January 1984).

Source: U.S. Office of Personnel Management, Office of Workforce Information, *The Fact Book, Federal Civilian Workforce Statistics*, annual. See also <http://www.opm.gov/feddata/>.

Federal Government Finances and Employment **321**

Table 489. **Federal Executive Branch (Nonpostal) Employment by Race and National Origin: 1990 to 2006**

[As of Sept. 30. Covers total employment for only Executive branch agencies participating in OPM's Central Personnel Data File (CPDF). For information on the CPDF, see <http://www.opm.gov/feddata/acpdf.pdf>]

Pay system	1990	1995	2000	2004	2005	2006
All personnel [1]	**2,150,359**	**1,960,577**	**1,755,689**	**1,851,349**	**1,856,966**	**1,848,339**
White, non-Hispanic	1,562,846	1,394,690	1,224,836	1,270,366	1,267,922	1,254,308
General schedule and related	1,218,188	1,101,108	961,261	972,737	973,767	948,740
Grades 1 to 4	132,028	79,195	55,067	48,798	46,671	43,450
Grades 5 to 8	337,453	288,755	239,128	231,765	227,387	219,168
Grades 9 to 12	510,261	465,908	404,649	405,825	408,111	399,400
Grades 13 to 15	238,446	267,250	262,417	286,349	291,598	286,722
Total executive/senior pay levels	9,337	13,307	14,332	16,337	16,409	16,118
Wage pay system	244,220	186,184	146,075	134,821	135,383	133,942
Other pay systems	91,101	94,091	103,168	146,471	142,363	155,508
Black	356,867	327,302	298,701	313,099	315,644	317,697
General schedule and related	272,657	258,586	241,135	244,736	246,691	246,248
Grades 1 to 4	65,077	41,381	26,895	20,797	19,774	18,326
Grades 5 to 8	114,993	112,962	99,937	95,798	94,655	93,717
Grades 9 to 12	74,985	79,795	82,809	88,813	90,809	91,869
Grades 13 to 15	17,602	24,448	31,494	39,328	41,453	42,336
Total executive/senior pay levels	479	942	1,180	1,238	1,270	1,218
Wage pay system	72,755	55,637	42,590	37,798	37,666	37,378
Other pay systems	10,976	12,137	13,796	29,327	30,017	32,853
Hispanic	115,170	115,964	115,247	135,533	138,507	138,596
General schedule and related	83,218	86,762	89,911	102,612	104,927	105,236
Grades 1 to 4	15,738	11,081	8,526	7,969	7,768	6,854
Grades 5 to 8	28,727	31,152	31,703	34,380	33,653	33,834
Grades 9 to 12	31,615	34,056	36,813	43,868	46,268	46,951
Grades 13 to 15	7,138	10,473	12,869	16,395	17,238	17,597
Total executive/senior pay levels	154	382	547	656	682	699
Wage pay system	26,947	22,128	16,926	15,915	15,945	15,822
Other pay systems	4,851	6,692	7,863	16,350	16,953	16,839
American Indian, Alaska Native, Asian, and Pacific Islander	115,476	122,621	116,905	132,351	134,893	136,593
General schedule and related	81,499	86,768	86,074	96,014	97,866	97,870
Grades 1 to 4	15,286	11,854	9,340	8,528	8,357	7,877
Grades 5 to 8	24,960	26,580	25,691	27,601	27,417	26,986
Grades 9 to 12	31,346	33,810	33,167	37,172	38,276	38,492
Grades 13 to 15	9,907	14,524	17,876	22,713	23,816	24,515
Total executive/senior pay levels	148	331	504	760	804	873
Wage pay system	24,927	21,553	17,613	16,760	16,938	16,728
Other pay systems	8,902	13,969	12,714	18,817	19,285	21,122

[1] Beginning 2006, includes persons classified as multiracial, not shown separately.

Source: U.S. Office of Personnel Management, Central Personnel Data File.

Table 490. **Area of Federally Owned Buildings in the United States by State: 2007**

[3,345.8 represents 3,345,800,000. As of September 30. For executive branch agencies. For data on federal land by state, see Table 353]

State	Total building area [1] (mil. sq. ft)	Owned building area (mil. sq. ft)	Leased building area (mil. sq. ft.)	State	Total building area [1] (mil. sq. ft)	Owned building area (mil. sq. ft)	Leased building area (mil. sq. ft.)
U.S. [2] ...	3,345.8	2,686.3	541.7	MO	56.8	43.0	11.5
				MT	17.1	14.4	2.1
AL	57.2	49.6	4.7	NE	15.0	12.1	1.9
AK	53.2	50.0	2.9	NV	32.0	28.7	2.4
AZ	58.0	52.3	4.7	NH	4.4	2.9	0.5
AR	23.6	19.5	1.5	NJ	47.7	39.4	6.3
CA	344.4	293.4	47.2	NM	62.8	56.3	5.1
CO	56.8	48.3	8.0	NY	102.6	82.2	15.8
CT	16.4	10.8	3.8	NC	90.5	74.8	13.5
DE	5.9	5.1	0.3	ND	22.7	20.1	1.0
DC	100.2	75.2	24.4	OH	71.2	62.7	6.3
FL	113.6	98.7	11.6	OK	64.5	55.2	7.1
GA	114.0	101.6	10.6	OR	25.3	20.1	2.8
HI	59.7	50.3	8.8	PA	75.9	64.0	9.7
ID	21.9	18.5	2.7	RI	12.5	11.6	0.4
IL	73.6	60.2	10.0	SC	59.8	53.4	4.3
IN	44.5	38.4	3.7	SD	18.6	16.3	0.9
IA	15.6	11.1	1.6	TN	71.5	63.9	4.5
KS	35.5	31.3	2.6	TX	205.6	174.1	27.8
KY	48.4	42.1	4.3	UT	33.6	28.6	3.1
LA	47.2	35.2	4.7	VT	4.0	2.5	1.0
ME	12.2	10.6	0.7	VA	174.6	134.0	39.3
MD	127.0	101.0	23.9	WA	89.0	76.3	11.2
MA	35.5	30.1	3.1	WV	19.9	15.5	3.0
MI	31.3	22.6	5.0	WI	25.2	20.2	2.6
MN	20.8	14.2	2.1	WY	15.1	13.3	0.8
MS	39.2	31.7	2.3				

[1] Includes otherwised managed square feet, not shown separately.   [2] Includes location not reported, not shown separately.

Source: U.S. General Services Administration, Federal Real Property Council, "Federal Real Property Report," July 2008 (revised since issued).

322   Federal Government Finances and Employment

Section 10
National Security and Veterans Affairs

This section displays data for national security (national defense and homeland security) and benefits for veterans. Data are presented on national defense and its human and financial costs; active and reserve military personnel; and federally sponsored programs and benefits for veterans, and funding, budget and selected agencies for homeland security. The principal sources of these data are the annual *Selected Manpower Statistics* and the *Atlas/Data Abstract for the United States, Annual Report of Secretary of Veterans Affairs*, U.S. Department of Veterans Affairs (VA), *Budget in Brief*, U.S. Department of Homeland Security; and *The Budget of the United States Government*, Office of Management and Budget. For data on international expenditures and personnel, see Table 1369, Section 30.

Department of Defense (DoD)—The U.S. Department of Defense is responsible for providing the military forces of the United States. It includes the Office of the Secretary of Defense, the Joint Chiefs of Staff, the Army, the Navy, the Air Force, and the defense agencies. The President serves as Commander-in-Chief of the Armed Forces; from him, the authority flows to the Secretary of Defense and through the Joint Chiefs of Staff to the commanders of unified and specified commands (e.g., U.S. Strategic Command).

Reserve components—The Reserve Components of the Armed Forces consist of the Army National Guard of the United States, Army Reserve, Naval Reserve, Marine Corps Reserve, Air National Guard, Air Force Reserve, and Coast Guard Reserve. They provide trained personnel and units available for active duty in the Armed Forces during times of war or national emergency, and at such other times as national security may require. The National Guard has dual federal/state responsibilities and uses jointly provided equipment, facilities, and budget support. The President is empowered to mobilize the National Guard and to use such of the Armed Forces as he considers necessary to enforce federal authority in any state. There is in each Armed Force a ready reserve, a standby reserve, and a retired reserve. The Ready Reserve includes the Selected Reserve, which provides trained and ready units and individuals to augment the active forces during times of war or national emergency, or at other times when required; and the Individual Ready Reserve, which is a manpower pool that can be called to active duty during times of war or national emergency and would normally be used as individual fillers for active, guard, and reserve units, and as a source of combat replacements. Most of the Ready Reserve serves in an active status. See Table 501 for Standby Reserve and Retired Reserve detail.

Department of Veterans Affairs (VA)—A veteran is someone 18 years and older (there are a few 17-year-old veterans) who is not currently on active duty, but who once served on active duty in the United States Army, Navy, Air Force, Marine Corps, or Coast Guard, or who served in the Merchant Marine during World War II. There are many groups whose active service makes them veterans including: those who incurred a service-connected disability during active duty for training in the Reserves or National Guard, even though that service would not otherwise have counted for veteran status; members of a national guard or reserve component who have been ordered to active duty by order of the President or who have a full-time military job. The latter are called AGRs (Active Guard and Reserve). No one who has received a dishonorable discharge is a veteran.

The VA administers laws authorizing benefits for eligible former and present members of the Armed Forces and for the beneficiaries of deceased members. Veterans' benefits available under various acts of Congress include compensation for service-connected disability or death;

U.S. Census Bureau, Statistical Abstract of the United States: 2010

pensions for non-service-connected disability or death; vocational rehabilitation, education and training; home loan insurance; life insurance; health care; special housing and automobiles or other conveyances for certain disabled veterans; burial and plot allowances; and educational assistance to families of deceased or totally disabled veterans, servicemen missing in action, or prisoners of war. Since these benefits are legislated by Congress, the dates they were enacted and the dates they apply to veterans may be different from the actual dates the conflicts occurred. VA estimates of veterans cover all persons discharged from active U.S. military service under conditions other than dishonorable.

Homeland Security—In an effort to increase homeland security following the September 11, 2001, terrorist attacks on the United States, President George W. Bush issued the *National Strategy for Homeland Security* in July 2002 and signed legislation creating the Department of Homeland Security (DHS) in November 2002.

The funding and activities of homeland security are not only carried out by DHS, but also by other federal agencies, state, and local entities. In addition to DHS, there are over 30 other federal agencies that comprise federal homeland security funding. DHS, along with four other agencies—Department of Defense (DoD), Energy (DoE), Health and Human Services (HHS), and Justice (DoJ)—account for most of the federal spending for homeland security.

Department of Homeland Security (DHS)—The mission of DHS is to lead the unified national effort to secure America. This effort is to prevent and deter terrorist attacks and to protect against and respond to threats and hazards to the nation. This effort is to secure our national borders while welcoming lawful immigrants, visitors, and trade.

The creation of DHS, which began operations in March 2003, represents a fusion of 22 federal agencies (legacy agencies) to coordinate and centralize the leadership of many homeland security activities

under a single department. Out of these agencies, the Secret Service and Coast Guard remain intact and report directly to the Secretary. Immigration and Naturalization Services (INS) adjudications and benefits programs report directly to the Deputy Secretary as the U.S. Citizenship and Immigration Services (USCIS).

The Customs and Border Protection (CBP) is responsible for managing, securing, and controlling U.S. borders. This includes carrying out traditional border-related responsibilities, such as stemming the tide of illegal drugs and illegal aliens; securing and facilitating legitimate global trade and travel; and protecting the food supply and agriculture industry from pests and disease. CBP is composed of the Border Patrol and Inspections (both moved from INS) along with Customs (absorbed from the U.S. Department of Treasury) and Animal and Plant Health Inspections Services (absorbed from the U.S. Department of Agriculture).

The Immigration and Customs Enforcement (ICE) mission is to protect America and uphold public safety by targeting the people, money, and materials crossing the nation's borders that support terrorist and criminal activities. ICE is the largest investigation arm of DHS. ICE is composed of five law enforcement divisions: Investigations, Intelligence, Federal Protective Service, International Affairs, and Detention and Removal Operations. ICE investigates a wide range of national security, financial and smuggling violations including drug smuggling, human trafficking, illegal arms exports, financial crimes, commercial fraud, human smuggling, document fraud, money laundering, child pornography/exploitation, and immigration fraud.

The Transportation Security Administration (TSA) was created as part of the Aviation and Transportation Security Act on November 19, 2001. TSA was originally part of the U.S. Department of Transportation, but was moved to DHS. TSA's mission is to provide security to our nation's transportation systems with a primary focus on aviation security.

U.S. Census Bureau, Statistical Abstract of the United States: 2010

Figure 10.1
Officers and Enlisted Personnel by Military Branch: 2008

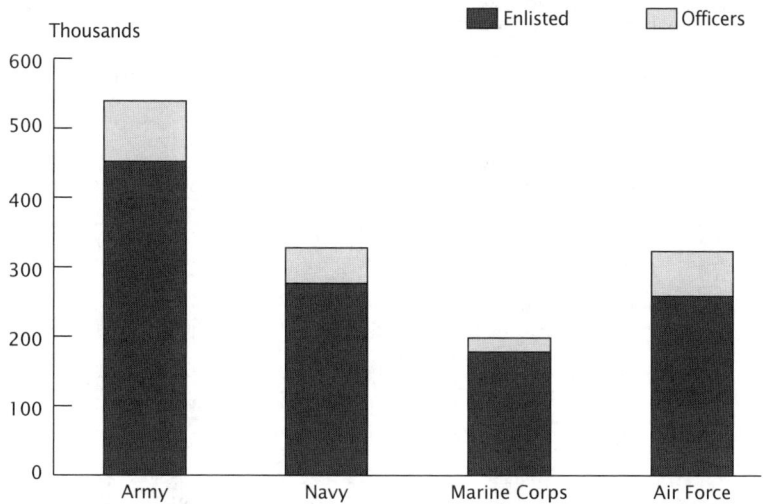

Source: Chart prepared by U.S. Census Bureau. For data, see Table 498.

Figure 10.2
Department of Defense Personnel by Sex: 2008

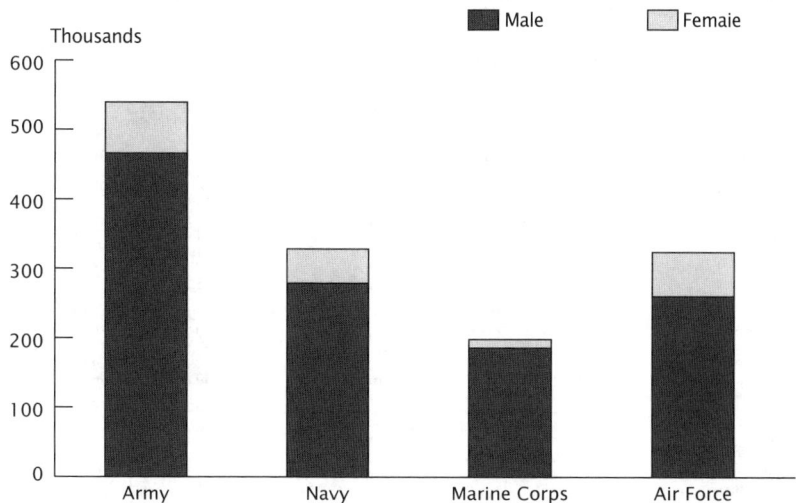

Source: Chart prepared by U.S. Census Bureau. For data, see Table 498.

National Security and Veterans Affairs   325

Table 491. National Defense Outlays and Veterans Benefits: 1960 to 2010

[In billions of dollars (53.5 represents $53,500,000,000), except percent. For fiscal year ending in year shown, see text, Section 8. Includes outlays of Department of Defense, Department of Veterans Affairs, and other agencies for activities primarily related to national defense and veterans programs. For explanation of average annual percent change, see Guide to Tabular Presentation. Minus sign (-) indicates decrease]

Year	National defense and veterans' outlays (bil. dol.)				Annual percent change [1]			Defense outlays percent of—	
	Defense outlays								
	Total outlays	Current dollars	Constant (FY2000) dollars	Veterans' outlays	Total outlays	Defense outlays	Veterans' outlays	Federal outlays	Gross domestic product [2]
1960	53.5	48.1	300.2	5.4	2.5	2.4	3.1	52.2	9.3
1970	90.4	81.7	375.1	8.7	0.3	-1.0	13.6	41.8	8.1
1980	155.1	134.0	267.1	21.1	13.9	15.2	6.3	22.7	4.9
1990	328.4	299.3	382.7	29.1	-1.6	-1.4	-3.2	23.9	5.2
1995	310.0	272.1	305.9	37.9	-2.9	-3.4	0.8	17.9	3.7
1997	309.8	270.5	288.4	39.3	2.3	1.8	6.3	16.9	3.3
1998	310.0	268.2	282.4	41.8	0.1	-0.8	6.3	16.2	3.1
1999	320.2	274.8	286.6	43.2	3.3	2.5	3.4	16.1	3.0
2000	341.5	294.4	294.4	47.1	6.6	7.1	9.0	16.5	3.0
2001	349.8	304.8	297.2	45.0	2.4	3.5	-4.3	16.4	3.0
2002	399.5	348.5	329.3	51.0	14.2	14.3	13.2	17.3	3.4
2003	461.8	404.8	364.4	57.0	15.6	16.2	11.8	18.7	3.7
2004	515.6	455.8	394.3	59.8	11.7	12.6	4.8	19.9	4.0
2005	565.5	495.3	407.3	70.2	9.7	8.7	17.4	20.0	4.0
2006	591.7	521.8	411.9	69.8	4.6	5.4	-0.4	19.7	4.0
2007	624.1	551.3	422.1	72.8	5.5	5.6	4.3	20.2	4.0
2008	700.8	616.1	461.3	84.7	12.3	11.8	16.3	20.7	4.3
2009, est.....	787.0	690.3	511.9	96.7	12.3	12.0	14.2	17.3	4.8
2010, est.....	821.8	712.9	522.2	108.9	4.4	3.3	12.7	19.9	4.8

[1] Change from immediate prior year; for 1960, change from 1955. [2] Represents fiscal year GDP; for definition, see text, Section 13.

Source: U.S. Office of Management and Budget, "Budget of the United States Government, Historical Tables," annual; <http://www.whitehouse.gov/omb/budget/>.

Table 492. National Defense Budget Authority and Outlays for Defense Functions: 1990 to 2009

[In billions of dollars (303.3 represents $303,300,000,000). For year ending September 30. Data includes defense budget authority and outlays by other departments. Minus sign (-) indicates decrease]

Function	1990	1995	2000	2002	2003	2004	2005	2006	2007	2008	2009, est.
Total budget authority	303.3	266.4	304.0	362.0	456.0	490.6	505.8	556.3	625.9	696.3	693.6
Department of Defense–Military ...	293.0	255.7	290.3	344.9	437.7	470.9	483.9	532.9	603.0	674.7	663.7
Military personnel	78.9	71.6	73.8	87.0	109.1	116.1	121.3	128.5	131.8	139.0	146.5
Operation and maintenance	88.4	93.7	108.7	133.2	178.3	189.8	179.2	213.5	240.2	256.2	272.4
Procurement	81.4	43.6	55.0	62.7	78.5	83.1	96.6	105.4	133.8	165.0	132.7
Research, development, test, and evaluation	36.5	34.5	38.7	48.7	58.1	64.6	68.8	72.9	77.5	79.6	80.9
Military construction..........	5.1	5.4	5.1	6.6	6.7	6.1	7.3	9.5	14.0	22.1	26.4
Family housing..............	3.1	3.4	3.5	4.0	4.2	3.8	4.1	4.4	4.0	2.9	3.8
Other	-0.4	3.4	5.5	2.6	2.9	7.4	6.6	-1.3	1.7	9.9	1.1
Atomic energy defense activities ...	9.7	10.1	12.4	15.2	16.4	16.8	17.9	17.4	17.2	16.6	22.9
Defense-related activities........	0.7	1.0	1.3	1.9	2.0	2.8	4.0	5.9	5.7	4.9	7.0
Total outlays	299.3	272.1	294.4	348.5	404.8	455.8	495.3	521.8	551.3	616.1	690.3
Department of Defense–Military ...	289.8	259.4	281.1	331.9	387.2	436.5	474.1	499.3	528.6	594.7	665.0
Military personnel	75.6	70.8	76.0	86.8	106.7	113.6	127.5	127.5	127.5	138.9	146.8
Operation and maintenance	88.3	91.0	105.8	130.0	151.4	174.0	188.1	203.8	216.6	244.8	271.8
Procurement	81.0	55.0	51.7	62.5	67.9	76.2	82.3	89.8	99.6	117.4	142.7
Research, development, test, and evaluation	37.5	34.6	37.6	44.4	53.1	60.8	65.7	68.6	73.1	75.2	78.2
Military construction..........	5.1	6.8	5.1	5.1	5.9	6.3	5.3	6.2	7.9	11.6	20.0
Family housing..............	3.5	3.6	3.4	3.7	3.8	3.9	3.7	3.7	3.5	3.6	3.9
Other	-1.2	-2.4	1.5	-0.6	-1.6	1.6	1.5	-0.4	0.2	3.2	1.7
Atomic energy activities........	9.0	11.8	12.1	14.8	16.0	16.6	18.0	17.5	17.1	17.1	18.5
Defense-related activities........	0.6	0.9	1.2	1.8	1.6	2.8	3.2	5.1	5.7	4.3	6.8

Source: U.S. Office of Management and Budget, "Budget Authority by Function and Subfunction, Outlay by Function and Subfunction," annual; <http://www.whitehouse.gov/omb/budget/>.

326 National Security and Veterans Affairs

Table 493. Military and Civilian Personnel and Expenditures: 1990 to 2006

[Personnel in thousands (3,693 represents 3,693,000); expenditures in millions of dollars (209,904 represents $209,904,000,000). For year ending September 30. For definitions, see headnote, Tables 494 and 496]

Item	1990	1995	2000	2003	2004	2005	2006
Personnel, total [1]	3,693	3,391	2,791	2,806	2,764	2,848	2,840
Active duty military (including afloat) . .	1,185	1,085	984	1,071	1,055	1,143	1,156
Civilian	931	768	634	631	634	639	642
Reserve and National Guard	1,577	1,538	1,173	1,105	1,074	1,065	1,042
Expenditures, total	209,904	209,695	229,072	316,648	345,891	381,290	408,249
Payroll outlays	88,650	98,396	103,447	122,270	139,490	141,018	146,858
Active duty military pay	33,705	35,188	36,872	46,614	50,489	50,482	55,829
Civilian pay	28,230	29,932	29,935	35,041	36,234	43,798	45,105
Reserve and National Guard pay . . .	5,556	5,681	4,646	7,306	10,303	11,087	10,123
Retired military pay	21,159	27,595	31,994	33,309	42,465	35,651	35,801
Prime contract awards [2]	121,254	109,005	123,295	191,222	203,389	236,987	257,457
Grants	6,329	7,543	2,330	3,156	3,012	3,285	3,934

[1] Members in a transient status are not included. [2] Represents contract awards over $25,000.

Source: U.S. Department of Defense, *DoD Personnel and Procurement Statistics, Personnel, Publications, Atlas/Data Abstract for the United States and Selected Areas*, annual; <http://siadapp.dmdc.osd.mil>.

Table 494. Department of Defense Payroll and Contract Awards—States: 2007

[(In millions of dollars (154,326 represents $154,326,000,000). For year ending September 30. Payroll outlays include the gross earnings of civilian, active duty military personnel, reserve and national guard, and retired military for services rendered to the government and for cash allowances for benefits. Excludes employer's share of employee benefits, accrued military retirement benefits and most permanent change of station costs. *Contracts,* refer to awards made in year specified; expenditures relating to awards may extend over several years. Military awards for supplies, services, and construction. Net value of contracts of over $25,000 for work in each state and DC. Figures reflect impact of prime contracting on state distribution of defense work. Often the state in which a prime contractor is located is not the state where the subcontracted work is done. Undistributed civilians and military personnel, their payrolls, and prime contract awards for performance in classified locations are excluded]

State	Payroll Total	Payroll Active duty military	Contract awards	Grants	State	Payroll Total	Payroll Active duty military	Contract awards	Grants
U.S. . . .	154,326	61,918	297,363	4,080	MO	2,513	806	10,131	46
AL	3,868	890	8,729	130	MT	557	289	206	38
AK	2,202	1,658	1,907	23	NE	1,277	682	686	60
AZ	3,035	1,342	11,409	107	NV	1,499	814	905	33
AR	1,389	511	695	47	NH	335	62	1,387	27
CA	13,008	4,874	36,135	443	NJ	2,255	608	6,884	59
CO	3,851	2,004	4,391	48	NM	1,854	912	1,263	33
CT	604	167	0,500	31	NY	2,852	1,339	7,676	238
DE	583	316	268	20	NC	6,570	3,745	2,991	76
DC	2,593	1,209	4,279	52	ND	751	533	413	30
FL	9,309	3,463	11,985	129	OH	3,416	838	6,434	94
GA	7,723	3,725	8,760	58	OK	3,430	1,387	2,110	37
HI	4,245	2,582	2,158	74	OR	821	105	1,131	72
ID	737	364	185	26	PA	3,177	335	11,564	243
IL	2,775	974	5,081	110	RI	626	97	511	24
IN	1,518	213	5,832	108	SC	3,112	1,335	3,977	43
IA	497	82	1,110	62	SD	490	256	347	11
KS	2,122	1,194	1,879	40	TN	1,687	204	3,258	46
KY	2,823	1,787	6,102	31	TX	13,822	7,145	30,799	211
LA	1,945	969	3,112	39	UT	1,958	500	3,052	27
ME	806	105	1,458	43	VT	170	41	807	16
MD	5,489	1,748	10,670	182	VA	17,310	5,361	34,014	126
MA	1,301	319	10,489	193	WA	5,661	2,542	5,432	109
MI	1,410	163	5,289	116	WV	419	69	301	36
MN	857	119	1,882	103	WI	756	137	3,608	45
MS	1,877	727	4,873	69	WY	441	269	209	18

Source: U.S. Department of Defense, *DoD Personnel and Procurement Statistics; Atlas/Data Abstract for the United States and Selected Areas,* annual; <http://siadapp.dmdc.osd.mil/>.

Table 495. Expenditures and Personnel by Selected Major Locations: 2007

[In thousands of dollars (9,923,355 represents $9,923,355,000), except for personnel. For year ending September 30. See headnote, Table 498]

Major locations	Expenditures Total	Expenditures Payroll outlays	Expenditures Contracts/ grants	Major locations	Military and civilian personnel Total	Military and civilian personnel Active duty military	Military and civilian personnel Civilian
Fort Worth, TX.	9,923,355	214,637	9,708,718	Camp Pendleton,CA . . .	58,981	56,658	2,323
St. Louis, MO	7,581,702	127,028	7,454,674	Camp Lejeune,NC.	27,958	25,134	2,824
Washington, DC.	6,923,030	2,592,616	4,330,414	Arlington,Va	23,065	7,901	15,164
San Diego, CA.	6,632,733	1,826,168	4,806,565	Lackland AFB,TX	19,959	15,958	4,001
Huntsville, AL	5,445,876	172,577	5,273,299	Tinker AFB,OK	19,676	5,957	13,719
Arlington, VA	5,325,803	2,582,763	2,743,040	San Diego,CA.	19,623	13,345	6,278
Long Beach, CA	5,063,024	46,447	5,016,547	Robins AFB,GA.	18,962	5,124	13,838
Marietta, GA	4,438,633	82,439	4,356,194	Wright Patterson,OH . . .	16,069	5,120	10,949
Sunnyvale, CA.	3,871,091	42,343	3,828,748	Hill AFB,UT	15,787	4,427	11,360
Louisville, KY.	3,649,256	122,429	3,526,827	Norfolk,VA	11,160	9,185	1,975

Source: U.S. Department of Defense, *DoD Personnel and Procurement Statistics, Personnel, Publications, Atlas/Data Abstract for the United States and Selected Areas,* annual; <http://siadapp.dmdc.osd.mil/>.

National Security and Veterans Affairs 327

Table 496. **Military and Civilian Personnel in Installations: 2006**

[As of September 30. *Civilian personnel* includes United States citizens and foreign national direct-hire civilians subject to Office of Management and Budget (OMB) ceiling controls and civilian personnel involved in civil functions in the United States. Excludes indirect-hire civilians and those direct-hire civilians not subject to OMB ceiling controls. Military personnel include active duty personnel based ashore or afloat, excludes personnel temporarily shore-based in a transient status]

State	Active military personnel				Reserve and National Guard, total	Civilian personnel			
	Total [1]	Army	Navy/ Marine Corps [2]	Air Force		Total [1]	Army	Navy/ Marine Corps	Air Force
United States.	1,156,308	423,825	443,658	288,825	1,041,542	642,214	232,243	170,667	157,270
Alabama	9,742	6,022	419	3,301	30,012	22,312	18,326	43	2,344
Alaska	20,363	11,183	101	9,079	5,845	4,894	2,689	17	1,844
Arizona	21,997	5,267	5,456	11,274	18,496	9,047	3,938	528	3,620
Arkansas.	4,905	88	59	4,758	17,798	3,977	2,944	5	894
California.	149,481	7,004	122,707	19,770	84,352	55,709	7,966	31,079	10,173
Colorado.	29,932	15,593	808	13,531	16,112	10,907	3,074	45	5,489
Connecticut	6,594	23	6,465	106	8,175	2,388	499	1,021	263
Delaware.	3,297	7	24	3,266	5,390	1,564	243	2	1,253
District of Columbia. . .	12,351	4,740	4,634	2,977	8,022	14,634	4,119	8,851	929
Florida	58,100	2,419	30,569	25,112	49,726	26,072	3,281	10,920	9,367
Georgia	68,928	52,107	6,907	9,914	36,150	32,862	11,697	4,216	14,729
Hawaii	45,366	18,687	21,561	5,118	11,337	17,079	4,750	9,130	2,109
Idaho	4,042	20	41	3,981	7,095	1,522	696	49	710
Illinois.	24,536	504	18,652	5,380	32,779	13,617	7,084	1,590	3,584
Indiana	805	420	275	110	22,628	9,281	1,949	3,067	1,027
Iowa.	390	190	141	59	14,342	1,582	1,032	5	501
Kansas	17,645	14,725	197	2,723	15,446	6,577	5,043	1	1,103
Kentucky.	38,799	38,335	266	198	15,555	9,170	7,817	193	228
Louisiana	15,069	7,999	1,303	5,767	22,081	6,212	3,511	870	1,518
Maine.	2,096	224	1,853	19	5,592	6,445	326	5,301	277
Maryland.	29,626	7,552	15,021	7,053	21,587	30,749	12,441	14,660	2,232
Massachusetts	2,175	208	576	1,391	18,916	6,491	2,339	218	2,986
Michigan	1,073	379	562	132	22,874	8,147	5,336	22	1,108
Minnesota	729	25	389	85	24,637	2,522	1,523	17	794
Mississippi.	10,158	401	3,729	6,028	19,136	8,630	3,444	2,211	2,708
Missouri	16,241	11,053	1,537	3,651	25,726	9,483	6,421	444	1,258
Montana	3,589	15	28	3,546	5,761	1,358	560	1	745
Nebraska	6,784	136	469	6,179	8,553	3,774	1,360	12	2,082
Nevada	9,127	97	1,003	8,027	7,394	2,178	384	278	1,353
New Hampshire	912	3	861	48	4,550	1,069	542	46	329
New Jersey	6,293	888	6,964	4,741	20,060	13,959	9,773	1,907	1,545
New Mexico.	10,834	444	158	10,232	7,342	6,863	2,919	44	3,431
New York	26,240	23,464	2,376	400	39,353	11,145	6,946	141	2,414
North Carolina	102,845	43,384	49,775	9,686	30,031	17,447	6,837	7,273	1,370
North Dakota	7,013	23	11	6,979	5,640	1,853	526	2	1,237
Ohio.	6,745	539	608	5,698	35,074	21,789	1,455	79	12,422
Oklahoma	25,064	14,297	1,953	8,814	18,399	21,539	4,763	78	15,479
Oregon	558	190	306	62	13,421	3,241	2,411	18	787
Pennsylvania	2,979	1,075	1,655	249	43,478	25,266	9,048	6,440	1,547
Rhode Island	2,403	109	2,214	80	5,112	4,213	298	3,586	230
South Carolina	38,090	12,372	16,695	9,023	21,677	9,640	3,115	3,501	1,899
South Dakota.	3,150	23	4	3,123	5,668	1,237	507	1	683
Tennessee.	2,441	302	1,918	221	23,695	5,334	2,419	1,004	1,081
Texas	119,176	73,654	6,986	38,536	72,955	41,462	21,777	1,352	14,758
Utah.	5,188	291	163	4,734	13,770	15,081	2,377	26	11,930
Vermont	70	16	31	23	4,130	608	312	1	263
Virginia	128,515	24,084	90,758	13,673	35,668	81,342	21,247	35,582	4,763
Washington	49,887	22,787	20,285	6,815	25,925	24,501	6,928	14,682	1,957
West Virginia	373	30	308	35	10,068	1,745	1,213	90	423
Wisconsin	449	193	176	80	20,270	2,695	1,802	18	773
Wyoming.	3,043	4	1	3,038	3,739	1,002	236	−	721

− Represents zero.   [1] Includes Other Defense Activities (ODA) not shown separately.   [2] Navy and Marine Corps personnel who are in afloat duty status at the time of the report are included in the strength counts of their homeport locations.

Source: U.S. Department of Defense, DoD Personnel and Procurement Statistics, Personnel, Publications, *Atlas/Data Abstract for the United States and Selected Areas,* annual; <http://siadapp.dmdc.osd.mil/>.

Table 497. **Military Personnel on Active Duty by Location: 1980 to 2008**

[In thousands (2,051 represents 2,051,000). As of September 30]

Location	1980	1990	1995	2000	2003	2004	2005	2006	2007	2008
Total	2,051	2,046	1,518	1,384	1,434	1,427	1,389	1,385	1,380	1,402
Shore-based [1]	1,840	1,794	1,351	1,237	1,287	1,291	1,262	1,263	1,264	1,294
Afloat [2]	211	252	167	147	148	136	127	121	115	108
United States [3]	1,562	1,437	1,280	1,127	1,182	1,139	1,098	1,100	1,085	1,113
Foreign countries	489	609	238	258	253	288	291	285	295	289

[1] Includes Navy personnel temporarily on shore.   [2] Includes Marine Corps.   [3] Includes Puerto Rico and Island areas.

Source: U.S. Department of Defense, DoD Personnel and Procurement Statistics, Personnel, Publications, *Atlas/Data Abstract for the United States and Selected Areas,* annual; <http://siadapp.dmdc.osd.mil>.

328   National Security and Veterans Affairs

Table 498. Department of Defense Personnel: 1960 to 2008

[In thousands (2,475 represents 2,475,000). As of end of fiscal year; see text, Section 8. Includes National Guard, Reserve, and retired regular personnel on extended or continuous active duty. Excludes Coast Guard. Other officer candidates are included under enlisted personnel]

Year	Total[1]	Army Total[1]	Army Male Officers	Army Male Enlisted	Army Female Officers	Army Female Enlisted	Navy[2] Total[1]	Navy Male Officers	Navy Male Enlisted	Navy Female Officers	Navy Female Enlisted	Marine Corps Total[1]	MC Male Officers	MC Male Enlisted	MC Female Officers	MC Female Enlisted	Air Force Total[1]	AF Male Officers	AF Male Enlisted	AF Female Officers	AF Female Enlisted
1960	2,475	873	97	762	4.3	8.3	617	67	540	2.7	5.4	171	16	153	0.1	1.5	815	126	677	3.7	5.7
1965	2,654	969	108	846	3.8	8.5	670	75	583	2.6	5.3	190	17	172	0.1	1.4	825	128	685	4.1	4.7
1970	3,065	1,323	162	1,142	5.2	11.5	691	78	600	2.9	5.8	260	25	233	0.3	2.1	791	125	648	4.7	9.0
1975	2,128	784	98	640	4.6	37.7	535	62	449	3.7	17.5	196	19	174	0.3	2.8	613	100	478	5.0	25.2
1980	2,051	777	91	612	7.6	61.7	527	58	430	4.9	30.1	189	18	164	0.5	6.2	558	90	404	8.5	51.9
1981	2,083	781	94	610	8.3	65.3	540	60	435	5.3	34.6	191	17	165	0.5	7.1	570	90	413	9.1	54.4
1982	2,109	780	94	609	9.0	64.1	553	61	444	5.7	37.3	192	18	165	0.6	7.9	583	92	421	9.9	54.5
1983	2,123	780	97	602	9.5	66.5	558	62	444	6.3	40.8	194	19	166	0.6	8.3	592	94	428	10.6	55.3
1984	2,138	780	98	601	10.2	67.1	565	62	448	6.6	42.6	196	19	167	0.6	8.6	597	95	430	11.2	55.9
1985	2,151	781	99	599	10.8	68.4	571	64	449	6.9	45.7	198	19	169	0.7	9.0	602	96	431	11.9	58.1
1986	2,169	781	99	597	11.3	69.7	581	65	457	7.3	47.2	200	19	170	0.6	9.2	608	97	434	12.4	61.2
1987	2,174	781	96	596	11.6	71.6	587	65	462	7.2	47.7	200	19	170	0.6	9.1	607	94	432	12.6	63.2
1988	2,138	772	95	588	11.8	72.0	593	65	466	7.3	49.7	197	19	168	0.7	9.0	576	92	405	12.9	61.5
1989	2,130	770	95	584	12.2	74.3	593	65	464	7.5	52.1	197	19	168	0.7	9.0	571	91	399	13.4	63.7
1990	2,044	732	92	553	12.4	71.2	579	64	451	7.8	52.1	197	19	168	0.7	8.7	535	87	370	13.3	60.8
1991	1,986	711	91	535	12.5	67.8	570	63	444	8.0	51.4	194	18	166	0.7	8.3	510	84	350	13.3	59.1
1992	1,807	610	83	449	11.7	61.7	542	61	417	8.3	51.0	185	18	157	0.6	7.9	470	77	320	12.7	56.1
1993	1,705	572	77	420	11.1	60.2	510	58	390	8.3	49.3	178	17	153	0.6	7.2	444	72	302	12.3	54.5
1994	1,610	541	74	394	10.9	59.0	469	54	355	8.0	47.9	174	17	149	0.6	7.0	426	69	287	12.3	54.0
1995	1,518	509	72	365	10.8	57.3	435	51	324	7.9	47.9	175	17	150	0.7	7.4	400	66	266	12.1	52.1
1996	1,472	491	70	347	10.6	59.0	417	50	308	7.8	46.9	175	17	149	0.8	7.8	389	64	256	12.0	52.8
1997	1,439	492	69	346	10.4	62.4	396	48	290	7.8	44.8	174	17	148	0.8	8.5	377	62	246	12.0	53.8
1998	1,407	484	68	340	10.4	61.4	382	47	280	7.8	42.9	173	17	146	0.8	8.9	368	60	237	12.0	54.2
1999	1,386	479	67	337	10.5	61.5	373	46	271	7.7	43.9	173	17	145	0.9	9.3	361	58	232	11.8	54.6
2000	1,384	482	66	339	10.8	62.9	373	46	272	7.8	43.8	173	17	146	0.9	9.5	356	57	227	11.8	55.0
2001	1,385	481	65	337	11.0	63.4	378	46	273	8.0	46.6	173	17	145	1.0	9.6	354	57	224	12.0	55.6
2002	1,414	487	66	341	11.5	63.2	385	47	279	8.2	47.3	174	17	146	1.0	9.5	368	59	233	13.5	58.6
2003	1,434	499	68	352	12.0	63.5	382	47	276	8.2	47.3	178	18	149	1.1	9.6	375	61	237	13.6	60.0
2004	1,427	500	69	358	12.4	61.9	373	46	273	8.1	46.1	178	18	149	1.0	9.7	377	61	242	13.4	60.2
2005	1,389	493	69	353	12.5	57.9	363	45	266	7.8	44.5	180	18	151	1.0	9.8	354	60	225	13.4	55.6
2006	1,385	505	69	365	13.0	58.5	350	44	255	7.6	43.2	180	18	151	1.1	10.0	349	58	223	12.8	55.8
2007	1,380	522	71	379	13.0	58.8	338	44	244	7.6	42.2	186	18	156	1.1	10.5	333	54	214	12.8	53.4
2008	1,402	544	74	392	13.5	59.7	332	44	235	7.7	41.4	199	19	167	1.2	11.1	327	53	207	11.9	51.4

[1] Includes cadets, midshipmen, and others not shown separately. [2] Beginning 1980, excludes Navy Reserve personnel on active duty for Training and Administration of Reserves (TARS).

Source: U.S. Dept. of Defense, Selected Manpower Statistics, annual; and unpublished data.

National Security and Veterans Affairs   329

Table 499. **Military Personnel on Active Duty by Rank or Grade: 1990 to 2008**

[In thousands (2,043.7 represents 2,043,700). As of Sept. 30]

Rank/grade	1990	2000	2004	2005	2006	2007	2008
Total	**2,043.7**	**1,384.3**	**1,426.8**	**1,389.4**	**1,385.0**	**1,379.6**	**1,401.8**
Total Officers	**296.6**	**217.2**	**226.7**	**226.6**	**223.2**	**221.3**	**223.7**
General-Admiral	(Z)	(Z)	(Z)	(Z)	(Z)	(Z)	(Z)
Lieutenant General-Vice Admiral . . .	0.1	0.1	0.1	0.1	0.1	0.1	0.1
Major General-Rear Admiral (U). . . .	0.4	0.3	0.3	0.3	0.3	0.3	0.3
Brigadier General-Rear Admiral (L). .	0.5	0.4	0.4	0.4	0.5	0.4	0.5
Colonel-Captain	14.0	11.3	11.5	11.4	11.3	11.3	11.6
Lieutenant Colonel-Commander. . . .	32.3	27.5	28.4	28.1	27.5	27.7	28.1
Major-LT Commander	53.2	43.2	44.0	44.4	45.1	44.2	43.4
Captain-Lieutenant	106.6	68.1	69.5	72.5	71.9	70.6	71.0
1st Lieutenant-Lieutenant (JG)	37.9	24.7	31.1	27.5	24.9	23.4	23.9
2nd Lieutenant-Ensign.	31.9	26.4	26.9	25.9	25.2	26.0	26.4
Chief Warrant Officer W-5.	(Z)	0.1	0.1	0.5	0.6	0.6	0.6
Chief Warrant Officer W-4.	3.0	2.0	1.9	2.2	2.4	2.9	3.1
Chief Warrant Officer W-3.	5.0	3.8	4.1	4.6	4.6	4.6	4.7
Chief Warrant Officer W-2.	8.4	6.7	6.0	6.2	6.0	5.7	6.4
Warrant Officer W-1.	3.2	2.1	3.1	2.5	2.9	3.4	3.4
Total Enlisted	**1,733.8**	**1,154.6**	**1,172.0**	**1,149.9**	**1,148.6**	**1,145.0**	**1,164.7**
E-9.	15.3	10.2	10.7	10.5	10.4	10.6	10.5
E-8.	38.0	26.0	27.1	27.1	26.7	27.4	27.4
E-7.	134.1	97.7	99.6	97.8	99.3	97.1	97.2
E-6.	239.1	164.9	173.1	172.4	170.3	168.4	170.3
E-5.	361.5	229.5	251.1	248.5	248.8	247.4	249.0
E-4.	427.8	251.0	264.1	261.7	261.4	260.1	266.1
E-3.	280.1	196.3	220.1	201.7	185.4	192.5	194.9
E-2.	140.3	99.0	84.3	70.8	83.5	79.9	83.6
E-1.	97.6	80.0	55.8	59.5	62.8	61.7	65.6
Cadets and Midshipmen	**13.3**	**12.5**	**12.6**	**12.9**	**13.2**	**13.2**	**13.4**

Z Fewer than 50.

Source: U.S. Department of Defense, DoD Personnel and Procurement Statistics, Personnel, Military, *Military Personnel Statistics,* annual; <http://siadapp.dmdc.osd.mil>.

Table 500. **Military Retirement System: 2008**

[**Payment in millions of dollars (3,567 represents $3,567,000,000). As of September 30.** The data published in this report are produced from the files maintained by the Defense Manpower Data Center (DMDC). This report compiles data primarily from the "Retiree Pay and Survivor Pay" files. Any grouping of members by address reflects mailing, not necessarily residence address. Only those members in plans administered by the Department of Defense (DoD) are included in this table. The data are preliminary because of reporting delays due to the information about many members who retired or died within one month of the September 30 reporting date. These data were not processed in time to be included in this report. For more information, please see *Introduction and Overview* at <http://www.defenselink.mil/actuary/statbook2008.pdf>]

State or other area	Retired military personnel [1]				State or other area	Retired military personnel [1]			
	Total	Disabled [2]	Non-disabled	Monthly payment		Total	Disabled [2]	Non-disabled	Monthly payment
Total[3] . . .	**2,002,852**	**179,129**	**1,823,723**	**3,567**	MO	36,436	3,769	32,667	57
U.S.	**1,962,806**	**175,873**	**1,786,933**	**3,502**	MT	8,527	782	7,745	14
AL	55,056	4,426	50,630	96	NE	13,721	1,023	12,698	25
AK	9,429	594	8,835	16	NV	27,225	1,811	25,414	49
AZ	53,873	4,518	49,355	100	NH	9,429	783	8,646	17
AR	25,564	2,336	23,228	41	NJ	20,374	2,606	17,768	30
CA	168,647	15,735	152,912	306	NM	21,350	1,703	19,647	40
CO	48,165	3,760	44,405	99	NY	37,480	5,726	31,754	49
CT	10,711	1,320	9,391	17	NC	83,688	7,212	76,476	150
DE	8,146	539	7,607	13	ND	4,738	360	4,378	7
DC	2,953	427	2,526	5	OH	43,965	5,569	38,396	69
FL	185,582	15,197	170,385	353	OK	34,432	2,833	31,599	56
GA	88,355	7,354	81,001	155	OR	21,366	2,496	18,870	35
HI	15,832	1,020	14,812	30	PA	48,837	5,885	42,952	75
ID	12,657	1,067	11,590	21	RI	5,552	534	5,018	10
IL	35,146	4,420	30,726	57	SC	54,718	4,199	50,519	95
IN	23,765	2,979	20,786	34	SD	7,025	571	6,454	11
IA	11,734	1,276	10,458	16	TN	50,496	4,537	45,959	84
KS	20,515	1,600	18,915	36	TX	185,400	15,206	170,194	349
KY	26,324	2,729	23,595	42	UT	14,707	1,123	13,584	25
LA	25,570	2,686	22,884	41	VT	3,641	336	3,305	5
ME	12,130	1,121	11,009	19	VA	143,582	7,836	135,746	341
MD	50,439	3,805	46,634	98	WA	70,403	5,155	65,248	128
MA	19,155	2,510	16,645	28	WV	10,737	1,308	9,429	16
MI	27,486	4,092	23,394	38	WI	19,403	2,339	17,064	27
MN	17,369	2,014	15,355	24	WY	4,951	408	4,543	8
MS	26,020	2,238	23,782	41					

[1] Represents military personnel (officers and enlisted) receiving and not receiving pay from DoD. [2] A disabled military member is entitled to disability retired pay if the disability is not the result of the member's intentional misconduct or willful neglect, was not incurred during a period of unauthorized absence, and either: (1) the member has at least 20 years of service; or (2) at the time of determination, the disability is at least 30 percent (under a standard schedule of rating disabilities by the Veterans Administration) and one of three additional conditions are met—For the continuation of this footnote, see U.S. Census Bureau, Statistical Abstract, National Security and Veterans Affairs, Military Personnel and Expenditures, Military Retirement System; <http://www.census.gov/compendia/statab/>. [3] Includes states, U.S. territories, and retirees living in foreign countries.

Source: U.S. Department of Defense, Office of the Actuary, Statistical Report, Fiscal Year 2008 (issued May 2009); <http://www.defenselink.mil/actuary/>.

Table 501. Military Reserve Personnel: 1995 to 2008

[As of September 30. The Ready Reserve data include the Selected Reserve which is scheduled to augment active forces during times of war or national emergency, and the Individual Ready Reserve, which, during times of war or national emergency, would be used to fill out Active, Guard, and Reserve units, and which would also be a source for casualty replacements; Ready Reservists serve in an active status (except for the Inactive National Guard—a very small pool within the Army National Guard). The Standby Reserve cannot be called to active duty, other than for training, unless authorized by Congress under "full mobilization," and a determination is made that there are not enough qualified members in the Ready Reserve in the required categories who are readily available. The Retired Reserve represents a lower potential for involuntary mobilization]

Reserve status and branch of service	1995	2000	2004	2005	2006	2007	2008
Total reserves [1]	**1,674,164**	**1,276,843**	**1,166,937**	**1,136,200**	**1,119,902**	**1,109,805**	**1,099,915**
Ready reserve	1,648,388	1,251,452	1,145,035	1,113,427	1,101,565	1,088,587	1,080,617
Army [2]	999,462	725,771	663,209	636,355	631,856	621,422	626,892
Navy	267,356	184,080	148,643	140,821	131,802	128,421	123,159
Marine Corps..........	103,668	99,855	101,443	99,820	100,522	100,787	95,748
Air Force [3]...........	263,011	229,009	219,159	223,551	224,637	226,806	224,545
Coast Guard	14,891	12,737	12,581	12,880	12,748	11,151	10,273
Standby reserve	25,776	25,391	21,902	22,773	18,337	21,218	19,298
Army	1,128	701	715	1,668	1,586	[4]5,294	2,136
Navy	12,707	7,213	2,502	4,038	4,514	3,046	3,310
Marine Corps..........	216	895	992	1,129	1,210	1,372	1,691
Air Force.............	11,453	16,429	17,340	15,897	10,932	10,154	10,384
Coast Guard	272	153	353	41	95	1,352	1,777
Retired reserve	505,905	573,305	614,904	627,424	637,262	648,346	658,251
Army	259,553	296,004	315,477	321,312	325,288	330,121	334,258
Navy	97,532	109,531	115,210	117,093	118,803	120,859	122,000
Marine Corps..........	11,319	12,937	14,319	14,693	15,000	15,264	15,558
Air Force.............	137,501	154,833	169,898	174,326	178,171	182,102	186,435

[1] Less retired reserves.   [2] Includes Army National Guard.   [3] Includes Air National Guard.   [4] The Army did a "scrub" of their Individual Ready Reserve (IRR) categories and dropped personnel awaiting retirement or discharge into the Standby Reserve during FY2007 in order to give them a better perspective on actual IRR members cleared for mobilization, if required.

Source: U.S. Department of Defense, DoD Personnel and Procurement Statistics, Personnel, Publications, Atlas/Data Abstract for the United States and Selected Areas, *Selected Manpower Statistics*, annual. See also <http://siadapp.dmdc.osd.mil>.

Table 502. Ready Reserve Personnel by Race, Hispanic Origin, and Sex: 1990 to 2008

[In thousands (1,658.7 represents 1,658,700). As of September 30]

Year		Race					Sex			
							Officer		Enlisted	
	Total [1]	White	Black	Asian	American Indian	Hispanic [2]	Male	Female	Male	Female
1990...	1,658.7	1,304.6	272.3	14.9	7.8	83.1	226.8	40.5	1,204.7	186.7
1995...	1,648.4	1,267.7	274.5	22.0	8.8	96.2	209.9	44.7	1,196.8	196.9
1997...	1,451.0	1,113.7	230.6	21.7	8.4	91.5	188.7	43.2	1,037.6	181.5
1998...	1,353.4	1,033.9	210.4	21.7	7.8	88.2	175.9	40.3	964.1	173.1
1999...	1,288.8	980.0	202.6	22.6	7.6	88.9	166.2	38.4	911.2	173.1
2000...	1,251.5	942.2	199.6	26.7	8.4	91.8	159.4	36.9	879.9	175.3
2001...	1,224.1	912.7	198.4	27.9	8.5	94.3	158.0	36.6	852.2	177.3
2002...	1,199.3	891.3	193.2	27.9	8.8	96.0	152.1	35.6	835.2	176.4
2003...	1,167.1	865.7	187.5	25.4	8.5	98.0	145.1	34.0	813.7	174.3
2004...	1,145.0	845.3	181.3	26.2	9.1	100.2	141.9	33.6	799.7	169.8
2005...	1,113.4	825.4	169.9	26.9	9.5	99.8	139.2	33.3	778.0	162.9
2006...	1,101.6	822.4	163.5	27.7	10.1	101.1	136.7	33.1	769.4	162.3
2007...	1,088.6	818.1	156.6	28.1	10.8	102.7	130.0	31.8	766.5	160.2
2008...	1,080.6	815.2	153.4	29.0	10.9	102.6	128.0	31.2	760.8	160.6

[1] Includes other races not shown separately.   [2] Persons of Hispanic origin may be any race.

Source: U.S. Department of Defense, DoD Personnel and Procurement Statistics, Personnel, Publications, Atlas/Data Abstract for the United States and Selected Areas, annual; <http://siadapp.dmdc.osd.mil>.

Table 503. National Guard by Sex and Race: 1995 to 2008

[In thousands (375 represents 375,000). As of September 30]

Year	Army National Guard					Air National Guard				
	Total	Male[1]	Female	White	Black	Total	Male[1]	Female	White	Black
1995	375	344	31	299	59	110	94	16	96	9
2000	353	313	40	278	55	106	88	18	90	10
2002	351	308	43	277	54	112	93	19	94	10
2003	351	307	44	277	52	108	89	19	91	10
2004	343	299	44	271	50	107	88	19	89	10
2005	333	290	43	264	46	106	87	19	89	9
2006	346	300	47	276	47	106	87	19	88	9
2007	353	304	49	283	47	106	87	19	88	9
2008	360	309	51	288	49	108	88	20	89	9

[1] Male population includes unknown sex.

Source: U.S. Department of Defense, DoD Personnel and Procurement Statistics, Personnel, Publications, Atlas/Data Abstract for the United States and Selected Areas, *Selected Manpower Statistics*, annual. See also <http://siadapp.dmdc.osd.mil>.

National Security and Veterans Affairs   331

Table 504. U.S. Active Duty Military Deaths by Manner of Death: 1980 to 2008

[As of December 31.]

Manner of death	1980–2008	1980	1990	1995	2000	2002	2003	2004	2005	2006	2007	2008
Deaths, total.	45,706	2,392	1,507	1,040	758	999	1,410	1,873	1,941	1,882	1,953	1,441
Accident	24,048	1,556	880	538	397	543	576	605	649	562	561	470
Hostile action	4,040	–	–	–	–	18	344	739	739	769	847	352
Homicide	2,195	174	74	67	34	54	43	45	52	47	47	43
Illness	8,011	419	277	174	139	195	234	272	289	256	235	235
Pending.	130	–	–	–	–	–	1	3	5	9	29	83
Self-inflicted	6,270	231	232	250	151	163	187	201	181	212	211	235
Terrorist attack	428	1	1	7	17	–	–	–	–	–	–	–
Undetermined.	584	11	43	4	20	26	25	8	26	27	23	23
Deaths per 100,000 of												
personnel strength. . . .	(X)	110.7	66.8	62.5	49.5	61.4	81.4	109.4	116.7	116.8	121.4	85.6
Accident	(X)	72.0	39.0	32.4	25.9	33.4	33.2	35.3	39.0	34.9	34.9	27.9
Hostile action	(X)	–	–	–	–	1.1	19.9	43.2	44.4	47.7	52.7	20.9
Homicide	(X)	8.1	3.3	4.0	2.2	3.3	2.5	2.6	3.1	2.9	2.9	2.6
Illness	(X)	19.4	12.3	10.5	9.1	12.0	13.5	15.9	17.4	15.9	14.6	14.0
Pending.	(X)	–	–	–	–	–	0.1	0.2	0.3	0.6	1.8	4.9
Self-inflicted	(X)	10.7	10.3	15.0	9.9	10.0	10.8	11.7	10.9	13.2	13.1	14.0
Terrorist attack	(X)	–	–	0.4	1.1	–	–	–	–	–	–	–
Undetermined.	(X)	0.5	1.9	0.2	1.3	1.6	1.4	0.5	1.6	1.7	1.4	1.4

– Represents zero.   X Not applicable.

U.S. Department of Defense, "Military Casualty Information"; <http://siadapp.dmdc.osd.mil/personnel/Pubs.htm>.

Table 505. U.S. Military Personnel on Active Duty in Selected Foreign Countries: 1995 to 2008

[As of September 30]

Country	1995	2000	2003	2004	2005	2006	2007	2008
In foreign countries [1] . . .	**238,064**	**257,817**	**252,764**	**287,802**	**290,997**	**284,967**	**295,003**	**288,550**
Ashore	208,836	212,858	226,570	265,594	268,214	262,586	272,124	269,260
Afloat	29,228	44,959	26,194	20,208	22,783	22,381	22,879	19,290
Australia	314	175	574	196	196	347	140	140
Bahrain.	618	949	1,514	1,712	1,641	1,357	1,495	1,545
Belgium	1,689	1,554	1,526	1,474	1,366	1,361	1,328	1,266
Bosnia and Herzegovina	1	5,708	3,041	951	263	232	209	14
Canada.	214	156	141	156	150	133	141	134
Colombia.	44	224	54	55	52	104	123	114
Cuba (Guantanamo)	5,129	688	697	682	950	953	932	969
Diego Garcia [2]	897	625	528	816	683	157	260	244
Djibouti	7	2	498	412	622	1,375	2,100	1,780
Egypt	1,123	499	385	348	410	360	250	284
Germany.	73,280	69,203	74,796	76,058	66,418	64,319	57,080	55,140
Greece	489	678	583	473	428	395	363	366
Greenland	131	125	139	133	146	137	126	134
Honduras	193	351	414	448	438	414	403	429
Italy	12,007	11,190	13,152	12,606	11,841	10,449	9,855	9,601
Korea, South	36,016	36,565	41,145	40,840	30,983	29,086	27,014	25,062
Kuwait	771	4,602	(3)	(3)	(3)	(3)	(3)	(3)
Netherlands.	687	659	703	701	583	591	579	547
Portugal	1,066	1,005	1,094	1,006	970	922	826	783
Qatar	2	52	2,997	273	463	446	411	433
Saudi Arabia	1,077	7,053	953	235	258	282	243	284
Senegal	13	10	8	9	42	7	11	7
Singapore	166	411	171	237	169	164	125	129
Spain	2,799	2,007	1,893	2,012	1,660	1,521	1,286	1,220
Turkey	3,111	2,006	2,021	1,762	1,780	1,810	1,594	1,575
United Kingdom	12,131	11,207	11,616	11,469	10,752	10,331	9,825	9,426
DEPLOYMENTS								
Operation Enduring Freedom (OEF) [4]	(X)	(X)	(NA)	(NA)	19,500	21,500	25,240	32,300
Operation Iraqi Freedom (OIF) [5]	(X)	(X)	183,002	170,647	192,600	185,500	218,500	190,400

X Not applicable.   NA Not available.   [1] Includes areas not shown separately.   [2] British Indian Ocean Territory.   [3] Military personnel data for Kuwait are included with the Operation Iraqi Freedom (OIF) data.   [4] Total (in/around Afghanistan as of September 30)—includes deployed Reserve/National Guard.   [5] Total (in/around Iraq as of September 30)—includes deployed Reserve/National Guard.

Source: U.S. Department of Defense, *DoD Personnel and Procurement Statistics*, "Active Duty Military Personnel Strengths by Regional Area and by Country." See also <http://siadapp.dmdc.osd.mil/personnel/MMIDHOME.HTM>.

Table 506. **U.S. Military Sales and Assistance to Foreign Governments: 1995 to 2007**

[In millions of dollars (8,495 represents $8,495,000,000). For year ending September 30. Department of Defense (DoD) sales deliveries cover deliveries against sales orders authorized under Arms Export Control Act, as well as earlier and applicable legislation. For details regarding individual programs, see source]

Item	1995	2000	2001	2002	2003	2004	2005	2006	2007
Military sales agreements	8,495	10,678	12,512	12,049	12,654	13,218	9,561	18,089	19,119
Military construction sales agreements	24	284	124	71	224	674	313	173	419
Military sales deliveries [1]	12,100	10,888	12,427	10,442	9,717	11,154	11,278	11,718	12,615
Military construction sales deliveries	(NA)	183	244	216	245	281	350	323	197
Military financing program	3,712	4,333	3,535	4,032	5,955	4,584	4,956	4,450	4,519
Commercial exports licensed under arms export control act [2] . .	(NA)	478	821	341	2,728	7,895	30,146	31,605	8,874
Military assistance program delivery [3]	20	14	21	34	182	28	62	46	14
IMET program/deliveries [4]	26	50	54	70	79	89	87	85	98

NA Not available. [1] Includes military construction sales deliveries. [2] The total dollar value of deliveries made against purchases of munitions-controlled items by foreign governments directly from U.S. manufacturers. [3] Includes Military Assistance Service Funded (MASF) program data and Section 506(a) drawdown authority. [4] International Military Education & Training. Includes military assistance service funded and emergency draw downs.

Source: U.S. Department of Defense, Defense Security Cooperation Agency, "DSCA Data and Statistics." See also <http://www.dsca.osd.mil/data_stats.htm>.

Table 507. **U.S. Military Sales Deliveries by Selected Country: 1995 to 2007**

[In millions of dollars (12,100 represents $12,100,000,000). For year ending September 30. Represents Department of Defense military sales.]

Country	1995	2000	2001	2002	2003	2004	2005	2006	2007
Total [1]	12,100	10,888	12,427	10,442	9,717	11,154	11,278	11,718	12,615
Australia	303	332	303	216	208	196	350	351	789
Bahrain	40	55	339	84	90	88	65	56	84
Belgium	8	61	169	68	71	42	50	53	49
Canada	127	84	113	85	155	144	151	183	281
Denmark	54	44	109	23	14	22	40	49	63
Egypt	1,479	1,092	875	1,860	1,081	1,518	1,459	1,219	1,281
France	64	217	142	206	276	99	69	43	47
Germany	257	131	330	221	241	264	208	149	206
Greece	220	389	448	469	1,324	1,225	468	180	222
Israel	327	585	778	630	927	1,204	1,524	1,286	1,269
Italy	54	52	188	103	185	281	127	300	158
Japan	693	458	491	466	430	392	410	769	654
Jordan	47	52	80	67	69	104	141	106	172
Korea, South	442	1,399	735	533	560	601	606	601	598
Kuwait	471	321	502	131	143	209	278	542	467
Netherlands	153	278	569	406	224	277	178	231	216
Norway	25	64	192	87	123	80	106	95	165
Portugal	88	20	42	28	116	30	84	83	46
Saudi Arabia	3,567	1,975	1,876	1,308	1,011	1,223	994	995	1,084
Singapore	59	131	244	407	168	205	229	355	174
Spain	193	141	467	178	160	188	124	105	151
Taiwan [2]	1,332	784	1,162	1,393	710	917	1,415	1,074	789
Thailand	356	114	119	171	153	180	92	83	50
Turkey	368	216	466	281	277	290	190	247	196
United Arab Emirates . . .	345	39	9	40	87	155	171	203	72
United Kingdom	419	347	525	386	350	453	384	295	430

[1] Includes countries not shown. [2] See footnote 4, Table 1296.

Source: U.S. Department of Defense, Defense Security Cooperation Agency, "DSCA Data and Statistics." See also <http://www.dsca.osd.mil/data_stats.htm>.

National Security and Veterans Affairs 333

Table 508. Veterans by Sex, Selected Period of Service, and State: 2008

[In thousands (23,215 represents 23,215,000). As of September 30. VetPop2007 is the Department of Veterans Affairs (VA) latest official estimate and projection of the veteran population. It is based on detailed tabulations of Census 2000 data (prepared for the VA Office of the Actuary by the Census Bureau) and on recent American Community Survey data. VetPop2007 also uses administrative data and projections of service member separations from active duty provided by the Department of Defense (the Defense Manpower Data Center and the Office of the Actuary), as well as VA administrative data on veterans benefits]

State	Total [1,2]	Gulf War [3]	Vietnam era	State	Total [1,2]	Gulf War [3]	Vietnam era
United States	23,215	5,193	7,700	Missouri	523	109	176
Alabama	414	105	140	Montana	104	22	36
Alaska	76	25	27	Nebraska	150	34	52
Arizona	565	125	181	Nevada	246	57	87
Arkansas	260	60	89	New Hampshire	131	23	46
California	2,078	464	678	New Jersey	485	73	150
Colorado	426	108	154	New Mexico	178	46	59
Connecticut	246	38	82	New York	1,026	165	324
Delaware	80	18	26	North Carolina	772	204	254
District of Columbia	39	9	12	North Dakota	58	14	18
Florida	1,715	365	522	Ohio	935	178	314
Georgia	770	222	260	Oklahoma	334	85	113
Hawaii	118	33	37	Oregon	346	65	123
Idaho	137	33	47	Pennsylvania	1,026	168	335
Illinois	822	172	264	Rhode Island	77	13	25
Indiana	509	102	171	South Carolina	410	107	141
Iowa	246	47	83	South Dakota	74	18	24
Kansas	233	57	77	Tennessee	507	116	179
Kentucky	344	80	117	Texas	1,705	471	576
Louisiana	319	85	101	Utah	156	36	52
Maine	142	28	51	Vermont	54	9	19
Maryland	480	127	153	Virginia	814	276	261
Massachusetts	425	64	136	Washington	640	159	227
Michigan	742	128	259	West Virginia	174	36	59
Minnesota	399	64	145	Wisconsin	437	80	147
Mississippi	213	56	69	Wyoming	56	14	21

[1] Veterans serving in more than one period of service are counted only once in the total.   [2] Current civilians discharged from active duty, other than for training only without service-connected disability.   [3] Service from August 2, 1990 to the present.

Source: Department of Veterans Affairs, Veteran Data and Information, Veteran Demographics; <http://www1.va.gov/vetdata/page.cfm?pg=15>.

Table 509. Employment Status of Persons 18 Years and Over by Veteran Status, Period of Service, and Sex: 2008

[The Current Population Study (CPS), defines veterans as men and women who have previously served on active duty in the U.S. Armed Forces and who were civilians at the time they were surveyed. Data about veteran status and period of service are collected monthly in the CPS; these data are the source for the 2008 annual averages presented. Period-of-service designations identify when the veteran served rather than where; thus, wartime veterans did not necessarily serve in a war zone. For more information on this report (technical note and definitions), go to <http://www.bls.gov/news.release/pdf/vet.pdf>]

Veteran status, period of service, and sex	Civilian noninstitutional population	Civilian labor force						Not in labor force
		Total	Percent of civilian noninstitutional population	Employed		Unemployed		
				Total	Percent of civilian noninstitutional population	Total	Percent of civilian labor force	
Total	224,655	151,735	67.5	143,373	63.8	8,361	5.5	72,920
Veterans.	22,429	12,368	55.1	11,795	52.6	573	4.6	10,061
Gulf War era, total.	4,592	3,989	86.9	3,782	82.4	207	5.2	604
Gulf War era I [1]	2,939	2,583	87.9	2,479	84.4	103	4.0	356
Gulf War era II [2]	1,653	1,406	85.0	1,303	78.8	103	7.3	247
WW II, Korean War, and Vietnam era [3] . .	11,855	4,690	39.6	4,492	37.9	198	4.2	7,165
Other service periods [4]	5,983	3,690	61.7	3,522	58.9	168	4.6	2,293
Nonveterans [5]	202,226	139,366	68.9	131,578	65.1	7,788	5.6	62,859
Male	108,488	81,282	74.9	76,560	70.6	4,722	5.8	27,206
Veterans.	20,712	11,253	54.3	10,739	51.8	515	4.6	9,458
Gulf War era, total.	3,848	3,425	89.0	3,256	84.6	169	4.9	423
Gulf War era I [1]	2,488	2,231	89.7	2,147	86.3	84	3.8	257
Gulf War era II [2]	1,359	1,193	87.8	1,109	81.6	84	7.1	166
WW II, Korean War, and Vietnam era [3] . .	11,455	4,542	39.7	4,349	38.0	193	4.3	6,913
Other service periods [4]	5,409	3,287	60.8	3,134	57.9	153	4.6	2,123
Nonveterans [5]	87,776	70,028	79.8	65,821	75.0	4,207	6.0	17,748
Female	116,167	70,453	60.6	66,813	57.5	3,639	5.2	45,715
Veterans.	1,718	1,115	64.9	1,057	61.5	58	5.2	603
Gulf War era, total.	745	564	75.7	526	70.6	38	6.8	181
Gulf War era I [1]	451	351	77.9	332	73.7	19	5.5	99
Gulf War era II [2]	294	212	72.3	194	65.9	19	8.9	81
WW II, Korean War, and Vietnam era [3] . .	399	148	37.0	143	35.8	5	3.2	252
Other service periods [4]	574	403	70.3	388	67.6	16	3.8	170
Nonveterans [5]	114,450	69,338	60.6	65,757	57.5	3,581	5.2	45,112

[1] Gulf War era I; August 1990–August 2001.   [2] Gulf War era II; September 2001–present.   [3] World War II; December 1941–December 1945, Korea War; July 1950–January 1955. Vietnam era; August 1964–April 1975.   [4] Other service periods; all other time periods.   [5] Nonveterans are men and women who never served on active duty in the U.S. Armed Forces.

Source: Bureau of Labor Statistics, "Current Population Study, CPS New Release, Employment Situation of Veterans" (released 20 March 2009); <http://www.bls.gov/news.release/vet.nr0.htm>.

334   National Security and Veterans Affairs

Table 510. Veterans by Sex, Race, and Hispanic or Latino Origin: 2007

[In thousands (22,892.1 represents 22,892,100). Data are based on the American Community Survey (ACS). The survey universe includes the household population and the population living in institutions, college dormitories, and other group quarters. Based on a sample and subject to sampling variability; see text of this section and Appendix III]

Characteristics	Total number	18 to 64 years	65 years and over
Total[1]	**22,892.1**	**13,906.3**	**8,985.8**
Male	21,334.5	12,628.4	8,706.1
Female	1,557.6	1,278.0	279.6
White alone	19,397.8	11,182.8	8,215.0
Male	18,224.7	10,268.0	7,956.6
Female	1,173.2	914.8	258.4
Black or African American alone	2,365.4	1,857.2	508.2
Male	2,083.7	1,588.6	495.0
Female	281.8	268.5	13.2
American Indian/Alaska Native alone	165.2	124.3	40.9
Male	150.1	110.7	39.4
Female	15.1	13.6	1.5
Asian alone	277.8	186.5	91.2
Male	254.1	165.4	88.6
Female	23.7	21.1	2.6
Native Hawaiian and Other Pacific Islander alone	26.9	21.0	5.9
Male	23.5	17.9	5.7
Female	3.3	3.1	0.2
Some other race alone	358.3	299.0	59.3
Male	327.6	269.6	58.0
Female	30.7	29.4	1.3
Hispanic or Latino origin [2]	1,096.4	839.2	257.2
Male	1,007.9	756.3	251.6
Female	88.5	82.9	5.6

[1] Includes data for two or more races not shown separately.   [2] Persons of Hispanic or Latino origin may be any race.

Source: U.S. Census Bureau, 2007 American Community Survey; using American FactFinder, tables B21001, B21001A, B21001B, B21001C, B21001D, B21001E, B21001F, and B21001I; <http://factfinder.census.gov/>.

Table 511. Veterans Benefits—Expenditures by Program and Compensation for Service-Connected Disabilities: 1990 to 2008

[In millions of dollars (28,998 represents $28,998,000,000). For years ending September 30. Minus sign (–) indicates decrease]

Program	1990	1995	2000	2004	2005	2006	2007	2008
Total expenditures	**28,998**	**37,775**	**47,086**	**59,555**	**69,564**	**69,950**	**72,805**	**84,410**
Medical programs	11,582	16,255	19,637	28,158	29,191	31,308	33,705	37,914
Construction	661	641	466	318	480	497	704	643
General operating expenses	811	954	1,016	1,252	1,285	1,545	1,476	1,253
Compensation and pension	14,674	17,765	22,012	29,937	32,131	34,681	34,600	40,241
Vocational rehabilitation and education	452	1,317	1,610	2,827	3,033	3,163	3,180	3,210
All other [1]	818	844	2,345	–2,937	3,445	–1,244	–860	1,149
Compensation for service-connected disabilities [2]	**9,284**	**11,644**	**15,511**	**22,387**	**24,515**	**26,551**	**28,200**	**36,255**

[1] Includes insurance, indemnities, and miscellaneous funds and expenditures and offsets from public receipts. (Excludes expenditures from personal funds of patients.)   [2] Represents veterans receiving compensation for service-connected disabilities.

Source: U.S. Department of Veterans Affairs, *Expenditures and Workload,* annual; <http://www1.va.gov/vetdata/page.cfm?pg=3>.

Table 512. Veterans Compensation and Pension Benefits—Number on Rolls by Period of Service and Status: 1990 to 2008

[In thousands (3,584 represents 3,584,000), except as indicated. As of September 30. Living refers to veterans receiving compensation for disability incurred or aggravated while on active duty and war veterans receiving pension and benefits for non-service connected disabilities. Deceased refers to deceased veterans whose dependents were receiving pensions and compensation benefits]

Period of service and veteran status	1990	1995	2000	2004	2005	2006	2007	2008
Total	**3,584**	**3,330**	**3,236**	**3,432**	**3,503**	**3,582**	**3,691**	**3,801**
Living veterans	2,746	2,669	2,672	2,899	2,973	3,056	3,167	3,268
Service-connected	2,184	2,236	2,308	2,556	2,637	2,726	2,844	2,952
Nonservice-connected	562	433	364	343	336	330	323	316
Deceased veterans	838	662	564	533	530	527	524	533
Service-connected	320	307	307	318	323	326	330	338
Nonservice-connected	518	355	257	215	207	201	195	196
World War I	198	89	34	16	13	11	9	8
Living	18	3	(Z)	(Z)	(Z)	(Z)	(Z)	(Z)
World War II	1,723	1,307	968	766	718	674	634	598
Living	1,294	961	676	506	466	430	397	362
Korean conflict [1]	390	368	323	302	295	290	287	282
Living	305	290	255	237	231	226	223	218
Vietnam era [2]	774	868	969	1,172	1,218	1,260	1,305	1,347
Living	685	766	848	1,028	1,068	1,104	1,142	1,175
Gulf War [3]	(X)	138	334	552	630	716	819	923
Living	(X)	134	326	540	617	701	802	904
Peacetime	495	559	607	624	627	631	637	644
Living	444	514	567	587	591	596	602	609

X Not applicable.   Z Fewer than 500.   [1] Service during period June 27, 1950 to January 31, 1955.   [2] Service from August 5, 1964 to May 7, 1975.   [3] Service from August 2, 1990 to the present.

Source: U.S. Department of Veterans Affairs, 1990 to 1995, *Annual Report of the Secretary of Veterans Affairs;* beginning 2000, *Annual Accountablility Report* and unpublished data; <http://www1.va.gov/vetdata/>.

National Security and Veterans Affairs   335

Table 513. **Homeland Security Funding by Agency: 2007 to 2009**

[In millions of dollars (56,925.9 represents $56,925,900,000). For year ending September 30. A total of 31 agencies comprise Federal homeland security funding for 2009. Department of Homeland Security (DHS) is the designated department to coordinate and centralize the leadership of many homeland security activities under a single department. In addition to DHS, the Departments of Defense (DoD), Energy (DoE), Health and Human Services (HHS), Justice (DoJ), and the State Department account for most of the total government-wide homeland security funding]

Agency	2007	2008	2009
Total budget authority, excluding BioShield [1,2]	56,925.9	61,227.8	68,818.5
Department of Agriculture	540.5	574.6	507.1
Department of Commerce	205.0	206.9	258.1
Department of Defense	16,538.3	17,374.4	19,413.5
Department of Education	26.2	27.1	31.8
Department of Energy	1,719.2	1,827.3	1,938.8
Department of Health and Human Services	4,327.0	4,300.6	4,626.8
Department of Homeland Security [3]	26,857.9	29,755.8	34,350.9
Department of Housing and Urban Development	1.9	1.9	4.8
Department of the Interior	47.8	50.2	52.7
Department of Justice	3,306.4	3,277.5	3,641.3
Department of Labor	49.4	47.8	48.5
Department of State	1,241.6	1,719.1	1,809.2
Department of Transportation	205.7	205.3	220.9
Department of the Treasury	126.8	120.0	133.7
Department of Veterans Affairs	259.8	308.9	304.6
Corps of Engineers	42.0	42.0	42.0
Environmental Protection Agency	166.7	138.1	157.0
Executive Office of the President	20.8	21.0	19.1
General Services Administration	168.2	143.0	159.4
National Aeronautics and Space Administration	199.2	205.2	221.8
National Science Foundation	385.4	365.1	377.2
Office of Personnel Management	2.8	2.3	1.9
Social Security Administration	194.0	184.2	214.6
District of Columbia	8.5	3.4	39.0
Federal Communications Commission	2.3	2.3	2.3
Intelligence Community Management Account	56.0	122.0	32.8
National Archives and Records Administration	17.9	17.7	20.7
Nuclear Regulatory Commission	72.2	72.1	72.8
Securities and Exchange Commission	14.3	13.4	14.0
Smithsonian Institution	80.7	91.0	92.3
United States Holocaust Memorial Museum	7.8	8.0	9.0
Corporation for National and Community Service	33.6	(NA)	(NA)

NA Not available. [1] The federal spending estimates are for the Executive Branch's homeland security efforts. These estimates do not include the efforts of the Legislative or Judicial Branches. [2] The Department of Homeland Security Appropriations Act, 2004, provided $5.6 billion for Project BioShield, to remain available through 2013. Including this uneven funding stream can distort year-over-year comparisons. [3] Not all actitivies carried out by DHS constitute homeland security funding (e.g. response to natural disasters and Coast Guard search and rescue activities), DHS estimates in this table do not represent the entire DHS budget. See Table 514.

Source: U.S. Office of Management and Budget, Budget of the United States Government Fiscal Year 2010, The Budget Documents, *Analytical Perspectives, Budget of the United States Government Fiscal Year 2010, Crosscutting Programs, Homeland Security Funding Analysis;* <http://www.whitehouse.gov/omb/budget/>.

Table 514. **Department of Homeland Security Total Budget Authority and Personnel by Organization: 2008 and 2009**

[In thousands of dollars (47,454,648 represents $47,454,648,000). For the fiscal year ending September 30. Not all activities carried out by DHS constitute homeland security funding (e.g., Coast Guard search and rescue activities)]

Organization	Budget authority		Full-time employees	
	2008	2009	2008	2009
Total [1]	47,454,648	52,543,592	195,865	203,554
Departmental operations [2]	573,983	644,553	1,119	1,307
Analysis and operations	304,500	327,373	518	594
Office of the Inspector General	108,711	98,513	551	577
U.S. Customs & Border Protection	9,285,001	11,274,783	50,417	54,868
U.S. Immigration & Customs Enforcement	5,054,317	5,928,210	17,938	18,965
Transportation Security Administration	6,809,359	6,990,778	50,871	51,488
U.S. Coast Guard	8,631,053	9,623,779	48,558	48,930
U.S. Secret Service	1,629,496	1,637,954	6,700	6,732
National Protection and Program Directorate	896,476	1,158,263	664	849
Office of Health Affairs	118,375	157,191	49	80
Federal Emergency Management Agency (FEMA)	5,515,178	5,985,805	6,689	6,917
FEMA Grants [3]	4,117,800	4,245,700	([4])	([4])
U.S. Citizenship & Immigration Services	2,822,012	2,690,926	10,264	10,623
Federal Law Enforcement Training Center	273,302	332,986	1,056	1,106
Science & Technology Directorate (S&T)	830,335	932,587	350	381
Domestic Nuclear Detection Office	484,750	514,191	121	137

[1] See footnote 3, Table 513. [2] Departmental operations is comprised of the Office of the Secretary & Executive Management, the Office of the Federal Coordinator for Gulf Coast Rebuilding, the Office of the Undersecretary for Management, the Office of the Chief Financial Officer, and the Office of the Chief Information Officer. [3] Includes the following FEMA appropriations: State and Local Programs & Emergency Management Perf. Grants, and Assistance to Firefighters Grants. [4] Employee data are included in the FEMA full-time employees.

Source: U.S. Department of Homeland Security, "Budget-in-Brief, Fiscal Year 2010"; <http://www.dhs.gov/xabout/budget/> (accessed 20 May 2009).

336 National Security and Veterans Affairs

Table 515. Homeland Security Funding by National Strategy Mission Area: 2006 to 2008

[In millions of dollars (54,639.4 represents $54,639,400,000). For Homeland Security funding analysis by OMB, agencies categorize their funding data based on the critical mission areas defined in the *National Strategy*]

Agency	2006 [1]	2007	2008
Total budget authority excluding BioShield [2, 3]	**54,639.4**	**56,925.9**	**61,808.4**
Intelligence and warning	443.0	670.8	682.7
Border and transportation security	18,042.3	19,365.3	22,286.8
Domestic counterterrorism	4,535.6	5,026.6	4,896.8
Protecting critical infrastructure and key assets	17,933.2	18,388.2	19,926.1
Defending against catastrophic threats	8,573.7	8,595.9	8,278.1
Emergency preparedness and response	4,992.3	4,822.2	5,551.4
Other	119.3	56.9	186.5

[1] FY 06 reflects the adjustments made for the Coast Guard and re-estimates for DoD. See "Source" for further details.
[2] Enacted budgets.   [3] See footnote 2 in Table 513.

Source: U.S. Office of Management and Budget, Budget of the United States Government Fiscal Year 2009, The Budget Documents, *Analytical Perspectives, Budget of the United States Government Fiscal Year 2009, Crosscutting Programs, Homeland Security Funding Analysis.* <http://www.whitehouse.gov/omb/budget/fy2009/>.

Table 516. Homeland Security Grants by State/Territories: 2007 and 2008

[In thousands of dollars (1,666,460 represents 1,666,460,000). For years ending September 30. Grants consist of the following programs: Citizen Corps Program (CCP), State Homeland Security Program (SHSP), Metropolitan Medical Response System (MMRS), and Urban Areas Security Initiative (UASI)]

State/Territory	2007	2008	State/Territory	2007	2008	State/Territory	2007	2008
Total . . .	**1,666,460**	**1,697,314**	KY	11,757	11,885			
			LA	21,873	23,663			
U.S.	**1,650,810**	**1,682,304**	ME	6,697	6,317	PA	61,306	56,291
			MD	32,670	30,145	RI	12,119	11,646
AL	11,574	12,698	MA	35,509	32,252	SC	11,001	9,538
AK	7,195	6,941	MI	39,237	36,984	SD	6,682	6,302
AZ	33,774	31,292	MN	20,504	21,367	TN	20,045	20,688
AR	7,238	6,682	MS	7,002	6,695	TX	121,629	142,270
CA	242,245	260,824	MO	31,244	30,884	UT	6,989	9,162
CO	19,899	20,708	MT	6,686	6,307	VT	6,677	6,297
CT	10,479	14,845	NE	7,226	6,973	VA	33,278	33,540
DE	6,684	6,304	NV	19,357	18,925	WA	28,926	31,379
DC	71,985	71,247	NH	6,955	6,638	WV	6,712	6,332
FL	84,743	77,483	NJ	61,109	63,770	WI	17,796	16,044
GA	39,959	37,127	NM	6,973	6,657	WY	6,674	6,294
HI	12,114	11,642	NY	208,039	233,090			
ID	6,701	6,322	NC	25,256	22,435	AS	2,218	1,888
IL	86,248	81,622	ND	6,678	6,298	GU	2,221	1,891
IN	23,397	21,063	OH	46,321	43,168	NMI	2,218	1,889
IA	7,043	6,687	OK	14,198	13,182	PR	6,773	8,352
KS	8,375	8,362	OR	16,033	17,035	VI	2,220	1,890

– Represents zero. [1] AS—America Samoa, GU—Guam, NMI—Northern Mariana Islands, PR—Puerto Rico, VI—Virgin Islands.

Source: U.S. Department of Homeland Security, State Contacts and Grants Award Administration. See <http://www.dhs.gov/xgovt /grants/index.shtm>.

Table 517. Urban Areas Security Initiative (UASI) Grant Program: 2008

[In thousands of dollars (781,630 represents $781,630,000). For year ending September 30. The UASI Program provides financial assistance to address the unique multi-disciplinary planning, operations, equipment, training, and exercise needs of high-threat, high-density urban areas. The sixty highest risk urban areas were eligible for funding. The seven highest risk urban areas are designated Tier 1. For a listing of all grant programs and their descriptions, see <http://www.dhs.gov/xgovt/grants/index.shtm>.]

State/ territory	Urban area	Amount	State/ territory	Urban area	Amount	State/ territory	Urban area	Amount
Total . . .		781,630		Jacksonville	5,723		Cleveland	5,355
				Miami	11,621		Columbus	4,579
TIER 1 .				Orlando	5,432		Toledo	1,265
CA	Bay Area	37,155		Tampa	8,352	OK	Oklahoma City	4,637
	Los Angeles/		GA	Atlanta	14,220	OR	Portland	7,557
	Long Beach	70,403	HI	Honolulu	5,005	PA	Philadelphia	18,139
DC	National Capital	59,801	IN	Indianapolis	7,479		Pittsburgh	6,732
IL	Chicago	45,862	KY	Louisville	1,422			
NJ	Jersey City/Newark	34,988	LA	Baton Rouge	1,787	PR	San Juan	2,033
NY	New York City	144,189		New Orleans	4,249	RI	Providence	5,015
TX	Houston	37,500	MD	Baltimore	11,553	TN	Memphis	4,453
			MA	Boston	13,784		Nashville	1,784
TIER 2			MI	Detroit	14,191	TX	Austin	1,823
AZ	Phoenix	11,563	MN	Twin Cities	8,206		Dallas/Fort	
	Tucson	4,753	MO	Kansas City	8,100		Worth/Arlington	20,322
CA	Anaheim/Santa Ana	13,425	. . . .	St. Louis	8,982		El Paso	5,665
	Riverside	3,252	NV	Las Vegas	9,031		San Antonio	6,548
	Sacramento	4,045	NY	Albany	1,757	UT	Salt Lake City	1,845
	San Diego	15,511		Buffalo	5,306	VA	Norfolk	7,760
CO	Denver	7,615		Rochester	1,466		Richmond	1,722
CT	Bridgeport	1,967		Syracuse	1,601	WA	Seattle	10,340
	Hartford	1,997	NC	Charlotte	4,821	WI	Milwaukee	4,491
FL	Fort Lauderdale	6,383	OH	Cincinnati	5,083			

Source: Department of Homeland Security, FEMA, Grants Program Directorate; <http://www.dhs.gov/xlibrary/assets /grant-program-overview-fy2008.pdf> (released July 25, 2008).

National Security and Veterans Affairs   337

Table 518.

Table 518. Coast Guard Migrant Interdictions by Nationality of Alien: 2000 to 2008

[For the year ending September 30]

Year	Total	Haiti	Dominican Republic	China [1]	Cuba	Mexico	Ecuador	Other
2000	4,210	1,113	499	261	1,000	49	1,244	44
2003	6,068	2,013	1,748	15	1,555	–	703	34
2004	10,899	3,229	5,014	68	1,225	86	1,189	88
2005	9,455	1,850	3,612	32	2,712	55	1,149	45
2006	7,886	1,198	3,011	31	2,810	52	693	91
2007	6,338	1,610	1,469	73	2,868	26	125	167
2008	4,802	1,582	688	1	2,199	47	220	65

– Represents zero. [1] See footnote 4, Table 1296.

Source: U.S. Department of Homeland Security, "United States Coast Guard, USCG Migrant Interdiction Statistics"; <http://www.uscg.mil/hq/cg5/cg531/AMIO/FlowStats/currentstats.asp/> (accessed 10 June 2009).

Table 519. Deportable Aliens Located by Program and Border Patrol Sector: 2000 to 2007

[As of the end of September. For purposes of statistical reporting there is no difference between the terms "apprehension" and "deportable alien located." For definitions for Immigration statistics, see <http://www.dhs.gov/ximgtn/statistics/stdfdef.shtm>]

Program and sector	2000	2003	2004	2005	2006	2007
Total	1,814,729	1,046,422	1,264,232	1,291,142	1,206,457	960,756
Investigations [1]	138,291	114,865	103,837	102,034	101,854	53,562
Detention and Removal Operations [2]	(X)	(X)	(X)	(X)	15,467	30,407
Border Patrol	1,676,438	931,557	1,160,395	1,189,108	1,089,136	876,787
All southwest sectors	1,643,679	905,065	1,139,282	1,171,428	1,072,018	858,722
San Diego, CA	151,681	111,515	138,608	126,909	142,122	152,459
El Centro, CA.	238,126	92,099	74,467	55,726	61,469	55,881
Yuma, AZ	108,747	56,638	98,060	138,438	118,537	37,994
Tucson, AZ	616,346	347,263	491,771	439,090	392,104	378,323
El Paso, TX	115,696	88,816	104,399	122,689	122,261	75,464
Marfa, TX	13,689	10,319	10,530	10,536	7,517	5,537
Del Rio, TX	157,178	50,145	53,794	68,510	42,634	22,919
Laredo, TX	108,973	70,521	74,706	75,342	74,843	56,715
Rio Grande Valley, TX	133,243	77,749	92,947	134,188	110,531	73,430
All other sectors.	32,759	26,492	21,113	17,680	17,118	18,065
Blaine, WA	2,581	1,380	1,354	1,001	809	749
Buffalo, NY	1,570	564	671	400	1,517	2,190
Detroit, MI	2,057	2,345	1,912	1,792	1,282	902
Grand Forks, ND	562	1,223	1,225	754	517	500
Havre, MT	1,568	1,406	986	949	567	486
Houlton, ME.	489	292	263	233	175	95
Livermore, CA [3]	6,205	3,565	1,850	117	(X)	(X)
Miami, FL	6,237	5,931	4,602	7,243	6,032	7,121
New Orleans, LA	6,478	5,151	2,889	1,358	3,054	4,018
Ramey, PR	1,731	1,688	1,813	1,619	1,436	548
Spokane, WA	1,324	992	847	279	185	337
Swanton, VT	1,957	1,955	2,701	1,935	1,544	1,119

X Not applicable. [1] The Immigration and Customs Enforcement (ICE) Office of Investigations focuses on the enforcement of a wide variety of laws that include immigration and customs statutes. [2] Include arrests of fugitive and nonfugitive aliens under the Office of Detention and Removal Operations (DRO) National Fugitive Operations Program. [3] Livermore sector closed July 30, 2004.

Source: U.S. Department of Homeland Security, Office of Immigration Statistics, Yearbook of Immigration Statistics, 2007. See also <http://www.dhs.gov/files/statistics/publications/yearbook.shtm/>.

Table 520. Deportable Aliens Located: 1925 to 2007

[See headnote, Table 519. Detention and Removal Operations (DRO) data are included beginning in Fiscal Year 2006.]

Year	Number	Year	Number	Year	Number	Year	Number
1925	22,199	1973	655,968	1985	1,348,749	1997	1,536,520
1930	20,880	1974	788,145	1986	1,767,400	1998	1,679,439
1935	11,016	1975	766,600	1987	1,190,488	1999	1,714,035
1940	10,492	1976 [1]	1,097,739	1988	1,008,145	2000	1,814,729
1945	69,164	1977	1,042,215	1989	954,243	2001	1,387,486
1950	468,339	1978	1,057,977	1990	1,169,939	2002	1,062,279
1955	254,096	1979	1,076,418	1991	1,197,875	2003	1,046,422
1960	70,684	1980	910,361	1992	1,258,481	2004	1,264,232
1965	110,371	1981	975,780	1993	1,327,261	2005	1,291,142
1970	345,353	1982	970,246	1994	1,094,719	2006	1,206,457
1971	420,126	1983	1,251,357	1995	1,394,554	2007	960,756
1972	505,949	1984	1,246,981	1996	1,649,986		

[1] Includes the 15 months from July 1, 1975 to September 30, 1976, because the end date of fiscal years was changed from June 30 to September 30.

Source: U.S. Department of Homeland Security, Office of Immigration Statistics, 2007 Yearbook of Immigration Statistics. See also <http://www.dhs.gov/files/statistics/publications/yearbook.shtm/>.

Table 521. Principal Immigration-Related Activities of Immigration and Customs Enforcement (ICE) Investigations: 2006

[Data refer to criminal cases only; administrative cases are not included due to changes in reporting]

Activities	Criminal arrests	Criminal indict-ments	Criminal con-victions	Number seizures	Value of seizures (dollars)
Total, all immigration-related categories	8,778	6,514	6,872	3,755	33,861,911
Financial investigations [1]	27	16	14	60	3,996,732
Human smuggling and trafficking investigations [2] . . .	2,154	1,585	1,596	1,609	11,046,622
General and criminal alien investigations [3]	4,589	3,434	3,689	532	4,804,781
Identity and benefit fraud (IBF) investigations [4]	1,272	1,032	1,073	1,281	12,230,727
Compliance and worksite enforcement [5]	20	6	7	12	602
Worksite enforcement [6]	716	441	493	261	1,782,447

[1] Financial investigations refer to cases developed to counteract organizations involved in money laundering and related financial crimes. [2] Human smuggling and trafficking investigations refer to cases targeted against persons or organizations that bring, transport, harbor, or smuggle illegal aliens into or within the United States. [3] General investigations refer to general investigative activities, including those targeting aliens who attempt illegal reentry, have absconded, or commit other crimes in the United States. Criminal alien investigations focus on large-scale organizations engaged in ongoing criminal activity. [4] Identity and benefit fraud investigations seek to penetrate fraud schemes that are used to violate immigration and related laws, or used to shield the true status of illegal aliens in order to obtain entitlement benefits from federal, state, or local agencies. [5] The compliance enforcement program focuses on preventing foreign nationals from exploiting the nations immigration system by developing cases for investigation from Department of Homeland Security systems containing information on the status of students and other nonimmigrants. [6] The worksite enforcement program focuses on monitoring and inspecting work sites to apprehend unauthorized alien workers and to provide for penalties and fines against employers who knowingly hire, recruit, or refer aliens for employment for a fee.

Source: U.S. Department of Homeland Security, Office of Immigration Statistics, *2006 Yearbook of Immigration Statistics*. See also <http://uscis.gov/graphics/shared/statistics/yearbook/index.htm>.(accessed 10 June 2008).

Table 522. Aliens Returned or Removed by Crime Categories and Country of Nationality: 2003 to 2007

[As of the end of September. For definitions of immigration enforcement terms, see "Immigration Enforcement Actions, 2007 Yearbook of Immigration Statistics"]

Crime category and country of nationality	2003	2004	2005	2006	2007
Total Aliens Returned or Removed:	1,152,725	1,403,508	1,343,351	1,324,355	1,210,772
Returns [1]	945,294	1,166,576	1,096,920	1,043,381	891,390
Removals [2]	207,431	236,932	246,431	280,974	319,382
Noncriminal	125,097	146,029	154,706	183,609	219,458
Criminal [3]	82,334	90,903	91,725	97,365	99,924
Leading crime categories					
Dangerous drugs.	32,441	34,071	34,215	33,485	33,449
Immigration	11,790	15,174	17,106	23,176	21,538
Assault	8,878	9,654	9,633	9,574	11,048
Burglary.	3,324	3,406	3,351	3,506	3,466
Robbery.	2,887	2,924	3,023	2,915	2,908
Larceny.	2,606	2,830	2,742	2,757	2,878
Sexual assault	2,316	2,777	2,649	2,571	2,786
Family offenses.	2,277	2,478	2,172	2,262	2,410
Stolen vehicles	1,577	1,797	1,806	1,934	1,875
Sex offenses.	1,631	1,984	1,922	1,868	1,874
Other	12,607	13,808	13,106	13,371	15,692
Leading country of nationality of criminals removed					
Mexico	64,641	70,113	70,178	72,157	75,243
Honduras.	1,996	2,483	2,659	5,674	5,032
El Salvador	2,066	2,768	2,808	3,731	4,669
Guatemala	1,565	1,937	1,935	3,649	3,477
Dominican Republic.	2,194	2,556	2,370	2,277	2,108
Colombia	1,380	1,493	1,393	1,322	1,226
Jamaica.	1,522	1,670	1,506	1,260	1,160
Canada	474	565	590	537	521
Nicaragua	323	407	357	593	498
Brazil.	220	763	1,433	563	328
Other	5,953	6,148	6,496	5,602	7,343

[1] Returns are the confirmed movement of an inadmissible or deportable alien out of the United States not based on an order of removal. Most of the voluntary departures are of Mexican nationals who have been apprehended by the U.S. Border Patrol and are returned to Mexico. [2] Removals are the compulsory and confirmed movement of an inadmissible or deportable alien out of the United States based on an order of removal. An alien who is removed has administrative or criminal consequences placed on subsequent reentry owing to the fact of the removal. [3] Refers to persons removed based on a criminal charge or those with a criminal conviction.

Source: U.S. Department of Homeland Security, Office of Immigration Statistics, *2007 Yearbook of Immigration Statistics* and unpublished data. See also <http://www.dhs.gov/ximgtn/statistics/publications/yearbook.shtm>.

National Security and Veterans Affairs **339**

Table 523. Customs and Border Protection (CBP)—Processed and Cleared Passengers, Planes, Vehicles, and Containers: 2000 to 2007

[In thousands (80,519 represents 80,519,000). For year ending September 30]

Characteristic	2000	2003	2004	2005	2006	2007
Air						
Passengers.	80,519	72,959	80,866	86,123	87,906	91,574
Commercial planes [1].	829	790	824	866	881	916
Private planes	146	132	140	135	139	139
Land						
Passengers [2, 3].	397,312	329,998	326,693	317,765	289,048	299,004
Autos [2].	127,095	120,376	121,419	121,654	119,372	112,428
Rail containers.	2,157	2,472	2,588	2,655	2,735	2,737
Truck containers [4].	10,397	11,163	11,252	11,308	11,489	11,459
Sea						
Passengers [5].	10,990	15,127	22,234	26,228	26,223	27,059
Vessels [6]	211	204	142	113	168	170
Vessel containers [7].	5,813	9,092	9,796	11,341	11,622	11,703

[1] A commercial aircraft is any aircraft transporting passengers and/or cargo for some payment or other consideration, including money or services rendered. [2] See Table 1234 for more details. [3] Includes pedestrians. [4] Truck containers—number of trucks entering the U.S. [5] Does not include passengers on ferries. [6] Number of vessels. Includes every description of water craft or other contrivance used or capable of being used as a means of transportation on water, does not include aircraft. [7] Number of vessel containers.

Source: U.S. Department of Homeland Security, Customs and Border Protection, *About CBP, Statistics and Accomplishments, National Workload Statistics, 2000–2007* and unpublished data.

Table 524. Prohibited Items Intercepted at U.S. Airport Screening Checkpoints: 2004 to 2008

[Passengers boarding aircraft in thousands (702,921 represents 702,921,000). Transportation Security Administration (TSA) assumed responsibility for airport security on February 17, 2002; and by November 19, 2002, TSA assumed control over all passenger screenings from private contractors]

Year	2004	2005	2006	2007	2008
Passengers boarding aircraft, total [1]	**702,921**	**738,327**	**744,242**	**769,370**	**741,450**
Domestic.	640,698	670,418	671,796	693,374	664,714
International.	62,222	67,908	72,445	75,996	76,735
Total prohibited items	**7,104,095**	**15,886,404**	**13,709,684**	**6,516,026**	**(NA)**
Knife [2].	2,055,404	1,822,892	1,607,125	1,056,691	[9]
Other cutting items [3]	3,409,888	3,276,941	163,419	101,387	[9]
Club [4].	28,998	20,531	12,296	9,443	[9]
Box cutter	22,430	21,319	15,999	11,908	[9]
Firearm [5].	254	850	820	1,416	902
Incendiary [6].	697,606	374,487	94,097	73,670	116,200
Lighters [7].	178	9,420,991	11,616,688	5,124,344	[9]
Other [8]	889,337	949,243	200,060	137,167	[9]

NA Not available. [1] Data comes from the Air Transport Association. Data are for U.S. passenger and cargo airlines only. [2] Knife includes any length and type except round-bladed, butter, and plastic cutlery. [3] Other cutting instruments refer to, e.g., scissors, screwdrivers, swords, sabers, and ice picks. [4] Club refers to baseball bats, night sticks, billy clubs, bludgeons; etc. [5] Firearm refers to items like pistols, revolvers, rifles, automatic weapons, shotguns, parts of guns and firearms. [6] Incendiaries refer to categories of ammunition and gunpowder, flammables/irritants, and explosives. [7] As of April 14, 2005, passengers are prohibited from carrying all lighters on their person or in carry-on luggage or onboard an airplane. [8] Other refer to categories of ammunition and gunpowder, dangerous objects, fireworks, replica weapons, and tools. [9] The data for this prohibited item category is no longer collected as of August 8, 2008.

Source: U.S. Department of Homeland Security, Transportation Security Administration, unpublished data (June 2009); <http://www.tsa.gov>; Air Transport Association of America, Washington, DC; Annual Traffic and Operations: U.S. Airlines; <http://www.airlines.org/economic/traffic/>.

Table 525. Seizure Statistics for Intellectual Property Rights (IPR) by Commodity and Trading Partner: 2007 and 2008

[In thousands of dollars (196,754 represents $196,754,000, except as indicated). Customs and Border Protection (CBP) is dedicated to protecting against the importation of goods which infringe/violate Intellectual Property Rights (IPR) by devoting substantial resources toward identifying and seizing shipments of infringing articles]

Commodity	2007	2008	Trading partner	2007	2008
Number of IPR seizures	13,657	14,992			
Total domestic value of IPR seizures [1]	196,754	272,729	China	158,083	221,662
Footwear.	77,781	102,317	India	855	16,258
Wearing apparel.	27,006	25,120	Hong Kong.	12,729	13,434
Handbags/wallets/backpacks.	14,214	29,609	Taiwan.	3,454	2,632
Computers/hardware	9,337	7,590	Korea, South	903	1,028
Pharmaceuticals	11,138	28,107	Dominican Republic	23	942
Consumer electronics [2]	16,042	22,998	Pakistan.	2,531	780
Sunglasses	3,952	7,919	Vietnam.	484	748
Computers/Technology Components.	9,337	7,590	United Arab Emirates	373	659
Media [3]	7,884	5,967	Indonesia	97	649
All others.	27,616	29,942	All other countries	17,223	13,938

[1] Domestic value is the cost of the seized goods, plus the costs of shipping and importing the goods into the U.S. and an amount for profit. [2] Consumer electronics includes cell phones and accessories, radios, power strips, electrical tools and appliances. [3] Includes motion pictures on tape, laser disc, and DVD; interactive and computer software on CD-ROM, and floppy discs; and music on CD or tape.

Source: U.S. Department of Homeland Security, Customs and Border Protection, "Import, Commercial Enforcement, Intellectual Property Rights, Seizure Statistics"; <http://www.cbp.gov/xp/cgov/trade/priority_trade/ipr/seizure/>.

340 National Security and Veterans Affairs

Section 11
Social Insurance and Human Services

This section presents data related to governmental expenditures for social insurance and human services; governmental programs for old-age, survivors, disability, and health insurance (OASDHI); governmental employee retirement; private pension plans; government unemployment and temporary disability insurance; federal supplemental security income payments and aid to the needy; child and other welfare services; and federal food programs. Also included here are selected data on workers' compensation and vocational rehabilitation, child support, child care, charity contributions, and philanthropic trusts and foundations.

The principal source for these data is the Social Security Administration's *Annual Statistical Supplement to the Social Security Bulletin* which presents current data on many of the programs.

Social insurance under the Social Security Act—Programs established by the Social Security Act provide protection against wage loss resulting from retirement, prolonged disability, death, or unemployment, and protection against the cost of medical care during old age and disability. The federal OASDI program provides monthly benefits to retired or disabled insured workers and their dependents and to survivors of insured workers. To be eligible, a worker must have had a specified period of employment in which OASDI taxes were paid. The age of eligibility for full retirement benefits had been 65 years old for many years. However, for persons born in 1938 or later that age gradually increases until it reaches age 67 for those born after 1959. Reduced benefits may be obtained as early as age 62. The worker's spouse is under the same limitations. Survivor benefits are payable to dependents of deceased insured workers. Disability benefits are payable to an insured worker under full retirement age with a prolonged disability and to the disabled worker's dependents on the same basis as

dependents of retired workers. Disability benefits are provided at age 50 to the disabled widow or widower of a deceased worker who was fully insured at the time of death. Disabled children, aged 18 or older, of retired, disabled, or deceased workers are also eligible for benefits. A lump-sum benefit is generally payable on the death of an insured worker to a spouse or minor children. For information on the Medicare program, see Section 3, Health and Nutrition.

Retirement, survivors, disability, and hospital insurance benefits are funded by a payroll tax on annual earnings (up to a maximum of earnings set by law) of workers, employers, and the self-employed. The maximum taxable earnings are adjusted annually to reflect increasing wage levels (see Table 532). Effective January 1994, there is no dollar limit on wages and self-employment income subject to the hospital insurance tax. Tax receipts and benefit payments are administered through federal trust funds. Special benefits for uninsured persons; hospital benefits for persons aged 65 and over with specified amounts of social security coverage less than that required for cash benefit eligibility; and that part of the cost of supplementary medical insurance not financed by contributions from participants are financed from federal general revenues.

Unemployment insurance is presently administered by the U.S. Employment and Training Administration and each state's employment security agency. By agreement with the U.S. Secretary of Labor, state agencies also administer unemployment compensation for eligible ex-military personnel and federal employees. Under state unemployment insurance laws, benefits related to the individual's past earnings are paid to unemployed eligible workers. State laws vary concerning the length of time benefits are paid and their amount. In most states, benefits are payable for 26 weeks and, during periods

Social Insurance and Human Services   341

U.S. Census Bureau, Statistical Abstract of the United States: 2010

of high unemployment, extended benefits are payable under a federal-state program to those who have exhausted their regular state benefits. Some states also supplement the basic benefit with allowances for dependents.

Unemployment insurance is funded by a federal unemployment tax levied on the taxable payrolls of most employers. Taxable payroll under the federal act and 12 state laws is the first $7,000 in wages paid each worker during a year. Forty-one states have taxable payrolls above $7,000. Employers are allowed a percentage credit of taxable payroll for contributions paid to states under state unemployment insurance laws. The remaining percent of the federal tax finances administrative costs, the federal share of extended benefits, and advances to states. About 97 percent of wage and salary workers are covered by unemployment insurance.

Retirement programs for government employees—The Civil Service Retirement System (CSRS) and the Federal Employees' Retirement System (FERS) are the two major programs providing age and service, disability, and survivor annuities for federal civilian employees. In general, employees hired after December 31, 1983, are covered under FERS and the social security program (OASDHI), and employees on staff prior to that date are members of CSRS and are covered under Medicare. CSRS employees were offered the option of transferring to FERS during 1987 and 1998. There are separate retirement systems for the uniformed services (supplementing OASDHI) and for certain special groups of federal employees. State and local government employees are covered for the most part by state and local retirement systems similar to the federal programs. In many jurisdictions these benefits supplement OASDHI coverage.

Workers' compensation—All states provide protection against work-connected injuries and deaths, although some states exclude certain workers (e.g., domestic workers). Federal laws cover federal employees, private employees in the District of Columbia, and longshoremen and harbor workers. In addition, the Department of Labor administers "black lung"

benefits programs for coal miners disabled by pneumoconiosis and for specified dependents and survivors. Specified occupational diseases are compensable to some extent. In most states, benefits are related to the worker's salary. The benefits may or may not be augmented by dependents' allowances or automatically adjusted to prevailing wage levels.

Income support—Income support programs are designed to provide benefits for persons with limited income and resources. The Supplemental Security Income (SSI) program and Temporary Assistance for Needy Families (TANF) program are the major programs providing monthly payments. In addition, a number of programs provide money payments or in-kind benefits for special needs or purposes. Several programs offer food and nutritional services. Also, various federal-state programs provide energy assistance, public housing, and subsidized housing to individuals and families with low incomes. General assistance may also be available at the state or local level.

The SSI program, administered by the Social Security Administration, provides income support to persons aged 65 or older and blind or disabled adults and children. Eligibility requirements and federal payment standards are nationally uniform. Most states supplement the basic SSI payment for all or selected categories of persons.

The Personal Responsibility and Work Opportunity Reconciliation Act of 1996 contained provisions that replaced the Aid to Families With Dependent Children (AFDC), Job Opportunities and Basic Skills (JOBS), and Emergency Assistance programs with the Temporary Assistance for Needy Families block grant program. This law contains strong work requirements, comprehensive child support enforcement, support for families moving from welfare to work, and other features. The TANF became effective as soon as each state submitted a complete plan implementing TANF, but no later than July 1, 1997. The AFDC program provided cash assistance based on need, income, resources, and family size.

Federal food stamp program—Under the food stamp program, single persons and those living in households meeting nationwide standards for income and assets may receive coupons redeemable for food at most retail food stores or provides benefits through electronic benefit transfer. The monthly amount of benefits or allotments a unit receives is determined by household size and income. Households without income receive the determined monthly cost of a nutritionally adequate diet for their household size. This amount is updated to account for food price increases. Households with income receive the difference between the amount of a nutritionally adequate diet and 30 percent of their income, after certain allowable deductions.

To qualify for the program, a household must have less than $2,000 in disposable assets ($3,000 if one member is aged 60 or older), gross income below 130 percent of the official poverty guidelines for the household size, and net income below 100 percent of the poverty guidelines. Households with a person aged 60 or older or a disabled person receiving SSI, social security, state general assistance, or veterans' disability benefits may have gross income exceeding 130 percent of the poverty guidelines. All households in which all members receive TANF or SSI are categorically eligible for food stamps without meeting these income or resource criteria. Households are certified for varying lengths of time, depending on their income sources and individual circumstances.

Health and welfare services—Programs providing health and welfare services are aided through federal grants to states for child welfare services, vocational rehabilitation, activities for the aged, maternal and child health services, maternity and infant care projects, comprehensive health services, and a variety of public health activities. For information about the Medicaid program, see Section 3, Health and Nutrition.

Noncash benefits—The U.S. Census Bureau annually collects data on the characteristics of recipients of noncash (in-kind) benefits to supplement the collection of annual money income data in the Current Population Survey (see text, Section 1, Population, and Section 13, Income, Expenditures, Poverty, and Wealth). Noncash benefits are those benefits received in a form other than money which serve to enhance or improve the economic well-being of the recipient. As for money income, the data for noncash benefits are for the calendar year prior to the date of the interview. The major categories of noncash benefits covered are public transfers (e.q., food stamps, school lunch, public housing, and Medicaid) and employer or union-provided benefits to employees.

Statistical reliability—For discussion of statistical collection, estimation, and sampling procedures and measures of statistical reliability applicable to HHS and Census Bureau data, see Appendix III.

U.S. Census Bureau, Statistical Abstract of the United States: 2010

Table 526. Selected Payments to Individuals by Function: 1970 to 2007

[In billions of dollars. (108 represents 108,000,000,000) The employee benefit system is composed of voluntary and mandatory programs which are employment-based and financed primarily from employment-based contributions]

Source and sector	1970	1980	1990	1995	1998	1999	2000	2001	2002	2003	2004	2005	2006	2007
All benefits	108	422	1,027	1,492	1,696	1,786	1,908	2,067	2,244	2,383	2,532	2,693	2,833	2,994
Retirement income benefits	51	202	482	661	775	813	863	918	974	1,020	1,068	1,132	1,192	1,254
Social Security Old-Age, Survivors, and Disability Insurance	31	119	244	328	369	380	401	425	447	463	485	513	544	576
Private employer pension and profit sharing	7	35	136	191	236	253	270	289	309	320	332	352	361	369
Public employer retirement plans	12	48	102	142	169	180	192	204	219	236	251	267	287	309
Federal civilian employee retirement[1]	3	16	32	40	46	47	50	52	53	55	58	62	67	72
State and local government retirement	4	15	41	66	84	92	100	110	121	132	141	150	162	175
Military retirement[2]	3	13	22	28	32	32	33	35	36	41	43	46	49	52
Railroad retirement	2	5	7	8	8	8	8	8	9	9	9	9	10	10
Health benefits	22	99	300	454	517	545	597	645	702	761	832	901	981	1,041
Medicare hospital insurance and supplementary medical insurance	7	36	108	179	206	209	220	244	261	278	303	332	395	424
Group health insurance	15	62	191	274	310	335	376	400	439	481	527	567	584	614
Military health insurance[3]	–	–	2	1	1	1	1	1	2	2	2	2	3	3
Other employee benefits	17	51	88	103	106	112	113	130	157	161	147	147	148	153
Unemployment insurance[4]	4	16	18	22	20	21	20	32	54	53	36	32	30	33
Workers' compensation[5]	3	13	38	43	44	46	48	52	54	55	56	56	55	55
Group life insurance	3	7	12	16	18	20	17	17	18	19	18	20	20	21
Miscellaneous disability[6]	1	3	4	3	3	3	4	4	4	4	5	5	5	5
Veterans' benefits[7]	7	13	16	19	21	22	23	25	28	30	32	35	38	40
Public assistance[8]	18	70	157	275	299	318	336	374	412	441	485	514	512	547

– Represents or rounds to zero. [1] Consists of civil service, foreign service, Public Health Service officers, Tennessee Valley Authority, and several small retirement programs. [2] Includes the U.S. Coast Guard. [3] Consists of payments for medical services for dependents of active duty military personnel at nonmilitary facilities. [4] Consists of state, railroad employee, and federal employee unemployment benefits; special unemployment benefits; and supplemental unemployment benefits. [5] Includes payments from private, federal, and state and local workers' compensation funds. [6] Includes federal black-lung payments and payments from state and local temporary disability insurance. [7] Consists of pension and disability, readjustment, and other veterans' benefits. [8] Consists of federal benefits (food stamp benefits, Supplemental Security Income, direct relief, earned income credit, payments to nonprofit institutions, aid to students, and payments for medical services for retired military personnel and their dependents at nonmilitary facilities) and state benefits (medical care, Aid to Families with Dependent Children, Supplemental Security Income, general assistance, energy assistance, emergency assistance, and medical insurance premium payments on behalf of indigents). Financed from state and federal general revenues.

Source: Employee Benefit Research Institute, Washington, DC, EBRI Databook on Employee Benefits, 12th ed. and unpublished data (copyright). EBRI tabulations based on U.S. Department of Commerce, Bureau of Economic Analysis. See also <http://www.ebri.org/publications/books/index.cfm?fa=databook>.

Table 527. **Government Transfer Payments to Individuals—Summary: 1990 to 2007**

[In billions of dollars (561.5 represents $561,500,000,000)]

Year	Total	Retirement & disability insurance benefits	Medical payments	Income mainte-nance benefits	Unemploy-ment insurance benefits	Veterans benefits	Federal education & training assistance payments[1]	Other[2]
1990	561.5	264.2	188.8	63.5	18.2	17.7	7.3	1.8
1995	840.0	350.3	336.5	100.4	21.8	20.5	9.0	1.4
1996	883.1	364.9	361.7	102.6	22.4	21.4	8.6	1.6
1997	912.8	379.3	377.3	100.5	20.3	22.2	11.5	1.6
1998	932.6	391.8	383.7	101.1	19.9	23.2	11.2	1.8
1999	966.5	402.5	401.1	104.8	20.8	24.1	11.4	1.9
2000	1,018.1	424.8	427.7	106.6	20.7	24.9	11.0	2.4
2001	1,117.2	450.4	482.5	109.4	32.2	26.5	13.1	3.1
2002	1,220.0	474.9	525.4	119.7	53.7	29.3	14.5	2.4
2003	1,286.0	493.8	556.8	133.2	53.6	31.6	13.9	3.0
2004	1,363.0	516.8	608.7	143.6	37.1	34.1	15.0	7.6
2005	1,446.4	545.1	653.5	158.1	32.3	36.4	16.1	5.0
2006	1,540.0	576.8	713.0	161.0	30.9	38.8	16.3	3.2
2007	1,641.2	609.4	767.3	169.5	33.3	41.5	17.4	2.8

[1] See footnote 9, Table 528.   [2] See footnote 10, Table 528.

Source: U.S. Bureau of Economic Analysis, "Regional Accounts Data, Annual State Personal Income"; <http://www.bea.gov/bea/regional/spi/> (accessed March 2009).

Table 528. **Government Transfer Payments to Individuals by Type: 1990 to 2007**

[In millions of dollars (561,484 represents $561,484,000,000)]

Item	1990	2000	2003	2004	2005	2006	2007
Total	561,484	1,018,106	1,286,001	1,362,992	1,446,373	1,540,004	1,641,228
Retirement & disability insurance benefit payments	264,230	424,810	493,780	516,830	545,069	576,751	609,445
Old age, survivors, & disability insurance	244,135	401,218	463,406	485,244	512,551	544,096	575,722
Railroad retirement and disability	7,221	8,265	8,855	9,009	9,194	9,519	9,813
Workers' compensation payments (federal & state)	8,618	10,845	14,547	15,240	15,499	15,285	15,725
Other government disability insurance & retirement[1]	4,256	4,482	6,972	7,337	7,825	7,851	8,185
Medical payments	188,808	427,689	556,843	608,682	653,498	713,015	767,270
Medicare	107,638	219,612	277,932	302,804	331,915	394,777	423,720
Public assistance medical care[2]	78,176	205,021	273,916	300,074	315,346	311,398	336,608
Military medical insurance[3]	2,994	3,056	4,995	5,804	6,237	6,840	6,942
Income maintenance benefit payments	63,481	106,616	133,199	143,631	158,118	161,006	169,513
Supplemental Security Income (SSI)	16,670	31,675	35,703	37,299	38,285	39,892	42,059
Family assistance[4]	19,187	18,440	18,367	18,371	18,216	18,304	18,799
Food stamps	14,741	14,896	22,127	25,631	29,492	29,390	30,926
Other income maintenance[5]	12,883	41,605	57,002	62,330	72,125	73,420	77,729
Unemployment insurance benefit payments	18,208	20,680	53,581	37,081	32,286	30,914	33,299
State unemployment insurance compensation	17,644	19,913	52,364	35,595	31,010	29,606	32,006
Unemployment compensation for federal civilian employees	215	226	333	281	225	218	216
Unemployment compensation for railroad employees	89	81	94	79	72	78	83
Unemployment compensation for veterans	144	182	365	431	446	449	406
Other unemployment compensation[6]	116	278	425	695	533	563	588
Veterans benefit payments	17,687	24,935	31,610	34,076	36,363	38,781	41,508
Veterans pension and disability	15,550	21,895	27,955	30,224	32,496	34,948	37,571
Veterans readjustment[7]	257	1,323	1,936	2,158	2,256	2,264	2,400
Veterans life insurance benefits	1,868	1,707	1,707	1,682	1,597	1,554	1,520
Other assistance to veterans[8]	12	10	12	12	14	15	17
Federal education & training assistance payments[9]	7,300	10,985	13,946	15,045	16,074	16,312	17,403
Other payments to individuals[10]	1,770	2,391	3,042	7,647	4,965	3,225	2,790

[1] Consists largely of temporary disability payments, pension benefit guaranty payments, and black lung payments. [2] Consists of medicaid and other medical vendor payments. [3] Consists of payments made under the TriCare Management Program (formerly called CHAMPUS) for the medical care of dependents of active duty military personnel and of retired military personnel and their dependents at nonmilitary medical facilities. [4] Through 1990, consists of emergency assistance and aid to families with dependent children. Beginning with 2000, consists of benefits—generally known as temporary assistance for needy families—provided under the Personal Responsibility and Work Opportunity Reconciliation Act of 1996. [5] Consists largely of general assistance, expenditures for food under the supplemental program for women, infants, and children; refugee assistance; foster home care and adoption assistance; earned income tax credits; and energy assistance. [6] Consists of trade readjustment allowance payments, Redwood Park benefit payments, public service employment benefit payments, and transitional benefit payments. [7] Consists largely of veterans' readjustment benefit payments, educational assistance to spouses and children of disabled or deceased veterans, payments to paraplegics, and payments for autos and conveyances for disabled veterans. [8] Consists largely of state and local government payments to veterans. [9] Excludes veterans. Consists largely of federal fellowship payments (National Science Foundation fellowships and traineeships, subsistence payments to state maritime academy cadets, and other federal fellowships), interest subsidy on higher education loans, basic educational opportunity grants, and Job Corps payments. [10] Consists largely of Bureau of Indian Affairs payments, education exchange payments, Alaska Permanent Fund dividend payments, compensation of survivors of public safety officers, compensation of victims of crime, disaster relief payments, compensation for Japanese internment, and other special payments to individuals.

Source: U.S. Bureau of Economic Analysis, "Regional Accounts Data, Annual State Personal Income"; <http://www.bea.gov/bea/regional/spi/> (accessed March 2009).

Social Insurance and Human Services   345

Table 529. **Government Transfer Payments to Individuals by State: 2000 to 2007**

[In millions of dollars (1,018,106 represents $1,018,106,000,000)]

State	2000, total	2006, total	2007							
			Total	Retirement & disability insurance benefits	Medical payments	Income maintenance benefits	Unemployment insurance benefits	Veterans benefits	Federal education & training assistance payments [1]	Other [2]
U.S.	1,018,106	1,540,004	1,641,228	609,445	767,270	169,513	33,299	41,508	17,403	2,790
AL.	16,643	25,602	27,274	10,836	11,726	3,097	251	1,024	322	17
AK.	2,966	3,767	4,209	793	1,493	400	90	142	18	1,273
AZ.	15,959	29,311	31,524	12,026	14,711	2,704	312	982	659	129
AR.	10,006	16,020	17,182	6,687	7,521	1,776	327	667	193	10
CA.	114,559	175,439	185,089	61,642	87,769	24,867	5,034	3,489	2,120	168
CO	11,169	17,703	18,862	7,836	8,070	1,577	314	769	268	29
CT.	14,086	19,531	20,452	7,786	10,192	1,477	563	289	134	11
DE.	2,857	4,606	4,935	2,018	2,267	391	112	109	33	4
DC	2,709	3,764	4,108	781	2,542	566	63	72	73	11
FL.	64,208	99,812	106,104	42,100	48,955	9,564	1,161	3,328	936	60
GA	23,696	38,573	41,335	15,396	17,718	5,476	689	1,500	516	39
HI	3,844	5,701	6,240	2,476	2,661	721	114	221	44	4
ID	3,804	6,242	6,725	2,987	2,725	521	139	240	104	9
IL	41,726	59,486	68,265	24,493	32,815	7,389	1,862	946	704	55
IN	20,081	30,805	31,423	13,988	12,763	2,896	765	624	366	21
IA	10,046	14,886	15,540	6,799	6,628	1,157	342	337	262	14
KS.	8,908	13,008	13,673	5,814	5,996	1,069	252	358	172	12
KY.	15,778	23,370	24,904	9,685	10,846	2,875	472	724	288	13
LA.	16,582	25,135	25,370	8,296	12,635	3,257	192	676	298	16
ME	5,307	8,010	8,460	3,136	4,032	725	125	368	68	5
MD	16,981	25,817	27,612	10,241	13,617	2,306	511	677	241	19
MA	26,471	39,697	42,604	13,103	22,189	4,799	1,433	745	316	19
MI	36,675	53,562	57,444	23,190	25,137	5,607	1,909	966	602	33
MN	15,748	24,719	26,418	10,125	12,610	1,953	750	689	269	22
MS	10,803	16,939	17,610	6,186	8,162	2,357	163	467	258	17
MO	20,904	31,610	33,503	13,128	15,774	2,922	463	838	356	23
MT	3,127	4,628	4,921	2,241	1,930	394	73	214	58	12
NE.	5,694	8,338	8,779	3,668	3,900	751	97	264	94	5
NV.	5,588	9,585	10,394	4,465	4,288	839	340	383	61	17
NH	3,918	5,873	6,133	2,881	2,514	384	101	202	48	4
NJ.	33,092	48,591	50,318	19,310	24,560	3,461	1,886	702	366	35
NM	6,014	9,956	10,742	3,691	5,024	1,190	137	473	134	92
NY.	95,735	134,860	140,641	40,958	78,807	15,714	2,179	1,591	1,324	70
NC	28,108	45,128	49,105	18,705	22,068	5,245	847	1,699	505	35
ND	2,322	3,138	3,321	1,439	1,420	239	48	109	46	21
OH	43,149	62,509	66,716	26,564	30,611	6,394	1,196	1,248	664	40
OK	11,999	18,970	20,362	7,863	8,991	2,032	179	1,032	242	24
OR	12,243	18,083	19,228	8,368	7,574	1,775	561	721	207	22
PA.	54,928	78,830	83,904	31,507	41,401	6,548	2,318	1,425	662	44
RI	4,748	6,799	7,359	2,554	3,744	600	233	150	74	4
SC.	14,340	22,855	24,396	9,902	10,162	2,756	413	897	245	20
SD.	2,490	3,714	3,946	1,625	1,715	319	25	164	56	43
TN.	21,864	32,415	35,453	13,388	16,341	3,932	485	931	350	26
TX.	59,911	97,451	106,086	36,525	49,810	13,157	1,260	3,842	1,374	117
UT.	4,962	7,924	8,321	3,763	3,296	702	107	226	204	22
VT.	2,245	3,582	3,846	1,383	1,912	331	90	96	32	2
VA.	19,916	32,051	34,153	14,353	13,946	3,647	418	1,420	345	25
WA	20,817	30,391	32,203	13,918	13,132	2,820	774	1,229	288	41
WV	8,894	12,483	13,152	5,506	5,635	1,233	182	461	127	7
WI	17,902	26,336	28,355	12,144	11,881	2,455	905	693	252	26
WY	1,583	2,405	2,532	1,175	1,056	146	37	87	27	5

[1] Excludes veterans. Consists largely of federal fellowship payments (National Science Foundation, fellowships and traineeships, subsistence payments to state maritime academy cadets, and other federal fellowships), interest subsidy on higher education loans, basic educational opportunity grants, and Job Corps payments.   [2] Consists largely of Bureau of Indian Affairs payments, education exchange payments, Alaska Permanent Fund dividend payments, compensation of survivors of public safety officers, compensation of victims of crime, disaster relief payments, compensation for Japanese internment, and other special payments to individuals.

Source: U.S. Bureau of Economic Analysis, "Regional Accounts Data, Annual State Personal Income"; <http://www.bea.gov/bea/regional/spi/> (accessed March 2009).

Table 530. **Number of Persons With Income by Specified Sources of Income: 2007**

[In thousands (210,019 represents 210,019,000). Persons 15 years old and over as of March of the following year. Based on Current Population Survey; see text, Sections 1 and 13, and Appendix III]

Source of income	Total persons with income	Under 65 years old	65 years old and over	White [1]	Black [2]	Hispanic origin [3]
Total	210,019	174,534	35,485	172,453	23,654	25,874
Earnings	158,777	151,541	7,236	129,975	17,748	21,887
Wages and salary	149,437	143,251	6,186	121,930	17,087	20,713
Nonfarm self-employment	12,499	11,450	1,049	10,708	938	1,455
Farm self-employment	2,048	1,801	247	1,859	109	111
Unemployment compensation	5,200	4,996	204	4,185	721	622
State or local only	4,942	4,762	180	3,987	666	593
Combinations	258	234	24	198	55	29
Worker's compensation	1,604	1,491	113	1,332	187	225
State payments	566	518	48	452	68	94
Employment insurance	682	652	30	570	82	94
Own insurance	56	53	3	44	10	5
Other.....................	370	337	32	324	34	50
Social security, railroad retirement	41,897	10,342	31,556	36,061	4,070	2,736
Supplemental Security Income (SSI)...	5,039	3,902	1,137	3,411	1,218	777
Public assistance	1,828	1,748	80	1,078	630	340
TANF/Welfare (AFDC) only [4]	1,191	1,160	30	677	430	236
Other assistance only..........	600	551	49	389	174	98
Both	37	37	–	11	25	6
Veterans payments	2,533	1,544	990	2,078	336	116
Disability only	1,532	1,040	492	1,281	185	76
Survivors only	169	52	116	135	23	9
Pension only.................	579	248	331	453	100	17
Education only	54	54	–	43	2	7
Other only	108	74	34	91	13	7
Combinations	92	77	16	74	13	6
Means-tested	478	281	198	356	87	37
Nonmeans-tested..............	2,055	1,263	792	1,722	250	79
Survivors benefits	2,906	1,031	1,875	2,619	192	94
Company or union	1,280	288	993	1,173	75	45
Federal government............	321	78	243	276	31	15
Military retirement	142	42	99	117	11	5
State or local government	244	91	153	210	25	4
Disability benefits	1,615	1,419	197	1,322	230	170
Workers' compensation..........	109	103	5	94	9	18
Company or union	441	371	71	361	65	45
Federal government............	122	94	28	96	19	13
Military retirement	58	48	9	51	7	3
State or local government	309	284	25	235	62	37
Pensions....................	15,845	5,177	10,669	14,015	1,322	589
Company or union	11,112	3,272	7,840	9,926	852	415
Federal Government............	1,678	543	1,135	1,421	183	76
Military retirement	1,121	664	457	945	129	48
State or local government	4,183	1,792	2,391	3,644	394	184
Property income [5]	96,484	77,694	18,790	84,884	5,686	5,315
Interest	90,998	73,230	17,768	80,147	5,302	4,870
Dividends..................	33,480	26,697	6,783	30,364	1,234	1,102
Rents, royalities, estates, or trusts...	9,894	7,414	2,480	8,844	413	582
Education	7,270	7,266	4	5,519	1,116	753
Pell grant only................	1,561	1,560	1	1,026	424	247
Other government only	1,181	1,181	–	904	177	128
Scholarships only..............	2,290	2,289	1	1,833	234	193
Child support	4,964	4,934	30	3,825	904	603
Alimony....................	411	362	49	368	14	24
Financial assistance from outside the household................	2,036	1,878	158	1,540	237	231
Other income	1,054	841	213	868	94	67
Combinations of income types:						
Government transfer payments.....	58,783	25,908	32,875	48,685	7,292	4,818
Public assistance or SSI	6,642	5,446	1,196	4,361	1,778	1,089

– Represents or rounds to zero. [1] Beginning with the 2003 CPS, respondents could choose one or more races. For example, "White" refers to people who reported White and did not report any other race category. The use of this single-race population does not imply that it is the preferred method of presenting or analyzing data. Information on people who reported more than one race, such as "Asian and Black or African American," is available from Census 2000 through American FactFinder. [2] "Black" refers to people who reported Black and did not report any other race category. [3] Persons of Hispanic origin may be of any race. [4] TANF—Temporary Assistance for Needy Families program; AFDC—Aid to Families with Dependent Children program. [5] Includes estates and trusts reported as survivor benefits.

Source: U.S. Census Bureau, "Table PINC-09. Source of Income in 2007—Number With Income and Mean Income of Specified Type in 2007 of People 15 Years Old and Over, by Age, Race, Hispanic Origin and Sex." See also <http://pubdb3.census.gov/macro/032008/perinc/new09_000.htm>.

Social Insurance and Human Services 347

Table 531. **Persons Living in Households Receiving Selected Noncash Benefits: 2007**

[In thousands (298,699 represents 298,699,000), except percent. Persons, as of March 2008, who lived with someone (a nonrelative or a relative) who received aid. Not every person tallied here received the aid themselves. Persons living in households receiving more than one type of aid are counted only once. Excludes members of the Armed Forces except those living off post or with their families on post. Population controls for 2008 based on Census 2000 and an expanded sample of households. Based on Current Population Survey; see text, Section 1 and Appendix III]

Age, Sex, and Race	Total	In household that received means-tested assistance [1]		In household that received means-tested cash assistance		In household that received food stamps		In household in which one or more persons were covered by Medicaid		Lived in public or authorized housing	
		Num-ber	Per-cent	Num-ber	Per-cent	Num-ber	Per-cent	Num-ber	Per-cent	Num-ber	Per-cent
Total	298,699	78,123	26.2	17,165	5.7	22,770	7.6	62,050	20.8	10,111	3.4
Under 18 years	73,996	29,243	39.5	4,969	6.7	9,860	13.3	23,270	31.4	3,748	5.1
18 to 24 years	28,398	7,965	28.0	1,604	5.6	2,292	8.1	6,605	23.3	996	3.5
25 to 34 years	40,146	10,801	26.9	1,962	4.9	3,180	7.9	8,783	21.9	1,222	3.0
35 to 44 years	42,132	9,900	23.5	1,950	4.6	2,445	5.8	7,605	18.1	932	2.2
45 to 54 years	43,935	8,425	19.2	2,629	6.0	2,188	5.0	6,746	15.4	926	2.1
55 to 59 years	18,371	2,985	16.3	1,072	5.8	769	4.2	2,415	13.1	391	2.1
60 to 64 years	14,931	2,403	16.1	881	5.9	533	3.6	1,929	12.9	366	2.5
65 years and over	36,790	6,401	17.4	2,098	5.7	1,503	4.1	4,696	12.8	1,530	4.2
65 to 74 years	19,588	3,283	16.8	1,056	5.4	822	4.2	2,504	12.8	686	3.5
75 years and over . . .	17,202	3,117	18.1	1,043	6.1	681	4.0	2,191	12.7	844	4.9
Male	146,655	36,251	24.7	7,957	5.4	9,815	6.7	28,891	19.7	3,895	2.7
Female	152,044	41,873	27.5	9,208	6.1	12,955	8.5	33,158	21.8	6,216	4.1
White alone [2]	239,133	54,551	22.8	10,899	4.6	13,904	5.8	43,641	18.2	4,929	2.1
Black alone [2].	37,665	17,049	45.3	4,822	12.8	7,204	19.1	13,121	34.8	4,275	11.4
Asian alone [2].	13,257	3,056	23.1	675	5.1	448	3.4	2,515	19.0	382	2.9
Hispanic [3]	45,933	21,839	47.5	3,212	7.0	5,392	11.7	16,886	36.8	2,106	4.6
White alone, Non-Hispanic [2].	196,583	34,543	17.6	7,984	4.1	9,099	4.6	28,214	14.4	3,198	1.6

[1] Means-tested assistance includes means-tested cash assistance, food stamps, Medicaid, and public or authorized housing. [2] Refers to people who reported specific race and did not report any other race category. [3] People of Hispanic origin may be of any race.

Source: U.S. Census Bureau, *Current Population Reports*, P60-235. See also <http:www.census.gov/prod/2008pubs /p60-235.pdf>.

Table 532. **Social Security—Covered Employment, Earnings, and Contribution Rates: 1990 to 2008**

[164.7 represents 164,700,000. Includes Puerto Rico, Virgin Islands, American Samoa, and Guam. Represents all reported employment. Data are estimated. OASDHI = Old-age, survivors, disability, and health insurance; SMI = Supplementary medical insurance]

Item	Unit	1990	1995	2000	2002	2003	2004	2005	2006	2007	2008
Workers with insured status [1]	Million . . .	164.7	173.6	185.8	190.3	192.0	193.7	195.8	198.4	200.9	203.4
Male	Million . . .	86.8	90.6	96.0	97.9	98.5	99.3	100.4	101.5	102.6	103.8
Female	Million . . .	77.9	83.1	89.9	92.4	93.4	94.4	95.7	96.9	98.3	99.7
Under 25 years	Million . . .	21.2	18.9	20.8	21.1	20.6	20.2	20.2	20.2	20.1	20.3
25 to 34 years	Million . . .	41.6	39.5	36.6	36.5	36.4	36.4	36.5	36.6	37.0	37.6
35 to 44 years	Million . . .	36.5	40.7	42.6	42.1	41.8	41.4	41.1	40.7	40.1	39.5
45 to 54 years	Million . . .	23.0	29.7	36.1	37.8	38.6	39.5	40.4	41.2	41.9	42.4
55 to 59 years	Million . . .	8.9	9.9	12.3	14.0	14.7	15.4	16.3	16.8	17.1	17.5
60 to 64 years	Million . . .	8.8	8.6	9.6	10.5	11.1	11.4	11.9	12.5	13.4	14.1
65 to 69 years	Million . . .	8.1	8.0	7.9	8.2	8.5	8.7	8.9	9.2	9.7	10.3
70 years and over	Million . . .	16.5	18.5	19.8	20.2	20.4	20.6	20.9	21.2	21.5	21.8
Workers reported with—											
Taxable earnings [2]	Million . . .	133	141	155	154	155	156	159	161	163	162
Maximum earnings [2]	Million . . .	8	8	10	8	8	9	10	10	10	10
Earnings in covered employment [2]	Bil. dol. . .	2,716	3,407	4,840	4,954	5,091	5,389	5,700	6,062	6,405	6,553
Reported taxable [2]	Bil. dol. . .	2,359	2,920	4,009	4,250	4,355	4,553	4,766	5,048	5,300	5,511
Percent of total	Percent . .	86.8	85.7	82.8	85.8	85.5	84.5	83.6	83.3	82.8	84.1
Average per worker:											
Total earnings [2]	Dollars . .	20,385	24,157	31,303	32,105	32,934	34,487	35,868	37,601	39,250	40,357
Taxable earnings [2]	Dollars . .	17,703	20,702	25,926	27,539	28,174	29,142	29,991	31,313	32,480	33,942
Annual maximum taxable earnings [3]	Dollars . .	51,300	61,200	76,200	84,900	87,000	87,900	90,000	94,200	97,500	102,000
Contribution rates for OASDHI: [4]											
Each employer and employee. . .	Percent . .	7.65	7.65	7.65	7.65	7.65	7.65	7.65	7.65	7.65	7.65
Self-employed [5]	Percent . .	15.30	15.30	15.30	15.30	15.30	15.30	15.30	15.30	15.30	15.30
SMI, monthly premium [6]	Dollars . .	28.60	46.10	45.50	54.00	58.70	66.60	78.20	88.50	93.50	96.40

[1] Estimated number fully insured for retirement and/or survivor benefits as of end of year. [2] Includes self-employment. Averages per worker computed with unrounded earnings and worker amounts, which may not agree with rounded table amounts. [3] Beginning 1995, upper limit on earnings subject to HI taxes was repealed. [4] As of January 1, 2006, each employee and employer pays 7.65 percent and the self-employed pay 15.3 percent. [5] Self-employed pays 15.3 percent, and half of the tax is deductible for income tax purposes and for computing self-employment income subject to social security tax. [6] As of January 1.

Source: U.S. Social Security Administration, *Annual Statistical Supplement* to the *Social Security Bulletin* and unpublished data (released March 2009). See also <http://www.ssa.gov/policy/docs/statcomps/supplement/2008/>.

348   Social Insurance and Human Services

Table 533. Social Security (OASDI)—Benefits by Type of Beneficiary: 1990 to 2007

[39,832 represents 39,832,000. A person eligible to receive more than one type of benefit is generally classified or counted only once as a retired-worker beneficiary. OASDI = Old-age, survivors, and disability insurance. See also headnote, Table 534, and Appendix III]

Type of beneficiary	1990	1995	2000	2001	2002	2003	2004	2005	2006	2007
Number of benefits [1] (1,000) . .	**39,832**	**43,387**	**45,415**	**45,878**	**46,444**	**47,038**	**47,688**	**48,434**	**49,123**	**49,865**
Retired workers [2] (1,000)	24,838	26,673	28,499	28,837	29,190	29,532	29,953	30,461	30,976	31,528
Disabled workers [3] (1,000)	3,011	4,185	5,042	5,274	5,544	5,874	6,198	6,519	6,807	7,099
Wives and husbands [2,4] (1,000) . . .	3,367	3,290	2,963	2,899	2,833	2,773	2,722	2,680	2,632	2,585
Children (1,000)	3,187	3,734	3,803	3,839	3,910	3,961	3,986	4,025	4,041	4,051
Under age 18	2,497	2,956	2,976	2,994	3,043	3,080	3,097	3,130	3,133	3,120
Disabled children [5]	600	686	729	737	745	753	759	769	777	795
Students [6]	89	92	98	109	123	128	130	127	131	136
Of retired workers	422	442	459	467	477	480	483	488	490	494
Of deceased workers	1,776	1,884	1,878	1,890	1,908	1,910	1,905	1,903	1,899	1,892
Of disabled workers	989	1,409	1,466	1,482	1,526	1,571	1,599	1,633	1,652	1,665
Widowed mothers [7] (1,000)	304	275	203	197	194	190	184	178	171	165
Widows and widowers [2,8] (1,000) . .	5,111	5,226	4,901	4,828	4,771	4,707	4,643	4,569	4,494	4,436
Parents [2] (1,000)	6	4	3	3	2	2	2	2	2	2
Special benefits [9] (1,000)	7	1	(Z)	(Z)	(Z)	(Z)	(Z)	(Z)	(Z)	(Z)
AVERAGE MONTHLY BENEFIT, CURRENT DOLLARS										
Retired workers [2]	603	720	844	874	895	922	955	1,002	1,044	1,079
Retired worker and wife [2]	1,027	1,221	1,420	1,466	1,494	1,535	1,586	1,660	1,726	1,776
Disabled workers [3]	587	682	786	814	834	862	894	938	978	1,004
Wives and husbands [2,4]	298	354	416	430	439	450	464	485	502	516
Children of retired workers	259	322	395	413	426	444	465	493	518	538
Children of deceased workers.	406	469	550	571	585	603	625	656	684	704
Children of disabled workers.	164	183	228	238	245	254	265	279	290	299
Widowed mothers [7]	409	478	595	621	640	664	689	725	757	782
Widows and widowers, nondisabled [2]	556	680	810	841	861	888	920	967	1,008	1,040
Parents [2]	482	591	704	729	753	779	810	851	892	918
Special benefits [9]	167	192	217	224	227	232	238	247	256	261
AVERAGE MONTHLY BENEFIT, CONSTANT (2007) DOLLARS [10]										
Retired workers [2]	909	947	979	999	998	1,010	1,013	1,027	1,087	1,079
Retired worker and wife [2]	1,549	1,605	1,647	1,674	1,667	1,681	1,682	1,702	1,796	1,776
Disabled workers [3]	885	897	912	930	930	943	948	962	1,017	1,004
Wives and husbands [2,4]	449	465	482	491	490	493	492	497	523	516
Children of deceased workers.	612	617	638	652	653	660	663	673	711	704
Widowed mothers [7]	617	628	690	709	714	727	731	743	787	782
Widows and widowers, nondisabled [2]	839	894	939	960	960	972	976	991	1,049	1,040
Number of benefits awarded (1,000).	**3,717**	**3,882**	**4,290**	**4,162**	**4,336**	**4,322**	**4,459**	**4,672**	**4,621**	**4,711**
Retired workers [2]	1,665	1,609	1,961	1,779	1,813	1,791	1,883	2,000	1,999	2,036
Disabled workers [3]	468	646	622	691	750	777	796	830	799	805
Wives and husbands [2,4]	379	322	385	358	363	353	367	379	378	364
Children	695	809	777	796	846	852	859	908	897	902
Widowed mothers [7]	58	52	40	41	41	39	40	38	36	34
Widows and widowers [2,8]	452	445	505	496	523	508	514	517	512	570
Parents [2]	(Z)	(Z)	(Z)	(Z)	(Z)	(Z)	(Z)	(Z)	(Z)	(Z)
Special benefits [9]	(Z)	(Z)	(Z)	(Z)	(Z)	(Z)	(Z)	(Z)	(Z)	(Z)
BENEFIT PAYMENTS DURING YEAR (bil. dol.)										
Total [11]	**247.8**	**332.6**	**407.6**	**431.9**	**453.8**	**470.8**	**493.3**	**520.8**	**552.8**	**585.0**
Monthly benefits [12]	247.6	332.4	407.4	431.7	453.6	470.6	493.1	520.6	552.6	584.8
Retired workers [2]	156.8	205.3	253.5	269.0	281.6	291.5	304.3	321.7	342.9	364.3
Disabled workers [3]	22.1	36.6	49.8	54.2	59.9	64.8	71.7	78.4	85.0	91.3
Wives and husbands [2,4]	14.5	17.9	19.4	19.9	20.3	20.4	20.6	20.5	21.5	22.1
Children	12.0	16.1	19.3	20.4	21.5	22.3	23.3	24.5	25.8	27.0
Under age 18	9.0	11.9	14.1	14.8	15.7	16.2	17.0	17.9	18.8	19.5
Disabled children [5]	2.5	3.6	4.6	4.8	5.1	5.2	5.5	5.8	6.1	6.5
Students [6]	0.5	0.6	0.7	0.7	0.8	0.8	0.9	1.0	1.0	1.0
Of retired workers	1.3	1.7	2.1	2.3	2.5	2.6	2.7	2.9	3.1	3.3
Of deceased workers	8.6	10.7	12.5	13.1	13.7	14.1	14.5	15.1	15.8	16.5
Of disabled workers	2.2	3.7	4.7	4.9	5.3	5.7	6.1	6.5	6.9	7.3
Widowed mothers [7]	1.4	1.6	1.4	1.4	1.5	1.5	1.5	1.5	1.6	1.6
Widows and widowers [2,8]	40.7	54.8	63.9	66.8	68.8	70.1	71.7	73.4	75.9	78.5
Parents [2]	(Z)	(Z)	(Z)	(Z)	(Z)	(Z)	(Z)	(Z)	(Z)	(Z)
Special benefits [9]	(Z)	(Z)	(Z)	(Z)	(Z)	(Z)	(Z)	(Z)	(Z)	(Z)
Lump sum	0.2	0.2	0.2	0.2	0.2	0.2	0.2	0.2	0.2	0.2

Z Fewer than 500 or less than $50 million.   [1] Number of benefit payments in current-payment status, i.e., actually being made at a specified time with no deductions or with deductions amounting to less than a month's benefit.   [2] 62 years and over.   [3] Disabled workers under age 65.   [4] Includes wife beneficiaries with entitled children in their care and entitled divorced wives.   [5] 18 years old and over. Disability began before age 18.   [6] Full-time students aged 18 and 19.   [7] Includes surviving divorced mothers with entitled children in their care and widowed fathers with entitled children in their care.   [8] Includes widows aged 60–61, surviving divorced wives aged 60 and over, disabled widows and widowers aged 50 and over; and widowers aged 60–61.   [9] Benefits for persons aged 72 and over not insured under regular or transitional provisions of Social Security Act.   [10] Constant dollar figures are based on the consumer price index (CPI-U) for December as published by the U.S. Bureau of Labor Statistics.   [11] Represents total disbursements of benefit checks by the U.S. Department of the Treasury during the years specified.   [12] Distribution by type estimated.

Source: U.S. Social Security Administration, Annual Statistical Supplement to the Social Security Bulletin, 2008 and unpublished data. See also <http://www.ssa.gov/policy/>.

Social Insurance and Human Services   349

Table 534. Social Security—Beneficiaries, Annual Payments, and Average Monthly Benefit, 1990 to 2008, and by State and Other Areas, 2008

[Number of beneficiaries in current-payment status (**39,832 represents** 39,832,000) and average monthly benefit as of December. Data based on 10-percent sample of administrative records. See also headnote, Table 533, and Appendix III]

Year, state, and other area	Number of beneficiaries (1,000) — Total	Retired workers and dependents[1]	Survivors	Disabled workers and dependents	Annual payments[2] (mil. dol.) — Total	Retired workers and dependents[1]	Survivors	Disabled workers and dependents	Avg. monthly benefit (dol.) — Retired workers[3]	Disabled workers[4]	Widows and widowers[4]
1990	39,832	28,369	7,197	4,266	247,796	172,042	50,951	24,803	603	587	557
2000	45,417	31,761	6,981	6,675	407,431	274,645	77,848	54,938	845	787	810
2004	47,707	33,025	6,730	7,952	493,078	327,139	87,737	78,202	955	894	920
2005	48,446	33,488	6,650	8,307	520,561	345,094	90,073	85,394	1,002	938	967
2006	49,123	33,945	6,566	8,612	552,636	366,952	93,300	92,384	1,044	978	1,007
2007	49,865	34,454	6,495	8,916	584,764	389,123	96,555	99,086	1,079	1,004	1,040
2008, total[5]	50,898	35,169	6,456	9,273	615,152	409,503	99,348	106,301	1,153	1,063	1,112
United States	49,600	34,477	6,236	9,050	605,117	403,813	97,110	104,192	(NA)	(NA)	(NA)
Alabama	953	523	136	245	11,089	6,440	1,922	2,727	1,116	1,040	1,042
Alaska	71	44	10	14	818	529	133	156	1,100	1,054	1,055
Arizona	987	657	110	166	12,162	8,465	1,719	1,977	1,178	1,101	1,151
Arkansas	602	341	78	155	6,807	4,059	1,079	1,669	1,085	1,015	1,022
California	4,679	3,050	554	759	56,447	38,714	8,732	9,002	1,148	1,084	1,134
Colorado	636	420	76	103	7,640	5,244	1,198	1,199	1,137	1,064	1,132
Connecticut	600	417	64	91	7,961	5,746	1,123	1,092	1,261	1,103	1,248
Delaware	161	107	18	29	2,081	1,426	298	357	1,224	1,121	1,201
District of Columbia	71	46	10	13	775	511	124	140	1,017	945	942
Florida	3,547	2,441	386	532	42,985	30,677	6,088	6,220	1,147	1,068	1,140
Georgia	1,348	825	184	277	15,908	10,158	2,614	3,136	1,132	1,055	1,065
Hawaii	213	154	22	26	2,557	1,915	336	305	1,140	1,097	1,083
Idaho	248	161	29	44	2,926	1,993	450	483	1,126	1,039	1,140
Illinois	1,949	1,271	257	314	24,565	16,680	4,199	3,686	1,192	1,086	1,186
Indiana	1,122	710	147	208	14,202	9,461	2,379	2,362	1,213	1,065	1,190
Iowa	564	378	72	81	6,864	4,800	1,172	892	1,150	1,014	1,149
Kansas	465	306	59	76	5,765	3,965	950	850	1,179	1,036	1,180
Kentucky	845	444	122	231	9,687	5,401	1,728	2,558	1,096	1,040	1,024
Louisiana	748	386	139	167	8,495	4,717	1,944	1,833	1,076	1,050	1,025
Maine	286	174	31	67	3,220	2,044	473	702	1,069	982	1,074
Maryland	802	535	103	125	10,010	6,881	1,619	1,510	1,176	1,094	1,142
Massachusetts	1,094	707	118	219	13,405	9,004	1,938	2,463	1,163	1,049	1,159
Michigan	1,841	1,151	238	345	23,903	15,802	3,966	4,135	1,246	1,122	1,205
Minnesota	832	563	96	129	10,228	7,200	1,558	1,470	1,167	1,054	1,142
Mississippi	568	307	84	150	6,325	3,628	1,103	1,595	1,073	1,008	989
Missouri	1,107	685	141	227	13,230	8,553	2,139	2,538	1,137	1,036	1,121
Montana	181	118	23	29	2,102	1,431	347	325	1,097	1,022	1,113
Nebraska	298	199	37	45	3,578	2,486	597	495	1,135	1,011	1,143
Nevada	374	256	39	62	4,614	3,226	621	767	1,158	1,128	1,156
New Hampshire	237	155	23	49	3,006	2,037	397	571	1,193	1,078	1,191
New Jersey	1,408	970	160	212	18,895	13,459	2,752	2,684	1,273	1,165	1,222
New Mexico	335	204	44	66	3,774	2,439	607	728	1,079	1,022	1,030
New York	3,144	2,046	358	572	39,929	27,255	5,843	6,831	1,214	1,113	1,169
North Carolina	1,631	1,032	190	346	19,473	12,763	2,740	3,971	1,141	1,051	1,062
North Dakota	117	75	18	15	1,346	906	273	167	1,074	987	1,067
Ohio	2,022	1,253	295	341	24,797	16,235	4,745	3,817	1,163	1,035	1,147
Oklahoma	670	406	92	136	7,836	4,965	1,353	1,518	1,110	1,036	1,082
Oregon	660	447	73	103	8,114	5,684	1,205	1,225	1,161	1,068	1,168
Pennsylvania	2,482	1,601	322	427	31,162	20,950	5,299	4,913	1,188	1,073	1,167
Rhode Island	196	130	20	40	2,387	1,628	313	446	1,156	1,028	1,156
South Carolina	850	528	106	182	10,155	6,546	1,505	2,104	1,142	1,067	1,056
South Dakota	147	98	20	20	1,663	1,160	289	214	1,070	983	1,052
Tennessee	1,169	698	156	258	13,778	8,669	2,240	2,868	1,133	1,030	1,066
Texas	3,192	1,907	470	597	37,403	23,792	6,965	6,647	1,122	1,050	1,080
Utah	299	194	37	48	3,608	2,500	578	530	1,162	1,054	1,181
Vermont	120	78	13	24	1,437	977	207	253	1,151	998	1,120
Virginia	1,207	765	150	231	14,588	9,620	2,280	2,688	1,149	1,072	1,087
Washington	1,009	668	112	172	12,899	8,788	1,857	2,054	1,199	1,077	1,191
West Virginia	430	219	67	114	5,167	2,807	1,014	1,346	1,137	1,108	1,074
Wisconsin	1,001	674	117	160	12,482	8,735	1,925	1,821	1,184	1,057	1,175
Wyoming	86	57	11	13	1,046	725	168	152	1,150	1,053	1,153
Puerto Rico	749	364	116	199	6,216	3,218	1,118	1,879	769	921	680
Guam	13	7	3	1	107	63	26	18	769	909	760
American Samoa	6	2	1	2	42	16	12	14	753	823	658
Virgin Islands	18	12	2	2	186	134	27	26	1,000	1,073	868
Northern Mariana Islands	2	1	1	(Z)	15	9	5	2	658	704	523
Abroad	510	307	97	17	3,469	2,250	1,050	170	626	958	699

NA Not available.   Z Less than 500.   [1] Includes special benefits for persons aged 72 years and over not insured under regular or transitional provisions of Social Security Act.   [2] Unnegotiated checks not deducted. 1990 and 1995 include lump-sum payments to survivors of deceased workers.   [3] Excludes persons with special benefits.   [4] Nondisabled only.   [5] Includes those with state or area unknown.

Source: U.S. Social Security Administration, *Annual Statistical Supplement to the Social Security Bulletin*, (released March 2009). See also <http://www.ssa.gov/policy/docs/statcomps/supplement/2008/supplement08.pdf>.

350   Social Insurance and Human Services

Table 535. **Social Security Trust Funds: 1990 to 2008**

[In billions of dollars (272.4 represents $272,400,000,000)]

Type of trust fund	1990	1995	2000	2003	2004	2005	2006	2007	2008
Old-age and survivors insurance (OASI):									
Net contribution income [1]	272.4	310.1	433.0	468.6	487.4	520.7	534.8	560.9	574.6
Interest received [2]	16.4	32.8	57.5	75.2	79.0	84.0	91.8	97.0	105.3
Benefit payments [3]	223.0	291.6	352.7	399.8	415.0	435.4	454.5	489.1	509.3
Assets, end of year	214.2	458.5	931.0	1,355.3	1,500.6	1,663.0	1,844.3	2,023.6	2,202.9
Disability insurance (DI):									
Net contribution income [1]	28.7	54.7	71.8	78.4	81.4	87.2	90.8	109.9	109.8
Interest received [2]	0.9	2.2	6.9	9.7	10.0	10.3	10.6	13.2	11.0
Benefit payments [3]	24.8	40.9	55.0	70.9	78.2	85.4	91.7	95.9	106.0
Assets, end of year	11.1	37.6	118.5	175.4	186.2	195.6	203.8	214.9	215.8

[1] Includes deposits by states and deductions for refund of estimated employee-tax overpayment. Includes government contributions on deemed wage credits for military service 1957–2001. Includes taxation of benefits. [2] In 1990, includes interest on advance tax transfers. Includes interest on reimbursement for unnegotiated checks. [3] Includes payments for vocational rehabilitation services furnished to disabled persons receiving benefits because of their disabilities. Amounts reflect deductions for unnegotiated benefit checks.

Source: U.S. Social Security Administration, *Annual Report of Board of Trustees, OASI, DI, HI, and SMI Trust Funds*; <http://www.ssa.gov/OACT/TR/TR08/>. Also published in *Social Security Bulletin*, quarterly.

Table 536. **Public Employee Retirement Systems—Participants and Finances: 1980 to 2007**

[4,629 represents 4,629,000. For fiscal year of retirement system, except data for the Thrift Savings Plan are for calendar year. For a definition of defined benefit, see headnote, Table 540]

Retirement plan	Unit	1980	1990	2000	2002	2003	2004	2005	2006	2007, proj.
TOTAL PARTICIPANTS [1]										
Federal retirement systems:										
Defined benefit:										
Civil Service Retirement System	1,000 ...	4,629	4,167	3,256	3,201	3,133	3,035	2,958	2,878	2,789
Federal Employees Retirement System [2]	1,000 ...	(X)	1,180	1,935	2,019	2,140	2,104	2,196	2,290	2,371
Military Service Retirement System [3]	1,000 ...	3,380	3,763	3,397	3,453	3,457	3,545	3,536	3,560	3,585
Thrift Savings Plan [4]	1,000 ...	(X)	1,625	2,500	3,000	3,200	3,400	3,600	3,700	3,900
State and local retirement systems [5,6]	1,000 ...	(NA)	16,858	16,834	17,264	17,650	17,890	17,932	18,484	18,583
ACTIVE PARTICIPANTS										
Federal retirement systems:										
Defined benefit:										
Civil Service Retirement System	1,000 ...	2,700	1,826	978	906	854	788	722	650	580
Federal Employees Retirement System [2]	1,000 ...	(X)	1,136	1,668	1,717	1,808	1,882	1,952	2,014	2,066
Military Service Retirement System [3]	1,000 ...	2,050	2,130	1,437	1,465	1,468	1,480	1,445	1,443	1,438
Thrift Savings Plan [4]	1,000 ...	(X)	1,419	1,900	2,300	2,400	2,500	2,800	2,600	2,600
State and local retirement systems [5,6]	1,000 ...	(NA)	11,345	13,917	14,123	14,249	14,181	14,116	14,529	14,422
ASSETS										
Total	Bil. dol. ...	258	1,047	2,950	3,016	3,092	3,472	3,697	4,023	4,537
Federal retirement systems	Bil. dol. ...	73	326	782	858	920	977	1,039	1,111	1,160
Defined benefit	Bil. dol. ...	73	318	684	756	791	825	866	904	928
Civil Service Retirement System	Bil. dol. ...	73	220	395	417	425	433	440	442	428
Federal Employees Retirement System [2]	Bil. dol. ...	(X)	18	126	162	183	204	228	254	282
Military Service Retirement System [3]	Bil. dol. ...	(7)	80	163	177	183	188	198	208	218
Thrift Savings Plan [4]	Bil. dol. ...	(X)	8	98	102	129	152	173	207	232
State and local retirement systems [5]	Bil. dol. ...	185	721	2,168	2,158	2,172	2,495	2,658	2,912	3,377
CONTRIBUTIONS										
Total	Bil. dol. ...	83	103	143	151	161	187	189	205	222
Federal retirement systems	Bil. dol. ...	19	61	78	85	86	95	98	108	115
Defined benefit	Bil. dol. ...	19	59	69	73	72	79	82	88	94
Civil Service Retirement System	Bil. dol. ...	19	28	33	34	29	34	33	34	35
Federal Employees Retirement System [2]	Bil. dol. ...	(X)	4	8	10	11	13	13	15	16
Military Service Retirement System [3]	Bil. dol. ...	(7)	27	28	30	32	32	38	39	43
Thrift Savings Plan [4]	Bil. dol. ...	(X)	2	9	12	14	16	16	20	21
State and local retirement systems [5]	Bil. dol. ...	64	42	65	66	75	92	91	97	107
BENEFITS										
Total	Bil. dol. ...	39	89	172	196	211	226	240	257	274
Federal retirement systems	Bil. dol. ...	27	53	81	86	89	93	99	105	112
Defined benefit	Bil. dol. ...	27	53	78	84	86	89	94	98	104
Civil Service Retirement System	Bil. dol. ...	15	31	44	47	48	50	52	54	57
Federal Employees Retirement System [2]	Bil. dol. ...	(X)	(Z)	1	2	2	2	3	3	4
Military Service Retirement System [3]	Bil. dol. ...	12	22	33	35	36	37	39	41	43
Thrift Savings Plan [4]	Bil. dol. ...	(X)	(Z)	3	3	3	4	5	7	8
State and local retirement systems [5]	Bil. dol. ...	12	36	91	110	122	133	141	152	160

NA Not available. X Not applicable. Z Less than $500 million. [1] Includes active, separated vested, retired employees and survivors. [2] The Federal Employees Retirement System was established June 6, 1986. [3] Includes nondisability and disability retirees, surviving families, and all active personnel with the exception of active reserves. [4] The Thrift Savings Plan (a defined contribution plan) was established April 1, 1987. [5] Excludes state and local plans that are fully supported by employee contributions. [6] Not adjusted for double counting of individuals participating in more than one plan. [7] The Military Retirement System was unfunded until October 1, 1984.

Source: Employee Benefit Research Institute, Washington, DC, *EBRI Databook on Employee Benefits, 12th ed.* and unpublished data (copyright). See also <http://www.ebri.org/>.

Social Insurance and Human Services **351**

Table 537. **Federal Civil Service Retirement: 1990 to 2008**

[As of September 30 or for year ending September 30 (2,945 represents 2,945,000). Covers both Civil Service Retirement System and Federal Employees Retirement System]

Item	Unit	1990	1995	2000	2003	2004	2005	2006	2007	2008
Employees covered [1]	1,000	2,945	2,668	2,764	2,662	2,670	2,674	2,611	2,618	2,613
Annuitants, total	1,000	2,143	2,311	2,376	2,389	2,404	2,433	2,449	2,463	2,471
Age and service	1,000	1,288	1,441	1,501	1,523	1,544	1,568	1,602	1,625	1,643
Disability	1,000	297	263	242	234	231	229	226	222	218
Survivors	1,000	558	607	633	632	629	636	621	616	610
Receipts, total [2]	Mil. dol. . . .	52,689	65,684	75,967	78,366	82,412	83,691	87,164	89,860	90,892
Employee contributions	Mil. dol. . . .	4,501	4,498	4,637	4,522	4,483	4,353	4,304	4,205	4,111
Federal government contributions	Mil. dol. . . .	27,368	33,130	37,722	36,583	42,240	43,093	46,427	48,397	49,547
Disbursements, total [3] . . . . , . . .	Mil. dol. . . .	31,416	38,435	45,194	50,368	52,277	54,790	57,983	78,146	63,687
Age and service annuitants [4] . .	Mil. dol. . . .	26,495	32,070	37,546	42,018	43,727	46,029	48,895	68,776	54,202
Survivors	Mil. dol. . . .	4,366	5,864	7,210	7,951	8,127	8,338	8,642	8,905	9,011
Average monthly benefit:										
Age and service	Dollars	1,369	1,643	1,885	2,085	2,154	2,240	2,363	2,473	2,550
Disability	Dollars	1,008	1,164	1,240	1,291	1,305	1,327	1,366	1,394	1,409
Survivors	Dollars	653	819	952	1,044	1,073	1,106	1,157	1,200	1,232
Cash and security holdings	Bil. dol. . . .	238.0	366.2	508.1	601.7	631.8	660.8	690.0	701.7	728.9

[1] Excludes employees in leave-without-pay status. [2] Includes interest on investments. [3] Includes refunds, death claims, and administration. [4] Includes disability annuitants.

Source: U.S. Office of Personnel Management, *Civil Service Retirement and Disability Trust Fund Annual Report.*

Table 538. **State and Local Government Retirement Systems—Beneficiaries and Finances: 1990 to 2007**

[In billions of dollars (111.3 represents $111,300,000,000), except as indicated. For fiscal years closed during the 12 months ending June 30]

Year and level of government	Num- ber of benefi- ciaries (1,000)	Receipts					Benefits and withdrawals			Cash and security holdings
		Total	Employee contribu- tions	Government contributions		Earn- ings on invest- ments	Total	Ben- efits	With- drawals	
				State	Local					
1990: All systems	4,026	111.3	13.9	14.0	18.6	64.9	38.4	36.0	2.4	721
State-administered	3,232	89.2	11.6	14.0	11.5	52.0	29.6	27.6	2.0	575
Locally administered . . .	794	22.2	2.2	(Z)	7.0	12.9	8.8	8.4	0.4	145
2000: All systems	6,292	297.0	25.0	17.5	22.6	231.9	95.7	91.3	4.4	2,169
State-administered	4,786	247.4	20.7	17.2	16.7	192.8	76.0	72.2	3.8	1,798
Locally administered . . .	1,506	49.7	4.3	0.4	5.9	39.1	19.8	19.1	0.7	371
2005: All systems	6,946	353.5	31.5	24.0	35.7	262.2	156.0	142.1	3.7	2,672
State-administered	5,846	293.4	26.8	23.6	22.1	220.9	126.8	115.2	3.1	2,226
Locally administered . . .	1,100	60.1	4.8	0.4	13.6	41.3	29.3	26.9	0.5	445
2006: All systems	7,301	392.8	32.7	26.4	38.1	295.6	166.3	152.1	4.1	2,912
State-administered	6,184	326.2	27.7	25.9	23.7	248.9	135.6	124.1	3.4	2,424
Locally administered . . .	1,117	66.5	5.0	0.5	14.3	46.7	30.7	28.0	0.7	488
2007: All systems	7,464	580.5	34.1	30.6	42.3	473.5	183.0	162.7	5.2	3,377
State-administered	6,353	486.8	29.1	30.0	26.4	401.3	148.4	131.2	4.6	2,819
Locally administered . . .	1,110	93.7	5.0	0.6	15.9	72.2	34.6	31.5	0.7	558

Z Less than $50 million.

Source: U.S. Census Bureau, through 1990, *Finances of Employee-Retirement Systems of State and Local Governments,* Series GF, No. 2, annual; beginning 2000, "Federal, State, and Local Governments, State and Local Government Public Employee Retirement Systems"; <http://www.census.gov/govs/www/retire.html>.

Table 539. **Percent of Workers Participating in Retirement Benefits by Worker Characteristics: 2005 to 2008**

[Based on National Compensation Survey, a sample survey of 10,370 private industry establishments of all sizes, representing over 105 million workers; see Appendix III. Survey covers all 50 states and the District of Columbia. For a definition of defined benefit and defined contribution, see headnote, Table 540. See also Table 640]

Characteristic	Total [1]				Defined benefit				Defined contribution			
	2005	2006	2007	2008	2005	2006	2007	2008	2005	2006	2007	2008
Total	50	51	51	51	21	20	20	20	42	43	43	43
White-collar occupations. . .	61	60	69	68	24	22	28	28	53	53	60	60
Blue-collar occupations. . . .	51	52	51	52	26	25	25	25	38	40	40	41
Service occupations.	22	24	25	25	7	7	7	8	18	20	20	20
Full-time	60	60	60	60	25	23	23	24	50	51	50	51
Part-time	19	21	23	23	9	8	9	10	14	16	18	18
Union	85	80	81	80	72	68	67	67	43	44	41	42
Nonunion.	46	47	47	48	15	14	15	15	41	43	43	43

[1] Total is less than the sum of the individual retirement items because many employees participated in both types of plans.

Source: U.S. Bureau of Labor Statistics, *Employee Benefits in Private Industry in the United States, March 2008,* Summary 03-08. See also <http://www.bls.gov/ncs/ebs/benefits/2008/ownership_private.htm>.

352   Social Insurance and Human Services

Table 540. Private Pension Plans—Summary by Type of Plan: 1990 to 2006

[712.3 represents 712,300. "**Pension plan**" is defined by the Employee Retirement Income Security Act (ERISA) as "any plan, fund, or program which was heretofore or is hereafter established or maintained by an employer or an employee organization, or by both, to the extent that such plan (a) provides retirement income to employees, or (b) results in a deferral of income by employees for periods extending to the termination of covered employment or beyond, regardless of the method of calculating the contributions made to the plan, the method of calculating the benefits under the plan, or the method of distributing benefits from the plan." A **defined benefit** plan provides a definite benefit formula for calculating benefit amounts—such as a flat amount per year of service or a percentage of salary times years of service. A **defined contribution** plan is a pension plan in which the contributions are made to an individual account for each employee. The retirement benefit is dependent upon the account balance at retirement. The balance depends upon amounts contributed, investment experience, and, in the case of profit sharing plans, amounts which may be allocated to the account due to forfeitures by terminating employees. Employee Stock Ownership Plans (ESOP) and 401(k) plans are included among defined contribution plans. Data are based on Form 5500 series reports filed with the U.S. Department of Labor]

Item	Unit	Total				Defined contribution plan				Defined benefit plan			
		1990	2000	2005	2006	1990	2000	2005	2006	1990	2000	2005	2006
Number of plans [1]	1,000 ...	712.3	735.7	679.1	694.6	599.2	686.9	631.5	646.0	113.1	48.8	47.6	48.6
Total participants [2]	Million ...	76.9	103.3	117.4	122.0	38.1	61.7	75.5	79.8	38.8	41.6	41.9	42.1
Active participants [3]	Million ...	61.5	73.1	82.7	85.8	35.3	50.9	62.4	65.8	26.2	22.2	20.3	19.9
Assets [4]	Bil. dol. ...	1,674	4,203	5,062	5684.3	712	2,216	2,808	3,216.2	962	1,986	2,254	2,468.1
Contributions [5]	Bil. dol. ...	98.8	231.9	341.4	364.7	75.8	198.5	248.8	275.4	23.0	33.4	92.7	89.3
Benefits [6]	Bil. dol. ...	129.4	341.0	354.5	408.2	63.0	213.5	218.0	259.0	66.4	127.5	136.6	149.2

[1] Excludes all plans covering only one participant. [2] Includes active, retired, and separated vested participants not yet in pay status. Also includes double counting of workers in more than one plan. [3] Includes any workers currently in employment covered by a plan and who are earning or retaining credited service under a plan. Also includes any individuals who are eligible to elect to have the employer make payments to a Code section 401(k) plan. Also includes any nonvested former employees who have not yet incurred breaks in service. [4] Asset amounts shown exclude funds held by life insurance companies under allocated group insurance contracts for payment of retirement benefits. These excluded funds make up roughly 10 to 15 percent of total private fund assets. [5] Includes both employer and employee contributions. [6] Includes benefits paid directly from trust and premium payments made from plans to insurance carriers. Excludes benefits paid directly by insurance carriers.

Source: U.S. Department of Labor, Employee Benefits Security Administration, *Private Pension Plan Bulletin* (published February 2009). See also <http://www.dol.gov/ebsa/pdf/privatepensionplanbulletinhistoricaltables.pdf>.

Table. 541. Defined Benefit Retirement Plans—Selected Features: 2006

[**In percent.** Covers full-time employees in private industry. Based on National Compensation Survey, a sample survey of 3,227 private industry establishments of all sizes, representing over 102 million workers; see Appendix III. For definition of defined benefit, see headnote, Table 540. See also Table 640]

Feature	All workers	White collar	Blue collar	Serv-ice	Goods pro-ducing	Serv-ice pro-ducing	1–99 work-ers	100 work-ers or more	Union	Non-union
Plan provisions:										
Benefits based on earnings	53	56	43	73	39	59	48	54	37	61
Early retirement benefits available	82	82	89	94	90	79	76	84	87	80
Availability of lump sum benefits at retirement	52	64	34	57	40	59	49	54	40	59
Benefit formula:										
Percent of terminal earnings	39	46	10	41	32	42	27	42	21	48
Percent of career earnings	14	10	16	32	7	17	21	12	15	13
Dollar amount formula	18	6	37	12	42	6	16	19	15	13
Percent of contribution formula	4	3	7	(Z)	7	3	9	3	10	1
Cash balance	23	33	12	14	10	30	25	23	12	29
Pension equity	2	2	1	1	2	2	1	2	(Z)	3
Requirements for normal retirement: [1]										
No age requirement	11	15	7	3	6	13	20	8	8	12
Less than 30 years of service	9	13	4	3	4	11	14	7	5	11
30 years of service	2	2	3	–	3	2	6	1	3	2
At age 55	1	1	2	(Z)	2	1	1	1	2	1
At age 60	9	8	10	16	7	10	8	10	14	7
At age 62	15	11	23	7	24	11	15	15	21	12
At age 65	59	63	48	74	55	60	47	62	43	67
Sum of age plus service [2]	1	1	1	–	2	(Z)	1	1	1	1

– Represents or rounds to zero. Z Less than 0.5 percent. [1] Normal retirement is defined as the point at which the participant could retire and immediately receive all accrued benefits by virtue of service and earnings, without reduction due to age. If a plan had alternative age and service requirements, the earliest age and associated service were tabulated; if one alternative did not specify an age, it was the requirement tabulated. Some age and service requirements are not shown separately. [2] In some plans, participants must also satisfy a minimum age or service requirement.

Source: U.S. Bureau of Labor Statistics, *National Compensation Survey: Employee Benefits in Private Industry in the United States* and unpublished data.

Social Insurance and Human Services   353

Table 542. Percent of U.S. Households Owning Individual Retirement Accounts (IRAs): 2000 to 2008

[Incidence of IRA ownership is based on an annual tracking survey of 3,000 randomly selected, representative U.S. households; see source for details]

Year and characteristic	Any type of IRA[1]	Tradi-tional IRA	Roth IRA	Employer-spon-sored IRA[2]	Year and characteristic	Any type of IRA[1]	Tradi-tional IRA	Roth IRA	Employer-spon-sored IRA[2]
2000	35.7	28.7	9.2	6.8	2008, total	40.5	32.1	15.9	8.6
2001	36.2	28.9	9.8	8.0					
2002	34.8	28.2	10.8	7.7	Under 35 years	28.0	17.0	13.0	10.0
2003	36.7	29.6	12.5	7.5	35 to 44 years	40.0	27.0	21.0	10.0
2004	36.5	29.6	11.6	8.0	45 to 54 years	46.0	37.0	19.0	10.0
2005	37.9	30.0	12.8	7.4	55 to 64 years	50.0	44.0	20.0	9.0
2006	38.3	31.7	13.4	7.7	65 years and over	40.0	38.0	8.0	4.0
2007	39.8	32.5	14.9	7.9					

[1] Excludes ownership of Coverdell Education Savings Accounts, which were referred to as Education IRAs before July 2001. [2] Employee-sponsored Individual Retirement Accounts (IRAs) include SIMPLE IRAs, Simplified Employee Pension IRAs (SEP-IRAs), and SAR-SEP IRAs (SEP IRAs with salary reduction plans included).

Source: Investment Company Institute, Washington, DC, *Research Fundamentals*, "Appendix: Additional Data on IRA Ownership in 2008"; Vol 18, No. 1A, January 2008 (copyright). See also <http://www.ici.org/statements/fundamentals/fm-v18n1appendix.pdf>.

Table 543. Characteristics of U.S. Households Owning Individual Retirement Accounts (IRAs): 2008

[See headnote, Table 542]

Characteristic	Households owning IRAs			Households not owning IRAs[2]
	Total[1]	Traditional IRA	Roth IRA	
MEDIAN PER HOUSEHOLD				
Age of household sole or co-decision-maker for investing	51	53	47	47
Household income	75,000	75,000	87,500	35,000
Household financial assets[3]	200,000	250,000	214,000	32,000
Household financial assets in all types of IRAs	55,000	75,000	55,000	(X)
Share of household financial assets in type of IRA indicated	31	25	10	(X)
PERCENT OF HOUSEHOLDS				
Household has defined contribution account or defined benefit plan coverage (total)[4]	79	80	83	49
Defined contribution retirement plan account	70	69	77	40
Defined benefit plan coverage	44	46	46	24
Types of IRAs owned:[4, 5]				
Traditional IRA	79	100	68	(X)
Roth IRA	39	34	100	(X)
Employer-sponsored IRA[6]	21	14	15	(X)

X Not applicable.   [1] Households owning IRAs include households that own Traditional or Roth IRAs. Households owning only employer-sponsored IRAs are not included.   [2] Households not owning IRAs exclude households with traditional, Roth, or employer-sponsored IRAs.   [3] Household financial assets include assets in employer-sponsored defined contribution retirement plans but exclude primary residence.   [4] Multiple responses are included.   [5] Data are from ICI's 2007 Mutual Fund Shareholder Tracking Survey.   [6] Employer-sponsored IRAs include SEP IRAs, SAR-SEP IRAs, and SIMPLE IRAs. Among households owning employer-sponsored IRAs, 63 percent have traditional IRAs and 31 percent have Roth IRAs.

Source: Investment Company Institute, Washington, DC, *Research Fundamentals*, "Appendix: Additional Data on IRA Ownership in 2008"; Vol 18, No. 1A, January 2009 (copyright). See also <http://www.ici.org/statements/fundamentals/>.

Table 544. **Percent Distribution of Assets in Individual Retirement Accounts (IRAs) by Type of IRA: 2008**

[See headnote, Table 542]

Assets category	Unit	Total assets in IRAs	Type of IRA owned — Traditional IRAs	Type of IRA owned — Roth IRAs
PERCENT DISTRIBUTION OF ASSETS IN IRAs				
Less than $10,000	Percent	16	16	30
$10,000 to $24,999	Percent	14	14	24
$25,000 to $49,999	Percent	17	14	20
$50,000 to $99,999	Percent	17	19	14
$100,000 to $249,999	Percent	20	20	10
$250,000 or more	Percent	16	17	3
TOTAL ASSETS IN IRAs				
Mean	Dollars	140,000	136,400	51,500
Median	Dollars	55,000	60,000	20,000

Source: Investment Company Institute, Washington, DC, *Research Fundamentals*, "Appendix: Additional Data on IRA Ownership in 2008"; Vol. 18, No. 1A, January 2009 (copyright). See also <www.ici.org/pdf/fm-v18n1_appendix.pdf/>.

Table 545. **401(k) Plans— Participants, Assets, Contributions, and Benefits by Type of Plan: 2006**

Type of Plan [1]	Total plans [2]	Total participants (thousands) [3]	Total assets (millions)	Total contributions (millions) [4]	Total benefits (millions) [5]
Total	465,653	70,295	58,351	251,233	229,217
Profit Sharing and thrift-savings	463,875	68,854	57,257	245,721	222,575
Stock bonus	304	1,090	827	4,535	5,782
Target benefit	150	15	12	28	11
Money Purchase	1,045	330	249	939	843
Annuity - 403(b)(1)	192	4	4	9	5
Custodial account - 403(b)(7)	87	1	1	2	1

[1] About 1% of defined contribution plans report more than one plan type.   [2] Excludes plans covering only one participant.   [3] Includes active, retired, and seperated vested participants not yet in pay status.   [4] Includes both employer and employee contributions.   [5] Amounts shown include benefits paid directly from trust funds and premium payments made by plans to insurance carriers.

Source: U.S. Department of Labor, *Private Pension Plan Bulletin: 2006* (published December 2008). See also <http://www.dol.gov /ebsa/pdf/2006pensionplanbulletin.pdf>.

Table 546. **State Unemployment Insurance—Summary: 1990 to 2007**

[**2,522 represents 2,522,000**. Includes unemployment compensation for state and local government employees where covered by state law]

Item	Unit	1990	1995	2000	2002	2003	2004	2005	2006	2007
Insured unemployment, average weekly	1,000	2,522	2,572	2,110	3,585	3,531	2,950	2,661	2,475	2,571
Percent of covered employment [1]	Percent	2.4	2.3	1.7	2.8	2.8	2.3	2.1	1.9	2.0
Percent of civilian unemployed	Percent	35.8	34.7	37.6	43.2	40.7	36.8	35.7	35.3	36.3
Unemployment benefits, average weekly	Dollars	161	187	221	257	262	263	267	277	288
Percent of weekly wage	Percent	36.0	35.5	32.9	36.8	36.5	35.2	34.6	34.3	35.1
Weeks compensated	Million	116.2	118.3	96.0	166.3	163.2	135.1	121.2	112.2	116.3
Beneficiaries, first payments	1,000	8,629	8,035	7,033	10,088	9,935	8,369	7,922	7,350	7,641
Average duration of benefits [2]	Weeks	13.4	14.7	13.7	16.5	16.4	16.1	15.3	15.2	15.3
Claimants exhausting benefits	1,000	2,323	2,662	2,144	4,416	4,417	3,532	2,856	2,676	2,670
Percent of first payment [3]	Percent	29.4	34.3	31.8	42.5	43.4	39.0	35.9	35.4	35.3
Contributions collected [4]	Bil. dol.	15.2	22.0	19.9	19.7	25.3	31.2	34.8	34.1	34.5
Benefits paid	Bil. dol.	18.1	21.2	20.5	42.0	41.4	34.4	31.2	29.8	30.1
Funds available for benefits [5]	Bil. dol.	37.9	35.4	53.4	35.2	23.4	23.0	29.0	35.8	32.5
Average employer contribution rate [6]	Percent	1.95	2.44	1.75	1.80	2.20	2.68	2.86	2.68	2.61

[1] Insured unemployment as percent of average covered employment in preceding year.   [2] Weeks compensated divided by first payment.   [3] Based on first payments for 12-month period ending June 30.   [4] Contributions from employers; also employees in states which tax workers.   [5] End of year. Sum of balances in state clearing accounts, benefit-payment accounts, and state accounts in federal unemployment trust funds.   [6] As percent of taxable wages.

Source: U.S. Department of Labor, Employment and Training Administration, *Unemployment Insurance Financial Data Handbook*. See also <http://www.ows.doleta.gov/unemploy/hb394.asp>.

Social Insurance and Human Services   355

Table 547. **State Unemployment Insurance by State and Other Area: 2007**

[7,642 represents 7,642,000. See headnote, Table 546. For state data on insured unemployment, see Table 616]

State or other area	Beneficiaries, first payments (1,000)	Benefits paid (mil. dol.)	Avg. weekly unemploy- ment benefits (dol.)	State or other area	Beneficiaries, first payments (1,000)	Benefits paid (mil. dol.)	Avg. weekly unemploy- ment benefits (dol.)
Total . . .	7,642	32,247	288	MT	21	70	228
AL	102	219	188	NE	32	93	234
AK	38	102	200	NV	81	339	284
AZ	84	278	202	NH	26	89	264
AR	83	284	257	NJ	312	1,925	359
CA	1,018	5,157	298	NM	30	130	256
CO	71	301	327	NY	458	2,274	295
CT	121	575	310	NC	243	718	276
DE	24	109	256	ND	13	45	268
DC	17	90	286	OH	278	1,151	290
FL.	330	1,123	237	OK	42	156	251
GA	212	583	263	OR	138	524	286
HI	23	115	384	PA	462	2,149	323
ID.	45	122	255	RI	41	229	359
IL	353	1,850	305	SC	114	354	230
IN	187	725	290	SD	8	22	227
IA.	91	330	293	TN	143	441	222
KS	58	224	302	TX	280	1,110	287
KY	115	412	284	UT	26	99	294
LA	55	176	204	VT	23	91	287
ME	33	115	254	VA	112	380	267
MD	106	447	282	WA	169	711	335
MA	219	1,357	379	WV	43	148	240
MI.	436	1,853	293	WI.	280	877	267
MN	142	746	341	WY	10	36	278
MS	54	143	177	PR	99	204	111
MO	139	438	225	VI.	2	9	319

Source: U.S. Employment and Training Administration, *Unemployment Insurance Financial Data Handbook*. See also <http://www.ows.doleta.gov/unemploy/hb394.asp>.

Table 548. **Persons With Work Disability by Selected Characteristics: 2008**

[In thousands, except percent (20,213 represents 20,213,000). As of March. Covers civilian noninstitutional population and members of Armed Forces living off post or with their families on post. Persons are classified as having a work disability if they (1) have a health problem or disability which prevents them from working or which limits the kind or amount of work they can do; (2) have a service-connected disability or ever retired or left a job for health reasons; (3) did not work in survey reference week or previous year because of long-term illness or disability; or (4) are under age 65, and are covered by medicare or receive supplemental security income. Based on Current Population Survey; see text, Section 1 and Appendix III]

Age and participation status in assistance programs	Total [1]	Male	Female	White alone [2]	Black alone [3]	Hispanic [4]
Persons with work disability	20,213	9,861	10,352	15,219	3,841	2,255
16 to 24 years old.	1,562	757	805	1,073	380	230
25 to 34 years old.	2,176	1,083	1,094	1,509	536	290
35 to 44 years old.	3,522	1,764	1,758	2,621	698	472
45 to 54 years old.	5,711	2,679	3,032	4,289	1,100	597
55 to 64 years old.	7,242	3,578	3,664	5,727	1126	666
Percent work disabled of total population						
16 to 24 years old.	4.2	4.0	4.3	3.7	6.8	3.5
25 to 34 years old.	5.5	5.4	5.5	4.9	10.3	3.6
35 to 44 years old.	8.4	8.5	8.3	7.9	13.4	6.9
45 to 54 years old.	13.0	12.5	13.5	12.0	21.3	12.2
55 to 64 years old.	21.8	22.3	21.3	20.5	33.4	23.9
Percent of work disabled—						
Receiving social security income	35.5	36.0	35.0	36.7	31.7	26.7
Receiving food stamps	19.3	15.0	23.3	16.6	29.5	22.6
Covered by medicaid.	65.4	68.9	62.0	67.8	60.7	56.6
Residing in public housing	5.9	4.7	7.1	4.4	11.1	7.5
Residing in subsidized housing	3.4	2.3	4.4	2.7	6.1	4.4

[1] Includes other races not shown separately. [2] Beginning with the 2003 Current Population Survey asked respondents to choose one or more races. White alone refers to people who reported White and did not report any other race category. The use of this single-race population does not imply that it is the preferred method of presenting or analyzing reported more than one race, such as "White and American Indian and Alaska Native" or "Asian and Black or African American," is available from Census 2000 through American Factfinder. About 2.6 percent of people reported more than one race in 2000. [3] Black alone refers to people who reported Black and did not report any other race category. [4] Hispanic persons may be of any race.

Source: U.S. Census Bureau, unpublished data.

Table 549. **Workers' Compensation Payments: 1990 to 2006**

[In billions of dollars, except as indicated (53.1 represents $53,100,000,000). See headnote, Table 550]

Item	1990	1995	1999	2000	2001	2002	2003	2004	2005	2006
Workers covered (mil.)	106	113	124	127	127	126	125	126	128	130
Premium amounts paid [1]	53.1	57.1	55.8	60.1	66.6	73.4	82.0	86.8	88.8	87.6
Private carriers [1]	35.1	31.6	33.4	35.7	37.8	41.4	45.3	48.0	50.9	52.1
State funds	8.0	10.5	7.5	8.8	11.5	14.6	17.8	19.1	18.2	15.6
Federal programs [2]	2.2	2.6	3.5	3.6	3.8	3.9	4.0	4.1	4.1	4.1
Self-insurers	7.9	12.5	11.4	11.9	13.6	13.6	14.9	15.8	15.7	15.7
Annual benefits paid [1]	38.2	42.1	46.3	47.7	50.8	52.4	55.1	56.1	55.5	54.7
By private carriers [1]	22.2	20.1	26.4	26.9	27.9	28.2	28.6	28.1	28.1	27.5
From state funds [3]	8.8	10.8	9.9	10.3	11.1	12.5	13.7	14.4	14.0	10.8
Employers' self-insurance [4]	7.2	11.2	10.0	10.5	11.8	11.8	12.8	13.6	13.2	13.1
Type of benefit:										
Medical/hospitalization	15.2	16.7	20.1	20.9	23.1	24.3	25.8	26.4	26.3	26.5
Compensation payments	23.1	25.4	26.3	26.8	27.7	28.1	29.2	29.7	29.2	28.2
Percent of covered payroll: [1]										
Workers' compensation costs [5, 6] . . .	2.18	1.82	1.35	1.34	1.45	1.59	1.74	1.75	1.71	1.58
Benefits [6]	1.53	1.34	1.12	1.06	1.10	1.14	1.17	1.13	1.07	0.99

[1] Premium and benefit amounts include estimated payments under insurance policy deductible provisions. Deductible benefits are allocated to private carriers and state funds.   [2] Years 1990–1995 includes federal employer compensation program and that portion of federal black lung benefits program financed from employer contributions. Years 1997–2000 includes federal employer compensation program only due to changes in reporting methods.   [3] Net cash and medical benefits paid by competitive and exclusive state funds and by federal workers' compensation programs.   [4] Cash and medical benefits paid by self-insurers, plus value of medical benefits paid by employers carrying workers' compensation policies that exclude standard medical coverage.   [5] Premiums written by private carriers and state funds, and benefits paid by self-insurers increased by 5–10 prior to 1995 and by 11 percent for 1995–2002 for administrative costs. Also includes benefits paid and administrative costs of federal system for government employees.   [6] Excludes programs financed from general revenue—black lung benefits and supplemental pensions in some states.

Source: National Academy of Social Insurance, Washington, DC, *Workers' Compensation: Benefits, Coverage, and Costs*, annual. See also <http://www.nasi.org/>.

Table 550. **Workers' Compensation Payments by State: 2000 to 2006**

[In millions of dollars (47,699 represents $47,699,000,000). Calendar-year data. Payments represent compensation and medical benefits and include insurance losses paid by private insurance carriers (compiled from state workers' compensation agencies and A.M. Best Co.); disbursements of state funds (compiled from the A.M. Best Co. and state workers' compensation agencies); and self-insurance payments (compiled from state workers' compensation agencies and authors' estimates)]

State	2000	2003	2004	2005	2006	State	2000	2003	2004	2005	2006
Total	47,699	55,066	56,074	55,307	54,686	Montana	155	217	223	239	248
						Nebraska	230	267	283	298	263
Alabama	529	580	576	609	609	Nevada	347	329	359	394	394
Alaska	139	182	187	189	182	New Hampshire	177	221	212	217	214
Arizona	498	515	548	536	608	New Jersey	1,378	1,660	1,479	1,608	1,672
Arkansas	214	224	227	208	219	New Mexico	144	189	196	231	248
California	9,449	12,410	12,460	10,938	10,149	New York	2,761	3,143	3,279	2,895	3,324
Colorado	810	753	843	896	871	North Carolina	865	1,077	1,160	1,398	1,358
Connecticut	638	677	711	713	713	North Dakota	70	78	83	82	81
Delaware	118	156	157	168	207	Ohio	2,099	2,442	2,435	2,447	2,384
District of Columbia .	78	84	96	91	92	Oklahoma	485	555	580	588	628
Florida	2,577	2,806	2,710	2,899	2,533	Oregon	425	498	534	551	613
Georgia	965	981	1,114	1,198	1,210	Pennsylvania	2,379	2,565	2,594	2,678	2,685
Hawaii	231	275	271	251	243	Rhode Island	127	134	148	142	156
Idaho	114	214	236	243	238	South Carolina	515	657	688	770	796
Illinois	1,944	2,147	2,246	2,404	2,488	South Dakota	63	74	77	86	91
Indiana	545	564	595	610	615	Tennessee	774	783	819	880	794
Iowa	343	427	447	474	492	Texas	2,160	1,968	1,641	1,555	1,398
Kansas	323	296	371	383	398	Utah	172	187	217	241	245
Kentucky	584	717	720	706	710	Vermont	101	120	124	122	124
Louisiana	547	669	726	667	579	Virginia	597	706	753	854	838
Maine	245	233	268	269	283	Washington	1,527	1,801	1,836	1,864	1,927
Maryland	641	723	787	770	815	West Virginia	661	823	797	696	696
Massachusetts	801	1,059	968	904	935	Wisconsin	765	844	1,039	1,188	1,043
Michigan	1,474	1,477	1,517	1,474	1,464	Wyoming	89	114	120	117	117
Minnesota	798	885	931	946	921						
Mississippi	293	291	310	312	341	Federal total [1] . . .	2,957	3,185	3,256	3,258	3,270
Missouri	780	1,081	1,120	1,051	1,175	Federal employees . .	2,119	2,368	2,445	2,462	2,455

[1] Federal benefits include: those paid under the Federal Employees Compensation Act for civilian employees; the portion of the Black Lung benefit program that is financed by employers; and a portion of benefits under the Longshore and Harbor Workers Compensation Act that are not reflected in state data, namely, benefits paid by self-insured employers and by special funds under the LHWCA. See Appendix H of source for more information about federal programs.

Source: National Academy of Social Insurance, Washington, DC, *Workers' Compensation: Benefits, Coverage, and Costs*, annual. See also <http://www.nasi.org/>.

Social Insurance and Human Services   **357**

Table 551. **Supplemental Security Income—Recipients and Payments: 1990 to 2007**

[In thousands (4,817 represents 4,817,000), except as noted. Recipients and monthly payment as of December. Payments for calendar year. Persons with a federal SSI payment and/or federally administered state supplementation. See also Appendix III]

Program	Unit	1990	2000	2002	2003	2004	2005	2006	2007
Recipients, total	1,000.....	4,817	6,602	6,788	6,902	6,988	7,114	7,236	7,360
Aged..............	1,000....	1,454	1,289	1,252	1,233	1,211	1,214	1,212	1,205
Blind.............	1,000....	84	79	78	77	76	75	73	72
Disabled...........	1,000....	3,279	5,234	5,459	5,593	5,701	5,825	5,951	6,083
Payments, total [1]....	Mil. dol....	16,133	30,672	33,719	34,693	36,065	37,236	38,889	41,205
Aged..............	Mil. dol....	3,559	4,540	4,803	4,857	4,894	4,965	5,116	5,301
Blind.............	Mil. dol....	329	386	416	409	412	414	409	419
Disabled...........	Mil. dol....	12,245	25,746	28,500	29,429	30,745	31,857	33,364	35,485
Average monthly payment, total	Dollars....	276	379	407	417	428	439	455	468
Aged..............	Dollars....	208	300	330	342	351	360	373	384
Blind.............	Dollars....	319	413	445	455	463	475	488	500
Disabled...........	Dollars....	303	398	425	433	444	455	471	485

[1] Includes payments not distributed by reason for eligibility.

Source: U.S. Social Security Administration, *Social Security Bulletin*, quarterly and *Annual Statistical Supplement to the Social Security Bulletin* (released March 2009). See also <http://www.ssa.gov/policy/docs/statcomps/supplement/>.

Table 552. **Supplemental Security Income (SSI)—Recipients and Payments by State and Other Area: 2000 to 2007**

[Recipients as of December; payments for calendar year (6,602 represents 6,602,000). Data cover federal SSI payments and/or federally administered state supplementation. For explanation of methodology, see Appendix III]

State and other area	Recipients (1,000) 2000	2007	Payments for year (mil. dol.) 2000	2005	2007	State and other area	Recipients (1,000) 2000	2007	Payments for year (mil. dol.) 2000	2005	2007
Total ...	6,602	7,360	30,672	37,236	41,205	MO........	112	122	471	573	629
U.S.....	6,601	7,360	30,669	37,232	41,205	MT........	14	16	57	70	79
AL........	159	166	659	776	841	NE........	21	23	85	103	115
AK........	9	11	37	53	60	NV........	25	36	108	163	185
AZ........	81	101	355	482	534	NH........	12	15	49	67	79
AR........	85	96	333	407	479	NJ........	146	156	672	763	844
CA........	1,088	1,247	6,386	8,146	8,734	NM........	47	56	193	248	282
CO........	54	58	228	264	301	NY........	617	649	3,197	3,561	3,882
CT........	49	54	216	260	292	NC........	191	206	732	894	1,009
DE........	12	14	50	66	74	ND........	8	8	30	33	37
DC........	20	22	93	113	126	OH........	240	258	1,114	1,295	1,430
FL........	377	431	1,621	2,031	2,225	OK........	72	85	302	381	443
GA........	197	208	785	944	1,059	OR........	52	64	228	298	336
HI........	21	23	104	119	134	PA........	284	334	1,367	1,659	1,884
ID........	18	24	76	106	121	RI........	28	31	130	161	174
IL........	249	262	1,174	1,337	1,450	SC........	107	106	429	488	527
IN........	88	104	382	488	557	SD........	13	13	48	55	61
IA........	40	45	158	193	217	TN........	164	163	664	752	842
KS........	36	40	151	187	212	TX........	409	545	1,575	2,191	2,620
KY........	174	184	741	862	952	UT........	20	24	87	110	127
LA........	166	162	715	771	824	VT........	13	14	51	63	72
ME........	30	33	116	146	165	VA........	132	140	535	632	697
MD........	88	98	400	481	535	WA........	101	122	484	616	704
MA........	168	179	807	902	1,014	WV........	71	79	318	376	419
MI........	210	228	988	1,157	1,271	WI........	85	96	357	437	496
MN........	64	78	272	355	415	WY........	6	6	23	26	29
MS........	129	123	512	572	607	N. Mariana...	1	1	3	4	5

Source: U.S. Social Security Administration, *Annual Statistical Supplement* to the *Social Security Bulletin* (released March 2009). See also <http://www.ssa.gov/policy/docs/statcomps/supplement/>.

Table 553. **Temporary Assistance for Needy Families (TANF)—Families and Recipients: 1980 to 2007**

[In thousands (3,712 represents 3,712,000). Average monthly families and recipients for calendar year. Prior to TANF, the cash assistance program to families was called Aid to Families with Dependent Children (1980-1996). Under the new welfare law (Personal Responsibility and Work Opportunity Reconciliation Act of 1996), the program became TANF. See text, this section. Includes Puerto Rico, Guam, and Virgin Islands]

Year	Families	Recipients	Year	Families	Recipients	Year	Families	Recipients
1980	3,712	10,774	1992	4,829	13,773	2000	2,215	5,778
1985	3,701	10,855	1993	5,012	14,205	2001	2,104	5,359
1986	3,763	11,038	1994	5,033	14,161	2002	2,048	5,069
1987	3,776	11,027	1995	4,791	13,418	2003	2,024	4,929
1988	3,749	10,915	1996	4,434	12,321	2004	1,979	4,748
1989	3,799	10,993	1997	3,740	10,376	2005	1,894	4,469
1990	4,057	11,695	1998	3,050	8,347	2006	1,767	4,125
1991	4,497	12,930	1999	2,554	6,824	2007	1,673	3,896

Source: U.S. Department of Health and Human Services, Administration for Children and Families, unpublished data.

Table 554. Temporary Assistance for Needy Families (TANF)—Recipients by State and Other Areas: 2000 to 2007

[In thousands (2,265 represents 2,265,000). Average monthly families and recipients for calendar year. See headnote, Table 553]

State or other area	Families			Recipients			State or other area	Families			Recipients		
	2000	2005	2007	2000	2005	2007		2000	2005	2007	2000	2005	2007
Total...	2,215	1,894	1,673	5,778	4,469	3,896	MT	5	4	3	13	12	8
U.S.....	2,181	1,876	1,659	5,678	4,418	3,859	NE	9	10	6	24	25	14
AL	19	20	18	45	47	42	NV	6	6	7	16	15	17
AK	7	4	3	21	11	8	NH	6	6	5	14	14	10
AZ	33	42	36	84	96	78	NJ	50	43	34	125	104	81
AR	12	8	9	29	18	20	NM	23	18	13	69	45	34
CA	489	461	472	1,262	1,078	1,161	NY	250	140	120	695	321	265
CO	11	15	10	28	39	25	NC	45	33	25	98	64	47
CT	27	19	18	64	39	36	ND	3	3	2	7	7	5
DE	6	6	4	12	13	9	OH	95	82	78	235	177	168
DC	17	17	6	45	41	14	OK	14	11	9	35	26	20
FL.	65	58	47	142	100	75	OR	17	19	19	38	44	42
GA	52	39	24	125	82	43	PA	88	97	61	241	254	146
HI	14	8	6	46	19	14	RI	16	10	8	44	26	20
ID	1	2	2	2	3	2	SC	18	16	15	42	36	34
IL	78	38	27	234	96	68	SD	3	3	3	7	6	6
IN	37	44	39	101	124	111	TN	57	70	59	147	184	154
IA	20	17	17	53	42	42	TX	129	82	59	347	189	133
KS	13	18	14	32	46	36	UT	8	9	5	21	22	12
KY	38	34	30	87	74	60	VT	6	5	4	16	11	11
LA	27	15	11	71	36	24	VA	31	10	30	69	28	66
ME	11	9	10	28	25	24	WA	56	57	50	148	136	117
MD	29	23	19	71	53	42	WV	13	12	9	33	26	22
MA	43	48	45	100	102	91	WI.	17	19	17	38	44	37
MI.	72	81	73	198	215	189	WY	1	–	–	1	1	–
MN	39	28	26	114	71	63	PR.	30	15	13	88	41	34
MS	15	15	11	34	33	23	GU	3	3	1	10	9	2
MO	47	40	38	125	96	91	VI	1	–	–	3	1	1

– Represents or rounds to zero.

Source: U.S. Department of Health and Human Services, Administration for Children and Families, unpublished data.

Table 555. Temporary Assistance for Needy Families (TANF)—Expenditures by State: 2000 to 2007

[In millions of dollars (24,781 represents $24,781,000,000). Represents federal and state funds expended in fiscal year]

State	2000, total	2005, total	2007		State	2000, total	2005, total	2007	
			Total [1]	Expenditures on assistance				Total [1]	Expenditures on assistance
U.S.	24,781	25,580	26,922	10,654	MO	321	299	341	115
AL......	96	123	156	50	MT......	44	44	40	18
AK......	93	74	78	46	NE......	79	78	108	43
AZ......	261	299	325	133	NV......	69	70	69	42
AR......	139	67	107	16	NH.....	73	63	88	36
CA......	6,481	5,882	6,586	3,718	NJ......	321	994	831	269
CO......	205	214	200	52	NM.....	149	127	96	65
CT......	436	459	485	114	NY......	3,512	3,970	4,400	1,846
DE......	55	61	64	9	NC......	440	448	435	86
DC......	157	156	149	19	ND.....	33	34	36	19
FL......	781	868	834	168	OH.....	995	990	1,339	339
GA......	386	520	500	85	OK.....	130	174	153	103
HI......	162	128	202	115	OR.....	169	269	257	171
ID	43	40	37	6	PA.....	1,327	1,190	898	271
IL......	879	998	1,025	99	RI......	172	168	84	52
IN......	342	307	285	108	SC.....	245	230	142	63
IA	163	162	166	78	SD.....	21	30	152	33
KS......	151	154	169	74	TN.....	293	233	29	21
KY......	203	216	199	137	TX.....	727	851	284	109
LA......	118	186	201	43	UT.....	100	108	790	160
ME.....	108	127	110	78	VT.....	62	68	90	33
MD......	336	349	384	94	VA.....	418	290	70	37
MA......	690	689	869	295	WA	535	525	255	93
MI	1,264	1,175	1,134	551	WV	134	124	615	266
MN......	381	392	394	106	WI	382	446	107	52
MS......	62	79	83	21	WY	34	32	446	89

[1] Includes other items not shown separately.

Source: U.S. Administration for Children and Families, *Temporary Assistance for Needy Families (TANF) Program, Annual Report to Congress.*

Social Insurance and Human Services 359

[In thousands except as noted (13,605 represents 13,605,000). Custodial parents 15 years and older with own children under 21 years of age present from absent parents as of spring 2006. Covers civilian noninstitutional population. Based on Current Population Survey; see text, Section 1 and Appendix III. For definition of mean, see Guide to Tabular Presentation]

Award and recipiency status	All custodial parents				Custodial parents below the poverty level			
	Total				Total			
	Number	Percent distri-bution	Mothers	Fathers	Number	Percent distri-bution	Mothers	Fathers
Total	13,605	(X)	11,406	2,199	3,406	(X)	3,160	245
With child support agreement or award[1] . . .	7,802	(X)	7,002	800	1,796	(X)	1,710	85
Supposed to receive payments in 2005. . .	6,809	100.0	6,131	678	1,502	100.0	1,427	75
Actually received payments in 2005 . . .	5,259	77.2	4,754	505	1,090	72.6	1,036	53
Received full amount	3,192	46.9	2,900	292	595	39.6	566	29
Received partial payments	2,068	30.4	1,855	213	495	33.0	470	24
Did not receive payments in 2005.	1,550	22.8	1,377	174	412	27.4	390	22
Child support not awarded	5,803	(X)	4,404	1,399	1,610	(X)	1,450	160
MEAN INCOME AND CHILD SUPPORT								
Received child support payments in 2005:								
Mean total money income (dol.).	29,454	(X)	28,018	42,977	7,799	(X)	7,773	8,295
Mean child support received (dol.)	4,717	(X)	4,719	4,691	3,372	(X)	3,369	3,428
Received the full amount due:								
Mean total money income (dol.)	31,934	(X)	30,403	47,134	7,766	(X)	7,698	9,112
Mean child support received (dol.). . . .	6,002	(X)	5,981	6,210	4,683	(X)	4,686	4,615
Received partial payments:								
Mean total money income (dol.)	25,626	(X)	24,288	37,278	7,838	(X)	7,864	7,328
Mean child support received (dol.). . . .	2,733	(X)	2,747	2,608	1,796	(X)	1,784	2,022
Received no payments in 2005:								
Mean total money income (dol.).	25,961	(X)	24,475	37,751	7,706	(X)	7,559	10,315
Without child support agreement or award:								
Mean total money income (dol.).	29,787	(X)	23,127	50,756	6,488	(X)	6,217	8,952

X Not applicable.   [1] As of April 2006.

Source: U.S. Census Bureau, unpublished data.

Table 557. **Child Support Enforcement Program—Caseload and Collections: 1990 to 2008**

[For years ending Sept. 30 (12,796 represents 12,796,000). Includes Puerto Rico, Guam, and the Virgin Islands. The child support enforcement program locates absent parents, establishes paternity of children born out of wedlock, and establishes and enforces support orders. By law, these services are available to all families that need them. The program is operated at the state and local government level, but 66 percent of administrative costs are paid by the federal government. Child support collected for families not receiving Temporary Assistance for Needy Families (TANF) goes to the family to help it remain self-sufficient. Most of the child support collected on behalf of TANF families goes to federal and state governments to offset TANF payments. Some states pass-through a portion of the CS collections to help families become self-sufficient. Based on data reported by state agencies. Minus sign (–) indicates net outlay]

Item	Unit	1990	2000	2003	2004	2005	2006	2007	2008, prel.
Total cases[1] . . . . . .₂.	1,000	12,796	17,334	15,923	15,854	15,861	15,844	15,755	15,676
Paternities established, total[2]. .ˌ. . . .	1,000	393	867	663	692	690	675	640	629
Support orders established, total[3]. . . .	1,000	1,022	1,175	1,161	1,181	1,180	1,159	1,178	1,193
FINANCES									
Collections, total	Mil. dol. . . .	6,010	17,854	21,176	21,861	23,006	23,933	24,855	26,561
TANF/FC collections[4]	Mil. dol. . . .	1,750	2,593	2,972	2,221	2,191	2,112	2,050	2,254
State share	Mil. dol. . . .	620	1,080	947	927	911	875	852	948
Estimated incentive payments to states	Mil. dol. . . .	264	353	356	361	365	402	431	NA
Federal share[5]	Mil. dol. . . .	533	968	1,167	1,147	1,129	1,086	1,054	1,170
Current Assistance Medical Support Collections	Mil. dol. . . .	(NA)	27	20	12	11	12	11	12
Current Assistance Payments to Families or Foster Care	Mil. dol. . . .	(NA)	165	837	136	140	139	133	124
Non-TANF collections	Mil. dol. . . .	4,260	15,261	18,204	19,641	20,815	21,822	22,804	24,307
Administrative expenditures, total. . .	Mil. dol. . . .	1,606	4,526	5,215	5,322	5,353	5,561	5,594	5,878
State share	Mil. dol. . . .	545	1,519	1,765	1,803	1,813	1,884	1,902	2,221
Federal share	Mil. dol. . . .	1,061	3,006	3,450	3,519	3,540	3,677	3,692	3,657
Program savings, total.	Mil. dol. . . .	–190	–2,125	–3,098	–3,249	–3,312	–3,600	–3,687	–3,780
State share	Mil. dol. . . .	338	–87	–461	–515	–537	–607	–619	–700
Federal share	Mil. dol. . . .	–528	–2,038	–2,637	–2,734	–2,776	–2,993	–3,068	–3,080

NA Not Available.   [1] Passage of the Personal Responsibility and Work Opportunity Reconciliation Act of 1996 (PRWORA) mandated new categories in 1999 and cases were no longer double counted resulting in a 2 million case reduction.   [2] Does not include in-hospital paternities.   [3] Includes modifications to orders.   [4] Collections for current assistance cases where the children are: (1) recipients of TANF under title IV-A of the Social Security Act or (2) entitled to Foster Care (FC) maintenance under title IV-E of the Social Security Act plus collections distributed as assistance reimbursements. Includes assistance reimbursements, which are collections that will be divided between the state and federal governments to reimburse their respective shares of either Title IV-A assistance payments or Title IV-E Foster Care maintenance payments.   [5] Prior to fiscal year 2002, incentives were paid out of the federal share of collections and the net federal share was reported.

Source: U.S. Department of Health and Human Services, Office of Child Support Enforcement, *Annual Report to Congress.*

Table 558. **Federal Food Programs: 1990 to 2008**

[20.0 represents 20,000,000, except as noted. For years ending September 30. Program data include Puerto Rico, Virgin Islands, Guam, American Samoa, Northern Marianas, and the former Trust Territory when a federal food program was operated in these areas. Participation data are average monthly figures except as noted. Participants are not reported for the commodity distribution programs. Cost data are direct federal benefits to recipients; they exclude federal administrative payments and applicable state and local contributions. Federal costs for commodities and cash in-lieu of commodities are shown separately from direct cash benefits for those programs receiving both]

Program	Unit	1990	2000	2003	2004	2005	2006	2007	2008
Food Stamp:									
Participants	Million	20.0	17.2	21.3	23.9	25.7	26.7	26.5	28.4
Federal cost	Mil. dol. . . .	14,143	14,983	21,404	24,619	28,568	30,187	30,373	34,611
Monthly average coupon value per									
recipient	Dollars . . .	58.78	72.62	83.90	85.99	92.57	94.32	95.63	101.53
Nutrition assistance program for Puerto Rico:									
Federal cost	Mil. dol. . . .	937	1,268	1,395	1,413	1,495	1,518	1,551	1,623
National school lunch program (NSLP):									
Free lunches served	Million	1,662	2,205	2,335	2,397	2,478	2,494	2,506	2,609
Reduced-price lunches served	Million	273	409	453	465	478	478	488	521
Children participating [1]	Million	24.1	27.3	28.4	29.0	29.6	30.1	30.5	31.0
Federal cost	Mil. dol. . . .	3,214	5,493	6,341	6,663	7,055	7,389	7,707	8258
School breakfast (SB):									
Children participating [1]	Million	4.1	7.6	8.4	8.9	9.4	9.8	10.1	10.6
Federal cost	Mil. dol. . . .	596	1,393	1,652	1,776	1,927	2,043	2,164	2,364
Special supplemental food program (WIC): [2]									
Participants	Million	4.5	7.2	7.6	7.9	8.0	8.1	8.3	8.7
Federal cost	Mil. dol. . . .	1,637	2,853	3,230	3,562	3,603	3,598	3,880	4,535
Child and adult care (CAC): [3]									
Participants [4]	Million	1.5	2.7	2.9	3.0	3.1	3.1	3.2	3.2
Federal cost	Mil. dol. . . .	719	1,500	1,726	1,812	1,904	1,944	2,024	2,167
Federal cost of commodities donated to— [5]									
Child nutrition (NSLP, CACFP, SFS, and									
SBP)	Mil. dol. . . .	644	704	909	1,028	1,045	875	1,110	1,138
Emergency feeding [6]	Mil. dol. . . .	282	182	396	361	314	243	198	227

[1] Average monthly participation (excluding summer months of June through August). Includes children in public and private elementary and secondary schools and in residential child care institutes. [2] WIC serves pregnant and postpartum women, infants, and children up to age 5. [3] CACFP provides year-round subsidies to feed preschool children in child care centers and family day care homes. Certain care centers serving disabled or elderly adults also receive meal subsidies. [4] Average quarterly daily attendance at participating institutions. [5] Includes the federal cost of commodity entitlements, cash-in-lieu of commodities, and bonus foods. [6] Provides free commodities to needy persons for home consumption through food banks, hunger centers, soup kitchens, and similar nonprofit agencies. Includes the Emergency Food Assistance Program, the commodity purchases for soup kitchens/food banks program (FY 1989-96), and commodity disaster relief.

Source: U.S. Department of Agriculture, Food and Nutrition Service, "Food and Nutrition Service, Program Data"; <http://www.fns.usda.gov/pd/>; updated monthly.

Table 559. **Federal Food Stamp Program by State: 2000 to 2008**

[Participation data are average monthly numbers (17,194 represents 17,194,000). For years ending September 30. Food stamp costs are for benefits only and exclude administrative expenditures]

State	Persons (1,000)			Benefits (mil. dol.)			State	Persons (1,000)			Benefits (mil. dol.)		
	2000	2005	2008	2000	2005	2008		2000	2005	2008	2000	2005	2008
Total [1] .	17,194	25,718	28,408	14,983	28,568	34,611	MO	423	766	889	358	736	810
U.S.	17,156	25,306	27,921	14,927	28,149	34,072	MT	59	81	80	51	89	94
AL.	396	559	572	344	616	664	NE.	82	117	121	61	120	141
AK.	38	56	57	46	80	94	NV.	61	122	144	57	129	170
AZ.	259	550	628	240	634	772	NH	36	52	64	28	51	71
AR.	247	374	378	206	401	432							
CA.	1,831	1,992	2,220	1,639	2,315	2,998	NJ.	345	392	438	304	437	533
CO	156	246	253	127	313	325	NM	169	241	240	140	251	269
CT.	165	204	225	138	223	285	NY.	1,439	1,755	1,953	1,361	2,136	2,573
DE.	32	62	74	31	65	86	NC	488	800	947	403	856	1,104
DC	81	89	89	77	103	112	ND	32	42	48	25	45	59
FL.	882	1,382	1,455	771	1,598	1,779	OH	610	1,007	1,151	520	1,155	1,495
GA	559	921	1,021	489	1,048	1,277	OK	253	424	419	208	440	491
HI	118	94	97	166	156	185	OR	234	429	469	198	456	542
ID	58	93	100	46	103	117	PA.	777	1,043	1,188	656	1,105	1,387
IL	817	1,158	1,299	777	1,400	1,718	RI	74	76	85	59	79	108
IN	300	556	623	268	627	773	SC	295	521	590	249	566	707
IA	123	207	256	100	220	306	SD	43	56	63	37	61	78
KS.	117	178	188	83	180	211	TN.	496	850	911	415	942	1,115
KY.	403	570	633	337	611	742	TX.	1,333	2,442	2,532	1,215	2,659	3,068
LA	500	808	791	448	979	1,025	UT.	82	133	134	68	141	151
ME	102	153	173	81	162	196	VT.	41	45	56	32	45	62
MD	219	289	360	199	320	432	VA.	336	488	545	263	500	610
MA	232	368	506	182	363	587	WA	295	508	581	241	539	681
MI	603	1,048	1,256	457	1,099	1,506	WV	227	262	277	185	258	304
MN	196	260	294	165	275	330	WI	193	346	423	129	317	430
MS	276	435	447	226	463	497	WY	22	25	23	19	27	26

[1] Includes Guam and the Virgin Islands. Several outlying areas receive nutrition assistance grants in lieu of food stamps (Puerto Rico, American Samoa, and the Northern Marianas).

Source: U.S. Department of Agriculture, Food and Nutrition Service. "Food and Nutrition Service, Program Data"; <http://www.fns.usda.gov/pd/>; updated monthly.

Social Insurance and Human Services 361

Table 560. Selected Characteristics of Food Stamp Households and Participants: 1990 to 2007

[7,796 represents 7,796,000. For years ending September 30. Data for 1990 exclude Guam and the Virgin Islands. Based on a sample of households from the Food Stamp Quality Control System]

Year	Households				Participants		
	Total [1] (1,000)	Percent of total			Total [1] (1,000)	Percent of total	
		With children	With elderly [2]	With disabled [3]		Children	Elderly [2]
1990	7,796	60.3	18.1	8.9	20,049	49.6	7.7
1995	10,879	59.7	16.0	18.9	26,619	51.5	7.1
2000	7,325	53.9	21.0	27.5	17,139	51.3	10.0
2003	9,154	54.7	18.0	23.3	21,260	50.8	8.5
2004	10,279	54.3	17.3	22.9	23,858	50.2	8.2
2005	11,184	53.8	17.1	23.1	25,683	50.0	8.2
2006	11,315	52.2	17.9	23.1	25,595	49.2	8.7
2007	11,563	51.3	17.9	23.9	25,926	49.1	8.7

[1] Total does not include those who are ineligible or those receiving disaster benefits. [2] Persons 60 years old and over. [3] The substantial increase in 1995 and decrease in 2003 are due in part to the changes in definition of a diasbled household. Prior to 1995, disabled households were defined as households with SSI income but no members over age 59. In 1995, that definition changed to households with at least one member under 65 who received SSI, or at least one member age 18–61 who received social security, veterans benefits, or other government benefits as a result of a disability. Because of changes to the QC data in 2003, the definition of a disabled household changed to households either SSI income or a medical expense deduction and without an elderly person, and households containing a nonelderly adult who does not appear to be working and who is receiving social security, veterans benefits, or workers' compensation.

Source: U.S. Department of Agriculture, Food and Nutrition Service, Totals obtained from the National Data Bank. Percentages obtained from *Characteristics of Food Stamp Households: Fiscal Year 2007*, September 2008. See also <http://www.fns.usda.gov /ora/MENU/Published/snap/snapparthh.htm>.

Table 561. Food Stamp Households and Participants—Summary: 2007

[11,563 represents 11,563,000. For year ending September 30. Based on a sample of households from the Food Stamp Quality Control System. Figures are lower than official participation counts because they do not include ineligible participants or those receiving disaster food stamp assistance]

Household type and income source	Households		Age, sex, race, and Hispanic origin	Participants	
	Number (1,000)	Percent		Number (1,000)	Percent
Total	**11,563**	100.0	**Total**	**25,926**	100.0
With children	5,927	51.3	Children	12,720	49.1
Single-parent households	3,714	32.1	Under 5 years old	4,345	16.8
Married-couple households	1,002	8.7	5 to 17 years old	8,375	32.3
Other	1,210	10.5	Adults	13,206	50.9
With elderly	2,065	17.9	18 to 35 years old	5,587	21.5
Living alone	1,655	14.3	36 to 59 years old	5,354	20.7
Not living alone	410	3.5	60 years old and over	2,265	8.7
Disabled	2,767	23.9			
Living alone	1,585	13.7	Male	10,730	41.4
Not living alone	1,182	10.2	Female	14,102	54.4
Earned income	3,445	29.8	White, non-Hispanic	7,344	28.3
Wages and salaries	3,088	26.7	Black, non-Hispanic	5,141	19.8
Unearned income	7,764	67.1	Hispanic	3,684	14.2
TANF [1]	1,399	12.1	Asian	742	2.9
Supplemental security income	3,207	27.7	Native American	1,230	4.7
Social security	2,881	24.9	Other [2]	7,786	30.0
No income	1,669	14.4			

[1] Temporary Assistance for Needy Families (TANF) program. [2] For FY 2007, this category includes repondents who recorded more than one race, and those with no racial/ethnic data.

Source: U.S. Department of Agriculture, Food and Nutrition Service, *Characteristics of Food Stamp Households: Fiscal Year 2007*, September 2008. See also <http://www.fns.usda.gov/ora/menu/Published/snapparthh.htm>.

Table 562. Head Start—Summary: 1980 to 2007

[For years ending September 30 (376 represents 376,000)]

Year	Enrollment (1,000)	Appropriation (mil. dol.)	Age and race	Enrollment, 2007 (percent)	Item	Number
1980 . . .	376	735	Under 3 years old	10	Average cost per child:	
1990 . . .	541	1,552	3 years old	36	1995	$4,534
1995 . . .	751	3,534	4 years old	51	2000	$5,951
1998 . . .	822	4,347	5 years old and over . . .	3	2007	$7,326
1999 . . .	826	4,658				
2000 . . .	858	5,267	White	40	Paid staff (1,000):	
2001 . . .	905	6,200	Black	30	1995	147
2002 . . .	912	6,537	Hispanic	35	2000	180
2003 . . .	910	6,668	American Indian/		2007	220
2004 . . .	906	6,775	Alaska Native	4	Volunteers (1,000):	
2005 . . .	907	6,843	Asian	2	1995	1,235
2006 . . .	909	6,872	Hawaiian/		2000	1,252
2007 . . .	908	6,888	Pacific Islander	1	2007	1,384

Source: U.S. Department of Health and Services, Administration for Children and Families, "Head Start Statistical Fact Sheet"; <http://www.acf.hhs.gov/programs/ohs/about/>.

Table 563. Number of Emergency and Transitional Beds in Homeless Assistance Systems Nationwide: 2007

[Data include beds located in Puerto Rico, Guam, and the Virgin Islands. Data are based on a nationally representative sample of 80 jurisdictions that collect data from emergency shelters and transitional providers. The data estimate homeless persons who used emergency shelters or transitional housing from January 1 through June 30, 2007. As a compliment to the survey, a "Continuum of Care" community was derived from each jurisdiction in order to estimate the number of unsheltered homeless persons and the number of emergency shelter and transitional housing beds available on a single night in January 2007. The data do not include homeless individuals living outside a sampled jurisdiction or homeless individuals not using an emergency shelter or a transitional housing program. For more information on data collection and methodology, see Appendix B of source]

Homeless programs	Year-round units/beds [1]				Other beds	
	Family units	Family beds	Individual beds	Total year-round beds	Seasonal beds [2]	Overflow/ voucher [3]
Emergency shelters	29,949	98,287	113,164	211,451	21,025	36,477
Transitional housing	34,621	111,368	99,837	211,205	(NA)	(NA)
Total inventory	64,570	209,655	213,001	422,656	21,025	36,477
Permanent supportive housing	25,141	72,481	116,155	188,636	(NA)	(NA)

NA Not available.   [1] Year-round beds are available for use throughout the year and are considered part of the stable inventory of beds for homeless persons.   [2] Seasonal beds are typically available during particularly high-demand seasons of the year (e.g. winter months in the North or summer months in the South) to accommodate increased need for emergency shelters to prevent illness or death due to the weather.   [3] Overflow beds are typically used during unanticipated emergencies (e.g., precipitous temperature drops or a natural disaster that displaces residents). Voucher beds are made available in a hotel or motel, and often function like overflow beds.

Source: U.S. Department of Housing and Urban Development, *The Second Annual Homeless Assessment Report to Congress* (released March 2009). See also <http://www.hudhre.info/documents/2ndHomelessAssessmentReport.pdf>.

Table 564. Social Assistance Services—Revenue for Employer Firms: 2000 to 2007

[In millions of dollars (77,032 represents $77,032,000,000). Based on the North American Industry Classification System, 2002, (NAICS), see text, Section 15. See Appendix III]

Kind of business	2002 NAICS code	2000, total	2005, total	2007		
				Total	Taxable firms	Tax-exempt firms
Social assistance, total.	624	77,032	110,493	124,521	32,122	92,399
Individual and family services	6241	37,311	52,806	61,558	10,252	51,306
Child and youth services	62411	7,517	10,367	11,292	1,270	10,022
Services for elderly and disabled persons	62412	12,804	19,310	23,237	4,501	10,040
Other individual and family services	62419	16,990	23,129	27,029	4,391	22,638
Community, emergency and other relief services . . .	6242	12,281	18,935	18,579	(S)	18,401
Community food services	62421	2,835	3,784	4,161	39	4,122
Community housing services.	62422	4,888	6,683	7,510	111	7,399
Emergency and other relief services.	62423	4,558	8,468	6,908	(S)	6,880
Vocational rehabilitation services.	6243	9,458	13,921	13,425	2,715	10,710
Child day care services	6244	17,982	24,831	30,959	18,977	11,982

S Figure does not meet publication standards.

Source: U.S. Census Bureau, *Service Annual Survey*, 2007. See also <http://www.census.gov/svsd/www/services/sas/sas_data/sas62.htm>.

Table 565. Social Assistance—Nonemployer Establishments and Receipts: 2000 to 2006

[Receipts in millions of dollars (7,539 represents $7,539,000,000). Includes only firms subject to federal income tax. Nonemployers are businesses with no paid employees. Data for 2000 based on the North American Industry Classification System (NAICS), 1997; 2004 and 2005 based on NAICS 2002, see text, Section 15]

Kind of business	NAICS code	Establishments			Receipts		
		2000	2005	2006	2000	2005	2006
Social assistance, total	624	642,946	807,729	822,099	7,539	10,265	10,911
Individual and family services	6241	72,433	112,909	121,153	1,106	1,920	2,106
Community/emergency and other relief services. . . .	6242	3,560	5,533	5,740	54	81	85
Vocational rehabilitation services.	6243	7,314	11,022	11,345	151	245	253
Child day care services	6244	559,639	678,265	683,861	6,228	8,018	8,467

Source: U.S. Census Bureau, "Nonemployer Statistics"; <http://www.census.gov/econ/nonemployer/index.html> (released July 2008).

Social Insurance and Human Services **363**

Table 566. Child Care Arrangements of Preschool Children by Type of Arrangement: 1991 to 2005

[In percent, except as indicated (8,428 represents 8,428,000). Estimates are based on children 3 to 5 years old who have not entered kindergarten. Based on interviews from a sample survey of the civilian, noninstitutional population in households with telephones; see source for details. See also Appendix III]

Characteristic	Children		Type of nonparental arrangement [1]			
	Number (1,000)	Percent distribution	In relative care	In nonrelative care	In center-based program [2]	With parental care only
1991, total	8,428	100.0	16.9	14.8	52.8	31.0
1995, total	9,232	100.0	19.4	16.9	55.1	25.9
2005, total	**9,066**	**100.0**	**22.6**	**11.6**	**57.2**	**26.3**
Age:						
3 years old	4,070	44.9	24.0	14.4	42.5	33.4
4 years old	3,873	42.7	20.8	9.2	69.2	20.6
5 years old	1,123	12.4	23.8	9.9	68.7	20.4
Race-ethnicity:						
White, non-Hispanic	5,177	57.1	21.4	15.0	59.1	24.1
Black, non-Hispanic.	1,233	13.6	25.0	5.2	66.5	19.5
Hispanic	1,822	20.1	22.7	8.1	43.4	38.0
Other	834	9.2	26.4	8.1	61.5	24.7
Household income:						
Less than $10,001	795	8.8	25.1	8.6	53.4	33.4
$10,001 to $20,000	978	10.8	26.0	7.8	49.2	27.2
$20,001 to $30,000	1,183	13.1	25.4	6.3	43.9	38.5
$30,001 to $40,000	1,124	12.4	23.8	6.9	48.7	33.4
$40,001 to $50,000	808	8.9	21.8	11.6	50.0	35.4
$50,001 to $75,000	1,849	20.4	21.1	13.3	57.1	25.5
$75,001 or more	2,329	25.7	19.8	18.0	75.1	11.4

[1] Columns do not add to 100.0 because some children participated in more than one type of nonparental arrangement. [2] Center-based programs include day care centers, Head Start programs, preschools, prekindergarten, and nursery schools.

Source: U.S. Department of Education, National Center for Education Statistics, Early Childhood Program Participation Survey of the National Household Education Surveys Program (NHES), 2005.

Table 567. Children in Foster Care and Awaiting Adoption: 2000 and 2007

[Data are preliminary and cover the period from October 1 of prior year through September 30 of year shown]

Characteristic	In foster care		Entered foster care		Exited foster care		Waiting to be adopted		Adopted from foster care	
	2000	2007	2000	2007	2000	2007	2000	2007	2000	2007
Total	**552,000**	**491,000**	**293,000**	**293,000**	**272,000**	**293,000**	**131,000**	**132,000**	**51,000**	**52,000**
AGE										
Under 1 year.	22,839	29,214	37,996	49,353	11,025	14,251	3,957	5,700	939	965
1 to 5 years	134,378	138,182	72,365	81,589	70,667	91,217	44,126	49,455	23,135	27,748
6 to 10 years	136,003	97,319	63,346	54,810	63,228	58,898	44,980	34,396	17,831	13,912
11 to 15 years.	160,077	125,130	86,555	73,165	65,550	58,266	33,143	32,249	7,946	7,371
16 to 20 years [1]	98,701	100,027	32,737	34,077	61,531	70,392	4,793	10,086	1,149	1,635
RACE										
White [2]	207,970	196,017	136,214	129,573	121,322	130,770	44,898	50,597	19,462	23,300
Black [2].	217,615	152,032	84,460	75,227	84,065	78,521	57,345	40,115	19,566	13,111
Asian [2]	4,370	2,775	3,565	2,361	3,307	2,332	664	676	290	266
Hispanic [3]	81,823	96,393	42,769	58,501	39,909	55,676	17,050	27,929	7,430	10,474
SEX										
Male	289,187	257,200	(NA)	150,750	(NA)	150,189	68,620	69,493	25,472	26,205
Female	262,813	233,332	(NA)	142,328	(NA)	142,865	62,380	62,382	25,528	25,425

NA Not available. [1] For children waiting to be adopted, includes ages 16 to 17 years only. [2] Beginning with the 2000 census, respondents could choose more than one race. Data represent persons who selected this race group only and exclude persons reporting more than one race. The census in prior years only allowed respondents to report one race group. See also comments on race in text, Section 1. [3] Hispanic persons may be any race.

Source: U.S. Department of Health and Human Services, Administration for Children and Families, Adoption and Foster Care Analysis and Reporting System Reports, annual. See also <http://www.acf.hhs.gov/programs/cb/stats_research/index.htm#afcars>.

Table 568. Private Philanthropy Funds by Source and Allocation: 1990 to 2007

[In billions of dollars (101.4 represents $101,400,000,000). Estimates for sources of funds based on U.S. Internal Revenue Service reports of individual charitable deductions and household surveys of giving by Independent Sector and the Center on Philanthropy at Indiana University. For corporate giving, data are corporate charitable deductions from the U.S. Internal Revenue Service and the contributions made by corporate foundations as reported by the Foundation Center. Data about foundation donations are based upon surveys of foundations and data provided by the Foundation Center. Estimates of the allocation of funds were derived from surveys of nonprofits conducted by various sources]

Source and allocation	1990	1995	1998	1999	2000	2001	2002	2003	2004	2005	2006	2007
Total funds	101.4	123.7	176.8	202.7	229.7	231.1	231.5	236.3	260.5	293.8	294.9	306.4
Individuals.	81.0	95.4	138.4	154.6	174.5	172.4	172.8	180.2	202.2	221.4	223.0	229.0
Foundations [1]	7.2	10.6	17.0	20.5	24.6	27.2	27.0	26.8	28.4	32.4	34.9	38.5
Corporations	5.5	7.4	8.5	10.2	10.7	11.6	10.8	11.1	11.4	16.6	15.4	15.7
Charitable bequests	7.6	10.4	13.0	17.4	19.9	19.8	20.9	18.2	18.5	23.5	21.7	23.2
Allocation:												
Religion.	49.8	58.1	68.3	71.3	77.0	79.9	82.9	84.6	88.0	93.0	97.7	102.3
Health.	9.9	13.9	13.2	15.2	16.4	18.3	17.8	17.8	20.2	22.5	22.0	23.2
Education	12.4	15.6	23.8	27.2	29.7	32.7	30.0	30.0	33.8	37.3	40.7	43.3
Human service	11.8	9.7	15.6	17.9	20.0	21.8	24.4	24.4	24.4	26.1	27.4	29.6
Arts, culture, and humanities. . .	7.9	5.7	9.9	9.2	10.5	11.4	10.8	10.8	11.8	11.8	12.7	13.7
Public/societal benefit	4.9	11.3	14.0	13.0	15.4	16.5	18.0	16.4	18.8	21.3	21.4	22.7
Environment/wildlife.	2.5	2.3	3.5	4.2	4.8	5.3	5.3	5.4	5.5	6.0	6.3	7.0
International.	1.3	3.0	5.1	6.6	7.2	8.3	8.7	9.8	11.6	15.2	11.4	13.2
Gifts to foundations [1].	3.8	8.5	19.9	28.8	24.7	25.7	19.2	21.6	20.3	27.5	30.6	27.7
Unallocated [2]	-3.0	-4.4	3.6	9.4	24.2	11.3	14.6	13.8	26.2	33.2	24.8	23.7

[1] Data are from the Foundation Center through 2001. [2] Money deducted as a charitable contribution by donors but not allocated to sources. May include gifts to governmental entities, in-kind giving, gifts to new charities.

Source: Giving USA Foundation, Glenview, IL, researched and written by the Center on Philanthropy at Indiana University, *Giving USA*, annual (copyright).

Table 569. Foundations—Number and Finances by Asset Size: 1990 to 2007

[Figures are for latest year reported by foundations (142,500 represents $142,500,000,000). Covers nongovernmental nonprofit organizations with funds and programs managed by their own trustees or directors, whose goals were to maintain or aid social, educational, religious, or other activities deemed to serve the common good. Excludes organizations that make general appeals to the public for funds, act as trade associations for industrial or other special groups, or do not currently award grants]

Asset size	Number	Assets (mil. dol.)	Gifts received (mil. dol.)	Total giving [1] (mil. dol.)
1990	32,401	142,500	5,000	8,700
2000	56,582	486,100	27,600	27,600
2005	71,095	550,600	31,500	36,400
2006	72,477	614,656	36,569	40,287
2007, total	**75,187**	**682,222**	**46,844**	**44,394**
Under $50,000	12,173	178	1,999	2,325
$50,000-$99,999.	4,658	344	219	255
$100,000-$249,999	9,403	1,578	416	485
$250,000-$499,999	8,942	3,263	497	558
$500,000-$999,999	10,337	7,498	923	1,024
$1,000,000-$4,999,999.	18,520	42,090	4,425	4,300
$5,000,000-$9,999,999.	4,512	31,554	2,680	2,373
$10,000,000-$49,999,999	4,966	105,617	9,610	8,269
$50,000,000-$99,999,999	831	57,950	4,793	3,878
$100,000,000-$249,999,999 . . .	540	82,484	5,757	4,671
$250,000,000 or more	305	349,666	15,525	16,255

[1] Includes grants, scholarships, and employee matching gifts; excludes set-asides, loans, program-related investments (PRIs), and program expenses.

Source: The Foundation Center, New York, NY, *Foundation Yearbook*, annual (copyright).

Table 570. Domestic Private Foundations—Information Returns: 1990 to 2005

[Money amounts in billions of dollars (122.4 represents $122,400,000,000). Minus sign (–) indicates loss]

Item	1990	1995	1998	1999	2000	2001	2002	2003	2004	2005
Number of returns.	40,105	47,917	56,658	62,694	66,738	70,787	73,255	76,348	76,897	79,535
Nonoperating foundations [1] . . .	36,880	43,966	52,460	58,840	61,501	63,650	67,101	70,004	70,613	72,800
Operating foundations [2]	3,226	3,951	4,198	3,854	5,238	7,137	6,154	6,344	6,284	6,734
Total assets, book value.	122.4	195.6	325.7	384.6	409.5	413.6	383.5	418.5	455.5	481.8
Total assets, fair market value. . . .	151.0	242.9	397.1	466.9	471.6	455.4	413.0	475.0	509.9	545.9
Investments in securities.	115.0	190.7	317.9	363.4	361.4	329.4	294.4	344.3	361.2	373.1
Total revenue.	19.0	30.8	59.7	83.3	72.8	45.3	27.8	48.4	58.7	76.4
Total expenses.	11.3	17.2	25.9	33.9	37.4	36.7	34.4	35.1	36.6	42.8
Contributions, gifts, and grants paid	8.6	12.3	19.4	22.8	27.6	27.4	26.3	26.7	27.6	31.9
Excess of revenue over expenses (net)	7.7	13.6	33.8	49.4	35.3	8.6	–6.6	13.3	22.1	33.5
Net investment income [3]	11.9	20.4	39.3	57.1	48.8	25.7	17.6	25.2	34.0	44.3

[1] Generally provide charitable support through grants and other financial means to charitable organizations; the majority of foundations are nonoperating. [2] Generally conduct their own charitable activities, e.g., museums. [3] Represents income not considered related to a foundation's charitable purpose, e.g., interest, dividends, and capital gains. Foundations could be subject to an excise tax on such income.

Source: Internal Revenue Service, Statistics of Income, SOI Tax Stats—Charities & Other Tax-Exempt Organizations; (accessed 17 January 2009). <http://www.irs.gov/taxstats/charitablestats/article/0,,id=97176,00.html>.

Social Insurance and Human Services 365

Table 571. **Nonprofit Charitable Organizations—Information Returns: 2000 and 2005**

[In billions of dollars (1,562.5 represents $1,562,500,000,000), except as indicated. Categories based on The National Taxonomy of Exempt Entities (NTEE), a classification system that uses 26 major field areas that are aggregated into 10 categories. Includes data reported by organizations described in Internal Revenue Code section 501(3), excluding private foundations and most religious organizations. Organizations with receipts under $25,000 were not required to file]

Year and category	Number of returns (1,000)	Total assets	Total fund balance or net worth	Revenue Total	Revenue Program service revenue [1]	Contributions, gifts, and grants	Total expenses	Excess of revenue over expenses (net)
2000	230.2	1,562.5	1,023.2	866.2	579.1	199.1	796.4	69.8
2005, total	**286.6**	**2,241.9**	**1,411.3**	**1,252.9**	**852.6**	**276.3**	**1,137.9**	**115.0**
Arts, culture, and humanities. . .	29.0	89.2	72.6	29.2	7.0	15.9	23.79	5.4
Education	52.5	744.5	548.6	243.1	126.8	69.9	201.456	41.6
Environment, animals	12.4	33.5	27.5	12.4	2.7	7.7	10.352	2.0
Health.	35.7	860.8	463.3	698.5	607.5	52.1	660.35	38.2
Human services	108.3	251.2	123.5	171.5	86.3	70.1	161.401	10.1
International, foreign affairs. . . .	4.2	17.6	12.8	19.2	1.6	16.7	17.388	1.8
Mutual, membership benefit . . .	25.7	208.4	138.2	67.4	17.8	37.5	53.119	14.2
Public, societal benefit.	18.2	21.5	17.5	9.0	1.4	6.2	7.803	1.2
Religion related	0.7	15.2	7.3	2.7	1.6	0.2	2.249	0.4

[1] Represents fees collected by organizations in support of their tax-exempt purposes, and income such as tuition and fees at educational institutions, hospital patient charges, and admission and activity fees collected by museums and other nonprofit organizations or institutions.

Source: Internal Revenue Service, Statistics of Income, SOI Tax Stats - Charities & Other Tax-Exempt Organizations Statistics. See also <http://www.irs.gov/taxstats/charitablestats/article/0,,id=97176,00.html> (accessed 17 January 2009).

Table 572. **Individual Charitable Contributions by State: 2006**

[In millions of dollars (182,131 represents $182,131,000,000). For tax year. Data will not agree with data in other tables due to differing survey methodology used to derive state data]

State	Charitable contribution Number of returns (1,000)	Charitable contribution Amount (mil. dol.)	State	Charitable contribution Number of returns (1,000)	Charitable contribution Amount (mil. dol.)	State	Charitable contribution Number of returns (1,000)	Charitable contribution Amount (mil. dol.)	State	Charitable contribution Number of returns (1,000)	Charitable contribution Amount (mil. dol.)
U.S.[1,2]. .	41,367	182,131	IL	1,860	7,512	NE	226	989	SC	562	2,639
AL	551	2,951	IN	738	2,948	NV	368	1,479	SD	61	285
AK	71	287	IA	372	1,311	NH	201	621	TN	600	3,437
AZ	836	3,262	KS	339	1,629	NJ	1,686	5,833	TX	2,138	12,274
AR	247	1,302	KY	475	1,836	NM	186	699	UT	387	2,901
CA	5,257	24,359	LA	368	1,866	NY	3,046	15,456	VT	77	253
CO	771	3,119	ME	164	487	NC	1,273	5,623	VA	1,270	5,360
CT	677	2,819	MD	1,183	5,196	ND	50	206	WA	920	3,784
DE	134	548	MA	1,142	4,431	OH	1,543	5,236	WV	110	434
DC	104	729	MI	1,462	5,229	OK	390	2,338	WI	871	3,020
FL.	2,328	11,362	MN	913	3,336	OR	572	2,053	WY	45	450
GA	1,382	6,608	MS	259	1,405	PA	1,675	6,270			
HI	181	687	MO	709	2,893	RI	172	464			
ID	186	861	MT	117	416						

[1] The sum for the states does not add to the total because other components are not shown in this table. [2] See footnote, Table 477.

Source: Internal Revenue Service, *Statistics of Income Bulletin*, Spring issue. See also <http://www.irs.gov/taxstats/article/0,,id=171535,00.html>.

Table 573. **Volunteers by Selected Characteristics: 2008**

[In percent, except as noted. Data on volunteers relate to persons who performed unpaid volunteer activities for an organization at any point from September 1, 2007, through September 2008. Data represent the percent of the population involved in the activity]

Type of main organization [1]	Total, both sexes	Sex Men	Sex Women	Educational attainment [2] Less than a high school diploma	Educational attainment [2] High school graduate, no college [3]	Educational attainment [2] Less than a bachelor's degree [4]	Educational attainment [2] College graduates
Total volunteers (1,000)	**61,803**	**26,268**	**35,535**	**2,427**	**10,998**	**15,519**	**24,620**
Percent of population [5]	26.4	23.2	29.4	9.4	19.1	30.0	42.2
Median annual hours [5]	52	52	52	48	52	52	60
Civic and political [6]	5.5	6.8	4.4	3.4	4.6	5.5	6.3
Educational or youth service.	26	24.8	27	21.9	23.2	25.1	27.8
Environmental or animal care	2.0	2.0	2.0	0.6	1.1	2.1	2.1
Hospital or other health	8.2	6.4	9.5	6.0	8.7	8.0	8.0
Public safety	1.3	2.1	0.6	1.5	1.8	1.3	0.8
Religious	35.1	34.6	35.5	47.0	40.6	36.4	32.1
Social or community service.	13.5	13.7	13.4	12.5	12.6	13.7	13.8
Sport and hobby [7]	3.3	3.8	2.8	1.2	3.0	3.2	3.6

[1] Main organization is defined as the organization for which the volunteer worked the most hours during the year. See headnote for more details. [2] Data refer to persons 25 years and over. [3] Includes high school diploma or equivalent. [4] Includes the categories, some college, no degree; and associate's degree. [5] For those reporting annual hours. [6] Includes professional and/or international. [7] Includes cultural and/or arts.

Source: U.S. Bureau of Labor Statistics, *News*, USDL 09-0078, 23 January 2009. See also <http://www.bls.gov/news.release/pdf /volun.pdf>.

366   Social Insurance and Human Services

Section 12
Labor Force, Employment, and Earnings

This section presents statistics on the labor force; its distribution by occupation and industry affiliation; and the supply of, demand for, and conditions of labor. The chief source of these data is the Current Population Survey (CPS) conducted by the U.S. Census Bureau for the Bureau of Labor Statistics (BLS). Comprehensive historical and current data are available from the BLS Internet site <http://www.bls.gov/cps/>. These data are published on a current basis in the BLS monthly publication *Employment and Earnings Online*. Detailed data on the labor force are also available from the Census Bureau's decennial census of population.

Types of data—Most statistics in this section are obtained by two methods: household interviews or questionnaires and reports of establishment payroll records. Each method provides data that the other cannot suitably supply. Population characteristics, for example, are readily obtainable only from the household survey, while detailed industrial classifications can be readily derived only from establishment records.

Household data are obtained from a monthly sample survey of the population. The CPS is used to gather data for the calendar week including the 12th of the month and provides current comprehensive data on the labor force (see text, Section 1, Population). The CPS provides information on the work status of the population without duplication since each person is classified as employed, unemployed, or not in the labor force. Employed persons holding more than one job are counted only once, according to the job at which they worked the most hours during the survey week.

Monthly, quarterly, and annual data from the CPS are published by BLS in *Employment and Earnings Online*. Data presented include national totals of the number of persons in the civilian labor force by sex, race, Hispanic or Latino origin, and age; the number employed; hours of work; industry and occupational groups; and the number unemployed, reasons for, and duration of unemployment. Annual data shown in this section are averages of monthly figures for each calendar year, unless otherwise specified. Historical national CPS data are available at <http://www.bls.gov/cps/>.

The CPS also produces annual estimates of employment and unemployment for each state, 50 large metropolitan statistical areas, and selected cities. These estimates are published by BLS in its annual *Geographic Profile of Employment and Unemployment* available at <http://www.bls.gov/gps/>. More detailed geographic data (e.g., for counties and cities) are provided by the decennial population censuses.

Data based on establishment records are compiled by BLS and cooperating state agencies as part of an ongoing Current Employment Statistics program. Survey data, gathered monthly from a sample of employers through electronic interviewing (including electronic data interchange, touchtone data entry, and computer-assisted telephone interviewing) or by mail, fax, on magnetic tape or computer diskette, are supplemented by data from other government agencies and adjusted at intervals to data from government social insurance program reports. The estimates exclude self-employed persons, private household workers, unpaid family workers, agricultural workers, and the Armed Forces. In March 2008, reporting establishments employed 3.2 million manufacturing workers (24 percent of the total manufacturing employment at the time), 20.3 million workers in private nonmanufacturing industries (20.2 percent of the total in private nonmanufacturing), and 15.2 million federal, state, and local government employees (67 percent of total government).

Labor Force, Employment, and Earnings   367

The establishment survey counts workers each time they appear on a payroll during the reference period (the payroll period that includes the 12th of the month). Thus, unlike the CPS, a person with two jobs is counted twice. The establishment survey is designed to provide detailed industry information for the nation, states, and metropolitan areas on non-farm wage and salary employment, average weekly hours, and average hourly and weekly earnings. Establishment survey data also are published in *Employment and Earnings Online*. Historical national data are available at <http://www.bls.gov/ces/>. Historical data for states and metropolitan areas are available at <http://www.bls.gov/sae/>.

In June 2003, BLS completed a comprehensive sample redesign of the establishment survey begun in June 2000, changing from a quota-based sample to a probability-based sample. Also in June 2003, all establishment survey employment, hours, and earnings series were converted from being classified by the 1987 Standard Industrial Classification (SIC) system to being classified by the 2002 North American Industry Classification System (NAICS). The NAICS conversion resulted in major definitional changes to many of the previously published SIC-based series. All establishment survey historical time series were reconstructed as part of the NAICS conversion process and all published series have a NAICS-based history extending back to at least 1990. For total nonfarm industries and other high-level aggregates, NAICS history was reconstructed back to the previously existing start date for the series, 1939 in most cases. More information on the sample redesign, the conversion to NAICS, and other changes to the establishment survey implemented in June 2003 appears in "Revisions to the Current Employment Statistics National Estimates Effective May 2003" in the June 2003 issue of *Employment and Earnings*, as well as the Establishment Data portion of the Explanatory Notes and Estimates of Error section of *Employment and Earnings Online*.

The completion of the sample redesign and the conversion to NAICS for state and metropolitan area establishment survey data were implemented in March 2003 with the release of January 2003 estimates. For a discussion of the changes to the state and area establishment survey data, see "Revisions to the Current Employment Statistics State and Area Estimates Effective January 2003" in the March 2003 issue of *Employment and Earnings Online*.

Labor force—According to the CPS definitions, the civilian labor force comprises all civilians in the noninstitutionalized population 16 years and over classified as "employed" or "unemployed" according to the following criteria: Employed civilians comprise (a) all civilians, who, during the reference week, did any work for pay or profit (minimum of an hour's work) or worked 15 hours or more as unpaid workers in a family enterprise and (b) all civilians who were not working but who had jobs or businesses from which they were temporarily absent for noneconomic reasons (illness, weather conditions, vacation, labor-management dispute, etc.) whether they were paid for the time off or were seeking other jobs. Unemployed persons comprise all civilians who had no employment during the reference week, who made specific efforts to find a job within the previous 4 weeks (such as applying directly to an employer or to a public employment service or checking with friends) and who were available for work during that week, except for temporary illness. Persons on layoff from a job and expecting recall also are classified as unemployed. All other civilian persons, 16 years old and over, are classified as "not in the labor force."

Various breaks in the CPS data series have occurred over time due to the introduction of population adjustments and other changes. For details on these breaks in series and the effect that they had on the CPS data, see the section on noncomparability of labor force levels in the Household Data portion of the Explanatory Notes and Estimates of Error section of *Employment and Earnings Online* available on the site <http://www.bls.gov/cps/eetech_methods.pdf>.

Beginning in January 2006, the CPS data reflect the introduction of revised population controls. The effect of the revised population controls on the monthly CPS estimates was to decrease the December 2005 employment level by 123,000 and the civilian noninstitutional population by 67,000. The updated controls had little or no effect on unemployment rates and other ratios. For additional information on the effects of the revised population controls on estimates from the CPS, see "Adjustments to Household Survey Population Estimates in January 2006" in the February 2006 issue of *Employment and Earnings Online* at <http://www.bls.gov/cps/cps06adj.pdf>.

Hours and earnings—Average hourly earnings, based on establishment data, are gross earnings (i.e., earnings before payroll deductions) and include overtime premiums; they exclude irregular bonuses and value of payments in kind. Hours are those for which pay was received. Wages and salaries from the CPS consist of total monies received for work performed by an employee during the income year. It includes wages, salaries, commissions, tips, piece-rate payments, and cash bonuses earned before deductions were made for taxes, bonds, union dues, etc. Persons who worked 35 hours or more are classified as working full-time.

Industry and occupational groups— Industry data derived from the CPS for 1983–91 utilize the 1980 census industrial classification developed from the 1972 SIC. CPS data from 1971 to 1982 were based on the 1970 census classification system, which was developed from the 1967 SIC. Most of the industry categories were not affected by the change in classification.

The occupational classification system used in the 1980 census and in the CPS for 1983–91, evolved from the 1980 Standard Occupational Classification (SOC) system, first introduced in 1977. Occupational categories used in the 1980 census classification system are so radically different from the 1970 census system used in the CPS through 1982, that their implementation represented a break in historical data series.

Beginning in January 1992, the occupational and industrial classification systems used in the 1990 census were introduced into the CPS. (These systems were largely based on the 1980 SOC and the 1987 SIC systems, respectively.)

Beginning in 2003, the 2002 Census Bureau occupational and industrial classification systems were introduced into the CPS. These systems were derived from the 2000 SOC and the 2002 NAICS. The composition of detailed occupational and industrial classifications in the new classification systems was substantially changed from the previous systems in use, as was the structure for aggregating them into broad groups. Consequently, the use of the new classification systems created breaks in existing data series at all levels of aggregation. CPS data using the new classification systems are available beginning 2000. Additional information on the 2002 Census Bureau occupational and industrial classifications systems appears in "Revisions to the Current Population Survey Effective in January 2003" in the February 2003 issue of *Employment and Earnings Online*, available on the BLS Web site <http://www.bls.gov /cps/rvcps03.pdf>.

For details on the changes over time in the industrial and occupational classification systems used in the CPS, see the section on changes in the occupational and industrial classification systems in the Household Data portion of the Explanatory Notes and Estimates of Error section of *Employment and Earnings Online* available on the site <http://www.bls.gov/cps/eetech _methods.pdf>.

Establishments responding to the establishment survey are classified according to the 2007 NAICS. Previously they were classified according to the SIC manual. See text, Section 15, Business Enterprise, for information about the SIC manual and NAICS.

Productivity—BLS publishes data on productivity as measured by output per hour (labor productivity), output per combined unit of labor and capital input (multifactor productivity), and, for industry groups and industries, output per combined unit of capital, labor, energy, materials, and purchased service inputs. Labor productivity and related indexes are published for the business sector as a whole and its major subsectors: nonfarm business,

Labor Force, Employment, and Earnings 369

manufacturing, and nonfinancial corporations, and for over 200 detailed industries. Productivity indexes that take into account capital, labor, energy, materials, and service inputs are published for 18 major manufacturing industry groups, 86 detailed manufacturing industries, utility services, and air and railroad transportation. The major sector data are published in the BLS quarterly news release *Productivity and Costs* and in the annual *Multifactor Productivity Trends* release. Industry productivity measures are updated and published annually in the news releases *Productivity and Costs by Industry* and *Multifactor Productivity Trends by Industry*. The latest data are available at the Labor Productivity and Costs Web site <http://www.bls.gov/lpc/> and the Multifactor Productivity Web site <http://www.bls.gov/mfp>. Detailed information on methods, limitations, and data sources appears in the BLS *Handbook of Methods*, BLS Bulletin 2490 (1997), Chapters 10 and 11 <http://www.bls.gov/opub/hom/home.htm>.

Unions—As defined here, unions include traditional labor unions and employee associations similar to labor unions. Data on union membership status provided by BLS are for employed wage and salary workers and relate to their principal job. Earnings by union membership status are usual weekly earnings of full-time wage and salary workers. The information is collected through the Current Population Survey.

Work stoppages—Work stoppages include all strikes and lockouts known to BLS that last for at least 1 full day or shift and involve 1,000 or more workers. All stoppages, whether or not authorized by a union, legal or illegal, are counted. Excluded are work slowdowns and instances where employees report to work late or leave early to attend mass meetings or mass rallies.

Seasonal adjustment—Many economic statistics reflect a regularly recurring seasonal movement that can be estimated on the basis of past experience. By eliminating that part of the change which can be ascribed to usual seasonal variation (e.g., climate or school openings and closings), it is possible to observe the cyclical and other nonseasonal movements in the series. However, in evaluating deviations from the seasonal pattern—that is, changes in a seasonally adjusted series—it is important to note that seasonal adjustment is merely an approximation based on past experience. Seasonally adjusted estimates have a broader margin of possible error than the original data on which they are based, since they are subject not only to sampling and other errors, but also are affected by the uncertainties of the adjustment process itself. Consistent with BLS practices, annual estimates will be published only for not-seasonally-adjusted data.

Statistical reliability—For discussion of statistical collection, estimation, sampling procedures, and measures of statistical reliability applicable to Census Bureau and BLS data, see Appendix III.

U.S. Census Bureau, Statistical Abstract of the United States: 2010

Table 574. **Civilian Population—Employment Status: 1970 to 2008**

[In thousands (137,085 represents 137,085,000), except as indicated. Annual averages of monthly figures. Civilian noninstitutional population 16 years old and over. Based on Current Population Survey; see text, Section 1, and Appendix III]

Year	Civilian noninsti- tutional population	Civilian labor force							Not in labor force	
					Employ- ment/ population ratio[1]	Unemployed				
		Total	Percent of population	Employed		Number	Percent of labor force		Number	Percent of population
1970	137,085	82,771	60.4	78,678	57.4	4,093	4.9		54,315	39.6
1980	167,745	106,940	63.8	99,303	59.2	7,637	7.1		60,806	36.2
1990 [2]	189,164	125,840	66.5	118,793	62.8	7,047	5.6		63,324	33.5
1991	190,925	126,346	66.2	117,718	61.7	8,628	6.8		64,578	33.8
1992	192,805	128,105	66.4	118,492	61.5	9,613	7.5		64,700	33.6
1993	194,838	129,200	66.3	120,259	61.7	8,940	6.9		65,638	33.7
1994 [2]	196,814	131,056	66.6	123,060	62.5	7,996	6.1		65,758	33.4
1995	198,584	132,304	66.6	124,900	62.9	7,404	5.6		66,280	33.4
1996	200,591	133,943	66.8	126,708	63.2	7,236	5.4		66,647	33.2
1997 [2]	203,133	136,297	67.1	129,558	63.8	6,739	4.9		66,837	32.9
1998 [2]	205,220	137,673	67.1	131,463	64.1	6,210	4.5		67,547	32.9
1999 [2]	207,753	139,368	67.1	133,488	64.3	5,880	4.2		68,385	32.9
2000 [2]	212,577	142,583	67.1	136,891	64.4	5,692	4.0		69,994	32.9
2001	215,092	143,734	66.8	136,933	63.7	6,801	4.7		71,359	33.2
2002	217,570	144,863	66.6	136,485	62.7	8,378	5.8		72,707	33.4
2003 [2]	221,168	146,510	66.2	137,736	62.3	8,774	6.0		74,658	33.8
2004 [2]	223,357	147,401	66.0	139,252	62.3	8,149	5.5		75,956	34.0
2005 [2]	226,082	149,320	66.0	141,730	62.7	7,591	5.1		76,762	34.0
2006 [2]	228,815	151,428	66.2	144,427	63.1	7,001	4.6		77,387	33.8
2007 [2]	231,867	153,124	66.0	146,047	63.0	7,078	4.6		78,743	34.0
2008 [2]	233,788	154,287	66.0	145,362	62.2	8,924	5.8		79,501	34.0

[1] Civilian employed as a percent of the civilian noninstitutional population.   [2] Data not strictly comparable with data for earlier years. See text, this section, and February 1994, March 1996, February 1997–99, and February 2003–09 issues of *Employment and Earnings.*

Source: U.S. Bureau of Labor Statistics, "Employment and Earnings Online," January 2009; <http://www.bls.gov/opub/ee /home.htm> and <http://www.bls.gov/cps/home.htm>.

Table 575. **Civilian Labor Force and Participation Rates With Projections: 1980 to 2016**

[106.9 represents 106,900,000. Civilian noninstitutional population 16 years old and over. Annual averages of monthly figures. Rates are based on annual average civilian noninstitutional population of each specified group and represent proportion of each specified group in the civilian labor force. Based on Current Population Survey; see text, Section 1, and Appendix III]

Race, Hispanic origin, sex, and age	Civilian labor force (millions)						Participation rate (percent) [1]					
	1980	1990 [2]	2000 [2]	2005 [2]	2008 [2]	2016, proj.	1980	1990 [2]	2000 [2]	2005 [2]	2008 [2]	2016, proj.
Total [3]	106.9	125.8	142.6	149.3	154.3	164.2	63.8	66.5	67.1	66.0	66.0	65.5
White [4]	93.6	107.4	118.5	122.3	125.6	130.7	64.1	66.9	67.3	66.3	66.3	65.5
Male	54.5	59.6	64.5	66.7	68.4	71.3	78.2	77.1	75.5	74.1	73.7	72.9
Female	39.1	47.8	54.1	55.6	57.3	59.4	51.2	57.4	59.5	58.9	59.2	58.4
Black [4]	10.9	13.7	16.4	17.0	17.7	20.1	61.0	64.0	65.8	64.2	63.7	64.9
Male	5.6	6.8	7.7	8.0	8.3	9.4	70.3	71.0	69.2	67.3	66.7	67.1
Female	5.3	6.9	8.7	9.0	9.4	10.7	53.1	58.3	63.1	61.6	61.3	63.1
Asian [4, 5]	(NA)	(NA)	6.3	6.5	7.2	8.7	(NA)	(NA)	67.2	66.1	67.0	65.9
Male	(NA)	(NA)	3.4	3.5	3.9	4.6	(NA)	(NA)	76.1	74.8	75.3	74.1
Female	(NA)	(NA)	2.9	3.0	3.4	4.1	(NA)	(NA)	59.2	58.2	59.4	67.1
Hispanic [6]	6.1	10.7	16.7	19.8	22.0	26.9	64.0	67.4	69.7	68.0	68.5	68.6
Male	3.8	6.5	9.9	12.0	13.3	15.8	81.4	81.4	81.5	80.1	80.2	79.0
Female	2.3	4.2	6.8	7.8	8.8	11.1	47.4	53.1	57.5	55.3	56.2	57.8
Male	61.5	69.0	76.3	80.0	82.5	87.8	77.4	76.4	74.8	73.3	73.0	72.3
16 to 19 years	5.0	4.1	4.3	3.6	3.5	2.9	60.5	55.7	52.8	43.2	40.1	36.8
20 to 24 years	8.6	7.9	7.5	8.1	8.1	8.0	85.9	84.4	82.6	79.1	78.7	76.4
25 to 34 years	17.0	19.9	17.8	17.8	18.3	20.9	95.2	94.1	93.4	91.7	91.5	95.7
35 to 44 years	11.8	17.5	20.1	19.5	19.0	18.4	95.5	94.3	92.7	92.1	92.2	91.7
45 to 54 years	9.9	11.1	16.3	18.1	18.9	18.2	91.2	90.7	88.6	87.7	88.0	86.6
55 to 64 years	7.2	6.6	7.8	10.0	11.3	13.9	72.1	67.8	67.3	69.3	70.4	70.1
65 years and over . . .	1.9	2.0	2.5	3.0	3.4	5.5	19.0	16.3	17.7	19.8	21.5	27.1
Female	45.5	56.8	66.3	69.3	71.8	76.5	51.5	57.5	59.9	59.3	59.5	59.2
16 to 19 years	4.4	3.7	4.0	3.6	3.4	3.0	52.9	51.6	51.2	44.2	40.2	38.3
20 to 24 years	7.3	6.8	6.7	7.1	7.1	7.0	68.9	71.3	73.1	70.1	70.0	67.2
25 to 34 years	12.3	16.1	14.9	14.5	15.0	16.4	65.5	73.5	76.1	73.9	75.2	75.0
35 to 44 years	8.6	14.7	17.5	16.5	16.1	15.3	65.5	76.4	77.2	75.8	76.1	75.1
45 to 54 years	7.0	9.1	14.8	16.3	17.1	16.9	59.9	71.2	76.8	76.0	76.1	77.8
55 to 64 years	4.7	4.9	6.6	8.9	10.3	13.4	41.3	45.2	51.9	57.0	59.1	63.5
65 years and over . . .	1.2	1.5	1.8	2.3	2.8	4.6	8.1	8.6	9.4	11.5	13.3	17.5

NA Not available.   [1] Civilian labor force as a percent of the civilian noninstitutional population.   [2] See footnote 2, Table 574.   [3] Includes other races, not shown separately.   [4] The 2003 Current Population Survey (CPS) allowed respondents to choose more than one race. Beginning 2003, data represent persons who selected this race group only and exclude persons reporting more than one race. Prior to 2003 the CPS only allowed respondents to report one race group. See also comments on race in the text for Section 1.   [5] Prior to 2005, includes Pacific Islanders.   [6] Persons of Hispanic or Latino origin may be any race.

Source: U.S. Bureau of Labor Statistics, "Employment and Earnings Online," January 2009; <http://www.bls.gov/opub/ee /home.htm>; *Monthly Labor Review*, November 2007; and <http://www.bls.gov/emp/emplab1.htm>.

Labor Force, Employment, and Earnings   371

Table 576. Civilian Population—Employment Status by Sex, Race, and Ethnicity: 1970 to 2008

[In thousands (64,304 represents 64,304,000), except as indicated. Annual averages of monthly figures. See Table 574 for U.S. totals and coverage]

Year, sex, race, and Hispanic origin	Civilian noninstitutional population	Civilian labor force — Total	Percent of population	Employed	Employment/ population ratio[1]	Unemployed — Number	Unemployed — Percent of labor force	Not in labor force — Number	Not in labor force — Percent of population
Male:									
1970	64,304	51,228	79.7	48,990	76.2	2,238	4.4	13,076	20.3
1980 [2]	79,398	61,453	77.4	57,186	72.0	4,267	6.9	17,945	22.6
1990 [2]	90,377	69,011	76.4	65,104	72.0	3,906	5.7	21,367	23.6
2000 [2]	101,964	76,280	74.8	73,305	71.9	2,975	3.9	25,684	25.2
2005 [2]	109,151	80,033	73.3	75,973	69.6	4,059	5.1	29,119	26.7
2006 [2]	110,605	81,255	73.5	77,502	70.1	3,753	4.6	29,350	26.5
2007 [2]	112,173	82,136	73.2	78,254	69.8	3,882	4.7	30,036	26.8
2008 [2]	113,113	82,520	73.0	77,486	68.5	5,033	6.1	30,593	27.0
Female:									
1970	72,782	31,543	43.3	29,688	40.8	1,855	5.9	41,239	56.7
1980 [2]	88,348	45,487	51.5	42,117	47.7	3,370	7.4	42,861	48.5
1990 [2]	98,787	56,829	57.5	53,689	54.3	3,140	5.5	41,957	42.5
2000 [2]	110,613	66,303	59.9	63,586	57.5	2,717	4.1	44,310	40.1
2005 [2]	116,931	69,288	59.3	65,757	56.2	3,531	5.1	47,643	40.7
2006 [2]	118,210	70,173	59.4	66,925	56.6	3,247	4.6	48,037	40.6
2007 [2]	119,694	70,988	59.3	67,792	56.6	3,196	4.5	48,707	40.7
2008 [2]	120,675	71,767	59.5	67,876	56.2	3,891	5.4	48,908	40.5
White: [3]									
1980 [2]	146,122	93,600	64.1	87,715	60.0	5,884	6.3	52,523	35.9
1990 [2]	160,625	107,447	66.9	102,261	63.7	5,186	4.8	53,178	33.1
2000 [2]	176,220	118,545	67.3	114,424	64.9	4,121	3.5	57,675	32.7
2005 [2]	184,446	122,299	66.3	116,949	63.4	5,350	4.4	62,148	33.7
2006 [2]	186,264	123,834	66.5	118,833	63.8	5,002	4.0	62,429	33.5
2007 [2]	188,253	124,935	66.4	119,792	63.6	5,143	4.1	63,319	33.6
2008 [2]	189,540	125,635	66.3	119,126	62.8	6,509	5.2	63,905	33.7
Black: [3]									
1980 [2]	17,824	10,865	61.0	9,313	52.2	1,553	14.3	6,959	39.0
1990 [2]	21,477	13,740	64.0	12,175	56.7	1,565	11.4	7,737	36.0
2000 [2]	24,902	16,397	65.8	15,156	60.9	1,241	7.6	8,505	34.2
2005 [2]	26,517	17,013	64.2	15,313	57.7	1,700	10.0	9,504	35.8
2006 [2]	27,007	17,314	64.1	15,765	58.4	1,549	8.9	9,693	35.9
2007 [2]	27,485	17,496	63.7	16,051	58.4	1,445	8.3	9,989	36.3
2008 [2] [4]	27,843	17,740	63.7	15,953	57.3	1,788	10.1	10,103	36.3
Asian: [3] [4]									
2000 [2]	9,330	6,270	67.2	6,043	64.8	227	3.6	3,060	32.8
2005 [2]	9,842	6,503	66.1	6,244	63.4	259	4.0	3,339	33.9
2006 [2]	10,155	6,727	66.2	6,522	64.2	205	3.0	3,427	33.7
2007 [2]	10,633	7,067	66.5	6,839	64.3	229	3.2	3,566	33.5
2008 [2] [5]	10,751	7,202	67.0	6,917	64.3	285	4.0	3,549	33.0
Hispanic: [5]									
1980 [2]	9,598	6,146	64.0	5,527	57.6	620	10.1	3,451	36.0
1990 [2]	15,904	10,720	67.4	9,845	61.9	876	8.2	5,184	32.6
2000 [2]	23,938	16,689	69.7	15,735	65.7	954	5.7	7,249	30.3
2005 [2]	29,133	19,824	68.0	18,632	64.0	1,191	6.0	9,310	32.0
2006 [2]	30,103	20,694	68.7	19,613	65.2	1,081	5.2	9,409	31.3
2007 [2]	31,383	21,602	68.8	20,382	64.9	1,220	5.6	9,781	31.2
2008 [2]	32,141	22,024	68.5	20,346	63.3	1,678	7.6	10,116	31.5
Mexican:									
1990 [2]	9,752	6,707	68.8	6,146	63.0	561	8.4	3,045	31.2
2000 [2]	15,333	10,783	70.3	10,144	66.2	639	5.9	4,550	29.7
2005 [2]	18,523	12,671	68.4	11,887	64.2	784	6.2	5,851	31.6
2006 [2]	19,036	13,158	69.1	12,477	65.5	681	5.2	5,877	30.9
2007 [2]	19,770	13,672	69.2	12,908	65.3	764	5.6	6,098	30.8
2008 [2]	20,474	14,009	68.4	12,931	63.2	1,078	7.7	6,465	31.6
Puerto Rican:									
1990 [2]	1,718	960	55.9	870	50.6	91	9.5	758	44.1
2000 [2]	2,193	1,411	64.3	1,318	60.1	92	6.6	783	35.7
2005 [2]	2,654	1,619	61.0	1,492	56.2	126	7.8	1,035	39.0
2006 [2]	2,600	1,599	61.5	1,484	57.1	115	7.2	1,001	38.5
2007 [2]	2,711	1,684	62.1	1,551	57.2	133	7.9	1,027	37.9
2008 [2]	2,854	1,822	63.9	1,634	57.3	188	10.3	1,032	36.2
Cuban:									
1990 [2]	918	603	65.7	559	60.9	44	7.2	315	34.3
2000 [2]	1,174	740	63.1	707	60.3	33	4.5	434	37.0
2005 [2]	1,259	755	60.0	730	58.0	25	3.3	503	40.0
2006 [2]	1,326	807	60.9	778	58.7	29	3.6	519	39.1
2007 [2]	1,421	898	63.2	862	60.7	36	4.0	523	36.8
2008 [2]	1,422	897	63.1	841	59.1	57	6.3	525	36.9

[1] Civilian employed as a percent of the civilian noninstitutional population.   [2] See footnote 2, Table 574.   [3] Beginning 2005, for persons in this race group only. See footnote 3, Table 575.   [4] Prior to 2005, includes Pacific Islanders.   [5] Persons of Hispanic or Latino ethnicity may be any race. Includes persons of other Hispanic or Latino ethnicity, not shown separately.

Source: U.S. Bureau of Labor Statistics, "Employment and Earnings Online," January 2009; <http://www.bls.gov/opub/ee/home.htm> and <http://www.bls.gov/cps/home.htm>.

Table 577. **Foreign-Born and Native-Born Populations—Employment Status by Selected Characteristics: 2008**

[233,788 represents 233,788,000. For civilian noninstitutional population 16 years old and over, except as indicated. Annual averages of monthly figures. Based on Current Population Survey; see text, Section 1, and Appendix III]

Characteristic	Civilian noninstitutional population (1,000)	Civilian labor force			Unemployed (1,000)	
		Total (1,000)	Partici-pation rate [1]	Employed (1,000)	Number (1,000)	Unemploy-ment rate
Total.........................	233,788	154,287	66.0	145,362	8,924	5.8
Male........................	113,113	82,520	73.0	77,486	5,033	6.1
Female......................	120,675	71,767	59.5	67,876	3,891	5.4
FOREIGN BORN						
Total [2].....................	35,317	24,063	68.1	22,660	1,403	5.8
Sex:						
Male.......................	17,688	14,400	81.4	13,578	822	5.7
Female	17,629	9,663	54.8	9,082	581	6.0
Presence of children:						
With own children under 18............	13,864	10,626	76.6	10,047	580	5.5
With own children under 3	3,923	2,727	69.5	2,558	169	6.2
With no own children under 18	21,453	13,436	62.6	12,613	823	6.1
Age:						
16 to 24 years old...............	3,845	2,211	57.5	1,979	232	10.5
25 to 34 years old...............	7,992	6,236	78.0	5,866	371	5.9
35 to 44 years old...............	8,327	6,814	81.8	6,473	341	5.0
45 to 54 years old...............	6,602	5,380	81.5	5,083	297	5.5
55 to 64 years old...............	4,126	2,700	65.4	2,580	120	4.5
65 years old and over	4,424	721	16.3	679	42	5.9
Race and Hispanic ethnicity:						
White non-Hispanic	7,517	4,531	60.3	4,305	226	5.0
Black non-Hispanic	2,743	2,007	73.2	1,863	144	7.2
Asian non-Hispanic	7,894	5,382	68.2	5,185	197	3.7
Hispanic [3]	16,816	11,889	70.7	11,067	822	6.9
Educational attainment:						
Total 25 years old and over..........	31,472	21,852	69.4	20,681	1,171	5.4
Less than a high school diploma.	9,420	5,759	61.1	5,316	443	7.7
High school graduates, no college [4] ...	8,098	5,514	68.1	5,201	312	5.7
Some college or associate's degree ...	4,951	3,648	73.7	3,457	190	5.2
Bachelor's degree and higher [5].......	9,003	6,931	77.0	6,705	226	3.3
NATIVE BORN						
Total [2].....................	198,471	130,224	65.6	122,703	7,521	5.8
Sex:						
Male.......................	95,424	68,119	71.4	63,908	4,211	6.2
Female	103,047	62,104	60.3	58,795	3,310	5.3
Presence of children:						
With own children under 18............	51,642	42,762	82.8	40,859	1,903	4.5
With own children under 3	13,358	10,419	78.0	9,841	578	5.5
With no own children under 18	146,829	87,462	59.6	81,844	5,618	6.4
Age:						
16 to 24 years old...............	33,639	19,821	58.9	17,223	2,599	13.1
25 to 34 years old...............	32,001	27,096	84.7	25,517	1,579	5.8
35 to 44 years old...............	33,372	28,247	84.6	26,984	1,264	4.5
45 to 54 years old...............	37,357	30,623	82.0	29,446	1,177	3.8
55 to 64 years old...............	29,364	18,915	64.4	18,232	682	3.6
65 years old and over	32,737	5,522	16.9	5,300	222	4.0
Race and Hispanic ethnicity:						
White non-Hispanic	152,157	100,679	66.2	95,909	4,770	4.7
Black non-Hispanic	24,157	15,101	62.5	13,524	1,577	10.4
Asian non-Hispanic	2,669	1,674	62.7	1,600	74	4.4
Hispanic [3]	15,325	10,135	66.1	9,279	856	8.4
Educational attainment:						
Total, 25 years and over............	164,832	110,403	67.0	105,480	4,923	4.5
Less than a high school diploma.	16,702	6,406	38.4	5,757	649	10.1
High school graduates, no college [4] ...	53,017	32,749	61.8	30,896	1,854	5.7
Some college or associate's degree ...	46,153	33,070	71.7	31,582	1,488	4.5
Bachelor's degree and higher [5].......	48,959	38,177	78.0	37,245	932	2.4

[1] Civilian labor force as a percent of the civilian noninstitutional population.   [2] Includes other races not shown separately.   [3] Persons of Hispanic origin may be any race.   [4] Includes persons with a high school diploma or equivalent.   [5] Includes persons with bachelor's, master's, professional, and doctoral degrees.

Source: U.S. Bureau of Labor Statistics, *Foreign-Born Workers: Labor Force Characteristics in 2008*, News, USDL 09-0303, March 26, 2009. See also <http://www.bls.gov/news.release/forbrn.toc.htm>.

Table 578. **Civilian Labor Force—Percent Distribution by Sex and Age: 1980 to 2008**

[106,940 represents 106,940,000. Civilian noninstitutional population 16 years old and over. Annual averages of monthly figures. Based on Current Population Survey; see text, Section 1, and Appendix III]

Year and sex	Civilian labor force (1,000)	Percent distribution						
		16 to 19 years	20 to 24 years	25 to 34 years	35 to 44 years	45 to 54 years	55 to 64 years	65 years and over
Total: 1980	106,940	8.8	14.9	27.3	19.1	15.8	11.2	2.9
1990 [1]	125,840	6.2	11.7	28.6	25.5	16.1	9.2	2.7
2000 [1]	142,583	5.8	10.0	23.0	26.3	21.8	10.1	3.0
2005 [1]	149,320	4.8	10.1	21.7	24.1	23.0	12.7	3.5
2008 [1]	154,287	4.4	9.8	21.6	22.7	23.3	14.0	4.0
Male: 1980	61,453	8.1	14.0	27.6	19.3	16.1	11.8	3.1
1990 [1]	69,011	5.9	11.4	28.8	25.3	16.1	9.6	2.9
2000 [1]	76,280	5.6	9.9	23.4	26.3	21.3	10.2	3.3
2005 [1]	80,033	4.5	10.1	22.3	24.4	22.6	12.6	3.7
2008 [1]	82,520	4.2	9.8	22.2	23.0	22.9	13.7	4.2
Female: 1980	45,487	9.6	16.1	26.9	19.0	15.4	10.4	2.6
1990 [1]	56,829	6.5	12.0	28.3	25.8	16.1	8.7	2.6
2000 [1]	66,303	6.0	10.2	22.5	26.4	22.3	9.9	2.7
2005 [1]	69,288	5.2	10.2	20.9	23.9	23.6	12.9	3.3
2008 [1]	71,767	4.7	9.9	20.9	22.4	23.8	14.3	3.9

[1] See footnote 2, Table 574.

Source: U.S. Bureau of Labor Statistics, "Employment and Earnings Online," January 2009; <http://www.bls.gov/opub/ee/home.htm> and <http://www.bls.gov/cps/home.htm>.

Table 579. **Civilian Labor Force and Participation Rates by Educational Attainment, Sex, Race, and Hispanic Origin: 2000 to 2008**

[120,061 represents 120,061,000. Civilian noninstitutional population 25 years old and over. Annual averages of monthly figures. See Table 614 for unemployment data. Rates are based on annual average civilian noninstitutional population of each specified group and represent proportion of each specified group in the civilian labor force]

Year, sex, and race	Civilian labor force					Participation rate [1]				
		Percent distribution								
	Total (1,000)	Less than high school diploma	High school graduates, no degree	Less than a bachelor's degree	College graduate	Total	Less than high school diploma	High school graduates, no degree	Less than a bachelor's degree	College graduate
Total: [2]										
2000 [3]	120,061	10.4	31.4	27.7	30.5	67.3	43.5	64.4	73.9	79.4
2005 [3]	127,030	10.0	30.1	27.5	32.4	67.1	45.5	63.2	72.5	77.9
2007 [3]	130,908	9.3	29.2	28.0	34.5	67.3	46.6	62.8	72.0	77.8
2008 [3]	132,255	9.2	28.9	27.8	34.1	67.4	46.6	62.6	71.8	77.8
Male:										
2000 [3] . .	64,490	11.8	31.1	25.9	31.2	76.1	56.0	75.1	80.9	84.4
2005 [3] . .	68,389	11.7	30.9	25.4	32.1	75.4	58.6	73.6	79.3	82.9
2007 [3] . .	70,501	11.0	30.3	25.8	33.5	75.6	60.2	73.2	78.7	82.9
2008 [3] . .	70,982	11.0	30.1	25.7	33.3	75.3	60.0	72.9	78.3	82.4
Female:										
2000 [3] . .	55,572	8.8	31.8	29.7	29.7	59.4	32.3	55.5	68.0	74.0
2005 [3] . .	58,641	8.0	29.2	30.0	32.8	59.4	32.9	53.8	66.8	72.9
2007 [3] . .	60,406	7.2	28.0	30.6	35.6	59.7	33.1	53.4	66.4	72.9
2008 [3] . .	61,273	7.1	27.6	30.2	35.1	60.0	33.3	53.1	66.4	73.4
White: [4]										
2000 [3] . .	99,964	10.1	31.4	27.5	31.0	67.0	44.1	63.6	73.1	79.0
2005 [3] . .	104,240	9.8	29.9	27.6	32.7	66.9	46.4	62.5	72.0	77.5
2007 [3] . .	106,962	9.2	29.0	27.9	34.7	67.2	47.9	62.3	71.4	77.4
2008 [3] . .	107,849	9.1	28.8	27.7	34.4	67.2	47.7	62.0	71.2	77.5
Black: [4]										
2000 [3] . .	13,582	12.4	36.0	31.2	20.5	68.2	39.3	69.9	79.3	84.4
2005 [3] . .	14,252	11.2	36.4	30.2	22.2	67.2	39.8	67.9	75.6	82.0
2007 [3] . .	14,720	9.8	35.3	32.4	24.2	67.3	39.1	65.4	75.3	83.0
2008 [3] . .	14,973	9.6	34.7	31.8	23.8	67.3	39.8	65.7	75.2	81.5
Asian: [4,5]										
2000 [3] . .	5,402	9.1	20.7	20.2	50.1	70.9	46.0	65.6	76.4	79.1
2005 [3] . .	5,805	8.0	17.7	17.3	57.0	69.4	45.3	61.8	71.6	77.5
2006 [3] . .	6,065	7.5	17.8	17.2	57.5	69.9	44.4	62.8	72.6	77.5
2007 [3] . .	6,378	7.4	18.7	17.3	58.9	70.5	43.8	63.2	72.5	77.5
2008 [3] . .	6,518	7.2	18.3	16.9	57.6	70.5	45.6	64.4	72.7	77.4
Hispanic: [6]										
2000 [3] . .	12,975	36.7	29.3	20.6	13.4	71.5	61.9	75.0	80.8	83.5
2005 [3] . .	16,135	35.5	29.4	20.9	14.2	70.8	61.4	74.3	78.8	81.7
2007 [3] . .	17,783	33.2	31.4	22.0	15.9	71.6	62.6	74.3	79.1	82.2
2008 [3] . .	18,235	32.4	30.6	21.5	15.5	71.6	61.9	74.1	78.6	83.0

[1] See footnote 1, Table 575. [2] Includes other races, not shown separately. [3] See footnote 2, Table 574. [4] Beginning 2005, for persons in this race group only. See footnote 4, Table 575. [5] 2000 data include Pacific Islanders. [6] Persons of Hispanic or Latino origin may be any race.

Source: U.S. Bureau of Labor Statistics, "Employment and Earnings Online," January 2009; <http://www.bls.gov/opub/ee/home.htm> and <http://www.bls.gov/cps/home.htm>.

Table 580. **Characteristics of the Civilian Labor Force by State: 2008**

[In thousands (154,287 represents 154,287,000), except ratio and rate. Civilian noninstitutional population, 16 years old and over. Annual averages of monthly figures. Data for states may not sum to national totals, due to rounding]

State	Total Number	Total Female	Employed Total	Employed Female	Employed popu-lation ratio [1]	Unemployed Total Number	Unemployed Total Female	Unemployed Rate [2] Total	Unemployed Rate [2] Male	Unemployed Rate [2] Female	Participation rate [3] Male	Participation rate [3] Female
United States . .	154,287	71,767	145,362	67,876	62.2	8,924	3,891	5.8	6.1	5.4	73.0	59.5
Alabama	2,185	1,027	2,062	979	57.4	123	48	5.6	6.5	4.7	68.1	54.3
Alaska.	360	165	335	155	66.3	24	11	6.8	7.1	6.4	76.2	65.9
Arizona	3,133	1,410	2,948	1,336	60.6	185	75	5.9	6.4	5.3	71.8	57.1
Arkansas	1,374	650	1,303	621	59.7	71	29	5.2	5.8	4.5	69.0	57.4
California	18,431	8,222	17,113	7,657	61.1	1,318	565	7.1	7.4	6.9	74.2	57.7
Colorado	2,735	1,222	2,603	1,169	68.6	132	53	4.8	5.2	4.3	80.2	64.1
Connecticut	1,891	907	1,782	857	65.1	109	50	5.7	6.0	5.5	74.9	63.6
Delaware	447	213	425	204	62.7	22	9	5.0	5.5	4.4	72.7	59.9
District of Columbia.	332	167	310	155	64.7	22	12	6.6	6.2	7.0	74.7	64.5
Florida.	9,214	4,319	8,654	4,080	59.6	560	239	6.1	6.6	5.5	70.0	57.4
Georgia.	4,904	2,281	4,588	2,124	63.4	316	157	6.4	6.0	6.9	75.9	60.4
Hawaii.	660	307	633	296	63.3	28	11	4.2	4.7	3.6	72.5	59.9
Idaho	756	342	715	325	62.9	41	16	5.4	5.9	4.8	73.4	59.6
Illinois	6,704	3,112	6,263	2,918	63.2	440	194	6.6	6.9	6.2	74.6	61.0
Indiana	3,251	1,521	3,056	1,440	62.5	194	81	6.0	6.5	5.3	72.8	60.5
Iowa	1,691	803	1,623	774	69.7	68	29	4.0	4.3	3.6	77.9	67.5
Kansas	1,509	707	1,442	675	68.0	67	33	4.5	4.3	4.6	77.5	65.2
Kentucky	2,022	937	1,895	880	57.4	127	57	6.3	6.5	6.1	68.5	54.6
Louisiana	2,045	968	1,943	924	59.4	102	44	5.0	5.4	4.6	69.9	55.9
Maine	707	336	669	320	62.8	38	16	5.4	5.9	4.7	72.4	60.7
Maryland	3,004	1,472	2,877	1,416	66.0	128	55	4.2	4.7	3.8	74.4	64.0
Massachusetts . . .	3,421	1,644	3,238	1,565	63.1	183	79	5.3	5.9	4.8	72.3	61.4
Michigan	4,952	2,330	4,542	2,159	58.1	410	171	8.3	9.1	7.4	69.3	57.8
Minnesota	2,905	1,381	2,744	1,312	67.6	161	69	5.5	6.0	5.0	76.0	67.1
Mississippi	1,314	626	1,229	590	56.1	86	37	6.5	7.2	5.8	67.0	53.9
Missouri.	3,023	1,440	2,840	1,356	62.3	183	84	6.1	6.3	5.8	72.5	60.7
Montana	509	242	483	230	63.5	26	12	5.2	5.5	4.8	73.6	63.0
Nebraska	1001	471	969	457	71.3	33	14	3.3	3.5	3.0	79.5	68.1
Nevada	1,390	614	1305	577	65.3	85	37	6.1	6.2	6.0	76.8	62.2
New Hampshire . .	743	352	715	339	68.1	28	13	3.8	4.0	3.6	76.3	65.6
New Jersey	4,529	2,122	4,285	2,017	63.1	244	106	5.4	5.8	5.0	73.6	60.2
New Mexico	971	456	928	435	61.0	43	22	4.4	4.2	4.7	70.0	58.0
New York.	9,604	4,538	9,074	4,311	59.6	530	227	5.5	6.0	5.0	69.8	56.9
North Carolina . . .	4,548	2,146	4,258	2,016	60.5	290	130	6.4	6.7	6.0	71.8	58.2
North Dakota	374	177	363	172	72.5	12	5	3.2	3.5	2.8	79.7	70.1
Ohio	5,981	2,887	5,595	2,712	62.8	386	175	6.5	6.8	6.1	72.4	62.4
Oklahoma	1,761	801	1,696	773	61.4	66	28	3.7	3.9	3.5	72.1	56.0
Oregon	1,973	918	1,845	869	61.8	127	49	6.4	7.4	5.4	72.0	60.3
Pennsylvania	6,416	3,048	6,075	2,904	61.8	341	143	5.3	5.9	4.7	71.7	59.5
Rhode Island	567	272	522	254	62.4	45	18	7.9	9.1	6.7	74.1	62.0
South Carolina . . .	2,134	1031	1,992	960	58.1	142	71	6.7	6.4	6.9	68.0	57.0
South Dakota	449	215	436	209	71.1	14	6	3.0	3.1	2.9	77.9	68.9
Tennessee	3,047	1,423	2,847	1,326	59.1	200	98	6.6	6.3	6.9	70.4	56.6
Texas	11,733	5,190	11,166	4,933	62.5	567	258	4.8	4.7	5.0	74.9	56.8
Utah	1,374	588	1,326	571	68.6	49	16	3.5	4.1	2.8	81.5	60.7
Vermont	354	170	336	162	66.6	17	8	4.9	5.0	4.9	74.4	66.0
Virginia	4,160	1,995	3,994	1,920	67.2	166	74	4.0	4.2	3.7	76.4	64.2
Washington	3,483	1,605	3,297	1,529	64.6	186	76	5.3	5.8	4.8	74.9	61.9
West Virginia	822	377	786	363	54.2	36	14	4.4	4.9	3.8	63.4	50.3
Wisconsin	3,098	1,488	2,953	1,427	67.2	145	62	4.7	5.2	4.1	74.6	66.6
Wyoming	294	131	285	127	69.4	9	4	3.0	2.8	3.1	79.0	64.0

[1] Civilian employment as a percent of civilian noninstitutional population.   [2] Percent unemployed of the civilian labor force.
[3] Percent of civilian noninstitutional population of each specified group in the civilian labor force.

Source: U.S. Bureau of Labor Statistics, Current Population Survey, *"Geographic Profile of Employment and Unemployment, 2008 Annual Averages"*; <http://www.bls.gov/gps/>.

Labor Force, Employment, and Earnings   375

Table 581. **Civilian Labor Force by Selected Metropolitan Area: 2008**

[154,287 represents 154,287,000. Civilian noninstitutional population 16 years old and over. Annual averages of monthly figures. Data are derived from the Local Area Unemployment Statistics Program. For metro areas with a 2000 Census population of one million or more. For definition of metropolitan areas, see Appendix II. Metropolitan areas defined as of November 2008]

Metropolitan areas ranked by population, 2000	Civilian labor force (1,000)	Unemployment rate [1]	Metropolitan areas ranked by population, 2000	Civilian labor force (1,000)	Unemployment rate [1]
United States	154,287	5.8	Cincinnati-Middletown, OH-KY-IN	1,128	5.8
New York-Northern New Jersey-Long Island, NY-NJ-PA	9,466	5.3	Portland-Vancouver-Beaverton, OR-WA	1,171	5.8
Los Angeles-Long Beach-Santa Ana, CA	6,611	7.0	Kansas City, MO-KS	1,040	5.7
Chicago-Naperville-Joliet, IL-IN-WI	4,923	6.2	Sacramento—Arden-Arcade—Roseville, CA	1,059	7.1
Philadelphia-Camden-Wilmington, PA-NJ-DE-MD	2,986	5.4	San Jose-Sunnyvale-Santa Clara, CA	905	6.1
Dallas-Fort Worth-Arlington, TX	3,137	5.0	San Antonio, TX	946	4.7
Miami-Fort Lauderdale-Pompano Beach, FL	2,850	5.8	Orlando-Kissimmee, FL	1,120	5.9
Washington-Arlington-Alexandria, DC-VA-MD-WV	3,028	3.8	Columbus, OH	966	5.5
Houston-Sugar Land-Baytown, TX	2,781	4.8	Virginia Beach-Norfolk-Newport News, VA-NC	825	4.2
Boston-Cambridge-Quincy, MA-NH NECTA	2,500	4.8	Indianapolis-Carmel, IN	905	5.1
Detroit-Warren-Livonia, MI	2,107	8.8	Milwaukee-Waukesha-West Allis, WI	806	4.8
Atlanta-Sandy Springs-Marietta, GA	2,746	6.2	Las Vegas-Paradise, NV	988	6.6
San Francisco-Oakland-Fremont, CA	2,268	5.7	Charlotte-Gastonia-Concord, NC-SC	861	6.4
Riverside-San Bernardino-Ontario, CA	1,795	8.3	New Orleans-Metairie-Kenner, LA	533	4.4
Phoenix-Mesa-Scottsdale, AZ	2,115	4.9	Nashville-Davidson—Murfreesboro—Franklin, TN	797	5.5
Seattle-Tacoma-Bellevue, WA	1,856	4.8	Providence-Fall River-Warwick, RI-MA NECTA [2]	701	7.7
Minneapolis-St. Paul-Bloomington, MN-WI	1,845	5.2	Austin-Round Rock, TX	868	4.4
San Diego-Carlsbad-San Marcos, CA	1,566	6.0	Memphis, TN-MS-AR	618	6.7
St. Louis, MO-IL	1,440	6.6	Buffalo-Niagara Falls, NY	586	6.0
Baltimore-Towson, MD	1,405	4.6	Louisville-Jefferson County, KY-IN	628	6.3
Pittsburgh, PA	1,218	5.1	Jacksonville, FL	684	5.8
Tampa-St. Petersburg-Clearwater, FL	1,324	6.5	Richmond, VA	650	4.3
Denver-Aurora-Broomfield, CO	1,400	5.0	Oklahoma City, OK	566	3.8
Cleveland-Elyria-Mentor, OH	1,081	6.6	Hartford-West Hartford-East Hartford, CT NECTA [2]	591	5.8
			Birmingham-Hoover, AL	529	4.5
			Rochester, NY	535	5.6

[1] Percent unemployed of the civilian labor force.   [2] New England City and Town Areas. See Appendix II.

Source: U.S. Bureau of Labor Statistics, Local Area Unemployment Statistics (LAUS); <http://www.bls.gov/lau/data.htm>.

Table 582. **School Enrollment and Labor Force Status: 2008**

[In thousands (37,569 represents 37,569,000), except percent. As of October. Civilian noninstitutional population. Based on Current Population Survey; see text, Section 1, and Appendix III]

Characteristic	Population	Civilian labor force	Employed	Unemployed Total	Unemployed Rate [1]	Not in labor force
Total, 16 to 24 years [2]	37,569	21,931	19,020	2,911	13.3	15,637
Enrolled in school [2]	21,348	8,974	7,907	1,067	11.9	12,374
Enrolled in high school	9,677	2,661	2,099	562	21.1	7,016
Male	4,991	1,272	960	311	24.5	3,720
Female	4,686	1,389	1,139	251	18.0	3,297
Enrolled in college	11,671	6,313	5,809	505	8.0	5,358
Enrolled in 2 year college	3,521	2,229	2,035	194	8.7	1,292
Enrolled in 4 year college	8,150	4,084	3,773	311	7.6	4,065
Race/ethnicity:						
White [3]						
Enrolled in high school	7,274	2,153	1,729	424	19.7	5,120
Enrolled in college	9,283	5,289	4,900	389	7.4	3,994
Black [3]						
Enrolled in high school	1,604	339	236	104	30.5	1,264
Enrolled in college	1,381	630	540	90	14.3	751
Asian [3]						
Enrolled in high school	349	66	57	9	([4])	283
Enrolled in college	680	238	223	16	6.6	441
Hispanic or Latino ethnicity						
Enrolled in high school	1,804	365	238	127	34.8	1,439
Enrolled in college	1,385	775	682	93	12.0	610
Not enrolled [2]						
White [3]	12,485	10,244	8,971	1,273	12.4	2,242
Black [3]	2,630	1,878	1,433	446	23.7	752
Asian [3]	435	320	297	23	7.3	114
Hispanic or Latino ethnicity	3,531	2,684	2,279	405	15.1	848

[1] Percent unemployed of civilian labor force in each category.   [2] Includes other races not shown separately.   [3] Data for persons in this race group only. See footnote 4, Table 575.   [4] Data not shown where base is less than 75,000.

Source: U.S. Bureau of Labor Statistics; College Enrollment and Work Activity of High School Graduates, News, USDL 09-0454, April 28, 2009. See also <http://www.bls.gov/news.release/hsgec.nro.htm>.

Table 583. Labor Force Participation Rates by Marital Status, Sex, and Age: 1970 to 2008

[For the civilian noninstitutional population 16 years old and over. Annual averages of monthly figures. See Table 580 for definition of participation rate. Based on Current Population Survey; see text, Section 1 and Appendix III]

Marital status and year	Male participation rate							Female participation rate						
	Total	16–19 years	20–24 years	25–34 years	35–44 years	45–64 years	65 years and over	Total	16–19 years	20–24 years	25–34 years	35–44 years	45–64 years	65 years and over
Single:														
1970	65.5	54.6	73.8	87.9	86.2	75.7	25.2	56.8	44.7	73.0	81.4	78.6	73.0	19.7
1980	72.6	59.9	81.3	89.2	82.2	66.9	16.8	64.4	53.6	75.2	83.3	76.9	65.6	13.9
1990 [1]	74.8	55.1	81.6	89.9	84.5	67.3	15.7	66.7	51.7	74.5	80.9	80.8	66.2	12.1
2000 [1]	73.6	52.5	80.5	89.4	82.9	69.7	17.3	68.9	51.1	76.1	83.9	80.9	69.9	10.8
2001	72.7	50.0	79.6	89.0	83.2	69.8	15.4	68.1	49.1	75.3	83.2	81.3	69.9	12.1
2002	71.7	47.2	78.7	88.7	83.1	69.6	16.9	67.4	47.3	74.5	83.3	79.9	69.6	14.3
2003 [1]	70.4	44.0	77.9	87.7	82.9	67.6	19.4	66.2	44.8	72.9	82.2	79.8	69.9	15.2
2004 [1]	70.2	43.6	77.7	87.9	82.7	67.8	20.3	65.9	43.8	73.1	81.8	80.5	70.9	14.7
2005 [1]	70.1	42.9	77.0	87.9	82.9	68.6	18.8	66.0	44.2	72.6	81.4	80.7	70.9	15.5
2006 [1]	70.7	43.4	77.8	87.7	83.5	69.9	19.3	65.7	43.7	71.8	81.4	79.8	70.5	15.0
2007 [1]	70.1	40.8	76.9	88.5	84.0	70.3	22.6	65.3	41.4	72.6	82.1	78.0	70.4	18.4
2008 [1]	69.9	39.8	77.1	87.9	84.3	69.5	24.7	65.3	40.3	71.9	82.6	79.6	70.4	20.5
Married: [2]														
1970	86.1	92.3	94.7	98.0	98.1	91.2	29.9	40.5	37.8	47.9	38.8	46.8	44.0	7.3
1980	80.9	91.3	96.9	97.5	97.2	84.3	20.5	49.8	49.3	61.4	58.8	61.8	46.9	7.3
1990 [1]	78.6	92.1	95.6	96.9	96.7	82.6	17.5	58.4	49.5	66.1	69.6	74.0	56.5	8.5
2000 [1]	77.3	79.5	94.1	96.7	95.8	83.0	19.2	61.1	53.2	63.8	70.3	74.8	65.4	10.1
2001	77.4	77.7	94.2	95.9	95.6	83.7	19.1	61.2	45.1	63.9	69.9	74.5	66.1	10.3
2002	77.4	81.1	93.3	95.7	95.1	83.8	19.4	61.0	49.6	63.4	69.3	73.8	66.5	10.7
2003 [1]	77.3	76.6	93.2	95.3	95.1	83.5	19.9	61.0	46.7	62.6	68.5	73.3	67.4	11.3
2004 [1]	77.1	77.4	92.4	95.6	95.1	83.1	20.4	60.5	41.1	60.9	67.6	72.7	67.0	11.6
2005 [1]	77.2	71.4	93.4	95.3	95.2	83.6	21.4	60.7	44.1	61.1	68.4	73.0	67.0	12.5
2006 [1]	77.1	79.2	93.3	95.5	95.2	83.6	21.8	61.0	39.6	59.8	68.6	73.8	67.8	12.4
2007 [1]	76.9	86.9	92.9	95.7	95.3	83.6	21.8	61.0	43.3	61.7	68.6	73.1	67.7	13.6
2008 [1]	76.8	83.4	92.0	95.3	95.2	84.0	22.8	61.4	38.0	62.3	69.5	73.8	68.3	14.1
Other: [3]														
1970	60.7	(B)	90.4	93.7	91.1	78.5	19.3	40.3	48.6	60.3	64.6	68.8	61.9	10.0
1980	66.0	(B)	92.6	94.1	91.9	73.3	13.7	43.6	50.0	68.4	76.5	77.1	60.2	8.2
1990 [1]	68.9	(B)	93.1	93.0	90.7	74.9	12.0	47.2	53.9	65.4	77.0	82.1	65.0	8.4
2000 [1]	66.8	60.5	88.1	93.2	89.9	73.9	12.9	49.0	46.0	74.0	83.1	82.9	69.8	8.7
2001	66.0	57.3	85.4	92.4	89.4	73.5	13.9	49.0	47.2	75.6	83.8	82.6	69.9	8.9
2002	65.5	57.5	87.4	91.2	89.6	74.1	13.2	49.2	46.2	74.7	80.7	82.7	69.7	8.9
2003 [1]	65.0	45.6	88.0	91.4	89.3	72.4	14.3	49.6	44.1	71.4	79.1	81.9	70.7	9.8
2004 [1]	64.9	53.1	87.2	90.6	88.6	72.8	14.3	49.6	48.7	70.0	79.4	81.7	69.8	10.4
2005 [1]	64.9	54.9	86.4	90.4	89.4	72.7	15.1	49.4	46.8	67.4	78.1	80.9	69.4	10.5
2006 [1]	65.6	47.8	86.0	91.5	88.9	73.8	16.3	49.6	45.3	71.5	78.2	80.9	69.3	10.9
2007 [1]	65.6	43.4	82.5	92.1	89.4	73.7	16.1	49.5	44.6	63.8	78.4	81.4	69.3	11.4
2008 [1]	65.0	43.2	84.9	90.7	89.4	73.2	16.8	49.2	39.7	64.9	77.4	81.4	69.1	12.1

B Percentage not shown where base is less than 35,000.   [1] See footnote 2, Table 574.   [2] Spouse present.   [3] Widowed, divorced, and married (spouse absent).

Source: U.S. Bureau of Labor Statistics, Bulletin 2217; and unpublished Basic Tabulations, Table 12.

Table 584. Marital Status of Women in the Civilian Labor Force: 1970 to 2008

[31,543 represents 31,543,000. For civilian noninstitutional population 16 years and over. Annual averages of monthly figures. Based on the Current Population Survey; see text, Section 1, and Appendix III]

Year	Female civilian labor force (1,000)				Female participation rate [3]			
	Total	Never married	Married [1]	Other [2]	Total	Never married	Married [1]	Other [2]
1970	31,543	7,265	18,475	5,804	43.3	56.8	40.5	40.3
1980	45,487	11,865	24,980	8,643	51.5	64.4	49.8	43.6
1985	51,050	13,163	27,894	9,993	54.5	66.6	53.8	45.1
1990 [4]	56,829	14,612	30,901	11,315	57.5	66.7	58.4	47.2
1995	60,944	15,467	33,359	12,118	58.9	66.8	61.0	47.4
2000 [4]	66,303	17,849	35,146	13,308	59.9	68.9	61.1	49.0
2001	66,848	18,021	35,236	13,592	59.8	68.1	61.2	49.0
2002	67,363	18,203	35,477	13,683	59.6	67.4	61.0	49.2
2003 [4]	68,272	18,397	36,046	13,828	59.5	66.2	61.0	49.6
2004 [4]	68,421	18,616	35,845	13,961	59.2	65.9	60.5	49.6
2005 [4]	69,288	19,183	35,941	14,163	59.3	66.0	60.7	49.4
2006 [4]	70,173	19,474	36,314	14,385	59.4	65.7	61.0	49.6
2007 [4]	70,988	19,745	36,881	14,362	59.3	65.3	61.0	49.5
2008 [4]	71,767	20,231	37,194	14,342	59.5	65.3	61.4	49.2

[1] Husband present.   [2] Widowed, divorced, or separated.   [3] See footnote 3, Table 580 for definition of participation rate.   [4] See footnote 2, Table 574.

Source: U.S. Bureau of Labor Statistics, Women in the Labor Force: A Databook, Report 1011, December 2008 and unpublished Basic Tabulations, Table 12. See also <http://www.bls.gov/cps/wlf-databook2008.htm>.

Labor Force, Employment, and Earnings   377

Table 585. Employment Status of Women by Marital Status and Presence and Age of Children: 1970 to 2007

[As of March (7.0 represents 7,000,000). Annual Social and Economic Supplement (ASEC) includes Civilian noninstitutional population, 16 years old and over. Based on the Current Population Survey; see text, Section 1 and Appendix III]

Item	Total Single	Total Married[1]	Total Other[2]	With any children Total Single	With any children Total Married[1]	With any children Total Other[2]	Children 6 to 17 yrs. only Single	Children 6 to 17 yrs. only Married[1]	Children 6 to 17 yrs. only Other[2]	Children under 6 yrs. Single	Children under 6 yrs. Married[1]	Children under 6 yrs. Other[2]
IN LABOR FORCE (mil.)												
1970	7.0	18.4	5.9	(NA)	10.2	1.9	(NA)	6.3	1.3	(NA)	3.9	0.6
1980	11.2	24.9	8.8	0.6	13.7	3.6	0.2	8.4	2.6	0.3	5.2	1.0
1990	14.0	31.0	11.2	1.5	16.5	4.2	0.6	9.3	3.0	0.9	7.2	1.2
1995	15.0	33.6	12.0	2.1	18.0	4.6	0.8	10.2	3.3	1.3	7.8	1.3
2000	17.8	35.0	13.2	3.1	18.2	4.5	1.2	10.8	3.4	1.8	7.3	1.1
2005 [3]	18.6	35.7	14.3	3.4	18.0	4.6	1.4	10.8	3.4	1.9	7.2	1.2
2006 [3]	19.0	36.2	14.2	3.3	18.1	4.6	1.4	10.7	3.5	1.9	7.4	1.1
2007 [3]	19.2	37.3	14.3	3.5	18.6	4.8	1.4	10.9	3.6	2.1	7.7	1.2
PARTICIPATION RATE [4]												
1970	53.0	40.8	39.1	(NA)	39.7	60.7	(NA)	49.2	66.9	(NA)	30.3	52.2
1980	61.5	50.1	44.0	52.0	54.1	69.4	67.6	61.7	74.6	44.1	45.1	60.3
1990	66.4	58.2	46.8	55.2	66.3	74.2	69.7	73.6	79.7	48.7	58.9	63.6
1995	65.5	61.1	47.3	57.5	70.2	75.3	67.0	76.2	79.5	53.0	63.5	66.3
2000	68.6	62.0	50.2	73.9	70.6	82.7	79.7	77.2	84.9	70.5	62.8	76.6
2005 [3]	65.1	60.2	49.8	72.9	68.1	79.8	79.7	75.0	82.2	68.5	59.8	73.5
2006 [3]	64.7	60.9	49.1	71.5	68.4	80.4	76.2	75.3	82.5	68.6	60.3	74.3
2007 [3]	64.7	61.6	49.5	71.4	69.3	80.0	78.0	76.2	82.9	67.4	61.5	72.2
EMPLOYMENT (mil.)												
1970	6.5	17.5	5.6	(NA)	9.6	1.8	(NA)	6.0	1.2	(NA)	3.6	0.6
1980	10.1	23.6	8.2	0.4	12.8	3.3	0.2	8.1	2.4	0.2	4.8	0.9
1990	12.9	29.9	10.5	1.2	15.8	3.8	0.5	8.9	2.7	0.7	6.9	1.1
1995	13.7	32.3	11.3	1.8	17.2	4.2	0.7	9.8	3.1	1.1	7.3	1.2
2000	16.4	34.0	12.7	2.7	17.6	4.3	1.1	10.6	3.2	1.6	7.1	1.1
2005 [3]	17.0	34.6	13.5	2.9	17.4	4.3	1.3	10.4	3.2	1.6	7.0	1.1
2006 [3]	17.4	35.2	13.5	2.9	17.5	4.3	1.2	10.4	3.3	1.7	7.1	1.0
2007 [3]	17.9	36.4	13.6	3.1	18.0	4.5	1.3	10.6	3.4	1.8	7.4	1.1
UNEMPLOYMENT RATE [5]												
1970	7.1	4.8	4.8	(NA)	6.0	7.2	(NA)	4.8	5.9	(NA)	7.9	9.8
1980	10.3	5.3	6.4	23.2	5.9	9.2	15.6	4.4	7.9	29.2	8.3	12.8
1990	8.2	3.5	5.7	18.4	4.2	8.5	14.5	3.8	7.7	20.8	4.8	10.2
1995	8.7	3.9	5.8	16.6	4.3	8.1	11.8	3.6	7.1	19.5	5.3	10.8
2000	7.3	2.7	4.3	11.0	2.9	5.1	8.7	2.6	4.8	12.6	3.5	5.9
2005 [3]	8.9	3.0	5.3	15.1	3.1	6.9	10.9	2.9	5.8	18.2	3.4	9.8
2006 [3]	8.1	2.8	4.8	12.7	3.2	6.2	10.4	2.8	5.4	14.2	3.7	8.9
2007 [3]	6.7	2.6	4.9	10.8	2.8	6.0	9.8	2.5	5.3	11.6	3.4	8.1

NA Not available.   [1] Husband present.   [2] Widowed, divorced, or separated.   [3] See footnote 2, Table 574.   [4] Percent of women in each specific category in the labor force.   [5] Unemployed as a percent of civilian labor force in specified group.

Source: U.S. Bureau of Labor Statistics, Bulletin 2307 and unpublished data.

Table 586. Labor Force Participation Rates for Wives, Husband Present by Age of Own Youngest Child: 1990 to 2007

[As of March. Annual Social and Economic Supplement (ASEC) includes Civilian noninstitutional population, 16 years old and over, and military personnel who live in households with at least one other civilian adult. Based on Current Population Survey; see text, Section 1 and Appendix III]

Presence and age of child	1990 total	2000 [1] total	2005 [1] total	2006 [1] total	2007 [1] Total	2007 [1] White [2]	2007 [1] Black [2]	2007 [1] Asian [2,3]	2007 [1] Hispanic [4]
Wives, total	58.3	62.2	60.4	61.1	61.8	61.3	68.3	60.2	55.4
No children under 18 years.	51.1	54.8	54.1	55.1	55.7	55.5	58.3	56.4	52.1
With children under 18 years	66.5	70.9	68.3	68.5	69.4	68.9	78.8	63.4	57.1
Under 6 years, total	59.1	63.1	60.3	60.6	61.6	60.9	72.2	55.4	48.4
Under 3 years	55.9	59.4	57.3	58.2	58.8	58.3	68.8	51.4	44.2
1 year or under	53.9	58.4	55.8	56.7	57.8	57.6	65.8	48.9	42.8
2 years	60.9	61.9	60.8	62.0	61.4	60.0	75.7	57.9	47.1
3 to 5 years	64.1	68.6	64.8	64.1	65.6	64.7	76.6	60.1	54.2
3 years	63.0	66.0	62.7	60.8	64.4	64.5	78.4	47.4	52.9
4 years	65.0	69.6	64.9	65.7	63.4	62.0	71.5	67.8	55.9
5 years	64.4	70.7	67.5	66.3	69.4	68.0	79.8	72.4	54.2
6 to 13 years	73.1	76.0	73.2	74.1	74.5	73.9	84.7	69.6	65.8
14 to 17 years	75.0	80.8	79.6	78.2	79.8	80.0	81.5	75.1	71.1

[1] See footnote 2, Table 574.   [2] For persons in this race group only. See footnote 4, Table 575.   [3] Excludes Pacific Islanders.   [4] Persons of Hispanic or Latino origin may be any race.

Source: U.S. Bureau of Labor Statistics, Bulletin 2307 and unpublished data.

Table 587. Married-Couple Households by Labor Force Status of Spouse: 1990 to 2008

[52,317 represents 52,317,000. Data represent married couple households. Based on the Current Population Survey; for details see source and Appendix III]

Year	Number (1,000)					Percent distribution			
	All married couples	In labor force			Husband and wife not in labor force	In labor force			Husband and wife not in labor force
		Husband and wife	Husband only	Wife only		Husband and wife	Husband only	Wife only	
TOTAL									
1990	52,317	28,056	13,013	2,453	8,794	53.6	24.9	4.7	16.8
2000	55,311	31,095	11,815	3,301	9,098	56.2	21.4	6.0	16.4
2001	56,592	31,794	12,213	3,274	9,311	56.2	21.6	5.8	16.5
2002	56,747	31,637	12,327	3,388	9,395	55.8	21.7	6.0	16.6
2003	57,320	31,951	12,443	3,553	9,373	55.7	21.7	6.2	16.4
2004	57,719	31,536	12,980	3,684	9,519	54.6	22.5	6.4	16.5
2005	57,975	31,398	13,385	3,641	9,551	54.2	23.1	6.3	16.5
2006	58,179	31,783	12,990	3,754	9,652	54.6	22.3	6.5	16.6
2007	60,676	33,337	13,351	4,031	9,958	54.9	22.0	6.6	16.4
2008	60,129	32,988	13,141	4,118	9,882	54.8	21.8	6.8	16.4
WITH CHILDREN UNDER 18									
1990	24,537	15,768	7,667	558	544	64.3	31.2	2.3	2.2
2000	25,248	17,116	6,950	795	387	67.8	27.5	3.1	1.5
2001	25,980	17,563	7,210	784	422	67.6	27.8	3.0	1.6
2002	25,792	17,233	7,301	777	482	66.8	28.3	3.0	1.9
2003	25,914	17,065	7,499	893	457	65.9	28.9	3.4	1.8
2004	25,793	16,691	7,715	952	433	64.7	29.9	3.7	1.7
2005	25,919	16,789	7,806	925	400	64.8	30.1	3.6	1.5
2006	25,982	16,909	7,754	900	420	65.1	29.9	3.5	1.6
2007	26,802	17,670	7,743	920	469	65.9	28.9	3.4	1.7
2008	25,778	16,977	7,398	932	471	65.9	28.7	3.6	1.8
WITH CHILDREN UNDER 6									
1990	12,051	6,932	4,692	192	235	57.5	38.9	1.6	2.0
2000	11,393	6,984	4,077	211	121	61.3	35.8	1.9	1.1
2001	11,732	7,054	4,296	247	134	60.1	36.6	2.1	1.1
2002	11,531	6,796	4,311	250	175	58.9	37.4	2.2	1.5
2003	11,743	6,747	4,507	298	191	57.5	38.4	2.5	1.6
2004	11,711	6,657	4,579	317	158	56.8	39.1	2.7	1.3
2005	11,802	6,813	4,553	299	137	57.7	38.6	2.5	1.2
2006	11,984	6,939	4,572	324	149	57.9	38.2	2.7	1.2
2007	12,468	7,337	4,633	331	167	58.8	37.2	2.7	1.3
2008	11,848	6,976	4,382	321	168	58.9	37.1	2.7	1.4

Source: U.S. Census Bureau, "Table MC-1, Married Couples by Labor Force Status of Spouses: 1986 to Present"; <http://www.census.gov/population/www/socdemo/hh-fam.html>.

Table 588. Employed Civilians and Weekly Hours: 1980 to 2008

[In thousands (99,303 represents 99,303.000), except as indicated. Annual averages of monthly figures. Civilian noninstitutional population 16 years old and over. Based on Current Population Survey; see text, Section 1 and Appendix III]

Item	1980	1990 [1]	2000 [1]	2005 [1]	2006 [1]	2007 [1]	2008 [1]
Total employed	99,303	118,793	136,891	141,730	144,427	146,047	145,362
Age:							
16 to 19 years old	7,710	6,581	7,189	5,978	6,162	5,911	5,573
20 to 24 years old	14,087	13,401	13,229	13,792	13,878	13,964	13,629
25 to 34 years old	27,204	33,935	31,549	30,680	31,051	31,586	31,383
35 to 44 years old	19,523	30,817	36,433	34,630	34,569	34,302	33,457
45 to 54 years old	16,234	19,525	30,310	33,207	34,052	34,562	34,529
55 to 64 years old	11,586	11,189	14,002	18,349	19,389	20,108	20,812
65 years old and over.	2,960	3,346	4,179	5,094	5,325	5,613	5,979
Class of worker:							
Nonagricultural industries . .[2]	95,938	115,570	134,427	139,532	142,221	143,952	143,194
Wage and salary worker [2]	88,525	106,598	125,114	129,931	132,449	134,283	133,882
Self-employed	7,000	8,719	9,205	9,509	9,685	9,557	9,219
Unpaid family workers	413	253	108	93	87	112	93
Agriculture and related industries	3,364	3,223	2,464	2,197	2,206	2,095	2,168
Wage and salary worker [2]	1,425	1,740	1,421	1,212	1,287	1,220	1,279
Self-employed	1,642	1,378	1,010	955	901	856	860
Unpaid family workers	297	105	33	30	18	19	28
Weekly hours:							
Nonagricultural industries:							
Wage and salary workers [2].	38.1	39.2	39.6	39.1	39.2	39.2	39.0
Self-employed	41.2	40.8	39.7	38.4	38.4	38.0	37.0
Unpaid family workers	34.7	34.0	32.5	32.2	32.7	33.4	33.4
Agriculture and related industries:							
Wage and salary workers [2].	41.6	41.2	43.2	43.6	42.8	42.1	42.3
Self-employed	49.3	46.8	45.3	44.0	43.8	45.2	44.2
Unpaid family workers	38.6	38.5	38.3	41.1	33.1	32.7	41.0

[1] See footnote 2, Table 574.   [2] Includes the incorporated self-employed.

Source: U.S. Bureau of Labor Statistics, "Employment and Earnings Online," January 2009; <http://www.bls.gov /opub/ee/home.htm> and <http://www.bls.gov/cps/home.htm>.

Labor Force, Employment, and Earnings   379

Table 589. **Persons at Work by Hours Worked: 2008**

[In thousands (139,824 represents 139,824,000), except as indicated. Persons "at work" are a subgroup of employed persons "at work," excluding those absent from their jobs during reference period for reasons such as vacation, illness, or industrial dispute. Annual averages of monthly figures. Civilian noninstitutional population 16 years old and over. Based on Current Population Survey; see text, Section 1, and Appendix III. See headnote, Table 592, regarding industries]

Hours of work	Persons at work (1,000)			Percent distribution		
	Total	Agriculture and related industries	Non-agricultural industries	Total	Agriculture and related industries	Non-agricultural industries
Total.....................	**139,824**	**2,085**	**137,739**	**100.0**	**100.0**	**100.0**
1 to 34 hours...................	33,384	548	32,836	23.9	26.3	23.8
1 to 4 hours..................	1,415	43	1,371	1.0	2.1	1.0
5 to 14 hours.................	5,216	124	5,091	3.7	6.0	3.7
15 to 29 hours................	16,487	256	16,232	11.8	12.3	11.8
30 to 34 hours................	10,267	125	10,141	7.3	6.0	7.4
35 hours and over	106,439	1,536	104,903	76.1	73.7	76.2
35 to 39 hours................	9,656	93	9,563	6.9	4.5	6.9
40 hours.....................	59,732	570	59,162	42.7	27.3	43.0
41 hours and over.............	37,052	874	36,178	26.5	41.9	26.3
41 to 48 hours	13,014	145	12,870	9.3	6.9	9.3
49 to 59 hours	14,102	256	13,846	10.1	12.3	10.1
60 hours and over	9,935	473	9,462	7.1	22.7	6.9
Average weekly hours: Persons at work . . .	38.9	43.0	38.8	(X)	(X)	(X)
Persons usually working full-time [1]	42.6	48.7	42.5	(X)	(X)	(X)

X Not applicable. [1] Full-time workers are those who usually worked 35 hours or more (at all jobs combined).

Source: U.S. Bureau of Labor Statistics, "Employment and Earnings Online," January 2009; <http://www.bls.gov/opub/ee/home.htm> and <http://www.bls.gov/cps/home.htm>.

Table 590. **Persons With a Job, But Not at Work: 1980 to 2008**

[In thousands (5,881 represents 5,881,000), except percent. For civilian noninstitutional population 16 years old and over. Annual averages of monthly figures. Based on Current Population Survey; see text, Section 1 and Appendix III]

Reason for not working	1980	1990 [1]	2000 [1]	2001	2002	2003 [1]	2004 [1]	2005 [1]	2006 [1]	2007 [1]	2008 [1]
All industries, number	**5,881**	**6,160**	**5,681**	**5,631**	**5,394**	**5,469**	**5,482**	**5,511**	**5,746**	**5,719**	**5,539**
Percent of employed	5.9	5.2	4.2	4.1	4.0	4.0	3.9	3.9	4.0	3.9	3.8
Reason for not working:											
Vacation................	3,320	3,529	3,109	3,039	2,929	2,922	2,923	2,892	3,101	3,056	2,916
Illness	1,426	1,341	1,156	1,095	1,072	1,090	1,058	1,088	1,096	1,064	1,026
Bad weather	155	90	89	100	97	123	133	145	117	140	141
Industrial dispute	105	24	14	9	7	18	10	6	7	10	7
All other	876	1,177	1,313	1,388	1,289	1,316	1,358	1,381	1,425	1,449	1,449

[1] See footnote 2, Table 574.

Source: U.S. Bureau of Labor Statistics, Current Population Survey, unpublished data; <http://www.bls.gov/cps/home.htm>.

Table 591. **Class of Worker by Sex and Selected Characteristic: 2008**

[In percent, except as indicated (10,079 represents 10,079,000). Civilian noninstitutional population 16 years old and over. Annual averages of monthly figures. Based on Current Population Survey; see text, Section 1 and Appendix III]

Characteristic	Unincorporated self-employed			Incorporated self-employed			Wage and salary workers[1]		
	Total	Male	Female	Total	Male	Female	Total	Male	Female
Total (1,000)	**10,079**	**6,373**	**3,707**	**5,784**	**4,223**	**1,561**	**129,377**	**66,846**	**62,531**
PERCENT DISTRIBUTION	100.0	100.0	100.0	100.0	100.0	100.0	100.0	100.0	100.0
Age: 16 to 19 years old	0.7	0.8	0.6	0.1	0.1	0.1	4.2	4.0	4.5
20 to 24 years old	3.1	3.4	2.6	1.2	1.2	1.3	10.2	10.3	10.2
25 to 34 years old	14.4	14.5	14.2	11.2	11.2	11.1	22.6	23.6	21.6
35 to 44 years old	22.7	22.1	23.7	24.9	24.5	25.8	23.0	23.4	22.5
45 to 54 years old	28.1	27.8	28.7	32.6	32.2	33.6	23.0	22.4	23.7
55 to 64 years old	21.0	21.0	21.0	21.5	21.7	21.0	13.5	13.0	14.0
65 years old and over	10.0	10.5	9.2	8.5	9.0	7.2	3.5	3.3	3.6
Race/ethnicity: White [2].	87.4	88.1	86.2	88.2	89.0	86.2	81.2	82.6	79.8
Black [2]	6.2	6.1	6.4	5.1	4.8	6.0	11.6	10.2	13.1
Asian [2] .,...............	4.4	4.0	5.2	5.6	5.3	6.5	4.7	4.8	4.7
Hispanic [3]	12.2	13.8	9.3	7.3	7.3	7.2	14.4	16.5	12.2
Country of birth: U.S. born	83.1	81.9	85.2	(NA)	(NA)	(NA)	(NA)	(NA)	(NA)
Foreign born...............	16.9	18.1	14.8	(NA)	(NA)	(NA)	(NA)	(NA)	(NA)

NA Not available. [1] Excludes the incorporated self-employed. [2] For persons in this race group only. [3] Persons of Hispanic or Latino origin may be any race.

Source: U.S. Bureau of Labor Statistics, Current Population Survey, unpublished data.

Table 592. **Self-Employed Workers by Industry and Occupation: 2000 to 2008**

[In thousands (10,214 represents 10,214,000). Civilian noninstitutional population 16 years old and over. Annual averages of monthly figures. Data represent the unincorporated self-employed; the incorporated self-employed are considered wage and salary workers. Based on the occupational and industrial classification derived from those used in the 2000 census. See text, this section. Based on the Current Population Survey; see text, section 1, and Appendix III]

Item	2000	2004 [1]	2005 [1]	2006 [1]	2007 [1]	2008 [1]
Total self-employed	**10,214**	**10,431**	**10,464**	**10,586**	**10,413**	**10,080**
Industry:						
Agriculture and related industries	1,010	964	955	901	856	860
Mining	12	13	11	10	19	15
Construction	1,728	1,848	1,830	1,910	1,890	1,817
Manufacturing	334	316	327	326	348	308
Wholesale and retail trade	1,221	1,153	1,251	1,139	1,116	1,059
Transportation and utilities	348	410	442	428	405	405
Information	139	146	126	120	135	125
Financial activities [2]	735	792	785	841	829	749
Professional and business services [2]	1,927	1,993	1,957	1,992	2,009	1,980
Education and health services [2]	1,107	1,105	1,071	1,158	1,102	1,071
Leisure and hospitality [2]	660	660	674	685	679	693
Other services [3]	993	1,031	1,036	1,076	1,026	997
Occupation:						
Management, professional, and related occupations . . .	4,169	4,179	4,085	4,069	4,024	4,043
Service occupations	1,775	1,757	1,774	1,905	1,872	1,847
Sales and office occupations	1,982	1,909	1,986	1,971	1,936	1,771
Natural resources, construction, and maintenance occupations	1,591	1,847	1,864	1,879	1,860	1,707
Production, transportation, and material moving occupations	698	739	756	763	721	712

[1] See footnote 2, Table 574.   [2] For composition of industries, see Table 612.   [3] Includes private households.

Source: U.S. Bureau of Labor Statistics, "Employment and Earnings Online," January 2009 issue; <http://www.bls.gov/opub/ee/home.htm> and <http://www.bls.gov/cps/home.htm>.

Table 593. **Type of Work Flexibility Provided to Employees: 2008**

[In percent. The National Study of Employers does not ask employers to report on whether they have "written policies," but rather whether their organization "allows employees to" or "provides the following benefits or programs." The wording is used for two reasons. First, employers may have written policies, but not "allow" employees to use them. Second, smaller employers are less likely to have written policies than larger ones. For methodology, see source]

Type of work flexibility provided (to employee)	Employer allows all or most employees	Employer size	
		50 to 99 employees	1,000 or more employees
FLEX TIME AND PLACE			
Periodically change starting and quitting times within some range of hours	37	40	37
Change starting and quitting times on a daily basis	10	11	7
Compress workweek by working longer hours on fewer days for at least part of the year	8	10	5
Work some regular paid hours at home occasionally	3	3	2
Work some regular paid hours at home on regular basis	1	1	1
CHOICES IN MANAGING TIME			
Have control over when to take breaks	55	54	51
Have choices about and control over which shifts to work	16	16	16
Have control over paid and unpaid overtime hours	13	14	15
REDUCED TIME			
Move from full time to part time and back again while remaining in same position or level	13	12	12
Share jobs	8	9	5
Work part year (work reduced time on annual basis)	11	10	11
CAREGIVING LEAVE			
Return to work gradually after childbirth or adoption	57	56	54
TIME OFF			
Family or personal time off without loss of pay	45	46	47
Compensatory time off program	18	21	9
Do volunteer work during regular work hours	21	24	20
FLEX CAREERS			
Phase into retirement by working reduced hours over time prior to full retirement	25	25	20
Take sabbaticals (paid or unpaid for six months or more)	21	24	14
Take paid or unpaid time off for education or job training skills	40	41	33
Take extended career breaks for caregiving or other personal or family reasons	47	48	44
Receive special consideration when returning to the organization after an extended career break	28	29	21

Source: Families and Work Institute, "2008 National Study of Employers" (copyright); <http://familiesandwork.org/site/research/reports/main.html>.

U.S. Census Bureau, Statistical Abstract of the United States: 2010

Table 594. **Persons on Flexible Schedules: 2004**

[In thousands, except percent. (99,778 represents 99,778,000.) As of May. For employed full-time wage and salary workers 16 years old and over. Excludes all self-employed persons, regardless of whether or not their businesses were incorporated. Data related to the primary job. Based on the Current Population Survey; see text, Section 1 and Appendix III]

Item	Total			Male			Female		
		With flexible schedules [2]			With flexible schedules			With flexible schedules [2]	
	Total [1]	Number	Percent	Total [1]	Number	Percent	Total [1]	Number	Percent
Total	99,778	27,411	27.5	56,412	15,853	28.1	43,366	11,558	26.7
AGE									
16 to 19 years old.	1,427	336	23.6	903	185	20.5	524	151	28.9
20 years and over.	98,351	27,075	27.5	55,509	15,668	28.2	42,842	11,406	26.6
20 to 24 years old	9,004	2,058	22.9	5,147	1,065	20.7	3,856	993	25.8
25 to 34 years old	24,640	6,902	28.0	14,358	4,051	28.2	10,283	2,851	27.7
35 to 44 years old	26,766	7,807	29.2	15,424	4,605	29.9	11,342	3,202	28.2
45 to 54 years old	24,855	6,651	26.8	13,440	3,769	28.0	11,415	2,882	25.2
55 to 64 years old	11,745	3,181	27.1	6,383	1,865	29.2	5,361	1,316	24.5
65 years old and over	1,341	475	35.4	757	314	41.4	585	161	27.6
RACE AND HISPANIC ORIGIN									
White [3]	80,498	23,121	28.7	46,222	13,582	29.4	34,276	9,539	27.8
Black [3]	12,578	2,476	19.7	6,447	1,193	18.5	6,131	1,283	20.9
Asian [3]	4,136	1,132	27.4	2,300	720	31.3	1,836	412	22.4
Hispanic origin [4]	14,110	2,596	18.4	8,621	1,430	16.6	5,489	1,166	21.2
MARITAL STATUS									
Married, spouse present.	57,630	16,270	28.2	34,926	10,382	29.7	22,704	5,888	25.9
Not married	42,148	11,141	26.4	21,486	5,471	25.5	20,662	5,670	27.4
Never married.	25,144	6,693	26.6	14,469	3,605	24.9	10,676	3,088	28.9
Other marital status	17,004	4,448	26.2	7,018	1,866	26.6	9,986	2,582	25.9
PRESENCE AND AGE OF CHILDREN									
Without own children under 18	61,761	16,759	27.1	34,680	9,410	27.1	27,081	7,349	27.1
With own children under 18	38,018	10,652	28.0	21,733	6,443	29.6	16,285	4,209	25.8
With youngest child 6 to 17.	21,739	5,960	27.4	11,477	3,341	29.1	10,262	2,619	25.5
With youngest child under 6	16,279	4,692	28.8	10,256	3,102	30.2	6,023	1,590	26.4

[1] Includes persons who did not provide information on flexible schedules. [2] Allowed to vary or make changes when work begins or ends. [3] For persons in the race group only. See footnote 4, Table 575. [4] Persons of Hispanic origin may be any race.

Source: U.S. Bureau of Labor Statistics, *Workers on Flexible and Shift Schedules in May 2004, News*, USDL 05-1198, July 1, 2005. See also <http://www.bls.gov/bls/newsrels.htm#OEUS>.

Table 595. **Employed Workers With Alternative and Traditional Work Arrangements: 2005**

[In thousands (138,952 represents 138,952,000). As of February. For employed workers 16 years old and over. Based on the Current Population Survey; see text, Section 1 and Appendix III]

Characteristic	Total employed [1]	Workers with alternative arrangements				Workers with traditional arrangements
		Independent contractors	On-call workers	Temporary help agency workers	Workers provided by contract firms	
Total employed.	138,952	10,342	2,454	1,217	813	123,843
16 to 19 years old.	5,510	89	133	33	7	5,194
20 to 24 years old.	13,114	356	355	202	87	12,055
25 to 34 years old.	30,103	1,520	535	362	205	27,427
35 to 44 years old.	34,481	2,754	571	253	196	30,646
45 to 54 years old.	32,947	2,799	417	200	186	29,324
55 to 64 years old.	17,980	1,943	267	135	114	15,496
65 years old and over	4,817	881	175	33	18	3,701
Male.	73,946	6,696	1,241	574	561	64,673
16 to 19 years old	2,579	32	82	24	7	2,389
20 to 24 years old	6,928	194	200	107	61	6,331
25 to 34 years old	16,624	1,006	299	185	138	14,950
35 to 44 years old	18,523	1,824	252	120	140	16,130
45 to 54 years old	17,193	1,764	209	71	143	15,003
55 to 64 years old	9,485	1,287	108	52	70	7,954
65 years old and over	2,615	589	91	16	3	1,917
Female	65,006	3,647	1,212	643	252	59,170
16 to 19 years old	2,931	57	52	9	–	2,805
20 to 24 years old	6,186	162	155	95	27	5,724
25 to 34 years old	13,480	514	236	177	67	12,477
35 to 44 years old	15,958	930	319	133	57	14,516
45 to 54 years old	15,754	1,035	208	129	43	14,322
55 to 64 years old	8,495	656	158	83	44	7,542
65 years old and over	2,202	292	84	17	15	1,785
Full-time workers	113,798	7,732	1,370	979	695	102,889
Part-time workers.	25,154	2,611	1,084	238	119	20,954

– Represents zero. [1] Includes day laborers (an alternative arrangement) and a small number of workers who were both "on call" and "provided by contract firms," not shown separately.

Source: U.S. Bureau of Labor Statistics, *Contingent and Alternative Employment Arrangements, February 2005, News*, USDL 05-1443, July 27, 2005. See also <http://www.bls.gov/bls/newsrels.htm#OEUS>.

382   Labor Force, Employment, and Earnings

Table 596. **Multiple Jobholders: 2008**

[**Annual average of monthly figures (7,620 represents 7,620,000).** Civilian noninstitutional population 16 years old and over. Multiple jobholders are employed persons who, either 1) had jobs as wage or salary workers with two employers or more; 2) were self-employed and also held a wage and salary job; or 3) were unpaid family workers on their primary jobs but also held a wage and salary job. Based on the Current Population Survey; see text, Section 1 and Appendix III]

Characteristic	Total		Male		Female	
	Number (1,000)	Percent of employed	Number (1,000)	Percent of employed	Number (1,000)	Percent of employed
Total [1]	7,620	5.2	3,837	5.0	3,783	5.6
Age:						
16 to 19 years old	225	4.0	94	3.4	131	4.6
20 to 24 years old	752	5.5	329	4.6	423	6.5
25 to 54 years old	5,354	5.4	2,746	5.1	2,608	5.7
55 to 64 years old	1,067	5.1	539	4.9	528	5.3
65 years old and over	223	3.7	129	3.9	94	3.5
Race and Hispanic ethnicity:						
White [2]	6,405	5.4	3,255	5.0	3,151	5.8
Black [2]	756	4.7	371	5.0	385	4.5
Asian [2]	254	3.7	118	3.2	136	4.2
Hispanic [3]	671	3.3	377	3.1	294	3.6
Marital status:						
Married, spouse present	4,166	5.1	2,386	5.2	1,780	5.0
Widowed, divorced, or separated	1,365	5.9	462	4.8	903	6.7
Single, never married	2,089	5.2	989	4.5	1,100	5.9
Full- or part-time status:						
Primary job full-time, secondary job part-time . .	4,165	(X)	2,289	(X)	1,876	(X)
Both jobs part-time	1,791	(X)	588	(X)	1,203	(X)
Both jobs full-time	284	(X)	192	(X)	92	(X)
Hours vary on primary or secondary job	1,338	(X)	747	(X)	591	(X)

X Not applicable.   [1] Includes a small number of persons who work part-time on their primary job and full-time on their secondary job(s), not shown separately. Includes other races not shown separately.   [2] For persons who selected this race group only. See footnote 4, Table 575.   [3] Persons of Hispanic or Latino ethnicity may be any race.

Source: U.S. Bureau of Labor Statistics, "Employment and Earnings Online," January 2009; <http://www.bls.gov/opub/ee/home.htm>; and <http://www.bls.gov/cps/home.htm>.

Table 597. **Average Number of Jobs Held From Ages 18 to 42: 1978 to 2006**

[**For persons aged 41 to 50 in 2006–07.** A job is an uninterrupted period of work with a particular employer. Educational attainment as of 2006–07. Based on the National Longitudinal Survey of Youth 1979; see source for details]

Sex and educational attainment	Total [1]	Number of jobs held by age				
		18 to 22 years old	23 to 27 years old	28 to 32 years old	33 to 37 years old	38 to 42 years old
Total [2]	10.8	4.4	3.3	2.6	2.2	1.9
Less than a high school diploma	10.9	3.9	3.2	2.6	2.2	1.9
High school graduates, no college	10.5	4.2	3.1	2.6	2.2	1.9
Some college or associate's degree	11.1	4.5	3.4	2.7	2.3	2.0
Bachelor's degree or more	11.1	5.0	3.6	2.6	2.1	1.9
Male	11.0	4.6	3.5	2.8	2.3	2.0
Less than a high school diploma	12.5	4.6	3.8	3.0	2.4	2.0
High school graduate, no college	10.7	4.5	3.4	2.8	2.2	1.9
Some college or associate's degree	11.1	4.5	3.5	2.8	2.4	2.0
Bachelor's degree or more	10.7	4.6	3.4	2.6	2.2	1.9
Female	10.6	4.3	3.1	2.4	2.1	1.9
Less than a high school diploma	8.7	2.9	2.3	2.1	1.9	1.6
High school graduate, no college	10.2	3.9	2.7	2.3	2.2	1.9
Some college or associate's degree	11.0	4.5	3.3	2.5	2.2	1.9
Bachelor's degree or more	11.5	5.3	3.7	2.6	2.0	1.8
White, non-Hispanic	10.9	4.6	3.3	2.6	2.2	1.9
Less than a high school diploma	11.5	4.2	3.3	2.7	2.3	1.9
High school graduate, no college	10.4	4.4	3.1	2.6	2.2	1.9
Some college or associate's degree	11.3	4.7	3.4	2.7	2.3	1.9
Bachelor's degree or more	11.1	5.1	3.6	2.6	2.1	1.8
Black, non-Hispanic	10.4	3.6	3.1	2.6	2.3	2.0
Less than a high school diploma	9.8	2.9	2.9	2.6	2.0	1.8
High school graduate, no college	10.6	3.5	3.0	2.6	2.3	2.0
Some college or associate's degree	10.4	3.8	3.1	2.7	2.4	2.1
Bachelor's degree or more	10.9	4.2	3.6	2.8	2.4	2.2
Hispanic or Latino [3]	10.5	4.1	3.0	2.5	2.2	1.9
Less than a high school diploma	10.4	4.0	2.8	2.4	2.0	1.7
High school graduate, no college	10.6	4.0	3.0	2.5	2.2	1.9
Some college or associate's degree	10.3	4.2	3.0	2.5	2.2	2.1
Bachelor's degree or more	10.7	4.4	3.3	2.7	2.3	1.9

[1] Jobs held in more than one age category were counted in each category, but only once in the total.   [2] Includes other races not shown separately.   [3] Persons of Hispanic or Latino origin may be any race.

Source: U.S. Bureau of Labor Statistics, Number of Jobs Held, Labor Market Activity, and *Earnings Growth Among the Youngest Baby Boomers: Results from a Longitudinal Survey, News,* USDL 08-0860, June 27, 2008. See also <http://www.bls.gov/nls/home.htm>.

Labor Force, Employment, and Earnings   **383**

Table 598. Distribution of Workers by Tenure With Current Employer: 2008

[129,276 represents 129,276,000. As of January. For employed wage and salary workers 16 years old and over. Data exclude the incorporated and unincorporated self-employed. Based on the Current Population Survey, see source and Appendix III]

Characteristic	Number employed (1,000)	Percent distribution by tenure with current employer									Median years [1]
		12 months or less	13 to 23 months	2 years	3 to 4 years	5 to 9 years	10 to 14 years	15 to 19 years	20 years or more	
Total [2]	129,276	22.9	7.4	5.6	16.9	20.2	10.6	6.2	10.3	4.1
AGE AND SEX										
16 to 19 years old	5,200	73.8	11.5	7.5	7.0	0.3	–	–	–	(NA)
20 to 24 years old	13,139	49.9	13.2	10.2	20.4	6.4	(Z)	–	–	1.3
25 to 34 years old	29,097	28.2	10.4	8.5	23.4	23.5	5.4	0.6	(Z)	2.7
35 to 44 years old	30,150	17.1	6.6	4.8	18.1	25.3	15.3	8.2	4.5	4.9
45 to 54 years old	30,151	12.9	4.4	3.5	13.7	21.6	14.4	9.9	19.4	7.6
55 to 64 years old	17,242	9.4	4.3	2.6	11.2	19.7	14.1	10.9	27.8	9.9
65 years old and over	4,297	8.9	2.5	2.8	10.6	18.9	16.6	10.4	29.2	10.2
Male	66,660	22.4	6.9	5.6	16.9	19.9	10.7	6.1	11.5	4.2
16 to 19 years old	2,423	72.5	11.8	8.4	7.0	0.3	–	–	–	(NA)
20 to 24 years old	6,856	49.6	12.2	10.2	21.3	6.6	–	–	–	1.4
25 to 34 years old	15,709	27.4	9.7	8.3	23.3	24.6	5.8	0.9	(Z)	2.8
35 to 44 years old	15,755	16.7	6.0	4.8	17.6	24.4	16.6	8.7	5.3	5.2
45 to 54 years old	15,289	12.7	3.9	3.3	13.1	20.4	14.0	10.0	22.7	8.2
55 to 64 years old	8,513	8.5	4.7	2.3	11.6	18.8	13.4	9.9	30.7	10.1
65 years old and over	2,115	8.5	2.7	2.0	10.5	17.6	15.8	9.1	33.9	10.4
Female	62,616	23.5	7.8	5.7	16.9	20.4	10.5	6.2	9.0	3.9
16 to 19 years old	2,776	74.9	11.2	6.8	6.9	0.3	–	–	–	(NA)
20 to 24 years old	6,283	50.2	14.2	10.1	19.3	6.1	0.1	–	–	1.3
25 to 34 years old	13,388	29.2	11.2	8.6	23.5	22.3	5.0	0.3	–	2.6
35 to 44 years old	14,395	17.5	7.4	4.8	18.7	26.3	13.9	7.6	3.8	4.7
45 to 54 years old	14,862	13.2	5.1	3.8	14.4	22.9	15.0	9.8	16.0	7.0
55 to 64 years old	8,729	10.3	3.9	2.8	10.8	20.5	14.9	11.8	25.1	9.8
65 years old and over	2,182	9.3	2.3	3.6	10.6	20.3	17.4	11.7	24.7	9.9
RACE AND HISPANIC ORIGIN										
White [3]	105,246	22.6	7.3	5.4	16.4	20.2	10.8	6.4	10.8	4.2
Male	55,008	22.0	6.8	5.4	16.5	19.8	10.9	6.4	12.2	4.4
Female	50,238	23.2	7.9	5.5	16.3	20.6	10.7	6.4	9.3	4.0
Black [3]	14,497	24.5	7.1	6.8	18.0	19.7	10.3	4.7	8.8	3.6
Male	6,704	25.4	7.2	6.7	17.0	19.5	10.6	4.0	9.6	3.5
Female	7,793	23.7	7.0	6.9	18.9	19.9	10.1	5.4	8.2	3.7
Asian [3]	6,283	21.5	7.6	5.4	21.8	22.4	9.6	5.5	6.2	3.7
Male	3,316	19.8	7.5	5.0	23.2	24.0	9.5	5.6	5.4	3.9
Female	2,967	23.4	7.7	5.8	20.3	20.5	9.7	5.3	7.2	3.5
Hispanic origin [4]	18,645	26.9	7.1	7.2	19.9	20.2	9.3	4.5	4.9	3.2
Male	10,886	25.9	6.3	7.6	20.5	20.1	9.2	4.8	5.6	3.3
Female	7,759	28.3	8.2	6.8	19.1	20.4	9.4	4.0	3.9	3.1

– Represents zero.   NA Not available.   Z Less that .05 percent.   [1] For definition of median, see Guide to Tabular Presentation.   [2] Includes other races, not shown separately.   [3] For persons in this race group only. See footnote 4, Table 575.   [4] Persons of Hispanic or Latino origin may be any race.

Source: U. S. Bureau of Labor Statistics, News, *Employee Tenure in 2008, News*, USDL 08-1344, September 26, 2008. See also <http://www.bls.gov/news.release/tenure.toc.htm>.

Table 599. Part-Time Workers by Reason: 2008

[In thousands (33,384 represents 33,384,000), except hours. For persons working 1 to 34 hours per week. For civilian noninstitutional population 16 years old and over. Annual average of monthly figures. Based on the Current Population Survey, see text, Section 1 and Appendix III]

Reason	All industries			Nonagriculture industries			
	Total	Usually work—			Total	Usually work—	
		Full-time	Part-time		Full-time	Part-time
Total working fewer than 35 hours	33,384	10,426	22,959	32,836	10,256	22,580
Economic reasons	5,875	2,259	3,616	5,773	2,198	3,575
Slack work or business conditions	4,169	2,006	2,163	4,097	1,962	2,135
Could find only part-time work	1,389	(S)	1,389	1,380	(S)	1,380
Seasonal work	190	126	64	171	111	60
Job started or ended during the week	127	127	(S)	125	125	(S)
Noneconomic reasons	27,509	8,166	19,343	27,063	8,058	19,005
Child-care problems	753	70	683	750	70	680
Other family or personal obligations	5,425	725	4,700	5,354	716	4,638
Health or medical limitations	834	(S)	834	814	(S)	814
In school or training	6,057	98	5,959	5,985	96	5,888
Retired or social security limit on earnings	2,185	(S)	2,185	2,089	(S)	2,089
Vacation or personal day	3,431	3,431	(S)	3,399	3,399	(S)
Holiday, legal, or religious	844	844	(S)	836	836	(S)
Weather-related curtailment	454	454	(S)	433	433	(S)
Other	7,525	2,543	4,982	7,404	2,508	4,896
Average hours per week:						
Economic reasons	22.9	23.8	22.4	23.0	23.8	22.4
Noneconomic reasons	21.4	25.1	19.8	21.4	25.1	19.8

S No data or data do not meet publication standards.

Source: U.S. Bureau of Labor Statistics, "Employment and Earnings Online," January 2009; <http://www.bls.gov/opub/ee/home.htm> and <http://www.bls.gov/cps/home.htm>.

384   Labor Force, Employment, and Earnings

Table 600. Displaced Workers by Selected Characteristics: 2008

[In percent, except total (3,641 represents 3,641,000). As of January. For persons 20 years old and over with tenure of 3 years or more who lost or left a job between January 2005 and December 2007 because of plant closings or moves, slack work, or the abolishment of their positions. Based on Current Population Survey see source and Appendix III]

Characteristic	Total (1,000)	Employment status in January 2008			Reason for job loss, 2005–2007		
		Employed	Unem-ployed	Not in the labor force	Plant or company closed down or moved	Slack/ insufficient work	Position or shift abolished
Total [1]	**3,641**	**67.1**	**18.0**	**15.0**	**45.3**	**23.9**	**30.8**
20 to 24 years old	127	67.5	22.8	9.7	42.4	39.8	17.7
25 to 54 years old	2,602	72.6	17.4	10.0	44.8	25.2	30.0
55 to 64 years old	708	60.8	20.7	18.5	45.7	17.6	36.7
65 years old and over . . .	204	18.4	12.6	69.0	52.2	19.2	28.5
Males	2,024	69.9	18.8	11.2	43.6	27.9	28.5
20 to 24 years old	75	66.4	22.5	11.1	34.2	52.6	13.2
25 to 54 years old	1,490	74.4	19.1	6.5	42.0	29.1	28.9
55 to 64 years old	356	68.0	17.9	14.0	49.7	18.7	31.6
65 years old and over . . .	103	14.4	15.4	70.2	52.3	24.3	23.4
Females	1,617	63.5	16.9	19.6	47.4	19.0	33.6
20 to 24 years old	53	(2)	(2)	(2)	(2)	(2)	(2)
25 to 54 years old	1,112	70.1	15.1	14.8	48.5	20.1	31.4
55 to 64 years old	352	53.4	23.6	23.0	41.6	16.5	41.9
65 years old and over . . .	101	22.4	9.8	67.8	52.2	14.1	33.8
White [3]	3,032	67.9	16.8	15.3	45.4	23.5	31.1
Black [3]	408	58.6	28.2	13.3	46.6	26.9	26.4
Asian [3]	122	67.3	11.7	21.0	44.7	15.7	39.5
Hispanic origin [4]	423	68.4	17.4	14.1	43.5	39.5	17.0

[1] Includes other races, not shown separately. [2] Data not shown where base is less than 75,000. [3] For persons in this race group only. See footnote 3, Table 575. [4] Persons of Hispanic or Latino origin may any race.

Source: U.S. Bureau of Labor Statistics, *Worker Displacement, 2005–2007*, News, USDL 08-1183, August 20, 2008. See also <http://www.bls.gov/news.release/disp.toc.htm>.

Table 601. Labor Force Status of Persons With a Work Disability by Age: 2008

[In percent, except as indicated (24,504 represents 24,504,000). As of March. For civilians 16 to 74 who have a condition which prevents them from working or limits the amount of work they can do. Data from the Current Population Survey; see text, Section 1 and Appendix III]

Labor force status	Total	Age						
		16 to 24 years old	25 to 34 years old	35 to 44 years old	45 to 54 years old	55 to 64 years old	65 to 69 years old	70 to 74 years old
Number (1,000)	**24,504**	**1,562**	**2,176**	**3,522**	**5,710**	**7,242**	**2,406**	**1,885**
In labor force.	21.4	29.4	32.4	30.9	24.6	17.2	9.9	6.0
Employed	18.8	22.3	27.7	27.2	21.6	15.8	9.1	5.3
Full-time.	10.9	8.7	16.9	17.9	13.7	8.9	3.0	1.9
Not in labor force	78.6	70.6	67.6	69.1	75.4	82.8	90.1	94.0
Unemployment rate	12.3	24.2	14.5	11.9	12.1	8.1	7.6	10.2

Source: U.S. Census Bureau, "Disability Data from the Current Population Survey"; <http://www.census.gov/hhes/www /disability/disabcps.html>.

Table 602. Persons Not in the Labor Force: 2008

[In thousands (79,501 represents 79,501,000). Annual average of monthly figures. Civilian noninstitutional population 16 years old and over. Based on the Current Population Survey; see text, Section 1 and Appendix III]

Status and reason	Total	Age			Sex	
		16 to 24 years old	25 to 54 years old	55 years old and over	Male	Female
Total not in the labor force	**79,501**	**15,452**	**21,255**	**42,794**	**30,593**	**48,908**
Do not want a job now [1]	74,519	13,719	19,087	41,712	28,365	46,154
Want a job now	4,983	1,733	2,168	1,082	2,228	2,755
In the previous year—						
Did not search for a job	2,826	913	1,145	768	1,187	1,639
Did search for a job [2]	2,157	819	1,023	314	1,041	1,115
Not available for work now.	543	252	244	48	214	329
Available for work now, not looking for work [3] . . .	1,614	568	780	266	827	787
Reason for not currently looking for work:						
Discouraged over job prospects [4]	462	145	226	90	282	180
Family responsibilities.	171	35	111	25	45	126
In school or training	218	173	42	3	108	109
Ill health or disability.	124	16	68	40	55	69
Other [5]	640	199	332	108	337	303

[1] Includes some persons who are not asked if they want a job. [2] Persons who had a job in the prior 12 months must have searched since the end of that job. [3] Persons who have searched for work in the previous year and are available to work now also are referred to as "marginally attached to the labor force." [4] Includes such things as believes no work available, could not find work, lacks necessary schooling or training, employer thinks too young or old, and other types of discrimination. [5] Includes such things as child care and transportation problems.

Source: U.S. Bureau of Labor Statistics, "Employment and Earnings Online," January 2009; <http://www.bls.gov/opub/ee /home.htm> and<http://www.bls.gov/cps/tables.htm#annual>.

Labor Force, Employment, and Earnings 385

Table 603. Employed Civilians by Occupation, Sex, Race, and Hispanic Origin: 2008

[145,362 represents 145,362,000. Civilian noninstitutional population 16 years old and over. Annual average of monthly figures. Based on Current Population Survey; see text, Section 1 and Appendix III. Occupational classifications are those used in the 2000 census]

Occupation	Total employed (1,000)	Percent of total			
		Female	Black[1]	Asian[1]	Hispanic[2]
Total, 16 years and over	**145,362**	**46.7**	**11.0**	**4.8**	**14.0**
Management, professional and related occupations	**52,761**	**50.8**	**8.3**	**6.3**	**7.1**
Management, business, and financial operations occupations	22,059	42.7	7.2	5.2	7.5
Management occupations [3]	15,852	37.4	6.4	4.6	7.3
Chief executives	1,655	23.4	3.9	4.0	4.8
General and operations managers	985	30.1	5.4	4.3	6.2
Advertising and promotions managers	77	62.1	7.6	5.8	9.7
Marketing and sales managers	922	42.0	4.9	4.1	6.2
Administrative services managers	100	32.6	8.9	2.3	5.7
Computer and information systems managers	475	27.2	7.7	10.2	5.3
Financial managers	1,168	54.8	7.9	5.7	8.6
Human resources managers	293	66.3	8.2	4.0	7.3
Industrial production managers	243	14.5	4.9	3.8	9.6
Purchasing managers	193	40.4	12.9	2.5	3.7
Transportation, storage, and distribution managers	239	17.0	7.7	1.7	12.7
Farm, ranch, and other agricultural managers	217	23.9	0.9	1.7	4.6
Farmers and ranchers	751	24.4	1.0	0.7	2.4
Construction managers	1,244	8.2	3.7	1.4	9.1
Education administrators	829	65.1	12.2	2.6	7.6
Engineering managers	109	6.3	1.1	8.0	4.9
Food service managers	1,039	44.8	7.3	11.8	12.9
Lodging managers	177	46.7	5.5	12.2	9.1
Medical and health services managers	561	69.4	10.1	4.2	7.3
Property, real estate, and community association managers	558	49.6	7.7	3.1	8.2
Social and community service managers	338	68.1	10.1	2.2	7.7
Business and financial operations occupations [3]	6,207	56.2	9.4	6.5	7.9
Wholesale and retail buyers, except farm products	191	47.6	7.6	6.1	12.2
Purchasing agents, except wholesale, retail, and farm products	264	56.5	6.7	4.8	11.2
Claims adjusters, appraisers, examiners, and investigators	312	65.7	14.6	3.6	7.6
Compliance officers, except agriculture, construction, health and safety, and transportation	179	52.3	7.9	3.1	6.4
Cost estimators	100	10.0	0.7	1.2	5.3
Human resources, training, and labor relations specialists	803	70.7	14.0	3.5	7.9
Management analysts	731	43.5	6.2	5.8	4.6
Accountants and auditors	1,762	61.1	8.3	10.2	7.6
Appraisers and assessors of real estate	102	33.4	5.2	2.0	7.2
Financial analysts	110	38.8	6.0	12.9	9.8
Personal financial advisors	430	34.3	5.9	5.9	6.1
Insurance underwriters	82	80.3	13.3	5.5	7.1
Loan counselors and officers	392	58.0	10.6	4.4	11.5
Tax preparers	105	66.6	9.1	5.7	12.6
Professional and related occupations [3]	30,702	56.7	9.0	7.1	6.7
Computer and mathematical occupations [3]	3,676	24.8	7.2	16.7	5.1
Computer scientists and systems analysts	837	27.5	9.7	13.7	5.3
Computer programmers	534	22.4	5.7	14.1	4.0
Computer software engineers	1,034	20.9	4.7	29.0	3.7
Computer support specialists	382	27.7	11.1	8.2	7.9
Database administrators	93	29.2	6.3	13.5	3.8
Network and computer systems administrators	227	21.4	8.0	9.8	7.4
Network systems and data communications analysts	422	23.7	7.1	9.2	6.4
Operations research analysts	75	47.6	8.6	4.1	8.3
Architecture and engineering occupations [3]	2,931	13.5	5.1	9.6	6.7
Architects, except naval	233	24.8	3.3	6.1	8.2
Aerospace engineers	137	10.3	6.1	11.1	5.0
Civil engineers	346	10.4	3.2	11.2	9.2
Electrical and electronics engineers	350	7.7	3.0	13.4	5.3
Industrial engineers, including health and safety	177	14.9	5.9	7.6	5.2
Mechanical engineers	318	6.7	4.5	10.6	4.1
Drafters	162	23.4	3.0	7.2	9.0
Engineering technicians, except drafters	416	18.5	10.9	5.4	10.3
Surveying and mapping technicians	105	4.9	1.5	1.2	8.0
Life, physical, and social science occupations [3]	1,307	46.1	7.1	12.0	4.7
Biological scientists	101	52.9	4.2	13.3	3.9
Medical scientists	132	52.3	8.1	24.8	2.7
Chemists and materials scientists	118	33.1	4.7	22.3	6.9
Environmental scientists and geoscientists	85	29.3	4.0	2.7	4.1
Market and survey researchers	134	57.0	5.7	3.3	5.8
Psychologists	176	66.9	7.2	3.1	6.6
Community and social services occupations [3]	2,293	60.3	19.0	2.5	8.9
Counselors	674	68.0	20.5	2.2	8.9
Social workers	729	79.4	24.5	2.9	10.0
Miscellaneous community and social service specialists	303	61.4	20.9	2.6	14.5
Clergy	441	14.8	10.2	2.7	3.6

See footnotes at end of table.

[145,362 represents 145,362,000. Civilian noninstitutional population 16 years old and over. Annual average of monthly figures. Based on Current Population Survey; see text, Section 1 and Appendix III. Occupational classifications are those used in the 2000 census]

Occupation	Total employed (1,000)	Percent of total			
		Female	Black [1]	Asian [1]	Hispanic [2]
Legal occupations	1,671	51.9	7.0	2.8	6.6
Lawyers	1,014	34.4	4.6	2.9	3.8
Paralegals and legal assistants.	346	87.7	11.6	2.2	10.3
Miscellaneous legal support workers	257	74.5	10.0	3.9	13.3
Education, training, and library occupations [3]	8,605	74.0	9.2	3.8	7.5
Postsecondary teachers	1,218	46.1	5.2	11.9	4.0
Preschool and kindergarten teachers	685	97.6	11.7	3.5	9.8
Elementary and middle school teachers	2,958	81.2	9.9	2.2	6.8
Secondary school teachers	1,210	56.0	7.2	1.8	6.5
Special education teachers	387	84.9	8.0	1.3	3.7
Other teachers and instructors	751	66.9	9.3	3.8	8.2
Librarians	197	83.5	6.7	3.5	3.7
Teacher assistants	1,020	91.7	13.9	2.8	15.0
Arts, design, entertainment, sports, and media occupations [3]	2,820	47.8	6.1	4.1	8.3
Artists and related workers.	213	48.6	2.0	3.7	5.4
Designers	834	57.5	5.6	6.1	8.2
Producers and directors	154	38.5	8.9	4.0	7.3
Athletes, coaches, umpires, and related workers	252	32.5	10.3	2.3	8.3
Musicians, singers, and related workers	186	29.3	9.7	1.6	10.8
News analysts, reporters and correspondents	94	45.4	2.1	3.9	2.9
Public relations specialists	135	61.6	5.1	1.7	7.3
Editors	171	54.8	3.5	2.5	2.2
Writers and authors	186	57.3	4.1	1.1	3.3
Miscellaneous media and communication workers	83	72.2	6.1	12.1	27.4
Broadcast and sound engineering technicians and radio operators .	98	16.1	11.0	5.9	12.9
Photographers	181	44.1	4.3	3.9	10.1
Healthcare practitioner and technical occupations [3]	7,399	74.6	10.2	8.0	5.9
Dentists	152	27.2	3.3	12.0	5.2
Dietitians and nutritionists	100	90.0	20.3	3.7	7.1
Pharmacists	243	51.8	8.7	12.6	2.5
Physicians and surgeons.	877	30.5	6.2	16.6	5.8
Physician assistants	99	66.9	6.6	5.2	9.3
Registered nurses	2,778	91.7	10.0	7.8	4.7
Occupational therapists.	87	95.9	1.2	6.3	5.5
Physical therapists	197	69.0	3.9	13.0	3.5
Respiratory therapists	109	68.3	10.4	4.6	7.4
Speech-language pathologists	133	98.1	2.3	4.8	6.2
Clinical laboratory technologists and technicians	351	75.7	14.6	8.8	9.0
Dental hygienists	143	97.7	4.1	2.0	5.3
Diagnostic-related technologists and technicians	298	72.0	8.8	5.3	5.0
Emergency medical technicians and paramedics	138	30.2	4.7	0.1	6.6
Health diagnosing and treating practitioner support technicians. . . .	447	76.7	10.8	5.2	10.8
Licensed practical and licensed vocational nurses	566	93.3	22.1	3.6	7.1
Medical records and health information technicians	98	95.0	13.9	4.0	9.9
Service occupations	**24,451**	57.2	15.9	4.6	20.2
Healthcare support occupations [3]	3,212	88.8	25.8	4.2	13.6
Nursing, psychiatric, and home health aides.	1,889	88.7	34.5	4.3	13.1
Massage therapists	147	84.5	7.0	8.0	7.4
Dental assistants.	263	96.3	6.9	2.0	17.3
Medical assistants and other healthcare support occupations	831	88.8	16.9	4.2	15.3
Protective service occupations [3]	3,047	22.8	19.1	1.8	10.9
First-line supervisors/managers of police and detectives	117	14.7	12.5	2.9	6.1
Fire-fighters	293	4.8	8.2	0.3	9.4
Bailiffs, correctional officers, and jailers	403	30.0	22.0	0.6	10.4
Detectives and criminal investigators.	139	19.2	10.6	2.3	9.5
Police and sheriff's patrol officers	674	14.7	13.6	1.8	11.6
Private detectives and investigators	89	39.4	13.8	0.8	6.5
Security guards and gaming surveillance officers.	867	23.6	31.0	3.0	12.4
Lifeguards and other protective service workers	148	52.3	5.7	0.8	9.6
Food preparation and serving related occupations	7,824	56.0	12.1	5.4	21.0
Chefs and head cooks	351	17.0	10.3	14.1	22.7
First-line supervisors/managers of food preparation and serving workers.	635	57.8	14.4	3.8	14.1
Cooks	1,997	40.1	18.1	5.0	30.2
Food-preparation workers	724	60.7	9.8	6.6	24.6
Bartenders.	365	58.3	3.5	2.3	9.6
Combined food preparation and serving workers, including fast food. .	323	68.5	15.6	2.0	17.2
Counter attendants, cafeteria, food concession, and coffee shop	323	64.1	12.2	4.5	15.4
Waiters and waitresses.	2,010	73.2	7.3	6.2	14.6
Food servers, nonrestaurant	187	70.5	20.5	6.5	18.0
Dining room and cafeteria attendants and bartender helpers	349	47.8	13.1	5.6	26.9
Dishwashers.	289	22.7	12.0	3.4	35.7
Hosts and hostesses, restaurant, lounge, and coffee shop	263	88.7	6.2	3.0	11.6
Building and grounds cleaning and maintenance occupations	5,445	40.2	15.0	2.8	33.4
First-line supervisors/managers of housekeeping and janitorial workers.	296	39.9	18.6	1.1	23.7
First-line supervisors/managers of landscaping, lawn service, and groundskeeping workers	258	7.5	4.5	0.6	16.8
Janitors and building cleaners	2,125	32.2	18.4	3.4	28.2
Maids and housekeeping cleaners	1,434	89.8	18.1	3.7	40.5
Grounds maintenance workers.	1,262	6.1	7.7	1.6	41.0

See footnotes at end of table.

U.S. Census Bureau, Statistical Abstract of the United States: 2010

[145,362 represents 145,362,000. Civilian noninstitutional population 16 years old and over. Annual average of monthly figures. Based on Current Population Survey; see text, Section 1 and Appendix III. Occupational classifications are those used in the 2000 census]

Occupation	Total employed (1,000)	Percent of total			
		Female	Black [1]	Asian [1]	Hispanic [2]
Personal care and service occupations [3]	4,923	78.4	14.7	7.4	14.2
First-line supervisors/managers of gaming workers	155	38.6	7.2	3.2	10.3
First-line supervisors/managers of personal service workers	174	73.2	11.1	13.8	7.5
Nonfarm animal caretakers	157	73.5	2.9	1.9	12.3
Gaming services workers	111	51.5	13.1	21.8	3.5
Barbers	87	20.8	33.3	4.1	20.2
Hairdressers, hairstylists, and cosmetologists	773	90.6	11.3	6.5	11.0
Miscellaneous personal appearance workers	229	82.3	4.4	55.0	6.3
Baggage porters, bellhops, and concierges	72	17.3	23.9	8.1	19.9
Transportation attendants	139	71.0	16.8	3.3	13.1
Child care workers	1,314	95.6	17.4	2.7	20.0
Personal and home care aides	871	85.4	21.8	6.7	17.4
Recreation and fitness workers	353	68.1	9.6	3.3	9.5
Residential advisors	70	65.8	28.1	0.1	4.7
Sales and office occupations	**35,544**	**63.2**	**11.5**	**4.2**	**12.3**
Sales and related occupations [3]	16,295	49.5	9.7	4.7	11.7
First-line supervisors/managers of retail sales workers	3,471	43.3	7.3	5.2	10.4
First-line supervisors/managers of non retail sales workers	1,287	26.1	6.9	4.9	11.0
Cashiers	3,031	75.5	16.3	6.4	16.6
Counter and rental clerks	161	50.4	14.8	7.9	13.7
Parts salespersons	119	10.8	7.5	1.7	14.7
Retail salespersons	3,416	52.2	10.7	4.1	12.3
Advertising sales agents	216	54.7	10.3	2.2	8.4
Insurance sales agents	573	46.9	7.6	2.7	9.4
Securities, commodities, and financial services sales agents	388	27.9	7.2	5.1	9.2
Travel agents	98	71.6	9.8	10.3	6.4
Sales representatives, services, all other	521	34.4	8.9	4.5	8.8
Sales representatives, wholesale and manufacturing	1,343	27.3	3.9	3.8	8.6
Models, demonstrators, and product promoters	74	79.0	8.0	6.7	6.6
Real estate brokers and sales agents	962	54.4	7.2	3.5	8.6
Telemarketers	139	66.3	23.6	0.7	16.6
Door-to-door sales workers, news and street vendors, and related workers	243	62.2	9.5	3.7	14.4
Office and administrative support occupations [3]	19,249	74.8	13.0	3.7	12.8
First-line supervisors/managers of office and administrative support workers	1,641	71.2	10.4	3.4	10.5
Bill and account collectors	232	68.0	20.0	2.2	18.2
Billing and posting clerks and machine operators	516	90.9	13.5	3.6	12.6
Bookkeeping, accounting, and auditing clerks	1,434	91.5	6.9	4.4	8.0
Payroll and timekeeping clerks	158	90.1	11.8	4.1	10.8
Tellers	466	84.8	12.3	6.1	15.8
Court, municipal, and license clerks	100	75.6	11.1	3.7	10.5
Customer service representatives	1,908	68.3	18.3	3.7	14.5
File clerks	364	83.8	15.5	4.4	12.0
Hotel, motel, and resort desk clerks	120	71.9	19.1	3.9	9.6
Interviewers, except eligibility and loan	146	82.2	18.4	1.9	17.7
Library assistants, clerical	107	83.8	8.9	4.5	5.7
Loan interviewers and clerks	122	84.7	7.1	2.4	18.3
Order clerks	112	58.8	11.8	1.5	18.0
Receptionists and information clerks	1,413	93.6	9.8	3.8	15.2
Reservation and transportation ticket agents and travel clerks	136	60.9	14.3	6.5	14.8
Couriers and messengers	261	17.4	13.9	1.7	21.1
Dispatchers	286	57.4	15.9	1.9	11.8
Postal service clerks	167	53.7	27.0	8.5	10.5
Postal service mail carriers	373	33.0	14.5	6.4	9.8
Postal service mail sorters, processors, and processing machine operators	90	42.7	34.1	10.9	11.4
Production, planning, and expediting clerks	269	58.2	8.9	3.7	7.3
Shipping, receiving, and traffic clerks	543	32.8	11.6	2.8	20.2
Stock clerks and order fillers	1,481	35.4	16.8	3.6	18.6
Secretaries and administrative assistants	3,296	96.1	8.1	2.3	9.6
Computer operators	134	51.4	19.9	4.3	5.1
Data entry keyers	415	77.3	17.6	5.2	12.9
Word processors and typists	149	92.9	17.3	3.6	13.1
Insurance claims and policy processing clerks	275	83.4	19.4	2.8	12.2
Mail clerks and mail machine operators, except postal service	123	49.0	20.8	7.1	12.9
Office clerks, general	1,176	84.4	15.4	4.7	14.1
Natural resources, construction, and maintenance occupations	**14,806**	**4.2**	**6.9**	**1.9**	**25.0**
Farming, fishing, and forestry occupations [3]	988	21.1	4.5	1.7	39.3
Logging workers	73	1.0	5.9	–	12.3
Construction and extraction occupations [3]	8,667	2.5	6.3	1.4	29.6
First-line supervisors/managers of construction trades and extraction workers	844	2.7	3.0	1.2	16.1
Brickmasons, blockmasons, and stonemasons	230	0.4	7.4	1.2	39.9
Carpenters	1,562	1.5	6.0	1.3	25.7

See footnotes at end of table.

U.S. Census Bureau, Statistical Abstract of the United States: 2010

Table 603. **Employed Civilians by Occupation, Sex, Race, and Hispanic Origin: 2008**—Con.

[145,362 represents 145,362,000. Civilian noninstitutional population 16 years old and over. Annual average of monthly figures. Based on Current Population Survey; see text, Section 1 and Appendix III. Occupational classifications are those used in the 2000 census]

Occupation	Total employed (1,000)	Percent of total			
		Female	Black [1]	Asian [1]	Hispanic [2]
Carpet, floor, and tile installers and finishers.................	224	2.3	1.9	1.0	42.7
Cement masons, concrete finishers, and terrazzo workers........	90	(−)	7.4	0.1	57.7
Construction laborers.................................	1,651	3.1	7.7	1.9	44.1
Operating engineers and other construction equipment operators....	398	1.5	5.1	0.5	17.4
Drywall installers, ceiling tile installers, and tapers.............	209	2.1	3.6	0.4	56.9
Electricians.......................................	874	1.0	5.9	2.7	16.2
Painters, construction and maintenance....................	647	6.3	7.3	2.2	40.1
Pipelayers, plumbers, pipefitters, and steamfitters.............	606	1.4	6.4	0.6	19.5
Roofers..	234	1.3	8.4	0.4	42.9
Sheet metal workers.................................	136	4.8	6.2	1.2	11.8
Structural iron and steel workers	77	0.9	2.2	0.3	14.4
Helpers, construction trades	113	4.1	18.1	0.3	41.3
Construction and building inspectors......................	93	9.5	9.2	1.6	5.4
Highway maintenance workers...........................	103	1.9	17.2	(−)	10.2
Installation, maintenance, and repair occupations [3].............	5,152	3.9	8.5	2.8	14.5
First-line supervisors/managers of mechanics, installers, and repairers	300	8.0	6.7	1.0	8.7
Computer, automated teller, and office machine repairers.........	335	10.5	10.8	7.5	13.0
Radio and telecommunications equipment installers and repairers ...	200	11.4	13.7	4.4	11.8
Electronic home entertainment equipment installers and repairers	75	1.6	13.5	8.0	16.2
Aircraft mechanics and service technicians..................	153	1.7	5.5	6.4	13.8
Automotive body and related repairers....................	157	2.1	5.2	0.7	27.2
Automotive service technicians and mechanics................	852	1.6	6.5	2.9	19.7
Bus and truck mechanics and diesel engine specialists	358	0.9	7.5	1.7	11.6
Heavy vehicle and mobile equipment service technicians and mechanics	217	1.1	5.0	0.4	10.5
Heating, air conditioning, and refrigeration mechanics and installers	397	2.0	8.6	2.2	13.2
Industrial and refractory machinery mechanics	439	2.6	8.8	3.0	13.0
Maintenance and repair workers, general...................	461	3.5	10.2	2.4	13.7
Electrical power-line installers and repairers................	109	1.4	8.7	0.3	8.9
Telecommunications line installers and repairers	204	3.3	16.2	1.1	15.0
Production, transportation, and material occupations	**17,800**	**22.4**	**14.5**	**3.8**	**20.4**
Production occupations [3].............................	8,973	29.7	12.2	5.2	21.1
First-line supervisors/managers of production and operating workers	874	18.1	9.5	5.0	14.9
Electrical, electronics, and electromechanical assemblers	203	57.8	12.2	17.5	19.4
Bakers..	194	55.7	12.1	5.0	28.9
Butchers and other meat, poultry, and fish processing workers......	309	26.8	14.6	6.7	38.4
Food batchmakers...................................	73	53.5	11.7	6.2	29.0
Cutting, punching, and press machine setters, operators, and tenders, metal and plastic	105	20.2	9.1	4.0	22.0
Machinists..	409	6.9	7.0	4.2	12.1
Tool and die makers.................................	71	1.0	0.9	1.2	5.9
Welding, soldering, and brazing workers	598	4.7	8.7	3.7	21.0
Printing machine operators	213	19.8	9.1	2.9	20.5
Laundry and dry-cleaning workers	239	60.8	22.4	7.7	29.3
Sewing machine operators	226	78.2	9.4	14.1	36.8
Tailors, dressmakers, and sewers........................	71	84.2	6.1	12.2	24.4
Cabinetmakers and bench carpenters	85	6.5	2.8	5.7	13.0
Stationary engineers and boiler operators	101	1.7	13.1	2.4	7.2
Water and liquid waste treatment plant and system operators	71	8.6	12.3	(−)	7.0
Crushing, grinding, polishing, mixing, and blending workers.......	108	13.3	14.5	1.4	20.6
Cutting workers....................................	80	26.7	8.0	5.1	27.4
Inspectors, testers, sorters, samplers, and weighers	751	41.3	13.4	5.8	14.2
Medical, dental, and ophthalmic laboratory technicians	95	56.9	6.2	6.9	13.8
Packaging and filling machine operators and tenders	261	51.5	15.0	5.0	42.5
Painting workers	183	13.6	13.2	1.1	26.2
Transportation and material-moving occupations [3].............	8,827	14.9	16.9	2.5	19.7
Supervisors, transportation and material-moving workers	208	20.5	14.4	5.5	12.0
Aircraft pilots and flight engineers.......................	141	2.6	1.8	2.4	2.5
Bus drivers.......................................	651	49.0	30.4	1.8	12.2
Driver/sales workers and truck drivers....................	3,388	4.9	14.3	1.5	17.8
Taxi drivers and chauffeurs............................	373	13.3	26.3	10.5	18.9
Parking lot attendants................................	83	12.6	15.7	8.7	27.3
Service station attendants.............................	87	14.8	10.3	4.4	12.4
Industrial truck and tractor operators.....................	568	8.9	23.4	1.5	26.7
Cleaners of vehicles and equipment	317	9.5	15.4	0.9	28.8
Laborers and freight, stock, and material movers, hand	1,889	17.1	15.9	2.4	21.2
Packers and packagers, hand	391	58.1	15.3	4.6	43.7
Refuse and recyclable material collectors..................	98	14.0	16.4	2.4	31.1

− Represents or rounds to zero.   [1] The Current Population Survey (CPS) allowes respondents to choose more than one race. Data represent persons who selected this race group only and exclude persons reporting more than one race. See also comments on race in the text for Section 1.   [2] Persons of Hispanic or Latino ethnicity may be any race.   [3] Includes other occupations not shown separately.

Source: U.S. Bureau of Labor Statistics, "Employment and Earnings Online," January 2009; <http://www.bls.gov/opub/ee /home.htm> and <http://www.bls.gov/cps/home.htm>.

Labor Force, Employment, and Earnings   **389**

Table 604. **Employed Civilians by Occupation—States: 2008**

[In thousands (145,362 represents 145,362,000). Occupation classifications are those used in the 2000 Census. Because of separate processing and weighting procedures, totals for the United States differ from the results obtained by aggregating the totals for the States. For details see source. Based on the Current Population Survey and subject to sampling error; see text, Section 1 and Appendix III]

State	Total	Management, professional, and related occupations			Sales and office occupations		Natural resources, construction, and maintenance occupations			Production, transportation, and material moving occupations	
		Management, business, and financial operations	Professional and related occupations	Service occupations	Sales and related occupations	Office and administrative support occupations	Farming, fishing, and forestry occupations	Construction and extraction occupations	Installation, maintenance, and repair occupations	Production occupations	Transportation and material moving occupations
Total ...	145,362	22,059	30,702	24,451	16,295	19,249	988	8,667	5,152	8,973	8,827
AL.......	2,061	253	399	311	234	296	6	135	84	196	147
AK.......	332	47	65	59	31	47	4	30	14	10	24
AZ.......	2,954	435	557	488	419	433	13	185	96	145	185
AR.......	1,301	172	242	182	140	171	21	94	58	123	97
CA.......	17,045	2,732	3,685	2,913	1,939	2,144	214	981	541	946	951
CO	2,594	469	592	396	298	317	9	188	91	108	126
CT.......	1,775	310	424	291	193	224	2	97	52	101	81
DE.......	424	61	96	70	47	63	2	25	15	20	24
DC	312	72	107	47	21	38	(Z)	9	3	4	11
FL.......	8,618	1,347	1,666	1,581	1,122	1,209	24	558	331	320	459
GA	4,569	743	964	667	543	607	17	284	175	275	293
HI	627	88	105	149	79	87	6	39	21	17	35
ID	711	106	130	119	91	89	18	46	26	38	48
IL	6,246	929	1,268	1,037	716	879	22	327	175	438	457
IN	3,047	413	557	472	339	396	21	167	137	325	220
IA	1,620	255	336	249	161	207	16	73	56	143	123
KS.......	1,440	224	311	240	151	178	12	77	55	105	85
KY.......	1,896	234	370	299	202	251	19	120	86	161	154
LA.......	1,981	257	402	345	220	248	10	151	86	124	137
ME	666	89	145	113	70	86	12	45	25	39	42
MD	2,875	531	758	450	282	357	7	162	100	94	133
MA	3,246	536	915	548	316	388	9	148	99	163	125
MI	4,522	623	989	787	499	582	30	188	168	397	260
MN	2,731	453	641	414	298	336	19	138	84	199	149
MS	1,230	139	239	204	114	170	16	84	51	121	91
MO	2,835	385	557	481	334	390	21	165	111	210	180
MT	481	85	88	89	54	58	7	40	14	18	28
NE.......	967	162	196	151	107	122	11	55	29	73	60
NV.......	1,288	177	202	310	163	167	2	114	46	36	71
NH	712	119	166	104	78	97	3	40	25	47	33
NJ.......	4,261	743	989	703	511	577	8	203	107	171	248
NM	919	119	214	149	95	131	10	81	37	38	45
NY.......	9,145	1,321	2,124	1,805	997	1,223	25	489	253	397	510
NC	4,245	611	896	715	466	504	25	301	169	302	255
ND	361	60	69	63	37	49	8	24	12	19	20
OH	5,593	783	1,138	964	572	778	16	236	213	496	396
OK	1,687	249	335	277	171	224	13	109	90	100	118
OR	1,842	310	406	295	192	233	37	104	47	121	97
PA	6,063	865	1,296	1,048	607	886	32	306	214	396	411
RI	520	69	122	95	56	71	3	27	16	33	27
SC.......	1,993	266	393	331	221	257	10	123	98	182	113
SD.......	434	75	80	68	46	59	8	24	15	34	24
TN.......	2,840	384	523	484	333	360	8	209	110	222	207
TX.......	11,126	1,638	2,066	1,836	1,325	1,521	80	861	413	662	724
UT.......	1,333	198	259	190	171	196	10	99	51	81	79
VT.......	336	52	83	54	34	38	4	23	10	23	14
VA.......	3,984	733	976	582	422	493	25	233	130	175	216
WA	3,286	546	734	526	320	413	52	192	139	161	202
WV	785	82	149	137	89	113	5	71	33	42	65
WI	2,949	420	579	476	306	418	25	137	111	291	186
WY	284	45	46	43	29	32	5	29	17	15	24

Z Less than 500.

Source: U.S. Bureau of Labor Statistics, Local Area Unemployment Statistics, *Geographic Profile of Employment and Unemployment, 2008.* See also <http://www.bls.gov/gps/>.

U.S. Census Bureau, Statistical Abstract of the United States: 2010

Table 605. Employment Projections by Occupation: 2006 and 2016

[In thousands (262 represents 262,000), except percent and rank. Estimates based on the Current Employment Statistics Program; the Occupational Employment Statistics Survey; and the Current Population Survey. See source for methodological assumptions. Occupations based on the 2000 Standard Occupational Classification system]

Occupation	Employment (1,000) 2006	Employment (1,000) 2016	Change 2006–2016 Number (1,000)	Change 2006–2016 Percent	Quartile rank by 2006 median annual earnings[1]	Most significant source of postsecondary education or training
FASTEST GROWING						
Network systems and data communications analysts	262	402	140	53.4	VH	Bachelor's degree
Personal and home care aides	767	1,156	389	50.6	VL	Short-term on-the-job training
Home health aides	787	1,171	384	48.7	VL	Short-term on-the-job training
Computer software engineers, applications . .	507	733	226	44.6	VH	Bachelor's degree
Veterinary technologists and technicians	71	100	29	41.0	L	Associate's degree
Personal financial advisors	176	248	72	41.0	VH	Bachelor's degree
Makeup artists, theatrical and performance . .	2	3	1	39.8	H	Postsecondary
Medical assistants.	417	565	148	35.4	L	Moderate-term on-the-job training
Veterinarians	62	84	22	35.0	VH	First professional degree
Substance abuse and behavioral disorder counselors.	83	112	29	34.3	H	Bachelor's degree
Skin care specialists	38	51	13	34.3	L	Postsecondary vocational award
Financial analysts	221	295	75	33.8	VH	Bachelor's degree
Social and human service assistants	339	453	114	33.6	L	Moderate-term on-the-job training
Gaming surveillance officers and gaming investigators	9	12	3	33.6	L	Moderate-term on-the-job training
Physical therapist assistants	60	80	20	32.4	H	Associate degree
Pharmacy technicians	285	376	91	32.0	L	Moderate-term on-the-job training
Forensic science technicians.	13	17	4	30.7	H	Bachelor's degree
Dental hygienists	167	217	50	30.1	VH	Associate's degree
Mental health counselors	100	130	30	30.0	H	Master's degree
Mental health and substance abuse social workers.	122	159	37	29.9	H	Master's degree
Marriage and family therapists.	25	32	7	29.8	H	Master's degree
Dental assistants	280	362	82	29.2	L	Moderate-term on-the-job training
Computer systems analysts	504	650	146	29.0	VH	Bachelor's degree
Database administrators.	119	154	34	28.6	VH	Bachelor's degree
Computer software engineers, systems software	350	449	99	28.2	VH	Bachelor's degree
Gaming and sports book writers and runners .	18	24	5	28.0	VL	Short-term on-the-job training
Environmental science and protection technicians, including health	36	47	10	28.0	H	Associate's degree
Manicurists and pedicurists.	78	100	22	27.6	VL	Postsecondary vocational award
Physical therapists	173	220	47	27.1	VH	Master's degree
Physician assistants	66	83	18	27.0	VH	Master's degree
LARGEST JOB GROWTH						
Registered nurses.	2,505	3,092	587	23.5	VH	Associate's degree
Retail salespersons.	4,477	5,034	557	12.4	VL	Short-term on-the-job training
Customer service representatives	2,202	2,747	545	24.8	L	Moderate-term on-the-job training
Combined food preparation and serving workers, including fast food	2,503	2,955	452	18.1	VL	Short-term on-the-job training
Office clerks, general.	3,200	3,604	404	12.6	L	Short-term on-the-job training
Personal and home care aides	767	1,156	389	50.6	VL	Short-term on-the-job training
Home health aides	787	1,171	384	48.7	VL	Short-term on-the-job training
Postsecondary teachers.	1,672	2,054	382	22.9	VH	Doctoral degree
Janitors and cleaners, except maids and housekeeping cleaners	2,387	2,732	345	14.5	VL	Short-term on-the-job training
Nursing aides, orderlies, and attendants	1,447	1,711	264	18.2	L	Postsecondary vocational award
Bookkeeping, accounting, and auditing clerks	2,114	2,377	264	12.5	L	Moderate-term on-the-job training
Waiters and waitresses	2,361	2,615	255	10.8	VL	Short-term on-the-job training
Child care workers	1,388	1,636	248	17.8	VL	Short-term on-the-job training
Executive secretaries and administrative assistants	1,618	1,857	239	14.8	H	Work experience in a related occupation
Computer software engineers, applications . .	507	733	226	44.6	VH	Bachelor's degree
Accountants and auditors	1,274	1,500	226	17.7	VH	Bachelor's degree
Landscaping and groundskeeping workers . .	1,220	1,441	221	18.1	L	Short-term on-the-job training
Elementary school teachers except special education	1,540	1,749	209	13.6	H	Bachelor's degree
Receptionsts and information clerks	1,173	1,375	202	17.2	L	Short-term on-the-job training
Truck drivers, heavy and tractor-trailer	1,860	2,053	193	10.4	H	Moderate-term on-the-job training
Maids and housekeeping cleaners	1,470	1,656	186	12.7	VL	Short-term on-the-job training
Security guards	1,040	1,216	175	16.9	L	Short-term on-the-job training
Carpenters	1,462	1,612	150	10.3	H	Long-term on-the-job training
Management analysts	678	827	149	21.9	VH	Bachelor's or higher degree, plus work experience
Medical assistants.	417	565	148	35.4	L	Moderate-term on-the-job training
Computer systems analysts	504	650	146	29.0	VH	Bachelor's degree
Maintenance and repair workers, general . . .	1,391	1,531	140	10.1	H	Moderate-term on-the-job training
Network systems and data communications analysts	262	402	140	53.4	VH	Bachelor's degree
Food preparation worker	902	1,040	138	15.3	VL	Short-term on-the-job training
Teacher assistants	1,312	1,449	137	10.4	VL	Short-term on-the-job training

[1] Quartile ranks based on the Occupational Employment Statistics annual earnings. VH = very high ($46,360 and over), H = high ($30,630 to $46,300), L = low ($21,260 to $30,560), and VL = very low (up to $21,220). The rankings were based on quartiles using one-fourth of total employment to define each quartile. Earnings are for wage and salary workers.

Source: U.S. Bureau of Labor Statistics "Occupational employment projections to 2016," *Monthly Labor Review,* November 2007. See <http://www.bls.gov/emp/home.htm>.

Labor Force, Employment, and Earnings   391

Table 606. Occupations of the Employed by Selected Characteristic: 2008

[In thousands (126,161 represents 126,161,000). Annual averages of monthly figures. Civilian noninstitutional population 25 years old and over. Based on Current Population Survey; see text, Section 1 and Appendix III. See headnote Table, 592, regarding occupations]

Race, and educational attainment	Total employed	Managerial, professional, and related	Service	Sales and office	Natural resources, construction, and maintenance	Production, transportation, and material moving
Total [1]	126,161	49,629	18,647	29,353	12,878	15,654
Less than a high school diploma	11,073	716	3,323	1,411	2,699	2,924
High school graduates, no college	36,097	5,748	7,276	9,901	5,626	7,545
Less than a bachelor's degree	35,040	11,468	5,507	10,640	3,531	3,894
College graduates	43,951	31,696	2,541	7,401	1,023	1,290
White [2]	103,373	41,487	13,918	24,265	11,346	12,357
Less than a high school diploma	9,036	612	2,465	1,148	2,418	2,393
High school graduates, no college	29,495	4,914	5,258	8,330	4,996	5,997
Less than a bachelor's degree	28,615	9,650	4,202	8,700	3,085	2,978
College graduates	36,228	26,310	1,993	6,088	848	988
Black [2]	13,786	4,096	3,224	3,221	928	2,317
Less than a high school diploma	1,234	58	547	152	150	327
High school graduates, no college	4,719	584	1,467	1,100	413	1,156
Less than a bachelor's degree	4,411	1,185	927	1,335	272	692
College graduates	3,423	2,269	284	634	94	143
Asian [2]	6,290	3,168	978	1,253	262	629
Less than a high school diploma	439	32	177	62	38	130
High school graduates, no college	1,139	144	372	294	87	242
Less than a bachelor's degree	1,061	332	218	318	75	117
College graduates	3,651	2,660	210	579	61	140
Hispanic [3]	17,115	3,424	4,038	3,298	3,169	3,186
Less than a high school diploma	5,426	169	1,745	497	1,595	1,420
High school graduates, no college	5,232	567	1,298	1,170	1,012	1,185
Less than a bachelor's degree	3,721	1,012	706	1,135	433	434
College graduates	2,736	1,676	289	496	129	147

[1] Includes other races not shown separately.   [2] For persons in this race group only. See footnote 4, Table 575.   [3] Persons of Hispanic or Latino ethnicity may be any race.

Source: U.S. Bureau of Labor Statistics, Current Population Survey, unpublished data.

Table 607. Employment by Industry: 2000 to 2008

[In thousands (136,891 represents 136,891,000), except percent. See headnote Table 592]

Industry	2000	2005 [1]	2007 [1]	2008 [1]	2008, percent [1] Female	Black [2]	Asian [2]	Hispanic [3]
Total employed	136,891	141,730	146,047	145,362	46.7	11.0	4.8	14.0
Agriculture and related industries	2,464	2,197	2,095	2,168	23.9	2.5	1.2	20.4
Mining	475	624	736	819	12.9	5.5	1.5	15.5
Construction	9,931	11,197	11,856	10,974	9.7	5.6	1.6	24.6
Manufacturing	19,644	16,253	16,302	15,904	29.3	9.5	5.9	14.6
Durable goods	12,519	10,333	10,363	10,273	25.5	8.4	6.2	12.3
Nondurable goods	7,125	5,919	5,938	5,631	36.1	11.6	5.3	18.9
Wholesale trade	4,216	4,579	4,367	4,052	29.5	8.3	4.2	14.5
Retail trade	15,763	16,825	16,570	16,533	48.8	10.4	4.4	13.6
Transportation and utilities	7,380	7,360	7,650	7,727	23.1	15.9	3.5	15.0
Transportation and warehousing	6,096	6,184	6,457	6,501	23.8	17.0	3.7	15.8
Utilities	1,284	1,176	1,193	1,225	19.5	10.3	2.4	10.6
Information	4,059	3,402	3,566	3,481	41.6	11.7	5.0	9.1
Financial activities	9,374	10,203	10,488	10,228	54.8	9.8	5.1	10.6
Finance and insurance	6,641	7,035	7,306	7,279	58.0	9.9	5.7	9.8
Real estate and rental and leasing	2,734	3,168	3,182	2,949	46.9	9.7	3.5	12.6
Professional and business services	13,649	14,294	15,621	15,540	42.4	9.3	6.1	13.8
Professional and technical services	8,266	8,584	9,208	9,362	44.1	6.3	8.2	7.2
Management, administrative, and waste services	5,383	5,709	6,412	6,178	39.7	13.9	3.0	23.8
Education and health services	26,188	29,174	30,662	31,402	75.2	14.2	4.8	9.7
Educational services	11,255	12,264	12,828	13,169	69.7	11.1	3.8	8.8
Health care and social assistance	14,933	16,910	17,834	18,233	79.1	16.4	5.5	10.3
Hospitals	5,202	5,719	5,955	6,241	76.7	15.3	7.2	7.9
Health services, except hospitals	7,009	8,332	8,733	8,865	78.6	15.9	5.0	10.7
Social assistance	2,722	2,860	3,147	3,127	85.5	20.2	3.7	13.9
Leisure and hospitality	11,186	12,071	12,415	12,767	51.5	11.0	6.2	18.4
Arts, entertainment, and recreation	2,539	2,765	2,833	2,972	46.2	8.4	4.3	10.7
Accommodation and food services	8,647	9,306	9,582	9,795	53.1	11.7	6.8	20.8
Other services	6,450	7,020	6,972	7,005	51.6	9.8	5.9	17.1
Other services, except private households	5,731	6,208	6,159	6,200	46.5	9.9	6.3	14.4
Private households	718	812	813	805	91.3	9.7	3.1	37.6
Government workers	6,113	6,530	6,746	6,763	45.2	15.3	3.6	9.3

[1] See footnote 2, Table 574.   [2] Persons in this race group only. See footnote 4, Table 575.   [3] Persons of Hispanic or Latino origin may be any race.

Source: U.S. Bureau of Labor Statistics, "Employment and Earnings Online," January 2009; <http://www.bls.gov/opub/ee/home.htm> and <http://www.bls.gov/cps/home.htm>.

Table 608. **Employment Projections by Industry: 2006 to 2016**

[**9,382.9 represents 9,382,900.** Estimates based on the Current Employment Statistics program. See source for methodological assumptions. Minus sign (–) indicates decline]

Industry	2002 NAICS code [1]	Employment (1,000) 2006	Employment (1,000) 2016	Change, 2006–2016 (1,000)	Average annual rate of change 2006–2016
LARGEST GROWTH					
Food service and drinking places.	722	9,382.9	10,406.5	1,023.6	1.0
Offices of health practitioners	6211-6213	3,508.3	4,365.4	857.1	2.2
Construction	23	7,688.9	8,469.6	780.7	1.0
Management, scientific, and technical consulting services	5416	920.9	1,638.7	717.8	5.9
Individual and family services	6241	973.6	1,687.0	713.4	5.7
Hospitals, private	622	4,427.1	5,118.9	691.8	1.5
Employment services.	5613	3,656.6	4,348.1	691.5	1.7
Retail trade	44, 45	15,319.4	16,006.4	687.0	0.4
Residential care facilities	6232, 6233, 6239	1,316.7	1,829.2	512.5	3.3
Local government educational services.	(X)	7,938.5	8,450.1	511.6	0.6
Computer systems design and related services	5415	1,278.2	1,767.6	489.4	3.3
Home health care services	6216	867.1	1,347.6	480.5	4.5
Amusement, gambling, and recreation industries.	713	1,404.4	1,876.8	472.4	2.9
Wholesale trade	42	5,897.7	6,326.2	428.5	0.7
Securities, commodity contracts, and other financial investments and related activities.	523	816.3	1,192.4	376.1	3.9
Services to buildings and dwellings	5617	1,797.0	2,160.8	363.8	1.9
Architectural, engineering, and related services	5413	1,385.6	1,731.0	345.4	2.3
MOST RAPID GROWTH					
Management, scientific, and technical consulting services	5416	920.9	1,638.7	717.8	5.9
Individual and family services	6241	973.6	1,687.0	713.4	5.7
Home health care services	6216	867.1	1,347.6	480.5	4.5
Securities, commodity contracts, and other financial investment and related activities	523	816.3	1,192.4	376.1	3.9
Facilities support services.	5612	122.8	179.1	56.3	3.8
Residential care facilities	6232, 6233, 6239	1,316.7	1,829.2	512.5	3.3
Independent artists, writers, and performers.	7115	46.8	64.8	18.0	3.3
Computer systems design and related services	5415	1,278.2	1,767.6	489.4	3.3
Museums, historical sites, and similar institutions.	712	123.9	167.4	43.5	3.1
Child day care services	6244	806.7	1,078.4	271.7	2.9
Amusement, gambling, and recreation industries	713	1,404.4	1,876.8	472.4	2.9
Specialized design services	5414	135.8	179.3	43.5	2.8
Software publishers.	5112	243.4	321.3	77.9	2.8
Funds, trusts, and other financial vehicles	525	93.1	122.4	29.3	2.8
Other educational services	6114, 6117	534.2	702.5	168.3	2.8
Promoters of events, and agents and managers.	7114	100.0	131.3	31.3	2.8
Local government excluding enterprises, educational services, and hospitals	(X)	1,027.1	1,347.0	319.9	2.7
Other support services.	5619	305.4	399.0	93.6	2.7
Scenic and sightseeing transportation.	487	27.0	34.7	7.7	2.5
Lessors of nonfinancial intangible assets (except copyrighted works)	533	28.9	36.6	7.7	2.4
MOST RAPID DECLINE					
Cut and sew apparel manufacturing	3152	185.5	77.2	–108.3	–8.4
Footwear manufacturing.	3162	17.4	8.1	–9.3	–7.3
Federal enterprises except the Postal Service and electric utilities	(X)	45.1	26.5	–18.6	–5.2
Apparel knitting mills	3151	34.0	20.1	–13.9	–5.1
Textile and fabric finishing and fabric coating mills.	3133	57.6	34.4	–23.2	–5.0
Leather and hide tanning and finishing, and other leather and allied product manufacturing	3169	20.0	12.1	–7.9	–4.9
Apparel accessories and other apparel manufacturing	3159	18.9	12.4	–6.5	–4.1
Tobacco manufacturing	3122	23.4	15.5	–7.9	–4.0
Computer and peripheral equipment manufacturing. . .	3341	198.8	132.3	–66.5	–4.0
Iron and steel mills and ferroalloy manufacturing	3311	94.4	63.7	–30.7	–3.9
Pipeline transportation.	486	39.0	26.4	–12.6	–3.8
Fabric mills	3132	89.9	61.2	–28.7	–3.8
Nonferrous metal (except aluminum) production and processing.	3314	73.0	50.3	–22.7	–3.7
Pulp, paper, and paperboard mills	3221	136.0	93.8	–42.2	–3.6
Hardware manufacturing	3325	34.0	23.5	–10.5	–3.6
Alumina and aluminum production and processing . . .	3313	72.7	50.3	–22.4	–3.6
Rubber product manufacturing	3262	159.3	113.8	–45.5	–3.3
Electric lighting equipment manufacturing	3351	58.9	42.5	–16.4	–3.2
Spring and wire product manufacturing	3326	58.2	42.1	–16.1	–3.2
Cutlery and handtool manufacturing	3322	54.1	39.7	–14.4	–3.0
Foundries	3315	162.1	119.8	–42.3	–3.0

X Not applicable.   [1] Based on the North American Industry Classification System, 2002; see text, this section.

Source: U.S. Bureau of Labor Statistics, "Industry output and employment projections to 2016," *Monthly Labor Review*, November 2007. See also <http://www.bls.gov/emp/home.htm>.

Labor Force, Employment, and Earnings   393

Table 609. **Unemployed Workers—Summary: 1980 to 2008**

[In thousands (7,637 represents 7,637,000), except as indicated. For civilian noninstitutional population 16 years old and over. Annual averages of monthly figures. Based on the Current Population Survey; see text Section 1 and Appendix III. For data on unemployment insurance, see Table 546]

Age, sex, race, Hispanic origin	1980	1990 [1]	2000 [1]	2004 [1]	2005 [1]	2006 [1]	2007 [1]	2008 [1]
UNEMPLOYED								
Total [2]	7,637	7,047	5,692	8,149	7,591	7,001	7,078	8,924
16 to 19 years old	1,669	1,212	1,081	1,208	1,186	1,119	1,101	1,285
20 to 24 years old	1,835	1,299	1,022	1,431	1,335	1,234	1,241	1,545
25 to 44 years old	2,964	3,323	2,340	3,362	3,061	2,800	2,769	3,553
45 to 64 years old	1,075	1,109	1,117	1,970	1,825	1,689	1,777	2,276
65 years and over	94	105	132	179	184	159	190	264
Male	4,267	3,906	2,975	4,456	4,059	3,753	3,882	5,033
16 to 19 years old	913	667	599	664	667	622	623	736
20 to 24 years old	1,076	715	547	811	775	705	721	920
25 to 44 years old	1,619	1,803	1,159	1,819	1,559	1,452	1,490	1,994
45 to 64 years old	600	662	587	1,057	955	887	940	1,229
65 years and over	58	59	83	104	102	88	108	153
Female	3,370	3,140	2,717	3,694	3,531	3,247	3,196	3,891
16 to 19 years old	755	544	483	543	519	496	478	549
20 to 24 years old	760	584	475	619	560	530	520	625
25 to 44 years old	1,345	1,519	1,181	1,543	1,502	1,348	1,279	1,560
45 to 64 years old	473	447	529	914	870	801	837	1,046
65 years and over	36	46	50	75	82	71	81	111
White [3]	5,884	5,186	4,121	5,847	5,350	5,002	5,143	6,509
16 to 19 years old	1,291	903	795	890	845	794	805	947
20 to 24 years old	1,364	899	682	959	878	832	851	1,087
Black [3]	1,553	1,565	1,241	1,729	1,700	1,549	1,445	1,788
16 to 19 years old	343	268	230	241	267	253	235	246
20 to 24 years old	426	349	281	353	358	318	300	355
Asian [3, 4]	(NA)	(NA)	227	277	259	205	229	285
16 to 19 years old	(NA)	(NA)	40	20	20	22	20	23
20 to 24 years old	(NA)	(NA)	41	46	35	28	30	33
Hispanic [5]	620	876	954	1,342	1,191	1,081	1,220	1,678
16 to 19 years old	145	161	194	203	191	170	197	251
20 to 24 years old	138	167	190	255	227	194	213	307
Full-time workers	6,269	5,677	4,538	6,762	6,175	5,675	5,789	7,446
Part-time workers	1,369	1,369	1,154	1,388	1,415	1,326	1,289	1,478
UNEMPLOYMENT RATE (percent) [6]								
Total [2]	7.1	5.6	4.0	5.5	5.1	4.6	4.6	5.8
16 to 19 years old	17.8	15.5	13.1	17.0	16.6	15.4	15.7	18.7
20 to 24 years old	11.5	8.8	7.2	9.4	8.8	8.2	8.2	10.2
25 to 44 years old	6.0	4.9	3.3	4.9	4.5	4.1	4.0	5.2
45 to 64 years old	3.7	3.5	2.5	3.8	3.4	3.1	3.1	4.0
65 years and over	3.1	3.0	3.1	3.6	3.5	2.9	3.3	4.2
Male	6.9	5.7	3.9	5.6	5.1	4.6	4.7	6.1
16 to 19 years old	18.3	16.3	14.0	18.4	18.6	16.9	17.6	21.2
20 to 24 years old	12.5	9.1	7.3	10.1	9.6	8.7	8.9	11.4
25 to 44 years old	5.6	4.8	3.1	4.9	4.2	3.9	4.0	5.3
45 to 64 years old	3.5	3.7	2.4	3.9	3.4	3.1	3.2	4.1
65 years and over	3.1	3.0	3.3	3.7	3.4	2.8	3.4	4.5
Female	7.4	5.5	4.1	5.4	5.1	4.6	4.5	5.4
16 to 19 years old	17.2	14.7	12.1	15.5	14.5	13.8	13.8	16.2
20 to 24 years old	10.4	8.5	7.1	8.7	7.9	7.6	7.3	8.8
25 to 44 years old	6.4	4.9	3.6	5.0	4.8	4.3	4.1	5.0
45 to 64 years old	4.0	3.2	2.5	3.7	3.4	3.1	3.1	3.8
65 years and over	3.1	3.1	2.7	3.4	3.5	3.0	3.1	3.9
White [3]	6.3	4.8	3.5	4.8	4.4	4.0	4.1	5.2
16 to 19 years old	15.5	13.5	11.4	15.0	14.2	13.2	13.9	16.8
20 to 24 years old	9.9	7.3	5.9	7.9	7.2	6.9	7.0	9.0
Black [3]	14.3	11.4	7.6	10.4	10.0	8.9	8.3	10.1
16 to 19 years old	38.5	30.9	24.5	31.7	33.3	29.1	29.4	31.2
20 to 24 years old	23.6	19.9	15.0	18.4	18.3	16.2	15.2	17.9
Asian [3, 4]	(NA)	(NA)	3.6	4.4	4.0	3.0	3.2	4.0
16 to 19 years old	(NA)	(NA)	14.2	11.5	12.4	14.0	12.7	14.6
20 to 24 years old	(NA)	(NA)	6.9	8.6	6.5	5.6	5.6	6.3
Hispanic [5]	10.1	8.2	5.7	7.0	6.0	5.2	5.6	7.6
16 to 19 years old	22.5	19.5	16.6	20.4	18.4	15.9	18.1	22.4
20 to 24 years old	12.1	9.1	7.5	9.3	8.6	7.2	7.8	11.5
Percent without work for—								
Fewer than 5 weeks	43.2	46.3	44.9	33.1	35.1	37.3	35.9	32.8
5 to 10 weeks	32.3	32.0	31.9	29.2	30.4	30.3	31.5	31.4
15 to 26 weeks	13.8	11.7	11.8	15.9	14.9	14.7	15.0	16.0
27 weeks and over	10.7	10.0	11.4	21.8	19.6	17.6	17.6	19.7
Unemployment duration, average (weeks)	11.9	12.0	12.6	19.6	18.4	16.8	16.8	17.9

NA Not available.   [1] See footnote 2, Table 574.   [2] Includes other races not shown separately.   [3] Includes other ages not shown separately.   Beginning 2003, for this race group only. See footnote 4, Table 575.   [4] Prior to 2004, includes Pacific Islanders.   [5] Persons of Hispanic or Latino origin may be any race. Also includes ages not shown separately.   [6] Unemployed as percent of civilian labor force in specified group.

Source: U.S. Bureau of Labor Statistics, "Employment and Earnings Online," January 2009; <http://www.bls.gov/opub/ee/home.htm> and <http://www.bls.gov/cps/home.htm/>.

Table 610. **Unemployed Jobseekers' Job Search Activities: 2008**

[8,924 represents 8,924,000. For the civilian noninstitutional population 16 years old and over. Annual average of monthly data. Based on the Current Population Survey; see text, Section 1 and Appendix III]

Characteristic	Population (1,000)		Jobseekers' job search methods (percent)						Average number of methods used
	Total unem- ployed	Total job- seekers [1]	Employer directly	Sent out a resume or filled out appli- cations	Placed or answer- ed ads	Friends or relatives	Public employ- ment agency	Private employ- ment agency	
Total, 16 years and over [2] ...	8,924	7,749	56.9	52.3	17.1	23.8	18.9	8.0	1.92
16 to 19 years old........	1,285	1,212	54.9	58.8	11.3	16.3	8.2	2.4	1.61
20 to 24 years old........	1,545	1,406	57.0	53.1	15.7	20.4	16.3	6.2	1.83
25 to 34 years old........	1,949	1,689	58.6	51.7	18.0	24.9	21.7	8.6	1.98
35 to 44 years old........	1,604	1,344	57.8	52.4	18.9	27.2	22.9	11.1	2.07
45 to 54 years old........	1,473	1,242	57.6	49.3	19.8	27.3	23.4	11.0	2.05
55 to 64 years old........	803	654	54.2	49.3	20.0	28.6	22.5	10.1	2.03
65 years old and over	264	201	53.7	38.7	14.7	24.2	11.6	4.9	1.61
Male.................	5,033	4,234	58.7	49.8	17.1	26.1	19.3	8.1	1.94
16 to 19 years old	736	688	56.2	57.2	12.4	18.0	8.5	2.5	1.64
20 to 24 years old	920	814	57.0	51.2	15.4	22.2	15.9	6.5	1.81
25 to 34 years old	1,119	928	60.8	49.1	18.7	27.5	22.5	8.8	2.02
35 to 44 years old	875	699	59.9	48.8	18.9	31.5	24.8	11.3	2.13
45 to 54 years old	804	644	61.4	46.1	19.9	29.5	24.5	11.3	2.09
55 to 64 years old	425	344	56.2	46.2	18.7	30.4	22.3	9.2	2.02
65 years old and over ...	153	116	54.6	37.8	14.4	26.0	11.9	5.0	1.63
Female...............	3,891	3,515	54.7	55.3	17.0	21.0	18.4	8.0	1.89
16 to 19 years old	549	525	53.2	60.9	10.0	14.0	7.9	2.4	1.57
20 to 24 years old	625	592	56.9	55.8	16.0	17.9	16.8	5.8	1.85
25 to 34 years old	830	761	55.9	54.8	17.1	21.7	20.7	8.3	1.94
35 to 44 years old	730	645	55.4	56.3	18.9	22.4	20.9	10.8	1.99
45 to 54 years old	669	598	53.5	52.8	19.7	24.9	22.3	10.6	2.01
55 to 64 years old	377	309	52.0	52.7	21.5	26.6	22.6	11.1	2.05
65 years old and over ...	111	85	52.4	40.0	15.1	21.6	11.3	4.7	1.59
White [3]	6,509	5,540	57.3	53.0	17.1	23.4	17.4	7.8	1.91
Male	3,727	3,057	59.2	50.5	17.4	25.8	18.0	7.9	1.94
Female	2,782	2,483	54.9	56.1	16.8	20.5	16.7	7.7	1.87
Black [3]	1,788	1,646	56.0	50.2	17.1	23.9	24.8	8.3	1.93
Male	949	862	57.5	47.6	16.2	26.1	25.2	8.1	1.92
Female	839	784	54.3	53.2	18.1	21.5	24.5	0.4	1.94
Asian [3]	285	266	57.7	47.0	16.3	31.6	14.7	12.7	1.99
Male	160	149	59.4	46.1	16.7	33.9	13.6	11.4	1.99
Female	125	117	55.6	48.3	15.9	28.6	16.1	14.3	1.98
Hispanic [4]	1,678	1,421	56.9	45.7	13.1	30.5	18.0	7.6	1.84
Male	1,007	818	59.7	42.3	13.9	32.8	17.5	7.4	1.86
Female	672	603	53.2	50.4	12.0	27.4	18.7	8.0	1.80

[1] Excludes persons on temporary layoff. [2] Includes other races not shown separately. [3] Data for this race group only. See footnote 4, Table 575. [4] Persons of Hispanic or Latino origin may be any race.

Source: U.S. Bureau of Labor Statistics, "Employment and Earnings Online," January 2009; <http://www.bls.gov/opub/ee/home.htm> and <http://www.bls.gov/cps/home.htm>.

Table 611. **Unemployed Persons by Sex and Reason: 1980 to 2008**

[In thousands (4,267 represents 4,267,000). For civilian noninstitutional population 16 years old and over. Annual averages of monthly figures. Based on Current Population Survey; see text, Section 1 and Appendix III]

Sex and reason	1980	1990 [1]	1995	2000 [1]	2001	2002	2003 [1]	2004 [1]	2005 [1]	2006 [1]	2007 [1]	2008 [1]
Male, total	4,267	3,906	3,983	2,975	3,690	4,597	4,906	4,456	4,059	3,753	3,882	5,033
Job losers [2]	2,649	2,257	2,190	1,516	2,119	2,820	3,024	2,603	2,188	2,021	2,175	3,055
Job leavers	438	528	407	387	422	434	422	437	445	406	408	458
Reentrants.......	776	806	1,113	854	925	1,068	1,141	1,070	1,067	1,015	956	1,128
New entrants	405	315	273	217	223	274	320	346	359	312	343	393
Female, total...	3,370	3,140	3,421	2,717	3,111	3,781	3,868	3,694	3,531	3,247	3,196	3,891
Job losers [2]	1,297	1,130	1,286	1,001	1,356	1,787	1,814	1,595	1,479	1,300	1,340	1,735
Job leavers	453	513	417	393	413	432	397	421	427	421	385	438
Reentrants.......	1,152	1,124	1,412	1,107	1,105	1,300	1,336	1,338	1,319	1,223	1,186	1,345
New entrants	468	373	306	217	237	262	321	340	306	304	285	374

[1] See footnote 2, Table 574. [2] Beginning 1995, persons who completed temporary jobs are identified separately and are included as job losers.

Source: U.S. Bureau of Labor Statistics, "Employment and Earnings Online," January 2009; <http://www.bls.gov/opub/ee/home.htm> and <http://www.bls.gov/cps/home.htm>.

Labor Force, Employment, and Earnings   **395**

Table 612. Unemployment Rates by Industry, and by Sex, 2000 and 2008

[In percent. Civilian noninstitutional population 16 years old and over. Annual averages of monthly figures. Rate represents unemployment as a percent of labor force in each specified group. Based on Current Population Survey; See headnote, Table 592, regarding industries; see text, Section 1 and Appendix III.]

Industry	2000	2005 [1]	2007 [1]	2008 [1]	Male 2000	Male 2008 [1]	Female 2000	Female 2008 [1]
All unemployed [2]	4.0	5.1	4.6	5.8	3.9	6.1	4.1	5.4
Wage and salary workers:								
Agriculture and related industries	9.0	8.3	6.3	9.2	8.3	8.9	11.5	10.3
Mining	4.4	3.1	3.4	3.1	4.6	3.2	2.8	2.0
Construction	6.2	7.4	7.4	10.6	6.4	11.0	5.1	7.1
Manufacturing	3.5	4.9	4.3	5.8	3.0	5.3	4.5	6.9
Wholesale trade	3.3	4.0	3.3	4.5	2.8	4.1	4.4	5.4
Retail trade	4.6	5.7	5.1	6.2	4.0	5.6	5.1	6.8
Transportation and utilities	3.4	4.1	3.9	5.1	3.2	4.9	4.2	5.8
Transportation and warehousing	3.8	4.5	4.3	5.6	1.9	5.5	4.6	5.9
Utilities	1.9	1.9	1.5	2.6	2.8	1.9	2.1	5.4
Information	3.2	5.0	3.6	5.0	2.7	4.9	3.7	5.2
Telecommunications	2.3	5.2	3.1	4.4	1.5	3.3	3.3	6.2
Financial activities	2.4	2.9	3.0	3.9	2.1	3.8	2.6	4.1
Finance and insurance	2.2	2.7	2.7	3.6	1.7	3.3	2.5	3.8
Real estate and rental and leasing	3.1	3.3	3.7	4.8	2.9	4.7	3.2	5.0
Professional and business services	4.8	6.2	5.3	6.5	4.4	6.6	5.2	6.5
Professional and technical services	2.5	3.5	3.0	3.8	2.2	3.6	2.9	4.0
Management, administrative, and waste services	8.1	10.2	8.5	10.5	7.6	10.5	8.8	10.5
Education and health services	2.5	3.4	3.0	3.5	2.2	3.4	2.5	3.5
Educational services	2.4	3.7	3.8	4.8	2.1	4.9	2.5	4.7
Health care and social assistance	2.5	3.3	2.8	3.2	2.3	2.9	2.5	3.3
Leisure and hospitality	6.6	7.8	7.4	8.6	6.2	8.5	7.0	8.8
Arts, entertainment, and recreation	5.9	6.9	7.3	8.2	6.1	9.1	5.7	7.1
Accommodation and food services	6.8	8.0	7.4	8.8	6.2	8.3	7.3	9.1
Other services [3]	3.9	4.8	3.9	5.3	3.7	5.7	4.0	4.9
Government workers	2.1	2.6	2.3	2.4	2.1	2.5	2.2	2.4

[1] See footnote 2, Table 574. [2] Includes the self-employed, unpaid family workers, and persons with no previous work experience not shown separately. [3] Includes private household workers.

Source: U.S. Bureau of Labor Statistics, "Employment and Earnings Online," January 2009; <http://www.bls.gov/opub/ee/home.htm> and <http://www.bls.gov/cps/home.htm>.

Table 613. Unemployment by Occupation, 2000 to 2008, and by Sex, 2008

[5,692 represents 5,692,000. Civilian noninstitutional population 16 years old and over. Annual averages of monthly data. Rate represents unemployment as a percent of the labor force for each specified group. Based on Current Population Survey; see text, Section 1 and Appendix III. See also headnote, Table 592, regarding occupations]

Occupation	Number (1,000) 2000	2005 [1]	2008 [1]	Unemployment rate 2000	2005 [1]	2008[1] Total	2008[1] Male	2008[1] Female
Total [2]	5,692	7,591	8,924	4.0	5.1	5.8	6.1	5.4
Management, professional, and related occupations	827	1,172	1,463	1.8	2.3	2.7	2.6	2.8
Management, business, and financial operations	320	464	619	1.6	2.2	2.7	2.6	2.9
Management	214	322	407	1.5	2.1	2.5	2.4	2.6
Business and financial operations	106	142	212	2.0	2.4	3.3	3.1	3.4
Professional and related occupations	507	708	844	1.9	2.4	2.7	2.6	2.7
Computer and mathematical	74	96	97	2.2	2.9	2.6	2.4	3.2
Architecture and engineering	51	60	95	1.7	2.1	3.1	3.0	3.7
Life, physical, and social science	18	39	32	1.4	2.7	2.4	2.3	2.5
Community and social services	40	52	63	2.0	2.4	2.7	2.1	3.0
Legal	18	27	44	1.2	1.6	2.6	2.2	2.9
Education, training, and library	136	210	247	1.8	2.5	2.8	2.6	2.9
Arts, design, entertainment, sports, and media	97	135	156	3.5	4.7	5.3	5.4	5.1
Healthcare practitioner and technical	73	90	110	1.2	1.3	1.5	0.8	1.7
Service occupations	1,132	1,587	1,769	5.2	6.4	6.7	7.2	6.4
Healthcare support	101	154	150	4.0	4.7	4.5	5.6	4.3
Protective service	70	121	109	2.7	4.0	3.5	3.1	4.6
Food preparation and serving-related	469	615	742	6.6	7.7	8.7	9.1	8.3
Building and grounds cleaning and maintenance	301	429	470	5.8	7.6	7.9	8.2	7.5
Personal care and service	190	268	298	4.4	5.6	5.7	6.5	5.5
Sales and office occupations	1,446	1,820	2,006	3.8	4.8	5.3	5.2	5.5
Sales and related	673	874	980	4.1	5.0	5.7	4.7	6.7
Office and administrative support	773	946	1,026	3.6	4.6	5.1	6.0	4.8
Natural resources, construction, and maintenance	758	1,069	1,421	5.3	6.5	8.8	8.7	11.0
Farming, fishing, and forestry	133	103	112	10.2	9.6	10.2	9.2	13.5
Construction and extraction	507	751	1,067	6.2	7.6	11.0	10.9	13.4
Installation, maintenance, and repair	119	214	243	2.4	3.9	4.5	4.5	5.4
Production, transportation, and material moving	1,081	1,245	1,474	5.1	6.5	7.6	7.2	9.3
Production	575	677	746	4.8	6.7	7.7	7.0	9.4
Transportation and material moving	505	568	727	5.6	6.2	7.6	7.3	9.1

[1] See footnote 2, Table 574. [2] Includes persons with no previous work experience and those whose last job was in the Armed Forces.

Source: U.S. Bureau of Labor Statistics, "Employment and Earnings Online," January 2009; <http://www.bls.gov/opub/ee/home.htm> and <http://www.bls.gov/cps/home.htm>.

Table 614. Unemployed and Unemployment Rates by Educational Attainment, Sex, Race, and Hispanic Origin: 2000 to 2008

[3,589 represents 3,589,000. Annual averages of monthly figures. Civilian noninstitutional population 25 years old and over. See Table 579 for civilian labor force and participation rate data. Based on Current Population Survey; see text, Section 1 and Appendix III]

Year, sex, and race	Unemployed (1,000)					Unemployment rate [1]				
	Total	Less than high school diploma	High school gradu- ates, no college	Some college or- associ- ate's degree	Bach- elor's degree or more	Total	Less than high school diploma	High school gradu- ates, no college	Some college or- associ- ate's degree	Bach- elor's degree or more
Total: [2]										
2000 [3] ..	3,589	791	1,298	890	610	3.0	6.3	3.4	2.7	1.7
2005 [3] ..	5,070	967	1,798	1,349	955	4.0	7.6	4.7	3.9	2.3
2008 [3] ..	6,094	1,092	2,166	1,678	1,158	4.6	9.0	5.7	4.6	2.6
Male:										
2000 [3]	1,829	411	682	427	309	2.8	5.4	3.4	2.6	1.5
2005 [3]	2,617	514	973	636	494	3.8	6.4	4.6	3.7	2.3
2008 [3]	3,377	682	1,270	839	585	4.8	8.8	5.9	4.6	2.5
Female:										
2000 [3]	1,760	380	616	463	301	3.2	7.8	3.5	2.8	1.8
2005 [3]	2,453	453	826	713	461	4.2	9.7	4.8	4.0	2.4
2008 [3]	2,717	410	896	838	573	4.4	9.4	5.3	4.5	2.7
White: [4]										
2000 [3]	2,644	564	924	667	489	2.6	5.6	2.9	2.4	1.6
2005 [3]	3,627	669	1,257	973	729	3.5	6.5	4.0	3.4	2.1
2008 [3]	4,475	807	1,570	1,211	888	4.1	8.2	5.1	4.1	2.4
Black: [4]										
2000 [3]	731	179	315	169	68	5.4	10.7	6.4	4.0	2.5
2005 [3]	1,075	231	440	295	110	7.5	14.4	8.5	6.9	3.5
2008 [3]	1,187	209	482	355	141	7.9	14.5	9.3	7.4	4.0
Asian: [4, 5]										
2000 [3]	146	28	34	35	49	2.7	5.7	3.0	3.2	1.8
2005 [3]	203	26	47	32	99	3.5	5.5	4.6	3.2	3.0
2008 [3]	229	30	51	42	106	3.5	6.4	4.3	3.8	2.8
Hispanic: [6]										
2000 [3]	569	297	150	85	38	4.4	6.2	3.9	3.2	2.2
2005 [3]	773	354	216	138	66	4.8	6.2	4.5	4.1	2.9
2008 [3]	1,120	485	344	195	97	6.1	8.2	6.2	5.0	3.4

[1] Percent unemployed of the civilian labor force. [2] Includes other races not shown separately. [3] See footnote 2, Table 574. [4] Beginning 2005 data are for persons in this race group only. See footnote 4, Table 575. [5] 2000 data include Pacific Islanders. [6] Persons of Hispanic or Latino origin may be any race.

Source: U.S. Bureau of Labor Statistics, "Employment and Earnings Online," January 2009; <http://www.bls.gov/opub/ee/home.htm> and <http://www.bls.gov/cps/home.htm>.

Table 615. Unemployed Persons by Reason of Unemployment: 2008

[8,924 represents 8,924,000. Annual averages of monthly data. Based on Current Population Survey; see text, Section 1, and Appendix III]

Age, sex, and reason	Total unem- ployed (1,000)	Percent distribution by duration				
		Less than 5 weeks	5 to 14 weeks	15 weeks and over		
				Total	15 to 26 weeks	27 weeks or longer
Total 16 years old and over	8,924	32.8	31.4	35.7	16.0	19.7
16 to 19 years old	1,285	42.2	34.2	23.6	12.3	11.4
Total 20 years old and over	7,639	31.3	31.0	37.8	16.6	21.1
Males	4,297	31.8	29.9	38.3	16.9	21.4
Job losers and persons who completed temporary jobs	2,918	34.2	30.3	35.4	16.6	18.8
On temporary layoff	751	56.3	31.1	12.6	9.8	2.8
Not on temporary layoff	2,167	26.6	30.1	43.4	19.0	24.4
Permanent job losers	1,574	24.3	29.9	45.8	19.6	26.2
Persons who completed temporary jobs	593	32.6	30.5	36.9	17.3	19.6
Job leavers	410	30.9	31.4	37.7	18.5	19.1
Reentrants	856	24.7	27.3	48.0	17.2	30.9
New entrants	113	26.4	31.9	41.6	16.3	25.3
Females	3,342	30.6	32.4	37.0	16.3	20.8
Job losers and persons who completed temporary jobs	1,668	32.8	32.0	35.2	16.3	18.9
On temporary layoff	352	55.8	31.3	12.9	7.9	5.0
Not on temporary layoff	1,316	26.6	32.2	41.2	18.6	22.6
Permanent job losers	1,013	25.2	31.6	43.2	19.2	24.0
Persons who completed temporary jobs	302	31.5	34.1	34.3	16.3	18.0
Job leavers	406	33.6	37.1	29.3	14.8	14.6
Reentrants	1,126	27.2	31.1	41.8	16.5	25.2
New entrants	143	23.8	33.4	42.7	17.7	25.0

Source: U.S. Bureau of Labor Statistics, "Employment and Earnings Online," January 2009; <http://www.bls.gov/opub/ee/home.htm> and <http://www.bls.gov/cps/home.htm>.

Labor Force, Employment, and Earnings   **397**

Table 616. **Total Unemployed and Insured Unemployed by State: 2000 to 2008**

[5,692 represents 5,692,000. Civilian noninstitutional population 16 years old and over. Annual averages of monthly figures. U.S. totals derived by independent population controls; therefore state data may not add to U.S. totals. Unemployment data are based on population controls from Census 2000. State total unemployment estimates come from the Local Area Unemployment Statistics program, while U.S. totals come from the Current Population Survey; see text, Section 1 and Appendix III]

State	Total unemployed								Insured unemployed [3]			
	Number (1,000)				Percent [1]				Number (1,000)		Percent [4]	
	2000	2005 [2]	2007 [2]	2008 [2]	2000	2005 [2]	2007 [2]	2008 [2]	2000	2008	2000	2008
United States ...	5,692	7,591	7,078	8,924	4.0	5.1	4.6	5.8	[5]2,130.2	[5]3,299.5	[5]1.7	[5]2.5
Alabama.........	87	81	76	109	4.1	3.8	3.5	5.0	29.4	36.7	1.6	1.9
Alaska	20	24	22	24	6.2	6.9	6.2	6.7	12.2	10.9	4.9	3.7
Arizona.........	100	133	116	172	4.0	4.6	3.8	5.5	20.5	47.0	1.0	1.8
Arkansas	53	68	69	70	4.2	5.1	5.1	5.1	24.2	33.8	2.2	2.9
California	833	957	969	1,332	4.9	5.4	5.4	7.2	339.6	498.8	2.4	3.2
Colorado........	65	133	104	134	2.7	5.1	3.9	4.9	14.7	29.9	0.7	1.3
Connecticut......	39	88	85	107	2.3	4.9	4.6	5.7	28.9	47.9	1.8	2.9
Delaware	14	17	15	21	3.3	4.0	3.4	4.8	6.0	10.3	1.5	2.4
District of Columbia .	18	21	18	23	5.7	6.5	5.5	7.0	5.5	4.8	1.3	1.0
Florida	300	331	372	572	3.8	3.8	4.1	6.2	70.8	173.8	1.1	2.2
Georgia	148	240	219	302	3.5	5.2	4.6	6.2	34.8	82.4	0.9	2.1
Hawaii	24	17	17	26	4.0	2.7	2.6	3.9	8.4	11.4	1.7	1.9
Idaho..........	31	27	23	37	4.6	3.7	3.0	4.9	12.3	18.7	2.3	2.9
Illinois	291	372	341	434	4.5	5.8	5.1	6.5	105.7	155.9	1.8	2.7
Indiana.........	92	172	147	191	2.9	5.4	4.6	5.9	32.3	72.8	1.1	2.5
Iowa	45	70	62	69	2.8	4.3	3.7	4.1	19.5	28.6	1.4	2.0
Kansas.........	53	75	60	66	3.8	5.1	4.1	4.4	15.9	21.9	1.3	1.7
Kentucky	83	121	113	132	4.2	6.1	5.5	6.4	25.4	39.0	1.5	2.2
Louisiana	101	139	76	96	5.0	6.7	3.8	4.6	24.2	25.5	1.3	1.4
Maine..........	22	34	33	38	3.3	4.9	4.6	5.4	8.9	12.4	1.6	2.1
Maryland	100	121	105	131	3.6	4.1	3.5	4.4	29.0	48.9	1.3	2.0
Massachusetts.....	92	164	153	180	2.7	4.8	4.5	5.3	59.9	95.1	1.9	3.0
Michigan........	190	347	357	416	3.7	6.8	7.1	8.4	83.3	160.7	1.9	3.9
Minnesota.......	87	120	135	160	3.1	4.2	4.6	5.4	31.8	56.8	1.3	2.2
Mississippi	74	103	82	91	5.7	7.8	6.3	6.9	19.9	24.3	1.8	2.2
Missouri	98	161	153	183	3.3	5.4	5.1	6.1	43.8	59.0	1.7	2.2
Montana........	22	18	17	23	4.8	3.7	3.4	4.5	7.7	9.8	2.2	2.3
Nebraska	27	38	29	33	2.8	3.9	2.9	3.3	7.4	10.7	0.9	1.2
Nevada	48	55	62	91	4.5	4.5	4.7	6.7	19.6	39.2	2.1	3.1
New Hampshire....	19	26	26	28	2.7	3.6	3.5	3.8	3.1	10.1	0.5	1.6
New Jersey.......	157	198	191	246	3.7	4.5	4.3	5.5	84.6	129.8	2.3	3.3
New Mexico	42	47	34	40	5.0	5.2	3.5	4.2	9.5	14.0	1.4	1.8
New York	416	475	434	527	4.5	5.0	4.5	5.4	147.4	205.3	1.8	2.4
North Carolina.....	155	229	213	287	3.7	5.3	4.7	6.3	55.0	105.9	1.5	2.7
North Dakota......	10	12	11	12	2.9	3.4	3.1	3.2	3.9	3.6	1.3	1.1
Ohio	234	345	336	390	4.0	5.9	5.6	6.5	72.8	126.7	1.4	2.4
Oklahoma........	52	77	71	67	3.1	4.5	4.1	3.8	12.2	16.6	0.9	1.1
Oregon.........	93	115	99	125	5.1	6.2	5.1	6.4	41.6	60.7	2.7	3.6
Pennsylvania......	255	311	274	344	4.2	5.0	4.4	5.4	131.4	192.2	2.5	3.5
Rhode Island.....	23	28	30	44	4.2	5.1	5.2	7.8	12.3	15.9	2.8	3.4
South Carolina.....	71	139	119	149	3.6	6.7	5.6	6.9	27.6	53.9	1.6	2.9
South Dakota	11	16	13	14	2.7	3.6	2.9	3.0	2.1	2.4	0.6	0.6
Tennessee	115	163	146	195	4.0	5.6	4.8	6.4	42.9	52.2	1.7	1.9
Texas..........	452	602	503	575	4.4	5.4	4.4	4.9	107.4	123.2	1.2	1.3
Utah	38	53	37	48	3.4	4.1	2.7	3.4	10.7	15.2	1.1	1.3
Vermont	9	12	14	17	2.7	3.5	4.0	4.8	4.8	7.9	1.7	2.7
Virginia.........	82	138	122	165	2.3	3.5	3.0	4.0	22.5	42.3	0.7	1.2
Washington......	151	179	154	186	5.0	5.5	4.5	5.3	70.1	66.7	2.7	2.3
West Virginia.....	44	39	35	34	5.5	4.9	4.3	4.3	14.2	14.6	2.1	2.1
Wisconsin.......	101	145	146	146	3.4	4.8	4.7	4.7	54.1	86.5	2.0	3.2
Wyoming........	10	10	8	9	3.8	3.7	2.9	3.1	2.9	2.9	1.3	1.1

[1] Total unemployment as percent of civilian labor force. [2] See footnote 2, Table 574. [3] Number of jobless workers who are receiving state unemployment benefits. Source: U.S. Employment and Training Administration, Unemployment Insurance, Financial Handbook, annual updates. See <http://www.ows.doleta.gov/unemply/claims.asp>. [4] Those currently collecting unemployment insurance as a percent of the total number of eligible workers. [5] U.S. totals include Puerto Rico and the Virgin Islands.

Source: Except as noted, U.S. Bureau of Labor Statistics, "Local Area Unemployment Statistics"; <http://www.bls.gov/lau/>.

[Annual averages of monthly data. (109,487 represents 109,487,000). Based on data from establishment reports. Includes all full- and part-time employees who worked during, or received pay for, any part of the pay period reported. Excludes proprietors, the self-employed, farm workers, unpaid family workers, private household workers, and Armed Forces. Establishment data shown here conform to industry definitions in the 2007 North American Industry Classification System (NAICS) and are adjusted to March 2008 employment benchmarks. Based on the Current Employment Statistics Program; see source and Appendix III]

Item and year	Total nonfarm	Private industry																	Govern-ment
		Total [1]	Con-struc-tion	Manu-fac-turing	Whole-sale trade	Retail trade	Trans-portation and ware-housing	Utilities	Infor-mation	Finance and insur-ance	Real estate and rental and leasing	Profes-sional and tech-nical services	Adminis-trative and waste services	Educa-tional services	Health care and social assist-ance	Arts, entertain-ment, and recre-ation	Accom-moda-tions and food services	
EMPLOYEES (1,000)																		
1990	109,487	91,072	5,263	17,695	5,268	13,182	3,476	720	2,688	4,976	1,637	4,538	4,643	1,688	9,296	1,132	8,156	18,415
2000	131,785	110,995	6,787	17,263	5,933	15,280	4,410	601	3,630	5,677	2,011	6,702	8,168	2,390	12,718	1,788	10,074	20,790
2004	131,435	109,814	6,976	14,315	5,663	15,058	4,249	564	3,118	5,945	2,086	6,747	7,923	2,763	14,190	1,850	10,643	21,621
2005	133,703	111,899	7,336	14,226	5,764	15,280	4,361	554	3,061	6,019	2,134	7,025	8,170	2,836	14,536	1,892	10,923	21,804
2006	136,086	114,113	7,691	14,155	5,905	15,353	4,470	549	3,038	6,156	2,173	7,357	8,398	2,901	14,925	1,929	11,181	21,974
2007	137,598	115,380	7,630	13,879	6,015	15,520	4,541	553	3,032	6,132	2,169	7,660	8,416	2,941	15,380	1,969	11,457	22,218
2008	137,066	114,566	7,215	13,431	5,964	15,356	4,505	560	2,997	6,015	2,130	7,830	8,054	3,037	15,819	1,969	11,489	22,500
WEEKLY EARNINGS [2] (dol.)																		
1990	(NA)	349.75	513.43	436.16	444.48	235.62	471.72	670.43	479.50	378.21	286.96	504.83	273.60	(NA)	319.80	219.02	147.89	(NA)
2000	(NA)	481.01	685.78	590.77	631.40	333.38	562.31	955.63	700.86	589.64	396.38	745.77	387.49	(NA)	449.27	273.79	207.44	(NA)
2004	(NA)	529.09	735.55	658.49	667.09	371.13	614.82	1,048.44	777.25	683.78	455.44	828.25	425.64	(NA)	537.87	313.01	221.68	(NA)
2005	(NA)	544.33	750.22	673.33	685.00	377.58	618.58	1,095.90	805.08	703.51	487.99	862.79	431.92	(NA)	560.43	330.19	226.48	(NA)
2006	(NA)	567.87	781.21	691.02	718.63	383.02	636.97	1,135.34	850.42	738.17	496.59	907.74	464.97	(NA)	581.55	332.66	236.70	(NA)
2007	(NA)	590.04	816.66	711.56	748.94	385.11	654.95	1,182.65	874.65	774.63	518.37	956.42	485.15	(NA)	606.74	348.35	251.52	(NA)
2008	(NA)	607.99	842.36	724.23	769.91	386.39	670.33	1,231.19	908.44	797.79	535.58	996.06	500.55	(NA)	630.51	354.71	259.74	(NA)
WEEKLY HOURS [2]																		
1990	(NA)	34.3	38.3	40.5	38.4	30.6	37.7	41.5	35.8	36.4	33.1	36.1	32.3	(NA)	31.8	26.1	25.9	(NA)
2000	(NA)	34.3	39.2	41.3	38.8	30.7	37.4	42.0	36.8	37.1	32.6	36.2	33.1	(NA)	32.1	25.6	26.2	(NA)
2004	(NA)	33.7	38.3	40.8	37.8	30.7	37.2	40.9	36.3	36.6	32.8	35.6	32.9	(NA)	32.7	25.7	25.6	(NA)
2005	(NA)	33.8	38.6	40.7	37.7	30.6	37.0	41.1	36.5	36.8	33.5	35.9	32.8	(NA)	32.9	25.7	25.7	(NA)
2006	(NA)	33.9	39.0	41.1	38.0	30.5	36.9	41.4	36.6	36.8	32.9	35.9	33.4	(NA)	32.8	25.2	25.8	(NA)
2007	(NA)	33.9	39.0	41.2	38.2	30.2	37.0	42.4	36.5	36.5	32.9	36.0	33.5	(NA)	32.8	24.7	25.6	(NA)
2008	(NA)	33.6	38.5	40.8	38.2	30.0	36.4	42.7	36.7	37.0	32.7	35.8	33.6	(NA)	32.8	24.1	25.4	(NA)
HOURLY EARNINGS [2] (dol.)																		
1990	(NA)	10.20	13.42	10.78	11.58	7.71	12.50	16.14	13.40	10.40	8.66	13.99	8.48	(NA)	10.05	8.41	5.70	(NA)
2000	(NA)	14.02	17.48	14.32	16.28	10.86	15.05	22.75	19.07	15.90	12.15	20.61	11.69	(NA)	13.98	10.68	7.92	(NA)
2004	(NA)	15.69	19.23	16.14	17.65	12.08	16.52	25.61	21.40	18.70	13.89	23.23	12.94	(NA)	16.45	12.17	8.65	(NA)
2005	(NA)	16.13	19.46	16.56	18.16	12.36	16.70	26.68	22.06	19.09	14.57	24.15	13.16	(NA)	17.05	12.85	8.80	(NA)
2006	(NA)	16.76	20.02	16.81	18.91	12.57	17.28	27.40	23.23	20.05	15.08	25.27	13.93	(NA)	17.75	13.16	9.19	(NA)
2007	(NA)	17.43	20.95	17.26	19.59	12.75	17.72	27.88	23.96	20.92	15.76	26.58	14.47	(NA)	18.48	13.21	9.82	(NA)
2008	(NA)	18.08	21.87	17.74	20.14	12.87	18.41	28.84	24.77	21.54	16.38	27.83	14.88	(NA)	19.25	14.74	10.23	(NA)

NA Not available. [1] Includes other industries not shown separately. [2] Average hours and earnings of production workers for natural resources and mining, manufacturing, and construction; average hours and earnings of nonsupervisory workers for the service-providing industries.

Source: U.S. Bureau of Labor Statistics, Current Employment Statistics, "Employment, Hours, and Earnings—National"; <http://www.bls.gov/ces/data.htm>.

Labor Force, Employment, and Earnings 399

Table 618. **Employees in Nonfarm Establishments—States: 2008**

[In thousands (137,066 represents 137,066,000). For coverage, see headnote, Table 617. National totals differ from the sum of the state figures because of differing benchmarks among states and differing industrial and geographic stratification. Compiled from data supplied by cooperating state agencies. Based on North American Industry Classification System, 2007; see text, this section]

State	Total [1]	Construction	Manufacturing	Trade, transportation, and utilities	Information	Financial activities [2]	Professional and business services [3]	Education and health services [4]	Leisure and hospitality [5]	Other services [6]	Government
U.S. . . .	137,066	7,215	13,431	26,385	2,997	8,146	17,778	18,855	13,459	5,528	22,500
AL.	1,994.2	108.8	284.7	390.1	27.1	99.6	220.2	211.7	174.9	81.3	383.2
AK.	322.4	17.3	13.2	64.8	7.0	14.9	25.9	37.5	32.2	11.5	82.8
AZ.	2,616.3	187.8	174.5	515.2	42.1	176.1	385.5	319.1	268.8	100.3	433.6
AR.	1,204.3	56.3	182.6	247.0	18.6	52.3	117.3	158.2	101.3	45.7	214.3
CA.	14,994.1	785.8	1425.4	2854.7	474.7	849.9	2244.4	1725.3	1570.6	515.4	2519.3
CO	2,349.3	161.2	144.3	429.8	77.1	155.6	350.1	250.3	273.5	95.1	384.2
CT.	1,699.5	65.2	187.5	309.7	37.6	143.4	205.3	296.3	138.1	63.4	252.3
DE.	432.5	[7]25.4	31.5	80.7	7.1	45.5	58.7	60.3	40.9	20.4	62.0
DC	704.8	12.9	1.6	27.9	20.7	28.3	153.1	102.2	58.1	65.5	234.6
FL.	7,763.8	513.0	372.9	1581.3	155.6	527.0	1148.0	1047.5	942.7	341.3	1128.1
GA	4,102.5	204.7	408.3	874.7	108.7	224.1	557.4	465.8	394.5	160.4	693.5
HI	619.2	[7]38.0	14.9	118.3	10.0	29.4	75.3	74.0	107.2	27.2	125.0
ID	648.4	45.2	63.4	131.1	11.8	31.7	80.3	77.6	63.5	20.5	119.2
IL	5,948.3	257.9	659.5	1203.9	115.2	392.4	860.9	799.1	530.5	263.9	855.0
IN	2,958.2	143.8	522.2	580.3	39.7	135.8	284.6	407.9	285.6	111.7	439.9
IA	1,523.2	73.0	227.8	309.5	33.4	103.0	121.5	206.9	135.4	57.7	252.9
KS.	1,391.1	64.4	187.5	263.3	38.7	73.2	148.0	176.5	116.0	53.6	260.2
KY.	1,854.0	84.1	245.0	381.8	29.9	92.1	183.0	244.5	172.7	74.8	322.5
LA.	1,940.0	135.4	152.4	382.9	28.6	95.2	205.6	256.4	196.4	68.8	363.3
ME	615.9	29.2	58.9	124.6	10.8	32.6	56.0	117.7	59.6	19.9	104.1
MD	2,598.4	[7]179.9	128.4	465.5	49.9	152.5	399.2	382.4	235.2	118.0	487.3
MA	3,285.0	132.0	286.2	568.2	89.1	219.6	486.2	639.9	305.1	120.2	437.1
MI	4,159.2	153.7	575.3	769.4	61.8	204.4	557.0	608.3	398.1	175.6	647.9
MN	2,758.8	109.8	335.1	523.2	57.7	177.1	326.3	442.5	245.0	117.7	418.1
MS	1,147.0	60.6	160.0	223.8	13.4	46.8	94.5	128.2	124.9	37.1	248.2
MO	2,792.3	141.4	289.3	542.6	64.3	165.4	342.8	392.9	281.1	121.2	446.0
MT	446.5	29.8	20.0	92.3	7.6	21.9	40.7	61.1	59.3	17.6	88.0
NE.	964.7	[7]50.0	101.6	204.8	18.8	69.1	105.8	132.8	82.8	35.1	164.0
NV.	1,266.4	117.3	48.3	232.0	15.0	61.5	152.6	95.4	333.3	37.0	161.6
NH	645.7	25.8	75.6	140.1	12.5	38.0	66.6	105.3	63.8	22.1	94.8
NJ.	4,058.3	164.8	298.9	864.0	92.4	269.3	614.9	592.0	344.2	165.0	651.2
NM	846.8	57.2	35.2	145.1	16.1	34.7	108.1	115.0	86.8	30.1	197.6
NY.	8,794.9	360.1	534.1	1524.3	263.3	722.4	1156.8	1631.2	715.6	368.5	1512.2
NC	4,130.1	236.3	514.4	767.3	71.5	211.5	501.1	535.5	398.0	180.4	707.5
ND	367.0	20.8	26.4	78.1	7.4	20.3	30.3	52.0	33.5	15.4	76.1
OH	5,368.0	209.9	739.6	1035.2	86.1	290.9	666.4	816.5	495.7	219.6	796.4
OK	1,595.4	75.6	150.7	289.6	28.9	83.1	184.8	198.2	144.0	63.5	325.4
OR	1,720.7	94.6	195.1	335.4	36.1	101.8	195.6	220.0	173.7	61.0	298.8
PA.	5,800.9	255.8	644.2	1125.5	105.4	330.4	709.2	1100.3	504.2	254.5	749.4
RI	481.7	20.4	48.0	77.3	10.6	33.5	54.7	99.9	50.9	22.8	63.5
SC.	1,927.7	114.2	242.4	372.8	28.8	106.2	220.4	207.4	215.6	71.1	344.5
SD.	411.4	[7]23.3	42.6	82.2	7.0	31.1	27.8	62.1	43.3	15.9	76.0
TN.	2,776.2	[7]133.4	361.8	601.2	50.3	145.0	321.6	357.7	275.5	103.6	426.1
TX.	10,616.8	671.5	924.0	2147.3	217.2	648.8	1339.2	1292.8	1007.6	360.8	1777.0
UT.	1,255.2	90.9	126.1	248.7	30.7	74.1	163.2	146.3	114.7	35.8	212.0
VT.	306.1	15.4	34.8	58.7	5.8	12.9	22.6	58.8	32.5	9.8	54.0
VA.	3,757.5	222.2	264.6	658.2	87.6	188.8	655.1	438.2	348.5	188.7	694.6
WA	2,959.4	201.4	291.0	552.8	105.5	152.4	349.3	361.5	285.0	107.6	545.4
WV	761.1	38.4	56.3	141.9	11.2	29.7	60.6	116.9	72.8	55.8	146.7
WI	2,870.2	118.0	492.6	539.7	50.2	163.5	279.3	405.5	258.3	139.2	420.5
WY	298.5	28.3	9.9	56.1	4.0	11.7	18.6	24.5	34.6	12.1	69.4

[1] Includes mining and logging, not shown separately. [2] Finance and insurance; real estate and rental and leasing. [3] Professional, scientific, and technical services; management of companies and enterprises; administrative and support and waste management and remediation services. [4] Education services; health care and social assistance. [5] Arts, entertainment, and recreation; accommodations and food services. [6] Includes repair and maintenance; personal and laundry services; and membership associations and organizations. [7] Mining and Logging included with construction.

Source: U.S. Bureau of Labor Statistics, Current Employment Statistics, "State and Metro Area Employment, Hours, and Earnings (SAU)"; <http://www.bls.gov/sae/data.htm>.

U.S. Census Bureau, Statistical Abstract of the United States: 2010

Table 619. Nonfarm Industries—Employees and Earnings: 1990 to 2008

[Annual averages of monthly figures (109,487 represents 109,487,000). Covers all full- and part-time employees who worked during, or received pay for, any part of the pay period including the 12th of the month. See also headnote, Table 617]

Industry	2007 NAICS [1] code	All employees (1,000)					Average hourly earnings [2] (dol.)		
		1990	2000	2005	2007	2008	2000	2005	2008
Total nonfarm	(X)	109,487	131,785	133,703	137,598	137,066	(NA)	(NA)	(NA)
Goods-producing [3]	(X)	23,723	24,649	22,190	22,233	21,419	15.27	17.60	19.33
Service-providing [4]	(X)	85,764	107,136	111,513	115,366	115,646	(NA)	(NA)	(NA)
Total private	(X)	91,072	110,995	111,899	115,380	114,566	14.02	16.13	18.08
Natural resources and mining	(X)	765	599	628	724	774	16.55	18.72	22.50
Logging	1133	85	79	65	60	57	13.70	15.74	16.64
Mining	21	680	520	562	664	717	16.94	19.04	23.01
Oil and gas extraction	211	190	125	126	146	162	19.43	19.34	27.28
Mining, except oil and gas	212	302	225	213	223	228	18.07	20.18	22.01
Support activities for mining	213	188	171	224	294	328	14.55	17.89	22.40
Construction	23	5,263	6,787	7,336	7,630	7,215	17.48	19.46	21.87
Construction of buildings	236	1,413	1,633	1,712	1,774	1,659	16.74	19.05	21.39
Residential building	2361	673	823	960	949	832	15.18	17.72	19.47
Nonresidential building	2362	741	809	752	825	827	18.18	20.55	23.10
Heavy and civil engineering construction . . .	237	813	937	951	1,005	970	16.80	19.60	22.00
Highway, street, and bridge construction. .	2373	289	340	351	345	329	18.17	20.12	22.11
Specialty trade contractors [5]	238	3,037	4,217	4,673	4,850	4,585	17.91	19.55	21.99
Building foundation and exterior contractors	2381	703	919	1,083	1,080	988	16.93	18.44	20.54
Building equipment contractors	2382	1,282	1,897	1,918	2,057	2,023	19.52	21.01	23.56
Building finishing contractors	2383	665	857	992	1,003	913	16.44	18.02	20.87
Manufacturing	31–33	17,695	17,263	14,226	13,879	13,431	14.32	16.56	17.74
Durable goods	(X)	10,737	10,877	8,956	8,808	8,476	14.92	17.33	18.70
Wood products	321	541	613	559	515	460	11.63	13.16	14.20
Nonmetallic mineral products	327	528	554	505	501	468	14.53	16.61	16.90
Cement and concrete products	3273	195	234	240	242	223	14.64	16.68	17.57
Primary metals	331	689	622	466	456	443	16.64	18.94	20.18
Iron and steel mills and ferroalloy production	3311	187	135	96	100	99	20.97	23.55	25.46
Foundries	3315	214	217	164	155	149	14.72	17.50	18.69
Fabricated metal products [5]	332	1,610	1,753	1,522	1,563	1,528	13.77	15.80	16.99
Architectural and structural metals	3323	357	428	398	417	409	13.43	15.10	16.61
Machine shops and threaded products . . .	3327	309	365	345	361	360	14.53	16.43	17.79
Machinery [5]	333	1,410	1,457	1,166	1,187	1,186	15.21	17.02	17.97
Agricultural, construction, and mining machinery	3331	229	222	208	229	242	14.21	15.91	16.90
HVAC and commercial refrigeration equip.	3304	165	194	154	154	150	13.10	14.60	15.90
Metalworking machinery	3335	267	274	202	194	192	16.66	17.86	18.73
Computer and electronic products [5]	334	1,903	1,820	1,316	1,273	1,248	14.73	18.39	21.03
Computer and peripheral equipment	3341	367	302	205	186	183	18.39	22.75	21.72
Communications equipment	3342	223	239	141	128	129	14.39	18.05	20.86
Semiconductors and electronic components	3344	574	676	452	448	432	13.46	17.03	19.66
Electronic instruments	3345	635	488	441	443	442	15.80	17.71	22.67
Electrical equipment and appliances	335	633	591	434	429	425	13.23	15.24	15.78
Household appliances	3352	114	106	85	76	72	13.49	14.28	14.85
Electrical equipment	3353	244	210	152	157	159	13.28	15.31	15.71
Transportation equipment [5]	336	2,135	2,057	1,772	1,712	1,607	18.89	22.09	23.83
Motor vehicles	3361	271	291	248	220	191	24.45	29.01	29.18
Motor vehicle parts	3363	653	840	678	608	544	17.95	21.10	20.99
Aerospace products and parts	3364	841	517	455	489	504	20.52	24.82	29.92
Ship and boat building	3366	174	154	154	160	157	14.84	17.26	19.64
Furniture and related products	337	604	683	568	531	481	11.73	13.45	14.54
Household and institutional furniture	3371	401	443	383	349	306	11.39	13.15	14.25
Miscellaneous manufacturing	339	686	728	647	642	631	11.93	14.07	15.19
Medical equipment and supplies	3391	283	305	300	306	310	12.70	14.71	15.79
Nondurable goods	(X)	6,958	6,386	5,271	5,071	4,955	13.31	15.27	16.15
Food manufacturing [5]	311	1,507	1,553	1,478	1,484	1,485	11.77	13.04	14.00
Fruit and vegetable preserving and specialty	3114	218	197	174	173	174	11.90	12.81	14.21
Fruit and vegetable canning and drying . .	31142	127	96	85	85	87	13.23	13.70	15.45
Animal slaughtering and processing	3116	427	507	504	508	512	10.27	11.47	12.34
Bakeries and tortilla manufacturing	3118	292	306	280	280	281	11.45	12.57	13.40
Beverages and tobacco products	312	218	207	192	198	199	17.40	18.76	19.35
Beverages	3121	173	175	167	176	177	17.19	18.28	18.31
Textile mills	313	492	378	218	170	151	11.23	12.38	13.57
Textile product mills	314	236	230	176	158	148	10.43	11.61	11.73
Apparel	315	903	484	251	215	198	8.60	10.26	11.40
Cut and sew apparel	3152	750	380	193	166	155	8.40	10.05	11.43
Leather and allied products	316	133	69	40	34	34	10.35	11.50	12.96
Paper and paper products	322	647	605	484	458	446	15.91	17.99	18.88
Printing and related support activities	323	809	807	646	622	594	14.09	15.74	16.75
Petroleum and coal products	324	153	123	112	115	117	22.80	24.47	27.46
Chemicals [5]	325	1,036	980	872	861	850	17.09	19.67	19.49
Basic chemicals	3251	249	188	150	149	152	21.06	23.80	23.30
Resin, rubber, and artificial fibers	3252	158	136	108	106	105	17.09	19.03	20.54
Pharmaceuticals and medicines	3254	207	274	288	295	290	17.27	21.31	20.10
Plastics and rubber products	326	825	951	802	757	734	12.70	14.80	15.85
Plastics products	3261	618	737	634	609	589	12.04	14.01	15.15
Rubber products	3262	207	214	168	148	145	14.83	17.58	18.47

See footnotes at end of table.

Table 619. **Nonfarm Industries—Employees and Earnings: 1990 to 2008**—Con.

[Annual averages of monthly figures (109,487 represents 109,487,000). Covers all full- and part-time employees who worked during, or received pay for, any part of the pay period including the 12th of the month. See also headnote, Table 617]

Industry	2007 NAICS [1] code	All employees (1,000)					Average hourly earnings [2] (dol.)		
		1990	2000	2005	2007	2008	2000	2005	2008
Trade, transportation, and utilities	(X)	22,666	26,225	25,959	26,630	26,385	13.31	14.92	16.16
Wholesale trade.	42	5,268	5,933	5,764	6,015	5,964	16.28	18.16	20.14
Durable goods [5].	423	2,834	3,251	2,999	3,122	3,061	16.71	18.88	20.22
Motor vehicles and parts	4231	309	356	344	350	339	14.27	16.18	16.32
Lumber and construction supplies	4233	181	227	254	260	236	13.61	16.78	18.42
Commercial equipment	4234	597	722	639	660	655	20.29	23.67	24.25
Electric goods	4236	357	425	342	354	351	19.43	21.78	23.52
Hardware and plumbing	4237	216	247	245	257	253	15.07	16.47	19.05
Machinery and supplies	4238	690	725	659	692	685	16.47	18.71	20.16
Nondurable goods [5]	424	1,900	2,065	2,022	2,062	2,053	14.33	16.15	18.19
Paper and paper products	4241	162	177	152	144	140	15.65	17.23	18.79
Druggists' goods.	4242	136	192	213	212	208	18.98	19.20	22.57
Grocery and related products	4244	623	689	699	724	731	13.57	15.38	17.34
Electronic markets and agents and brokers.	425	535	618	743	832	850	20.79	20.71	24.83
Retail trade	44,45	13,182	15,280	15,280	15,520	15,356	10.86	12.36	12.87
Motor vehicle and parts dealers [5]	441	1,494	1,847	1,919	1,908	1,845	14.94	16.33	16.15
Automobile dealers	4411	983	1,217	1,261	1,242	1,186	16.95	17.85	17.13
Auto parts, accessories, and tire stores	4413	418	499	491	495	493	11.04	12.74	13.65
Furniture and home furnishings stores . . .	442	432	544	576	575	543	12.33	14.23	15.02
Furniture stores	4421	244	289	298	286	267	13.37	14.87	15.13
Home furnishings stores	4422	188	254	278	288	275	11.06	13.46	14.88
Electronics and appliance stores.	443	382	564	536	549	550	13.67	17.73	17.61
Building material and garden supply stores.	444	891	1,142	1,276	1,309	1,253	11.25	13.14	13.83
Building material and supplies dealers .	4441	753	982	1,134	1,145	1,115	11.30	13.24	13.85
Food and beverage stores.	445	2,779	2,993	2,818	2,844	2,858	9.76	10.85	11.56
Grocery stores	4451	2,406	2,582	2,446	2,481	2,497	9.71	10.80	11.59
Specialty food stores.	4452	232	270	236	226	223	9.97	11.04	11.07
Health and personal care stores	446	792	928	954	993	1,002	11.68	14.03	16.28
Gasoline stations	447	910	936	871	862	843	8.05	8.92	9.46
Clothing & clothing accessories stores . . .	448	1,313	1,322	1,415	1,500	1,484	9.96	11.07	11.57
Clothing stores.	4481	930	954	1,066	1,147	1,134	9.88	10.63	10.83
Shoe stores.	4482	216	193	180	189	192	8.96	10.05	12.58
Jewelry, luggage, and leather goods stores	4483	167	175	169	164	159	11.48	14.10	14.36
Sporting goods, hobby, book, and music stores.	451	532	686	647	656	647	9.33	10.35	11.70
Sporting goods and musical instrument stores	4511	352	437	447	475	472	9.55	10.68	11.94
Book, periodical, and music stores. . . .	4512	180	249	200	181	175	8.91	9.59	10.99
General merchandise stores	452	2,500	2,820	2,934	3,021	3,047	9.22	10.53	10.73
Department stores	4521	1,494	1,755	1,595	1,592	1,557	(NA)	(NA)	(NA)
Miscellaneous store retailers [5]	453	738	1,007	900	865	848	10.20	11.22	11.70
Office supplies, stationery, and gift stores.	4532	358	471	391	361	352	10.46	11.65	12.85
Used merchandise stores.	4533	56	107	113	117	119	8.07	8.96	8.94
Nonstore retailers.	454	419	492	435	438	436	13.22	14.56	16.42
Electronic shopping and mail-order houses	4541	157	257	240	247	251	13.38	14.52	16.47
Transportation and warehousing.	48,49	3,476	4,410	4,361	4,541	4,505	15.05	16.70	18.41
Air transportation	481	529	614	501	492	493	(NA)	(NA)	(NA)
Scheduled air transportation	4811	503	570	456	446	446	(NA)	(NA)	(NA)
Rail transportation	482	272	232	228	234	230	(NA)	(NA)	(NA)
Water transportation	483	57	56	61	66	65	(NA)	(NA)	(NA)
Truck transportation	484	1,122	1,406	1,398	1,439	1,391	15.86	16.74	17.99
General freight trucking	4841	807	1,013	981	1,007	977	16.37	17.20	17.99
Specialized freight trucking	4842	315	393	417	432	414	14.51	15.60	17.97
Transit and ground passenger transportation [5].	485	274	372	389	412	418	11.88	13.00	13.94
Urban transit, interurban and rural bus transportation.	4851,2	46	59	60	61	64	(NA)	(NA)	(NA)
Taxi and limousine service	4853	57	72	66	73	72	(NA)	(NA)	(NA)
Pipeline transportation	486	60	46	38	40	42	19.86	24.33	26.44
Scenic and sightseeing transportation . . .	487	16	28	29	29	28	12.49	13.75	15.77
Support activities for transportation [5] . . .	488	364	537	552	584	590	14.57	17.66	19.52
Support activities for air transportation .	4881	96	141	148	163	167	13.42	15.07	17.54
Support activities for water transportation	4883	91	97	94	100	97	19.57	27.08	29.06
Support activities for road transportation	4884	35	66	79	84	86	13.98	15.41	15.01
Freight transportation arrangement . . .	4885	111	178	177	184	187	13.46	16.94	18.95
Couriers and messengers	492	375	605	571	581	576	13.51	15.33	17.60
Couriers and express delivery services. .	4921	340	546	522	531	525	13.92	15.76	18.28
Warehousing and storage	493	407	514	595	665	673	14.46	15.06	15.14
Utilities.	22	740	601	554	553	560	22.75	26.68	28.84
Power generation and supply	2211	550	434	401	398	405	23.13	27.63	30.26
Natural gas distribution	2212	155	121	107	107	107	23.41	26.86	26.82
Water, sewage and other systems.	2213	35	46	45	49	48	16.93	17.70	21.47

See footnotes at end of table.

U.S. Census Bureau, Statistical Abstract of the United States: 2010

Table 619. **Nonfarm Industries—Employees and Earnings: 1990 to 2008**—Con.

[Annual averages of monthly figures (109,487 represents 109,487,000). Covers all full- and part-time employees who worked during, or received pay for, any part of the pay period including the 12th of the month. See also headnote, Table 617]

Industry	2007 NAICS [1] code	All employees (1,000)					Average hourly earnings [2] (dol.)		
		1990	2000	2005	2007	2008	2000	2005	2008
Information.	51	**2,688**	**3,630**	**3,061**	**3,032**	**2,997**	**19.07**	**22.06**	**24.77**
Publishing industries, except Internet	511	871	1,035	904	901	883	20.18	24.20	25.78
Newspaper, book, and directory publishers.	5111	773	774	666	646	619	15.06	18.57	20.03
Software publishers	5112	98	261	238	255	264	28.48	38.11	38.08
Motion picture and sound recording industries.	512	255	383	378	381	382	21.25	18.75	20.99
Motion picture and video industries	5121	232	352	357	359	362	21.33	18.88	21.19
Broadcasting, except Internet	515	284	344	328	325	316	16.74	21.22	23.84
Radio and television broadcasting.	5151	232	253	239	237	231	17.13	22.15	24.22
Cable and other subscription programming.	5152	52	91	89	89	85	(NA)	(NA)	(NA)
Telecommunications [5]	517	980	1,397	1,071	1,031	1,021	18.59	22.13	25.74
Wired telecommunications carriers	5171	673	922	690	665	666	18.62	22.46	25.01
Wireless telecommunications carriers (except satellite).	5172	36	186	191	203	203	14.40	20.40	29.59
Data processing, hosting and related services.	518	211	316	263	268	262	16.97	19.97	22.65
Financial activities	(X)	**6,614**	**7,687**	**8,153**	**8,301**	**8,146**	**14.98**	**17.94**	**20.27**
Finance and insurance [5].	52	**4,979**	**5,680**	**6,023**	**6,132**	**6,015**	**15.90**	**19.09**	**21.54**
Monetary authorities–central bank.	521	24	23	21	22	22	(NA)	(NA)	(NA)
Credit intermediation and related activities.	522	2,425	2,548	2,869	2,866	2,736	13.14	15.85	17.49
Depository credit intermediation.	5221	1,909	1,681	1,769	1,824	1,820	11.97	14.13	16.68
Commercial banking	52211	1,362	1,251	1,296	1,351	1,360	11.83	13.79	16.42
Nondepository credit intermediation . . .	5222	398	644	770	716	631	15.30	19.24	19.62
Activities related to credit intermediation.	5223	119	222	330	327	286	15.39	16.48	17.57
Securities, commodity contracts, investments.	523	458	805	786	849	858	20.20	26.59	30.58
Securities and commodity contracts brokerage and exchanges	5231,2	338	566	499	519	511	20.07	27.68	30.82
Other financial investment activities . . .	5239	120	239	287	330	347	20.48	24.69	30.20
Insurance carriers and related activities . .	524	2,016	2,221	2,259	2,307	2,309	17.37	20.66	22.83
Insurance carriers.	5241	1,338	1,433	1,386	1,397	1,402	17.92	21.67	23.96
Insurance agencies, brokerages, and related services	5242	678	788	874	910	907	16.28	18.88	20.95
Funds, trusts, and other financial vehicles	525	56	85	88	89	90	17.66	21.12	22.74
Real estate and rental and leasing [5]	53	**1,637**	**2,011**	**2,134**	**2,169**	**2,130**	**12.14**	**14.55**	**16.38**
Real estate	531	1,107	1,312	1,457	1,500	1,481	12.24	14.67	16.62
Lessors of real estate	5311	564	607	600	599	598	11.16	13.75	15.79
Offices of real estate agents and brokers	5312	217	281	356	368	345	12.57	14.90	17.12
Activities related to real estate	5313	327	424	502	533	539	13.60	15.64	17.21
Rental and leasing services [5]	532	514	667	646	640	621	11.69	14.05	15.38
Automotive equipment rental and leasing	5321	163	208	199	196	195	10.70	13.64	14.32
Consumer goods rental	5322	220	292	275	261	246	9.53	12.39	13.23
Professional and business services	(X)	**10,848**	**16,666**	**16,954**	**17,942**	**17,778**	**15.52**	**18.08**	**21.19**
Professional and technical services [5] . . .	54	**4,557**	**6,734**	**7,053**	**7,660**	**7,830**	**20.61**	**24.15**	**27.83**
Legal services	5411	944	1,066	1,168	1,175	1,164	21.38	23.96	28.68
Accounting and bookkeeping services . . .	5412	664	866	849	936	950	14.42	17.45	19.78
Architectural and engineering services . . .	5413	942	1,238	1,311	1,432	1,445	20.49	23.96	27.77
Computer systems design and related services	5415	410	1,254	1,195	1,372	1,450	27.13	31.64	36.10
Management and technical consulting services	5416	305	673	824	953	1,009	20.83	23.97	26.09
Scientific research and development services	5417	494	515	577	602	622	21.39	28.33	32.89
Advertising and related services	5418	382	497	446	471	462	16.99	19.49	21.73
Management of companies and enterprises	55	**1,667**	**1,796**	**1,759**	**1,866**	**1,895**	**15.28**	**18.08**	**22.05**
Administrative and waste services	56	**4,624**	**8,136**	**8,142**	**8,416**	**8,054**	**11.69**	**13.16**	**14.88**
Administrative and support services [5]	561	4,395	7,823	7,804	8,061	7,694	11.53	12.93	14.65
Office administrative services	5611	211	264	345	390	403	14.68	17.82	21.14
Employment services	5613	1,494	3,817	3,578	3,546	3,144	11.89	13.04	15.00
Temporary help services.	56132	1,156	2,636	2,549	2,597	2,343	11.79	12.00	13.74
Business support services	5614	505	787	766	817	823	11.08	13.14	13.85
Travel arrangement and reservation services	5615	250	299	224	227	228	12.72	14.55	16.07
Investigation and security services. . . .	5616	507	689	737	784	807	9.78	11.64	13.28
Services to buildings and dwellings . . .	5617	1,175	1,571	1,738	1,850	1,847	10.02	11.44	12.71
Waste management and remediation services	562	229	313	338	355	360	15.29	17.69	19.06
Waste collection	5621	82	100	124	137	141	12.97	15.54	17.22
Waste treatment and disposal.	5622	77	119	103	100	101	15.02	17.76	20.30

See footnotes at end of table.

U.S. Census Bureau, Statistical Abstract of the United States: 2010

Table 619. Nonfarm Industries—Employees and Earnings: 1990 to 2008—Con.

[Annual averages of monthly figures (109,487 represents 109,487,000). Covers all full- and part-time employees who worked during, or received pay for, any part of the pay period including the 12th of the month. See also headnote, Table 617]

Industry	2007 NAICS [1] code	All employees (1,000)					Average hourly earnings [2] (dol.)		
		1990	2000	2005	2007	2008	2000	2005	2008
Education and health services	(X)	10,984	15,109	17,372	18,322	18,855	13.95	16.71	18.88
Educational services	61	1,688	2,390	2,836	2,941	3,037	(NA)	(NA)	(NA)
Elementary and secondary schools	6111	461	716	837	829	855	(NA)	(NA)	(NA)
Junior colleges	6112	44	79	100	74	80	(NA)	(NA)	(NA)
Colleges and universities.	6113	939	1,196	1,393	1,483	1,523	(NA)	(NA)	(NA)
Business, computer, and management training.	6114	60	86	77	77	76	(NA)	(NA)	(NA)
Technical and trade schools.	6115	72	91	102	110	115	(NA)	(NA)	(NA)
Other schools and instruction	6116	96	184	250	282	294	(NA)	(NA)	(NA)
Educational support services	6117	17	39	78	87	94	(NA)	(NA)	(NA)
Health care and social assistance	62	9,296	12,718	14,536	15,380	15,819	13.98	17.05	19.25
Ambulatory health care services [5].	621	2,842	4,320	5,114	5,474	5,661	14.99	17.86	20.49
Offices of physicians	6211	1,278	1,840	2,094	2,202	2,266	15.65	18.95	22.09
Offices of dentists.	6212	513	688	774	808	819	15.96	19.40	22.36
Offices of other health practitioners . . .	6213	276	438	549	600	629	14.24	16.70	19.35
Outpatient care centers	6214	261	386	473	512	533	15.29	18.96	21.13
Medical and diagnostic laboratories . . .	6215	129	162	198	211	219	15.74	18.67	23.21
Home health care services	6216	288	633	821	914	958	12.86	14.42	16.17
Hospitals [5]	622	3,513	3,954	4,345	4,515	4,641	16.71	21.30	23.99
General medical and surgical hospitals.	6221	3,305	3,745	4,096	4,242	4,351	16.75	21.40	24.14
Psychiatric and substance abuse hospitals	6222	113	86	93	99	102	14.97	17.79	18.29
Nursing and residential care facilities [5]. .	623	1,856	2,583	2,855	2,958	3,008	10.67	12.37	13.70
Nursing care facilities	6231	1,170	1,514	1,577	1,603	1,614	11.08	13.08	14.37
Residential mental health facilities	6232	269	437	497	528	542	9.96	11.30	13.01
Community care facilities for the elderly.	6233	330	478	615	663	685	9.83	11.33	12.63
Social assistance	624	1,085	1,860	2,222	2,433	2,509	9.78	11.35	12.47
Individual and family services	6241	389	678	921	1,050	1,109	10.57	12.44	13.13
Emergency and other relief services. . .	6242	67	117	129	134	138	10.95	13.48	14.72
Vocational rehabilitation services	6243	242	370	383	399	403	9.57	10.67	12.45
Child day care services	6244	388	696	790	850	859	8.88	10.14	11.32
Leisure and hospitality	(X)	9,288	11,862	12,816	13,427	13,459	8.32	9.38	10.84
Arts, entertainment, and recreation	71	1,132	1,788	1,892	1,969	1,969	10.68	12.85	14.74
Performing arts and spectator sports	711	273	382	376	405	406	13.11	18.67	20.66
Museums, historical sites, zoos, and parks	712	68	110	121	130	132	12.21	13.67	15.14
Amusements, gambling, and recreation . .	713	791	1,296	1,395	1,434	1,431	9.86	11.08	12.87
Accommodations and food services	72	8,156	10,074	10,923	11,457	11,489	7.92	8.80	10.23
Accommodations	721	1,616	1,884	1,819	1,867	1,857	9.48	10.75	12.89
Traveler and other longer-term accommodations.	7211	1,582	1,837	1,765	1,812	1,804	9.49	10.78	12.94
Food services and drinking places	722	6,540	8,189	9,104	9,590	9,632	7.49	8.34	9.59
Full-service restaurants	7221	3,070	3,845	4,316	4,572	4,598	7.78	8.84	10.21
Limited-service eating places	7222	2,765	3,462	3,889	4,106	4,137	6.87	7.49	8.62
Special food services	7223	392	491	538	555	544	9.45	10.48	11.49
Drinking places, alcoholic beverages . .	7224	312	391	361	358	352	7.24	7.89	9.57
Other services	81	4,261	5,168	5,395	5,494	5,528	12.73	14.34	16.08
Repair and maintenance.	811	1,009	1,242	1,236	1,253	1,228	13.28	14.82	16.5
Automotive repair and maintenance.	8111	659	888	886	885	858	12.45	14.11	15.24
Personal and laundry services	812	1,120	1,243	1,277	1,310	1,327	10.18	11.81	12.88
Personal care services	8121	430	490	577	609	622	10.18	12.44	13.53
Death care services	8122	123	136	137	134	136	13.04	15.34	16.82
Dry-cleaning and laundry services.	8123	371	388	347	338	335	9.17	10.18	11.42
Dry-cleaning and laundry services, except coin-operated	81232	215	211	180	170	165	8.14	9.14	9.93
Other personal services	8129	196	229	216	230	234	10.52	11.29	11.75
Pet care services, except veterinary . . .	81291	23	31	44	52	56	(NA)	(NA)	(NA)
Parking lots and garages	81293	68	93	103	111	113	8.81	9.89	10.86
Membership associations & organizations [5] .	813	2,132	2,683	2,882	2,931	2,973	13.66	15.20	17.31
Grantmaking and giving services	8132	113	116	137	149	156	14.65	18.80	21.91
Social advocacy organizations	8133	126	143	174	190	195	12.08	13.89	15.63
Civic and social organizations.	8134	377	404	409	415	415	9.85	11.16	12.1
Professional and similar organizations . . .	8139	379	473	492	508	523	15.98	18.60	21.04
Government.	(X)	18,415	20,790	21,804	22,218	22,500	(NA)	(NA)	(NA)
Federal.	(X)	3,196	2,865	2,732	2,734	2,764	(NA)	(NA)	(NA)
State	(X)	4,305	4,786	5,032	5,122	5,178	(NA)	(NA)	(NA)
Local	(X)	10,914	13,139	14,041	14,362	14,557	(NA)	(NA)	(NA)

NA Not available.   X Not applicable.   [1] Based on the North American Industry Classification System, 2007. See text, Section 15.   [2] Production workers in the goods-producing industries and nonsupervisory workers in service-producing industries. See footnotes 3 and 4.   [3] Natural resources and mining, construction, and manufacturing.   [4] Trade, transportation and utilities, information, financial activities, professional and business services, education and health services, leisure and hospitality, other services, and government.   [5] Includes other industries not shown separately.

Source: U.S. Bureau of Labor Statistics, Current Employment Statistics, "Employment, Hours, and Earnings—National"; <http://www.bls.gov/ces/data.htm>.

Table 620. Private Nonfarm Extended Mass Layoff Activity by Industry and Reason: 2000 to 2008

[The Mass Layoff Statistics (MLS) program is a federal-state program which collects reports on mass layoff actions that result in workers being separated from their jobs using data from each state's unemployment insurance (UI) database. Employers which have at least 50 initial claims filed against them during a consecutive 5-week period are contacted by the state agency to determine whether these separations are of at least 31 days duration, and if so, information is obtained on the total number of persons separated and the reasons for these separations. Employers are identified according to industry classification and location, and unemployment insurance claimants are identified by demographic factors. The program yields information on an individual's entire spell of unemployment, to the point when regular unemployment insurance benefits are exhausted]

Industry	2007 NAICS code [1]	Extended mass layoff events	Separations	Initial claimants [2]
Total, 2000	(X)	4,591	915,962	846,267
Total, 2005	(X)	4,881	884,661	834,533
Total, 2006	(X)	4,885	935,969	951,155
Total, 2007	(X)	5,363	965,935	978,712
Total, 2008.	**(X)**	**8,263**	**1,517,857**	**1,665,377**
Mining, quarrying, and gas extraction.	21	55	9,218	9,756
Utilities.	22	11	2,032	2,122
Construction	23	1,724	205,327	256,109
Manufacturing	31–33	2,589	484,187	638,346
Wholesale trade.	42	190	25,247	25,057
Retail trade	44,45	482	121,385	126,326
Transportation and warehousing	48,49	489	102,087	97,906
Information	51	204	37,988	39,258
Finance and Insurance	52	405	92,782	86,609
Real estate and rental and leasing	53	51	6,385	6,970
Professional and technical services	54	257	67,400	51,071
Management of companies and enterprises . . .	55	30	4,611	4,799
Administrative and waste services.	56	671	141,034	150,870
Educational services.	61	43	5,504	5,623
Health care and social assistance	62	319	44,229	36,249
Arts, entertainment, and recreation	71	179	52,643	22,081
Accommodation and food services	72	458	102,325	92,605
Other services	81	102	12,722	13,123
Unclassified.	(X)	4	841	497
Reasons for layoff:				
Business demand.	(X)	3,389	516,922	731,804
Disaster/safety.	(X)	58	9,165	8,442
Financial issues.	(X)	764	165,652	145,769
Organizational changes.	(X)	517	123,349	119,929
Production specific	(X)	107	27,181	25,512
Seasonal	(X)	1,982	393,109	348,835
Other/miscellaneous	(X)	1,446	285,086	285,086

X Not applicable. [1] Based on the North American Industry Classification System, 2007. See text, Section 1b. [2] A person who files any notice of unemployment to initiate a request either for a determination of entitlement to and eligibility for compensation, or for a subsequent period of unemployment within a benefit year or period of eligibility.

Source: U.S. Bureau of Labor Statistics, Extended Mass Layoffs in the First Quarter of 2009, USDL 09-0506, May 12, 2009. See also <http://www.bls.gov/mls/home.htm>.

Table 621. Women Employees on Nonfarm Payrolls by Major Industry: 1980 to 2008

[Annual averages of monthly data. For coverage see headnote, Table 617]

Industry	Women employees (1,000s)				Percent of total employees			
	1980	1990	2000	2008	1980	1990	2000	2008
Total nonfarm	**37,813**	**51,587**	**63,223**	**67,194**	**41.8**	**47.1**	**48.0**	**49.0**
Total private	29,783	41,732	51,452	54,291	40.2	45.8	46.4	47.4
Mining and logging	123	112	92	102	11.4	14.6	15.4	13.2
Construction	458	656	846	923	10.3	12.5	12.5	12.8
Manufacturing	5,676	5,702	5,359	3,855	30.3	32.2	31.0	28.7
Trade, transportation, and utilities	6,799	9,363	10,859	10,826	36.9	41.3	41.4	41.0
Wholesale trade	1,179	1,611	1,827	1,827	25.9	30.6	30.8	30.6
Retail trade	4,980	6,696	7,680	7,750	48.6	50.8	50.3	50.5
Transportation and warehousing	506	879	1,202	1,097	17.1	25.3	27.3	24.4
Utilities	134	177	151	151	20.6	24.0	25.1	27.0
Information	1,118	1,324	1,697	1,265	47.4	49.3	46.7	42.2
Financial activities	2,848	4,055	4,638	4,816	56.7	61.3	60.3	59.1
Finance and insurance.	(NA)	3,345	3,744	3,815	(NA)	67.2	66.0	63.4
Real estate and rental and leasing.	(NA)	710	894	1,001	(NA)	43.4	44.4	47.0
Professional and business services	3,096	5,105	7,680	7,962	41.0	47.1	46.1	44.8
Professional and technical services	(NA)	2,209	3,146	3,733	(NA)	48.7	46.9	47.7
Management of companies and enterprises. .	(NA)	849	924	966	(NA)	50.9	51.4	51.0
Administrative and waste services	(NA)	2,048	3,610	3,262	(NA)	44.1	44.2	40.5
Education and health services	5,459	8,422	11,586	14,586	77.2	76.7	76.7	77.4
Educational services	(NA)	958	1,417	1,855	(NA)	56.8	59.3	61.1
Health care and social assistance	(NA)	7,464	10,168	12,732	(NA)	80.3	79.9	80.5
Leisure and hospitality.	3,021	4,829	6,082	7,067	44.9	52.0	51.3	52.5
Arts, entertainment, and recreation.	(NA)	516	815	933	(NA)	45.6	45.6	47.4
Accommodation and food services.	(NA)	4,312	5,267	6,134	(NA)	52.9	52.3	53.4
Other services	1,185	2,164	2,614	2,889	43.0	50.8	50.6	52.3
Government.	8,029	9,855	11,771	12,904	49.0	53.5	56.6	57.4

NA Not available.

Source: U.S. Bureau of Labor Statistics, Current Employment Statistics, "Employment, Hours, and Earnings—National"; <http://www.bls.gov/ces/data.htm>.

Labor Force, Employment, and Earnings   405

Table 622. Hires and Separations Affecting Establishment Payrolls: 2005 to 2008

[64,502 represents 64,502,000. Hires represent any additions to payrolls, including new and rehired employees, full- and part-time workers, short-term and seasonal workers, etc. Separations represent terminations of employment, including quits, layoffs, and discharges etc. Based on a monthly survey of private nonfarm establishments and governmental entities]

Industry	Annual hires (1,000)				Annual separations (1,000)			
	2005	2006	2007	2008	2005	2006	2007	2008
Total............................	64,502	64,911	63,381	56,496	62,087	62,626	62,104	59,343
Total Private industry...................	60,455	60,478	58,833	52,807	58,221	58,435	57,860	55,808
Mining and Logging..................	303	312	347	382	253	256	311	334
Construction	5,885	5,398	4,811	4,618	5,484	5,220	4,971	5,242
Manufacturing	4,540	4,605	4,617	3,651	4,630	4,750	4,871	4,475
Durable goods	2,896	2,737	2,687	2,089	2,883	2,766	2,880	2,695
Nondurable goods	1,643	1,869	1,930	1,561	1,745	1,985	1,988	1,780
Trade, transportation, and utilities	13,688	13,802	13,215	11,602	13,299	13,454	12,889	12,488
Wholesale trade	2,010	2,044	2,212	1,892	1,914	1,894	2,126	2,093
Retail trade	9,443	9,596	9,121	7,876	9,235	9,522	8,928	8,424
Transportation, warehousing, and utilities..	2,234	2,160	1,881	1,833	2,149	2,034	1,835	1,970
Information	1,044	1,121	983	814	1,076	1,139	999	897
Financial activities..................	2,865	3,098	3,158	2,649	2,712	2,946	3,259	2,870
Finance and insurance	1,849	1,992	2,089	1,704	1,736	1,866	2,181	1,856
Real estate and rental and leasing	1,017	1,105	1,070	945	976	1,081	1,078	1,013
Professional and business services	12,153	11,955	11,475	10,112	11,467	11,415	11,183	10,823
Education and health services...........	6,210	6,385	6,438	6,553	5,767	5,907	5,911	6,055
Educational services	826	879	910	939	754	834	850	858
Health care and social assistance......	5,386	5,506	5,529	5,616	5,012	5,070	5,060	5,199
Leisure and hospitality...............	10,948	11,245	11,194	9,965	10,709	10,856	10,938	10,158
Arts, entertainment, and recreation	1,641	1,572	1,639	1,473	1,587	1,491	1,601	1,509
Accommodation and food services	9,306	9,674	9,554	8,492	9,123	9,365	9,341	8,648
Other services	2,817	2,560	2,600	2,462	2,825	2,493	2,529	2,467
Government workers..................	4,046	4,434	4,549	3,688	3,868	4,191	4,242	3,534
Federal	511	711	844	335	502	721	825	322
State and local...................	3,537	3,721	3,705	3,351	3,363	3,470	3,420	3,210

Source: U.S. Bureau of Labor Statistics, *Job Openings and Labor Turnover*, News, USDL 09-0245, March 10, 2009. See also <http://www.bls.gov/jlt.htm>.

Table 623. Hires and Separations Affecting Establishment Payrolls: 2008

[31,004 represents 31,004,000. Covers all private nonfarm establishments. Separations are the total number of terminations of employment occuring at any time during the reference month, and are reported by type of separation—quits, layoffs and discharges, and other separations. Annual rate estimates are computed by dividing annual levels by the Current Employment Statistics (CES) annual average employment level, see Table 619, and multiplying that quotient by 100]

Industry	Number (1,000)			Rate		
	Annual quits level [1]	Annual lay-offs and discharge levels [2]	Annual other sep-erations [3]	Annual quits level [1]	Annual lay-offs and discharge levels [2]	Annual other sep-erations [3]
Total.........................	31,004	24,370	3,969	22.6	17.8	2.9
Total private industry...................	29,344	23,146	3,319	25.6	20.2	2.9
Natural resources and mining	187	117	28	24.2	15.1	3.6
Construction	1,664	3,347	233	23.1	46.4	3.2
Manufacturing	1,929	2,217	332	14.4	16.5	2.5
Durable goods	1,072	1,413	209	12.6	16.7	2.5
Nondurable goods	855	801	124	17.3	16.2	2.5
Trade, transportation, and utilities	6,824	4,691	974	25.9	17.8	3.7
Wholesale trade	999	973	120	16.8	16.3	2.0
Retail trade	4,861	2,907	658	31.7	18.9	4.3
Transportation, warehousing, and utilities..	965	811	196	19.1	16.0	3.9
Information	465	365	68	15.5	12.2	2.3
Financial activities..................	1,528	1,100	245	18.8	13.5	3.0
Finance and insurance	1,047	640	172	17.4	10.6	2.9
Real estate and rental and leasing	481	461	73	22.6	21.6	3.4
Professional and business services	5,145	5,110	568	28.9	28.7	3.2
Education and health services...........	3,531	2,069	454	18.7	11.0	2.4
Educational services	386	426	48	12.7	14.0	1.6
Health care and social assistance......	3,148	1,644	406	19.9	10.4	2.6
Leisure and hospitality...............	6,685	3,152	322	49.7	23.4	2.4
Arts, entertainment, and recreation	570	898	42	28.9	45.6	2.1
Accommodation and food services	6,115	2,256	278	53.2	19.6	2.4
Other services	1,387	977	102	25.1	17.7	1.8
Government workers..................	1,661	1,227	647	7.4	5.5	2.9
Federal	105	109	110	3.8	3.9	4.0
State and local...................	1,555	1,114	538	7.9	5.6	2.7

[1] Quits are voluntary separations by employees (except for retirements, which are reported as other separations). [2] Layoffs and discharges are involuntary separations initiated by the employer and include layoffs with no intent to rehire; formal layoffs lasting or expected to last more than seven days; discharges resulting from mergers, downsizing, or closings, firings or other discharges for cause; terminations of permanent or short term employees; and terminations of seasonal employees. [3] Other separations include retirements, transfers to other locations, deaths, and separations due to disability.

Source: U.S. Bureau of Labor Statistics, *Job Openings and Labor Turnover*, News, USDL 09-0245, March 10, 2009. See also <http://bls.gov/news.release/archives/jolts_03102009.htm>.

Table 624. Adults in Selected Work-Related Formal Learning Activities by Type of Educational Activity: 2004-2005

[(211,607 represents 211,607,000). Civilian noninstitutional population 16 years old and over not enrolled in elementary or secondary school. Based on the Adult Education Survey of the National Household Education Survey Program; see source and Appendix III for details]

Characteristic	Total adults (1,000)	Any activities	College degree program	Vocational degree/ diploma program	Apprenticeship	Work-related courses
		\multicolumn{5}{c}{Adults participating in work-related formal learning activities (percent)}				
Total	211,607	33	7	1	1	27
Age:						
16 to 24 years old	25,104	46	28	3	3	21
25 to 44 years old	81,674	39	7	2	2	33
45 to 64 years old	70,908	34	2	1	–	33
65 years old and over	33,922	5	–	–	–	5
Sex:						
Male	101,596	31	6	2	2	24
Female	110,011	35	8	1	1	29
Race/ethnicity:						
White, non-Hispanic	146,614	34	7	1	1	29
Black, non-Hispanic	23,467	34	6	2	2	27
Asian or Pacific Islander, non-Hispanic	7,080	35	12	1	1	24
Other, non-Hispanic	8,346	34	11	2	2	23
Hispanic [1]	26,101	23	4	2	2	17
Educational attainment:						
Less than high school	38,538	8	1	1	2	6
High school diploma or equivalent	63,701	23	2	2	1	18
Some college	51,657	43	14	2	2	32
BA degree	37,244	49	9	1	–	44
Graduate degree or higher	20,466	55	8	1	1	51

– Represents or rounds to zero.   [1] Persons of Hispanic Origin may be any race.

Source: U.S. National Center for Education Statistics, Adult Education Survey of the National Household Education Surveys Program 2005, unpublished data.

Table 625. Average Hours Worked Per Day by Employed Persons: 2008

[(155,371 represents 155,371,000). Civilian noninstitutional population 15 years old and over, except as indicated. Includes work at main and any other job(s). Excludes travel related to work. Based on the American Time Use Survey; see source for details]

Characteristic	Total employed (1,000)	Number (1,000)	Percent of employed	Hours of work	Percent of employed [3]	Hours of work	Percent of employed [3]	Hours of work
		\multicolumn{8}{c}{Employed persons who worked on their diary day [1]}							
					\multicolumn{2}{c}{Worked at workplace}	\multicolumn{2}{c}{Worked at home [2]}		
Total	155,371	105,735	68.1	7.59	85.5	7.88	21.1	2.90
Work status: [4]								
Full-time workers [5]	121,122	87,297	72.1	8.05	86.7	8.31	20.9	3.01
Part-time workers [5]	34,250	18,439	53.8	5.37	80.2	5.73	21.9	2.36
Male [4]	83,045	58,744	70.7	7.97	86.6	8.17	20.0	3.03
Full-time workers [5]	71,006	52,368	73.8	8.27	87.3	8.44	20.1	3.13
Part-time workers [5]	12,039	6,376	53.0	5.47	81.3	5.77	19.3	2.23
Female [4]	72,326	46,991	65.0	7.11	84.2	7.52	22.4	2.74
Full-time workers [5]	50,115	34,928	69.7	7.73	85.7	8.10	22.1	2.86
Part-time workers [5]	22,211	12,063	54.3	5.33	79.7	5.71	23.3	2.42
Jobholding status:								
Single-jobholders	140,936	93,810	66.6	7.57	86.7	7.86	19.2	2.88
Multiple-jobholders	14,436	11,925	82.6	7.73	76.5	8.13	35.6	2.95
Educational attainment: [6]								
Less than high school	11,659	7,955	68.2	8.17	91.0	8.34	8.6	(B)
High school diploma [7]	36,749	24,843	67.6	7.86	89.0	8.03	12.9	3.49
Some college	33,637	22,655	67.4	7.63	85.9	7.95	20.5	3.03
BA degree or higher	48,938	35,669	72.9	7.42	78.5	7.90	35.3	2.70

B Percent not shown where base is less than 1.2 million.   [1] Individuals may have worked at more than one location.   [2] "Working at home" includes any time persons did work at home and is not restricted to persons whose usual workplace is their home.   [3] Percent of employed who worked on their diary day.   [4] Includes workers whose hours vary.   [5] Full-time workers usually worked 35 or more hours per week at all jobs combined; part-time workers fewer than 35 hours per week.   [6] For those 25 years old and over.   [7] Includes persons with a high school diploma or equivalent.

Source: U.S. Bureau of Labor Statistics, American Time Use Survey—2008 Results, News, USDL 09-0704, June 24, 2009. See also <http://www.bls.gov/tus/home.htm>.

Table 626. **Productivity and Related Measures for Selected NAICS Industries: 1987 to 2007 and 2001 to 2007**

[For a discussion of productivity measures, see text, this section and BLS Handbook of Methods; <http://www.bls.gov/opub/hom/homch11a.htm>. Minus sign (–) indicates decrease]

Industry	2002 NAICS [1] code	Average annual percent change [2]							
		1987–2007 [3]				2001–2007 [4]			
		Output per hour	Output	Hours	Unit labor costs	Output per hour	Output	Hours	Unit labor costs
Mining	21	−0.2	−0.3	−0.1	5.1	−4.7	−1.0	3.9	10.2
Oil and gas extraction	2111	1.0	−0.9	−1.8	5.9	−3.7	−1.2	2.5	10.5
Mining, except oil and gas	212	2.1	0.9	−1.2	0.9	−0.6	0.0	0.6	3.8
Support activities for mining	2131	3.5	5.9	2.3	2.5	6.0	14.2	7.8	−0.2
Utilities:									
Power generation and supply	2211	2.8	1.2	−1.5	1.6	1.0	−0.3	−1.3	3.8
Natural gas distribution	2212	2.9	1.3	−1.5	2.1	1.4	0.5	-0.9	2.8
Manufacturing:									
Food	311	1.3	1.7	0.3	1.4	2.0	1.5	−0.5	1.0
Animal slaughtering and processing	3116	1.0	2.5	1.5	1.0	2.4	2.0	−0.4	0.4
Bakeries and tortilla manufacturing	3118	0.5	0.6	0.2	1.9	0.1	–	−0.1	0.4
Beverages and tobacco products	312	1.0	0.2	−0.8	1.5	1.0	−0.5	−1.4	2.0
Textile mills	313	3.8	−1.5	−5.2	−0.4	6.6	-3.9	−9.8	−2.2
Textile product mills	314	1.4	0.2	−1.1	1.0	3.0	−1.1	−4.0	−1.4
Apparel	315	2.5	−4.8	−7.1	−0.1	−0.4	−11.1	−10.7	−0.5
Cut-and-sew apparel	3152	2.8	−5.0	−7.5	−0.1	−0.3	−11.4	−11.2	1.0
Leather and allied products	316	3.3	−3.8	−6.9	1.0	1.6	−6.4	−7.9	0.9
Wood products	321	1.4	1.2	−0.2	2.2	3.3	2.6	−0.7	1.0
Other wood products	3219	1.0	1.0	–	2.9	3.7	2.8	−0.8	1.3
Paper and paper products	322	2.1	0.5	−1.6	1.2	3.6	−0.2	−3.7	−0.5
Converted paper products	3222	1.4	0.6	−0.8	1.9	3.0	−0.3	−3.2	0.2
Printing and related support activities	3231	1.1	0.3	−0.8	1.5	2.8	−0.8	−3.6	−0.4
Petroleum and coal products	3241	2.9	1.3	−1.6	2.8	1.8	1.1	−0.7	6.1
Chemicals	325	2.5	1.9	−0.6	1.3	5.5	3.6	−1.8	−1.8
Pharmaceuticals and medicines	3254	1.5	4.2	2.7	2.1	2.9	3.7	0.7	1.1
Plastics and rubber products	326	2.6	2.6	−0.1	0.9	3.4	0.9	−2.4	−0.1
Plastics products	3261	2.5	3.0	0.4	1.1	3.2	1.2	−1.9	0.1
Nonmetallic mineral products	327	1.4	1.4	0.0	1.4	2.8	2.0	−0.7	0.4
Cement and concrete products	3273	0.5	2.1	1.6	2.1	1.0	2.9	1.9	1.8
Primary metals	331	2.7	0.8	−1.8	0.3	5.9	2.1	−3.6	−2.4
Fabricated metal products	332	1.7	1.7	–	1.2	2.7	1.5	−1.1	–
Architectural and structural metals	3323	1.3	2.2	0.9	1.6	2.2	1.9	−0.3	1.0
Machine shops and threaded products	3327	2.2	3.5	1.2	0.9	1.5	2.5	1.0	−0.4
Other fabricated metal products	3329	1.4	0.6	−0.7	1.2	4.0	2.0	−1.9	−0.9
Machinery	333	2.7	2.0	−0.7	0.2	4.7	2.3	−2.3	−2.0
Agriculture, construction, and mining machinery	3331	2.9	3.3	0.4	−0.5	5.2	6.5	1.2	−2.7
Metalworking machinery	3335	2.2	0.8	−1.4	0.9	4.4	0.5	−3.7	−2.0
Other general purpose machinery	3339	2.9	2.0	−0.9	0.9	5.4	2.3	−3.0	−0.9
Computer and electronic products	334	12.8	10.3	−2.3	−8.4	9.2	3.3	−5.4	−7.2
Computer and peripheral equipment	3341	24.6	19.4	−4.1	−18.5	23.2	13.0	−8.3	−19.4
Semiconductors and electronic components	3344	17.8	16.3	−1.2	−12.4	10.6	3.7	−6.3	−8.0
Electronic instruments	3345	4.1	1.8	−2.2	−0.2	4.8	3.4	−1.3	−1.3
Electrical equipment and appliances	335	2.9	0.6	−2.2	0.7	3.0	−1.3	−4.2	–
Transportation equipment	336	3.0	1.9	−1.1	−0.4	4.6	2.9	−1.6	−1.8
Motor vehicles	3361	4.2	2.6	−1.5	−0.7	8.3	4.5	−3.6	−2.7
Motor vehicle parts	3363	3.2	3.3	0.1	−1.1	4.6	1.3	−3.2	−2.5
Aerospace products and parts	3364	1.6	−1.2	−2.7	1.1	0.4	−1.1	−1.5	2.9
Furniture and related products	337	2.2	1.7	−0.5	1.3	4.3	1.8	−2.4	−0.8
Household and institutional furniture	3371	2.0	1.4	−0.6	1.6	3.3	1.3	−1.9	0.2
Miscellaneous manufacturing	339	3.3	3.3	–	1.3	5.1	3.1	−2.0	0.5
Medical equipment and supplies	3391	3.7	4.8	1.1	0.8	4.8	4.5	−0.3	0.4
Other miscellaneous manufacturing	3399	2.8	1.9	−0.8	1.6	5.1	1.6	−3.4	0.7
Wholesale trade	42	3.3	4.1	0.7	0.9	3.1	3.6	0.5	0.6
Durable goods	423	5.4	6.0	0.6	−0.9	5.6	5.4	−0.2	−2.0
Nondurable goods	424	1.2	1.6	0.4	3.4	1.5	1.3	−0.2	2.5
Electronic markets and agents and brokers	4251	2.1	4.8	2.6	0.1	−2.0	3.8	5.9	6.1
Retail trade	44-45	3.3	4.1	0.7	−0.2	4.1	3.9	−0.1	−1.2
Motor vehicle and parts dealers	441	2.6	3.7	1.1	0.4	2.2	2.6	0.4	−0.4
Automobile dealers	4411	2.5	3.7	1.1	0.6	2.0	2.4	0.5	−0.5
Other motor vehicle dealers	4412	3.5	5.9	2.3	0.4	2.8	7.3	4.4	−0.2
Auto parts, accessories, and tire stores	4413	2.2	2.8	0.6	0.4	1.7	0.9	−0.8	0.9
Furniture and home furnishings stores	442	4.1	5.1	0.9	−0.8	5.5	5.6	0.1	−3.0
Furniture stores	4421	3.6	4.4	0.8	−0.6	4.6	4.8	0.2	−2.5
Home furnishings stores	4422	4.9	6.0	1.1	−1.2	6.6	6.6	0.1	−3.5
Electronics and appliance stores	4431	13.4	15.4	1.7	−9.1	15.7	16.1	0.4	−13.6
Building material and garden supply stores	444	3.2	4.9	1.6	−0.5	3.3	4.7	1.4	−0.5
Building material and supplies dealers	4441	3.0	5.0	2.0	−0.3	3.1	4.8	1.7	−0.3
Lawn and garden equipment and supplies stores	4442	4.5	4.1	−0.4	−1.4	5.4	4.3	−1.0	−2.4
Food and beverage stores	445	0.6	0.4	−0.1	2.9	3.0	0.8	−2.1	0.9
Grocery stores	4451	0.4	0.4	–	3.1	2.6	0.6	−1.9	1.6
Specialty food stores	4452	0.2	−0.2	−0.4	2.5	5.0	2.1	−2.8	0.9
Beer, wine, and liquor stores	4453	2.6	1.0	−1.6	1.4	6.6	3.1	−3.3	−3.4
Health and personal care stores	4461	2.5	3.9	1.4	1.3	3.0	3.8	0.8	1.2
Gasoline stations	4471	2.2	1.6	−0.6	0.9	2.3	1.1	−1.2	−0.2

See footnotes at end of table.

408   Labor Force, Employment, and Earnings

[For a discussion of productivity measures, see text, this section and BLS Handbook of Methods; <http://www.bls.gov/opub
/hom/homch11a.htm>. Minus sign (−) indicates decrease]

Industry	2002 NAICS [1] code	Average annual percent change [2]							
		1987–2007 [3]				2001–2007 [4]			
		Output per hour	Output	Hours	Unit labor costs	Output per hour	Output	Hours	Unit labor costs
Retail Trade—Con.									
Clothing and clothing accessories stores	448	5.0	5.0	−	−1.6	5.7	6.1	0.4	−2.4
Clothing stores	4481	5.3	5.6	0.3	−1.8	6.2	7.1	0.8	−2.7
Shoe stores	4482	3.9	2.7	−1.2	−0.8	4.1	2.8	−1.3	−1.3
Jewelry, luggage, and leather goods stores.	4483	4.7	4.4	−0.3	−1.3	4.7	4.7	−	−1.7
Sporting goods, hobby, book, and music stores.	451	4.1	4.9	0.8	−0.7	4.7	3.6	−1.1	−2.4
Sporting goods and musical instrument stores. . .	4511	4.9	5.7	0.8	−1.2	5.8	5.7	−0.1	−3.2
Book, periodical, and music stores	4512	2.5	3.2	0.7	0.3	2.1	−1.4	−3.4	−0.6
General merchandise stores	452	3.7	5.5	1.7	−1.3	3.4	5.4	2.0	−0.9
Department stores	4521	1.0	2.4	1.4	0.6	0.5	−0.3	−0.8	1.4
Other general merchandise stores.	4529	7.2	9.4	2.1	−3.4	4.9	10.3	5.2	−1.2
Miscellaneous store retailers	453	4.6	4.9	0.3	−1.9	6.1	2.8	−3.1	−3.2
Florists.	4531	2.7	0.9	−1.7	0.2	4.4	−0.9	−5.0	−1.0
Office supplies, stationery, and gift stores	4532	6.7	6.7	0.0	−3.2	9.2	4.3	−4.5	−5.9
Used merchandise stores	4533	5.3	6.5	1.1	−2.6	6.9	4.5	−2.3	−5.3
Other miscellaneous store retailers	4539	2.7	4.0	1.3	−1.1	3.0	1.8	−1.1	−0.2
Nonstore retailers	454	9.1	9.5	0.3	−4.9	10.1	9.3	−0.7	−4.6
Electronic shopping and mail-order houses	4541	12.2	16.1	3.4	−7.1	14.1	13.5	−0.5	−7.3
Vending machine operators	4542	1.6	−0.5	−2.1	2.3	5.6	1.4	−3.9	−1.1
Direct selling establishments	4543	3.4	2.2	−1.2	−0.3	1.3	1.3	−	2.5
Transportation and warehousing:									
Air transportation	481	3.2	3.4	0.3	−0.3	7.8	4.0	−3.5	−5.9
General freight trucking, long-distance.	48412	1.5	3.2	1.7	0.5	1.9	3.0	1.1	0.1
Used household and office goods moving	48421	−0.7	0.3	1.0	3.8	1.8	−0.3	−2.0	1.8
Postal service	4911	1.1	1.0	0.0	3.5	0.9	−1.0	−1.9	4.9
Couriers and messengers	492	−0.6	2.5	3.1	2.8	−	−1.2	−1.2	1.0
Warehousing and storage	4931	2.8	6.2	3.3	−0.1	−	4.5	4.5	2.7
Information:									
Publishing	511	4.3	4.9	0.5	1.0	4.3	1.5	−2.7	−0.2
Newspaper, book, and directory publishers	5111	0.4	−0.4	−0.8	4.1	1.3	−1.7	−3.0	3.4
Software publishers	5112	15.6	23.5	6.9	−8.9	7.8	5.4	−2.2	−4.5
Motion picture and video exhibition	51213	1.0	1.7	0.7	2.2	1.4	−1.7	−3.1	5.0
Broadcasting, except Internet	515	1.5	2.7	1.3	2.6	5.0	4.7	−0.2	0.2
Radio and television broadcasting.	5151	0.0	0.0	0.2	3.0	3.6	3.0	−0.6	0.7
Cable and other subscription programming	5152	3.0	8.2	5.0	2.3	7.0	7.7	0.6	1.9
Wired telecommunications carriers	5171	4.7	2.9	−1.7	−1.0	3.3	−3.8	−6.9	1.0
Wireless telecommunications carriers	5172	9.4	23.3	12.7	−6.0	15.5	17.0	1.3	−6.7
Cable and other program distribution.	5175	0.8	6.0	5.1	3.9	5.9	7.0	1.0	−0.3
Finance and insurance:									
Commercial banking	52211	2.6	2.6	−	3.1	3.2	4.1	0.9	3.0
Real estate and rental and leasing:									
Truck, trailer, and RV rental and leasing	53212	5.4	4.6	−0.7	−1.0	7.4	4.6	−2.6	−2.1
Video tape and disc rental.	53223	5.5	5.9	0.4	−1.9	9.0	1.4	−7.0	−3.3
Professional and technical services:									
Architectural services	54131	1.6	4.3	2.6	2.0	1.9	4.2	2.2	1.5
Engineering services	54133	1.0	3.3	2.3	3.4	1.6	3.6	2.0	2.6
Advertising agencies	54181	1.9	2.4	0.5	2.7	4.5	4.7	0.2	−2.6
Administrative and waste services:									
Employment placement agencies	56131	3.2	5.5	2.3	4.3	4.9	3.4	−1.5	2.0
Travel agencies.	56151	3.9	2.9	−1.0	1.3	8.8	3.0	−5.3	−4.1
Janitorial services	56172	2.5	4.6	2.1	1.4	3.1	4.6	1.5	−0.6
Health care and social assistance:									
Medical and diagnostic laboratories	6215	3.1	6.6	3.4	−0.3	0.1	4.2	4.1	2.5
Medical laboratories	621511	2.7	5.6	2.8	−0.1	0.3	3.2	2.9	2.5
Diagnostic imaging centers	621512	3.4	8.4	4.8		−1.1	5.7	6.8	2.8
Arts, entertainment, and recreation:									
Amusement and theme parks	71311	−0.4	2.7	3.1	3.7	1.7	1.0	−0.8	2.2
Bowling centers.	71395	0.7	−0.9	−1.7	2.4	4.5	2.2	−2.2	−0.4
Accommodation and food services.	72	0.7	2.4	1.6	3.2	0.5	2.1	1.6	2.7
Accommodation	721	1.2	2.5	1.3	3.0	0.2	0.9	0.8	2.9
Traveler accommodation	7211	1.3	2.6	1.3	3.0	0.1	0.9	0.9	3.0
Food services and drinking places	722	0.6	2.4	1.7	3.2	0.8	2.6	1.8	2.6
Full-service restaurants	7221	0.6	2.4	1.8	4.1	0.1	2.2	2.1	3.7
Limited-service eating places	7222	0.6	2.5	1.9	2.8	1.1	3.3	2.2	1.7
Special food services	7223	1.5	2.6	1.1	1.4	0.7	1.9	1.2	3.3
Drinking places, alcoholic beverages	7224	−	−0.1	−0.1	2.5	5.9	2.0	−3.6	−1.7
Other services:									
Automotive repair and maintenance	8111	1.3	2.2	0.9	2.3	0.2	−0.3	−0.5	3.3
Reupholstery and furniture repair	81142	0.0	−1.8	−1.8	3.1	0.1	−3.8	−3.9	3.8
Hair, nail, and skin care services	81211	2.4	3.4	0.9	2.1	2.7	3.9	1.1	1.6
Funeral homes and funeral services	81221	−0.3	−0.2	0.2	4.6	0.9	−2.3	−3.2	4.1
Drycleaning and laundry services	8123	0.8	0.5	−0.3	2.7	0.6	−0.9	−1.5	3.3
Photofinishing.	81292	0.7	−4.6	−5.3	2.8	5.2	−7.5	−12.1	−3.1

− Represents zero or rounds to less than half the unit of measurement shown. [1] North American Industry Classification
System, 2002 (NAICS); see text, this section. [2] Average annual percent changes based on compound rate formula. Rates of
change are calculated using index numbers to three decimal places. [3] For industries in the manufacturing sector (NAICS 31–33),
rates are for 1987–2006. For NAICS industries 4931, 49311, and 49312, annual percent changes are for 1992–2007, and for
NAICS industries 56131, 6215, 621511, and 621512, annual percent changes are for 1994–2007. [4] For industries in the
manufacturing sector (NAICS 31–33), rates are for 2001–2006.
Source: U.S. Bureau of Labor Statistics, Labor Productivity and Costs; <http://www.bls.gov/lpc/data.htm> (accessed May
2009).

Labor Force, Employment, and Earnings 409

Table 627. Productivity and Related Measures: 1990 to 2008

[See text, Section 12. Minus sign (–) indicates decrease]

Item	1990	2000	2002	2003	2004	2005	2006	2007	2008
INDEXES (1992 = 100)									
Output per hour, business sector.	94.4	116.1	123.9	128.7	132.4	134.8	136.1	138.2	141.9
Nonfarm business.	94.5	115.7	123.5	128.0	131.6	133.9	135.1	137.0	140.9
Manufacturing.	93.9	139.1	151.0	160.4	164.0	171.9	173.7	179.2	180.7
Output, [1] business sector.	96.9	140.5	143.1	147.5	153.7	159.1	163.9	167.3	168.6
Nonfarm business.	97.1	140.8	143.4	147.8	153.9	159.2	164.2	167.5	168.8
Manufacturing.	98.5	144.2	136.0	137.3	139.7	144.8	147.5	149.5	144.9
Hours, [2] business sector	102.7	121.0	115.4	114.6	116.1	118.0	120.5	121.1	118.8
Nonfarm business.	102.7	121.7	116.1	115.4	116.9	118.9	121.5	122.2	119.8
Manufacturing.	104.9	103.7	90.1	85.6	85.2	84.3	84.9	83.4	80.2
Compensation per hour, [3] business sector	90.6	134.7	145.3	151.2	157.0	163.2	169.4	176.5	182.8
Nonfarm business.	90.4	134.2	144.6	150.4	156.0	162.1	168.3	175.2	181.7
Manufacturing.	90.5	134.7	147.8	158.2	161.5	164.5	171.2	177.4	184.7
Real hourly compensation, [3] business sector. . .	96.2	112.0	115.7	117.7	119.0	119.7	120.3	121.9	121.6
Nonfarm business.	96.0	111.6	115.1	117.1	118.2	118.9	119.5	121.0	120.8
Manufacturing.	96.1	112.0	117.7	123.2	122.5	120.7	121.6	122.5	122.8
Unit labor costs, [4] business sector.	96.0	116.0	117.3	117.5	118.5	121.0	124.5	127.7	128.8
Nonfarm business.	95.7	116.0	117.1	117.5	118.5	121.1	124.5	127.9	129.0
Manufacturing.	96.4	96.9	97.9	98.7	98.5	95.7	98.6	99.0	102.2
ANNUAL PERCENT CHANGE [5]									
Output per hour, business sector.	2.1	2.9	4.1	3.8	2.9	1.8	0.9	1.6	2.7
Nonfarm business.	1.9	2.8	4.1	3.7	2.8	1.7	0.9	1.4	2.8
Manufacturing.	2.2	4.1	6.9	6.2	2.3	4.8	1.0	3.2	0.9
Output, [1] business sector.	1.5	3.9	1.5	3.1	4.2	3.5	3.0	2.0	0.8
Nonfarm business.	1.5	3.8	1.5	3.1	4.1	3.4	3.2	2.0	0.8
Manufacturing.	–0.3	2.7	–0.7	1.0	1.7	3.7	1.8	1.3	–3.1
Hours, [2] business sector	–0.6	1.0	–2.5	–0.7	1.2	1.7	2.1	0.5	–1.9
Nonfarm business.	–0.4	1.0	–2.6	–0.6	1.3	1.7	2.2	0.5	–1.9
Manufacturing.	–2.5	–1.3	–7.1	–4.9	–0.5	–1.1	0.8	–1.8	–3.9
Compensation per hour, [3] business sector	6.3	7.1	3.5	4.1	3.8	3.9	3.8	4.2	3.6
Nonfarm business.	6.1	7.2	3.6	4.0	3.7	4.0	3.8	4.1	3.7
Manufacturing.	4.4	9.1	7.2	7.0	2.1	1.8	4.1	3.6	4.1
Real hourly compensation, [3] business sector. . .	1.3	3.6	1.9	1.8	1.1	0.6	0.5	1.3	–0.2
Nonfarm business.	1.0	3.7	2.0	1.8	1.0	0.6	0.5	1.3	–0.2
Manufacturing.	–0.5	5.6	5.5	4.7	–0.6	–1.5	0.8	0.7	0.3
Unit labor costs, [4] business sector.	4.1	4.1	–0.5	0.2	0.9	2.1	2.9	2.6	0.9
Nonfarm business.	4.1	4.2	–0.5	0.3	0.9	2.2	2.8	2.7	0.9
Manufacturing.	2.2	4.9	0.3	0.8	–0.2	–2.8	3.0	0.4	3.2

[1] Refers to gross sectoral product, annual weighted. [2] Hours at work of all persons engaged in the business and nonfarm business sectors (employees, proprietors, and unpaid family workers); employees' and proprietors' hours in manufacturing. [3] Wages and salaries of employees plus employers' contributions for social insurance and private benefit plans. Also includes an estimate of same for self-employed. Real compensation deflated by the consumer price index for all urban consumers, see text, Section 14. [4] Hourly compensation divided by output per hour. [5] All changes are from the immediate prior year.

Source: U.S. Bureau of Labor Statistics, *Productivity and Costs*, News, USDL 09-0587, June 4, 2009. See also <http://www.bls.gov/lpc/data.htm>.

Table 628. Annual Total Compensation and Wages and Salary Accruals Per Full-Time Equivalent Employee by Industry: 2000 to 2007

[In dollars. Wage and salary accruals include executives' compensation, bonuses, tips, and payments-in-kind; total compensation includes in addition to wages and salaries, employer contributions for social insurance, employer contributions to private and welfare funds, director's fees, jury and witness fees, etc. Based on the 1997 North American Industry Classification System (NAICS); see text, this section]

Industry	Annual total compensation				Annual wages and salary			
	2000	2005	2006	2007	2000	2005	2006	2007
Domestic industries	46,407	55,491	57,682	60,016	38,762	44,813	46,787	48,836
Private industries	45,240	53,260	55,382	57,615	38,446	43,996	45,992	48,035
Agriculture, forestry, fishing, and hunting	29,332	31,274	32,640	34,329	25,847	27,790	28,969	30,409
Mining.	70,413	89,215	94,639	98,417	58,291	72,829	78,841	82,687
Utilities	78,147	102,580	103,072	109,476	64,271	76,267	79,021	83,237
Construction	44,764	53,317	55,807	58,342	37,196	43,579	46,275	48,430
Manufacturing.	54,219	64,700	68,192	70,766	44,216	50,140	52,315	54,482
Wholesale trade	56,264	68,434	71,525	74,765	48,017	57,194	60,079	62,988
Retail trade	30,225	33,981	34,817	35,567	26,307	28,664	29,391	30,066
Transportation and warehousing.	48,336	54,800	55,725	57,610	39,463	43,097	44,641	46,559
Information	74,196	82,696	86,366	90,527	63,217	67,508	70,714	74,180
Finance and insurance	74,821	93,163	97,852	103,261	64,049	77,347	81,759	86,898
Real estate and rental and leasing . . .	41,906	50,912	53,913	55,938	36,178	43,313	46,075	47,831
Professional, scientific, and technical services	68,436	81,807	85,352	89,215	58,886	69,047	72,417	76,053
Management of companies and enterprises [1]	89,496	104,230	107,893	115,204	75,984	86,656	91,035	98,262
Administrative and waste management services.	28,540	35,766	37,032	38,655	25,181	30,685	31,943	33,437
Educational services	32,736	39,783	40,932	42,644	28,974	34,362	35,558	37,140
Health care and social assistance. . . .	40,897	49,473	50,669	52,602	35,127	41,332	42,747	44,470
Arts, entertainment, and recreation . . .	35,898	41,672	43,536	44,667	31,259	35,357	37,327	37,982
Accommodation and food services . . .	19,092	23,583	24,401	25,260	16,830	20,240	21,060	21,873
Other services, except government. . . .	28,630	34,316	35,423	36,772	25,495	29,852	31,063	32,280
Government.	52,845	67,450	70,202	73,096	40,501	49,192	51,113	53,200

[1] Consists of offices of bank and other holding companies and of corporate, subsidiary, and regional managing offices.

Source: U.S. Bureau of Economic Analysis, *Survey of Current Business*, April 2009 and <http://www.bea.gov/bea/dn/nipaweb/SelectTable.asp?Selected=N> (accessed 15 May 2009).

410   Labor Force, Employment, and Earnings

Table 629. **Average Hourly Earnings by Private Industry Group: 1990 to 2008**

[**In dollars.** Average earnings include overtime. Data are for production workers in natural resources and mining, manufacturing, and construction, and nonsupervisory employees in the service providing industries. See headnote, Table 617]

Private industry group	Current dollars					Constant (1982) dollars [1]				
	1990	2000	2005	2007	2008	1990	2000	2005	2007	2008
AVERAGE HOURLY EARNINGS										
Total private..............	10.20	14.02	16.13	17.43	18.08	7.66	8.04	8.18	8.33	8.30
Natural resources and mining.......	13.40	16.55	18.72	20.97	22.50	10.07	9.50	9.50	10.02	10.33
Construction.................	13.42	17.48	19.46	20.95	21.87	10.08	10.03	9.87	10.01	10.04
Manufacturing................	10.78	14.32	16.56	17.26	17.74	8.10	8.22	8.40	8.25	8.14
Trade, transportation, and utilities.....	9.83	13.31	14.92	15.78	16.16	7.39	7.64	7.57	7.54	7.42
Information .....,.............	13.40	19.07	22.06	23.96	24.77	10.07	10.94	11.19	11.45	11.37
Financial activities [2] ....₂...	9.99	14.98	17.95	19.64	20.27	7.51	8.59	9.11	9.39	9.31
Professional and business services [2] ...	11.14	15.52	18.08	20.15	21.19	8.37	8.90	9.17	9.63	9.73
Education and health services [2]......	10.00	13.95	16.71	18.11	18.88	7.51	8.00	8.48	8.65	8.67
Leisure and hospitality [2]...........	6.02	8.32	9.38	10.41	10.84	4.52	4.77	4.76	4.97	4.98
Other services................	9.08	12.73	14.34	15.42	16.08	6.82	7.30	7.28	7.37	7.38
AVERAGE WEEKLY EARNINGS										
Total private..............	350	481	544	590	608	263	276	276	282	279
Natural resources and mining.......	603	735	854	963	1014	453	422	433	460	465
Construction.................	513	686	750	817	842	386	393	381	390	387
Manufacturing................	436	591	673	712	724	328	339	342	340	333
Trade, transportation, and utilities.....	332	450	498	526	536	249	258	253	251	246
Information .....,.............	480	701	805	875	908	360	402	408	418	417
Financial activities [2] ....₂...	355	537	645	705	726	266	308	327	337	334
Professional and business services [2] ...	381	535	619	701	738	286	307	314	335	339
Education and health services [2]......	319	449	545	590	614	240	258	276	282	282
Leisure and hospitality [2]...........	156	217	241	266	273	117	125	122	127	125
Other services................	298	413	443	477	495	224	237	225	228	227

[1] Earnings in current dollars divided by the Consumer Price Index (CPI-W) on a 1982 base; see text, Section 14.   [2] For composition of industries, see Table 612.

Source: U.S. Bureau of Labor Statistics, Current Employment Statistics, "Employment, Hours, and Earnings—National"; <http://www.bls.gov/ces/data.htm>.

Table 630. **Mean Hourly Earnings and Weekly Hours by Selected Characteristics: 2007**

[Covers civilian workers in private industry establishments and state and local governments in the 50 states and DC. Excludes private households, federal government and agriculture. Based on survey of 37,760 establishments representing over 129 million workers; see source and Appendix III for details about the National Compensation Survey]

Item	Mean hourly earnings (dol.) [1]			Mean weekly hours		
	Total	Private industry	State and local govern- ment	Total	Private industry	State and local govern- ment
Total.........................	19.88	19.21	24.15	35.5	35.4	36.3
WORKER CHARACTERISTIC						
Management, professional and related.......	32.38	32.96	30.63	37.1	37.5	36.0
Management, business, and financial.......	35.97	36.54	32.65	39.6	40.0	37.5
Professional and related..............	30.63	30.83	30.16	36.0	36.1	35.6
Service.............................	11.36	10.06	17.77	31.4	30.5	36.5
Sales and office.....................	15.98	15.97	16.17	34.9	34.7	36.5
Sales and related	17.27	17.29	15.62	32.7	32.7	34.3
Office and administrative support.........	15.27	15.14	16.19	36.2	36.1	36.6
Natural resources, construction, and mainte-						
nance...........................	20.09	20.15	19.37	39.4	39.4	38.8
Construction and extraction.............	20.14	20.27	18.69	39.4	39.4	38.6
Installation, maintenance, and repair........	20.20	20.19	20.29	39.5	39.6	39.2
Production, transportation, and material moving ..	15.12	15.03	18.02	37.2	37.3	34.4
Production........................	15.44	15.38	19.96	38.9	38.9	39.0
Transportation and material moving	14.78	14.65	17.40	35.6	35.8	33.1
Full-time [2].........................	21.08	20.46	24.76	39.6	39.7	38.9
Part-time [2].........................	11.34	11.02	15.57	20.6	20.7	18.6
Union [3]............................	23.96	21.9	27.17	36.7	36.4	37.0
Nonunion	19.14	18.89	21.73	35.3	35.3	35.7
Time [4]	19.46	18.69	24.14	35.4	35.3	36.3
Incentive [4].........................	26.94	26.90	97.34	38.1	38.1	25.4
ESTABLISHMENT CHARACTERISTIC						
Goods producing [5]...................	(X)	20.79	(X)	(X)	39.5	(X)
Service producing [5]..................	(X)	18.74	(X)	(X)	34.4	(X)
1 to 49 workers	16.84	16.80	18.02	34.2	34.2	33.2
50 to 99 workers	18.06	17.99	19.24	34.9	34.9	35.8
100 to 499 workers...................	19.46	19.09	22.51	36.1	36.2	36.1
500 workers or more..................	24.75	24.60	25.71	37.0	37.1	36.7

X Not applicable.   [1] Earnings are straight time hourly wages or salary, including incentive pay, cost-of-living adjustments, and hazard pay. Excludes premium pay for overtime, vacations and holidays, nonproduction bonuses and tips.   [2] Based on definition used by each establishment.   [3] Workers whose wages are determined through collective bargaining.   [4] Time worker wages are based solely on an hourly rate or salary. Incentive workers wages are based at least in part on productivity payments such as piece rates or commissions.   [5] For private industry only. See footnotes 3 and 4, Table 619, for composition of goods and service producing industries.

Source: U.S. Bureau of Labor Statistics, *National Compensation Survey: Occupational Earnings in the United States*, Bulletin 2704, August 2008. See also <http://www.bls.gov/ncs/ncswage2007.htm#Wage_Tables>.

Labor Force, Employment, and Earnings   411

Table 631. **Employment and Wages: 2000 to 2007**

[**(129,877 represents 129,877,000).** See headnote, Table 632]

Employment and wages	Unit	2000	2002	2003	2004	2005	2006	2007
Average annual employment:								
Total	1,000	129,877	128,234	127,796	129,278	131,572	133,834	135,366
Excluding federal	1,000	127,006	125,475	125,032	126,539	128,838	131,105	132,640
Private	1,000	110,015	107,577	107,066	108,490	110,611	112,719	114,012
State government	1,000	4,370	4,485	4,482	4,485	4,528	4,566	4,611
Local governments	1,000	12,620	13,413	13,484	13,564	13,699	13,820	14,016
Federal government	1,000	2,871	2,759	2,764	2,740	2,734	2,729	2,726
Annual wages:								
Total	Bil. dol.	4,588	4,714	4,826	5,088	5,352	5,693	6,018
Excluding federal	Bil. dol.	4,455	4,571	4,676	4,929	5,188	5,523	5,841
Private	Bil. dol.	3,888	3,931	4,016	4,246	4,480	4,781	5,058
State government	Bil. dol.	159	176	180	184	191	200	212
Local governments	Bil. dol.	409	464	481	499	517	541	572
Federal government	Bil. dol.	133	144	150	158	164	170	177
Average wage per employee:								
Total	Dol.	35,323	36,764	37,765	39,354	40,677	42,535	44,458
Excluding federal	Dol.	35,077	36,428	37,401	38,955	40,270	42,124	44,038
Private	Dol.	35,337	36,539	37,508	39,134	40,505	42,414	44,362
State government	Dol.	36,296	39,212	40,057	41,118	42,249	43,875	45,903
Local governments	Dol.	32,387	34,605	35,669	36,805	37,718	39,179	40,790
Federal government	Dol.	46,228	52,050	54,239	57,782	59,864	62,274	64,871
Average weekly wage per employee:								
Total	Dol.	679	707	726	757	782	818	855
Excluding federal	Dol.	675	701	719	749	774	810	847
Private	Dol.	680	703	721	753	779	816	853
State government	Dol.	698	754	770	791	812	844	883
Local governments	Dol.	623	665	686	708	725	753	784
Federal government	Dol.	889	1,001	1,043	1,111	1,151	1,198	1,248

Source: U.S. Bureau of Labor Statistics, USDL news release, Average Annual Pay by State and Industry, annual through 2000 data; 2002 Annual Wages for All Covered Workers by State; thereafter Employment and Wages, Annual Averages, 2007, Bulletin 2718, January, 2009 and previous years. See <http://www.bls.gov/cew/home.htm>.

Table 632. **Average Annual Wage by State: 2006 and 2007**

[**In dollars, except percent change.** Based on federal-state cooperative program, the Quarterly Census of Employment and Wages (QCEW), also referenced as ES-202. For workers covered by state unemployment insurance laws and for federal civilian workers covered by unemployment compensation for federal employees, approximately 97 percent of employees on nonfarm payrolls in 2007. Excludes most agricultural workers on small farms, all Armed Forces, elected officials in most states, railroad employees, most domestic workers, most student workers at school, value of meals and lodging, and tips and other gratuities]

State	Average wage per employee		Percent change, 2006–07	State	Average wage per employee		Percent change, 2006–07
	2006	2007			2006	2007	
United States	42,535	44,458	4.5	Missouri	37,143	38,603	3.9
Alabama	36,204	37,492	3.6	Montana	30,596	32,224	5.3
Alaska	41,750	43,972	5.3	Nebraska	33,814	35,238	4.2
Arizona	40,019	41,551	3.8	Nevada	40,070	42,149	5.2
Arkansas	32,389	34,118	5.3	New Hampshire	42,447	43,863	3.3
California	48,345	50,538	4.5	New Jersey	51,645	53,853	4.3
Colorado	43,506	45,396	4.3	New Mexico	34,567	36,379	5.2
Connecticut	54,814	58,029	5.9	New York	55,479	59,439	7.1
Delaware	46,285	47,308	2.2	North Carolina	37,439	38,909	3.9
District of Columbia	70,151	73,450	4.7	North Dakota	31,316	33,086	5.7
Florida	38,485	39,746	3.3	Ohio	38,568	39,917	3.5
Georgia	40,370	42,178	4.5	Oklahoma	34,022	35,491	4.3
Hawaii	37,799	39,466	4.4	Oregon	38,077	39,569	3.9
Idaho	32,580	33,544	3.0	Pennsylvania	41,349	43,239	4.6
Illinois	45,650	47,685	4.5	Rhode Island	40,454	41,646	2.9
Indiana	36,553	37,528	2.7	South Carolina	34,281	35,393	3.2
Iowa	34,320	35,738	4.1	South Dakota	30,291	31,655	4.5
Kansas	35,696	37,044	3.8	Tennessee	37,564	39,082	4.0
Kentucky	35,201	36,480	3.6	Texas	42,458	44,695	5.3
Louisiana	36,604	38,229	4.4	Utah	35,130	37,054	5.5
Maine	33,794	35,129	3.9	Vermont	35,542	36,956	4.0
Maryland	46,162	48,241	4.5	Virginia	44,051	45,995	4.4
Massachusetts	52,435	55,244	5.4	Washington	42,897	45,021	5.0
Michigan	42,157	43,357	2.8	West Virginia	32,728	34,106	4.2
Minnesota	42,185	44,375	5.2	Wisconsin	36,821	38,050	3.3
Mississippi	31,194	32,291	3.5	Wyoming	36,662	39,254	7.1

Source: U.S. Bureau of Labor Statistics, Employment and Wages, Annual Averages, 2007, Bulletin 2718, January 2009 and computed by U.S. Census Bureau. See also <http://www.bls.gov/cew/home.htm>.

Table 633. **Full-Time Wage and Salary Workers—Number and Earnings: 2000 to 2008**

[In current dollars of usual weekly earnings. Data represent annual averages (101,210 represents 101,210,000). Full-time workers are those who usually worked 35 hours or more (at all jobs combined). Occupational classifications are those used in the 2000 census; see text this section. Based on the Current Population Survey; see text, Section 1 and Appendix III. For definition of median, see Guide to Tabular Presentation]

Characteristic	Number of workers (1,000)			Median weekly earnings (dol.)		
	2000	2005 [1]	2008 [1]	2000	2005 [1]	2008 [1]
All workers [2]	**101,210**	**103,560**	**106,648**	**576**	**651**	**722**
SEX						
Male	57,107	58,406	59,439	641	722	798
16 to 24 years old.	6,770	6,396	5,996	375	409	461
25 years old and over	50,337	52,010	53,444	693	771	857
Female.	44,103	45,154	47,209	493	585	638
16 to 24 years old.	5,094	4,711	4,625	344	381	420
25 years old and over	39,009	40,443	42,584	516	612	670
RACE/ETHNICITY						
White [3].	83,228	84,110	86,022	590	672	742
Male.	48,085	48,572	49,082	662	743	825
Female	35,143	35,538	36,940	502	596	654
Black [3].	12,410	12,388	12,821	474	520	589
Male.	5,911	5,916	6,031	510	559	620
Female	6,500	6,472	6,790	429	499	554
Asian [3][4].	4,598	4,651	5,266	615	753	861
Male.	2,538	2,597	2,919	685	825	966
Female	2,060	2,054	2,347	547	665	753
Hispanic origin [5].	12,761	14,673	15,807	399	471	529
Male.	8,077	9,433	9,961	417	489	559
Female	4,684	5,241	5,846	366	429	501
OCCUPATION						
Management, professional and related occupations	34,831	36,908	40,154	810	937	1,025
Management, business, and financial operations	14,240	14,977	16,310	877	997	1,128
Management occupations	9,952	10,340	11,223	937	1,083	1,204
Business and financial operations occupations	4,200	4,637	5,087	760	871	974
Professional and related occupations	20,590	21,931	23,845	770	902	980
Computer and mathematical occupations.	3,051	2,924	3,344	938	1,132	1,242
Architecture and engineering occupations	2,781	2,509	2,652	949	1,105	1,244
Life, physical, and social science occupations	989	1,164	1,080	811	965	1,035
Community and social services occupations.	1,641	1,797	1,908	629	725	788
Legal occupations	1,039	1,162	1,199	919	1,052	1,174
Education, training, and library occupations	5,467	6,066	6,677	704	798	866
Arts, design, entertainment, sports, and media	1,488	1,488	1,570	724	819	882
Healthcare practitioner and technical occupations	4,134	4,821	5,415	727	878	962
Service occupations	12,595	14,123	14,814	365	413	475
Healthcare support occupations.	1,731	2,085	2,222	358	410	465
Protective service occupations	2,281	2,549	2,683	591	678	748
Food preparation and serving-related occupations	3,483	4,007	4,153	317	356	402
Building and grounds cleaning and maintenance	3,354	3,425	3,506	351	394	431
Personal care and service occupations	1,746	2,057	2,250	351	409	475
Sales and office occupations	25,606	25,193	25,232	492	575	614
Sales and related occupations.	9,650	10,031	10,113	525	622	656
Office and administrative support occupations	15,956	15,161	15,119	480	550	601
Natural resources, construction, and maintenance occupations.	10,958	12,086	11,609	582	623	702
Farming, fishing, and forestry occupations	842	755	756	310	372	420
Construction and extraction occupations	5,852	6,826	6,432	580	604	688
Installation, maintenance, and repair occupations	4,263	4,504	4,420	628	705	774
Production, transportation, and material-moving occupations.	17,221	15,251	14,840	475	540	594
Production occupations	10,378	8,403	8,008	471	538	595
Transportation and material-moving occupations.	6,843	6,848	6,832	481	543	593

[1] See footnote 2, Table 574.   [2] Includes other races, not shown separately.   [3] Beginning 2005, for persons in this race group only. See footnote 4, Table 575.   [4] 2000, includes Pacific Islanders.   [5] Persons of Hispanic or Latino origin may be any race.

Source: U.S. Bureau of Labor Statistics, "Employment and Earnings Online," January 2009; <http://www.bls.gov/opub/ee/home.htm> and <http://www.bls.gov/cps/home.htm>.

Table. 634. **Workers With Earnings by Occupation of Longest Held Job and Sex: 2007**

[As of March. (74,295 represents 74,295,000). For definition of median, see Guide to Tabular Presentation. Annual Social and Economic Supplement (ASEC) includes Civilian noninstitutional population, 15 years old and over, and military personnel who live in households with at least one other civilian adult. Based on Current Population Survey; see text, Section 1 and Appendix III]

Major occupation of longest job held in 2007	All workers				Full-time, year-round			
	Women		Men		Women		Men	
	Number (1,000)	Median earnings (dol.)	Number (1,000)	Median earnings (dol.)	Number (1,000)	Median earnings (dol.)	Number (1,000)	Median earnings (dol.)
Total	74,295	25,878	84,482	36,635	45,613	35,102	62,984	45,113
Management, business, and financial occupations	9,793	45,394	12,621	65,020	7,683	50,303	11,023	70,008
Professional and related occupations . . .	18,393	38,250	13,680	56,710	11,962	45,842	10,833	62,426
Service occupations	15,482	14,879	11,801	20,892	7,356	22,023	7,270	29,657
Sales and office occupations.	25,196	23,272	14,244	33,375	15,204	30,950	10,377	42,033
Natural resources, construction, and maintenance	776	21,640	16,042	31,153	443	36,246	11,364	36,590
Production, transportation, and material-moving occupations.	4,590	20,416	15,404	30,873	2,917	26,014	11,456	36,017
Armed Forces	64	(B)	692	41,778	49	(B)	660	42,064

B Data not shown where base is less than 75,000.

Source: U.S. Census Bureau, Table PINC-06, "Occupation of Longest Job in 2007—People 15 years Old and Over, by Total Money Earnings in 2007, Work Experience in 2007 Race, Hispanic Origin, and Sex" (accessed 17 July 2009); <http://www.census.gov/hhes/www/macro/032008/perinc/new06—000.htm>.

Table. 635. **Employment Cost Index (ECI), Total Compensation by Occupation and Industry: 2003 to 2008**

[As of December. The ECI is a measure of the rate of change in employee compensation (wages, salaries, and employer costs for employee benefits). Data are not seasonally adjusted: 2001 to 2005, based on the Standard Instustry Classification System (SIC); beginning in 2006, based on the 2007 North American Industry Classification (NAICS) for classifying by industry and based on the 2000 Standard Occupational Classification (SOC) for classifying by occupation. See Chapter 8 of the BLS Handbook of Methods at <http://www.bls.gov/opub/hom/homch8_a.htm>]

Item	Indexes (December 2005 = 100)					Percent change for 12 months ending Dec.—				
	2003	2004	2006	2007	2008	2003	2004	2006	2007	2008
Civilian workers [1]	93.5	97.0	103.3	106.7	109.5	3.9	3.7	3.3	3.3	2.6
State and local government. . .	92.8	96.1	104.1	108.4	111.6	3.5	3.6	4.1	4.1	3.0
Workers, by occupational group:										
Management, professional and related occupations.	93.1	96.2	104.0	108.3	111.6	3.1	3.3	4.0	4.1	3.0
Sales and office occupations	92.8	96.5	104.1	108.6	111.3	4.2	4.0	4.1	4.3	2.5
Service occupations	91.6	95.5	104.5	109.1	112.4	4.1	4.3	4.5	4.4	3.0
Workers, by industry division:										
Service-providing industries										
Education and health services.	93.2	96.1	104.3	108.2	111.5	3.1	3.1	4.3	3.7	3.0
Schools.	93.1	96.1	104.1	108.0	111.2	3.0	3.2	4.1	3.7	3.0
Elementary and secondary	92.7	96.0	104.2	108.0	111.4	3.1	3.6	4.2	3.6	3.1
Health care and social assistance .	93.5	96.5	105.7	109.3	113.2	3.2	3.2	5.7	3.4	3.6
Hospitals	93.4	96.7	104.3	108.2	111.3	3.1	3.5	4.3	3.7	2.9
Public administration [2]	92.0	95.8	103.8	109.1	112.0	4.2	4.1	3.8	5.1	2.7
Private industry workers [3]	93.6	97.2	103.2	106.3	108.9	4.0	3.8	3.2	3.0	2.4
Workers, by occupational group:										
Management, professional, and related occupations.	93.8	97.1	103.5	106.8	109.9	4.6	3.5	3.5	3.2	2.9
Sales and office occupations	93.1	96.8	102.9	106.1	107.9	3.7	4.0	2.9	3.1	1.7
Natural resources, construction, and maintenance occupations.	93.3	97.1	103.6	106.7	109.6	4.0	4.1	3.6	3.0	2.7
Production, transportation, and material moving occupations	93.6	97.8	102.3	104.5	106.9	3.7	4.5	2.3	2.2	2.3
Service occupations	95.0	97.7	103.1	107.0	109.8	3.3	2.8	3.1	3.8	2.6
Workers, by industry division:										
Goods-producing industries [4]	92.6	96.9	102.5	105.0	107.5	4.0	4.6	2.5	2.4	2.4
Manufacturing	92.4	96.9	101.8	103.8	105.9					
Service-providing industries [5]	94.0	97.3	103.4	106.7	109.4	4.0	3.5	3.4	3.2	2.5
Trade, transportation, and utilities. .	94.0	97.0	103.0	105.5	107.5	3.4	3.2	3.0	2.4	1.9
Information	94.5	96.8	103.2	106.1	107.4	3.8	2.4	3.2	2.8	1.2
Financial activities.	93.8	96.8	102.5	105.6	107.1	6.8	3.2	2.5	3.0	1.4
Professional and business services.	94.7	98.5	103.5	107.5	111.6	4.1	4.0	3.5	3.9	3.8
Education and health services.	93.0	96.7	104.1	107.7	110.6	3.8	4.0	4.1	3.5	2.7
Leisure and hospitality	96.3	97.7	103.7	108.1	111.4	2.0	1.5	3.7	4.2	3.1
Bargaining status										
Union	92.3	97.3	103.0	105.1	108.0	4.6	5.4	3.0	2.0	2.8
Nonunion.	93.9	97.2	103.2	106.5	109.1	4.0	3.5	3.2	3.2	2.4

[1] Includes private industry and state and local government workers and excludes farm, household, and federal government workers. [2] Consists of executive, legislative, judicial, administrative, and regulatory activities. [3] Excludes farm and household workers. [4] Includes the following NAICS industries: construction and manufacturing. [5] Includes all other service industries not shown seperately. For a description of NAICS industries, see text this section.

Source: U.S. Bureau of Labor Statistics, "Employment Cost Index Current-Dollar Historical Listings"; <http://www.bls.gov/ncs/ect/home.htm>.

414   Labor Force, Employment, and Earnings

Table 636. **Federal and State Minimum Wage Rates: 1940 to 2009**

[**In current dollars.** Where an employee is subject to both the state and federal minimum wage laws, the employee is entitled to the higher minimum wage rate]

Year	Federal minimum wage rates per hour	State	2009 minimum wage rates per hour	State	2009 minimum wage rates per hour	State	2009 minimum wage rates per hour
1940 ...	0.30	KY	7.25	ND	7.25		
1945 ...	0.40	AL	([1])	LA	([1])	OH	7.30
1950 ...	0.75	AK	7.15	ME	7.50	OK	[7]7.25
1955 ...	0.75	AZ	7.25	MD	7.25	OR	8.40
1960 ...	1.00	AR	[3]6.25	MA	8.00	PA	7.25
1965 ...	1.25	CA	8.00	MI.....	[4]7.40	RI.....	7.40
1970 ...	1.60	CO	7.28	MN	[5]6.15/5.25	SC	([1])
1975 ...	2.10	CT	8.00	MS	([1])	SD	7.25
1980 ...	3.10	DE	7.15	MO	7.05	TN	([1])
1985 ...	3.35	DC	7.55	MT	[6]7.25	TX	7.25
1990 ...	3.80	FL.....	7.21	NE	[2]7.25	UT	7.25
1995 ...	4.25	GA	[3]5.15	NV	2.85	VT	[4]8.06
2000 ...	5.15	HI.....	7.25	NH	7.25	VA	[2]7.25
2005 ...	5.15	ID.....	7.25	NJ.....	7.25	WA	8.55
2006 ...	5.15	IL.....	[2]8.00	NM	7.50	WV....	[3]7.25
2007 ...	5.85	IN.....	[4]7.25	NY	7.25	WI.....	6.50
2008 ...	6.55	IA.....	7.25	NC	7.25	WY....	5.15
2009 ...	7.25	KS	2.65				

[1] No state minimum wage law.   [2] Employers of 4 or more, Illinois excluding family members.   [3] Employers of 6 or more.   [4] Employers of 2 or more.   [5] Large employer (receipts of $625.000 or more) and small employer (with annual receipts of less than $625,000).   [6] Except businesses with gross annual sales of $110,000 or less.   [7] Employees of 10 or more full-time employees at any one location and employers with gross sales over $100,000 regardless of number of full-time employees.

Source: U.S. Department of Labor, Wage and Hour Division, "Minimum Wage Laws in the States—January 1, 2009"; <http://www.dol.gov/esa/minwage/america.htm>.

Table 637. **Workers Paid Hourly Rates by Selected Characteristics: 2008**

[**Data are annual averages (75,305 represents 75,305,000).** For employed wage and salary workers, excluding the incorporated self-employed. Based on the Current Population Survey; see text, Section 1 and Appendix III]

Characteristic	Number of workers paid hourly rates (1,000)			Number of workers at or below prevailing federal minimum wage	
	Total	Below (federal min wage)	At (federal min wage)	Number (1,000)	Percent of hourly paid workers
Total, 16 years and over [1]	**75,305**	**1,940**	**286**	**2,226**	**3.0**
16 to 24 years	15,680	961	161	1,122	7.2
25 years and over	59,626	979	125	1,104	1.9
Male, 16 years old and over ...	37,334	638	90	728	2.0
16 to 24 years	7,978	326	58	384	4.8
25 years and over	29,356	313	32	345	1.2
Female, 16 years old and over .	37,972	1,302	196	1,497	3.9
16 to 24 years	7,701	635	103	738	9.6
25 years and over	30,270	666	93	759	2.5
White [2].................	60,464	1,568	215	1,783	2.9
Black [2].................	9,866	259	49	308	3.1
Asian [2].................	2,844	58	11	69	2.4
Hispanic origin [3]............	13,070	285	39	324	2.5
Full-time workers	56,837	778	95	873	1.5
Part-time workers [4]...........	18,334	1,162	191	1,353	7.4
Private sector industries	65,758	1,832	261	2,093	3.2
Public sector industries	9,547	108	25	133	1.4

[1] Includes races not shown separately. Also includes a small number of multiple jobholders whose full- or part-time status can not be determined for their principal job.   [2] For persons in this race group only. See footnote 4, Table 575.   [3] Persons of Hispanic or Latino origin may be any race.   [4] Working fewer than 35 hours per week.

Source: U.S. Bureau of Labor Statistics, "Employment and Earnings Online," January 2009; <http://www.bls.gov/opub/ee/home.htm> and <http://www.bls.gov/cps/home.htm>.

Labor Force, Employment, and Earnings   **415**

Table 638. **Employer Costs for Employee Compensation Per Hour Worked: 2008**

[In dollars. As of December, for civilian workers. Based on a sample of establishments from the National Compensation Survey; see source for details. See also Appendix III]

Compensation component	Total civilian workers	State and local government workers	Private industry workers Total	Goods producing [1]	Service providing [2]	Union workers	Non-union workers	Full-time workers	Part-time workers
Total compensation	**29.18**	**39.25**	**27.35**	**32.14**	**26.22**	**36.22**	**26.31**	**31.07**	**15.32**
Wages and salaries	20.37	25.87	19.37	21.54	18.86	22.53	19.00	21.64	12.04
Total benefits	8.81	13.38	7.98	10.59	7.36	13.69	7.31	9.43	3.28
Paid leave.	2.06	3.21	1.85	2.05	1.81	2.65	1.76	2.28	0.47
Vacation	0.98	1.14	0.95	1.09	0.92	1.36	0.91	(NA)	(NA)
Holiday	0.67	1.05	0.60	0.74	0.57	0.79	0.58	(NA)	(NA)
Sick	0.32	0.81	0.23	0.18	0.24	0.36	0.21	(NA)	(NA)
Supplemental pay.	0.74	0.34	0.81	1.27	0.71	1.20	0.77	0.98	0.26
Overtime [3]	0.26	0.17	0.28	0.58	0.20	0.77	0.22	(NA)	(NA)
Insurance	2.45	4.43	2.09	2.91	1.90	4.27	1.83	2.51	0.73
Health insurance.	2.31	4.25	1.95	2.71	1.77	3.99	1.71	(NA)	(NA)
Retirement and savings. . . .	1.29	3.07	0.96	1.47	0.85	2.46	0.79	1.18	0.25
Defined benefit	0.78	2.76	0.42	0.83	0.32	1.74	0.26	(NA)	(NA)
Defined contributions	0.51	0.32	0.55	0.64	0.53	0.73	0.53	(NA)	(NA)
Legally required	2.27	2.32	2.26	2.90	2.11	3.11	2.16	2.47	1.57
Social security.	1.32	1.40	1.30	1.48	1.26	1.58	1.27	(NA)	(NA)
Medicare	0.33	0.42	0.32	0.36	0.31	0.38	0.31	(NA)	(NA)
Federal unemployment. . .	0.03	(−)	0.03	0.03	0.03	0.03	0.03	(NA)	(NA)
State unemployment	0.14	0.06	0.15	0.20	0.14	0.22	0.14	(NA)	(NA)
Workers' compensation . .	0.45	0.44	0.46	0.84	0.36	0.90	0.40	(NA)	(NA)

− Represents or rounds to zero.   NA Not available.   [1] Based on the North American Industry Classification System, 2002 (NAICS). See text, this section. Includes mining, construction, and manufacturing. The agriculture, forestry, farming, and hunting sector is excluded.   [2] Based on the 2002 NAICS. Includes utilities; wholesale and retail trade; transportation and warehousing; information; finance and insurance; real estate and rental and leasing; professional and technical services; management of companies and enterprises, administrative and waste services; education services; health care and social assistance; arts, entertainment, and recreation; accommodations and food services; and other services, except public administration.   [3] Includes premium pay for work in addition to regular work schedule, such as, overtime, weekends, and holidays.

Source: U.S. Bureau of Labor Statistics, Employer Costs for Employee Compensation, News, USDL 09-0247, March 12, 2009. See also <http://www.bls.gov/ncs/ect/home.htm>.

Table 639. **Percent of Workers in Private Industry With Access to Retirement and Health Care Benefits by Selected Characteristics: 2008**

[As of March. Based on National Compensation Survey. See headnote, Table 640]

Characteristic	Retirement benefits All plans [1]	Defined benefit	Defined contri-bution	Healthcare benefits Medical care	Dental care	Vision care	Outpatient prescription drug coverage
Total	**61**	**21**	**56**	**71**	**47**	**28**	**68**
WORKER CHARACTERISTICS							
Management, professional, and related occupations.	76	29	72	86	62	37	83
Service occupations	37	9	33	46	29	20	45
Sales and office occupations	65	20	61	71	47	25	68
Natural resources, construction, and maintenance occupations	62	26	53	77	44	31	72
Production, transportation, and material moving occupations	65	26	57	78	49	30	74
Full-time [2]	71	25	65	85	56	34	82
Part-time [2]	32	11	27	24	16	10	23
Union [3]	85	69	50	88	68	54	86
Nonunion [3]	59	16	57	69	44	25	66
AVERAGE HOURLY WAGE [4]							
Less than $7.85	25	4	24	25	(S)	(S)	24
$7.85 to under $10.13	41	9	38	48	27	15	45
$10.13 to under$15.00	63	16	58	77	48	27	73
$15.00 to under $23.25	70	25	63	84	53	32	80
$23.25 to under $34.79	79	40	70	88	62	42	84
$34.79 or greater	84	39	80	91	71	43	88
ESTABLISHMENT CHARACTERISTIC							
Goods producing [5]	71	30	64	85	55	34	81
Service producing [5]	59	19	54	68	44	27	65

S Figure does not meet publication standards.   [1] Employees may have access to both defined benefit and defined contribution plans. Total excludes duplication.   [2] Employees are classified as working either a full-time or part-time schedule based on the definition used by each establishment.   [3] See footnote 3, Table 640.   [4] The National Compensation Survey—Benefits program presents wage data in percentiles rather than dollar amounts; see "Technical Note" in source.   [5] See footnotes 3 and 4, Table 619, for composition of goods and service producing industries.

Source: U.S. Bureau of Labor Statistics, Employee Benefits in the United States, March 2008 News, USDL 08-1122, August 7, 2008. See also <http://www.bls.gov/ncs/ebs/home.htm>.

Table 640. **Percent of Workers in Private Industry With Access to Selected Employee Benefits: 2008**

[As of March. Based on National Compensation Survey. The NCS benefits survey obtained data from 12,872 private industry establishments of all sizes, representing over 107 million workers: An employee has access to a benefit plan if the plan is made available by the employer, regardless of whether the employee actually participates in the plan. see Appendix III. See also Chapter 8 of the BLS Handbook of Methods at <http://www.bls.gov/opub/hom/homch8a.htm>]

Characteristic	Paid holidays	Paid vacation	Paid personal leave	Family leave Paid	Family leave Unpaid	Paid jury duty leave	Paid military leave	Employer assistance for child care [1] Total	Employer-provided funds	On-site and off-site child care	Flexible work place [2]	Subsidized commuting [3]	All non-production bonuses [4]
Total	**77**	**78**	**37**	**8**	**83**	**71**	**48**	**15**	**3**	**5**	**5**	**6**	**47**
WORKER CHARACTERISTIC													
Management, professional, and related occupations	89	87	55	15	90	88	66	28	6	11	11	11	55
Service occupations	52	61	26	5	78	55	34	10	2	5	1	2	33
Sales and office occupations	81	80	39	8	85	75	50	14	3	3	5	6	49
Natural resources, construction, and maintenance occupations	76	76	26	6	76	56	38	7	1	2	2	4	48
Production, transportation, and material moving occupations	85	83	32	4	84	71	46	10	2	2	2	3	49
Full-time [5]	89	90	42	9	86	79	54	17	4	6	5	6	52
Part-time [5]	40	39	21	4	73	48	30	10	1	4	2	3	31
Union [6]	85	84	47	7	90	83	56	21	4	6	2	7	39
Nonunion [6]	76	77	36	8	83	70	47	14	3	5	5	5	48
AVERAGE HOURLY WAGE [7]													
Less than $7.85	38	43	17	2	71	(NA)	(NA)	(NA)	(NA)	(NA)	1	1	29
$7.85 to under $10.13	61	63	25	5	79	(NA)	(NA)	(NA)	(NA)	(NA)	1	2	37
$10.13 to under $15.00	84	84	38	7	84	(NA)	(NA)	(NA)	(NA)	(NA)	3	3	48
$15.00 to under $23.25	89	88	39	9	85	(NA)	(NA)	(NA)	(NA)	(NA)	5	6	52
$23.25 to under $34.79	88	87	52	13	88	(NA)	(NA)	(NA)	(NA)	(NA)	8	9	55
$34.79 or greater	89	88	54	14	90	(NA)	(NA)	(NA)	(NA)	(NA)	14	15	59
ESTABLISHMENT CHARACTERISTIC													
Goods producing [8]	86	86	33	6	84	70	51	12	2	3	3	4	52
Service producing [8]	75	76	38	9	83	72	48	16	3	6	5	6	46
GEOGRAPHIC AREA [9]													
New England division	78	75	42	9	88	82	53	16	3	8	6	9	53
Middle Atlantic	80	79	46	8	84	81	53	15	5	7	7	7	44
East North Central	76	76	43	9	81	71	49	18	3	6	5	3	48
West North Central	74	77	31	7	82	68	48	15	2	5	5	6	48
South Atlantic	78	79	33	9	84	73	50	12	2	4	5	3	51
East South Central	80	81	37	6	89	70	43	8	(-)	3	3	2	52
West South Central	80	79	34	8	81	67	46	16	3	5	3	3	45
Mountain	75	75	35	5	80	68	44	16	3	3	5	9	45
Pacific	74	77	34	10	85	64	44	16	2	4	3	10	43

NA Not available. [1] Employer assistance of child care includes employer provided funds, on-site and off-site child care, and child care resource and referral services. [2] Arrangements permitting employees to work at home several days of the workweek. [3] Employers subsidize employees' cost of commuting to and from work via public transportation, company-sponsored van pool, discounted subway fares, etc. [4] All nonproduction bonuses include cash profit sharing bonuses, holiday bonuses, referral bonuses, and stock options. [5] Employees are classified as working either a full-time or part-time schedule based on the definition used by each establishment. [6] Union workers are those whose wages are determined through collective bargaining. [7] See footnotes 4, Table 639. Table 619, for composition of goods and service producing industries. [8] See footnotes 3 and 4. [9] For composition of divisions, see map, inside front cover.

Source: U.S. Bureau of Labor Statistics, *Employee Benefits in the United States, March 2008*, News, USDL 08-1122, August 7, 2008. See also <http://www.bls.gov/news.release/archives/ebs2_08072008.htm>.

Labor Force, Employment, and Earnings   417

Table 641. Workers Killed or Disabled on the Job: 1970 to 2007

[Data for 2007 are preliminary estimates (1.7 represents 1,700). Excludes homicides and suicides. Estimates based on data from the U.S. National Center for Health Statistics, state vital statistics departments, state industrial commissions and beginning 1995, Bureau of Labor Statistics, Census of Occupational Fatalities. Numbers of workers based on data from the U.S. Bureau of Labor Statistics]

Year	Deaths Manufacturing Number (1,000)	Rate[1]	Deaths Non-manufacturing Number (1,000)	Rate[1]	Disabling injuries[2] (mil.)
1970 ...	1.7	9	12.1	21	2.2
1980 ...	1.7	8	11.5	15	2.2
1990 ...	1.0	5	9.1	9	3.9
1995 ...	0.6	3	4.4	4	3.6
1996 ...	0.7	3	4.4	4	3.9
1997 ...	0.7	3	4.5	4	3.8
1998 ...	0.6	3	4.5	4	3.8
1999 ...	0.6	3	4.6	4	3.8
2000 ...	0.6	3	4.4	4	3.9
2001 ...	0.5	3	4.5	4	3.9
2002 ...	0.5	3	4.2	3	3.7
2003 ...	0.4	2	4.3	4	3.4
2004 ...	0.4	3	4.6	4	3.7
2005 ...	0.4	2	4.6	4	3.7
2006 ...	0.4	3	4.7	4	3.7
2007 ...	0.4	2	4.3	3	3.5

Year and industry group	Deaths, 2007 Number	Rate[1]	Disabling injuries 2007[2] (1,000)
Total, 2007[3] ...	4,689	3.2	3,500
Agriculture[4] ...	552	26.3	70
Mining[5] ...	178	24.4	20
Construction ...	1,140	10.0	420
Manufacturing ...	358	2.2	410
Wholesale trade ...	183	4.2	110
Retail trade ...	156	0.9	450
Transportation and warehousing ...	766	14.5	280
Utilities ...	32	3.8	20
Information ...	70	2.1	50
Financial activities[6] ...	69	0.7	100
Professional & business services[6] ...	407	2.7	180
Educational & health services ...	121	0.6	500
Leisure & hospitality[6] ...	130	1.1	250
Other services[7] ...	113	1.6	130
Government ...	412	1.8	510

[1] Per 100,000 workers. [2] Disabling injury defined as one which results in death, some degree of physical impairment, or renders the person unable to perform regular activities for a full day beyond the day of the injury. Due to change in methodology, data beginning 1990 not comparable with prior years. [3] Includes deaths where industry is not known. [4] Includes forestry, fishing, and hunting. [5] Includes oil and gas extraction. [6] For composition of industry, see Table 618. [7] Excludes public service administration.

Source: National Safety Council, Itasca, IL, *Accident Facts*, annual through 1998 edition; thereafter, *Injury Facts*, annual (copyright).

Table 642. Worker Deaths, Injuries, and Production Time Lost: 2000 to 2007

[47.0 represents 47,000. Data may not agree with Table 644 because data here are not revised]

Item	Deaths (1,000)			Disabling injuries[1] (mil.)			Production time lost (mil. days) In current year			In future years[2]		
	2000	2005	2007	2000	2005	2007	2000	2005	2007	2000	2005	2007
All accidents	47.0	54.3	57.2	10.5	11.9	12.9	240	275	300	460	535	565
On the job	5.2	5.0	4.7	3.9	3.7	3.5	80	80	75	60	65	60
Off the job	41.8	49.3	52.5	6.6	8.2	9.4	160	195	225	400	470	505
Motor vehicle	22.8	24.1	23.2	1.2	1.3	1.2	(NA)	(NA)	(NA)	(NA)	(NA)	(NA)
Public nonmotor vehicle. .	8.3	10.0	12.3	2.8	3.3	4.1	(NA)	(NA)	(NA)	(NA)	(NA)	(NA)
Home	10.7	15.2	17.0	2.6	3.6	4.1	(NA)	(NA)	(NA)	(NA)	(NA)	(NA)

NA Not available. [1] See footnote 2, Table 641, for a definition of disabling injuries. [2] Based on an average of 5,850 days lost in future years per fatality and 565 days lost in future years per permanent injury.
Source: National Safety Council, Itasca, IL, *Injury Facts*, annual (copyright).

Table 643. Industries With the Highest Total Case Incidence Rates for Nonfatal Injuries and Illnesses: 2007

[Rates per 100 full-time employees. Rates refer to any Occupational Safety and Health Administration (OSHA)-recordable occupational injury or illness, whether or not it resulted in days away from work, job transfer, or restriction. Incidence rates were calculated as: Number of injuries and illnesses divided by total hours worked by all employees during the year multiplied by 200,000 as base for 100 full-time equivalent workers (working 40 hours per week, 50 weeks per year)]

Industry	2002 NAICS[1] code	Incidence rate	Industry	2002 NAICS[1] code	Incidence rate
Private industry[2]	(X)	4.2	Sawmill and woodworking machinery manufacturing	33321	11.2
Skiing facilities	71392	16.5	Seafood canning	311711	11.1
Sports teams and clubs	711211	16.2	Copper foundries	331525	10.9
Beet sugar manufacturing	311313	13.8	Scheduled passenger air transportation .	481111	10.9
Steel foundries (except investment). . . .	331513	13.8	Couriers	4291	10.5
Iron foundries	331511	13.6	Truck trailer manufacturing	336212	10.4
Manufactured (mobile) home manufacturing	321991	13.0	Ornamental and architectural metal work manufacturing	332323	10.3
Motor home manufacturing	336213	12.5	Wood container and pallet manufacturing	32192	10.1
Animal (except poultry) slaughtering ...	311611	12.1	Concrete pipe manufacturing	327332	10.1
Rolling mill machinery and equipment manufacturing	333516	11.9	Elevator and moving stairway manufacturing	333921	10.1
Light truck and utility vehicle manufacturing	336112	11.9	Soft drink manufacturing	312111	10.0
Ambulance services	62191	11.8	Iron and steel forging	332111	10.0
Travel trailer and camper manufacturing	336214	11.3	Fabricated structural metal manufacturing	332312	10.0

X Not applicable. [1] Based on the North American Industry Classification System, 2002 (NAICS). See text, this section. [2] Excludes farms with fewer than 11 employees.
Source: U.S. Bureau of Labor Statistics, *Workplace Injuries and Illnesses in 2007*, USDL 08-1498, October 23, 2008. See also <http://www.bls.gov/iif/oshsum.htm#07Summary%20News%20Release>.

418   Labor Force, Employment, and Earnings

Table 644. **Nonfatal Occupational Injury and Illness Incidence Rates: 2007**

[Rates per 100 full-time employees. Except as noted, data refer to any Occupational Safety and Health Administration (OSHA) recordable occupational injury or illness, whether or not it resulted in days away from work, job transfer, or restriction. Incidence rates were calculated as: Number of injuries and illnesses divided by total hours worked by all employees during the year multiplied by 200,000 as base for 100 full-time equivalent workers (working 40 hours, per week, 50 weeks per year)]

Industry	2002 NAICS code [1]	Incidence rate	Industry	2002 NAICS code [1]	Incidence rate
Private industry [2]	(X)	4.2	Truck transportation	484	5.6
Agriculture, forestry, fishing hunting [2,3]	11	5.4	Transit and ground passenger transportation	485	5.3
Crop production [2]	111	5.2	Support activities for transportation	488	4.9
Mining [3,4]	21	3.1	Couriers and messengers	492	9.8
Construction	23	5.4	Warehousing and storage	493	7.7
Construction of buildings	236	4.7	Utilities	22	4.0
Heavy and civil engineering const.	237	4.9	Information [3]	51	2.0
Specialty trade contractors	238	5.7	Telecommunications	517	2.5
Manufacturing [3]	31–33	5.6	Finance and insurance [3]	52	0.9
Food manufacturing	311	6.8	Credit intermediation and related activities	522	1.0
Wood product manufacturing	321	7.8	Insurance carriers and related activities	524	1.1
Paper manufacturing	322	4.0	Real estate and rental and leasing [3]	53	2.9
Printing and related support activities	323	3.8	Real estate	531	2.7
Chemical manufacturing	325	3.1	Rental and leasing services	532	3.5
Plastics and rubber products mfg	326	6.4	Professional, scientific, and technical services	54	1.3
Nonmetallic mineral product mfg	327	6.5	Management of companies and enterprises	55	1.9
Primary metal manufacturing	331	8.1	Administrative and support and waste management and remediation services	56	3.3
Fabricated metal product mfg	332	7.2	Administrative and support services	561	3.1
Machinery manufacturing	333	5.8	Waste management and remediation services	562	6.4
Computer and electronic product mfg	334	2.0	Educational services	61	2.4
Electrical equipment, appliance, and component manufacturing	335	4.7	Health care and social assistance	62	5.6
Transportation equipment mfg	336	6.9	Ambulatory health care services	621	3.0
Furniture and related product mfg.	337	6.7	Hospitals	622	7.7
Miscellaneous manufacturing	339	3.9	Nursing and residential care facilities	623	8.8
Wholesale trade [3]	42	4.0	Social assistance	624	3.9
Merchant wholesalers, durable goods	423	3.9	Arts, entertainment, and recreation [3]	71	5.3
Merchant wholesalers, nondurable goods	424	5.1	Performing arts, spectator sports, and related industries	711	6.8
Retail trade [3]	44–45	4.8	Amusement, gambling, and recreation industries	713	5.0
Motor vehicle and parts dealers	441	4.5	Accommodation and food services	72	4.4
Furniture and home furnishings stores.	442	4.5	Accommodation	721	5.6
Building material and garden equipment and supplies dealers	444	6.6	Food services and drinking places	722	4.1
Food and beverage stores	445	5.9	Other services, (except public admin.)	81	3.1
Health and personal care stores.	446	2.4	Repair and maintenance	811	3.9
Gasoline stations	447	3.2	Personal and laundry services	812	2.6
Clothing and clothing access. stores	448	2.9	Religious, grantmaking, civic, professional, and similar organizations	813	2.8
Sporting goods, hobby, book, and music stores	451	3.6			
General merchandise stores	452	6.4			
Miscellaneous store retailers	453	3.7			
Nonstore retailers	454	5.0			
Transportation and warehousing [3,5]	48–49	6.4			
Air transportation	481	9.9			

X Not applicable. [1] North American Industry Classification System, 2002; see text, this section. [2] Excludes farms with fewer than 11 employees. [3] Includes other industries, not shown separately. [4] Data for mining operators in coal, metal, and nonmetal mining are provided to BLS by the Mine Safety and Health Administration (MHSA), U.S. Department of Labor. Independent mining contractors are excluded. Data provided by MSHA do not reflect 2002 OSHA recordkeeping requirements; therefore, estimates for these industries are not comparable with estimates for other industries. [5] Data for employers in railroad transportation are provided to BLS by the Federal Railroad Administration, U.S. Department of Transportation.

Source: U.S. Bureau of Labor Statistics, *Workplace Injuries and Illnesses in 2007*, USDL 08-1498, October 23, 2008. See also <http://www.bls.gov/iif/>.

Table 645. **Fatal Work Injuries by Event or Exposure: 2007**

[For the 50 states and DC. Based on the Census of Fatal Occupational Injuries. For details, see source. Due to methodological differences, data differ from National Safety Council data]

Event or exposure	Number of fatalities	Percent distribution	Event or exposure	Number of fatalities	Percent distribution
Total	5,657	100	Struck by object or equipment [1]	504	9
Transportation accidents [1]	2,351	42	Struck by falling object or equipment	328	6
Highway accidents [1]	1,414	25	Struck by flying object	58	1
Collision between vehicles, mobile equipment	687	12	Caught in or compressed by— equipment or objects	296	5
Noncollision accidents	308	5	Caught in or crushed in collapsing materials	108	2
Nonhighway accident (farm, industrial premises)	296	5	Falls	847	15
Aircraft accidents	174	3	Exposure to harmful substances or environments [1]	497	9
Workers struck by a vehicle	345	6	Contact with electric current	212	4
Water vehicle accidents	71	1	Exposure to caustic, noxious or allergenic substances	161	3
Railway accidents	49	1	Oxygen deficiency	82	1
Assaults and violent acts [1]	864	15	Drowning, submersion	62	1
Homicides [1]	628	11	Fires and explosions	152	3
Shooting	503	9	Other events and exposures	26	(Z)
Stabbing	45	1			
Self-inflicted injury	196	3			
Contacts with objects and equipment [1]	920	16			

Z Less than 0.5 percent. [1] Includes other causes, not shown separately.
Source: U.S. Bureau of Labor Statistics, "Census of Fatal Occupational Injuries (CFOI)—Current and Revised Data"; <http://www.bls.gov/iif/oshcfoi1.htm>.

Labor Force, Employment, and Earnings 419

Table 646. Workplace Violence Incidence and Security Measures: 2005

[In percent. Covers period September 2004 to June 2005. Based on establishment survey and subject to sampling error; see source for details]

Incident or security measure	All establishments	Industry			Employment size class				
		Private industry [1]	State government	Local government	1 to 10 employees	11 to 49 employees	50 to 249 employees	250 to 999 employees	1,000 or more employees
Any workplace violence incidents	5.3	4.8	32.2	14.7	2.4	9.1	16.0	28.8	49.9
Criminal	2.2	2.1	8.7	3.7	1.4	3.5	4.7	6.8	17.2
Customer or client	2.2	1.9	15.4	10.3	1.0	3.9	6.4	12.2	28.3
Co-worker	2.3	2.1	17.7	4.3	0.6	4.6	8.1	16.8	34.1
Domestic violence	0.9	0.8	5.5	2.1	0.1	2.0	2.9	9.0	24.1
No incident	92.1	92.5	65.3	85.1	95.6	87.8	77.8	63.9	43.8
Selected types of security provided:									
Intruder/burglar systems	41.8	42.1	29.1	35.5	35.7	53.9	57.5	54.2	61.0
Surveillance cameras	22.6	22.2	45.2	32.7	17.0	29.2	47.9	69.1	77.9
Motion detectors	26.9	27.1	14.8	21.3	24.0	32.9	33.7	28.3	36.4
Metal detectors	0.9	0.7	16.0	4.3	0.5	1.1	2.5	7.2	15.7
Electronic badges [2]	6.3	6.0	35.6	9.0	3.9	7.2	20.8	45.1	60.1
Security guards	9.5	9.1	48.6	10.5	6.4	11.7	24.8	53.9	65.3
Limited access [3]	30.7	30.0	58.0	50.7	26.0	35.9	52.5	68.3	83.2
Physical barriers [4]	13.4	13.1	27.2	23.6	10.2	18.2	24.5	33.5	46.5
Lighting of work areas	39.1	38.7	55.8	48.5	32.2	50.0	62.1	71.9	80.4
Workplace violence training provided:									
Any training	20.8	20.2	58.0	32.3	14.6	29.1	45.7	64.2	67.8
No training	78.4	78.9	42.0	67.6	84.3	70.5	54.0	35.6	32.0

[1] Excludes farms with fewer than 11 employees.   [2] Or ID scanner at entry or exit.   [3] Secured entry/locked doors.   [4] Between work areas and the public.

Source: U.S. Bureau of Labor Statistics, *Survey of Workplace Violence and Prevention, 2005 News*, USDL 06-1860, October, 27, 2006. See also <http://www.bls.gov/iif/home.htm> and <http://www.bls.gov/iif/osh_wpvs.htm>.

Table 647. Work Stoppages: 1960 to 2008

[896 represents 896,000. Excludes work stoppages involving fewer than 1,000 workers and lasting less than 1 day. Information is based on reports of labor disputes appearing in daily newspapers, trade journals, and other public sources. The parties to the disputes are contacted by telephone, when necessary, to clarify details of the stoppages]

Year	Number of stoppages [1]	Workers involved [2] (1,000)	Days idle Number [3] (1,000)	Percent estimated working time [4]	Year	Number of stoppages [1]	Workers involved [2] (1,000)	Days idle Number [3] (1,000)	Percent estimated working time [4]
1960	222	896	13,260	0.09	1991	40	392	4,584	0.02
1965	268	999	15,140	0.10	1992	35	364	3,989	0.01
1970	381	2,468	52,761	0.29	1993	35	182	3,981	0.01
1975	235	965	17,563	0.09	1994	45	322	5,021	0.02
1976	231	1,519	23,962	0.12	1995	31	192	5,771	0.02
1977	298	1,212	21,258	0.10	1996	37	273	4,889	0.02
1978	219	1,006	23,774	0.11	1997	29	339	4,497	0.01
1979	235	1,021	20,409	0.09	1998	34	387	5,116	0.02
1980	187	795	20,844	0.09	1999	17	73	1,996	0.01
1981	145	729	16,908	0.07	2000	39	394	20,419	0.06
1982	96	656	9,061	0.04	2001	29	99	1,151	(Z)
1983	81	909	17,461	0.08	2002	19	46	660	(Z)
1984	62	376	8,499	0.04	2003	14	129	4,091	0.01
1985	54	324	7,079	0.03	2004	17	171	3,344	0.01
1986	69	533	11,861	0.05	2005	22	100	1,736	0.01
1987	46	174	4,481	0.02	2006	20	70	2,688	0.01
1988	40	118	4,381	0.02	2007	21	189	1,265	(Z)
1989	51	452	16,996	0.07	2008	15	72	1,954	0.01
1990	44	185	5,926	0.02					

Z Less than 0.005 percent.   [1] Beginning in year indicated.   [2] Workers counted more than once if involved in more than one stoppage during the year.   [3] Resulting from all stoppages in effect in a year, including those that began in an earlier year.   [4] Agricultural and government employees are included in the total working time; private household and forestry and fishery employees are excluded.

Source: U.S. Bureau of Labor Statistics, *Major Work Stoppages in 2008, News*, USDL 09-0150, February 11, 2009. See also <http://www.bls.gov/wsp/>.

Table 648. **Labor Union Membership by Sector: 1985 to 2008**

[See headnote, Table 650. **(16,996 represents 16,996,000)**]

Sector	1985	1990	1995	2000	2004	2005	2006	2007	2008
TOTAL (1,000)									
Wage and salary workers:									
Union members	16,996	16,740	16,360	16,258	15,472	15,685	15,359	15,670	16,098
Covered by unions	19,358	19,058	18,346	17,944	17,087	17,223	16,860	17,243	17,761
Public sector workers:									
Union members.	5,743	6,485	6,927	7,111	7,267	7,430	7,378	7,557	7,832
Covered by unions.	6,921	7,691	7,987	7,976	8,131	8,262	8,172	8,373	8,676
Private sector workers:									
Union members.	11,253	10,255	9,432	9,148	8,205	8,255	7,981	8,114	8,265
Covered by unions.	12,438	11,366	10,360	9,969	8,956	8,962	8,688	8,870	9,084
PERCENT									
Wage and salary workers:									
Union members	18.0	16.1	14.9	13.5	12.5	12.5	12.0	12.1	12.4
Covered by unions	20.5	18.3	16.7	14.9	13.8	13.7	13.1	13.3	13.7
Public sector workers:									
Union members.	35.7	36.5	37.7	37.5	36.4	36.5	36.2	35.9	36.8
Covered by unions.	43.1	43.3	43.5	42.0	40.7	40.5	40.1	39.8	40.7
Private sector workers:									
Union members.	14.3	11.9	10.3	9.0	7.9	7.8	7.4	7.5	7.6
Covered by unions.	15.9	13.2	11.3	9.8	8.6	8.5	8.1	8.2	8.4

Source: The Bureau of National Affairs, Inc., Washington, DC, *Union Membership and Earnings Data Book: Compilations from the Current Population Survey (2009 edition)*, (copyright by BNA PLUS); authored by Barry Hirsch of Georgia State University and David Macpherson of Florida State University. See also <http://bnaplus.bna.com/LaborReports.aspx> and <http://www.unionstats.com>.

Table 649. **Union Members by Selected Characteristics: 2008**

[**Annual averages of monthly data (129,377 represents 129,377,000).** Covers employed wage and salary workers 16 years old and over. Excludes self-employed workers whose businesses are incorporated although they technically qualify as wage and salary workers. Based on Current Population Survey, see text, Section 1 and Appendix III]

Characteristic	Employed wage and salary workers			Median usual weekly earnings [3] (dol.)			
		Percent					Not
	Total (1,000)	Union members [1]	Represented by unions [2]	Total	Union members [1]	Represented by unions [2]	repre- sented by unions
Total [4].	129,377	12.4	13.7	722	886	880	691
16 to 24 years old	18,705	5.0	5.7	443	560	549	434
25 to 34 years old	29,276	10.7	11.8	666	801	793	645
35 to 44 years old	29,708	13.4	14.7	804	933	926	775
45 to 54 years old	29,787	16.0	17.6	822	944	941	785
55 to 64 years old	17,430	16.6	18.4	825	927	922	790
65 years and over	4,471	9.0	10.2	644	771	773	627
Men.	66,846	13.4	14.5	798	939	937	766
Women	62,532	11.4	12.9	638	809	800	615
White [5].	105,052	12.2	13.5	742	914	907	712
Men.	55,197	13.2	14.4	825	967	965	789
Women	49,855	11.1	12.6	654	837	828	627
Black [5].	15,030	14.5	15.8	589	720	712	564
Men.	6,809	15.9	17.0	620	756	751	598
Women	8,221	13.3	14.7	554	674	668	523
Asian [5].	6,157	10.6	11.6	861	902	908	852
Men.	3,216	9.6	10.6	966	927	939	973
Women	2,941	11.7	12.7	753	880	880	737
Hispanic [6].	18,572	10.6	11.7	529	733	724	512
Men.	10,998	11.0	12.0	559	778	765	526
Women	7,574	10.0	11.2	501	654	656	487
Private sector industry.	108,073	7.6	8.4	694	838	829	680
Agriculture and related industries.	1,057	2.8	3.4	444	(B)	(B)	446
Nonagriculture and related industries . . .	107,016	7.7	8.5	698	840	831	683
Mining.	776	6.9	7.9	1,007	1024	1,032	1,003
Construction.	7,652	15.6	16.2	712	1,014	1,012	668
Manufacturing.	15,131	11.4	12.3	741	796	795	733
Wholesale and retail trade.	18,622	5.2	5.9	603	643	638	601
Transportation and utilities.	5,544	22.2	23.4	787	958	950	747
Information.	3,056	12.7	13.7	898	1,011	1,001	871
Financial activities [7]	8,654	1.8	2.3	814	782	782	816
Professional and business services [7] .	11,967	2.1	2.7	835	814	817	836
Education and health services [7]	18,841	9.1	10.3	685	795	798	671
Leisure and hospitality [7]	11,187	3.2	3.6	470	584	575	462
Other services	5,585	3.1	3.6	610	878	810	606
Public sector.	21,305	36.8	40.7	842	923	918	766

B Data not shown where base is less than 50,000. [1] Members of a labor union or an employee association similar to a labor union. [2] Members of a labor union or an employee association similar to a union as well as workers who report no union affiliation but whose jobs are covered by a union or an employee association contract. [3] For full-time employed wage and salary workers. [4] Includes races not shown separately. Also includes a small number of multiple jobholders whose full- and part-time status cannot be determined for their principal job. [5] For persons in this race group only. See footnote 4, Table 575. [6] Persons of Hispanic or Latino ethnicity may be any race. [7] For composition of industries, see Table 612.

Source: U.S. Bureau of Labor Statistics, *Union Members in 2008*, News, USDL-09-0095, January 28, 2009. See also <http://www.bls.gov/cps/home.htm>.

Labor Force, Employment, and Earnings 421

Table 650. **Labor Union Membership by State: 1985 and 2008**

[Annual averages of monthly figures (16,996.1 represents 16,996,100). For wage and salary workers in agriculture and non-agriculture. Data represent union members by place of residence. Based on the Current Population Survey and subject to sampling error. For methodological details, see source]

State	Union members (1,000)		Workers covered by unions (1,000)		Percent of workers					
					Union members		Covered by unions		Private sector union members	
	1985	2008	1985	2008	1985	2008	1985	2008	1985	2008
United States.	16,996.1	16,097.5	19,358.1	17,760.6	18.0	12.4	20.5	13.7	14.3	7.6
Alabama [1].	226.6	181.4	254.9	199.4	15.7	9.8	17.6	10.7	13.5	5.1
Alaska	47.7	67.8	53.4	71.3	25.0	23.5	28.0	24.7	17.0	11.2
Arizona [1]	115.6	227.4	145.7	253.9	9.5	8.8	12.0	9.8	7.9	7.0
Arkansas [1]	91.6	67.9	108.4	85.1	11.2	5.9	13.3	7.3	9.5	3.6
California	2,123.1	2,739.9	2,485.8	2,909.5	20.4	18.4	23.9	19.5	15.8	10.7
Colorado.	165.2	181.1	191.1	208.1	11.8	8.0	13.7	9.2	8.9	5.5
Connecticut.	306.5	275.2	325.9	290.9	20.9	16.9	22.2	17.9	14.4	8.3
Delaware	45.6	52.3	50.9	57.4	16.6	13.4	18.5	14.7	12.8	8.2
District of Columbia	45.2	35.2	58.2	41.1	16.5	12.2	21.2	14.3	13.9	8.8
Florida [1]	395.2	482.3	515.7	600.5	9.1	6.4	11.9	7.9	5.3	2.3
Georgia [1]	239.5	150.7	273.1	189.3	10.0	3.7	11.4	4.6	9.1	2.6
Hawaii	109.6	136.3	121.2	143.0	27.8	24.3	30.8	25.5	19.7	16.4
Idaho [1].	41.7	42.5	48.4	48.1	11.7	7.1	13.6	8.0	9.8	4.8
Illinois	1,031.7	939.2	1,124.9	993.3	22.2	16.6	24.3	17.5	19.2	11.0
Indiana.	476.7	349.3	524.4	385.6	21.3	12.4	23.4	13.7	20.8	10.1
Iowa [1]	181.7	152.6	212.8	186.7	17.0	10.6	20.0	13.0	14.5	6.6
Kansas [1]	129.0	89.3	157.3	110.8	12.8	7.0	15.6	8.7	11.4	4.9
Kentucky	219.2	145.9	250.8	163.0	16.5	8.6	18.8	9.6	16.4	6.9
Louisiana [1]	147.9	80.0	172.8	96.7	9.6	4.6	11.2	5.6	7.9	3.0
Maine.	77.5	70.7	90.0	84.1	17.1	12.3	19.8	14.7	11.2	5.5
Maryland	329.9	329.4	412.9	379.7	16.7	12.6	20.9	14.5	13.0	6.6
Massachusetts.	495.4	457.6	548.4	491.4	18.5	15.7	20.4	16.9	13.0	7.8
Michigan.	1,004.5	770.5	1,071.0	801.1	28.4	18.8	30.3	19.6	23.5	13.1
Minnesota	407.5	391.7	452.7	412.2	22.6	16.1	25.1	17.0	16.7	9.4
Mississippi [1]	81.3	57.3	94.5	79.0	9.3	5.3	10.8	7.3	8.4	4.1
Missouri	378.3	284.6	418.9	326.5	18.7	11.2	20.7	12.8	19.1	9.3
Montana	57.3	47.3	66.9	61.1	19.4	12.2	22.7	15.7	14.9	5.9
Nebraska [1]	78.8	70.0	99.0	90.3	12.7	8.3	16.0	10.7	10.3	4.2
Nevada [1]	89.7	199.0	102.1	216.7	21.6	16.7	24.6	18.2	19.5	13.9
New Hampshire	48.8	67.0	54.8	78.8	17.7	10.6	12.0	12.4	6.9	4.0
New Jersey.	821.0	703.1	937.2	731.1	24.9	18.3	28.4	19.0	19.0	10.3
New Mexico	49.4	58.4	62.4	94.0	10.0	7.2	12.7	11.6	8.9	4.1
New York	2,102.3	2,029.3	2,298.3	2,170.4	30.2	24.9	33.0	26.6	21.3	14.4
North Carolina [1].	167.0	132.5	209.5	189.1	6.4	3.5	8.0	5.0	4.7	2.0
North Dakota [1].	27.9	18.9	34.2	25.2	11.4	6.1	14.0	8.2	6.4	3.1
Ohio . . . . . [2].	999.0	715.8	1,090.9	782.7	23.6	14.2	25.7	15.5	20.7	9.3
Oklahoma [2].	128.4	101.6	151.0	126.8	10.5	6.6	12.3	8.3	8.2	3.8
Oregon.	231.6	259.2	260.8	271.8	22.7	16.6	25.6	17.4	16.7	9.0
Pennsylvania.	1,055.4	847.1	1,174.7	898.9	22.8	15.4	25.4	16.3	19.1	10.3
Rhode Island.	90.2	77.7	97.7	81.8	21.1	16.5	22.9	17.4	12.7	8.7
South Carolina [1]	58.8	69.9	72.5	104.7	4.5	3.9	5.6	5.8	3.8	2.4
South Dakota [1]	27.9	18.4	34.5	23.7	11.2	5.0	13.8	6.4	7.5	2.5
Tennessee [1]	236.8	138.7	281.8	166.2	13.1	5.5	15.6	6.6	10.9	3.5
Texas [1].	474.8	448.6	626.2	559.2	7.4	4.5	9.7	5.6	5.6	2.5
Utah [1]	69.9	67.9	91.9	83.8	11.4	5.8	14.9	7.1	8.0	3.4
Vermont	28.5	29.4	35.4	36.4	12.8	10.4	15.9	12.8	7.1	4.7
Virginia [1]	236.0	145.8	296.7	178.0	9.7	4.1	12.2	5.0	8.6	2.6
Washington.	405.8	577.9	469.2	626.4	25.0	19.8	28.9	21.5	18.6	13.0
West Virginia.	134.7	101.3	148.3	112.5	22.7	13.8	25.0	15.3	22.2	10.7
Wisconsin.	435.9	395.9	463.9	422.0	22.3	15.0	23.8	16.0	17.8	9.7
Wyoming [1]	26.8	18.6	34.2	21.4	13.8	7.7	17.6	8.9	11.2	6.2

[1] Right to work state.   [2] Passed right to work law in 2001.

Source: The Bureau of National Affairs (BNA), Inc., Washington, DC, *Union Membership and Earnings Data Book: Compilations from the Current Population Survey (2009 edition)*, (copyright by BNA PLUS); authored by Barry Hirsch of Georgia State University and David Macpherson of Florida State University. See <http://bnaplus.bna.com/LaborReports.aspx> and <http://www.unionstats.com>.

Section 13
Income, Expenditures, Poverty, and Wealth

This section presents data on gross domestic product (GDP), gross national product (GNP), national and personal income, saving and investment, money income, poverty, and national and personal wealth. The data on income and expenditures measure two aspects of the U.S. economy. One aspect relates to the National Income and Product Accounts (NIPA), a summation reflecting the entire complex of the nation's economic income and output and the interaction of its major components; the other relates to the distribution of money income to families and individuals or consumer income.

The primary source for data on GDP, GNP, national and personal income, gross saving and investment, and fixed assets and consumer durables is the *Survey of Current Business*, published monthly by the Bureau of Economic Analysis (BEA). A comprehensive revision to the NIPA was released beginning in December 2003. Discussions of the revision appeared in the January, June, August, September, and December 2003 issues of the *Survey of Current Business*. Summary historical estimates appeared in the August 2008 issue of the *Survey of Current Business*. Detailed historical data can be found on BEA's Web site at <http://www.bea.gov/>.

Sources of income distribution data are the decennial censuses of population, the Current Population Survey (CPS), and the American Community Survey, all products of the U.S. Census Bureau (see text, Section 1 and Section 4). Annual data on income of families, individuals, and households are presented in *Current Population Reports, Consumer Income*, P60 Series, in print. Many data series are also found on the Census Web site at <http://www.census.gov/hhes/www /income/income.html>. Data on the household sector's saving and assets are published by the Board of Governors of the Federal Reserve System in the quarterly statistical release *Flow of Funds Accounts*. The Federal Reserve Board also

periodically conducts the *Survey of Consumer Finances*, which presents financial information on family assets and net worth. The most recent survey is available at <http:www.federal.reserve.gov /pubs/oss/oss2/scfindex.html>. Detailed information on personal wealth is published periodically by the Internal Revenue Service (IRS) in *SOI Bulletin*.

National income and product—GDP is the total output of goods and services produced by labor and property located in the United States, valued at market prices. GDP can be viewed in terms of the expenditure categories that comprise its major components: personal consumption expenditures, gross private domestic investment, net exports of goods and services, and government consumption expenditures and gross investment. The goods and services included are largely those bought for final use (excluding illegal transactions) in the market economy. A number of inclusions, however, represent imputed values, the most important of which is the rental value of owner-occupied housing. GDP, in this broad context, measures the output attributable to the factors of production located in the United States. GDP by state is the gross market value of the goods and services attributable to labor and property located in a state. It is the state counterpart of the nation's GDP.

The featured measure of real GDP is an index based on chain-type annual weights. Changes in this measure of real output and prices are calculated as the average of changes based on weights for the current and preceding years. (Components of real output are weighted by price, and components of prices are weighted by output.) These annual changes are "chained" (multiplied) together to form a time series that allows for the effects of changes in relative prices and changes in the composition of output over time. Quarterly and monthly changes are based on quarterly and monthly weights, respectively. The output indexes are expressed as 2000 = 100, and for recent years, in 2000 dollars; the price indexes are also based to 2000 = 100. For more information on chained-dollar indexes, see the article on this subject in the November 2003 issue of the *Survey of Current Business.*

Chained (2000) dollar estimates of most components of GDP are not published for periods prior to 1990, because during periods far from the base period, the levels of the components may provide misleading information about their contributions to an aggregate. Values are published in index form (2000 = 100) for 1929 to the present to allow users to calculate the percent changes for all components, which are accurate for all periods. In addition, BEA publishes estimates of contributions of major components to the percent change in GDP for all periods.

Gross national product measures the output attributable to all labor and property supplied by United States residents. GNP differs from "national income" mainly in that GNP includes allowances for depreciation—that is, consumption of fixed capital.

National income includes all net incomes net of consumption of fixed capital (CFC), earned in production. National income is the sum of compensation of employees, proprietors' income with inventory valuation adjustment (IVA) and capital consumption adjustment (CCAdj), rental income of persons with CCAdj, corporate profits with IVA and CCAdj, net interest and miscellaneous payments, taxes on production and imports, business current transfer payments (net), and current surplus of government enterprises, less subsidies.

Capital consumption adjustment for corporations and for nonfarm sole proprietorships and partnerships is the difference between capital consumption based on income tax returns and capital consumption measured using empirical evidence on prices of used equipment and structures in resale markets, which have shown that depreciation for most types of assets approximates a geometric pattern.

The tax-return data are valued at historical costs and reflect changes over time in service lives and depreciation patterns as permitted by tax regulations. *Inventory valuation adjustment* represents the difference between the book value of inventories used up in production and the cost of replacing them.

Personal income is the current income received by persons from all sources minus their personal contributions for government social insurance. Classified as "persons" are individuals (including owners of unincorporated firms), nonprofit institutions that primarily serve individuals, private trust funds, and private noninsured welfare funds. Personal income includes personal current transfer receipts (payments not resulting from current production) from government and business such as social security benefits, public assistance, etc., but excludes transfers among persons. Also included are certain nonmonetary types of income chiefly, estimated net rental value to owner-occupants of their homes and the value of services furnished without payment by financial intermediaries. Capital gains (and losses) are excluded.

Disposable personal income is personal income less personal current taxes. It is the income available to persons for spending or saving. Personal current taxes are tax payments (net of refunds) by persons (except personal contributions for government social insurance) that are not chargeable to business expense. Personal taxes include income taxes, personal property taxes, motor vehicle licenses, and other miscellaneous taxes.

Gross domestic product by industry—The BEA also prepares estimates of value added by industry. *Value added* is a measure of the contribution of each private industry and of government to the nation's GDP. It is defined as an industry's gross output (which consists of sales or receipts and other operating income, commodity taxes, and inventory change) minus its intermediate inputs (which consists of energy, raw materials, semi-finished goods, and services that are purchased from domestic industries or from foreign sources). These estimates of value added are produced for 61 private

424   Income, Expenditures, Poverty, and Wealth

industries and for 4 government classifications—federal general government and government enterprises and state and local general government and government enterprises.

The estimates by industry are available in current dollars and are derived from the estimates of gross domestic income, which consists of three components—the compensation of employees, gross operating surplus, and taxes on production and imports, less subsidies. Real, or inflation-adjusted, estimates are also prepared.

Regional Economic Accounts—These accounts consist of estimates of state and local area personal income and of gross domestic product by state and are consistent with estimates of personal income and gross domestic product in the Bureau's national economic accounts. BEA's estimates of state and local area personal income provide a framework for analyzing individual state and local economies, and they show how the economies compare with each other. The *personal income* of a state and/or local area is the income received by, or on behalf of, the residents of that state or area. Estimates of labor and proprietors' earnings by place of work indicate the economic activity of business and government within that area, and estimates of personal income by place of residence indicate the income within the area that is available for spending. BEA prepares estimates for states, counties, metropolitan areas, and BEA economic areas.

Gross domestic product by state estimates measure the value added to the nation's production by the labor and property in each state. GDP by state is often considered the state counterpart of the nation's GDP. The GDP by state estimates provide the basis for analyzing the regional impacts of national economic trends. GDP by state is measured as the sum of the distributions by industry and state of the components of gross domestic income; that is, the sum of the costs incurred and incomes earned in the production of GDP by state. The GDP estimates are presented in current dollars and in real (chained dollars) for 63 industries.

Consumer Expenditure Survey—The Consumer Expenditure Survey program was begun in 1980. The principal objective of the survey is to collect current consumer expenditure data, which provide a continuous flow of data on the buying habits of American consumers. The data are necessary for future revisions of the Consumer Price Index.

The survey conducted by the Census Bureau for the Bureau of Labor Statistics consists of two components: (1) an interview panel survey in which the expenditures of consumer units are obtained in five interviews conducted every 3 months, and (2) a diary or recordkeeping survey completed by participating households for two consecutive 1-week periods.

Each component of the survey queries an independent sample of consumer units representative of the U.S. total population. Over 52 weeks of the year, 7,000 consumer units are sampled for the diary survey. Each consumer unit keeps a diary for two 1-week periods yielding approximately 14,000 diaries a year. The interview sample is selected on a rotating panel basis, targeted at 7,000 consumer units per quarter. Data are collected in 91 areas of the country that are representative of the U.S. total population. The survey includes students in student housing. Data from the two surveys are combined; integration is necessary to permit analysis of total family expenditures because neither the diary nor quarterly interview survey was designed to collect a complete account of consumer spending.

Distribution of money income to families and individuals—Money income statistics are based on data collected in various field surveys of income conducted since 1936. Since 1947, the Census Bureau has collected the data on an annual basis and published them in *Current Population Reports*, P60 Series. In each of the surveys, field representatives interview samples of the population with respect to income received during the previous year. *Money income* as defined by the Census Bureau differs from the BEA concept of "personal income." Data on consumer income collected in the CPS by

Income, Expenditures, Poverty, and Wealth 425

the Census Bureau cover money income received (exclusive of certain money receipts such as capital gains) before payments for personal income taxes, social security, union dues, medicare deductions, etc. Therefore, money income does not reflect the fact that some families receive part of their income in the form of noncash benefits (see Section 11) such as food stamps, health benefits, and subsidized housing; that some farm families receive noncash benefits in the form of rent-free housing and goods produced and consumed on the farm; or that noncash benefits are also received by some nonfarm residents, which often take the form of the use of business transportation and facilities, full or partial payments by business for retirement programs, medical and educational expenses, etc. These elements should be considered when comparing income levels. None of the aggregate income concepts (GDP, national income, or personal income) is exactly comparable with money income, although personal income is the closest.

Poverty—Families and unrelated individuals are classified as being above or below poverty following the Office of Management and Budget's Statistical Policy Directive 14. The Census Bureau uses a set of thresholds that vary by family size and composition.

The poverty calculation is based solely on money income and does not reflect the fact that many low-income persons receive noncash benefits such as food stamps, medicaid, and public housing. The original thresholds were based on the U.S. Department of Agriculture's 1961 Economy Food Plan and reflected the different consumption requirements of families. The poverty thresholds are updated every year to reflect changes in the Consumer Price Index. The following technical changes to the thresholds were made in 1981: (1) distinctions based on sex of householder were eliminated, (2) separate thresholds for farm families were dropped, and (3) the matrix was expanded to families of nine or more persons from the old cutoff of seven or more persons. These changes were incorporated in the calculation of poverty data beginning with 1981. Besides the Census Bureau Web site at <http://www.census .gov/hhes/www/poverty/poverty.html>, information on poverty guidelines and research may be found at the U.S. Department of Human Services Web site at <http://aspe.hhs.gov/poverty/index .shtml>.

In the recent past, the Census Bureau has published a number of technical papers and reports that presented experimental poverty estimates based on income definitions that counted the value of selected government noncash benefits. The Census Bureau has also published reports on aftertax income.

Statistical reliability—For a discussion of statistical collection and estimation, sampling procedures, and measures of statistical reliability pertaining to Census Bureau data, see Appendix III.

Table 651. **Gross Domestic Product in Current and Chained (2000) Dollars: 1970 to 2008**

[In billions of dollars (1,039 represents $1,039,000,000,000). For explanation of gross domestic product and chained dollars, see text, this section. Minus sign (-) indicates decline in inventories or net imports]

Item	1970	1980	1990	1995	1996	1997	1998	1999	2000	2001	2002	2003	2004	2005	2006	2007	2008
CURRENT DOLLARS																	
Gross domestic product	1,039	2,790	5,803	7,398	7,817	8,304	8,747	9,268	9,817	10,128	10,470	10,961	11,686	12,422	13,178	13,808	14,265
Personal consumption expenditures	649	1,757	3,840	4,976	5,257	5,547	5,880	6,283	6,739	7,055	7,351	7,704	8,196	8,694	9,207	9,710	10,058
Durable goods	85	214	474	612	653	693	750	818	863	884	924	943	984	1,021	1,052	1,083	1,023
Nondurable goods	272	696	1,250	1,485	1,556	1,619	1,684	1,805	1,947	2,017	2,080	2,190	2,344	2,514	2,685	2,833	2,965
Services	292	847	2,116	2,879	3,049	3,236	3,446	3,660	3,929	4,154	4,347	4,571	4,868	5,159	5,470	5,794	6,070
Gross private domestic investment	152	479	861	1,144	1,240	1,390	1,509	1,626	1,736	1,614	1,582	1,664	1,889	2,086	2,220	2,130	1,994
Fixed investment	150	486	846	1,113	1,210	1,318	1,438	1,559	1,679	1,646	1,570	1,650	1,830	2,043	2,171	2,134	2,041
Change in private inventories	2	-6	15	31	31	72	71	67	57	-32	12	14	59	43	49	-4	-47
Net exports of goods and services	4	-13	-78	-91	-96	-102	-160	-261	-380	-367	-424	-499	-615	-714	-757	-708	-669
Exports	60	281	552	812	869	955	956	991	1,096	1,033	1,006	1,041	1,182	1,312	1,481	1,662	1,859
Imports	56	294	630	904	965	1,057	1,116	1,252	1,476	1,400	1,430	1,540	1,798	2,025	2,238	2,370	2,529
Government consumption expenditures and gross investment	234	566	1,180	1,369	1,416	1,469	1,518	1,621	1,722	1,826	1,961	2,093	2,217	2,355	2,508	2,675	2,882
Federal	114	244	508	519	527	531	530	556	579	613	680	756	826	876	932	979	1,072
National defense	88	168	374	349	355	350	346	361	370	393	437	497	551	588	624	662	735
Nondefense	26	76	134	171	173	181	185	195	209	220	243	259	275	287	308	317	337
State and local	120	322	672	850	889	938	988	1,065	1,143	1,213	1,282	1,336	1,391	1,480	1,576	1,696	1,810
CHAINED (2000) DOLLARS																	
Gross domestic product	3,772	5,162	7,113	8,032	8,329	8,704	9,067	9,470	9,817	9,891	10,049	10,301	10,676	10,990	11,295	11,524	11,652
Personal consumption expenditures	2,452	3,374	4,770	5,434	5,619	5,832	6,126	6,439	6,739	6,910	7,099	7,295	7,561	7,792	8,029	8,253	8,272
Durable goods	(NA)	(NA)	454	553	596	647	720	805	863	901	965	1,021	1,085	1,134	1,185	1,242	1,189
Nondurable goods	(NA)	(NA)	1,484	1,639	1,680	1,725	1,794	1,877	1,947	1,987	2,037	2,103	2,178	2,253	2,335	2,393	2,378
Services	(NA)	(NA)	2,852	3,260	3,356	3,468	3,615	3,758	3,929	4,023	4,100	4,179	4,311	4,421	4,530	4,646	4,714
Gross private domestic investment	427	645	895	1,134	1,234	1,388	1,524	1,643	1,736	1,598	1,557	1,613	1,770	1,874	1,913	1,810	1,689
Fixed investment	(NA)	(NA)	887	1,110	1,209	1,321	1,455	1,576	1,679	1,629	1,545	1,597	1,713	1,830	1,866	1,809	1,719
Change in private inventories	(NA)	(NA)	15	30	29	71	73	69	57	-32	13	14	54	39	42	-3	-29
Net exports of goods and services	(NA)	(NA)	-55	-71	-80	-105	-204	-296	-380	-399	-471	-519	-594	-617	-616	-547	-390
Exports	161	324	553	778	843	944	967	1,008	1,096	1,037	1,013	1,026	1,126	1,205	1,315	1,426	1,514
Imports	213	311	607	849	923	1,048	1,170	1,304	1,476	1,436	1,485	1,545	1,720	1,822	1,931	1,972	1,904
Government consumption expenditures and gross investment	1,013	1,115	1,530	1,550	1,565	1,594	1,624	1,687	1,722	1,780	1,859	1,905	1,932	1,939	1,971	2,012	2,070
Federal	(NA)	(NA)	659	580	574	568	561	574	579	601	643	687	716	725	741	753	798
National defense	(NA)	(NA)	479	389	384	373	365	372	370	385	413	449	475	482	490	502	538
Nondefense	(NA)	(NA)	179	191	190	195	196	202	209	217	230	238	241	242	251	250	260
State and local	(NA)	(NA)	868	968	991	1,026	1,063	1,113	1,143	1,179	1,215	1,218	1,216	1,214	1,230	1,259	1,273
Residual	-68	14	-91	-51	-39	-24	-15	-6	–	2	3	3	–	-12	-35	-55	-25

– Represents or rounds to zero.   NA Not available.

Source: U.S. Bureau of Economic Analysis, *Survey of Current Business*, April 2009. See also <http://www.bea.gov/national/nipaweb/SelectTable.asp?Selected=N>.

Table 652. **Real Gross Domestic Product, Chained (2000) Dollars—Annual Percent Change: 1990 to 2008**

[Change from immediate previous year; for example, 1990, change from 1989. Minus sign (–) indicates decrease]

Component	1990	2000	2001	2002	2003	2004	2005	2006	2007	2008
Gross domestic product (GDP)...	1.9	3.7	0.8	1.6	2.5	3.6	2.9	2.8	2.0	1.1
Personal consumption expenditures....	2.0	4.7	2.5	2.7	2.8	3.6	3.0	3.0	2.8	0.2
Durable goods..............	–0.3	7.3	4.3	7.1	5.8	6.3	4.6	4.5	4.8	–4.3
Nondurable goods..............	1.6	3.8	2.0	2.5	3.2	3.5	3.4	3.7	2.5	–0.6
Services..................	2.9	4.5	2.4	1.9	1.9	3.2	2.5	2.5	2.6	1.5
Gross private domestic investment.....	–3.4	5.7	–7.9	–2.6	3.6	9.7	5.8	2.1	–5.4	–6.7
Fixed investment..............	–2.1	6.5	–3.0	–0.5	3.4	7.3	6.8	2.0	–3.1	–5.0
Nonresidential..............	0.5	8.7	–4.2	–9.2	1.0	5.8	7.2	7.5	4.9	1.6
Structures..............	1.5	6.8	–2.3	–17.1	–4.1	1.3	1.3	8.2	12.7	11.2
Equipment and software.......	–	9.4	–4.9	–6.2	2.8	7.4	9.3	7.2	1.7	–3.0
Residential	–8.6	0.7	0.4	4.8	8.4	10.0	6.3	–7.1	–17.9	–20.8
Exports	9.0	8.7	–5.4	–2.3	1.3	9.7	7.0	9.1	8.4	6.2
Goods	8.4	11.2	–6.1	–4.0	1.8	9.0	7.7	9.9	7.5	6.0
Services..................	10.5	2.9	–3.7	1.9	–	11.5	5.6	7.2	10.5	6.6
Imports	3.6	13.1	–2.7	3.4	4.1	11.3	5.9	6.0	2.2	–3.5
Goods	3.0	13.5	–3.2	3.7	4.9	11.3	6.8	5.9	1.7	–4.1
Services..................	6.5	11.1	–0.3	2.1	–	11.5	1.4	6.0	4.5	0.2
Government consumption expenditures and gross investment.............	3.2	2.1	3.4	4.4	2.5	1.4	0.4	1.7	2.1	2.9
Federal	2.0	0.9	3.9	7.0	6.8	4.2	1.2	2.3	1.6	6.0
National defense	–	–0.5	3.9	7.4	8.7	5.8	1.5	1.6	2.5	7.2
Nondefense.................	8.3	3.5	3.8	6.3	3.4	1.1	0.5	3.6	–0.2	3.6
State and local	4.1	2.7	3.2	3.1	0.2	–0.2	–0.1	1.3	2.3	1.1

– Represents or rounds to zero.

Source: U.S. Bureau of Economic Analysis, *Survey of Current Business*, April 2009. See also <http://www.bea.gov/national/nipaweb/SelectTable.asp?Selected=N>.

Table 653. **Gross Domestic Product in Current and Chained (2000) Dollars by Type of Product and Sector: 1990 to 2008**

[In billions of dollars (5,803 represents $5,803,000,000,000). For explanation of chained dollars, see text, this section]

Type of product and sector	1990	2000	2002	2003	2004	2005	2006	2007	2008
CURRENT DOLLARS									
Gross domestic product	5,803	9,817	10,470	10,961	11,686	12,422	13,178	13,808	14,265
PRODUCT									
Goods	2,156	3,449	3,442	3,524	3,707	3,874	4,109	4,273	4,296
Durable goods	958	1,689	1,575	1,585	1,651	1,752	1,836	1,885	1,881
Nondurable goods............	1,198	1,760	1,867	1,939	2,056	2,121	2,273	2,387	2,416
Services [1]	3,114	5,426	6,031	6,367	6,778	7,200	7,645	8,135	8,619
Structures	534	942	996	1,069	1,201	1,348	1,424	1,400	1,350
SECTOR									
Business....................	4,463	7,667	8,041	8,412	8,988	9,592	10,184	10,642	10,918
Nonfarm	4,386	7,595	7,970	8,323	8,873	9,488	10,093	10,505	10,791
Farm......................	77	72	71	88	115	104	91	137	126
Households and institutions	619	1,081	1,227	1,269	1,350	1,405	1,497	1,582	1,674
General government	722	1,070	1,202	1,280	1,348	1,425	1,497	1,583	1,673
Federal	259	315	353	384	413	438	460	484	516
State and local	463	754	849	896	936	987	1,037	1,099	1,157
CHAINED (2000) DOLLARS									
Gross domestic product	7,113	9,817	10,049	10,301	10,676	10,990	11,295	11,524	11,652
PRODUCT									
Goods	2,253	3,449	3,433	3,538	3,705	3,865	4,074	4,202	4,243
Durable goods	877	1,689	1,627	1,682	1,782	1,898	1,998	2,082	2,112
Nondurable goods............	1,407	1,760	1,805	1,856	1,925	1,974	2,083	2,131	2,144
Services [1]	4,170	5,426	5,693	5,811	5,973	6,101	6,243	6,416	6,558
Structures	718	942	922	952	1,001	1,034	1,011	960	911
SECTOR									
Business....................	5,287	7,667	7,807	8,050	8,387	8,681	8,946	9,128	9,199
Nonfarm	5,238	7,595	7,737	7,974	8,304	8,590	8,861	9,035	9,108
Farm......................	49	72	70	76	82	90	83	92	90
Households and institutions	841	1,081	1,131	1,129	1,166	1,182	1,219	1,252	1,281
General government	1,004	1,070	1,110	1,124	1,129	1,138	1,144	1,160	1,184
Federal	372	315	323	332	335	337	337	340	352
State and local	634	754	787	792	794	800	807	820	832

[1] Includes government consumption expenditures, which are for services (such as education and national defense) produced by government. In current dollars, these services are valued at their cost of production.

Source: U.S. Bureau of Economic Analysis, *Survey of Current Business*, April 2009. See also <http://www.bea.gov/national/nipaweb/SelectTable.asp?Selected=N>.

428   Income, Expenditures, Poverty, and Wealth

Table 654. Gross Domestic Product in Current and Chained (2000) Dollars by Industry: 2000 to 2008

[In billions of dollars (9,817 represents $9,817,000,000,000). Data are based on the 1997 North American Industry Classification System (NAICS); see text, Section 15. Data include nonfactor charges (capital consumption allowances, indirect business taxes, etc.) as well as factor charges against gross product; corporate profits and capital consumption allowances have been shifted from a company to an establishment basis]

Industry	Current dollars				Chained (2000) dollars			
	2000	2005	2007	2008	2000	2005	2007	2008
Gross domestic product	**9,817**	**12,422**	**13,808**	**14,265**	**9,817**	**10,990**	**11,524**	**11,652**
Private industries	8,614	10,853	12,065	12,425	8,614	9,740	10,250	10,309
Agriculture, forestry, and fishing	98	133	168	158	98	120	122	121
Farms	72	104	137	(NA)	72	90	92	(NA)
Agricultural services	27	29	31	(NA)	27	30	30	(NA)
Mining	121	224	275	325	121	104	111	110
Oil and gas extraction	81	150	165	(NA)	81	69	70	(NA)
Mining, except oil and gas	27	37	45	(NA)	27	25	25	(NA)
Mining support activities	13	37	65	(NA)	13	10	15	(NA)
Utilities	189	239	281	306	189	200	204	208
Construction	436	605	611	582	436	418	356	336
Manufacturing	1,426	1,481	1,617	1,638	1,426	1,491	1,619	1,574
Durable goods	865	845	922	915	865	949	1,075	1,061
Wood products	31	38	31	(NA)	31	32	32	(NA)
Nonmetallic mineral products	46	53	54	(NA)	46	48	44	(NA)
Primary metals	48	56	62	(NA)	48	44	41	(NA)
Fabricated metal products	122	124	140	(NA)	122	113	123	(NA)
Machinery	109	112	126	(NA)	109	110	121	(NA)
Computer and electronic products	186	134	146	(NA)	186	304	456	(NA)
Electrical equipment, appliances, and components	51	46	58	(NA)	51	46	52	(NA)
Motor vehicles, bodies & trailers, & parts	118	98	98	(NA)	118	129	155	(NA)
Other transportation equipment	64	81	96	(NA)	64	68	78	(NA)
Furniture and related products	33	35	35	(NA)	33	33	32	(NA)
Miscellaneous manufacturing	58	68	73	(NA)	58	66	71	(NA)
Nondurable goods	561	636	695	723	561	551	566	539
Food & beverage & tobacco	155	159	175	(NA)	155	146	166	(NA)
Textile mills and textile product mills	27	23	20	(NA)	27	24	20	(NA)
Apparel and leather and allied products	25	17	16	(NA)	25	18	17	(NA)
Paper products	56	50	51	(NA)	56	53	51	(NA)
Printing and related support activities	49	46	48	(NA)	49	45	47	(NA)
Petroleum and coal products	26	71	70	(NA)	26	30	22	(NA)
Chemical products	157	201	249	(NA)	157	172	198	(NA)
Plastics and rubber products	67	67	66	(NA)	67	67	61	(NA)
Wholesale trade	592	722	805	819	592	688	698	688
Retail trade	662	825	893	885	662	841	928	923
Transportation and warehousing	302	365	407	415	302	348	364	350
Air transportation	58	48	55	(NA)	58	81	90	(NA)
Rail transportation	26	34	41	(NA)	26	27	29	(NA)
Water transportation	7	10	11	(NA)	7	6	8	(NA)
Truck transportation	93	118	128	(NA)	93	101	105	(NA)
Transit & ground passenger transport	15	18	19	(NA)	15	15	15	(NA)
Pipeline transportation	9	9	12	(NA)	9	12	12	(NA)
Other transportation & support	70	92	101	(NA)	70	77	77	(NA)
Warehousing and storage	25	36	40	(NA)	25	32	35	(NA)
Information	458	558	586	622	458	609	676	711
Publishing industries (includes software)	117	143	139	(NA)	117	150	144	(NA)
Motion picture and sound recording	33	42	43	(NA)	33	35	37	(NA)
Broadcasting and telecommunications	271	310	342	(NA)	271	362	411	(NA)
Information and data processing services	38	62	62	(NA)	38	62	88	(NA)
Finance and insurance	741	989	1,091	1,065	741	890	946	917
Real estate and rental and leasing	1,191	1,538	1,720	1,784	1,191	1,333	1,414	1,440
Professional, scientific, and technical services	675	859	1,008	1,096	675	792	897	974
Legal services	136	180	198	(NA)	136	140	135	(NA)
Computer systems design, related services	126	135	169	(NA)	126	142	174	(NA)
Miscellaneous services	413	545	640	(NA)	413	512	597	(NA)
Management of companies & enterprises	183	236	271	284	183	186	179	180
Admin/support waste management/remediation services	282	368	415	426	282	321	331	335
Educational services	79	114	130	138	79	85	90	93
Health care and social assistance	599	856	957	1,020	599	724	763	798
Ambulatory health care services	308	439	498	(NA)	308	392	423	(NA)
Hospitals, nursing, residential care	239	341	374	(NA)	239	262	265	(NA)
Social assistance	53	76	86	(NA)	53	72	79	(NA)
Arts, entertainment, and recreation	89	118	134	140	89	100	106	108
Performing arts, spectator sports, museums, and related activities	40	54	62	(NA)	40	44	46	(NA)
Amusements, gambling, & recreation	49	64	72	(NA)	49	56	60	(NA)
Accommodation and food services	261	334	379	396	261	286	300	305
Accommodation	91	106	121	(NA)	91	92	95	(NA)
Food services and drinking places	171	228	259	(NA)	171	194	205	(NA)
Other services, except government	229	287	316	327	229	235	235	236
Government	1,203	1,569	1,743	1,840	1,203	1,262	1,286	1,311
Federal	379	502	554	587	379	394	396	408
State and local	824	1,067	1,189	1,253	824	868	890	904

NA Not available.

Source: U.S. Bureau of Economic Analysis, *Survey of Current Business*, May 2009. See also <http://www.bea.gov/newsreleases/industry/gdpindustry/gdpindnewsrelease.htm>.

Income, Expenditures, Poverty, and Wealth 429

Table 655. **Gross Domestic Product by State in Current and Chained (2000) Dollars: 2000 to 2008**

[In billions of dollars (9,749.1 represents $9,749,100,000,000). For definition of gross domestic product by state or chained dollars, see text, this section]

State	Current dollars					Chained (2000) dollars				
	2000	2005	2006	2007	2008, prel.	2000	2005	2006	2007	2008, prel.
United States [1]	9,749.1	12,339.0	13,090.8	13,715.7	14,165.6	9,749.1	10,912.2	11,218.8	11,439.2	11,523.6
Alabama.	114.6	150.6	158.9	164.5	170.0	114.6	132.3	134.9	136.1	137.1
Alaska	27.0	39.4	43.3	44.9	47.9	27.0	29.3	30.6	30.6	30.0
Arizona.	158.5	215.2	236.4	246.0	248.9	158.5	196.2	208.6	211.6	210.2
Arkansas	66.8	86.5	90.7	95.1	98.3	66.8	76.5	77.5	78.7	79.2
California	1,287.1	1,628.6	1,727.6	1,801.8	1,846.8	1,287.1	1,467.9	1,512.9	1,539.4	1,546.1
Colorado.	171.9	212.6	225.1	235.8	248.6	171.9	188.4	193.4	197.3	203.0
Connecticut.	160.4	190.5	201.6	212.3	216.2	160.4	169.1	174.3	178.5	177.7
Delaware	41.5	57.6	59.2	61.5	61.8	41.5	49.9	49.6	50.1	49.2
District of Columbia	58.7	83.4	88.1	92.5	97.2	58.7	70.0	71.4	72.6	74.8
Florida	471.3	670.0	721.4	741.9	744.1	471.3	589.3	613.6	613.4	603.5
Georgia	290.9	359.5	375.6	391.2	397.8	290.9	322.6	326.5	331.3	329.5
Hawaii	40.2	54.9	59.1	62.0	63.8	40.2	46.9	48.7	49.4	49.8
Idaho	35.0	46.6	48.6	52.1	52.7	35.0	42.9	43.8	45.5	45.5
Illinois	464.2	553.0	588.9	617.4	633.7	464.2	490.3	505.3	514.8	516.1
Indiana	194.4	232.9	239.9	249.2	254.9	194.4	208.1	208.3	211.1	209.9
Iowa	90.2	115.8	121.1	129.9	135.7	90.2	102.6	104.5	108.1	110.4
Kansas.	82.8	102.9	109.9	117.0	122.7	82.8	90.0	93.1	96.0	98.1
Kentucky	111.9	138.6	146.4	152.1	156.4	111.9	122.9	125.8	127.0	127.0
Louisiana	131.5	183.0	197.6	207.4	222.2	131.5	140.3	143.1	144.4	144.9
Maine.	35.5	44.5	46.3	48.0	49.7	35.5	39.0	39.4	39.8	40.3
Maryland	180.4	241.5	253.0	264.4	273.3	180.4	211.4	214.2	217.9	220.9
Massachusetts.	274.9	317.4	334.5	352.2	365.0	274.9	289.9	297.6	306.5	312.5
Michigan.	337.2	372.0	375.1	379.9	382.5	337.2	339.9	334.8	331.0	326.1
Minnesota.	185.1	232.8	240.9	252.5	262.8	185.1	208.4	209.4	212.8	217.0
Mississippi	64.3	79.5	83.8	87.7	91.8	64.3	68.4	69.6	70.5	71.7
Missouri	176.7	213.2	219.7	229.0	237.8	176.7	189.1	188.8	191.2	193.8
Montana	21.4	29.8	31.8	34.3	35.9	21.4	25.2	25.8	26.8	27.3
Nebraska	55.5	71.0	75.0	80.4	83.3	55.5	62.2	63.8	65.7	66.6
Nevada	73.7	112.4	121.7	129.3	131.2	73.7	97.2	101.1	103.9	103.2
New Hampshire	43.5	53.5	56.1	57.8	60.0	43.5	48.5	49.3	49.6	50.6
New Jersey	344.8	425.5	445.7	461.3	474.9	344.8	379.1	384.6	388.0	390.4
New Mexico	50.7	68.0	71.8	75.2	79.9	50.7	57.6	59.0	60.2	61.4
New York	777.2	956.4	1,034.1	1,105.0	1,144.5	777.2	865.7	912.9	949.5	964.8
North Carolina	273.7	348.4	378.6	390.5	400.2	273.7	309.7	326.9	329.1	329.4
North Dakota.	17.8	24.3	25.4	28.5	31.2	17.8	20.9	21.1	22.6	24.3
Ohio	372.0	438.8	449.0	462.5	471.5	372.0	390.6	387.3	388.3	385.6
Oklahoma.	89.8	120.6	129.6	136.4	146.4	89.8	99.2	102.2	104.1	106.9
Oregon.	112.4	138.0	151.2	158.3	161.6	112.4	129.4	139.6	144.8	147.1
Pennsylvania.	389.6	482.0	509.0	533.2	553.3	389.6	422.5	431.0	438.9	443.7
Rhode Island.	33.6	43.1	45.5	46.7	47.4	33.6	37.8	38.5	38.5	38.1
South Carolina.	112.5	138.6	146.5	151.7	156.4	112.5	122.8	125.2	126.3	127.1
South Dakota	23.1	30.7	31.2	35.2	37.0	23.1	27.4	27.1	29.3	30.3
Tennessee	174.9	223.8	236.1	245.2	252.1	174.9	200.9	206.4	209.1	210.2
Texas.	727.2	982.1	1,070.3	1,148.5	1,223.5	727.2	828.4	869.4	907.4	925.5
Utah	67.6	89.1	98.3	105.6	109.8	67.6	77.8	82.7	86.5	87.7
Vermont	17.8	22.8	23.7	24.6	25.4	17.8	20.7	21.0	21.3	21.7
Virginia.	260.7	350.9	368.0	384.1	397.0	260.7	303.1	314.5	320.3	324.5
Washington.	222.0	272.7	289.1	310.3	322.8	222.0	241.8	248.5	259.4	264.6
West Virginia.	41.5	52.9	55.8	57.9	61.7	41.5	44.7	44.9	45.2	46.3
Wisconsin.	175.7	214.8	224.9	233.4	240.4	175.7	191.7	195.0	197.0	198.3
Wyoming	17.3	26.4	30.1	31.5	35.3	17.3	19.3	20.7	20.8	21.8

[1] For chained (2000) dollar estimates, states will not add to U.S. total.

Source: U.S. Bureau of Economic Analysis, *Survey of Current Business*, June 2009 and "Gross Domestic Product by State" (published 2 June 2009); <http://www.bea.gov/regional/gsp/>.

Table 656. Gross Domestic Product by Selected Industries and State: 2008

[In billions of dollars (14,165.6 represents $14,165,600,000,000). Preliminary data. For definition of gross domestic product by state, see text, this section. Industries based on 1997 North American Industry Classification System; see text, Section 15]

State	Total [1]	Manu-facturing	Whole-sale trade	Retail trade	Infor-mation	Finance and insur-ance	Real estate, rental, and leasing	Profes-sional and tech-nical ser-vices	Health care and social assis-tance	Govern-ment [2]
United States.	14,165.6	1,637.7	818.8	885.5	622.0	1,064.9	1,783.5	1,095.6	1,019.7	1,740.9
Alabama.	170.0	29.3	9.9	13.2	4.4	9.1	15.1	10.6	12.3	27.8
Alaska	47.9	1.0	0.9	2.0	1.0	1.3	3.5	1.7	2.4	8.4
Arizona.	248.9	19.5	13.9	19.5	6.7	17.7	40.0	15.7	19.4	32.4
Arkansas	98.3	17.1	6.4	7.2	3.9	3.7	8.4	3.9	7.7	13.7
California	1,846.8	181.1	105.1	118.6	112.8	107.6	308.7	174.6	115.6	216.8
Colorado.	248.6	15.9	13.8	14.7	21.1	14.7	31.5	24.3	14.9	30.6
Connecticut.	216.2	28.9	11.3	11.9	8.2	33.7	27.4	16.9	17.0	20.4
Delaware	61.8	4.6	2.0	2.6	1.3	20.0	7.5	4.0	3.6	5.4
District of Columbia	97.2	0.2	0.9	1.2	5.6	4.0	9.7	21.0	4.3	31.7
Florida	744.1	35.7	46.6	55.8	30.5	47.4	134.0	50.7	57.6	90.6
Georgia	397.8	43.3	31.0	26.0	25.3	23.9	45.3	29.2	24.6	55.4
Hawaii	63.8	1.1	2.1	4.5	1.4	2.5	11.4	3.0	4.2	15.1
Idaho	52.7	5.2	2.8	4.5	1.2	2.5	6.5	4.0	3.9	7.5
Illinois	633.7	78.8	44.0	35.2	23.1	58.0	79.2	57.6	42.9	61.3
Indiana.	254.9	63.8	14.4	15.9	5.6	14.8	23.4	11.1	20.1	25.9
Iowa	135.7	28.2	7.7	7.9	3.9	14.2	10.4	4.6	9.2	15.8
Kansas.	122.7	18.6	7.6	8.1	7.2	6.9	10.0	6.8	8.8	17.4
Kentucky	156.4	28.8	9.7	10.4	4.1	7.4	12.9	6.9	13.0	24.6
Louisiana	222.2	40.5	9.7	13.6	4.4	6.7	15.6	9.8	12.8	24.6
Maine.	49.7	5.5	2.5	4.4	1.3	3.1	6.8	2.6	5.6	7.0
Maryland	273.3	15.2	13.5	16.1	10.1	15.3	38.6	30.5	21.4	51.1
Massachusetts.	365.0	34.8	20.7	17.7	17.6	35.5	51.8	44.5	34.6	33.1
Michigan.	382.5	61.8	23.3	25.8	10.5	23.1	44.0	32.5	32.9	44.5
Minnesota.	262.8	33.7	18.4	15.0	9.1	23.0	30.6	17.3	22.8	27.8
Mississippi	91.8	13.7	4.5	7.5	2.1	3.8	7.6	3.4	6.7	16.1
Missouri	237.8	32.0	15.3	16.1	11.1	13.4	22.7	16.1	18.8	29.6
Montana	35.9	1.5	1.9	2.5	0.9	1.7	3.9	1.9	3.3	5.6
Nebraska	83.3	9.9	4.7	5.0	2.8	6.2	6.7	4.2	6.1	11.7
Nevada	131.2	5.7	5.1	9.9	2.4	10.0	18.6	6.8	6.6	13.4
New Hampshire	60.0	6.5	3.7	4.7	2.2	4.9	8.9	4.5	5.5	5.8
New Jersey	474.9	43.9	37.7	29.6	22.1	36.4	74.4	45.8	35.5	49.3
New Mexico	79.9	5.3	2.7	5.2	2.1	2.4	7.7	6.5	5.4	13.9
New York	1,144.5	69.1	53.2	57.3	80.1	187.2	176.0	103.1	82.6	117.5
North Carolina	400.2	78.0	21.7	25.0	12.1	39.9	36.7	21.7	26.6	56.0
North Dakota.	31.2	2.8	2.2	2.1	1.0	1.7	2.5	1.1	2.6	4.4
Ohio	471.5	84.1	30.1	30.3	12.4	34.7	46.7	29.0	40.2	54.1
Oklahoma.	146.4	15.7	7.1	9.8	4.5	6.2	11.3	6.5	9.9	23.0
Oregon.	161.6	30.2	10.5	8.7	5.4	7.9	21.2	8.6	13.0	20.7
Pennsylvania.	553.3	75.5	33.0	33.3	20.2	40.3	65.3	43.6	53.6	54.0
Rhode Island.	47.4	4.7	2.4	2.8	1.8	5.3	7.0	2.7	4.5	6.1
South Carolina.	156.4	25.2	9.0	12.3	4.3	7.3	16.5	8.2	9.7	27.1
South Dakota	37.0	3.5	2.0	2.5	1.0	6.5	2.4	1.0	3.2	4.5
Tennessee	252.1	40.6	17.0	20.6	8.4	14.4	24.3	14.8	22.9	28.6
Texas.	1,223.5	158.8	76.4	72.0	46.3	66.8	104.6	83.3	69.5	130.0
Utah	109.8	13.0	5.5	8.0	3.8	9.5	12.3	7.9	6.2	15.2
Vermont	25.4	2.9	1.2	2.1	0.9	1.5	3.1	1.6	2.6	3.5
Virginia.	397.0	34.1	16.5	22.7	18.8	23.1	50.3	52.6	22.5	72.9
Washington	322.8	32.0	19.5	22.7	25.5	17.1	45.3	22.0	22.5	46.9
West Virginia	61.7	6.6	2.9	4.6	1.5	5.1	5.1	2.5	5.7	11.0
Wisconsin	240.4	48.9	13.6	14.6	7.3	17.7	27.5	11.3	20.9	26.5
Wyoming	35.3	1.1	1.2	1.9	0.5	0.9	2.5	1.0	1.4	4.5

[1] Includes industries not shown separately. [2] Includes federal civilian and military and state and local government.

Source: U.S. Bureau of Economic Analysis, *Survey of Current Business,* June 2009; and "Gross Domestic Product by State" (published 2 June 2009); <http://www.bea.gov/regional/gsp/>.

Income, Expenditures, Poverty, and Wealth   431

Table 657. **Relation of GDP, GNP, Net National Product, National Income, Personal Income, Disposable Personal Income, and Personal Saving: 1990 to 2008**

[In billions of dollars (5,803 represents $5,803,000,000,000). For definitions, see text, this section. Minus sign (−) indicates deficit or net disbursement]

Item	1990	2000	2003	2004	2005	2006	2007	2008
Gross domestic product (GDP)	5,803	9,817	10,961	11,686	12,422	13,178	13,808	14,265
Plus: Income receipts from the rest of the world.	189	383	337	438	574	725	862	798
Less: Income payments to the rest of the world.	154	344	280	361	481	647	759	665
Equals: Gross national product (GNP) . . .	5,838	9,856	11,018	11,762	12,515	13,257	13,910	14,398
Less: Consumption of fixed capital	683	1,188	1,337	1,436	1,612	1,624	1,721	1,832
Equals: Net national product.	5,155	8,668	9,681	10,326	10,903	11,633	12,190	12,566
Less: Statistical discrepancy	*66*	*−127*	*49*	*19*	*−71*	*−163*	*−81*	*136*
Equals: National income.	5,089	8,795	9,632	10,307	10,974	11,796	12,271	12,430
Less: Corporate profits [1]	438	818	993	1,231	1,448	1,669	1,642	1,477
Taxes on production and imports less subsidies	399	665	759	819	869	926	963	983
Contributions for government social insurance	410	703	779	829	874	926	965	996
Net interest and miscellaneous payments on assets	442	559	525	491	569	631	664	683
Business current transfer payments (net).	39	87	84	83	70	85	100	104
Current surplus of government enterprises	2	5	2	−4	−13	−9	−8	−8
Wage accruals less disbursements	−	−	15	−15	5	1	−6	−
Plus: Personal income receipts on assets	924	1,387	1,337	1,432	1,597	1,825	2,000	2,038
Personal current transfer receipts	595	1,084	1,351	1,423	1,521	1,603	1,713	1,869
Equals: Personal income	4,879	8,430	9,164	9,727	10,270	10,994	11,663	12,103
Less: Personal current taxes.	593	1,236	1,001	1,046	1,208	1,353	1,493	1,461
Equals: Disposable personal income	4,286	7,194	8,163	8,681	9,062	9,641	10,171	10,642
Less: Personal outlays	3,986	7,026	7,988	8,499	9,030	9,570	10,113	10,451
Equals: Personal saving	299	169	175	182	33	71	57	191

− Represents or rounds to zero. [1] Corporate profits with inventory valuation and capital consumption adjustments.

Source: U.S. Bureau of Economic Analysis, *Survey of Current Business,* April 2009. See also <http://www.bea.gov/national /nipaweb/SelectTable.asp?Selected=N>.

Table 658. **Gross Saving and Investment: 1990 to 2008**

[In billions of dollars (940 represents $940,000,000,000)]

Item	1990	2000	2003	2004	2005	2006	2007	2008
Gross saving	940	1,771	1,459	1,618	1,844	2,039	1,956	1,700
Net saving.	258	583	123	182	232	415	236	−132
Net private saving	423	343	515	551	494	570	455	469
Personal saving.	299	169	175	182	33	71	57	191
Undistributed corporate profits with IVA and CCA [1].	123	175	325	384	457	498	403	278
Wage accruals less disbursements	−	−	15	−15	5	1	−6	−
Net government saving.	−165	239	−393	−369	−262	−155	−219	−602
Federal	−172	190	−372	−371	−292	−201	−229	−522
State and local	7	50	−20	2	30	46	10	−80
Consumption of fixed capital.	683	1,188	1,337	1,436	1,612	1,624	1,721	1,832
Private	552	991	1,118	1,206	1,360	1,356	1,431	1,523
Domestic business.	466	836	917	970	1,062	1,086	1,147	1,225
Households and institutions	85	155	202	236	297	271	284	298
Government.	131	197	218	230	252	268	289	309
Federal	68	87	90	94	99	106	112	118
State and local	63	110	128	136	153	162	178	191
Gross domestic investment, capital acct. transactions, and net lending. . .	1,007	1,643	1,508	1,637	1,773	1,876	1,875	1,836
Gross domestic investment.	1,077	2,040	2,020	2,261	2,484	2,647	2,593	2,490
Gross private domestic investment	861	1,736	1,664	1,889	2,086	2,220	2,130	1,994
Gross government investment	216	305	356	373	398	427	463	496
Capital account transactions (net)	7	1	3	2	4	4	2	2
Net lending or net borrowing.	−77	−397	−516	−627	−715	−776	−720	−656
Statistical discrepancy.	66	−127	49	19	−71	−163	−81	136
Addenda:								
Gross private saving	974	1,334	1,633	1,757	1,854	1,926	1,886	1,992
Gross government saving	−34	436	−174	−139	−10	113	70	−292
Federal	−104	277	−282	−277	−193	−96	−118	−404
State and local	70	160	107	138	183	209	188	111
Net domestic investment.	394	852	684	825	872	1,023	873	657
Gross saving as a percentage of gross national income	16.3	17.7	13.3	13.8	14.7	15.2	14.0	11.9
Net saving as a percentage of gross national income	4.5	5.8	1.1	1.5	1.8	3.1	1.7	−0.9

− Represents or rounds to zero. [1] IVA and CCA = Inventory valuation adjustment and capital consumption adjustment.

Source: U.S. Bureau of Economic Analysis, *Survey of Current Business,* April 2009. See also <http://www.bea.gov/national /nipaweb/SelectTable.asp?Selected=N>.

Table 659. **Flow of Funds Accounts—Composition of Individuals' Savings: 1990 to 2008**

[In billions of dollars (511.0 represents $511,000,000,000). Combined statement for households, farm business, and nonfarm noncorporate business. Minus sign (–) indicates decrease]

Composition of savings	1990	2000	2003	2004	2005	2006	2007	2008
Net acquisition of financial assets	511.0	372.6	908.8	1,407.8	1,197.2	1,211.4	1,327.1	606.8
Foreign deposits	1.4	7.6	2.2	5.4	2.4	5.3	13.0	–18.3
Checkable deposits and currency	–8.4	–73.9	–34.2	58.6	–49.0	33.0	–67.6	108.1
Time and savings deposits	33.1	348.8	332.2	450.0	510.7	506.6	499.9	119.6
Money market fund shares	30.6	152.4	–109.2	–50.6	50.0	171.8	249.4	236.4
Securities	202.5	–641.0	247.1	189.0	47.0	–280.4	–209.6	–4.2
Open market paper	5.8	12.4	–4.5	30.2	28.1	23.4	–38.0	–139.2
U.S. savings bonds	8.5	–1.7	8.9	0.6	–0.7	–2.7	–6.0	–2.4
Other Treasury securities	89.3	–204.3	22.0	31.7	–93.1	–76.5	–143.5	88.0
Agency and GSE-backed securities [1]	36.3	38.6	148.0	29.8	99.1	–40.3	336.8	180.7
Municipal securities	34.7	4.6	24.7	40.3	78.7	54.0	34.1	53.4
Corporate and foreign bonds	47.1	80.3	–144.6	98.3	120.3	205.2	154.0	–241.2
Corporate equities [2]	–50.8	–637.6	–81.7	–258.2	–414.9	–665.9	–805.9	112.5
Mutual fund shares	31.5	66.7	274.4	216.4	228.1	222.4	258.8	–55.9
Life insurance reserves	26.5	50.2	66.8	33.1	16.1	65.6	34.2	35.7
Pension fund reserves	191.0	271.6	258.5	288.4	238.3	197.1	162.9	20.9
Miscellaneous and other assets	34.3	256.9	145.5	433.7	381.7	512.4	644.9	108.6
Gross investment in tangible assets	808.0	1,487.2	1,680.7	1,818.8	1,964.0	1,997.8	1,933.1	1,769.2
Minus: Consumption of fixed capital	*558.8*	*940.9*	*1,057.6*	*1,141.7*	*1,274.5*	*1,264.2*	*1,317.8*	*1,346.1*
Equals: Net investment in tangible assets. . .	249.2	546.3	623.2	677.1	689.5	733.7	615.3	423.1
Net increase in liabilities	229.7	931.6	1,110.6	1,512.9	1,698.9	1,828.5	1,468.3	130.8
Mortgage debt on nonfarm homes	206.2	425.2	799.9	1,020.6	1,108.3	1,038.2	685.4	–90.3
Other mortgage debt [3]	–1.9	109.5	130.0	151.7	117.1	241.6	264.0	113.2
Consumer credit	15.1	176.5	104.4	115.0	94.5	104.4	133.6	44.3
Policy loans	4.1	2.8	–0.7	1.6	0.8	3.3	3.6	4.6
Security credit	–3.7	7.2	34.3	81.5	–31.6	59.7	33.4	–160.7
Other liabilities [3]	10.0	210.3	42.6	142.5	409.8	381.3	348.3	219.8
Personal saving with consumer durables [4] . . .	545.5	23.8	436.2	587.9	204.0	135.2	479.2	900.1
Personal saving without consumer durables [4] . .	469.6	–182.2	230.5	381.4	2.9	–61.2	280.0	758.8
Personal saving (NIPA, excludes consumer durables) [5]	299.4	168.5	174.9	181.7	32.5	70.7	57.4	192.9

[1] GSE = government-sponsored enterprises.   [2] Only directly held and those in closed-end and exchange-traded funds. Other equities are included in mutual funds and life insurance and pension reserves.   [3] Includes corporate farms.   [4] Flow of Funds measure.   [5] National Income and Product Accounts measure.

Source: Board of Governors of the Federal Reserve System, "Federal Reserve Statistical Release, Z.1, Flow of Funds Accounts of the United States" (published 12 March 2009), <http://www.federalreserve.gov/releases/z1/20090312>.

Table 660. **Government Consumption Expenditures and Gross Investment by Level of Government and Type: 2000 to 2008**

[In billions of dollars (1,721.6 represents $1,721,600,000,000). Government consumption expenditures are services (such as education and national defense) produced by government that are valued at their cost of production. Excludes government sales to other sectors and government own-account investment (construction and software). Gross government investment consists of general government and government enterprise expenditures for fixed assets; inventory investment is included in government consumption expenditures. For explanation of national income and chained dollars, see text, Section 13]

Item	Current dollars				Chained (2000) dollars			
	2000	2005	2007	2008	2000	2005	2007	2008
Government consumption expenditures and gross investment, total	1,721.6	2,355.3	2,674.8	2,882.4	1,721.6	1,939.0	2,012.1	2,070.2
Consumption expenditures	1,417.1	1,957.5	2,212.0	2,386.4	1,417.1	1,590.9	1,646.3	1,692.4
Gross investment	304.5	397.8	462.8	496.0	304.5	348.0	366.0	378.2
Structures	189.3	250.1	299.4	318.0	189.3	198.2	203.0	205.0
Equipment and software	115.2	147.7	163.5	178.0	115.2	153.1	168.3	181.4
Federal	578.8	875.5	979.3	1,071.9	578.8	724.5	752.9	798.2
Consumption expenditures	499.3	766.3	856.1	931.9	499.3	618.5	637.8	671.0
Gross investment	79.5	109.2	123.2	140.0	79.5	107.1	117.3	131.1
Structures	13.3	14.2	18.4	22.4	13.3	11.4	13.0	15.3
Equipment and software	66.2	94.9	104.9	117.6	66.2	96.7	105.1	116.4
National defense	370.3	588.1	662.2	734.9	370.3	482.2	502.1	538.1
Consumption expenditures	321.5	515.2	580.1	639.7	321.5	411.6	425.8	452.5
Gross investment	48.8	72.9	82.1	95.2	48.8	71.7	78.0	88.6
Structures	5.0	6.0	7.5	9.8	5.0	4.7	5.2	6.7
Equipment and software	43.8	66.9	74.6	85.4	43.8	67.2	72.9	81.8
Nondefense	208.5	287.4	317.1	337.0	208.5	242.0	250.4	259.5
Consumption expenditures	177.8	251.1	276.0	292.2	177.8	206.7	211.7	217.9
Gross investment	30.7	36.3	41.1	44.8	30.7	35.5	39.3	42.6
Structures	8.3	8.3	10.9	12.6	8.3	6.6	7.7	8.6
Equipment and software	22.3	28.0	30.3	32.2	22.3	29.5	32.3	34.5
State and local	1,142.8	1,479.8	1,695.5	1,810.4	1,142.8	1,214.3	1,259.0	1,273.0
Consumption expenditures	917.8	1,191.2	1,355.9	1,454.4	917.8	971.9	1,008.0	1,021.2
Gross investment	225.0	288.6	339.6	356.0	225.0	242.3	250.9	251.7
Structures	176.0	235.9	281.0	295.6	176.0	186.9	190.1	189.8
Equipment and software	49.0	52.7	58.6	60.4	49.0	56.2	63.1	64.6

Source: U.S. Bureau of Economic Analysis, *Survey of Current Business*, April 2009. See also <http://www.bea.gov/national/nipaweb/SelectTable.asp?Selected=N>.

Income, Expenditures, Poverty, and Wealth   433

Table 661. **Personal Consumption Expenditures by Type of Expenditure: 2000 to 2007**

[In billions of dollars (6,739.4 represents $6,739,400,000,000). For definition of "chained" dollars, see text, this section]

Expenditure	Current dollars				Chained (2000) dollars			
	2000	2005	2006	2007	2000	2005	2006	2007
Total expenditures [1]	6,739.4	8,694.1	9,207.2	9,710.2	6,739.4	7,791.7	8,029.0	8,252.8
Food and tobacco [1]	1,003.7	1,269.5	1,347.2	1,422.5	1,003.7	1,115.3	1,156.1	1,174.3
Food purchased for off-premise consumption	566.7	719.7	762.7	809.8	566.7	646.3	673.1	688.3
Purchased meals and beverages [2]	348.8	449.2	480.3	504.0	348.8	390.7	405.0	409.9
Tobacco products	78.5	88.3	89.8	93.4	78.5	69.3	68.2	66.5
Clothing, accessories, and jewelry [1]	397.0	464.5	492.6	511.9	397.0	489.0	515.7	533.0
Shoes	47.0	54.9	58.1	59.2	47.0	55.4	58.2	59.8
Clothing and accessories	250.4	286.3	301.8	314.4	250.4	316.8	336.1	353.0
Jewelry and watches	50.6	58.4	62.8	65.5	50.6	62.7	65.9	65.4
Personal care	93.4	111.9	115.9	120.4	93.4	105.4	107.3	109.0
Toilet articles and preparations	55.0	60.9	64.9	68.4	55.0	60.8	64.3	66.8
Barbershops, beauty parlors, and health clubs. .	38.4	51.0	51.0	52.0	38.4	44.5	43.4	42.8
Housing [1]	1,006.5	1,298.7	1,388.7	1,460.9	1,006.5	1,118.4	1,154.6	1,171.7
Owner-occupied nonfarm dwellings-space rent	712.2	951.4	1,020.2	1,063.3	712.2	821.9	851.7	858.7
Tenant-occupied nonfarm dwellings-space rent	227.5	262.9	277.2	299.1	227.5	223.6	227.7	235.7
Household operation [1]	719.3	875.3	922.2	959.5	719.3	824.1	844.1	868.1
Furniture [3]	67.6	79.4	83.3	85.0	67.6	84.7	88.1	90.7
Cleaning and polishing preparations	61.6	76.9	81.7	84.3	61.6	73.0	74.5	75.6
Household utilities [1]	209.9	283.3	300.8	318.0	209.9	217.9	213.6	218.5
Electricity	102.3	133.4	146.1	153.8	102.3	113.2	110.6	112.0
Gas	41.0	64.9	63.5	65.0	41.0	40.3	38.5	39.8
Water and other sanitary services	50.8	64.0	68.8	72.9	50.8	52.1	53.4	53.8
Telephone and telegraph	125.1	133.0	135.8	141.7	125.1	140.8	142.7	146.0
Medical care [1]	1,218.3	1,781.0	1,888.4	2,008.0	1,218.3	1,503.8	1,546.4	1,591.8
Drug preparations and sundries [4]	169.4	265.3	287.1	298.7	169.4	223.9	233.1	239.1
Physicians [5]	236.8	344.0	362.3	387.5	236.8	317.5	331.4	340.7
Dentists	61.8	85.0	91.1	96.8	61.8	67.8	69.1	69.1
Other professional services	161.6	230.8	242.3	261.5	161.6	204.3	210.4	221.6
Hospitals and nursing homes [6]	482.6	690.2	733.3	783.1	482.6	564.0	576.2	594.0
Health insurance	84.0	141.3	146.7	153.2	84.0	105.9	106.3	106.5
Medical care [7]	68.4	117.6	121.2	127.3	68.4	84.7	84.7	85.6
Personal business [1]	539.1	646.0	680.9	741.0	539.1	576.7	591.2	627.2
Brokerage charges and investment counseling	100.6	91.7	102.3	114.5	100.6	98.6	106.8	116.3
Bank service charges, trust services, and safe deposit box rental	64.2	99.0	107.1	115.9	64.2	88.2	92.8	99.1
Services furnished without payment [8]	167.2	201.1	205.2	227.6	167.2	182.5	183.5	201.5
Expense of handling life insurance [9]	96.1	106.8	110.7	117.7	96.1	88.7	88.5	89.7
Legal services	63.9	86.1	91.9	97.7	63.9	67.7	69.9	71.4
Transportation [1]	853.4	1,051.0	1,089.0	1,138.0	853.4	924.9	916.1	929.0
User-operated transportation [1]	793.8	989.6	1,024.6	1,072.0	793.8	861.7	853.3	865.4
New autos	103.6	103.1	106.5	102.0	103.6	106.6	109.1	105.0
Net purchases of used autos.	60.7	57.2	57.9	56.5	60.7	56.8	56.8	56.1
Other motor vehicles	173.2	225.1	209.0	219.1	173.2	233.1	217.8	231.7
Tires, tubes, accessories, etc.	49.0	57.7	60.6	62.8	49.0	53.4	53.9	54.0
Repair, greasing, washing, parking, storage, rental, and leasing	183.5	198.6	212.7	224.2	183.5	176.0	182.2	186.9
Gasoline and oil	175.7	283.6	313.8	340.6	175.7	187.4	184.2	184.5
Insurance	43.0	57.8	57.2	59.4	43.0	44.1	43.9	43.9
Purchased intercity transportation	47.4	46.8	48.7	49.7	47.4	52.3	51.1	51.6
Recreation [1, 10]	585.7	745.3	796.7	841.0	585.7	791.4	854.1	917.0
Nondurable toys and sport supplies	56.6	66.2	70.6	74.3	56.6	84.7	93.8	102.5
Wheel goods, sports and photographic equipment, boats, and pleasure aircraft	57.6	75.7	82.2	87.0	57.6	80.0	87.1	94.2
Video and audio goods, including musical instruments.	72.8	86.8	95.0	97.5	72.8	119.4	142.1	163.0
Computers, peripherals, and software	43.8	55.5	59.1	63.3	(NA)	(NA)	(NA)	(NA)
Commercial participant amusements	75.8	107.1	114.6	120.0	75.8	94.0	97.3	99.0
Education and research	163.8	226.3	240.9	257.3	163.8	175.4	177.8	182.2
Higher education	86.4	127.0	134.7	143.0	86.4	96.1	96.7	98.3
Religious and welfare activities.	172.3	224.5	240.6	252.7	172.3	193.1	198.7	202.1
Foreign travel and other, net [1]	–13.0	0.1	3.9	–2.9	–13.0	–10.7	–8.0	–15.9
Foreign travel by U.S. residents	84.4	99.9	108.7	113.6	84.4	78.8	81.9	80.7
Less: Expenditures in the United States by nonresidents.	100.7	104.9	110.0	122.6	100.7	92.3	92.6	99.2

NA Not available.   [1] Includes other expenditures not shown separately.   [2] Consists of purchases (including tips) of meals and beverages from retail, service, and amusement establishments; hotels; dining and buffet cars; schools; school fraternities; institutions; clubs; and industrial lunch rooms. Includes meals and beverages consumed both on- and off-premise.   [3] Includes mattresses and bedsprings.   [4] Excludes drug preparations and related products dispensed by physicians, hospitals, and other medical services.   [5] Consists of offices of physicians, HMO medical centers, and freestanding ambulatory surgical and emergency centers.   [6] Consists of (1) current expenditures (including consumption of fixed capital) of nonprofit hospitals and nursing homes and (2) payments by patients to proprietary and government hospitals and nursing homes.   [7] Consists of premiums less benefits for health, hospitalization, and accidental death and dismemberment insurance.   [8] By financial intermediaries except life insurance carriers and private noninsured pension plans.   [9] Consists of (1) operating expenses of commercial life insurance carriers and fraternal benefit life insurance and (2) administrative expenses of private noninsured pension plans and publicly administered government employee retirement plans.   [10] For additional details, see Table 1202.

Source: U.S. Bureau of Economic Analysis, *Survey of Current Business*, August 2008. See also <http://www.bea.gov/national/nipaweb/SelectTable.asp?Selected=N>.

434   Income, Expenditures, Poverty, and Wealth

Table 662. **Personal Income and Its Disposition: 1990 to 2008**

[In billions of dollars (4,879 represents $4,879,000,000,000), except as indicated. For definition of personal income and chained dollars, see text, this section]

Item	1990	2000	2003	2004	2005	2006	2007	2008
Personal income.	**4,879**	**8,430**	**9,164**	**9,727**	**10,270**	**10,994**	**11,663**	**12,103**
Compensation of employees, received . .	3,338	5,783	6,310	6,671	7,026	7,433	7,819	8,055
Wage and salary disbursements.	2,754	4,829	5,113	5,395	5,672	6,027	6,362	6,550
Supplements to wages and salaries . .	584	953	1,198	1,277	1,354	1,405	1,457	1,505
Proprietors' income [1]	381	728	811	912	960	1,015	1,056	1,072
Farm.	32	23	29	37	34	16	44	35
Nonfarm	349	706	782	874	926	999	1,012	1,038
Rental income of persons [1].	51	150	133	118	41	44	40	64
Personal income receipts on assets	924	1,387	1,337	1,432	1,597	1,825	2,000	2,038
Personal interest income.	755	1,011	914	895	1,022	1,125	1,214	1,209
Personal dividend income	169	376	423	537	575	699	786	829
Personal current transfer receipts.	595	1,084	1,351	1,423	1,521	1,603	1,713	1,869
Government social benefits to persons	573	1,042	1,317	1,396	1,482	1,578	1,681	1,834
Old-age, survivors, disability, and health insurance benefits	352	621	741	788	845	939	999	1,058
Other current transfer receipts, from business (net)	22	42	34	26	39	25	32	35
Less: Contributions for government social insurance	410	703	779	829	874	926	965	996
Less: Personal current taxes	*593*	*1,236*	*1,001*	*1,046*	*1,208*	*1,353*	*1,493*	*1,461*
Equals: Disposable personal income . . .	**4,286**	**7,194**	**8,163**	**8,681**	**9,062**	**9,641**	**10,171**	**10,642**
Less: Personal outlays	*3,986*	*7,026*	*7,988*	*8,499*	*9,030*	*9,570*	*10,113*	*10,451*
Personal consumption expenditures	3,840	6,739	7,704	8,196	8,694	9,207	9,710	10,058
Personal interest payments.	116	205	183	191	215	235	265	248
Personal current transfer payments	30	82	102	112	120	127	138	145
Equals: Personal saving	**299**	**169**	**175**	**182**	**33**	**71**	**57**	**191**
Personal saving as a percentage of disposable personal income	7.0	2.3	2.1	2.1	0.4	0.7	0.6	1.8
Addenda: Disposable personal income:								
Total, billions of chained (**2000**) dollars . .	5,324	7,194	7,730	8,009	8,121	8,407	8,644	8,753
Per capita:								
Current dollars	17,131	25,473	28,076	29,592	30,611	32,263	33,706	34,946
Chained (**2000**) dollars	21,281	25,473	26,588	27,302	27,434	28,134	28,648	28,741

[1] With inventory valuation adjustments and capital consumption adjustment.

Source: U.S. Bureau of Economic Analysis, *Survey of Current Business,* April 2009. See also <http://www.bea.gov /national/nipaweb/SelectTable.asp?Selected=N>.

Table 663. **Selected Per Capita Income and Product Measures in Current and Chained (2000) Dollars: 1960 to 2008**

[In dollars. Based on U.S. Census Bureau estimated population including Armed Forces abroad; based on quarterly averages. For explanation of chained dollars, see text, this section]

Year	Current dollars					Chained (**2000**) dollars			
	Gross domestic product	Gross national product	Personal income	Disposable personal income	Personal consumption expenditures	Gross domestic product	Gross national product	Disposable personal income	Personal consumption expenditures
1960	2,912	2,929	2,277	2,022	1,835	13,840	13,938	9,735	8,837
1970	5,064	5,095	4,090	3,587	3,162	18,391	18,520	13,563	11,955
1975	7,586	7,646	6,181	5,498	4,789	19,961	20,133	15,291	13,320
1980	12,249	12,400	10,134	8,822	7,716	22,666	22,956	16,940	14,816
1985	17,695	17,806	14,787	13,037	11,406	25,382	25,548	19,476	17,040
1990	23,195	23,335	19,500	17,131	15,349	28,424	28,600	21,281	19,067
1991	23,650	23,770	19,923	17,609	15,722	28,007	28,150	21,109	18,848
1992	24,668	24,783	20,870	18,494	16,485	28,556	28,693	21,548	19,208
1993	25,578	25,700	21,356	18,872	17,204	28,940	29,079	21,493	19,553
1994	26,844	26,944	22,176	19,555	18,004	29,741	29,850	21,812	20,082
1995	27,749	27,884	23,078	20,287	18,665	30,128	30,271	22,153	20,382
1996	28,982	29,112	24,176	21,091	19,490	30,881	31,015	22,546	20,835
1997	30,424	30,544	25,334	21,940	20,323	31,886	32,010	23,065	21,365
1998	31,674	31,752	26,880	23,161	21,291	32,833	32,912	24,131	22,183
1999	33,181	33,302	27,933	23,968	22,491	33,904	34,027	24,564	23,050
2000	34,761	34,899	29,849	25,473	23,864	34,761	34,899	25,473	23,864
2001	35,500	35,653	30,579	26,243	24,729	34,668	34,819	25,704	24,222
2002	36,346	36,452	30,834	27,183	25,518	34,885	34,990	26,253	24,646
2003	37,701	37,896	31,519	28,076	26,498	35,432	35,618	26,588	25,093
2004	39,836	40,096	33,159	29,592	27,939	36,393	36,632	27,302	25,776
2005	41,961	42,275	34,691	30,611	29,368	37,122	37,401	27,434	26,320
2006	44,101	44,363	36,791	32,263	30,812	37,798	38,024	28,134	26,869
2007	45,760	46,100	38,654	33,706	32,181	38,192	38,476	28,648	27,351
2008	46,842	47,279	39,742	34,946	33,028	38,262	38,624	28,741	27,164

Source: U.S. Bureau of Economic Analysis, *Survey of Current Business,* April 2009. See also <http://www.bea.gov /national/nipaweb/SelectTable.asp?Selected=N>.

Income, Expenditures, Poverty, and Wealth   435

Table 664. **Personal Income in Current and Constant (2000) Dollars by State: 2000 to 2008**

[In billions of dollars (8,422.1 represents $8,422,100,000,000). Represents a measure of income received from all sources during the calendar year by residents of each state. Data exclude federal employees overseas and U.S. residents employed by private U.S. firms on temporary foreign assignment. Totals may differ from those in Tables 657, 662, and 663]

State	Current dollars					Constant (2000) dollars [1]				
	2000	2005	2006	2007	2008, prel.	2000	2005	2006	2007	2008, prel.
United States.....	8,422.1	10,253.0	10,978.1	11,634.3	12,086.5	8,422.1	9,188.8	9,573.2	9,888.2	9,939.9
Alabama..........	105.8	133.7	141.6	150.0	156.8	105.8	119.8	123.5	127.5	129.0
Alaska...........	18.7	24.1	25.9	27.3	29.7	18.7	21.6	22.6	23.2	24.5
Arizona..........	132.6	182.5	199.5	208.6	214.2	132.6	163.6	173.9	177.3	176.2
Arkansas.........	58.7	74.9	79.8	85.4	89.3	58.7	67.1	69.6	72.6	73.4
California........	1,103.8	1,342.8	1,445.6	1,520.8	1,569.4	1,103.8	1,203.4	1,260.6	1,292.5	1,290.6
Colorado.........	144.4	175.4	188.2	199.5	209.3	144.4	157.2	164.1	169.5	172.1
Connecticut.......	141.6	167.1	180.0	191.9	196.9	141.6	149.7	156.9	163.1	162.0
Delaware.........	24.3	30.9	32.9	34.6	35.7	24.3	27.6	28.7	29.4	29.3
District of Columbia...	23.1	31.8	34.4	36.7	38.5	23.1	28.5	30.0	31.2	31.6
Florida...........	457.5	614.4	668.5	699.2	716.1	457.5	550.7	582.9	594.2	588.9
Georgia..........	230.4	284.3	301.0	319.0	329.1	230.4	254.8	262.5	271.1	270.6
Hawaii...........	34.5	44.1	47.3	50.1	52.2	34.5	39.5	41.3	42.6	42.9
Idaho	31.3	40.8	44.4	47.6	49.0	31.3	36.6	38.7	40.4	40.3
Illinois..........	400.4	463.1	490.7	526.0	547.0	400.4	415.0	427.9	447.1	449.8
Indiana	165.3	191.2	201.5	210.4	217.5	165.3	171.3	175.7	178.9	178.8
Iowa............	77.8	93.2	97.2	104.2	110.1	77.8	83.5	84.7	88.5	90.6
Kansas..........	74.6	88.1	95.2	101.4	106.4	74.6	79.0	83.0	86.2	87.5
Kentucky.........	98.8	116.9	124.1	130.6	135.9	98.8	104.8	108.2	111.0	111.7
Louisiana.........	103.2	110.8	139.3	153.5	160.0	103.2	99.3	121.5	130.5	131.6
Maine...........	33.2	40.4	42.4	44.7	46.6	33.2	36.2	37.0	38.0	38.3
Maryland.........	182.0	233.0	245.9	261.1	270.9	182.0	208.8	214.4	221.9	222.8
Massachusetts......	240.2	278.7	298.4	316.9	329.7	240.2	249.8	260.2	269.3	271.1
Michigan	294.2	325.3	332.6	345.9	353.1	294.2	291.5	290.1	294.0	290.4
Minnesota	158.0	190.3	200.3	213.0	223.3	158.0	170.5	174.7	181.0	183.6
Mississippi........	59.8	73.3	78.4	83.4	86.9	59.8	65.7	68.4	70.9	71.5
Missouri..........	152.7	180.5	189.7	199.7	208.3	152.7	161.8	165.4	169.7	171.3
Montana	20.7	27.5	29.4	31.8	33.1	20.7	24.7	25.6	27.0	27.3
Nebraska.........	47.3	57.5	59.9	64.4	67.3	47.3	51.5	52.3	54.7	55.3
Nevada..........	61.4	90.0	96.5	101.8	104.9	61.4	80.7	84.2	86.5	86.3
New Hampshire	41.4	48.7	52.0	54.6	56.4	41.4	43.6	45.3	46.4	46.3
New Jersey	323.6	376.9	404.5	428.4	442.1	323.6	337.8	352.7	364.1	363.6
New Mexico.......	40.3	53.4	56.9	60.3	63.7	40.3	47.8	49.6	51.3	52.4
New York.........	663.0	788.6	846.8	900.8	937.0	663.0	706.7	738.4	765.6	770.6
North Carolina	218.7	268.5	285.4	305.0	317.6	218.7	240.6	248.9	259.2	261.2
North Dakota	16.1	20.1	20.5	23.0	25.2	16.1	18.0	17.9	19.6	20.7
Ohio............	320.5	362.7	378.1	395.6	407.9	320.5	325.0	329.7	336.2	335.4
Oklahoma	84.3	106.7	116.9	126.3	134.4	84.3	95.7	101.9	107.3	110.5
Oregon	96.4	114.4	123.9	131.3	136.3	96.4	102.5	108.0	111.6	112.1
Pennsylvania	364.8	429.5	455.9	481.8	501.2	364.8	384.9	397.5	409.5	412.2
Rhode Island	30.7	37.9	39.9	41.9	43.1	30.7	33.9	34.8	35.7	35.4
South Carolina	98.3	120.2	129.9	137.0	142.8	98.3	107.7	113.3	116.4	117.5
South Dakota	19.4	25.1	25.4	28.5	30.1	19.4	22.5	22.2	24.2	24.7
Tennessee	148.8	183.7	195.2	205.4	213.4	148.8	164.6	170.2	174.5	175.5
Texas	593.1	758.4	821.6	884.2	938.4	593.1	679.7	716.5	751.5	771.7
Utah............	53.6	69.7	75.6	79.6	82.9	53.6	62.5	65.9	67.7	68.2
Vermont	16.9	20.3	21.8	23.3	24.2	16.9	18.2	19.0	19.8	19.9
Virginia	220.8	286.7	306.9	321.2	333.1	220.8	256.9	267.6	273.0	273.9
Washington	187.9	226.6	245.8	265.7	277.4	187.9	203.1	214.3	225.9	228.1
West Virginia	39.6	47.6	50.5	53.2	55.9	39.6	42.6	44.0	45.2	46.0
Wisconsin	153.5	181.2	191.9	203.1	210.0	153.5	162.4	167.3	172.6	172.7
Wyoming	14.1	19.6	22.2	24.6	26.5	14.1	17.6	19.4	20.9	21.8

[1] Constant dollar estimates are computed by the U.S. Census Bureau using the national implicit price deflator for personal consumption expenditures from the Bureau of Economic Analysis. Any regional differences in the rate of inflation are not reflected in these constant dollar estimates.

Source: Except as noted, U.S. Bureau of Economic Analysis, *Survey of Current Business*, April 2009, and unpublished data. See also <http://www.bea.gov/regional/spi>.

Table 665. **Personal Income Per Capita in Current and Constant (2000) Dollars by State: 2000 to 2008**

[In dollars, except as indicated. 2008 preliminary. See headnote, Table 664]

State	Current dollars				Constant (2000) dollars [1]				Income rank	
	2000	2005	2007	2008	2000	2005	2007	2008	2000	2008
United States.	29,847	34,690	38,615	39,751	29,847	31,090	32,819	32,691	(X)	(X)
Alabama	23,768	29,468	32,419	33,643	23,768	26,410	27,553	27,668	44	41
Alaska	29,870	36,084	40,042	43,321	29,870	32,339	34,032	35,627	15	7
Arizona	25,656	30,620	32,833	32,953	25,656	27,442	27,905	27,100	37	42
Arkansas.	21,927	27,035	30,177	31,266	21,927	24,229	25,648	25,713	48	47
California.	32,467	37,418	41,805	42,696	32,467	33,534	35,531	35,113	8	11
Colorado.	33,364	37,611	41,192	42,377	33,364	33,707	35,010	34,851	7	13
Connecticut	41,495	48,032	54,981	56,248	41,495	43,047	46,729	46,258	1	1
Delaware.	30,871	36,793	40,112	40,852	30,871	32,974	34,092	33,596	13	16
District of Columbia. . .	40,408	54,715	62,484	64,991	40,408	49,036	53,106	53,448	(X)	(X)
Florida	28,512	34,709	38,417	39,070	28,512	31,107	32,651	32,131	20	21
Georgia	27,990	31,260	33,499	33,975	27,990	28,016	28,471	27,941	26	40
Hawaii	28,437	34,885	39,242	40,490	28,437	31,264	33,352	33,299	22	17
Idaho	24,079	28,681	31,804	32,133	24,079	25,704	27,031	26,426	42	43
Illinois	32,190	36,452	41,012	42,397	32,190	32,669	34,857	34,867	9	12
Indiana	27,134	30,593	33,215	34,103	27,134	27,418	28,230	28,046	31	39
Iowa.	26,558	31,575	34,916	36,680	26,558	28,298	29,676	30,165	33	29
Kansas	27,693	32,130	36,525	37,978	27,693	28,795	31,043	31,233	27	24
Kentucky	24,413	28,071	30,824	31,826	24,413	25,158	26,198	26,174	40	46
Louisiana	23,082	24,651	35,100	36,271	23,082	22,092	29,832	29,829	45	30
Maine.	25,974	30,798	33,991	35,381	25,974	27,601	28,889	29,097	35	33
Maryland.	34,264	41,781	46,471	48,091	34,264	37,445	39,496	39,550	5	5
Massachusetts	37,753	43,315	48,995	50,735	37,753	38,819	41,642	41,724	3	3
Michigan	29,555	32,229	34,423	35,299	29,555	28,884	29,257	29,030	17	34
Minnesota	32,017	37,275	41,105	42,772	32,017	33,406	34,936	35,175	10	10
Mississippi.	21,008	25,289	28,541	29,569	21,008	22,664	24,257	24,317	50	50
Missouri	27,243	31,202	33,964	35,228	27,243	27,964	28,866	28,971	30	35
Montana	22,934	29,436	33,225	34,256	22,934	26,381	28,238	28,172	46	38
Nebraska	27,626	32,847	36,372	37,730	27,626	29,438	30,913	31,029	29	25
Nevada.	30,436	37,481	39,853	40,353	30,436	33,591	33,872	33,186	14	18
New Hampshire	33,401	37,432	41,639	42,830	33,401	33,547	35,300	35,223	6	9
New Jersey	38,377	43,651	49,511	50,919	38,377	39,120	42,080	41,876	2	2
New Mexico.	22,144	27,907	30,706	32,091	22,144	25,011	26,097	26,391	47	44
New York	34,898	40,781	46,364	48,076	34,898	36,548	39,405	39,537	4	6
North Carolina	27,067	31,002	33,735	34,439	27,067	27,784	28,672	28,322	32	36
North Dakota	25,105	31,571	36,082	39,321	25,105	28,294	30,667	32,337	38	20
Ohio.	28,207	31,672	34,468	35,511	28,207	28,385	29,295	29,204	24	32
Oklahoma	24,410	30,237	34,997	36,899	24,410	27,099	29,744	30,346	41	28
Oregon	28,099	31,580	35,143	35,956	28,099	28,302	29,869	29,570	25	31
Pennsylvania	29,698	34,774	38,793	40,265	29,698	31,165	32,971	33,114	16	19
Rhode Island	29,215	35,575	39,829	41,008	29,215	31,883	33,851	33,725	18	15
South Carolina	24,425	28,292	31,103	31,884	24,425	25,356	26,435	26,221	39	45
South Dakota.	25,723	32,193	35,760	37,375	25,723	28,852	30,393	30,737	36	26
Tennessee.	26,097	30,705	33,395	34,330	26,097	27,518	28,383	28,233	34	37
Texas	28,317	33,249	37,083	38,575	28,317	29,798	31,517	31,724	23	23
Utah.	23,866	27,885	29,831	30,291	23,866	24,991	25,354	24,911	43	49
Vermont.	27,683	32,736	37,483	38,880	27,683	29,338	31,857	31,975	28	22
Virginia	31,086	37,988	41,727	42,876	31,086	34,045	35,464	35,261	12	8
Washington	31,780	36,227	41,203	42,356	31,780	32,467	35,019	34,833	11	14
West Virginia	21,905	26,366	29,385	30,831	21,905	23,629	24,975	25,355	49	48
Wisconsin	28,572	32,706	36,272	37,314	28,572	29,311	30,828	30,687	19	27
Wyoming.	28,470	38,755	47,047	49,719	28,470	34,733	39,986	40,889	21	4

X Not applicable.   [1] Constant dollar estimates are computed by the U.S. Census Bureau using the national implicit price deflator for personal consumption expenditures from the Bureau of Economic Analysis. Any regional differences in the rate of inflation are not reflected in these constant dollar estimates.

Source: Except as noted, U.S. Bureau of Economic Analysis, *Survey of Current Business*, April 2009. See also <http://www.bea.gov/bea/regional/spi>.

Income, Expenditures, Poverty, and Wealth   437

Table 666. **Disposable Personal Income Per Capita in Current and Constant (2000) Dollars by State: 2000 to 2008**

[In dollars, except percent. 2008 preliminary. Disposable personal income is the income available to persons for spending or saving; it is calculated as personal income less personal tax and nontax payments. See headnote, Table 664]

State	Current dollars				Constant (2000) dollars [1]				Index, compared to U.S. average	
	2000	2005	2007	2008	2000	2005	2007	2008	2000	2008
United States.....	25,472	30,608	33,665	34,949	25,472	27,431	28,612	28,742	100.0	100.0
Alabama..........	21,049	26,672	28,977	30,297	21,049	23,904	24,628	24,916	82.6	86.7
Alaska...........	26,429	32,887	36,126	39,458	26,429	29,474	30,704	32,450	103.8	112.9
Arizona..........	22,322	27,285	29,006	29,391	22,322	24,453	24,653	24,171	87.6	84.1
Arkansas.........	19,377	24,471	27,114	28,270	19,377	21,931	23,045	23,249	76.1	80.9
California.........	26,719	32,490	35,863	37,041	26,719	29,118	30,480	30,462	104.9	106.0
Colorado.........	28,230	33,221	35,697	37,039	28,230	29,773	30,339	30,461	110.8	106.0
Connecticut.......	33,388	40,189	45,179	46,775	33,388	36,018	38,398	38,468	131.1	133.8
Delaware.........	26,279	32,041	34,954	35,880	26,279	28,715	29,708	29,508	103.2	102.7
District of Columbia ...	33,369	47,389	53,606	56,245	33,369	42,470	45,560	46,256	131.0	160.9
Florida...........	24,812	30,837	33,920	34,880	24,812	27,636	28,829	28,685	97.4	99.8
Georgia..........	24,054	27,770	29,361	30,082	24,054	24,888	24,954	24,739	94.4	86.1
Hawaii...........	24,855	30,846	34,524	35,939	24,855	27,644	29,342	29,556	97.6	102.8
Idaho	20,962	25,683	28,040	28,638	20,962	23,017	23,832	23,552	82.3	81.9
Illinois...........	27,416	32,201	35,778	37,298	27,416	28,859	30,408	30,674	107.6	106.7
Indiana	23,650	27,387	29,452	30,437	23,650	24,545	25,032	25,031	92.8	87.1
Iowa	23,393	28,484	31,134	32,919	23,393	25,528	26,461	27,072	91.8	94.2
Kansas	24,047	28,701	32,111	33,642	24,047	25,722	27,292	27,667	94.4	96.3
Kentucky.........	21,345	25,073	27,390	28,424	21,345	22,471	23,279	23,376	83.8	81.3
Louisiana.........	20,577	21,964	31,471	32,651	20,577	19,684	26,748	26,852	80.8	93.4
Maine	22,493	27,495	30,120	31,593	22,493	24,641	25,599	25,982	88.3	90.4
Maryland.........	28,806	36,052	39,576	41,325	28,806	32,310	33,636	33,985	113.1	118.2
Massachusetts	30,308	37,094	41,366	43,134	30,308	33,244	35,158	35,473	119.0	123.4
Michigan	25,438	28,879	30,684	31,719	25,438	25,882	26,079	26,086	99.9	90.8
Minnesota	27,186	32,590	35,574	37,300	27,186	29,207	30,235	30,675	106.7	106.7
Mississippi	18,938	23,380	26,024	27,077	18,938	20,953	22,118	22,268	74.3	77.5
Missouri..........	23,678	27,913	30,022	31,339	23,678	25,016	25,516	25,773	93.0	89.7
Montana	20,238	26,487	29,507	30,627	20,238	23,738	25,078	25,188	79.5	87.6
Nebraska.........	24,090	29,520	32,237	33,678	24,090	26,456	27,399	27,697	94.6	96.4
Nevada	26,322	33,110	34,936	35,768	26,322	29,674	29,693	29,415	103.3	102.3
New Hampshire	28,571	33,585	36,957	38,304	28,571	30,099	31,410	31,501	112.2	109.6
New Jersey	32,020	37,762	42,327	43,921	32,020	33,843	35,974	36,120	125.7	125.7
New Mexico........	19,586	25,303	27,481	28,922	19,586	22,677	23,356	23,785	76.9	82.8
New York..........	28,881	34,646	38,553	40,254	28,881	31,050	32,767	33,105	113.4	115.2
North Carolina	23,395	27,509	29,486	30,311	23,395	24,654	25,061	24,928	91.8	86.7
North Dakota	22,594	28,910	32,604	35,824	22,594	25,909	27,711	29,461	88.7	102.5
Ohio	24,264	27,963	30,223	31,370	24,264	25,061	25,687	25,799	95.3	89.8
Oklahoma	21,520	27,183	31,195	33,143	21,520	24,362	26,513	27,257	84.5	94.8
Oregon	23,906	27,616	30,487	31,643	23,906	24,750	25,911	26,023	93.9	90.5
Pennsylvania	25,576	30,747	33,919	35,413	25,576	27,556	28,828	29,123	100.4	101.3
Rhode Island	25,059	31,495	34,990	36,336	25,059	28,226	29,738	29,883	98.4	104.0
South Carolina	21,501	25,375	27,633	28,556	21,501	22,741	23,486	23,484	84.4	81.7
South Dakota	23,165	29,694	32,545	34,216	23,165	26,612	27,660	28,139	90.9	97.9
Tennessee........	23,409	28,211	30,267	31,327	23,409	25,283	25,724	25,763	91.9	89.6
Texas	24,968	30,243	33,248	34,850	24,968	27,104	28,258	28,660	98.0	99.7
Utah	20,792	24,832	25,979	26,641	20,792	22,255	22,080	21,909	81.6	76.2
Vermont	24,012	29,212	33,188	34,634	24,012	26,180	28,207	28,483	94.3	99.1
Virginia	26,214	33,061	35,877	37,194	26,214	29,630	30,492	30,588	102.9	106.4
Washington	27,309	32,703	36,685	38,009	27,309	29,309	31,179	31,258	107.2	108.8
West Virginia	19,540	23,935	26,496	27,926	19,540	21,451	22,519	22,966	76.7	79.9
Wisconsin	24,499	28,911	31,748	32,835	24,499	25,910	26,983	27,003	96.2	94.0
Wyoming	24,505	34,685	40,935	43,607	24,505	31,085	34,791	35,862	96.2	124.8

[1] Constant dollar estimates are computed by the U.S. Census Bureau using the national implicit price deflator for personal consumption expenditures from the Bureau of Economic Analysis. Any regional differences in the rate of inflation are not reflected in these constant dollar estimates.

Source: Except as noted, U.S. Bureau of Economic Analysis, *Survey of Current Business*, April 2009, and earlier reports. See also <http://www.bea.gov/regional/spi>.

438   Income, Expenditures, Poverty, and Wealth

Table 667. **Personal Income by Selected Large Metropolitan Area: 2005 to 2007**

[**10,252,973** represents $10,252,973,000,000. Metropolitan areas as defined November 2008. MSA = Metropolitan Statistical Area. See Appendix II]

Metropolitan area ranked by **2007** population	Personal income				Per capita personal income			
	2005 (mil. dol.)	**2006** (mil. dol.)	**2007** (mil. dol.)	Annual percent change, 2006-2007	**2005** (dol.)	**2006** (dol.)	**2007** (dol.)	Index (U.S.= 100) **2007**
United States................	10,252,973	10,978,053	11,634,322	6.0	34,690	36,794	38,615	100.0
New York-Northern New Jersey-Long Island, NY-NJ-PA MSA....................	865,850	935,656	1,000,151	6.9	46,026	49,642	52,855	136.9
Los Angeles-Long Beach-Santa Ana, CA MSA	481,124	518,758	540,510	4.2	37,543	40,538	42,278	109.5
Chicago-Naperville-Joliet, IL-IN-WI MSA......	370,077	393,208	421,143	7.1	39,409	41,654	44,346	114.8
Dallas-Fort Worth-Arlington, TX MSA	221,568	239,169	255,363	6.8	38,085	39,891	41,499	107.5
Philadelphia-Camden-Wilmington, PA-NJ-DE-MD MSA...................	235,630	251,380	264,951	5.4	40,720	43,301	45,499	117.8
Houston-Sugar Land-Baytown, TX MSA	215,111	238,607	260,140	9.0	40,565	43,497	46,471	120.3
Miami-Fort Lauderdale-Pompano Beach, FL MSA..........................	205,656	222,600	232,522	4.5	38,259	41,204	43,123	111.7
Washington-Arlington-Alexandria, DC-VA-MD-WV MSA..............	259,040	276,061	291,471	5.6	49,606	52,485	54,971	142.4
Atlanta-Sandy Springs-Marietta, GA MSA	175,197	186,590	198,580	6.4	35,424	36,487	37,744	97.7
Boston-Cambridge-Quincy, MA-NH MSA.....	209,954	225,661	240,085	6.4	47,128	50,515	53,443	138.4
Detroit-Warren-Livonia, MI MSA	164,985	167,398	173,885	3.9	36,692	37,310	39,009	101.0
San Francisco-Oakland-Fremont, CA MSA ...	222,667	241,665	257,111	6.4	53,557	57,848	60,983	157.9
Phoenix-Mesa-Scottsdale, AZ MSA	128,077	140,540	146,578	4.3	33,066	34,829	35,185	91.1
Riverside-San Bernardino-Ontario, CA MSA. ..	103,716	111,762	117,134	4.8	26,789	28,063	28,804	74.6
Seattle-Tacoma-Bellevue, WA MSA	136,859	149,858	162,935	8.7	42,804	46,054	49,401	127.9
Minneapolis-St. Paul-Bloomington, MN-WI MSA........................	132,708	140,158	149,496	6.7	42,377	44,295	46,752	121.1
San Diego-Carlsbad-San Marcos, CA MSA ...	118,458	125,472	131,500	4.8	40,406	42,721	44,430	115.1
St. Louis, MO-IL MSA	98,872	104,204	110,192	5.7	35,653	37,339	39,278	101.7
Tampa-St. Petersburg-Clearwater, FL MSA ...	88,623	95,333	99,253	4.1	33,607	35,478	36,554	94.7
Baltimore-Towson, MD MSA	108,790	115,091	122,235	6.2	41,099	43,299	45,887	118.8
Denver-Aurora-Broomfield, CO MSA	100,386	108,312	114,529	5.7	42,567	45,072	46,682	120.9
Pittsburgh, PA MSA...................	85,636	91,566	97,007	5.9	36,097	38,787	41,206	106.7
Portland-Vancouver-Beaverton, OR-WA MSA. .	73,287	79,014	84,151	6.5	35,115	37,157	38,842	100.6
Cincinnati-Middletown, OH-KY-IN MSA......	73,561	76,952	80,997	5.3	35,009	36,299	37,782	97.8
Cleveland-Elyria-Mentor, OH MSA	74,752	77,966	81,622	4.7	35,322	37,059	38,963	100.9
Sacramento-Arden-Arcade-Roseville, CA MSA.	71,855	76,563	80,006	4.5	35,355	37,239	38,424	99.5
Orlando-Kissimmee, FL MSA	61,591	67,103	70,047	4.4	31,822	33,653	34,528	89.4
San Antonio, TX MSA	58,569	62,964	67,179	6.7	31,168	32,590	33,845	87.6
Kansas City, MO-KS MSA	68,958	73,510	77,717	5.7	35,593	37,552	39,222	101.6
Las Vegas-Paradise, NV MSA............	62,786	67,833	71,622	5.6	36,869	38,309	39,188	101.5
San Jose-Sunnyvale-Santa Clara, CA MSA . .	89,615	98,252	105,999	7.9	51,418	55,754	59,338	153.7
Columbus, OH MSA	59,262	62,112	65,611	5.6	34,610	35,852	37,428	96.9
Indianapolis-Carmel, IN MSA	58,743	62,301	65,094	4.5	35,752	37,345	38,455	99.6
Virginia Beach-Norfolk-Newport News, VA-NC MSA.......................	54,644	58,509	61,138	4.5	33,129	35,212	36,837	95.4
Charlotte-Gastonia-Concord, NC-SC MSA....	55,973	60,661	64,591	6.5	36,861	38,391	39,231	101.6
Providence-New Bedford-Fall River, RI-MA MSA........................	56,519	59,632	62,762	5.3	35,106	37,185	39,267	101.7
Austin-Round Rock, TX MSA	51,059	55,636	59,306	6.6	34,863	36,434	37,238	96.4
Milwaukee-Waukesha-West Allis, WI MSA....	57,060	61,083	64,472	5.5	37,193	39,697	41,774	108.2
Nashville-Davidson-Murfreesboro-Franklin, TN MSA	51,733	55,842	59,059	5.8	35,692	37,587	38,851	100.6
Jacksonville, FL MSA	44,088	48,583	50,862	4.7	35,333	38,060	39,191	101.5
Memphis, TN-MS-AR MSA..............	42,666	45,139	47,516	5.3	34,057	35,535	37,147	96.2
Louisville/Jefferson County, KY-IN MSA	40,744	43,726	46,179	5.6	33,751	35,871	37,473	97.0
Richmond, VA MSA	43,399	46,457	48,790	5.0	36,995	38,913	40,286	104.3
Oklahoma City, OK MSA	38,545	42,677	46,180	8.2	33,387	36,373	38,834	100.6
Hartford-West Hartford-East Hartford, CT MSA	50,449	53,891	57,343	6.4	42,797	45,543	48,330	125.2
Buffalo-Niagara Falls, NY MSA	36,298	38,047	39,471	3.7	31,832	33,611	35,038	90.7
New Orleans-Metairie-Kenner, LA MSA......	24,913	42,038	49,141	16.9	18,983	42,381	44,295	114.7
Birmingham-Hoover, AL MSA	38,981	41,069	43,683	6.4	35,818	37,326	39,401	102.0
Salt Lake City, UT MSA	34,815	37,789	39,442	4.4	33,287	35,177	36,008	93.2
Raleigh-Cary, NC MSA	34,312	37,506	41,104	9.6	36,001	37,614	39,373	102.0
Rochester, NY MSA	35,179	36,772	38,231	4.0	33,996	35,602	37,028	95.9
Tucson, AZ MSA	27,814	30,170	31,647	4.9	29,354	30,971	31,755	82.2
Tulsa, OK MSA	31,261	34,543	37,356	8.1	35,483	38,761	41,307	107.0
Honolulu, HI MSA....................	33,457	35,766	37,835	5.8	37,188	39,558	42,015	108.8
Fresno, CA MSA	22,592	23,965	25,214	5.2	25,950	27,166	28,181	73.0
Bridgeport-Stamford-Norwalk, CT MSA......	61,573	67,497	72,651	7.6	69,040	75,796	81,576	211.3
Albany-Schenectady-Troy, NY MSA	30,453	32,103	33,301	3.7	35,981	37,755	39,105	101.3
New Haven-Milford, CT MSA	33,203	35,339	37,424	5.9	39,522	41,976	44,322	114.8
Dayton, OH MSA	26,452	27,694	28,597	3.3	31,376	32,930	34,091	88.3
Albuquerque, NM MSA	24,616	26,408	27,744	5.1	30,880	32,364	33,305	86.2
Omaha-Council Bluffs, NE-IA MSA.........	30,637	32,461	34,476	6.2	37,816	39,631	41,655	107.9
Allentown-Bethlehem-Easton, PA-NJ MSA ...	26,320	28,022	29,722	6.1	33,537	35,273	37,037	95.9
Oxnard-Thousand Oaks-Ventura, CA MSA ...	32,127	34,505	36,210	4.9	40,741	43,609	45,694	118.3
Bakersfield, CA MSA..................	18,649	19,927	21,325	7.0	24,906	25,872	27,090	70.2
Worcester, MA MSA	28,489	30,460	32,365	6.3	36,636	39,019	41,380	107.2
Grand Rapids-Wyoming, MI MSA	24,312	25,197	26,231	4.1	31,661	32,670	33,849	87.7
Baton Rouge, LA MSA.................	22,011	24,578	26,341	7.2	30,179	32,187	34,236	88.7
El Paso, TX MSA	16,951	18,193	19,406	6.7	23,875	25,182	26,585	68.8
Columbia, SC MSA...................	21,252	23,012	24,211	5.2	30,768	32,738	33,829	87.6
McAllen-Edinburg-Mission, TX MSA	11,244	11,930	12,922	8.3	16,854	17,390	18,316	47.4

Source: U.S. Bureau of Economic Analysis, *Survey of Current Business*, May 2009. See also <http://www.bea.gov/regional/reis>.

Table 668. **Average Annual Expenditures of All Consumer Units by Selected Major Types of Expenditure: 1990 to 2007**

[In dollars, except as indicated (96,968 represents $96,968,000). Based on Consumer Expenditure Survey. Data are averages for the noninstitutional population. Expenditures reported here are out-of-pocket]

Type	1990	1995	2000	2003	2004	2005	2006	2007
Number of consumer units (1,000)	96,968	103,123	109,367	115,356	116,282	117,356	118,843	120,171
Expenditures, total [1]	$28,381	$32,264	$38,045	$40,817	$43,395	$46,409	$48,398	$49,638
Food.	4,296	4,505	5,158	5,340	5,781	5,931	6,111	6,133
Food at home [1]	2,485	2,803	3,021	3,129	3,347	3,297	3,417	3,465
Meats, poultry, fish, and eggs	668	752	795	825	880	764	797	777
Dairy products	295	297	325	328	371	378	368	387
Fruits and vegetables	408	457	521	535	561	552	592	600
Other food at home.	746	856	927	999	1,075	1,158	1,212	1,241
Food away from home.	1,811	1,702	2,137	2,211	2,434	2,634	2,694	2,668
Alcoholic beverages.	293	277	372	391	459	426	497	457
Housing [1].	8,703	10,458	12,319	13,432	13,918	15,167	16,366	16,920
Shelter.	4,836	5,928	7,114	7,887	7,998	8,805	9,673	10,023
Utilities, fuels, and public services . . .	1,890	2,191	2,489	2,811	2,927	3,183	3,397	3,477
Apparel and services	1,618	1,704	1,856	1,640	1,816	1,886	1,874	1,881
Transportation [1].	5,120	6,014	7,417	7,781	7,801	8,344	8,508	8,758
Vehicle purchases	2,129	2,638	3,418	3,732	3,397	3,544	3,421	3,244
Gasoline and motor oil	1,047	1,006	1,291	1,333	1,598	2,013	2,227	2,384
Other vehicle expenses	1,642	2,015	2,281	2,331	2,365	2,339	2,355	2,592
Health care.	1,480	1,732	2,066	2,416	2,574	2,664	2,766	2,853
Entertainment	1,422	1,612	1,863	2,060	2,218	2,388	2,376	2,698
Reading.	153	162	146	127	130	126	117	118
Tobacco products, smoking supplies . . .	274	269	319	290	288	319	327	323
Personal insurance and pensions	2,592	2,964	3,365	4,055	4,823	5,204	5,270	5,336
Life and other personal insurance . . .	345	373	399	397	390	381	322	309
Pensions and Social Security	2,248	2,591	2,966	3,658	4,433	4,823	4,948	5,027

[1] Includes expenditures not shown separately.

Source: U.S. Bureau of Labor Statistics, *Consumer Expenditures in 2007*, News, USDL-08-1746 (25 November 2008). See also <http://stats.bls.gov/cex/home.htm>.

Table 669. **Average Annual Expenditures of All Consumer Units by Metropolitan Area: 2006 to 2007**

[In dollars. Covers 2-year period, 2006–2007. Metropolitan areas defined 30 June 1983, CMSA = Consolidated Metropolitan Statistical Area; MSA = Metropolitan Statistical Area; PMSA = Primary Metropolitan Statistical Area. See text, Section 1 and Appendix II. See headnote, Table 668]

Metropolitan area	Total expendi-tures [1]	Food	Housing			Transportation			Health care
			Total [1]	Shelter	Utility, fuels [2]	Total [1]	Vehicle purchases	Gasoline and motor oil	
Atlanta, GA MSA	46,705	5,646	17,716	10,860	3,874	8,053	2,957	2,407	2,355
Baltimore, MD MSA.	53,244	6,222	19,123	11,930	3,951	8,673	3,562	2,508	2,431
Boston-Lawrence-Salem, MA-NH CMSA.	55,189	6,700	20,174	13,068	3,850	8,707	3,420	2,026	2,809
Chicago-Gary-Lake County, IL-IN-WI CMSA.	57,304	7,202	20,238	12,612	3,761	8,846	3,084	2,322	3,020
Cleveland-Akron-Lorain, OH CMSA . .	47,890	5,514	16,602	9,719	3,768	8,371	3,296	2,177	3,293
Dallas-Fort Worth, TX CMSA	54,334	6,160	18,169	9,843	4,551	10,764	4,866	2,559	2,967
Detroit-Ann Arbor, MI CMSA	48,348	6,550	15,995	9,568	3,637	8,743	2,201	2,602	2,307
Houston-Galveston-Brazoria, TX CMSA.	55,381	6,547	17,752	9,965	4,297	11,119	4,544	2,936	3,293
Los Angeles-Long Beach, CA PMSA .	60,932	7,785	23,336	15,271	3,125	10,141	3,338	2,712	2,324
Miami-Fort Lauderdale, FL CMSA . . .	46,201	5,728	18,708	12,190	3,611	7,938	2,859	2,457	2,167
Minneapolis-St. Paul, MN-WI MSA. . .	60,059	6,848	20,819	11,559	3,294	8,694	3,689	2,151	3,705
New York-Northern New Jersey-Long Island, NY-NJ-CT CMSA.	56,683	7,023	22,295	14,848	3,879	8,048	2,349	1,892	2,674
Philadelphia-Wilmington-Trenton, PA-NJ-DE-MD CMSA.	48,649	5,600	18,411	10,755	3,981	7,345	2,244	2,106	2,175
Phoenix-Mesa, AZ MSA	57,657	7,156	18,591	10,615	3,628	12,424	6,383	2,594	3,058
San Diego, CA MSA	54,648	5,312	22,670	16,174	2,837	7,258	2,090	2,504	2,613
San Francisco-Oakland-San Jose, CA CMSA.	69,559	8,369	27,310	19,519	3,199	10,792	3,564	2,489	3,224
Seattle-Tacoma, WA CMSA	59,384	6,486	20,671	13,530	3,322	10,047	3,917	2,288	3,127
Washington, DC-MD-VA MSA	65,894	7,533	25,525	17,040	4,037	9,531	3,319	2,272	2,641

[1] Includes expenditures not shown separately.   [2] Includes public services.

Source: U.S. Bureau of Labor Statistics, *Consumer Expenditures in 2007*, News, USDL-08-1746 (25 November 2008). See also <http://stats.bls.gov/cex/home.htm>.

Table 670. **Average Annual Expenditures of All Consumer Units by Race, Hispanic Origin, and Age of Householder: 2007**

[**In dollars.** Based on Consumer Expenditure Survey. Data are averages for the noninstitutional population. Expenditures reported here are out-of-pocket]

Type	All consumer units [1]	White and all other races	Asian	Black or African American	Hispanic or Latino	Age of householder Under 25 years	Age of householder 65 years and over
Expenditures, total	**49,638**	**51,120**	**60,402**	**36,067**	**41,501**	**29,457**	**36,530**
Food	6,133	6,312	7,139	4,601	5,933	4,141	4,515
Food at home	3,465	3,539	3,890	2,831	3,424	2,265	2,905
Cereals and bakery products	460	473	469	365	410	274	405
Cereals and cereal products	143	143	195	127	154	93	116
Bakery products	317	330	275	237	255	180	289
Meats, poultry, fish, and eggs [2]	777	760	1,026	834	890	491	634
Beef	216	220	221	185	255	155	174
Pork	150	144	160	185	162	84	135
Poultry	142	135	158	189	193	90	101
Fish and seafood	122	112	321	138	119	64	103
Dairy products	387	407	349	259	368	238	332
Fresh milk and cream	154	160	154	111	168	103	126
Other dairy products	234	247	196	147	200	136	206
Fruits and vegetables [2]	600	610	887	455	652	340	557
Fresh fruits	202	208	309	131	227	112	193
Fresh vegetables	190	192	369	133	229	103	175
Processed fruits	112	113	116	107	106	66	106
Other food at home [2]	1,241	1,290	1,159	919	1,104	922	976
Sugar and other sweets	124	129	133	88	97	69	118
Nonalcoholic beverages	333	340	343	279	345	255	247
Food away from home	2,668	2,773	3,249	1,771	2,508	1,876	1,610
Alcoholic beverages	457	499	290	198	262	461	285
Housing	16,920	17,169	22,554	13,494	15,573	9,598	12,396
Shelter	10,023	10,074	15,383	8,084	9,794	6,220	6,656
Owned dwellings	6,730	6,950	10,387	4,110	5,419	1,398	4,414
Mortgage interest and charges	3,890	3,952	6,383	2,723	3,609	919	1,320
Property taxes	1,709	1,781	2,754	893	1,218	325	1,651
Maintenance, repair, insurance, other expenses	1,131	1,217	1,249	494	592	154	1,443
Rented dwellings	2,602	2,389	4,073	3,669	4,135	4,649	1,639
Other lodging	691	736	923	305	239	173	604
Utilities, fuels, and public services	3,477	3,476	3,436	3,500	3,274	1,813	3,117
Natural gas	480	477	577	475	378	169	497
Electricity	1,303	1,301	1,169	1,355	1,258	706	1,175
Fuel oil and other fuels	151	168	[3]44	56	62	28	208
Telephone	1,110	1,095	1,172	1,196	1,167	744	800
Water and other public services	434	434	475	418	409	166	431
Household operations	984	1,029	1,157	616	681	363	825
Personal services	415	428	529	297	348	174	205
Other household expenses	569	602	627	319	333	189	620
Housekeeping supplies [2]	639	680	496	383	571	278	562
Laundry and cleaning supplies	140	141	103	142	170	84	115
Postage and stationery	152	165	155	58	157	60	150
Household furnishings and equipment [2]	1,797	1,910	2,081	910	1,253	925	1,235
Household textiles	133	145	125	51	112	65	117
Furniture	446	448	858	313	364	281	235
Major appliances	231	249	196	119	136	122	180
Miscellaneous household equipment	840	913	765	336	528	394	558
Apparel and services [2]	1,881	1,869	2,709	1,743	1,994	1,477	1,040
Men and boys	435	442	602	344	539	323	209
Women and girls	749	742	1,234	671	636	535	487
Footwear	327	312	514	387	408	237	160
Other apparel products and services	276	283	252	238	272	237	160
Transportation	8,758	8,996	10,921	6,458	8,035	5,708	5,785
Vehicle purchases (net outlay) [2]	3,244	3,357	4,007	2,223	2,876	2,273	1,977
Cars and trucks, new	1,572	1,640	2,797	729	1,271	1,058	1,209
Cars and trucks, used	1,567	1,597	1,210	1,460	1,541	1,126	740
Gasoline and motor oil	2,384	2,447	2,391	1,935	2,304	1,760	1,461
Other vehicle expenses	2,592	2,662	2,978	2,001	2,525	1,365	1,928
Vehicle finance charges	305	316	236	252	314	221	122
Maintenance and repair	738	771	729	505	557	437	543
Vehicle insurance	1,071	1,082	1,550	872	1,280	492	975
Vehicle rental, leases, licenses, other charges	478	494	463	371	375	216	287
Public transportation	538	530	1,545	299	330	310	420
Health care [4]	2,853	3,046	2,170	1,689	1,486	800	4,631
Entertainment [5]	2,698	2,908	2,454	1,288	1,674	1,448	1,966
Personal care products and services	588	603	564	485	526	337	528
Reading	118	129	98	46	38	51	143
Education	945	952	1,627	700	415	1,787	292
Tobacco products and smoking supplies	323	346	135	219	165	290	176
Miscellaneous	808	861	719	453	478	368	672
Cash contributions	1,821	1,899	2,153	1,178	1,083	549	2,282
Personal insurance and pensions	5,336	5,531	6,868	3,515	3,837	2,440	1,819
Life and other personal insurance	309	317	353	245	109	39	329
Pensions and social security	5,027	5,214	6,515	3,271	3,729	2,401	1,491
Personal taxes	**2,233**	**2,439**	**2,295**	**771**	**703**	**641**	**1,126**

[1] Includes other householders not shown separately. [2] Includes other types not shown separately. [3] Data are likely to have large sampling errors. [4] For additional health care expenditures, see Table 136. [5] For additional recreation expenditures, see Section 26.

Source: U.S. Bureau of Labor Statistics, *Consumer Expenditures in 2007*, News, USDL-08-1746 (25 November 2008). See also <http://www.bls.gov/cex/2007 /Standard/race.pdf>; <http://www.bls.gov/cex/2007/Standard/hispanic.pdf>; and <http://www.bls .gov/cex/2007/Standard /age.pdf>.

Table 671. **Average Annual Expenditures of All Consumer Units by Region and Size of Unit: 2007**

[In dollars. For composition of regions, see map, inside front cover. See headnote, Table 668]

Type	Region				Size of consumer unit				
	North-east	Mid-west	South	West	One person	Two persons	Three persons	Four persons	Five or more
Expenditures, total	51,624	48,014	45,464	56,291	29,285	53,091	57,326	66,476	65,042
Food	6,419	5,793	5,780	6,811	3,328	6,209	7,251	8,671	9,220
Food at home	3,595	3,252	3,311	3,822	1,814	3,375	4,227	4,967	5,564
Cereals and bakery products	495	444	438	480	238	437	563	654	783
Cereals and cereal products	157	131	134	157	72	130	174	210	262
Bakery products	339	313	304	323	166	308	389	444	521
Meats, poultry, fish, and eggs [1]	832	691	770	830	390	744	940	1,146	1,310
Beef.	207	201	219	235	104	202	272	325	370
Pork.	149	140	160	144	69	149	190	221	236
Poultry	151	112	148	154	70	128	158	225	270
Fish and seafood	159	96	103	148	67	128	146	151	188
Dairy products.	400	375	366	422	201	385	449	562	628
Fresh milk and cream	151	145	156	161	80	140	180	235	272
Other dairy products	249	230	211	261	121	245	270	327	356
Fruits and vegetables [1]	647	546	552	693	322	616	708	832	903
Fresh fruits	216	191	177	241	111	209	240	268	302
Fresh vegetables	205	161	175	233	100	202	229	258	271
Processed fruits	133	105	102	119	62	110	122	170	177
Other food at home [1]	1,221	1,196	1,185	1,396	662	1,193	1,567	1,775	1,939
Sugar and other sweets	125	125	117	136	66	127	148	171	195
Nonalcoholic beverages	333	313	325	366	180	321	406	482	523
Food away from home	2,824	2,541	2,470	2,988	1,514	2,834	3,024	3,704	3,656
Alcoholic beverages	508	501	382	488	428	528	448	429	353
Housing	19,085	15,380	14,911	19,885	11,269	17,248	19,035	22,635	21,789
Shelter	11,640	8,839	8,233	12,729	7,212	9,923	11,116	13,123	12,914
Owned dwellings	7,616	6,238	5,723	8,097	3,628	6,770	7,879	10,134	9,541
Mortgage interest and charges . . .	3,715	3,310	3,420	5,366	1,818	3,470	4,812	6,633	6,334
Property taxes	2,649	1,801	1,259	1,555	1,030	1,908	1,846	2,330	2,050
Maintenance, repair, insurance, other expenses.	1,252	1,126	1,044	1,176	780	1,392	1,221	1,170	1,157
Rented dwellings	3,036	1,883	2,072	3,811	3,228	2,153	2,559	2,258	2,710
Other lodging	988	717	437	821	356	1,001	678	731	663
Utilities, fuels, and public services	3,832	3,323	3,547	3,229	2,206	3,577	4,068	4,481	4,722
Natural gas.	653	689	285	437	325	497	528	616	639
Electricity	1,276	1,116	1,568	1,093	804	1,349	1,532	1,670	1,811
Fuel oil and other fuels	455	116	71	62	107	175	172	155	167
Telephone.	1,120	1,025	1,167	1,095	706	1,104	1,341	1,459	1,514
Water and other public services	330	377	456	541	264	452	495	582	591
Household operations	1,011	855	933	1,174	486	823	1,361	1,800	1,303
Personal services.	434	394	400	447	92	154	755	1,098	776
Other household expenses	577	462	533	727	394	669	607	702	527
Housekeeping supplies [1]	576	620	595	782	316	825	647	775	780
Laundry and cleaning supplies	121	145	152	132	69	137	180	197	227
Postage and stationery	152	155	134	179	91	200	144	185	141
Household furnishings and equipment [1] .	2,026	1,742	1,604	1,970	1,049	2,100	1,842	2,456	2,070
Household textiles	148	107	129	155	88	146	118	210	147
Furniture	589	401	382	472	228	512	521	640	507
Major appliances	240	233	222	237	112	294	239	309	268
Miscellaneous household equipment .	877	866	741	936	525	992	812	1,096	955
Apparel and services [1].	2,068	1,866	1,692	2,042	971	1,848	2,330	2,859	2,719
Men and boys.	450	379	425	498	267	397	510	631	692
Women and girls.	812	821	638	800	352	801	924	1,109	1,014
Footwear	350	334	297	350	158	292	413	548	529
Other apparel products and services. . .	374	244	246	275	175	310	312	398	243
Transportation	8,014	8,684	8,485	9,882	4,539	9,274	10,801	11,655	12,754
Vehicle purchases (net outlay) [1]	2,508	3,407	3,216	3,729	1,478	3,361	4,121	4,338	5,388
Cars and trucks, new	1,373	1,532	1,524	1,852	743	1,908	1,717	1,891	2,344
Cars and trucks, used.	1,095	1,698	1,597	1,776	683	1,324	2,266	2,283	2,989
Gasoline and motor oil	2,080	2,408	2,522	2,389	1,276	2,452	2,804	3,364	3,531
Other vehicle expenses	2,678	2,418	2,378	3,042	1,461	2,740	3,330	3,329	3,382
Vehicle finance charges	250	281	342	318	122	323	383	468	458
Maintenance and repair.	716	694	689	876	471	796	848	924	927
Vehicle insurance.	1,069	908	1,041	1,290	621	1,127	1,461	1,211	1,463
Vehicle rental, leases, licenses, other charges	642	536	306	558	247	494	638	726	534
Public transportation	749	451	368	721	324	722	546	624	453
Health care [2]	2,645	3,097	2,800	2,860	1,790	3,709	2,876	3,147	2,840
Entertainment [3]	2,811	2,585	2,320	3,319	1,413	3,079	3,009	3,785	3,373
Personal care products and services	609	544	565	650	364	650	653	756	725
Reading	135	126	89	140	97	140	114	131	94
Education	1,163	1,187	744	842	621	777	1,242	1,483	1,277
Tobacco products and smoking supplies . .	361	365	332	234	223	350	417	335	378
Miscellaneous	826	778	652	1,071	533	977	836	935	863
Cash contributions	1,421	1,792	1,762	2,275	1,219	2,512	1,655	1,819	1,663
Personal insurance and pensions	5,558	5,315	4,948	5,791	2,491	5,789	6,659	7,835	6,994
Life and other personal insurance.	342	347	298	262	146	349	394	432	378
Pensions and social security	5,216	4,968	4,650	5,529	2,345	5,441	6,265	7,403	6,616
Personal taxes.	**2,497**	**1,875**	**2,048**	**2,674**	**1,423**	**3,070**	**2,332**	**2,309**	**1,707**

[1] Includes other types not shown separately. [2] For additional health care expenditures, see Table 136. [3] For additional recreation expenditures, see Section 26.

Source: U.S. Bureau of Labor Statistics, *Consumer Expenditures in 2007, News, USDL-08-1746, 25, November 2008.* See also <http://www.bls.gov/cex/2007/Standard/cusize.pdf> and <http://www.bls.gov/cex/2007/Standard/region.pdf>.

Table 672. **Average Annual Expenditures of All Consumer Units by Income Level: 2007**

[In dollars. Based on Consumer Expenditure Survey. Data are averages for the noninstitutional population. Expenditures reported here are out-of-pocket]

Income level	Total expendi- tures [1]	Food	Housing			Transportation			Health care	Pen- sions and social security
			Total [1]	Shelter	Utility fuels [2]	Total [1]	Vehicle pur- chases	Gaso- line and motor oil		
All consumer units	49,638	6,133	16,920	10,023	3,477	8,758	3,244	2,384	2,853	5,027
Consumer units with complete reporting:										
Less than $70,000	34,109	4,625	12,193	7,166	2,894	6,232	2,185	1,887	2,368	2,322
$70,000 to $79,999	58,005	7,541	19,178	11,396	4,129	10,886	4,046	3,041	3,136	6,321
$80,000 to $99,999	67,640	8,128	21,703	12,850	4,256	13,039	5,386	3,243	3,619	7,924
$100,000 and over.	101,041	10,890	32,965	19,710	5,234	16,163	6,217	3,751	4,348	14,096
$100,000 to $119,999 . . .	77,838	8,856	24,952	15,064	4,657	13,892	5,626	3,600	3,794	10,173
$120,000 to $149,999 . . .	91,864	10,567	30,391	18,543	5,077	16,050	6,198	3,772	4,297	12,168
$150,000 and over	126,443	12,849	41,294	24,274	5,809	18,074	6,708	3,859	4,836	18,604

[1] Includes expenditures not shown separately.   [2] Includes public service.

Source: U.S. Bureau of Labor Statistics, Consumer Expenditures in 2007, News, USDL-08-1746 (25 November 2008). See also <http://www.bls.gov/cex/2007/share /higherincome.pdf>.

Table 673. **Annual Expenditure Per Child by Husband-Wife Families by Family Income and Expenditure Type: 2008**

[In dollars. Data are for a child in a two-child family. Excludes expenses for college. Expenditures based on data from the 2005–06 Consumer Expenditure Survey updated to 2008 dollars using the Consumer Price Index. For more on the methodology, see report cited below]

Family income and age of child	Expenditure type							
	Total	Housing	Food	Trans- por- tation	Clothing	Health care	Child care and educa- tion [1]	Miscel- lan- eous [2]
INCOME: LESS THAN $56,870								
Less than 2 years old	8,500	2,950	1,090	1,080	620	570	1,780	410
3 to 5 years old.	8,570	2,950	1,190	1,130	490	540	1,670	600
6 to 8 years old.	8,330	2,950	1,610	1,240	560	600	750	620
9 to 11 years old.	9,010	2,950	1,850	1,250	570	650	1,130	610
12 to 14 years old.	9,430	2,950	2,010	1,360	670	990	770	680
15 to 17 years old.	9,450	2,950	2,000	1,510	710	920	790	570
INCOME: $56,870 TO $98,470								
Less than 2 years old	11,610	3,870	1,310	1,550	740	770	2,500	870
3 to 5 years old.	11,650	3,870	1,400	1,600	600	730	2,390	1,060
6 to 8 years old.	11,620	3,870	1,970	1,720	670	850	1,460	1,080
9 to 11 years old.	12,350	3,870	2,250	1,720	690	910	1,840	1,070
12 to 14 years old.	13,020	3,870	2,420	1,830	820	1,280	1,660	1,140
15 to 17 years old.	13,480	3,870	2,410	1,980	880	1,210	2,100	1,030
INCOME: MORE THAN $98,470								
Less than 2 years old	19,250	7,010	1,790	2,350	1,020	890	4,440	1,750
3 to 5 years old.	19,270	7,010	1,880	2,400	860	850	4,330	1,940
6 to 8 years old.	19,280	7,010	2,470	2,510	940	980	3,410	1,960
9 to 11 years old.	20,090	7,010	2,800	2,520	980	1,040	3,790	1,950
12 to 14 years old.	21,370	7,010	3,000	2,630	1,140	1,470	4,100	2,020
15 to 17 years old.	22,960	7,010	2,990	2,780	1,240	1,390	5,640	1,910

[1] Includes only families with child care and education expenses.   [2] Expenses include personal care items, entertainment, and reading materials.

Source: U.S. Department of Agriculture, Center for Nutrition Policy and Promotion, Expenditures on Children by Families, 2008, Annual Report, Miscellaneous Publication number 1528-2008, July 2009. See also <http://www.cnpp.usda.gov/Publications /CRC/crc2008.pdf>.

Income, Expenditures, Poverty, and Wealth   443

Table 674. **Money Income of Households—Percent Distribution by Income Level, Race, and Hispanic Origin in Constant (2007) Dollars: 1980 to 2007**

[Constant dollars based on CPI-U-RS deflator. Households as of March of following year. (82,368 represents 82,368,000). Based on Current Population Survey, Annual Social and Economic Supplement (ASEC); see text, Sections 1 and 13, and Appendix III. For data collection changes over time, see <http://www.census.gov/hhes/www/income/histinc/hstchg.html>. For definition of median, see Guide to Tabular Presentation]

Year	Number of house- holds (1,000)	Percent distribution							Median income (dollars)
		Under $15,000	$15,000- $24,999	$25,000- $34,999	$35,000- $49,999	$50,000- $74,999	$75,000- $99,999	$100,000 and over	
ALL HOUSEHOLDS [1]									
1980	82,368	16.1	13.2	12.2	16.8	21.4	10.8	9.4	42,429
1990	94,312	14.5	12.4	11.6	15.9	19.9	11.7	13.9	46,049
2000 [2]	108,209	12.6	11.4	10.9	14.7	18.5	12.5	19.3	50,557
2006	116,011	13.1	11.6	11.4	14.3	18.1	11.5	19.9	49,568
2007	116,783	13.2	11.6	10.7	14.1	18.2	11.9	20.2	50,233
WHITE									
1980	71,872	14.2	12.6	12.1	17.1	22.4	11.4	10.2	44,762
1990	80,968	12.5	12.0	11.6	16.2	20.5	12.4	14.8	48,029
2000 [2]	90,030	11.3	11.0	10.7	14.7	18.8	13.0	20.4	52,876
2006 [3, 4]	94,705	11.5	11.2	11.3	14.4	18.6	12.0	21.1	52,111
2007 [3, 4]	95,112	11.6	11.3	10.5	14.1	18.6	12.4	21.4	52,115
BLACK									
1980	8,847	31.5	18.2	13.1	14.6	14.1	5.6	2.9	25,788
1990	10,671	30.1	15.5	12.4	14.2	15.1	6.6	6.1	28,721
2000 [2]	13,174	21.7	14.6	13.0	15.9	16.9	8.4	9.5	35,720
2006 [3, 5]	14,354	24.0	15.1	13.4	14.7	15.3	7.9	9.5	32,876
2007 [3, 5]	14,551	24.0	14.2	12.8	14.5	16.2	8.3	9.8	33,916
ASIAN AND PACIFIC ISLANDER									
1990	1,958	11.1	9.7	8.3	13.1	21.1	13.3	21.7	59,131
2000 [2]	3,963	9.5	7.8	8.1	12.6	17.3	14.9	28.2	67,133
2006 [3, 6]	4,454	10.2	7.7	8.4	12.0	17.1	13.0	31.4	66,060
2007 [3, 6]	4,494	10.5	8.5	7.6	11.4	17.1	13.7	31.3	66,103
HISPANIC [7]									
1980	3,906	20.9	17.8	15.1	17.4	17.4	6.9	4.5	32,704
1990	6,220	20.5	16.9	13.5	17.4	17.8	7.1	6.9	34,341
2000 [2]	10,034	15.1	15.1	13.6	17.5	18.8	10.2	9.8	39,935
2006	12,973	16.0	15.3	13.7	17.4	17.3	9.1	11.1	38,853
2007	13,339	16.0	14.8	14.3	16.6	18.3	9.7	10.4	38,679

[1] Includes other races not shown separately. [2] Data reflect implementation of Census 2000-based population controls and a 28,000 household sample expansion to 78,000 households. [3] Beginning with the 2003 Current Population Survey (CPS), the questionnaire allowed respondents to choose more than one race. For 2002 and later, data represent persons who selected this race group only and exclude persons reporting more than one race. The CPS in prior years allowed respondents to report only one race group. See also comments on race in the text for Section 1. [4] Data represent White alone, which refers to people who reported White and did not report any other race category. [5] Data represent Black alone, which refers to people who reported Black and did not report any other race category. [6] Data represent Asian alone, which refers to people who reported Asian and did not report any other race category. [7] People of Hispanic origin may be any race.

Source: U.S. Census Bureau, *Current Population Reports*, P60-235 (published August 2008). See also <http://www.census.gov /prod/2008pubs /p60-235.pdf> and <http://www.census.gov/hhes/www/income/histinc/h17.html>.

Table 675. **Money Income of Households—Median Income by Race and Hispanic Origin in Current and Constant (2007) Dollars: 1980 to 2007**

[In dollars. See headnote, Table 674]

Year	Median income in current dollars					Median income in constant (2007) dollars				
	All house- holds [1]	White [2]	Black [3]	Asian, Pacific Islander [4]	His- panic [5]	All house- holds [1]	White [2]	Black [3]	Asian, Pacific Islander [4]	His- panic [5]
1980	17,710	18,684	10,764	(NA)	13,651	42,429	44,762	25,788	(NA)	32,704
1990 [6]	29,943	31,231	18,676	38,450	22,330	46,049	48,029	28,721	59,131	34,341
1995 [6]	34,076	35,766	22,393	40,614	22,860	46,034	48,317	30,251	54,867	30,882
1999 [7]	40,696	42,325	27,910	50,960	30,746	50,641	52,668	34,731	63,414	38,260
2000 [8]	41,990	43,916	29,667	55,757	33,168	50,557	52,876	35,720	67,133	39,935
2001	42,228	44,517	29,470	53,635	33,565	49,455	52,136	34,514	62,815	39,310
2002 [9]	42,409	45,086	29,026	52,626	33,103	48,878	51,963	33,454	60,653	38,152
2003	43,318	45,631	29,645	55,699	32,997	48,835	51,443	33,421	62,793	37,200
2004 [10]	44,334	46,658	30,095	57,504	34,271	48,665	51,216	33,035	63,122	37,619
2005	46,326	48,554	30,858	61,094	35,967	49,202	51,569	32,774	64,887	38,200
2006	48,201	50,673	31,969	64,238	37,781	49,568	52,111	32,876	66,060	38,853
2007	50,233	52,115	33,916	66,103	38,679	50,233	52,115	33,916	66,103	38,679

NA Not available. [1] Includes other races not shown separately. [2] Beginning with 2002, data represents White alone, which refers to people who reported White and did not report any other race category. [3] Beginning with 2002, data represents Black alone, which refers to people who reported Black and did not report any other race category. [4] Beginning with 2002, data represents Asian alone, which refers to people who reported Asian and did not report any other race category. [5] People of Hispanic origin may be any race. [6] Data reflect full implementation of the 1990 census-based sample design and metropolitan definitions, 7,000 household sample reduction, and revised race edits. [7] Implementation of Census 2000-based population controls. [8] Implementation of a 28,000 household sample expansion. [9] See footnote 3, Table 674. See also comments on race in the text for Section 1. [10] Data have been revised to reflect a correction to the weights in the 2005 ASEC.

Source: U.S. Census Bureau, *Current Population Reports*, P60-235 (published August 2008). See also <http://www.census.gov/prod /2008pubs/p60-235.pdf> and <http://www.census.gov/hhes/www/income/histinc/h05.html>.

Table 676. **Money Income of Households—Distribution by Income Level and Selected Characteristics: 2007**

[116,783 represents 116,783,000. Households as of **March of the following year**. Based on Current Population Survey, Annual Social and Economic Supplement (ASEC), see text, Sections 1 and 13, and Appendix III. For definition of median, see Guide to Tabular Presentation]

Characteristic	Number of households (1,000)								Median income (dollars)
	Total	Under $15,000	$15,000- $24,999	$25,000- $34,999	$35,000- $49,999	$50,000- $74,999	$75,000- $99,999	$100,000 and over	
Total	116,783	15,506	13,528	12,532	16,521	21,268	13,841	23,586	50,233
Age of householder:									
15 to 24 years old	6,554	1,441	1,065	1,024	1,177	1,079	416	351	31,790
25 to 34 years old	19,225	1,941	2,007	2,256	3,146	4,160	2,543	3,172	51,016
35 to 44 years old	22,448	1,838	1,772	1,972	3,034	4,679	3,296	5,854	62,124
45 to 54 years old	24,536	2,201	1,852	1,916	3,191	4,730	3,688	6,959	65,476
55 to 64 years old	19,909	2,432	1,862	1,736	2,677	3,737	2,449	5,016	57,386
65 years old and over	24,113	5,653	4,973	3,626	3,298	2,881	1,451	2,233	28,305
Region: [1]									
Northeast	21,351	3,039	2,301	2,034	2,814	3,605	2,563	4,994	52,274
Midwest	26,266	3,227	3,102	2,866	3,851	5,060	3,257	4,900	50,277
South	43,062	6,240	5,355	4,944	6,291	7,829	4,693	7,711	46,186
West	26,105	2,998	2,770	2,688	3,564	4,772	3,327	5,981	54,138
Size of household:									
One person	32,167	9,500	6,176	4,547	4,707	4,067	1,443	1,726	25,703
Two people	38,737	3,131	4,060	4,285	6,119	7,754	5,031	8,354	54,841
Three people	18,522	1,341	1,453	1,638	2,442	3,915	2,947	4,786	64,403
Four people	15,865	823	1,002	1,119	1,759	3,190	2,674	5,298	75,263
Five people	7,332	438	530	571	882	1,489	1,161	2,258	70,977
Six people	2,694	171	190	235	397	557	368	775	64,827
Seven or more people	1,467	100	120	136	213	293	216	388	63,823
Type of household:									
Family household	77,873	5,549	6,772	7,366	10,679	15,635	11,387	20,484	62,359
Married-couple	58,370	2,066	3,845	4,635	7,402	12,106	9,698	18,615	72,785
Male householder, wife absent	5,100	485	521	639	911	1,162	571	809	49,839
Female householder, husband absent	14,404	2,997	2,406	2,090	2,368	2,365	1,118	1,060	33,370
Nonfamily household	38,910	9,957	6,757	5,165	5,841	5,632	2,456	3,102	30,176
Male householder	17,872	3,380	2,588	2,468	2,980	3,117	1,436	1,903	36,767
Female householder	21,038	6,575	4,170	2,698	2,862	2,517	1,017	1,199	24,294
Educational attainment of householder: [2]									
Total	110,230	14,065	12,465	11,508	15,344	20,188	13,425	23,235	51,427
Less than 9th grade	5,507	1,924	1,327	765	598	544	203	145	20,805
9th to 12th grade (no diploma) .	8,621	2,650	1,736	1,223	1,143	1,082	443	344	24,492
High school graduate	32,422	5,053	4,779	4,251	5,352	6,196	3,311	3,480	40,456
Some college, no degree	20,152	2,185	2,232	2,294	3,265	4,062	2,746	3,365	50,419
Associate's degree	9,968	763	843	1,061	1,461	2,168	1,592	2,081	60,132
Bachelor's degree or more . . .	33,560	1,490	1,547	1,913	3,522	6,137	5,132	13,820	84,508
Bachelor's degree	21,454	1,044	1,097	1,410	2,486	4,188	3,343	7,883	77,605
Master's degree	8,785	328	354	387	818	1,572	1,423	3,906	90,660
Professional degree	1,727	50	52	71	85	168	184	1,119	100,000
Doctoral degree	1,593	68	46	45	133	208	180	912	100,000
Number of earners:									
No earners	24,541	10,415	5,647	3,180	2,451	1,620	542	687	17,492
One earner	43,318	4,563	6,517	6,997	8,509	8,177	3,504	5,049	40,710
Two earners and more	48,924	527	1,365	2,353	5,562	11,472	9,797	17,850	82,044
Two earners	39,093	500	1,264	2,141	4,944	9,610	7,688	12,943	77,758
Three earners	7,352	23	91	182	542	1,524	1,628	3,360	95,026
Four earners or more	2,480	2	9	31	74	336	483	1,547	100,000
Work experience of householder:									
Total	116,783	15,506	13,528	12,532	16,521	21,268	13,841	23,586	50,233
Worked	81,048	4,385	6,672	7,848	11,969	17,278	11,930	20,966	62,209
Worked at full-time jobs . . .	68,881	2,395	5,034	6,516	10,351	15,113	10,653	18,820	65,538
50 weeks or more	59,353	1,196	3,737	5,324	8,795	13,316	9,642	17,346	69,257
27 to 49 weeks	6,178	505	818	757	1,034	1,258	729	1,078	49,568
26 weeks or less	3,350	695	480	435	523	542	280	395	36,379
Worked at part-time jobs . .	12,167	1,989	1,638	1,331	1,616	2,166	1,279	2,146	44,742
50 weeks or more	6,822	860	949	707	903	1,281	803	1,323	49,910
27 to 49 weeks	2,616	448	343	310	346	429	287	451	42,286
26 weeks or less	2,729	682	349	315	366	456	188	372	35,715
Did not work	35,736	11,122	6,856	4,684	4,553	3,989	1,913	2,620	24,805
Tenure:									
Owner occupied	79,330	6,703	7,324	7,275	10,442	15,454	11,210	20,923	61,581
Renter occupied	35,845	8,277	5,920	5,045	5,881	5,594	2,549	2,579	31,811
Occupier paid no cash rent .	1,608	528	285	210	197	219	84	84	24,682

[1] For composition of regions, see map, inside front cover.   [2] People 25 years old and over.

Source: U.S. Census Bureau, *Current Population Reports*, P60-235 (published August 2008). See also <http://www.census.gov /hhes/www/macro/032008/hhinc/toc.htm>.

Income, Expenditures, Poverty, and Wealth   445

Table 677. **Money Income of Households—Number and Distribution by Race and Hispanic Origin: 2007**

[Households as of **March of the following year. (116,783 represents 116,783,000).** Based on Current Population Survey (CPS); see text, Sections 1 and 13, and Appendix III. The 2008 CPS allowed respondents to choose more than one race. Data represent persons who selected this race group only and excludes persons reporting more than one race. See also comments on race in the text for Section 1]

Income interval	Number (1,000)					Percent distribution				
	All races	White alone	Black alone	Asian alone	Hispanic [1]	All races	White alone	Black alone	Asian alone	Hispanic [1]
All households......	116,783	95,112	14,551	4,494	13,339	100.0	100.0	100.0	100.0	100.0
Under $10,000.........	8,455	5,661	2,201	296	1,184	7.2	6.0	15.1	6.6	8.9
$10,000 to $14,999......	7,051	5,392	1,298	174	945	6.0	5.7	8.9	3.9	7.1
$15,000 to $19,999......	6,727	5,331	1,076	178	956	5.8	5.6	7.4	4.0	7.2
$20,000 to $24,999......	6,801	5,434	992	203	1,021	5.8	5.7	6.8	4.5	7.7
$25,000 to $29,999......	6,314	5,044	954	164	940	5.4	5.3	6.6	3.6	7.0
$30,000 to $34,999......	6,218	4,979	907	179	965	5.3	5.2	6.2	4.0	7.2
$35,000 to $39,999......	5,788	4,683	780	157	822	5.0	4.9	5.4	3.5	6.2
$40,000 to $44,999......	5,750	4,677	752	185	759	4.9	4.9	5.2	4.1	5.7
$45,000 to $49,999......	4,983	4,095	585	168	628	4.3	4.3	4.0	3.7	4.7
$50,000 to $59,999......	9,565	7,893	1,141	320	1,119	8.2	8.3	7.8	7.1	8.4
$60,000 to $74,999......	11,703	9,796	1,223	446	1,324	10.0	10.3	8.4	9.9	9.9
$75,000 to $84,999......	6,404	5,414	573	285	651	5.5	5.7	3.9	6.3	4.9
$85,000 to $99,999......	7,437	6,346	636	331	639	6.4	6.7	4.4	7.4	4.8
$100,000 to $149,999	14,214	12,163	1,028	785	939	12.2	12.8	7.1	17.5	7.0
$150,000 to $199,999	5,115	4,446	241	343	275	4.4	4.7	1.7	7.6	2.1
$200,000 to $249,999	2,012	1,757	86	139	73	1.7	1.8	0.6	3.1	0.5
$250,000 and above	2,245	2,000	77	141	99	1.9	2.1	0.5	3.1	0.7

[1] Persons of Hispanic origin may be any race.

Source: U.S. Census Bureau, *Current Population Reports*, P60-235 (published August 2008). See also <http://www.census.gov/hhes/www/macro/032008/hhinc/new06_000.htm>.

Table 678. **Share of Aggregate Income Received by Each Fifth and Top 5 Percent of Households: 1990 to 2007**

[Households as of **March of the following year (94,312 represents 94,312,000).** Income in constant **2007** CPI-U-RS-adjusted dollars. Based on the Current Population Survey; see text, Sections 1 and 13, and Appendix III. For data collection changes over time, see <http://www.census.gov/hhes/www/income/histinc/hstchg.html>]

Year	Number of households (1,000)	Income at selected positions (dollars)					Percent distribution of aggregate income					
		Upper limit of each fifth				Top 5 percent	Lowest 5th	Second 5th	Third 5th	Fourth 5th	Highest 5th	Top 5 percent
		Lowest	Second	Third	Fourth							
1990	94,312	19,223	36,389	55,671	84,899	145,711	3.8	9.6	15.9	24.0	46.6	18.5
1995 [1]	99,627	19,453	36,359	56,742	87,978	152,655	3.7	9.1	15.2	23.3	48.7	21.0
2000 [2, 3] ...	108,209	21,576	39,733	62,819	98,449	174,850	3.6	8.9	14.8	23.0	49.8	22.1
2002	111,278	20,649	38,468	61,271	96,831	172,883	3.5	8.8	14.8	23.3	49.7	21.7
2003	112,000	20,274	38,330	61,388	97,930	173,749	3.4	8.7	14.8	23.4	49.8	21.4
2004 [4] ...	113,343	20,292	38,063	60,626	96,599	172,505	3.4	8.7	14.7	23.2	50.1	21.8
2005	114,384	20,369	38,235	61,240	97,399	176,306	3.4	8.6	14.6	23.0	50.4	22.2
2006	116,011	20,603	38,846	61,702	99,785	178,949	3.4	8.6	14.5	22.9	50.5	22.3
2007	116,783	20,291	39,100	62,000	100,000	177,000	3.4	8.7	14.8	23.4	49.7	21.2

[1] Data reflect full implementation of the 1990 census-based sample design and metropolitan definitions, 7,000 household sample reduction, and revised race edits. [2] Implementation of Census 2000-based population controls. [3] Implementation of a 28,000 household sample expansion. [4] Data have been revised to reflect a correction to the weights in the 2005 ASEC.

Source: U.S. Census Bureau, *Current Population Reports*, P60-235 (published August 2008). See also <http://www.census.gov/prod/2008pubs/p60-235.pdf>; <http://www.census.gov/hhes/www/income/histinc/h01AR.html>, and <http://www.census.gov/hhes/www/income/histinc/h02AR.html>.

Table 679. **Money Income of Families—Number and Distribution by Race and Hispanic Origin: 2007**

[Families as of **March of the following year. (77,908 represents 77,908,000).** Based on Current Population Survey (CPS); see text, Sections 1 and 13, and Appendix III. The 2008 CPS allowed respondents to choose more than one race. Data represent persons who selected this race group only and excludes persons reporting more than one race. See also comments on race in the text for Section 1]

Income interval	Number (1,000)					Percent distribution				
	All races	White alone	Black alone	Asian alone	Hispanic [1]	All races	White alone	Black alone	Asian alone	Hispanic [1]
All families [1]	**77,908**	**63,595**	**9,259**	**3,302**	**10,397**	**100.0**	**100.0**	**100.0**	**100.0**	**100.0**
Under $10,000.........	3,606	2,281	1,078	112	776	4.6	3.6	11.6	3.4	7.5
$10,000 to $14,999......	2,578	1,782	627	84	594	3.3	2.8	6.8	2.5	5.7
$15,000 to $19,999......	3,262	2,446	642	103	746	4.2	3.8	6.9	3.1	7.2
$20,000 to $24,999......	3,773	2,915	617	120	839	4.8	4.6	6.7	3.6	8.1
$25,000 to $29,999......	3,754	2,976	571	115	754	4.8	4.7	6.2	3.5	7.3
$30,000 to $34,999......	3,727	2,949	561	123	764	4.8	4.6	6.1	3.7	7.3
$35,000 to $39,999......	3,700	2,968	518	101	637	4.7	4.7	5.6	3.1	6.1
$40,000 to $44,999......	3,665	2,949	473	143	614	4.7	4.6	5.1	4.3	5.9
$45,000 to $49,999......	3,301	2,715	385	104	493	4.2	4.3	4.2	3.1	4.7
$50,000 to $59,999......	6,527	5,368	760	240	925	8.4	8.4	8.2	7.3	8.9
$60,000 to $74,999......	8,755	7,378	859	345	1,051	11.2	11.6	9.3	10.4	10.1
$75,000 to $84,999......	5,077	4,284	456	231	529	6.5	6.7	4.9	7.0	5.1
$85,000 to $99,999......	6,073	5,198	534	247	503	7.8	8.2	5.8	7.5	4.8
$100,000 to $149,999....	11,958	10,253	835	674	794	15.3	16.1	9.0	20.4	7.6
$150,000 to $199,999....	4,383	3,800	202	310	224	5.6	6.0	2.2	9.4	2.2
$200,000 to $249,999....	1,804	1,582	73	123	63	2.3	2.5	0.8	3.7	0.6
$250,000 and above.....	1,969	1,753	67	125	89	2.5	2.8	0.7	3.8	0.9

[1] Persons of Hispanic origin may be any race.

Source: U.S. Census Bureau, *Current Population Reports,* P60-235 (published August 2008). See also <http://www.census.gov/hhes/www/macro/032008/faminc/new07_000.htm>.

Table 680. **Money Income of Families—Percent Distribution by Income Level in Constant (2007) Dollars: 1980 to 2007**

[Constant dollars based on CPI-U-RS deflator. Families as of March of following year (60,309 represents 60,309,000). Based on Current Population Survey, Annual Social and Economic Supplement (ASEC); see text, Sections 1 and 13, and Appendix III. For data collection changes over time, see <http://www.census.gov/hhes/www/income/histinc/hstchg.html>. For definition of median, see Guide to Tabular Presentation]

Year	Number of families (1,000)	Percent distribution							Median income (dollars)
		Under $15,000	$15,000– $24,999	$25,000– $34,999	$35,000– $49,999	$50,000– $74,999	$75,000– $99,999	$100,000 and over	
ALL FAMILIES [1]									
1980	60,309	9.3	11.1	11.7	17.7	25.1	13.3	11.7	50,366
1990	66,322	9.1	10.0	10.7	15.8	22.7	14.1	17.6	54,369
2000 [2]	73,778	7.3	8.9	9.9	14.6	20.1	15.0	24.2	61,083
2006	78,454	8.1	9.0	10.3	14.2	19.5	13.7	25.3	60,064
2007	77,908	8.0	9.0	9.6	13.7	19.6	14.3	25.8	61,355
WHITE									
1980	52,710	7.9	10.7	12.0	18.4	26.0	13.5	11.6	51,029
1990	56,803	7.4	9.6	10.8	16.6	23.4	14.6	17.5	55,205
2000 [2]	61,330	6.3	8.7	9.6	14.9	20.8	15.5	24.3	62,087
2006 [3, 4]	64,120	6.6	8.3	9.9	14.2	19.9	14.3	26.7	63,018
2007 [3, 4]	63,595	6.4	8.4	9.3	13.6	20.0	14.9	27.3	64,427
BLACK									
1980	6,317	24.0	18.7	13.8	15.5	16.9	7.3	3.7	30,364
1990	7,471	25.0	15.0	12.9	14.2	17.4	7.8	7.7	32,946
2000 [2]	8,731	16.4	14.1	13.3	16.1	18.4	9.9	11.9	40,547
2006 [3, 5]	9,274	18.4	13.7	13.2	15.3	17.4	9.6	12.6	39,355
2007 [3, 5]	9,259	18.5	13.6	12.2	14.9	17.5	10.7	12.7	40,143
ASIAN AND PACIFIC ISLANDER									
1990	1,536	8.2	8.4	8.1	12.3	21.3	15.0	26.7	64,969
2000 [2]	2,982	6.4	6.4	7.3	12.0	17.7	16.1	34.1	75,393
2006 [3, 6]	3,346	6.4	6.3	7.9	11.2	17.4	13.8	36.9	76,729
2007 [3, 6]	3,302	5.9	6.8	7.2	10.6	17.7	14.5	37.3	77,133
HISPANIC ORIGIN [7]									
1980	3,235	16.9	17.7	15.5	18.6	19.1	7.4	4.9	35,256
1990	4,981	17.8	16.9	14.0	17.1	19.0	7.6	7.6	36,034
2000 [2]	8,017	13.2	14.8	13.8	17.9	19.4	10.3	10.5	41,469
2006	10,155	13.4	15.3	14.2	17.8	17.8	9.6	11.9	41,135
2007	10,397	13.2	15.2	14.6	16.8	19.0	9.9	11.3	40,566

[1] Includes other races not shown separately. [2] Data reflect implementation of Census 2000-based population controls and a 28,000 household sample expansion to 78,000 households. [3] Beginning with the 2003 Current Population Survey (CPS), the questionnaire allowed respondents to choose more than one race. For 2002 and later, data represent persons who selected this race group only and excludes persons reporting more than one race. The CPS in prior years allowed respondents to report only one race group. See also comments on race in the text for Section 1. [4] Data represent White alone, which refers to people who reported White and did not report any other race category. [5] Data represent Black alone, which refers to people who reported Black and did not report any other race category. [6] Data represent Asian alone, which refers to people who reported Asian and did not report any other race category. [7] People of Hispanic origin may be any race.

Source: U.S. Census Bureau, *Current Population Reports,* P60-235 (published August 2008). See also <http://www.census.gov/prod/2008pubs/p60-235.pdf> and <http://www.census.gov/hhes/www/income/histinc/f23.html>.

Income, Expenditures, Poverty, and Wealth   447

Table 681. Money Income of Families—Median Income by Race and Hispanic Origin in Current and Constant (2007) Dollars: 1990 to 2007

[See headnote, Table 680]

Year	Median income in current dollars					Median income in constant (2007) dollars				
	All families [1]	White [2]	Black [3]	Asian, Pacific Islander [4]	Hispanic [5]	All families [1]	White [2]	Black [3]	Asian, Pacific Islander [4]	Hispanic [5]
1990 [6]	35,353	36,915	21,423	42,246	23,431	54,369	56,771	32,946	64,969	36,034
1995 [6]	40,611	42,646	25,970	46,356	24,570	54,863	57,612	35,084	62,624	33,192
2000 [7,8] ...	50,732	53,029	33,676	62,617	34,442	61,083	63,849	40,547	75,393	41,469
2002 [9]	51,680	54,633	33,525	60,984	34,185	59,563	62,966	38,639	70,286	39,399
2003	52,680	55,768	34,369	63,251	34,272	59,389	62,871	38,746	71,307	38,637
2004 [10] ...	54,061	56,723	35,148	65,420	35,440	59,342	62,264	38,582	71,811	38,902
2005	56,194	59,317	35,464	68,957	37,867	59,683	63,000	37,666	73,238	40,218
2006	58,407	61,280	38,269	74,612	40,000	60,064	63,018	39,355	76,729	41,135
2007	61,355	64,427	40,143	77,133	40,566	61,355	64,427	40,143	77,133	40,566

[1] Includes other races not shown separately. [2] Beginning with 2002, data represent White alone, which refers to people who reported White and did not report any other race category. [3] Beginning with 2002, data represent Black alone, which refers to people who reported Black and did not report any other race category. [4] Beginning with 2002, data represent Asian alone, which refers to people who reported Asian and did not report any other race category. [5] People of Hispanic origin may be any race. [6] Data reflect full implementation of the 1990 census-based sample design and metropolitan definitions, 7,000 household sample reduction, and revised race edits. [7] Implementation of Census 2000-based population controls. [8] Implementation of a 28,000 household sample expansion. [9] See footnote 3, Table 680. See also comments on race in the text for Section 1. [10] Data have been revised to reflect a correction to the weights in the 2005 ASEC.

Source: U.S. Census Bureau, *Current Population Reports*, P60-235 (published August 2008). See also <http://www.census.gov /prod/2008pubs/p60-235.pdf> and <http://www.census.gov/hhes/www/income/histinc/f05.html>.

Table 682. Money Income of Families—Distribution by Family Characteristics and Income Level: 2007

[77,908 represents 77,908,000. See headnote, Table 680. For composition of regions, see map inside front cover]

Characteristic	Number of families (1,000)								Median income (dollars)
	Total	Under $15,000	$15,000 to $24,999	$25,000 to $34,999	$35,000 to $49,999	$50,000 to $74,999	$75,000 to $99,999	$100,000 and over	
All families	77,908	6,184	7,035	7,481	10,666	15,282	11,150	20,113	61,355
Age of householder:									
15 to 24 years old.	3,359	853	513	467	569	527	206	226	31,283
25 to 34 years old.	13,269	1,496	1,399	1,390	1,981	2,787	1,864	2,353	52,291
35 to 44 years old.	17,601	1,217	1,268	1,411	2,221	3,560	2,745	5,180	67,849
45 to 54 years old.	17,954	945	1,048	1,097	1,955	3,545	3,183	6,180	77,440
55 to 64 years old.	13,225	749	855	928	1,667	2,686	2,005	4,335	72,286
65 years old and over	12,500	925	1,953	2,190	2,272	2,180	1,145	1,839	41,851
Region:									
Northeast	13,910	1,091	1,128	1,187	1,791	2,488	2,011	4,214	66,687
Midwest	17,408	1,196	1,425	1,626	2,382	3,780	2,691	4,308	62,874
South	29,189	2,718	2,959	3,013	4,193	5,682	3,896	6,723	56,538
West.	17,402	1,178	1,522	1,654	2,300	3,333	2,547	4,868	63,423
Type of family:									
Married-couple families	58,395	2,081	3,869	4,655	7,428	12,114	9,690	18,557	72,589
Male householder, no spouse present.	5,103	616	610	692	952	1,042	512	678	44,358
Female householder, no spouse present.	14,411	3,488	2,557	2,134	2,284	2,125	949	877	30,296
Unrelated subfamilies	609	211	100	106	87	61	27	13	24,139
Educational attainment of householder:									
Persons 25 years old and over, total	74,550	5,330	6,522	7,015	10,095	14,755	10,943	19,887	62,831
Less than 9th grade	3,509	627	952	666	504	463	168	130	26,963
9th to 12th grade (no diploma) . . .	5,617	1,123	1,044	951	930	895	382	294	31,190
High school graduate (includes equivalency)	21,820	1,960	2,466	2,712	3,823	4,912	2,939	3,010	49,739
Some college, no degree.	13,543	821	1,060	1,272	2,186	2,968	2,279	2,960	60,955
Associate's degree	6,940	290	394	579	917	1,641	1,327	1,792	69,600
Bachelor's degree or more.	23,121	510	608	834	1,739	3,876	3,853	11,701	100,000
Bachelor's degree.	14,701	361	430	647	1,310	2,688	2,554	6,714	92,327
Master's degree	6,032	106	130	139	320	953	1,049	3,336	100,000
Professional degree	1,294	19	32	39	49	101	141	912	100,000
Doctoral degree	1,093	25	15	9	59	134	110	739	100,000
Number of earners:									
No earners	10,831	3,110	2,333	1,855	1,563	1,093	382	496	24,875
One earner	24,963	2,676	3,654	3,788	4,623	4,566	2,183	3,472	41,603
Two earners or more	42,115	397	1,047	1,838	4,480	9,622	8,586	16,145	84,713

Source: U.S. Census Bureau, *Current Population Reports*, P60-235 (published August 2008). See also <http://www.census.gov /hhes/www/macro/032008/faminc/new01_000.htm> (released 26 August 2008).

Table 683. Median Income of Families by Type of Family in Current and Constant (2007) Dollars: 1990 to 2007

[In dollars. See headnote, Table 680. For definition of median, see Guide to Tabular Presentation]

Year	Current dollars						Constant (2007) dollars					
	Married-couple families				Male house-holder, no spouse present	Female house-holder, no spouse present		Married-couple families			Male house-holder, no spouse present	Female house-holder, no spouse present
	Total	Total	Wife in paid labor force	Wife not in paid labor force			Total	Total	Wife in paid labor force	Wife not in paid labor force		
1990 ...	35,353	39,895	46,777	30,265	29,046	16,932	54,369	61,354	71,937	46,544	44,669	26,039
1995 [1] ..	40,611	47,062	55,823	32,375	30,358	19,691	54,863	63,578	75,413	43,736	41,012	26,601
2000 [2,3].	50,732	59,099	69,235	39,982	37,727	25,716	61,083	71,157	83,361	48,140	45,425	30,963
2002 ...	51,680	61,130	72,806	40,102	37,739	26,423	59,563	70,455	83,912	46,219	43,496	30,453
2003 ...	52,680	62,281	75,170	41,122	38,032	26,550	59,389	70,213	84,744	46,359	42,876	29,931
2004 [4] ..	54,061	63,626	76,854	42,215	40,361	26,969	59,342	69,842	84,362	46,339	44,304	29,604
2005 ...	56,194	65,906	78,755	44,457	41,111	27,244	59,683	69,998	83,645	47,217	43,663	28,935
2006 ...	58,407	69,404	82,788	45,757	41,844	28,829	60,064	71,373	85,137	47,055	43,031	29,647
2007 ...	61,355	72,589	86,435	47,329	44,358	30,296	61,355	72,589	86,435	47,329	44,358	30,296

[1] Data reflect full implementation of the 1990 census-based sample design and metropolitan definitions, 7,000 household sample reduction, and revised race edits. [2] Implementation of Census 2000-based population controls. [3] Implementation of a 28,000 household sample expansion. [4] Data have been revised to reflect a correction to the weights in the 2005 ASEC.

Source: U.S. Census Bureau, *Current Population Reports*, P60-235 (published August 2008). See also <http://www.census.gov/prod/2008pubs/p60-235.pdf> and <http://www.census.gov/hhes/www/income/histinc/f07AR.html>.

Table 684. Married-Couple Families—Number and Median Income by Work Experience of Husbands and Wives and Presence of Children: 2007

[58,395 represents 58,395,000. See headnote, Table 680. For definition of median, see Guide to Tabular Presentaton]

Work experience of husband or wife	Number (1,000)					Median income (dollars)				
	All married-couple families	No related children	One or more related children under 18 years old			All married-couple families	No related children	One or more related children under 18 years old		
			Total	One child	Two or more			Total	One child	Two or more
All married-couple families ...	58,395	31,944	26,450	10,269	16,182	72,589	68,957	76,711	77,669	76,072
Husband worked	45,898	21,109	24,789	9,401	15,388	82,873	87,316	79,276	81,111	77,660
Wife worked.	33,743	15,943	17,800	7,211	10,589	90,299	93,942	86,842	87,553	86,374
Wife did not work	12,155	5,166	6,989	2,190	4,798	60,050	64,765	55,638	54,621	56,075
Husband year-round, full-time worker..	38,565	16,855	21,710	8,193	13,516	86,654	92,275	82,145	8,193	13,516
Wife worked	28,685	13,104	15,581	6,289	9,293	93,575	97,904	89,951	90,458	89,593
Wife did not work	9,880	3,752	6,129	1,905	4,224	62,558	70,482	60,274	58,169	60,534
Husband did not work	12,497	10,835	1,661	867	794	36,528	36,522	36,575	38,909	34,567
Wife worked	3,848	2,887	960	520	440	51,313	52,807	45,079	47,563	42,162
Wife did not work	8,649	7,948	701	347	354	31,838	32,520	21,909	23,183	19,368

Source: U.S. Census Bureau, *Current Population Reports*, P60-235 (published August 2008). See also <http://www.census.gov/hhes/www/macro/032008/faminc/new04_000.htm>.

Table 685. Median Income of People With Income in Constant (2007) Dollars by Sex, Race, and Hispanic Origin: 1990 to 2007

[In dollars. People as of March of following year. People 15 years old and over. Constant dollars based on CPI-U-RS deflator. Based on the Current Population Survey; see text, Sections 1 and 13, and Appendix III. For data collection changes over time, see <http://www.census.gov/hhes/www/income/histinc/hstchg.html>]

Race and Hispanic origin	Male					Female				
	1990	2000 [1]	2005 [2]	2006	2007	1990	2000 [1]	2005 [2]	2006	2007
All races [3]	31,208	34,126	33,217	33,180	33,196	15,486	19,340	19,729	20,582	20,922
White [4]	32,557	35,877	34,177	34,803	35,141	15,866	19,360	19,828	20,652	21,069
Black [5]	19,789	25,698	24,059	25,775	25,822	12,807	19,121	18,726	19,645	19,752
Asian [6]	(NA)	(NA)	36,339	38,478	37,193	(NA)	(NA)	22,985	22,831	24,355
Hispanic [7]	20,715	23,476	23,460	24,117	24,451	11,583	14,747	15,970	16,205	16,748
White non-Hispanic......	33,769	37,937	37,539	37,601	37,373	16,272	20,065	20,659	21,315	21,687

NA Not available. [1] Implementation of Census 2000-based population controls and sample expanded by 28,000 households. [2] Beginning with the 2003 Current Population Survey (CPS), the questionnaire allowed respondents to choose more than one race. For 2002 and later, data represent persons who selected this race group only and excludes persons reporting more than one race. The CPS in prior years allowed respondents to report only one race group. See also comments on race in the text for Section 1. [3] Includes other races not shown separately. [4] Beginning with 2002, data represent White alone, which refers to people who reported White and did not report any other race category. [5] Beginning with 2002, data represent Black alone, which refers to people who reported Black and did not report any other race category. [6] Beginning with 2002, data represent Asian alone, which refers to people who reported Asian and did not report any other race category. [7] People of Hispanic origin may be any race.

Source: U.S. Census Bureau, *Current Population Reports*, P60-235. See also <http://www.census.gov/prod/2008pubs/p60-235.pdf> (released August 2008) and <http://www.census.gov/hhes/www/income/histinc/p02.html>.

Income, Expenditures, Poverty, and Wealth 449

Table 686. **Money Income of People—Selected Characteristics by Income Level: 2007**

[People as of March 2008 (115,678 represents 115,678,000). Covers people 15 years old and over. Median income in constant dollars based on CPI-U-RS deflator. For definition of median, see Guide to Tabular Presentation. For composition of regions, see map, inside front cover. Based on the Current Population Survey (CPS), see Appendix III]

Characteristic	All persons (1,000)	Persons with income — Number (1,000) Total (1,000)	Under $5,000 [1]	$5,000 to $9,999	$10,000 to $14,999	$15,000 to $24,999	$25,000 to $34,999	$35,000 to $49,999	$50,000 to $74,999	$75,000 and over	Median income (dollars)
MALE											
Total	115,678	104,789	6,700	7,289	8,440	16,719	14,739	16,835	16,680	17,390	33,196
15 to 24 years old	21,208	14,142	4,155	2,361	1,713	2,962	1,618	860	342	132	11,209
25 to 34 years old	20,210	19,017	695	1,032	1,340	3,317	3,482	3,879	3,220	2,051	32,875
35 to 44 years old	20,880	20,108	449	834	992	2,368	2,779	3,782	4,276	4,628	45,018
45 to 54 years old	21,539	20,682	573	988	980	2,245	2,578	3,830	4,332	5,154	45,849
55 to 64 years old	16,079	15,522	500	751	1,033	2,014	1,936	2,617	2,956	3,713	42,129
65 years old and over . .	15,762	15,317	329	1,323	2,383	3,809	2,344	1,867	1,552	1,712	24,323
Region:											
Northeast	21,128	19,099	1,368	1,296	1,561	2,881	2,456	2,923	3,108	3,507	34,921
Midwest	25,337	23,303	1,536	1,519	1,680	3,625	3,441	3,995	3,871	3,636	34,324
South	41,917	37,742	2,269	2,854	3,180	6,307	5,532	6,039	5,789	5,772	31,887
West	27,295	24,645	1,528	1,622	2,020	3,905	3,310	3,876	3,910	4,473	34,609
Educational attainment of householder: [2]											
Total	94,470	90,647	2,545	4,928	6,727	13,755	13,121	15,975	16,336	17,258	37,828
Less than 9th grade. . . .	5,446	5,036	244	823	1,100	1,482	713	386	207	81	16,625
9th to 12th grade [3] . . .	7,853	7,200	377	987	1,128	1,834	1,192	903	563	217	20,643
High school graduate [4] . .	29,491	27,988	863	1,704	2,429	5,389	5,257	5,779	4,410	2,159	31,337
Some college, no degree.	15,810	15,321	419	681	990	2,259	2,531	3,270	3,050	2,119	37,447
Associate's degree	7,436	7,244	169	209	333	791	1,100	1,624	1,759	1,257	43,006
Bachelor's degree or more	28,433	27,857	474	524	748	2,000	2,329	4,010	6,349	11,423	62,421
Bachelor's degree . . .	18,042	17,654	333	376	509	1,401	1,715	2,947	4,183	6,187	56,826
Master's degree.	6,886	6,759	104	90	166	425	461	808	1,559	3,146	71,097
Professional degree . .	1,877	1,843	21	32	36	103	74	129	293	1,155	100,000
Doctoral degree.	1,628	1,601	15	24	38	70	78	130	314	931	86,171
Tenure:											
Owner-occupied	83,090	75,998	4,924	4,511	5,095	10,376	9,908	12,399	13,464	15,320	37,926
Renter-occupied	31,203	27,583	1,694	2,603	3,209	6,051	4,636	4,288	3,093	2,008	25,355
Occupier paid no cash rent	1,384	1,207	82	176	134	292	194	147	122	59	21,534
FEMALE											
Total	122,470	105,230	12,498	14,433	13,137	19,578	14,498	14,143	10,356	6,586	20,922
15 to 24 years old	20,635	13,155	4,378	2,634	1,866	2,261	1,140	625	202	49	8,959
25 to 34 years old	19,937	17,240	1,877	1,330	1,547	3,501	3,115	3,087	1,949	833	25,884
35 to 44 years old	21,252	18,824	2,038	1,526	1,654	3,177	3,013	3,199	2,558	1,659	27,702
45 to 54 years old	22,396	20,243	1,684	1,809	1,712	3,494	3,165	3,486	2,838	2,054	29,453
55 to 64 years old	17,223	15,601	1,498	1,912	1,660	2,661	2,155	2,404	1,965	1,349	25,262
65 years old and over . .	21,028	20,167	1,023	5,223	4,698	4,481	1,911	1,342	843	646	14,021
Region:											
Northeast	22,834	20,014	2,371	2,683	2,427	3,437	2,653	2,730	2,195	1,521	21,691
Midwest	26,897	24,054	2,941	3,226	3,012	4,675	3,575	3,261	2,200	1,165	20,557
South	44,890	37,814	4,301	5,500	4,912	7,336	5,244	5,020	3,452	2,048	20,337
West	27,849	23,348	2,885	3,025	2,786	4,128	3,027	3,133	2,509	1,855	21,673
Educational attainment of householder: [2]											
Total	101,835	92,075	8,120	11,799	11,272	17,316	13,359	13,518	10,152	6,539	23,052
Less than 9th grade. . . .	5,379	4,070	508	1,393	1,051	774	214	72	49	9	10,539
9th to 12th grade [3] . . .	7,663	6,286	707	1,812	1,413	1,429	526	241	119	39	11,982
High school graduate [4] . .	31,692	28,134	2,544	4,539	4,400	7,017	4,580	3,099	1,363	593	18,162
Some college, no degree.	18,002	16,600	1,398	1,859	1,958	3,467	2,955	2,714	1,596	651	23,532
Associate's degree	9,746	9,166	701	737	908	1,739	1,656	1,711	1,228	485	27,668
Bachelor's degree or more	29,354	27,820	2,261	1,458	1,544	2,891	3,428	5,680	5,796	4,763	40,712
Bachelor's degree . . .	19,517	18,347	1,712	1,137	1,188	2,173	2,544	3,826	3,358	2,410	36,167
Master's degree.	7,879	7,590	458	277	278	606	752	1,583	2,022	1,618	48,077
Professional degree . .	1,114	1,060	55	16	47	60	78	152	220	432	61,875
Doctoral degree.	844	823	36	28	32	54	54	119	198	305	61,554
Tenure:											
Owner-occupied	87,585	76,461	9,154	9,723	8,853	13,286	10,454	10,775	8,478	5,738	22,238
Renter-occupied	33,473	27,604	3,153	4,485	4,108	6,065	3,903	3,262	1,818	812	17,639
Occupier paid no cash rent	1,411	1,165	191	225	176	228	143	107	60	36	14,704

[1] Includes persons with income deficit.   [2] Persons 25 years and over.   [3] No diploma attained.   [4] Includes high school equivalency.

Source: U.S. Census Bureau, *Current Population Reports*, series P60-235 (published August 2008). See also <http://www.census.gov/hhes/www/macro/032008/perinc/new01_000.htm>.

Table 687. **Average Earnings of Year-Round, Full-Time Workers by Educational Attainment: 2007**

[In dollars. For people 18 years old and over as of March 2008. See headnote, Table 685]

Sex and Age	All workers	Less than 9th grade	High school 9th to 12th grade (no diploma)	High school graduate [1]	College Some college, no degree	College Associate's degree	College Bachelor's degree or more
Male, total.	58,373	27,561	32,379	42,042	48,993	52,322	88,641
18 to 24 years old	26,260	18,020	22,095	25,153	25,739	29,542	37,429
25 to 34 years old	46,688	26,624	28,475	35,995	41,551	45,691	66,731
35 to 44 years old	63,611	25,877	34,094	47,149	55,232	55,394	92,776
45 to 54 years old	66,285	30,127	35,858	46,677	57,991	56,903	100,260
55 to 64 years old	68,281	32,337	40,983	46,037	53,532	56,808	97,029
65 years old and over. . . .	65,586	33,540	40,922	47,557	45,505	54,063	97,614
Female, total.	42,219	21,320	22,171	30,657	36,836	41,097	58,000
18 to 24 years old	24,619	(B)	18,013	21,389	23,748	25,130	33,693
25 to 34 years old	40,204	19,341	20,899	30,092	34,561	39,606	49,966
35 to 44 years old	44,528	23,120	23,344	30,854	38,419	40,762	62,358
45 to 54 years old	45,878	20,279	23,822	33,079	39,509	45,759	64,429
55 to 64 years old	43,869	21,428	23,153	31,828	40,648	41,133	61,580
65 years old and over. . . .	39,668	(B)	20,480	29,610	50,688	40,408	52,344

B Base figure too small to meet statistical standards for reliability of derived figure.   [1] Includes equivalency.

Source: U.S. Census Bureau, *Current Population Reports*, series P60-235 (published August 2008). See also <http://www.census.gov/hhes/www/macro/032008/perinc/new04_000.htm>.

Table 688. **Per Capita Money Income in Current and Constant (2007) Dollars by Race and Hispanic Origin: 1990 to 2007**

[In dollars. Constant dollars based on CPI-U-RS deflator. People as of March of following year. Based on the Current Population Survey, Annual Social and Economic Supplement (ASEC); see text, Sections 1 and 13, and Appendix III. For data collection changes over time, see <http://www.census.gov/hhes/www/income/histinc/hstchg.html>]

Year	Current dollars All races [1]	White [2]	Black [3]	Asian, Pacific Islander [4]	His-panic [5]	Constant (2007) dollars All races [1]	White [2]	Black [3]	Asian, Pacific Islander [4]	His-panic [5]
1990	14,387	15,265	9,017	(NA)	8,424	22,125	23,476	13,867	(NA)	12,955
1995 [6] . . .	17,227	18,304	10,982	16,567	9,300	23,273	24,727	14,836	22,381	12,564
2000 [7, 8] . . .	22,346	23,582	14,796	23,350	12,651	26,905	28,394	17,815	28,114	15,232
2002 [9]	22,794	24,142	14,131	24,131	13,487	26,271	27,825	17,796	27,812	15,544
2003 [10]	23,276	24,626	15,775	24,604	13,492	26,240	27,762	17,784	27,738	15,210
2004 [10] . . .	23,857	25,223	16,025	26,165	14,105	26,188	27,687	17,591	28,721	15,403
2005	25,036	26,496	16,874	27,331	14,483	26,590	28,141	17,922	29,028	15,382
2006	26,352	27,821	17,902	30,474	15,421	27,100	28,610	18,410	31,339	15,858
2007	26,804	28,325	18,428	29,901	15,603	26,804	28,325	18,428	29,901	15,603

NA Not available.   [1] Includes other races not shown separately.   [2] Beginning with 2002, data represents White alone, which refers to people who reported White and did not report any other race category.   [3] Beginning with 2002, data represents Black alone, which refers to people who reported Black and did not report any other race category.   [4] Beginning with 2002, data represents Asian alone, which refers to people who reported Asian and did not report any other race category.   [5] People of Hispanic origin may be any race.   [6] Data reflect full implementation of the 1990 census-based sample design and metropolitan definitions, 7,000 household sample reduction, and revised race edits.   [7] Implementation of Census 2000-based population controls.   [8] Implementation of a 28,000 household sample expansion.   [9] See footnote 3, Table 680. See also comments on race in the text for Section 1.   [10] Data have been revised to reflect a correction to the weights in the 2005 ASEC.

Source: U.S. Census Bureau, *Current Population Reports*, P60-235. See also <http://www.census.gov/prod/2008pubs/p60-235.pdf> (released August 2008) and <http://www.census.gov/hhes/www/income/histinc/incpertoc.html>.

Table 689. **Money Income of People—Number by Income Level and by Sex, Race, and Hispanic Origin: 2007**

[In thousands (115,678 represents 115,678,000). People as of March of the following year. Based on Current Population Survey (CPS); see text, Sections 1 and 13, and Appendix III]

Income interval	Male All races [1]	White [2]	Black [3]	Asian [4]	His-panic [5]	Female All races [1]	White [2]	Black [3]	Asian [4]	His-panic [5]
All households [1]. . . .	115,678	94,769	12,888	5,112	16,837	122,470	98,197	15,618	5,677	15,853
Under $10,000 [6].	24,878	18,221	4,504	1,242	4,363	44,171	34,448	6,069	2,292	7,985
$10,000 to $19,999.	16,953	13,788	2,067	605	3,548	23,616	19,194	3,079	831	2,967
$20,000 to $29,999.	15,483	12,805	1,644	611	3,168	16,710	13,490	2,247	590	1,973
$30,000 to $39,999.	13,877	11,519	1,514	505	2,143	12,457	10,070	1,610	485	1,284
$40,000 to $49,999.	10,420	8,835	965	403	1,209	8,573	7,025	982	404	675
$50,000 to $59,999.	8,291	7,083	735	323	809	5,461	4,510	578	273	359
$60,000 to $74,999.	8,389	7,183	661	415	692	4,895	3,964	550	297	291
$75,000 to $84,999.	3,985	3,465	252	217	270	1,833	1,510	169	134	96
$85,000 to $99,999.	3,456	3,025	183	187	209	1,507	1,240	122	117	76
$100,000 to $149,999	6,135	5,377	261	407	273	2,282	1,911	154	185	99
$150,000 to $199,999	1,999	1,816	61	97	84	540	474	19	43	31
$200,000 to $249,999	728	654	26	37	24	186	162	9	14	4
$250,000 and above	1,086	997	18	65	44	238	195	31	12	14

[1] Includes races not shown separately.   [2] White alone refers to people who reported White and did not report any other race category.   [3] Black alone refers to people who reported Black and did not report any other race category.   [4] Asian alone refers to people who reported Asian and did not report any other race category.   [5] Persons of Hispanic origin may be any race.   [6] Includes persons without income.

Source: U.S. Census Bureau, *Current Population Reports*, P60-235 (published August 2008). See also <http://www.census.gov/hhes/www/macro/032008/perinc/new11_000.htm>.

Income, Expenditures, Poverty, and Wealth   451

Table 690. Household Income—Distribution by Income Level and State: 2007

[In thousands (112,378 represents 112,378,000), except as indicated. The American Community Survey universe includes the household population and the population living in institutions, college dormitories, and other group quarters. Based on a sample and subject to sampling variability; see Appendix III. For definition of median, see Guide to Tabular Presentation]

State	Number of households (1,000)								Median income (dollars)
	Total	Under $25,000	$25,000– $49,999	$50,000– $74,999	$75,000– $99,999	$100,000– $149,999	$150,000– $199,999	$200,000 and over	
United States. .	112,378	26,924	28,379	21,288	13,676	13,152	4,508	4,449	50,740
Alabama.	1,816	580	487	318	195	155	44	37	40,554
Alaska	236	40	49	48	37	41	14	9	64,333
Arizona.	2,252	514	614	438	281	251	77	76	49,889
Arkansas	1,103	366	321	193	102	80	20	21	38,134
California	12,201	2,453	2,726	2,195	1,549	1,786	734	757	59,948
Colorado.	1,860	389	454	363	247	245	85	76	55,212
Connecticut.	1,321	232	268	238	183	216	78	105	65,967
Delaware	328	66	82	65	43	45	16	11	54,610
District of Columbia .	251	63	54	38	27	32	17	21	54,317
Florida	7,089	1,721	1,955	1,380	816	736	230	251	47,804
Georgia	3,417	834	899	657	404	375	127	121	49,136
Hawaii	440	73	92	91	66	73	25	20	63,746
Idaho	561	132	170	117	66	48	14	14	46,253
Illinois	4,760	1,058	1,132	926	623	603	209	208	54,124
Indiana.	2,462	591	697	516	310	235	61	53	47,448
Iowa	1,214	302	334	261	152	111	28	26	47,292
Kansas.	1,089	263	306	213	131	110	34	31	47,451
Kentucky	1,656	528	454	292	180	135	35	32	40,267
Louisiana	1,597	514	418	267	169	149	43	37	40,926
Maine.	544	144	149	113	63	50	12	12	45,888
Maryland	2,082	334	415	388	297	355	151	143	68,080
Massachusetts.	2,449	502	490	428	338	389	149	152	62,365
Michigan.	3,849	971	1,020	741	460	428	125	104	47,950
Minnesota.	2,063	409	508	427	289	267	85	78	55,802
Mississippi	1,080	386	297	180	97	76	23	21	36,338
Missouri	2,310	623	638	456	264	211	64	54	45,114
Montana.	372	105	106	73	42	29	8	7	43,531
Nebraska	700	172	199	144	87	65	18	16	47,085
Nevada	954	177	248	205	130	120	38	36	55,062
New Hampshire	502	82	113	103	75	79	27	21	62,369
New Jersey.	3,150	552	620	555	431	528	228	235	67,035
New Mexico	735	220	207	130	77	66	20	16	41,452
New York	7,100	1,715	1,603	1,270	844	910	358	399	53,514
North Carolina.	3,541	982	961	670	389	330	105	103	44,670
North Dakota.	272	79	73	56	31	23	5	5	43,753
Ohio	4,506	1,171	1,219	893	531	449	134	109	46,597
Oklahoma.	1,400	418	398	256	148	120	30	29	41,567
Oregon.	1,472	358	395	297	183	154	44	41	48,730
Pennsylvania.	4,873	1,233	1,262	948	583	533	156	158	48,576
Rhode Island.	403	98	91	70	56	53	20	15	53,568
South Carolina.	1,703	485	471	316	196	150	46	40	43,329
South Dakota	313	84	96	63	34	24	6	6	43,424
Tennessee	2,408	703	681	457	243	201	62	61	42,367
Texas.	8,244	2,118	2,178	1,485	935	908	307	314	47,548
Utah	835	147	223	190	118	106	28	24	55,109
Vermont	253	58	69	51	32	28	7	7	49,907
Virginia.	2,932	563	672	555	385	419	173	166	59,562
Washington.	2,502	507	608	504	336	341	106	100	55,591
West Virginia.	734	258	203	130	73	48	12	10	37,060
Wisconsin.	2,242	506	600	477	300	241	63	56	50,578
Wyoming	206	45	54	41	29	25	7	5	51,731

Source: U.S. Census Bureau, *2007 American Community Survey,* series ACS-01; B19001. "Household Income in the Past 12 Months"; B19013. "Median Household Income in the Past 12 Months (In 2007 Inflation-Adjusted Dollars)"; using American FactFinder (published online 25 September 2008); <http://factfinder.census.gov/>.

452   Income, Expenditures, Poverty, and Wealth

Table 691. **Family Income—Distribution by Income Level and State: 2007**

[In thousands (75,119 represents 75,119,000), except as indicated. The American Community Survey universe includes the household population and the population living in institutions, college dormitories, and other group quarters. Based on a sample and subject to sampling variability; see Appendix III. For definition of median, see Guide to Tabular Presentation]

State	Number of families (1,000)								Median income (dollars)
	Total	Under $25,000	$25,000– $49,999	$50,000– $74,999	$75,000– $99,999	$100,000– $149,999	$150,000– $199,999	$200,000 and over	
United States. .	75,119	12,339	17,742	15,441	10,918	10,999	3,858	3,822	61,173
Alabama.	1,245	281	332	248	171	141	39	34	50,770
Alaska	162	18	30	35	26	34	12	7	72,865
Arizona.	1,492	245	380	313	217	206	64	66	58,627
Arkansas	756	179	222	155	89	74	18	18	47,021
California	8,331	1,268	1,780	1,533	1,141	1,387	594	628	67,484
Colorado.	1,202	167	255	249	191	202	72	66	67,491
Connecticut.	885	90	154	159	140	180	68	94	81,421
Delaware	224	30	51	45	36	39	14	10	66,198
District of Columbia .	108	22	22	14	12	14	10	15	66,672
Florida	4,626	773	1,219	993	634	600	197	210	56,966
Georgia	2,329	418	571	477	329	320	110	104	58,403
Hawaii	307	30	59	66	53	60	21	17	73,879
Idaho	398	66	113	92	58	43	13	12	54,342
Illinois	3,180	465	693	658	493	510	179	182	65,761
Indiana.	1,662	259	436	391	266	209	54	48	57,734
Iowa	794	112	203	200	131	99	25	23	59,587
Kansas.	728	106	186	164	114	99	31	28	60,510
Kentucky	1,114	256	298	226	154	121	32	28	50,291
Louisiana	1,080	256	276	206	140	131	39	32	50,727
Maine.	356	58	95	86	53	43	10	11	56,266
Maryland	1,392	135	239	253	219	289	131	127	82,404
Massachusetts.	1,561	194	272	273	251	313	126	132	78,497
Michigan.	2,561	433	617	547	384	376	113	91	59,618
Minnesota.	1,353	153	287	301	237	230	75	71	69,172
Mississippi	754	208	206	146	86	68	21	19	44,769
Missouri	1,534	268	406	350	222	185	56	48	55,947
Montana.	241	43	68	57	34	25	7	6	53,497
Nebraska	460	71	118	109	74	58	15	14	58,587
Nevada	632	85	147	143	102	96	30	29	62,842
New Hampshire	342	32	65	75	62	66	24	18	74,626
New Jersey.	2,185	237	378	378	339	444	202	209	81,823
New Mexico	483	113	129	96	61	53	17	13	49,658
New York	4,595	773	990	863	636	728	289	316	64,602
North Carolina	2,367	450	613	507	324	290	92	91	55,028
North Dakota.	168	25	43	43	27	21	5	5	58,827
Ohio	2,962	497	741	666	446	395	121	96	58,374
Oklahoma.	936	193	256	201	126	107	27	26	51,787
Oregon.	941	149	238	209	144	129	38	34	59,152
Pennsylvania.	3,198	484	786	709	479	462	137	140	60,825
Rhode Island.	254	38	51	46	44	44	18	13	70,187
South Carolina.	1,152	234	304	243	164	129	41	36	52,913
South Dakota	205	34	59	50	30	22	5	5	53,910
Tennessee	1,606	332	438	349	203	175	54	55	51,945
Texas.	5,791	1,160	1,447	1,105	761	776	266	276	55,742
Utah	630	75	156	153	104	96	25	22	62,432
Vermont	164	23	41	36	27	24	6	7	61,561
Virginia.	1,964	249	404	388	294	337	147	146	70,894
Washington.	1,620	220	347	347	256	274	92	84	66,642
West Virginia	491	118	145	105	62	42	10	9	46,338
Wisconsin.	1,462	197	341	355	252	212	55	50	62,804
Wyoming	135	16	33	31	23	21	6	4	63,947

Source: U.S. Census Bureau, *2007 American Community Survey*, series ACS-01; B19101. "Family Income in the Past 12 Months"; B19113. "Median Family Income in the Past 12 Months" (In 2007 Inflation-Adjusted Dollars); using American FactFinder (published online 29 September 2008); <http://factfinder.census.gov/>.

Income, Expenditures, Poverty, and Wealth   453

Table 692. **Household Income, Family Income, and Per Capita Income and Individual and Family Below Poverty Level by City: 2007**

[For number and percent below poverty, see headnote, Table 693. The American Community Survey universe includes the household population and the population living in institutions, college dormitories, and other group quarters. Based on a sample and subject to sampling variability; see Appendix III. For definition of median, see Guide to Tabular Presentation]

City	Median household income (dol.)	Median family income (dol.)	Per capita income (dol.)	Number below poverty level [1] Individuals	Number below poverty level [1] Families	Percent below poverty level [1] Individuals	Percent below poverty level [1] Families
Albuquerque, NM	43,677	56,062	24,242	79,178	13,823	15.8	11.4
Anaheim, CA	57,059	60,552	22,490	42,475	7,376	12.5	9.8
Anchorage municipality, AK	68,726	80,325	32,225	20,113	4,056	7.3	5.7
Arlington, TX	50,447	60,932	24,626	46,621	9,492	13.0	10.8
Atlanta, GA	47,153	57,367	36,038	87,273	12,875	21.1	17.4
Aurora, CO	46,937	56,668	22,565	56,280	10,806	18.4	14.3
Austin, TX	48,966	63,116	29,443	129,220	18,468	17.5	11.5
Bakersfield, CA	51,664	56,782	22,278	49,518	10,609	15.5	13.6
Baltimore, MD	36,949	45,353	21,887	123,353	19,682	20.0	15.4
Boston, MA	50,476	55,998	30,976	118,125	18,672	20.4	17.3
Buffalo, NY	29,706	36,696	19,474	72,269	14,084	28.7	23.6
Charlotte, NC	52,690	65,261	31,306	81,737	14,833	12.4	9.0
Chicago, IL	45,505	51,472	26,229	550,580	99,101	20.5	16.7
Cincinnati, OH	33,006	46,945	23,960	66,425	10,661	23.5	18.3
Cleveland, OH	28,512	34,363	16,177	113,815	22,557	29.5	24.7
Colorado Springs, CO	50,479	64,382	26,705	45,212	8,311	11.8	8.6
Columbus, OH	42,253	51,888	22,597	150,323	25,548	21.0	15.4
Corpus Christi, TX	41,416	49,821	21,943	53,399	11,526	18.8	15.6
Dallas, TX	40,986	43,408	26,298	257,788	50,078	21.1	18.8
Denver, CO	44,444	54,798	29,091	102,292	16,341	17.7	13.6
Detroit, MI	28,097	33,922	15,284	269,011	46,681	33.8	28.2
El Paso, TX	35,646	40,558	16,912	164,748	34,929	27.4	23.4
Fort Wayne, IN	43,685	54,158	22,704	31,375	5,878	12.8	9.6
Fort Worth, TX	47,104	53,073	22,708	102,890	20,514	16.2	13.2
Fresno, CA	44,513	50,194	19,771	101,956	18,809	21.9	17.6
Honolulu, HI [2]	55,536	71,378	31,667	30,064	3,558	8.6	4.3
Houston, TX	40,856	44,940	25,719	417,160	81,079	20.7	17.5
Indianapolis, IN [3]	44,325	54,558	24,840	124,176	23,188	16.0	12.3
Jacksonville, FL	48,699	57,533	25,530	99,507	18,229	12.6	8.7
Kansas City, MO	42,123	51,526	24,299	74,657	14,560	17.4	13.9
Las Vegas, NV	54,357	61,556	27,239	66,069	12,503	11.9	9.0
Lexington-Fayette, KY	46,296	62,919	28,093	43,484	7,255	16.1	10.5
Long Beach, CA	48,290	54,331	24,323	81,905	14,480	18.2	14.9
Los Angeles, CA	47,781	51,371	26,896	691,887	119,798	18.5	15.1
Memphis, TN	35,143	42,866	21,532	162,209	32,326	26.2	22.0
Mesa, AZ	49,778	58,915	24,316	48,618	8,524	10.2	7.5
Miami, FL	29,075	32,176	19,948	86,848	15,873	25.5	20.0
Milwaukee, WI	35,281	40,433	18,018	138,769	24,582	24.4	19.7
Minneapolis, MN	44,423	62,427	30,343	68,460	10,271	20.4	14.8
Nashville-Davidson, TN [3]	45,844	56,603	26,668	87,541	13,934	15.3	10.6
New Orleans, LA	38,614	45,902	23,476	47,487	6,753	20.6	15.3
New York, NY	48,631	52,871	29,523	1,507,696	286,451	18.5	15.6
Newark, NJ	34,452	41,058	16,782	61,406	11,811	23.9	20.1
Oakland, CA	46,475	52,020	30,123	62,388	10,756	17.6	14.1
Oklahoma City, OK	41,899	53,143	24,808	87,016	17,130	16.2	12.4
Omaha, NE	45,170	56,418	24,565	53,901	11,269	14.7	12.7
Philadelphia, PA	35,365	44,855	20,542	333,142	58,305	23.8	18.8
Phoenix, AZ	48,061	54,164	23,101	266,702	44,543	17.8	14.0
Pittsburgh, PA	32,363	47,658	23,309	56,847	8,871	21.0	14.2
Plano, TX	84,492	101,616	41,534	15,453	2,344	5.9	3.4
Portland, OR	47,143	61,419	28,305	81,112	12,352	15.1	10.2
Raleigh, NC	51,071	66,373	30,625	41,030	7,143	12.2	8.7
Riverside, CA	55,999	61,938	22,001	37,591	6,380	12.2	9.6
Sacramento, CA	49,849	55,762	25,536	63,386	10,568	14.3	10.6
San Antonio, TX	41,593	50,285	20,808	227,135	40,878	18.2	14.0
San Diego, CA	61,863	72,980	31,924	148,170	22,527	12.1	8.2
San Francisco, CA	68,023	82,320	45,410	79,536	9,775	10.5	6.9
San Jose, CA	76,963	86,822	33,265	90,330	14,574	9.9	6.9
Santa Ana, CA	53,661	52,062	16,663	54,902	8,137	17.1	14.0
Seattle, WA	57,849	83,861	40,010	73,325	9,139	13.1	7.9
St. Louis, MO	34,191	42,115	19,699	76,872	13,253	22.4	18.9
St. Paul, MN	46,579	57,078	24,934	48,734	8,276	18.9	14.2
St. Petersburg, FL	42,008	54,970	25,560	30,385	4,753	13.1	8.7
Stockton, CA	48,132	51,632	20,567	50,388	9,283	17.6	14.0
Tampa, FL	44,079	52,220	28,694	55,313	10,409	17.4	13.7
Toledo, OH	35,216	46,141	18,641	62,322	12,044	22.6	17.9
Tucson, AZ	36,096	46,269	20,337	93,090	14,475	18.4	12.9
Tulsa, OK	38,270	50,308	25,928	72,567	14,783	19.1	16.0
Virginia Beach, VA	61,462	70,173	29,511	26,705	4,622	6.4	4.2
Washington, DC	54,317	66,672	40,379	91,934	14,098	16.4	13.0
Wichita, KS	42,696	57,732	24,980	51,844	9,614	14.7	10.6

[1] See headnote, Table 693.   [2] Data shown for census designated place (CDP).   [3] Represents the portion of a consolidated city that is not within one or more separately incorporated places.

Source: U.S. Census Bureau, *2007 American Community Survey*, series ACS-01; B19013, B19113, B19301, B17001, and B17010 (published 30 September 2008); using American FactFinder; <http://factfinder.census.gov/>.

Table 693. **Individuals and Families Below Poverty Level—Number and Rate by State: 2000 and 2007**

[**In thousands (33,311 represents 33,311,000), except as indicated.** Represents number and percent below poverty in the past 12 months. Prior to 2006, the American Community Survey universe was limited to the household population and excluded the population living in institutions, college dormitories, and other group quarters. Poverty status was determined for all people except institutionalized people, people in military group quarters, people in college dormitories, and unrelated individuals under 15 years old. These groups were excluded from the numerator and denominator when calculating poverty rates. Based on a sample and subject to sampling variability; see Appendix III]

State	Number below poverty level (1,000)				Percent below poverty level			
	Individuals		Families		Individuals		Families	
	2000	2007	2000	2007	2000	2007	2000	2007
United States........	33,311	38,052	6,615	7,162	12.2	13.0	9.3	9.5
Alabama..............	672	760	146	163	15.6	16.9	12.4	13.1
Alaska	55	60	11	10	9.1	8.9	6.8	6.5
Arizona.............	780	881	150	152	15.6	14.2	11.6	10.2
Arkansas	439	492	96	104	17.0	17.9	13.0	13.7
California	4,520	4,433	832	774	13.7	12.4	10.7	9.3
Colorado.............	363	569	64	101	8.7	12.0	5.7	8.4
Connecticut...........	254	269	51	50	7.7	7.9	5.8	5.7
Delaware	70	88	14	17	9.3	10.5	6.7	7.5
District of Columbia	94	92	17	14	17.5	16.4	15.4	13.0
Florida	1,987	2,159	387	398	12.8	12.1	9.3	8.6
Georgia	999	1,324	206	249	12.6	14.3	10.0	10.7
Hawaii	103	100	19	16	8.8	8.0	6.8	5.4
Idaho...............	144	178	26	35	11.4	12.1	7.7	8.9
Illinois	1,335	1,496	262	280	11.1	11.9	8.6	8.8
Indiana..............	592	758	113	145	10.1	12.3	7.1	8.7
Iowa	281	318	53	58	10.0	11.0	7.0	7.4
Kansas..............	247	300	43	56	9.5	11.2	6.2	7.7
Kentucky	640	714	148	147	16.4	17.3	13.5	13.2
Louisiana	862	775	182	158	20.0	18.6	16.0	14.6
Maine...............	124	154	22	28	10.1	12.0	6.6	7.9
Maryland	477	454	89	76	9.3	8.3	6.6	5.4
Massachusetts........	586	621	110	113	9.6	9.9	7.1	7.3
Michigan.............	975	1,377	196	257	10.1	14.0	7.7	10.1
Minnesota............	328	482	66	87	6.9	9.5	5.1	6.5
Mississippi	498	582	104	123	18.2	20.6	14.2	16.3
Missouri	000	742	118	146	11.2	13.0	7.7	9.5
Montana.............	117	132	23	23	13.4	14.1	9.5	9.7
Nebraska	158	193	28	38	9.6	11.2	6.5	8.2
Nevada	194	270	34	47	9.9	10.7	6.9	7.5
New Hampshire.........	63	90	11	16	5.3	7.1	3.5	4.6
New Jersey...........	651	729	126	138	7.9	8.6	6.0	6.3
New Mexico	320	349	64	69	18.0	18.1	14.2	14.2
New York	2,391	2,570	491	474	13.1	13.7	10.7	10.3
North Carolina	1,018	1,259	203	252	13.1	14.3	9.6	10.6
North Dakota..........	71	74	14	13	11.6	12.1	8.1	7.5
Ohio	1,216	1,464	246	287	11.1	13.1	8.4	9.7
Oklahoma............	459	557	100	111	13.8	15.9	11.0	11.9
Oregon..............	439	474	84	83	13.2	12.9	9.5	8.9
Pennsylvania..........	1,240	1,393	247	259	10.5	11.6	7.8	8.1
Rhode Island..........	108	122	23	21	10.7	12.0	8.5	8.3
South Carolina.........	557	642	123	129	14.4	15.0	11.7	11.2
South Dakota.........	83	101	16	18	11.5	13.1	8.4	8.9
Tennessee	745	954	158	192	13.5	15.9	10.5	12.0
Texas...............	3,056	3,791	639	738	15.1	16.3	12.3	12.8
Utah	192	251	40	43	8.8	9.7	7.2	6.9
Vermont	63	61	12	11	10.7	10.1	7.5	6.4
Virginia..............	630	743	124	140	9.2	9.9	6.8	7.1
Washington...........	667	725	127	127	11.6	11.4	8.6	7.8
West Virginia..........	327	298	72	64	18.6	16.9	14.7	13.0
Wisconsin............	461	588	75	104	8.9	10.8	5.6	7.1
Wyoming	55	44	10	7	11.4	8.7	7.9	5.2

Source: U.S. Census Bureau, 2007 American Community Survey; B17001. "Poverty Status in the Past 12 Months by Sex and Age," and B17010. "Poverty Status in the Past 12 Months of Familes by Family Type by Presence of Related Children under 18 Years by Age of Related Children"; using American FactFinder (published online 1 October 2008); <http://factfinder.census.gov/>.

Income, Expenditures, Poverty, and Wealth   455

Table 694. **Poverty Thresholds by Size of Unit: 1980 to 2007**

[In dollars. For information on the official poverty thresholds; see text, this section. For data collection changes over time, see <http://www.census.gov/hhes/www/income/histinc/hstchg.html>]

Size of family unit	1980	1990	1995	2000 [1]	2003	2004 [2]	2005	2006	2007
One person (unrelated individual)	4,190	6,652	7,763	8,791	9,393	9,646	9,973	10,294	10,590
Under 65 years old	4,290	6,800	7,929	8,959	9,573	9,827	10,160	10,488	10,787
65 years old and over	3,949	6,268	7,309	8,259	8,825	9,060	9,367	9,669	9,944
Two persons	5,363	8,509	9,933	11,235	12,015	12,335	12,755	13,167	13,540
Householder under 65 years old	5,537	8,794	10,259	11,589	12,384	12,714	13,145	13,569	13,954
Householder 65 years old and over . .	4,983	7,905	9,219	10,418	11,133	11,430	11,815	12,201	12,550
Three persons	6,565	10,419	12,158	13,740	14,680	15,066	15,577	16,079	16,530
Four persons	8,414	13,359	15,569	17,604	18,810	19,307	19,971	20,614	21,203
Five persons	9,966	15,792	18,408	20,815	22,245	22,830	23,613	24,382	25,080
Six persons	11,269	17,839	20,804	23,533	25,122	25,787	26,683	27,560	28,323
Seven persons	12,761	20,241	23,552	26,750	28,544	29,233	30,249	31,205	32,233
Eight persons	14,199	22,582	26,237	29,701	31,589	32,641	33,610	34,774	35,816
Nine or more persons	16,896	26,848	31,280	35,150	37,656	39,062	40,288	41,499	42,739

[1] Implementation of Census 2000-based population controls and sample expanded by by 28,000 households. [2] The 2004 data have been revised to reflect a correction to the weights in the 2005 Annual Social and Economic Supplement (ASEC).

Source: U.S. Census Bureau, *Current Population Reports*, P60-235 (published August 2008). See also <http://www.census.gov /prod/2008pubs> and <http://www.census.gov/hhes/www/poverty/histpov/hstpov1.xls>.

Table 695. **People Below Poverty Level and Below 125 Percent of Poverty Level by Race and Hispanic Origin: 1980 to 2007**

[29,272 represents 29,272,000 People as of March of the following year. Based on Current Population Survey, Annual Social and Economic Supplement (ASEC); See text, Section 1, and Appendix III. For data collection changes over time, see <http://www.census.gov/hhes/www/income/histinc/hstchg.html>]

Year	Number below poverty level (1,000)					Percent below poverty level					Below 125 percent of poverty level	
	All races [1]	White [2]	Black [3]	Asian and Pacific Islander [4]	His-panic [5]	All races [1]	White [2]	Black [3]	Asian and Pacific Islander [4]	His-panic [5]	Num-ber (1,000)	Percent of total popu-lation
1980. . . .	29,272	19,699	8,579	(NA)	3,491	13.0	10.2	32.5	(NA)	25.7	40,658	18.1
1985. . . .	33,064	22,860	8,926	(NA)	5,236	14.0	11.4	31.3	(NA)	29.0	44,166	18.7
1986. . . .	32,370	22,183	8,983	(NA)	5,117	13.6	11.0	31.1	(NA)	27.3	43,486	18.2
1987 [6]. . .	32,221	21,195	9,520	1,021	5,422	13.4	10.4	32.4	16.1	28.0	43,032	17.9
1988. . . .	31,745	20,715	9,356	1,117	5,357	13.0	10.1	31.3	17.3	26.7	42,551	17.5
1989. . . .	31,528	20,785	9,302	939	5,430	12.8	10.0	30.7	14.1	26.2	42,653	17.3
1990. . . .	33,585	22,326	9,837	858	6,006	13.5	10.7	31.9	12.2	28.1	44,837	18.0
1991. . . .	35,708	23,747	10,242	996	6,339	14.2	11.3	32.7	13.8	28.7	47,527	18.9
1992 [7]. . .	38,014	25,259	10,827	985	7,592	14.8	11.9	33.4	12.7	29.6	50,592	19.7
1993 [8]. . .	39,265	26,226	10,877	1,134	8,126	15.1	12.2	33.1	15.3	30.6	51,801	20.0
1994. . . .	38,059	25,379	10,196	974	8,416	14.5	11.7	30.6	14.6	30.7	50,401	19.3
1995. . . .	36,425	24,423	9,872	1,411	8,574	13.8	11.2	29.3	14.6	30.3	48,761	18.5
1996. . . .	36,529	24,650	9,694	1,454	8,697	13.7	11.2	28.4	14.5	29.4	49,310	18.5
1997. . . .	35,574	24,396	9,116	1,468	8,308	13.3	11.0	26.5	14.0	27.1	47,853	17.8
1998 [9]. . .	34,476	23,454	9,091	1,360	8,070	12.7	10.5	26.1	12.5	25.6	46,036	17.0
1999 [9]. . .	32,791	22,169	8,441	1,285	7,876	11.9	9.8	23.6	10.7	22.7	45,050	16.3
2000 [10]. .	31,581	21,645	7,982	1,258	7,747	11.3	9.5	22.5	9.9	21.5	43,612	15.6
2001. . . .	32,907	22,739	8,136	1,275	7,997	11.7	9.9	22.7	10.2	21.4	45,320	16.1
2002 [11]. .	34,570	23,466	8,602	1,161	8,555	12.1	10.2	24.1	10.1	21.8	47,084	16.5
2003 [12]. .	35,861	24,272	8,781	1,401	9,051	12.5	10.5	24.4	11.8	22.5	48,687	16.9
2004 [12]. .	37,040	25,327	9,014	1,201	9,122	12.7	10.8	24.7	9.8	21.9	49,693	17.1
2005. . . .	36,950	24,872	9,168	1,402	9,368	12.6	10.6	24.9	11.1	21.8	49,327	16.8
2006. . . .	36,460	24,416	9,048	1,353	9,243	12.3	10.3	24.3	10.3	20.6	49,688	16.8
2007. . . .	37,276	25,120	9,237	1,349	9,890	12.5	10.5	24.5	10.2	21.5	50,876	17.0

NA Not available. [1] Includes other races not shown separately. [2] Beginning 2002, data represent White alone, which refers to people who reported White and did not report any other race category. [3] Beginning 2002, data represent Black alone, which refers to people who reported Black and did not report any other race category. [4] Beginning 2002, data represent Asian alone, which refers to people who reported Asian and did not report any other race category. [5] People of Hispanic origin may be any race. [6] Implementation of a new March CPS processing system. [7] Implementation of 1990 census population controls. [8] The March 1994 income supplement was revised to allow for the coding of different income amounts on selected questionnaire items. Limits either increased or decreased in the following categories: earnings increased to $999,999; social security increased to $49,999; supplemental security income and public assistance increased to $24,999; veterans benefits increased to $99,999; child support and alimony decreased to $49,999. [9] Implementation of Census-2000-based population controls. [10] Implementation of sample expansion by 28,000 households. [11] Beginning with the 2003 Current Population Survey (CPS), the questionnaire allowed respondents to choose more than one race. For 2002 and later, data represent persons who selected this race group only and exclude persons reporting more than one race. The CPS in prior years allowed respondents to report only one race group. See also comments on race in the text for Section 1, Population. [12] Data have been revised to reflect a correction to the weights in the 2005 ASEC.

Source: U.S. Census Bureau, *Current Population Reports*, P60-235 (published August 2008). See also <http://www.census.gov /prod/2008pubs/p60-235.pdf> and <http://www.census.gov/hhes/www/poverty/histpov/perindex.html>.

Table 696. Children Below Poverty Level by Race and Hispanic Origin: 1980 to 2007

[11,114 represents 11,114,000. Persons as of March of the following year. Covers only related children in families under 18 years old. Based on Current Population Survey; see text, this section and Section 1, and Appendix III. For data collection changes over time, see <http://www.census.gov/hhes/www/income/histinc/hstchg.html>]

Year	Number below poverty level (1,000)					Percent below poverty level				
	All races [1]	White [2]	Black [3]	Asian and Pacific Islander [4]	His-panic [5]	All races [1]	White [2]	Black [3]	Asian and Pacific Islander [4]	His-panic [5]
1980	11,114	6,817	3,906	(NA)	1,718	17.9	13.4	42.1	(NA)	33.0
1985	12,483	7,838	4,057	(NA)	2,512	20.1	15.6	43.1	(NA)	39.6
1988	11,935	7,095	4,148	458	2,576	19.0	14.0	42.8	23.5	37.3
1989	12,001	7,164	4,257	368	2,496	19.0	14.1	43.2	18.9	35.5
1990	12,715	7,696	4,412	356	2,750	19.9	15.1	44.2	17.0	37.7
1991	13,658	8,316	4,637	348	2,977	21.1	16.1	45.6	17.1	39.8
1992 [6] . . .	14,521	8,752	5,015	352	3,440	21.6	16.5	46.3	16.0	39.0
1993 [7]	14,961	9,123	5,030	358	3,666	22.0	17.0	45.9	17.6	39.9
1994	14,610	8,826	4,787	308	3,956	21.2	16.3	43.3	17.9	41.1
1995	13,999	8,474	4,644	532	3,938	20.2	15.5	41.5	18.6	39.3
1996	13,764	8,488	4,411	553	4,090	19.8	15.5	39.5	19.1	39.9
1997	13,422	8,441	4,116	608	3,865	19.2	15.4	36.8	19.9	36.4
1998 [8]	12,845	7,935	4,073	542	3,670	18.3	14.4	36.4	17.5	33.6
1999 [8]	11,678	7,194	3,698	367	3,561	16.6	13.1	32.8	11.5	29.9
2000 [9]	11,005	6,834	3,495	407	3,342	15.6	12.4	30.9	12.5	27.6
2001	11,175	7,086	3,423	353	3,433	15.8	12.8	30.0	11.1	27.4
2002 [10] . . .	11,646	7,203	3,570	302	3,653	16.3	13.1	32.1	11.4	28.2
2003 [11] . . .	12,340	7,624	3,750	331	3,982	17.2	13.9	33.6	12.1	29.5
2004 [11] . . .	12,473	7,876	3,702	265	3,985	17.3	14.3	33.4	9.4	28.6
2005	12,335	7,652	3,743	312	3,977	17.1	13.9	34.2	11.0	27.7
2006	12,299	7,522	3,690	351	3,959	16.9	13.6	33.0	12.0	26.6
2007	12,802	8,002	3,838	345	4,348	17.6	14.4	34.3	11.8	28.3

NA Not available. [1] Includes other races not shown separately. [2] Beginning 2002, data represent White alone, which refers to people who reported White and did not report any other race category. [3] Beginning 2002, data represent Black alone, which refers to people who reported Black and did not report any other race category. [4] Beginning 2002, data represent Asian alone, which refers to people who reported Asian and did not report any other race category. [5] People of Hispanic origin may be any race. [6] Implementation of 1990 census population controls. [7] The March 1994 income supplement was revised to allow for the coding of different income amounts on selected questionnaire items. Limits either increased or decreased in the following categories: earnings increased to $999,999; social security increased to $49,999; supplemental security income and public assistance increased to $24,999; veterans' benefits increased to $99,999; child support and alimony decreased to $49,999. [8] Implementation of Census 2000-based population controls. [9] Implementation of sample expansion to 28,000 households. [10] Beginning with the 2003 Current Population Survey (CPS), the questionnaire allowed respondents to choose more than one race. For 2002 and later, data represent persons who selected this race group only and excludes persons reporting more than one race. The CPS in prior years allowed respondents to report only one race group. See also comments on race in the text for Section 1. [11] Data have been revised to reflect a correction to the weights in the 2005 Annual Social and Economic Supplement (ASEC).

Source: U.S. Census Bureau, *Current Population Reports*, P60-235 (published August 2008). See also <http://www.census.gov /prod/2008pubs /p60-235.pdf> and <http://www.census.gov/hhes/www/poverty/histpov/hstpov3.xls>.

Table 697. Persons Below Poverty Level by Selected Characteristics: 2007

[37,276 represents 37,276,000. People as of March 2008. Based on Current Population Survey (CPS); see text, this section and Section 1, and Appendix III. The 2008 CPS allowed respondents to choose more than one race. For 2007, data represent persons who selected this race group only and exclude persons reporting more than one race. The CPS in prior years allowed respondents to report only one race group. See also comments on race in the text for Section 1. For composition of regions, see map, inside front cover]

Characteristic	Number below poverty level (1,000)					Percent below poverty level				
	All races [1]	White alone	Black alone	Asian alone	His-panic [2]	All races [1]	White alone	Black alone	Asian alone	His-panic [2]
Total	37,276	25,120	9,237	1,349	9,890	12.5	10.5	24.5	10.2	21.5
Male	16,302	11,090	3,907	615	4,627	11.1	9.4	22.3	9.7	19.6
Female.	20,973	14,030	5,330	734	5,263	13.8	11.6	26.5	10.7	23.6
Under 18 years old. . . .	13,324	8,395	3,904	374	4,482	18.0	14.9	34.5	12.5	28.6
18 to 24 years old	4,901	3,376	1,134	159	1,105	17.3	15.3	27.6	13.6	22.0
25 to 34 years old	4,930	3,353	1,151	230	1,516	12.3	10.7	21.8	10.1	18.6
35 to 44 years old	3,971	2,756	892	174	1,154	9.4	8.2	17.0	7.4	16.7
45 to 54 years old	3,722	2,632	810	142	760	8.5	7.3	15.6	7.5	15.6
55 to 59 years old	1,471	989	368	58	241	8.0	6.5	18.5	7.6	15.0
60 to 64 years old	1,402	1,028	247	70	194	9.4	8.1	17.9	12.7	16.4
65 years old and over . .	3,556	2,590	731	143	438	9.7	8.1	23.2	11.3	17.1
65 to 74 years old. . . .	1,726	1,168	431	71	253	8.8	7.0	23.5	9.4	16.5
75 years old and over .	1,829	1,422	301	72	185	10.6	9.4	22.8	14.1	18.0
Northeast	6,166	4,181	1,469	377	1,512	11.4	9.6	22.2	13.1	24.5
Midwest	7,237	4,849	1,887	150	839	11.1	8.7	28.3	9.5	20.9
South.	15,501	9,505	5,207	264	3,616	14.2	11.4	25.0	9.4	22.0
West	8,372	6,585	674	558	3,923	12.0	11.6	19.2	9.3	20.3
Native	31,126	20,630	8,661	438	5,975	11.9	9.6	25.1	9.1	21.3
Foreign born	6,150	4,489	575	911	3,915	16.5	18.1	18.1	10.8	22.0
Naturalized citizen. . . .	1,426	873	171	352	629	9.5	9.6	11.8	8.2	13.0
Not a citizen.	4,724	3,616	405	560	3,286	21.3	23.1	23.4	13.4	25.3

[1] Includes other races not shown separately. [2] Persons of Hispanic origin may be any race.

Source: U.S. Census Bureau, *Current Population Reports*, P60-235 (published August 2008). See also <http://www.census.gov /hhes/www/macro/032008/pov/toc.htm>.

Income, Expenditures, Poverty, and Wealth   457

Table 698. **Work Experience of People During 2007 by Poverty Status, Sex, and Age: 2007**

[108,617 represents 108,617,000. Covers only persons 16 years old and over. Based on Current Population Survey; see text, this section and Section 1, and Appendix III]

Sex and age	Worked full-time year-round Number (1,000)	Below poverty level Number (1,000)	Percent	Did not work full-time year-round Number (1,000)	Below poverty level Number (1,000)	Percent	Did not work Number (1,000)	Below poverty level Number (1,000)	Percent
BOTH SEXES									
Total............	108,617	2,768	2.5	49,851	6,320	12.7	75,417	16,208	21.5
16 to 17 years old	99	8	8.4	2,516	184	7.3	6,567	1,152	17.5
18 to 64 years old	105,244	2,740	2.6	43,359	6,030	13.9	39,310	11,627	29.6
18 to 24 years old....	8,140	458	5.6	12,105	1,961	16.2	8,153	2,482	30.4
25 to 34 years old....	24,472	814	3.3	9,320	1,709	18.3	6,354	2,407	37.9
35 to 54 years old....	56,075	1,299	2.3	15,700	1,866	11.9	14,292	4,527	31.7
55 to 64 years old....	16,558	168	1.0	6,234	494	7.9	10,510	2,211	21.0
65 years old and over...	3,274	20	0.6	3,976	107	2.7	29,540	3,429	11.6
MALE									
Total............	62,994	1,534	2.4	21,298	2,665	12.5	29,210	5,988	20.5
16 to 17 years old	59	8	(B)	1,264	96	7.6	3,318	555	16.7
18 to 64 years old	60,927	1,514	2.5	18,100	2,518	13.9	14,073	4,464	31.7
18 to 24 years old....	4,775	232	4.9	5,952	777	13.1	3,665	1,005	27.4
25 to 34 years old....	14,309	449	3.1	3,977	687	17.3	1,923	796	41.4
35 to 54 years old....	32,497	742	2.3	5,619	832	14.8	4,303	1,734	40.3
55 to 64 years old....	9,346	91	1.0	2,551	222	8.7	4,182	929	22.2
65 years old and over...	2,008	13	0.6	1,934	51	2.6	11,820	969	8.2
FEMALE									
Total............	45,622	1,234	2.7	28,554	3,656	12.8	46,207	10,220	22.1
16 to 17 years old	40	–	(B)	1,252	88	7.0	3,250	598	18.4
18 to 64 years old	44,317	1,226	2.8	25,259	3,512	13.9	25,238	7,163	28.4
18 to 24 years old....	3,365	226	6.7	6,152	1,183	19.2	4,489	1,477	32.9
25 to 34 years old....	10,163	365	3.6	5,343	1,022	19.1	4,431	1,611	36.3
35 to 54 years old....	23,577	558	2.4	10,081	1,034	10.3	9,989	2,793	28.0
55 to 64 years old....	7,211	77	1.1	3,683	272	7.4	6,329	1,282	20.3
65 years old and over...	1,266	8	0.6	2,043	56	2.7	17,720	2,459	13.9

– Represents zero.   B Base figure too small to meet statistical standards for reliability of a derived figure.

Source: U.S. Census Bureau, *Current Population Reports*, series P60-235 (published August 2008). See also <http://www.census.gov /hhes/www/macro/032008/pov/new22_100.htm>.

Table 699. **Families Below Poverty Level and Below 125 Percent of Poverty by Race and Hispanic Origin: 1980 to 2007**

[6,217 represents 6,217,000. Families as of March of the following year. Based on Current Population Survey. See text, this section and Section 1, and Appendix III. For data collection changes over time, see <http://www.census.gov/hhes/www/income /histinc/hstchg.html>]

Year	Number below poverty level (1,000) All races [1]	White [2]	Black [3]	Asian and Pacific Islander [4]	His-panic [5]	Percent below poverty level All races [1]	White [2]	Black [3]	Asian and Pacific Islander [4]	His-panic [5]	Below 125 percent of poverty level Number (1,000)	Percent
1980 ...	6,217	4,195	1,826	(NA)	751	10.3	8.0	28.9	(NA)	23.2	8,764	14.5
1985 ...	7,223	4,983	1,983	(NA)	1,074	11.4	9.1	28.7	(NA)	25.5	9,753	15.3
1990 ...	7,098	4,622	2,193	169	1,244	10.7	8.1	29.3	11.0	25.0	9,564	14.4
1995 ...	7,532	4,994	2,127	264	1,695	10.8	8.5	26.4	12.4	27.0	10,223	14.7
1998 ...	7,186	4,829	1,981	270	1,648	10.0	8.0	23.4	11.0	22.7	9,714	13.6
1999 [6] ...	6,792	4,447	1,887	258	1,593	9.3	7.3	21.8	10.3	20.5	9,320	12.9
2000 [7] ...	6,400	4,333	1,686	233	1,540	8.7	7.1	19.3	7.8	19.2	9,032	12.2
2001 ...	6,813	4,579	1,829	234	1,649	9.2	7.4	20.7	7.8	19.4	9,525	12.8
2002 [8] ...	7,229	4,862	1,923	210	1,792	9.6	7.8	21.5	7.4	19.7	9,998	13.2
2003 ...	7,607	5,058	1,986	311	1,925	10.0	8.1	22.3	10.2	20.8	10,360	13.6
2004 [9] ...	7,835	5,293	2,035	232	1,953	10.2	8.4	22.8	7.4	20.5	10,499	13.7
2005 ...	7,657	5,068	1,997	289	1,948	9.9	8.0	22.1	9.0	19.7	10,442	13.5
2006 ...	7,668	5,118	2,007	260	1,922	9.8	8.0	21.6	7.8	18.9	10,531	13.4
2007 ...	7,623	5,046	2,045	261	2,045	9.8	7.9	22.1	7.9	19.7	10,551	13.5

NA Not available.   [1] Includes other races not shown separately.   [2] Beginning 2002, data represent White alone, which refers to people who reported White and did not report any other race category.   [3] Beginning 2002, data represent Black alone, which refers to people who reported Black and did not report any other race category.   [4] Beginning 2002, data represent Asian alone, which refers to people who reported Asian and did not report any other race category.   [5] People of Hispanic origin may be any race.   [6] Implementation of Census 2000-based population controls.   [7] Implementation of a 28,000 household sample expansion.   [8] Beginning with the 2003 Current Population Survey (CPS), the questionnaire allowed respondents to choose more than one race. For 2002 and later, data represent persons who selected this race group only and excludes persons reporting more than one race. The CPS in prior years allowed respondents to report only one race group. See also comments on race in the text for Section 1, Population.   [9] Data have been revised to reflect a correction to the weights in the 2005 Annual Social and Economic Supplement (ASEC).

Source: U.S. Census Bureau, *Current Population Reports*, P60-235 (published August 2008). See also <http://www.census.gov /prod/2008pubs/p60-235.pdf> and <http://www.census.gov/hhes/www/poverty/histpov/hstpov4.xls>.

Table 700. **Families Below Poverty Level by Selected Characteristics: 2007**

[7,623 represents 7,623,000. Families as of March 2008. Based on Current Population Survey (CPS); see text, this section, Section 1, and Appendix III. The 2008 CPS allowed respondents to choose more than one race. For 2007, data represent persons who selected this race group only and exclude persons reporting more than one race. See also comments on race in the text for Section 1. For composition of regions, see map, inside front cover]

Characteristic	Number below poverty level (1,000)					Percent below poverty level				
	All races [1]	White alone	Black alone	Asian alone	His- panic [2]	All races [1]	White alone	Black alone	Asian alone	His- panic [2]
Total families	7,623	5,046	2,045	261	2,045	9.8	7.9	22.1	7.9	19.7
Age of householder:										
15 to 24 years old	940	580	304	21	264	29.8	25.1	49.3	19.9	32.3
25 to 34 years old	2,093	1,352	618	55	638	15.8	13.0	33.3	8.7	23.1
35 to 44 years old	1,802	1,226	432	71	584	10.2	8.8	18.7	7.8	20.3
45 to 54 years old	1,226	846	301	46	299	6.8	5.8	14.2	5.8	15.2
55 to 64 years old	805	526	210	36	148	6.1	4.7	16.0	7.1	13.7
65 years old and over	717	495	166	31	101	5.7	4.5	16.6	8.6	12.2
Region:										
Northeast.	1,272	847	332	70	353	9.1	7.4	20.7	9.8	24.3
Midwest.	1,464	959	426	31	166	8.4	6.4	25.5	7.3	19.0
South	3,285	1,987	1,145	59	750	11.3	8.7	22.4	8.7	19.6
West.	1,601	1,253	142	101	775	9.2	8.8	16.4	6.8	18.3
Type of family:										
Married couple	2,849	2,265	295	175	926	4.9	4.5	6.8	6.6	13.4
Male householder, no spouse present	4,078	2,330	1,544	69	968	28.3	24.7	37.3	16.1	38.4
Female householder, no spouse present	696	451	205	17	151	13.6	11.6	25.7	7.6	15.3

[1] Includes other races not shown separately.　　[2] Hispanic persons may be any race.

Source: U.S. Census Bureau, *Current Population Reports*, P60-235 (published August 2008). See also <http://www.census.gov/hhes/www/macro/032008/pov/toc.htm>.

Table 701. **Top Wealth Holders With Gross Assets of $1.5 Million or More— Debts, Mortgages, and Net Worth: 2004**

[2,728 represents 2,728,000. Net worth is defined as assets minus liabilities. Figures are estimates based on a sample of federal estate tax returns (Form 706). Based on the estate multiplier technique; for more information on this methodology, see source]

Sex and net worth	Total assets		Debts and mortgages		Net worth	
	Number of top wealth holders (1,000)	Amount [1] (mil. dol.)	Number of top wealth holders (1,000)	Amount (mil. dol.)	Number of top wealth holders (1,000)	Amount (mil. dol.)
Both sexes, total	2,728	11,076,759	2,099	850,622	2,728	10,201,246
Size of net worth:						
Under $1.5 million [2].	531	736,039	468	231,035	531	480,113
$1.5 million under $2.0 million	746	1,386,077	544	98,187	746	1,287,890
$2.0 million under $3.5 million	846	2,316,701	614	147,370	846	2,169,331
$3.5 million under $5.0 million	247	1,082,889	192	58,950	247	1,023,939
$5.0 million under $10.0 million.	231	1,668,002	176	104,811	231	1,563,191
$10.0 million under $20.0 million.	79	1,155,326	64	69,849	79	1,085,477
$20.0 million or more	47	2,731,726	40	140,421	47	2,591,305
Males, total	1,555	6,471,540	1,208	583,805	1,555	5,862,844
Size of net worth:						
Under $1.5 million [2].	389	528,017	339	184,673	389	318,454
$1.5 million under $2.0 million	359	675,321	258	54,149	359	621,172
$2.0 million under $3.5 million	465	1,289,522	346	96,654	465	1,192,868
$3.5 million under $5.0 million	131	578,304	102	37,496	131	540,808
$5.0 million under $10.0 million.	135	989,077	100	74,003	135	915,074
$10.0 million under $20.0 million.	47	679,613	38	41,466	47	638,146
$20.0 million or more	30	1,731,686	25	95,364	30	1,636,322
Females, total	1,173	4,605,219	891	266,817	1,173	4,338,402
Size of net worth:						
Under $1.5 million [2].	143	208,021	129	46,362	143	161,659
$1.5 million under $2.0 million	387	710,757	286	44,038	387	666,719
$2.0 million under $3.5 million	380	1,027,179	268	50,716	380	976,463
$3.5 million under $5.0 million	116	504,585	89	21,454	116	483,131
$5.0 million under $10.0 million.	96	678,924	77	30,808	96	648,116
$10.0 million under $20.0 million.	33	475,713	27	28,382	33	447,331
$20.0 million or more	18	1,000,040	15	45,057	18	954,983

[1] Includes other types of assets not shown separately.　　[2] Includes individuals with zero net worth.

Source: U.S. Internal Revenue Service, Statistics of Income Division, "SOI Data Tables" (published July 2008); <http://www.irs.gov/taxstats/indtaxstats/article/0,,id=96426,00.html>.

Income, Expenditures, Poverty, and Wealth　**459**

Table 702. **Top Wealth Holders With Gross Assets of $1.5 Million or More by Type of Property, Sex, and Size of Net Worth: 2004**

[2,728 represents 2,728,000. Net worth is defined as assets minus liabilities. Figures are estimates based on a sample of federal estate tax returns (Form 706). Based on the estate multiplier technique; for more information on this methodology, see source]

Sex and net worth	Number of top wealth holders (1,000)	Assets (mil. dol.)				
		Total [1]	Personal residences	Other real estate	Closely held stock	Publicly traded stock
Both sexes, total	**2,728**	**11,076,759**	**1,185,941**	**1,402,029**	**1,127,194**	**2,247,269**
Size of net worth:						
Under $1.5 million [2]	531	736,039	176,105	134,674	42,431	63,062
$1.5 million under $2.0 million	746	1,386,077	229,369	206,626	69,066	219,818
$2.0 million under $3.5 million	846	2,316,701	342,206	329,893	141,272	415,249
$3.5 million under $5.0 million	247	1,082,889	127,444	152,634	95,958	209,459
$5.0 million under $10.0 million	231	1,668,002	148,543	230,146	165,781	373,575
$10.0 million under $20.0 million	79	1,155,326	76,472	137,770	136,144	246,824
$20.0 million or more	47	2,731,726	85,802	210,286	476,542	719,282
Males, total	**1,555**	**6,471,540**	**597,971**	**828,055**	**833,929**	**1,140,665**
Size of net worth:						
Under $1.5 million [2]	389	528,017	117,554	96,796	36,177	42,494
$1.5 million under $2.0 million	359	675,321	97,605	105,224	44,376	94,788
$2.0 million under $3.5 million	465	1,289,522	163,984	179,481	102,116	199,844
$3.5 million under $5.0 million	131	578,304	60,123	80,919	63,006	95,417
$5.0 million under $10.0 million	135	989,077	68,653	151,731	110,961	200,003
$10.0 million under $20.0 million	47	679,613	38,710	75,459	97,601	135,157
$20.0 million or more	30	1,731,686	51,342	138,446	379,692	372,962
Females, total	**1,173**	**4,605,219**	**587,970**	**573,974**	**293,264**	**1,106,604**
Size of net worth:						
Under $1.5 million [2]	143	208,021	58,550	37,879	6,255	20,568
$1.5 million under $2.0 million	387	710,757	131,764	101,402	24,690	125,030
$2.0 million under $3.5 million	380	1,027,179	178,222	150,412	39,155	215,405
$3.5 million under $5.0 million	116	504,585	67,321	71,714	32,953	114,042
$5.0 million under $10.0 million	96	678,924	79,890	78,416	54,820	173,572
$10.0 million under $20.0 million	33	475,713	37,762	62,312	38,543	111,667
$20.0 million or more	18	1,000,040	34,461	71,840	96,849	346,320

[1] Includes other types of assets not shown separately. [2] Includes individuals with zero net worth.

Source: U.S. Internal Revenue Service, Statistics of Income Division, "SOI Data Tables" (published July 2008); <http://www.irs.gov/taxstats/indtaxstats/article/0,,id=96426,00.html>.

Table 703. **Top Wealth Holders With Net Worth of $1.5 Million or More—Number and Net Worth by State: 2004**

[2,196 represents 2,196,000. Estimates based on a sample of federal estate tax returns (Form 706). Estimates of wealth by state can be subject to significant year-to-year fluctuations and this is especially true for individuals at the extreme tail of the net worth distribution and for states with relatively small decedent populations. Based on the estate mulitiplier technique; for more information on this methodology, see source]

State	Number of top wealth holders (1,000)	Net worth (mil. dol.)	State	Number of top wealth holders (1,000)	Net worth (mil. dol.)
Total	**2,196**	**9,721,133**	Montana	7	23,966
Alabama	18	79,123	Nebraska	13	83,265
Alaska	1	4,776	Nevada	15	80,768
Arizona	36	139,861	New Hampshire	7	27,342
Arkansas	11	94,704	New Jersey	79	324,712
California	428	1,793,642	New Mexico	9	28,107
Colorado	32	163,324	New York	168	942,812
Connecticut	47	197,801	North Carolina	59	223,408
Delaware	8	30,923	North Dakota	1	3,988
District of Columbia	7	27,850	Ohio	61	228,532
Florida	199	904,014	Oklahoma	17	58,554
Georgia	56	270,677	Oregon	15	61,328
Hawaii	7	22,552	Pennsylvania	86	399,312
Idaho	5	23,982	Rhode Island	8	30,782
Illinois	101	476,354	South Carolina	14	67,856
Indiana	32	112,272	South Dakota	6	18,850
Iowa	18	55,332	Tennessee	25	100,778
Kansas	21	65,084	Texas	108	492,663
Kentucky	18	65,404	Utah	8	52,674
Louisiana	22	92,315	Vermont	4	20,584
Maine	8	35,173	Virginia	59	223,984
Maryland	50	191,279	Washington	50	180,008
Massachusetts	83	335,482	West Virginia	12	28,415
Michigan	47	261,085	Wisconsin	26	127,515
Minnesota	33	135,682	Wyoming	5	106,698
Mississippi	8	61,786			
Missouri	33	115,716	Other areas [1]	5	28,042

[1] Includes U.S. territories and possessions.

Source: U.S. Internal Revenue Service, Statistics of Income Division, "SOI Data Tables" (published July 2008); <http://www.irs.gov/taxstats/indtaxstats/article/0,,id=96426,00.html>.

Table 704. **Nonfinancial Assets Held by Families by Type of Asset: 2007**

[221.5 represents $221,500. Families include one-person units and, as used in this table, are comparable to the U.S. Census Bureau's household concept. For definition of family, see text, Section 1. Based on Survey of Consumer Finance; see Appendix III. For data on financial assets, see Table 1133. For definition of median, see Guide to Tabular Presentation]

Family characteristic	Any financial or non-financial asset	Any non-financial asset	Vehicles	Primary residence	Other residential property	Equity in nonresidential property	Business equity	Other
PERCENT OF FAMILIES HOLDING ASSET								
All families, total	97.7	92.0	87.0	68.6	13.7	8.1	13.6	7.2
Age of family head:								
Under 35 years old	97.1	88.2	85.4	40.7	5.6	3.2	8.0	5.9
35 to 44 years old.	96.9	91.3	87.5	66.1	12.0	7.5	18.2	5.5
45 to 54 years old.	97.6	95.0	90.3	77.3	15.7	9.5	17.2	8.7
55 to 64 years old.	99.1	95.6	92.2	81.0	20.9	11.5	18.1	8.5
65 to 74 years old.	98.4	94.5	90.6	85.5	18.9	12.3	11.2	9.1
75 years old and over	98.1	87.3	71.5	77.0	13.4	6.8	4.5	5.8
Race or ethnicity of respondent:								
White non-Hispanic	98.9	94.6	89.6	75.6	15.3	9.0	15.8	8.4
Non White or Hispanic	94.9	85.8	80.9	51.9	10.0	5.9	8.2	4.3
Tenure:								
Owner-occupied	100.0	100.0	93.8	100.0	17.5	10.8	17.5	8.0
Renter-occupied or other	92.8	74.5	72.3	(B)	5.6	2.1	5.0	5.3
MEDIAN VALUE [1] ($1,000)								
All families, total	221.5	177.4	15.5	200.0	146.0	75.0	92.2	14.0
Age of family head:								
Under 35 years old	38.8	30.9	13.3	175.0	85.0	50.0	35.0	8.0
35 to 44 years old.	222.3	182.6	17.4	205.0	150.0	50.0	59.0	10.0
45 to 54 years old.	306.0	224.9	18.7	230.0	150.0	80.0	76.8	15.0
55 to 64 years old.	347.0	233.1	17.4	210.0	157.0	90.0	100.0	20.0
65 to 74 years old.	303.3	212.2	14.6	200.0	150.0	75.0	300.0	20.0
75 years old and over	219.3	157.1	9.4	150.0	100.0	110.0	225.0	25.0
Race or ethnicity of respondent:								
White non-Hispanic	271.0	203.8	17.1	200.0	136.5	75.0	100.0	15.0
Non White or Hispanic	89.2	102.0	12.0	180.0	175.0	62.7	50.0	8.0
Tenure:								
Owner occupied	344.2	253.5	18.4	200.0	150.0	80.0	100.0	20.0
Renter occupied or other	13.6	10.1	8.6	(B)	85.0	38.0	33.0	5.4

B Base too small to meet statistical standards for reliability of derived figure.   [1] Median value of asset for families holding such assets.

Source: Board of Governors of the Federal Reserve System, "2007 Survey of Consumer Finances" (published 7 May 2009); <http://www.federalreserve.gov/pubs/oss/oss2/2007/scf2007home.html>.

Table 705. **Family Net Worth—Mean and Median Net Worth in Constant (2007) Dollars by Selected Family Characteristics: 1998 to 2007**

[Net worth in thousands of constant (2007) dollars (359.7 represents $359,700). Constant dollar figures are based on consumer price index for all urban consumers published by U.S. Bureau of Labor Statistics. Families include one-person units and as used in this table are comparable to the U.S. Census Bureau's, household concept. Based on Survey of Consumer Finance; see Appendix III. For definition of mean and median, see Guide to Tabular Presentation]

Family characteristic	1998 Mean	1998 Median	2001 Mean	2001 Median	2004 Mean	2004 Median	2007 Mean	2007 Median
All families.	359.7	91.3	464.4	101.2	492.3	102.2	556.3	120.3
Age of family head:								
Under 35 years old.	81.3	11.6	106.1	13.7	80.7	15.6	106.0	11.8
35 to 44 years old	249.9	80.8	303.7	90.7	328.6	76.2	325.6	86.6
45 to 54 years old	461.5	134.5	568.4	155.4	596.1	158.9	661.2	182.5
55 to 64 years old	677.6	162.8	856.0	216.8	926.7	273.1	935.8	253.7
65 to 74 years old	594.2	186.5	793.5	207.9	758.8	208.8	1,015.2	239.4
75 years old and over.	395.7	159.9	548.6	181.6	580.0	179.1	638.2	213.5
Race or ethnicity of respondent:								
White non-Hispanic	429.5	121.9	571.2	143.0	617.0	154.5	692.2	170.4
Non-White or Hispanic	128.0	21.2	137.4	21.0	168.2	27.2	228.5	27.8
Tenure:								
Owner occupied	514.7	168.2	655.5	201.8	686.3	202.6	778.2	234.2
Renter occupied or other. . . .	55.3	5.4	64.4	5.6	59.4	4.4	70.6	5.1

Source: Board of Governors of the Federal Reserve System, "2007 Survey of Consumer Finances" (published 7 May 2009); <http://www.federalreserve.gov/pubs/oss/oss2/2007/scf2007home.html>.

U.S. Census Bureau, Statistical Abstract of the United States: 2010

Table 706. **Household and Nonprofit Organization Sector Balance Sheet: 1990 to 2008**

[In billions of dollars (23,951 represents $23,951,000,000,000). **As of December 31.** For details of financial assets and liabilities, see Table 1132]

Item	1990	1995	2000	2004	2005	2006	2007	2008
Assets	**23,951**	**32,753**	**49,419**	**62,910**	**70,286**	**75,731**	**77,019**	**65,719**
Tangible assets [1]	9,355	11,243	16,237	23,969	27,391	28,360	27,265	24,905
Real estate	7,381	8,767	13,078	20,205	23,451	24,252	22,993	20,512
Households [2,3]	6,580	7,984	11,841	18,619	21,381	21,887	20,488	18,335
Consumer durable goods [4]	1,899	2,371	3,015	3,565	3,726	3,877	4,025	4,131
Financial assets [1]	14,596	21,510	33,182	38,940	42,895	47,371	49,754	40,814
Deposits [1]	3,326	3,357	4,377	5,743	6,154	6,779	7,330	7,685
Time and savings deposits	2,490	2,300	3,034	4,411	4,888	5,363	5,804	5,891
Money market fund shares	391	472	960	904	949	1,114	1,347	1,578
Credit market instruments [1]	1,748	2,242	2,481	3,102	3,452	3,626	3,942	3,876
Agency and GSE-backed securities [5]	119	223	609	405	501	434	740	920
Municipal securities	648	533	531	742	821	874	907	960
Corporate and foreign bonds	238	467	554	1,145	1,304	1,564	1,842	1,601
Corporate equities [2]	1,961	4,434	8,147	7,496	8,004	9,199	9,158	5,502
Mutual fund shares [6]	512	1,253	2,704	3,417	3,839	4,410	4,873	3,254
Security credit	62	128	412	578	575	656	866	743
Life insurance reserves	392	566	819	1,060	1,083	1,164	1,202	1,156
Pension fund reserves	3,308	5,715	9,166	10,633	11,369	12,613	13,247	10,280
Equity in noncorporate business [7]	3,033	3,487	4,695	6,369	7,828	8,294	8,436	7,538
Liabilities [1]	**3,720**	**5,054**	**7,400**	**11,036**	**12,188**	**13,431**	**14,329**	**14,242**
Credit market instruments [1]	3,598	4,857	7,011	10,576	11,747	12,916	13,765	13,821
Home mortgages [8]	2,506	3,334	4,821	7,839	8,879	9,843	10,495	10,454
Consumer credit	824	1,168	1,741	2,219	2,314	2,418	2,552	2,596
Net worth	**20,232**	**27,699**	**42,019**	**51,874**	**58,098**	**62,300**	**62,690**	**51,477**
Replacement cost value of structures:								
Residential [1]	4,624	6,105	8,468	11,998	13,431	14,387	14,593	13,926
Households	4,367	5,817	8,106	11,545	12,942	13,878	14,085	13,447
Nonresidential (nonprofits)	472	591	813	1,062	1,179	1,285	1,359	1,479
Owners' equity in household real estate	4,075	4,650	7,020	10,781	12,501	12,044	9,993	7,881
Owners' equity as percentage of household real estate	61.9	58.2	59.3	57.9	58.5	55.0	48.8	43.0

[1] Includes types of assets and/or liabilities not shown separately. [2] At market value. [3] Includes all types of owner-occupied housing including farm houses and mobile homes, as well as second homes that are not rented, vacant homes for sale, and vacant land. [4] At replacement (current) cost. [5] GSE = Government-sponsored enterprises. [6] Value based on the market values of equities held and the book value of other assets held by mutual funds. [7] Net worth of noncorporate business and owners equity in farm business and unincorporated security brokers and dealers. [8] Includes loans made under home equity lines of credit and home equity loans secured by junior liens.

Source: Board of Governors of the Federal Reserve System, "Federal Reserve Statistical Release, Z.1, Flow of Funds Accounts of the United States" (published 12 March 2009); <http://www.federalreserve.gov/releases/z1/20090312/>.

Table 707. **Net Stock of Fixed Reproducible Tangible Wealth in Current and Real (2000) Dollars: 1990 to 2007**

[In billions of dollars (18,111 represents $18,111,000,000,000). **As of December 31.** For explanation of chained dollars, see text, this section]

Item	1990	1995	2000	2003	2004	2005	2006	2007
CURRENT DOLLARS								
Net stock, total	**18,111**	**22,670**	**29,917**	**34,805**	**38,202**	**41,894**	**45,053**	**46,618**
Fixed assets	16,212	20,299	26,902	31,424	34,637	38,168	41,175	42,592
Private	12,611	15,794	21,190	24,917	27,423	30,224	32,429	33,381
Nonresidential	6,500	7,954	10,514	11,692	12,620	13,726	14,788	15,512
Equipment and software	2,469	3,067	4,077	4,381	4,549	4,760	5,044	5,286
Structures	4,031	4,887	6,437	7,311	8,071	8,966	9,744	10,226
Residential	6,111	7,840	10,676	13,225	14,803	16,498	17,641	17,869
Government	3,601	4,505	5,713	6,508	7,214	7,944	8,746	9,211
Nonresidential	3,452	4,317	5,481	6,228	6,918	7,609	8,400	8,887
Equipment and software	551	675	703	738	784	818	864	897
Structures	2,900	3,642	4,778	5,490	6,134	6,792	7,535	7,990
Residential	149	188	232	280	296	335	346	324
Federal	1,079	1,291	1,425	1,499	1,591	1,723	1,831	1,701
Defense	735	865	896	928	983	1,059	1,123	1,054
State and local	2,522	3,213	4,288	5,009	5,623	6,221	6,915	7,510
Consumer durable goods	1,899	2,371	3,015	3,380	3,565	3,726	3,877	4,026
Motor vehicles and parts	670	842	1,092	1,256	1,326	1,372	1,381	1,402
Furniture and household equipment	814	1,011	1,260	1,366	1,439	1,506	1,583	1,647
Other	415	518	662	759	800	848	913	977
CHAINED (2000) DOLLARS								
Net stock, total	**22,580**	**25,156**	**29,528**	**32,004**	**32,865**	**33,709**	**34,623**	**35,443**
Fixed assets	20,726	22,939	26,498	28,368	29,025	29,680	30,411	31,049
Private	16,029	17,804	20,880	22,384	22,915	23,459	24,071	24,587
Nonresidential	7,809	8,638	10,392	10,986	11,147	11,333	11,584	11,849
Equipment and software	2,532	2,972	4,091	4,422	4,523	4,663	4,841	4,991
Structures	5,347	5,702	6,302	6,568	6,632	6,690	6,784	6,910
Residential	8,223	9,174	10,488	11,401	11,763	12,114	12,469	12,722
Government	4,700	5,137	5,618	5,984	6,110	6,221	6,339	6,462
Nonresidential	4,507	4,926	5,390	5,747	5,869	5,978	6,095	6,216
Equipment and software	631	686	706	739	757	779	806	830
Structures	3,872	4,237	4,684	5,007	5,112	5,199	5,292	5,391
Residential	201	220	227	238	241	243	245	247
Consumer durable goods	1,903	2,242	3,030	3,662	3,886	4,106	4,324	4,548

Source: U.S. Bureau of Economic Analysis, *Survey of Current Business* (published 21 August 2008). See also <http://www.bea.gov /national/FA2004/SelectTable.asp>.

462 Income, Expenditures, Poverty, and Wealth

Section 14
Prices

This section presents indexes of producer and consumer prices, actual prices for selected commodities, and energy prices. The primary sources of these data are monthly publications of the U.S. Department of Labor, Bureau of Labor Statistics (BLS), which include *Monthly Labor Review, Consumer Price Index, Detailed Report, Producer Price Indexes,* and *U.S. Import and Export Price Indexes.* The U.S. Department of Commerce, Bureau of Economic Analysis is the source for gross domestic product measures. Cost of living data for many urban and metropolitan areas are provided by The Council for Community and Economic Research, a private organization in Arlington, VA. Table 713 on housing price indexes appears in this edition from the Office of Federal Housing Enterprise Oversight, *Housing Price Index.* Other commodity, housing, and energy prices may be found in the Energy and Utilities, Natural Resources, and Construction and Housing sections.

Consumer price indexes (CPI)—The CPI is a measure of the average change in prices over time in a "market basket" of goods and services purchased either by urban wage earners and clerical workers or by all urban consumers. In 1919, BLS began to publish complete indexes at semiannual intervals, using a weighting structure based on data collected in the expenditure survey of wage-earner and clerical-worker families in 1917–19 (BLS Bulletin 357, 1924). The first major revision of the CPI occurred in 1940, with subsequent revisions in 1953, 1964, 1978, 1987, and 1998.

Beginning with the release of data for January 1988 in February 1988, most consumer price indexes shifted to a new reference base year. All indexes previously expressed on a base of 1967 = 100, or any other base through December 1981, have been rebased to 1982–84 = 100. The expenditure weights are based upon data tabulated from the Consumer Expenditure Surveys.

BLS publishes CPIs for two population groups: (1) a CPI for all urban consumers (CPI-U), which covers approximately 80 percent of the total population; and (2) a CPI for urban wage earners and clerical workers (CPI-W), which covers 32 percent of the total population. The CPI-U includes, in addition to wage earners and clerical workers, groups which historically have been excluded from CPI coverage, such as professional, managerial, and technical workers; the self-employed; short-term workers; the unemployed; and retirees and others not in the labor force.

The current CPI is based on prices of food, clothing, shelter, fuels, transportation fares, charges for doctors' and dentists' services, drugs, etc. purchased for day-to-day living. Prices are collected in 87 areas across the country from over 50,000 housing units and 23,000 establishments. Area selection was based on the 1990 census. All taxes directly associated with the purchase and use of items are included in the index. Prices of food, fuels, and a few other items are obtained every month in all 87 locations. Prices of most other commodities and services are collected monthly in the three largest geographic areas and every other month in other areas.

In calculating the index, each item is assigned a weight to account for its relative importance in consumers' budgets. Price changes for the various items in each location are then averaged. Local data are then combined to obtain a U.S. city average. Separate indexes are also published for regions, area size-classes, cross-classifications of regions and size-classes, and for 26 local areas, usually consisting of the Metropolitan Statistical Area (MSA); see Appendix II. Area definitions are those established by the Office of Management and Budget in 1983. Definitions do not include revisions made since 1992. Area indexes do not measure differences in the level of prices among cities; they only measure the average

U.S. Census Bureau, Statistical Abstract of the United States: 2010

change in prices for each area since the base period. For further detail regarding the CPI, see the BLS *Handbook of Methods,* Bulletin 2490 (June 2008), Chapter 17; the *Consumer Price Index,* and the CPI home page: <http://www.bls.gov/cpi/>. In January 1983, the method of measuring homeownership costs in the CPI-U was changed to a rental equivalence approach. This treatment calculates homeowner costs of shelter based on the implicit rent owners would pay to rent the homes they own. The rental equivalence approach was introduced into the CPI-W in 1985. The CPI-U was used to prepare the consumer price tables in this section.

Producer price index (PPI)—This index, dating from 1890, is the oldest continuous statistical series published by BLS. It is designed to measure average changes in prices received by domestic producers of all commodities, at various stages of processing.

The index has undergone several revisions (see *Monthly Labor Review,* February 1962, April 1978, and August 1988). It is now based on approximately 10,000 individual products and groups of products along with about 100,000 quotations per month. Indexes for the net output of manufacturing and mining industries have been added in recent years. Prices used in constructing the index are collected from sellers and generally apply to the first significant large-volume commercial transaction for each commodity—i.e., the manufacturer's or other producer's selling price or the selling price on an organized exchange or at a central market.

The weights used in the index represent the total net selling value of commodities produced or processed in this country. Values are f.o.b. (free on board) production point and are exclusive of excise taxes. Effective with the release of data for January 1988, many important producer price indexes were changed to a new reference base year, 1982 = 100, from 1967 = 100. The reference year of the PPI shipment weights has been taken primarily from the 2002 Census of Manufactures. For further detail regarding the PPI, see the BLS *Handbook of Methods,* Bulletin 2490 (June 2008), Chapter 14. The PPI Web page is <http://www.bls.gov/ppi/>.

BEA price indexes—Chain-weighted price indexes, produced by the Bureau of Economic Analysis (BEA), are weighted averages of the detailed price indexes used in the deflation of the goods and services that make up the gross domestic product (GDP) and its major components. Growth rates are constructed for years and quarters using quantity weights for the current and preceding year or quarter; these growth rates are used to move the index for the preceding period forward a year or quarter at a time. All chain-weighted price indexes are expressed in terms of the reference year value 2000 = 100.

Personal consumption expenditures (PCE) price and quantity indexes are based on market transactions for which there are corresponding price measures. The price index provides a measure of the prices paid by persons for domestic purchases of goods and services, which may be a useful measure of consumer prices for some analytical purposes. PCEs are defined as market value of spending by individuals and not-for-profit institutions on all goods and services. Personal consumption expenditures also include the value of certain imputed goods and services—such as the rental value of owner-occupied homes and compensation paid in kind—such as employer-paid health and life insurance premiums. More information on this index may be found at <http://www.bea.gov/bea/mp_National.htm>.

Measures of inflation—Inflation is defined as a time of generally rising prices for goods and factors of production. The BLS samples prices of items in a representative market basket and publishes the result as the CPI. The media invariably announce the inflation rate as the percent change in the CPI from month to month. A much more meaningful indicator of inflation is the percent change from the same month of the prior year. The PPI measures prices at the producer level only. The PPI shows the same general pattern of inflation as does the CPI but is more volatile. The PPI can be often tends to foreshadow trends that later occur in the CPI.

Other measures of inflation include the gross domestic purchases chain-weighted price index, the index of industrial materials prices; the Futures Price and Spot Market prices from the Commodity Research Bureau; the Employment Cost Index, the Hourly Compensation Index, or the Unit Labor Cost Index found in Section 12, Labor Force, Employment, and Earnings, as a measure of the change in cost of the labor factor of production; and changes in long-term interest rates that are often used to measure changes in the cost of the capital factor of production.

International price indexes—The BLS International Price Program produces export and import price indexes for non-military goods traded between the United States and the rest of the world.

The export price index provides a measure of price change for all products sold by U.S. residents to foreign buyers. The

import price index provides a measure of price change for goods purchased from other countries by U.S. residents. The reference period for the indexes is 2000 = 100, unless otherwise indicated. The product universe for both the import and export indexes includes raw materials, agricultural products, semifinished manufactures, and finished manufactures, including both capital and consumer goods. Price data for these items are collected primarily by mail questionnaire. In nearly all cases, the data are collected directly from the exporter or importer, although in a few cases, prices are obtained from other sources.

To the extent possible, the data gathered refer to prices at the U.S. border for exports and at either the foreign border or the U.S. border for imports. For nearly all products, the prices refer to transactions completed during the first week of the month. Survey respondents are asked to indicate all discounts, allowances, and rebates applicable to the reported prices, so that the price used in the calculation of the indexes is the actual price for which the product was bought or sold.

Table 708. Purchasing Power of the Dollar: 1950 to 2008

[Indexes: PPI, 1982 = $1.00; CPI, 1982–84 = $1.00. Producer prices prior to 1961, and consumer prices prior to 1964, exclude Alaska and Hawaii. Producer prices based on finished goods index. Obtained by dividing the average price index for the 1982 = 100, PPI; 1982–84 = 100, CPI base periods (100.0) by the price index for a given period and expressing the result in dollars and cents. Annual figures are based on average of monthly data]

Year	Annual average as measured by—		Year	Annual average as measured by—	
	Producer prices	Consumer prices		Producer prices	Consumer prices
1950	3.546	4.151			
1951	3.247	3.846	1980	1.136	1.215
1952	3.268	3.765	1981	1.041	1.098
1953	3.300	3.735	1982	1.000	1.035
1954	3.289	3.717	1983	0.984	1.003
			1984	0.964	0.961
1955	3.279	3.732			
1956	3.195	3.678	1985	0.955	0.928
1957	3.077	3.549	1986	0.969	0.913
1958	3.012	3.457	1987	0.949	0.880
1959	3.021	3.427	1988	0.926	0.846
			1989	0.880	0.807
1960	2.994	3.373			
1961	2.994	3.340	1990	0.839	0.766
1962	2.985	3.304	1991	0.822	0.734
1963	2.994	3.265	1992	0.812	0.713
1964	2.985	3.220	1993	0.802	0.692
			1994	0.797	0.675
1965	2.933	3.166			
1966	2.841	3.080	1995	0.782	0.656
1967	2.809	2.993	1996	0.762	0.638
1968	2.732	2.873	1997	0.759	0.623
1969	2.632	2.726	1998	0.765	0.613
			1999	0.752	0.600
1970	2.545	2.574			
1971	2.469	2.466	2000	0.725	0.581
1972	2.392	2.391	2001	0.711	0.565
1973	2.193	2.251	2002	0.720	0.556
1974	1.901	2.029	2003	0.698	0.543
			2004	0.673	0.529
1975	1.718	1.859			
1976	1.645	1.757	2005	0.642	0.512
1977	1.546	1.649	2006	0.623	0.496
1978	1.433	1.532	2007 [1]	0.600	0.482
1979	1.289	1.380	2008 [1]	0.565	0.464

[1] PPI data are preliminary.

Source: U.S. Bureau of Labor Statistics. *CPI Detailed Report*, monthly, and at <http://www.bls.gov/cpi/cpi_dr.htm> See also *Monthly Labor Review* at <http://www.bls.gov/opub/mlr/welcome.htm> and *Producer Price Indexes*, monthly and annual.

Table 709. **Consumer Price Indexes (CPI-U) by Major Groups: 1990 to 2008**

[1982-84 = 100, except as indicated. Represents annual averages of monthly figures. Reflects buying patterns of all urban consumers. Minus sign (−) indicates decrease. See text, this section]

Year	All items	Com- mod- ities	Ser- vices	Food	Energy	All items less food and energy	Food and bever- ages	Hous- ing	Apparel	Trans- por- tation	Med- ical care	Education and commun- ication [1]
1990	130.7	122.8	139.2	132.4	102.1	135.5	132.1	128.5	124.1	120.5	162.8	(NA)
1994	148.2	133.8	163.1	144.3	104.6	156.5	144.9	144.8	133.4	134.3	211.0	88.8
1995	152.4	136.4	168.7	148.4	105.2	161.2	148.9	148.5	132.0	139.1	220.5	92.2
1996	156.9	139.9	174.1	153.3	110.1	165.6	153.7	152.8	131.7	143.0	228.2	95.3
1997	160.5	141.8	179.4	157.3	111.5	169.5	157.7	156.8	132.9	144.3	234.6	98.4
1998	163.0	141.9	184.2	160.7	102.9	173.4	161.1	160.4	133.0	141.6	242.1	100.3
1999	166.6	144.4	188.8	164.1	106.6	177.0	164.6	163.9	131.3	144.4	250.6	101.2
2000	172.2	149.2	195.3	167.8	124.6	181.3	168.4	169.6	129.6	153.3	260.8	102.5
2001	177.1	150.7	203.4	173.1	129.3	186.1	173.6	176.4	127.3	154.3	272.8	105.2
2002	179.9	149.7	209.8	176.2	121.7	190.5	176.8	180.3	124.0	152.9	285.6	107.9
2003	184.0	151.2	216.5	180.0	136.5	193.2	180.5	184.8	120.9	157.6	297.1	109.8
2004	188.9	154.7	222.8	186.2	151.4	196.6	186.6	189.5	120.4	163.1	310.1	111.6
2005	195.3	160.2	230.1	190.7	177.1	200.9	191.2	195.7	119.5	173.9	323.2	113.7
2006	201.6	164.0	238.9	195.2	196.9	205.9	195.7	203.2	119.5	180.9	336.2	116.8
2007	207.3	167.5	246.8	202.9	207.7	210.7	203.3	209.6	119.0	184.7	351.1	119.6
2008	215.3	174.8	255.5	214.1	236.7	215.6	214.2	216.3	118.9	195.5	364.1	123.6
PERCENT CHANGE [2]												
1990	5.4	5.2	5.5	5.8	8.3	5.0	5.8	4.5	4.6	5.6	9.0	(NA)
1994	2.6	1.7	3.3	2.4	0.4	2.8	2.3	2.5	−0.2	3.0	4.8	3.9
1995	2.8	1.9	3.4	2.8	0.6	3.0	2.8	2.6	−1.0	3.6	4.5	3.8
1996	3.0	2.6	3.2	3.3	4.7	2.7	3.2	2.9	−0.2	2.8	3.5	3.4
1997	2.3	1.4	3.0	2.6	1.3	2.4	2.6	2.6	0.9	0.9	2.8	3.3
1998	1.6	0.1	2.7	2.2	−7.7	2.3	2.2	2.3	0.1	−1.9	3.2	1.9
1999	2.2	1.8	2.5	2.1	3.6	2.1	2.2	2.2	−1.3	2.0	3.5	0.9
2000	3.4	3.3	3.4	2.3	16.9	2.4	2.3	3.5	−1.3	6.2	4.1	1.3
2001	2.8	1.0	4.1	3.2	3.8	2.6	3.1	4.0	−1.8	0.7	4.6	2.6
2002	1.6	−0.7	3.1	1.8	−5.9	2.4	1.8	2.2	−2.6	−0.9	4.7	2.6
2003	2.3	1.0	3.2	2.2	12.2	1.4	2.1	2.5	−2.5	3.1	4.0	1.8
2004	2.7	2.3	2.9	3.4	10.9	1.8	3.4	2.5	−0.4	3.5	4.4	1.6
2005	3.4	3.6	3.3	2.4	17.0	2.2	2.5	3.3	−0.7	6.6	4.2	1.9
2006	3.2	2.4	3.8	2.4	11.2	2.5	2.4	3.8	−	4.0	4.0	2.7
2007	2.8	2.1	3.3	4.0	5.5	2.3	3.9	3.1	−0.4	2.1	4.4	2.4
2008	3.8	4.3	3.5	5.5	13.9	2.3	5.4	3.2	−0.1	5.9	3.7	3.4

− Represents zero. NA Not available. [1] Dec. 1997 = 100. [2] Change from immediate prior year. 1990 change from 1989.
Source: U.S. Bureau of Labor Statistics, *CPI Detailed Report*, monthly, and at <http://www.bls.gov/cpi/cpi_dr.htm>. See also *Monthly Labor Review* at <http://www.bls.gov/opub/mlr/welcome.htm>.

Table 710. **Annual Percent Changes From Prior Year in Consumer Price Indexes (CPI-U)—Selected Areas: 2008**

[Percent changes computed from annual averages of monthly figures published by source. Local area CPI indexes are by-products of the national CPI program. Each local index has a smaller sample size than the national index and is therefore subject to substantially more sampling and other measurement error. As a result, local area indexes show greater volatility than the national index, although their long-term trends are similar. Area definitions are those established by the Office of Management and Budget in 1983. For further detail, see the U.S. Bureau of Labor Statistics Handbook of Methods, Bulletin 2285, Chapter 19, the Consumer Price Index, and Report 736, the CPI: 1987 Revision. Minus sign (−) indicates decrease. See also text, this section and Appendix III]

Area	All items	Food and bever- ages	Food	Hous- ing	Apparel	Trans- porta- tion	Medi- cal care	Fuel and other utilities
U.S. city average	3.8	5.4	5.5	3.2	−0.1	5.9	3.7	9.7
Anchorage, AK MSA	4.6	4.4	4.7	2.5	6.1	10.5	3.7	1.2
Atlanta, GA MSA	3.2	4.9	5.2	2.8	−0.6	6.3	1.5	11.0
Boston, MA MSA	3.5	5.0	4.9	2.2	−2.0	4.7	3.9	16.1
Chicago-Gary, IL-IN CMSA	3.8	5.1	5.1	2.8	−2.8	6.6	4.5	14.0
Cincinnati-Hamilton, OH-KY-IN CMSA	3.9	6.9	7.2	2.1	10.7	5.4	2.9	8.6
Cleveland-Akron-Lorain, OH CMSA	3.6	5.2	5.4	2.2	7.0	5.3	6.3	12.1
Dallas-Fort Worth, TX CMSA	4.4	6.1	6.3	3.9	−0.4	7.0	3.3	9.1
Denver-Boulder-Greely, CO CMSA	3.9	4.8	5.2	2.4	3.4	6.3	7.5	10.5
Detroit-Ann Arbor-Flint, MI CMSA	2.3	3.0	3.2	1.4	3.2	5.6	0.2	8.5
Honolulu, HI MSA	4.3	5.7	5.8	4.3	1.1	4.4	(NA)	32.6
Houston-Galveston-Brazoria, TX CMSA	3.3	6.0	6.2	3.9	−4.7	3.5	2.8	6.4
Kansas City, MO-KS CMSA	3.4	6.3	6.3	3.1	−2.7	6.3	−1.5	12.0
Los Angeles-Anaheim-Riverside, CA CMSA	3.5	4.5	4.6	2.9	1.9	5.1	3.8	4.9
Miami-Fort Lauderdale, FL CMSA	4.6	5.6	5.9	4.3	−2.8	6.4	5.6	4.4
Milwaukee, WI PMSA	4.6	4.8	5.1	3.9	4.3	6.9	4.4	11.6
Minneapolis-St. Paul, MN-WI MSA	3.8	7.2	7.6	3.5	−2.2	4.1	4.8	9.2
New York-Northern New Jersey-Long Island, NY-NJ-CT CMSA	3.9	5.6	5.7	3.6	0.0	6.2	2.3	12.6
Philadelphia-Wilmington-Trenton, PA-NJ-DE-MD CMSA. . .	3.4	3.7	3.8	2.5	−0.1	6.9	3.6	8.0
Pittsburgh, PA MSA	4.9	5.5	5.6	3.3	2.2	7.6	6.7	13.0
Portland, OR MSA	3.3	5.4	5.4	2.6	−2.5	4.8	5.5	2.3
San Diego, CA MSA	3.9	4.6	4.7	3.8	1.7	3.9	(NA)	5.1
San Francisco-Oakland-San Jose, CA CMSA	3.1	4.4	4.3	1.9	−1.7	5.8	3.5	4.2
Seattle-Tacoma, WA CMSA	3.7	5.4	5.6	4.5	−1.4	5.6	1.9	2.2
St. Louis-East St. Louis, MO-IL CMSA	2.8	4.4	4.5	2.0	1.6	3.4	0.4	3.7
Tampa-St. Petersburg-Clearwater, FL MSA	3.2	6.1	6.2	2.4	4.5	4.3	0.6	3.6
Washington-Baltimore, DC-MD-VA-WV CMSA	4.5	4.8	5.1	4.7	0.3	6.7	5.2	17.8

NA Not available.
Source: U.S. Bureau of Labor Statistics, *CPI Detailed Report*, monthly, and at <http://www.bls.gov/cpi/cpi_dr.htm>. See also *Monthly Labor Review* at <http://www.bls.gov/opub/mlr/welcome.htm>.

Table 711. Consumer Price Indexes for All Urban Consumers (CPI-U) for Selected Items and Groups: 2000 to 2008

[1982–84 = 100, except as noted. Annual averages of monthly figures. Minus sign (−) indicates decrease. See headnote, Table 709]

Item	2000	2003	2004	2005	2006	2007	2008	Annual percentage change, 2007–2008
All items	**172.2**	**184.0**	**188.9**	**195.3**	**201.6**	**207.3**	**215.3**	**3.8**
Food and beverages	168.4	180.5	186.6	191.2	195.7	203.3	214.2	5.4
Food	167.8	180.0	186.2	190.7	195.2	202.9	214.1	5.5
Food at home	167.9	179.4	186.2	189.8	193.1	201.2	214.1	6.4
Cereals and bakery products	188.3	202.8	206.0	209.0	212.8	222.1	244.9	10.2
Cereals and cereal products	175.9	185.2	186.2	186.7	187.3	194.7	214.4	10.1
Bakery products	194.1	211.7	216.2	220.5	226.4	236.6	261.0	10.3
Bread [1]	107.4	118.5	121.1	126.2	130.4	140.1	160.6	14.6
Cakes, cupcakes, and cookies	187.9	202.8	206.4	209.8	214.2	221.7	239.9	8.2
Other bakery products	191.5	207.3	211.8	211.4	215.5	220.5	236.5	7.3
Meats, poultry, fish, and eggs	154.5	169.3	181.7	184.7	186.6	195.6	204.7	4.6
Meats, poultry, and fish	155.5	169.7	182.3	186.7	188.2	195.4	203.6	4.2
Meats	150.7	169.0	183.2	187.5	188.8	195.0	201.8	3.5
Beef and veal	148.1	175.1	195.3	200.4	202.1	211.1	220.6	4.5
Uncooked ground beef	125.2	149.2	166.3	175.1	176.3	184.3	196.4	6.6
Uncooked beef steaks [1]	109.1	127.6	144.7	145.1	146.1	151.8	155.3	2.3
Pork	156.5	164.9	174.2	177.7	177.3	180.9	185.0	2.3
Other meats	152.0	166.0	173.4	177.5	180.7	184.8	190.6	3.1
Poultry	159.8	169.1	181.7	185.3	182.0	191.4	200.9	5.0
Chicken [1]	102.5	108.9	118.2	120.6	117.6	124.4	130.7	5.1
Fish and seafood	190.4	190.0	194.3	200.1	209.5	219.1	232.1	5.9
Dairy products	160.7	167.9	180.2	182.4	181.4	194.8	210.4	8.0
Milk [1]	107.8	111.5	125.0	127.0	125.5	140.1	148.5	6.0
Cheese and related products	162.8	169.4	180.8	183.3	180.8	191.5	214.5	12.1
Fruits and vegetables	204.6	225.9	232.7	241.4	252.9	262.6	278.9	6.2
Fresh fruits and vegetables	238.8	265.3	274.7	285.3	300.4	312.1	328.3	5.2
Fresh fruits	258.3	279.1	286.8	297.4	315.2	329.5	345.4	4.8
Fresh vegetables	219.4	250.5	261.2	271.7	284.3	293.5	309.8	5.6
Processed fruits and vegetables [1]	105.6	114.1	115.5	119.3	122.8	127.2	139.3	9.5
Nonalcoholic beverages and beverage materials	137.8	139.8	140.4	144.4	147.4	153.4	160.0	4.3
Juices and nonalcoholic drinks [1]	105.6	108.0	108.5	110.6	113.2	117.9	123.1	4.4
Carbonated drinks	123.4	125.6	127.9	131.9	134.2	140.1	147.0	4.9
Nonfrozen noncarbonated juices and drinks [1]	104.2	106.5	105.7	106.5	109.5	112.9	117.5	4.1
Beverage materials including coffee and tea [1]	97.9	97.4	97.6	102.4	104.1	108.2	112.8	4.2
Other food at home	155.6	162.6	164.9	167.0	169.6	173.3	184.2	6.3
Sugar and sweets	154.0	162.0	163.2	165.2	171.5	176.8	186.6	5.5
Candy and chewing gum [1]	103.8	107.8	108.4	109.5	112.2	116.1	123.2	6.1
Fats and oils	147.4	157.4	167.8	167.7	168.0	172.9	196.8	13.8
Other food	172.2	178.8	179.7	182.5	185.0	188.2	198.1	5.2
Frozen and freeze dried prepared food	148.5	150.6	152.5	153.2	153.7	156.7	163.5	4.3
Snacks	166.3	173.1	173.7	178.5	181.2	184.9	199.8	8.1
Spices, seasonings, condiments, sauces	175.6	185.5	185.3	188.0	190.3	195.5	204.6	4.7
Other miscellaneous food [1]	107.5	110.3	110.4	111.3	113.9	115.1	119.9	4.2
Food away from home	169.0	182.1	187.5	193.4	199.4	206.7	215.8	4.4
Full service meals and snacks [1]	106.8	115.3	118.4	121.9	125.7	130.2	135.4	4.0
Limited service meals and snacks [1]	106.3	114.9	118.8	122.4	126.0	130.6	136.9	4.9
Food at employee sites and schools [1]	104.4	112.4	115.5	118.6	122.6	126.8	131.8	4.0
Other food away from home [1]	109.0	121.3	125.3	131.3	136.6	144.1	150.6	4.6
Alcoholic beverages	174.7	187.2	192.1	195.9	200.7	207.0	214.5	3.6
Alcoholic beverages at home	158.1	166.5	170.2	172.3	174.9	179.1	184.9	3.2
Beer, ale, and other malt beverages at home	156.8	168.5	174.6	176.4	178.1	184.1	190.3	3.4
Wine at home	151.6	153.1	153.8	156.2	159.8	162.9	168.7	3.6
Alcoholic beverages away from home	207.1	228.6	236.6	244.5	254.6	266.0	277.4	4.3
Housing	169.6	184.8	189.5	195.7	203.2	209.6	216.3	3.2
Shelter	193.4	213.1	218.8	224.4	232.1	240.6	246.7	2.5
Rent of primary residence	183.9	205.5	211.0	217.3	225.1	234.7	243.3	3.7
Lodging away from home [1]	117.5	119.3	125.9	130.3	136.0	142.8	143.7	0.6
Other lodging away from home including hotels and motels	252.4	252.2	265.3	274.2	285.6	299.9	301.0	0.4
Owners' equivalent rent of primary residence [2]	198.7	219.9	224.9	230.2	238.2	246.2	252.4	2.5
Tenants' and household insurance [1]	103.7	114.8	116.2	117.6	116.5	117.0	118.8	1.6
Fuels and utilities	137.9	154.5	161.9	179.0	194.7	200.6	220.0	9.7
Household energy	122.8	138.2	144.4	161.6	177.1	181.7	200.8	10.5
Fuel oil and other fuels	129.7	139.5	160.5	208.6	234.9	251.5	334.4	33.0
Fuel oil	130.3	136.6	160.0	216.4	244.6	262.6	365.0	39.0
Propane, kerosene, and firewood [3]	155.5	181.9	202.1	240.6	268.8	286.0	344.2	20.4

See footnotes at end of table.

Prices 467

Table 711. Consumer Price Indexes for All Urban Consumers (CPI-U) for Selected Items and Groups: 2000 to 2008—Con.

[1982-84 = 100, except as noted. Annual averages of monthly figures. Minus sign (–) indicates decrease. See headnote, Table 709]

Item	2000	2003	2004	2005	2006	2007	2008	Annual percentage change, 2007–2008
Gas (piped) and electricity	128.0	145.0	150.6	166.5	182.1	186.3	202.2	8.6
Electricity	128.5	139.5	142.1	150.8	169.2	175.8	187.1	6.4
Utility (piped) gas service	132.0	166.3	180.1	215.4	220.8	217.7	247.8	13.8
Water and sewer and trash collection services [1]	106.5	117.2	124.0	130.3	136.8	143.7	152.1	5.9
Water and sewerage maintenance	227.5	251.7	268.1	283.4	297.2	312.6	331.3	6.0
Garbage and trash collection [4]	269.8	291.9	303.3	314.0	330.1	345.6	364.7	5.5
Household furnishings and operations	128.2	126.1	125.5	126.1	127.0	126.9	127.8	0.7
Window and floor coverings and other linens [1]	100.9	91.5	88.8	87.4	84.2	80.7	78.2	–3.1
Furniture and bedding	134.4	127.7	127.3	125.9	127.0	125.8	124.5	–1.0
Bedroom furniture	138.4	133.9	137.3	142.7	145.4	144.7	143.7	–0.7
Living room, kitchen, and dining room furniture [1]	102.4	97.2	95.9	92.7	92.8	91.6	90.5	–1.3
Appliances [1]	96.3	89.5	85.9	86.9	88.1	89.8	89.9	0.1
Other household equipment and furnishings [1]	98.0	89.3	87.4	85.5	80.4	76.9	75.6	–1.7
Clocks, lamps, and decorator items	111.7	96.2	91.4	88.0	79.6	73.6	69.9	–5.1
Tools, hardware, outdoor equipment, and supplies [1]	97.0	94.0	93.5	94.4	94.6	94.6	93.5	–1.2
Tools, hardware, and supplies [1]	97.3	93.3	94.8	98.1	99.4	99.7	99.0	–0.8
Outdoor equipment and supplies [1]	96.8	94.2	92.6	92.4	92.1	92.0	90.7	–1.4
Housekeeping supplies	153.4	157.5	157.4	159.9	166.6	169.4	176.5	4.2
Household cleaning products [1]	105.1	108.2	107.0	107.9	111.6	112.3	115.9	3.2
Household paper products [1]	113.8	117.2	120.8	125.4	132.0	135.6	146.8	8.3
Miscellaneous household products [1]	104.3	106.1	105.3	106.4	111.0	113.6	116.3	2.4
Household operations	110.5	121.8	125.0	130.3	136.6	140.6	147.5	4.9
Domestic services [1]	109.7	121.3	123.8	128.3	133.1	138.1	142.8	3.4
Gardening and lawncare services [1]	111.4	120.2	122.9	127.9	136.6	140.5	(NA)	(NA)
Apparel	129.6	120.9	120.4	119.5	119.5	119.0	118.9	–0.1
Men's and boys' apparel	129.7	118.0	117.5	116.1	114.1	112.4	113.0	0.6
Men's apparel	133.1	122.1	121.4	121.4	119.8	118.2	118.4	0.2
Men's shirts and sweaters [1]	98.3	85.2	85.3	84.2	84.7	82.5	80.4	–2.5
Women's and girls' apparel	121.5	113.1	113.0	110.8	110.7	110.3	107.5	–2.6
Women's apparel	121.9	113.1	113.3	111.8	112.5	112.1	109.3	–2.5
Women's suits and separates [1]	98.2	88.1	89.8	87.3	88.2	88.9	85.7	–3.6
Women's underwear, nightwear, sportswear, and accessories [1]	101.8	95.9	94.2	95.4	94.4	91.8	90.4	–1.6
Footwear	123.8	119.6	119.3	122.6	123.5	122.4	124.2	1.5
Men's footwear	129.5	120.7	119.7	121.3	123.5	120.9	122.9	1.7
Women's footwear	119.6	118.4	118.4	121.9	122.8	122.5	122.6	0.1
Jewelry and watches [3]	137.0	128.7	129.5	127.6	130.7	137.1	146.5	6.9
Jewelry [3]	141.2	133.2	133.6	131.3	134.8	142.4	153.8	8.0
Transportation	153.3	157.6	163.1	173.9	180.9	184.7	195.5	5.9
Private transportation	149.1	153.6	159.4	170.2	177.0	180.8	191.0	5.7
New and used motor vehicles [1]	100.8	96.5	94.2	95.6	95.6	94.3	93.3	–1.1
New vehicles	142.8	137.9	137.1	137.9	137.6	136.3	134.2	–1.5
Used cars and trucks	155.8	142.9	133.3	139.4	140.0	135.7	134.0	–1.3
Leased cars and trucks [5]	(NA)	96.8	93.6	92.7	93.1	92.6	95.1	2.6
Motor fuel	129.3	135.8	160.4	195.7	221.0	239.1	279.7	17.0
Gasoline (all types)	128.6	135.1	159.7	194.7	219.9	238.0	277.5	16.6
Motor vehicle parts and equipment	101.5	107.8	108.7	111.9	117.3	121.6	128.7	5.9
Motor vehicle maintenance and repair	177.3	195.6	200.2	206.9	215.6	223.0	233.9	4.9
Motor vehicle maintenance and servicing	162.7	179.5	182.8	189.2	195.7	202.1	213.1	5.4
Motor vehicle repair [1]	108.2	119.6	122.7	126.7	132.7	137.4	143.8	4.7
Motor vehicle insurance	256.7	314.4	323.2	329.9	331.8	333.1	341.5	2.5
Motor vehicle fees [1]	107.3	116.5	131.0	134.7	138.8	141.2	145.8	3.3
State and local registration and license [1]	105.1	112.7	131.3	133.2	137.3	138.8	141.9	2.3
Public transportation	209.6	209.3	209.1	217.3	226.6	230.0	250.5	8.9
Airline fare	239.4	231.3	227.2	236.6	247.3	251.7	282.0	12.0
Medical care	260.8	297.1	310.1	323.2	336.2	351.1	364.1	3.7
Medical care commodities	238.1	262.8	269.3	276.0	285.9	290.0	296.0	2.1
Prescription drugs	285.4	326.3	337.1	349.0	363.9	369.2	378.3	2.5
Nonprescription drugs and medical supplies [3]	149.5	152.0	152.3	151.7	154.6	156.8	158.3	0.9
Internal and respiratory over-the-counter drugs	176.9	181.2	180.9	179.7	183.4	186.4	188.7	1.2
Medical care services	266.0	306.0	321.3	336.7	350.6	369.3	384.9	4.2
Professional medical services	237.7	261.2	271.5	281.7	289.3	300.8	311.0	3.4
Physicians' services	244.7	267.7	278.3	287.5	291.9	303.2	311.3	2.7
Dental services	258.5	292.5	306.9	324.0	340.9	358.4	376.9	5.1
Services by other medical professionals [3]	161.9	177.1	181.9	186.8	192.2	197.4	205.5	4.1
Hospital and related services	317.3	394.8	417.9	439.9	468.1	498.9	534.0	7.0
Hospital services [6]	115.9	144.7	153.4	161.6	172.1	183.6	197.2	7.4

See footnotes at end of table.

U.S. Census Bureau, Statistical Abstract of the United States: 2010

Table 711. **Consumer Price Indexes for All Urban Consumers (CPI-U) for Selected Items and Groups: 2000 to 2008**—Con.

[1982-84 = 100, except as noted. Annual averages of monthly figures. Minus sign (–) indicates decrease. See headnote, Table 709]

Item	2000	2003	2004	2005	2006	2007	2008	Annual percentage change, 2007–2008
Recreation [1]	103.3	107.5	108.6	109.4	110.9	111.4	113.3	1.6
Video and audio [1]	101.0	103.6	104.2	104.2	104.6	102.9	102.6	–0.3
Cable and satellite television and radio service [4]	266.8	309.5	322.4	331.9	344.9	351.5	359.9	2.4
Pets, pet products, and services [1]	106.1	115.7	120.1	123.6	128.4	133.8	144.5	7.9
Pets and pet products	144.3	150.3	154.5	155.8	161.7	166.6	181.9	9.2
Pet services including veterinary [1]	114.6	134.9	142.3	150.3	156.5	165.7	176.0	6.2
Sporting goods	119.0	115.3	115.0	115.5	117.1	116.4	118.4	1.7
Sports vehicles, including bicycles	130.9	130.3	130.8	133.2	138.0	137.9	139.4	1.1
Other recreational goods [1]	87.8	76.1	73.3	69.5	67.2	64.3	62.1	–3.4
Recreation services [1]	111.7	124.5	127.5	130.5	135.1	139.4	142.9	2.5
Club membership dues and fees for participant sports [1]	108.9	116.1	116.7	117.4	121.9	123.7	125.8	1.7
Admissions	230.5	263.2	272.9	282.3	291.9	303.8	312.3	2.8
Education and communication [1]	102.5	109.8	111.6	113.7	116.8	119.6	123.6	3.4
Education [1]	112.5	134.4	143.7	152.7	162.1	171.4	181.3	5.8
Tuition/child care fees and other school fees	324.0	386.7	414.3	440.9	468.1	494.1	522.1	5.7
College tuition and fees	331.9	403.9	442.1	475.1	507.0	538.7	572.3	6.2
Elementary and high school tuition and fees	349.9	424.9	453.5	483.2	511.2	539.4	570.6	5.8
Child care and nursery school [7]	156.3	180.3	187.1	195.4	206.0	214.9	224.6	4.5
Communication [1]	93.6	89.7	86.7	84.7	84.1	83.4	84.2	1.0
Information and information processing [1]	92.8	87.8	84.6	82.6	81.7	80.7	81.4	0.8
Telephone services [1]	98.5	98.3	95.8	94.9	95.8	98.2	100.5	2.2
Land-line telephone services, local charges	175.6	201.1	204.1	209.6	213.9	222.1	230.0	3.6
Land-line telephone services, long distance charges [1]	91.8	77.8	70.9	67.5	68.3	71.5	74.8	4.7
Wireless telephone services [1]	76.0	66.8	66.2	65.0	64.6	64.4	64.2	–0.2
Information technology, hardware, and services [8]	25.9	16.1	14.8	13.6	12.5	10.6	10.1	–5.1
Other goods and services	271.1	298.7	304.7	313.4	321.7	333.3	345.4	3.6
Tobacco and smoking products	394.9	469.0	478.0	502.8	519.9	554.2	588.7	6.2
Cigarettes [1]	159.9	190.4	193.5	203.5	210.4	224.8	239.0	6.3
Personal care	165.6	178.0	181.7	185.6	190.2	195.6	201.3	2.9
Personal care products	153.7	153.5	153.9	154.4	155.8	158.3	159.3	0.6
Hair, dental, shaving, and miscellaneous personal care products [1]	103.3	102.5	102.1	101.8	102.6	103.6	104.3	0.7
Cosmetics, perfume, bath, nail preparations, and implements	166.8	168.0	169.5	171.3	173.1	177.0	178.0	0.6
Personal care services [1]	178.1	193.2	197.6	203.9	209.7	216.6	223.7	3.3
Haircuts and other personal care services [1]	108.7	117.9	120.6	124.4	127.9	132.1	136.5	3.3
Miscellaneous personal services	252.3	283.5	293.9	303.0	313.6	325.0	338.9	4.3
Legal services [3]	189.3	221.7	232.3	241.8	250.0	260.3	270.7	4.0
Funeral expenses [3]	187.8	212.1	221.3	228.8	240.6	252.6	265.4	5.1
SPECIAL AGGREGATE INDEXES								
Commodities	**149.2**	**151.2**	**154.7**	**160.2**	**164.0**	**167.5**	**174.8**	**4.3**
Commodities less food and beverages	137.7	134.5	136.7	142.5	145.9	147.5	153.0	3.7
Nondurables less food and beverages	147.4	149.7	157.2	168.4	176.7	182.5	196.2	7.5
Nondurables less food, beverages, and apparel	162.5	171.5	183.9	202.6	216.3	226.2	248.8	10.0
Durables	125.4	117.5	114.8	115.3	114.5	112.5	110.9	–1.4
Services	195.3	216.5	222.8	230.1	238.9	246.8	255.5	3.5
Rent of shelter [2]	201.3	221.9	227.9	233.7	241.9	250.8	257.2	2.5
Transportation services	196.1	216.3	220.6	225.7	230.8	233.7	244.1	4.4
Other services	229.9	254.4	261.3	268.4	277.5	285.6	295.8	3.6
All items less food	173.0	184.7	189.4	196.0	202.7	208.1	215.5	3.6
All items less shelter	165.7	174.6	179.3	186.1	191.9	196.6	205.5	4.5
All items less medical care	167.3	178.1	182.7	188.7	194.7	200.1	207.8	3.8
Commodities less food	139.2	136.5	138.8	144.5	148.0	149.7	155.3	3.7
Nondurables less food	149.1	151.9	159.3	170.1	178.2	184.0	197.3	7.2
Nondurables less food and apparel	162.9	172.1	183.8	201.2	213.9	223.4	244.4	9.4
Nondurables	158.2	165.3	172.2	180.2	186.7	193.5	205.9	6.4
Apparel less footwear [1]	126.2	116.8	116.3	114.4	114.1	113.8	113.4	–0.4
Services less rent of shelter [2]	202.9	226.4	233.5	243.2	253.3	260.8	273.0	4.7
Services less medical care services	188.9	208.7	214.5	221.2	229.6	236.8	245.0	3.4
Energy	124.6	136.5	151.4	177.1	196.9	207.7	236.7	13.9
All items less energy	178.6	190.6	194.4	198.7	203.7	208.9	214.8	2.8
All items less food and energy	181.3	193.2	196.6	200.9	205.9	210.7	215.6	2.3
Commodities less food and energy commodities	144.9	140.9	139.6	140.3	140.6	140.1	140.2	0.1
Energy commodities	129.5	136.7	161.2	197.4	223.0	241.0	284.4	18.0
Services less energy services	202.1	223.8	230.2	236.6	244.7	253.1	261.0	3.1
Domestically produced farm food	170.1	183.7	191.7	195.0	198.1	206.5	220.1	6.6
Utilities and public transportation	152.6	164.3	167.5	176.6	186.7	191.3	202.8	6.0

NA Not available. [1] December 1997=100. [2] December 1982=100. [3] December 1986=100. [4] December 1983=100. [5] December 2001=100. [6] December 1996=100. [7] December 1990=100. [8] December 1988=100.

Source: U.S. Bureau of Labor Statistics, *CPI Detailed Report,* monthly; <http://www.bls.gov/cpi/cpi_dr.htm>. See also *Monthly Labor Review;* <http://www.bls.gov/opub/mlr/welcome.htm>.

Prices   469

Table 712. **Cost of Living Index—Selected Urban Areas: Annual Average 2008**

[Measures relative price levels for consumer goods and services in participating areas for a mid-management standard of living. **The nationwide average equals 100 and each index is read as a percent of the national average.** The index does not measure inflation, but compares prices at a single point in time. Percents in parentheses represent share of consumer spending devoted to the category and consequently the category's importance or weight in the index. Excludes taxes. For definition of urban areas, see source. For international comparisons, see Table 1322, Section 30]

Urban areas	Composite index (100%)	Grocery items (12%)	Housing (29%)	Utilities (10%)	Transportation (11%)	Health care (4%)	Misc. goods and services (33%)
Akron, OH.	94.4	99.3	84.6	102.8	103.4	92.6	95.8
Albuquerque, NM.	96.7	95.0	99.2	87.1	95.8	97.4	98.4
Amarillo, TX.	87.9	87.8	84.8	84.0	96.4	95.4	88.0
Anchorage, AK.	125.5	142.5	136.4	97.7	106.9	130.1	123.7
Asheville, NC.	99.7	100.2	101.8	100.0	96.8	101.7	98.4
Atlanta, GA.	97.2	98.9	91.3	87.6	103.0	102.0	102.1
Austin, TX.	95.5	92.5	84.9	88.4	98.0	96.5	107.2
Baltimore, MD.	121.9	105.6	160.7	124.7	105.9	102.1	100.7
Baton Rouge, LA.	89.6	94.8	80.0	90.0	92.9	96.6	93.9
Bergen-Passaic, NJ.	132.7	114.7	176.8	115.6	104.2	110.3	118.2
Bethesda-Gaithersburg-Frederick, MD.	133.4	105.9	197.2	114.0	110.7	106.3	104.5
Boston, MA.	133.6	115.9	156.7	140.6	108.1	133.6	126.4
Bradenton, FL.	98.2	97.8	101.1	89.8	101.4	103.6	96.6
Brownsville, TX.	86.7	87.2	74.3	96.1	100.1	96.8	88.9
Burlington-Chittenden Co, VT.	117.9	107.2	130.3	127.0	106.5	103.3	113.9
Camden, SC.	93.6	98.4	82.7	90.1	91.2	92.6	103.4
Cedar Rapids, IA.	93.0	86.4	78.8	106.9	96.2	108.1	100.8
Champaign-Urbana, IL.	96.7	90.2	88.3	103.1	98.6	98.9	103.7
Charleston, WV.	92.3	93.5	86.3	93.6	97.9	95.4	94.5
Charleston-N Charleston, SC.	96.8	100.0	89.4	100.0	98.0	105.4	99.7
Charlotte, NC.	94.2	102.2	79.9	91.8	97.1	109.5	101.7
Cheyenne, WY.	101.5	110.0	104.5	108.9	95.9	97.9	95.7
Chicago, IL.	112.5	106.9	129.2	117.9	108.7	103.1	100.8
Cincinnati, OH.	92.6	90.8	84.7	104.4	98.2	92.0	94.7
Cleveland, OH.	96.3	103.2	87.2	105.9	100.1	103.1	96.8
Colorado Springs, CO.	92.8	98.4	90.4	84.7	99.2	104.8	91.6
Columbia, SC.	95.2	108.0	77.1	105.6	98.8	110.8	100.0
Columbus, OH.	95.6	98.5	92.8	100.7	99.0	104.8	93.3
Conroe, TX.	88.6	87.6	78.4	91.6	95.1	95.6	94.0
Corpus Christi, TX.	89.9	81.8	78.2	114.8	95.8	89.7	93.8
Covington, KY.	89.9	84.7	79.6	96.1	102.4	98.1	93.9
Dallas, TX.	92.1	99.8	70.8	105.3	102.9	104.3	98.9
Davenport-Moline-Rock Island, IA-IL.	94.8	94.7	89.6	98.5	98.9	92.1	97.2
Dayton, OH.	92.0	92.6	73.1	102.0	99.6	96.9	102.3
Denver, CO.	105.0	108.5	110.3	96.3	97.2	105.8	104.0
Des Moines, IA.	91.6	88.2	87.4	99.8	94.0	90.2	93.8
Dover, DE.	101.7	108.1	90.6	125.9	103.8	101.6	100.9
Durham, NC.	93.5	99.1	79.9	94.5	99.8	100.7	100.1
El Paso, TX.	92.5	109.2	85.7	94.4	96.7	95.3	89.9
Eugene, OR.	112.5	96.6	142.0	84.2	104.2	115.1	103.6
Fargo-Moorhead ND-MN.	93.3	99.4	83.7	102.1	94.8	98.4	95.8
Fayetteville, AR.	90.7	94.9	79.8	95.1	98.6	93.5	94.4
Fort Lauderdale, FL.	122.0	106.7	165.7	94.2	107.3	102.7	105.1
Fort Smith, AR.	87.6	90.3	70.9	99.3	88.3	92.2	97.1
Fort Worth, TX.	89.2	93.0	71.1	108.5	99.7	90.5	94.2
Fresno, CA.	120.6	117.5	145.6	113.5	111.3	108.6	106.7
Gastonia, NC.	88.5	97.0	75.6	91.9	95.0	96.7	92.4
Grand Rapids, MI.	95.2	100.1	96.6	107.2	95.2	86.8	89.5
Greeley, CO.	97.6	111.1	91.6	86.2	93.4	105.7	101.6
Green Bay, WI.	92.4	90.3	83.9	106.8	99.1	97.8	93.5
Greenville, NC.	98.1	107.9	80.2	102.7	95.2	114.3	107.9
Hampton Roads-SE Virginia, VA.	108.5	101.2	117.0	98.0	102.0	105.7	109.4
Harlingen, TX.	85.3	83.4	72.7	115.5	89.4	97.0	85.2
Hickory, NC.	94.6	101.8	90.7	96.2	93.3	97.8	94.9
Honolulu, HI.	162.8	155.8	252.5	134.4	116.5	111.4	116.8
Houston, TX.	90.7	85.7	75.8	103.8	98.9	100.2	97.9

See footnotes at end of table.

U.S. Census Bureau, Statistical Abstract of the United States: 2010

Table 712. Cost of Living Index—Selected Urban Areas: Annual Average 2008—Con.

[Measures relative price levels for consumer goods and services in participating areas for a mid-management standard of living. **The nationwide average equals 100 and each index is read as a percent of the national average.** The index does not measure inflation, but compares prices at a single point in time. Excludes taxes. For definition of urban areas, see source. For international comparisons, see Table 1322, Section 30]

Urban areas	Composite index (100%)	Grocery items (13%)	Housing (29%)	Utilities (10%)	Transportation (10%)	Health care (4%)	Misc. goods and services (35%)
Huntsville, AL	92.5	94.7	81.3	83.1	99.1	94.0	101.9
Indianapolis, IN	91.7	93.4	88.6	89.4	102.0	99.0	90.2
Jackson, MS	95.5	92.6	90.1	109.4	95.6	100.5	96.5
Jacksonville, FL	97.1	100.2	88.4	87.4	106.5	99.1	103.2
Joliet-Will County, IL	100.0	102.6	94.4	110.5	109.6	101.3	97.6
Kalamazoo, MI	95.6	101.3	89.7	100.9	101.0	94.6	95.3
Kansas City, MO-KS	96.8	93.3	88.2	98.1	99.7	97.0	104.3
Knoxville, TN	89.4	91.5	76.2	94.3	91.2	90.4	97.9
Lafayette, LA	98.6	91.9	105.0	89.6	107.2	86.5	96.9
Las Vegas, NV	107.9	101.0	129.1	93.8	102.6	104.3	98.2
Lawrence, KS	93.4	90.4	89.2	95.8	96.3	95.3	96.3
Little Rock-North Little Rock, AR	93.9	98.0	79.7	108.6	98.1	96.9	98.5
Los Angeles-Long Beach, CA	147.7	111.2	250.8	89.0	112.8	108.3	104.8
Louisville, KY	92.9	84.9	81.8	108.1	103.1	91.8	97.8
Loveland, CO	95.3	104.6	78.4	95.8	101.1	99.7	104.1
Lubbock, TX	87.4	92.5	73.6	81.9	100.1	99.5	93.4
McAllen, TX	87.6	80.0	73.4	109.1	98.1	100.4	91.4
Memphis, TN	88.2	94.2	74.2	87.6	93.8	97.2	95.4
Miami-Dade County, FL	116.6	106.7	142.4	96.9	107.9	107.1	107.5
Middlesex-Monmouth, NJ	126.2	111.9	157.1	115.9	104.5	109.3	116.8
Missoula, MT	105.0	125.2	96.0	108.3	103.3	105.6	104.9
Mobile, AL	94.2	101.4	81.0	103.9	96.5	87.9	100.2
Montgomery, AL	98.0	98.4	98.6	101.6	102.2	88.4	96.0
Murfreesboro-Smyrna, TN	91.1	94.2	74.3	91.5	100.8	100.8	100.1
Myrtle Beach, SC	92.5	100.8	78.8	84.7	97.8	103.0	100.6
Nassau County, NY	151.4	115.1	232.7	140.5	107.4	116.2	115.8
New Haven, CT	122.3	117.9	140.9	137.0	104.7	111.0	110.3
New York (Manhattan), NY	219.8	142.4	409.6	167.3	120.2	132.6	141.8
New York (Queens), NY	156.0	130.1	232.0	146.3	110.0	106.3	123.4
Newark-Elizabeth, NJ	129.2	113.2	167.2	116.1	103.6	105.9	117.2
Oakland, CA	147.9	128.6	224.5	89.4	111.7	119.1	120.9
Oklahoma City, OK	88.7	90.2	79.4	89.7	96.2	99.2	92.2
Olympia, WA	104.8	110.8	100.7	84.5	107.9	122.2	109.0
Omaha, NE	86.9	89.6	72.8	88.8	97.2	95.9	93.1
Orlando, FL	101.0	101.5	89.9	102.1	104.6	96.3	109.6
Palm Springs, CA	127.2	112.9	170.1	105.6	115.2	103.2	108.4
Peoria, IL	100.8	105.3	93.0	112.9	106.6	98.9	100.6
Philadelphia, PA	123.9	124.9	144.5	118.2	104.1	109.0	115.7
Phoenix, AZ	101.1	103.4	100.1	90.9	100.2	99.4	104.8
Pittsburgh, PA	92.8	97.8	77.5	104.4	105.8	89.7	97.0
Plano, TX	94.1	100.9	81.8	108.8	102.3	101.6	94.3
Portland, OR	116.1	106.9	132.2	92.9	108.6	106.5	116.2
Providence, RI	122.0	109.4	134.8	130.2	103.1	123.4	119.2
Raleigh, NC	102.6	104.1	99.3	94.3	97.8	107.3	108.4
Reno-Sparks, NV	110.6	110.4	123.7	94.4	102.1	110.0	106.8
Richmond, VA	104.2	97.1	109.4	108.5	104.6	108.2	100.4
Riverside City, CA	119.5	111.0	157.6	88.5	114.4	105.6	102.0
Roanoke, VA	92.6	91.7	94.7	73.6	95.2	96.6	95.5
Rochester, MN	96.7	89.9	86.9	101.3	100.7	104.9	104.2
Rochester, NY	104.1	95.0	92.3	138.6	106.6	104.6	106.6
Round Rock, TX	91.6	80.5	73.1	113.1	98.6	105.3	101.6
Sacramento, CA	118.9	121.8	148.4	100.5	112.0	109.0	101.1
Salt Lake City, UT	99.7	104.2	99.9	71.8	101.6	101.6	105.4
San Antonio, TX	95.6	82.8	87.8	88.1	99.5	107.3	106.7
San Diego, CA	136.4	111.9	210.9	94.7	110.3	113.7	104.2
San Francisco, CA	172.1	128.6	292.9	98.6	113.4	120.3	130.5
San Jose, CA	156.0	138.9	249.5	113.5	114.2	119.3	111.3
Sarasota, FL	107.2	101.9	123.0	91.7	108.1	107.1	99.8
Savannah, GA	94.0	90.6	87.3	90.1	99.4	96.5	100.2
Seattle, WA	123.0	117.2	151.2	83.8	110.5	120.8	116.5

Source: C2ER, Arlington, VA, *ACCRA Cost of Living Index*, Annual Average 2008 (copyright)

Prices **471**

Table 713. Single-Family Housing Price Indexes by State: 2000 to 2008

[Index 1980, 1st quarter = 100. The index reflects average price changes in repeat sales or refinancings on the same properties. Since the data are for the fourth quarter, the index represents the annual percentage change in home values in the fourth quarter of the year shown relative to the fourth quarter of the previous year. The information is obtained by reviewing repeat mortgage transactions on single-family properties whose mortages have been purchased or securitized by either Fannie Mae or Freddie Mac; for more information on methodology, see Appendix III. Minus sign (–) indicates decrease]

State	2000	2005	2007	2008	Percent change 2008	State	2000	2005	2007	2008	Percent change 2008
U.S.	241	366	390	378	-3.1	MT......	218	333	395	394	-0.3
AL......	204	262	297	300	1.0	NE......	205	249	261	258	-1.0
AK......	170	257	285	282	-1.3	NV......	194	396	387	300	-22.4
AZ......	207	394	420	352	-16.3	NH......	296	493	499	470	-5.7
AR......	184	240	264	262	-0.8	NJ......	295	547	577	542	-6.2
CA......	285	617	602	464	-22.9	NM.....	203	290	346	334	-3.3
CO.....	280	355	370	367	-0.8	NY.....	361	627	664	630	-5.2
CT.....	276	457	477	453	-5.2	NC.....	243	307	348	346	-0.5
DE.....	279	475	522	494	-5.4	ND.....	167	229	261	268	2.7
DC.....	267	614	670	615	-8.2	OH.....	223	268	270	263	-2.6
FL.....	214	445	464	368	-20.6	OK.....	150	190	210	211	0.6
GA.....	250	322	348	325	-6.5	OR.....	256	400	472	448	-5.2
HI	238	501	549	517	-5.9	PA.....	244	376	413	409	-0.9
ID	201	299	358	348	-2.9	RI	296	586	585	530	-9.4
IL.......	252	358	385	370	-4.0	SC.....	220	287	322	325	0.9
IN	211	251	260	258	-1.0	SD.....	203	269	298	304	2.0
IA	192	241	255	254	-0.3	TN......	221	279	314	315	0.4
KS.....	186	231	248	248	0.1	TX......	166	204	229	233	1.9
KY	221	274	295	296	0.3	UT......	242	306	394	378	-3.9
LA.....	164	219	253	253	0.1	VT......	263	432	475	470	-1.1
ME.....	295	489	521	504	-3.2	VA......	243	441	478	449	-6.2
MD.....	248	493	542	493	-9.0	WA	279	429	514	491	-4.5
MA......	440	725	708	669	-5.5	WV	161	217	236	229	-2.7
MI......	264	321	305	281	-7.7	WI	231	316	334	329	-1.6
MN.....	239	362	368	352	-4.4	WY	157	235	290	291	0.6
MS.....	186	233	266	268	1.0						
MO	215	288	308	303	-1.7						

Source: Federal Housing Finance Agency, *Housing Price Index, 4th quarter 2008;* <http://www.fhfa.gov/webf.les/1346/4q08hpi.pdf> (released 26 February 2009). For most recent release, see <http://www.fhfa.gov>.

Table 714. Average Prices of Selected Fuels and Electricity: 1990 to 2008

[In dollars per unit, except electricity, in cents per kWh. Represents price to end-users, except as noted]

Type	Unit	1990	2000	2001	2002	2003	2004	2005	2006	2007	2008
Crude oil, composite [1].....	Barrel.....	22.22	28.26	22.95	24.10	28.53	36.98	50.24	60.24	67.94	94.73
Motor gasoline: [2]											
Unleaded regular	Gallon.....	1.16	1.51	1.46	1.36	1.59	1.88	2.30	2.59	2.80	3.27
Unleaded premium	Gallon.....	1.35	1.69	1.66	1.56	1.78	2.07	2.49	2.81	3.03	3.52
No. 2 heating oil.........	Gallon	0.73	0.93	0.83	0.74	0.93	1.17	1.71	1.98	2.24	2.99
No. 2 diesel fuel.........	Gallon.....	0.73	0.94	0.84	0.76	0.94	1.24	1.79	2.10	2.27	3.15
Propane, consumer grade ..	Gallon.....	0.75	0.60	0.51	0.42	0.58	0.84	1.09	1.36	1.49	1.84
Residual fuel oil	Gallon.....	0.44	0.60	0.53	0.57	0.70	0.74	1.05	1.22	1.37	1.96
Natural gas, residential	1,000 cu/ft .	5.80	7.76	9.63	7.89	9.63	10.75	12.70	13.73	13.06	13.68
Electricity, residential......	kWh......	7.83	8.24	8.58	8.44	8.72	8.95	9.45	10.40	10.65	11.36

[1] Refiner acquisition cost. [2] Average, all service.

Source: U.S. Energy Information Administration, *Monthly Energy Review.* For most current issue, see <http://www.eia.doe.gov/emeu/mer/>.

Table 715. Retail Gasoline Prices—Selected Areas: 2006 to 2008

[In cents per gallon. Prices are annual averages]

Area	Regular			Midgrade			Premium		
	2006	2007	2008	2006	2007	2008	2006	2007	2008
Boston, MA..........	256.3	271.0	317.2	268.2	283.6	330.2	278.7	294.2	340.7
Chicago, IL..........	266.3	294.1	340.7	276.6	305.1	352.0	286.8	315.4	362.3
Cleveland, OH........	249.4	275.9	317.1	259.7	286.4	327.7	270.6	297.2	338.4
Denver, CO..........	253.1	276.8	315.4	264.7	289.0	327.8	274.5	299.7	338.8
Houston, TX	246.6	260.6	308.1	256.7	272.1	321.8	266.6	283.1	334.1
Los Angeles, CA	283.3	304.7	350.6	293.4	315.5	361.6	303.3	325.7	372.0
Miami, FL...........	267.1	286.0	337.7	277.9	299.1	351.9	286.9	309.8	362.6
New York, NY	263.1	278.9	327.1	275.8	293.3	344.5	286.4	304.4	355.9
San Francisco, CA	279.1	317.1	356.4	291.0	329.7	369.3	301.1	340.0	379.7
Seattle, WA..........	268.3	294.7	339.0	278.9	305.1	350.8	289.1	315.4	361.2

Source: U.S. Energy Information Administration, *Weekly U.S. Retail Gasoline Prices,* Gasoline Historical Data. See also <http://www.eia.doe.gov/oil_gas/petroleum/data_publications/wrgp/mogas_history.html>.

472 Prices

Table 716. **Weekly Food Cost of a Nutritious Diet by Type of Family and Individual: 2008**

[In dollars, As of December. Assumes that food for all meals and snacks is purchased at the store and prepared at home. See source for details on estimation procedures]

Family type	Thrifty plan	Low-cost plan	Moderate-cost plan	Liberal plan
FAMILIES				
Family of two:				
19 to 50 years	83.00	105.60	131.00	163.70
51 to 70 years	79.10	101.50	124.90	150.10
Family of four:				
Couple, 19 to 50 years and children—				
2 to 3 and 4 to 5 years	120.60	152.90	188.60	233.40
6 to 8 and 9 to 11 years	138.70	179.60	224.10	272.20
INDIVIDUALS [1]				
Child:				
1 year	20.70	27.50	31.40	38.00
2 to 3 years	22.10	27.80	33.60	40.90
4 to 5 years	23.00	29.10	35.90	43.70
6 to 8 years	29.30	39.60	48.60	57.20
9 to 11 years	33.90	44.00	56.40	66.30
Male:				
12 to 13 years	35.90	50.20	62.40	73.50
14 to 18 years	37.30	52.00	64.80	74.60
19 to 50 years	40.00	51.30	64.10	78.40
51 to 70 years	36.60	48.70	59.50	72.10
71 years and over	36.70	48.20	59.70	73.30
Female:				
12 to 13 years	36.00	43.90	52.50	63.80
14 to 18 years	35.70	44.10	53.20	65.40
19 to 50 years	35.50	44.70	54.90	70.40
51 to 70 years	35.20	43.60	54.10	64.40
71 years and over	34.60	43.20	53.90	64.70

[1] The costs given are for individuals in 4-person families. For individuals in other size families, the following adjustments are suggested: 1-person, add 20 percent; 2-person, add 10 percent; 3-person, add 5 percent; 5- or 6-person, subtract 5 percent; 7- (or more) person, subtract 10 percent.

Source: U.S. Department of Agriculture, *Official USDA Food Plans: Cost of Food at Home at Four Levels*, monthly. See also <http://www.cnpp.usda.gov/Publications/FoodPlans/2008/CostofFoodDec08.pdf> (released January 2009).

Table 717. **Food—Retail Prices of Selected Items: 2000 to 2008**

[In dollars per pound, except as indicated. As of December. See Appendix III]

Food	2000	2007	2008	Food	2000	2007	2008
Cereals and bakery products:				Fresh fruits and vegetables:			
Flour, white, all purpose	0.28	0.40	0.50	Apples, Red Delicious	0.82	1.12	1.18
Rice, white, lg. grain, raw	(NA)	0.55	0.81	Bananas	0.49	0.53	0.62
Spaghetti and macaroni	0.88	0.85	1.13	Oranges, navel	0.62	0.91	0.93
Bread, white, pan	0.99	1.28	1.42	Grapefruit	0.58	0.91	0.91
Bread, whole wheat	1.36	1.81	1.95	Grapes, Thompson seedless	2.36	2.72	2.46
Beef:				Lemons	1.11	2.05	1.62
Ground beef, 100% beef	1.63	2.23	2.41	Pears, Anjou	(NA)	1.27	1.37
Ground chuck, 100% beef	1.98	2.70	3.00	Potatoes, white	0.35	0.52	0.68
Ground beef, lean and extra lean	2.33	3.07	3.44	Lettuce, iceberg	0.85	0.95	0.88
Round steak, USDA Choice	3.28	4.04	4.37	Tomatoes, field grown	1.57	2.15	1.73
Sirloin steak, boneless	4.81	5.91	6.07				
Pork:				Processed fruits and vegetables:			
Bacon, sliced	3.03	3.69	3.67	Orange juice, frozen concentrate,			
Chops, center cut, bone-in	3.46	3.38	3.54	12 oz. can, per 16 oz.	1.88	2.53	2.56
Ham, boneless, excluding canned	2.75	3.04	3.41	Sugar and sweets:			
Poultry, fish, and eggs:				Sugar, white, all sizes	0.41	0.50	0.53
Chicken, fresh, whole	1.08	1.17	1.31	Sugar, white, 33-80 oz. pkg	0.40	0.48	0.50
Chicken legs, bone-in	1.26	1.36	1.50				
Turkey, frozen, whole	0.99	1.01	1.33	Fats and oils:			
Eggs, Grade A, large, (dozen)	0.96	2.10	1.83	Margarine, stick	(NA)	1.01	1.18
Dairy products:				Margarine, tubs, soft	0.84	1.24	1.57
Milk, fresh, whole, fortified (per gal.)	2.79	3.87	3.68	Peanut butter, creamy, all sizes	1.96	1.88	2.15
Butter, salted, grade AA, stick	2.80	2.98	3.13	Nonalcoholic beverages:			
American processed cheese	3.69	3.91	4.14	Coffee, 100% ground roast, all sizes	3.21	3.69	(NA)
Cheddar cheese, natural	3.76	4.45	4.95	Other prepared foods:			
Ice cream, prepack., bulk, reg.				Potato chips, per 16 oz.	3.44	3.65	4.48
(1/2 gal.)	3.66	4.08	4.28				

NA Not available.

Source: U.S. Bureau of Labor Statistics, *CPI Detailed Report*, monthly, and <http://www.bls.gov/cpi/cpi_dr.htm>. See also *Monthly Labor Review*, <http://www.bls.gov/opub/mlr/welcome.htm>.

Prices 473

Table 718. **Producer Price Indexes by Stage of Processing: 1990 to 2008**

[1982 = 100, **except as indicated**. See Appendix III. Minus sign (–) indicates decrease]

Year	Crude materials Total	Crude materials Foodstuffs and feedstuffs	Crude materials Fuel	Crude nonfood materials except fuel	Intermediate materials, supplies, and components	Finished goods Consumer goods	Finished goods Capital equipment	Finished consumer foods Crude	Finished consumer foods Processed	Finished consumer goods excl. food
1990	108.9	113.1	84.8	107.3	114.5	118.2	122.9	123.0	124.4	115.3
1995	102.7	105.8	72.1	105.8	124.9	125.6	136.7	118.8	129.8	124.0
1996	113.8	121.5	92.6	105.7	125.7	129.5	138.3	129.2	133.8	127.6
1997	111.1	112.2	101.3	103.5	125.6	130.2	138.2	126.6	135.1	128.2
1998	96.8	103.9	86.7	84.5	123.0	128.9	137.6	127.2	134.8	126.4
1999	98.2	98.7	91.2	91.1	123.2	132.0	137.6	125.5	135.9	130.5
2000	120.6	100.2	136.9	118.0	129.2	138.2	138.8	123.5	138.3	138.4
2001	121.0	106.1	151.4	101.5	129.7	141.5	139.7	127.7	142.4	141.4
2002	108.1	99.5	117.3	101.0	127.8	139.4	139.1	128.5	141.0	138.8
2003	135.3	113.5	185.7	116.9	133.7	145.3	139.5	130.0	147.2	144.7
2004	159.0	127.0	211.4	149.2	142.6	151.7	141.4	138.2	153.9	150.9
2005	182.2	122.7	279.7	176.7	154.0	160.4	144.6	140.2	156.9	161.9
2006	184.8	119.3	241.5	210.0	164.0	166.0	146.9	151.3	157.1	169.2
2007	207.1	146.7	236.8	238.7	170.7	173.5	149.5	170.2	166.7	175.6
2008 [1]	251.7	163.5	296.7	309.0	188.6	186.3	153.7	175.5	178.8	189.0
PERCENT CHANGE [2]										
1990	5.6	1.7	-0.6	12.0	2.2	5.4	3.5	2.8	4.9	5.9
1995	0.9	-0.7	-12.5	9.1	5.4	1.9	1.9	6.7	1.5	2.0
1996	10.8	14.8	28.4	-0.1	0.6	3.1	1.2	8.8	3.1	2.9
1997	-2.4	-7.7	9.4	-2.1	-0.1	0.5	-0.1	-2.0	1.0	0.5
1998	-12.9	-7.4	-14.4	-18.4	-2.1	-1.0	-0.4	0.5	-0.2	-1.4
1999	1.4	-5.0	5.2	7.8	0.2	2.4	–	-1.3	0.8	3.2
2000	22.8	1.5	50.1	29.5	4.9	4.7	0.9	-1.6	1.8	6.1
2001	0.3	5.9	10.6	-14.0	0.4	2.4	0.6	3.4	3.0	2.2
2002	-10.7	-6.2	-22.5	-0.5	-1.5	-1.5	-0.4	0.6	-1.0	-1.8
2003	25.2	14.1	58.3	15.7	4.6	4.2	0.3	1.2	4.4	4.3
2004	17.5	11.9	13.8	27.6	6.7	4.4	1.4	6.3	4.6	4.3
2005	14.6	-3.4	32.3	18.4	8.0	5.7	2.3	1.4	1.9	7.3
2006	1.4	-2.8	-13.7	18.8	6.5	3.5	1.6	7.9	0.1	4.5
2007	12.1	23.0	-1.9	13.7	4.1	4.5	1.8	12.5	6.1	3.8
2008 [1] . . .	21.5	11.5	25.3	29.5	10.5	7.4	2.8	3.1	7.3	7.6

– Represents or rounds to zero. [1] Preliminary. [2] Change from immediate prior year. 1990, change from 1989.

Source: U.S. Bureau of Labor Statistics, *Producer Price Indexes*, monthly and annual. See also *Monthly Labor Review* <http://www.bls.gov/opub/mlr/welcome.htm>.

Table 719. **Commodity Research Bureau Futures Price Index: 1990 to 2008**

[1967 = 100. Index computed daily. Represents unweighted geometric average of commodity futures prices (through 6 months forward) of 17 major commodity futures markets. Represents end of year index]

Item	1990	1995	1999	2000	2001	2002	2003	2004	2005	2006	2007	2008
All commodities	222.6	243.2	205.1	227.8	190.6	234.5	255.3	283.9	347.9	394.9	476.1	363.1
Softs [1]	276.0	354.4	280.9	254.4	252.8	303.7	250.5	343.5	420.5	475.9	467.5	487.2
Industrials	245.5	272.5	192.9	211.0	141.8	176.6	256.6	232.1	302.5	368.8	418.3	475.4
Grains and oilseeds [2]	171.2	218.6	156.6	174.9	159.0	188.2	225.8	177.0	193.8	279.1	427.0	545.5
Energy	246.0	180.0	221.0	355.8	204.9	320.7	358.7	457.3	705.3	591.6	825.1	1263.2
Livestock and meats	226.2	192.4	239.6	253.6	247.4	251.0	237.8	303.6	300.3	294.6	297.7	337.0
Metals (precious)	257.8	276.0	253.4	265.7	246.8	289.1	364.1	396.6	478.1	611.9	773.6	894.6

[1] Prior to 1997, reported as imported. Softs include commodities that are grown and not mined such as coffee, cocoa, lumber, cotton, and sugar. [2] Prior to 1997, reported as grains.

Source: Commodity Research Bureau (CRB), Chicago, IL, *CRB Commodity Index Report*, weekly (copyright).

Table 720. **Indexes of Spot Primary Market Prices: 1990 to 2008**

[1967 = 100. Computed daily Represents unweighted geometric average of price quotations of 23 commodities; much more sensitive to changes in market conditions than is a monthly producer price index]

Items and number of commodities	1990	1995	1999	2000	2001	2002	2003	2004	2005	2006	2007	2008
All commodities (23)	258.1	289.1	227.3	224.0	212.1	244.3	283.6	293.0	303.3	362.4	413.4	315.1
Foodstuffs (10)	206.4	236.4	178.1	184.7	201.6	238.1	250.2	256.0	241.7	276.0	335.9	294.2
Raw industrials (13)	301.2	332.2	268.9	255.8	217.3	248.6	309.1	321.5	354.7	437.3	477.0	330.2
Livestock and products (5)	292.7	307.4	265.7	265.5	257.2	317.8	365.9	365.0	326.6	378.6	402.6	310.8
Metals (5)	283.2	300.6	261.6	214.0	172.5	184.5	276.7	357.7	440.9	693.9	811.9	402.6
Textiles and fibers (4)	257.6	274.3	223.8	245.7	217.4	230.2	255.2	237.9	252.5	254.4	267.5	241.3
Fats and oils (4)	188.7	226.7	174.8	163.6	175.8	234.0	297.2	262.6	223.4	273.9	363.4	268.0

Source: Commodity Research Bureau, Chicago, IL, *CRB Commodity Index Report*, weekly (copyright).

Table 721. **Producer Price Indexes by Stage of Processing and Commodity: 1990 to 2008**

[1982 = 100, except as indicated. See Appendix III]

Stage of processing	1990	1995	2000	2004	2005	2006	2007	2008 [1]
Finished goods	119.2	127.9	138.0	148.5	155.7	160.4	166.6	177.1
Finished consumer goods	118.2	125.6	138.2	151.7	160.4	166.0	173.5	186.3
Finished consumer foods.	124.4	129.0	137.2	152.7	155.7	156.7	167.0	178.4
Fresh fruits and melons.	118.1	85.8	91.4	104.9	102.8	111.0	123.4	123.0
Fresh and dry vegetables	118.1	144.4	126.7	129.4	142.6	153.3	165.5	172.9
Eggs for fresh use (Dec. 1991 = 100)	(NA)	86.3	84.9	100.0	79.6	90.0	132.6	152.4
Bakery products.	141.0	164.3	182.3	196.3	201.1	207.7	216.6	237.5
Milled rice	102.5	113.1	101.2	135.5	120.1	136.1	155.0	251.6
Pasta products (June 1985 = 100).	114.1	125.0	121.6	127.3	127.9	128.3	136.3	183.4
Beef and veal	116.0	100.9	113.7	141.2	147.4	142.3	146.1	155.6
Pork.	119.8	101.5	113.4	132.7	131.9	128.0	133.3	131.8
Processed young chickens.	111.0	113.5	110.4	138.9	136.2	118.1	139.0	143.1
Processed turkeys	107.6	104.9	98.7	107.8	105.1	103.6	110.2	120.2
Finfish and shellfish	147.2	170.8	198.1	206.3	222.6	237.4	242.8	255.1
Dairy products	117.2	119.7	133.7	155.9	154.5	147.5	175.7	182.8
Processed fruits and vegetables	124.7	122.4	128.6	135.2	140.4	148.9	157.4	167.0
Soft drinks	122.3	133.1	144.1	156.5	159.1	162.8	166.7	174.2
Roasted coffee	113.0	146.5	133.5	130.1	151.1	153.6	163.7	179.5
Shortening and cooking oils	123.2	142.5	132.4	193.7	176.7	183.7	211.7	291.4
Finished consumer goods excluding foods . . .	115.3	124.0	138.4	150.9	161.9	169.2	175.6	189.0
Alcoholic beverages	117.2	128.5	140.6	152.8	158.5	160.1	160.2	166.2
Apparel	117.5	124.2	127.4	125.6	125.6	125.9	127.0	127.8
Women's/girls/infants' cut & sew apparel (Dec. 2003 = 100).	(NA)	(NA)	(NA)	100.2	100.3	100.3	101.1	100.8
Men's and boy's cut and sew apparel (Dec. 2003 = 100).	(NA)	(NA)	(NA)	99.9	98.7	98.0	98.6	99.6
Textile house furnishings	109.5	119.5	122.0	123.4	122.9	123.2	125.3	126.9
Footwear	125.6	139.2	144.9	146.2	148.1	149.3	151.6	157.0
Residential electric power (Dec. 1990 = 100).	(NA)	111.8	110.8	121.4	126.4	134.8	138.8	146.0
Residential gas (Dec. 1990 = 100)	(NA)	104.4	135.5	183.2	216.8	226.7	224.9	250.4
Gasoline.	78.7	63.7	94.6	128.1	168.6	197.2	221.9	263.0
Fuel oil No. 2.	73.3	56.6	93.5	120.7	178.4	207.4	223.7	306.8
Soaps and synthetic detergents	117.7	122.9	128.2	132.9	134.6	142.7	144.9	154.4
Cosmetics and other toilet preparations	121.6	129.0	137.4	140.6	143.0	145.2	147.6	147.8
Tires, tubes, and tread	96.8	100.2	93.0	102.5	108.1	114.7	118.5	128.0
Sanitary papers and health products	135.3	144.4	146.7	148.5	154.6	160.1	161.8	170.9
Book publishing	150.4	185.0	218.2	253.1	264.0	275.2	285.0	296.6
Household furniture	125.1	141.8	152.7	160.5	166.5	172.3	174.6	181.0
Floor coverings	119.0	123.7	129.6	136.7	146.4	154.5	156.6	160.5
Household appliances	110.8	112.4	107.3	101.5	103.3	104.1	105.2	107.2
Home electronic equipment	82.7	78.9	71.8	65.2	62.6	60.3	58.2	57.0
Household glassware	132.5	153.2	166.0	171.4	174.7	172.3	177.0	(NA)
Household flatware	122.1	138.3	142.6	145.4	147.7	152.7	186.8	(NA)
Lawn and garden equipment, except tractors . . .	123.0	130.4	132.0	134.5	134.5	134.9	137.0	140.4
Passenger cars	118.3	134.1	132.8	131.7	131.8	128.0	126.2	128.6
Toys, games, and children's vehicles	118.1	124.3	121.9	125.1	127.0	128.5	131.0	134.4
Sporting and athletic goods	112.6	122.0	126.1	123.4	124.6	126.1	129.9	129.8
Tobacco products.	221.4	231.3	397.2	434.0	457.8	460.0	489.1	508.7
Mobile homes	117.5	145.6	161.3	186.6	200.8	208.8	211.0	219.1
Jewelry, platinum, and karat gold	122.8	127.8	127.2	135.3	138.6	148.6	153.2	164.2
Costume jewelry and novelties	125.3	135.1	141.6	147.9	153.5	154.2	156.7	159.5
Capital Equipment	122.9	136.7	138.8	141.4	144.6	146.9	149.5	153.7
Agricultural machinery and equipment	121.7	142.9	153.7	165.9	174.7	178.9	184.3	192.6
Construction machinery and equipment	121.6	136.7	148.6	158.5	168.3	175.4	179.6	185.4
Metal cutting machine tools	129.8	148.0	161.9	151.4	155.1	163.4	165.8	170.4
Metal forming machine tools.	128.7	145.7	161.8	171.6	178.9	183.3	184.4	193.6
Pumps, compressors, and equipment	119.2	139.4	154.1	167.5	178.5	186.0	195.0	205.9
Electronic computers (Dec. 2004 = 100).	(NA)	850.1	261.6	107.3	85.5	66.5	51.6	40.8
Textile machinery.	128.8	146.7	156.2	158.1	160.5	161.7	162.5	165.0
Paper industries machinery (June 1982 = 100)	134.8	151.0	164.7	173.7	178.1	180.6	183.4	188.5
Printing trades machinery	124.9	133.6	142.1	143.4	144.3	146.5	150.5	152.3
Transformers and power regulators	120.9	128.9	135.8	135.7	150.3	172.5	194.9	216.0
Communication/related equip.(Dec. 1985 = 100) . . .	106.1	112.1	110.6	103.3	102.5	102.4	103.2	104.8
X-ray and electromedical equipment	109.8	111.8	101.5	97.5	95.7	94.9	92.8	91.6
Mining machinery and equipment	121.0	135.6	146.1	163.4	175.9	183.9	190.9	205.2
Office and store machines and equipment	109.5	115.5	112.7	113.2	115.1	114.7	114.6	121.2
Commercial furniture.	133.4	148.2	158.4	165.6	172.7	177.0	181.5	189.9
Light motor trucks.	130.0	159.0	157.6	151.3	148.4	143.3	145.3	145.4
Heavy motor trucks.	120.3	144.1	148.0	155.7	162.4	169.1	177.2	182.0
Truck trailers	110.8	131.7	139.4	148.1	157.1	164.5	169.4	176.9
Civilian aircraft (Dec. 1985 = 100).	115.3	141.8	159.6	190.5	202.2	212.4	219.6	230.1
Ships (Dec. 1985 = 100)	110.1	132.8	146.9	171.4	176.6	183.2	192.1	199.2
Railroad equipment.	118.6	134.8	135.7	143.9	160.4	169.4	176.4	180.7
Intermediate materials, supplies, and components.	114.5	124.9	129.2	142.6	154.0	164.0	170.7	188.6
Intermediate foods and feeds	113.3	114.8	111.7	137.1	133.8	135.2	154.4	182.2
Flour	103.6	123.0	103.8	129.0	133.6	145.8	178.4	239.4
Refined sugar	122.7	119.3	110.6	120.7	124.9	149.9	132.6	137.6
Soft drink beverage bases (December 1985 = 100) .	126.2	148.3	167.1	176.2	180.4	188.4	196.0	210.2
Prepared animal feeds	107.4	109.1	102.9	124.8	115.6	118.7	142.7	183.9

See footnotes at end of table.

U.S. Census Bureau, Statistical Abstract of the United States: 2010

[1982 = 100, except as indicated. See Appendix III]

Stage of processing	1990	1995	2000	2004	2005	2006	2007	2008 [1]
Intermediate materials less foods and feeds.	114.5	125.5	130.1	143.0	155.1	165.4	171.5	189.0
Synthetic fibers	106.7	109.4	107.2	106.6	112.3	115.0	114.2	116.3
Processed yarns and threads	112.6	112.8	107.9	108.7	111.7	114.0	116.9	123.7
Leather	177.5	191.4	182.2	220.6	219.6	223.7	230.6	234.6
Liquefied petroleum gas	77.4	65.1	127.1	193.3	244.7	268.5	316.1	373.5
Commercial electric power	115.3	131.7	131.5	142.8	149.8	161.3	165.4	173.9
Industrial electric power	119.6	130.8	131.5	147.2	156.2	172.8	180.4	189.3
Commercial natural gas (Dec. 1990 = 100)	(NA)	96.5	134.7	194.9	232.5	239.9	235.6	271.6
Industrial natural gas (Dec. 1990 = 100)	(NA)	90.9	139.0	201.7	249.4	246.2	242.3	281.0
Natural gas to electric utilities (Dec. 1990 = 100)	(NA)	87.7	120.7	171.6	204.0	191.4	186.0	203.6
Jet fuels	76.0	55.0	88.5	112.6	169.6	199.1	211.2	301.3
No. 2 Diesel fuel	74.1	57.0	93.3	128.2	189.1	216.9	235.5	325.3
Residual fuel	57.7	52.6	84.7	100.2	148.9	161.1	173.4	229.7
Industrial chemicals	113.2	128.4	129.1	162.8	188.5	212.4	226.4	277.4
Prepared paint	124.8	142.1	160.8	175.7	187.9	201.3	208.8	222.4
Fats and oils, inedible	88.1	126.9	70.1	153.6	146.9	147.9	189.4	296.0
Mixed fertilizers	103.3	111.1	112.4	127.8	138.9	144.9	161.2	249.7
Plastic resins and materials	124.1	143.5	141.6	163.1	193.0	198.4	195.9	218.1
Synthetic rubber	111.9	126.3	119.1	132.4	151.3	162.0	169.3	206.3
Plastic construction products	117.2	133.8	135.8	144.6	158.8	181.8	179.2	185.4
Unsupported plastic film, sheet, and shapes	119.0	135.6	133.2	149.1	164.8	175.1	176.0	195.5
Plastic parts and components for manufacturing	112.9	115.9	117.3	116.5	119.8	130.3	130.0	132.5
Softwood lumber	123.8	178.5	178.6	209.8	203.6	189.4	170.5	156.0
Hardwood lumber	131.0	167.0	185.9	199.3	196.6	195.3	192.4	184.7
Plywood	114.2	165.3	157.6	198.5	186.8	172.7	176.1	174.5
Paper	128.8	159.0	149.8	149.4	159.6	167.4	169.3	184.4
Paperboard	135.7	183.1	176.7	170.2	175.5	192.0	201.7	217.8
Paper boxes and containers	129.9	163.8	172.6	177.6	183.7	192.5	197.8	208.2
Building paper and board	112.2	144.9	138.8	192.4	184.9	173.0	155.2	164.1
Commercial printing (June 1982 = 100)	128.0	144.5	155.2	159.4	161.6	165.0	166.0	169.2
Foundry and forge shop products	117.2	129.3	136.5	144.0	156.2	163.0	170.7	189.6
Primary nonferrous metals	133.4	146.8	113.6	133.6	158.2	236.0	268.6	267.4
Nonferrous wire and cable	142.6	151.5	143.7	152.5	169.4	226.9	238.7	249.1
Metal containers	114.0	117.2	106.8	116.2	123.9	126.9	133.4	144.1
Hardware	125.9	141.1	151.2	161.6	168.0	174.0	179.7	189.9
Plumbing fixtures and brass fittings	144.3	166.0	180.4	188.3	197.6	207.2	220.6	226.8
Heating equipment	131.6	147.5	155.6	169.5	179.9	185.7	195.5	208.6
Fabricated ferrous wire products (June 1982 = 100)	114.6	125.7	130.0	149.3	157.1	162.6	166.7	201.6
Mechanical power transmission equipment	125.3	146.9	163.9	179.3	189.5	197.0	205.2	219.8
Air conditioning and refrigeration equipment	122.1	130.2	135.3	139.4	146.2	150.1	157.3	162.8
Ball and roller bearings	130.6	152.0	168.8	177.1	187.1	193.1	199.8	212.5
Wiring devices	132.2	147.2	152.9	169.0	176.6	188.2	194.5	206.6
Motors, generators, motor generator sets	132.9	143.9	146.2	149.8	157.8	165.0	172.9	181.4
Switchgear and switchboard equipment	124.4	140.3	153.0	163.8	170.2	178.6	188.5	195.3
Electronic components and accessories	118.4	113.6	97.1	88.8	87.0	88.5	82.3	77.2
Internal combustion engines	120.2	135.6	143.8	145.8	147.7	152.5	154.7	157.1
Flat glass	107.5	113.2	109.7	108.6	111.0	113.5	114.2	115.9
Cement	103.7	128.1	150.1	156.8	176.4	199.3	209.7	209.7
Concrete products	113.5	129.4	147.8	161.2	177.2	195.1	203.5	210.7
Asphalt felts and coatings	97.1	100.0	104.1	117.7	130.8	144.5	145.7	186.3
Gypsum products	105.2	154.5	201.4	198.8	229.6	274.9	233.0	213.0
Glass containers	120.4	130.5	127.4	144.4	146.4	152.8	162.0	171.8
Motor vehicle parts	111.2	116.0	113.6	112.0	113.1	116.3	117.9	119.8
Aircraft engines and engine parts (Dec. 1985 = 100)	113.5	132.8	141.0	163.0	165.9	172.4	178.9	185.8
Photographic supplies	127.6	126.8	125.2	115.1	120.1	121.6	122.9	125.5
Medical/surgical/personal aid devices	127.3	141.3	146.0	157.8	159.2	161.4	163.1	165.7
Crude materials for further processing .	108.9	102.7	120.6	159.0	182.2	184.8	207.1	251.7
Crude foodstuffs and feedstuffs	113.1	105.8	100.2	127.0	122.7	119.3	146.7	163.5
Wheat	87.6	118.6	80.3	106.0	102.7	116.9	172.1	235.5
Corn	100.9	109.0	76.4	97.5	75.9	95.6	141.5	199.1
Slaughter cattle	122.5	99.5	104.1	126.2	131.5	126.2	136.1	136.1
Slaughter hogs	94.1	70.2	72.7	87.8	82.7	77.2	76.1	78.0
Slaughter broilers/fryers	119.5	129.1	127.6	188.5	181.0	156.1	199.9	210.7
Slaughter turkeys	116.9	120.3	120.7	122.0	131.1	140.5	153.3	165.9
Fluid milk	100.8	93.6	92.0	120.1	113.5	96.7	143.3	137.5
Soybeans	100.8	102.2	83.4	130.0	102.6	96.8	137.9	203.9
Crude nonfood materials	101.5	96.8	130.4	179.2	223.4	230.6	246.3	313.5
Raw cotton	118.2	156.2	95.2	85.6	78.9	79.7	83.1	99.1
Coal	97.5	95.0	87.9	109.2	116.8	126.6	130.7	161.7
Natural gas	80.4	66.6	155.5	245.9	335.4	280.3	273.8	341.9
Crude petroleum	71.0	51.1	85.2	108.2	150.1	176.0	192.6	275.6
Logs and timber	142.8	220.4	196.4	193.3	197.4	201.2	217.1	216.8
Wastepaper	138.9	371.1	282.5	231.4	230.9	234.8	368.7	368.5
Iron ore	83.3	91.8	94.8	98.2	116.9	132.5	128.8	142.5
Iron and steel scrap	166.0	202.7	142.1	323.7	289.8	335.2	408.8	565.6
Nonferrous metal ores (Dec. 1983 = 100)	98.3	101.6	68.0	113.7	150.0	215.9	243.5	256.5
Copper base scrap	181.3	193.5	123.7	186.5	258.6	436.8	485.2	492.6
Aluminum base scrap	172.6	209.4	177.0	194.1	210.1	275.7	274.7	272.7
Construction sand, gravel, and crushed stone	125.4	142.3	163.1	183.3	195.8	213.9	232.4	247.8
Industrial sand	117.6	132.5	146.0	165.3	174.4	183.2	190.9	217.9

NA Not available.   [1] Preliminary data.

Source: U.S. Bureau of Labor Statistics, *Producer Price Indexes*, monthly and annual. See also *Monthly Labor Review* at <http://www.bls.gov/opub/mlr/welcome.htm>.

Table 722. **Producer Price Indexes for the Net Output of Selected Industries: 2004 to 2008**

[Indexes are based on selling prices reported by establishments of all sizes by probability sampling. Manufacturing industries selected by shipment value. N.e.c.= not elsewhere classified. See text, Section 22. See Appendix III]

Industry	2002 NAICS code [1]	Index base [2]	2004	2005	2006	2007	2008 [3]
Logging industries	113310	12/81	175.3	179.2	176.6	175.1	171.5
Total mining industries	**21**	**12/84**	**153.4**	**201.0**	**209.6**	**220.1**	**274.2**
Crude petroleum & natural gas extraction	211111	06/02	183.4	253.5	254.2	261.5	348.3
Natural gas liquid extraction	211112	06/02	216.5	285.4	259.4	286.7	345.0
Bituminous coal & lignite surface mining	212111	12/01	107.1	111.9	117.3	120.9	140.3
Anthracite mining	212113	12/79	180.9	205.4	234.7	240.9	268.1
Iron ore mining	212210	12/84	97.2	115.7	132.1	127.5	141.0
Gold ore mining	212221	06/85	121.6	131.7	177.2	203.0	208.4
Crushed and broken granite mining and quarrying	212313	12/83	203.7	217.3	243.6	279.3	305.9
Construction sand and gravel mining	212321	06/82	195.0	209.9	229.2	247.0	262.7
Clay and ceramic and refractory minerals mining	212325	06/84	144.4	148.3	156.9	163.4	174.8
Drilling oil and gas wells	213111	12/85	168.0	258.8	376.6	360.6	367.7
Nonmetallic minerals support activity (except fuels)	213115	06/85	119.6	127.5	137.1	140.2	146.1
Total manufacturing industries.	**31–33**	**12/84**	**142.9**	**150.8**	**156.9**	**162.9**	**175.8**
Dog & cat food mfg.	311111	12/85	144.0	145.8	147.7	155.2	175.9
Flour milling	311211	06/83	117.4	117.5	127.5	153.9	202.4
Rice milling	311212	06/84	113.1	102.1	114.2	129.2	209.4
Chocolate & confectionery mfg. from cacao beans	311320	06/83	155.0	157.5	161.1	166.0	181.4
Frozen fruit, juice, & vegetable mfg.	311411	06/81	149.3	156.0	170.7	174.9	178.9
Frozen specialty food mfg.	311412	12/82	142.1	143.6	144.3	145.5	154.2
Fruit and vegetable canning	311421	06/81	146.5	151.4	155.8	165.3	177.3
Ice cream and frozen dessert mfg.	311520	06/83	166.0	168.2	171.5	177.7	184.4
Animal (except poultry) slaughtering	311611	12/80	137.8	141.0	136.4	142.7	151.1
Meat processed from carcasses.	311612	12/82	132.9	136.6	137.2	139.5	144.8
Poultry processing	311615	12/81	137.5	135.3	123.7	139.5	145.0
Coffee and tea manufacturing	311920	06/81	142.2	161.0	164.3	173.8	189.9
Spice and extracts manufacturing.	311942	12/03	100.3	99.1	99.7	102.3	108.4
Soft drinks manufacturing	312111	06/81	165.3	168.6	173.3	177.4	185.6
Breweries	312120	06/82	151.9	158.4	158.2	156.0	163.3
Wineries	312130	12/83	140.0	144.8	152.7	155.7	159.5
Distilleries	312140	06/83	164.7	165.5	167.6	175.3	187.5
Cigarettes	312221	12/82	412.6	437.0	440.1	470.2	489.5
Men's/boys' cut & sew trouser/slack/jean mfg.	315224	12/81	126.6	123.2	121.0	122.3	123.0
Women's/girls' cut & sew dress mfg.	315233	12/80	124.9	123.7	123.2	120.8	122.7
Sawmills	321113	12/80	163.4	162.0	158.1	152.0	143.4
Wood preservation	321114	00/05	107.7	175.7	169.5	163.8	165.6
Hardwood veneer & plywood manufacturing.	321211	06/85	143.6	146.2	149.8	151.1	153.0
Wood window & door mfg.	321911	12/03	101.9	103.1	106.8	107.3	107.7
Manufactured homes (mobile homes) mfg.	321991	06/81	190.0	204.4	212.5	214.7	222.9
Paper (except newsprint) mills	322121	12/03	102.4	108.4	112.5	116.2	125.0
Newsprint mills	322122	12/03	104.0	115.7	124.7	106.8	119.2
Paperboard mills	322130	12/82	190.1	196.2	212.9	224.4	242.9
Book printing	323117	12/83	151.5	154.9	158.3	158.6	159.1
Petroleum refineries.	324110	06/85	151.5	205.3	240.9	266.9	338.6
Petroleum lubricating oils and greases	324191	12/80	199.4	231.2	284.8	304.8	356.4
Plastics material and resins manufacturing.	325211	12/80	192.0	228.5	236.1	232.4	256.5
Synthetic rubber manufacturing	325212	06/81	131.6	150.6	161.6	170.2	213.0
Nitrogenous fertilizer manufacturing	325311	12/79	203.9	236.9	245.9	278.5	419.7
Phosphatic fertilizer manufacturing	325312	12/79	161.3	173.3	183.8	257.4	575.5
Pharmaceutical preparation mfg.	325412	06/81	360.1	378.7	398.0	413.8	440.9
Plastics pipe and pipe fitting manufacturing	326122	06/93	140.8	171.9	214.0	197.2	214.3
Cement manufacturing	327310	06/82	154.4	175.2	197.6	208.4	207.7
Steel investment foundries	331512	06/81	197.7	204.8	216.7	235.4	235.7
Steel foundries (except investment)	331513	06/81	146.2	160.1	170.1	183.7	193.7
Aluminum die-casting foundries	331521	06/91	114.1	116.4	125.1	126.4	132.8
Iron & steel forging	332111	12/83	117.5	128.1	133.4	140.4	150.6
Hand and edge tools, except machine tools and handsaws	332212	06/83	168.8	177.0	183.7	188.9	196.8
Saw blade & handsaw mfg.	332213	06/83	142.9	146.0	150.2	152.8	158.2
Metal window and door manufacturing	332321	06/83	166.5	175.2	183.6	188.1	196.1
Sheetmetal work mfg.	332322	12/82	159.4	165.6	171.4	176.8	187.8
Heating equipment (except warm air furnaces) mfg.	333414	06/80	206.2	215.4	222.0	231.2	245.6
Laboratory apparatus and furniture.	339111	12/91	141.2	148.1	152.5	158.8	165.9
Surgical and medical instrument mfg.	339112	06/82	134.6	135.2	133.9	134.5	136.2
Services industries							
Grocery (except convenience) stores.	445110	12/99	123.6	132.1	135.6	140.7	150.6
Beer, wine, and liquor stores	445310	06/00	110.7	111.0	111.4	113.2	120.6
Gasoline stations with convenience stores	447110	12/03	102.5	104.3	109.9	123.0	139.3
Scheduled passenger air transportation.	481111	12/89	205.8	217.1	227.7	234.5	257.6
Scheduled freight air transportation	481112	12/03	100.2	104.9	108.5	109.0	128.5
General freight trucking, long-distance.	484121	12/03	102.7	108.6	112.0	186.1	217.0
Pipeline transportation of crude oil	486110	06/86	115.2	125.5	135.3	114.2	126.8
Pipeline transportation of refined petroleum products	486910	06/86	116.0	120.3	123.7	114.8	123.5
Marine cargo handling	488320	12/91	113.2	115.1	117.9	112.9	116.7
United States Postal Service	491110	06/89	155.0	155.0	164.7	158.2	175.3
Nursing care facilities.	623110	12/94	155.6	161.4	166.1	158.8	163.5

[1] North American Industry Classification System, 2002.   [2] Index base year equals 100.   [3] Preliminary data.

Source: U.S. Bureau of Labor Statistics, *Producer Price Indexes*, monthly and annual. See also *Monthly Labor Review* at <http://www.bls.gov/opub/mlr/welcome.htm>.

Prices   477

Table 723. Chain-Type Price Indexes for Personal Consumption Expenditures by Type of Expenditure: 1990 to 2007

[2000 = 100. For explanation of "chain-type," see text, Section 13. See also Table 661]

Type of expenditure	1990	1995	2003	2004	2005	2006	2007
Total expenditures [1]	80.5	91.6	105.6	108.4	111.6	114.7	117.7
Food and tobacco [1]	78.2	86.8	107.9	111.1	113.8	116.5	121.1
Food purchased for off-premise consumption.	82.7	90.4	106.2	109.5	111.4	113.3	117.7
Purchased meals and beverages [2]	78.6	88.2	108.2	111.5	115.0	118.6	123.0
Tobacco products	46.7	57.6	118.8	121.0	127.3	131.6	140.3
Clothing, accessories, and jewelry [1]	105.6	105.7	95.1	95.3	95.0	95.5	96.0
Shoes	103.7	106.2	96.6	96.3	99.0	99.8	98.9
Clothing.	109.4	106.3	92.3	92.0	90.4	89.8	89.1
Jewelry and watches	114.4	117.9	93.9	94.5	93.1	95.4	100.1
Personal care [1]	83.1	91.8	103.4	104.6	106.1	108.0	110.4
Housing [1]	74.5	86.1	110.4	113.2	116.1	120.3	124.7
Owner-occupied nonfarm dwellings— space rent	74.8	86.2	110.7	113.2	115.7	119.8	123.8
Tenant-occupied nonfarm dwellings—space rent	75.4	86.2	111.3	114.1	117.6	121.7	126.9
Household operation [1]	89.3	96.6	102.0	102.8	106.2	109.2	110.5
Furniture [3]	91.9	99.6	95.0	94.7	93.7	94.5	93.6
Semidurable house furnishings [4]	112.0	111.0	87.7	83.9	81.7	76.1	70.9
Cleaning and polishing preparations	84.2	89.5	102.8	103.2	105.3	109.7	111.5
Household utilities.	80.9	90.3	112.3	118.1	130.1	140.9	145.5
Electricity	91.5	100.9	109.3	111.4	118.1	132.4	137.3
Gas.	73.2	77.3	123.8	134.3	160.0	163.8	163.1
Water and other sanitary services	66.1	87.1	110.2	116.7	123.1	129.1	135.4
Fuel oil and coal	76.9	69.9	109.7	125.4	159.6	180.3	192.3
Telephone and telegraph	103.8	107.0	97.2	95.2	94.4	95.1	97.0
Medical care [1]	70.1	88.0	110.3	114.6	118.4	122.1	126.1
Drug preparations and sundries [5]	72.7	87.2	112.0	115.1	118.5	123.2	124.9
Physicians	71.2	92.3	104.3	106.5	108.5	109.4	113.7
Dentists.	60.6	80.1	113.2	118.7	125.3	131.8	138.7
Hospitals and nursing homes [6]	70.1	87.7	112.8	117.6	122.4	127.2	131.8
Health insurance.	62.0	82.4	114.2	126.8	133.5	137.5	143.8
Medical care [7]	60.3	84.2	120.0	134.4	139.1	143.2	148.7
Personal business [1]	76.0	90.3	105.9	109.2	112.3	115.3	118.1
Expense of handling life insurance [8]	61.7	75.2	110.4	116.6	120.0	124.3	131.2
Legal services	65.7	80.5	116.5	122.0	127.1	131.5	136.9
Funeral and burial expenses	63.7	82.1	113.0	117.8	121.8	128.1	134.4
Transportation [1]	79.9	90.8	101.8	106.1	113.6	119.2	122.5
User-operated transportation [1]	79.5	90.8	102.4	107.0	114.8	120.5	123.9
New autos	87.5	99.9	96.6	96.0	96.7	97.6	97.2
Net purchases of used autos	69.1	95.6	97.4	98.0	101.0	102.7	100.6
Tires, tubes, accessories, etc.	102.2	101.8	105.2	105.7	108.2	112.6	116.4
Repair, greasing, washing, parking, storage, rental, and leasing	77.6	90.4	108.0	109.6	112.8	116.7	120.0
Gasoline and oil	78.4	77.8	105.2	123.9	150.8	170.5	184.6
Purchased local transportation.	77.0	90.2	112.8	119.5	125.0	129.2	131.9
Mass transit systems	77.9	90.9	112.8	119.5	125.0	129.2	131.9
Taxicab	75.0	88.7	112.8	119.5	125.0	129.2	131.9
Purchased intercity transportation [1]	87.9	91.4	88.9	87.8	89.8	94.8	96.2
Railway (commutation)	76.2	85.7	107.6	98.4	99.2	107.8	105.7
Bus.	86.8	86.6	110.5	114.8	118.9	127.5	128.5
Airline	91.5	93.0	84.8	83.3	84.9	89.7	91.1
Recreation [1]	104.9	109.0	95.8	95.2	94.2	93.3	91.7
Magazines, newspapers, and sheet music .	73.9	89.4	105.9	109.0	111.8	113.6	114.8
Nondurable toys and sport supplies	115.9	118.4	85.8	82.4	78.2	75.3	72.5
Video and audio products, including musical instruments and computer goods	284.8	205.9	68.7	62.9	56.8	51.1	45.9
Computers, peripherals, and software	1,516.2	516.5	49.2	43.6	37.6	32.6	29.6
Education and research.	66.6	82.6	115.4	122.2	129.0	135.5	141.2
Higher education.	62.9	82.8	117.0	124.7	132.0	139.3	145.5
Religious and welfare activities	73.1	84.5	109.3	112.6	116.2	121.0	125.1
Foreign travel and other, net:							
Foreign travel by U.S. residents	80.1	95.1	111.6	117.1	125.6	128.1	140.8
Expenditures abroad by U.S. residents . . .	102.0	124.1	124.3	137.8	145.4	153.9	172.3
Less: Expenditures in the United States by nonresidents.	76.9	87.3	104.5	109.0	113.8	119.0	123.6
Less: Personal remittances in kind to nonresidents.	87.8	93.8	101.3	103.7	107.4	109.9	112.1

[1] Includes other types not shown separately. [2] Consists of purchases (including tips) of meals and beverages from retail, service, and amusement establishments; hotels; dining and buffet cars; schools; school fraternities; institutions; clubs; and industrial lunch rooms. Includes meals and beverages consumed both on and off-premise. [3] Includes mattresses and bedsprings. [4] Consists largely of textile house furnishings including piece goods allocated to house furnishing use. Also includes lamp shades, brooms, and brushes. [5] Excludes drug preparations and related products dispensed by physicians, hospitals, and other medical services. [6] Consists of (1) current expenditures (including consumption of fixed capital) of nonprofit hospitals and nursing homes and (2) payments by patients to proprietary and government hospitals and nursing homes. [7] Consists of (1) premiums, less benefits and dividends, for health hospitalization and accidental death and dismemberment insurance provided by commercial insurance carriers and (2) administrative expenses (including consumption of fixed capital) of Blue Cross and Blue Shield plans and of other independent prepaid and self-insured health plans. [8] Consists of (1) operating expenses of life insurance carriers and private noninsured pension plans and (2) premiums less benefits and dividends of fraternal benefit societies. Excludes expenses allocated by commercial carriers to accident and health insurance.

Source: U.S. Bureau of Economic Analysis, *Survey of Current Business*, April 2009. See also <http://www.bea.doc.gov /bea/dn/nipaweb/SelectTable.asp?Selected=N> (released 4 April 2009).

Table 724. Chain-Type Price Indexes for Gross Domestic Product: 1990 to 2008

[2000 = 100. For explanation of "chain-type," see text, Section 13]

Component	1990	1995	2003	2004	2005	2006	2007	2008
Gross domestic product	81.6	92.1	106.4	109.5	113.0	116.7	119.8	122.5
Personal consumption expenditures. . . .	80.5	91.6	105.6	108.4	111.6	114.7	117.7	121.6
Durable goods	104.6	110.7	92.4	90.7	90.0	88.8	87.2	86.1
Nondurable goods.	84.2	90.6	104.1	107.6	111.6	115.0	118.4	124.7
Services	74.2	88.3	109.4	112.9	116.7	120.8	124.7	128.8
Gross private domestic investment	96.4	100.9	103.2	106.7	111.2	116.1	117.7	118.5
Fixed investment	95.5	100.3	103.3	106.8	111.4	116.4	118.0	118.7
Nonresidential.	104.7	106.2	99.6	100.9	103.8	107.3	108.7	110.5
Structures.	74.0	83.9	113.9	120.9	135.0	151.8	157.7	163.3
Equipment and software	118.2	115.2	94.9	94.6	94.5	94.6	94.9	95.5
Residential	74.9	85.8	112.4	120.6	128.7	136.9	138.9	135.6
Net exports of goods and services:								
Exports	100.0	104.4	101.4	105.0	108.8	112.6	116.6	122.8
Goods	108.0	109.2	100.6	104.3	107.5	111.1	115.1	121.1
Services	82.5	93.1	103.3	106.6	111.8	116.2	120.2	126.7
Imports	103.8	106.4	99.7	104.5	111.1	115.9	120.2	132.7
Goods	108.2	108.6	98.1	102.9	109.6	114.2	118.3	131.4
Services	85.7	96.1	108.3	113.0	119.3	125.3	129.9	139.2
Government consumption expenditures and gross investment	77.1	88.4	109.8	114.8	121.4	127.2	132.9	139.2
Federal	77.1	89.5	110.1	115.3	120.9	125.8	130.1	134.3
National defense	78.0	89.6	110.8	115.9	122.0	127.4	131.9	136.6
Nondefense	75.3	89.4	108.9	114.2	118.8	122.8	126.6	129.9
State and local	77.4	87.8	109.7	114.4	121.8	128.1	134.7	142.2

Source: U.S. Bureau of Economic Analysis, *Survey of Current Business*, April 2009. See also <http://www.bea.gov /bea/dn/nipaweb/SelectTable.asp?Selected=N> (released April 2009).

Table 725. Import and Export Price Indexes by End-Use Category: 1990 to 2008

[**As of June**. Import indexes are weighted by the 2000 Tariff Schedule of the United States Annotated, a scheme for describing and reporting product composition and value of U.S. imports. Import prices are based on U.S. dollar prices paid by importer. Export indexes are weighted by 2000 export values according to the Schedule B classification system of the U.S. Census Bureau. Prices used in these indexes were collected from a sample of U.S. manufacturers of exports and are factory transaction prices, except as noted. Minus sign (–) indicates decrease]

Year	Index (2000 = 100)					Percent change [1]				
	Imports			Exports		Imports			Exports	
	Total imports	Petro-leum imports	Non-petro-leum imports	Total exports	Agri-cul-tural exports	Non-agri-cul-tural exports	Total imports	Petro-leum imports	Non-petro-leum imports	Total exports	Agri-cul-tural exports	Non-agricul-tural exports

Year	Total imports	Petro-leum imports	Non-petro-leum imports	Total exports	Agri-cul-tural exports	Non-agri-cul-tural exports	Total imports	Petro-leum imports	Non-petro-leum imports	Total exports	Agri-cul-tural exports	Non-agricul-tural exports
1990	90.8	55.4	96.4	95.1	107.7	93.5	–0.8	–13.4	0.5	–0.1	–4.0	0.5
1995	101.4	62.9	107.6	104.5	117.0	103.3	5.3	9.2	4.9	6.1	7.0	5.9
2000	100.2	101.9	99.9	100.1	100.5	100.0	7.9	87.0	1.1	1.9	–0.6	2.1
2001	97.6	89.4	98.9	99.4	100.9	99.3	–2.6	–12.3	–1.0	–0.7	0.4	–0.7
2002	94.1	85.3	96.2	98.0	100.7	97.8	–3.6	–4.6	–2.7	–1.4	–0.2	–1.5
2003	96.2	96.4	97.3	99.5	110.0	98.7	2.2	13.0	1.1	1.5	9.2	0.9
2004	101.7	129.7	99.7	103.4	127.4	101.5	5.7	34.5	2.5	3.9	15.8	2.8
2005	109.2	181.5	102.0	106.7	123.9	105.4	7.4	39.9	2.3	3.2	–2.7	3.8
2006	117.3	242.6	104.2	111.2	124.1	110.3	7.4	33.7	2.2	4.2	0.2	4.6
2007	120.0	245.6	107.1	116.0	146.7	113.8	2.3	1.2	2.8	4.3	18.2	3.2
2008	145.5	450.3	114.9	126.1	195.2	121.2	21.3	83.3	7.3	8.7	33.1	6.5

[1] Percent change from immediate prior year.

Source: U.S. Bureau of Labor Statistics, *US Import and Export Price Indexes*, monthly. See also <http://www.bls.gov/web /ximpim.supp.toc.htm#longtables>.

Prices   479

Table 726. **Export Price Indexes—Selected Commodities: 2000 to 2008**

[2000 = 100. As of June. Indexes are weighted by 2000 export values according to the Schedule B classification system of the U.S. Census Bureau. Prices used in these indexes were collected from a sample of U.S. manufacturers of exports and are factory transaction prices, except as noted]

Commodities	2000 [1]	2002	2003	2004	2005	2006	2007	2008
All commodities.	**100.1**	**98.0**	**99.5**	**103.4**	**106.7**	**111.2**	**116.0**	**126.1**
Animal products	102.2	94.3	104.5	121.5	130.9	125.1	153.2	174.5
Fish	99.1	98.4	109.6	105.2	114.2	122.8	124.3	149.1
Vegetable products	100.0	105.0	115.0	140.3	130.3	131.0	159.3	239.3
Fruit and nuts	94.8	97.6	97.3	109.2	126.5	114.5	117.5	123.0
Cereals	100.0	106.6	119.3	143.3	118.1	136.9	179.2	293.6
Wheat.	99.4	113.4	121.4	136.2	130.0	154.3	180.4	276.7
Corn (maize)	101.0	104.8	121.3	146.9	111.8	127.1	189.8	286.4
Oilseeds	102.8	104.7	121.5	161.0	136.2	121.5	157.4	259.3
Beverages and tobacco	100.0	99.3	102.8	110.7	110.3	112.5	120.5	136.3
Mineral products	97.8	92.8	106.4	129.7	182.3	238.4	243.4	360.5
Fuels	97.4	92.1	106.2	127.9	172.8	219.6	230.5	361.9
Chemicals and related products	100.3	96.7	102.4	107.7	115.3	122.8	130.1	145.4
Plastics and rubber products	101.5	97.2	102.6	105.7	118.4	128.7	131.3	142.2
Hides, skins, and leather products	95.7	102.6	104.3	108.6	113.0	116.8	122.6	117.3
Wood products	100.0	89.9	93.0	103.8	104.3	107.8	113.5	112.3
Woodpulp and paper products	101.6	92.7	95.1	98.1	101.9	105.5	110.6	117.5
Textiles.	100.2	95.0	97.7	98.8	100.8	101.9	101.9	108.0
Stone and glass products	100.7	100.7	100.2	99.0	103.5	104.1	110.1	111.1
Gems and precious metals.	98.1	89.7	92.1	101.6	106.5	141.8	162.7	183.1
Base metals	100.5	98.4	100.2	119.6	131.8	151.9	169.3	181.2
Iron and steel.	101.7	96.8	102.7	152.9	164.0	173.7	209.2	243.3
Articles of iron and steel.	100.2	102.0	104.7	115.3	124.8	134.6	148.5	156.6
Copper	98.7	92.7	93.4	122.7	143.1	230.6	243.9	261.2
Aluminum	98.4	94.3	94.6	107.3	113.2	146.0	149.5	150.6
Machinery.	99.9	97.2	95.4	94.9	94.9	93.8	94.3	95.3
Nonelectrical machinery	100.0	98.9	99.1	99.9	100.5	101.5	102.7	103.7
Electrical machinery	99.8	95.1	91.2	89.4	88.6	85.3	85.2	86.2
Transportation equipment	100.0	102.9	104.5	106.5	108.8	111.5	113.8	116.6
Motor vehicles	100.0	100.3	101.1	102.4	103.2	104.6	105.6	106.7
Instruments	100.0	100.6	101.2	101.2	101.3	102.4	103.3	107.1
Miscellaneous manufactured articles	100.4	101.5	100.5	99.2	100.6	101.1	104.7	108.6

[1] June 2000 may not equal 100 because indexes were reweighted to an "average" trade value in 2000.

Source: U.S. Bureau of Labor Statistics, *U.S. Import and Export Price Indexes,* monthly. See also <http://stats.bls.gov/news.release /ximpim.toc.htm>.

Table 727. **Import Price Indexes—Selected Commodities: 2000 to 2008**

[2000 = 100. As of June. Indexes are weighted by the 2000 Tariff Schedule of the United States Annotated, a scheme for describing and reporting product composition and value of U.S. imports. Import prices are based on U.S. dollar prices paid by importer]

Commodity	2000 [1]	2002	2003	2004	2005	2006	2007	2008
All commodities.	**100.2**	**94.1**	**96.2**	**101.7**	**109.2**	**117.1**	**120.0**	**145.5**
Animal products	99.9	88.2	95.1	107.8	112.7	118.2	127.4	141.6
Meat.	100.5	104.1	104.1	130.8	138.7	137.2	146.8	165.4
Fish	100.2	79.8	81.9	83.4	88.3	96.6	100.2	106.3
Vegetable products.	97.1	94.7	102.7	103.0	116.9	108.6	129.3	159.5
Vegetables	93.9	106.7	122.7	113.8	136.8	143.6	175.3	202.6
Fruit and nuts	96.9	97.5	96.5	96.3	89.7	81.7	90.9	112.8
Beverages and tobacco.	100.0	101.8	105.4	108.9	114.0	119.8	124.3	140.0
Mineral products	101.3	85.5	100.6	130.9	178.1	229.2	234.0	418.5
Fuels	101.3	84.4	99.5	130.0	177.5	229.0	233.7	421.6
Chemicals and related products	99.8	96.3	99.1	103.6	111.3	114.5	123.8	139.2
Organic chemicals.	100.6	95.7	97.0	100.1	109.6	118.0	120.5	132.9
Pharmaceutical products	99.8	98.8	101.8	106.9	111.0	106.5	107.6	114.1
Plastics and rubber products	99.9	98.6	103.9	105.9	113.5	120.1	121.7	133.2
Hides, skins, and leather products.	100.2	97.9	99.9	101.5	104.0	105.2	107.0	112.4
Wood products	100.5	99.8	96.1	129.5	124.2	120.7	113.5	118.5
Woodpulp and paper products	100.0	91.3	95.2	98.2	102.3	107.9	108.0	115.3
Textiles.	99.7	98.5	99.8	100.3	100.4	100.7	102.1	103.5
Footwear and clothing accessories	99.6	99.1	99.4	99.8	99.9	100.6	101.5	105.8
Footwear.	99.6	99.2	100.0	100.2	100.3	101.0	101.3	104.7
Stone and glass products	99.5	101.0	102.4	103.8	105.4	108.6	110.4	115.4
Gems and precious metals.	99.3	87.5	87.8	93.5	98.3	125.1	132.8	157.1
Gold.	98.3	112.3	127.0	137.1	150.7	241.2	238.2	317.4
Platinum	(NA)	111.2	89.9	116.2	125.7	230.1	257.2	368.6
Base metals	101.5	93.4	96.5	118.9	132.1	157.9	176.7	206.9
Iron and steel.	104.1	94.3	103.3	155.1	170.6	173.8	206.2	308.8
Articles of iron and steel.	100.6	95.6	96.8	109.0	122.7	125.1	129.0	159.7
Copper	97.2	93.0	94.3	119.0	142.7	291.6	307.5	326.2
Aluminum	97.9	97.5	96.8	103.5	113.2	150.0	146.8	155.8
Machinery.	100.2	95.0	92.8	90.7	89.7	88.1	87.8	88.9
Nonelectrical machinery	99.8	94.7	92.9	90.9	90.1	88.3	88.2	89.3
Electrical machinery	100.5	95.4	92.8	90.5	89.4	87.9	87.5	88.5
Transportation equipment	100.0	100.4	101.0	102.8	104.4	104.9	105.9	109.5
Motor vehicles	100.1	100.2	100.7	102.3	103.8	104.3	105.1	108.7
Instruments	99.8	97.9	99.6	99.1	100.1	99.6	99.4	101.5
Miscellaneous manufactured articles	99.7	97.2	97.5	97.4	99.4	99.5	101.1	106.4
Furniture	99.5	97.7	98.3	99.7	103.4	103.3	104.6	111.9

NA Not available. [1] June 2000 may not equal 100 because indexes were reweighted to an "average" trade value in 2000.

Source: U.S. Bureau of Labor Statistics, *U.S. Import and Export Price Indexes,* monthly. See also <http://stats.bls.gov/news .release/ximpim.toc.htm>.

Business Enterprise

This section relates to the place and behavior of the business firm and to business initiative in the American economy. It includes data on the number, type, and size of businesses; financial data of domestic and multinational U.S. corporations; business investments, expenditures, and profits; and sales and inventories.

The principal sources of these data are the *Survey of Current Business*, published by the Bureau of Economic Analysis (BEA), the Web site of the Board of Governors of the Federal Reserve System, (<http:// www.federalreserve.gov/econresdata /default.htm>), the annual *Statistics of Income (SOI)* reports of the Internal Revenue Service (IRS), and the Census Bureau's Economic Census, *County Business Patterns, Quarterly Financial Report for Manufacturing, Mining, and Trade Corporations (QFR), Survey of Business Owners*, and *Annual Capital Expenditures Survey*.

Business firms—A firm is generally defined as a business organization under a single management and may include one or more establishments. The terms firm, business, company, and enterprise are used interchangeably throughout this section. A firm doing business in more than one industry is classified by industry according to the major activity of the firm as a whole.

The IRS concept of a business firm relates primarily to the legal entity used for tax reporting purposes. A sole proprietorship is an unincorporated business owned by one person and may include large enterprises with many employees and hired managers and part-time operators. A partnership is an unincorporated business owned by two or more persons, each of whom has a financial interest in the business. A corporation is a business that is legally incorporated under state laws. While many corporations file consolidated tax returns, most corporate tax returns represent individual corporations, some of which are affiliated through common ownership or control with other corporations filing separate returns.

Economic census—The economic census is the major source of facts about the structure and functioning of the nation's economy. It provides essential information for government, business, industry, and the general public. It furnishes an important part of the framework for such composite measures as the gross domestic product estimates, input/output measures, production and price indexes, and other statistical series that measure short-term changes in economic conditions. The Census Bureau takes the economic census every 5 years, covering years ending in "2" and "7."

The economic census is collected on an establishment basis. A company operating at more than one location is required to file a separate report for each store, factory, shop, or other location. Each establishment is assigned a separate industry classification based on its primary activity and not that of its parent company. Establishments responding to the establishment survey are classified into industries on the basis of their principal product or activity (determined by annual sales volume). The statistics issued by industry in the 2007 Economic Census are classified primarily on the 2007 North American Industry Classification System (NAICS), and, to a lesser extent, on the 2002 NAICS used in the previous census (see below).

More detailed information about the scope, coverage, methodology, classification system, data items, and publications for each of the economic censuses and related surveys is published in the *2007 Economic Census User Guide* at <http:// www.census.gov/econ/census07/www /user_guide/>.

Data from the 2007 Economic Census are released through the Census Bureau's American FactFinder® service on the Census Bureau Web site. For more information, see <http://www.census.gov/econ/census07/>.

Survey of Business Owners—The Survey of Business Owners (SBO) provides statistics that describe the composition of U.S. businesses by gender, Hispanic or Latino origin, and race. Data from SBO are published in a series of reports: *American Indian- and Alaska Native-Owned Firms, Asian-Owned Firms, Black-Owned Firms, Hispanic-Owned Firms, Native Hawaiian- and Other Pacific Islander-Owned Firms, Women-Owned Firms,* and *Company Summary.* Data are presented by industry classifications and/or geographic area and size of firm (employment and receipts). The reports include totals for all U.S. businesses based on the 2002 Economic Census and estimates of business ownership by gender, Hispanic or Latino origin, and race based on the 2002 SBO. Each owner had the option of selecting more than one race and therefore is included in each race selected. For more information, see <http://www.census.gov/econ/sbo/>.

North American Industry Classification System (NAICS)—NAICS is the standard used by Federal statistical agencies in classifying business establishments for the purpose of collecting, analyzing, and publishing statistical data related to the U.S. business economy. NAICS was developed under the auspices of the Office of Managemnet and Budget (OMB), and adopted in 1997 to replace the Standard Industrial Classification (SIC) system. The official 2007 U.S. NAICS Manual includes definitions for each industry, background information, tables showing changes between 2002 and 2007, and a comprehensive index. For more information, see <http://www.census.gov/eos/www/naics/>.

Changes between 2002 NAICS and 2007 NAICS are relatively minor, but do affect totals for sectors 52 (finance and insurance), 53 (real estate, rental, and leasing),

54 (professional, scientific, and technical services), and 56 (admin/support waste mgt/remediation services). Nearly all industries are comparable from 2002 to 2007 NAICS classifications. Several industries in the Information sector have been consolidated.

Quarterly Financial Report—The Quarterly Financial Report (QFR) program publishes quarterly aggregate statistics on the financial conditions of U.S. corporations. The QFR requests companies to report estimates from their statements of income and retained earnings, and balance sheets. The statistical data are classified and aggregated by type of industry and asset size. The QFR sample includes manufacturing companies with assets of $250 thousand and above, and mining, wholesale, and retail companies with assets of $50 million and above. The data are available quarterly in the *Quarterly Financial Report for Manufacturing, Mining, and Trade Corporations* on the Internet at <http://www.census.gov/econ/qfr/>.

Multinational Companies—BEA collects financial and operating data on U.S. multinational companies. These data provide a picture of the overall activities of foreign affiliates and U.S. parent companies, using a variety of indicators of their financial structure and operations. The data on foreign affiliates cover the entire operations of the affiliate, irrespective of the percentage of U.S. ownership. These data cover items such as sales, value added, employment and compensation of employees, capital expenditures, exports and imports, and research and development expenditures. Separate tabulations are available for all affiliates and for affiliates that are majority-owned by their U.S. parent(s). More information is available at <http://www.bea.gov/international/index.htm#omc>.

Statistical reliability—For a discussion of statistical collection, estimation, and sampling procedures and measures of reliability applicable to data from the Census Bureau and the Internal Revenue Service, see Appendix III.

Table 728. **Number of Tax Returns, Receipts, and Net Income by Type of Business: 1990 to 2006**

[14,783 represents 14,783,000. Covers active enterprises only. Figures are estimates based on sample of unaudited tax returns; see Appendix III]

Item	Number of returns (1,000)			Business receipts [1] (bil. dol.)			Net income (less loss) [2] (bil. dol.)		
	Nonfarm proprietorships	Partnerships	Corporations	Nonfarm proprietorships	Partnerships	Corporations	Nonfarm proprietorships	Partnerships	Corporations
1990	14,783	1,554	3,717	731	541	10,914	141	17	371
1991	15,181	1,515	3,803	713	539	10,963	142	21	345
1992	15,495	1,485	3,869	737	571	11,272	154	43	402
1993	15,848	1,468	3,965	757	627	11,814	156	67	498
1994	16,154	1,494	4,342	791	732	12,858	167	82	577
1995	16,424	1,581	4,474	807	854	13,969	169	107	714
1996	16,955	1,654	4,631	843	1,042	14,890	177	145	806
1997	17,176	1,759	4,710	870	1,297	15,890	187	168	915
1998	17,409	1,855	4,849	918	1,534	16,543	202	187	838
1999	17,576	1,937	4,936	969	1,829	18,009	208	228	929
2000	17,905	2,058	5,045	1,021	2,316	19,593	215	269	928
2001	18,338	2,132	5,136	1,017	2,569	19,308	217	276	604
2002	18,926	2,242	5,267	1,030	2,669	18,849	221	271	564
2003	19,710	2,375	5,401	1,050	2,818	19,755	230	301	780
2004	20,591	2,547	5,558	1,140	3,142	21,717	248	385	1,112
2005	21,468	2,764	5,671	1,223	3,719	24,060	270	546	1,949
2006	22,075	2,947	5,841	1,278	4,131	26,070	278	667	1,933

[1] Excludes investment income except for partnerships and corporations in finance, insurance, and real estate before 1998. Beginning 1998, finance and insurance, real estate, and management of companies included investment income for partnerships and corporations. Excludes investment income for S corporations; for definition, see footnote 1, Table 737.   [2] Net income (less loss) is defined differently by form of organization, basically as follows: (a) Proprietorships: Total taxable receipts less total business deductions, including cost of sales and operations, depletion, and certain capital expensing, excluding charitable contributions and owners' salaries; (b) Partnerships: Total taxable receipts (including investment income except capital gains) less deductions, including cost of sales and operations and certain payments to partners, excluding charitable contributions, oil and gas depletion, and certain capital expensing; (c) Corporations: Total taxable receipts (including investment income, capital gains, and income from foreign subsidiaries deemed received for tax purposes, except for S corporations) less business deductions, including cost of sales and operations, depletion, certain capital expensing, and officers' compensation excluding S corporation charitable contributions and investment expenses; net income is before income tax.

Source: U.S. Internal Revenue Service, *Statistics of Income,* various publications.

Table 729. **Number of Tax Returns and Business Receipts by Size of Receipts: 2000 to 2006**

[5,045 represents 5,045,000. Covers active enterprises only. Figures are estimates based on sample of unaudited tax returns; see Appendix III]

Size-class of receipts	Returns (1,000)					Business receipts [1] (bil. dol.)				
	2000	2003	2004	2005	2006	2000	2003	2004	2005	2006
Corporations	5,045	5,401	5,558	5,671	5,841	19,593	19,755	21,717	24,060	26,070
Under $25,000 [2]	1,220	1,280	1,317	1,300	1,363	4	3	4	4	3
$25,000 to $49,999	302	346	334	340	341	10	13	12	12	13
$50,000 to $99,999	477	522	545	544	554	35	39	40	40	41
$100,000 to $499,999	1,515	1,649	1,703	1,755	1,780	397	412	424	437	443
$500,000 to $999,999	582	623	635	644	668	407	441	448	458	473
$1,000,000 or more	946	981	1,023	1,088	1,135	18,738	18,848	20,788	23,108	25,097
Partnerships	2,058	2,375	2,547	2,764	2,947	2,316	2,818	3,142	3,719	4,131
Under $25,000 [2]	1,105	1,284	1,373	1,465	1,568	5	5	5	5	6
$25,000 to $49,999	183	192	193	218	240	7	7	7	8	9
$50,000 to $99,999	187	206	226	233	245	13	15	16	17	18
$100,000 to $499,999	353	410	436	489	498	82	95	102	114	118
$500,000 to $999,999	92	111	121	131	149	66	78	86	92	106
$1,000,000 or more	137	172	198	227	248	2,143	2,619	2,925	3,482	3,875
Nonfarm proprietorships	17,905	19,710	20,591	21,468	22,075	1,021	1,050	1,140	1,223	1,278
Under $25,000 [2]	11,997	13,308	13,916	14,456	14,867	82	93	97	100	104
$25,000 to $49,999	2,247	2,450	2,536	2,587	2,721	80	87	90	92	96
$50,000 to $99,999	1,645	1,805	1,792	1,981	1,983	117	128	128	140	140
$100,000 to $499,999	1,733	1,851	2,020	2,091	2,139	355	373	405	425	437
$500,000 to $999,999	190	200	218	235	236	126	135	147	160	161
$1,000,000 or more	92	96	109	117	128	261	235	273	306	340

[1] Finance and insurance, real estate, and management of companies included investment income for partnerships and corporations.   [2] Includes firms with no receipts.

Source: U.S. Internal Revenue Service, *Statistics of Income Bulletin;* and unpublished data.

Business Enterprise   483

Table 730. **Number of Tax Returns, Receipts, and Net Income by Type of Business and Industry: 2006**

[22,075 represents 22,075,000. Covers active enterprises only. Figures are estimates based on sample of unaudited tax returns; see Appendix III. Based on the North American Industry Classification System (NAICS), 2002; see text, this section]

Industry	2002 NAICS code	Number of returns (1,000)			Business receipts [1] (bil. dol.)			Net income (less loss) (bil. dol.)		
		Non-farm propri-etor-ships	Partner-ships	Corpo-rations	Non-farm propri-etor-ships	Partner-ships	Corpo-rations	Non-farm propri-etor-ships	Partner-ships	Corpo-rations
Total	(X)	**22,075**	**2,947**	**5,841**	**1,278**	**4,131**	**26,070**	**278**	**667**	**1,933**
Agriculture, forestry, fishing, and hunting [2]	11	275	132	141	15	23	128	1	2	3
Mining.	21	135	35	37	13	96	327	2	46	59
Utilities	22	14	3	8	(Z)	144	585	(Z)	9	37
Construction.	23	2,916	192	781	236	310	1,582	38	24	74
Special trade contractors.	238	2,287	70	471	158	60	634	29	4	29
Manufacturing.	31–33	325	43	279	26	776	6,940	3	62	481
Wholesale and retail trade [3]	(X)	2,845	200	1,000	243	815	7,087	14	20	228
Wholesale trade	42	379	49	383	48	466	3,600	5	16	115
Retail trade [4]	44–45	2,466	151	615	195	349	3,486	9	3	112
Motor vehicle and parts dealers	441	132	16	94	39	114	883	1	1	10
Food and beverage stores.	445	106	18	94	27	49	482	1	(Z)	11
Gasoline stations	447	21	8	39	25	68	275	(Z)	(Z)	2
Transportation and warehousing.	48–49	1,084	43	200	76	101	712	11	7	26
Information [4]	51	334	39	128	11	218	943	2	32	101
Broadcasting (except Internet).	515	[5]52	2	7	[5]2	38	103	[5](Z)	2	6
Telecommunications.	517	(5)	6	18	(5)	131	400	(5)	26	48
Finance and insurance.	52	688	295	250	82	562	3,748	20	282	632
Real estate and rental and leasing	53	1,381	1,395	655	77	308	286	27	59	24
Professional, scientific, and technical services [4]	54	2,930	186	813	156	309	888	67	75	36
Legal services.	5411	349	28	102	37	124	84	16	45	7
Accounting, tax preparation, bookkeeping, and payroll services.	5412	370	22	71	12	48	35	5	10	3
Management, scientific, and technical consulting services	5416	800	38	230	40	42	184	22	8	11
Management of companies and enterprises.	55	(NA)	29	50	(NA)	49	1,094	(NA)	18	157
Administrative and support and waste management and remediation services	56	2,141	60	268	57	70	449	16	5	14
Educational services	61	607	12	47	9	4	37	3	(Z)	2
Health care and social assistance.	62	1,874	64	401	110	143	558	45	20	28
Arts, entertainment, and recreation.	71	1,238	50	120	30	44	86	7	(Z)	5
Accommodation and food services.	72	390	105	289	45	135	417	2	3	21
Accommodation.	721	61	33	31	6	59	87	(Z)	1	5
Food services and drinking places	722	330	72	258	40	76	330	2	2	15
Other services [4]	81	2,544	64	369	86	23	202	20	1	7
Auto repair and maintenance	8111	370	21	112	25	8	72	3	(Z)	1
Personal and laundry services	812	1,401	35	154	38	10	76	11	1	3
Religious, grantmaking, civic, professional, and similar organizations.	813	262	1	46	4	(Z)	13	2	(Z)	(Z)
Unclassified	(X)	354	1	5	5	(Z)	(Z)	2	(Z)	(Z)

NA Not available.   X Not applicable.   Z Less than $500 million.   [1] Includes investment income for partnerships and corporations in finance and insurance, real estate, and management of companies' industries. Excludes investment income for S corporations; for definition, see footnote 1, Table 737.   [2] For corporations, represents agricultural services only.   [3] For corporations, includes trade business not identified as wholesale or retail.   [4] Includes other industries not shown separately.   [5] Broadcasting includes telecommunications.

Source: U.S. Internal Revenue Service, *Statistics of Income,* various publications.

Table 731. **Nonfarm Sole Proprietorships—Selected Income and Deduction Items: 1990 to 2006**

[In billions of dollars (731 represents $731,000,000,000) except as indicated. All figures are estimates based on samples. Tax law changes have affected the comparability of the data over time; see *Statistics of Income* reports for a description. See Appendix III]

Item	1990	1995	2000	2001	2002	2003	2004	2005	2006
Number of returns (1,000)	14,783	16,424	17,905	18,338	18,926	19,710	20,591	21,468	22,075
Returns with net income (1,000).	11,222	12,213	13,308	13,604	13,751	14,448	15,053	15,750	16,207
Business receipts	731	807	1,021	1,017	1,030	1,050	1,140	1,223	1,278
Income from sales and operations . . .	719	797	1,008	1,002	1,015	1,034	1,122	1,205	1,259
Business deductions [1]	589	638	806	800	809	820	892	953	1,001
Cost of goods sold/operations [1]	291	307	387	363	352	338	371	397	410
Purchases	210	219	269	247	227	218	239	253	260
Labor costs.	23	24	29	28	30	28	32	32	32
Materials and supplies	30	34	43	44	46	47	53	56	60
Advertising	(NA)	(NA)	10	11	11	12	13	14	15
Car and truck expenses	22	33	46	47	50	53	59	71	75
Commissions	9	10	12	12	14	14	13	15	16
Contract labor.	(NA)	(NA)	(NA)	(NA)	(NA)	(NA)	25	28	35
Depreciation	24	27	32	33	37	42	43	39	39
Insurance.	13	13	14	14	16	17	19	19	19
Interest paid [2].	13	10	12	13	11	11	11	12	14
Office expenses	(NA)	(NA)	10	11	11	12	12	13	13
Rent paid [3].	23	28	33	34	35	36	37	39	41
Repairs	9	10	12	12	13	13	15	15	16
Salaries and wages (net)	47	54	63	64	66	68	71	75	77
Supplies	(NA)	(NA)	22	23	25	26	27	29	32
Taxes paid	10	13	14	14	15	15	16	17	18
Utilities	14	17	19	20	21	22	21	23	24
Net income (less loss) [4]	141	169	215	217	221	230	248	270	278
Net income [4]	162	192	245	250	257	269	291	315	327
Constant (2000) Dollars [5]									
Business receipts	896	877	1,021	993	991	991	1,045	1,085	1,097
Business deductions	722	693	806	781	778	774	818	846	859
Net income (less loss)	173	184	215	212	213	217	227	239	239
Net income.	198	208	245	244	248	254	266	279	280

NA Not available. [1] Includes other amounts not shown separately. [2] Interest paid includes "mortgage interest" and "other interest paid on business indebtedness." [3] Rent paid includes "Rent on machinery and equipment" and "Rent on other business property." [4] After adjustment for the passive loss carryover from prior years. Therefore, "business receipts" minus "total deductions" do not equal "net income." [5] Based on the overall implicit price deflator for gross domestic product.

Source: U.S. Internal Revenue Service, *Statistics of Income Bulletin.*

Table 732. **Partnerships—Selected Income and Balance Sheet Items: 1990 to 2006**

[In billions of dollars (1,735 represents $1,735,000,000,000), except as indicated. Covers active partnerships only. All figures are estimates based on samples. See Appendix III]

Item	1990	1995	2000	2001	2002	2003	2004	2005	2006
Number of returns (1,000)	1,554	1,581	2,058	2,132	2,242	2,375	2,547	2,764	2,947
Returns with net income (1,000).	854	955	1,261	1,301	1,325	1,357	1,441	1,580	1,623
Number of partners (1,000).	17,095	15,606	13,660	14,232	14,328	14,108	15,557	16,212	16,728
Assets [1,2]	1,735	2,719	6,694	8,428	8,867	9,675	11,608	13,734	17,146
Depreciable assets (net)	681	767	1,487	1,646	1,792	1,846	1,988	2,176	2,490
Inventories, end of year	57	88	150	208	203	214	276	315	446
Land.	215	221	359	392	423	455	509	607	731
Liabilities [1,2].	1,415	1,886	3,696	4,835	4,972	5,303	6,248	7,483	9,350
Accounts payable	67	91	230	362	346	276	336	400	505
Short-term debt [3]	88	124	252	289	283	274	296	373	456
Long-term debt [4]	498	544	1,132	1,286	1,375	1,389	1,546	1,772	2,227
Nonrecourse loans	470	466	639	700	770	800	854	914	1,103
Partners' capital accounts [2]	320	832	2,999	3,593	3,895	4,372	5,360	6,251	7,796
Receipts [1]	566	890	2,405	2,665	2,773	2,923	3,260	3,863	4,301
Business receipts [5]	483	854	2,316	2,569	2,669	2,818	3,142	3,719	4,131
Interest received	21	31	82	85	70	71	88	134	193
Deductions [1]	550	784	2,136	2,389	2,502	2,621	2,876	3,317	3,634
Cost of goods sold/operations	243	395	1,226	1,338	1,430	1,523	1,666	1,976	2,109
Salaries and wages	56	80	201	231	238	245	269	293	332
Taxes paid	9	13	31	35	36	39	42	47	53
Interest paid	30	43	93	97	68	65	64	103	137
Depreciation	60	23	59	72	83	84	90	71	79
Net income (less loss)	17	107	269	276	271	301	385	546	667
Net income.	116	179	410	446	440	469	566	724	871

[1] Includes items not shown separately. [2] Assets, liabilities, and partners' capital accounts are understated because not all partnerships file complete balance sheets. [3] Mortgages, notes, and bonds payable in less than 1 year. [4] Mortgages, notes, and bonds payable in 1 year or more. [5] Excludes investment income except for partnerships in finance, insurance, and real estate in 1995. Beginning 2000, finance and insurance, real estate, and management of companies included investment income for partnerships.

Source: U.S. Internal Revenue Service, *Statistics of Income,* various issues.

Business Enterprise 485

Table 733. **Partnerships—Selected Items by Industry: 2006**

[In billions of dollars (17,146 represents $17,146,000,000,000), except as indicated. Covers active partnerships only. Figures are estimates based on samples. Based on the North American Industry Classification System (NAICS), 2002; see text, this section. See Appendix III]

| Industry | 2002 NAICS code | Number of partnerships (1,000) | | | Total assets [1] | Business receipts [2] | Total deductions | Net income less loss | Net income | Net loss |
		Total	With net income	With net loss						
Total [3]	(X)	2,947	1,623	1,324	17,146	4,131	3,634	666.7	871.1	204.3
Agriculture, forestry, fishing, and hunting	11	132	77	55	134	23	30	2.1	9.0	7.0
Mining	21	35	21	14	229	96	65	45.9	52.7	6.8
Utilities	22	3	1	2	202	144	141	9.2	13.5	4.3
Construction	23	192	110	82	323	310	294	24.4	32.8	8.4
Manufacturing	31-33	43	19	25	492	776	738	62.2	74.0	11.7
Wholesale trade	42	49	26	23	132	466	456	16.2	18.5	2.4
Retail trade	44-45	151	67	84	117	349	354	3.5	9.5	6.1
Transportation and warehousing	48-49	43	22	21	159	101	101	6.6	10.7	4.1
Information	51	39	16	23	573	218	216	32.1	44.6	12.5
Finance and insurance	52	295	215	80	10,085	562	280	281.8	303.9	22.1
Real estate and rental and leasing	53	1,395	722	672	3,725	308	257	59.4	144.1	84.7
Professional, scientific, and technical services	54	186	118	68	157	309	253	75.2	82.3	7.1
Management of companies and enterprises	55	29	17	12	399	49	30	18.2	24.0	5.8
Admin/support waste mgt/ remediation services	56	60	36	24	42	70	69	5.0	7.0	2.0
Educational services	61	12	5	6	4	4	5	0.1	0.7	0.6
Health care and social assistance	62	64	40	24	87	143	132	20.4	24.5	4.0
Arts, entertainment, and recreation	71	50	20	30	82	44	50	0.3	5.9	5.6
Accommodation and food services	72	105	54	51	186	135	138	2.8	10.8	8.0
Other services	81	64	37	27	17	23	23	1.4	2.6	1.2

X Not applicable.   [1] Total assets are understated because not all partnerships file complete balance sheets.   [2] Finance and insurance, real estate, and management of companies include investment income for partnerships.   [3] Includes businesses not allocable to individual industries.

Source: U.S. Internal Revenue Service, *Statistics of Income*, various issues.

Table 734. **Nonfarm Noncorporate Business-Sector Balance Sheet: 1990 to 2008**

[In billions of dollars (3,707 represents $3,707,000,000,000), except as noted. Represents year-end outstandings]

Item	1990	1995	2000	2003	2004	2005	2006	2007	2008
Assets	3,707	4,108	6,385	7,579	8,541	10,353	11,212	11,752	10,944
Tangible assets	3,351	3,560	4,963	5,842	6,435	7,811	8,155	8,172	7,168
Real estate [1]	3,040	3,210	4,525	5,366	5,932	7,273	7,582	7,569	6,543
Residential	2,121	2,365	3,338	4,130	4,620	5,594	5,655	5,550	4,792
Nonresidential	919	845	1,187	1,237	1,312	1,679	1,927	2,020	1,751
Equipment and software [2]	263	294	367	405	426	454	484	508	533
Residential [3]	32	36	39	40	42	45	48	50	51
Nonresidential	232	259	329	365	384	409	436	458	482
Inventories [2]	47	56	70	71	78	84	89	95	92
Financial assets	356	548	1,423	1,737	2,106	2,542	3,057	3,580	3,776
Checkable deposits and currency	71	105	164	173	259	323	382	436	453
Time and savings deposits	51	71	248	314	318	352	383	453	485
Money market fund shares	7	17	49	64	69	74	81	98	103
Treasury securities	13	24	40	45	50	56	56	66	70
Municipal securities	–	2	2	3	4	4	6	7	7
Mortgages	31	22	23	26	31	36	35	41	43
Trade receivables	98	140	342	338	364	431	471	551	581
Miscellaneous assets	86	167	554	775	1,010	1,266	1,644	1,929	2,034
Insurance receivables	39	44	46	57	60	65	67	69	72
Equity investment in GSEs [4]	1	1	2	2	2	2	2	2	3
Other	47	122	506	716	947	1,198	1,576	1,858	1,960
Liabilities	1,349	1,397	2,673	3,172	3,517	4,052	4,635	5,190	5,409
Credit market instruments	1,093	1,062	1,796	2,199	2,444	2,775	3,184	3,595	3,767
Bank loans n.e.c. [5]	136	165	361	442	469	623	729	863	968
Other loans and advances	94	92	127	132	133	137	150	162	173
Mortgages	863	805	1,308	1,625	1,842	2,016	2,305	2,570	2,626
Trade payables	60	86	260	255	277	329	349	396	413
Taxes payable	32	33	65	70	78	87	96	103	106
Miscellaneous liabilities	164	215	553	649	718	860	1,005	1,096	1,123
Net worth	2,358	2,712	3,713	4,406	5,024	6,301	6,577	6,562	5,535
Debt/net worth (percent)	46.4	39.2	48.4	49.9	48.6	44.0	48.4	54.8	68.1

– Represents or rounds to zero.   [1] At market value.   [2] At replacement (current) cost.   [3] Durable goods in rental properties.   [4] GSEs = government-sponsored enterprises. Equity in the Farm Credit System.   [5] Not elsewhere classified.

Source: Board of Governors of the Federal Reserve System, "Federal Reserve Statistical Release, Z.1, Flow of Funds Accounts of the United States"; published 12 March 2009; <http://www.federalreserve.gov/releases/z1/20090312/>.

Table 735. **Nonfinancial Corporate Business-Sector Balance Sheet: 1990 to 2008**

[In billions of dollars (9,683 represents $9,683,000,000,000). Represents year-end outstandings]

Item	1990	1995	2000	2003	2004	2005	2006	2007	2008
Assets	9,683	11,461	19,018	20,074	21,698	24,750	27,108	29,113	28,277
Tangible assets	6,108	6,502	9,246	9,965	10,766	12,841	14,423	15,332	14,228
Real estate [1]	3,388	3,146	4,846	5,370	5,935	7,738	9,010	9,634	8,397
Equipment and software [2]	1,819	2,287	3,067	3,250	3,351	3,501	3,715	3,896	4,083
Inventories [2]	901	1,070	1,334	1,345	1,480	1,602	1,698	1,802	1,748
Financial assets [3]	3,575	4,959	9,772	10,109	10,932	11,909	12,685	13,781	14,049
Checkable deposits and currency...	166	205	246	191	178	252	134	185	166
Time and savings deposits	75	100	272	363	400	450	497	443	467
Money market fund shares	20	60	191	299	324	366	433	567	675
Treasury securities	38	57	18	33	33	51	44	49	41
Mortgages	53	58	44	52	67	68	60	51	43
Consumer credit	67	85	81	58	59	59	57	55	56
Trade receivables	967	1,185	1,939	1,702	1,831	2,109	2,091	2,293	2,385
Mutual fund shares [1]	10	46	122	126	140	156	204	225	160
Liabilities [3]	4,729	6,010	9,611	9,867	10,349	11,145	11,782	12,553	12,888
Credit market instruments........	2,536	2,940	4,638	4,974	5,178	5,511	5,977	6,785	7,104
Commercial paper.	117	157	278	82	98	90	113	124	132
Municipal securities [4]	115	135	154	164	169	177	182	190	193
Corporate bonds [5]	1,008	1,357	2,271	2,900	2,976	3,032	3,248	3,559	3,764
Bank loans n.e.c. [6]	545	602	853	548	547	515	532	631	704
Other loans and advances	473	469	716	750	805	911	1,024	1,284	1,272
Mortgages	277	220	366	529	583	785	879	998	1,041
Trade payables	626	878	1,541	1,403	1,500	1,699	1,813	1,999	2,106
Taxes payable	38	40	78	81	88	93	93	94	95
Net worth (market value)	4,954	5,451	9,407	10,207	11,348	13,605	15,326	16,559	15,390
Debt/net worth (percent).	51.2	53.9	49.3	48.7	45.6	40.5	39.0	41.0	46.2

[1] At market value. [2] At replacement (current) cost. [3] Includes items not shown separately. [4] Industrial revenue bonds. Issued by state and local governments to finance private investment and secured in interest and principal by the industrial user of the funds. [5] Through 1992, corporate bonds include net issues by Netherlands Antillean financial subsidiaries. [6] Not elsewhere classified.

Source: Board of Governors of the Federal Reserve System, "Federal Reserve Statistical Release, Z.1, Flow of Funds Accounts of the United States"; published 12 March 2009; <http://www.federalreserve.gov/releases/z1/20090312/>.

Table 736. **Corporate Funds—Sources and Uses: 1990 to 2008**

[In billions of dollars (238 represents $238,000,000,000). Covers nonfarm nonfinancial corporate business]

Item	1990	1995	2000	2003	2004	2005	2006	2007	2008
Profits before tax (book)	238	419	422	424	660	953	1,126	1,090	938
− Taxes on corporate income	98	141	170	135	190	274	309	320	277
− Net dividends	117	177	250	291	364	181	472	501	498
+ Capital consumption allowance [1].......	365	463	629	733	745	622	621	644	812
= U.S. internal funds, book	388	564	632	732	851	1,120	966	913	974
+ Foreign earnings retained abroad	45	53	100	113	121	−17	159	185	147
+ Inventory valuation adjustment (IVA)	−13	−18	−14	−14	−43	−38	−39	−51	−76
= Internal funds + IVA	420	598	718	831	928	1,065	1,086	1,047	1,045
Gross investment	369	653	900	819	1,000	919	936	1,165	1,018
Capital expenditures	429	618	929	750	826	922	1,059	1,047	1,069
Fixed investment [2].	422	577	882	748	788	890	1,005	1,062	1,093
Inventory change + IVA	12	40	55	13	48	41	51	−5	−41
Nonproduced nonfinancial assets	−5	1	−9	−11	−11	−9	4	−10	17
Net financial investment	−59	36	−28	69	174	−3	−123	118	−50
Net acquisition of financial assets [3].....	124	426	1,209	83	783	958	713	1,074	487
Foreign deposits	(Z)	2	−7	18	16	7	−11	−1	−26
Checkable deposits and currency	6	4	15	50	−13	74	−119	52	−19
Time and savings deposits..........	−6	3	35	71	38	50	47	−54	24
Money market fund shares..........	9	23	37	−37	25	42	67	133	108
Commercial paper	(Z)	1	10	11	19	16	12	−64	−54
Municipal securities	−8	−20	7	3	−4	(Z)	−4	2	−19
Mortgages	−2	2	2	2	15	2	−8	−8	−8
Mutual fund shares...............	−1	5	4	11	1	7	31	9	9
Trade receivables.	29	78	282	−17	129	278	−18	202	92
Miscellaneous assets [3]	114	320	819	−10	555	450	728	805	391
U.S. direct investment abroad [4]	36	90	128	123	270	21	218	264	252
Insurance receivables	13	8	(Z)	18	19	21	7	7	13
Net increase in liabilities [3]	184	391	1,237	13	609	961	836	956	537
Net funds raised in markets	73	179	244	46	80	−28	−133	−30	−71
Net new equity issues	−63	−58	−118	−41	−124	−361	−603	−831	−395
Credit market instruments [3]	136	238	362	87	204	332	469	801	324
Corporate bonds [4]	47	104	164	152	75	57	216	311	205
Bank loans n.e.c [5]	3	75	44	−99	−1	−32	17	92	73
Other loans and advances [6]	56	30	83	7	55	106	116	260	−12
Mortgages	22	8	22	61	54	202	94	119	47
Trade payables	28	81	313	−55	97	199	110	186	107
Miscellaneous liabilities [3]	82	131	673	34	425	785	860	798	501
Foreign direct investment in U.S.....	59	53	192	24	29	43	105	143	154

Z Less than $500 million. [1] Consumption of fixed capital plus capital consumption adjustment. [2] Nonresidential fixed investment plus residential fixed investment. [3] Includes other items not shown separately. [4] 1990, corporate bonds include net issues by Netherlands Antillean financial subsidiaries, and U.S. direct investment abroad excludes net inflows from those bond issues. [5] Not elsewhere classified. [6] Loans from rest of the world, U.S. government, and nonbank financial institutions.

Source: Board of Governors of the Federal Reserve System, "Federal Reserve Statistical Release, Z.1, Flow of Funds Accounts of the United States"; published 12 March 2009; <http://www.federalreserve.gov/releases/z1/20090312/>.

Table 737. Corporations—Selected Financial Items: 1990 to 2006

[In billions of dollars (18,190 represents $18,190,000,000,000), except as noted. Covers active corporations only. All corporations are required to file returns except those specifically exempt. See source for changes in law affecting comparability of historical data. Based on samples; see Appendix III]

Item	1990	1995	2000	2001	2002	2003	2004	2005	2006
Number of returns (1,000)	3,717	4,474	5,045	5,136	5,267	5,401	5,558	5,671	5,841
Number with net income (1,000) . . .	1,911	2,455	2,819	2,822	2,801	2,932	3,116	3,324	3,367
S Corporation returns [1] (1,000)	1,575	2,153	2,860	2,986	3,154	3,342	3,518	3,684	3,873
Assets [2]	18,190	26,014	47,027	49,154	50,414	53,645	60,118	66,445	73,081
Cash	771	962	1,820	1,926	1,923	2,120	2,730	2,823	2,902
Notes and accounts receivable	4,198	5,307	8,754	8,756	8,886	8,995	10,691	11,962	13,611
Inventories.	894	1,045	1,272	1,208	1,221	1,267	1,386	1,505	1,613
Investments in government obligations	921	1,363	1,236	1,392	1,527	1,656	1,571	1,613	1,714
Mortgage and real estate	1,538	1,713	2,822	3,229	3,687	4,073	4,627	4,777	5,232
Other investments.	4,137	7,429	17,874	18,344	18,728	20,536	22,657	25,162	27,903
Depreciable assets	4,318	5,571	7,292	7,614	7,678	7,805	7,974	8,416	8,817
Depletable assets	129	154	191	199	226	237	270	310	382
Land.	210	242	303	320	326	342	363	407	457
Liabilities [2]	18,190	26,014	47,027	49,154	50,414	53,645	60,118	66,445	73,081
Accounts payable	1,094	1,750	3,758	3,927	4,074	4,338	5,645	6,029	7,779
Short-term debt [3]	1,803	2,034	4,020	4,132	3,814	4,002	4,399	4,192	4,709
Long-term debt [4].	2,665	3,335	6,184	6,782	7,185	7,384	8,154	8,332	9,399
Net worth	4,739	8,132	17,349	17,615	17,545	18,819	20,814	23,525	25,996
Capital stock.	1,585	2,194	3,966	4,253	4,000	3,151	2,308	2,482	2,513
Paid-in or capital surplus.	2,814	5,446	12,265	13,920	15,287	15,258	16,160	17,828	19,142
Retained earnings [5]	1,410	2,191	3,627	2,132	1,111	2,282	3,278	4,331	5,764
Receipts [2, 6]	11,410	14,539	20,606	20,273	19,749	20,690	22,712	25,505	27,402
Business receipts [6, 7].	9,860	12,786	17,637	17,504	17,297	18,264	19,976	21,800	23,310
Interest [8]	977	1,039	1,628	1,549	1,282	1,182	1,368	1,773	2,307
Rents and royalties	133	145	254	251	252	270	274	290	299
Deductions [2, 6].	11,033	13,821	19,692	19,683	19,199	19,941	21,636	23,613	25,502
Cost of sales and operations [7]	6,611	8,206	11,135	11,042	10,607	11,319	12,498	13,816	14,800
Compensation of officers	205	304	401	383	381	389	417	445	474
Rent paid on business property	185	232	380	398	411	407	420	439	462
Taxes paid.	251	326	390	392	397	417	447	473	497
Interest paid.	825	744	1,272	1,203	913	818	939	1,287	1,787
Depreciation	333	437	614	650	711	692	691	531	564
Advertising	126	163	234	220	218	225	239	253	277
Net income (less loss) [6, 9]	371	714	928	604	564	780	1,112	1,949	1,933
Net income	553	881	1,337	1,112	1,053	1,176	1,456	2,235	2,240
Deficit.	182	166	409	509	489	396	344	286	306
Income subject to tax	366	565	760	635	601	699	857	1,201	1,291
Income tax before credits [10]	119	194	266	221	210	244	300	419	453
Tax credits	32	42	62	54	56	66	75	107	100
Foreign tax credit	25	30	49	41	42	50	57	82	78
Income tax after credits [11]	96	156	204	167	154	178	224	312	353

[1] Represents certain small corporations with up to 75 shareholders (35 for 1990 and 1995), mostly individuals, electing to be taxed at the shareholder level. [2] Includes items not shown separately. [3] Payable in less than 1 year. [4] Payable in 1 year or more. [5] Appropriated and unappropriated and "adjustments to shareholders' equity." [6] Receipts, deductions, and net income of S corporations are limited to those from trade or business. Those from investments are excluded. [7] Includes gross sales and cost of sales of securities, commodities, and real estate by exchanges, brokers, or dealers selling on their own accounts. Excludes investment income. [8] Includes tax-exempt interest in state and local government obligations. [9] Excludes regulated investment companies. [10] Consists of regular (and alternative tax) only. [11] Includes minimum tax, alternative minimum tax, adjustments for prior year credits, and other income-related taxes.

Source: U.S. Internal Revenue Service, *Statistics of Income, Corporation Income Tax Returns*, annual.

Table 738. **Corporations by Receipt-Size Class and Industry: 2006**

[**Number of returns in thousands (5,841 represents 5,841,000); receipts and net income in billions of dollars (26,070 represents $26,070,000,000,000).** Covers active enterprises only. Figures are estimates based on a sample of unaudited tax returns; see Appendix III. Numbers in parentheses represent North American Industry Classification System 2002 codes, see text, this section]

Industry	Total	Under $1 mil.[1]	$1 mil.–$4.9 mil.	$5 mil.–$9.9 mil.	$10 mil.–$49.9 mil.	$50 mil. or more
Total: [2]						
Number of returns..............	5,841	4,706	836	136	128	34
Business receipts [3].............	26,070	973	1,801	950	2,631	19,715
Net income (less loss)...........	1,933	32	72	41	142	1,646
Agriculture, forestry, fishing, and hunting (11):						
Number...........	141	122	15	2	1	(Z)
Business receipts [3]	128	19	32	11	23	43
Mining (21):						
Number...........	37	28	6	1	1	(Z)
Business receipts [3]	327	5	14	10	21	277
Utilities (22):						
Number...........	8	7	1	(Z)	(Z)	(Z)
Business receipts [3]	585	1	1	1	3	579
Construction (23):						
Number...........	781	588	147	24	19	3
Business receipts [3]	1,582	142	316	168	380	577
Manufacturing (31–33):						
Number...........	279	166	70	18	19	7
Business receipts [3]	6,940	45	159	127	399	6,210
Wholesale and retail trade (42,44–45):						
Number...........	1,000	674	220	44	50	13
Business receipts [3]	7,087	176	504	307	1,045	5,055
Transportation and warehousing (48–49):						
Number...........	200	159	30	6	5	1
Business receipts [3]	712	31	66	40	94	482
Information (51):						
Number...........	128	107	15	3	3	1
Business receipts [3]	943	17	35	17	54	820
Finance and insurance (52):						
Number...........	250	205	28	6	8	4
Business receipts [3]	3,748	39	61	40	162	3,446
Real estate and rental and leasing (53):						
Number...........	655	623	27	4	2	(Z)
Business receipts [3]	286	60	53	24	36	112
Professional, scientific, and technical services (54):						
Number...........	813	708	86	10	8	1
Business receipts [3]	888	124	175	71	155	363
Management of companies and enterprises (55):						
Number...........	50	43	3	1	2	1
Business receipts [3]	1,094	(Z)	6	10	46	1,031
Administrative and support and waste management and remediation services (56):						
Number...........	268	223	36	5	2	1
Business receipts [3]	449	48	75	34	48	244
Educational services (61):						
Number...........	47	43	4	(Z)	(Z)	(Z)
Business receipts [3]	37	7	7	2	4	17
Health care and social assistance (62):						
Number...........	401	321	68	6	5	1
Business receipts [3]	558	98	135	37	91	198
Arts, entertainment, and recreation (71):						
Number...........	120	110	8	1	1	(Z)
Business receipts [3]	86	19	18	5	11	33
Accommodation and food services (72):						
Number...........	289	239	44	4	2	(Z)
Business receipts [3]	417	73	86	26	34	199
Other services (81):						
Number...........	369	335	30	3	2	(Z)
Business receipts [3]	202	69	58	19	27	29

Z Less than 500 returns or $500 million.   [1] Includes businesses without receipts.   [2] Includes businesses not allocable to individual industries.   [3] Includes investment income for corporations in finance and insurance and management of companies' industries. Excludes investment income for S corporations (certain small corporations with up to 75 shareholders, mostly individuals, electing to be taxed at the shareholder level).

Source: U.S. Internal Revenue Service, *Statistics of Income, Corporation Income Tax Returns*, annual.

Table 739. **Corporations by Asset-Size Class and Industry: 2006**

[**In billions of dollars (142 represents $142,000,000,000), except number of returns.** Covers active corporations only. Excludes corporations not allocable by industry. Numbers in parentheses represent North American Industry Classification System 2002 codes, see text, this section]

Industry	Total	Asset-size class					
		Under $10 mil. [1]	$10–$24.9 mil.	$25–$49.9 mil.	$50–$99.9 mil.	$100–$249.9 mil.	$250 mil. and over
Agriculture, forestry, fishing, and hunting (11):							
Returns....................	140,525	139,353	793	181	106	57	35
Total receipts	142	87	14	5	8	11	18
Mining (21):							
Returns....................	36,946	35,317	740	322	196	152	219
Total receipts	367	42	12	8	11	14	279
Utilities (22):							
Returns....................	7,636	7,204	129	53	41	45	163
Total receipts	626	10	4	2	3	7	601
Construction (23):							
Returns....................	780,579	771,229	6,459	1,672	690	353	176
Total receipts	1,608	893	183	104	76	85	266
Manufacturing (31–33):							
Returns....................	279,430	263,781	7,579	3,160	1,779	1,371	1,760
Total receipts	7,576	561	222	192	181	285	6,135
Wholesale and retail trade (42, 44–45):							
Returns....................	999,869	980,853	11,965	3,716	1,534	940	859
Total receipts	7,256	2,083	617	391	290	368	3,506
Transportation and warehousing (48–49):							
Returns....................	199,912	197,772	1,281	352	177	157	173
Total receipts	757	219	40	21	21	32	424
Information (51):							
Returns....................	128,343	125,524	1,182	579	363	273	423
Total receipts	1,128	108	20	19	20	28	934
Finance and insurance (52):							
Returns....................	249,876	229,744	3,796	2,576	2,806	3,521	7,433
Total receipts	3,748	280	26	26	35	64	3,316
Real estate and rental and leasing (53):							
Returns....................	655,389	648,176	4,755	1,361	584	311	203
Total receipts	338	168	20	13	11	13	113
Professional, scientific, and technical services (54):							
Returns....................	813,266	809,165	2,255	781	466	318	282
Total receipts	929	519	52	37	37	49	234
Management of companies and enterprises (55):							
Returns....................	50,261	43,388	1,225	1,000	1,258	1,642	1,749
Total receipts	1,094	18	2	3	7	19	1,046
Administrative and support and waste management and remediation services (56):							
Returns....................	267,624	266,347	645	247	153	109	124
Total receipts	461	229	27	16	19	25	146
Educational services (61):							
Returns....................	47,349	47,141	109	28	28	27	16
Total receipts	38	18	2	1	2	5	10
Health care and social assistance (62):							
Returns....................	400,591	399,563	490	215	131	96	95
Total receipts	579	382	18	17	14	19	130
Arts, entertainment, and recreation (71):							
Returns....................	120,163	119,352	452	190	68	51	50
Total receipts	95	49	5	4	4	7	26
Accommodation and food services (72):							
Returns....................	288,783	287,422	747	248	136	98	130
Total receipts	454	209	15	10	14	19	186
Other services (81):							
Returns....................	369,214	368,661	371	84	53	23	21
Total receipts	208	169	8	5	6	4	16

[1] Includes returns with zero assets.

Source: U.S. Internal Revenue Service, *Statistics of Income, Corporation Income Tax Returns*, annual.

Table 740. Economic Census Summary (NAICS 2002 Basis): 2002 and 2007

[24 represents 24,000. 2007 data are preliminary. Covers establishments with payroll. Data are based on the 2002 and 2007 economic censuses which are subject to nonsampling error. Data for the construction sector are also subject to sampling errors. For details on survey methodology and nonsampling and sampling errors, see Appendix III]

Kind of business	2002 NAICS code [1]	Establishments (1,000)		Sales, receipts or shipments (bil. dol.)		Annual payroll (bil. dol.)		Paid employees [2] (1,000)	
		2002	2007	2002	2007	2002	2007	2002	2007
Mining	21	24	21	183	369	21.0	37.3	475	703
Oil & gas extraction	211	8	6	113	231	5.3	9.5	99	162
Mining (except oil & gas)	212	7	6	48	81	8.9	11.5	196	220
Mining support activities	213	9	8	22	57	6.8	16.3	180	322
Utilities	22	17	17	399	582	42.4	50.9	663	632
Construction	23	710	725	1,209	1,782	254.3	348.1	7,193	7,399
Manufacturing	31-33	351	294	3,915	5,339	568.5	612.5	14,664	13,333
Wholesale trade	42	436	432	4,635	6,039	259.7	336.1	5,878	6,295
Merchant wholesalers, durable goods	423	260	253	2,171	2,709	157.2	205.8	3,357	3,637
Merchant wholesalers, nondurable goods	424	143	133	1,980	2,754	92.6	116.7	2,273	2,367
Wholesale electronic markets and agents and brokers	425	32	46	483	576	9.9	13.6	249	292
Retail trade	44-45	1,115	1,123	3,056	3,932	302.1	365.0	14,648	15,611
Motor vehicle & parts dealers	441	125	126	802	893	64.5	72.8	1,845	1,916
Furniture & home furnishings stores	442	65	65	92	110	12.8	15.2	535	589
Electronics & appliance stores	443	47	50	82	111	9.3	11.1	391	484
Bldg. material & garden equipment & supplies dealers	444	(NA)	90	(NA)	323	(NA)	38.2	(NA)	1,340
Food & beverage stores	445	149	147	457	541	48.7	55.7	2,839	2,879
Health & personal care stores	446	82	87	178	239	20.3	28.5	1,024	1,012
Gasoline stations	447	121	117	249	447	13.7	14.7	927	887
Clothing & clothing accessories stores	448	150	155	168	213	21.4	26.9	1,427	1,689
Sporting goods, hobby, book, & music stores	451	62	57	73	82	8.7	9.6	611	626
General merchandise stores	452	41	46	445	578	42.6	54.5	2,525	2,770
Miscellaneous store retailers	453	129	120	91	103	12.8	14.4	792	791
Nonstore retailers	454	55	61	173	292	17.1	23.3	571	628
Transportation & warehousing [3]	48-49	200	218	382	656	116.0	172.2	3,651	4,436
Information	51	138	141	892	1,075	194.7	223.4	3,736	3,428
Publishing industries (except Internet)	511	32	30	242	273	65.7	75.8	1,090	1,028
Motion picture & sound recording industries	512	22	24	78	95	12.6	17.2	303	326
Broadcasting (except Internet)	515	10	10	74	99	14.4	17.6	291	291
Internet publishing and broadcasting	516	2	3	6	15	2.3	4.5	40	55
Telecommunications	517	49	49	412	485	72.2	72.3	1,440	1,210
Internet service providers, Web search portals, and data processing	518	19	21	75	101	25.7	33.8	514	463
Other information services	519	3	4	5	7	1.7	2.0	58	55
Finance & insurance [4]	52	438	503	2,781	3,641	376.5	494.5	6,560	6,563
Real estate & rental & leasing [4]	53	323	377	336	452	60.2	85.2	1,949	2,249
Professional, scientific, & technical services	54	771	852	887	1,352	376.1	515.1	7,244	8,121
Management of companies & enterprises	55	49	(S)	107	(S)	179.0	(S)	2,605	(S)
Admin/support waste management/remediation services	56	351	382	433	629	206.4	290.5	8,742	10,154
Administrative & support services	561	332	360	381	556	194.2	274.7	8,410	9,787
Waste management & remediation services	562	19	21	51	73	12.2	15.9	332	367
Educational services	61	49	61	31	47	10.2	14.6	430	562
Health care and social assistance	62	705	779	1,207	1,697	495.8	665.8	15,052	16,860
Ambulatory health care services	621	489	545	489	692	203.3	280.1	4,925	5,791
Hospitals	622	6	7	500	713	197.2	263.3	5,174	5,536
Nursing & residential care facilities	623	69	76	127	168	59.0	74.0	2,831	3,056
Social assistance	624	140	152	91	124	36.4	48.4	2,123	2,477
Arts, entertainment, & recreation	71	110	124	142	189	45.2	57.5	1,849	2,071
Performing arts, spectator sports, & related industries	711	38	44	58	76	21.2	27.3	423	441
Museums, historical sites, & like institutions	712	7	7	9	13	2.9	3.6	123	129
Amusement, gambling, & recreation industries	713	66	73	75	99	21.0	26.7	1,303	1,500
Accommodation & food services	72	566	627	449	613	127.6	169.8	10,121	11,588
Accommodation	721	61	63	128	180	35.0	45.9	1,813	1,980
Food services & drinking places	722	505	564	321	433	92.6	124.0	8,308	9,608
Other services (except public administration)	81	538	538	307	418	83.0	99.8	3,475	3,516
Repair & maintenance	811	231	223	118	143	35.1	41.7	1,285	1,305
Personal and laundry services	812	201	208	72	84	22.9	26.8	1,297	1,341
Religious/grantmaking/prof/like organizations	813	106	107	117	190	24.9	31.2	893	870

NA Not available. S Estimates did not meet publication standards. [1] Based on North American Industry Classification System, 2002; see text, this section. [2] For pay period including March 12. [3] For detailed industries, see Table 1034. [4] For detailed industries, see Table 1126.

Source: U.S. Census Bureau, "2007 Economic Census, Comparative Statistics for United States, Summary Statistics by 2002 NAICS"; published 17 March 2009; using American FactFinder;<http://factfinder.census.gov/>.

Business Enterprise 491

Table 741. Nonemployer Establishments and Receipts by Industry: 2000 to 2006

[Establishments: 16,530 represents 16,530,000. Includes only firms subject to federal income tax. Nonemployers are businesses with no paid employees. Data originate chiefly from administrative records of the Internal Revenue Service; see Appendix III. Data for 2000 based on the North American Industry Classification System (NAICS), 1997; 2005 and 2006 based on NAICS 2002, see text, this section]

Kind of business	NAICS code	Establishments (1,000)			Receipts (mil. dol.)		
		2000	2005	2006	2000	2005	2006
All industries	(X)	**16,530**	**20,392**	**20,769**	**709,379**	**951,206**	**970,384**
Forestry, fishing & hunting, & agricultural support services	113–115	223	231	229	9,196	10,567	10,670
Mining	21	86	100	102	5,227	8,739	9,026
Utilities	22	14	15	17	504	671	698
Construction	23	2,014	2,531	2,549	107,538	153,760	159,432
Manufacturing	31–33	285	298	311	13,022	15,064	15,469
Wholesale trade	42	388	381	387	31,684	34,091	34,804
Retail trade	44–45	1,743	1,881	1,858	73,810	83,599	83,933
Transportation & warehousing	48–49	747	962	1,002	37,824	58,650	62,928
Information	51	238	291	318	7,620	10,158	10,776
Finance & insurance	52	692	742	758	49,058	47,244	52,768
Real estate & rental & leasing	53	1,696	2,442	2,421	133,398	207,688	193,105
Professional, scientific, & technical services	54	2,420	2,854	2,904	90,272	118,575	124,237
Admin/support waste mgt/ remediation services	56	1,032	1,417	1,482	23,754	33,028	34,989
Educational services	61	283	454	482	3,736	6,028	6,509
Health care & social assistance	62	1,317	1,669	1,728	36,550	50,307	52,579
Arts, entertainment, & recreation	71	782	972	1,002	17,713	23,704	24,782
Accommodation & food services	72	218	279	287	13,418	15,307	15,694
Other services (except public administration)	81	2,350	2,873	2,931	55,056	74,025	77,986

X Not applicable.

Source: U.S. Census Bureau, "Nonemployer Statistics"; <http://www.census.gov/econ/nonemployer/>.

Table 742. Establishments, Employees, and Payroll by Employment-Size Class: 1990 to 2006

[6,176 represents 6,176,000. Excludes most government employees, railroad employees, self-employed persons. Employees are for the week including March 12. Covers establishments with payroll. An *establishment* is a single physical location where business is conducted or where services or industrial operations are performed. For statement on methodology, see Appendix III]

Employment-size class	Unit	1990	1995	2000	2002	2003	2004	2005	2006
Establishments, total	1,000	**6,176**	**6,613**	**7,070**	**7,201**	**7,255**	**7,388**	**7,500**	**7,601**
Under 20 employees	1,000	5,354	5,733	6,069	6,199	6,240	6,359	6,468	6,533
20 to 99 employees	1,000	684	730	826	835	845	856	856	886
100 to 499 employees	1,000	122	135	157	149	151	154	157	163
500 to 999 employees	1,000	10	10	12	11	11	12	12	12
1,000 or more employees	1,000	6	6	7	7	7	7	7	7
Employees, total	1,000	**93,476**	**100,335**	**114,065**	**112,401**	**113,398**	**115,075**	**116,317**	**119,917**
Under 20 employees	1,000	24,373	25,785	27,569	28,116	28,313	28,701	28,874	29,429
20 to 99 employees	1,000	27,414	29,202	33,147	33,335	33,760	34,288	34,302	35,504
100 to 499 employees	1,000	22,926	25,364	29,736	28,101	28,549	28,976	29,591	30,616
500 to 999 employees	1,000	6,551	7,021	8,291	7,743	7,638	7,815	8,053	8,248
1,000 or more employees	1,000	12,212	12,962	15,322	15,105	15,138	15,295	15,497	16,120
Annual payroll, total	Bil. dol.	**2,104**	**2,666**	**3,879**	**3,943**	**4,041**	**4,254**	**4,483**	**4,792**
Under 20 employees	Bil. dol.	485	608	818	866	885	926	970	1,021
20 to 99 employees	Bil. dol.	547	696	1,006	1,041	1,068	1,124	1,177	1,260
100 to 499 employees	Bil. dol.	518	675	1,031	1,021	1,054	1,106	1,176	1,264
500 to 999 employees	Bil. dol.	174	219	336	329	334	355	376	401
1,000 or more employees	Bil. dol.	381	467	690	685	700	743	784	848

Source: U.S. Census Bureau, "County Business Patterns"; <http://www.census.gov/econ/cbp/>.

492   Business Enterprise

Table 743. Establishments, Employees, and Payroll by Employment-Size Class and Industry: 2000 to 2006

[Establishments and employees in thousands (7,070.0 represents 7,070,000); payroll in billions of dollars. See headnote, Table 742. Data for 2000 based on the North American Industry Classification System (NAICS), 1997; 2005 and 2006 data based on NAICS 2002. See text, this section]

Industry	NAICS code	2000, total	2005, total	2006					
				Total	Under 20 employ-ees	20 to 99 employ-ees	100 to 499 employ-ees	500 to 999 employ-ees	1,000 or more employ-ees
Establishments, total [1]	(X)	7,070.0	7,499.7	7,601.2	6,533.4	885.8	162.8	12.1	7.1
Forestry, fishing & hunting, & ag support services	113–115	26.1	24.1	23.6	22.1	1.3	0.2	(Z)	(Z)
Mining	21	23.7	24.7	26.2	21.1	4.2	0.8	0.1	(Z)
Utilities	22	17.3	17.3	17.2	12.1	3.8	1.1	0.1	(Z)
Construction	23	709.6	787.7	802.3	729.2	64.1	8.5	0.5	0.2
Manufacturing	31–33	354.5	333.5	331.1	226.2	75.6	25.8	2.4	1.1
Wholesale trade	42	446.2	429.8	430.0	366.4	55.1	7.9	0.5	0.2
Retail trade	44–45	1,113.6	1,123.2	1,120.3	960.6	132.1	27.0	0.6	(Z)
Transportation and warehousing	48–49	190.0	211.2	215.1	179.2	28.6	6.3	0.6	0.3
Information	51	133.6	141.3	141.9	114.9	20.9	5.3	0.6	0.3
Finance and insurance	52	423.7	476.8	494.3	446.4	39.5	6.9	1.0	0.5
Real estate and rental and leasing.	53	300.2	370.7	382.1	365.4	14.8	1.8	0.1	(Z)
Professional, scientific, and technical services.	54	722.7	826.1	846.5	780.5	55.8	9.1	0.7	0.4
Management of companies and enterprises.	55	47.4	47.6	48.3	31.9	11.0	4.3	0.6	0.4
Admin/support waste mgt/remediation services.	56	351.5	369.5	378.3	314.7	45.5	15.9	1.4	0.9
Educational services	61	68.0	80.5	82.6	62.9	15.8	3.2	0.4	0.4
Health care and social assistance	62	658.6	746.6	762.5	646.1	91.4	21.3	1.7	1.9
Arts, entertainment, and recreation	71	103.8	121.8	123.0	103.5	16.4	2.8	0.2	0.1
Accommodation and food services.	72	542.4	603.4	612.3	436.6	164.2	10.8	0.4	0.2
Other services [2]	81	723.3	740.0	736.4	686.7	45.7	3.9	0.2	0.1
Unclassified establishments	99	99.0	24.0	27.0	26.9	0.1	–	–	–
Employees, total [1]	(X)	114,065	116,317	119,917	29,429	35,504	30,616	8,248	16,120
Forestry, fishing & hunting, & ag support services.	113–115	184	169	166	(NA)	(NA)	28	(NA)	(NA)
Mining	21	456	497	554	100	168	161	57	69
Utilities	22	655	633	614	65	168	225	85	72
Construction	23	6,573	6,781	7,339	2,749	2,487	1,532	298	273
Manufacturing	31–33	16,474	13,667	13,632	1,313	3,324	5,149	1,629	2,216
Wholesale trade	42	6,112	5,969	6,031	1,764	2,156	1,467	329	315
Retail trade	44–45	14,841	15,339	15,768	5,144	5,319	4,846	369	90
Transportation and warehousing	48–49	3,790	4,168	4,306	732	1,187	1,206	419	762
Information	51	3,546	3,403	3,396	514	886	1,044	405	547
Finance and insurance	52	5,963	6,432	6,647	1,957	1,524	1,391	666	1,109
Real estate and rental and leasing.	53	1,942	2,144	2,217	1,195	559	324	82	57
Professional, scientific, and technical services.	54	6,816	7,689	8,054	2,667	2,171	1,739	476	1,003
Management of companies and enterprises.	55	2,874	2,856	2,916	174	495	922	446	879
Admin/support waste mgt/remediation services.	56	9,138	9,280	10,004	1,233	1,999	3,161	981	2,629
Educational services	61	2,532	2,879	2,980	304	667	611	279	1,118
Health care and social assistance	62	14,109	16,025	16,451	3,402	3,670	3,954	1,222	4,204
Arts, entertainment, and recreation	71	1,741	1,936	1,974	394	686	525	141	228
Accommodation and food services.	72	9,881	11,026	11,381	2,702	6,323	1,673	(NA)	(NA)
Other services [2]	81	5,293	5,391	5,459	2,916	1,665	657	(NA)	(NA)
Unclassified establishments	99	144	31	30	(NA)	(NA)	–	–	–
Annual payroll, total [1]	(X)	3,879	4,483	4,792	1,021	1,260	1,264	401	848
Forestry, fishing & hunting, & ag support services.	113–115	5	5	5	(D)	(D)	1	(D)	(D)
Mining	21	22	31	37	6	10	12	4	5
Utilities	22	41	46	48	4	11	18	8	7
Construction	23	240	293	322	103	114	77	14	14
Manufacturing	31–33	644	601	620	48	133	224	79	136
Wholesale trade	42	270	309	323	85	110	80	23	25
Retail trade	44–45	303	348	368	113	127	115	9	3
Transportation and warehousing	48–49	126	154	166	27	44	46	16	33
Information	51	209	203	213	28	50	68	26	40
Finance and insurance	52	347	447	481	102	112	115	49	104
Real estate and rental and leasing.	53	59	82	88	42	24	15	4	3
Professional, scientific, and technical services.	54	362	456	497	136	140	123	34	64
Management of companies and enterprises.	55	211	243	266	17	42	83	41	83
Admin/support waste mgt/remediation services.	56	210	255	283	43	62	80	24	74
Educational services	61	62	83	88	7	17	19	7	39
Health care and social assistance	62	431	590	627	138	125	119	49	195
Arts, entertainment, and recreation	71	43	53	57	14	14	19	5	6
Accommodation and food services.	72	126	156	167	39	81	28	(D)	(D)
Other services [2]	81	110	127	134	66	41	20	(D)	(D)
Unclassified establishments	99	4	1	1	(D)	(D)	–	–	–

– Represents zero.   D Data withheld to avoid disclosure.   NA Not available.   X Not applicable.   Z Less than 50 establishments.   [1] Totals for 2000 include auxiliaries. Beginning 2005, cases previously classified under NAICS code 95 (auxiliaries) are coded in the operating NAICS sector of the establishment.   [2] Except public administration.

Source: U.S. Census Bureau, "County Business Patterns"; <http://www.census.gov/econ/cbp/>.

U.S. Census Bureau, Statistical Abstract of the United States: 2010

Table 744. **Employer Firms, Establishments, Employment, and Annual Payroll by Firm Size: 1990 to 2006**

[In thousands except as noted (5,074 represents 5,074,000). Firms are an aggregation of all establishments owned by a parent company with some annual payroll. Establishments are locations with active payroll in any quarter. This table illustrates the changing importance of enterprise sizes over time, not job growth, as enterprises can grow or decline and change enterprise size cells over time]

Item	Total	0 to 4 [1]	5 to 9	10 to 19	20 to 99	100 to 499	Less than 500	500 or more
Firms:								
1990............	5,074	3,021	952	563	454	70	5,060	14
1995............	5,369	3,250	981	577	470	76	5,354	15
2000............	5,653	3,397	1,021	617	516	84	5,635	17
2002............	5,698	3,466	1,011	614	508	82	5,681	17
2003............	5,767	3,504	1,025	620	515	85	5,750	17
2004............	5,886	3,580	1,043	633	526	87	5,869	17
2005............	5,984	3,678	1,050	630	521	87	5,966	17
2006............	6,022	3,670	1,061	647	536	91	6,004	18
Establishments:								
1990............	6,176	3,032	971	600	590	255	5,448	728
1995............	6,613	3,260	998	618	639	284	5,799	814
2000............	7,070	3,406	1,035	652	674	312	6,080	990
2002............	7,201	3,471	1,024	653	693	333	6,173	1,028
2003............	7,255	3,510	1,038	655	687	331	6,222	1,033
2004............	7,388	3,586	1,056	667	693	330	6,331	1,056
2005............	7,500	3,684	1,063	662	679	332	6,421	1,079
2006............	7,601	3,677	1,073	679	698	346	6,473	1,129
Employment:								
1990............	93,469	5,117	6,252	7,543	17,710	13,545	50,167	43,302
1995............	100,314	5,395	6,440	7,734	18,422	14,660	52,653	47,662
2000............	114,065	5,593	6,709	8,286	20,277	16,260	57,124	56,941
2002............	112,401	5,698	6,640	8,246	19,874	15,909	56,366	56,034
2003............	113,398	5,768	6,732	8,330	20,187	16,430	57,448	55,950
2004............	115,075	5,845	6,853	8,500	20,643	16,758	58,597	56,477
2005............	116,317	5,937	6,898	8,454	20,444	16,911	58,645	57,672
2006............	119,917	5,960	6,974	8,676	21,077	17,537	60,224	59,693
Annual payroll (bil. dol.):								
1990............	2,104	117	114	144	352	279	1,007	1,097
1995............	2,666	142	137	175	437	361	1,252	1,414
2000............	3,879	186	174	231	608	528	1,727	2,152
2002............	3,943	194	182	241	624	536	1,777	2,166
2003............	4,041	197	187	247	635	552	1,818	2,222
2004............	4,254	206	196	258	670	588	1,917	2,337
2005............	4,483	220	206	269	700	617	2,013	2,470
2006............	4,792	230	214	282	742	661	2,129	2,664

[1] Employment is measured in March, thus some firms (start-ups after March, closures before March, and seasonal firms) will have zero employment and some annual payroll.

Source: U.S. Small Business Administration, Office of Advocacy, "Statistics of U.S. Businesses"; <http://www.sba.gov/advo/research/data.html>; accessed 3 February 2009.

Table 745. **Firm Births and Deaths by Employment Size of Enterprise: 1990 to 2006**

[In thousands (541.1 represents 541,100). Data represent activity from March of the beginning year to March of the ending year. Establishments with no employment in the first quarter of the beginning year were excluded. This table provides the number of births and deaths of initial establishments (based on Census ID) as an approximation of firm births and deaths]

Item	Births (initial locations)				Deaths (initial locations)			
	Total	Less than 20 employees	Less than 500 employees	500 employees or more	Total	Less than 20 employees	Less than 500 employees	500 employees or more
Firms:								
1990 to 1991.......	541.1	515.9	540.9	0.3	546.5	517.0	546.1	0.4
1995 to 1996.......	597.8	572.4	597.5	0.3	512.4	485.5	512.0	0.4
2000 to 2001.......	585.1	558.0	584.8	0.3	553.3	524.0	552.8	0.5
2001 to 2002 [1].....	569.8	541.5	568.3	1.5	586.9	557.1	586.5	0.4
2002 to 2003.......	612.3	585.6	612.0	0.3	540.7	514.6	540.3	0.3
2003 to 2004.......	628.9	601.9	628.7	0.3	541.0	515.0	540.7	0.3
2004 to 2005.......	644.1	616.0	643.9	0.3	565.7	539.1	565.5	0.3
2005 to 2006.......	670.1	640.7	669.8	0.2	599.3	573.3	599.1	0.3
Employment:								
1990 to 1991.......	3,105	1,713	2,907	198	3,208	1,723	3,044	164
1995 to 1996.......	3,256	1,845	3,056	200	3,100	1,560	2,808	291
2000 to 2001.......	3,418	1,821	3,109	310	3,262	1,701	3,050	212
2001 to 2002 [1].....	3,370	1,748	3,034	336	3,660	1,755	3,257	403
2002 to 2003.......	3,667	1,856	3,174	493	3,324	1,608	2,880	445
2003 to 2004.......	3,575	1,889	3,241	334	3,221	1,615	2,868	353
2004 to 2005.......	3,609	1,931	3,279	330	3,307	1,685	2,981	326
2005 to 2006.......	3,682	1,999	3,412	270	3,220	1,711	2,964	256

[1] A change in methodology ("based on Census ID" rather than "plant number") has affected the allocation of firms by employment size.

Source: U.S. Small Business Administration, Office of Advocacy, "Firm Size Data, Statistics of U.S. Businesses and Nonemployer Statistics"; <http://www.sba.gov/advo/research/data.html>.

Table 746. **Employer Firms, Employment, and Annual Payroll by Employment Size of Firm and Industry: 2006**

[6,022 represents 6,022,000. A firm is an aggregation of all establishments owned by a parent company (within a geographic location and/or industry) with some annual payroll. A firm may be a single location or it can include multiple locations. Employment is measured in March and payroll annual leading to some firms with zero employment. Numbers in parentheses represent North American Industry Classification System codes, 2002; see text this section]

Industry and data type	Unit	Total	All industries—employment size of firm						
			0 to 4	5 to 9	10 to 19	20 to 99	100 to 499	Less than 500	500 or more
Total [1]:									
Firms	1,000	6,022	3,670	1,061	647	536	91	6,004	18
Employment	1,000	119,917	5,960	6,974	8,676	21,077	17,537	60,224	59,693
Annual payroll	Bil. dol. . . .	4,792	230	214	282	742	661	2,129	2,664
Construction (23):									
Firms	1,000	792	513	132	78	60	8	790	1
Employment	1,000	7,339	796	867	1,038	2,268	1,296	6,265	1,074
Annual payroll	Bil. dol. . . .	322	31	29	40	101	62	262	60
Manufacturing (31-33):									
Firms	1,000	286	113	53	45	57	14	282	4
Employment	1,000	13,632	209	354	618	2,338	2,538	6,056	7,575
Annual payroll	Bil. dol. . . .	620	9	11	21	90	103	235	385
Wholesale trade (42):									
Firms	1,000	335	189	58	40	37	8	332	3
Employment	1,000	6,031	320	381	531	1,389	1,064	3,686	2,345
Annual payroll	Bil. dol. . . .	323	15	17	24	67	53	176	147
Retail trade (44-45):									
Firms	1,000	726	424	150	82	58	9	723	2
Employment	1,000	15,768	764	980	1,085	2,174	1,312	6,314	9,454
Annual payroll	Bil. dol. . . .	368	18	21	26	64	41	169	199
Transportation & warehousing (48-49):									
Firms	1,000	172	110	25	16	15	4	170	2
Employment	1,000	4,306	160	161	220	577	510	1,630	2,677
Annual payroll	Bil. dol. . . .	166	6	5	7	20	19	56	110
Information (51):									
Firms	1,000	75	44	11	8	8	2	74	1
Employment	1,000	3,396	65	74	111	319	325	894	2,502
Annual payroll	Bil. dol. . . .	213	5	3	5	16	19	48	166
Finance & insurance (52):									
Firms	1,000	263	186	38	17	16	4	261	2
Employment	1,000	6,647	313	244	232	645	750	2,184	4,463
Annual payroll	Bil. dol. . . .	481	14	12	14	43	49	133	348
Professional, scientific & technical services (54):									
Firms	1,000	772	556	106	59	41	7	769	3
Employment	1,000	8,054	818	694	783	1,526	1,138	4,958	3,096
Annual payroll	Bil. dol. . . .	497	42	32	41	94	74	283	215
Management of companies & enterprises (55):									
Firms	1,000	27	4	1	1	6	8	20	7
Employment	1,000	2,916	5	3	7	69	268	352	2,564
Annual payroll	Bil. dol. . . .	266	1	(Z)	(Z)	4	17	23	243
Admin/support waste mgt/ remediation services (56):									
Firms	1,000	323	203	49	30	28	9	320	4
Employment	1,000	10,004	299	321	409	1,142	1,562	3,733	6,271
Annual payroll	Bil. dol. . . .	283	12	9	12	35	40	107	176
Educational services (61):									
Firms	1,000	74	36	11	9	13	3	73	1
Employment	1,000	2,980	54	76	129	540	535	1,334	1,646
Annual payroll	Bil. dol. . . .	88	2	2	3	13	16	35	53
Health care and social assistance (62):									
Firms	1,000	606	308	140	79	59	16	602	4
Employment	1,000	16,451	565	925	1,054	2,345	3,057	7,946	8,505
Annual payroll	Bil. dol. . . .	627	28	36	42	85	91	282	345
Accommodation & food services (72):									
Firms	1,000	467	200	90	83	84	9	465	2
Employment	1,000	11,381	320	603	1,132	3,161	1,632	6,849	4,532
Annual payroll	Bil. dol. . . .	167	8	7	13	40	22	90	77
Other services (except public administration) (81):									
Firms	1,000	672	421	137	67	41	4	671	1
Employment	1,000	5,459	775	892	880	1,482	635	4,664	795
Annual payroll	Bil. dol. . . .	134	18	19	20	35	18	109	24

Z Less than $500 million.　　[1] Includes other industries not shown separately.

Source: U.S. Small Business Administration, Office of Advocacy, "Statistics of U.S. Businesses"; <http://www.sba.gov/advo/research/data.html>; accessed 3 February 2009.

Table 747. **Employer Firms, Employment, and Payroll by Employment Size of Firm and State: 2000 and 2006**

[5,652.5 represents 5,652,500. A firm is an aggregation of all establishments owned by a parent company (within a state) with some annual payroll. A firm may be a single location or it can include multiple locations. Employment is measured in March and payroll is annual leading to some firms with zero employment]

State	Employer firms (1,000)					Employment, 2006 (mil.)			Annual payroll, 2006 (bil. dol.)		
	2000		2006								
	Total	Less than 20 employ- ees	Total	Less than 20 employ- ees	Less than 500 employ- ees	Total	Less than 20 employ- ees	Less than 500 employ- ees	Total	Less than 20 employ- ees	Less than 500 employ- ees
U.S....	5,652.5	5,035.0	6,022.1	5,377.6	6,004.1	119.9	21.6	60.2	4,792.4	726.1	2,128.8
AL	79.9	68.2	80.7	68.5	78.4	1.7	0.3	0.9	55.9	8.6	25.6
AK	15.9	14.0	16.7	14.7	16.2	0.2	0.1	0.1	10.8	2.2	5.3
AZ	93.0	79.3	110.4	94.1	107.5	2.3	0.4	1.1	85.1	12.6	37.6
AR	52.4	45.4	53.5	46.0	51.9	1.0	0.2	0.5	31.7	5.0	13.6
CA	664.6	581.1	723.9	637.7	718.2	13.8	2.5	7.2	633.8	98.3	287.8
CO	116.2	101.5	129.9	114.5	127.0	2.0	0.4	1.0	82.3	14.1	37.4
CT	78.5	67.2	77.6	66.3	75.6	1.6	0.3	0.8	78.8	11.6	34.4
DE	20.2	16.6	21.1	17.1	19.8	0.4	0.1	0.2	17.4	2.3	6.8
DC	16.3	12.4	17.1	12.9	15.9	0.4	0.1	0.2	27.1	3.3	11.9
FL......	354.0	319.3	430.4	390.8	426.1	7.5	1.3	3.3	260.4	44.4	112.4
GA	160.4	138.3	181.3	157.3	177.4	3.6	0.6	1.7	137.9	19.9	57.2
HI......	24.3	20.8	26.7	22.6	25.9	0.5	0.1	0.3	17.3	3.2	9.2
ID......	32.2	28.0	39.7	34.8	38.6	0.5	0.1	0.3	17.2	3.7	9.0
IL......	254.1	218.1	262.9	227.6	258.6	5.4	0.9	2.6	231.1	33.2	101.9
IN......	116.3	98.1	118.2	100.2	115.3	2.7	0.4	1.3	92.3	12.4	39.8
IA......	65.6	56.2	65.8	56.4	64.1	1.3	0.2	0.7	42.1	6.1	19.1
KS	61.6	52.4	61.9	52.6	60.0	1.1	0.2	0.6	39.3	6.0	18.8
KY	72.3	61.0	73.0	61.5	70.8	1.6	0.3	0.8	50.2	7.3	22.1
LA	81.7	69.5	81.4	69.2	79.4	1.6	0.3	0.9	55.5	9.1	27.3
ME	34.1	30.1	35.7	31.4	34.8	0.5	0.1	0.3	16.7	3.5	9.3
MD	106.0	90.4	115.1	98.4	112.5	2.2	0.4	1.2	93.7	14.8	46.0
MA	148.2	127.8	144.9	125.0	142.0	3.0	0.5	1.5	148.1	20.7	63.7
MI......	193.9	167.2	190.4	165.5	187.4	3.8	0.7	2.0	151.5	22.4	66.7
MN	116.2	99.4	124.2	107.0	121.7	2.5	0.4	1.3	100.6	13.5	43.4
MS	48.3	41.5	48.0	41.0	46.4	0.9	0.2	0.5	27.4	4.5	12.6
MO	118.1	101.1	124.1	106.7	121.4	2.5	0.4	1.2	87.7	12.4	37.8
MT	28.0	25.0	32.3	28.9	31.5	0.3	0.1	0.2	9.8	2.8	6.3
NE	41.4	35.5	42.6	36.5	41.3	0.8	0.1	0.4	25.7	3.8	11.6
NV	40.3	33.4	50.7	42.1	48.6	1.2	0.2	0.5	41.7	6.4	18.3
NH	32.1	27.3	33.2	28.1	32.1	0.6	0.1	0.3	21.9	4.2	11.6
NJ......	202.2	178.4	208.5	184.1	205.3	3.6	0.7	1.9	175.5	28.1	77.1
NM	35.5	30.1	37.9	31.9	36.4	0.6	0.1	0.4	19.8	3.8	10.4
NY	424.8	379.2	444.7	399.0	440.5	7.5	1.5	3.9	398.2	58.3	171.2
NC	163.6	142.0	176.8	153.4	173.4	3.5	0.6	1.7	124.1	18.7	52.7
ND	17.2	14.7	17.9	15.2	17.2	0.3	0.1	0.2	8.4	1.6	4.7
OH	212.5	180.5	207.8	176.9	204.0	4.8	0.8	2.3	176.1	23.7	75.4
OK	70.2	61.0	72.9	63.0	71.0	1.3	0.3	0.7	41.4	7.2	19.9
OR	85.1	74.2	92.7	81.0	90.7	1.5	0.3	0.8	53.6	9.5	26.9
PA	237.5	204.6	240.6	207.2	236.8	5.2	0.9	2.6	200.5	27.9	87.2
RI......	25.2	21.5	26.7	22.8	25.8	0.4	0.1	0.3	17.1	3.0	8.7
SC	78.4	67.2	83.9	72.0	81.7	1.6	0.3	0.8	52.2	8.4	23.4
SD	20.6	17.7	21.9	18.9	21.2	0.3	0.1	0.2	9.4	1.9	5.4
TN	102.4	86.7	103.6	87.3	100.6	2.5	0.4	1.1	86.5	11.7	36.5
TX	369.0	321.3	391.5	340.0	386.4	8.7	1.4	4.1	347.7	49.1	143.1
UT	46.2	39.3	58.5	50.5	56.7	1.0	0.2	0.5	35.2	5.6	16.5
VT	19.1	16.7	19.6	17.0	18.9	0.3	0.1	0.2	8.6	2.0	5.2
VA	139.7	120.3	156.2	134.6	153.0	3.2	0.6	1.6	129.0	18.9	57.3
WA	138.2	120.9	150.6	132.5	147.9	2.4	0.5	1.3	104.2	17.0	48.6
WV	33.5	28.8	32.3	27.5	31.2	0.6	0.1	0.3	17.3	2.9	8.2
WI......	115.6	98.2	117.9	100.2	115.5	2.5	0.4	1.3	89.0	12.8	41.5
WY	15.9	13.9	17.7	15.5	17.1	0.2	0.1	0.1	7.3	1.8	4.1

Source: U.S. Small Business Administration, Office of Advocacy, "Statistics of U.S. Businesses"; <http://www.sba.gov/advo/research /data.html>; accessed 3 February 2009.

Table 748. **Employer Firm Births and Deaths and Business Bankruptcies by State: 2005 to 2008**

[Births represent an employing unit which is determined, for the first time, as meeting the definition of "employer" in the state unemployment compensation law or a previously terminated employing unit, which again is determined as meeting the definition of employer]

State	Births			Deaths			Business bankruptcies [1]		
	2005	2007	2008	2005	2007	2008	2005	2007	2008
United States [2]	938,927	923,932	874,816	935,736	926,283	966,647	32,406	23,889	33,822
Alabama.	10,575	9,813	9,194	10,168	10,710	11,468	322	285	395
Alaska	1,982	1,777	1,922	2,294	3,615	2,879	67	63	78
Arizona.	21,339	18,208	15,847	18,249	16,019	21,219	522	332	691
Arkansas	7,591	8,157	8,499	7,021	7,596	7,511	363	335	429
California	121,482	113,829	103,572	151,944	143,591	150,314	3,576	2,697	4,697
Colorado.	26,610	23,035	21,921	14,035	23,080	27,591	748	536	756
Connecticut.	9,220	9,265	9,164	11,131	11,052	11,488	104	250	366
Delaware	3,299	2,921	2,980	3,355	2,775	3,698	190	243	361
District of Columbia	4,316	4,302	3,939	3,952	3,378	2,765	46	35	42
Florida	84,890	75,533	72,203	58,737	60,724	72,003	1,278	1,455	2,759
Georgia	29,804	30,062	28,980	29,315	29,517	29,945	2,161	1,316	1,714
Hawaii	3,763	3,611	3,475	3,794	4,185	3,973	55	43	51
Idaho.	9,312	8,065	6,854	6,334	6,995	7,273	141	79	167
Illinois	30,445	30,013	31,493	32,846	33,213	35,689	901	868	1,178
Indiana.	14,545	13,863	13,959	16,504	12,826	14,380	586	484	692
Iowa	6,004	5,903	5,893	6,802	7,601	7,679	367	227	270
Kansas.	7,095	7,799	8,156	7,330	8,376	7,648	313	196	244
Kentucky	9,617	8,816	8,821	8,515	8,320	8,790	297	258	390
Louisiana	9,393	10,356	9,527	9,123	8,334	7,656	683	451	571
Maine.	4,251	4,243	4,202	4,711	4,565	5,095	98	118	154
Maryland	22,083	20,168	18,392	21,769	20,835	21,251	493	406	405
Massachusetts.	19,723	18,427	18,581	18,878	21,695	20,223	350	297	334
Michigan.	24,642	23,166	22,090	26,971	20,359	34,272	757	1,019	1,394
Minnesota.	12,555	12,313	11,811	15,302	12,004	12,597	1,400	473	656
Mississippi	6,071	6,871	5,776	6,823	7,550	6,800	186	234	298
Missouri	17,239	15,510	15,061	20,109	19,422	21,290	368	316	534
Montana.	4,768	4,751	4,181	4,394	4,476	4,771	116	47	71
Nebraska	5,127	4,752	4,602	4,982	5,092	5,200	265	202	221
Nevada	11,299	11,057	10,202	8,485	9,222	10,771	292	234	395
New Hampshire	4,758	4,588	4,587	5,406	5,523	5,515	441	306	318
New Jersey.	33,022	36,381	26,774	32,751	34,183	31,167	661	705	925
New Mexico	5,272	6,158	5,971	5,670	6,003	5,972	755	102	185
New York	62,045	67,577	65,624	62,667	65,500	69,267	1,488	1,235	1,534
North Carolina	26,906	29,042	24,150	22,867	23,570	23,734	537	473	738
North Dakota.	1,893	1,812	1,842	2,512	2,192	2,344	74	57	54
Ohio	22,542	21,900	20,361	23,429	23,434	21,038	1,590	1,172	1,436
Oklahoma.	8,609	8,961	8,943	7,231	7,777	7,787	751	315	392
Oregon.	14,445	14,333	13,952	14,804	13,479	14,182	871	298	283
Pennsylvania.	36,609	34,558	35,587	36,989	34,528	42,318	1,159	889	1,078
Rhode Island.	3,677	3,460	3,310	4,164	4,536	4,459	75	65	122
South Carolina	12,341	12,554	11,634	10,681	11,603	11,657	163	118	196
South Dakota	2,102	2,124	2,127	2,354	2,442	2,311	149	74	95
Tennessee	17,484	17,619	17,167	17,135	17,602	18,614	542	483	653
Texas.	55,858	55,865	55,214	55,039	55,269	36,108	2,964	2,241	2,728
Utah	11,536	13,403	11,228	11,871	11,419	8,105	427	139	302
Vermont	1,911	2,228	2,146	2,346	2,374	2,555	65	56	52
Virginia.	25,061	28,174	25,517	21,359	21,726	23,971	527	436	798
Washington.	30,353	33,191	33,701	40,944	35,077	37,955	681	439	565
West Virginia.	3,493	3,434	3,363	4,869	4,824	4,644	229	117	169
Wisconsin.	13,656	12,663	12,905	13,397	12,920	12,711	785	363	525
Wyoming	2,632	2,707	2,593	2,689	2,903	2,703	60	35	42

[1] For year ending June 30. See headnote, Table 753. [2] Includes Puerto Rico and Virgin Islands, not shown separately. Bankruptcy data also includes Guam and Northern Mariana Islands.

Source: U.S. Small Business Administration, unpublished data, and Administrative Office of the U.S. Courts, "Bankruptcy Statistics"; <http://www.uscourts.gov/bnkrpctystats/statistics.htm>.

Table 749. **Small Business Administration Loans to Minority-Owned Small Businesses: 2000 to 2008**

[**3,634 represents $3,634,000,000.** For year ending September 30. A small business must be independently owned and operated, must not be dominant in its particular industry, and must meet standards set by the Small Business Administration as to its annual receipts or number of employees]

Minority group	Number of loans					Amount (mil. dol.)				
	2000	2005	2006	2007	2008	2000	2005	2006	2007	2008
Total minority loans	11,999	29,721	33,782	36,330	24,851	3,634	6,132	6,607	6,853	5,674
Percent of all loans	24.8	28.3	31.5	32.9	31.7	29.4	30.2	32.6	33.3	31.6
African American	2,120	6,635	7,238	8,919	7,127	388	627	694	919	1,009
Asian American	5,838	13,457	14,449	15,433	10,813	2,383	4,056	4,238	4,324	3,517
Hispanic American	3,500	8,794	11,214	11,049	6,249	761	1,325	1,561	1,482	1,037
Native American	541	835	881	929	662	101	123	114	128	111

Source: U.S. Small Business Administration, Management Information Summary, unpublished data.

U.S. Census Bureau, Statistical Abstract of the United States: 2010

Table 750. **U.S. Firms—Ownership by Women, Race, and Hispanic or Latino Origin: 2002**

[**22,975 represents 22,975,000.** A Hispanic firm may be of any race and, therefore may be included in more than one race group. See text, this section]

Group	All firms [1]		Firms with paid employees			
	Firms (1,000)	Sales and receipts (bil. dol.)	Firms (1,000)	Sales and receipts (bil. dol.)	Employees (1,000)	Annual payroll (bil. dol.)
All firms [2]	**22,975**	**22,604**	**5,525**	**21,836**	**110,767**	**3,812**
Female-owned.....................	6,489	940	917	803	7,141	174
Male-owned	13,184	7,061	3,525	6,564	42,429	1,320
Equally male-/female-owned............	2,693	732	718	627	5,665	130
Publicly held and other firms [3]	494	13,820	353	13,797	55,398	2,186
Hispanic or Latino origin	1,573	222	200	180	1,537	37
Black...........................	1,198	89	95	66	754	18
American Indian and Alaska Native	201	27	24	22	191	5
Asian...........................	1,104	327	319	291	2,214	56
Native Hawaiian and Other Pacific Islander...	29	4	4	4	29	1

[1] Both firms with paid employees and firms with no paid employees. [2] U.S. totals are based on the 2002 Economic Census, whereas the gender, Hispanic or Latino origin, and race estimates are based on the 2002 Survey of Business Owners. [3] Publicly held and other firms not classifiable by gender, Hispanic or Latino origin, and race.

Source: U.S. Census Bureau, *2002 Economic Census, Survey of Business Owners, Women-Owned Firms: 2002* (SB02-00CS-WMN)(RV); *Hispanic-Owned Firms: 2002* (SB02-00CS-HISP)(RV); *Black-Owned Firms: 2002* (SB02-00CS-BLK)(RV); *American Indian- and Alaska Native-Owned Firms: 2002* (SB02-00CS-AIAN)(RV); *Asian-Owned Firms: 2002* (SB02-00CS-ASIAN)(RV); and *Native Hawaiian- and Other Pacific Islander-Owned Firms: 2002* (SB02-00CS-NHPI)(RV).

Table 751. **Women-Owned and Minority-Owned Firms With Paid Employees by Employment Size: 2002**

[**917 represents 917,000.** Employment reflects number of paid employees during the March 12 pay period. Based on the 2002 Survey of Business Owners; see text, this section]

Item	Unit		Number of employees							
		Total	None [1]	1 to 4	5 to 9	10 to 19	20 to 49	50 to 99	100 to 499	500 or more
WOMEN-OWNED										
Firms.....................	1,000...	917	161	462	149	83	43	11	7	1
Sales and receipts	Mil. dol...	802,851	23,539	113,447	96,282	103,160	117,875	74,053	114,484	160,012
Employees	1,000...	7,141	–	939	971	1,105	1,269	750	1,194	913
Annual payroll	Mil. dol...	173,529	3,953	20,483	21,360	25,946	31,578	19,316	30,015	20,877
HISPANIC-OWNED										
Firms.....................	1,000...	200	37	100	31	18	9	3	1	(Z)
Sales and receipts	Mil. dol...	179,508	6,703	28,292	26,627	26,945	29,496	19,447	27,206	14,792
Employees	1,000...	1,537	–	202	205	248	267	185	244	186
Annual payroll	Mil. dol...	36,712	1,153	4,568	4,958	5,705	6,393	4,817	5,900	3,217
BLACK-OWNED										
Firms.....................	1,000...	95	19	47	14	7	4	1	1	(Z)
Sales and receipts	Mil. dol...	65,799	2,986	10,679	7,773	7,769	10,912	9,697	11,193	4,790
Employees	1,000...	754	–	96	92	100	133	87	162	82
Annual payroll	Mil. dol...	17,550	541	2,251	2,133	2,279	3,034	2,154	3,623	1,535
AMERICAN INDIAN- AND ALASKA NATIVE-OWNED										
Firms.....................	1,000...	24	5	12	4	2	1	(Z)	(Z)	(Z)
Sales and receipts	Mil. dol...	21,987	1,021	3,378	2,411	2,996	3,814	3,092	2,842	2,433
Employees	1,000...	191	–	26	23	28	36	23	26	29
Annual payroll	Mil. dol...	5,135	137	578	528	706	945	675	773	793
ASIAN-OWNED										
Firms.....................	1,000...	319	54	161	55	30	15	3	2	(Z)
Sales and receipts	Mil. dol...	291,163	10,287	56,967	46,155	44,109	50,950	30,759	32,955	18,980
Employees	1,000...	2,214	–	347	353	393	437	226	302	155
Annual payroll	Mil. dol...	56,045	1,616	7,946	7,992	9,130	10,947	6,048	8,211	4,154
NATIVE HAWAIIAN- AND OTHER PACIFIC ISLANDER-OWNED										
Firms.....................	1,000...	4	1	2	1	(Z)	(Z)	(Z)	(Z)	–
Sales and receipts	Mil. dol...	3,502	73	520	413	574	805	420	698	–
Employees	1,000...	29	–	4	4	5	7	4	5	–
Annual payroll	Mil. dol...	826	12	133	99	123	228	100	132	–

– Represents zero. Z Less than 500. [1] Firms reported annual payroll, but did not report any employees on their payroll during specified period in 2002.

Source: U.S. Census Bureau, *2002 Economic Census, Survey of Business Owners, Women-Owned Firms: 2002* (SB02-00CS-WMN)(RV). *Hispanic-Owned Firms: 2002* (SB02-00CS-HISP)(RV); *Black-Owned Firms: 2002* (SB02-00CS-BLK)(RV); *American Indian- and Alaska Native-Owned Firms: 2002* (SB02-00CS-AIAN)(RV); *Asian-Owned Firms: 2002* (SB02-00CS-ASIAN)(RV); and *Native Hawaiian- and Other Pacific Islander-Owned Firms: 2002* (SB02-00CS-NHPI)(RV).

Table 752. **Bankruptcy Petitions Filed and Pending by Type and Chapter: 1990 to 2008**

[For years ending June 30. Covers only bankruptcy cases filed under the Bankruptcy Reform Act of 1978. *Bankruptcy:* legal recognition that a company or individual is insolvent and must restructure or liquidate. Petitions "filed" means the commencement of a proceeding through the presentation of a petition to the clerk of the court; "pending" is a proceeding in which the administration has not been completed]

Item	1990	1995	2000	2003	2004	2005	2006	2007	2008
Total filed.	725,484	858,104	1,276,922	1,650,279	1,635,725	1,637,254	1,484,570	751,056	967,831
Business [1].	64,688	51,288	36,910	37,182	35,739	32,406	31,562	23,889	33,822
Nonbusiness [2].	660,796	806,816	1,240,012	1,613,097	1,599,986	1,604,848	1,453,008	727,167	934,009
Chapter 7 [3].	468,171	552,244	864,183	1,144,658	1,146,761	1,174,681	1,142,958	435,064	592,376
Chapter 11 [4].	2,116	1,755	722	966	935	847	749	540	780
Chapter 13 [5].	190,509	252,817	375,107	467,466	452,286	429,315	309,298	291,560	340,852
Voluntary.	723,886	856,991	1,276,146	1,649,543	1,635,099	1,636,678	1,484,085	750,577	967,248
Involuntary	1,598	1,113	776	736	626	576	485	479	583
Chapter 7 [3].	505,337	581,390	885,447	1,165,993	1,167,101	1,196,212	1,164,815	450,332	615,748
Chapter 9 [6].	7	12	8	7	7	6	10	7	4
Chapter 11 [4].	19,591	13,221	9,947	10,602	11,048	6,703	6,224	5,586	7,293
Chapter 12 [7].	1,351	904	732	775	302	290	360	386	314
Chapter 13 [5].	199,186	262,551	380,770	472,811	457,171	433,945	313,085	294,693	344,421
Section 304 [8].	12	26	18	91	96	98	[9]36	(X)	(X)
Chapter 15 [9].	(X)	(X)	(X)	(X)	(X)	(X)	40	52	51
Total pending. . .	961,919	1,090,446	1,400,416	1,729,139	1,697,267	1,750,562	1,411,212	1,312,016	1,362,236

X Not applicable.   [1] Business bankruptcies include those filed under Chapters 7, 9, 11, 12, 13, or 15.   [2] Includes other petitions not shown separately.   [3] Chapter 7, liquidation of nonexempt assets of businesses or individuals.   [4] Chapter 11, individual or business reorganization.   [5] Chapter 13, adjustment of debts of an individual with regular income.   [6] Chapter 9, adjustment of debts of a municipality.   [7] Chapter 12, adjustment of debts of a family farmer with regular income, effective November 26, 1986.   [8] Chapter 11, U.S.C., Section 304, cases ancillary to foreign proceedings.   [9] Chapter 15 was added and Section 304 was terminated by changes in the Bankruptcy Laws effective October 17, 2005.

Source: Administrative Office of the U.S. Courts, *Statistical Tables for the Federal Judiciary* and "Bankruptcy Statistics"; <http://www.uscourts.gov/bnkrpctystats/statistics.htm>.

Table 753. **Bankruptcy Cases Filed by State: 2000 to 2008**

[In thousands (1,276.9 represents 1,276,900). For years ending June 30. Covers only bankruptcy cases filed under the Bankruptcy Reform Act of 1978. *Bankruptcy:* legal recognition that a company or individual is insolvent and must restructure or liquidate. Petitions "filed" means the commencement of a proceeding through the presentation of a petition to the clerk of the court]

State	2000	2005	2007	2008	State	2000	2005	2007	2008
Total [1].	1,276.9	1,637.3	751.1	967.8	Missouri	26.3	39.2	19.0	23.1
					Montana	3.3	4.4	2.0	1.7
Alabama	31.4	42.6	22.5	25.8	Nebraska	5.6	9.6	5.0	5.9
Alaska	1.4	1.6	0.7	0.7	Nevada	14.3	16.3	8.1	14.4
Arizona	21.7	32.4	8.8	14.3	New Hampshire	3.9	4.9	2.6	3.5
Arkansas.	16.3	25.5	11.1	12.8					
California.	160.6	122.6	55.1	98.7	New Jersey	38.7	40.7	17.3	22.9
					New Mexico.	7.1	10.1	3.0	4.0
Colorado	15.6	30.2	13.0	17.9	New York	61.7	81.7	37.0	42.4
Connecticut	11.4	11.8	5.2	7.1	North Carolina	25.8	37.5	18.9	20.8
Delaware.	4.9	3.6	1.8	2.3	North Dakota	2.0	2.5	1.0	1.3
District of Columbia. . .	2.6	1.9	0.6	0.8					
Florida	74.0	85.8	32.7	52.7	Ohio.	53.6	95.8	45.5	54.2
					Oklahoma	19.3	28.2	8.7	9.9
Georgia	57.9	77.3	45.7	55.0	Oregon	18.1	25.3	8.6	10.5
Hawaii	5.0	3.2	1.2	1.6	Pennsylvania	43.8	62.3	28.1	31.5
Idaho	7.3	9.7	3.5	4.2	Rhode Island	4.8	4.4	2.2	3.6
Illinois.	62.3	83.6	36.8	48.5					
Indiana	37.5	55.9	27.7	35.0	South Carolina	11.7	15.2	6.9	7.6
					South Dakota.	2.1	2.9	1.2	1.4
Iowa.	8.2	14.3	6.2	7.5	Tennessee.	47.1	60.8	36.2	42.9
Kansas	11.4	17.3	7.5	8.2	Texas	62.9	97.5	41.4	44.2
Kentucky	20.8	29.2	15.5	19.2	Utah.	14.4	20.5	6.0	7.7
Louisiana	23.1	31.1	13.1	15.1					
Maine	4.1	4.7	1.9	2.6	Vermont	1.6	1.7	0.8	1.1
					Virginia	37.1	38.8	16.5	23.9
Maryland.	31.1	28.5	11.2	16.3	Washington	31.2	37.7	13.9	18.1
Massachusetts	16.7	19.6	11.7	15.0	West Virginia	8.2	12.6	4.0	4.9
Michigan	36.4	68.5	41.1	51.3	Wisconsin	18.0	29.0	13.9	18.8
Minnesota	15.4	19.4	10.4	14.2	Wyoming.	2.0	2.5	0.8	0.8
Mississippi	17.9	21.8	10.5	11.6					

[1] Includes island areas not shown separately.

Source: Administrative Office of the U.S. Courts, *Statistical Tables for the Federal Judiciary* and "Bankruptcy Statistics"; <http://www.uscourts.gov/bnkrpctystats/statistics.htm>.

U.S. Census Bureau, Statistical Abstract of the United States: 2010

Table 754. **Patents and Trademarks: 1990 to 2008**

[In thousands (99.2 represents 99,200). Calendar year data. Covers U.S. patents issued to citizens of the United States and residents of foreign countries. For data on foreign countries, see Table 1355]

Type	1990	1995	2000	2003	2004	2005	2006	2007	2008
Patents issued	99.2	113.8	176.0	187.0	181.3	157.7	196.4	182.9	185.2
Inventions	90.4	101.4	157.5	169.0	164.3	143.8	173.8	157.3	157.8
Individuals	17.3	17.4	22.4	19.6	17.6	14.7	16.6	14.0	12.6
Corporations:									
United States	36.1	44.0	70.9	75.3	73.0	65.2	78.9	70.5	70.0
Foreign [1]	36.0	39.1	63.3	73.2	72.9	63.2	77.4	72.0	74.5
U.S. government	1.0	1.0	0.9	0.9	0.8	0.7	0.8	0.7	0.7
Designs	8.0	11.7	17.4	16.6	15.7	13.0	21.0	24.1	25.6
Botanical plants	0.3	0.4	0.5	1.0	1.0	0.7	1.1	1.0	1.2
Reissues	0.4	0.3	0.5	0.4	0.3	0.2	0.5	0.5	0.6
U.S. residents	52.8	64.4	96.9	98.6	94.1	82.6	102.2	93.7	92.0
Foreign country residents	46.2	49.4	79.1	88.5	87.2	75.2	94.2	89.2	93.2
Percent of total	46.7	43.4	44.9	47.3	48.1	47.6	48.0	48.8	50.3
Trademarks:									
Applications filed	127.3	181.0	361.8	271.7	304.5	334.7	362.3	401.0	390.8
Issued	60.8	92.5	115.2	166.6	146.0	154.8	193.7	218.8	233.9
Trademarks	53.6	85.6	106.4	130.9	113.7	121.6	153.3	170.8	194.4
Trademark renewals	7.2	6.9	8.8	35.6	32.3	33.3	40.4	48.1	39.5

[1] Includes patents to foreign governments.

Source: U.S. Patent and Trademark Office, "Statistical Reports Available For Viewing, Calendar Year Patent Statistics"; <http://www.uspto.gov/web/offices/ac/ido/oeip/taf/reports.htm> and unpublished data.

Table 755. **Patents by State and Island Areas: 2008**

[Includes only U.S. patents granted to residents of the United States and territories]

State	Total	Inventions	Designs	Botanical plants	Reissues	State	Total	Inventions	Designs	Botanical plants	Reissues
Total	91,980	77,501	13,713	433	333	Missouri	786	615	161	4	6
Alabama	354	279	68	6	1	Montana	115	91	24	–	–
Alaska	28	20	8	–	–	Nebraska	214	191	23	–	–
Arizona	1,892	1,584	303	–	5	Nevada	464	375	86	–	3
Arkansas	152	108	40	2	2	New Hampshire	526	477	43	2	4
California	22,200	19,181	2,766	180	73	New Jersey	3,247	2,722	506	11	8
Colorado	1,868	1,622	237	1	8	New Mexico	295	280	14	–	1
Connecticut	1,595	1,356	231	2	6	New York	5,905	4,885	993	4	23
Delaware	353	325	28	–	–	North Carolina	2,157	1,841	289	18	9
District of Columbia	71	68	3	–	–	North Dakota	72	63	9	–	–
Florida	2,808	2,046	680	70	12	Ohio	3,153	2,227	910	4	12
Georgia	1,585	1,344	224	14	3	Oklahoma	474	417	57	–	–
Hawaii	101	77	23	1	–	Oregon	2,173	1,781	343	42	7
Idaho	1,207	1,162	41	–	4	Pennsylvania	2,850	2,414	424	6	6
Illinois	3,580	2,741	815	16	8	Rhode Island	303	218	84	–	1
Indiana	1,195	985	202	–	8	South Carolina	524	395	124	4	1
Iowa	644	561	78	–	5	South Dakota	60	54	6	–	–
Kansas	543	425	114	–	4	Tennessee	798	586	207	2	3
Kentucky	469	413	54	–	2	Texas	6,184	5,712	448	2	22
Louisiana	322	260	55	3	4	Utah	727	642	85	–	–
Maine	136	113	22	–	1	Vermont	514	437	76	–	1
Maryland	1,427	1,232	185	4	6	Virginia	1,180	1,030	144	1	5
Massachusetts	3,896	3,516	355	8	17	Washington	4,158	3,517	626	5	10
Michigan	3,583	2,996	563	10	14	West Virginia	91	74	16	–	1
Minnesota	2,869	2,535	311	5	18	Wisconsin	1,921	1,349	557	5	10
Mississippi	142	102	40	–	–	Wyoming	41	35	6	–	–
						Island areas	28	22	6	–	–

– Represents zero.

Source: U.S. Patent and Trademark Office, "Statistical Reports Available For Viewing, Calendar Year Patent Statistics"; <http://www.uspto.gov/web/offices/ac/ido/oeip/taf/reports.htm>.

Table 756. **Copyright Registration by Subject Matter: 2000 to 2008**

[In thousands (497.6 represents 497,600). For years ending September 30. Comprises claims to copyrights registered for both U.S. and foreign works. Semiconductor chips and renewals are not considered copyright registration claims]

Subject matter	2000	2005	2007	2008	Subject matter	2000	2005	2007	2008
Total copyright claims	497.6	515.2	524.7	232.1	Works of the visual arts [3]	85.8	82.5	89.2	42.1
Monographs [1]	169.7	191.4	198.6	78.7					
Serials	69.0	57.7	52.6	22.0	Semiconductor chip				
Sound recordings	34.2	49.9	53.7	24.2	products	0.7	0.5	0.3	0.2
Musical works [2]	138.9	133.7	130.6	65.1	Renewals	16.8	15.8	1.3	0.4

[1] Includes computer software and machine readable works. [2] Includes dramatic works, accompanying music, choreography, pantomimes, motion pictures, and filmstrips. [3] Two-dimensional works of fine and graphic art, including prints and art reproductions; sculptural works; technical drawings and models; photographs; commercial prints and labels; works of applied arts, cartographic works, and multimedia works.

Source: The Library of Congress, Copyright Office, *Annual Report.*

Table 757. **Net Stock of Private Fixed Assets by Industry: 2000 to 2007**

[In billions of dollars (21,190 represents $21,190,000,000,000). **Estimates as of Dec. 31**. Net stock estimates are presented in terms of current cost and cover equipment, software, and structures]

Industry	1997 NAICS code [1]	2000	2005	2006	2007
Private fixed assets	(X)	21,190	30,224	32,429	33,381
Agriculture, forestry, fishing, and hunting..........	11	406	522	549	566
Farms [2].............................	111, 112	379	488	512	528
Forestry, fishing, and related activities..........	113–115	27	34	37	38
Mining.................................	21	580	1,024	1,194	1,253
Oil and gas extraction	211	442	844	986	1,025
Mining, except oil and gas	212	92	117	132	143
Mining support activities..................	213	46	63	76	85
Utilities.................................	22	1,039	1,376	1,477	1,568
Construction	23	173	221	239	249
Manufacturing	31–33	1,759	1,957	2,042	2,110
Durable goods	(X)	996	1,111	1,157	1,194
Wood products	321	31	35	37	38
Nonmetallic mineral products...........	327	55	64	67	70
Primary metals	331	124	127	130	132
Fabricated metal products.............	332	112	124	128	132
Machinery	333	140	164	173	181
Computer and electronic products	334	245	269	279	287
Electrical equipment, appliances, and components	335	45	49	51	53
Motor vehicles, bodies and trailers, and parts	3361-3363	105	118	121	123
Other transportation equipment	3364, 3365, 3369	79	93	98	102
Furniture and related products	337	16	19	20	21
Miscellaneous manufacturing...........	339	43	51	53	56
Nondurable goods......................	(X)	763	846	885	916
Food and beverage and tobacco products	311, 312	182	204	213	220
Textile mills and textile product mills	313, 314	44	42	42	42
Apparel and leather and allied products ...	315, 316	17	17	18	18
Paper products	322	100	100	103	106
Printing and related support activities ...	323	41	47	49	51
Petroleum and coal products..........	324	92	112	122	130
Chemical products...................	325	220	250	261	270
Plastics and rubber products	326	67	74	77	79
Wholesale trade...........................	42	348	432	469	497
Retail trade.............................	44–45	641	874	943	994
Transportation and warehousing	48–49	805	947	992	1,029
Air transportation.......................	481	196	241	243	245
Railroad transportation...................	482	267	292	302	313
Water transportation	483	39	49	54	57
Truck transportation.....................	484	68	79	89	95
Transit and ground passenger transportation ...	185	31	39	42	44
Pipeline transportation...................	486	74	112	120	128
Other transportation and support activites [3] ...	487, 488, 492	105	107	112	114
Warehousing and storage.................	493	22	29	32	34
Information	51	817	979	1,061	1,109
Publishing industries (includes software)....	511	50	54	57	59
Motion picture and sound recording industries ...	512	32	36	37	38
Broadcasting and telecommunications	513	716	859	934	976
Information and data processing services ...	514	19	30	34	37
Finance and insurance	52	822	1,065	1,145	1,205
Federal Reserve banks	521	11	15	16	17
Credit intermediation and related activities....	522	465	589	629	659
Securities, commodity contracts, and investments....	523	86	108	118	125
Insurance carriers and related activities.....	524	165	201	211	217
Funds, trusts, and other financial vehicles ...	525	95	151	171	188
Real estate and rental and leasing	53	11,476	17,543	18,769	19,051
Real estate	531	11,233	17,217	18,416	18,683
Rental and leasing services and lessors of intangible assets [4]	532, 533	243	326	353	368
Professional, scientific, and technical services....	54	205	305	328	350
Legal services	5411	20	25	26	27
Computer systems design and related services	5415	50	67	73	79
Miscellaneous professional, scientific, and technical services [5] ...	([5])	135	213	228	243
Management of companies and enterprises [6] ...	551111, 551112	269	364	388	403
Admin/support waste mgt/remediation services ...	56	153	204	220	233
Administrative and support services......	561	84	123	133	141
Waste management and remediation services ...	562	68	81	88	92
Educational services.......................	61	213	330	362	392
Health care and social assistance	62	693	1,010	1,099	1,162
Ambulatory health care services	621	190	266	284	297
Hospitals.............................	622	449	669	733	780
Nursing and residential care facilities.....	623	29	42	46	48
Social assistance	624	24	33	36	38
Arts, entertainment, and recreation	71	128	193	211	224
Performing arts, spectator sports, museums, and related activities..	711, 712	48	76	83	89
Amusements, gambling, and recreation industries....	713	80	117	128	136
Accommodation and food services	72	336	439	471	497
Accommodation	721	177	218	236	250
Food services and drinking places	722	160	220	236	247
Other services, except public administration ...	81	329	440	471	488

X Not applicable.   [1] Based on North American Industry Classification System, 1997; see text this section.   [2] NAICS crop and animal production.   [3] Consists of scenic and sightseeing transportation; transportation support services; and couriers and messengers.   [4] Intangible assets include patents, trademarks, and franchise agreements, but not copyrights.   [5] Consists of accounting, tax preparation, bookkeeping, and payroll services (NAICS code 5412); architectural, engineering, and related services (5413); specialized design services (5414); management, scientific, and technical consulting services (5416); scientific research and development services (5417); advertising and related services (5418); and other professional, scientific, and technical services (5419).   [6] Consists of bank and other holding companies.

Source: U.S. Bureau of Economic Analysis, "Table 3.1ES. Current-Cost Net Stock of Private Fixed Assets by Industry"; published 21 August 2008; <http://www.bea.gov/bea/dn/FA2004/SelectTable.asp#S3>.

Business Enterprise 501

Table 758. **Private Domestic Investment in Current and Chained (2000) Dollars: 1990 to 2007**

[In billions of dollars (861 represents $861,000,000,000). Covers equipment, software, and structures. For explanation of chained dollars, see text, Section 13]

Item	1990	2000	2002	2003	2004	2005	2006	2007
CURRENT DOLLARS								
Gross private domestic investment . . .	861	1,736	1,582	1,664	1,889	2,086	2,220	2,130
Less: Consumption of fixed capital	552	991	1,080	1,118	1,206	1,360	1,356	1,431
Equals: Net private domestic investment	309	745	502	546	683	726	864	699
Fixed investment	846	1,679	1,570	1,650	1,830	2,043	2,171	2,134
Less: Consumption of fixed capital . . .	552	991	1,080	1,118	1,206	1,360	1,356	1,431
Equals: Net fixed investment	295	688	490	532	624	683	815	703
Nonresidential	622	1,232	1,066	1,077	1,155	1,273	1,414	1,504
Residential	224	447	504	572	676	770	757	630
Change in private inventories.	15	57	12	14	59	43	49	−4
CHAINED (2000) DOLLARS								
Gross private domestic investment . . .	895	1,736	1,557	1,613	1,770	1,874	1,913	1,810
Less: Consumption of fixed capital	572	991	1,080	1,108	1,167	1,267	1,216	1,263
Equals: Net private domestic investment	323	745	477	505	603	607	696	547
Fixed investment	887	1,679	1,545	1,597	1,713	1,830	1,866	1,809
Nonresidential	595	1,232	1,072	1,082	1,144	1,226	1,318	1,383
Residential	299	447	470	509	560	595	553	454
Change in private inventories.	15	57	13	14	54	39	42	−3

Source: U.S. Bureau of Economic Analysis, "Table 5.2.5. Gross and Net Domestic Investment by Major Type" and "Table 5.2.6. Real Gross and Net Domestic Investment by Major Type, Chained Dollars"; published 6 August 2008; <http://www.bea.gov/national/nipaweb/SelectTable.asp?Selected=N>.

Table 759. **Information and Communications Technology (ICT) Equipment and Computer Software Expenditures: 2006 and 2007**

[In millions of dollars (92,636 represents $92,636,000,000). Covers only companies with employees. The Information and Communication Technology Survey collects noncapitalized and capitalized data on information and communication technology equipment, including computer software. This survey is sent to a sample of approximately 46,000 private nonfarm employer businesses operating in the United States]

Type of expenditure and industry	2002 NAICS code [1]	Noncapitalized expenditures [2]		Capitalized expenditures [3]	
		2006	2007	2006	2007
Total expenditures for ICT equipment and computer software	(X)	92,636	94,401	160,381	169,812
Total equipment expenditures.	(X)	37,187	38,018	(NA)	(NA)
Purchases.	(X)	18,901	20,233	101,118	106,493
Computer and peripheral equipment	(X)	12,932	13,538	57,449	58,593
Information and communication technology equipment	(X)	5,685	6,432	39,055	42,758
Electromedical and electrotherapeutic apparatus	(X)	284	262	4,615	5,141
Operating leases and rental payments	(X)	18,286	17,785	(NA)	(NA)
Computer and peripheral equipment	(X)	11,791	12,125	(NA)	(NA)
Information and communication technology equipment	(X)	5,453	4,459	(NA)	(NA)
Electromedical and electrotherapeutic apparatus	(X)	1,042	1,201	(NA)	(NA)
Total computer software expenditures	(X)	55,449	56,383	(NA)	(NA)
Purchases and payroll for developing software.	(X)	32,200	30,476	59,263	63,319
Software licensing and service/maintenance agreements	(X)	23,249	25,907	(NA)	(NA)
Forestry, fishing, and agricultural services.	113–115	51	51	46	60
Mining.	21	696	1,224	1,268	1,343
Utilities.	22	1,469	1,375	2,364	2,548
Construction	23	1,002	1,188	1,521	1,748
Manufacturing	31–33	17,273	17,699	18,060	18,547
Durable goods industries	321, 327, 33	11,339	11,101	10,468	10,922
Nondurable goods industries.	31, 322-326	5,934	6,598	7,592	7,625
Wholesale trade.	42	2,625	3,074	5,257	6,119
Retail trade.	44–45	3,918	4,716	10,915	12,408
Transportation and warehousing	48–49	1,514	1,785	3,114	3,333
Information	51	14,159	12,666	49,084	51,097
Finance and insurance	52	22,130	23,412	27,362	29,116
Real estate and rental and leasing	53	1,267	1,509	2,004	1,964
Professional, scientific, and technical services	54	12,046	11,307	13,698	13,608
Management of companies and enterprises	55	697	681	1,049	1,385
Admin/support and waste management/remediation services	56	2,406	2,135	4,460	4,116
Educational services.	61	1,637	1,640	1,880	1,997
Health care and social assistance	62	5,986	6,911	13,057	14,483
Arts, entertainment, and recreation	71	532	532	885	1,159
Accommodation and food services	72	1,008	849	1,727	1,802
Other services (except public administration).	81	1,954	1,335	2,306	2,612
Equipment expenditures serving multiple industry codes . . .	(X)	265	312	322	363

NA Not available.   X Not applicable.   [1] Based on North American Industry Classification System, 2002; see text, this section.   [2] Expenses for ICT equipment including computer software not charged to asset accounts for which depreciation or amortization accounts are ordinarily maintained.   [3] Expenses for ICT equipment including computer software chargeable to asset accounts for which depreciation or amortization accounts are ordinarily maintained.

Source: U.S. Census Bureau, "2007 Information and Communication Technology Survey"; published 26 February 2009; <http://www.census.gov/econ/ict/xls/2007/Full%20Report.htm>.

502   Business Enterprise

Table 760. Capital Expenditures: 2000 to 2007

[In billions of dollars (1,161 represents $1,161,000,000,000). Based on a sample survey and subject to sampling error; see source for details]

Item	All companies				Companies with employees				Companies without employees			
	2000	2005	2006	2007	2000	2005	2006	2007	2000	2005	2006	2007
Capital expenditures, total.	1,161	1,145	1,310	1,362	1,090	1,063	1,217	1,277	71	82	93	84
Structures	364	402	489	529	338	369	454	495	26	33	35	34
New	329	366	449	484	309	341	420	460	20	25	29	24
Used.	35	36	40	45	29	28	34	34	6	8	6	11
Equipment and software.	797	743	821	832	752	694	763	783	45	49	58	50
New	751	701	777	792	718	665	734	752	32	37	43	40
Used.	46	42	44	40	34	29	29	30	12	13	15	10
Capital leases	20	18	24	20	19	18	24	19	(Z)	(Z)	1	1

Z Less than $500 million.

Source: U.S. Census Bureau, "2007 Annual Capital Expenditures Survey"; published 22 January 2009; <http://www.census.gov/econ/aces/> and earlier reports.

Table 761. Capital Expenditures by Industry: 2000 and 2007

[In billions of dollars (1,090 represents $1,090,000,000,000). Covers only companies with employees. Data for 2000 based on the North American Industry Classification System (NAICS), 1997; 2007 based on NAICS, 2002; see text this section. Based on a sample survey and subject to sampling error; see source for details]

Industry	NAICS code	2000	2007	Industry	NAICS code	2000	2007
Total expenditures	(X)	1,090	1,277	Professional, scientific, and technical services	54	34	32
Forestry, fishing, and agricultural services.	113–115	1	2	Management of companies and enterprises.	55	5	4
Mining	21	43	122	Admin/support waste mgt/ remediation services	56	18	19
Utilities	22	61	84	Educational services	61	18	23
Construction	23	25	37	Health care and social assistance	62	52	84
Manufacturing	31–33	215	197	Arts, entertainment, and recreation	71	19	19
Durable goods	321, 327, 33	134	108	Accommodation and food services.	72	26	38
Nondurable goods.	31, 322-326	81	89	Other services (except public administration)	81	21	30
Wholesale trade	42	34	32	Structure and equipment expenditures serving multiple industry categories. . .	(X)	2	2
Retail trade	44–45	70	84				
Transportation and warehousing	48–49	60	69				
Information	51	160	105				
Finance and insurance	52	134	172				
Real estate and rental and leasing	53	92	123				

X Not applicable.

Source: U.S. Census Bureau, "2007 Annual Capital Expenditures Survey"; published 22 January 2009; <http://www.census.gov/econ/aces/> and earlier reports.

Table 762. Business Cycle Expansions and Contractions—Months of Duration: 1945 to 2007

[A trough is the low point of a business cycle; a peak is the high point. Contraction, or recession, is the period from peak to subsequent trough; expansion is the period from trough to subsequent peak. Business cycle reference dates are determined by the National Bureau of Economic Research, Inc.]

Business cycle reference date				Contraction (peak to trough)	Expansion (previous trough to this peak)	Length of cycle	
Peak		Trough				Trough from previous trough	Peak from previous peak
Month	Year	Month	Year				
February	1945	October	1945	8	[1]80	[1]88	[2]93
November	1948	October	1949	11	37	48	45
July	1953	May.	1954	10	45	55	56
August	1957	April	1958	8	39	47	49
April	1960	February	1961	10	24	34	32
December	1969	November	1970	11	106	117	116
November	1973	March	1975	16	36	52	47
January.	1980	July.	1980	6	58	64	74
July	1981	November	1982	16	12	28	18
July	1990	March	1991	8	92	100	108
March	2001	November	2001	8	120	128	128
December	2007				73		81
Average, all cycles: 1945 to 2001 (10 cycles). . .				10	57	67	67

[1] Previous trough: June 1938.   [2] Previous peak: May 1937.

Source: National Bureau of Economic Research, Inc., Cambridge, MA, "Business Cycle Expansions and Contractions"; <http://www.nber.org/cycles.html>; (accessed 17 April 2009).

Business Enterprise   503

Table 763. **The Conference Board Leading, Coincident, and Lagging Economic Indexes: 2000 to 2008**

[299.4 represents 299,400]

Item	Unit	2000	2004	2005	2006	2007	2008
The Conference Board Leading Economic Index (LEI), composite.............	2004 = 100	86.3	100.0	102.7	104.3	104.0	101.1
Average weekly hours, manufacturing ...	Hours........	41.2	40.8	40.6	41.2	41.2	40.8
Average weekly initial claims for unemployment insurance	1,000........	299.4	342.4	330.9	313.0	322.0	421.7
Manufacturers' new orders, consumer goods and materials (1982 dol.)......	Mil. dol.	152,049	145,264	150,291	149,994	145,548	132,132
Index of supplier deliveries— vendor performance [1]............	Percent	53.4	62.6	54.1	54.3	51.2	51.6
Manufacturers' new orders, nondefense capital goods (1982 dol.)...........	Mil. dol.	49,808	39,499	45,323	48,821	49,631	45,033
Building permits, new private housing units	1,000........	1,598	2,058	2,160	1,844	1,392	895
Stock prices, 500 common stocks [1]	1941–43 = 10 ..	1,426.8	1,130.6	1,207.1	1,310.0	1,476.7	1,220.9
Money supply, M2 (chain 2000 dol.)	Bil. dol.........	4,778	5,763	5,838	5,965	6,147	6,348
Interest rate spread, 10-year Treasury bonds less federal funds	Percent	−0.21	2.93	1.08	−0.17	−0.39	1.74
Index of consumer expectations [1]......	1966:1 = 100...	102.7	88.5	77.4	75.9	75.6	57.3
The Conference Board Coincident Economic Index (CEI), composite.......	2004 = 100	98.8	100.0	102.4	105.0	106.7	105.8
Employees on nonagricultural payrolls...	1,000........	131,794	131,419	133,699	136,098	137,604	137,046
Personal income less transfer payments (chain 2000 dol.).........	Bil. dol.	7,345	7,647	7,845	8,190	8,456	8,415
Industrial production...............	2002 = 100	103.7	103.8	107.2	109.7	111.3	108.8
Manufacturing and trade sales (chain 2000 dol.)	Mil. dol.	844,794	888,784	926,999	956,413	967,661	940,481
The Conference Board Lagging Economic Index (LAG), composite.........	2004 = 100	99.9	100.0	103.1	106.5	109.4	112.7
Average duration of unemployment.....	Weeks	12.7	19.6	18.4	16.9	16.9	17.8
Inventories to sales ratio, manufacturing and trade (chain 2000 dol.)	Ratio	1.38	1.35	1.33	1.33	1.32	1.36
Change in labor cost per unit of output, manufacturing..................	Percent	2.3	−0.8	−3.4	2.1	–	6.6
Average prime rate	Percent	9.2	4.3	6.2	8.0	8.1	5.1
Commercial and industrial loans outstanding (chain 2000 dol.)........	Mil. dol.	957,110	571,959	608,176	646,257	724,756	797,960
Consumer installment credit to personal income ratio...........	Percent	19.2	22.0	21.9	21.3	21.1	21.2
Change in consumer price index for services....................	Percent	3.8	3.0	3.5	3.7	3.3	3.6

– Represents or rounds to zero. [1] Data are from private sources and provided through the courtesy of the compilers and are subject to their copyrights: stock prices, Standard & Poor's Corporation; index of consumer expectations, University of Michigan's Survey Research Center; index of supplier deliveries, Institute for Supply Management.

Source: The Conference Board, New York, NY 10022-6601, *Business Cycle Indicators,* monthly, <http://www.conference-board.org/economics/bci/>. Reproduced with permission from The Conference Board, Inc. 2009, The Conference Board, Inc. (copyright).

Table 764. **Manufacturing and Trade—Sales and Inventories: 1992 to 2008**

[In billions of dollars (541 represents $541,000,000,000), except ratios. Based on North American Industry Classification System (NAICS) 2002; see text, this section]

Year	Sales, average monthly [1]				Inventories [2]				Inventory-sales ratios [3]			
	Total	Manu-facturing	Retail trade	Merchant whole-salers	Total	Manu-facturing	Retail trade	Merchant whole-salers	Total	Manu-facturing	Retail trade	Merchant whole-salers
1992	541	242	151	147	837	379	261	197	1.53	1.57	1.67	1.31
1993	568	252	162	154	864	380	280	205	1.50	1.50	1.68	1.30
1994	610	270	176	165	927	400	305	222	1.46	1.44	1.66	1.29
1995	655	290	185	180	986	425	323	238	1.48	1.44	1.72	1.29
1996	687	300	197	190	1,006	430	334	241	1.46	1.43	1.67	1.27
1997	724	320	206	198	1,047	444	345	259	1.42	1.37	1.64	1.26
1998	743	325	216	202	1,079	449	357	272	1.43	1.39	1.62	1.31
1999	787	336	234	217	1,139	464	385	290	1.40	1.35	1.59	1.30
2000	834	351	249	235	1,198	482	407	309	1.41	1.35	1.59	1.29
2001	819	331	256	232	1,121	428	395	298	1.43	1.38	1.58	1.32
2002	824	326	261	236	1,141	423	416	302	1.36	1.28	1.55	1.26
2003	854	335	272	247	1,148	408	432	308	1.34	1.24	1.56	1.23
2004	923	359	290	275	1,240	441	461	338	1.30	1.19	1.56	1.18
2005	1,000	395	307	298	1,307	473	472	362	1.27	1.17	1.51	1.18
2006	1,064	418	322	323	1,391	511	488	392	1.28	1.19	1.50	1.17
2007	1,102	423	333	346	1,447	531	500	417	1.28	1.23	1.49	1.16
2008	1,137	432	330	375	1,456	542	484	430	1.31	1.28	1.52	1.17

[1] Averages of monthly not-seasonally-adjusted figures. [2] Seasonally adjusted end-of-year data. [3] Averages of seasonally adjusted monthly ratios.

Source: U.S. Council of Economic Advisors, *Economic Indicators,* May 2009.

U.S. Census Bureau, Statistical Abstract of the United States: 2010

Table 765. **Industrial Production Indexes by Industry: 1990 to 2008**

[2002 = 100. Except as noted, based on the North American Industry Classification System (NAICS); 2002; see text, this section]

Industry	2002 NAICS code	1990	2000	2003	2004	2005	2006	2007	2008
Total index	(X)	69.7	103.7	101.3	103.8	107.2	109.7	111.3	108.8
Manufacturing (SIC) [1]	(X)	67.0	104.4	101.3	104.3	108.5	111.2	112.7	109.2
Manufacturing (NAICS)	31–33	65.5	103.9	101.6	104.7	109.1	112.1	113.8	110.4
Durable goods	(X)	52.8	105.2	102.7	107.0	112.8	117.8	120.2	116.3
Wood products	321	84.1	103.7	100.7	104.4	110.4	110.0	99.2	84.8
Nonmetallic mineral products	327	83.3	103.6	100.5	103.6	108.1	109.9	106.9	100.7
Primary metals	331	96.7	111.4	99.1	110.0	108.0	112.6	110.0	102.6
Fabricated metal products	332	80.3	110.7	98.7	98.9	103.4	109.0	112.1	110.1
Machinery	333	86.7	117.7	99.7	103.7	110.2	115.5	116.4	109.3
Computers and electronic products	334	13.8	101.4	114.3	129.9	144.5	163.8	176.7	193.2
Electrical equipment, appliances, and components . . .	335	87.5	121.3	97.3	99.0	100.7	101.4	104.8	104.5
Motor vehicles and parts	3361–3	55.8	99.9	103.5	103.7	103.9	100.2	97.4	83.4
Aerospace and other misc. transportation equipment	3364–9	123.0	99.3	95.8	94.3	105.0	110.9	121.7	119.2
Furniture and related products . . .	337	75.2	103.3	98.2	100.9	104.6	104.2	101.0	90.4
Miscellaneous products.	339	67.3	96.7	103.0	103.2	109.9	113.3	118.3	117.7
Nondurable goods.	(X)	87.7	102.2	100.1	102.0	104.8	105.7	106.7	103.7
Food, beverage, and tobacco products.	311,2	90.0	101.2	102.0	102.5	106.2	106.7	109.6	109.4
Textile and product mills	313,4	99.2	111.9	96.0	94.6	96.7	88.0	81.2	72.8
Apparel and leather	315,6	172.4	150.8	93.3	82.0	80.4	79.1	79.3	75.9
Paper	322	97.4	105.3	96.8	97.6	97.5	97.6	95.9	92.1
Printing and related support.	323	102.1	113.1	96.2	96.9	99.2	99.8	100.6	94.0
Petroleum and coal products	324	86.9	96.9	97.9	106.0	110.1	109.7	109.1	110.0
Chemical	325	78.3	95.0	101.3	105.6	109.3	112.7	114.1	108.8
Plastics and rubber products	326	67.2	102.9	100.3	101.5	102.3	102.9	104.7	99.1
Other manufacturing (non-NAICS) [2] . . .	1133, 5111	100.9	112.6	97.1	97.9	97.6	96.6	95.3	89.9
Mining.	21	107.8	104.2	100.2	99.6	98.3	101.5	102.1	104.2
Utilities.	2211,2	77.9	97.4	101.9	103.3	105.4	104.8	108.3	108.4
Electric power generation, transmission, and distribution	2211	76.7	97.2	102.1	104.2	107.2	107.8	110.5	110.2
Natural gas distribution	2212	85.6	98.6	100.9	98.8	97.1	91.3	98.1	100.2

X Not applicable.   [1] Standard Industrial Classification (SIC); see text, this section.   [2] Those industries—logging and newspaper, periodical, book, and directory publishing   that have traditionally been considered to be manufacturing.

Source: Board of Governors of the Federal Reserve System, *Industrial Production and Capacity Utilization*, Statistical Release G.17, monthly. See also <http://www.federalreserve.gov/releases/g17/>.

Table 766. **Index of Industrial Capacity: 1990 to 2008**

[2002 output = 100. Annual figures are averages of monthly data. Capacity represents estimated quantity of output relative to output in 2002 which the current stock of plant and equipment was capable of producing]

Year	Index of capacity		Relation of output to capacity (percent)				
	Total industry	Manufacturing	Total industry	Stage of process			Manufacturing
				Crude [1]	Primary and semifinished [2]	Finished [3]	
1990	84.5	82.0	82.5	88.2	82.7	80.6	81.7
1995	95.7	94.3	84.0	89.0	86.6	79.7	83.2
1999	121.4	123.8	81.9	86.6	84.2	78.3	80.7
2000	126.9	130.4	81.7	88.5	84.4	77.1	80.1
2001	131.5	135.7	76.1	85.3	77.4	72.5	73.8
2002	134.0	137.6	74.6	82.7	76.6	70.7	72.7
2003	133.7	137.4	75.8	84.4	77.7	71.6	73.7
2004	133.4	137.0	77.9	86.1	79.8	73.3	76.2
2005	133.8	138.1	80.1	86.5	81.7	76.0	78.6
2006	135.7	140.1	80.9	88.3	81.7	77.1	79.4
2007	138.1	142.7	80.6	87.8	81.0	77.5	79.0
2008	140.3	145.4	77.6	86.6	77.3	74.1	75.1

[1] Crude processing, covers a relatively small portion of total industrial capacity and consists of logging (NAICS 1133), much of mining (excluding stone, sand, and gravel mining, and oil and gas drilling, which are NAICS 21231, 21221–2, and 213111) and some basic manufacturing industries, including basic chemicals (NAICS 3251); fertilizers, pesticides, and other agricultural chemicals (NAICS 32531,2); pulp, paper, and paperboard mills (NAICS 3221); and alumina, aluminum, and other nonferrous production and processing mills (NAICS 3313,4).   [2] Primary and semifinished processing loosely corresponds to the previously published aggregate, primary processing. Includes utilities and portions of several 2-digit SIC industries included in the former advanced processing group. These include printing and related support activities (NAICS 3231); paints and adhesives (NAICS 3255); and newspaper, periodical, book, and directory publishers (NAICS 5111).   [3] Finished processing generally corresponds to the previously published aggregate, advanced processing. Includes oil and gas well drilling and carpet and rug mills.

Source: Board of Governors of the Federal Reserve System, *Industrial Production and Capacity Utilization*, Statistical Release G.17, monthly. (Based on data from Federal Reserve Board, U.S. Dept. of Commerce, U.S. Bureau of Labor Statistics, and McGraw-Hill Information Systems Company, New York, NY; and other sources.)

U.S. Census Bureau, Statistical Abstract of the United States: 2010

Table 767. **Corporate Profits, Taxes, and Dividends: 1990 to 2008**

[In billions of dollars (438 represents $438,000,000,000). Covers corporations organized for profit and other entities treated as corporations. Represents profits to U.S. residents, without deduction of depletion charges and exclusive of capital gains and losses; intercorporate dividends from profits of domestic corporations are eliminated; net receipts of dividends, reinvested earnings of incorporated foreign affiliates, and earnings of unincorporated foreign affiliates are added. CCA = capital consumption adjustment]

Item	1990	2000	2004	2005	2006	2007	2008
Corporate profits with IVA and CCA	438	818	1,231	1,448	1,669	1,642	1,477
Taxes on corporate income	145	265	307	414	469	450	367
Profits after tax with IVA and CCA	292	553	924	1,034	1,200	1,192	1,110
Net dividends	169	378	540	577	702	789	832
Undistributed profits with IVA and CCA. . .	123	175	384	457	498	403	278
Cash flow:							
Net cash flow with IVA and CCA	491	865	1,182	1,316	1,390	1,349	1,289
Undistributed profits with IVA and CCA. . .	123	175	384	457	498	403	278
Consumption of fixed capital	368	690	797	859	893	945	1,011
Less: Inventory valuation adjustment (IVA). .	−13	−14	−43	−38	−40	−51	−49
Equals: Net cash flow.	504	879	1,225	1,354	1,430	1,400	1,338

Source: U.S. Bureau of Economic Analysis, *Survey of Current Business*, monthly. See also <http://www.bea.gov /national/nipaweb/Index.asp>.

Table 768. **Corporate Profits With Inventory Valuation and Capital Consumption Adjustments—Financial and Nonfinancial Industries: 2000 to 2008**

[In billions of dollars (818 represents $818,000,000,000). Based on the North American Industry Classification System 1997; see text, this section. Minus sign (−) indicates loss. See headnote, Table 767]

Item	2000	2004	2005	2006	2007	2008
Corporate profits with IVA/CCA [1]	818	1,231	1,448	1,669	1,642	1,477
Domestic industries	672	1,038	1,209	1,401	1,298	1,090
Rest of the world	146	193	239	268	345	387
Corporate profits with IVA [1]	759	1,162	1,583	1,834	1,835	1,548
Domestic industries	614	968	1,343	1,567	1,491	1,162
Financial [2]	200	349	425	479	450	309
Nonfinancial.	413	619	918	1,088	1,041	853
Utilities	24	19	29	56	59	55
Manufacturing.	144	153	244	304	317	240
Wholesale trade	60	79	97	108	103	77
Retail trade	60	91	120	132	132	92
Transportation and warehousing.	15	14	29	43	43	25
Information.	−18	44	80	91	103	102
Other nonfinancial [3]	128	220	319	355	285	264
Rest of the world	146	193	239	268	345	387

[1] Inventory valuation adjustment and capital consumption adjustment. [2] Consists of finance and insurance and bank and other holding companies. [3] Consists of agriculture, forestry, fishing, and hunting; mining; construction; real estate and rental and leasing; professional, scientific, and technical services; administrative and waste management services; educational services; health care and social assistance; arts, entertainment, and recreation; accommodation and food services; and other services, except government.

Source: U.S. Bureau of Economic Analysis, *Survey of Current Business*, April 2009. See also <http://www.bea.gov/national /nipaweb/Index.asp>.

Table 769. **Corporate Profits Before Taxes by Industry: 2000 to 2007**

[In billions of dollars (773 represents $773,000,000,000). Profits are without inventory valuation and capital consumption adjustments. Minus sign (−) indicates loss. See headnote, Table 767]

Industry	1997 NAICS code [1]	2000	2004	2005	2006	2007
Corporate profits before tax	(X)	773	1,205	1,621	1,874	1,886
Domestic industries	(X)	628	1,011	1,381	1,606	1,542
Agriculture, forestry, fishing, and hunting	11	2	3	5	4	4
Mining.	21	15	24	44	57	55
Utilities	221	25	19	30	55	59
Construction	23	42	56	84	86	6
Manufacturing.	31–33	153	175	262	326	339
Wholesale trade	42	62	89	105	119	119
Retail trade	44–45	61	98	127	137	140
Transportation and warehousing	48–49	15	14	30	43	44
Information	51	−18	43	80	91	103
Finance and insurance.	52	113	210	264	307	286
Real estate and rental and leasing	53	9	13	28	27	27
Professional, scientific, and technical services . .	54	1	35	41	49	58
Management of companies and enterprises [2]	551111,551112	87	139	161	172	164
Admin/support waste mgt/remediation services. . .	56	9	15	23	22	24
Educational services	61	2	4	5	6	6
Health care and social assistance	62	25	43	53	59	61
Arts, entertainment, and recreation.	71	2	5	6	7	6
Accommodation and food services	72	14	16	22	25	27
Other services, except public administration.	81	8	8	12	14	14
Rest of the world [3]	(X)	146	193	239	268	345

X Not applicable. [1] Based on North American Industry Classification System, 1997; see text, this section. [2] Consists of bank and other holding companies. [3] Consists of receipts by all U.S. residents, including both corporations and persons, of dividends from foreign corporations, and for U.S. corporations, their share of reinvested earnings of their incorporated foreign affiliates, and earnings of unincorporated foreign affiliates, net of corresponding payments.

Source: U.S. Bureau of Economic Analysis, *Survey of Current Business*, August 2008. See also <http://www.bea.gov/national /nipaweb/Index.asp>.

506   Business Enterprise

Table 770. **Manufacturing, Mining, and Trade Corporations—Profits and Stockholders' Equity by Industry: 2007 and 2008**

[Averages of quarterly figures at annual rates. Manufacturing data exclude estimates for corporations with less than $250,000 in assets at time of sample selection. Mining, wholesale and retail trade data excludes estimates for corporations with less than $50 million in assets at time of sample selection. Based on sample; see source for discussion of methodology. Based on North American Industry Classification System (NAICS), 2002; see text, this section. Minus sign (–) indicates loss]

Industry	2002 NAICS code	Ratio of profits after taxes to stockholders' equity (percent)		Profits after taxes per dollar of sales (cents)		Ratio of stockholders' equity to debt	
		2007	2008	2007	2008	2007	2008
Manufacturing.	31–33	15.2	9.2	7.3	4.3	2.0	1.8
Nondurable manufacturing	(X)	19.9	14.9	9.3	6.4	1.8	1.7
Food	311	16.8	13.5	5.9	4.9	1.4	1.4
Beverage and tobacco products	312	30.4	20.8	19.8	11.5	1.3	1.1
Textile mills and textile product mills	313, 314	6.9	–9.9	2.7	–3.8	1.9	1.9
Apparel and leather products	315, 316	17.4	12.1	6.9	5.0	2.1	2.1
Paper	322	10.0	–0.1	3.9	0.4	1.1	0.9
Printing and related support activities	323	14.8	–0.3	3.3	0.1	0.7	0.6
Petroleum and coal products	324	25.5	17.6	9.6	4.5	3.0	2.9
Chemicals	325	17.3	15.8	13.1	12.4	1.9	1.8
Plastics and rubber products	326	15.0	4.5	4.1	1.3	0.9	0.9
Durable manufacturing.	(X)	10.7	3.5	5.3	2.1	2.1	1.9
Wood products	321	7.0	–3.2	2.0	–1.5	1.2	1.3
Nonmetallic mineral products	327	13.9	2.7	6.7	1.2	1.3	1.1
Primary metals	331	17.0	–2.7	7.9	–1.7	2.4	2.2
Fabricated metal products	332	22.9	18.2	7.5	6.1	1.5	1.5
Machinery	333	19.1	17.1	8.4	6.6	1.9	1.8
Computer and electronic products	334	9.7	2.5	9.2	2.5	4.0	3.3
Electrical equipment, appliances, & components	335	18.2	14.4	14.7	11.4	3.8	3.5
Transportation equipment	336	–13.9	–40.4	–2.9	–5.8	1.0	0.8
Furniture and related products	337	13.8	5.7	4.1	1.7	1.2	1.1
Miscellaneous manufacturing	339	14.7	13.4	10.8	10.0	2.4	2.2
All mining	21	15.4	10.7	21.9	12.5	2.1	2.0
All wholesale trade	42	13.9	9.0	2.0	1.2	1.5	1.4
Durable goods	421	12.4	6.6	2.4	1.3	1.7	1.6
Nondurable goods	422	16.8	13.7	1.6	1.1	1.2	1.1
All retail trade.	44–45	15.2	9.7	3.0	1.8	1.6	1.4
Food and beverage stores	445	19.5	9.9	2.4	1.2	1.1	1.1
Clothing and general merchandise stores	448, 452	16.0	12.7	3.8	3.1	1.8	1.6
All other retail trade	(X)	13.4	6.3	2.6	1.1	1.6	1.3

X Not applicable.

Source: U.S. Census Bureau, *Quarterly Financial Report for Manufacturing, Mining, and Trade Corporations.*

Table 771. **Value Added, Employment, and Capital Expenditures of Nonbank U.S. Multinational Companies: 1999 to 2006**

[Value added and capital expenditures in billions of dollars (2,481 represents $2,481,000,000,000); employees in thousands. See headnote, Table 772. MNC = Multinational company. MOFA = Majority-owned foreign affiliate. Minus sign (–) indicates decrease]

Item	1999	2000	2002	2003	2004	2005	2006	Percent change at annual rates	
								1999–2005	2005–2006
VALUE ADDED									
MNCs worldwide:									
Parents and MOFAs	2,481	2,748	2,460	2,656	2,992	3,233	3,505	4.5	8.4
Parents	1,914	2,141	1,859	1,958	2,173	2,321	2,509	3.3	8.1
MOFAs	566	607	602	698	818	911	996	8.3	9.2
EMPLOYEES									
MNCs worldwide:									
Parents and all affiliates	32,227	33,598	31,894	30,762	31,245	32,094	32,683	–0.1	1.8
Parents and MOFAs	30,773	32,057	30,373	29,347	29,843	30,573	31,245	–0.1	2.2
Parents	23,007	23,885	22,118	21,105	21,177	21,472	21,748	–1.1	1.3
Affiliates, total	9,220	9,713	9,776	9,658	10,068	10,622	10,935	2.4	3.0
MOFAs	7,766	8,171	8,256	8,242	8,667	9,101	9,498	2.7	4.4
Other	1,454	1,542	1,520	1,415	1,402	1,520	1,438	0.7	–5.4
CAPITAL EXPENDITURES									
MNCs worldwide:									
Parents and all affiliates	550	(NA)	(NA)	(NA)	487	(NA)	(NA)	(NA)	(NA)
Parents and MOFAs	519	548	478	444	463	507	596	–0.4	17.4
Parents	406	438	367	335	339	377	443	–1.2	17.3
Affiliates, total	144	(NA)	(NA)	(NA)	147	(NA)	(NA)	(NA)	(NA)
MOFAs	113	111	110	110	123	130	153	2.3	17.7
Other	31	(NA)	(NA)	(NA)	24	(NA)	(NA)	(NA)	(NA)

NA Not available.

Source: U.S. Bureau of Economic Analysis, *Survey of Current Business*, November 2008.

Table 772. **U.S. Multinational Companies—Selected Characteristics: 2006**

[Preliminary. In billions of dollars (18,521 represents $18,521,000,000,000), except as indicated. Consists of nonbank U.S. parent companies and their nonbank foreign affiliates. U.S. parent comprises the domestic operations of a multinational and is a U.S. person that owns or controls, directly or indirectly, 10 percent or more of the voting securities of an incorporated foreign business enterprise, or an equivalent interest in an unincorporated foreign business enterprise. A U.S. person can be an incorporated business enterprise. A majority-owned foreign affiliate (MOFA) is a foreign business enterprise in which a U.S. parent company owns or controls more than 50 percent of the voting securities]

Industry [1]	2002 NAICS code	U.S. parents				MOFAs		
		Total assets	Capital expen-ditures	Value added	Employ-ment (1,000)	Capital expen-ditures	Value added	Employ-ment (1,000)
All industries...............	(X)	18,521	442.6	2,509	21,748	153.2	996	9,498
Mining........................	21	326	34.1	65	179	42.5	130	168
Utilities......................	22	570	29.0	75	226	3.0	11	46
Manufacturing [2].............	31–33	4,868	168.3	1,046	7,546	59.6	455	4,536
Petroleum and coal products.......	324	590	23.5	155	263	5.4	70	38
Chemicals...................	325	882	21.5	185	893	9.4	86	580
Transportation equipment..........	336	1,363	66.2	184	1,821	13.8	63	953
Wholesale trade................	42	722	25.8	133	1,061	7.4	143	763
Information [2].................	51	1,487	57.1	288	1,865	5.6	41	331
Broadcasting (except Internet) and telecommunications............	515, 517	1,135	47.4	200	1,170	3.4	8	73
Finance (except depository institutions) and insurance.................	521, 522 52 exc.	8,754	39.6	231	1,148	9.3	38	293
Professional, scientific, and technical services	54	344	9.0	142	1,158	3.8	58	586
Other industries [2]...............	(X)	1,451	79.7	530	8,564	21.9	120	2,776
Retail trade	44–45	435	27.3	201	3,927	5.7	48	890

X Not applicable.   [1] Represents North American Industry Classification System 2002-based industry of U.S. parent or industry of foreign affiliate.   [2] Includes other industries not shown separately.

Source: U.S. Bureau of Economic Analysis, *Survey of Current Business*, November 2008 and unpublished data.

Table 773. **U.S. Multinational Companies—Value Added: 2000 and 2006**

[In billions of dollars (2,748 represents $2,748,000,000,000). See headnote, Table 772. Data are by industry of U.S. parent. Based on the North American Industry Classification System, 2002 (NAICS); see text, this section]

Industry	2002 NAICS code	U.S. multinationals		U.S. parents		Majority-owned foreign affiliates	
		2000	2006	2000	2006	2000	2006
All industries.....................	(X)	2,748	3,505	2,141	2,509	607	996
Mining	21	39	100	28	65	11	35
Utilities	22	86	84	81	75	5	8
Manufacturing [1]	31–33	1,410	1,711	995	1,046	415	666
Petroleum and coal products	324	232	363	112	155	120	208
Chemicals	325	212	298	141	185	71	112
Transportation equipment	336	271	268	209	184	62	84
Wholesale trade	42	133	170	99	133	34	37
Information [1]	51	325	338	302	288	22	51
Broadcasting (except Internet) and telecommunications.................	515, 517 52 exc.	(NA)	212	(NA)	200	(NA)	12
Finance (except depository institutions) and insurance	521, 522	181	270	157	231	24	38
Professional, scientific, and technical services ...	54	141	200	101	142	41	59
Other industries [1]	(X)	433	631	379	530	54	101
Retail trade	44–45	166	237	149	201	18	37

NA Not available.   X Not applicable.   [1] Includes other industries not shown separately.

Source: U.S. Bureau of Economic Analysis, *Survey of Current Business*, November 2003 and November 2008.

Table 774. **U.S. Majority-Owned Foreign Affiliates—Value Added by Industry of Affiliate and Country: 2006**

[Preliminary. In millions of dollars (995,638 represents $995,638,000,000. See headnote, Table 772. Numbers in parentheses represent North American Industry Classification System 2002 codes; see text, this section]

Country	All industries [1]	Mining (21)	Manufacturing (31–33)			Wholesale trade (42)	Professional, scientific, and technical services (54)
			Total [1]	Chemicals (325)	Transporta-tion equip-ment (336)		
All countries [2]......	995,638	129,703	455,497	86,228	62,687	142,512	57,745
United Kingdom.......	154,818	(D)	60,882	8,489	6,150	23,504	14,272
Canada	114,247	19,104	50,962	5,906	11,744	9,621	5,062
Germany	85,285	1,703	56,425	5,910	11,472	10,444	4,144
France	50,013	47	26,170	4,910	3,074	7,493	2,712
Ireland	48,594	158	27,500	12,483	52	6,129	1,277
Japan	39,380	4	11,518	4,707	575	8,578	5,413
Australia	39,040	8,299	14,544	1,756	1,390	5,552	2,787
Italy	30,911	29	19,901	4,055	988	4,858	2,060
Mexico	28,353	2,030	16,937	3,395	(D)	1,792	643
Netherlands	26,610	975	15,516	4,919	1,564	4,243	2,205

D Data withheld to avoid disclosure.   [1] Includes other industries not shown separately.   [2] Includes other countries not shown separately.

Source: U.S. Bureau of Economic Analysis, *Survey of Current Business*, November 2008.

Section 16
Science and Technology

This section presents statistics on scientific, engineering, and technological resources, with emphasis on patterns of research and development (R&D) funding and on scientific, engineering, and technical personnel; education; and employment. Also included are statistics on space program outlays. Principal sources of these data are the National Science Foundation (NSF) and the National Aeronautics and Space Administration (NASA).

NSF gathers data chiefly through recurring surveys. Current NSF publications containing data on funds for research and development and on scientific and engineering personnel include detailed statistical tables; info briefs; and annual, biennial, and special reports <http://www.nsf.gov/statistics>. Titles or the areas of coverage of these reports include the following: *Science and Engineering Indicators; National Patterns of R&D Resources; Women, Minorities, and Persons with Disabilities in Science and Engineering, Federal Funds for Research and Development*; Federal R&D Funding by Budget Function; Federal Support to Universities, Colleges, and Selected Nonprofit Institutions; *Research and Development in Industry;* R&D expenditures and graduate enrollment and support in academic science and engineering; and characteristics of doctoral scientists and engineers and of recent graduates in the United States. Statistical surveys in these areas pose problems of concept and definition and the data should therefore be regarded as broad estimates rather than precise, quantitative statements. See sources for methodological and technical details.

The National Science Board's biennial *Science and Engineering Indicators* <http://www.nsf.gov/statistics/seind08/> contains data and analysis of international and domestic science and technology, including measures of inputs and outputs.

Research and development outlays—NSF defines research as "systematic study directed toward fuller scientific knowledge of the subject studied" and development as "the systematic use of scientific knowledge directed toward the production of useful materials, devices, systems, or methods, including design and development of prototypes and processes."

National coverage of R&D expenditures is developed primarily from periodic surveys in four principal economic sectors: (1) *Government,* made up primarily of federal executive agencies; (2) *industry,* consisting of manufacturing and nonmanufacturing firms and the federally funded research and development centers (FFRDCs) they administer; (3) *universities and colleges,* composed of universities, colleges, and their affiliated institutions, agricultural experiment stations, and associated schools of agriculture and of medicine, and FFRDCs administered by educational institutions; and (4) *other nonprofit institutions,* consisting of such organizations as private philanthropic foundations, nonprofit research institutes, voluntary health agencies, and FFRDCs administered by nonprofit organizations.

The R&D funds reported consist of current operating costs, including planning and administration costs, except as otherwise noted. They exclude funds for routine testing, mapping and surveying, collection of general-purpose data, dissemination of scientific information, and training of scientific personnel.

Scientists, engineers, and technicians—Scientists and engineers are defined as persons engaged in scientific and engineering work at a level requiring a knowledge of sciences equivalent at least to that acquired through completion of a 4-year college course. Technicians are defined as persons engaged in technical work at a level requiring knowledge acquired through a technical institute, junior college, or other type of training less extensive than 4-year college training. Craftsmen and skilled workers are excluded.

U.S. Census Bureau, Statistical Abstract of the United States: 2010

Table 775. **Research and Development (R&D) Expenditures by Source and Objective: 1980 to 2007**

[In millions of dollars (63,225 represents $63,225,000,000), except as indicated]

Year	Total	Sources of funds					Objective (percent of total)			Character of work		
		Federal govern-ment	Indus-try	Univer-sities/ col-leges	Non-profit	Non-federal govern-ment[1]	Defense related[2]	Space related[3]	Other	Basic research	Applied research	Devel-opment
1980....	63,225	29,986	30,929	920	871	519	24	5	70	8,745	13,714	40,765
1981....	72,293	33,739	35,948	1,058	967	581	24	5	70	9,658	16,329	46,305
1982....	80,748	37,133	40,692	1,207	1,095	621	26	5	69	10,651	18,218	51,879
1983....	89,950	41,451	45,264	1,357	1,220	658	28	4	68	11,880	20,298	57,771
1984....	102,243	46,470	52,187	1,514	1,351	721	29	3	68	13,332	22,451	66,461
1985....	114,671	52,641	57,962	1,743	1,491	834	30	3	67	14,748	25,401	74,522
1986....	120,248	54,622	60,991	2,019	1,647	969	31	3	66	17,154	27,240	75,855
1987....	126,361	58,609	62,576	2,262	1,849	1,065	32	3	65	18,481	27,951	79,929
1988....	133,880	60,130	67,977	2,527	2,081	1,165	30	4	66	19,786	29,528	84,566
1989....	141,889	60,464	74,966	2,852	2,333	1,274	28	4	69	21,889	32,277	87,723
1990....	151,990	61,607	83,208	3,187	2,589	1,399	25	4	71	23,028	34,896	94,067
1991....	160,872	60,780	92,300	3,457	2,852	1,483	22	5	73	27,139	38,629	95,104
1992....	165,347	60,912	96,229	3,568	3,113	1,525	22	4	74	27,604	37,933	99,810
1993....	165,727	60,524	96,549	3,709	3,388	1,557	21	4	74	28,743	37,280	99,704
1994....	169,202	60,773	99,203	3,938	3,665	1,623	20	5	76	29,651	36,615	102,936
1995....	183,620	62,964	110,870	4,110	3,925	1,751	19	5	77	29,610	40,933	113,077
1996....	197,340	63,389	123,416	4,435	4,239	1,861	18	4	78	32,799	43,165	121,375
1997....	212,144	64,568	136,227	4,837	4,590	1,922	17	4	79	36,917	46,551	128,676
1998....	226,457	66,376	147,845	5,162	5,102	1,972	16	4	80	35,333	46,388	144,735
1999....	245,041	67,046	164,660	5,618	5,619	2,098	15	3	82	38,875	52,097	154,069
2000....	267,562	66,406	186,136	6,231	6,542	2,247	13	2	84	42,767	56,932	167,863
2001....	277,746	72,826	188,440	6,826	7,257	2,397	14	2	84	47,792	64,708	165,245
2002....	276,602	77,699	180,711	7,343	8,292	2,557	15	2	82	51,410	51,035	174,157
2003....	289,039	83,606	186,174	7,649	8,868	2,742	16	2	82	54,839	61,690	172,509
2004....	299,905	88,749	191,377	7,933	8,962	2,884	17	2	81	56,378	70,172	173,354
2005....	323,005	93,734	207,841	8,575	9,905	2,950	17	2	81	60,003	70,355	192,647
2006....	347,872	97,701	227,276	9,282	10,542	3,071	17	2	81	61,721	76,788	209,362
2007 [4]...	368,097	98,331	245,027	9,866	11,647	3,226	16	2	82	64,417	81,211	222,470

[1] Nonfederal R&D expenditures to university and college performers. [2] R&D spending by the Department of Defense, including space activities, and a portion of the Department of Energy funds. [3] For the National Aeronautics and Space Administration only. [4] Preliminary.

Source: U.S. National Science Foundation, NSF 08-318, *National Patterns of R&D Resources*, November 2008, annual. See also <http://www.nsf.gov/statistics/nsf083181/>.

Table 776. **National Research and Development (R&D) Expenditures as a Percent of Gross Domestic Product by Country: 1990 to 2007**

Year	United States	Japan[1]	Germany[2]	France	United Kingdom	Italy	Canada	Russia	Total OECD[3]
1990	2.65	2.81	2.61	2.32	2.14	1.25	1.51	2.03	2.25
1995	2.51	2.71	2.19	2.29	1.94	0.97	1.70	0.85	2.06
2000	2.75	3.04	2.45	2.15	1.85	1.05	1.91	1.05	2.21
2002	2.66	3.17	2.49	2.23	1.82	1.13	2.04	1.25	2.22
2003	2.66	3.20	2.52	2.17	1.78	1.11	2.03	1.28	2.22
2004	2.59	3.17	2.49	2.15	1.71	1.10	2.05	1.15	2.19
2005	2.62	3.32	2.48	2.10	1.76	1.09	2.01	1.07	2.23
2006	2.66	3.39	2.54	2.10	1.78	1.14	1.94	1.07	2.26
2007	2.68	(NA)	2.53	2.08	(NA)	(NA)	1.89	1.12	(NA)

NA Not available. [1] Data on Japanese research and development in 1996 and later years may not be consistent with data in earlier years because of changes in methodology. [2] Data for 1990 are for West Germany only. [3] Organization for Economic Cooperation and Development.

Source: Organization for Economic Cooperation and Development, Paris, France, *Main Science and Technology Indicators*, 2008/2nd edition (copyright); <http://www.oecd.org/>.

510   Science and Technology

Table 777. Performance Sector of Research and Development (R&D) Expenditures: 2000 to 2007

[In millions of dollars (267,562 represents $267,562,000,000). FFRDCs are federally funded research and development centers]

Year	Total	Federal government	Industry — Total	Industry — Funded by Federal government	Industry — Funded by Industry[1]	Industry FFRDCs	Univ. & colleges — Total	Univ. — Funded by Federal government	Univ. — Funded by Non-federal government[2]	Univ. — Funded by Industry	Univ. — Funded by Universities & colleges	Univ. — Funded by Non-profits	University & college FFRDCs[3]	Other nonprofit — Total	Other nonprofit — Funded by Federal government	Other nonprofit — Funded by Industry	Other nonprofit — Funded by Non-profits
RESEARCH AND DEVELOPMENT TOTAL																	
2000	267,562	17,917	199,961	17,117	182,844	2,001	30,693	17,717	2,247	2,174	6,231	2,325	5,742	9,782	4,447	1,118	4,217
2003	289,038	22,752	200,724	17,798	182,926	2,458	40,470	25,116	2,742	2,129	7,649	2,833	7,301	12,839	5,686	1,118	6,035
2004	299,905	22,844	208,301	20,266	188,035	2,485	43,111	27,157	2,884	2,191	7,933	2,946	7,658	12,862	5,695	1,151	6,016
2005	323,005	24,459	226,159	21,909	204,250	2,601	45,191	28,203	2,950	2,338	8,575	3,126	7,812	13,954	5,922	1,253	6,779
2006	347,872	25,327	247,669	24,304	223,365	2,562	46,987	28,784	3,071	2,536	9,282	3,314	7,866	14,507	5,905	1,374	7,228
2007 [4]	368,097	24,744	265,193	24,450	240,743	2,539	48,913	29,468	3,226	2,799	9,866	3,553	8,126	15,346	5,767	1,485	8,094
BASIC RESEARCH																	
2000	42,767	3,765	7,040	925	6,115	547	22,854	13,915	1,549	1,499	4,297	1,603	2,874	5,062	2,099	621	2,341
2003	54,839	4,664	8,330	1,386	6,944	299	30,034	19,600	1,872	1,454	5,223	1,935	3,747	6,686	2,714	621	3,351
2004	56,378	4,697	7,835	1,072	6,763	175	32,105	21,143	1,981	1,506	5,450	2,024	3,729	6,768	2,788	639	3,341
2005	60,003	4,826	8,667	1,108	7,559	136	34,009	22,159	2,057	1,631	5,982	2,180	3,814	7,370	2,910	696	3,764
2006	61,721	4,952	8,384	1,444	6,940	131	35,413	22,661	2,151	1,777	6,502	2,322	3,907	7,680	2,904	763	4,013
2007 [4]	64,417	4,869	8,933	1,453	7,480	130	36,801	23,199	2,257	1,958	6,901	2,485	4,047	8,260	2,941	824	4,494
APPLIED RESEARCH																	
2000	56,932	6,105	39,176	2,682	36,494	269	6,653	3,350	572	553	1,586	592	1,329	3,183	1,831	283	1,069
2003	61,690	7,672	37,334	4,473	32,861	1,434	8,832	4,838	713	554	1,989	737	1,756	4,300	2,487	283	1,529
2004	70,172	7,455	45,432	4,775	40,657	1,509	9,230	5,136	740	562	2,035	756	1,920	4,264	2,448	292	1,525
2005	70,355	7,594	45,284	5,289	39,995	1,487	9,284	5,070	732	580	2,126	775	1,858	4,439	2,403	318	1,718
2006	76,788	7,692	51,173	6,140	45,033	1,446	9,623	5,153	754	623	2,279	814	1,779	4,635	2,455	348	1,832
2007 [4]	81,211	7,839	54,713	6,177	48,537	1,414	10,102	5,310	795	690	2,431	875	1,844	4,844	2,417	376	2,051
DEVELOPMENT																	
2000	167,863	8,047	153,745	13,510	140,235	1,185	1,177	452	126	121	348	130	1,539	1,537	517	214	807
2003	172,509	10,416	155,060	11,939	143,121	725	1,555	678	157	122	437	162	1,798	1,853	485	214	1,155
2004	173,354	10,692	155,034	14,419	140,615	801	1,776	878	163	123	447	166	2,008	1,830	459	220	1,151
2005	192,647	12,039	172,208	15,512	156,696	979	1,859	974	161	127	467	170	2,140	2,145	609	240	1,297
2006	209,362	12,682	188,112	16,720	171,392	985	1,951	970	166	137	500	179	2,180	2,192	546	263	1,383
2007 [4]	222,470	12,037	201,547	16,820	184,726	995	2,010	958	175	151	534	192	2,236	2,242	409	284	1,549

[1] Includes all nonfederal sources of industry R&D expenditures. [2] Includes all nonfederal sources. [3] Includes all R&D expenditures of FFRDCs administered by academic institutions and funded by the federal government. [4] Preliminary

Source: National Science Foundation. Data derived from: Research and Development in Industry, annual; Academic Research and Development Expenditures, annual; and Federal Funds For Research and Development, annual. See also <http://www.nsf.gov/statistics/>.

U.S. Census Bureau, Statistical Abstract of the United States: 2010

Table 778. Federal Obligations for Research in Current and Constant (2000) Dollars by Field of Science: 2005 to 2008

[In millions of dollars (53,738 represents $53,738,000,000). For years ending September 30. Excludes R&D plant]

Field of science	Current dollars				Constant (2000) dollars [1]			
	2005	2006	2007, prel.	2008, prel.	2005	2006	2007, prel.	2008, prel.
Research, total	53,738	53,536	55,075	54,709	48,032	47,658	45,966	44,689
Basic	27,140	26,585	27,477	27,721	24,258	24,001	22,932	22,644
Applied	26,598	26,951	27,598	26,988	23,774	23,657	23,034	22,045
Life sciences	28,543	27,928	27,814	27,533	25,327	23,987	23,214	22,490
Psychology	1,916	1,747	1,757	1,758	1,700	1,501	1,466	1,436
Physical sciences	5,473	5,351	5,468	5,607	4,857	4,596	4,564	4,580
Environmental sciences	3,876	3,431	3,343	3,408	3,439	2,946	2,790	2,784
Mathematics and computer sciences . .	3,115	2,815	3,194	3,129	2,764	2,418	2,665	2,556
Engineering	9,481	8,679	9,426	9,258	8,412	7,454	7,867	7,563
Social sciences	1,132	1,124	1,141	1,146	1,004	965	952	936
Other sciences, n.e.c. [2]	2,010	2,461	2,932	2,869	1,784	2,114	2,447	2,343

[1] Based on gross domestic product implicit price deflator.   [2] Not elsewhere classified.

Source: U.S. National Science Foundation, NSF 09-300 *Federal Funds for Research and Development*, November 2008, annual. See also <http://www.nsf.gov/statistics/nsf09300/>.

Table 779. Federal Budget Authority for Research and Development (R&D) in Current and Constant (2000) Dollars by Selected Budget Functions: 2005 to 2008

[In millions of dollars (126,601 represents $126,601,000,000). For year ending September 30. Excludes R&D plant. Represents budget authority. Functions shown are those for which $1 billion or more was authorized since 2001]

Function	Current dollars				Constant (2000) dollars [1]			
	2005	2006	2007	2008, prel.	2005	2006	2007	2008, prel.
Total [2]	126,601	131,624	138,087	137,972	112,003	112,812	115,248	112,702
National defense	74,047	78,037	82,272	81,050	65,509	66,884	68,665	66,205
Health	28,824	28,797	29,461	29,634	25,500	24,681	24,588	24,206
Space research and technology	7,300	8,204	9,024	9,233	6,458	7,031	7,531	7,542
Energy	1,296	1,195	1,893	2,374	1,147	1,024	1,580	1,939
General science	6,570	6,691	7,809	7,915	5,812	5,735	6,517	6,465
Natural resources and environment . . .	2,168	2,120	1,936	2,008	1,918	1,817	1,616	1,640
Transportation	1,847	1,711	1,361	1,340	1,634	1,466	1,136	1,095
Agriculture	1,820	1,869	1,857	1,852	1,610	1,602	1,550	1,513

[1] Based on gross domestic product implicit price deflator.   [2] Includes other functions, not shown separately.

Source: U.S. National Science Foundation, NSF 08-315 *Federal R&D Funding by Budget Function*, annual. See also <http://www.nsf.gov/statistics/nsf083151/>.

Table 780. Federal Research and Development (R&D) by Federal Agency: 2007 and 2008

[In millions of dollars (141,933 represents $144,933,000,000). For years ending September 30. R&D refers to actual research and development activities as well as R&D facilities. R&D facilities (also known as R&D plant) includes construction, repair, or alteration of physical plant used in the conduct of R&D. Based on Office of Management and Budget data]

Federal agency	2007	2008, est.	Federal agency	2007	2008, est.
Total research and development . .	141,933	144,354	National Institute of Standards and		
Defense R&D	82,658	83,065	Technology	487	521
Nondefense R&D	59,276	61,288	Department of Interior	647	676
Department of Defense	79,009	79,347	U.S. Geological Survey	574	586
Science and technology	13,518	13,456	Department of Transportation	767	820
All other Department of Defense R&D .	65,490	65,891	Environmental Protection Agency	557	548
Health and Human Services	29,621	29,966	Department of Veterans Affairs	819	891
National Institute of Health	28,350	28,826	Department of Education	327	321
All other Health and Human Services			Department of Homeland Security	996	992
R&D	1,271	1,140	International Assistance Programs	246	223
NASA	11,582	12,251	Smithsonian	186	203
Department of Energy	9,035	9,724	Tennessee Valley Authority	20	20
Atomic Energy Defense	3,649	3,718	Department of Labor	24	57
Office of Science	3,560	3,637	Nuclear Regulatory Commission	76	71
Energy R&D	1,826	2,369	Army Corps of Engineers	11	11
National Science Foundation	4,440	4,501	Department of Housing and Urban		
Department of Agriculture	2,275	2,359	Development	49	51
Department of Commerce	1,073	1,138	Department of Justice	104	81
National Oceanic and Atmospheric			Social Security Administration	27	27
Administration	557	581	U.S. Postal Service	43	43

Source: American Association for the Advancement of Science (AAAS), *AAAS Report XXXIII Research and Development FY 2009*, annual. See also <http://www.aaas.org/spp/rd/rd09main.htm>.

Table 781. Research and Development (R&D) Funds in R&D-Performing Manufacturing and Nonmanufacturing Companies by Industry: 2005 to 2007

Industry	NAICS [1] code	Total R&D funds as a percent of net sales			Company R&D funds as a percent of net sales		
		2005	2006	2007	2005	2006	2007
All industries, total.	(X)	**3.7**	**3.7**	**3.8**	**3.3**	**3.4**	**3.5**
All manufacturing industries, total.	(X)	**4.0**	**4.0**	**4.1**	**3.6**	**3.6**	**3.7**
Food	311	0.7	0.7	(D)	0.7	0.7	0.7
Paper, printing, and support activities.	322, 323	(D)	(D)	(D)	1.5	1.2	1.3
Petroleum and coal products	324	(D)	0.3	(D)	0.4	0.3	0.3
Chemicals.	325	6.9	7.6	(D)	6.9	7.5	7.9
Plastic and rubber products	326	2.0	2.0	(D)	1.9	1.9	1.5
Nonmetallic mineral products	327	1.8	2.1	1.8	1.8	1.9	1.8
Primary metals.	331	0.6	0.5	0.6	0.5	0.5	0.6
Fabricated metal products	332	0.8	1.4	1.7	0.8	1.4	1.6
Machinery.	333	3.7	3.6	3.7	3.6	3.6	3.7
Navigational, measuring, electromedical, and control instruments	3345	12.8	13.1	10.2	7.0	7.5	6.1
Electrical equipment, appliances, and components. .	335	2.4	2.6	3.1	2.3	2.5	3.0
Transportation equipment	336	(D)	(D)	(D)	3.0	2.9	3.1
Motor vehicles, trailers, and parts	3361–3363	(D)	(D)	(D)	2.5	2.4	2.4
Aerospace products and parts	3364	6.6	6.7	7.0	4.8	4.9	5.1
All nonmanufacturing industries, total	(X)	**3.2**	**3.2**	**3.4**	**2.9**	**2.9**	**3.0**
Information	51	5.4	5.3	(D)	5.3	5.2	5.1
Internet service and data processing providers. . . .	518	9.1	9.6	(D)	8.7	9.4	9.6
Software publishing	5112	21.9	(D)	(D)	21.9	19.9	19.6
Professional, scientific, and technical services	54	12.2	9.5	11.7	10.0	7.6	9.5
Architectural, engineering, and related services . . .	5413	9.4	14.4	12.0	4.9	10.7	8.1
Computer systems design and related services	5415	10.0	5.3	7.0	9.6	4.9	6.6
Scientific R&D services	5417	35.6	35.1	42.0	27.4	24.2	30.0

D Figure withheld to avoid disclosure of information pertaining to a specific organization or individual.   X Not applicable.
[1] North American Industry Classification System 1997 (NAICS); see text, Section 15.

Source: U.S. National Science Foundation, *Research and Development in Industry,* annual. See also <http://www.nsf.gov /statistics/>.

Table 782. Funds for Performance of Industrial Research and Development (R&D) by Source of Funds and Selected Industries: 2004 to 2007

[In millions of dollars (208,301 represents $208,301,000,000). For calendar years. Covers basic research, applied research, and development. Based on the Survey of Industry Research and Development]

Industry	NAICS [1] code	2004	2005	2006	2007
CURRENT DOLLARS					
Total funds [2]	(X)	**208,301**	**226,159**	**247,669**	**269,267**
Company and other funds	(X)	**188,035**	**204,250**	**223,365**	**242,682**
Federal funds	(X)	**20,266**	**21,909**	**24,304**	**26,585**
Petroleum and coal products	324	1,603	(D)	1,432	(D)
Chemicals and allied products	325	(D)	42,995	46,329	(D)
Pharmaceuticals and medicines	3254	31,477	34,839	38,901	(D)
Machinery	333	6,579	8,531	9,848	9,865
Computer and electronic products	334	48,296	(D)	56,773	58,599
Navigational, measuring, electromedical, and control instruments . .	3345	15,214	15,204	18,300	20,438
Electrical equipment, appliances, and components	335	2,664	2,424	2,281	(D)
Motor vehicles, trailers, and parts.	3361–3363	15,677	(D)	(D)	(D)
Aerospace products and parts	3364	13,086	15,055	16,367	18,436
Information.	51	22,593	23,836	26,883	(D)
Professional, scientific, and technical services	54	28,709	32,021	38,049	40,533
Computer systems design and related services	5415	11,575	13,592	14,841	14,407
Scientific R&D services	5417	11,355	12,299	14,525	16,849
CONSTANT (2000) DOLLARS [3]					
Total funds [2]	(X)	**190,351**	**200,088**	**212,271**	**224,732**
Company and other funds	(X)	**171,831**	**180,704**	**191,440**	**202,544**
Federal funds	(X)	**18,520**	**19,383**	**20,830**	**22,188**
Petroleum and coal products	324	1,465	(D)	1,227	(D)
Chemicals	325	(D)	38,039	39,707	(D)
Pharmaceuticals and medicines	3254	28,765	30,823	33,341	(D)
Machinery	333	6,012	7,548	8,440	8,233
Computer and electronic products	334	44,134	(D)	48,659	48,907
Navigational, measuring, electromedical, and control instruments . .	3345	13,903	13,451	15,684	17,058
Electrical equipment, appliances, and components	335	2,434	2,145	1,955	(D)
Motor vehicles, trailers, and parts.	3361–3363	14,326	(D)	(D)	(D)
Aerospace products and parts	3364	11,958	13,319	14,028	15,387
Information.	51	20,646	21,088	23,041	(D)
Professional, scientific, and technical services	54	26,235	28,330	32,611	33,829
Computer systems design and related services	5415	10,578	12,025	12,720	12,024
Scientific R&D services.	5417	10,376	10,881	12,449	14,062

D Figure withheld to avoid disclosure of information pertaining to a specific organization or individual.   X Not applicable.
[1] North American Industry Classification System, 1997; see text, Section 15.   [2] Includes other industries not shown separately.
[3] Based on gross domestic product implicit price deflator.

Source: U.S. National Science Foundation, *Research and Development in Industry,* annual. See also <http://www.nsf.gov /statistics/>.

Table 783. **Academic and Industrial Research and Development (R&D) Performed by State: 2006**

[In millions of dollars (46,917 represents 46,917,000,000). For definition of research and development (R&D), see text this section]

State	Academic R&D (mil. dol.)	Academic R&D per $1,000 of GDP	Industry-performed R&D (mil. dol.)	Industry-performed R&D per private-industry output (percent) [1]	State	Academic R&D (mil. dol.)	Academic R&D per $1,000 of GDP	Industry-performed R&D (mil. dol.)	Industry-performed R&D per private-industry output (percent) [1]
U.S. [2] ..	46,917	3.56	247,669	1.88	MT......	173	5.40	[4]103	[4]0.32
AL.....	602	3.80	1,835	1.16	NE......	359	4.77	447	0.59
AK.....	163	3.78	[3]49	[3]0.11	NV......	194	1.58	535	0.43
AZ.....	765	3.22	3,590	1.51	NH......	315	5.62	[4]1,774	[4]3.16
AR.....	237	2.61	285	0.31					
CA.....	6,493	3.73	58,424	3.35	NJ......	858	1.91	14,606	3.26
					NM......	425	5.90	676	0.94
CO.....	821	3.63	4,657	2.06	NY......	3,790	3.69	9,518	0.93
CT.....	693	3.38	8,273	4.04	NC.....	1,710	4.49	5,486	1.44
DE.....	122	2.05	1,446	2.43	NC.....	160	6.19	120	0.46
DC.....	296	3.36	276	0.31					
FL.....	1,528	2.13	4,139	0.58	OH......	1,636	3.62	6,852	1.52
GA.....	1,303	3.46	2,786	0.74	OK.....	298	2.29	474	0.36
HI.....	257	4.39	155	0.26	OR.....	557	3.69	3,419	2.26
ID.....	111	2.30	625	1.29	PA.....	2,428	4.77	9,819	1.93
IL.....	1,824	3.12	10,765	1.84	RI.....	230	5.03	[4]1,330	[4]2.91
IN.....	823	3.45	4,858	2.04					
IA.....	573	4.70	1,055	0.87	SC......	524	3.58	1,396	0.95
KS.....	354	3.20	[4]2,064	[4]1.87	SD......	73	2.27	95	0.30
KY.....	479	3.27	839	0.57	TN......	743	3.15	1,428	0.61
LA.....	539	2.65	367	0.18	TX......	3,271	3.06	13,334	1.25
ME.....	120	2.59	253	0.55	UT......	413	4.21	1,274	1.30
MD.....	[5]1,821	[5]7.07	3,421	1.33	VT......	122	5.16	360	1.52
MA.....	2,159	6.44	15,562	4.64	VA......	947	2.57	4,816	1.31
MI.....	1,473	3.92	16,477	4.38	WA	988	3.39	11,320	3.89
MN.....	605	2.50	6,296	2.60	WV	149	2.65	221	0.39
MS.....	369	4.36	231	0.27	WI	1,040	4.65	3,020	1.35
MO	900	4.09	2,675	1.22	WY	89	2.99	[4]27	[4]0.09

[1] Gross Domestic Product (GDP) by state for private industries. [2] National totals for calendar year 2006. The industrial totals include $3.8 billion of R&D expenditures in 2006 that could not be allocated to specific states. The academic totals incorporate adjustments to convert fiscal year academic data to calendar year and to eliminate double counting of funds passed through one academic institution to another. [3] More than 50 percent of industrial R&D value imputed. [4] More than 50 percent of industrial R&D value imputed because of raking of state data. [5] For Maryland, academic R&D excludes R&D performed by the Applied Physics Laboratory (APL) at the Johns Hopkins University. APL performed $709 million of R&D in 2006.

Source: National Science Foundation, NSF-08-318, *National Patterns of R&D Resources*, annual. See also <http://www.nsf.gov/statistics/natlpatterns/>.

Table 784. **Research and Development (R&D) Expenditures in Science and Engineering at Universities and Colleges in Current and Constant (2000) Dollars: 2000 to 2007**

[In millions of dollars (30,073 represents $30,073,000,000)]

Characteristic	Current dollars				Constant (2000) dollars [1]			
	2000	2005	2006	2007	2000	2005	2006	2007
Total	30,073	45,793	47,743	49,431	30,073	40,513	40,921	41,255
Basic research [2]	22,456	34,358	36,063	37,609	22,456	30,396	30,910	31,389
Applied R&D [2]	7,617	11,434	11,680	11,822	7,617	10,116	10,011	9,867
Source of funds:								
Federal government........	17,538	29,203	30,124	30,441	17,538	25,836	25,820	25,406
State and local government...	2,200	2,942	2,963	3,145	2,200	2,603	2,540	2,625
Institutions' own funds	5,924	8,261	9,057	9,655	5,924	7,308	7,763	8,058
Industry................	2,156	2,294	2,404	2,672	2,156	2,029	2,061	2,230
Other	2,254	3,093	3,196	3,517	2,254	2,736	2,739	2,935
Fields:								
Physical sciences	2,712	3,702	3,812	3,842	2,712	3,275	3,267	3,207
Environmental sciences	1,765	2,554	2,601	2,725	1,765	2,259	2,229	2,274
Mathematical sciences	342	495	533	572	342	438	457	477
Computer sciences	876	1,406	1,438	1,417	876	1,244	1,233	1,183
Life sciences	17,471	27,603	28,802	29,764	17,471	24,420	24,687	24,841
Psychology	517	826	875	863	517	731	750	720
Social sciences...........	1,299	1,685	1,702	1,781	1,299	1,491	1,459	1,486
Other sciences	535	778	888	949	535	688	761	792
Engineering	4,555	6,745	7,092	7,517	4,555	5,967	6,079	6,274

[1] Based on gross domestic product implicit price deflator. [2] Basic research and applied R&D statistics were reestimated for FY 2001 and forward. These data are not directly comparable to those from earlier years.

Source: U.S. National Science Foundation, NSF-09-303, *Survey of Research and Development Expenditures at Universities and Colleges*, annual. See also <http://www.nsf.gov/statistics/srvyrdexpenditures/>.

514   Science and Technology

Table 785. Federal Research and Development (R&D) Obligations to Selected Universities and Colleges: 2006 and 2007

[In millions of dollars (25,361.0 represents $25,361,000,000). For years ending September 30. For the top 40 institutions receiving federal R&D funds in 2007. Awards to the administrative offices of university systems are excluded from totals for individual institutions because that allocation of funds is unknown, but those awards are included in "total all institutions"]

Major institution ranked by total 2007 federal R&D obligations	2006	2007	Major institution ranked by total 2007 federal R&D obligations	2006	2007
Total, all institutions [1]	25,361.6	25,419.4	University of Colorado	340.3	330.3
Johns Hopkins University	1,251.5	1,186.8	Cornell University	299.3	326.4
University of Washington	615.6	612.5	Case Western Reserve University	277.9	278.9
University of Michigan	516.4	501.8	University Southern California	266.5	262.2
University of Pennsylvania	497.7	498.5	University of Rochester	252.3	255.2
University of California—Los Angeles	478.7	480.7	Northwestern University	222.6	255.0
Duke University	472.7	470.8	University of Chicago	219.8	248.6
University of California—San Diego	401.8	433.8	Emory University	228.1	247.9
University of California—San Francisco	441.9	433.4	University of California—Davis	236.4	243.1
Harvard University	420.8	429.7	University of Alabama—Birmingham	235.4	235.1
University of Pittsburgh	426.9	426.8	Baylor College of Medicine	236.5	227.9
Columbia University—City of NY	467.8	426.4	Ohio State University	206.7	217.6
Stanford University	458.3	425.9	University of California—Berkeley	228.8	214.5
Washington University	410.7	407.8	University of Arizona	201.5	212.5
Yale University	361.9	387.3	University of Illinois—Urbana Champaign	185.6	210.5
Massachusetts Institute of Technology	405.5	381.8	Boston University	204.7	208.7
University of Minnesota	331.6	371.3	University of Iowa	193.0	208.4
University of Wisconsin—Madison	373.8	369.3	The Scripps Research Institute	217.5	199.0
Pennsylvania State University	302.6	355.3	University of Virginia	176.4	199.0
University of North Carolina at Chapel Hill	343.4	353.5	Oregon Health & Science University	193.6	189.7
Vanderbilt University	306.4	331.2	Mt. Sinai School of Medicine	177.0	187.3

[1] Includes other institutions, not shown separately.

Source: U.S. National Science Foundation, NSF 09-313, *Federal S&E Support to Universities and Colleges and Nonprofit Institutions*, March 2009, annual. See also <http://www.nsf.gov/statistics/fedsupport/>.

Table 786. Graduate Science/Engineering Students in Doctorate-Granting Colleges by Characteristic and Field: 1990 to 2006

[In thousands (409.4 represents 409,400). As of fall. Includes outlying areas]

Field of science or engineering	Total			Female			Foreign		Part-time		
	1990	2000	2006	1990	2000	2006	2000	2006	1990	2000	2006
Total, all surveyed fields	409.4	443.5	542.1	155.5	201.8	263.6	123.3	144.5	130.8	123.6	148.9
Science/engineering	360.6	374.8	445.0	117.9	150.3	188.9	118.0	136.6	107.5	99.3	113.7
Engineering, total	101.0	98.8	116.6	13.8	19.7	26.3	46.3	52.9	36.7	28.2	31.5
Sciences, total	259.6	275.9	328.4	104.2	130.7	162.6	71.7	83.7	70.8	71.1	82.2
Physical sciences	32.9	29.6	35.9	7.7	8.8	11.6	11.5	14.5	3.9	3.5	3.6
Environmental	13.1	13.0	14.0	3.8	5.3	6.5	2.6	2.7	3.2	2.8	2.9
Mathematical sciences	18.1	14.4	19.0	5.6	5.2	6.8	5.9	7.4	4.7	3.0	4.0
Computer sciences	29.2	40.3	43.0	6.8	11.7	10.8	19.7	19.1	14.1	16.7	16.1
Agricultural sciences	11.0	11.3	12.1	3.2	4.8	5.8	2.4	2.6	2.0	2.4	3.2
Biological sciences	46.7	53.1	65.9	21.4	27.8	36.9	11.6	16.6	7.2	7.6	8.8
Psychology	38.5	40.3	47.2	25.5	29.0	35.5	2.1	2.6	12.0	10.8	14.3
Social sciences	70.0	73.9	91.2	30.1	38.1	48.6	15.8	18.1	23.8	24.3	29.3
Health fields, total	48.8	68.8	97.0	37.6	51.5	74.7	5.4	7.9	23.3	24.3	35.3

Source: U.S. National Science Foundation, *Survey of Graduate Science Engineering Students and Postdoctorates*, annual. See also <http://www.nsf.gov/statistics/gradpostdoc>.

Table 787. Non-U.S. Citizens Awarded Doctorates in Science and Engineering by Visa Type and Country of Citizenship: 1998 to 2007

[For description of science and engineering fields, see Table 792]

Visa and country	1998	1999	2000	2001	2002	2003	2004	2005	2006	2007
All non-U.S. citizens	9,736	8,894	9,070	9,217	8,867	9,483	10,158	11,519	12,777	13,545
Canada	286	289	294	306	316	324	380	368	362	397
Mexico	176	172	208	206	182	218	181	206	182	182
Brazil	164	164	131	142	126	108	136	156	139	122
France	76	79	83	85	92	87	92	113	124	129
Germany	210	183	229	220	197	192	185	182	176	162
China	2,503	2,234	2,379	2,407	2,402	2,503	2,878	3,482	4,279	4,395
Japan	155	158	201	149	157	201	186	211	222	235
Korea	822	760	754	865	856	958	1,057	1,179	1,220	1,137
Taiwan	910	746	676	539	469	440	394	444	431	462
Thailand	122	134	153	237	264	314	272	252	199	224
India	1,134	915	834	818	681	773	864	1,110	1,525	1,956
Iran	93	92	80	100	59	68	60	136	148	156
Turkey	172	192	275	307	345	374	344	342	357	436
Science	6,678	6,299	6,269	6,129	5,945	6,305	6,605	7,481	8,209	8,676
Engineering	3,058	2,595	2,801	3,088	2,922	3,178	3,553	4,038	4,568	4,869
Permanent visa	1,991	1,654	1,409	1,271	1,173	1,099	1,003	1,113	1,252	1,222
Temporary visa	7,745	7,240	7,661	7,946	7,694	8,384	9,155	10,406	11,525	12,323

Source: U.S. National Science Foundation, NSF 09-311, *Science and Engineering Doctorate Awards*, March 2009, annual. See also <http://www.nsf.gov/statistics/nsf09311/>.

Science and Technology 515

Table 788. Science and Engineering (S&E) Degrees Awarded by Degree Level and Sex of Recipient: 1990 to 2007

[For a description of science and engineering degree categories, see Appendix B of source <http://www.nsf.gov/statistics/nsf07307/content.cfm?pubid=3634&id=4>]

Academic year ending	Bachelor's degree				Master's degree				Doctoral degree			
	Total S&E	Men	Women	Percent women	Total S&E	Men	Women	Percent women	Total S&E	Men	Women	Percent women
1990	329,094	189,082	140,012	42.5	77,788	51,230	26,558	34.1	22,867	16,498	6,369	27.9
2000	400,059	198,060	201,999	50.5	95,194	53,616	41,578	43.7	25,912	16,518	9,394	36.2
2004	485,488	239,580	245,908	50.7	119,090	66,555	52,535	44.1	26,272	16,418	9,854	37.5
2005	499,133	246,356	252,777	50.6	121,180	67,067	54,113	44.7	27,941	17,404	10,537	37.7
2006	507,175	250,017	257,158	50.7	120,733	66,042	54,691	45.3	29,836	18,367	11,469	38.4
2007	514,509	253,934	260,575	50.6	119,685	64,695	54,990	45.9	31,768	19,509	12,259	38.5

Source: U.S. National Science Foundation, NSF-08-321, *Science and Engineering Degrees: 1966–2006*, October, 2008. See also <http://www.nsf.gov/statistics/degrees/>.

Table 789. Doctorates Conferred by Characteristics of Recipients: 2000 and 2007

[In percent, except as indicated. Based on the Survey of Earned Doctorate Awards; for description of methodology, see source]

Characteristic	2000, total [1]	2007									
		All fields [1]	Engin-eer-ing	Physi-cal sci-ences [2]	Earth sci-ences	Mathe-matics	Com-puter sci-ences	Biologi-cal sci-ences [3]	Agri-cul-tural	Social sci-ences [4]	Psy-chol-ogy
Total conferred (number).	41,365	48,079	7,745	4,106	876	1,393	1,662	7,173	1,137	4,415	3,294
Male	56.0	54.4	79.2	71.1	61.8	70.9	79.8	51.2	59.6	52.2	28.7
Female.	43.8	45.5	20.7	28.8	38.1	28.9	20.0	48.7	40.1	47.7	71.3
CITIZENSHIP [5]											
Total conferred (number).	39,596	44,515	7,111	3,812	834	1,299	1,543	6,797	1,059	4,086	3,026
U.S. citizen	70.7	61.9	31.5	49.3	62.5	41.9	35.1	65.9	56.2	61.0	89.9
Foreign citizen	29.3	38.1	68.5	50.7	37.5	58.1	64.9	34.1	43.8	39.0	10.1
RACE/ETHNICITY [6]											
Total conferred (number).	29,936	29,400	2,532	2,027	550	605	644	4,781	625	2,690	2,790
White [7]	79.2	75.9	71.1	77.6	84.9	77.7	71.9	75.6	85.9	75.8	76.8
Black [7]	5.8	6.6	3.6	4.1	1.6	3.1	4.8	3.9	2.7	7.0	5.8
Asian/Pacific [7]	7.6	7.9	15.6	9.4	2.0	11.6	16.5	11.7	3.5	6.7	5.5
Indian/Alaskan [7]	0.6	0.5	0.3	0.3	0.0	0.3	0.2	0.3	1.3	0.7	0.8
Hispanic	4.4	5.6	5.0	4.7	3.6	3.8	2.8	5.4	3.8	5.9	7.3
Other/unknown [8] . . .	2.4	3.5	4.4	3.9	4.2	3.5	3.9	3.2	2.7	3.9	3.6

[1] Includes other fields, not shown separately. [2] Astronomy, physics, and chemistry. [3] Biochemistry, botany, microbiology, physiology, zoology, and related fields. [4] Anthropology, sociology, political science, economics, international relations and related fields. [5] For those with known citizenship. Includes those with temporary visas. [6] Excludes those with temporary visas. [7] Non-Hispanic. [8] 2007 data includes Native Hawaiians and Other Pacific Islanders, respondents choosing multiple races (excluding those selecting an Hispanic ethnicity), and respondents with unknown race/ethnicity.

Source: U.S. National Science Foundation, NSF-09-307, *Science and Engineering Doctorate Awards,* annual. See also <http://www.nsf.gov/statistics/nsf07305/>.

Table 790. Science and Engineering (S&E) Doctorates by State: 2006

[Data on U.S. S&E doctorate holders classified by the state where the doctorate holder resides, if known; otherwise data are classified by employer's location. Population of doctorate holders consisted of all individuals under age 76 years of age who received a research doctorate in S&E from a U.S. institution and were residing in the United States. Excludes medical doctorates]

State	S&E doctorates con-ferred [1]	S&E doctor-ate holders [1]	Doctor-ate holders per capita [1]	State	S&E doctorates con-ferred [1]	S&E doctor-ate holders [1]	Doctor-ate holders per capita [1]	State	S&E doctorates con-ferred [1]	S&E doctor-ate holders [1]	Doctor-ate holders per capita [1]
US. . .	29,777	708,080	2.4	KS	268	4,830	1.8	ND [2] . . .	51	1,550	2.4
				KY	255	5,760	1.4	OH	1,197	23,630	2.1
AL [2]	338	7,090	1.5	LA	303	6,290	1.5	OK	220	5,290	1.5
AK [2] . . .	21	1,330	2.0	ME [2] . . .	27	2,930	2.2	OR	317	10,900	3.0
AZ	507	10,050	1.6	MD	840	29,870	5.3	PA	1,472	32,780	2.6
AR	107	3,250	1.2	MA	1,724	35,440	5.5	RI	222	3,290	3.1
CA	4,005	99,110	2.7	MI	1,066	19,790	2.0	SC [2] . . .	238	6,920	1.6
CO	477	16,080	3.4	MN	533	13,220	2.6	SD [2] . . .	36	1,220	1.5
CT	443	11,830	3.4	MS	169	3,910	1.3	TN	395	11,380	1.9
DE	146	3,880	4.6	MO	503	10,340	1.8	TX	1,930	41,420	1.8
DC	338	13,750	23.5	MT	65	2,480	2.6	UT	238	6,730	2.6
FL.	1,082	22,020	1.2	NE	149	3,320	1.9	VT [2] . . .	49	2,070	3.3
GA	791	14,890	1.6	NV	99	2,940	1.2	VA	727	22,800	3.0
HI	91	3,230	2.5	NH	96	2,760	2.1	WA [2] . . .	544	19,900	3.1
ID	67	3,190	2.2	NJ.	670	23,610	2.7	WV [2] . . .	117	2,510	1.4
IL	1,466	26,800	2.1	NM	193	9,960	5.1	WI.	577	11,200	2.0
IN	762	11,380	1.8	NY	2,530	50,760	2.6	WY [2] . . .	38	990	1.9
IA	402	5,740	1.9	NC	876	21,670	2.4				

[1] Estimates for S&E doctorate holders may vary between 10 percent and 25 percent because geography is not part of sample design. [2] Data for 2006 S&E doctorate holders are preliminary.

Source: National Science Foundation, *Science and Engineering Indicators, 2008,* January 2008, biennial.

516   Science and Technology

Table 791. **Scientists and Engineers by Selected Demographic Characteristics: 2006**

[In thousands (22,630 represents 22,630,000). Scientists and engineers refer to all persons who have received a bachelor's degree or higher in science and engineering (S&E), or S&E related field, plus persons holding a non-S&E degree or higher, employed in S&E or S&E related field]

Characteristic	Both sexes	Female	Male	Characteristic	Both sexes	Female	Male
All scientists and engineers	**22,630**	**10,230**	**12,400**	Highest degree attained:			
Age:				Bachelor's	13,228	6,223	7,005
29 or younger	2,732	1,542	1,190	Master's	6,411	3,039	3,373
30–39 years	5,302	2,596	2,705	Doctorate	1,018	308	710
40–49 years	5,849	2,699	3,150	Professional	1,973	660	1,312
50–59 years	5,400	2,303	3,097				
60–69 years	2,497	835	1,662	Citizenship status:			
70 or older	851	254	596	U.S. citizen, native	19,131	8,743	10,387
Race/ethnicity:				U.S. citizen, naturalized	2,373	1,062	1,311
American Indian/Alaska Native	102	51	50	Non-U.S. citizen, permanent resident	835	330	505
Asian	2,255	994	1,261	Non-U.S. citizen, temporary resident	291	95	196
Black	1,258	738	520				
Native Hawaiian/Other Pacific Islander	85	33	53	Marital status:			
White	17,420	7,670	9,751	Married	16,100	6,655	9,445
Multiple race	316	156	159	Living in marriage-like relationship	892	482	410
Hispanic, any race	1,193	588	605	Widowed	356	245	111
Children in the home?				Separated	243	131	111
Yes	10,966	5,015	5,951	Divorced	1,518	887	631
No	11,664	5,215	6,449	Never married	3,521	1,829	1,692

Source: National Science Foundation/Division of Science Resource Statistics, Scientists and Engineers Statistical Data System (SESTAT), March 2008; <http://www.nsf.gov/statistics/sestat/>.

Table 792. **Doctorates Awarded by Field of Study and Year of Doctorate: 2000 to 2007**

Field of study	2000	2002	2003	2004	2005	2006	2007
Total, all fields	**41,365**	**40,024**	**40,757**	**42,117**	**43,378**	**45,598**	**48,079**
Science and engineering, total	**25,971**	**24,608**	**25,282**	**26,273**	**27,984**	**29,855**	**31,801**
Engineering, total	5,323	5,081	5,281	5,777	6,427	7,183	7,745
Aeronautical/astronautical	214	209	200	201	219	238	267
Chemical	720	705	648	726	875	891	921
Civil	556	630	674	673	758	803	865
Electrical	1,544	1,393	1,466	1,651	1,851	2,132	2,408
Industrial/manufacturing	176	230	214	217	221	234	280
Materials/metallurgical	451	396	475	510	540	625	679
Mechanical	864	827	814	852	978	1,146	1,129
Other	792	691	790	947	985	1,114	1,196
Science, total	20,648	19,527	20,001	20,496	21,557	22,672	24,056
Biological/agricultural sciences	6,895	6,704	6,757	6,987	7,404	7,674	8,310
Agricultural sciences	1,042	1,010	1,061	1,045	1,038	1,033	1,137
Biological sciences	5,853	5,694	5,696	5,942	6,366	6,641	7,173
Earth, atmospheric, and ocean sciences, total	694	689	683	686	714	757	876
Atmospheric	143	117	139	126	145	147	167
Earth	387	426	374	420	420	469	522
Ocean sciences	164	146	170	140	149	141	187
Mathematical/computer sciences, total	1,911	1,728	1,860	2,024	2,334	2,778	3,055
Computer sciences	861	809	867	948	1,129	1,453	1,662
Mathematics	1,050	919	993	1,076	1,205	1,325	1,393
Physical sciences, total	3,378	3,187	3,287	3,335	3,643	3,929	4,106
Astronomy	185	141	167	165	186	197	224
Chemistry	1,989	1,923	2,040	1,986	2,126	2,363	2,328
Physics	1,204	1,123	1,080	1,184	1,331	1,369	1,554
Psychology	3,615	3,206	3,275	3,325	3,321	3,258	3,294
Social sciences, total	4,155	4,013	4,139	4,139	4,141	4,276	4,415
Economics	1,086	1,027	1,050	1,069	1,183	1,142	1,179
Political science	986	939	1,025	946	990	998	1,256
Sociology	637	567	612	599	556	602	591
Other social sciences	1,446	1,481	1,452	1,524	1,412	1,533	1,389
Nonscience and engineering, total	**15,394**	**15,416**	**15,475**	**15,844**	**15,394**	**15,743**	**16,278**
Education	6,436	6,503	6,643	6,633	6,224	6,120	6,429
Health	1,591	1,655	1,633	1,719	1,784	1,905	2,134
Humanities	5,213	5,050	5,020	5,012	4,950	5,125	4,890
Professional/other/unknown	2,154	2,208	2,179	2,480	2,436	2,593	2,825

Source: U.S. National Science Foundation, NSF 09-311, *Science and Engineering Doctorate Awards*, annual. See also <http://www.nsf.gov/statistics/nsf07305/>.

U.S. Census Bureau, Statistical Abstract of the United States: 2010

Table 793. Civilian Employment of Scientists, Engineers, and Related Occupations by Occupation and Industry: 2006

[In thousands (263.7 represents 263,700). Standard Occupational Classification (SOC) system categorizes workers in 1 of 801 detailed occupations. Industry classifications correspond to 2002 North American Industry Classification System (NAICS) industrial groups. For definition of scientists and engineers, see text this section and Table 784]

Occupation	Total employment, all workers	Wage and salary workers						Self employ- ed [2]
		Mining (NAICS 21) [1]	Construction (NAICS 23)	Manu- facturing (NAICS 31–33)	Informa- tion (NAICS 51)	Profes- sional, scientific and technical services (NAICS 54)	Govern- ment (NAICS 99)	
Computer and information systems managers	263.7	0.5	0.7	24.7	31.0	65.3	18.1	3.6
Engineering managers	187.1	2.1	5.4	80.9	5.2	55.9	16.5	0.1
Natural science managers	40.7	0.3	(NA)	5.5	0.2	14.6	14.3	0.2
Computer and mathematical scientists...	3,313.2	8.4	7.7	268.3	413.2	1,004.6	240.5	130.9
Computer specialists.............	3,199.6	0.4	7.5	262.4	406.2	978.8	221.5	129.5
Mathematical science occupations....	113.6	(NA)	0.2	5.9	7.1	25.7	19.0	1.5
Surveyors, cartographers, and photogrammetrists	72.2	0.8	4.1	(NA)	(NA)	52.2	9.5	2.6
Engineers [3]	1,511.5	21.0	40.3	563.7	41.3	430.6	180.0	45.7
Aerospace engineers	89.8	(NA)	(NA)	58.4	(NA)	15.9	9.1	1.3
Civil engineers.................	256.3	0.5	24.3	2.7	1.1	130.9	69.1	12.5
Computer and hardware engineers ...	78.5	(NA)	(NA)	33.8	(NA)	23.3	4.5	2.8
Electrical and electronics engineers...	291.2	0.2	4.9	103.2	30.6	70.8	26.1	6.3
Industrial engineers [4]	226.7	2.3	5.9	149.5	3.0	29.2	5.2	2.1
Mechanical engineers	225.8	0.8	2.9	120.6	0.3	63.2	11.9	5.1
Drafters, engineering, and mapping technicians [5]	839.8	4.9	25.2	240.4	24.2	309.3	107.6	20.9
Engineering technicians..........	511.0	3.6	4.8	178.0	21.8	126.5	90.7	4.4
Surveying and mapping technicians...	75.6	0.6	0.9	0.2	0.4	54.2	11.6	3.2
Life, physical, and social science occupations	1,406.9	18.3	3.6	151.1	30.0	346.1	302.4	97.4
Life scientists.................	258.5	(NA)	(NA)	31.1	(NA)	60.8	66.9	11.5
Physical scientists	266.8	8.7	0.4	42.4	1.9	98.4	73.9	4.7
Social scientists and related occupations	530.2	(NA)	2.9	24.2	27.4	100.0	75.4	77.7
Life, physical, and social science technicians	351.4	9.2	0.4	53.5	(NA)	86.9	86.2	3.5

NA Not available. [1] Includes oil and gas extraction. [2] Includes secondary jobs and unpaid private household employment. [3] Includes kinds of engineers not shown separately. [4] Includes health and safety engineers. [5] Includes other drafters, technicians, and mapping technicians.

Source: U.S. Bureau of Labor Statistics, *National Employment Matrix*, February 2008. (Data collected biennially.) For more information see <http://www.bls.gov/emp/nioem/empioan.htm>.

Table 794. Employment and Earnings in Science and Engineering (S&E) Occupations by Industry: 2006

[As of May 2006. Industries ordered by Science and Engineering share of total employment. See headnote, Table 795]

Industry	2002 NAICS code [1]	Workers employed (number)		S&E workers as percent of all employed	Mean earnings in S&E occupations (dollars)
		All occupations	S&E occupations		
Computer systems design and related services	5415	1,254,320	609,590	48.6	75,040
Software publishers	5112	240,130	116,260	48.4	79,120
Scientific research and development services	5417	586,220	247,310	42.2	81,220
Computer and peripheral equipment manufacturing	3341	199,370	79,040	39.6	90,710
Internet service providers and Web search portals	5181	119,560	46,120	38.6	69,720
Data processing, hosting, and related services	5182	264,320	83,470	31.6	70,460
Internet publishing and broadcasting	5161	33,220	9,810	29.5	69,800
Architectural, engineering, and related services	5413	1,361,280	397,910	29.2	74,570
Communications equipment manufacturing	3342	144,200	39,270	27.2	83,400
Navigational, measuring, electromedical, and control instruments manufacturing	3345	435,510	117,950	27.1	82,190
Aerospace product and parts manufacturing	3364	464,990	114,620	24.6	80,410
Securities and commodity exchanges	5232	8,850	1,930	21.8	74,000
Semiconductor and other electronic component manufacturing	3344	452,060	93,940	20.8	83,490
Pharmaceutical and medicine manufacturing........	3254	288,270	55,640	19.3	73,710
Other telecommunications	5179	5,300	980	18.5	73,820

[1] North American Industry Classification System (NAICS) 2002; see text, Section 15.

Source: National Science Foundation, *Science and Engineering Indicators 2008*, January 2008. See also <http://nsf.gov/statistics/seind08/>.

Table 795. **Individuals Employed in Science and Engineering (S&E) Occupations as Share of Workforce by State and Other Areas: 2008**

[In thousands (7,628.9 represents 7,628,900), except as noted. As of May 2008. The Occupational Employment Statistics Survey (OES) collects data in six semiannual panels over a 3-year (November 2005 through May 2008) period on occupational employment and wages of wage and salary workers in nonfarm establishments in the United States, Guam, Puerto Rico, and the Virgin Islands. U.S. totals include data items that are not released seperately at the state level due to confidentiality and quality issues. The OES survey uses the Standard Occupational Classification (SOC) system to categorize workers in 1 of 801 detailed occupations. Excludes self employed. For a list of occupations see <http://www.bls.gov/oes/current/oesstru.htm>. For more information about methodology, see <http://www.bls.gov/oes/current/oestec.htm/]

State	Employed in S&E occu- pations [1]	Employed workforce	Work- force in S&E occupa- tions [1] (percent)	State	Employed in S&E occu- pations [1]	Employed workforce	Work- force in S&E occupa- tions [1] (percent)
United States.	7,628.9	135,185.2	5.6	Nebraska	41.6	928.1	4.5
Alabama	88.9	1,945.3	4.6	Nevada.	40.2	1,278.2	3.1
Alaska	18.9	307.8	6.1	New Hampshire	37.8	634.6	6.0
Arizona.	147.1	2,637.8	5.6	New Jersey	261.1	3,986.3	6.5
Arkansas.	41.5	1,176.1	3.5	New Mexico.	49.2	819.5	6.0
California.	1,004.1	15,212.6	6.6	New York	446.9	8,633.6	5.2
Colorado.	182.6	2,302.3	7.9	North Carolina	207.5	4,063.4	5.1
Connecticut	108.3	1,697.8	6.4	North Dakota	13.5	350.4	3.8
Delaware.	30.6	425.2	7.2	Ohio.	264.2	5,323.1	5.0
District of Columbia. . .	73.6	635.5	11.6	Oklahoma	65.1	1,557.8	4.2
Florida	336.8	7,771.7	4.3	Oregon	100.5	1,706.7	5.9
Georgia	193.7	4,068.3	4.8	Pennsylvania	295.1	5,705.2	5.2
Hawaii	24.8	612.4	4.0	Rhode Island	23.3	478.4	4.9
Idaho	39.2	650.2	6.0	South Carolina	81.3	1,892.7	4.3
Illinois.	300.0	5,910.6	5.1	South Dakota.	14.9	396.0	3.8
Indiana	121.4	2,927.6	4.1	Tennessee.	98.1	2,755.8	3.6
Iowa.	63.1	1,502.6	4.2	Texas	630.2	10,391.4	6.1
Kansas	71.1	1,374.6	5.2	Utah.	73.7	1,230.3	6.0
Kentucky	67.1	1,817.9	3.7	Vermont	16.5	301.1	5.5
Louisiana	66.1	1,887.4	3.5	Virginia	315.1	3,671.0	8.6
Maine.	24.5	604.2	4.0	Washington	245.5	2,868.9	8.6
Maryland	209.5	2,561.5	8.2	West Virginia	24.2	717.7	3.4
Massachusetts	272.5	3,234.9	8.4	Wisconsin	138.3	2,776.7	5.0
Michigan	267.5	4,142.8	6.5	Wyoming.	12.7	284.0	4.5
Minnesota	177.9	2,704.9	6.6				
Mississippi.	39.5	1,138.2	3.5	Guam	1.8	58.8	3.0
Missouri	138.4	2,740.2	5.1	Puerto Rico	33.2	999.0	3.3
Montana	22.3	444.1	5.0	Virgin Islands	0.9	44.9	2.0

[1] Science and Engineering includes those occupations listed under SOC11-3021, SOC11-0041, SOC11-9121, SOC15-0000, SOC17-0000, and SOC19-0000.

Source: U.S. Bureau of Labor Statistics, "Employment and Wages from Occupational Employment Statistics (OES) Survey," January 2008; <http://www.bls.gov/oes/data.htm> (accessed 21 May 2009).

Table 796. **Research and Development (R&D) Scientists and Engineers— Employment and Cost by Industry: 2005 to 2007**
[1,104.5 represents 1,104,500]

Industry	NAICS [1] code	Employed scientists and engineers [2] (1,000)			Cost per scientist or engineer, constant (2000) dollars [3, 4] ($1,000)		
		2005	2006	2007	2005	2006	2007
All industries [5]	(X)	1,104.5	1,116.6	1,133.0	192.4	201.6	211.9
Chemicals	325	118.3	123.2	134.0	328.5	330.1	356.4
Machinery	333	61.1	62.3	61.9	125.2	141.1	144.4
Electrical equipment, appliances, and components . . .	335	18.7	16.9	15.8	(D)	(D)	(D)
Motor vehicles, trailers, and parts.	3361–3363	42.0	42.0	(NA)	(D)	(D)	(D)
Aerospace products and parts	3364	39.7	39.5	40.2	335.4	359.4	380.5
Software publishing	5112	93.4	46.5	(NA)	162.5	174.0	175.4
Architectural, engineering, and related services.	5413	35.8	41.2	48.5	129.3	146.4	113.9
Computer systems design and related services.	5415	82.4	93.1	88.1	158.5	157.2	160.3
Scientific R&D services	5417	43.7	44.3	50.4	264.0	298.2	308.7

D Withheld to avoid disclosure.   NA Not available.   X Not applicable.   [1] North American Industry Classification System 1997 (NAICS); see text, Section 15.   [2] The mean number of full-time equivalent R&D scientists and engineers employed in January of the year shown and the following January.   [3] Based on gross domestic product implicit price deflator.   [4] Represents the arithmetic mean of the numbers of R&D scientists and engineers reported in each industry for January in 2 consecutive years divided into total R&D expenditures in each industry.   [5] Includes other industries not shown separately.

Source: U.S. National Science Foundation, NSF 09-301, *Research and Development in Industry.* See also <http://www.nsf.gov/statistics/nsf09301/>.

Table 797. **World-Wide Space Launch Events: 2000 to 2008**

[(2,729 represents $2,729,000,000)

Country	Non-commercial launches				Commercial launches				Launch revenues for commercial events (million dollars)			
	2000	2005	2007	2008	2000	2005	2007	2008	2000	2005	2007	2008
Total	50	37	45	41	35	18	23	28	2,729	1,190	1,548	1,971
United States	21	11	16	9	7	1	3	6	370	70	150	215
Russia	23	18	14	15	13	8	12	11	671	350	477	700
Europe	–	–	–	1	12	5	6	5	1,433	490	840	581
China [1]	5	5	10	11	–	–	–	–	(X)	(X)	(X)	(X)
India	–	1	2	3	–	–	1	–	(X)	(X)	11	(X)
Japan	1	2	2	1	–	–	–	–	(X)	(X)	(X)	(X)
Israel	–	–	1	–	–	–	–	–	(X)	(X)	(X)	(X)
Iran	–	–	–	1	–	–	–	–	(X)	(X)	(X)	(X)
Multinational	–	–	–	–	3	4	1	6	255	280	70	475

– Represents zero.   X Not applicable.   [1] See footnote 4, Table 1296.

Source: Federal Aviation Administration, *Commercial Space Transportation: 2008 Year in Review*, and prior years. See also <http://www.faa.gov/about/office_org/headquarters_offices/ast/reports_studies/year_review/>.

Table 798. **U.S. and Worldwide Commercial Space Industry Revenue by Type: 2000 to 2008**

[In billions of dollars (19.3 represents $19,300,000,000). For calendar years]

Industry	U.S.				World			
	2000	2005	2007	2008	2000	2005	2007	2008
Revenue, total	19.3	30.8	(NA)	(NA)	64.2	88.8	121.7	144.4
Satellite manufacturing [1]	6.0	3.2	4.8	3.1	11.5	7.8	11.6	10.5
Launch industry [2]	2.7	1.5	1.0	1.1	5.3	3.0	3.2	3.9
Satellite services [2]	10.6	26.1	(NA)	(NA)	28.9	52.8	72.6	84.0
Ground equipment manufacturing [3]	(NA)	(NA)	(NA)	(NA)	18.5	25.2	34.3	46.0

NA Not available.   [1] Includes revenues from the construction and sale of satellites to both commercial and government. [2] Includes revenues derived from transponder leasing and subscription/retail services such as direct-to-home television, satellite radio, remote sensing, and satellite mobile and data communications.   [3] Includes revenues from the manufacture of gateways and satellite control stations, satellite news-gathering trucks, very small aperture terminals, direct-to-home television equipment and mobile satellite phones.

Source: Satellite Industry Association/Futron Corporation, *State of the Satellite Industry Report*, June 2009 (copyright). See also <http://sia.org/IndustryReport.htm>.

Table 799. **National Aeronautics and Space Administration—Budget Appropriations: 2008 and 2009**

[In millions of dollars (17,401.9 represents $17,401,900,000).

Budget function/category	2008	2009
Appropriations, total	17,401.9	17,782.4
Science	4,733.2	4,503.0
Earth science	1,237.4	1,379.6
Heliophysics	787.6	591.6
Planetary Science	1,312.6	1,325.6
Astrophysics	1,395.6	1,206.2
Exploration	3,299.4	3,505.5
Constellation systems	2,675.9	3,033.1
Advanced capabilities	623.5	472.3
Aeronautics	511.4	500.0
Space operations	5,427.2	5,764.7
Space shuttle	3,295.4	2,981.7
International space station	1,685.5	2,060.2
Space & flight support	446.2	722.8

Source: U.S. National Aeronautics and Space Administration, "Fiscal Year 2010 Budget Request Summary" <http://www.nasa.gov/about/budget/index.html> (accessed 15 May 2009).

Section 17
Agriculture

This section presents statistics on farms and farm operators; land use; farm income, expenditures, and debt; farm output, productivity, and marketings; foreign trade in agricultural products; specific crops; and livestock, poultry, and their products.

The principal sources are the reports issued by the National Agricultural Statistics Service (NASS) and the Economic Research Service (ERS) of the U.S. Department of Agriculture (USDA). The information from the 2007 Census of Agriculture is available in printed form in the Volume 1, Geographic Area Series; in electronic format on CD-ROM; and on the Internet site <http://www.agcensus.usda.gov /Publications/2007/Full_Report/index.asp>. The Department of Agriculture publishes annually *Agricultural Statistics,* a general reference book on agricultural production, supplies, consumption, facilities, costs, and returns. The ERS publishes data on farm assets, debt, and income on the Internet site <http://www.ers.usda .gov/briefing/farmincome/>. Sources of current data on agricultural exports and imports include *Outlook for U.S. Agricultural Trade,* published by the ERS; the ERS Internet site <http://www.ers.usda.gov /briefing/AgTrade/>; and the foreign trade section of the U.S. Census Bureau Web site <http://www.census.gov /foreign-trade/statistics/index.html>.

The field offices of the NASS collect data on crops, livestock and products, agricultural prices, farm employment, and other related subjects mainly through sample surveys. Information is obtained on crops and livestock items as well as scores of items pertaining to agricultural production and marketing. State estimates and supporting information are sent to the Agricultural Statistics Board of NASS, which reviews the estimates and issues reports containing state and national data. Among these reports are annual summaries such as *Crop Production, Crop Values, Agricultural Prices,* and *Livestock Production, Disposition and Income.*

Farms and farmland—The definitions of a farm have varied through time. Since 1850, when minimum criteria defining a farm for census purposes first were established, the farm definition has changed nine times. The current definition, first used for the 1974 census, is any place from which $1,000 or more of agricultural products were produced and sold, or normally would have been sold, during the census year.

Acreage designated as "land in farms" consists primarily of agricultural land used for crops, pasture, or grazing. It also includes woodland and wasteland not actually under cultivation or used for pasture or grazing, provided it was part of the farm operator's total operation. Land in farms Includes acres set aside under annual commodity acreage programs as well as acres in the Conservation Reserve and Wetlands Reserve Programs for places meeting the farm definition. Land in farms is an operating unit concept and includes land owned and operated as well as land rented from others. All grazing land, except land used under government permits on a per-head basis, was included as "land in farms" provided it was part of a farm or ranch.

An evaluation of coverage has been conducted for each census of agriculture since 1945 to provide estimates of the completeness of census farm counts. Beginning with the 1997 Census of Agriculture, census farm counts and totals were statistically adjusted for coverage and reported at the county level. The size of the adjustments varies considerably by state. In general, farms not on the census mail list tended to be small in acreage, production, and sales of farm products. The response rate for the 2007 Census of Agriculture was 85.2 percent as compared with a response rate of 88.0 for the

2002 Census of Agriculture and 86.2 percent for the 1997 Census of Agriculture. For more explanation about census mail list compilation, collection methods, coverage measurement, and adjustments, see Appendix A, 2007 Census of Agriculture, Volume 1 reports.

Farm income—The final agricultural sector output comprises cash receipts from farm marketings of crops and livestock, federal government payments made directly to farmers for farm-related activities, rental value of farm homes, value of farm products consumed in farm homes, and other farm-related income such as machine hire and custom work. Farm marketings represent quantities of agricultural products sold by farmers multiplied by prices received per unit of production at the local market. Information on prices received for farm products is generally obtained by the NASS Agricultural Statistics Board from surveys of firms (such as grain elevators, packers, and processors) purchasing agricultural commodities directly from producers. In some cases, the price information is obtained directly from the producers.

Crops—Estimates of crop acreage and production by the NASS are based on current sample survey data obtained from individual producers and objective yield counts, reports of carlot shipments, market records, personal field observations by field statisticians, and reports from other sources. Prices received by farmers are marketing year averages. These averages are based on U.S. monthly prices weighted by monthly marketings during specific periods. U.S. monthly prices are state average prices weighted by marketings during the month. Marketing year average prices do not include allowances for outstanding loans, government purchases, deficiency payments or disaster payments.

All state prices are based on individual state marketing years, while U.S. marketing year averages are based on standard marketing years for each crop. For a listing of the crop marketing years and the participating states in the monthly program, see *Crop Values*. Value of production is computed by multiplying state prices by each state's production. The U.S. value of production is the sum of state values for all states. Value of production figures shown in Tables 830–834 and 836 should not be confused with cash receipts from farm marketings which relate to sales during a calendar year, irrespective of the year of production.

Livestock—Annual inventory numbers of livestock and estimates of livestock, dairy, and poultry production prepared by the Department of Agriculture are based on information from farmers and ranchers obtained by probability survey sampling methods.

Statistical reliability—For a discussion of statistical collection and estimation, sampling procedures, and measures of statistical reliability pertaining to Department of Agriculture data, see Appendix III.

Figure 17.1
Farms and Market Value of Farm Sales by Sales Class: 2007

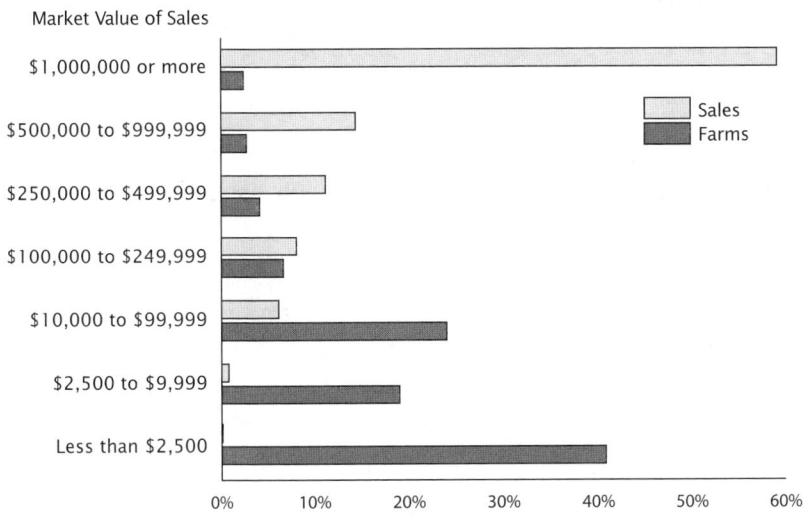

Source: Chart prepared by U.S. Census Bureau. For data, see Table 808.

Figure 17.2
**Consumer Expenditures for Farm Foods:
2000 to 2007**

☐ Marketing Bill
■ Farm Value

Billions of Dollars

¹ Food purchased from retail food stores for use at home.

Source: Chart prepared by U.S. Census Bureau. For data, see Table 819.

Agriculture   523

Table 800. **Farms—Number and Acreage: 1990 to 2008**

[**As of June 1 (2,146 represents 2,146,000**). Based on 1974 census definition; for definition of farms and farmland, see text of this section. Activities included as agriculture have undergone changes in recent years. Data for period 2000 to 2008 are not directly comparable with data for 1990. Data for 2002 and 2007 have been adjusted for underenumeration]

Item	Unit	1990	2000	2002	2003	2004	2005	2006	2007	2008
Number of farms.....	1,000......	2,146	2,167	2,135	2,127	2,113	2,099	2,089	2,205	2,200
Land in farms.......	Mil. acres...	987	945	940	937	932	928	926	921	920
Average per farm...	Acres......	460	436	440	440	441	442	443	418	418

Source: U.S. Dept. of Agriculture, National Agricultural Statistics Service, *Farms and Land in Farms, Final Estimates, 1988–1992; Farm Numbers and Land in Farms, Final Estimates, 1998–2002; Farms and Land in Farms, Final Estimates, 2003–2007;* and *Farms, Land in Farms, and Livestock Operations,* annual.

Table 801. **Farms—Number and Acreage by State: 2000 and 2008**

[**2,167 represents 2,167,000**. See headnote, Table 800]

State	Farms (1,000) 2000	Farms (1,000) 2008	Acreage (mil.) 2000	Acreage (mil.) 2008	Acreage per farm 2000	Acreage per farm 2008	State	Farms (1,000) 2000	Farms (1,000) 2008	Acreage (mil.) 2000	Acreage (mil.) 2008	Acreage per farm 2000	Acreage per farm 2008
U.S.	**2,167**	**2,200**	**945**	**920**	**436**	**418**	Montana.	28	30	59	61	2,133	2,061
Alabama.	47	49	9	9	191	185	Nebraska	52	47	46	46	887	962
Alaska	1	1	1	1	1,569	1,309	Nevada	3	3	6	6	2,065	1,903
Arizona.	11	16	27	26	2,514	1,673	New						
Arkansas	48	49	15	14	304	278	Hampshire.	3	4	(Z)	(Z)	133	113
California	83	82	28	25	337	312	New Jersey.	10	10	1	1	86	71
Colorado.	30	37	32	31	1,053	858	New Mexico	18	21	45	43	2,494	2,087
Connecticut.	4	5	(Z)	(Z)	86	82	New York	38	37	8	7	205	194
Delaware	3	3	1	1	215	200	North Carolina. . . .	56	53	9	9	166	164
Florida	44	48	10	9	236	195	North Dakota. . . .	31	32	39	40	1,279	1,238
Georgia	49	48	11	10	222	218	Ohio	79	75	15	14	187	185
Hawaii	6	8	1	1	251	148	Oklahoma.	85	87	34	35	400	405
Idaho	25	25	12	11	486	452	Oregon.	40	39	17	16	433	425
Illinois	77	76	28	27	357	352	Pennsylvania. . . .	59	63	8	8	130	123
Indiana.	63	61	15	15	240	243	Rhode Island. . . .	1	1	(Z)	(Z)	75	57
Iowa	94	93	33	31	346	333	South Carolina. . . .	24	27	5	5	203	182
Kansas.	65	66	48	46	736	705	South Dakota. . . .	32	31	44	44	1,358	1,396
Kentucky	90	85	14	14	152	164	Tennessee	88	79	12	11	134	138
Louisiana	29	30	8	8	277	268	Texas.	228	248	131	130	573	527
Maine.	7	8	1	1	190	169	Utah	16	17	12	11	748	673
Maryland	12	13	2	2	172	160	Vermont	7	7	1	1	192	174
Massachusetts. . .	6	8	1	1	89	66	Virginia.	49	47	9	8	180	170
Michigan.	53	55	10	10	192	182	Washington.	37	40	16	15	420	375
Minnesota.	81	81	28	27	344	332	West Virginia. . . .	21	23	4	4	173	159
Mississippi	42	42	11	11	266	262	Wisconsin.	78	78	16	15	206	195
Missouri	109	108	30	29	277	269	Wyoming	9	11	35	30	3,750	2,736

Z Less than 500,000 acres.

Source: U.S. Department of Agriculture, National Agricultural Statistics Service, *Farm Numbers and Land in Farms, Final Estimates, 1998–2002* and *Farms, Land in Farms, and Livestock Operations,* annual.

Table 802. **Farms by Size and Type of Organization: 1978 to 2007**

[**2,258 represents 2,258,000**. For comments on adjustment, see text this section]

Size and type of organization	Unit	Not adjusted for coverage 1978	Not adjusted for coverage 1982	Not adjusted for coverage 1987	Not adjusted for coverage 1992	Not adjusted for coverage 1997	Adjusted for coverage 1997[1]	Adjusted for coverage 2002[1]	Adjusted for coverage 2007[1]
Farms.	1,000	2,258	2,241	2,088	1,925	1,912	2,216	2,129	2,205
Land in farms.	Mil. acres...	1,015	987	964	946	932	955	938	922
Average size of farm	Acres	449	440	462	491	487	431	441	418
Farms by size:									
Under 10 acres.	1,000	151	188	183	166	154	205	179	233
10 to 49 acres	1,000	392	449	412	388	411	531	564	620
50 to 179 acres.	1,000	759	712	645	584	593	694	659	661
180 to 499 acres.	1,000	582	527	478	428	403	428	389	368
500 to 999 acres.	1,000	213	204	200	186	176	179	162	150
1,000 to 1,999 acres	1,000	98	97	102	102	101	103	99	93
2,000 acres or more	1,000	63	65	67	71	75	74	78	80
Farms by type of organization:									
Family or individual	1,000	1,966	1,946	1,809	1,653	1,643	1,923	1,910	1,906
Partnership	1,000	233	223	200	187	169	186	130	174
Corporation	1,000	50	60	67	73	84	90	74	96
Other [2]	1,000	9	12	12	12	15	17	16	28

[1] Data have been adjusted for coverage; see text, this section.   [2] Cooperative, estate or trust, institutional, etc.

Source: U.S. Department of Agriculture, National Agricultural Statistics Service, *2007 Census of Agriculture,* Vol. 1.

Table 803. **Farms—Number and Acreage by Size of Farm: 2002 and 2007**

[2,129 represents 2,129,000. Data have been adjusted for coverage; see text, this section]

Size of farm	Number of farms (1,000)		Land in farms (mil. acres)		Cropland harvested (mil. acres)		Percent distribution, 2007		
	2002	2007	2002	2007	2002	2007	Number of farms	All land in farms	Cropland harvested
Total	2,129	2,205	938.3	922.1	302.7	309.6	100.0	100.0	100.0
Under 10 acres	179	233	0.8	1.1	0.2	0.3	10.6	0.1	0.1
10 to 49 acres.	564	620	14.7	15.9	4.1	4.3	28.1	1.7	1.4
50 to 69 acres.	152	154	8.8	8.9	2.5	2.5	7.0	1.0	0.8
70 to 99 acres.	191	192	15.7	15.8	4.7	4.5	8.7	1.7	1.5
100 to 139 acres	175	175	20.2	20.3	6.1	5.8	7.9	2.2	1.9
140 to 179 acres	142	139	22.3	22.0	7.3	6.6	6.3	2.4	2.1
180 to 219 acres	91	88	18.0	17.3	6.2	5.6	4.0	1.9	1.8
220 to 259 acres	72	68	17.1	16.3	6.5	5.7	3.1	1.8	1.9
260 to 499 acres	226	213	80.6	75.9	34.1	30.4	9.6	8.2	9.8
500 to 999 acres	162	150	112.4	104.1	56.7	51.6	6.8	11.3	16.7
1,000 to 1,999 acres. . .	99	93	135.7	127.6	72.8	69.8	4.2	13.8	22.6
2,000 acres or more . . .	78	80	491.9	496.9	101.6	122.5	3.6	53.9	39.6

Source: U.S. Department of Agriculture, National Agricultural Statistics Service, *2007 Census of Agriculture*, Vol. 1.

Table 804. **Farms—Number, Acreage, and Value by Tenure of Principal Operator and Type of Organization: 2002 and 2007**

[2,129 represents 2,129,000. Full owners own all the land they operate. Part owners own a part and rent from others the rest of the land they operate. A principal operator is the person primarily responsible for the on-site, day-to-day operation of the farm or ranch business. Data have been adjusted for coverage; see text, this section]

Item and year	Unit	Total [1]	Tenure of operator			Type of organization		
			Full owner	Part owner	Tenant	Family or indi- vidual	Partner- ship	Corpora- tion
NUMBER OF FARMS								
2002, total	1,000	2,129	1,428	551	150	1,910	130	74
2007, total.	1,000	2,205	1,522	542	141	1,906	174	96
Under 50 acres	1,000	853	739	70	44	774	45	26
50 to 179 acres	1,000	661	492	130	38	588	45	18
180 to 499 acres	1,000	368	198	143	27	312	34	16
500 to 999 acres	1,000	150	51	84	14	118	18	12
1,000 acres or more.	1,000	173	41	114	17	114	32	24
LAND IN FARMS								
2002.	Mil. acres. . .	938	357	495	87	622	146	108
2007.	Mil. acres. . .	922	344	496	82	574	161	125
Value of land and buildings, **2007** [2] . . .	Bil. dol.	1,744	726	868	150	1,203	277	227
Value of farm products sold, **2007**	Bil. dol.	297	117	148	32	148	62	84

[1] Includes other types, not shown separately.   [2] Based on a sample of farms.

Source: U.S. Department of Agriculture, National Agricultural Statistics Service, *2007 Census of Agriculture*, Vol. 1.

Table 805. **Corporate Farms—Characteristics by Type: 2007**

[125.3 represents 125,300,000. Data have been adjusted for coverage; see text, this section and Appendix III]

Item	Unit	All corpora- tions	Family held corporations			Other corporations		
			Total	1 to 10 stock- holders	11 or more stock- holders	Total	1 to 10 stock- holders	11 or more stock- holders
Farms	Number. . .	96,074	85,837	83,796	2,041	10,237	9,330	907
Percent distribution	Percent . . .	100	89	87	2	11	10	1
Land in farms	Mil. acres. . .	125.3	114.3	106.4	7.8	11.1	7.7	3.3
Average per farm	Acres	1,304	1,331	1,270	3,834	1,080	829	3,657
Value of—								
Land and buildings [1]	Bil. dol. . . .	226.6	200.6	189.5	11.0	26.0	20.2	5.8
Average per farm.	$1,000 . . .	2,358	2,336	2,262	5,399	2,542	2,170	6,371
Farm products sold	Bil. dol. . . .	84.1	65.8	58.9	6.9	18.3	12.2	6.2
Average per farm.	$1,000 . . .	876	766	703	3,378	1,791	1,305	6,787

[1] Based on a sample of farms.

Source: U.S. Department of Agriculture, National Agricultural Statistics Service, *2007 Census of Agriculture*, Vol. 1.

Agriculture   525

Table 806. **Farm Operators—Tenure and Characteristics: 2002 and 2007**

[In thousands, except as indicated (3,054 represents 3,054,000). An "operator" is a person who operates a farm, either doing the work or making day-to-day decisions. A family operation may have more than one operator. A principal operator is the person primarily responsible for the on-site, day-to-day operation of the farm or ranch business. Data on operator characteristics were collected up to a maximum of three operators per farm, though operations were asked to report the total number of operators. Data have been adjusted for coverage; see text, this section and Appendix III]

Characteristic	Total opera- tors, 2002	2007			Characteristic	Total opera- tors, 2002	2007		
		Total opera- tors	Princi- pal opera- tors	Other opera- tors			Total opera- tors	Princi- pal opera- tors	Other opera- tors
Total	3,054	3,282	2,205	1,077	Full owner	(NA)	(NA)	1,522	(NA)
					Part owner	(NA)	(NA)	542	(NA)
White	2,966	3,141	2,114	1,026	Tenant	(NA)	(NA)	141	(NA)
Black or									
African American	36	40	31	9	Principal occupation:				
American Indian or					Farming	1,658	1,400	994	406
Alaska Native	24	56	35	21	Other	1,396	1,882	1,211	671
Asian	13	18	11	7					
Native Hawaiian or					Place of residence:				
Other Pacific Islander	2	2	1	1	On farm operated	2,391	2,492	1,693	799
More than one race					Not on farm operated	662	789	511	278
reported	12	25	13	12	Years on present farm:				
Operators of Hispanic					2 years or less	143	163	85	78
origin [1]	72	82	56	27	3 to 4 years	251	240	139	101
					5 to 9 years	587	593	360	233
Female	822	985	306	679	10 years or more	2,073	2,286	1,622	664
Under 25 years old	60	54	12	42	Average years on				
25 to 34 years old	201	209	107	103	present farm	(NA)	(NA)	22	(NA)
35 to 44 years old	590	469	269	200	Days worked off farm:				
45 to 54 years old	838	878	565	312	None	1,354	1,118	778	340
55 to 64 years old	690	848	596	252	1 to 49 days	183	364	238	125
65 to 74 years old	439	533	412	121	50 to 99 days	102	181	116	65
75 years old and over	236	290	243	47	100 to 199 days	224	305	197	108
Average age (years)	53.2	54.9	57.1	(NA)	200 days or more	1,190	1,314	876	438

NA Not available.   [1] Operators of Hispanic origin may be any race.

Source: U.S. Department of Agriculture, National Agricultural Statistics Service, *2007 Census of Agriculture*, Vol. 1.

Table 807. **Organic Agriculture—Number of Farms, Acreage, and Value of Sales: 2007**

[2,577 represents 2,577,000. Data have been adjusted for coverage; see text, this section and Appendix III]

Size and usage	Number of farms	Acreage (1,000)	Sales value of organically produced commodities and commodity	Number of farms	Value (mil. dol.)
Total acres used for organic production . .	20,437	2,577	Organic product sales, total . . .	18,211	1,709
1 to 9 organic acres	9,251	29	$1 to $4,999	8,285	13
10 to 49 organic acres	4,994	115	$5,000 to $9,999	1,935	13
50 to 179 organic acres	3,498	348	$10,000 to $24,999	2,318	37
180 to 499 organic acres	1,808	528	$25,000 to $49,999	1,515	54
500 organic acres or more	886	1,557	$50,000 or more	4,158	1,593
Acres from which organic crops harvested . .	16,778	1,288	Crops [1]	14,968	1,122
Acres of organic pastureland	7,268	975	Livestock and poultry	2,496	110
Acres being converted to organic production.	11,901	616	Livestock and poultry products . . .	3,191	477

[1] Includes nursery and greenhouse crops.

Source: U.S. Department of Agriculture, National Agricultural Statistics Service, *2007 Census of Agriculture*, Vol. 1.

Table 808. **Farms—Number, Acreage, and Value of Sales by Size of Sales: 2007**

[2,205 represents 2,205,000. Data have been adjusted for coverage; see text, this section and Appendix III]

Market value of agricultural products sold	Farms (1,000)	Acreage		Value of sales		Percent distribution		
		Total (mil.)	Average per farm	Total (mil. dol.)	Average per farm (dol.)	Farms	Acreage	Value of sales
Total	2,205	922.1	418	297,220	134,807	100.0	100.0	100.0
Less than $2,500	900	121.5	135	435	483	40.8	13.2	0.1
$2,500 to $4,999	200	17.5	87	718	3,585	9.1	1.9	0.2
$5,000 to $9,999	219	27.6	126	1,553	7,104	9.9	3.0	0.5
$10,000 to $24,999	248	65.8	265	3,960	15,949	11.3	7.1	1.3
$25,000 to $49,999	155	59.8	386	5,480	35,419	7.0	6.5	1.8
$50,000 to $99,999	125	78.2	623	8,961	71,429	5.7	8.5	3.0
$100,000 to $249,999	148	147.6	1,000	24,213	164,156	6.7	16.0	8.1
$250,000 to $499,999	93	140.7	1,507	33,410	357,811	4.2	15.3	11.2
$500,000 to $999,999	61	119.4	1,965	42,691	702,417	2.8	13.0	14.4
$1,000,000 or more	56	144.0	2,593	175,800	3,167,050	2.5	15.6	59.1

Source: U.S. Department of Agriculture, National Agricultural Statistics Service, *2007 Census of Agriculture*, Vol. 1.

Table 809. **Farms—Number, Value of Sales, and Government Payments by Economic Class of Farm: 2002 and 2007**

[2,129 represents 2,129,000. Economic class of farm is a combination of value of agricultural products sold and federal farm program payments. Data have been adjusted for coverage; see text, this section and Appendix III]

Economic class of farm	Number of farms (1,000)			Market value of agricultural products sold and government payments (mil. dol.)		
		2007			2007	
	2002, total	Total	Receiving government payments	2002, total	Total	Agricultural products sold	Government payments
Total	2,129	2,205	838	207,192	305,204	297,220	7,984
Less than $1,000	431	500	42	72	96	77	19
$1,000 to $2,499.	307	271	85	508	448	332	116
$2,500 to $4,999.	243	246	80	870	884	685	199
$5,000 to $9,999.	247	255	87	1,746	1,811	1,488	323
$10,000 to $24,999 . . .	272	274	110	4,320	4,364	3,810	554
$25,000 to $49,999 . . .	164	164	87	5,804	5,795	5,286	508
$50,000 to $99,999 . . .	143	129	83	10,202	9,219	8,644	575
$100,000 to $249,999 .	163	149	110	26,119	24,401	23,256	1,145
$250,000 to $499,999 .	86	96	75	30,084	34,367	32,980	1,387
$500,000 to $999,999 .	44	64	46	30,598	44,578	43,156	1,422
$1,000,000 to $2,499,999.	21	42	27	31,701	62,751	61,508	1,243
$2,500,000 to $4,999,999.	5	10	6	16,056	33,190	32,839	352
$5 million or more	3	6	2	49,112	83,300	83,159	141

Source: U.S. Department of Agriculture, National Agricultural Statistics Service, *2007 Census of Agriculture*, Vol. 1.

Agriculture   527

Table 810. **Farms—Number, Acreage, and Value by State: 2002 and 2007**

[**2,129 represents 2,129,000**. Data have been adjusted for coverage; see text, this section and Appendix III]

State	Number of farms (1,000) 2002	Number of farms (1,000) 2007	Land in farms (mil. acres) 2002	Land in farms (mil. acres) 2007	Average size of farm (acres) 2002	Average size of farm (acres) 2007	Total value of land and buildings [1] (bil. dol.) 2002	Total value of land and buildings [1] (bil. dol.) 2007	Market value of agricultural products sold and government payments, **2007** (mil. dol.)	Total number of operators, **2007** (1,000)
U.S....	2,129	2,205	938.3	922.1	441	418	1,144.9	1,744.3	305,204	3,337
AL........	45	49	8.9	9.0	197	185	15.1	20.7	4,540	71
AK........	1	1	0.9	0.9	1,479	1,285	0.3	0.3	59	1
AZ........	7	16	26.6	26.1	3,645	1,670	10.6	19.5	3,290	26
AR........	47	49	14.5	13.9	305	281	21.2	32.5	7,778	75
CA........	80	81	27.6	25.4	346	313	96.1	162.5	34,125	131
CO........	31	37	31.1	31.6	991	853	23.8	33.1	6,217	61
CT........	4	5	0.4	0.4	85	83	3.5	5.1	556	8
DE........	2	3	0.5	0.5	226	200	2.3	5.3	1,092	4
FL........	44	47	10.4	9.2	236	195	29.3	52.1	7,831	73
GA........	49	48	10.7	10.2	218	212	22.6	31.6	7,337	69
HI........	5	8	1.3	1.1	241	149	4.6	8.6	516	11
ID........	25	25	11.8	11.5	470	454	15.3	22.7	5,788	40
IL........	73	77	27.3	26.8	374	348	66.7	101.5	13,816	111
IN........	60	61	15.1	14.8	250	242	38.4	52.9	8,532	92
IA........	91	93	31.7	30.7	350	331	64.2	104.2	21,124	136
KS........	64	66	47.2	46.3	733	707	32.6	42.2	14,840	97
KY........	87	85	13.8	14.0	160	164	25.5	37.5	4,928	124
LA........	27	30	7.8	8.1	286	269	12.2	16.7	2,787	44
ME........	7	8	1.4	1.3	190	166	2.3	3.0	626	13
MD........	12	13	2.1	2.1	170	160	8.5	14.4	1,868	20
MA........	6	8	0.5	0.5	85	67	4.6	6.4	494	12
MI........	53	56	10.1	10.0	190	179	27.1	34.2	5,872	85
MN........	81	81	27.5	26.9	340	332	41.8	69.2	13,626	120
MS........	42	42	11.1	11.5	263	273	15.6	21.4	5,108	61
MO........	107	108	29.9	29.0	280	269	45.3	63.2	7,832	164
MT........	28	30	59.6	61.4	2,139	2,079	23.3	47.6	3,025	47
NE........	49	48	45.9	45.5	930	953	35.7	52.7	15,893	72
NV........	3	3	6.3	5.9	2,118	1,873	2.8	3.6	517	5
NH........	3	4	0.4	0.5	132	113	1.4	2.3	202	7
NJ........	10	10	0.8	0.7	81	71	7.4	11.3	994	16
NM........	15	21	44.8	43.2	2,954	2,066	10.6	14.6	2,218	32
NY........	37	36	7.7	7.2	206	197	12.9	16.3	4,481	58
NC........	54	53	9.1	8.5	168	160	28.0	34.7	10,461	77
ND........	31	32	39.3	39.7	1,283	1,241	15.8	30.6	6,444	45
OH........	78	76	14.6	14.0	187	184	39.6	49.2	7,302	114
OK........	83	87	33.7	35.1	404	405	23.8	40.6	6,016	131
OR........	40	39	17.1	16.4	427	425	20.4	31.0	4,463	65
PA........	58	63	7.7	7.8	133	124	26.3	37.3	5,885	95
RI........	1	1	0.1	0.1	71	56	0.6	1.1	67	2
SC........	25	26	4.8	4.9	197	189	10.1	14.0	2,420	37
SD........	32	31	43.8	43.7	1,380	1,401	19.6	39.1	6,841	47
TN........	88	79	11.7	11.0	133	138	28.5	37.1	2,713	117
TX........	229	247	129.9	130.4	567	527	100.5	165.6	21,722	373
UT........	15	17	11.7	11.1	768	664	9.0	13.9	1,438	26
VT........	7	7	1.2	1.2	189	177	2.5	3.6	680	11
VA........	48	47	8.6	8.1	181	171	23.3	34.1	2,961	71
WA........	36	39	15.3	15.0	426	381	22.4	29.8	6,931	64
WV........	21	24	3.6	3.7	172	157	4.8	8.8	595	35
WI........	77	78	15.7	15.2	204	194	35.8	49.0	9,163	123
WY........	9	11	34.4	30.2	3,651	2,726	10.2	15.5	1,186	19

[1] Based on reports for a sample of farms.

Source: U.S. Department of Agriculture, National Agricultural Statistics Service, *2007 Census of Agriculture*, Vol. 1.

Table 811. **Balance Sheet of the Farming Sector: 1990 to 2007**

[In billions of dollars, except as indicated (841 represents $841,000,000,000). As of December 31. Minus sign (–) represents capital loss]

Item	1990	1995	1999	2000	2001	2002	2003	2004	2005	2006	2007
Assets	**841**	**966**	**1,139**	**1,203**	**1,256**	**1,304**	**1,379**	**1,618**	**1,835**	**2,047**	**2,210**
Real estate	619	740	887	946	996	1,046	1,112	1,341	1,549	1,756	1,912
Livestock and poultry [1]	71	58	73	77	79	76	79	79	81	81	81
Machinery, motor vehicles [2]	86	88	90	90	93	94	96	102	107	108	109
Crops [3]	23	27	28	28	25	23	24	24	24	23	23
Purchased inputs	3	3	4	5	4	6	6	6	6	6	7
Financial assets	38	49	57	57	59	60	62	66	67	74	79
Claims	841	966	1,139	1,203	1,256	1,304	1,379	1,618	1,835	2,047	2,210
Debt [4]	131	143	168	164	171	177	175	183	193	196	212
Real estate debt	68	72	87	85	89	95	94	97	102	101	108
Nonreal estate debt	63	71	80	79	82	82	81	86	92	95	104
Equity	**709**	**823**	**971**	**1,039**	**1,085**	**1,127**	**1,204**	**1,435**	**1,642**	**1,851**	**1,998**
FINANCIAL RATIOS (percent)											
Farm debt/equity ratio	18.5	17.4	17.3	15.9	15.8	15.8	14.6	12.8	11.8	10.6	10.6
Farm debt/asset ratio	15.6	14.8	14.7	13.7	13.7	13.6	12.7	11.3	10.5	9.6	9.6
Rate of return on assets from:											
Total	3.5	4.3	5.3	7.9	6.9	4.8	8.1	22.5	17.6	13.1	10.2
Current income [5]	4.1	2.2	1.8	2.2	2.6	1.0	2.3	4.2	3.6	1.2	2.1
Real capital gains [6]	–0.7	2.1	3.4	5.7	4.4	3.8	5.7	18.3	14.0	11.9	8.0
Rate of return on equity from:											
Total	3.0	3.9	5.1	8.2	6.2	3.9	8.7	23.5	18.1	13.6	9.6
Current income [7]	3.0	1.1	0.7	1.2	1.8	0.1	1.7	3.1	2.7	0.5	1.5
Real capital gains [8]	0.1	2.8	4.3	7.1	4.4	3.8	6.9	20.4	15.4	13.1	8.1

[1] Excludes horses, mules, and broilers.   [2] Includes only farm share value for trucks and autos.   [3] All non-CCC crops held on farms plus the value above loan rate for crops held under Commodity Credit Corporation.   [4] Excludes debt for nonfarm purposes.   [5] Returns to farm assets from current income/farm business assets. Measures how efficiently the farm business uses its assets; the per dollar return on farm assets from current income only.   [6] Real capital gains on farm business assets/farm business assets. The per dollar return on farm assets from real capital gains.   [7] Returns to farm assets from current income minus interest/farm business equity. Measures the returns to equity capital employed in farm business from current income less interest.   [8] Real capital gains on farm business assets/farm business equity. The per dollar return on farm equity from real capital gains.

Source: U.S. Department of Agriculture, Economic Research Service, "Farm Balance Sheet"; <http://www.ers.usda.gov/Data /FarmBalanceSheet/FBSDMU.HTM> (accessed 26 October 2008).

Table 812. **Farm Sector Output and Value Added: 1990 to 2007**

[In billions of dollars (180.1 represents $180,100,000,000). For definition of value added, see text, Section 13. Minus sign (–) indicates decrease]

Item	1990	1995	1999	2000	2001	2002	2003	2004	2005	2006	2007
CURRENT DOLLARS											
Farm output, total	**180.1**	**192.0**	**198.5**	**203.6**	**210.8**	**202.1**	**227.7**	**260.5**	**255.8**	**253.8**	**307.0**
Cash receipts from farm marketings . . .	172.1	194.3	190.2	196.6	200.1	194.6	214.8	238.0	239.9	240.6	284.7
Farm products consumed on farms . . .	0.7	0.5	0.5	0.6	0.5	0.5	0.5	0.5	0.5	0.6	0.6
Other farm income	4.9	6.3	9.4	8.4	9.5	10.6	11.8	13.8	15.3	16.3	19.8
Change in farm finished goods inventories	2.4	–9.2	–1.6	–2.0	0.6	–3.7	0.7	8.2	–	–3.6	1.9
Less: Intermediate goods and services consumed [1]	103.5	123.5	129.8	132.1	137.7	131.2	139.5	145.8	151.6	162.7	169.8
Equals: **Gross farm value added**	**76.6**	**68.5**	**68.8**	**71.5**	**73.1**	**70.8**	**88.3**	**114.7**	**104.1**	**91.1**	**137.3**
Less: Consumption of fixed capital	18.6	19.6	21.2	21.3	27.4	27.0	27.7	29.6	31.6	33.3	34.7
Equals: Net farm value added	58.0	48.9	47.6	50.2	45.7	43.9	60.6	85.1	72.5	57.8	102.6
Compensation of employees	13.4	15.4	18.9	19.7	20.9	20.8	20.0	22.0	21.9	22.0	23.3
Taxes on production and imports	3.8	4.2	4.9	4.7	4.8	5.0	4.9	5.0	5.4	5.9	6.5
Less: Subsidies to operators	7.6	6.1	18.6	19.6	18.3	9.6	14.9	11.8	21.6	13.4	10.2
Net operating surplus	48.5	35.4	42.4	45.4	38.3	27.7	50.6	69.9	66.8	43.3	82.9
CHAINED (2000) DOLLARS [2]											
Farm output, total	**164.5**	**179.6**	**200.5**	**203.6**	**200.7**	**201.4**	**207.9**	**211.5**	**217.4**	**214.8**	**218.4**
Cash receipts from farm marketings . . .	159.0	183.5	192.0	196.6	190.1	194.1	195.5	191.9	202.2	202.2	200.6
Farm products consumed on farms . . .	0.7	0.5	0.6	0.6	0.5	0.5	0.4	0.4	0.4	0.5	0.5
Other farm income	4.8	5.8	9.5	8.4	9.4	10.1	10.7	11.8	13.7	13.7	14.4
Change in farm finished goods inventories	2.1	–8.8	–1.8	–2.0	0.6	–3.6	0.6	6.0	–0.1	–3.0	1.3
Less: Intermediate goods and services consumed [1]	117.5	134.4	138.1	132.1	135.3	131.3	131.7	128.4	126.3	129.5	125.1
Equals: **Gross farm value added**	**49.3**	**49.6**	**62.9**	**71.5**	**65.6**	**70.1**	**76.0**	**82.1**	**89.6**	**83.4**	**91.5**
Less: Consumption of fixed capital	23.0	21.3	21.6	21.3	27.0	26.2	26.5	27.3	27.9	28.5	28.8
Equals: Net farm value added	29.4	30.4	41.5	50.2	39.0	44.2	49.7	54.8	61.4	54.6	62.0

– Represents zero.   [1] Includes rent paid to nonoperator landlords.   [2] See text, Section 13.

Source: U.S. Bureau of Economic Analysis, *Survey of Current Business*, August 2008. See also <http://www.bea.gov /national/nipaweb/SelectTable.asp?Selected=N>.

Agriculture   529

Table 813. **Value Added to Economy by Agricultural Sector: 1990 to 2007**

[In billions of dollars (188.5 represents $188,500,000,000). Data are consistent with the net farm income accounts and include income and expenses related to the farm operator dwellings. The concept presented is consistent with that employed by the Organization for Economic Cooperation and Development. Minus sign (−) indicates decrease]

Item	1990	1995	1999	2000	2001	2002	2003	2004	2005	2006	2007
Value of agricultural sector production	188.5	203.6	213.4	220.4	229.3	220.2	243.5	282.7	276.7	276.6	329.2
Value of crop production	83.2	95.9	92.8	94.8	95.0	98.3	108.6	124.4	115.2	119.2	150.8
Food grains	7.5	10.4	6.9	6.5	6.4	6.8	8.0	8.9	8.6	9.1	12.8
Feed crops	18.7	24.5	19.5	20.5	21.5	24.0	24.7	27.4	24.7	29.4	42.5
Cotton	5.5	6.9	4.6	2.9	3.6	3.4	6.4	4.8	6.3	5.6	6.2
Oil crops	12.3	15.5	13.4	13.5	13.3	15.0	18.0	17.9	18.5	18.5	22.6
Tobacco	2.7	2.5	2.3	2.3	1.9	1.7	1.6	1.6	1.1	1.2	1.3
Fruits and tree nuts	9.4	11.0	12.0	12.4	11.9	12.6	13.4	15.5	17.4	17.2	17.8
Vegetables	11.3	15.0	15.0	15.5	15.4	17.1	16.9	16.2	17.0	18.5	20.0
All other crops	12.9	15.2	18.4	18.7	19.3	20.2	21.0	21.4	22.3	23.2	23.8
Home consumption	0.1	0.2	0.2	0.2	0.2	0.2	0.1	0.1	0.1	0.1	0.1
Value of inventory adjustment	2.8	−5.3	0.5	2.2	1.5	−2.9	−1.6	10.7	−0.8	−3.5	3.8
Value of livestock production	90.0	87.8	95.2	99.1	106.4	93.5	104.9	124.4	126.5	119.0	138.1
Meat animals	51.1	44.9	45.7	53.0	53.3	48.1	56.2	62.4	64.8	63.6	65.0
Dairy products	20.2	19.9	23.2	20.6	24.7	20.6	21.2	27.4	26.7	23.4	35.4
Poultry and eggs	15.3	19.1	22.9	21.9	24.6	21.1	24.0	29.5	28.7	26.5	32.6
Miscellaneous livestock	2.5	3.4	3.9	4.2	4.1	4.1	4.2	4.3	4.6	4.8	4.9
Home consumption	0.5	0.3	0.1	0.1	0.1	0.1	0.1	0.2	0.3	0.3	0.3
Value of inventory adjustment	0.4	0.2	−0.7	−0.6	−0.4	−0.6	−0.8	0.6	1.3	0.5	−0.1
Services and forestry	15.3	19.9	25.4	26.5	28.0	28.5	30.0	33.9	35.0	38.4	40.3
Machine hire and customwork	1.8	1.9	2.0	2.2	2.1	2.2	3.0	3.4	2.8	2.7	2.5
Forest products sold	1.8	2.8	2.7	2.8	2.6	2.5	2.2	2.4	2.5	2.5	2.4
Other farm income	4.5	5.8	10.1	8.7	10.1	10.2	10.5	11.3	10.9	12.3	11.8
Gross imputed rental value of farm dwellings	7.2	9.4	10.6	12.7	13.1	13.6	14.3	16.8	18.8	20.9	23.6
Less: Purchased inputs	92.2	108.8	118.7	121.8	125.7	123.3	130.3	137.4	144.0	153.6	171.4
Farm origin	39.5	41.8	45.5	47.9	48.2	48.3	53.7	57.5	56.9	61.0	68.8
Feed purchased	20.4	23.8	24.5	24.5	24.8	24.9	27.5	29.7	28.0	31.4	38.1
Livestock and poultry purchased	14.6	12.5	13.8	15.9	15.2	14.4	16.7	18.1	18.5	18.5	18.8
Seed purchased	4.5	5.5	7.2	7.5	8.2	8.9	9.4	9.6	10.4	11.0	11.9
Manufactured inputs	22.0	26.1	27.1	28.7	29.4	28.5	28.8	31.6	35.4	37.5	43.7
Fertilizers and lime	8.2	10.0	9.9	10.0	10.3	9.6	10.0	11.4	12.8	13.3	16.7
Pesticides	5.4	7.7	8.6	8.5	8.6	8.3	8.4	8.6	8.8	9.0	10.0
Petroleum fuel and oils	5.8	5.4	5.6	7.2	6.9	6.6	6.8	8.2	10.3	11.3	13.0
Electricity	2.6	3.0	3.0	3.0	3.6	3.9	3.5	3.4	3.5	3.8	3.9
Other purchased inputs	30.7	40.9	46.1	45.2	48.1	46.6	47.9	48.3	51.6	55.2	58.9
Repair and maintenance of capital items	8.6	9.6	10.7	10.9	11.2	10.5	11.0	11.9	11.9	12.5	13.6
Machine hire and custom work	3.0	3.9	4.4	4.1	4.0	4.0	3.5	3.6	3.5	3.5	3.7
Marketing, storage, and transportation expenses	4.2	7.2	7.3	7.5	7.8	7.6	7.1	7.2	8.8	9.0	9.8
Contract labor	1.6	2.0	2.5	2.7	3.1	2.7	3.3	3.1	3.1	3.0	3.8
Miscellaneous expenses	13.4	18.2	21.3	19.9	21.9	21.7	22.9	22.4	24.4	27.2	28.0
Plus: Net government transactions [1]	3.1	0.4	14.3	15.8	15.0	5.2	9.2	5.4	15.8	6.2	1.5
Direct Government payments	9.3	7.3	21.5	23.2	22.4	12.4	16.5	13.0	24.4	15.8	11.9
Motor vehicle registration and licensing fees	0.4	0.4	0.4	0.5	0.5	0.4	0.5	0.5	0.6	0.6	0.6
Property taxes	5.8	6.4	6.8	6.9	6.9	6.8	6.8	7.0	8.0	9.0	9.8
Equals: Gross value added	99.3	95.1	109.0	114.4	118.7	102.1	122.4	150.7	148.6	129.2	159.3
Less: Capital consumption	18.1	18.9	19.8	20.1	20.6	20.9	21.4	23.1	24.9	26.1	26.9
Equals: Net value added	81.2	76.2	89.2	94.3	98.2	81.1	100.9	127.6	123.6	103.1	132.5
Less: Employee compensation	12.4	14.3	17.4	17.9	18.8	19.1	18.7	20.2	20.5	21.2	21.8
Less: Net rent received by nonoperator landlords	9.0	9.6	10.4	11.2	11.2	9.6	10.1	10.0	10.6	9.4	8.8
Less: Real estate and nonreal estate interest	13.5	12.6	13.8	14.6	13.3	12.8	11.6	11.6	13.2	14.0	15.1
Equals: Net farm income	46.3	39.8	47.7	50.6	54.9	39.6	60.5	85.8	79.3	58.5	86.8

[1] Direct government payments minus motor vehicle registration and licensing fees and property taxes.

Source: U.S. Dept. of Agriculture, Economic Research Service, "United States and State Farm Income Data"; <http://www.ers.usda.gov/Data/farmincome/finfidmu.htm> (accessed 29 April 2009).

Table 814. **Cash Receipts for Selected Commodities—Leading States: 2007**

[In millions of dollars (49,722 represents $49,722,000,000). See headnote, Table 815]

State	Value	State	Value	State	Value	State	Value
Cattle and calves	49,722	**Dairy products**	35,425	**Corn**	33,923	**Broilers**	21,460
Texas	7,631	California	7,328	Iowa	6,351	Georgia	3,188
Nebraska	7,138	Wisconsin	4,593	Illinois	5,681	Arkansas	2,610
Kansas	6,318	New York	2,378	Nebraska	3,682	North Carolina	2,480
Colorado	3,175	Pennsylvania	2,219	Minnesota	3,055	Alabama	2,400
Iowa	2,676	Idaho	2,050	Indiana	2,714	Mississippi	1,984

Source: U.S. Department of Agriculture, Economic Research Service, "Farm Income" (published 28 August 2008); <http://www.ers.usda.gov/Data/FarmIncome/firkdmuXls.htm>.

Table 815. Farm Income—Cash Receipts From Farm Marketings: 2000 to 2007

[In millions of dollars (191,999 represents $191,999,000,000). Represents gross receipts from commercial market sales as well as net Commodity Credit Corporation loans. The source estimates and publishes individual cash receipt values only for major commodities and major producing states. The U.S. receipts for individual commodities, computed as the sum of the reported states, may understate the value of sales for some commodities. The degree of underestimation in some of the minor commodities can be substantial]

Commodity	2000	2005	2006	2007
Total	191,999	240,891	240,828	284,844
Livestock and products [1]	99,618	124,918	118,227	137,889
Cattle and calves	40,783	49,295	48,974	49,722
Hogs	11,758	14,992	14,091	14,786
Sheep and lambs . . .	470	560	485	485
Dairy products	20,587	26,698	23,405	35,425
Broilers	13,989	20,878	17,739	21,460
Chicken eggs	4,289	4,007	4,432	6,678
Turkeys	2,771	3,108	3,574	3,711
Horses/mules	1,239	1,125	1,209	1,219
Aquaculture [2]	798	1,055	1,072	1,126
Crops [1]	92,382	115,972	122,601	146,954
Rice	837	1,591	1,773	2,083
Wheat	5,672	6,994	7,298	10,686
Barley	556	676	443	654
Corn	15,162	18,480	22,886	33,923
Hay	3,855	4,712	5,195	6,281
Sorghum grain	864	693	778	1,423
Cotton	2,950	6,320	5,566	6,172
Tobacco	2,316	1,097	1,156	1,277
Peanuts	897	843	613	763
Soybeans	12,047	16,906	17,232	21,113
Vegetables [1]	15,530	17,030	18,457	19,965
Beans, dry	436	487	470	627
Potatoes	2,375	2,466	2,906	2,960
Beans, snap	393	416	445	522
Broccoli	622	570	674	737
Carrots	390	597	565	619
Corn, sweet	709	814	817	862

Commodity	2000	2005	2006	2007
Lettuce	1,863	1,940	2,453	2,757
Head	1,202	1,017	1,062	1,389
Romaine	299	386	594	708
Leaf	356	534	798	660
Onions	713	809	920	1,318
Tomatoes	1,845	2,237	2,330	2,188
Fresh	1,195	1,616	1,626	1,287
Processing	650	621	705	902
Watermelons	240	446	437	476
Fruits/nuts	12,385	17,440	17,195	17,802
Oranges	1,775	1,876	1,895	1,481
Apples	1,466	1,721	2,007	2,175
Cherries	327	548	519	625
Grapes [1]	3,100	3,491	3,302	3,452
Wine	1,909	2,215	1,848	1,855
Table	437	384	641	625
Raisins	487	595	509	602
Peaches	470	512	513	505
Strawberries	1,045	1,399	1,524	1,749
Blueberries	223	382	558	602
Almonds	666	2,526	2,259	2,127
Walnuts	296	557	564	754
Pistachios	245	580	450	562
Sugar beets	1,113	1,193	1,526	1,428
Cane for sugar	881	812	807	908
Greenhouse/nursery [1] .	13,710	16,823	17,027	17,179
Floriculture	4,576	5,435	4,027	4,096
Christmas trees	502	497	370	493
Mushrooms	867	913	913	900

[1] Includes other commodities not shown separately.   [2] See also Table 864.

Source: U.S. Department of Agriculture, Economic Research Service, "United States and State Farm Income Data"; <http://www.ers.usda.gov/Data/farmincome/finfidmu.htm> (accessed 4 September 2008).

Table 816. Farm Output, Income, and Government Payments by State: 2006 and 2007

[In millions of dollars (276,591 represents $276,591,000,000). Farm income data are after inventory adjustment and include income and expenses related to the farm operator's dwelling]

State	Final agricultural sector output		Net farm income		Government payments, 2007	State	Final agricultural sector output		Net farm income		Government payments, 2007
	2006	2007	2006	2007			2006	2007	2006	2007	
U.S. . . .	276,591	329,245	58,509	86,778	11,902						
AL	4,719	5,049	1,403	1,438	181	MT	2,832	3,372	324	761	258
AK	40	42	11	11	4	NE	13,173	16,121	1,994	3,392	441
AZ	3,405	4,058	707	1,158	93	NV	577	624	99	128	25
AR	6,866	7,820	1,656	2,161	484	NH	201	240	36	66	42
CA	34,616	39,094	8,012	12,747	479	NJ	1,062	1,121	266	312	13
CO	6,555	7,326	878	1,535	199	NM	2,749	3,294	429	822	53
CT	631	673	168	208	11	NY	3,912	4,964	779	1,609	48
DE	983	1,144	288	353	18	NC	10,018	10,569	3,256	2,807	570
FL	7,904	8,496	2,326	1,911	121	ND	4,475	6,342	680	1,992	390
GA	7,165	8,159	2,061	2,635	373	OH	6,779	8,437	1,388	1,950	269
HI	649	605	129	77	5	OK	5,611	6,462	762	1,069	249
ID	5,143	6,346	889	1,785	122	OR	4,874	5,402	986	1,483	124
IL	10,156	13,279	1,759	3,244	601	PA	5,689	6,726	1,489	2,155	77
IN	6,880	8,863	1,482	2,315	303	RI	80	90	22	38	11
IA	16,236	21,155	3,015	5,334	776	SC	2,270	2,377	610	535	165
KS	11,119	13,567	1,173	2,156	520	SD	4,903	7,212	707	2,302	317
KY	5,171	5,331	1,658	1,506	338	TN	3,432	3,270	645	375	307
LA	2,610	3,146	681	949	286	TX	19,382	23,851	4,860	7,181	1,346
ME	660	755	190	262	11	UT	1,622	1,831	250	400	37
MD	2,070	2,385	565	730	44	VT	554	758	94	263	14
MA	551	602	98	143	8	VA	3,448	3,791	663	800	133
MI	5,471	6,650	1,315	1,538	141	WA	6,835	8,210	1,050	2,449	185
MN	11,223	13,894	2,583	3,439	480	WV	640	691	30	49	13
MS	4,283	5,206	929	1,434	591	WI	8,127	10,313	1,374	2,654	208
MO	6,959	8,283	1,626	2,027	382	WY	1,282	1,248	118	90	35

Source: U.S. Department of Agriculture, Economic Research Service, "United States and State Farm Income Data"; <http://www.ers.usda.gov/Data/farmincome/finfidmu.htm> (accessed 2 September 2008).

Agriculture 531

Table 817. **Farm Income—Farm Marketings, 2006 and 2007, and Principal Commodities, 2007, by State**

[In millions of dollars (240,828 represents $240,828,000,000). Cattle include calves; and greenhouse includes nursery]

State	2006			2007			
	Total	Crops	Live-stock	Total	Crops	Live-stock	State rank for total farm marketings and four principal commodities in order of marketing receipts
U.S....	240,828	122,601	118,227	284,844	146,954	137,889	Cattle, dairy products, corn, broilers
AL	3,743	788	2,955	4,166	796	3,371	28-Broilers, cattle, greenhouse, chicken eggs
AK	32	25	8	33	26	7	50-Greenhouse, hay, potatoes, cattle
AZ	2,852	1,525	1,328	3,420	1,843	1,577	29-Dairy products, cattle, lettuce, hay
AR	5,995	2,357	3,638	7,138	3,038	4,100	13-Broilers, rice, soybeans, cotton
CA	31,816	24,269	7,547	36,575	25,840	10,735	1-Dairy products, greenhouse, grapes, lettuce
CO	5,796	1,687	4,109	6,290	2,019	4,271	17-Cattle, dairy products, wheat, corn
CT	529	375	154	564	361	202	43-Greenhouse, dairy products, chicken eggs, aquaculture
DE	842	182	660	1,005	209	795	39-Broilers, corn, soybeans, greenhouse
FL.	7,184	5,901	1,284	7,646	6,183	1,463	11-Greenhouse, oranges, tomatoes, dairy products
GA	5,696	2,108	3,588	6,814	2,452	4,362	16-Broilers, cotton, chicken eggs, greenhouse
HI	579	499	80	533	457	76	45-Greenhouse, sugar cane, coffee, cattle
ID......	4,542	2,123	2,418	5,682	2,413	3,269	21-Dairy products, cattle, potatoes, hay
IL	8,937	7,131	1,806	11,679	9,605	2,073	7-Corn, soybeans, hogs, cattle
IN	6,084	4,045	2,039	7,776	5,211	2,565	10-Corn, soybeans, hogs, dairy products
IA	15,262	7,490	7,772	19,037	10,180	8,857	3-Corn, hogs, soybeans, cattle
KS	10,335	3,359	6,976	11,729	4,518	7,212	6-Cattle, wheat, corn, soybeans
KY	4,031	1,358	2,673	4,432	1,475	2,958	25-Horses/mules, broilers, cattle, corn
LA	2,140	1,282	858	2,710	1,769	941	33-Sugar cane, corn, cotton, rice
ME	587	301	286	684	340	345	41-Dairy products, potatoes, blueberries, chicken eggs
MD	1,668	720	948	1,972	828	1,144	36-Broilers, greenhouse, dairy products, corn
MA	435	347	88	450	350	100	47-Greenhouse, cranberries, dairy products, sweet corn
MI.	4,587	2,931	1,656	5,742	3,375	2,367	19-Dairy products, corn, greenhouse, soybeans
MN	10,137	5,502	4,635	12,538	6,910	5,629	5-Corn, soybeans, hogs, dairy products
MS	3,663	1,212	2,450	4,342	1,588	2,754	27-Broilers, cotton, soybeans, corn
MO	5,562	2,523	3,039	6,920	3,469	3,451	14-Soybeans, cattle, corn, hogs
MT	2,335	1,056	1,279	2,394	1,237	1,157	34-Cattle, wheat, barley, hay
NE	12,193	4,523	7,670	14,556	6,198	8,358	4-Cattle, corn, soybeans, hogs
NV	464	185	279	553	216	337	44-Cattle, hay, dairy products, onions
NH	161	97	64	184	105	80	48-Greenhouse, dairy products, apples, cattle
NJ.	928	765	163	946	769	177	40-Greenhouse, horses/mules, blueberries, peaches
NM	2,467	605	1,862	3,058	700	2,358	30-Dairy products, cattle, hay, pecans
NY	3,485	1,534	1,951	4,447	1,724	2,723	24-Dairy products, greenhouse, apples, corn
NC	7,978	2,854	5,124	8,691	2,924	5,768	9-Broilers, hogs, greenhouse, tobacco
ND	4,108	3,210	898	5,490	4,534	957	22-Wheat, soybeans, cattle, corn
OH	5,614	3,630	1,984	6,898	4,372	2,526	15-Soybeans, corn, dairy products, greenhouse
OK	4,988	894	4,094	5,158	1,180	3,977	23-Cattle, hogs, broilers, wheat
OR	4,011	2,981	1,030	4,365	3,298	1,067	26-Greenhouse, cattle, dairy products, wheat
PA	4,740	1,776	2,963	5,760	1,929	3,831	18-Dairy products, cattle, mushrooms, corn
RI	65	55	10	70	59	11	49-Greenhouse, dairy products, sweet corn, aquaculture
SC	1,851	788	1,063	2,028	785	1,242	35-Broilers, greenhouse, turkeys, cattle
SD	4,743	2,081	2,662	5,734	3,029	2,705	20-Cattle, corn, soybeans, wheat
TN	2,466	1,298	1,168	2,741	1,342	1,399	32-Cattle, broilers, cotton, greenhouse
TX	16,315	5,959	10,356	19,075	7,688	11,386	2-Cattle, cotton, greenhouse, dairy products
UT	1,192	331	861	1,340	389	951	37-Dairy products, cattle, hay, hogs
VT	501	85	416	674	93	581	42-Dairy products, cattle, greenhouse, hay
VA	2,682	852	1,830	2,950	887	2,064	31-Broilers, cattle, dairy products, turkeys
WA....	6,110	4,491	1,619	7,450	5,323	2,127	12-Apples, dairy products, wheat, cattle
WV	432	72	360	480	81	399	46-Broilers, cattle, turkeys, dairy products
WI.	6,921	2,272	4,649	8,858	2,654	6,204	8-Dairy products, corn, cattle, soybeans
WY	1,042	166	876	1,066	184	882	38-Cattle, hay, hogs, sheep

Source: U.S. Department of Agriculture, Economic Research Service, "Farm Income: Cash Receipts" (published 28 August 2008); <http://www.ers.usda.gov/Data/FarmIncome/firkdmuXls.htm>.

Table 818. **Indexes of Prices Received and Paid by Farmers: 2000 to 2008**

[1990-1992 = 100, except as noted]

Item	2000	2005	2007	2008	Item	2000	2005	2007	2008
Prices received, all products	96	114	136	149	Prices paid, total [2].........	118	142	161	184
					Production	116	140	160	190
Crops	96	110	142	168	Feed	102	117	149	191
Food grains	85	111	186	258	Livestock and poultry	110	138	131	125
Feed grains and hay......	86	95	152	206	Seed	124	168	205	254
Cotton	82	70	82	100	Fertilizer..............	110	164	216	375
Tobacco	107	94	92	93	Agricultural chemicals	120	123	129	139
Oil-bearing crops	85	106	137	202	Fuels.................	134	216	264	372
Fruits and nuts	98	128	158	147	Supplies and repairs......	124	140	150	153
Commercial vegetables [1]...	121	130	158	151	Autos and trucks	119	114	111	109
Potatoes and dry beans ...	93	109	126	161	Farm machinery.........	139	173	191	204
All other crops..........	110	113	118	123	Building materials........	121	142	155	164
					Farm services	119	134	146	154
Livestock and products......	97	119	130	130	Rent	110	129	148	163
Meat animals	94	118	118	117	Interest	113	114	154	164
Dairy products..........	94	116	146	140	Taxes	123	154	187	203
Poultry and eggs	106	123	140	151	Wage rates	140	165	177	183
					Parity ratio (1910–14 = 100) [3]...	38	39	40	39

[1] Excludes potatoes and dry beans. [2] Includes production items, interest, taxes, wage rates, and a family living component. The family living component is the Consumer Price Index for all urban consumers from the Bureau of Labor Statistics. See text, Section 14 and Table 709. [3] Ratio of prices received by farmers to prices paid.

Source: U.S. Department of Agriculture, National Agricultural Statistics Service, *Agricultural Prices: Annual Summary*.

532 Agriculture

Table 819. **Civilian Consumer Expenditures for Farm Foods: 1990 to 2007**

[In billions of dollars, except percent (449.8 represents $449,800,000,000). Excludes imported and nonfarm foods, such as coffee and seafood, as well as food consumed by the military, or exported]

Item	1990	1995	1999	2000	2001	2002	2003	2004	2005	2006	2007
Consumer expenditures, total. . .	**449.8**	**529.5**	**625.3**	**661.1**	**687.5**	**709.4**	**744.2**	**788.9**	**830.7**	**880.7**	**925.2**
Farm value, total	106.2	113.8	122.2	123.3	130.0	132.5	140.2	155.5	157.8	163.2	194.3
Marketing bill, total [1]	343.6	415.7	503.1	537.8	557.5	576.9	604.0	633.4	672.9	717.5	731.0
Percent of total consumer expenditures	76.4	78.5	80.5	81.3	81.1	81.3	81.2	80.3	81.0	81.5	79.0
At-home expenditures [2]	276.2	316.9	370.7	390.2	403.9	416.8	437.2	463.5	488.1	517.5	543.7
Farm value	80.2	76.1	78.7	79.6	83.9	85.7	91.4	98.5	99.3	103.2	128.3
Marketing bill [1]	196.0	240.8	292.0	310.6	320.0	331.1	345.8	365.0	388.8	414.3	415.4
Away-from-home expenditures	173.6	212.6	254.6	270.9	283.6	292.6	307.0	325.4	342.6	363.2	381.5
Farm value	26.0	37.7	43.5	43.7	46.1	46.8	48.8	57.0	58.5	60.0	66.0
Marketing bill [1]	147.6	174.9	211.1	227.2	237.5	245.8	258.2	268.4	284.1	303.2	315.5
Marketing bill cost components:											
Labor cost	154.0	196.6	241.5	252.9	263.8	273.1	285.9	303.7	319.8	341.0	347.4
Packaging materials	36.5	48.2	50.9	53.5	55.0	56.8	59.5	63.1	66.5	70.5	71.8
Rail and truck transport	19.8	22.3	25.2	26.4	27.5	28.4	29.7	31.6	33.2	35.2	35.9
Corporate profits before taxes	13.2	19.5	29.2	31.1	32.0	33.0	34.6	35.5	37.4	39.7	40.4
Fuels and electricity.	15.2	18.6	22.0	23.1	24.1	24.9	26.1	27.6	31.6	33.5	34.1
Advertising	17.1	19.8	24.8	26.1	27.5	28.1	29.4	30.8	32.7	34.9	35.6
Depreciation	16.3	18.9	23.0	24.2	24.5	25.3	26.5	27.8	29.5	31.5	32.1
Net interest	13.5	11.6	14.4	16.9	18.6	19.2	20.1	21.1	22.4	23.9	24.3
Net rent	13.9	19.8	25.3	26.7	29.4	30.3	31.7	33.2	35.3	37.6	38.3
Repairs.	6.2	7.9	9.6	10.1	10.6	10.9	11.4	12.0	12.7	13.5	13.8
Taxes	15.7	19.1	22.2	23.5	24.1	24.9	26.1	27.4	29.1	31.0	31.6
Other	22.2	13.4	15.0	23.3	20.4	22.0	23.0	19.6	22.7	25.2	25.7

[1] The difference between expenditures for domestic farm-originated food products and the farm value or payment farmers received for the equivalent farm products.   [2] Food primarily purchased from retail food stores for use at home.

Source: U.S. Department of Agriculture, Economic Research Service, *Food Cost Review, 1950–97*, ERS Agricultural Economic Report No. AER780, June 1999; and "ERS/USDA Briefing Room—Food Marketing System in the U.S.: Price Spreads from Farm to Consumer"; <http://www.ers.usda.gov/Briefing/FoodMarketingSystem/pricespreads.htm>.

Table 820. **Agricultural Exports and Imports—Volume by Principal Commodities: 1990 to 2008**

[In thousands of metric tons (7,703 represents 7,703,000), except fruit juices, wine and malt beverages in thousands of hectoliters (1,000 hectoliters equals 264.18 gallons). Includes Puerto Rico, U.S. territories, and shipments under foreign aid programs. Excludes fish, forest products, distilled liquors, manufactured tobacco, and products made from cotton; but includes raw tobacco, raw cotton, rubber, beer and wine, and processed agricultural products]

Commodity	1990	2000	2004	2005	2006	2007	2008
EXPORTS							
Fruit juices and wine	7,703	14,356	15,383	13,982	14,438	14,470	14,977
Beef, pork, lamb, and poultry meats [1]. . .	1,451	4,935	3,844	4,343	4,617	5,103	6,574
Wheat, unmilled	27,384	27,568	31,044	27,040	23,208	32,991	30,066
Wheat products	863	844	381	313	281	448	389
Rice, paddy, milled	2,534	3,241	3,518	4,388	3,779	3,477	3,937
Feed grains	61,066	54,946	53,324	50,865	62,555	63,215	59,861
Feed grain products	1,430	2,062	2,566	3,442	4,153	4,002	1,478
Feeds and fodders [2]	10,974	13,065	11,393	11,422	11,372	11,823	15,833
Fresh fruits and nuts	2,648	3,450	3,501	3,675	3,569	3,553	4,040
Fruit products.	390	471	442	394	419	460	540
Vegetables, fresh	1,297	2,029	2,034	2,077	1,982	1,938	2,022
Vegetables, frozen and canned	529	1,112	1,046	1,086	1,150	1,261	1,603
Oilcake and meal	5,079	6,462	5,526	6,905	7,943	8,272	8,445
Oilseeds	15,820	28,017	26,091	26,462	29,373	31,077	35,097
Vegetable oils	1,226	2,043	1,939	1,937	2,222	2,539	2,900
Tobacco, unmanufactured	223	180	164	154	180	187	169
Cotton, excluding linters.	1,696	1,485	2,885	3,405	3,507	3,258	3,011
IMPORTS							
Fruit juices.	33,116	31,154	34,380	41,488	39,002	49,710	47,387
Wine	2,510	4,584	6,549	7,262	7,950	8,615	8,488
Malt beverages	10,382	23,464	27,946	29,947	34,356	34,749	33,667
Coffee, including products	1,214	1,370	1,323	1,307	1,359	1,393	1,393
Rubber and allied gums, crude	840	1,232	1,158	1,169	1,012	1,028	1,053
Beef, pork, lamb, and poultry meats [1]. . .	1,169	1,579	1,820	1,778	1,608	1,610	1,394
Grains [3]	2,071	4,622	3,701	3,726	4,718	5,576	6,435
Biscuits, pasta, and noodles	300	711	934	1,001	1,033	1,084	1,038
Feeds and fodders [2]	959	1,224	1,063	963	1,022	1,236	1,299
Fruits, nuts, and preparations [4]	5,401	8,354	9,122	9,570	9,897	10,706	10,546
Vegetables, fresh or frozen.	1,898	3,763	5,061	5,183	5,404	5,965	6,125
Tobacco, unmanufactured	173	216	254	233	249	243	220
Oilseeds and oilnuts	509	1,056	800	818	1,091	1,276	1,555
Vegetable oils and waxes.	1,204	1,846	2,274	2,386	2,897	3,117	3,708
Oilcake and meal	316	1,254	1,779	1,541	1,663	1,716	1,964

[1] Includes variety meats.   [2] Excluding oil meal.   [3] Includes wheat, corn, oats, barley, and rice.   [4] Includes bananas and plantains.

Source: U.S. Department of Agriculture, Economic Research Service, "Foreign Agricultural Trade of the United States (FATUS)"; <http://www.ers.usda.gov/data/fatus/> and "U.S. Trade Internet System"; <http://www.fas.usda.gov/ustrade>.

Agriculture   533

Table 821. **Agricultural Exports and Imports—Value: 1990 to 2008**

[In billions of dollars, except percent (16.6 represents $16,600,000,000). Includes Puerto Rico, U.S. territories, and shipments under foreign aid programs. Excludes fish, forest products, distilled liquors, manufactured tobacco, and products made from cotton; but includes raw tobacco, raw cotton, rubber, beer and wine, and processed agricultural products]

Year	Trade balance	Exports, domestic products	Percent of all exports	Imports for consumption	Percent of all imports	Year	Trade balance	Exports, domestic products	Percent of all exports	Imports for consumption	Percent of all imports
1990...	16.6	39.5	11	22.9	5	2002...	11.2	53.1	8	41.9	4
1995...	26.0	56.3	10	30.3	4	2003...	12.0	59.4	9	47.4	4
1997...	21.0	57.2	9	36.1	4	2004...	7.4	61.4	8	54.0	4
1998...	14.9	51.8	8	36.9	4	2005...	3.9	63.2	8	59.3	4
1999...	10.7	48.4	8	37.7	4	2006...	5.6	70.9	8	65.3	4
2000...	12.3	51.3	7	39.0	3	2007...	18.1	90.0	9	71.9	4
2001...	14.3	53.7	8	39.4	3	2008...	34.9	115.4	10	80.5	4

Source: U.S. Department of Agriculture, Economic Research Service, "Foreign Agricultural Trade of the United States (FATUS)"; <http://www.ers.usda.gov/data/fatus/> and U.S. Department of Agriculture, Foreign Agricultural Service, "U.S. Trade Internet System"; <http://www.fas.usda.gov/ustrade>.

Table 822. **Agricultural Imports—Value by Selected Commodity: 1990 to 2008**

[22,918 represents $22,918,000,000. See headnote, Table 821]

Commodity	Value (mil. dol.)							Percent distribution		
	1990	2000	2004	2005	2006	2007	2008	1990	2000	2008
Total [1]............	22,918	38,974	53,989	59,291	65,326	71,913	80,465	100.0	100.0	100.0
Cattle, live...........	978	1,152	543	1,039	1,546	1,878	1,761	4.3	3.0	2.2
Beef and veal	1,872	2,399	3,626	3,651	3,221	3,285	3,057	8.2	6.2	3.8
Pork...............	938	997	1,367	1,281	1,197	1,162	1,060	4.1	2.6	1.3
Dairy products	891	1,671	2,424	2,686	2,711	2,883	3,138	3.9	4.3	3.9
Grains and feeds	1,188	3,075	4,291	4,527	5,321	6,422	8,260	5.2	7.9	10.3
Fruits and preparations ...	2,167	3,851	5,079	5,842	6,517	7,439	7,896	9.5	9.9	9.8
Vegetables and preparations [2]........	1,979	3,958	6,077	6,410	7,008	7,713	8,314	8.6	10.2	10.3
Sugar and related products	1,213	1,555	2,107	2,494	3,046	2,592	2,967	5.3	4.0	3.7
Wine	917	2,207	3,416	3,762	4,155	4,638	4,635	4.0	5.7	5.8
Malt beverages	923	2,179	2,767	3,096	3,583	3,625	3,668	4.0	5.6	4.6
Oilseeds and products....	952	1,773	2,944	2,998	3,505	4,329	6,767	4.2	4.5	8.4
Coffee and products	1,915	2,700	2,263	2,976	3,313	3,768	4,412	8.4	6.9	5.5
Cocoa and products	1,072	1,404	2,484	2,751	2,659	2,662	3,299	4.7	3.6	4.1
Rubber, crude natural	707	842	1,466	1,552	2,029	2,119	2,857	3.1	2.2	3.6

[1] Includes other commodities not shown separately.   [2] Includes pulses.

Source: U.S. Department of Agriculture, Economic Research Service, "Foreign Agricultural Trade of the United States (FATUS)"; <http://www.ers.usda.gov/data/fatus/> and U.S. Department of Agriculture, Foreign Agricultural Service, "U.S. Trade Internet System"; <http://www.fas.usda.gov/ustrade>.

Table 823. **Agricultural Imports—Value by Selected Countries of Origin: 1990 to 2008**

[22,918 represents $22,918,000,000. See headnote, Table 821]

Country	Value (mil. dol.)							Percent distribution		
	1990	2000	2004	2005	2006	2007	2008	1990	2000	2008
Total [1]............	22,918	38,974	53,989	59,291	65,326	71,913	80,465	100.0	100.0	100.0
Canada..............	3,171	8,661	11,453	12,270	13,432	15,244	18,009	13.8	22.2	22.4
European Union [2]......	5,016	8,303	12,402	13,410	14,465	15,282	15,505	21.9	21.3	19.3
Mexico..............	2,614	5,077	7,262	8,331	9,391	10,169	10,900	11.4	13.0	13.5
China [3]............	273	812	1,615	1,872	2,265	2,916	3,454	1.2	2.1	4.3
Indonesia	683	998	1,490	1,702	2,042	2,081	2,816	3.0	2.6	3.5
Brazil	1,563	1,144	1,674	1,952	2,231	2,644	2,616	6.8	2.9	3.3
Australia	1,174	1,592	2,486	2,421	2,487	2,633	2,424	5.1	4.1	3.0
Chile	481	1,026	1,342	1,521	1,777	1,837	2,049	2.1	2.6	2.5
Thailand	470	779	1,083	1,094	1,330	1,507	1,917	2.0	2.0	2.4
Malaysia	308	353	577	666	829	1,139	1,867	1.3	0.9	2.3
New Zealand	855	1,132	1,598	1,712	1,669	1,733	1,828	3.7	2.9	2.3
Colombia............	790	1,123	1,162	1,437	1,480	1,539	1,769	3.4	2.9	2.2
India...............	285	826	858	923	1,042	1,166	1,603	1.2	2.1	2.0
Guatemala	497	710	784	920	924	1,064	1,313	2.2	1.8	1.6
Argentina	389	672	616	831	992	1,079	1,257	1.7	1.7	1.6
Costa Rica	400	812	899	916	1,163	1,236	1,206	1.7	2.1	1.5
Philippines...........	418	468	553	568	640	704	916	1.8	1.2	1.1
Peru...............	90	196	348	448	602	683	817	0.4	0.5	1.0
Vietnam	(NA)	200	376	422	495	663	760	(NA)	0.5	0.9
Ecuador	482	451	581	596	669	691	746	2.1	1.2	0.9

NA Not available.   [1] Includes other countries not shown separately.   [2] For consistency, data for all years are shown on the basis of 27 countries in the European Union; see footnote 5, Table 1339.   [3] See footnote 4, Table 1296.

Source: U.S. Department of Agriculture, Foreign Agricultural Service, "U.S. Trade Internet System"; <http://www.fas.usda.gov/ustrade>; (accessed 13 April 2009).

Table 824. Selected Farm Products—U.S. and World Production and Exports: 2000 to 2008

[In metric tons, except as indicated (61 represents 61,000,000). Metric ton = 1.102 short tons or .984 long tons]

Commodity	Unit	Amount						United States as percent of world		
		United States			World					
		2000	2005	2008	2000	2005	2008	2000	2005	2008
PRODUCTION [1]										
Wheat	Million	61	57	68	581	620	682	10.4	9.2	10.0
Corn for grain	Million	252	282	307	590	698	786	42.7	40.4	39.1
Soybeans	Million	75	84	81	176	221	219	42.6	37.8	36.8
Rice, milled	Million	5.9	7.1	6.5	398	418	441	1.5	1.7	1.5
Cotton [2]	Million bales [3] . . .	17.0	23.3	19.2	87.7	121.4	120.6	19.3	19.1	15.9
EXPORTS [4]										
Wheat [5]	Million	28.0	27.4	26.5	104.0	113.9	130.6	26.9	24.1	20.3
Corn	Million	48.3	56.1	44.0	76.4	82.6	76.1	63.3	67.9	57.8
Soybeans	Million	27.1	25.6	32.9	53.9	63.8	74.1	50.3	40.1	44.5
Rice, milled basis	Million	2.8	3.9	3.4	22.8	29.2	29.4	12.5	13.2	11.5
Cotton [2]	Million bales [3] . . .	6.8	14.4	13.7	27.1	35.0	38.4	24.9	41.2	35.5

[1] Production years vary by commodity. In most cases, includes harvests from July 1 of the year shown through June 30 of the following year.   [2] For production and trade years ending in year shown.   [3] Bales of 480 lb. net weight.   [4] Trade years may vary by commodity. Wheat, corn, and soybean data are for trade year beginning in year shown. Rice data are for calendar year.   [5] Includes wheat flour on a grain equivalent.

Source: U.S. Department of Agriculture, Foreign Agricultural Service, *Foreign Agricultural Commodity Circular Series*, periodic; <http://www.fas.usda.gov/commodities.asp>.

Table 825. Percent of U.S. Agricultural Commodity Output Exported: 1990 to 2007

[All export shares are estimated from export and production volumes]

Commodity group	1990–94, average	1995–99, average	2000–04, average	2000	2004	2005	2006	2007
Total agriculture	**25.7**	**24.9**	**24.5**	**24.6**	**24.0**	**22.6**	**24.1**	**25.2**
Livestock [1]	5.5	6.1	6.1	6.1	5.3	5.5	5.8	7.2
Red meat	4.1	7.1	8.0	8.1	5.8	7.4	8.7	9.4
Poultry meat	7.4	15.5	14.9	15.5	13.7	14.4	14.3	15.7
Dairy products	3.5	1.4	1.3	1.3	1.3	1.3	1.3	2.6
Crops [2]	30.4	29.1	28.8	28.8	28.3	26.2	28.3	29.6
Grains, food and feed	30.2	27.3	25.9	26.7	25.7	21.8	25.0	25.6
Oilseeds & products [3]	24.8	26.7	27.4	27.4	24.5	26.2	23.8	27.9
Fruit and nuts	16.4	17.7	18.4	17.0	18.9	20.2	21.6	21.0
Vegetables	4.9	5.6	5.8	5.6	5.5	6.3	6.5	6.1
Other field crops [4]	24.9	22.6	25.5	19.0	32.4	32.6	37.0	29.0

[1] Includes eggs, animal fat, and inedible animal products. Excludes live animals, hides, and skins.   [2] Includes wine, beer, and essential oils. Excludes nursery products.   [3] Includes flaxseed, corn oil, linseed meal and oil, and olive oil.   [4] Includes cotton, sugar, tobacco, and seeds.

Source: U.S. Department of Agriculture, Economic Research Service, "Food Availability (Per Capita) Data System, Food Availability: Spreadsheets"; <http://www.ers.usda.gov/Data/FoodConsumption/FoodAvailSpreadsheets.htm>; and USDA Foreign Agricultural Service, "Production, Supply, and Distribution"; and trade data <http://www.fas.usda.gov/>.

Table 826. Top 10 U.S. Export Markets for Selected Commodities: 2008

[In thousands of metric tons (53,879 represents 53,879,000)]

Corn		Wheat [1]		Soybeans		Poultry meat	
Country	Amount	Country	Amount	Country	Amount	Country	Amount
World, total	**53,879**	**World, total . . .**	**30,066**	**World, total . . .**	**33,894**	**World, total . . .**	**3,564**
Japan	15,181	Japan	3,676	China [2]	16,516	Russia	836
Mexico	9,153	Mexico	2,804	Mexico	3,552	Mexico	484
Korea, South	7,950	Nigeria	2,607	Japan	2,815	China [2]	376
Taiwan [2]	3,245	Egypt	2,161	Taiwan [2]	1,886	Ukraine	179
Canada	2,644	Iraq	2,018	Germany	1,750	Canada	165
Colombia	2,567	Philippines	1,775	Indonesia	1,323	Cuba	146
Egypt	2,438	Iran	1,645	Egypt	772	Angola	106
Venezuela	1,142	Korea, South	1,321	Spain	657	Lithuania	90
Dominican Republic . .	1,042	Colombia	954	Netherlands	601	Hong Kong	69
Israel	812	Indonesia	927	Turkey	497	Turkey	68
Rest of world	7,705	Rest of world	10,177	Rest of world	3,525	Rest of world	1,046

[1] Unmilled.   [2] See footnote 4, Table 1296.   [3] Includes Gaza Strip and West Bank.

Source: U.S. Department of Agriculture, Foreign Agricultural Service, "FAS Online, U.S. Trade Exports—FATUS Commodity Aggregations"; <http://www.fas.usda.gov/ustrade/USTExFatus.asp>; (accessed 13 April 2009).

Agriculture   535

Table 827. **Agricultural Exports—Value by Principal Commodities: 1990 to 2008**

[(39,495 represents $39,495,000,000). See headnote, Table 821]

Commodity	Value (mil. dol.)							Percent distribution		
	1990	2000	2004	2005	2006	2007	2008	1990	2000	2008
Total agricultural exports . . .	39,495	51,265	61,426	63,182	70,948	89,990	115,439	100.0	100.0	100.0
Animals and animal products [1]	6,636	11,600	10,369	12,226	13,495	17,188	21,831	16.8	22.6	18.9
Meat and meat products	2,558	5,276	3,240	4,299	5,183	6,122	8,783	6.5	10.3	7.6
Poultry and poultry products. . . .	910	2,235	2,577	3,138	2,932	4,092	5,053	2.3	4.4	4.4
Grains and feeds [1]	14,386	13,620	17,636	16,364	19,142	27,896	36,952	36.4	26.6	32.0
Wheat and products	4,035	3,578	5,273	4,520	4,359	8,616	11,604	10.2	7.0	10.1
Corn	6,037	4,469	5,875	4,789	6,992	9,763	13,454	15.3	8.7	11.7
Fruits and preparations.	2,007	2,743	3,162	3,468	3,760	4,155	4,841	5.1	5.4	4.2
Nuts and preparations	978	1,322	2,276	2,992	3,153	3,387	3,781	2.5	2.6	3.3
Vegetables and preparations [2]	1,836	3,112	3,258	3,571	3,913	4,307	5,130	4.6	6.1	4.4
Oilseeds and products [1]	5,725	8,584	10,439	10,229	11,307	15,601	23,712	14.5	16.7	20.5
Soybeans	3,550	5,258	6,668	6,274	6,936	9,992	15,469	9.0	10.3	13.4
Vegetable oils and waxes	832	1,259	1,677	1,656	1,832	2,503	3,892	2.1	2.5	3.4
Tobacco, unmanufactured	1,441	1,204	1,044	990	1,141	1,208	1,238	3.6	2.3	1.1
Cotton, excluding linters	2,783	1,873	4,226	3,921	4,502	4,578	4,829	7.0	3.7	4.2
Other.	3,702	7,207	9,016	9,421	10,533	11,671	13,125	9.4	14.1	11.4

[1] Includes commodities not shown separately. [2] Includes pulses.

Source: U.S. Department of Agriculture, Economic Research Service, "Foreign Agricultural Trade of the United States (FATUS)"; <http://www.ers.usda.gov/data/fatus/> and U.S. Department of Agriculture, Foreign Agricultural Service, "U.S. Trade Internet System"; <http://www.fas.usda.gov/ustrade>.

Table 828. **Agricultural Exports—Value by Selected Countries of Destination: 1990 to 2008**

[(39,495 represents $39,495,000,000). See headnote, Table 821]

Country	Value (mil. dol.)							Percent distribution		
	1990	2000	2004	2005	2006	2007	2008	1990	2000	2008
Total agricultural exports [1] . . .	39,495	51,265	61,426	63,182	70,948	89,990	115,439	100.0	100.0	100.0
Canada	4,214	7,643	9,742	10,618	11,951	14,062	16,240	10.7	14.9	14.1
Mexico	2,560	6,410	8,510	9,429	10,881	12,692	16,027	6.5	12.5	13.9
Caribbean.	1,015	1,408	1,850	1,913	2,114	2,575	3,598	2.6	2.7	3.1
Central America	483	1,121	1,429	1,589	1,832	2,363	3,099	1.2	2.2	2.7
South America	1,063	1,704	1,955	1,943	2,364	3,510	5,336	2.7	3.3	4.6
Asia, excluding Middle East [2]	15,857	19,877	23,009	22,543	25,743	32,427	44,355	40.1	38.8	38.4
Japan	8,142	9,292	8,147	7,931	8,390	10,159	13,265	20.6	18.1	11.5
Korea, South	2,650	2,546	2,489	2,233	2,851	3,528	5,568	6.7	5.0	4.8
Taiwan [3]	1,663	1,996	2,065	2,301	2,477	3,097	3,419	4.2	3.9	3.0
China [3, 4].	818	1,716	5,542	5,233	6,711	8,314	12,165	2.1	3.3	10.5
Indonesia	275	668	925	958	1,102	1,542	2,230	0.7	1.3	1.9
Europe/Eurasia [2]	10,162	7,676	8,319	8,569	8,761	10,815	12,942	25.7	15.0	11.2
European Union [5]	7,474	6,515	6,953	7,052	7,408	8,754	10,095	18.9	12.7	8.7
Russia	(X)	580	802	972	820	1,329	1,838	(X)	1.1	1.6
Middle East.	1,728	2,323	2,833	2,844	3,332	4,952	6,659	4.4	4.5	5.8
Africa [2].	1,848	2,308	2,953	2,773	3,087	5,188	5,810	4.7	4.5	5.0
Egypt	687	1,050	935	819	1,022	1,801	2,050	1.7	2.0	1.8
Oceania	343	490	601	742	760	963	1,190	0.9	1.0	1.0

X Not applicable. [1] Totals include transshipments through Canada, but transshipments are not distributed by country after 1998. [2] Includes areas not shown separately. [3] See footnote 4, Table 1296. [4] China includes Macao. However Hong Kong remains separate economically until 2050 and is not included. [5] For consistency, data for all years are shown on the basis of 27 countries in the European Union; see footnote 5, Table 1339.

Source: U.S. Department of Agriculture, Economic Research Service, "Foreign Agricultural Trade of the United States (FATUS)"; <http://www.ers.usda.gov/data/fatus/> and U.S. Department of Agriculture, Foreign Agricultural Service, "U.S. Trade Internet System"; <http://www.fas.usda.gov/ustrade>.

Table 829. **Cropland Used for Crops and Acreages of Crops Harvested: 1990 to 2008**

[In millions of acres, except as indicated (341 represents 341,000,000)]

Item	1990	1995	2000	2002	2003	2004	2005	2006	2007	2008
Cropland used for crops.	341	332	345	340	342	336	337	330	336	340
Index (1977 = 100)	90	88	91	90	90	89	89	87	89	90
Cropland harvested [1]	310	302	314	307	316	312	314	303	312	316
Crop failure	6	8	11	17	10	9	6	11	7	8
Cultivated summer fallow	25	22	20	16	16	15	16	15	16	16
Cropland idled by all federal programs	62	55	31	34	34	35	35	37	37	34
Acres of crops harvested [2] . . .	322	314	325	316	324	321	321	312	321	325

[1] Land supporting one or more harvested crops. [2] Area in principal crops harvested as reported by Crop Reporting Board plus acreages in fruits, vegetables for sale, tree nuts, and other minor crops.

Source: U.S. Department of Agriculture, Economic Research Service, *Major Uses of Land in the United States, 2002*, 2006; Also in *Agricultural Statistics*, annual. Beginning 1995, *Agricultural Resources and Environmental Indicators*, periodic, and *AREI Updates: Cropland Use.* See also ERS Briefing Room at <http://www.ers.usda.gov/Briefing/LandUse/majorlandusechapter .htm#trends>.

536   Agriculture

Table 830. **Principal Crops—Production, Supply, and Disappearance: 2000 to 2008**

[72.4 represents 72,400,000. Marketing year beginning January 1 for potatoes, May 1 for hay, June 1 for wheat, August 1 for cotton, September 1 for soybeans and corn. Acreage, production, and yield of all crops periodically revised on basis of census data]

Item	Unit	2000	2003	2004	2005	2006	2007	2008
CORN FOR GRAIN								
Acreage harvested	Million	72.4	70.9	73.6	75.1	70.6	86.5	78.6
Yield per acre	Bushel.	137	142	160	148	149	151	154
Production	Mil. bu.	9,915	10,087	11,806	11,112	10,531	13,038	12,101
Farm price [1]	Dol./bu.	1.85	2.42	2.06	2.00	3.04	4.20	3.90
Farm value	Mil. dol.	18,499	24,472	24,378	22,194	32,083	54,667	47,378
Total supply [2]	Mil. bu.	11,639	11,189	12,775	13,235	12,510	14,362	13,740
Total disappearance [3] . . .	Mil. bu.	9,740	10,230	10,661	11,268	11,207	12,737	12,000
Ethanol.	Mil. bu.	(NA)	1,168	1,323	1,603	2,119	3,026	3,700
Exports	Mil. bu.	1,941	1,900	1,818	2,134	2,125	2,436	1,700
Ending stocks	Mil. bu.	1,899	958	2,114	1,967	1,304	1,624	1,740
SOYBEANS								
Acreage harvested	Million	72.4	72.5	74.0	71.3	74.6	64.1	74.6
Yield per acre	Bushel.	38.1	33.9	42.2	43.1	42.9	41.7	39.6
Production	Mil. bu.	2,758	2,454	3,124	3,068	3,197	2,677	2,959
Farm price [1]	Dol./bu.	4.54	7.34	5.74	5.66	6.43	10.10	9.25
Farm value	Mil. dol.	12,467	18,015	17,896	17,297	20,468	26,974	27,399
Total supply [2]	Mil. bu.	3,052	2,638	3,242	3,327	3,655	3,261	3,173
Total disappearance [3] . . .	Mil. bu.	2,804	2,525	2,986	2,878	3,081	3,056	2,988
Exports.	Mil. bu.	996	887	1,097	940	1,116	1,161	1,185
Ending stocks	Mil. bu.	248	112	256	449	574	205	185
HAY								
Acreage harvested	Million	60.4	63.4	61.9	61.6	60.6	61.0	60.1
Yield per acre	Sh. tons.	2.54	2.48	2.55	2.44	2.32	2.41	2.43
Production	Mil. sh. tons . . .	154	157	158	150	141	147	146
Farm price [4], [5]	Dol./ton	84.60	85.50	92.00	98.20	110.00	128.00	157.00
Farm value	Mil. dol.	11,557	11,987	12,198	12,534	13,634	16,842	18,777
WHEAT								
Acreage harvested	Million	53.1	53.1	50.0	50.1	46.8	51.0	55.7
Yield per acre	Bushel.	42.0	44.2	43.2	42.0	38.6	40.2	44.9
Production	Mil. bu.	2,228	2,344	2,157	2,103	1,808	2,051	2,500
Farm price [1]	Dol./bu.	2.62	3.40	3.40	3.42	4.26	6.48	6.80
Farm value	Mil. dol.	5,782	7,928	7,278	7,167	7,695	13,289	16,568
Total supply [2]	Mil. bu.	3,268	2,899	2,774	2,725	2,501	2,620	2,925
Total disappearance [3] . . .	Mil. bu.	2,392	2,352	2,234	2,154	2,045	2,314	2,213
Exports.	Mil. bu.	1,062	1,158	1,066	1,003	908	1,264	980
Ending stocks	Mil. bu.	876	546	540	571	456	306	712
COTTON								
Acreage harvested	Million	13.1	12.0	13.1	13.8	12.7	10.5	7.7
Yield per acre	Pounds	632	730	855	831	814	879	810
Production [6]	Mil. bales [7]. . . .	17.2	18.3	23.3	23.9	21.6	19.2	13.0
Farm price [1]	Cents/lb.	51.6	63.0	43.5	49.7	48.4	61.3	56.6
Farm value	Mil. dol.	4,260	5,517	4,854	5,695	5,013	5,653	3,539
Total supply [2]	Mil. bales [7]. . . .	21.1	23.7	26.7	29.4	27.7	28.7	23.1
Total disappearance [3] . . .	Mil. bales [7]. . . .	15.6	20.0	21.1	23.4	17.9	18.3	15.8
Exports.	Mil. bales [7]. . . .	6.7	13.8	14.4	17.5	13.0	13.7	12.0
Ending stocks [8]	Mil. bales [7]. . . .	6.0	3.4	5.5	6.1	9.5	10.0	7.3
POTATOES								
Acreage harvested	Million [9]	1.3	1.2	1.2	1.1	1.1	1.1	1.0
Yield per acre	Cwt. [9]	381	367	391	390	393	396	395
Production	Mil. cwt. [9]	514	458	456	424	441	445	413
Farm price [1]	Dol./cwt. [9]	5.08	5.88	5.65	7.04	7.31	7.51	9.46
Farm value	Mil. dol.	2,591	2,677	2,565	2,982	3,209	3,340	3,899

NA Not available.   [1] Marketing year average price. U.S. prices are computed by weighting U.S. monthly prices by estimated monthly marketings and do not include an allowance for outstanding loans and government purchases and payments.   [2] Comprises production, imports, and beginning stocks.   [3] Includes feed, residual, and other domestic uses not shown separately.   [4] Prices are for hay sold baled.   [5] Season average prices received by farmers. U.S. prices are computed by weighting state prices by estimated sales.   [6] State production figures, which conform with annual ginning enumeration with allowance for cross-state ginnings, rounded to thousands and added for U.S. totals.   [7] Bales of 480 pounds, net weight.   [8] Stock estimates based on Census Bureau data which results in an unaccounted difference between supply and use estimates and changes in ending stocks.   [9] Cwt = hundredweight (100 pounds).

Source: Production—U.S. Department of Agriculture, National Agricultural Statistics Service, *Crop Production*, annual; and *Crop Values*, annual. Supply and disappearance—U.S. Department of Agriculture, Economic Research Service, *Feed Situation*, quarterly; *Fats and Oils Situation*, quarterly; *Wheat Situation*, quarterly; *Cotton and Wool Outlook Statistics*, periodic; and *Agricultural Supply and Demand Estimates*, periodic. Data are also in *Agricultural Statistics*, annual; and "Agricultural Outlook: Statistical Indicators"; <http://www.ers.usda.gov/publications/agoutlook/aotables/>.

Agriculture   537

Table 831. Corn—Acreage, Production, and Value by Leading States: 2006 to 2008

[70,638 represents 70,638,000. One bushel of corn = 56 pounds]

State	Acreage harvested (1,000 acres)			Yield per acre (bu.)			Production (mil. bu.)			Price ($/bu.)			Farm value (mil. dol.)		
	2006	2007	2008	2006	2007	2008	2006	2007	2008	2006	2007	2008	2006	2007	2008
U.S. [1]..	70,638	86,520	78,640	149	151	154	10,531	13,038	12,101	3.04	4.20	3.90	32,083	54,667	47,378
IA	12,350	13,900	12,800	166	171	171	2,050	2,377	2,189	3.03	4.29	3.95	6,212	10,197	8,646
IL	11,150	13,050	11,900	163	175	179	1,817	2,284	2,130	3.07	4.09	3.80	5,580	9,341	8,094
NE	7,750	9,200	8,550	152	160	163	1,178	1,472	1,394	3.00	4.14	3.90	3,534	6,094	5,435
MN	6,850	7,850	7,200	161	146	164	1,103	1,146	1,181	2.89	4.13	3.80	3,187	4,733	4,487
IN	5,380	6,370	5,460	157	154	160	845	981	874	3.17	4.39	3.75	2,678	4,307	3,276
SD	3,220	4,480	4,400	97	121	133	312	542	585	2.88	4.17	3.60	900	2,260	2,107
KS	3,000	3,680	3,630	115	138	134	345	508	486	3.08	4.13	4.25	1,063	2,097	2,067
OH	2,960	3,610	3,120	159	150	135	471	542	421	3.08	4.29	3.95	1,450	2,323	1,664
WI	2,800	3,280	2,880	143	135	137	400	443	395	3.04	4.11	3.50	1,217	1,820	1,381
MO	2,630	3,270	2,650	138	140	144	363	458	382	3.06	4.17	4.00	1,111	1,909	1,526
MI	1,950	2,340	2,140	147	123	138	287	288	295	3.10	4.37	3.60	889	1,258	1,063
ND	1,400	2,350	2,300	111	116	124	155	273	285	2.77	4.06	3.85	430	1,107	1,098
TX	1,450	1,970	2,030	121	148	125	175	292	254	3.20	4.35	4.80	561	1,268	1,218
KY	1,040	1,340	1,120	146	128	136	152	172	152	3.18	4.14	4.05	483	710	617
CO	860	1,060	1,080	156	140	137	134	148	148	3.02	3.96	3.95	405	588	584
PA	960	980	880	122	124	133	117	122	117	3.54	4.56	3.75	415	554	439
MS	325	910	700	107	148	140	35	135	98	2.84	3.68	4.60	99	496	451
NY	480	550	640	129	128	144	62	70	92	3.42	5.05	4.30	212	356	396
TN	500	790	630	125	106	118	63	84	74	2.93	3.80	4.50	183	318	335
LA	290	730	510	140	163	144	41	119	73	2.80	3.80	4.45	114	452	327
AR	180	590	430	146	169	155	26	100	67	2.73	3.80	4.35	72	379	290

[1] Includes other states, not shown separately.

Source: U.S. Department of Agriculture, National Agricultural Statistics Service, *Crop Production*, annual; and *Crop Values*, annual.

Table 832. Soybeans—Acreage, Production, and Value by Leading States: 2006 to 2008

[74,602 represents 74,602,000. One bushel of soybeans = 60 pounds]

State	Acreage harvested (1,000 acres)			Yield per acre (bu.)			Production (mil. bu.)			Price ($/bu.)			Farm value (mil. dol.)		
	2006	2007	2008	2006	2007	2008	2006	2007	2008	2006	2007	2008	2006	2007	2008
U.S. [1]..	74,602	64,146	74,641	43	42	40	3,197	2,677	2,959	6.43	10.10	9.25	20,468	26,974	27,399
IA	10,100	8,630	9,670	51	52	46	510	449	445	6.58	10.50	9.65	3,356	4,712	4,293
IL	10,050	8,280	9,100	48	44	47	482	360	428	6.68	10.40	9.35	3,222	3,746	3,999
MN	7,250	6,290	6,950	45	43	38	323	267	264	6.26	10.20	9.60	2,020	2,727	2,535
IN	5,680	4,790	5,430	50	46	45	284	220	244	6.53	10.20	9.30	1,855	2,247	2,272
NE	5,010	3,850	4,860	50	51	47	251	196	226	6.05	9.92	9.40	1,516	1,948	2,124
MO	5,110	4,670	5,030	38	38	38	194	175	191	6.47	10.10	9.00	1,256	1,769	1,720
OH	4,620	4,240	4,480	47	47	36	217	199	161	6.46	9.93	9.60	1,403	1,979	1,548
SD	3,850	3,240	4,060	34	42	34	131	136	138	6.03	9.60	9.05	789	1,306	1,249
AR	3,070	2,820	3,250	35	36	38	107	102	124	6.41	9.02	8.85	689	916	1,093
KS	3,080	2,610	3,250	32	33	37	99	86	120	6.37	10.10	8.60	628	870	1,034
ND	3,870	3,060	3,760	32	36	28	122	109	105	5.98	9.63	9.10	729	1,046	958
MS	1,650	1,440	1,960	26	41	40	43	58	78	6.23	8.36	8.75	267	488	686
MI	1,990	1,790	1,890	46	40	37	92	72	70	6.27	9.69	9.20	574	694	643
WI	1,640	1,380	1,590	44	41	35	72	56	56	6.04	9.83	9.20	436	549	512

[1] Includes other states, not shown separately.

Source: U.S. Department of Agriculture, National Agricultural Statistics Service, *Crop Production*, annual; and *Crop Values*, annual.

Table 833. Wheat—Acreage, Production, and Value by Leading States: 2006 to 2008

[46,800 represents 46,800,000. One bushel of wheat = 60 pounds]

State	Acreage harvested (1,000 acres)			Yield per acre (bu.)			Production (mil. bu.)			Price ($/bu.)			Farm value (mil. dol.)		
	2006	2007	2008	2006	2007	2008	2006	2007	2008	2006	2007	2008	2006	2007	2008
U.S. [1]..	46,800	50,999	55,685	38.6	40.2	44.9	1,808	2,051	2,500	4.26	6.48	6.80	7,695	13,289	16,568
KS	9,100	8,600	8,900	32.0	33.0	40.0	291	284	356	4.56	5.93	7.15	1,328	1,683	2,545
ND	8,290	8,405	8,640	30.3	35.6	36.0	252	299	311	4.50	7.74	7.20	1,130	2,340	2,299
SD	2,576	3,327	3,420	32.6	43.1	50.5	84	144	173	4.44	6.42	6.80	374	899	1,175
OK	3,400	3,500	4,500	24.0	28.0	37.0	82	98	167	4.70	6.22	6.50	384	610	1,082
MT	5,215	5,065	5,470	29.4	29.6	30.1	153	150	165	4.54	7.14	6.55	694	1,076	1,091
WA	2,225	2,137	2,225	62.1	58.7	52.8	138	125	118	4.49	7.58	6.40	618	949	755
MN	1,695	1,710	1,870	47.4	47.9	55.9	80	82	104	4.55	7.28	6.80	364	595	714
TX	1,400	3,800	3,300	24.0	37.0	30.0	34	141	99	4.47	6.40	7.45	150	900	738

[1] Includes other states, not shown separately.

Source: U.S. Department of Agriculture, National Agricultural Statistics Service, *Crop Production*, annual; and *Crop Values*, annual.

Table 834. Commercial Vegetable and Other Specified Crops—Area, Production, and Value, 2006 to 2008, and Leading Producing States, 2008

[297 represents 297,000. Except as noted, relates to commercial production for fresh market and processing combined. Includes market garden areas but excludes minor producing acreage in minor producing states. Excludes production for home use in farm and nonfarm gardens. Value is for season or crop year and should not be confused with calendar-year income]

Crop	Area [1] (1,000 acres)			Production [2] (1,000 short tons)			Value [3] (mil. dol.)			Leading states in order of production, 2008
	2006	2007	2008	2006	2007	2008	2006	2007	2008	
Beans, snap	297	295	293	1,097	1,079	1,118	434	524	508	(NA)
Fresh market	94	96	95	311	325	310	310	398	331	FL, GA
Processed	203	199	198	786	754	808	123	127	177	WI, OR
Broccoli	131	130	125	952	959	988	634	695	708	CA, AZ
Cabbage [4]	69	69	67	1,171	1,194	1,246	324	386	367	NY, CA, FL
Cantaloupes [4]	79	74	72	975	1,021	965	336	302	371	CA, AZ, GA
Carrots	93	94	89	1,618	1,599	1,633	529	568	634	CA [4]
Cauliflower	39	38	37	348	341	340	219	233	270	CA
Celery	28	28	28	962	1,001	1,001	350	408	338	CA, MI
Corn, sweet.	603	602	593	4,373	4,323	4,286	797	883	1,083	(NA)
Fresh market	218	234	233	1,287	1,425	1,453	591	646	753	FL, CA, GA
Processed	385	368	361	3,086	2,897	2,832	206	237	330	MN, WI, WA
Cucumbers	154	152	147	959	1,026	1,062	384	415	421	FL, GA [4]
Garlic.	26	25	25	216	205	214	127	169	187	CA, OR
Lettuce, head [4]	179	162	149	3,125	2,874	2,648	1,055	1,248	1,059	CA, AZ
Lettuce, leaf [4]	56	55	53	666	612	597	464	374	387	CA, AZ
Lettuce, Romaine [4] . . .	86	82	81	1,325	1,320	1,286	594	656	533	CA, AZ
Onions	164	160	153	3,653	3,982	3,692	1,084	816	865	CA, WA
Peas, green [5]	196	202	210	392	419	412	97	109	148	MN, WA, WI
Peppers, bell	53	54	54	786	805	833	529	533	672	CA, FL, NJ
Spinach	46	43	47	372	324	365	190	174	187	CA, AZ [4]
Squash	48	42	42	397	313	334	192	174	204	MI, CA, FL
Tomatoes	420	422	402	12,426	14,341	13,863	2,289	2,070	2,365	(NA)
Fresh market	120	108	105	1,814	1,681	1,557	1,585	1,169	1,414	CA, FL
Processed	299	314	297	10,612	12,660	12,306	705	902	950	CA
Watermelons [4]	131	129	126	1,993	1,867	1,978	414	423	492	FL, CA, TX

NA Not available.   [1] Area of crops for harvest for fresh market, including any partially harvested or not harvested because of low prices or other factors, plus area harvested for processing.   [2] Excludes some quantities not marketed.   [3] Fresh market vegetables valued at f.o.b. shipping point. Processing vegetables are equivalent returns at packinghouse door.   [4] Fresh market only.   [5] Processed only.

Source: U.S. Department of Agriculture, National Agricultural Statistics Service, *Vegetables, 2008 Summary*, January 2009.

Table 835. Fresh Fruits and Vegetables—Supply and Use: 2000 to 2008

[In millions of pounds, except per capita in pounds (8,355 represents 8,355,000,000)]

Year	Utilized production [1]	Imports [2]	Supply, [1] total	Exports [2]	Consumption Total	Consumption Per capita [3]
FRUITS						
Citrus:						
2000.	8,355	720	9,075	2,445	6,630	23.5
2003.	8,442	969	9,411	2,456	6,955	23.9
2004.	8,156	993	9,149	2,495	6,654	22.7
2005.	7,320	1,123	8,443	2,040	6,403	21.6
2006.	7,304	1,169	8,473	2,045	6,428	21.5
2007.	5,811	1,408	7,219	1,782	5,437	18.0
Noncitrus: [4]						
2000.	13,850	11,225	25,074	3,389	21,685	76.6
2003.	13,386	12,164	25,550	2,835	22,716	77.9
2004.	14,335	12,325	26,660	3,079	23,581	80.1
2005.	14,369	12,442	26,811	3,477	23,335	78.6
2006.	13,882	13,136	27,018	3,056	23,962	80.0
2007.	13,996	13,436	27,433	3,321	24,112	79.7
VEGETABLES AND MELONS						
2000.	46,995	7,231	55,570	4,200	49,147	174.0
2003.	46,670	8,743	56,663	4,252	50,383	173.3
2004.	48,614	8,902	58,769	4,366	51,786	176.6
2005.	46,539	9,559	57,590	4,266	51,297	173.3
2006.	46,609	10,201	58,089	3,951	52,185	174.7
2007.	46,554	10,918	58,634	3,823	52,458	173.9
2008.	45,309	11,207	57,988	3,985	51,915	170.5
POTATOES						
2000.	13,185	806	13,990	677	13,313	47.1
2003.	13,349	872	14,221	590	13,631	46.8
2004.	13,181	755	13,936	479	13,457	45.8
2005.	12,095	788	12,883	639	12,244	41.4
2006.	11,333	817	12,150	631	11,519	38.6
2007.	11,326	1,106	12,432	640	11,792	39.1
2008.	10,630	1,178	11,808	640	11,168	36.7

[1] Crop-year basis for fruits. Supply data for vegetables include ending stocks of previous year.   [2] Fiscal year for fruits; calendar year for vegetables and potatoes.   [3] Based on Census Bureau estimated total population.   [4] Includes bananas.

Source: U.S. Department of Agriculture, Economic Research Service, *Fruit and Tree Nuts Situation and Outlook Yearbook*, and *Vegetables and Melons Situation and Outlook Yearbook*.

Agriculture   539

Table 836. **Fruits and Nuts—Utilized Production and Value, 2006 to 2008, and Leading Producing States, 2008**

[4,865 represents 4,865,000]

Fruit or nut	Unit	Utilized production [1]			Farm value (mil. dol.)			Leading states in order of production, 2008
		2006	2007	2008	2006	2007	2008	
Apples [2]	1,000 tons	4,865	4,523	4,970	2,213	2,608	2,599	WA, NY, MI
Apricots	1,000 tons	45	89	77	30	42	41	CA, WA
Avocados	1,000 tons	147	188	(NA)	263	328	(NA)	CA, FL
Blackberries, cultivated (OR)	1,000 tons	21	30	19	36	29	23	OR
Blueberries	1,000 tons	179	182	219	560	614	593	MI, ME, NJ
Cherries, sweet	1,000 tons	288	306	240	465	557	571	WA, CA, OR
Cherries, tart	1,000 tons	124	124	107	53	68	82	MI
Cranberries	1,000 tons	339	328	380	279	307	444	WI, MA, NJ
Dates (California)	1,000 tons	18	16	18	38	37	26	CA
Figs (fresh) (California)	1,000 tons	43	48	40	18	19	26	CA
Grapefruit	1,000 tons	1,232	1,627	1,569	345	312	265	FL, TX, CA
Grapes (13 states)	1,000 tons	6,366	7,036	7,421	3,305	3,452	3,342	CA, WA, NY
Lemons	1,000 tons	980	798	703	410	449	589	CA
Nectarines	1,000 tons	232	283	294	121	96	107	CA, WA
Olives (California)	1,000 tons	24	133	67	18	87	51	CA
Oranges [3]	1,000 tons	9,021	7,625	10,167	1,830	2,216	2,135	FL, CA
Peaches	1,000 tons	987	1,116	1,100	513	502	539	CA, SC, NJ
Pears	1,000 tons	831	872	818	330	363	387	WA, CA, OR
Plums (CA)	1,000 tons	158	152	154	109	101	55	CA
Prunes (dried basis) (CA)	1,000 tons	189	81	126	263	117	192	CA
Raspberries	1,000 tons	83	71	60	244	263	284	CA, WA
Strawberries	1,000 tons	1,202	1,223	1,266	1,519	1,751	1,885	CA, FL
Tangerines	1,000 tons	417	361	490	138	156	219	CA, FL
Almonds (shelled basis) (CA)	Mil. lb.	1,120	1,390	1,550	2,259	2,402	2,229	CA
Hazelnuts (in the shell)	1,000 tons	43	37	32	46	75	52	OR
Macadamia nuts	1,000 tons	29	21	27	39	25	31	HI
Pecans (in the shell) (11 states)	1,000 tons	104	194	96	322	434	270	GA, NM, TX
Pistachios	1,000 tons	119	208	139	450	587	539	CA
Walnuts, English (in the shell)	1,000 tons	346	328	375	564	751	(NA)	CA

NA Not available.   [1] Excludes quantities not harvested or not marketed.   [2] Production in commercial orchards with 100 or more bearing age trees.   [3] Temples included in early, midseason, and Navel varieties beginning with the 2006–2007 season.

Source: U.S. Department of Agriculture, National Agricultural Statistics Service, *Noncitrus Fruits and Nuts, 2008 Preliminary Summary*, January 2009; and *Citrus Fruits, 2008 Summary*, September 2008.

Table 837. **Nuts—Supply and Use: 2000 to 2007**

[In millions of pounds (shelled) (331 represents 331,000,000). For marketing season beginning in year shown]

Year	Beginning stocks	Marketable production [1]	Imports	Supply, total	Consumption	Exports	Ending stocks
2000	331	1,117	293	1,741	723	781	237
2001	237	1,335	339	1,911	810	849	252
2002	252	1,562	363	2,177	926	928	323
2003	323	1,504	431	2,258	998	963	297
2004	299	1,546	504	2,348	1,000	1,040	308
2005	280	1,499	434	2,213	804	1,126	283
2006	283	1,652	441	2,377	989	1,130	258
2007, total [2]	258	2,097	488	2,843	1,129	1,306	408
Almonds	134	1,340	8	1,482	365	891	226
Pecans	31	180	77	288	131	73	84
Pistachios	57	207	1	265	69	128	67
Hazelnuts	2	71	13	87	67	19	2
Walnuts	35	280	9	323	150	144	29

[1] Utilized production minus inedibles and noncommercial usage.   [2] Includes macadamia nuts, Brazil nuts, cashew nuts, pine nuts, chestnuts, and mixed nuts not shown separately.

Source: U.S. Department of Agriculture, Economic Research Service, *Fruit and Tree Nuts Situation and Outlook Yearbook*.

Table 838. **Meat Supply and Use: 1990 to 2008**

[**In millions of pounds** (carcass weight equivalent) (**62,255 represents 62,255,000,000**). 2008 data are forecasts. Carcass weight equivalent is the weight of the animal minus entrails, head, hide, and internal organs; includes fat and bone. Covers federal and state inspected, and farm slaughter]

Year and type of meat	Production	Imports	Supply [1]	Exports	Consumption [2]	Ending stocks
RED MEAT AND POULTRY						
1990	62,255	3,295	66,673	2,472	62,937	1,263
2000	82,372	4,136	88,480	9,344	77,068	2,069
2005	86,783	4,845	93,819	9,274	82,333	2,212
2006	88,907	4,326	95,445	10,070	83,240	2,135
2007	90,934	4,297	97,365	11,069	84,102	2,194
2008	93,681	4,130	100,004	12,014	85,816	2,174
ALL RED MEATS						
1990	38,787	3,295	42,742	1,250	40,784	707
2000	46,299	4,127	51,340	3,760	46,559	1,021
2005	45,848	4,803	51,838	3,373	47,385	1,080
2006	47,675	4,265	53,020	4,158	47,696	1,166
2007	48,817	4,223	54,206	4,579	48,435	1,192
2008	50,567	4,055	55,814	5,259	49,333	1,222
Beef:						
1990.	22,743	2,356	25,434	1,006	24,031	397
2000.	26,888	3,032	30,332	2,468	27,338	525
2005.	24,787	3,599	29,023	697	27,754	571
2006.	26,256	3,085	29,912	1,145	28,137	630
2007.	26,523	3,052	30,205	1,431	28,144	630
2008.	26,682	2,930	30,242	1,515	28,127	600
Pork:						
1990.	15,354	898	16,565	238	16,031	296
2000.	18,952	965	20,406	1,287	18,642	478
2005.	20,705	1,024	22,272	2,666	19,112	494
2006.	21,074	990	22,558	2,995	19,048	514
2007.	21,962	968	23,444	3,138	19,763	542
2008.	23,554	925	25,021	3,735	20,686	600
Veal:						
1990.	327	(NA)	331	(NA)	325	6
2000.	225	(NA)	230	(NA)	225	5
2005.	165	(NA)	169	(NA)	164	5
2006.	156	(NA)	161	(NA)	155	6
2007.	145	(NA)	151	(NA)	144	7
2008.	150	(NA)	157	(NA)	153	4
Lamb and mutton:						
1990.	363	41	412	6	397	8
2000.	234	130	372	5	354	13
2005.	191	180	375	9	355	10
2006.	190	190	390	18	356	16
2007.	188	202	406	10	384	13
2008.	181	200	394	9	367	18
POULTRY, TOTAL						
1990	23,468	–	23,931	1,222	22,153	556
2000	36,073	9	37,140	5,584	30,508	1,048
2005	40,935	42	41,981	5,902	34,949	1,132
2006	41,231	61	42,425	5,911	35,544	969
2007	42,117	74	43,159	6,490	35,667	1,002
2008	43,114	75	44,190	6,755	36,483	952
Broilers:						
1990.	18,430	–	18,651	1,143	17,266	242
2000.	30,209	6	31,011	4,918	25,295	798
2005.	34,986	34	35,733	5,203	29,609	924
2006.	35,120	47	36,090	5,205	30,139	745
2007.	35,739	61	36,545	5,772	30,034	739
2008.	36,505	60	37,304	6,000	30,629	674
Mature chicken:						
1990.	523	–	530	25	496	9
2000.	531	2	540	220	311	9
2005.	516	1	520	130	388	2
2006.	504	3	509	159	345	5
2007.	498	4	507	165	341	2
2008.	525	3	529	150	377	2
Turkeys:						
1990.	4,514	–	4,750	54	4,390	306
2000.	5,333	1	5,589	445	4,902	241
2005.	5,432	8	5,728	570	4,952	206
2006.	5,607	12	5,825	547	5,060	218
2007.	5,880	9	6,107	554	5,292	261
2008.	6,084	12	6,357	605	5,477	275

– Represents zero.   NA Not available.   [1] Total supply equals production plus imports plus ending stocks of previous year. [2] Includes shipments to territories.

Source: U.S. Department of Agriculture, Economic Research Service, *Food Consumption, Prices, and Expenditures, 1970–1997*; and "Agricultural Outlook: Statistical Indicators"; <http://www.ers.usda.gov/publications/agoutlook/aotables/>.

Table 839. **Livestock Inventory and Production: 1990 to 2008**

[95.8 represents 95,800,000. **Production in live weight**; includes animals-for-slaughter market, younger animals shipped to other states for feeding or breeding purposes, farm slaughter and custom slaughter consumed on farms where produced, minus livestock shipped into states for feeding or breeding with an adjustment for changes in inventory]

Type of livestock	Unit	1990	1995	2000	2002	2003	2004	2005	2006	2007	2008
ALL CATTLE [1]											
Inventory: [2] Number on farms	Mil	95.8	102.8	98.2	96.7	96.1	94.4	95.0	96.3	96.6	96.0
Total value.	Bil. dol. . . .	59.0	63.2	67.1	72.3	69.9	77.2	87.0	97.2	89.1	95.1
Value per head.	Dol.	616	615	683	747	728	818	916	1,009	922	990
Production: Quantity	Bil. lb.	39.2	42.5	43.0	42.4	42.2	41.6	41.2	41.8	41.4	40.7
Beef, price per 100 lb.	Dol.	74.60	61.80	68.60	66.50	79.70	85.80	89.70	87.20	89.90	89.10
Calves, price per 100 lb. . . .	Dol.	95.60	73.10	104.00	96.40	102.00	119.00	135.00	133.00	119.00	110.00
Value of production	Bil. dol. . . .	29.3	24.7	28.5	27.1	32.1	34.9	36.3	35.5	36.0	34.9
HOGS AND PIGS											
Inventory: [3] Number on farms	Mil	53.8	59.7	59.3	59.7	59.6	60.5	61.0	61.5	62.5	68.2
Total value.	Bil. dol. . . .	4.3	3.2	4.3	4.6	4.2	4.0	6.3	5.8	5.6	5.0
Value per head.	Dol.	79	53	72	77	71	67	103	95	90	73
Production: Quantity	Bil. lb.	21.3	24.4	25.7	26.3	26.3	26.7	27.4	28.2	29.6	31.4
Price per 100 lb.	Dol.	53.70	40.50	42.30	33.40	37.20	49.30	50.20	46.00	46.60	47.00
Value of production	Bil. dol. . . .	11.3	9.8	10.8	8.7	9.7	13.1	13.6	12.7	13.5	14.4
SHEEP AND LAMBS											
Inventory: [2] Number on farms	Mil	11.4	9.0	7.0	6.6	6.3	6.1	6.1	6.2	6.1	6.0
Total value.	Mil. dol. . . .	901	663	670	614	657	720	798	872	818	823
Value per head.	Dol.	79	75	95	92	104	119	130	141	134	138
Production: Quantity	Mil. lb.	781	602	512	485	467	466	472	461	440	417
Value of production	Mil. dol. . . .	374	414	365	314	389	413	451	368	363	350

[1] Includes milk cows. [2] As of January 1. [3] As of December 1 of preceding year.

Source: U.S. Department of Agriculture, National Agricultural Statistics Service, *Meat Animals—Production, Disposition, and Income Final Estimates 1998–2002*, May 2004; *Meat Animals—Production, Disposition, and Income Final Estimates 2003–2007*, May 2009; *Meat Animals Production, Disposition, and Income*, annual; and annual livestock summaries. Also in *Agricultural Statistics*, annual.

Table 840. **Livestock Operations by Size of Herd: 2000 to 2008**

[In thousands (1,076 represents 1,076,000). An operation is any place having one or more head on hand at any time during the year]

Size of herd	2000	2005	2007	2008	Size of herd	2000	2005	2007	2008
CATTLE [1]									
					MILK COWS [2]				
Total operations	1,076	983	966	957	Total operations	105	78	70	67
1 to 49 head.	671	612	646	646	1 to 49 head.	53	37	34	33
50 to 99 head.	186	164	138	133	50 to 99 head.	31	23	19	18
100 to 499 head	192	178	152	148	100 head or more	21	18	17	16
500 to 999 head	19	19	19	19	HOGS AND PIGS				
1,000 head or more	10	10	11	11	Total operations	87	67	75	73
BEEF COWS [2]					1 to 99 head.	50	41	52	51
Total operations	831	770	766	757	100 to 499 head	17	10	7	7
1 to 49 head.	655	597	606	601	500 to 999 head	8	5	4	3
50 to 99 head.	100	95	86	83	1,000 to 1,999 head.	6	4	4	4
100 to 499 head	71	73	68	67	2,000 to 4,999 head.	5	5	5	5
500 head or more	6	5	6	6	5,000 head or more	2	2	3	3

[1] Includes calves. [2] Included in operations with cattle.

Source: U.S. Department of Agriculture, National Agricultural Statistics Service, *Livestock Operations Final Estimates 1998–2002*, April 2004; *Livestock Operations Final Estimates 2003–2007*, March 2009; *Farms, Land in Farms, and Livestock Operations 2008 Summary*, February 2009.

Table 841. **Hogs and Pigs—Number, Production, and Value by State: 2006 to 2008**

[62,516 represents 62,516,000. See headnote, Table 839]

State	Number on farms [1] (1,000)			Quantity produced (mil. lb.)			Value of production (mil. dol.)			Commercial slaughter [2] (mil. lb.)	
	2006	2007	2008	2006	2007	2008	2006	2007	2008	2007	2008
U.S. [3]	62,516	68,177	66,768	28,182	29,606	31,384	12,714	13,468	14,435	29,314	31,199
IA.	17,300	19,400	19,800	8,021	8,444	9,395	3,417	3,632	4,024	8,074	8,744
NC	9,500	10,200	9,600	3,779	3,815	4,186	1,890	1,931	2,108	2,926	3,160
MN	6,900	7,700	7,500	3,327	3,540	3,752	1,502	1,646	1,750	2,492	2,594
MO.	2,800	3,150	3,100	1,464	1,806	1,749	589	716	766	1,906	2,160
IN.	3,350	3,700	3,500	1,485	1,607	1,730	643	713	820	2,034	2,182
IL.	4,200	4,350	4,350	1,523	1,513	1,702	781	786	912	2,798	2,989
NE	3,050	3,350	3,300	1,412	1,438	1,377	699	727	711	1,995	2,122

[1] As of December 1. [2] Includes slaughter in federally inspected and other slaughter plants; excludes animals slaughtered on farms. [3] Includes other states not shown separately.

Source: U.S. Department of Agriculture, National Agricultural Statistics Service, *Meat Animals—Production, Disposition and Income*, annual; and *Livestock Slaughter*, annual.

Table 842. **Cattle and Calves—Number, Production, and Value by State: 2006 to 2009**

[96,573 represents 96,573,000. Includes milk cows. See headnote, Table 839]

State	Number on farms [1] (1,000)			Quantity produced (mil. lb.)			Value of production (mil. dol.)			Commercial slaughter [2] (mil. lb.)	
	2007	2008	2009	2006	2007	2008	2006	2007	2008	2007	2008
U.S. [3]	96,573	96,035	94,491	41,825	41,437	40,679	35,491	35,973	34,859	43,483	43,895
TX	13,900	13,600	13,600	6,694	6,728	6,453	5,705	6,026	5,714	7,446	8,269
NE	6,650	6,450	6,350	4,863	4,697	4,622	4,095	4,246	4,203	9,262	9,415
KS	6,400	6,650	6,300	4,132	4,069	3,892	2,971	3,328	3,321	9,700	8,296
OK	5,300	5,400	5,400	2,128	1,977	2,036	2,105	2,002	1,954	24	30
CA	5,500	5,450	5,250	1,994	1,977	1,887	1,173	1,289	1,303	2,054	1,999
CO	2,700	2,750	2,600	1,921	1,898	1,871	1,914	1,915	1,850	2,862	3,272
IA	3,900	4,000	3,950	1,729	1,732	1,845	1,387	1,446	1,606	([4])	([4])
SD	3,700	3,700	3,700	1,529	1,472	1,480	1,488	1,410	1,392	([4])	([4])
MO	4,400	4,250	4,250	1,368	1,333	1,335	1,407	1,320	1,221	105	108
ID	2,180	2,210	2,110	1,065	1,102	1,140	858	918	936	277	382
MN	2,440	2,400	2,400	1,061	1,094	1,108	821	886	896	1,049	1,175

[1] As of January 1.   [2] Data cover cattle only. Includes slaughter in federally inspected and other slaughter plants; excludes animals slaughtered on farms.   [3] Includes other states not shown separately.   [4] Included in U.S. total. Not printed to avoid disclosing individual operation.

Source: U.S. Department of Agriculture, National Agricultural Statistics Service, *Meat Animals—Production, Disposition and Income*, annual; and *Livestock Slaughter*, annual.

Table 843. **Milk Cows—Number, Production, and Value by State: 2006 to 2008**

[9,137 represents 9,137,000]

State	Number on farms [1] (1,000)			Milk produced on farms (mil. lb.)			Value of production [2] (mil. dol.)		
	2006	2007	2008	2006	2007	2008	2006	2007	2008
United States [3] . . .	9,137	9,189	9,315	181,782	185,654	189,992	23,556	35,666	34,977
California	1,780	1,813	1,844	38,830	40,683	41,203	4,497	7,343	6,930
Wisconsin	1,243	1,247	1,252	23,398	24,080	24,472	3,112	4,647	4,625
New York	638	627	626	12,045	12,103	12,432	1,614	2,384	2,312
Idaho	488	513	549	10,905	11,549	12,315	1,287	2,056	2,106
Pennsylvania	554	550	549	10,742	10,682	10,575	1,568	2,233	2,115
Minnesota	450	460	464	8,369	8,656	8,782	1,088	1,714	1,677
Texas	367	389	418	7,157	7,384	8,416	952	1,455	1,574
New Mexico	348	332	338	7,605	7,290	7,865	920	1,371	1,376
Michigan	320	335	350	7,115	7,625	7,763	946	1,502	1,490

[1] Average number during year. Represents cows and heifers that have calved, kept for milk; excluding heifers not yet fresh.   [2] Valued at average returns per 100 pounds of milk in combined marketings of milk and cream. Includes value of milk fed to calves.   [3] Includes other states not shown separately.

Source: U.S. Department of Agriculture, National Agricultural Statistics Service, *Milk Disposition and Income Final Estimates 2003–2007*, May 2009; *Milk Cows and Production, Final Estimates 2003–2007*, March 2009; and *Milk: Production, Disposition, and Income*, annual.

Table 844. **Milk Production and Manufactured Dairy Products: 1990 to 2008**

[193 represents 193,000]

Item	Unit	1990	2000	2002	2003	2004	2005	2006	2007	2008
Number of farms with milk cows	1,000	193	105	91	86	82	78	75	70	67
Cows and heifers that have calved, kept for milk	Mil. head. . .	10.0	9.2	9.1	9.1	9.0	9.1	9.1	9.2	9.3
Milk produced on farms	Bil. lb. . . .	148	167	170	170	171	177	182	186	190
Production per cow	1,000 lb. . .	14.8	18.2	18.6	18.8	19.0	19.6	19.9	20.2	20.4
Milk marketed by producers [1]	Bil. lb. . . .	146	166	169	169	170	176	181	185	189
Value of milk produced	Bil. dol.	20.4	20.8	20.7	21.4	27.6	26.9	23.6	35.7	35.0
Cash receipts from marketing of milk and cream [1]	Bil. dol.	20.1	20.6	20.6	21.2	27.4	26.7	23.4	35.5	34.8
Number of dairy manufacturing plants	Number. . . .	1,723	1,164	1,149	1,119	1,093	1,088	1,094	1,123	1,116
Manufactured dairy products:										
Butter (incl. whey butter)	Mil. lb.	1,302	1,256	1,355	1,242	1,247	1,347	1,448	1,533	1,644
Cheese, total [2]	Mil. lb.	6,059	8,258	8,547	8,557	8,873	9,149	9,525	9,777	9,935
American (excl. full-skim American) . . .	Mil. lb.	2,894	3,642	3,691	3,622	3,739	3,808	3,913	3,877	4,071
Cream and Neufchatel	Mil. lb.	431	687	686	677	699	715	756	773	764
All Italian varieties	Mil. lb.	2,207	3,289	3,470	3,524	3,662	3,803	3,973	4,199	4,158
Cottage cheese: Creamed [3]	Mil. lb.	832	735	748	769	788	784	778	774	715
Condensed bulk milk	Mil. lb.	1,426	1,202	1,191	1,047	1,021	1,182	1,427	1,853	1,756
Nonfat dry milk [4]	Mil. lb.	902	1,457	1,596	1,589	1,412	1,210	1,244	1,298	1,519
Dry whey [5]	Mil. lb.	1,143	1,188	1,115	1,085	1,035	1,041	1,110	1,134	1,108
Yogurt, plain and fruit-flavored	Mil. lb.	(NA)	1,837	2,311	2,507	2,707	3,058	3,301	3,476	3,599
Ice cream, regular	Mil. gal. . . .	824	980	1,005	993	920	960	982	956	943
Ice cream, lowfat [6]	Mil. gal. . . .	352	373	339	398	387	360	377	383	377

NA Not available.   [1] Comprises sales to plants and dealers, and retail sales by farmers direct to consumers.   [2] Includes varieties not shown separately.   [3] Includes partially creamed (low fat).   [4] Includes dry skim milk for animal feed through 2000.   [5] Includes animal but excludes modified whey production.   [6] Includes freezer-made milkshake in most states.

Source: U.S. Department of Agriculture, National Agricultural Statistics Service, *Milk Disposition and Income Final Estimates 2003–2007*, May 2009; *Dairy Products*, annual; and *Milk: Production, Disposition, and Income*, annual.

Agriculture   543

Table 845. **Milk Production and Commercial Use: 1990 to 2008**

[In billions of pounds milkfat basis (147.7 represents 147,700,000,000) except as noted]

Year	Produc-tion	Farm use	Commercial Farm market-ings	Commercial Begin-ning stock	Imports	Com-mercial supply, total	Ending stock	Exports	Disappear-ance[1]	Milk price per 100 lb.[2] (dol.)
1990	147.7	2.0	145.7	4.1	2.7	152.5	5.1	(NA)	138.8	13.68
2000	167.4	1.3	166.1	6.1	4.4	176.7	6.8	(NA)	169.0	12.40
2003	170.4	1.1	169.3	9.9	5.0	184.2	8.3	(NA)	174.7	12.52
2004	170.9	1.1	169.8	8.3	5.3	183.4	7.2	(NA)	176.4	16.05
2005	176.9	1.1	175.8	7.2	5.0	188.0	8.0	3.3	176.7	15.13
2006	181.8	1.1	180.6	8.0	5.0	193.6	9.5	3.4	180.7	12.88
2007	185.7	1.1	184.5	9.5	4.6	198.6	10.4	5.7	182.6	19.13
2008	190.0	1.1	188.8	10.4	3.9	203.1	10.0	8.7	184.3	18.32

NA Not available. [1] Prior to 2005, disappearance represents domestic disappearance plus exports. [2] Wholesale price received by farmers for all milk delivered to plants and dealers.

Source: U.S. Department of Agriculture, Economic Research Service, "Agricultural Outlook: Statistical Indicators"; <http://www.ers.usda.gov/publications/agoutlook/aotables/>.

Table 846. **Broiler, Turkey, and Egg Production: 1990 to 2008**

[For year ending November 30 (353 represents 353,000,000)]

Item	Unit	1990	2000	2001	2002	2003	2004	2005	2006	2007	2008
Chickens:[1]											
Number [2]	Million	353	437	444	444	450	454	456	458	459	446
Value per head [2]	Dollars . . .	2.29	2.44	2.41	2.38	2.48	2.48	2.52	2.60	2.95	3.38
Value, total [2]	Mil. dol . . .	808	1,064	1,069	1,055	1,116	1,126	1,150	1,190	1,352	1,507
Number sold	Million	208	218	202	200	190	192	194	174	168	176
Price per lb.	Cents	9.6	5.7	4.5	4.8	4.9	5.8	6.5	5.9	5.6	6.6
Value of sales	Mil. dol . . .	94	64	47	50	48	58	65	54	51	62
PRODUCTION											
Broilers: [3]											
Number.	Million	5,864	8,284	8,390	8,591	8,493	8,741	8,872	8,868	8,907	9,009
Weight	Bil. lb.	25.6	41.6	42.5	44.1	44.0	45.8	47.9	48.8	49.3	50.4
Price per lb.	Cents	32.6	33.6	39.3	30.5	34.6	44.6	43.6	36.3	43.6	45.8
Production value. . . .	Mil. dol . . .	8,366	13,989	16,696	13,437	15,215	20,446	20,878	17,739	21,514	23,118
Turkeys:											
Number.	Million	282	270	273	275	270	256	250	256	267	273
Weight	Bil. lb.	6.0	7.0	7.2	7.5	7.2	6.9	7.0	7.2	7.6	7.9
Price per lb.	Cents	39.6	40.6	39.0	36.5	34.6	41.5	44.5	48.0	52.3	57.0
Production value. . . .	Mil. dol . . .	2,393	2,828	2,797	2,732	2,504	2,887	3,108	3,468	3,954	4,477
Eggs:											
Number.	Billion	68.1	84.7	86.1	87.3	87.5	89.2	90.3	91.8	91.1	90.2
Price per dozen	Cents	70.8	61.6	62.0	58.9	73.1	71.3	54.0	58.3	88.5	109.0
Production value. . . .	Mil. dol . . .	4,021	4,346	4,446	4,281	5,334	5,303	4,067	4,460	6,719	8,225

[1] Excludes commercial broilers. [2] As of December 1. [3] Young chickens of the heavy breeds and other meat-type birds, to be marketed at 2–5 lbs. live weight and from which no pullets are kept for egg production.

Source: U.S. Department of Agriculture, National Agricultural Statistics Service, *Poultry Production and Value Final Estimates 2003–2007*, May 2009; *Chickens and Eggs Final Estimates 2003–2007*, March 2009; *Poultry—Production and Value*, annual; and *Chickens and Eggs*, annual.

Table 847. **Broiler and Turkey Production by State: 2006 to 2008**

[In millions of pounds, live weight production (48,830 represents 48,830,000,000)]

State	Broilers 2006	2007	2008	Turkeys 2006	2007	2008	State	Broilers 2006	2007	2008	Turkeys 2006	2007	2008
U.S. [1] . . .	48,830	49,331	50,441	7,224	7,566	7,922	MS	4,662	4,614	4,876	(NA)	(NA)	(NA)
AL	5,688	5,625	5,846	(NA)	(NA)	(NA)	MO	(NA)	(NA)	(NA)	618	646	651
AR	6,283	6,232	6,380	543	572	611	NC	5,099	5,390	5,493	1,095	1,147	1,208
CA	(NA)	(NA)	(NA)	402	450	435	OH	242	274	328	217	227	230
DE	1,614	1,598	1,580	(NA)	(NA)	(NA)	OK	1,352	1,288	1,260	(NA)	(NA)	(NA)
FL.	443	418	376	(NA)	(NA)	(NA)	PA	829	847	933	203	199	216
GA	7,066	7,414	7,469	(NA)	(NA)	(NA)	SC	1,408	1,480	1,516	356	382	478
IL	(NA)	(NA)	(NA)	74	77	(NA)	SD	(NA)	(NA)	(NA)	150	173	189
IN	(NA)	(NA)	(NA)	459	481	519	TN	1,089	1,050	1,019	(NA)	(NA)	(NA)
IA	(NA)	(NA)	(NA)	281	325	360	TX	3,330	3,266	3,460	(NA)	(NA)	(NA)
KY	1,590	1,668	1,653	(NA)	(NA)	(NA)	UT	(NA)	(NA)	(NA)	(NA)	(NA)	105
MD	1,607	1,592	1,612	14	13	(NA)	VA	1,332	1,301	1,252	480	483	484
MI.	(NA)	(NA)	(NA)	179	192	(NA)	WV	359	356	351	98	97	102
MN	230	242	238	1,197	1,218	1,306	WI	169	203	217	(NA)	(NA)	(NA)

NA Not available. [1] Includes other states not shown separately.

Source: U.S. Department of Agriculture, National Agricultural Statistics Service, *Poultry Production and Value Final Estimates 2003–2007*, May 2009; *Poultry—Production and Value*, annual.

Section 18
Forestry, Fishing, and Mining

This section presents data on the area, ownership, production, trade, reserves, and disposition of natural resources. Natural resources is defined here as including forestry, fisheries, and mining and mineral products.

Forestry—Presents data on the area, ownership, and timber resource of commercial timberland; forestry statistics covering the National Forests and Forest Service cooperative programs; product data for lumber, pulpwood, woodpulp, paper and paperboard, and similar data.

The principal sources of data relating to forests and forest products are *Forest Resources of the United States, 2007; Timber Demand and Technology Assessment; U.S. Timber Production, Trade, Consumption, and Price Statistics, 1965–2005; Land Areas of the National Forest System,* issued annually by the Forest Service of the U.S. Department of Agriculture; *Agricultural Statistics* issued by the Department of Agriculture; and reports of the annual survey of manufactures, and the annual *Current Industrial Reports,* issued by the U.S. Census Bureau on the Internet and in print in the annual *Manufacturing Profiles.* Additional information is published in the monthly *Survey of Current Business* of the Bureau of Economic Analysis, and the annual *Wood Pulp* and *Fiber Statistics* and *The Annual Statistics of Paper, Paperboard, and Wood Pulp* of the American Forest and Paper Association, Washington, DC.

The completeness and reliability of statistics on forests and forest products vary considerably. The data for forest land area and stand volumes are much more reliable for areas that have been recently surveyed than for those for which only estimates are available. In general, more data are available for lumber and other manufactured products such as particle board and softwood panels, etc., than for the primary forest products such as poles and piling and fuelwood.

Fisheries—The principal source of data relating to fisheries is *Fisheries of the United States,* issued annually by the National Marine Fisheries Service (NMFS), National Oceanic and Atmospheric Administration (NOAA). The NMFS collects and disseminates data on commercial landings of fish and shellfish. Annual reports include quantity and value of commercial landings of fish and shellfish disposition of landings and number and kinds of fishing vessels and fishing gear. Reports for the fish-processing industry include annual output for the wholesaling and fish processing establishments, annual and seasonal employment. The principal source for these data is the annual *Fisheries of the United States.*

Mining and mineral products—
Presents data relating to mineral industries and their products, general summary measures of production and employment, and more detailed data on production, prices, imports and exports, consumption, and distribution for specific industries and products. Data on mining and mineral products may also be found in Sections 19, 21, and 28 of this *Abstract;* data on mining employment may be found in Section 12.

Mining comprises the extraction of minerals occurring naturally (coal, ores, crude petroleum, natural gas) and quarrying, well operation, milling, refining and processing, and other preparation customarily done at the mine or well site or as a part of extraction activity. (Mineral preparation plants are usually operated together with mines or quarries.) Exploration for minerals is included as is the development of mineral properties.

The principal governmental sources of these data are the *Minerals Yearbook* and *Mineral Commodity Summaries,* published by the U.S. Geological Survey, U.S. Department of the Interior, and various monthly and annual publications of the Energy

Information Administration, U.S. Department of Energy. See text, Section 19, for a list of Department of Energy publications. In addition, the Census Bureau conducts a census of mineral industries every 5 years.

Nongovernment sources include the *Annual Statistical Report* of the American Iron and Steel Institute, Washington, DC; *Metals Week* and the monthly *Engineering and Mining Journal,* issued by the McGraw-Hill Publishing Co., New York, NY; *The Iron Age,* issued weekly by the Chilton Co., Philadelphia, PA; and the *Joint Association Survey of the U.S. Oil and Gas Industry,* conducted jointly by the American Petroleum Institute, Independent Petroleum Association of America, and Mid-Continent Oil and Gas Association.

Mineral statistics, with principal emphasis on commodity detail, have been collected by the U.S. Geological Survey and the former Bureau of Mines since 1880. Current data in U.S. Geological Survey publications include quantity and value of non-fuel minerals produced, sold, or used by producers, or shipped; quantity of minerals stocked; crude materials treated and prepared minerals recovered; and consumption of mineral raw materials.

The Economic Census, conducted by the Census Bureau at various intervals since 1840, collects data on mineral industries. Beginning with the 1967 census, legislation provides for a census to be conducted every 5 years for years ending in "2" and "7." The most recent results, published for 2002, are based on the North American Industry Classification System (NAICS). The censuses provide, for the various types of mineral establishments, information on operating costs, capital expenditures, labor, equipment, and energy requirements in relation to their value of shipments and other receipts.

Table 848. **Gross Domestic Product of Natural Resource-Related Industries in Current and Real (2000) Dollars by Industry: 2000 to 2008**

[In billions of dollars (9,817.0 represents $9,817,000,000,000). Data are based on the 1997 North American Industry Classification System (NAICS); see text, Section 15. Data include nonfactor charges (capital consumption allowances, indirect business taxes, etc.) as well as factor charges against gross product; corporate profits and capital consumption allowances have been shifted from a company to an establishment basis]

Industry	Current dollars				Chained (2000) dollars			
	2000	2005	2007	2008	2000	2005	2007	2008
All industries, total [1]	9,817.0	12,421.9	13,807.5	14,264.6	9,817.0	10,989.5	11,523.9	11,652.0
Industries covered	306.3	445.7	525.0	(NA)	306.3	309.3	316.3	(NA)
Percent of all industries	3.1	3.6	3.8	(NA)	3.1	2.8	2.7	(NA)
Agriculture, forestry, fishing, and hunting. .	98.0	133.3	167.9	157.7	98.0	120.5	122.1	121.4
Farms	71.5	104.1	137.3	(NA)	71.5	89.6	91.5	(NA)
Forestry, fishing, and related activities. .	26.5	29.2	30.7	(NA)	26.5	30.2	29.5	(NA)
Mining	121.3	223.8	275.0	325.3	121.3	103.7	111.4	110.5
Oil and gas extraction	81.0	150.5	164.7	(NA)	81.0	69.5	69.5	(NA)
Mining, except oil and gas	27.0	36.8	45.3	(NA)	27.0	25.2	24.8	(NA)
Support activities for mining	13.4	36.6	65.0	(NA)	13.4	10.3	14.7	(NA)
Timber-related manufacturing	87.0	88.6	82.1	(NA)	87.0	85.1	82.8	(NA)
Wood products	31.4	38.4	31.4	(NA)	31.4	32.0	31.7	(NA)
Paper products	55.6	50.2	50.7	(NA)	55.6	53.1	51.1	(NA)

NA Not available.   [1] Includes industries not shown separately.

Source: U.S. Bureau of Economic Analysis, *Survey of Current Business,* May 2009. See also <http://www.bea.gov /industry/gdpbyind_data.htm> (published 28 April 2009).

Table 849. **Natural Resource-Related Industries—Establishments, Sales, Payroll, and Employees by Industry: 2002 and 2007**

[183 represents $183,000,000,000. Includes only establishments of firms with payroll. Data are based on the 2002 and 2007 economic censuses, which are subject to nonsampling error. For details on methodology and nonsampling and sampling errors, see Appendix III]

Industry	2002 NAICS code [1]	Establishments (number)		Value of shipments (bil. dol.)		Annual payroll (bil. dol.)		Paid employees [2] (1,000)	
		2002	2007	2002	2007	2002	2007	2002	2007
Mining	21	24,087	21,169	183	369	21	37	475	703
Oil & gas extraction	211	7,730	6,293	113	231	5	10	99	162
Mining (except oil & gas) . . .	212	7,253	6,465	48	81	9	11	196	220
Mining support activities	213	9,104	8,411	22	57	7	16	180	322
Manufacturing [3]	31-33	350,728	293,919	3,915	5,339	568	612	15	13
Wood product mfg	321	17,192	14,862	89	102	16	17	540	520
Paper mfg	322	5,520	4,803	154	176	21	21	491	417
Petroleum & coal products manufacturing	324	2,268	2,284	216	606	6	8	104	105

[1] North American Industry Classification System, 2002.   [2] For pay period including March 12.   [3] Includes other industries not shown separately.

Source: U.S. Census Bureau, 2007 Economic Census, *Comparative Statistics* (published 17 March 2009); using American FactFinder; <http://www.census.gov/econ/census07/www/get_data.html>.

Table 850. **Natural Resource-Related Industries—Establishments, Employees, and Annual Payroll, by Industry: 2000 and 2006**

[1,791.3 represents 1,791,300. Excludes government employees, railroad employees, self-employed persons, etc. See "General Explanation" in source for definitions and statement on reliability of data. An establishment is a single physical location where business is conducted or where services or industrial operations are performed]

Industry	2002 NAICS code [1]	Establishments (number)		Number of employees [2] (1,000)		Annual payroll (bil. dol.)	
		2000	2006	2000	2006	2000	2006
Natural resource-related industries, total . . .	(X)	72,932	71,673	1,791.3	1,737.9	66.58	82.93
Forestry, fishing, hunting, and agriculture support	11	26,076	23,551	183.6	165.7	4.68	5.20
Forestry and logging	113	13,347	10,723	83.1	66.3	2.26	2.21
Timber tract operations	1131	469	454	3.3	2.8	0.13	0.13
Forest nurseries and gathering forest products	1132	258	231	1.7	2.1	0.07	0.07
Logging	1133	12,620	10,038	78.1	61.4	2.06	2.01
Fishing, hunting and trapping	114	2,671	2,372	10.0	7.5	0.34	0.35
Fishing	1141	2,308	2,024	7.5	5.6	0.27	0.29
Hunting and trapping	1142	363	348	2.5	1.9	0.08	0.06
Agriculture and forestry support activities	115	10,058	10,456	90.4	91.8	2.08	2.64
Crop production support activities	1151	5,061	4,557	57.6	59.3	1.35	1.70
Animal production support activities	1152	3,450	4,217	18.2	19.1	0.38	0.51
Forestry support activities	1153	1,547	1,682	14.7	13.5	0.35	0.44
Mining	21	23,738	26,248	456.1	554.3	22.09	37.49
Oil and gas extraction	211	7,740	7,803	83.0	92.7	5.39	9.57
Mining (except oil and gas)	212	7,231	7,278	204.3	205.3	9.34	11.68
Coal mining	2121	1,253	1,147	70.7	77.9	3.54	4.92
Metal ore mining	2122	522	307	34.8	27.7	1.72	1.83
Nonmetallic mineral mining and quarrying	2123	5,456	5,824	98.8	99.7	4.08	4.93
Mining support activities	213	8,767	11,167	168.8	256.3	7.35	16.24
Timber-related manufacturing	(X)	23,118	21,874	1,151.6	1,017.9	39.80	40.24
Wood product manufacturing	321	17,328	16,735	597.7	576.5	16.51	18.58
Sawmills and wood preservation	3211	4,695	4,223	131.4	118.5	3.78	4.02
Veneer, plywood and engineered wood product manufacturing	3212	1,904	1,956	120.6	124.5	3.75	4.36
Other wood product manufacturing	3219	10,729	10,556	345.8	333.6	8.95	10.21
Paper manufacturing	322	5,790	5,139	553.9	441.4	23.29	21.66
Pulp, paper and paperboard mills	3221	597	597	177.1	138.8	9.48	8.59
Converted paper product manufacturing	3222	5,193	4,542	376.8	302.7	13.82	13.06

X Not applicable.   [1] North American Industry Classification System, 2002.   [2] Covers full- and part-time employees who are on the payroll in the pay period including March 12.

Source: U.S. Census Bureau, "County Business Patterns," annual. See also <http://www.census.gov/econ/cbp/index.html>.

U.S. Census Bureau, Statistical Abstract of the United States: 2010

Table 851. **Timber-Based Manufacturing Industries—Employees, Payroll, and Shipments: 2006**

[In thousands (12,990 represents 12,990,000). Based on the Annual Survey of Manufactures; see Appendix III]

Selected industry	2002 NAICS code [1]	All employees			Produc-tion workers, total (1,000)	Value added by manufactures		Value of ship-ments (mil. dol.)
		Number (1,000)	Payroll			Total (mil. dol.)	Per produc-tion worker (dol.)	
			Total (mil. dol.)	Per employee (dol.)				
Manufacturing, all industries [2] . . .	31–33	12,990	592,342	45,599	9,179	2,305,589	251,179	5,019,963
Timber-based manufacturing, total	321–322	950	38,781	40,816	754	125,032	165,826	282,765
Percent of total manufacturing .	(X)	7.31	6.55	(X)	8.21	5.42	(X)	5.63
Wood product manufacturing	321	536	18,141	33,839	432	44,432	102,776	112,404
Sawmills and wood preservation . . .	3211	104	3,863	37,146	87	9,854	112,833	32,163
Veneer, plywood, and engineered wood product	3212	115	4,171	36,360	92	10,475	113,662	25,746
Other wood product.	3219	317	10,107	31,844	253	24,103	95,334	54,496
Millwork	32191	160	5,355	33,524	127	12,781	100,684	30,436
Wood container and pallet.	32192	52	1,398	27,064	43	3,016	69,885	6,542
All other wood products	32199	106	3,354	31,640	83	8,306	100,402	17,518
Paper manufacturing.	322	414	20,640	49,849	322	80,601	250,558	170,361
Pulp, paper, and paperboard mills . .	3221	128	8,015	62,687	102	42,047	414,237	79,961
Pulp mills.	32211	7	486	72,161	5	1,767	331,685	4,257
Paper mills.	32212	85	5,227	61,430	68	28,494	420,245	52,485
Paperboard mills	32213	36	2,302	63,884	28	11,787	415,361	23,219
Converted paper product	3222	286	12,625	44,114	220	38,554	175,101	90,400
Paperboard container.	32221	162	7,226	44,655	124	18,631	149,807	48,733
Paper bag and coated and treated paper	32222	56	2,618	46,338	42	9,033	216,072	19,858
Stationery product	32223	32	1,230	39,005	25	3,470	140,136	8,360
Other converted paper products . .	32229	36	1,551	42,683	29	7,419	253,696	13,448

X Not applicable.   [1] North American Industry Classification System, 2002; see text, Section 15.   [2] Includes other industries not shown separately.

Source: U.S. Census Bureau, "Annual Survey of Manufactures, 2006" (published 31 December 2006); <http://www.census.gov/mcd/asm-as1.html>.

Table 852. **Forest Land and Timberland by Type of Owner and Region: 2007**

[In thousands of acres (751,228 represents 751,228,000). As of January 1. Forest land is land at least 10 percent stocked by forest trees of any size, including land that formerly had such tree cover and that will be naturally or artificially regenerated. The minimum area for classification of forest land is 1 acre or strips of timber with a crown width of at least 120 feet wide. Timberland is forest land that is producing or is capable of producing crops of industrial wood and that is not withdrawn from timber utilization by statute or administrative regulation]

Region	Forest land, total	Timberland				State, county, and municipal	Private [1]
		Total	Federal				
			Total	National forest	Other		
Total	751,228	514,213	112,733	98,721	14,015	44,994	356,485
North	172,039	164,018	11,897	10,126	1,771	7,098	126,868
Northeast	84,796	79,803	2,971	2,401	570	1,838	67,523
North Central	87,243	84,215	8,926	7,725	1,201	5,260	59,345
South.	214,644	204,030	17,164	12,225	4,940	2,015	178,986
Southeast	87,889	85,665	7,559	4,970	2,590	1,202	73,417
South Central.	126,756	118,365	9,605	7,255	2,350	813	105,569
Rocky Mountains	150,661	70,968	48,612	45,386	252	119	19,169
Great Plains.	5,757	5,287	1,294	1,056	199	45	3,795
Intermountain.	144,905	65,681	47,318	44,330	53	74	15,374
Pacific Coast.	213,883	75,197	35,060	30,984	349	621	31,462
Alaska	126,869	11,865	4,750	3,772	173	62	2,771
Pacific Northwest . . .	52,449	43,489	20,403	17,937	133	452	19,383
Pacific Southwest [2] . . .	34,565	19,843	9,907	9,275	43	107	9,308

[1] Includes Indian lands.   [2] Includes Hawaii.

Source: U.S. Forest Service, "RPA Assessment Tables," 2007; <http://www.fs.fed.us/research/rpa/>.

Table 853. **Timber Volume, Growth, and Removal on Timberland by Species, Group, and Region: 2007**

[932,096 represents 932,096,000,000]

| Region | Net volume [1] | | | | | | Timber growth [4] (mil. cu. ft.) | | | Timber removals [5] (mil. cu. ft.) | | |
| | Growing stock [2] (mil. cu. ft.) | | | Sawtimber [3] (bil. board ft.) | | | | | | | | |
	All species	Soft- woods	Hard- woods	All spe- cies	Soft- woods	Hard- woods	All spe- cies	Soft- woods	Hard- woods	All spe- cies	Soft- woods	Hard- woods
Total	932,096	529,203	402,893	1,013	558	455	26,744	15,241	11,503	15,533	9,859	5,675
North	248,007	55,866	192,141	268	60	209	6,576	1,489	5,087	2,820	677	2,143
Northeast	137,585	34,252	103,333	146	37	109	3,249	836	2,412	1,169	353	815
North Central	110,422	21,614	88,808	122	23	99	3,327	652	2,675	1,651	324	1,328
South	288,522	118,471	170,051	325	123	202	13,272	7,632	5,640	9,696	6,317	3,379
Southeast	126,747	56,722	70,025	143	58	84	6,115	3,876	2,239	4,306	2,961	1,345
South Central	161,775	61,749	100,026	182	64	118	7,157	3,756	3,401	5,391	3,357	2,034
Rocky Mountains	137,263	124,809	12,454	159	144	15	1,761	1,577	184	543	521	22
Great Plains	4,539	1,641	2,898	7	2	5	72	27	45	41	25	16
Intermountain	132,724	123,168	9,556	153	142	11	1,689	1,550	139	502	496	6
Pacific Coast	258,304	230,057	28,247	261	232	29	5,135	4,543	593	2,474	2,344	131
Alaska	31,998	29,125	2,873	34	31	3	248	130	118	66	59	7
Pacific Northwest . . .	158,896	146,006	12,890	159	146	13	3,340	3,039	301	1,939	1,818	121
Pacific Southwest [6] . . .	67,410	54,926	12,484	68	55	13	1,548	1,374	174	469	466	3

[1] As of January 1. [2] Live trees of commercial species meeting specified standards of quality or vigor. Cull trees are excluded. Includes only trees 5.0-inches in diameter or larger at 4 1/2 feet above ground. [3] Live trees of commercial species containing at least one 12-foot sawlog or two noncontiguous 8-foot logs, and meeting regional specifications for freedom from defect. Softwood trees must be at least 9.0 inches in diameter and hardwood trees must be at least 11.0-inches in diameter at 4 1/2 feet above ground. [4] The net increase in the volume of trees during a specified year. Components include the increment in net volume of trees at the beginning of the specific year surviving to its end, plus the net volume of trees reaching the minimum size class during the year, minus the volume of trees that died during the year, and minus the net volume of trees that became cull trees during the year. [5] The net volume of trees removed from the inventory during a specified year by harvesting, cultural operations such as timber stand improvement, or land clearing. [6] Includes Hawaii.

Source: U.S. Forest Service, "RPA Assessment Tables," 2007; <http://www.fs.fed.us/research/rpa/>.

Table 854. **Timber Products—Production, Foreign Trade, and Consumption by Type of Product: 1990 to 2008**

[In millions of cubic feet, roundwood equivalent (15,577 represents 15,577,000,000)]

Type of product	1990	1995	2000	2001	2002	2003	2004	2005	2006	2007	2008
Industrial roundwood:											
Domestic production	15,577	15,537	15,436	14,634	14,902	14,571	15,139	15,465	14,836	13,932	12,493
Softwoods	10,968	10,191	10,201	9,859	10,124	10,290	10,710	11,002	10,413	9,566	8,389
Hardwoods	4,609	5,347	5,235	4,775	4,778	4,282	4,428	4,463	4,423	4,366	4,104
Imports	3,091	3,907	4,529	4,605	4,505	5,096	5,805	5,802	5,292	4,147	3,065
Exports	2,307	2,282	1,996	1,759	1,769	1,535	1,604	1,646	1,596	1,481	1,517
Consumption	16,361	17,161	17,969	17,481	17,637	18,132	19,339	19,622	18,841	16,598	14,041
Softwoods	11,779	11,961	12,659	12,552	12,790	13,398	14,357	14,652	13,732	12,009	9,845
Hardwoods	4,582	5,200	5,310	4,929	4,847	4,734	4,983	4,970	4,799	4,589	4,197
Lumber:											
Domestic production . . .	7,317	6,815	7,199	6,820	7,060	7,131	7,510	7,889	7,552	6,964	5,928
Imports	1,909	2,522	2,845	2,903	3,036	3,193	3,704	3,737	3,415	2,743	1,922
Exports	589	460	428	354	353	347	348	389	390	359	345
Consumption	8,637	8,877	9,616	9,369	9,744	9,977	10,866	11,237	10,577	9,347	7,506
Plywood and veneer:											
Domestic production . . .	1,423	1,303	1,187	1,067	1,074	1,054	1,086	1,068	1,003	912	743
Imports	97	107	155	173	205	240	354	373	339	265	185
Exports	109	89	42	32	31	35	43	37	35	40	45
Consumption	1,410	1,321	1,300	1,208	1,249	1,259	1,397	1,403	1,308	1,136	882
Pulp products:											
Domestic production . . .	5,313	6,079	5,881	5,691	5,708	5,557	5,692	5,679	5,470	5,176	4,926
Imports	1,038	1,248	1,459	1,458	1,180	1,579	1,669	1,570	1,440	1,071	918
Exports	646	905	842	801	810	643	680	708	681	526	556
Consumption	5,704	6,422	6,498	6,348	6,078	6,493	6,680	6,541	6,229	5,721	5,288
Logs:											
Imports	4	13	68	70	81	80	73	114	94	67	35
Exports	674	451	331	307	309	356	366	345	339	350	313
Pulpwood chips, exports . . .	288	377	353	265	265	155	168	166	151	205	257
Fuelwood consumption	3,019	2,937	2,561	2,571	2,581	1,515	1,540	1,550	1,555	1,605	1,605

Source: U.S. Forest Service, *U.S. Timber Production, Trade, Consumption, and Price Statistics, 1965–2005*, Research Paper RP-FPL-637 and unpublished data. See also <http://www.treesearch.fs.fed.us/pubs/28972>.

Forestry, Fishing, and Mining **549**

Table 855. **Selected Timber Products—Imports and Exports: 1990 to 2008**

[In million board feet (13,063 represents 13,063,000,000) except as indicated]

Product	Unit	1990	1995	2000	2003	2004	2005	2006	2007	2008
IMPORTS [1]										
Lumber, total [2]	Mil. bd. ft.	13,063	17,524	19,906	21,981	25,493	25,738	23,037	25,807	(NA)
From Canada	Percent	91	97	92	90	83	85	86	89	(NA)
Logs, total	Mil. bd. ft. [3]. .	23	80	435	497	454	710	585	418	253
From Canada . . .	Percent	84	70	96	98	97	85	85	91	(NA)
Paper and board [4]. . .	1,000 tons . . .	12,195	14,292	17,555	20,034	21,146	20,438	20,293	18,634	16,872
Woodpulp	1,000 tons . . .	4,893	5,969	7,227	6,691	6,726	6,762	6,939	6,793	6,272
Plywood	Mil. sq. ft. [5]. . .	1,687	1,951	2,917	4,489	5,896	6,325	6,324	4,969	3,722
EXPORTS										
Lumber, total [2]	Mil. bd. ft.	4,623	2,958	2,700	2,193	3,842	2,682	2,651	2,613	(NA)
To: Canada.	Percent	14	22	26	29	12	28	28	27	(NA)
Japan.	Percent	28	33	12	7	11	3	4	4	(NA)
Europe	Percent	15	17	19	16	9	15	16	16	(NA)
Logs, total	Mil. bd. ft. [3]. . .	4,213	2,820	2,068	2,224	2,287	2,157	2,120	2,189	2,240
To: Canada.	Percent	9	25	41	54	49	54	52	43	(NA)
Japan.	Percent	62	61	45	29	28	27	26	26	(NA)
China	Percent	9	1	–	2	3	4	5	7	(NA)
Paper and board [4]. . .	1,000 tons . . .	5,163	7,621	10,003	11,868	12,566	13,434	13,349	14,582	12,907
Woodpulp	1,000 tons . . .	5,905	8,261	6,409	5,847	6,225	6,413	6,606	6,831	7,790
Plywood	Mil. sq. ft. [5]. . .	1,766	1,517	754	640	783	568	749	501	621

– Represents zero.   NA Not available.   [1] Customs value of imports; see text, Section 28.   [2] Includes railroad ties.   [3] Log scale.   [4] Includes paper and board products. Excludes hardboard.   [5] 3/8 inch basis.

Source: U.S. Forest Service, *U.S. Timber Production, Trade, Consumption, and Price Statistics, 1965–2005,* Research Paper RP-FPL-637 and unpublished data. See also <http://www.treesearch.fs.fed.us/pubs/28972>.

Table 856. **Lumber Consumption by Species Group and End Use: 1995 to 2008**

[In billion board feet (59.3 represents 59,300,000,000), **except per capita in board feet.** Per capita consumption based on estimated resident population as of **July 1**]

Item	1995	1999	2000	2001	2002	2003	2004	2005	2006	2007	2008
Consumption, total	**59.3**	**68.3**	**66.1**	**64.6**	**67.5**	**67.0**	**73.1**	**75.6**	**71.3**	**62.7**	**49.7**
Per capita	225	250	240	227	235	230	249	255	238	208	163
SPECIES GROUP											
Softwoods.	47.6	54.5	54.0	53.7	56.4	56.5	62.0	64.4	60.4	52.6	40.7
Hardwoods	11.7	13.8	12.2	11.0	11.1	10.5	11.1	11.2	10.9	10.2	9.0
END USE											
New housing	18.1	22.6	21.1	21.6	22.5	24.0	25.4	27.7	23.8	17.5	11.2
Residential upkeep and improvements	15.0	14.7	15.3	15.3	16.4	16.2	17.6	18.3	18.6	17.8	16.1
New nonresidential construction [1]	4.7	5.4	5.5	5.3	4.8	4.4	4.5	4.7	5.2	4.9	5.2
Manufacturing	7.7	8.2	7.9	6.9	6.4	5.9	5.7	5.6	5.3	4.9	4.2
Shipping.	6.9	7.4	7.6	6.9	7.1	7.0	7.7	8.1	8.6	7.9	6.8
Other [2]	7.2	8.5	8.7	8.9	9.9	9.8	13.2	11.3	9.8	10.0	6.0

[1] In addition to new construction, includes railroad ties laid as replacements in existing track and lumber used by railroads for railcar repair.   [2] Includes upkeep and improvement of nonresidential buildings and structures; made-at-home projects, such as furniture, boats, and picnic tables; made-on-the-job items such as advertising and display structures; and miscellaneous products and uses.

Source: U.S. Forest Service, *U.S. Timber Production, Trade, Consumption, and Price Statistics, 1965–2005,* Research Paper RP-FPL-637 and unpublished data. See also <http://www.treesearch.fs.fed.us/pubs/28972>.

Table 857. **Selected Species—Stumpage Prices in Current and Constant (1996) Dollars: 2000 to 2008**

[In dollars per 1,000 board feet. Stumpage prices are based on sales of sawtimber from national forests]

Species	Current dollars				Constant (1996) dollars [1]			
	2000	2005	2007	2008	2000	2005	2007	2008
Softwoods:								
Douglas fir [2].	433	321	103	(NA)	397	260	76	(NA)
Southern pine [3]	258	193	176	173	237	157	130	133
Sugar pine [4]	187	114	81	130	172	93	60	100
Ponderosa pine [4, 5]	155	103	61	162	142	84	45	124
Western hemlock [6]	46	70	26	(NA)	42	57	15	(NA)
Hardwoods:								
All eastern hardwoods [7]	341	415	277	(NA)	313	337	277	(NA)
Oak, white, red, and black [7]	258	329	220	(NA)	237	267	220	(NA)
Maple, sugar [8]	314	648	362	(NA)	288	526	267	(NA)

NA Not available.   [1] Deflated by the producer price index, all commodities.   [2] Western Washington and western Oregon.   [3] Southern region.   [4] Pacific Southwest region (formerly California region).   [5] Includes Jeffrey pine.   [6] Pacific Northwest region.   [7] Eastern and Southern regions.   [8] Eastern region.

Source: U.S. Forest Service, "RPA Assessment Tables," 2007; <http://www.fs.fed.us/research/rpa/>.

Table 858. **Selected Timber Products—Producer Price Indexes: 1990 to 2008**

[1982 = 100. For information about producer prices, see text, Section 14]

Product	1990	1995	2000	2003	2004	2005	2006	2007	2008
Lumber and wood products [1]	129.7	178.1	178.2	177.4	195.6	196.5	194.4	192.4	191.3
Lumber	124.6	173.4	178.8	174.3	203.6	198.6	188.6	174.7	163.4
Softwood lumber.	123.8	178.5	178.6	170.8	209.8	203.6	189.4	170.5	156.0
Hardwood lumber	131.0	167.0	185.9	188.8	199.3	196.6	195.3	192.4	184.7
Millwork [1]	130.4	163.8	176.4	181.8	191.9	197.2	201.8	201.4	204.8
General millwork.	132.0	165.4	178.0	185.4	193.1	196.1	201.3	203.9	207.6
Prefabricated structural members.	122.3	163.5	175.1	171.0	193.7	206.9	206.6	189.5	188.9
Plywood	114.2	165.3	157.6	167.0	198.5	186.8	172.7	176.1	174.5
Softwood plywood.	119.6	188.1	173.3	195.9	250.9	223.5	190.5	197.8	192.5
Hardwood plywood and related products	102.7	122.2	130.2	129.0	134.4	138.1	(NA)	(NA)	(NA)
Other wood products [1]	114.7	143.7	130.5	129.9	134.3	139.2	142.8	142.1	144.7
Boxes.	119.1	145.0	155.2	157.6	163.1	164.9	167.2	170.3	174.5
Pulp, paper, and allied products [1]	141.2	172.2	183.7	190.0	195.7	202.6	209.8	216.9	226.7
Pulp, paper, and prod., excl. bldg. paper [1]	132.9	163.4	161.4	157.1	162.1	169.8	178.4	186.7	199.0
Woodpulp	151.3	183.2	145.3	121.4	132.2	138.0	144.1	161.5	171.7
Wastepaper	138.9	371.1	282.5	197.3	231.4	230.9	234.8	368.7	368.5
Paper [1]	128.8	159.0	149.8	146.1	149.4	159.6	167.4	169.3	184.4
Writing and printing papers	129.1	158.4	146.6	144.7	146.0	156.1	162.8	166.7	181.7
Newsprint	119.6	161.8	127.5	112.1	124.5	138.5	151.8	131.6	147.6
Paperboard	135.7	183.1	176.7	162.7	170.2	175.5	192.0	201.7	217.8
Converted paper and paperboard products [1] . .	135.2	157.0	162.7	165.3	168.3	176.1	184.1	187.8	199.1
Office supplies and accessories	121.4	134.9	133.8	137.4	137.6	143.1	146.2	151.0	158.4
Building paper & building board mill prods.	112.2	144.9	138.8	159.9	192.4	184.9	173.0	155.2	164.1

NA Not available. [1] Includes other products not shown separately.

Source: U.S. Bureau of Labor Statistics, *Producer Price Indexes*, monthly.

Table 859. **Pulpwood Consumption, Woodpulp Production, and Paper and Board Production and Consumption: 1995 to 2008**

[Revised to match data from American Forest and Paper Association and American Pulpwood Association]

Item	Unit	1995	2000	2002	2003	2004	2005	2006	2007	2008
Pulpwood consumption [1] . .	1,000 cords [2] . .	97,052	95,904	90,500	85,436	87,110	88,595	86,284	84,076	80,461
Woodpulp production [3] . . .	1,000 tons	67,103	62,758	58,069	53,197	54,301	60,267	60,568	60,568	57,964
Paper and board [4]:										
Production	1,000 tons	89,509	94,491	89,636	80,712	83,612	91,031	91,800	91,570	87,632
Consumption or new supply [5]	1,000 tons	96,126	103,147	97,227	94,422	95,068	101,864	102,948	99,825	95,533
Per capita.	Pounds	731	731	676	629	627	687	688	661	625

[1] Includes changes in stocks. [2] One cord equals 128 cubic feet. [3] Excludes defibrated and exploded woodpulp used for hard pressed board. [4] Excludes hardboard. [5] Production plus imports, minus exports (excludes products); changes in inventories not taken into account.

Source: U.S. Forest Service, *U.S. Timber Production, Trade, Consumption and Price Statistics*, 1965–2005, Research Paper RP-FPL-637 and unpublished data. See also <http://www.treesearch.fs.fed.us/pubs/28972>.

Table 860. **Paper and Paperboard—Production and New Supply: 1990 to 2007**

[In millions of short tons (80.45 represents 80,450,000). 1 short ton = 2,000 lbs.]

Item	1990	1995	2000	2002	2003	2004	2005	2006	2007
Production, total	80.45	91.33	96.05	91.11	89.81	93.41	92.61	93.72	92.96
Paper, total.	39.36	42.87	45.52	41.56	40.37	41.82	41.40	41.81	41.27
Paperboard, total	39.32	46.64	48.97	48.13	48.02	50.08	49.71	50.41	50.40
Unbleached kraft	20.36	22.70	21.80	21.09	21.73	22.67	22.58	23.41	23.54
Semichemical	5.64	5.66	5.95	5.84	6.10	6.53	6.41	6.22	6.16
Bleached kraft	4.40	5.30	5.44	5.30	5.36	5.65	5.66	5.71	5.81
Recycled.	8.92	12.98	15.79	15.91	14.83	15.24	15.05	15.07	14.89
Wet machine board	0.15	0.15	0.06	0.05	0.05	0.05	0.05	0.05	0.03
Building paper	0.81	0.81	0.64	0.55	0.55	0.58	0.57	0.56	0.54
Insulating board	0.86	0.86	0.86	0.83	0.83	0.88	0.88	0.88	0.71
New supply, all grades, excluding products	87.68	98.16	105.02	100.57	99.76	103.74	101.81	101.69	98.85
Paper, total.	49.49	52.77	57.13	53.66	53.22	54.88	53.69	52.97	50.88
Newsprint	13.41	12.76	12.92	11.18	11.05	10.84	10.12	9.49	8.35
Printing/writing papers	25.46	29.55	32.99	31.09	31.03	32.68	31.99	31.78	31.05
Packaging and ind. conv. papers . . .	4.72	4.24	4.27	4.20	3.96	4.14	4.05	4.10	4.07
Tissue	5.90	6.22	6.95	7.20	7.18	7.22	7.53	7.60	7.42
Paperboard, total	36.30	43.45	46.02	45.29	44.95	47.20	46.51	47.11	46.61
Construction and other	1.90	1.95	1.88	1.62	1.59	1.66	1.61	1.62	1.36

Source: American Forest and Paper Association, Washington, DC, *Monthly Statistical Summary of Paper, Paperboard and Woodpulp.*

Forestry, Fishing, and Mining 551

Table 861. **Fishery Products—Domestic Catch, Imports, and Disposition: 1990 to 2007**

[Live weight, in millions of pounds (16,349 represents 16,349,000,000). For data on commercial catch for selected countries, see Table 1337, Section 30]

Item	1990	1995	2000	2002	2003	2004	2005	2006	2007
Total	16,349	16,484	17,340	19,028	19,850	20,412	20,612	20,960	20,484
For human food	12,662	13,584	14,738	16,007	17,187	17,648	18,147	18,594	18,228
For industrial use	3,687	2,900	2,599	3,021	2,663	2,765	2,382	2,366	2,255
Domestic catch.	9,404	9,788	9,069	9,397	9,507	9,683	9,707	9,483	9,232
For human food	7,041	7,667	6,912	7,205	7,521	7,794	7,997	7,842	7,466
For industrial use.	2,363	2,121	2,157	2,192	1,986	1,889	1,710	1,641	1,766
Imports [1]	6,945	6,696	8,271	9,631	10,343	10,729	10,905	11,477	11,252
For human food	5,621	5,917	7,828	8,802	9,666	9,854	10,158	10,752	10,763
For industrial use [2]	1,324	779	443	829	677	875	747	725	489
Exports [1]	4,627	5,166	5,758	6,979	6,756	8,203	8,420	7,710	7,057
For human food	3,832	4,175	4,587	5,587	5,392	6,462	6,385	6,250	5,761
For industrial use [2]	795	991	1,171	1,392	1,364	1,741	2,035	1,459	1,297
Disposition of domestic catch	9,404	9,788	9,069	9,397	9,507	9,683	9,707	9,483	9,232
Fresh and frozen	6,501	7,099	6,657	6,826	7,266	7,488	7,776	7,627	7,387
Canned.	751	769	530	652	498	552	563	573	501
Cured.	126	90	119	117	119	137	160	117	121
Reduced to meal, oil, etc.. . .	2,026	1,830	1,763	1,802	1,624	1,506	1,208	1,166	1,223

[1] Excludes imports of edible fishery products consumed in Puerto Rico; includes landings of tuna caught by foreign vessels in American Samoa.   [2] Fish meal and sea herring.

Source: U.S. National Oceanic and Atmospheric Administration, National Marine Fisheries Service, *Fisheries of the United States*, annual (published July 2008). See also <http://www.st.nmfs.noaa.gov/st1/fus/fus07/index.html>.

Table 862. **Fisheries—Quantity and Value of Domestic Catch: 1980 to 2007**

[In millions of pounds (6,482 represents 6,482,000,000), except as noted]

Year	Quantity (mil. lb. [1])			Value (mil. dol.)	Average price per lb. (cents)	Year	Quantity (mil. lb. [1])			Value (mil. dol.)	Average price per lb. (cents)
	Total	For human food	For industrial products [2]				Total	For human food	For industrial products [2]		
1980 . . .	6,482	3,654	2,828	2,237	34.5	2000 . . .	9,069	6,912	2,157	3,550	39.1
1985 . . .	6,258	3,294	2,964	2,326	37.2	2001 . . .	9,489	7,311	2,178	3,218	33.9
1990 . . .	9,404	7,041	2,363	3,522	37.5	2002 . . .	9,397	7,205	2,192	3,092	32.9
1995 . . .	9,788	7,667	2,121	3,770	38.5	2003 . . .	9,507	7,521	1,986	3,347	35.2
1996 . . .	9,565	7,474	2,091	3,487	36.5	2004 . . .	9,683	7,794	1,889	3,756	38.8
1997 . . .	9,842	7,244	2,598	3,448	35.0	2005 . . .	9,707	7,997	1,710	3,942	40.6
1998 . . .	9,194	7,173	2,021	3,126	34.0	2006 . . .	9,483	7,842	1,641	4,024	42.4
1999 . . .	9,339	6,832	2,507	3,467	37.1	2007 . . .	9,232	7,466	1,766	4,089	44.3

[1] Live weight.   [2] Meal, oil, fish solubles, homogenized condensed fish, shell products, bait, and animal food.

Source: U.S. National Oceanic and Atmospheric Administration, National Marine Fisheries Service, *Fisheries of the United States*, annual (published July 2008). See also <http://www.st.nmfs.noaa.gov/st1/fus/fus07/index.html>.

Table 863. **Domestic Fish and Shellfish Catch and Value by Major Species Caught: 2000 to 2007**

[In thousands (9,068,985 represents 9,068,985,000)]

Species	Quantity (1,000 lb.)				Value ($1,000)			
	2000	2005	2006	2007	2000	2005	2006	2007
Total [1]	9,068,985	9,707,275	9,482,996	9,231,833	3,549,481	3,942,376	4,024,445	4,089,012
Fish, total [1]	7,689,661	8,462,473	8,287,267	8,210,777	1,594,815	1,836,448	1,930,725	2,076,083
Cod: Atlantic	25,060	13,920	12,618	16,948	26,384	20,828	20,484	27,050
Pacific.	530,505	548,746	518,733	488,293	142,330	150,738	197,243	224,635
Flounder.	412,723	419,430	445,913	485,830	109,910	135,176	151,589	153,476
Halibut	75,190	76,263	71,429	70,107	143,826	177,593	202,099	226,732
Herring, Atlantic	160,269	215,565	207,915	162,657	9,972	20,467	21,907	19,486
Herring, Pacific.	74,835	87,295	81,935	69,304	12,043	13,799	8,042	15,315
Menhaden.	1,760,498	1,243,723	1,306,761	1,481,672	112,403	62,465	65,597	125,285
Pollock, Alaska.	2,606,802	3,411,307	3,400,812	3,066,152	160,525	306,072	329,879	297,417
Salmon.	628,638	899,457	663,654	884,983	270,213	330,699	310,900	381,110
Tuna	50,779	44,316	49,958	50,785	95,176	85,922	86,996	93,132
Whiting (Atlantic, silver) . . .	26,855	16,561	12,350	14,044	11,370	8,284	6,762	7,906
Whiting (Pacific, hake).	452,718	569,381	570,489	455,295	18,809	29,145	35,234	34,228
Shellfish, total [1]	1,379,324	1,244,802	1,195,729	1,021,056	1,954,666	2,105,928	2,093,720	2,012,929
Clams.	118,482	105,640	110,912	116,100	153,973	173,655	188,601	187,703
Crabs.	299,006	299,137	339,944	284,797	405,006	415,057	413,744	453,966
Lobsters: American	83,180	88,032	92,615	75,192	301,300	416,597	395,175	349,056
Oysters.	41,146	33,963	34,409	35,142	90,667	110,679	121,493	126,903
Scallops, sea	32,747	56,702	59,005	58,423	164,609	433,512	384,809	385,037
Shrimp	332,486	260,884	320,176	231,553	690,453	406,344	440,651	369,788
Squid, Pacific.	259,508	126,107	113,266	109,170	27,077	31,601	27,188	29,214

[1] Includes other landings not shown separately.

Source: U.S. National Oceanic and Atmospheric Administration, National Marine Fisheries Service, *Fisheries of the United States*, annual (published July 2008). See also <http://www.st.nmfs.noaa.gov/st1/fus/fus07/index.html>.

552   Forestry, Fishing, and Mining

Table 864. **U.S. Private Aquaculture—Trout and Catfish Production and Value: 1990 to 2008**

[67.8 represents 67,800,000. Data are for calendar year and foodsize fish (those over 12 inches long)]

Item	Unit	1990	1995	2000	2004	2005	2006	2007	2008
TROUT FOODSIZE									
Number sold.	Mil.	67.8	60.2	58.4	49.6	55.5	52.5	58.7	40.4
Total weight	Mil. lb.	56.8	55.6	59.0	57.6	59.7	65.3	66.9	52.4
Total value of sales	Mil. dol. . . .	64.6	60.8	63.3	59.4	62.7	72.7	79.5	72.4
Avg. price received by processors. . .	Dol./lb. . . .	1.14	1.09	1.07	1.03	1.05	1.11	1.19	1.38
Percent sold to processors	Percent . . .	58	68	70	73	66	69	64	58
CATFISH FOODSIZE									
Number sold.	Mil.	272.9	321.8	420.1	389.3	405.4	370.9	365.8	304.0
Total weight	Mil. lb.	392.4	481.5	633.8	682.2	638.9	587.0	563.9	514.9
Total value of sales	Mil. dol. . . .	305.1	378.1	468.8	450.9	450.2	455.1	423.7	389.3
Avg. price received by processors. . .	Dol./lb.	0.78	0.79	0.74	0.66	0.70	0.78	0.75	0.76
Fish sold to processors.	Mil. lb. . . .	360.4	446.9	593.6	630.5	600.7	566.1	496.2	509.6
Avg. price paid by processors	Cents/lb. . . .	75.8	78.6	75.1	69.7	72.5	79.5	76.7	77.6
Processor sales.	Mil. lb.	183.1	227.0	297.2	306.8	300.0	284.0	252.5	251.2
Avg. price received by processors. . .	Dol./lb.	2.24	2.40	2.36	2.23	2.29	2.46	2.44	2.44
Inventory (Jan. 1)	Mil. lb.	9.4	10.9	13.6	15.2	13.7	18.2	15.1	15.5

Source: U.S. Department of Agriculture, National Agricultural Statistics Service, *Trout Production*, published February 2009; *Catfish Production*, published January 2009; and *Catfish Processing*, published February 2009. See also <http://usda.mannlib.cornell.edu/reports/nassr/other/>. Also in *Agricultural Statistics*, annual.

Table 865. **Supply of Selected Fishery Items: 1990 to 2007**

[In millions of pounds (734 represents 734,000,000). Totals available for U.S. consumption are supply minus exports plus imports. Round weight is the complete or full weight as caught]

Species	Unit	1990	1995	2000	2002	2003	2004	2005	2006	2007
Shrimp	Heads-off weight. . .	734	832	1,173	1,430	1,608	1,670	1,559	1,879	1,712
Tuna, canned	Canned weight	856	875	980	922	982	874	895	858	812
Snow crab	Round weight	37	42	122	172	198	168	171	187	208
Clams.	Meat weight	152	144	133	144	143	132	120	125	128
Salmon, canned	Canned weight	148	147	95	135	111	98	123	56	91
American lobster.	Round weight	95	94	125	135	128	138	144	150	122
Spiny lobster , ...	Round weight	89	89	99	87	93	93	83	77	78
Scallops	Meat weight	74	62	70	91	91	94	86	94	92
Sardines, canned	Canned weight	61	44	(NA)	(NA)	(NA)	(NA)	(NA)	(NA)	(NA)
Oysters	Meat weight	56	63	71	62	69	53	47	49	48
King crab	Round weight	19	21	41	47	47	52	78	110	134
Crab meat, canned . . .	Canned weight	9	12	29	44	47	56	59	58	66

NA Not available.

Source: U.S. National Oceanic and Atmospheric Administration, National Marine Fisheries Service, *Fisheries of the United States*, annual (published July 2008). See also <http://www.st.nmfs.noaa.gov/st1/fus/fus07/index.html>.

Table 866. **Canned, Fresh, and Frozen Fishery Products—Production and Value: 1990 to 2007**

[In millions of pounds (1,178 represents 1,178,000,000). Fresh fishery products exclude Alaska and Hawaii. Canned fishery products data are for natural pack only]

Product	Production (mil. lb.)					Value (mil. dol.)				
	1990	2000	2005	2006	2007	1990	2000	2005	2006	2007
Canned, total [1]	**1,178**	**1,747**	**1,082**	**1,081**	**1,099**	**1,562**	**1,626**	**1,211**	**1,330**	**1,352**
Tuna	581	671	446	445	436	902	856	628	705	702
Salmon	196	171	219	152	183	366	288	301	250	283
Clam products.	110	127	123	112	100	76	120	127	123	109
Sardines, Maine	13	(Z)	(NA)	(NA)	(NA)	17	(Z)	(NA)	(NA)	(NA)
Shrimp.	1	2	1	(Z)	(Z)	3	11	3	1	1
Crabs	1	(Z)	(Z)	(Z)	(Z)	4	(Z)	(Z)	(Z)	(Z)
Oysters [2]	1	(Z)	(Z)	(Z)	(Z)	1	1	(Z)	(Z)	(Z)
Fish fillets and steaks [3] . . .	**441**	**368**	**615**	**631**	**622**	**843**	**823**	**1,136**	**1,300**	**1,287**
Cod.	65	56	47	42	32	132	167	116	123	102
Flounder	54	27	20	18	20	154	71	65	73	68
Haddock	7	6	24	16	10	24	24	89	70	57
Ocean perch, Atlantic	1	(Z)	1	1	1	1	1	4	3	3
Rockfish.	33	11	3	3	3	53	25	8	5	6
Pollock, Atlantic.	12	2	3	2	2	21	4	6	4	5
Pollock, Alaska	164	160	383	398	396	174	178	404	488	485
Other.	105	106	134	152	158	284	353	444	534	561

NA Not available. Z Less than 500,000 pounds or $500,000. [1] Includes other products not shown separately. [2] Includes oyster specialties. [3] Fresh and frozen.

Source: U.S. National Oceanic and Atmospheric Administration, National Marine Fisheries Service, *Fisheries of the United States*, annual (published July 2008). See also <http://www.st.nmfs.noaa.gov/st1/fus/fus07/index.html>.

Forestry, Fishing, and Mining   553

Table 867. Mineral Industries—Employment, Hours, and Earnings: 1990 to 2008

[In thousands (680 represents 680,000), except as noted. Based on the Current Employment Statistics Program, see Appendix III]

Industry and item	Unit	1990	1995	2000	2004	2005	2006	2007	2008
All mining: [1]									
All employees.	1,000	680	558	520	523	562	620	664	717
Production workers	1,000	469	391	383	384	419	466	497	531
Avg. weekly hours	Number. . .	46.1	46.8	45.5	45.4	46.4	46.3	46.2	45.3
Avg. weekly earnings . . .	Dollars . . .	630	711	771	837	884	938	989	1,043
Coal mining:									
All employees.	1,000	136	97	72	71	74	78	77	81
Production workers	1,000	110	78	59	59	61	67	68	71
Avg. weekly hours	Number. . .	44.7	45.7	45.6	47.7	48.5	49.5	47.9	49.0
Avg. weekly earnings . . .	Dollars . . .	822	929	945	1,029	1,071	1,093	1,052	1,140
Oil and gas extraction:									
All employees.	1,000	190	152	125	123	126	135	146	162
Production workers	1,000	84	73	67	70	72	78	83	90
Avg. weekly hours	Number. . .	44.4	43.6	41.3	43.5	44.3	43.0	41.9	41.1
Avg. weekly earnings . . .	Dollars . . .	591	677	802	808	856	921	1,015	1,120
Metal ore mining:									
All employees.	1,000	53	48	38	28	29	32	36	40
Production workers	1,000	43	39	29	20	22	25	28	32
Avg. weekly hours	Number. . .	42.5	43.4	43.4	45.2	44.2	43.5	45.9	46.1
Avg. weekly earnings . . .	Dollars . . .	646	788	871	1,035	1,001	974	1,077	1,195
Nonmetallic minerals mining, and quarrying:									
All employees.	1,000	113	108	115	107	110	110	110	107
Production workers	1,000	85	81	87	81	84	82	82	81
Avg. weekly hours	Number. . .	45.0	46.3	46.1	44.6	45.9	46.1	46.3	43.9
Avg. weekly earnings . . .	Dollars . . .	532	632	722	791	830	863	872	840

[1] Includes other industries not shown separately.

Source: U.S. Bureau of Labor Statistics, Current Employment Statistics, "Employment, Hours, and Earnings—National"; <http://www.bls.gov/ces/data.htm> (accessed 10 April 2009).

Table 868. Mine Safety: 2000 to 2008

[Reported injury rates per 200,000 employee hours]

Item	All mines			Coal			Metal and nonmetal		
	2000	2007	2008 [1]	2000	2007	2008 [1]	2000	2007	2008 [1]
Number of mines.	14,413	14,786	14,880	2,124	2,030	2,122	12,289	12,841	12,758
Number of miners	348,548	376,386	392,012	108,098	122,936	133,493	240,450	255,186	258,519
Fatalities	85	64	52	38	34	30	47	33	22
Fatal injury rate.	0.03	0.02	0.02	0.04	0.03	0.02	0.02	0.01	0.01
All injury rate	5.13	3.43	3.24	6.64	4.21	3.88	4.45	3.02	2.86
Coal production (mil. tons)	1,078	1,147	1,172	1,078	1,147	1,172	(X)	(X)	(X)
Total mining area inspection hours/mine.	57	44	56	178	169	227	28	19	21
Citations and orders.	120,269	144,735	174,522	58,394	84,544	107,441	61,875	60,191	67,081
S&S [2] citations and orders (percent). . .	36	31	30	42	37	35	31	22	21
Amount assessed [3] (mil. dol.)	24.7	74.5	194.3	12.0	53.5	152.7	12.7	21.0	41.6

X Not applicable. [1] Preliminary. [2] A violation that "significantly and substantially" contributes to the cause and effect of a coal or other mine safety or health hazard. [3] Government penalties or fines.

Source: U.S. Mine Safety and Health Administration, Office of Program Education and Outreach Services, "Mine Safety and Health At a Glance" (published 27 March 2009); <http://www.msha.gov/MSHAINFO/FactSheets/MSHAFCT10.HTM>.

Table 869. Mining and Primary Metal Production Indexes: 1990 to 2008

[Index 2002 = 100]

Industry group	NAICS code [1]	1990	1995	2000	2003	2004	2005	2006	2007	2008
Mining [2]	21	**107.8**	**105.3**	**104.2**	**100.2**	**99.6**	**98.3**	**101.5**	**102.1**	**104.2**
Oil and gas extraction [2].	211	107.2	104.0	101.0	99.0	96.0	92.0	93.5	95.0	97.5
Crude oil and natural gas.	211111	109.2	104.8	100.9	99.7	95.9	92.1	93.5	95.0	97.7
Coal mining	2121	98.3	96.8	99.2	97.5	100.8	102.5	105.2	103.6	105.9
Metal ore mining	2122	113.1	123.8	120.5	95.4	98.2	106.1	109.1	106.0	109.6
Iron ore	21221	109.8	121.8	122.2	94.1	106.0	105.2	102.3	100.4	102.1
Gold ore and silver ore	21222	99.9	106.9	119.0	92.9	86.8	86.1	84.5	80.4	77.4
Copper, nickel, lead, and zinc. .	21223	122.2	140.0	122.9	98.5	100.6	99.2	103.4	102.4	112.1
Oil and gas drilling	213111	102.3	89.5	114.4	116.2	126.9	142.5	164.4	170.3	177.8
Primary metal manufacturing [2] . . .	331	**96.7**	**106.0**	**111.4**	**99.1**	**110.0**	**108.0**	**112.6**	**110.0**	**102.6**
Iron and steel	3311	95.1	105.6	110.8	101.2	118.2	110.1	119.3	115.8	105.8
Aluminum	3313	103.3	99.1	104.7	95.8	96.4	102.7	105.1	102.5	100.1
Nonferrous metals [2]	3314	111.4	123.9	115.5	100.3	103.7	103.4	99.8	101.6	98.0
Copper	33142	142.5	263.1	133.8	86.9	90.7	81.8	68.0	72.2	65.1

[1] Based on the 2002 North American Industry Classification System (NAICS). [2] Includes other industries not shown separately.

Source: Board of Governors of the Federal Reserve System, The Statistical Supplement to the Federal Reserve Bulletin, monthly; and Industrial Production and Capacity Utilization, Statistical Release G.17, monthly.

Table 870. **Mineral Production: 1990 to 2008**

[**1,029.1 represents 1,029,100,000.** Data represent production as measured by mine shipments, mine sales, or marketable production; see Appendix IV]

Minerals and Metals	Unit	1990	2000	2006	2007	2008, est.
FUEL MINERALS						
Coal, total [1]	Mil. sh. tons	1,029.1	1,073.6	1,162.7	1,146.6	1,171.5
Bituminous [1]	Mil. sh. tons	693.2	574.3	561.6	542.8	559.4
Subbituminous	Mil. sh. tons	244.3	409.2	515.3	523.7	534.7
Lignite.	Mil. sh. tons	88.1	85.6	84.2	78.6	75.7
Anthracite [1]	Mil. sh. tons	3.5	4.6	1.5	1.6	1.7
Natural gas (marketed production).	Tril. cu. ft.	18.59	20.20	19.41	20.02	21.46
Petroleum (crude).	Mil. bbl. [2]	2,685	2,131	1,862	1,848	1,814
Uranium (recoverable content)	Mil. lb.	8.9	4.0	4.1	4.5	3.9
NONFUEL MINERALS						
Asbestos (sales).	1,000 metric tons . .	(D)	5	–	–	–
Barite, primary, sold/used by producers. .	1,000 metric tons . .	430	392	589	455	615
Boron minerals, sold or used by producers	1,000 metric tons . .	1,090	1,070	(D)	(D)	(D)
Bromine, sold or used by producers. . . .	1,000 metric tons . .	177	228	243	(D)	(D)
Cement:						
Portland [3]	Mil. metric tons . . .	67	84	93	90	85
Masonry [3]	Mil. metric tons . . .	3	4	5	4	3
Clays	1,000 metric tons . .	42,900	40,800	41,200	36,800	33,200
Diatomite.	1,000 metric tons . .	631	677	799	687	653
Feldspar [4]	1,000 metric tons . .	630	790	760	730	600
Fluorspar, finished shipments	1,000 metric tons . .	64	–	–	–	(NA)
Garnet (industrial).	1,000 metric tons . .	47	60	34	61	61
Gypsum, crude.	Mil. metric tons . . .	15	20	21	18	13
Helium [5]	Mil. cu. meters . . .	65	98	79	77	78
Lime, sold or used by producers	Mil. metric tons . . .	16	20	21	20	20
Mica, scrap & flake, sold/used by producers	1,000 metric tons . .	109	101	110	97	99
Peat, sales by producers	1,000 metric tons . .	721	847	734	694	700
Perlite, processed, sold or used.	1,000 metric tons . .	576	672	454	409	449
Phosphate rock (marketable)	Mil. metric tons . . .	46	39	30	30	31
Potash (K$_2$O equivalent) sales.	1,000 metric tons . .	1,710	1,300	1,100	1,100	1,200
Pumice & pumicite, producer sales	1,000 metric tons . .	443	1,050	1,540	1,270	1,140
Salt, common, sold/used by producers . .	Mil. metric tons . . .	37	46	44	45	46
Sand & gravel, sold/used by producer . .	Mil. metric tons . . .	855	1,148	1,349	1,260	1,070
Construction.	Mil. metric tons . . .	829	1,120	1,320	1,230	1,040
Industrial	Mil. metric tons . . .	26	28	29	30	30
Sodium carbonate (natural) (soda ash) . .	1,000 metric tons	9,100	10,200	11,000	11,100	11,300
Sodium sulfate (natural).	1,000 metric tons . .	349	(NA)	290	312	320
Stone [6]	Mil. metric tons . . .	2,230	2,810	3,100	2,990	2,790
Crushed and broken	Mil. metric tons . . .	1,110	1,560	1,770	1,600	1,340
Dimension [7]	1,000 metric tons . .	1,120	1,250	1,330	1,390	1,450
Sulfur: Total shipments.	1,000 metric tons . .	11,500	10,700	8,960	9,120	9,200
Sulfur: Frasch mines (shipments).	1,000 metric tons . .	3,680	900	–	–	–
Talc and pyrophyllite, crude	1,000 metric tons . .	1,270	851	895	769	645
Vermiculite concentrate	1,000 metric tons . .	209	150	100	100	100
METALS						
Antimony ore and concentrate.	Metric tons.	(D)	(D)	–	(D)	(D)
Aluminum	1,000 metric tons . .	4,048	3,668	2,284	2,554	2,640
Bauxite (dried)	1,000 metric tons . .	(D)	(NA)	(NA)	(NA)	(NA)
Copper (recoverable content)	1,000 metric tons . .	1,590	1,450	1,200	1,170	1,310
Gold (recoverable content)	Metric tons.	294	353	252	238	230
Iron ore (gross weight) [8]	Mil. metric tons . . .	57	61	53	51	56
Lead (recoverable content).	1,000 metric tons . .	484	449	419	434	420
Magnesium metal	1,000 metric tons . .	139	(D)	(D)	(D)	(D)
Manganiferous ore (gross weight) [9]	1,000 metric ton . . .	(D)	–	(NA)	(NA)	(NA)
Mercury [10]	Metric tons.	(NA)	(NA)	(NA)	(NA)	(NA)
Molybdenum (concentrate)	1,000 metric tons . .	62	41	60	57	61
Nickel ore (recovered Ni content).	1,000 metric tons . .	330	–	–	–	–
Palladium metal	Kilograms	5,930	10,300	14,400	12,800	12,400
Platinum metal	Kilograms	1,810	3,110	4,290	[11]3,860	[11]3,700
Silicon (Si content)	1,000 metric tons . .	418	367	146	[11]155	[11]166
Silver (recoverable content)	Metric tons.	2,120	1,860	1,140	1,260	1,120
Titanium concentrate (TiO$_2$ content)	1,000 metric tons . .	(D)	300	300	300	200
Tungsten ore and concentrate [12]	Metric tons.	(D)	–	–	(D)	(D)
Zinc (recoverable content)	1,000 metric tons . .	508	796	699	769	794

– Represents or rounds to zero.   D Withheld to avoid disclosing individual company data.   NA Not available.   [1] Beginning 2006, includes a small amount of refuse recovery.   [2] 42 gal. bbl.   [3] Excludes Puerto Rico.   [4] Beginning 2000, includes aplite.   [5] Refined.   [6] Excludes abrasive stone, bituminous limestone and sandstone, and ground soapstone, all included elsewhere in table; includes calcareous marl and slate.   [7] Includes Puerto Rico in 1990.   [8] Represents shipments; includes byproduct ores.   [9] 5- to 35-percent manganiferous ore.   [10] Mercury recovered as a byproduct of gold ores only, 1990.   [11] Ferrosilocon only; silicon metal withheld to avoid disclosing proprietary data.   [12] Content of ore and concentrate.

Source: Nonfuels, 1990 only, U.S. Bureau of Mines, thereafter, U.S. Geological Survey, *Minerals Yearbook* and *Mineral Commodities Summaries,* annual. See also <http://minerals.er.usgs.gov/minerals/pubs/mcs/>. Fuels, U.S. Energy Information Administration, *Annual Energy Review*, 2008. See also <http://www.eia.doe.gov/emeu/aer/contents.html>.

Forestry, Fishing, and Mining   555

Table 871. Nonfuel Mineral Commodities—Summary: 2008

[2,640 represents 2,640,000. Preliminary estimates. Average price in dollars per metric tons except as noted]

Mineral	Unit	Mineral disposition Production	Exports	Net import reliance [1] (percent)	Consumption, apparent	Average price per unit (dollars)	Employment (number)
Aluminum	1,000 metric tons	2,640	3,800	(²)	3,700	[3]1.21	55,000
Antimony (contained)	Metric tons	[4]−	2,050	86	23,800	[3]2.84	10
Asbestos	1,000 metric tons	−	−	100	2	(NA)	−
Barite	1,000 metric tons	615	52	79	2,960	[5]49.00	350
Bauxite and alumina (metal equivalent)	1,000 metric tons	(NA)	680	100	3,600	[5]31.00	(NA)
Beryllium (contained)	Metric tons	155	130	(²)	141	[3]162	(NA)
Bismuth (contained)	Metric tons	−	566	97	3,000	[3]12.13	(NA)
Boron (B₂O₃ content)	1,000 metric tons	(D)	260	(²)	(D)	[5, 6](NA)	1,420
Bromine (contained)	1,000 metric tons	(D)	11	25	(D)	[7, 8](NA)	1,000
Cadmium (contained)	Metric tons	[4]745	360	(²)	564	[3, 9]6.86	(NA)
Cement	1,000 metric tons	[10]87,700	950	12	98,600	[5]107	15,000
Chromium	1,000 metric tons	[11](D)	250	54	630	(NA)	(NA)
Clays	1,000 metric tons	33,200	5,200	(²)	28,100	(NA)	900
Cobalt (contained)	Metric tons	[11]1,900	2,900	81	10,200	[3]40.40	(NA)
Copper (mine, recoverable)	1,000 metric tons	1,300	1,000	31	1,980	319	11.2
Diamond (industrial)	Mil. carats	296	122	56	671	[12]0.20	(NA)
Diatomite	1,000 metric tons	653	152	(²)	504	[5]249	1,020
Feldspar	1,000 metric tons	600	11	(²)	591	[5]60.00	400
Fluorspar	1,000 metric tons	−	15	100	460	(NA)	−
Garnet (industrial)	Metric tons	61,000	13,900	40	102,000	[5]50-2,000	160
Gemstones	Mil. dol.	55.8	16,400	99	6,420	(NA)	1,200
Germanium (contained)	Kilograms	4,600	18,200	(NA)	(NA)	[7]1,600	70
Gold (contained)	Metric tons	230	595	(²)	(NA)	[13]900	9,200
Graphite (crude)	1,000 metric tons	−	16	100	39	[5, 14]669	(NA)
Gypsum (crude)	1,000 metric tons	12,700	159	27	28,000	[5]7.25	5,400
Iodine	Metric tons	(D)	1,200	(D)	(D)	[7, 15]22.20	30
Iron ore (usable)	Mil. metric tons	[16]56.0	9.0	(²)	52.0	[5]66.00	4,450
Iron and steel scrap (metal)	Mil. metric tons	87	23	(²)	(NA)	[5, 17]390	30,000
Iron and steel slag (metal)	1,000 metric tons	[18]15,000	1,000	8	15,000	[5]25.00	2,400
Lead (contained)	1,000 metric tons	440	300	(²)	1,600	[3]120	3,040
Lime	1,000 metric tons	19,800	175	1	20,000	[19]89.20	5,400
Magnesium compounds	1,000 metric tons	340	26	52	704	(NA)	370
Magnesium metal	1,000 metric tons	(D)	14	50	140	[3]3.15	400
Manganese (gross weight)	1,000 metric tons	−	42	100	1000	[20]12.97	(NA)
Mercury	Metric tons	[11](NA)	900	(²)	(NA)	[21]600	(NA)
Mica, scrap and flake	1,000 metric tons	99	9	16	118	[5]213	(NA)
Molybdenum (contained)	Metric tons	61,400	32,300	(²)	43,500	[7]62.99	940
Nickel (contained)	Metric tons	(D)	106,000	[22]33	118,000	[23]21,104	−
Niobium (contained)	Metric tons	−	1,100	100	9,910	(NA)	(NA)
Nitrogen (fixed)-ammonia	1,000 metric tons	8,240	166	48	15,800	[24]500	1,100
Peat	1,000 metric tons	650	79	58	1,560	[5]26.10	620
Perlite	1,000 metric tons	449	28	19	556	[5]49.93	103
Phosphate rock	1,000 metric tons	30,900	−	9	(NA)	[5]113	2,350
Platinum-group metals	Kilograms	[25]16,100	77,200	91	(NA)	[13, 26]1,680	[27]1,700
Potash (K₂O equivalent)	1,000 metric tons	1,200	275	81	6,200	[5, 28]717	1,130
Pumice and pumicite	1,000 metric tons	1,140	17	6	1,210	[5]25.00	110
Salt	1,000 metric tons	46,000	800	17	55,200	[5, 29]155	4,100
Silicon (contained)	Metric tons	[30](D)	35	[31](²)	374	[32]374	(NA)
Silver (contained)	Metric tons	1,120	520	60	6,740	[13]15.85	850
Sodium carbonate (soda ash)	1,000 metric tons	11,200	5,200	(²)	6,000	[34]260	2,500
Sodium sulfate	1,000 metric tons	320	120	(²)	270	[35]134	225
Stone (crushed)	Mil. metric tons	1,340	1	1	1,360	[5]8.98	81,000
Sulfur (all forms)	1,000 metric tons	9,200	820	28	12,800	[5, 36]100	2,600
Talc	1,000 metric tons	645	220	(²)	615	[5]121	440
Thallium (contained)	Kilograms	−	540	100	(NA)	[7]4,900	(NA)
Tin (contained)	Metric tons	[11]2,600	4,700	80	59,500	[3]12.40	−
Titanium dioxide	1,000 metric tons	1,500	770	(²)	930	[3, 37]0.91	4,200
Tungsten (contained)	Metric tons	[11]5,000	5,675	61	14,200	[38]185	(NA)
Vermiculite	1,000 metric tons	100	5	35	155	[5]140	100
Zinc (contained)	1,000 metric tons	829	816	73	1,010	[3, 39]0.89	1,130
Zirconium (ZrO₂)	Metric tons	(D)	34,100	(²)	(D)	[5, 40]890	(NA)

− Represents zero.   D Withheld to avoid disclosure.   NA Not available.   [1] Calculated as a percent of apparent consumption.   [2] Net exporter.   [3] Dollars per pound.   [4] Refinery production.   [5] Dollars per metric ton.   [6] Granulated pentahydrate borax in bulk, f.o.b mine.   [7] Dollars per kilogram.   [8] Bulk, purified bromine.   [9] 1- to 5-short ton lots.   [10] Excludes Puerto Rico.   [11] Secondary production.   [12] Value of imports, dollars per carat.   [13] Dollars per troy ounce.   [14] Price of flake imports.   [15] C.i.f. value, crude, per kilogram.   [16] Shipments of usable ore.   [17] Delivered, No. 1 Heavy Melting composite price.   [18] Sales of processed slag.   [19] Quicklime only.   [20] 46–48 percent Mn metallurgical ore, per unit contained Mn, c.i.f. U.S. ports.   [21] Dollars per 76-pound flask.   [22] Exports include both primary and secondary materials.   [23] London Metal Exchange cash price; dollars per metric ton.   [24] F.o.b. Gulf Coast.   [25] Platinum and palladium only.   [26] Dealer price of platinum.   [27] Platinum only.   [28] Price of K₂O, muriate.   [29] Vacuum and open pan, bulk, pellets and packaged, f.o.b. mine and plant.   [30] Silicon metal only.   [31] Value less than or equal to 50,000 metric tons. Ferrosilicon statistics include: production (156,001 tons), exports (6,000 tons), and net import reliance (56%).   [32] Ferrosilicon only.   [33] Ferrosilicon, 50 percent; cents per pound.   [34] Quoted year-end price, dense, bulk, f.o.b. Green River, WY, dollars per short ton.   [35] Quoted price, bulk, f.o.b. works, East, dollars per short ton.   [36] Elemental sulfur, f.o.b. plant.   [37] Yearend. Unit value based on landed-duty-paid U.S. imports for consumption of pigment with 80 percent or more TiO₂.   [38] Dollars per metric ton unit WO₃ (7.93 kilograms of contained tungsten per metric ton unit).   [39] Platts Metals Week North American price for Special High Grade zinc.   [40] Price for imported zircon, f.o.b. U.S. East Coast.

Source: U.S. Geological Survey, Mineral Commodity Summaries, annual. See also <http://minerals.er.usgs.gov/minerals/pubs/mcs/2009/mcs2009.pdf> (released 29 January 2009).

Table 872. **Selected Mineral Products—Average Prices: 1990 to 2008**

[Excludes Alaska and Hawaii, except as noted]

Year	Nonfuels								Fuels		
	Copper, cathode [1] (cents per lb.)	Plati-num [2] (dol./ troy oz.)	Gold (dol./ troy oz.[3])	Silver (dol./ troy oz.[3])	Lead [4] (cents per lb.)	Tin (New York) [5] (cents per lb.)	Zinc [6] (cents per lb.)	Sulfur, crude [7] (dol./ metric ton)	Bitumi-nous coal [8] (dol./ short ton)	Crude petro-leum [8] (dol./ bbl.)	Natural gas [8] (dol./ 1,000 cu. ft.)
1990	123	467	385	4.82	46	386	75	80.14	27.43	20.03	1.71
1995	138	425	386	5.15	42	416	56	44.46	25.56	14.62	1.55
1996	109	398	389	5.19	49	412	51	34.11	25.17	18.46	2.17
1997	107	397	332	4.89	47	381	65	36.06	24.64	17.23	2.32
1998	79	375	295	5.54	45	373	51	29.14	24.87	10.87	1.96
1999	76	379	280	5.25	44	366	53	37.81	23.92	15.56	2.19
2000	88	549	280	5.00	44	370	56	24.73	24.15	26.72	3.68
2001	77	533	272	4.39	44	315	44	10.01	25.36	21.84	4.00
2002	76	543	311	4.62	44	292	39	11.84	26.57	22.51	2.95
2003	85	694	365	4.91	44	340	41	28.70	26.73	27.56	4.88
2004	134	849	411	6.69	55	547	52	32.62	30.56	36.77	5.46
2005	174	900	446	7.34	61	483	67	30.88	36.80	50.28	7.33
2006	315	1,144	606	11.61	77	565	159	32.85	39.32	59.69	6.39
2007	328	1,308	699	13.38	124	899	154	36.29	40.80	66.52	6.37
2008	319	1,680	900	15.85	120	1,240	89	100.00	51.45	94.04	8.07

[1] U.S. producer price. [2] Average annual dealer prices. [3] 99.95 percent purity. [4] Nationwide delivered basis. [5] Composite price. [6] Platt's Metals Week price for North American Special High Grade zinc. Average prices for 1990 are for U.S. High Grade Zinc. [7] F.o.b. (Free on Board) works. [8] Average value at the point of production or domestic first purchase price.

Source: Nonfuels, 1990, U.S. Bureau of Mines, thereafter, U.S. Geological Survey, *Minerals Yearbook* and *Mineral Commodities Summaries*, annual. See also <http://minerals.er.usgs.gov/minerals/pubs/mcs/>. Fuels, U.S. Energy Information Administration, *Annual Energy Review*. See also <http://www.eia.doe.gov/emeu/mer/prices.html>.

Table 873. **Value of Domestic Nonfuel Mineral Production by State: 2000 to 2008**

[In millions of dollars (39,400 represents $39,400,000,000). For similar data on fuels, see Table 878]

State	2000	2007 [1]	2008 [1]	State	2000	2007 [1]	2008 [1]
United States [2] . .	39,400	69,600	71,100	Montana	596	1,360	1,380
				Nebraska	[3]84	[3]147	[3]138
Alabama	930	1,350	1,220	Nevada	2,980	5,370	6,480
Alaska	1,140	3,530	2,740	New Hampshire	[3]57	[3]118	119
Arizona	2,510	7,260	7,840	New Jersey	[3]291	342	326
Arkansas	484	768	843				
California	3,270	4,380	4,000	New Mexico	786	1,560	1,810
				New York	1,020	1,530	1,520
Colorado	592	2,040	2,050	North Carolina	744	1,200	[3]876
Connecticut	[3]112	[3]166	140	North Dakota	35	[3]50	45
Delaware	[3]14	[3]25	[3]22	Ohio	999	1,270	1,120
Florida	1,820	3,380	4,200				
Georgia	1,620	2,060	1,850	Oklahoma	473	731	746
				Oregon	299	493	419
Hawaii	[3]92	150	158	Pennsylvania	[3]1,250	[3]1,840	1,680
Idaho	358	774	1,220	Rhode Island	[3]20	[3]52	56
Illinois	913	1,220	1,110	South Carolina	[3]551	[3]789	617
Indiana	695	991	932				
Iowa	503	688	782	South Dakota	233	270	270
				Tennessee	737	975	856
Kansas	629	1,070	1,060	Texas	1,950	3,240	3,300
Kentucky	501	786	772	Utah	1,430	3,880	4,170
Louisiana	325	567	508	Vermont	[3]67	[3]102	99
Maine	96	188	229				
Maryland	[3]358	[3]673	548				
Massachusetts	[3]200	[3]277	246	Virginia	710	1,150	1,090
Michigan	1,640	1,970	2,050	Washington	607	748	619
Minnesota	1,460	[3]2,690	3,210	West Virginia	172	268	276
Mississippi	149	238	228	Wisconsin	[3]372	[3]540	575
Missouri	1,370	2,270	2,080	Wyoming	978	1,750	1,890

[1] Preliminary. [2] Includes undistributed not shown separately. [3] Partial data only; excludes values withheld to avoid disclosing individual company data.

Source: U.S. Geological Survey, *Minerals Yearbook*, annual, (published 29 January 2009) and *Mineral Commodities Summaries*, annual. See also <http://minerals.er.usgs.gov/minerals/pubs/mcs/2009/mcs2009.pdf>.

Forestry, Fishing, and Mining **557**

Table 874. **Principal Fuels, Nonmetals, and Metals—World Production and the U.S. Share: 1990 to 2008**

[In millions of short tons (4,937 represents 4,937,000,000), except as indicated; see Appendix IV]

Mineral	Unit	World production				Percent U.S. of world			
		2000	2005	2007	2008 [1]	2000	2005	2007	2008 [1]
Fuels: [2]									
Coal	Mil. sh. tons	4,937	6,465	7,080	(NA)	22	18	16	(NA)
Petroleum (crude)	Bil. bbl.	24.7	26.5	26.3	26.6	8	7	7	7
Natural gas (dry, marketable)	Tril. cu. ft.	88.4	101.5	(NA)	(NA)	22	18	(NA)	(NA)
Natural gas plant liquids	Bil. bbl.	2.3	2.8	2.9	2.9	30	22	22	22
Nonmetals:									
Asbestos	1,000 metric tons . .	2,110	2,250	2,200	2,200	–	–	–	–
Barite	1,000 metric tons . .	6,470	8,110	7,630	7,770	6	6	6	8
Cement	Mil. metric tons . . .	(NA)	101	97	89	(NA)	4	4	3
Feldspar	1,000 metric tons . .	9,580	16,200	18,100	18,300	8	5	4	3
Fluorspar	1,000 metric tons . .	4,470	5,280	5,690	5,840	–	–	–	–
Gypsum	Mil. metric tons . . .	106	118	154	151	19	21	18	13
Mica (incl. scrap)	1,000 metric tons . .	328	294	380	390	31	27	26	25
Nitrogen (N content)	Mil. metric tons . . .	108	123	131	136	11	7	7	6
Phosphate rock (gross wt.)	Mil. metric tons . . .	132	147	156	167	30	25	19	19
Potash (K₂O equivalent)	Mil. metric tons . . .	27	31	35	36	4	4	3	3
Sulfur, elemental basis	Mil. metric tons . . .	58	67	68	69	19	14	13	13
Metals, mine basis:									
Bauxite	Mil. metric tons . . .	136	179	199	205	(NA)	(NA)	(NA)	(NA)
Copper	1,000 metric tons . .	13,200	15,000	15,400	15,500	11	8	8	8
Gold	Metric tons	2,590	2,470	2,380	2,330	14	10	10	10
Iron ore (gross wt.)	Mil. metric tons . . .	1,070	1,540	2,000	2,200	6	4	3	2
Lead [3]	1,000 metric tons . .	3,184	3,450	3,770	3,800	15	13	12	12
Mercury	Metric tons	1,350	1,680	1,170	950	(NA)	(D)	(NA)	(NA)
Molybdenum	1,000 metric tons . .	133	186	205	212	31	31	28	29
Nickel [3]	1,000 metric tons . .	1,270	1,460	1,660	1,610	(Z)	–	–	–
Silver	1,000 metric tons . .	18	19	21	21	11	6	6	5
Tantalum concentrates (Ta content) .	Metric tons	1,040	1,260	815	815	–	–	–	–
Titanium mineral concentrates (titanium content) [4]	1,000 metric tons . .	(NA)	5,200	6,300	6,300	(NA)	6	5	3
Tungsten [3]	1,000 metric tons . .	44	60	55	55	(NA)	–	(D)	(D)
Vanadium [3]	1,000 metric tons . .	56	56	59	60	–	–	–	–
Zinc [3]	1,000 metric tons . .	8,788	9,530	10,900	11,300	10	8	7	7
Metals, smelter basis:									
Aluminum	1,000 metric tons . .	24,400	31,900	37,900	39,700	15	8	7	7
Cadmium	1,000 metric tons . .	20	20	20	21	10	7	4	4
Copper	1,000 metric tons . .	11,000	13,600	15,400	15,700	9	4	8	8
Iron, pig	Mil. metric tons . . .	573	825	947	927	8	4	4	4
Lead [4]	1,000 metric tons . .	6,580	7,640	8,280	8,750	22	17	16	15
Magnesium [5]	1,000 metric tons . .	428	622	749	808	(D)	(D)	(D)	(D)
Raw Steel	Mil. metric tons . . .	845	1,130	1,340	1,310	12	8	7	7
Tin [6]	1,000 metric tons . .	271	290	320	333	2	–	–	–
Zinc	1,000 metric tons . .	9,137	10,400	11,500	11,300	4	3	2	2

– Represents or rounds to zero. D Withheld to avoid disclosing company data. NA Not available. Z Less than half the unit of measure. [1] Preliminary. [2] Source: Energy Information Administration, "International Energy Statistics." [3] Content of ore and concentrate. [4] Refinery production. [5] Primary production; no smelter processing necessary. [6] Production from primary sources only.

Source: Nonfuels, U.S. Geological Survey, *Minerals Yearbook*, annual, and *Mineral Commodities Summaries*, annual (published 29 January 2009); <http://minerals.er.usgs.gov/minerals/pubs/mcs/2009/mcs2009.pdf>; fuels, U.S. Energy Information Administration, "International Energy Statistics"; <http://tonto.eia.doe.gov/cfapps/ipdbproject/IEDIndex3.cfm> (accessed 10 June 2009).

Table 875. **Net U.S. Imports of Selected Minerals and Metals as Percent of Apparent Consumption: 1980 to 2008**

[In percent. Based on net imports which equal the difference between imports and exports plus or minus government stockpile and industry stock changes]

Minerals and metals	1980	1990	1995	2000	2004	2005	2006	2007	2008 [1]
Bauxite [2]	(NA)	98	99	100	100	100	100	100	100
Fluorspar	87	91	92	100	100	100	100	100	100
Manganese	98	100	100	100	100	100	100	100	100
Strontium	100	100	100	100	100	100	100	100	100
Tantalum	90	86	80	80	100	100	100	100	100
Vanadium	35	(D)	84	100	100	100	100	100	100
Platinum	(NA)	(NA)	(NA)	78	92	93	90	94	91
Mica (sheet)	100	100	100	100	100	100	100	100	86
Potash	65	68	75	80	80	80	79	81	81
Cobalt	93	84	79	78	77	83	82	78	81
Tin	79	71	84	88	92	78	79	79	80
Barite	44	71	65	84	78	84	81	83	79
Titanium	(NA)	(NA)	70	79	58	71	71	82	77
Zinc	60	64	71	72	72	68	78	73	73
Tungsten	53	81	90	66	73	68	68	70	61
Silver	7	(NA)	(NA)	43	54	54	38	55	60
Nickel	76	64	60	55	49	48	49	17	33
Iron and steel	13	13	21	18	14	15	17	12	9
Aluminum	(3)	(3)	23	33	44	45	41	26	(3)
Iron ore	25	21	14	10	6	4	8	–	(3)

– Represents or rounds to zero. D Withheld to avoid disclosure. NA Not available. [1] Preliminary. [2] Includes alumina. [3] Net exporter.

Source: Through 1990, U.S. Bureau of Mines; thereafter, U.S. Geological Survey, *Mineral Commodity Summaries* and *Minerals Yearbook*, annual and *Historical Statistics for Mineral and Material Commodities in the United States*; import and export data from U.S. Census Bureau.

558 Forestry, Fishing, and Mining

Table 876. Petroleum Industry—Summary: 1990 to 2008

[602 represents 602,000. Includes all costs incurred for drilling and equipping wells to point of completion as productive wells or abandonment after drilling becomes unproductive. Based on sample of operators of different size drilling establishments]

Item	Unit	1990	1995	2000	2003	2004	2005	2006	2007	2008 [1]
Crude oil producing wells (Dec. 31)..	1,000 ...	602	574	534	513	510	498	497	500	525
Daily output per well [2]	Bbl.	12.2	11.4	10.9	11.1	10.7	10.4	10.3	10.1	9.5
Completed wells drilled, total	1,000 ...	26.58	17.55	26.78	29.96	33.38	39.61	46.05	44.98	50.00
Crude oil.	1,000 ...	11.70	7.35	7.70	7.70	8.32	10.12	12.46	12.18	16.40
Natural gas	1,000 ...	10.30	7.42	16.28	19.63	22.38	26.30	29.89	29.24	29.74
Dry holes	1,000 ...	4.58	2.78	2.79	2.64	2.68	3.19	3.70	3.56	3.86
Average depth per well	Feet....	4,645	5,546	4,782	5,309	5,442	5,428	5,554	6,040	5,923
Average cost per well	$1,000 ..	384	513	755	1,200	1,673	1,721	2,102	4,172	(NA)
Average cost per foot	Dollars..	76.07	87.22	142.16	216.27	292.57	306.50	378.03	688.30	(NA)
Crude oil production, total [3]	Mil. bbl..	2,685	2,394	2,131	2,073	1,983	1,890	1,862	1,848	1,814
Value at wells [3, 4]	Bil. dol..	53.77	35.00	56.93	57.14	72.93	95.03	111.16	122.96	170.56
Average price per barrel	Dollars..	20.03	14.62	26.72	27.56	36.77	50.28	59.69	66.52	94.04
Lower 48 states [5]	Mil. bbl..	2,037	1,853	1,776	1,718	1,651	1,575	1,592	1,585	1,564
Alaska	Mil. bbl..	647	542	355	356	332	315	270	264	250
Onshore	Mil. bbl..	2,290	1,838	1,482	1,339	1,294	1,265	1,241	1,244	1,312
Offshore	Mil. bbl..	395	557	649	735	689	625	621	605	502
Imports: Crude oil [3, 6]	Mil. bbl..	2,151	2,639	3,320	3,528	3,692	3,696	3,693	3,661	3,571
Refined petroleum products	Mil. bbl..	775	586	874	949	1,119	1,310	1,310	1,255	1,140
Exports: Crude oil [3]	Mil. bbl..	39.7	34.5	18.4	4.5	9.8	11.6	9.0	10.0	10.5
Proved reserves	Bil. bbl..	26.3	22.4	22.0	21.9	21.4	21.8	21.0	21.3	(NA)
Operable refineries	Number.	205	175	158	149	149	148	149	149	150
Capacity (Jan. 1)	Mil. bbl..	5,684	5,633	6,027	6,116	6,166	6,251	6,329	6,367	6,422
Refinery input, total.	Mil. bbl..	5,325	5,555	5,964	6,027	6,135	6,136	6,198	6,205	6,224
Crude oil [3]	Mil. bbl..	4,894	5,100	5,514	5,586	5,664	5,555	5,563	5,532	5,360
Natural gas plant liquids	Mil. bbl..	171	172	139	153	154	161	183	184	178
Other liquids [7]	Mil. bbl..	260	283	311	289	317	420	452	488	686
Refinery output, total [8]	Mil. bbl..	5,574	5,838	6,311	6,383	6,520	6,497	6,561	6,568	6,579
Motor gasoline [9]	Mil. bbl..	2,540	2,722	2,910	2,991	3,025	3,036	3,053	3,051	3,072
Jet fuel [10]	Mil. bbl..	543	517	588	543	566	564	541	528	540
Distillate fuel oil	Mil. bbl..	1,067	1,152	1,310	1,353	1,396	1,443	1,475	1,509	1,570
Residual fuel oil	Mil. bbl..	347	288	255	241	240	229	232	246	227
Liquefied petroleum gases	Mil. bbl..	182	239	258	240	236	209	229	239	230
Utilization rate	Percent..	87.1	92.0	92.6	92.6	93.0	90.6	89.7	88.5	85.4

NA Not available. [1] Preliminary. [2] Based on number of wells producing at end of year. [3] Includes lease condensate. [4] Values based on domestic first purchase price. [5] Excluding Alaska and Hawaii. [6] Includes imports for the Strategic Petroleum Reserve. [7] Unfinished oils (net), other hydrocarbons, hydrogen, aviation and motor gasoline blending components (net). Beginning 1995, also includes oxygenates (net). [8] Includes other products not shown separately. [9] Finished motor gasoline. Beginning 1995, also includes ethanol blended into motor gasoline. [10] Prior to 2005, kerosene-type jet fuel is included in kerosene in "Other products." Beginning 2005, naphtha-type jet fuel is also included in "Other products."

Source: U.S. Energy Information Administration, *Annual Energy Review 2008.* See also <http://www.eia.doe.gov/emcu/aer/contents.html>.

Table 877. Supply, Disposition, and Ending Stocks of Crude Oil and Petroleum Products: 2008

[In millions of barrels (1,813.7 represents 1,813,700,000). Minus sign (–) indicates decrease]

Commodity	Supply				Disposition				
	Field production	Refinery and blender net production	Imports	Adjustments [1]	Stock change	Refinery and blender net inputs	Exports	Products supplied [2]	Ending stocks
Crude oil	1,813.7	(X)	3,570.8	29.4	43.3	5,360.2	10.5	–	1,026.1
Commercial	1,813.7	(X)	3,568.2	29.4	38.4	(X)	10.5	(X)	324.2
Alaskan	249.9	(X)	(X)	(X)	(X)	(X)	(X)	(X)	(X)
Lower 48 states	1,563.8	(X)	(X)	(X)	(X)	(X)	(X)	(X)	(X)
SPR	(X)	(X)	2.6	(X)	4.9	(X)	(X)	(X)	701.8
Imports by SPR	(X)	(X)	(NA)	(X)	(X)	(X)	(X)	(X)	(X)
Imports into SPR by others	(X)	(X)	2.6	(X)	(X)	(X)	(X)	(X)	(X)
Natural gas liquids and LRGs	651.9	229.9	97.9	(X)	21.4	178.3	37.0	743.1	126.9
Pentanes plus	95.7	(X)	8.0	(X)	3.4	56.2	12.4	31.6	13.7
Liquefied petroleum gases	556.2	229.9	89.9	(X)	18.0	122.0	24.6	711.5	113.2
Ethane/ethylene	256.9	6.7	0.1	(X)	12.7	(NA)	(NA)	250.9	27.6
Propane/propylene	187.2	190.0	66.7	(X)	3.2	(NA)	19.3	421.4	55.4
Normal butane/butylene	48.9	30.7	15.6	(X)	1.8	49.9	5.3	38.3	23.1
Isobutane/isobutylene	63.2	2.6	7.5	(X)	0.9	72.1	(NA)	0.9	7.1
Finished motor gasoline	(X)	3,072.4	111.3	148.3	–11.8	(X)	62.8	3,281.0	98.2
Kerosene-type jet fuel	(X)	539.5	37.2	(X)	–1.2	(X)	22.4	555.6	38.2
Distillate fuel oil [3]	(X)	1,569.5	77.2	–	12.4	(X)	193.0	1,441.4	145.9

– Represents zero. NA Not available. X Not applicable. [1] Includes an adjustment for crude oil, previously referred to as "Unaccounted For Crude Oil." Also included is an adjustment for motor gasoline blending components, fuel ethanol, and distillate fuel oil. See Appendix B of source for more details. [2] Products supplied is equal to field production, plus refinery and blender net production, plus imports, plus adjustments, minus stock change, minus refinery and blender net imputs, minus exports. [3] Distillate stocks located in the "Northeast Heating Oil Reserve" are not included. For details, see Appendix C of source.

Source: U.S. Energy Information Administration, "Petroleum Supply Annual, Volume 1"; <http://www.eia.doe.gov/oil_gas/petroleum/data_publications/petroleum_supply_annual/psa_volume1/psa_volume1.html>.

Forestry, Fishing, and Mining 559

[1,890 represents 1,890,000,000 barrels]

State	Crude petroleum Quantity (mil. bbl.)			Value (mil. dol.)			Natural gas marketed production [1] Quantity (bil. cu. ft.)			Value (mil. dol.)		
	2005	2006	2007	2005	2006	2007	2005	2006	2007	2005	2006	2007
Total [2]	1,890	1,862	1,848	95,035	111,158	122,959	18,927	19,410	20,019	138,751	124,074	127,531
AL	8	8	7	419	476	510	297	286	270	2,751	2,168	2,011
AK	315	270	264	14,841	15,380	16,788	487	445	433	2,313	2,576	2,439
AR	6	6	6	323	358	387	191	270	270	1,383	1,739	1,868
CA	230	223	217	10,842	12,813	14,106	318	315	307	2,365	2,039	2,033
CO	23	23	23	1,263	1,492	1,558	1,133	1,203	1,243	8,418	7,362	5,680
FL	3	2	2	(NA)	(NA)	(NA)	3	3	2	(NA)	(NA)	(NA)
IL	10	10	10	523	616	631	(Z)	(Z)	(Z)	(NA)	(NA)	(NA)
IN	2	2	2	88	103	113	3	3	4	29	18	21
KS	34	36	36	1,806	2,165	2,439	377	371	366	2,456	2,082	2,082
KY	3	2	3	125	136	170	93	95	95	634	842	701
LA	75	74	77	4,080	4,745	5,491	1,296	1,361	1,364	11,305	9,429	9,577
MI	6	5	5	298	310	348	261	263	265	1,383	(NA)	(NA)
MS	18	17	20	877	1,030	1,400	53	61	73	452	414	492
MT	33	36	35	1,730	2,056	2,251	108	113	117	709	624	668
NE	2	2	2	126	134	147	1	1	2	5	(NA)	(NA)
NM	61	60	59	3,205	3,693	4,056	1,645	1,609	1,545	11,369	9,947	10,633
NY	(Z)	(Z)	(Z)	(NA)	(NA)	(NA)	55	56	55	429	399	486
ND	36	40	45	1,868	2,263	2,942	53	55	55	441	361	365
OH	6	5	5	302	341	371	84	86	88	754	669	669
OK	62	63	61	3,384	3,966	4,225	1,639	1,689	1,744	11,821	10,671	10,884
PA	4	4	4	215	232	256	169	176	182	(NA)	(NA)	(NA)
TX	388	397	397	20,396	24,354	27,108	5,276	5,548	6,092	39,813	36,591	42,514
UT	17	18	20	899	1,069	1,220	301	348	376	2,157	1,913	(NA)
WV	2	2	2	84	110	106	221	226	231	(NA)	(NA)	(NA)
WY	52	53	54	2,356	2,817	3,158	1,639	1,816	1,923	11,245	10,627	8,951
Federal offshore	131	121	114	80,118	93,384	103,032	(NA)	(NA)	(NA)	(NA)	(NA)	(NA)
Lower 48 states	1,575	1,592	1,585	80,194	95,778	106,171	18,440	18,965	19,586	136,437	121,498	125,091

NA Not available. Z Less than 500,000 barrels or 500 million cubic feet. [1] Excludes nonhydrocarbon gases. [2] Includes other states not shown separately. State production does not include state offshore production. U.S. level totals shown in Tables 876 and 882 may contain revisions not carried to state level.

Source: U.S. Energy Information Administration, "Petroleum Supply Annual, Vol. 1"; "Petroleum Marketing Annual"; "Natural Gas Annual"; and "Natural Gas Monthly."

Table 879. **Crude Oil, Natural Gas, and Natural Gas Liquids—Reserves by State: 2005 to 2007**

[21,757 mil. bbl. represents 21,757,000,000 bbl. As of **December 31.** Proved reserves are estimated quantities of the mineral, which geological and engineering data demonstrate with reasonable certainty, to be recoverable in future years from known reservoirs under existing economic and operating conditions. Based on a sample of operators of oil and gas wells]

Area	2005			2006			2007		
	Crude oil proved reserves (mil. bbl.)	Natural gas (bil. cu. ft.)	Natural gas liquids (mil. bbl.)	Crude oil proved reserves (mil. bbl.)	Natural gas (bil. cu. ft.)	Natural gas liquids (mil. bbl.)	Crude oil proved reserves (mil. bbl.)	Natural gas (bil. cu. ft.)	Natural gas liquids (mil. bbl.)
United States [1]	21,757	204,385	8,165	20,972	211,085	8,472	21,317	237,726	9,143
Alabama	55	3,965	61	45	3,911	56	42	3,994	53
Alaska	4,171	8,171	352	3,879	10,245	338	4,163	11,917	325
Arkansas	40	1,964	3	37	2,269	4	31	3,305	3
California	3,435	3,228	137	3,389	2,794	132	3,322	2,740	126
Colorado	250	16,596	484	274	17,149	478	304	21,851	559
Florida	59	77	7	38	45	3	32	108	2
Illinois	95	(NA)	(NA)	89	(NA)	(NA)	101	(NA)	(NA)
Indiana	16	(NA)	(NA)	12	(NA)	(NA)	17	(NA)	(NA)
Kansas	281	4,314	224	263	3,931	209	206	3,982	198
Kentucky	23	2,151	70	25	2,227	105	24	2,469	89
Louisiana	432	10,447	292	428	10,474	280	458	10,045	303
Michigan	62	2,910	39	63	3,065	42	55	3,630	55
Mississippi	189	755	7	186	813	8	200	954	9
Montana	427	986	9	419	1,057	10	410	1,052	11
Nebraska	16	(NA)	(NA)	14	(NA)	(NA)	12	(NA)	(NA)
New Mexico	690	18,201	840	705	17,934	861	735	17,245	844
New York	(NA)	349	(NA)	(NA)	363	(NA)	(NA)	376	(NA)
North Dakota	418	453	49	412	479	55	482	511	58
Ohio	46	898	(NA)	49	975	(NA)	48	1,027	(NA)
Oklahoma	630	17,123	839	569	17,464	892	530	19,031	949
Pennsylvania	14	2,782	(NA)	20	3,050	(NA)	12	3,361	(NA)
Texas	4,919	56,507	3,080	4,871	61,836	3,335	5,122	72,091	3,658
Utah	256	4,295	[2]	334	5,146	[2]	355	6,391	(NA)
Virginia	(NA)	2,018	(NA)	(NA)	2,302	(NA)	(NA)	2,529	(NA)
West Virginia	21	4,459	85	23	4,509	110	28	4,729	115
Wyoming	704	23,774	[3]879	706	23,549	[3]887	690	29,710	(NA)
Federal offshore	4,483	17,831	696	4,096	15,360	653	3,905	14,439	624
Lower 48 states	17,586	196,214	7,813	17,093	200,840	8,134	17,154	225,809	8,818

NA Not available. [1] Includes states not shown separately. [2] Included with Wyoming. [3] Includes Utah.

Source: Energy Information Administration, "U.S. Crude Oil, Natural Gas, and Natural Gas Liquids Reserves, 2007 Annual Report" (published 10 February 2009); <http://www.eia.doe.gov/oil_gas/natural_gas/data_publications/crude_oil_natural_gas_reserves/cr.html>.

Table 880. **Federal Offshore Leasing, Exploration, Production, and Revenue: 1990 to 2008**

[In millions (56.79 represents 56,790,000), except as indicated. Data presented by fiscal year. See source for explanation of terms and for reliability statement]

Item	Unit	1990	1995	2000	2004	2005	2006	2007	2008
Tracts offered...............	Number....	10,459	10,995	7,992	9,123	11,447	7,905	4,992	19,812
Tracts leased................	Number....	825	835	553	888	989	763	360	2,121
Acres offered...............	Millions....	56.79	59.70	42.89	48.35	61.08	42.24	26.63	106.76
Acres leased................	Millions....	4.30	4.34	2.92	4.69	5.24	4.12	2.01	11.73
New wells being drilled:									
Active....................	Number....	120	124	224	156	242	209	164	190
Suspended................	Number....	266	247	146	67	67	61	76	67
Cumulative wells (since 1953):									
Wells completed	Number....	13,167	13,475	13,718	18,260	18,001	17,801	17,429	16,410
Wells plugged and abandoned...	Number....	14,677	18,008	22,814	33,746	34,878	36,407	38,351	39,378
Revenue, total [1].............	Bil. dol.....	3.4	2.7	5.2	5.3	6.3	7.6	7.0	18.0
Bonuses	Bil. dol.....	0.8	0.4	0.4	0.5	0.6	0.9	0.4	9.5
Oil and gas royalties [1]	Bil. dol.....	2.6	2.1	4.1	4.6	5.5	6.5	6.4	8.3
Rentals	Bil. dol.....	0.09	0.09	0.21	0.21	0.22	0.22	0.20	0.24
Sales value [2]................	Bil. dol.....	17.0	13.8	27.4	30.6	37.2	45.6	45.5	57.2
Oil	Bil. dol.....	7.0	6.3	11.5	8.4	15.4	24.2	27.8	35.9
Natural gas	Bil. dol.....	9.5	7.5	15.9	22.2	21.8	21.4	17.7	21.3
Sales volume: [3]									
Oil	Mil. bbls....	324	409	566	248	332	391	471	358
Natural gas	Bil. cu. ft....	5,093	4,692	4,723	3,941	3,504	2,581	2,547	1,573

[1] Includes condensate royalties. [2] Production value is value at time of production, not current value. [3] Excludes sales volumes for gas lost, gas plant products, or sulfur.

Source: U.S. Dept. of the Interior, Minerals Management Service, *Federal Offshore Statistics*, annual; for revenue, sales value, and sales volume data after 2000, Minerals Revenue Management, Annual Reported Royalty Revenue Statistical Information; <http://www.mrm.mms.gov/MRMWebStats/Home.aspx>.

Table 881. **Oil and Gas Extraction Industry—Establishments, Employees, and Payroll by State: 2006**

[8,297,839 represents 8,297,839,000. Excludes government employees, railroad employees, self-employed persons, etc. See "General Explanation" in source for definitions and statement on reliability of data. An establishment is a single physical location where business is conducted or where services or industrial operations are performed. See Appendix III]

State	Crude petroleum and natural gas extraction (211111) [1]			State	Natural gas liquid extraction (211112)[1]		
	Establish-ments	Number of employees [2]	Annual payroll ($1,000)		Establish-ments	Number of employees [2]	Annual payroll ($1,000)
United States ..	7,276	78,367	8,297,839	United States...	527	14,316	1,269,014
Alabama	26	398	22,672	Alabama.........	7	48	3,780
Colorado	378	4,160	500,680	Colorado..........	24	715	84,646
Kansas	397	2,755	157,924	Kansas...........	13	228	15,903
Kentucky	81	754	38,600	Kentucky	5	46	2,825
Louisiana	364	8,004	725,431	Louisiana	68	3,188	229,506
Mississippi	64	321	22,374	Mississippi	7	164	13,190
Montana	79	531	42,964	Montana.........	6	72	4,517
Nebraska	24	114	3,217	New Mexico	28	577	48,000
New Mexico	159	2,262	172,407	Oklahoma........	44	492	32,950
Oklahoma	1,092	10,873	1,382,971	Texas............	151	5,954	594,132
Texas	2,985	30,527	3,773,052	Utah	7	68	6,212
Utah	48	971	76,025	Wyoming	25	585	48,221
Wyoming	182	2,617	212,230				

[1] Based on North American Industry Classification System, 2002. [2] Covers full- and part-time employees who are on the payroll in the pay period including March 12.

Source: U.S. Census Bureau, "County Business Patterns." See also <http://www.census.gov/econ/cbp/index.html>.

Table 882. **Natural Gas—Supply, Consumption, Reserves, and Marketed Production: 1990 to 2008**

[**269 represents 269,000**]. Data are for natural gas, plus a small amount of supplemental gaseous fuels]

Item	Unit	1990	1995	2000	2003	2004	2005	2006	2007	2008
Producing wells (year-end)......	1,000.....	269	299	342	393	406	426	441	453	468
Production value at wells........	Bil. of dol...	31.8	30.2	74.3	97.5	106.6	138.7	124.0	127.5	(NA)
Avg. per 1,000 cu. ft..........	Dollars....	1.71	1.55	3.68	4.88	5.46	7.33	6.39	6.37	(NA)
Proved reserves [1]	Tril. cu. ft...	169	165	177	189	193	204	211	238	(NA)
Marketed production [2].......	**Bil. cu. ft..**	**18,594**	**19,506**	**20,198**	**19,974**	**19,517**	**18,927**	**19,410**	**20,019**	**21,455**
Minus: Extraction losses [3]	Bil. cu. ft...	784	908	1,016	876	927	876	906	930	881
Equals: Dry production	Bil. cu. ft...	17,810	18,599	19,182	19,099	18,591	18,051	18,504	19,089	20,574
Plus: Supplemental gas supplies...	Bil. cu. ft...	123	110	90	68	60	64	66	63	55
Equals: Dry production with supplemental gas	Bil. cu. ft...	17,932	18,709	19,272	19,166	18,651	18,114	18,570	19,152	20,629
Plus: Withdrawals from storage....	Bil. cu. ft...	1,986	3,025	3,550	3,161	3,088	3,107	2,527	3,380	3,367
Plus: Imports..............	Bil. cu. ft...	1,532	2,841	3,782	3,944	4,259	4,341	4,186	4,608	3,962
Plus: Balancing item [4].......	Bil. cu. ft...	307	396	-306	44	448	232	89	-83	-380
Equals: Total supply	Bil. cu. ft...	21,758	24,971	26,298	26,314	26,445	25,794	25,372	27,057	27,578
Minus: Exports.............	Bil. cu. ft...	86	154	244	680	854	729	724	822	1,000
Minus: Additions to storage [5]	Bil. cu. ft...	2,499	2,610	2,721	3,358	3,202	3,055	2,963	3,187	3,335
Equals: Consumption, total.....	**Bil. cu. ft..**	**19,174**	**22,207**	**23,333**	**22,277**	**22,389**	**22,011**	**21,685**	**23,047**	**23,243**
Lease and plant fuel	Bil. cu. ft...	1,236	1,220	1,151	1,122	1,098	1,112	1,142	1,199	1,285
Pipeline fuel [6]	Bil. cu. ft...	660	700	642	591	566	584	584	623	628
Residential...............	Bil. cu. ft...	4,391	4,850	4,996	5,079	4,869	4,827	4,368	4,717	4,866
Commercial [7].............	Bil. cu. ft...	2,623	3,031	3,182	3,179	3,129	2,999	2,832	3,017	3,122
Industrial................	Bil. cu. ft...	8,255	9,384	9,293	8,273	8,341	7,709	7,654	7,823	7,937
Vehicle fuel	Bil. cu. ft...	(Z)	5	13	18	21	23	24	25	30
Electric power sector	Bil. cu. ft...	3,245	4,237	5,206	5,135	5,464	5,869	6,222	6,841	6,661
World production (dry).........	Tril. cu. ft...	73.7	78.1	88.4	95.5	98.5	101.5	104.0	106.0	(NA)
U.S. production (dry)........	Tril. cu. ft...	17.8	18.6	19.2	19.1	18.6	18.1	18.5	19.1	20.5
Percent U.S. of world.......	Percent ...	24.2	23.8	21.7	20.0	18.9	17.8	17.8	18.0	(NA)

NA Not available. Z Less than 500 million cubic feet. [1] Estimated, end of year. Source: U.S. Energy Information Administration, *U.S. Crude Oil, Natural Gas, and Natural Gas Liquids Reserves,* annual. [2] Marketed production includes gross withdrawals from reservoirs less quantities used for reservoir repressuring and quantities vented or flared. Excludes nonhydrocarbon gases subsequently removed. [3] Volumetric reduction in natural gas resulting from the removal of natural gas plant liquids, which are transferred to petroleum supply. [4] Quantities lost and imbalances in data due to differences among data sources. Since 1980, excludes intransit shipments that cross U.S.-Canada border (i.e., natural gas delivered to its destination via the other country). [5] Underground storage. Through 2004, includes liquefied natural gas (LNG) storage in above-ground tanks. [6] Natural gas consumed in the operation of pipelines and delivery to consumers. [7] Includes deliveries to municipalities and public authorities for institutional heating and other purposes.

Source: Except as noted, U.S. Energy Information Administration, *Annual Energy Review;* "International Energy Annual"; "U.S. Crude Oil, Natural Gas, and Natural Gas Liquids Reserves"; "Natural Gas Annual" and "International Energy Statistics"; <http://www.eia.doe.gov>.

Table 883. **Natural Gas Plant Liquids—Production and Value: 1990 to 2008**

[Barrels of 42 gallons (566 represents 566,000,000)]

Item	Unit	1990	1995	2000	2003	2004	2005	2006	2007	2008
Field production [1]	Mil. bbl.....	566	643	699	686	662	627	635	651	652
Pentanes plus...........	Mil. bbl.....	112	122	112	109	101	97	96	96	96
Liquefied petroleum gases...	Mil. bbl.....	454	521	587	577	561	529	539	555	556
Natural gas processed	Tril. cu. ft...	15	17	17	15	15	15	15	16	(NA)

NA Not available. [1] Includes other finished petroleum products, not shown separately.

Source: U.S. Energy Information Administration, "Petroleum Supply Annual" and "Natural Gas Annual"; <http://www.eia.doe.gov>.

Table 884. Coal Supply, Disposition, and Prices: 2000 to 2008

[In millions of short tons (1,073.6 represents 1,073,600,000). 1 short ton = 2,000 lbs.]

Item	2000	2003	2004	2005	2006	2007	2008
United States, total supply	1,073.6	1,071.8	1,112.1	1,131.5	1,162.8	1,146.6	1,171.5
Consumption by sector:							
Total	1,084.1	1,094.9	1,107.3	1,126.0	1,112.3	1,128.0	1,121.7
Electric power	985.8	1,005.1	1,016.3	1,037.5	1,026.6	1,045.1	1,041.6
Coke plants	28.9	24.2	23.7	23.4	23.0	22.7	22.1
Other industrial plants	65.2	61.3	62.2	60.3	59.5	56.6	54.5
Combined heat and power (CHP)	28.0	24.8	26.6	25.9	25.3	22.5	23.6
Noncombined heat and power	37.2	36.4	35.6	34.5	34.2	34.1	31.0
Residential/commercial users	4.1	4.2	5.1	4.7	3.2	3.5	3.5
Year-end coal stocks:							
Total [1]	140.0	165.5	154.0	144.3	186.9	192.8	199.2
Electric power	102.0	121.6	106.7	101.1	141.0	151.2	163.1
Coke plants	1.5	0.9	1.3	2.6	2.9	1.9	2.3
Other industrial plants	4.6	4.7	4.8	5.6	6.5	5.6	6.0
Producers/distributors	31.9	38.3	41.2	35.0	36.5	34.0	27.3
U.S. coal trade:							
Net exports [2]	46.0	18.0	20.7	19.5	13.4	22.8	47.3
Exports	58.5	43.0	48.0	49.9	49.6	59.2	81.5
Steam coal	25.7	20.9	21.2	21.3	22.1	27.0	39.0
Metallurgical coal	32.8	22.1	26.8	28.7	27.5	36.3	42.5
Imports	12.5	25.0	27.3	30.5	36.2	36.3	34.2
Average delivered price (dollars per short ton):							
Electric utilities	24.28	25.82	27.30	31.22	34.26	36.06	41.23
Independent power producers	(NA)	26.2	27.27	30.39	33.04	33.11	39.31
Coke plants	44.38	50.63	61.50	83.79	92.87	94.97	118.09
Other industrial plants	31.46	34.70	39.30	47.63	51.67	54.42	63.44
Average free alongside ship (f.a.s.):							
Exports	34.90	35.98	54.11	67.10	70.93	70.25	97.68
Steam coal	29.67	26.94	42.03	47.64	46.25	47.90	57.35
Metallurgical coal	38.99	44.55	63.63	81.56	90.81	88.99	134.62
Imports	30.10	31.45	37.52	46.71	49.10	47.64	59.83

NA Not available.   [1] Includes other stocks not shown separately.   [2] Exports minus imports.

Source: U.S. Energy Information Administration, "U.S. Coal Supply and Demand: 2008 Review," annual; <http://www.eia.doe.gov/cneaf/coal/page/special/feature.html> (released 14 April 2009).

Table 885. Coal and Coke—Summary: 1990 to 2008

[In millions of short tons (1,029 represents 1,029,000,000), except as indicated. Includes coal consumed at mines. Recoverability varies between 40 and 90 percent for individual deposits; 50 percent or more of overall U.S. coal reserve base is believed to be recoverable]

Item	Unit	1990	1995	2000	2004	2005	2006	2007	2008
COAL									
Coal production, total [1, 2] . . .	Mil. sh. tons . . .	1,029	1,033	1,074	1,112	1,131	1,163	1,147	1,171
Value [3]	Bil. dol	22.39	19.45	18.02	22.16	26.69	29.25	30.04	38.18
Anthracite production [2]	Mil. sh. tons . . .	3.5	4.7	4.6	1.7	1.7	1.5	1.6	1.7
Bituminous coal and lignite [4]	Mil. sh. tons . . .	1,026	1,028	1,069	1,110	1,130	1,161	1,145	1,170
Underground	Mil. sh. tons . . .	425	396	374	368	369	359	352	358
Surface [2]	Mil. sh. tons . . .	605	637	700	745	763	804	795	814
Exports	Mil. sh. tons . . .	106	89	58	48	50	50	59	82
Imports	Mil. sh. tons . . .	3	9	13	27	30	36	36	34
Consumption [5]	Mil. sh. tons . . .	904	962	1,084	1,107	1,126	1,112	1,128	1,122
Electric power sector [6]	Mil. sh. tons . . .	783	850	986	1,016	1,037	1,027	1,045	1,042
Industrial	Mil. sh. tons . . .	115	106	94	86	84	82	79	77
Number of mines	Number	3,243	2,104	1,453	1,379	1,415	1,438	1,374	(NA)
Daily employment	1,000	131	90	72	74	79	83	81	(NA)
Production, by state:									
Alabama	Mil. sh. tons . . .	29	25	19	22	21	19	19	21
Illinois	Mil. sh. tons . . .	60	48	33	32	32	33	32	33
Indiana	Mil. sh. tons . . .	36	26	28	35	34	35	35	36
Kentucky	Mil. sh. tons . . .	173	154	131	114	120	121	115	120
Montana	Mil. sh. tons . . .	38	39	38	40	40	42	43	45
Ohio	Mil. sh. tons . . .	35	26	22	23	25	23	23	26
Pennsylvania	Mil. sh. tons . . .	71	62	75	66	67	66	65	65
Virginia	Mil. sh. tons . . .	47	34	33	31	28	30	25	25
West Virginia	Mil. sh. tons . . .	169	163	158	148	154	152	153	158
Wyoming	Mil. sh. tons . . .	184	264	339	396	404	447	454	468
Other states	Mil. sh. tons . . .	187	192	197	204	206	196	181	175
World production	Mil. sh. tons . . .	5,354	5,107	4,951	6,093	6,491	6,807	7,081	(NA)
Percent U.S. of world	Percent	19.2	20.2	21.7	18.3	17.4	17.1	16.2	(NA)
COKE									
Production	Mil. sh. tons . . .	27.6	23.7	20.8	16.9	16.7	16.4	16.2	15.6
Imports	Mil. sh. tons . . .	0.8	3.8	3.8	6.9	3.5	4.1	2.5	3.6
Exports	Mil. sh. tons . . .	0.6	1.4	1.1	1.3	1.7	1.6	1.4	2.0
Consumption [7]	Mil. sh. tons . . .	27.8	25.8	23.2	22.5	18.2	18.8	17.3	17.0

NA Not available.   [1] Includes bituminous coal, subbituminous coal, lignite, and anthracite.   [2] Beginning 2002, includes a small amount of refuse recovery.   [3] Coal values are based on free-on-board rail/barge prices, which are the free-on-board prices of coal at the point of first sale, excluding freight or shipping and insurance costs.   [4] Includes subbituminous.   [5] Includes some categories not shown separately.   [6] Electricity-only and combined-heat-and-power (CHP) plants whose primary business is to sell electricity and/or heat to the public.   [7] Consumption is calculated as the sum of production and imports minus exports and stock change.

Source: U.S. Energy Information Administration, *Annual Energy Review*, "International Energy Annual", "Annual Coal Report", "Monthly Coal Report" and "International Energy Statistics"; <http://www.eia.doe.gov>.

Forestry, Fishing, and Mining   563

Table 886. **Demonstrated Coal Reserves by Major Producing State: 2006 and 2007**

[In millions of short tons (491,076 represents 491,076,000,000), except as noted. As of January 1. The demonstrated reserve base represents the sum of coal in both measured and indicated resource categories of reliability. Measured resources of coal are estimates that have a high degree of geologic assurance from sample analyses and measurements from closely spaced and geological well-known sample sites. Indicated resources are estimates based partly from sample and analyses and measurements and partly from reasonable geologic projections]

State	2006				2007			
	Number of mines	Total reserves	Method of mining		Number of mines	Total reserves	Method of mining	
			Underground	Surface			Underground	Surface
United States[1]	1,438	491,076	333,991	157,085	1,374	489,395	333,277	156,118
Alabama	57	4,174	986	3,188	49	4,141	963	3,178
Alaska	1	6,108	5,423	685	1	6,107	5,423	684
Arkansas	2	417	272	144	2	417	272	144
Colorado	12	16,158	11,397	4,761	12	16,092	11,331	4,761
Illinois	22	104,408	87,865	16,543	21	104,347	87,811	16,536
Indiana	28	9,431	8,720	711	27	9,379	8,699	681
Iowa	(NA)	2,189	1,732	457	(NA)	2,189	1,732	457
Kansas	2	972	(NA)	972	2	971	(NA)	971
Kentucky	442	29,814	16,909	12,906	417	29,618	16,770	12,848
Kentucky, Eastern	416	10,362	1,080	9,282	394	10,219	990	9,229
Kentucky, Western	26	19,452	15,829	3,624	23	19,399	15,780	3,619
Maryland	19	634	572	62	19	631	571	60
Missouri	2	5,989	1,479	4,510	2	5,988	1,479	4,509
Montana	6	119,177	70,957	48,220	6	119,123	70,957	48,166
New Mexico	4	12,093	6,142	5,951	4	12,057	6,128	5,929
North Dakota	4	9,015	(NA)	9,015	4	8,978	(NA)	8,978
Ohio	52	23,260	17,515	5,745	57	23,220	17,484	5,736
Oklahoma	10	1,551	1,230	321	9	1,549	1,229	320
Pennsylvania	270	27,349	23,113	4,236	264	27,228	23,006	4,222
Anthracite	74	7,196	3,843	3,353	72	7,195	3,843	3,352
Bituminous	196	20,153	19,270	883	192	20,034	19,164	870
Tennessee	23	770	508	262	17	766	506	260
Texas	12	12,328	(NA)	12,328	11	12,276	(NA)	12,276
Utah	13	5,344	5,076	268	10	5,295	5,028	268
Virginia	127	1,642	1,093	548	118	1,598	1,062	536
Washington	1	1,340	1,332	8	(NA)	1,340	1,332	8
West Virginia	290	32,706	29,015	3,691	282	32,450	28,845	3,605
Wyoming	21	63,261	42,499	20,762	20	62,692	42,493	20,198

NA Not available.   [1] Includes other states not shown separately.

Source: U.S. Energy Information Administration, *Annual Coal Report*, 2007. See also <http://www.eia.doe.gov/cneaf/coal/page/acr/acr_sum.html>.

Table 887. **Uranium Concentrate (U_3O_8) Industry—Summary: 1990 to 2008**

[In millions of feet (1.7 represents 1,700,000), except as indicated. See also Table 908 in Section 19]

Item	Unit	1990	1995	2000	2003[1]	2004	2005	2006	2007	2008
Exploration and development, surface drilling	Mil. ft.	1.7	1.3	1.0	(D)	1.2	1.7	2.7	5.1	5.1
Expenditures	Mil. dol.	(NA)	2.6	5.6	(D)	10.6	18.1	40.1	67.5	81.9
Number of mines operated	Number	39	12	10	4	6	10	11	12	17
Underground	Number	27	–	1	1	2	4	5	6	10
Openpit	Number	2	–	–	–	–	–	–	–	–
In situ leaching	Number	7	5	4	2	3	4	5	5	6
Other sources[2]	Number	3	7	5	1	1	2	1	1	1
Mine production	1,000 pounds	5,876	3,528	3,123	2,200	2,452	3,045	4,692	4,541	3,879
Underground	1,000 pounds	(D)	–	(D)	(D)	(D)	(D)	(D)	(D)	(D)
Openpit	1,000 pounds	1,881	–	–	–	–	–	–	–	–
In situ leaching	1,000 pounds	(D)	3,372	2,995	(D)	(D)	2,681	4,259	(D)	(D)
Other sources[2]	1,000 pounds	3,995	156	128	(D)	(D)	(D)	(D)	(D)	(D)
Uranium concentrate production	1,000 pounds	8,886	6,043	3,958	2,000	2,282	2,689	4,106	4,534	3,092
Concentrate shipments from mills and plants	1,000 pounds	12,957	5,500	3,187	1,600	2,280	2,702	3,838	4,050	4,130
Employment	Person-years	1,335	1,107	627	321	420	648	755	1,231	1,563

– Represents zero.   D Data withheld to avoid disclosing figures for individual companies.   NA Not available.   [1] Estimate.
[2] Includes mine water, mill site cleanup and mill tailings, and well field restoration as sources of uranium.

Source: U.S. Department of Energy, through 2002, *Uranium Industry*, annual. Thereafter, "Domestic Uranium Production Report," annual. See also <http://www.eia.doe.gov/cneaf/nuclear/dupr/dupr.html>.

Section 19
Energy and Utilities

This section presents statistics on fuel resources, energy production and consumption, electric energy, hydroelectric power, nuclear power, solar and wind energy, wood energy (biomass), and the electric and gas utility industries. The principal sources are the U.S. Department of Energy's Energy Information Administration (EIA), the Edison Electric Institute, Washington, DC, and the American Gas Association, Arlington, VA. The Department of Energy was created in October 1977 and assumed and centralized the responsibilities of all or part of several agencies including the Federal Power Commission (FPC), the U.S. Bureau of Mines, the Federal Energy Administration, and the U.S. Energy Research and Development Administration. For additional data on transportation, see Section 23; on fuels, see Section 18; and on energy-related housing characteristics, see Section 20.

The EIA, in its *Annual Energy Review,* provides statistics and trend data on energy supply, demand, and prices. Information is included on petroleum and natural gas, coal, electricity, hydroelectric power, nuclear power, solar, wind, wood, and geothermal energy. Among its annual reports are *Annual Energy Review; Electric Power Annual; Natural Gas Annual; Petroleum Supply Annual; State Energy Consumption, Price, and Expenditure Data; U.S. Crude Oil, Natural Gas, and Natural Gas Liquids Reserves; Electric Sales and Revenue; Annual Energy Outlook;* and *International Energy Annual.* These various reports contain state, national, and international data on production of electricity, net summer capability of generating plants, fuels used in energy production, energy sales and consumption, and hydroelectric power. The EIA also issues the *Monthly Energy Review,* which presents current supply, disposition, and price data and monthly publications on

petroleum, coal, natural gas, and electric power. Data on residential energy consumption, expenditures, and conservation activities are available from EIA's Residential Energy Consumption Survey and are published every 4 years.

The Edison Electric Institute's monthly bulletin and annual *Statistical Year Book of the Electric Utility Industry for the Year* contain data on the distribution of electric energy by public utilities; information on the electric power supply, expansion of electric generating facilities, and the manufacture of heavy electric power equipment is presented in the annual *Year-End Summary of the Electric Power Situation in the United States.* The American Gas Association, in its monthly and quarterly bulletins and its yearbook, *Gas Facts,* presents data on gas utilities and financial and operating statistics.

Btu conversion factors—Various energy sources are converted from original units to the thermal equivalent using British thermal units (Btu). A Btu is the amount of energy required to raise the temperature of 1 pound of water 1 degree Fahrenheit (F) at or near 39.2 degrees F. Factors are calculated annually from the latest final annual data available; some are revised as a result. The following list provides conversion factors used in 2008 for production and consumption, in that order, for various fuels: Petroleum, 5.800 and 5.339 mil. Btu per barrel; total coal, 20.219 and 19.988 mil. Btu per short ton; and natural gas (dry), 1,028 Btu per cubic foot for both. The factors for the production of nuclear power and geothermal power were 10,488 and 21,017 Btu per kilowatt-hour, respectively. The fossil fuel steam-electric power plant generation factor of 9,884 Btu per kilowatt-hour was used for hydroelectric power generation and for wood and waste, wind, photovoltaic, and solar thermal energy consumed at electric utilities.

U.S. Census Bureau, Statistical Abstract of the United States: 2010

In the past few years, EIA has restructured the industry categories it once used to gather and report electricity statistics. The electric power industry, previously divided into electric utilities and non-utilities, now consists of the Electric Power Sector, the Commercial Sector, and the Industrial Sector.

The Electric Power Sector is composed of electricity-only and combined-heat-and-power plants (CHPs) whose primary business is to sell electricity, or electricity and heat, to the public.

Electricity-only plants are composed of traditional electric utilities, and nontraditional participants, including energy service providers, power marketers, independent power producers (IPPs), and the portion of CHPs that produce only electricity.

A utility is defined as a corporation, person, agency, authority, or other legal entity or instrumentality aligned with distribution facilities for delivery of electric energy for use primarily by the public. Electric utilities include investor-owned electric utilities, municipal and state utilities, federal electric utilities, and rural electric cooperatives. In total, there are more than 3,100 electric utilities in the United States.

An independent power producer is an entity defined as a corporation, person, agency, authority, or other legal entity or instrumentality that owns or operates facilities whose primary business is to produce electricity for use by the public. They are not generally aligned with distribution facilities and are not considered electric utilities.

Combined-heat-and-power producers are plants designed to produce both heat and electricity from a single heat source. These types of electricity producers can be independent power producers or industrial or commercial establishments. As some independent power producers are CHPs, their information is included in the data for the combined-heat-and-power sector. There are approximately 2,800 unregulated independent power producers and CHPs in the United States.

The Commercial Sector consists of commercial CHPs and commercial electricity-only plants. Industrial CHPs and industrial electricity-only plants make up the Industrial Sector. For more information, please refer to the *Electric Power Annual 2007* Web site located at <http://www.eia.doe.gov/cneaf/electricity/epa/epa_sum.html>.

Table 888. **Utilities—Employees, Annual Payroll, and Establishments by Industry: 2006**

[47,692 represents $47,692,000,000. Excludes government employees, railroad employees, self-employed persons, etc. An establishment is a single physical location where business is conducted or where services or industrial operations are performed. See Appendix III]

Year and industry	2002 NAICS code [1]	Number of employees [2]	Annual payroll (mil. dol.)	Average payroll per employee (dol.)	Establishments by employment size-class				
					Total	Under 20 employees	20 to 99 employees	100 to 499 employees	500 and over employees
Utilities, total	22	614,427	47,692	77,621	17,174	12,093	3,782	1,132	167
Electric power generation, transmission and distribution	2211	493,670	39,900	80,824	9,494	5,506	2,926	907	155
Electric power generation	22111	117,236	9,869	84,184	2,101	1,264	573	220	44
Hydroelectric power generation. . . .	221111	5,652	401	70,941	371	301	61	9	–
Fossil fuel electric power generation.	221112	73,258	5,915	80,740	1,285	684	404	187	10
Nuclear electric power generation . .	221113	26,863	2,631	97,931	72	22	12	8	30
Other electric power generation . . .	221119	11,463	923	80,507	373	257	96	16	4
Electric power transmission, control & distribution.	22112	376,434	30,031	79,778	7,393	4,242	2,353	687	111
Electric bulk power transmission & control	221121	4,943	426	86,283	111	78	20	11	2
Electric power distribution	221122	371,491	29,605	79,691	7,282	4,164	2,333	676	109
Natural gas distribution	2212	78,813	5,945	75,433	2,458	1,734	535	178	11
Water, sewage, & other systems	2213	41,944	1,847	44,033	5,222	4,853	321	47	1
Water supply & irrigation systems. . . .	22131	34,129	1,497	43,858	4,406	4,128	234	44	–
Sewage treatment facilities	22132	6,115	241	39,463	726	662	60	3	1
Steam & air-conditioning supply	22133	1,700	109	63,991	90	63	27	–	–

– Represents zero. [1] North American Industry Classification System, 2002; see text, Section 15. [2] Covers full- and part-time employees who are on the payroll in the pay period including March 12.

Source: U.S. Census Bureau, "County Business Patterns"; <http://www.census.gov/econ/cbp/index.html>.

Table 889. **Fossil Fuel Prices by Type of Fuel: 1990 to 2008**

[In dollars per million British thermal units (Btu), except as indicated. For definition of Btu and mineral fuel conversions, see source and text, this section. All fuel prices taken as close to the point of production as possible]

Fuel	Current dollars					Constant (2000) dollars				
	1990	2000	2006	2007	2008 [1]	1990	2000	2006	2007	2008 [1]
Composite [2]. . .	1.84	2.60	4.73	4.99	6.58	2.26	2.60	4.05	4.16	5.38
Crude oil [3]	3.45	4.61	10.29	11.47	16.21	4.23	4.61	8.82	9.57	13.24
Natural gas [4]	1.55	3.32	5.79	5.77	7.31	1.90	3.32	4.97	4.82	5.97
Coal [5]	1.00	0.80	1.24	1.29	1.61	1.22	0.80	1.06	1.08	1.32

[1] Preliminary. [2] Derived by multiplying the price per Btu of each fossil fuel by the total Btu content of the production of each fossil fuel and dividing this accumulated value of total fossil fuel production by the accumulated Btu content of total fossil fuel production. [3] Domestic first purchase prices. [4] Wellhead prices. [5] Free-on-board (f.o.b.) rail/barge prices, which are the f.o.b. prices of coal at the point of first sale, excluding freight or shipping and insurance costs. Includes bituminous coal, subbituminous coal, and lignite.

Source: U.S. Energy Information Administration, *Annual Energy Review 2008;* (published 26 June 2009). See also <http://www.eia.doe.gov/emeu/aer/txt/ptb0301.html>.

Table 890. Energy Supply and Disposition by Type of Fuel: 1960 to 2008

[In quadrillion British thermal units (Btu) (42.80 represents 42,800,000,000,000,000). For definition of Btu, see source and text, this section]

Year	Production Total [1]	Crude oil [2]	Natural gas	Coal [3]	Nuclear power	Renewable energy [4] Total [1,5]	Hydro-electric power [6]	Biofuel [7]	Solar/photo-voltaic	Wind	Net imports, total [8]	Consumption Total [1]	Petroleum [9]	Natural gas [10]	Coal	Nuclear power	Renewable energy [4] total
1960	42.80	14.93	12.66	10.82	0.01	2.93	1.61	1.32	(NA)	(NA)	2.71	45.09	19.92	12.39	9.84	0.01	2.93
1970	63.50	20.40	21.67	14.61	0.24	4.08	2.63	1.43	(NA)	(NA)	5.71	67.84	29.52	21.79	12.26	0.24	4.08
1975	61.36	17.73	19.64	14.99	1.90	4.72	3.15	1.50	(NA)	(NA)	11.71	72.00	32.73	19.95	12.66	1.90	4.72
1980	67.23	18.25	19.91	18.60	2.74	5.49	2.90	2.48	(NA)	(NA)	12.10	78.12	34.20	20.24	15.42	2.74	5.49
1983	64.18	18.39	16.59	17.25	3.20	6.56	3.53	2.91	(NA)	(Z)	8.06	73.04	30.05	17.22	15.89	3.20	6.56
1984	68.93	18.85	18.01	19.72	3.55	6.52	3.39	2.97	(Z)	(Z)	8.68	76.72	31.05	18.39	17.07	3.55	6.52
1985	67.80	18.99	16.98	19.33	4.08	6.19	2.97	3.02	(Z)	(Z)	7.58	76.49	30.92	17.70	17.48	4.08	6.19
1986	67.18	18.38	16.54	19.51	4.38	6.22	3.07	2.93	(Z)	(Z)	10.13	76.76	32.20	16.59	17.26	4.38	6.22
1987	67.66	17.67	17.14	20.14	4.75	5.74	2.63	2.88	(Z)	(Z)	11.59	79.18	32.87	17.64	18.01	4.75	5.74
1988 [11]	69.03	17.28	17.60	20.74	5.59	5.57	2.33	3.02	(Z)	(Z)	12.93	82.82	34.22	18.45	18.85	5.59	5.57
1989	69.48	16.12	17.85	21.36	5.60	6.39	2.84	3.16	0.06	0.02	14.11	84.95	34.21	19.60	19.07	5.60	6.39
1990	70.87	15.57	18.33	22.49	6.10	6.21	3.05	2.74	0.06	0.03	14.06	84.65	33.55	19.60	19.17	6.10	6.21
1991	70.53	15.70	18.23	21.64	6.42	6.24	3.02	2.78	0.06	0.03	13.19	84.61	32.85	20.03	18.99	6.42	6.24
1992	70.13	15.22	18.38	21.69	6.48	6.00	2.62	2.93	0.06	0.03	14.44	85.96	33.53	20.71	19.12	6.48	6.00
1993	68.50	14.49	18.58	20.34	6.41	6.26	2.89	2.91	0.07	0.03	17.01	87.61	33.74	21.23	19.84	6.41	6.26
1994	70.89	14.10	19.35	22.20	6.69	6.16	2.68	3.03	0.07	0.04	18.33	89.26	34.56	21.73	19.91	6.69	6.16
1995	71.32	13.89	19.08	22.13	7.08	6.70	3.21	3.10	0.07	0.03	17.75	91.17	34.44	22.67	20.09	7.08	6.71
1996	72.64	13.72	19.34	22.79	7.09	7.17	3.59	3.16	0.07	0.03	19.07	94.18	35.67	23.08	21.00	7.09	7.17
1997	72.63	13.66	19.39	23.31	6.60	7.18	3.64	3.11	0.07	0.03	20.70	94.77	36.16	23.22	21.45	6.60	7.18
1998	73.04	13.24	19.61	24.05	7.07	6.66	3.30	2.93	0.07	0.03	22.28	95.18	36.82	22.83	21.66	7.07	6.66
1999	71.91	12.45	19.34	23.30	7.61	6.68	3.27	2.97	0.07	0.05	23.54	96.82	37.84	22.91	21.62	7.61	6.68
2000	71.49	12.36	19.66	22.74	7.86	6.26	2.81	3.01	0.07	0.06	24.97	98.98	38.26	23.82	22.58	7.86	6.26
2001	71.89	12.28	20.17	23.55	8.03	5.32	2.24	2.63	0.07	0.07	26.39	96.33	38.19	22.77	21.91	8.03	5.32
2002	70.94	12.16	19.44	22.73	8.14	5.90	2.69	2.71	0.06	0.11	25.74	97.86	38.23	23.56	21.90	8.14	5.89
2003	70.26	12.03	19.69	22.09	7.96	6.15	2.82	2.81	0.06	0.11	27.01	98.21	38.81	22.90	22.32	7.96	6.15
2004	70.38	11.50	19.09	22.85	8.22	6.25	2.69	3.01	0.06	0.14	29.11	100.35	40.29	22.93	22.47	8.22	6.26
2005	69.63	10.96	18.57	23.19	8.16	6.41	2.70	3.12	0.07	0.18	30.15	100.48	40.39	22.58	22.80	8.16	6.42
2006	71.04	10.80	19.02	23.79	8.21	6.86	2.87	3.31	0.07	0.26	29.81	99.88	39.96	22.22	22.45	8.21	6.91
2007	71.50	10.72	19.62	23.49	8.46	6.80	2.45	3.58	0.08	0.34	29.24	101.55	39.77	23.63	22.75	8.46	6.81
2008 [12]	73.71	10.52	21.15	23.86	8.46	7.32	2.45	3.90	0.09	0.51	25.78	99.30	37.14	23.84	22.42	8.46	7.30

NA Not available. Z Less than 5 trillion. [1] Includes other types of fuel not shown separately. [2] Includes lease condensate. [3] Beginning 1989, includes waste coal supplied. Beginning 2001, also includes a small amount of refuse recovery. [4] Electricity net generation from conventional hydroelectric power, geothermal, solar, and wind; consumption of electricity from wood, waste, and alcohol fuels; geothermal heat pump and direct use energy; and solar thermal direct use energy. [5] Production equals consumption for all renewable energy sources except biofuels. [6] Conventional hydroelectricity net generation. [7] Wood and wood-derived fuels, biomass waste, fuel ethanol, and biodiesel. [8] Imports minus exports. [9] Petroleum products supplied, including natural gas plant liquids and crude oil burned as fuel. [10] Includes supplemental gaseous fuels. [11] There is a discontinuity in this time series between 1989 and 1990. [12] Preliminary.

Source: U.S. Energy Information Administration, Annual Energy Review 2008 (published 26 June 2009). See also <http://www.eia.doe.gov/emeu/aer/overview.html>.

Table 891. **Energy Supply and Disposition by Type of Fuel—
Estimates, 2006 and 2007, and Projections, 2008 to 2020**

[Quadrillion Btu (71.35 represents 71,350,000,000,000,000) per year. Btu = British thermal unit. For definition of Btu, see source and text, this section. Mcf = 1,000 cubic feet. Projections are "reference" or mid-level forecasts. See report for methodology and assumptions used in generating projections]

Type of fuel	2006	2007	Projections			
			2008	2010	2015	2020
Production, total	**71.35**	**72.52**	**74.92**	**77.45**	**79.76**	**84.19**
Crude oil and lease condensate	10.80	10.73	10.75	12.18	12.40	14.02
Natural gas plant liquids	2.36	2.41	2.46	2.52	2.50	2.52
Natural gas, dry	18.99	19.84	21.08	20.87	20.83	22.02
Coal [1]	23.79	23.50	24.06	24.21	24.56	24.41
Nuclear power	8.21	8.41	8.34	8.45	8.68	9.00
Renewable energy [2]	6.72	6.66	7.61	8.40	9.73	11.18
Other [3]	0.48	0.97	0.63	0.83	1.07	1.05
Imports, total	**34.57**	**34.59**	**30.90**	**27.79**	**28.16**	**26.44**
Crude oil [4]	22.08	21.90	21.20	18.21	17.94	16.42
Petroleum products [5]	7.22	6.97	4.83	5.45	5.74	5.43
Natural gas	4.29	4.72	3.94	3.24	3.59	3.37
Other imports [6]	0.98	0.99	0.92	0.89	0.90	1.22
Exports, total	**4.58**	**5.17**	**5.65**	**5.33**	**5.45**	**5.58**
Petroleum [7]	2.59	2.84	2.68	2.58	2.65	2.82
Natural gas	0.73	0.83	0.96	0.70	1.16	1.44
Coal	1.26	1.51	2.01	2.05	1.65	1.33
Consumption, total	**100.08**	**101.92**	**100.88**	**99.95**	**102.91**	**105.41**
Petroleum products [8]	40.63	40.75	38.84	38.10	38.97	38.97
Natural gas	22.26	23.70	24.10	23.09	23.34	24.03
Coal	22.46	22.74	22.60	22.91	23.59	23.98
Nuclear power	8.21	8.41	8.34	8.45	8.68	9.00
Renewable energy [9]	6.33	6.08	6.75	7.19	8.14	9.24
Other [10]	0.19	0.23	0.25	0.21	0.19	0.20
Net imports of petroleum	**26.71**	**26.03**	**23.35**	**21.08**	**21.03**	**19.04**
Prices (2006 dollars per unit):						
Imported crude oil price [11]	60.70	63.83	96.57	71.97	107.64	110.34
Gas wellhead price (dol. per 1,000 cu. ft.) [12] . .	6.48	6.22	7.78	5.76	6.09	6.57
Coal minemouth price (dol. per ton) [13]	25.29	25.82	28.50	29.40	28.98	27.94
Average electric price (cents per kWh)	8.86	9.11	9.86	9.44	10.47	12.14

[1] Includes waste coal. [2] Includes grid-connected electricity from conventional hydroelectric; wood and wood waste; landfill gas; municipal solid waste; other biomass; wind; photovoltaic and solar thermal sources; nonelectric energy from renewable sources, such as active and passive solar systems, and wood. Excludes electricity imports using renewable sources and nonmarketed renewable energy. [3] Includes nonbiogenic municipal solid waste, liquid hydrogen, methanol, and some domestic inputs to refineries. [4] Includes imports of crude oil for the Strategic Petroleum Reserve. [5] Includes imports of finished petroleum products, imports of unfinished oils, alcohols, ethers, blending components, and renewable fuels such as ethanol. [6] Includes coal, coal coke (net), and electricity (net). [7] Includes crude oil and petroleum products. [8] Includes petroleum-derived fuels and non-petroleum-derived fuels, such as ethanol, biodiesel, and coal-based synthetic liquids. Petroleum coke, which is a solid, is included. Also included are natural gas plant liquids, crude oil consumed as a fuel, and liquid hydrogen. [9] Includes grid-connected electricity from wood and wood waste, non-electric energy from wood, and biofuels heat and coproducts used in the production of liquid fuels, but excludes the energy content of the liquid fuels. Also includes non-biogenic municipal solid waste and net electricity imports. [10] Includes non-biogenic municipal solid waste and net electricity imports. [11] Weighted average price delivered to U.S. refiners. [12] Represents lower 48 onshore and offshore supplies. [13] Includes reported prices for both open market and captive mines.

Source: U.S. Energy Information Administration, *Annual Energy Outlook 2009 Early Release* (published December 2008). See also <http://www.eia.doe.gov/oiaf/aeo/overview.html>.

Table 892. **Energy Consumption by End-Use Sector: 1970 to 2008**

[67.84 represents 67,840,000,000,000,000 Btu. Btu = British thermal units. For definition of Btu, see source and text, this section. See Appendix III. Total energy consumption in the end-use sectors consists of primary energy consumption, electricity retail sales, and electrical system energy losses]

Year	Total (quad. Btu)	Residential and commercial [1] (quad. Btu)	Industrial [2] (quad. Btu)	Trans- portation (quad. Btu)	Percent of total		
					Residential and commercial [1]	Industrial [2]	Transpor- tation
1970	67.84	22.11	29.64	16.10	32.6	43.7	23.7
1975	72.00	24.31	29.45	18.24	33.8	40.9	25.3
1980	78.12	26.35	32.08	19.70	33.7	41.1	25.2
1985	76.49	27.53	28.88	20.09	36.0	37.8	26.3
1990	84.65	30.35	31.90	22.42	35.8	37.7	26.5
1995	91.17	33.28	34.05	23.85	36.5	37.3	26.2
2000	98.98	37.66	34.76	26.55	38.1	35.1	26.8
2001	96.33	37.25	32.81	26.28	38.7	34.1	27.3
2002	97.86	38.24	32.76	26.85	39.1	33.5	27.4
2003	98.21	38.56	32.65	27.00	39.3	33.2	27.5
2004	100.35	38.84	33.61	27.90	38.7	33.5	27.8
2005	100.48	39.57	32.55	28.36	39.4	32.4	28.2
2006	99.88	38.49	32.54	28.84	38.5	32.6	28.9
2007	101.55	39.91	32.52	29.13	39.3	32.0	28.7
2008 [3]	99.30	40.18	31.21	27.92	40.5	31.4	28.1

[1] Commercial sector fuel use, including that at commercial combined-heat-and-power (CHP) and industrial electricity-only plants. [2] Industrial sector fuel use, including that at industrial combined-heat-and-power (CHP) and industrial electricity-only plants. [3] Preliminary.

Source: U.S. Energy Information Administration, *Annual Energy Review 2008* (published 26 June 2009). See also <http://www.eia.doe.gov/emeu/aer/txt/ptb0201a.html>.

Energy and Utilities   569

Table 893. **Energy Consumption—End-Use Sector and Selected Source by State: 2007**

[In trillions of Btu (101,468 represents 101,468,000,000,000,000), except as indicated. For definition of Btu, see source and text, this section. Data are preliminary. U.S. totals may not equal sum of states due to independent rounding and/or interstate flows of electricity that are not allocated to the states. For technical notes and documentation, see source <http://www.eia.doe.gov/emeu/states/_seds_tech_notes.html>]

State	Total [1,2]	Per capita [3] (mil. Btu)	End-use sector [4]				Source				
			Resi-dential	Com-mercial	Indus-trial [2]	Trans-por-tation	Petro-leum [5]	Natural gas (dry) [6]	Coal	Hydro electric power [7]	Nuclear electric power
U.S....	101,468	337	21,604	18,279	32,494	29,091	40,358	23,678	22,740	2,446	8,458
AL........	2,132	461	406	281	942	504	626	431	888	41	360
AK........	724	1,062	54	62	356	251	324	372	13	13	–
AZ........	1,578	248	430	369	232	547	595	402	438	65	281
AR........	1,149	406	229	162	464	295	387	228	275	32	162
CA........	8,492	233	1,535	1,614	1,956	3,387	3,946	2,440	66	270	375
CO........	1,479	305	343	291	399	446	525	516	389	17	–
CT........	871	249	277	219	115	261	397	184	40	4	172
DE........	302	350	67	58	101	76	136	50	64	–	–
DC........	187	318	37	125	4	22	23	34	(Z)	–	–
FL........	4,602	253	1,340	1,089	559	1,614	1,984	950	721	2	307
GA........	3,133	329	744	566	887	936	1,100	454	935	22	341
HI	344	269	38	42	68	195	306	3	19	1	–
ID	530	354	122	84	187	137	166	84	10	89	–
IL........	4,043	315	997	780	1,203	1,064	1,418	979	1,090	2	1,004
IN	2,904	458	552	360	1,346	647	878	548	1,574	4	–
IA	1,235	414	235	192	492	316	442	262	464	10	47
KS........	1,136	409	226	203	426	282	425	292	396	(Z)	109
KY........	2,023	478	373	261	892	498	747	236	1,020	16	–
LA........	3,766	861	356	292	2,404	714	1,600	1,423	250	8	179
ME........	456	346	107	76	147	127	236	48	7	37	–
MD........	1,489	265	426	416	184	463	557	209	328	16	151
MA........	1,515	234	443	384	196	492	685	417	120	8	54
MI	3,027	301	786	625	819	798	987	848	800	13	331
MN........	1,875	362	414	352	578	531	706	396	366	6	137
MS........	1,240	424	234	175	454	376	471	375	185	–	98
MO	1,964	334	521	407	429	607	759	278	802	12	98
MT........	462	483	79	68	186	128	211	75	202	93	–
NE........	693	392	155	136	224	178	235	146	217	3	116
NV........	777	304	183	134	201	259	293	264	83	20	–
NH........	314	239	92	70	45	107	170	65	45	13	113
NJ........	2,744	317	616	639	452	1,037	1,373	641	112	(Z)	336
NM........	711	362	114	125	252	220	285	240	296	3	–
NY........	4,064	209	1,202	1,257	505	1,101	1,633	1,219	258	250	445
NC........	2,700	299	716	574	644	767	971	245	828	29	420
ND........	428	671	64	61	199	105	143	63	420	13	–
OH........	4,049	353	956	708	1,348	1,038	1,357	836	1,462	4	165
OK........	1,609	446	306	250	588	464	578	691	373	30	–
OR........	1,108	297	268	209	284	347	385	258	45	332	–
PA........	4,006	323	967	719	1,289	1,032	1,456	782	1,491	22	812
RI	218	207	72	58	24	65	92	91	(Z)	(Z)	–
SC........	1,692	384	359	264	621	449	577	180	444	15	558
SD........	292	367	66	59	75	93	121	54	33	29	–
TN........	2,331	379	546	387	740	658	827	230	672	49	301
TX........	11,835	496	1,594	1,382	5,951	2,908	5,887	3,641	1,609	16	430
UT........	806	302	166	152	225	262	306	232	391	5	–
VT........	162	261	48	31	29	54	88	9	(Z)	6	49
VA........	2,611	339	628	601	567	815	1,017	333	458	12	286
WA	2,067	321	490	384	521	672	847	280	96	779	85
WV........	851	470	164	112	396	179	289	123	983	12	–
WI	1,846	330	419	357	624	447	620	404	465	15	135
WY	496	949	46	60	263	127	176	118	495	7	–

- Represents zero. Z Less than 50 billion Btu. [1] Includes other sources, not shown separately. [2] U.S. total energy and U.S. industrial sector include 60.8 trillion Btu of net imports of coal coke that is not allocated to the states. [3] Based on estimated resident population as of July 1. [4] End-use sector data include electricity sales and associated electrical system energy losses. [5] Includes fuel ethanol blended into motor gasoline. [6] Includes supplemental gaseous fuels. [7] Conventional hydroelectric power. Does not include pumped-storage hydroelectricity.

Source: U.S. Energy Information Administration, "State Energy Data, 2007" (published 28 August 2009); <http://www.eia.doe.gov/emeu/states/_seds.html>.

Table 894. **Residential Energy Consumption, Expenditures, and Average Price: 1980 to 2005**

[9.32 represents 9,320,000,000,000,000 Btu. For period April to March for 1980; January to December for 1990 to 2005. Excludes Alaska and Hawaii in 1980. Covers occupied units only. Excludes household usage of gasoline for transportation and the use of wood or coal. Based on Residential Energy Consumption Survey; see source. Btu = British thermal unit; see text, this section]

Type of fuel	Unit	1980	1990	1993	1997	2001	2005
CONSUMPTION							
Total [1]	Quad. Btu	9.32	9.22	10.01	10.25	9.86	10.55
Average per household . . .	Mil. Btu	114	98	104	101	92	95
Natural gas	Quad. Btu.	4.97	4.86	5.27	5.28	4.84	4.79
Electricity, site	Quad. Btu.	2.48	3.03	3.28	3.54	3.89	4.35
Fuel oil, kerosene [2]	Quad. Btu.	1.52	1.04	1.07	1.07	0.76	0.88
Liquid petroleum gas	Quad. Btu.	0.35	0.28	0.38	0.36	0.38	0.52
EXPENDITURES							
Total	Bil. dol.	75.6	110.2	123.9	135.8	159.7	201.1
Average per household . . .	Dollars	926	1,172	1,282	1,338	1,493	1,810
Natural gas	Bil. dol.	19.8	27.3	32.0	35.8	47.0	52.3
Electricity	Bil. dol.	40.8	71.5	81.1	88.3	100.3	124.7
Fuel oil, kerosene	Bil. dol.	12.2	8.3	7.0	7.6	6.8	13.0
Liquid petroleum gas	Bil. dol.	2.8	3.1	3.8	4.0	5.6	11.0
AVERAGE PRICE							
Total	Dol./mil. Btu . .	8.12	11.95	12.38	13.25	16.19	19.07
Natural gas	Dol./mil. Btu . . .	3.98	5.61	6.07	6.78	9.70	10.93
Electricity	Dol./mil. Btu . . .	16.46	23.60	24.69	24.97	25.80	28.67
Fuel oil, kerosene	Dol./mil. Btu . . .	8.03	7.92	6.53	7.13	9.05	28.79
Liquid petroleum gas	Dol./mil. Btu . . .	8.00	11.18	10.04	11.23	14.87	20.97

[1] Total excludes primary electricity and wood.   [2] Kerosene consumption and expenditure estimates could only be calculated for space heating since too few cases in the sample had viable data for water heating and appliances. Therefore, total estimates for kerosene equal space heating estimates for kerosene.

Source: U.S. Energy Information Administration, "Residential Energy Consumption Survey: Household Energy Consumption and Expenditures" 1980, 1990, 1993, 1997, 2001, and 2005; <http://www.eia.doe.gov/emeu/recs/contents.html>.

Table 895. **Residential Energy Consumption and Expenditures by Type of Fuel and Selected Household Characteristics: 2005**

[**Quad. = quadrillion. (10.55 represents 10,550,000,000,000,000 Btu).** See headnote, Table 894]

Characteristic	Consumption (Btu's)					Expenditures				
	Total [1] (quad.)	Avg. per house-hold [1,2] (mil.)	Natural gas (quad.)	Electric-ity (quad.)	Fuel oil [3] (quad.)	Total [1] (bil. dol.)	Avg. per house-hold [1,2] (dol.)	Natural gas (bil. dol.)	Electric-ity (bil. dol.)	Fuel oil [3] (bil. dol.)
Total households . . .	10.55	94.9	4.79	4.35	0.88	201.07	1,810	52.34	124.74	12.99
Single family.	7.81	108.4	3.49	3.24	0.65	148.42	2,060	38.31	91.59	9.58
Single family, attached	0.68	89.3	0.40	0.24	0.04	12.14	1,598	4.38	7.08	0.52
Apartment (two-to-four unit building). .	0.66	85.0	0.38	0.20	0.08	12.06	1,556	4.40	6.45	1.12
Apartment (five-or-more unit building).	0.91	54.4	0.40	0.40	0.10	18.03	1,077	4.00	12.28	1.43
Mobile home	0.49	70.4	0.12	0.28	0.03	10.42	1,501	1.26	7.33	0.35
Year house built:										
1949 or earlier.	2.54	114.9	1.35	0.68	0.40	43.46	1,967	14.81	20.47	5.87
1950 to 1959	1.23	98.3	0.64	0.41	0.15	22.17	1,770	7.12	12.19	2.17
1960 to 1969	1.18	94.9	0.59	0.46	0.11	21.98	1,764	6.47	13.21	1.57
1970 to 1979	1.58	83.4	0.65	0.73	0.12	31.25	1,654	7.14	20.85	1.74
1980 to 1989	1.51	81.4	0.59	0.79	0.05	31.31	1,685	6.29	22.39	0.78
1990 to 1999	1.64	94.4	0.63	0.85	0.04	33.06	1,907	6.82	23.27	0.62
2000 to 2005	0.87	94.7	0.34	0.79	0.02	17.84	1,936	3.69	12.37	0.25

[1] Includes liquid petroleum gas, primary electricity, and wood.   [2] The averages are over the set of all households; otherwise the averages are over the set of households using a given fuel or enduse.   [3] Includes kerosene.

Source: U.S. Energy Information Administration, "Residential Energy Consumption Survey: Household Energy Consumption and Expenditures" 2005; <http://www.eia.doe.gov/emeu/recs/contents.html>.

Energy and Utilities   **571**

Table 896. **Energy Expenditures—End-Use Sector and Selected Source by State: 2007**

[In millions of dollars (1,233,059 represents $1,233,059,000,000). Data are preliminary. End-use sector and electric utilities exclude expenditures on energy sources such as hydroelectric, photovoltaic, solar thermal, wind, and geothermal. Also excludes expenditures for reported amounts of energy consumed by the energy industry for production, transportation, and processing operations. For technical notes and documentation, see source <http://www.eia.doe.gov/emeu/states/_seds_tech_notes.html>]

State	Total [1,2]	End-use sector				Source			
		Resi-dential	Com-mercial	Industrial [2]	Trans-portation	Petroleum products [3]	Natural gas [4]	Coal	Electricity sales
U.S.	1,233,059	238,695	174,108	235,692	584,564	739,856	196,482	42,673	340,928
AL	21,606	3,922	2,505	5,042	10,138	12,009	3,399	1,924	6,771
AK	6,260	694	640	450	4,476	5,198	461	30	831
AZ	20,198	4,141	3,034	1,854	11,169	12,199	3,218	705	6,590
AR	12,533	2,079	1,185	3,188	6,082	7,664	1,919	454	3,183
CA	121,829	19,515	18,788	14,702	68,825	73,781	19,816	164	33,546
CO	17,033	3,088	2,179	2,566	9,201	10,593	2,971	495	3,943
CT	15,146	4,982	3,098	1,456	5,610	8,227	1,981	114	5,613
DE	3,849	904	651	751	1,543	2,104	526	151	1,336
DC	2,392	457	1,440	43	452	505	471	1	1,428
FL	60,747	13,993	10,178	4,568	32,008	36,406	8,910	1,857	23,878
GA	35,678	7,388	4,572	5,776	17,942	20,353	4,889	2,458	10,800
HI	6,174	838	862	769	3,705	4,877	78	37	2,213
ID	5,418	937	512	1,099	2,870	3,480	726	21	1,204
IL	48,297	9,999	6,770	9,355	22,174	26,834	9,377	1,532	12,269
IN	28,627	4,920	2,781	7,636	13,290	16,052	4,818	3,004	7,040
IA	14,334	2,454	1,599	3,880	6,400	8,939	2,373	569	3,093
KS	12,803	2,115	1,489	3,613	5,586	8,026	2,190	493	2,729
KY	20,316	2,921	1,854	5,287	10,255	12,912	2,013	1,897	5,333
LA	33,624	3,310	2,751	15,526	12,037	20,978	7,571	534	6,498
ME	6,696	1,925	1,007	1,026	2,738	4,680	420	21	1,731
MD	21,490	5,265	4,586	1,689	9,950	11,579	2,567	707	7,523
MA	25,862	7,320	5,485	2,630	10,427	13,868	5,068	336	8,664
MI	36,882	8,310	5,445	6,417	16,710	20,456	7,657	1,475	9,251
MN	21,708	4,095	2,875	3,888	10,851	13,389	3,425	568	5,035
MS	13,392	2,226	1,572	2,569	7,024	8,221	2,622	543	3,775
MO	23,342	4,535	2,793	3,454	12,560	14,830	3,112	1,086	5,614
MT	5,265	772	570	1,243	2,681	3,573	572	228	1,092
NE	7,877	1,302	933	1,866	3,776	4,903	1,271	201	1,775
NV	10,571	2,115	1,332	1,705	5,419	6,016	2,104	158	3,494
NH	5,335	1,505	958	538	2,333	3,436	662	130	1,571
NJ	39,609	8,634	7,767	4,460	18,748	23,080	7,196	323	10,614
NM	7,877	1,171	982	1,178	4,546	5,536	1,079	530	1,619
NY	63,642	19,153	17,390	4,831	22,269	30,892	13,779	635	22,553
NC	32,574	7,080	4,431	4,868	16,195	19,639	2,702	2,280	10,332
ND	4,110	556	414	1,181	1,959	2,780	298	597	759
OH	48,190	10,078	6,375	9,699	22,039	26,242	9,139	2,682	12,692
OK	17,027	2,761	1,919	3,380	8,967	10,316	4,560	448	3,998
OR	13,175	2,375	1,593	1,890	7,317	8,026	2,247	64	3,419
PA	49,301	11,974	6,901	9,264	21,162	27,798	8,283	2,957	13,619
RI	3,567	1,122	729	302	1,414	1,963	962	(Z)	1,051
SC	18,130	3,371	2,068	3,696	8,995	10,653	1,782	1,057	5,880
SD	3,585	591	410	706	1,878	2,459	426	55	730
TN	25,462	4,476	3,186	4,590	13,211	15,438	2,283	1,340	7,493
TX	140,651	18,472	12,872	54,350	54,958	94,946	21,460	2,663	33,964
UT	8,739	1,382	1,013	1,077	5,266	5,891	1,356	543	1,763
VT	2,687	813	405	293	1,176	1,865	112	(Z)	706
VA	30,509	6,166	4,089	3,786	16,469	19,689	3,427	1,176	7,904
WA	23,224	4,059	2,746	2,580	13,840	15,212	2,770	184	5,404
WV	8,369	1,318	796	2,716	3,539	5,422	981	1,875	1,801
WI	22,455	4,715	3,171	4,579	9,990	12,673	3,999	831	5,997
WY	4,546	403	413	1,333	2,396	3,248	454	542	806

Z Less than $500,000. [1] Total expenditures are the sum of purchases for each source (including retail electricity sales) less electric power sector purchases of fuel. [2] Includes sources not shown separately, such as electricity imports and exports and coal coke net imports ($508.5 million in 2006), which are not allocated to the States. [3] Includes fuel ethanol blended into motor gasoline. [4] Includes supplemental gaseous fuels.

Source: U.S. Energy Information Administration, "State Energy Data, 2007" (published 28 August 2009); <http://www.eia.doe.gov/emeu/states/_seds.html>.

Table 897. **Energy Expenditures and Average Fuel Prices by Source and Sector: 1980 to 2006**

[In millions of dollars (373,790 represents $373,790,000,000), except as indicated. For definition of Btu, see text, this section. End-use sector and electric utilities exclude expenditures and prices on energy sources such as hydropower, solar, wind, and geothermal. Also excludes expenditures for reported amounts of energy consumed by the energy industry for production, transportation, and processing operations]

Source and sector	1980	1985	1990	1995	2000	2002	2003	2004	2005	2006
EXPENDITURES (mil. dol.)										
Total [1, 2, 3]	373,790	437,517	472,030	513,587	688,774	661,496	754,147	868,595	1,044,898	1,157,910
Natural gas [4]	50,488	72,255	64,752	74,544	118,530	110,948	143,952	162,166	199,605	189,640
Petroleum products	237,676	223,928	235,368	236,905	360,864	319,841	378,967	468,351	595,862	681,443
Motor gasoline [5]	124,408	118,048	126,558	136,647	193,947	179,511	209,592	253,218	311,082	357,119
Coal	22,607	29,678	28,602	27,431	28,080	28,511	29,402	31,764	36,932	40,004
Electricity sales	98,095	149,233	176,691	205,876	231,577	247,598	257,995	268,136	295,789	323,965
Residential sector [6]	69,138	99,453	110,863	128,181	155,829	160,994	179,069	189,913	215,879	226,272
Commercial sector [2, 3]	46,796	70,219	79,143	91,658	112,725	119,609	129,317	137,762	154,390	166,758
Industrial sector [2, 3]	94,176	106,361	102,281	106,934	141,374	129,308	150,579	176,473	208,003	226,871
Transportation sector [2]	163,680	161,484	179,743	186,813	278,846	251,585	295,182	364,448	466,626	538,008
Motor gasoline [5]	121,809	115,205	123,845	134,641	191,620	175,729	204,878	247,181	303,931	348,534
Electric utilities [3]	38,010	43,953	40,609	39,058	60,026	54,215	64,669	71,699	95,927	90,058
AVERAGE FUEL PRICES (dol. per mil. Btu)										
All sectors	6.90	8.37	8.25	8.29	10.34	10.04	11.38	12.87	15.52	17.35
Residential sector [6]	7.49	10.94	11.91	12.65	14.29	14.73	15.87	17.13	19.21	21.56
Commercial sector [3]	7.87	11.68	11.92	12.66	13.95	14.70	15.63	16.61	18.60	20.64
Industrial sector [3]	4.71	6.04	5.23	4.98	6.49	6.24	7.39	8.46	10.36	11.33
Transportation sector	8.61	8.27	8.28	8.09	10.79	9.63	11.21	13.37	16.85	19.11
Electric utilities [3]	1.77	1.90	1.48	1.29	1.71	1.54	1.84	2.00	2.61	2.48

[1] Includes other sources not shown separately.   [2] Through 1990, total also includes ethanol blended into gasoline that is not included in motor gasoline for those years.   [3] There are no direct fuel costs for hydroelectric, geothermal, wind, photovoltaic, or solar thermal energy.   [4] Excludes supplemental gaseous fuels.   [5] Beginning 1995, includes fuel ethanol blended into motor gasoline.   [6] There are no direct fuel costs for geothermal, photovoltaic, or solar thermal energy.
Source: U.S. Energy Information Administration, "State Energy Data: Prices and Expenditures," annual (published 28 November 2008); <http://www.eia.doe.gov/emeu/states/state.html?q_state_a=us&q_state=UNITED%20STATES>.

Table 898. **Renewable Energy Consumption Estimates by Source: 1990 to 2008**

[In quadrillion Btu (6.21 represents 6,210,000,000,000,000). For definition of Btu, see source and text, this section. Renewable energy is obtained from sources that are essentially inexhaustible, unlike fossil fuels of which there is a finite supply]

Source and sector	1990	2000	2004	2005	2006	2007	2008 [1]
Consumption, total	6.21	6.26	6.26	6.42	6.91	6.81	7.30
Conventional hydroelectric power [2]	3.05	2.81	2.69	2.70	2.87	2.45	2.45
Geothermal energy [3]	0.34	0.32	0.34	0.34	0.34	0.35	0.36
Biomass [4]	2.74	3.01	3.02	3.13	3.36	3.60	3.88
Solar energy [5]	0.06	0.07	0.06	0.07	0.07	0.08	0.09
Wind energy [6]	0.03	0.06	0.14	0.18	0.26	0.34	0.51
Residential [7]	0.64	0.49	0.48	0.51	0.48	0.53	0.60
Biomass [4]	0.58	0.42	0.41	0.43	0.39	0.43	0.49
Geothermal [3]	0.01	0.01	0.01	0.02	0.02	0.02	0.03
Solar [5]	0.06	0.06	0.06	0.06	0.07	0.07	0.08
Commercial [8]	0.10	0.13	0.12	0.12	0.12	0.12	0.12
Biomass [4]	0.09	0.12	0.11	0.10	0.10	0.10	0.11
Geothermal [3]	(Z)	0.01	0.01	0.01	0.01	0.01	0.01
Hydroelectric [2]	(Z)	(Z)	(Z)	(Z)	(Z)	(Z)	(Z)
Industrial [9]	1.72	1.93	1.86	1.88	2.01	2.05	2.06
Biomass [4]	1.69	1.88	1.82	1.85	1.97	2.03	2.03
Geothermal [3]	(Z)	(Z)	(Z)	(Z)	(Z)	(Z)	0.01
Hydroelectric [2]	0.03	0.04	0.03	0.03	0.03	0.02	0.02
Transportation	0.06	0.14	0.30	0.35	0.48	0.61	0.83
Fuel ethanol [10]	0.06	0.14	0.29	0.33	0.45	0.57	0.79
Biodiesel [11]	(NA)	(NA)	(Z)	0.01	0.03	0.05	0.04
Electric power [12]	3.69	3.58	3.50	3.57	3.83	3.51	3.69
Biomass [4]	0.32	0.45	0.39	0.41	0.41	0.42	0.42
Geothermal [3]	0.33	0.30	0.31	0.31	0.31	0.31	0.31
Hydroelectric [2]	3.01	2.77	2.66	2.67	2.84	2.43	2.43
Solar [5]	(Z)	0.01	0.01	0.01	0.01	0.01	0.01

Z Less than 5 trillion Btu.   [1] Preliminary.   [2] Power produced from natural stream flow as regulated by available storage.   [3] As used at electric power plants, hot water or steam extracted from geothermal reservoirs in the Earth's crust that is supplied to steam turbines at electric power plants that drive generators to produce electricity.   [4] Wood and wood-derived fuels, municipal solid waste (from biogenic sources, landfill gas, sludge waste, agricultural byproducts, and other biomass), fuel ethanol, and biodiesel.   [5] The radiant energy of the sun, which can be converted into other forms of energy, such as heat or electricity. Solar thermal and photovoltaic electricity net generation and solar thermal direct use energy.   [6] Energy present in wind motion that can be converted to mechanical energy for driving pumps, mills, and electric power generators. Wind pushes against sails, vanes, or blades radiating from a central rotating shaft.   [7] Consists of living quarters for private households, but excludes institutional living quarters.   [8] Consists of service-providing facilities and equipment of businesses, governments, and other private and public organizations. Includes institutional living quarters and sewage treatment facilities. Includes commercial combined-heat-and-power and commercial electricity-only plants.   [9] Consists of all facilities and equipment used for producing, processing, or assembling goods. Includes industrial combined-heat-and-power and industrial electricity-only plants.   [10] Ethanol primarily derived from corn.   [11] Any liquid biofuel suitable as a diesel fuel substitute, additive, or extender.   [12] Consists of electricity-only and combined-heat-and-power plants whose primary business is to sell electricity and/or heat to the public. Includes sources not shown separately.
Source: U.S. Energy Information Administration, *Annual Energy Review, 2008* (published 26 June 2008). See also <http://www.eia.doe.gov/emeu/aer/renew.html>

Energy and Utilities   573

Table 899. Fuel Ethanol and Biodiesel—Summary: 1981 to 2008

[13 represents 13,000,000,000,000. Data from 1981 to 1992 are estimates. Beginning 1993, only feedstock data are estimates. Minus sign (–) indicates an excess of exports over imports, except where noted]

Year	Fuel ethanol Feedstock[1] (tril. Btu)	Production (1,000 bbl)	Production (Tril. Btu)	Net imports[2] (1,000 bbl)	Stocks[3] (1,000 bbl)	Stock change[4] (1,000 bbl)	Consumption (1,000 bbl)	Consumption (Tril. Btu)	Biodiesel Feedstock[5] (tril. Btu)	Production (1,000 bbl)	Production (Tril. Btu)	Net imports[2] (1,000 bbl)	Consumption (1,000 bbl)	Consumption (Tril. Btu)
1981	13	1,978	7	(NA)	(NA)	(NA)	1,978	7	(NA)	(NA)	(NA)	(NA)	(NA)	(NA)
1982	35	5,369	19	(NA)	(NA)	(NA)	5,369	19	(NA)	(NA)	(NA)	(NA)	(NA)	(NA)
1983	64	9,890	35	(NA)	(NA)	(NA)	9,890	35	(NA)	(NA)	(NA)	(NA)	(NA)	(NA)
1984	79	12,150	43	(NA)	(NA)	(NA)	12,150	43	(NA)	(NA)	(NA)	(NA)	(NA)	(NA)
1985	95	14,693	52	(NA)	(NA)	(NA)	14,693	52	(NA)	(NA)	(NA)	(NA)	(NA)	(NA)
1986	109	16,954	60	(NA)	(NA)	(NA)	16,954	60	(NA)	(NA)	(NA)	(NA)	(NA)	(NA)
1987	125	19,497	69	(NA)	(NA)	(NA)	19,497	69	(NA)	(NA)	(NA)	(NA)	(NA)	(NA)
1988	127	19,780	70	(NA)	(NA)	(NA)	19,780	70	(NA)	(NA)	(NA)	(NA)	(NA)	(NA)
1989	128	20,062	71	(NA)	(NA)	(NA)	20,062	71	(NA)	(NA)	(NA)	(NA)	(NA)	(NA)
1990	113	17,802	63	(NA)	(NA)	(NA)	17,802	63	(NA)	(NA)	(NA)	(NA)	(NA)	(NA)
1991	131	20,627	73	(NA)	(NA)	(NA)	20,627	73	(NA)	(NA)	(NA)	(NA)	(NA)	(NA)
1992	148	23,453	83	(NA)	(NA)	(NA)	23,453	83	(NA)	(NA)	(NA)	(NA)	(NA)	(NA)
1993	173	27,484	97	244	1,791	323	27,405	97	(NA)	(NA)	(NA)	(NA)	(NA)	(NA)
1994	192	30,689	109	279	2,114	279	30,689	109	(NA)	(NA)	(NA)	(NA)	(NA)	(NA)
1995	202	32,325	114	387	2,393	-207	32,919	117	(NA)	(NA)	(NA)	(NA)	(NA)	(NA)
1996	144	23,178	82	313	2,186	-121	23,612	84	(NA)	(NA)	(NA)	(NA)	(NA)	(NA)
1997	190	30,674	109	85	2,065	860	29,899	106	(NA)	(NA)	(NA)	(NA)	(NA)	(NA)
1998	207	33,453	118	66	2,925	481	33,038	117	(NA)	(NA)	(NA)	(NA)	(NA)	(NA)
1999	215	34,881	123	87	3,406	618	34,350	122	(NA)	(NA)	(NA)	(NA)	(NA)	(NA)
2000	238	38,627	137	116	4,024	-624	39,367	139	(NA)	(NA)	(NA)	(NA)	(NA)	(NA)
2001	259	42,028	149	315	3,400	898	41,445	147	1	204	1	39	243	1
2002	313	50,956	180	306	4,298	1,902	49,360	175	1	250	1	135	385	2
2003	410	66,772	236	292	6,200	-222	67,286	238	2	338	2	-16	322	2
2004	497	81,058	287	3,542	5,978	24	84,576	299	4	666	4	-26	640	3
2005	569	92,961	329	3,234	6,002	-439	96,634	342	12	2,162	12	1	2,163	12
2006	711	116,294	412	17,408	5,563	3,197	130,505	462	32	5,963	32	242	6,204	33
2007	948	155,263	549	10,457	8,760	1,775	163,945	580	63	11,662	62	-3,135	8,528	46
2008[6]	1,340	219,927	778	12,347	10,535	[7]3,710	228,564	809	88	16,251	87	-8,626	7,624	41

NA Not available. [1] Total corn and other biomass inputs to the production of fuel ethanol. [2] Net imports equal imports minus exports. [3] Stocks are at end of year. [4] A negative number indicates a decrease in stocks. [5] Total vegetable oil and other biomass inputs to the production of biodiesel. [6] Preliminary. [7] Derived from preliminary 2007 stock value, not final 2007 value.

Source: U.S. Energy Information Administration, *Annual Energy Review 2008* (published 26 June 2009). See also <http://www.eia.doe.gov/emeu/aer/renew.html>.

574   Energy and Utilities

Table 900. **Energy Imports and Exports by Type of Fuel: 1980 to 2008**

[In quadrillion of Btu. (12.10 represents 12,100,000,000,000,000 Btu). Minus sign (–) indicates an excess of exports over imports. For definition of Btu, see source and text, this section]

Type of fuel	1980	1990	1995	2000	2002	2003	2004	2005	2006	2007	2008 [1]
Net imports, total [2]	12.10	14.06	17.75	24.97	25.74	27.01	29.11	30.15	29.81	29.24	25.78
Coal	–2.39	–2.70	–2.08	–1.21	–0.61	–0.49	–0.57	–0.51	–0.36	–0.60	–1.22
Natural gas (dry).	0.96	1.46	2.74	3.62	3.58	3.36	3.50	3.71	3.56	3.89	3.05
Petroleum [3]	13.50	15.29	16.89	22.38	22.63	24.07	25.99	26.81	26.42	25.79	23.79
Other [4]	0.04	0.01	0.19	0.18	0.13	0.07	0.18	0.13	0.12	0.13	0.15
Imports, total	15.80	18.82	22.26	28.97	29.41	31.06	33.54	34.71	34.67	34.69	32.84
Coal	0.03	0.07	0.24	0.31	0.42	0.63	0.68	0.76	0.91	0.91	0.86
Natural gas (dry).	1.01	1.55	2.90	3.87	4.10	4.04	4.37	4.45	4.29	4.72	4.06
Petroleum [3]	14.66	17.12	18.88	24.53	24.67	26.22	28.20	29.25	29.16	28.76	27.56
Other [4]	0.10	0.08	0.24	0.26	0.21	0.17	0.29	0.24	0.25	0.24	0.28
Exports, total	3.69	4.75	4.51	4.01	3.67	4.05	4.43	4.56	4.87	5.45	7.06
Coal	2.42	2.77	2.32	1.53	1.03	1.12	1.25	1.27	1.26	1.51	2.07
Natural gas (dry).	0.05	0.09	0.16	0.25	0.52	0.69	0.86	0.74	0.73	0.83	1.01
Petroleum	1.16	1.82	1.99	2.15	2.04	2.15	2.21	2.44	2.75	2.97	3.77
Other [4]	0.07	0.07	0.05	0.08	0.07	0.10	0.11	0.11	0.12	0.10	0.13

[1] Preliminary.   [2] Net imports equals imports minus exports.   [3] Includes imports into the Strategic Petroleum Reserve.
[4] Coal coke, small amounts of electricity transmitted across U.S. borders with Canada and Mexico, and small amounts of biodiesel.

Source: U.S. Energy Information Administration, *Annual Energy Review, 2008* (published 26 June 2009). See also <http://www.eia.doe.gov/emeu/aer/txt/ptb0104.html>.

Table 901. **U.S. Foreign Trade in Selected Mineral Fuels: 1980 to 2008**

[985 represents 985,000,000,000 cu. ft. Minus sign (–) indicates an excess of imports over exports]

Mineral fuel	Unit	1980	1990	1995	2000	2004	2005	2006	2007	2008 [1]
Natural gas:										
Imports	Bil. cu. ft.	985	1,532	2,841	3,782	4,259	4,341	4,186	4,608	3,962
Exports	Bil. cu. ft.	49	86	154	244	854	729	724	822	1,000
Net trade [2]	Bil. cu. ft.	–936	–1,447	–2,687	–3,538	–3,404	–3,612	–3,462	–3,785	–2,962
Crude oil [3]:										
Imports [4]	Mil. bbl.	1,926	2,151	2,639	3,320	3,692	3,696	3,693	3,661	3,571
Exports	Mil. bbl.	105	40	35	18	10	12	9	10	10
Net trade [2]	Mil. bbl.	–1,821	–2,112	–2,604	–3,301	–3,682	–3,684	–3,684	–3,651	–3,560
Petroleum products:										
Imports	Mil. bbl.	603	775	586	874	1,119	1,310	1,310	1,255	1,140
Exports	Mil. bbl.	94	273	312	362	374	414	472	513	660
Net trade [2]	Mil. bbl.	508	–502	–274	–512	–745	–896	–838	–742	–481
Coal:										
Imports	Mil. sh. tons . . .	1	3	9	13	27	30	36	36	34
Exports	Mil. sh. tons . . .	92	106	89	58	48	50	50	59	82
Net trade [2]	Mil. sh. tons . . .	90.5	103.1	79.1	46.0	20.7	19.5	13.4	22.8	47.3

[1] Preliminary.   [2] Exports minus imports.   [3] Includes lease condensate.   [4] Includes strategic petroleum reserve imports.

Source: U.S. Energy Information Administration, *Annual Energy Review, 2008* (published 26 June 2009). See also <http://www.eia.doe.gov/emeu/aer/contents.html>.

Table 902. **Crude Oil Imports Into the U.S. by Country of Origin: 1980 to 2008**

[In millions of barrels (1,921 represents 1,921,000,000). Barrels contain 42 gallons. Crude oil imports are reported by the Petroleum Administration for Defense (PAD) District in which they are to be processed. A PAD District is a geographic aggregation of the 50 states and D.C. into 5 districts. Includes crude oil imported for storage in the Strategic Petroleum Reserve (SPR). Total OPEC excludes, and Non-OPEC includes, petroleum imported into the United States indirectly from members of OPEC, primarily from Carribean and West European areas, as petroleum products that were refined from crude oil produced by OPEC]

Country of origin	1980	1990	1995	2000	2002	2003	2004	2005	2006	2007	2008
Total imports . . .	1,921	2,151	2,639	3,311	3,336	3,521	3,674	3,670	3,685	3,656	3,571
OPEC, total [1, 2, 3, 4]	1,410	1,283	1,219	1,659	1,490	1,671	2,032	1,738	1,745	1,969	1,984
Algeria	166	23	10	(Z)	11	41	79	83	130	162	114
Angola [2]	(NA)	86	131	108	117	132	112	164	187	181	184
Ecuador [3]	6	(NA)	35	46	37	50	83	101	99	72	78
Iraq	10	188	–	226	168	171	238	190	202	177	229
Kuwait [5]	10	29	78	96	79	75	88	79	65	64	75
Nigeria	307	286	227	319	215	306	389	387	381	395	338
Saudi Arabia [5]	456	436	460	556	554	629	547	525	519	530	551
Venezuela	57	243	420	446	438	436	473	449	416	420	381
Non-OPEC, total [2, 3, 4, 6] .	511	869	1,419	1,652	1,846	1,850	1,838	1,932	1,940	1,687	1,587
Brazil	(NA)	–	–	2	21	17	19	34	49	61	84
Canada	73	235	380	492	527	565	590	600	651	681	707
Chad	(NA)	(NA)	(NA)	(NA)	(NA)	(NA)	(NA)	(NA)	35	28	37
Colombia	(NA)	51	76	116	86	59	51	57	52	50	65
Mexico	185	251	375	479	548	580	584	566	575	514	434
Russia	(NA)	(Z)	5	3	31	54	55	70	39	41	41
United Kingdom	63	57	124	106	148	127	86	80	47	37	27

– Represents zero.   NA Not available.   Z Represents less than 500,000 barrels.   [1] OPEC (Organization of Petroleum Exporting Countries) includes the nations shown, as well as Iran, Libya, Qatar, United Arab Emirates, and Indonesia.   [2] Angola joined OPEC at the beginning of 2007. Prior to 2007, it is included in the non-OPEC total.   [3] Ecuador withdrew from OPEC on Dec. 31, 1992; therefore, it is included under OPEC prior to 1995. From 1995 through 2007, it is included in the Non-OPEC total. In Nov. 2007, Ecuador rejoined OPEC; imports for 2008 are included in the OPEC total.   [4] Gabon withdrew from OPEC on Dec. 31, 1994; therefore, it is included under OPEC prior to 1995. Beginning 1995, it is included in the Non-OPEC total.   [5] Imports from the Neutral Zone between Kuwait and Saudi Arabia are included in Saudi Arabia.   [6] Non-OPEC total includes nations not shown.

Source: U.S. Energy Information Administration, "Petroleum Supply Monthly," February 2009; <http://www.eia.doe.gov /pub/oil_gas/petroleum/data_publications/petroleum_supply_monthly/historical/2009/2009_02/pdf/table38.pdf>.

Energy and Utilities   575

Table 903. Crude Oil and Refined Products—Summary: 1980 to 2008

[13,481 represents 13,481,000 bbl. Barrels (bbl.) of 42 gallons. Data are averages]

Year	Crude oil [1] (1,000 bbl. per day)					Refined oil products (1,000 bbl. per day)			Total oil imports [4] (1,000 bbl. per day)	Crude oil stocks [1,5] (mil. bbl.)	
	Input to refineries	Domestic production	Imports Total [2]	Strategic reserve [3]	Exports	Domestic demand	Imports	Exports		Total	Strategic reserve [6]
1980 . . .	13,481	8,597	5,263	44	287	17,056	1,646	258	6,909	[7]466	108
1985 . . .	12,002	8,971	3,201	118	204	15,726	1,866	577	5,067	814	493
1990 . . .	13,409	7,355	5,894	27	109	16,988	2,123	748	8,018	908	586
1995 . . .	13,973	6,560	7,230	–	95	17,725	1,605	855	8,835	895	592
2000 . . .	15,067	5,822	9,071	8	50	19,701	2,389	990	11,459	826	541
2002 . . .	14,947	5,746	9,140	16	9	19,761	2,390	975	11,530	877	599
2003 . . .	15,304	5,681	9,665	–	12	20,034	2,599	1,014	12,264	907	638
2004 . . .	15,475	5,419	10,088	77	27	20,731	3,057	1,021	13,145	961	676
2005 . . .	15,220	5,178	10,126	52	32	20,802	3,588	1,133	13,714	1,008	685
2006 . . .	15,242	5,102	10,118	8	25	20,687	3,589	1,292	13,707	1,001	689
2007 . . .	15,156	5,064	10,031	7	27	20,680	3,422	1,371	13,468	1,015	691
2008 . . .	14,645	4,955	9,756	7	29	19,419	(NA)	(NA)	12,872	1,010	703

– Represents zero. NA Not available. [1] Includes lease condensate. [2] Includes Strategic Petroleum Reserve. [3] SPR is the Strategic Petroleum Reserve. Through 2003, includes imports by SPR only; beginning in 2004, includes imports by SPR, and imports into SPR by others. [4] Crude oil (including Strategic Petroleum Reserve imports) plus refined products. [5] Crude oil at end of period. Includes commercial and Strategic Petroleum Reserve stocks. [6] Crude oil stocks in the Strategic Petroleum Reserve include non-U.S. stocks held under foreign or commercial storage agreements. [7] Stocks of Alaskan crude oil in transit are included from January 1985 forward.

Source: U.S. Energy Information Administration, "Monthly Energy Review," March 2009.

Table 904. Petroleum and Coal Products Corporations—Sales, Net Profit, and Profit Per Dollar of Sales: 1990 to 2008

[318.5 represents $318,500,000,000. Represents SIC group 29 (NAICS group 324). Through 2000, based on Standard Industrial Classification (SIC) code; beginning 2001, based on North American Industry Classification System, 1997 (NAICS). Profit rates are averages of quarterly figures at annual rates. Beginning 1990, excludes estimates for corporations with less than $250,000 in assets]

Item	Unit	1990	1995	2000	2001	2002	2003	2004	2005	2006	2007	2008
Sales.	Bil. dol. . .	318.5	283.1	455.2	472.5	474.9	597.8	767.7	956.0	1,037.8	1,113.2	1,370.5
Net profit:												
Before income taxes	Bil. dol. . .	23.1	16.5	55.5	47.2	22.4	52.8	89.7	120.2	139.8	127.0	102.9
After income taxes	Bil. dol. . .	17.8	13.9	42.6	35.8	19.5	43.6	71.8	96.3	111.0	105.4	82.1
Depreciation [1]	Bil. dol. . .	18.7	16.7	15.5	17.2	17.8	19.4	18.5	18.6	20.0	22.6	22.8
Profits per dollar of sales:												
Before income taxes	Cents . . .	7.3	5.8	12.2	9.7	4.6	8.8	11.6	12.6	13.4	11.6	6.0
After income taxes	Cents . . .	5.6	4.9	9.4	7.4	4.2	7.3	9.3	10.1	10.6	9.6	4.5
Profits on stockholders' equity:												
Before income taxes	Percent. .	16.4	12.6	29.4	21.8	9.7	20.8	32.9	38.0	36.3	30.7	22.2
After income taxes	Percent. .	12.7	10.6	22.6	16.5	8.4	17.1	26.3	30.4	28.8	25.5	17.6

[1] Includes depletion and accelerated amortization of emergency facilities.

Source: U.S. Census Bureau, Quarterly Financial Report for Manufacturing, Mining and Trade Corporations.

Table 905. Major Petroleum Companies—Financial Summary: 1980 to 2008

[32.9 represents $32,900,000,000. Data represent a composite of approximately 42 major worldwide petroleum companies aggregated on a consolidated total company basis. Minus sign (–) indicates deficit]

Item	1980	1990	1995	2000	2003	2004	2005	2006	2007	2008
FINANCIAL DATA (bil. dol.)										
Net income	32.9	26.8	24.3	76.4	85.5	120.5	170.6	187.6	237.6	198.1
Depreciation, depletion, etc.	32.5	38.7	43.1	53.3	68.0	76.9	76.5	85.8	114.3	156.8
Cash flow [1]	65.4	65.5	67.4	129.7	157.7	205.1	239.9	261.2	327.1	440.7
Dividends paid	9.3	15.9	17.6	23.0	27.5	33.5	37.5	39.2	62.2	74.8
Net internal funds available for investment or debt repayment [2]	56.1	49.6	49.8	106.7	130.2	171.6	202.4	222.0	264.9	365.9
Capital and exploratory expenditures	62.1	59.6	59.8	72.8	90.7	112.4	140.4	193.1	221.7	328.0
Long-term capitalization	211.4	300.0	304.3	516.9	606.1	700.1	800.4	910.6	1,211.8	1,362.0
Long-term debt	49.8	90.4	85.4	112.8	142.1	161.0	165.2	177.4	240.1	299.4
Preferred stock	2.0	5.2	5.7	5.4	2.2	1.3	3.5	3.4	1.9	1.4
Common stock and retained earnings [3] . .	159.6	204.4	213.2	398.7	461.8	537.8	631.7	729.8	969.8	1,061.2
Excess of expenditures over cash income [4]	6.0	10.0	10.0	–33.9	–39.5	–59.2	–62.0	–28.9	–43.2	–37.9
RATIOS [5] (percent)										
Long-term debt to long-term capitalization. .	23.6	30.1	28.1	21.8	26.5	24.1	23.5	19.9	19.1	19.8
Net income to total average capital	17.0	9.1	8.1	15.7	15.2	18.9	23.0	22.3	21.2	15.2
Net income to average common equity. . . .	22.5	13.5	11.6	20.5	20.1	24.2	29.3	27.8	26.3	19.2

[1] Generally represents internally generated funds from operations. Sum of net income and noncash charges such as depreciation, depletion, amortization, ceiling tests, and mark-to-market accounting. [2] Cash flow minus dividends paid. [3] Includes common stock, capital surplus, and earned surplus accounts after adjustments. [4] Capital and exploratory expenditures plus dividends paid minus cash flow. [5] Represents approximate year-to-year comparisons because of changes in the makeup of the group due to mergers and other corporate changes.

Source: Carl H. Pforzheimer & Co., New York, NY, Comparative Oil Company Statements, annual.

Table 906. **Nuclear Power Plants—Number, Capacity, and Generation: 1980 to 2008**

[51.8 represents 51,800,000 kW]

Item	1980	1990	1995	2000	2001	2002	2003	2004	2005	2006	2007	2008
Operable generating units [1, 2] . . .	71	112	109	104	104	104	104	104	104	104	104	104
Net summer capacity [2, 3] (mil. kW).	51.8	99.6	99.5	97.9	98.2	98.7	99.2	99.6	100.0	100.3	100.3	100.3
Net generation (bil. kWh).	251.1	576.9	673.4	753.9	768.8	780.1	763.7	788.5	782.0	787.2	806.4	809.0
Percent of total electricity net generation	11.0	19.0	20.1	19.8	20.6	20.2	19.7	19.9	19.3	19.4	19.4	19.7
Capacity factor [4] (percent)	56.3	66.0	77.4	88.1	89.4	90.3	87.9	90.1	89.3	89.6	91.8	91.9

[1] Total of nuclear generating units holding full-power licenses, or equivalent permission to operate, at the end of the year. Although Browns Ferry 1 was shut down in 1985, the unit has remained fully licensed and thus has continued to be counted as operable during the shutdown. [2] As of year-end. [3] Net summer capacity is the peak steady hourly output that generating equipment is expected to supply to system load, exclusive of auxiliary and other power plant, as demonstrated by test at the time of summer peak demand. [4] Weighted average of monthly capacity factors. Monthly factors are derived by dividing actual monthly generation by the maximum possible generation for the month (number of hours in the month multiplied by the net summer capacity at the end of the month).

Source: U.S. Energy Information Administration, "Monthly Energy Review," March 2009; <http://www.eia.doe.gov/emeu/mer/nuclear.html> (accessed 2 April 2009).

Table 907. **Nuclear Power Plants—Number of Units, Net Generation, and Net Summer Capacity by State: 2007**

[806,425 represents 806,425,000,000 kWh]

State	Number of units	Net generation		Net summer capacity		State	Number of units	Net generation		Net summer capacity	
		Total (mil. kWh)	Percent of total [1]	Total (mil. kW)	Percent of total [1]			Total (mil. kWh)	Percent of total [1]	Total (mil. kW)	Percent of total [1]
U.S. . . .	104	806,425	19.4	100.3	10.1	MS	1	9,359	18.7	1.3	7.8
AL	5	34,325	23.9	5.0	16.3	MO	1	9,372	10.3	1.2	5.8
AZ	3	26,782	23.6	3.9	15.1	NE	2	11,042	34.0	1.2	17.8
AR	2	15,486	28.4	1.8	12.0	NH	1	10,764	46.2	1.2	29.1
CA	4	35,792	17.0	4.4	6.9	NJ	1	32,010	51.1	4.0	21.7
CT	2	16,386	49.4	2.0	26.2	NY	6	42,453	29.1	5.2	13.2
FL.	5	29,289	13.0	3.9	7.0	NC	5	40,045	30.8	5.0	18.0
GA	4	32,545	22.4	4.0	11.0	OH	3	15,764	10.2	2.1	6.3
IL	11	95,729	47.8	11.4	26.6	PA	9	77,376	34.2	9.3	20.6
IA	1	4,519	9.1	0.6	4.7	SC	7	53,200	51.4	6.5	27.5
KS	1	10,369	20.7	1.2	10.4	TN	3	28,700	30.2	3.4	16.3
LA	2	17,078	18.4	2.1	8.1	TX	4	40,955	10.1	4.9	4.8
MD	2	14,353	28.6	1.7	13.9	VT	1	4,704	80.8	0.6	55.8
MA	1	5,120	10.9	0.7	5.1	VA	4	27,268	34.8	3.4	14.8
MI	3	31,517	26.4	4.0	13.1	WA	1	8,109	7.6	1.1	4.0
MN	3	13,103	24.1	1.7	12.9	WI	3	12,910	20.4	1.6	9.7

[1] For total generation and capacity, see Table 913.

Source: U.S. Energy Information Administration, "Electric Power Annual 2007" (published 26 January 2009); <http://www.eia.doe.gov/cneaf/electricity/epa/epa_sprdshts.html>.

Table 908. **Uranium Concentrate—Supply, Inventories, and Average Prices: 1980 to 2008**

[43.70 represents 43,700,000 pounds (lbs.). Years ending Dec. 31. For additional data on uranium, see Section 18]

Item	Unit	1980	1990	1995	2000	2004	2005	2006	2007	2008
Production [1]	Mil. lb. . . .	43.70	8.89	6.04	3.96	2.28	2.69	4.11	4.53	3.90
Exports [2]	Mil. lb. . . .	5.8	2.0	9.8	13.6	13.2	20.5	18.7	14.8	17.2
Imports [2]	Mil. lb. . . .	3.6	23.7	41.3	44.9	66.1	65.5	64.8	54.1	57.1
Electric plant purchases from domestic suppliers.	Mil. lb. . . .	(NA)	20.5	22.3	24.3	28.2	27.3	27.9	18.5	20.4
Loaded into U.S. nuclear reactors [3] . . .	Mil. lb. . . .	(NA)	(NA)	51.1	51.5	50.1	58.3	51.7	45.5	51.3
Inventories, total	Mil. lb. . . .	(NA)	129.1	72.5	111.3	95.2	93.8	106.6	112.4	108.8
At domestic suppliers	Mil. lb. . . .	(NA)	26.4	13.7	56.5	37.5	29.1	29.1	31.2	26.9
At electric plants	Mil. lb. . . .	(NA)	102.7	58.7	54.8	57.7	64.7	77.5	81.2	81.9
Average price per pound: Purchased imports.	Dollars. . .	(NA)	12.55	10.20	9.84	12.25	14.83	19.31	34.18	41.30
Domestic purchases	Dollars. . .	(NA)	15.70	11.11	11.45	11.91	13.98	18.54	33.13	43.43

NA Not available. [1] Data are for uranium concentrate, a yellow or brown powder obtained by the milling of uranium ore, processing of in situ leach mining solutions, or as a by-product of phosphoric acid production. [2] Trade data prior to 1990 were for transactions conducted by uranium suppliers only. For 1990 forward, transactions by uranium buyers (consumers) have been included. Buyer imports and exports prior to 1990 are believed to be small. [3] Does not include any fuel rods removed from reactors and later reloaded into the reactor.

Source: U.S. Energy Information Administration, *Annual Energy Review 2008* (published 26 June 2009). See also <http://www.eia.doe.gov/emeu/aer/txt/ptb0903.html>.

Energy and Utilities **577**

Table 909. **Solar Collector Shipments by Type, End Use, and Market Sector: 1980 to 2007**

[Shipments in thousands of square feet (19,398 represents 19,398,000). Solar collector is a device for intercepting sunlight, converting the light to heat, and carrying the heat to where it will be either used or stored. 1985 data are not available. Based on the Annual Solar Thermal Collector Manufacturers Survey]

Year	Number of manufacturers	Total shipments [1,2,3]	Collector type Low temperature [1,2]	Collector type Medium temperature, special, other [2]	End use Pool heating	End use Hot water	End use Space heating	Market sector Residential	Market sector Commercial	Market sector Industrial
1980	233	19,398	12,233	7,165	12,029	4,790	1,688	16,077	2,417	488
1990	51	11,409	3,645	2,527	5,016	1,091	2	5,835	294	22
1995	36	7,666	6,813	840	6,763	755	132	6,966	604	82
2000	26	8,354	7,948	400	7,863	367	99	7,473	810	57
2005	25	16,041	15,224	702	15,041	640	228	14,681	1,160	31
2006	44	20,744	15,546	1,346	15,362	1,136	330	15,123	1,626	42
2007	60	15,153	13,323	1,797	12,076	1,393	189	12,799	931	46

[1] Includes shipments of high temperature collectors to the government, including some military, but excluding space applications. Also includes end uses such as process heating, utility, and other market sectors not shown separately. [2] Includes imputation of shipment data to account for nonrespondents. [3] Total shipments include all domestic and export shipments and may include imported collectors that subsequently were shipped to domestic or foreign customers.

Source: U.S. Energy Information Administration, 1980–1990, "Solar Collector Manufacturing Activity", annual reports; 1995–2002, "Renewable Energy Annual"; thereafter, "Solar Thermal and Photovoltaic Collector Manufacturing Activities 2007" (published October 2008); <http://www.eia.doe.gov/cneaf/solar.renewables/page/solarreport/solar.html>.

Table 910. **Electricity Net Generation by Sector and Fuel Type: 1990 to 2008**

[3,037.8 represents 3,037,800,000,000 kWh. Data are for fuels consumed to produce electricity. Also includes fuels consumed to produce useful thermal output at a small number of electric utility combined-heat-and-power (CHP) plants]

Source and sector	Unit	1990	1995	2000	2005	2007	2008 [1]
Net generation, total.............	Bil. kWh.	3,037.8	3,353.5	3,802.1	4,055.4	4,156.7	4,110.3
Electric power sector, total	Bil. kWh.....	2,901.3	3,194.2	3,637.5	3,902.2	4,005.3	3,966.7
Electricity-only plants [2].........	Bil. kWh.....	2,840.0	3,052.8	3,472.9	3,721.8	3,828.0	3,801.4
Combined-heat-and-power plants [3]..	Bil. kWh.....	61.3	141.5	164.6	180.4	177.4	165.3
Commercial sector [4]	Bil. kWh.....	5.8	8.2	7.9	8.5	8.3	7.9
Industrial sector [5]	Bil. kWh.....	130.7	151.0	156.7	144.7	143.1	135.7
Net generation by source, all sectors:							
Fossil fuels, total	Bil. kWh.....	2,103.6	2,293.9	2,692.5	2,909.5	2,992.2	2,928.3
Coal [6]	Bil. kWh.....	1,594.0	1,709.4	1,966.3	2,012.9	2,016.5	1,994.4
Petroleum [7]	Bil. kWh.....	126.5	74.6	111.2	122.2	65.7	45.4
Natural gas [8]	Bil. kWh.....	372.8	496.1	601.0	761.0	896.6	876.9
Other gases [9]	Bil. kWh.....	10.4	13.9	14.0	13.5	13.5	11.6
Nuclear electric power..........	Bil. kWh.....	576.9	673.4	753.9	782.0	806.4	806.2
Hydroelectric pumped storage [10]	Bil. kWh.....	-3.5	-2.7	-5.5	-6.6	-6.9	-6.2
Renewable energy, total	Bil. kWh.....	357.2	384.8	356.5	357.7	352.7	371.7
Conventional hydroelectric power...	Bil. kWh.....	292.9	310.8	275.6	270.3	247.5	248.1
Biomass, total	Bil. kWh.....	45.8	56.9	60.7	54.3	55.5	55.9
Wood [11]	Bil. kWh.....	32.5	36.5	37.6	38.9	39.0	38.8
Waste [12]	Bil. kWh.....	13.3	20.4	23.1	15.4	16.5	17.1
Geothermal	Bil. kWh.....	15.4	13.4	14.1	14.7	14.6	14.9
Solar [13]	Bil. kWh.....	0.4	0.5	0.5	0.6	0.6	0.8
Wind....................	Bil. kWh.....	2.8	3.2	5.6	17.8	34.4	52.0
Other [14]	Bil. kWh.....	3.6	4.1	4.8	12.8	12.2	10.4
Consumption of fuels for electricity generation:							
Coal [6]	Mil. sh. tons..	792.5	860.6	994.9	1,041.4	1,046.8	1,043.6
Petroleum, total	Mil. bbl.....	218.8	132.6	195.2	206.8	112.6	79.2
Distillate fuel oil [15]	Mil. bbl.....	18.1	19.6	31.7	20.7	15.7	12.4
Residual fuel oil [16]	Mil. bbl.....	190.7	95.5	143.4	141.5	63.8	37.6
Other liquids [17]	Mil. bbl....	0.4	0.7	1.4	3.0	2.9	2.3
Petroleum coke	Mil. sh. Tons [18].	1.9	3.4	3.7	8.3	6.0	5.4
Natural gas [8]	Bil. cu. ft....	3,691.6	4,737.9	5,691.5	6,036.4	7,089.3	6,833.4
Other gases [9]	Tril. Btu	111.8	132.5	126.0	109.9	114.9	95.4
Biomass......................	Tril. Btu	653.5	795.6	825.9	585.3	598.1	595.1
Wood [11]...................	Tril. Btu	442.3	479.9	495.8	355.3	353.0	345.5
Waste [12]	Tril. Btu	211.2	315.7	330.1	230.1	245.1	249.6
Other [14]	Tril. Btu	36.0	42.0	46.2	173.0	167.9	153.7

[1] Preliminary. [2] Electricity-only plants within the NAICS 22 category whose primary business is to sell electricity to the public. Data also include a small number of electric utility combined-heat-and-power plants (CHP). [3] Combined-heat-and-power plants within the NAICS 22 category whose primary business is to sell electricity and/or heat to the public. Data do not include electric utility CHP plants—these are included under electricity-only plants. [4] Commercial combined-heat-and-power (CHP) and commercial electricity-only plants. [5] Industrial combined-heat-and-power (HCP) and industrial electricity-only plants. [6] Anthracite, bituminous coal, subbituminous coal, lignite, waste coal, and coal synfuel. [7] Distillate fuel oil, residual fuel oil, petroleum coke, jet fuel, kerosene, other petroleum, and waste oil. [8] Includes a small amount of supplemental gaseous fuels that cannot be identified separately. [9] Blast furnace gas, propane gas, and other manufactured and waste gases derived from fossil fuels. [10] Pumped storage facility production minus energy used for pumping. [11] Wood and wood-derived fuels. [12] Municipal solid waste from biogenic sources, landfill gas, sludge waste, tires, agricultural by-products, and other biomass. Through 2000, also includes nonrenewable waste (municipal solid waste from nonbiogenic sources, and tire-derived fuels). [13] Solar thermal and photovoltaic energy. [14] Batteries, chemicals, hydrogen, pitch, purchased steam, sulfur, miscellaneous technologies, and beginning 2005, nonrenewable waste (municipal solid waste from nonbiogenic sources, and tire-derived fuels). [15] Fuel oil numbers 1, 2, and 4. Prior to 2005, electric utility data also include small amounts of kerosene and jet fuel. [16] Fuel oil numbers 5 and 6. Prior to 2005, electric utility data also include a small amount of fuel oil number 4. [17] Jet fuel, kerosene, other petroleum liquids, and waste oil. [18] Short tons.

Source: U.S. Energy Information Administration, Annual Energy Review 2008 (published 26 June 2009). See also <http://www.eia.doe.gov/emeu/aer/contents.html>.

Table 911. **Total Electric Net Summer Capacity, All Sectors: 1990 to 2007**

[In million kilowatts (734.1 represents 734,100,000). Data are at end of year. For plants that use multiple sources of energy, capacity is assigned to the predominant energy source]

Source	1990	1995	2000	2002	2003	2004	2005	2006	2007
Net summer capacity, total	734.1	769.5	811.7	905.3	948.4	962.9	978.0	986.2	994.9
Fossil fuels, total	527.8	554.2	598.9	689.5	731.2	745.4	757.1	761.6	764.0
Coal [1]	307.4	311.4	315.1	315.4	313.0	313.0	313.4	313.0	312.7
Petroleum [2]	77.9	66.6	61.8	59.7	60.7	59.1	58.5	58.1	56.1
Natural gas [3]	140.8	174.5	219.6	312.5	355.4	371.0	383.1	388.3	392.9
Dual fired [4]	113.6	122.0	149.8	162.3	171.3	172.2	174.7	(NA)	(NA)
Other gases [5]	1.6	1.7	2.3	2.0	2.0	2.3	2.1	2.3	2.3
Nuclear electric power	99.6	99.5	97.9	98.7	99.2	99.6	100.0	100.3	100.3
Hydroelectric pumped storage	19.5	21.4	19.5	20.4	20.5	20.8	21.3	21.5	21.9
Renewable energy, total	86.8	93.9	94.9	96.1	96.8	96.4	98.7	101.9	108.0
Conventional hydroelectric power . . .	73.9	78.6	79.4	79.4	78.7	77.6	77.5	77.8	77.9
Biomass, total	8.1	10.3	10.0	9.6	9.6	9.7	9.8	10.1	10.8
Wood [6]	5.5	6.7	6.1	5.8	5.9	6.2	6.2	6.4	6.7
Waste [7]	2.5	3.5	3.9	3.8	3.8	3.5	3.6	3.7	4.1
Geothermal	2.7	3.0	2.8	2.3	2.1	2.2	2.3	2.3	2.2
Solar [8]	0.3	0.3	0.4	0.4	0.4	0.4	0.4	0.4	0.5
Wind	1.8	1.7	2.4	4.4	6.0	6.5	8.7	11.3	16.5
Other [9]	0.5	0.5	0.5	0.7	0.7	0.7	0.9	0.9	0.8

NA Not available. [1] Anthracite, bituminous coal, subbituminous coal, lignite, waste coal, and coal synfuel. [2] Distillate fuel oil, residual fuel oil, petroleum coke, jet fuel, kerosene, other petroleum, and waste oil. [3] Includes a small amount of supplemental gaseous fuels that cannot be identified separately. [4] Petroleum and natural gas. [5] Blast furnace gas, propane gas, and other manufactured and waste gases derived from fossil fuels. [6] Wood and wood-derived fuels. [7] Municipal solid waste from biogenic sources, landfill gas, sludge waste, tires, agricultural byproducts, and other biomass. Also includes nonrenewable waste (municipal solid waste from nonbiogenic sources, and tire-derived fuels). [8] Solar thermal and photovoltaic energy. [9] Batteries, chemicals, hydrogen, pitch, purchased steam, sulfur, and miscellaneous technologies.

Source: U.S. Energy Information Administration, *Annual Energy Review 2008* (published 26 June 2009). See also <http://www.eia.doe.gov/emeu/aer/elect.html>.

Table 912. **Electricity—End Use and Average Retail Prices: 1980 to 2008**

[Beginning 2003, the category "other" has been replaced by "transportation," and the categories "commercial" and "industrial" have been redefined. Data represent revenue from electricity retail sales divided by the amount of retail electricity sold (in kilowatt-hours). Prices include state and local taxes, energy or demand charges, customer service charges, environmental surcharges, franchise fees, fuel adjustments, and other miscellaneous charges applied to end-use customers during normal billing operations. Prices do not include deferred charges, credits, or other adjustments, such as fuel or revenue from purchased power, from previous reporting periods. Data are for a census of electric utilities. Beginning in 2000, data also include energy service providers selling to retail customers]

Item	1990	1995	2000	2003	2004	2005	2006	2007	2008 [1]
END USE (Billion kilowatt-hours)									
Total end use [2]	2,837.1	3,164.0	3,592.4	3,662.0	3,715.9	3,811.0	3,816.8	3,923.8	3,872.6
Direct use [3]	124.5	150.7	170.9	168.3	168.5	150.0	146.9	159.3	151.0
Retail sales, total [4]	2,712.6	3,013.3	3,421.4	3,493.7	3,547.5	3,661.0	3,669.9	3,764.6	3,721.6
Residential	924.0	1,042.5	1,192.4	1,275.8	1,292.0	1,359.2	1,351.5	1,392.2	1,379.3
Commercial [5]	838.3	953.1	1,159.3	1,198.7	1,230.4	1,275.1	1,299.7	1,336.3	1,352.5
Industrial [6]	945.5	1,012.7	1,064.2	1,012.4	1,017.8	1,019.2	1,011.3	1,027.8	982.1
Transportation [7]	4.8	5.0	5.4	6.8	7.2	7.5	7.4	8.2	7.7
AVERAGE RETAIL PRICES (Cents per kilowatt-hour)									
Total:									
Nominal	6.57	6.89	6.81	7.44	7.61	8.14	8.90	9.13	9.82
Real	8.05	7.48	6.81	6.99	6.95	7.20	7.63	7.62	8.02
Residential:									
Nominal	7.83	8.40	8.24	8.72	8.95	9.45	10.40	10.65	11.36
Real	9.60	9.12	8.24	8.20	8.18	8.36	8.91	8.89	9.28
Commercial: [8]									
Nominal	7.34	7.69	7.43	8.03	8.17	8.67	9.46	9.65	10.28
Real	9.00	8.35	7.43	7.55	7.46	7.67	8.11	8.05	8.40
Industrial: [6]									
Nominal	4.74	4.66	4.64	5.11	5.25	5.73	6.16	6.39	7.01
Real	5.81	5.06	4.64	4.80	4.80	5.07	5.28	5.33	5.73
Transportation: [7]									
Nominal	(NA)	(NA)	(NA)	7.54	7.18	8.57	9.54	9.70	11.28
Real	(NA)	(NA)	(NA)	7.09	6.56	7.58	8.18	8.10	9.21
Other: [9]									
Nominal	6.40	6.88	6.56	(X)	(X)	(X)	(X)	(X)	(X)
Real	7.84	7.47	6.56	(X)	(X)	(X)	(X)	(X)	(X)

NA Not available. X Not applicable. [1] Preliminary. [2] The sum of "total retail sales" and "direct use." [3] Use of electricity that is 1) self-generated, 2) produced by either the same entity that consumes the power or an affiliate, and 3) used in direct support of a service or industrial process located within the same facility or group of facilities that house the generating equipment. Direct use is exclusive of station use. [4] Electricity retail sales to ultimate customers reported by electric utilities and, beginning in 2000, other energy service providers. [5] Includes public street and highway lighting, interdepartmental sales, and other sales to public authorities. [6] Beginning 2003, includes agriculture and irrigation. [7] Includes sales to railroads and railways. [8] Beginning 2003, includes public street and highway lighting, interdepartmental sales, and other sales to public authorities. [9] Public street and highway lighting, interdepartmental sales, other sales to public authorities, agriculture and irrigation, and transportation including railroads and railways.

Source: U.S. Energy Information Administration, *Annual Energy Review 2008* (published 26 June 2009). See also <http://www.eia.doe.gov/emeu/aer/elect.html>.

Energy and Utilities 579

Table 913. Electric Power Industry—Net Generation and Net Summer Capacity by State: 2000 to 2007

[Capacity as of December 31. (3,802.1 represents 3,802,100,000,000). Covers utilities for public use]

State	Net generation (bil. kWh) 2000	2005	Total (bil. kWh) 2007	Percent from— Petro-leum	Natural gas	Renewable Hydro-electric	Non-hydro-electric	Nuclear	Coal	Net summer capacity (mil. kW) 2000	2007
U.S. ...	3,802.1	4,055.4	4,156.7	1.6	21.6	6.0	2.5	19.4	48.5	811.7	994.9
AL	124.4	137.9	143.8	0.1	16.2	2.9	2.6	23.9	54.2	23.5	30.6
AK	6.2	6.6	6.8	14.8	56.7	18.9	0.2	–	9.4	2.1	2.0
AZ	88.9	101.5	113.3	(Z)	33.9	5.8	(Z)	23.6	36.4	15.3	25.6
AR	43.9	47.8	54.6	0.2	15.3	5.9	3.0	28.4	47.2	9.7	15.3
CA	208.1	200.3	210.8	1.1	54.9	13.0	11.8	17.0	1.1	51.9	63.8
CO	44.2	49.6	53.9	0.1	27.9	3.2	2.5	–	66.7	8.4	12.3
CT	33.0	33.5	33.2	4.0	29.9	1.1	2.2	49.4	11.3	6.4	7.7
DE	6.0	8.1	8.5	2.8	22.3	–	0.6	–	65.9	2.1	3.4
DC	0.1	0.2	0.1	100.0	–	–	–	–	–	0.8	0.8
FL	191.8	220.3	225.4	9.0	44.5	0.1	1.9	13.0	30.1	41.5	55.5
GA	123.9	136.7	145.2	0.5	11.1	1.5	2.4	22.4	62.2	27.8	36.5
HI	10.6	11.5	11.5	77.3	–	0.8	6.5	–	13.7	2.4	2.4
ID	11.9	10.8	11.5	(Z)	14.4	78.6	5.7	–	0.7	3.0	3.2
IL	178.5	194.1	200.3	0.1	3.8	0.1	0.6	47.8	47.6	36.3	42.7
IN	127.8	130.4	130.6	0.1	3.1	0.3	0.2	–	94.0	23.3	27.0
IA	41.5	44.2	49.8	0.6	6.2	1.9	5.8	9.1	76.3	9.1	12.3
KS	44.8	45.9	50.1	0.4	4.3	(Z)	2.3	20.7	72.3	10.1	11.2
KY	93.0	97.8	97.2	2.9	1.8	1.7	0.5	–	93.1	16.8	20.0
LA	92.9	92.6	92.6	2.4	47.4	0.9	3.2	18.4	24.9	21.0	26.3
ME	14.0	18.8	16.1	5.1	41.4	23.2	26.1	–	2.3	4.2	4.2
MD	51.1	52.7	50.2	2.0	4.5	3.3	1.2	28.6	59.2	10.4	12.5
MA	38.7	47.5	47.1	6.5	52.9	1.7	2.6	10.9	25.5	12.4	13.6
MI	104.2	121.6	119.3	0.6	11.0	1.1	2.0	26.4	59.4	25.8	30.3
MN	51.4	53.0	54.5	0.7	7.1	1.2	7.2	24.1	59.1	10.3	12.9
MS	37.6	45.1	50.0	0.8	42.6	–	3.0	18.7	34.8	9.0	16.2
MO	76.6	90.8	91.2	0.1	5.5	1.3	(Z)	10.3	82.4	17.3	20.6
MT	26.5	27.9	28.9	1.7	0.4	32.4	2.1	–	63.4	5.2	5.5
NE	29.1	31.5	32.4	0.1	3.4	1.1	0.9	34.0	60.5	6.0	7.0
NV	35.5	40.2	32.7	(Z)	68.1	6.1	4.0	–	21.7	6.7	10.0
NH	15.0	24.5	23.3	1.7	24.7	5.4	4.8	46.2	16.9	2.9	4.3
NJ	58.1	60.5	62.7	0.7	29.9	(Z)	1.3	51.1	16.3	16.5	18.4
NM	34.0	35.1	36.0	0.1	18.5	0.7	3.9	–	76.7	5.6	7.2
NY	138.1	146.9	145.9	5.6	31.3	17.3	1.9	29.1	14.7	35.6	39.1
NC	122.3	129.7	130.1	0.4	3.4	2.3	1.3	30.8	61.5	24.5	27.6
ND	31.3	31.9	31.2	0.2	0.1	4.2	2.0	–	93.4	4.7	5.1
OH	149.1	157.0	155.2	0.7	2.6	0.3	0.3	10.2	85.8	28.4	33.8
OK	55.6	68.6	72.8	0.2	45.5	4.2	2.9	–	47.3	14.1	20.0
OR	51.8	49.3	55.1	(Z)	27.0	61.0	4.0	–	7.9	11.3	13.2
PA	201.7	218.1	226.1	0.7	8.5	1.0	1.1	34.2	54.3	36.7	45.1
RI	6.0	6.1	7.0	0.5	97.3	0.1	2.2	–	–	1.2	1.8
SC	93.3	102.5	103.4	0.2	5.8	1.5	1.9	51.4	40.2	18.7	23.6
SD	9.7	6.5	6.1	1.0	5.7	47.5	2.4	–	43.3	2.8	2.9
TN	95.8	97.1	95.1	0.2	0.8	5.2	1.0	30.2	63.3	19.5	20.9
TX	377.7	396.7	405.5	0.3	49.2	0.4	2.5	10.1	36.3	81.7	101.9
UT	36.6	38.2	45.4	0.1	16.4	1.2	0.4	–	81.9	5.2	7.1
VT	6.3	5.7	5.8	0.1	(Z)	11.1	8.0	80.8	–	1.0	1.1
VA	77.2	78.9	78.4	2.7	13.9	1.6	3.3	34.8	45.2	19.4	23.0
WA	108.2	102.0	107.0	(Z)	6.8	73.7	3.5	7.6	8.0	26.1	28.6
WV	92.9	93.6	93.9	0.2	0.4	1.3	0.2	–	97.8	15.0	16.1
WI	59.6	61.8	63.4	1.6	10.2	2.4	2.1	20.4	63.1	13.6	16.4
WY	45.5	45.6	45.6	0.1	1.3	1.6	1.7	–	94.5	6.2	6.7

– Represents zero.   Z Represents less than 50 million kWh or 50,000 kW.

Source: U.S. Energy Information Administration, "Electric Power Annual 2007" (published 26 January 2009); <http://www.eia.doe.gov/cneaf/electricity/epa/epa_sprdshts.html>.

580   Energy and Utilities

Table 914. **Electric Power Industry—Capability, Peak Load, and Capacity Margin: 1980 to 2008**

[558,237 represents 558,237,000 kW. Excludes Alaska and Hawaii. Capability represents the maximum kilowatt output with all power sources available and with hydraulic equipment under actual water conditions, allowing for maintenance, emergency outages, and system operating requirements. Capacity margin is the difference between capability and peak load. Minus sign (–) indicates decrease]

Year	Capability at the time of— Summer peak load (1,000 kW) Amount	Change from prior year	Capability at the time of— Winter peak load (1,000 kW) Amount	Change from prior year	Noncoincident peak load Summer (1,000 kW)	Noncoincident peak load Winter (1,000 kW)	Capacity margin Summer Amount (1,000 kW)	Capacity margin Summer Percent of capability	Capacity margin Winter Amount (1,000 kW)	Capacity margin Winter Percent of capability
1980	558,237	13,731	572,195	17,670	427,058	384,567	131,179	23.5	187,628	32.8
1985	621,597	17,357	636,475	14,350	460,503	423,660	161,094	25.9	212,815	33.4
1988	661,580	13,462	676,940	13,963	529,460	466,533	132,120	20.0	210,407	31.1
1989	673,316	11,736	685,249	8,309	524,110	496,378	149,206	22.2	188,871	27.6
1990	685,091	11,775	696,757	11,508	546,331	484,231	138,760	20.3	212,526	30.5
1991	690,915	5,824	703,212	6,455	551,418	485,761	139,497	20.2	217,451	30.9
1992	695,436	4,521	707,752	4,540	548,707	492,983	146,729	21.1	214,769	30.3
1993	694,250	–1,186	711,957	4,205	575,356	521,733	118,894	17.1	190,224	26.7
1994	702,985	8,735	715,090	3,133	585,320	518,253	117,665	16.7	196,837	27.5
1995	714,222	11,237	727,679	12,589	620,249	544,684	93,973	13.2	182,995	25.1
1996	730,376	16,154	737,637	9,958	616,790	554,081	113,586	15.6	183,556	24.9
1997	737,855	7,479	736,666	–971	637,677	529,874	100,178	13.6	206,792	28.1
1998	744,670	6,815	735,090	–1,576	660,293	567,558	84,377	11.3	167,532	22.8
1999	765,744	21,074	748,271	13,181	682,122	570,915	83,622	10.9	177,356	23.7
2000	808,054	42,310	767,505	19,234	678,413	588,426	129,641	16.0	179,079	23.3
2001	788,990	–19,064	806,598	39,093	687,812	576,312	101,178	12.8	230,286	28.6
2002	833,380	44,390	850,984	44,386	714,565	604,986	118,815	14.3	245,998	28.9
2003	856,131	22,751	882,120	31,136	709,375	593,874	146,756	17.1	288,246	32.7
2004	875,870	19,739	864,849	–17,271	704,459	618,701	171,411	19.6	246,148	28.5
2005	882,125	6,255	878,110	13,261	758,876	626,365	123,249	14.0	251,745	28.7
2006	906,155	24,030	899,551	21,441	789,475	640,981	116,680	12.9	258,570	28.7
2007 [1]	915,292	9,137	913,650	14,099	782,227	637,905	133,065	14.5	275,745	30.2
2008 [1]	929,338	14,046	927,781	14,131	789,915	656,989	139,423	15.0	270,792	29.2

[1] Preliminary.

Source: Edison Electric Institute, Washington, DC, *Statistical Yearbook of the Electric Power Industry,* annual.

Table 915. **Electric Energy Retail Sales by Class of Service and State: 2007**

[In billions of kilowatt–hours (3,764.6 represents 3,764,600,000,000)]

State	Total [1]	Resi- dential	Com- mercial	Indus- trial	State	Total [1]	Resi- dential	Com- mercial	Indus- trial
United States ...	3,764.6	1,392.2	1,336.3	1,027.8	Missouri	85.5	35.9	31.1	18.5
Alabama	91.8	32.8	22.9	36.2	Montana	15.5	4.5	4.8	6.2
Alaska	6.3	2.1	2.8	1.4	Nebraska	28.2	9.7	9.4	9.1
Arizona	77.2	34.4	30.5	12.3	Nevada	35.6	12.4	9.4	13.9
Arkansas	47.1	17.4	11.8	17.8	New Hampshire	11.2	4.5	4.6	2.2
California	264.2	89.2	123.7	50.5	New Jersey	81.9	29.8	40.9	11.0
Colorado	51.3	17.6	20.5	13.1	New Mexico	22.3	6.4	8.9	6.9
Connecticut	34.1	13.4	15.1	5.4	New York	148.2	50.2	74.3	20.2
Delaware	11.9	4.5	4.3	3.1	North Carolina	131.9	56.1	46.8	29.0
District of Columbia ...	12.1	2.0	9.5	0.3	North Dakota	11.9	4.1	4.2	3.6
Florida	231.1	117.8	93.9	19.2	Ohio	161.8	54.4	48.1	59.2
Georgia	137.5	56.2	47.0	34.1	Oklahoma	55.2	21.4	18.6	15.2
Hawaii	10.6	3.2	3.5	3.9	Oregon	48.7	19.4	16.2	13.1
Idaho	23.8	8.3	6.0	9.4	Pennsylvania	151.6	54.6	47.5	48.6
Illinois	146.1	48.0	52.0	45.4	Rhode Island	8.0	3.1	3.7	1.2
Indiana	109.4	34.6	24.8	50.0	South Carolina	81.9	29.6	21.7	30.6
Iowa	45.3	14.1	12.1	19.1	South Dakota	10.6	4.3	4.2	2.2
Kansas	40.2	13.8	15.5	10.9	Tennessee	106.7	42.9	30.0	33.9
Kentucky	92.4	28.0	20.0	44.4	Texas	343.8	124.9	110.5	108.3
Louisiana	79.6	28.9	22.9	27.8	Utah	27.8	8.8	10.2	8.8
Maine	11.9	4.4	4.2	3.3	Vermont	5.9	2.2	2.1	1.6
Maryland	65.4	28.2	30.7	6.0	Virginia	111.6	45.5	47.0	18.9
Massachusetts	57.1	20.1	27.1	9.5	Washington	85.7	35.4	29.6	20.8
Michigan	109.3	35.4	40.0	33.9	West Virginia	34.2	11.7	7.8	14.7
Minnesota	68.2	22.6	22.5	23.0	Wisconsin	71.3	22.4	23.5	25.4
Mississippi	48.2	18.6	13.4	16.2	Wyoming	15.5	2.6	4.2	8.7

[1] Includes transportation, not shown separately.

Source: U.S. Energy Information Administration, "Electric Sales and Revenue 2007" (published January 2009); <http://www.eia.doe.gov/cneaf/electricity/esr/table2.xls>.

Table 916. **Electric Energy Price by Class of Service and State: 2007**

[Revenue (in cents) per kilowatt-hour (kWh). Data include both bundled and unbundled consumers]

State	Total [1]	Residential	Commercial	Industrial
United States . . .	9.13	10.65	9.65	6.39
Alabama	7.57	9.32	8.70	5.27
Alaska	13.28	15.18	12.19	12.63
Arizona	8.54	9.66	8.27	6.05
Arkansas	6.96	8.73	6.91	5.25
California	12.80	14.42	12.82	9.98
Colorado	7.76	9.25	7.62	5.97
Connecticut	16.45	19.11	15.39	12.92
Delaware	11.35	13.16	11.21	8.93
District of Columbia . . .	11.79	11.18	12.01	9.32
Florida	10.33	11.22	9.75	7.76
Georgia	7.86	9.10	8.07	5.53
Hawaii	21.29	24.12	21.91	18.38
Idaho	5.07	6.36	5.14	3.87
Illinois	8.46	10.12	8.57	6.61
Indiana	6.50	8.26	7.29	4.89
Iowa	6.83	9.45	7.11	4.74
Kansas	6.84	8.19	6.83	5.13
Kentucky	5.84	7.34	6.76	4.47
Louisiana	8.39	9.37	9.13	6.77
Maine	14.59	16.52	12.94	14.11
Maryland	11.50	11.89	11.58	9.41
Massachusetts	15.16	16.23	15.20	13.03
Michigan	8.53	10.21	8.77	6.47
Minnesota	7.44	9.18	7.48	5.69
Mississippi.	8.03	9.36	8.92	5.75
Missouri	6.56	7.69	6.34	4.76
Montana	7.13	8.77	8.10	5.16
Nebraska	6.28	7.59	6.39	4.78
Nevada	9.99	11.82	10.09	8.28
New Hampshire	13.98	14.88	13.91	12.27
New Jersey	13.01	14.14	12.99	10.08
New Mexico	7.44	9.12	7.66	5.60
New York	15.22	17.10	15.92	8.71
North Carolina	7.83	9.40	7.43	5.47
North Dakota	6.42	7.30	6.58	5.24
Ohio	7.91	9.57	8.67	5.76
Oklahoma	7.29	8.58	7.33	5.41
Oregon	7.02	8.19	7.20	5.06
Pennsylvania	9.08	10.95	9.20	6.87
Rhode Island	13.12	14.05	12.67	12.04
South Carolina	7.18	9.19	7.74	4.83
South Dakota	6.89	8.07	6.61	5.09
Tennessee	7.07	7.84	8.09	5.19
Texas	10.11	12.34	9.87	7.79
Utah	6.41	8.15	6.54	4.52
Vermont	12.04	14.15	12.29	8.92
Virginia	7.12	8.74	6.38	5.07
Washington	6.37	7.26	6.55	4.57
West Virginia	5.34	6.73	5.85	3.95
Wisconsin	8.48	10.87	8.71	6.16
Wyoming	5.29	7.75	6.25	4.10

[1] Includes transportation, not shown separately.

Source: U.S. Energy Information Administration, "Electric Sales and Revenue 2007" (published January 2009); <http://www.eia.doe .gov/cneaf/electricity/esr/esr_sum.html>.

Table 917. **Total Electric Power Industry—Generation, Sales, Revenue, and Customers: 1990 to 2008**

[2,808 represents 2,808,000,000,000 kWh. Sales and revenue are to and from ultimate customers. Commercial and Industrial are not wholly comparable on a year-to-year basis due to changes from one classification to another. For the 2003 period forward, the Energy Information Administration replaced the "Other" sector with the Transportation sector. The Transportation sector consists entirely of electrified rail and urban transit systems. Data previously reported in "Other" have been relocated to the Commercial sector, except for Agriculture (i.e., irrigation load), which have been relocated to the Industrial sector]

Class	Unit	1990	1995	2000	2003	2004	2005	2006	2007	2008 [1]
Generation [2]	Bil. kWh . .	2,808	3,353	3,802	3,883	3,971	4,055	4,065	4,157	4,110
Sales [3]	Bil. kWh .	2,713	3,013	3,421	3,489	3,548	3,661	3,670	3,765	3,722
Residential or domestic . .	Bil. kWh . .	924	1,043	1,192	1,274	1,294	1,359	1,352	1,392	1,379
Percent of total	Percent . . .	34.1	34.6	34.9	36.5	36.5	37.1	36.8	37.0	37.1
Commercial [4]	Bil. kWh . .	751	863	1,055	1,197	1,229	1,275	1,300	1,336	1,352
Industrial [5]	Bil. kWh . .	946	1,013	1,064	1,019	1,019	1,019	1,011	1,028	982
Revenue [3]	Bil. dol. . .	178.2	207.7	233.2	258.9	270.5	298.0	326.5	343.7	365.4
Residential or domestic . .	Bil. dol. . .	72.4	87.6	98.2	110.8	116.0	128.4	140.6	148.3	156.6
Percent of total	Percent . . .	40.6	42.2	42.1	42.8	42.9	43.1	43.1	43.1	42.9
Commercial [4]	Bil. dol. . .	55.1	66.4	78.4	95.8	100.3	110.5	122.9	128.9	139.0
Industrial [5]	Bil. dol. . .	44.9	47.2	49.4	51.8	53.7	58.4	62.3	65.7	68.9
Ultimate customers, Dec. 31 [3]	Million. . . .	110.6	118.3	127.6	134.5	136.1	138.4	140.4	142.1	143.0
Residential or domestic . .	Million . . .	97.1	103.9	111.7	117.3	118.8	120.8	122.5	123.9	124.7
Commercial [4]	Million . . .	12.1	12.9	14.3	16.5	16.6	16.9	17.2	17.4	17.5
Industrial [5]	Million . . .	0.5	0.6	0.5	0.7	0.7	0.7	0.8	0.8	0.8
Avg. kWh used per customer.	1,000. . . .	24.5	25.5	26.8	25.9	26.1	26.5	26.1	26.5	26.0
Residential	1,000. . . .	9.5	10.0	10.7	10.9	10.9	11.3	11.0	11.2	11.1
Commercial [4]	1,000. . . .	62.2	66.6	73.5	72.3	74.0	75.6	75.7	76.9	77.2
Avg. annual bill per customer.	Dollar . . .	1,612	1,756	1,828	1,924	1,987	2,154	2,325	2,418	2,555
Residential	Dollar . . .	745	843	879	945	977	1,063	1,148	1,196	1,256
Commercial [4]	Dollar . . .	4,562	5,124	5,464	5,786	6,037	6,551	7,158	7,418	7,929
Avg. revenue per kWh sold.	Cents . . .	6.57	6.89	6.81	7.42	7.62	8.14	8.90	9.13	9.82
Residential	Cents . . .	7.83	8.40	8.24	8.70	8.97	9.45	10.40	10.65	11.36
Commercial [4]	Cents . . .	7.34	7.69	7.43	8.00	8.16	8.67	9.46	9.65	10.28
Industrial [5]	Cents . . .	4.74	4.66	4.64	5.12	5.27	5.73	6.16	6.39	7.01

[1] Preliminary. [2] "Generation" includes batteries, chemicals, hydrogen, pitch, sulfur, purchased steam, and miscellaneous technologies, which are not separately displayed. [3] Includes other types not shown separately. Data for 1990 are as of December 31, data for following years are average yearly customers. [4] Small light and power. [5] Large light and power.

Source: Edison Electric Institute, Washington, DC, Statistical Yearbook of the Electric Power Industry, annual.

Table 918. **Revenue and Expense Statistics for Major U.S. Investor-Owned Electric Utilities: 1995 to 2007**

[In millions of nominal dollars (199,967 represents $199,967,000,000). Covers approximately 180 investor-owned electric utilities that during each of the last 3 years met any one or more of the following conditions—1 mil. megawatt-hours of total sales; 100 megawatt-hours of sales for resale, 500 megawatt-hours of gross interchange out, and 500 megawatt-hours of wheeling for others. Missing or erroneous respondent data may result in slight imbalances in some of the expense account subtotals]

Item	1995	2000	2003	2004	2005	2006	2007
Utility operating revenues	199,967	235,336	226,227	240,318	267,534	277,142	282,875
Electric utility	183,655	214,707	202,369	213,539	235,570	247,503	251,959
Other utility	16,312	20,630	23,858	26,779	31,964	29,639	30,305
Utility operating expenses	165,321	210,324	197,459	207,161	238,590	247,170	252,216
Electric utility	150,599	191,329	175,473	182,337	208,461	219,171	223,297
Operation	91,881	132,662	122,723	131,962	151,150	159,472	161,939
Production	68,983	107,352	96,181	104,287	121,058	128,016	128,914
Cost of fuel	29,122	32,555	26,476	28,678	36,161	38,158	42,178
Purchased power	29,981	61,969	62,173	67,354	78,279	79,485	78,124
Other	9,880	12,828	7,532	8,256	6,638	10,399	8,632
Transmission	1,425	2,699	3,585	4,519	5,687	6,185	6,095
Distribution	2,561	3,115	3,185	3,301	3,517	3,658	3,870
Customer accounts	3,613	4,246	4,180	4,087	4,243	4,424	4,843
Customer service	1,922	1,839	1,893	2,012	2,289	2,533	2,959
Sales	348	403	234	238	219	241	249
Administrative and general	13,028	13,009	13,466	13,519	14,113	14,618	14,933
Maintenance	11,767	12,185	11,141	11,774	12,058	12,879	13,675
Depreciation	19,885	22,761	16,962	16,373	17,177	17,438	18,662
Taxes and other	27,065	23,721	24,648	22,228	26,848	28,187	27,839
Other utility	14,722	18,995	21,986	24,823	30,129	27,999	28,347
Net utility operating income . . .	34,646	25,012	28,768	33,158	28,944	29,972	30,659

Source: U.S. Energy Information Administration, "Electric Power Annual 2007" (published 21 January 2009); <http://www.eia.doe.gov/cneaf/electricity/epa/epat8p1.html>.

Table 919. **Total Renewable Energy Net Generation of Electricity by Source and State: 2007**

[In millions of kilowatt-hours (352,747 represents 352,747,000,000). MSW = municipal solid waste. For more on net generation, see Table 916]

State	Total [1]	Hydro-electric	Bio-mass [2]	Wind	Wood/wood waste [3]	State	Total [1]	Hydro-electric	Bio-mass [2]	Wind	Wood/wood waste [3]
U.S...	352,747	247,510	16,525	34,450	39,014	MO	1,234	1,204	29	(NA)	(Z)
AL	7,937	4,136	17	(NA)	3,784	MT	9,971	9,364	(NA)	496	111
AK	1,302	1,291	10	1	(Z)	NE	625	347	61	217	(NA)
AZ	6,639	6,598	33	(NA)	(NA)	NV	3,300	2,003	(NA)	(NA)	(NA)
AR	4,860	3,237	43	(NA)	1,581	NH	2,389	1,265	153	(NA)	970
CA	52,173	27,328	2,305	5,585	3,407	NJ	864	21	823	20	(NA)
CO	3,054	1,730	31	1,292	(NA)	NM	1,677	268	16	1,393	(NA)
CT	1,093	363	728	(NA)	2	NY	28,028	25,253	1,449	833	492
DE	48	(NA)	48	(NA)	(NA)	NC	4,656	2,984	87	(NA)	1,585
DC	(NA)	(NA)	(NA)	(NA)	(NA)	ND	1,940	1,305	14	621	(NA)
FL	4,457	154	2,373	(NA)	1,930	OH	846	410	21	15	399
GA	5,652	2,236	53	(NA)	3,362	OK	5,195	3,066	4	1,849	276
HI	846	92	285	238	(NA)	OR	35,816	33,587	139	1,247	843
ID	9,675	9,022	(NA)	172	481	PA	4,782	2,236	1,457	470	620
IL	1,438	154	620	664	(NA)	RI	159	4	155	(NA)	(NA)
IN	681	450	231	(NA)	(NA)	SC	3,552	1,556	101	(NA)	1,895
IA	3,870	962	151	2,757	(Z)	SD	3,067	2,917	(NA)	150	(NA)
KS	1,163	11	(NA)	1,153	(NA)	TN	5,910	4,940	52	50	868
KY	2,134	1,669	95	(NA)	370	TX	11,932	1,644	367	9,006	914
LA	3,807	827	82	(NA)	2,898	UT	734	539	31	(NA)	(NA)
ME	7,945	3,738	260	99	3,848	VT	1,110	647	(NA)	11	453
MD	2,256	1,652	400	(NA)	203	VA	3,814	1,248	773	(NA)	1,792
MA	2,038	797	1,121	(NA)	119	WA	82,560	78,829	176	2,438	1,116
MI	3,687	1,270	722	3	1,692	WV	1,422	1,254	(NA)	168	(NA)
MN	4,586	654	566	2,639	727	WI	2,846	1,516	435	109	785
MS	1,493	(NA)	5	(NA)	1,488	WY	1,484	729	(NA)	755	(NA)

NA Not available. Z Less than 500,000 million kilowatt-hours. [1] Includes types not shown separately. [2] Includes landfill gas and municipal solid waste biogenic (paper and paper board, wood, food, leather, textiles, and yard trimmings). Also includes agriculture by-products/crops, sludge waste, and other biomass solids, liquids, and gases. Excludes wood and wood waste. [3] Black liquor and wood/woodwaste solids and liquids.

Source: Energy Information Administration, "Renewable Energy Trends 2007" (published April 2009); <http://www.eia.doe.gov/cneaf/solar.renewables/page/trends/table20.html>.

Energy and Utilities 583

Table 920. Gas Utility Industry—Summary: 1990 to 2007

[54,261 represents 54,261,000. Covers natural, manufactured, mixed, and liquid petroleum gas. Based on a questionnaire mailed to all privately and municipally owned gas utilities in the United States, except those with annual revenues less than $25,000]

Item	Unit	1990	1995	2000	2003	2004	2005	2006	2007
End users [1]	1,000	54,261	58,728	61,262	62,610	63,297	64,395	65,020	65,389
Residential	1,000	49,802	53,955	56,494	57,802	58,501	59,569	60,147	60,534
Commercial	1,000	4,246	4,530	4,610	4,661	4,641	4,678	4,734	4,718
Industrial and other	1,000	214	242	159	147	155	147	140	137
Sales [2]	Tril. Btu [3]	9,842	9,221	9,232	8,927	8,766	8,848	8,222	8,565
Residential	Tril. Btu	4,468	4,803	4,741	4,722	4,566	4,516	4,117	4,418
Percent of total	Percent	45	52	51	53	52	51	50	52
Commercial	Tril. Btu	2,192	2,281	2,077	2,125	2,075	2,056	1,861	1,943
Industrial	Tril. Btu	3,010	1,919	1,698	1,672	1,763	1,654	1,576	1,522
Other	Tril. Btu	171	218	715	408	363	622	668	682
Revenues [2]	Mil. dol.	45,153	46,436	59,243	72,606	79,929	96,909	91,928	92,131
Residential	Mil. dol.	25,000	28,742	35,828	43,664	47,275	55,680	53,961	55,027
Percent of total	Percent	55	62	60	60	59	57	59	60
Commercial	Mil. dol.	10,604	11,573	13,339	17,349	18,689	22,653	21,557	21,248
Industrial	Mil. dol.	8,996	5,571	7,432	9,478	11,230	13,751	12,006	11,323
Other	Mil. dol.	553	549	2,645	2,115	2,735	4,825	4,405	4,533
Prices per mil. Btu [3]	Dollars	4.59	5.05	6.42	8.13	9.13	10.95	11.18	10.76
Residential	Dollars	5.60	6.00	7.56	9.25	10.37	12.33	13.11	12.46
Commercial	Dollars	4.84	5.07	6.42	8.17	9.01	11.02	11.58	10.93
Industrial	Dollars	2.99	2.98	4.38	5.67	6.37	8.31	7.62	7.44
Gas mains mileage	1,000	1,189	1,278	1,369	1,424	1,462	1,438	1,534	1,520
Field and gathering	1,000	32	31	27	22	24	23	20	19
Transmission	1,000	292	297	297	304	299	297	300	300
Distribution	1,000	865	950	1,046	1,098	1,140	1,118	1,214	1,201
Construction expenditures [4]	Mil. dol.	7,899	10,760	8,624	13,034	16,567	10,089	10,218	10,987
Transmission	Mil. dol.	2,886	3,380	1,590	7,317	3,205	3,368	3,316	4,327
Distribution	Mil. dol.	3,714	5,394	5,437	3,870	11,636	5,129	5,165	4,851
Production and storage	Mil. dol.	309	367	138	258	181	179	240	107
General	Mil. dol.	770	1,441	1,273	1,350	1,271	1,070	1,119	1,146
Underground storage	Mil. dol.	219	177	185	239	274	343	379	556

[1] Annual average.   [2] Excludes sales for resale.   [3] For definition of Btu, see text, this section.   [4] Includes general.

Source: American Gas Association, Arlington, VA, *Gas Facts*, annual (copyright).

Table 921. Gas Utility Industry—Customers, Sales, and Revenues by State: 2007

[65,389 represents 65,389,000. See headnote, Table 920. For definition of Btu, see text, this section]

State	Customers [1] (1,000) Total	Customers [1] (1,000) Residential	Sales [2] (tril. Btu) Total	Sales [2] (tril. Btu) Residential	Revenues [2] (mil. dol.) Total	Revenues [2] (mil. dol.) Residential	State	Customers [1] (1,000) Total	Customers [1] (1,000) Residential	Sales [2] (tril. Btu) Total	Sales [2] (tril. Btu) Residential	Revenues [2] (mil. dol.) Total	Revenues [2] (mil. dol.) Residential
U.S.	65,389	60,534	8,565	4,418	92,131	55,027	MO	1,499	1,354	162	105	2,004	1,364
							MT	279	247	31	20	299	195
AL	864	796	93	37	1,241	643	NE	463	424	63	34	614	369
AK	128	116	70	20	439	172	NV	791	751	87	39	1,005	540
AZ	1,177	1,119	83	40	1,167	659	NH	111	95	16	8	239	124
AR	628	558	61	34	690	428	NJ	2,777	2,565	340	231	4,436	3,241
CA	10,871	10,413	739	506	7,663	5,667	NM	592	545	53	34	576	400
CO	1,725	1,584	205	135	1,683	1,157	NY	4,210	3,900	539	344	7,322	5,168
CT	533	482	87	44	1,172	698	NC	1,178	1,064	120	60	1,594	916
DE	158	145	19	10	269	162	ND	135	118	30	11	238	98
DC	136	129	14	11	214	160	OH	2,007	1,861	226	164	2,795	2,073
FL	710	669	42	15	635	303	OK	1,012	920	100	62	1,059	722
GA	366	331	54	17	592	235	OR	747	664	89	44	1,121	628
HI	28	26	3	1	79	17	PA	2,654	2,439	320	220	4,380	3,099
ID	357	323	37	24	402	269	RI	246	224	27	18	416	294
IL	3,876	3,623	511	396	5,248	4,132	SC	610	553	83	25	1,011	422
IN	1,759	1,614	223	142	2,322	1,549							
IA	963	866	117	70	1,240	797	SD	185	163	25	13	236	130
KS	942	858	94	65	1,115	818	TN	1,200	1,071	147	63	1,705	815
KY	829	746	99	51	1,066	597	TX	4,490	4,155	1,499	206	11,302	2,397
LA	929	871	334	38	2,659	523	UT	837	779	98	63	842	571
ME	27	19	4	1	61	20	VT	40	35	8	3	106	51
MD	996	938	95	72	1,335	1,039	VA	1,133	1,047	126	75	1,698	1,120
MA	1,485	1,361	175	119	2,771	1,956	WA	1,124	1,025	147	83	1,836	1,111
MI	3,289	3,048	446	320	4,677	3,433	WV	381	347	47	27	613	387
MN	1,531	1,402	268	133	2,658	1,436	WI	1,797	1,632	239	135	2,561	1,577
MS	495	439	58	23	621	288	WY	89	79	13	7	104	59

[1] Averages for the year.   [2] Excludes sales for resale.

Source: American Gas Association, Arlington, VA, *Gas Facts*, annual (copyright).

Table 922. **Privately Owned Gas Utility Industry—Balance Sheet and Income Account: 1990 to 2007**

[In millions of dollars (121,686 represents $121,686,000,000). The gas utility industry consists of pipeline and distribution companies. Excludes operations of companies distributing gas in bottles or tanks]

Item	1990	1995	2000	2002	2003	2004	2005	2006	2007
COMPOSITE BALANCE SHEET									
Assets, total	121,686	141,965	165,709	185,064	174,756	168,306	196,215	203,135	205,345
Total utility plant.	112,863	143,636	162,206	197,717	188,807	180,884	207,976	212,500	213,516
Depreciation and amortization. . . .	*49,483*	*62,723*	*69,366*	*85,038*	*76,642*	*79,889*	*91,794*	*91,804*	*86,244*
Utility plant (net).	63,380	80,912	92,839	112,679	112,165	100,996	116,183	120,696	127,272
Investment and fund accounts . . .	23,872	26,489	10,846	13,000	13,430	12,716	16,331	17,309	13,677
Current and accrued assets	23,268	18,564	35,691	25,786	22,905	22,107	32,325	26,955	28,871
Deferred debits [1]	9,576	13,923	24,279	31,928	24,663	31,033	29,574	36,278	34,608
Liabilities, total	121,686	141,965	165,709	185,064	174,756	168,709	196,215	203,135	205,345
Capitalization, total	74,958	90,581	96,079	117,362	112,089	105,799	120,949	126,842	127,609
Capital stock	43,810	54,402	47,051	58,067	57,605	54,252	62,470	66,153	71,038
Long-term debts	31,148	35,548	48,267	58,962	54,179	51,327	58,264	60,632	56,538
Current and accrued liabilities. . . .	29,550	28,272	42,312	30,856	28,599	25,515	34,936	32,417	34,017
Deferred income taxes [2]	11,360	14,393	17,157	24,612	23,888	23,944	24,937	27,454	27,009
Other liabilities and credits	5,818	8,715	10,161	12,235	10,179	13,049	15,393	16,422	16,709
COMPOSITE INCOME ACCOUNT									
Operating revenues, total . .	66,027	58,390	72,042	68,352	75,527	80,194	102,018	97,156	97,195
Minus: Operating expenses [3]	*60,137*	*50,760*	*64,988*	*60,041*	*66,677*	*71,719*	*89,385*	*87,013*	*85,050*
Operation and maintenance . . .	51,627	37,966	54,602	48,521	55,036	59,920	77,673	73,459	71,011
Federal, state, and local taxes. .	4,957	6,182	6,163	6,249	6,581	6,472	7,513	7,350	7,803
Equals: Operating income	5,890	7,630	7,053	8,310	8,852	8,475	12,632	10,144	12,146
Utility operating income.	6,077	7,848	7,166	8,564	9,198	8,619	12,812	10,185	12,472
Income before interest charges. . .	8,081	9,484	7,589	9,305	10,053	9,609	13,972	11,586	14,329
Net income	4,410	5,139	4,245	4,792	6,198	5,942	9,777	6,931	9,758
Dividends	3,191	4,037	3,239	3,887	3,765	2,111	2,419	2,304	2,253

[1] Includes capital stock discount and expense and reacquired securities. [2] Includes reserves for deferred income taxes. [3] Includes expenses not shown separately.

Source: American Gas Association, Arlington, VA, *Gas Facts,* annual (copyright).

Table 923. **Sewage Treatment Facilities: 2006**

[Based on the North American Industry Classification System (NAICS), 2002; see text, Section 15]

State	Sewage treatment facilities (NAICS 22132)		State	Sewage treatment facilities (NAICS 22132)	
	Number of establishments	Paid employees		Number of establishments	Paid employees
U.S.	**726**	**6,115**	MO	20	[1]
AL	8	[1]	MT	8	[1]
AK	2	[2]	NE	3	[3]
AZ	10	30	NV	3	[2]
AR	6	[1]	NH	2	[2]
CA	28	[3]	NJ	11	[3]
CO	11	29	NM	5	[1]
CT	7	[1]	NY	34	317
DE	1	[2]	NC	21	[1]
DC	(NA)	(NA)	ND	(NA)	(NA)
FL	67	866	OH	15	91
GA	8	117	OK	9	56
HI	14	[1]	OR	6	[1]
ID	8	[1]	PA	84	561
IL	40	[4]	RI	3	[1]
IN	39	168	SC	11	[1]
IA	4	[1]	SD	1	[2]
KS	4	[1]	TN	11	[1]
KY	10	[3]	TX	67	[5]
LA	25	237	UT	2	[2]
ME	3	[2]	VT	3	[2]
MD	6	[2]	VA	8	[1]
MA	10	[3]	WA	7	[1]
MI	26	[1]	WV	15	78
MN	4	31	WI	12	30
MS	22	122	WY	2	[2]

NA Not available. [1] 20–99 employees. [2] 0–19 employees. [3] 100–249 employees. [4] 250–499 employees. [5] 1,000–2,499 employees.

Source: U.S. Census Bureau, "County Business Patterns" (accessed 1 October 2008); <http://www.census.gov/econ/cbp/index.html>.

Table 924. **Public Drinking Water Systems by Size of Community Served and Source of Water: 2008**

[As of **September.** Covers systems that provide water for human consumption through pipes and other constructed conveyances to at least 15 service connections or serve an average of at least 25 persons for at least 60 days a year. Based on reported data in the Safe Drinking Water Information System maintained by the Environmental Protection Agency]

Type of system	Total [1]	Size of community served					Water source	
		500 or fewer persons	501 to 3,300 persons	3,301 to 10,000 persons	10,001 to 100,000	100,001 persons or more	Ground water	Surface water
Total systems	**154,879**	**126,438**	**19,204**	**5,069**	**3,761**	**407**	**140,468**	**14,369**
COMMUNITY WATER SYSTEMS [2]								
Number of systems..............	51,988	29,160	13,858	4,838	3,728	404	40,301	11,671
Percent of systems	100	56	27	9	7	1	78	22
Population served (1,000)	292,300	4,857	19,869	28,135	106,311	133,129	88,039	204,095
Percent of population............	100	2	7	10	36	46	30	70
NONTRANSIENT NONCOMMUNITY WATER SYSTEM [3]								
Number of systems..............	18,742	15,954	2,641	130	16	1	18,041	688
Percent of systems	100	85	14	1	–	–	96	4
Population served (1,000)	6,254	2,235	2,702	702	412	203	5,462	788
Percent of population............	100	36	43	11	7	3	87	13
TRANSIENT NONCOMMUNITY WATER SYSTEM [4]								
Number of systems..............	84,149	81,324	2,705	101	17	2	82,126	2,010
Percent of systems	100	97	3	–	–	–	98	2
Population served (1,000)	13,573	7,197	2,626	542	482	2,725	11,037	2,535
Percent of population............	100	53	19	4	4	20	81	19

– Represents zero.   [1] Includes a small number of systems for which the water source (ground vs. surface) is unknown.
[2] A public water system that supplies water to the same population year-round.   [3] A public water system that regularly supplies water to at least 25 of the same people at least 6 months per year, but not year-round. Some examples are schools, factories, and office buildings which have their own water systems.   [4] A public water system that provides water in a place such as a gas station or campground where people do not remain for long periods of time and is open at least 60 day per year.

Source: U.S. Environmental Protection Agency, *Factoids: Drinking Water and Ground Water Statistics for 2008*, annual reports (pubished November 2008). See also <http://www.epa.gov/safewater/data/getdata.html>.

Table 925. **Public Drinking Water Systems—Number and Population Served by State: 2008**

[**312,127 represents 312,127,000.** See headnote, Table 924]

State	Number of sys-tems	Population served (1,000)				State	Number of sys-tems	Population served (1,000)			
		Total	Commu-nity [1]	Non-tran-sient, non-com-mu-nity [2]	Tran-sient, non-com-mu-nity [3]			Total	Commu-nity [1]	Non-tran-sient, non-com-mu-nity [2]	Tran-sient, non-com-mu-nity [3]
U.S. [4] ..	**154,879**	**312,127**	**292,300**	**6,254**	**13,573**	MO	2,791	5,264	5,074	77	114
AL	625	5,416	5,393	16	7	MT	2,109	970	717	80	174
AK	1,579	730	563	62	105	NE	1,328	1,525	1,415	52	58
AZ	1,605	6,262	6,014	134	113	NV	569	2,611	2,546	42	23
AR	1,113	2,649	2,618	10	21	NH	2,412	1,265	850	96	320
CA	7,209	41,168	39,338	385	1,444	NJ	3,868	9,493	8,718	355	421
CO	1,998	5,511	5,183	68	260	NM	1,262	1,821	1,697	51	73
CT	2,700	2,851	2,681	111	58	NY	9,490	21,040	17,872	323	2,845
DE	499	976	894	27	55	NC	6,477	7,595	7,140	134	322
DC	6	607	607	(Z)	(NA)	ND	515	580	562	4	14
FL.......	5,852	19,303	18,780	253	271	OH	5,139	11,008	10,346	218	444
GA	2,482	8,339	8,196	65	78	OK	1,574	3,518	3,460	29	29
HI	130	1,333	1,318	11	4	OR	2,627	3,369	3,080	73	216
ID	1,983	1,220	1,060	52	109	PA	9,462	12,011	10,705	523	783
IL.......	5,764	12,496	12,003	128	364	RI	479	1,074	992	28	55
IN	4,297	5,272	4,692	198	382	SC	1,508	3,812	3,731	41	40
IA	1,967	2,782	2,649	48	85	SD	657	715	682	8	25
KS	1,037	2,596	2,571	21	4	TN	896	5,896	5,812	26	58
KY	487	4,923	4,904	13	7	TX	6,761	25,297	24,536	512	248
LA	1,467	5,003	4,885	56	62	UT	964	2,710	2,608	29	73
ME	1,950	919	660	69	189	VT	1,366	594	450	43	101
MD	3,528	5,594	5,127	159	308	VA	2,930	6,968	6,489	300	179
MA	1,735	9,576	9,314	74	188	WA	4,170	6,491	5,944	139	408
MI.......	11,595	8,983	7,613	328	1,042	WV	1,102	1,567	1,493	41	33
MN	7,313	4,790	4,171	84	536	WI.......	11,512	4,860	3,940	206	713
MS	1,287	3,084	2,998	75	11	WY	767	533	438	22	73

NA Not available.   Z Less than 500.   [1] A public water system that supplies water to the same population year-round.
[2] A public water system that regularly supplies water to at least 25 of the same people at least 6 months per year, but not year-round. Some examples are schools, factories, and office buildings which have their own water systems.   [3] A public water system that provides water in a place such as a gas station or campground where people do not remain for long periods of time and is open at least 60 day per year.   [4] U.S. total does not equal sum of states due to incomplete reporting of a small number of systems.

Source: U.S. Environmental Protection Agency, *Factoids: Drinking Water and Ground Water Statistics for 2008*, annual reports (published November 2008). See also <http://www.epa.gov/safewater/data/getdata.html>.

586   Energy and Utilities

Section 20
Construction and Housing

This section presents data on the construction industry and on various indicators of its activity and costs; on housing units and their characteristics and occupants; and on the characteristics and vacancy rates for commercial buildings. This edition contains data from the 2005 American Housing Survey.

The principal source of these data is the U.S. Census Bureau, which issues a variety of current publications, as well as data from the decennial census. Current construction statistics compiled by the Census Bureau appear in its *New Residential Construction* and *New Residential Sales* press releases and Web site <http://www.census.gov/const/www/>. Statistics on expenditures by owners of residential properties are issued quarterly and annually in *Expenditures for Residential Improvements and Repairs. Value of New Construction Put In Place* presents data on all types of construction. Reports of the censuses of construction industries (see below) are also issued on various topics.

Other Census Bureau publications include the *Current Housing Reports* series, which comprise the quarterly *Housing Vacancies,* the quarterly *Market Absorption of Apartments,* the biennial *American Housing Survey* (formerly *Annual Housing Survey),* and reports of the censuses of housing and of construction industries.

Other sources include the monthly *Dodge Construction Potentials* of McGraw-Hill Construction, New York, NY, which present national and state data on construction contracts; the National Association of Home Builders with state-level data on housing starts; the NATIONAL ASSOCIATION OF REALTORS®, which presents data on existing home sales; the Bureau of Economic Analysis, which presents data on residential capital and gross housing product; and the U.S. Energy Information Administration, which provides data on commercial buildings through its periodic sample surveys.

Censuses and surveys—Censuses of the construction industry were first conducted by the Census Bureau for 1929, 1935, and 1939; beginning in 1967, a census has been taken every 5 years (through 2002, for years ending in "2" and "7"). The latest reports are part of the 2002 Economic Census. See text, Section 15, Business Enterprise.

The construction sector of the economic census, covers all employer establishments primarily engaged in (1) building construction by general contractors or operative builders; (2) heavy (nonbuilding) construction by general contractors; and (3) construction by special trade contractors. This sector includes construction management and land subdividers and developers. The 2002 census was conducted in accordance with the 2002 North American Industrial Classification System (NAICS). See text, Section 15, Business Enterprise.

From 1850 through 1930, the Census Bureau collected some housing data as part of its censuses of population and agriculture. Beginning in 1940, separate censuses of housing have been taken at 10-year intervals. For the 1970 and 1980 censuses, data on year-round housing units were collected and issued on occupancy and structural characteristics, plumbing facilities, value, and rent; for 1990 such characteristics were presented for all housing units.

The American Housing Survey (*Current Housing Reports* Series H-150 and H-170), which began in 1973, provided an annual and ongoing series of data on selected housing and demographic characteristics until 1983. In 1984, the name of the survey was changed from the Annual Housing Survey. Currently, national data are collected every other year, and data for

U.S. Census Bureau, Statistical Abstract of the United States: 2010

selected metropolitan areas are collected on a rotating basis. All samples represent a cross section of the housing stock in their respective areas. Estimates are subject to both sampling and nonsampling errors; caution should therefore be used in making comparisons between years.

Data on residential mortgages were collected continuously from 1890 to 1970, except 1930, as part of the decennial census by the Census Bureau. Since 1973, mortgage status data, limited to single family homes on less than 10 acres with no business on the property, have been presented in the American Housing Survey. Data on mortgage activity are covered in Section 25, Banking and Finance.

Housing units—In general, a housing unit is a house, an apartment, a group of rooms or a single room occupied or intended for occupancy as separate living quarters; that is, the occupants live separately from any other individual in the building, and there is direct access from the outside or through a common hall. Transient accommodations, barracks for workers, and institutional-type quarters are not counted as housing units.

Statistical reliability—For a discussion of statistical collection and estimation, sampling procedures, and measures of statistical reliability applicable to Census Bureau data, see Appendix III.

Table 926. **Construction—Establishments, Employees, and Payroll by Kind of Business (NAICS Basis): 2005 and 2006**

[6,781 represents 6,781,000. Covers establishments with payroll. Excludes most government employees, railroad employees, and self-employed persons. Kind-of-business classification based on North American Industry Classification System (NAICS) 2002. For statement on methodology, see Appendix III]

Industry	2002 NAICS code [1]	Establishments		Paid employees [2] (1,000)		Annual payroll (mil. dol.)	
		2005	2006	2005	2006	2005	2006
Construction	23	787,672	802,349	6,781	7,339	292,519	322,004
Construction of buildings	236	243,567	243,614	1,613	1,708	76,180	82,560
Residential building construction	2361	200,826	198,912	919	966	40,451	42,481
New single-family housing construction (except operative builders).	236115	111,872	62,108	464	305	18,173	12,546
Nonresidential building construction	2362	42,741	44,702	694	742	35,728	40,079
Heavy and civil engineering construction	237	50,827	51,122	908	989	47,153	52,681
Utility system construction	2371	20,945	21,232	446	497	21,558	25,067
Land subdivision.	2372	12,448	12,469	69	77	3,792	4,098
Highway, street, and bridge construction	2373	11,940	11,860	311	325	17,517	18,542
Other heavy and civil engineering construction. . .	2379	5,494	5,561	82	90	4,286	4,974
Specialty trade contractors.	238	493,278	507,613	4,260	4,641	169,187	186,763
Foundation, structure, and building exterior contractors	2381	115,719	117,456	1,065	1,168	38,122	41,956
Poured concrete foundation and structures contractors	23811	26,646	26,951	283	319	10,850	12,232
Structural steel and precast concrete contractors	23812	3,524	3,608	65	72	2,815	3,237
Framing contractors.	23813	18,732	18,632	169	185	5,305	5,276
Masonry contractors.	23814	26,997	27,430	229	249	7,792	8,483
Glass and glazing contractors	23815	5,328	5,469	48	53	1,905	2,211
Roofing contractors	23816	19,344	19,660	185	195	6,488	7,127
Siding contractors	23817	10,425	10,543	49	52	1,596	1,679
Other foundation, structure, and building exterior contractors	23819	4,723	5,163	37	43	1,370	1,711
Building equipment contractors	2382	177,316	182,368	1,806	1,940	78,955	86,667
Electrical contractors	23821	75,325	77,558	760	815	33,126	36,296
Plumbing, heating, and air-conditioning contractors	23822	95,478	98,147	936	1,001	40,073	43,763
Other building equipment contractors	23829	6,513	6,663	110	124	5,756	6,608
Building finishing contractors.	2383	129,107	133,343	894	975	31,247	34,454
Drywall and insulation contractors.	23831	21,368	22,237	304	331	11,040	12,300
Painting and wall covering contractors.	23832	41,172	41,477	225	243	7,144	7,791
Flooring contractors.	23833	16,354	16,630	85	87	3,136	3,294
Tile and terrazzo contractors.	23834	10,971	11,572	66	72	2,275	2,503
Finish carpentry contractors.	23835	32,921	34,738	156	174	5,403	6,009
Other building finishing contractors	23839	6,321	6,689	59	68	2,249	2,556
Other specialty trade contractors	2389	71,136	74,446	495	558	20,863	23,685
Site preparation contractors.	23891	37,749	39,265	289	322	12,590	14,208
All other specialty trade contractors.	23899	33,387	35,181	206	235	8,273	9,477

[1] North American Industry Classification System code, 2002; see text, Section 15. [2] Employees on the payroll for the pay period including March 12.

Source: U.S. Census Bureau, "County Business Patterns"; annual. See <http://www.census.gov/epcd/cbp/view/cbpview.html>.

Table 927. **Construction Materials—Producer Price Indexes: 1990 to 2008**

[1982 = 100, except as noted. Data for 2008 are preliminary. For discussion of producer price indexes, see text, Section 14. This index, more formally known as the special commodity grouping index for construction materials, covers materials incorporated as integral part of a building or normally installed during construction and not readily removable. Excludes consumer durables such as kitchen ranges, refrigerators, etc. This index is not the same as the stage-of-processing index of intermediate materials and components for construction]

Commodity	1990	2000	2002	2003	2004	2005	2006	2007	2008
Construction materials	119.6	144.1	144.0	147.1	161.5	169.6	180.2	183.2	196.5
Interior solvent-based paint	133.0	191.1	190.5	198.0	(NA)	(NA)	(NA)	(NA)	(NA)
Architectural coatings	132.7	168.7	175.2	180.6	187.4	203.3	220.2	230.5	248.1
Construction products from plastics	117.2	135.8	136.1	138.6	144.6	158.8	181.8	179.2	185.4
Douglas fir, dressed	138.4	185.2	178.5	176.7	(NA)	(NA)	(NA)	(NA)	(NA)
Southern pine, dressed	111.2	161.0	145.2	145.4	(NA)	(NA)	(NA)	(NA)	(NA)
Softwood lumber	123.8	178.6	170.8	170.8	209.8	203.6	189.4	170.5	156.0
Millwork	130.4	176.4	179.8	181.8	191.9	197.2	201.8	201.4	204.8
Softwood plywood	119.6	173.3	164.1	195.9	250.9	223.5	190.5	197.8	192.5
Hardwood plywood and related products	102.7	130.2	131.5	129.0	134.4	138.1	(NA)	(NA)	(NA)
Hardwood veneer and plywood [1]	(NA)	(NA)	(NA)	(NA)	(NA)	(NA)	101.4	102.4	103.8
Softwood plywood veneer, excluding reinforced/backed	142.3	182.2	172.8	184.1	209.5	206.2	(NA)	(NA)	(NA)
Building paper and building board mill products	112.2	138.8	129.3	159.9	192.4	184.9	173.0	155.2	164.1
Steel pipe and tubes [2]	102.6	106.6	106.7	113.3	166.3	193.3	200.9	202.4	251.8
Builders' hardware	133.0	163.8	169.3	170.3	172.9	179.2	187.8	198.1	215.2
Plumbing fixtures and brass fittings	144.3	180.4	181.9	183.4	188.3	197.6	207.2	220.6	226.8
Heating equipment	131.6	155.6	157.9	163.2	169.5	179.9	185.7	195.5	208.6
Metal doors, sash, and trim	131.4	165.1	168.0	169.9	175.8	184.9	192.9	197.3	205.2
Siding, aluminum [3]	(NA)	142.2	141.0	152.6	(NA)	(NA)	(NA)	(NA)	(NA)
Sheet metal products . . . . [4]	129.2	144.0	145.2	146.6	162.6	169.4	176.1	181.2	192.7
Outdoor lighting equipment, including parts [4]	113.0	124.7	126.2	126.9	129.4	131.8	137.7	140.1	145.4
Commercial fluorescent fixtures [5]	113.0	117.7	114.0	115.2	113.6	(NA)	(NA)	(NA)	(NA)
Commercial and industrial lighting fixtures	127.5	140.3	139.5	141.9	142.3	147.0	151.9	158.3	165.0
Architectural and ornamental metalwork [6]	118.7	139.8	144.2	147.2	172.5	185.4	191.5	200.1	227.2
Fabricated ferrous wire products [2]	114.6	130.0	129.7	131.3	149.3	157.1	162.6	166.7	201.6
Elevators, escalators, and other lifts	110.1	118.7	120.0	118.7	120.5	123.5	126.0	129.3	134.9
Stamped metal switch and receptacle box	158.0	183.0	195.4	196.1	205.2	(NA)	(NA)	(NA)	(NA)
Electrical conduit and conduit fittings [7]	(NA)	(NA)	(NA)	(NA)	(NA)	106.6	116.6	112.1	123.7
Other noncurrent-carrying wiring devices [7]	(NA)	(NA)	(NA)	(NA)	(NA)	102.3	108.0	114.3	123.4
Concrete ingredients and related products	115.3	155.6	162.6	164.8	170.4	185.3	204.9	220.2	229.7
Concrete products	113.5	147.8	152.7	153.6	161.2	177.2	195.1	203.5	210.7
Clay construction products excluding refractories . . .	129.9	152.8	152.8	154.2	156.6	165.4	176.8	178.7	180.1
Prep asphalt and tar roofing and siding products . . .	95.8	100.0	106.6	110.6	111.3	125.0	137.0	139.7	175.7
Gypsum products	105.2	201.4	168.9	171.5	198.8	229.6	274.9	233.0	213.0
Insulation materials	108.4	128.6	128.3	128.8	137.2	142.2	149.9	145.3	141.8
Paving mixtures and blocks	101.2	130.4	136.2	142.6	144.9	156.9	200.5	218.9	273.3

NA Not available. [1] December 2005 = 100. [2] June 1982 = 100. [3] December 1982 = 100. [4] June 1985 = 100. [5] Recessed nonair. [6] December 1983 = 100. [7] December 2004 = 100

Source: U.S. Bureau of Labor Statistics, *Producer Price Indexes,* monthly and annual. See also <http://www.bls.gov/ppi/home.htm>.

Table 928. **Value of New Construction Put in Place: 1980 to 2008**

[In millions of dollars (273,936 represents $273,936,000,000). Represents value of construction put in place during year; differs from building permit and construction contract data in timing and coverage. Includes installed cost of normal building service equipment and selected types of industrial production equipment (largely site fabricated). Excludes cost of shipbuilding, land, and most types of machinery and equipment. For methodology, see Appendix III. For details, see Tables 929 and 930]

Year		Private			Public		
	Total	Total	Residential buildings	Non-residential	Total	Federal	State and local
1980	273,936	210,290	100,381	109,909	63,646	9,642	54,004
1990	476,778	369,300	191,103	178,197	107,478	12,099	95,379
1991	432,592	322,483	166,251	156,232	110,109	12,845	97,264
1992	463,661	347,814	199,393	148,421	115,847	14,376	101,471
1993	502,435	375,073	225,067	150,006	127,362	14,424	112,938
1994	549,420	418,999	258,561	160,438	130,421	14,440	115,981
1995	567,896	427,885	247,351	180,534	140,011	15,751	124,260
1996	623,313	476,638	281,115	195,523	146,675	15,325	131,350
1997	656,171	502,734	289,014	213,720	153,437	14,087	139,350
1998	706,779	552,001	314,607	237,394	154,778	14,318	140,460
1999	768,811	599,729	350,562	249,167	169,082	14,025	155,057
2000	831,075	649,750	374,457	275,293	181,325	14,166	167,157
2001	864,159	662,247	388,324	273,922	201,912	15,081	186,830
2002	847,873	634,435	396,696	237,739	213,438	16,578	196,860
2003	891,497	675,370	446,035	229,335	216,127	17,913	198,214
2004	991,561	771,378	532,900	238,478	220,183	18,342	201,841
2005	1,102,703	868,543	611,989	256,644	234,160	17,300	216,860
2006	1,167,554	912,169	613,731	298,438	255,385	17,555	237,831
2007	1,137,152	850,009	492,499	357,510	287,143	20,328	266,815
2008	1,074,093	766,603	355,883	410,720	307,490	24,013	283,477

Source: U.S. Census Bureau, "Construction Spending"; <http://www.census.gov/const/www/c30index.html>.

Construction and Housing **589**

Table 929. **Value of Private Construction Put in Place: 2000 to 2008**

[In millions of dollars (649,750 represents $649,750,000,000). Represents value of construction put in place during year; differs from building permit and construction contract data in timing and coverage. See Appendix III and Tables 928 and 930]

Type of construction	2000	2001	2002	2003	2004	2005	2006	2007	2008
Total construction [1]	649,750	662,247	634,435	675,370	771,378	868,543	912,169	850,009	766,603
Residential	374,457	388,324	396,696	446,035	532,900	611,899	613,731	492,499	355,883
New single family	236,788	249,086	265,889	310,575	377,557	433,510	415,997	305,184	186,111
New multifamily	28,259	30,305	32,952	35,116	39,944	47,297	52,803	48,209	44,105
Improvements	109,410	108,933	97,855	100,344	115,399	131,092	144,931	139,106	125,668
Nonresidential [1]	275,293	273,922	237,739	229,335	238,478	256,644	298,438	357,510	410,720
Lodging	16,304	14,519	10,467	9,930	11,982	12,666	17,624	27,503	36,237
Office [1]	52,407	49,745	35,296	30,579	32,879	37,276	45,680	53,377	57,455
General	49,637	47,136	32,356	27,380	28,679	32,962	41,085	48,397	52,036
Financial	2,689	2,586	2,857	3,174	4,186	4,285	4,542	4,887	5,062
Commercial [1]	64,055	63,606	59,008	57,505	63,195	66,584	73,368	84,999	81,891
Automotive [1]	5,967	5,650	5,807	5,039	5,235	5,614	5,528	6,373	5,502
Sales	1,629	2,014	2,235	2,099	2,443	2,834	2,285	2,587	2,397
Service/parts	3,009	2,394	2,308	1,866	1,978	1,805	2,184	2,407	1,754
Parking	1,330	1,242	1,265	1,074	814	975	1,059	1,379	1,351
Food/beverage [1]	8,786	8,765	7,914	8,369	8,232	7,795	7,442	7,929	8,318
Food	4,792	4,300	4,207	4,234	3,590	3,128	2,752	2,771	3,363
Dining/drinking	2,935	3,441	2,916	3,321	3,937	4,078	3,780	3,816	4,038
Fast food	1,058	1,024	792	813	705	590	910	1,342	918
Multiretail [1]	14,911	16,373	15,581	15,400	18,828	22,750	29,218	34,249	32,293
General merchandise	5,100	5,066	6,009	5,341	6,416	6,740	5,699	6,827	4,792
Shopping center	6,803	7,769	6,605	6,867	9,256	12,462	18,417	22,213	22,531
Shopping mall	2,523	2,701	2,108	2,231	2,138	2,631	3,616	4,253	4,163
Other commercial [1]	13,537	11,945	12,083	11,249	13,341	11,744	10,874	12,799	12,054
Drug store	1,682	1,185	1,644	1,790	1,427	1,315	1,238	1,516	1,864
Building supply store	2,592	3,016	2,471	2,268	2,521	2,416	2,594	3,567	2,789
Other stores	8,136	6,995	7,145	6,214	8,229	7,075	6,135	6,938	6,294
Warehouse	14,822	15,691	11,908	12,345	12,074	12,827	14,491	16,368	16,395
General commercial	13,511	14,440	10,934	11,004	10,830	11,468	13,493	15,098	15,154
Farm	5,988	5,135	5,611	5,103	5,485	5,854	5,817	7,281	7,330
Health care	19,455	19,506	22,438	24,217	26,272	28,495	32,016	34,776	37,883
Hospital	10,183	11,313	13,925	15,234	16,147	18,250	21,914	24,285	26,078
Medical building	5,066	4,638	4,924	6,068	7,615	8,031	7,165	7,582	8,203
Special care	4,206	3,555	3,538	2,915	2,510	2,213	2,937	2,909	3,603
Educational [1]	11,683	12,846	13,109	13,424	12,701	12,788	13,839	17,071	18,806
Preschool	770	874	593	711	674	516	487	726	729
Primary/secondary	2,948	3,536	3,605	3,204	3,202	2,718	3,240	4,036	3,832
Higher education [1]	6,333	6,597	6,875	7,259	6,496	6,946	7,611	9,668	11,757
Instructional	3,058	3,210	3,619	3,701	3,200	3,556	3,501	4,307	5,598
Dormitory	1,356	1,555	1,528	1,761	1,669	1,537	2,065	2,954	3,797
Sports/recreation	645	755	772	677	739	821	858	848	844
Other educational	1,318	1,421	1,651	1,785	1,998	2,294	2,090	2,212	2,075
Gallery/museum	920	990	1,312	1,371	1,335	1,745	1,697	1,975	1,793
Religious	8,030	8,393	8,335	8,559	8,153	7,715	7,740	7,429	7,074
House of worship	5,656	6,040	6,021	6,238	6,015	5,992	6,262	6,212	5,822
Other religious	2,347	2,330	2,312	2,322	2,138	1,723	1,478	1,217	1,253
Auxiliary building	1,280	1,247	1,358	1,296	1,258	1,251	1,219	1,068	1,070
Public safety	423	274	217	185	289	408	419	495	681
Amusement and recreation [1]	8,768	7,828	7,478	7,781	8,432	7,507	9,326	10,352	10,948
Theme/amusement park	747	462	230	270	198	200	417	540	268
Sports	1,068	1,067	1,427	1,306	900	807	959	2,024	2,529
Fitness	1,152	1,294	1,286	1,262	1,141	1,425	2,028	1,954	2,183
Performance/meeting center	732	977	900	844	1,054	1,072	737	853	1,158
Social center	2,368	2,337	2,285	1,996	2,594	1,626	1,538	1,640	1,624
Movie theater/studio	1,461	792	568	855	1,218	1,248	1,309	1,197	623
Transportation [1]	6,879	7,058	6,773	6,568	6,841	7,124	8,654	9,444	10,128
Air	1,804	1,993	1,281	1,012	869	748	719	584	692
Land	4,907	4,883	5,325	5,462	5,800	6,214	7,764	8,543	9,175
Railroad	4,263	4,456	4,584	4,851	5,392	5,816	7,313	7,969	8,596
Communication	18,799	19,596	18,384	14,456	15,468	18,846	22,187	26,947	24,726
Power [1]	29,344	31,499	32,608	33,619	27,360	26,304	31,164	41,481	60,115
Electricity	23,374	25,270	24,998	25,592	20,431	19,192	22,804	29,523	44,804
Gas	4,891	5,078	6,080	6,358	5,096	5,239	5,528	7,369	8,664
Oil	1,003	943	1,193	1,068	1,579	1,293	1,831	3,651	4,323
Sewage and waste disposal	508	402	246	278	331	240	305	383	602
Water supply	714	563	397	393	405	326	477	460	712
Manufacturing [1]	37,583	37,815	22,744	21,434	23,667	29,886	35,086	42,229	63,189
Food/beverage/tobacco	3,985	4,088	2,817	2,695	3,157	4,677	4,707	4,254	4,948
Textile/apparel/leather & allied	413	307	284	218	188	415	144	42	290
Wood	483	343	477	376	485	982	1,465	856	409
Paper	479	1,265	584	818	548	467	559	493	497
Print/publishing	848	1,232	666	630	654	777	727	279	332
Petroleum/coal	1,255	1,171	887	717	1,204	771	1,799	2,541	17,420
Chemical	3,798	4,896	5,625	5,368	5,507	6,588	9,235	14,521	15,216
Plastic/rubber	1,645	1,379	776	659	936	877	884	1,034	1,225
Nonmetallic mineral	1,898	2,216	536	865	896	1,163	2,603	4,243	4,117
Primary metal	1,976	773	241	436	312	836	1,441	1,442	3,169
Fabricated metal	2,148	1,447	833	662	595	699	562	966	1,780
Machinery	864	863	797	707	645	917	935	568	985
Computer/electronic/electrical	6,392	6,029	1,918	1,444	2,835	4,247	4,347	2,992	2,730
Transportation equipment	6,318	6,901	3,832	3,314	2,610	3,702	2,631	3,881	5,752
Furniture	148	232	148	278	217	96	122	194	47

[1] Includes other types of construction not shown separately.

Source: U.S. Census Bureau, "Construction Spending"; <http://www.census.gov/const/www/c30index.html>.

Table 930. **Value of State and Local Government Construction Put in Place: 2000 to 2008**

[In millions of dollars (167,157 represents $167,157,000,000). See Tables 928 and 929]

Type of construction	2000	2001	2002	2003	2004	2005	2006	2007	2008
Total construction [1]	167,157	186,830	196,860	198,214	201,841	216,860	237,831	266,815	283,477
Residential	2,962	3,493	3,754	3,724	4,110	4,047	4,349	5,092	4,908
Multifamily	2,945	3,440	3,671	3,593	3,956	3,740	3,990	4,500	4,090
Nonresidential	164,196	183,337	193,106	194,490	197,731	212,813	233,482	261,723	278,569
Office	4,494	5,557	6,274	6,116	6,024	5,211	5,588	7,112	9,548
Commercial [1]	1,820	2,462	2,422	2,207	1,979	1,882	1,567	1,744	1,742
Automotive	1,233	1,927	1,714	1,599	1,501	1,490	1,152	978	1,179
Parking	1,143	1,913	1,693	1,562	1,356	1,357	1,011	910	980
Warehouse	330	301	293	318	276	218	230	555	319
Health care	2,829	2,942	3,490	4,005	5,025	5,059	5,615	6,975	7,157
Hospital	1,949	2,124	2,539	2,685	3,324	3,429	4,085	5,250	5,449
Medical building	490	487	509	876	1,211	1,168	919	951	909
Special care	390	331	442	444	490	463	611	774	800
Educational [1]	46,818	52,813	59,463	59,340	59,741	65,750	69,790	77,604	83,608
Primary/secondary [1]	33,764	36,670	41,972	40,316	40,990	44,184	47,846	54,561	57,335
Elementary	12,274	14,105	15,154	13,430	14,308	14,251	13,870	16,828	18,563
Middle/junior high	5,820	6,923	8,410	7,921	8,132	9,069	10,764	11,432	10,762
High	13,326	14,072	17,142	18,561	17,950	19,892	22,631	25,625	27,473
Higher education [1]	10,749	13,365	14,280	15,451	15,864	18,033	18,961	20,278	23,033
Instructional	6,317	7,874	7,982	9,042	8,699	9,275	9,434	11,117	13,083
Parking	514	561	432	508	765	1,013	909	823	701
Administration	294	199	456	236	303	387	657	499	292
Dormitory	1,078	1,429	1,620	2,074	2,673	2,918	3,409	2,609	2,852
Library	308	374	440	544	524	588	493	699	831
Student union/cafeteria	322	618	1,031	702	632	880	1,028	1,543	1,375
Sports/recreation	966	1,287	1,546	1,329	1,370	1,769	1,748	1,712	2,477
Infrastructure	835	835	545	613	867	1,138	1,227	1,209	1,228
Other educational	1,645	2,164	2,629	2,687	2,357	2,735	2,312	1,857	2,542
Library/archive	976	1,675	2,118	1,815	1,501	2,098	1,857	1,292	1,591
Public safety [1]	5,854	6,056	5,960	5,844	5,477	6,013	6,608	8,429	9,501
Correctional	4,754	4,894	4,554	4,204	3,771	3,958	4,611	5,392	6,257
Detention	3,907	3,838	3,418	3,148	2,787	2,936	3,305	4,053	4,416
Police/sheriff	848	1,057	1,135	1,056	985	1,022	1,307	1,339	1,841
Other public safety	1,100	1,161	1,406	1,640	1,705	2,055	1,997	3,037	3,244
Fire/rescue	994	991	1,227	1,359	1,441	1,675	1,615	2,399	2,350
Amusement and recreation [1]	7,583	9,143	9,215	8,354	7,794	7,340	9,444	11,015	11,494
Sports	2,289	2,709	2,569	2,065	1,746	1,587	1,853	2,125	2,727
Performance/meeting center	2,075	2,915	2,915	2,260	2,061	1,921	2,292	1,774	1,774
Convention center	1,397	2,268	2,130	1,545	1,350	1,350	1,422	1,088	1,129
Social center	1,152	1,432	1,446	1,606	1,476	1,006	1,285	1,383	1,616
Neighborhood center	886	1,065	934	1,221	1,312	866	1,098	1,058	1,237
Park/camp	1,930	1,846	1,928	1,999	2,303	2,728	3,887	5,425	5,232
Transportation	13,000	15,868	17,312	16,483	16,440	16,256	17,695	21,197	22,558
Air [1]	6,700	7,849	8,123	8,146	8,715	8,993	9,676	11,507	11,559
Passenger terminal	2,930	2,770	3,040	3,778	3,972	3,310	3,766	5,289	6,154
Runway	3,196	4,354	4,305	3,793	4,049	4,861	4,898	5,228	4,513
Land [1]	5,165	6,253	7,291	7,207	6,415	5,936	6,629	7,516	9,203
Passenger terminal	1,253	1,557	1,860	2,099	1,368	907	969	1,230	1,633
Mass transit	1,484	2,492	3,375	3,160	3,067	3,208	3,228	3,577	4,246
Railroad	1,471	1,095	674	449	349	552	320	518	592
Water [1]	1,136	1,766	1,899	1,130	1,309	1,327	1,391	2,173	1,795
Dock/marina	863	1,258	1,203	894	1,028	930	971	1,459	1,394
Dry dock/marine terminal	236	483	695	235	281	397	420	715	402
Power	5,501	5,267	3,771	6,785	7,044	8,320	7,766	11,411	10,757
Electrical	5,257	4,963	3,244	6,041	5,851	7,091	7,195	10,082	9,800
Distribution	2,087	1,397	1,158	2,144	1,856	1,786	2,187	2,576	3,424
Highway and street [1]	51,574	56,428	56,660	56,251	57,351	63,157	71,032	74,779	79,473
Pavement	37,929	41,125	40,962	39,294	40,274	45,177	45,933	47,185	51,789
Lighting	856	1,228	888	1,156	1,146	1,232	1,057	1,710	1,544
Retaining wall	1,099	624	742	565	552	675	1,546	1,075	952
Tunnel	894	1,069	657	619	521	373	224	231	256
Bridge	9,302	10,910	11,741	12,980	13,150	14,244	20,057	22,649	23,715
Toll/weigh	325	104	217	180	233	320	657	417	206
Maintenance building	293	407	297	244	170	96	213	102	89
Rest facility/streetscape	878	961	1,155	1,213	1,306	1,042	1,347	1,411	922
Sewage and waste disposal [1]	14,000	14,157	15,334	15,625	17,084	18,336	21,524	23,123	24,230
Sewage/dry waste [1]	9,338	9,038	9,956	9,812	10,836	11,717	13,401	13,946	14,013
Plant	2,765	2,404	2,680	2,735	3,095	3,369	3,410	3,842	3,851
Line/pump station	6,326	6,375	7,082	6,934	7,574	8,243	9,820	9,796	9,901
Waste water	4,663	5,120	5,378	5,813	6,248	6,620	8,124	9,177	10,217
Plant	3,229	3,818	4,227	4,403	4,658	5,231	6,039	7,218	8,837
Line/drain	1,434	1,302	1,151	1,410	1,591	1,389	2,085	1,959	1,380
Water supply [1]	9,528	11,447	11,674	11,711	11,977	13,483	14,299	14,880	15,718
Plant	3,067	4,070	3,824	4,309	4,418	4,943	5,005	5,554	6,446
Well	378	394	555	365	318	360	623	655	458
Line	4,644	5,300	5,195	4,944	5,307	6,234	5,922	6,091	5,942
Pump station	625	684	852	767	705	776	1,285	1,135	1,282
Reservoir	266	410	463	450	503	502	700	581	644
Tank/tower	548	588	785	876	727	668	764	865	947
Conservation and development [1] . .	933	1,077	1,012	1,020	1,466	1,752	2,000	2,179	2,223
Dam/levee	303	242	279	231	297	405	591	634	765
Breakwater/jetty	270	490	397	514	654	726	809	624	634

[1] Includes other types of construction, not shown separately.

Source: U.S. Census Bureau, Construction Spending; <http://www.census.gov/const/www/c30index.html>.

Construction and Housing   591

Table 931. **Construction Contracts—Value of Construction and Floor Space of Buildings by Class of Construction: 1990 to 2008**

[246.0 reresents $246,000,000,000. Building construction includes new structures and additions; nonbuilding construction includes major alterations to existing structures which affect only valuation, since no additional floor area is created by "alteration"]

Year	Total	Resi-dential build-ings	Nonresidential buildings									Non-build-ing con-struc-tion
			Total	Com-mer-cial[1]	Manu-fac-turing	Educa-tional[2]	Health	Public build-ings	Reli-gious	Social and recrea-tional	Mis-cella-neous	
VALUE (bil. dol.)												
1990	246.0	100.9	95.4	44.8	8.4	16.6	9.2	5.7	2.2	5.3	3.1	49.7
1995	306.5	127.9	114.2	46.6	13.8	22.9	10.8	6.3	2.8	7.1	3.8	64.4
1998	405.6	179.8	154.5	74.0	12.1	30.1	12.9	6.6	4.3	10.8	3.6	71.3
1999	447.2	195.0	168.7	77.2	11.3	37.1	13.6	8.2	4.5	11.6	5.1	83.5
2000	472.9	208.3	173.3	80.9	8.9	40.9	12.4	7.5	4.6	13.8	4.4	91.3
2001	496.5	219.7	169.1	70.2	8.0	47.0	14.4	7.8	4.8	12.0	4.8	107.7
2002	504.0	248.7	155.1	59.6	5.5	45.3	16.1	7.3	5.1	11.5	4.7	100.2
2003	531.7	283.4	156.1	58.8	6.9	47.7	15.8	7.1	4.5	11.0	4.3	92.3
2004	593.2	333.1	164.4	67.3	8.0	44.0	17.6	7.2	4.5	11.6	4.4	95.6
2005	670.3	384.0	182.4	72.2	10.1	49.1	22.3	7.9	4.1	11.7	5.0	103.8
2006	689.4	342.1	217.2	92.9	13.5	53.9	24.3	8.3	4.1	14.3	5.9	130.0
2007	639.7	263.1	238.5	100.8	20.2	58.0	24.2	12.3	3.8	13.7	5.5	138.2
2008	554.7	162.2	243.6	84.3	30.3	63.2	30.6	13.1	3.5	13.3	5.2	148.9
FLOOR SPACE (mil. sq. ft.)												
1990	3,020	1,817	1,203	694	128	152	69	47	29	51	32	(X)
1995	3,454	2,172	1,281	700	163	186	70	40	33	56	33	(X)
1998	4,812	3,015	1,797	1,107	166	219	96	42	47	85	34	(X)
1999	5,091	3,253	1,838	1,115	141	261	98	49	48	87	39	(X)
2000	4,982	3,113	1,869	1,180	111	273	88	44	49	94	29	(X)
2001	4,828	3,159	1,669	988	93	295	92	44	50	81	27	(X)
2002	4,792	3,356	1,436	810	68	277	97	37	52	71	26	(X)
2003	5,093	3,689	1,404	794	75	270	92	35	45	67	26	(X)
2004	5,518	4,061	1,457	875	86	231	94	34	43	68	27	(X)
2005	5,873	4,346	1,527	927	79	246	108	33	37	67	29	(X)
2006	5,284	3,648	1,637	1,017	83	254	110	34	34	73	33	(X)
2007	4,325	2,656	1,669	1,055	91	247	103	50	31	66	27	(X)
2008	2,962	1,583	1,379	777	76	252	111	48	27	59	27	(X)

X Not applicable.   [1] Includes nonindustrial warehouses.   [2] Includes science.

Source: McGraw-Hill Construction, a Division of the McGraw-Hill Companies, New York, NY (copyright).

Table 932. **Construction Contracts—Value by Region: 2004 to 2008**

[In millions of dollars (593,208 represents $593,208,000,000). Represents value of construction in regions in which work was actually done. See headnote, Table 931]

Region	2004	2005	2006	2007	2008		
					Total[1]	Residen-tial	Nonresi-dential
U.S.	593,208	670,257	689,369	639,742	554,718	162,222	243,564
New England	22,418	25,236	23,272	24,640	20,997	5,696	9,964
Middle Atlantic	50,208	58,873	67,003	64,879	67,055	16,672	31,982
East North Central	80,386	83,673	82,169	72,433	74,657	15,202	35,529
West North Central	38,450	40,849	40,839	43,305	32,773	8,759	12,704
South Atlantic	147,639	172,149	165,374	150,216	113,465	41,221	48,094
East South Central	31,969	35,016	39,822	36,849	37,408	10,435	16,521
West South Central	65,219	75,479	92,103	85,247	85,531	26,943	39,505
Mountain	63,244	74,159	76,382	68,594	50,656	15,875	18,216
Pacific	93,674	104,824	102,406	93,578	72,176	21,419	31,049

[1] Includes nonbuilding construction, not shown separately.

Source: McGraw-Hill Construction, a Division of the McGraw-Hill Companies, New York, NY, (copyright).

592   Construction and Housing

Table 933. **New Privately Owned Housing Units Authorized by State: 2007 and 2008**

[**1,398.4 represents 1,398,400.** Based on about 20,000 places in United States having building permit systems in 2007 and 20,000 in 2008]

State	Housing units (1,000) 2007	Housing units (1,000) 2008 Total	Housing units (1,000) 2008 1 unit	Valuation (mil. dol.) 2007	Valuation (mil. dol.) 2008 Total	Valuation (mil. dol.) 2008 1 unit	State	Housing units (1,000) 2007	Housing units (1,000) 2008 Total	Housing units (1,000) 2008 1 unit	Valuation (mil. dol.) 2007	Valuation (mil. dol.) 2008 Total	Valuation (mil. dol.) 2008 1 unit
U.S..	1,398.4	905.4	575.6	225,237	141,633	110,687	MO ...	21.5	13.3	7.8	3,128	1,890	1,455
							MT ...	4.2	2.4	1.9	624	359	312
AL ...	25.8	17.5	12.0	3,200	2,144	1,751	NE ...	7.6	6.3	4.7	970	860	727
AK ...	1.7	0.9	0.7	329	209	167	NV ...	27.2	14.9	7.1	4,150	1,653	1,032
AZ ...	49.6	26.1	19.2	8,213	4,483	3,917	NH ...	4.6	3.2	2.3	856	593	492
AR ...	11.0	8.8	5.2	1,437	994	765	NJ ...	25.4	18.4	9.2	3,675	2,801	1,902
CA ...	110.1	62.7	32.4	21,335	12,301	8,373	NM ...	9.2	6.1	5.2	1,694	1,066	994
CO ...	29.5	19.0	11.1	6,131	3,999	2,904	NY ...	54.1	51.6	12.7	7,091	6,304	2,804
CT ...	7.7	5.2	3.1	1,736	1,158	868	NC ...	85.8	54.7	39.1	14,298	8,432	7,279
DE ...	5.3	3.3	2.7	636	394	336	ND ...	3.4	2.8	1.9	446	399	328
DC ...	1.9	0.5	0.2	217	67	41	OH ...	27.1	17.7	12.9	4,704	2,928	2,580
FL ...	102.6	61.0	38.7	17,999	10,769	8,485	OK ...	14.7	10.5	8.4	2,137	1,591	1,440
GA ...	73.2	35.4	24.9	10,439	4,955	4,040	OR ...	21.1	11.7	7.5	4,000	2,247	1,645
HI....	7.0	4.1	2.5	1,724	1,171	814	PA ...	33.7	24.6	20.2	5,362	4,145	3,733
ID ...	12.1	6.5	5.7	2,111	1,130	1,049	RI ...	1.9	1.1	0.9	329	232	204
IL	43.0	22.5	11.8	6,936	3,783	2,661	SC ...	40.6	25.9	19.8	6,319	4,239	3,651
IN ...	23.8	16.6	11.8	3,893	2,470	2,137	SD ...	5.1	3.9	2.7	638	500	400
IA....	11.2	8.4	6.3	1,746	1,319	1,107	TN ...	37.4	22.4	16.2	5,337	3,078	2,639
KS ...	11.5	8.2	5.4	1,741	1,173	947	TX ...	177.0	129.5	79.6	24,778	17,582	13,856
KY ...	14.9	10.5	6.9	1,984	1,298	1,057	UT ...	20.3	10.9	7.1	3,966	1,827	1,447
LA ...	23.4	16.3	11.7	3,154	2,220	1,804	VT ...	2.1	1.4	1.1	350	241	208
ME ...	5.9	3.6	3.1	934	582	539	VA ...	38.4	27.6	19.9	6,357	4,078	3,460
MD ...	18.6	13.0	8.9	3,769	2,230	1,744	WA ...	47.4	28.9	17.4	8,130	5,063	3,656
MA ...	15.4	9.9	5.4	2,913	1,899	1,412	WV ...	4.8	3.5	2.6	720	483	431
MI....	17.8	10.9	9.0	2,908	1,792	1,631	WI. ...	21.8	15.5	10.1	3,624	2,507	2,083
MN ...	17.9	11.6	8.9	3,375	2,153	1,861	WY ...	4.6	2.7	2.2	812	567	519
MS ...	16.8	11.4	7.4	1,885	1,274	999							

Source: U.S. Census Bureau, Construction Reports, "New Residential Construction"; <http://www.census.gov/const/www /newresconstindex.html>.

Table 934. **New Privately Owned Housing Units Started—Selected Characteristics: 1970 to 2008**

[**In thousands (1,434 represents 1,434,000).** For composition of regions, see map inside front cover]

Year	Total units	Structures with— 1 unit	Structures with— 2 to 4 units	Structures with— 5 or more units	Region North-east	Region Mid-west	Region South	Region West	Units for sale Total	Units for sale Single-family	Units for sale Multi-family
1970	1,434	813	85	536	218	294	612	311	(NA)	(NA)	(NA)
1980	1,292	852	110	331	125	218	643	306	689	526	163
1981	1,084	705	91	288	117	165	562	240	584	426	158
1982	1,062	663	80	320	117	149	591	205	549	409	140
1983	1,703	1,068	113	522	168	218	935	382	923	713	210
1984	1,750	1,084	121	544	204	243	866	436	934	728	206
1985	1,742	1,072	93	576	252	240	782	468	867	713	154
1986	1,805	1,179	84	542	294	296	733	483	925	782	143
1987	1,621	1,146	65	409	269	298	634	420	862	732	130
1988	1,488	1,081	59	348	235	274	575	404	808	709	99
1989	1,376	1,003	55	318	179	266	536	396	735	648	87
1990	1,193	895	38	260	131	253	479	329	585	529	56
1991	1,014	840	36	138	113	233	414	254	531	490	41
1992	1,200	1,030	31	139	127	288	497	288	659	618	41
1993	1,288	1,126	29	133	127	298	562	302	760	716	44
1994	1,457	1,198	35	224	138	329	639	351	815	763	52
1995	1,354	1,076	34	244	118	290	615	331	763	712	51
1996	1,477	1,161	45	271	132	322	662	361	833	774	59
1997	1,474	1,134	45	296	137	304	670	363	843	784	59
1998	1,617	1,271	43	303	149	331	743	395	941	882	59
1999	1,641	1,302	32	307	156	347	746	392	981	912	69
2000	1,569	1,231	39	299	155	318	714	383	946	871	75
2001	1,603	1,273	37	293	149	330	732	391	990	919	71
2002	1,705	1,359	39	308	158	350	782	416	1,070	999	71
2003	1,848	1,499	34	315	163	374	839	472	1,207	1,120	87
2004	1,956	1,611	42	303	175	356	909	516	1,360	1,240	120
2005	2,068	1,716	41	311	190	357	996	525	1,508	1,358	150
2006	1,801	1,465	43	293	167	280	910	444	1,272	1,121	151
2007	1,355	1,046	32	277	143	210	681	321	875	760	115
2008	906	622	18	266	121	135	453	196	472	408	64

NA Not available.

Source: U.S. Census Bureau, Construction Reports, "New Residential Construction"; <http://www.census.gov/const/www /newresconstindex.html>.

Construction and Housing 593

[In thousands of units (1,573 represents 1,573,000)]

State	2000	2004, est.	2005, est.	2006, est. Total units	2006, est. Single-family units	State	2000	2004, est.	2005, est.	2006, est. Total units	2006, est. Single-family units
U.S.	1,573	1,724	1,658	1,614	1,319	MO	27.4	27.7	27.5	27.5	24.3
AL......	21.2	20.8	20.9	21.1	18.2	MT......	2.4	2.9	2.9	2.8	2.0
AK......	2.0	2.3	2.3	2.3	1.6	NE......	9.2	10.5	10.0	9.7	8.5
AZ......	59.4	64.4	61.9	60.1	53.2	NV......	31.0	37.8	36.1	35.0	27.9
AR......	12.5	13.8	13.6	13.6	10.4	NH......	6.4	7.4	7.0	6.6	5.6
CA......	137.1	177.7	165.0	154.2	120.3	NJ......	31.4	27.2	26.5	26.1	20.7
CO......	52.5	35.9	36.8	37.7	31.7	NM......	7.3	10.6	10.3	10.1	8.9
CT......	8.9	8.6	8.5	8.5	7.7	NY......	41.1	41.0	38.8	37.5	22.0
DE......	4.4	6.2	5.9	5.7	5.4	NC......	76.1	72.8	71.1	70.2	59.3
DC......	0.4	0.4	0.4	0.4	0.1	ND......	2.4	3.6	3.4	3.3	2.3
FL......	147.9	185.7	173.6	165.4	123.7	OH......	47.8	51.2	49.7	48.8	41.7
GA......	90.4	89.3	86.1	84.1	71.0	OK......	14.1	14.6	14.3	14.2	12.6
HI	4.7	6.8	6.5	6.2	5.1	OR......	18.8	19.2	19.6	20.0	15.6
ID	11.3	13.5	13.1	12.8	11.1	PA	39.2	40.4	39.4	39.0	34.6
IL......	51.3	61.5	58.5	56.6	45.2	RI	2.6	2.4	2.4	2.4	2.0
IN	38.2	40.4	39.4	38.8	33.5	SC	31.6	35.1	33.4	32.3	27.2
IA	12.8	15.3	14.6	14.1	11.5	SD	4.4	5.2	4.9	4.8	4.0
KS......	13.4	14.0	13.8	13.8	11.7	TN	34.6	34.3	34.2	34.3	30.4
KY......	21.8	20.4	20.4	20.5	17.9	TX	145.0	163.3	154.9	149.1	117.8
LA......	15.5	18.7	18.0	17.7	15.2	UT	18.1	20.2	19.9	19.8	16.7
ME......	6.3	7.3	6.8	6.5	6.0	VT	2.6	2.8	2.7	2.6	2.4
MD......	28.7	27.4	27.1	27.0	22.5	VA	47.5	53.4	51.8	50.6	43.2
MA......	17.1	16.2	16.0	16.0	12.8	WA	36.9	38.8	38.3	38.2	29.9
MI......	50.4	53.4	51.7	50.7	45.2	WV	5.3	5.4	5.4	5.4	5.1
MN......	32.9	41.7	39.0	37.1	31.9	WI......	32.6	38.1	36.7	35.8	27.9
MS......	14.1	12.8	12.8	12.9	11.1	WY	1.9	2.2	2.2	2.3	2.1

Source: National Association of Home Builders, Economics Division, Washington, DC. Data provided by the Econometric Forecasting Service.

Table 936. **Characteristics of New Privately Owned One-Family Houses Completed: 1990 to 2008**

Percent distribution, except total houses. (966 represents 966,000). Data are percent distribution of characteristics for all houses completed (includes new houses completed, houses built for sale completed, contractor-built and owner-built houses completed, and houses completed for rent). Percents exclude houses for which characteristics specified were not reported]

Characteristic	1990	2000	2005	2008	Characteristic	1990	2000	2005	2008
Total houses (1,000)	966	1,242	1,636	819	Bedrooms.............	100	100	100	100
					2 or less.............	15	11	12	14
Construction type	100	100	100	100	3.................	57	54	49	50
Site built.............	(NA)	94	96	95	4 or more	29	35	39	36
Modular..............	(NA)	3	3	3					
Other...............	(NA)	3	2	2	Bathrooms	100	100	100	100
					1-1/2 or less	13	7	4	7
Exterior wall material	100	100	100	100	2.................	42	39	36	35
Brick	18	20	20	24	2-1/2 or more	45	54	59	59
Wood................	39	14	7	9					
Stucco..............	18	17	22	21	Heating fuel...........	100	100	100	100
Vinyl siding [1]	(NA)	39	34	31	Gas...............	59	70	66	59
Aluminum siding	5	1	1	(NA)	Electricity	33	27	31	38
Other [1].............	20	7	16	12	Oil................	5	3	2	1
					Other...............	3	1	1	2
Floor area............	100	100	100	100					
Under 1,200 sq. ft	11	6	4	13	Heating system	100	100	100	100
1,200 to 1,599 sq. ft	22	18	18	18	Warm air furnace	65	71	67	60
1,600 to 1,999 sq. ft	22	23	20	26	Electric heat pump	23	23	29	34
2,000 to 2,399 sq. ft	17	18	18	17	Other..............	12	6	4	6
2,400 sq. ft. and over	29	35	42	25					
Average (sq. ft.)........	2,080	2,266	2,434	2534	Central air-conditioning ...	100	100	100	100
Median (sq. ft.)	1,905	2,057	2,227	2219	With................	76	85	89	89
					Without	24	15	11	11
Number of stories	100	100	100	100					
1..................	46	47	44	44	Fireplaces.............	100	100	100	100
2 or more	49	52	55	56	No fireplace	34	40	45	48
Split level	4	1	(Z)	(Z)	1 or more	66	60	55	53
Foundation	100	100	100	100	Parking facilities	100	100	100	100
Full or partial basement...	38	37	31	29	Garage..............	82	89	91	87
Slab................	40	46	53	51	Carport..............	2	1	1	1
Crawl space	21	17	16	19	No garage or carport	16	11	8	12

NA Not available.   Z Less than 0.5 percent.   [1] Prior to 2000, "other" includes vinyl siding.

Source: U.S. Census Bureau, "Characteristics of New Housing"; <http://www.census.gov/const/www/charindex.html>.

Table 937. **Housing Starts and Average Length of Time From Start to Completion of New Privately Owned One-Unit Residential Buildings: 1980 to 2008**

[852 represents 852,000. For buildings started in permit-issuing places]

Year	Total [1]	Purpose of construction			Region [2]			
		Built for sale	Contractor built	Owner built	North-east	Midwest	South	West
STARTS (1,000)								
1980	852	526	149	164	87	142	428	196
1990	895	529	196	147	104	193	371	226
1995	1,076	712	199	133	102	234	485	256
1997	1,134	784	189	131	111	238	507	278
1998	1,271	882	209	144	122	273	574	303
1999	1,302	912	208	142	126	289	580	308
2000	1,231	871	195	128	118	260	556	297
2001	1,273	919	186	129	111	269	590	303
2002	1,359	999	198	125	118	277	628	336
2003	1,499	1,120	205	127	116	309	686	388
2004	1,611	1,240	198	130	128	306	743	433
2005	1,716	1,358	197	129	138	306	831	441
2006	1,465	1,121	189	119	118	235	757	356
2007	1,046	760	151	104	93	171	540	242
2008	622	408	107	74	63	102	324	133
COMPLETION (months)								
1980	6.9	6.2	5.5	10.1	7.7	8.0	6.1	7.4
1990	6.4	5.9	5.3	10.3	9.3	5.6	5.7	6.9
1995	5.9	5.2	5.8	9.5	7.4	6.0	5.4	6.0
1997	6.0	5.2	5.9	9.8	7.3	6.2	5.6	5.8
1998	6.0	5.4	6.0	9.5	7.1	6.2	5.5	6.1
1999	6.1	5.5	6.4	9.2	7.0	6.4	5.7	6.3
2000	6.2	5.6	6.5	9.2	7.5	6.4	5.9	6.0
2001	6.2	5.6	7.0	9.2	7.6	6.5	5.8	6.3
2002	6.1	5.5	6.6	9.6	7.3	6.4	5.6	6.2
2003	6.2	5.5	6.8	9.9	7.5	6.7	5.7	6.2
2004	6.2	5.7	7.0	9.1	7.3	6.7	5.8	6.3
2005	6.4	5.9	7.6	9.8	7.7	6.6	6.0	6.8
2006	6.9	6.3	7.8	10.7	8.3	7.1	6.3	7.4
2007	7.1	6.5	7.9	10.2	8.5	7.4	6.5	8.0
2008	7.7	6.8	8.5	11.1	8.9	8.2	6.7	9.0

[1] Includes units built for rent not shown separately. [2] For composition of regions, see map inside front cover.

Source: U.S. Census Bureau, "New Residential Construction"; <http://www.census.gov/const/www/newresconstindex.html>.

Table 938. **Price Indexes of New One-Family Houses Sold by Region: 1980 to 2008**

1996 = 100. Based on kinds of homes sold in 1996. Includes value of the lot. For composition of regions, see map, inside front cover]

Year	Total	Northeast	Midwest	South	West
1980	38.9	30.2	41.2	44.4	31.9
1983	43.9	36.1	46.2	51.2	34.9
1984	45.7	39.2	49.0	52.8	36.2
1985	46.2	43.1	48.2	53.9	36.4
1986	48.0	49.5	51.0	55.5	37.3
1987	50.6	56.2	54.4	57.6	39.3
1988	52.5	57.6	56.8	58.8	41.4
1989	54.6	59.2	58.1	60.5	44.0
1990	55.7	58.0	58.6	60.6	46.2
1991	56.4	56.2	60.1	61.8	46.4
1992	57.2	60.5	61.2	62.4	46.7
1993	59.4	57.4	65.2	65.5	47.8
1994	62.9	62.0	69.4	68.1	51.9
1995	64.3	62.3	70.9	70.1	52.7
1996	66.0	63.2	72.5	71.2	55.3
1997	67.5	65.9	74.3	72.7	56.5
1998	69.2	66.1	76.0	74.4	58.4
1999	72.8	69.1	79.5	78.1	62.0
2000	75.6	73.0	83.5	80.6	64.4
2001	77.9	76.7	84.4	82.8	67.1
2002	81.4	80.2	86.1	86.3	71.5
2003	86.0	84.3	90.6	89.4	78.2
2004	92.8	91.6	96.7	94.4	88.2
2005	100.0	100.0	100.0	100.0	100.0
2006	104.7	102.6	102.9	105.4	105.2
2007	104.8	101.5	102.8	107.5	102.6
2008	99.7	99.8	98.4	104.5	92.7

Source: U.S. Census Bureau, "Construction Price Indexes"; <http://www.census.gov/const/www/constpriceindex.html>.

Construction and Housing 595

Table 939. New Privately Owned One-Family Houses Sold by Region and Type of Financing, 1980 to 2008, and by Sales-Price Group, 2008

[In thousands (545 represents 545,000). Based on a national probability sample of monthly interviews with builders or owners of one-family houses for which building permits have been issued or, for nonpermit areas on which construction has started. For details, see source and Appendix III. For composition of regions, see map inside front cover]

Year and sales-price group	Total sales	Region				Financing type			
		North-east	Midwest	South	West	Conven-tional [1]	FHA and VA	Rural Housing Service [2]	Cash
1980	545	50	81	267	145	302	196	14	32
1985	688	112	82	323	170	403	208	11	64
1990	534	71	89	225	149	337	138	10	50
1995	667	55	125	300	187	490	129	9	39
2000	877	71	155	406	244	695	138	4	40
2001	908	66	164	439	239	726	141	2	39
2002	973	65	185	450	273	788	140	4	42
2003	1,086	79	189	511	307	911	130	4	41
2004	1,203	83	210	562	348	1,047	105	6	46
2005	1,283	81	205	638	358	1,150	79	1	52
2006	1,051	63	161	559	267	948	63	1	38
2007	776	65	118	411	181	693	52	2	30
2008.	**485**	**35**	**70**	**266**	**114**	**358**	**104**	**(NA)**	**23**
Under $200,000	183	13	35	128	16	(NA)	(NA)	(NA)	(NA)
$200,000 to $299,999 . . .	149	10	21	76	42	(NA)	(NA)	(NA)	(NA)
$300,000 to $499,999 . . .	104	12	18	45	38	(NA)	(NA)	(NA)	(NA)
$500,000 and over	49	9	4	17	18	(NA)	(NA)	(NA)	(NA)

NA Not available. [1] Includes houses reporting other types of financing [2] Prior to 2000, the Farmers Home Administration.

Source: U.S. Census Bureau and U.S. Department of Housing and Urban Development, Current Construction Reports, Series C25, *Characteristics of New Housing,* annual; and *New One-Family Houses Sold,* monthly; publications discontinued in 2001. See "New Residential Sales" at <http://www.census.gov/const/www/newressalesindex.html>.

Table 940. Median Sales Price of New Privately Owned One-Family Houses Sold by Region: 1990 to 2008

[In dollars. For definition of median, see Guide to Tabular Presentation. For composition of regions, see map inside front cover. See Appendix III. See also headnote, Table 939]

Year	U.S.	North-east	Mid-west	South	West	Year	U.S.	North-east	Mid-west	South	West
1990	122,900	159,000	107,900	99,000	147,500	2004	221,000	315,800	205,000	181,100	283,100
1995	133,900	180,000	134,000	124,500	141,400	2005	240,900	343,800	216,900	197,300	332,600
2000	169,000	227,400	169,700	148,000	196,400	2006	246,500	346,000	213,500	208,200	337,700
2001	175,200	246,400	172,600	155,400	213,600	2007	247,900	320,200	208,600	217,700	330,900
2002	187,600	264,300	178,000	163,400	238,500	2008	232,100	343,600	198,900	203,700	294,800
2003	195,000	264,500	184,300	168,100	260,900						

Source: U.S. Census Bureau and U.S. Department of Housing and Urban Development, Current Construction Reports, Series C25, *Characteristics of New Housing,* annual; and *New One-Family Houses Sold,* monthly; publications discontinued in 2001. See New Residential Sales at <http://www.census.gov/const/www/newressalesindex.html>.

Table 941. New Manufactured (Mobile) Homes Placed for Residential Use and Average Sales Price by Region: 1980 to 2008

[233.7 represents 233,700. A mobile home is a moveable dwelling, 8 feet or more wide and 40 feet or more long, designed to be towed on its own chassis, with transportation gear integral to the unit when it leaves the factory, and without need of permanent foundation. Excluded are travel trailers, motor homes, and modular housing. Data are based on a probability sample and subject to sampling variability; see source. For composition of regions, see map inside front cover]

Year	Units placed (1,000)					Average sales price (dol.)				
	Total	North-east	Mid-west	South	West	U.S.	North-east	Mid-west	South	West
1980	233.7	12.3	32.3	140.3	48.7	19,800	18,500	18,600	18,200	25,400
1985	283.4	20.2	38.6	187.6	36.9	21,800	22,700	21,500	20,400	28,700
1990	195.4	18.8	37.7	108.4	30.6	27,800	30,000	27,000	24,500	39,300
1995	319.4	15.0	57.5	203.2	43.7	35,300	35,800	35,700	33,300	44,100
1997	336.3	14.3	55.3	219.4	47.3	39,800	41,300	40,000	38,000	47,300
1998	373.7	14.7	58.3	250.3	50.4	41,600	42,200	42,400	40,100	48,400
1999	338.3	14.1	53.6	227.2	43.5	43,300	44,000	44,400	41,900	49,600
2000	280.9	14.9	48.7	178.7	38.6	46,400	47,000	47,900	44,300	54,100
2002	174.3	11.8	34.2	101.0	27.2	51,300	53,200	51,700	48,000	62,600
2003	139.8	11.2	25.2	77.2	26.1	54,900	57,300	55,100	50,500	67,700
2004	124.4	11.0	20.6	67.4	25.5	58,200	60,200	58,800	52,300	73,200
2005	122.9	9.2	17.1	68.1	28.5	62,600	67,000	60,600	55,700	79,900
2006	112.4	7.9	14.5	66.1	23.9	64,300	65,300	59,100	58,900	83,400
2007	94.8	7.0	10.8	59.4	17.7	65,400	66,100	64,900	59,900	85,500
2008	79.3	5.0	8.2	53.0	13.1	64,900	68,400	65,700	59,700	85,100

Source: U.S. Census Bureau, "Manufactured Housing"; <http://www.census.gov/const/www/mhsindex.html>.

Table 942. **Existing One-Family Homes Sold and Price by Region: 1990 to 2008**

[**3,186 represents 3,186,000.** Includes existing detached single-family homes and townhomes; excludes condos and co-ops. Based on data (adjusted and aggregated to regional and national totals) reported by participating real estate multiple listing services. For definition of median, see Guide to Tabular Presentation. See Table 945 for data on condos and co-ops. For composition of regions, see map inside front cover]

Year	Homes sold (1,000)					Median sales price (dol.)				
	Total	North-east	Mid-west	South	West	Total	North-east	Mid-west	South	West
1990	3,186	586	859	1,088	653	96,400	141,400	76,300	84,700	138,600
1991	3,147	592	862	1,065	628	101,400	143,600	80,500	88,100	144,500
1992	3,433	665	968	1,124	676	104,000	142,600	84,200	91,100	141,100
1993	3,739	712	1,027	1,256	744	107,200	142,000	87,000	93,700	141,800
1994	3,887	726	1,029	1,314	818	111,300	141,500	90,600	94,900	149,200
1995	3,852	723	1,006	1,308	815	114,600	138,400	96,100	96,900	150,600
1996	4,167	776	1,058	1,388	945	119,900	139,600	102,300	102,400	157,100
1997	4,371	817	1,083	1,467	1,004	126,000	143,500	108,200	108,400	165,700
1998	4,965	902	1,221	1,718	1,124	132,800	147,300	115,600	115,000	175,900
1999	5,183	910	1,247	1,849	1,177	138,000	150,500	121,000	118,900	185,300
2000	5,174	912	1,222	1,867	1,173	143,600	149,800	125,300	126,300	194,600
2001	5,336	913	1,270	1,969	1,184	153,100	158,700	132,500	135,500	207,000
2002	5,631	951	1,346	2,065	1,269	165,000	179,300	139,300	146,000	230,100
2003	6,178	1,020	1,469	2,284	1,405	178,800	209,900	145,600	156,700	251,800
2004	6,778	1,113	1,550	2,540	1,575	195,400	243,800	154,600	170,400	286,400
2005	7,076	1,169	1,588	2,702	1,617	219,600	271,300	170,600	181,700	335,300
2006	6,478	1,086	1,483	2,563	1,346	221,900	271,900	167,800	183,700	342,700
2007	5,652	1,006	1,327	2,235	1,084	219,000	279,100	165,100	179,300	335,000
2008	4,913	849	1,129	1,865	1,070	198,100	266,400	154,100	169,200	271,500

Source: NATIONAL ASSOCIATION OF REALTORS, Washington, DC, *Real Estate Outlook; Market Trends & Insights*, monthly, (copyright). See also <http://www.realtor.org/research>.

Table 943. **Median Sales Price of Existing One-Family Homes by Selected Metropolitan Area: 2005 and 2008**

[In thousands of dollars (219.0 represents $219,000). Includes existing detached single-family homes and townhouses. Areas are metropolitan statistical areas defined by Office of Management and Budget as of 2004, except as noted]

Metropolitan area	2005	2008	Metropolitan area	2005	2008
United States, total	**219.0**	**196.6**	New York-Wayne-White Plains, NY-NJ. .	495.2	494.3
Allentown-Bethlehem-Easton, PA-NJ	243.4	243.6	NY: Edison, NJ	375.5	365.2
Anaheim-Santa Ana-Irvine, CA [1]	691.9	530.2	NY: Nassau-Suffolk, NY	465.2	435.8
Atlantic City, NJ	256.1	253.3	NY: Newark-Union, NJ-PA.	416.8	417.2
Baltimore-Towson, MD.	265.3	274.1	Norwich-New London, CT.	255.9	236.6
Barnstable Town, MA.	398.3	341.9	Orlando, FL	243.6	208.9
Boston-Cambridge-Quincy, MA-NH [2]	413.2	361.1	Palm Bay-Melbourne-Titusville, FL.	209.7	144.7
Boulder, CO.	348.4	359.6	Philadelphia-Camden-		
Bridgeport-Stamford-Norwalk, CT.	482.4	437.9	Wilmington, PA-NJ-DE-MD	215.3	231.4
Cape Coral-Fort Myers, FL.	269.2	152.6	Phoenix-Mesa-Scottsdale, AZ	247.4	191.3
Charleston-North Charleston, SC.	197.0	206.2	Pittsfield, MA	207.3	212.6
Chicago-Naperville-Joliet, IL	264.2	245.6	Portland-South Portland-Biddeford, ME. . .	246.6	229.3
Colorado Springs, CO	205.9	205.5	Portland-Vancouver-Beaverton, OR-WA . .	244.9	280.1
Deltona-Daytona Beach-			Providence-New Bedford-		
Ormond Beach, FL	192.5	164.1	Fall River, RI-MA.	293.4	250.6
Denver-Aurora, CO	247.1	219.3	Raleigh-Cary, NC	194.9	223.4
Dover, DE	180.4	206.2	Reno-Sparks, NV	349.9	259.1
Eugene-Springfield, OR	197.6	224.7	Richmond, VA	201.9	223.5
Gainesville, FL	184.0	188.6	Riverside-San Bernardino-Ontario, CA [1] . .	374.2	234.2
Hagerstown-Martinsburg, MD-WV	208.7	185.8	Sacramento-Arden-Arcade-		
Hartford-West Hartford-			Roseville, CA [1]	375.9	216.7
East Hartford, CT	253.3	246.2	Salem, OR	177.7	208.8
Honolulu, HI.	590.0	624.0	San Diego-Carlsbad-San Marcos, CA [1]. . .	604.3	385.6
Kingston, NY	251.0	242.1	San Francisco-Oakland-Fremont, CA [1] . . .	715.7	622.0
Las Vegas-Paradise, NV	304.7	220.5	San Jose-Sunnyvale-Santa Clara, CA [1] . .	744.5	668.0
Los Angeles-Long Beach-			Sarasota-Bradenton-Venice, FL.	354.2	240.6
Santa Ana, CA [1]	529.0	402.1	Seattle-Tacoma-Bellevue, WA	316.8	357.2
Madison, WI	218.3	226.6	Springfield, MA.	201.8	200.6
Miami-Fort Lauderdale-			Tampa-St.Petersburg-Clearwater, FL	205.3	173.0
Miami Beach, FL.	363.9	285.1	Trenton-Ewing, NJ	261.1	303.2
Milwaukee-Waukesha-West Allis, WI	215.7	212.3	Tucson, AZ	231.6	204.3
Minneapolis-St. Paul-			Virginia Beach-Norfolk-		
Bloomington, MN-WI	234.8	202.0	Newport News, VA-NC.	197.2	220.0
New Haven-Milford, CT	279.1	263.8	Washington-Arlington-		
New York-Northern New Jersey-			Alexandria, DC-VA-MD-WV	425.8	343.4
Long Island, NY-NJ-PA.	445.2	437.9	Worcester, MA	290.7	237.1

[1] California data supplied by the California Association of REALTORS.   [2] Excludes areas in New Hampshire.

Source: NATIONAL ASSOCIATION OF REALTORS, Washington, DC, *Real Estate Outlook: Market Trends & Insights*, monthly, (copyright). See also <http://www.realtor.org/research>.

Construction and Housing   597

Table 944. **Existing Home Sales by State: 2000 to 2008**

[In thousands (5,174 represents 5,174,000). Includes condos and co-ops as well as single-family homes. Data shown here reflect revisions from prior estimates]

State	2000	2005	2007	2008	State	2000	2005	2007	2008
United States . . .	5,174	7,076	5,652	4,913	Missouri	110.2	142.9	123.7	108.7
Alabama	67.0	128.0	118.0	86.0	Montana	17.4	25.4	24.1	19.9
Alaska	14.3	24.6	26.4	23.2	Nebraska	32.3	41.2	36.8	30.9
Arizona	104.8	199.2	105.5	116.1	Nevada	44.6	98.0	45.3	65.5
Arkansas	45.0	75.3	78.6	64.2	New Hampshire	26.7	(NA)	(NA)	18.4
California	573.5	601.1	355.0	439.9	New Jersey	161.1	184.4	139.7	112.6
Colorado	111.5	130.4	118.2	106.8	New Mexico	29.9	57.5	44.5	33.3
Connecticut	61.5	78.0	62.6	47.4	New York	273.3	319.8	295.9	255.4
Delaware	12.9	19.3	15.7	11.5	North Carolina	134.2	215.7	214.0	157.1
District of Columbia . . .	10.6	12.1	9.6	7.1	North Dakota	10.8	15.8	14.4	12.4
Florida	393.6	547.1	286.4	262.5	Ohio	216.4	286.9	250.8	229.7
Georgia	143.6	242.1	209.9	174.9	Oklahoma	67.3	104.6	102.0	87.7
Hawaii	22.1	36.8	27.8	20.0	Oregon	62.6	100.5	74.3	54.8
Idaho	24.1	49.8	36.3	26.5	Pennsylvania	195.9	255.2	214.0	174.7
Illinois	246.8	315.3	239.7	183.1	Rhode Island	17.0	19.8	16.4	13.4
Indiana	111.0	138.3	148.3	118.6	South Carolina	64.3	114.6	105.0	80.3
Iowa	53.3	74.9	70.5	55.7	South Dakota	12.6	18.3	18.5	16.3
Kansas	52.6	77.9	70.5	60.4	Tennessee	100.4	170.9	145.7	118.0
Kentucky	66.0	96.2	91.8	75.3	Texas	381.8	532.5	557.8	474.8
Louisiana	66.8	87.7	75.9	59.1	Utah	35.5	51.7	41.9	30.8
Maine	27.6	33.3	25.5	20.6	Vermont	12.1	15.3	14.4	10.7
Maryland	100.5	135.5	86.4	63.8	Virginia	130.0	182.5	116.5	112.7
Massachusetts	112.3	148.6	122.4	103.8	Washington	112.4	167.8	133.5	86.9
Michigan	185.0	208.6	172.4	155.6	West Virginia	22.9	38.6	29.0	25.5
Minnesota	96.3	134.9	99.8	96.2	Wisconsin	91.6	122.8	104.6	84.5
Mississippi	38.7	61.2	59.7	50.4	Wyoming	9.6	14.3	12.9	10.0

NA Not available.

Source: NATIONAL ASSOCIATION OF REALTORS, Washington, DC, *Real Estate Outlook: Market Trends & Insights*, monthly (copyright). See also <http://www.realtor.org/research>.

Table 945. **Existing Apartment Condos and Co-Ops—Units Sold and Median Sales Price by Region: 1990 to 2008**

[272 represents 272,000. Data shown here reflect revisions from prior estimates. For definition of median, see Guide to Tabular Presentation. For composition of regions, see map inside front cover]

Year	Units sold (1,000)					Median sales price (dol.)				
	U.S.	North-east	Mid-west	South	West	U.S.	North-east	Mid-west	South	West
1990	272	73	55	80	64	86,900	107,500	70,200	64,200	114,600
1995	333	108	66	96	63	89,000	92,500	90,700	67,800	114,800
1999	534	182	102	145	105	110,100	109,800	114,600	80,700	143,900
2000	571	197	106	160	108	114,000	108,500	121,700	84,200	149,100
2001	601	203	116	174	108	125,600	121,200	134,800	93,200	160,400
2002	657	221	129	193	114	144,900	143,500	148,600	109,900	187,000
2003	732	250	146	211	125	168,500	178,100	162,600	126,900	222,400
2004	820	292	161	230	137	197,100	214,100	181,000	156,600	258,000
2005	896	331	177	245	143	223,900	245,100	189,100	187,300	283,800
2006	801	299	169	211	122	221,900	249,700	190,900	184,000	264,700
2007	713	283	146	182	102	226,300	256,100	195,200	185,100	263,300
2008	563	226	107	144	86	209,800	252,500	188,200	166,800	218,500

Source: NATIONAL ASSOCIATION OF REALTORS, Washington, DC, *Real Estate Outlook: Market Trends & Insights*, monthly (copyright). See also <http://www.realtor.org/research>.

Table 946. **New Unfurnished Apartments Completed and Rented in 3 Months by Region: 2000 to 2007**

[226.2 represents 226,200. Structures with five or more units, privately financed, nonsubsidized, unfurnished rental apartments. Based on sample and subject to sampling variability; see source for details. For composition of regions, see map, inside front cover]

Year and rent	Number (1,000)					Percent rented in 3 months				
	U.S.	North-east	Mid-west	South	West	U.S.	North-east	Mid-west	South	West
2000	226.2	14.8	39.5	125.9	45.9	72	85	76	67	77
2004	153.8	13.1	31.7	72.7	36.3	62	75	59	60	65
2005	113.0	4.7	20.5	57.8	30.0	64	75	64	62	64
2006	117.2	6.0	12.6	69.9	28.6	55	41	58	60	56
2007	104.8	5.6	9.5	61.8	28.0	55	66	58	52	58
2008, prel.	**145.7**	**8.5**	**17.4**	**87.7**	**32.1**	**50**	**54**	**58**	**48**	**50**
Less than $750										
Less than $850	31.0	1.3	6.9	20.2	2.7	55	97	62	50	50
$850 to $949	18.3	0.1	1.4	14.2	2.6	53	30	73	49	66
$950 to $1,049	17.8	0.9	2.4	11.5	3.0	54	45	53	54	60
$1,050 to $1,149	13.8	0.5	0.6	10.6	2.1	49	14	34	49	62
$1,150 or more	64.7	5.7	6.0	31.3	21.8	46	50	53	43	46
Median monthly asking rent (dollars) . .	1,091	(¹)	964	1,032	(¹)	(X)	(X)	(X)	(X)	(X)

X Not applicable.   Z Fewer than 50 units or less than one-half of 1 percent.   ¹ Over $1,150.

Source: U.S. Census Bureau, *Current Housing Reports*, Series H130, *Market Absorption of Apartments,* and unpublished data. See also <http://www.census.gov/prod/www/abs/apart.html>.

Table 947. Total Housing Inventory for the United States: 1990 to 2008

[In thousands (106,283 represents 106,283,000), except percent. Based on the Current Population Survey and the Housing Vacancy Survey and subject to sampling error; see source and Appendix III for details]

Item	1990	1995	2000	2002 [1]	2003	2004	2005	2006	2007	2008
All housing units	**106,283**	**112,655**	**119,628**	**119,297**	**120,834**	**122,187**	**123,925**	**126,012**	**127,958**	**130,113**
Vacant	12,059	12,669	13,908	14,332	15,274	15,599	15,694	16,437	17,652	18,704
Year-round vacant.	9,128	9,570	10,439	10,771	11,631	11,884	11,916	12,459	13,276	13,936
For rent	2,662	2,946	3,024	3,347	3,676	3,802	3,721	3,737	3,848	4,056
For sale only.	1,064	1,022	1,148	1,220	1,308	1,307	1,451	1,836	2,117	2,226
Rented or sold	660	810	856	842	976	991	1,060	1,108	1,130	1,075
Held off market	4,742	4,793	5,411	5,362	5,671	5,784	5,684	5,778	6,181	6,579
Occasional use	1,485	1,667	1,892	1,819	1,989	1,967	1,884	1,858	1,993	2,071
Usual residence elsewhere	1,068	801	1,037	995	994	1,068	1,128	1,198	1,139	1,170
Other	2,189	2,325	2,482	2,548	2,688	2,749	2,672	2,722	3,049	3,338
Seasonal [2]	2,931	3,099	3,469	3,561	3,643	3,715	3,778	3,978	4,376	4,768
Total occupied	94,224	99,985	105,720	104,965	105,560	106,588	108,231	109,575	110,306	111,409
Owner	60,248	64,739	71,250	71,278	72,054	73,575	74,553	75,380	75,159	75,566
Renter	33,976	35,246	34,470	33,687	33,506	33,013	33,678	34,195	35,147	35,843
PERCENT DISTRIBUTION										
All housing units	100.0	100.0	100.0	100.0	100.0	100.0	100.0	100.0	100.0	100.0
Vacant	11.3	11.2	11.6	12.0	12.6	12.8	12.7	13.0	13.8	14.4
Total occupied	88.7	88.8	88.4	88.0	87.4	87.2	87.3	87.0	86.2	85.6
Owner	56.7	57.5	59.6	59.7	59.6	60.2	60.2	60.3	58.7	58.1
Renter	32.0	31.3	28.8	28.2	27.7	27.0	27.2	27.5	27.5	27.5

[1] Revised. Based on 2000 census controls. [2] Beginning 1990, includes vacant seasonal mobile homes. For years shown, seasonal vacant housing units were underreported prior to 1990.

Source: U.S. Census Bureau, "Housing Vacancies and Home Ownership"; <http://www.census.gov/hhes/www/housing/hvs/hvs.html>.

Table 948. Occupied Housing Inventory by Age of Householder: 1990 to 2008

[In thousands (94,224 represents 94,224,000). Based on the Current Population Survey/Housing Vacancy Survey; see source for details]

Age of householder	1990	1995	2000	2002 [1]	2003	2004	2005	2006	2007	2008
Total.	**94,224**	**99,986**	**105,719**	**104,965**	**105,560**	**106,588**	**108,231**	**109,576**	**110,306**	**111,409**
Under 25 years old	5,143	5,502	6,221	6,372	6,441	6,538	6,536	6,578	6,494	6,272
25 to 29 years old	9,508	8,662	8,482	8,231	8,213	8,491	8,790	8,975	9,170	9,094
30 to 34 years old	11,213	11,206	10,219	10,176	10,084	9,865	9,583	9,423	9,349	9,343
35 to 39 years old	10,914	11,993	11,834	10,924	10,777	10,438	10,526	10,520	10,499	10,550
40 to 44 years old	9,893	11,151	12,377	11,839	11,748	11,768	11,722	11,484	11,125	10,974
45 to 49 years old	8,038	10,080	11,164	11,204	11,341	11,583	11,780	11,988	12,007	11,968
50 to 54 years old	6,532	7,882	9,834	10,123	10,194	10,316	10,595	10,896	11,082	11,415
55 to 59 years old	6,182	6,355	7,602	8,261	8,550	8,928	9,504	9,919	10,013	10,217
60 to 64 years old	6,446	5,860	6,215	6,422	6,776	7,112	7,336	7,604	8,108	8,601
65 to 69 years old	6,407	6,088	5,816	5,644	5,570	5,656	5,900	6,074	6,330	6,642
70 to 74 years old	5,397	5,693	5,567	5,137	5,163	5,065	5,016	5,057	5,063	5,114
75 years old and over. . . .	8,546	9,514	10,388	10,632	10,703	10,827	10,943	11,058	11,065	11,219

[1] Revised. Based on 2000 census controls.

Source: U.S. Census Bureau, "Housing Vacancies and Home Ownership"; <http://www.census.gov/hhes/www/housing/hvs/hvs.html>.

Table 949. Vacancy Rates for Housing Units—Characteristics: 2000 to 2008

[In percent. Rate is relationship between vacant housing for rent or for sale and the total rental and homeowner supply, which comprises occupied units, units rented or sold and awaiting occupancy, and vacant units available for rent or sale. Based on the Current Population/ Housing Vacancy Survey; see source for details. For composition of regions, see map, inside front cover]

Characteristic	Rental units				Homeowner units			
	2000	2005	2007	2008	2000	2005	2007	2008
Total units	**8.0**	**9.8**	**9.7**	**10.0**	**1.6**	**1.9**	**2.7**	**2.8**
Northeast	5.6	6.5	7.0	6.9	1.2	1.5	2.0	2
Midwest	8.8	12.6	11.5	10.8	1.3	2.2	2.8	2.9
South	10.5	11.8	12.3	13.0	1.9	2.1	3.1	3.1
West	5.8	7.3	6.7	7.5	1.5	1.4	2.5	2.9
Units in structure:								
1 unit	7.0	9.9	9.6	9.8	1.5	1.7	2.4	2.5
2 units or more	8.7	10.0	10.0	10.4	4.7	6.2	8.3	8.8
5 units or more	9.2	10.4	10.3	10.8	5.8	6.6	8.5	8.8
Units with—								
3 rooms or less	10.3	12.1	11.9	12.2	10.4	12.0	14.9	12.4
4 rooms	8.2	9.6	10.0	10.0	2.9	3.3	4.9	4.7
5 rooms	6.9	9.3	8.6	9.1	2.0	2.2	3.0	3.3
6 rooms or more	5.2	8.1	7.9	8.7	1.1	1.4	2.0	2.2

Source: U.S. Census Bureau, "Housing Vacancies and Home Ownership"; <http://www.census.gov/hhes/www/housing/hvs/hvs.html>.

Construction and Housing **599**

Table 950. **Housing Units and Tenure—States: 2007**

[**127,895 represents 127,895,000.** The American Community Survey universe includes the household population and the population living in institutions, college dormitories, and other group quarters. Based on a sample and subject to sampling variability; see Appendix III]

State	Housing units						Housing tenure			
			Vacant (1,000)		Vacancy rate		Owner-occupied units		Renter-occupied units	
	Total (1,000)	Occu-pied (1,000)	Total	For sea-sonal use [1]	Home-owner [2]	Renter [3]	Total (1,000)	Average house-hold size	Total (1,000)	Average house-hold size
United States . . .	127,895	112,378	15,517	4,430	2.5	8.0	75,515	2.70	36,863	2.42
Alabama	2,137	1,816	321	63	2.4	9.5	1,288	2.54	528	2.34
Alaska.	282	236	46	23	1.4	6.1	149	2.97	87	2.51
Arizona	2,668	2,252	416	165	4.0	9.4	1,533	2.81	718	2.68
Arkansas	1,287	1,103	185	41	2.6	8.8	747	2.55	356	2.38
California	13,309	12,201	1,108	303	2.2	4.8	7,077	3.01	5,124	2.80
Colorado	2,127	1,860	267	96	3.3	8.8	1,280	2.63	580	2.39
Connecticut	1,439	1,321	118	23	1.3	7.5	925	2.71	396	2.22
Delaware	389	328	60	33	2.4	9.5	238	2.61	90	2.42
District of Columbia . . .	284	251	33	2	3.0	5.3	112	2.36	139	2.08
Florida.	8,717	7,089	1,628	716	4.5	11.7	5,006	2.53	2,083	2.49
Georgia	3,962	3,417	545	91	3.5	10.7	2,342	2.77	1,075	2.60
Hawaii.	507	440	67	27	1.2	10.0	262	2.99	178	2.62
Idaho	631	561	70	31	2.2	6.3	404	2.67	157	2.46
Illinois	5,246	4,760	487	39	2.3	7.8	3,335	2.75	1,425	2.35
Indiana	2,778	2,462	316	35	2.9	9.9	1,764	2.61	699	2.22
Iowa	1,329	1,214	115	19	2.0	7.6	895	2.49	320	2.04
Kansas	1,219	1,089	130	12	2.0	8.3	764	2.61	325	2.17
Kentucky	1,906	1,656	250	31	3.0	10.0	1,171	2.56	485	2.33
Louisiana	1,859	1,597	261	51	1.9	7.3	1,085	2.70	512	2.43
Maine	697	544	153	105	2.1	8.3	402	2.47	142	2.03
Maryland	2,318	2,082	236	46	1.9	8.9	1,456	2.75	626	2.35
Massachusetts	2,722	2,449	273	107	1.4	6.3	1,594	2.74	855	2.18
Michigan	4,527	3,849	678	259	3.5	9.8	2,880	2.64	969	2.27
Minnesota	2,304	2,063	242	112	1.9	7.2	1,552	2.59	511	2.04
Mississippi	1,255	1,080	175	30	2.3	10.4	770	2.64	310	2.56
Missouri.	2,647	2,310	338	74	2.7	8.5	1,632	2.60	678	2.17
Montana	436	372	64	31	1.8	4.3	259	2.57	113	2.35
Nebraska	781	700	81	14	2.3	9.0	481	2.59	219	2.18
Nevada	1,102	954	148	35	4.5	10.2	576	2.71	378	2.57
New Hampshire	594	502	93	59	2.2	5.4	372	2.68	130	2.16
New Jersey	3,499	3,150	349	121	1.9	6.4	2,119	2.84	1,031	2.41
New Mexico	862	735	127	42	2.0	9.8	514	2.70	220	2.43
New York.	7,940	7,100	840	273	1.8	4.8	3,942	2.80	3,158	2.42
North Carolina	4,124	3,541	583	172	2.5	9.4	2,418	2.55	1,123	2.33
North Dakota	310	272	39	12	1.1	7.6	179	2.47	93	1.83
Ohio	5,065	4,506	559	52	2.9	10.2	3,140	2.61	1,366	2.18
Oklahoma	1,623	1,400	223	36	2.3	9.5	955	2.57	445	2.35
Oregon	1,610	1,472	138	46	2.2	5.1	951	2.60	521	2.30
Pennsylvania	5,478	4,873	605	158	1.9	7.5	3,491	2.59	1,382	2.12
Rhode Island	451	403	48	15	1.4	7.9	256	2.72	147	2.20
South Carolina	2,022	1,703	319	99	2.5	12.1	1,192	2.55	510	2.39
South Dakota	356	313	43	14	1.7	6.9	213	2.56	100	2.20
Tennessee	2,725	2,408	317	58	2.4	9.4	1,684	2.56	724	2.34
Texas	9,433	8,244	1,189	214	2.5	10.8	5,374	2.96	2,870	2.59
Utah	925	835	90	38	1.8	5.7	599	3.24	236	2.80
Vermont	311	253	59	44	1.0	4.9	184	2.47	69	2.12
Virginia	3,273	2,932	341	74	1.9	7.3	2,038	2.62	894	2.37
Washington	2,744	2,502	243	78	2.0	4.9	1,653	2.65	849	2.30
West Virginia	883	734	149	41	2.3	9.0	549	2.48	184	2.19
Wisconsin	2,558	2,242	317	154	1.8	7.0	1,571	2.55	671	2.14
Wyoming	242	206	36	16	2.3	5.5	143	2.54	63	2.30

[1] For seasonal, recreational, or occasional use. [2] Proportion of the homeowner housing inventory which is vacant for sale.
[3] Proportion of the rental inventory which is vacant for rent.

Source: U.S. Census Bureau, 2007 American Community Survey; B25002. Occupancy Status; B25003. Tenure; B25004. Vacancy Status; and B25010. Average Household Size of Units by Tenure; using American FactFinder; <http://factfinder.census.gov/> (accessed March 2009).

600   Construction and Housing

Table 951. **Homeownership and Rental Vacancy Rates by State: 2008**

[The American Community Survey universe is limited to the household population and excludesthe population living in institutions, college dormitories, and other group quarters. Based on a sample and subject to sampling variability; see Appendix III. FIPS means Federal Information Processing Standards]

State	Home-ownership vacancy rate	Rental vacancy rate	State	Home-ownership vacancy rate	Rental vacancy rate	State	Home-ownership vacancy rate	Rental vacancy rate
U.S.	2.8	10.0	KS	2.0	10.3	ND	1.3	8.2
			KY	2.7	9.9	OH	2.9	10.5
AL	3.3	15.3	LA	1.9	10.3	OK	2.7	9.0
AK	2.0	8.7	ME	2.3	7.6	OR	2.0	5.4
AZ	3.8	14.1	MD	2.6	11.3	PA	2.4	9.5
AR	2.9	13.4	MA	1.6	6.5	RI	2.1	8.7
CA	3.1	6.4	MI	3.7	14.6	SC	3.1	13.4
CO	3.1	8.3	MN	2.8	6.8	SD	1.4	8.5
CT	2.2	8.6	MS	2.6	11.4	TN	3.0	12.1
DE	2.4	13.4	MO	2.6	11.3	TX	2.3	12.3
DC	3.0	8.6	MT	2.1	5.6	UT	2.0	7.4
FL	4.7	16.9	NE	2.3	9.0	VT	1.6	3.5
GA	4.3	14.5	NV	5.3	14.0	VA	2.6	10.0
HI	1.7	7.2	NH	1.8	7.5	WA	1.9	5.3
ID	3.1	10.3	NJ	1.6	6.4	WV	2.2	11.4
IL	3.2	10.0	NM	2.0	7.6	WI	2.1	8.8
IN	2.8	14.8	NY	2.1	5.7	WY	1.6	4.7
IA	2.4	8.9	NC	3.2	12.8			

Source: U.S. Census Bureau, "Housing Vacancies and Home Ownership"; <http://www.census.gov/hhes/www/housing/hvs/annual08/ann08ind.html>.

Table 952. **Homeownership and Rental Vacancy Rates by Metropolitan Area: 2008**

[Based on the Current Population Survey and the Housing Vacancy Survey and subject to sampling error; see source and Appendix III for details]

Metropolitan area	Home-ownership vacancy rates	Rental vacancy rates	Metropolitan area	Home-ownership vacancy rates	Rental vacancy rates
Inside Metropolitan Areas	3.7	10.0	Minneapolis-St. Paul-Bloomington, MN-WI .	2.8	7.2
Akron, OH	3.0	11.7	Nashville-Davidson-Murfreesboro, TN	2.2	10.6
Albany-Schenectady-Troy, NY	2.3	4.6	New Haven-Milford, CT	2.6	8.4
Albuquerque, NM	1.9	8.1	New Orleans-Metairie-Kenner, LA	3.7	12.3
Allenton-Bethleham-Easton, PA-NJ	1.3	11.1	New York-Northern New Jersey-Long		
Atlanta-Sandy Springs-Marietta, GA	4.8	16.1	Island, NY	1.9	5.2
Austin-Round Rock, TX	2.3	11.8	Oklahoma City, OK	3.5	9.9
Bakersfield, CA	2.8	8.7	Omaha-Council Bluffs, NE-IA	3.2	12.6
Baltimore-Towson, MD	2.3	12.4	Orlando, FL	6.8	21.9
Baton Rouge, LA	0.9	9.2	Oxnard-Thousand Oaks-Ventura, CA	2.0	4.2
Birmingham-Hoover, AL	3.3	10.6	Philadelphia-Camden-Wilmington, PA	2.5	11.8
Boston-Cambridge-Quincy, MA-NH	1.5	5.9	Phoenix-Mesa-Scottsdale, AZ	3.7	15.0
Bridgeport-Stamford-Norwalk, CT	2.9	7.2	Pittsburgh, PA	2.6	7.8
Buffalo-Cheektowaga-Tonawanda, NY . . .	2.2	7.0	Portland-Vancouver-Beaverton, OR-WA . .	1.9	5.5
Charlotte-Gastonia-Concord, NC-SC	4.0	12.1	Poughkeepsie-Newburg-Middletown, NJ . .	0.7	9.1
Chicago-Naperville-Joliet, IL	3.1	9.9	Providence-New Bedford-Fall River		
Cincinnati-Middletown, OH-KY-IN	4.4	8.5	RI-MA	1.9	9.6
Cleveland-Elyria-Mentor, OH	2.7	13.4	Raleigh-Cary, NC	3.2	9.9
Columbia, SC	3.2	6.8	Richmond, VA	2.0	20.8
Columbus, OH	3.2	9.2	Riverside-San Bernardino-Ontario, CA . . .	5.2	9.4
Dallas-Ft. Worth-Arlington, TX	2.8	10.5	Rochester, NY	1.7	7.0
Dayton, OH	2.9	16.5	Sacramento-Arden-Arade-Roseville, CA . .	4.8	10.4
Denver-Aurora, CO	3.1	7.1	St. Louis, MO-IL	3.1	10.7
Detroit-Warren-Livonia, MI	4.6	18.3	Salt Lake City, UT	1.8	9.2
El Paso, TX	3.0	9.5	San Antonio, TX	1.5	11.5
Fresno, CA	2.0	8.9	San Diego-Carlsbad-San Marcos, CA. . . .	2.7	7.2
Grand Rapids-Wyoming, MI	2.3	7.4	San Francisco-Oakland-Fremont, CA	2.1	5.4
Greensboro-High Point, NC	5.6	17.6	San Jose-Sunnyvale-Santa Clara, CA. . . .	2.0	5.6
Hartford-West Hartford-East Hartford, CT .	1.4	9.6	Seattle-Bellevue-Everett, WA	1.9	4.5
Honolulu, HI.	1.0	5.1	Springfield, MA.	1.9	4.6
Houston-Baytown-Sugar Land, TX	2.7	15.6	Syracuse, NY	2.3	12.9
Indianapolis, IN	4.2	19.3	Tampa-St. Petersburg-Clearwater, FL. . . .	3.0	15.4
Jacksonville, FL	5.4	15.3	Toledo, OH	2.1	10.5
Kansas City, MO-KS	3.4	14.1	Tucson, AZ	1.8	7.1
Las Vegas-Paradise, NV	6.1	14.9	Tulsa, OK	3.0	9.8
Los Angeles-Long Beach-Santa Ana, CA . .	1.5	5.3	Virginia Beach-Norfolk-Newport News, VA. .	3.2	6.7
Louisville, KY-IN	2.5	10.2	Washington-Arlington-Alexandria, DC-VA-		
Memphis, TN-AR-MS.	3.3	16.6	MD-WV	2.7	10.0
Miami-Fort Lauderdale-Miami Beach, FL. . .	3.8	12.1	Worchester, MA	1.3	9.7
Milwaukee-Waukesha-West Allis, WI	1.1	7.8			

Source: U.S. Census Bureau, "Housing Vacancies and Home Ownership"; <http://www.census.gov/hhes/www/housing/hvs/annual08/ann08ind.html>.

Construction and Housing 601

Table 953. **Housing Units—Characteristics by Tenure and Region: 2007**

[In thousands of units (128,203 represents 128,203,000), except as indicated. As of fall. Based on the American Housing Survey; see Appendix III. For composition of regions, see map, inside front cover]

Characteristic	Total housing units	Seasonal	Year-round units Occupied — Total	Owner	Renter	North-east	Mid-west	South	West	Vacant
Total units	**128,203**	**4,402**	**110,692**	**75,647**	**35,045**	**20,392**	**25,292**	**40,609**	**24,400**	**13,109**
Percent distribution	100.0	3.4	86.3	59.0	27.3	15.9	19.7	31.7	19.0	10.2
Units in structure:										
Single family detached	80,406	2,651	71,435	62,512	8,923	11,106	17,655	27,213	15,460	6,320
Single family attached.	7,135	210	6,083	4,042	2,040	1,836	1,080	1,963	1,203	843
2 to 4 units	10,515	196	8,790	1,414	7,376	2,635	2,027	2,167	1,961	1,528
5 to 9 units	6,200	107	5,258	571	4,686	906	1,110	1,810	1,431	835
10 to 19 units	5,808	108	4,697	476	4,221	838	908	1,773	1,178	1,003
20 or more units	9,435	397	7,511	1,212	6,298	2,518	1,359	1,756	1,876	1,527
Manufactured/mobile home [1]	8,705	733	6,919	5,419	1,500	552	1,151	3,925	1,290	1,053
Year structure built:										
Median year	1973	1974	1973	1975	1971	1957	1969	1978	1976	1973
1980 or later.	46,141	1,615	39,866	29,950	9,915	4,119	7,588	18,553	9,606	4,660
1970 to 1979	25,373	950	21,847	13,619	8,228	2,889	4,836	8,736	5,386	2,578
1960 to 1969	15,292	523	13,397	8,979	4,418	2,470	2,993	4,774	3,160	1,372
1950 to 1959	12,994	396	11,501	8,382	3,120	2,485	2,972	3,456	2,589	1,097
1949 and earlier	28,402	917	24,081	14,716	9,364	8,428	6,903	5,091	3,660	3,403
Stories in structure: [2]										
1 story	41,469	1,788	35,578	26,487	9,091	1,139	4,093	19,680	10,666	4,103
2 stories.	42,643	1,116	37,065	24,378	12,687	6,160	10,127	11,537	9,241	4,462
3 stories.	26,948	419	24,127	16,640	7,487	8,660	8,563	4,393	2,511	2,402
4 or more stories	8,437	345	7,004	2,723	4,281	3,881	1,357	1,074	692	1,088
Foundation: [3]										
Full basement	27,759	322	25,658	23,019	2,639	8,702	11,035	3,894	2,026	1,779
Partial building.	9,052	177	8,299	7,523	776	2,313	3,262	1,643	1,081	576
Crawlspace.	21,087	1,032	18,098	14,943	3,155	722	2,564	9,570	5,243	1,957
Concrete slab	28,052	1,003	24,400	20,226	4,174	1,119	1,698	13,500	8,084	2,649
Equipment:										
Lacking complete facilities	5,511	544	1,725	304	1,421	372	374	508	472	3,242
With complete facilities	122,692	3,857	108,967	75,343	33,624	20,020	24,918	40,101	23,929	9,867
Kitchen sink	126,830	4,192	110,339	75,518	34,821	20,319	25,245	40,494	24,282	12,300
Refrigerator.	124,647	3,982	110,455	75,543	34,912	20,338	25,235	40,530	24,352	10,210
Cooking stove or range.	124,885	3,979	109,977	75,415	34,562	20,268	25,154	40,366	24,189	10,928
Dishwasher.	79,186	1,949	70,830	55,681	15,149	11,489	14,854	27,381	17,106	6,407
Washing machine	98,687	2,324	91,364	72,897	18,467	15,144	21,279	35,339	19,602	4,999
Clothes dryer	95,638	2,240	88,506	71,443	17,063	14,140	21,030	34,249	19,087	4,892
Disposal in kitchen sink.	61,798	1,393	55,026	39,619	15,406	5,177	12,749	19,395	17,705	5,380
Safety Equipment:										
Smoke detector:										
Working	112,984	2,601	102,249	70,431	31,817	19,371	23,844	36,565	22,469	8,134
Powered by:										
Electricity	10,361	289	9,115	6,087	3,028	1,906	1,565	3,727	1,917	957
Batteries	73,238	1,371	67,497	44,426	23,072	13,150	16,792	23,271	14,284	4,371
Both	27,379	831	24,212	19,310	4,903	4,058	5,215	9,064	5,875	2,335
Not working.	10,214	854	7,017	4,203	2,815	782	1,096	3,462	1,677	2,343
Not reported	5,005	947	1,426	1,013	413	238	351	582	255	2,632
Batteries:										
Replaced in last 6 months	74,021	1,309	68,317	48,299	20,018	13,787	16,890	23,688	13,953	4,395
Not replaced in last 6 months . .	22,634	476	20,894	14,170	6,724	3,057	4,487	7,730	5,620	1,264
Not reported	3,962	417	2,499	1,266	1,232	364	630	917	587	1,046
Fire extinguisher purchased or recharged in last 2 years	48,270	–	48,270	37,215	11,055	8,832	10,922	18,074	10,443	–
Sprinkler system inside home.	5,479	314	4,288	1,766	2,523	676	695	1,515	1,402	876
Working carbon monoxide detector . .	38,484	595	36,076	28,325	7,751	11,164	11,568	8,520	4,824	1,812
Main heating equipment: [4]										
Warm-air furnace	78,624	1,842	69,582	50,952	18,630	8,587	20,517	24,333	16,145	7,200
Steam or hot water system	13,878	104	12,760	7,520	5,240	9,335	2,072	569	785	1,014
Electric heat pump	15,348	729	12,996	9,562	3,434	372	706	10,478	1,439	1,623
Built-in electric units	5,735	342	4,802	2,147	2,656	1,126	1,109	881	1,687	591
Floor, wall, or pipeless furnace	5,597	128	4,994	2,055	2,940	425	415	1,204	2,951	475
Room heaters with flue	1,350	78	1,135	676	459	168	124	570	273	137
Room heaters without flue.	1,403	68	1,188	746	442	21	52	1,074	41	147
Portable electric heaters	1,180	73	1,036	447	589	21	33	732	250	71
Stoves	1,240	209	945	793	152	191	150	297	307	86
Fireplaces [5]	279	46	216	188	27	26	29	73	89	17
None	2,679	665	478	244	234	23	31	87	336	1,537
Central air conditioning:	85,243	2,148	75,492	57,618	17,874	6,817	17,912	37,445	13,318	7,602
One or more room units	27,437	589	25,191	13,938	11,253	10,525	5,820	5,332	3,513	1,657
Source of water: [4]										
Public system or private company. . .	111,727	2,953	97,054	63,571	33,482	17,059	21,349	35,726	22,920	11,720
Well serving 1 to 5 units	15,623	1,135	13,249	11,752	1,497	3,250	3,880	4,683	1,436	1,239
Means of sewage disposal: [4]										
Public sewer.	101,760	2,333	88,723	56,238	32,485	16,195	20,499	30,504	21,525	10,704
Septic tank, cesspool, chemical toilet	26,121	1,841	21,927	19,382	2,546	4,189	4,787	10,077	2,875	2,353

– Represents or rounds to zero. [1] Includes trailers. Includes width not reported, not shown separately. [2] Excludes mobile homes; includes basements and finished attics. [3] Limited to single-family units. [4] Includes other items, not shown separately. [5] With and without inserts.

Source: U.S. Census Bureau, Current Housing Reports, Series H150/07, *American Housing Survey for the United States: 2007* (published September 2008). See also <http://www.census.gov/hhes/www/housing/ahs/nationaldata.html>.

602   Construction and Housing

Table 954. Housing Units by Units in Structure and State: 2007

[In percent, except as indicated (127,895 represents 127,895,000). The American Community Survey universe includes the household population and the population living in institutions, college dormitories, and other group quarters. Based on a sample and subject to sampling variability; see Appendix III]

State	Total housing units (1,000)	Percent of units by units in structure—								
		1-unit detached	1-unit attached	2 units	3 or 4 units	5 to 9 units	10 to 19 units	20 or more units	Mobile homes	Boat, RV van, etc.
U.S.....	**127,895**	**61.7**	**5.7**	**4.0**	**4.5**	**4.9**	**4.5**	**7.9**	**6.7**	**0.1**
AL	2,137	68.1	1.8	2.1	3.0	4.4	2.8	2.9	14.7	0.1
AK	282	60.5	8.0	5.0	7.3	5.8	2.5	5.7	5.1	0.1
AZ	2,668	62.8	5.0	1.5	3.4	4.5	5.3	5.9	11.1	0.5
AR	1,287	70.5	1.9	3.2	3.0	3.4	2.9	2.3	12.7	0.1
CA	13,309	58.3	7.0	2.6	5.6	6.3	5.4	10.8	4.0	0.1
CO	2,127	63.2	7.0	1.7	3.6	4.5	6.0	9.3	4.7	(Z)
CT	1,439	59.2	5.1	7.9	9.2	5.4	3.6	8.6	0.9	(Z)
DE	389	57.1	15.2	1.8	2.5	3.8	5.0	4.5	10.0	0.1
DC	284	12.1	27.2	3.2	7.5	6.4	11.0	32.4	(Z)	0.1
FL	8,717	54.1	6.1	2.3	3.8	5.1	6.1	12.2	10.1	0.1
GA	3,962	66.4	3.5	2.5	3.0	5.3	5.0	4.3	10.1	(Z)
HI	507	54.0	6.7	2.4	4.3	7.1	5.4	19.8	0.2	(Z)
ID	631	73.2	2.9	2.8	4.1	2.7	1.7	2.6	9.7	0.1
IL	5,246	58.6	5.8	6.4	6.7	6.0	4.0	9.6	2.8	(Z)
IN	2,778	72.5	3.4	2.9	3.6	4.7	3.7	3.7	5.5	(Z)
IA	1,329	74.0	3.1	2.6	3.7	4.0	3.9	4.7	4.0	(Z)
KS	1,219	73.3	4.2	2.4	3.9	3.9	3.2	4.0	5.2	(Z)
KY	1,906	68.4	2.2	3.0	3.7	4.4	3.3	2.8	12.2	(Z)
LA	1,859	66.0	2.3	3.5	4.1	3.4	2.8	3.7	14.0	0.1
ME	697	69.5	2.1	4.9	5.7	4.1	1.6	2.9	9.2	(Z)
MD	2,318	51.8	21.4	1.8	2.4	5.3	8.2	7.2	1.8	(Z)
MA	2,722	52.5	4.5	11.2	11.0	6.2	4.2	9.6	0.8	(Z)
MI	4,527	71.6	4.5	2.9	2.7	4.2	3.8	4.5	5.7	(Z)
MN	2,304	68.2	7.0	2.4	2.1	2.3	3.6	10.6	3.7	(Z)
MS	1,255	69.8	1.2	2.3	3.3	4.5	1.7	1.6	15.4	0.3
MO	2,647	70.2	3.3	3.8	4.8	4.0	3.3	3.9	6.7	(Z)
MT	436	70.3	2.4	3.3	4.8	3.4	1.9	2.7	11.1	0.1
NE	781	73.0	3.9	2.3	2.5	3.7	4.9	5.3	4.2	0.1
NV	1,102	58.9	4.6	1.3	5.9	10.0	6.3	6.0	6.8	0.2
NH	594	04.4	5.2	5.3	5.4	4.6	3.0	6.0	6.0	(Z)
NJ	3,499	53.8	9.2	9.6	6.5	5.0	5.1	9.8	1.0	(Z)
NM	862	63.3	4.0	1.8	3.7	3.1	3.0	4.1	16.8	0.1
NY	7,940	41.7	4.8	11.3	7.2	5.3	4.2	23.0	2.5	(Z)
NC	4,124	65.3	3.5	2.4	2.7	4.4	3.9	3.3	14.5	(Z)
ND	310	61.2	4.3	2.4	4.2	4.7	6.1	9.6	7.4	(Z)
OH	5,065	68.2	4.6	4.7	4.5	4.8	3.9	5.1	4.1	(Z)
OK	1,623	73.5	2.0	2.0	2.7	4.1	3.6	2.9	9.1	0.1
OR	1,610	64.2	4.0	3.1	4.2	4.7	3.9	7.0	8.6	0.3
PA	5,478	56.8	18.4	4.9	4.3	3.4	2.6	5.2	4.4	(Z)
RI	451	55.0	3.5	12.4	13.4	4.7	3.1	6.9	0.9	0.1
SC	2,022	62.5	2.2	2.5	3.0	4.9	3.3	3.3	18.2	(Z)
SD	356	69.0	2.8	2.4	3.2	3.4	3.6	5.9	9.7	(Z)
TN	2,725	68.5	3.2	3.0	3.4	4.4	4.1	3.3	10.2	0.1
TX	9,433	65.7	2.6	2.1	3.3	5.0	6.6	7.0	7.7	0.1
UT	925	69.7	5.4	2.9	4.9	3.9	4.0	5.2	3.9	0.1
VT	311	67.7	3.3	6.2	6.3	4.7	2.0	2.6	7.2	(Z)
VA	3,273	63.2	10.1	1.7	2.7	4.4	5.9	6.1	5.7	(Z)
WA	2,744	63.5	3.4	2.8	3.8	4.5	5.6	8.9	7.4	0.2
WV	883	71.0	1.9	2.3	2.9	2.9	1.6	2.3	15.1	(Z)
WI	2,558	66.5	4.3	7.1	3.8	4.6	3.5	6.4	3.9	(Z)
WY	242	65.9	3.8	2.7	5.3	3.1	2.2	2.2	14.7	0.1

Z Less than .05 percent.

Source: U.S. Census Bureau, 2007 American Community Survey, "Table B25024, Units in Structure"; using American FactFinder; <http://factfinder.census.gov/> (accessed March 2009).

Construction and Housing   603

Table 955. Housing Units—Size of Units and Lot: 2007

[In thousands (128,203 represents 128,203,000), except as indicated. As of fall. Based on the American Housing Survey; see Appendix III. For composition of regions, see map inside front cover]

Item	Total housing units	Sea-sonal	Year-round units Occupied Total	Owner	Renter	North-east	Mid-west	South	West	Vacant
Total units	128,203	4,402	110,692	75,647	35,045	20,392	25,292	40,609	24,400	13,109
Rooms:										
1 room	689	111	420	51	370	104	53	56	207	159
2 rooms	1,385	157	943	66	877	256	143	254	289	285
3 rooms	11,050	519	8,837	992	7,845	2,196	1,841	2,486	2,314	1,694
4 rooms	23,290	1,440	18,330	6,666	11,664	3,315	4,121	6,594	4,300	3,520
5 rooms	29,186	1,158	24,773	16,817	7,956	3,883	5,754	9,824	5,312	3,255
6 rooms	27,146	497	24,362	20,392	3,970	4,434	5,544	9,547	4,837	2,286
7 rooms	17,631	320	16,265	14,772	1,493	3,020	3,837	6,001	3,407	1,046
8 rooms or more	17,825	200	16,763	15,892	871	3,184	3,998	5,847	3,734	1,046
Complete bathrooms:										
No bathrooms	1,753	539	493	189	304	140	91	164	98	721
1 bathroom	47,694	1,801	39,771	16,268	23,503	9,523	10,199	12,017	8,033	6,122
1 and one-half bathrooms	17,150	361	15,465	11,964	3,500	3895	4796	4,125	2,649	1,324
2 or more bathrooms	61,606	1,700	54,963	47,226	7,737	6,833	10,206	24,303	13,621	4,942
Square footage of unit:										
Single detached and mobile homes	89,111	3,384	78,354	67,931	10,423	11,658	18,807	31,138	16,750	7,373
Less than 500	1,004	232	630	361	269	91	89	289	161	143
500 to 749	2,725	510	1,821	1,108	712	229	389	868	335	394
750 to 999	6,443	602	5,071	3,605	1,466	632	1,346	2,075	1,017	770
1,000 to 1,499	20,725	711	18,169	14,864	3,305	2,050	4,270	7,610	4,239	1,845
1,500 to 1,999	20,061	457	18,192	16,220	1,973	2,428	4,098	7,279	4,387	1,412
2,000 to 2,499	13,960	260	12,870	11,957	914	2,028	3,278	4,868	2,696	830
2,500 to 2,999	7,320	108	6,757	6,438	320	1,207	1,602	2,622	1,326	455
3,000 to 3,999	6,845	103	6,300	6,028	271	1,187	1,660	2,138	1,315	442
4,000 or more	4,285	68	3,920	3,708	212	782	964	1,468	707	297
Other [1]	5,742	334	4,624	3,642	981	1,023	1,111	1,921	568	785
Median square footage	1,769	1,128	1,807	1,876	1,344	1,977	1,836	1,759	1,767	1,550
Lot size:										
Single detached and attached units and mobile homes	93,208	3,388	82,031	69,921	12,110	12,999	19,331	32,391	17,311	7,789
Less than one-eighth acre	13,614	585	11,397	8,779	2,618	2,205	2,619	3,296	3,277	1,631
One-eighth to one-quarter acre	25,775	836	22,758	18,782	3,976	2,717	5,470	7,607	6,963	2,182
One-quarter to one-half acre	17,703	477	16,053	14,077	1,975	2,399	4,047	6,394	3,212	1,174
One-half up to one acre	11,216	368	9,995	8,891	1,104	1,905	2,039	4,813	1,238	853
1 up to 5 acres	17,713	696	15,670	13,783	1,886	2,828	3,295	7,777	1,769	1,348
5 up to 10 acres	2,785	119	2,492	2,323	169	392	670	1,071	359	174
10 acres or more	4,402	308	3,668	3,285	382	552	1,191	1,432	493	426
Median acreage	0.35	0.39	0.36	0.38	0.23	0.41	0.35	0.46	0.22	0.27

[1] Represents units not reported or size unknown.

Source: U.S. Census Bureau, Current Housing Reports, Series H150/07, American Housing Survey for the United States: 2007 (published September 2008). See also <http://www.census.gov/hhes/www/housing/ahs/nationaldata.html>.

Table 956. Occupied Housing Units—Tenure by Race of Householder: 1991 to 2007

[In thousands (93,147 represents 93,147,000), except percent. As of fall. Based on the American Housing Survey; see Appendix III]

Race of householder and tenure	1991	1995	1997	1999	2001	2003 [1]	2005	2007
ALL RACES [2]								
Occupied units, total	93,147	97,693	99,487	102,803	106,261	105,842	108,871	110,692
Owner-occupied	59,796	63,544	65,487	68,796	72,265	72,238	74,931	75,647
Percent of occupied	64.2	65.0	65.8	66.9	68.0	68.3	68.8	68.3
Renter-occupied	33,351	34,150	34,000	34,007	33,996	33,604	33,940	35,045
WHITE [3]								
Occupied units, total	79,140	81,611	82,154	83,624	85,292	87,483	89,449	90,413
Owner-occupied	53,749	56,507	57,781	60,041	62,465	63,126	65,023	65,554
Percent of occupied	67.9	69.2	70.3	71.8	73.2	72.2	72.7	72.5
Renter-occupied	25,391	25,104	24,372	23,583	22,826	24,357	24,426	24,859
BLACK [3]								
Occupied units, total	10,832	11,773	12,085	12,936	13,292	13,004	13,447	13,856
Owner-occupied	4,635	5,137	5,457	6,013	6,318	6,193	6,471	6,464
Percent of occupied	42.8	43.6	45.2	46.5	47.5	47.6	48.1	46.7
Renter-occupied	6,197	6,637	6,628	6,923	6,974	6,811	6,975	7,392
HISPANIC ORIGIN [4]								
Occupied units, total	6,239	7,757	8,513	9,041	9,814	11,038	11,651	12,609
Owner-occupied	2,423	3,245	3,646	4,087	4,731	5,106	5,752	6,364
Percent of occupied	38.8	41.8	42.8	45.2	48.2	46.3	49.4	50.5
Renter-occupied	3,816	4,512	4,867	4,955	5,083	5,931	5,899	6,244

[1] Based on 2000 census controls. [2] Includes other races not shown separately. [3] The 2003 American Housing Survey (AHS) allowed respondents to choose more than one race. Beginning in 2003, data represent householders who selected this race group only and exclude householders reporting more than one race. The AHS in prior years only allowed respondents to report one race group. See also comments on race in the text for Section 1 and the below cited source. [4] Persons of Hispanic origin may be any race.

Source: U.S. Census Bureau, Current Housing Reports, Series H150/91, H150/93, H150/95RV, H150/97, H150/99, H150/01, H150/03, H150/05, and H150/07, American Housing Survey for the United States. See also <http://www.census.gov/hhes/www/housing/ahs/nationaldata.html>.

Table 957. **Homeownership Rates by Age of Householder and Household Type: 1990 to 2008**

[In percent. Represents the proportion of owner households to the total number of occupied households. Based on the Current Population Survey/Housing Vacancy Survey; see source and Appendix III for details]

Age of householder and household type	1990	1995	2000	2002	2003	2004	2005	2006	2007	2008
United States.	**63.9**	**64.7**	**67.4**	**67.9**	**68.3**	**69.0**	**68.9**	**68.8**	**68.1**	**67.8**
AGE OF HOUSEHOLDER										
Less than 25 years old	15.7	15.9	21.7	22.9	22.8	25.2	25.7	24.8	24.8	23.6
25 to 29 years old	35.2	34.4	38.1	38.8	39.8	40.2	40.9	41.8	40.6	40.0
30 to 34 years old	51.8	53.1	54.6	54.9	56.5	57.4	56.8	55.9	54.4	53.5
35 to 39 years old	63.0	62.1	65.0	65.2	65.1	66.2	66.6	66.4	65.0	64.6
40 to 44 years old	69.8	68.6	70.6	71.7	71.3	71.9	71.7	71.2	70.4	69.4
45 to 49 years old	73.9	73.7	74.7	74.8	75.4	76.3	75.0	74.9	74.0	73.6
50 to 54 years old	76.8	77.0	78.5	77.9	77.9	78.2	78.3	77.7	76.9	76.4
55 to 59 years old	78.8	78.8	80.4	80.8	80.9	81.2	80.6	80.4	79.9	79.4
60 to 64 years old	79.8	80.3	80.3	81.6	81.9	82.4	81.9	81.5	81.5	80.9
65 to 69 years old	80.0	81.0	83.0	82.9	82.5	83.2	82.8	82.4	81.7	81.6
70 to 74 years old	78.4	80.9	82.6	82.5	82.0	84.4	82.9	83.0	82.4	81.7
75 years old and over.	72.3	74.6	77.7	78.4	78.7	78.8	78.4	79.1	78.7	78.6
Less than 35 years old	38.5	38.6	40.8	41.3	42.2	43.1	43.0	42.6	41.7	41.0
35 to 44 years old	66.3	65.2	67.9	68.6	68.3	69.2	69.3	68.9	67.8	67.0
45 to 54 years old	75.2	75.2	76.5	76.3	76.6	77.2	76.6	76.2	75.4	75.0
55 to 64 years old	79.3	79.5	80.3	81.1	81.4	81.9	81.2	80.9	80.6	80.1
65 years and over	76.3	78.1	80.4	80.6	80.5	81.1	80.6	80.9	80.4	80.1
TYPE OF HOUSEHOLD										
Family households:										
Married-couple families . . .	78.1	79.6	82.4	82.9	83.3	84.0	84.2	84.1	83.8	83.4
Male householder, no spouse present.	55.2	55.3	57.5	57.3	57.9	59.6	59.1	58.9	57.4	57.6
Female householder, no spouse present.	44.0	45.1	49.1	49.2	49.6	50.9	51.0	51.3	49.9	49.5
Nonfamily households:										
One-person	49.0	50.5	53.6	54.9	55.2	55.8	55.6	55.7	55.2	55.0
Male householder	42.4	43.8	47.4	48.6	50.0	50.5	50.3	50.5	50.2	50.6
Female householder . . .	53.6	55.4	58.1	59.6	59.1	59.9	59.6	59.8	59.1	58.6
Other:										
Male householder	31.7	34.2	38.0	38.7	40.0	41.7	41.7	40.8	40.0	41.3
Female householder . . .	32.5	33.0	40.6	41.9	43.1	43.5	44.8	45.5	42.9	42.5

Source: U.S. Census Bureau, "Housing Vacancies and Home Ownership"; <http://www.census.gov/hhes/www/hvs.html>.

Table 958. **Homeownership Rates by State: 1990 to 2008**

[In percent. See headnote, Table 957]

State	1990	2000	2005	2006	2007	2008	State	1990	2000	2005	2006	2007	2008
United States .	**63.9**	**67.4**	**68.9**	**68.8**	**68.1**	**67.8**	Missouri	64.0	74.2	72.3	71.9	70.4	71.4
Alabama	68.4	73.2	76.6	74.2	73.3	73.0	Montana	69.1	70.2	70.4	69.5	67.3	70.3
Alaska	58.4	66.4	66.0	67.2	66.6	66.4	Nebraska	67.3	70.2	70.2	67.6	68.2	69.6
Arizona	64.5	68.0	71.1	71.6	70.4	69.1	Nevada.	55.8	64.0	63.4	65.7	63.3	63.6
Arkansas.	67.8	68.9	69.2	70.8	69.5	68.9	New Hampshire . . .	65.0	69.2	74.0	74.2	73.8	75.0
California.	53.8	57.1	59.7	60.2	58.3	57.5	New Jersey	65.0	66.2	70.1	69.0	68.3	67.3
Colorado	59.0	68.3	71.0	70.1	70.2	69.0	New Mexico.	68.6	73.7	71.4	72.0	71.5	70.4
Connecticut	67.9	70.0	70.5	71.1	70.3	70.7	New York	53.3	53.4	55.9	55.7	55.9	55.0
Delaware.	67.7	72.0	75.8	76.8	76.8	76.2	North Carolina	69.0	71.1	70.9	70.2	70.3	69.4
Dist. of Columbia . . .	36.4	41.9	45.8	45.9	47.2	44.1	North Dakota	67.2	70.7	68.5	68.3	66.0	66.6
Florida	65.1	68.4	72.4	72.4	71.8	71.1	Ohio	68.7	71.3	73.3	72.1	71.4	70.8
Georgia	64.3	69.8	67.9	68.5	67.6	68.2	Oklahoma	70.3	72.7	72.9	71.6	70.3	70.4
Hawaii	55.5	55.2	59.8	59.9	60.1	59.1	Oregon	64.4	65.3	68.2	68.1	65.7	66.2
Idaho	69.4	70.5	74.2	75.1	74.5	75.0	Pennsylvania	73.8	74.7	73.3	73.2	72.9	72.6
Illinois	63.0	67.9	70.9	70.4	69.4	68.9	Rhode Island	58.5	61.5	63.1	64.6	64.9	64.5
Indiana	67.0	74.9	75.0	74.2	73.8	74.4	South Carolina	71.4	76.5	73.9	74.2	74.1	73.9
Iowa	70.7	75.2	73.9	74.0	73.7	74.0	South Dakota	66.2	71.2	68.4	70.6	70.4	70.4
Kansas	69.0	69.3	69.5	70.0	69.4	68.8	Tennessee.	68.3	70.9	72.4	71.3	70.2	71.7
Kentucky.	65.8	73.4	71.6	71.7	72.9	72.8	Texas	59.7	63.8	65.9	66.0	66.0	65.5
Louisiana	67.8	68.1	72.5	71.3	71.5	73.5	Utah	70.1	72.7	73.9	73.5	74.9	76.2
Maine	74.2	76.5	73.9	75.3	74.3	73.9	Vermont	72.6	68.7	74.2	74.0	73.7	72.8
Maryland	64.9	69.9	71.2	72.6	71.7	70.6	Virginia	69.8	73.9	71.2	71.1	71.5	70.6
Massachusetts	58.6	59.9	63.4	65.2	64.3	65.7	Washington	61.8	63.6	67.6	66.7	66.8	66.2
Michigan	72.3	77.2	76.4	77.4	76.4	75.9	West Virginia	72.0	75.9	81.3	78.4	77.6	77.8
Minnesota	68.0	76.1	76.5	75.6	73.5	73.1	Wisconsin	68.3	71.8	71.1	70.2	70.5	70.4
Mississippi.	69.4	75.2	78.8	76.2	74.0	75.4	Wyoming.	68.9	71.0	72.8	73.7	73.2	73.3

Source: U.S. Census Bureau, "Housing Vacancies and Home Ownership"; <http://www.census.gov/hhes/www/hvs.html>.

Construction and Housing   605

Table 959. **Occupied Housing Units—Costs by Region: 2007**

[75,647 represents 75,647,000. As of fall. See headnote, Table 960, for an explanation of housing costs. Based on the American Housing Survey; see Appendix III. For composition of regions, see map inside front cover]

Category	Number (1,000)					Percent distribution				
	Total units	North-east	Mid-west	South	West	Total units	North-east	Mid-west	South	West
OWNER-OCCUPIED UNITS										
Total	75,647	13,339	18,194	28,508	15,607	100.0	100.0	100.0	100.0	100.0
Monthly housing costs:										
Less than $300	9,613	722	1,986	5,080	1,823	12.7	5.4	10.9	17.8	11.7
$300 to $399	6,383	829	1,752	2,785	1,017	8.4	6.2	9.6	9.8	6.5
$400 to $499	5,387	906	1,577	1,989	913	7.1	6.8	8.7	7.0	5.8
$500 to $599	4,394	892	1,208	1,635	659	5.8	6.7	6.6	5.7	4.2
$600 to $699	3,912	828	996	1,563	526	5.2	6.2	5.5	5.5	3.4
$700 to $799	3,701	777	997	1,488	439	4.9	5.8	5.5	5.2	2.8
$800 to $999	6,992	1,231	1,994	2,703	1,064	9.2	9.2	11.0	9.5	6.8
$1,000 to $1,249	7,766	1,301	2,250	3,038	1,177	10.3	9.8	12.4	10.7	7.5
$1,250 to $1,499	6,501	1,128	1,858	2,178	1,336	8.6	8.5	10.2	7.6	8.6
$1,500 or more	20,999	4,723	3,575	6,048	6,653	27.8	35.4	19.6	21.2	42.6
Median (dol.) [1]	927	1,093	858	781	1,285	(X)	(X)	(X)	(X)	(X)
RENTER-OCCUPIED UNITS										
Total	35,045	7,052	7,097	12,101	8,794	100.0	100.0	100.0	100.0	100.0
Monthly housing costs:										
Less than $300	2,649	655	666	875	454	7.6	9.3	9.4	7.2	5.2
$300 to $399	1,552	278	393	614	266	4.4	3.9	5.5	5.1	3.0
$400 to $499	2,689	490	797	942	460	7.7	6.9	11.2	7.8	5.2
$500 to $599	3,416	559	910	1,335	611	9.7	7.9	12.8	11.0	6.9
$600 to $699	4,002	643	1,041	1,582	736	11.4	9.1	14.7	13.1	8.4
$700 to $799	3,711	624	806	1,352	928	10.6	8.8	11.4	11.2	10.6
$800 to $999	5,902	1,303	1,091	1,934	1,574	16.8	18.5	15.4	16.0	17.9
$1,000 to $1,249	4,090	976	508	1,274	1,333	11.7	13.8	7.2	10.5	15.2
$1,250 to $1,499	2,095	477	180	587	850	6.0	6.8	2.5	4.9	9.7
$1,500 or more	2,578	667	216	541	1,154	7.4	9.5	3.0	4.5	13.1
No cash rent	2,361	380	490	1,064	427	6.7	5.4	6.9	8.8	4.9
Median (dol.) [1]	755	813	652	713	893	(X)	(X)	(X)	(X)	(X)

X Not applicable. [1] For explanation of median, see Guide to Tabular Presentation.

Source: U.S. Census Bureau, Current Housing Reports, Series H150/05, *American Housing Survey for the United States:*
2007 (published September 2008). See also <http://www.census.gov/hhes/www/housing/ahs/nationaldata.html>.

Table 960. **Occupied Housing Units—Financial Summary by Selected Characteristics of the Householder: 2007**

[In thousands of units (110,692 represents 110,692,000), except as indicated. As of fall. Housing costs include real estate taxes, property insurance, utilities, fuel, water, garbage collection, homeowner association fees, mobile home fees, and mortgage. Based on the American Housing Survey; see Appendix III]

Characteristic	Total occu-pied units	Tenure		Black [1]		Hispanic origin [2]		Elderly [3]		Households below poverty level	
		Owner	Renter	Owner	Renter	Owner	Renter	Owner	Renter	Owner	Renter
Total units [4]	110,692	75,647	35,045	6,464	7,392	6,364	6,244	18,271	4,594	5,566	8,591
Monthly housing costs:											
Less than $300	12,263	9,613	2,649	976	810	763	368	4,503	822	1,824	1,813
$300 to $399	7,935	6,383	1,552	590	399	479	198	2,959	304	769	704
$400 to $499	8,076	5,387	2,689	452	541	334	402	2,448	521	551	876
$500 to $599	7,809	4,394	3,416	393	707	353	593	1,571	392	370	845
$600 to $699	7,914	3,912	4,002	390	884	253	712	1,197	384	244	865
$700 to $799	7,411	3,701	3,711	339	872	232	764	915	357	302	743
$800 to $999	12,894	6,992	5,902	696	1,305	527	1,209	1,348	548	397	977
$1,000 or more	44,028	35,266	8,763	2,629	1,419	3,424	1,753	3,332	805	1,111	959
Median amount (dol.) [5]	843	927	755	827	715	1097	795	464	607	430	559
Monthly housing costs as percent of income: [6]											
Less than 5 percent	3,767	3,557	210	265	32	229	18	702	34	18	19
5 to 9 percent	11,430	10,483	947	671	150	651	120	2,893	95	59	29
10 to 14 percent	13,684	11,471	2,213	858	382	723	303	3,102	145	101	84
15 to 19 percent	14,357	11,132	3,225	793	525	753	509	2,573	198	248	105
20 to 24 percent	12,787	9,312	3,476	716	654	684	586	1,793	242	219	162
25 to 29 percent	10,455	6,736	3,719	595	844	560	649	1,379	521	229	431
30 to 34 percent	7,918	4,822	3,096	405	698	506	577	939	403	225	362
35 to 39 percent	6,116	3,657	2,459	395	579	380	523	836	372	225	340
40 percent or more	25,998	13,727	12,271	1,653	2,769	1,812	2,562	3,938	2,058	3,535	5,332
Median amount (percent) [5] . .	24	20	33	24	35	26	37	20	41	82	79

[1] For persons who selected this race group only. See footnote 3, Table 956.   [2] Persons of Hispanic origin may be any race.
[3] Householders 65 years old and over.   [4] Includes units with no cash rent not shown separately.   [5] For explanation of median,
see Guide to Tabular Presentation.   [6] Money income before taxes.

Source: U.S. Census Bureau, Current Housing Reports, Series H150/07, *American Housing Survey for the United States:*
2007 (published September 2008). See also <http://www.census.gov/hhes/www/housing/ahs/nationaldata.html>.

Table 961. **Owner-Occupied Housing Units—Value and Costs by State: 2007**

[In percent, except as indicated (75,515 represents 75,515,000). The American Community Survey universe includes the household population and the population living in institutions, college dormitories, and other group quarters. Based on a sample and subject to sampling variability; see Appendix III. For definition of median, see Guide to Tabular Presentation]

State	Total (1,000)	Percent of units with value of— $99,999 or less	$100,000 to $199,999	$200,000 or more	Median value (dol.)	Median selected monthly owner costs [1] (dol.)	Selected monthly owner costs as a percent of household income in the past 12 months [1] Less than 15 percent	15.0 to 24.9 percent	25.0 to 29.9 percent	30 percent or more
U.S. ...	75,515	22.1	29.2	48.6	194,300	1,464	17.0	32.6	12.4	37.5
AL......	1,288	43.3	34.4	22.3	115,600	1,049	23.5	36.3	10.6	29.1
AK......	149	12.5	26.4	61.1	231,300	1,711	17.6	35.1	12.3	34.9
AZ......	1,533	13.4	23.3	63.4	237,700	1,464	16.3	31.2	12.6	39.5
AR......	747	49.6	33.2	17.3	101,000	920	27.1	36.2	10.0	26.5
CA......	7,077	4.8	4.5	90.6	532,300	2,314	11.0	23.7	11.9	53.0
CO......	1,280	8.4	28.5	63.1	233,900	1,569	15.6	32.2	14.0	37.9
CT......	925	2.9	18.3	78.8	309,200	1,971	14.2	31.6	13.7	40.3
DE......	238	10.1	25.3	64.7	239,700	1,478	18.5	31.5	13.4	35.9
DC	112	1.3	7.8	90.8	450,900	2,094	19.7	29.5	11.9	38.7
FL......	5,006	13.7	27.0	59.3	230,400	1,577	12.2	26.2	12.0	48.9
GA	2,342	22.3	40.6	37.1	164,500	1,343	18.6	34.5	11.9	34.6
HI	262	2.4	5.3	92.3	555,400	2,099	13.4	27.5	12.8	45.8
ID	404	17.7	39.6	42.7	178,100	1,162	18.5	35.7	12.1	33.1
IL	3,335	19.4	28.2	52.4	208,800	1,625	15.3	32.6	13.0	38.7
IN	1,764	36.3	44.7	19.1	122,900	1,098	22.4	38.5	12.1	26.9
IA	895	40.1	41.1	18.8	117,900	1,100	22.7	40.2	11.6	25.3
KS......	764	40.8	37.6	21.6	121,200	1,169	22.6	39.2	12.5	25.7
KY......	1,171	42.8	37.7	19.5	114,300	1,021	23.9	37.8	11.0	27.0
LA......	1,085	39.0	36.7	24.2	126,800	1,074	26.8	32.9	10.2	29.6
ME	402	22.5	34.8	42.6	176,000	1,249	17.9	33.8	12.6	35.4
MD	1,456	5.8	13.8	80.4	347,000	1,881	16.4	32.2	13.1	37.9
MA	1,594	2.0	10.6	87.4	366,400	2,021	14.0	30.7	13.8	41.3
MI	2,880	24.2	44.7	31.1	153,100	1,332	16.1	34.2	13.1	36.3
MN	1,552	13.3	31.3	55.5	213,600	1,500	16.7	34.9	13.6	34.6
MS	770	52.1	31.6	16.3	96,000	956	21.3	34.2	11.3	32.6
MO	1,632	31.9	41.5	26.6	138,600	1,152	21.3	36.8	12.4	29.1
MT	259	24.8	35.0	40.2	170,000	1,141	19.7	34.9	11.5	33.6
NE......	481	36.7	43.9	19.4	122,200	1,199	20.0	38.6	13.5	26.9
NV......	576	7.9	12.5	79.7	311,300	1,779	11.1	27.5	12.1	49.0
NH	372	8.0	20.9	71.2	261,800	1,830	12.5	32.0	14.8	40.5
NJ......	2,119	4.0	11.4	84.6	372,300	2,278	12.4	27.6	13.6	46.1
NM	514	30.4	34.4	35.2	155,400	1,130	21.2	33.1	11.3	34.0
NY......	3,942	18.9	19.6	61.6	311,000	1,865	16.9	29.7	11.6	41.5
NC......	2,418	29.6	39.1	31.3	145,700	1,189	20.9	35.6	12.1	30.7
ND	179	46.8	38.2	15.0	106,800	1,093	26.0	39.9	12.5	21.4
OH	3,140	28.8	46.5	24.7	137,800	1,242	18.2	37.8	13.1	30.7
OK	955	48.5	36.3	15.2	103,000	1,015	24.8	37.8	10.9	26.2
OR	951	9.3	21.5	69.2	257,300	1,508	13.7	31.8	13.2	40.8
PA......	3,491	29.4	34.5	36.2	155,000	1,324	18.5	35.5	12.7	32.9
RI	256	2.1	12.0	85.9	292,800	1,788	12.8	30.0	14.2	42.3
SC......	1,192	36.1	35.4	28.5	133,900	1,117	22.0	35.1	11.0	31.3
SD......	213	40.9	39.0	20.0	118,700	1,104	19.8	41.6	12.8	25.8
TN......	1,684	34.8	40.1	25.0	130,800	1,105	19.6	36.9	11.6	31.5
TX......	5,374	39.4	38.9	21.7	120,900	1,342	19.4	36.1	12.2	31.9
UT......	599	7.8	35.4	56.8	218,700	1,358	17.5	34.4	14.4	33.5
VT......	184	13.2	34.9	51.9	205,400	1,391	16.1	31.8	12.5	39.5
VA......	2,038	13.6	23.2	63.2	262,100	1,655	17.7	33.5	13.1	35.5
WA	1,653	7.8	18.4	73.8	300,800	1,675	13.5	31.7	14.1	40.6
WV	549	52.3	30.9	16.8	96,000	881	27.9	36.7	9.4	25.5
WI......	1,571	17.0	45.8	37.2	168,800	1,374	15.2	37.0	14.1	33.5
WY	143	21.4	38.5	40.1	172,300	1,162	28.2	36.8	10.5	24.4

[1] For homes with a mortgage. Includes all forms of debt where the property is pledged as security for repayment of the debt, including deeds of trust, land contracts, home equity loans. Also includes cost of property insurance, utilities, real estate taxes, etc.

Source: U.S. Census Bureau, 2007 American Community Survey, Tables B25075. Value for Owner-Occupied Housing Units; B25077. Median Value for Owner-Occupied Housing Units; B25088. Median Selected Monthly Owner Costs by Mortgage Status; B25091. Mortgage Status by Selected Monthly Owner Cost as a Percentage of Household Income; using American FactFinder; <http://factfinder.census.gov/> (accessed May 17, 2008).

U.S. Census Bureau, Statistical Abstract of the United States: 2010

Table 962. **Renter-Occupied Housing Units—Gross Rent by State: 2007**

[In percent, except as indicated (36,863 represents 36,863,000. The American Community Survey universe includes the household population and the population living in institutions, college dormitories, and other group quarters. Based on a sample and subject to sampling variability; see Appendix III]

State	Total [1] (1,000)	Percent of units with gross rent of— $299 or less	$300 to $499	$500 to $749	$750 to $999	$1,000 or more	Median gross rent (dol.)	Gross rent as a percent of household income in the past 12 months Less than 15 percent	15.0 to 24.9 percent	25.0 to 29.9 percent	30 percent or more
U.S. ...	36,863	6.0	11.1	25.9	22.6	28.5	789	12.1	24.0	10.8	45.6
AL	528	9.5	19.7	32.4	16.9	8.0	601	12.4	21.9	9.5	40.6
AK	87	3.0	7.0	19.2	22.8	36.5	918	15.3	26.0	9.5	37.2
AZ	718	3.3	8.0	27.6	26.2	30.0	819	11.3	24.5	10.9	46.8
AR	356	9.2	23.3	35.2	15.3	5.7	573	13.2	22.5	10.4	41.6
CA	5,124	3.0	4.4	13.0	22.2	54.0	1,078	9.9	22.7	11.4	51.2
CO	580	4.7	8.2	30.4	25.3	27.3	788	11.8	24.8	11.1	46.2
CT	396	6.3	6.9	15.4	26.4	40.4	931	11.9	23.7	11.2	47.5
DE	90	5.2	5.0	17.6	27.5	36.9	910	8.7	23.6	11.9	46.5
DC	139	8.0	5.8	19.2	20.3	43.6	934	12.7	24.6	11.5	45.8
FL.	2,083	3.8	5.2	18.5	28.0	39.5	925	7.9	21.6	11.2	52.7
GA	1,075	5.6	11.1	27.8	28.1	20.8	768	11.9	24.2	10.5	44.8
HI.	178	4.3	4.5	8.3	16.9	58.1	1,194	9.2	21.7	11.3	47.9
ID.	157	6.9	16.9	36.3	18.7	13.2	654	14.3	27.6	10.5	38.8
IL.	1,425	6.0	10.2	27.3	27.2	24.9	783	12.3	24.1	10.5	46.6
IN	699	7.4	17.3	39.1	20.6	9.4	638	14.2	26.2	10.1	41.8
IA	320	8.3	26.4	36.3	13.3	7.2	567	16.5	25.4	10.4	38.4
KS	325	7.8	21.0	34.2	18.5	11.1	623	14.9	27.7	10.4	37.8
KY	485	10.8	23.7	34.9	15.0	5.7	563	15.7	22.5	10.9	39.5
LA	512	7.6	16.0	31.1	19.4	12.1	651	13.1	19.3	8.5	42.4
ME	142	13.2	13.9	31.6	20.2	13.2	650	11.7	24.1	13.7	42.1
MD	626	5.4	5.1	13.3	23.9	47.7	1,000	11.4	24.7	11.8	46.3
MA	855	9.5	8.3	14.0	20.9	43.4	946	10.9	23.9	12.8	47.2
MI.	969	7.6	13.6	35.2	21.8	15.6	683	11.6	22.0	10.2	48.0
MN	511	8.4	12.9	31.5	22.1	20.1	711	11.6	26.5	11.7	43.9
MS	310	10.1	17.8	31.2	17.6	8.2	609	11.2	21.0	8.3	42.4
MO	678	8.7	19.6	36.3	18.3	10.0	618	13.9	24.1	10.6	42.9
MT	113	9.7	22.8	32.2	15.8	9.0	579	15.3	26.8	9.2	36.4
NE	219	7.7	21.2	35.5	16.5	10.9	614	15.0	27.0	10.8	38.3
NV	378	1.7	4.2	16.8	27.8	46.2	980	9.8	25.5	12.2	47.7
NH	130	7.1	6.0	17.1	30.0	35.9	892	10.9	29.1	13.2	42.2
NJ	1,031	5.3	4.4	11.0	25.2	50.7	1,026	11.4	23.6	11.2	48.5
NM	220	6.8	18.3	34.0	17.4	14.0	637	14.0	23.1	9.9	42.1
NY	3,158	6.5	8.6	19.7	21.0	40.3	907	13.8	22.8	10.4	47.6
NC	1,123	6.2	14.6	35.4	22.9	12.6	678	13.2	24.7	9.5	42.7
ND	93	12.7	29.7	34.1	9.4	6.0	516	21.1	22.4	10.1	36.9
OH	1,366	8.1	17.4	37.7	20.9	10.2	643	13.1	24.0	10.0	45.1
OK	445	7.0	21.8	37.2	15.9	7.6	588	15.2	23.8	10.0	38.8
OR	521	4.1	10.0	34.7	26.4	20.1	743	11.9	26.0	11.0	45.1
PA	1,382	8.0	15.6	30.7	22.3	17.0	685	13.2	24.5	11.1	43.3
RI.	147	11.1	8.2	20.4	29.2	27.3	830	12.1	21.9	13.2	47.1
SC	510	6.8	15.9	33.1	20.6	11.6	645	12.5	23.0	10.9	39.2
SD	100	11.1	29.8	30.8	11.4	5.6	526	16.6	25.4	11.8	34.4
TN	724	8.4	17.2	36.1	19.0	10.1	634	12.7	25.4	10.1	40.8
TX	2,870	4.4	11.0	33.4	25.5	19.0	734	12.4	25.2	10.4	43.5
UT	236	4.7	9.9	35.1	24.6	20.2	733	14.9	27.6	11.6	39.4
VT	69	8.1	8.1	29.4	25.6	21.4	756	10.2	23.5	13.0	45.0
VA	894	5.4	8.7	19.6	21.8	38.1	892	12.7	26.2	10.7	42.7
WA	849	5.0	8.6	25.9	26.6	29.9	816	11.6	26.7	11.8	44.8
WV	184	12.8	25.2	30.8	9.8	4.7	525	14.2	21.2	9.1	36.5
WI.	671	6.3	14.6	38.7	23.0	12.8	673	13.4	27.4	11.6	41.8
WY	63	8.0	17.6	33.4	18.7	11.8	636	21.8	29.2	10.2	28.3

[1] Includes units with no cash rent.

Source: U.S. Census Bureau, 2007 American Community Survey, Tables B25063. Gross Rent; B25064. Median Gross Rent; B25070. Gross Rent as a Percentage of Household Income; using American FactFinder; <http://factfinder.census.gov/> (accessed 17 May 2009).

Table 963. Mortgage Characteristics—Owner-Occupied Units: 2007

[In thousands (75,647 represents 75,647,000). As of fall. Based on the American Housing Survey; see Appendix III]

Mortgage characteristic	Total owner-occupied units	Housing unit characteristics — New construction[1]	Housing unit characteristics — Mobile homes	Household characteristics — Black[2]	Household characteristics — Hispanic[3]	Household characteristics — Elderly[4]	Household characteristics — Moved in past year	Household characteristics — Below poverty level
ALL OWNERS								
Total	75,647	4,710	5,419	6,464	6,364	18,271	5,501	5,566
Mortgages currently on property:								
None, owned free and clear.........	24,885	716	3,161	2,021	1,691	12,467	951	3,191
Regular and home equity mortgages....	48,742	3,884	2,129	4,216	4,511	5,281	4,423	2,152
Regular mortgage...............	45,156	3,801	2,034	3,953	4,340	4,162	4,345	1,989
Home equity lump sum mortage	4,148	241	66	303	290	464	200	129
Home equity line of credit.........	9,818	554	132	513	613	1,464	368	243
Not reported	1,861	111	127	214	139	376	127	202
Number of regular and home equity mortgages:[5]								
1 mortgage..................	32,963	2,619	1,830	3,172	3,201	3,856	3,210	1,534
2 mortgages	11,741	969	119	684	994	781	883	218
3 mortgages or more	847	71	3	62	85	67	76	20
Type of mortgage:								
Regular and home equity lump sum [5] ...	2,843	211	26	173	238	167	166	51
With home equity line of credit	446	28	-	18	26	43	33	7
No home equity line of credit	2,377	180	26	153	208	124	133	44
Regular no home equity lump sum [5]	42,313	3,590	2,008	3,780	4,102	3,996	4,179	1,938
With home equity line of credit	6,845	470	74	332	460	541	289	140
No home equity line of credit	32,399	2,908	1,760	3,163	3,424	2,902	3,644	1,425
Home equity lump sum no regular [5] ...	1,305	30	39	129	53	298	35	78
With home equity line of credit	246	3	3	30	9	58	3	11
No home equity line of credit	1,038	26	36	94	44	234	29	67
No regular or home equity lump sum [5]...	29,186	879	3,346	2,381	1,972	13,811	1,121	3,499
With home equity line of credit	2,281	53	56	134	119	821	43	86
No home equity line of credit	25,044	716	3,164	2,033	1,715	12,613	951	3,212
OWNERS WITH ONE OR MORE REGULAR OR LUMP SUM HOME EQUITY MORTGAGES								
Total [5]	46,461	3,831	2,073	4,083	4,392	4,460	4,380	2,067
Type of primary mortgage:								
FHA	4,649	385	101	792	654	279	518	186
VA........................	3,295	266	81	285	260	363	368	125
RHS/RD [6]...................	426	54	42	51	37	39	45	57
Other types.................	34,585	2,895	1,631	2,592	3,176	3,164	3,162	1,288
Mortgage origination:								
Placed new mortgage(s)	46,123	3,804	2,027	4,010	4,345	4,424	4,328	2,024
Primary obtained when property acquired	30,871	3,570	1,679	2,957	3,241	2,512	4,237	1,586
Obtained later	15,251	234	348	1,053	1,104	1,912	92	439
Assumed	271	20	47	62	33	33	42	37
Wrap-around.................	22	6	-	-	6	-	7	6
Combination of the above	45	1	-	11	8	3	3	-
Payment plan of primary mortgage:								
Fixed payment, self amortizing	37,876	3,030	1,585	3,180	3,573	3,436	3,536	1,392
Adjustable rate mortgage	2,261	239	120	272	249	201	197	92
Adjustable term mortgage	53	10	-	3	10	14	9	2
Graduated payment mortgage	815	93	21	74	83	44	106	32
Balloon.....................	382	69	29	27	37	27	46	12
Combination of the above	180	46	4	6	21	5	26	20
Payment plan of secondary mortgage:								
Units with two or more mortgages [5].....	5,777	613	48	406	650	263	698	97
Fixed payment, self amortizing	4,762	523	46	338	547	223	573	85
Adjustable rate mortgage	391	35	-	29	55	18	46	3
Adjustable term mortgage	51	2	3	8	3	4	3	-
Graduated payment mortgage.......	56	8	-	3	11	-	9	-
Balloon.....................	210	29	-	14	12	5	29	3
Other	3	-	-	-	-	-	-	-
Combination of the above	85	-	-	9	3	6	15	-
Reason primary refinanced:								
Units with a refinanced primary mortgage [7]	15,087	275	346	957	1,176	1,394	121	322
To get a lower interest rate.........	11,216	190	212	658	723	931	82	226
To increase payment period	196	9	11	18	19	9	-	11
To reduce payment period	780	5	9	49	69	37	-	10
To renew or extend a loan that has fall	118	3	4	5	13	16	3	3
To receive cash	2,209	41	72	200	223	264	25	46
Other reason.................	1,883	54	64	111	193	202	17	46
Cash received in primary mortgage refinance:								
Units receiving refinance cash	2,209	41	72	200	223	264	25	46
Median amount received (dol.)........	31,275	-	18,363	22,223	30,791	40,309	-	-

– Represents or rounds to zero.   NA Not available.   [1] Constructed in the past 4 years.   [2] For persons who selected this race group only. See footnote 3, Table 949.   [3] Persons of Hispanic origin may be of any race.   [4] 65 years old and over.   [5] Includes "don't know" and "not reported."   [6] Rural Housing Service/Rural Development Mortgage, formerly Farmers Home Administration.   [7] Persons reporting more than one reason are counted once in the total.

Source: U.S. Census Bureau, Current Housing Reports, Series H150/07, *American Housing Survey for the United States: 2007* (published September 2008). See also <http://www.census.gov/hhes/www/housing/ahs/nationaldata.html>.

Construction and Housing 609

Table 964. **Home Purchase Loans by Race and Sex: 2007**

[Applications in thousands (2,218.7 represents 2,218,700), payroll in millions of dollars (187,476 represents $187,476,000,000). Data is the final 2007 National Aggregates data]

Race and Sex [1,2,3]	Application received Number (1,000)	Application received Amount (mil. dol.)	Loans originated Number (1,000)	Loans originated Amount (mil. dol.)	Applications approved but not accepted Number (1,000)	Applications approved but not accepted Amount (mil. dol.)	Applications denied Number (1,000)	Applications denied Amount (mil. dol.)	Applications withdrawn Number (1,000)	Applications withdrawn Amount (mil. dol.)	Files closed for incompleteness Number (1,000)	Files closed for incompleteness Amount (mil. dol.)
Total	**2,218.7**	**187,476**	**958.1**	**79,606**	**190.3**	**16,238**	**866.1**	**66,757**	**166.1**	**19,948**	**38.1**	**4,926**
White	4,996.4	1,000,132	3,202.0	637,296	47.3	95,609	839.6	163,286	375.0	81,052	106.5	22,889
Male	1,867.6	372,756	1,107.9	214,655	184.5	37,234	377.3	77,537	150.7	33,073	47.3	10,258
Female	1,157.8	202,575	705.3	119,496	111.9	19,743	223.5	40,861	90.3	17,300	26.8	5,175
Joint (male/female)	1,959.1	422,369	1,383.1	301,988	175.7	38,387	236.0	44,335	132.2	30,284	32.1	7,375
Black	632.3	113,866	280.3	48,926	64.6	11,265	206.0	37,865	58.6	11,417	22.9	4,393
Male	253.9	46,689	105.1	18,150	26.3	467	86.8	17,230	24.0	4,764	9.6	1,874
Female	266.5	44,828	118.6	19,088	27.1	4,440	88.9	15,084	24.2	4,433	9.8	1,784
Joint (male/female)	109.6	21,922	55.9	11,545	10.9	2,100	29.5	5,407	9.9	2,150	3.4	719
Asian	340.6	98,935	204.6	57,841	41.2	12,453	57.9	17,640	29.1	8,544	7.8	2,458
Male	142.5	39,286	82.5	21,749	17.1	4,859	26.7	7,982	12.6	3,588	3.6	1,109
Female	93.9	25,391	53.6	13,949	11.3	3,138	18.7	5,519	8.2	2,229	2.2	675
Joint (male/female)	103.1	33,952	68.0	22,143	12.7	4,418	12.3	4,061	8.2	2,666	1.9	664
Native Hawaiian/Other Pacific Islander	34.1	8,464	17.4	4,144	3.9	951	8.8	2,297	3.2	843	0.8	228
Male	14.4	3,445	7.0	1,581	1.7	378	4.0	1,009	1.4	370	0.4	108
Female	10.4	2,492	5.1	1,142	1.4	294	2.9	761	1.0	234	0.2	62
Joint (male/female)	9.2	2,492	5.2	1,409	1.0	276	1.9	517	0.8	239	0.2	56
American Indian/Alaska Native	40.5	7,668	19.8	3,747	4.7	917	11.4	2,010	3.6	775	1.0	218
Male	19.3	3,687	9.3	1,740	2.3	429	5.6	1,023	1.7	388	0.5	106
Female	12.3	2,236	5.8	1,037	1.4	276	3.7	627	1.1	223	0.3	73
Joint (male/female)	8.7	1,705	4.6	955	1.1	207	2.1	348	0.7	160	0.2	36
Two or more minority races	4.6	1,010	2.6	576	0.4	94	1.0	229	0.4	90	0.1	22
Male	1.9	403	1.1	225	0.2	36	0.5	99	0.2	35	(Z)	7
Female	1.5	316	0.8	157	0.1	36	0.4	90	0.1	29	(Z)	10
Joint (male/female)	1.1	281	0.7	186	0.1	27	0.2	38	0.1	25	(Z)	5
Joint [4]	8.7	1,705	4.6	955	1.1	207	2.1	348	0.7	160	0.2	36
Race Not Available [5]	863.0	206,725	451.7	111,076	93.0	22,456	181.0	40,963	107.3	255,077	30.0	7,153
Male	173.9	40,654	81.2	18,478	18.6	4,373	44.8	10,842	22.9	5,394	6.5	1,567
Female	113.5	23,667	53.7	10,735	11.7	2,458	29.6	6,498	14.4	3,116	4.1	861
Joint (male/female)	15.0	38,523	89.7	23,665	14.8	3,854	23.5	5,444	18.0	4,567	4.0	994

Z Rounds to zero. [1] Applicants are shown in only one race category. [2] Total includes those cases in which gender was reported and that information was not reported and that information was not available. [3] Applicants are shown in only one gender category. [4] "Joint" means with two applicants, one reported a single designation of "White" and the other applicant reports one or more minority racial designations. [5] "Not Available" includes situations where information was reported as not provided or not applicable.

Source: Federal Financial Institutions Examination Council, "HMDA National Aggregate Report," annual. See also <http://www.ffiec.gov/hmdaadwebreport/nataggwelcome.aspx>.

Table 965. Occupied Housing Units—Neighborhood Indicators by Selected Characteristics of the Householder: 2007

[In thousands (110,692 represents 110,692,000). As of fall. Based on the American Housing Survey; see Appendix III]

Characteristic	Total occu-pied units	Tenure Owner	Tenure Renter	Black [1] Owner	Black [1] Renter	Hispanic origin [2] Owner	Hispanic origin [2] Renter	Elderly [3] Owner	Elderly [3] Renter	Households below poverty level Owner	Households below poverty level Renter
Total units	**110,692**	**75,647**	**35,045**	**6,464**	**7,392**	**6,364**	**6,244**	**18,271**	**4,594**	**5,566**	**8,591**
Bothersome street noise or heavy traffic present [4]	110,692	75,647	35,045	6,464	7,392	6,364	6,244	18,271	4,594	5,566	8,591
Yes	25,978	15,611	10,367	1,647	2,486	1,418	1,741	3,864	1,137	1,362	2,844
No	83,435	59,110	24,326	4,741	4,800	4,902	4,466	14,174	3,433	4,061	5,629
Serious crime in past 12 months [4]	110,692	75,647	35,045	6,464	7,392	6,364	6,244	18,271	4,594	5,566	8,591
Yes	17,156	9,797	7,360	1,172	2,043	1,102	1,322	1,822	620	846	2,074
No	90,920	64,203	26,717	5,125	5,092	5,157	4,780	16,047	3,851	4,474	6,224
Bothersome smoke, gas, or bad smell [4]	110,692	75,647	35,045	6,464	7,392	6,364	6,244	18,271	4,594	5,566	8,591
Yes	6,001	3,668	2,333	341	595	364	425	720	235	364	799
No	103,374	71,014	32,360	6,040	6,695	5,956	5,778	17,301	4,337	5,050	7,672
Other problems:											
Noise	1,906	1,132	774	113	177	86	133	283	56	138	247
Litter or housing deterioration	1,626	1,073	553	179	202	83	82	234	33	108	181
Poor city or county services	673	424	249	68	94	46	42	74	8	31	80
People	5,189	3,239	1,950	358	494	286	315	585	137	322	582
With public transportation [4]											
With public transportation	59,195	34,797	24,398	3,673	5,824	3,946	4,942	8,271	3,230	2,372	6,026
Household uses public transportation regularly for commuting to school or work	9,862	3,612	6,251	750	1,879	517	1,656	537	640	283	1,882
Household does not use public transportation regularly for commuting to school or work	48,960	31,038	17,922	2,888	3,862	3,421	3,267	7,707	2,567	2,065	4,063
No public transportation	48,171	38,549	9,622	2,644	1,409	2,275	1,183	9,496	1,261	2,940	2,321
Not reported	3,326	2,302	1,024	146	160	143	118	504	103	254	245
Police protection:											
Satisfactory	99,311	68,254	31,057	5,575	6,247	5,562	5,481	16,621	4,244	4,661	7,363
Unsatisfacory	8,029	5,307	2,722	699	822	655	616	1,136	228	597	899
Secured communities [5]:											
Community access secured with walls or fences	10,393	5,086	5,300	411	1,162	621	1,325	1,480	845	328	1,202
Community access not secured	99,406	69,960	29,446	6,001	6,136	5,718	4,876	16,649	3,731	5,142	7,299
Secured multiunits: [5]											
Multiunit access secured	6,892	1,228	5,664	100	1,280	112	909	412	1,408	99	1,535
Multiunit access not secured	17,836	2,313	15,523	217	3,409	257	3,088	662	1,688	194	3,921
Senior citizen communities:											
Households with persons 55 years	44,984	35,993	8,992	2,979	1,777	2,273	1,219	18,271	4,594	3,401	2,620
Community age restricted [6]	3,152	1,569	1,584	88	250	79	157	1,181	1,329	184	551
Access to structure:											
Enter building from outside [4, 7]	26,256	3,674	22,582	324	5,085	372	4,288	1,123	3,347	305	5,817
Use of steps not required	9,595	1,406	8,190	99	1,744	166	1,629	512	1,745	122	2,272
Use of steps required [4, 8]	16,649	2,266	14,383	225	3,337	207	2,659	611	1,597	180	3,537
Enter home from outside [7]	84,436	71,973	12,463	6,140	2,307	5,992	1,956	17,148	1,247	5,261	2,774
Use of steps not required	36,988	31,960	5,028	2,612	875	3,361	906	7,945	581	2,138	1,044
Use of steps required	47,262	39,835	7,427	3,513	1,429	2,623	1,050	9,167	663	3,090	1,730
Community quality:											
Some or all activities present	47,629	31,530	16,098	2,512	3,389	2,503	2,438	8,040	2,589	1,953	3,879
Community center or clubhouse	24,546	14,836	9,710	1,137	2,093	1,133	1,410	4,313	1,935	955	2,336
Golf in the community	13,679	10,478	3,202	615	585	321	388	2,813	458	542	642
Trails in the community	20,833	14,940	5,893	955	951	1,017	762	3,423	833	716	1,136
Shuttle bus	10,014	5,966	4,048	430	657	501	606	2,133	1,224	415	1,113
Daycare	16,303	10,892	5,411	1,271	1,453	839	916	2,474	584	738	1,495
Private or restricted beach,	20,252	14,405	5,847	867	977	1,095	986	3,284	643	726	1,311
Trash, litter, or junk on street: [9]											
None	98,294	69,019	29,275	5,634	5,745	5,699	5,133	16,905	4,143	4,800	6,891
Minor accumulation	7,166	3,399	3,767	444	1,039	377	744	641	282	344	1,092
Major accumulation	2,595	1,386	1,209	177	350	164	256	336	87	173	396

[1] For persons who selected this race group only. See footnote 3, Table 956. [2] Persons of Hispanic origin may be any race. [3] Householders 65 years old and over. [4] Includes those not reporting. [5] Public access is restricted (walls, gates, private security). Includes high rise apartments, retirement communities, resorts, etc. [6] At least one family member must be aged 55 years old or older. [7] Restricted to multiunits. [8] Restricted to single units. [9] Or on any properties within 300 feet.

Source: U.S. Census Bureau, Current Housing Reports, Series H150/07, *American Housing Survey for the United States: 2007* (published September 2008). See also <http://www.census.gov/hhes/www/housing/ahs/nationaldata.html>.

Construction and Housing 611

Table 966. Heating Equipment and Fuels for Occupied Units: 1995 to 2007

[97,693 represents 97,693,000. As of fall. Based on American Housing Survey. See Appendix III]

Type of equipment or fuel	Number (1,000)					Percent distribution		
	1995	2001	2003 [1]	2005	1995	2005	2007
Occupied units, total.	97,693	106,261	105,842	108,871	110,692	100.0	100.0
Heating equipment:							
Warm air furnace.	53,165	65,262	65,380	68,275	69,582	54.4	62.9
Steam or hot water	13,669	13,441	13,257	12,880	12,760	14.0	11.5
Heat pumps	9,406	11,080	11,347	12,484	12,996	9.6	11.7
Built-in electric units.	7,035	5,063	4,760	4,699	4,802	7.2	4.3
Floor, wall, or pipeless furnace. . .	4,963	5,343	5,322	5,102	4,994	5.1	4.5
Room heaters with flue.	1,620	1,542	1,432	1,294	1,135	1.7	1.0
Room heaters without flue.	1,642	1,558	1,509	1,327	1,188	1.7	1.1
Fireplaces, stoves, portable.	5,150	2,571	2,396	2,411	2,756	5.3	2.5
None.	1,044	401	439	399	478	1.1	0.4
House main heating fuel:							
Electricity	26,771	32,590	32,341	34,263	36,079	27.4	32.6
Utility gas.	49,203	54,689	54,928	56,317	56,681	50.4	51.2
Bottled, tank, or LP gas	4,251	6,079	6,134	6,228	6,095	4.4	5.5
Fuel oil, kerosene, etc.	12,029	10,473	10,136	9,929	9,317	12.3	8.4
Coal or coke.	210	128	126	95	91	(Z)	(Z)
Wood and other fuel	4,186	1,902	1,735	1,640	1,487	4.3	1.3
None.	1,042	400	441	398	464	1.1	0.4
Cooking fuel:							
Electricity	57,621	63,685	62,859	65,297	66,276	59.0	59.9
Gas [2]	39,218	42,161	42,612	43,316	44,194	40.1	39.9
Other fuel	566	66	62	51	26	0.6	(Z)
None.	287	349	309	206	17	0.3	(Z)

Z Less than 0.05 percent.   [1] Based on 2000 census controls.   [2] Includes utility, bottled, tank, and LP gas.

Source: U.S. Census Bureau, Current Housing Reports, Series H150/95RV, H150/01, H150/03, H150/05, and H150/07, *American Housing Survey for the United States: 2007* (published September 2008). See also <http://www.census.gov /hhes/www/housing/ahs/nationaldata.html>.

Table 967. Occupied Housing Units—Housing Indicators by Selected Characteristics of the Householder: 2007

[In thousands of units (110,692 represents 110,692,000). As of fall. Based on the American Housing Survey; see Appendix III]

Characteristic	Total occu- pied units	Tenure		Black [1]		Hispanic origin [2]		Elderly [3]		Households below poverty level	
		Owner	Renter	Owner	Renter	Owner	Renter	Owner	Renter	Owner	Renter
Total units	110,692	75,647	35,045	6,464	7,392	6,364	6,244	18,271	4,594	5,566	8,591
Amenities:											
Porch, deck, balcony or patio	94,456	69,899	24,557	5,623	4,989	5,798	3,995	16,706	2,786	4,903	5,444
Telephone available	108,226	74,455	33,771	6,334	7,083	6,234	6,043	18,054	4,479	5,423	8,230
Usable fireplace	38,189	34,070	4,118	2,147	616	2,136	541	7,164	346	1,420	540
Separate dining room.	54,083	44,094	9,989	3,922	2,380	3,486	1,656	10,242	1,000	2,652	2,043
With 2 or more living rooms or rec. rooms.	33,156	30,515	2,641	2,161	449	1,801	269	6,636	298	1,238	371
Garage or carport with home.	72,317	60,059	12,258	4,084	1,610	4,995	2,333	14,745	1,447	3,565	1,954
Cars and trucks available:											
No cars, trucks, or vans . . .	8,658	2,073	6,584	386	2,107	118	1,160	1,311	1,866	700	3,084
Other households without cars	13,719	9,266	4,454	522	695	1,028	913	1,665	299	779	906
1 car with or without trucks or vans	52,515	35,339	17,177	3,202	3,531	2,772	2,840	10,730	2,081	3,042	3,699
2 cars	27,576	21,816	5,760	1,753	917	1,841	1,108	3,872	332	840	785
3 or more cars	8,224	7,154	1,070	601	143	606	224	692	16	205	116
Selected deficiencies:											
Signs of rats in last 3 months	760	406	354	35	138	55	134	73	34	54	149
Signs of mice in last 3 months	6,052	3,962	2,090	315	601	238	447	915	221	417	727
Holes in floors.	1,083	477	607	78	180	71	101	92	36	137	241
Open cracks or holes	5,310	2,772	2,538	342	675	248	410	520	176	335	801
Broken plaster or peeling paint (interior of unit)	2,186	1,075	1,110	193	291	88	186	267	89	154	369
No electrical wiring	54	44	10	–	–	–	4	–	–	10	4
Exposed wiring	1,082	608	475	48	121	51	117	173	54	69	143
Rooms without electric outlet.	1,414	797	617	78	190	91	113	200	36	103	218
Water leakage from inside structure [4]	8,785	5,030	3,755	480	943	332	557	884	235	409	1,007
Water leakage from outside structure [4]	11,347	8,171	3,176	733	667	480	409	1,622	220	588	776

– Represents or rounds to zero.   [1] For persons who selected this race group only. See footnote 3, Table 956.   [2] Persons of Hispanic origin may be any race.   [3] Householders 65 years old and over.   [4] During the 12 months prior to the survey.

Source: U.S. Census Bureau, Current Housing Reports, Series H150/07, *American Housing Survey for the United States: 2007* (published September 2008). See also <http://www.census.gov/hhes/www/housing/ahs/nationaldata.html>.

Table 968. Home Remodeling—Number of Households With Work Done by Amount Spent: 2008

[In thousands, except percent (3,149 represents 3,149,000). As of fall 2007. For work done in the prior 12 months. Based on household survey and subject to sampling error; see source]

Remodeling project	Total households with work done [1]		Households with work done by outside contractor	Number of households by amount spent (dol.)		
	Number	Percent of all households		Under $1,000	$1,000 to $2,999	Over $3,000
Conversion of garage/attic/basement into living space	3,149	1.41	647	546	681	1,118
Remodel bathroom	16,760	7.49	4,874	6,626	3,400	3,446
Remodel kitchen	11,611	5.19	3,759	3,357	1,810	4,062
Remodel bedroom	8,237	3.68	1,260	4,561	1,122	905
Convert room to home office	3,321	1.48	310	1,691	275	297
Convert room to home theater	991	0.44	125	153	282	230
Remodel other rooms	8,664	3.87	1,576	3,655	1,464	1,256
Add bathroom	1,337	0.60	355	287	186	400
Add/extend garage	886	0.40	355	94	102	412
Add other rooms—exterior addition	1,436	0.64	553	175	211	674
Add deck/porch/patio	6,668	2.98	2,378	1,831	1,534	2,051
Roofing	7,874	3.52	4,543	1,655	1,583	3,099
Siding—vinyl/metal	2,790	1.25	1,315	630	461	1,084
Aluminum windows	1,476	0.66	604	388	204	380
Clad-wood/wood windows	1,111	0.50	474	143	138	529
Vinyl windows	4,755	2.13	2,456	1,119	1,085	1,652
Ceramic tile floors	8,118	3.63	3,030	3,376	1,539	1,139
Hardwood floors	5,470	2.45	2,204	1,149	1,601	1,461
Laminate flooring	5,772	2.58	1,484	2,399	1,722	591
Vinyl flooring	3,282	1.47	820	1,837	487	89
Carpeting	9,655	4.32	5,663	3,171	2,638	1,639
Kitchen cabinets	5,497	2.46	2,002	1,402	815	1,865
Kitchen counter tops	6,203	2.77	3,104	1,680	1,467	1,687
Skylights	1,034	0.46	515	316	166	181
Exterior doors	6,736	3.01	2,543	3,398	1,101	536
Interior doors	4,985	2.23	1,211	2,676	671	283
Garage doors	3,364	1.50	1,916	1,414	956	103
Concrete or masonry work	5,003	2.24	2,018	1,444	1,020	1,205
Swimming pool—inground	1,079	0.48	472	49	113	512
Wall paneling	1,417	0.63	143	590	120	27
Ceramic wall tile	2,746	1.23	1,008	1,408	461	229

[1] Includes no response and amount unknown.

Source: Mediamark Research Inc., New York, NY, *Top-Line Reports,* (copyright). See also <http://www.mediamark.com/>.

Table 969. Home Improvement Loans by Race: 2007

[Applications in thousands (6,991.8 represents 6,991,800), loan amount in millions of dollars (1,456,549.3 represents $1,456,549,300,000). For purposes of categorization, the general rule is: The race (including situations where race was reported as not provided or not applicable) of the application is categorized by the race of the first person listed on the application unless the "joint" race definition applies]

Item	Unit	Total	White	Black	Asian	Joint [1]	Race not available [2]
Applications received							
Number	1,000	6,991.8	1,528.7	261.4	48.2	29.8	301.9
Amount	Mil. dol. . .	1,456,549.3	125,470.2	19,758.4	7,711.2	3,059.2	26,440.0
Loans originated							
Number	1,000	4,230.9	733.2	75.7	18.4	11.6	106.0
Amount	Mil. dol. . .	876,755.2	57,923.9	5,698.7	3,179.9	1,153.6	10,353.1
Applications approved but not accepted							
Number	1,000	689.0	127.9	17.3	5.6	2.3	33.7
Amount	Mil. dol. . .	145,784.7	10,804.5	1,289.0	890.3	231.8	2,670.3
Applications denied							
Number	1,000	1,318.1	536.0	145.3	19.3	12.7	126.2
Amount	Mil. dol. . .	266,917.8	40,966.6	10,119.0	2,652.2	1,254.2	9,137.1
Applications withdrawn							
Number	1,000	583.3	107.3	19.5	3.8	2.7	28.3
Amount	Mil. dol. . .	129,372.3	12,655.1	2,249.4	734.3	354.8	3,299.3
Files closed for incompleteness							
Number	1,000	170.5	24.2	3.6	1.2	0.5	7.7
Amount	Mil. dol. . .	37,719.3	3,120.2	402.3	254.5	64.7	980.1

[1] Joint means one applicant reports a single designation of "White" and the other applicant reports one or more minority racial designations. [2] "Not available" includes situations where information was not provided or not applicable.

Source: Federal Financial Institutions Examination Council, "HMDA National Aggregate Report," annual. See also <http://www.ffiec.gov/hmdaadwebreport/nataggwelcome.aspx>.

Construction and Housing   613

Table 970. Net Stock of Residential Fixed Assets: 1990 to 2007

[In billions of dollars (6,260 represents $6,260,000,000,000). End of year estimates]

Item	1990	1995	2000	2002	2003	2004	2005	2006	2007
Total residential fixed assets. . .	**6,260**	**8,028**	**10,907**	**12,457**	**13,504**	**15,098**	**16,832**	**17,987**	**18,193**
By type of owner and legal form of organization:									
Private	6,111	7,840	10,676	12,193	13,225	14,803	16,498	17,641	17,869
Corporate.	66	77	100	110	116	127	141	151	153
Noncorporate	6,045	7,763	10,576	12,083	13,109	14,676	16,357	17,490	17,716
Government.	149	188	232	264	280	296	335	346	324
Federal	52	62	75	83	88	94	102	104	90
State and local	97	127	156	181	192	202	233	242	234
By industry:									
Private	6,111	7,840	10,676	12,193	13,225	14,803	16,498	17,641	17,869
Farm	49	51	72	81	86	91	97	100	101
Nonfarm	6,062	7,789	10,603	12,113	13,139	14,712	16,401	17,541	17,768
By tenure group: [1]									
Owner-occupied	4,516	5,988	8,329	9,614	10,499	11,826	13,245	14,190	14,396
Farm	49	51	72	81	86	91	97	100	101
Nonfarm	4,467	5,937	8,256	9,534	10,413	11,735	13,147	14,090	14,295
Tenant-occupied	1,719	2,011	2,543	2,802	2,962	3,224	3,536	3,742	3,741

[1] Excludes stocks of other nonfarm residential assets, which consists primarily of dormitories, and of fraternity and sorority houses.

Source: U.S. Bureau of Economic Analysis, "Table 5.1 Current-Cost Net Stock of Residential Fixed Assets by Type of Owner, Legal Form of Organization, Industry, and Tenure Group" (published 21 August 2008); <http://www.bea.gov/national/FA2007/SelectTable.asp#S5>.

Table 971. Commercial Buildings—Summary: 2003

[4,645 represents 4,645,000. Excludes mall buildings. Building type based on predominant activity in which the occupants were engaged. Based on a sample survey of building representatives conducted in 2003, therefore subject to sampling variability.

Characteristic	All buildings (1,000)	Total floor-space (mil. sq.ft.)	Total workers in all buildings (1,000)	Mean square foot per building [1] (1,000)	Mean square foot per worker [1]	Mean operating hours per week [1]
All buildings	**4,645**	**64,783**	**72,807**	**13.9**	**890**	**61**
Building floorspace (sq. ft.):						
1,001 to 5,000	2,552	6,789	9,936	2.7	683	57
5,001 to 10,000	889	6,585	7,512	7.4	877	61
10,001 to 25,000	738	11,535	10,787	15.6	1,069	67
25,001 to 50,000	241	8,668	8,881	35.9	976	72
50,001 to 100,000.	129	9,057	8,432	70.4	1,074	80
100,001 to 200,000.	65	9,064	11,632	138.8	779	89
200,001 to 500,000.	25	7,176	6,883	289.0	1,043	100
Over 500,000.	7	5,908	8,744	896.1	676	115
Principal activity within building:						
Education	386	9,874	12,489	25.6	791	50
Food sales	226	1,255	1,430	5.6	877	107
Food service	297	1,654	3,129	5.6	528	86
Health care	129	3,163	6,317	24.6	501	59
Inpatient	8	1,905	3,716	241.4	513	168
Outpatient	121	1,258	2,600	10.4	484	52
Lodging.	142	5,096	2,457	35.8	2,074	167
Retail (other than mall).	443	4,317	3,463	9.7	1,246	59
Office	824	12,208	28,154	14.8	434	55
Public assembly	277	3,939	2,395	14.2	1,645	50
Public order and safety	71	1,090	1,347	15.5	809	103
Religious worship	370	3,754	1,706	10.1	2,200	32
Service	622	4,050	3,667	6.5	1,105	55
Warehouse and storage	597	10,078	4,369	16.9	2,306	66
Other	79	1,738	1,819	21.9	956	63
Vacant	182	2,567	(NA)	14.1	(NA)	(NA)
Energy sources: [2]						
Electricity.	4,404	63,307	72,708	14.4	871	62
Natural gas	2,391	43,468	51,956	18.2	837	65
Fuel oil	451	15,157	19,625	33.6	772	68
District heat	67	5,443	10,190	81.4	534	79
District chilled water	33	2,853	7,189	86.7	397	79
Propane	502	7,076	5,858	14.1	1,208	60
Wood	62	289	262	4.6	1,105	46

NA Not available. [1] For explanation of mean, see Guide to Tabular Presentation. [2] More than one type may apply.

Source: U.S. Energy Information Administration, "2003 Commercial Buildings Energy Consumption Buildings (CBECS) Detailed Tables"; Table B1.; <http://www.eia.doe.gov/emeu/cbecs/cbecs2003/detailedtables2003/detailedtables2003.html> (accessed 11 July 2007).

Section 21
Manufactures

This section presents summary data for manufacturing as a whole and more detailed information for major industry groups and selected products. The types of measures shown at the different levels include data for establishments, employment and payroll, value and quantity of production and shipments, value added by manufacture, inventories, and various indicators of financial status.

The principal sources of these data are U.S. Census Bureau reports of the censuses of manufactures conducted every 5 years, the *Annual Survey of Manufactures*, and *Current Industrial Reports*. Reports on current activities of industries or current movements of individual commodities are compiled by such government agencies as the Bureau of Economic Analysis; Bureau of Labor Statistics; the Department of Commerce, International Trade Administration; and by private research or trade associations.

The Quarterly Financial Report publishes up-to-date aggregate statistics on the financial results and position of U.S. corporations. Based upon a sample survey, the QFR presents estimated statements of income and retained earnings, balance sheets, and related financial and operating ratios for manufacturing corporations with assets of $250,000 or over, and mining, wholesale trade and retail trade corporations with assets of $50 million and over or above industry specific receipt cut-off values. These statistical data are classified by industry and by asset size.

Several private trade associations provide industry coverage for certain sections of the economy. They include the Aluminum Association (Table 995), American Iron and Steel Institute (Table 993), Consumer Electronics Association (Table 999), and the Aerospace Industries Association (Tables 1004 and 1006).

Censuses and annual surveys—The first census of manufactures covered the year 1809. Between 1809 and 1963, a census was conducted at periodic intervals. Since 1967, it has been taken every 5 years (for years ending in "2" and "7"). Results from the 2002 census are presented in this section utilizing the North American Industry Classification System (NAICS). For additional information see text, Section 15, Business Enterprise, and the Census Bureau Web site at <http://www.census.gov/econ/census07/>. Census data, either directly reported or estimated from administrative records, are obtained for every manufacturing plant with one or more paid employees.

The *Annual Survey of Manufactures* (ASM), conducted for the first time in 1949, collects data for the years between censuses for the more general measure of manufacturing activity covered in detail by the censuses. The annual survey data are estimates derived from a scientifically selected sample of establishments. The 2004 annual survey is based on a sample of about 50,000 from a universe of 346,000 establishments. These establishments represent all manufacturing establishments of multiunit companies and all single-establishment manufacturing companies mailed schedules in the 2002 Census of Manufactures. For the current panel of the ASM sample, all establishments of companies with 2002 shipments in manufacturing in excess of $500 million were included in the survey with certainty. For the remaining portion of the mail survey, the establishment was defined as the sampling unit. For this portion, all establishments with 500 employees or more and establishments with a very large value of shipments also were included. Therefore, of the 50,000 establishments included in the ASM panel, approximately 24,000 are selected with certainty. Smaller establishments in the remaining portion of the mail survey were selected by sample.

Establishments and classification— Each of the establishments covered in the 2002 Economic Census—Manufacturing

U.S. Census Bureau, *Statistical Abstract of the United States: 2010*

was classified in 1 of 480 industries (473 manufacturing industries and 7 former manufacturing industries) in accordance with the industry definitions in the 2002 NAICS manual. In the NAICS system, an industry is generally defined as a group of establishments that have similar production processes. To the extent practical, the system uses supply-based or production-oriented concepts in defining industries. The resulting group of establishments must be significant in terms of number, value added by manufacture, value of shipments, and number of employees.

Establishments frequently make products classified both in their industry (primary products) and other industries (secondary products). Industry statistics (employment, payroll, value added by manufacture, value of shipments, etc.) reflect the activities of the establishments, which may make both primary and secondary products. Product statistics, however, represent the output of all establishments without regard for the classification of the producing establishment. For this reason, when relating the industry statistics, especially the value of shipments, to the product statistics, the composition of the industry's output should be considered.

Establishment—Establishment signifies a single physical plant site or factory. It is not necessarily identical to the business unit or company, which may consist of one or more establishments. A company operating establishments at more than one location is required to submit a separate report for each location and include establishments with payroll at any time during the year. An establishment engaged in distinctly different lines of activity and maintaining separate payroll and inventory records is also required to submit separate reports.

Durable goods—Items with a normal life expectancy of 3 years or more. Automobiles, furniture, household appliances, and mobile homes are common examples.

Nondurable goods—Items which generally last for only a short time (3 years or less). Food, beverages, clothing, shoes, and gasoline are common examples.

Statistical reliability—For a discussion of statistical collection and estimation, sampling procedures, and measures of statistical reliability applicable to Census Bureau data, see Appendix III.

Table 972. **Gross Domestic Product in Current and Real (2000) Dollars by Industry: 2000 to 2008**

[In billions of dollars (9,817.0 represents $9,817,000,000,000). Data include nonfactor charges (capital consumption allowances, indirect business taxes, etc.) as well as factor charges against gross product; corporate profits and capital consumption allowances have been shifted from a company to an establishment basis]

Industry	1997 NAICS code[1]	2000	2004	2005	2006	2007	2008
CURRENT DOLLARS							
Gross domestic product, total[2]	(X)	**9,817.0**	**11,685.9**	**12,421.9**	**13,178.4**	**13,807.5**	**14,264.6**
Private industries	(X)	8,614.3	10,194.3	10,853.1	11,529.3	12,064.6	12,424.6
Manufacturing	31–33	1,426.2	1,427.9	1,480.6	1,577.4	1,616.8	1,637.7
Durable goods	(X)	865.3	807.5	845.1	899.4	922.0	914.7
Wood products	321	31.4	37.5	38.4	33.8	31.4	(NA)
Nonmetallic mineral products	327	45.7	49.3	53.0	58.0	54.4	(NA)
Primary metals	331	48.2	54.5	56.4	63.4	62.4	(NA)
Fabricated metal products	332	121.7	115.2	123.7	131.6	140.4	(NA)
Machinery	333	109.3	103.4	111.6	119.5	125.7	(NA)
Computer and electronic products. . .	334	185.6	125.5	133.7	144.4	146.3	(NA)
Electrical equipment, appliances, and components	335	50.6	45.7	46.3	55.3	58.4	(NA)
Motor vehicles, bodies and trailers, and parts	3361–63	118.1	106.9	98.2	98.3	98.5	(NA)
Other transportation equipment	3364, 66 69	64.4	70.9	80.6	87.7	96.1	(NA)
Furniture and related products	337	32.7	31.2	34.7	36.6	35.4	(NA)
Miscellaneous manufacturing	339	57.5	67.4	68.3	70.8	73.0	(NA)
Nondurable goods.	(X)	561.0	620.4	635.5	678.0	694.9	723.0
Food and beverage and tobacco products.	311, 312	154.8	161.0	159.2	160.2	174.7	(NA)
Textile mills and textile product mills.	313, 314	26.5	23.1	23.2	21.7	19.8	(NA)
Apparel and leather and allied products.	315, 316	25.1	17.3	17.1	16.7	16.1	(NA)
Paper products	322	55.6	50.7	50.2	56.9	50.7	(NA)
Printing and related support activities.	323	49.0	45.6	46.3	47.5	47.9	(NA)
Petroleum and coal products	324	26.2	56.6	70.9	73.6	70.4	(NA)
Chemical products	325	157.1	198.7	201.5	236.0	249.2	(NA)
Plastics and rubber products	326	66.7	67.3	67.1	65.4	66.2	(NA)
CHAINED (2000) DOLLARS							
Gross domestic product, total[2]	(X)	**9,817.0**	**10,675.8**	**10,989.5**	**11,294.8**	**11,523.9**	**11,652.0**
Private industries.	(X)	8,614.3	9,406.6	9,740.0	10,043.5	10,250.1	10,309.4
Manufacturing	31–33	1,426.2	1,478.3	1,491.0	1,573.3	1,618.6	1,574.3
Durable goods	(X)	865.3	898.8	948.5	1,025.7	1,074.6	1,061.0
Wood products	321	31.4	30.7	32.0	29.9	31.7	(NA)
Nonmetallic mineral products	327	45.7	48.2	48.3	47.3	44.3	(NA)
Primary metals	331	48.2	48.8	44.1	42.2	41.1	(NA)
Fabricated metal products	332	121.7	110.4	113.1	120.0	123.4	(NA)
Machinery	333	109.3	103.7	109.6	116.9	121.0	(NA)
Computer and electronic products. . .	334	185.6	248.9	304.4	380.3	456.0	(NA)
Electrical equipment, appliances, and components	335	50.6	46.6	46.1	51.8	51.7	(NA)
Motor vehicles, bodies and trailers, and parts	3361–63	118.1	125.4	128.6	148.2	155.2	(NA)
Other transportation equipment	3364, 66 69	64.4	61.3	67.7	71.6	77.7	(NA)
Furniture and related products	337	32.7	30.4	32.8	33.8	31.8	(NA)
Miscellaneous manufacturing	339	57.5	64.6	66.2	69.1	70.8	(NA)
Nondurable goods.	(X)	561.0	580.4	551.4	563.1	565.5	539.4
Food and beverage and tobacco products.	311, 312	154.8	149.4	145.9	152.6	166.2	(NA)
Textile mills and textile product mills.	313, 314	26.5	23.2	23.5	21.3	19.8	(NA)
Apparel and leather and allied products.	315, 316	25.1	17.8	17.8	17.4	16.7	(NA)
Paper products	322	55.6	54.0	53.1	57.6	51.1	(NA)
Printing and related support activities.	323	49.0	44.5	45.5	46.2	47.0	(NA)
Petroleum and coal products	324	26.2	39.7	30.1	26.3	21.7	(NA)
Chemical products	325	157.1	182.6	172.3	191.3	197.6	(NA)
Plastics and rubber products	326	66.7	68.3	66.9	58.5	60.7	(NA)

NA Not available.   X Not applicable.   [1] North American Industry Classification System, 1997; see text Section 15. [2] Includes industries, not shown separately. For additional industries, see Table 654.

Source: U.S. Bureau of Economic Analysis, *Survey of Current Business,* May 2009. See also <http://www.bea.gov/newsreleases/industry/gdpindustry/gdpindnewsrelease.htm>.

Manufactures 617

Table 973. **Manufacturing—Establishments, Employees, and Annual Payroll by Industry: 2005 and 2006**

[(116,317 represents 116,317,000). Excludes self-employed, individual employees on private households, railroad employees, agricultural production employees, and most government employees]

Kind of business	2002 NAICS code [1]	Establishments (number)		Employees (1,000) [2]		Payroll (mil. dol.)	
		2005	2006	2005	2006	2005	2006
All industries, total	(X)	7,499,702	7,601,160	116,317	119,917	4,482,722	4,792,430
Manufacturing, total	31–33	333,460	331,062	13,667	13,632	600,696	620,224
Percent of all industries	(X)	4.4	4.4	11.8	11.4	13.4	12.9
Food manufacturing.	311	25,785	25,382	1,470	1,459	48,474	50,219
Beverage & tobacco products	312	3,516	3,684	154	155	7,263	7,552
Textile mills	313	3,411	3,243	209	188	6,518	6,028
Textile product mills.	314	6,891	6,726	164	156	4,649	4,632
Apparel manufacturing	315	11,165	10,967	243	216	5,607	5,344
Leather & allied products	316	1,414	1,398	41	39	1,254	1,174
Wood products	321	16,707	16,735	556	577	18,232	18,584
Paper	322	5,273	5,139	454	441	21,560	21,656
Printing & related support activities.	323	34,385	33,433	658	641	25,060	25,335
Petroleum & coal products	324	2,362	2,448	102	103	8,201	8,151
Chemical	325	13,220	13,247	810	805	49,210	51,084
Plastics & rubber products	326	14,707	14,592	902	901	33,391	34,075
Nonmetallic mineral products.	327	16,908	17,350	469	482	19,691	20,598
Primary metal	331	5,362	5,285	451	450	22,108	22,784
Fabricated metal products.	332	59,053	59,064	1,520	1,564	60,693	64,905
Machinery	333	26,723	26,317	1,107	1,127	52,653	55,289
Computer & electronic products	334	14,741	14,548	1,059	1,057	65,601	69,826
Electrical equip, appliance & component	335	6,201	6,109	427	420	17,885	18,416
Transportation equipment	336	12,694	12,707	1,636	1,623	86,006	86,459
Furniture & related products	337	21,563	21,449	548	543	17,560	17,897
Miscellaneous.	339	31,379	31,239	688	686	29,078	30,213

X Not applicable.   [1] North American Industry Classification System, 2002; see text, Section 15.   [2] Covers full- and part-time employees who are on the payroll in the pay period including March 12.

Source: U.S. Census Bureau, "County Business Patterns" (published June 2008); <http://www.census.gov/econ/cbp/index.html>.

Table 974. **Manufacturing—Establishments, Employees, and Annual Payroll by State: 2006**

[(13,632 represents 13,632,000). Data are for North American Industry Classification System (NAICS), 2002 codes 31–33. See headnote, Table 973]

State	Establishments (number)	Employees (1,000) [1]	Payroll (mil. dol.)	State	Establishments (number)	Employees (1,000) [1]	Payroll (mil. dol.)
United States	331,062	13,632	620,224	Missouri	6,885	305	12,984
Alabama	4,901	291	11,028	Montana	1,274	20	763
Alaska	515	10	423	Nebraska	1,996	105	3,789
Arizona	4,971	179	8,512	Nevada	1,933	47	2,075
Arkansas	3,109	201	6,657	New Hampshire	2,139	76	3,746
California	44,474	1,450	75,714	New Jersey	9,346	297	15,591
Colorado	5,223	135	6,477	New Mexico	1,518	35	1,446
Connecticut	4,937	182	9,941	New York	18,812	551	24,832
Delaware	651	33	1,703	North Carolina	10,130	536	20,683
District of Columbia. . . .	130	2	77	North Dakota	744	26	916
Florida	14,181	372	15,488	Ohio.	16,401	788	36,125
Georgia	8,623	431	16,605	Oklahoma	3,915	142	5,871
Hawaii	953	15	507	Oregon	5,632	189	8,368
Idaho	1,870	64	2,751	Pennsylvania	15,430	664	29,913
Illinois.	15,822	667	31,246	Rhode Island	1,861	54	2,363
Indiana	8,957	557	24,933	South Carolina	4,323	264	10,950
Iowa.	3,795	227	9,582	South Dakota	1,005	42	1,454
Kansas	3,165	176	7,622	Tennessee.	6,659	393	16,004
Kentucky	4,131	257	10,842	Texas	20,691	846	40,922
Louisiana	3,323	141	7,085	Utah.	3,241	118	4,960
Maine	1,800	59	2,447	Vermont	1,094	37	1,664
Maryland.	3,633	131	6,614	Virginia	5,780	289	12,378
Massachusetts	7,680	275	15,696	Washington	7,505	258	13,203
Michigan	13,740	615	30,905	West Virginia	1,437	64	2,668
Minnesota	7,935	337	15,788	Wisconsin	9,670	493	21,546
Mississippi	2,585	173	5,876	Wyoming.	537	10	489

[1] Covers full- and part-time employees who are on the payroll in the pay period including March 12.

Source: U.S. Census Bureau, "County Business Patterns" (published June 2008); <http://www.census.gov/econ/cbp/index.html>.

Table 975. **Manufactures—Summary by Selected Industry: 2006**

[12,984.7 represents 12,984,700. Based on the Annual Survey of Manufactures; see Appendix III]

Industry based on shipments	2002 NAICS code [1]	All employees [2]			Produc- tion workers (1,000) [2]	Value added by manufac- tures [3] (mil.dol.)	Value of ship- ments [4] (mil. dol.)
		Number (1,000)	Payroll				
			Total (mil. dol.)	Per employee (dol.)			
Manufacturing, total	31-33	12,984.7	592,119	45,601	9,175.3	2,285,929	5,015,553
Food [5]	311	1,416.9	48,842	34,470	1,089.6	233,407	536,939
Grain and oilseed milling	3112	52.6	2,647	50,340	39.6	19,974	56,978
Sugar and confectionery products	3113	65.2	2,724	41,742	50.9	15,748	28,225
Fruit and vegetable preserving and specialty foods	3114	160.6	5,757	35,857	133.1	27,732	56,161
Dairy products	3115	121.7	5,277	43,371	85.8	24,143	75,252
Animal slaughtering and processing	3116	488.5	13,563	27,765	421.9	52,793	149,577
Bakeries and tortillas	3118	273.6	9,153	33,455	173.5	34,417	54,245
Beverage and tobacco products	312	143.9	7,183	49,912	83.7	79,168	124,033
Beverage	3121	124.3	5,927	47,694	69.2	42,906	82,443
Tobacco	3122	19.6	1,256	63,940	14.5	36,262	41,589
Textile mills	313	174.0	5,778	33,208	145.1	17,140	38,829
Textile product mills	314	145.5	4,407	30,290	114.2	15,121	33,264
Apparel	315	199.9	5,013	25,074	155.1	15,968	30,325
Cut and sew apparel	3152	155.3	3,870	24,923	119.2	12,695	23,610
Leather and allied products	316	36.1	1,078	29,844	27.8	3,011	5,941
Wood products [5]	321	536.2	18,144	33,838	432.4	44,267	112,403
Sawmills and wood preservation	3211	104.0	3,863	37,141	87.4	9,787	32,153
Veneer, plywood, and engineered wood products	3212	114.7	4,171	36,364	92.2	10,447	25,749
Paper.	322	413.4	20,587	49,802	321.3	79,952	169,033
Pulp, paper, and paperboard mills	3221	127.9	8,019	62,683	101.5	41,531	78,926
Converted paper products	3222	285.4	12,567	44,029	219.7	38,421	90,107
Printing and related support activities.	323	620.0	25,110	40,502	443.6	60,357	99,800
Petroleum and coal products	324	101.0	8,078	79,974	65.8	125,792	546,811
Chemical [5]	325	748.5	45,861	61,274	431.9	340,038	657,082
Basic chemical	3251	153.3	10,420	67,966	91.8	82,690	195,007
Resin, syn rubber, and artificial and syn. fibers and filaments	3252	78.5	4,945	62,992	55.1	31,494	94,313
Pharmaceutical and medicine	3254	233.5	16,108	68,997	114.0	134,143	180,934
Plastics and rubber products	326	867.6	33,323	38,407	676.1	99,451	211,299
Plastics products	3261	715.2	26,727	37,368	557.1	82,762	174,143
Nonmetallic mineral products	327	473.8	20,201	42,658	368.3	72,132	126,263
Cement and concrete products	3273	231.2	9,892	42,794	178.6	35,334	64,463
Primary metal [5]	331	422.2	21,906	51,892	336.6	84,343	234,384
Iron and steel mills and ferroalloy.	3311	101.6	7,011	69,002	81.9	34,367	93,320
Foundries	3315	162.9	7,078	43,437	133.2	17,632	33,457
Fabricated metal products [5]	332	1,491.8	63,170	42,344	1,110.9	169,322	317,214
Architectural and structural metals	3323	371.0	15,114	40,743	267.1	40,145	83,539
Machine shops, turned product and screw, nut, and bolt.	3327	378.0	16,143	42,701	286.8	34,739	56,195
Coating, engraving, heat treating, and allied activities	3328	127.7	4,979	39,001	98.9	13,914	24,280
Machinery [5]	333	1,070.4	52,597	49,137	693.4	154,460	326,583
Agriculture, construction, and mining machinery	3331	181.1	8,348	46,101	124.7	32,431	77,458
Metalworking machinery.	3335	163.7	8,300	50,709	115.1	16,553	28,096
Computer and electronic products [5]	334	1,002.1	61,832	61,703	468.9	230,762	390,813
Computer and peripheral equipment.	3341	96.2	5,809	60,383	35.2	35,049	67,403
Communications equipment	3342	127.2	8,336	65,534	51.4	36,906	70,195
Semiconductor and other electronic components	3344	346.7	18,739	54,055	201.5	76,460	117,688
Navigational, measuring, medical, control instruments	3345	385.1	26,805	69,607	150.2	75,808	118,994
Electrical equipment, appliance, and component	335	410.4	17,763	43,284	292.9	57,520	119,402
Electrical equipment	3353	142.7	6,340	44,421	96.0	18,477	36,926
Transportation equipment [5]	336	1,525.0	83,837	54,974	1,093.4	260,883	699,034
Motor vehicles	3361	205.8	14,019	68,106	179.1	66,046	261,860
Motor vehicle bodies and trailers	3362	150.2	5,573	37,111	120.3	13,475	36,016
Motor vehicle parts	3363	577.7	28,699	49,676	450.7	80,486	202,299
Aerospace products and parts.	3364	381.1	26,392	69,249	191.8	75,906	143,003
Ship and boat building	3366	139.6	5,896	42,249	101.5	14,064	26,511
Furniture and related products [5]	337	519.0	17,699	34,102	404.1	46,390	85,618
Household and institutional furniture and kitchen cabinets	3371	342.9	10,813	31,533	272.8	26,218	48,931
Miscellaneous manufacturing	339	667.0	29,702	44,533	420.2	96,447	150,481
Medical equipment and supplies	3391	305.0	15,413	50,533	180.6	55,891	78,486

[1] North American Industry Classification System, 2002; see text, Section 15.   [2] Includes employment and payroll at administrative offices and auxiliary units. All employees represents the average of production workers plus all other employees for the payroll period ended nearest the 12th of March. Production workers represent the average of the employment for the payroll periods ended nearest the 12th of March, May, August, and November.   [3] Adjusted value added; takes into account (a) value added by merchandising operations (that is, difference between the sales value and cost of merchandise sold without further manufacture, processing, or assembly), plus (b) net change in finished goods and work-in-process inventories between beginning and end of year.   [4] Includes extensive and unmeasurable duplication from shipments between establishments in the same industry classification.   [5] Includes industries not shown separately.

Source: U.S. Census Bureau, *Annual Survey of Manufactures*, "Statistics for Industry Groups and Industries: 2006" (published November 18, 2008); using American FactFinder; <http://www.census.gov/manufacturing/asm/index.html>.

Manufactures   619

Table 976. **Manufactures—Summary by State: 2006**

[**12,984.7 represents 12,984,700**. Data are for North American Industry Classification System (NAICS) 2002 codes 31–33. See Appendix III]

State	All employees [1]			Production workers [1]		Value added by manufactures [2]		Value of ship-ments [3] (mil. dol.)
	Number (1,000)	Payroll		Total (1,000)	Wages (mil. dol.)	Total (mil. dol.)	Per production worker (dol.)	
		Total (mil. dol.)	Per employee (dol.)					
United States	12,984.7	592,119	45,601	9,175.3	344,193	2,285,929	249,139	5,015,553
Alabama	265.0	10,557	39,841	206.1	7,186	40,508	196,539	102,049
Alaska	11.0	401	36,598	9.2	284	1,592	173,902	7,015
Arizona	161.9	8,188	50,577	101.4	3,826	27,434	270,500	50,289
Arkansas	188.5	6,575	34,880	153.1	4,702	27,227	177,880	60,186
California	1,385.4	67,753	48,907	884.9	31,734	237,840	268,768	466,237
Colorado	128.0	6,145	47,996	86.5	3,296	20,828	240,677	40,430
Connecticut	175.6	9,416	53,619	107.1	4,549	32,714	305,584	52,513
Delaware	33.5	1,667	49,803	24.2	993	8,862	366,192	24,424
District of Columbia . . .	1.7	71	41,663	1.0	40	171	169,516	271
Florida	342.1	14,717	43,025	225.4	7,490	50,784	225,281	97,856
Georgia	408.4	16,148	39,536	314.5	10,592	61,846	196,668	140,972
Hawaii	13.9	504	36,156	9.0	299	2,049	228,537	7,301
Idaho	55.4	2,399	43,283	37.4	1,351	7,242	193,720	14,904
Illinois	638.8	29,840	46,715	445.2	17,138	107,367	241,162	242,291
Indiana	527.3	24,425	46,321	401.3	16,428	90,203	224,781	207,514
Iowa	224.6	9,289	41,360	165.2	5,989	40,931	247,798	91,386
Kansas	173.3	7,550	43,565	125.1	4,667	26,021	207,944	68,999
Kentucky	243.1	10,623	43,690	185.7	7,230	42,967	231,319	112,682
Louisiana	138.7	6,973	50,270	101.7	4,528	64,355	632,814	182,868
Maine	54.4	2,318	42,648	40.4	1,515	7,747	191,684	15,201
Maryland	132.1	6,698	50,688	82.4	3,224	22,808	276,952	42,120
Massachusetts	282.6	15,017	53,144	172.0	6,782	48,427	281,498	83,777
Michigan	577.2	29,831	51,682	424.6	19,640	88,161	207,642	214,431
Minnesota	325.9	15,170	46,547	220.4	8,127	48,943	222,051	100,772
Mississippi	160.0	5,612	35,062	128.4	3,884	20,698	161,151	56,316
Missouri	285.0	12,559	44,070	214.6	8,284	45,148	210,336	103,950
Montana	17.0	729	42,877	12.5	473	3,474	277,485	9,555
Nebraska	100.6	3,759	37,348	77.5	2,561	15,442	199,160	40,075
Nevada	44.3	2,051	46,322	29.9	1,076	7,461	249,431	12,841
New Hampshire	74.5	3,838	51,499	46.5	1,724	9,185	197,355	16,967
New Jersey	290.2	15,280	52,657	190.1	7,501	51,717	272,023	107,325
New Mexico	32.3	1,418	43,899	23.0	844	9,556	415,974	16,963
New York	525.9	24,111	45,847	345.9	12,884	92,046	266,100	161,220
North Carolina	501.8	19,228	38,314	382.4	12,419	106,996	279,819	200,992
North Dakota	23.0	900	39,047	17.6	604	3,874	220,641	9,789
Ohio	755.7	35,137	46,496	552.7	22,698	124,941	226,072	283,928
Oklahoma	134.6	5,678	42,181	100.2	3,579	23,846	237,894	55,972
Oregon	172.3	7,771	45,092	124.7	4,642	39,461	316,417	65,511
Pennsylvania	643.2	29,013	45,111	455.7	17,073	108,927	239,018	227,879
Rhode Island	53.2	2,414	45,340	33.1	1,151	7,829	236,340	14,181
South Carolina	248.4	10,538	42,416	188.2	6,782	38,049	202,183	90,509
South Dakota	38.2	1,390	36,370	28.8	910	5,386	186,916	11,209
Tennessee	373.9	15,315	40,963	277.6	9,804	62,013	223,380	141,268
Texas	808.1	38,196	47,265	560.6	21,202	194,846	347,557	528,831
Utah	111.9	4,819	43,059	76.1	2,692	17,668	232,281	38,248
Vermont	34.4	1,607	46,692	22.0	852	5,079	230,655	10,704
Virginia	272.2	11,655	42,814	202.0	7,401	50,649	250,794	93,909
Washington	254.3	12,968	50,999	165.3	6,653	48,862	295,559	105,628
West Virginia	59.5	2,594	43,624	45.3	1,738	10,468	231,181	23,915
Wisconsin	471.3	20,775	44,084	342.9	12,813	71,865	209,585	153,782
Wyoming	10.3	488	47,467	7.8	335	3,418	437,637	7,598

[1] Includes employment and payroll at administrative offices and auxiliary units. All employees represents the average of production workers plus all other employees for the payroll period ended nearest the 12th of March. Production workers represent the average of the employment for the payroll periods ended nearest the 12th of March, May, August, and November. [2] Adjusted value added; takes into account (a) value added by merchandising operations (that is, difference between the sales value and cost of merchandise sold without further manufacture, processing, or assembly), plus (b) net change in finished goods and work-inprocess inventories between beginning and end of year. [3] Includes extensive and unmeasurable duplication from shipments between establishments in the same industry classification.

Source: U.S. Census Bureau, *Annual Survey of Manufactures*, "Geographic Area Statistics: 2006" (published November 18, 2008); using American FactFinder; <http://www.census.gov/manufacturing/asm/index.html>.

Table 977. Manufacturers' E-Commerce Shipments by Industry: 2006 and 2007

[(5,015,553 represents $5,015,553,000,000). Based on the 2007 Economic Census—Manufacturing and the 2006 Annual Survey of Manufactures; subject to sampling variability. For businesses with paid employees. E-commerce is the value of goods and services sold online whether over open networks computer-mediated networks such as the Internet, or proprietary networks running systems such as Electronic Data Interchange (EDI)]

Industry	2002 NAICS code [1]	2006				2007 [2]			
		Ship-ments, total (mil. dol).	E-commerce			Ship-ments, total (mil.dol).	E-commerce		
			Ship-ments, total (mil.dol.)	Percent of total ship-ments	Percent distri-bution		Ship-ments, total (mil. dol).	Percent of total ship-ments	Percent distri-bution
Manufacturing, total . . .	31–33	5,015,553	1,566,799	31.2	100.0	5,305,935	1,855,719	35.0	100.0
Food products	311	536,939	153,996	28.7	9.8	586,907	202,684	34.5	9.8
Beverage and tobacco	312	124,033	68,046	54.9	4.3	127,625	72,049	56.5	4.3
Textile mills	313	38,829	12,377	31.9	0.8	35,857	14,188	39.6	0.8
Textile product mills	314	33,264	11,588	34.8	0.7	28,677	13,499	47.1	0.7
Apparel	315	30,325	9,182	30.3	0.6	24,318	7,280	29.9	0.6
Leather and allied products . . .	316	5,941	926	15.6	0.1	5,652	1,347	23.8	0.1
Wood products	321	112,403	14,960	13.3	1.0	101,958	19,422	19.0	1.0
Paper	322	169,033	40,842	24.2	2.6	176,103	61,128	34.7	2.6
Printing and related support activities	323	99,800	19,181	19.2	1.2	103,488	25,645	24.8	1.2
Petroleum and coal products . .	324	546,811	160,177	29.3	10.2	606,144	189,934	31.3	10.2
Chemicals	325	657,082	203,168	30.9	13.0	725,057	247,150	34.1	13.0
Plastics and rubber products . .	326	211,299	48,686	23.0	3.1	211,416	61,405	29.0	3.1
Nonmetallic mineral products. .	327	126,263	20,726	16.4	1.3	127,271	22,669	17.8	1.3
Primary metals	331	234,384	59,376	25.3	3.8	259,607	79,431	30.6	3.8
Fabricated metal products. . . .	332	317,214	64,109	20.2	4.1	343,541	82,062	23.9	4.1
Machinery	333	326,583	93,763	28.7	6.0	347,892	109,197	31.4	6.0
Computer and electronic products.	334	390,813	120,947	30.9	7.7	398,157	141,551	35.6	7.7
Electrical equipment, appli-ances, and components	335	119,402	34,211	28.7	2.2	129,200	40,606	31.4	2.2
Transportation equipment	336	699,034	383,560	54.9	24.5	735,829	409,424	55.6	24.5
Furniture and related products	337	85,618	18,187	21.2	1.2	84,978	22,489	26.5	1.2
Miscellaneous.	339	150,481	28,790	19.1	1.8	146,257	32,558	22.3	1.8

[1] North American Industry Classification System, 2002; see text, Section 15.   [2] Establishments representing approximately 5 percent of 2007 value of shipments did not have opportunity to report e-commerce receipts.

Source: U.S. Census Bureau, "E-Stats" (published 28 May 2008). See <http://www.census.gov/eos/www/ebusiness614.htm>.

Table 978. Manufacturing Employer Costs for Employee Compensation Per Hour Worked: 2000 to 2009

[As of March, for private industry workers. Based on a sample of establishments in the National Compensation Survey; see Appendix III and source for details. See also Table 638, Section 12]

Compensation component	Cost (dol.)					Percent distribution				
	2000	2005	2007	2008	2009	2000	2005	2007	2008	2009
Total compensation	23.41	28.48	30.37	31.42	32.03	100.0	100.0	100.0	100.0	100.0
Wages and salaries.	16.01	18.26	20.00	20.66	21.20	68.4	64.1	65.8	65.7	66.2
Total benefits	7.40	10.21	10.38	10.76	10.83	31.6	35.9	34.2	34.3	33.8
Paid leave	1.74	2.07	2.37	2.38	2.45	7.4	7.3	7.8	7.6	7.7
Vacation.	0.86	1.04	1.23	1.25	1.28	3.7	3.7	4.0	4.0	4.0
Holiday	0.65	0.76	0.85	0.86	0.89	2.8	2.7	2.8	2.7	2.8
Sick.	0.13	0.16	0.21	0.21	0.23	0.6	0.6	0.7	0.7	0.7
Other.	0.10	0.10	0.09	0.05	0.06	0.4	0.3	0.3	0.2	0.2
Supplemental pay	1.04	1.25	1.23	1.35	1.20	4.4	4.4	4.1	4.3	3.8
Overtime and premium pay	0.58	0.61	0.52	0.54	0.53	2.5	2.1	1.7	1.7	1.7
Shift differentials	0.10	0.12	0.14	0.14	0.13	0.4	0.4	0.5	0.4	0.4
Nonproduction bonuses. . .	0.36	0.53	0.57	0.68	0.54	1.5	1.8	1.9	2.10	1.7
Insurance.	1.85	2.68	2.97	3.13	3.26	7.9	9.4	9.8	10.0	10.2
Health insurance	1.69	2.48	2.76	2.91	3.03	7.2	8.7	9.1	9.3	9.5
Retirement and savings	0.75	1.64	1.24	1.32	1.30	3.2	5.8	4.1	4.2	4.1
Defined benefit	0.34	1.13	0.67	0.68	0.67	1.5	4.0	2.2	2.1	2.1
Defined contributions	0.41	0.51	0.57	0.65	0.63	1.8	1.8	1.9	2.1	2.0
Legally required benefits. . . .	1.92	2.45	2.56	2.58	2.62	8.2	8.6	8.4	8.2	8.2
Social Security.	1.38	1.60	1.74	1.79	1.84	5.9	5.6	5.7	5.7	5.7
Federal unemployment . . .	0.03	0.03	0.03	0.03	0.03	0.1	0.1	0.1	0.1	0.1
State unemployment.	0.11	0.19	0.19	0.18	0.18	0.5	0.7	0.6	0.6	0.6
Workers compensation . . .	0.40	0.64	0.60	0.58	0.57	1.7	2.2	2.0	1.8	1.8
Other benefits [1].	0.09	0.12	(NA)	(NA)	(NA)	0.4	0.4	(NA)	(NA)	(NA)

NA Not available.   [1] Includes severance pay, and supplemental unemployment benefits.

Source: U.S. Bureau of Labor Statistics, News, USDL 09-0634, Employer Costs for Employee Compensation (published June 2009). See also <http://www.bls.gov/ncs/ect/home.htm>.

Table 979. **Manufacturing Industries—Employment by Industry: 1990 to 2008**

[Annual averages of monthly figures (109,487 represents 109,487,000). Covers all full- and part-time employees who worked during, or received pay for, any part of the pay period including the 12th of the month. Minus sign (–) indicates decrease. See also headnote, Table 619]

Industry	2007 NAICS code[1]	All employees (1,000) 1990	2000	2005	2006	2007	2008	Percent change 1990–2000	2000–2008
All industries	(X)	109,487	131,785	133,703	136,086	137,598	137,066	20.4	4.0
Manufacturing.	31–33	17,695	17,263	14,226	14,155	13,879	13,431	–2.4	–22.2
Percent of all industries.	(X)	16	13	11	10	10	10	(X)	(X)
Durable goods	(X)	10,736	10,877	8,956	8,981	8,808	8,476	1.3	–22.1
Wood products	321	541	613	559	559	515	460	13.4	–25.0
Sawmills & wood preservation	3211	148	134	119	118	111	104	–9.6	–22.6
Plywood & engineered wood products . .	3212	96	122	123	120	108	91	28.2	–25.8
Nonmetallic mineral products.	327	528	554	505	510	501	468	4.9	–15.5
Cement & concrete products	3273	195	234	240	248	242	223	20.1	–4.6
Lime, gypsum, & other nonmetallic mineral products	3274,9	98	97	96	99	102	96	–0.3	–1.4
Primary metals	331	689	622	466	464	456	443	–9.7	–28.7
Iron & steel mills & ferroalloy production.	3311	187	135	96	97	100	99	–27.7	–26.7
Foundries	3315	214	217	164	161	155	149	1.4	–31.3
Fabricated metal products.	332	1,610	1,753	1,522	1,553	1,563	1,528	8.9	–12.8
Forging & stamping	3321	128	138	111	113	110	108	7.9	–21.9
Architectural & structural metals	3323	357	428	398	412	417	409	20.0	–4.4
Machine shops & threaded products . . .	3327	309	365	345	352	361	360	18.4	–1.5
Coating, engraving, & heat treating metals.	3328	143	175	145	149	148	144	22.7	–17.8
Machinery	333	1,408	1,457	1,166	1,183	1,187	1,186	3.5	–18.6
Agricultural, construction, & mining machinery.	3331	229	222	208	220	229	242	–2.8	8.9
Industrial machinery	3332	152	164	124	124	125	121	8.0	–26.3
Commercial & service industry machinery.	3333	147	147	111	109	108	105	0.3	–28.4
HVAC & commercial refrigeration equipment.	3334	165	194	154	157	154	150	17.9	–23.1
Metalworking machinery	3335	267	274	202	200	194	192	2.5	–29.9
Turbine & power transmission equipment.	3336	114	111	98	100	102	104	–2.4	–7.1
Computer & electronic products	334	1,903	1,820	1,316	1,308	1,273	1,248	–4.3	–31.5
Computer & peripheral equipment. . . .	3341	367	302	205	196	186	183	–17.8	–39.5
Communications equipment.	3342	232	239	141	136	128	129	3.1	–45.9
Semiconductors & electronic components	3344	574	676	452	458	448	432	17.8	–36.1
Electronic instruments.	3345	626	488	441	445	443	442	–22.1	–9.5
Electrical equipment & appliances	335	633	591	434	433	429	425	–6.7	–28.1
Electrical equipment	3353	244	210	152	155	157	159	–13.9	–24.4
Transportation equipment [2]	336	2,133	2,057	1,772	1,769	1,712	1,607	–3.6	–21.9
Motor vehicles.	3361	271	291	248	237	220	191	7.4	–34.6
Motor vehicle bodies & trailers	3362	130	183	171	179	166	142	40.8	–22.3
Motor vehicle parts.	3363	653	840	678	655	608	544	28.6	–35.2
Aerospace products & parts.	3364	841	517	455	474	489	504	–38.5	–2.5
Ship & boat building	3366	173	154	154	157	160	157	–10.7	1.7
Furniture & related products	337	601	683	568	560	531	481	13.5	–29.5
Household & institutional furniture	3371	398	443	383	374	349	306	11.3	–30.9
Office furniture & fixtures	3372	156	181	133	136	135	131	16.0	–27.6
Miscellaneous manufacturing.	339	690	728	647	644	642	631	5.4	–13.4
Medical equipment & supplies	3391	288	305	300	303	306	310	5.9	1.6
Other miscellaneous manufacturing. . . .	3399	403	423	347	341	336	321	5.1	–24.1
Nondurable goods	(X)	6,959	6,386	5,271	5,174	5,071	4,955	–8.2	–22.4
Food manufacturing.	311	1,507	1,553	1,478	1,479	1,484	1,485	3.0	–4.4
Fruit & vegetable preserving & specialty.	3114	218	197	174	176	173	174	–9.5	–12.0
Dairy products	3115	145	136	132	131	131	129	–5.9	–5.1
Animal slaughtering & processing	3116	427	507	504	506	508	512	18.6	1.0
Bakeries & tortilla manufacturing.	3118	292	306	280	280	280	281	4.9	–8.3
Beverages & tobacco products	312	218	207	192	194	198	199	–4.9	–3.9
Beverages	3121	173	175	167	171	176	177	1.2	1.3
Textile mills	313	492	378	218	195	170	151	–23.1	–60.1
Textile product mills	314	209	230	176	167	158	148	9.7	–35.8
Apparel	315	929	484	251	232	215	198	–48.0	–59.0
Leather & allied products	316	133	69	40	37	34	34	–48.3	–51.2
Paper & paper products	322	647	605	484	471	458	446	–6.6	–26.3
Pulp, paper, & paperboard mills	3221	238	191	142	136	132	126	–19.7	–34.1
Converted paper products	3222	409	413	343	334	326	320	1.1	–22.6
Printing & related support activities.	323	809	807	646	634	622	594	–0.2	–26.4
Petroleum & coal products	324	153	123	112	113	115	117	–19.4	–5.0
Chemicals	325	1,036	980	872	866	861	850	–5.3	–13.3
Basic chemicals.	3251	249	188	150	147	149	152	–24.4	–19.3
Resin, rubber, & artificial fibers	3252	158	136	108	105	106	105	–14.2	–23.3
Pharmaceuticals & medicines.	3254	207	274	288	292	295	290	32.4	5.6
Soaps, cleaning compounds, and toiletries	3256	132	129	114	111	110	108	–2.4	–15.8
Plastics & rubber products	326	826	951	802	786	757	734	15.1	–22.8
Plastics products	3261	619	737	634	630	609	589	19.1	–20.1
Rubber products	3262	207	214	168	156	148	145	3.3	–32.1

X Not applicable.   [1] Based on the North American Industry Classification System, 2007 (NAICS); see text, this section and Section 15.   [2] Includes railroad rolling stock manufacturing not shown separately.

Source: U.S. Bureau of Labor Statistics, Current Employment Statistics, "Employment, Hours, and Earnings—National"; <http://www.bls.gov/ces/data.htm>.

Table 980. **Average Hourly Earnings of Production Workers in Manufacturing Industries by State: 2005 to 2008**

[In dollars. Data are based on the North American Industry Classification System (NAICS) 2007. Based on the Current Employment Statistics Program; see headnote Table 619 and Appendix III]

State	2005	2006	2007	2008	State	2005	2006	2007	2008
United States	16.56	16.81	17.26	17.74	Montana	15.62	15.90	15.88	16.66
Alabama	14.93	15.56	15.75	15.68	Nebraska	15.44	15.04	15.19	15.26
Alaska	14.22	14.31	16.37	17.31	Nevada	14.98	15.46	15.54	15.56
Arizona	14.55	14.88	15.61	16.45	New Hampshire	15.87	16.57	17.09	17.31
Arkansas	13.71	13.35	14.06	14.17	New Jersey	16.33	16.56	17.22	17.88
California	15.70	15.77	16.28	16.79	New Mexico	13.66	14.06	14.40	14.72
Colorado	15.91	16.59	17.77	19.78	New York	17.77	18.29	18.49	18.58
Connecticut	18.96	19.78	20.63	21.42	North Carolina	14.38	14.57	15.08	15.49
Delaware	17.74	18.11	17.83	17.24	North Dakota	15.29	14.98	14.70	15.14
District of Columbia [1] . . .	(NA)	(NA)	(NA)	(NA)	Ohio	19.07	19.17	19.35	19.37
Florida	13.89	14.75	16.12	18.31	Oklahoma	14.56	14.77	14.56	14.74
Georgia	14.56	14.74	14.88	14.83	Oregon	15.49	15.57	16.45	16.91
Hawaii	14.34	15.89	17.06	18.93					
Idaho	14.96	16.89	19.01	19.94	Pennsylvania	15.26	15.38	15.48	15.77
Illinois	15.84	16.03	16.47	16.44	Rhode Island	13.12	13.42	13.78	13.94
Indiana	18.14	18.57	18.70	18.47	South Carolina	15.23	15.03	15.72	15.92
Iowa	16.25	16.40	16.84	16.63	South Dakota	13.47	13.75	14.27	14.64
Kansas	17.14	17.69	18.07	18.73	Tennessee	14.02	14.04	14.39	14.69
Kentucky	16.65	16.92	16.92	17.38	Texas	14.03	14.00	14.07	14.37
Louisiana	17.30	17.94	19.34	19.99	Utah	14.73	15.25	16.71	17.87
Maine	17.28	18.58	19.19	19.72	Vermont	15.06	15.79	16.49	16.51
Maryland	16.98	17.88	17.65	17.97	Virginia	16.40	16.75	17.60	18.33
Massachusetts	17.66	18.26	19.26	20.33	Washington	18.83	19.91	20.51	21.06
Michigan	21.50	21.84	22.06	22.11	West Virginia	17.14	17.89	18.71	19.02
Minnesota	16.63	17.24	17.39	17.74	Wisconsin	16.29	16.54	17.37	17.94
Mississippi	13.53	13.78	13.79	14.43	Wyoming	17.08	17.44	18.02	20.36
Missouri	17.42	17.16	16.99	17.70					

NA Not available.   [1] Represents the Washington-Arlington-Alexandria Metropolitan Area.

Source: U.S. Bureau of Labor Statistics, Current Employment Statistics, "State and Metro Area Employment, Hours, and Earnings (SAE)"; <http://www.bls.gov/sae/data.htm>.

Table 981. **Manufacturing Full-Time Equivalent Employees and Wages by Industry: 2000 to 2007**

[124,707 represents 124,707,000. Full-time equivalent employees equals the number of employees on full-time schedules plus the number of employees for part-time schedules converted to full-time basis]

Industry	1997 NAICS code [1]	Full-time equivalent (FTE) employees (1,000)				Wage and salary accruals per FTE worker (dol.)			
		2000	2005	2006	2007	2000	2005	2006	2007
All domestic industries, total . .	(X)	124,707	126,817	128,991	130,288	38,762	44,813	46,787	48,836
Manufacturing	31–33	16,947	14,041	13,977	13,692	44,216	50,140	52,315	54,482
Percent of all industries	(X)	13.6	11.1	10.8	10.5	114.1	111.9	111.8	111.6
Durable goods	(X)	10,713	8,870	8,880	8,703	47,007	52,383	54,953	57,083
Wood products	321	606	566	566	523	30,360	35,094	35,381	36,120
Nonmetallic mineral products	327	545	495	505	498	38,879	44,899	46,101	47,121
Primary metals	331	611	461	457	447	45,745	52,666	55,528	57,736
Fabricated metal products	332	1,738	1,503	1,525	1,530	37,688	43,020	45,063	46,948
Machinery	333	1,420	1,147	1,164	1,173	46,882	52,965	55,203	57,176
Computer and electronic products	334	1,813	1,296	1,288	1,256	71,372	78,032	83,186	86,792
Electrical equipment, appliances, and components	335	568	429	429	423	42,732	48,159	50,439	52,555
Motor vehicles, bodies and trailers, and parts	3361–3363	1,283	1,094	1,058	983	49,727	54,042	56,405	58,061
Other transportation equipment	3364–3365	736	671	688	709	52,612	64,162	68,597	70,115
Furniture and related products	337	664	555	549	520	29,660	33,976	35,162	36,607
Miscellaneous manufacturing	339	728	652	651	641	38,504	45,998	48,144	50,952
Nondurable goods	(X)	6,235	5,172	5,097	4,989	39,420	46,293	47,719	49,945
Food and beverage and tobacco products	311–312	1,719	1,628	1,632	1,636	34,110	38,659	39,647	40,955
Textile mills and textile product mills	313–314	584	374	345	321	29,018	33,545	34,621	35,716
Apparel and leather and allied products	315	538	301	280	253	24,769	31,161	32,654	34,714
Paper products	322	596	469	458	447	45,578	52,983	54,255	55,758
Printing and related support activities	323	767	641	635	625	38,966	41,887	43,034	44,078
Petroleum and coal products	324	120	111	110	113	62,310	81,403	87,360	93,651
Chemical products	325	968	861	853	848	60,928	72,126	73,993	78,717
Plastics and rubber products	326	942	787	784	744	35,375	40,341	41,451	43,008

X Not applicable   [1] North American Industry Classification System, 1997; see text, this section.

Source: U.S. Bureau of Economic Analysis, *Survey of Current Business*, August 2008. See also <http://www.bea.gov/bea /dn/nipaweb/SelectTable.asp?Selected=N>

Manufactures   623

Table 982. **Manufacturers' Shipments, Inventories, and New Orders: 1995 to 2008**

[In billions of dollars (3,480 represents $3,480,000,000,000), except ratio. Based on a sample survey; for methodology, see source]

Year	Shipments	Inventories (Dec. 31) [1]	Ratio of inventories to shipments [2]	New orders	Unfilled orders (Dec. 31)
1995	3,480	415	1.47	3,427	443
1996	3,597	421	1.44	3,567	485
1997	3,835	433	1.39	3,780	508
1998	3,900	439	1.38	3,808	492
1999	4,032	453	1.38	3,957	501
2000	4,209	470	1.37	4,161	545
2001	3,970	417	1.29	3,873	510
2002	3,915	412	1.30	3,802	458
2003	4,015	398	1.22	3,964	474
2004	4,309	429	1.23	4,255	493
2005	4,742	460	1.20	4,745	570
2006	5,020	497	1.22	5,038	658
2007	5,081	516	1.25	5,131	772
2008	5,183	528	1.25	5,152	799

[1] Inventories are stated at current cost.   [2] Ratio based on December seasonally adjusted data.

Source: U.S. Census Bureau, *Current Industrial Reports, Benchmark Report for Manufacturers' Shipments, Inventories, and Orders: January 2004 through December 2007*, Series M3-3 (07) (released May 2009); U.S. Census Bureau, "Full Report on Manufacturers' Shipments, Inventories and Orders: February 2008–January 2009." See also <http://www.census.gov/indicator/www/m3/>.

Table 983. **Ratios of Manufacturers' Inventories to Shipments and Unfilled Orders to Shipments by Industry Group: 2000 to 2008**

[Based on a sample survey; for methodology, see source]

Industry	2002 NAICS code [1]	2000	2003	2004	2005	2006	2007	2008
INVENTORIES-TO-SHIPMENTS RATIO								
All manufacturing industries	(X)	1.37	1.22	1.23	1.20	1.22	1.25	1.25
Durable goods	(X)	1.55	1.38	1.40	1.40	1.45	1.50	1.65
Wood products	321	1.32	1.25	1.26	1.24	1.27	1.31	1.28
Nonmetallic mineral products	327	1.23	1.17	1.16	1.09	1.11	1.19	1.31
Primary metals	331	1.69	1.61	1.60	1.53	1.60	1.52	1.51
Fabricated metals	332	1.56	1.46	1.57	1.53	1.57	1.55	1.61
Machinery	333	2.08	1.81	1.85	1.78	1.82	1.89	1.91
Computers and electronic products . . .	334	1.54	1.40	1.28	1.45	1.39	1.40	1.51
Electrical equipment, appliances, and components	335	1.44	1.42	1.41	1.37	1.44	1.40	1.42
Transportation equipment	336	1.35	1.14	1.19	1.17	1.27	1.41	1.85
Furniture and related products	337	1.35	1.19	1.23	1.19	1.16	1.17	1.20
Miscellaneous products	339	1.90	1.68	1.70	1.70	1.76	1.80	1.85
Nondurable goods	(X)	1.14	1.03	1.03	0.98	0.98	1.00	0.89
Food products	311	0.88	0.77	0.75	0.75	0.78	0.77	0.72
Beverages and tobacco products	312	1.51	1.61	1.63	1.40	1.42	1.36	1.33
Textile mills	313	1.49	1.24	1.26	1.18	1.25	1.24	1.30
Textile product mills	314	1.75	1.29	1.20	1.17	1.26	1.32	1.44
Apparel	315	1.89	1.45	1.58	1.53	1.61	1.76	1.64
Leather and allied products	316	2.10	1.65	1.79	1.74	2.11	1.95	2.23
Paper products	322	1.11	1.08	1.11	1.07	1.06	1.09	1.04
Printing	323	0.79	0.76	0.80	0.79	0.81	0.84	0.86
Petroleum and coal products	324	0.71	0.83	0.79	0.75	0.70	0.76	0.45
Basic chemicals	325	1.40	1.21	1.22	1.17	1.18	1.19	1.15
Plastics and rubber products	326	1.21	1.08	1.16	1.15	1.17	1.24	1.20
UNFILLED ORDERS-TO-SHIPMENTS RATIO								
All manufacturing industries	(X)	1.57	1.43	1.38	1.45	1.58	1.83	1.85
Durable goods	(X)	2.78	2.67	2.63	2.83	3.09	3.62	3.85
Primary metals	331	1.45	1.58	1.49	1.59	1.42	1.38	0.89
Fabricated metals	332	2.02	1.81	1.93	2.07	2.16	2.25	2.12
Machinery	333	2.51	2.41	2.37	2.54	2.92	3.31	3.44
Computers and electronic products . . .	334	3.08	3.30	3.31	3.19	3.54	3.79	3.95
Electrical equipment, appliances, and components	335	1.77	1.72	1.80	1.98	2.26	2.26	2.16
Transportation equipment	336	4.91	4.52	4.50	5.24	5.94	7.50	8.98
Furniture and related products	337	1.14	1.07	1.12	1.08	0.98	1.05	0.99
Miscellaneous products	339	0.62	0.54	0.54	0.41	0.45	0.50	0.46

X Not applicable.   [1] Based on the North American Industry Classification System, 2002; see text, this section and Section 15.

Source: U.S. Census Bureau, *Current Industrial Reports, Benchmark Report for Manufacturers' Shipments, Inventories, and Orders: January 2004 through December 2007*, Series M3-3 (07) (released May 2008); U.S. Census Bureau , "Full Report on Manufacturers' Shipments, Inventories and Orders: February 2008–January 2009." See also <http://www.census.gov/indicator/www/m3/>.

Table 984. **Value of Manufacturers' Shipments, Inventories, and New Orders by Industry: 2000 to 2008**

[In billions of dollars (4,209 represents $4,209,000,000,000). Based on a sample survey; for methodology, see source]

Industry	2002 NAICS code [1]	2000	2004	2005	2006	2007	2008
SHIPMENTS							
All manufacturing industries	(X)	4,209	4,309	4,742	5,020	5,081	5,183
Durable goods	(X)	2,374	2,265	2,425	2,561	2,563	2,494
Wood products	321	94	104	112	112	102	97
Nonmetallic mineral products	327	97	103	115	126	119	109
Primary metals	331	157	182	203	233	242	255
Fabricated metals.	332	268	261	289	317	327	331
Machinery.	333	292	272	303	326	331	347
Computers and electronic products	334	511	366	373	391	387	380
Electrical equipment, appliances, and components.	335	125	105	112	120	127	125
Transportation equipment	336	640	662	691	698	693	619
Furniture and related products	337	75	78	84	87	82	76
Miscellaneous products.	339	115	132	143	150	153	155
Nondurable goods.	(X)	1,835	2,044	2,317	2,459	2,518	2,690
Food products	311	435	512	532	538	574	611
Beverages and tobacco products	312	112	114	124	125	132	138
Textile mills	313	52	41	42	39	37	34
Textile product mills	314	34	34	35	33	30	27
Apparel	315	60	33	31	30	30	31
Leather and allied products	316	10	6	6	6	6	6
Paper products	322	165	155	162	170	169	172
Printing	323	104	94	97	100	102	98
Petroleum and coal products	324	235	330	476	549	564	674
Basic chemicals.	325	449	541	611	658	664	689
Plastics and rubber products	326	178	185	200	211	211	211
INVENTORIES (Dec. 31)							
All manufacturing industries	(X)	470	429	460	497	516	528
Durable goods	(X)	298	258	276	301	312	334
Wood products	321	10	11	12	12	11	10
Nonmetallic mineral products	327	10	10	10	11	12	12
Primary metals	331	22	24	26	31	31	32
Fabricated metals.	332	34	33	36	40	41	43
Machinery.	333	49	41	43	48	50	53
Computers and electronic products	334	63	38	44	44	44	47
Electrical equipment, appliances, and components.	335	15	12	12	14	14	14
Transportation equipment	336	69	63	65	71	78	92
Furniture and related products	337	8	8	8	8	8	7
Miscellaneous products.	339	18	18	20	21	22	23
Nondurable goods.	(X)	172	171	184	196	204	194
Food products	311	32	32	33	35	36	36
Beverages and tobacco products	312	14	15	14	15	15	15
Textile mills	313	6	4	4	4	4	4
Textile product mills	314	5	3	3	3	3	3
Apparel	315	9	4	4	4	4	4
Leather and allied products	316	2	1	1	1	1	1
Paper products	322	15	14	14	15	15	15
Printing	323	6	6	6	6	7	7
Petroleum and coal products	324	13	20	27	29	33	24
Basic chemicals.	325	52	54	58	63	65	65
Plastics and rubber products	326	18	17	19	20	21	21
NEW ORDERS							
All manufacturing industries	(X)	4,161	4,255	4,745	5,038	5,131	5,152
Durable goods	(X)	2,327	2,211	2,428	2,578	2,613	2,463
Wood products	321	94	104	112	112	102	97
Nonmetallic mineral products	327	97	103	115	126	119	109
Primary metals	331	154	186	208	233	242	247
Fabricated metals.	332	270	266	297	324	331	328
Machinery.	333	295	274	313	342	343	355
Computers and electronic products	334	436	297	297	337	330	325
Electrical equipment, appliances, and components.	335	126	107	115	124	128	124
Transportation equipment	336	663	663	745	743	781	650
Furniture and related products	337	75	79	84	86	82	75
Miscellaneous products.	339	117	132	142	151	154	154
Nondurable goods.	(X)	1,835	2,044	2,317	2,459	2,518	2,690

X Not applicable.   [1] Based on the North American Industry Classification System, 2002; see text, this section and Section 15.

Source: U.S. Census Bureau, Current Industrial Reports, *Benchmark Report for Manufacturers' Shipments, Inventories, and Orders: January 2004 through December 2007*, Series M3-3 (07) (released May 2008) and U.S. Census Bureau, *Full Report on Manufacturers' Shipments, Inventories and Orders: February 2008–January 2009*. See also <http://www.census.gov/indicator/www/m3/>.

Manufactures   625

Table 985. **Value of Manufacturers' Shipments, Inventories, and New Orders by Market Grouping: 2000 to 2008**

[In billions of dollars (4,029 represents $4,029,000,000,000). Based on a sample survey; for methodology, see source]

Market grouping	2000	2003	2004	2005	2006	2007	2008
SHIPMENTS							
All manufacturing industries	4,209	4,015	4,309	4,742	5,020	5,081	5,183
Consumer goods	1,501	1,584	1,701	1,895	1,989	2,038	2,121
Consumer durable goods	391	419	419	423	422	418	354
Consumer nondurable goods.	1,109	1,166	1,282	1,473	1,567	1,619	1,766
Aircraft and parts	112	103	106	114	124	141	152
Defense aircraft and parts.	25	39	42	38	39	40	56
Nondefense aircraft and parts	87	64	64	76	86	101	97
Construction materials and supplies. . . .	445	429	463	510	546	533	520
Motor vehicles and parts	471	492	495	501	500	480	387
Computers and related products	110	69	63	65	67	66	60
Information technology industries.	400	275	288	295	320	322	321
Nondefense capital goods	808	634	661	730	796	796	800
Excluding aircraft.	758	601	629	687	745	740	749
Defense capital goods.	67	86	92	92	90	93	107
Durables excluding capital goods.	1,498	1,423	1,512	1,603	1,675	1,673	1,586
INVENTORIES (Dec. 31)							
All manufacturing industries	470	398	429	460	497	516	528
Consumer goods	128	121	130	140	147	153	144
Consumer durable goods	26	24	25	27	28	28	27
Consumer nondurable goods.	102	98	105	113	120	125	117
Aircraft and parts	36	32	30	33	37	44	60
Defense aircraft and parts.	9	10	10	12	12	13	14
Nondefense aircraft and parts	27	22	20	22	25	31	46
Construction materials and supplies. . . .	49	44	50	53	58	58	59
Motor vehicles and parts	22	21	22	23	25	23	21
Computers and related products	8	4	4	4	5	5	5
Information technology industries.	51	34	32	38	39	39	42
Nondefense capital goods	127	96	96	108	117	124	142
Excluding aircraft.	107	80	82	91	98	101	106
Defense capital goods.	17	15	18	16	17	18	19
Durables excluding capital goods.	154	128	143	152	168	169	172
NEW ORDERS							
All manufacturing industries	4,161	3,964	4,255	4,745	5,038	5,131	5,152
Consumer goods	1,502	1,585	1,701	1,894	1,989	2,038	2,119
Consumer durable goods	393	420	420	421	422	419	353
Consumer nondurable goods.	1,109	1,166	1,282	1,473	1,567	1,619	1,766
Aircraft and parts	131	100	105	149	166	225	185
Defense aircraft and parts.	31	45	32	30	38	41	61
Nondefense aircraft and parts	99	55	73	119	128	184	124
Construction materials and supplies. . . .	447	429	466	518	549	540	520
Motor vehicles and parts	468	494	495	504	503	478	384
Computers and related products	108	68	62	64	67	66	60
Information technology industries.	410	277	294	297	338	328	323
Nondefense capital goods	831	635	673	789	861	891	830
Excluding aircraft.	768	609	631	702	776	755	753
Defense capital goods.	80	97	92	93	88	97	116
Durables excluding capital goods.	1,416	1,360	1,446	1,545	1,630	1,624	1,517

Source: U.S. Census Bureau, *Current Industrial Reports, Benchmark Report for Manufacturers' Shipments, Inventories, and Orders: January 2004 through December 2007,* Series M3-3 (07) (released May 2008) and U.S. Census Bureau, *Full Report on Manufacturers' Shipments, Inventories and Orders: February 2008–January 2009.* See also <http://www.census.gov/indicator/www/m3/>.

Table 986. **Finances and Profits of Manufacturing Corporations: 2000 to 2008**

[In billions of dollars (4,548 represents $4,548,000,000,000). Data exclude estimates for corporations with less than $250,000 in assets at time of sample selection. See Table 770 for individual industry data]

Item	2000 [1]	2001 [1]	2001 [2]	2002 [2]	2003 [2]	2004 [2]	2005 [2]	2006 [2]	2007 [2]	2008 [3]
Net sales.	4,548	4,308	4,295	4,217	4,397	4,934	5,411	5,783	6,060	6,483
Net operating profit	348	185	186	225	237	320	359	405	416	362
Net profit:										
Before taxes	381	82	83	196	306	447	524	605	603	418
After taxes	275	36	36	135	237	348	401	470	443	294
Cash dividends.	132	102	103	106	115	143	179	178	178	186
Net income retained in business . .	143	−67	−66	28	122	205	222	292	265	108

[1] Based on the Standard Industrial Classification system.   [2] Based on the North American Industry Classification System, 2002; see text, Section 15.   [3] Based on the North American Industry Classification System, 2007; see text, Section 15.

Source: U.S. Census Bureau, *Quarterly Financial Report for Manufacturing, Mining, and Trade Corporations.* See also Fourth Quarter 2008 QFR Press Release (published March 2009). See <http://webdev.ssd.census.gov/econ/qfr/index.html>.

[In millions of dollars (2,629,458 represents $2,629,458,000,000). Corporations and assets as of end of 4th quarter; profits for entire year. Through 2000, based on Standard Industrial Classification code; beginning 2001, based on the North American Industry Classification System; see text, Section 15. For corporations above a certain asset value based on complete canvass. The asset value for complete canvass was raised in 1995 to $250 million. Asset sizes less than these values are sampled, except as noted. For details regarding Survey description, data analysis and methodology, see <http://www.census.gov/econ/qfr/collection.html>. Minus sign (–) indicates loss]

Year	Total [1]	Asset-size class						
		Under $10 mil. [1]	$10– $25 mil.	$25– $50 mil.	$50– $100 mil.	$100– $250 mil.	$250– $1 bil.	$1 bil. and over
Assets:								
1990.......	2,629,458	142,498	74,477	55,914	72,554	123,967	287,512	1,872,536
1994.......	3,080,231	148,751	81,505	66,405	82,116	138,950	358,100	2,204,404
1995.......	3,345,229	155,618	87,011	68,538	87,262	159,133	370,263	2,417,403
1996.......	3,574,407	163,928	87,096	69,722	93,205	156,702	398,651	2,605,102
1997.......	3,746,797	167,921	87,398	76,034	85,186	157,130	397,559	2,775,570
1998.......	3,967,309	170,068	87,937	69,627	86,816	148,060	419,153	2,985,647
1999.......	4,382,814	170,058	85,200	67,352	97,810	138,143	398,881	3,425,370
2000.......	4,852,106	171,666	85,482	72,122	90,866	149,714	389,537	3,892,720
2001 [2]	4,747,789	169,701	84,664	67,493	88,088	131,617	393,752	3,812,474
2002.......	4,823,219	166,191	82,369	62,654	81,667	134,821	407,423	3,888,095
2003.......	5,162,852	161,462	80,681	62,592	77,205	126,826	392,192	4,261,894
2004.......	5,538,113	163,072	80,085	71,674	81,741	126,950	414,144	4,600,447
2005.......	5,828,716	165,195	85,785	68,731	87,818	142,900	423,917	4,854,370
2006.......	6,179,142	168,537	93,786	72,494	91,877	146,651	418,501	5,187,295
2007.......	6,891,131	180,319	98,348	80,400	93,017	144,254	433,634	5,861,160
2008.......	6,842,856	185,286	105,176	83,225	97,418	146,676	416,299	5,808,777
Net profit: [3]								
1990.......	110,128	8,527	5,160	2,769	2,661	3,525	7,110	80,377
1994.......	174,874	14,131	7,057	4,072	4,996	6,745	14,626	123,250
1995.......	198,151	13,224	5,668	3,767	5,771	7,000	16,549	146,172
1996.......	224,869	15,802	6,872	4,266	5,664	7,935	16,059	168,271
1997.......	244,505	17,948	8,383	4,153	4,675	7,074	18,433	183,836
1998.......	234,386	18,350	6,421	3,790	4,681	5,610	14,364	181,170
1999.......	257,805	17,398	7,618	3,504	4,798	4,795	12,756	206,934
2000.......	275,313	16,578	6,820	3,403	2,742	3,510	15,121	227,136
2001 [2]	36,168	8,387	3,366	–408	403	–543	–6,782	31,746
2002.......	134,686	10,003	2,784	807	1,699	3,356	–1,227	117,262
2003.......	237,041	9,821	3,374	2,005	2,256	2,973	4,115	212,497
2004.......	348,151	14,970	5,745	3,858	3,080	5,140	12,787	302,571
2005.......	401,344	17,357	6,057	4,066	3,781	7,678	15,967	346,438
2006.......	470,282	22,301	8,685	5,260	4,601	8,901	21,405	399,131
2007.......	442,734	22,930	9,006	4,402	6,518	8,400	17,565	373,915
2008.......	293,700	20,209	7,788	6,411	3,686	3,891	0,563	245,153

[1] Excludes estimates for corporations with less than $250,000 in assets at time of sample selection. [2] Beginning 2001, data reported on a NAICS basis. [3] After taxes.

Source: U.S. Census Bureau, *Quarterly Financial Report for Manufacturing, Mining, and Trade Corporations.* See also Fourth Quarter 2008 QFR Press Release (published 30 March 2009); <http://webdev.ssd.census.gov/econ/qfr/index.html>.

Table 988. **Manufacturing Corporations—Selected Finances: 1990 to 2008**

[In billions of dollars (2,811 represents $2,811,000,000,000). Data are not necessarily comparable from year to year due to changes in accounting procedures, industry classifications, sampling procedures, etc.; for detail, see source. See headnote, Table 987. Minus sign (–) indicates loss]

Year	All manufacturing corps.			Durable goods industries			Nondurable goods industries		
		Profits [1]			Profits [1]			Profits [1]	
	Sales	Before taxes	After taxes	Sales	Before taxes	After taxes	Sales	Before taxes	After taxes
1990	2,811	158	110	1,357	57	41	1,454	101	69
1994	3,256	244	175	1,658	121	87	1,598	123	88
1995	3,528	275	198	1,808	131	94	1,721	144	104
1996	3,758	307	225	1,942	147	106	1,816	160	119
1997	3,922	331	244	2,076	167	121	1,847	164	123
1998	3,949	315	234	2,169	175	128	1,781	140	107
1999	4,149	355	258	2,314	199	140	1,835	157	117
2000 [2]	4,548	381	275	2,457	191	132	2,091	190	144
2001 [2]	4,295	83	36	2,321	–69	–76	1,974	152	112
2002	4,217	196	135	2,261	45	21	1,955	149	113
2003	4,397	306	237	2,283	118	88	2,114	188	149
2004	4,934	447	348	2,537	200	157	2,397	248	192
2005	5,411	524	401	2,731	211	161	2,681	313	240
2006	5,783	605	470	2,910	249	193	2,873	356	278
2007	6,060	603	443	3,016	247	159	3,044	356	283
2008	6,483	418	294	3,080	117	62	3,403	301	232

[1] Beginning 1998, profits before and after income taxes reflect inclusion of minority stockholders' interest in net income before and after income taxes. [2] Beginning 2001, data reported on a NAICS basis.

Source: U.S. Census Bureau, *Quarterly Financial Report for Manufacturing, Mining, and Trade Corporations.* See also Fourth Quarter 2008 QFR Press Release (published 30 March 2009); <http://webdev.ssd.census.gov/econ/qfr/index.html>.

Manufactures 627

Table 989. **Cotton, Wool, and Manmade Fibers—Consumption by End-Use: 2003 to 2007**

[14,081 represents 14,081,000,000. Based on U.S. Manufactured Fiber, Cotton and Wool End Use Survey. Represents raw fiber which was put into process in order to manufacture end products manufactured by U.S. mills. Excludes glass fiber]

Year	Total [1] (mil. lb.)	Cotton [2] Total (mil. lb.)	Cotton Percent of end-use	Wool [3] Total (mil. lb.)	Wool Percent of end-use	Manufactured fibers Total (mil. lb.)	Manufactured fibers Percent of end-use	Cellulosic [4] Total (mil. lb.)	Cellulosic Percent of end-use	Synthetic [5] Total (mil. lb.)	Synthetic Percent of end-use
Total:											
2003......	14,081	3,465	24.6	112	0.8	11,163	79.3	227	1.6	10,964	77.9
2004......	13,454	2,744	20.4	107	0.8	11,125	82.7	218	1.6	10,911	81.1
2005......	13,127	2,548	19.4	95	0.7	10,924	83.2	210	1.6	10,697	81.5
2006......	11,696	1,914	16.4	97	0.8	10,057	86.0	189	1.6	9,869	84.4
2007......	10,940	1,724	15.8	91	0.8	9,126	83.4	209	1.9	8,917	81.5
Apparel:											
2003......	3,426	1,902	55.5	65	1.9	1,459	42.6	93	2.7	1,366	39.9
2004......	2,873	1,443	50.2	60	2.1	1,371	47.7	76	2.6	1,295	45.1
2005......	2,738	1,415	51.7	51	1.8	1,273	46.5	62	2.3	1,210	44.2
2006......	2,143	1,019	47.5	51	2.4	1,074	50.1	41	1.9	1,033	48.2
2007......	2,016	963	47.7	47	2.3	1,007	49.9	40	2.0	967	48.0
Home textiles:											
2003......	2,069	1,180	57.0	12	0.6	877	42.4	43	2.1	834	40.3
2004......	1,741	937	53.8	10	0.6	794	45.6	40	2.3	753	43.3
2005......	1,492	791	53.0	9	0.6	691	46.3	31	2.1	660	44.3
2006......	1,140	568	49.8	12	1.0	561	49.2	23	2.0	538	47.2
2007......	941	440	46.8	10	1.1	491	52.2	22	2.3	469	49.9
Floor coverings:											
2003......	4,417	32	0.7	28	0.6	4,357	98.7	–	–	4,357	98.7
2004......	4,494	32	0.7	29	0.6	4,433	98.7	–	–	4,433	98.7
2005......	4,558	32	0.7	29	0.6	4,497	98.7	–	–	4,497	98.7
2006......	4,229	32	0.8	29	0.7	4,169	98.6	–	–	4,169	98.6
2007......	3,840	30	0.8	29	0.8	3,781	98.5	–	–	3,781	98.5
Industrial: [6]											
2003......	4,170	351	8.4	8	0.2	3,811	91.4	92	2.2	3,719	89.2
2004......	4,346	333	7.7	8	0.2	4,006	92.2	102	2.3	3,904	89.8
2005......	4,340	310	7.2	5	0.1	4,024	92.7	112	2.6	3,912	90.1
2006......	4,184	296	7.1	6	0.1	3,882	92.8	117	2.8	3,765	90.0
2007......	4,143	291	7.0	5	0.1	3,847	92.9	147	3.5	3,700	89.3

– Represents or rounds to zero. [1] Includes other fibers such as silk, linen, jute and sisal. [2] Raw cotton. [3] Wool data includes virgin, noils, reprocessed and reused wool. [4] Includes rayon and acetate. [5] Includes acrylic, nylon, polyester, olefin, and spandex. [6] Includes consumer type products, such as, narrow fabrics, medical, sanitary, tires, hose, belting, felts, sewing thread, filtration, etc. See source.

Source: Fiber Economics Bureau, Inc., Arlington, VA, *Fiber Organon*, Vol. 79, No. 10, October 2008 (copyright).

Table 990. **Textiles—Production and Foreign Trade: 2008**

[1,308,598 represents 1,308,598,000. Fabric blends as shown in the report are reported based on the chief weight of the fiber; whereas, fabrics blends as shown for imports are based on the chief value of the fiber]

Product description	Unit	Quanity (1,000) Manufacturers' production	Imports for consumption	Exports of domestic merchandise	Percent Imports to manufacturers' production	Exports to manufacturers' production	Value ($1,000) Imports for consumption [1]	Exports of domestic merchandise
YARN								
Spun yarn..............	kilograms .	1,308,598	131,655	(S)	10.1	(S)	557,379	(S)
Textured, crimped, twisted, or bulked filament yarn	kilograms .	1,166,076	86,018	60,981	7.4	5.2	310,163	270,649
BROADWOVEN FABRICS [2]								
Spun yarn fabrics.........	sq.meters .	1,361,242	1,030,573	228,345	75.7	16.8	1,533,903	471,600
85 percent or more filament yarn fabrics, manmade	sq.meters .	1,662,442	1,023,469	(S)	61.6	(S)	718,745	(S)
Spun/filament combinations (except blue denim and other yarn dyed).........	sq.meters .	137,397	128,008	38,850	93.2	28.3	232,899	91,774
Silk fabrics	sq.meters .	(D)	27,611	(S)	(D)	(S)	245,942	(S)
KNIT FABRICS								
Pile fabrics	kilograms.	34,155	143,678	32,363	420.7	94.8	185,487	172,773
Elastic fabric	kilograms.	17,156	18,291	(S)	106.6	(S)	205,981	(S)
Other warp knit fabrics	kilograms.	35,082	29,614	12,668	84.4	36.1	190,428	132,832
Other weft knit fabrics......	kilograms.	138,740	56,166	(S)	40.5	(S)	299,247	(S)
Other narrow knit fabrics	kilograms.	2,224	763	(S)	34.3	(S)	11,998	(S)
SHEETS, PILLOWCASES, AND TOWELS								
Sheets and pillowcases	dozens...	1,598	52,880	501	3,309.2	31.4	2,123,896	40,374
Finished towels	dozens...	4,963	152,644	663	3,075.6	13.4	1,747,248	31,624

D Withheld to avoid disclosing data for individual companies. S Does not meet publication standards. [1] Dollar value represents the c.i.f. (cost, insurance, and freight) at the first port of entry in the United States plus calculated import duty. [2] Represents production of gray broadwoven fabrics; import and export data represent gray as well as finished broadwoven fabrics.

Source: U.S. Census Bureau, Current Industrial Reports, "Textiles," Series MQ313A; <http://www.census.gov/manufacturing/cir/historical-data/mq313a/index.html>.

628 Manufactures

Table 991. **Pharmaceutical Preparations—Value of Shipments: 2000 to 2008**

[In millions of dollars (79,262 represents 79,262,000,000]

Product description	Product code	2000	2004	2005	2006	2007	2008
Pharmaceutical preparations, except biologicals	(X)	79,262	109,852	118,647	123,118	(NA)	(NA)
Affecting neoplasms, endocrine systems, and metabolic disease	3254121	9,784	20,789	23,779	25,721	28,497	33,229
Acting on the central nervous system and sense organs	3254124	18,508	25,001	25,627	29,882	28,714	26,480
Acting on the cardiovascular system	3254127	8,993	10,224	10,232	10,874	11,969	11,545
Acting on the respiratory system	325412A	10,179	15,148	16,367	18,350	16,177	16,277
Acting on the digestive system.	325412D	10,046	15,252	16,829	11,775	9,822	10,183
Acting on the skin	325412G	2,941	3,283	3,657	3,303	3,498	3,324
Vitamin, nutrient, and hematinic preparations .	325412L	5,676	6,683	7,556	7,711	8,062	8,735
Affecting parasitic and infective disease.	325412P	11,037	10,819	11,228	11,693	11,014	9,021
Pharmaceutical preps. for veterinary use	325412T	2,096	2,653	3,371	3,808	3,206	3,280

X Not applicable.   NA Not available.

Source: U.S. Census Bureau, Current Industrial Reports, "Pharmaceutical Preparations, Except Biologicals," Series MA325G, (published August 2009); <http://www.census.gov/manufacturing/cir/historical_data/ma325g/index.html>.

Table 992. **Inorganic Chemicals and Fertilizers—Production: 2000 to 2008**

[(15,809 represents 15,809,000)].

Product description	Product code	2000	2004	2005	2006	2007	2008
INORGANIC FERTILIZERS 1,000 short tons (2,000 lbs.)							
Ammonia, synthetic anhydrous	3253111120	15,809	12,058	11,181	10,981	11,448	10,550
Ammonium nitrate, original solution	3253111201	7,979	7,229	7,212	7,068	8,236	7,841
Ammonium sulfate.	3253111240	2,808	3,005	2,906	2,870	3,145	2,771
Urea (100%).	3253114100	7,682	6,344	5,807	5,934	6,156	5,777
Nitric acid (100%)	3253111111	8,708	7,129	7,398	7,245	8,623	7,986
Phosphoric acid (100% P2O5).	3253121100	12,492	12,693	12,621	11,797	12,081	10,158
Sulfuric acid, gross (100%)	3251881100	43,643	41,934	40,996	39,578	39,745	35,692
Superphosphates and other fertilizer materials (100% P2O5).	3253124100	8,899	8,737	8,141	7,184	7,241	6,105
INORGANIC CHEMICALS 1,000 short tons (2,000 lbs.)							
Chlorine gas [1]	3251811111	14,000	12,329	10,272	12,443	11,895	10,669
Sodium hydroxide, total liquid [2]	3251814111	11,523	9,620	8,517	9,735	8,869	8,111
Potassium hydroxide liquid [2]	3251817111	539	525	527	610	621	582
Finished sodium bicarbonate.	3251817131	536	579	581	644	663	682
Hydrochloric acid [3]	3251884131	4,717	5,302	4,619	4,391	4,331	3,902
Aluminum oxide	3313110100	(D)	(D)	(D)	(D)	(D)	(D)
Aluminum sulfate (commercial) [4]	3251887151	1,076	972	967	1,022	967	(S)
Sodium chlorate	325188A141	940	556	523	615	617	607
Sodium phosphate tripoly	325188A174	(D)	(D)	(D)	(D)	(D)	(D)
Sodium silicates [5]	325188A181	1,136	1,112	1,309	1,270	1,182	1,106
Sodium metasilicates.	325188A187	72	58	59	28,772	(D)	(D)
Sodium sulfate	325188A1A7	509	86	93	101	93	87
Carbon activated, Granular carbons (dry weight) [6, 7]	325998H1E4	95	(D)	(D)	24	27	(S)
Pulverized carbons	325998H1E7	71	39	(D)	64	98	(S)
Hydrogen peroxide	325188G181	1,083	357	365	390	429	437
Phosphorous, oxychloride, and trichlorde. . .	325188G1F1	(D)	(D)	(D)	(D)	(D)	(D)

D Withheld to avoid disclosing data for individual companies.   S Does not meet publication standards.   [1] Production includes amounts liquefied.   [2] Liquid production figures represent total production, including quantities later evaporated to solid caustic.   [3] Includes production from salt and acid.   [4] Excludes quantities produced and consumed in municipalities.   [5] Excludes amounts produced and consumed in making meta, ortho, and sesquisilicates.   [6] Excludes reactivated carbon.   [7] Includes pelleted carbon.

Source: U.S. Census Bureau, Current Industrial Reports, "Inorganic Chemicals," Series MQ325A, July 2009 and Current Industrial Reports, "Fertilizers and Related Chemicals," Series MQ325B (published June 2009); <http://www.census.gov/cir/www/325/mq325a.html> and <http://www.census.gov/manufacturing/cir/historical_data/mq325b/index.html>.

Manufactures   629

Table 993. Iron and Steel Industry—Summary: 1990 to 2008

[95.5 represents 95,500,000 tons. Comprises carbon, alloy, and stainless steel]

Item	Unit	1990	1995	2000	2004	2005	2006	2007	2008
Steel mill products, apparent supply	Mil. tons [1] . . .	95.5	109.6	131.9	131.8	120.8	135.7	121.9	111.0
Net shipments, total	Mil. tons [1] . . .	85.0	97.5	109.1	111.4	105.0	109.5	106.4	98.5
STEEL MARKETS									
Automotive	Mil. tons [1] . . .	11.1	14.6	16.1	13.9	14.5	15.5	13.6	12.8
Steel service centers, distributors . .	Mil. tons [1] . . .	21.1	23.8	30.1	34.7	30.6	30.1	26.5	25.5
Construction, including mainte- nance [2]	Mil. tons [1] . . .	9.2	14.9	20.3	23.8	24.0	21.0	23.8	20.4
Containers, packaging, shipping . . .	Mil. tons [1] . . .	4.5	4.1	3.7	2.6	3.0	3.1	2.9	2.8
Machinery, industrial equipment, tools	Mil. tons [1] . . .	2.4	2.3	1.8	1.9	1.7	1.5	1.4	1.1
Steel for converting and processing	Mil. tons [1] . . .	9.4	10.4	12.7	8.2	5.6	8.5	8.0	6.0
Rail transportation	Mil. tons [1] . . .	1.1	1.4	1.3	1.2	1.3	1.4	1.2	1.5
Contractors' products	Mil. tons [1] . . .	2.9	(2)	(2)	(2)	(2)	(2)	(2)	(2)
Oil and gas industries	Mil. tons [1] . . .	1.9	2.6	2.9	2.5	3.1	2.7	2.6	2.4
Electrical equipment	Mil. tons [1] . . .	2.5	2.4	2.1	2.0	1.2	1.1	0.8	0.9
Appliances, utensils, and cutlery . . .	Mil. tons [1] . . .	1.5	1.6	1.9	0.9	1.9	1.7	2.0	1.8
Other	Mil. tons [1] . . .	17.4	19.3	16.2	19.8	18.3	22.8	23.7	23.3
Exports of steel mill products	Mil. tons [1] . . .	4.3	7.1	6.5	7.9	9.4	9.7	11.2	13.5
Imports of steel mill products	Mil. tons [1] . . .	17.2	24.4	29.4	35.8	32.1	45.3	33.2	31.9
Raw steel production [3]	Mil. tons [1] . . .	(NA)	(NA)	112.2	109.9	104.6	108.2	108.1	101.3
Basic oxygen furnaces	Percent	(NA)	(NA)	53.0	47.9	45.0	42.9	41.8	43.1
Electric arc furnaces	Percent	(NA)	(NA)	47.0	52.1	55.0	57.1	58.2	58.2
Steel employment [4]	Thousands. . .	169	123	151	123	122	124	127	(NA)

[1] In millions of short tons. Short ton = 2,000 lbs.   [2] Beginning 1995, contractors' products included with construction.   [3] Raw steel is defined as steel in the first solid state after melting suitable for further processing or sale, including ingots, steel for foundry castings and strand or pressure cast blooms, slabs or other product forms.   [4] Covering only those employees engaged in the production and sale of iron and steel products, excludes mining and quarrying operations, transportation, warehousing and other non-steel producing activities.

Source: American Iron and Steel Institute, Washington, DC, Annual Statistical Report (copyright). See also <http://www.steel.org>.

Table 994. Metalworking Machinery—Value of Shipments: 2006 to 2008

[In thousands of dollars (3,094,478 represents $3,094,478,000)]

Product description	Product code	2006	2007	2008
Metalworking machinery	(X)	3,094,478	3,318,208	3,576,882
Metal cutting type [1, 2, 3, 4]	(X)	2,293,813	2,533,389	2,758,378
Boring and drilling machines	333512A1	178,487	130,220	167,355
Gear cutting machines [1]	33351212	(D)	(D)	(D)
Grinding and polishing machines	33351221	259,063	237,928	304,588
Lathes [2]	33351231	295,651	375,871	320,515
Milling machines [3]	33351241	56,082	81,294	80,952
Machining centers	33351271	703,045	807,425	766,791
Station type machines [4]	33351281	79,153	(D)	(D)
Other metal cutting machine tools	33351291	464,779	585,522	608,576
Remanufactured metal cutting machine tools	3335126111	90,172	81,004	56,589
Metal forming type [5]	(X)	800,665	784,819	818,504
Punching and shearing machines	33351311 part	130,126	145,530	135,773
Bending and forming machines	33351311 part	273,235	264,261	272,795
Presses (excluding forging) [5]	33351331	128,599	135,292	142,282
Other metal forming type machines [5]	33351351	228,880	209,309	219,706
Remanufactured metal forming machine tools	3335137121	15,081	10,382	19,732

D Withheld to avoid disclosing data for individual companies.   X Not applicable.   [1] Data for "Gear cutting machines" are included in total "Metal cutting type."   [2] Data for product code 3335123126, "Vertical NC turning machines" are included in total "Metal cutting type," but excluded from product code 33351231.   [3] Data for product code 3335124101, "All milling machines valued under $3,025 each" are included in total "Metal cutting type," but excluded from product code 33351241.   [4] Data for "Station type machines" are included in total "Metal cutting type."   [5] Data for product codes 3335133101 "All presses valued under $3,025 each" and 3335135101 "All other metal forming type machine tools valued under $3,025 each," are included in total "Metal forming type," but excluded from product codes 33351331 and 33351351, respectively.

Source: U.S. Census Bureau, Current Industrial Reports, "Metalworking Machinery," Series MQ333W (published June 2009); <http://www.census.gov/manufacturing/cir/historical_data/mq333w/index.html>.

Table 995. **Aluminum—Supply, Shipments, and Foreign Trade: 1990 to 2008**

[In millions of pounds (17,334 represents 17,334,000,000)]

Item	1990	1995	2000	2004	2005	2006	2007	2008 prel.
SUPPLY								
Aluminum supply, total	17,334	20,425	23,586	22,292	23,659	24,020	23,787	23,100
Primary production	8,925	7,441	8,087	5,549	5,468	5,029	5,643	5,862
Recovery from scrap.	5,276	7,030	7,606	6,680	6,680	7,842	8,497	7,590
Imports of ingot and mill products	3,133	5,956	7,893	10,063	11,510	11,149	9,648	9,648
Aluminum net shipments, total	17,188	21,019	24,496	24,924	25,520	25,967	24,656	21,869
PRODUCT [1]								
Mill products, total	13,013	15,716	17,676	17,122	17,738	17,956	16,455	15,281
Sheet, plate, and foil	9,297	11,168	12,116	11,463	11,810	11,794	11,009	10,514
Rod, bar, and wire.	370	534	690	631	664	718	702	680
Electrical conductor	542	566	681	763	794	850	818	700
Extruded shapes and tube	2,546	3,102	3,792	3,821	4,018	4,137	3,485	3,030
Powder and paste.	106	108	142	155	144	140	151	135
Forgings and impacts	152	238	255	289	308	317	290	222
Ingot for castings and other [2]	4,175	5,303	6,820	7,802	7,782	8,011	8,201	6,588
MARKET [1]								
Domestic, total.	14,637	18,152	21,680	22,901	23,064	23,168	21,457	18,595
Building and construction	2,663	2,679	3,204	3,692	3,681	3,627	3,100	2,600
Transportation	3,205	5,749	7,947	8,509	8,685	8,670	7,885	6,092
Consumer durables.	1,122	1,369	1,692	1,585	1,561	1,644	1,474	1,357
Electrical	1,309	1,395	1,704	1,580	1,646	1,707	1,679	1,522
Machinery and equipment	992	1,257	1,496	1,610	1,636	1,680	1,623	1,403
Containers and packaging	4,772	5,088	4,992	5,098	5,115	5,113	4,904	4,908
Other	574	615	645	827	740	727	792	713
Exports	2,551	2,867	2,816	2,023	2,456	2,799	3,199	3,274
FOREIGN TRADE [3]								
Exports	3,753	3,846	4,100	4,416	5,629	6,592	6,704	7,621
Imports.	3,718	6,899	9,358	11,221	12,607	12,322	10,737	10,126

[1] Statistics on shipments and markets for 1990 to 2000 represent total U.S. producer's shipments plus imports by consumers. Beginning 2003 figures include Canada. [2] Net ingot for foundry castings, export, and destructive uses. [3] U.S. imports and exports of aluminum ingot, mill products, and scrap.

Source: The Aluminum Association, Inc., Washington, DC, *Aluminum Statistical Review,* annual. See also <http://www.aluminum.org/>.

Table 996. **Semiconductors, Electronic Components, and Semiconductor Manufacturing Equipment—Value of Shipments: 2004 to 2008**

[In millions of dollars (9,728 represents $9,728,000,000)]

Product description	Product code	2004	2005	2006	2007	2008
Semiconductor machinery	3332950	(NA)	9,728	12,598	13,190	10,064
Transmitting, industrial, and special purpose electron tubes [1]	3344111	641	652	690	734	792
Receiving type electron tubes [2].	3344114	1,049	621	216	(D)	(D)
Electron tube parts	3344117	78	72	49	36	31
Bare printed circuit boards	3344120	4,709	4,856	4,933	4,443	4,547
Integrated microcircuits [3]	3344131	60,097	61,631	54,963	41,271	35,013
Transistors	3344134	656	603	679	599	401
Diodes and rectifiers.	3344137	305	372	467	457	457
Other semiconductor devices [4]	334413A	7,247	8,330	10,483	10,176	9,122
Capacitors for electronic circuitry.	3344140	1,184	1,113	1,064	945	937
Resistors for electronic circuitry.	3344150	744	653	660	645	720
Electronic coils, transformers, and other inductors . .	3344160	1,116	1,216	1,231	1,393	1,389
Connectors for electronic circuitry	3344170	3,416	3,589	3,980	4,189	3,994
Printed circuit assemblies, loaded boards and modules [5]	334418B	19,566	20,106	19,591	20,382	19,999
Crystals, filters, piezoelectric, and other related electronic devices [6].	3344191	654	779	754	689	648
All other miscellaneous transducers [7].	3344194	1,495	1,401	1,323	1,466	1,439
Switches, mechanical types for electronic circuitry . .	3344197	716	794	645	662	732
Microwave components and devices [8]	334419A	1,326	1,306	1,470	1,541	1,460
All other miscellaneous electronic components	334419E	4,158	4,040	4,346	4,831	4,609

NA Not available. [1] Except X-ray. [2] Including cathode ray (new and rebuilt). [3] Includes semiconductor networks, microprocessors, and MOS memories. [4] Includes semiconductor parts such as chips, wafers, and heat sinks. [5] Printed circuit boards with inserted electronic components. [6] Except microwave filters. [7] Includes electrical-electronic input/output transducers. [8] Except antennae, tubes, and semiconductors

Source: U.S. Census Bureau, *Current Industrial Reports,* "Semiconductors, Electronic Components, and Semiconductor Manufacturing Equipment," Series MA334Q (published August 2009); <http://www.census.gov/manufacturing/cir/historical_data/ma334q/index.html>.

U.S. Census Bureau, Statistical Abstract of the United States: 2010

Table 997. **Computers and Peripheral Equipment—Value of Shipments: 2000 to 2007**

[In millions of dollars (62,857 represents $62,857,000,000)]

Product description	Product code	2000	2003	2004	2005	2006	2007
Electronic computers [1]	334111	62,857	38,271	37,895	38,386	37,657	36,859
Host computers (multiusers).	3341111	22,877	12,237	10,993	11,759	(D)	(D)
Single user computers	3341117	38,981	25,164	26,309	25,906	(D)	(D)
Other computers	334111D	998	870	593	721	(D)	299
Computer storage devices (except parts, attachments and accessories)	3341121	8,995	5,101	5,034	6,100	6,956	7,872
Parts, attachments, and accessories for computer storage devices	3341124	1,692	1,130	1,039	1,441	1,929	1,426
Computer terminals [1]	3341131	415	258	274	245	268	331
Parts, attachments, and accessories for computer terminals [1]	3341134	(D)	1	2	(D)	(D)	(D)
All other miscellaneous computer peripheral equipment	3341191	(S)	(S)	4,705	4,425	4,517	4,428
Parts, subassemblies, and accessories for computer peripheral equipment	3341194	2,766	1,849	2,257	2,743	2,720	3,171
Point-of-sale terminals and funds-transfer devices.	3341197	852	732	513	497	621	1,034
Parts and attachments for point-of-sale terminals and funds-transfer devices	334119D	(NA)	(NA)	(D)	(D)	35	12
Magnetic and optical recording media	3346130	3,206	2,271	1,586	1,303	1,364	1,381

D Withheld to avoid disclosing data for individual companies.   NA Not available.   S Does not meet publication standards.
[1] Excludes point-of-sale and funds transfer devices.

Source: U.S. Census Bureau, Current Industrial Reports, "Computers and Peripheral Equipment," Series MA334R; <http://www.census.gov/manufacturing/cir/historical_data/mq334r/index.html>.

Table 998. **Computers and Peripheral Equipment—Shipments: 2006 and 2007**

[26,926 represents 26,926,000]

Product description	Product code	Number of compa- nies, 2007	Quantity (1,000)		Value (mil. dol.)	
			2006	2007	2006	2007
Electronic computers [1]	334111	90	26,926	25,657	37,657	36,859
Host computers, multiusers	3341111	42	(D)	(D)	(D)	(D)
Single-user computers, microprocessor-based, capable of supporting attached peripherals [1]	3341117	52	(D)	(D)	(D)	(D)
Personal computers	3341117107	25	(D)	(D)	(D)	(D)
Workstations	3341117109	25	(D)	(D)	(D)	2,442
Other computers (array, analog, hybrid, and special-use computers)	334111D	28	(D)	135	(D)	299
Computer storage devices (except parts, attach- ments, and accessories).	3341121	42	(X)	(X)	6,956	7,872
Disk subsystem and disk arrays for multiuser- computer systems	3341121109	14	(D)	(X)	(D)	2,531
Disk drives (all sizes)	3341121112	15	(X)	(X)	(D)	150
Storage Area Networks(SANs).	3341121123	10	(D)	(X)	(D)	2,892
Tape drives (all sizes)	3341121138	9	(X)	(X)	285	239
Other computer storage devices.	3341121145	16	1,134	(X)	3,795	2,061
Parts, attachments, and accessories for computer storage devices	3341124	12	(X)	(X)	1,929	1,426
Computer terminals (except point-of-sale and funds-transfer devices, parts, attachments, and accessories)	3341131	17	(X)	(X)	268	330,640
Parts, attachments, and accessories for com- puter terminals (except point-of-sale and funds-transfer devices)	3341134	4	(X)	(X)	(D)	(D)
All other miscellaneous computer peripheral (input/output) equipment (except parts, attach- ments and accessories)	3341191	111	(X)	(X)	4,517	4,427
Parts, subassemblies, and accessories for computer peripheral equipment	3341194	34	(X)	(X)	2,719	3,171
devices	3341197	14	378	(X)	621	1,034
Magnetic and optical recording media	3346130	18	(X)	(X)	1,364	1,381

D Withheld to avoid disclosing data for individual companies.   X Not applicable.   [1] Includes other products, not shown separately.

Source: U.S. Census Bureau, Current Industrial Reports, "Computers and Peripheral Equipment," Series MA334R; <http://www.census.gov/manufacturing/cir/historical_data/mq334r/index.html>.

Table 999. **U.S. Consumer Electronics Sales and Forecasts by Product Category: 2005 to 2009**

[In millions of dollars (137,345 represents $137,345,000,000). Represents shipment volumes from manufacturers to U.S. dealers. Includes both domestic production and imports of products to consumer-oriented channels, regardless of retail type, including distribution and direct-to-consumer sales]

Product category	2005	2006	2007	2008	2009, proj.
Total	137,345	156,441	168,919	178,649	164,915
In-home technologies, total	70,611	76,960	79,561	82,765	75,483
TV sets and displays	18,502	24,042	24,661	25,931	24,355
Digital TV sets and displays [1]	15,043	22,696	24,519	25,931	24,355
LCD flat panel	3,258	8,430	14,520	17,962	18,363
Plasma flat panel	3,609	5,302	4,488	3,689	2,907
Front projection	2,914	2,943	2,996	2,841	2,197
OLED	(X)	(X)	(X)	113	233
Analog displays	3,459	1,346	142	(X)	(X)
Video components [1]	4,206	4,747	4,911	6,846	6,636
Component DVD players/recorders	2,053	2,228	1,765	1,388	1,167
Next generation DVD players [2]	(X)	65	345	739	1,097
Set-top boxes [1]	2,074	2,409	2,798	4,719	4,373
Direct broadcast satellite (DBS) receivers . . .	1,366	1,278	1,220	1,064	958
Cable/multi-system operator (MSO) receivers.	643	874	1,085	1,300	1,618
Digital Media Adapters (DMAs)	40	53	152	563	859
IPTV.	26	69	187	318	438
Digital video recorders (DVRs)	532	975	1,580	3,237	2,764
Audio separates/systems detail [1]	4,904	4,810	4,962	4,429	3,940
Audio separates components.	1,116	1,152	1,258	1,081	959
Home technologies	2,042	2,047	1,996	1,962	1,707
Home information technologies and security [1]	40,083	40,682	42,783	43,547	38,781
Desktop computers.	7,672	8,956	8,500	6,744	4,806
Notebook computers.	11,727	10,597	12,656	14,187	11,675
Personal computer software	6,173	6,655	7,084	7,406	7,821
Home security systems.	2,322	2,786	3,204	3,558	3,725
Communications [1].	2,915	2,678	2,244	2,012	1,770
Phones	1,135	968	576	435	420
Telephone answering devices	1,279	1,162	1,030	954	747
VIOP adapters	312	390	492	517	515
In-vehicle technologies total	8,992	10,712	12,257	12,782	9,381
Entertainment devices	8,272	9,358	9,501	8,706	6,259
Aftermarket autosound equipment [3]	2,270	2,654	1,974	1,516	1,344
Mobile video devices [4]	552	630	713	539	467
Factory-installed autosound.	5,450	6,074	6,814	6,651	4,448
Information and security [1].	720	1,354	2,756	4,076	3,122
Portable and transportable navigation	349	988	2,387	3,731	2,807
Anywhere technologies total	39,921	49,588	57,900	63,546	60,689
Digital imaging [1]	7,315	9,827	9,107	9,416	8,688
Digital cameras	5,611	7,819	6,517	6,813	5,969
All camcorders	1,704	1,828	2,112	1,885	1,897
Portable entertainment [1].	5,003	6,722	7,349	7,325	6,667
Portable Media/MP3 players	4,229	5,559	5,968	5,844	5,207
Electronic gaming [1]	12,550	14,662	19,738	23,558	24,070
Electronic gaming hardware.	3,087	4,477	6,710	7,780	7,037
Electronic gaming software	8,041	8,450	11,154	14,166	15,582
Portable communication [1]	15,053	18,377	21,616	23,247	21,265
Wireless communication technologies [1]	14,365	17,836	21,162	22,814	20,811
Smartphones.	3,795	5,192	8,645	11,393	11,729
Consumer electronic enhancements.	17,821	19,181	19,201	19,556	19,362
Accessories [1]	12,117	13,614	14,299	14,777	14,249
Primary batteries	5,902	6,155	6,421	6,565	6,247
Blank media [1]	5,704	5,567	4,902	4,779	5,113
Flash media	3,087	3,374	3,441	3,904	4,400

X Not applicable.   [1] Includes categories, not shown separately.   [2] Includes HD-DVD and Blu-Ray.   [3] Includes satellite radio receivers, satellite radio accessories and satellite radio kits, does not include Bluetooth headsets.   [4] Includes all fixed navigation units.

Source: Consumer Electronics Association, Arlington, VA, *U.S. Consumer Electronics Sales and Forecasts, 2005–2010*, July 2009 (copyright). See also <http://www.ce.org>

Table 1000. **Telecommunication Equipment—Value of Shipments: 2000 to 2008**

[In millions of dollars (15,174 represents $15,174,000,000)]

Product description	Product code	2000	2004	2005	2006	2007	2008
Telephone switching and switchboard equipment	3342101	15,174	3,294	1,576	1,812	1,959	1,643
Carrier line equipment and nonconsumer modems	3342104	13,112	3,598	2,824	2,912	3,512	3,137
Wireline voice and data network equipment.	3342107	28,971	12,052	12,289	18,563	11,181	4,595
Broadcast, studio, and related electronic equipment	3342202	4,029	2,763	3,289	3,653	3,350	3,484
Wireless networking equipment.	3342203	(NA)	(NA)	(NA)	(NA)	6,159	4,768
Radio station equipment	3342205	(NA)	(NA)	(NA)	(NA)	17,824	16,467
Other communications systems equipment	3342209	(NA)	(NA)	(NA)	(NA)	6,355	10,879
Alarm systems	3342901	2,755	2,014	1,910	1,526	2,044	2,090
Vehicular and pedestrian traffic control equipment	3342902	838	898	1,020	1,048	1,239	1,235
Intercommunications systems	3342903	447	455	416	433	438	458
Modems, consumer type	3344184	95	100	98	79	82	87

NA Not available.

Source: U.S. Census Bureau, Current Industrial Reports, "Telecommunications," Series MQ334P; <http://www.census.gov /manufacturing/cir/historical_data/mq334p/index.html>.

Manufactures   633

Table 1001. **Motor Vehicle Manufactures—Summary by Selected Industry: 2006**

[48,290 represents $48,290,000,000. Based on the Annual Survey of Manufactures; see Appendix III]

Industry	2002 NAICS code [1]	All employees [2]			Produc- tion workers[2]	Value of ship- ments [3] (mil. dol.)
		Number	Payroll			
			Total (mil. dol.)	Per employee (dol.)		
Motor vehicle manufacturing, total	3361–3363	933,738	48,291	51,718	750,113	500,175
Motor vehicle, total	3361	205,843	14,019	68,106	179,052	261,860
Automobile & light duty motor vehicle	33611	173,658	12,524	72,117	152,516	232,471
Automobile	336111	74,335	5,352	71,999	64,049	94,229
Light truck & utility vehicle	336112	99,323	7,172	72,205	88,467	138,242
Heavy duty truck	33612	32,185	1,496	46,468	26,536	29,389
Motor vehicle body & trailer.	3362	150,166	5,573	37,111	120,336	36,016
Motor vehicle body.	336211	50,906	1,944	38,185	38,509	11,855
Truck trailer	336212	30,527	1,051	34,427	25,652	8,165
Motor home	336213	18,932	729	38,510	15,425	5,519
Travel trailer & camper	336214	49,801	1,849	37,125	40,751	10,477
Motor vehicle parts	3363	577,729	28,699	49,676	450,725	202,299
Motor vehicle gasoline engine & engine parts	33631	69,087	3,927	56,841	53,249	32,835
Motor vehicle electrical and electronic equipment. .	33632	72,621	3,350	46,127	52,684	21,545
Motor vehicle steering and suspension	33633	35,695	1,800	50,417	28,242	10,595
Motor vehicle brake system	33634	32,569	1,341	41,174	25,050	12,676
Motor vehicle transmission & power train parts . . .	33635	76,874	5,193	67,553	62,719	34,974
Motor vehicle seating & interior trim.	33636	47,321	1,943	41,067	33,539	18,866
Motor vehicle metal stamping.	33637	95,398	5,117	53,633	77,737	25,978
Other motor vehicle parts	33639	148,164	6,029	40,689	117,504	44,831

[1] North American Industry Classification System, 2002; see text, Section 15.   [2] Production workers represent average number of production workers for March 12, June 12, September 12, and December 12 pay periods. All employees include production workers and other employees for the pay period that includes the 12th of March.   [3] Includes extensive and unmeasurable duplication from shipments between establishments in the same industry classification.

Source: U.S. Census Bureau, Annual Survey of Manufactures, "Statistics for Industry Groups and Industries: 2006" (published November 2008); using American FactFinder; <http://www.census.gov/manufacturing/asm/index.html>.

Table 1002. **Motor Vehicle Manufactures—Employees, Payroll, and Shipments by Major State: 2006**

[14,019 represents $14,019,000,000. Industry based on the North American Industry Classification System (NAICS), 2002; see text, Section 15. See footnote 3, Table 1001 for information regarding shipments. Based on the Annual Survey of Manufactures; see Apppendix III]

Major state based on employment	Motor vehicle manufacturing (NAICS 3361)			Motor vehicle parts manufacturing (NAICS 3363)		
	Employees	Payroll (mil. dol.)	Shipments (mil. dol.)	Employees	Payroll (mil. dol.)	Shipments (mil. dol.)
United States [1]	205,843	14,019	261,860	577,729	28,699	202,299
Alabama.	11,050	718	14,235	15,844	667	5,735
Arkansas	([2])	(D)	(D)	5,366	172	1,156
California	6,538	476	7,500	21,161	875	6,362
Connecticut.	–	–	–	([3])	(D)	(D)
Delaware	([3])	(D)	(D)	–	–	–
Florida	–	–	–	3,736	147	979
Georgia	5,435	324	5,703	8,903	350	3,016
Illinois	7,068	494	7,774	24,454	1,046	6,929
Indiana.	13,855	887	18,088	71,743	3,745	23,125
Iowa	–	–	–	6,413	270	1,773
Kansas.	([3])	(D)	(D)	2,169	86	–
Kentucky	17,778	1,313	24,492	28,631	1,180	9,851
Maryland	–	–	–	2,050	107	754
Michigan.	36,796	2,937	49,878	122,262	7,355	47,710
Minnesota.	2,636	127	1,846	2,772	96	538
Mississippi	([3])	(D)	(D)	5,525	195	1,814
Missouri	13,682	1,063	17,457	13,136	521	3,940
Nebraska	–	–	–	3,104	154	928
New York	–	–	–	19,906	1,329	7,556
North Carolina	([4])	(D)	(D)	17,422	666	7,450
Ohio	24,664	1,762	37,119	82,352	4,561	27,868
Oklahoma.	1,852	101	1,775	3,840	154	997
Pennsylvania.	([2])	(D)	(D)	11,510	470	2,924
South Carolina.	([4])	(D)	(D)	14,278	679	6,559
Tennessee	12,764	801	13,236	34,982	1,457	16,294
Texas.	6,831	462	13,010	12,603	505	3,594
Utah	–	–	–	4,386	179	1,759
Virginia.	5,113	274	6,295	6,751	289	1,982
Washington.	([2])	(D)	(D)	2,132	94	513
Wisconsin.	([4])	(D)	(D)	13,359	604	4,360

– Represents zero.   D Withheld to avoid disclosing data on individual companies.   [1] Includes states not shown separately.   [2] Employee class size of 1,000 to 2,499.   [3] Employee class size of 2,500 to 4,999.   [4] Employee class size of 5,000 to 9,999.

Source: U.S. Census Bureau, Annual Survey of Manufactures, "Geographic Area Statistics: Statistics for all Manufacturing by State: 2006" (published November 2008); using American FactFinder; <http://factfinder.census.gov/home/saff/main.htm/?_lang=en /SAFFInfo.jsp?content=sp8annualeconomicsurveys.html&submenuId=aboutdata0>.

Table 1003. **Aerospace—Sales, New Orders, and Backlog: 2000 to 2008**

[In billions of dollars (109.3 represents $109,300,000,000), except as indicated. Reported by establishments in which the principal business is the development and/or production of aerospace products]

Item	2000	2003	2004	2005	2006	2007	2008
Net sales..........................	109.3	116.4	124.3	124.2	155.9	126.8	118.7
Percent U.S. government. ;	37.5	52.9	51.7	50.6	44.7	38.2	40.7
Complete aircraft and parts [1]	57.2	49.6	49.6	49.9	(D)	(D)	(D)
Aircraft engines and parts	12.5	13.8	16.1	18.5	28.6	15.5	(D)
Missiles and space vehicles, parts.......	15.6	15.6	14.2	(S)	(D)	(D)	(D)
Other products, services	24.0	37.4	44.4	45.8	(D)	43.70	(D)
Net, new orders...................	140.1	117.7	131.7	186.4	202.8	231.6	162.0
Backlog, Dec. 31....................	215.0	226.9	234.3	290.0	334.5	437.1	466.5

D Withheld to avoid disclosing data of individual companies.   S Does not meet publication standards.

Source: U.S. Census Bureau, "Current Industrial Reports, Civil Aircraft and Aircraft Engines, and Aerospace Industry," Series MA336G. See <http://www.census.gov/manufacturing/cir/historical_data/ma336/index.html>.

Table 1004. **Net Orders for U.S. Civil Jet Transport Aircraft: 1990 to 2008**

[1990 data are net new firm orders; beginning 1995, net announced orders. Minus sign (−) indicates net cancellations. In 1997, Boeing acquired McDonnell Douglas]

Type of aircraft and customer	1990	2000	2003	2004	2005	2006	2007	2008
Total number [1]	670	585	237	267	1,004	1,058	1,417	662
U.S. customers...............	259	412	84	23	220	321	281	112
Foreign customers.............	411	193	185	204	811	737	1,136	550
Boeing 737, total	189	378	204	142	571	739	846	484
U.S. customers...............	38	302	74	16	152	242	164	107
Foreign customers.............	151	86	145	92	439	497	682	377
Boeing 747, total	153	24	4	10	43	72	25	3
U.S. customers...............	24	1	–	1	13	18	–	–
Foreign customers.............	129	18	9	10	30	54	25	3
Boeing 757, total	66	43	−1	–	–	–	–	–
U.S. customers...............	33	38	−7	–	–	–	–	–
Foreign customers.............	33	14	6	–	–	–	–	–
Boeing 767, total	60	6	10	9	15	10	36	28
U.S. customers...............	23	−2	–	–	–	–	27	–
Foreign customers.............	37	14	15	1	20	10	9	28
Boeing 777, total	34	113	12	42	154	76	141	54
U.S. customers...............	34	60	11	–	10	35	23	11
Foreign customers.............	–	53	8	43	146	41	118	43
Boeing 787, total	–	–	–	66	235	161	369	93
U.S. customers...............	–	–	–	–	45	26	67	−6
Foreign customers.............	–	–	–	56	190	135	302	99
McDonnell Douglas MD-11, total	52	–	–	–	–	–	–	–
U.S. customers...............	16	–	–	–	–	–	–	–
Foreign customers.............	36	–	–	i	–	–	–	–
McDonnell Douglas MD-80/90, total	116	–	–	–	–	–	–	–
U.S. customers...............	91	–	–	–	–	–	–	–
Foreign customers.............	25	–	–	–	–	–	–	–
McDonnell Douglas MD-95, total	–	21	8	8	–	–	–	–
U.S. customers...............	–	13	6	6	–	–	–	–
Foreign customers.............	–	8	2	2	–	–	–	–

− Represents zero.   [1] Beginning 2000, includes unidentified customers.

Source: Aerospace Industries Association of America, Washington, DC, "Orders: U.S. Civil Jet Transport Aircraft," Series 22. See also <http://www.aia-aerospace.org/industry_information/economics/aerospace_statistics>.

Table 1005. **U.S. Aircraft Shipments: 1990 to 2008**

[Value in millions of dollars (64,567 represents $64,567,000,000)]

Year	Total		Civil						Military	
			Large transports		General aviation [1]		Rotocraft			
	Units	Value	Units	Value	Units	Value	Units	Value	Units	Value
1990	3,321	64,567	521	22,215	1,144	2,007	603	254	1,053	40,091
1995	2,436	49,381	256	15,263	1,077	2,842	292	194	816	31,082
1996	2,220	55,583	269	18,915	1,115	3,048	278	193	558	33,427
1997	2,757	65,129	374	26,929	1,549	4,593	346	231	511	33,376
1998	3,533	75,724	559	35,663	2,193	5,534	363	252	419	34,275
1999	3,799	80,974	620	38,171	2,475	6,803	345	200	357	35,800
2000	4,113	72,669	485	30,327	2,802	8,040	493	270	333	34,032
2001	3,902	77,608	526	34,155	2,616	7,991	415	247	347	35,215
2002	3,251	73,112	379	27,547	2,196	7,261	318	157	359	38,147
2003	3,221	68,006	281	21,033	2,080	6,205	517	366	383	40,402
2004	3,804	74,526	283	20,484	2,296	6,918	805	515	418	46,609
2005	4,649	81,515	290	22,116	2,853	8,632	947	815	587	49,952
2006	5,126	86,014	398	25,875	3,134	9,550	898	802	996	49,757
2007	5,378	101,419	441	29,160	3,279	11,941	1,009	1,385	915	54,200
2008, proj.	5,087	93,478	373	24,700	3,079	13,348	1,115	1,530	520	53,900

[1] Excludes off-the-shelf military aircraft.

Source: U.S. Department of Commerce, International Trade Administration, "Shipments of Complete U.S. Aircraft, 1971–2008"; <http://trade.gov/mas/manufacturing/OAAI/aero_stats.asp>.

Manufactures   635

Table 1006. Aerospace Industry Sales by Product Group and Customer: 1990 to 2009

[In billions of dollars (134.4 represents $134,400,000,000). Due to reporting practices and tabulating methods, figures may differ from those in Table 1003]

Group	1990	2000	2003	2004	2005 [1]	2006	2007	2008 [2]	2009 [3]
CURRENT DOLLARS									
Total sales	134.4	144.7	146.6	155.7	173.3	186.9	200.3	204.4	214.3
Product group:									
Aircraft, total	71.4	81.6	72.8	79.1	112.2	126.4	134.4	135.3	143.5
Civil [4]	31.3	47.6	32.4	32.5	62.1	72.6	80.2	80.6	86.6
Military	40.1	34.0	40.4	46.6	50.1	53.8	54.2	54.7	57.0
Missiles	14.2	9.3	13.5	14.7	9.1	11.3	12.4	13.2	13.3
Space	26.4	29.7	35.9	35.9	33.5	32.9	32.0	33.4	34.1
Related products and services [5] . . .	22.4	24.1	24.4	26.0	18.6	16.3	21.5	22.5	23.3
Customer group:									
Aerospace products & services, total.	112.0	120.6	122.2	129.8	154.8	170.6	178.8	181.9	191.0
DOD [6]	60.5	47.5	64.0	70.1	80.0	86.8	87.6	89.3	91.8
NASA [7] and other agencies	11.1	13.4	15.5	16.0	11.0	9.5	9.9	10.4	10.7
Other customers [8]	40.4	59.7	42.7	43.7	63.7	74.3	81.3	82.2	88.5
Related products and services [5] . . .	22.4	24.1	24.4	26.0	18.6	16.3	21.5	22.5	23.3
CONSTANT (1987) DOLLARS [9]									
Total sales	123.5	144.7	137.0	141.2	151.4	157.5	163.7	162.0	164.8
Product group:									
Aircraft, total	65.6	81.6	68.1	71.7	98.0	106.5	109.9	107.2	110.4
Civil [4]	28.7	47.6	30.3	29.5	54.2	61.2	65.5	63.8	66.6
Military	36.8	34.0	37.8	42.3	43.7	45.3	44.3	43.4	43.8
Missiles	13.0	9.3	12.6	13.3	8.0	9.5	10.1	10.5	10.3
Space	24.3	29.7	33.5	32.6	29.2	27.7	26.2	26.4	26.3
Related products and services [5] . . .	20.6	24.1	22.8	23.5	16.2	13.8	17.6	17.8	17.9
Customer group:									
Aerospace products & services, total.	102.9	120.6	114.2	117.6	135.1	143.8	146.2	144.1	146.9
DOD [6]	55.6	47.5	59.8	63.5	69.9	73.1	71.7	70.7	70.6
NASA [7] and other agencies	10.2	13.4	14.5	14.5	9.6	8.0	8.1	8.2	8.2
Other customers [8]	37.1	59.7	39.9	39.6	55.7	62.7	66.4	65.2	68.1
Related products and services [5] . . .	20.6	24.1	22.8	23.5	16.2	13.8	17.6	17.8	17.9

[1] Beginning in 2005, sales numbers for individual product groups are not comparable to figures in prior years due to revised survey methodology. However, total annual sales data remain comparable across all years of the time series.   [2] Preliminary.   [3] Estimate.   [4] All civil sales of aircraft (domestic and export sales of jet transports, commuters, business, and personal aircraft and helicopters).   [5] Electronics, software, and ground support equipment, plus sales of nonaerospace products which are produced by aerospace-manufacturing use technology, processes, and materials derived from aerospace products.   [6] Department of Defense.   [7] National Aeronautics and Space Administration.   [8] Includes civil aircraft sales (see footnote 4), commercial space sales, all exports of military aircraft and missiles, and related propulsion and parts.   [9] Based on AIA's aerospace composite price deflator.

Source: Aerospace Industries Association of America, Inc., Washington, DC, *2008 Year-end Review and Forecast* (published 10 December 2008). See also <http://www.aia-aerospace.org/industry_information/economics/year_end_review_and_forecast/>.

Table 1007. Major Household Appliances—Value of Shipments: 2000 to 2008

[In millions of dollars (2,170 represents $2,170,000,000)]

Product description	Product code	2000	2004	2005	2006	2007	2008
Electric household ranges, ovens and surface cooking units, equipment and parts	3352211	2,170	2,285	2,577	2,541	2,736	2,360
Gas household ranges, ovens, and surface cooking units, equipment, and parts	3352213	779	1,120	1,392	1,363	1,541	1,279
Other household ranges, cooking equipment, and outdoor cooking equipment [1]	3352215	1,251	914	965	784	491	509
Household refrigerators, including combination refrigerator-freezers	3352221	5,396	5,002	5,405	5,427	5,440	4,879
Parts and attachments for household refrigerators and freezers	3352223	(D)	(D)	(D)	(D)	159	106
Household laundry machines and parts	3352240	4,047	5,130	5,236	5,184	5,232	4,844
Water heaters, electric	3352281	573	545	638	652	950	953
Water heaters, except electric	3352283	844	884	970	903	1,572	1,547
Household appliances, n.e.c. [2]	3352285	2,066	2,297	2,433	2,413	2,717	2,445

D Withheld to avoid disclosing data of individual companies.

[1] Includes parts and accessories.   [2] n.e.c. means not elsewhere classified.

Source: U.S. Census Bureau, Current Industrial Reports, "Major Household Appliances," Series MA335F (published July 2009). See <http://www.census.gov/manufacturing/cir/historical_data/ma335f/index.html>.

Section 22
Wholesale and Retail Trade

This section presents statistics relating to the distributive trades, specifically wholesale trade and retail trade. Data shown for the trades are classified by kind of business and cover sales, establishments, employees, payrolls, and other items. The principal sources of these data are from the Census Bureau and include the *2007 Economic Census*, annual and monthly surveys, and the *County Business Patterns* program. These data are supplemented by several tables from trade associations, such as the National Automobile Dealers Association (Table 1023). Several notable research groups are also represented, such as Claritas, Inc. (Table 1025).

Data on wholesale and retail trade also appear in several other sections. For instance, labor force employment and earnings data appear in Section 12, Labor Force, Employment, and Earnings; gross domestic product of the industry (Table 652) appears in Section 13, Income, Expenditures, Poverty, and Wealth; financial data (several tables) from the quarterly *Statistics of Income Bulletin*, published by the Internal Revenue Service, appear in Section 15, Business Enterprise.

Censuses—Censuses of wholesale trade and retail trade have been taken at various intervals since 1929. Beginning with the 1967 census, legislation provides for a census of each area to be conducted every 5 years (for years ending in "2" and "7"). For more information on the most recent census, see the *Guide to the 2007 Economic Census* found at <http://www .census.gov/econ/census02/guide/>. The industries covered in the censuses and surveys of business are defined in the *North American Industry Classification System*, (NAICS). *Retail trade* refers to places of business primarily engaged in retailing merchandise to the general public; and *wholesale trade,* to establishments primarily engaged in selling goods to other businesses and normally operating from a warehouse or office that have little or no display of merchandise. Most

Census Bureau tables in this section utilize the 2002 NAICS codes, which replaced the Standard Industrial Classification (SIC) system. NAICS made substantial structural improvements and identifies over 350 new industries. At the same time, it causes breaks in time series far more profound than any prior revision of the previously used SIC system. For information on this system and how it affects the comparability of wholesale and retail statistics historically, see text, Section 15, Business Enterprise, and especially the Census Bureau Web site at <http://www .census .gov/epcd/www/naics.html>. In general, the 2007 Economic Census has three series of publications for these two sectors: 1) subject series with reports such as product lines and establishment and firm sizes, 2) geographic reports with individual reports for each state, and 3) industry series with individual reports for industry groups. For information on these series, see the Census Bureau Web site at <http://www.census.gov/econ/census07/>.

Current surveys—Current sample surveys conducted by the Census Bureau cover various aspects of wholesale and retail trade. Its *Monthly Retail Trade and Food Services* release <http://www.census .gov/mrts/www/mrts.html> contains monthly estimates of sales, inventories, and inventory/sales ratios for the United States, by kind of business. Annual figures on retail sales, year-end inventories, purchases, accounts receivable, and gross margins by kind of business are located on the Census Bureau Web site at <http://www.census.gov/svsd/www /artstbl.html>. Additionally, annual data for accommodation and food services are located at the same site.

Statistics from the Bureau's monthly wholesale trade survey include national estimates of sales, inventories, and inventory/sales ratios for merchant wholesalers excluding manufacturers' sales branches and offices. Data are presented by major summary groups

U.S. Census Bureau, Statistical Abstract of the United States: 2010

"durable and nondurable," and 4-digit NAICS industry groups. Merchant wholesalers excluding manufacturers' sales branches and offices are those wholesalers who take title to the goods they sell (e.g., jobbers, exporters, importers, industrial distributors). These data, based on reports submitted by a sample of firms, appear in the *Monthly Wholesale Trade Report* <http://www.census.gov /Wholesale/index.htm>. This report, along with monthly sales, inventories, and inventories/sales ratios, also provides data on annual sales, inventories, and year-end inventories/sales ratios. The Annual Wholesale Trade Survey provides data on merchant wholesalers excluding manufacturer sales branches and offices as well as summary data for all merchant wholesalers. This report also provides separate data for manufacturer sales branches and offices, and electronic markets, agents, brokers, and commission merchants. This report provides data on annual sales, year-end inventories, inventories/sales ratios, operating expenses, purchases, and gross margins. Data are presented by major summary groups "durable and nondurable" and 4-digit NAICS industry groups for sales, end-of-year inventories, and operating expenses. The reports are available as documents on the Census Bureau Web site at <http://www.census.gov/econ/www /retmenu.html>.

E-commerce—Electronic commerce (or e-commerce) is sales of goods and services over the Internet and extranet, electronic data interchange (EDI), or other online systems. Payment may or may not be made online. E-commerce data were collected in four separate Census Bureau surveys. These surveys used different measures of economic activity such as shipments for manufacturing, sales for wholesale and retail trade, and revenues for service industries. Consequently, measures of total economic and e-commerce activity vary by economic sector, are conceptually and definitionally different, and therefore, are not additive. This edition has several tables on e-commerce sales, such as Tables 1011, 1021, and 1022 in this section, 977 in Section 21, Manufactures, and 1242 in Section 27, Accommodation, Food Services, and Other Services.

Statistical reliability—For a discussion of statistical collection and estimation, sampling procedures, and measures of statistical reliability applicable to Census Bureau data, see Appendix III.

Table 1008. **Wholesale and Retail Trade—Establishments, Sales, Payroll, and Employees: 2002 and 2007**

[4,635 represents $4,635,000,000,000. Covers establishments with payroll. For statement on methodology, see Appendix III]

Kind of business	2002 NAICS code [1]	Establishments (1,000)		Sales (bil. dol.)		Annual payroll (bil. dol.)		Paid employees (1,000)	
		2002	2007	2002	2007	2002	2007	2002	2007
Wholesale trade	42	**435.5**	**432.1**	**4,635**	**6,039**	**260**	**336**	**5,878**	**6,295**
Wholesale trade, durable goods	423	260.4	253.0	2,171	2,709	157	206	3,357	3,637
Wholesale trade, nondurable goods.	424	142.7	133.2	1,980	2,754	93	117	2,273	2,367
Wholesale electronic markets and agents and brokers.	425	32.4	45.9	483	576	10	14	249	292
Retail trade.	**44–45**	**1,114.6**	**1,122.7**	**3,056**	**3,932**	**302**	**365**	**14,648**	**15,611**
Motor vehicle and parts dealers	441	125.1	125.9	802	893	65	73	1,845	1,916
Furniture and home furnishings stores	442	65.2	65.3	92	110	13	15	535	589
Electronics and appliance stores.	443	46.8	50.0	82	111	9	11	391	484
Building material and garden equipment and supplies dealers	444	(NA)	90.4	(NA)	323	(NA)	38	(NA)	1,340
Food and beverage stores	445	148.8	147.0	457	541	49	56	2,839	2,879
Health and personal care stores	446	81.8	87.3	178	239	20	29	1,024	1,012
Gasoline stations	447	121.4	117.0	249	447	14	15	927	887
Clothing and clothing accessories stores . .	448	149.8	154.9	168	213	21	27	1,427	1,689
Sporting goods, hobby, book, and music stores.	451	62.2	57.2	73	82	9	10	611	626
General merchandise stores.	452	40.7	46.1	445	578	43	55	2,525	2,770
Miscellaneous store retailers	453	129.5	120.3	91	103	13	14	792	791
Nonstore retailers.	454	54.9	61.3	173	292	17	23	571	628

NA Not available. [1] North American Industry Classification System; see text, Section 15.

Source: U.S. Census Bureau, "2007 Economic Census, Advance Comparative Statistics for the United States, (2002 NAICS Basis): 2007 and 2002" (published 17 March 2009); <http://www.census.gov/econ/census07/>.

Table 1009. **Wholesale Trade—Nonemployer Establishments and Receipts by Kind of Business: 2004 to 2006**

[33,227 represents 33,227,000,000. Includes only firms subject to federal income tax. Nonemployers are businesses with no paid employees. Based on NAICS 2002, see text, Section 15]

Kind of business	2002 NAICS code	Establishments (number)			Receipts (mil. dol.)		
		2004	2005	2006	2004	2005	2006
Wholesale trade, total.	**42**	**384,333**	**381,137**	**387,022**	**33,227**	**34,091**	**34,804**
Durable goods merchant wholesalers.	423	204,896	203,327	203,501	18,860	19,240	19,649
Motor vehicle and motor vehicle parts and supplies merchant wholesalers	4231	16,130	16,470	16,826	2,268	2,300	2,374
Furniture and home furnishing merchant wholesalers	4232	16,667	16,286	16,049	1,293	1,317	1,296
Lumber and other construction materials- merchant wholesalers	4233	7,658	7,859	8,704	938	1,032	1,037
Professional and commercial equipment and supplies merchant wholesalers	4234	10,546	10,386	10,419	1,007	1,034	1,079
Metal and mineral (except petroleum) merchant wholesalers	4235	3,341	3,175	3,184	466	461	494
Electrical goods merchant wholesalers	4236	10,664	10,885	11,057	1,122	1,180	1,200
Hardware and plumbing and heating equip- ment and supplies merchant wholesalers. . .	4237	5,600	5,514	5,429	552	557	564
Machinery, equipment, and supplies merchant wholesalers	4238	20,899	20,318	19,649	2,576	2,627	2,651
Miscellaneous durable goods merchant wholesalers	4239	113,391	112,434	112,184	8,639	8,732	8,956
Nondurable goods merchant wholesalers	424	153,828	150,848	154,295	12,640	12,865	12,936
Paper and paper product merchant wholesalers	4241	7,041	6,831	7,069	568	551	544
Drugs and druggists' sundries merchant wholesalers	4242	3,519	3,180	3,091	266	250	239
Apparel, piece goods, and notions merchant wholesalers	4243	22,956	23,201	23,859	1,703	1,733	1,736
Grocery and related products merchant wholesalers	4244	27,706	27,529	28,085	3,428	3,508	3,559
Farm product raw material merchant wholesalers	4245	4,122	3,936	4,331	496	495	485
Chemical and allied products merchant wholesalers	4246	4,281	4,086	3,940	435	441	437
Petroleum and petroleum products merchant wholesalers	4247	2,382	2,354	2,348	277	283	286
Beer, wine, and distilled alcoholic beverage merchant wholesalers	4248	3,277	3,456	3,778	281	320	335
Miscellaneous nondurable goods merchant wholesalers	4249	78,544	76,275	77,794	5,185	5,285	5,314
Wholesale electronic markets and agents and brokers.	425	25,608	26,959	29,226	1,725	1,981	2,219

Source: U.S. Census Bureau, "Nonemployer Statistics" (published June 2008); <http://www.census.gov/econ/nonemployer/index.html>.

U.S. Census Bureau, Statistical Abstract of the United States: 2010

Table 1010. **Wholesale Trade—Establishments, Employees, and Payroll: 2005 and 2006**

[429.8 represents 429,800. Covers establishments with payroll. Employees are for the week including March 12. Excludes self-employed individuals, employees of private households, railroad employees, agricultural production employees, and most government employees. Kind-of-business classification based on North American Industry Classification System (NAICS), 2002. See text, Section 15. For statement on methodology, see Appendix III]

Kind of business	2002 NAICS code	Establishments (1,000)		Employees (1,000)		Payroll (bil. dol.)	
		2005	2006	2005	2006	2005	2006
Wholesale trade	42	429.8	430.0	5,969	6,031	308.9	323.3
Merchant wholesalers, durable goods.	423	245.9	244.7	3,365	3,430	185.3	195.0
Motor vehicles and motor vehicle parts & supplies. . . .	4231	24.8	24.5	366	368	15.7	16.0
Furniture & home furnishing	4232	12.8	12.6	155	158	6.9	7.3
Lumber & other construction materials.	4233	18.5	18.9	263	275	12.3	12.9
Professional & commercial equipment & supplies	4234	37.0	36.6	724	724	48.7	50.4
Metal & mineral (except petroleum).	4235	10.3	10.7	151	158	8.3	9.1
Electrical goods.	4236	29.5	29.2	466	466	33.4	34.6
Hardware, & plumbing & heating equipment & supplies	4237	19.1	19.2	222	231	10.7	11.5
Machinery, equipment, & supplies.	4238	59.4	59.0	689	714	34.9	38.0
Miscellaneous durable goods.	4239	34.6	34.0	330	336	14.4	15.2
Merchant wholesalers, nondurable goods	424	132.9	130.8	2,289	2,268	109.5	112.4
Paper & paper product.	4241	12.2	11.8	201	180	9.8	9.0
Drugs & druggists' sundries.	4242	7.7	7.6	263	258	19.0	20.0
Apparel, piece goods & notions	4243	16.0	15.7	200	201	10.0	10.4
Grocery & related product.	4244	33.9	33.5	764	771	32.2	33.1
Farm product raw material	4245	6.8	6.6	64	62	2.3	2.4
Chemical & allied products	4246	12.6	12.5	143	141	8.1	8.4
Petroleum & petroleum products	4247	7.3	7.2	103	103	5.3	5.8
Beer, wine, and distilled alcoholic beverages	4248	4.2	4.1	172	179	8.3	8.7
Miscellaneous nondurable goods	4249	32.3	31.8	380	373	14.4	14.6
Wholesale electronic markets and agents and brokers. . .	425	51.0	54.5	314	333	14.1	15.8

Source: U.S. Census Bureau, "County Business Patterns" (published July 2008); <http://www.census.gov/econ/cbp/index.html>.

Table 1011. **Merchant Wholesale Trade Sales—Total and E-Commerce: 2007**

[4,150,455 represents $4,150,455,000,000. Covers only businesses with paid employees. Excludes manufacturers' sales branches and offices. Based on the Annual Wholesale Trade Survey, see Appendix III]

Kind of business	2002 NAICS code [1]	Value of sales (mil. dol.)		E-commerce as percent of total sales	Percent distribution of E-commerce sales
		Total	E-commerce		
Merchant wholesalers, total	42	4,150,455	689,319	16.6	100.0
Durable goods.	423	1,997,552	283,425	14.2	41.1
Motor vehicles and motor vehicle parts and supplies.	4231	324,957	102,303	31.5	14.8
Furniture and home furnishings.	4232	65,548	7,465	11.4	1.1
Lumber and other construction materials	4233	129,267	6,002	4.6	0.9
Professional & commercial equipment & supplies . . .	4234	344,740	83,604	24.3	12.1
Computer, peripheral equipment, and software . . .	42343	175,143	54,534	31.1	7.9
Metals and minerals (except petroleum)	4235	162,289	3,779	2.3	0.5
Electrical goods	4236	311,441	35,746	11.5	5.2
Hardware, & plumbing & heating equipment & supplies	4237	88,890	9,650	10.9	1.4
Machinery, equipment and supplies	4238	329,983	12,148	3.7	1.8
Miscellaneous durable goods	4239	240,437	22,728	9.5	3.3
Nondurable goods	424	2,152,903	405,894	18.9	58.9
Paper and paper products	4241	92,809	14,644	15.8	2.1
Drugs and druggists' sundries.	4242	358,632	(S)	(S)	(S)
Apparel, piece goods and notions	4243	120,315	28,766	23.9	4.2
Grocery and related products	4244	501,127	52,594	10.5	7.6
Farm product raw materials	4245	171,962	(S)	(S)	(S)
Chemical and allied products	4246	95,126	4,921	5.2	0.7
Petroleum and petroleum products	4247	491,834	(S)	(S)	(S)
Beer, wine, and distilled alcoholic beverages	4248	100,894	3,327	3.3	0.5
Miscellaneous nondurable goods.	4249	220,204	27,706	12.6	4.0

S Figure does not meet publication standards.   [1] North American Industry Classification System, 2002. See text, Section 15.

Source: U.S. Census Bureau, "E-Stats, 2007 E-commerce Multi-sector Report" (published 28 May 2009); <http://www.census.gov/econ/estats/index.html>.

Table 1012. **Merchant Wholesalers—Summary: 2000 to 2008**

[In billions of dollars (2,814.6 represents $2,814,600,000,000), except ratios. Inventories and inventories/sales ratios, as of December, seasonally adjusted. Excludes manufacturers' sales branches and offices. Data reflect latest revision. Based on data from the Annual Wholesale Trade Survey and the Monthly Wholesale Trade Survey; see Appendix III]

Kind of business	2002 NAICS code [1]	2000	2003	2004	2005	2006	2007	2008
SALES								
Merchant wholesalers	42	2,814.6	2,962.3	3,296.5	3,575.0	3,880.8	4,150.5	4,500.7
Durable goods	423	1,486.7	1,448.9	1,654.6	1,771.8	1,929.3	1,997.6	2,049.3
Motor vehicles, parts, and supplies	4231	222.2	257.3	277.8	294.0	324.9	325.0	294.0
Furniture and home furnishings.	4232	52.7	54.8	58.3	60.9	66.0	65.5	60.9
Lumber and construction materials	4233	87.2	105.7	128.6	141.1	145.0	129.3	117.7
Professional and commercial equipment.	4234	282.2	272.6	296.3	309.5	324.3	344.7	360.1
Computer, peripheral equipment and software	42343	174.8	144.3	157.5	163.1	162.0	175.1	181.5
Metal and mineral (except petroleum)	4235	93.8	81.4	121.2	135.9	156.6	162.3	174.6
Electrical and electronic goods	4236	260.0	227.1	253.8	265.9	294.0	311.4	322.7
Hardware, plumbing and heating equipment . . .	4237	72.1	71.2	77.5	83.2	90.7	88.9	84.5
Machinery, equipment and supplies	4238	256.1	230.8	260.2	288.4	313.0	330.0	362.1
Miscellaneous durable goods	4239	160.3	148.0	181.0	193.0	214.8	240.4	272.7
Nondurable goods.	424	1,327.9	1,513.3	1,641.9	1,803.1	1,951.5	2,152.9	2,451.4
Paper and paper products	4241	77.8	73.9	81.6	87.5	91.0	92.8	96.6
Drugs and druggists' sundries.	4242	176.0	273.5	296.6	329.1	347.0	358.6	386.4
Apparel, piece goods, and notions.	4243	96.5	104.4	108.4	112.9	117.8	120.3	124.7
Grocery and related products	4244	374.7	405.3	409.7	428.4	448.8	501.1	524.1
Farm-product raw materials	4245	102.7	115.1	123.0	118.6	130.8	172.0	234.9
Chemical and allied products	4246	62.3	69.7	76.4	88.2	89.6	95.1	103.7
Petroleum and petroleum products	4247	195.8	225.7	274.9	350.1	426.1	491.8	641.4
Beer, wine, and distilled beverages	4248	71.3	82.2	85.6	90.4	96.4	100.9	105.3
Miscellaneous nondurable goods	4249	170.9	163.4	185.7	198.1	204.0	220.2	234.2
INVENTORIES								
Merchant wholesalers	42	310.0	309.6	339.6	363.9	393.8	418.8	429.8
Durable goods	423	199.3	186.6	212.1	228.0	247.6	251.5	267.9
Motor vehicles, parts, and supplies	4231	28.9	31.6	33.5	36.8	38.8	39.4	43.7
Furniture and home furnishings.	4232	6.3	6.5	6.8	7.3	7.7	7.7	7.7
Lumber and construction materials	4233	8.4	10.4	13.4	14.5	14.8	14.0	13.4
Professional and commercial equipment.	4234	27.9	25.0	27.0	27.7	30.0	30.8	31.4
Computer, peripheral equipment and software	42343	12.1	9.4	10.1	10.1	10.5	10.5	10.4
Metal and mineral (except petroleum)	4235	13.5	12.4	19.5	20.0	25.3	23.9	27.9
Electrical and electronic goods	4236	31.1	24.4	26.7	28.3	31.4	32.8	33.8
Hardware, plumbing and heating equipment . . .	4237	11.5	11.1	12.3	13.1	14.1	14.5	13.7
Machinery, equipment and supplies	4238	51.3	45.3	50.6	56.3	61.3	64.1	71.2
Miscellaneous durable goods	4239	20.5	19.9	22.4	24.1	24.1	24.2	25.0
Nondurable goods.	424	110.6	123.0	127.4	135.9	146.3	167.2	161.9
Paper and paper products	4241	6.6	5.4	6.2	6.6	6.8	7.0	7.3
Drugs and druggists' sundries.	4242	24.1	33.2	33.2	31.5	32.5	33.6	33.5
Apparel, piece goods, and notions.	4243	13.7	13.2	13.4	14.2	15.5	15.8	16.7
Grocery and related products	4244	20.4	20.2	20.8	22.9	24.9	27.5	28.8
Farm-product raw materials	4245	11.8	15.2	12.0	13.9	18.9	28.0	21.0
Chemical and allied products	4246	6.1	6.8	7.4	8.2	8.2	9.1	9.3
Petroleum and petroleum products	4247	5.2	6.5	9.2	11.5	12.3	15.9	12.3
Beer, wine, and distilled beverages	4248	6.5	7.2	7.7	8.2	8.7	9.6	10.5
Miscellaneous nondurable goods	4249	16.2	15.4	17.6	18.8	18.6	20.7	22.5
INVENTORIES/SALES RATIO								
Merchant wholesalers	42	1.34	1.18	1.16	1.18	1.23	1.21	1.31
Durable goods	423	1.71	1.46	1.44	1.49	1.56	1.58	1.77
Motor vehicles, parts, and supplies	4231	1.55	1.33	1.36	1.40	1.32	1.52	2.20
Furniture and home furnishings.	4232	1.56	1.45	1.41	1.43	1.49	1.62	1.75
Lumber and construction materials	4233	1.42	1.33	1.40	1.37	1.62	1.79	2.01
Professional and commercial equipment.	4234	1.22	0.96	0.94	0.94	1.01	0.98	0.97
Computer, peripheral equipment and software	42343	0.87	0.66	0.62	0.65	0.66	0.61	0.59
Metal and mineral (except petroleum)	4235	1.98	1.86	1.91	1.85	2.26	2.21	2.52
Electrical and electronic goods	4236	1.50	1.27	1.25	1.30	1.26	1.32	1.35
Hardware, plumbing and heating equipment . . .	4237	2.20	2.00	2.01	1.97	2.13	2.31	2.28
Machinery, equipment and supplies	4238	2.55	2.20	2.04	2.18	2.39	2.30	2.38
Miscellaneous durable goods	4239	1.65	1.49	1.33	1.44	1.44	1.28	1.54
Nondurable goods.	424	0.97	0.92	0.88	0.88	0.91	0.89	0.92
Paper and paper products	4241	1.06	0.84	0.85	0.89	0.95	0.94	0.96
Drugs and druggists' sundries.	4242	1.52	1.30	1.22	1.08	1.11	1.10	0.98
Apparel, piece goods, and notions.	4243	2.12	1.69	1.64	1.70	1.91	1.93	2.03
Grocery and related products	4244	0.64	0.60	0.58	0.62	0.65	0.64	0.66
Farm-product raw materials	4245	1.23	1.20	1.07	1.29	1.61	1.63	1.24
Chemical and allied products	4246	1.25	1.20	1.14	1.17	1.19	1.23	1.28
Petroleum and petroleum products	4247	0.28	0.33	0.39	0.37	0.36	0.34	0.41
Beer, wine, and distilled beverages	4248	0.98	0.85	0.86	0.94	0.94	0.99	1.00
Miscellaneous nondurable goods	4249	1.16	1.06	1.10	1.19	1.18	1.17	1.32

[1] North American Industry Classification System, 2002; see text, Section 15.

Source: U.S. Census Bureau, "Annual Revision of Monthly Wholesale Distributors: Sales and Inventories—January 1992 Through January 2009"; (published 31 March 2009); <http://www.census.gov/wholesale/www/historic_releases/>.

Wholesale and Retail Trade   641

Table 1013. **Wholesale and Retail Trade—Establishments, Employees, and Payroll by State: 2000 and 2006**

[**6,112 represents 6,112,000.** Covers establishments with payroll. Employees are for the week including March 12. Excludes self-employed, employees of private households, railroad employees, agricultural production employees, and most government employees. Kind-of-business classification for 2000 based on North American Industry Classification System (NAICS) 1997; data for 2006 based on NAICS 2002. See text, Section 15, see Appendix III]

State	Wholesale trade (NAICS 42)						Retail trade (NAICS 44, 45)					
	Establishments		Employees (1,000)		Annual payroll (mil. dol.)		Establishments		Employees (1,000)		Annual payroll (mil. dol.)	
	2000	2006	2000	2006	2000	2006	2000	2006	2000	2006	2000	2006
U.S.	446,237	429,952	6,112	6,031	270,122	323,270	1,113,573	1,120,319	14,841	15,768	302,553	368,278
AL.	6,132	5,660	82	79	2,892	3,470	19,723	19,497	230	247	4,074	5,182
AK.	752	738	7	9	281	413	2,733	2,655	33	35	790	940
AZ.	6,731	6,791	86	97	3,627	4,870	16,911	18,693	255	331	5,694	8,088
AR.	3,505	3,514	45	49	1,402	1,987	12,211	11,653	135	145	2,268	2,868
CA.	58,326	59,935	808	826	40,011	50,038	107,987	113,307	1,491	1,701	36,073	45,772
CO	7,452	7,350	97	100	4,906	5,681	18,748	19,309	252	257	5,883	6,396
CT.	5,076	4,687	77	80	4,481	5,243	14,111	13,752	191	201	4,540	5,313
DE.	1,009	1,019	19	20	1,117	1,511	3,742	3,955	52	56	1,048	1,375
DC	372	434	5	6	282	362	1,945	1,934	19	20	431	517
FL.	30,671	31,567	315	320	12,536	15,023	67,396	72,986	903	1,057	18,044	25,287
GA	13,892	14,097	199	207	9,064	10,882	33,788	35,371	464	478	9,365	11,045
HI	1,809	1,873	19	21	627	819	4,924	5,045	63	73	1,313	1,770
ID	2,012	2,012	24	24	845	976	5,871	6,145	70	81	1,347	1,875
IL	21,509	19,847	344	315	16,683	18,387	43,800	42,941	637	652	12,992	15,412
IN	8,642	8,179	120	118	4,607	5,369	24,261	23,469	354	351	6,332	7,144
IA	5,155	4,857	65	64	2,173	2,686	14,382	13,495	184	181	3,169	3,591
KS.	4,876	4,517	62	57	2,333	2,592	12,261	11,367	153	151	2,747	3,126
KY.	4,939	4,517	74	69	2,536	2,891	16,988	16,485	221	228	3,804	4,529
LA.	6,192	5,533	79	72	2,723	3,312	17,755	16,691	232	230	4,032	5,114
ME	1,740	1,644	22	19	744	832	7,015	6,980	77	85	1,436	1,899
MD	6,098	6,057	95	98	4,526	5,466	19,539	19,590	285	307	6,062	7,544
MA	9,735	8,655	156	145	9,114	9,924	25,813	25,625	353	368	7,729	9,263
MI	13,576	11,785	191	174	8,887	9,338	38,862	38,102	545	489	10,667	10,429
MN	9,294	8,646	137	137	6,399	8,438	20,862	20,868	304	313	5,980	7,165
MS	3,116	2,918	40	38	1,222	1,477	12,794	12,248	141	149	2,384	2,975
MO	9,072	8,259	146	128	5,458	5,504	23,911	23,299	318	326	6,258	7,042
MT	1,537	1,480	15	15	433	569	5,101	5,192	52	58	920	1,261
NE.	3,061	2,956	41	38	1,346	1,691	8,248	7,981	110	109	1,895	2,204
NV.	2,556	2,919	31	39	1,238	1,967	6,940	8,304	108	143	2,533	3,805
NH	2,105	1,965	25	25	1,184	1,414	6,545	6,657	93	100	1,930	2,412
NJ	17,157	16,012	279	271	14,724	17,776	34,841	34,925	439	462	9,897	11,840
NM	2,162	1,991	22	22	753	876	7,249	7,260	91	100	1,745	2,272
NY.	36,606	34,864	422	405	20,941	23,058	75,500	76,982	844	901	18,116	22,553
NC	12,364	11,983	173	170	7,153	8,431	35,785	36,148	450	467	8,739	10,292
ND	1,543	1,476	18	17	532	688	3,435	3,419	42	45	719	914
OH	16,646	15,437	261	238	10,437	11,618	42,708	40,312	644	609	11,903	12,795
OK	5,005	4,583	62	61	2,126	2,656	14,147	13,493	168	176	2,913	3,595
OR	5,836	5,681	79	77	3,266	3,876	14,256	14,522	193	208	4,126	5,030
PA.	16,796	15,805	243	242	10,287	12,600	48,518	46,660	668	679	12,556	14,873
RI	1,530	1,436	21	19	768	947	4,342	4,182	53	56	1,149	1,487
SC.	5,091	4,808	65	68	2,353	3,071	18,619	18,598	224	229	4,083	4,860
SD.	1,390	1,315	16	15	472	552	4,181	4,220	50	51	879	1,053
TN.	8,006	7,378	127	121	4,848	5,888	24,624	23,718	311	333	5,908	7,267
TX.	32,631	31,411	458	464	20,176	26,082	74,758	76,527	1,021	1,128	21,846	26,068
UT.	3,294	3,558	44	48	1,583	2,194	7,952	8,602	124	139	2,455	3,149
VT.	889	863	11	11	401	441	3,974	3,878	38	41	750	951
VA.	7,893	7,750	110	121	4,651	6,061	28,794	29,345	399	441	7,949	10,074
WA	9,869	9,562	125	130	5,412	6,698	22,700	22,761	313	329	7,181	8,570
WV	1,869	1,625	22	21	698	806	7,788	7,118	92	96	1,493	1,777
WI.	7,928	7,241	119	115	4,636	5,487	21,354	21,102	322	322	5,891	6,787
WY	790	762	7	7	229	329	2,881	2,951	28	32	515	728

Source: U.S. Census Bureau, "County Business Patterns" (published June 2008); <http://www.census.gov/econ/cbp/>.

U.S. Census Bureau, Statistical Abstract of the United States: 2010

Table 1014. **Retail Trade—Establishments, Employees, and Payroll: 2000 and 2006**

[1,113.6 **represents 1,113,600.** Covers establishments with payroll. Employees are for the week including March 12. See headnote Table 1013. For statement on methodology, see Appendix III]

Kind of business	NAICS code [1]	Establishments (1,000)		Employees (1,000)		Payroll (bil. dol.)	
		2000	2006	2000	2006	2000	2006
Retail trade, total	44–45	1,113.6	1,120.3	14,841	15,768	302.6	368.3
Motor vehicle & parts dealers	441	124.5	128.4	1,866	1,948	63.9	75.0
Automobile dealers	4411	50.9	52.2	1,222	1,287	47.8	55.5
New car dealers	44111	26.2	26.0	1,112	1,158	44.8	51.3
Used car dealers	44112	24.7	26.2	110	129	3.1	4.2
Other motor vehicle dealers	4412	14.5	16.8	127	167	3.8	5.9
Recreational vehicle dealers	44121	3.1	3.1	36	44	1.1	1.7
Motorcycle and boat and other motor vehicle dealers	44122	11.4	13.7	91	124	2.7	4.3
Automotive parts, accessories, & tire stores .	4413	59.1	59.4	517	493	12.2	13.5
Automotive parts, accessories and tire stores . .	44131	41.1	40.4	355	327	7.8	8.1
Tire dealers	44132	18.0	19.1	162	167	4.4	5.4
Furniture & home furnishings stores.	442	64.8	65.9	549	578	13.4	15.6
Furniture stores	4421	29.7	29.2	284	283	7.5	8.4
Home furnishings stores.	4422	35.1	36.6	265	295	5.9	7.3
Floor covering stores	44221	15.8	14.6	103	99	3.2	3.6
Other home furnishings stores	44229	19.3	22.0	162	196	2.7	3.7
Electronics & appliance stores [2]	443	45.6	49.3	407	489	11.2	13.0
Appliance, TV, & other electronics stores.	44311	29.6	36.4	279	379	6.6	9.8
Household appliance stores.	443111	9.8	9.1	62	71	1.5	2.1
Radio, television, and other electronics stores. .	443112	19.8	27.3	217	308	5.1	7.6
Computer & software stores	44312	12.9	10.7	106	95	4.2	2.8
Bldg material & garden equip & supp dealers	444	91.9	87.8	1,235	1,366	32.5	40.7
Building material & supplies dealers [2].	4441	70.9	67.3	1,055	1,191	28.4	36.2
Home centers	44411	4.4	6.7	351	573	7.6	14.9
Hardware stores	44413	15.0	14.0	146	142	2.5	3.0
Lawn & garden equip, & supplies stores [2].	4442	21.0	20.5	180	175	4.0	4.5
Nursery and garden centers	44422	16.5	16.3	152	149	3.4	3.7
Food & beverage stores	445	154.5	152.4	3,004	2,926	48.4	54.5
Grocery stores	4451	98.3	94.2	2,717	2,615	44.0	48.9
Supermarkets & other grocery (except convenience) stores	44511	68.8	66.1	2,544	2,474	41.8	46.8
Convenience stores	44512	29.5	28.1	173	142	2.2	2.2
Specialty food stores	4452	27.8	28.0	154	169	2.4	2.9
Beer, wine, & liquor stores [3]	4453	28.5	30.2	134	143	2.1	2.6
Health & personal care stores [2]	446	81.2	87.0	914	1,114	19.3	29.7
Pharmacies & drug stores	44611	40.6	41.8	680	851	14.5	23.2
Cosmetics, beauty supplies, & perfume stores . . .	44612	9.6	13.6	61	86	0.8	1.6
Optical goods stores	44613	14.3	12.6	74	66	1.7	1.8
Gasoline stations	447	119.6	116.9	937	913	13.3	15.0
Gasoline stations with convenience stores.	44711	80.5	93.7	653	731	8.9	11.4
Other gasoline stations	44719	39.1	23.1	284	183	4.4	3.6
Clothing & clothing accessories stores	448	150.9	152.0	1,369	1,631	20.2	26.5
Clothing stores [2]	4481	90.0	95.7	1,015	1,260	13.7	18.9
Men's clothing stores	44811	10.7	9.0	85	68	1.6	1.5
Women's clothing stores.	44812	35.6	34.5	302	336	3.9	4.9
Family clothing stores.	44814	20.6	25.4	453	650	5.9	9.2
Shoe stores	4482	29.7	26.7	185	201	2.6	3.2
Jewelry, luggage, & leather goods stores.	4483	31.3	29.7	168	171	3.9	4.4
Jewelry stores.	44831	29.3	28.3	156	162	3.6	4.1
Sporting goods, hobby, book, & music stores	451	65.0	60.5	616	638	8.8	10.1
Sporting goods/hobby/musical instrument stores [2].	4511	43.6	43.0	389	442	6.0	7.4
Sporting goods stores	45111	22.6	23.3	185	223	2.9	4.2
Hobby, toy, and game stores	45112	10.9	9.5	131	132	1.8	1.8
Book, periodical, & music stores [2]	4512	21.4	17.5	228	196	2.8	2.7
Book stores	451211	11.7	11.0	142	143	1.7	2.0
Prerecorded tape, CD, & record stores	45122	7.7	4.9	76	43	0.9	0.6
General merchandise stores.	452	39.6	46.7	2,526	2,802	39.8	53.4
Department stores	4521	10.4	10.0	1,766	1,532	27.2	28.6
Other general merchandise stores.	4529	29.2	36.7	760	1,270	12.6	24.8
Warehouse clubs & superstores	45291	2.0	3.2	478	965	8.7	20.5
All other general merchandise stores.	45299	27.2	33.5	283	305	3.8	4.3
Miscellaneous store retailers [2]	453	131.0	125.1	850	840	13.8	15.5
Florists	4531	24.2	20.2	122	98	1.6	1.4
Office supplies, stationery, and gift stores	4532	43.0	41.2	350	338	5.2	5.7
Used merchandise stores.	4533	17.5	17.7	114	134	1.6	2.2
Other miscellaneous store retailers [2]	4539	46.4	46.0	264	270	5.4	6.3
Nonstore retailers [2].	454	44.8	48.3	567	522	18.1	19.3
Electronic shopping & mail-order houses.	4541	11.8	16.2	277	264	10.4	10.8
Direct selling establishments	4543	26.8	26.8	223	206	6.1	7.0
Fuel dealers	45431	11.8	10.2	106	94	3.1	3.3

[1] Data for 2000 based on North American Industry Classification System 1997; 2006 data based on NAICS 2002. See text, Section 15. [2] Includes other kinds of business not shown separately. [3] Includes government employees.

Source: U.S. Census Bureau, "County Business Patterns" (published June 2008); <http://www.census.gov/econ/cbp/>.

Wholesale and Retail Trade **643**

Table 1015. **Retail Trade—Nonemployer Establishments and Receipts by Kind of Business: 2004 to 2006**

[**1,893 represents 1,893,000.** Includes only firms subject to federal income tax. Nonemployers are businesses with no paid employees. Based on NAICS 2002, see text, Section 15]

Kind of business	2002 NAICS code	Establishments (1,000)			Receipts (mil. dol.)		
		2004	2005	2006	2004	2005	2006
Retail trade, total [1]	44–45	1,893	1,881	1,858	82,916	83,599	83,933
Motor vehicle & parts dealers	441	145	147	141	20,097	20,072	19,789
Furniture & home furnishings stores.	442	43	41	39	3,049	3,088	2,965
Electronics and appliance stores	443	28	27	26	1,704	1,701	1,645
Bldg material & garden equip & supp dealers . .	444	32	31	32	2,603	2,710	2,723
Food & beverage stores [1]	445	89	89	87	8,951	9,027	8,983
Grocery stores	4451	40	39	38	4,567	4,518	4,448
Specialty food stores	4452	39	39	39	2,522	2,584	2,607
Health & personal care stores.	446	118	114	122	2,487	2,510	2,673
Clothing & clothing accessories stores [1]	448	106	109	111	5,023	5,231	5,327
Clothing stores	4481	70	73	74	3,067	3,239	3,319
Jewelry, luggage, and leather goods stores . .	4483	32	32	33	1,674	1,702	1,712
Sporting goods, hobby, book, & music stores [1] .	451	95	93	90	3,873	3,882	3,882
Book, periodical, and music stores	4512	31	30	29	962	944	912
General merchandise stores.	452	35	36	36	1,559	1,632	1,640
Miscellaneous store retailers [1]	453	325	313	301	13,719	13,625	13,656
Gift, novelty, & souvenir stores	45322	72	68	63	2,172	2,095	2,028
Nonstore retailers [1]	454	867	873	865	18,218	18,608	19,189
Electronic shopping & mail-order houses. . . .	4541	67	73	77	2,310	2,587	2,854
Direct selling establishments	4543	769	771	759	15,002	15,144	15,466

[1] Includes other kinds of business not shown separately.

Source: U.S. Census Bureau, "Nonemployer Statistics"; (published June 2008); <http://www.census.gov/econ/nonemployer/index.html>.

Table 1016. **Retail Industries—Employees, Average Weekly Hours, and Average Hourly Earnings: 2000 to 2008**

[**Annual averages of monthly figures (15,280 represents 15,280,000).** Covers all full- and part-time employees who worked during, or received pay for, any part of the pay period including the 12th of the month]

Industry	2007 NAICS code [1]	Employees (1,000)			Average weekly hours			Average hourly earnings (dol.)	
		2000	2005	2008	2000	2005	2008	2000	2008
Retail trade, total.	(X)	15,280	15,280	15,356	30.7	30.6	30.0	10.86	12.87
Motor vehicle and parts dealers [2]	441	1,847	1,919	1,845	35.9	35.8	35.7	14.94	16.15
Automobile dealers	4411	1,217	1,261	1,186	35.1	35.8	35.6	16.95	17.13
Other motor vehicle dealers	4412	132	166	165	35.1	34.7	34.7	12.35	16.75
Auto parts, accessories, and tire stores.	4413	499	491	493	38.2	36.0	36.4	11.04	13.65
Furniture and home furnishings stores [2]	442	544	576	543	31.2	30.7	29.5	12.33	15.02
Furniture stores	4421	289	298	267	31.7	31.7	32.4	13.37	15.13
Home furnishings stores.	4422	254	278	275	30.7	29.5	26.7	11.06	14.88
Electronics and appliance stores [2]	443	564	536	550	31.4	32.8	30.6	13.67	17.61
Building material and garden suply stores [2].	444	1,142	1,276	1,253	35.7	36.8	34.5	11.25	13.83
Building material and supplies dealers	4441	982	1,134	1,115	36.2	37.3	34.7	11.30	13.85
Lawn and garden equipment and supplies stores .	4442	160	142	139	32.5	32.6	32.4	10.89	13.63
Food and beverage stores	445	2,993	2,818	2,858	31.7	30.1	29.3	9.76	11.56
Grocery stores	4451	2,582	2,446	2,497	31.9	30.0	29.4	9.71	11.59
Specialty food stores	4452	270	236	223	31.6	33.0	29.9	9.97	11.07
Beer, wine, and liquor stores.	4453	141	136	138	28.6	27.1	27.4	10.40	11.85
Health and personal care stores [2]	446	928	954	1,002	29.8	29.3	29.7	11.68	16.28
Gasoline stations [2]	447	936	871	843	31.6	31.6	30.7	8.05	9.46
Clothing and clothing accessories stores	448	1,322	1,415	1,484	24.9	24.4	21.3	9.96	11.57
Clothing stores	4481	954	1,066	1,134	24.4	23.1	19.7	9.88	10.83
Shoe stores	4482	193	180	192	24.9	26.0	24.8	8.96	12.58
Jewelry, luggage, and leather goods stores	4483	175	169	159	27.7	31.9	29.0	11.48	14.36
Sporting goods, hobby, book, and music stores . .	451	686	647	647	26.4	23.3	24.4	9.33	11.70
Sporting goods and musical instrument stores . . .	4511	437	447	472	27.0	23.5	24.9	9.55	10.94
Book, periodical, and music stores	4512	249	200	175	25.4	23.0	23.3	8.91	10.99
General merchandise stores.	452	2,820	2,934	3,047	27.8	29.4	30.6	9.22	10.73
Miscellaneous store retailers [2]	453	1,007	900	848	29.2	28.5	28.4	10.20	11.70
Office supplies, stationary, and gift stores	4532	471	391	352	29.7	27.8	27.5	10.46	12.85
Used merchandise stores.	4533	107	113	119	26.7	27.8	29.3	8.07	8.94
Nonstore retailers [2].	454	492	435	436	35.4	34.5	34.0	13.22	16.42
Electronic shopping and mail-order houses	4541	257	240	251	36.2	33.0	34.1	13.38	16.47
Direct selling establishments	4543	169	145	140	34.1	36.0	34.6	13.70	16.56

X Not applicable. [1] Based on the North American Industry Classification System, 2007 (NAICS); see text, this section and Section 15. [2] Includes other kinds of business not shown separately.

Source: U.S. Bureau of Labor Statistics, Current Employment Statistics, "Employment, Hours, and Earnings—National," See <http://www.bls.gov/ces/data.htm>.

Table 1017. **Retail Trade and Food Services—Sales by Kind of Business: 2000 to 2008**

[In billions of dollars (3,294.2 represents $3,294,200,000,000)]

Kind of business	2002 NAICS code [1]	2000	2003	2004	2005	2006	2007	2008
Retail & food services sales, total ..	44, 45, 722	3,294.2	3,615.2	3,846.3	4,080.7	4,287.4	4,432.6	4,412.9
Retail sales, total	44, 45	2,988.8	3,265.5	3,474.3	3,687.4	3,869.5	3,994.8	3,960.0
GAFO, total [2]	(X)	863.9	948.2	1,007.2	1,062.3	1,116.9	1,154.2	1,155.7
Motor vehicle and parts dealers	441	797.6	841.2	864.5	885.9	896.4	906.9	792.9
Automobile and other motor vehicle dealers	4411, 4412	733.9	776.6	797.3	814.8	821.9	830.2	714.3
Automobile dealers	4411	688.7	721.0	734.7	748.0	752.9	758.9	645.8
New car dealers.............	44111	630.1	656.9	665.9	675.2	676.0	677.2	569.8
Used car dealers	44112	58.6	64.1	68.8	72.8	76.9	81.7	76.0
Automotive parts, accessories, and tire stores	4413	63.7	64.6	67.2	71.2	74.5	76.7	78.6
Furniture, home furnishings, electronics and appliance stores..............	442, 443	173.7	184.5	200.1	213.4	226.0	227.2	216.6
Furniture and home furnishings stores ..	442	91.3	97.5	105.3	111.8	117.7	115.3	105.5
Furniture stores...............	4421	50.7	52.1	56.5	59.8	61.9	61.1	56.4
Home furnishings stores	4422	40.6	45.5	48.8	51.9	55.7	54.2	49.1
Electronics and appliance stores [3]	443	82.4	87.0	94.8	101.6	108.4	111.9	111.1
Appliance, television, and other electronics stores.............	44311	58.3	66.1	72.2	77.6	83.1	85.0	84.6
Household appliance stores......	443111	12.6	14.5	15.7	17.0	18.1	17.9	17.3
Radio, television, and other electronics stores	443112	45.6	51.6	56.5	60.5	65.1	67.0	67.3
Computer and software stores......	44312	20.7	17.5	19.1	20.5	21.7	23.3	22.9
Building materials, garden equipment & supply stores	444	229.3	265.1	298.8	327.2	344.7	335.5	323.3
Building materials & supply dealers	4441	197.9	232.0	263.6	290.4	306.9	293.9	274.9
Hardware stores	44413	16.2	17.6	18.1	18.6	19.4	19.8	19.7
Food and beverage stores [3]..........	445	445.7	477.1	495.0	515.0	533.8	559.6	587.7
Grocery stores	4451	403.0	430.0	446.9	462.6	477.7	500.5	526.5
Beer, wine and liquor stores	4453	28.7	30.7	32.4	33.9	36.7	38.8	41.3
Health and personal care stores	446	155.4	192.2	198.9	209.0	224.8	236.4	245.8
Pharmacies and drug stores	44611	130.9	164.6	167.2	175.8	189.1	197.7	203.8
Gasoline stations	447	250.0	273.6	320.4	373.9	416.2	437.0	478.9
Clothing and clothing accessories stores [3]	448	168.0	178.8	190.1	201.5	214.9	221.1	216.0
Clothing stores [3]................	4481	118.2	128.3	137.1	146.1	156.2	162.1	158.6
Women's clothing stores.........	44812	31.5	32.5	34.7	36.8	39.1	39.3	37.8
Family clothing stores..........	44814	58.9	67.3	72.0	77.4	82.0	84.2	83.2
Shoe stores	4482	22.9	23.2	23.7	25.3	26.7	26.7	26.8
Jewelry stores	44831	25.0	25.5	27.5	28.2	29.9	30.1	28.3
Sporting goods, hobby, book & music stores [3]................	451	76.1	77.3	80.1	81.8	84.8	86.9	87.7
Sporting goods stores	45111	25.4	27.2	28.9	30.9	34.3	36.3	37.1
Book stores	451211	14.9	16.2	16.8	16.9	16.7	17.0	16.7
General merchandise stores.	452	404.3	468.7	497.2	525.2	552.1	577.0	596.0
Department stores (excl. L.D.) [4].......	4521	232.5	214.4	215.7	214.3	212.7	209.7	200.0
Department stores (incl. L.D.) [4].......	4521	239.9	221.0	222.0	220.7	219.0	215.9	206.1
Other general merchandise stores	4529	171.9	254.3	281.5	310.9	339.4	367.3	396.0
Warehouse clubs and superstores ..	45291	139.6	216.3	242.4	270.2	296.7	323.8	351.2
Miscellaneous store retailers	453	108.1	103.1	105.3	108.4	115.8	117.4	117.5
Nonstore retailers [3]...............	454	180.7	203.9	224.0	246.7	275.7	289.8	297.6
Electronic shopping & mail order houses.	4541	113.9	131.2	147.2	164.3	190.9	199.2	204.2
Fuel dealers..................	45431	26.7	29.0	31.9	37.0	39.3	42.5	47.1
Food services and drinking places [5] ..	**722**	**305.5**	**349.7**	**372.0**	**393.6**	**420.4**	**437.8**	**452.9**

X Not applicable. [1] North American Industry Classification System, 2002; see text, Section 15. [2] GAFO (General Merchandise, Apparel, Furniture, and Office Supplies) represents stores classified in the following NAICS codes: 442, 443, 448, 451, 452, and 4532. [3] Includes other kinds of business not shown separately. [4] L.D. represents leased departments. [5] See also Table 1245.

Source: U.S. Census Bureau, "Annual Revision of Monthly Retail and Food Services: Sales and Inventories—January 1992 Through March 2009" (published April 2009); <http://www.census.gov/retail/mrts/www/benchmark/2009/html/annrev09.html>.

Table 1018. **Retail Trade Corporations—Sales, Net Profit, and Profit Per Dollar of Sales: 2007 and 2008**

[Represents North American Industry Classification System, 2007 (NAICS) groups 44 and 45. Profit rates are averages of quarterly figures at annual rates. Covers corporations with assets of $50,000,000 or more]

Item	Unit	Total retail trade		Food and beverage stores (NAICS 445)		Clothing and general merchandise stores (NAICS 448 and 452)		All other retail stores	
		2007	2008	2007	2008	2007	2008	2007	2008
Sales	Bil. dol ..	2,062	2,089	379	397	741	745	942	947
Net profit:									
Before income taxes	Bil. dol ..	94.3	63.2	12.3	8.1	44.4	34.0	37.6	21.1
After income taxes...........	Bil. dol ..	62.2	38.1	9.0	4.8	28.8	22.8	24.5	10.6
Profits per dollar of sales:									
Before income taxes	Cents...	4.6	3.0	3.2	2.1	5.9	4.6	4.0	2.2
After income taxes...........	Cents...	2.6	1.8	2.4	1.2	3.8	3.1	2.6	1.1
Profits on stockholders' equity:									
Before income taxes	Percent .	23.1	16.0	26.7	16.9	24.6	19.0	20.7	12.5
After income taxes...........	Percent .	15.2	9.7	19.5	9.9	16.0	12.7	13.4	6.3

Source: U.S. Census Bureau, *Quarterly Financial Report for Manufacturing, Mining and Trade Corporations*, annual; <http://webdev.ssd.census.gov/econ/qfr/index.html>.

Wholesale and Retail Trade 645

Table 1019. Retail Trade and Food Services—Estimated Per Capita Sales by Kind of Business: 2000 to 2008

[In dollars. As of Dec. 31. Based on estimated resident population estimates as of July. For statement on methodology, see Appendix III]

Kind of business	2002 NAICS code [1]	2000	2003	2004	2005	2006	2007	2008
Retail and food service sales	44–45,722	11,675	12,457	13,132	13,807	14,370	14,712	14,513
Retail sales, total	44–45	10,592	11,252	11,862	12,476	12,969	13,259	13,024
Total (excluding motor vehicle and parts dealers)	*44–45 ex 441*	*7,765*	*8,353*	*8,910*	*9,478*	*9,965*	*10,249*	*10,416*
Motor vehicle and parts dealers	441	2,827	2,899	2,952	2,997	3,004	3,010	2,608
Furniture and home furnishings stores	442	324	336	360	378	390	383	347
Electronics and appliance stores	443	292	300	324	343	363	371	365
Building material and garden equipment and supplies dealers	444	813	913	1,020	1,105	1,153	1,113	1,063
Food and beverage stores	445	1,579	1,644	1,690	1,743	1,789	1,857	1,933
Health and personal care stores	446	551	662	679	709	751	785	808
Gasoline stations	447	886	943	1,094	1,261	1,383	1,450	1,575
Clothing and clothing accessories stores . .	448	595	616	649	681	715	734	710
Sporting goods, hobby, book, and music stores	451	270	266	273	277	283	288	288
General merchandise stores	452	1,433	1,615	1,697	1,778	1,852	1,915	1,960
Miscellaneous store retailers	453	383	355	359	366	383	390	387
Nonstore retailers	454	640	703	765	836	902	962	979
Food services and drinking places . . .	722	1,083	1,205	1,270	1,331	1,401	1,453	1,490

[1] North American Industry Classification System, 2002; see text, Section 15.

Source: U.S. Census Bureau, "Annual Retail Trade Report" (published April 2009); <http://www.census.gov/retail/index.html>.

Table 1020. Retail Trade—Merchandise Inventories and Inventory/Sales Ratio by Kind of Business: 2000 to 2008

[Inventories in billions of dollars (406.9 represents $406,900,000,000). As of Dec. 31. Estimates exclude food services. Includes warehouses. Adjusted for seasonal variations. Sales data also adjusted for holiday and trading-day differences. Based on data from the Monthly Retail Trade Survey, Annual Retail Trade Survey, and administrative records; see Appendix III. Data have been adjusted using results of the 2002 Economic Census]

Kind of business	2002 NAICS code [1]	Inventories				Inventory/sales ratio			
		2000	2005	2007	2008	2000	2005	2007	2008
Total [2]	44–45	406.9	472	499.7	484.4	1.62	1.50	1.47	1.62
Excluding motor vehicle and parts dealers	*44–45 ex 441*	*278.6*	*319.1*	*342.9*	*336.6*	*1.49*	*1.33*	*1.30*	*1.39*
Motor vehicle and parts dealers	441	128.3	152.6	156.8	147.8	2.01	2.07	2.09	2.62
Furniture, home furnishings, electronics, and appliance stores	442,443	25.7	31.1	32.8	30.6	1.85	1.72	1.74	1.84
Building material and garden equipment and supplies dealers	444	34.5	46.4	49.4	49.9	1.76	1.65	1.81	2.00
Food and beverage stores	445	32.2	34.1	36.2	37.6	0.85	0.78	0.75	0.78
Clothing and clothing accessories stores	448	36.9	43.5	47.9	46.7	2.61	2.52	2.60	2.80
General merchandise stores	452	64.9	73.3	75.9	73.7	1.87	1.64	1.54	1.50
Department stores	4521	42.7	37.5	37.1	33.8	2.17	2.10	2.14	2.11

[1] North American Industry Classification System, 2002; see text, Section 15.   [2] Includes kind of business not shown separately.

Source: U.S. Census Bureau, "Annual Revision of Monthly Retail and Food Services: Sales and Inventories—January 1992 Through March 2009" (published April 2009); <http://www.census.gov/retail/mrts/www/benchmark/2009/html/annrev09.html>.

Table 1021. Retail Trade Sales—Total and E-Commerce by Kind of Business: 2007

[3,994,823 represents $3,994,823,000,000. Covers retailers with and without payroll. Based on the Annual Retail Trade Survey; see Appendix III]

Kind of business	2002 NAICS code [1]	Value of sales (mil. dol.)		E-commerce as percent of total sales	Percent distribution of E-commerce sales
		Total	E-commerce		
Retail trade, total [2]	44–45	3,994,823	126,697	3.2	100.0
Motor vehicle and parts dealers	441	906,923	23,600	2.6	18.6
Furniture and home furnishings stores	442	115,349	796	0.7	0.6
Electronics and appliance stores	443	111,893	1,301	1.2	1.0
Food and beverage stores	445	559,625	1,022	0.2	0.8
Clothing and clothing accessories stores	448	221,097	2,115	1.0	1.7
Sporting goods, hobby, book, and music stores . . .	451	86,906	1,686	1.9	1.3
Miscellaneous store retailers	453	117,447	1,963	1.7	1.5
Nonstore retailers	454	289,808	93,026	32.1	73.4
Electronic shopping and mail-order houses	45411	199,199	88,915	44.6	70.2

[1] North American Industry Classification System, 2002; see text, Section 15.   [2] Includes other kinds of businesses not shown separately.

Source: U.S. Census Bureau, "E-Stats, 2007 E-commerce Multi-sector Report" (published 28 May 2009); <http://www.census.gov/econ/estats/index.html>.

Table 1022. **Electronic Shopping and Mail-Order Houses—Total and E-Commerce Sales by Merchandise Line: 2006 and 2007**

[183,273 represents $183,273,000,000. Represents NAICS code 454110, which comprises establishments primarily engaged in retailing all types of merchandise using nonstore means, such as catalogs, toll-free telephone numbers, or electronic media, such as interactive television or computer. Covers businesses with and without paid employees. Based on the Annual Retail Survey; see Appendix III]

Merchandise line	Value of sales, total, 2006 (mil. dol.)	2007					
		Value of sales (mil. dol.)		E-commerce as percent of total sales	Percent distribution		
		Total	E-commerce		Total	E-commerce
Total	183,273	199,199	88,915	44.6	100.0	100.0
Books and magazines............	5,982	6,861	4,200	61.0	3.4	4.7
Clothing and clothing accessories (includes footwear)	18,451	20,609	13,585	65.9	10.3	15.3
Computer hardware	20,243	23,059	11,097	48.1	11.6	12.5
Computer software	4,084	5,000	2,849	57.0	2.5	3.2
Drugs, health aids, beauty aids......	57,056	54,848	4,806	8.8	27.5	5.4
Electronics and appliances.........	10,079	11,318	8,382	74.1	5.7	9.4
Food, beer, and wine	3,548	4,034	2,335	57.9	2.0	2.6
Furniture and home furnishings......	10,849	11,913	7,841	65.8	6.0	8.8
Music and videos...............	3,599	4,025	2,979	74.0	2.0	3.4
Office equipment and supplies	7,436	8,445	5,722	67.8	4.2	6.4
Sporting goods	4,281	5,199	3,027	58.2	2.6	3.4
Toys, hobby goods, and games	3,718	4,465	2,740	61.4	2.2	3.1
Other merchandise [1]...........	24,981	29,030	12,549	43.2	14.6	14.1
Nonmerchandise receipts [2]	8,966	10,393	6,803	65.5	5.2	7.7

[1] Includes other merchandise such as jewelry, collectibles, souvenirs, auto parts and accessories, hardware, and lawn and garden equipment and supplies. [2] Includes nonmerchandise receipts such as auction commissions, shipping and handling, customer training, customer support, and advertising.

Source: U.S. Census Bureau, "E-Stats, 2007 E-commerce Multi-sector Report" (published 28 May 2009); <http://www.census .gov/econ/estats/index.html>.

Table 1023. **Franchised New Car Dealerships—Summary: 1990 to 2008**

[316 represents $316,000,000,000]

Item	Unit	1990	2000	2001	2002	2003	2004	2005	2006	2007	2008
Dealerships [1]	Number..	24,825	22,250	21,800	21,725	21,650	21,640	21,495	21,200	20,770	20,010
Sales	Bil. dol. ...	316	650	690	680	699	714	699	675	693	576
New cars sold [2]	Millions ..	9.3	8.8	8.4	8.1	7.6	7.5	7.7	7.0	7.6	6.0
Used vehicles sold	Millions ..	14.2	20.5	21.4	19.4	19.5	19.7	19.7	19.2	18.5	15.0
Employment...........	1,000 ...	924	1,114	1,130	1,130	1,130	1,130	1,138	1,120	1,115	1,057
Dealer pretax profits as a percentage of sales.....	Percent ..	1.0	1.6	2.0	1.9	1.7	1.7	1.6	1.5	1.5	1.0
Inventory: [3] Domestic: [4]											
Total	1,000 ...	2,537	3,183	2,824	2,727	3,085	3,267	2,991	2,943	2,712	2,478
Days' supply	Days....	73	68	63	63	63	75	70	71	67	80
Imported: [4]											
Total	1,000 ...	707	468	508	521	618	646	566	605	619	687
Days' supply	Days....	72	50	51	49	49	59	52	51	51	65

[1] At beginning of year. [2] Data provided by "Ward's Automotive Reports." [3] Annual average. Includes light trucks. [4] Classification based on where automobiles are produced (i.e., automobiles manufactured by foreign companies but produced in the U.S. are classified as domestic).

Source: National Automobile Dealers Association, McLean, VA, *NADA Data*, annual. See also <http://www.nada.org/Publications /NADADATA/>.

Table 1024. **Retail Sales and Leases of New and Used Vehicles: 1990 to 2008**

[In thousands, except as noted (51,390 represents 51,390,000)]

Item	1990	2000	2002	2003	2004	2005	2006	2007	2008
Vehicle sales and leases, total	51,390	58,964	59,835	60,215	59,411	61,086	59,070	57,507	(NA)
New vehicle sales and leases..........	13,860	17,344	16,810	16,643	16,866	16,948	16,504	16,089	13,195
New vehicle sales [1]...............	13,285	13,181	13,639	13,594	13,609	13,551	13,271	13,671	10,933
Passenger cars.................	8,766	6,580	6,370	5,932	5,737	5,806	6,088	6,342	5,642
Light trucks	4,519	6,601	7,269	7,663	7,872	7,745	7,184	7,329	5,291
New vehicle leases [2]..............	575	4,163	3,171	3,049	3,257	3,397	3,233	3,458	2,262
Passenger cars.................	534	2,272	1,732	1,683	1,768	1,861	1,693	1,743	1,164
Light trucks	41	1,891	1,439	1,366	1,489	1,536	1,540	1,715	1,098
Used vehicle sales [3]...............	37,530	41,620	43,025	43,572	42,545	44,138	42,566	41,418	(NA)
New and used vehicle sales, total value (bil. dol.) [4]...........	446	736	721	738	765	776	786	774	(NA)
New vehicle sales (bil. dol.)..........	227	380	371	382	407	421	445	435	(NA)
Used vehicle sales (bil. dol.)..........	219	356	350	356	358	355	341	339	(NA)

NA Not available. [1] New vehicle sales data is calculated by subtracting CNW Marketing's vehicle leasing data from Bureau of Economic Analysis' data which combines sales and leases. [2] Consumer leases only. [3] Used car sales include sales from franchised dealers, independent dealers, and casual sales. [4] Includes leased vehicles.

Source: U.S. Bureau of Transportation Statistics, *National Transportation Statistics*, annual. See also <http://www.bts.gov /publications/national_transportation_statistics/>. Data supplied by following sources: New vehicle sales and leases— U.S. Department of Commerce, Bureau of Economic Analysis; New vehicle leases—<http://bea.doc.gov/>, CNW Marketing/Research, "Personal Communication," March 30, 2009; Used vehicle sales and value: Manheim, *Used Car Market Report*, Atlanta, GA; <http://www.manheimconsulting.com/>.

Wholesale and Retail Trade 647

Table 1025. **Retail Trade and Food Services—Sales by Type of Store and State: 2008**

[In millions of dollars (4,593,507 represents $4,593,507,000,000). Based on North American Industry Classification System (NAICS), 2002; see text, Section 15]

State	Total retail sales plus food services and drinking places (NAICS 44–45, 722)	All retail stores [1] (NAICS 44–45)	Motor vehicle and parts dealers (NAICS 441)	Furniture and home furnishings (NAICS 442)	Electronics and appliances (NAICS 443)	Building material & garden equip. & supplies dealers (NAICS 444)	Food and beverage stores (NAICS 445)	Health and personal care (NAICS 446)
U.S....	4,593,507	4,124,924	693,211	96,552	110,275	488,997	617,207	255,492
AL	70,059	64,415	11,556	1,504	1,838	8,985	7,113	4,474
AK	11,562	10,263	1,525	177	212	1,112	1,820	193
AZ	105,584	96,094	16,774	2,469	3,443	10,488	13,038	4,149
AR	40,183	36,919	7,187	645	603	5,069	3,872	2,141
CA	562,603	502,877	82,265	12,254	18,840	52,736	85,076	28,237
CO	79,338	70,657	12,671	1,976	2,339	8,527	11,789	2,587
CT	56,710	51,190	7,914	1,269	1,228	6,799	8,719	3,515
DE	16,905	15,344	2,743	532	439	2,290	2,684	976
DC	6,608	4,034	65	160	94	196	1,262	696
FL.....	309,065	275,198	53,589	8,433	6,731	28,054	39,853	18,656
GA	142,167	127,091	22,790	3,327	2,925	17,707	17,432	7,927
HI......	22,864	19,212	2,649	385	390	1,826	3,486	1,352
ID......	24,797	23,017	4,684	618	362	3,362	3,018	747
IL......	191,824	170,808	24,839	3,383	5,013	18,677	23,315	9,476
IN......	88,925	79,869	13,758	1,555	1,877	10,472	8,873	5,025
IA......	40,982	37,424	6,190	709	760	5,424	5,374	1,856
KS	37,033	33,786	5,781	647	1,109	3,838	4,890	1,685
KY	57,876	52,314	7,793	1,186	1,038	7,102	6,786	3,850
LA	68,434	62,360	10,630	1,693	1,420	9,389	6,602	3,881
ME	23,039	21,216	3,029	289	273	2,828	3,673	926
MD	88,991	79,556	14,587	2,145	2,226	10,384	15,675	4,109
MA	99,088	85,836	13,184	2,279	2,137	10,648	17,574	7,352
MI......	133,535	119,962	20,618	2,308	3,168	15,475	15,712	9,131
MN	79,945	71,933	10,872	1,530	2,215	9,288	11,134	3,888
MS	41,172	37,859	6,003	754	642	5,655	3,694	2,509
MO	89,498	80,402	12,731	1,373	1,675	9,625	8,536	4,746
MT	18,115	16,668	2,778	456	389	2,666	2,101	564
NE	28,825	26,468	4,245	518	587	3,218	2,631	1,178
NV	49,038	42,832	7,240	863	1,221	3,578	5,766	1,750
NH	28,873	26,720	4,146	406	949	3,661	5,066	1,192
NJ......	139,811	125,910	21,283	2,856	3,282	13,181	26,974	10,725
NM	29,169	26,289	4,507	517	478	2,911	2,624	1,069
NY	277,951	248,079	32,017	6,173	9,833	27,138	44,315	25,614
NC	136,348	123,249	22,642	3,277	2,418	17,827	15,008	9,209
ND	12,228	11,429	2,046	194	271	1,716	1,282	568
OH	149,005	131,073	21,089	2,354	2,896	14,359	21,129	7,861
OK	47,818	43,310	8,575	881	691	5,089	3,966	2,447
OR	59,315	53,021	9,205	1,249	1,445	6,114	8,787	2,121
PA	180,948	163,605	26,431	3,024	3,071	17,666	25,364	11,909
RI......	15,070	13,205	1,865	270	210	1,344	3,942	1,920
SC	63,402	56,857	9,366	1,223	858	8,194	7,775	4,368
SD	14,948	13,902	2,441	228	299	2,071	1,282	526
TN	98,901	89,784	14,917	1,954	1,703	12,177	11,133	7,361
TX	349,238	313,639	62,847	8,234	8,091	34,097	43,524	13,739
UT	44,759	42,022	7,296	1,185	962	5,170	4,896	953
VT	11,015	10,174	1,526	180	160	1,455	1,847	629
VA	130,064	117,019	18,833	2,889	2,960	14,404	19,074	6,065
WA	104,065	94,747	14,985	2,291	1,936	11,214	14,105	3,950
WV	25,237	23,081	3,461	329	368	2,923	2,614	1,770
WI......	80,609	73,025	11,322	1,274	2,054	9,749	10,085	3,714
WY	9,968	9,175	1,719	128	147	1,120	916	206

See footnotes at end of table.

U.S. Census Bureau, Statistical Abstract of the United States: 2010

[See headnote, page 648]

State	Gasoline stations (NAICS 447)	Clothing and clothing accessories (NAICS 448)	Sporting goods, hobby, book & music stores (NAICS 451)	General merchandise (NAICS 452)	Miscellaneous stores (NAICS 453)	Nonstore retailers (NAICS 454)	Food services & drinking places (NAICS 722)
U.S....	**524,739**	**210,946**	**88,519**	**615,759**	**117,651**	**305,575**	**468,583**
AL	9,600	2,685	1,138	11,621	1,545	2,357	5,644
AK	1,155	388	344	2,373	368	597	1,298
AZ	13,112	3,828	1,724	15,617	2,670	8,782	9,490
AR	5,757	1,268	650	7,498	1,190	1,039	3,264
CA	50,588	28,241	11,530	86,520	13,658	32,932	59,726
CO	7,108	3,032	2,306	11,550	2,205	4,565	8,681
CT	5,003	3,529	1,247	5,279	1,227	5,462	5,520
DE	1,315	784	354	1,913	652	663	1,561
DC	225	476	192	257	102	310	2,573
FL......	31,316	16,960	5,473	40,174	7,206	18,752	33,868
GA	19,339	6,401	2,386	18,463	3,568	4,824	15,075
HI......	1,710	2,320	447	3,489	839	317	3,652
ID......	3,439	551	676	3,664	672	1,223	1,780
IL......	18,325	7,939	3,615	26,396	4,146	25,685	21,016
IN......	13,031	3,698	1,794	13,048	2,403	4,335	9,056
IA......	6,719	1,089	690	5,660	700	2,252	3,558
KS	5,392	1,384	703	5,816	869	1,672	3,246
KY	8,894	1,902	816	9,759	1,706	1,481	5,562
LA	10,263	2,623	1,188	10,594	2,086	1,991	6,074
ME	3,203	820	397	2,545	566	2,667	1,823
MD	7,135	4,830	1,827	9,626	1,837	5,174	9,434
MA	8,218	5,184	2,224	7,617	2,027	7,394	13,252
MI......	15,203	5,531	2,715	20,103	4,046	5,954	13,573
MN	9,367	2,943	1,516	11,100	1,717	6,361	8,012
MS	7,225	1,742	609	7,138	1,096	792	3,312
MO	13,798	2,954	1,449	13,076	2,447	7,994	9,095
MT	3,306	420	462	2,483	569	474	1,447
NE	3,862	749	843	3,613	518	4,507	2,358
NV	4,796	3,535	692	6,613	1,436	5,345	6,206
NH	2,733	1,122	612	3,263	595	2,976	2,153
NJ.....	11,751	7,763	3,516	10,775	3,334	10,470	13,900
NM	4,621	854	443	5,140	1,030	2,096	2,880
NY	19,232	23,075	5,990	25,786	11,485	17,422	29,872
NC	17,615	5,178	1,957	17,801	3,274	7,041	13,100
ND	2,331	327	218	1,562	267	647	799
OH	22,706	4,799	2,595	17,853	3,353	10,081	17,931
OK	8,563	1,638	818	8,090	1,922	628	4,509
OR	5,204	2,119	1,388	9,086	1,781	4,520	6,294
PA	20,549	6,880	3,170	20,584	4,720	20,237	17,343
RI......	1,145	589	212	629	284	795	1,865
SC	9,885	3,129	996	8,420	1,540	1,102	6,545
SD	2,294	263	244	1,987	285	1,982	1,046
TN	13,661	4,486	1,558	14,038	2,319	4,477	9,116
TX	43,146	15,461	6,608	48,533	7,733	21,629	35,599
UT	5,354	1,330	1,065	5,754	916	7,141	2,737
VT	1,721	333	283	597	370	1,073	841
VA	16,424	5,916	2,461	19,210	2,833	5,950	13,045
WA	8,830	4,444	2,224	15,950	2,853	11,965	9,318
WV	4,234	588	314	4,770	658	1,052	2,155
WI.....	11,883	2,678	1,668	10,987	1,702	5,908	7,584
WY	2,453	167	169	1,338	329	482	793

[1] Excluding food services and drinking places (NAICS 722). Includes other types of stores, not shown separately.

Source: Nielsen Claritas Retail Market Power 2009 (copyright).

U.S. Census Bureau, Statistical Abstract of the United States: 2010

Table 1026. New Motor Vehicle Sales and Car Production: 1990 to 2008

[In thousands (14,137 represents 14,137,000). Includes leases]

Type of vehicle	1990	2000	2003	2004	2005	2006	2007	2008
New motor vehicle sales	**14,137**	**17,806**	**16,971**	**17,297**	**17,445**	**17,048**	**16,460**	**13,493**
New-car sales and leases.	9,300	8,852	7,615	7,505	7,667	7,781	7,588	6,806
Domestic	6,897	6,833	5,527	5,350	5,480	5,436	5,221	4,528
Import	2,403	2,019	2,087	2,155	2,187	2,345	2,367	2,278
New-truck sales and leases.	4,837	8,954	9,356	9,792	9,777	9,268	8,872	6,687
Light	4,560	8,492	9,028	9,361	9,281	8,723	8,501	6,388
Domestic	3,957	7,651	7,801	8,115	8,065	7,377	7,113	5,292
Import	603	841	1,227	1,246	1,216	1,347	1,388	1,096
Other.	278	462	328	432	497	544	371	299
Domestic-car production	6,231	5,542	4,510	4,230	4,321	4,367	3,924	3,777
Average expenditure per new car [1] (dollars)	14,371	20,600	21,169	21,367	22,497	23,140	23,336	23,051

[1] Estimate based on the manufacturer's suggested retail price.

Source: U.S. Bureau of Economic Analysis, "Auto and Truck Seasonal Adjustment"; <http://www.bea.gov/national/xls/gap_hist.xls> (accessed May 2009). Data are mainly from "Ward's Automotive Reports" published by Ward's Communications, Southfield, MI.

Table 1027. Retail Foodstores—Number and Sales by Type: 2000 to 2007

[119.6 represents 119,600. Based on North American Industry Classification System (NAICS), 2002; see text, Section 15]

Type of foodstore	Number [1] (1,000)				Sales [2]						
					Amount (bil.dol.)				Percent distribution		
	2000	2005	2006	2007	2000	2005	2006	2007	2000	2005	2007
Total	**119.6**	**(NA)**	**(NA)**	**(NA)**	**417.3**	**484.3**	**504.0**	**521.1**	**100.0**	**100.0**	**100.0**
Grocery stores.	95.9	(NA)	(NA)	(NA)	403.1	463.6	482.8	501.1	96.6	95.7	96.2
Supermarkets [3]	21.9	20.2	18.6	20.0	310.3	321.8	317.8	339.3	74.4	66.4	65.1
Conventional	7.2	3.0	(NA)	(NA)	58.3	67.0	(NA)	(NA)	14.0	13.8	(NA)
Superstore [4]	7.9	8.0	(NA)	(NA)	131.0	130.9	(NA)	(NA)	31.4	27.0	(NA)
Warehouse [5]	2.4	2.7	(NA)	(NA)	20.2	12.3	(NA)	(NA)	4.8	2.5	(NA)
Combination food and drug [6]	3.7	5.6	(NA)	(NA)	75.3	89.1	(NA)	(NA)	18.0	18.4	(NA)
Super warehouse [7]	0.5	0.5	(NA)	(NA)	16.0	11.5	(NA)	(NA)	3.8	2.4	(NA)
Hypermarket [8]	0.2	0.3	(NA)	(NA)	9.5	10.9	(NA)	(NA)	2.3	2.3	(NA)
Convenience stores [9]	28.2	26.1	27.2	28.1	19.2	19.9	20.5	18.3	4.6	4.1	3.5
Superette [10]	45.8	(NA)	(NA)	(NA)	73.6	121.9	144.5	143.5	17.6	25.2	27.5
Specialized food stores [11]	23.7	(NA)	(NA)	(NA)	14.2	20.4	21.2	20.0	3.4	4.2	3.8

NA Not available. [1] Estimated. [2] Includes nonfood items. [3] A grocery store, primarily self-service in operation, providing a full range of departments, and having at least $2.5 million in annual sales in 1985 dollars. [4] Contains greater variety of products than conventional supermarkets, including specialty and service departments, and considerable nonfood (general merchandise) products. [5] Contains limited product variety and fewer services provided, incorporating case lot stocking and shelving practices. [6] Contains a pharmacy, a nonprescription drug department, and a greater variety of health and beauty aids than that carried by conventional supermarkets. [7] A larger warehouse store that offers expanded product variety and often service meat, deli, or seafood departments. [8] A very large store offering a greater variety of general merchandise—like clothes, hardware, and seasonal goods—and personal care products than other grocery stores. [9] A small grocery store selling a limited variety of food and nonfood products, typically open extended hours. [10] A grocery store, primarily self-service in operation, selling a wide variety of food and nonfood products with annual sales below $2.5 million (1985 dollars). [11] Primarily engaged in the retail sale of a single food category such as meat and seafood stores and retail bakeries.

Source: U.S. Department of Agriculture, Economic Research Service, The U.S. Food Marketing System, 2002, Agricultural Economic Report 811, August 2002 and unpublished data.

Table 1028. Food and Alcoholic Beverage Sales by Sales Outlet: 1990 to 2008

[In billions of dollars (553.4 represents $553,400,000,000)]

Sales outlet	1990	2000	2002	2003	2004	2005	2006	2007	2008
Food sales, total [1]	**553.4**	**814.6**	**879.3**	**917.9**	**960.4**	**1,011.9**	**1,075.0**	**1,128.0**	**1,165.3**
Food at home	305.3	423.2	457.8	476.2	494.3	520.5	553.2	580.8	600.0
Food stores [2]	256.4	303.5	312.4	323.7	333.9	347.2	359.7	377.2	397.2
Other stores [3]	32.3	89.4	116.4	122.6	129.4	142.4	160.5	167.4	165.3
Home-delivered, mail order.	5.3	19.2	17.9	18.2	18.8	19.2	21.1	23.2	24.1
Farmers, manufacturers, wholesalers . . .	3.5	4.6	4.6	4.9	5.0	5.2	5.5	6.2	6.5
Home production and donations	7.7	6.5	6.6	6.8	7.2	6.5	6.5	6.7	6.9
Food away from home [4]	248.1	391.5	421.3	441.7	466.2	491.4	521.8	547.3	565.3
Alcoholic beverage sales, total	**72.6**	**111.6**	**128.0**	**126.2**	**137.0**	**142.8**	**155.1**	**163.2**	**168.0**
Packaged alcoholic beverages	38.0	52.7	57.0	57.5	59.8	62.2	69.7	72.8	72.8
Liquor stores	18.6	24.5	25.5	26.0	27.7	29.4	31.4	32.9	34.7
Food stores	10.8	15.9	17.4	17.8	18.5	19.3	20.0	20.9	22.0
All other	8.6	12.3	14.2	13.7	13.5	13.6	18.4	18.9	16.2
Alcoholic drinks	34.5	58.9	70.9	68.7	77.2	80.5	85.4	90.4	95.1
Eating and drinking places [5]	26.5	41.6	47.3	44.6	52.5	55.2	59.5	63.9	67.9
Hotels and motels [5]	3.8	11.3	17.5	17.7	18.0	18.3	18.5	18.5	19.0
All other	4.2	6.0	6.1	6.4	6.7	7.0	7.4	7.9	8.3

[1] Includes taxes and tips. [2] Excludes sales to restaurants and institutions. [3] Includes eating and drinking establishments, trailer parks, commissary stores, and military exchanges. [4] Includes food furnished and donations. [5] Includes tips.

Source: U.S. Department of Agriculture, Economic Research Service, "Food CPI, Prices, and Expenditures: Food Expenditure Tables" (published 17 June 2009); <http://www.ers.usda.gov/briefing/CPIFoodAndExpenditures/Data/>.

Section 23
Transportation

This section presents data on civil air transportation, both passenger and cargo, and on water transportation, including inland waterways, oceanborne commerce, the merchant marine, cargo, and vessel tonnages.

This section also presents statistics on revenues, passenger and freight traffic volume, and employment in various revenue-producing modes of the transportation industry, including motor vehicles, trains, and pipelines. Data are also presented on highway mileage and finances, motor vehicle travel, accidents, and registrations; and characteristics of public transit, railroads, and pipelines.

Principal source of transportation data is the annual *National Transportation Statistics* publication of the U.S. Bureau of Transportation Statistics. Principal sources of air and water transportation data are the *Annual Report* issued by the Air Transport Association of America, Washington, DC and the annual *Waterborne Commerce of the United States* issued by the Corps of Engineers of the Department of Army. In addition, the U.S. Census Bureau in its commodity flow survey (part of the census of transportation, taken every 5 years through 2007, for years ending in "2" and "7") provides data on the type, weight, and value of commodities shipped by manufacturing establishments in the United States, by means of transportation, origin, and destination. The advance reports for 2007 are part of the 2007 Economic Census. This census was conducted in accordance with the 2002 North American Industry Classification System (NAICS). See text, Section 15, Business Enterprise, for a discussion of the Economic Census and NAICS.

The Bureau of Transportation Statistics (BTS) was established within the U.S. Department of Transportation (USDOT) in 1992 to collect, report, and analyze transportation data. Today, BTS is a component of the USDOT Research and Innovative

Technology Administration (RITA). BTS products include reports to Congress, the Secretary of Transportation, and stakeholders in the nation's transportation community. These stakeholders include: federal agencies, state and local governments, metropolitan planning organizations, universities, the private sector and general public. Congress requires the BTS to report (congressional mandate, laid out in 49 U.S.C. 111 (1)) on transportation statistics to the President and Congress. *The Transportation Statistics Annual Report (TSAR),* provides a data overview of U.S. transportation issues. As required by Congress, each TSAR has two essential components: a review of the state of transportation statistics with recommendations for improvements and a presentation of the data. The BTS publication *National Transportation Statistics (NTS),* a companion report to the TSAR, has more comprehensive and longer time-series data. NTS presents information on the U.S. transportation system, including its physical components, safety record, economic performance, energy use, and environmental impacts. The BTS publication *State Transportation Statistics* presents a statistical profile of transportation in the 50 states and the District of Columbia. This profile includes infrastructure, freight movement and passenger travel, system safety, vehicles, transportation-related economy and finance, energy usage and the environment.

The principal compiler of data on public roads and on operation of motor vehicles is the U.S. Department of Transportation's (DOT) Federal Highway Administration (FHWA). These data appear in FHWA's annual *Highway Statistics* and other publications.

The U.S. National Highway Traffic Safety Administration (NHTSA), through its *Traffic Safety Facts FARS/GES Annual Report,* presents descriptive statistics about traffic crashes of all severities, from those that result in property damage to those

U.S. Census Bureau, Statistical Abstract of the United States: 2010

that result in the loss of human life. The data for this report is a compilation of motor vehicle crash data from the *Fatality Analysis Reporting System (FARS)* and the *General Estimates System (GES)*. For other publications and reports, go to the National Center for Statistics and Analysis (NCSA), Publications and Data Request. The Web site is located at <http://www-nrd.nhtsa.dot.gov/CAT/index.aspx>.

DOT's Federal Railroad Administration (FRA), Office of Safety Analysis presents railroad safety information including accidents and incidents, inspections and highway-rail crossing data in its annual report *Railroad Safety Statistics*. The Web site is located at <http://safetydata.fra.dot.gov/officeofsafety>.

Data are also presented in many nongovernment publications. Among them are the weekly and annual *Cars of Revenue Freight Loaded* and the annual *Yearbook of Railroad Facts,* both published by the Association of American Railroads, Washington, DC; *Public Transportation Fact Book,* containing electric railway and motorbus statistics, published annually by the American Public Transportation Association, Washington, DC; and *Injury Facts,* issued by the National Safety Council, Chicago, IL.

Civil aviation—Federal promotion and regulation of civil aviation have been carried out by the Federal Aviation Administration (FAA) and the Civil Aeronautics Board (CAB). The CAB promoted and regulated the civil air transportation industry within the United States and between the United States and foreign countries. The Board granted licenses to provide air transportation service, approved or disapproved proposed rates and fares, and approved or disapproved proposed agreements and corporate relationships involving air carriers. In December 1984, the CAB ceased to exist as an agency. Some of its functions were transferred to the DOT, as outlined below. The responsibility for investigation of aviation accidents resides with the National Transportation Safety Board.

The Office of the Secretary, DOT aviation activities include: negotiation of international air transportation rights, selection of U.S. air carriers to serve capacity-controlled international markets, oversight of international rates and fares, maintenance of essential air service to small communities, and consumer affairs. DOT's Bureau of Transportation Statistics (BTS) handles aviation information functions formerly assigned to CAB. Prior to BTS, the Research and Special Programs Administration handled these functions.

The principal activities of the FAA include: the promotion of air safety; controlling the use of navigable airspace; prescribing regulations dealing with the competency of airmen, airworthiness of aircraft and air traffic control; operation of air route traffic control centers, airport traffic control towers, and flight service stations; the design, construction, maintenance, and inspection of navigation, traffic control, and communications equipment; and the development of general aviation.

The CAB published monthly and quarterly financial and traffic statistical data for the certificated route air carriers. BTS continues these publications, including both certificated and noncertificated (commuter) air carriers. The FAA annually publishes data on the use of airway facilities; data related to the location of airmen, aircraft, and airports; the volume of activity in the field of nonair carrier (general aviation) flying; and aircraft production and registration.

General aviation comprises all civil flying (including such commercial operations as small demand air taxis, agriculture application, powerline patrol, etc.) but excludes certificated route air carriers, supplemental operators, large-aircraft commercial operators, and commuter airlines.

Air carriers and service—The CAB previously issued "certificates of public convenience and necessity" under Section 401 of the Federal Aviation Act of 1958 for scheduled and nonscheduled (charter) passenger services and cargo services. It also issued certificates under Section 418 of the Act to cargo air carriers for domestic all-cargo service only. The DOT Office of the Secretary now issues the certificates under a "fit, willing, and able" test of air carrier operations. Carriers operating only a 60-seat-or-less aircraft are given exemption authority to carry passengers, cargo, and mail in scheduled and nonscheduled service under Part 298 of the DOT (formerly CAB) regulations. Exemption authority carriers who offer scheduled passenger service to an essential air service point must meet the "fit, willing, and able" test.

Vessel shipments, entrances, and clearances—Shipments by dry cargo vessels comprise shipments on all types of watercraft, except tanker vessels; shipments by tanker vessels comprise all types of cargo, liquid and dry, carried by tanker vessels.

A vessel is reported as entered only at the first port which it enters in the United States, whether or not cargo is unloaded at that port. A vessel is reported as cleared only at the last port at which clearance is made to a foreign port, whether or not it takes on cargo. Army and Navy vessels entering or clearing without commercial cargo are not included in the figures.

Units of measurement—Cargo (or freight) tonnage and shipping weight both represent the gross weight of the cargo including the weight of containers, wrappings, crates, etc. However, shipping weight excludes lift and cargo vans and similar substantial outer containers. Other tonnage figures generally refer to stowing capacity of vessels, 100 cubic feet being called 1 ton. Gross tonnage comprises the space within the frames and the ceiling of the hull, together with those closed-in spaces above deck available for cargo, stores, passengers, or crew, with certain minor exceptions. Net or registered tonnage is the gross tonnage less the spaces occupied by the propelling machinery, fuel, crew quarters, master's cabin, and navigation spaces. Substantially, it represents space available for cargo and passengers. The net tonnage capacity of a ship may bear little relation to weight of cargo. Deadweight tonnage is the weight in long tons required to depress a vessel from light water line (that is, with only the machinery and equipment on board)

to load line. It is, therefore, the weight of the cargo, fuel, etc., which a vessel is designed to carry with safety.

Federal-aid highway systems—The Intermodal Surface Transportation Efficiency Act (ISTEA) of 1991 eliminated the historical Federal-Aid Highway Systems and created the National Highway System (NHS) and other federal-aid highway categories. The final NHS was approved by Congress in December of 1995 under the National Highway System Designation Act.

Functional systems—Roads and streets are assigned to groups according to the character of service intended. The functional systems are (1) arterial highways that generally handle the long trips, (2) collector facilities that collect and disperse traffic between the arterials and the lower systems, and (3) local roads and streets that primarily serve direct access to residential areas, farms, and other local areas.

Regulatory bodies— The Federal Energy Regulatory Commission (FERC) is an independent agency that regulates the interstate transmission of electricity, natural gas, and oil. FERC also reviews proposals to build liquefied natural gas (LNG) terminals and interstate natural gas pipelines as well as licensing hydropower projects. The Energy Policy Act of 2005 gave FERC additional responsibilities such as regulating the transmission and wholesale sales of electricity in interstate commerce. See source for more details.

Railroads—The Surface Transportation Board (STB) was created in the Interstate Commerce Commission Termination Act of 1995, Pub. L. No.104-88, 109 Stat. 803 (1995) (ICCTA), and is the successor agency to the Interstate Commerce Commission. The STB is an economic regulatory agency that Congress charged with the fundamental missions of resolving railroad rate and service disputes and reviewing proposed railroad mergers. The STB is decisionally independent, although it is administratively affiliated with the Department of Transportation.

The STB serves as both an adjudicatory and a regulatory body. The agency has jurisdiction over railroad rate and service issues and rail restructuring transactions (mergers, line sales, line construction, and line abandonments); certain trucking company, moving van, and non-contiguous ocean shipping company rate matters; certain intercity passenger bus company structure, financial, and operational matters; and rates and services of certain pipelines not regulated by the Federal Energy Regulatory Commission. Other ICC regulatory functions were either eliminated or transferred to the Federal Highway Administration or the Bureau of Transportation Statistics within DOT.

Class I Railroads are regulated by the STB and subject to the Uniform System of Accounts and required to file annual and periodic reports. Railroads are classified based on their annual operating revenues. The class to which a carrier belongs is determined by comparing its adjusted operating revenues for 3 consecutive years to the following scale: Class I, $250 million or more; Class II, $20 million to $250 million; and Class III, $0 to $20 million. Operating revenue dollar ranges are indexed for inflation.

Postal Service—The U.S. Postal Service provides mail processing and delivery services within the United States. The Postal Reorganization Act of 1970 created the Postal Service, effective July 1971, as an independent establishment of the Federal Executive Branch.

Revenue and cost analysis describes the Postal Service's system of attributing revenues and costs to classes of mail and service. This system draws primarily upon probability sampling techniques to develop estimates of revenues, volumes, and weights, as well as costs by class of mail and special service. The costs attributed to classes of mail and special services are primarily incremental costs which vary in response to changes in volume; they account for roughly 60 percent of the total costs of the Postal Service. The balance represents "institutional costs." Statistics on revenues, volume of mail, and distribution of expenditures are presented in the Postal Service's annual report, *Cost and Revenue Analysis,* and its *Annual Report of the Postmaster General* and its annual *Comprehensive Statement on Postal Operations.*

Statistical reliability—For a discussion of statistical collection and estimation, sampling procedures, and measures of statistical reliability applicable to Census Bureau data, see Appendix III.

Table 1029. **Transportation and Warehousing—Establishments, Revenue, Payroll, and Employees by Industry: 2002 and 2007**

[**382,152 represents $382,152,000,000.** For establishments with payroll. Based on the 2002 and 2007 Economic Censuses. 2007 data are preliminary. See Appendix III]

Kind of business	2002 NAICS code [1]	Number of establish-ments	Revenue (mil. dol.)	Annual payroll (mil. dol.)	Paid employees (1,000)
Transportation and warehousing total, 2002	48–49	199,618	382,152	115,989	3,650.9
Air transportation [2]	481	3,847	19,735	3,805	99.1
Water transportation	483	1,890	23,331	3,194	66.2
Truck transportation	484	112,642	164,219	47,750	1,435.2
Transit and ground passenger transportation [3]	485	17,260	18,850	7,675	398.4
Pipeline transportation [3]	486	2,188	22,031	2,477	36.8
Scenic and sightseeing transportation	487	2,523	1,859	526	22.5
Support activities for transportation [3]	488	33,942	57,414	16,202	465.6
Couriers and messengers	492	12,655	58,165	17,175	561.5
Warehousing and storage	493	12,671	16,548	17,183	565.5
Transportation and warehousing total, 2007	48–49	217,926	655,857	172,166	4,435.8
Air transportation [2]	481	5,763	146,567	25,639	477.4
Water transportation	483	1,814	36,057	4,048	70.0
Truck transportation	484	119,694	221,737	59,146	1,520.6
Transit and ground passenger transportation [3]	485	17,769	26,967	10,012	453.4
Pipeline transportation [3]	486	2,644	24,666	3,273	38.2
Scenic and sightseeing transportation	487	2,440	2,661	661	24.1
Support activities for transportation [3]	488	41,189	96,256	25,129	615.4
Couriers and messengers	492	12,788	76,286	19,972	550.4
Warehousing and storage	493	13,825	24,660	24,285	686.2

[1] North American Industry Classification System, 2002; see text, Section 15. [2] Excludes large certificated passenger carriers that do not report to the Office of Airline Information, U.S. Department of Transportation. [3] Includes other industries not shown separately.

Source: U.S. Census Bureau, "2007 Economic Census, Core Business Statistics Series: Advance Comparative Statistics for the United States (2002 NAICS Basis): 2007 and 2002" (published 17 March 2009); using American FactFinder; <http://www.census.gov/econ/census07/>.

Table 1030. **Transportation-Related Components of U.S. Gross Domestic Product: 2000 to 2007**

[In billions of dollars (1,089.5 represents $1,089,500,000,000), except percent]

Item	2000	2003	2004	2005	2006	2007
CURRENT DOLLARS						
Total transportation-related final demand [1]	**1,089.5**	**1,156.9**	**1,227.7**	**1,325.0**	**1,394.4**	**1,469.4**
Total gross domestic product (GDP)	9,817.0	10,971.2	11,734.3	12,421.9	13,178.4	13,807.5
Transportation as a percent of GDP	11.1	10.5	10.5	10.7	10.6	10.6
Personal consumption of transportation	853.5	928.5	979.1	1,051.0	1,089.0	1,138.0
Motor vehicles and parts	386.5	439.1	441.8	443.1	434.0	440.4
Gasoline and oil	175.7	192.6	230.4	283.6	313.8	340.6
Transportation services	291.3	296.8	306.9	324.3	341.2	357.0
Gross private domestic investment	167.4	133.9	158.4	171.4	185.5	166.4
Transportation structures	6.6	6.0	6.5	7.0	8.5	9.2
Transportation equipment	160.8	127.9	151.9	164.4	177.0	157.2
Net exports of transportation–related goods and service [2] ...	–109.0	–125.6	–135.3	–131.7	–127.3	–103.4
Exports (+)	179.0	174.4	195.1	221.5	250.5	285.5
Civilian aircraft, engines, and parts	48.1	46.7	50.0	60.8	75.2	87.3
Automotive vehicles, engines, and parts	80.4	80.7	89.3	98.4	107.0	121.0
Passenger fares	20.7	15.7	18.9	21.0	22.0	25.6
Other transportation	29.8	31.3	36.9	41.3	46.3	51.6
Imports (–)..............................	288.0	300.0	330.4	353.2	377.8	388.9
Civilian aircraft, engines, and parts	26.4	24.1	24.3	25.8	28.4	34.4
Automotive vehicles, engines, and parts	195.9	210.2	228.2	239.4	256.6	258.9
Passenger fares	24.3	21.0	23.7	26.1	27.5	28.5
Other transportation.......................	41.4	44.7	54.2	61.9	65.3	67.1
Government transportation–related purchases...........	177.6	220.1	225.5	234.3	247.2	268.4
Federal purchases [3]	19.2	30.6	29.7	30.2	32.1	32.1
State and local purchases [3]	149.4	173.3	179.2	188.2	200.2	216.6
Defense–related purchases [4]	9.0	16.2	16.6	15.9	14.9	19.7
CHAINED (2000) DOLLARS						
Total transportation-related final demand [1]	**1,089.5**	**1,117.1**	**1,139.8**	**1,138.3**	**1,136.2**	**1,148.4**
Total gross domestic product (GDP)	9,817.0	10,320.6	10,755.7	10,989.5	11,294.8	11,523.9
Transportation as a percent of GDP	11.1	10.8	10.6	10.4	10.1	10.0
Personal consumption of transportation	853.5	913.0	926.3	925.2	915.8	930.4
Motor vehicles and parts	386.5	449.7	457.0	449.9	437.9	446.7
Gasoline and oil	175.7	183.2	185.9	187.4	184.2	184.5
Transportation services	291.3	280.1	283.4	287.9	293.7	299.2
Gross private domestic investment	167.4	128.6	144.4	155.5	166.6	146.9
Transportation structures	6.6	5.5	5.7	6.0	7.1	7.5
Transportation equipment	160.8	123.1	138.7	149.5	159.5	139.4
Net exports of transportation–related goods and service [2] ...	–109.0	–126.6	–132.9	–130.9	–131.3	–113.9
Exports (+)	179.0	164.2	178.6	193.5	212.5	235.0
Civilian aircraft, engines, and parts	48.1	41.5	42.6	50.1	59.6	66.3
Automotive vehicles, engines, and parts	80.4	79.4	87.2	95.1	102.1	114.2
Passenger fares	20.7	13.5	14.8	15.2	15.9	17.1
Other transportation.......................	29.8	29.8	34.0	32.1	34.9	37.4
Imports (–)..............................	288.0	290.8	311.5	324.4	343.8	348.9
Civilian aircraft, engines, and parts	26.4	22.8	22.2	22.9	24.3	28.0
Automotive vehicles, engines, and parts	195.9	208.6	222.7	231.2	246.8	246.5
Passenger fares	24.3	17.9	20.6	21.8	21.7	21.1
Other transportation.......................	41.4	41.5	46.0	48.5	51.0	53.3
Government transportation–related purchases...........	177.6	202.1	202.0	188.5	185.1	185.0
Federal purchases [3]	19.2	28.2	26.2	25.3	25.9	24.9
State and local purchases [3]	149.4	159.9	161.9	150.4	147.6	144.9
Defense–related purchases [4]	9.0	14.0	13.9	12.8	11.6	15.2

[1] Sum of total personal consumption of transportation, total gross private domestic investment, net exports of transportation-related goods and services, and total government transportation-related purchases.   [2] Sum of exports and imports.   [3] Federal purchases and state and local purchases are the sum of consumption expenditures and gross investment.   [4] Defense-related purchases are the sum of transportation of material and travel.

Source: U.S. Bureau of Transportation Statistics, "National Transportation Statistics"; <http://www.bts.gov/publications /national_transportation_statistics/>.

Table 1031. **Employment in Transportation and Warehousing: 1990 to 2008**

[In thousands (3,476 represents 3,476,000). Annual average of monthly figures. Based on Current Employment Statistics program; see Appendix III]

Industry	2007 NAICS code [1]	1990	1995	2000	2005	2006	2007	2008
Transportation and warehousing . . .	48,49	3,476	3,838	4,410	4,361	4,470	4,541	4,505
Air transportation	481	529	511	614	501	487	492	493
Rail transportation	482	272	233	232	228	228	234	230
Water transportation	483	57	51	56	61	63	66	65
Truck transportation	484	1,122	1,249	1,406	1,398	1,436	1,439	1391
Transit and ground	485	274	328	372	389	399	412	418
Pipeline transportation.	486	60	54	46	38	39	40	42
Scenic and sightseeing	487	16	22	28	29	28	29	28
Support activities	488	364	430	537	552	571	584	590
Couriers and messengers	492	375	517	605	571	582	581	576
Warehousing and storage	493	407	444	514	595	638	665	673

[1] North American Industry Classification System 2007, see text, Sections 12 and 15.

Source: U.S. Bureau of Labor Statistics, Current Employment Statistics, "Employment, Hours, and Earnings—National"; <http://www.bls.gov/ces/data.htm>.

Transportation   655

Table 1032. **Transportation and Warehousing—Establishments, Employees, and Payroll by Kind of Business (NAICS Basis): 2000 and 2006**

[3,790.0 represents 3,790,000. Covers establishments with payroll. Excludes most government employees, railroad employees, and self-employed persons. For statement on methodology, see Appendix III. County Business Patterns excludes rail transportation (NAICS 482) and the National Postal Service (NAICS 491)]

Industry	2002 NAICS code [1]	Establishments		Paid employees [2] (1,000)		Annual payroll (mil. dol.)	
		2000	2006	2000	2006	2000	2006
Transportation & warehousing	48–49	190,044	215,117	3,790.0	4,306.4	125,592.4	166,173.9
Air transportation	481	5,429	5,610	615.6	474.8	26,569.3	24,509.7
Scheduled air transportation	4811	3,324	3,072	570.9	432.5	24,484.5	22,141.4
Scheduled passenger air transportation...	481111	2,740	2,616	536.2	414.4	23,470.7	21,438.7
Scheduled freight air transportation......	481112	584	456	34.7	18.1	1,013.8	702.7
Nonscheduled air transportation	4812	2,105	2,538	44.7	42.3	2,084.8	2,368.3
Water transportation	483	1,900	1,925	67.6	68.4	3,003.2	4,084.1
Deep sea, coastal, & Great Lakes water transportation	4831	1,254	1,262	47.8	47.5	2,214.2	2,988.9
Inland water transportation	4832	646	663	19.7	20.9	789.0	1,095.2
Inland water freight transportation.......	483211	402	396	16.3	17.2	673.9	949.9
Inland water passenger transportation	483212	244	267	3.5	3.7	115.1	145.4
Truck transportation	484	110,416	120,263	1,415.8	1,532.3	46,451.5	58,935.0
General freight trucking	4841	55,874	67,305	922.7	1,050.0	31,614.0	41,465.8
General freight trucking, local.	48411	20,329	27,682	153.2	205.1	4,529.8	7,458.4
General freight trucking, long distance....	48412	35,545	39,623	769.5	844.9	27,084.2	34,007.4
Specialized freight trucking	4842	54,542	52,958	493.1	482.4	14,837.5	17,469.2
Used household & office goods moving ...	48421	9,147	8,683	128.9	109.1	3,661.4	3,430.5
Specialized freight (except used goods) trucking, local	48422	32,493	32,598	200.4	218.7	5,692.4	7,870.5
Specialized freight (except used goods) trucking, long-distance	48423	12,902	11,677	163.7	154.6	5,483.7	6,168.1
Transit & ground passenger transportation	485	16,383	17,224	386.9	418.7	7,214.7	9,079.6
Urban transit systems	4851	705	912	43.1	49.4	1,295.8	1,680.3
Mixed mode systems	485111	152	63	6.2	1.3	146.9	40.4
Commuter rail	485112	15	25	(D)	0.5	(D)	20.5
Bus and other motor vehicle mode systems...................	485113	505	778	31.4	44.6	925.1	1,474.6
Other	485119	33	46	(D)	3.0	(D)	144.8
Interurban & rural bus transportation	4852	444	475	26.8	16.5	709.7	464.7
Taxi & limousine service..............	4853	6,806	7,013	67.8	69.2	1,244.3	1,542.7
Taxi service	48531	3,116	2,878	30.4	30.7	485.2	603.1
Limousine service	48532	3,690	4,135	37.5	38.5	759.1	939.6
School & employee bus transportation	4854	4,217	4,321	162.9	194.8	2,322.6	3,392.8
Charter bus industry	4855	1,451	1,207	34.1	27.9	668.7	647.8
Other transit & ground passenger transportation	4859	2,760	3,296	52.2	60.9	973.6	1,351.3
Special needs transportation	485991	1,914	2,166	34.8	45.4	648.9	1,031.6
Pipeline transportation................	486	2,802	2,653	53.0	39.2	3,828.6	3,173.5
Pipeline transportation of crude oil	4861	307	373	6.7	7.5	425.6	727.8
Pipeline transportation of natural gas	4862	1,938	1,363	39.2	22.2	2,961.1	1,709.5
Other pipeline transportation	4869	557	917	7.0	9.4	441.9	736.2
Scenic & sightseeing transportation	487	2,254	2,720	23.6	26.7	583.5	788.8
Scenic & sightseeing transportation, land ...	4871	454	678	8.7	9.2	192.8	232.5
Scenic & sightseeing transportation, water...	4872	1,642	1,857	13.0	15.3	331.2	463.8
Scenic & sightseeing transportation, other..	4879	158	185	2.0	2.2	59.5	92.5
Support activities for transportation	488	31,440	37,083	472.4	579.6	16,507.0	24,124.8
Support activities for air transportation	4881	4,368	5,174	126.7	158.3	3,634.0	5,431.9
Airport operations	48811	1,834	1,619	67.9	70.0	1,569.5	1,764.6
Air traffic control.................	488111	137	171	0.8	1.7	29.9	63.0
Other support activities for air transportation	48819	2,534	3,555	58.8	88.3	2,064.6	3,667.3
Support activities for rail transportation	4882	821	962	21.4	28.1	714.4	1,048.5
Support activities for water transportation ...	4883	2,543	2,331	81.6	91.8	3,250.7	4,798.3
Port and harbor operations	48831	196	229	7.4	7.0	265.8	323.6
Marine cargo handling	48832	607	540	53.5	61.9	2,194.7	3,262.0
Navigational services to shipping	48833	863	802	11.8	12.0	478.7	699.4
Other	48839	877	760	8.9	10.8	311.5	513.4
Support activities for road transportation	4884	7,010	9,545	56.2	71.8	1,308.8	2,133.2
Motor vehicle towing	48841	6,078	7,789	41.8	50.8	961.7	1,524.1
Freight transportation arrangement........	4885	15,177	17,434	161.7	198.3	6,620.3	9,452.0
Other support activities for transportation ...	4889	1,521	1,637	24.7	31.2	978.6	1,264.9
Couriers & messengers.................	492	12,297	13,790	619.3	571.4	17,399.4	19,984.2
Couriers	4921	6,667	8,724	548.9	525.6	15,890.5	18,856.7
Local messengers & local delivery	4922	5,630	5,066	70.5	45.8	1,508.9	1,127.5
Warehousing & storage.................	493	7,123	13,849	135.9	595.3	4,035.3	21,490.3

D Figure withheld to avoid disclosure pertaining to individual companies. [1] Based on the North American Industry Classification System (NAICS), 2002; see text, Section 15. [2] For employees on the payroll for the pay period including March 12.

Source: U.S. Census Bureau, "County Business Patterns" (published June 2008); <http://www.census.gov/econ/cbp/>.

Table 1033. **Transportation System Mileage Within the United States: 1980 to 2007**

[3,860 represents 3,860,000]

System	1980	1985	1990	1995	2000	2004	2005	2006	2007
Highway (1,000)........	3,860	3,864	3,867	3,912	3,936	3,982	3,996	4,017	4,032
Class 1 rail..........	164,822	145,764	119,758	108,264	99,250	97,662	95,830	94,942	94,440
Amtrak.............	24,000	24,000	24,000	24,000	23,000	22,256	22,007	21,708	21,708
Transit:									
Commuter rail [1]	(NA)	3,574	4,132	4,160	5,209	6,875	7,118	6,972	7,135
Heavy rail [2]	(NA)	1,293	1,351	1,458	1,558	1,596	1,601	1,603	1,603
Light rail [3]	(NA)	384	483	568	834	1,187	1,188	1,280	1,341
Navigable channels	26,000	26,000	26,000	26,000	26,000	26,000	26,000	26,000	(NA)
Oil pipeline [4]	218,393	213,605	208,752	181,912	176,996	161,670	159,512	169,346	(NA)
Gas pipeline [5] (1,000)...	1,052	1,119	1,189	1,278	1,369	1,462	1,438	1,534	(NA)

NA Not available. [1] Also called metropolitan rail or regional rail. [2] Also called metro, subway, rapid transit, or rapid rail. [3] Also called streetcar, tramway, or trolley. [4] Includes trunk and gathering lines for crude-oil pipeline. [5] Excludes service pipelines.

Source: U.S. Bureau of Transportation Statistics, "National Transportation Statistics"; <http://www.bts.gov/publications/national_transportation_statistics>.

Table 1034. **U.S. Aircraft, Vehicles, and Other Conveyances: 1980 to 2007**

[121,601 represents 121,601,000]

System	1980	1990	1995	2000	2003	2004	2005	2006	2007
Air:									
Air carrier [1].................	3,808	6,083	7,411	8,055	8,176	8,186	8,225	(NA)	(NA)
General aviation [2] (active fleet).....	211,045	198,000	188,089	217,533	209,708	219,426	224,352	221,943	231,607
Highway, registered vehicles (1,000):									
Passenger car.................	121,601	133,700	128,387	133,621	135,670	136,431	136,568	135,400	135,933
Motorcycle...................	5,694	4,259	3,897	4,346	5,370	5,768	6,227	6,679	7,138
Van, pick-up, SUV..............	27,876	48,275	65,738	79,085	87,187	91,845	95,337	99,125	101,470
Truck.......................	5,791	6,196	6,719	8,023	7,757	8,171	8,482	8,819	9,028
Bus........................	529	627	686	746	777	795	807	822	834
Transit: [3]									
Motor bus..................	50,411	58,714	67,107	75,013	77,328	81,033	82,027	83,080	65,249
Light rail cars [3]	1,013	910	1,048	1,327	1,482	1,622	1,645	1,001	1,810
Heavy rail cars [4]	9,641	10,567	10,166	10,311	10,754	10,858	11,110	11,052	11,222
Trolley bus	823	610	695	652	672	597	615	609	559
Commuter rail cars and									
locomotives...............	4,500	4,982	5,164	5,498	5,959	6,228	6,392	6,403	6,391
Demand response	(X)	16,471	29,352	33,080	35,954	37,078	41,958	43,509	64,865
Other [5].....................	(NA)	1,197	2,809	5,208	6,272	6,566	7,080	8,741	13,877
Rail:									
Class I, freight cars (1,000)	1,168	659	583	560	467	474	475	475	460
Class I, locomotive.............	28,094	18,835	18,812	20,028	20,774	22,015	22,779	23,732	24,143
Nonclass I freight cars	102,161	103,527	84,724	132,448	124,580	120,169	120,195	120,688	120,463
Car companies' and shippers'									
freight cars	440,552	449,832	550,717	688,194	687,337	693,978	717,211	750,404	805,074
Amtrak, passenger train car.......	2,128	1,863	1,722	1,894	1,623	1,211	1,186	1,191	1,164
Amtrak, locomotive.............	419	318	313	378	442	276	258	319	270
Water:									
Non-self-propelled vessels [6].......	31,662	31,209	31,360	33,152	31,335	31,296	32,052	32,211	31,654
Self-propelled vessels [7]..........	7,126	8,236	8,281	8,202	8,648	8,994	8,976	8,898	9,041
Ocean-going steam and motor ships									
(1,000 gross tons and over)	849	635	512	461	416	412	357	286	(NA)
Recreational boats (1,000)........	8,578	10,997	11,735	12,782	12,795	12,781	12,942	12,746	12,876

NA Not available. [1] Air carrier aircraft are those carrying passengers or cargo for hire under 14 CFR 121 and 14 CFR 135. [2] Includes air taxi aircraft. [3] Fixed rail streetcar or trolley, for example. [4] Metro, subway, or rapid transit, for example. [5] Includes aerial tramway, automated guideway transit, cablecar, ferry boat, inclined plane, monorail, and vanpool. [6] Includes dry-cargo barges, tank barges, and railroad-car floats. [7] Includes dry-cargo and/or passenger, offshore supply vessels, railroad-car ferries, tankers, and towboats.

Source: U.S. Bureau of Transportation Statistics, "National Transportation Statistics"; <http://www.bts.gov/publications/national_transportation_statistics/>.

U.S. Census Bureau, Statistical Abstract of the United States: 2010

Table 1035. Transportation Accidents, Deaths, and Injuries: 1990 to 2007

[6,471 represents 6,471,000. Numbers, except as indicated]

Mode	Accidents					Deaths					Injuries				
	1990	1995	2000	2005	2007	1990	1995	2000	2005	2007	1990	1995	2000	2005	2007
Transit type:															
Air:															
Air carrier [1]	24	36	56	40	26	39	168	92	22	1	29	25	29	14	15
Commuter [2]	15	12	12	6	3	6	9	5	–	–	11	17	7	–	–
On-demand [3]	107	75	80	65	62	51	52	71	18	43	36	14	12	23	20
General aviation	2,242	2,056	1,837	1,670	1,631	770	735	596	563	491	409	396	309	267	260
Land:															
Highway crashes (1,000) [4]	6,471	6,699	6,394	6,159	6,024	44.6	41.8	41.9	43.5	41.1	3,231	3,465	3,189	2,699	2,491
Passenger car occupants	5,561	5,594	4,926	4,499	(NA)	24.1	22.4	20.7	18.5	16.5	2,376	2,469	2,052	1,573	1,379
Motorcyclists	103	66	69	101	(NA)	3.2	2.9	2.9	4.6	5.2	84	57	58	87	103
Light truck occupants	2,152	2,750	3,208	3,382	(NA)	8.6	9.6	11.5	13.0	12.4	505	722	887	872	841
Large truck occupants	372	363	438	423	(NA)	0.7	0.6	0.6	0.1	(Z)	42	30	31	27	23
Bus occupants	60	59	56	50	(NA)	(Z)	(Z)	(Z)	0.1	(Z)	33	19	18	11	12
Pedestrians	(NA)	(NA)	(NA)	(NA)	(NA)	6.5	5.6	4.8	4.9	4.7	105	86	78	64	70
Pedacyclists	(NA)	(NA)	(NA)	(NA)	(NA)	0.9	0.8	0.7	0.8	0.7	75	67	51	45	43
Other	(NA)	(NA)	(NA)	(NA)	(NA)	0.6	0.5	0.6	0.8	0.8	11	14	15	18	18
Railroad [5]	8,594	7,092	6,485	6,319	5,399	1,297	1,146	937	883	845	25,143	14,440	11,643	9,495	9,343
Highway-rail grade crossing	5,715	4,633	3,502	3,058	2,752	698	579	425	358	335	2,407	1,894	1,219	1,049	1,043
Railroad	2,879	2,459	2,983	3,261	2,647	599	567	512	525	510	22,736	12,546	10,424	8,446	8,300
Transit [6]	58,002	25,683	24,261	8,151	9,398	339	274	295	236	214	54,556	57,196	56,697	18,131	20,625
Waterborne:															
Waterborne (vessel related) [7]	3,613	5,349	5,403	4,977	(NA)	85	53	53	45	52	175	154	150	140	167
Recreational boating [8]	6,411	8,019	7,740	4,969	5,191	865	829	701	697	685	3,822	4,141	4,355	3,451	3,673
Pipeline: [9]	378	349	380	490	402	9	21	38	16	15	76	64	81	48	53
Hazard liquid	180	188	146	138	116	3	3	1	2	4	7	11	4	2	10
Gas	198	161	234	352	286	6	18	37	14	11	69	53	77	46	43
Other transit [10]	77,985	48,144	47,116	138	116	9	3	215	2	4	7	11	4	2	10
Hazardous materials [11]	8,879	14,853	17,557	352	286	6	7	16	14	11	69	53	77	46	43

– Represents or rounds to zero. Z Less than 50. NA Not available. [1] See footnote 1, Table 1042. Injuries classified as serious. [2] See footnote 2, Table 1042. Injuries classified as serious. [3] See footnote 3, Table 1042. Injuries classified as serious. [4] Data on deaths are from U.S. National Highway Traffic Safety Administration and are based on deaths within 30 days of the accident. Includes only police reported crashes. For more details, see Table 1075. [5] Accidents which result in damages to railroad property. Grade crossing accidents are also included when classified as a train accident. Deaths exclude fatalities in railroad-highway grade crossing accidents. [6] Includes motor bus, commuter rail, heavy rail, light rail, demand response, van pool, and automated guideway. Starting with 2002, only injuries requiring immediate medical treatment away from the scene now qualify as reportable. [7] Accidents resulting in death, injury, or requiring medical treatment beyond first aid; damages exceeding $500; or a person's disappearance. [8] Covers accidents involving commercial vessels which must be reported to U.S. Coast Guard if there is property damage exceeding $25,000; material damage affecting the seaworthiness or efficiency of a vessel; stranding or grounding; loss of life; or injury causing a person's incapacity for more than 3 days. [9] Beginning 1990, pipeline accidents/incidents are credited to year of occurrence; prior data are credited to the year filed. [10] Other transit includes bus, light rail, commuter rail, demand response, van pool, and automated guideway. Excludes cable car, inclined plane, jitney, and ferry boat. [11] Incidents, deaths, and injuries involving hazardous materials cover all types of transport, excludes pipelines and bulk, nonpackaged water incidents.

Source: U.S. Bureau of Transportation Statistics, "National Transportation Statistics"; <http://www.bts.gov/publications/national_transportation_statistics/>.

Table 1036. Shipment Characteristics by Mode of Transportation: 2007

[11,831,503 represents $11,831,503,000,000. Estimates are based on preliminary data from the 2007 Commodity Fund Survey. For business establishments in mining, manufacturing, wholesale trade, and selected retail industries. Selected auxiliary establishments are also included.]

Mode of transportation	Value (mil. dol.)		Tons (1,000)		Ton-miles (mil.)		Average miles per shipment
	Total	Percent	Total	Percent	Total	Percent	
All modes	**11,831,503**	**100.0**	**13,016,610**	**100.0**	**3,490,806**	**100.0**	**580**
Single modes	**9,554,880**	**80.8**	**12,087,756**	**92.9**	**2,953,076**	**84.6**	**213**
Truck [1]	8,363,657	70.7	8,957,687	68.8	1,390,102	39.8	187
For-hire truck	4,764,442	40.3	4,029,016	31.0	1,011,018	29.0	527
Private truck.	3,599,215	30.4	4,928,670	37.9	379,084	10.9	82
Rail	387,567	3.3	1,928,530	14.8	1,294,921	37.1	691
Water.	106,905	0.9	423,282	3.3	175,973	5.0	330
Shallow draft	95,420	0.8	381,566	2.9	163,571	4.7	284
Great lakes	705	–	13,261	0.1	4,830	0.1	(S)
Deep draft	10,779	0.1	28,455	0.2	(S)	(S)	390
Air (includes truck and air)	209,611	1.8	3,525	–	4,014	0.1	1,299
Pipeline [2]	487,140	4.1	774,732	6.0	(S)	(S)	(S)
Multiple modes	**1,938,884**	**16.4**	**626,539**	**4.8**	**489,767**	**14.0**	**915**
Parcel, U.S. Postal Service or courier .	1,597,931	13.5	36,029	0.3	29,535	0.8	914
Truck and rail	197,748	1.7	213,411	1.6	188,547	5.4	1,053
Truck and water.	31,112	0.3	74,421	0.6	48,870	1.4	1,347
Rail and water	7,744	0.1	44,979	0.3	30,444	0.9	2,608
Other multiple modes	104,350	0.9	257,698	2.0	192,372	5.5	2,190
Other and unknown modes	**337,739**	**2.9**	**302,315**	**2.3**	**47,964**	**1.4**	**149**

– Rounds to zero.   S Data do not meet publication standards due to high sampling variability or other reasons.   [1] Truck as a single mode includes shipments that went by private truck only, for-hire truck only, or a combination of private truck and for-hire truck.   [2] Commodity Flow Survey data exclude shipments of crude oil.

Source: U.S. Department of Transportation, Research and Innovative Technology Administration, Bureau of Transportation Statistics, and U.S. Census Bureau, 2007 Commodity Flow Survey; Transportation Commodity Flow Survey, preliminary (released December 2008); <http://factfinder.census.gov/home/saff/main.html?lang=en>.

Table 1037. U.S. Scheduled Airline Industry—Summary: 1995 to 2008

[For calendar years or Dec. 31, (547.8 represents 547,800,000). For domestic and international operations. Covers carriers certificated under Section 401 of the Federal Aviation Act. Minus sign (–) indicates loss]

Item	Unit	1995	2000	2003 [1]	2004	2005	2006	2007	2008
SCHEDULED SERVICE									
Revenue passengers enplaned. . .	Mil.	547.8	666.2	646.3	702.9	738.6	744.2	769.4	741.4
Revenue passenger miles	Bil.	540.7	692.8	656.9	733.6	779.0	796.8	829.1	811.4
Available seat miles	Bil.	807.1	957.0	893.8	971.4	1,003.3	1,005.5	1,037.2	1,020.1
Revenue passenger load factor . .	Percent . . .	67.0	72.4	73.5	75.5	77.6	79.2	79.9	79.5
Mean passenger trip length [2]	Miles.	987	1,040	1,016	1,044	1,055	1,071	1,078	1,094
Cargo ton miles	Mil.	16,921	23,888	26,735	27,978	28,036	29,339	29,570	28,383
Aircraft departures	1,000	8,062	9,035	10,839	11,398	11,562	11,264	11,397	10,841
FINANCES [3]									
Total operating revenue [4]	Mil. dol. . .	95,117	130,839	117,920	134,300	151,255	164,912	174,696	185,979
Passenger revenue	Mil. dol.	69,835	93,622	77,379	85,669	93,500	101,419	107,678	111,535
Cargo revenue.	Mil. dol.	9,882	14,456	15,003	17,146	20,704	22,848	24,531	29,852
Charter revenue.	Mil. dol.	3,742	4,913	5,589	5,503	6,074	6,026	5,544	4,268
Total operating expense	Mil. dol.	89,266	123,840	120,028	135,782	150,828	157,398	163,353	189,645
Operating profit (or loss)	Mil. dol.	5,852	6,999	–2,108	–1,491	427	7,514	9,344	–3,666
Interest income (or expense)	Mil. dol.	–2,426	–2,193	–3,442	–3,715	–4,209	–4,150	–3,915	–3,743
Net profit (or loss)	Mil. dol.	2,314	2,618	–1,700	–9,061	–27,217	18,183	7,691	–23,562
Adjusted Net Profit (or loss)[5]	Mil. dol.	2,283	2,486	–2,371	–7,643	–5,782	3,123	4,998	–9,464
Revenue per passenger mile	Cents	12.9	13.5	11.8	11.7	12.0	12.7	13.0	13.8
Operating profit margin	Percent . . .	6.2	5.3	–1.8	–1.1	0.3	4.6	5.3	–2.0
Net profit margin	Percent . . .	2.4	1.9	–1.4	–6.7	–18.0	11.0	4.4	–12.7
Adjusted Net Profit (or loss)[5]	Percent . . .	2.4	1.9	–2.0	–5.7	-3.8	1.9	2.9	–5.1
EMPLOYEES [6]									
Total	1,000	547.0	680.0	569.8	569.5	562.5	545.7	561.0	556.9
Pilots and copilots.	1,000	55.4	72.4	67.8	82.0	74.5	71.1	69.4	(NA)

NA Not available.   [1] Includes security costs reimbursements remitted to carriers under the Emergency Wartime Supplemental Appropriations Act (P.L. 108-11).   [2] For definition of mean, see Guide to Tabular Presentation.   [3] 2008 data are preliminary.   [4] Includes other types of revenues not shown separately.   [5] Excludes special items: bankruptcy-related reorganization charges and fresh-start acconting gains; special goodwill charges.   [6] Average full-time equivalents.

Source: Air Transport Association of America, Washington, DC, Air Transport Annual Report.

U.S. Census Bureau, Statistical Abstract of the United States: 2010

Table 1038. **Airline Cost Indexes: 1980 to 2008**

[2000 = 100. Data prior to 1990 excludes passenger airlines with annual revenue less than $100 million]

Index	1980	1990	1995	2000	2002	2003	2004	2005	2006	2007	2008
Composite index [1]	81.5	104.5	99.8	100.0	110.9	116.6	133.7	166.0	184.3	188.4	249.0
Labor costs.............	84.7	72.7	91.0	100.0	118.2	122.2	122.1	116.2	117.8	117.4	117.8
Fuel..................	123.4	101.9	71.1	100.0	93.9	113.7	151.1	215.0	261.4	273.5	389.9
Aircraft ownership [2]	25.8	57.4	72.8	100.0	90.6	86.9	91.5	85.9	84.0	82.3	80.7
Nonaircraft ownership	37.8	88.8	104.0	100.0	112.0	112.9	105.0	102.3	100.4	101.8	113.3
Professional services	28.8	68.3	86.9	100.0	96.4	96.5	97.1	105.4	110.9	114.8	124.2
Food and beverage	91.4	125.9	107.6	100.0	86.8	72.7	67.3	62.6	58.8	58.1	60.3
Landing fees............	55.6	83.2	97.7	100.0	117.1	108.7	118.6	126.1	133.2	131.5	143.9
Maintenance material	65.1	136.7	93.1	100.0	74.0	62.8	61.6	52.7	54.8	61.7	67.5
Aircraft insurance	221.8	117.1	264.7	100.0	218.3	151.2	149.0	125.0	143.8	129.2	103.0
Nonaircraft insurance	71.1	70.4	229.4	100.0	540.0	423.9	352.2	307.4	245.8	207.4	182.2
Passenger commissions	121.8	237.0	184.8	100.0	57.3	41.8	37.3	32.5	29.9	29.7	28.4
Communication	53.3	86.9	88.2	100.0	101.4	85.1	77.3	74.4	69.7	71.8	80.3
Advertising and promotion ...	117.4	165.8	108.5	100.0	74.3	68.2	77.1	75.5	81.2	66.4	58.5
Utilities and office supplies...	65.8	94.2	84.6	100.0	90.1	79.7	80.0	84.1	91.3	97.5	103.7
Transportation-related expenses	(NA)	45.4	47.8	100.0	107.0	202.2	285.4	379.5	408.3	408.2	483.8
Other operating expenses ...	85.5	101.9	93.9	100.0	112.9	91.6	96.1	111.6	102.1	110.1	153.7
Interest [3]	153.1	170.6	165.3	100.0	87.9	91.6	91.5	124.8	123.6	114.1	101.9

NA Not available. [1] Weighted average of all components, including interest. [2] Includes lease, aircraft and engine rentals, depreciation, and amortization. [3] Interest on long-term debt and capital and other interest expense.

Source: Air Transport Association of America, Washington, DC, *U.S. Passenger Airline Cost Index, Major and National Carriers.* See also <http://www.airlines.org/economics/>.

Table 1039. **Top 40 Airports in 2007—Passengers Enplaned: 1997 and 2007**

[In thousands (605,361 represents 605,361,000), except rank. For calendar year. Airports ranked by total passengers enplaned by large certificated air carriers on scheduled and nonscheduled operations, 2007]

Airport	1997 Total	1997 Rank	2007 Total	2007 Rank	Airport	1997 Total	1997 Rank	2007 Total	2007 Rank
All airports........	605,361	(X)	726,429	(X)	Washington, DC (Dulles Intl)..............	4,970	34	10,393	23
Total, top 40	403,888	(X)	552,062	(X)	Baltimore, MD (BWI Intl).....	6,231	28	10,293	24
Atlanta, GA (Hartsfield Intl).	32,693	1	42,704	1	Chicago, IL (Midway).....	4,230	37	9,128	25
Chicago, IL (O'Hare Intl)...	31,154	2	34,213	2	Tampa Intl, FL	5,851	30	9,126	26
Dallas/Ft. Worth Intl, TX ...	27,294	3	28,184	3	Honolulu Intl, HI	8,939	24	9,090	27
Los Angeles, Intl, CA	22,352	4	23,796	4	San Diego, CA (Lindbergh Field)	6,545	27	9,047	28
Denver, Intl, CO	16,002	6	23,731	5	Washington, DC (Ronald Reagan Washington Natl.)	7,010	26	8,934	29
Las Vegas, NV (McCarran Intl).................	13,689	12	21,490	6	Cincinnati, OH (Cincinnati/ Northern Kentucky Intl.....	7,641	25	7,727	30
Phoenix Sky Harbor Intl, AZ	14,331	8	20,564	7	Portland Intl, OR.........	6,182	29	7,130	31
Houston, Intercontinental, TX..................	12,695	13	20,092	8	St. Louis, MO (Lambert -St Louis Intl)	13,836	10	7,087	32
Detroit, MI (Wayne County).	14,822	7	17,279	9	Oakland Intl, CA	4,151	39	7,066	33
Minneapolis-St. Paul Intl, MN	13,864	9	16,896	10	Kansas City Intl, MO	5,071	33	5,817	34
New York, NY (JFK Intl)..	9,757	20	16,759	11	Cleveland, OH (Cleveland-Hopkins Intl)...........	5,550	31	5,555	35
Newark Intl, NJ.........	13,800	11	16,614	12	Memphis Intl, TN.	4,157	38	5,545	36
Orlando Intl, FL.........	11,701	15	16,590	13	Sacramento Intl, CA	3,215	47	5,315	37
Charlotte-Douglas Intl, NC .	10,358	18	16,507	14	San Jose Intl, CA	4,724	36	5,184	38
Philadelphia Intl, PA.	9,716	21	15,315	15	San Juan, PR (Luis Munoz Marin Intl)	4,725	35	5,052	39
Seattle-Tacoma Intl, WA	11,688	16	14,912	16	Santa Ana, CA (John Wayne-Orange County) ..	3,675	42	4,946	40
San Francisco Intl, CA	16,820	5	14,849	17					
Miami Intl, FL...........	12,097	14	13,479	18					
Boston, MA (Logan Intl) ...	10,463	17	12,485	19					
New York, NY (La Guardia).	9,868	19	12,108	20					
Salt Lake City Intl, UT	9,340	22	10,560	21					
Fort Lauderdale-Hollywood Intl, FL.	5,371	32	10,501	22					

X Not applicable.

Source: U.S. Bureau of Transportation Statisics, Office of Airline Information, BTS Form 41, Schedule T-3, unpublished data.

Table 1040. **Domestic Airline Markets: 2008**

[In thousands (4,450 represents 4,450,000). For calendar year. Data are for the 25 top markets and include all commercial airports in each metro area. Data represent origin and final destination of travel]

Market	Passengers	Market	Passengers
Fort Lauderdale-New York	4,450	Boston-New York	1,943
New York-Orlando................	4,126	Chicago-Los Angeles............	1,879
Chicago-New York	4,044	Chicago-Las Vegas.............	1,869
Los Angeles-New York............	3,912	Dallas/Fort Worth-New York	1,831
Atlanta-New York	3,409	Chicago-Orlando...............	1,771
New York- San Francisco	3,135	Orlando-Philadelphia	1,769
Los Angeles-San Francisco	2,421	New York-San Juan	1,712
Las Vegas-New York	2,310	Chicago-Washington	1,705
Miami-New York	2,205	New York-Washington	1,658
New York-West Palm Beach	2,153	Chicago-Denver	1,624
Honolulu-Kahului	2,091	Chicago-Phoenix	1,621
New York-Tampa	2,045	Boston-Washington	1,603
Dallas/Fort Worth-Houston	2,002		

Source: Air Transport Association of America, Washington, DC, *Annual Report.*

Table 1041. **Worldwide Airline Fatalities: 1990 to 2008**

[For scheduled air transport operations. **Excludes accidents due to acts of unlawful interference**]

Year	Fatal accidents	Passenger deaths	Death rate [1]	Year	Fatal accidents	Passenger deaths	Death rate [1]
1990	27	544	0.05	2000	18	757	0.04
1992	28	1,070	0.09	2001	13	577	0.03
1993	33	864	0.07	2002	14	791	0.04
1994	27	1,170	0.09	2003	7	466	0.02
1995	25	711	0.05	2004	9	203	0.01
1996	24	1,146	0.07	2005	17	712	0.03
1997	25	921	0.06	2006	23	755	0.02
1998	20	904	0.05	2007	11	587	0.01
1999	21	499	0.03	2008	11	439	0.01

[1] Rate per 100 million passenger kilometers flown.

Source: International Civil Aviation Organization, Montreal, Canada, *Civil Aviation Statistics of the World*, annual.

Table 1042. **Aircraft Accidents: 1990 to 2008**
[For years ending December 31]

Item	Unit	1990	1995	2000	2005	2006	2007	2008, prel.
Air carrier accidents, all services [1]	Number...	24	36	56	40	33	28	28
Fatal accidents.................	Number...	6	3	3	3	2	1	2
Fatalities	Number...	39	168	92	22	50	1	3
Aboard...................	Number...	12	162	92	20	49	1	1
Rates per 100,000 flight hours:								
Accidents....................	Rate.....	0.198	0.267	0.306	0.206	0.171	0.144	0.145
Fatal accidents...............	Rate.....	0.049	0.022	0.016	0.015	0.010	0.005	0.010
Commuter air carrier accidents [2]	Number...	15	12	12	6	3	3	7
Fatal accidents.................	Number...	3	2	1	–	1	–	–
Fatalities	Number...	6	9	5	–	2	–	–
Aboard...................	Number...	4	9	5	–	2	–	–
Rates per 100,000 flight hours:								
Accidents....................	Rate.....	0.641	0.457	3.247	2.002	0.995	1.028	2.410
Fatal accidents	Rate.....	0.128	0.076	0.271	–	0.332	–	–
On-demand air taxi accidents [3]	Number...	107	75	80	65	52	62	56
Fatal accidents.................	Number...	29	24	22	11	10	14	19
Fatalities	Number...	51	52	71	18	16	43	66
Aboard...................	Number...	49	52	68	16	16	43	66
Rates per 100,000 flight hours:								
Accidents....................	Rate.....	4.76	3.02	2.04	1.70	1.42	1.54	1.52
Fatal accidents	Rate.....	1.29	0.97	0.56	0.29	0.27	0.35	0.52
General aviation accidents [4]	Number...	2,242	2,056	1,837	1,670	1,520	1,650	1,559
Fatal accidents.................	Number...	444	413	345	321	307	288	275
Fatalities	Number...	770	735	596	563	705	496	491
Aboard...................	Number...	765	728	585	558	546	495	486
Rates per 100,000 flight hours:								
Accidents....................	Rate.....	7.85	8.21	6.57	7.20	6.33	6.92	7.11
Fatal accidents	Rate.....	1.55	1.63	1.21	1.38	1.28	1.20	1.25

– Represents zero. [1] U.S. air carriers operating under 14 CFR 121. Beginning 2000, includes aircraft with 10 or more seats, previously operating under 14 CFR 135. [2] All scheduled service of U.S. air carriers operating under 14 CFR 135. Beginning 2000, only aircraft with fewer than 10 seats. [3] All nonscheduled service of U.S. air carriers operating under 14 CFR 135. [4] U.S. civil registered aircraft not operated under 14 CFR 121 or 135. Data from 2006 include 154 deaths aboard a foreign registered aircraft when it collided with a business general aviation aircraft over the Brazilian Amazon jungle. There were no fatalities in the general aviation aircraft.

Source: U.S. National Transportation Safety Board, "Aviation Accident Statistics" (published 01 June 2009); <http://www.ntsb.gov/aviation/stats.htm>.

Table 1043. **U.S. Carrier Delays, Cancellations, and Diversions: 1995 to 2007**
[In thousands (5,327.4 represents 5,327,400). For calendar year. See headnote, Table 1044]

Item	1995	1999	2000	2001	2002	2003	2004	2005	2006	2007
Total operations	5,327.4	5,527.9	5,683.0	5,967.8	5,271.4	6,488.5	7,129.3	7,140.6	7,141.9	7,453.2
Delays:										
Late departures [1]	827.9	937.3	1,131.7	953.8	717.4	834.4	1,187.6	1,279.4	1,424.8	1,572.3
Late arrivals [2].......	1,039.3	1,152.7	1,356.0	1,104.4	868.2	1,057.8	1,421.4	1,466.1	1,615.5	1,803.3
Cancellations [3]	91.9	154.3	187.5	231.2	65.1	101.5	127.8	133.7	121.9	160.7
Diversions [4]	10.5	13.6	14.3	12.9	8.4	11.4	13.8	14.0	16.2	17.2

[1] Late departures comprise flights departing 15 minutes or more after the scheduled departure time. [2] Late arrivals comprise flights arriving 15 minutes or more after the scheduled arrival time. [3] A cancelled flight is one that was not operated, but was listed in a carrier's computer reservation system within seven days of the scheduled departure. [4] A diverted flight is one that left from the scheduled departure airport but flew to a destination point other than the scheduled destination point.

Source: U.S. Bureau of Transportation Statistics, "National Transportation Statistics"; <http://www.bts.gov/publications/national_transportation_statistics/>.

Transportation **661**

Table 1044. On-Time Flight Arrivals and Departures at Major U.S. Airports: 2008

[In percent. Quarterly, based on gate arrival and departure times for domestic scheduled operations of U.S. major airlines. All U.S. airlines with 1 percent or more of total U.S. domestic scheduled airline passenger revenues are required to report on-time data. A flight is considered on time if it operated less than 15 minutes after the scheduled time shown in the carrier's computerized reservation system. See source for data on individual airlines]

Airport	On-time arrivals				On-time departures			
	1st qtr.	2d qtr.	3d qtr.	4th qtr.	1st qtr.	2d qtr.	3d qtr.	4th qtr.
Total, all airports	71.4	73.9	74.2	74.2	74.7	77.3	77.2	77.7
Atlanta, Hartsfield.	72.2	79.8	76.8	73.1	72.6	80.3	76.7	77.8
Boston, Logan International	72.6	73.1	71.7	76.3	78.2	80.3	77.8	82.1
Baltimore/Washington International	76.5	80.6	81.4	82.9	76.9	80.0	81.2	82.3
Charlotte, Douglas	74.5	79.2	78.3	81.1	76.3	79.6	79.5	84.2
Cincinnati, Greater Cincinnati	72.4	80.9	82.2	81.8	74.7	81.9	81.6	82.2
Washington, Reagan National.	75.5	76.2	78.6	81.6	81.2	81.5	83.0	85.8
Denver International	75.0	76.4	81.6	80.2	75.7	77.9	80.9	80.2
Dallas-Fort Worth International	70.7	70.5	80.9	82.9	69.4	69.3	76.6	80.7
Detroit, Metro Wayne County	71.8	79.9	86.6	82.2	73.4	79.8	85.6	82.9
Newark International.	59.6	61.2	66.2	62.6	66.5	67.9	69.7	72.4
Fort Lauderdale-Hollywood International. . .	69.5	77.7	77.9	76.2	74.2	81.4	81.3	81.0
Washington/Dulles	71.1	72.0	74.2	79.6	73.4	73.6	76.0	81.5
Houston, George Bush	74.1	78.4	80.4	80.5	75.7	78.5	79.4	83.2
New York, JFK International	70.1	70.3	61.9	73.0	76.1	78.1	70.6	78.3
Las Vegas, McCarran International	73.4	76.3	84.0	77.4	74.1	77.9	82.7	77.7
Los Angeles International.	70.9	74.4	82.4	80.4	75.9	80.6	84.5	82.9
New York, La Guardia.	57.9	57.1	65.5	71.7	71.3	71.9	76.2	81.3
Orlando International	72.5	78.8	80.1	80.2	75.9	80.4	81.1	83.9
Chicago, Midway	72.8	81.9	86.5	81.9	67.9	78.9	83.1	77.7
Miami International	66.0	70.7	71.7	75.8	68.6	71.2	70.5	76.8
Minneapolis-St. Paul International	73.5	78.0	85.1	79.5	77.1	82.3	86.4	82.6
Oakland International	74.2	79.1	87.0	82.0	76.4	82.2	87.0	81.5
Chicago, O'Hare	55.5	66.7	74.6	74.6	56.2	68.5	74.7	74.9
Portland International	74.2	76.5	83.2	76.7	81.8	84.1	87.9	81.7
Philadelphia International.	71.3	72.8	74.5	73.5	74.5	77.3	78.0	77.9
Phoenix, Sky Harbor International	78.0	80.1	84.1	81.6	78.8	81.1	83.1	82.2
San Diego, Lindbergh Field	73.5	75.7	84.1	79.0	76.9	81.4	86.2	81.7
Seattle-Tacoma International	72.8	74.4	80.4	74.2	78.1	81.0	84.1	79.1
San Francisco International	61.9	68.5	73.6	72.0	69.3	76.5	77.9	77.0
Salt Lake City International	75.5	86.5	89.1	83.4	81.0	89.6	89.5	85.8
St. Louis, Lambert	70.8	75.9	81.4	81.1	73.3	78.2	83.5	81.7
Tampa, Tampa International	73.3	79.0	80.1	80.1	77.7	81.8	82.6	84.0

Source: U.S. Department of Transportation, Aviation Consumer Protection Division, *Air Travel Consumer Report*, monthly. See also <http://airconsumer.ost.dot.gov>.

Table 1045. Consumer Complaints Against U.S. Airlines: 1990 to 2008

[Calendar year data. Represents complaints filed by consumers to the U.S. Department of Transportation, Aviation Consumer Protection Division, regarding service problems with air carrier personnel. See source for data on individual airlines]

Complaint category	1990	2000	2002	2003	2004	2005	2006	2007	2008
Total	7,703	20,564	7,697	4,601	5,839	6,900	6,452	10,960	9,194
Flight problems [1]	3,034	8,698	1,808	1,049	1,462	1,942	1,845	4,097	3,011
Customer service [2]	758	4,074	1,478	584	742	800	870	1,214	1,201
Baggage.	1,329	2,753	1,082	802	1,085	1,586	1,400	2,154	1,671
Ticketing/boarding [3]	624	1,405	898	643	637	679	708	1,136	1,147
Refunds	701	803	737	428	376	530	485	745	632
Fares [4]	312	708	436	243	180	219	173	315	324
Disability [5]	(NA)	612	420	325	467	430	368	428	428
Oversales [6]	399	759	364	223	263	284	275	420	370
Discrimination [7]	(NA)	(NA)	176	71	96	100	90	82	99
Advertising	96	42	43	13	41	45	30	34	28
Tours	29	25	(8)	(8)	(8)	(8)	(8)	(8)	(8)
Animals	(NA)	1	—	2	3	3	3	7	5
Smoking.	74	(9)	(9)	(9)	(9)	(9)	(9)	(9)	(9)
Credit.	5	(9)	(9)	(9)	(9)	(9)	(9)	(9)	(9)
Other	342	684	255	218	487	282	205	328	278

– Represents zero. NA Not available. [1] Cancellations, delays, etc. from schedule. [2] Unhelpful employees, inadequate meals or cabin service, treatment of delayed passengers. [3] Errors in reservations and ticketing; problems in making reservations and obtaining tickets. Includes disability complaints prior to 1998. [4] Incorrect or incomplete information about fares, discount fare conditions, and availability, etc. [5] Prior to 2000, included in ticketing/boarding. [6] All bumping problems, whether or not airline complied with DOT regulations. [7] Allegations of discrimination by airlines due to factors other than disability, such as race, religion, national origin or sex. [8] Included in "Other" beginning 2002. [9] Included in "Other" beginning 2000.

Source: U.S. Department of Transportation, Aviation Consumer Protection Division, *Air Travel Consumer Report*, monthly. See also <http://airconsumer.ost.dot.gov>.

Table 1046. **Commuter/Regional Airline Operations Summary: 2003 to 2007**

[Calendar year data (112.6 represents 112,600,000). Commuter/regional airlines operate primarily aircraft of predominately 75 passengers or less and 18,000 pounds of payload capacity serving short haul and small community markets. Represents operations within all North America by U.S. Regional Carriers. Averages are means. For definition of mean, see Guide to Tabular Presentation]

Item	Unit	2003	2004	2005	2006	2007
Passenger carriers operating	Number. . .	73	75	75	71	72
Passengers enplaned	Millions . . .	112.6	134.1	154.2	153.9	159.0
Average passengers enplaned per carrier. . .	1,000	1,542.5	1,787.7	2,055.6	2,168.0	2,208.5
Revenue passenger miles (RPM)	Billions . . .	47.7	62.6	73.8	70.8	73.8
Average RPMs per carrier	Millions . . .	652.8	835.1	983.7	997.2	1,024.7
Available seat miles	Billions . . .	72.2	91.6	104.8	94.8	99.0
Average load factor	Percent . . .	66.0	68.4	70.4	74.7	74.6
Departures completed.	Millions . . .	4.6	5.0	5.3	5.0	5.0
Airports served	Number. . .	823	846	846	688	666
Average trip length	Miles.	423.2	467.1	478.5	460.0	464.0
Average seating capacity (seats).	Number. . .	48.9	52.4	54.4	51.0	52.4
Fleet flying hours	1,000	5,940.3	6,595.5	7,333.0	7,133.1	7,306.7

Source: Compiled by the Regional Airline Association and BACK Aviation from DOT Form 41 data, *Annual Report of the Regional Airline Industry* (copyright). See <http://www.raa.org/>.

Table 1047. **Airports, Aircraft, and Airmen: 1980 to 2007**

[As of December 31 or for years ending December 31]

Item	1980	1990	1995	2000	2004	2005	2006	2007
Public [1].	4,814	5,589	5,415	5,317	5,288	5,270	5,233	5,221
Percent—with lighted runways . . .	66.2	71.4	74.3	75.9	76.3	76.8	77.2	(NA)
With paved runways	72.3	70.7	73.3	74.3	74.5	74.8	75.3	(NA)
Private	10,347	11,901	12,809	13,964	14,532	14,584	14,757	14,839
Percent—with lighted runways . . .	15.2	7.0	6.4	7.2	9.0	9.2	9.5	(NA)
With paved runways	13.3	31.5	33.0	32.0	32.8	33.2	33.3	(NA)
Certificated [2]	730	680	667	651	599	575	604	565
Civil	(X)	(X)	572	563	542	(NA)	(NA)	(NA)
Civil military	(X)	(X)	95	88	57	(NA)	(NA)	(NA)
General aviation	14,431	16,810	17,557	18,630	19,221	19,279	19,379	19,776
Active air carrier fleet [3]	3,805	6,083	7,411	8,055	8,186	8,225	(NA)	(NA)
Fixed wing.	3,803	6,072	7,293	8,016	8,150	8,182	(NA)	(NA)
Helicopter	2	11	118	39	36	43	(NA)	(NA)
General aviation fleet [4]	211,043	198,000	188,089	217,533	219,426	224,352	221,943	231,607
Fixed-wing.	200,094	184,500	162,342	183,276	182,007	185,373	182,186	186,806
Turbojet	2,992	4,100	4,559	7,001	9,298	9,823	10,379	10,385
Turboprop	4,089	5,300	4,995	5,762	8,379	7,942	8,063	9,514
Piston	193,013	175,200	152,788	170,513	165,189	167,608	163,743	166,907
Rotocraft	6,001	6,900	5,830	7,150	7,821	8,728	9,159	9,567
Other	4,945	6,600	4,741	6,700	5,939	6,454	6,277	5,940
Gliders	(X)	(X)	2,182	2,041	2,116	2,074	1,975	1,947
Lighter than air	(X)	(X)	2,559	4,660	3,823	4,380	4,303	3,993
Experimental	(X)	(X)	15,176	20,407	22,800	23,627	23,047	23,228
Airman certificates held: [5]								
Pilot, total	827,071	702,659	639,184	625,581	618,633	609,737	597,109	590,349
Women	52,902	40,515	38,032	36,757	37,243	36,584	36,101	35,784
Student	199,833	128,663	101,279	93,064	87,910	87,213	84,866	84,339
Recreational	(X)	87	232	340	291	278	239	239
Airplane:								
Private.	357,479	299,111	261,399	251,561	235,994	228,619	219,233	211,096
Commercial.	183,442	149,666	133,980	121,858	122,592	120,614	117,610	115,127
Air transport	69,569	107,732	123,877	141,596	142,160	141,992	141,935	143,953
Rotorcraft only [6]	6,030	9,567	7,183	7,775	8,586	9,518	10,690	12,290
Glider only	7,039	7,833	11,234	9,387	21,100	21,369	21,597	21,274
Flight instructor certificates	60,440	63,775	77,613	80,931	89,596	90,555	91,343	92,175
Instrument ratings	260,462	297,073	298,798	311,944	313,546	311,828	309,333	309,865
Nonpilot [7]	368,356	492,237	651,341	547,453	515,293	644,016	656,227	666,559
Mechanic.	250,157	344,282	405,294	344,434	317,111	320,293	323,097	322,852
Repairmen.	(X)	(X)	61,233	38,208	39,231	40,030	40,329	40,277
Parachute rigger	9,547	10,094	11,824	10,477	8,011	8,150	8,252	8,186
Ground instructor.	61,550	66,882	96,165	72,326	73,735	74,378	74,849	74,544
Dispatcher	6,799	11,002	15,642	16,340	17,493	18,079	18,610	19,043
Flight navigator	1,936	1,290	916	570	336	298	264	250
Flight engineer	38,367	58,687	60,267	65,098	59,376	57,756	55,952	54,394

NA Not available.   X Not applicable.   [1] Existing airports, heliports, seaplane bases, etc. recorded with FAA. Includes military airports with joint civil and military use. Includes U.S. outlying areas. Airport-type definitions: Public—publicly owned and under control of a public agency; private—owned by a private individual or corporation. May or may not be open for public use. [2] Certificated airports serve air-carriers with aircraft seating more than 30 passengers.   [3] Air-carrier aircraft are aircraft carrying passengers or cargo for hire under 14 CFR 121 (large aircraft—more than 30 seats) and 14 CFR 135 (small aircraft—30 seats or fewer).   [4] Beginning 1995 excludes commuters.   [5] Source: U.S. Federal Aviation Administration. See <http://www.faa.gov /data_research/>. Prior years in the *Statistical Handbook of Aviation*, annual.   [6] Data for 1980 are for helicopters only.   [7] All certificates on record. No medical examination required.

Source: Except as noted, U.S. Bureau of Transportation Statistics, *National Transportation Statistics*, annual. See also <http://www.bts.gov/publications/national_transportation_statistics/>.

Transportation   663

Table 1048. **Freight Carried on Major U.S. Waterways: 1980 to 2007**

[In millions of tons (4.0 represents 4,000,000)]

Item	1980	1990	1995	2000	2003	2004	2005	2006	2007
Atlantic intracoastal waterway	4.0	4.2	3.5	3.1	1.9	2.3	2.7	2.6	2.5
Great Lakes.	183.5	167.1	177.8	187.5	156.5	178.4	169.4	173.0	161.0
Gulf intracoastal waterway	94.5	115.4	118.0	113.8	117.8	123.3	116.1	122.6	125.1
Mississippi River system [1]	584.2	659.1	707.2	715.5	676.8	699.8	678.0	702.1	699.0
Mississippi River mainstem	441.5	475.3	520.3	515.6	478.0	496.9	464.6	497.7	500.5
Ohio River system [2]	179.3	260.0	267.6	274.4	261.3	271.5	280.1	270.7	260.2
Columbia River.	49.2	51.4	57.1	55.2	47.2	53.5	51.5	52.3	58.1
Snake River.	5.1	4.8	6.8	6.7	5.3	5.7	5.3	5.2	5.4

[1] Main channels and all tributaries of the Mississippi, Illinois, Missouri, and Ohio Rivers. [2] Main channels and all navigable tributaries and embayments of the Ohio, Tennessee, and Cumberland Rivers.

Source: U.S. Army Corps of Engineers, *Waterborne Commerce of the United States,* annual. See also <http://www.iwr.usace.army.mil /ndc/wcsc/wcsc.htm>.

Table 1049. **Waterborne Commerce by Type of Commodity: 1995 to 2007**

[In millions of short tons (2,240.4 represents 2,240,400,000). One short ton equals 2,000 pounds. Domestic trade includes all commercial movements between United States ports and on inland rivers, Great Lakes, canals, and connecting channels of the United States, Puerto Rico, and Virgin Islands]

Commodity	1995	2000	2005	2007 Total	2007 Domestic	2007 Foreign imports	2007 Foreign exports
Total	2,240.4	2,424.6	2,527.6	2,564.0	1,021.5	1,075.7	466.8
Coal	324.5	297.0	316.6	326.1	231.8	38.6	55.7
Petroleum and petroleum products	907.1	1,044.0	1,111.4	1,133.0	367.5	683.1	82.4
Crude petroleum	504.6	571.4	602.7	593.9	71.8	521.9	0.1
Petroleum products [1]	402.5	472.4	508.8	539.1	295.6	161.2	82.3
Gasoline.	114.4	125.2	156.1	151.7	80.4	58.6	12.7
Distillate fuel oil	76.7	91.7	141.1	167.4	84.7	55.6	27.1
Residual fuel oil	111.9	131.6	96.1	97.3	81.1	10.8	5.4
Chemicals and related products.	153.7	172.4	174.9	178.2	71.1	46.9	60.2
Fertilizers.	35.7	35.1	34.5	35.7	14.5	10.2	11.0
Other chemicals and related products	118.0	137.3	140.4	142.5	56.6	36.7	49.2
Crude material, inedible	381.7	380.3	386.0	362.4	201.9	101.9	58.6
Forest products, wood and chips	47.2	33.1	29.4	25.5	8.5	7.9	9.2
Pulp and waste paper.	14.9	13.6	18.7	19.8	0.1	2.0	17.6
Soil, sand, gravel, rock, and stone [1]	152.5	165.0	177.9	166.4	119.7	42.4	4.2
Limestone.	54.0	67.4	73.5	69.0	49.5	16.5	3.1
Phosphate rock	10.7	3.4	6.0	5.6	2.7	2.9	–
Sand & gravel	77.0	79.0	80.2	75.3	63.8	10.6	0.9
Iron ore and scrap	104.9	97.9	85.7	85.5	54.3	12.3	19.0
Marine shells	0.5	0.3	–	0.1	0.1	–	–
Nonferrous ores and scrap	27.9	29.2	29.2	27.9	6.6	18.4	2.9
Sulphur, clay, and salt.	23.4	11.3	8.7	7.7	0.7	2.2	4.8
Slag	1.9	4.0	6.0	6.0	2.7	3.1	0.1
Other nonmetal minerals.	8.4	25.9	30.4	23.6	9.2	13.6	0.8
Primary manufactured goods.	106.3	153.0	166.4	154.2	44.0	88.1	22.2
Papers products	13.1	12.1	13.7	15.0	0.3	6.7	8.0
Lime, cement, and glass	33.9	55.9	62.4	50.4	18.6	30.3	1.6
Primary iron and steel products	44.1	57.1	52.1	49.5	14.5	32.2	2.8
Primary nonferrous metal products	12.3	25.5	33.5	36.1	10.5	16.0	9.5
Primary wood products	2.9	2.5	4.8	3.3	0.1	2.9	0.4
Food and farm products	303.2	283.3	251.3	285.1	84.4	37.0	163.7
Fish	3.6	2.4	3.0	3.1	0.1	1.8	1.2
Grain [1].	167.9	145.2	124.0	149.0	52.6	1.1	95.4
Wheat	48.5	43.4	36.4	43.7	10.7	0.1	32.9
Corn	105.0	88.2	75.2	92.9	38.1	0.1	54.8
Oilseeds	46.1	57.6	47.2	53.2	19.3	0.3	33.6
Soybeans	42.0	47.3	40.8	45.1	16.4	0.1	28.6
Vegetables products.	9.0	8.9	8.3	9.8	1.0	4.9	3.9
Processed grain and animal feed	33.0	23.1	18.4	17.2	4.9	0.8	11.5
Other agricultural products	43.5	46.1	50.5	52.8	6.5	28.2	18.2
All manufactured equip, machinery and products	57.0	83.6	110.3	113.7	19.1	74.3	20.3
Waste and scrap, n.e.c. [2]	5.4	4.3	2.0	1.7	1.7	–	–
Unknown or not elsewhere classified	1.6	6.8	8.7	9.6	0.1	5.9	3.7

– Represents or rounds to zero. [1] Includes commodities not shown separately. [2] Not elsewhere classified.

Source: U.S. Army Corps of Engineers, *Waterborne Commerce of the United States,* annual. See also <http://www.iwr.usace.army.mil /ndc/wcsc/wcsc.htm>.

U.S. Census Bureau, Statistical Abstract of the United States: 2010

Table 1050. **Selected U.S. Ports by Tons of Traffic: 2007**

[In thousands of short tons (41,251 represents 41,251,000), except rank. One short ton equals 2,000 lbs. For calendar year for the top 30 ports. Represents tons of cargo shipped from or received by the specified port. Excludes cargo carried on general ferries; coal and petroleum products loaded from shore facilities directly onto bunkers of vessels for fuel; and amounts of less than 100 tons of government-owned equipment in support of Corps of Engineers projects]

| Port name | Rank | Total | Foreign | | | Domestic |
			Total	Inbound	Outbound	
Baltimore, MD	17	41,251	26,748	16,044	10,704	14,502
Baton Rouge, LA	14	54,624	18,543	13,720	4,823	36,080
Beaumont, TX	5	81,384	57,044	50,456	6,588	24,340
Corpus Christi, TX	6	81,073	58,365	48,025	10,340	22,707
Duluth-Superior, MN and WI.	16	46,498	15,139	258	14,880	31,359
Freeport, TX	27	29,598	24,065	20,967	3,098	5,533
Houston, TX	2	216,064	145,342	94,692	50,651	70,722
Huntington - Tristate [1]	7	76,489	–	–	–	76,489
Lake Charles, LA	11	64,234	39,712	34,457	5,256	24,522
Long Beach, CA	4	85,940	70,556	49,706	20,850	15,384
Los Angeles, CA	9	65,502	57,341	40,466	16,875	8,161
Mobile, AL.	10	64,494	34,816	22,973	11,842	29,679
New Orleans, LA	8	76,046	37,791	21,653	16,138	38,255
New York, NY and NJ	3	157,202	91,422	74,958	16,464	65,780
Norfolk Harbor, VA	18	39,737	32,055	10,179	21,877	7,681
Pascagoula, MS.	23	35,195	23,367	18,961	4,406	11,828
Paulsboro, NJ	20	37,984	24,158	22,797	1,361	13,826
Philadelphia, PA.	24	35,149	21,666	21,101	565	13,483
Pittsburgh, PA	19	38,086	–	–	–	38,086
Plaquemines, LA, Port of	12	58,817	23,996	8,468	15,528	34,821
Port Arthur, TX.	28	29,262	17,647	11,851	5,796	11,614
Portland, OR	26	31,119	18,810	4,661	14,149	12,309
Savannah, GA	22	36,486	34,795	21,981	12,814	1,691
Seattle, WA.	29	28,169	21,328	9,512	11,817	6,841
South Louisiana, LA, Port of.	1	229,040	107,490	47,343	60,147	121,550
St. Louis, MO and IL.	25	32,125	–	–	–	32,125
Tacoma, WA	30	26,944	19,347	6,845	12,502	7,597
Tampa, FL	15	46,857	15,154	8,848	6,307	31,703
Texas City, TX	13	56,787	40,479	35,919	4,561	16,307
Valdez, AK	21	37,775	–	–	–	37,775

– Represents zero. [1] The Port of Huntington is the largest inland shipping port in the United States.

Source: U.S. Army Corps of Engineers, *"Waterborne Commerce of the United States, 2007."* See also <http://www.iwr.usace.army.mil/ndc/wcsc/wcsc.htm> (accessed 2 June 2009).

Table 1051. **Selected U.S. Ports/Waterways by Container Traffic: 2007**

[In thousands of twenty-foot equivalent units (TEUS). 32,567.3 represents 32,567,300. For calendar year. For the 30 leading ports/waterways in total TEUS. A TEUS is a measure of containerized cargo capacity equal to 1 standard 20'0foot length by 8'0foot width by 8'0foot 6'0inch height container]

| Port/waterway name | Rank | Total loaded | Domestic | | | Foreign loaded | |
			Total [1]	Inbound loaded	Outbound loaded	Total	Inbound
Total [2]	(X)	32,567.3	5,280.2	2,173.2	2,173.2	28,220.8	17,871.2
Anchorage, AK	17	275.6	276.8	223.9	49.5	2.2	–
Baltimore, MD	16	501.3	95.2	39.1	40.0	422.3	246.0
Boston, MA	21	173.9	28.9	12.5	8.1	153.4	89.9
Camden-Gloucester, NJ. .	28	90.4	60.9	21.6	39.3	29.5	25.8
Charleston, SC	10	1,369.2	–	–	–	1,369.2	747.4
Chester, PA.	26	101.3	–	–	–	101.3	53.6
Gulfport, MS	22	169.4	–	–	–	169.4	102.1
Honolulu, HI	11	889.4	1,142.1	546.6	307.3	35.5	22.0
Houston, TX	9	1,399.9	52.4	17.4	29.7	1,352.8	595.3
Jacksonville, FL.	15	580.6	449.8	88.0	361.8	130.8	39.8
Kahului, Maui, HI	27	93.4	142.2	76.4	17.0	–	–
Kawaihae Harbor, HI. . . .	29	65.0	96.0	50.6	14.4	–	–
Long Beach, CA	2	5,130.9	364.7	53.2	265.3	4,812.4	3,540.5
Los Angeles, CA	1	5,496.7	–	–	–	5,496.7	4,141.3
Miami, FL.	14	669.4	–	–	–	669.4	339.2
Mobile, AL.	30	62.6	–	–	–	62.6	34.2
New Orleans, LA	18	254.9	14.5	4.8	6.2	243.9	70.1
New York (NY and NJ) . .	3	4,047.3	280.5	102.5	132.4	3,812.4	2,560.3
Norfolk Harbor, VA	5	1,625.9	102.1	44.0	41.4	1,540.6	830.0
Oakland, CA	6	1,578.7	265.2	29.4	165.7	1,383.7	769.4
Palm Beach, FL.	25	141.7	–	–	–	141.7	39.1
Philadelphia, PA.	23	167.4	–	–	–	167.4	130.8
Port Everglades, FL	13	676.4	9.5	–	9.5	666.9	304.9
Portland, OR	19	213.5	30.0	18.9	0.9	193.6	98.4
San Juan, PR	12	792.1	600.4	469.7	130.7	191.7	142.1
Savannah, GA.	4	1,980.3	0.0	0.0	0.0	1,980.3	1,045.9
Seattle, WA.	7	1,416.1	324.2	49.5	160.1	1,206.4	708.6
Tacoma, WA	8	1,415.5	296.0	56.1	238.7	1,120.7	713.4
Wilmington, DE	20	179.4	–	–	–	179.4	136.3
Wilmington, NC	24	148.7	–	–	–	148.7	84.4

– Represents zero. [1] Includes empty TEUS. [2] Includes other ports/waterways not shown separately.

Source: U.S. Army Corps of Engineers, "U.S. Waterborne Container Traffic for U.S. Port/Waterway in 2007." See also <http://www.iwr.usace.army.mil/ndc/wcsc/wcsc.htm> (published 2 June 2009).

Transportation   665

Table 1052. **Highway Mileage—Urban and Rural by Ownership: 1980 to 2007**

[In thousands (3,955 represents 3,955,000). As of Dec. 31. Includes Puerto Rico beginning 2000]

Type and control	1980	1990	1995	2000	2003	2004	2005	2006	2007
Total mileage [1,2]	[3]3,955	3,880	3,912	3,951	3,991	3,997	4,012	4,033	4,032
Urban mileage [1]	624	757	819	859	954	994	1,023	1,043	1,044
Under state control	79	96	112	112	127	130	144	148	145
Under local control	543	661	706	746	828	862	874	890	894
Rural mileage	[3]3,331	3,123	3,093	3,092	3,036	3,003	2,989	2,990	2,988
Under state control	702	703	691	664	653	650	637	635	634
Under local control	2,270	2,242	2,231	2,311	2,263	2,236	2,228	2,231	2,228
Under federal control	262	178	170	117	120	118	123	123	126

[1] Includes State park, State toll, other State agency, other local agency and other roadways not identified by ownership.
[2] Roadways in federal parks, forest, and reservations that are not part of the state and local highway system.   [3] Includes 98,000 miles of nonpublic road mileage previously contained

Source: U.S. Federal Highway Administration, *Highway Statistics,* annual. See also <http://www.fhwa.dot.gov/policy/ohpi/hss /hsspubs.htm>.

Table 1053. **Highway Mileage by State—Functional Systems and Urban/Rural: 2007**

[As of Dec. 31. Excludes Puerto Rico. For definition of functional systems see text, this section]

State	Total	Functional systems					Urban	Rural
		Interstate	Other free-ways and express-ways	Arterial	Collector	Local		
U.S.	**4,032,126**	**46,672**	**10,913**	**397,377**	**791,891**	**2,785,273**	**1,044,368**	**2,987,758**
AL.	97,323	905	41	9,220	20,473	66,684	22,024	75,299
AK.	14,438	1,081	–	1,518	2,829	9,010	2,357	12,081
AZ.	60,593	1,168	171	5,716	8,117	45,421	22,918	37,675
AR.	99,558	656	100	6,901	20,369	71,532	11,966	87,592
CA.	171,154	2,461	1,550	27,167	32,060	107,916	87,709	83,445
CO	88,163	954	315	8,924	16,241	61,729	19,229	68,934
CT.	21,295	346	237	2,758	3,201	14,753	15,108	6,187
DE.	6,242	41	30	638	1,052	4,481	2,963	3,279
DC	1,505	13	20	266	156	1,050	1,505	–
FL.	121,526	1,471	576	12,871	14,304	92,304	81,270	40,256
GA	118,779	1,243	114	14,022	22,766	80,634	37,683	81,096
HI	4,341	55	34	752	826	2,674	2,300	2,041
ID	48,416	613	–	4,114	10,362	33,327	5,606	42,810
IL	139,157	2,170	116	14,513	21,741	100,617	40,952	98,205
IN [1]	95,469	1,172	136	7,960	22,683	63,518	22,149	73,320
IA	114,193	781	–	9,730	31,557	72,125	11,288	102,905
KS.	140,271	874	187	9,534	33,525	96,151	12,659	127,612
KY.	78,587	762	66	5,867	16,084	55,808	12,479	66,108
LA.	61,008	905	50	5,527	10,046	44,480	16,277	44,731
ME	22,792	367	20	2,174	5,951	14,280	2,987	19,805
MD	31,300	481	294	3,787	5,050	21,688	17,276	14,024
MA	36,008	573	313	6,177	4,825	24,120	28,041	7,967
MI	121,593	1,242	328	14,618	24,503	80,902	35,756	85,837
MN [2]	137,693	914	161	13,489	30,409	92,720	18,383	119,310
MS	74,622	698	70	7,443	15,449	50,962	10,779	63,843
MO	129,122	1,181	400	10,183	24,964	92,394	22,710	106,412
MT	73,203	1,192	–	6,036	16,194	49,781	2,983	70,220
NE.	93,398	481	21	8,087	20,746	64,063	6,222	87,176
NV.	33,872	571	71	3,077	4,997	25,156	7,078	26,794
NH	15,839	226	57	1,546	2,755	11,255	4,822	11,017
NJ.	38,752	431	404	5,760	4,151	28,006	31,455	7,297
NM	68,339	1,000	5	5,097	8,513	53,724	7,988	60,351
NY.	113,740	1,688	798	13,827	20,699	76,728	47,866	65,874
NC	104,412	1,109	398	9,509	17,601	75,795	33,106	71,306
ND	86,842	571	–	5,911	11,813	68,547	1,897	84,945
OH	125,160	1,574	483	10,947	22,628	89,528	44,682	80,478
OK	112,922	933	191	8,197	25,292	78,309	15,633	97,289
OR	59,758	729	58	7,020	17,579	34,372	12,783	46,975
PA.	121,581	1,758	549	13,301	19,807	86,166	45,130	76,451
RI	6,510	72	87	836	884	4,631	5,240	1,270
SC.	66,248	843	84	7,146	15,084	43,091	16,422	49,826
SD.	83,744	679	11	6,392	19,107	57,555	2,878	80,866
TN.	91,058	1,105	148	9,069	17,838	62,898	21,713	69,345
TX.	305,855	3,233	1,245	29,235	63,437	208,681	84,194	221,661
UT.	44,221	936	12	3,670	7,850	31,753	11,549	32,672
VT.	14,400	320	20	1,302	3,113	9,645	1,421	12,979
VA.	72,662	1,119	269	8,321	14,075	48,878	22,312	50,350
WA	83,431	764	375	7,726	16,714	57,852	22,551	60,880
WV	38,274	555	9	3,464	8,618	25,628	5,279	32,995
WI	114,705	743	286	12,418	21,663	79,595	22,148	92,557
WY	28,052	913	3	3,590	11,190	12,356	2,642	25,410

– Represents zero.   [1] Excludes 788 miles of Federal agency owned roads.   [2] Includes 274 miles of miscoded non-Interstate functional system length or rural/urban categorization or both.

Source: U.S. Federal Highway Administration, *Highway Statistics,* annual. See also <http://www.fhwa.dot.gov/policy/ohpi/hss /hsspubs.htm>.

666   Transportation

Table 1054. **Bridge Inventory—Total, Deficient and Obsolete, 1996 to 2008, and by State, 2008**

[Based on the National Bridge Inventory program; for details, see source]

State and year	Number of bridges	Total number	Percent	Deficient and obsolete			
				Structurally deficient [1]		Functionally obsolete [2]	
				Number	Percent	Number	Percent
1996	581,862	182,726	31.4	101,518	17.4	81,208	14.0
1997	582,751	175,885	30.2	98,475	16.9	77,410	13.3
1998	582,984	172,582	29.6	93,076	16.0	79,506	13.6
1999	585,542	170,050	29.0	88,150	15.1	81,900	14.0
2000	587,755	167,993	28.6	87,106	14.8	80,887	13.8
2001	590,066	165,099	28.0	83,630	14.2	81,469	13.8
2002	591,220	163,010	27.6	81,437	13.8	81,573	13.8
2003	592,246	160,819	27.2	79,811	13.5	81,008	13.7
2004	593,885	158,318	26.7	77,758	13.1	80,560	13.6
2005	594,616	156,177	26.3	75,871	12.8	80,306	13.5
2006	596,842	153,990	25.8	73,764	12.4	80,226	13.4
2007	599,766	152,316	25.4	72,524	12.1	79,792	13.3
U.S. total, 2008	**601,411**	**151,391**	**25.2**	**71,469**	**11.9**	**79,922**	**13.3**
Alabama	15,909	3,927	24.7	1,783	11.2	2,144	13.5
Alaska	1,201	321	26.7	143	11.9	178	14.8
Arizona	7,374	828	11.2	204	2.8	624	8.5
Arkansas	12,539	2,846	22.7	944	7.5	1,902	15.2
California	24,411	7,085	29.0	3,199	13.1	3,886	15.9
Colorado	8,408	1,411	16.8	597	7.1	814	9.7
Connecticut	4,180	1,409	33.7	368	8.8	1,041	24.9
Delaware	857	133	15.5	22	2.6	111	13.0
District of Columbia	243	147	60.5	20	8.2	127	52.3
Florida	11,678	1,920	16.4	292	2.5	1,628	13.9
Georgia	14,578	2,869	19.7	991	6.8	1,878	12.9
Hawaii	1,120	487	43.5	136	12.1	351	31.3
Idaho	4,125	792	19.2	344	8.3	448	10.9
Illinois	26,102	4,269	16.4	2,454	9.4	1,815	7.0
Indiana	18,543	4,177	22.5	2,005	10.8	2,172	11.7
Iowa	24,798	6,545	26.4	5,164	20.8	1,381	5.6
Kansas	25,514	5,196	20.4	2,877	11.3	2,319	9.1
Kentucky	13,630	4,412	32.4	1,310	9.6	3,102	22.8
Louisiana	13,320	3,909	29.3	1,748	13.1	2,161	16.2
Maine	2,392	789	33.0	345	14.4	444	18.6
Maryland	5,166	1,357	26.3	396	7.7	961	18.6
Massachusetts	5,042	2,581	51.2	604	12.0	1,977	39.2
Michigan	10,937	2,830	25.9	1,520	13.9	1,310	12.0
Minnesota	13,125	1,568	11.9	1,163	8.9	405	3.1
Mississippi	17,024	4,201	24.7	2,891	17.0	1,310	7.7
Missouri	24,204	7,396	30.6	4,333	17.9	3,063	12.7
Montana	4,968	942	19.0	403	8.1	539	10.8
Nebraska	15,471	3,564	23.0	2,397	15.5	1,167	7.5
Nevada	1,735	215	12.4	49	2.8	166	9.6
New Hampshire	2,371	751	31.7	382	16.1	369	15.6
New Jersey	6,474	2,172	33.5	710	11.0	1,462	22.6
New Mexico	3,866	702	18.2	401	10.4	301	7.8
New York	17,366	6,525	37.6	2,135	12.3	4,390	25.3
North Carolina	17,889	5,131	28.7	2,448	13.7	2,683	15.0
North Dakota	4,451	966	21.7	716	16.1	250	5.6
Ohio	28,065	6,761	24.1	2,809	10.0	3,952	14.1
Oklahoma	23,587	7,223	30.6	5,566	23.6	1,657	7.0
Oregon	7,292	1,633	22.4	466	6.4	1,167	16.0
Pennsylvania	22,349	10,403	46.5	6,106	27.3	4,297	19.2
Rhode Island	741	397	53.6	165	22.3	232	31.3
South Carolina	9,221	2,027	22.0	1,231	13.3	796	8.6
South Dakota	5,920	1,473	24.9	1,224	20.7	249	4.2
Tennessee	19,880	4,007	20.2	1,274	6.4	2,733	13.7
Texas	50,599	9,819	19.4	1,873	3.7	7,946	15.7
Utah	2,853	450	15.8	184	6.4	266	9.3
Vermont	2,715	969	35.7	498	18.3	471	17.3
Virginia	13,447	3,490	26.0	1,231	9.2	2,259	16.8
Washington	7,656	2,024	26.4	422	5.5	1,602	20.9
West Virginia	7,038	2,592	36.8	1,064	15.1	1,528	21.7
Wisconsin	13,831	2,021	14.6	1,256	9.1	765	5.5
Wyoming	3,036	658	21.7	381	12.5	277	9.1
Puerto Rico	2,170	1,071	49.4	225	10.4	846	39.0

[1] Bridges are structurally deficient if they have been restricted to light vehicles, require immediate rehabilitation to remain open, or are closed. [2] Bridges are functionally obsolete if they have deck geometry, load carrying capacity, clearance or approach roadway alignment that no longer meet the criteria for the system of which the bridge is carrying a part.

Source: U.S. Federal Highway Administration, Office of Bridge Technology, "National Bridge Inventory";<http://www.fhwa.dot.gov/bridge/nbi.htm>.

Transportation 667

Table 1055. **Funding for Highways and Disposition of Highway-User Revenue: 1990 to 2007**

[In millions of dollars (75,444 represents $75,444,000,000). Data compiled from reports of state and local authorities]

Type	1990	1995	2000	2002	2003	2004	2005	2006	2007
Total receipts	75,444	96,269	131,115	138,878	139,246	145,315	154,690	165,443	192,714
Current income.	69,880	87,620	119,815	123,802	124,593	129,521	137,668	147,615	167,983
Highway-user revenues	44,346	59,331	81,335	79,487	79,280	83,006	90,343	93,648	97,916
Other taxes and fees	19,827	21,732	31,137	36,168	37,783	38,956	39,214	44,455	55,584
Investment income, other receipts . . .	5,707	6,557	7,342	8,147	7,530	7,560	8,111	9,512	14,484
Bond issue proceeds [1]	5,564	8,649	11,301	15,076	14,654	15,794	17,022	17,828	24,730
Funds drawn from or placed in reserves [2] . .	−36	−2,791	−8,418	−239	4,359	2,174	−1,990	−4,382	−20,961
Total funds available	75,408	93,478	122,697	138,639	143,605	147,489	152,700	161,061	171,753
Total disbursements	75,408	93,478	122,697	138,639	143,605	147,489	152,700	161,061	171,753
Current disbursements.	72,457	88,994	117,592	131,694	136,213	139,478	144,629	153,413	163,721
Capital outlay	35,151	44,228	61,323	68,794	70,004	70,274	75,162	78,676	81,098
Maintenance and traffic services.	20,365	24,319	30,636	33,893	35,011	36,327	37,882	40,426	45,759
Administration and research	6,501	8,419	10,020	10,934	11,986	12,737	11,126	13,189	14,370
Highway law enforcement and safety . .	7,235	8,218	11,031	12,548	13,501	14,322	14,066	14,482	15,074
Interest on debt.	3,205	3,810	4,583	5,526	5,711	5,819	6,392	6,639	7,420
Bond retirement [1]	2,951	4,484	5,105	6,945	7,393	8,011	8,071	7,648	8,032

[1] Proceeds and redemptions of short-term notes and refunding issues are excluded. [2] Negative numbers indicate that funds were placed in reserves.

Source: U.S. Federal Highway Administration, *Highway Statistics*, annual. See also <http://www.fhwa.dot.gov/policy/ohpi/hss/hsspubs.htm>.

Table 1056. **Federal Aid to State and Local Governments for Highway Trust Fund by State: 2007**

[Year ending Sept. 30. (33,694 represents $33,694,000,000)]

State	Total (mil. dol.)	Per capita (dol.)[1]	State	Total (mil. dol.)	Per capita (dol.)[1]	State	Total (mil. dol.)	Per capita (dol.)[1]	State	Total (mil. dol.)	Per capita (dol.)[1]
U.S.[2] . .	33,694	111	ID	347	232	MT.	331	346	RI	228	216
U.S.[3] . .	33,447	112	IL	1,144	89	NE	241	136	SC	565	128
AL	768	166	IN	660	104	NV	300	117	SD	214	269
AK	410	600	IA	347	116	NH	179	136	TN	730	119
AZ	436	69	KS	514	185	NJ	917	106	TX	1,887	79
AR	377	133	KY	678	160	NM	316	161	UT	282	106
CA	2,660	73	LA	661	154	NY	1,555	81	VT	163	263
CO	486	100	ME	171	130	NC	899	99	VA	693	90
CT	336	96	MD	601	107	ND	231	361	WA	745	115
DE	101	117	MA	465	72	OH	1,164	102	WV	388	214
DC	132	225	MI	1,084	108	OK	507	140	WI	641	114
FL	2,123	116	MN	587	113	OR	400	107	WY	218	417
GA	1,296	136	MS	921	315	PA	1,398	112			
HI	115	90	MO	832	142						

[1] Based on estimated population as of July 1. [2] Includes outlying areas and undistributed funds, not shown separately. [3] For the 50 states and DC.

Source: U.S. Census Bureau, *Federal Aid to States for Fiscal Year, 2007* (published September 2008). See also <http://www.census.gov/prod/www/abs/fas.html>.

Table 1057. **State Motor Fuel Tax Receipts, 2006 and 2007, and Gasoline Tax Rates, 2007**

[680 represents $680,000,000]

State	Net receipts (mil. dol.) 2006	Net receipts (mil. dol.) 2007	Tax rate,[1] 2007	State	Net receipts (mil. dol.) 2006	Net receipts (mil. dol.) 2007	Tax rate,[1] 2007	State	Net receipts (mil. dol.) 2006	Net receipts (mil. dol.) 2007	Tax rate,[1] 2007
AL	680	620	18.00	KY	528	563	21.00	ND	136	124	23.00
AK	29	31	8.00	LA	603	640	20.00	OH	1,873	1,877	28.00
AZ	705	717	18.00	ME	227	233	27.60	OK	441	411	17.00
AR	436	462	21.50	MD	746	755	23.50	OR	400	397	24.00
CA	3,303	3,266	18.00	MA	671	668	21.00	PA	2,092	2,107	31.20
CO	603	568	22.00	MI	1,037	1,010	19.00	RI	144	146	30.00
CT	581	677	25.00	MN	659	659	20.00	SC	504	532	16.00
DE	118	117	23.00	MS	423	431	18.40	SD	129	128	22.00
DC	25	27	20.00	MO	708	704	17.00	TN	832	850	20.00
FL	2,183	2,233	15.30	MT	196	191	27.75	TX	2,998	3,065	20.00
GA	811	934	7.50	NE	310	332	27.00	UT	342	369	24.50
HI	81	85	17.00	NV	481	521	24.00	VT	92	93	20.00
ID	221	233	25.00	NH	151	152	19.60	VA	907	927	17.50
IL	1,313	1,333	19.00	NJ	579	590	10.50	WA	1,004	1,107	36.00
IN	879	880	18.00	NM	283	289	18.88	WV	298	316	31.50
IA	430	441	21.00	NY	1,595	2,198	24.65	WI	944	986	30.90
KS	429	440	24.00	NC	1,532	1,654	29.95	WY	97	104	14.00

[1] State gasoline tax rates in cents per gallon. In effect December 31.

Source: U.S. Federal Highway Administration, *Highway Statistics*, annual. See also <http://www.fhwa.dot.gov/policy/ohpi/hss/hsspubs.htm>.

Table 1058. **Public Obligations for Highways—Changes in Indebtedness During the Year: 1995 to 2007**

[In millions of dollars (37,449 represents $37,449,000,000). Table summarizes state indebtedness from all state bond issues, including the toll facility issues and the state issues for local roads. This table is compiled from reports of state authorities. Table also summarizes the change in status of the highway obligations of local governments including toll authorities]

Item	1995	2000	2002	2003	2004	2005	2006	2007
STATE GOVERNMENT								
Obligations outstanding, beginning of year	37,449	56,264	67,564	72,175	80,513	82,476	89,642	89,899
Obligations issued	4,718	9,067	13,250	16,571	13,344	19,784	15,651	20,924
Obligations retired	2,940	3,897	9,988	11,541	8,291	14,072	8,780	7,108
Obligations outstanding, end of year .... [1]	39,228	61,434	70,826	77,205	85,565	88,187	96,513	103,715
LOCAL GOVERNMENT [1, 2]								
Obligations outstanding, beginning of year	26,393	34,904	38,896	40,901	42,733	44,406	47,346	(NA)
Bonds outstanding, beginning of year..............	25,613	34,229	38,110	40,091	41,979	43,403	46,344	(NA)
Bonds outstanding, end of year	29,505	34,949	40,400	41,979	44,368	46,168	49,130	(NA)
Obligations outstanding, end of year	30,295	35,557	41,210	42,734	45,331	47,170	50,366	(NA)

NA Not available. [1] Short-term notes data not shown. The data are included in beginning and ending year obligations. [2] The number of local government data estimated varied year to year.

Source: U.S. Federal Highway Administration, *Highway Statistics,* annual. See also <http://www.fhwa.dot.gov/policy/ohpi/hss/hsspubs.htm>.

Table 1059. **State Disbursements for Highways by State: 1995 to 2007**

[In millions of dollars (67,615 represents $67,615,000,000). Comprise disbursements from current revenues or loans for construction, maintenance, interest and principal payments on highway bonds, transfers to local units, and miscellaneous. Includes transactions by state toll authorities. Excludes amounts allocated for collection expenses and nonhighway purposes, and mass transit]

State	1995	2000	2002	2003	2004	2005	2006	2007
United States........	67,615	89,832	104,977	109,403	104,677	116,517	117,048	130,306
Alabama...............	1,002	1,246	1,575	1,572	1,562	1,519	1,684	1,752
Alaska................	438	501	541	618	623	643	654	710
Arizona...............	1,199	2,040	2,445	2,453	2,569	2,458	2,662	2,335
Arkansas.............	666	817	1,161	1,176	1,219	1,078	1,134	1,036
California	5,966	6,750	8,570	9,349	7,967	8,308	10,571	13,288
Colorado.	922	1,392	2,195	1,788	1,870	1,652	1,490	1,601
Connecticut..........	1,153	1,304	1,848	1,743	1,677	1,434	1,223	1,265
Delaware	441	595	738	929	798	1,104	804	676
District of Columbia	140	244	336	368	369	327	287	334
Florida	3,421	4,208	4,985	6,664	5,804	7,369	7,725	8,069
Georgia	1,437	1,567	1,945	1,756	1,935	2,070	2,655	2,878
Hawaii	360	272	275	375	314	506	323	352
Idaho................	350	492	508	547	568	608	622	758
Illinois	3,006	3,447	4,286	4,595	4,289	4,201	4,974	5,424
Indiana...............	1,433	1,932	1,975	2,445	2,578	2,235	2,416	3,251
Iowa	1,078	1,494	1,405	1,419	1,401	1,392	1,515	1,564
Kansas...............	1,019	1,206	1,951	1,891	1,387	1,394	1,521	1,414
Kentucky	1,397	1,651	1,776	2,152	1,907	1,723	1,635	2,194
Louisiana	1,198	1,301	1,287	1,498	1,576	1,387	1,866	1,923
Maine................	379	488	744	579	702	616	628	584
Maryland	1,289	1,599	1,803	1,885	1,831	2,049	2,304	2,689
Massachusetts..........	2,501	3,524	3,783	3,547	3,612	3,196	2,723	2,815
Michigan..............	1,974	2,748	2,859	2,799	2,930	3,561	3,263	3,240
Minnesota............	1,210	1,692	1,866	1,969	1,995	2,131	2,143	2,168
Mississippi	662	1,039	1,040	1,014	1,087	1,081	1,272	1,647
Missouri	1,313	1,818	2,110	2,120	2,135	2,069	2,430	3,955
Montana..............	388	474	535	578	657	664	696	622
Nebraska	578	745	867	839	859	876	882	1,436
Nevada	484	651	631	807	1,045	865	1,144	1,063
New Hampshire........	328	387	522	453	389	389	524	693
New Jersey...........	2,102	4,503	4,863	6,364	3,849	7,119	5,561	4,018
New Mexico...........	535	1,162	983	862	1,164	911	942	942
New York	4,584	5,307	7,161	6,592	6,094	9,638	5,659	7,459
North Carolina.........	1,871	2,621	3,001	3,013	3,557	3,698	3,330	3,385
North Dakota..........	270	385	385	379	388	456	506	441
Ohio	2,637	3,351	3,580	3,660	3,657	4,040	4,251	4,418
Oklahoma.............	828	1,417	1,839	1,379	1,175	1,163	2,001	1,282
Oregon...............	888	1,010	1,029	1,183	1,000	1,628	1,254	1,736
Pennsylvania..........	3,153	4,517	5,365	5,258	4,283	4,567	5,537	5,999
Rhode Island..........	290	256	380	299	373	407	488	494
South Carolina.........	668	970	1,201	1,191	1,254	1,360	1,476	1,472
South Dakota..........	286	466	437	441	455	466	491	402
Tennessee	1,230	1,440	1,622	1,661	1,549	1,718	1,658	1,657
Texas................	3,593	5,665	6,019	6,758	7,134	8,918	9,101	13,136
Utah	431	1,072	956	879	1,871	986	1,128	1,335
Vermont..............	194	287	265	312	297	310	335	368
Virginia...............	2,107	2,678	3,185	3,419	3,002	3,384	3,195	3,228
Washington...........	1,909	1,871	2,276	2,288	2,469	2,625	2,656	3,057
West Virginia..........	781	1,170	1,210	1,169	1,056	1,425	1,117	1,057
Wisconsin............	1,252	1,663	2,204	1,904	1,942	2,363	2,161	2,279
Wyoming	272	396	460	468	458	429	434	484

Source: U.S. Federal Highway Administration, *Highway Statistics,* annual. See <http://www.fhwa.dot.gov/policy/ohpi/hss/hsspubs.htm>.

Transportation   669

Table 1060. State Motor Vehicle Registrations: 1990 to 2007

[In thousands (188,798 represents 188,798,000). Compiled principally from information obtained from state authorities, but it was necessary to draw on other sources and to make numerous estimates in order to complete series. Excludes motorcycles; see Table 1062]

Item	1990	1995	2000	2004	2005	2006	2007
All motor vehicles	188,798	201,530	221,475	237,243	241,194	244,166	247,265
Private and commercial	185,541	197,941	217,567	233,266	237,140	240,059	243,094
Publicly owned	3,257	3,589	3,908	3,977	4,054	4,106	4,170
Automobiles [1]	133,700	128,387	133,621	136,431	136,568	135,400	135,933
Private and commercial	132,164	126,900	132,247	135,077	135,192	134,012	134,510
Publicly owned	1,536	1,487	1,374	1,354	1,376	1,388	1,423
Buses	627	686	746	795	807	822	834
Private and commercial	275	288	314	330	331	339	345
Publicly owned	351	398	432	465	476	483	490
Trucks [1]	54,470	72,458	87,108	100,017	103,819	107,944	110,497
Private and commercial	53,101	70,754	85,005	97,860	101,616	105,708	108,239
Publicly owned	1,369	1,704	2,103	2,157	2,203	2,235	2,258

[1] Trucks include pickups, panels, and delivery vans. Personal passenger vans, passenger minivans, and utility-type vehicles are no longer included in automobiles but are included in trucks.

Source: U.S. Federal Highway Administration, *Highway Statistics,* annual. See also <http://www.fhwa.dot.gov/policy/ohpi /hss/hsspubs.htm>.

Table 1061. Alternative Fueled Vehicles and Estimated Consumption of Vehicle Fuels by Fuel Type: 2004 to 2007

[In thousands,(428,532 represents 428,532,000). Vehicles in use do not include concept and demonstration vehicles that are not ready for delivery to end users. Vehicles in use represent accumulated acquisitions, less retirements, as of the end of each calendar year]

Vehicles and fuel consumption	Unit	2004	2005	2006	2007
ALTERNATIVE FUELED VEHICLES IN USE					
Total.	Number	565,492	592,125	634,562	695,766
Compressed Natural Gas (CNG)	Number	118,532	117,699	116,131	114,391
Electric [1]	Number	49,536	51,398	53,526	55,730
Ethanol, 85 percent (E85)[2, 3]	Number	211,800	246,363	297,099	364,384
Hydrogen.	Number	43	119	159	223
Liquefied Natural Gas (LNG)	Number	2,717	2,748	2,798	2,781
Liquefied Petroleum Gas (LPG)	Number	182,864	173,795	164,846	158,254
Other fuels [4]	Number	–	3	3	3
FUEL CONSUMPTION					
Alternative fuels:					
Compressed Natural Gas (CNG)	1,000 gal.(g-e-g)[5]	428,532	420,778	417,803	414,715
Compressed Natural Gas (CNG)	1,000 gal.(g-e-g)[5]	158,903	166,878	172,011	178,565
Electric [1]	1,000 gal.(g-e-g)[5]	5,269	5,219	5,104	5,037
Ethanol, 85 percent (E85)[2]	1,000 gal.(g-e-g)[5]	31,581	38,074	44,041	54,091
Hydrogen.	1,000 gal.(g-e-g)[5]	8	25	41	66
Liquefied Natural Gas (LNG)	1,000 gal.(g-e-g)[5]	20,888	22,409	23,474	24,594
Liquefied Petroleum Gas (LPG)	1,000 gal.(g-e-g)[5]	211,883	188,171	173,130	152,360
Other fuels [4]	1,000 gal.(g-e-g)[5]	–	2	2	2
Biodiesel.	1,000 gal.(g-e-g)[5]	28,244	91,649	260,606	(NA)
Oxygenates:					
Methyl Tertiary Butyl Ether (MTBE)	1,000 gal.(g-e-g)[5]	1,877,300	1,654,500	435,000	618,000
Ethanol in Gasohol	1,000 gal.(g-e-g)[5]	2,414,167	2,756,663	3,729,168	4,694,304
Total alternative and replacement fuels	1,000 gal.(g-e-g)[5]	4,748,243	4,923,590	4,842,577	(NA)
FUEL CONSUMPTION IN NATIVE UNITS					
Alternative fuels:					
Compressed Natural Gas (CNG)	million cubic feet	19,145	20,106	20,724	21,514
Electric [1]	1,000 kwh	175,633	173,967	170,133	167,900
Ethanol, 85 percent (E85)[2]	1,000 gallons	43,862	52,881	61,168	75,126
Hydrogen.	1,000 kilograms	7	23	37	60
Liquefied Natural Gas (LNG)	1,000 gallons	31,648	33,953	35,567	37,264
Liquefied Petroleum Gas (LPG)	1,000 gallons	286,328	254,285	233,959	205,892
Biodiesel.	1,000 gallons	27,980	90,790	250,426	(NA)
Oxygenates:					
Methyl Tertiary Butyl Ether (MTBE)	1,000 gallons	2,309,160	2,035,320	534,912	76,314
Ethanol in Gasohol	1,000 gallons	3,514,909	4,013,679	5,429,217	6,885,690
Total alternative and replacement fuels	(X)	(X)	(X)	(X)	(X)

– Represents zero. X Not applicable. [1] Excludes gasoline-electric and diesel-electric hybrids because the input fuel is gasoline or diesel rather than an alternative transportation fuel. [2] The remaining portion of E85 percent ethanol is gasoline. Consumption data include the gasoline portion of the fuel. [3] For 2007, the EIA estimates that the number of E85 vehicles that are capable of operating on E85, gasoline, or both, is about 7.1 million. Many of these alternative-fueled vehicles (AFVs) are sold and used as traditional gasoline-powered vehicles. In this table, AFVs in use include only those E85 vehicles believed to be used as AFVs. These are primarily fleet-operated vehicles. [4] May include P-Series fuel or any other fuel designated by the Secretary of Energy as an alternative fuel in accordance with the Energy Policy Act of 1995. [5] Gasoline equivalent gallons.

Source: U.S. Energy Information Administration, *Renewable and Alternative Fuels.* See also <http://www.eia.doe.gov /fuelrenewable.html>.

Table 1062. **State Motor Vehicle Registrations, 1990 to 2007, Motorcycle Registrations and Licensed Drivers by State: 2007**

[In thousands (188,798 represents 188,798,000). Motor vehicle registrations cover publicly, privately, and commercially owned vehicles. For uniformity, data have been adjusted to a calendar-year basis as registration years in states differ; figures represent net numbers where possible, excluding reregistrations and nonresident registrations. See also Table 1060]

State	Motor vehicle registrations [1]						2007		Motor-cycle registra-tions [2] 2007	Licensed drivers, 2007
	1990	1995	2000	2004	2005	2006	Total	Auto-mobiles (incl. taxis)		
U.S.	188,798	201,530	221,475	237,243	241,194	244,166	247,265	134,510	7,093	205,742
AL.	3,744	3,553	3,960	4,508	4,545	4,630	4,678	1,960	110	3,692
AK.	477	542	594	660	673	675	680	238	26	495
AZ.	2,825	2,873	3,795	3,776	3,972	4,182	4,372	2,220	124	4,154
AR.	1,448	1,613	1,840	1,918	1,940	1,994	2,010	934	64	2,046
CA.	21,926	22,432	27,698	31,400	32,487	33,182	33,935	19,829	751	23,467
CO	3,155	2,812	3,626	2,023	1,808	1,808	1,707	775	111	3,503
CT.	2,623	2,622	2,853	3,042	3,059	3,052	3,047	1,977	64	2,849
DE.	526	592	630	711	737	813	851	465	23	624
DC	262	243	242	239	237	219	218	161	1	396
FL.	10,950	10,369	11,781	15,057	15,691	16,374	16,474	7,075	619	14,139
GA	5,489	6,120	7,155	7,882	8,063	8,286	8,513	4,125	171	6,134
HI	771	802	738	947	948	1,009	993	514	30	863
ID	1,054	1,043	1,178	1,344	1,374	1,275	1,282	519	44	1,028
IL	7,873	8,973	8,973	9,232	9,458	9,876	9,757	5,738	308	8,190
IN	4,366	5,072	5,571	5,525	4,955	4,955	4,956	2,670	147	4,309
IA	2,632	2,814	3,106	3,369	3,398	3,346	3,360	1,715	161	2,094
KS.	2,012	2,085	2,296	2,347	2,368	2,389	2,429	871	77	2,018
KY.	2,909	2,631	2,826	3,319	3,428	3,558	3,547	1,911	62	2,933
LA.	2,995	3,286	3,557	3,767	3,819	3,873	3,927	1,884	64	3,034
ME	977	967	1,024	1,068	1,075	1,072	1,080	563	50	1,010
MD	3,607	3,654	3,848	4,120	4,322	4,488	4,510	2,639	78	3,738
MA	3,726	4,502	5,265	5,456	5,420	5,385	5,367	3,255	144	4,699
MI	7,209	7,674	8,436	8,399	8,247	8,154	8,192	4,922	267	7,059
MN	3,508	3,882	4,630	4,593	4,647	4,705	4,756	2,539	229	3,149
MS	1,875	2,144	2,200	1,964	1,978	1,998	2,008	1,127	28	1,927
MO	3,905	4,255	4,580	4,812	4,589	4,957	4,917	2,668	92	4,162
MT	783	968	1,026	1,009	1,009	1,067	949	384	20	736
NE.	1,384	1,467	1,619	1,689	1,703	1,733	1,739	801	40	1,331
NV.	853	1,047	1,220	1,281	1,349	1,367	1,424	689	61	1,662
NH	946	1,122	1,052	1,178	1,174	1,060	1,185	639	76	1,027
NJ.	5,652	5,906	6,390	6,224	6,262	5,958	6,247	3,784	163	5,782
NM	1,301	1,484	1,529	1,543	1,548	1,581	1,599	687	46	1,365
NY.	10,196	10,274	10,235	11,099	11,863	11,284	11,495	8,785	315	11,369
NC	5,162	5,682	6,223	6,198	6,148	6,301	6,317	3,569	116	6,384
ND	630	695	694	701	695	712	711	340	28	471
OH	8,410	9,810	10,467	10,636	10,634	10,829	10,848	6,297	346	7,976
OK	2,649	2,856	3,014	3,151	3,725	3,202	3,225	1,592	101	2,283
OR	2,445	2,785	3,022	3,003	2,897	2,981	3,088	1,433	96	2,827
PA.	7,971	8,481	9,260	9,821	9,864	9,894	9,938	5,756	353	8,601
RI	672	699	760	808	812	806	797	486	31	744
SC.	2,521	2,833	3,095	3,257	3,339	3,454	3,521	1,929	95	3,127
SD.	704	709	793	841	854	844	865	368	58	589
TN.	4,444	5,400	4,820	5,035	4,980	5,091	5,340	2,996	144	4,426
TX.	12,800	13,682	14,070	16,907	17,470	17,538	18,072	8,681	384	15,184
UT.	1,206	1,447	1,628	2,084	2,210	2,236	2,320	1,127	54	1,652
VT.	462	492	515	523	508	588	565	294	26	534
VA.	4,938	5,613	6,046	6,497	6,591	6,636	6,614	3,923	80	5,260
WA	4,257	4,503	5,116	5,535	5,598	5,689	5,758	3,124	205	4,880
WV	1,225	1,425	1,442	1,396	1,352	1,441	1,413	694	45	1,359
WI	3,815	3,993	4,366	4,705	4,725	4,971	5,018	2,628	325	4,066
WY	528	601	586	641	646	645	652	210	38	398

[1] Automobiles, trucks, and buses (excludes motorcycles). Excludes vehicles owned by military services. [2] Private and commercial.

Source: U.S. Federal Highway Administration, *Highway Statistics,* annual. See also <http://www.fhwa.dot.gov/policy/ohpi/hss/hsspubs.htm>.

Transportation 671

Table 1063. Roadway Congestion by Urbanized Area: 2007

[16,437 represents 16,437,000. Various federal, state, and local information sources were used to develop the data base with the primary source being the Federal Highway Administration's Highway Performance Monitoring System]

Urbanized area	Freeway daily vehicle miles of travel		Annual person hours of delay		Annual congestion cost [1]		
	Total miles (1,000)	Per lane-mile of freeway	Total hours (1,000)	Per person [2]	Per person (dol.)	Delay and fuel cost (mil. dol.)	Fuel wasted (gal. per person)
Total, average............	16,437	16,239	39,915	22	472	842	15
Akron, OH..................	5,530	12,860	3,031	5	102	63	4
Albany-Schenectady, NY........	7,005	11,390	6,082	10	220	131	6
Albuquerque, NM	4,875	14,552	11,095	19	416	244	12
Allentown-Bethlehem, PA-NJ......	4,935	11,892	7,571	12	247	154	7
Atlanta, GA	47,830	18,943	135,335	30	671	2,981	22
Austin, TX..................	9,400	16,068	22,777	22	455	471	15
Baltimore, MD................	26,670	17,096	56,964	25	550	1,276	18
Beaumont, TX	2,400	11,707	1,425	6	126	28	4
Birmingham, AL	9,715	14,287	12,605	18	373	267	12
Boston, MA-NH-RI.............	40,000	15,686	91,052	22	475	1,996	15
Bridgeport-Stamford, CT-NY	10,550	17,438	16,077	18	400	350	15
Buffalo, NY	6,760	10,400	6,185	5	119	134	3
Cape Coral, FL...............	1,845	16,773	7,451	16	331	152	9
Charleston-North, Charleston, SC. . .	3,645	13,500	9,944	21	431	207	13
Charlotte, NC-SC	11,775	14,905	24,237	23	491	525	15
Chicago, IL-IN	55,150	18,507	189,201	22	498	4,207	15
Cincinnati, OH-KY-IN	18,990	15,377	23,832	14	304	508	10
Cleveland, OH	18,120	12,851	12,037	7	134	241	5
Colorado Springs, CO	4,065	12,318	6,457	13	253	129	8
Columbus, OH	15,210	15,844	20,428	17	346	424	12
Dallas-Fort, Worth- Arlington, TX...............	55,300	17,390	140,744	32	641	2,849	22
Dayton, OH	7,360	13,027	5,800	8	161	120	5
Denver-Aurora, CO	20,395	15,934	61,345	28	569	1,240	19
Detroit, MI	32,780	17,117	116,981	29	610	2,472	19
El Paso, TX-NM	5,505	12,233	7,185	10	210	147	7
Fresno, CA	3,740	12,678	7,032	11	236	151	7
Grand Rapids, MI	5,090	11,311	7,324	12	247	148	7
Hartford, CT................	10,840	13,722	10,147	11	227	203	8
Honolulu, HI................	6,275	15,120	10,076	14	283	199	10
Houston, TX................	48,000	18,824	123,915	32	651	2,482	23
Indianapolis, IN..............	13,000	14,444	23,505	22	488	522	15
Jacksonville, FL	12,460	15,974	22,491	22	439	457	15
Kansas City, MO-KS	21,015	10,917	12,703	8	175	267	5
Las Vegas, NV	11,510	20,017	34,521	25	502	705	17
Los Angeles-Long Beach- Santa Ana, CA	140,815	23,806	485,022	38	807	10,328	29
Louisville, KY-IN	12,085	15,106	19,015	21	447	409	14
Memphis, TN-MS-AR...........	8,640	13,292	14,633	14	301	311	9
Miami, FL	41,035	19,494	145,608	27	545	2,955	19
Milwaukee, WI	11,055	14,740	14,860	10	210	307	7
Minneapolis-St. Paul, MN	28,385	17,308	55,287	22	455	1,148	15
Nashville-Davidson, TN	14,150	13,349	20,215	20	428	426	13
New Haven, CT	7,565	14,410	5,728	10	208	117	8
New Orleans, LA.............	5,340	14,240	11,327	10	222	244	6
New York-Newark, NY-NJ-CT	119,240	16,527	379,328	21	449	8,180	13
Oklahoma City, OK	9,770	12,855	12,826	15	294	257	9
Omaha, NE-IA	4,140	13,143	9,298	14	285	184	9
Orlando, FL	13,540	15,563	41,791	30	605	850	20
Oxnard-Ventura, CA	7,125	18,038	14,258	21	435	298	15
Pensacola, FL-AL	1,520	10,857	5,469	15	300	106	9
Philadelphia, PA-NJ-DE-MD	36,400	15,167	112,074	21	436	2,316	13
Phoenix, AZ................	29,450	19,186	80,456	23	552	1,891	17
Pittsburgh, PA.	12,405	9,729	15,334	8	168	304	5
Portland, OR-WA	13,625	17,357	34,418	19	395	712	13
Providence, RI-MA	11,735	12,825	19,937	16	310	386	10
Raleigh-Durham, NC	11,300	14,037	19,588	19	411	421	12
Richmond, VA...............	11,960	11,390	10,212	11	216	202	7
Riverside-San Bernardino, CA....	24,210	21,713	48,135	24	534	1,083	19
Sacramento, CA	15,955	19,339	39,197	21	433	806	15
Salem, OR.................	1,505	12,040	2,069	9	177	41	5
Salt Lake City, UT............	7,945	13,939	14,557	15	294	287	10
San Antonio, TX	18,300	16,561	31,026	21	428	621	15
San Diego, CA	38,400	19,296	85,392	29	605	1,786	22
San Francisco-Oakland, CA	49,850	20,101	129,393	29	597	2,675	21
San Jose, CA...............	16,680	18,330	51,070	30	594	1,013	21
Sarasota-Bradenton, FL........	2,575	15,606	9,030	14	264	176	8
Seattle, WA	30,670	16,578	73,636	24	513	1,591	16
St. Louis, MO-IL	29,610	12,600	32,863	15	315	697	9
Tampa-St. Petersburg, FL........	14,100	15,932	61,018	26	519	1,205	17
Toledo, OH-MI	4,025	12,015	3,916	8	160	83	5
Tucson, AZ	3,510	14,040	17,321	22	508	393	14
Tulsa, OK	7,140	9,520	9,826	12	237	192	7
Virginia Beach, VA............	13,115	13,878	24,665	16	324	501	11
Washington, DC-VA-MD........	39,045	18,817	133,862	31	638	2,762	21

[1] Value of extra time (delay) and the extra fuel consumed by vehicles traveling at slower speeds. Fuel cost per gallon is the average price for each state.   [2] The hours of extra travel time divided by the number of urban area peak period travelers. This is an annual measure indicating the sum of all extra travel time that would occur during the year for the average traveler.

Source: Texas Transportaton Institute, College Station, Texas; 2009 Urban Mobility Study (published Summer 2009) (copyright). See <http://mobility.tamu.edu/ums/>.

672   Transportation

Table 1064. **Commuting to Work by State: 2007**

[In percent, except as indicated (139,260 represents 139,260,000). **For workers 16 years old and over.** The American Community Survey universe includes the household population and the population living in institutions, college dormitories, and other group quarters. Based on a sample and subject to sampling variability; see Appendix III]

State	Total workers (1,000)	Percent of workers who—						Mean travel time to work (min.)
		Commuted by car, truck, or van		Used public transpor- tation [1]	Walked	Used other means [2]	Worked at home	
		Drove alone	Car- pooled					
U.S.	139,260	76.1	10.4	4.9	2.8	1.7	4.1	25.3
AL.	1,982	83.4	11.2	0.4	1.3	1.1	2.5	24.1
AK.	330	66.2	13.4	1.4	8.4	4.6	5.9	18.0
AZ.	2,778	74.8	13.5	2.1	2.2	2.5	4.8	25.1
AR.	1,210	80.8	12.1	0.5	1.6	1.5	3.5	21.0
CA.	16,422	73.2	11.9	5.1	2.8	2.2	4.8	27.3
CO	2,446	74.5	10.5	3.4	3.2	2.4	6.0	24.2
CT.	1,720	79.6	7.8	4.4	3.1	1.4	3.8	24.6
DE.	406	79.9	10.2	2.7	2.7	1.2	3.2	24.0
DC	290	38.2	6.8	36.4	11.1	2.5	5.0	30.1
FL.	8,173	79.6	10.5	1.9	1.6	2.1	4.2	25.9
GA	4,332	78.7	11.1	2.2	1.7	2.0	4.4	27.1
HI	627	68.0	15.2	5.6	4.4	2.6	4.2	26.4
ID	698	76.4	11.6	0.8	3.1	2.8	5.3	20.5
IL	6,008	73.7	9.3	8.8	3.1	1.5	3.7	28.2
IN	2,953	83.1	9.5	1.0	2.1	1.2	3.2	22.7
IA	1,509	78.7	10.2	1.1	3.9	1.3	4.9	18.3
KS.	1,375	81.3	9.6	0.5	2.7	1.4	4.4	18.8
KY.	1,864	81.3	11.0	1.2	2.2	1.2	3.2	22.2
LA.	1,849	80.9	11.2	1.1	2.0	1.9	2.7	24.9
ME	643	79.2	9.8	0.6	4.1	1.5	4.8	22.7
MD	2,783	74.3	10.2	8.4	2.6	0.9	3.6	31.1
MA	3,182	73.0	8.1	9.1	4.3	1.5	4.0	27.4
MI	4,401	83.1	8.9	1.2	2.3	1.2	3.4	23.9
MN	2,681	77.8	9.3	3.2	3.1	1.6	5.1	22.3
MS	1,183	82.7	11.1	0.4	1.8	1.6	2.4	23.9
MO	2,752	80.7	10.4	1.5	2.0	1.3	4.1	23.5
MT	461	73.7	10.5	1.3	4.8	2.5	7.2	17.6
NE.	908	79.9	9.2	0.7	3.0	1.6	5.6	17.6
NV.	1,223	77.8	11.5	3.4	2.3	1.9	3.0	23.5
NH	678	81.4	8.4	0.7	3.4	1.2	5.0	25.3
NJ.	4,123	71.8	9.2	10.4	3.2	2.1	3.3	29.8
NM	867	77.2	12.4	1.0	2.2	1.9	5.2	21.5
NY.	8,817	54.1	7.4	26.5	6.3	1.9	3.8	31.5
NC	4,163	79.8	11.9	0.9	1.9	1.5	3.9	23.3
ND	336	78.6	9.3	0.5	4.4	1.5	5.7	16.1
OH	5,288	83.0	8.2	1.9	2.3	1.1	3.5	22.8
OK	1,637	80.5	11.9	0.5	1.9	1.3	3.9	20.6
OR	1,757	73.2	11.3	3.7	3.6	2.8	5.4	22.1
PA	5,746	76.7	9.4	5.1	4.0	1.2	3.6	25.4
RI	503	80.7	8.8	2.7	3.4	1.2	3.3	23.0
SC.	1,964	81.1	11.0	0.7	1.8	1.4	3.9	23.2
SD.	406	77.3	10.1	0.4	4.6	1.4	6.2	16.3
TN.	2,775	83.4	10.0	0.8	1.4	1.0	3.4	23.8
TX.	10,743	78.9	12.2	1.7	1.8	1.9	3.6	25.0
UT.	1,245	74.9	13.0	2.4	2.6	1.8	5.3	21.4
VT.	326	74.6	10.4	0.9	6.2	1.5	6.4	21.2
VA.	3,791	77.5	10.8	3.8	2.2	1.3	4.5	26.8
WA	3,089	73.1	11.4	5.4	3.4	1.8	4.8	25.9
WV	738	81.2	11.0	1.2	2.6	1.3	2.8	25.5
WI	2,808	79.8	9.4	1.7	3.3	1.7	4.0	21.4
WY	274	74.8	13.2	1.5	4.0	2.0	4.6	18.6

[1] Excluding taxicabs.   [2] Includes taxicabs, motorcycles, bicycles, and other means.

Source: U.S. Census Bureau; 2007 American Community Survey; B08006. Sex of Worker by Means of Transportation to Work; and R0801. Mean Travel Time to Work of Workers 16 Years Old and Over Who Did Not Work At Home (minutes); using American FactFinder; <http://factfinder.census.gov/> (published 23 September 2008).

Transportation   673

Table 1065. **Motor Vehicle Distance Traveled by Type of Vehicle: 1970 to 2007**

[1,110 represents 1,110,000,000,000. The travel data by vehicle type and stratification of trucks are estimated by the Federal Highway Administration (FHWA)]

Year	Vehicle-miles of travel (bil.)					Average miles traveled per vehicle (1,000)				
	Total [1]	Cars [1]	Buses [2]	Vans, pickups, SUVs [3]	Trucks [4]	Total [1]	Cars [1]	Buses [2]	Vans, pickups, SUVs [3]	Trucks [4]
1970 . . .	1,110	920	4.5	123	62	10.0	10.0	12.0	8.7	13.6
1980 . . .	1,527	1,122	6.1	291	108	9.5	8.8	11.5	10.4	18.7
1985 . . .	1,775	1,256	4.5	391	124	10.0	9.4	7.5	10.5	20.6
1987 . . .	1,921	1,325	5.3	457	134	10.5	9.7	8.9	11.1	23.3
1988 . . .	2,026	1,380	5.5	502	138	10.7	10.0	8.9	11.5	22.5
1989 . . .	2,096	1,412	5.7	536	143	10.9	10.2	9.1	11.7	22.9
1990 . . .	2,144	1,418	5.7	575	146	11.1	10.3	9.1	11.9	23.6
1991 . . .	2,172	1,367	5.8	649	150	11.3	10.3	9.1	12.2	24.2
1992 . . .	2,247	1,381	5.8	707	153	11.6	10.6	9.0	12.4	25.4
1993 . . .	2,296	1,385	6.1	746	160	11.6	10.5	9.4	12.4	26.3
1994 . . .	2,358	1,416	6.4	765	170	11.7	10.8	9.6	12.2	25.8
1995 . . .	2,423	1,438	6.4	790	178	11.8	11.2	9.4	12.0	26.5
1996 . . .	2,486	1,470	6.6	817	183	11.8	11.3	9.4	11.8	26.1
1997 . . .	2,562	1,503	6.8	851	191	12.1	11.6	9.8	12.1	27.0
1998 . . .	2,632	1,550	7.0	868	196	12.2	11.8	9.8	12.2	25.4
1999 . . .	2,691	1,569	7.7	901	203	12.2	11.9	10.5	12.0	26.0
2000 . . .	2,747	1,600	7.6	923	206	12.2	11.9	10.2	11.7	25.7
2001 . . .	2,797	1,628	7.1	943	209	11.9	11.8	9.4	11.2	26.6
2002 . . .	2,856	1,658	6.8	966	215	12.2	12.2	9.0	11.4	27.1
2003 . . .	2,890	1,672	6.8	984	218	12.2	12.3	8.7	11.3	28.1
2004 . . .	2,965	1,700	6.8	1,027	221	12.2	12.5	8.5	11.2	27.0
2005 . . .	2,989	1,708	7.0	1,041	223	12.1	12.5	8.6	10.9	26.2
2006 . . .	3,014	1,691	6.8	1,082	223	12.0	12.5	8.3	10.9	25.1
2007 . . .	3,030	1,671	7.0	1,111	227	11.9	12.3	8.4	11.0	25.2

[1] Motorcycles included with cars through 1994; thereafter in total, not shown separately.   [2] Includes school buses.   [3] SUV = Sport utility vehicles.   [4] Includes combinations.

Source: U.S. Federal Highway Administration, *Highway Statistics*, annual. See also <http://www.fhwa.dot.gov/policy/ohpi/hss/hsspubs.htm>.

Table 1066. **Domestic Motor Fuel Consumption by Type of Vehicle: 1970 to 2007**

[92.3 represents 92,300,000,000. Comprises all fuel types used for propulsion of vehicles under state motor fuels laws. Excludes federal purchases for military use. Minus sign (−) indicates decrease]

Year	Annual fuel consumption (bil. gal.)						Average miles per gallon				
	All vehicles [1]	Annual percent change [2]	Cars [1]	Buses [3]	Vans, pickups, SUVs [4]	Trucks [5]	All vehicles [1]	Cars [1]	Buses [3]	Vans, pickups, SUVs [4]	Trucks [5]
1970	92.3	4.8	67.8	0.8	12.3	11.3	12.0	13.5	5.5	10.0	5.5
1980	115.0	−5.9	70.2	1.0	23.8	20.0	13.3	16.0	6.0	12.2	5.4
1985	121.3	2.2	71.7	0.8	27.4	21.4	14.6	17.5	5.4	14.3	5.8
1987	127.5	1.8	73.5	0.9	30.6	22.5	15.1	18.0	5.8	14.9	5.9
1988	130.1	2.0	73.5	0.9	32.7	22.9	15.6	18.8	5.8	15.4	6.0
1989	131.9	1.4	74.1	0.9	33.3	23.5	15.9	18.0	6.0	16.1	6.1
1990	130.8	−0.8	69.8	0.9	35.6	24.5	16.4	20.3	6.4	16.1	6.0
1991	128.6	−1.7	64.5	0.9	38.2	25.0	16.9	21.2	6.7	17.0	6.0
1992	132.9	3.3	65.6	0.9	40.9	25.5	16.9	21.0	6.6	17.3	6.0
1993	137.3	3.3	67.2	0.9	42.9	26.2	16.7	20.6	6.6	17.4	6.1
1994	140.8	2.5	68.1	1.0	44.1	27.7	16.7	20.8	6.6	17.3	6.1
1995	143.8	2.1	68.1	1.0	45.6	29.0	16.8	21.1	6.6	17.3	6.1
1996	147.4	2.5	69.2	1.0	47.4	29.6	16.9	21.2	6.6	17.2	6.2
1997	150.4	2.0	69.9	1.0	49.4	29.9	17.0	21.5	6.7	17.2	6.4
1998	155.4	3.3	71.7	1.1	50.5	32.0	16.9	21.6	6.7	17.2	6.1
1999	161.4	3.9	73.2	1.1	52.8	33.9	16.7	21.4	6.7	17.0	6.0
2000	162.5	0.7	73.1	1.1	52.9	35.2	16.9	21.9	6.8	17.4	5.8
2001	163.5	0.6	73.6	1.0	53.5	35.2	17.1	22.1	6.9	17.6	5.9
2002	168.7	3.2	75.5	1.0	55.2	36.8	16.9	22.0	6.8	17.5	5.8
2003	170.0	0.8	75.5	1.0	60.7	32.7	17.0	22.2	7.0	16.2	6.7
2004	173.5	2.1	75.4	1.3	63.4	33.1	17.1	22.5	5.0	16.2	6.7
2005	174.8	0.7	77.4	1.1	58.9	37.2	17.2	22.1	6.2	17.7	6.0
2006	175.0	0.1	75.0	1.1	60.7	38.0	17.2	22.5	5.9	17.8	5.9
2007	176.1	0.6	74.4	1.1	61.8	38.6	17.2	22.5	6.1	18.0	5.9

[1] Motorcycles included with cars through 1994; thereafter in total, not shown separately.   [2] Change from immediate prior year.   [3] Includes school buses.   [4] SUV = Sport utility vehicles.   [5] Includes combinations.

Source: U.S. Federal Highway Administration, *Highway Statistics*, annual. See also <http://www.fhwa.dot.gov/policy/ohpi/hss/hsspubs.htm>.

674   Transportation

Table 1067. **Motor Vehicle Accidents—Number and Deaths: 1980 to 2007**

[17.9 represents 17,900,000]

Item	Unit	1980	1990	1995	2000	2003	2004	2005	2006	2007
ACCIDENTS										
Motor vehicle accidents [1]	Million . . .	17.9	11.5	10.7	13.4	11.8	10.9	10.7	10.4	10.6
DEATHS										
Motor vehicle deaths within 1 yr. [2] . . .	1,000 . . .	53.2	46.8	43.4	43.4	44.1	44.9	45.3	44.6	43.1
Noncollision accidents	1,000 . . .	(NA)	4.9	4.4	4.8	5.1	5.1	5.3	5.3	5.2
Collision accidents:										
With other motor vehicles	1,000 . . .	23.0	19.9	19.0	19.1	19.8	19.6	19.4	18.5	17.2
With pedestrians	1,000 . . .	9.7	7.3	6.4	5.9	5.7	6.0	6.2	6.1	5.9
With fixed objects.	1,000 . . .	(NA)	13.1	12.1	12.3	12.4	13.0	13.3	13.4	13.5
Deaths within 30 days [3]	1,000 . . .	51.1	44.6	41.8	41.9	42.9	42.8	43.5	42.7	41.1
Occupants	1,000 . . .	36.8	33.9	33.1	33.5	33.6	33.3	33.1	32.1	30.4
Passenger cars	1,000 . . .	27.4	24.1	22.4	20.7	19.7	19.2	18.5	17.9	16.5
Light trucks [4]	1,000 . . .	7.5	8.6	9.6	11.5	12.5	12.7	13.0	12.8	12.4
Large trucks [4]	1,000 . . .	1.3	0.7	0.6	0.8	0.7	0.8	0.8	0.8	0.8
Buses	1,000 . . .	(Z)	(Z)	(Z)	(Z)	(Z)	0.0	0.1	(Z)	(Z)
Other/unknown	1,000 . . .	0.5	0.5	0.4	0.5	0.6	0.6	0.7	0.6	0.6
Motorcycle riders [5]	1,000 . . .	5.1	3.2	2.2	2.9	3.7	4.0	4.6	4.8	5.2
Nonoccupants.	1,000 . . .	9.2	7.5	6.5	5.6	5.5	5.5	5.9	5.8	5.5
Pedestrians.	1,000 . . .	8.1	6.5	5.6	4.8	4.8	4.7	4.9	4.8	4.7
Pedalcyclist.	1,000 . . .	1.0	0.9	0.8	0.7	0.6	0.7	0.8	0.8	0.7
Other/unknown	1,000 . . .	0.1	0.1	0.1	0.1	0.1	0.1	0.2	0.2	0.2
Traffic death rates: [3, 6]										
Per 100 million vehicle miles	Rate	3.3	2.1	1.7	1.5	1.5	1.4	1.5	1.4	1.4
Per 100,000 licensed drivers	Rate	35.2	26.7	23.7	22.0	21.9	21.5	21.7	21.1	20.0
Per 100,000 registered vehicles . . .	Rate	34.8	24.2	21.2	19.3	18.6	18.0	17.7	17.0	16.1
Per 100,000 resident population. . .	Rate	22.5	17.9	15.9	14.9	14.8	14.6	14.7	14.3	13.6

NA Not available.   Z Fewer than 50.   [1] Covers only accidents occurring on the road. Data are estimated. Year-to-year comparisons should be made with caution.   [2] Deaths that occur within 1 year of accident. Includes collision categories not shown separately.   [3] Within 30 days of accident. Source: U.S. National Highway Traffic Safety Administration, *Traffic Safety Facts*, annual; and unpublished data. See Internet site <http://www-nrd.nhtsa.dot.gov/CATS/index.aspx>.   [4] See footnotes 2 and 3 in Table 1071.   [5] Includes motorized cycles.   [6] Based on 30-day definition of traffic deaths.

Source: Except as noted, National Safety Council, Itasca, IL, *Injury Facts*, annual (copyright). See <http://www.nsc.org/>.

Table 1068. **Traffic Fatalities by State: 1990 to 2007**

[For deaths within 30 days of the accident]

State	1990	2000	2005	2007	Fatality rate [1] 1990	Fatality rate [1] 2007	State	1990	2000	2005	2007	Fatality rate [1] 1990	Fatality rate [1] 2007
U.S...	**44,599**	**41,945**	**43,510**	**41,059**	**2.1**	**1.4**	MO	1,097	1,157	1,257	992	2.2	1.4
AL	1,121	996	1,148	1,110	2.6	1.8	MT	212	237	251	277	2.5	2.5
AK	98	106	73	84	2.5	1.6	NE	262	276	276	256	1.9	1.3
AZ	869	1,036	1,179	1,066	2.5	1.7	NV	343	323	427	373	3.4	1.7
AR	604	652	654	650	2.9	2.0	NH	158	126	166	129	1.6	1.0
CA	5,192	3,753	4,333	3,974	2.0	1.2	NJ. . . .	886	731	747	724	1.5	1.0
CO	544	681	606	554	2.0	1.1	NM	499	432	488	413	3.1	1.5
CT	385	341	278	277	1.5	0.9	NY	2,217	1,460	1,434	1,333	2.1	1.0
DE	138	123	133	117	2.1	1.2	NC	1,385	1,557	1,547	1,675	2.2	1.6
DC	48	48	48	44	1.4	1.2	ND	112	86	123	111	1.9	1.4
FL.	2,891	2,999	3,518	3,214	2.6	1.6	OH	1,638	1,366	1,321	1,257	1.8	1.1
GA	1,562	1,541	1,729	1,641	2.2	1.5	OK	641	650	803	754	1.9	1.6
HI	177	132	140	138	2.2	1.3	OR	579	451	487	455	2.2	1.3
ID	244	276	275	252	2.5	1.6	PA	1,646	1,520	1,616	1,491	1.9	1.4
IL	1,589	1,418	1,363	1,249	1.9	1.2	RI	84	80	87	69	1.1	0.8
IN	1,049	886	938	898	2.0	1.3	SC	979	1,065	1,094	1,066	2.8	2.1
IA	465	445	450	445	2.0	1.4	SD	153	173	186	146	2.2	1.6
KS	444	461	428	416	1.9	1.4	TN	1,177	1,307	1,270	1,210	2.5	1.7
KY	849	820	985	864	2.5	1.8	TX	3,250	3,779	3,536	3,363	2.1	1.4
LA	959	938	963	985	2.5	2.2	UT	272	373	282	299	1.9	1.1
ME	213	169	169	183	1.8	1.2	VT	90	76	73	66	1.5	0.9
MD	707	588	614	614	1.7	1.1	VA	1,079	929	947	1,027	1.8	1.3
MA	605	433	441	417	1.3	0.8	WA	825	631	649	568	1.8	1.0
MI	1,571	1,382	1,129	1,088	1.9	1.0	WV	481	411	374	431	3.1	2.1
MN	566	625	559	504	1.5	0.9	WI. . . .	769	799	815	756	1.7	1.3
MS	750	949	931	884	3.1	2.0	WY	125	152	170	150	2.1	1.6

[1] Deaths per 100 million vehicle miles traveled.

Source: U.S. National Highway Traffic Safety Administration, *Traffic Safety Facts*, annual. See <http://www-nrd.nhtsa.dot.gov /CATS/index.aspx>.

Transportation   675

Table 1069. Fatal Motor Vehicle Accidents—National Summary: 1990 to 2007

[Based on data from the Fatality Analysis Reporting System (FARS). FARS gathers data on accidents that result in loss of human life. FARS is operated and maintained by National Highway Traffic Safety Administration's (NHTSA), National Center for Statistics and Analysis (NCSA). FARS data are gathered on motor vehicle accidents that occurred on a roadway customarily open to the public, resulting in the death of a person within 30 days of the accident. Collection of these data depend on the use of police, hospital, medical examiner/coroner, and Emergency Medical Services reports; state vehicle registration, driver licensing, and highway department files; and vital statistics documents and death certificates. See source for further detail]

Item	1990	1995	2000	2003	2004	2005	2006	2007
Fatal crashes, total	**39,836**	**37,241**	**37,526**	**38,477**	**38,444**	**39,252**	**38,648**	**37,428**
One vehicle involved	23,445	21,250	21,117	21,775	21,836	22,678	22,701	22,054
Two or more vehicles involved.	16,391	15,991	16,409	16,702	16,608	16,574	15,947	15,194
Persons killed in fatal crashes [1]	**44,599**	**41,817**	**41,945**	**42,884**	**42,836**	**43,510**	**42,708**	**41,059**
Occupants	37,134	35,291	36,348	37,341	37,304	37,646	36,956	30,401
Drivers.	25,750	24,390	25,567	26,779	26,871	27,491	27,348	26,480
Passengers	11,276	10,782	10,695	10,458	10,355	10,069	9,507	8,977
Other	108	119	86	104	78	86	101	98
Nonoccupants	7,465	6,526	5,597	5,543	5,532	5,864	5,752	5,504
Pedestrians	6,482	5,584	4,763	4,774	4,675	4,892	4,795	4,654
Pedalcyclists.	859	833	693	629	727	786	772	698
Other	124	109	141	140	130	186	185	152
Occupants killed by vehicle type:								
Passenger cars	24,092	22,423	20,699	19,725	19,192	18,512	17,925	16,520
Mini–compact (95 inches)	3,556	2,207	1,113	636	599	452	416	346
Subcompact (95 to 99 inches)	4,753	4,584	3,660	3,081	2,718	2,536	2,228	1,915
Compact (100 to 104 inches)	5,310	6,899	7,022	6,769	6,650	6,288	6,015	5,501
Intermediate (105 to 109) inches	4,849	4,666	5,204	5,583	5,667	5,571	5,461	5,195
Full-size (110 to 114) inches	2,386	2,116	2,287	2,451	2,354	2,491	2,520	2,396
Largest (115 inches and over)	2,249	1,297	897	782	807	796	773	774
Unknown	989	654	516	423	397	378	422	393
Motorcycles and Other Motorized Cycles . .	3,129	2,114	2,897	3,714	4,028	4,576	4,837	5,154
Motorcycles	3,014	2,001	2,783	3,583	3,827	4,418	4,679	4,973
Other motorized cycles	115	113	114	131	201	158	158	181
Light trucks [2]	8,601	9,568	11,526	12,546	12,674	13,037	12,761	12,413
Pickup.	5,979	5,938	6,003	5,957	5,838	6,067	5,993	5,830
Utility.	1,214	1,935	3,358	4,483	4,760	4,831	4,928	4,809
Van	1,154	1,639	2,129	2,080	2,046	2,112	1,815	1,760
Other	254	56	36	26	30	27	25	14
Large trucks [3]	705	648	754	726	766	804	805	802
Medium trucks	134	96	106	82	99	118	107	111
Heavy trucks	571	552	648	644	667	686	698	691
Buses.	32	33	22	41	42	58	27	37
Other vehicles	296	307	401	477	512	492	500	539
Unknown.	164	85	49	112	90	167	101	90
Persons involved in fatal crashes.	**107,777**	**102,102**	**100,716**	**101,862**	**100,760**	**101,262**	**98,356**	**93,722**
Occupants	99,297	94,621	94,325	95,470	94,579	94,614	91,860	87,581
Drivers.	58,893	56,164	57,280	58,517	58,395	59,220	57,846	55,681
Passengers	40,229	38,252	36,889	36,743	35,992	35,231	33,826	31,701
Other	175	205	156	210	192	163	188	199
Nonoccupants	8,480	7,481	6,391	6,392	6,181	6,648	6,496	6,141
Vehicle miles traveled (VMT) (bil.) [5]	2,144	2,423	2,747	2,890	2,965	2,989	3,014	3,030
Licensed drivers (1,000)	167,015	176,628	190,625	196,166	198,889	200,549	212,810	205,742
Registered vehicles (1,000)	184,275	197,065	217,028	230,788	237,949	245,628	251,415	255,748
Percent distribution of fatal crashes by the highest driver (BAC) in accident: [4]								
0.00 percent	54.0	62.1	62.7	64.1	64.3	63.3	62.6	62.5
0.01 to 0.07 percent	6.3	5.5	5.6	5.3	5.1	5.4	5.7	5.7
0.08 percent and over	39.4	32.1	31.4	30.3	30.4	31.1	31.4	31.6
Percent distribution of fatal crashes by the highest (BAC): [4]								
0.00 percent	49.5	57.7	58.7	60.2	60.5	59.5	58.4	58.4
0.01 to 0.07 percent	6.5	5.7	5.9	5.6	5.4	5.6	6.0	5.9
0.08 percent and over	44.0	36.7	35.4	34.3	34.2	34.9	35.6	35.7
Fatalities per 100,000 resident population .								
Under 5 years old	4.90	4.30	3.70	3.06	3.16	2.94	2.83	2.45
5 to 9 years old	5.14	4.48	3.55	3.01	3.13	3.00	2.64	2.37
10 to 15 years old	7.60	7.23	5.65	5.45	5.43	4.67	4.33	4.25
16 to 20 years old.	36.66	31.59	29.38	29.48	28.80	27.48	26.79	24.97
21 to 24 years old	33.47	29.68	27.02	26.50	26.66	27.73	27.99	26.86
25 to 34 years old	22.78	19.44	17.29	16.96	17.28	17.82	17.88	16.74
35 to 44 years old	16.11	15.10	15.08	15.27	14.55	15.08	14.68	14.09
45 to 54 years old	14.83	13.39	13.79	14.27	14.47	14.59	14.43	13.97
55 to 64 years old	15.00	13.92	13.61	13.59	13.19	13.88	13.29	12.54
65 to 74 years old	17.03	16.64	15.29	14.92	14.87	15.16	13.84	13.45
75 years old and over	25.45	26.09	23.29	22.51	21.36	20.47	18.69	17.97
Fatalities per 100 million VMT [5]	2.1	1.7	1.5	1.5	1.4	1.5	1.4	1.4
Fatalities per 100,000 licensed drivers	26.7	23.7	22.0	21.9	21.5	21.7	21.1	20.0
VMT [5] per registered vehicle	11,637	12,294	12,657	12,522	12,461	12,168	11,990	11,847
Fatalities per 100,000 registered vehicles . .	24.2	21.2	19.3	18.6	18.0	17.7	17.0	16.1
Fatal crashes per 100 million VMT [5]	2.08	1.73	1.53	1.5	1.44	1.5	1.4	1.4
Involved vehicles per fatal crash	1.5	1.5	1.5	1.5	1.4	1.5	1.5	1.5
Fatalities per 100,000 resident population .	17.9	15.9	14.9	14.8	14.6	14.7	14.4	13.6

[1] Deaths within 30 days of the accident. [2] Trucks with a gross vehicle weight rating of 10,000 pounds or less, including pickups, vans, truck-based station wagons, and utility vehicles. [3] Trucks with a gross vehicle weight rating of over 10,000 pounds. [4] BAC = blood alcohol concentration. [5] VMT = vehicle miles of travel.

Source: U.S. National Highway Traffic Safety Administration, *Fatality Analysis Reporting System*, annual. See also <http://www-nrd.nhtsa.dot.gov/CATS/index.aspx>.

Table 1070. **Motor Vehicle Occupants and Nonoccupants Killed and Injured: 1980 to 2007**

[For deaths within 30 days of the accident. (3,231 represents 3,231,000)]

Year	Total	Occupants						Motor-cycle riders [3]	Nonoccupants			
		Total	Pas-senger cars	Light trucks [1]	Large trucks [1]	Buses	Other/unknown [2]		Total	Pedes-trian	Pedal-cyclist	Other/unknown [2]
KILLED												
1980	51,091	36,783	27,449	7,486	1,262	46	540	5,144	9,164	8,070	965	129
1985	43,825	31,479	23,212	6,689	977	57	544	4,564	7,782	6,808	890	84
1990	44,599	33,890	24,092	8,601	705	32	460	3,244	7,465	6,482	859	124
1995	41,817	33,064	22,423	9,568	648	33	392	2,227	6,526	5,584	833	109
1997	42,013	33,609	22,199	10,249	723	18	420	2,116	6,288	5,321	814	153
1998	41,501	33,088	21,194	10,705	742	38	409	2,294	6,119	5,228	760	131
1999	41,717	33,392	20,862	11,265	759	59	447	2,483	5,842	4,939	754	149
2000	41,945	33,451	20,699	11,526	754	22	450	2,897	5,597	4,763	693	141
2001	42,196	33,243	20,320	11,723	708	34	458	3,197	5,756	4,901	732	123
2002	43,005	34,105	20,569	12,274	689	45	528	3,270	5,630	4,851	665	114
2003	42,884	33,627	19,725	12,546	726	41	589	3,714	5,543	4,774	629	140
2004	42,836	33,276	19,192	12,674	766	42	602	4,028	5,532	4,675	727	130
2005	43,510	33,070	18,512	13,037	804	58	659	4,576	5,864	4,892	786	186
2006	42,708	32,119	17,925	12,761	805	27	601	4,837	5,752	4,795	772	185
2007	41,059	30,401	16,520	12,413	802	37	629	5,154	5,504	4,654	698	152
INJURED (1,000)												
1990	3,231	2,960	2,376	505	42	33	4	84	187	105	75	7
1995	3,465	3,246	2,469	722	30	19	4	57	162	86	67	10
1997	3,348	3,149	2,341	755	31	17	6	53	146	77	58	11
1998	3,192	3,012	2,201	763	29	16	4	49	131	69	53	8
1999	3,236	3,047	2,138	847	33	22	7	50	140	85	51	3
2000	3,189	2,997	2,052	887	31	18	10	58	134	78	51	5
2001	3,033	2,841	1,927	861	29	15	9	60	131	78	45	8
2002	2,926	2,735	1,805	879	26	19	6	65	126	71	48	7
2003	2,889	2,697	1,756	889	27	18	7	67	124	70	46	8
2004	2,788	2,594	1,643	900	27	16	7	76	118	68	41	9
2005	2,699	2,494	1,573	872	27	11	10	87	118	64	45	8
2006	2,575	2,375	1,475	857	23	10	11	88	112	61	44	7
2007	2,491	2,264	1,379	841	23	12	8	103	124	70	43	10

[1] See footnotes 2 and 3 in Table 1071. [2] Includes combination trucks. [3] Includes motorized cycles.

Source: U.S. National Highway Traffic Safety Administration, *Traffic Safety Facts*, annual; and unpublished data. See <http://www-nrd.nhtsa.dot.gov/CATS/index.aspx>.

Table 1071. **Vehicles Involved in Crashes by Vehicle Type, Rollover Occurrence, and Crash Severity: 2007**

[10,427.9 represents 10,427,900. Excludes motorcycles]

Crash severity by vehicle type	Total		Rollover occurrence			
			Yes		No	
	Number (1,000)	Percent	Number (1,000)	Percent	Number (1,000)	Percent
Vehicles involved in all crashes [1]	10,427.9	100.0	282.3	2.7	10,145.6	97.3
Passenger cars	5,745.4	100.0	104.6	1.8	5,640.8	98.2
Light trucks: [2]						
Pickup.	1,560.3	100.0	63.7	4.1	1,496.6	95.9
Utility	1,773.5	100.0	82.2	4.6	1,691.4	95.4
Van.	759.7	100.0	12.7	1.7	747.0	98.3
Other	98.2	100.0	1.1	1.2	97.0	98.8
Large truck [3]	413.4	100.0	14.7	3.5	398.8	96.5
Bus	56.8	100.0	(Z)	0.2	56.6	99.8
Other/unknown.	20.6	100.0	3.1	15.1	17.5	84.9
Fatal crashes	50.6	100.0	10.9	21.5	39.8	78.5
Passenger cars	22.7	100.0	3.8	16.8	18.9	83.2
Light trucks: [2]						
Pickup.	10.3	100.0	2.8	27.6	7.4	72.4
Utility	8.2	100.0	2.8	33.7	5.4	66.3
Van.	3.2	100.0	0.6	17.1	2.7	82.9
Other	0.1	100.0	(Z)	15.1	(Z)	84.9
Large truck [3]	4.6	100.0	0.6	13.9	3.9	86.1
Bus	0.3	100.0	(Z)	5.4	0.3	94.6
Other/unknown.	1.4	100.0	0.3	19.2	1.1	80.8

Z Less than 50. [1] Includes injury and property-only crashes, not shown separately. [2] Trucks of 10,000 pounds gross vehicle weight rating or less, including pickups, vans, truck-based station wagons and utility vehicles. [3] Trucks over 10,000 pounds gross vehicle weight rating.

Source: U.S. National Highway Traffic Safety Administration, *Traffic Safety Facts,* annual. See <http://www-nrd.nhtsa.dot.gov/CATS/index.aspx>.

Table 1072. Speeding-Related Traffic Fatalities by Road Type, Speed Limit, and State: 2007

[Speeding consists of exceeding the posted speed limit or driving too fast for the road conditions or any speed-related violation charged (racing, driving above speed limit, speed greater than reasonable, exceeding special speed limit)]

State	Traffic fatalities, total	Total [1]	Interstate Over 55 mph	Interstate At or under 55 mph	Noninterstate 55 mph	50 mph	45 mph	40 mph	35 mph	Under 35 mph
United States.....	41,059	13,040	1,204	353	3,386	464	1,798	917	1,517	1,485
Alabama.........	1,110	497	38	8	118	9	158	45	47	29
Alaska..........	84	20	1	–	6	–	3	4	–	4
Arizona...........	1,066	447	65	15	41	21	81	53	53	40
Arkansas.........	650	64	5	–	27	1	5	2	10	7
California.........	3,974	1,464	194	18	340	49	150	126	190	176
Colorado.........	554	224	16	11	30	16	28	31	34	24
Connecticut.......	277	94	9	6	3	2	10	16	18	26
Delaware.........	117	44	1	–	3	24	5	5	4	2
District of Columbia ...	44	8	–	2	–	–	–	–	–	6
Florida............	3,214	611	52	12	82	16	123	56	78	106
Georgia...........	1,641	384	24	14	117	7	58	12	68	28
Hawaii...........	138	69	1	5	7	–	8	–	19	23
Idaho	252	77	21	–	14	12	6	1	5	2
Illinois...........	1,249	523	64	26	176	6	44	38	59	107
Indiana	898	199	26	4	62	9	32	10	26	25
Iowa............	445	38	2	2	16	4	4	–	5	4
Kansas..........	416	112	12	–	33	4	4	7	4	17
Kentucky.........	864	132	6	2	85	–	10	–	22	4
Louisiana.........	985	251	19	5	96	7	38	17	31	25
Maine	183	86	3	–	6	14	20	8	15	12
Maryland.........	614	216	5	20	20	36	11	43	38	42
Massachusetts	417	140	18	5	8	4	8	18	19	55
Michigan..........	1,088	242	14	8	119	7	29	6	17	31
Minnesota	504	108	8	2	15	–	–	–	–	–
Mississippi........	884	349	38	4	131	14	61	14	28	19
Missouri..........	992	434	37	15	149	10	28	14	53	43
Montana	277	96	13	1	6	–	11	1	10	8
Nebraska.........	256	44	8	–	9	11	3	–	4	5
Nevada..........	373	97	2	–	2	–	25	1	36	12
New Hampshire	129	41	5	2	2	3	1	6	12	8
New Jersey	724	61	2	1	2	13	10	4	8	13
New Mexico........	413	159	19	2	25	5	17	7	15	20
New York.........	1,333	417	11	9	157	2	32	28	20	50
North Carolina	1,675	620	34	6	331	14	146	2	63	14
North Dakota	111	45	4	–	15	–	5	1	2	6
Ohio............	1,257	277	30	5	133	6	22	6	38	26
Oklahoma	754	209	34	3	24	5	45	10	14	13
Oregon..........	455	121	3	1	55	2	14	12	11	8
Pennsylvania	1,491	783	52	47	189	8	149	98	128	89
Rhode Island	69	14	–	–	–	–	1	1	–	5
South Carolina	1,066	454	48	5	144	14	74	26	46	38
South Dakota	146	49	7	–	16	1	6	1	11	1
Tennessee........	1,210	268	14	9	57	10	59	32	37	41
Texas	3,363	1,343	127	45	173	40	117	93	110	132
Utah	299	110	27	1	10	3	10	16	6	11
Vermont	66	23	2	–	2	6	–	7	2	4
Virginia	1027	341	32	22	156	6	56	7	22	23
Washington	568	224	16	3	22	39	13	14	54	32
West Virginia	431	76	7	–	20	3	9	6	8	14
Wisconsin	756	279	11	7	130	1	40	8	17	48
Wyoming..........	150	56	17	–	2	–	6	4	–	7

– Represents zero.   [1] Includes fatalities that occurred on roads for which the speed limit was unknown.

Source: U.S. National Highway Traffic Safety Administration, *Traffic Safety Facts, Speeding,* DOT HS 810 998, annual. See <http://www-nrd.nhtsa.dot.gov/CATS/index.aspx>.

Table 1073. **Fatalities by Highest Driver Blood Alcohol Concentration (BAC) in the Crash: 1990 to 2007**

[g/dl means grams per deciliter. A motor vehicle crash is considered to be alcohol-impaired if at least one driver involved in the crash is determined to have had a BAC of .08 g/dL or higher. Thus, any fatality that occurs in an alcohol-impaired crash is considered an alcohol-impaired-driving fatality. The term alcohol-impaired does not indicate that a crash or fatality was caused by the presence of alcohol. A person is considered to be legally impaired with a BAC of .08 g/dl or more]

Item	1990	1995	2000	2003	2004	2005	2006	2007
Total Fatalities	**44,599**	**41,817**	**41,945**	**42,884**	**42,836**	**43,510**	**42,708**	**41,059**
BAC=.00								
Number	23,823	25,768	26,082	27,328	27,413	27,423	26,633	25,555
Percent	53.4	61.6	62.2	63.7	64.0	63.0	62.4	62.2
BAC=.01-.07								
Number	2,901	2,416	2,422	2,327	2,212	2,404	2,479	2,388
Percent	6.5	5.8	5.8	5.4	5.2	5.5	5.8	5.8
Alcohol-Impaired-Driving Fatalities BAC=.08+								
Number	17,705	13,478	13,324	13,096	13,099.0	13,582.0	13,491	12,998
Percent	39.7	32.2	31.8	30.5	30.6	31.2	31.6	31.7

Source: U.S. National Highway Traffic Safety Administration, *Traffic Safety Facts*, annual; and unpublished data. See also <http://www-nrd.nhtsa.dot.gov/CATS/index.aspx>.

Table 1074. **Traffic Fatalities by State and Highest Driver Blood Alcohol Concentration (BAC) in the Crash: 2007**

[See headnote, Table 1073]

State	Traffic fatalities, total	BAC = 0.00		BAC = 0.01-0.07		Alcohol impaired driving fatalities (BAC = 0.08 or more)		BAC = 0.01 or more	
		Number	Percent	Number	Percent	Number	Percent	Number	Percent
United States . . .	**41,059**	**25,555**	**62**	**2,388**	**6**	**12,998**	**32**	**15,387**	**37**
Alabama	1,110	653	59	67	6	389	35	456	41
Alaska	84	49	58	5	6	30	36	35	42
Arizona	1,066	649	61	61	6	336	32	396	37
Arkansas	650	424	65	44	7	182	28	226	35
California	3,974	2,564	65	251	6	1,155	29	1,405	35
Colorado	554	355	64	29	5	170	31	199	36
Connecticut	277	157	57	18	7	101	36	119	43
Delaware	117	59	50	9	7	50	43	59	50
District of Columbia . . .	44	26	59	3	6	15	35	18	41
Florida	3,214	2,119	66	187	6	890	28	1,078	34
Georgia	1,641	1,122	68	78	5	441	27	519	32
Hawaii	138	73	53	21	15	45	32	66	47
Idaho	252	161	64	17	7	70	28	88	35
Illinois	1,249	742	59	73	6	434	35	507	41
Indiana	898	631	70	37	4	230	26	267	30
Iowa	445	307	69	32	7	106	24	137	31
Kansas	416	273	66	27	7	114	27	142	34
Kentucky	864	614	71	40	5	210	24	250	29
Louisiana	985	550	56	67	7	368	37	435	44
Maine	183	108	59	9	5	66	36	76	41
Maryland	614	389	63	46	8	179	29	225	37
Massachusetts	417	240	58	31	7	146	35	177	42
Michigan	1,088	707	65	72	7	305	28	377	35
Minnesota	504	324	64	23	4	158	31	180	36
Mississippi	884	546	62	36	4	302	34	338	38
Missouri	992	595	60	55	5	338	34	392	40
Montana	277	149	54	18	6	106	38	124	45
Nebraska	256	156	61	21	8	77	30	97	38
Nevada	373	230	62	25	7	118	32	143	38
New Hampshire	129	85	66	11	8	34	26	45	34
New Jersey	724	471	65	54	7	199	27	253	35
New Mexico	413	261	63	19	5	133	32	152	37
New York	1,333	860	65	89	7	384	29	473	35
North Carolina	1,675	1,102	66	83	5	487	29	570	34
North Dakota	111	46	42	5	5	53	48	59	53
Ohio	1,257	781	62	82	7	391	31	473	38
Oklahoma	754	511	68	21	3	219	29	240	32
Oregon	455	272	60	31	7	150	33	181	40
Pennsylvania	1,491	909	61	78	5	500	34	578	39
Rhode Island	69	35	50	8	11	25	36	32	47
South Carolina	1,066	541	51	57	5	463	43	520	49
South Dakota	146	90	61	9	6	45	31	54	37
Tennessee	1,210	763	63	54	4	390	32	444	37
Texas	3,363	1,873	56	193	6	1,292	38	1,485	44
Utah	299	237	79	11	4	51	17	63	21
Vermont	66	39	60	3	5	22	34	26	39
Virginia	1,027	629	61	64	6	332	32	397	39
Washington	568	337	59	34	6	195	34	230	40
West Virginia	431	265	62	24	6	142	33	166	38
Wisconsin	756	387	51	52	7	313	41	365	48
Wyoming	150	95	63	6	4	49	33	55	37

Source: U.S. National Highway Traffic Safety Administration, *Traffic Safety Facts*, annual. See also <http://www-nrd.nhtsa.dot.gov/CATS /index.aspx>.

Table 1075. **Crashes by Crash Severity: 1990 to 2007**

[6,471 represents 6,471,000. A crash is a police-reported event that produces injury and/or property damage, involves a vehicle in transport and occurs on a trafficway or while the vehicle is in motion after running off the trafficway]

Item	1990	1995	2000	2002	2003	2004	2005	2006	2007
Crashes (1,000)	6,471	6,699	6,394	6,316	6,328	6,181	6,159	5,973	6,024
Fatal.	39.8	37.2	37.5	38.5	38.5	38.4	39.3	38.6	37.2
Nonfatal injury	2,122	2,217	2,070	1,929	1,925	1,862	1,816	1,746	1,711
Property damage only	4,309	4,446	4,286	4,348	4,365	4,281	4,304	4,189	4,275
Percent of total crashes:									
Fatal.	0.6	0.6	0.6	0.6	0.6	0.6	0.6	0.6	0.6
Nonfatal injury	32.8	33.1	32.4	30.5	30.4	30.1	29.5	29.2	28.4
Property damage only	66.6	66.4	67.0	68.8	69.0	69.3	69.9	70.1	71.0

Source: U.S. National Highway Safety Traffic Administration, *Traffic Safety Facts*, annual. See <http://www-nrd.nhtsa.dot.gov/CATS/index.aspx>.

Table 1076. **Alcohol Involvement for Drivers in Fatal Crashes: 1997 and 2007**

[BAC = blood alcohol concentration]

Age, sex, and vehicle type	1997		2007	
	Number of drivers	Percentage with BAC of .08% or greater	Number of drivers	Percentage with BAC of .08% or greater
Total drivers involved in fatal crashes [1]	**56,688**	**20.4**	**55,681**	**21.7**
Drivers by age group:				
Under 16 years old	345	7.7	239	11.5
16 to 20 years old.	7,719	17.1	6,851	17.6
21 to 24 years old.	5,705	29.9	6,256	34.5
25 to 34 years old.	12,453	27.4	10,692	29.2
35 to 44 years old.	10,904	25.6	9,862	24.5
45 to 54 years old.	7,522	17.2	8,982	20.4
55 to 64 years old.	4,394	10.9	6,011	12.2
65 to 74 years old.	3,401	7.6	3,025	7.5
75 years old and over	3,314	4.2	2,855	4.1
Drivers by sex:				
Male.	40,954	23.5	40,804	24.5
Female	14,954	12.2	14,099	13.2
Drivers by vehicle type:				
Passenger cars	29,896	21.6	22,621	22.8
Light trucks [2]	18,502	22.6	21,591	23.3
Large trucks [2]	4,859	1.7	4,551	0.9
Motorcycles	2,159	32.4	5,286	27.1
Buses.	297	1.1	275	1.3

[1] Includes age and sex unknown, and other and unknown types of vehicles. [2] See footnotes 2 and 3 in Table 1071.

Source: U.S. National Highway Traffic Safety Administration, *Traffic Safety Facts*, annual. See <http://www-nrd.nhtsa.dot.gov/CATS/index.aspx>.

Table 1077. **Licensed Drivers and Number in Accidents by Age: 2007**

[205,100 represents 205,100,000]

Age group	Licensed drivers		Drivers in accidents				Accident rates per number of drivers	
			Fatal		All			
	Number	Percent	Number	Percent	Number	Percent	Fatal [1]	All [2]
Total	**205,100**	**100.0**	**58,400**	**100.0**	**18,100**	**100.0**	**28**	**9**
19 years old and under	10,034	4.9	5,400	9.2	2,150	11.9	54	21
Under 16 years old	419	0.2	300	0.5	70	0.4	(3)	(3)
16 years old.	1,307	0.6	700	1.2	360	2.0	54	28
17 years old.	2,283	1.1	1,100	1.9	530	2.9	48	23
18 years old.	2,870	1.4	1,600	2.7	620	3.4	56	22
19 years old.	3,155	1.5	1,700	2.9	570	3.1	54	18
20 to 24 years old	17,173	8.4	8,700	14.9	2,620	14.5	51	15
20 years old.	3,291	1.6	1,700	2.9	690	3.8	52	21
21 years old.	3,362	1.6	1,800	3.1	530	2.9	54	16
22 years old.	3,400	1.7	1,800	3.1	480	2.7	53	14
23 years old.	3,517	1.7	1,600	2.7	470	2.6	45	13
24 years old.	3,603	1.8	1,800	3.1	450	2.5	50	12
25 to 34 years old	35,712	17.4	10,700	18.3	3,740	20.7	30	10
35 to 44 years old	40,322	19.7	9,600	16.4	3,220	17.8	24	8
45 to 54 years old	40,937	20.0	9,400	16.1	3,030	16.7	23	7
55 to 64 years old	30,355	14.8	6,500	11.1	1,990	11.0	21	7
65 to 74 years old	17,246	8.4	3,800	6.5	790	4.4	22	5
75 years old and over	13,321	6.5	4,300	7.4	560	3.1	32	4

[1] Per 100,000 licensed drivers. [2] Per 100 licensed drivers. [3] Rates for drivers under age 16 are substantially overstated due to the high proportion of unlicensed drivers involved.

Source: National Safety Council, Itasca, IL, *Injury Facts, 2009*, (copyright). See <http://www.nsc.org/>.

Table 1078. **Passenger Transit Industry—Summary: 1980 to 2007**

[**6,510 represents $6,510,000,000.** Includes Puerto Rico. Includes aggregate information for all transit systems in the United States. Excludes nontransit services such as taxicab, school bus, unregulated jitney(a small bus or automobile that transport passengers on a route for a small fare), sightseeing bus, intercity bus, and special application mass transportation systems (e.g., amusement parks, airports, island, and urban park ferries). Includes active vehicles only]

Item	Unit	1980	1990	1995	2000	2005	2006	2007
Operating systems	Number. . .	1,044	5,078	5,973	6,000	6,429	6,435	7,700
Motor bus systems	Number. . .	1,040	2,688	2,250	2,262	1,500	1,500	1,200
Revenue vehicles, active	Number. . .	75,388	93,553	116,473	131,918	150,827	155,195	163,973
Motor bus	Number. . .	59,411	58,714	67,107	75,013	82,027	83,080	65,249
Commuter rail . . . ,̇.	Number. . .	4,500	5,007	5,164	5,498	6,392	6,403	6,391
Demand response [5]	Number. . .	(NA)	16,471	29,352	33,080	41,958	43,509	64,865
Heavy rail	Number. . .	9,641	10,419	10,157	10,591	11,110	11,052	11,222
Light rail	Number. . .	1,013	913	999	1,577	1,645	1,801	1,810
Trolley bus.	Number. . .	823	832	885	951	615	609	559
Other	Number. . .	(NA)	1,197	2,809	5,208	7,080	8,741	13,877
Operating funding, total	Mil. dol. . .	6,510	16,053	18,241	24,243	31,708	33,713	35,541
Agency funds	Mil. dol. . .	2,805	6,786	8,069	11,004	12,559	13,545	13,473
Passenger funding.	Mil. dol. . .	2,557	5,891	6,801	8,746	10,269	11,195	11,145
Other	Mil. dol. . .	248	895	1,268	2,258	2,290	2,350	2,328
Government funds [1]	Mil. dol. . .	3,705	9,267	10,172	13,239	19,149	20,168	22,068
Directly generated [2]	Mil. dol. . .	([3])	([3])	1,544	1,959	2,694	2,797	2,698
Local [4].	Mil. dol. . .	2,611	5,327	3,981	5,319	6,658	7,105	8,322
State [4].	Mil. dol. . .	(NA)	2,970	3,830	4,967	7,495	7,674	8,371
Federal	Mil. dol. . .	1,094	970	817	994	2,303	2,592	2,678
Operating expense	Mil. dol. . .	6,247	15,742	17,849	22,646	30,295	32,037	33,877
Vehicle operations.	Mil. dol. . .	3,248	6,654	8,282	10,111	13,793	14,743	15,560
Maintenance	Mil. dol. . .	1,774	4,631	5,047	6,445	8,259	8,690	9,136
General administration	Mil. dol. . .	1,224	3,450	2,590	3,329	4,075	4,301	4,779
Purchased transportation	Mil. dol. . .	(NA)	1,008	1,930	2,761	4,168	4,304	4,402
Capital expenditures	Mil. dol. . .	(NA)	(NA)	7,230	9,587	12,383	13,340	14,528
Vehicle-miles operated	Million	2,287	3,242	3,550	4,081	4,601	4,684	5,038
Motor bus	Million	1,677	2,130	2,184	2,315	2,485	2,495	2,302
Trolley bus.	Million	13	14	14	14	13	12	11
Heavy rail	Million	385	537	537	595	646	652	657
Light rail	Million	18	24	35	53	69	74	84
Commuter rail . . . ,̇.	Million	179	213	238	271	303	315	326
Demand response [5]	Million	(NA)	306	507	759	978	1,013	1,471
Other	Million	15	18	37	74	107	123	186
Trips taken	Million	8,567	8,799	7,763	9,363	9,815	10,017	10,247
Motor bus	Million	5,837	5,677	4,848	5,678	5,855	5,894	5,413
Trolley bus.	Million	142	126	119	122	107	100	97
Heavy rail	Million	2,108	2,346	2,033	2,632	2,808	2,927	3,460
Light rail	Million	133	175	251	320	381	407	419
Commuter rail . . . ,̇.	Million	280	328	344	413	423	441	459
Demand response [5]	Million	(NA)	68	88	105	125	126	209
Other	Million	67	79	80	93	117	121	190
Avg. fare per trip . . . . ,̇. .	Cents	30	67	88	93	102	112	109
Employees, number (avg.) [6]	1,000	187	273	311	360	367	369	383
Payroll, employee.	Mil. dol. . . .	3,281	7,226	8,213	10,400	12,177	12,764	13,205
Fringe benefits, employee	Mil. dol. . . .	1,353	3,986	4,484	5,413	8,093	8,424	9,092

NA Not available.　[1] Represents the sum of federal, state, and local assistance, and that portion of directly generated funds that accrue from tax collections, toll transfers from other sectors of operations, and bond proceeds.　[2] These are any funds generated from taxes controlled by the transit agency.　[3] Funds data are included in local government data through 1993; [4] Through 1985, data for state and local are combined.　[5] This operation (also called paratransit or dial-a-ride) is comprised of passenger cars, vans or small buses operating in response to calls from passengers or their agents to the transit operator, who then dispatches a vehicle to pick up the passengers and transport them to their destinations.　[6] Through 1990, represents employee equivalents of 2,080 hours = one employee; beginning 1995, equals actual employees.

Source: American Public Transportation Association, Washington, DC, *Public Transportation Fact Book,* annual. See also <http://www.apta.com/resources/statistics/Pages/default.aspx>.

Table 1079. **Transit Buses Equipped for Disabilities: 1995 to 2007**

[Represents ADA (Americans with Disabilities Act of 1992). Lift- or ramp-equipped buses. Includes buses of transit agencies receiving federal funding for bus purchases and buses of agencies not receiving federal funds that voluntarily report data to the Federal Transit Administration]

Item	1995	2000	2002	2003	2004	2005	2006	2007
Transit buses, total	**57,322**	**65,324**	**68,418**	**68,596**	**68,789**	**69,504**	**70,227**	**73,397**
Percent ADA equipped . .	61.7	83.6	94.1	95.3	98.1	96.5	98.1	98.1
Small buses, total [1]	5,372	8,850	9,822	10,084	10,248	11,118	11,537	13,699
Percent ADA equipped.	84.5	94.5	99.2	99.2	98.5	97.6	98.1	98.3
Medium buses, total [1]	3,879	7,455	8,693	9,346	10,031	10,631	10,993	11,306
Percent ADA equipped.	66.0	92.9	98.4	97.7	100.0	98.8	99.1	99.1
Large buses, total [1]	46,355	47,017	47,764	46,608	45,919	45,524	45,403	46,125
Percent ADA equipped.	59.2	79.9	92.2	93.9	97.4	95.5	97.8	97.6
Articulated buses, total [1]	1,716	2,002	2,139	2,558	2,591	2,231	2,294	2,267
Percent ADA equipped.	50.2	85.5	97.2	96.4	99.8	99.7	99.8	100

[1] Small buses have fewer than 25 seats; medium buses have 25 to 35 seats; large ones have more than 35 seats; articulated buses are extra long and measure between 54 and 60 feet.

Source: U.S. Bureau of Transportation Statistics, *National Transportation Statistics,* annual. See also <http://www.bts.gov/publications /national_transportation_statistics>.

Transportation　681

Table 1080. Characteristics of Rail Transit by Transit Authority: 2007

Mode and transit agency	Primary city served	States served	Directional route-miles [1,2]	Number of highway-rail crossings [1]	Number of stations	Number of ADA-accessible stations [3]
Total [4]	35	31	11,046.2	5,746	3,010	1,883
Heavy rail	11	12	1,602.8	27	1,026	477
Chicago Transit Authority	Chicago	IL	207.8	25	144	80
Greater Cleveland Regional Transit Authority	Cleveland	OH	38.1	–	18	13
L.A. County Metropolitan Transportation Authority	Los Angeles	CA	31.9	–	16	16
Maryland Transit Administration	Baltimore	MD	29.4	–	14	14
Massachusetts Bay Transportation Authority	Boston	MA	76.3	–	53	49
Metropolitan Atlanta Rapid Transit Authority	Atlanta	GA	96.1	–	38	38
Miami-Dade Transit Agency	Miami	FL	45.0	–	22	22
MTA New York City Transit	New York	NY	493.8	–	468	75
Port Authority Trans-Hudson Corporation	New York	NY, NJ	28.6	2	13	7
Port Authority Transit Corporation	Philadelphia	PA, NJ	31.5	–	13	5
San Francisco Bay Area Rapid Transit District	San Francisco	CA	209.0	–	43	43
Southeastern Pennsylvania Transportation Authority	Philadelphia	PA	74.9	–	75	24
Staten Island Rapid Transit Operating Authority . .	New York	NY	28.6	–	23	5
Washington Metropolitan Area Transit Authority . .	Washington	DC, MD, VA	211.8	–	86	86
Commuter rail [5]	16	21	8,092.9	3,111	1,182	735
Alaska Railroad Corporation	Anchorage	AK	958.0	161	10	10
Altamont Commuter Express Authority	San Jose	CA	172.0	127	10	10
Central Puget Sound Regional Transit Authority	Seattle	WA	146.9	45	9	9
Connecticut Department of Transportation	New Haven	CT	101.2	3	8	8
Dallas Area Rapid Transit	Dallas	TX	29.0	15	4	4
Fort Worth Transportation Authority	Dallas	TX	40.5	19	5	5
Maryland Transit Administration	Baltimore	MD, DC, WV	400.4	40	42	24
Massachusetts Bay Transportation Authority	Boston	MA, RI	702.1	233	126	88
MTA Long Island Rail Road	New York	NY	638.2	346	124	99
MTA Metro-North Railroad	New York	NY, NJ, CT	545.7	158	109	38
Northern New England Passenger Rail Authority	Boston	MA, ME, NH	230.4	65	10	10
NE Illinois Regional Commuter Rail Corporation	Chicago	IL, WI	980.4	532	239	163
New Jersey Transit Corporation	New York	NY, NJ, PA	996.8	316	162	67
North	San Diego County Transit District	CA	82.2	34	8	8
Northern Indiana Commuter Transportation District	Chicago	IL, IN	179.8	117	20	13
Peninsula Corridor Joint Powers Board	San Francisco	CA	153.7	46	32	24
Pennsylvania Department of Transportation	Philadelphia	PA	144.4	7	12	4
Regional Transportation Authority	Nashville	TN	62.8	35	6	6
South Florida Regional Transportation Authority	Miami	FL	142.2	73	18	18
Southeastern Pennsylvania Transportation Authority	Philadelphia	PA	446.9	283	156	55
Southern California Regional Rail Authority	Los Angeles	CA	777.8	436	54	54
Virginia Railway Express	Washington	DC, VA	161.5	20	18	18

– Represents zero.   [1] Vehicles operated in maximun services (VOMS) include directly operated (DO) and Purchase Transportation (PT) by mode.   [2] The mileage in each direction over which public transportation vehicles travel while in revenue service. The mileage is computed without regard to the number of traffic lanes or rail tracks existing in the right-of-way.   [3] Number of stations that comply with the American with Disabilities Act of 1992 (ADA). Additional stations may be wheelchair accessible but not comply with other provisions of the ADA.   [4] Includes light rail, not shown separately.   [5] Excludes commuter-type services operated independently by AMTRAK.

Source: U.S. Bureau of Transportation Statistics, *"State Transportation Statistics, 2007"*; <http://www.bts.gov/publications/state_transportation _statistics/> and *"Top transit cities"*; <http://www.ntdprogram.gov/ntdprogram/data.htm>.

682   Transportation

Table 1081. **Transit Ridership in Selected Urbanized Areas: 2006**

Urbanized areas	Annual unlinked passenger trips [1] (mil.)	Area rank based on trips per capita [2]	Unlinked passenger trips per capita	Percent distribution				
				Motor bus	Heavy rail [3]	Light rail [4]	Commuter rail [5]	Other [6]
U.S. urbanized areas	9,888,416	(X)	51	53.2	34.9	4.2	4.6	3.1
Atlanta, GA	158,478	14	45	50.0	49.0	–	–	1.0
Austin, TX	34,040	16	37.7	97.1	–	–	–	2.9
Baltimore, MD	110,366	11	53.2	74.0	11.9	6.1	6.8	1.1
Boston, MA-NH-RI	364,193	4	90.3	28.9	39.4	19.3	10.7	1.7
Buffalo, NY	24,146	29	24.7	75.4	–	24.2	–	0.4
Charlotte, NC-SC	20,398	25	26.9	97.3	–	–	–	2.7
Chicago, IL-IN	619,411	5	74.6	55.6	30.7	–	12.7	0.9
Cincinnati, OH-KY-IN	29,977	32	19.9	98.5	–	–	–	1.5
Cleveland, OH	61,179	21	34.2	81.5	12.2	5.0	–	1.4
Dallas-Fort Worth-Arlington, TX. . .	82,189	33	19.8	72.4	–	21.8	3.0	2.8
Denver-Aurora, CO.	94,196	12	47.5	78.5	–	19.8	–	1.7
Houston, TX	100,987	26	26.4	85.0	–	11.6	–	3.4
Las Vegas, NV	73,064	10	55.6	86.0	–	–	–	14.0
Los Angeles-Long Beach-Santa Ana, CA.	717,411	9	60.9	86.0	5.7	5.8	1.7	0.9
Miami, FL	168,943	20	34.3	80.2	10.4	–	2.0	7.4
Milwaukee, WI.	48,387	19	37.0	97.3	–	–	–	2.7
Minneapolis-St. Paul, MN.	88,866	17	37.2	87.4	–	10.2	–	2.3
New York-Newark, NY-NJ-CT	4,053,990	1	227.8	31.1	61.1	0.5	6.5	0.9
Orlando, FL.	26,078	31	22.5	97.1	–	–	–	2.9
Philadelphia, PA-NJ-DE-MD	340,748	8	66.2	52.5	28.7	8.1	9.9	0.8
Phoenix-Mesa, AZ	65,827	30	22.6	96.7	–	–	–	3.3
Pittsburgh, PA	71,712	15	40.9	85.6	–	9.9	–	4.5
Portland, OR-WA	106,660	6	67.4	64.9	–	33.9	–	1.3
Sacramento, CA.	35,777	27	25.7	58.3	–	40.5	–	1.2
Salt Lake City, UT	41,350	13	46.6	56.3	–	39.4	–	4.3
San Antonio, TX.	41,718	22	31.4	97.2	–	–	–	2.8
San Diego, CA.	99,344	18	37.1	60.5	–	35.3	1.6	2.6
San Francisco-Oakland, CA.	422,803	2	131.0	43.2	25.8	9.9	2.4	18.8
San Jose, CA	43,434	23	28.2	74.0	–	23.7	–	2.4
Seattle, WA.	181,903	7	67.1	68.2	–	0.5	1.2	30.2
St. Louis, MO-IL.	56,486	24	27.2	59.5	–	38.6	–	2.0
Tucson, AZ	18,206	28	25.3	97.6	–	–	–	2.4
Virginia Beach, VA	26,895	34	19.3	96.8	–	–	–	3.2
Washington, DC-VA-MD	465,131	3	118.2	39.5	59.4	–	0.7	0.4

– Represents zero.   X Not applicable.   [1] The number of times passengers board public transportation vehicles. A passenger is counted each time he or she boards a vehicle even if the boarding is part of the same journey from origin to destination.   [2] As of April 1. Based on the 2000 decennial census.   [3] Also called metro, subway, rapid transit, or rapid rail.   [4] Also called streetcar, tramway, or trolley.   [5] Also called metropolitan rail or regional rail.   [6] Includes such modes as trolley bus, ferry, cable car, vanpool, and demand response (see footnote 5, Table 1078).

Source: U.S. Bureau of Transportation Statistics, *"State Transportation Statistics, 2006"*; <http://www.bts.gov/publications /state_transportation_statistics/>. National Transit database; Access NTD data; Top transit cities; <http://www.ntdprogram.gov/ntdprogram /data.htm>.

Table 1082. **Federal Aid to State and Local Governments for Federal Transit Administration (FTA) by State: 2007**

[Year ending Sept. 30. (9,286 represents $9,286,000,000)]

State	Total (mil.- dol.)	Per capita (dol.)[1]	State	Total (mil.- dol.)	Per capita (dol.)[1]	State	Total (mil.- dol.)	Per capita (dol.)[1]	State	Total (mil.- dol.)	Per capita (dol.)[1]
U.S. [2] . .	9,286	31	ID	13	9	MT.	13	14	SC	36	8
U.S. [3] . .	9,234	31	IL.	546	42	NE.	20	11	SD	12	14
AL.	64	14	IN	70	11	NV.	52	20	TN	57	9
AK.	53	78	IA	43	14	NH.	13	10	TX	450	19
AZ	209	33	KS	27	10	NJ.	676	78	UT	128	48
AR	22	8	KY	54	13	NM.	31	16	VT	16	25
CA	1,290	35	LA	75	18	NY	1,647	85	VA	122	16
CO.	185	38	ME.	21	16	NC.	168	19	WA	319	49
CT	63	18	MD.	181	32	ND.	14	21	WV	22	12
DE.	13	15	MA.	275	43	OH.	183	16	WI	94	17
DC.	309	525	MI	154	15	OK.	43	12	WY	9	17
FL.	341	19	MN.	110	21	OR.	205	55			
GA.	124	13	MS.	17	6	PA	475	38			
HI	47	37	MO	96	16	RI	30	28			

[1] Based on estimated population as of July 1.   [2] Includes outlying areas and undistributed funds, not shown separately.   [3] For the 50 states and DC.

Source: U.S. Census Bureau, Federal, State, and Local Governments, *Federal Aid to States for Fiscal Year, 2007* (published September 2008). See also <http://www.census.gov/prod/www/abs/fas.html>.

Transportation   683

Table 1083. Truck Transportation, Couriers and Messengers, and Warehousing and Storage—Estimated Revenue: 2000 to 2007

[In millions of dollars (237,812 represents $237,812,000,000). For taxable and tax-exempt employer firms. Estimates have been adjusted to the results of the 2002 Economic Census. Based on the North American Industry Classification System, 2002; see text, Section 15]

Kind of business	2002 NAICS code [1]	2000	2005	2007
Selected transportation and warehousing industries...............................	48, 49	237,812	292,385	325,298
Truck transportation........................	484	165,421	206,512	228,907
General freight trucking.....................	4841	108,051	139,133	152,550
General freight trucking, local	48411	17,254	22,467	25,906
General freight trucking, long-distance	48412	90,797	116,666	126,644
General freight trucking, long-distance, truckload	484121	61,562	84,647	92,678
General freight trucking, long-distance, less than truckload....	484122	29,235	32,019	33,966
Specialized freight trucking	4842	57,370	67,379	76,357
Used household and office goods moving	48421	14,484	15,135	15,127
Specialized freight (except used goods) trucking, local	48422	21,912	28,018	32,976
Specialized freight (except used goods) trucking, long-distance	48423	20,974	24,226	28,254
Couriers and messengers.....................	492	57,776	66,908	74,704
Couriers....................................	4921	54,114	63,497	70,983
Local messengers and local delivery	4922	3,662	3,411	3,721
Warehousing and storage.....................	493	14,615	18,965	21,687
General warehousing and storage..............	49311	8,967	11,656	13,653
Refrigerated warehousing and storage.........	49312	2,859	3,018	3,235
Farm product warehousing and storage.........	49313	776	772	836
Other warehousing and storage	49319	2,013	3,519	3,963

[1] Based on the 2002 North American Industry Classification System; see text, Section 15.

Source: U.S. Census Bureau, "2007 Service Annual Survey, Truck Transportation, Messenger Services and Warehousing" (published March 2008); <http://www.census.gov/services>.

Table 1084. Truck Transportation—Summary: 2000 to 2007

[In millions of dollars (165,421 represents $165,421,000,000, except where noted). For taxable and tax-exempt employer firms. Covers NAICS 484. Estimates have been adjusted to the results of the 2002 Economic Census. Based on the North American Industry Classification System, 2002; see text, Section 15]

Item	2000	2005	2006	2007
Total operating revenue	**165,421**	**206,512**	**221,871**	**228,907**
Total motor carrier revenue	152,810	193,298	207,121	213,622
Local trucking [1]	48,837	63,741	69,165	72,635
Long-distance trucking [1]......................	103,973	129,557	137,956	140,987
Size of shipments:				
Less-than-truckload	36,453	42,596	51,303	52,691
Truckload..................................	116,357	150,702	155,818	160,931
Commodities handled:				
Agricultural and fish products................	13,666	17,389	18,496	18,924
Grains, alcohol, and tobacco products.............	4,912	7,101	9,137	10,175
Stone, nonmetallic minerals, and metallic ores	8,703	13,395	15,384	15,732
Coal and petroleum products....................	5,812	7,036	7,550	8,303
Pharmaceutical and chemical products	9,929	10,382	10,943	12,038
Wood products, textiles, and leathers	14,281	17,386	17,666	18,775
Base metal and machinery.....................	12,239	16,289	18,072	18,533
Electronic, motorized vehicles, and precision instruments ...	11,999	15,119	15,945	15,333
Used household and office goods................	11,078	11,807	12,326	12,907
New furniture and miscellaneous manufactured products ...	17,244	22,090	22,251	20,781
Other goods	43,007	55,304	59,351	62,121
Origin and destination of shipments:				
U.S. to U.S.................................	145,985	185,906	198,781	205,023
U.S. to Canada.............................	1,390	1,561	1,834	1,997
U.S. to Mexico.............................	1,434	1,604	1,697	1,662
Canada to U.S..............................	1,184	1,328	1,335	1,226
Mexico to U.S..............................	1,283	1,371	1,817	2,100
All other destinations	1,534	1,528	1,657	1,614
Inventory of revenue-generating equipment (1,000):				
Trucks	201	222	248	256
Owned and/or leased with drivers..............	168	197	221	227
Leased without drivers	33	25	27	29
Truck-tractors..............................	916	881	898	927
Owned and/or leased with drivers..............	772	743	748	771
Leased without drivers	144	137	150	156
Trailers	1,893	1,958	1,978	2,018
Owned and/or leased with drivers..............	1,572	1,603	1,631	1,657
Leased without drivers	321	355	347	360
Highway miles traveled (mil.):				
Total.......................................	84,910	91,220	92,654	93,512
By loaded or partially loaded vehicles	67,558	73,702	74,687	75,718
By empty vehicles	17,352	17,518	17,966	17,794

[1] Local trucking is the carrying of goods within a single metro area and its adjacent nonurban areas; long-distance trucking is the carrying of goods between metro areas.

Source: U.S. Census Bureau, "2007 Service Annual Survey, Truck Transportation, Messenger Services, and Warehousing" (published March 2009); <http://www.census.gov/services/>.

684   Transportation

Table 1085. **Railroads, Class I—Summary: 1990 to 2007**

[As of Dec. 31, or calendar year data, except as noted (216 represents 216,000). Compiled from annual reports of class I railroads only, except where noted. Minus sign (–) indicates deficit]

Item	Unit	1990	2000	2002	2003	2004	2005	2006	2007
Class I line-hauling companies [1]	Number. .	14	8	7	7	7	7	7	7
Employees [2]	1,000 . .	216	168	157	155	158	162	168	167
Compensation	Mil. dol..	8,654	9,623	9,387	9,576	10,337	10,879	11,419	11,599
Average per hour	Dollars . .	15.8	21.5	22.7	23.4	24.2	25.7	26.0	27.3
Average per year	Dollars . .	39,987	57,157	59,650	61,920	65,550	66,975	68,141	69,367
Mileage:									
Railroad line owned [3]	1,000 . . .	146	121	118	117	123	121	120	120
Railroad track owned [4]	1,000 . . .	244	205	200	200	211	208	206	212
Equipment:									
Locomotives in service	Number. .	18,835	20,028	20,506	20,774	22,015	22,779	23,730	24,143
Average horsepower	1,000 lb..	2,665	3,261	3,378	3,415	3,458	3,467	3,485	3,518
Cars in service:									
Freight train [5]	1,000 . . .	1,212	1,381	1,300	1,279	1,288	1,312	1,347	1,386
Freight cars [6]	1,000 . . .	659	560	478	467	474	475	475	460
Average capacity	Tons. . . .	87.5	92.3	93.1	93.7	94.3	97.2	98.8	99.5
Income and expenses:									
Operating revenues	Mil. dol..	28,370	34,102	35,327	36,639	40,517	46,118	52,152	54,600
Operating expenses	Mil. dol..	24,652	29,040	29,592	31,440	35,107	37,843	40,980	42,747
Net revenue from operations	*Mil. dol..*	*3,718*	*5,062*	*5,735*	*5,199*	*5,410*	*8,275*	*11,172*	*11,852*
Income before fixed charges	Mil. dol..	4,627	5,361	6,179	5,220	5,523	8,361	11,276	12,084
Provision for taxes [7]	Mil. dol..	1,088	1,430	1,823	1,494	1,543	2,224	3,643	4,108
Ordinary income	Mil. dol..	1,961	2,501	3,201	2,683	2,867	4,917	6,482	6,797
Net income	Mil. dol..	1,977	2,500	3,201	2,687	2,867	4,917	6,482	6,797
Net railway operating income	Mil. dol..	2,648	3,924	4,248	4,078	4,147	6,075	7,560	7,765
Total taxes [8]	Mil. dol..	3,780	4,379	4,724	4,316	4,480	5,176	6,830	7,272
Indus. return on net investment	Percent..	8.1	6.5	7.0	6.3	6.1	8.5	10.2	9.9
Gross capital expenditures	Mil. dol..	3,591	5,290	5,605	5,989	6,345	7,068	8,159	9,853
Equipment.	Mil. dol..	996	1,508	1,021	1,300	1,301	1,026	1,470	2,213
Roadway and structures	Mil. dol..	2,644	4,549	4,645	4,561	4,941	5,364	6,982	6,944
Other	Mil. dol..	–49	–767	–61	128	102	678	–293	696
Balance sheet:									
Total property investment	Mil. dol..	70,348	106,136	117,770	122,902	135,941	141,400	148,320	156,666
Accrued depreciation and									
amortization	Mil. dol..	22,222	23,989	26,649	29,215	29,771	32,508	35,763	38,702
Net investment	Mil. dol..	48,126	82,147	91,121	93,686	106,170	108,892	112,556	117,963
Shareholder's equity.	Mil. dol..	23,662	32,401	39,675	41,151	51,955	55,828	58,901	59,300
Net working capital.	Mil. dol..	–3,505	–5,783	–6,037	–6,750	–5,171	–4,729	–4,461	–5,482
Cash dividends	Mil. dol..	2,074	819	870	1,406	1,888	1,267	1,089	6,427
Amtrak passenger traffic:									
Passenger revenue	Mil. dol..	941.9	1,201.6	1,304.3	1,421.1	1,432.6	1,461.7	1,606.0	1,774.7
Revenue passengers carried	1,000 . . .	22,382	22,985	23,269	24,595	25,215	25,076	24,549	26,550
Revenue passenger miles	Million. . .	6,125	5,574	5,314	5,680	5,511	5,381	5,410	5,784
Averages:									
Revenue per passenger.	Dollars . .	42.1	52.3	56.1	57.8	56.8	58.3	65.4	66.8
Revenue per passenger mile	Cents . . .	15.4	21.6	24.5	25.0	26.0	27.2	27.2	30.7
Freight service:									
Freight revenue	Mil. dol..	24,471	33,083	34,110	35,413	39,131	44,457	50,315	52,932
Per ton-mile.	Cents . . .	2.7	2.3	2.3	2.3	2.4	2.6	2.8	3.0
Per ton originated	Dollar . . .	19.3	19.0	19.3	19.7	21.2	23.4	25.7	27.3
Revenue-tons originated	Million. . .	1,425	1,738	1,767	1,799	1,844	1,899	1,957	1,940
Revenue-tons carried	Million. . .	2,024	2,179	2,207	2,240	2,398	2,448	2,517	2,431
Tons carried one mile	Billion . . .	1,034	1,466	1,507	1,551	1,663	1,696	1,772	1,771
Average miles of road operated	1,000 . . .	133	121	123	122	121	121	120	120
Revenue ton-miles per mile of									
road.	1,000 . . .	7,763	12,156	12,245	12,686	13,695	14,071	14,805	14,801
Revenue per ton-mile	Cents . . .	3	2	2	2	2	3	3	3
Train miles	Million. . .	380	504	500	516	535	548	563	543
Net ton-miles per train-mile [9]	Number. .	2,755	2,923	3,030	3,024	3,126	3,115	3,163	3,274
Net ton-miles per loaded									
car-mile [9]	Number. .	69.1	73.1	71.5	71.4	78.5	79.0	82	84
Train-miles per train-hour	Miles . . .	24	21	21	20	19	19	18	19
Haul per ton, U.S. as a system. . .	Miles . . .	726	843	853	862	902	893	906	913
Accidents/incidents: [10]									
Casualties—all railroads:									
Persons killed	Number. .	1,297	937	951	868	895	888	910	845
Persons injured	Number. .	25,143	11,643	11,103	9,251	9,178	9,463	8,432	9,461
Class I railroads: [11]									
Persons killed	Number. .	1,166	778	796	749	782	738	787	706
Persons injured	Number. .	19,284	7,655	7,722	6,161	6,186	6,238	5,442	6,088

[1] See text, this section, for definition of Class I. [2] Average midmonth count. [3] Represents the aggregate length of roadway of all line-haul railroads. Excludes yard tracks, sidings, and parallel lines. (Includes estimate for Class II and III railroads). [4] Includes multiple main tracks, yard tracks, and sidings owned by both line-haul and switching and terminal. (Includes estimate for Class II and III railroads). [5] Includes cars owned by all railroads, private car companies, and shippers. [6] Class I railroads only. [7] Includes state income taxes. [8] Includes payroll, income, and other taxes. [9] Revenue and nonrevenue freight. [10] Source: Federal Railroad Admin., *Railroad Safety Statistics*, annual. [11] Includes Amtrack data. Includes highway grade crossing casualties. See Internet site <http://www.fra.dot.gov/>.

Source: Except as noted, Association of American Railroads, Washington, DC, *Industry Information, Industry Statistics, Railroad Statistics*. See also <http://www.aar.org/Resources/Resources%20Landing.aspx>.

Transportation 685

Table 1086. Railroads, Class-I Line-Haul-Revenue Freight Originated by Commodity Group: 1990 to 2008

[21,401 represents 21,401,000]

Commodity group	1990	1995	2000	2003	2004	2005	2006	2007	2008
Carloads (1,000) [1]	**21,401**	**23,726**	**27,763**	**28,870**	**30,095**	**31,142**	**32,114**	**31,459**	**30,625**
Farm products	1,689	1,692	1,437	1,519	1,519	1,510	1,590	1,681	1,726
Metallic ores	508	463	322	331	339	662	674	662	671
Coal.	5,912	6,095	6,954	7,037	7,102	7,202	7,574	7,480	7,713
Nonmetallic minerals	1,202	1,159	1,309	1,370	1,430	1,488	1,470	1,398	1,325
Food and kindred products	1,307	1,377	1,377	1,478	1,461	1,448	1,487	1,493	1,501
Lumber and wood products	780	719	648	612	616	611	548	456	391
Pulp, paper, allied products	611	628	633	667	669	679	671	652	666
Chemicals, allied products	1,531	1,642	1,820	1,913	1,981	1,937	1,943	2,050	2,040
Petroleum and coal products	573	596	565	606	651	689	689	691	578
Stone, clay, and glass products	539	516	541	581	594	603	570	513	467
Primary metal products	477	575	723	648	701	680	728	666	634
Fabricated metal products	31	32	30	36	39	36	50	55	58
Machinery, exc. electrical	39	41	35	38	45	42	43	40	44
Transportation equipment.	1,091	1,473	1,984	1,811	1,849	1,923	1,871	1,810	1,521
Waste and scrap materials	439	623	619	651	725	706	701	726	729
Tons (mil.) [1]	**1,425**	**1,550**	**1,738**	**1,799**	**1,844**	**1,899**	**1,957**	**1,940**	**1,934**
Farm products	147	154	136	141	142	140	149	152	156
Metallic ores	47	44	32	33	33	60	61	59	60
Coal.	579	627	758	784	792	804	852	850	879
Nonmetallic minerals	109	110	126	133	140	146	141	138	132
Food and kindred products	81	91	94	102	100	102	105	105	105
Lumber and wood products	53	51	49	47	47	48	43	36	31
Pulp, paper, allied products	33	36	36	39	38	38	37	35	34
Chemicals, allied products	126	138	155	162	167	165	167	176	175
Petroleum and coal products	40	43	42	49	54	57	57	57	46
Stone, clay, and glass products	44	43	48	51	53	55	52	48	45
Primary metal products	38	47	60	54	59	57	61	56	54
Fabricated metal products	1	1	1	1	1	1	1	1	1
Machinery, exc. electrical	1	1	1	1	1	1	1	1	1
Transportation equipment.	23	30	42	36	37	38	36	34	27
Waste and scrap materials	28	38	40	41	46	47	48	48	49
Gross revenue (mil. dol.) [1] . . .	**29,775**	**33,782**	**36,331**	**38,434**	**41,622**	**46,743**	**52,639**	**54,637**	**60,513**
Farm products	2,422	3,020	2,673	2,870	3,176	3,628	4,205	4,529	5,403
Metallic ores	408	394	338	289	317	485	529	542	637
Coal.	6,954	7,356	7,794	7,890	8,418	9,393	10,821	11,471	14,200
Nonmetallic minerals	885	875	969	1,041	1,131	1,293	1,462	1,527	1,749
Food and kindred products	2,188	2,464	2,424	2,760	2,892	3,253	3,730	4,041	4,610
Lumber and wood products	1,390	1,385	1,524	1,745	1,924	2,278	2,335	1,987	1,684
Pulp, paper, allied products	1,486	1,543	1,526	1,646	1,730	1,953	2,124	2,100	2,228
Chemicals, allied products	3,933	4,553	4,636	4,779	5,100	5,432	6,049	6,830	7,655
Petroleum and coal products	918	997	1,010	1,123	1,268	1,500	1,722	1,853	1,930
Stone, clay, and glass products	931	1,044	1,113	1,211	1,323	1,505	1,664	1,607	1,636
Primary metal products	979	1,199	1,371	1,349	1,518	1,734	2,157	2,267	2,572
Fabricated metal products	42	44	48	47	50	55	79	86	92
Machinery, exc. electrical	67	69	61	60	72	91	109	126	166
Transportation equipment.	3,100	3,269	3,843	3,707	3,746	3,960	4,228	4,292	3,964
Waste and scrap materials	504	685	706	799	956	1,070	1,190	1,276	1,415

[1] Includes commodity groups and small packaged freight shipments, not shown separately.

Source: Association of American Railroads, Washington, DC, *Freight Commodity Statistics*, annual; <http://www.aar.org/Resources/Resources%20Landing.aspx>.

Table 1087. Railroads, Class-I Cars of Revenue Freight Loaded, 1990 to 2008, and by Commodity Group, 2007 and 2008

[In thousands (16,177 represents 16,177,000). Figures are 52-week totals]

Year	Car-loads [1]	Commodity group	Carloads 2007	Carloads 2008 [2]	Commodity group	Carloads 2007	Carloads 2008 [2]
1990	16,177	Coal	7,164	7,406	Metals and products	616	574
2000 [2] . . .	16,354	Metallic ores.	240	248	Stone, clay, and glass products. . .	454	416
2002 [2] . . .	16,101	Grain	1,178	1,215	Nonmetallic minerals.	312	287
2003 [2] . . .	16,159	Motor vehicles and equipment.	1,029	811	Waste and scrap materials.	501	486
2004 [2] . . .	16,600	Pulp, paper, allied products. .	392	367	Lumber, wood products	227	179
2005 [2] . . .	16,691	Primary forest products	122	109	Coke	277	185
2006 [2] . . .	16,936	Food and kindred products . .	449	444	Petroleum products	334	313
2007 [2] . . .	16,564	Grain mill products	466	446	All other carloads	304	318
2008 [2, 3] . .	16,208						

[1] Excludes intermodal.　[2] Excludes 3 Class I railroads.　[3] 2008 data preliminary.

Source: Association of American Railroads, Washington, DC, *Weekly Railroad Traffic*, annual. See also <http://www.aar.org/NewsAndEvents/NewsAndEvents.aspx>.

Table 1088. Petroleum Pipeline Companies—Characteristics: 1980 to 2007

[173 represents 173,000. Covers pipeline companies operating in interstate commerce and subject to the jurisdiction of the Federal Energy Regulatory Commission]

Item	Unit	1980	1990	1995	2000	2003	2004	2005	2006	2007
Miles of pipeline, total . . .	1,000	173	168	177	152	140	142	131	140	147
Gathering lines.	1,000	36	32	35	18	14	15	14	12	15
Trunk lines.	1,000	136	136	142	134	126	127	118	129	132
Total deliveries.	Mil. Bbl.	10,600	11,378	12,862	14,450	13,236	13,394	12,732	12,768	13,934
Crude oil	Mil. Bbl.	6,405	6,563	6,952	6,923	6,941	6,612	6,675	6,668	7,038
Products	Mil. Bbl.	4,195	4,816	5,910	7,527	6,295	6,782	6,057	6,101	6,896
Total trunk line traffic. . .	Bil. Bbl.-miles . .	3,405	3,500	3,619	3,508	3,591	3,652	3,485	3,536	3,459
Crude oil	Bil. Bbl.-miles . .	1,948	1,891	1,899	1,602	1,609	1,604	1,571	1,578	1,451
Products	Bil. Bbl.-miles . .	1,458	1,609	1,720	1,906	1,982	2,049	1,914	1,958	2,008
Carrier property value . . .	Mil. dol.	19,752	25,828	27,460	29,648	32,018	29,552	29,526	32,686	35,863
Operating revenues	Mil. dol.	6,356	7,149	7,711	7,483	7,704	8,020	7,917	8,517	8,996
Net income	Mil. dol.	1,912	2,340	2,670	2,705	3,470	3,323	3,076	3,743	3,757

Source: PennWell Publishing Co., Houston, Texas, *Oil & Gas Journal*, annual (copyright).

Table 1089. U.S. Postal Service Rates for Letters and Postcards: 1991 to 2009

[In dollars. International rates exclude Canada and Mexico]

Domestic mail date of rate change	Letters First ounce	Letters Each added ounce	Postcards	Express mail— first 1/2 pound	International air mail date of rate change	Let-ters— first ounce [1]	Post-cards	Aero-grammes
1991 (Feb. 3)	0.29	0.23	0.19	9.95	First 1/2 ounce . . .			
1995 (Jan. 1).	0.32	0.23	0.20	10.75	1991 (Feb. 3) . . .	0.50	0.40	0.45
1999 (Jan. 10).	0.33	0.22	0.20	11.75	1995 (July 9). . . .	0.60	0.40	0.45
2001 (Jan. 7).	0.34	0.21	0.20	12.25	1999 (Jan. 10). . .	0.60	0.50	0.50
2001 (July 1).	0.34	0.23	0.21	12.45	First ounce [1]			
2002 (June 30)	0.37	0.23	0.23	13.65	2001 (Jan. 7) . . .	0.80	0.70	0.70
2006 (Jan. 8).	0.39	0.24	0.24	14.40	2006 (Jan. 8) . . .	0.84	0.75	0.75
2007 (May 14).	0.41	0.17	0.26	16.25	2007 (May 14). . .	0.90	0.90	[2]
2008 (May 12).	0.42	0.17	0.27	[3]12.60	2008 (May 12). . .	0.94	0.94	[2]
2009 (May 11).	0.44	0.17	0.28	[4]13.05	2009 (May 11). . .	0.98	0.98	[2]

[1] International letter prices after the first ounce vary according to the price group that is applicable to each destination country.　[2] Aerogrammes were discontinued on May 14, 2007.　[3] On May 12, 2008, the Postal Service initiated a zoned pricing structure for Express Mail. Prices for a mail piece weighing up to a half-pound range from $12.60 to zones 1 and 2 to $19.50 to zone 8.　[4] Express Mail prices increased on January 18, 2009. Prices for a mail piece weighing up to a half-pound range from $13.05 to zones 1 and 2 to $21.20 to zone 8.

Source: U.S. Postal Service, *"United States Domestic Postage Rate: Recent History"* and unpublished data. See also <http://www.usps.com/rates/welcome.htm>.

Table 1090. U.S. Postal Service—Summary: 1990 to 2008

[166,301 represents 166,301,000,000. For years ending September 30. Includes Puerto Rico and all outlying areas. See text, this section]

Item	1990	1995	2000	2005	2006	2007	2008
Offices, stations, and branches	**40,067**	**39,149**	**38,060**	**37,142**	**36,826**	**36,721**	**36,723**
Number of post offices	28,959	28,392	27,876	27,385	27,318	27,276	27,232
Number of stations and branches	11,108	10,757	10,184	9,757	9,508	9,445	9,491
Delivery Points (mil.)	(NA)	(NA)	135.9	144.3	146.2	148.0	149.0
Residential	(NA)	(NA)	123.9	131.3	133.0	134.6	135.7
City	(NA)	(NA)	76.1	78.5	78.9	79.5	79.8
P.O. Box	(NA)	(NA)	15.9	15.6	15.6	15.6	15.6
Rural/highway contract	(NA)	(NA)	31.9	37.2	38.4	39.5	40.2
Business	(NA)	(NA)	12.1	13.0	13.2	13.4	13.5
Pieces of mail handled (mil.)	**166,301**	**180,734**	**207,882**	**211,743**	**213,138**	**212,234**	**202,703**
Domestic	165,503	179,933	206,782	210,891	212,345	210,604	201,128
First class mail [1]	89,270	96,296	103,526	98,071	97,618	96,297	91,697
Priority mail [6]	59	57	71	56	56	(2)	(2)
Express mail [7]	518	869	1,223	888	924	(2)	(2)
Periodicals (formerly 2d class)	10,680	10,194	10,365	9,070	9,023	8,796	8,605
Standard Mail (formerly Standard A)	63,725	71,112	90,057	100,942	102,460	103,516	99,084
Package Services (formerly Standard B)	663	936	1,128	1,166	1,175	915	846
U.S. Postal Service	538	412	363	621	1,016	1,008	824
Free for the blind	35	52	47	76	75	72	72
Shipping Services Volume [2]	(X)	(X)	(X)	(X)	(X)	1,630	1,575
International economy mail (surface)	166	106	79	23	155	(2)	(2)
International airmail	632	696	1,021	829	638	(2)	(2)
Employees, total (1,000)	**843**	**875**	**901**	**803**	**796**	**786**	**765**
Career	761	753	788	705	696	685	663
Headquarters	2	2	2	3	3	3	3
Headquarters support	6	4	6	4	4	5	4
Inspection Service	4	4	4	3	3	3	3
Inspector General	(X)	(X)	1	1	1	1	1
Field Career	749	743	775	693	685	673	652
Postmasters	27	27	26	25	25	25	25
Supervisors/managers	43	35	39	33	33	33	32
Professional, administrative, and technical	10	11	10	9	9	8	8
Clerks	290	274	282	222	214	204	195
Mail handlers	51	57	61	56	57	58	56
City carriers	236	240	241	228	224	222	212
Motor vehicle operators	7	8	9	9	9	9	9
Rural carriers	42	46	57	64	66	68	69
Special delivery messengers	2	2	(X)	(X)	(X)	(X)	(X)
Building and equipment maintenance	33	38	42	40	40	40	40
Vehicle maintenance	5	5	6	5	6	5	5
Other [3]	1	2	2	2	2	1	1
Noncareer	83	122	114	98	100	101	102
Casuals	27	26	30	19	23	22	12
Transitional	(X)	32	13	8	5	5	18
Rural substitutes	43	50	58	57	59	60	58
Relief/Leave replacements	12	13	12	12	12	12	12
Nonbargaining temporary	(Z)	1	1	1	1	1	1
Compensation and employee benefits (mil. dol.)	34,214	41,931	49,532	53,932	56,302	64,270	60,992
Avg. salary per employee (dol.) [4]	37,570	45,001	50,103	62,635	64,992	65,905	67,076
Pieces of mail per employee, (1,000)	197	207	231	264	268	270	265
Total revenue (mil. dol.) [5]	**40,074**	**54,509**	**64,540**	**69,993**	**72,817**	**74,973**	**74,968**
Operating postal revenue	39,201	54,176	64,476	69,798	72,551	74,715	74,829
Mail revenue	37,892	52,490	62,284	66,649	69,144	71,035	71,261
First class mail	24,023	31,955	35,516	36,062	37,039	38,405	38,179
Priority mail [6]	1,555	3,075	4,837	4,634	5,043	(2)	(2)
Express mail [7]	630	711	996	872	918	(2)	(2)
Periodicals (formerly 2d class)	1,509	1,972	2,171	2,161	2,215	2,188	2,295
Standard Mail (formerly Standard A)	8,082	11,792	15,193	18,954	19,877	20,779	20,586
Package Services (formerly Standard B)	919	1,525	1,912	2,201	2,259	1,812	1,845
Shipping Services [2]	(X)	(X)	(X)	(X)	(X)	7,852	8,355
International economy mail (surface)	222	205	180	134	118	(2)	(2)
International airmail	941	1,254	1,477	1,631	1,678	(2)	(2)
Service revenue	1,310	1,687	2,191	3,150	3,407	3,743	3,671
Registry [8]	174	118	98	77	73	53	57
Certified [8]	310	560	385	601	632	698	718
Insurance [8]	47	52	109	132	137	157	145
Collect-on-delivery	26	21	22	9	10	(NA)	(NA)
Money orders	155	196	235	208	193	211	205
Other [8]	592	737	1,342	2,122	2,363	2,624	2,547
Operating expenses (million dollars) [9]	40,490	50,730	62,992	68,283	71,681	80,105	77,738

NA Not available.   X Not applicable.   Z Fewer than 500.   [1] Items mailed at 1st class rates and weighing 11 ounces or less.   [2] "Volume" and "Mailing & Shipping Revenue" restructured for the "Postal Accountability and Enhancement Act (PAEA) of 2006."   [3] Includes discontinued operations, area offices, and nurses.   [4] For career bargaining unit employees. Includes fringe benefits.   [5] Net revenues after refunds of postage. Includes operating reimbursements, stamped envelope purchases, indemnity claims, and miscellaneous revenue and expenditure offsets. Shown in year which gave rise to the earnings.   [6] Provides 2 to 3 day delivery service.   [7] Overnight delivery of packages weighing up to 70 pounds.   [8] Beginning 2000, return receipt revenue broken out from registry, certified, and insurance and included in "other."   [9] Shown in year in which obligation was incurred.

Source: U.S. Postal Service, *Annual Report of the Postmaster General* and *Comprehensive Statement on Postal Operations,* annual and unpublished data.

Section 24
Information and Communications

This section presents statistics on the various information and communications media: publishing, including newspapers, periodicals, books, and software; motion pictures, sound recordings, broadcasting, and telecommunications; and information services, such as libraries. Statistics on computer use and Internet access are also included. Data on the usage, finances, and operations of the U.S. Postal Service previously shown in this section are now presented in Section 23, Transportation.

Information industry—The U.S. Census Bureau's *Service Annual Survey, Information Services Sector,* provides estimates of operating revenue of taxable firms and revenues and expenses of firms exempt from federal taxes for industries in the information sector of the economy. Similar estimates were previously issued in the *Annual Survey of Communications Services.* Data are based on the North American Industry Classification System (NAICS), and the information sector is a newly created economic sector. It comprises establishments engaged in the following processes: (a) producing and distributing information and cultural products, (b) providing the means to transmit or distribute these products as well as data or communications, and (c) processing data. It includes establishments previously classified in the Standard Industrial Classification (SIC) in manufacturing (publishing); transportation, communications, and utilities (telecommunications and broadcasting); and services (software publishing, motion picture production, data processing, online information services, and libraries).

This new sector is comprised of industries which existed previously, were revised from previous industry definitions, or are completely new industries. Among those which existed previously are newspaper publishers, motion picture and video production, and online information services. Revised industries include book publishers, libraries, and archives. Newly created industries include database and directory publishers, record production, music publishers, sound recording studios, cable networks, wired telecommunications carriers, paging, and satellite telecommunications.

Data from 1998 to 2003 are based on the 1997 NAICS; beginning 2004, data are based on the 2002 NAICS. Major revisions in many communications industries affect the comparability of these data. The following URL contains detailed information about NAICS <http://www.census.gov/epcd/www/naics.html>. See also the text in Section 15, Business Enterprise.

Several industries in the information sectors have been consolidated: paging is now included in Wireless Telecommunications Carriers (except Satellite). Cable and other program distribution and most Internet service providers are now included in Wired Telecommunications Carriers.

The 1997 Economic Census was the first economic census to cover the new information sector of the economy. The census, conducted every 5 years, for the years ending "2" and "7," provides information on the number of establishments, receipts, payroll, and paid employees for the United States and various geographic levels. The most recent reports are from the 2007 Economic Census. This census was conducted in accordance with the 2007 NAICS.

The Federal Communications Commission (FCC), established in 1934, regulates wire and radio communications. Only the largest carriers and holding companies file annual financial reports which are publically available. The FCC has jurisdiction over interstate and foreign communication services but not over intrastate or local services. The gross operating revenues of the telephone carriers reporting publically available data annually to the FCC, however, are estimated to cover

Information and Communications   689

about 90 percent of the revenues of all U.S. telephone companies. Data are not service comparable with Census Bureau's *Annual Survey* because of coverage and different accounting practices for those telephone companies which report to the FCC.

Reports filed by the broadcasting industry cover all radio and television stations operating in the United States. The private radio services represent the largest and most diverse group of licensees regulated by the FCC. These services provide voice, data communications, point-to-point, and point-to-multipoint radio communications for fixed and mobile communicators. Major users of these services are small businesses, the aviation industry, the maritime trades, the land transportation industry, the manufacturing industry, state and local public safety and governmental authorities, emergency medical service providers, amateur radio operators, and personal radio operations (CB and the General Mobile Radio Service). The FCC also licenses entities as private and common carriers. Private and common carriers provide fixed and land mobile communications service on a for-profit basis. Principal sources of wire,

radio, and television data are the FCC's *Annual Report* and its annual *Statistics of Communications Common Carriers* <http://fcc.gov/wcb/iatd/stats.html/>.

Statistics on publishing are available from the Census Bureau, as well as from various private agencies. Editor & Publisher Co., New York, NY, presents annual data on the number and circulation of daily and Sunday newspapers in its *International Year Book*. The Book Industry Study Group, New York, NY, collects data on books sold and domestic consumer expenditures. Data on academic and public libraries are collected by the Institute of Museums and Library Services. Data on Internet use by adults are collected by the Pew Internet and American Life Project, Washington, DC, and Mediamark Research, Inc., New York, NY.

Advertising—Data on advertising previously shown in this section are now presented in Section 27, Accommodation, Food Services, and Other Services.

Statistical reliability—For a discussion of statistical collection and estimation, sampling procedures, and measures of statistical reliability applicable to Census Bureau data, see Appendix III.

Table 1091. **Information Industries—Establishments, Employees, and Payroll: 2005 and 2006**

[For establishments with payroll (3,402.6 represents 3,402,600). Excludes most government employees, railroad employees, and self-employed persons. For statement on methodology, see Appendix III]

Industry	2002 NAICS code [1]	Establishments (number)		Paid employees [2] (1,000)		Annual payroll (mil. dol.)	
		2005	2006	2005	2006	2005	2006
Information industries	51	**141,290**	**141,945**	**3,402.6**	**3,396.2**	**203,130**	**213,277**
Publishing industries	511	31,538	31,821	1,032.3	1,039.7	67,094	72,651
Newspaper, periodical, book, and database publishers	5111	22,745	23,080	704.6	699.9	33,111	34,857
Newspaper publishers	51111	8,395	8,547	380.1	372.0	14,376	14,401
Periodical publishers	51112	7,846	7,932	158.8	161.8	9,940	10,886
Book publishers	51113	3,359	3,335	83.6	83.5	4,656	4,994
Database and directory publishers	51114	1,824	1,834	57.0	56.5	3,030	3,365
Other publishers	51119	1,321	1,432	25.0	26.1	1,109	1,212
Greeting card publishers	511191	120	132	12.5	12.8	580	631
All other publishers	511199	1,201	1,300	12.6	13.4	529	581
Software publishers	5112	8,793	8,741	327.6	339.8	33,983	37,793
Motion picture and sound recording industries	512	23,579	23,961	314.4	331.2	14,040	15,263
Motion picture and video industries	5121	20,131	20,396	292.1	308.8	12,404	13,450
Motion picture and video production	51211	12,419	12,776	131.6	145.4	9,301	10,143
Motion picture and video distribution	51212	457	412	4.3	4.6	257	270
Motion picture and video exhibition	51213	5,129	5,049	134.0	134.5	1,288	1,283
Motion picture theaters (except drive-ins) . .	512131	4,854	4,771	132.2	132.8	1,260	1,257
Drive-in motion picture theaters.	512132	275	278	1.7	1.8	27	26
Post production and other motion picture and video industries	51219	2,126	2,159	22.3	24.3	1,559	1,754
Teleproduction and other post-production services	512191	1,804	1,841	17.5	19.6	1,201	1,382
Other motion picture and video industries . .	512199	322	318	4.7	4.7	358	371
Sound recording industries	5122	3,448	3,565	22.3	22.5	1,636	1,813
Record production	51221	349	375	1.5	1.5	72	79
Integrated record production/distribution.	51222	402	421	7.8	8.1	891	1,024
Music publishers	51223	645	671	4.6	4.2	337	337
Sound recording studios	51224	1,561	1,608	4.9	5.5	204	235
Other sound recording industries	51229	491	490	3.4	3.2	132	137
Broadcasting (except Internet)	515	10,342	10,583	287.0	302.0	17,354	18,180
Radio and television broadcasting	5151	9,685	9,910	248.3	262.2	13,200	14,516
Radio broadcasting	51511	7,697	7,611	124.1	126.7	6,136	6,100
Radio networks	515111	743	782	11.9	11.9	797	837
Radio stations	515112	6,954	6,829	112.2	114.8	5,339	5,263
Television broadcasting.	51512	1,988	2,299	124.2	135.6	7,064	8,416
Cable and other subscription programming	5152	657	673	38.8	39.7	4,154	3,664
Internet publishing and broadcasting	516	2,343	2,653	36.1	41.6	2,687	3,164
Telecommunications	517	49,431	47,762	1,226.5	1,161.8	69,687	69,821
Wired telecommunications carriers	5171	26,744	27,159	693.7	634.5	41,799	41,102
Wireless telecommunications carriers (except satellite).	5172	14,173	12,108	250.0	241.4	14,035	13,578
Paging.	517211	788	623	7.6	4.8	359	240
Cellular and other wireless telecommunications	517212	13,385	11,485	242.3	236.6	13,676	13,339
Telecommunications resellers	5173	2,778	2,557	33.7	32.4	1,762	1,791
Satellite telecommunications	5174	605	581	15.4	11.5	992	1,119
Cable and other program distribution	5175	4,561	4,816	224.6	231.8	10,512	11,586
Other telecommunications	5179	570	541	9.2	10.2	587	646
Internet service providers, Web search portals, and data processing service	518	20,142	21,002	452.2	465.3	30,292	32,151
Internet service providers and Web search portals.	5181	5,579	5,572	72.7	80.2	7,588	8,036
Internet service providers	518111	4,948	4,839	57.6	58.0	3,701	4,145
Web search portals	518112	631	733	15.1	22.2	3,887	3,890
Data processing, hosting, and related services . .	5182	14,563	15,430	379.4	385.1	22,704	24,116
Other information services	519	3,915	4,163	54.1	54.6	1,975	2,047
News syndicates.	51911	606	764	11.8	11.6	705	746
Libraries and archives	51912	2,593	2,650	30.5	31.5	720	768
All other information services	51919	716	749	11.7	11.5	550	533

[1] North American Industry Classification System, 2002; see text, this section and Section 15.   [2] For employees on the payroll for the pay period including March 12.

Source: U.S. Census Bureau, "County Business Patterns" (published June 2009); <http://www.census.gov/econ/cbp/index.html>.

Information and Communications   691

Table 1092. **Information Sector Services—Estimated Revenue and Expenses: 2005 to 2007**

[In millions of dollars (1,003,262 represents $1,003,262,000,000). For taxable and tax-exempt employer firms. Estimates have been adjusted to the results of the 2002 Economic Census. Based on the Service Annual Survey; see Appendix III.

Industry	2002 NAICS code [1]	Operating revenue			Operating expenses		
		2005	2006	2007	2005	2006	2007
Information industries.	51	**1,003,262**	**1,057,430**	**1,114,883**	**803,658**	**836,794**	**864,642**
Publishing industries (except Internet).	511	269,715	282,880	297,709	196,848	204,741	213,829
Newspaper, periodical, book, and directory publishers	5111	148,381	150,623	154,005	110,054	113,759	117,715
Newspaper publishers.	51111	49,958	49,601	48,274	41,221	44,134	42,291
Periodical publishers.	51112	44,315	46,948	49,292	35,188	36,540	39,615
Book publishers.	51113	27,904	28,237	29,296	16,997	16,053	16,954
Directory and mailing list publishers.	51114	19,413	18,915	19,890	12,222	12,443	14,135
Other publishers	51119	6,791	6,922	7,253	4,426	4,589	4,720
Greeting card publishers	511191	4,553	4,631	4,799	2,759	2,814	2,913
All other publishers	511199	2,238	2,291	2,454	1,667	1,775	1,807
Software publishers	5112	121,334	132,257	143,704	86,794	90,982	96,114
Motion picture and sound recording industries	512	93,655	98,392	102,166	72,576	74,257	75,885
Motion picture and video industries.	5121	74,789	77,576	82,066	57,568	57,826	60,399
Motion picture and video production and distribution	51211,12	59,760	61,847	65,922	45,219	45,407	48,085
Motion picture and video exhibition	51213	10,789	11,194	11,341	8,501	8,454	8,208
Motion picture theaters (except drive-ins)	512131	10,669	10,983	11,123	8,422	8,343	8,075
Drive-in motion picture theaters	512132	120	(S)	(S)	79	(S)	(S)
Postproduction services and other motionpicture and video industries.	51219	4,240	4,535	4,803	3,848	3,965	4,106
Teleproduction and other postproduction services.	512191	3,379	3,624	3,822	3,078	3,145	3,344
Other motion picture and video industries.	512199	861	911	981	770	820	762
Sound recording industries	5122	18,866	20,816	20,100	15,008	16,431	15,486
Record production	51221	410	285	350	296	317	310
Integrated record production/distribution	51222	12,856	14,405	13,591	10,993	12,150	(S)
Music publishers	51223	4,260	4,544	4,432	2,444	2,552	2,692
Sound recording studios	51224	766	928	998	672	772	879
Other sound recording industries	51229	574	654	729	603	640	685
Broadcasting (except Internet).	515	87,694	93,134	96,728	67,015	69,710	72,926
Radio and television broadcasting	5151	52,308	55,153	55,858	43,546	44,869	46,198
Radio broadcasting	51511	17,059	18,181	18,850	15,013	16,388	16,395
Radio networks	515111	3,347	4,474	5,226	4,858	6,481	6,407
Radio stations	515112	13,712	13,707	13,624	10,155	9,907	9,988
Television broadcasting	51512	35,249	36,972	37,008	28,533	28,481	29,803
Cable and other subscription programming. . . .	5152	35,386	37,981	40,870	23,469	24,841	26,728
Internet publishing and broadcasting	516	10,391	12,862	15,480	9,084	11,272	13,784
Telecommunications	517	446,220	463,253	490,761	380,731	391,733	397,903
Wired telecommunications carriers	5171	206,622	195,092	192,779	176,407	168,750	158,626
Wireless telecommunications carriers (except satellite)	5172	140,025	158,577	174,085	122,543	135,043	137,818
Paging.	517211	1,990	1,874	1,557	1,750	1,528	1,221
Cellular and other wireless telecommunications	517212	138,035	156,703	172,528	120,793	133,515	136,597
Telecommunications resellers	5173	11,228	12,224	13,606	6,832	6,839	7,414
Satellite telecommunications	5174	5,808	6,667	7,393	4,447	5,093	5,756
Cable and other program distribution.	5175	80,492	88,788	100,849	69,030	74,536	86,481
Other telecommunications.	5179	2,045	1,905	2,049	1,472	1,472	1,808
Internet service providers, Web search portals, and data processing services	518	88,598	99,546	104,050	71,943	79,290	84,120
Internet service providers and Web search portals.	5181	25,969	28,749	31,168	17,497	19,229	19,709
Internet service providers	518111	18,977	19,092	19,086	14,253	14,318	13,607
Web search portals	518112	6,992	9,657	12,082	3,244	4,911	6,102
Data processing, hosting, and related services.	5182	62,629	70,797	72,882	54,446	60,061	64,411
Other information services	519	6,989	7,363	7,989	5,461	5,791	6,195
News syndicates	51911	2,098	2,209	2,418	1,836	1,880	1,911
Libraries and archives.	51912	1,967	2,077	2,288	1,720	1,788	1,969
Other information services	51919	2,924	3,077	3,283	1,905	2,123	2,315

S Data do not meet publication standards.   [1] North American Industry Classification System (NAICS), 2002; see text this section and Section 15.

Source: U.S. Census Bureau, "2007 Service Annual Survey, Information Sector Services" (published March 2009). See <http://www.census.gov/services/>.

Table 1093. **Information Industries—Establishments, Revenue, Payroll and Employees by Kind of Business: 2007**

[For establishments with payroll. (1,075,154 represents $1,075,154,000,000). Based on the 2007 Economic Census; see Appendix III]

Kind of business	2007 NAICS code [1]	Number of establishments	Receipts (mil. dol.)	Annual payroll (mil. dol.)	Paid employees (1,000)
Information industries	51	141,034	1,075,154	223,377	3,428
Publishing industries (except Internet)	511	30,016	273,416	75,847	1,028
Motion picture & sound recording industries	512	23,542	95,164	17,230	326
Broadcasting (except Internet)	515	10,030	98,663	17,647	291
Telecommunications	517	52,614	498,256	75,228	1,250
Data processing, hosting and related services	518	16,911	71,308	26,841	400
Other information services	519	7,921	38,346	10,584	133

[1] North American Industry Classification System, 2007; see text, this section and Section 15.

Source: U.S. Census Bureau, "2007 Economic Census, Advance Summary Statistics for the United States (2007 NAICS Basis)," <http://www.census.gov/econ/census07/>.

Table 1094. **Media Usage and Consumer Spending: 2004 to 2012**

[Estimates for time spent were derived using rating data for television and cable television, survey research for radio, mobile, out-of-home media and yellow pages, and consumer purchase data (units, admissions, access) for books, home video, in-flight entertainment, Internet, newspapers, magazines, box office, recorded music, videogames. Adults 18 and older were the basis for estimates for newspapers, consumer books, consumer magazines, in-flight entertainment, out-of-home media, yellow pages and home video. Persons 12 and older were the basis for the estimates for box office, broadcast TV, cable TV Internet, mobile, radio recorded, music and videogames]

Item	2004	2005	2006	2007	2008, proj.	2009, proj.	2010, proj.	2011, proj.	2012, proj.
HOURS PER PERSON PER YEAR [1]									
Total [2]	3,475	3,501	3,499	3,496	3,493	3,493	3,509	3,502	3,515
Television	1,550	1,596	1,612	1,613	1,603	1,606	1,607	1,602	1,597
Broadcast Television	679	655	650	639	639	642	643	644	644
Network - affliated stations.	584	561	577	577	577	582	583	584	585
Independent and public stations [4]	95	94	73	63	62	60	60	60	59
Cable networks	871	942	962	973	964	964	964	958	952
Basic cable networks	719	778	805	824	817	822	827	832	831
Premium cable networks [4]	152	164	157	149	147	142	137	126	122
Broadcast and satellite radio.	821	807	791	782	777	758	751	735	729
Recorded music	100	107	187	177	173	177	184	192	200
Newspapers.	192	187	178	171	164	159	155	152	150
Pure-play internet services [3]	166	173	182	189	193	195	197	197	197
Consumer magazines	125	124	125	125	126	124	124	122	123
Consumer books	110	109	110	109	109	108	108	108	107
Videogames.	79	73	76	85	101	116	125	131	142
Home video [5]	67	63	62	61	60	59	59	60	59
Yellow Pages	12	12	12	13	13	13	12	12	12
Box office	13	12	12	12	12	12	12	12	12
Pure-play mobile services [3]	7	9	12	15	19	24	29	32	36
Educational books [6]	8	8	8	8	8	8	8	9	9
CONSUMER SPENDING PER PERSON PER YEAR (dol.)									
Total	770.95	784.24	813.19	851.57	903.30	950.64	997.07	1,038.70	1,077.66
Television	256.39	280.21	307.58	332.78	357.67	383.06	407.59	431.75	454.67
Cable and satellite TV	256.30	279.81	306.60	330.93	354.51	378.15	400.78	422.82	443.61
Broadcast Television	0.09	0.39	0.98	1.86	3.16	4.90	6.81	8.93	11.06
Home video [5]	125.36	114.77	114.12	109.52	107.24	105.82	105.93	105.78	105.22
Consumer books	94.60	98.01	99.56	103.60	105.52	107.96	110.75	114.03	117.45
Pure-play internet services [3]	60.31	57.88	54.06	55.45	59.53	63.88	67.42	70.65	73.48
Recorded music	51.97	50.59	49.48	44.72	43.11	42.37	42.63	43.04	43.33
Newspapers.	51.92	50.32	49.23	47.74	45.78	44.61	43.85	44.20	44.41
Consumer magazines	47.33	47.42	44.46	44.35	44.42	43.97	44.31	43.10	43.49
Box office	37.50	35.54	36.38	38.01	38.16	37.66	38.80	39.29	39.66
Videogames.	33.61	32.15	33.91	43.91	55.77	67.60	75.36	80.76	90.59
Pure-play mobile services [3]	7.54	9.59	12.33	15.66	19.47	23.42	27.22	30.70	33.60
Broadcast and satellite radio	1.19	3.03	5.76	7.59	9.31	10.93	12.25	13.34	14.26

[1] Can include concurrent use of media, such as watching television and reading e-mail simultaneously. Does not include media use at work. [2] Includes other media not shown seperately. [3] Online and mobile use and spending on traditional media platforms, such as downloaded music, newspaper websites or info alerts, e-books, cable modems, online video of television programs and Internet radio were included in the traditional media segment, not in pure-play Internet services or pure-play mobile content. Pure-play Internet services and pure-play mobile content included telecommunications access, such as DSL and dial up, but not cable modems, pure play content such as MobiTV, GameSpy, eHarmony, and mobile instant messaging and email alerts. [4] Telemundo and Univision affiliates included in independent and public stations. Pay-per-view, interactive channels, home shopping, and audio-only feeds included in premium cable and satellite services. [5] Playback of prerecorded VHS cassettes and DVDs only. [6] Grades 9–12 and college only. Not included in consumer spending.

Source: Veronis Suhler Stevenson, New York, NY, *Communications Industry Forecast & Report*, annual (copyright).

Information and Communications 693

Table 1095. **Utilization of Selected Media: 1980 to 2007**

[78.6 represents 78,600,000]

Item	Unit	1980	1990	2000	2001	2002	2003	2004	2005	2006	2007
Households with—											
Telephone service [1]	Percent . . .	93.0	93.3	94.6	94.6	95.5	95.5	94.2	92.4	92.8	94.6
Radio [2]	Millions . . .	78.6	94.4	100.5	101.9	105.1	106.7	108.3	109.9	110.5	110.5
Percent of total households. . . .	Percent . . .	99.0	99.0	99.0	99.0	99.0	99.0	99.0	99.0	99.0	99.0
Average number of sets	Number . . .	5.5	5.6	5.6	5.6	5.6	8.0	8.0	8.0	8.0	8.0
Television [3]	Millions . . .	76	92	101	102	106	107	109	110	110	111
Percent of total households. . . .	Percent . . .	97.9	98.2	98.2	98.2	98.2	98.2	98.2	98.2	98.2	98.2
Television sets in homes.	Millions . . .	128	193	245	248	254	260	268	287	301	311
Average number of sets per home	Number . . .	1.7	2.0	2.4	2.4	2.4	2.4	2.5	2.6	2.7	2.8
Wired cable television [4]	Millions . . .	15.2	51.9	68.6	69.5	73.2	74.4	73.8	73.9	62.1	61.3
Percent of TV households. . . .	Percent . . .	19.9	56.4	68.0	68.0	69.4	69.8	68.1	67.5	72.4	69.3
Alternative delivery system (ADS) households [4]	Millions . . .	(NA)	(NA)	11.7	14.7	17.4	19.7	21.2	23.3	24.5	28.0
Percent of TV households. . . .	Percent . . .	(NA)	(NA)	11.4	14.1	16.3	18.2	19.3	20.8	28.5	31.6
Commercial radio stations: [2, 5]											
AM	Number . . .	4,589	4,987	4,685	4,727	4,804	4,802	4,770	4,758	4,751	4,776
FM	Number . . .	3,282	4,392	5,892	6,051	6,161	6,207	6,217	6,215	6,252	6,290
Television stations: [5] Total	Number . . .	1,011	1,442	1,663	1,686	1,714	1,730	1,748	1,749	1,754	1,759
Commercial.	Number . . .	734	1,092	1,288	1,309	1,333	1,349	1,366	1,370	1,373	1,379
VHF	Number . . .	516	547	567	572	581	587	589	589	786	796
UHF	Number . . .	218	545	721	737	752	762	777	781	587	583
Cable television systems [6].	Number . . .	4,225	9,575	10,400	10,300	9,900	9,400	8,875	7,926	7,090	6,101
Daily newspaper circulation [7]	Millions . . .	62.2	62.3	55.8	55.6	55.2	55.2	54.6	53.3	52.3	50.7

NA Not available. [1] For occupied housing units. 1980 as of April 1; all other years as of March. Source: U.S. Census Bureau, *1980 Census of Housing,* vol. 1; thereafter, Federal Communications Commission, *Trends in Telephone Service,* annual. [2] 1980–1995 as of December 31. Source: M Street Corp. as reported by Radio Advertising Bureau New York, NY; through 1990, Radio Facts, annual (copyright); beginning 1995, Radio Marketing Guide and Fact Book for Advertisers, annual (copyright). **Number of stations** on the air compiled from Federal Communications Commission reports. Beginning 1999, Federal Communications Commission. See <http://www.fcc.gov/mb/audio/totals>. [3] As of January of year shown. Excludes Alaska and Hawaii. Source: Television Bureau of Advertising, Inc., *Trends in Television,* annual (copyright). [4] Wired cable as of February; ADS for fourth quarter. Excludes Alaska and Hawaii. Source: See footnote 3. [5] Source: Beginning 1999, Federal Communications Commission, unpublished data. See <http://www.fcc.gov/mb/audio/totals>. Broadcast Station Totals as of December, Federal Communications Commission. [6] As of January 1. Source: Warren Communications News, Washington DC, *Television and Cable Factbook* (copyright). [7] As of September 30. Source: Editor & Publisher, Co., New York, NY, *Editor & Publisher International Year Book,* annual (copyright).

Source: Compiled from sources mentioned in footnotes.

Table 1096. **Multimedia Audiences—Summary: 2008**

[In percent, except total (223,672 represents 223,672,000). As of fall. For persons 18 years old and over. Represents the percent of persons participating during the prior week, except as indicated. Based on sample and subject to sampling error; see source for details]

Item	Total population (1,000)	Television viewing	Television prime time viewing	Cable viewing [1]	Radio listening	Newspaper reading	Accessed Internet [2]
Total	223,672	94.1	84.5	81.0	82.7	74.5	71.6
18 to 24 years old	28,532	90.2	72.6	73.1	87.2	67.9	85.1
25 to 34 years old	40,028	92.4	80.8	78.1	88.6	70.0	82.8
35 to 44 years old	42,939	94.1	85.8	82.8	90.3	73.3	81.7
45 to 54 years old	43,634	94.8	87.7	83.5	86.1	78.3	76.3
55 to 64 years old	32,324	96.0	88.6	85.1	81.3	78.0	66.7
65 years old and over	36,215	96.5	88.8	81.5	60.9	78.3	35.1
Male	108,031	94.3	84.4	81.7	84.5	74.3	70.9
Female.	115,641	94.0	84.6	80.3	81.1	74.7	72.2
Not high school graduate. . . .	33,953	94.3	84.0	69.0	75.5	59.6	32.9
High school graduate	70,385	95.4	85.7	81.5	81.0	73.5	60.9
Attended college	60,791	93.7	83.6	82.7	85.7	77.2	84.1
College graduate	58,543	92.9	84.2	85.5	85.8	81.5	93.8
Household income:							
Less than $10,000	11,548	90.4	77.7	57.7	74.8	60.9	38.9
$10,000 to $19,999.	19,649	94.0	85.2	64.0	72.5	66.8	37.0
$20,000 to $29,999.	22,199	93.8	83.7	71.1	76.8	69.9	47.9
$30,000 to $34,999.	11,787	94.6	86.9	74.2	76.8	70.6	57.3
$35,000 to $39,999.	11,010	94.2	84.2	78.4	79.0	73.9	61.0
$40,000 to $49,999.	20,909	94.6	84.3	81.4	82.3	72.4	67.6
$50,000 to $74,999.	43,699	94.8	85.1	84.8	85.0	77.3	78.5
$75,000 to $99,999.	29,331	94.3	85.3	88.6	88.0	76.2	87.6
$100,000 or more	53,541	94.1	84.7	90.8	88.1	80.7	93.6

[1] In the past 7 days. [2] In the last 30 days.

Source: Mediamark Research Inc., New York, NY, *Multimedia Audiences,* fall 2008 (copyright).

Table 1097. **Publishing Industries—Estimated Revenue by Source and Media Type: 2004 to 2007**

[In millions of dollars (256,301 represents $256,301,000,000). For taxable and tax-exempt employer firms. Covers NAICS 5111. Estimates have been adjusted to the results of the 2002 Economic Census. Based on the North American Industry Classification System (NAICS). See also Appendix III]

Source of revenue and media type	2004	2005	2006	2007
Publishing industries (except Internet) [1]	**256,301**	**269,715**	**282,880**	**297,709**
Newspaper publishers	**48,366**	**49,958**	**49,601**	**48,274**
General newspapers.	40,810	42,080	41,564	40,083
Subscription and sales.	8,884	9,207	9,276	8,918
Advertising space	31,926	32,873	32,289	31,165
Specialized newspapers	2,439	2,524	2,637	2,574
Subscription and sales.	(S)	(S)	(S)	(S)
Advertising space	2,149	2,242	2,294	2,202
Other operating revenue	5,117	5,354	5,400	5,617
Printing services.	1,310	1,404	1,326	1,240
Distribution services.	2,024	2,094	2,022	1,911
All other	1,783	1,856	2,052	2,466
Print newspapers.	41,319	42,468	42,118	40,638
Online newspapers	1,308	1,537	1,450	1,728
Other media newspapers	621	600	633	291
Periodical publishers	**42,290**	**44,315**	**46,948**	**49,292**
General interest periodicals	21,420	22,451	24,025	25,062
Subscription and sales.	7,467	7,497	7,856	8,211
Advertising space	13,952	14,954	16,168	16,851
Professional and academic periodicals.	6,878	7,009	7,083	7,882
Subscription and sales.	3,785	3,924	3,985	4,343
Advertising space	3,093	3,085	3,098	3,540
Other periodicals	3,819	4,176	4,247	3,823
Subscription and sales.	1,933	2,081	2,111	1,870
Advertising space	1,886	2,095	2,136	(S)
Other operating revenue	10,173	10,679	11,593	12,524
Printing services for others	887	896	858	808
Licensing of rights to content.	237	298	377	333
All other.	9,049	9,485	10,358	11,384
Print	29,886	31,113	32,042	32,684
Online	1,848	2,063	2,765	3,271
Other media	382	460	548	813
Book publishers.	**27,904**	**27,904**	**28,237**	**29,296**
Books, print.	24,475	24,330	24,600	24,891
Textbooks	9,554	10,038	10,408	10,450
Children's books	3,117	3,082	3,104	3,249
General reference books	1,848	1,415	1,331	972
Professional, technical, and scholarly books.	2,745	3,261	3,335	3,044
Adult trade books	7,210	6,535	6,421	7,176
All other operating revenue	3,429	3,574	3,637	4,405
Print books	23,241	23,013	23,163	23,501
Online books.	620	654	705	585
Other media books	614	664	731	805
Directory and mailing list publishers	**18,040**	**19,413**	**18,915**	**19,890**
Directories.	13,195	13,873	13,660	13,790
Subscription and sales.	340	365	358	329
Advertising space	12,855	13,509	13,301	13,461
Database and other collections	2,894	3,337	3,174	3,828
Subscription and sales.	2,323	2,684	2,550	2,853
Advertising space	572	653	624	975
Other operating revenue	1,951	2,203	2,082	2,272
Rental or sale of mailing lists.	495	583	557	731
All other	1,456	1,620	1,525	(S)
Print directories, databases, and other collections of information	13,127	13,685	13,483	13,380
Online directories, databases, and other collections of information	2,540	3,243	3,038	3,586
Other media directories, databases, and other collections of information	423	282	313	652

S Figure does not meet publication standards. [1] Includes other industries not shown seperately.

Source: U.S. Census Bureau, "2007 Service Annual Survey, Information Sector Services" (published March 2009). See <http://www.census.gov/services/>.

Information and Communications **695**

Table 1098. **Daily and Sunday Newspapers—Number and Circulation: 1970 to 2008**

[Number of newspapers as of February 1 the following year. Circulation figures as of September 30 of year shown (62.1 represents 62,100,000). For English language newspapers only]

Type	1970	1980	1990	1995	2000	2002	2003	2004	2005	2006	2007	2008
NUMBER												
Daily: Total [1]	1,748	1,745	1,611	1,533	1,480	1,457	1,456	1,457	1,452	1,437	1,422	1,408
Morning	334	387	559	656	766	777	787	814	817	833	867	872
Evening	1,429	1,388	1,084	891	727	692	680	653	645	614	565	546
Sunday	586	736	863	888	917	913	917	915	914	907	907	902
NET PAID CIRCULATION (mil.)												
Daily: Total [1]	62.1	62.2	62.3	58.2	55.8	55.2	55.2	54.6	53.3	52.3	50.7	48.6
Morning	25.9	29.4	41.3	44.3	46.8	46.6	46.9	46.9	46.1	45.4	44.5	42.8
Evening	36.2	32.8	21.0	13.9	9.0	8.6	8.3	7.7	7.2	6.9	6.2	5.8
Sunday	49.2	54.7	62.6	61.5	59.4	58.8	58.5	57.8	55.3	53.2	51.2	49.1
PER CAPITA CIRCULATION [2]												
Daily: Total [1]	0.30	0.27	0.25	0.22	0.20	0.19	0.19	0.19	0.18	0.18	0.17	0.16
Morning	0.13	0.13	0.17	0.17	0.17	0.16	0.16	0.16	0.16	0.15	0.15	0.14
Evening	0.18	0.14	0.08	0.05	0.03	0.03	0.03	0.03	0.02	0.02	0.02	0.02
Sunday	0.24	0.24	0.25	0.23	0.21	0.21	0.20	0.20	0.19	0.18	0.17	0.16

[1] All-day newspapers are counted in both morning and evening columns but only once in total. Circulation is divided equally between morning and evening.　[2] Based on U.S. Census Bureau estimated resident population as of July 1.

Source: Editor & Publisher Co., New York, NY, *Editor & Publisher International Year Book,* annual (copyright).

Table 1099. **Daily and Sunday Newspapers—Number and Circulation, Total: 1991 to 2008 and by State, 2008**

[Number of newspapers as of February 1 the following year. Circulation as of September 30 (60,687 represents 60,687,000). For English language newspapers only. California, New York, Massachusetts, and Virginia Sunday newspapers include national circulation]

State	Daily Number	Daily Circulation [1] Net paid (1,000)	Daily Per capita [2]	Sunday Number	Sunday Net paid circulation (1,000)	State	Daily Number	Daily Circulation [1] Net paid (1,000)	Daily Per capita [2]	Sunday Number	Sunday Net paid circulation (1,000)
1991	1,586	60,687	0.24	875	62,068	KY	23	524	0.12	14	577
1992	1,570	60,164	0.23	891	62,160	LA	24	573	0.13	18	624
1993	1,556	59,812	0.23	884	62,566	ME	7	205	0.16	4	168
1994	1,548	59,305	0.23	886	62,294	MD	10	438	0.08	8	568
1995	1,533	58,193	0.22	888	61,529	MA	32	1,212	0.19	16	1,154
1996	1,520	56,983	0.21	890	60,798	MI	48	1,426	0.14	27	1,628
1997	1,509	56,728	0.21	903	60,484	MN	25	779	0.15	15	976
1998	1,489	56,182	0.20	898	60,066	MS	22	317	0.11	19	327
1999	1,483	55,979	0.20	905	59,894	MO	42	817	0.14	21	1,032
2000	1,480	55,773	0.20	917	59,421	MT	11	180	0.19	7	178
2001	1,468	55,578	0.19	913	59,090	NE	16	374	0.21	6	357
2002	1,457	55,186	0.19	913	58,780	NV	7	253	0.10	5	286
2003	1,456	55,185	0.19	917	58,495	NH	11	193	0.15	8	195
2004	1,457	54,626	0.19	915	57,753	NJ	18	1,052	0.12	15	1,264
2005	1,452	53,345	0.18	914	55,270	NM	17	258	0.13	12	257
2006	1,437	52,329	0.18	907	53,175	NY	59	6,379	0.33	38	4,543
2007	1,422	50,742	0.17	907	51,246	NC	47	1,164	0.13	39	1,294
						ND	10	148	0.23	7	151
Total, 2008	**1,408**	**48,598**	**0.16**	**902**	**49,115**	OH	82	1,986	0.17	41	2,215
AL	24	575	0.12	20	638	OK	37	532	0.15	30	635
AK	7	98	0.14	4	102	OR	19	592	0.16	12	616
AZ	16	628	0.10	12	754	PA	80	2,353	0.19	42	2,647
AR	26	453	0.16	16	524	RI	6	170	0.16	3	208
CA	83	4,855	0.13	59	5,184	SC	16	550	0.12	14	632
CO	30	887	0.18	15	914	SD	11	141	0.18	4	119
CT	17	579	0.17	13	642	TN	26	781	0.13	19	893
DE	2	117	0.13	2	142	TX	81	2,408	0.10	78	3,004
DC	3	964	1.63	2	904	UT	6	319	0.12	6	353
FL	38	2,672	0.15	36	3,360	VT	8	98	0.16	3	72
GA	34	857	0.09	29	1,108	VA	23	3,115	0.40	17	862
HI	6	259	0.20	6	277	WA	22	894	0.14	16	999
ID	11	200	0.13	7	214	WV	20	351	0.19	14	367
IL	63	1,921	0.15	30	2,119	WI	33	779	0.14	17	950
IN	67	1,178	0.18	25	1,106	WY	9	84	0.16	5	69
IA	37	552	0.18	13	585						
KS	36	356	0.13	13	321						

[1] Circulation figures based on the principal community served by a newspaper which is not necessarily the same location as the publisher's office.　[2] Per capita based on estimated resident population as of July 1, except 2000, enumerated resident population as of April 1.

Source: Editor & Publisher Co., New York, NY, *Editor & Publisher International Year Book,* annual (copyright).

U.S. Census Bureau, Statistical Abstract of the United States: 2010

Table 1100. **Net Book Publishers' Shipments: 2007 to 2010**

[(3,126.8 represents 3,126,800,000). Represents net publishers' shipments after returns. Includes all titles released by publishers in the United States and imports which appear under the imprints of American publishers. Multivolume sets, such as encyclopedias, are counted as one unit. Due to changes in methodology and scope, these data are not comparable to those previously published]

Type of publication	2007	2008, proj.	2009, proj.	2010, proj.
Total.	3,126.8	3,078.9	3,101.3	3,168.9
Trade	2,281.7	2,237.7	2,248.3	2,294.3
Adult	1,380.8	1,348.5	1,360.8	1,393.4
Juvenile	900.9	889.2	887.5	900.8
Religious	274.5	247.1	239.2	246.8
Professional	245.9	255.8	264.5	269.0
Scholarly	72.1	74.9	76.2	77.5
Elementary and high school.	175.0	182.3	188.7	194.1
College	77.6	81.1	84.5	87.2

Source: Book Industry Study Group, Inc., New York, NY, *Book Industry Trends, 2009*, annual (copyright).

Table 1101. **Software Publishers—Estimated Revenue by Source of Revenue and Software Type: 2004 to 2007**

[In millions of dollars (112,261 represents $112,261,000,000). For taxable and tax-exempt employer firms. Covers NAICS 5112. Estimates have been adjusted to the results of the 2002 Economic Census. Based on the North American Industry Classification System, System (NAICS), 2002. See text, this section and Section 15]

Source of revenue	2004	2005	2006	2007
Software publishers.	112,261	121,334	132,257	143,704
System software publishing [1]	40,845	44,367	46,507	51,668
Operating system software.	16,553	16,460	16,282	18,714
Network software	9,982	12,618	13,533	14,599
Database management software	6,778	7,204	8,693	9,836
Development tools and programming languages software . .	3,483	3,366	3,227	3,148
Application software publishing [1]	41,316	44,466	46,856	49,621
General business productivity and home use applications . .	19,430	21,710	21,219	22,889
Cross-industry application software	11,626	11,701	13,423	13,174
Vertical market application software	6,590	6,981	7,165	7,987
Utilities application software	1,034	1,184	1,441	1,409
Other services [1]	30,101	32,501	38,894	42,415
Customization and integration of packaged software	4,433	4,962	6,159	5,496
Information technology technical consulting services	4,193	4,500	4,480	5,100
Application service provisioning.	784	(S)	(S)	(S)
Resale of computer hardware and software.	2,620	2,253	3,275	4,207
Information technology-related training services	1,465	1,527	1,749	2,690
System software [1]	40,845	44,367	46,507	51,668
Personal computer software	14,444	15,071	15,221	18,280
Enterprise or network software	14,333	16,520	18,315	18,587
Mainframe computer software.	9,111	9,138	9,737	10,200
Application software [1]	41,316	44,466	46,856	49,621
Personal computer software	19,609	22,299	(S)	22,086
Enterprise or network software	14,258	15,209	17,099	19,133
Mainframe computer software.	2,648	2,737	2,685	2,756

S Data do not meet publication standards.   [1] Includes other sources of revenue and other expenses, not shown separately.

Source: U.S. Census Bureau, "2007 Service Annual Survey, Information Sector Services" (published March 2009); <http://www.census.gov/services/>.

U.S. Census Bureau, Statistical Abstract of the United States: 2010

Table 1102. **Motion Picture and Sound Recording Industries—Estimated Revenue: 2004 to 2007**

[In millions of dollars (88,269 represents $88,269,000,000). For taxable and tax-exempt employer firms. For NAICS 512. Estimates have been adjusted to the results of the 2002 Economic Census. Based on the North American Industry Classification System (NAICS), 2002. See text, this section, and Section 15. See also Appendix III]

Source of revenue	2004	2005	2006	2007
Motion picture and Sound Recording Industries	**88,269**	**93,655**	**98,392**	**102,166**
Motion picture and video industries	**71,774**	**74,789**	**77,576**	**82,066**
Motion picture and video production and distribution [1]	56,605	59,760	61,847	65,922
Domestic licensing of rights to motion picture films	14,884	16,244	16,241	15,505
Domestic licensing of rights to television programs	10,526	9,348	9,479	10,421
International licensing of rights to motion picture films	5,446	6,862	8,525	8,733
International licensing of rights to television programs	2,673	2,948	3,514	3,581
Contract production of audiovisual works	4,446	4,376	4,725	4,570
Sale of audiovisual works for wholesale, retail, and rental markets.	6,309	7,853	7,251	8,910
Motion picture and video exhibition [1]	11,180	10,789	11,194	11,341
Admissions to domestic films	7,358	6,996	7,312	7,470
Admissions to foreign films	165	182	(S)	55
Food and beverage sales	3,124	3,049	3,225	3,313
Coin-operated games and rides	43	41	52	44
Postproduction services and other motion picture and video industries [1]	3,989	4,240	4,535	4,803
Audiovisual postproduction services	2,525	2,650	2,750	2,845
Motion picture film laboratory services	576	605	686	704
Duplication and copying services	373	376	392	395
Sound recording industries	**16,495**	**18,866**	**20,816**	**20,100**
Integrated record production and distribution [1]	11,021	12,856	14,405	13,591
Licensing of rights to use musical compositions.	(S)	(S)	1,410	(S)
Sales of recordings	9,806	(S)	(S)	11,281
Music publishers [1]	3,885	4,260	4,544	4,432
Licensing of rights to use musical compositions.	2,025	2,259	2,372	(S)
Print music.	1,591	1,748	1,894	1,684
Sound recording studios [1]	724	766	928	998
Studio recording	504	529	592	631

S Data do not meet publication standards. [1] Includes other sources of revenue not shown seperately.

Source: U.S. Census Bureau, "2007 Service Annual Survey, Information Sector Services" (published March 2009); <http://www.census.gov/services/>.

Table 1103. **Recording Media—Manufacturers' Shipments and Value: 2000 to 2008**

[1,079.2 represents 1,079,200,000. Based on reports of RIAA member companies who distributed about 84 percent of the prerecorded music in 2008. These data are supplemented by other sources]

Medium	2000	2001	2002	2003	2004	2005	2006	2007	2008
UNIT SHIPMENTS (mil.)									
Total [1]	**1,079.2**	**968.5**	**859.7**	**798.4**	**958.0**	**1,301.8**	**1,588.5**	**1,774.3**	**1,852.5**
Physical:									
Compact disks [2]	942.5	881.9	803.3	746.0	767.0	705.4	619.7	511.1	384.7
Cassette	76.0	45.0	31.1	17.2	5.2	2.5	0.7	0.4	0.1
Music video [3]	18.2	17.7	14.7	19.9	32.8	33.8	23.2	27.5	12.8
LP/EP	2.2	2.3	1.7	1.5	1.4	1.0	0.9	1.3	2.9
Digital:									
Download single	(X)	(X)	(X)	(X)	139.4	366.9	586.4	809.9	1,033.0
Download album	(X)	(X)	(X)	(X)	4.6	13.6	27.6	42.5	56.9
Kiosk [4]	(X)	(X)	(X)	(X)	(X)	0.7	1.4	1.8	1.6
Music video	(X)	(X)	(X)	(X)	(X)	1.9	9.9	14.2	20.8
Mobile [5]	(X)	(X)	(X)	(X)	(X)	170.0	315.0	362.0	338.4
Subscription [6]	(X)	(X)	(X)	(X)	(X)	1.3	1.3	1.8	1.6
VALUE (mil. dol.)									
Total [1]	**14,323.7**	**13,740.9**	**12,614.2**	**11,854.4**	**12,345.0**	**12,296.9**	**11,758.2**	**10,372.1**	**8,480.2**
Physical:									
Compact discs [2]	13,214.5	12,909.4	12,044.1	11,232.9	11,446.5	10,520.2	9,372.6	7,452.3	5,471.3
Cassette	626.0	363.4	209.8	108.1	23.7	13.1	3.7	3.0	0.9
Music video [3]	281.9	329.2	288.4	399.9	607.2	602.2	451.1	484.9	218.9
LP/EP	27.7	27.4	20.5	21.7	19.3	14.2	15.7	22.9	56.7
Digital:									
Download single	(X)	(X)	(X)	(X)	138.0	363.3	580.6	801.8	1,022.7
Download album	(X)	(X)	(X)	(X)	45.5	135.7	275.9	424.9	568.9
Kiosk [4]	(X)	(X)	(X)	(X)	(X)	1.0	1.9	2.6	2.6
Music video	(X)	(X)	(X)	(X)	(X)	3.7	19.7	28.2	41.3
Mobile [5]	(X)	(X)	(X)	(X)	(X)	421.6	773.8	880.8	816.3
Subscription [6]	(X)	(X)	(X)	(X)	(X)	149.2	206.2	201.3	188.2

X Not applicable.   [1] Net, after returns.   [2] Includes DualDisc.   [3] Includes DVD video.   [4] Includes singles and albums.
[5] Includes Master Ringtunes, Ringbacks, full length downloads and other mobile.   [6] Weighted annual average. Number of units not included in total.

Source: Recording Industry Association of America, Washington, DC, 2008 Year-end Statistics (copyright); <http://www.riaa.com>.

Table 1104. **Radio and Television Broadcasting—Estimated Revenue and Expenses: 2005 and 2007**

[In millions of dollars (3,347 represents $3,347,000,000). For taxable and tax-exempt employer firms. Estimates have been adjusted to the results of the 2002 Economic Census. Based on the North American Industry Classification System (NAICS), 2002. See text, this section and Section 15]

Item	Radio networks (NAICS 515111)		Radio stations (NAICS 515112)		TV broadcasting (NAICS 51512)	
	2005	2007	2005	2007	2005	2007
Operating revenue	3,347	5,226	13,712	13,624	35,249	37,008
Air time	1,187	1,271	12,084	11,924	29,106	29,798
National/regional air time	639	648	2,683	2,885	18,233	18,224
Local air time	548	623	9,401	9,039	10,873	11,574
Other operating revenue	2,160	3,955	1,627	1,700	6,143	7,211
Network compensation	122	324	223	252	1,659	1,524
Public and noncommercial programming services	375	455	(S)	(S)	1,767	2,066
All other operating revenue	1,663	3,177	835	905	2,717	3,620
Operating expenses	4,858	6,407	10,155	9,988	28,533	29,803
Personnel costs	1,013	1,307	5,120	5,326	7,796	8,869
Gross annual payroll	867	1,120	4,408	4,502	6,646	7,371
Employer's cost for fringe benefits	104	164	612	650	1,049	1,337
Temporary staff and leased employee expense	42	(S)	100	174	100	161
Expensed materials, parts and supplies (not for resale)	35	28	123	107	241	207
Expensed equipment	8	(S)	41	35	66	68
Expensed purchase of other materials, parts and supplies	27	17	82	72	175	139
Expensed purchased services	602	(S)	1,046	1,126	1,889	2,028
Expensed purchases of software	20	26	(S)	40	43	70
Purchased electricity and fuels (except motor fuel)	13	24	144	148	255	331
Lease and rental payments	65	129	342	355	415	502
Purchased repair and maintenance	18	26	85	91	177	210
Purchased advertising and promotional services	487	(S)	429	492	999	914
Other operating expenses	3,207	4,478	3,867	3,429	18,607	18,699
Broadcast rights and music license fees	407	(S)	491	461	10,937	11,216
Network compensation fees	143	205	(S)	(S)	668	463
Depreciation and amortization fees	401	581	587	768	1,526	1,675
Government taxes and license fees	17	20	489	395	168	126
All other operating expenses	2,240	3,159	2,219	1,755	5,308	5,220

S Data do not meet publication standards.

Source: U.S. Census Bureau, 2007 Service Annual Survey, "Information Sector Services" (published March 2009); <http://www.census.gov/econ/services/>.

Table 1105. **Cable and Premium TV Summary: 1980 to 2008**

[17,500 represents 17,500,000. Cable TV for calendar year. Premium TV as of December 31 of year shown]

Year	Cable TV				Premium TV					
	Avg. basic subscribers (1,000)	Avg. monthly basic rate (dol.)	Revenue [1] (mil. dol.)		Units [2] (1,000)			Monthly rate (dol.)		
			Total	Basic	Total premium [3]	Premium cable	Non cable delivered premium	All premium weighted average [3]	Premium cable	Non cable delivered premium
1980	17,500	7.69	2,609	1,615	8,581	7,336	(NA)	8.91	8.62	(NA)
1985	35,440	9.73	8,831	4,138	29,885	29,418	(NA)	10.29	10.25	(NA)
1990	50,520	16.78	17,582	10,174	39,902	39,751	(NA)	10.35	10.30	(NA)
1995	60,550	23.07	24,137	16,763	46,823	46,798	8,925	8.29	8.54	6.99
1996	62,300	24.41	26,195	18,249	50,722	49,607	13,265	7.98	8.12	7.50
1997	63,600	26.48	28,931	20,213	55,660	51,600	17,810	8.31	8.43	8.00
1998	64,650	27.81	31,191	21,574	59,751	54,528	21,673	8.58	8.74	8.22
1999	65,500	28.92	34,095	22,732	64,477	57,095	25,864	8.74	8.85	8.50
2000	66,250	30.37	36,723	24,142	70,730	62,715	30,535	8.72	8.81	8.48
2001	66,732	32.87	42,159	26,324	74,649	68,441	33,035	8.97	9.10	8.66
2002	66,472	34.71	48,295	27,690	77,751	71,732	37,314	9.19	9.29	9.00
2003	66,050	36.59	53,536	29,000	75,197	71,841	36,681	9.38	9.45	9.23
2004	65,727	38.14	58,889	30,080	80,384	76,948	41,203	9.91	9.92	9.88
2005	65,337	39.63	64,832	31,075	81,983	81,910	44,157	9.95	9.97	9.93
2006	65,319	41.17	71,668	32,274	86,218	85,193	47,890	10.01	10.02	9.98
2007	65,141	42.72	78,462	33,393	89,623	91,032	51,977	10.05	10.06	10.02
2008	64,274	44.28	85,371	34,151	93,149	92,539	57,209	10.08	10.10	10.06

NA Not available. [1] Includes installation revenue, subscriber revenue, and nonsubscriber revenue; excludes telephony and high-speed access. [2] Individual program services sold to subscribers. [3] Includes multipoint distribution service (MDS), satellite TV (STV), multipoint multichannel distribution service (MMDS), satellite master antenna TV (SMATV), C-band satellite, and DBS satellite and Telco Video. Includes average pay unit price based on data for major premium pay movie services.

Source: SNL Kagan, a division of SNL Financial LC. From the *Broadband Cable Financial Databook* 2004, 2005, 2006, 2007, 2008 (copyright); the Cable *Cable Program Investor and Cable TV Investor: Deals & Finance* newsletters (monthly); and various other SNL Kagan publications.

Information and Communications   699

Table 1106. Cable and Other Subscription Programming—Estimated Revenue and Expenses: 2004 to 2007

[In millions of dollars (31,373 represents $31,373,000,000). For taxable and tax-exempt employer firms. Covers NAICS 51521. This industry comprises establishments engaged in operating studios and facilities for the broadcasting of programs on a subscription or fee basis. Estimates have been adjusted to the results of the 2002 Economic Census. Based on the North American Industry Classification System (NAICS), 2002. See text, this section and Section 15]

Item	2004	2005	2006	2007
Operating revenue.	31,373	35,386	37,981	40,870
Source of revenue:				
Licensing of rights to broadcast specialty programming [1] . . .	16,323	17,704	18,989	20,644
Air time.	13,129	14,921	15,588	16,653
All other operating services revenue	1,921	2,761	3,404	3,573
Operating expenses.	21,003	23,469	24,841	26,728
Personnel costs:				
Gross annual payroll.	4,021	4,677	4,588	5,242
Employer's cost for fringe benefits.	3,205	3,737	3,550	3,907
Temporary staff and leased employee expense	539	619	627	824
Expensed materials, parts and supplies (not for resale)	276	321	411	511
Expensed equipment	255	265	305	405
Expensed purchase of other materials, parts and supplies . .	58	53	48	63
	197	212	256	342
Expensed purchased services	1,872	2,224	2,643	2,245
Expensed purchases of software.	36	43	52	50
Purchased electricity and fuels (except motor fuel)	49	48	50	50
Lease and rental payments	432	515	457	335
Purchased repair and maintenance	(S)	97	93	84
Purchased advertising and promotional services	1,235	1,521	1,992	1,725
Other operating expenses	14,856	16,303	17,305	18,835
Depreciation and amortization charges.	(S)	(S)	2,591	2,714
Government taxes and license fees.	120	133	103	77
Program and production costs	10,063	10,452	11,227	12,394
All other operating expenses	2,294	3,098	3,384	3,650

S Data do not meet publication standards.   [1] Protected by copyright.

Source: U.S. Census Bureau, "2007 Service Annual Survey, Information Sector Services" (published March 2009); <http://www.census.gov/services/>.

Table 1107. Internet Publishing and Broadcasting—Estimated Revenue and Expenses: 2004 to 2007

[In millions of dollars (8,695 represents $8,695,000,000). For taxable and tax-exempt employer firms. Covers NAICS 516. Establishments engaged in publishing and/or broadcasting on the Internet exclusively. Estimates have been adjusted to the results of the 2002 Economic Census. Based on the North American Industry Classification System (NAICS), 2002. See text, this section and Section 15]

Item	2004	2005	2006	2007
Operating revenue.	8,695	10,391	12,862	15,480
Source of revenue:				
Publishing and broadcasting of content on the Internet	5,278	6,068	7,109	8,478
Online advertising space	1,607	1,976	2,879	3,642
Licensing of rights to use intellectual property	401	433	527	556
All other operating revenue	1,410	1,912	2,347	2,804
Breakdown of revenue by type of customer:				
Government	446	(S)	(S)	(S)
Business firms and not-for-profit organizations.	6,310	7,315	8,810	10,307
Household consumers and individual users.	1,939	2,479	3,392	4,461
Operating expenses.	7,056	9,084	11,272	13,784
Personnel.	3,087	3,936	4,901	5,732
Gross annual payroll.	2,394	3,138	3,917	4,447
Employer's cost for fringe benefits.	479	562	712	968
Temporary staff and leased employee expense	214	236	272	(S)
Expensed materials, parts and supplies (not for resale)	239	317	327	(S)
Expensed equipment	104	134	140	(S)
Expensed purchase of other materials, parts and supplies . .	135	183	187	(S)
Expensed purchased services	1,218	1,547	2,000	2,472
Expensed purchases of software.	78	194	275	(S)
Purchased electricity and fuels (except motor fuel)	14	16	23	22
Lease and rental payments	281	344	383	455
Purchased repair and maintenance	105	100	107	(S)
Purchased advertising and promotional services	741	893	1,211	1,607
Other operating expenses	2,512	3,285	4,044	5,190
Depreciation and amortization charges.	767	792	910	(S)
Government taxes and license fees.	53	62	73	90
All other operating expenses	1,692	(S)	3,061	4,076

S Data do not meet publication standards.

Source: U.S. Census Bureau, "2007 Service Annual Survey, Information Sector Services" (published March 2009); <http://www.census.gov/services/>.

Table 1108. **Telecommunications Industry—Carriers and Revenue: 1995 to 2006**

[Revenue in millions of dollars (190,076 represents $190,076,000,000). Data based on carrier filings to the FCC. Because of reporting changes, data beginning 2000 are not strictly comparable with previous years; see source for details]

Category	Carriers					Telecommunications revenue				
	1995	2000	2004	2005	2006	1995	2000	2004	2005	2006
Total [1]	3,058	4,879	5,031	5,005	6,222	190,076	292,762	291,734	297,921	295,742
Local service providers.	1,675	2,641	2,864	2,922	3,540	103,792	128,075	123,067	122,609	119,905
Incumbent local exchange carriers (ILECs)	1,347	1,335	1,304	1,303	1,311	102,820	116,158	105,496	103,561	99,997
Pay telephone providers . . .	271	699	642	576	595	349	972	445	481	435
Competitors of ILECs.	57	607	918	1,043	1,634	623	10,945	17,126	18,568	19,473
CAPs and CLECs [2].	57	479	690	734	985	623	9,814	15,112	16,930	17,276
Local resellers	([3])	105	136	122	186	([3])	879	1,215	630	460
Other local exchange carriers	([3])	23	92	187	212	([3])	11	245	216	124
Private carriers.	([3])	([3])	([3])	([3])	([3])	([3])	39	532	770	1,080
Shared tenant service providers	([3])	([3])	([3])	([3])	([3])	([3])	202	22	22	19
Wireless service providers [4] . .	930	1,430	963	905	1,045	18,627	63,280	99,465	108,809	117,752
Telephony [5]	792	783	396	402	467	17,208	59,823	98,329	107,834	116,971
Paging service providers . . .	138	425	360	300	315	([3])	3,102	872	579	555
Toll service providers	453	808	1,204	1,178	1,637	76,447	101,407	69,204	66,503	59,611
Interexchange carriers	130	212	257	262	361	70,938	87,311	51,589	46,856	44,083
Operator service providers. .	25	20	19	23	29	500	635	523	548	631
Prepaid service providers . .	8	23	67	69	154	16	727	1,635	1,828	1,713
Satellite service carriers . . .	([3])	25	40	40	43	([3])	336	721	714	444
Toll resellers	260	493	751	721	923	4,220	10,641	12,192	13,362	9,943
Other toll carriers	30	35	70	63	127	773	1,758	2,543	3,195	2,798

[1] Revenue data include adjustments, not shown separately. For 1995, revenue data include some nontelecommunications revenue, formerly reported as local exchange wireless revenue. [2] Competitive access providers (CAPs) and competitive local exchange carriers (CLECs). [3] Data not available separately. [4] Beginning 2000, includes specialized mobile radio services and other services, not shown separately. [5] Cellular service, personal communications service, and specialized mobile radio.

Source: U.S. Federal Communications Commission, Telecommunications Industry Revenue; <http://www.fcc.gov/wcb/iatd /stats.html>.

Table 1109. **Wired and Wireless Telecommunications Carriers— Estimated Revenue: 2004 to 2007**

[In millions of dollars (211,176 represents $211,176,000,000). For taxable and tax-exempt employer firms. Covers NAICS 5171 Wired Telecommunications, NAICS 517211 Paging, and NAICS 517212 Cellular and Other Wireless (except Paging). See Table 1092 for industry composition. Estimates have been adjusted to the results of the 2002 Economic Census. Based on the North American Industry Classification System NAICS, 2002. See text, this section]

Item	2004	2005	2006	2007
Wired telecommunications carriers operating revenue	211,176	206,622	195,092	192,779
Fixed total [1]	101,627	94,422	89,905	90,675
Fixed local	61,316	58,928	57,327	58,516
Fixed long-distance.	38,420	33,802	31,252	30,498
Fixed all distance	1,891	1,692	(S)	1,661
Other telecommunication services.	94,609	96,295	89,629	88,833
Carrier services	37,656	37,423	31,387	27,410
Private network services	26,144	26,678	23,279	23,472
Subscriber line charges	8,520	8,204	7,692	6,043
Internet access services	12,616	14,374	15,350	18,609
Intrernet telephony	798	938	1,663	1,855
Telecommunications network installation services	(S)	(S)	5,948	6,314
Reselling services for telecommunications equipment, retail .	3,878	3,560	3,364	3,350
Rental of telecommunications equipment	291	251	(S)	982
Repair and maintenance services for telecommunications equipment.	851	802	740	797
All other.	14,941	15,905	15,558	13,272
Wireless telecommunications carriers operating revenue [2]	127,602	140,025	158,577	174,085
Paging.	1,909	1,990	1,874	1,557
Messaging (paging) services	1,472	1,584	1,469	1,252
Mobile services	99,949	111,663	124,645	133,912
Mobile telephony	54,114	57,097	53,820	54,516
Mobile long distance	3,267	4,398	4,804	5,312
Mobile all-distance	35,783	42,292	(S)	60,310
Other mobile services	6,785	7,875	(S)	(S)
Other telecommunications services	8,258	9,508	11,888	14,312
Internet access services	659	1,124	(D)	(D)
Installation services for telecommunications networks	(S)	(S)	146	181
Reselling services for telecommunications equipment, retail .	6,980	7,377	8,585	9,382
Rental of telecommunications equipment	74	(S)	110	70
Repair and maintenance services for telecommunications equipment.	431	732	(D)	(D)
All other operating revenue	17,485	16,865	20,170	24,304

S Estimate does not meet publication standard.   D Estimate withheld to avoid disclosing data of individual companies, data are included in higher level totals.   [1] No distinction between local or long distance.   [2] Excludes satelite.

Source: U.S. Census Bureau, "2007 Service Annual Survey, Information Sector Services" (published March 2009); <http://www.census.gov/services/>.

Information and Communications   701

Table 1110. **Telephone Systems—Summary: 1990 to 2006**

[**130 represents 130,000,000.** Covers principal carriers filing annual reports with Federal Communications Commission]

Item	Unit	1990	1995	2000	2001 [1]	2002 [1]	2003 [1]	2004 [1]	2005 [1]	2006 [1]
LOCAL EXCHANGE CARRIERS [2]										
Carriers [3]	Number. . .	51	53	52	52	53	54	56	56	56
Access lines	Millions . . .	130	166	245	253	264	275	286	349	379
Business access lines	Millions . . .	36	46	58	54	53	49	48	47	46
Residential access lines	Millions . . .	89	101	115	112	104	99	94	89	82
Other access lines (public, mobile, special).	Millions . . .	6	19	72	87	107	127	144	213	251
Number of local calls (originating) . . .	Billions . . .	402	484	537	515	454	418	381	330	280
Number of toll calls (originating)	Billions . . .	63	94	106	98	96	88	82	79	73
INTERNATIONAL TELEPHONE SERVICE [4]										
Number of U.S. billed calls.	Millions . . .	984	2,830	5,742	6,265	5,926	7,350	10,895	13,134	13,673
Number of U.S. billed minutes	Millions . . .	8,030	15,889	30,135	33,287	35,064	42,664	63,553	70,064	72,440
U.S. billed revenues	Mil. dol. . . .	8,059	14,335	14,909	11,380	9,956	8,944	9,178	7,976	7,299
U.S. carrier revenue net of settlements with foreign carriers . . .	Mil. dol. . . .	5,188	9,397	10,982	8,034	7,114	6,167	5,546	4,514	4,277
Revenue from private-line service . . .	Mil. dol. . . .	201	514	1,480	1,419	988	743	574	628	678
Revenue from resale service	Mil. dol. . . .	167	1,756	7,600	5,341	4,871	5,760	5,226	5,750	6,077

[1] Beginning 2001, detailed financial data are only filed by regional Bell-operating companies. Access lines and calls reported by all subject reporting companies. [2] Gross operating revenues, gross plant, and total assets of reporting carriers estimated at more than 90 percent of total industry. New accounting rules became effective in 1990; prior years may not be directly comparable on a one-to-one basis. Includes Virgin Islands, and prior to 1995, Puerto Rico. [3] The reporting threshold for carriers is $100 million in annual operating revenue. [4] Beginning 1995, data are for all U.S. points, and include calls to and from Alaska, Hawaii, Puerto Rico, Guam, the U.S. Virgin Islands, and offshore U.S. points. Beginning 1995, carriers first started reporting traffic to and from Canada and Mexico. Data for Canada and Mexico in prior years are staff estimates.

Source: U.S. Federal Communications Commission, *Statistics of Communications Common Carriers; Trends in Telephone Service;* and *Trends in the International Telecommunications Industry;* <http://www.fcc.gov/wcb/iatd/stats.html>.

Table 1111. **Average Annual Telephone Service Expenditures by All Consumer Units: 2001 to 2007**

[Based on Consumer Expenditure Survey. A consumer unit is defined as members of a household related by blood, marriage, adoption, or some other legal arrangement; a single person living alone or sharing a household with others, but who is financially independent; or two or more persons living together who share responsibility for at least two out of the three major types of expenses: food, housing, and other expenses]

Year	Average annual expenditure (dollars)				Percent distribution			
	Total telephone services	Residential tele-phone/pay phone	Cellular phone service	Other services [1]	Total telephone services	Residential tele-phone/pay phone	Cellular phone service	Other services [1]
2001	914	686	210	19	100.0	75.0	23.0	2.0
2002	957	641	294	22	100.0	67.0	30.7	2.3
2003	956	620	316	20	100.0	64.8	33.1	2.1
2004	990	592	378	20	100.0	59.8	38.2	2.0
2005	1,048	570	455	23	100.0	54.4	43.4	2.2
2006	1,087	542	524	21	100.0	49.9	48.2	2.0
2007	1,110	482	608	20	100.0	43.4	54.8	1.8

[1] Phone cards and pager services.

Source: Bureau of Labor Statistics, *Consumer Expenditures in 2007* (published November 25, 2008); <http://www.bls.gov/cex/cellphones.htm>

Table 1112. **Cellular Telecommunications Industry: 1990 to 2008**

[Calendar year data, except as noted (**5,283 represents 5,283,000**). Based on a survey sent to all facilities-based cellular, personal communications services, and enhanced special mobile radio (ESMR) systems. The number of operational systems beginning 2000 differs from that reported for previous periods as a result of the consolidated operation of ESMR systems in a broader service area instead of by a city-to-city basis]

Item	Unit	1990	2000	2003	2004	2005	2006	2007	2008
Subscribers	1,000	5,283	109,478	158,722	182,140	207,896	233,041	255,396	270,334
Employees	Number	21,382	184,449	205,629	226,016	233,067	253,793	266,782	268,528
Service revenue	Mil. dol.	4,548	52,466	87,624	102,121	113,538	125,457	138,869	148,084
Roamer revenue [1]	Mil. dol.	456	3,883	3,766	4,210	3,786	3,494	3,742	3,739
Capital investment [2]	Mil. dol.	6,282	89,624	145,867	173,794	199,025	223,449	244,591	264,761
Average monthly bill [3]	Dollars	80.90	45.27	49.91	50.64	49.98	50.56	49.79	50.07
Average length of call [3]	Minutes	2.20	2.56	2.87	3.05	3.00	3.03	(NA)	2.27
Number of text messages [4]	Billions	(NA)	(Z)	2.1	4.7	9.8	18.7	48.1	110.4
Number of MMS [4, 5]	Billions	(NA)	(NA)	(NA)	(NA)	0.2	0.3	0.8	1.6

NA Not available. Z Entry less than half the unit of measurement shown. [1] Service revenue generated by subscribers' calls outside of their system areas. [2] Beginning 2005, cumulative capital investment figure reached by summing the incremental capital investment in year shown with cumulative capital investment of prior year. [3] As of December 31. [4] Number of messages in final month of survey, in billions. [5] Multimedia Messaging Service.

Source: CTIA-The Wireless Association, Washington, DC, *Semi-annual Wireless Survey* (copyright).

U.S. Census Bureau, Statistical Abstract of the United States: 2010

Table 1113. **Cable and Other Programming Distribution—Estimated Revenue and Expenses: 2004 to 2007**

[In millions of dollars (73,317 represents $73,317,000,000). For taxable and tax-exempt employer firms. Covers NAICS 5175. Estimates have been adjusted to the results of the 2002 Economic Census. Based on the North American Industry Classification System (NAICS), 2002; See text, this section, and Section 15]

Item	2004	2005	2006	2007
Operating revenue.	73,317	80,492	88,788	100,849
Multichannel programming distribution services	48,336	52,158	56,080	61,561
Basic programming package	36,498	39,639	42,440	45,971
Premium programming package	9,312	9,816	10,489	11,859
Pay-per-view	2,525	2,703	3,151	3,731
Other revenue	24,982	28,334	32,708	39,288
Air time.	3,933	4,144	4,565	4,671
Rental and reselling services for program distribution equipment.	2,376	2,581	3,158	3,990
Installation services for connections to program distribution networks. . . .	621	668	735	954
Internet access services	9,924	11,651	13,778	16,501
Internet telephony	698	318	1,048	2,708
Fixed local telephony	1,445	1,478	1,754	(S)
Fixed long-distance telephony.	531	648	418	(S)
All other operating revenue	5,454	6,846	7,251	8,164

S Data do not meet publication standards.

Source: U.S. Census Bureau, "2007 Service Annual Survey, Information Sector Services" (published March 2009); <http://www.census.gov/services/>.

Table 1114. **Internet Service Providers and Data Processing, Hosting, and Related Services—Estimated Revenue: 2005 to 2007**

[In millions of dollars (18,977 represents $18,977,000,000). For taxable and tax-exempt employer firms. Estimates have been adjusted to the results of the 2002 Economic Census. Based on the North American Industry Classification System (NAICS), 2002. See text, this section, and Section 15]

Item	Internet service providers (NAICS 518111)			Data processing, hosting, and related services (NAICS 5182)		
	2005	2006	2007	2005	2006	2007
Operating revenue, (NAICS 518111) [1]	**18,977**	**19,092**	**19,086**	**(X)**	**(X)**	**(X)**
Internet access service.	12,465	11,492	10,379	(X)	(X)	(X)
Online advertising space	3,442	(S)	(S)	(X)	(X)	(X)
Internet backbone services	335	407	477	(X)	(X)	(X)
Internet telephony	(S)	(S)	168	(X)	(X)	(X)
Web Site hosting services.	818	1,077	969	(X)	(X)	(X)
Information technology design and development services	(S)	(S)	(S)	(X)	(X)	(X)
Operating revenue, (NAICS 5182)	**(X)**	**(X)**	**(X)**	**62,629**	**70,797**	**72,882**
Data processing IT infrastructure provisioning, and hosting services [1] . .	(X)	(X)	(X)	31,875	37,428	37,249
Business processing management services	(X)	(X)	(X)	17,841	21,183	19,742
Data management services	(X)	(X)	(X)	5,867	6,231	6,007
Application service provisioning	(X)	(X)	(X)	4,933	6,063	6,672
Web Site hosting services	(X)	(X)	(X)	2,514	2,745	(S)
Collocation services	(X)	(X)	(X)	(S)	(S)	(S)
Other operating revenue [1]	(X)	(X)	(X)	30,753	33,368	35,633
IT design and development services	(S)	(S)	(S)	6,578	6,161	6,154
IT technical support services	(X)	(X)	(X)	1,458	1,495	1,450
IT technical consulting services	(X)	(X)	(X)	1,247	1,553	1,927
Information and document transformation services.	(X)	(X)	(X)	3,212	3,431	3,563
Software publishing	(X)	(X)	(X)	1,872	2,061	2,358
Reselling services for computer hardware and software, retail	(X)	(X)	(X)	1,224	2,092	2,157

S Data do not meet publication standards.   X Not applicable.   [1] Includes other sources of revenue, not shown separately.

Source: U.S. Census Bureau, "2007 Service Annual Survey, Information Sector Services" (published March 2009); <http://www.census.gov/services/>.

Information and Communications   703

Table 1115. **Public Libraries by Selected Characteristics: 2007**

[**10,998 represents $10,998,000,000.** Based on survey of public libraries. Data are for public libraries in the 50 states and the District of Columbia. The response rates for these items are between 97 and 100 percent]

Population of service area	Number of—		Operating income—			Paid staff [3]		Average number of public use Internet computers per stationary outlet [5]
	Public libraries	Stationary outlets [1]	Total (mil. dol.) [2]	Source (percent)		Total	Librarians with ALA-MLS [4]	
				State government	Local government			
Total	**9,214**	**16,604**	**10,998**	**6.7**	**84.1**	**144,655**	**32,173**	**12.5**
1,000,000 or more . . .	26	1,077	1,694	6.5	80.9	18,856	4,749	21.7
500,000 to 999,000. . .	58	1,181	1,769	6.2	85.8	20,566	5,006	22.0
250,000 to 499,999. . .	104	1,137	1,312	9.5	82.9	16,233	4,026	18.1
100,000 to 249,999. . .	335	2,004	1,720	6.4	86.2	23,214	4,989	16.2
50,000 to 99,999	556	1,633	1,377	8.4	84.0	18,908	4,253	15.6
25,000 to 49,999	952	1,690	1,322	5.6	86.0	18,109	4,281	13.8
10,000 to 24,999	1,764	2,261	1,112	5.3	84.6	16,211	3,445	11.1
5,000 to 9,999	1,483	1,632	404	4.6	83.5	6,741	1,014	8.1
2,500 to 4,999	1,340	1,373	167	4.4	79.4	3,117	271	5.9
1,000 to 2,499	1,524	1,543	93	4.6	74.8	1,995	114	4.3
Fewer than 1,000	1,072	1,073	27	7.4	72.8	707	24	3.2

[1] The sum of central and branch libraries. The total number of central libraries was 9,040; the total of branch libraries was 7,564.   [2] Includes income from the federal government (0.4%) and other sources (8.7%), not shown separately.   [3] Full-time equivalents.   [4] Librarians with master's degrees from a graduate library education program accredited by the American Library Association (ALA). Total librarians, including those without ALA-MLS, were 47,151.   [5] See footnote 2, Table 1115.

Source: Institute of Museum and Library Services, "Public Libraries Survey Fiscal Year 2007" (published June 2009); <http://harvester.census.gov/imls/pubs/pls/index.asp>.

Table 1116. **Number of Public Library Service Outlets and Library Services by State: 2007**

[For Fiscal Year. **1,433,734 represents 1,433,734,000.** Based on Public Libraries Survey. Public libraries can have one or more outlets that provide direct service to the public. The three types of outlets include central libraries, branch libraries, and bookmobiles]

State	Stationary outlets [1]	Library visits (1,000)	Total circulation (1,000)	Average number of public use Internet computers per stationary outlet [2]	State	Stationary outlets [1]	Library visits (1,000)	Total circulation (1,000)	Average number of public use Internet computers per stationary outlet [2]
U.S.	**16,604**	**1,433,734**	**2,166,787**	**12.5**	MO	360	27,033	47,691	12.9
AL	286	15,306	18,712	14.3	MT	109	3,935	5,606	7.2
AK	104	3,432	4,257	4.9	NE	288	9,568	13,312	6.4
AZ	198	24,754	44,755	18.3	NV	85	10,406	16,147	12.3
AR	214	9,405	12,612	7.7	NH	235	6,769	10,499	4.5
CA	1,107	159,252	204,758	14.3	NJ	454	46,604	56,541	13.7
CO	248	28,943	53,731	15.1	NM	117	7,141	9,338	11.3
CT	245	22,895	31,544	12.7	NY	1,067	112,989	146,709	12.6
DE	33	4,417	7,814	13.4	NC	388	36,290	49,416	15.7
DC	27	2,144	1,463	12.0	NC	89	2,669	3,960	5.7
FL	507	78,934	109,634	24.4	OH	720	87,764	182,648	15.3
GA	385	35,704	40,816	15.5	OK	204	14,276	20,388	10.5
HI	51	5,730	6,792	9.7	OR	215	21,344	50,441	10.3
ID	139	7,939	11,310	7.8	PA	629	47,199	66,659	11.1
IL	781	75,079	101,711	11.7	RI	73	6,147	7,184	13.2
IN	433	39,220	74,212	16.0	SC	186	15,731	22,477	15.6
IA	559	17,872	28,391	5.9	SD	145	4,013	5,405	6.2
KS	375	14,939	26,073	7.2	TN	290	19,707	24,312	12.3
KY	196	17,769	26,542	15.1	TX	864	72,002	105,933	16.0
LA	327	14,450	17,619	12.8	UT	116	16,730	32,143	12.8
ME	278	6,964	8,898	4.9	VT	183	3,819	4,464	4.7
MD	183	28,843	53,244	19.4	VA	342	36,786	65,179	14.1
MA	476	39,539	52,312	10.2	WA	332	39,543	74,353	14.3
MI	658	51,777	74,998	14.5	WV	173	5,905	7,542	6.4
MN	359	28,866	53,992	12.0	WI	458	34,300	59,611	9.6
MS	238	8,211	8,298	8.3	WY	75	3,281	4,340	7.6

[1] The sum of central and branch libraries (does not include bookmobiles).   [2] The average per stationary outlet was calculated by dividing the total number of public use Internet computers in central and branch outlets by the total number of such outlets.

Source: Institute of Museum and Library Services, "Public Libraries Survey Fiscal Year 2007" (published June 2009); <http://harvester.census.gov/imls/data/pls/index.asp>.

Table 1117. **Public Library Use of the Internet: 2009**

[In percent, except number of outlets. As of spring. Based on sample survey; see source for details]

Item	Total	Metropolitan status [1]			Poverty status [2]		
		Urban	Sub-urban	Rural	Less than 20 percent	20 to 40 percent	More than 40 percent
All libraries' outlets [3]	16,620	2,940	5,421	8,259	13,943	2,490	187
Connected with public access	98.7	98.7	99.3	98.5	99.0	98.0	100.0
Average number of workstations	11.0	18.7	12.7	7.6	10.4	12.9	22.0
Speed of access:							
Less than 256kbps	3.4	([4])	2.4	5.1	3.2	4.8	([4])
257kbps to 768kbps	9.2	3.2	5.8	13.7	9.4	8.5	5.5
769kbps to 1.4mbps	9.3	3.9	7.8	12.2	9.7	7.6	([4])
1.5Mbps	25.5	26.9	27.2	23.8	24.9	28.7	30.7
1.6mbps to 3mbps	10.0	8.0	9.5	11.1	10.0	10.5	5.5
3.1mbps to 6mbps	11.2	14.0	11.6	10.0	11.4	10.2	17.1
6.1mbps to 10mbps	11.0	16.5	15.7	5.9	11.0	10.8	16.5
Greater than 10mbps	12.3	23.9	12.4	7.9	11.8	14.1	20.9
Don't Know	8.1	2.8	7.6	10.3	8.7	4.8	3.7
Public library availability of wireless Internet access:							
Currently available	76.4	83.0	81.9	70.5	77.2	71.9	73.2
Plan to make available within the next year	9.2	8.1	7.6	10.7	9.1	9.2	17.7

[1] Urban = inside central city; Suburban = in metro area, outside of a central city; Rural = outside a metro area.   [2] Determined by the 2000 poverty status of the service area of the outlet.   [3] Central libraries and branches; excludes bookmobiles.   [4] Less than 1 percent.

Source: Center for Library and Information Innovation, College of Information Studies, University of Maryland, College Park, MD, *Public Libraries and the Internet 2009: Survey Results and Findings,* by John Carlo Bertot, et al., University of Maryland, College Park, MD. Study funded by the American Library Association.

Table 1118. **Household Internet Usage In and Outside of the Home by Selected Characteristics: 2007**

[As of October. Civilian noninstitutional population 16 years and older. Based on the Current Population Survey. Householder refers to the person (or one of the persons) in whose name the housing unit is owned or rented (maintained) or, if there is no such person, any adult member, excluding roomers, boarders, or paid employees. If the house is owned or rented jointly by a married couple, the householder may be either the husband or the wife. The person designated as the householder is the "reference person" to whom the relationship of all other household members, if any, is recorded]

Characteristics	Total house-holds	In the home				Anywhere		No internet use	
		Percent				Total house-holds	Percent of total	Total house-holds	Percent of total
		All house-hold	Dial-up	Broad-band					
All households	117,840	61.7	10.7	50.8		83,708	71.0	34,132	29.0
Age of householder									
Under 25 years old	7,028	57.7	5.6	51.9		5,238	74.5	1,791	25.5
25 to 34 years old	19,718	65.6	7.0	58.3		15,566	78.9	4,152	21.1
35 to 44 years old	22,854	71.8	10.1	61.4		18,862	82.5	3,992	17.5
45 to 54 years old	24,773	70.7	12.4	58.0		19,763	79.8	5,010	20.2
55 years and older	43,467	50.2	12.4	37.5		24,280	55.9	19,188	44.1
Sex of householder									
Male	59,871	65.3	10.6	54.4		43,985	73.5	15,887	26.5
Female	57,969	58.0	10.8	47.0		39,723	68.5	18,245	31.5
Race and ethnicity of householder [1]									
White	83,294	67.0	11.8	54.9		62,593	75.2	20,701	24.9
Black	14,303	44.9	8.4	36.4		8,433	59.0	5,870	41.0
American Indian/Alaskan Native	643	41.5	11.2	29.8		385	59.9	258	40.1
Asian	4,477	75.5	6.1	69.1		3,672	82.0	805	18.0
Hispanic	13,619	43.4	8.0	35.2		7,463	54.8	6,156	45.2
Educational attainment of householder									
Elementary	5,812	18.5	5.4	13.1		1,490	25.6	4,322	74.4
Some high school	9,264	28.2	7.4	20.5		3,542	38.2	5,721	61.8
High school diploma/GED	35,295	49.1	12.1	36.8		20,973	59.4	14,322	40.6
Some college	33,078	68.9	12.1	56.5		26,498	80.1	6,580	19.9
Bachelors degree or more	34,392	84.1	9.7	74.2		31,205	90.7	3,187	9.3
Family Income of householder [1]									
Less than $15,000	13,939	82.7	18.5	63.9		5,433	120.9	8,506	179.1
$15,000 to 24,999	10,848	76.2	20.2	55.7		5,468	100.3	5,382	99.7
$25,000 to 34,999	11,650	50.9	11.2	39.7		7,565	64.9	4,085	35.1
$35,000 to 49,999	13,718	65.7	14.4	51.0		10,723	78.2	2,995	21.8
$50,000 to 74,999	17,101	80.2	13.8	66.0		15,151	88.6	1,949	11.4
$75,000 to 99,999	9,872	88.6	11.4	76.8		9,326	94.5	546	5.5
$100,000 to 149,000	8,481	92.1	8.0	83.7		8,118	95.7	363	4.3
$150,000 and over	5,570	95.5	5.0	90.3		5,450	97.9	120	2.2

[1] Includes other groups not shown seperately.

Source: U.S. Department of Commerce, National Telecommunications and Information Administration, *Networked Nation: Broadband in America 2007,* January 2008. See also <http://www.ntia.doc.gov/reports/2008/NetworkedNation.html>.

Information and Communications   705

Table 1119. **Household Internet Usage by Type of Internet Connection and State: 2007**

[**In percent. As of October.** See headnote, Table 1118. Based on the Current Population Survey. See Appendix III]

State	Any-where	In the home Total	In the home Broad-band	In the home Dial-up	No Internet use	State	Any-where	In the home Total	In the home Broad-band	In the home Dial-up	No Internet use
U.S.	71.0	61.7	50.8	10.7	29.0	MO	67.3	56.1	45.3	10.6	32.7
AL	60.6	49.8	37.4	12.4	39.4	MT......	68.6	56.9	40.2	16.7	31.4
AK......	84.3	73.4	62.5	10.4	15.8	NE......	73.9	63.8	54.1	9.6	26.2
AZ......	71.7	62.5	53.9	8.2	28.3	NV......	73.4	65.4	54.4	10.6	26.6
AR......	62.0	51.2	38.2	11.9	38.0	NH......	80.6	74.9	64.9	9.9	19.4
CA......	73.6	66.1	56.4	9.4	26.4	NJ	74.1	68.4	57.1	11.3	25.9
CO......	78.9	69.1	58.0	10.8	21.1	NM......	67.4	54.8	43.2	11.2	32.6
CT......	73.4	66.3	59.7	6.4	26.6	NY......	68.0	61.5	54.1	7.3	32.0
DE......	72.8	65.7	50.4	14.9	27.3	NC......	67.8	56.8	47.1	9.5	32.2
DC......	74.7	58.9	52.0	6.6	25.3	ND......	72.6	59.3	48.7	10.4	27.4
FL......	69.7	64.8	53.2	11.0	30.3	OH......	69.1	58.6	48.8	9.5	30.9
GA......	72.0	61.7	53.9	7.7	28.1	OK......	63.7	53.1	38.8	14.0	36.3
HI	72.5	64.1	57.6	5.9	27.5	OR......	75.3	68.2	57.5	10.3	24.7
ID	69.9	57.9	45.6	12.0	30.1	PA	69.3	60.1	47.7	12.1	30.7
IL.......	73.4	63.0	51.6	11.0	26.6	RI	72.5	66.1	59.3	6.6	27.5
IN	68.0	58.1	42.3	15.6	32.0	SC......	66.8	54.7	39.1	15.3	33.3
IA	73.6	62.4	46.8	15.5	26.4	SD......	73.6	60.8	47.5	13.2	26.4
KS......	76.7	62.8	55.2	7.2	23.3	TN......	65.9	53.5	41.6	11.9	34.2
KY......	66.7	54.9	40.0	14.4	33.3	TX......	68.1	57.3	47.6	9.6	31.9
LA......	63.2	53.9	42.9	11.0	36.9	UT......	82.0	69.5	59.3	10.0	18.0
ME......	74.5	65.1	48.4	16.5	25.5	VT......	79.4	70.2	46.8	21.8	20.6
MD......	76.8	66.4	56.1	9.9	23.2	VA......	75.0	68.0	53.3	14.6	25.0
MA......	72.9	66.4	61.1	5.2	27.1	WA......	81.7	71.6	58.4	12.6	18.3
MI	70.7	58.5	45.9	12.5	29.3	WV......	58.2	49.1	32.7	16.1	41.8
MN......	78.6	66.6	53.0	13.4	21.4	WI	76.6	65.0	52.6	12.3	23.4
MS......	59.7	46.0	33.2	12.5	40.3	WY	76.4	61.4	50.4	10.9	23.6

Source: U.S. Department of Commerce, *National Telecommunications and Information Administration, Networked Nation: Broadband in America 2007*, (published January 2008). See also <http://www.ntia.doc.gov/reports/2008/NetworkedNation.html>.

Table 1120. **Internet Access and Usage: 2008**

[**For persons 18 years old and over (223,672 represents 223,672,000). As of fall.** Based on sample and subject to sampling error; see source for details]

Item	Total adults	Have Internet access Home or work or other	Have Internet access Home	Have Internet access Work	Used the Internet in the last 30 days Home or work or other	Used the Internet in the last 30 days Home	Used the Internet in the last 30 days Work
Total adults [1] (1,000)	**223,672**	**190,646**	**160,757**	**85,342**	**160,093**	**141,444**	**72,841**
PERCENT DISTRIBUTION							
Total	100.00	100.00	100.00	100.00	100.00	100.00	100.00
Age:							
18 to 34 years old	30.65	33.02	31.57	33.03	35.88	33.97	32.72
35 to 54 years old	38.71	41.21	43.03	50.69	42.71	43.84	51.66
55 years old and over	30.64	25.77	25.40	16.29	21.41	22.20	15.62
Sex:							
Male	48.30	48.44	49.03	50.62	47.84	48.15	50.42
Female..................	51.70	51.56	50.97	49.38	52.16	51.85	49.58
Census region: [2]							
Northeast	18.62	19.05	19.97	19.48	19.31	19.96	19.34
Midwest	22.28	22.32	21.64	21.27	21.93	21.59	20.66
South	36.59	36.09	35.04	36.39	35.59	34.75	36.18
West	22.51	22.54	23.35	22.85	23.17	23.70	23.81
Household size:							
1 to 2 persons	47.19	43.74	41.85	41.48	42.34	41.84	41.82
3 to 4 persons	36.60	39.37	40.80	42.71	40.97	41.44	42.84
5 or more persons	16.22	16.89	17.34	15.81	16.70	16.72	15.34
Any child in household	41.45	44.21	45.11	46.90	45.67	45.58	46.98
Marital status:							
Single	25.21	25.90	23.73	23.80	27.24	25.21	23.16
Married..................	56.05	58.54	62.88	63.04	59.05	61.92	63.76
Other	18.74	15.57	13.39	13.16	13.71	12.87	13.08
Educational attainment:							
Graduated college plus	26.17	29.97	33.64	45.09	34.31	36.73	48.13
Attended college	27.18	29.81	30.51	31.03	31.94	31.73	30.74
Did not attend college	46.65	40.22	35.85	23.88	33.76	31.53	21.13
Employed full-time	53.47	58.25	59.77	86.62	62.16	61.56	87.73
Employed part-time	11.09	11.77	11.94	12.75	12.33	12.46	11.70
Household income:							
Less than $50,000	43.41	36.55	29.99	19.79	31.24	27.89	17.76
$50,000 to $74,999...........	19.54	20.99	21.89	21.12	21.43	21.45	20.68
$75,000 to $149,999...........	26.95	30.72	34.45	40.79	33.88	35.86	42.12
$150,000 or more.............	10.10	11.74	13.66	18.29	13.44	14.80	19.44

[1] Includes other labor force status, not shown separately.   [2] For composition of regions, see map inside front cover.

Source: Mediamark Research & Intelligence, LLC, New York, NY, *CyberStats*, fall 2008 (copyright); <http://www.mriplus.com /site/index.aspx>.

706 Information and Communications

Table 1121. **Adult Computer and Adult Internet Users by Selected Characteristics: 2000 to 2009**

[**Percent of persons 18 years old and over.** Represents persons who use a computer or the Internet at a workplace, school, home, or anywhere else, on at least an occasional basis. Based on telephone surveys of persons with landline telephones. In 2009, 2,253 persons were interviewed, including 651 cell phone users. The response rate for the landline sample was 20.6 percent and 18.2 percent for the cell sample. For 2000, Internet users include persons who ever go online to access the Internet or World Wide Web or to send and receive e-mail. For 2005, 2008 and 2009 Internet users include those who at least occasionally use the Internet or send and receive e-mail]

Characteristic	Adult computer users				Adult Internet users				Adult broad-band users, 2009
	2000	2005	2008	2009	2000	2005	2008	2009	2009
Total adults.	65	71	74	78	53	69	73	79	63
Age:									
18 to 29 years old	82	83	90	88	72	82	90	92	77
30 to 49 years old	76	81	86	87	62	80	85	87	72
50 to 64 years old	61	72	70	78	48	68	70	79	61
65 years old and over	21	31	35	42	15	28	35	42	30
Sex:									
Male	66	72	74	78	56	70	73	81	64
Female.	64	70	74	77	51	67	73	77	63
Race/ethnicity:									
White, non-Hispanic	66	72	75	78	55	70	75	79	65
Black, non-Hispanic	59	60	65	66	42	54	59	67	46
English-speaking Hispanic . . .	64	75	77	84	48	73	80	84	68
Educational attainment:									
Less than high school	28	36	46	47	19	35	44	50	30
High school graduate [1]	56	63	65	67	41	59	63	69	52
Some college	80	81	83	89	69	80	84	88	71
College graduate or higher. . .	88	90	92	94	79	88	91	94	83
Annual household income:									
Less than $30,000	48	52	55	56	35	50	53	60	42
$30,000 to $49,999.	74	76	78	82	61	74	76	80	62
$50,000 to $74,999.	85	88	84	93	74	86	85	94	80
$75,000 or more	90	92	95	95	81	91	95	95	85

[1] Includes those with a GED certificate.

Source: Pew Internet & American Life Project Surveys from September–December 2000; September and December of 2005; April–May 2008 and April 2009; <http://www.pewinternet.org/index.asp>.

Table 1122. **Internet Activities of Adults by Type of Home Internet Connection: 2008 and 2009**

[**In percent. For Internet users 18 years old and over.** For persons who have ever performed the activity. Based on telephone surveys of persons with land-line telephones, unless otherwise noted. In May 2008, 2,251 persons were interviewed. The response rate was 25 percent. In April 2009, 2,253 persons were interviewed, including 651 cell phone users. The response rate for the landline sample was 20.6 percent and 18.2 percent for the cell sample]

Activity	Survey date (month,year)	American adults performing activity	Internet users performing activity	Home broadband users performing activity
Send or read e-mail	April, 09	71	90	94
Use a search engine to find information	April, 09	69	88	91
Check weather reports and forecasts online	April, 09	60	76	81
Get news online.	April, 09	57	72	79
Buy a product online.	April, 09	59	75	80
Visit a local, state, or federal government Web site.	Nov, 08	44	59	64
Buy or make a reservation for travel	April, 09	52	66	71
Look for news or information about politics	April, 09	47	60	66
Do any banking online.	April, 09	45	57	65
Watch a video on a video-sharing site	April, 09	49	62	69
Look online for info about a job.	April, 09	41	52	54
Look for information on Wikipedia	Dec, 08	35	47	54
Send instant messages.	Nov, 08	29	38	41
Get financial information online.	April, 09	31	39	43
Use online classified ads or sites like Craig's List.	April, 09	39	49	53
Rate a product, service, or person.	April, 09	24	31	34
Use a social networking site.	April, 09	36	46	50
Participate in an online auction	April, 09	21	27	30
Look for religious or spiritual information online	April, 09	22	28	30
Download a podcast so you can listen to it or view it later . . .	May, 08	14	19	22
Make a donation to a charity online	April, 09	15	19	23
Create or work on your own online journal or blog	Dec, 08	8	11	12

Source: Pew Internet & American Life Project Surveys; <http://www.pewinternet.org/>.

Information and Communications 707

Table 1123. **Typical Daily Internet Activities of Adult Internet Users: 2008 and 2009**

[Percent of Internet users 18 years old and over. Represents persons who reported doing the activity "yesterday." Based on telephone surveys of persons with landline telephones unless otherwise noted. In May 2008, 2,251 persons were interviewed. The response rate was 25 percent. In November 2008, 2,254 persons were interviewed. The response rate was 23 percent. In April 2009, 2,253 persons were interviewed, including 561 cell phone users. The response rate for the landline sample was 20.6 percent and 18.2 percent for the cell sample]

Activity	Survey date (month-year)	Total Internet users	Age				Sex	
			18 to 29 years old	30 to 49 years old	50 to 64 years old	65 years old and over	Male	Female
Send or read e-mail	April, 09	57	57	62	53	46	53	61
Use a search engine to find information	April, 09	50	56	56	41	30	51	49
Get news online	April, 09	38	35	44	37	28	42	35
Check weather reports and forecasts online	April, 09	33	31	38	29	27	35	30
Look for news or information about politics	April, 09	25	24	27	28	20	32	19
Do any banking online	April, 09	24	24	30	19	14	25	24
Watch a video on a video-sharing site	April, 09	19	36	17	10	10	23	15
Use a social networking site	April, 09	27	51	28	10	4	23	31
Send instant messages	Nov., 08	11	20	12	4	3	14	8
Visit a local, state or federal government Web site	Nov., 08	10	9	12	9	2	11	8
Get financial information online	April, 09	12	6	14	13	15	16	8
Buy a product online	April, 09	8	9	8	7	6	9	7
Look online for information about a job	April, 09	9	16	10	5	1	9	10
Use online classified ads or sites	April, 09	9	12	11	6	3	12	7
Create or work on your own online journal or blog	Dec., 08	3	5	3	2	2	3	3
Buy or make a reservation for travel	April, 09	3	4	4	3	(Z)	3	3
Rate a product, service, or person	April, 09	3	3	2	3	5	4	2
Participate in an online auction	April, 09	3	3	3	3	1	4	1
Download a podcast so you can listen to it or view it later	May, 08	3	6	3	2	1	3	3
Make a donation to a charity online	April, 09	(Z)	1	1	(Z)	(Z)	(Z)	(Z)

Z Less than .05 percent.

Source: Pew Internet & American Life Project Surveys; <http://www.pewinternet.org/>.

Table 1124. **Online News Consumption by Selected Characteristics: 2000 to 2009**

[Percent of internet users 18 years old and over. Represents persons who report getting news online "ever" or "yesterday." Based on telephone surveys of persons with landline telephones. In 2008, 2,251 persons were interviewed. The response rate was 25 percent. In April 2009, 2,253 persons were interviewed, including 561 cell phone users. The response rate for the landline sample was 20.6 percent and 18.2 percent for the cell sample]

Characteristic	"Ever" get news online			Got news online "yesterday"		
	2000	2008	2009	2000	2008	2009
Total adult Internet users	**60**	**73**	**72**	**22**	**39**	**38**
Age:						
18 to 29 years old	56	73	74	16	41	35
30 to 49 years old	63	77	76	25	44	44
50 to 64 years old	57	72	71	25	35	37
65 years old and over	53	61	56	28	25	28
Sex:						
Male	66	75	73	29	48	42
Female	53	72	72	16	31	35
Race/ethnicity:						
White, non-Hispanic	60	73	73	23	41	40
Black, non-Hispanic	63	69	72	13	37	32
English-speaking Hispanic	57	69	67	23	31	34
Annual household income:						
Less than $30,000	55	63	59	21	21	28
$30,000 to $49,999	57	73	69	20	33	33
$50,000 to $74,999	63	78	75	22	46	40
$75,000 or more	69	79	84	31	53	53
Frequency of Internet use:						
Daily	66	83	81	33	52	50
Several times per week	59	59	59	17	15	13
Less Often	51	38	30	12	3	2

Source: Pew Internet & American Life Project Surveys from March 2000, April–May 2008, and April 2009; <http://www.pewinternet.org/>.

708 Information and Communications

Section 25
Banking, Finance, and Insurance

This section presents data on the nation's finances, various types of financial institutions, money and credit, securities, insurance, and real estate. The primary sources of these data are publications of several departments of the federal government, especially the U.S. Treasury Department, and independent agencies such as the Federal Deposit Insurance Corporation, the Board of Governors of the Federal Reserve System, and the Securities and Exchange Commission. National data on insurance are available primarily from private organizations, such as the American Council of Life Insurers and the Insurance Information Institute.

Flow of funds—The flow of funds accounts of the Federal Reserve Board bring together statistics on all of the major forms of financial instruments to present an economy-wide view of asset and liability relationships. In flow form, the accounts relate borrowing and lending to one another and to the nonfinancial activities that generate income and production. Each claim outstanding is included simultaneously as an asset of the lender and as a liability of the debtor. The accounts also indicate the balance between asset totals and liability totals over the economy as a whole. Several publications of the Federal Reserve Board contain information on the flow of funds accounts: Summary data on flows and outstandings, in the statistical release *Flow of Funds Accounts of the United States* (quarterly); and concepts and organization of the accounts in *Guide to the Flow of Funds Accounts* (2000). Data are also available on the Federal Reserve Board's Web site <http://www.federalreserve.gov/>.

Survey of Consumer Finances (SCF)—The Federal Reserve Board, in cooperation with the Treasury Department, sponsors this survey, which is conducted every 3 years to provide detailed information on the finances of U.S. families. Among the topics covered are the balance sheet, pension, income, and other demographic characteristics of U.S. families. The survey also gathers information on the use of financial institutions. Since 1992, data for the SCF have been collected by the National Organization for Social Science and Survey Research at the University of Chicago. Data and information on the survey are available on the Web site of the Federal Reserve Board: <http://www.federalreserve.gov/pubs/oss/oss2/scfindex.html>.

Banking system—Banks in this country are organized under the laws of both the states and the federal government and are regulated by several bank supervisory agencies. National banks are supervised by the Comptroller of the Currency. *Reports of Condition* have been collected from national banks since 1863. Summaries of these reports are published in the Comptroller's *Annual Report,* which also presents data on the structure of the national banking system.

The Federal Reserve System was established in 1913 to exercise central banking functions, some of which are shared with the U.S. Treasury. It includes national banks and such state banks that voluntarily join the system. Statements of state bank members are consolidated by the Federal Reserve Board with data for national banks collected by the Comptroller of the Currency into totals for all member banks of the system. Balance sheet data for member banks and other commercial banks are available on the Federal Reserve Board's Web site at <http://www.federalreserve.gov/econresdata/releases/statisticsdata.htm>.

The Federal Deposit Insurance Corporation (FDIC), established in 1933, insures each depositor up to $250,000. Major item balance sheet and income data for all insured financial institutions are published in the *FDIC Quarterly Banking Profile.* This publication is also available on the Internet at the following address: <http://www.fdic.gov>. Quarterly financial information for individual institutions is available through the FDIC and Federal

Financial Institutions Examination Council Web sites at <http://www.fdic.gov> and <http://www.ffiec.gov>.

Credit unions—Federally chartered credit unions are under the supervision of the National Credit Union Administration. State-chartered credit unions are supervised by the respective state supervisory authorities. The administration publishes comprehensive program and statistical information on all federal and federally insured state credit unions in the *Annual Report of the National Credit Union Administration.*

Other credit agencies—Insurance companies, finance companies dealing primarily in installment sales financing, and personal loan companies represent important sources of funds for the credit market. Statistics on loans, investments, cash, etc., of life insurance companies are published principally by the American Council of Life Insurers in its *Life Insurers Fact Book.* Consumer credit data are available on the Federal Board's Web site at <http://www.federalreserve.gov /econresdata/releases/statisticsdata.htm>.

Government corporations and credit agencies make available credit of specified types or to specified groups of private borrowers, either by lending directly or by insuring or guaranteeing loans made by private lending institutions. Data on operations of government credit agencies, along with other government corporations, are available in reports of individual agencies.

Securities—The Securities and Exchange Commission (SEC) was established in 1934 to protect the interests of the public and investors against malpractices in the securities and financial markets and to provide the fullest possible disclosure of information regarding securities to the investing public.

Data on the securities industry and securities transactions are also available from a number of private sources. The Securities Industry and Financial Markets Association, New York, NY, <http://www.sifma .org/>, publishes the *Securities Industry*

Fact Book and *Securities Industry Year-book.* The Investment Company Institute, Washington, DC, <http://www.ici.org/>, publishes a reference book, research newsletters, and a variety of research reports that examine the industry, its shareholders, or industry issues. The annual *Mutual Fund Fact Book* is a guide to trends and statistics observed in the investment company industry. *Fundamentals* is a newsletter summarizing the findings of major Institute research projects. Institute research reports provide a detailed examination of shareholder demographics and other aspects of fund ownership.

Among the many sources of data on stock and bond prices and sales are the New York Stock Exchange, New York, NY, <http://www.nyse.com/>; NASDAQ, Washington, DC, <http://www.nasdaq .com/>; Global Financial Data, Los Angeles, CA, <http://www.globalfinancialdata .com/>; and Dow-Jones & Company, Inc., New York, NY, <http://www.djindexes .com>.

Insurance—Insuring companies, which are regulated by the various states or the District of Columbia, are classified as either life or property. Both life and property insurance companies may underwrite health insurance. Insuring companies, other than those classified as life, are permitted to underwrite one or more property lines provided they are so licensed and have the necessary capital or surplus.

There are a number of published sources for statistics on the various classes of insurance—life, health, fire, marine, and casualty. Organizations representing certain classes of insurers publish reports for these classes. The American Council of Life Insurers publishes statistics on life insurance purchases, ownership, benefit payments, and assets in its *Life Insurers Fact Book.*

Statistical reliability—For a discussion of statistical collection, estimation, and sampling procedures and measures of reliability applicable to data from the Census Bureau and the Federal Reserve Board's Survey of Consumer Finances, see Appendix III.

Figure 25.1
Interest Rates and Bond Yields: 1990 to 2008
(Annual averages)

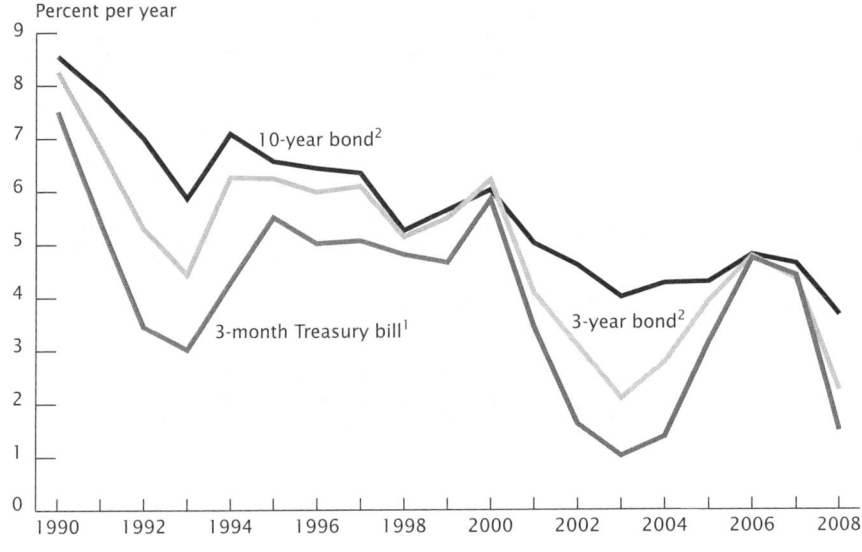

¹New issues.   ² U.S. Treasury, constant maturities.

Source: Chart prepared by U.S. Census Bureau. For data, see Tables 1160 and 1161.

Figure 25.2
Foreign Holdings of U.S. Treasury Securities by Country: 2008
(In billions of dollars)

Total = 3,211

¹Comprises Indonesia, Iran, Iraq, Kuwait, Qatar, Saudi Arabia, and the United Arab Emirates.

Source: Chart prepared by U.S. Census Bureau. For data, see Table 1169.

U.S. Census Bureau, Statistical Abstract of the United States: 2010

Table 1125. **Gross Domestic Product in Finance, Insurance, Real Estate, Rental, and Leasing in Current and Chained (2000) Dollars: 2000 to 2008**

[In billions of dollars, except percent (741 represents $741,000,000,000). Represents value added by industry. For definition of gross domestic product and explanation of chained dollars, see text, Section 13]

Industry	1997 NAICS code [1]	Current dollars				Chained (2000) dollars			
		2000	2005	2007	2008	2000	2005	2007	2008
Finance & insurance, total	52	741	989	1,091	1,065	741	890	946	917
Percent of gross domestic product ...		7.5	8.0	7.9	7.5	7.5	8.1	8.2	7.9
Monetary authorities—central bank, credit intermediation & related activities......	521, 522	319	496	504	(NA)	319	428	412	(NA)
Security, commodity contracts, & like activity.....................	523	168	189	238	(NA)	168	231	292	(NA)
Insurance carriers & related activities.....	524	238	280	332	(NA)	238	221	254	(NA)
Funds, trusts, & other financial vehicles (part)..................	525	16	25	17	(NA)	16	18	12	(NA)
Real estate & rental & leasing, total ..	53	1,191	1,538	1,720	1,784	1,191	1,333	1,414	1,440
Percent of gross domestic product ...		12.1	12.4	12.5	12.5	12.1	12.1	12.3	12.4
Real estate.............	531	1,082	1,428	1,587	(NA)	1,082	1,233	1,300	(NA)
Rental & leasing services [2]	532, 533	108	110	133	(NA)	108	98	113	(NA)

NA Not available.   [1] See footnote 1, Table 1126.   [2] Includes lessors of other nonfinancial intangible assets.

Source: U.S. Bureau of Economic Analysis, *Survey of Current Business*, May 2009.

Table 1126. **Finance and Insurance/Real Estate and Rental and Leasing— Establishments, Revenue, Payroll, and Employees by Kind of Business (2002 NAICS Basis): 2002 and 2007**

[2,781 represents $2,781,000,000,000. Preliminary. For establishments with payroll. Based on the 2002 and 2007 Economic Censuses; see Appendix III]

Kind of business	2002 NAICS code [1]	Number of establishments		Revenue (bil. dol.)		Annual payroll (bil. dol.)		Paid employees (1,000)	
		2002	2007	2002	2007	2002	2007	2002	2007
Finance & insurance [2]	52	438,356	503,156	2,781	3,641	376.5	494.5	6,560	6,563
Monetary authorities—central bank	521	47	47	29	45	1.2	1.3	22	19
Credit intermediation & related activities.....................	522	196,451	235,440	1,056	1,327	151.2	178.1	3,300	3,203
Security, commodity contracts, & like activity	523	72,338	84,829	316	632	103.4	161.1	832	931
Insurance carriers & related activities...	524	169,520	182,840	1,380	1,637	120.6	154.0	2,406	2,409
Real estate & rental & leasing.....	53	322,815	376,799	336	452	60.2	85.2	1,949	2,249
Real estate..................	531	256,086	308,004	224	303	41.7	60.8	1,305	1,551
Rental & leasing services..........	532	64,344	66,067	95	127	16.9	22.1	617	666
Lessors of other nonfinancial intangible assets	533	2,385	2,728	17	23	1.7	2.4	27	32

[1] Based on North American Industry Classification System (NAICS); see text, Section 15.   [2] Total does not include NAICS 525, Funds, trusts, and other financial vehicles, not published in the 2007 Economic Census.

Source: U.S. Census Bureau, "2007 Economic Census; Core Business Statistics Series: Advance Comparative Statistics for the United States (2002 NAICS Basis): 2007 and 2002" (published 17 March 2009); using American FactFinder; <http://factfinder .census.gov>.

Table 1127. **Finance and Insurance—Nonemployer Establishments and Receipts by Kind of Business: 2000 to 2006**

[691.8 represents 691,800. Includes only firms subject to federal income tax. Nonemployers are businesses with no paid employees. Data originate chiefly from administrative records of the Internal Revenue Service; see Appendix III. Data for 2000 based on the 1997 North American Industry Classification System (NAICS); beginning 2005 based on 2002 NAICS. See text, Section 15]

Kind of business	NAICS code	Establishments (1,000)			Receipts (mil. dol.)		
		2000	2005	2006	2000	2005	2006
Finance and insurance	52	691.8	741.9	758.2	49,058	47,244	52,768
Credit intermediation & related activities	522	165.3	82.5	89.7	4,848	5,046	4,983
Depository credit intermediation................	5221	6.5	7.3	7.4	197	240	232
Nondepository credit intermediation	5222	134.1	29.4	30.3	3,624	2,541	2,489
Activities related to credit intermediation	5223	24.7	45.8	51.9	1,028	2,265	2,262
Security, commodity contracts, & like activity	523	181.5	276.2	280.3	29,379	23,405	28,113
Securities & commodity contracts interm & brokerage .	5231	29.6	33.4	32.9	6,395	5,017	4,983
Investment banking and securities dealing	52311	5.6	8.0	8.3	2,043	1,499	1,480
Securities brokerage	52312	19.5	20.5	19.6	3,712	2,872	2,829
Commodity contracts dealing.............	52313	1.0	1.2	1.3	238	211	169
Commodity contracts brokerage.............	52314	3.6	3.7	3.7	402	435	506
Securities & commodity exchanges	5232	1.6	2.0	2.1	1,495	571	529
Other financial investment activities	5239	150.2	240.7	246.3	21,488	17,817	22,600
Insurance carriers & related activities.............	524	345.0	383.3	388.3	14,831	18,793	19,672
Insurance carriers................	5241	1.0	0.5	0.5	98	37	32
Agencies & other insurance-related activities	5242	344.0	382.7	387.8	14,733	18,756	19,640
Insurance agencies & brokerages	52421	245.5	256.5	263.0	11,570	13,933	14,593
Other insurance related activities	52429	98.5	126.2	125.2	3,163	4,824	5,047

Source: U.S. Census Bureau, "Nonemployer Statistics"; <http://www.census.gov/econ/nonemployer/>.

Table 1128. **Finance and Insurance—Establishments, Employees, and Payroll: 2000 and 2006**

[423.7 represents 423,700. Covers establishments with payroll. Kind-of-business classification for 2000 based on North American Industry Classification System (NAICS) 1997; data for 2006 based on NAICS 2002. See text, Section 15. Employees are for the week including March 12. Most government employees are excluded. For statement on methodology, see Appendix III]

Kind of business	NAICS code	Establishments (1,000)		Employees (1,000)		Payroll (bil. dol.)	
		2000	2006	2000	2006	2000	2006
Finance & insurance, total [1]	52	423.7	494.3	5,963	6,647	346.8	481.0
Monetary authorities—central bank	521	0.1	0.1	22	20	1.1	1.3
Credit intermediation & related activities	522	176.3	224.6	2,753	3,282	116.1	181.3
Depository credit intermediation [1]	5221	105.6	120.6	1,935	2,155	78.5	114.7
Commercial banking	52211	73.9	87.7	1,493	1,634	63.6	91.5
Savings institutions	52212	15.9	16.5	244	263	9.2	13.0
Credit unions	52213	15.6	16.1	192	250	5.4	9.5
Nondepository credit intermediation [1]	5222	49.3	59.4	621	765	29.6	49.5
Real estate credit	522292	19.8	29.9	238	402	10.8	26.5
Activities related to credit intermediation	5223	21.4	44.6	198	361	7.9	17.2
Security, commodity contracts & like activity	523	72.9	86.6	866	941	119.5	148.7
Security & commodity contracts intermediation & brokerage [1]	5231	38.1	39.4	539	516	80.2	89.9
Investment banking & securities dealing	52311	6.3	7.6	138	156	31.2	38.2
Securities brokerage	52312	29.5	29.2	378	339	47.0	49.2
Securities & commodity exchanges	5232	(Z)	0.4	7	9	0.5	1.0
Other financial investment activities	5239	34.8	46.8	320	417	38.8	57.8
Insurance carriers & related activities	524	172.2	180.2	2,290	2,378	108.1	146.4
Insurance carriers [1]	5241	37.4	34.4	1,489	1,439	74.7	97.1
Direct life insurance carriers	524113	10.7	8.3	491	354	25.7	26.3
Direct health & medical insurance carriers	524114	3.1	4.1	322	422	14.3	27.1
Direct property & casualty insurance carriers	524126	19.8	14.0	609	528	31.1	34.3
Agencies & other insurance-related activities [1]	5242	134.8	145.7	801	939	33.3	49.3
Insurance agencies & brokerages	52421	121.5	132.4	596	713	24.7	37.3

Z Less than 50. [1] Includes industries not shown separately.

Source: U.S. Census Bureau, "County Business Patterns"; <http://www.census.gov/econ/cbp/view/cbpview.html>.

Table 1129. **Flow of Funds Accounts—Financial Assets of Financial and Nonfinancial Institutions by Holder Sector: 1990 to 2008**

[In billions of dollars (35,844 represents $35,844,000,000,000). As of Dec. 31]

Sector	1990	1995	2000	2002	2003	2004	2005	2006	2007	2008
All sectors	35,844	53,484	89,868	90,516	101,524	112,448	123,106	137,413	149,379	141,512
Households [1]	14,596	21,510	33,182	30,094	35,071	38,940	42,895	47,371	49,754	40,814
Nonfinancial business	3,970	5,556	11,252	11,659	11,908	13,103	14,518	15,816	17,439	17,908
Farm business	38	49	57	60	62	66	67	74	79	82
Nonfarm noncorporate	356	548	1,423	1,657	1,737	2,106	2,542	3,057	3,580	3,776
Nonfinancial corporations	3,575	4,959	9,772	9,942	10,109	10,932	11,909	12,685	13,781	14,049
State and local government	1,020	1,122	1,662	1,800	1,908	2,030	2,247	2,461	2,635	2,554
U.S. Government	442	432	545	629	630	610	615	625	659	1,261
Monetary authorities	342	472	636	754	797	841	879	908	951	2,271
Commercial banking	3,337	4,494	6,469	7,329	7,825	8,560	9,320	10,203	11,192	13,417
U.S.-chartered commercial banks	2,644	3,322	4,774	5,427	5,838	6,399	6,906	7,614	8,269	9,676
Foreign banking offices in U.S.	367	666	789	801	750	633	782	785	1,002	1,570
Bank-holding companies	298	467	842	1,026	1,153	1,429	1,524	1,695	1,813	2,063
Banks in U.S.-affiliated areas	28	39	63	75	84	100	109	108	108	107
Savings institutions	1,323	1,013	1,218	1,349	1,466	1,650	1,789	1,715	1,815	1,526
Credit unions	217	311	441	564	617	655	686	716	759	814
Life insurance companies	1,351	2,064	3,136	3,335	3,773	4,130	4,351	4,685	4,950	4,411
Property-casualty insurance companies	533	740	862	940	1,060	1,157	1,240	1,329	1,359	1,288
Private pension funds	1,629	2,899	4,468	3,677	4,520	4,915	5,296	6,014	6,392	4,595
Defined benefit plans	900	1,466	1,979	1,639	1,995	2,132	2,281	2,530	2,666	1,930
Defined contribution plans	729	1,433	2,489	2,038	2,526	2,783	3,014	3,485	3,726	2,665
State and local government employee retirement funds	730	1,327	2,293	1,930	2,349	2,578	2,721	3,050	3,157	2,311
Federal government retirement funds	340	541	797	894	958	1,023	1,072	1,141	1,197	1,221
Money market mutual funds	493	741	1,812	2,224	2,016	1,880	2,007	2,312	3,033	3,757
Mutual funds	608	1,853	4,433	3,638	4,654	5,436	6,049	7,068	7,829	5,274
Closed-end funds	53	136	142	151	206	246	271	294	317	207
Exchange-traded funds	–	1	66	102	151	227	301	423	607	529
Government-sponsored enterprises (GSE)	478	897	1,965	2,549	2,794	2,883	2,819	2,873	3,174	3,459
Agency- and GSE-backed mortgage pools	1,020	1,571	2,493	3,159	3,327	3,375	3,542	3,837	4,464	4,965
Asset-backed securities issuers	268	663	1,497	1,977	2,212	2,650	3,375	4,182	4,500	4,058
Finance companies	596	705	1,213	1,446	1,679	1,858	1,857	1,891	1,911	1,912
Real estate investment trusts	28	33	66	101	135	251	304	344	317	276
Security brokers and dealers	262	568	1,221	1,335	1,613	1,845	2,127	2,742	3,092	2,217
Funding corporations	251	384	1,172	1,084	1,065	1,084	1,310	1,453	1,836	3,570
Rest of the world	1,954	3,452	6,828	7,795	8,791	10,523	11,516	13,960	16,041	16,897

– Represents zero. [1] Includes nonprofit organizations.

Source: Board of Governors of the Federal Reserve System, "Federal Reserve Statistical Release, Z.1, Flow of Funds Accounts of the United States"; published 12 March 2009; <http://www.federalreserve.gov/releases/z1/20090312>.

Banking, Finance, and Insurance 713

Table 1130. **Flow of Funds Accounts—Credit Market Debt Outstanding: 1990 to 2008**

[In billions of dollars (13,769 represents $13,769,000,000,000). As of December 31. Represents credit market debt owed by sectors shown]

Item	1990	1995	2000	2002	2003	2004	2005	2006	2007	2008
Credit market debt..........	13,769	18,475	27,157	31,843	34,622	37,808	41,269	45,325	49,866	52,593
Domestic nonfinancial.............	10,837	13,674	18,184	20,732	22,442	24,450	26,777	29,166	31,673	33,518
Households [1]................	3,598	4,857	7,011	8,514	9,500	10,576	11,747	12,916	13,765	13,821
Corporations.................	2,536	2,940	4,638	4,857	4,974	5,178	5,511	5,977	6,785	7,104
Nonfarm noncorporate business	1,093	1,062	1,796	2,107	2,199	2,444	2,775	3,184	3,595	3,767
Farm business................	124	131	156	170	168	174	187	198	214	225
State and local government	987	1,047	1,198	1,448	1,568	1,683	1,855	2,006	2,192	2,240
U.S. government	2,498	3,637	3,385	3,637	4,033	4,395	4,702	4,885	5,122	6,362
Rest of the world................	318	568	815	1,073	1,253	1,438	1,512	1,880	2,016	1,858
Financial sectors................	2,614	4,234	8,158	10,038	10,928	11,921	12,980	14,279	16,176	17,216
Commercial banking	198	251	509	612	660	739	824	998	1,261	1,422
Savings institutions	140	115	301	278	313	405	427	319	423	411
Credit unions................	–	–	3	7	9	11	15	19	32	45
Life insurance companies	–	1	2	5	8	11	11	14	29	45
Government-sponsored enterprises (GSE)...................	399	807	1,826	2,350	2,601	2,676	2,592	2,628	2,910	3,224
Agency- and GSE-backed mortgage pools	1,020	1,571	2,493	3,159	3,327	3,375	3,542	3,837	4,464	4,965
Asset-backed securities issuers.....	269	666	1,504	1,983	2,217	2,655	3,379	4,186	4,503	4,061
Finance companies............	398	500	807	884	995	1,130	1,109	1,144	1,280	1,272
Real estate investment trusts	28	45	168	198	230	340	396	412	422	377
Brokers and dealers	15	29	41	41	47	62	62	69	65	143
Funding corporations	147	249	503	521	519	517	623	653	788	1,250

– Represents or rounds to zero.   [1] Includes nonprofit organizations.

Source: Board of Governors of the Federal Reserve System, "Federal Reserve Statistical Release, Z.1, Flow of Funds Accounts of the United States"; published 12 March 2009; <http://www.federalreserve.gov/releases/z1/20090312>.

Table 1131. **Flow of Funds Accounts—Financial Assets and Liabilities of Foreign Sector: 1990 to 2008**

[In billions of dollars (1,954 represents $1,954,000,000,000). As of December 31]

Type of instrument	1990	1995	2000	2002	2003	2004	2005	2006	2007	2008
Total financial assets [1].....	1,954	3,452	6,828	7,795	8,791	10,523	11,516	13,960	16,041	16,897
Net interbank assets.............	53	229	161	120	110	118	106	97	-57	289
U.S. checkable deposits and currency ..	86	158	236	273	263	285	300	312	306	375
U.S. time deposits...............	40	40	102	143	115	149	156	167	208	253
Security RPs [2]................	20	68	91	190	460	665	713	1,029	1,109	578
Credit market instruments [1]	882	1,465	2,451	3,303	3,836	4,635	5,188	6,198	7,369	7,831
Open market paper	11	43	114	127	193	230	240	288	278	233
Treasury securities	438	817	1,021	1,285	1,514	1,814	1,984	2,126	2,432	3,187
Official...................	286	490	640	812	986	1,252	1,341	1,558	1,697	2,125
Private...................	152	327	382	474	527	562	644	568	735	1,062
Agency- and GSE-backed securities [3].	49	123	348	631	655	875	1,013	1,262	1,572	1,331
Official...................	5	18	116	214	263	373	487	694	956	935
Private...................	44	106	232	416	392	503	526	568	615	396
U.S. corporate bonds [4]...........	209	355	842	1,123	1,330	1,559	1,763	2,321	2,781	2,813
Loans to U.S. corporate business....	172	122	117	126	125	131	160	167	274	225
U.S. corporate equities	243	485	1,483	1,222	1,675	1,905	2,039	2,472	2,750	1,813
Mutual fund shares	–	60	149	98	146	196	242	294	325	219
Trade receivables	46	49	49	49	50	49	57	63	84	88
Miscellaneous assets.............	584	893	2,094	2,381	2,117	2,499	2,691	3,302	3,914	5,409
Foreign direct investment in U.S. [5]...	505	680	1,421	1,500	1,581	1,743	1,906	2,152	2,423	2,799
Other	78	212	673	881	536	756	785	1,151	1,491	2,610
Total liabilities...........	1,359	2,104	3,788	4,298	4,759	5,856	6,488	7,420	7,989	10,441
U.S. official foreign exchange and net IMF [6] position	61	64	46	56	62	62	46	46	50	57
U.S. private deposits..............	298	419	803	831	867	957	998	1,086	1,303	1,039
Credit market instruments [1]	318	568	815	1,073	1,253	1,438	1,512	1,880	2,016	1,858
Commercial paper.............	75	56	121	257	275	344	382	480	412	342
Bonds....................	145	413	573	703	869	985	1,012	1,276	1,478	1,386
Bank loans n.e.c. [7]	19	35	71	69	66	70	84	98	103	108
Trade payables	29	47	51	39	45	48	54	61	72	61
Miscellaneous liabilities [1]...........	653	1,008	2,073	2,300	2,532	3,351	3,878	4,348	4,548	7,425
U.S. equity in IBRD [8], etc.........	20	27	35	39	40	42	43	45	47	49
Nonofficial foreign currencies.	1	2	3	3	3	3	1	1	24	554
U.S. direct investment abroad [4, 5]....	630	886	1,532	1,867	2,054	2,498	2,652	2,936	3,333	3,632

– Represents zero.   [1] Includes other items not shown separately.   [2] Repurchase agreements.   [3] GSE = Government-sponsored enterprises.   [4] Through 1992, corporate bonds include net issues by Netherlands Antillean financial subsidiaries; U.S. direct investment abroad excludes net inflows from those bond issues.   [5] Direct investment is valued on a current-cost basis.   [6] IMF = International Monetary Fund.   [7] Not elsewhere classified.   [8] International Bank for Reconstruction and Development.

Source: Board of Governors of the Federal Reserve System, "Federal Reserve Statistical Release, Z.1, Flow of Funds Accounts of the United States"; published 12 March 2009; <http://www.federalreserve.gov/releases/z1/20090312>.

Table 1132. **Flow of Funds Accounts—Assets of Households and Nonprofit Organizations: 1990 to 2008**

[As of December 31 (14,596 represents $14,596,000,000,000). See also Table 706]

Type of instrument	Total (bil. dol.)							Percent distribution		
	1990	2000	2004	2005	2006	2007	2008	1990	2000	2008
Total financial assets	14,596	33,182	38,940	42,895	47,371	49,754	40,814	100.0	100.0	100.0
Deposits	3,326	4,377	5,743	6,154	6,779	7,330	7,685	22.8	13.2	18.8
Foreign deposits	13	48	57	60	65	78	60	0.1	0.1	0.1
Checkable deposits and currency	433	335	370	257	236	101	156	3.0	1.0	0.4
Time and savings deposits	2,490	3,034	4,411	4,888	5,363	5,804	5,891	17.1	9.1	14.4
Money market fund shares	391	960	904	949	1,114	1,347	1,578	2.7	2.9	3.9
Credit market instruments	1,748	2,481	3,102	3,452	3,626	3,942	3,876	12.0	7.5	9.5
Open-market paper	94	97	136	164	188	150	10	0.6	0.3	–
Treasury securities	509	585	535	511	440	191	273	3.5	1.8	0.7
Agency and GSE-backed securities [1] . .	119	609	405	501	434	740	920	0.8	1.8	2.3
Municipal securities	648	531	742	821	874	907	960	4.4	1.6	2.4
Corporate and foreign bonds	238	554	1,145	1,304	1,564	1,842	1,601	1.6	1.7	3.9
Other loans and advances [2]	-	2	6	9	8	16	17	–	–	–
Mortgages	141	103	132	142	117	97	94	1.0	0.3	0.2
Corporate equities [3]	1,961	8,147	7,496	8,004	9,199	9,158	5,502	13.4	24.6	13.5
Mutual fund shares	512	2,704	3,417	3,839	4,410	4,873	3,254	3.5	8.1	8.0
Security credit	62	412	578	575	656	866	743	0.4	1.2	1.8
Life insurance reserves	392	819	1,060	1,083	1,164	1,202	1,156	2.7	2.5	2.8
Pension fund reserves [4]	3,308	9,166	10,633	11,369	12,613	13,247	10,280	22.7	27.6	25.2
Equity in noncorporate business	3,033	4,695	6,369	7,828	8,294	8,436	7,538	20.8	14.2	18.5
Miscellaneous assets	254	379	542	591	631	698	779	1.7	1.1	1.9

– Represents or rounds to zero.   [1] GSE = government-sponsored enterprises.   [2] Syndicated loans to nonfinancial corporate business by nonprofits and domestic hedge funds.   [3] Only those directly held and those in closed-end and exchange-traded funds. Other equities are included in mutual funds and life insurance and pension reserves.   [4] See also Table 1180.

Source: Board of Governors of the Federal Reserve System, "Federal Reserve Statistical Release, Z.1, Flow of Funds Accounts of the United States"; published 12 March 2009; <http://www.federalreserve.gov/releases/z1/20090312/>.

Table 1133. **Financial Assets Held by Families by Type of Asset: 2004 and 2007**

[Median value in thousands of constant 2007 dollars (25.3 represents $25,300). All dollar figures are adjusted to 2007 dollars using the "current methods" version of the consumer price index for all urban consumers published by U.S. Bureau of Labor Statistics. Families include one-person units; for definition of family, see text, Section 1. Based on Survey of Consumer Finances; see Appendix III]

Age of family head and family income	Any financial asset [1]	Trans-action accounts [2]	Certifi-cates of deposit	Savings bonds	Stocks [3]	Pooled invest-ment funds [4]	Retirement accounts [5]	Life insur-ance [6]	Other man-aged [7]
PERCENT OF FAMILIES OWNING ASSET									
2004, total	93.8	91.3	12.7	17.6	20.7	15.0	49.7	24.2	7.3
2007, total	93.9	92.1	16.1	14.9	17.9	11.4	52.6	23.0	5.8
Under 35 years old	89.2	87.3	6.7	13.7	13.7	5.3	41.6	11.4	(B)
35 to 44 years old	93.1	91.2	9.0	16.8	17.0	11.6	57.5	17.5	2.2
45 to 54 years old	93.3	91.7	14.3	19.0	18.6	12.6	64.7	22.3	5.1
55 to 64 years old	97.8	96.4	20.5	16.2	21.3	14.3	60.9	35.2	7.7
65 to 74 years old	96.1	94.6	24.2	10.3	19.1	14.6	51.7	34.4	13.2
75 years old and over	97.4	95.3	37.0	7.9	20.2	13.2	30.0	27.6	14.0
Percentiles of income: [8]									
Less than 20	79.1	74.9	9.4	3.6	5.5	3.4	10.7	12.8	2.7
20 to 39.9	93.2	90.1	12.7	8.5	7.8	4.6	35.6	16.4	4.7
40 to 59.9	97.2	96.4	15.4	15.2	14.0	7.1	55.2	21.6	5.3
60 to 79.9	99.7	99.3	19.3	20.9	23.2	14.6	73.3	29.4	5.7
80 to 89.9	100.0	100.0	19.9	26.2	30.5	18.9	86.7	30.6	7.6
90 to 100	100.0	100.0	27.7	26.1	47.5	35.5	89.6	38.9	13.6
MEDIAN VALUE [9]									
2004, total	25.3	4.1	16.5	1.1	16.5	44.4	38.7	6.6	49.4
2007, total	28.8	4.0	20.0	1.0	17.0	56.0	45.0	8.0	70.0
Under 35 years old	6.8	2.4	5.0	0.7	3.0	18.0	10.0	2.8	(B)
35 to 44 years old	25.8	3.4	5.0	1.0	15.0	22.5	36.0	8.3	24.0
45 to 54 years old	54.0	5.0	15.0	1.0	18.5	50.0	67.0	10.0	45.0
55 to 64 years old	72.4	5.2	23.0	1.9	24.0	112.0	98.0	10.0	59.0
65 to 74 years old	68.1	7.7	23.2	1.0	38.0	86.0	77.0	10.0	70.0
75 years old and over	41.5	6.1	10.0	20.0	40.0	75.0	35.0	5.0	100.0

B Base figure too small.   [1] Includes other types of financial assets, not shown separately.   [2] Checking, savings, and money market deposit accounts, money market mutual funds, and call accounts at brokerages.   [3] Covers only those stocks that are directly held by families outside mutual funds, retirement accounts, and other managed assets.   [4] Excludes money market mutual funds and indirectly held mutual funds and includes all other types of directly held pooled investment funds, such as traditional open-ended and closed-end mutual funds, real estate investment trusts, and hedge funds.   [5] The tax-deferred retirement accounts consist of IRAs, Keogh accounts, and certain employer-sponsored accounts. Employer-sponsored accounts include 401(k), 403(b), and thrift saving accounts from current or past jobs; other current job plans from which loans or withdrawals can be made; and accounts from past jobs from which the family expects to receive the account balance in the future.   [6] The value of such policies according to their current cash value, not their death benefit.   [7] Includes personal annuities and trusts with an equity interest and managed investment accounts.   [8] Percentiles of income distribution in 2007 dollars: 20th: $20,600; 40th: $36,500; 60th: $59,600; 80th: $98,200; 90th: $140,900. Percentile: A value on a scale of zero to 100 that indicates the percent of a distribution that is equal to or below it. For example, a family with income in the 80th percentile has income equal to or better than 80 percent of all other families.   [9] Median value of financial asset for families holding such assets.

Source: Board of Governors of the Federal Reserve System, "2007 Survey of Consumer Finances"; published February 2009; <http://www.federalreserve.gov/pubs/oss/oss2/2007/scf2007home.html>.

Banking, Finance, and Insurance   715

Table 1134. **Flow of Funds Accounts—Liabilities of Households and Nonprofit Organizations: 1990 to 2008**

[As of December 31 (3,720 represents $3,720,000,000,000). See also Table 706]

Type of instrument	Total (bil. dol.)							Percent distribution		
	1990	2000	2004	2005	2006	2007	2008	1990	2000	2008
Total liabilities	3,720	7,400	11,036	12,188	13,431	14,329	14,242	100.0	100.0	100.0
Credit market instruments	3,598	7,011	10,576	11,747	12,916	13,765	13,821	96.7	94.7	97.0
Home mortgages [1]	2,506	4,821	7,839	8,879	9,843	10,495	10,454	67.4	65.1	73.4
Consumer credit	824	1,741	2,219	2,314	2,418	2,552	2,596	22.2	23.5	18.2
Municipal securities	86	138	189	205	227	250	271	2.3	1.9	1.9
Bank loans, not elsewhere classified . .	18	65	35	48	96	108	124	0.5	0.9	0.9
Other loans and advances	82	119	119	119	124	127	132	2.2	1.6	0.9
Commercial mortgages	83	127	175	181	208	234	244	2.2	1.7	1.7
Security credit	39	235	264	232	292	326	165	1.0	3.2	1.2
Trade payables	67	135	173	186	200	215	230	1.8	1.8	1.6
Unpaid life insurance premiums [2]	16	20	22	22	23	24	26	0.4	0.3	0.2

[1] Includes loans made under home equity lines of credit and home equity loans secured by junior liens. [2] Includes deferred premiums.

Source: Board of Governors of the Federal Reserve System, "Federal Reserve Statistical Release, Z.1, Flow of Funds Accounts of the United States" (published 12 March 2009); <http://www.federalreserve.gov/releases/z1/20090312/>.

Table 1135. **Financial Debt Held by Families by Type of Debt: 2004 and 2007**

[Median debt in thousands of constant 2007 dollars (60.7 represents $60,700). See headnote, Table 1133]

Age of family head and family income	Any debt	Secured by residential property		Lines of credit not secured by residential property	Installment loans	Credit card balances [2]	Other [3]
		Primary residence [1]	Other				
PERCENT OF FAMILIES HOLDING DEBT							
2004, total	76.4	47.9	4.0	1.6	46.0	46.2	7.6
2007, total	77.0	48.7	5.5	1.7	46.9	46.1	6.8
Under 35 years old	83.5	37.3	3.3	2.1	65.2	48.5	5.9
35 to 44 years old	86.2	59.5	6.5	2.2	56.2	51.7	7.5
45 to 54 years old	86.8	65.5	8.0	1.9	51.9	53.6	9.8
55 to 64 years old	81.8	55.3	7.8	1.2	44.6	49.9	8.7
65 to 74 years old	65.5	42.9	5.0	1.5	26.1	37.0	4.4
75 years old and over	31.4	13.9	0.6	(B)	7.0	18.8	1.3
Percentiles of income: [4]							
Less than 20	51.7	14.9	1.1	(B)	27.8	25.7	3.9
20 to 39.9	70.2	29.5	1.9	1.8	42.3	39.4	6.8
40 to 59.9	83.8	50.5	2.6	(B)	54.0	54.9	6.4
60 to 79.9	90.9	69.7	6.8	2.1	59.2	62.1	8.7
80 to 89.9	89.6	80.8	8.5	(B)	57.4	55.8	9.6
90 to 100	87.6	76.4	21.9	2.1	45.0	40.6	7.0
MEDIAN DEBT [5]							
2004, total	60.7	104.3	95.6	3.3	12.7	2.4	4.4
2007, total	67.3	107.0	100.0	3.8	13.0	3.0	5.0
Under 35 years old	36.2	135.3	78.0	1.0	15.0	1.8	4.5
35 to 44 years old	106.2	128.0	101.6	4.6	13.5	3.5	5.0
45 to 54 years old	95.9	110.0	82.0	6.0	12.9	3.6	4.5
55 to 64 years old	60.3	85.0	130.0	10.0	10.9	3.6	6.0
65 to 74 years old	40.1	69.0	125.0	30.0	10.3	3.0	5.0
75 years old and over	13.0	40.0	50.0	(B)	8.0	0.8	4.5

B Base figure too small. [1] First and second mortgages and home equity loans and lines of credit secured by the primary residence. [2] Families that had an outstanding balance on any of their credit cards after paying their most recent bills. [3] Includes loans on insurance policies, loans against pension accounts, borrowing on margin accounts and unclassified loans. [4] See footnote 8, Table 1133. [5] Median amount of financial debt for families holding such debts.

Source: Board of Governors of the Federal Reserve System, "2007 Survey of Consumer Finances" (published February 2009); <http://www.federalreserve.gov/pubs/oss/oss2/2007/scf2007home.html>.

Table 1136. **Amount of Debt Held by Families—Percent Distribution: 2004 and 2007**

[See headnote, Table 1133]

Type of debt	2004	2007	Purpose of debt	2004	2007	Type of lending institution	2004	2007
Total	100.0	100.0	Total	100.0	100.0	Total	100.0	100.0
Secured by residential property:			Primary residence:			Commercial bank	35.1	37.3
Primary residence . .	75.2	74.7	Purchase	70.2	69.5	Thrift institution	7.3	4.2
Other	8.5	10.1	Improvement	1.9	2.3	Credit union	3.6	4.2
Lines of credit not			Other residential			Finance or loan company.	4.1	3.4
secured by			property	9.5	10.8	Brokerage	2.5	1.6
residential property . .	0.7	0.4	Investments, excluding			Real estate lender [1]	39.4	41.6
Installment loans.	11.0	10.2	real estate	2.2	1.6	Individual lender	1.7	1.4
Credit card balances . .	3.0	3.5	Vehicles	6.7	5.5	Other nonfinancial	2.0	2.0
Other	1.6	1.1	Goods and services . .	6.0	6.2	Government	0.7	0.4
			Education	3.0	3.6	Credit card issuer	3.0	3.6
			Other loans	0.6	0.5	Other loans	0.5	0.4

[1] Includes mortgage lender.

Source: Board of Governors of the Federal Reserve System, "2007 Survey of Consumer Finances" (published February 2009); <http://www.federalreserve.gov/pubs/oss/oss2/2007/scf2007home.html>.

Table 1137. **Ratios of Debt Payments to Family Income: 2001 to 2007**

[In percent. All dollar figures are adjusted to 2007 dollars using the "current methods" version of the consumer price index for all urban consumers published by U.S. Bureau of Labor Statistics. Families include one-person units; for definition of family, see text, Section 1. Based on Survey of Consumer Finance; see Appendix III. For definition of median, see Guide to Tabular Presentation]

Age of family head and family income (constant (2007) dollars)	Ratio of debt payments to family income						Percent of debtors with—					
	Aggregate			Median for debtors			Ratios above 40 percent			Any payment 60 days or more past due		
	2001	2004	2007	2001	2004	2007	2001	2004	2007	2001	2004	2007
All families	12.9	14.4	14.5	16.7	18.0	18.6	11.8	12.2	14.7	7.0	8.9	7.1
Under 35 years old.	17.2	17.8	19.7	17.7	18.0	17.5	12.0	12.8	15.1	11.9	13.7	9.4
35 to 44 years old	15.1	18.2	18.5	17.8	20.6	20.3	10.1	12.5	12.7	5.9	11.7	8.6
45 to 54 years old	12.8	15.3	14.9	17.4	18.4	19.3	11.6	13.1	16.0	6.2	7.6	7.3
55 to 64 years old	10.9	11.5	12.5	14.3	15.7	17.5	12.3	10.2	14.5	7.1	4.2	4.9
65 to 74 years old	9.2	8.7	9.6	16.0	15.6	17.9	14.7	11.6	15.6	1.5	3.4	4.4
75 years old and over	3.9	7.1	4.4	8.0	12.8	13.0	14.6	10.7	13.9	0.8	3.9	1.0
Percentiles of income: [1]												
Less than 20	16.1	18.2	17.6	19.2	19.7	19.0	29.3	26.8	26.9	13.4	15.9	15.1
20 to 39.9	15.8	16.6	17.2	16.7	17.4	17.0	16.6	18.5	19.5	11.7	13.8	11.5
40 to 59.9	17.1	19.4	19.8	17.6	19.5	20.3	12.3	13.7	14.5	7.9	10.4	8.3
60 to 79.9	16.8	18.5	21.7	18.1	20.6	21.9	6.5	7.1	12.7	4.0	7.1	4.1
80 to 89.9	17.0	17.3	19.7	17.2	18.1	19.3	3.5	2.4	8.1	2.6	2.3	2.1
90 to 100	8.1	9.3	8.4	11.2	12.7	12.5	2.0	1.8	3.8	1.3	0.3	0.2

[1] See footnote 8, Table 1133.

Source: Board of Governors of the Federal Reserve System, "2007 Survey of Consumer Finances"; published February 2009; <http://www.federalreserve.gov/pubs/oss/oss2/2007/scf2007home.html>.

Table 1138. **Household Debt-Service Payments and Financial Obligations as a Percentage of Disposable Personal Income: 1990 to 2008**

[As of end of year, seasonally adjusted. Household debt service ratio is an estimate of the ratio of debt payments to disposable personal income. Debt payments consist of the estimated required payments on outstanding mortgage and consumer debt. The financial obligations ratio adds automobile lease payments, rental payments on tenant-occupied property, homeowners' insurance, and property tax payments to the debt service ratio]

Year	Household debt service ratio	Financial obligations ratio			Year	Household debt service ratio	Financial obligations ratio		
		Total	Renter	Home-owner			Total	Renter	Home-owner
1990. . .	11.99	17.37	24.71	15.51	2004. . .	13.56	18.46	26.10	16.98
1995. . .	11.82	17.43	26.82	15.15	2005. . .	13.99	18.96	25.96	17.59
2000. . .	12.86	18.22	30.47	15.75	2006. . .	14.29	19.33	26.11	18.02
2002. . .	13.61	18.88	29.05	16.80	2007. . .	14.28	19.39	26.35	18.03
2003. . .	13.54	18.57	26.76	16.91	2008. . .	13.90	18.97	26.31	17.52

Source: Board of Governors of the Federal Reserve System, "Household Debt Service and Financial Obligations Ratios"; <http://www.federalreserve.gov/releases/housedebt/default.htm>.

Table 1139. **FDIC-Insured Financial Institutions—Deposit Insurance Fund (DIF): 1990 to 2008**

[In billions of dollars, except as indicated (4,735 represents $4,735,000,000,000). As of December 31. Includes island areas. Includes insured branches of foreign banks]

Item	1990	2000	2002	2003	2004	2005	2006	2007	2008
Number of institutions	15,369	9,920	9,369	9,194	8,988	8,845	8,691	8,544	8,314
Assets, total	4,735	7,472	8,447	9,086	10,117	10,894	11,881	13,051	13,900
Domestic deposits, total [1]	3,415	4,212	4,916	5,224	5,725	6,230	6,640	6,922	7,505
Estimated insured deposits [2].	2,697	3,055	3,384	3,452	3,622	3,891	4,154	4,292	4,757
DIF balance [3]	4	42	44	46	48	49	50	52	19
Reserve ratio [4]	0.15	1.36	1.29	1.33	1.31	1.25	1.21	1.22	0.40
Number of problem institutions	1,496	94	136	116	80	52	50	76	252
Assets of problem institutions	646.8	23.8	38.9	29.9	28.2	6.6	8.3	22.2	159.4
Number of assisted institutions	1	–	–	–	–	–	–	–	5
Assets of assisted institutions	(Z)	–	–	–	–	–	–	–	1,306.0
Number of failed institutions	381	7	11	3	4	–	–	3	25
Assets of failed institutions.	146.6	0.4	3.4	0.9	0.2	–	–	2.6	371.9

– Represents zero.   Z Less than $50 million.   [1] Excludes foreign office deposits, which are uninsured.   [2] The Emergency Economic Stabilization Act of 2008 directs the FDIC not to consider the temporary coverage increase to $250,000 in setting assessments. Therefore, additional insured deposits are not included in calculating the fund reserve ratio.   [3] Prior to 2006 Bank Insurance Fund and Savings Association Insurance Fund.   [4] DIF balance as percent of DIF-insured deposits.

Source: U.S. Federal Deposit Insurance Corporation, *The FDIC Quarterly Banking Profile*.

Banking, Finance, and Insurance   717

Table 1140. **FDIC-Insured Financial Institutions—Number, Assets, and Liabilities: 1990 to 2008**

[In billions of dollars, except as indicated (4,649 represents $4,649,000,000,000). As of Dec. 31. 2008 data preliminary. Includes island areas. Excludes insured branches of foreign banks. Except as noted, includes foreign branches of U.S. banks]

Item	1990	2000	2002	2003	2004	2005	2006	2007	2008
Commercial bank offices, total [1]	63,205	73,174	74,790	75,985	78,473	80,967	83,860	86,150	97,103
Number of main offices	12,347	8,315	7,888	7,770	7,631	7,526	7,401	7,283	7,085
Number of branches	50,858	64,859	66,902	68,215	70,842	73,441	76,459	78,867	90,018
Savings institutions, total	2,815	1,589	1,466	1,411	1,345	1,307	1,279	1,251	1,220
Number of financial institutions reporting	15,158	9,905	9,354	9,181	8,976	8,833	8,680	8,534	8,305
Assets, total [2]	4,649	7,462	8,436	9,075	10,106	10,878	11,862	13,034	13,847
Net loans and leases	2,867	4,576	4,968	5,349	6,037	6,640	7,156	7,804	7,702
Real estate loans	1,586	2,396	2,850	3,144	3,680	4,141	4,508	4,782	4,704
1–4 family residential mortgages ..	859	1,340	1,513	1,611	1,833	2,042	2,735	2,241	2,045
Commercial real estate.........	328	525	628	682	752	826	904	969	1,068
Construction and development....	171	197	245	272	338	450	590	629	590
Home equity loans [3]	86	151	256	346	491	534	559	611	668
Commercial and industrial loans	646	1,086	953	922	968	1,086	1,215	1,439	1,496
Loans to individuals..............	451	672	772	848	930	949	955	1,058	1,089
Credit cards and related plans	142	266	292	339	399	396	385	422	445
Farm loans	33	49	47	47	49	52	54	57	60
Other loans and leases	245	448	435	478	496	494	504	573	531
Less: Reserve for losses	65	71	85	86	82	77	78	103	173
Less: Unearned income	29	3	4	3	3	3	2	2	5
Securities	890	1,361	1,633	1,771	1,860	1,893	1,981	1,954	2,036
Domestic office assets	4,259	6,702	7,684	8,251	9,160	9,824	10,557	11,475	12,326
Foreign office assets.............	390	760	752	824	945	1,054	1,304	1,559	1,521
Liabilities and capital, total	4,649	7,462	8,436	9,075	10,106	10,878	11,862	13,034	13,847
Noninterest-bearing deposits	511	802	1,002	1,028	1,173	1,267	1,270	1,260	1,484
Interest-bearing deposits	3,127	4,113	4,566	4,926	5,412	5,874	6,555	7,156	7,551
Other borrowed funds.............	569	1,467	1,571	1,735	1,905	2,063	2,121	2,517	2,575
Subordinated debt	28	90	99	107	119	131	161	185	185
Other liabilities.................	128	356	422	450	459	424	507	569	755
Equity capital.................	286	634	776	831	1,039	1,119	1,248	1,347	1,296
Domestic office deposits	3,344	4,208	4,911	5,213	5,719	6,221	6,631	6,913	7,496
Foreign office deposits	293	707	658	741	866	921	1,194	1,503	1,539

[1] Includes insured branches of foreign banks that file a Call Report. [2] Includes other items not shown separately. [3] For one- to four-family residential properties.

Source: U.S. Federal Deposit Insurance Corporation, *The FDIC Quarterly Banking Profile, Historical Statistics on Banking,* annual; *Statistics on Banking,* annual; and *FDIC Quarterly Banking Profile Graph Book.*

Table 1141. **FDIC-Insured Financial Institutions—Income and Selected Measures of Financial Condition: 1990 to 2008**

[In billions of dollars, except as indicated (437.7 represents $437,700,000,000). 2008 data preliminary. Includes island areas. Includes foreign branches of U.S. banks]

Item	1990	2000	2002	2003	2004	2005	2006	2007	2008
Interest income	437.7	512.2	429.5	404.6	418.4	522.0	643.5	724.9	603.4
Interest expense	295.9	276.5	152.9	122.6	123.3	205.0	313.4	372.1	245.6
Net interest income...............	141.8	235.7	276.6	281.9	295.2	317.0	330.1	352.7	357.7
Provisions for loan losses	41.4	32.0	51.5	37.3	29.0	29.7	29.5	69.2	174.4
Noninterest income.................	62.2	164.8	183.5	202.7	202.6	223.4	240.4	233.1	207.5
Percent of net operating revenue [1] .	30.5	41.1	39.9	41.8	40.7	41.3	42.1	39.8	36.7
Noninterest expense...............	144.2	241.6	263.7	279.7	295.5	317.4	332.3	367.0	364.9
Income taxes....................	9.1	43.7	51.9	58.9	58.6	64.6	68.1	46.5	6.2
Net income	11.3	81.7	105.0	120.5	122.3	133.9	145.3	99.9	10.2
PERFORMANCE RATIOS									
Return on assets [2] (percent)	0.24	1.14	1.30	1.38	1.28	1.28	1.28	0.81	0.08
Return on equity [3] (percent)	3.95	13.55	14.12	15.04	13.20	12.43	12.30	7.75	0.79
Net interest margin [4] (percent)	3.47	3.78	3.96	3.73	3.54	3.47	3.31	3.29	3.18
Net charge-offs [5]	34.8	26.3	47.0	40.8	32.0	31.6	27.0	44.1	99.5
Net charge-offs to loans and leases, total (percent)................................	1.19	0.59	0.97	0.78	0.56	0.49	0.39	0.59	1.28
Net charge-off rate, credit card loans (percent). . .	3.39	4.37	5.47	5.75	4.99	4.74	3.44	4.06	5.44
CONDITION RATIOS									
Equity capital to assets (percent).............	6.16	8.49	9.20	9.15	10.28	10.28	10.52	10.34	9.36
Noncurrent assets plus other real estate owned to assets [6] (percent)	3.16	0.71	0.90	0.75	0.53	0.50	0.54	0.94	1.88

[1] Net operating revenue equals net interest income plus noninterest income. [2] Net income (including securities transactions and nonrecurring items) as a percentage of average total assets. [3] Net income as a percentage of average total equity capital. [4] Interest income less interest expense as a percentage of average earning assets (i.e. the profit margin a bank earns on its loans and investments). [5] Total loans and leases charged off (removed from balance sheet because of uncollectibility), less amounts recovered on loans and leases previously charged off. [6] Noncurrent assets: the sum of loans, leases, debt securities and other assets that are 90 days or more past due, or in nonaccrual status. Other real estate owned: primarily foreclosed property.

Source: U.S. Federal Deposit Insurance Corporation, *Annual Report; Statistics on Banking,* annual; and *FDIC Quarterly Banking Profile.*

718   Banking, Finance, and Insurance

Table 1142. **FDIC-Insured Financial Institutions by Asset Size: 2008**

[(12,313 represents $12,313,000,000,000). Preliminary. Minus sign (–) indicates loss. See headnote, Table 1141]

Item	Unit	Total	Less than $100 million	$100 million to $1 billion	$1 billion to $10 billion	Greater than $10 billion
COMMERCIAL BANKS						
Institutions reporting	Number . . .	7,085	2,784	3,790	425	86
Assets, total	Bil. dol. . . .	12,313	153	1,106	1,143	9,912
Deposits	Bil. dol. . . .	8,082	125	887	831	6,239
Net income	Bil. dol. . . .	19	1	4	–1	15
Return on assets	Percent . . .	0.16	0.36	0.38	–0.10	0.16
Return on equity	Percent . . .	1.62	2.76	3.68	–0.90	1.70
Equity capital to assets	Percent . . .	9.40	12.57	9.95	10.93	9.12
Noncurrent assets plus other real estate owned to assets	Percent . . .	1.82	1.66	2.24	2.49	1.70
Net charge–offs to loans and leases	Percent . . .	1.31	0.47	0.68	1.15	1.44
Percentage of banks losing money	Percent . . .	22.1	23.1	20.3	28.9	36.1
SAVINGS INSTITUTIONS						
Institutions reporting	Number . . .	1,220	347	709	136	28
Assets, total	Bil. dol. . . .	1,534	18	250	349	917
Deposits	Bil. dol. . . .	954	14	185	250	506
Net income	Bil. dol. . . .	–9	(–Z)	(Z)	–2	–7
Return on assets	Percent . . .	–0.57	–0.20	0.09	–0.81	–0.45
Return on equity	Percent . . .	–6.15	–1.25	0.80	–9.84	–4.19
Equity capital to assets	Percent . . .	9.04	15.48	10.59	8.05	10.18
Noncurrent assets plus other real estate owned to assets	Percent . . .	2.38	1.66	1.70	2.73	1.97
Net charge–offs to loans and leases	Percent . . .	1.13	0.30	0.40	1.52	0.70
Percentage of banks losing money	Percent . . .	32.5	36.3	30.6	58.6	27.9

Z Less than $500 million.

Source: U.S. Federal Deposit Insurance Corporation, *Annual Report; Statistics on Banking*, annual; and *FDIC Quarterly Banking Profile*. See also <http://www.fdic.gov/bank/index.html>.

Table 1143. **FDIC-Insured Financial Institutions—Number and Assets by State and Island Areas: 2008**

[In billions of dollars, except as indicated (13,848.3 represents $13,848,300,000,000). As of Dec. 31. Information is obtained primarily from the Federal Financial Institutions Examination Council (FFIEC) Call Reports and the Office of Thrift Supervision's Thrift Financial Reports. Data are based on the location of each reporting institution's main office. Reported data may include assets located outside of the reporting institution's home state]

State or island area	Number of insti- tutions	Assets by asset size of bank				State or island area	Number of insti- tutions	Assets by asset size of bank			
		Total	Less than $1 bil.	$1 bil. to $10 bil.	Greater than $10 bil.			Total	Less than $1 bil.	$1 bil. to $10 bil.	Greater than $10 bil.
Total . . .	8,305	13,848.3	1,527.5	1,491.7	10,829.2	NV	41	1,353.3	5.9	25.8	1,321.6
						NH	25	10.9	8.7	2.2	–
AL	157	272.1	29.4	12.8	230.0	NJ	126	159.5	30.7	49.9	78.9
AK	7	31.5	1.1	3.4	26.9	NM	54	19.4	9.2	10.2	–
AZ	57	16.2	9.3	6.9	–	NY	196	609.1	47.2	114.6	447.3
AR	143	53.0	28.8	14.0	10.2	NC	110	2,351.7	27.3	24.5	2,299.8
CA	311	458.7	64.4	149.0	245.3	ND	96	22.0	12.7	9.3	–
CO	153	53.3	29.8	23.6	–	OH	252	2,488.5	40.5	31.6	2,416.5
CT	58	74.5	15.0	22.7	36.7	OK	253	79.8	33.8	14.8	31.3
DE	31	552.8	4.2	21.5	527.1	OR	40	35.4	6.7	17.2	11.5
DC	6	1.6	1.6	–	–	PA	232	415.6	58.2	90.1	267.3
FL	307	168.0	69.0	73.4	25.7	RI	13	173.2	2.4	5.6	165.1
GA	334	300.5	68.6	46.7	185.1	SC	88	56.0	23.5	18.9	13.6
HI	9	37.0	1.4	12.1	23.6	SD	87	653.2	13.1	14.5	625.6
ID	19	8.1	5.8	2.3	–	TN	198	98.7	43.9	24.0	30.8
IL	655	367.1	108.3	104.4	154.4	TX	644	365.1	105.1	77.1	182.8
IN	158	70.4	31.7	38.7	–	UT	69	514.4	13.7	31.0	469.7
IA	379	63.5	50.0	13.5	–	VT	15	9.0	3.9	5.1	–
KS	348	63.0	41.3	21.7	–	VA	118	576.1	30.1	29.4	516.6
KY	198	51.0	34.7	16.3	–	WA	97	80.0	24.3	30.9	24.8
LA	160	54.7	34.4	7.9	12.4	WV	66	25.0	10.2	14.8	–
ME	30	18.5	12.6	5.9	–	WI	283	158.7	56.6	22.8	79.3
MD	95	40.2	21.4	18.8	–	WY	39	6.7	6.7	–	–
MA	175	268.6	52.2	45.2	171.2						
MI	159	129.0	29.2	19.3	80.5						
MN	431	78.1	54.8	6.6	16.7	AS	1	0.1	0.1	–	–
MS	95	57.1	19.5	24.1	13.5	GU	3	1.1	1.1	–	–
MO	352	129.0	56.5	44.4	28.2	FM	1	0.9	0.9	–	–
MT	77	19.1	10.7	8.4	–	PR	10	99.5	–	40.2	59.3
NE	242	48.5	25.2	23.3	–	VI	2	0.2	0.2	–	–

– Represents zero.

Source: U.S. Federal Deposit Insurance Corporation, *Statistics on Banking*, annual.

Banking, Finance, and Insurance   719

Table 1144. **FDIC-Insured Financial Institutions—Number of Offices and Deposits by State: 2008**

[As of June 30 (7,025.8 represents $7,025,800,000,000). Includes insured U.S. branches of foreign banks. The term "offices" includes both main offices and branches. "Banking office" is defined to include all offices and facilities that actually hold deposits, and does not include loan production offices, computer centers, and other nondeposit installations, such as automated teller machines (ATMs). Several institutions have designated home offices that do not accept deposits; these have been included to provide a more complete listing of all offices. The figures for each geographical area only include deposits of offices located within that area. Based on the Summary of Deposits survey]

State	Number of offices	Total deposits (bil. dol.)	State	Number of offices	Total deposits (bil. dol.)	State	Number of offices	Total deposits (bil. dol.)
Total [1]..	99,161	7,025.8	IA	1,639	60.1	NC........	2,746	219.5
U.S.	98,525	6,956.6	KS	1,556	57.9	ND........	445	15.3
			KY........	1,828	64.4	OH........	4,066	227.8
AL........	1,564	76.6	LA	1,606	74.7	OK........	1,383	63.0
AK........	134	13.7	ME........	518	19.5	OR........	1,104	49.2
AZ........	1,379	78.7	MD........	1,829	96.6	PA........	4,822	271.7
AR........	1,513	47.1	MA........	2,228	185.3	RI........	247	29.6
CA........	7,313	762.8	MI	3,125	157.2	SC........	1,440	66.5
CO........	1,664	83.1	MN........	1,862	101.1	SD........	482	74.9
CT........	1,305	83.2	MS........	1,181	45.5	TN........	2,302	104.8
DE........	272	176.9	MO........	2,427	110.7	TX........	6,887	484.2
DC........	228	23.4	MT........	387	15.5	UT........	621	229.3
FL........	5,771	380.3	NE........	1,080	38.8	VT........	272	9.9
GA........	2,873	184.3	NV........	603	199.8	VA........	2,649	193.9
HI	288	26.2	NH........	433	23.0	WA........	1,925	112.3
ID	541	17.2	NJ........	3,381	227.2	WV	664	26.9
IL........	5,046	344.6	NM........	512	22.3	WI	2,389	114.8
IN........	2,401	90.6	NY........	5,364	763.3	WY	230	11.1

[1] Includes Puerto Rico and other areas, not shown separately.

Source: U.S. Federal Deposit Insurance Corporation, *Bank and Thrift Branch Office Data Book*, annual.

Table 1145. **U.S. Banking Offices of Foreign Banks—Summary: 1990 to 2008**

[In billions of dollars, except as indicated (834 represents $834,000,000,000). As of December. Covers the U.S. offices of foreign banking organizations that are located in the 50 states and the District of Columbia. Offices located in Puerto Rico, American Samoa, Guam, the Virgin Islands and other U.S.-affiliated insular areas are excluded. Foreign-owned institutions are those owned by a bank located outside of the United States and its affiliated insular areas. The U.S. offices of foreign banking organizations consist of U.S. branches and agencies of foreign banks and bank subsidiaries of foreign banking organizations. The latter are U.S. commercial banks of which more than 25 percent is owned by a foreign banking organization or where the relationship is reported as being a controlling relationship by the filer of the FR Y-10 (Report of Changes in Organizational Structure) report form]

Item	1990	2000	2003	2004	2005	2006	2007	2008	Share [1] 1990	2000	2005	2008
Assets	834	1,358	1,556	1,808	2,123	2,515	2,871	3,032	20.9	18.9	20.6	21.2
Loans, total..........	412	557	549	656	802	913	1,055	1,164	17.2	13.5	14.1	15.7
Business..........	199	309	221	231	276	342	412	485	27.7	25.0	24.5	28.4
Deposits............	425	770	885	1,025	1,162	1,375	1,629	1,610	14.6	16.5	17.3	17.9

[1] Foreign owned banks plus U.S. branches and offices of foreign banks as percent of all banks in the U.S.

Source: Board of Governors of the Federal Reserve System, "Share Data for U.S. Offices of Foreign Banks" (published March 2009); <http://www.federalreserve.gov/Releases/iba/fboshr.htm>.

Table 1146. **Federal and State-Chartered Credit Unions—Summary: 1990 to 2008**

[Except as noted, as of December 31 (36,241 represents 36,241,000). Federal data include District of Columbia, Puerto Rico, Guam, and Virgin Islands. Excludes state-insured, privately insured, and noninsured state-chartered credit unions and corporate central credit unions, which have mainly other credit unions as members]

Year	Operating credit unions Federal	State	Number of failed institu- tions [1]	Members (1,000) Federal	State	Assets (mil. dol.) Federal	State	Loans outstanding (mil. dol.) Federal	State	Savings (mil. dol.) Federal	State
1990...	8,511	4,349	164	36,241	19,454	130,073	68,133	83,029	44,102	117,892	62,082
2000...	6,336	3,980	29	43,883	33,705	242,881	195,363	163,851	137,485	210,188	169,053
2001...	6,118	3,866	22	43,817	35,560	270,123	231,432	170,326	152,112	235,201	201,923
2002...	5,953	3,735	15	44,600	36,300	301,238	255,837	181,768	160,881	261,819	222,372
2003...	5,776	3,593	13	46,153	36,287	336,611	273,572	202,898	173,236	291,484	236,856
2004...	5,572	3,442	21	46,858	36,710	358,701	288,294	223,878	190,376	308,317	247,804
2005...	5,393	3,302	27	47,612	36,895	377,804	300,868	249,515	208,728	321,820	255,804
2006...	5,189	3,173	22	48,262	37,487	394,125	315,817	270,420	223,917	333,914	267,275
2007...	5,036	3,065	12	48,474	38,363	417,578	335,885	289,169	237,755	349,100	283,298
2008...	4,847	2,959	19	49,129	39,437	447,484	364,404	309,275	256,721	373,369	307,762

[1] 1990 for year ending September 30; beginning 2000, reflects calendar year. A failed institution is defined as a credit union which has ceased operation because it was involuntarily liquidated or merged with assistance from the National Credit Union Share Insurance Fund.

Source: National Credit Union Administration, *Annual Report of the National Credit Union Administration*, and unpublished data.

720   Banking, Finance, and Insurance

Table 1147. **Noncash Payments by Method of Payment and ATM Cash Withdrawals: 2003 and 2006**

[**81.4 represents 81,400,000,000**. Based on two data collection efforts to estimate the annual number and value of significant types of noncash payments. Estimates of check payments and ATM withdrawals were based on findings from the Depository Institutions Payments Study (2007 DI study). Electronic payments volume estimates were based on findings from the Electronic Payments Study and supplemented by the 2007 DI study. The Depository Institutions Payments Study collected the number and value of different types of payments from deposit accounts at a representative, random sample of depository institutions. A total of 1,437 depository institutions (commercial banks, savings institutions, and credit unions) from a stratified random sample of 2,700 institutions provided data for the survey. The Electronic Payments Study estimated the number and value of electronic payments in the United States for calendar year 2006. Data were collected by surveying payment networks and card issuers. Of the 73 organizations asked to participate, 65 of the largest organizations provided data. Respondents to this study collectively accounted for an estimated 99.8 percent of the electronic transactions and 99.9 percent of the electronic payments value in the United States]

Method of payment	Transactions (bil.)		Value (tril. dol.)		Average value per transaction (dol.)	
	2003	2006	2003	2006	2003	2006
Noncash payments, total	**81.4**	**93.3**	**67.6**	**75.8**	**830**	**813**
Checks (paid)	37.3	30.5	41.1	41.6	1,104	1,363
Commercial checks	36.8	30.1	40.8	41.4	1,108	1,371
Commercial banks	29.7	25.1	38.4	39.0	1,293	1,550
Credit unions.	4.2	2.7	0.9	0.8	219	288
Savings institutions.	3.0	2.3	1.5	1.6	511	696
U.S. Treasury checks.	0.3	0.2	0.3	0.2	1,154	1,203
Postal money orders	0.2	0.2	(Z)	(Z)	146	164
Electronic payments	44.1	62.8	26.4	34.1	599	544
Automated Clearing House (ACH)	8.8	14.6	24.1	31.0	2,754	2,122
Debit cards	15.6	25.3	0.6	1.0	40	39
Signature [1]	10.3	16.0	0.4	0.6	42	40
PIN [2]	5.3	9.4	0.2	0.3	38	37
Credit cards [3]	19.0	21.7	1.7	2.1	89	98
Electronic benefits transfer cards	0.8	1.1	(Z)	(Z)	26	27
Memo:						
ATM cash withdrawals	**5.9**	**5.8**	**0.5**	**0.6**	**85**	**99**
Checks (written) [4]	37.6	33.1	41.2	42.4	1,096	1,280
Checks converted to ACH	0.3	2.6	0.1	0.7	187	267

Z Less than $50 billion.   [1] Signature debit card payments are made like credit card payments, but use funds from transaction deposit accounts.   [2] PIN debit card payments also use funds from transaction deposit accounts and typically require the entry of the same personal identification number (PIN) used to access automated teller machines (ATMs). Excludes a portion estimated to have been returned to the customer as cash.   [3] Credit cards include both general purpose and private-label cards.   [4] Includes the use of checks as source documents to initiate electronic payments.

Source: Board of Governors of the Federal Reserve System, "Recent Payment Trends in the United States"; Federal Reserve Bulletin, October 2008; <http://www.federalreserve.gov/pubs/bulletin/2008/default.htm> and "The 2007 Federal Reserve Payments Study"; published 10 December 2007; <http://www.frbservices.org/files/communications/pdf/research/2007_payments_study.pdf>.

Table 1148. **Percentage of Households Using Selected Electronic Banking Technologies: 1995 to 2007**

[Covers only those households that access services (other than by check or credit card) at a bank, thrift institution, or credit union. Based on sample surveys. For details on the Survey of Consumer Finances, see Appendix III and the Web site of the Federal Reserve Board: <www.federalreserve.gov/boarddocs/surveys>. The Reuters/University of Michigan Surveys of Consumers is based on data from approximately 1,000 respondents. For details, see the Web site of the University of Michigan Survey Research Center: <http://www.sca.isr.umich.edu/>]

Technology	Survey of Consumer Finances					Reuters/ University of Michigan Surveys of Consumers		
	1995	1998	2001	2004	2007	1999	2003	2006
ELECTRONIC								
Direct deposit of any type	53	67	71	75	80	65	70	77
ATM card.	35	55	57	65	76	59	65	69
Debit card [1]	20	37	50	62	71	(NA)	54	62
Preauthorized debts.	25	40	43	50	49	31	46	57
Automated phone system	(NA)	26	22	20	25	40	44	46
Computer banking.	4	7	19	34	53	10	32	51
Smart card [2]	1	2	3	(NA)	(NA)	(NA)	6	12
Prepaid card [2]	(NA)	(NA)	(NA)	(NA)	(NA)	(NA)	73	73
NONELECTRONIC								
In person.	87	81	78	78	85	(NA)	(NA)	(NA)
Mail	59	55	51	51	59	(NA)	(NA)	(NA)
Phone (talk in person)	(NA)	43	42	42	57	(NA)	(NA)	(NA)

NA Not available.   [1] A debit card is a card that automatically deducts the amount of a purchase from the money in an account.   [2] A smart card is a type of payment card containing a computer chip which is set to hold a sum of money. As the card is used, purchases are subtracted from that sum. Prepaid cards are cards that contain a stored value, or a value that has been paid up-front, allowing you to use the card much like cash. As you use the card, the prepaid value is drawn down. Examples are phone cards and gift cards. Smart cards are different from prepaid cards in that you can add money to the card at special machines designed for smart cards or sometimes at ATMs.

Source: Board of Governors of the Federal Reserve System, *Federal Reserve Bulletin*, July 2009.

Banking, Finance, and Insurance   721

Table 1149. **Percent of U.S. Households That Use Selected Payment Instruments: 2001 and 2007**

[In percent. Based on Survey of Consumer Finances conducted by the Board of Governors of the Federal Reserve System; see Appendix III]

Characteristic of head of household	Any of these instruments		ATM [1]		Debit card		Direct deposit		Automatic bill paying		Software [2]	
	2001	2007	2001	2007	2001	2007	2001	2007	2001	2007	2001	2007
All households	88.9	91.8	69.8	79.7	47.0	67.0	67.3	74.9	40.3	45.5	18.0	19.1
Under 30 years old.	83.8	88.6	78.1	84.8	60.6	78.3	48.8	61.3	32.1	35.7	17.0	21.4
30 to 60 years old	89.9	92.4	76.8	85.9	53.4	74.9	64.8	72.6	44.1	48.8	22.0	21.6
61 years old and over . . .	89.4	92.1	48.9	63.5	24.6	43.9	83.2	86.4	35.9	42.9	9.0	12.3
Household income: [3]												
Low income	74.3	79.7	46.8	58.8	29.2	48.1	51.9	60.5	18.2	23.8	6.1	7.7
Moderate income	88.6	91.1	67.4	78.5	46.3	68.0	63.1	68.5	35.1	37.8	10.7	10.7
Middle income	92.5	96.4	75.2	87.5	50.0	75.0	65.7	76.8	45.1	50.2	16.3	18.8
Upper income.	97.1	98.4	83.7	91.0	57.8	75.8	80.2	86.6	55.2	61.6	29.9	30.5
No college degree	85.1	88.4	63.7	74.0	42.3	63.7	61.8	68.9	33.7	38.0	10.9	11.9
College degree	96.4	98.2	81.6	90.3	56.2	72.9	78.0	85.9	53.2	59.3	31.8	32.2

[1] The question on ATM cards asked whether any member of the household had an ATM card, not whether the member used it. The other questions asked about usage of other instruments. [2] The question on software asked whether the respondent or spouse/partner uses any type of computer software to help in managing their money. [3] Low income is defined as less than 50 percent of the median household income; moderate income is 50 to 80 percent of the median; middle income is 80 to 120 percent of the median; and upper income is greater than 120 percent of the median. Each survey refers to income in the previous year. Median income was $41,990 in 2000 and $48,201 in 2006.

Source: Mester, Loretta J., "Changes in the Use of Electronic Means of Payment: 1995–2007," *Business Review*, Third Quarter 2009, published by Federal Reserve Bank of Philadelphia. See also <http://www.philadelphiafed.org/research -and-data/publications/business-review/2009/q3/brq309_changes-in-electronic-payment>.

Table 1150. **Debit Cards—Holders, Number, Transactions, and Volume, 2000 and 2007, and Projections, 2010**

[160 represents 160,000,000]

Type of debit card	Cardholders (mil.)			Number of cards (mil.)		Number of point-of-sale transactions (mil.)			Purchase volume (bil. dol.)		
	2000	2007	2010, proj.	2007	2010, proj.	2000	2007	2010, proj.	2000	2007	2010, proj.
Total [1]	160	179	185	440	525	8,291	30,312	40,622	311	1,186	1,646
Bank [2]	137	158	164	398	481	5,290	25,062	33,818	210	995	1,387
EFT systems [3]	159	177	184	274	281	2,979	5,229	6,771	100	190	257
Other [4]	11	11	13	11	13	22	21	32	1	1	1

[1] Cardholders may hold more than one type of card. Bank cards and EFT cards are the same pieces of plastic that carry multiple brands. The total card figure shown does not include any duplication. [2] Visa and MasterCard debit cards. [3] Cards issued by financial institution members of regional and national switches such as Star, Interlink (for 2000), Pulse, Nyce, etc. EFT = Electronic funds transfer. [4] Retail cards such as those issued by supermarkets.

Source: The Nilson Report, Carpinteria, CA, Twice-monthly newsletter. (Copyright used by permission.)

Table 1151. **Credit Cards—Holders, Number, Spending, and Debt, 2000 and 2007, and Projections, 2010**

[159 represents 159,000,000]

Type of credit card	Cardholders (mil.)			Number of cards (mil.)			Credit card purchase volume (bil. dol.)			Credit card debt outstanding (bil. dol.)		
	2000	2007	2010, proj.	2000	2007	2010, proj.	2000	2007	2010, proj.	2000	2007	2010, proj.
Total [1]	159	176	181	1,425	1,493	1,416	1,242	2,109	2,119	680	962	929
Bank [2]	(NA)	(NA)	(NA)	455	599	563	768	1,355	1,330	480	692	672
Store	114	114	114	597	546	513	120	139	121	92	102	93
Oil company	76	58	55	98	73	72	45	56	59	9	9	9
Other [3]	133	120	113	275	275	267	308	560	608	103	159	154

NA Not available. [1] Cardholders may hold more than one type of card. [2] Visa and MasterCard credit cards. [3] Includes Universal Air Travel Plan (UATP), phone cards, automobile rental, and miscellaneous cards; credit card purchase volume excludes phone cards. Except for data on cardholders, also includes Discover and American Express.

Source: The Nilson Report, Carpinteria, CA, Twice-monthly newsletter. (Copyright used by permission.)

722 Banking, Finance, and Insurance

Table 1152. **Usage of General Purpose Credit Cards by Families: 1995 to 2007**

[General purpose credit cards include Mastercard, Visa, Optima, and Discover cards. Excludes cards used only for business purposes. All dollar figures are given in constant 2007 dollars based on consumer price index data as published by U.S. Bureau of Labor Statistics. Families include one-person units; for definition of family, see text, Section 1. Based on Survey of Consumer Finances; see Appendix III. For definition of median, see Guide to Tabular Presentation]

Age of family head, family income, and housing tenure	Percent having a general purpose credit card	Median number of cards	Median new charges on last month's bills (dol.)	Percent having a balance after last month's bills	Median balance (dol.) [1]	Percent of cardholding families who—		
						Almost always pay off the balance	Some-times pay off the balance	Hardly ever pay off the balance
1995, total	66.4	2	200	56.0	2,000	52.4	20.1	27.5
2001, total	72.7	2	200	53.6	2,100	55.3	19.1	25.6
2004, total	71.5	2	300	56.2	2,300	55.7	20.3	24.0
2007, total	**70.2**	**2**	**300**	**58.3**	**3,000**	**55.3**	**19.4**	**25.4**
Under 35 years old	58.9	2	100	70.9	2,000	47.1	22.9	30.0
35 to 44 years old.	68.1	2	300	68.2	3,400	46.9	22.5	30.6
45 to 54 years old.	74.3	2	300	64.6	4,000	48.8	19.4	31.8
55 to 64 years old.	78.9	3	300	58.6	3,500	56.0	20.0	24.0
65 to 74 years old.	79.5	2	300	39.9	3,900	70.4	16.7	12.9
75 years old and over	66.0	1	200	23.9	900	80.8	8.8	10.4
Less than $10,000	27.7	2	200	56.8	1,200	59.2	20.7	20.1
$10,000 to $24,999.	44.5	2	100	55.9	1,000	54.4	19.4	26.2
$25,000 to $49,999.	66.4	2	100	60.3	2,100	49.7	20.5	29.8
$50,000 to $99,999.	85.8	2	200	66.2	3,900	50.4	20.7	29.0
$100,000 and more.	94.3	3	1,000	47.1	6,000	67.3	16.3	16.3
Owner occupied	81.5	2	300	55.3	4,000	57.5	19.4	23.1
Renter occupied or other . .	45.4	2	100	70.2	1,400	46.6	19.2	34.2

[1] Among families having a balance.

Source: Board of Governors of the Federal Reserve System, unpublished data.

Table 1153. **Consumer Credit Outstanding and Finance Rates: 1990 to 2008**

[In billions of dollars, except percent (808 represents $808,000,000,000). Covers most short- and intermediate-term credit extended to individuals, excluding loans secured by real estate. Estimated amounts of seasonally adjusted credit outstanding as of end of year; finance rates, annual averages]

Type of credit	1990	2000	2001	2002	2003	2004	2005	2006	2007	2008
Total	**808**	**1,718**	**1,867**	**1,974**	**2,078**	**2,192**	**2,285**	**2,388**	**2,519**	**2,563**
Revolving	239	684	717	749	770	800	824	875	940	960
Nonrevolving [1]	570	1,034	1,151	1,226	1,308	1,392	1,461	1,513	1,580	1,602
FINANCE RATES (percent)										
Commercial banks:										
New automobiles (48 months)	11.78	9.34	8.50	7.62	6.93	6.60	7.08	7.72	7.77	7.02
Other consumer goods (24 months)	15.46	13.90	13.22	12.54	11.95	11.89	12.05	12.41	12.39	11.35
Credit card plans.	18.17	15.78	14.87	13.40	12.30	12.72	12.51	13.21	13.38	12.07
Finance companies:										
New automobiles.	12.54	6.85	5.76	4.50	3.81	4.92	6.02	4.99	4.87	5.52
Used automobiles.	15.99	13.47	12.45	11.18	9.86	8.81	8.81	9.61	9.24	8.74

[1] Comprises automobile loans and all other loans not included in revolving credit, such as loans for mobile homes, education, boats, trailers, or vacations. These loans may be secured or unsecured.

Source: Board of Governors of the Federal Reserve System, "Consumer Credit-G.19"; <http://www.federalreserve.gov/releases /g19/current/g19.htm> and "Finance Companies-G.20"; <http://www.federalreserve.gov/releases/g20/current/g20.htm>.

Table 1154. **Consumer Credit by Type of Holder: 1990 to 2008**

[In billions of dollars (824 represents $824,000,000,000). As of December 31. Not seasonally adjusted]

Type of holder	1990	2000	2001	2002	2003	2004	2005	2006	2007	2008
Total.	**824**	**1,741**	**1,892**	**2,000**	**2,104**	**2,219**	**2,314**	**2,418**	**2,552**	**2,596**
Nonfinancial corporations.	67	81	73	75	58	59	59	57	55	56
U.S. government	–	60	72	80	82	86	90	92	98	111
Commercial banking	382	551	568	603	669	704	707	741	804	878
Savings institutions.	50	65	71	69	78	91	109	96	91	86
Credit unions.	92	184	190	196	206	215	229	235	236	238
Government–sponsored enterprises. . .	19	37	39	37	21	–	–	–	–	–
Asset–backed securities issuers	77	528	598	633	597	571	604	664	684	655
Finance companies	138	234	280	308	393	492	517	534	584	573

– Represents or rounds to zero.

Source: Board of Governors of the Federal Reserve System, "Federal Reserve Statistical Release, Z.1, Flow of Funds Accounts of the United States"; published 12 March 2009; <http://www.federalreserve.gov/releases/z1/20090312>.

Banking, Finance, and Insurance **723**

Table 1155. **Mortgage Debt Outstanding by Type of Property and Holder: 1990 to 2008**

[In billions of dollars (3,800 represents $3,800,000,000,000). As of December 31]

Type of property and holder	1990	2000	2001	2002	2003	2004	2005	2006	2007	2008
Total mortgages [1]	**3,800**	**6,789**	**7,498**	**8,400**	**9,399**	**10,666**	**12,108**	**13,488**	**14,562**	**14,640**
Home [2]	2,623	5,129	5,681	6,437	7,231	8,272	9,387	10,434	11,122	11,030
Multifamily residential	288	405	446	485	565	618	689	744	843	900
Commercial	821	1,171	1,282	1,382	1,509	1,680	1,930	2,209	2,489	2,599
Farm	68	85	89	95	94	97	102	101	108	111
Household sector	141	103	109	116	121	132	142	117	97	94
State and local government	110	131	130	124	133	141	152	166	177	173
Commercial banking	849	1,660	1,790	2,058	2,256	2,596	2,958	3,403	3,646	3,841
Savings institutions	802	723	758	781	871	1,057	1,153	1,074	1,095	860
Credit unions	50	125	141	159	183	213	246	277	308	348
Life insurance companies	268	236	243	250	261	273	285	304	326	338
Government-sponsored enterprises (GSE)	156	264	297	357	622	629	589	607	643	699
Agency- and GSE-backed mortgage pools	1,020	2,493	2,832	3,159	3,327	3,375	3,542	3,837	4,464	4,965
Asset-backed securities issuers	68	618	740	851	1,023	1,455	2,142	2,770	2,951	2,585
Finance companies	114	238	258	330	370	476	541	594	532	448
Real estate investment trusts	8	19	18	28	49	118	146	136	121	89
HOME MORTGAGES [2]										
Total [1]	**2,623**	**5,129**	**5,681**	**6,437**	**7,231**	**8,272**	**9,387**	**10,434**	**11,122**	**11,030**
State and local government	61	67	66	63	68	72	77	85	90	88
Commercial banking	433	970	1,028	1,227	1,356	1,581	1,793	2,085	2,208	2,251
Savings institutions	600	594	620	631	703	874	954	868	879	666
Credit unions	50	125	141	159	183	213	246	277	308	348
Government-sponsored enterprises (GSE)	119	210	231	277	515	508	455	460	449	462
Agency- and GSE-backed mortgage pools	991	2,426	2,749	3,064	3,211	3,256	3,420	3,711	4,320	4,811
Asset-backed securities issuers	55	386	463	544	666	1,046	1,618	2,128	2,163	1,839
Finance companies	80	187	210	286	320	422	490	538	473	376
Memo:										
Home equity loans included above [1,3]	215	408	439	501	593	776	915	1,065	1,130	1,115
Commercial banking	115	235	259	303	366	484	549	654	692	775
Savings institutions	60	73	78	78	96	121	152	138	180	119
Credit unions	20	41	45	48	52	64	76	87	94	100

[1] Includes other holders not shown separately. [2] Mortgages on one- to four-family properties including mortgages on farm houses. [3] Loans made under home equity lines of credit and home equity loans secured by junior liens. Excludes home equity loans held by individuals.

Source: Board of Governors of the Federal Reserve System, "Federal Reserve Statistical Release, Z.1, Flow of Funds Accounts of the United States"; published 12 March 2009; <http://www.federalreserve.gov/releases/z1/20090312>.

Table 1156. **Characteristics of Conventional First Mortgage Loans for Purchase of Single-Family Homes: 2000 to 2008**

[In percent, except as indicated (234.9 represents $234,900). Annual averages. Covers fully amortized conventional mortgage loans used to purchase single-family nonfarm homes. Excludes refinancing loans, nonamortized and balloon loans, loans insured by the Federal Housing Administration, and loans guaranteed by the Veterans Administration. Based on a sample of mortgage lenders, including savings and loans associations, savings banks, commercial banks, and mortgage companies]

Loan characteristics	New homes						Previously occupied homes					
	2000	2004	2005	2006	2007	2008	2000	2004	2005	2006	2007	2008
Contract interest rate, [1]												
all loans	7.4	5.7	5.9	6.5	6.3	5.9	7.9	5.7	5.8	6.5	6.5	6.1
Fixed-rate loans	8.0	6.0	6.1	6.6	6.3	5.9	8.2	6.0	6.0	6.6	6.5	6.1
Adjustable-rate loans [2]	6.5	5.4	5.3	6.2	6.2	5.7	7.2	5.1	5.6	6.4	6.3	5.7
Initial fees, charges [3]	0.69	0.50	0.54	0.67	0.81	0.84	0.66	0.37	0.33	0.33	0.40	0.46
Effective interest rate, [4]												
all loans	7.5	5.8	5.9	6.6	6.4	6.1	8.1	5.7	5.9	6.6	6.5	6.2
Fixed-rate loans	8.2	6.0	6.2	6.7	6.4	6.1	8.3	6.0	6.0	6.6	6.5	6.2
Adjustable-rate loans [2]	6.5	5.4	5.3	6.2	6.3	5.8	7.2	5.2	5.6	6.4	6.4	5.8
Term to maturity (years)	29.2	28.8	29.2	29.5	29.4	29.1	28.6	27.7	28.3	28.9	29.3	28.3
Purchase price ($1,000)	234.9	293.6	328.5	346.4	360.4	350.6	191.8	253.2	291.3	295.9	286.2	296.4
Loan-to-price ratio	77.4	76.0	75.2	75.4	77.1	76.2	77.9	74.6	74.6	76.9	79.9	77.0
Percent of number of loans with adjustable rates	40	42	29	21	11	4	21	33	30	22	11	8

[1] Initial interest rate paid by the borrower as specified in the loan contract. [2] Loans with a contractual provision for periodic adjustments in the contract interest rate. [3] Includes all fees, commissions, discounts, and "points" paid by the borrower, or seller, in order to obtain the loan. Excludes those charges for mortgage, credit, life, or property insurance; for property transfer; and for title search and insurance. [4] Contract interest rate plus fees and charges amortized over a 10-year period.

Source: U.S. Federal Housing Finance Board, *Rates & Terms on Conventional Home Mortgages, Annual Summary.*

724 Banking, Finance, and Insurance

Table 1157. **Mortgage Originations and Delinquency and Foreclosure Rates: 1990 to 2008**

[In percent, except as indicated (459 represents $459,000,000,000). Covers one- to four-family residential nonfarm mortgage loans. Mortgage origination is the making of a new mortgage, including all steps taken by a lender to attract and qualify a borrower, process the mortgage loan, and place it on the lender's books. Based on the National Delinquency Survey which covers 45 million loans on one- to four-unit properties, representing between 80 to 85 percent of all 'first-lien' residential mortgage loans outstanding. Loans surveyed were reported by approximately 120 lenders, including mortgage bankers, commercial banks, and thrifts]

Item	1990	2000	2002	2003	2004	2005	2006	2007	2008
MORTGAGE ORIGINATIONS									
Total (bil. dol.)	459	1,139	2,854	3,812	2,773	2,908	2,726	2,306	1,618
Purchase (bil. dol.)	389	905	1,097	1,280	1,309	1,512	1,399	1,140	854
Refinance (bil. dol.)	70	234	1,757	2,532	1,463	1,397	1,326	1,166	765
DELINQUENCY RATES [1]									
Total	4.7	4.4	5.1	4.7	4.5	4.5	4.6	5.4	7.0
Prime conventional loans	(NA)	2.3	2.6	2.5	2.3	2.3	2.4	2.9	4.3
Subprime conventional loans. . . .	(NA)	11.9	14.3	12.2	10.8	10.8	12.3	15.6	19.9
Federal Housing Administration loans.	6.7	9.1	11.5	12.2	12.2	12.5	12.7	12.7	13.0
Veterans Administration loans	6.3	6.8	7.9	8.0	7.3	7.0	6.7	6.4	7.2
FORECLOSURE RATES									
Total loans in foreclosure process [2].	0.9	1.2	1.5	1.3	1.2	1.0	1.2	2.0	3.3
Prime conventional loans	(NA)	0.4	0.5	0.6	0.5	0.4	0.5	1.0	1.9
Subprime conventional loans.	(NA)	9.4	8.0	5.6	3.8	3.3	4.5	8.7	13.7
Federal Housing Administration loans.	1.3	1.7	2.8	2.9	2.7	2.3	1.9	2.3	2.4
Veterans Administration loans	1.2	1.2	1.6	1.6	1.5	1.1	1.0	1.1	1.7
Loans entering foreclosure process: [3]									
Prime conventional loans	(NA)	0.6	0.8	0.8	0.8	0.7	0.8	1.3	4.2
Subprime conventional loans.	(NA)	9.2	8.5	6.6	5.9	5.6	7.3	11.7	16.5
Federal Housing Administration loans.	1.7	2.3	3.3	3.6	3.9	3.4	3.3	3.6	3.8
Veterans Administration loans	1.6	1.5	1.8	1.9	2.0	1.5	1.4	1.6	2.3

NA Not available. [1] Number of loans delinquent 30 days or more as percentage of mortgage loans serviced in survey. Annual average of quarterly figures. Delinquency rate does not include loans in the process of foreclosure. [2] Percentage of loans in the foreclosure process at year-end, not seasonally adjusted. [3] Percentage of loans entering foreclosure process at year-end, not seasonally adjusted.

Source: Mortgage Bankers Association of America, Washington, DC, "MBA Mortgage Originations Estimates"; <http://www.mortgagebankers.org/files/Research/HistoricalMortgageOriginationEstimates032409.xls> (accessed 12 May 2009); National Delinquency Survey, quarterly; <http://www.mortgagebankers.org/>; and unpublished data.

Table 1158. **Delinquency Rates and Charge-Off Rates on Loans at Insured Commercial Banks: 1990 to 2008**

[In percent. Annual averages of quarterly figures, not seasonally adjusted. Delinquent loans are those past due 30 days or more and still accruing interest as well as those in nonaccrual status. They are measured as a percentage of end-of-period loans. Charge-offs, which are the value of loans removed from the books and charged against loss reserves, are measured net of recoveries as a percentage of average loans and annualized. Includes only U.S.-chartered commercial banks]

Type of loan	1990	2000	2002	2003	2004	2005	2006	2007	2008
DELINQUENCY RATES									
Total loans.	5.33	2.18	2.69	2.33	1.80	1.57	1.57	2.06	3.65
Real estate	6.10	1.89	1.99	1.76	1.44	1.37	1.49	2.27	4.63
Residential [1].	(NA)	2.11	2.11	1.83	1.55	1.55	1.73	2.55	4.96
Commercial [2]	(NA)	1.49	1.71	1.54	1.20	1.07	1.12	1.94	4.42
Consumer.	3.83	3.55	3.51	3.28	3.08	2.81	2.90	3.13	3.77
Credit cards	(NA)	4.50	4.87	4.47	4.11	3.70	4.01	4.25	5.04
Other	(NA)	2.98	2.79	2.67	2.46	2.24	2.21	2.46	3.00
Leases	1.97	1.59	2.24	1.91	1.34	1.28	1.26	1.20	1.58
Commercial and industrial	5.34	2.22	3.84	3.34	2.18	1.51	1.27	1.22	1.88
Agricultural	3.84	2.54	2.51	2.50	1.68	1.30	1.11	1.21	1.18
CHARGE-OFF RATES									
Total loans.	1.44	0.66	1.07	0.86	0.60	0.54	0.42	0.61	1.42
Real estate	0.85	0.10	0.16	0.17	0.09	0.06	0.09	0.23	1.19
Residential [1].	(NA)	0.12	0.16	0.19	0.10	0.08	0.11	0.26	1.27
Commercial [2]	(NA)	0.05	0.15	0.13	0.07	0.05	0.06	0.20	1.17
Consumer.	1.82	2.36	3.16	2.90	2.68	2.75	2.05	2.48	3.51
Credit cards	3.46	4.46	6.42	5.84	5.04	4.84	3.64	3.99	5.52
Other	1.03	1.14	1.45	1.41	1.31	1.38	1.06	1.56	2.31
Leases	0.66	0.31	1.08	0.86	0.42	0.58	0.17	0.24	0.53
Commercial and industrial	1.29	0.76	1.75	1.24	0.53	0.26	0.29	0.49	0.98
Agricultural	0.21	0.25	0.45	0.35	0.19	0.07	0.10	0.10	0.17

NA Not available. [1] Residential real estate loans include loans secured by one- to four-family properties, including home equity lines of credit, booked in domestic offices, only. [2] Commercial real estate loans include construction and land development loans, loans secured by multifamily residences, and loans secured by nonfarm, nonresidential real estate, booked in domestic offices, only.

Source: Federal Financial Institutions Examination Council (FFIEC), *Consolidated Reports of Condition and Income* (1990–2000: FFIEC 031 through 034; beginning 2002: FFIEC 031 & 041).

Banking, Finance, and Insurance 725

Table 1159. **Money Stock: 1990 to 2008**

[In billions of dollars (825 represents $825,000,000,000). As of December. Seasonally adjusted averages of daily figures]

Item	1990	2000	2001	2002	2003	2004	2005	2006	2007	2008
M1, total	**825**	**1,088**	**1,182**	**1,220**	**1,307**	**1,376**	**1,374**	**1,366**	**1,365**	**1,596**
Currency [1]	246	531	581	626	662	697	724	748	758	812
Travelers' checks [2]	8	8	8	8	8	8	7	7	6	6
Demand deposits [3]	277	310	336	307	326	343	325	305	293	466
Other checkable deposits [4]	294	238	257	280	310	328	319	306	308	312
M2, total	**3,277**	**4,911**	**5,418**	**5,765**	**6,055**	**6,400**	**6,661**	**7,021**	**7,417**	**8,154**
M1	825	1,088	1,182	1,220	1,307	1,376	1,374	1,366	1,365	1,596
Non-M1 components of M2	2,453	3,823	4,236	4,544	4,748	5,023	5,287	5,656	6,053	6,558
Retail money funds	356	898	951	875	767	688	690	794	967	1,091
Savings deposits (including MMDAs [5])	923	1,878	2,309	2,774	3,163	3,506	3,602	3,693	3,869	4,097
Commercial banks	581	1,424	1,738	2,060	2,338	2,631	2,774	2,910	3,041	3,328
Thrift institutions	342	454	571	714	825	875	828	783	827	769
Small time deposits [6]	1,173	1,047	976	896	818	829	995	1,170	1,217	1,370
Commercial banks	611	700	635	590	541	551	644	758	821	1,016
Thrift institutions	563	347	341	305	277	279	351	412	395	354

[1] Currency outside U.S. Treasury, Federal Reserve Banks and the vaults of depository institutions. [2] Outstanding amount of U.S. dollar-denominated travelers' checks of nonbank issuers. Travelers' checks issued by depository institutions are included in demand deposits. [3] Demand deposits at domestically chartered commercial banks, U.S. branches and agencies of foreign banks, and Edge Act corporations (excluding those amounts held by depository institutions, the U.S. government, and foreign banks and official institutions) less cash items in the process of collection and Federal Reserve float. [4] Negotiable order of withdrawal (NOW) and automatic transfer service (ATS) balances at domestically chartered commercial banks, U.S. branches and agencies of foreign banks, Edge Act corporations, and thrift institutions, credit union share draft balances, and demand deposits at thrift institutions. [5] Money market deposit accounts (MMDAs). [6] Small-denomination time deposits are those issued in amounts of less than $100,000. All Individual Retirement Account (IRA) and Keogh account balances at commercial banks and thrift institutions are subtracted from small time deposits.

Source: Board of Governors of the Federal Reserve System, Federal Reserve Statistical Release H.6, weekly.

Table 1160. **Money Market Interest Rates and Mortgage Rates: 1990 to 2008**

[Percent per year. Annual averages of monthly data, except as indicated]

Type	1990	1995	2000	2001	2002	2003	2004	2005	2006	2007	2008
Federal funds, effective rate	8.10	5.83	6.24	3.88	1.67	1.13	1.35	3.22	4.97	5.02	1.92
Prime rate charged by banks	10.01	8.83	9.23	6.91	4.67	4.12	4.34	6.19	7.96	8.05	5.09
Discount rate [1]	6.98	5.21	5.73	3.40	1.17	2.12	2.34	4.19	5.96	5.86	2.39
Eurodollar deposits, 3-month	8.16	5.93	6.45	3.70	1.73	1.14	1.55	3.51	5.19	5.32	3.31
Large negotiable CDs:											
3-month, secondary market	8.15	5.92	6.46	3.71	1.73	1.15	1.57	3.51	5.16	5.27	2.97
6-month, secondary market	8.17	5.98	6.59	3.66	1.81	1.17	1.74	3.73	5.24	5.23	3.14
Taxable money market funds [2]	7.82	5.48	5.89	3.67	1.29	0.64	0.82	2.66	4.51	4.70	2.05
Tax-exempt money market funds [2]	5.45	3.39	3.54	2.24	0.94	0.53	0.66	1.87	2.90	3.13	1.77
Certificates of deposit (CDs): [3]											
6-month	7.79	4.92	5.09	3.43	1.67	1.02	1.14	2.37	3.29	3.46	2.12
1-year	7.92	5.39	5.46	3.60	1.98	1.20	1.45	2.77	3.64	3.65	2.36
2½-year	7.96	5.69	5.64	3.97	2.74	1.77	2.21	3.18	3.75	3.65	2.43
5-year	8.06	6.00	5.97	4.58	3.96	2.93	3.34	3.75	4.02	3.89	3.17
U.S. government securities:											
Secondary market: [4]											
3-month Treasury bill	7.50	5.49	5.82	3.40	1.61	1.01	1.37	3.15	4.73	4.36	1.37
6-month Treasury bill	7.46	5.56	5.90	3.34	1.68	1.05	1.58	3.39	4.81	4.44	1.62
Auction average: [5]											
3-month Treasury bill	7.51	5.51	5.85	3.45	1.62	1.02	1.38	3.16	4.73	4.41	1.48
Home mortgages:											
New-home mortgage yields [6]	10.05	7.87	7.52	7.00	6.43	5.80	5.77	5.94	6.63	6.41	6.05
Conventional, 15 yr. fixed [3]	9.73	7.39	7.76	6.53	6.02	5.25	5.23	5.50	6.13	6.11	5.83
Conventional, 30 yr. fixed [3]	9.97	7.86	8.08	7.01	6.56	5.89	5.86	5.93	6.47	6.40	6.23

[1] Rate for the Federal Reserve Bank of New York. Beginning 2003, the rate charged for discounts made and advances extended under the Federal Reserve's primary credit discount window program, which became effective January 9, 2003. The rate replaced that for adjustment credit, which was discontinued after January 8, 2003. [2] 12-month return for period ending December 31. Source: iMoneyNet, Inc., Westborough, MA, *Money Market Insight*, monthly, <http://www.imoneynet.com> (copyright). [3] Annual averages. Source: Bankrate, Inc., North Palm Beach, FL, *Bank Rate Monitor*, weekly (copyright); <http://www.bankrate.com>. [4] Averages based on daily closing bid yields in secondary market, bank discount basis. [5] Averages computed on an issue-date basis; bank discount basis. Source: U.S. Council of Economic Advisors, *Economic Indicators*, monthly. [6] Effective rate (in the primary market) on conventional mortgages, reflecting fees and charges as well as contract rate and assumed, on the average, repayment at end of ten years. Source: U.S. Federal Housing Finance Board, *Rates & Terms on Conventional Home Mortgages, Annual Summary.*

Source: Except as noted, Board of Governors of the Federal Reserve System, "H15, Selected Interest Rates"; <http://www.federalreserve.gov/releases/h15/data.htm>.

Table 1161. Bond Yields: 1990 to 2008

[**Percent per year**. Annual averages of daily figures, except as indicated]

Type	1990	1995	2000	2001	2002	2003	2004	2005	2006	2007	2008
U.S. Treasury, constant maturities: [1,2]											
1-year	7.89	5.94	6.11	3.48	2.00	1.24	1.89	3.62	4.93	4.52	1.82
2-year	8.16	6.15	6.26	3.82	2.64	1.65	2.38	3.85	4.82	4.36	2.00
3-year	8.26	6.25	6.22	4.08	3.10	2.11	2.78	3.93	4.77	4.34	2.24
5-year	8.37	6.38	6.15	4.55	3.82	2.97	3.43	4.05	4.75	4.43	2.80
7-year	8.52	6.50	6.20	4.88	4.30	3.52	3.87	4.15	4.76	4.50	3.17
10-year	8.55	6.57	6.03	5.02	4.61	4.02	4.27	4.29	4.80	4.63	3.66
20-year	(NA)	6.95	6.23	5.63	5.43	4.96	5.05	4.65	4.99	4.91	4.36
State and local govt. bonds, Aaa rating [3]	6.96	5.79	5.58	5.01	4.87	4.52	4.51	4.28	4.15	4.13	4.58
State and local govt. bonds, Baa rating [3]	7.30	6.05	6.19	5.75	5.63	5.20	5.09	4.86	4.71	4.59	5.64
Municipal (Bond Buyer, 20 bonds)	7.27	5.95	5.71	5.15	5.04	4.75	4.68	4.40	4.40	4.40	4.85
High-grade municipal bonds (Standard & Poor's) [4]	7.25	5.95	5.77	5.19	5.05	4.73	4.63	4.29	4.42	4.42	4.80
Corporate Aaa rating seasoned [3,5]	9.32	7.59	7.62	7.08	6.49	5.66	5.63	5.23	5.59	5.56	5.63
Corporate Baa rating seasoned [3]	10.36	8.20	8.37	7.95	7.80	6.76	6.39	6.06	6.48	6.48	7.44
Corporate seasoned, all industries [3]	9.77	7.83	7.98	7.49	7.10	6.24	6.00	5.57	5.98	6.01	6.44

NA Not available. [1] Yields on actively traded non-inflation-indexed issues adjusted to constant maturities. Data from U.S. Treasury. [2] Through 1995, yields are based on closing bid prices quoted by at least five dealers. Beginning 2000, yields are based on closing indicative prices quoted by secondary market participants. [3] Data from Moody's Investors Service, New York, NY. [4] Source: U.S. Council of Economic Advisors, *Economic Indicators*, monthly. [5] Moody's Aaa rates through December 6, 2001, are average of Aaa utility and Aaa industrial bond rates. As of December 7, 2001, these rates are averages of Aaa industrial bonds only.

Source: Except as noted, Board of Governors of the Federal Reserve System, "H15, Selected Interest Rates"; <http://www.federalreserve.gov/releases/h15/data.htm>.

Table 1162. Volume of Debt Markets by Type of Security: 1990 to 2008

[**In billions of dollars (1,081 represents $1,081,000,000,000)**. Covers debt markets as represented by the source]

Type of security	1990	2000	2003	2004	2005	2006	2007	2008
NEW ISSUE VOLUME [1]								
Total	1,081	2,513	6,704	5,306	5,296	5,723	5,811	4,727
U.S. Treasury securities [2]	398	312	745	853	746	789	752	1,037
Federal agency debt [3]	55	447	1,268	882	669	747	942	1,115
Municipal	128	201	383	360	408	387	429	391
Mortgage-backed securities [4]	380	684	3,071	1,779	1,967	1,988	2,050	1,340
Asset-backed securities [5]	44	282	462	652	754	754	510	137
Corporate debt [6]	77	588	776	781	753	1,059	1,128	706
DAILY TRADING VOLUME								
Total	111	358	752	819	919	893	1,015	1,036
U.S. Treasury securities [2,7]	111	207	434	499	555	525	570	553
Federal agency debt [7]	(NA)	73	82	79	79	74	83	105
Municipal [8]	(NA)	9	13	15	17	23	25	19
Mortgage-backed securities [4,7]	(NA)	70	206	207	252	255	320	345
Corporate [6]	(NA)	(NA)	18	19	17	17	16	14
VOLUME OF SECURITIES OUTSTANDING								
Total	7,745	17,203	22,288	24,393	26,899	29,722	31,999	33,491
U.S. Treasury securities [2]	2,196	3,210	3,819	4,256	4,561	4,719	4,917	5,912
Federal agency debt	435	1,854	2,626	2,701	2,616	2,651	2,933	3,247
Municipal	1,184	1,481	1,901	2,031	2,226	2,403	2,619	2,690
Mortgage-backed securities [4]	1,333	3,566	5,239	5,862	7,128	8,453	8,931	8,897
Asset-backed securities [5]	90	1,072	1,694	1,828	1,955	2,130	2,472	2,672
Money market instruments [9]	1,157	2,663	2,520	2,904	3,434	4,009	4,172	3,791
Corporate debt [6]	1,350	3,358	4,490	4,811	4,979	5,356	5,955	6,281

NA Not available. [1] Covers only long-term issuance. [2] Marketable public debt. [3] Includes overnight discount notes. Beginning 2004 excludes Sallie Mae. [4] Includes only Government National Mortgage Association (GNMA), Federal National Mortgage Association (FNMA), Federal Home Loan Mortgage Corporation (FHLMC) mortgage-backed securities (MBS) and collateralized mortgage obligations (CMOs) and private-label MBS/CMOs. [5] Excludes mortgage-backed assets. [6] Includes nonconvertible corporate debt, Yankee bonds, and MTNs (Medium-Term Notes), but excludes all issues with maturities of one year or less, agency debt, and all certificates of deposit. [7] Primary dealer transactions. [8] Beginning 2000 includes customer-to-dealer and dealer-to-dealer transactions. [9] Commercial paper, bankers acceptances, and large time deposits.

Source: The Securities Industry and Financial Markets Association, New York, NY; <http://www.sifma.org/research/research.html>. Copyright. Based on data supplied by Board of Governors of the Federal Reserve System, U.S. Dept. of Treasury, Thompson Reuters, FHLMC, FNMA, GNMA, Federal Home Loan Banks, Student Loan Marketing Association, Federal Farm Credit Banks, Tennessee Valley Authority, Bloomberg, Loan Performance, Dealogic and Municipal Securities Rulemaking Board.

Banking, Finance, and Insurance 727

Table 1163. **Total Returns of Stocks, Bonds, and Treasury Bills: 1980 to 2008**

[In percent. Average annual percent change. Stock return data are based on the Standard & Poor's 500 index. Minus sign (−) indicates loss]

Period	Stocks				Treasury bills, total return	Bonds (10–year), total return
	Total return	Capital gains	Dividends and reinvestment	Total return after inflation		
1980 to 1989.........	17.55	12.59	4.40	11.85	9.13	13.01
1990 to 1999.........	18.21	15.31	2.51	14.85	4.95	8.02
2000 to 2006.........	1.13	−0.49	1.63	−1.10	3.07	6.76
2001	−11.89	−13.04	1.32	−13.68	3.32	5.51
2002	−22.10	−23.37	1.65	−23.91	1.61	15.15
2003	28.68	26.38	1.82	26.31	1.03	0.54
2004	10.88	8.99	1.73	7.38	1.43	4.59
2005	4.91	3.00	1.85	1.45	3.30	3.16
2006	15.80	13.62	1.91	11.97	4.97	2.36
2007	5.49	3.53	1.89	1.35	4.52	10.17
2008	−37.00	−38.49	1.88	−37.10	1.24	19.24

Source: Global Financial Data, Los Angeles, CA, "GFD Guide to Total Returns"; <http://www.globalfinancialdata.com/articles/total_return_worksheet.xls>; and unpublished data. (copyright).

Table 1164. **Equities, Corporate Bonds, and Treasury Securities—Holdings and Net Purchases by Type of Investor: 2000 to 2008**

[In billions of dollars (17,575 represents $17,575,000,000,000). Holdings as of Dec. 31. Minus sign (−) indicates net sales]

Type of investor	Holdings					Net purchases				
	2000	2005	2006	2007	2008	2000	2005	2006	2007	2008
EQUITIES [1]										
Total [2].............	17,575	20,643	24,066	25,196	15,190	5.4	−95.5	−405.6	−535.1	254.2
Household sector [3]	8,147	8,004	9,199	9,158	5,502	−637.6	−414.9	−665.9	−805.9	112.5
Rest of the world [4]	1,483	2,039	2,472	2,750	1,813	199.7	56.9	119.0	175.5	20.5
Life insurance companies........	892	1,162	1,365	1,465	930	111.3	65.9	71.4	84.1	52.8
Private pension funds	1,971	2,537	2,871	2,850	1,654	62.8	−18.5	−94.2	−249.6	−263.6
State and local government retirement funds	1,299	1,716	1,928	1,987	1,238	11.6	−5.6	−41.2	−18.9	−13.4
Mutual funds	3,227	4,176	4,990	5,477	2,852	193.1	129.6	131.3	91.3	−41.3
Exchange-traded funds	66	286	402	574	474	42.4	50.0	68.3	137.2	154.2
CORPORATE & FOREIGN BONDS										
Total [2]................	4,830	8,697	9,982	11,294	11,169	358.2	863.5	1,248.0	1,152.9	−124.2
Household sector [3]	554	1,304	1,564	1,842	1,601	80.3	120.3	205.2	154.0	−241.2
Rest of the world [4]	842	1,763	2,321	2,781	2,813	168.2	328.5	541.0	425.0	32.4
Commercial banking	266	687	780	979	989	56.0	123.4	93.3	198.4	9.8
Property-casualty insurance companies...............	188	263	277	283	275	6.4	17.5	14.2	5.9	−8.2
Life insurance companies........	1,215	1,825	1,823	1,865	1,861	47.9	74.7	32.9	42.4	−3.9
Private pension funds	266	288	316	353	395	−76.3	20.9	27.9	37.4	41.6
State and local government retirement funds	314	228	266	257	258	4.2	14.5	37.6	−8.1	0.7
Mutual funds	338	663	769	908	988	−10.6	65.9	106.2	139.5	79.5
Government-sponsored enterprises .	135	466	483	464	376	23.3	50.9	17.1	−18.4	−87.9
Funding corporations	25	67	60	170	667	−8.9	−29.4	−7.1	109.6	497.3
TREASURY SECURITIES										
Total [2]..................	3,358	4,678	4,862	5,099	6,338	−294.9	307.3	183.7	237.5	1,239.0
State and local governments......	310	481	517	531	523	5.5	92.3	35.5	14.5	−8.7
Rest of the world [4]	1,021	1,984	2,126	2,432	3,187	−75.2	245.1	150.4	215.7	755.2
Monetary authority.............	512	744	779	741	476	33.7	26.4	34.7	−38.3	−264.7
Money market mutual funds	92	89	83	178	578	−12.9	−9.6	−5.9	95.2	399.8

[1] Excludes mutual fund shares; see Table 1178. [2] Includes other types not shown separately. [3] Includes nonprofit organizations. [4] Holdings and net purchases of U.S. issues by foreign residents.

Source: Board of Governors of the Federal Reserve System, "Federal Reserve Statistical Release, Z.1, Flow of Funds Accounts of the United States"; published 12 March 2009; <http://www.federalreserve.gov/releases/z1/20090312>.

Table 1165. **New Security Issues of Corporations by Type of Offering: 2000 to 2008**

[In billions of dollars (1,082 represents $1,082,000,000,000). Represents gross proceed of issues maturing in more than one year. Figures are the principal amount or the number of units multiplied by the offering price. Excludes secondary offerings, employee stock plans, investment companies other than closed–end, intracorporate transactions, and Yankee bonds. Stock data include ownership securities issued by limited partnerships]

Type of offering	2000	2005	2007	2008	Type of offering	2000	2005	2007	2008
Total	1,082	2,439	2,389	1,072	Nonfinancial	259	216	405	318
					Financial.............	688	2,108	1,816	547
Bonds, total	947	2,324	2,221	866	Stocks, total	135	115	168	207
Sold in the U.S.........	825	2,141	2,003	749	Nonfinancial	118	55	65	45
Sold abroad	123	182	218	117	Financial.............	17	61	103	162

Source: Board of Governors of the Federal Reserve System, "New Security Issues, U.S. Corporations"; <http://www.federalreserve.gov/econresdata/releases/corpsecure/current.htm>.

728 Banking, Finance, and Insurance

Table 1166. **U.S. Purchases and Sales of Foreign Bonds and Stocks, 1990 to 2008, and by Selected Country, 2008**

[In billions of dollars (31.2 represents $31,200,000,000). Covers transactions in all types of long-term foreign securities by foreigners as reported to the Treasury International Capital Reporting System by banks, brokers, and other entities in the United States. Data cover new issues of securities, transactions in outstanding issues, and redemptions of securities. Includes transactions executed in the United States for the account of foreigners, and transactions executed abroad for the account of reporting institutions and their domestic customers. Data by country show the country of location of the foreign buyers and sellers who deal directly with reporting institutions in the United States. The data do not necessarily indicate the country of beneficial owner or issuer. The term "foreigner" covers all institutions and individuals domiciled outside the United States, including U.S. citizens domiciled abroad, and the foreign branches, subsidiaries, and other affiliates abroad of U.S. banks and businesses; the central governments, central banks, and other official institutions of foreign countries; and international and regional organizations. "Foreigner" also includes persons in the United States to the extent that they are known by reporting institutions to be acting on behalf of foreigners. Excludes acquisitions of foreign stocks through mergers that involve stock swaps. Including stock swaps, net sales of foreign securities was $98 billion in 2008. Minus sign (–) indicates net sales by U.S. investors or a net inflow of capital into the United States]

Year and country	Net purchases			Total transactions [1]			Bonds		Stocks	
	Total	Bonds	Stocks	Total	Bonds	Stocks	Purchases	Sales	Purchases	Sales
1990	31.2	21.9	9.2	907	652	255	337	315	132	123
2000	17.1	4.1	13.1	5,539	1,922	3,617	963	959	1,815	1,802
2001	19.6	–30.5	50.1	5,135	2,290	2,845	1,130	1,160	1,448	1,398
2002	–27.0	–28.5	1.5	5,253	2,716	2,537	1,344	1,372	1,269	1,268
2003	56.5	–32.0	88.6	5,580	2,883	2,698	1,425	1,457	1,393	1,305
2004	152.8	67.9	85.0	6,399	2,986	3,413	1,527	1,459	1,749	1,664
2005	172.4	45.1	127.3	7,572	2,965	4,608	1,505	1,460	2,367	2,240
2006	250.9	144.5	106.5	11,283	3,904	7,379	2,024	1,880	3,743	3,636
2007	229.2	133.9	95.3	16,604	6,078	10,527	3,106	2,972	5,311	5,216
2008, total [2]	–102.1	–82.0	–20.1	15,287	4,445	10,842	2,182	2,264	5,411	5,431
United Kingdom.	–1.9	–4.0	2.1	5,127	1,615	3,512	805	809	1,757	1,755
Cayman Islands.	15.9	–17.9	33.8	2,489	344	2,144	163	181	1,089	1,055
Canada	–3.1	–5.1	2.0	1,107	502	606	248	253	304	302
Japan	–18.3	3.3	–21.6	968	183	785	93	90	381	403
Hong Kong.	–13.5	–1.0	–12.4	662	13	648	6	7	318	330
Ireland.	0.4	–2.4	2.8	654	591	63	294	297	33	30
Bermuda	13.5	15.0	–1.4	452	71	380	43	28	189	191
France.	–26.6	–26.2	–0.4	431	161	270	68	94	135	135
British Virgin Islands. . .	7.4	0.2	7.2	343	58	285	29	29	146	139
Australia.	11.8	11.1	0.7	296	66	230	39	27	115	115
Netherlands	–4.0	–4.5	0.5	232	48	184	22	26	92	92
Sweden	–19.5	–5.9	–13.7	227	32	195	13	19	91	104
Germany	–15.9	–12.0	–3.9	221	113	108	51	63	52	56
Bahamas, The.	–0.1	0.1	–0.2	189	45	145	22	22	72	72

[1] Total purchases plus total sales. [2] Includes other countries not shown separately.

Source: U.S. Dept. of Treasury, *Treasury Bulletin*, quarterly.

Table 1167. **U.S. Holdings of Foreign Stocks and Bonds by Country: 2006 to 2008**

[In billions of dollars (4,329.0 represents $4,329,000,000,000). See also Table 1253]

Country	Stocks			Country	Bonds		
	2006	2007	2008, prel.		2006	2007	2008, prel.
Total holdings	4,329.0	5,248.0	2,851.4	Total holdings	1,275.5	1,587.1	1,392.9
Europe [1]	2,191.1	2,569.4	1,336.0	Europe [1]	646.9	798.7	691.1
United Kingdom	689.1	734.7	376.8	United Kingdom	256.1	296.7	257.8
France	306.9	347.8	196.5	Belgium and Luxembourg . .	42.8	48.9	118.3
Switzerland	262.9	281.0	195.9	Germany	58.2	84.6	66.7
Germany	220.4	329.2	177.0	Netherlands.	67.9	76.4	66.5
Netherlands	161.5	154.0	80.1	France	58.9	78.3	46.5
Spain	85.6	106.6	60.8	Ireland	38.3	50.2	43.0
Italy	92.7	96.9	49.0	Sweden	23.8	29.1	21.0
Finland	55.9	90.2	40.8	Canada	162.1	185.2	165.2
Belgium and Luxembourg . . .	44.4	71.7	33.6	Caribbean financial centers [1] . .	199.0	296.3	280.7
Canada.	298.1	379.0	212.5	Cayman Islands	177.9	271.3	243.0
Caribbean financial centers [1] . .	418.1	588.6	373.4	Bermuda.	13.6	16.7	29.7
Cayman Islands	160.6	231.9	165.9	Latin America, excluding			
Bermuda	191.9	256.1	145.1	Mexico	82.1	79.1	47.8
Latin America, excluding				Mexico	23.8	23.9	15.5
Caribbean financial centers [1] . .	207.0	293.8	150.3	Asia [1]	93.4	118.9	93.0
Brazil	92.0	172.6	82.8	Japan.	35.5	49.1	48.6
Mexico	84.6	85.4	46.8	Africa.	6.7	9.0	4.6
Asia [1]	1,050.2	1,193.7	661.3	Other countries [1]	85.4	99.8	110.5
Japan	543.5	529.2	355.6	Australia	61.6	73.3	77.0
Korea, South	114.2	129.2	55.9				
Hong Kong.	85.8	119.5	48.6				
China [2]	73.9	95.7	48.1				
Taiwan [2]	74.2	81.0	42.1				
Africa [1]	49.4	65.6	39.5				
South Africa	39.6	49.1	30.7				
Other countries [1]	115.1	157.9	78.5				
Australia	102.0	138.1	69.0				

[1] Includes other countries not shown separately. [2] See footnote 3, Table 1169.

Source: U.S. Bureau of Economic Analysis, *Survey of Current Business*, July 2009.

Banking, Finance, and Insurance   729

Table 1168. **Foreign Purchases and Sales of U.S. Securities by Type of Security, 1990 to 2008, and by Selected Country, 2008**

[In billions of dollars (18.7 represents $18,700,000,000). Covers transactions in all types of long-term domestic securities by foreigners as reported to the Treasury International Capital Reporting System by banks, brokers, and other entities in the United States (except nonmarketable U.S. Treasury notes, foreign series; and nonmarketable U.S. Treasury bonds and notes, foreign currency series). See headnote, Table 1166. Excludes U.S. equities acquired through mergers and reincorporations that involve stock swaps. Also excludes principal repayment flows on foreign holdings of U.S. government agency and corporate asset-backed securities (ABS). Including stock swaps and accounting for ABS repayment flows, net purchases of U.S. securities was $219 billion in 2008. Minus sign (−) indicates net sales by foreigners or a net outflow of capital from the United States]

Year and country	Net purchases					Total transactions [4]				
	Total	Treasury bonds and notes [1]	U.S. govt. corporations [2] bonds	Corporate bonds [3]	Corporate stocks	Total	Treasury bonds and notes [1]	U.S. govt. corporations [2] bonds	Corporate bonds [3]	Corporate stocks
1990	18.7	17.9	6.3	9.7	−15.1	4,204	3,620	104	117	362
2000	457.8	−54.0	152.8	184.1	174.9	16,910	7,795	1,305	775	7,036
2001	520.8	18.5	164.0	222.0	116.4	20,003	10,517	2,239	1,260	5,986
2002	547.6	119.9	195.1	182.3	50.2	25,498	14,409	3,261	1,459	6,369
2003	719.9	263.6	155.8	265.7	34.7	26,332	15,739	2,725	1,694	6,174
2004	916.5	352.1	226.4	309.5	28.5	29,441	17,520	2,192	2,033	7,696
2005	1,011.5	338.1	219.3	372.2	82.0	33,303	19,764	1,976	2,182	9,382
2006	1,143.2	195.5	286.5	510.8	150.4	41,011	21,720	2,858	2,846	13,587
2007	1,005.8	198.0	219.0	393.4	195.5	58,455	30,057	3,882	3,433	21,083
2008, total [5]	412.5	316.0	−37.8	93.5	40.8	60,936	28,939	5,216	2,841	23,941
United Kingdom	328.6	188.6	78.1	31.9	29.9	19,668	13,775	933	1,289	3,671
Cayman Islands	−17.1	34.5	−51.4	29.0	−29.2	14,963	3,202	2,276	646	8,839
France	−21.8	−15.4	2.8	−2.0	−7.2	8,832	4,312	77	42	4,401
Bermuda	−30.3	9.2	−38.0	−0.4	−1.2	2,343	364	164	88	1,728
Canada	14.1	−5.9	5.4	7.2	7.4	1,987	1,044	121	66	756
Japan	55.8	6.1	6.1	22.3	21.4	1,580	1,097	281	99	102
British Virgin Islands .	−8.0	2.3	0.6	−6.3	−4.6	1,256	152	9	73	1,023
Bahamas, The	−12.2	−12.7	2.1	0.2	−1.8	1,054	632	19	42	361
Ireland	−22.1	−4.3	−3.4	−15.3	0.8	936	677	112	57	91
China [6]	130.4	84.7	16.7	29.6	−0.7	817	487	243	55	32
Anguilla	−3.5	−0.8	−0.2	−0.3	−2.2	746	39	2	2	704
Germany	−17.1	0.7	−3.4	5.0	−19.3	640	221	54	40	326

[1] Marketable bonds and notes.   [2] Includes federally sponsored agencies.   [3] Includes transactions in directly placed issues abroad by U.S. corporations and issues of states and municipalities.   [4] Total purchases plus total sales.   [5] Includes other countries, not shown separately.   [6] See footnote 3, Table 1169.

Source: U.S. Department of Treasury, *Treasury Bulletin*, quarterly.

Table 1169. **Foreign Holdings of U.S. Securities by Country: 2006 to 2008**

[In billions of dollars (2,126.2 represents $2,126,200,000,000). Covers only private holdings of U.S. securities, except as noted. See also Table 1253]

Type of security and country	2006	2007	2008, prel.	Type of security and country	2006	2007	2008, prel.
U.S. Treasury securities [1, 2] .	2,126.2	2,376.4	3,210.6				
China [3]	445.2	486.8	807.5	China [3]	65.6	56.1	33.8
Japan	636.4	616.8	668.9	Taiwan [3]	30.1	30.7	33.8
OPEC Asia [4]	101.5	116.1	173.4	OPEC Asia [4]	7.3	16.0	22.7
Brazil	53.0	135.5	136.7	Hong Kong	26.2	35.1	20.0
Russia	18.3	41.1	134.7	Africa	3.1	3.5	2.1
Cayman Islands	33.8	50.4	124.9	Other countries [2]	32.7	44.7	42.5
Belgium and Luxembourg	72.8	94.6	119.9	Australia	22.7	32.2	30.2
Hong Kong	53.2	54.5	81.6				
Taiwan [3]	54.3	52.6	75.8	**Corporate stocks**	2,547.5	2,901.0	1,837.6
Switzerland	37.4	42.0	65.1	Europe [2]	1,396.7	1,560.7	981.0
				United Kingdom	377.8	443.7	295.0
Corporate and agency bonds	2,824.9	3,289.1	2,865.9	Belgium and Luxembourg	243.5	246.3	144.5
Europe [2]	1,762.4	2,068.3	1,792.4	Netherlands	167.6	193.1	126.7
Belgium and Luxembourg	648.3	753.0	671.9	Switzerland	162.2	173.2	113.9
United Kingdom	593.4	709.3	595.9	France	116.1	144.1	88.4
Ireland	120.8	168.7	142.6	Ireland	75.3	82.1	53.3
Germany	90.4	113.4	104.3	Germany	84.3	99.2	48.2
Switzerland	88.6	97.7	95.4	Sweden	50.6	50.2	31.7
Netherlands	103.3	104.2	89.9	Canada	318.4	353.0	225.0
France	54.6	58.4	47.3	Caribbean financial centers [2]	391.7	500.8	303.3
Canada	77.3	78.0	72.0	Cayman Islands	220.8	324.4	212.3
Caribbean financial centers [2]	503.9	590.4	505.6	Bermuda	72.0	76.0	39.6
Cayman Islands	353.7	430.7	365.9	Latin America, excluding Caribbean financial centers	40.2	49.5	37.1
Bermuda	110.8	119.8	106.3	Asia [2]	309.8	332.4	227.8
Latin America, excluding Caribbean financial centers [2]	38.3	50.0	51.8	Japan	213.3	217.0	153.9
Mexico	11.6	24.8	27.4	Singapore	45.5	44.7	21.4
Asia [2]	407.2	454.2	399.5	Africa	5.4	9.2	4.6
Japan	253.3	286.7	268.2	Other countries [2]	85.3	95.4	58.8
				Australia	74.8	88.0	55.0

[1] Includes foreign official holdings.   [2] Includes other countries not shown separately.   [3] With the establishment of diplomatic relations with China on January 1, 1979, the U.S. government recognized the People's Republic of China as the sole legal government of China and acknowledged the Chinese position that there is only one China and that Taiwan is part of China.   [4] Comprises Indonesia, Iran, Iraq, Kuwait, Qatar, Saudi Arabia, and the United Arab Emirates.

Source: U.S. Bureau of Economic Analysis, *Survey of Current Business*, July 2009.

Table 1170. **Stock Prices and Yields: 2000 to 2008**

[Closing values as of end of December, except as noted]

Index	2000	2003	2004	2005	2006	2007	2008
STOCK PRICES							
Standard & Poor's indices: [1]							
S&P 500 composite (1941–43 = 10)	1,320	1,112	1,212	1,248	1,418	1,468	903
S&P 400 MidCap Index (1982 = 100)	517	576	663	738	804	858	538
S&P 600 SmallCap Index (Dec. 31, 1993 = 100)	220	270	329	351	400	395	269
S&P 500 Citigroup Value Index (Dec. 31, 1974 = 35) . . .	636	552	626	648	764	761	447
S&P 500 Citigroup Growth Index (Dec. 31, 1974 = 35) . .	688	556	582	597	653	703	451
Russell indices: [2]							
Russell 1000 (Dec. 31, 1986 = 130)	700	595	651	679	770	800	488
Russell 2000 (Dec. 31, 1986 = 135)	484	557	652	673	788	766	499
Russell 3000 (Dec. 31, 1986 = 140)	726	630	694	723	822	849	521
N.Y. Stock Exchange common stock index:							
Composite (Dec. 31, 2002 = 5000)	6,946	6,440	7,250	7,754	9,139	9,740	5,757
Yearly high	7,165	6,470	7,373	7,868	9,188	10,387	9,713
Yearly low	6,095	4,419	6,211	6,903	7,708	8,344	4,607
American Stock Exchange Composite Index (Dec. 29, 1995 = 550)	898	1,174	1,434	1,759	2,056	2,410	2,174
NASDAQ Composite Index (Feb. 5, 1971 = 100)	2,471	2,003	2,175	2,205	2,415	2,653	1,577
Nasdaq-100 (Jan. 31, 1985 = 125)	2,342	1,468	1,621	1,645	1,757	2,085	1,212
Industrial (Feb. 5, 1971 = 100)	1,483	1,604	1,858	1,860	2,090	2,179	1,191
Banks (Feb. 5, 1971 = 100)	1,939	2,899	3,218	3,078	3,417	2,663	2,026
Computers (Oct. 29, 1993 = 200)	1,295	935	965	992	1,053	1,283	684
Transportation (Feb. 5, 1971 = 100)	1,160	1,754	2,229	2,438	2,582	2,673	1,885
Telecommunications (Oct. 29, 1993 = 200)	463	184	198	184	235	257	146
Biotech (Oct. 29, 1993 = 200)	1,085	724	769	790	798	835	730
Dow-Jones and Co., Inc.:							
Composite (65 stocks)	3,317	3,001	3,396	3,638	4,121	4,394	3,086
Industrial (30 stocks)	10,787	10,454	10,783	10,718	12,463	13,265	8,776
Transportation (20 stocks)	2,947	3,007	3,798	4,196	4,560	4,571	3,537
Utility (15 stocks)	412	267	335	405	457	533	371
Dow Jones Wilshire 5000 Composite Index [3] (Dec. 31, 1980 = 1404.596)	12,176	10,800	11,971	12,518	14,258	14,820	9,087
COMMON STOCK YIELDS (percent) Standard & Poor's Composite Index (500 stocks): [4]							
Dividend-price ratio [5]	1.15	1.77	1.72	1.83	1.87	1.80	2.37
Earnings-price ratio [6]	3.63	3.84	4.89	5.36	5.78	5.29	3.54

[1] Standard & Poor's Indices are market-value weighted and are chosen for market size, liquidity, and industry group representation. The S&P 500 index represents 500 large publicly-traded companies. The S&P MidCap Index tracks mid-cap companies. The S&P SmallCap Index consists of 600 domestic small-cap stocks. [2] The Russell 1000 and 3000 indices show respectively the 1000 and 3000 largest capitalization stocks in the United States. The Russell 2000 index shows the 2000 largest capitalization stocks in the United States after the first 1000. [3] The Dow Jones Wilshire 5000 Composite Index measures the performance of all U.S. headquartered equity securities with readily available prices. Source: Dow Jones & Company, Inc., New York, NY, Dow Jones Indexes, (copyright). [4] Source: U.S. Council of Economic Advisors, Economic Indicators, monthly. [5] Aggregate cash dividends (based on latest known annual rate) divided by aggregate market value based on Wednesday closing prices. Averages of monthly figures. [6] Averages of quarterly ratios which are ratio of earnings (after taxes) for four quarters ending with particular quarter-to-price index for last day of that quarter.

Source: Except as noted, Global Financial Data, Los Angeles, CA, <http://www.globalfinancialdata.com/> (copyright).

Table 1171. **Dow Jones U.S. Total Market Index by Industry: 2000 to 2008**

[As of end of year]

Industry	2000	2003	2004	2005	2006	2007	2008
U.S. Total Market Index, total	306.88	262.68	289.38	302.37	343.25	357.48	219.66
Basic materials	154.49	181.10	200.33	205.79	236.22	307.92	147.91
Consumer goods	219.82	240.91	266.44	265.88	298.60	320.39	231.71
Consumer services	279.11	280.07	306.85	298.62	338.32	310.76	211.93
Oil and gas	272.96	246.08	319.76	422.12	510.72	679.31	429.60
Financial	440.91	445.96	492.54	510.02	592.98	474.23	226.52
Health care	360.18	286.04	295.22	315.50	332.38	354.89	268.73
Industrials	276.11	235.69	272.24	280.72	314.41	351.44	207.77
Technology	749.01	493.02	499.78	513.48	561.85	645.98	365.85
Telecommunications	210.38	119.12	136.84	126.90	168.11	179.65	115.34
Utilities	177.80	114.54	136.79	152.41	178.78	204.52	137.79

Source: Dow Jones & Company, Inc., New York, NY, Dow Jones Indexes (copyright).

Table 1172. **Transaction Activity in Equities, Options, and Security Futures, 1990 to 2008, and by Exchange, 2008**

[In billions of dollars (2,229 represents $2,229,000,000,000). Market value of all sales of equities and options listed on an exchange or subject to last-sale reporting. Also reported are the value of such options that were exercised and the value of single-stock futures that were delivered. Excludes options and futures on indexes]

Year and exchange	Total	Equity trading	Option trading	Option exercises and futures deliveries
1990	2,229	2,154	27	48
2000	36,275	35,557	485	233
2001	26,138	25,636	278	224
2002	23,028	22,658	161	209
2003	22,737	22,292	164	282
2004	27,876	27,158	223	495
2005	34,568	33,223	350	995
2006	43,941	41,798	531	1,611
2007	66,136	63,064	861	2,211
2008, total [1]	82,012	78,653	1,096	2,264
BATS Exchange, Inc.	1,090	1,090	–	–
Chicago Board Options Exchange, Inc.	1,018	192	268	559
FINRA, Inc. [2]	21,561	21,561	–	–
International Securities Exchange, Inc.	1,557	759	269	529
The Nasdaq Stock Market LLC	25,000	24,975	9	15
National Stock Exchange	1,043	1,043	–	–
New York Stock Exchange, Inc	12,767	12,767	–	–
NYSE Arca, Inc. [3]	16,116	15,429	222	465
Philadelphia Stock Exchange, Inc.	762	43	230	490
U.S. Alternext [4]	549	377	56	116

– Represents zero. [1] Includes other exchanges not shown separately. [2] Financial Industry Regulatory Authority. [3] NYSE Arca, formerly Archipelago, is a fully electronic stock exchange. [4] NYSE Euronext completed its acquisition of the American Stock Exchange (Amex) on October 1, 2008. Post merger, the Amex equities business was branded NYSE Alternext US.

Source: U.S. Securities and Exchange Commission, "Select SEC and Market Data"; <http://www.sec.gov/about.shtml>.

Table 1173. **Volume of Trading on New York Stock Exchange: 1990 to 2008**

[39,946 represents 39,946,000,000. Round lot: A unit of trading or a multiple thereof. On the NYSE the unit of trading is generally 100 shares in stocks. For some inactive stocks, the unit of trading is 10 shares. Odd lot: An amount of stock less than the established 100-share unit or 10-share unit of trading]

Item	Unit	1990	2000	2002	2003	2004	2005	2006	2007	2008
Shares traded	Million .	39,946	265,499	369,069	356,767	372,718	410,832	523,811	597,720	671,402
Round lots [1]	Million ..	39,665	262,478	363,136	352,398	367,099	403,764	516,743	588,127	664,020
Average daily shares	Million .	157	1,042	1,441	1,398	1,457	1,602	2,051	2,343	2,645
High day	Million .	292	1,561	2,813	1,886	2,690	3,116	3,628	3,853	5,505
Low day	Million .	57	403	462	360	509	545	694	797	917
Odd lots	Million ..	282	3,021	5,933	4,370	5,619	7,068	7,068	9,593	7,383
Value of shares traded .	Bil. dol..	1,336	11,205	10,491	9,847	11,841	14,441	18,174	22,247	28,805
Round lots [1]	Bil. dol. .	1,325	11,060	10,278	9,692	11,618	14,125	17,858	21,790	28,428
Odd lots	Bil. dol. .	11	145	213	154	223	316	316	458	378

[1] Beginning 2005, reflects trades of NYSE Group.

Source: New York Stock Exchange, Inc., New York, NY, "Facts & Figures"; <http://www.nyxdata.com/factbook> (copyright).

Table 1174. **Stock Ownership by Age of Family Head and Family Income: 2001 to 2007**

[Median value in thousands of constant 2007 dollars (40.4 represents $40,400). Constant dollar figures are based on consumer price index data published by U.S. Bureau of Labor Statistics. Families include one-person units; for definition of family, see text, Section 1. Based on Survey of Consumer Finance; see Appendix III. For definition of median, see Guide to Tabular Presentation]

Age of family head and family income (constant (2007) dollars)	Families having direct or indirect stock holdings [1] (percent)			Median value among families with holdings			Stock holdings' share of total financial assets (percent)		
	2001	2004	2007	2001	2004	2007	2001	2004	2007
All families	52.2	50.2	51.1	40.4	35.7	35.0	56.1	51.3	53.3
Under 35 years old	49.0	40.8	38.6	8.2	8.8	7.0	52.5	40.3	44.3
35 to 44 years old	59.5	54.5	53.5	32.2	22.0	26.0	57.2	53.5	53.7
45 to 54 years old	59.3	56.5	60.4	58.5	54.9	45.0	59.1	53.8	53.0
55 to 64 years old	57.4	62.8	58.9	94.2	78.0	78.0	56.2	55.0	55.0
65 to 74 years old	40.0	46.9	52.1	175.8	76.9	57.0	55.4	51.5	55.3
75 years old and over	35.7	34.8	40.1	128.7	94.3	41.0	51.8	39.3	48.1
Percentiles of income: [2]									
Less than 20	12.9	11.7	13.6	8.8	8.2	6.5	37.4	32.0	39.0
20 to 39.9	34.1	29.6	34.0	9.1	11.0	8.8	35.6	30.9	34.3
40 to 59.9	52.5	51.7	49.5	17.5	16.5	17.7	46.8	43.4	38.3
60 to 79.9	75.7	69.9	70.5	33.5	28.7	34.1	52.0	41.7	52.5
80 to 89.9	82.0	83.8	84.4	75.6	60.9	62.0	57.3	48.8	49.3
90 to 100	89.7	92.7	91.0	289.7	225.2	219.0	60.5	57.5	57.6

[1] Indirect holdings are those in retirement accounts and other managed assets. [2] See footnote 8, Table 1133.

Source: Board of Governors of the Federal Reserve System, "2007 Survey of Consumer Finances" (published February 2009); <http://www.federalreserve.gov/pubs/oss/oss2/2007/scf2007home.html>.

Table 1175. **Households Owning Mutual Funds by Age and Income: 2000 and 2008**

[In percent. Ownership includes money market, stock, bond, and hybrid mutual funds, variable annuities, and mutual funds owned through Individual Retirement Accounts (IRAs), Keoghs, and employer-sponsored retirement plans. In 2008, an estimated 52,500,000 households own mutual funds. The May 2008 survey included a sample of 4,100 randomly selected households; for details, see source. For definition of mutual fund, see headnote, Table 1177]

Age of household head and household income	Percent distribution, 2008	As percent of all households 2000	As percent of all households 2008	Age of household head and household income	Percent distribution, 2008	As percent of all households 2000	As percent of all households 2008
Total	100	45	45	Less than $25,000.	5	13	10
Less than 35 years old. . .	17	36	34	$25,000 to $34,999	5	33	22
35 to 44 years old	22	55	52	$35,000 to $49,999	12	46	39
45 to 54 years old	26	59	56	$50,000 to $74,999	21	66	53
55 to 64 years old	20	50	51	$75,000 to $99,999	20	75	73
65 years old and over . . .	15	26	33	$100,000 to $199,999 . . .	29	84	80
				$200,000 and over	8	56	87

Source: Investment Company Institute, Washington, DC, *Fundamentals, Investment Company Institute Research in Brief*, Vol. 17, No. 6, December 2008 (copyright).

Table 1176. **Characteristics of Mutual Fund Owners: 2008**

[In percent, except as indicated. Mutual fund ownership includes holdings of money market, stock, bond, and hybrid mutual funds; and funds owned through variable annuities, Individual Retirement Accounts (IRAs), Keoghs, and employer-sponsored retirement plans. Based on a national probability sample of 1,844 primary financial decision-makers in households with mutual fund investments. For definition of mutual fund, see headnote, Table 1177. For definition of median, see Guide to Tabular Presentation]

Characteristic	Total	Age Under 40 years old	Age 40 to 64 years old	Age 65 years old and over	Household income Less than $50,000	Household income $50,000 to $99,999	Household income $100,000 to $149,999	Household income $150,000 or more
Median household income (dol.) . . .	80,000	79,000	87,500	50,000	35,000	72,000	115,000	190,000
Median household financial assets [1] (dol.)	200,000	70,000	250,000	300,000	70,000	125,000	350,000	500,000
Own an IRA	68	61	69	77	60	66	76	75
Household with defined contribution retirement plan(s) [2] . . .	78	83	83	53	58	79	92	88
401(k) plan	64	74	69	28	44	66	76	74
403(b), state, local, or federal government plan	34	31	36	33	22	32	46	41
Median mutual fund assets (dol.). . .	100,000	45,000	150,000	150,000	35,000	73,000	200,000	350,000
Own:								
Equity funds	80	78	83	75	66	80	87	91
Bond funds	48	42	52	45	38	45	54	62
Own mutual funds bought:								
Outside employer-sponsored retirement plan(s)	73	62	73	88	72	68	75	81
Inside employer-sponsored retirement plan(s)	68	74	74	35	50	67	81	79

[1] Includes assets in employer-sponsored retirement plans but excludes value of primary residence. [2] For definition of defined contribution plan, see headnote, Table 540.

Source: Investment Company Institute, Washington, DC, *Profile of Mutual Fund Shareholders, 2008*, Winter 2009 (copyright).

Table 1177. **Mutual Funds—Summary: 1990 to 2008**

[Number of funds and assets as of December 31 (1,065 represents $1,065,000,000,000). A mutual fund is an open-end investment company that continuously issues and redeems shares that represent an interest in a pool of financial assets. Excludes data for funds that invest in other mutual funds. Minus sign (–) indicates net redemptions]

Type of fund	Unit	1990	2000	2002	2003	2004	2005	2006	2007	2008
Number of funds, total	Number. . .	3,079	8,155	8,244	8,126	8,041	7,975	8,117	8,024	8,022
Equity funds	Number. . .	1,099	4,385	4,747	4,599	4,547	4,586	4,769	4,764	4,830
Hybrid funds	Number. . .	193	523	473	508	510	505	508	488	492
Bond funds	Number. . .	1,046	2,208	2,035	2,045	2,041	2,013	1,993	1,967	1,916
Money market funds, taxable [1]	Number. . .	506	703	679	662	639	595	574	546	536
Money market funds, tax-exempt [2] . . .	Number. . .	235	336	310	312	304	276	273	259	248
Assets, total	Bil. dol.	1,065	6,965	6,390	7,414	8,107	8,905	10,397	12,000	9,601
Equity funds	Bil. dol. . . .	239	3,962	2,662	3,684	4,384	4,940	5,911	6,516	3,704
Hybrid funds	Bil. dol. . . .	36	346	325	430	519	567	653	719	499
Bond funds	Bil. dol. . . .	291	811	1,130	1,248	1,290	1,357	1,494	1,679	1,566
Money market funds, taxable [1]	Bil. dol. . . .	415	1,607	1,997	1,764	1,603	1,707	1,972	2,621	3,341
Money market funds, tax-exempt [2] . . .	Bil. dol. . . .	84	238	275	288	310	334	366	465	491
Net sales:										
Equity, hybrid and bond funds	Bil. dol. . . .	51	300	206	282	293	303	369	404	-10
Money market funds, taxable [1]	Bil. dol. . . .	36	192	–63	–252	–157	67	255	623	604
Money market funds, tax-exempt [2] . . .	Bil. dol. . . .	7	31	14	7	16	24	33	90	26

[1] Funds invest in short-term, high-grade securities sold in the money market. [2] Funds invest in municipal securities with relatively short maturities.

Source: Investment Company Institute, Washington, DC, *Mutual Fund Fact Book*, annual (copyright).

Banking, Finance, and Insurance   733

Table 1178. **Mutual Fund Shares—Holdings and Net Purchases by Type of Investor: 2000 to 2008**

[In billions of dollars (4,433 represents $4,433,000,000,000). Holdings as of Dec. 31. For definition of mutual fund, see headnote, Table 1177. Excludes money market mutual funds. Minus sign (–) indicates net sales]

Type of investor	Holdings					Net purchases				
	2000	2005	2006	2007	2008	2000	2005	2006	2007	2008
Total	4,433	6,049	7,068	7,829	5,274	237.6	260.2	336.8	364.7	28.9
Households, nonprofit organizations	2,704	3,839	4,410	4,873	3,254	66.7	228.1	222.4	258.8	-55.9
Nonfinancial corporate business. . .	122	156	204	225	160	3.5	6.7	30.7	9.4	9.4
State and local governments	31	30	32	34	28	1.2	0.8	-1.3	0.7	8.0
Rest of the world.	149	242	294	325	219	-9.2	32.2	24.0	14.0	1.2
Commercial banking	15	17	25	30	20	2.5	-1.8	3.9	3.6	1.3
Credit unions	2	2	2	2	2	-0.3	-1.0	-0.1	–	–
Property-casualty insurance companies	3	6	7	7	5	0.4	0.3	0.5	-0.5	0.1
Life insurance companies	97	109	149	188	159	5.6	-9.9	26.9	31.3	27.0
Private pension funds	1,132	1,399	1,658	1,848	1,230	117.3	10.2	28.6	50.2	39.9
State and local government retirement funds	178	248	288	297	199	49.9	-5.5	1.3	-2.8	-2.0

– Represents or rounds to zero.

Source: Board of Governors of the Federal Reserve System, "Federal Reserve Statistical Release, Z.1, Flow of Funds Accounts of the United States"; published 12 March 2009; <http://www.federalreserve.gov/releases/z1/20090312>.

Table 1179. **Retirement Assets by Type of Asset: 1990 to 2008**

[In billions of dollars, except as indicated (3,921 represents $3,921,000,000,000). As of December 31. Estimated]

Type of asset	1990	2000	2003	2004	2005	2006	2007	2008
Retirement assets, total.	3,921	11,690	12,545	13,778	14,862	16,680	17,916	13,985
IRA assets	637	2,629	2,993	3,299	3,652	4,220	4,747	3,610
Bank and thrift deposits [1]	266	250	268	269	278	313	340	391
Life insurance companies [2]	40	203	285	282	308	318	325	301
Mutual funds	140	1,249	1,327	1,521	1,700	2,028	2,304	1,596
Securities held in brokerage accounts [3] . .	190	928	1,114	1,227	1,366	1,562	1,778	1,321
Traditional	(NA)	2,407	2,719	2,957	3,259	3,749	4,208	3,221
Roth	(X)	78	106	140	160	195	225	165
SEP and SAR-SEP [4]	(NA)	134	145	169	191	223	253	180
SIMPLE [5]	(X)	10	23	34	42	53	61	44
Defined contribution plans.	892	2,969	3,043	3,335	3,620	4,154	4,502	3,517
401(k) plans	(NA)	1,725	1,922	2,189	2,396	2,768	3,025	2,350
403(b) plans	(NA)	517	533	571	616	687	729	572
457 plans	(NA)	110	117	130	143	158	173	140
Other defined contribution plans [6]	(NA)	618	472	446	465	541	575	455
State and local government pension plans. .	739	2,335	2,399	2,626	2,765	3,087	3,186	2,328
Private defined benefit plans	922	2,009	2,025	2,162	2,310	2,557	2,691	1,957
Federal pension plans [7]	340	797	958	1,023	1,072	1,141	1,197	1,221
Annuities [8]	391	951	1,125	1,332	1,443	1,521	1,592	1,351
Memo:								
Mutual fund retirement assets	206	2,497	2,674	3,090	3,460	4,111	4,613	3,143
Percent of total retirement assets	5	21	21	22	23	25	26	22
Percent of all mutual funds	19	36	36	38	39	40	38	33

NA Not available.   X Not applicable.   [1] Includes Keogh deposits.   [2] Annuities held by IRAs, excluding variable annuity mutual fund IRA assets.   [3] Excludes mutual fund assets held through brokerage accounts, which are included in mutual funds.   [4] Simplified Employee Pension IRAs and salary reduction (SAR) SEP IRAs.   [5] Savings Incentive Match Plan for Employees (SIMPLE) IRAs.   [6] Includes Keoghs and other defined contribution plans (profit-sharing, thrift-savings, stock bonus, and money purchase) without 401(k) features.   [7] Federal pension plans include U.S. Treasury security holdings of the civil service retirement and disability fund, the military retirement fund, the judicial retirement funds, the Railroad Retirement Board, and the foreign service retirement and disability fund. These plans also include securities held in the National Railroad Retirement Investment Trust and Federal Employees Retirement System (FERS) Thrift Savings Plan (TSP).   [8] Annuities include all fixed and variable annuity reserves at life insurance companies less annuities held by IRAs, 403(b) plans, 457 plans, and private pension funds. Some of these annuity reserves represent assets of individuals held outside retirement plan arrangements and IRAs; however, information to separate out such reserves is not available.

Source: Investment Company Institute, Washington, DC, *Research Fundamentals,* "The U.S. Retirement Market, 2008", Vol. 18, No. 5, June 2009 and *Research Fundamentals,* "Appendix: Additional Data on the U.S. Retirement Market, 2008", Vol. 18, No. 5A, June 2009 (copyright).

Table 1180. **Assets of Private and Public Pension Funds by Type of Fund: 1990 to 2008**

[In billions of dollars (3,269 represents $3,269,000,000,000). As of end of year. Except for corporate equities, represents book value. Excludes social security trust funds; see Table 535]

Type of pension fund	1990	2000	2002	2003	2004	2005	2006	2007	2008
Total, all types.	3,269	9,084	8,106	9,631	10,544	11,286	12,538	13,184	10,226
Private funds	2,199	5,994	5,282	6,323	6,943	7,493	8,347	8,830	6,694
Insured [1]	570	1,526	1,605	1,803	2,028	2,197	2,332	2,438	2,099
Noninsured [2, 3]	1,629	4,468	3,677	4,520	4,915	5,296	6,014	6,392	4,595
Credit market instruments [3]	464	622	577	646	646	691	752	853	941
Agency- and GSE-backed securities [4] . . .	133	197	183	221	233	251	267	296	315
Corporate and foreign bonds	158	266	254	275	267	288	316	353	395
Corporate equities	606	1,971	1,589	2,097	2,334	2,537	2,871	2,850	1,654
Mutual fund shares	40	1,132	932	1,127	1,278	1,399	1,658	1,848	1,230
Unallocated insurance contracts [5]	215	308	250	317	328	338	388	444	352
State and local government employee retirement funds [3]	730	2,293	1,930	2,349	2,578	2,721	3,050	3,157	2,311
Credit market instruments [3]	402	743	639	658	675	693	770	800	796
Agency- and GSE-backed securities [4]	63	179	193	235	259	258	295	317	323
Corporate and foreign bonds	142	314	217	207	213	228	266	257	258
Corporate equities	285	1,299	1,057	1,421	1,601	1,716	1,928	1,987	1,238
Federal government retirement funds [6]	340	797	894	958	1,023	1,072	1,141	1,197	1,221

[1] Annuity reserves held by life insurance companies, excluding unallocated contracts held by private pension funds. [2] Private benefit plans and defined contribution plans (including 401(k) type plans). [3] Includes other types of assets not shown separately. [4] GSE = Government-sponsored enterprises. [5] Assets held at life insurance companies (e.g., guaranteed investment contracts (GICs), variable annuities). [6] Includes the Federal Employees Thrift Savings Plan, the National Railroad Retirement Investment Trust, and nonmarketable government securities held by federal government retirement funds.

Source: Board of Governors of the Federal Reserve System, "Federal Reserve Statistical Release, Z.1, Flow of Funds Accounts of the United States"; published 12 March 2009; <http://www.federalreserve.gov/releases/z1/20090312>.

Table 1181. **Annual Revenues of Selected Securities Industries: 2000 to 2007**

[In millions of dollars (384,992 represents $384,992,000,000). Covers taxable and tax-exempt employer firms only. Based on the North American Industry Classification System (NAICS), 2002; see text, Section 15. Based on Service Annual Survey. Estimates have been adjusted to the results of the 2002 Economic Census. See Appendix III]

Kind of business	2002 NAICS code	2000	2004	2005	2006	2007
Total.	523x	384,992	349,166	392,734	467,702	461,096
Securities and commodity contracts intermediation and brokerage	5231	296,045	250,080	279,101	335,703	312,790
Investment banking & securities dealing	52311	145,416	127,257	140,411	170,328	145,576
Securities brokerage	52312	144,631	115,626	131,053	156,549	156,109
Commodity contracts dealing	52313	2,945	3,858	4,385	4,704	5,335
Commodity contracts brokerage	52314	3,053	(S)	3,252	4,122	5,770
Other financial investment activities [1]	5239x	88,947	99,086	113,633	131,999	148,306
Portfolio management	52392	75,349	80,872	90,675	104,718	118,901
Investment advice	52393	13,598	18,214	22,958	27,281	29,405

S Estimate does not meet publication standards. [1] Excludes NAICS 52391 (miscellaneous intermediation) and NAICS 52399 (all other financial investment activities).

Source: U.S. Census Bureau, "Service Annual Survey: 2007" (published March 2009); <http://www.census.gov/services/>.

Table 1182. **Securities Industry—Financial Summary: 1990 to 2007**

[In billions of dollars, except as indicated. (71.4 represents $71,400,000,000)]

Type	1990	2000	2001	2002	2003	2004	2005	2006	2007
Number of firms	8,437	7,258	7,002	6,768	6,565	6,284	6,016	5,808	5,562
Revenues, total	71.4	349.5	280.1	221.8	219.0	242.9	332.5	458.5	496.5
Commissions	12.0	54.1	44.8	45.0	45.5	47.6	46.8	49.7	54.4
Trading/investment gains	15.7	70.8	39.0	24.2	38.8	30.7	30.7	55.2	4.1
Underwriting profits	3.7	18.7	16.9	14.7	17.2	19.1	19.9	23.6	26.5
Margin interest	3.2	24.5	13.9	6.4	5.3	7.0	13.3	23.7	32.3
Mutual fund sales	3.2	19.4	16.4	15.7	16.2	18.5	20.7	23.3	26.2
Other	33.4	161.9	149.1	115.8	96.0	120.1	201.2	282.9	353.0
Expenses, total	70.6	310.4	260.7	206.5	193.3	219.7	311.3	419.9	491.5
Interest expense	28.1	131.9	98.9	56.4	44.4	59.7	140.2	226.1	282.2
Compensation	22.9	95.2	83.5	74.9	77.4	83.5	88.8	103.4	106.3
Commissions/clearance paid	3.0	15.5	14.0	15.0	16.3	17.4	18.6	22.0	25.9
Other	16.6	67.8	64.2	60.3	55.1	59.2	63.6	68.4	77.0
Net income, pretax	0.8	39.1	19.4	15.3	25.7	23.2	21.2	38.6	5.1
Pre-tax profit margin (percent)	1.1	11.2	6.9	6.9	11.7	9.5	6.4	8.4	1.0
Pre-tax return on equity (percent). . .	2.2	31.1	13.8	10.7	17.6	15.0	13.1	22.1	2.7
Assets.	657	2,866	3,371	3,261	3,980	4,831	5,215	6,222	6,777
Liabilities	623	2,728	3,227	3,119	3,831	4,671	5,051	6,037	6,591
Ownership equity	34	138	144	142	149	160	164	185	186

Source: U.S. Securities and Exchange Commission, "Select SEC and Market Data Fiscal 2008"; <http://www.sec.gov/about/secstats2008.pdf>.

Banking, Finance, and Insurance 735

Table 1183. Life Insurance in Force and Purchases in the United States— Summary: 1990 to 2007

[As of December 31 or calendar year, as applicable (389 represents 389,000,000). Covers life insurance with life insurance companies only. Represents all life insurance in force on lives of U.S. residents whether issued by U.S. or foreign companies]

Year	Number of policies, total (mil.)	Life insurance in force			Life insurance purchases [2]					
		Value (bil. dol.)			Number (1,000)			Amount (bil. dol.)		
		Total [1]	Individual	Group	Total	Individual	Group	Total	Individual	Group
1990	389	9,393	5,391	3,754	28,791	14,199	14,592	1,529	1,070	459
2000	369	15,953	9,376	6,376	34,882	13,345	21,537	2,515	1,594	921
2001	377	16,290	9,346	6,765	40,095	14,059	26,036	2,773	1,600	1,172
2002	375	16,346	9,312	6,876	38,713	14,692	24,020	2,767	1,753	1,014
2003	379	17,044	9,655	7,236	35,767	13,821	21,946	2,823	1,773	1,050
2004	373	17,508	9,717	7,631	38,453	12,581	25,872	2,948	1,846	1,102
2005	373	18,399	9,970	8,263	34,519	11,407	23,112	2,836	1,796	1,040
2006	375	19,112	10,057	8,906	29,287	10,908	18,378	2,835	1,813	1,022
2007	374	19,539	10,232	9,158	30,788	10,826	19,962	2,994	1,891	1,103

[1] Includes other types of policies not shown separately. [2] Excludes revivals, increases, dividend additions, and reinsurance acquired. Includes long-term credit insurance (life insurance on loans of more than 10 years' duration).

Source: American Council of Life Insurers, Washington, DC, *Life Insurers Fact Book*, annual (copyright).

Table 1184. U.S. Life Insurance Companies—Summary: 1990 to 2007

[As of December 31 or calendar year, as applicable (402.2 represents $402,200,000,000). Covers domestic and foreign business of U.S. companies. Beginning 2000, includes annual statement data for companies that primarily are health insurance companies. Beginning 2003 includes fraternal benefit societies]

Item	Unit	1990	2000	2001	2002	2003	2004	2005	2006	2007
U.S. companies [1]	Number .	2,195	1,269	1,341	1,284	1,227	1,179	1,119	1,072	1,009
Income	**Bil. dol.**	**402.2**	**811.5**	**724.4**	**734.0**	**727.0**	**756.8**	**779.0**	**883.6**	**950.4**
Life insurance premiums	Bil. dol . .	76.7	130.6	125.3	134.5	127.3	139.7	142.3	149.2	142.7
Annuity considerations [2]	Bil. dol . .	129.1	306.7	251.3	269.3	268.6	276.7	277.1	302.7	314.2
Health insurance premiums. . . .	Bil. dol . .	58.3	105.6	103.4	108.7	115.8	125.8	118.3	141.2	151.5
Investment and other.	Bil. dol . .	138.2	268.5	244.5	221.5	215.3	214.7	241.4	290.4	342.0
Payments under life insurance and annuity contracts	Bil. dol . .	88.4	375.2	304.9	301.3	307.1	331.7	365.7	422.7	461.0
Payments to life insurance beneficiaries.	Bil. dol . .	24.6	44.1	46.5	48.2	51.7	51.6	53.0	55.7	58.0
Surrender values under life insurance [3]	Bil. dol . .	18.0	27.2	30.7	32.9	35.9	35.5	39.2	38.5	47.7
Surrender values under annuity contracts [3, 4]	Bil. dol . .	(NA)	214.0	151.3	142.9	140.3	162.9	190.3	237.8	262.3
Policyholder dividends	Bil. dol . .	12.0	20.0	20.0	21.0	20.8	19.0	17.9	18.4	19.5
Annuity payments [4]	Bil. dol . .	32.6	68.7	55.2	55.0	57.1	61.2	63.9	71.1	72.3
Matured endowments	Bil. dol . .	0.7	0.6	0.5	0.6	0.6	0.6	0.6	0.6	0.6
Other payments	Bil. dol . .	0.6	0.6	0.6	0.6	0.7	0.9	0.7	0.6	0.6
Health insurance benefit payments.	Bil. dol . .	40.0	78.8	76.3	78.7	81.9	88.5	79.6	97.0	106.1
BALANCE SHEET										
Assets.	**Bil. dol. .**	**1,408**	**3,182**	**3,269**	**3,380**	**3,887**	**4,253**	**4,482**	**4,823**	**5,092**
Government bonds	Bil. dol . .	211	364	377	481	538	563	590	579	561
Corporate securities	Bil. dol . .	711	2,238	2,263	2,266	2,666	2,965	3,136	3,413	3,628
Percent of total assets . . .	Percent .	50	70	69	67	69	70	70	71	71
Bonds	Bil. dol . .	583	1,241	1,354	1,475	1,644	1,785	1,850	1,882	1,957
Stocks.	Bil. dol . .	128	997	909	791	1,022	1,180	1,285	1,531	1,670
Mortgages.	Bil. dol . .	270	237	244	251	269	283	295	314	336
Real estate	Bil. dol . .	43	36	32	33	31	31	33	33	35
Policy loans	Bil. dol . .	63	102	104	105	107	109	110	113	117
Other	Bil. dol . .	110	204	248	244	276	303	319	371	415
Interest earned on assets [5]	Percent .	8.89	7.05	6.31	5.38	5.03	4.80	4.90	5.35	5.71
Obligations and surplus funds [6] . .	Bil. dol . .	1,408	3,182	3,269	3,380	3,888	4,253	4,482	4,823	5,092
Policy reserves	**Bil. dol.**	**1,197**	**2,712**	**2,446**	**2,507**	**2,895**	**3,160**	**3,360**	**3,608**	**3,791**
Annuities [7]	Bil. dol . .	798	1,841	1,516	1,550	1,835	2,024	2,174	2,328	2,458
Group	Bil. dol . .	516	960	571	570	662	712	758	807	843
Individual	Bil. dol . .	282	881	945	980	1,173	1,312	1,415	1,521	1,615
Supplementary contracts [8] . .	Bil. dol . .	17	34	13	14	15	16	16	17	18
Life insurance	Bil. dol . .	349	742	816	833	921	988	1,029	1,110	1,148
Health insurance	Bil. dol . .	33	96	101	111	123	134	141	153	166
Liabilities for deposit-type contracts [9]	Bil. dol . .	18	21	338	364	405	445	456	487	517
Capital and surplus	Bil. dol . .	91	188	191	202	231	250	256	266	282

NA Not available. [1] Beginning 2000, includes life insurance companies that sell accident and health insurance. [2] Beginning 2001, excludes certain deposit-type funds from income due to codification. [3] Beginning with 2000, "surrender values" include annuity withdrawals of funds, which were not included in 1990. [4] Beginning 2001, excludes payments under deposit-type contracts. [5] Net rate. [6] Includes other obligations not shown separately. [7] Beginning 2001, excludes reserves for guaranteed interest contracts (GICs). [8] Through 2000, includes reserves for contracts with and without life contingencies; beginning 2001, includes only reserves for contracts with life contingencies. [9] Policyholder dividend accumulations for all years. Beginning 2001, also includes liabilities for guaranteed interest contracts, supplementary contracts without life contingencies, and premium and other deposits.

Source: American Council of Life Insurers, Washington, DC, *Life Insurers Fact Book*, annual (copyright).

736 Banking, Finance, and Insurance

Table 1185. **Property and Casualty Insurance—Summary: 2000 to 2007**

[In billions of dollars (305.1 represents $305,100,000,000). Minus sign (–) indicates loss]

Item	2000	2002	2003	2004	2005	2006	2007
Premiums, net written [1]	305.1	373.1	407.5	425.7	427.6	447.8	447.9
Automobile, private [2]	120.0	139.6	151.3	157.6	159.6	160.5	159.7
Automobile, commercial [2]	19.8	24.6	25.5	26.7	26.8	26.7	25.7
Homeowners' multiple peril	32.7	40.2	46.0	50.0	53.0	55.8	57.1
Commercial multiple peril	(NA)	25.4	27.4	29.1	29.7	31.9	31.3
Marine, inland and ocean	8.3	9.4	10.4	10.8	11.2	12.3	13.1
Workers' compensation	26.2	30.6	32.9	36.7	39.7	41.8	40.9
Medical malpractice	(NA)	7.4	8.8	9.1	9.7	10.4	10.0
Other liability [3]	(NA)	29.3	36.1	39.8	39.4	42.2	41.4
Reinsurance	(NA)	15.1	15.5	13.7	6.6	12.9	11.6
Losses and expenses	321.3	377.4	389.4	407.7	421.4	401.0	417.6
Underwriting gain/loss	−27.3	−28.3	−3.0	6.0	−3.7	34.5	21.4
Net investment income	42.0	39.8	38.6	40.0	49.7	52.3	54.6
Operating earnings after taxes	4.4	4.3	23.5	29.4	34.4	62.2	53.0

NA Not available.   [1] Excludes state funds. Includes other lines of insurance not shown separately.   [2] Includes premiums for automobile liability and physical damage.   [3] Coverages protecting against legal liability resulting from negligence, carelessness, or failure to act.

Source: Insurance Information Institute, New York, NY, *The III Insurance Fact Book*, annual; and *Financial Services Fact Book*, annual (copyright). Data from ISO and Highline Data LLC. See also <http://www.iii.org>.

Table 1186. **Automobile Insurance—Average Expenditures Per Insured Vehicle by State: 2000 and 2006**

[In dollars. Average expenditure equals total premiums written divided by liability car-years. A car-year is equal to 365 days of insured coverage for a single vehicle. The average expenditures for automobile insurance in a state are affected by a number of factors, including the underlying rate structure, the coverages purchased, the deductibles and limits selected, the types of vehicles insured, and the distribution of driver characteristics. The NAIC does not rank state average expenditures and does not endorse any conclusions drawn from this data]

State	2000	2006	State	2000	2006	State	2000	2006	State	2000	2006
U.S.	690	817	ID	505	577	MT	530	661	SC	620	756
			IL	652	740	NE	533	584	SD	482	554
AL	594	684	IN	570	631	NV	829	1,006	TN	592	654
AK	770	955	IA	479	536	NH	665	793	TX	678	820
AZ	792	913	KS	540	579	NJ	977	1,152	UT	620	702
AR	606	684	KY	616	739	NM	674	737	VT	568	687
CA	672	843	LA	806	1,094	NY	939	1,083	VA	576	685
CO	755	785	ME	528	634	NC	564	596	WA	722	830
CT	871	981	MD	757	949	ND	477	530	WV	680	827
DE	849	1,024	MA	946	1,042	OH	579	654	WI	545	590
DC	996	1,164	MI	702	925	OK	603	659	WY	496	639
FL	781	1,069	MN	696	753	OR	625	726			
GA	674	788	MS	654	746	PA	699	832			
HI	702	853	MO	612	673	RI	825	1,038			

Source: National Association of Insurance Commissioners (NAIC), Kansas City, MO, *Auto Insurance Database Report*, annual (copyright). Reprinted with permission of the NAIC. Further reprint or distribution strictly prohibited without prior written permission of the NAIC.

Table 1187. **Renters and Homeowners Insurance—Average Premiums by State: 2006**

[In dollars. Average premium equals premiums divided by exposure per house-years. A house-year is equal to 365 days of insured coverage for a single dwelling and is the standard measurement for homeowners insurance. The NAIC does not rank state average expenditures and does not endorse any conclusions drawn from these data]

State	Renters [1]	Homeowners [2]	State	Renters [1]	Homeowners [2]	State	Renters [1]	Homeowners [2]
U.S.	188	804	KS	170	866	ND	119	742
			KY	161	637	OH	163	530
AL	223	894	LA	245	1,257	OK	230	1,018
AK	182	850	ME	145	573	OR	162	502
AZ	207	640	MD	160	721	PA	148	643
AR	217	802	MA	223	925	RI	189	919
CA	244	937	MI	164	715	SC	189	851
CO	169	813	MN	139	788	SD	120	628
CT	197	878	MS	252	998	TN	208	706
DE	159	530	MO	166	707	TX [3]	261	1,409
DC	185	1,012	MT	160	666	UT	139	494
FL	201	1,386	NE	148	783	VT	160	677
GA	215	703	NV	205	693	VA	147	662
HI	213	776	NH	157	669	WA	170	603
ID	153	477	NJ	179	726	WV	177	650
IL	168	674	NM	200	638	WI	122	490
IN	173	638	NY	220	869	WY	155	648
IA	132	596	NC	144	649			

[1] Based on the HO-4 renters insurance policy for tenants. Includes broad named-peril coverage for the personal property of tenants.   [2] Based on the HO-3 homeowner package policy for owner-occupied dwellings, 1–4 family units. Provides "all risks" coverage (except those specifically excluded in the policy) on buildings, broad named-peril coverage on personal property, and is the most common package written.   [3] The Texas Insurance Commissioner promulgates residential policy forms which are similar but not identical to the standard forms.

Source: National Association of Insurance Commissioners (NAIC), Kansas City, MO, *Dwelling Fire, Homeowners Owner-Occupied, and Homeowners Tenant and Condominium/Cooperative Unit Owners Insurance* (copyright). Reprinted with permission of the NAIC. Further reprint or distribution strictly prohibited without prior written permission of the NAIC.

Banking, Finance, and Insurance   737

Table 1188. **Real Estate and Rental and Leasing—Nonemployer Establishments and Receipts by Kind of Business: 2000 to 2006**

[1,696 represents 1,696,000. Includes only firms subject to federal income tax. Nonemployers are businesses with no paid employees. Data originate chiefly from administrative records of the Internal Revenue Service; see Appendix III. Data for 2000 based on the North American Industry Classification System (NAICS), 1997; beginning 2005, based on NAICS 2002. See text, Section 15]

Kind of business	NAICS code	Establishments (1,000)			Receipts (mil. dol.)		
		2000	2005	2006	2000	2005	2006
Real estate & rental & leasing, total . . .	53	1,696	2,442	2,421	133,398	207,688	193,105
Real estate	531	1,616	2,357	2,338	127,862	201,075	186,400
Lessors of real estate.	5311	714	869	804	86,934	117,430	105,927
Offices of real estate agents & brokers	5312	522	808	830	22,623	39,346	36,214
Activities related to real estate	5313	380	680	704	18,305	44,299	44,259
Rental & leasing services.	532	79	83	81	5,440	6,465	6,564
Automotive equipment rental & leasing	5321	19	20	20	995	1,023	1,023
Consumer goods rental	5322	17	18	18	766	837	862
General rental centers	5323	3	4	4	252	375	358
Commercial/industrial equipment rental & leasing.	5324	41	41	39	3,426	4,230	4,320
Lessors of other nonfinancial intangible assets.	533	1	2	1	96	152	141

Source: U.S. Census Bureau, "Nonemployer Statistics"; <http://www.census.gov/econ/nonemployer/>.

Table 1189. **Real Estate and Rental and Leasing—Establishments, Employees, and Payroll: 2000 and 2006**

[300.2 represents 300,200. Covers establishments with payroll. Kind-of-business classification for 2000 based on North American Industry Classification System (NAICS) 1997; data for 2006 based on NAICS 2002. See text, Section 15, Business Enterprise. Employees are for the week including March 12. Most government employees are excluded. For statement on methodology, see Appendix III]

Kind of business	NAICS code	Establishments (1,000)		Employees (1,000)		Payroll (bil. dol.)	
		2000	2006	2000	2006	2000	2006
Real estate & rental & leasing, total . . .	53	300.2	382.1	1,942	2,217	59.2	87.5
Real estate	531	234.9	313.5	1,280	1,553	40.4	64.0
Lessors of real estate.	5311	108.2	117.6	501	545	12.5	18.6
Offices of real estate agents & brokers	5312	65.1	114.0	271	377	10.6	18.6
Activities related to real estate	5313	61.6	81.8	507	631	17.3	26.8
Rental & leasing services.	532	63.2	66.3	636	634	17.2	21.2
Automotive equipment rental & leasing	5321	11.1	13.6	182	184	5.1	6.3
Passenger car rental & leasing.	53211	5.2	7.4	129	129	3.4	4.1
Truck, utility trailer & RV rental & leasing.	53212	5.8	6.3	53	55	1.7	2.2
Consumer goods rental [1]	5322	33.1	33.3	255	254	4.2	5.4
Video tape & disc rental	53223	19.6	17.8	152	137	1.6	1.7
General rental centers	5323	6.4	5.6	42	36	1.2	1.2
Commercial/industrial equipment rental & leasing.	5324	12.6	13.8	157	160	6.7	8.3
Lessors of other nonfinancial intangible assets.	533	2.1	2.3	26	29	1.6	2.3

[1] Includes other kinds of business not shown separately.

Source: U.S. Census Bureau, "County Business Patterns"; <http://www.census.gov/econ/cbp/index.html>.

Table 1190. **Rental and Leasing Services—Revenue by Kind of Business: 2000 to 2007**

[In millions of dollars (98,504 represents $98,504,000,000). Based on the North American Industry Classification System (NAICS) 2002; see text, Section 15. Covers taxable and tax-exempt employer firms. Estimates have been adjusted using the results of the 2002 Economic Census. Based on Service Annual Survey; see Appendix III]

Kind of business	2002 NAICS code	2000	2003	2004	2005	2006	2007
Rental & leasing services	532	98,504	96,387	102,863	108,612	118,507	123,041
Automotive equipment rental & leasing	5321	37,231	37,007	41,126	43,737	46,872	48,063
Passenger car rental & leasing	53211	22,949	23,007	24,793	25,925	27,649	28,578
Truck, utility trailer, & RV rental & leasing. . .	53212	14,282	14,000	16,333	17,812	19,223	19,485
Consumer goods rental [1]	5322	20,159	21,923	23,412	22,747	23,245	23,844
Video tape & disc rental	53223	9,569	10,053	10,604	9,507	9,844	10,069
General rental centers.	5323	3,636	3,611	3,710	3,784	4,104	4,417
Commercial/industrial equip. rental & leasing. .	5324	37,478	33,846	34,615	38,344	44,286	46,717

[1] Includes other kinds of business not shown separately.

Source: U.S. Census Bureau, "Service Annual Survey: 2007" (published March 2009); <http://www.census.gov/services/>.

Section 26
Arts, Recreation, and Travel

This section presents data on the arts, entertainment, and recreation economic sector of the economy, and personal recreational activities, the arts and humanities, and domestic and foreign travel.

Arts, Entertainment, and Recreation Industry—The U.S. Census Bureau's *Service Annual Survey, Arts, Entertainment, and Recreation Sector,* provides estimates of operation revenue of taxable firms and revenues and expenses of firms exempt from federal taxes for industries in this sector of the economy. Data beginning 1998 are based on the North American Industry Classification System (NAICS). Most establishments were previously classified in the Standard Industrial Classification (SIC) in services, some in retail trade. The following URL contains detailed information about NAICS and provides a comparison of the SIC and NAICS <http://www.census.gov/eos/www /naics/>. See also the text in Section 15, Business Enterprise.

The Economic Census, conducted every 5 years, for the years ending "2" and "7," provides information on the number of establishments, receipts, payroll, and paid employees for the U.S. and various geographic levels.

Recreation and leisure activities— Data on the participation in various recreation and leisure time activities are based on several sample surveys. Data on the public's involvement with arts events and activities are published by the National Endowment for Arts (NEA). The NEA's Survey of Public Participation in the Arts remains the largest periodic study of arts participation in the United States. The most recent data are from the 2008 survey. Data on participation in fishing,

hunting, and other forms of wildlife-associated recreation are published periodically by the U.S. Department of Interior, Fish and Wildlife Service. The most recent data are from the 2006 survey. Data on participation in various sports recreation activities are published by the National Sporting Goods Association. Mediamark, Inc. also conducts periodic surveys on sports and leisure activities, as well as other topics.

Parks and recreation—The Department of the Interior has responsibility for administering the national parks. The National Park Service publishes information on visits to national park areas in its annual report, *National Park Statistical Abstract. The National Parks: Index (year)* is an annual report which contains brief descriptions, with acreages and visits for each area administered by the service, plus certain "related" areas. This information can be found at: <http://www.nature .nps.gov/stats>. Statistics for state parks are compiled by the National Association of State Park Directors.

Travel—Statistics on arrivals and departures to the United States are reported by the International Trade Administration (ITA), Office of Travel & Tourism Industries (OTTI). Data on domestic travel, business receipts and employment of the travel industry, and travel expenditures are published by the research department of the U.S. Travel Association. Other data on household transportation characteristics are in Section 23, Transportation.

Statistical reliability—For a discussion of statistical collection and estimation, sampling procedures, and measures of statistical reliability applicable to Census Bureau data, see Appendix III.

U.S. Census Bureau, Statistical Abstract of the United States: 2010

Table 1191. **Arts, Entertainment, and Recreation Services—Estimated Revenue: 2000 to 2007**

[In millions of dollars (127,394 represents $127,394,000,000), except percent. For taxable and tax-exempt employer firms. Except where indicated, estimates adjusted using the results of the 2002 Economic Census. Based on the Service Annual Survey, see Appendix III]

Industry	2002 NAICS code [1]	2000	2003	2004	2005	2006	2007
Arts, entertainment, and recreation	71	127,394	149,360	158,557	166,561	180,383	191,005
Performing arts, spectator sports, and related industries.	711	51,149	60,367	62,796	65,235	71,365	75,853
Performing arts companies	7111	10,746	11,070	11,554	11,978	11,987	11,734
Spectator sports	7112	19,339	22,445	23,659	24,402	26,531	28,757
Sports teams and clubs.	711211	10,739	13,257	14,115	14,067	15,742	17,418
Racetracks	711212	6,349	6,582	7,022	7,358	7,584	7,877
Other spectator sports	711219	2,251	2,606	2,522	2,977	3,205	3,462
Promoters of performing arts, sports, and similar events	7113	10,098	12,872	13,571	14,338	17,187	18,830
Agents and managers for artists, athletes, entertainers and other public figures	7114	3,184	3,604	3,819	3,909	4,089	4,633
Independent artists, writers, and performers.	7115	7,782	10,376	10,193	10,608	11,571	11,899
Museums, historical sites, and similar institutions	712	9,350	9,082	9,688	10,256	11,967	12,978
Amusement, gambling, and recreation industries	713	66,895	79,911	86,073	91,070	97,051	102,174
Amusement parks and arcades	7131	9,441	9,930	10,561	11,181	11,365	12,050
Amusement and theme parks.	71311	8,245	8,737	9,344	9,882	9,963	10,746
Amusement arcades.	71312	1,196	1,193	1,217	1,299	1,402	1,304
Gambling industries	7132	14,621	22,370	25,698	28,094	31,127	33,021
Casinos (except casino hotels)	71321	9,592	14,601	16,664	18,010	19,746	20,485
Other gambling industries	71329	5,029	7,769	9,034	10,084	11,381	12,536
Other amusement and recreation industries	7139	42,833	47,611	49,814	51,795	54,559	57,103
Golf courses and country clubs.	71391	16,692	16,987	17,880	18,533	19,082	19,279
Skiing facilities.	71392	1,551	1,839	1,980	2,049	2,234	2,414
Marinas	71393	3,379	3,382	3,393	3,663	4,018	4,187
Fitness and recreational sports centers	71394	12,543	16,130	16,839	17,620	18,519	19,507
Bowling centers.	71395	2,762	3,293	3,505	3,427	3,347	3,738
All other amusement and recreation	71399	5,906	5,980	6,217	6,503	7,359	7,978

[1] Based on the North American Industry Classification System (NAICS) 2002; see text, this section and Section 15.

Source: U.S. Census Bureau, "Service Annual Survey, Arts, Entertainment, and Recreation Services" (published March 2009); <http://www.census.gov/econ/www/servmenu.html>.

Table 1192. **Arts, Entertainment, and Recreation—Nonemployer Establishments and Receipts by Kind of Business (NAICS Basis): 2000 to 2006**

[(781.7 represents 781,700). Includes only firms subject to federal income tax. Nonemployers are businesses with no paid employees]

Kind of business	2002 NAICS code [1]	Establishments (1,000)			Receipts (mil. dol.)		
		2000	2005	2006	2000	2005	2006
Arts, entertainment, and recreation	71	781.7	972.5	1,001.8	17,713	23,704	24,782
Performing arts, spectator sports, and related industries	711	645.4	828.8	855.7	13,008	17,741	18,733
Performing arts companies	7111	19.3	30.0	41.7	576	827	944
Spectator sports	7112	67.3	91.6	95.6	1,481	1,877	1,993
Promoters of performing arts, sports, and similar events	7113	23.1	35.5	37.8	851	1,434	1,475
Agents/managers for artists, athletes, and other public figures	7114	27.1	32.6	33.7	857	1,183	1,253
Independent artists, writers, and performers	7115	508.6	639.1	646.9	9,244	12,419	13,067
Museums, historical sites, and similar institutions.	712	3.6	5.6	5.9	52	91	88
Amusement, gambling, and recreation industries	713	132.7	138.1	140.1	4,653	5,873	5,961
Amusement parks and arcades	7131	5.4	5.4	5.6	291	346	337
Gambling industries.	7132	5.9	8.4	8.8	532	1,064	1,122
Other amusement and recreation services. . .	7139	121.3	124.2	125.6	3,830	4,463	4,503

[1] Based on the 2002 North American Industry Classification System (NAICS); see text, Section 15.

Source: U.S. Census Bureau, "Nonemployer Statistics"; <http://www.census.gov/epcd/nonemployer/>.

Table 1193. Arts, Entertainment, and Recreation—Establishments, Employees, and Payroll by Kind of Business (NAICS Basis): 2001 and 2006

[(1,780.4 represents 1,780,400). For establishments with payroll. See Appendix III]

Kind of business	2002 NAICS [1] code	Establishments 2001	Establishments 2006	Paid employees [2] (1,000) 2001	Paid employees [2] (1,000) 2006	Annual payroll (mil. dol.) 2001	Annual payroll (mil. dol.) 2006
Arts, entertainment, & recreation	71	105,961	123,048	1,780.4	1,973.7	46,133	56,839
Performing arts, spectator sports	711	34,840	42,430	361.7	424.9	20,393	26,636
Performing arts companies	7111	9,327	9,195	127.8	133.5	3,344	3,913
Theater companies & dinner theaters	71111	3,354	3,524	66.4	74.1	1,517	1,976
Dance companies	71112	604	620	10.9	9.3	218	225
Musical groups & artists	71113	4,562	4,522	43.0	43.3	1,349	1,470
Other performing arts companies	71119	807	529	7.5	6.8	260	243
Spectator sports	7112	4,584	4,564	104.4	120.3	9,955	13,298
Sports teams & clubs	711211	735	818	40.1	50.9	8,268	11,148
Racetracks	711212	881	741	45.2	48.3	989	1,229
Other spectator sports	711219	2,968	3,005	19.1	21.1	697	922
Promoters of performing arts, sports, and similar events	7113	4,456	5,779	43.0	107.1	1,349	2,665
Promoters of performing arts, sports, & similar events with facilities	71131	1,184	2,089	48.3	80.1	942	1,409
Promoters of performing arts, sports, & similar events without facilities	71132	3,272	3,690	25.6	27.0	1,068	1,256
Agents/managers for artists, athletes, and other public figures	7114	3,107	3,494	16.2	16.4	1,139	1,579
Independent artists, writers, & performers	7115	13,366	19,398	39.4	47.6	3,946	5,181
Museums, historical sites, & similar institutions . . .	712	6,032	7,089	113.5	123.2	2,781	3,360
Museums	71211	4,140	4,787	76.8	80.7	1,907	2,235
Historical sites	71212	893	979	8.4	9.4	154	208
Zoos & botanical gardens	71213	459	611	21.8	26.5	558	742
Nature parks & other similar institutions	71219	540	712	6.5	6.6	162	174
Amusement, gambling, & recreation industries . . .	713	65,089	73,529	1,305.1	1,425.6	22,958	26,843
Amusement parks & arcades	7131	2,783	2,927	119.3	136.4	2,314	2,662
Amusement & theme parks	71311	700	579	98.8	108.7	2,044	2,310
Amusement arcades	71312	2,083	2,348	20.5	27.6	270	352
Gambling industries	7132	2,175	2,600	215.6	196.0	5,400	5,540
Casinos (except casino hotels)	71321	562	468	156.2	133.6	4,007	3,861
Other gambling industries	71329	1,613	2,132	59.5	62.3	1,392	1,679
Other amusement & recreation services	7139	60,131	68,002	970.1	1,093.2	15,244	18,642
Golf courses & country clubs	71391	11,861	11,870	295.1	309.4	6,472	7,839
Skiing facilities	71392	404	381	63.9	75.3	495	624
Marinas	71393	4,121	4,025	24.7	28.3	675	894
Fitness & recreational sports centers	71394	24,068	32,432	399.4	507.9	4,844	6,478
Bowling centers	71395	5,059	4,615	84.6	81.3	889	1,000
All other amusement & recreation industries	71399	14,618	14,679	102.5	91.0	1,870	1,807

[1] North American Industry Classification System code (NAICS); see text, this section and Section 15.   [2] For employees on the payroll for the period including March 12.

Source: U.S. Census Bureau, "County Business Patterns." See <http://www.census.gov/econ/cbp/index.html>.

Table 1194. Personal Consumption Expenditures for Recreation: 1990 to 2007

[In billions of dollars (290.2 represents $290,200,000,000), except percent. Represents market value of purchases of goods and services by individuals and nonprofit institutions]

Type of product or service	1990	2000	2003	2004	2005	2006	2007
Total recreation expenditures	290.2	585.7	659.9	707.8	745.3	796.7	841.0
Percent of total personal consumption [1]	7.6	8.7	8.6	8.7	8.6	8.7	8.7
Books and maps	16.2	33.7	38.7	40.4	41.8	44.0	46.3
Magazines, newspapers, and sheet music	21.6	35.0	36.3	39.4	42.1	45.4	48.6
Nondurable toys and sport supplies	32.8	56.6	60.6	63.3	66.2	70.6	74.3
Wheel goods, sports, and photographic equipment [2]	29.7	57.6	65.6	71.3	75.7	82.2	87.0
Video and audio products, computer equipment, and musical instruments	53.0	116.6	123.1	133.3	142.4	154.1	160.8
Video and audio goods, including musical instruments	44.1	72.8	76.5	81.7	86.8	95.0	97.5
Computers, peripherals, and software	8.9	43.8	46.6	51.6	55.5	59.1	63.3
Radio and television repair	3.2	4.2	4.1	4.6	4.6	4.8	5.0
Flowers, seeds, and potted plants	10.9	18.0	17.9	18.3	19.3	20.3	20.6
Admissions to specified spectator amusements	15.1	30.4	36.0	37.6	38.4	41.2	43.6
Motion picture theaters	5.1	8.6	9.9	9.9	9.1	9.4	9.7
Legitimate theaters and opera, and entertainments of nonprofit institutions [3]	5.2	10.3	11.9	12.5	13.2	14.3	15.5
Spectator sports [4]	4.8	11.5	14.3	15.3	16.1	17.4	18.5
Clubs and fraternal organizations except insurance [5]	13.5	19.0	22.2	22.3	23.2	25.6	26.3
Commercial participant amusements [6]	25.2	75.8	91.2	100.9	107.1	114.6	120.0
Parimutuel net receipts	3.5	5.0	5.2	5.7	6.2	6.0	6.3
Other [7]	65.4	133.9	158.9	170.8	178.3	188.0	202.3

[1] See Table 661.   [2] Includes boats and pleasure aircraft.   [3] Except athletic.   [4] Consists of admissions to professional and amateur athletic events and to racetracks, including horse, dog, and auto.   [5] Consists of current expenditures (including consumption of fixed capital) of nonprofit clubs and fraternal organizations and dues and fees paid to proprietary clubs. [6] Consists of billiard parlors; bowling alleys; dancing, riding, shooting, skating, and swimming places; amusement devices and parks; golf courses; sightseeing buses and guides; private flying operations; casino gambling; and other commercial participant amusements.   [7] Consists of net receipts of lotteries and expenditures for purchases of pets and pet care services, cable TV, film processing, photographic studios, sporting and recreation camps, video cassette rentals, and recreational services, not elsewhere classified.

Source: U.S. Bureau of Economic Analysis, *Survey of Current Business*, August 2008. See also <http://www.bea.gov /national/nipaweb/SelectTable.asp?Selected=N\>.

Arts, Recreation, and Travel   741

Table 1195. **Expenditures Per Consumer Unit for Entertainment and Reading: 1985 to 2007**

[Data are annual averages. In dollars, except as indicated. Based on Consumer Expenditure Survey (CE); see text in Section 13, for description of survey. See also headnote, Table 670. For composition of regions, see map, inside front cover]

Year and characteristic	Entertainment and reading		Entertainment				Reading
	Total	Percent of total expenditures	Total	Fees and admissions	Audio and visual equipment, and services	Other entertainment supplies, equipment and services [1]	
1985	1,311	5.6	1,170	320	371	479	141
1990	1,575	5.6	1,422	371	454	597	153
1992	1,662	5.6	1,500	379	492	629	162
1993	1,792	5.8	1,626	414	590	621	166
1994	1,732	5.5	1,567	439	533	595	165
1995	1,775	5.5	1,612	433	542	637	163
1996	1,993	5.9	1,834	459	561	814	159
1997	1,977	5.7	1,813	471	577	766	164
1998	1,907	5.4	1,746	449	535	762	161
1999	2,050	5.5	1,891	459	608	824	159
2000	2,009	5.3	1,863	515	622	727	146
2001	2,094	5.3	1,953	526	660	767	141
2002	2,218	5.5	2,079	542	692	845	139
2003	2,187	5.4	2,060	494	730	835	127
2004	2,348	5.4	2,218	528	788	903	130
2005	2,514	5.4	2,388	588	888	912	126
2006	2,493	5.2	2,376	606	906	863	117
2007, total	2,816	5.7	2,698	658	987	1,053	118
Age of reference person:							
Under 25 years old	1,499	5.1	1,448	290	726	432	51
25 to 34 years old	2,534	5.3	2,462	500	1,034	928	72
35 to 44 years old	3,658	6.2	3,551	967	1,196	1,388	107
45 to 54 years old	3,300	5.7	3,163	823	1,126	1,215	137
55 to 64 years old	2,881	5.4	2,730	645	965	1,121	151
65 to 74 years old	2,787	6.6	2,636	575	812	1,250	151
75 years old and over	1,391	4.6	1,255	318	570	367	136
Hispanic or Latino Origin of reference person:							
Hispanic	1,712	3.3	1,674	316	815	544	38
Non-Hispanic	2,959	8.2	2,831	703	1,010	1,119	128
Race of reference person:							
White, Asian, and all other races.	3,017	7.3	2,890	719	1,021	1,175	127
Black	1,334	2.6	1,288	212	753	322	46
Region of residence:							
Northeast	2,946	5.7	2,811	803	1,010	998	135
Midwest	2,711	5.6	2,585	630	913	1,042	126
South	2,409	5.3	2,320	476	971	874	89
West	3,459	6.1	3,319	857	1,068	1,394	140
Size of consumer unit:							
One person	1,510	5.2	1,413	323	642	448	97
Two or more persons	3,365	5.8	3,238	799	1,132	1,306	127
Two persons	3,219	6.1	3,079	708	1,032	1,339	140
Three persons	3,123	5.4	3,009	646	1,141	1,221	114
Four persons	3,916	5.9	3,785	1,079	1,296	1,410	131
Five persons or more	3,467	5.3	3,373	942	1,227	1,204	94
Income before taxes:							
Quintiles of income:							
Lowest 20 percent	980	4.8	926	112	499	305	54
Second 20 percent	1,576	5.1	1,505	231	706	569	71
Third 20 percent	2,244	5.3	2,150	393	913	844	94
Fourth 20 percent	3,118	5.4	2,982	705	1,131	1,147	136
Highest 20 percent	6,155	6.4	5,921	1,838	1,684	2,400	234
Education:							
Less than a high school graduate	1,335	4.4	1,295	131	638	526	40
High school graduate	2,046	5.2	1,966	288	854	823	80
High school graduate with some college	2,581	5.6	2,481	551	975	955	100
Associate's degree	3,067	5.8	2,957	622	1,091	1,245	110
Bachelor's degree	3,903	5.9	3,727	1,234	1,241	1,252	176
Master's, professional, doctoral degree	5,137	6.5	4,873	1,544	1,297	2,032	264

[1] Other equipment and services include pets, toys, and playground equipment; sports, exercise, and photographic equipment; and recreational vehicles.

Source: U.S. Bureau of Labor Statistics, *Consumer Expenditure Survey,* "Consumer Expenditures in 2007," Report 1016; April 2009. See also <http://www.bls.gov/cex/home.htm#tables>.

Table 1196. **Performing Arts—Selected Data: 1990 to 2007**

[**Sales, receipts, and expenditures in millions of dollars (282 represents $282,000,000).** For season ending in year shown, except as indicated]

Item	1990	1995	2000	2001	2002	2003	2004	2005	2006	2007
Legitimate theater: [1]										
Broadway shows:										
New productions	40	33	37	28	37	36	39	39	39	35
Attendance (mil.)	8.0	9.0	11.4	11.9	11.0	11.4	11.6	11.5	12.0	12.3
Playing weeks [2,3]	1,070	1,120	1,464	1,484	1,434	1,544	1,451	1,494	1,501	1,509
Gross ticket sales	282	406	603	666	643	721	771	769	862	939
Broadway road tours: [4]										
Attendance (mil.)	11.1	15.6	11.7	11.0	11.7	12.4	12.9	18.2	17.1	16.7
Playing weeks	944	1,242	888	823	863	877	1,060	1,389	1,377	1,400
Gross ticket sales	367	701	572	541	593	642	714	934	915	950
Nonprofit professional theatres: [5]										
Companies reporting [6]	185	215	262	363	1,146	1,274	1,477	1,490	1,893	1,910
Gross income	308	444	791	961	1,436	1,481	1,571	1,647	1,791	1,881
Earned income	188	281	466	555	761	787	856	845	923	962
Contributed income	119	163	325	407	675	694	715	802	868	919
Gross expenses	306	445	708	924	1,405	1,476	1,464	1,530	1,667	1,742
Productions	2,265	2,646	3,241	4,787	10,000	13,000	11,000	12,000	14,000	17,000
Performances	46,131	56,608	66,123	81,828	157,000	170,000	169,000	169,000	172,000	197,000
Total attendance (mil.)	15.2	18.6	22.0	21.1	32.2	34.3	32.1	32.5	30.5	31.0
OPERA America professional member companies: [7]										
Number of companies reporting [8] . . .	98	88	98	99	86	91	95	93	94	97
Expenses [8]	321	435	637	685	684	692	678	742	752	872
Performances [9]	2,336	2,120	2,153	2,031	1,824.0	1,741	1,946	1,893	1,851	1,961
Total attendance (mil.) [9,10] . . .	7.5	4.1	6.7	5.9	4.9	5.8	5.1	5	5.3	5.3
Main season attendance (mil.) [9,11] . .	4.1	3.9	4.3	3.8	3.2	3.1	3.4	3.3	3.4	3.6
Symphony orchestras: [12]										
Concerts	18,931	29,328	33,154	36,437	37,118	38,182	37,263	37,196	36,731	(NA)
Attendance (mil.)	24.7	30.9	31.7	31.5	30.3	27.8	27.7	26.5	29.1	(NA)
Gross revenue	378	536	734	775	764	781	827	812	945	(NA)
Operating expenses	622	859	1,126	1,286	1,312	1,315	1,483	1,513	1,603	(NA)
Support	258	351	521	560	580	576	639	626	713	(NA)

NA Not available.   [1] Source: The Broadway League, New York, NY. For season ending in year shown.   [2] All shows (new productions and holdovers from previous seasons).   [3] Eight performances constitute one playing week.   [4] North American Tours include U.S. and Canadian companies.   [5] Source: Theatre Communications Group, New York, NY. For years ending on or prior to Aug. 31.   [6] Beginning in 2002, nonprofit theatre data is based on survey responses and extrapolated data from IRS Form 990.   [7] Source: OPERA America, New York, NY. For years ending on or prior to Aug 31.   [8] U.S. companies.   [9] Prior to 1993, and for 1999, U.S. and Canadian companies; 1993 to 1998 and 2000 to 2006, U.S. companies only.   [10] Includes educational performances, outreach, etc.   [11] For paid performances.   [12] Source: League of American Orchestras, New York, NY. For years ending Aug. 31. Prior to 1995, represents 254 U.S. orchestras; beginning 1995, represents all U.S. orchestras, excluding college/university and youth orchestras. Also, beginning 1995, data based on 1,200 orchestras.

Source: Compiled from sources listed in footnotes. See also <http://www.livebroadway.com>; <http://www.tcg.org>; <http://www.operaamerica.org/>; <http://www.americanorchestras.org/

Table 1197. **Arts and Humanities—Selected Federal Aid Programs: 1990 to 2007**

[**In millions of dollars (170.8 represents $170,800,000), except as indicated.** For fiscal year ending September 30]

Type of fund and program	1990	1995	2000	2002	2003	2004	2005	2006	2007
National Endowment for the Arts:									
Funds available [1]	170.8	152.1	85.2	100.5	101.0	105.5	108.8	112.8	111.7
Program appropriation [2]	152.3	109.0	79.6	95.8	95.2	99.3	99.5	100.7	100.3
Grants awarded (number) [3]	4,252	3,685	1,906	2,147	1,885	2,150	2,161	2,293	2,158
Funds obligated [4,5]	157.6	147.9	83.5	98.6	99.3	102.6	104.4	107.0	106.5
National Endowment for the Humanities:									
Funds available [1]	140.6	152.3	102.6	110.1	111.6	127.1	119.8	121.5	122.3
Program appropriation	114.2	125.7	82.7	89.9	89.3	98.7	99.9	102.2	102.2
Matching funds [6]	26.3	25.7	15.1	16.1	16.0	15.9	15.9	15.2	15.2
Grants awarded (number)	2,195	1,871	1,230	1,252	963	1,246	1,174	1,282	1,091
Funds obligated [4]	141.0	151.8	100.0	106.1	100.1	125.1	117.8	120.3	121.1
Education programs	16.3	19.2	13.0	12.1	11.3	17.4	14.6	14.4	16.6
State programs	29.6	32.0	30.6	32.8	33.0	36.3	36.9	38.7	38.8
Research grants	22.5	22.2	6.9	7.0	7.9	8.4	7.1	8.7	9.0
Fellowship program	15.3	16.5	6.1	7.7	6.9	8.1	8.9	7.2	6.8
Challenge [7]	14.6	13.8	10.8	13.4	8.3	12.6	12.7	10.5	10.3
Public programs	25.4	25.8	11.8	13.2	12.7	18.3	14.4	15.5	13.8
Preservation and access	17.5	22.2	20.7	19.8	20.7	23.7	22.4	24.5	23.9

[1] Includes other program funds (nonfederal gifts, interagency transfers, and unobligated balances from prior years) not shown separately. Excludes administrative funds.   [2] FY1990 and FY1995 include Regular Program Funds, Treasury Funds, Challenge Grant Funds, and Policy, Planning, and Research Funds. FY2000 includes Regular Program Funds and Matching Grant Funds.   [3] Excludes cooperative agreements and interagency agreements.   [4] Includes obligations for new grants, supplemental awards on previous years' grants, cooperative agreements, and interagency agreements.   [5] Beginning with 1997 data, the grantmaking structure changed from discipline-based categories to thematic ones.   [6] Represents federal funds obligated only upon receipt or certification by endowment of matching nonfederal gifts.   [7] Program designed to stimulate new sources and higher levels of giving to institutions for the purpose of guaranteeing long-term stability and financial independence. Program usually requires a match of at least 3 private dollars to each federal dollar. Funds for challenge grants are not allocated by program area because they are awarded on a grant-by-grant basis.

Source: U.S. National Endowment for the Arts, *Annual Report* and U.S. National Endowment for the Humanities, *Annual Report*. See also <http://arts.endow.gov/> and <http://www.neh.gov/>.

Arts, Recreation, and Travel   743

Table 1198. Budgets for Selected U.S. Federal and Quasi-Governmental Organizations Funding Arts and Culture: 2004 and 2006

[In millions of dollars (489 represents $489,000,000). Independent of the Arts Endowment and its state and regional partners, other public agencies also support arts and culture, along with legislative earmarks]

Organization	2004	2006	Organization	2004	2006
Smithsonian Institution [1].............	489	517	Department of Education (Arts in Education		
Corporation for Public Broadcasting........	377	460	Model Development Program)...........	10	13
Institute of Museum and Library Services....	262	247	Commission of Fine Arts..............	8	2
National Endowment for the Humanities.....	135	142	National Capital Planning Commission......	8	8
National Endowment for the Arts..........	121	124	General Services Administration (Art-in-		
National Gallery of Art...............	88	95	architecture Program)	5	7
Department of Interior (Save America's			Advisory Council on Historic Preservation....	4	5
Treasures).....................	30	28	Department of State (Bureau of Education and		
Kennedy Center for the Performing Arts.....	17	18	Cultural Affairs' culturalexchanges,		
			presentations, and diplomacy)..........	(NA)	5

NA Not available.   [1] Exclusive of buildings and facilities capital.

Source: National Endowment for the Arts, *How the United States Funds the Arts. Other Public Support for the Arts and Culture.* See also <http://www.nea.gov/pub/how.pdf>.

Table 1199. Total State Arts Agency Legislative Appropriations: 2008 to 2009

[In thousands of dollars (354,746 represents 354,746,000. For fiscal year ending September 30. The National Assembly of State Arts Agencies (NASAA) is the membership organization of the nations' state and jurisdictional arts agencies. Legislative appropriations include funds designated to the state arts agency by state legislatures. These include line items, which are not controlled by the agency but passed through to designated entities. State arts agencies also receive monies from other sources including other state funds, the federal government (primarily the National Endowment for the Arts), private funds, and legislative earmarks. Minus (–) sign indicates decrease in spending]

State	Legislative appropriation including line items		Per- cent change 2008 to 2009	State	Legislative appropriation including line items		Per- cent change 2008 to 2009	State	Legislative appropriation including line items		Per- cent change 2008 to 2009
	2008	2009	2009		2008	2009	2009		2008	2009	2009
U.S..	354,746	343,117	–3.3	KY...	4,183	3,552	–15.1	OH...	11,266	10,681	–5.2
AL...	5,824	5,470	–6.1	LA...	6,715	7,259	8.1	OK...	5,151	5,151	–
AK...	610	668	9.6	ME...	795	747	–6.1	OR...	2,115	2,115	–
AZ...	2,012	1,888	–6.2	MD...	15,197	14,183	–6.7	PA...	15,225	14,578	–4.2
AR...	1,566	1,597	2.0	MA...	12,298	12,659	2.9	RI...	2,504	2,095	–16.3
CA...	4,015	4,286	6.7	MI...	7,488	7,567	1.1	SC...	5,445	4,070	–25.3
CO...	1,531	1,600	4.5	MN...	10,215	10,227	0.1	SD...	636	644	1.2
CT...	9,880	9,442	–4.4	MS...	1,856	1,907	2.7	TN...	7,262	8,084	11.3
DE...	2,058	1,971	–4.2	MO...	10,665	14,545	36.4	TX...	3,481	3,688	6.0
DC...	9,530	13,227	38.8	MT...	544	459	–15.7	UT...	4,342	3,657	–15.8
FL...	15,091	7,160	–52.6	NE...	1,468	1,480	0.8	VT...	546	532	–2.6
GA...	4,189	3,781	–9.7	NV...	1,913	1,691	–11.6	VA...	6,213	5,263	–15.3
HI...	7,661	6,596	–13.9	NH...	840	780	–7.2	WA...	2,565	2,555	–0.4
ID...	957	951	–0.6	NJ...	28,498	22,134	–22.3	WV..	2,572	2,795	8.7
IL...	15,205	15,959	5.0	NM...	2,250	2,513	11.7	WI...	2,470	2,470	–
IN...	3,976	3,968	–0.2	NY...	49,810	49,810	–	WY..	705	1,254	77.7
IA...	1,246	1,261	1.2	NC...	10,514	10,685	1.6				
KS...	1,659	1,734	4.5	ND...	585	585	–				

– Represents zero.

Source: National Assembly of State Arts Agencies, *Legislative Appropriations Annual Survey,* February 2009. See also <http://www.nasaa-arts.org/nasaanews/nn_contents.shtml>.

Table 1200. Personal Participation in Various Arts or Creative Activities: 2008

[In percent, except as indicated (224.8 represents 224,800,000). For persons 18 years old and over. Represents participation at least once in the prior 12 months]

Item	Adult popu- lation (mil.)	Classical music [1]	Paint -ing [2]	Pottery	Sewing [3]	Photo- graphy	Creative writing	Pur- chased art [4]	Choir/ chorale
Total..............	224.8	3.1	9.0	6.0	13.1	14.7	6.9	28.7	5.2
Sex:									
Male...............	108.5	3.0	7.1	4.5	2.3	13.3	6.2	29.6	3.9
Female..............	116.3	3.2	10.7	7.4	23.2	16.1	7.5	27.9	6.3
Race and ethnicity:									
White alone..........	154.5	3.5	9.4	6.9	15.5	16.1	7.0	29.6	4.9
African American alone ...	25.6	2.0	6.8	3.5	7.6	10.0	7.5	20.1	10.3
Other alone..........	14.3	4.7	11.9	6.1	10.2	16.2	8.2	16.5	5.5
Hispanic............	30.4	1.1	7.4	3.6	7.1	10.9	5.3	30.6	2.2
Age:									
18 to 24 years old.......	28.9	5.9	14.7	6.4	9.0	17.8	11.3	37.2	6.1
25 to 34 years old.......	39.9	3.7	11.3	6.1	10.0	16.1	9.7	38.8	3.8
35 to 44 years old.......	41.8	3.0	9.9	7.5	11.4	18.6	6.2	27.1	4.3
45 to 54 years old.......	43.9	2.5	7.4	7.0	15.4	14.6	6.4	28.0	6.8
55 to 64 years old.......	33.3	2.4	6.8	5.4	15.7	13.0	4.4	25.6	5.3
65 to 74 years old.......	19.9	1.8	5.0	4.1	17.7	10.4	5.2	28.7	6.2
75 years old and older....	17.1	1.4	4.4	2.1	15.4	5.5	3.1	14.2	3.6

[1] Of those who reported playing a musical instrument in the last 12 months.   [2] Includes painting, drawing, sculpture, and printmaking.   [3] Includes weaving, crocheting, quilting, needlepoint, and sewing.   [4] Of those who reported owning original art.

Source: U.S. National Endowment for the Arts, 2008 Survey of Public Participation in the Arts; <http://www.nea.gov/research/index.html>.

744   Arts, Recreation, and Travel

Table 1201. **Attendance Participation Rates for Various Arts Activities: 2008**

[In percent, except as indicated (224.8 represents 224,800,000). For persons 18 years old and over. Represents attending visiting, or reading at least once in the prior twelve months. Excludes elementary and high school performances]

Item	Adult population (mil.)	Jazz concert	Classical music concert	Musicals	Nonmusical plays	Art museums/ galleries	Craft/ visual art festivals	Parks/ historic sites [1]	Read Literature [2]
Total.	**224.8**	**7.8**	**9.3**	**16.7**	**9.4**	**22.7**	**24.5**	**24.9**	**50.2**
Sex: Male	108.5	7.7	8.5	14.4	8.2	21.4	20.5	24.4	41.9
Female	116.3	7.9	10.0	18.9	10.6	24.0	28.3	25.4	58.0
Race and Ethnicity:									
White alone	154.5	8.8	11.3	20.0	11.4	26.0	29.3	29.5	55.7
African American alone. . .	25.6	8.6	4.3	8.6	5.5	12.0	12.2	12.6	42.6
Other alone	14.3	4.0	8.8	13.4	6.1	23.4	17.0	20.0	43.9
Hispanic	30.4	3.9	3.8	8.1	4.3	14.5	13.7	14.0	31.9
Age:									
18 to 24 years old	28.9	7.3	6.9	14.5	8.2	22.9	17.8	21.9	51.7
25 to 34 years old	39.9	7.7	7.0	16.0	9.2	24.3	22.7	25.7	50.1
35 to 44 years old	41.8	7.2	8.9	18.2	8.9	25.7	27.2	26.8	50.8
45 to 54 years old	43.9	9.8	10.2	17.4	8.7	23.3	29.1	28.0	50.3
55 to 64 years old	33.3	9.7	11.6	19.5	12.3	24.3	28.9	27.6	53.1
65 to 74 years old	19.9	6.1	12.2	18.0	11.0	19.9	24.8	24.1	49.1
75 years old and older . . .	17.1	4.0	9.7	10.0	7.4	10.5	12.7	11.2	42.3
Education:									
Grade school	11.2	1.5	1.8	1.7	0.7	3.8	4.9	3.8	18.5
Some high school	22.1	2.4	2.3	5.2	2.8	9.2	11.2	9.1	34.3
High school graduate. . . .	68.3	3.9	3.1	8.1	4.0	9.6	17.3	14.6	39.1
Some college	61.4	8.1	9.1	17.1	9.0	23.8	27.5	28.4	56.2
College graduate.	41.3	13.7	16.7	30.1	17.5	40.6	35.8	39.4	66.6
Graduate school	20.5	17.4	27.1	37.9	24.3	52.2	41.6	48.1	71.2
Income: [3]									
Less than $10,000.	11.6	4.3	4.0	6.6	4.2	9.4	10.7	10.3	38.6
$10,000 to $19,999	19.3	3.6	3.9	6.3	3.7	10.3	13.0	11.4	38.3
$20,000 to $29,999	23.4	4.1	4.4	7.7	4.1	11.9	15.5	13.9	41.7
$30,000 to $39,999	22.6	7.1	6.8	11.0	6.7	16.3	21.8	19.9	43.2
$40,000 to $49,999	18.8	8.9	8.7	15.4	7.4	20.2	24.7	23.2	51.9
$50,000 to $74,999	40.7	7.6	9.5	15.4	8.6	23.9	26.2	26.8	50.1
$75,000 to $99,999	27.2	8.7	11.7	21.8	13.4	31.3	33.8	32.6	59.1
$100,000 to $149,999 . . .	21.4	13.4	14.8	32.0	14.1	34.4	34.5	41.2	62.1
$150,000 and over	16.0	15.4	22.8	40.1	24.2	51.9	37.5	47.3	71.2

[1] Visiting historic parks or monuments or touring buildings or neighborhoods for the historic or design value.   [2] Literature is defined as poetry, novels, short stories, or plays.   [3] Excludes results for respondents who did not report income.

Source: U.S. National Endowment for the Arts, "2008 Survey of Public Participation in the Arts"; <http://www.nea.gov/pub/research/index.html>.

Table 1202. **Participation in Various Leisure Activities: 2008**

[In percent, except as indicated (224.8 represents 224,800,000). See headnote, Table 1200]

Item	Adult population (mil.)	Attendance at— Movies	Sports events	Exercise program	Participation in— Playing sports	Volunteering charity work	Gardening
Total.	**224.8**	**53.3**	**30.6**	**52.9**	**26.3**	**32.0**	**41.6**
Sex: Male.	108.5	52.7	34.9	52.1	33.2	28.9	33.6
Female	116.3	54.0	26.6	53.6	20.0	34.9	48.9
Race and Ethnicity:							
Hispanic	14.3	49.3	21.8	48.6	23.5	25.7	40.1
White alone	30.4	48.1	22.1	40.7	17.9	20.1	28.0
African American alone	154.5	55.7	34.0	57.4	29.2	35.8	47.2
Other alone	25.6	47.4	24.5	42.6	21.0	27.0	24.4
Age:							
18 to 24 years old.	28.9	74.2	37.4	57.4	42.0	27.2	15.1
25 to 34 years old.	39.9	64.5	37.3	57.5	34.9	29.4	34.8
35 to 44 years old.	41.8	59.5	36.7	59.5	32.0	37.6	43.9
45 to 54 years old.	43.9	52.6	31.3	51.8	23.9	35.7	49.1
55 to 64 years old.	33.3	46.2	25.9	51.8	17.1	33.4	52.4
65 to 74 years old.	19.9	31.7	18.2	47.6	13.3	30.2	54.5
75 years old and over	17.1	18.9	10.3	30.0	6.4	23.2	41.0
Education:							
Grade school	11.2	15.9	6.6	21.1	6.7	11.4	30.3
Some high school	22.1	37.9	17.8	35.7	19.0	17.7	29.5
High school graduate.	68.3	42.5	22.8	40.0	17.4	20.9	37.7
Some college.	61.4	60.8	33.7	58.5	29.1	35.6	43.2
College graduate	41.3	68.8	44.9	70.8	38.9	48.1	49.0
Graduate school	20.5	71.6	44.2	77.1	40.0	51.5	53.3
Income: [1]							
Less than $10,000	11.6	32.3	14.9	35.6	15.9	16.0	25.3
$10,000 to $19,999	19.3	32.4	13.4	35.3	14.5	18.8	30.4
$20,000 to $29,999	23.4	38.2	21.1	40.4	14.9	19.6	35.4
$30,000 to $39,999	22.6	48.6	22.3	46.8	23.3	29.2	37.7
$40,000 to $49,999	18.8	54.0	28.7	54.9	26.5	31.5	44.9
$50,000 to $74,999	40.7	58.5	33.3	55.6	26.0	32.2	42.8
$75,000 or more	27.2	67.5	42.2	66.2	37.0	42.0	50.2
$100,000 to $149,999	21.4	71.4	46.8	73.3	39.1	49.6	54.0
$150,000 and over	16.0	76.7	53.1	73.2	46.0	49.0	50.9

[1] Excludes results for respondents who did not report income.

Source: U.S. National Endowment for the Arts, "2008 Survey of Public Participation in the Arts"; <http://www.nea.gov/pub/research/index.html>.

U.S. Census Bureau, Statistical Abstract of the United States: 2010

Table 1203. **Adult Participation in Selected Leisure Activities by Frequency: 2008**

[In thousands (14,166 represents 14,466,000), except percent. For fall 2008. Percent is based on total projected population of 223,672,000. Based on sample and subject to sampling error; see source]

| Activity | Participated in the last 12 months [1] | | Frequency of participation | | | | | | | |
| | | | Two or more times a week | | Once a week | | Two to three times a month | | Once a month | |
	Number	Percent	Number	Percent	Number	Percent	Number	Percent	Number	Percent
Adult education courses	14,166	6.3	2,435	1.1	2,430	1.1	862	0.4	871	0.4
Attend auto shows	19,405	8.7	196	0.1	293	0.1	489	0.2	885	0.4
Attend art galleries or shows	18,669	8.4	204	0.1	236	0.1	684	0.3	2,151	1.0
Attend classical music/opera performances.	9,900	4.4	35	(Z)	117	0.1	321	0.1	1,265	0.6
Attend country music performances . . .	10,898	4.9	102	0.1	134	0.1	179	0.1	533	0.2
Attend dance performances	9,423	4.2	160	0.1	138	0.1	253	0.1	664	0.3
Attend horse races	6,277	2.8	215	0.1	71	(Z)	319	0.1	256	0.1
Attend other music performances [2] . . .	24,679	11.0	208	0.1	407	0.2	1,258	0.6	2,095	0.9
Attend rock music performances	24,278	10.9	193	0.1	226	0.1	913	0.4	1,257	0.6
Backgammon	3,948	1.8	340	0.2	431	0.2	445	0.2	279	0.1
Baking	52,228	23.4	8,947	4.0	8,048	3.6	11,991	5.4	7,473	3.3
Barbecuing	75,735	33.9	12,411	5.6	12,571	5.6	16,847	7.5	9,955	4.5
Billiards/pool	21,273	9.5	1,502	0.7	1,744	0.8	2,463	1.1	2,442	1.1
Bird watching.	14,377	6.4	5,953	2.7	1,253	0.6	1,373	0.6	1,262	0.6
Board games.	35,190	15.7	3,020	1.4	2,890	1.3	5,857	2.6	6,667	3.0
Book clubs	6,720	3.0	254	0.1	423	0.2	421	0.2	2,841	1.3
Chess	7,936	3.6	965	0.4	592	0.3	997	0.5	959	0.4
Concerts on radio.	7,966	3.6	1,349	0.6	1,339	0.6	990	0.4	791	0.4
Cooking for fun	46,205	20.7	15,977	7.1	7,156	3.2	7,688	3.4	4,307	1.9
Crossword puzzles	32,209	14.4	13,766	6.2	3,895	1.7	2,680	1.2	2,427	1.1
Dance/go dancing	20,203	9.0	1,211	0.5	2,266	1.0	2,760	1.2	2,863	1.3
Dining out	112,248	50.2	22,103	9.9	25,976	11.6	25,833	11.6	13,893	6.2
Electronic games (not TV)	20,377	9.1	6,593	3.0	2,074	0.9	2,585	1.2	1,880	0.8
Entertain friends or relatives at home. .	89,645	40.1	8,381	3.8	11,712	5.2	20,095	9.0	17,252	7.7
Fantasy sports league.	6,477	2.9	2,371	1.1	1,303	0.6	305	0.1	405	0.2
Fly kites	5,843	2.6	160	0.1	127	0.1	198	0.1	497	0.2
Furniture refinishing	6,928	3.1	174	0.1	231	0.1	325	0.2	616	0.3
Go to bars/night clubs	42,092	18.8	3,349	1.5	4,533	2.0	7,506	3.4	6,529	2.9
Go to beach	57,082	25.5	2,825	1.3	2,992	1.3	5,648	2.5	5,057	2.3
Go to live theater	27,625	12.4	411	0.2	259	0.1	1,124	0.5	2,766	1.2
Go to museums	27,874	12.5	212	0.1	320	0.1	813	0.4	2,558	1.1
Home decoration and furnishing	26,424	11.8	1,059	0.5	1,410	0.6	2,876	1.3	4,741	2.1
Karaoke	9,194	4.1	308	0.1	546	0.2	756	0.3	943	0.4
Painting, drawing	14,245	6.4	2,481	1.1	1,530	0.7	1,865	0.8	2,217	1.0
PC/Computer Games	42,884	19.2	20,182	9.0	5,278	2.4	4,254	1.9	2,656	1.2
Photo Album/scrap book	18,142	8.1	1,242	0.6	1,417	0.6	2,635	1.2	2,939	1.3
Photography	28,445	12.7	4,802	2.2	3,470	1.6	5,961	2.7	3,878	1.7
Picnic.	24,491	11.0	446	0.2	695	0.3	1,846	0.8	3,283	1.5
Play bingo.	8,861	4.0	471	0.2	1,062	0.5	493	0.2	917	0.4
Play cards.	45,677	20.4	4,998	2.2	5,504	2.5	6,254	2.8	7,669	3.4
Play musical instrument.	16,526	7.4	6,301	2.8	1,823	0.8	1,583	0.7	1,297	0.6
Reading books	91,372	40.9	48,492	21.7	9,491	4.2	7,820	3.5	6,483	2.9
Reading comic books	5,069	2.3	1,185	0.5	564	0.3	432	0.2	573	0.3
Trivia games	12,601	5.6	2,025	0.9	1,143	0.5	1,410	0.6	1,716	0.8
Video games.	28,950	12.9	9,785	4.4	3,786	1.7	3,462	1.6	2,347	1.1
Woodworking.	9,724	4.4	1,648	0.7	842	0.4	1,316	0.6	1,258	0.6
Word games	19,741	8.8	6,763	3.0	2,643	1.2	2,261	1.0	1,986	0.9
Zoo attendance	29,337	13.1	171	0.1	194	0.1	579	0.3	2,172	1.0

Z represents less than 0.05.   [1] Includes those participating less than once a month not shown separately.   [2] Excluding country and rock.

Source: Mediamark Research & Intelligence, LLC, New York, NY, *Top-line Reports* (copyright). See also <http://www.mediamark.com/mri/docs/TopLineReports.html>.

Table 1204. **Household Pet Ownership: 2006**

[Based on a sample survey of 47,000 households in 2006; For definition of mean, see source]

Item	Unit	Dogs	Cats	Birds	Horses
Total companion pet population [1]	Million	72.1	81.7	11.2	7.3
Number of households owning pets	Million	43.0	37.5	4.5	2.1
Percent of households owning companion pets [1]	Percent . . .	37.2	32.4	3.9	1.8
Average number owned per household	Number . . .	1.7	2.2	2.5	3.5
PERCENT OF HOUSEHOLDS OWNING PETS					
Annual household income:					
Under $20,000	Percent . . .	30.7	30.1	4.4	1.5
$20,000 to $34,999	Percent . . .	37.3	33.6	4.2	1.7
$35,000 to $54,999	Percent . . .	39.8	34.1	4.4	2.1
$55,000 to $84,999	Percent . . .	42.8	35.5	3.7	1.9
$85,000 and over	Percent . . .	42.1	33.3	3.7	2.3
Household size:[1]					
One person	Percent . . .	21.9	24.7	2.1	0.8
Two persons	Percent . . .	37.6	33.4	3.9	1.7
Three persons	Percent . . .	47.5	39.1	5.1	2.3
Four persons	Percent . . .	51.9	38.5	5.4	2.7
Five or more persons.	Percent . . .	54.3	40.0	6.6	3.6

[1] As of December 31, 2006.

Source: American Veterinary Medical Association, Schaumburg, IL, *U.S. Pet Ownership and Demographics Sourcebook, 2007* (copyright). See also <http://www.avma.org/>.

746   Arts, Recreation, and Travel

Table 1205. **Retail Sales and Household Participation in Lawn and Garden Activities: 2004 to 2008**

[(36,778 represents $36,778,000,000). For calendar year. Subject to sampling variability; see source]

Activity	Retail sales (mil. dol.)					Percent households engaged in activity				
	2004	2005	2006	2007	2008	2004	2005	2006	2007	2008
Total.............	36,778	35,208	34,077	35,102	36,060	75	83	74	71	70
Lawn care.............	8,887	9,657	8,558	10,754	9,638	48	54	48	48	46
Indoor houseplants........	1,495	1,464	1,156	988	1,177	39	42	35	31	31
Flower gardening..........	2,735	3,003	2,572	2,386	2,679	36	41	33	30	32
Insect control............	1,823	1,869	1,746	2,103	1,734	28	30	26	25	25
Shrub care.............	1,027	1,109	840	913	746	26	31	25	23	22
Vegetable gardening.......	1,058	1,154	1,164	1,421	1,402	22	25	22	22	23
Tree care..............	3,067	2,820	2,322	2,192	2,473	24	26	21	18	20
Landscaping............	11,346	9,078	10,893	9,874	11,712	33	31	30	27	28
Flower bulbs...........	892	945	786	811	796	26	29	22	20	20
Fruit trees.............	589	507	640	477	538	11	13	11	10	10
Container gardening.......	1,196	1,295	948	927	1,003	21	26	18	18	19
Raising transplants [1].......	258	237	257	320	220	9	11	9	7	8
Herb gardening..........	367	371	296	451	391	14	17	12	13	12
Growing berries..........	141	151	121	144	138	6	8	6	5	6
Ornamental gardening......	769	678	493	561	424	9	12	7	6	6
Water gardening	1,128	870	1,285	780	989	13	11	14	11	10

[1] Starting plants in advance of planting in ground.

Source: The National Gardening Association, Burlington, VT, *National Gardening Survey*, annual (copyright). See also <http://www.garden.org/home>.

Table 1206. **Selected Recreational Activities: 1990 to 2008**

[41 represents 41,000,000]

Activity	Unit	1990	2000	2003	2004	2005	2006	2007	2008
Softball, amateur: [1]									
Total participants [2]........	Million..	41	31	30	28	27	25	(NA)	(NA)
Youth participants.......	1,000 ..	1,100	1,370	1,351	1,356	1,447	1,459	(NA)	(NA)
Adult teams [3]...........	1,000 ..	188	155	119	132	128	127	(NA)	(NA)
Youth teams [3]...........	1,000 ..	46	81	79	80	85	86	(NA)	(NA)
Golf facilities [4]	Number.	12,846	15,489	15,899	16,057	16,052	15,990	15,970	15,979
Tennis players [5]...........	1,000 ..	21,000	22,900	24,100	24,000	24,720	24,200	25,130	26,880
Tenpin bowling [6]									
Establishments	Number.	7,611	6,247	5,811	5,761	5,818	5,566	5,498	(NA)
Membership, total [7]	1,000 ..	6,588	3,756	3,246	3,112	2,896	2,728	2,608	(NA)
Skiing: [8]									
Skier visits [9]	Million..	50.0	52.2	57.6	57.1	56.9	58.9	60.1	57.1
Operating resorts........	Number.	591	503	490	494	492	478	481	473
Motion picture screens [10].....	1,000 ..	24	37	36	37	39	39	39	(NA)
Receipts, box office	Mil. dol..	5,022	7,468	9,165	9,215	8,832	9,137	9,629	(NA)
Attendance............	Million..	1,189	1,385	1,520	1,484	1,378	1,395	1,400	(NA)
Boating: [11]									
People participating in recreational boating [12].....	Million..	67.4	67.5	63.0	63.4	57.9	60.2	66.4	70.1
Retail expenditures on boating [13]	Mil. dol..	13,731	27,065	30,283	32,953	37,317	39,493	37,416	33,624
Recreational boats in use by boat type [14]	Million..	16.0	16.8	17.2	17.4	17.7	16.8	16.9	16.9
Outboard..............	Million..	(NA)	8.3	8.4	8.4	8.5	8.3	8.3	8.3
Inboard	Million..	(NA)	1.0	1.1	1.1	1.1	1.1	1.1	1.1
Sterndrive.............	Million..	(NA)	1.6	1.6	1.7	1.7	1.6	1.7	1.7
Personal watercraft	Million..	(NA)	1.2	1.2	1.3	1.2	1.2	1.2	1.2
Sailboats	Million..	(NA)	1.6	1.6	1.6	1.6	1.6	1.6	1.6
Other................	Million..	(NA)	3.1	3.4	3.4	3.6	3.1	3.1	3.1

NA Not available. [1] Source: Amateur Softball Association, Oklahoma City, OK. [2] Amateur Softball Association teams and other amateur softball teams. [3] Amateur Softball Association teams only. [4] Source: National Golf Foundation, Jupiter, FL. [5] Source: Tennis Industry Association, Hilton Head, SC. Players for persons 12 years old and over who played at least once. 2008 data are for players 6 years old and over who played at least once. [6] Source: United States Bowling Congress, Greendale, WI. [7] Membership totals are for U.S., Canada, and for U.S. military personnel worldwide. [8] Source: National Ski Areas Association, Kottke National End of Season Survey Report (copyright). [9] Represents one person visiting a ski area for all or any part of a day or night, and includes full-and half-day, night, complimentary, adult, child, season, and other types of tickets. Data are estimated and are for the season ending in the year shown. 2007 data are preliminary. [10] Source: Motion Picture Association of America, Inc., Encino, CA. [11] Source: National Marine Manufacturers Association, Chicago, IL. (copyright). [12] People participating are now measured as adults 18 years and older. [13] Represents expenditures for new and used boats, motors and engines, accessories, safety equipment, fuel, insurance, docking, maintenance, launching, storage, repairs, and other expenses. [14] 2008 data are estimated.

Source: Compiled from sources listed in footnotes.

Arts, Recreation, and Travel 747

Table 1207. **College and Professional Football Summary: 1990 to 2008**

[35,330 represents 35,330,000. For definition of median, see Guide to Tabular Presentation]

Sport	Unit	1990	1995	2000	2004	2005	2006	2007	2008
NCAA college: [1]									
Teams.............	Number.	533	565	606	612	615	615	619	628
Attendance..........	1,000 ..	35,330	35,638	39,059	43,106	43,487	47,909	48,752	48,839
National Football League: [2]									
Teams.............	Number.	28	30	31	32	32	32	32	32
Attendance, total [3]......	1,000 ..	17,666	19,203	20,954	21,709	21,792	22,200	22,256	21,859
Regular season.......	1,000 ..	13,960	15,044	16,387	17,001	17,012	17,341	17,345	17,057
Average per game	Number.	62,321	62,682	66,078	66,409	66,455	67,738	67,755	66,629
Postseason games [4].....	1,000 ..	848	(NA)	809	789	802	776	792	807
Players' salaries: [5]									
Average.............	$1,000 .	354	584	787	1,331	1,400	1,700	1,750	1,824
Median base salary	$1,000 .	275	301	441	537	569	722	772	830

NA Not available. [1] Source: National Collegiate Athletic Assn., Indianapolis, IN (copyright); <http://www.ncaa.org/wps/portal>.
[2] Source: National Football League, New York, NY; <http://www.nfl.com/>. [3] Preseason attendance data are not shown.
[4] Includes Pro Bowl (a nonchampionship game) and Super Bowl. [5] Source: National Football League Players Association, Washington, DC; <http://www.nflpa.org/>.
Source: Compiled from sources listed in footnotes.

Table 1208. **Selected Spectator Sports: 1990 to 2008**

[55,512 represents 55,512,000]

Sport	Unit	1990	1995	2000	2004	2005	2006	2007	2008
Baseball, major leagues: [1]									
Attendance.............	1,000 ..	55,512	51,288	74,339	74,822	76,286	77,524	80,803	79,975
Regular season........	1,000 ..	54,824	50,469	72,748	73,023	74,926	76,043	79,503	78,588
Playoffs [2]..........	1,000 ..	479	533	1,314	1,625	1,191	1,218	1,083	1,167
World Series........	1,000 ..	209	286	277	174	168	225	173	219
Players' salaries: [3]									
Average............	$1,000 .	598	1,111	1,896	2,313	2,476	2,699	2,825	(NA)
Basketball: [4, 5]									
NCAA—Men's college:									
Teams.............	Number.	767	868	932	981	983	984	982	1,017
Attendance.........	1,000 ..	28,741	28,548	29,025	30,761	30,569	30,940	32,836	33,396
NCAA—Women's college:									
Teams.............	Number.	782	864	956	1,008	1,036	1,018	1,003	1,013
Attendance [6]........	1,000 ..	2,777	4,962	8,698	10,016	9,940	9,903	10,878	11,121
National Hockey League: [7]									
Regular season attendance..	1,000 ..	12,580	9,234	18,800	20,356	[8]	20,854	20,862	21,236
Playoffs attendance	1,000 ..	1,356	1,329	1,525	1,709	[8]	1,530	1,497	1,587
Professional rodeo: [9]									
Rodeos.............	Number.	754	739	688	671	662	649	592	609
Performances..........	Number.	2,159	2,217	2,081	1,982	1,940	1,884	1,733	1,861
Members............	Number.	5,693	6,894	6,255	6,247	6,127	5,892	5,528	5,825
Permit-holders (rookies)	Number.	3,290	3,835	3,249	2,990	2,701	2,468	2,186	2,233
Total prize money	Mil. dol..	18.2	24.5	32.3	35.5	36.6	36.2	40.5	39.1

[1] Source: Major League Baseball (previously, The National League of Professional Baseball Clubs), New York, NY, National League Green Book; and The American League of Professional Baseball Clubs, New York, NY, American League Red Book.
[2] Beginning 1997, two rounds of playoffs were played. Prior years had one round. [3] Source: Major League Baseball Players Association, New York, NY. [4] Season ending in year shown. [5] Source: National Collegiate Athletic Association, Indianapolis, IN (copyright). [6] For women's attendance total, excludes double-headers with men's teams. [7] For season ending in year shown. Source: National Hockey League, Montreal, Quebec. [8] In September 2004, franchise owners locked out their players upon the expiration of the collective bargaining agreement. The entire season was cancelled in February 2005. [9] Source: Professional Rodeo Cowboys Association, Colorado Springs, CO., Official Professional Rodeo Media Guide, annual (copyright).
Source: Compiled from sources listed in footnotes.

Table 1209. **Adult Attendance at Sports Events by Frequency: 2008**

[In thousands (2,124 represents 2,124,000), except percent. For fall 2008. Percent is based on total projected population of 223,672,000. Based on survey and subject to sampling error; see source]

Event	Attend one or more times a month		Attend less than once a month		Event	Attend one or more times a month		Attend less than once a month	
	Number	Percent	Number	Percent		Number	Percent	Number	Percent
Auto racing—NASCAR ..	2,124	1.0	15,052	6.7	Weekend				
Auto racing—Other.....	2,196	1.0	12,770	5.7	professional games ..	4,553	2.0	16,885	7.6
Baseball.............	8,584	3.8	25,744	11.5	Golf	2,379	1.1	11,709	5.2
Basketball:					High school sports	12,282	5.5	13,683	6.1
College games......	4,212	1.9	14,336	6.4	Horse racing:				
Professional games...	3,959	1.8	15,795	7.1	Flats, runners.......	1,262	0.6	11,176	5.0
Bowling	1,750	0.8	10,534	4.7	Trotters/harness	773	0.4	10,072	4.5
Boxing	1,118	0.5	10,053	4.5	Ice hockey	2,491	1.1	13,579	6.1
Equestrian events	950	0.4	10,539	4.7	Motorcycle racing.....	1,037	0.5	10,398	4.7
Figure skating	601	0.3	9,929	4.4	Pro beach volleyball	387	0.2	9,780	4.4
Fishing tournaments	881	0.4	10,152	4.5	Rodeo/bull riding	929	0.4	11,215	5.0
Football:					Soccer.............	3,330	1.5	11,252	5.0
College games......	6,387	2.9	17,053	7.6	Tennis	1,429	0.6	10,675	4.8
Monday night					Truck and tractor pull/				
professional games ..	2,775	1.2	11,473	5.1	mud racing	960	0.4	10,910	4.9
					Wrestling—professional..	1,289	0.6	10,270	4.6

Source: Mediamark Research & Intelligence. LLC, New York, NY, Top-line Reports (copyright). See <http://www.mediamark.com/mri/docs/TopLineReports.html>.

Table 1210. **Participation in NCAA Sports by Sex: 2007 to 2008**

[For the academic year]

Sport	Males			Females		
	Teams	Athletes	Average squad	Teams	Athletes	Average squad
Total [1]	**8,448**	**240,261**	**(X)**	**9,469**	**178,084**	**(X)**
Baseball	906	30,386	33.5	(X)	(X)	(X)
Basketball	1,031	17,081	16.6	1,057	15,307	14.5
Bowling [2]	–	–	(NA)	52	462	8.9
Cross country	912	12,478	13.7	988	13,491	13.7
Equestrian [2, 3]	2	4	2.0	45	1,388	30.8
Fencing [3]	35	625	17.9	43	655	15.2
Field hockey	(X)	(X)	(X)	258	5,633	21.8
Football	629	64,235	102.1	(X)	(X)	(X)
Golf [3]	795	8,315	10.5	516	4,096	7.9
Gymnastics	18	353	19.6	85	1,430	16.8
Ice hockey	138	4,006	29.0	81	1,896	23.4
Lacrosse	239	8,900	37.2	301	6,830	22.7
Rifle [3]	29	213	7.3	36	182	5.1
Rowing [2]	87	2,412	27.7	144	7,024	48.8
Rugby [2]	2	79	39.5	5	181	36.2
Sailing [2]	24	528	22.0	(X)	(X)	(X)
Skiing [3]	39	567	14.5	42	547	13.0
Soccer	775	21,031	27.1	956	22,682	23.7
Softball	(X)	(X)	(X)	950	17,154	18.1
Squash [2]	31	464	15.0	28	383	13.7
Swimming/diving [3]	389	8,382	21.5	509	11,238	22.1
Synchronized swimming [2] . . .	(X)	(X)	(X)	8	104	13.0
Tennis	754	7,850	10.4	898	8,721	9.7
Track, indoor [3]	575	20,346	35.4	645	20,413	31.6
Track, outdoor [3]	687	23,479	34.2	745	22,363	30.0
Volleyball	82	1,298	15.8	1,014	14,715	14.5
Water polo	42	919	21.9	60	1,155	19.3
Wrestling	227	6,310	27.8	(X)	(X)	(X)

– Represents zero.   NA Not available.   X Not applicable.   [1] Includes other sports, not shown separately.   [2] Sport recognized by the NCAA but does not have an NCAA championship.   [3] Co-ed championship sport.

Source: The National Collegiate Athletic Association (NCAA), Indianapolis, IN, *2007–08 Participation Study (copyright)*; <http://www.ncaa.org/wps/portal>.

Table 1211. **Participation in High School Athletic Programs by Sex: 1979 to 2008**

[Data based on number of state associations reporting and may underrepresent the number of schools with and participants in athletic programs]

Year	Participants [1]		Sex and sport	Most popular sports, 2007–2008 [2]	
	Males	Females		Schools	Participants
1979-80	3,517,829	1,750,264			
1985-86	3,344,275	1,807,121	MALE		
1986-87	3,364,082	1,836,356	Football (11-player)	13,987	1,108,286
1987-88	3,425,777	1,849,684	Basketball	17,861	552,935
1988-89	3,416,844	1,839,352	Track & field (outdoor)	15,835	548,821
1989-90	3,398,192	1,858,659	Baseball	15,720	478,029
1990-91	3,406,355	1,892,316	Soccer	11,122	383,561
1991-92	3,429,853	1,940,801	Wrestling	10,090	259,688
1992-93	3,416,389	1,997,489	Cross country	13,485	221,109
1993-94	3,472,967	2,130,315	Golf	13,647	159,958
1994-95	3,536,359	2,240,461	Tennis	9,576	156,285
1995-96	3,634,052	2,367,936	Swimming & diving	6,428	111,896
1996-97	3,706,225	2,474,043			
1997-98	3,763,120	2,570,333	FEMALE		
1998-99	3,832,352	2,652,726	Basketball	17,564	449,450
1999-20	3,861,749	2,675,874	Track & field (outdoor)	15,772	447,520
2000-01	3,921,069	2,784,154	Volleyball	15,009	397,968
2001-02	3,960,517	2,806,998	Softball (fast pitch)	14,846	371,293
2002-03	3,988,738	2,856,358	Soccer	10,543	346,545
2003-04	4,038,253	2,865,299	Cross country	13,294	190,349
2004-05	4,110,319	2,908,390	Tennis	9,694	172,455
2005-06	4,206,549	2,953,355	Swimming & diving	6,766	147,197
2006-07	4,321,103	3,021,807	Competitive spirit squads	4,510	111,307
2007-08	4,372,115	3,057,266	Golf	9,447	69,243

[1] A participant is counted in the number of sports participated in.   [2] Ten most popular sports for each sex in terms of number of participants.

Source: National Federation of State High School Associations, Indianapolis, IN, *The 2007–2008 High School Athletics Participation Survey (copyright)*; <http://www.nfhs.org/>.

Table 1212. **Participation in Selected Sports Activities: 2007**

[In thousands (265,381 represents 265,381,000), except rank. Data are based on a questionnaire mailed to 10,000 households. The questionnaire asked the male and female heads of households and up to two other household members who were at least seven years of age to indicate their age, the sports in which they participated in 2007, and the number of days of participation in 2007. A participant is defined as an individual seven years of age or older who participates in a sport more than once a year. See source for methodology.]

Activity	All persons		Sex		Age								Household income (dol.)					
	Number	Rank	Male	Female	7–11 years	12–17 years	18–24 years	25–34 years	35–44 years	45–54 years	55–64 years	65 years and over	Under 15,000	15,000–24,999	25,000–34,999	35,000–49,000	50,000–74,999	75,000 and over
Total	**265,381**	(X)	**129,201**	**136,180**	**19,410**	**25,341**	**28,959**	**37,285**	**41,600**	**43,343**	**32,066**	**37,377**	**27,497**	**23,309**	**27,441**	**38,546**	**57,397**	**91,192**
SERIES I SPORTS																		
Number participated in—																		
Aerobic exercising [1]	30,340	11	8,867	21,473	1,053	2,134	4,266	7,039	5,943	4,785	2,749	2,372	2,196	1,747	2,381	4,083	6,186	13,747
Backpacking [2]	12,980	18	7,623	5,357	1,187	1,636	1,903	1,993	3,057	2,061	835	308	1,167	834	876	1,280	2,600	6,223
Baseball	13,951	16	10,683	3,268	3,975	2,909	1,834	1,285	2,191	786	455	515	1,344	514	1,014	1,637	2,680	6,762
Basketball	24,145	14	16,651	7,494	4,923	6,952	3,496	3,360	2,524	1,662	733	495	2,602	1,496	2,099	3,111	4,462	10,374
Bicycle riding [1]	37,405	6	19,904	17,501	7,046	6,518	4,395	4,766	5,684	4,639	2,549	1,809	2,512	2,394	2,911	4,764	7,908	16,916
Billiards [1]	29,491	12	17,799	11,692	988	2,543	6,015	6,999	6,045	4,206	1,901	794	2,784	2,409	2,897	4,488	5,888	11,025
Bowling	43,466	5	21,542	21,925	5,091	6,813	7,720	7,207	7,575	5,277	2,113	1,669	3,031	2,617	3,955	5,640	9,522	18,702
Camping [3]	47,541	4	24,226	23,315	4,863	5,518	5,831	7,902	9,924	7,432	3,707	2,364	3,548	2,840	4,733	7,150	11,678	17,592
Dart throwing	12,093	20	7,114	4,979	652	937	1,803	3,285	2,969	1,699	498	251	909	734	1,176	1,674	3,185	4,415
Exercise walking [1]	89,794	1	33,660	56,133	3,676	5,185	6,740	13,742	16,270	17,944	13,295	12,942	8,379	6,065	8,088	12,131	19,858	35,272
Exercising with equipment [1]	52,827	2	25,858	26,969	817	4,301	8,070	10,581	9,559	9,618	5,518	4,363	2,565	3,032	4,553	6,314	11,237	25,126
Fishing (net) [1]	35,325	7	23,923	11,403	3,058	3,536	3,460	5,361	7,109	6,549	3,754	2,498	3,479	2,540	3,617	4,940	7,192	13,556
Fishing—fresh water	30,825	9	20,898	9,927	2,894	3,107	3,027	4,779	6,177	5,613	3,220	2,009	3,338	2,344	3,148	4,241	6,356	11,397
Fishing—salt water	10,414	23	6,985	3,429	368	1,094	1,195	1,627	2,302	1,915	1,109	803	1,420	532	918	1,456	1,827	4,261
Football—tackle	9,195	25	7,930	1,264	1,442	3,906	1,729	810	518	275	219	297	1,425	850	990	639	1,516	3,775
Golf [1]	22,729	15	17,583	5,147	654	1,441	2,165	3,765	5,169	4,535	2,845	2,154	757	854	1,033	2,093	4,912	13,080
Hiking	28,633	13	14,746	13,887	2,038	2,720	2,517	5,182	6,083	5,976	2,760	1,356	1,862	1,248	1,643	2,895	6,381	14,604
Lacrosse	1,218	28	572	646	256	411	212	49	274	–	–	15	–	–	15	30	138	1,035
Mountain/Rock climbing	4,594	26	2,705	1,894	457	535	1,240	777	745	549	274	22	514	178	281	547	1,234	1,845
Running/jogging [1]	30,372	10	15,852	14,519	2,211	5,071	5,904	6,978	5,087	3,547	950	623	1,892	1,641	1,975	3,918	6,321	14,624
Soccer	13,770	17	8,434	5,335	5,041	3,332	1,529	1,814	1,563	127	203	160	1,108	716	849	1,859	2,791	6,447
Softball	9,958	24	5,139	4,818	1,155	1,795	1,815	1,933	1,578	1,131	415	138	1,609	376	787	1,580	2,209	4,398
Swimming [1]	52,346	3	23,950	28,397	8,710	7,801	6,238	6,906	8,992	6,971	3,752	2,978	2,886	3,031	3,992	6,244	11,294	24,901
Tennis	12,290	19	6,542	5,747	1,446	1,883	2,139	2,253	2,018	1,536	556	460	661	914	622	747	2,536	6,810
Volleyball	12,029	21	5,108	6,921	1,189	3,041	2,713	1,696	1,502	1,192	555	142	763	1,122	734	1,764	2,590	5,056
Weightlifting	33,163	8	21,317	11,846	330	3,983	5,994	8,199	6,440	4,863	2,070	1,283	2,229	1,563	2,734	4,049	7,300	15,279
Wrestling	2,109	27	1,761	348	276	723	363	254	188	96	101	108	248	232	464	137	206	823
Yoga	10,683	22	1,574	9,109	179	278	1,332	3,179	2,276	1,981	955	505	542	343	1,046	1,803	2,083	4,866

See footnotes at end of table.

U.S. Census Bureau, Statistical Abstract of the United States: 2010

Table 1212. **Participation in Selected Sports Activities: 2007**—Con.

[See headnote, page 750]

Activity	All persons Number	All persons Rank	Sex Male	Sex Female	Age 7-11 years	Age 12-17 years	Age 18-24 years	Age 25-34 years	Age 35-44 years	Age 45-54 years	Age 55-64 years	Age 65 years and over	Household income (dol.) Under 15,000	Household income (dol.) 15,000-24,999	Household income (dol.) 25,000-34,999	Household income (dol.) 35,000-49,999	Household income (dol.) 50,000-74,999	Household income (dol.) 75,000 and over
Total	**265,377**	(X)	**129,196**	**136,182**	**19,409**	**25,340**	**28,958**	**37,285**	**41,600**	**43,341**	**32,065**	**37,378**	**26,184**	**24,651**	**27,942**	**41,191**	**57,310**	**88,100**
SERIES II SPORTS																		
Number participated in—																		
Archery (Target)	6,574	11	5,368	1,206	840	1,673	1,068	768	859	917	391	58	288	408	775	1,254	1,644	2,206
Boating-motor/power	31,854	2	18,269	13,585	3,029	3,465	4,285	4,978	5,174	5,788	3,245	1,891	1,138	1,650	2,727	5,017	7,659	13,664
Hockey (Ice)	2,071	18	1,697	374	254	419	500	225	342	228	73	32	125	140	61	257	546	941
Hunting with bow and arrow	5,744	13	5,299	445	107	482	808	1,122	1,092	1,119	672	343	317	450	801	1,212	1,248	1,716
Hunting with firearms	19,452	4	16,932	2,521	817	1,969	3,327	2,885	3,682	3,498	2,126	1,148	860	1,320	2,338	3,370	4,308	7,257
In-line roller skating	10,713	5	4,896	5,817	3,013	3,384	1,013	1,271	1,385	367	256	24	557	679	509	1,929	2,574	4,464
Kayaking	5,873	12	2,978	2,895	397	891	763	794	1,242	1,111	590	84	199	210	312	704	1,273	3,177
Mountain biking-off road	7,425	9	4,941	2,485	640	942	789	1,877	1,444	1,097	451	186	424	594	686	1,199	1,443	3,079
Muzzleloading	3,623	17	3,342	281	52	56	470	866	617	844	508	210	205	398	568	664	809	980
Paintball games	7,443	8	6,618	825	571	2,350	2,470	852	990	151	9	50	444	527	1,025	1,251	1,284	2,911
Scooter riding	10,631	6	5,823	4,808	4,697	3,434	603	313	734	398	296	151	629	830	595	1,928	2,305	4,345
Skateboarding	10,137	7	7,441	2,695	3,156	4,171	1,653	508	481	127	16	24	811	783	746	1,911	1,726	4,159
Skiing—alpine	5,494	14	3,333	2,160	533	821	607	648	1,078	1,120	535	151	72	92	253	794	938	3,345
Skiing—cross country	1,665	19	881	784	80	56	326	366	211	380	164	84	79	-	84	230	489	783
Snowboarding	5,063	16	3,724	1,339	782	1,352	1,902	454	376	146	12	39	422	109	259	1,103	1,103	2,469
Target shoot	20,537	3	15,800	4,737	891	2,177	3,319	4,034	4,113	3,310	1,862	832	925	1,300	2,800	3,220	4,716	7,577
Target shoot-airgun	6,590	10	5,706	884	1,435	1,740	623	925	754	452	420	237	405	433	926	1,589	1,196	2,041
Water skiing	5,265	15	3,106	2,158	325	1,261	1,034	721	903	695	188	136	304	203	264	694	820	2,979
Work-out at club	33,830	1	15,226	18,604	514	2,193	5,139	7,138	5,608	5,934	3,848	3,457	1,194	1,702	2,602	3,785	8,277	16,269

- Represents or rounds to zero. X Not applicable. [1] Participant engaged in activity at least six times in the year. [2] Includes wilderness camping. [3] Vacation/overnight

Source: National Sporting Goods Association, Mt. Prospect, IL, Sports Participation in 2007: Series 1 and Series II (copyright). See <http://www.nsga.org/public/pages/index.cfm?pageid=864>.

Table 1213. **Sporting Goods Sales by Product Category: 1990 to 2007, and Projection, 2008**

[In millions of dollars (50,725 represents $50,725,000,000), except percent. Based on a sample survey of consumer purchases of 80,000 households, (100,000 beginning 2000), except recreational transport, which was provided by industry associations. Excludes Alaska and Hawaii. Minus sign (−) indicates decrease]

Selected product category	1990	2000	2002	2003	2004	2005	2006	2007	2008, proj.
Sales, all products	50,725	74,442	77,726	79,779	85,811	88,434	90,472	90,802	87,348
Annual percent change [1] . . .	(NA)	4.6	4.6	2.6	7.6	3.1	2.3	0.4	−3.8
Percent of retail sales	(NA)	2.5	2.5	2.4	2.5	2.4	2.3	2.3	2.2
Athletic and sport clothing . [2]	10,130	11,030	9,801	10,543	11,201	10,898	10,580	10,834	10,770
Athletic and sport footwear [2]	11,654	13,026	14,144	14,446	14,752	15,719	16,910	17,366	17,715
Aerobic shoes	611	292	239	222	237	261	262	280	285
Basketball shoes	918	786	789	890	877	878	964	892	887
Cross training shoes	679	1,528	1,421	1,407	1,327	1,437	1,516	1,584	1,617
Golf shoes	226	226	243	222	230	259	232	244	247
Gym shoes, sneakers	2,536	1,871	2,042	2,059	2,221	2,314	2,434	2,699	2,745
Jogging and running shoes. . . .	1,110	1,638	1,733	1,802	1,989	2,157	2,260	2,193	2,239
Tennis shoes	740	533	503	544	508	528	505	452	471
Walking shoes . . . . [2] . . .	2,950	3,317	3,415	3,468	3,496	3,673	4,091	4,197	4,319
Athletic and sport equipment [2] . . .	14,439	21,608	21,699	22,394	23,328	23,735	24,497	25,267	24,884
Archery	265	259	279	320	332	372	396	402	396
Baseball and softball	217	319	334	340	352	372	388	401	396
Billiards and indoor games	192	516	574	625	622	572	574	543	527
Camping	1,072	1,354	1,442	1,487	1,531	1,447	1,526	1,453	1,410
Exercise	1,824	3,610	4,378	4,957	5,074	5,177	5,239	5,508	5,439
Fishing tackle	1,910	2,030	2,024	1,981	2,026	2,139	2,218	2,247	2,205
Golf	2,514	3,805	3,258	3,046	3,198	3,466	3,669	3,824	3,770
Hunting and firearms	2,202	2,274	2,449	2,654	3,175	3,563	3,732	3,977	3,921
Optics	438	729	826	847	859	887	1,014	1,049	1,033
Skin diving and scuba	294	355	348	338	351	358	369	376	367
Snow skiing [3]	475	495	527	462	452	643	501	531	518
Tennis	333	383	358	343	362	397	418	440	442
Recreational transport	14,502	28,779	32,083	32,397	36,531	38,082	38,485	37,334	33,979
Bicycles and supplies	2,423	5,131	4,961	4,736	4,898	5,343	5,161	5,393	5,285
Pleasure boats, motors, & accessories	7,644	13,224	15,382	14,705	16,054	17,634	17,907	17,549	15,800
Recreational vehicles	4,113	9,529	10,960	12,058	14,753	14,366	14,732	13,704	12,200
Snowmobiles	322	894	779	898	826	739	685	688	694

NA Not available. [1] Represents change from immediate prior year. [2] Includes other products not shown separately. [3] Data through 2004 categorized as "Skiing Downhill."

Source: National Sporting Goods Association, Mt. Prospect, IL, *The Sporting Goods Market in 2008*; and prior issues (copyright). See also <http://www.nsga.org/i4a/pages/index.cfm?pageid=3345>.

Table 1214. **Consumer Purchases of Sporting Goods by Consumer Characteristics: 2007**

[In percent. Based on sample survey of consumer purchases of 100,000 households. Excludes Alaska and Hawaii]

Characteristic	Total house-holds	Footwear						Equipment				
		Aero-bic shoes	Fit-ness shoes	Gym shoes/ sneak-ers	Trail running shoes	Walk-ing shoes	Multi pur-pose home gyms	Rod/ reel combi-nation	Golf club sets	Rifles	Soccer balls
Total	100	100	100	100	100	100	100	100	100	100	100
Age of user:											
Under 14 years old	18.9	9.5	7.5	42.1	2.1	5.0	(NA)	10.8	3.3	3.6	60.5
14 to 17 years old	5.8	3.7	8.3	10.4	17.5	2.6	0.6	1.1	2.6	2.6	11.5
18 to 24 years old	9.8	4.8	5.6	5.7	7.0	3.9	5.3	8.6	5.5	1.8	2.4
25 to 34 years old	13.5	24.2	20.4	14.5	31.9	9.9	16.6	22.2	27.1	23.1	10.8
35 to 44 years old	14.6	17.5	21.5	9.9	23.2	15.2	31.1	16.7	22.5	19.2	4.0
45 to 64 years old	25.0	27.6	29.8	13.7	17.9	42.6	42.2	35.3	30.6	42.8	5.9
65 years old and over. . .	12.4	12.7	6.9	3.7	0.4	20.8	4.2	4.4	8.4	6.6	0.4
Multiple ages.	−	−	−	−	−	−	−	0.9	−	0.3	4.5
Sex of user:											
Male	49.3	21.1	39.4	50.4	61.5	37.8	59.7	81.5	79.8	95.4	62.4
Female	50.7	78.9	60.6	49.6	38.5	62.2	32.6	13.2	20.2	3.1	32.6
Household use	−	−	−	−	−	−	7.7	5.3	−	1.5	5.0
Annual household income:											
Under $15,000	11.9	7.8	6.1	7.3	7.0	8.3	4.9	6.9	3.4	4.3	5.6
$15,000 to $24,999	12.9	9.2	6.8	9.3	5.7	11.0	2.3	8.4	2.9	10.3	4.3
$25,000 to $34,999	12.1	5.9	8.6	13.7	6.2	11.4	9.6	13.6	1.2	14.8	11.1
$35,000 to $49,999	15.2	18.2	14.8	16.0	17.6	14.6	15.5	13.0	11.2	13.4	10.0
$50,000 to $74,999	18.2	23.7	16.5	21.9	21.2	19.0	26.5	18.9	18.2	18.7	20.9
$75,000 to $99,999	14.2	17.5	20.0	15.0	19.4	17.6	15.4	14.3	24.6	12.8	26.3
$100,000 and over.	14.5	17.7	27.2	16.8	22.9	18.1	25.8	24.9	38.5	25.7	21.8

− Represents or rounds to zero.

Source: National Sporting Goods Association, Mt. Prospect, IL, *The Sporting Goods Market in 2008* (copyright). See also <http://www.nsga.org.public/pages/index.cfm?pageid=869>.

Table 1215. **National Park System—Summary: 1990 to 2008**

[For year ending September 30, except as noted. (986 represents $986,000,000). Includes data for five areas in Puerto Rico and Virgin Islands, one area in American Samoa, and one area in Guam]

Item	1990	1995	2000	2004	2005	2006	2007	2008
Finances (mil. dol.): [1]								
Expenditures reported	986	1,445	1,833	2,371	2,451	2,463	2,412	2,614
Salaries and wages	459	633	799	956	984	998	1,005	1,066
Improvements, maintenance	160	234	299	332	361	389	381	428
Construction	109	192	215	354	381	300	280	303
Other	259	386	520	729	725	776	746	817
Funds available	1,506	2,225	3,316	4,087	4,218	4,242	4,266	4,537
Appropriations.	1,053	1,325	1,881	2,388	2,425	2,450	2,484	2,636
Other [2]	453	900	1,435	1,699	1,793	1,792	1,782	1,901
Revenue from operations	79	106	234	264	286	308	346	404
Recreation visits (millions): [3]								
All areas	258.7	269.6	285.9	276.9	273.5	272.6	275.6	274.9
National parks [4]	57.7	64.8	66.1	63.8	63.5	60.4	62.3	61.2
National monuments	23.9	23.5	23.8	19.8	20.9	19.6	19.7	20.2
National historical, commemorative, archaeological [5].	57.5	56.9	72.2	77.0	74.9	73.6	75.1	76.2
National parkways	29.1	31.3	34.0	31.7	31.7	32.6	31.1	30.2
National recreation areas [4]	47.2	53.7	50.0	46.6	46.8	47.8	48.9	49.6
National seashores and lakeshores. . .	23.3	22.5	22.5	21.3	21.7	19.6	19.9	19.3
National Capital Parks	7.5	5.5	5.4	4.7	4.3	6.2	4.9	5.1
Recreation overnight stays (millions). . . .	17.6	16.8	15.4	13.7	13.5	13.2	13.8	13.7
In commercial lodgings.	3.9	3.8	3.7	3.5	3.4	3.4	3.6	3.6
In Park Service campgrounds	7.9	7.1	5.9	5.4	5.2	5.0	5.1	5.0
In backcountry	1.7	2.2	1.9	1.7	1.7	1.7	1.7	1.8
Other	4.2	3.7	3.8	3.1	3.2	3.1	3.4	3.3
Land (1,000 acres): [6, 7]								
Total.	76,362	77,355	78,153	79,023	79,048	78,810	78,845	78,859
Parks	46,089	49,307	49,785	49,892	49,910	49,912	49,911	49,916
Recreation areas.	3,344	3,353	3,388	3,391	3,391	3,391	3,413	3,413
Other	26,929	24,695	24,980	25,740	25,747	25,507	25,521	25,530
Acquisition, net.	21	27	186	12	17	17	16	7

[1] Financial data are those associated with the National Park System. Certain other functions of the National Park Service (principally the activities absorbed from the former Heritage Conservation and Recreation Service in 1981) are excluded. [2] Includes funds carried over from prior years. [3] For calendar year. Includes other areas, not shown separately. [4] For 1990, combined data for North Cascades National Park and two adjacent National Recreation Areas are included in National Parks total. [5] Includes military areas. [6] Federal land only, as of Dec. 31. Federal land acreages, in addition to National Park Service administered lands, also include lands within national park system area boundaries but under the administration of other agencies. Year-to-year changes in the federal lands figures includes changes in the acreages of these other lands and hence often differ from "net acquisition." [7] The decrease in the 2006 land total reflects corrected acreage by the Bureau of Land Management, not by the National Park Service lands.

Source: U.S. National Park Service, *National Park Statistical Abstract*, annual and unpublished data. See also <http://www2.nature.nps.gov/stats/>.

Table 1216. **State Parks and Recreation Areas by State: 2007**

[For year ending June 30 (13,922 represents 13,922,000). Data are shown as reported by state park directors. In some states, park agency has under its control forests, fish and wildlife areas, and/or other areas. In other states, agency is responsible for state parks only]

State	Acreage (1,000)	Visitors (1,000) [1]	Revenue Total ($1,000)	Percent of operating expenditures	State	Acreage (1,000)	Visitors (1,000) [1]	Revenue Total ($1,000)	Percent of operating expenditures
United States. . .	13,922	747,964	935,005	40.1	Missouri	204	15,142	8,095	27.5
					Montana	55	5,333	4,952	55.3
Alabama	48	5,142	22,567	57.0	Nebraska	135	10,236	16,681	84.7
Alaska	3,361	4,977	2,791	35.2	Nevada	139	3,132	2,748	18.3
Arizona.	64	2,348	9,639	38.9	New Hampshire . . .	233	1,626	4,324	58.7
Arkansas.	54	8,399	22,332	48.3	New Jersey	426	18,543	10,388	26.9
California.	1,566	79,854	90,672	21.3	New Mexico.	93	4,604	3,904	14.0
Colorado.	420	11,834	25,811	66.9	New York	1,348	61,771	88,000	43.2
Connecticut	206	7,504	5,104	29.9	North Carolina	202	12,868	5,317	13.8
Delaware.	26	5,022	12,397	53.6	North Dakota	18	879	1,585	47.0
Florida	700	20,737	42,779	54.8	Ohio.	174	49,659	27,530	37.3
Georgia.	86	10,351	35,272	56.2	Oklahoma	72	13,485	36,368	78.7
Hawaii	34	10,182	2,206	20.5	Oregon	99	42,605	17,187	36.1
Idaho	46	4,031	3,608	20.9	Pennsylvania	292	33,210	17,176	20.6
Illinois.	486	45,159	6,804	11.9	Rhode Island	9	6,217	4,322	47.6
Indiana	179	18,043	41,379	78.1	South Carolina	84	7,050	21,116	77.9
Iowa.	69	13,382	3,864	25.1	South Dakota	103	7,375	11,530	82.0
Kansas.	33	6,875	5,998	57.1	Tennessee.	174	32,264	37,770	44.6
Kentucky.	49	7,082	54,983	61.1	Texas	602	7,142	38,172	43.8
Louisiana	43	1,679	7,669	24.6	Utah.	151	4,554	10,694	34.3
Maine	100	2,124	3,027	34.4	Vermont	69	698	6,124	79.9
Maryland.	133	11,330	16,694	49.4	Virginia	68	7,040	14,214	45.5
Massachusetts	341	31,635	11,299	14.6	Washington	117	41,590	17,881	25.7
Michigan	273	19,309	38,639	86.7	West Virginia	177	7,324	20,390	57.7
Minnesota	279	8,380	15,694	44.9	Wisconsin	139	14,516	17,011	80.4
Mississippi	24	1,212	8,926	63.0	Wyoming.	122	2,511	1,371	19.0

[1] Includes overnight visitors.

Source: The National Association of State Park Directors, Raleigh, NC, *2007–2008 Annual Information Exchange (published February 2009)*. See <http://www.naspd.org/>.

Arts, Recreation, and Travel   753

Table 1217. **National Park Service (NPS) Visits and Acreage by State and Island Area: 2008**

[See headnote, table 1218]

| State and Island Area | Recreation visits [1] | Gross area acres | Federal land | | | Nonfederal land | |
			NPS fee acres [2]	NPS/OTFED less than fee acres [3]	Other federal fee acres [4]	Other public acres	Private acres
Total.	274,852,949	84,331,948	78,138,061	276,072	444,480	1,192,777	4,280,558
Alabama	789,451	21,081	16,715	202	8	3,295	869
Alaska	2,403,877	54,638,503	51,086,654	27,885	–	189,102	3,334,856
American Samoa	3,683	9,000	–	–	–	4,500	4,500
Arizona	10,681,127	2,962,853	2,618,735	115	76,937	57,067	209,999
Arkansas	2,873,026	104,976	98,319	3,395	6	2,736	521
California	34,374,981	8,107,457	7,560,571	22,437	13,061	313,662	197,726
Colorado	5,383,786	673,589	609,880	6,859	42,451	862	13,537
Connecticut	18,522	7,782	5,719	1,055	–	874	133
District of Columbia . .	33,165,410	7,088	6,951	7	–	126	4
Florida	7,937,737	2,637,762	2,437,026	1,330	45,907	129,192	24,308
Georgia	6,425,910	62,888	39,664	125	1,461	16,777	4,861
Guam	187,005	2,037	958	–	–	872	208
Hawaii	4,536,505	369,110	357,772	1	11	11,228	98
Idaho.	543,485	517,904	507,425	1,138	3,960	901	4,480
Illinois	335,473	13	12	–	–	–	1
Indiana	2,094,407	15,322	10,525	498	–	3,284	1,015
Iowa	211,352	2,713	2,708	–	–	5	1
Kansas	86,264	11,636	461	269	–	39	10,866
Kentucky	1,708,529	95,415	94,395	137	–	831	52
Louisiana	431,134	21,126	14,536	–	–	2,456	4,134
Maine	2,075,857	90,268	66,919	11,120	22	10,646	1,561
Maryland	3,544,992	71,822	39,584	5,909	395	23,269	2,665
Massachusetts	10,281,657	57,897	32,946	972	40	21,867	2,072
Michigan	1,420,947	718,188	631,717	732	42	58,515	27,182
Minnesota	640,843	301,333	139,509	3,193	141	98,811	59,678
Mississippi	5,898,917	118,749	103,698	5,261	–	55	9,735
Missouri	3,436,201	83,471	54,379	9,262	–	14,070	5,760
Montana	3,822,075	1,274,374	1,214,184	1,233	6,137	1,464	51,355
Nebraska	265,858	39,708	5,650	494	–	36	33,527
Nevada	5,770,632	778,512	774,509	–	2,508	81	1,415
New Hampshire.	29,819	15,897	8,403	1,556	5,772	162	5
New Jersey	5,811,657	99,206	35,267	140	3,208	59,000	1,592
New Mexico	1,556,586	391,029	376,528	5	2,524	3,365	8,607
New York	16,913,720	72,426	33,481	3,920	164	19,812	15,049
North Carolina.	17,984,028	405,920	363,042	12,272	20,782	3,289	6,536
North Dakota	553,135	72,581	71,252	258	151	56	865
Ohio	3,121,019	34,149	19,423	1,329	84	8,203	5,110
Oklahoma	1,245,188	10,241	10,008	9	189	8	27
Oregon	832,095	199,095	192,020	1,404	4,975	183	513
Pennsylvania	9,189,257	136,754	48,525	2,511	387	19,627	65,703
Puerto Rico	1,135,577	75	53	–	–	22	–
Rhode Island	46,154	5	5	–	–	–	–
South Carolina	1,441,433	32,618	30,288	61	5	51	2,213
South Dakota	3,501,677	297,417	141,317	122,327	–	79	33,693
Tennessee	7,733,826	384,445	356,168	1,679	9,629	3,616	13,353
Texas	5,804,179	1,238,198	1,193,022	85	1,013	5,079	38,999
Utah	8,451,252	2,117,043	2,097,106	833	1,142	12,803	5,160
Vermont.	37,121	22,178	8,830	3,874	8,809	544	120
Virgin Islands	622,379	48,924	14,035	3	18,135	14,677	2,073
Virginia	22,542,952	362,973	303,924	6,238	24,658	6,994	21,159
Washington	7,140,553	1,965,395	1,832,401	2,108	100,187	12,691	18,007
West Virginia	1,812,908	92,657	64,248	326	314	6,894	20,874
Wisconsin.	424,668	133,754	61,742	11,481	802	47,624	12,105
Wyoming	5,572,123	2,396,390	2,344,852	21	48,462	1,380	1,675

– Represents zero.   [1] See Table 1218, for footnotes 1, 2, 3, and 4.

Source: U.S. National Park Service, Land Resource Board and unpublished data. See also <http://www2.nature.nps.gov/stats/>.

Table 1218. **National Park Service (NPS) Visits and Acreage by Type of Area: 2008**

[Includes data for five areas in Puerto Rico and Virgin Islands, one area in American Samoa, and one area in Guam]

| Type of area | Recreation visits [1] | Gross area acres | Federal land | | | Nonfederal land | |
			NPS fee acres [2]	NPS/OTFED less than fee acres [3]	Other federal fee acres [4]	Other public acres	Private acres
Total [5]	274,852,949	84,331,948	78,138,061	276,072	444,480	1,192,777	4,280,558
National historic sites.	9,385,959	37,506	22,886	784	51	922	12,862
National historical parks. . .	27,304,519	173,709	124,290	3,556	360	28,532	16,971
National memorials	29,507,434	10,588	8,033	8	149	63	2,336
National monuments	21,610,296	2,027,865	1,802,847	14,830	30,671	19,777	159,740
National parks	61,159,714	52,095,046	49,717,998	148,822	49,499	498,132	1,680,595
National recreation areas . .	49,584,382	3,700,277	3,146,582	23,718	243,101	106,290	180,586
National seashores	15,909,135	595,014	403,240	14,890	61,226	106,131	9,527
National parkways.	30,165,232	177,340	158,204	8,530	125	294	10,187

[1] Recreation visit represents the entry of a person onto lands or waters administered by the National Park Service (NPS) for recreational purposes excluding government personnel, through traffic (commuters), trades–persons, and persons residing within park boundaries.   [2] Fee represents complete Federal ownership of all rights in the land.   [3] Represents Federal ownership of some rights in the land.   [4] NPS acreage lies under the jurisdiction of another federal agency (such as Bureau of Land Management).   [5] Includes other "type of areas" not shown separately.

Source: U.S. National Park Service, Land Resource Board and unpublished data. See also <http://www2.nature.nps.gov/stats/>.

754   Arts, Recreation, and Travel

Table 1219. **Participants in Wildlife-Related Recreation Activities: 2006**

[In thousands (33,916 represents 33,916,000). For persons 16 years old and over engaging in activity at least once in 2006. Based on survey and subject to sampling error; see source for details]

Participant	Number	Days of partici-pation	Trips	Participant	Number	Days of partici-pation
Total sportspersons [1] . .	**33,916**	**736,707**	**588,891**	**Wildlife watchers** [1]	**71,132**	**(X)**
Total anglers	29,952	516,781	403,492	Away from home [2]	22,977	352,070
Freshwater	25,431	433,337	336,528	Observe wildlife	21,546	291,027
Excluding Great Lakes . .	25,035	419,942	323,265	Photograph wildlife . . .	11,708	103,872
Great Lakes	1,420	18,016	13,264	Feed wildlife.	7,084	77,329
Saltwater.	7,717	85,663	66,963			
				Around home [3]	67,756	(X)
Total hunters	12,510	219,925	185,399	Observe wildlife	44,467	(X)
Big game	10,682	164,061	115,255	Photograph wildlife . .	18,763	(X)
Small game	4,797	52,395	40,856	Feed wild birds	55,512	(X)
Migratory birds	2,293	19,770	16,390	Visit public parks. . . .	13,271	(X)
Other animals hunted	1,128	15,205	12,898	Maintain plantings or .		
				natural areas	14,508	(X)

X Not applicable.   [1] Detail does not add to total due to multiple responses and nonresponse.   [2] Persons taking a trip of at least 1 mile from home for activity.   [3] Activity within 1 mile of home.

Source: U.S. Fish and Wildlife Service, *2006 National Survey of Fishing, Hunting, and Wildlife Associated Recreation,* October 2007. See also <http://wsfrprograms.fws.gov/Subpages/NationalSurvey/nat_survey2006_final.pdf> and <http://federalaid.fws.gov /surveys/surveys.html>.

Table 1220. **Expenditures for Wildlife-Related Recreation Activities: 2006**

[(42,011 represents $42,011,000,000). For persons 16 years old and over. Based on survey and subject to sampling error; see source for details]

Expenditure item	Fishing			Hunting			Wildlife watching		
		Spenders			Spenders			Spenders	
	Expendi-tures (mil.dol.)	Number (1,000)	Per-cent of an-glers	Expendi-tures (mil.dol.)	Number (1,000)	Per-cent of hunt-ers	Expendi-tures (mil.dol.)	Number (1,000)	Per-cent of watch-ers [2]
Total, all items [1]	42,011	28,307	95	22,893	12,153	97	45,655	55,979	79
Total trip-related [3]	17,879	26,318	88	6,679	10,828	87	12,875	19,443	85
Food and lodging	6,303	22,572	75	2,791	9,567	76	7,516	16,415	71
Food	4,327	22,415	75	2,177	9,533	76	4,298	16,261	71
Lodging	1,975	5,304	18	614	1,599	13	3,218	6,624	29
Transportation.	4,962	22,361	75	2,697	10,064	80	4,456	18,329	80
Public	524	1,163	4	214	401	3	1,567	2,902	13
Private	4,438	21,979	73	2,483	9,982	80	2,889	17,447	76
Other trip costs	6,614	22,275	74	1,190	3,416	27	903	7,681	33
Total equipment and other expenditures	24,133	25,355	85	16,215	11,745	94	32,780	52,178	73
Equipment [4]	5,332	19,082	64	5,366	9,287	74	9,870	49,040	69
Auxiliary equipment	779	3,837	13	1,330	4,196	34	1,033	4,848	7
Special equipment [5]	12,646	1,818	6	4,035	505	4	12,271	1,914	3
Other expenditures [6]	5,375	20,638	69	5,483	10,632	85	9,606	19,070	27
Magazines, books	115	2,944	10	84	1,767	14	360	9,490	13
Licenses, stamps, tags, and per-mits	503	16,259	54	743	9,862	79	(X)	(X)	(X)

X Not applicable.   [1] Total not adjusted for multiple responses or nonresponse.   [2] Percent of wildlife-watching participants column is based on away-from-home participants for trip-related expenditures. For equipment and other expenditures the percent of wildlife-watching participants is based on total participants.   [3] Information on trip-related expenditures for wildlife watching was collected for away-from-home participants only. Equipment and other expenditures for wildlife watching are based on information collected from both away-from-home and around-the-home participants.   [4] Includes fishing, hunting, and wildlife-watching.   [5] Special equipment includes boats, campers, cabins, trail bikes, etc.   [6] Other expenditures not shown.

Source: U.S. Fish and Wildlife Service, *2006 National Survey of Fishing, Hunting, and Wildlife Associated Recreation,* October 2007. See also <http://wsfrprograms.fws.gov/Subpages/NationalSurvey/nat_survey2006_final.pdf>

Table 1221. **Tribal Gaming Revenues: 2003 to 2008**

[In millions (16,826 represents $16,826,000,000). For year ending September 30]

	2003		2004		2005		2006		2007		2008	
	Num-ber of opera-tions	Rev-enue	Num-ber of opera-tions	Rev-enue	Num-ber of opera-tions	Rev-enue	Num-ber of opera-tions	Rev-enue	Num-ber of opera-tions	Rev-enue	Num-ber of opera-tions	Rev-enue
Total [1]	358	16,826	375	19,479	392	22,579	394	24,889	382	26,016	405	26,739
Region I	46	1,441	45	1,602	49	1,829	46	2,080	46	2,264	47	2,376
Region II	54	4,700	54	5,822	57	6,993	56	7,675	58	7,796	59	7,363
Region III	43	1,899	45	2,160	48	2,529	45	2,719	46	2,874	46	2,774
Region IV	109	3,597	117	3,816	118	3,984	122	4,070	111	4,225	115	4,402
Region V	82	867	87	1,259	92	1,730	98	2,126	102	2,584	110	3,047
Region VI	24	4,322	27	4,821	28	5,514	27	6,219	28	6,400	28	6,776

X Not applicable.   [1] Region 1: Alaska Idaho Oregon, and Washington. Region 2: California, and Northern Nevada. Region 3: Arizona, Colorado, New Mexico, and Southern Nevada. Region 4: Iowa, Michigan, Minnesota, Montana, North Dakota, Nebraska, South Dakota, Wisconsin, and Wyoming. Data for Montana not included for years 2004 and earlier. Region 5: Kansas, Oklahoma, and Texas. Region 6: Alabama, Connecticut, Florida, Louisiana, Mississippi, North Carolina, and New York.

Source: National Indian Gaming Commission, *Tribal Gaming Revenues,* annual. See also <http://www.nigc.gov>.

Arts, Recreation, and Travel   755

Table 1222. **Gaming Revenue by Industry: 2000 to 2007**

[In millions of dollars (62,154 represents $62,154,000,000). Data shown are for gross revenue. Gross gambling revenue (GGR) is the amount wagered minus the winnings returned to players, a true measure of the economic value of gambling. GGR is the figure used to determine what an operation earns before taxes, salaries, and other expenses are paid]

Industry	2000	2002	2003	2004	2005	2006	2007
Total [1]	62,154	68,783	73,062	78,589	84,433	90,931	92,272
Card rooms.	949	811	979	989	1,025	1,104	1,180
Commercial casinos . . . . . [2] . . .	26,455	28,144	28,669	[2]30,595	[2]31,775	[2]34,113	[2]34,407
Charitable games and bingo [3] . . .	2,466	2,671	2,331	2,336	2,338	2,237	2,220
Legal bookmaking	131	116	128	116	130	191	169
Lotteries	17,277	18,658	20,283	21,405	22,898	24,631	24,780
Parimutuel wagering	3,935	3,912	3,847	3,740	3,689	3,580	3,500

[1] Includes industry not shown separately.   [2] Amount includes deepwater cruise ships, curises-to-nowhere and noncasino devices.   [3] Data are estimated.

Source: Christiansen Capital Advisors LLC. Prepared for the American Gaming Association (AGA). Industry Information, Fact Sheets, *Gaming Revenue: Current-Year Data (copyright)*. See also <http://www.americangaming.org/Industry/factsheets/index.cfm> and <www.cca-i.com>.

Table 1223. **North America Cruise Industry in the United States: 2003 to 2007**

[The North American passenger cruise industry is defined as those cruise lines that primarily market their cruises in North America. These cruise lines offer cruises with destinations throughout the globe. While most of these cruises originate in ports throughout North America, cruises also originate at ports in other continents]

Item	Unit	2003	2004	2005	2006	2007
Capacity Measures:						
Number of ships	Number. . .	134	144	145	151	159
Lower berths [1]	Number. . .	212,004	225,714	230,891	249,691	268,062
Passenger embarkations, global: [2]	1,000	9,830	10,850	11,500	12,000	12,560
United States	1,000	7,113	8,100	8,612	9,001	9,184
Florida	1,000	4,676	4,791	4,875	4,994	4,977
California	1,000	807	1,095	1,301	1,241	1,334
New York	1,000	438	547	370	536	575
Other U.S. ports	1,000	1,192	1,667	2,066	2,230	2,298
Canada	1,000	482	454	455	423	477
San Juan	1,000	325	450	581	555	534
Rest of world	1,000	1,910	1,846	1,852	2,021	2,367
United States expenditures of the North American cruise industry: [3, 4]	Bil. dol. . . .	12.92	14.70	16.18	17.64	18.68
U.S. purchases of the cruise lines . .	Bil. dol. . . .	9.49	10.70	11.76	12.89	13.72
Passenger and crew	Bil. dol. . . .	2.36	2.88	3.23	3.48	3.63
Wages & taxes paid by cruise lines .	Bil. dol. . . .	1.07	1.12	1.19	1.27	1.33

[1] Single beds.   [2] Port of departure.   [3] See details in the report for the sources of U.S. expenditures of the North American cruise industry.   [4] Includes wages and salaries paid to U.S. employees of the cruise lines.

Source: Business Research & Economic Advisors (BREA), Exton, PA. The Contribution of the North American Cruise Industry to the U.S. Economy in 2007. Prepared for the Cruise Lines International Association, July 2008. See also <http://www.cruising.org>.

Table 1224. **Top States and Cities Visited by Overseas Travelers: 2000 to 2008**

[25,975 represents 25,975,000. Includes travelers for business and pleasure, international travelers in transit through the United States, and students. Excludes travel by international personnel and international businessmen employed in the United States. Starting with the 2006 data, the statistical policy for visitation estimates of international travelers to the U.S. has changed. For more information, go to <http://tinet.ita.doc.gov/outreachpages/2007statisticalpolicy.html/>. **States and Cities are ranked by the latest overseas visitors data**]

State and other area	Overseas visitors [1] (1,000)				City	Overseas visitors [1] (1,000)			
	2000	2005	2007	2008		2000	2005	2007	2008
Total overseas travelers [2, 3] . .	25,975	21,679	23,892	25,341	New York City, NY.	5,714	5,810	7,646	8,211
New York	5,922	6,092	7,908	8,413	Los Angeles, CA	3,533	2,580	2,652	2,788
California	6,364	4,791	5,185	5,296	San Francisco, CA	2,831	2,124	2,270	2,610
Florida	6,026	4,379	4,683	5,246	Miami, FL	2,935	2,081	2,341	2,585
Nevada	2,364	1,821	1,768	2,103	Orlando, FL.	3,013	2,016	2,055	2,433
Hawaiian Islands	2,727	2,255	1,864	1,825	Las Vegas, NV	2,260	1,778	1,720	2,027
Illinois	1,377	1,149	1,171	1,419	Oahu/Honolulu, HI	2,234	1,821	1,553	1,495
Massachusetts.	1,429	867	1,171	1,267	Washington, DC.	1,481	1,106	1,195	1,470
Guam	1,325	1,127	1,099	1,191	Chicago, IL	1,351	1,084	1,147	1,368
Texas.	1,169	954	1,003	1,090	Boston, MA	1,325	802	1,075	1,115
New Jersey.	909	997	956	1,039	Philadelphia, PA.	390	434	550	710
Pennsylvania.	649	629	812	1,014	San Diego, CA.	701	499	645	684
Arizona.	883	564	573	710	Atlanta, GA	701	564	478	532
Georgia	(B)	(B)	526	634	Houston, TX	442	369	478	481
Washington.	(B)	(B)	454	456	Flagstaff, AZ [4]	(B)	(B)	(B)	431
Michigan.	(B)	(B)	382	405	Seattle, WA.	416	347	406	405
Colorado.	(B)	(B)	311	380	Dallas-Plano-Irving, TX . .	493	347	358	380
Utah	(B)	(B)	(B)	380	Tampa/St. Petersburg, FL.	519	455	334	380
North Carolina	(B)	(B)	358	355	San Jose, CA	494	347	430	355

B Figure too small to meet statistical standards for reliability of a derived figure.   [1] Excludes Canada and Mexico.   [2] A person is counted in each area visited, but only once in the total.   [3] Includes other states and cities, not shown separately.   [4] Data include Flagstaff, Grand Canyon and Sedona grouped together.

Source: U.S. Department of Commerce; International Trade Administration; Office of Travel and Tourism Industries and Bureau of Economic Analysis (BEA) (released May 2009). See also http://www.tinet.ita.doc.gov/outreachpages/inbound .generalinformation.inboundoverview.html>.

Table 1225. **Domestic Travel by U.S. Resident Households—Summary: 2000 to 2006**

[In millions (1,008.9 represents 1,008,900,000). See headnote, Table 1226]

Type of trip	2000	2001	2002	2003	2004	2005	2006
All travel: [1]							
Household trips	1,008.9	993.8	994.9	978.2	1,002.6	1,019.1	1,034.3
Person-trips [2]	1,892.1	1,869.9	1,919.1	1,890.3	1,953.3	1,992.4	2,000.5
All overnight travel:							
Household trips	493.0	480.7	475.2	470.5	482.2	499.0	536.9
Person-trips.	895.6	878.3	884.1	903.2	941.8	968.3	969.0
Business travel:							
Household trips	401.0	393.0	364.8	346.8	349.5	345.7	346.5
Person-trips.	566.6	545.3	512.0	502.1	513.0	510.0	508.7
Leisure travel: [3]							
Household trips	607.9	600.8	630.1	631.4	653.1	673.5	687.8
Person-trips.	1,325.4	1,324.6	1,407.1	1,388.2	1,440.4	1,482.5	1,491.8

[1] Includes personal and other trips (e.g., medical, funerals, weddings), not shown separately. All domestic travel included. [2] One person on one trip 50 miles or more, one way, away from home or including one or more nights away from home. [3] Includes visiting friends/relatives, outdoor recreation, entertainment, and travel for other pleasure/personal reasons, etc., as the primary mode of transportation.

Source: U.S. Travel Association, Washington, DC, *TravelScope/Directions, annual* (copyright). See <http://www.ustravel.org/index.html>.

Table 1226. **Characteristics of Domestic Overnight Leisure Trips by U.S. Resident Households: 2000 to 2005**

[In millions except as indicated (317.4 represents 317,400,000). Represents household trips to destinations 50 miles or more, one-way, away from home and including one or more overnights. "Leisure" includes visiting friends/relatives, outdoor recreation, entertainment, and travel for other pleasure/personal reasons, etc. Other pleasure/personal trips are trips such as for medical reasons, funerals, weddings, etc. Based on a monthly mail panel survey of 25,000 U.S. households. For details, see source]

Overnight leisure trip characteristics	Unit	2000	2001	2002	2003	2004	2005
Total overnight leisure trips	Millions. . .	317.4	300.8	312.0	318.1	322.5	349.3
Average nights per trip	Number. . .	4.4	4.3	4.1	4.1	4.3	4.4
Traveled primarily by auto, truck, RV, or rental car.	Percent . . .	80.1	80.1	81.4	81.4	81.3	81.7
Traveled primarily by air	Percent . . .	17.1	16.7	15.3	15.1	15.3	14.8
Stayed in a hotel/motel/B&B while on trip . .	Poroont . . .	44.0	41.3	42.5	43.0	43.9	43.0
Household income:							
Less than $50,000	Percent . . .	43.6	41.6	39.5	37.1	38.5	35.2
$50,000 or more.	Percent . . .	56.4	58.4	60.5	62.9	61.5	64.8

Source: U.S. Travel Association, Washington, DC, *TravelScope/Directions, annual* (copyright). See <http://www.ustravel.org/index.html>.

Table 1227. **Domestic Travel Expenditures by State: 2007**

[641,289 represents $641,289,000,000. Represents U.S. spending on domestic overnight trips and day trips of 50 miles or more, one way, away from home. Excludes spending by foreign visitors and by U.S. residents in U.S. territories and abroad]

State	Total (mil. dol.)	Percent distri- bution	Rank	State	Total (mil. dol.)	Percent distri- bution	Rank	State	Total (mil. dol.)	Percent distri- bution	Rank
U.S., total . . .	**641,289**	**100.0**	**(X)**	KS.	5,223	0.8	38	ND	1,683	0.3	48
				KY.	7,253	1.1	30	OH	15,207	2.4	12
AL.	7,312	1.1	29	LA.	8,717	1.4	25	OK	5,867	0.9	33
AK.	1,778	0.3	47	ME	2,474	0.4	44	OR	7,394	1.2	28
AZ.	12,726	2.0	17	MD	11,463	1.8	19	PA.	18,773	2.9	7
AR.	5,366	0.8	37	MA	13,346	2.1	15	RI	1,663	0.3	49
CA.	80,442	12.5	1	MI	14,509	2.3	13	SC.	9,704	1.5	22
CO	12,854	2.0	16	MN	9,834	1.5	21	SD.	2,096	0.3	46
CT.	8,503	1.3	27	MS	5,999	0.9	32	TN.	13,796	2.2	14
DE.	1,382	0.2	51	MO	11,595	1.8	18	TX.	43,276	6.7	3
DC	5,656	0.9	34	MT	2,848	0.4	42	UT.	5,381	0.8	36
FL.	52,289	8.2	2	NE.	3,719	0.6	39	VT.	1,633	0.3	50
GA	18,680	2.9	9	NV.	31,458	4.9	5	VA.	18,691	2.9	8
HI	9,703	1.5	23	NH	3,265	0.5	40	WA	10,680	1.7	20
ID	3,237	0.5	41	NJ	17,862	2.8	10	WV	2,354	0.4	45
IL	27,920	4.4	6	NM	5,565	0.9	35	WI	8,844	1.4	24
IN	8,532	1.3	26	NY.	37,477	5.8	4	WY	2,482	0.4	43
IA	6,267	1.0	31	NC	16,511	2.6	11				

X Not applicable.

Source: U.S. Travel Association, Washington, DC, *Impact of Travel on State Economies, 2007* (copyright). See <http://www.ustravel.org/index.html>.

Arts, Recreation, and Travel   **757**

Table 1228. **Travel Forecast Summary: 2006 to 2012**

[In billions of dollars (11,295 represents $11,295,000,000,000)]

Measurement	Unit	2006	2007	2008 [1]	2009 [2]	2010 [2]	2011 [2]	2012 [2]
Real GDP	Billions . .	11,295	11,524	11,652	11,252	11,431	11,986	12,566
Unemployment rate	Percent. .	4.6	4.6	5.8	9.2	9.6	6.8	5.3
Consumer price index (CPI) [3]	Percent. .	201.6	207.4	215.2	214.0	217.3	222.9	229.4
Travel price index (TPI) [3]	Percent. .	233.5	244.0	263.0	243.1	252.5	264.8	275.2
Total travel expenditures in US . . .	Billions . .	695.8	737.8	772.9	704.8	748.3	800.8	843.5
US residents	Billions . .	610.1	641.0	662.4	608.5	647.4	693.7	729.1
International visitors [4]	Billions . .	85.7	96.7	110.5	96.2	100.9	107.1	114.4
Total international visitors to the United States	Millions. .	51.0	56.0	58.0	52.9	55.9	60.4	64.4
Total domestic person trips [5]	Millions. .	2,001	2,005	1,965	1,901	1,938	1,992	2,028

[1] Projected. [2] Forecast. [3] 1982 through 1984 = 100. [4] Excludes international visitors' spending on traveling to the U.S. on U.S. flag carriers, and other misc. transportation. [5] One person on one trip 50 miles or more, one way, away from home or including one or more nights away from home.

Source: U.S.Travel Association's Travel Forecast Model; Bureau of Labor Statistics; Department of Commerce, Bureau of Economic Analysis, Office of Travel and Tourism Industries. See <http://www.tia.org/index.html>.

Table 1229. **Chain-Type Price Indexes for Direct Tourism Output: 1999 to 2008**

[Index numbers, 2000=100. See headnote, Table 1230. For explanation of chain-type price indexes, see text, Section 13]

Tourism Goods and Services Group	1999	2000	2001	2002	2003	2004	2005	2006	2007	2008
Traveler accommodations	96.8	100.0	102.0	101.2	102.8	108.7	114.8	119.1	124.8	125.0
Transportation	93.8	100.0	97.8	95.1	98.9	102.7	109.8	117.4	121.5	132.2
Passenger air transportation	95.8	100.0	95.8	90.3	93.2	92.2	96.6	102.8	104.6	114.8
All other transportation-related commodities.	91.9	100.0	99.9	99.4	103.3	110.8	120.1	128.8	134.6	145.9
Food services and drinking places. . . .	97.3	100.0	103.2	106.0	108.2	111.5	115.0	118.6	122.9	128.4
Recreation, entertainment, and shopping.	97.3	100.0	102.5	104.0	105.4	110.2	113.0	115.7	118.4	122.7
Recreation and entertainment	96.1	100.0	103.4	105.9	108.6	110.2	114.0	117.7	120.8	124.7
Shopping.	98.2	100.0	101.8	102.6	103.1	104.9	106.5	108.4	110.7	115.1
All tourism goods and services	95.8	100.0	100.6	100.4	102.8	106.4	111.5	116.5	12 0.5	126.7

Source: U.S. Department of Commerce, Bureau of Economic Analysis, Office of Travel and Tourism Industries, *United States Travel and Tourism Satellite Accounts (TTSAs)*. See <http://www.bea.gov/industry/index.htm>.

Table 1230. **Tourism Sales by Commodity Group and Tourism Employment by Industry Group: 2005 to 2008**

[Sales in billions of dollars (660 represents $660,000,000,000). Employment in thousands (5,767 represents 5,767,000). Direct tourism-related sales comprise all output consumed directly by visitors (e.g., traveler accommodations, passenger air transportation, souvenirs). Direct tourism-related employment comprises all jobs where the workers are engaged in the production of direct tourism-related output (e.g., hotel staff, airline pilots, and souvenir sellers)]

Tourism commodity group	Direct tourism sales (bil. dol.)				Tourism industry group	Direct tourism employment			
	2005	2006	2007	2008		2005	2006	2007	2008
All commodities [1]	660	710	742	767	**All industries**	5,767	5,847	5,908	5,907
Traveler accommodations	115	124	134	137	Traveler accommodations.	1,358	1,363	1,376	1,377
Transportation.	253	275	287	301	Transportation	1,111	1,117	1,131	1,130
Passenger air transportation. .	98	105	109	112	Air transportation services. . .	452	447	452	454
All other transportation-related commodities	155	170	179	190	All other transportation-related industries	659	670	679	676
Food services and drinking places	110	118	123	128	Food and beverage services. . .	1,859	1,908	1,940	1,944
Recreation, entertainment, and shopping	181	192	197	200	Recreation, entertainment, and shopping	1,189	1,199	1,198	1,195
Recreation and entertainment	78	82	85	85	Recreation and entertainment	630	637	651	658
Shopping	103	110	112	115	Shopping	559	562	547	537
					All other industries	250	260	264	262

[1] Commodities that are typically purchased by visitors from the producer: such as airline passenger fares, meals, or hotel services.

Source: U.S. Bureau of Economic Analysis, "Industry Economic Accounts, Satellite Industry Accounts, Travel and Tourism." See also <http://www.bea.gov/bea/dn2/home/tourism.htm>.

Table 1231. **International Travelers and Payments: 1990 to 2008**

[(47,880 represents $47,880,000,000). For coverage, see Table 1232. Some traveler data revised since originally issued]

Year	Payments by U.S. travelers		Receipts from international visitors		U.S. net travel and passenger receipts (mil. dol.)	U.S. travelers to international countries (1,000)	International travelers to the U.S. (1,000)
	Total [1]	Travel payments	Total [1]	Travel receipts			
1990	47,880	37,349	58,305	43,007	10,425	44,624	39,363
1995	59,579	44,916	82,304	63,395	22,725	51,285	43,491
2000	88,979	64,705	103,087	82,400	14,108	61,327	51,238
2002	78,684	58,715	83,651	66,605	4,967	58,065	43,581
2003	78,436	57,447	80,250	64,359	1,814	56,250	41,218
2004	90,468	65,750	93,397	74,546	2,929	61,809	46,086
2005	95,119	68,970	102,769	81,799	7,650	63,503	49,206
2006	99,605	72,104	107,825	85,789	8,220	63,662	50,977
2007	104,791	76,354	122,686	97,050	17,895	64,024	55,979
2008 [2]	112,340	79,743	141,713	110,090	29,373	63,554	57,949

[1] Includes passenger fares not shown separately.   [2] Preliminary estimates for the receipts payment figures, and U.S. travelers to international countries.

Source: U.S. Department of Commerce; International Trade Administration; Office of Travel and Tourism Industries and Bureau of Economic Analysis (BEA) (released June 2009). See <http://www.tinet.ita.doc.gov>.

Table 1232. **International Travel: 1990 to 2008**

[In thousands (44,619 represents 44,619,000). U.S. travelers cover residents of the United States, its territories and possessions. International travelers to the U.S. include travelers for business and pleasure, excludes travel by international personnel and international businessmen employed in the United States. Some traveler data revised since originally issued]

Item and area	1990	1995	2000	2004	2005	2006	2007	2008
U.S. travelers to international countries [1,2]	44,619	51,285	61,327	61,809	63,503	63,662	64,024	63,554
Canada	12,252	13,005	15,188	15,088	14,391	13,855	13,371	12,495
Mexico	16,377	19,221	19,285	19,370	20,325	19,659	19,425	20,271
Total overseas	15,990	19,059	26,853	27,351	28,787	30,148	31,228	30,789
Europe	8,043	8,596	13,373	11,679	11,976	12,029	12,304	11,238
International travelers to the U.S.	39,363	43,491	51,238	46,086	49,206	51,063	55,979	57,949
Canada	17,263	14,663	14,667	13,857	14,862	15,992	17,760	18,922
Mexico	7,041	8,189	10,596	11,907	12,665	13,317	14,327	13,686
Total overseas	15,059	20,639	25,975	20,322	21,679	21,668	23,892	25,341
Europe	6,659	8,793	11,597	9,686	10,313	10,136	11,406	12,783
Asia	4,360	6,616	7,554	5,802	6,198	6,152	6,377	6,179
South America	1,328	2,449	2,941	1,645	1,820	1,928	2,274	2,556
Caribbean	1,137	1,044	1,331	1,095	1,135	1,198	1,317	1,201
Oceania	662	588	731	660	737	756	834	852
Central America	412	509	822	692	696	694	786	776
Middle East	365	454	702	502	527	553	620	681
Africa	137	186	295	241	252	253	278	315

[1] A person is counted in each area visited but only once in the total.   [2] 2008 U.S. outbound totals are preliminary estimates.

Source: U.S. Department of Commerce; International Trade Administration; Office of Travel and Tourism Industries and Bureau of Economic Analysis (BEA) (released June 2009). See <http://www.tinet.ita.doc.gov>.

Table 1233. **Top 20 U.S. Gateways for Nonstop International Air Travel: 2006 and 2007**

[155,394 represents 155,394,000. International passengers are residents of any country traveling nonstop to and from the United States on U.S. and foreign carriers. The data cover all passengers arriving and departing from U.S. airports on nonstop commercial international flights with 60 seats or more. Minus sign (–) indicates decrease in passengers]

Gateway airport	2006 [1]	2007	Percent change 2006-2007	Gateway airport	2006 [1]	2007	Percent change 2006-2007
Total	155,394	161,468	3.9	Washington (Dulles), DC	5,184	5,773	11.4
Total, top 20	135,487	142,251	5.0	Dallas-Ft. Worth, TX	5,288	5,105	–3.5
Top 20, percentage of				Detroit, MI	3,695	3,830	3.7
total	87.2	88.1	1.0	Boston, MA	3,776	3,808	0.8
New York (JFK), NY.	19,450	21,443	10.2	Honolulu, HI	4,050	3,757	–7.2
Los Angeles, CA	16,500	16,869	2.2	Philadelphia, PA	3,517	3,611	2.7
Miami, FL	14,852	15,586	4.9	Fort Lauderdale, FL	2,420	2,883	19.1
Chicago (OHare), IL.	11,517	11,539	0.2	Guam Island, GU	2,699	2,780	3.0
Newark, NJ	9,895	10,538	6.5	Seattle-Tacoma, WA	2,302	2,576	11.9
Atlanta, GA	8,482	9,113	7.4	Minneapolis-St. Paul, MN	2,487	2,522	1.4
San Francisco, CA	8,164	8,601	5.3	Las Vegas, NV	1,988	2,229	12.1
Houston (G. Bush), TX	7,147	7,476	4.6	Orlando, FL	2,073	2,214	6.8

[1] Data have been revised.

Source: U.S. Department of Transportation, Bureau of Transportation Statistics, Office of Airline Information, T-100 Segment data (published October 2008). See <http://www.bts.gov/publications/pocketguidetotransportation/2009/>.

Arts, Recreation, and Travel   759

Table 1234. **Selected U.S.-Canadian and U.S.-Mexican Border Land—Passenger Gateways: 2008**

[(28,674 represents 28,674,000)]

Item and gateway	Entering the U.S. (1,000)	Item and gateway	Entering the U.S. (1,000)
All U.S.-Canadian land gateways [1]		**All U.S.-Mexican land gateways** [1]	
Personal vehicles	28,674	Personal vehicles	78,857
Personal vehicle passengers	57,401	Personal vehicle passengers	157,982
Buses.	132	Buses.	266
Bus passengers	3,404	Bus passengers	3,456
Train passengers	239	Train passengers	22
Pedestrians	483	Pedestrians	44,842
Selected top five gateways:		**Selected top five gateways:**	
Personal vehicles		Personal vehicles	
Buffalo-Niagara Falls, NY	5,716	El Paso, TX.	13,716
Detroit, MI.	4,744	San Ysidro, CA	13,672
Blaine, WA	2,749	Hidalgo, TX.	6,983
Port Huron, MI.	1,667	Brownsville, TX	6,567
Massena, NY	1,003	Laredo, TX	6,105
Personal vehicle passengers		Personal vehicle passengers	
Buffalo-Niagara Falls, NY	13,102	San Ysidro, CA	25,319
Detroit, MI.	8,386	El Paso, TX.	21,806
Blaine, WA	5,755	Laredo, TX	15,398
Port Huron, MI.	3,500	Hidalgo, TX.	13,468
Champlain-Rouses Point, NY	1,946	Brownsville, TX	13,275
Pedestrians		Pedestrians	
Buffalo-Niagara Falls, NY.	334	El Paso, TX.	8,029
Sumas, WA.	38	San Ysidro, CA	7,290
Calais, ME	27	Nogales, AZ	6,568
Detroit, MI.	16	Calexico, CA	4,360
International Falls, MN.	15	Laredo, TX	3,874

[1] Data reflect all personal vehicles and buses, passengers, and pedestrians entering the U.S., regardless of nationality.

Source: U.S. Department of Transportation, Bureau of Transportation Statistics, based on data from the Department of Homeland Security, U.S. Customs and Border Protection, Office of Field Operations, Operations Management Reporting system. See <http://www.bts.gov/programs/international/border_crossing_entry_data/>.

Table 1235. **Foreign Visitors for Pleasure Admitted by Country of Citizenship: 2000 to 2007**

[In thousands (30,511 represents 30,511,000). For years ending September 30. Represents non-U.S. citizens (also known as nonimmigrants) admitted to the country for a temporary period of time]

Country	2000 [1]	2005	2006	2007	Country	2000 [1]	2005	2006	2007
All countries [2]	30,511	23,815	24,888	27,486	Thailand.	76	37	40	46
					Turkey.	93	57	59	64
Europe [3]	11,806	10,016	9,749	10,703	United Arab Emirates . . .	36	3	4	4
Austria.	182	116	115	124	Africa [3]	327	212	211	228
Belgium	254	154	153	175	Egypt.	44	19	20	24
Czech Republic.	44	26	27	30	Nigeria.	27	40	37	41
Denmark	150	153	166	191	South Africa	114	64	65	67
Finland	95	76	75	78	Oceania [3]	748	723	765	823
France.	1,113	1,007	875	1,073	Australia.	535	527	562	623
Germany	1,925	1,248	1,215	1,315	New Zealand.	170	184	192	188
Greece	60	40	38	42	North America [3, 5]	6,501	5,546	6,839	8,071
Hungary.	58	30	30	32	Canada.	277	23	29	36
Iceland.	27	34	41	44	Mexico.	3,972	4,070	5,262	6,326
Ireland.	325	398	417	501	Caribbean	1,404	876	978	1,081
Italy	626	636	579	700	Bahamas, The	24	257	318	334
Netherlands	559	483	480	515	Dominican Republic . .	195	189	198	228
Norway	144	117	123	143	Haiti.	72	65	56	82
Poland.	116	119	121	121	Jamaica	240	152	186	205
Portugal.	86	81	85	98	Trinidad and Tobago . .	133	106	113	122
Russia.	74	53	58	72	Central America.	792	578	570	628
Spain.	370	402	432	533	Costa Rica	172	109	105	122
Sweden	321	249	248	282	El Salvador	175	147	139	141
Switzerland.	400	207	217	232	Guatemala	177	135	136	148
United Kingdom.	4,671	4,232	4,088	4,211	Honduras	87	75	75	90
Asia [3]	7,853	5,688	5,636	5,745	Nicaragua	47	33	35	37
China [4]	656	221	248	278	Panama	106	64	65	72
India	253	247	265	379	South America [3]	2,867	1,498	1,583	1,856
Indonesia	62	42	43	45	Argentina	515	145	162	214
Israel.	319	220	220	241	Bolivia	48	18	18	23
Japan	4,946	3,758	3,620	3,446	Brazil.	706	385	431	491
Korea, South.	606	528	570	625	Chile	194	82	86	98
Malaysia	64	32	32	34	Colombia	411	282	310	353
Pakistan.	47	34	30	32	Ecuador.	122	119	121	137
Philippines	163	144	142	156	Peru	190	142	126	135
Saudi Arabia	67	10	10	13	Uruguay	66	24	24	27
Singapore.	131	57	59	64	Venezuela	570	270	276	348

[1] Due to the temporary expiration of the Visa Waiver Program from May through October 2000, data for business and pleasure not available separately for 2000 and 2001.   [2] Total includes unknown visitors by country of citizenship.   [3] Total includes other countries not shown separately.   [4] See Table 1296, footnote 4.   [5] The majority of short-term admissions from Canada and Mexico are excluded.

Source: U.S. Dept. of Homeland Security, Office of Immigration Statistics, *2007 Yearbook of Immigration Statistics*. See also <http://www.dhs.gov/ximgtn/statistics/publications/yearbook.shtm>.

760 Arts, Recreation, and Travel

Section 27
Accommodation, Food Services, and Other Services

This section presents statistics relating to services other than those covered in the previous few sections (22 to 26) on wholesale and retail trade, transportation, communications, financial services, and recreation services. Data shown for services are classified by kind of business and cover sales or receipts, establishments, employees, payrolls, and other items. The principal sources of these data are from the Census Bureau and include the *2007 Economic Census*, annual surveys, and the *County Business Patterns* program. These data are supplemented by data from several sources such as the National Restaurant Association on food and drink sales (Table 1247), the American Hotel & Lodging Association on lodging (Table 1246), and Universal McCann on advertising (Table 1243).

Data on these services also appear in several other sections. For instance, labor force employment and earnings data appear in Section 12, Labor Force, Employment, and Earnings; gross domestic product of the industry (Table 654) appears in Section 13, Income, Expenditures, Poverty, and Wealth; and financial data (several tables) from the quarterly *Statistics of Income Bulletin,* published by the Internal Revenue Service, appear in Section 15, Business Enterprise.

Censuses—Limited coverage of the service industries started in 1933. Beginning with the 1967 census, legislation provides for a census of each area to be conducted every 5 years (for years ending in "2" and "7"). For more information on the most current census, see the Economic Census, *Guide to Economic Census*, found at <http://www.census.gov/econ /census/guide/index.html>. The industries covered in the censuses and surveys

of business are defined in the *North American Industry Classification System* (NAICS). For information on NAICS, see the Census Web site at <http://www .census.gov/epcd/www/naics.html>.

In general, the 2007 Economic Census has two final series of publications for these sectors: 1) subject series with reports such as product lines, and establishment and firm sizes and 2) geographic reports with individual reports for each state. For information on these series, see the Census Bureau Web site at <http:// www.census.gov/econ/census07>.

Current surveys—The Service Annual Survey provides annual estimates of nationwide receipts for selected personal, business, leasing and repair, amusement and entertainment, social and health, and other professional service industries in the United States. For selected social, health, and other professional service industries, separate estimates are developed for receipts of taxable firms and revenue and expenses for firms and organizations exempt from federal income taxes. Several service sectors from this survey are covered in other sections of this publication. The estimates for tax exempt firms in these industries are derived from a sample of employer firms only. Estimates obtained from annual and monthly surveys are based on sample data and are not expected to agree exactly with results that would be obtained from a complete census of all establishments. Data include estimates for sampling units not reporting.

Statistical reliability—For a discussion of statistical collection and estimation, sampling procedures, and measures of statistical reliability applicable to Census Bureau data, see Appendix III.

Table 1236. **Selected Service-Related Industries—Establishments, Sales, Payroll, and Employees by Kind of Business: 2007**

[844,552 represents $844,552,000,000. Covers only establishments with payroll. For statement on methodology, see Appendix III]

Kind of business	2007 NAICS code [1]	Estab-lishments (number)	Sales or receipts (mil. dol.)	Annual payroll (mil. dol.)	Paid employ-ees [2] (1,000)
Professional, scientific, and technical services	54	844,552	1,344,761	511,818	8,079
Professional, scientific, and technical services	541	844,552	1,344,761	511,818	8,079
Management of companies and enterprises.	55	(S)	(S)	(S)	(S)
Administrative and support and waste management and remediation services.	56	389,073	636,657	293,803	10,196
Administrative and support services	561	367,819	563,259	277,916	9,829
Waste management and remediation services	562	21,254	73,399	15,887	367
Accommodation and food services.	72	626,558	612,949	169,846	11,588
Accommodation	721	62,774	180,044	45,872	1,980
Food services and drinking places	722	563,784	432,905	123,974	9,608
Other services (except public administration)	81	537,820	417,512	99,810	3,516
Repair and maintenance.	811	222,673	143,173	41,741	1,305
Personal and laundry services	812	208,403	84,245	26,849	1,341
Religious, grantmaking, civic, professional, and similar organizations.	813	106,744	190,094	31,220	870

S Figure does not meet statistical standards. [1] North American Industrial Classification System, 2007; see text, Section 15. [2] For employees on the payroll during the pay period including March 12.

Source: U.S. Census Bureau, "2007 Economic Census, Economy-Wide Key Statistics," June 2009, using American FactFinder; <http://factfinder.census.gov>.

Table 1237. **Selected Service-Related Industries—Nonemployer Establishments and Receipts by Kind of Business: 2002 to 2006**

[2,553 represents 2,553,000. Includes only firms subject to federal income tax. Nonemployers are businesses with no paid employees. Data originate chiefly from administrative records of the Internal Revenue Service; see Appendix III]

Kind of business	2002 NAICS code [1]	Establishments (1,000)			Receipts (mil. dol.)		
		2002	2005	2006	2002	2005	2006
Professional, scientific, and technical services. . . .	54	2,553	2,854	2,904	96,395	118,575	124,237
Professional, scientific, and technical services [2]. . . .	541	2,553	2,854	2,904	96,395	118,577	124,237
Accounting, tax preparation, bookeeping, and payroll services.	5412	325	338	348	6,423	7,371	7,714
Architectual, engineering [3]	5413	209	231	238	8,560	10,807	11,308
Management, scientific and technical consulting. .	5416	465	580	536	18,637	24,232	25,653
Scientific research and development services . . .	5417	25	28	31	799	987	1,086
Administrative and support and waste manage-ment and remediation services	56	1,263	1,417	1,482	26,910	33,028	34,989
Administrative and support services [2]	561	1,244	1,398	1,463	25,826	31,666	33,569
Office administrative services	5611	127	180	190	1,886	2,667	2,923
Business support services	5614	176	185	193	4,460	5,274	5,521
Services to buildings and dwellings	5617	722	816	850	13,261	16,548	17,702
Waste management and remediation services.	562	18	19	19	1,084	1,364	1,421
Accommodation and food services	72	242	279	287	14,178	15,307	15,694
Accommodation.	721	52	56	55	3,766	3,823	3,660
Food services and drinking places	722	190	223	232	10,412	11,483	12,034
Full-service restaurants	7221	34	37	38	3,561	3,815	3,972
Limited-service eating places	7222	43	47	48	2,978	3,168	3,376
Special food services	7223	90	115	122	2,358	2,917	3,085
Drinking places (alcoholic beverages).	7224	23	25	25	1,515	1,583	1,601
Other services (except public administration).	81	2,459	2,873	2,931	60,468	74,025	77,986
Repair and maintenance [2].	811	643	691	693	22,817	26,465	27,276
Automotive repair and maintenance	8111	271	289	289	12,182	13,706	13,987
Personal and household goods repair [4]	8114	274	302	303	6,831	8,397	8,765
Personal and laundry services	812	1,642	1,996	2,047	35,127	44,809	47,776
Personal care services	8121	666	827	870	13,582	17,707	19,266
Death care services	8122	14	15	15	746	816	802
Drycleaning and laundry services	8123	37	36	35	1,741	1,884	1,966
Other personal services.	8129	925	1,118	1,128	19,057	24,401	25,742
Religious, grantmaking, civic, professional, and similar organizations.	813	174	186	190	2,524	2,752	2,933

[1] Based on the North American Industry Classification System, 2002, see text, Section 15. [2] Includes other kinds of business not shown separately. [3] Includes related services. [4] Includes maintenance.

Source: U.S. Census Bureau, "Nonemployer Statistics"; <http://www.census.gov/econ/nonemployer/index.html>.

U.S. Census Bureau, Statistical Abstract of the United States: 2010

Table 1238. Selected Service-Related Industries—Establishments, Employees, and Payroll by Industry: 2005 and 2006

[826 represents 826,000. Covers establishments with payroll. Excludes most government employees, railroad employees, and self-employed persons. Kind-of-business classification based on North American Industry Classification System, 2002 (NAICS); see text, Section 15. For statement on methodology, see Appendix III]

Kind of business	2002 NAICS code	Establishments (1,000) 2005	Establishments (1,000) 2006	Employees (1,000) [1] 2005	Employees (1,000) [1] 2006	Annual payroll (bil. dol.) 2005	Annual payroll (bil. dol.) 2006
Professional, scientific, & technical services	54	**826**	**846**	**7,689**	**8,054**	**456.5**	**497.4**
Professional, scientific, & technical services	541	826	846	7,689	8,054	456.5	497.4
Legal services	5411	188	189	1,199	1,219	81.3	85.1
Offices of lawyers	54111	175	175	1,103	1,117	77.0	80.7
Accounting, tax preparation, bookkeeping, and payroll services	5412	119	121	1,330	1,357	48.6	53.2
Tax preparation services	541213	23	25	205	227	2.2	2.5
Architectural, engineering, & related services [2]	5413	112	115	1,298	1,391	81.7	91.3
Architectural services	54131	25	25	186	201	11.5	13.1
Engineering services	54133	56	57	882	933	59.7	66.3
Specialized design services [2]	5414	33	34	121	130	5.6	6.2
Graphic design services	54143	17	17	60	63	2.8	3.1
Computer systems design & related services [2]	5415	108	111	1,132	1,215	82.0	90.8
Custom computer programming services	541511	48	49	460	506	34.8	38.7
Computer systems design services	541512	44	47	457	487	32.2	35.8
Management, scientific, & technical consulting services [2]	5416	138	146	957	1,039	61.8	67.9
Management consulting services	54161	108	111	814	866	53.2	57.5
Environmental consulting services	54162	9	9	62	71	3.3	3.7
Scientific research & development services	5417	17	17	661	673	54.5	58.9
Research & development in the physical engineering & life sciences	54171	14	15	603	615	50.7	54.8
Advertising & related services [2]	5418	39	39	414	434	22.5	24.2
Advertising agencies	54181	13	14	156	167	11.4	12.2
Direct mail advertising	54186	3	3	71	73	2.9	3.0
Other professional, scientific, & tech services	5419	73	73	578	596	18.4	19.8
Veterinary services	54194	27	28	270	282	7.3	8.0
Management of companies and enterprises	55	**48**	**48**	**2,856**	**2,916**	**243.3**	**266.3**
Admin/support & waste mgmt & remediation service	56	**370**	**378**	**9,280**	**10,004**	**255.4**	**283.2**
Administrative & support services [2]	561	350	358	8,947	9,658	241.7	268.4
Employment services	5613	41	44	4,580	5,102	118.1	133.5
Temporary help services	56132	28	29	2,615	2,931	58.5	64.6
Business support services [2]	5614	36	36	764	779	20.8	22.2
Telephone call centers	56142	5	5	383	383	8.3	9.0
Collection agencies	56144	5	5	138	143	4.2	4.5
Credit bureaus	56145	1	1	22	22	1.5	1.6
Travel arrangement & reservation services	5615	24	23	254	254	10.9	10.7
Travel agencies	56151	17	17	127	129	5.0	5.3
Investigation & security services	5616	24	25	767	802	18.7	20.9
Investigation, guard, & armored car services	56161	14	15	651	680	14.1	15.7
Security systems services	56162	10	10	116	122	4.7	5.1
Services to buildings & dwellings	5617	173	176	1,624	1,707	35.4	38.0
Waste management & remediation services	562	19	20	333	345	13.7	14.9
Waste collection	5621	9	9	172	177	6.8	7.3
Waste treatment & disposal	5622	3	3	54	56	2.6	2.8
Remediation & other waste mgmt services	5629	8	8	108	112	4.3	4.8
Accommodation & food services	72	**603**	**612**	**11,026**	**11,381**	**156.0**	**167.2**
Accommodation	721	63	63	1,854	1,881	41.8	43.9
Traveler accommodation	7211	53	53	1,805	1,831	40.6	42.7
Hotels (except casino hotels) & motels	72111	48	48	1,414	1,436	29.2	30.6
RV (recreational vehicle) parks & recreational camps	7212	7	7	38	38	1.0	1.0
Rooming & boarding houses	7213	2	2	12	12	0.2	0.2
Food services & drinking places	722	541	550	9,171	9,501	114.2	123.3
Full-service restaurants	7221	210	214	4,340	4,519	58.1	62.9
Limited-service eating places	7222	250	256	3,927	4,074	42.8	45.3
Special food services	7223	33	33	552	546	9.2	10.7
Drinking places (alcoholic beverages)	7224	47	46	352	362	4.1	4.4
Other services (except public administration)	81	**740**	**736**	**5,391**	**5,459**	**127.5**	**133.6**
Repair & maintenance [2]	811	228	226	1,295	1,307	39.5	41.2
Automotive repair & maintenance	8111	166	164	880	888	23.7	24.6
Personal & household goods repair & maintenance	8114	24	23	104	98	2.8	2.7
Personal & laundry services [2]	812	210	210	1,337	1,358	26.4	27.6
Personal care services	8121	108	110	589	613	9.9	10.6
Death care services	8122	22	21	138	137	4.0	4.1
Drycleaning & laundry services	8123	43	42	382	374	7.9	8.1
Religious/grantmaking/civic/professional [3]	813	302	301	2,759	2,794	61.6	64.8
Religious organizations	8131	173	175	1,632	1,647	27.2	28.3
Grantmaking & giving services	8132	16	16	145	149	6.0	6.4
Social advocacy organizations	8133	14	14	121	123	3.9	4.2
Civic & social organizations	8134	32	31	327	328	5.0	5.2
Business/professional/labor/political [3]	8139	67	66	534	546	19.5	20.7
Labor unions [3]	81393	16	16	177	179	4.8	4.9

[1] Includes employees on the payroll for the pay period including March 12.   [2] Includes other kinds of business not shown separately.   [3] And similar organizations.

Source: U.S. Census Bureau, "County Business Patterns"; <http://www.census.gov/econ/cbp/>.

Accommodation, Food Services, and Other Services 763

Table 1239.

Table 1239. Employed Persons—Sex, Race, and Hispanic or Latino Origin by Industry: 2008

[15,540 represents 15,540,000. Civilian noninstitutional population 16 years and older. Based on the Current Population Survey; see text, Sections 1 and 13, and Appendix III. For information on employees in other sectors see Tables 603 and 619]

Industry	2002 NAICS code [1]	Total employed (1,000)	Percent of total Female	Percent of total Black [2]	Percent of total Asian [2]	Percent of total Hispanic or Latino [3]
Professional and business services	(X)	15,540	42.4	9.3	6.1	13.8
Professional and technical services	54	9,362	44.1	6.3	8.2	7.2
Legal services	5411	1,642	58.6	7.5	3.1	7.8
Accounting, tax preparation, bookkeeping, & payroll services	5412	1,002	62.8	7.7	6.9	8.7
Architectural, engineering, and related services	5413	1,615	25.8	4.8	5.9	7.8
Specialized design services.	5414	386	59.7	4.0	6.8	6.5
Computer systems design & related services	5415	1,945	25.5	6.4	17.8	5.0
Management, scientific, and technical consulting services.	5416	1,112	43.4	7.1	6.5	6.0
Scientific research & development services . .	5417	543	47.4	6.8	13.4	7.2
Advertising and related services.	5418	520	49.9	6.7	3.5	9.1
Other professional, scientific, and technical services [4].	5419	352	55.5	4.5	4.2	9.1
Veterinary services	54194	246	81.7	3.8	1.4	9.2
Management, administrative, and waste services	55-56	6,178	39.7	13.9	3.0	23.8
Management of companies and enterprises .	55	67	60.7	6.8	2.6	6.8
Employment services.	5613	984	58.5	18.6	3.2	17.3
Business support services.	5614	801	62.9	15.7	4.0	11.4
Travel arrangement & reservation services. .	5615	272	61.6	8.4	8.7	10.4
Investigations & security services.	5616	814	26.6	24.1	3.4	12.6
Services to buildings and dwellings [5]	5617	1,350	50.1	13.3	2.4	33.0
Landscaping services.	56173	1,229	8.6	5.6	1.4	40.3
Other administrative and support services . .	5611,2,9	226	45.3	10.2	3.7	16.6
Waste management and remediation services.	562	437	15.1	12.0	1.8	22.3
Accommodation and food services	72	9,795	53.1	11.7	6.8	20.8
Accommodation	721	1,523	56.9	16.1	7.6	21.5
Traveler accommodation.	7211	1,423	57.4	16.5	8.1	22.2
Recreational vehicle parks and camps, and rooming and board houses	7212,3	100	50.6	9.9	1.0	10.9
Food services and drinking places	722	8,272	52.4	10.9	6.6	20.7
Restaurants and other food services [6].	722	8,032	52.4	11.1	6.7	20.9
Drinking places, alcoholic beverages.	7224	240	54.6	5.8	2.4	13.0
Other services	81	7,005	51.6	9.8	5.9	17.1
Other services (except private households) . . .	81	6,200	46.5	9.9	6.3	14.4
Repair and maintenance.	811	2,086	12.3	7.8	3.2	20.7
Automotive repair and maintenance [7] . . .	8111	1,208	10.6	6.2	2.8	21.3
Car washes	811192	175	14.7	12.7	4.1	34.0
Electronic & precision equipment repair and maintenance	8112	177	14.8	13.1	8.2	13.1
Commercial and industrial machinery & equipment repair and maintenance	8113	320	6.9	7.4	1.2	16.3
Personal and household goods repair and maintenance [8]	8114	199	26.4	8.0	3.4	18.0
Footwear and leather goods repair	81143	6	(Z)	(Z)	(Z)	(Z)
Personal and laundry services.	812	2,240	71.3	11.3	12.5	14.2
Barber shops	812111	95	25.2	31.3	3.8	22.2
Beauty salons	812112	929	90.0	11.0	7.3	11.2
Nail salons and other personal care services	812113,81219	365	75.1	2.6	37.9	5.7
Drycleaning & laundry services.	8123	378	61.4	14.8	14.4	28.3
Funeral homes, cemeteries, and crematories	8122	124	27.6	11.4	0.4	8.8
Other personal services	8129	348	56.6	11.9	4.1	15.5
Membership associations and organizations.	813	1,874	54.8	10.4	2.3	7.8
Religious organizations	8131	1,060	48.0	8.9	1.9	6.8
Civic, social, advocacy organizations, grantmaking & giving services	8132,3,4	601	67.3	13.1	2.4	10.3
Business, professional, political, and similar organizations [9]	8139	155	54.6	7.9	4.3	4.8
Labor unions.	81393	59	49.4	15.0	2.1	8.0
Private households	814	805	91.3	9.7	3.1	37.6

Z Base less than 50,000.   X Not applicable.   [1] Based on the North American Industry Classification System, 2002; see Section 15.   [2] The Current Population Survey (CPS) allows respondents to choose more than one race. Data represents persons who selected this race group only and exclude persons reporting more than one race. See also comments on race in the text for Section 1.   [3] Persons of Hispanic or Latino ethnicity may be any race.   [4] Excludes NAICS 54194 (veterinary services).   [5] Excludes NAICS 56173 (landscaping services).   [6] Excludes NAICS 7224 (drinking places, alcoholic beverages).   [7] Excludes NAICS 811192 (car washes).   [8] Excludes NAICS 81143 (footwear and leather goods repair).   [9] Excludes NAICS 81393 (labor unions).

Source: U.S. Bureau of Labor Statistics, "Employment and Earnings Online," January 2009; <http://www.bls.gov/opub/ee/home.htm> and <http://www.bls.gov/cps/home.htm>.

Table 1240. **Selected Service-Related Industries—Establishments, Employees, and Annual Payroll by State: 2006**

[8,054 represents 8,054,000. Covers establishments with payroll. Excludes most government employees, railroad employees, and self-employed persons. Based on the North American Industry Classification System, 2002 (NAICS); see text, Section 15. For statement on methodology, see Appendix III]

State	Professional, scientific, & technical services (NAICS 54)			Admin./ support waste mgt./ remediation services (NAICS 56)			Accommodation and food services (NAICS 72)		
	Estab-lish-ments	Employ-ees [1] (1,000)	Annual payroll (mil. dol.)	Estab-lish-ments	Employ-ees [1] (1,000)	Annual payroll (mil. dol.)	Estab-lish-ments	Employ-ees [1] (1,000)	Annual payroll (mil. dol.)
United States. .	846,473	8,054	497,407	378,335	10,004	283,241	612,254	11,381	167,231
Alabama.	9,379	98	5,071	4,128	129	2,790	7,810	152	1,706
Alaska	1,849	14	871	1,022	19	762	1,977	24	521
Arizona.	16,165	134	6,892	8,195	240	6,615	10,926	254	3,539
Arkansas	5,583	38	1,575	2,464	53	1,107	5,052	90	960
California	112,691	1,225	83,746	42,546	1,153	34,730	72,849	1,322	21,244
Colorado.	22,429	164	10,380	7,986	187	6,127	11,829	229	3,327
Connecticut.	10,313	103	6,931	5,409	107	3,391	7,702	133	2,507
Delaware	2,523	28	2,045	1,308	24	683	1,748	32	505
District of Columbia .	4,728	89	8,600	1,017	30	1,145	2,016	49	1,185
Florida	68,350	455	24,343	32,116	1,408	38,945	33,677	742	11,626
Georgia	27,220	222	12,935	11,660	355	9,890	17,754	354	4,654
Hawaii	3,355	26	1,286	1,805	42	1,091	3,530	101	2,305
Idaho	4,090	34	1,497	2,093	48	1,080	3,317	54	644
Illinois	39,185	377	24,308	15,918	461	12,629	25,878	457	6,762
Indiana.	12,954	113	5,352	7,095	176	4,435	12,562	254	3,097
Iowa	6,260	43	1,865	3,464	72	1,549	6,906	112	1,189
Kansas.	7,231	58	2,656	3,395	67	1,801	5,745	106	1,185
Kentucky	8,142	64	2,603	3,759	92	1,906	7,078	150	1,761
Louisiana	11,057	86	4,042	4,399	111	2,901	7,601	166	2,266
Maine.	3,545	24	1,143	1,930	28	843	3,892	47	758
Maryland	19,507	228	14,511	7,961	177	5,483	10,429	194	2,896
Massachusetts.	22,215	261	20,220	9,320	186	6,701	15,500	248	4,335
Michigan.	22,727	302	18,992	12,628	342	10,933	19,198	338	4,040
Minnesota.	16,754	139	8,159	7,095	148	4,371	10,912	218	2,902
Mississippi . . .	4,675	33	1,379	2,223	49	993	4,608	112	1,575
Missouri	13,798	138	7,440	7,282	157	3,955	11,968	240	3,049
Montana.	3,412	23	816	1,548	14	299	3,375	45	523
Nebraska	4,239	46	2,282	2,517	66	1,657	4,159	68	718
Nevada	7,837	59	3,216	4,099	102	2,706	5,264	313	8,417
New Hampshire	4,086	30	1,756	2,100	41	1,473	3,407	56	830
New Jersey.	31,674	295	20,760	13,371	306	9,227	18,881	285	5,387
New Mexico	4,807	39	1,903	1,890	45	1,073	3,962	81	1,042
New York	58,818	600	42,983	23,955	513	18,572	42,493	569	10,751
North Carolina	22,054	196	11,047	11,095	278	6,966	17,491	331	4,215
North Dakota.	1,440	12	465	883	12	249	1,785	29	314
Ohio	25,636	250	13,262	13,747	356	9,037	23,410	441	5,011
Oklahoma	9,070	70	3,014	4,057	100	2,340	6,699	128	1,377
Oregon.	11,235	80	4,024	5,207	95	2,388	9,756	146	2,093
Pennsylvania.	29,942	316	19,625	14,346	306	8,205	26,218	411	5,420
Rhode Island.	3,198	22	1,151	1,704	23	614	2,898	42	626
South Carolina.	9,373	81	4,109	5,430	140	3,185	9,072	181	2,297
South Dakota	1,731	10	388	982	11	228	2,332	36	414
Tennessee	11,572	127	6,055	6,242	197	4,895	11,144	232	2,964
Texas.	56,918	552	35,551	24,350	869	23,979	41,243	851	11,408
Utah	7,877	71	3,291	3,668	101	2,758	4,463	91	1,115
Vermont	2,170	17	660	1,012	8	204	1,948	29	419
Virginia.	27,091	373	26,054	10,191	239	7,434	15,127	299	4,239
Washington	19,080	157	9,800	8,683	141	4,801	15,368	226	3,499
West Virginia.	3,039	25	891	1,463	33	678	3,459	60	689
Wisconsin	11,586	102	5,115	6,699	137	3,242	14,120	225	2,510
Wyoming	1,863	8	337	878	7	175	1,716	26	414

[1] For employees on the payroll for the pay period including March 12.

Source: U.S. Census Bureau, "County Business Patterns"; <http://www.census.gov/econ/cbp/>.

Accommodation, Food Services, and Other Services **765**

Table 1241. **Professional, Scientific, and Technical Services— Estimated Revenue: 2000 to 2007**

[In millions of dollars (803,527 represents $803,527,000,000). For taxable employer firms. Estimates have been adjusted to the results of the 2002 Economic Census. Based on the Service Annual Survey; see Appendix III]

Kind of business	2002 NAICS code [1]	2000	2003	2004	2005	2006	2007
Professional, scientific, and technical services (except notaries) [2]	54	803,527	879,725	966,437	1,052,303	1,137,804	1,247,590
Legal services (except notaries)	5411	160,619	199,915	209,475	221,852	235,768	251,532
Offices of lawyers	54111	152,834	187,819	197,385	207,925	221,301	237,432
Other legal services	54119	7,785	12,096	12,090	13,927	14,467	14,100
Accounting, tax preparation, bookkeeping and payroll services	5412	79,361	87,791	92,884	100,950	109,136	121,290
Offices of certified public accountants	541211	45,773	47,835	50,679	54,508	57,744	63,206
Tax preparation services	541213	3,347	4,468	4,944	5,416	5,977	6,686
Payroll services	541214	21,394	24,366	25,359	27,856	31,316	36,158
Other accounting services	541219	8,847	11,122	11,902	13,170	14,099	15,240
Architectural, engineering, & related services [3]	5413	150,269	160,917	184,292	204,983	223,004	243,843
Architectural services	54131	25,021	26,851	28,609	31,668	34,721	40,068
Landscape architectural services	54132	(NA)	(NA)	4,218	4,575	5,038	5,367
Engineering services	54133	111,929	117,509	132,814	148,352	161,099	172,744
Testing laboratories	54138	7,128	8,849	9,908	10,380	11,185	14,096
Other related services	54134,5,6,7	6,191	7,708	8,742	10,008	10,960	11,568
Specialized design services	5414	17,889	18,090	19,617	21,556	23,542	25,851
Interior design services	54141	6,798	7,497	8,061	8,838	10,037	11,281
Graphic design services	54143	8,962	8,269	8,528	9,221	9,595	9,874
All other design services	54142,9	(NA)	(NA)	3,028	3,497	3,910	4,695
Computer systems design and services	5415	186,402	171,393	173,525	188,266	202,281	228,623
Custom computer programming services	541511	70,004	58,140	58,303	64,289	68,323	79,751
Computer systems design services	541512	82,763	76,992	77,042	84,995	91,908	101,211
Computer facilities management services	541513	21,816	22,518	23,422	22,748	23,934	26,694
Other computer-related services	541519	11,819	13,743	14,758	16,234	18,116	20,967
Management, scientific, and technical consulting services	5416	90,129	108,783	121,709	137,364	149,767	165,248
Management consulting services	54161	78,250	92,129	102,452	115,877	125,546	137,119
Environmental consulting services	54162	5,578	7,902	8,748	9,094	10,416	12,022
Other scientific and technical consulting services	54169	6,301	8,752	10,509	12,393	13,805	16,107
Scientific research and development services	5417	35,587	48,142	54,272	60,169	68,607	75,171
Research and development in physical, engineering and life sciences	54171	34,029	46,104	51,994	57,679	66,183	72,427
Research and development in social sciences and humanities	54172	1,558	2,038	2,278	2,490	2,424	2,744
Advertising and related services	5418	59,680	58,629	63,585	67,045	72,911	79,033
Advertising agencies	54181	21,584	22,396	24,551	25,482	27,976	30,824
Public relations agencies	54182	6,501	6,305	6,954	7,546	8,635	9,361
Media buying agencies	54183	1,036	1,063	1,405	1,478	1,704	1,714
Media representatives	54184	3,247	2,712	2,096	2,267	2,352	2,655
Display advertising	54185	4,752	4,925	5,440	6,181	6,611	7,368
Direct mail advertising	54186	10,351	10,648	11,570	12,190	12,371	12,255
All other advertising	54187,9	(NA)	(NA)	11,568	11,901	13,262	14,856
Other professional, scientific, and technical services [4]	5419	23,591	26,065	47,080	50,119	52,788	56,998
Marketing research and public opinion polling	54191	11,683	11,118	11,851	12,283	13,170	13,872
Photographic services	54192	6,613	6,758	6,984	7,268	7,342	7,615
Photography studios, portrait	541921	4,642	4,879	5,031	5,262	5,272	5,579
Commercial photography	541922	1,971	1,879	1,953	2,006	2,070	2,036
Translation and interpretation services	54193	810	968	1,093	1,121	1,166	1,393
Veterinary services	54194	(NA)	(NA)	19,144	20,541	22,321	24,481
All other professional, scientific, and technical services	54199	4,485	7,221	8,008	8,905	8,789	9,637

NA Not available. [1] Based on the North American Industry Classification System, 2002; see Section 15. [2] Prior to 2004, excludes NAICS 54132 (landscape architecture services) and NAICS 54194 (veterinary services). [3] Prior to 2004, excludes NAICS 54132 (landscape architectural services). [4] Prior to 2004, excludes NAICS 54194 (veterinary services).

Source: U.S. Census Bureau, "Service Annual Survey" (published March 2009); <http://www.census.gov/services/>.

Table 1242. Selected Service Industries—E-Commerce Revenue: 2006 and 2007

[103,697 represents $103,697,000,000]. Includes data only for businesses with paid employees, except for accommodation and food services, which also includes businesses with and without paid employees. Except as noted, based on the Service Annual Survey]

Kind of business	2002 NAICS code [1]	E-commerce revenue (mil. dol.) 2006	E-commerce revenue (mil. dol.) 2007	E-commerce as percent of total revenue, 2007	E-commerce revenue, percent distribution, 2007
Selected service industries, total	(X)	103,697	124,123	1.8	100.0
Selected transportation and warehousing [2]	(X)	6,523	9,245	2.8	7.4
Truck transportation	484	5,617	8,164	3.6	6.6
Couriers and messengers	492	78	(S)	(S)	(S)
Warehousing and storage	493	828	987	4.6	0.8
Information	51	37,227	44,035	3.9	35.5
Publishing industries	511	16,520	18,581	6.2	15.0
Online information services	51811	4,637	(S)	(S)	(S)
Selected finance [3]	(X)	7,241	8,791	1.9	7.1
Securities and commodity contracts intermediation and brokerage	5231	7,018	8,507	2.7	6.9
Rental and leasing services	532	6,538	7,330	6.0	5.9
Selected professional, scientific, and technical services [4]	(X)	14,659	18,893	1.5	15.2
Computer systems design and related services	5415	3,829	4,580	2.0	3.7
Administrative and support and waste management and remediation services	56	13,333	12,759	2.1	10.3
Travel arrangements and reservation services	5615	6,470	7,308	22.8	5.9
Health care and social assistance services	62	1,034	1,048	0.1	0.8
Arts, entertainment, and recreation services	71	2,540	3,073	1.6	2.5
Accommodation and food services [5]	72	9,270	12,309	2.0	9.9
Selected other services [6]	(X)	5,332	6,640	1.6	5.3
Repair and maintenance	811	913	1,004	0.7	0.8
Religious, grantmaking, civic, professional, and similar organizations	813	3,156	4,044	2.2	3.3

S Data do not meet publication standards. X Not applicable. [1] North American Industry Classification System (NAICS), 2002; see text Section 15. [2] Excludes NAICS 481 (air transportation), 482 (rail transportation), 483 (water transportation), 485 (transit and good passenger transportation), 486 (pipeline transportation), 487 (scenic and sightseeing transportation), 488 (support activities for transportation) and 491 (postal service). [3] Excludes NAICS 521 (monetary authorities-central bank), 522 (credit intermediation and related activities), 5232 (securities and commodity exchanges), NAICS 52391 (miscellaneous intermediation), 52399 (all other financial investment activities), 524 (insurance carriers and related activities) and 525 (funds and trusts). [4] Excludes NAICS 54112 (offices of notaries). [5] Based on 2006 Annual Retail Trade Survey. [6] Excludes NAICS 81311 (religious organizations), 81393 (labor and similar organizations), 81394 (political organizations) and 814 (private households).

Source: U.S. Census Bureau, Internet site "E-Stats" (published 28 May 2009); <http://www.census.gov/ens/www/ebusiness614.htm>.

Table 1243. Advertising—Estimated Expenditures by Medium: 1990 to 2008

[In millions of dollars (129,968 represents $129,968,000,000). See source for definitions of types of advertising]

Medium	1990	2000	2002	2003	2004	2005	2006	2007	2008 [1]
Total	129,968	247,472	236,875	245,477	263,766	271,074	281,653	279,612	270,767
National	73,638	151,664	145,429	152,482	167,096	172,797	182,483	185,280	185,049
Local	56,330	95,808	91,446	92,995	96,670	98,277	99,170	94,332	85,718
Newspapers	32,281	49,050	44,031	44,843	46,614	47,335	46,555	42,133	35,788
National	3,867	7,229	6,806	7,357	7,629	7,465	7,084	6,609	5,948
Local	28,414	41,821	37,225	37,486	38,985	39,870	39,471	35,524	29,840
Magazines	6,803	12,370	10,995	11,435	12,247	12,847	13,168	13,787	12,960
Broadcast TV	26,616	44,802	42,068	41,932	46,264	44,293	46,880	44,521	43,734
Four TV networks	9,863	15,888	15,000	15,030	16,713	16,128	16,676	16,643	17,226
Syndication	1,109	3,108	3,034	3,434	3,674	3,865	3,691	3,329	3,560
Spot (national)	7,788	12,264	10,920	9,948	11,370	10,040	11,626	10,138	9,834
Spot (local)	7,856	13,542	13,114	13,520	14,507	14,260	14,887	14,411	13,114
Cable TV	2,631	15,455	16,297	18,814	21,527	23,654	25,025	26,319	27,544
Cable TV networks	2,000	11,765	12,071	13,954	16,424	18,296	19,320	20,614	21,440
Spot (local)	631	3,690	4,226	4,860	5,103	5,358	5,705	5,705	6,104
Radio	8,726	19,295	18,877	19,100	19,581	19,640	19,643	19,152	17,535
Network	482	780	775	798	836	814	798	830	765
Spot (national)	1,635	3,668	3,340	3,540	3,540	3,469	3,642	3,423	3,063
Spot (local)	6,609	14,847	14,762	14,762	15,205	15,357	15,203	14,899	13,707
Yellow Pages	8,926	13,228	13,776	13,896	14,002	14,229	14,393	14,250	13,844
National	1,132	2,093	2,087	2,114	2,110	2,163	2,206	2,185	2,141
Local	7,794	11,135	11,689	11,782	11,892	12,066	12,187	12,065	11,703
Direct mail	23,370	44,591	46,067	48,370	52,191	55,218	58,642	60,225	59,622
Business papers	2,875	4,915	3,976	4,004	4,072	4,170	4,195	4,111	4,111
Out-of-home [2]	1,084	5,176	5,175	5,443	5,770	6,232	6,731	7,202	7,562
National	640	2,068	2,061	2,298	2,530	2,736	2,955	3,027	3,178
Local	444	3,108	3,114	3,145	3,240	3,496	3,776	4,175	4,384
Internet [3]	(NA)	6,507	4,883	5,650	6,853	7,764	9,100	10,529	11,371
Miscellaneous [4]	16,656	32,083	30,730	31,990	34,645	35,692	37,321	37,383	36,696
National	12,074	24,418	23,414	24,550	26,907	27,822	29,380	29,830	29,830
Local	4,582	7,665	7,316	7,440	7,738	7,870	7,941	7,553	6,866

NA Not available. [1] Preliminary data. [2] Prior to 2000, represents only "outdoor" billboards. Beginning 2000, includes other forms of outdoor advertising (i.e. transportation vehicles, bus shelters, telephone kiosks, etc.) previously covered under "Miscellaneous." [3] Excludes search revenue. [4] Beginning 2000, part of miscellaneous now included under "Out-of-home" advertising. See footnote 2.

Source: Universal McCann, New York, N.Y. (copyright); <http://www.universalmccann.com>.

U.S. Census Bureau, Statistical Abstract of the United States: 2010

Table 1244. **Administrative and Support and Waste Management and Remediation Services—Estimated Revenue: 2000 to 2007**

[In millions of dollars (396,499 represents $396,499,000,000). For taxable and tax-exempt employer firms. Estimates have been adjusted to results of the 2002 Economic Census. Based on the Service Annual Survey; see Appendix III]

Kind of business	2002 NAICS code [1]	2000	2003	2004	2005	2006	2007
Administrative and support and waste management and remediation services [2] . .	56	396,499	414,988	484,309	527,647	563,729	594,820
Administrative and support services [2]	561	345,302	360,434	425,667	464,451	495,034	523,610
Office administrative services.	56111	26,288	34,556	38,014	43,073	47,156	49,776
Facilities support services.	56121	13,211	12,158	12,520	14,028	15,655	17,444
Employment services	5613	144,242	133,833	145,717	159,144	171,019	178,667
Employment placement agencies	56131	4,985	5,874	6,513	6,772	7,154	7,589
Temporary help services	56132	79,622	69,910	77,660	85,023	90,169	93,740
Professional employer organizations	56133	59,635	58,049	61,544	67,349	73,696	77,338
Business support services.	5614	41,203	46,111	48,166	50,948	54,353	55,250
Document preparation services.	56141	1,920	2,500	2,483	2,631	2,834	2,931
Telephone call centers	56142	14,805	13,273	13,843	14,545	15,528	15,791
Telephone answering services.	561421	2,135	1,897	1,783	1,907	1,849	2,039
Telemarketing bureaus.	561422	12,670	11,376	12,060	12,638	13,679	13,752
Business service centers.	56143	8,257	8,335	8,469	8,378	7,686	7,703
Private mail centers.	561431	1,692	2,187	2,274	2,234	2,410	2,562
Other business service centers (including copy shops)	561439	6,565	6,148	6,195	6,144	5,276	5,141
Collection agencies	56144	7,300	9,830	10,860	11,479	11,600	12,142
Credit bureaus.	56145	3,741	5,230	5,516	6,332	8,202	8,497
Other business support services	56149	5,180	6,943	6,995	7,583	8,503	8,186
Repossession services	561491	418	549	534	572	596	(S)
Court reporting and stenotype services.	561492	1,250	1,715	1,792	1,847	2,023	2,013
All other business support services	561499	3,512	4,679	4,669	5,164	5,884	5,525
Travel arrangement and reservation services	5615	26,119	26,594	28,200	29,117	30,201	32,072
Travel agencies	56151	11,639	9,759	10,101	10,431	11,058	11,374
Tour operators.	56152	3,564	3,212	3,515	3,621	3,534	3,962
Other travel arrangement and reservation services	56159	10,916	13,623	14,584	15,065	15,609	16,736
Convention and visitors bureaus	561591	1,020	1,227	1,256	1,313	1,408	1,600
All other travel arrangement and reservation services.	561599	9,896	12,396	13,328	13,752	14,201	15,136
Investigation and security services	5616	27,594	32,325	33,723	37,081	37,610	39,977
Investigation, guard, and armored car services	56161	17,581	20,920	21,754	24,416	24,864	26,143
Investigation services	561611	2,350	3,090	3,345	3,668	3,536	4,054
Security guards and patrol services	561612	13,393	15,551	16,321	18,624	19,147	20,106
Armored car services.	561613	1,838	2,279	2,088	2,124	2,181	1,983
Security systems services	56162	10,013	11,405	11,969	12,665	12,746	13,834
Security systems services (except locksmiths)	561621	8,683	9,987	10,488	11,083	10,961	11,937
Locksmiths	561622	1,330	1,418	1,481	1,582	1,785	1,897
Services to buildings and dwellings [2]	5617	35,790	43,697	86,013	93,520	99,137	107,959
Exterminating and pest control services	56171	5,723	7,206	7,673	8,144	8,535	8,789
Janitorial services.	56172	24,593	29,303	30,288	31,766	32,830	36,546
Landscaping services	56173	(NA)	(NA)	40,384	44,807	47,869	51,564
Carpet and upholstery cleaning services	56174	2,463	2,808	2,964	3,386	3,596	3,856
Other services to buildings and dwellings	56179	3,011	4,380	4,703	5,416	6,307	7,203
Other support services	5619	30,855	31,160	33,315	37,539	39,905	42,467
Packaging and labeling services	56191	4,432	5,021	5,591	6,709	7,151	7,636
Convention and trade show organizers	56192	8,410	9,083	9,517	10,710	11,377	11,402
All other support services	56199	18,013	17,056	18,207	20,120	21,377	23,429
Waste management and remediation services	562	51,197	54,554	58,643	63,196	68,695	71,211
Waste collection	5621	28,820	30,272	32,430	33,998	37,483	38,484
Solid waste collection	562111	27,032	28,363	30,436	31,900	35,059	35,834
Hazardous waste collection	562112	1,249	1,445	1,565	1,614	1,834	1,990
Other waste collection.	562119	539	464	429	484	590	660
Waste treatment and disposal	5622	11,025	11,173	11,398	12,543	13,280	13,308
Hazardous waste treatment and disposal	562211	3,155	3,351	3,264	3,730	4,037	4,427
Solid waste landfill	562212	5,965	5,802	6,168	6,439	6,704	6,692
Solid waste combustors and incinerators	562213	1,261	1,442	1,303	1,587	1,672	1,311
Other nonhazardous waste treatment and disposal	562219	644	578	663	787	867	878
Remediation and other waste management services.	5629	11,352	13,109	14,815	16,655	17,932	19,419
Remediation services	56291	6,750	7,745	8,834	10,204	11,078	11,475
Materials recovery facility.	56292	1,593	2,222	2,633	2,714	2,754	3,351
All other waste management services	56299	3,009	3,142	3,348	3,737	4,100	4,593
Septic tank and related services	562991	2,197	2,049	2,132	2,372	2,563	2,760
All other miscellaneous waste management services	562998	812	1,093	1,216	1,365	1,537	1,833

NA Not available.   S Data do not meet publication standards.   [1] North American Industry Classification System, 2002; see text, Section 15.   [2] Prior to 2004, excludes NAICS 56173 (Landscaping services).

Source: U.S. Census Bureau, "Service Annual Survey" (published March 2009); <http://www.census.gov/services/>.

Table 1245. **Estimated Accommodation and Food Services Sales by Kind of Business: 2000 to 2007**

[In millions of dollars (443,642 represents 443,642,000,000). Estimates are based on data from the Annual Retail Trade Survey and administrative records and have been adjusted to the results of the 2002 Economic Census]

Kind of business	NAICS code [1]	2000	2002	2003	2004	2005	2006	2007
Accommodation and food services, total ..	72	443,642	463,678	484,174	516,580	545,248	575,348	601,504
Accommodation	721	138,181	131,864	134,481	144,604	151,934	157,473	163,706
Traveler accommodation	7211	133,582	127,050	129,610	139,731	146,879	152,024	157,996
RV parks and recreational camps	7212	3,608	3,799	3,884	3,863	3,993	4,306	4,494
Rooming and boarding houses	7213	991	1,015	987	1,010	1,062	1,143	1,216
Food services and drinking places [2]	722	305,461	331,814	349,693	371,976	393,314	417,875	437,798
Full service restaurants	7221	134,204	148,211	155,085	163,834	171,666	182,144	190,417
Limited service eating places	7222	127,879	138,302	147,087	158,699	169,021	178,582	186,326
Drinking places	7224	15,415	16,417	17,580	18,168	18,953	20,762	21,835

[1] North American Industry Classification System, 2002; see text, Section 15.   [2] Includes other kinds of business not shown separately.

Source: U.S. Census Bureau, "Annual Revision of Monthly Retail and Food Services: Sales and Inventories—January 1992 Through March 2009"; <http://www.census.gov/retail/> (accessed 14 May 2009).

Table 1246. **Lodging Industry Summary: 1990 to 2007**

Year	Average occupancy rate (percent)	Average room rate (dol.)	Room size of property	2007 Estab-lish-ments	2007 Rooms (mil.)	Item	2007 Busi-ness traveler	2007 Leisure traveler
1990	63.3	57.96	Total	48,062	4.5	Typical night:		
1995	65.5	66.65				Made reservations		
2000	63.7	85.89	Percent:			(percent)	91	86
2003	61.6	82.52	Under 75 rooms . .	56.6	25.9	Amount paid (dol.)	$119.00	$109.00
2004	61.3	86.24	75–149 rooms . . .	31.4	35.6	Length of stay (percent):		
2005	63.1	90.88	150–299 rooms . .	8.6	18.6	One night	33	42
2006	63.3	97.78	300–500 rooms . .	2.3	9.1	Two nights	26	30
2007	63.1	103.87	Over 500 rooms . .	1.1	10.8	Three or more	41	28

Source: American Hotel & Lodging Association, Washington, DC Lodging Industry Profile, annual (copyright). See also <http://www.ahla.com>.

Table 1247. **Commercial and Noncommercial Groups—Food and Drink Establishments and Sales: 1990 to 2009**

[(238,149 represents $238,149,000,000). Excludes military. Data refer to sales to consumers of food and alcoholic beverages. Sales are estimated. For details, see source]

Type of group	Estab-lish-ments, 2006	Sales (mil. dol.) 1990	1995	2000	2005	2007	2008	2009 [1]
Total	921,442	238,149	294,631	377,652	486,494	532,534	550,146	563,744
Commercial restaurant services [2, 3]	720,628	211,606	265,910	345,345	445,078	487,909	503,403	515,965
Eating places [2]	458,527	155,552	198,293	259,743	329,598	360,621	369,907	377,899
Full-service restaurants	199,084	77,811	96,396	133,834	165,170	179,093	181,063	182,874
Limited-service restaurants [4]	201,269	[5]69,798	[5]92,901	107,147	136,903	150,821	157,457	163,755
Snack and nonalcoholic beverage bars	43,323	(5)	(5)	12,867	17,150	19,578	20,089	19,927
Bars and taverns [6]	48,856	9,533	9,948	12,412	15,002	16,148	16,632	17,098
Managed services [2]	20,693	14,149	18,186	24,841	32,030	36,162	38,257	40,113
Manufacturing and industrial plants . . .	(NA)	3,856	4,814	6,223	6,570	7,163	7,258	7,374
Colleges and universities	(NA)	2,788	3,989	5,879	9,283	10,949	11,913	12,914
Lodging places	14,991	13,568	15,561	19,438	23,854	26,262	27,328	27,950
Retail hosts [2, 7]	134,399	9,513	12,589	14,869	22,502	24,865	26,249	27,591
Department store restaurants	4,014	876	1,038	903	490	(NA)	(NA)	(NA)
Grocery store restaurants [7]	61,115	5,432	6,624	7,116	12,032	(NA)	(NA)	(NA)
Gasoline service stations	53,251	1,718	2,520	4,693	6,137	(NA)	(NA)	(NA)
Recreation and sports	36,080	2,871	3,866	4,772	11,397	12,735	13,171	13,332
Noncommercial restaurant services [2]	200,814	26,543	28,722	32,307	41,416	44,625	46,743	47,779
Employee restaurant services	3,261	1,864	1,364	986	548	472	463	443
Industrial, commercial organizations	975	1,603	1,129	717	260	(NA)	(NA)	(NA)
Educational restaurant services	105,070	7,671	9,059	9,977	11,007	11,395	11,728	11,833
Elementary and secondary schools . . .	100,847	3,700	4,533	5,039	5,320	5,582	5,916	6,083
Hospitals	5,728	8,968	9,219	9,982	12,332	13,454	14,482	15,114
Miscellaneous	50,009	2,892	3,673	4,898	9,703	10,606	11,004	11,149
Clubs	26,689	1,993	2,278	3,164	7,555	(NA)	(NA)	(NA)

NA Not available.   [1] Projection.   [2] Includes other types of groups, not shown separately.   [3] Data for establishments with payroll.   [4] Fast-food restaurants.   [5] Snack and nonalcoholic beverage bars included in limited service restaurants, prior to 1997.   [6] For establishments serving food.   [7] Includes a portion of delicatessen sales in grocery stores.

Source: National Restaurant Association, Washington, DC, *Restaurant Numbers: 25 Year History, 1970–1995*, 1998; *Restaurant Industry in Review*, annual; and *National Restaurant Association 2009 Restaurant Industry Forecast*, December 2008, (copyright).

Accommodation, Food Services, and Other Services   769

Table 1248. **Other Services—Estimated Revenue for Employer Firms by Kind of Business: 2000 to 2007**

[In millions of dollars (302,783 represents $302,783,000,000). For employer firms. Estimates have been adjusted to the results of the 2002 Economic Census. Based on the Service Annual Survey; see Appendix III]

Kind of business	2002 NAICS code [1]	2000	2005	2006	2007
Other services [2, 3]	81	302,783	357,288	384,188	410,950
Repair and maintenance [4]	811	112,719	133,483	138,271	142,611
Automotive repair and maintenance	8111	73,219	85,562	87,895	89,983
Automotive mechanical and electrical repair and maintenance	81111	37,879	43,941	45,226	46,606
General automotive repair	811111	30,988	37,179	38,347	39,698
Automotive body, paint, interior, and glass repair	81112	25,766	29,461	29,703	30,102
Automotive body, paint, and interior repair and maintenance	811121	22,018	25,781	26,017	26,584
Other automotive repair and maintenance	81119	9,574	12,160	12,966	13,275
Electronic and precision equipment repair and maintenance	8112	14,419	17,568	18,139	18,044
Commercial and industrial machinery and equipment (except automotive and electronic) repair and maintenance	8113	16,687	20,948	22,353	23,741
Personal and household goods repair and maintenance	8114	8,394	9,405	9,884	10,843
Home and garden equipment and appliance repair and maintenance	81141	3,866	4,341	4,548	5,283
Personal and laundry services [4]	812	(NA)	81,213	83,246	86,285
Personal care services	8121	18,264	25,362	26,758	28,682
Hair, nail, and skin care services	81211	15,553	20,168	20,826	21,875
Barber shops	812111	479	526	538	582
Beauty salons	812112	14,445	18,073	18,516	19,167
Nail salons	812113	629	1,569	1,772	2,126
Other personal care services	81219	2,711	5,194	5,932	6,807
Death care services	8122	13,707	15,731	15,311	14,744
Funeral homes and funeral services	81221	10,279	12,130	12,495	12,238
Cemeteries and crematories	81222	3,428	3,601	2,816	2,506
Drycleaning and laundry services	8123	19,950	21,194	22,278	22,579
Coin-operated laundries and drycleaners	81231	3,359	3,259	3,368	3,521
Drycleaning and laundry services (except coin-operated)	81232	7,846	7,928	8,547	8,882
Linen and uniform supply	81233	8,745	10,007	10,363	10,176
Pet care (except veterinary) services	81291	(NA)	1,990	2,215	2,410
Photofinishing	81292	3,809	2,609	2,219	2,197
Parking lots and garages	81293	6,389	7,608	7,523	7,516
All other personal services	81299	5,021	6,719	6,941	8,157
Religious, grantmaking, civic, professional, and similar organizations (except religious, labor, and political organizations) [5]	813	122,924	142,590	162,671	182,054
Grantmaking and giving services	8132	57,465	61,051	74,356	87,544
Social advocacy organizations	8133	10,852	13,908	15,359	16,998
Civic and social organizations	8134	13,703	17,180	18,606	19,498
Business, professional, and other organizations (except labor and political organizations)	8139	40,904	50,451	54,350	58,014

NA Not available.   [1] Based on the North American Industry Classification System, 2002; see Section 15.   [2] Except public administration, religious, labor, and political organizations, and private households.   [3] Prior to 2004, excludes NAICS 81291 (Pet care services).   [4] For taxable firms only.   [5] For tax-exempt firms only.

Source: U.S. Census Bureau, "2007 Service Annual Survey" (published March 2009); <http://www.census.gov/services/>.

Table 1249. **National Nonprofit Associations—Number by Type: 1980 to 2008**

[Data compiled during last few months of year previous to year shown and the beginning months of year shown]

Type	1980	1990	2000	2002	2003	2004	2005	2006	2007 [1]	2008
Total	14,726	22,289	21,840	22,141	22,464	22,659	22,720	23,772	25,048	25,176
Trade, business, commercial	3,118	3,918	3,880	3,883	3,818	3,812	3,789	3,942	4,072	4,003
Agriculture and environment	677	940	1,103	1,125	1,137	1,140	1,170	1,286	1,353	1,439
Legal, governmental, public admin., military	529	792	790	814	832	839	868	887	938	951
Scientific, engineering, technical	1,039	1,417	1,302	1,309	1,326	1,354	1,354	1,396	1,505	1,588
Educational	[2]2,376	1,291	1,297	1,307	1,301	1,313	1,318	1,365	1,471	1,530
Cultural	[2]	1,886	1,786	1,766	1,749	1,735	1,733	1,782	1,881	1,896
Social welfare	994	1,705	1,829	1,917	1,941	1,972	2,072	2,218	2,307	2,582
Health, medical	1,413	2,227	2,495	2,601	2,808	2,921	2,982	3,089	3,383	3,552
Public affairs	1,068	2,249	1,776	1,808	1,836	1,881	1,854	1,938	1,951	1,842
Fraternal, nationality, ethnic	435	573	525	529	557	547	550	567	580	523
Religious	797	1,172	1,123	1,154	1,155	1,157	1,147	1,162	1,204	1,146
Veteran, hereditary, patriotic	208	462	835	785	802	803	774	790	774	645
Hobby, avocational	910	1,475	1,330	1,380	1,435	1,449	1,433	1,525	1,615	1,511
Athletic sports	504	840	717	730	760	755	762	863	960	1,008
Labor unions	235	253	232	218	211	213	208	209	227	212
Chambers of Commerce [3]	105	168	143	141	139	136	135	137	169	162
Greek and non-Greek letter societies	318	340	296	301	309	305	349	302	335	325
Fan clubs	(NA)	581	381	373	348	327	314	314	323	261

NA Not available.   [1] The increase in the number of associations comes from the increase in newly discovered and established associations.   [2] Data for cultural associations included with educational associations.   [3] National and binational. Includes trade and tourism organizations.

Source: Gale, Cengage Learning, Farmington Hills, MI. Compiled from *Encyclopedia of Associations*, annual (copyright).

Section 28
Foreign Commerce and Aid

This section presents data on the flow of goods, services, and capital between the United States and other countries; changes in official reserve assets of the United States; international investments; and foreign assistance programs.

The Bureau of Economic Analysis publishes current figures on U.S. international transactions and the U.S. international investment position in its monthly *Survey of Current Business*. Statistics for the foreign aid programs are presented by the Agency for International Development (AID) in its annual *U.S. Overseas Loans and Grants and Assistance from International Organizations*.

The principal source of merchandise import and export data is the U.S. Census Bureau. Current data are presented monthly in *U.S. International Trade in Goods and Services* report Series FT 900. The *Guide to Foreign Trade Statistics*, found on the Census Bureau Web site at <http://www.census.gov/foreign-trade /guide/index.html>, lists the Bureau's monthly and annual products and services in this field. In addition, the International Trade Administration and the Bureau of Economic Analysis present summary as well as selected commodity and country data for U.S. foreign trade on their Web sites: <http://ita.doc.gov/td /industry/otea/> and <http://www.bea .gov/international/index>, respectively. The merchandise trade data published by the Bureau of Economic Analysis in the *Survey of Current Business* and on the Web include balance of payments adjustments to the Census Bureau data. The U.S. Treasury Department's *Monthly Treasury Statement of Receipts and Outlays of the United States Government* contains information on import duties. The International Trade Commission, U.S. Department of Agriculture (agricultural products), U.S. Department of Energy (mineral fuels, like petroleum and coal), and the U.S. Geological Survey (minerals) release various reports and specialized products on U.S. trade.

International accounts—The international transactions tables (Tables 1246 to 1248) show, for given time periods, the transfer of goods, services, grants, and financial assets and liabilities between the United States and the rest of the world. The international investment position table (Table 1253) presents, for specific dates, the value of U.S. investments abroad and of foreign investments in the United States. The movement of foreign and U.S. capital as presented in the balance of payments is not the only factor affecting the total value of foreign investments. Among the other factors are changes in the valuation of assets or liabilities, including changes in prices of securities, defaults, expropriations, and write-offs.

Direct investment abroad means the ownership or control, directly or indirectly, by one person of 10 percent or more of the voting securities of an incorporated business enterprise or an equivalent interest in an unincorporated business enterprise. Direct investment position is the value of U.S. parents' claims on the equity of and receivables due from foreign affiliates, less foreign affiliates' receivables due from their U.S. parents. Income consists of parents' shares in the earnings of their affiliates plus net interest received by parents on intercompany accounts, less withholding taxes on dividends and interest.

Foreign aid—Foreign assistance is divided into three major categories—grants (military supplies and services and other grants), credits, and other assistance (through net accumulation of foreign currency claims from the sale of agricultural commodities). *Grants* are transfers for which no payment is expected (other than a limited percentage of the foreign currency "counterpart" funds generated by the grant), or which at most involve an obligation on the part of the receiver to extend aid to the United States or other countries to achieve a common objective. *Credits* are loan disbursements or transfers under other agreements which give rise to specific obligations to repay, over a period of years, usually with interest. All known returns to the U.S. government stemming from grants and credits (reverse grants, returns of grants, and payments of principal) are taken into account in net grants and net credits, but no allowance is made for interest or commissions. *Other assistance* represents the transfer of U.S. farm products in exchange for foreign currencies (plus, since enactment of Public Law 87-128, currency claims from principal and interest collected on credits extended under the farm products program), less the government's disbursements of the currencies as grants, credits, or for purchases. The net acquisition of currencies represents net transfers of resources to foreign countries under the agricultural programs, in addition to those classified as grants or credits.

In 1952, economic, technical, and military aid programs were combined under the Mutual Security Act, which in turn was followed by the Foreign Assistance Act passed in 1961. Appropriations to provide military assistance were also made in the Department of Defense Appropriation Act (rather than the Foreign Assistance Appropriation Act) beginning in 1966 for certain countries in Southeast Asia and in other legislation concerning programs for specific countries (such as Israel). Figures on activity under the Foreign Assistance Act as reported in the *Foreign Grants and Credits* series differ from data published by AID or its immediate predecessors, due largely to differences in reporting, timing, and treatment of particular items.

Exports—The Census Bureau compiles export data primarily from Shipper's Export Declarations required to be filed with customs officials for shipments leaving the United States. They include U.S. exports under mutual security programs and exclude shipments to U.S. Armed Forces for their own use.

The value reported in the export statistics is generally equivalent to a free alongside ship (f.a.s.) value at the U.S. port of export, based on the transaction price, including inland freight, insurance, and

other charges incurred in placing the merchandise alongside the carrier at the U.S. port of exportation. This value, as defined, excludes the cost of loading merchandise aboard the exporting carrier and also excludes freight, insurance, and any other charges or transportation and other costs beyond the U.S. port of exportation. The country of destination is defined as the country of ultimate destination or country where the merchandise is to be consumed, further processed, or manufactured, as known to the shipper at the time of exportation. When ultimate destination is not known, the shipment is statistically credited to the last country to which the shipper knows the merchandise will be shipped in the same form as exported.

Effective January 1990, the United States began substituting Canadian import statistics for U.S. exports to Canada. As a result of the data exchange between the United States and Canada, the United States has adopted the Canadian import exemption level for its export statistics based on shipments to Canada.

Data are estimated for shipments valued under $2,501 to all countries, except Canada, using factors based on the ratios of low-valued shipments to individual country totals.

Prior to 1989, exports were based on Schedule B, Statistical Classification of Domestic and Foreign Commodities Exported from the United States. Beginning in 1989, Schedule B classifications are based on the Harmonized System and coincide with the Standard International Trade Classification, Revision 3. This revision will affect the comparability of most export series beginning with the 1989 data for commodities.

Imports—The Census Bureau compiles import data from various customs forms required to be filed with customs officials. Data on import values are presented on two valuations bases in this section: The c.i.f. (cost, insurance, and freight) and the customs import value (as appraised by the U.S. Customs Service in accordance with legal requirements of the Tariff Act of 1930, as amended). This latter valuation, primarily used for collection of import duties, frequently does not reflect the actual transaction value. Country of origin is defined as country where the merchandise was grown, mined, or manufactured. If country of origin is unknown, country of shipment is reported.

Imports are classified either as "General imports" or "Imports for consumption." *General imports* are a combination of entries for immediate consumption, entries into customs bonded warehouses, and entries into U.S. Foreign Trade Zones, thus generally reflecting total arrivals of merchandise. *Imports for consumption* are a combination of entries for immediate consumption, withdrawals from warehouses for consumption, and entries of merchandise into U.S. customs territory from U.S. Foreign Trade Zones, thus generally reflecting the total of the commodities entered into U.S. consumption channels.

Beginning in 1989, import statistics are based on the Harmonized Tariff Schedule of the United States, which coincides with import Standard International Trade Classification, Revision 3. This revision will affect the comparability of most import series beginning with the 1989 data.

Area coverage—Except as noted, the geographic area covered by the export and import trade statistics is the United States Customs area (includes the 50 states, the District of Columbia, and Puerto Rico), the U.S. Virgin Islands (effective January 1981), and U.S. Foreign Trade Zones (effective July 1982). Data for selected tables and total values for 1980 have been revised to reflect the U.S. Virgin Islands' trade with foreign countries, where possible.

Statistical reliability—For a discussion of statistical collection and estimation, sampling procedures, and measures of statistical reliability applicable to Census Bureau data, see Appendix III.

U.S. Census Bureau, Statistical Abstract of the United States: 2010

Table 1250. U.S. International Transactions by Type of Transaction: 1990 to 2008

[In millions of dollars (706,975 represents $706,975,000,000). Minus sign (−) indicates debits. N.i.e. = Not included elsewhere]

Type of transaction	1990	1995	2000	2001	2002	2003	2004	2005	2006	2007	2008
Exports of goods and services and income receipts	**706,975**	**1,004,631**	**1,421,515**	**1,295,692**	**1,258,411**	**1,340,647**	**1,572,971**	**1,816,723**	**2,133,905**	**2,462,099**	**2,591,233**
Exports of goods and services	535,233	794,387	1,070,597	1,004,895	977,469	1,020,191	1,159,233	1,281,460	1,451,684	1,643,168	1,826,596
Goods, balance of payments basis [1]	387,401	575,204	771,994	718,711	685,170	715,848	806,161	892,337	1,015,812	1,138,384	1,276,994
Services [2]	147,832	219,183	298,603	286,184	292,299	304,342	353,072	389,122	435,873	504,784	549,602
Transfers under U.S. military agency sales contracts [3]	9,932	14,643	13,790	12,539	11,943	13,315	15,781	19,539	23,913	25,436	22,571
Travel	43,007	63,395	82,400	71,893	66,605	64,359	74,546	81,799	85,789	97,050	110,090
Passenger fares	15,298	18,909	20,687	17,926	17,046	15,891	18,851	20,970	22,036	25,636	31,623
Other transportation	22,042	26,081	29,803	28,442	29,195	31,416	36,957	41,281	46,225	51,550	58,945
Royalties and license fees [4]	16,634	30,289	43,233	40,696	44,508	46,988	56,715	64,395	70,727	83,824	91,599
Other private services [4]	40,251	65,048	107,904	113,857	122,207	131,563	149,262	160,051	186,028	220,077	233,529
U.S. government miscellaneous services	668	818	786	831	795	810	959	1,087	1,155	1,212	1,245
Income receipts	171,742	210,244	350,918	290,797	280,942	320,456	413,739	535,263	682,221	818,931	764,637
Income receipts on U.S.-owned assets abroad	170,570	208,065	348,083	287,918	278,131	317,643	410,917	532,373	679,338	815,960	761,593
Direct investment receipts	65,973	95,260	151,839	128,665	145,590	186,417	250,606	294,538	324,816	363,247	370,747
Other private receipts	94,072	108,092	192,398	155,692	129,238	126,529	157,313	235,120	352,122	450,480	385,940
U.S. government receipts	10,525	4,713	3,846	3,561	3,303	4,697	2,998	2,715	2,400	2,233	4,906
Compensation of employees	1,172	2,179	2,835	2,879	2,811	2,813	2,822	2,890	2,883	2,971	3,044
Imports of goods and services and income payments	**−759,290**	**−1,080,124**	**−1,780,296**	**−1,629,475**	**−1,652,615**	**−1,790,372**	**−2,115,739**	**−2,459,633**	**−2,846,179**	**−3,072,675**	**−3,168,938**
Imports of goods and services	−616,097	−890,771	−1,450,432	−1,370,400	−1,399,071	−1,515,225	−1,769,220	−1,996,728	−2,212,043	−2,344,590	−2,522,532
Goods, balance of payments basis [1]	−498,438	−749,374	−1,226,684	−1,148,609	−1,168,002	−1,264,860	−1,477,996	−1,683,188	−1,863,072	−1,969,375	−2,117,245
Services [2]	−117,659	−141,397	−223,748	−221,791	−231,069	−250,365	−291,224	−313,540	−348,972	−375,215	−405,287
Direct defense expenditures	−17,531	−10,043	−13,473	−14,835	−19,101	−25,296	−29,299	−30,075	−31,032	−32,820	−36,452
Travel	−37,349	−44,916	−64,705	−60,200	−58,715	−57,447	−65,750	−68,970	−72,104	−76,354	−79,743
Passenger fares	−10,531	−14,663	−24,274	−22,633	−19,969	−20,989	−24,718	−26,149	−27,501	−28,437	−32,597
Other transportation	−24,966	−27,034	−41,425	−38,682	−38,407	−44,705	−54,161	−61,937	−65,318	−67,100	−72,143
Royalties and license fees [4]	−3,135	−6,919	−16,468	−16,538	−19,353	−19,033	−23,266	−24,612	−23,518	−24,656	−26,616
Other private services [4]	−22,228	−35,199	−60,520	−66,021	−72,604	−79,764	−90,252	−97,818	−125,478	−141,664	−153,267
U.S. government miscellaneous services	−1,919	−2,623	−2,883	−2,882	−2,920	−3,131	−3,778	−3,979	−4,021	−4,184	−4,469
Income payments	−143,192	−189,353	−329,864	−259,075	−253,544	−275,147	−346,519	−462,905	−634,136	−728,085	−646,406
Income payments on foreign-owned assets in the U.S.	−139,728	−183,090	−322,345	−250,989	−245,164	−266,635	−337,556	−453,615	−624,646	−718,019	−636,043
Direct investment payments	−3,450	−30,318	−56,910	−12,783	−43,244	−73,750	−99,754	−121,333	−150,770	−126,532	−120,862
Other private payments	−95,508	−97,149	−180,918	−159,825	−127,012	−119,051	−155,266	−228,408	−338,897	−427,159	−349,871
U.S. government payments	−40,770	−55,623	−84,517	−78,381	−74,908	−73,834	−82,536	−103,874	−134,979	−164,328	−165,310
Compensation of employees	−3,464	−6,263	−7,519	−8,086	−380	−8,512	−8,963	−9,290	−9,490	−10,066	−10,364
Unilateral current transfers, net	**−26,654**	**−38,074**	**−58,645**	**−64,487**	**−64,948**	**−71,794**	**−88,362**	**−105,772**	**−91,273**	**−115,996**	**−128,363**
U.S. government grants [3]	−10,359	−11,190	−16,714	−11,517	−17,097	−22,173	−23,823	−33,647	−27,733	−34,437	−36,003
U.S. government pensions and other transfers	−3,224	−3,451	−4,705	−5,798	−5,125	−5,341	−6,264	−6,303	−6,508	−7,323	−8,390
Private remittances and other transfers [5]	−13,070	−23,433	−37,226	−47,172	−42,726	−44,280	−58,275	−65,822	−57,032	−74,236	−83,970

See footnotes at end of table.

U.S. Census Bureau, Statistical Abstract of the United States: 2010

Table 1250. **U.S. International Transactions by Type of Transaction: 1990 to 2008**—Con.

[See headnote, page 774]

Type of transaction	1990	1995	2000	2001	2002	2003	2004	2005	2006	2007	2008
Capital account transactions, net	-6,579	-927	-1,010	11,922	-1,470	-3,480	1,323	11,344	-3,906	-1,895	953
U.S. assets abroad, net (increase/financial outflow (–))	**-81,234**	**-352,264**	**-560,523**	**-382,616**	**-294,646**	**-325,424**	**-1,000,870**	**-546,631**	**-1,285,729**	**-1,472,126**	**-106**
U.S. official reserve assets, net	-2,158	-9,742	-290	-4,911	-3,681	1,523	2,805	14,096	2,374	-122	-4,848
Special drawing rights	-192	-808	-722	-630	-475	601	-398	4,511	-223	-154	-106
Reserve position in the International Monetary Fund	731	-2,466	2,308	-3,600	-2,632	1,494	3,826	10,200	3,331	1,021	-3,473
Foreign currencies	-2,697	-6,468	-1,876	-681	-574	-572	-623	-615	-734	-989	-1,269
U.S. government assets, other than official reserve assets, net	2,317	-984	-941	-486	345	537	1,710	5,539	5,346	-22,273	-529,615
U.S. credits and other long-term assets	-8,410	-4,859	-5,182	-4,431	-5,251	-7,279	-3,044	-2,255	-2,992	-2,475	-2,200
Repayments on U.S. credits and other long-term assets [6]	10,856	4,125	4,265	3,873	5,701	7,981	4,716	5,603	8,329	4,104	2,354
U.S. foreign currency holdings and U.S. short-term assets, net.	-130	-250	-24	72	-105	-165	38	2,191	9	-23,902	-529,766
U.S. private assets, net	-81,393	-341,538	-559,292	-377,219	-291,310	-327,484	-1,005,385	-566,266	-1,293,449	-1,449,731	534,357
Direct investment	-37,183	-98,750	-159,212	-142,349	-154,460	-149,564	-316,223	-36,235	-244,922	-398,597	-332,012
Foreign securities	-28,765	-122,394	-127,908	-90,644	-48,568	-146,722	-170,549	-251,199	-365,129	-366,524	60,761
U.S. claims on unaffiliated foreigners reported by U.S. nonbanking concerns	-27,824	-45,286	-138,790	-8,520	-50,022	-18,184	-152,566	-71,207	-181,299	-40,517	372,229
U.S. claims reported by U.S. banks, n.i.e.	12,379	-75,108	-133,382	-135,706	-38,260	-13,014	-366,047	-207,625	-502,099	-644,093	433,379
Foreign-owned assets in the United States, net (increase/financial inflow (+))	**139,357**	**435,102**	**1,038,224**	**782,870**	**795,161**	**858,303**	**1,533,201**	**1,247,347**	**2,065,169**	**2,129,460**	**534,071**
Foreign official assets in the U.S., net	33,910	109,880	42,758	28,059	115,945	278,069	397,755	259,268	487,939	480,949	487,021
U.S. government securities	30,243	72,712	35,710	54,620	90,971	224,874	314,941	213,334	428,401	269,897	543,498
Other U.S. government liabilities	1,868	-105	-1,825	-2,309	137	-723	-134	-421	2,816	5,342	8,626
U.S. liabilities reported by U.S. banks, n.i.e.	3,385	34,008	5,746	-29,978	21,221	48,643	69,245	26,260	22,365	109,019	-153,443
Other foreign official assets	-1,586	3,265	3,127	5,726	3,616	5,275	13,703	20,095	34,357	96,691	88,340
Other foreign assets in the U.S., net	105,447	325,222	995,466	754,811	679,216	580,234	1,135,446	988,079	1,577,230	1,648,511	47,050
Direct investments in U.S	48,494	57,776	321,274	167,021	84,372	63,750	145,966	112,638	243,151	275,758	319,737
U.S. Treasury securities	-2,534	91,544	-69,983	-14,378	100,403	91,455	93,608	132,300	-58,229	66,807	196,619
U.S. securities other than U.S. Treasury securities	1,592	77,249	459,889	393,885	283,299	220,705	381,493	450,386	683,245	605,652	-126,737
U.S. currency flows	16,586	8,840	-3,357	23,794	18,861	10,591	13,301	8,447	2,227	-10,675	29,187
U.S. liabilities to unaffiliated foreigners reported by U.S. nonbanking concerns	45,133	59,637	170,672	66,110	95,871	96,526	165,872	69,572	244,793	201,681	-45,167
U.S. liabilities reported by U.S. banks, n.i.e.	-3,824	30,176	116,971	118,379	96,410	97,207	335,206	214,736	462,043	509,288	-326,589
Financial derivatives, net	**(NA)**	**(NA)**	**(NA)**	**(NA)**	**(NA)**	**(NA)**	**(NA)**	**(NA)**	**29,710**	**6,222**	**-28,905**
Statistical discrepancy	*27,425*	*31,656*	*-59,265*	*-13,906*	*-39,894*	*-7,880*	*97,476*	*36,623*	*-1,699*	*64,912*	*200,055*
Balance on goods	-111,037	-174,170	-454,690	-429,898	-482,831	-549,012	-671,835	-790,851	-847,260	-830,992	-840,252
Balance on services	30,173	77,786	74,855	64,393	61,230	53,977	61,848	75,582	86,901	129,569	144,316
Balance on income	28,550	20,891	21,054	31,722	27,398	45,309	67,219	72,358	48,085	90,845	118,231
Balance on current account [7]	-78,968	-113,567	-417,426	-398,270	-459,151	-521,519	-631,130	-748,683	-803,547	-726,573	-706,068

NA Not available. [1] Excludes exports of goods under U.S. military agency sales contracts identified in census export documents, excludes imports of goods under direct defense expenditures identified in census import documents, and reflects various other adjustments (for valuation, coverage, and timing) of census statistics to balance of payments basis. [2] Includes some goods: Mainly military equipment; major equipment, other materials, supplies, and petroleum products purchased abroad by U.S. military agencies; and fuels purchased by airline and steamship operators. [3] Includes transfers of goods and services under U.S. military grant programs. [4] These lines are presented on a gross basis. The definition of exports is revised to exclude U.S. parents' payments to foreign affiliates and to include U.S. affiliates' receipts from foreign parents. The definition of imports is revised to include U.S. parents' payments to foreign affiliates and to exclude U.S. affiliates' receipts from foreign parents. [5] The "other transfers" component includes taxes paid by U.S. private residents to foreign governments and taxes paid by private nonresidents to the U.S. government. [6] Includes sales of foreign obligations to foreigners. [7] Conceptually, 'Balance on current account' is equal to "net foreign investment" in the national income and product accounts (NIPAs). However, the foreign transactions account in the NIPAs (a) includes adjustments to the international transactions accounts for the treatment of gold, (b) includes adjustments for the different geographical treatment of transactions with U.S. territories and Puerto Rico, and (c) includes services furnished without payment by financial pension plans except life insurance carriers and private noninsured pension plans.

Source: U.S. Bureau of Economic Analysis, *Survey of Current Business* (publised July 2009). Also see <http://www.bea.gov/scb/index.htm>.

Figure 28.1
U.S. International Trade in Goods and Services: 2000 to 2008

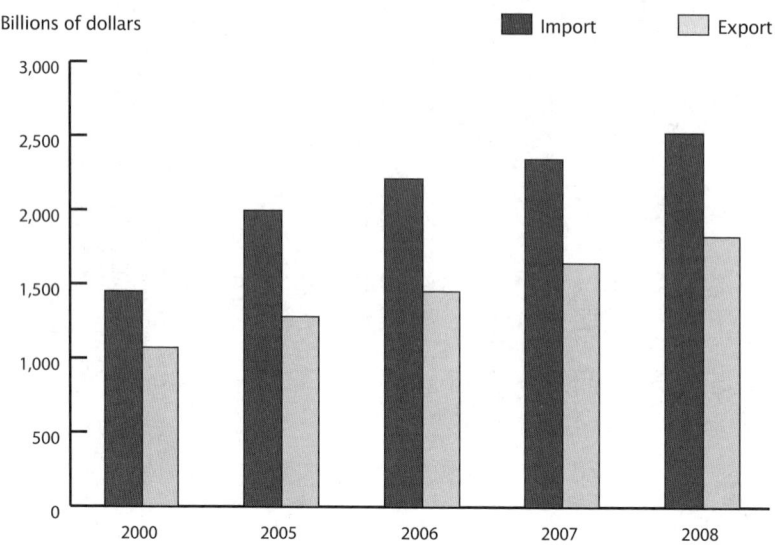

Source: Chart prepared by U.S. Census Bureau. For data, see Table 1264.

Figure 28.2
Top U.S. Trading Partners—Imports, Exports: 2008

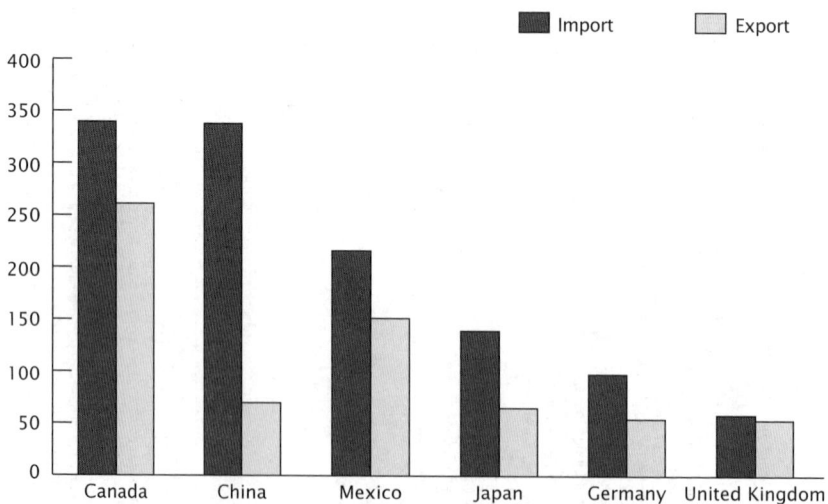

Source: Chart prepared by U.S. Census Bureau. For data, see Table 1271.

U.S. Census Bureau, Statistical Abstract of the United States: 2010

Table 1251. **U.S. Balances on International Transactions by Area and Selected Country: 2007 and 2008**

[In millions of dollars (–830,992 represents –$830,992,000,000). Minus sign (–) indicates debits]

Area or country	2007, balance on—				2008, balance on—			
	Goods [1]	Ser-vices	Income	Current account	Goods [1]	Ser-vices	Income	Current account
All areas	–830,992	129,569	90,845	–726,573	–840,252	144,316	118,231	–706,068
Europe	–131,729	41,712	57,193	–44,070	–119,651	51,466	47,868	–32,491
European Union	–115,353	37,512	44,513	–37,729	–98,688	44,453	49,749	–11,627
Euro Area	–92,313	15,049	49,956	–33,709	–79,190	21,143	52,748	–12,475
Germany	–45,200	–6,433	3,228	–48,813	–43,387	–5,768	5,870	–44,007
Italy	–21,024	833	4,765	–15,836	–20,810	1,103	4,308	–15,875
Netherlands	14,225	3,781	19,413	38,231	18,296	4,938	32,009	55,321
United Kingdom	–6,971	17,105	–9,061	4,035	–5,015	17,384	–4,477	8,776
Canada	–70,837	17,958	17,349	–37,217	–81,049	21,257	24,399	–37,207
Latin America, other Western Hemisphere	–107,097	24,207	28,692	–85,521	–91,977	24,884	41,667	–59,306
Mexico	–78,771	7,872	1,901	–82,250	–68,661	8,136	–298	–74,604
Venezuela	–29,717	3,249	–683	–27,140	–38,820	4,129	1,585	–33,183
Asia and Pacific	–417,375	38,019	–51,704	–452,594	–403,194	39,026	–41,647	–430,534
Australia	10,227	5,097	2,079	17,568	11,078	6,238	7,471	24,388
China [2]	–258,902	4,614	–36,336	–293,105	–268,411	6,039	–43,211	–308,474
Hong Kong	12,785	–1,326	4,471	15,871	14,945	–1,716	2,642	15,758
India	–9,217	–662	1,403	–11,067	–8,116	–1,532	893	–11,509
Japan [3]	–85,616	14,989	–41,155	–110,634	–75,130	15,452	–29,866	–90,532
Korea, South	–13,890	4,920	–350	–9,943	–14,149	5,756	515	–8,605
Singapore	6,956	4,288	13,647	24,904	11,741	4,237	14,760	30,677
Taiwan [2]	–13,074	179	–3,181	–16,541	–11,860	199	–3,427	–15,552
Middle East	–34,661	3,389	–3,255	–47,732	–58,764	2,755	–2,168	–71,402
Africa	–69,292	4,666	6,545	–67,202	–85,617	4,896	7,233	–83,190
International and unallocated	(X)	–381	36,028	7,766	(X)	32	40,880	8,059

X Not applicable. [1] Adjusted to balance of payments basis; excludes exports under U.S. military sales contracts and imports under direct defense expenditures. [2] See footnote 4, Table 1296. [3] Includes Ryukyu Islands.

Source: U.S. Bureau of Economic Analysis, *Survey of Current Business*, July 2009. See also <http://www.bea.gov/scb/index.htm>.

Table 1252. **Private International Service Transactions by Selected Type of Service and Selected Country: 2000 to 2008**

[In millions of dollars (284,027 represents $284,027,000,000). For all transactions, see Table 1250]

Type of service and country	Exports				Imports			
	2000	2005	2007	2008	2000	2005	2007	2008
Private services, total	284,027	368,496	478,136	525,786	207,392	279,486	338,211	364,366
TYPE OF SERVICE								
Travel	82,400	81,799	97,050	110,090	64,705	68,970	76,354	79,743
Passenger fares	20,687	20,970	25,636	31,623	24,274	26,149	28,437	32,597
Other transportation	29,803	41,281	51,550	58,945	41,425	61,937	67,100	72,143
Freight	12,547	16,470	19,830	22,430	27,388	43,920	45,576	45,248
Port services	17,256	24,811	31,720	36,515	14,037	18,017	21,524	26,895
Royalties and license fees	43,233	64,395	83,824	91,599	16,468	24,612	24,656	26,616
Other private services	107,904	160,051	220,077	233,529	60,520	97,818	141,664	153,267
By type								
Education	10,348	14,021	15,956	17,796	2,032	3,992	4,760	5,204
Financial services	(NA)	(NA)	61,393	60,190	(NA)	(NA)	19,750	19,143
Insurance services	3,631	7,566	10,184	10,756	11,284	28,710	41,666	42,939
AREA AND COUNTRY								
Europe	107,650	153,262	203,505	224,483	89,825	122,723	151,650	160,574
European Union	94,232	133,633	178,473	195,775	77,876	105,745	131,561	139,415
Euro Area	56,735	77,827	103,392	116,927	45,625	61,553	78,934	84,858
France	10,553	12,929	15,641	17,916	10,642	12,309	15,233	16,499
Germany	15,928	21,217	24,776	28,160	12,440	18,977	24,039	26,366
Italy	5,459	7,135	8,992	9,943	5,061	6,172	7,100	7,598
Netherlands	7,057	8,689	12,482	14,600	5,698	7,768	8,759	9,678
United Kingdom	31,973	45,125	60,289	62,545	28,304	35,240	42,022	43,537
Canada	24,559	32,671	42,777	45,775	17,711	21,809	24,629	24,421
Latin America, other Western Hemisphere	54,417	61,622	87,153	94,068	38,092	51,747	62,910	69,094
Mexico	14,334	20,366	23,364	24,040	11,023	14,184	15,343	15,758
Asia and Pacific	79,386	99,882	117,583	129,755	51,798	68,832	83,099	91,330
Australia	5,575	7,527	10,317	11,826	3,494	4,670	5,617	6,077
China [1]	5,211	9,015	13,453	15,870	3,259	6,627	8,827	9,810
India	2,546	5,173	8,850	10,532	1,892	5,031	9,606	12,123
Japan	33,411	41,513	39,606	41,245	17,405	22,276	23,810	24,483
Korea, South	7,287	10,466	12,894	14,260	4,617	6,036	6,568	7,195
Taiwan [1]	4,856	6,390	6,818	7,254	4,221	6,531	7,186	7,651
Middle East	6,852	9,279	13,809	16,290	3,310	5,271	6,041	7,971
Africa	4,957	6,321	9,154	10,603	2,710	3,950	5,257	6,083
International organizations and unallocated	6,206	5,458	4,152	4,812	3,946	5,155	4,623	4,893

NA Not available. [1] See footnote 4, Table 1296.

Source: U.S. Bureau of Economic Analysis, *Survey of Current Business*, July 2009. See also <http://www.bea.gov/scb/index.htm>.

Foreign Commerce and Aid **777**

Table 1253. **International Investment Position by Type of Investment: 2000 to 2008**

[In billions of dollars (–1,331 represents –$1,331,000,000,000). Estimates for end of year; subject to considerable error due to nature of basic data. Unless otherwise specified, types below refer to current-cost method. For information on current-cost method and market value, see article cited in source]

Type of investment	2000	2003	2004	2005	2006	2007	2008, prel.
Net international investment position	–1,331	–2,087	–2,245	–1,925	–2,184	–2,140	–3,469
Financial derivatives, net [1]	(X)	(X)	(X)	58	60	71	160
Net international investment position, excluding financial derivatives	–1,331	–2,087	–2,245	–1,983	–2,244	–2,211	–3,629
U.S.-owned assets abroad	6,239	7,638	9,341	11,962	14,428	18,279	19,888
Financial derivatives, gross positive fair value [1]	(X)	(X)	(X)	1,190	1,239	2,559	6,625
U.S.-owned assets abroad, excluding financial derivatives	6,239	7,638	9,341	10,772	13,189	15,720	13,264
U.S. official reserve assets	128	184	190	188	220	277	294
Gold	72	109	114	134	165	218	227
Special drawing rights	11	13	14	8	9	9	9
Reserve position in the International Monetary Fund	15	23	20	8	5	4	8
Foreign currencies	31	40	42	38	41	45	49
U.S. government assets, other than official reserve assets	85	85	83	78	72	94	624
U.S. credits and other long-term assets	83	82	80	77	72	70	70
U.S. foreign currency holdings and U.S. short-term assets	3	3	3	1	1	24	554
U.S. private assets	6,025	7,370	9,068	10,506	12,897	15,348	12,346
Direct investment at current cost	1,532	2,054	2,498	2,652	2,948	3,451	3,699
Foreign securities	2,426	2,948	3,545	4,329	5,604	6,835	4,244
Bonds	573	869	985	1,012	1,276	1,587	1,393
Corporate stocks	1,853	2,079	2,560	3,318	4,329	5,248	2,851
U.S. claims on unaffiliated foreigners [2]	837	594	794	1,018	1,184	1,240	992
U.S. claims reported by U.S. banks [3] .	1,232	1,773	2,231	2,507	3,160	3,822	3,411
Foreign-owned assets in the United States	7,569	9,725	11,586	13,887	16,612	20,419	23,357
Financial derivatives, gross negative fair value [1]	(X)	(X)	(X)	1,132	1,179	2,488	6,465
Foreign-owned assets in the United States, excluding financial derivatives	7,569	9,725	11,586	12,755	15,433	17,931	16,892
Foreign official assets in the United States	1,031	1,563	2,012	2,306	2,826	3,404	3,871
U.S. government securities	756	1,187	1,510	1,725	2,167	2,540	3,228
U.S. Treasury securities	640	986	1,252	1,341	1,558	1,737	2,326
Other	116	200	258	385	609	803	903
Other U.S. government liabilities	19	16	16	16	19	24	33
U.S. liabilities reported by U.S. banks [3]	153	201	270	297	297	406	253
Other foreign official assets	102	159	215	269	343	434	358
Other foreign assets	6,539	8,162	9,574	10,448	12,608	14,527	13,021
Direct investment at current cost	1,421	1,581	1,743	1,906	2,154	2,450	2,647
U.S. Treasury securities	382	527	562	644	568	640	885
U.S. securities other than U.S. Treasury securities	2,623	3,423	3,996	4,353	5,372	6,190	4,704
Corporate and other bonds	1,069	1,711	2,035	2,243	2,825	3,289	2,866
Corporate stocks	1,554	1,712	1,960	2,110	2,547	2,901	1,838
U.S. currency	205	259	272	280	283	272	301
U.S. liabilities to unaffiliated foreigners [2]	739	451	600	658	799	1,000	873
U.S. liabilities reported by U.S. banks [3]	1,169	1,921	2,402	2,607	3,431	3,975	3,611
Memoranda: Direct investment abroad at market value	2,694	2,729	3,363	3,638	4,470	5,228	3,071
Direct investment in the United States at market value	2,783	2,455	2,717	2,818	3,293	3,593	2,557

X Not applicable.   [1] A break in series in 2005 reflects the introduction of U.S. Department of the Treasury data on financial derivatives.   [2] Reported by U.S. nonbanking concerns.   [3] Not included elsewhere.

Source: U.S. Bureau of Economic Analysis, *Survey of Current Business*, July 2009. See also <http:www.bea.gov/scb/index.htm>.

Table 1254. **U.S. Reserve Assets: 1990 to 2008**

[In billions of dollars (83.3 represents $83,300,000,000). As of end of year, except as indicated]

Type	1990	2000	2002	2003	2004	2005	2006	2007	2008
Total	83.3	67.6	79.0	85.9	86.8	65.1	65.9	70.6	77.6
Gold stock	11.1	11.0	11.0	11.0	11.0	11.0	11.0	11.0	11.0
Special drawing rights	11.0	10.5	12.2	12.6	13.6	8.2	8.9	9.5	9.3
Foreign currencies	52.2	31.2	33.8	39.7	42.7	37.8	40.9	45.8	49.6
Reserve position in IMF [1]	9.1	14.8	22.0	22.5	19.5	8.0	5.0	4.2	7.7

[1] International Monetary Fund.

U.S. Department of the Treasury, *Treasury Bulletin,* quarterly. For latest issue, see <http://www.fms.treas.gov/bulletin/index.html>.

Table 1255. **Foreign Direct Investment Position in the United States on a Historical-Cost Basis by Selected Country, 2000 to 2008, and by Industry, 2008**

[In millions of dollars (1,256,867 represents $1,256,867,000,000)]

Country	2000	2005	2006	2007	2008 Total [1]	2008 Manufac- turing	2008 Whole- sale	2008 Finance [2] and insurance
All countries	1,256,867	1,634,121	1,840,463	2,109,876	2,278,892	795,336	312,583	248,888
Canada	114,309	165,667	165,281	207,925	221,870	42,851	4,758	62,132
Europe [3]	887,014	1,154,048	1,326,738	1,507,594	1,622,911	617,579	167,610	177,827
Austria	3,007	2,425	2,305	2,373	2,406	1,323	263	1
Belgium.	14,787	10,024	11,691	23,663	18,580	2,245	6,147	1,005
Denmark.	4,025	6,117	6,726	4,709	4,992	3,346	891	(Z)
Finland	8,875	5,938	7,129	5,413	12,499	3,495	(D)	(Z)
France	125,740	114,260	147,799	160,116	163,430	75,973	10,710	27,114
Germany.	122,412	177,176	205,969	214,506	211,521	55,598	16,415	36,254
Ireland	25,523	17,465	25,517	32,679	34,094	16,514	187	6,644
Italy	6,576	7,725	9,299	13,291	17,575	5,923	1,677	(D)
Luxembourg.	58,930	79,680	89,157	120,524	113,248	48,364	1,204	2,586
Netherlands	138,894	156,602	182,014	208,177	259,385	131,423	23,486	39,865
Norway	2,665	9,810	10,442	5,564	6,755	851	3,715	1
Spain	5,068	7,472	13,969	27,511	38,662	2,914	152	(D)
Sweden	21,991	22,269	20,098	42,129	35,020	24,660	8,070	248
Switzerland	64,719	133,387	134,568	153,277	165,697	107,154	7,184	31,522
United Kingdom	277,613	371,350	414,629	426,545	454,123	102,800	78,758	26,420
Latin America and other Western Hemisphere . . . . , . .	53,691	57,175	66,583	55,816	49,233	25,421	8,069	−19,829
South and Central America [3]. .	13,384	22,507	24,171	14,021	15,609	5,130	6,495	298
Brazil.	882	2,051	1,054	1,750	778	85	(D)	14
Mexico	7,462	3,595	5,310	6,287	7,948	5,126	1,760	77
Panama.	3,819	10,983	11,924	980	881	54	−11	198
Venezuela	792	5,292	5,380	4,196	4,563	−168	(D)	1
Other Western Hemisphere [3] .	40,307	34,668	42,412	41,795	33,623	20,291	1,575	−20,126
Bermuda	18,336	2,147	513	4,697	10,750	16,156	248	−11,965
Netherlands Antilles	3,807	5,531	9,223	5,574	6,266	(D)	(D)	1
U.K. Islands, Caribbean	15,191	23,063	28,367	34,423	21,604	3,858	(D)	(D)
Africa	2,700	2,341	1,976	1,396	2,002	427	493	(D)
Middle East [3]	6,506	8,306	10,112	15,058	14,676	2,747	5,868	(D)
Israel	3,012	4,231	5201	6,556	6,143	2,708	(D)	(D)
Saudi Arabia	(D)	(D)	(D)	(D)	(D)	14	(D)	2
Asia and Pacific [3]	192,647	246,585	269,772	322,087	368,200	106,312	125,785	28,501
Australia	18,775	36,392	38,777	50,233	64,316	5,224	1,469	4,922
Hong Kong	1,493	3,467	2,992	3,742	3,973	1,494	1,772	4
Japan	159,690	189,851	204,020	230,453	259,569	86,952	108,278	21,690
Korea, South	3,110	6,077	9,459	15,146	15,632	(D)	(D)	152
Singapore	5,087	3,338	6,458	11,707	12,718	(D)	251	(D)
Taiwan [4]	3,174	3,731	4,064	4,746	3,900	1,425	(D)	(D)

D Suppressed to avoid disclosure of data of individual companies. Z Less than $500,000. [1] Includes other industries not shown separately. [2] Excludes depository institutions. [3] Includes other countries not shown separately. [4] See footnote 4, Table 1296.

Source: U.S. Bureau of Economic Analysis, *Survey of Current Business*, July 2009 and previous issues. For most recent copy and previous issues, see <http://www.bea.gov/scb/index.htm>.

Table 1256. **U.S. Majority-Owned Affiliates of Foreign Companies—Assets, Sales, Employment, Value, Exports, and Imports by Industry: 2006**

[(6,807,654 represents $6,807,654,000,000). Preliminary. A U.S. affiliate is a U.S. business enterprise in which one foreign owner (individual, branch, partnership, association, trust, corporation, or government) has a direct or indirect voting interest of 10 percent or more. Estimates cover the universe of nonbank affiliates]

Industry	2002 NAICS code [1]	Total assets (mil. dol.)	Sales [2] (mil. dol.)	Employ- ment [3] (1,000)	Employee compen- sation (mil. dol.)	Gross book value, P & E [4] (mil. dol.)	Merchan- dise exports [5] (mil. dol.)	Merchan- dise imports [5] (mil. dol.)
All industries.	(X)	6,807,654	2,795,143	5,330.5	364,162	1,140,252	195,292	482,363
Manufacturing [6]	31–33	1,224,595	1,100,669	2,057.8	155,422	502,473	108,554	173,867
Petroleum and coal products.	324	(D)	136,657	33.2	4,510	(D)	(D)	(D)
Chemicals	325	266,995	212,418	287.8	32,178	93,322	19,481	33,617
Computers and electronic products .	334	(D)	63,940	168.7	14,467	20,804	(D)	(D)
Transportation equipment	336	274,463	246,663	420.3	25,551	133,835	36,033	59,277
Wholesale trade.	42	562,140	863,364	618.7	50,126	233,382	78,029	295,190
Retail trade	44–45	69,449	146,128	564.0	18,280	38,789	578	5,711
Information	51	207,114	81,894	223.5	20,998	44,546	972	235
Finance (except depository institutions) and insurance	52, exc. 521, 522	3,957,790	257,764	215.1	38,922	34,818	(D)	(D)
Real estate and rental and leasing . . .	53	115,945	34,883	46.0	3,254	79,449	(D)	541
Professional, scientific, and technical services	54	101,387	61,360	202.4	18,159	11,207	(D)	(D)
Other industries	(X)	569,234	249,082	1,403	59,001	195,588	6,382	6,547

D Withheld to avoid disclosure of data of individual companies. X Not applicable. [1] North American Industry Classification System, 2002. [2] Excludes returns, discounts, allowances, and sales and excise taxes. [3] Average number of full-time and part-time employees. [4] Plant and equipment (P & E). Includes mineral rights and minor amounts of property other than land. [5] F.a.s. value at port of exportation. Goods shipped by/to affiliates. [6] Includes industries not shown separately.

Source: U.S. Bureau of Economic Analysis, *Survey of Current Business*, August 2008 and *Foreign Direct Investment in the United States: Operations of U.S. Affiliates of Foreign Companies*, annual.

Foreign Commerce and Aid 779

Table 1257. **Foreign Direct Investment in the United States—Gross Book Value and Employment of U.S. Affiliates of Foreign Companies by State: 2000 to 2006**

[1,175,628 represents $1,175,628,000,000. A U.S. affiliate is a U.S. business enterprise in which one foreign owner (individual, branch, partnership, association, trust corporation, or government) has a direct or indirect voting interest of 10 percent or more. Estimates cover the universe of nonbank U.S. affiliates. Beginning 2003, data are on a majority-owned basis and not strictly comparable with 2000 data]

State and other area	Gross book value of property, plant, and equipment (mil. dol.)				Total employment				
								2006	
	2000	2004	2005	2006	2003 (1,000)	2004 (1,000)	2005 (1,000)	Total (1,000)	Percent of all businesses
Total	1,175,628	1,060,181	1,103,766	1,188,641	5,244.4	5,131.5	5,201.6	5,330.5	(X)
United States.	1,070,422	931,238	(D)	161,568	5,214.4	5,102.1	5,172.6	5,302.5	4.5
Alabama	16,646	16,857	20,247	20,457	72.6	72.4	69.6	73.6	4.4
Alaska.	28,964	31,121	(D)	32,216	11.7	12.2	12.0	12.2	5.1
Arizona	10,716	9,333	10,577	11,863	58.0	64.2	68.5	71.1	3.1
Arkansas	4,613	4,913	5,474	6,009	32.2	31.5	33.8	33.7	3.3
California	121,040	90,622	94,432	103,433	558.0	541.8	565.2	572.5	4.3
Colorado	15,319	16,115	22,438	24,711	72.3	71.7	73.8	75.9	3.8
Connecticut	13,604	12,517	12,641	13,427	105.5	102.1	102.0	104.9	7.1
Delaware	6,114	4,508	4,404	5,277	28.1	27.5	25.4	25.2	6.6
District of Columbia . . .	4,247	4,518	4,141	4,969	15.8	15.1	16.9	17.3	3.6
Florida.	38,755	26,819	27,418	30,322	247.8	237.6	230.7	248.0	3.5
Georgia	29,510	23,574	23,750	23,349	183.9	177.5	167.7	173.6	4.9
Hawaii.	10,369	6,948	5,806	5,607	35.2	31.1	28.6	28.5	5.6
Idaho	2,749	2,187	2,748	2,117	11.6	13.2	13.0	13.0	2.4
Illinois	48,425	39,276	39,809	43,340	252.5	232.4	228.6	243.1	4.7
Indiana	30,179	30,904	33,282	37,171	134.7	133.7	143.1	148.0	5.7
Iowa	7,186	6,391	6,376	6,781	38.7	37.4	39.5	40.2	3.1
Kansas	9,036	5,322	6,113	6,548	31.4	31.9	41.9	46.5	4.1
Kentucky	22,091	26,919	26,516	27,825	87.9	86.1	86.7	91.0	5.8
Louisiana	31,160	27,962	28,021	27,436	49.2	50.4	53.3	49.7	3.2
Maine	5,087	5,313	5,444	5,423	29.4	28.4	24.4	24.4	4.7
Maryland	13,157	11,172	11,637	12,075	102.9	100.6	105.2	104.1	4.8
Massachusetts	23,875	22,834	21,500	23,951	188.4	182.0	167.2	173.0	5.9
Michigan	39,238	38,886	38,621	41,449	204.6	202.4	202.4	195.5	5.2
Minnesota	13,472	10,926	12,011	12,916	85.5	85.2	84.8	86.5	3.6
Mississippi	4,121	6,777	7,159	7,197	21.7	25.4	25.4	25.7	2.7
Missouri.	15,773	16,027	15,421	17,435	87.2	84.0	82.7	85.7	3.6
Montana	3,099	2,233	3,295	2,939	5.5	6.5	6.5	6.8	1.9
Nebraska.	2,737	2,021	1,948	2,438	19.0	19.8	18.0	18.7	2.4
Nevada	10,128	6,530	7,087	7,523	26.1	26.7	31.9	35.9	3.1
New Hampshire	5,124	4,693	5,129	5,229	41.7	40.8	35.7	37.1	6.6
New Jersey	35,115	33,846	33,786	37,352	224.0	218.4	214.4	230.5	6.6
New Mexico	5,801	3,792	4,396	3,953	11.6	12.7	13.3	14.2	2.2
New York.	68,522	60,572	63,708	68,625	384.2	380.5	388.6	389.3	5.3
North Carolina	29,931	23,917	23,851	26,082	203.8	199.2	200.1	209.4	6.1
North Dakota	1,824	1,416	1,090	1,523	7.8	6.3	7.2	8.3	2.9
Ohio	37,530	32,898	35,873	38,592	208.0	207.8	211.3	213.3	4.5
Oklahoma	7,635	8,222	8,388	9,646	34.5	32.9	36.0	35.9	2.9
Oregon	13,178	11,749	12,000	8,850	47.9	47.1	50.7	44.0	3.0
Pennsylvania	34,106	30,237	31,959	35,129	233.1	226.5	242.6	249.0	4.8
Rhode Island	3,394	3,381	4,152	4,335	26.1	26.3	24.3	19.5	4.5
South Carolina	23,563	21,844	22,197	24,043	126.8	121.9	110.6	114.3	7.1
South Dakota	1,011	750	902	1,006	6.5	5.6	8.0	6.7	2.0
Tennessee	20,842	19,890	20,616	21,518	128.5	129.5	134.2	140.3	5.7
Texas	110,032	83,739	86,280	96,606	340.3	338.2	358.9	368.2	4.3
Utah	14,340	11,402	11,675	6,918	34.0	30.6	32.1	34.6	3.3
Vermont	2,146	1,357	1,342	1,461	10.3	11.0	9.9	9.8	3.7
Virginia	23,570	16,422	16,848	18,504	138.9	134.8	145.7	150.8	4.9
Washington	22,257	17,477	19,286	19,876	83.7	85.9	84.1	88.2	3.6
West Virginia	7,061	5,716	5,748	5,891	21.4	18.4	20.9	19.9	3.4
Wisconsin	13,961	15,949	15,664	16,124	95.6	87.9	86.2	87.2	3.5
Wyoming	8,072	12,444	11,549	9,346	8.4	9.0	9.0	8.0	3.7
Puerto Rico.	2,169	2,613	2,505	2,734	16.6	16.6	16.6	16.8	(NA)
Other territories and offshore	34,105	36,125	41,588	47,906	12.9	10.5	10.7	9.9	(NA)
Foreign	2,406	1,515	(D)	2,333	0.4	2.2	1.6	1.3	(NA)
Unspecified [1]	66,526	88,688	91,647	108,591	(NA)	(NA)	(NA)	(NA)	(NA)

D Data withheld to avoid disclosure.   NA Not available.   X Not applicable.   [1] Covers property, plant, and equipment not located in a particular state, including aircraft, railroad rolling stock, satellites, undersea cable, and trucks engaged in interstate transportation.

Source: U.S. Bureau of Economic Analysis, *Survey of Current Business*, August 2008 and *Foreign Direct Investment in the United States, Operations of U.S. Affiliates of Foreign Companies*, annual.

780 Foreign Commerce and Aid

Table 1258. **U.S. Businesses Acquired or Established by Foreign Direct Investors—Investment Outlays by Industry of U.S. Business Enterprise and Country of Ultimate Beneficial Owner: 2000 to 2008**

[In millions of dollars (335,629 represents $335,629,000,000). Foreign direct investment is the ownership or control directly or indirectly, by one foreign individual branch, partnership, association, trust, corporation, or government of 10 percent or more of the voting securities of a U.S. business enterprise or an equivalent interest in an unincorporated one. Data represent number and full cost of acquisitions of existing U.S. business enterprises, including business segments or operating units of existing U.S. business enterprises and establishments of new enterprises. Investments may be made by the foreign direct investor itself, or indirectly by an existing U.S. affiliate of the foreign direct investor. Covers investments in U.S. business enterprises with assets of over $1 million, or ownership of 200 acres of U.S. land]

Industry and country	2000	2002	2003	2004	2005	2006	2007	2008, prel.
Total [1]	335,629	54,519	63,591	86,219	91,390	165,603	251,917	260,362
By type of investment:								
U.S. businesses acquired	322,703	43,442	50,212	72,738	73,997	148,604	223,616	242,799
U.S. businesses established	12,926	11,077	13,379	13,481	17,393	16,999	28,301	17,564
By type of investor:								
Foreign direct investors	105,151	13,650	27,866	34,184	40,304	44,129	88,337	47,078
U.S. affiliates	230,478	40,869	35,725	52,035	51,086	121,474	163,580	213,284
INDUSTRY [2]								
Manufacturing	143,285	16,446	10,750	18,251	34,036	56,330	118,370	141,079
Wholesale trade	8,561	871	1,086	(D)	3,489	8,273	5,631	3,977
Retail trade	1,672	551	941	3,073	1,262	1,295	6,867	2,775
Information	67,932	14,181	9,236	4,315	8,487	10,341	8,585	22,214
Depository institutions	2,636	613	4,864	(D)	7,973	7,547	12,307	15,996
Finance (except depository institutions) and insurance	44,420	4,344	23,511	26,234	5,529	33,776	27,497	29,584
Real estate and rental and leasing	4,526	5,266	2,817	6,335	8,756	12,441	17,852	3,796
Professional, scientific, and technical services	32,332	4,012	1,955	(D)	6,407	8,923	9,018	15,167
Other industries	30,264	8,234	8,429	10,121	15,453	26,677	45,790	25,775
COUNTRY [3]								
Canada	28,346	4,333	9,157	31,502	13,640	12,121	38,502	25,181
Europe [1]	249,167	39,644	39,024	43,815	56,416	106,732	132,454	157,853
France	26,149	15,196	2,955	6,415	5,608	18,140	14,307	16,565
Germany	18,452	3,067	8,830	4,788	7,239	20,514	15,831	12,823
Netherlands	47,686	3,476	1,077	461	2,609	4,769	8,357	12,545
Switzerland	22,789	2,656	649	6,505	2,332	12,401	6,501	9,041
United Kingdom	110,208	12,188	20,373	23,288	30,420	26,261	56,051	19,657
Latin America and other Western Hemisphere	15,400	3,487	1,607	2,629	5,042	(D)	(D)	18,259
South and Central America	5,334	373	182	1,382	980	2,273	(D)	3,551
Other Western Hemisphere	10,066	3,144	1,425	1,247	4,062	(D)	1,933	14,708
Africa	(D)	(D)	(D)	(D)	(D)	(D)	(D)	129
Middle East	947	(D)	1,738	1,318	5,068	11,755	21,882	12,263
Asia and Pacific [1]	40,282	5,131	11,469	6,015	10,924	15,759	34,408	44,863
Australia	(D)	1,565	9,032	3,850	4,713	5,650	12,983	10,522
Japan	26,044	3,275	1,544	1,027	4,245	8,350	7,928	28,041

D Suppressed to avoid disclosure of data of individual companies. [1] Includes other countries not shown separately. [2] Based on 1997 North American Industry Classification System (NAICS). Beginning 2002, based on NAICS 2002; see text, Section 15. [3] For investments in which more than one investor participated, each investor and each investor's outlays are classified by country of each ultimate beneficial owner.

Source: U.S. Bureau of Economic Analysis, *Survey of Current Business*, June 2009. For most recent copy and historical issues, see <http://www.bea.gov/bea/pubs.htm>.

Table 1259. **U.S. Direct Investment Position Abroad, Capital Outflows, and Income by Industry of Foreign Affiliates: 2000 to 2008**

[In millions of dollars (1,316,247 represents $1,316,247,000,000). See footnote 2, Table 1258 and headnote, Table 1260]

Industry	Direct investment position on a historical-cost basis			Capital outflows [inflows (–)]			Income [1]		
	2000	2007	2008	2000	2007	2008	2000	2007	2008
All industries, total [2]	1,316,247	2,916,930	3,162,021	142,627	378,362	311,796	133,692	343,012	350,531
Mining	72,111	143,430	151,859	2,174	19,943	27,272	13,164	29,403	36,690
Manufacturing [2]	343,899	493,064	512,293	43,002	66,717	44,980	42,230	64,846	64,012
Food	23,497	39,100	41,802	2,014	10,701	4,530	2,681	4,441	5,128
Chemicals	75,807	102,678	108,049	3,812	7,937	13,018	(D)	15,340	17,467
Primary and fabricated metals	21,644	22,389	24,038	1,233	2,927	2,689	1,536	2,246	2,323
Machinery	22,229	32,397	36,807	2,659	5,421	7,239	2,257	5,796	5,616
Computer and electronic products	59,909	69,159	76,453	17,303	6,440	9,426	8,860	11,060	9,830
Electrical equipment, appliances, and components	10,005	18,909	24,095	2,100	2,255	5,458	1,079	1,807	2,778
Transportation equipment	49,887	58,768	51,774	7,814	11,820	-6,692	4,107	4,915	2,759
Wholesale trade	93,936	154,780	178,213	11,938	13,637	29,874	14,198	27,421	27,421
Information	52,345	114,578	121,864	16,531	9,219	10,551	-964	12,188	10,974
Finance and insurance	217,086	617,312	634,046	21,659	83,466	43,061	15,210	43,993	39,852
Professional, scientific, and technical services	32,868	68,978	81,242	5,441	7,767	7,427	3,548	8,606	9,377
Holding companies (nonbank)	(NA)	998,618	1,128,538	(NA)	148,753	123,806	(NA)	142,755	141,810

D Withheld to avoid disclosure of individual company data. NA Not available. [1] Prior to 2006, income is shown net of withholding taxes. For 2006, income is shown gross of withholding taxes. [2] Includes other industries not shown separately.

Source: U.S. Bureau of Economic Analysis, *Survey of Current Business*, September 2008. For most recent copy and historical issues, see <http://www.bea.gov/scb/index.htm>.

Foreign Commerce and Aid   781

Table 1260. **U.S. Direct Investment Position Abroad on a Historical-Cost Basis by Selected Country: 2000 to 2008**

[In millions of dollars (1,316,247 represents $1,316,247,000,000). U.S. investment abroad is the ownership or control by one U.S. person of 10 percent or more of the voting securities of an incorporated foreign business enterprise or an equivalent interest in an unincorporated foreign business enterprise. Negative position can occur when a U.S. parent company's liabilities to the foreign affiliate are greater than its equity in and loans to the foreign affiliate]

Country	2000	2002	2003	2004	2005	2006	2007	2008
All countries	1,316,247	1,616,548	1,769,613	2,160,844	2,241,656	2,477,268	2,916,930	3,162,021
Canada [1]	132,472	166,473	187,953	214,931	231,836	205,134	233,971	227,298
Europe [1]	687,320	859,378	976,889	1,180,130	1,210,679	1,397,704	1,659,499	1,809,876
Austria	2,872	4,011	6,366	9,264	11,236	14,897	16,527	17,518
Belgium.	17,973	25,727	27,415	41,840	49,306	51,862	62,959	65,054
Czech Republic	1,228	1,264	1,668	2,444	2,729	3,615	4,180	4,654
Denmark.	5,270	6,184	5,597	6,815	6,914	5,849	8,273	10,393
Finland	1,342	1,722	1,677	2,208	1,950	2,107	2,196	2,298
France	42,628	43,348	51,229	63,359	60,526	63,008	70,113	75,040
Germany.	55,508	61,073	72,262	79,467	100,473	93,620	100,806	110,784
Greece	795	981	1,431	1,899	1,884	1,804	2,116	2,125
Hungary	1,920	2,503	2,856	3,024	2,795	2,602	4,302	5,103
Ireland	35,903	51,598	60,604	72,907	55,173	86,372	114,876	146,194
Italy	23,484	23,771	23,092	25,184	24,528	25,435	26,731	28,653
Luxembourg.	27,849	62,181	68,298	83,634	79,937	125,146	153,639	163,167
Netherlands.	115,429	158,415	186,366	219,384	240,205	279,373	389,430	442,926
Norway.	4,379	6,045	7,511	8,491	8,533	9,667	12,044	10,889
Poland	3,884	4,231	4,382	7,256	5,575	6,934	15,239	15,597
Portugal	2,664	3,093	2,402	1,915	2,138	2,832	3,123	3,397
Russia	1,147	1,135	2,511	6,088	9,363	11,371	14,404	9,157
Spain	21,236	38,001	41,119	48,409	50,197	49,356	66,621	69,649
Sweden	25,959	30,114	27,004	29,730	30,153	33,857	35,120	43,391
Switzerland.	55,377	74,229	92,750	121,790	100,692	102,022	97,917	123,358
Turkey	1,826	1,869	2,213	2,682	2,563	3,141	5,974	6,089
United Kingdom	230,762	247,952	277,246	330,416	351,513	406,358	424,612	420,873
Latin America and other Western Hemisphere.	266,576	289,413	297,222	351,709	379,582	418,429	508,711	563,809
South America [1]	84,220	64,603	66,256	68,685	73,311	80,477	103,697	108,231
Argentina.	17,488	11,288	10,663	9,201	10,103	13,174	14,061	15,195
Brazil.	36,717	27,598	29,553	29,485	30,882	33,504	47,750	45,500
Chile.	10,052	8,928	9,021	10,804	11,127	10,927	11,568	12,613
Colombia	3,693	2,622	2,773	2,991	4,292	3,799	4,496	6,263
Ecuador.	832	809	975	881	941	904	977	1,276
Peru	3,130	3,310	3,401	4,773	5,542	5,561	7,551	8,458
Venezuela	10,531	8,671	8,438	9,109	8,934	10,922	15,748	17,332
Central America [1]	73,841	65,395	64,647	73,214	82,496	91,811	103,122	110,424
Costa Rica.	1,716	1,803	840	2,687	1,598	2,105	2,265	2,525
Honduras.	399	181	272	755	821	864	640	700
Mexico	39,352	56,303	56,851	63,384	73,687	82,965	91,259	95,618
Panama.	30,758	5,842	5,409	4,919	4,826	4,636	6,509	7,243
Other Western Hemisphere [1] . .	108,515	159,416	166,319	209,810	223,775	246,142	301,891	345,153
Bahamas, The	3,291	7,645	8,643	11,255	13,451	13,703	17,763	19,549
Barbados	2,141	1,817	984	3,249	3,881	4,831	674	873
Bermuda	60,114	89,473	84,508	100,856	113,222	133,480	162,286	165,857
Dominican Republic.	1,143	983	816	1,028	815	789	766	960
Jamaica.	2,483	3,097	3,406	3,551	1,018	940	749	901
Netherlands Antilles	3,579	4,753	2,926	4,712	5,607	3,924	6,493	11,476
Trinidad and Tobago	1,550	2,326	2,392	2,577	2,219	2,940	3,825	5,460
U.K. Islands, Caribbean	33,451	48,305	61,882	82,159	83,164	84,817	108,559	139,290
Africa [1].	11,891	16,040	19,835	20,356	22,756	28,158	32,496	36,640
Egypt	1,998	2,682	3,524	4,526	5,475	5,564	7,147	8,771
Nigeria	470	901	1,100	1,936	1,105	1,677	1,433	3,393
South Africa.	3,562	3,334	3,580	3,913	3,969	3,980	5,198	4,915
Middle East [1].	10,863	15,158	16,885	18,963	21,115	24,206	28,256	32,488
Israel	3,735	5,726	7,020	6,171	7,978	9,168	9,464	10,153
Saudi Arabia	3,661	4,930	3,140	3,657	3,830	4,410	5,013	5,382
United Arab Emirates.	683	1,087	1,934	2,962	2,285	2,670	2,969	3,423
Asia and Pacific [1].	207,125	270,086	270,830	374,754	375,689	403,637	453,997	491,910
Australia	34,838	39,074	48,447	(D)	75,669	67,632	83,346	88,549
China [2].	11,140	10,570	11,261	17,616	19,016	26,459	28,579	45,695
Hong Kong	27,447	40,329	36,426	32,735	36,415	39,636	50,199	51,505
India.	2,379	4,232	4,868	7,658	7,162	9,746	14,540	16,104
Indonesia	8,904	(D)	(D)	(D)	8,603	9,484	17,679	17,909
Japan.	57,091	66,468	57,794	71,005	81,175	84,428	81,923	79,235
Korea, South	8,968	11,856	13,063	17,747	19,760	27,299	26,854	27,673
Malaysia	7,910	7,101	7,057	8,909	11,097	11,185	13,037	13,291
New Zealand	4,271	3,926	3,859	4,620	5,191	5,933	5,395	5,266
Philippines.	3,638	5,964	6,390	6,176	6,522	6,948	7,066	5,914
Singapore	24,133	50,955	51,053	61,076	76,390	81,879	94,810	106,529
Taiwan [2]	7,836	10,144	11,983	(D)	14,356	16,999	15,711	16,604
Thailand	5,824	7,774	6,886	7,499	10,352	10,642	8,850	9,128

D Suppressed to avoid disclosure of data of individual companies.   [1] Includes other countries not shown separately.   [2] See footnote 4, Table 1296.

Source: U.S. Bureau of Economic Analysis, *Survey of Current Business*, July 2009. For most recent copy and historical issues, see <http://www.bea.gov/bea/pubs.htm>.

Table 1261. **U.S. Government Foreign Grants and Credits by Country: 2000 to 2008**

[In millions of dollars (17,858 represents $17,858,000,000). See text, this section. Negative figures (−) occur when the total of grant returns, principal repayments, and/or foreign currencies disbursed by the U.S. government exceeds new grants and new credits utilized and/or acquisitions of foreign currencies through new sales of farm products]

Country	2000	2002	2003	2004	2005	2006	2007	2008
Investment in financial institutions.	1,500	1,486	1,434	1,994	1,263	2,024	1,651	1,385
Western Europe.	**429**	**485**	**706**	**348**	**345**	**98**	**231**	**262**
Ireland	–	–	44	50	–	30	–	34
Spain	−19	−19	−19	−19	−19	−205	–	–
Yugoslavia	1	−54	231	13	4	−73	−2	3
Bosnia and Herzegovina	52	64	47	66	72	49	46	29
Macedonia	50	15	58	42	67	30	2	34
Former Yugoslavia - Regional [1]:	63	131	66	38	66	120	45	53
Other [2] and unspecified [1]	478	314	221	69	49	45	50	58
Eastern Europe	**2,220**	**1,689**	**1,492**	**1,273**	**−70**	**257**	**1,062**	**1,877**
Albania	26	40	42	43	53	31	36	30
Romania	38	48	66	34	57	41	41	9
Newly independent states:								
Armenia	20	54	74	66	85	61	68	63
Azerbaijan	8	32	35	47	74	52	44	36
Georgia	36	97	66	113	169	75	87	352
Kazakhstan	42	52	50	56	69	40	43	44
Kyrgyzstan	15	36	35	39	60	50	26	38
Moldova	32	28	23	27	38	26	20	40
Russia	797	266	192	251	−681	−920	−41	403
Tajikistan	8	18	25	40	61	35	33	24
Ukraine	138	118	96	114	145	119	69	66
Former Soviet Union—Regional [1] . .	501	510	364	372	456	470	461	508
Other [3] and unspecified [1]	419	232	214	107	153	76	73	76
Near East and South Asia.	**3,304**	**1,632**	**2,268**	**3,544**	**5,259**	**4,500**	**9,659**	**9,045**
Afghanistan	5	140	555	1,222	2,076	3,560	7,262	6,124
Bangladesh	43	45	29	50	48	45	81	75
Egypt	3,091	1,689	2,055	2,689	2,827	149	1,761	1,802
Greece	−169	−218	−287	−457	−114	−103	−74	−66
India	−64	−122	−150	−40	−70	61	46	28
Nepal	15	28	43	37	50	57	63	64
Pakistan	366	145	223	230	530	703	526	692
Turkey	−86	−138	−322	−299	−228	−194	−296	−43
UNRWA [4]	97	71	124	27	48	137	135	160
Other and unspecified [1]	21	2	14	79	54	47	117	150
Africa	**1,058**	**2,085**	**3,909**	**2,450**	**2,199**	**1,342**	**3,523**	**4,580**
Algeria	−53	−73	−123	−146	−173	−1,324	−19	−18
Burundi	3	3	18	27	6	37	18	16
Congo (Kinshasa) [5]	0	33	1,078	229	135	131	91	1
Ethiopia	142	86	138	234	308	233	278	446
Ghana	40	48	50	67	53	54	55	55
Guinea	19	41	30	33	36	29	15	75
Kenya	44	50	58	82	91	186	178	282
Liberia	19	10	13	50	40	61	81	261
Madagascar	21	36	31	34	35	44	48	40
Malawi	45	46	42	54	46	61	68	81
Mali	50	49	50	45	55	52	43	42
Mozambique	119	105	107	105	64	92	106	144
Nigeria	−17	45	472	41	67	−178	123	200
Rwanda	26	32	36	35	47	55	71	93
Senegal	27	42	45	53	39	34	39	75
Somalia	7	6	10	16	7	33	40	168
South Africa	68	98	115	332	103	106	155	243
Sudan	17	11	41	120	130	390	363	529
Tanzania	15	44	49	66	62	75	104	117
Uganda	92	71	86	120	148	154	183	190
Zambia	44	34	52	56	90	89	105	157
Zimbabwe	23	21	23	31	27	32	69	141
Other and unspecified [1]	164	181	278	407	513	621	1,060	777
Far East and Pacific.	**544**	**105**	**712**	**−129**	**42**	**−106**	**141**	**611**
Cambodia	23	35	32	44	58	56	61	60
Hong Kong	−15	−20	−23	−28	−28	−28	−28	−22
Indonesia	270	196	821	−157	−8	−71	−18	−108
Korea, South	−132	−134	−137	−110	−43	−43	−40	182
Malaysia	134	11	2	−45	−46	−45	−185	2
Philippines	20	−46	−35	−15	−36	−28	46	131
Thailand	−102	−27	−37	11	4	−67	–	18
Pacific Islands, Trust Territory of the [6] . .	145	193	103	204	190	174	195	182
Other and unspecified [1]	19	15	22	40	47	39	182	200

See footnotes at end of table.

U.S. Census Bureau, Statistical Abstract of the United States: 2010

Table 1261. **U.S. Government Foreign Grants and Credits by Country: 2000 to 2008**—Con.

[In millions of dollars. See headnote, page 783]

Country	2000	2002	2003	2004	2005	2006	2007	2008
Western Hemisphere	**1,621**	**1,590**	**1,658**	**1,986**	**2,164**	**1,537**	**1,409**	**2,023**
Bolivia	136	152	212	217	159	142	155	135
Brazil.	195	106	−78	−136	−93	−344	−181	−167
Colombia	33	76	328	467	598	613	771	914
Ecuador.	14	75	39	36	59	80	73	53
El Salvador.	27	45	56	104	52	27	40	52
Guatemala	49	54	42	40	21	34	25	55
Haiti	63	66	64	83	118	154	164	192
Honduras	100	85	51	84	70	60	75	62
Mexico.	−123	−13	5	14	40	30	50	51
Nicaragua.	53	60	41	28	36	53	71	57
Panama [7]	−13	(Z)	5	14	7	11	6	9
Peru	87	109	93	167	127	71	−258	127
Other [8] and unspecified [1]	1,100	925	868	806	815	510	447	406
Other international organizations	**2,837**	**4,405**	**3,207**	**2,485**	**4,201**	**3,770**	**4,843**	**5,324**
Middle East	**4,345**	**3,736**	**7,745**	**8,384**	**16,326**	**9,882**	**9,260**	**10,791**
Iraq [9]	(Z)	(Z)	3,235	5,011	10,481	8,822	6,102	6,227
Israel	3,932	3,061	2,761	2,163	4,953	390	2,373	2,955
Jordan	317	483	1,420	800	582	462	424	632
Lebanon	22	28	24	30	37	45	146	252
Yemen	16	1	17	31	24	30	40	22
West Bank-Gaza Regional	64	143	195	171	179	128	152	473

– Represents or rounds to zero.   Z Less than 5000,000.   [1] In recent years, significant amounts of foreign assistance has been reported on a regional, inter-regional, and worldwide basis. Country totals in this table may understate actual assistance to many countries.   [2] Includes European Atomic Energy Community, European Coal and Steel Community, European Payments Union, European Productivity Agency, North Atlantic Treaty Organization, and Organization for European Economic Cooperation.   [3] In 1992, some successor countries assumed portions of outstanding credits of the former Yugoslavia (assignment of the remaining portions is pending). Subsequent negative totals reflect payments to the United States on these assumed credits which were greater than the extension of new credits and grants to these countries.   [4] United Nations Relief and Works Agency for Palestine refugees.   [5] See footnote 5, Table 1296.   [6] Excludes transactions with Commonwealth of the Northern Mariana Islands after October 1986; includes transactions with Federated States of Micronesia, Republic of the Marshall Islands, and Republic of Palau.   [7] Includes transfer of Panama Canal to the Republic of Panama on Dec. 1999.   [8] Includes Andean Development Corporation, Caribbean Development Bank, Central American Bank for Economic Integration, Eastern Caribbean Central Bank, Inter-American Institute of Agricultural Science, Organizations of American States, and Pan American Health Organization.   [9] Foreign assistance to Iraq in 1991–96 was direct humanitarian assistance to ethnic minorities of Northern Iraq after the conflict in the Persian Gulf. Foreign assistance to Iraq in 2003, 2004, 2005, 2006 and 2007 includes Iraq Reconstruction and humanitarian assistance.

Source: U.S. Bureau of Economic Analysis, press releases and unpublished data.

Table 1262. **U.S. Foreign Economic and Military Aid Programs: 1980 to 2007**

[In millions of dollars (9,694 represents $9,694,000,000). For years ending September 30. Economic aid shown here represents U.S. economic aid—not just aid under the Foreign Assistance Act. Major components in recent years include AID, Food for Peace, Peace Corps, and paid-in subscriptions to international financial institutions. Annual figures are gross unadjusted program figures]

Year and region	Total foreign assistance	Military assistance	Economic assistance, by funding agency					
			Total	U.S. Agency for International Development	U.S. Department of Agriculture	State Department	Other U.S. agencies	Multilateral organizations
1980	9,694	2,122	7,572	4,062	1,437	459	137	1,478
1990	16,015	4,971	11,044	6,964	1,643	590	377	1,469
1995	16,408	4,165	12,242	7,281	1,401	763	1,016	1,781
2000	17,579	4,876	12,702	5,907	1,941	2,486	1,258	1,110
2002	20,023	4,797	15,226	8,419	1,433	2,340	1,442	1,591
2003	25,970	6,662	19,308	10,126	2,625	2,184	3,736	637
2004	33,627	6,146	27,481	11,208	2,150	4,026	7,212	2,885
2005	35,499	7,331	28,168	10,052	2,318	5,037	9,102	1,659
2006	39,144	12,260	26,884	9,610	2,033	5,375	8,375	1,492
2007, total	**41,940**	**13,025**	**28,915**	**11,941**	**1,835**	**5,657**	**7,750**	**1,733**
Asia	8,216	4,020	4,196	2,579	207	469	843	99
Central Asia	2,433	163	2,270	433	25	83	1,729	–
Eastern Europe.	527	120	407	293	–	25	89	–
Latin America and Caribbean	2,347	117	2,231	561	138	648	875	9
Middle East and North Africa	13,984	8,091	5,893	3,747	21	662	1,462	–
Oceania	191	1	190	2	–	–	188	–
Sub-Saharan Africa	7,980	396	7,583	2,189	1,360	2,236	1,660	137
Western Europe	134	19	115	42	–	11	62	–
Canada.	24	–	24	–	–	–	24	–
World not specified	6,105	98	6,006	2,095	85	1,522	816	1,488

– Represents or rounds to zero.

Source: U.S. Agency for International Development, *U.S. Overseas Loans, Grants, Obligations, and Loan Authorizations,* annual. See also <http://qesdb.cdie.org/gbk/index.html>.

Table 1263. **U.S. Foreign Economic and Military Aid by Major Recipient Country: 2000 to 2007**

[In millions of dollars (17,579 represents $17,579,000,000), except as indicated. For years ending Sept. 30]

Recipient country	2000	2004	2005	2006	2007 Total	2007 Economic aid	2007 Military aid
Total [1]	17,579	33,627	35,499	39,144	41,941	28,915	13,025
Afghanistan	54	2,032	2,252	3,740	5,816	2,174	3,642
Albania	72	59	43	54	40	36	4
Angola	105	116	67	52	48	48	–
Armenia.	104	80	76	321	82	78	5
Azerbaijan	55	60	64	56	57	52	5
Bangladesh	78	93	84	82	93	91	2
Bolivia.	241	183	162	224	181	181	–
Bosnia and Herzegovina.	181	85	47	53	52	43	10
Bulgaria.	49	43	44	39	43	19	24
Burundi	7	49	59	50	38	38	–
Cambodia	27	93	98	71	74	73	1
Chad	4	59	63	82	98	97	–
Colombia.	1,169	758	824	1,348	497	410	87
Congo (Kinshasa) [2]	33	117	121	171	149	148	1
Ecuador	77	91	87	76	66	66	–
Egypt	2,076	1,958	1,563	1,787	1,972	671	1,301
El Salvador	35	70	59	68	513	504	9
Eritrea	39	86	133	6	3	3	–
Ethiopia.	278	436	694	323	470	468	2
Georgia.	112	124	105	409	98	87	11
Ghana.	67	73	72	104	621	619	2
Guatemala.	72	77	96	102	84	83	–
Haiti	88	163	224	243	210	208	2
Honduras.	42	66	285	88	65	62	3
India	188	190	209	174	159	158	2
Indonesia.	242	161	587	269	244	235	9
Iraq	1	8,673	7,773	9,851	8,193	4,050	4,143
Israel	3,864	2,722	2,713	2,544	2,508	168	2,340
Jamaica.	22	41	66	36	36	34	2
Jordan	448	638	683	562	560	349	211
Kazakhstan	53	78	66	110	105	100	4
Kenya	94	187	263	390	522	522	–
Kosovo	260	53	43	51	93	93	–
Kyrgyzstan.	47	43	49	45	49	46	3
Liberia.	22	138	148	152	260	204	56
Macedonia.	63	50	48	45	38	34	4
Madagascar	27	47	155	55	67	66	–
Malawi	44	53	85	74	107	107	1
Mali	44	58	54	64	535	535	–
Marshall Islands	41	42	44	51	48	48	–
Mexico	44	94	98	184	88	88	–
Micronesia, Federated States of. . .	81	95	94	100	100	100	–
Morocco	51	35	55	53	88	74	14
Mozambique	88	114	127	161	261	259	1
Namibia.	16	31	50	64	89	89	–
Nepal	23	55	72	60	81	80	1
Nicaragua	34	62	95	248	58	56	2
Nigeria	113	133	151	188	338	336	2
Pakistan	24	441	757	957	977	665	312
Peru	204	273	191	338	165	165	–
Philippines	82	238	167	213	168	126	43
Poland	85	37	93	34	32	2	31
Romania	46	49	63	53	38	22	16
Russia.	709	941	1,584	1,529	1,594	1,481	112
Rwanda.	39	59	83	103	120	119	1
Senegal.	37	53	48	67	70	68	2
Serbia and Montenegro [3]	424	172	133	4	–	–	–
South Africa.	57	130	187	263	393	393	–
Sri Lanka.	11	39	160	49	44	42	1
Sudan	51	482	1,043	908	1,180	926	254
Tajikistan	37	50	64	48	34	33	1
Tanzania	44	100	137	187	253	253	–
Turkey.	5	50	54	23	30	12	18
Uganda	76	219	291	280	370	369	–
Ukraine	199	132	149	154	167	155	11
Uzbekistan	34	43	42	45	17	17	–
West Bank/Gaza [4].	122	139	350	274	165	165	–
Zambia	35	103	144	197	201	201	–
Zimbabwe	21	33	61	30	140	140	–

– Represents or rounds to zero.　　[1] Includes other countries not shown separately.　　[2] See Footnote 5, Table 1296.　　[3] See footnote 3, Table 1345.　　[4] See footnote 7, Table 1296.

Source: U.S. Agency for International Development, *U.S. Overseas Loans, Grants, Obligations, and Loan Authorizations*, annual. See also <http://qesdb.cdie.org/gbk/index.html>.

Table 1264. **U.S. International Trade in Goods and Services: 2000 to 2008**

[In millions of dollars (–379,835 represents –$379,835,000,000). Data presented on a balance of payments basis and will not agree with other merchandise trade tables in this section]

Category	2000	2002	2003	2004	2005	2006	2007	2008
TRADE BALANCE								
Total	–379,835	–423,725	–496,915	–609,987	–715,269	–760,359	–701,423	–695,937
Goods.	–454,690	–484,955	–550,892	–671,835	–790,851	–847,260	–830,992	–840,252
Services	74,855	61,230	53,977	61,848	75,582	86,901	129,569	144,315
Travel	17,695	7,890	6,912	8,796	12,829	13,685	20,696	30,347
Passenger fares	–3,587	–2,923	–5,098	–5,867	–5,179	–5,465	–2,801	–974
Other transportation	–11,622	–9,212	–13,289	–17,204	–20,656	–19,093	–15,550	–13,198
Royalties, license fees	26,765	25,155	27,955	33,449	39,783	47,209	59,168	64,983
Other private services.	47,384	49,603	51,799	59,010	62,233	60,550	78,413	80,262
Other [1].	317	–7,158	–11,981	–13,518	–10,536	–7,119	–7,384	–13,881
U.S. govt misc. services . . .	–2,097	–2,125	–2,321	–2,819	–2,892	–2,866	–2,972	–3,224
EXPORTS								
Total	1,070,597	974,721	1,017,757	1,159,233	1,281,459	1,451,685	1,643,168	1,826,596
Goods.	771,994	682,422	713,415	806,161	892,337	1,015,812	1,138,384	1,276,994
Services	298,603	292,299	304,342	353,072	389,122	435,873	504,784	549,602
Travel	82,400	66,605	64,359	74,546	81,799	85,789	97,050	110,090
Passenger fares	20,687	17,046	15,891	18,851	20,970	22,036	25,636	31,623
Other transportation	29,803	29,195	31,416	36,957	41,281	46,225	51,550	58,945
Royalties, license fees	43,233	44,508	46,988	56,715	64,395	70,727	83,824	91,599
Other private services.	107,904	122,207	131,563	149,262	160,051	186,028	220,077	233,529
Other [1].	13,790	11,943	13,315	15,781	19,539	23,913	25,436	22,571
U.S. govt misc. services . . .	786	795	810	959	1,087	1,155	1,212	1,245
IMPORTS								
Total	1,450,432	1,398,446	1,514,672	1,769,220	1,996,728	2,212,044	2,344,590	2,522,532
Goods.	1,226,684	1,167,377	1,264,307	1,477,996	1,683,188	1,863,072	1,969,375	2,117,245
Services	223,748	231,069	250,365	291,224	313,540	348,972	375,215	405,287
Travel	64,705	58,715	57,447	65,750	68,970	72,104	76,354	79,743
Passenger fares	24,274	19,969	20,989	24,718	26,149	27,501	28,437	32,597
Other transportation	41,425	38,407	44,705	54,161	61,937	65,318	67,100	72,143
Royalties, license fees	16,468	19,353	19,033	23,266	24,612	23,518	24,656	26,616
Other private services.	60,520	72,604	79,764	90,252	97,818	125,478	141,664	153,267
Other [1].	13,473	19,101	25,296	29,299	30,075	31,032	32,820	36,452
U.S. govt misc. services . . .	2,883	2,920	3,131	3,778	3,979	4,021	4,184	4,469

[1] Represents transfers under U.S. military sales contracts for exports and direct defense expenditures for imports.

Source: U.S. Census Bureau, *U.S. International Trade in Goods and Services, Annual Revision for 2008*, Series FT-900(07-04) and previous reports. See also <http://www.census.gov/foreign-trade/Press-Release/2008pr/final_revisions /08final.pdf> (released 10 June 2009).

Table 1265. **U.S. International Trade in Goods by Related Parties: 2000 to 2008**

[In millions of dollars (1,205,339 represents $1,205,339,000,000). "Related party trade" is trade by U.S. companies with their subsidiaries abroad as well as trade by U.S. subsidiaries of foreign companies with their parent companies. Based on the North American Industry Classification System (NAICS), 2002; see text, Section 15]

Country and commodity	2002 NAICS code	2000	2005	2006	2007	2008
IMPORTS FOR CONSUMPTION						
Total imports . . . . [1]	(X)	1,205,339	1,662,380	1,845,053	1,942,863	2,090,483
Related party trade, total [1]	(X)	563,084	775,730	862,657	920,369	975,096
Canada.	(X)	100,689	127,719	139,490	146,906	156,666
Japan.	(X)	108,290	108,322	116,690	116,304	111,898
Mexico.	(X)	89,068	99,709	114,504	120,551	111,979
China [2].	(X)	18,061	62,716	70,701	82,404	89,339
Germany.	(X)	37,781	30,792	54,972	61,318	64,058
Transportation equipment.	336	161,150	188,445	200,855	207,668	189,984
Computer & electronic products.	334	166,279	176,719	189,046	196,933	182,337
Chemicals	325	45,452	84,459	96,919	109,734	137,095
Machinery, except electrical	333	39,918	56,804	62,975	61,272	62,192
Oil & gas.	211	13,241	48,725	61,758	69,394	104,091
EXPORTS						
Total exports	(X)	780,418	904,380	1,037,143	1,162,708	1,300,136
Related party trade, domestic exports, total [1]	(X)	196,596	245,712	279,832	301,314	327,151
Canada.	(X)	64,133	76,331	80,687	88,396	89,928
Mexico.	(X)	34,249	44,570	49,801	52,470	51,789
Japan.	(X)	20,313	17,427	18,332	17,486	18,825
Netherlands.	(X)	6,845	9,308	13,835	12,812	16,364
Germany.	(X)	6,751	9,250	13,779	16,185	18,275
Transportation equipment.	336	46,288	52,513	58,379	63,885	63,946
Chemicals	325	26,376	48,121	55,349	58,343	61,497
Computer & electronic products.	334	51,210	41,863	47,140	47,127	47,027
Machinery, except electrical	333	19,831	25,492	27,627	30,231	32,978
Electrical equipment, appliances & components	335	7,575	9,888	11,642	12,205	11,806

X Not applicable.   [1] Includes other countries and other commodities not shown separately.   [2] See footnote 4, Table 1296.

Source: U.S. Census Bureau, "Related Party Trade—2008" (published 9 May 2009). See <http://www.census.gov /foreign-trade/Press-Release/2008pr/aip/related_party>.

786   Foreign Commerce and Aid

Table 1266. **U.S. Freight Gateways—Value of Shipments: 2007**

[In billions of dollars, except as indicated (2,892.3 represents $2,892,300,000,000). For the top 50 gateways ranked by value of shipments. Excludes imports of less than $1,250, exports less than $2,500, and intransit shipments]

Port	Mode	Rank	Total trade	Exports	Imports	Exports as a percent of total
Total U.S. merchandise trade	**(X)**	**(X)**	**3,116.4**	**1,162.7**	**1,953.7**	**37.3**
Top 50 gateways	(X)	(X)	2,444.9	901.9	1,543.0	36.9
As a percent of total	(X)	(X)	78.5	77.6	79.0	(X)
Port of Los Angeles, CA	Water	1	180.2	29.9	150.4	16.6
Port of New York, NY and NJ	Water	2	165.2	40.6	124.6	24.6
JFK International Airport, NY	Air	3	161.2	77.0	84.2	47.8
Port of Long Beach, CA	Water	4	147.1	26.7	120.4	18.2
Port of Detroit, MI.	Land	5	136.6	73.3	63.3	53.7
Port of Houston, TX	Water	6	114.6	53.4	61.2	46.6
Port of Laredo, TX	Land	7	110.4	47.4	63.0	42.9
Chicago, IL	Air	8	86.6	33.4	53.1	38.6
Los Angeles International Airport, CA	Air	9	79.6	41.6	38.0	52.3
Port of Buffalo-Niagara Falls, NY.	Land	10	78.6	38.6	40.0	49.1
Port of Huron, MI	Land	11	77.1	30.7	46.3	39.9
San Francisco International Airport, CA	Air	12	61.6	29.7	31.9	48.1
Port of Charleston, SC	Water	13	60.9	19.8	41.1	32.5
Port of Savannah, GA.	Water	14	49.6	18.3	31.3	36.9
Port of Norfolk Harbor, VA	Water	15	49.5	20.7	28.8	41.8
Port of El Paso, TX.	Land	16	49.1	20.0	29.1	40.8
Anchorage, AK	Air	17	45.3	10.7	34.5	23.7
Port of Baltimore, MD	Water	18	42.0	14.0	28.0	33.3
Dallas-Fort Worth, TX	Air	19	41.5	18.1	23.4	43.7
New Orleans, LA	Air	20	41.1	18.2	22.9	44.4
Port of Seattle, WA.	Water	21	37.6	9.2	28.4	24.5
Atlanta, GA.	Air	22	35.4	12.5	22.9	35.3
Port of Oakland, CA	Water	23	34.8	11.4	23.4	32.7
Miami International Airport, FL	Air	24	34.5	24.0	10.4	69.7
Port of Tacoma, WA	Water	25	33.8	6.0	27.8	17.8
Port of New Orleans, LA	Water	26	33.0	15.9	17.1	48.2
Port of Otay Mesa Station, CA	Land	27	30.7	9.9	20.8	32.4
Cleveland, OH.	Air	28	27.3	15.9	11.4	58.3
Port of Morgan City, LA	Water	29	26.5	0.1	26.4	0.4
Port of Beaumont, TX	Water	30	23.3	2.1	21.3	8.9
Port of Corpus Christi, TX	Water	31	22.8	4.2	18.7	18.2
Port of Hidalgo, TX.	Land	32	21.9	9.0	12.9	41.1
Port of Champlain-Rouses Pt., NY.	Land	33	21.5	8.1	13.4	37.7
Port of Jacksonville, FL	Water	34	21.0	9.0	12.0	42.8
Port of Port Everglades, FL	Water	35	20.9	10.1	10.9	48.2
Port of Miami, FL	Water	36	19.5	9.0	10.5	46.0
Port of Luis Munoz Marin International, PR	Air	37	18.8	10.3	8.5	54.8
Port of Philadelphia, PA.	Water	38	18.5	1.9	16.6	10.2
Port of Nogales, AZ	Land	39	18.2	6.0	12.1	33.1
Port of Blaine, WA	Land	40	17.9	9.9	7.9	55.6
Port of Texas City, TX	Water	41	17.6	2.5	15.1	14.0
Port of Pembina, ND.	Land	42	17.2	9.4	7.8	54.5
Port of Portland, OR.	Water	43	15.9	3.6	12.3	22.8
Port of Dulles Interational, DC	Air	44	14.9	5.2	9.7	34.9
Port of General Edward Lawrence Logan International, MA	Air	45	14.7	8.8	5.9	59.7
Port of Gramery, LA	Water	46	14.7	6.0	8.6	41.0
Port of Newark Liberty International, NJ	Air	47	14.1	3.7	10.4	26.5
Port of Sweetgrass, MT.	Land	48	13.7	6.8	6.9	49.4
Port of Lake Charles, LA	Water	49	13.4	1.5	12.0	10.9
Port of Portal, ND.	Land	50	13.4	7.7	5.7	57.6

X Not applicable.

Source: U.S. Bureau of Transportation Statistics, *National Transportation Statistics,* annual. See <http://www.bts.gov/publications/national_transportation_statistics/>.

Foreign Commerce and Aid   787

Table 1267. **U.S. Exports and Imports for Consumption of Merchandise by Customs District: 2000 to 2008**

[In billions of dollars (780.0 represents $780,000,000,000). Exports are f.a.s. (free alongside ship) value all years; imports are on customs-value basis. These data may differ from those in Tables 1265, 1271, and 1272. For methodology, see Foreign Trade Statistics in Appendix III]

Customs district	Exports					Imports for consumption				
	2000	2005	2006	2007	2008	2000	2005	2006	2007	2008
Total [1]	780.0	901.1	1,026.0	1,148.2	1,287.4	1,205.6	1,673.5	1,853.9	1,957.0	2,103.6
Anchorage, AK.	5.9	12.1	14.9	14.1	13.5	13.4	10.4	11.7	11.5	10.7
Baltimore, MD	6.2	9.0	10.0	14.4	16.5	18.6	29.6	29.7	30.3	31.3
Boston, MA	7.0	10.4	10.5	11.3	11.9	18.7	21.7	22.8	24.5	24.4
Buffalo, NY	38.2	35.0	38.0	41.4	43.5	38.4	42.6	44.1	45.1	46.0
Charleston, SC [2]	12.6	16.2	16.2	20.0	22.3	16.9	31.9	33.0	36.9	36.5
Chicago, IL	21.7	29.9	32.2	34.3	36.6	51.1	78.7	88.5	98.6	116.9
Cleveland, OH	22.7	20.8	21.4	22.3	23.8	36.5	49.0	56.1	61.3	70.4
Dallas/Fort Worth, TX	11.5	17.8	20.7	20.7	19.8	18.8	31.8	37.7	36.9	37.1
Detroit, MI	79.4	106.9	113.7	121.2	119.1	97.6	123.1	125.9	127.8	117.4
Duluth, MN	1.5	1.9	2.0	2.1	3.2	7.0	9.3	7.0	7.4	8.5
El Paso, TX	18.0	19.9	21.9	20.9	21.1	24.1	28.0	30.3	34.2	32.4
Great Falls, MT	5.0	9.8	12.4	14.8	18.0	14.3	27.1	28.1	30.1	34.9
Honolulu, HI.	0.7	2.4	3.1	3.7	5.6	2.9	3.7	4.9	5.2	6.0
Houston/Galveston, TX . . .	29.7	47.0	58.1	72.3	89.9	40.9	89.4	104.1	113.0	151.0
Laredo, TX	57.7	60.5	67.2	70.6	79.6	62.7	78.7	90.1	96.7	95.1
Los Angeles, CA.	77.6	78.4	90.4	100.0	110.0	150.1	215.5	239.0	249.0	247.1
Miami, FL	31.0	34.1	39.6	45.5	54.9	23.3	31.8	32.5	33.6	35.4
Milwaukee, WI	0.1	0.1	0.2	0.2	0.2	1.5	1.3	1.4	1.5	1.1
Minneapolis, MN.	1.4	2.3	2.5	3.3	2.3	4.3	6.9	12.0	13.1	16.6
Mobile, AL [2]	4.0	5.0	6.0	6.0	8.5	7.9	14.3	18.8	18.4	24.7
New Orleans, LA	35.9	32.6	39.8	52.1	65.6	54.0	97.8	113.0	123.7	151.3
New York, NY	79.5	90.9	106.3	123.7	143.7	145.6	176.7	188.7	200.0	209.5
Nogales, AZ.	7.3	6.9	8.3	8.0	9.2	14.1	13.0	16.3	16.4	16.8
Norfolk, VA [2]	12.4	16.8	18.1	22.1	25.8	13.6	23.5	26.3	28.4	29.6
Ogdensburg, NY.	12.4	13.3	14.3	15.4	16.5	23.7	28.2	30.1	30.9	33.0
Pembina, ND	8.7	13.6	16.1	18.0	22.0	11.0	12.8	14.0	15.1	17.4
Philadelphia, PA	6.0	10.2	13.1	14.3	19.4	28.3	47.8	56.2	60.4	73.3
Port Arthur, TX	1.2	2.1	3.0	3.1	5.3	10.9	20.9	24.2	25.1	32.4
Portland, ME	2.6	2.8	3.1	3.3	4.8	8.7	11.2	10.7	11.1	11.6
Portland, OR	7.2	6.3	7.6	9.9	14.3	12.5	14.2	16.3	18.2	16.9
Providence, RI	(Z)	0.1	0.1	0.2	0.3	1.3	4.4	6.0	4.5	5.7
San Diego, CA.	12.7	15.0	16.0	16.0	16.6	22.2	28.4	34.8	38.2	37.4
San Francisco, CA	58.3	36.6	41.4	43.3	43.7	68.6	62.4	69.7	68.9	71.6
San Juan, PR	4.8	9.7	11.8	14.9	17.2	11.8	19.5	20.7	21.7	21.6
Savannah, GA	15.9	24.7	27.9	33.6	38.3	26.1	47.9	54.6	60.3	62.7
Seattle, WA	40.4	44.1	54.7	61.2	59.9	40.5	51.7	54.4	58.5	60.7
St Albans, VT.	4.5	4.3	3.7	3.7	3.8	9.4	12.6	11.1	11.0	10.2
St Louis, MO	1.3	1.3	1.7	2.1	2.8	7.9	9.7	10.2	11.4	12.7
Tampa, FL.	4.8	10.1	12.1	13.5	18.1	14.7	19.3	24.9	22.3	22.2
Virgin Islands, VI.	0.3	0.5	0.5	0.8	2.7	4.8	9.1	10.3	11.0	16.6
Washington, DC	2.8	3.7	5.2	5.4	5.7	2.6	3.7	7.4	6.8	8.8
Wilmington, NC	2.5	2.2	2.3	2.8	3.2	10.6	15.4	16.3	16.9	15.3

Z Less than $50 million.   [1] Totals shown for exports reflect the value of estimated parcel post and Special Category shipments, and adjustments for undocumented exports to Canada are not distributed by coastal area or customs district. The value of bituminous coal exported through Norfolk, VA; Charleston, SC; and Mobile, AL, is reflected in the total but not distributed by district.   [2] Excludes exports of bituminous coal.

Source: U.S. Census Bureau, U.S. Highlights of Export and Import Trade, series FT 990; U.S. Merchandise Trade: Selected Highlights, series FT 920; 1991–2004, U.S. Export History and U.S. Import History on compact disc; beginning 2005, U.S. Merchandise Trade: Selected Highlights, December issues, series FT920. See also <http://www.census.gov/foreign-trade/Press-Release/ft920index.html>.

Table 1268. **Export and Import Unit Value Indexes—Selected Countries: 2004 to 2008**

[Indexes in U.S. dollars, 2000 = 100. A unit value is an implicit price derived from value and quantity data]

Country	Export unit value					Import unit value				
	2004	2005	2006	2007	2008	2004	2005	2006	2007	2008
United States	103.6	106.9	110.7	116.1	123.1	102.3	110.0	115.4	120.2	134.1
Australia	129.1	152.9	174.3	194.7	244.0	111.1	116.6	119.8	127.8	139.7
Belgium	134.9	142.0	149.1	169.8	189.5	136.1	142.8	150.5	167.9	191.9
Canada.	117.1	130.1	139.5	149.9	165.0	105.5	113.7	122.3	127.4	136.8
France	127.3	126.6	127.1	138.7	146.0	122.5	121.7	124.3	136.8	(NA)
Germany.	128.9	129.7	131.9	147.1	159.3	120.3	123.2	129.0	143.1	159
Greece	154.1	160.1	168.2	189.0	215.2	(NA)	(NA)	(NA)	(NA)	(NA)
Ireland	115.4	119.1	118.2	124.3	(NA)	119.6	120.7	125.2	136.2	(NA)
Italy	148.6	148.8	157.8	180.6	(NA)	143.8	149.0	164.6	184.2	(NA)
Japan.	96.1	96.1	93.9	94.8	101.5	103.9	115.4	124.6	132.1	163.9
Korea, South	91.5	92.8	93.3	96.3	100.0	107.3	117.4	126.4	133.8	160.6
Netherlands.	126.3	133.1	140.7	174.7	195.7	130.9	132.8	138.3	156.4	175.2
Norway.	126.8	160.9	193.4	211.9	258.5	126.5	132.4	138.9	158.2	168.8
Spain	133.4	139.9	147.8	165.3	180.2	130.6	137.4	142.8	157.9	175.4
Sweden	121.1	124.1	130.8	148.2	156.1	131.2	138.4	148.4	165.9	180.2
Switzerland	137.2	139.4	143.1	155.6	178.2	135.3	142.1	148.5	161.3	179.2
United Kingdom	121.5	125.9	131.3	144.5	153.4	115.6	119.6	125.5	138.4	144.1

NA Not available.

Source: International Monetary Fund, Washington, DC, *International Financial Statistics*, monthly, (copyright).

788   Foreign Commerce and Aid

Table 1269. U.S. Exports of Goods by State of Origin: 2000 to 2008

[In millions of dollars (782,429 represents $782,429,000,000), except as indicated. Exports are on a f.a.s. value basis. Exports are based on origin of movement]

State and other area	2000	2007	2008 Total	2008 Rank	State and other area	2000	2007	2008 Total	2008 Rank
Total	782,429	1,148,199	1,287,442	(X)	Montana	541	1,134	1,395	48
					Nebraska	2,511	4,266	5,412	36
United States	712,055	1,090,418	1,222,545	(X)	Nevada	1,482	5,714	6,121	33
					New Hampshire	2,373	2,914	3,752	40
Alabama	7,317	14,407	15,879	24					
Alaska	2,464	4,010	3,542	42	New Jersey	18,638	30,836	35,643	10
Arizona	14,334	19,228	19,784	19	New Mexico	2,391	2,585	2,783	44
Arkansas	2,599	4,887	5,776	34	New York	42,846	71,116	81,386	3
California	119,640	134,319	144,806	2	North Carolina	17,946	23,356	25,091	15
Colorado	6,593	7,352	7,713	31	North Dakota	626	2,047	2,772	45
Connecticut	8,047	13,799	15,384	25	Ohio	26,322	42,562	45,628	7
Delaware	2,197	4,024	4,898	39	Oklahoma	3,072	4,579	5,077	37
District of Columbia	1,003	1,082	1,196	49	Oregon	11,441	16,531	19,352	20
Florida	26,543	44,858	54,238	5	Pennsylvania	18,792	29,195	34,649	11
					Rhode Island	1,186	1,649	1,974	46
Georgia	14,925	23,366	27,514	13					
Hawaii	387	560	960	51	South Carolina	8,565	16,575	19,853	18
Idaho	3,559	4,703	5,005	38	South Dakota	679	1,510	1,654	47
Illinois	31,438	48,896	53,677	6	Tennessee	11,592	21,865	23,238	16
Indiana	15,386	25,956	26,502	14	Texas	103,866	168,229	192,222	1
Iowa	4,466	9,656	12,125	28	Utah	3,221	7,815	10,306	30
Kansas	5,145	10,277	12,514	27	Vermont	4,097	3,685	3,697	41
Kentucky	9,612	19,652	19,121	22	Virginia	11,698	16,864	18,942	23
Louisiana	16,814	30,319	41,908	9	Washington	32,215	52,089	54,498	4
Maine	1,779	2,750	3,016	43	West Virginia	2,219	3,987	5,643	35
					Wisconsin	10,508	18,825	20,570	17
Maryland	4,593	8,949	11,383	29	Wyoming	503	802	1,081	50
Massachusetts	20,514	25,351	28,369	12					
Michigan	33,845	44,555	45,136	8	Puerto Rico	9,735	18,078	19,961	(X)
Minnesota	10,303	18,062	19,186	21	Virgin Islands	174	808	2,747	(X)
Mississippi	2,726	5,184	7,323	32	Other [1]	60,810	38,894	42,188	(X)
Missouri	6,497	13,484	12,852	26	Timing adjustments	−346	(X)	(X)	(X)

X Not applicable.   [1] Includes unreported, not specified, special category, estimated shipments, and re-exports.

Source: U.S. Census Bureau, *U.S. International Trade in Goods and Services*, December issues, Series FT-900. See <http://www.census.gov/foreign-trade/Press-Release/2008pr/12/> (released 13 February 2009).

Table 1270. U.S. Agricultural Exports by State: 2000 to 2008

[In millions of dollars (50,762 represents $50,762,000,000). For years ending September 30]

State	2000	2005	2006	2007	2008	State	2000	2005	2006	2007	2008
U.S.	50,762	62,504	68,678	82,364	115,452	NE	2,816	2,816	3,213	4,054	5,945
						NV	39	42	38	43	57
AL	401	564	569	625	1,007	NH	14	15	18	22	25
AK	2	3	4	4	5	NJ	150	192	220	247	308
AZ	391	417	466	507	661						
AR	1,210	1,686	1,927	2,157	3,216	NM	82	153	240	272	385
CA	6,298	9,465	10,595	11,391	13,691	NY	515	622	721	867	1,203
CO	894	714	817	1,121	1,425	NC	1,525	1,801	2,059	2,068	3,118
CT	140	84	99	119	139	ND	1,475	1,739	1,852	2,578	3,949
DE	127	134	134	162	248	OH	1,348	1,563	1,752	2,196	2,915
FL	1,469	1,542	1,619	1,948	2,172	OK	534	765	669	879	1,631
GA	908	1,125	1,326	1,444	2,066	OR	749	902	979	1,189	1,557
						PA	989	1,123	1,304	1,471	1,911
HI	81	95	93	89	100	RI	7	11	11	12	14
ID	803	898	961	1,182	1,779	SC	333	382	411	393	659
IL	2,951	3,289	3,847	4,718	7,541						
IN	1,501	1,824	2,002	2,413	3,778	SD	1,094	1,233	1,087	1,822	3,044
IA	2,944	4,007	4,192	5,246	7,859	TN	561	816	931	771	1,356
KS	2,929	2,892	3,107	3,851	5,902	TX	2,877	3,622	3,632	5,201	6,007
KY	806	1,074	1,104	1,280	1,671	UT	246	249	285	343	448
LA	426	553	651	711	926	VT	14	16	35	49	63
ME	61	71	87	101	121	VA	490	575	563	623	907
MD	273	286	310	361	529	WA	1,595	1,943	2,193	2,662	3,169
						WV	36	39	40	48	66
MA	120	151	208	205	350	WI	1,283	1,518	1,713	2,104	3,010
MI	813	934	1,084	1,239	1,684	WY	48	50	52	63	114
MN	2,230	2,770	2,931	3,626	5,461						
MS	571	916	945	1,130	1,654	Unallocated	2,072	2,994	3,542	3,959	5,132
MO	1,204	1,249	1,483	2,049	3,219						
MT	319	583	561	749	1,256						

Source: U.S. Dept. of Agriculture, Economic Research Service, "State Export Data" (published 29 June 2009). See <http://www.ers.usda.gov/data/stateexports/>.

U.S. Census Bureau, Statistical Abstract of the United States: 2010

Table 1271. U.S. Exports, Imports, and Merchandise Trade Balance by Country: 2004 to 2008

[In millions of dollars (814,875 represents $814,875,000,000). Includes silver ore and bullion. Country totals include exports of special category commodities, if any. Data include nonmonetary gold and include trade of Virgin Islands with foreign countries. For methodology, see Foreign Trade Statistics in Appendix III. Minus sign (–) denotes an excess of imports over exports]

Country[1]	Exports, domestic and foreign					General imports					Merchandise trade balance				
	2004	2005	2006	2007	2008	2004	2005	2006	2007	2008	2004	2005	2006	2007	2008
Total[1]	814,875	901,082	1,025,968	1,148,199	1,287,442	1,469,704	1,673,455	1,853,938	1,956,962	2,201,151	-654,829	-772,373	-827,970	-808,763	-913,709
Afghanistan	150	262	417	495	482	25	67	45	74	85	126	195	372	421	397
Albania	20	19	28	34	40	11	37	24	10	12	9	-19	4	25	28
Algeria	972	1,106	1,102	1,652	1,243	7,410	10,446	15,456	17,816	19,355	-6,438	-9,340	-14,354	-16,164	-18,112
Angola	594	929	1,389	1,242	2,019	4,521	8,484	11,719	12,508	18,911	-3,927	-7,555	-10,330	-11,266	-16,892
Anguilla	21	32	43	93	81	1	4	4	5	5	20	28	39	88	77
Antigua and Barbuda	126	190	194	240	183	4	4	6	9	5	121	186	188	232	178
Argentina	3,388	4,122	4,776	5,856	7,536	3,746	4,584	3,979	4,487	5,822	-357	-462	797	1,369	1,714
Armenia	91	66	80	111	151	46	46	47	33	43	45	19	34	78	109
Aruba	384	559	511	529	680	1,776	2,920	2,845	2,995	3,179	-1,392	-2,361	-2,335	-2,466	-2,499
Australia	13,958	15,589	17,546	19,178	22,219	7,546	7,342	8,204	8,615	10,589	6,413	8,247	9,342	10,563	11,630
Austria	1,946	2,544	2,961	3,110	2,649	5,798	6,103	8,304	10,669	8,457	-3,853	-3,559	-5,343	-7,559	-5,808
Azerbaijan	159	133	231	178	239	38	45	716	1,887	4,361	121	87	-485	-1,710	-4,122
Bahamas, The	1,186	1,787	2,282	2,468	2,760	638	700	453	504	604	548	1,087	1,830	1,965	2,156
Bahrain	302	351	475	591	830	405	432	632	625	539	-104	-81	-158	-33	291
Bangladesh	289	320	333	456	468	2,303	2,693	3,271	3,432	3,748	-2,013	-2,373	-2,938	-2,976	-3,280
Barbados	348	395	443	457	497	37	32	34	38	40	312	363	409	419	457
Belarus	33	35	75	102	135	336	345	539	1,033	1,070	-303	-310	-465	-932	-935
Belgium	16,871	18,691	21,340	25,259	28,904	12,446	13,023	14,405	15,281	17,308	4,425	5,668	6,935	9,978	11,595
Belize	152	218	239	234	353	107	98	147	105	154	45	119	92	129	199
Benin	46	72	116	289	846	1	1	1	5	31	44	72	115	284	815
Bermuda	461	491	634	660	822	25	87	16	24	140	436	403	618	636	682
Bolivia	194	220	215	278	389	260	293	362	363	511	-67	-73	-147	-85	-122
Bosnia and Herzegovina	28	18	52	20	34	11	71	26	25	25	17	-53	26	-5	9
Botswana	54	67	27	54	62	74	178	252	188	219	-19	-111	-225	-134	-157
Brazil	13,886	15,372	18,887	24,172	32,299	21,160	24,436	26,367	25,644	30,453	-7,274	-9,064	-7,480	-1,472	1,846
Brunei	48	50	48	140	112	406	563	550	405	114	-358	-513	-502	-265	-3
Bulgaria	172	268	293	306	509	507	454	458	426	391	-335	-186	-165	-120	119
Cambodia	59	70	75	139	154	1,497	1,767	2,188	2,463	2,412	-1,439	-1,697	-2,114	-2,325	-2,257
Cameroon	100	117	120	133	125	308	158	273	297	614	-209	-41	-153	-164	-489
Canada	189,880	211,899	230,656	248,888	261,150	256,360	290,384	302,438	317,057	339,491	-66,480	-78,486	-71,782	-68,169	-78,342
Cayman Islands	400	681	632	640	746	13	54	15	21	14	387	627	617	619	732
Chad	41	54	61	66	63	756	1,498	1,918	2,145	3,334	-715	-1,444	-1,857	-2,079	-3,272
Chile	3,606	5,134	6,586	8,148	11,857	4,732	6,664	9,565	8,999	8,196	-1,126	-1,530	-2,979	-851	3,661
China[2]	34,428	41,192	53,673	62,937	69,733	196,682	243,470	287,774	321,443	337,773	-162,254	-202,278	-234,101	-258,506	-268,040
Colombia	4,505	5,462	6,709	8,558	11,437	7,256	8,849	9,266	9,434	13,093	-2,751	-3,387	-2,557	-876	-1,656
Congo (Brazzaville)[3]	66	104	138	140	185	858	1,623	3,097	3,071	5,074	-792	-1,519	-2,959	-2,931	-4,889
Congo (Kinshasa)[3]	67	65	71	113	130	124	264	85	207	266	-57	-199	-14	-94	-136
Costa Rica	3,306	3,599	4,132	4,581	5,680	3,333	3,415	3,844	3,942	3,938	-27	186	288	639	1,742
Cote d'Ivoire	118	124	148	162	254	715	1,198	702	600	1,092	-597	-1,074	-554	-439	-838
Croatia	130	159	147	247	467	291	364	353	332	271	-161	-206	-207	-85	196
Cuba	404	369	341	447	712	–	–	–	–	–	404	369	341	447	712
Cyprus	96	84	199	169	217	26	31	51	17	13	70	53	148	152	204
Czech Republic	827	1,054	1,123	1,262	1,378	1,756	2,193	2,349	2,431	2,569	-929	-1,139	-1,227	-1,168	-1,190

See footnotes at end of table.

U.S. Census Bureau, Statistical Abstract of the United States: 2010

Table 1271. **U.S. Exports, Imports, and Merchandise Trade Balance by Country: 2004 to 2008**—Con.

[See headnote, page 790]

Country	Exports, domestic and foreign					General imports					Merchandise trade balance				
	2004	2005	2006	2007	2008	2004	2005	2006	2007	2008	2004	2005	2006	2007	2008
Denmark	2,147	1,918	2,269	2,890	2,711	3,876	5,144	5,540	6,064	6,446	-1,730	-3,226	-3,272	-3,174	-3,735
Djibouti	44	48	48	59	141	1	1	3	5	7	43	47	44	54	134
Dominica	36	62	68	84	105	3	4	3	2	2	33	58	65	82	103
Dominican Republic	4,358	4,719	5,351	6,084	6,594	4,527	4,604	4,532	4,216	3,978	-169	115	818	1,869	2,617
Ecuador	1,669	1,964	2,727	2,936	3,450	4,283	5,759	7,094	6,135	9,048	-2,615	-3,795	-4,367	-3,199	-5,598
Egypt	3,078	3,159	4,029	5,259	6,002	1,284	2,091	2,396	2,377	2,370	1,794	1,068	1,633	2,882	3,632
El Salvador	1,868	1,854	2,152	2,313	2,462	2,052	1,989	1,857	2,044	2,228	-185	-135	295	270	234
Equatorial Guinea	215	282	552	236	185	1,170	1,561	1,733	1,777	3,367	-955	-1,280	-1,182	-1,541	-3,183
Estonia	134	145	221	242	226	393	511	526	296	392	-259	-366	-305	-54	-167
Ethiopia	303	456	137	168	302	41	62	81	88	152	262	394	56	79	149
Fiji	25	28	33	30	55	214	170	146	153	162	-188	-141	-113	-123	-107
Finland	2,069	2,254	2,648	3,133	3,761	3,887	4,342	4,974	5,266	5,903	-1,818	-2,088	-2,326	-2,133	-2,143
France	20,918	22,259	23,512	26,676	28,840	31,606	33,842	37,040	41,553	44,049	-10,688	-11,583	-13,528	-14,877	-15,209
French Guiana	228	27	33	31	18	—	—	—	—	—	228	27	33	31	18
French Polynesia	93	112	108	124	130	67	60	58	62	72	26	52	50	62	58
Gabon	93	99	135	478	284	2,467	2,816	1,361	2,182	2,279	-2,374	-2,717	-1,226	-1,704	-1,995
Georgia	227	214	264	364	587	78	194	105	212	208	149	20	158	153	379
Germany	—	—	—	—	54,505	77,266	84,751	89,082	94,164	97,497	-77,266	-84,751	-89,082	-94,164	-42,991
Ghana	310	337	290	416	608	145	158	192	199	222	165	179	97	218	386
Gibraltar	138	163	286	594	2,641	2	5	1	3	2	136	159	285	591	2,639
Greece	2,063	1,192	1,555	2,110	1,932	724	884	966	1,192	999	1,340	309	589	918	933
Grenada	70	82	74	83	84	5	5	5	8	7	65	77	70	75	77
Guadeloupe	38	55	55	139	384	3	3	5	5	7	35	52	50	134	377
Guatemala	2,551	2,835	3,511	4,065	4,718	3,154	3,137	3,102	3,026	3,463	-603	-302	409	1,039	1,256
Guinea	59	94	65	74	102	64	75	94	99	106	-5	19	-29	-26	-5
Guyana	138	177	179	188	289	122	120	125	123	146	16	57	54	65	143
Haiti	673	710	817	680	944	371	447	496	488	450	302	262	321	192	494
Honduras	3,078	3,254	3,687	4,461	4,846	3,640	3,749	3,718	3,912	4,041	-562	-495	-30	549	805
Hong Kong	15,827	16,351	17,742	19,902	21,499	9,314	8,892	7,947	7,026	6,483	6,514	7,459	9,795	12,876	15,015
Hungary	1,143	1,023	1,188	1,292	1,431	2,573	2,561	2,584	2,828	3,103	-1,430	-1,538	-1,397	-1,536	-1,672
Iceland	309	512	366	630	470	274	269	228	206	241	35	243	138	424	229
India	6,109	7,919	9,674	14,969	17,682	15,572	18,804	21,831	24,073	25,704	-9,463	-10,885	-12,157	-9,104	-8,022
Indonesia	2,671	3,054	3,079	3,970	5,645	10,811	12,014	13,425	14,301	15,799	-8,139	-8,960	-10,346	-10,331	-10,155
Iran	85	96	86	145	683	152	175	157	173	104	-67	-79	-71	-28	579
Iraq	857	1,374	1,491	1,560	2,070	8,514	9,054	11,546	11,396	22,080	-7,657	-7,680	-10,055	-9,835	-20,010
Ireland	7,552	8,447	7,621	7,777	7,611	27,448	28,733	28,526	30,445	31,347	-19,896	-20,286	-20,905	-22,668	-23,736
Israel	9,169	9,737	10,965	12,887	14,487	14,552	16,831	19,167	20,794	22,336	-5,382	-7,093	-8,202	-7,907	-7,849
Italy	10,685	11,524	12,546	14,150	15,461	28,097	31,009	32,655	35,028	36,135	-17,413	-19,485	-20,109	-20,878	-20,674
Jamaica	1,431	1,701	2,036	2,316	2,643	320	376	528	720	729	1,111	1,325	1,508	1,596	1,915
Japan	53,569	54,681	58,459	61,160	65,142	129,805	138,004	148,181	145,463	139,262	-76,236	-83,323	-89,722	-84,303	-74,120
Jordan	552	644	650	856	940	1,093	1,267	1,422	1,329	1,138	-542	-623	-772	-473	-197
Kazakhstan	320	538	646	753	986	539	1,101	961	1,252	1,603	-218	-563	-314	-499	-618
Kenya	348	573	431	520	442	352	348	354	325	344	-4	225	77	195	99
Korea, South	26,187	27,572	32,219	34,402	34,669	46,168	43,781	45,804	47,562	48,069	-19,981	-16,209	-13,585	-13,160	-13,400

See footnotes at end of table.

U.S. Census Bureau, Statistical Abstract of the United States: 2010

Table 1271. U.S. Exports, Imports, and Merchandise Trade Balance by Country: 2004 to 2008—Con.

[See headnote, page 790]

Country	Exports, domestic and foreign					General imports					Merchandise trade balance				
	2004	2005	2006	2007	2008	2004	2005	2006	2007	2008	2004	2005	2006	2007	2008
Kuwait	1,519	1,975	2,087	2,484	2,719	3,231	4,335	3,981	4,119	7,093	-1,712	-2,360	-1,894	-1,635	-4,374
Kyrgyzstan	29	31	71	49	44	11	27	4	3	3	19	27	63	42	42
Latvia	121	178	246	381	394	365	362	299	334	228	-244	-185	-53	47	166
Lebanon	464	466	931	826	1,464	75	86	89	104	104	390	379	842	722	1,365
Lesotho	6	4	4	8	1	467	404	408	443	374	-461	-400	-404	-436	-373
Liberia	61	69	68	76	157	84	91	140	115	144	-23	-22	-72	-39	13
Libya	39	84	384	511	721	332	1,590	2,472	3,385	4,179	-292	-1,507	-2,088	-2,874	-3,458
Liechtenstein	11	20	16	16	29	286	296	324	284	245	-276	-276	-309	-268	-216
Lithuania	295	390	567	720	831	482	634	570	456	750	-187	-244	-4	265	81
Luxembourg	640	711	581	926	988	290	389	534	526	536	350	322	265	400	452
Macau	86	102	200	226	307	1,487	1,249	1,230	1,095	915	-1,401	-1,147	47	-869	-609
Macedonia	21	32	22	34	36	78	48	42	73	78	-57	-17	-20	-39	-42
Madagascar	36	28	45	32	71	470	324	281	338	324	-34	-295	-236	-306	-254
Malawi	22	28	46	52	45	61	116	60	59	65	-39	-88	-14	-8	-20
Malaysia	10,850	10,461	12,444	11,680	12,950	28,179	33,685	36,533	32,629	30,736	-17,329	-23,224	-24,089	-20,948	-17,787
Mali	43	32	43	32	31	4	4	8	10	5	39	29	35	22	26
Malta	181	194	163	207	253	383	283	371	329	279	-202	-89	-208	-122	-25
Martinique	28	35	32	194	289	2	22	42	1	8	26	13	-9	187	281
Mauritania	34	86	90	103	107	7	1	51	7	46	27	85	39	102	60
Mauritiu	28	31	36	50	51	270	222	219	187	176	-242	-191	-183	-138	-125
Mexico	110,731	120,248	133,722	135,918	151,220	155,902	170,109	198,253	210,714	215,942	-45,171	-49,861	-64,531	-74,796	-64,722
Moldova	40	40	30	53	66	49	50	37	23	12	-10	-10	-7	30	54
Monaco	18	17	34	43	63	23	38	32	21	22	-5	-21	2	21	40
Mongolia	28	22	23	26	57	239	144	114	84	53	-211	-122	-91	-58	4
Morocco	498	481	838	1,294	1,436	515	446	521	610	879	-17	35	317	684	557
Mozambique	77	63	64	115	213	11	12	16	5	17	66	51	49	110	197
Namibia	75	112	127	128	280	238	130	116	220	301	-164	-17	11	-92	-21
Nepal	25	25	17	29	29	143	111	99	90	85	-118	-87	-83	-61	-56
Netherlands	24,140	26,468	30,960	32,837	39,720	12,451	14,862	17,342	18,403	21,123	11,690	11,606	13,618	14,434	18,597
Netherlands Antilles	824	1,138	1,485	2,082	2,952	435	922	1,119	782	809	390	215	366	1,300	2,142
New Caledonia	45	38	44	58	89	19	27	51	79	50	26	11	-7	-22	39
New Zealand	2,073	2,592	2,806	2,718	2,534	2,968	3,155	3,116	3,113	3,171	-895	-563	-310	-395	-637
Nicaragua	592	626	752	890	1,094	990	1,181	1,526	1,604	1,704	-398	-555	-774	-714	-609
Niger	34	79	129	69	50	27	66	124	10	44	7	13	5	60	6
Nigeria	1,554	1,620	2,234	2,778	4,102	16,249	24,239	27,863	32,770	38,068	-14,694	-22,619	-25,630	-29,992	-33,966
Norway	1,604	1,942	2,394	3,040	3,292	6,509	6,776	7,085	7,318	7,315	-4,904	-4,834	-4,691	-4,278	-4,023
Oman	330	571	829	1,059	1,382	418	555	909	1,041	852	-88	16	-80	18	530
Pakistan	1,680	1,252	1,723	1,944	1,898	2,875	3,253	3,672	3,578	3,591	-1,195	-2,002	-1,949	-1,634	-1,693
Panama	1,772	2,162	2,660	3,669	4,887	316	327	379	365	379	1,456	1,835	2,281	3,304	4,508
Papua New Guinea	43	55	44	66	70	54	59	84	109	106	-12	-4	-40	-43	-36
Paraguay	623	896	911	1,237	1,610	59	52	58	68	78	564	844	853	1,169	1,532
Peru	2,101	2,309	2,927	4,120	6,183	3,702	5,119	5,880	5,272	5,813	-1,601	-2,810	-2,954	-1,152	371
Philippines	7,087	6,895	7,617	7,712	8,295	9,137	9,250	9,694	9,408	8,713	-2,050	-2,355	-2,077	-1,696	-418
Poland	929	1,268	1,961	3,123	4,131	1,822	1,949	2,253	2,226	2,587	-892	-681	-292	897	1,544
Portugal	1,046	1,132	1,471	2,479	2,646	2,243	2,329	3,060	3,049	2,451	-1,197	-1,197	-1,590	-571	195
Qatar	455	987	1,279	2,524	2,716	387	448	262	477	484	68	539	539	2,047	2,232
Romania	525	609	554	677	1,048	853	1,208	1,119	1,054	1107	-328	-599	-565	-378	-59

See footnotes at end of table.

U.S. Census Bureau, Statistical Abstract of the United States: 2010

Table 1271. U.S. Exports, Imports, and Merchandise Trade Balance by Country: 2004 to 2008—Con.

[See headnote, page 790]

Country	Exports, domestic and foreign 2004	2005	2006	2007	2008	General imports 2004	2005	2006	2007	2008	Merchandise trade balance 2004	2005	2006	2007	2008
Russia	2,961	3,962	4,700	7,283	9,335	11,891	15,307	19,828	19,314	26,783	-8,930	-11,344	-15,128	-12,031	-17,448
Saudi Arabia	5,257	6,805	7,640	10,396	12,484	20,959	27,193	31,689	35,626	54,747	-15,702	-20,388	-24,050	-25,230	-42,263
Senegal	89	141	97	150	137	3	4	21	18	18	86	137	76	132	119
Serbia and Montenegro [4]	143	133	147	–	261	92	55	68	64	72	51	78	79	-64	189
Sierra Leone	41	38	38	55	59	11	9	35	48	47	30	29	3	7	12
Singapore	19,397	20,466	23,826	25,619	27,854	15,370	15,110	17,768	18,394	15,885	4,027	5,356	6,058	7,225	11,969
Slovakia	132	150	422	503	548	1,211	961	1,405	1,505	1,301	-1,080	-811	-983	-1,002	-754
Slovenia	192	234	239	297	310	510	413	483	488	467	-318	-179	-244	-192	-157
South Africa	3,179	3,907	4,462	5,521	6,491	5,945	5,886	7,501	9,054	9,948	-2,766	-1,979	-3,039	-3,533	-3,458
Spain	6,543	6,839	7,401	9,766	12,190	7,350	8,615	9,778	10,498	11,094	-807	-1,776	-2,377	-732	1,096
Sri Lanka	164	198	237	227	283	1,957	2,083	2,146	2,065	1,962	-1,793	-1,885	-1,909	-1,838	-1,679
St. Kitts and Nevis	60	127	111	111	124	4	50	50	54	54	56	77	61	57	70
St. Lucia	105	135	149	165	241	14	32	30	33	26	91	103	119	132	215
St. Vincent and the Grenadines	46	45	58	65	83	5	15	2	–	1	41	30	56	65	82
Sudan	68	108	77	79	143	3	13	6	7	5	65	95	71	72	138
Suriname	179	246	259	304	406	141	166	165	130	126	38	80	94	174	280
Swaziland	12	12	12	29	12	199	199	156	145	134	-186	-187	-144	-116	-122
Sweden	3,244	3,715	4,126	4,473	5,018	12,683	13,821	13,870	13,024	12,498	-9,439	-10,106	-9,745	-8,551	-7,480
Switzerland	9,280	10,718	14,375	17,033	22,024	11,628	13,000	14,230	14,760	17,782	-2,348	-2,282	145	2,279	4,242
Syria [2]	213	155	224	361	409	268	324	214	111	352	-55	-169	11	251	57
Taiwan [3]	21,585	21,614	22,709	25,829	24,926	34,624	34,826	38,212	38,278	36,326	-13,039	-13,212	-15,503	-12,449	-11,400
Tajikistan	56	29	43	53	51	8	241	61	53	8	48	-212	-18	(–)	43
Tanzania	128	96	161	174	169	24	34	35	46	56	103	63	126	128	114
Thailand	6,368	7,257	7,915	8,336	9,067	17,579	19,890	22,466	22,755	23,538	-11,211	-12,633	-14,551	-14,419	-14,472
Togo	24	28	108	288	117	2	6	4	5	11	22	22	105	283	106
Trinidad and Tobago	1,208	1,417	1,615	1,780	2,250	5,842	7,891	8,362	8,790	9,030	-4,635	-6,474	-6,748	-7,010	-6,780
Tunisia	258	261	363	403	502	209	264	470	458	644	49	-3	-107	-55	-142
Turkey	3,362	4,239	5,291	6,499	9,959	4,934	5,182	5,359	4,601	4,642	-1,572	-943	-68	1,898	5,317
Turkmenistan	262	215	113	127	60	81	135	76	219	140	181	80	37	-92	-80
Turks and Caicos Islands	137	238	366	396	434	7	10	12	13	10	130	228	354	383	424
Uganda	63	63	51	80	89	26	26	22	27	53	38	37	29	54	36
Ukraine	399	533	756	1,342	1,868	830	1,098	1,640	1,220	2,340	-400	-565	-884	122	-472
United Arab Emirates	4,080	8,120	10,277	10,787	14,417	1,143	1,468	1,385	1,338	1,286	2,937	6,652	8,892	9,450	13,131
United Kingdom	35,902	38,568	45,410	49,981	53,599	46,274	51,033	53,513	56,858	58,587	-10,372	-12,465	-8,103	-6,877	-4,988
Uruguay	326	357	482	641	893	580	732	512	492	244	-254	-376	-30	149	649
Uzbekistan	192	74	54	89	301	88	96	152	165	292	104	-22	-98	-76	9
Venezuela	4,767	6,421	9,002	10,201	12,610	24,921	33,978	37,134	39,910	51,424	-20,153	-27,557	-28,132	-29,709	-38,814
Vietnam	1,105	1,193	1,100	1,903	2,789	5,275	6,631	8,567	10,633	12,901	-4,170	-5,438	-7,466	-8,730	-10,112
Virgin Islands, British	–	–	–	–	310	17	34	26	43	11	-17	-34	-26	-43	299
Yemen	–	–	–	–	279	447	–	–	–	279	–	–	–	–	–
Zambia	26	29	52	69	79	33	32	28	49	52	-7	-3	23	21	27
Zimbabwe	47	46	48	105	93	76	94	103	73	112	-29	-49	-56	33	-19

– Represents or rounds to zero. [1] Includes timing adjustment and unidentified countries, not shown separately. [2] See footnote 4, Table 1296. [3] See footnote 5, Table 1296. [4] See footnote 3, Table 1345.

Source: U.S. Census Bureau, *U.S. International Trade in Goods and Services*, Series FT-900(09-04), and previous final reports. See also <http://www.census.gov/foreign-trade/Press-Release/2008pr/final_revisions/> (released 10 June 2009).

Table 1272. **U.S. Exports and General Imports by Selected SITC Commodity Groups: 2000 to 2008**

[In millions of dollars (781,918 represents $781,918,000,000). SITC = Standard International Trade Classification. For methodology, see Foreign Trade Statistics in Appendix III. N.e.s. = not elsewhere specified]

Selected commodity	Exports [1]				General imports [2]			
	2000	2006	2007	2008	2000	2006	2007	2008
Total	781,918	1,036,635	1,162,479	1,287,442	1,218,022	1,853,938	1,956,962	2,103,641
Agricultural commodities [3]	51,296	70,912	89,921	115,248	39,186	65,459	72,067	80,662
Animal feeds	3,780	4,534	5,506	7,610	597	828	1,008	1,258
Cereal flour	1,310	2,339	2,839	2,870	1,753	3,357	3,774	4,268
Corn.	4,695	7,251	10,095	13,931	160	179	257	350
Cotton, raw and linters.	1,893	4,514	4,589	4,812	28	15	14	12
Meat and preparations.	7,004	7,257	9,131	12,584	3,841	5,231	5,355	5,046
Soybeans	5,284	6,949	10,002	15,455	31	56	97	182
Vegetables and fruits.	7,477	11,071	12,125	14,040	9,286	15,455	17,671	19,145
Wheat.	3,374	4,205	8,328	11,294	229	311	501	1,080
Manufactured goods [3].	625,894	785,599	868,297	912,382	1,012,855	1,416,302	1,479,971	1,490,383
ADP equipment, office machinery . .	46,595	31,091	29,914	28,639	92,133	106,416	101,602	96,526
Airplane parts.	15,062	20,515	21,666	(X)	5,572	6,771	8,434	(X)
Airplanes.	24,777	43,933	51,854	(X)	12,412	10,604	13,286	(X)
Alcoholic beverages, distilled.	424	844	984	80,206	2,946	4,912	5,521	5,478
Aluminum	3,780	5,596	5,806	1,049	6,949	14,919	13,947	13,429
Artwork/antiques	1,387	3,250	4,335	6,204	5,864	6,633	8,740	7,513
Basketware, etc	3,309	6,200	6,995	5,409	4,840	9,093	10,810	12,196
Chemicals, cosmetics	5,292	9,100	10,120	7,692	3,539	8,333	8,872	9,577
Chemicals, dyeing.	4,089	5,337	5,807	11,534	2,667	3,054	3,115	3,073
Chemicals, fertilizers	2,249	2,941	3,339	6,238	1,684	3,438	4,981	8,377
Chemicals, inorganic	5,359	9,074	10,807	6,540	6,108	11,414	13,349	16,826
Chemicals, medicinal.	12,893	28,431	32,755	12,846	14,685	45,746	53,798	59,212
Chemicals, n.e.s.	12,264	17,860	20,730	37,379	5,725	9,477	10,851	12,713
Chemicals, organic	17,990	29,839	33,869	25,287	28,578	42,212	42,178	47,802
Chemicals, plastics	19,519	32,617	37,129	34,256	10,647	18,813	18,248	18,912
Clothing	8,191	3,849	3,209	3,169	64,296	79,149	81,176	78,893
Copper	1,425	3,266	3,489	3,439	4,471	12,888	11,532	10,358
Cork, wood, lumber.	4,320	4,273	4,412	4,241	8,227	10,386	8,282	5,704
Crude fertilizers	1,724	1,947	2,009	2,428	1,401	1,825	1,854	2,966
Electrical machinery	89,917	83,228	81,452	82,049	108,747	109,721	113,613	112,623
Fish and preparations	2,806	4,012	4,044	4,017	9,907	13,176	13,519	13,994
Footwear.	663	572	578	673	14,842	19,160	19,408	19,545
Furniture and bedding	4,744	4,877	5,123	5,170	18,923	32,788	33,853	31,371
Gem diamonds.	1,289	3,884	5,305	5,943	12,068	17,285	18,937	19,744
General industrial machinery.	33,094	44,089	48,641	55,192	34,667	59,710	63,940	66,910
Glass	2,502	3,041	3,350	3,317	2,248	2,956	2,885	2,653
Gold, nonmonetary	5,898	8,790	13,344	18,714	2,657	5,633	4,670	6,120
Iron and steel mill products.	5,715	11,799	14,018	18,493	15,807	32,904	30,890	38,910
Jewelry	1,574	4,033	4,538	4,834	6,459	11,222	11,193	9,615
Lighting, plumbing.	1,384	1,868	2,090	2,516	5,104	8,069	8,111	7,767
Metal manufactures, n.e.s.	13,453	15,860	17,315	18,743	16,204	27,893	29,929	30,403
Metal ores; scrap	4,234	16,617	22,999	29,431	3,817	6,533	7,549	9,309
Metalworking machinery.	6,191	8,228	5,351	6,074	7,726	8,644	7,723	8,548
Nickel	401	1,038	1,379	1,567	1,425	3,348	4,903	3,430
Optical goods.	3,246	3,173	3,210	2,860	4,019	4,378	4,698	5,090
Paper and paperboard.	10,640	12,337	13,480	14,668	15,185	18,503	17,913	18,073
Photographic equipment.	4,236	3,590	3,612	3,595	6,896	4,506	2,760	2,489
Plastic articles, n.e.s.	7,607	8,915	9,427	9,511	8,034	14,823	15,348	15,793
Platinum	888	1,739	1,615	1,161	5,566	5,833	7,716	7,115
Power generating machinery.	32,743	44,036	49,933	33,658	33,773	44,742	50,191	48,187
Printed materials.	4,776	5,748	6,190	6,355	3,680	5,142	5,548	5,372
Pulp and waste paper	4,576	5,738	6,906	7,744	3,381	3,181	3,734	4,004
Records/magnetic media	5,395	4,912	5,088	5,250	5,172	7,095	7,382	6,735
Rubber articles, n.e.s.	1,673	1,787	1,953	1,915	1,962	3,039	3,212	3,169
Rubber tires and tubes	2,379	3,007	3,517	3,981	4,785	8,662	9,380	9,705
Scientific instruments.	30,984	39,278	42,315	42,588	22,007	32,297	35,604	37,275
Ships, boats.	1,070	2,575	3,062	3,114	1,178	1,548	1,921	1,675
Specialized industrial machinery . . .	30,959	37,469	48,357	51,928	22,711	31,010	35,761	35,574
Television, VCR, etc.	27,921	22,515	24,735	24,379	70,468	115,327	129,796	133,187
Textile yarn, fabric.	10,534	12,106	11,861	11,860	15,171	22,184	22,759	21,854
Toys/games/sporting goods.	3,609	4,172	5,039	4,697	20,011	26,547	31,807	32,617
Travel goods	351	461	436	463	4,430	6,882	7,625	7,986
Vehicles	57,421	83,472	95,187	98,871	161,544	211,946	210,431	190,799
Watches/clocks/parts	348	304	392	416	3,481	4,082	4,454	4,340
Wood manufactures	1,842	2,007	2,125	2,270	7,228	12,539	10,390	8,446
Mineral fuel [3]	13,179	34,711	41,725	76,075	135,367	332,500	364,987	491,885
Coal.	2,162	3,663	4,288	8,196	805	2,639	2,451	3,958
Crude oil	463	853	1,015	2,270	89,876	225,156	245,771	353,537
Petroleum preparations	5,746	22,078	26,522	51,384	25,673	66,197	74,108	87,103
Liquified propane/butane	663	805	1,048	1,011	1,508	4,419	4,024	4,755
Natural gas	411	2,226	3,130	4,879	12,594	28,268	31,938	34,423
Mineral fuels, other mineral.	3,734	4,435	4,708	7,030	4,911	3,942	3,717	4,452
Reexports	68,203	108,070	117,177	131,066	(X)	(X)	(X)	(X)

X Not applicable. [1] F.a.s. basis. Exports by commodity are only for domestic exports. [2] Customs value basis. [3] Includes other commodities not shown separately.

Source: U.S. Census Bureau, *U.S. International Trade in Goods and Services*, Series FT-900(07-04), and previous final reports. See also <http://www.census.gov/foreign-trade/Press-Release/2008pr/final_revisions/> (released 10 June 2009).

Table 1273. **U.S. Total and Aerospace Foreign Trade: 1990 to 2007**

[In millions of dollars (–101,718 represents –$101,718,000,000), except percent. Data are reported as exports of domestic merchandise, including Department of Defense shipments and undocumented exports to Canada, f.a.s. (free alongside ship) basis, and imports for consumption, customs value basis. Minus sign (–) indicates deficit]

Year	Merchandise trade			Aerospace trade						
				Trade balance	Imports	Exports				
						Total	Percent of U.S. exports	Civil		Military
	Trade balance	Imports	Exports					Total	Trans-ports	
1990	–101,718	495,311	393,592	27,282	11,801	39,083	9.9	31,517	16,691	7,566
1991	–66,723	488,453	421,730	30,785	13,003	43,788	10.4	35,548	20,881	8,239
1992	–84,501	532,665	448,164	31,356	13,662	45,018	10.0	36,906	22,379	8,111
1993	–115,568	580,659	465,091	27,235	12,183	39,418	8.5	31,823	18,146	7,596
1994	–150,630	663,256	512,626	25,010	12,363	37,373	7.3	30,050	15,931	7,322
1995	–158,801	743,543	584,742	21,562	11,509	33,071	5.7	25,079	10,606	7,991
1996	–170,214	795,289	625,075	26,602	13,668	40,270	6.4	29,477	13,624	10,792
1997	–180,522	869,704	689,182	32,240	18,134	50,374	7.3	40,075	21,028	10,299
1998	–229,758	911,896	682,138	40,961	23,110	64,071	9.4	51,999	29,168	12,072
1999	–328,821	1,024,618	695,797	37,381	25,063	62,444	9.0	50,624	25,694	11,820
2000	–436,104	1,218,022	781,918	26,735	27,944	54,679	7.0	45,566	19,615	9,113
2001	–411,899	1,140,999	729,100	26,035	32,473	58,508	8.0	49,371	22,151	9,137
2002	–468,263	1,161,366	693,103	29,514	27,241	56,775	8.2	47,348	21,661	9,427
2003	–532,350	1,257,121	724,771	27,111	25,393	52,504	7.2	44,060	19,434	8,445
2004	–650,930	1,469,704	818,775	31,002	25,815	56,817	6.9	47,325	18,577	9,492
2005	–767,477	1,673,455	905,978	39,783	27,649	67,433	7.4	57,225	21,888	10,207
2006	–817,304	1,853,938	1,036,635	54,809	30,453	85,262	8.2	71,857	32,897	13,404
2007	–794,483	1,956,962	1,162,479	60,614	36,610	97,224	8.4	83,977	40,297	13,247

Source: Aerospace Industries Association of America, Washington, DC, *Aerospace Facts and Figures,* annual.

Table 1274. **U.S. High Technology Exports by Industry and Selected Major Country: 2000 to 2008**

[In billions of dollars (222.5 represents $222,500,000,000)]

Selected industry	2000	2007	2008	Selected country	2000	2007	2008
Total exports	222.5	214.3	218.8	Total exports	222.5	214.1	218.8
Computers and office equipment. . .	57.8	47.1	47.0	Canada	34.4	29.4	29.1
Consumer electronics	10.0	8.8	8.6	China [1]	4.6	14.5	15
Communications equipment	26.9	29.7	32.6	Japan	19.9	11.9	10.9
Electronic components	22.1	17.7	17.5	Korea, South	12.1	8.9	7.5
Semiconductors	60.0	50.0	50.2	Malaysia	7.8	7.4	8.3
Industrial electronics	30.5	38.5	38.7	Mexico	30.0	26.0	27.7
Electromedical equipment	8.1	16.6	18.3	Taiwan [1]	10.4	8.4	8.0
Photonics	7.1	5.9	5.9	European Union 27	51.5	46.6	46.9

[1] See footnote 4, Table 1296.

Source: AeA (formerly the American Electronics Association), *Cyberstates 2009,* annual, (copyright). See <http://www.aeanet.org>.

Table 1275. **U.S. Exporting Companies Profile by Employment-Size Class: 2000 and 2007**

[(668,310 represents $668,310,000,000). Based on data from export trade documents and the Business Register. For information on data limitations, see the Techical Documentation in the source]

Employment-size class	Number of exporters		Known export value [1] (mil. dol.)		Percent of—			
					Number of exporters		Known export value	
	2000	2007	2000	2007	2000	2007	2000	2007
All companies, total . . .	246,452	266,457	668,310	1,031,007	100.0	100.0	100.0	100.0
No employees	74,772	85,229	47,024	74,891	30.3	32.0	7.0	7.3
1 to 19 employees	96,268	107,550	45,272	71,248	39.1	40.4	6.8	6.9
20 to 49 employees	31,362	32,039	21,262	37,259	12.7	12.0	3.2	3.6
50 to 99 employees	16,988	16,815	19,711	32,897	6.9	6.3	2.9	3.2
100 to 249 employees.	13,685	12,806	32,192	53,882	5.6	4.8	4.8	5.2
250 to 499 employees.	5,454	4,942	27,397	41,507	2.2	1.9	4.1	4.0
500 or more employees.	7,923	7,076	475,453	719,322	3.2	2.7	71.1	69.8

[1] Known value is defined as the value of exports by known exporters, i.e., those export transactions that could be matched to specific companies. Export values are on f.a.s. or "free alongside ship basis."

Source: U.S. Census Bureau, *A Profile of U.S. Exporting Companies, 2000* and *2006–2007*. See also <http://www.census.gov /foreign-trade/Press-Release/edb/2007/edb-3a.pdf> (released 11 January 2009).

Table 1276. **Domestic Exports and Imports for Consumption of Merchandise by Selected NAICS Product Category: 2000 to 2008**

[In millions of dollars (712,285 represents $712,285,000,000). Includes nonmonetary gold. For methodology, see Foreign Trade Statistics in Appendix III. NAICS = North American Industry Classification System; see text, Section 15]

Product category	2000	2004	2005	2006	2007	2008
Domestic exports, total	712,285	724,494	798,997	917,087	1,030,116	1,155,576
Agricultural, forestry, and fishery products	29,153	37,870	37,109	41,518	53,517	68,233
Agricultural products, total	23,596	31,978	30,683	34,768	46,436	61,073
Livestock and livestock products.	1,255	962	1,118	1,285	1,362	1,520
Forestry products, not elsewhere specified	1,644	1,662	1,686	1,713	1,925	1,894
Fish, fresh or chilled; and other marine products . .	2,658	3,268	3,622	3,752	3,795	3,746
Mining, total	6,187	8,764	12,629	13,968	17,013	24,751
Oil and gas.	1,706	3,040	4,547	4,225	5,689	8,706
Minerals and ores	4,481	5,725	8,082	9,743	11,324	16,045
Manufacturing, total	644,440	641,856	708,205	810,606	897,516	987,582
Food and kindred products	24,966	25,996	28,937	32,151	38,793	48,476
Beverages and tobacco products	5,568	3,648	3,423	3,850	4,193	4,793
Textiles and fabrics.	7,010	8,375	8,483	8,523	8,251	8,213
Textile mill products	2,236	2,091	2,344	2,573	2,651	2,611
Apparel and accessories	8,104	4,359	4,075	3,792	3,133	3,055
Leather and allied products	2,322	2,194	2,300	2,451	2,355	2,266
Wood products	4,854	4,265	4,463	4,915	4,973	5,041
Paper products	15,539	15,257	16,640	18,032	19,738	21,713
Printed, publishing, & similar products	4,869	5,006	5,526	5,816	6,321	6,504
Petroleum and coal products	8,862	12,594	17,979	25,943	30,976	58,440
Chemicals	77,649	105,461	114,821	129,615	147,596	166,249
Plastics and rubber products	16,970	17,320	18,784	20,551	22,041	23,403
Nonmetallic mineral products	7,830	6,341	6,663	7,555	8,372	8,927
Primary metal products	20,126	21,219	27,455	37,120	44,623	54,713
Fabricated metal products	21,737	20,872	23,370	27,281	29,878	32,483
Machinery, except electrical	85,038	86,496	97,001	109,430	122,669	134,117
Computers and electronic products	161,449	121,272	122,744	133,788	135,429	134,757
Electrical equipment, appliances and components	25,401	23,584	26,457	31,177	33,422	34,548
Transportation equipment	121,701	128,498	144,985	169,382	190,474	192,296
Furniture and fixtures	2,882	2,648	2,844	3,162	3,511	3,999
Miscellaneous manufactured commodities	19,327	24,360	28,909	33,498	38,117	40,978
Special classification provisions	32,505	36,004	41,055	50,995	62,069	75,010
Waste & scrap.	4,948	8,595	10,389	15,806	22,020	28,943
Used or second-hand merchandise	1,950	1,966	2,570	4,228	5,708	7,326
Goods returned or reimported	333	152	65	57	36	47
Special classification provision, not elsewhere specified	25,274	25,291	28,030	30,905	34,305	38,693
Imports for consumption, total	1,205,339	1,460,501	1,664,497	1,843,900	1,946,288	2,093,540
Agricultural, forestry, and fishery products	24,378	27,801	30,761	34,621	37,678	41,068
Agricultural products, total	11,771	14,339	15,818	17,333	19,677	22,477
Livestock and livestock products.	3,085	2,497	3,277	4,105	4,691	4,435
Forestry products not elsewhere specified	1,409	2,018	2,250	2,757	2,745	3,417
Fish, fresh or chilled; and other marine products . .	8,113	8,947	9,416	10,427	10,565	10,739
Mining, total	79,841	139,192	192,115	221,903	241,494	341,123
Oil and gas.	76,166	134,374	185,621	214,130	233,384	329,397
Minerals and ores	3,675	4,818	6,494	7,772	8,110	11,726
Manufacturing, total	1,040,329	1,231,034	1,372,004	1,512,070	1,585,062	1,627,042
Food and kindred products	18,944	27,719	29,779	31,803	34,706	39,987
Beverages and tobacco products	8,350	11,644	12,849	14,616	15,937	15,877
Textiles and fabrics.	7,042	7,388	7,450	7,364	7,451	6,943
Textile mill products	7,347	11,705	13,508	14,680	15,410	14,984
Apparel and accessories	62,928	70,536	74,478	77,007	78,947	76,182
Leather and allied products	21,463	24,546	26,559	28,467	29,400	29,479
Wood products	15,388	22,869	23,654	22,740	18,540	14,142
Paper products	19,080	20,645	22,094	23,467	23,472	24,014
Printed, publishing, & similar products	4,197	5,149	5,599	5,805	6,347	6,170
Petroleum and coal products	40,156	54,606	81,359	93,022	102,303	130,639
Chemicals	76,606	115,437	131,936	146,612	160,297	195,731
Plastics and rubber products	17,362	24,054	28,072	30,567	32,039	33,006
Nonmetallic mineral products	14,740	16,532	18,445	20,278	19,683	18,070
Primary metal products	43,833	56,515	64,666	88,622	88,928	99,327
Fabricated metal products	27,974	35,961	41,026	46,061	50,011	51,934
Machinery, except electrical	79,366	94,380	109,619	121,334	121,276	123,669
Computers and electronic products	250,694	248,003	269,921	295,214	312,769	300,391
Electrical equipment, appliances and components	39,567	48,796	55,179	62,269	67,115	67,758
Transportation equipment	213,110	239,511	251,386	269,391	277,450	254,296
Furniture and fixtures	15,607	22,561	25,096	27,027	27,674	26,321
Miscellaneous manufactured commodities	56,577	72,476	79,329	85,724	95,307	98,121
Special classification provisions	60,791	62,474	69,617	75,306	82,054	84,308
Waste & scrap.	1,875	3,050	3,207	4,788	5,031	5,669
Used or second-hand merchandise	6,345	5,715	6,026	7,127	8,994	7,757
Goods returned or reimported	33,851	33,789	37,024	38,436	39,494	40,134
Special classification provision, not elsewhere specified	18,720	19,920	23,359	24,954	28,535	30,747

Source: U.S. Census Bureau, *U.S. International Trade in Goods and Services,* Series FT-900, December issues. For most recent, see <http://www.census.gov/foreign-trade/Press-Release/2008pr/12/#exhibits> (released 14 February 2009), and previous December or final reports.

796   Foreign Commerce and Aid

Section 29
Puerto Rico and the Island Areas

This section presents summary economic and social statistics for Puerto Rico, the U.S. Virgin Islands, Guam, American Samoa, and the Northern Mariana Islands. Primary sources are the decennial censuses of population and housing, county business patterns, and the Puerto Rico Community Survey conducted by the U.S. Census Bureau; the annual *Vital Statistics of the United States,* issued by the National Center for Health Statistics; and the annual *Income and Product* of the Puerto Rico Planning Board.

Jurisdiction—The United States gained jurisdiction over these areas as follows: the islands of *Puerto Rico* and *Guam,* surrendered by Spain to the United States in December 1898, were ceded to the United States by the Treaty of Paris, ratified in 1899. Puerto Rico became a commonwealth on July 25, 1952, thereby achieving a high degree of local autonomy under its own constitution. The *U.S. Virgin Islands,* comprising 50 islands and cays, was purchased by the United States from Denmark in 1917. *American Samoa,* a group of seven islands, was acquired by the United States in accordance with a convention among the United States, Great Britain, and Germany, ratified in 1900 (Swains Island was annexed in 1925). By an agreement approved by the Security Council and the United States, the Northern Mariana Islands, previously under Japanese mandate, was administered by the United States between 1947 and 1986 under the United Nations trusteeship system. The Northern Mariana Islands became a commonwealth in 1986.

Censuses—Because characteristics of the Puerto Rico and the Island Areas differ, the presentation of census data for them is not uniform. The 1960 Census of Population covered all of the places listed above except the Northern Mariana Islands (their census was conducted in April 1958 by the Office of the High Commissioner), while the 1960 Census of Housing excluded American Samoa. The 1970, 1980, 1990, and 2000 Censuses of Population and Housing covered all five areas. Beginning in 1967, Congress authorized the economic censuses, to be taken at 5-year intervals, for years ending in "2" and "7." Prior economic censuses were conducted in Puerto Rico for 1949, 1954, 1958, and 1963 and in Guam and the U.S. Virgin Islands for 1958 and 1963. In 1967, the census of construction industries was added for the first time in Puerto Rico; in 1972, the U.S. Virgin Islands and Guam were covered; and in 1982, the economic census was taken for the first time for the Northern Mariana Islands.

Puerto Rico Community Survey—The Puerto Rico Community Survey (PRCS) began in 2005 and is a critical element in the Census Bureau's reengineered 2010 census plan. The American Community Survey is the equivalent of the PRCS for the United States (50 states, and District of Columbia). The PRCS collects and produces population and housing information every year instead of every 10 years. About 36,000 households are surveyed each year from across every municipio in Puerto Rico.

Information in other sections—In addition to the statistics presented in this section, other data are included as integral parts of many tables showing distribution by states in various sections of the *Abstract.* See "Puerto Rico and the Island Areas" in the Index. For definition and explanation of terms used, see Sections 1, 2, 4, 17, 20, 21, and 22.

U.S. Census Bureau, Statistical Abstract of the United States: 2010

Selected Island Areas of the United States

Caribbean Region

United States

The Bahamas

ATLANTIC OCEAN

Turks and Caicos Islands (U.K.)

Cuba

Cayman Islands
(U.K.)

Jamaica

Haiti

Dominican
Republic

PUERTO RICO (U.S.)

*B.V.I.
(U.K.)*

VIRGIN ISLANDS (U.S.)

Caribbean Sea

Pacific Region

NORTHERN
MARIANA
ISLANDS (U.S.)

· Wake Island (U.S.)

Johnston Atoll (U.S.)·

GUAM (U.S.)

PACIFIC OCEAN

Marshall
Islands

Kingman Reef (U.S.)

Palmyra Atoll (U.S.) ·

Federated States of Micronesia

Kiribati

Howland Island (U.S.)

· Nauru

·Baker Island (U.S.)

Papua
New
Guinea

Solomon Islands

Tuvalu

Coral Sea

Vanuatu

Samoa

Australia

Fiji

AMERICAN SAMOA (U.S.)

798 Puerto Rico and the Island Areas

U.S. Census Bureau, Statistical Abstract of the United States: 2010

Table 1277. **Estimated Resident Population With Projections: 1990 to 2025**

[In thousands (3,537 represents 3,537,000). **Population as of July 1.** Population data generally are de-facto figures for the present territory. Data for 1990 to 2000 are adjusted to the 2000 Census of Population for Puerto Rico only. See text, Section 30, for general comments regarding the data. For details of methodology, coverage, and reliability, see source]

Area	1990	2000	2005	2007	2008	2009	Projected 2010	2015	2020	2025
Puerto Rico...............	3,537	3,814	3,911	3,941	3,954	3,966	3,978	4,025	4,053	4,059
American Samoa............	47	58	62	64	65	66	66	71	75	79
Guam	134	155	169	174	176	178	181	193	204	214
Virgin Islands..............	104	109	110	110	110	110	110	109	109	107
Northern Mariana Islands.......	44	70	71	59	55	51	48	44	49	53

Source: U.S. Census Bureau, International Data Base; <http://www.census.gov/ipc/www/idb/>.

Table 1278. **Vital Statistics—Specified Areas: 1990 to 2007**

[Births, deaths, and infant deaths by place of residence. Rates for 1990 and 2000 based on population enumerated as of **April 1;** for other years, on population estimated as of **July 1**]

Area and year	Births Number	Births Rate [1]	Deaths Number	Deaths Rate [1]	Infant deaths Number	Infant deaths Rate [2]
Puerto Rico:						
1990.............	66,417	18.8	25,957	7.3	888	13.4
1995.............	63,425	17.0	30,032	8.1	804	12.7
2000.............	59,333	15.2	28,369	7.2	574	9.7
2004.............	51,127	13.1	28,922	7.4	409	8.0
2005.............	50,564	12.9	29,531	7.5	466	9.2
2006.;............	48,597	12.4	28,206	7.2	426	8.8
2007 [3]	46,636	11.8	28,975	7.4	(NA)	(NA)
Guam:						
1990.............	3,839	28.6	520	3.9	31	8.1
1995.............	4,180	29.0	592	4.1	38	9.4
2000.............	3,766	24.4	648	4.2	22	5.8
2004.............	3,410	20.5	683	4.1	40	11.7
2005.............	3,187	18.9	677	4.0	34	10.7
2006.;............	3,391	19.8	679	4.0	45	13.3
2007 [3]	(NA)	(NA)	778	4.5	(NA)	(NA)
Virgin Islands:						
1990.............	2,267	21.8	480	4.6	33	14.6
1995.............	2,063	18.1	664	5.8	34	16.6
2000.............	1,564	12.9	641	5.3	21	13.4
2004.............	1,674	14.5	626	5.8	13	(NA)
2005.............	1,605	14.8	663	6.1	11	(B)
2006.;............	1,687	15.5	624	5.7	9	(B)
2007 [3]	1,674	15.2	699	6.4	(NA)	(NA)
American Samoa:						
2000.............	1,731	26.4	219	3.3	11	(NA)
2005.............	1,720	27.6	272	4.4	12	(B)
2006.;............	1,442	25.0	266	4.6	16	(B)
2007 [3]	1,288	20.1	250	3.9	(NA)	(NA)
Northern Marianas:						
2000.............	1,431	19.9	136	1.9	11	(NA)
2005.............	1,335	16.6	186	2.3	6	(B)
2006.;............	1,422	17.2	170	2.1	9	(B)
2007 [3]	1,345	15.9	141	1.7	(NA)	(NA)

B Base figure too small to meet statistical standards of reliability. NA Not available. [1] Per 1,000 population. [2] Rates are infant deaths (under 1 year) per 1,000 live births. [3] Data for 2007 are preliminary.

Source: U.S. National Center for Health Statistics, National Vital Statistics Reports (NVSR), *Births: Preliminary Data for 2007,* Vol. 57, No. 12, March 18, 2009, and *Deaths: Preliminary Data for 2007,* Vol. 58, No. 1 August 19, 2009. See also <http://www.cdc.gov/nchs/nvss.htm>.

Table 1279. **Public Elementary and Secondary Schools by Area: 2006**

[For school year ending in year shown, unless otherwise indicated. (3,082,295 represents $3,082,295,000)]

Item	Puerto Rico	Guam	U.S. Virgin Islands	American Samoa	Item	Puerto Rico	Guam	U.S. Virgin Islands	American Samoa
Enrollment, fall......	544,138	(NA)	16,284	16,427	Teachers	40,163	(NA)	1,531	971
Elementary (kindergarten- grade 8).......	382,600	(NA)	11,237	11,755	Student support staff...........	4,628	(NA)	170	218
Secondary (grades 9–12 and post graduates)	161,538	(NA)	5,047	4,672	Other support services staff.....	17,016	(NA)	417	101
Staff, fall..........	71,962	(NA)	3,020	1,869	Current expendi- tures [1] ($1,000)	3,082,295	210,119	146,872	58,539
School district staff .	1,064	(NA)	263	186	Per pupil [2] (dol.) ...	5,654	6,907	9,529	3,837
School staff	49,254	(NA)	2,170	1,364					

NA Not available. [1] Public elementary and secondary day schools. [2] Per pupil expenditures include current expenditures, capital expenditures, and interest on school debt and excludes "other current expenditures" such as community services, private school programs, adult education, and other programs not allocable to expenditures per pupil in public schools.

Source: U.S. National Center for Education Statistics, *Digest of Education Statistics,* annual, and unpublished data. See also <http://nces.ed.gov/annuals>.

Puerto Rico and the Island Areas **799**

Table 1280. **Occupational Employment and Average Annual Wages in Guam, Puerto Rico, and Virgin Islands: 2008**

[The Occupational Employment Survey (OES) program conducts a semiannual mail survey designed to produce estimates of employment and wages for specific occupations. For more details on the survey, see <http://www.bls.gov/oes/oesemp.htm#scope>]

Selected occupations	SOC code[1]	Guam		Puerto Rico		Virgin Islands	
		Employ-ment	Average annual wages[2]	Employ-ment	Average annual wages[2]	Employ-ment	Average annual wages[2]
Total, all occupations [3, 4]	(X)	58,810	29,400	999,010	24,650	44,910	33,470
Management	11	4,590	55,600	35,740	65,370	1,950	75,950
Business and financial operations	13	2,060	43,710	42,310	34,440	1,530	47,330
Computer and mathematical	15	460	43,980	9,090	41,830	340	52,420
Architecture and engineering	17	810	47,340	12,610	50,170	350	60,880
Life, physical, and social science	19	370	44,230	9,590	40,510	230	46,210
Community and social services	21	710	32,540	18,740	25,390	430	35,430
Legal	23	(NA)	68,170	4,470	55,800	480	72,280
Education, training, and library	25	4,170	38,130	68,340	31,990	(NA)	42,340
Arts, design, entertainment sports	27	540	27,650	7,320	29,520	370	38,160
Healthcare practitioner and technical	29	1,500	54,310	45,400	30,760	1,300	51,410
Healthcare support	31	620	23,000	14,380	16,450	420	22,150
Protective service	33	2,420	27,360	67,190	21,620	2,480	29,700
Food preparation and serving related	35	5,790	16,720	67,140	15,540	4,360	20,620
Buildings and grounds cleaning and maintenance	37	3,360	18,000	44,990	16,440	3,070	20,840
Personal care and service	39	2,430	29,270	(NA)	16,990	970	21,810
Sales and related occupations	41	5,500	19,390	108,140	20,270	4,750	25,430
Office and administrative support	43	10,660	25,930	191,710	21,690	8,450	27,960
Farming, fishing, and forestry	45	(NA)	(NA)	1,640	19,390	(NA)	(NA)
Construction and extraction	47	4,510	26,420	62,440	19,120	3,070	36,700
Installation, maintenance, and repair	49	3,140	28,330	34,580	25,700	2,560	36,290
Production	51	1,510	25,250	80,150	20,690	2,010	39,450
Transportation and material moving	53	3,420	22,890	60,460	18,340	2,650	26,780

NA Not available. X Not applicable. [1] Office of Management and Budget's Standard Occupational Classification (SOC) is used to define occupations. SOC categorizes workers into 1 of 801 detailed occupations and aggregates; the detailed occupations into 23 major occupational groups. [2] Annual wages have been calculated by multiplying the hourly mean wage by a "year-round, full-time" hours figure of 2,080 hours; for those occupations where there is not an hourly mean wage published, the annual wage has been directly calculated from the reported survey data. [3] Estimates for detailed occupations do not sum to the totals because the totals include occupations not shown separately. [4] Estimates do not include self-employed workers.

Source: U.S. Department of Labor, Bureau of Labor Statistics; "Employment Statistics," <http://www.bls.gov/oes/home.htm> (accessed 8 June 2009) .

Table 1281. **Prisoners in Custody of Correctional Authorities in U.S. Territories and Commonwealths: 2006 and 2007**

[As of December 31. Minus sign (–) indicates decrease]

Jurisdiction	Total inmates			Sentenced to more than 1 year			
	2006	2007	Percent change 2006–2007	2006	2007	Percent change 2006–2007	Incar-ceration rate, 2007 [1]
Total	15,205	14,678	–3.5	11,743	11,465	–2.4	261
American Samoa	210	236	12.4	113	122	8.0	188
Guam	495	535	8.1	337	320	–5.0	182
Northern Mariana Islands	126	137	8.7	76	78	2.6	90
Puerto Rico	13,788	13,215	–4.2	10,789	10,553	–2.2	267
U.S. Virgin Islands	586	555	–5.3	428	392	–8.4	357

[1] The number of prisoners with a sentence of more than 1 year per 100,000 persons in the resident population.

Source: U.S. Department of Justice, Office of Justice Programs, Bureau of Justice Statistics, *Prisoners in 2007*, December 2008, NCJ 224280. See also <http://www.ojp.usdoj.gov/bjs/abstract/p07.htm>.

Table 1282. **Federal Direct Payments: 2007**

[In thousands of dollars (6,764,230 represents $6,764,230,000). For fiscal years ending September 30]

Selected program payments	Puerto Rico	Guam	Virgin Islands	American Samoa	Northern Mariana Islands
Direct payments to individuals for retirement and disability [1]	6,764,230	250,399	193,764	50,797	28,145
Social security:					
Retirement insurance	2,827,137	86,661	115,199	13,464	7,182
Survivors' insurance	1,228,969	38,589	29,056	13,339	5,434
Disability insurance	1,814,670	21,630	23,550	12,541	1,961
Federal retirement and disability:					
Civilian [2]	258,677	56,352	16,820	1,824	6,998
Military	20,607	21,890	1,915	1,723	860
Veterans benefits:					
Service connected disability	357,896	20,462	4,793	6,359	1,048
Other benefit payments	225,392	3,750	1,376	1,373	112
Other	30,880	1,065	1,057	173	23

[1] Includes other payments, not shown separately. [2] Includes retirement and disability payments to former U.S. Postal Service employees.

Source: U.S. Census Bureau, *Consolidated Federal Funds Report for Fiscal Year, 2007* (published September 2008); <http://www.census.gov/govs/cffr/>.

Table 1283. **Selected Social, Demographic, and Housing Charecteristics in Puerto Rico: 2007**

[The Puerto Rico Community Survey universe includes the household population and the population living in institutions, college dormitories, and other group quarters. Based on a sample and subject to sampling variability; see text, this section and Appendix III]

Characteristic	Estimate	Per-cent	Characteristic	Estimate	Per-cent
Total	**3,942,375**	**100.0**	Never married	545,183	33.1
			Now married, except separated	625,243	37.9
SEX AND AGE			Separated	69,560	4.2
			Widowed	180,557	11.0
Male	1,893,735	48.0	Divorced	228,263	13.8
Female	2,048,640	52.0			
			HOUSEHOLDS		
Under 5 years	245,185	6.2			
5 to 9 years	271,211	6.9	**Total households**	**1,204,285**	**100.0**
10 to 14 years	304,894	7.7	Family households (families)	898,030	74.6
15 to 19 years	299,448	7.6	With own children under 18 years . .	374,023	31.1
20 to 24 years	282,355	7.2	Married-couple families	548,833	45.6
25 to 34 years	546,787	13.9	With own children under 18 years . .	210,950	17.5
35 to 44 years	533,880	13.5	Male householder, no wife present . . .	65,643	5.5
45 to 54 years	499,791	12.7	With own children under 18 years . .	23,783	2.0
55 to 59 years	225,423	5.7	Female householder, no husband		
60 to 64 years	210,508	5.3	present	283,554	23.5
65 to 74 years	294,961	7.5	With own children under 18 years . .	139,290	11.6
75 to 84 years	164,690	4.2	Nonfamily households	306,255	25.4
85 years and over	63,242	1.6	Householder living alone	270,300	22.4
			65 years and over	111,652	9.3
MARITAL STATUS			Average household size	3.24	(X)
Males 15 years and over	1,472,279	100.0	Average family size	3.81	(X)
Never married	597,549	40.6			
Now married, except separated	625,647	42.5	DISABILITY STATUS OF THE CIVILIAN		
Separated	50,827	3.5	NONINSTITUTIONALIZED POPULATION		
Widowed	48,154	3.3			
Divorced	150,102	10.2	Population 5 years and over	3,670,864	100.0
Females 15 years and over	1,648,806	100.0	With a disability	954,577	26.0

X Not applicable.

Source: U.S. Census Bureau, 2007 Puerto Rico Community Survey; "DP-2 PR. Selected Social Charecteristics Puerto Rico: 2007"; using American FactFinder; <http://factfinder.census.gov/> (accessed 1 October 2008).

Table 1284. **Tenure by Household Type in Puerto Rico: 2007**

[The Puerto Rico Community Survey universe includes the household population and the population living in institutions, college dormitories, and other group quarters. Based on a sample and subject to sampling variability; see text, this section and Appendix III]

Household type	Owner Occupied	Renter Occu-pied	Household type	Owner Occupied	Renter Occu-pied
Total households.	**1,204,285**	**309,977**	Householder 15 to 34 years . . .	20,782	39,552
Family households	686,016	212,014	Householder 35 to 64 years . . .	109,765	59,292
Married-couple family	462,224	86,609	Householder 65 years and over .	47,370	6,793
Householder 15 to 34 years	46,416	30,105	Nonfamily households	208,292	97,963
Householder 35 to 64 years	298,442	48,819	Householder living alone	186,641	83,659
Householder 65 years and over . .	117,366	7,685	Householder 15 to 34 years . . .	11,566	12,388
Other family	223,792	125,405	Householder 35 to 64 years . . .	88,998	45,696
Male householder, no wife present.	45,875	19,768	Householder 65 years and over .	86,077	25,575
Householder 15 to 34 years . . .	7,337	6,617	Householder not living alone	21,651	14,304
Householder 35 to 64 years . . .	27,347	10,184	Householder 15 to 34 years . . .	2,455	6,261
Householder 65 years and over .	11,191	2,967	Householder 35 to 64 years . . .	13,723	6,664
Female householder, no husband			Householder 65 years and over .	5,473	1,379
present	177,917	105,637			

Source: U.S. Census Bureau, 2007 Puerto Rico Community Survey; "B25011. Tenure by Household Type and Age of House-holder"; using American FactFinder; <http://factfinder.census.gov/> (accessed 1 October 2008).

Table 1285. **Puerto Rico—Summary: 1990 to 2008**

[3,512.4 represents 3,512,400]

Item	Unit	1990	2000	2003	2004	2005	2006	2007	2008
POPULATION									
Total [1]	1,000	3,512.4	3,808.0	3,869.0	3,886.7	3,903.5	3,919.9	3,934.6	3,947.5
Persons per family	Number...	3.7	3.4	3.3	3.3	3.3	3.2	3.2	3.2
EDUCATION [2]									
Enrollment, total	1,000	953.0	971.5	1,172.3	(NA)	959.0	1,016.9	1,009.5	962.0
Public (except public colleges or universities)....	1,000	651.2	612.3	596.3	584.9	575.9	563.5	548.1	526.5
College and university	1,000	156.0	175.5	199.8	207.1	208.0	209.5	225.4	225.4
Expenses	Mil. dol....	1,686.4	4,254.1	4,962.3	5,230.5	5,902.4	6,353.4	6,656.5	6,821.8
As percent of GNP	Percent ...	7.8	10.3	10.5	10.3	11.0	11.2	11.4	11.2
Public	Mil. dol....	1,054.2	3,160.4	3,617.0	3,641.2	4,274.6	4,533.9	4,811.9	4,965.4
Private	Mil. dol....	644.2	1,093.7	1,345.3	1,589.3	1,627.8	1,819.5	1,844.5	1,856.4
LABOR FORCE [3]									
Total [4]	1,000	1,124	1,303	1,352	1,360	1,385	1,422	1,409	1,368
Employed [5]	1,000	963	1,159	1,188	1,206	1,238	1,256	1,263	1,218
Agriculture [6]	1,000	36	24	24	25	26	22	16	15
Manufacturing	1,000	168	159	134	136	138	136	135	129
Trade	1,000	185	239	252	253	261	271	260	257
Government	1,000	222	249	269	268	274	280	296	279
Unemployed [7]	1,000	161	143	164	155	147	166	147	151
Unemployment rate [7]	Rate.....	14.0	11.0	12.1	11.4	10.6	11.7	10.4	11.0
Compensation of employees...	Mil. dol....	13,639	23,504	26,183	27,769	29,372	30,027	30,500	31,164
Average compensation	Dollar	14,854	20,280	22,039	23,026	23,725	23,907	24,149	25,586
Salary and wages	Mil. dol....	13,639	23,504	22,670	24,016	25,393	25,844	26,286	27,008
INCOME [8]									
Personal income:									
Current dollars	Mil. dol....	21,105	38,856	44,216	45,566	48,820	50,842	52,295	56,201
Constant (1954) dollars	Mil. dol....	5,551	8,491	9,155	9,289	9,611	9,555	9,560	9,783
Disposable personal income:									
Current dollars	Mil. dol....	19,914	36,239	41,120	42,476	45,488	47,333	48,933	53,074
Constant (1954) dollars	Mil. dol....	5,238	7,919	8,514	8,659	8,955	8,896	8,945	9,239
Average family income:									
Current dollars	Dollar	22,232	34,693	37,716	38,688	41,273	41,505	42,531	45,629
Constant (1954) dollars	Dollar	5,847	7,581	7,809	7,887	8,125	7,800	7,775	7,956
BANKING [9]									
Assets	Mil. dol....	27,902	58,813	74,315	94,427	109,292	112,658	109,320	110,558
TOURISM [8]									
Number of visitors	1,000	3,426	4,566	4,402	4,889	5,073	5,022	5,062	5,391
Visitor expenditures	Mil. dol....	1,366	2,388	2,677	3,024	3,239	3,369	3,414	3,644
Average per visitor	Dollar	399	523	608	619	638	671	674	676
Net income from tourism	Mil. dol....	383	615	678	735	771	806	830	(NA)

NA Not available.   [1] 1990, and 2000 enumerated as of April 1; all other years estimated as of July 1.   [2] Enrollment for the first school month. Expenses for school year ending in year shown. "Public" includes: Public Preschool, Public Elementary, Public Intermediate, Public High School, Public Post-High School, Public Technological, Public Adult Education, Public Vocational Education, and Public Special Education. "College and university" includes both public and private colleges and universities.   [3] Annual average of monthly figures. For fiscal years.   [4] For population 16 years old and over.   [5] Includes other employment not shown separately.   [6] Includes forestry and fisheries.   [7] Percent unemployed of the labor force.   [8] For fiscal years.   [9] As of June 30. Does not include federal savings banks and international banking entities.

Source: Puerto Rico Planning Board, San Juan, PR, *Economic Report of the Governor*, annual. See also <http://www.gobierno.pr /gprportal/inicio>.

Table 1286. **Puerto Rico—Economic Summary by Industry: 2006**

[In thousands of dollars, (16,439,908 represents $16,439,908,000). Covers establishments with payroll. Employees are for the pay period including March 12. See headnote, Table 742. Based on the County Business Patterns (CBP). This annual series is used as a benchmark for statistical series, surveys, and databases between economic censuses. For a description of CBP; see Appendix III. Starting with the 2003 CBP series, the data are tabulated using the 2002 North American Industial Classification System (NAICS)]

Industry	2002 NAICS code [1]	Total number of establishments	Number of employees	Annual payroll (1,000)
Establishments, total [2]	(X)	46,300	762,730	16,439,908
Construction	23	2,956	61,751	1,009,598
Manufacturing	31–33	2,118	110,050	3,585,032
Wholesale trade	42	2,303	37,187	1,169,744
Retail trade	44–45	10,851	136,502	2,035,162
Transportation and warehousing	48–49	1,062	16,369	394,958
Information	51	491	20,477	734,955
Finance and insurance	52	1,934	40,304	1,406,578
Real estate and rental and leasing	53	1,771	16,353	316,635
Professional, scientific, and technical services	54	4,196	29,835	902,536
Management of companies and enterprises	55	106	6,039	251,495
Admin/support waste mgt/remediation services	56	1,780	70,491	1,095,409
Educational services	61	741	33,800	627,355
Health care and social assistance	62	6,649	73,877	1,412,039
Arts, entertainment, and recreation	71	453	4,330	65,182
Accommodation and food services	72	4,033	76,317	914,442

X Not Applicable.   [1] See text, Section 12, for more information on NAICS.   [2] Includes other industries not shown separately.

Source: U.S. Census Bureau, "County Business Patterns"; <http://www.census.gov/econ/cbp/>.

802   Puerto Rico and the Island Areas

Table 1287. **Puerto Rico—Gross Product and Net Income: 1990 to 2008**

[In millions of dollars (21,619 represents $21,619,000,000). For fiscal years ending June 30. Data for 2008 are preliminary. Minus sign (–) indicates decrease]

Item	1990	1995	2000	2005	2006	2007	2008
Gross product...............	21,619	28,452	41,419	53,752	56,732	58,563	60,787
Agriculture........................	434	318	529	375	394	418	444
Manufacturing......................	12,126	17,867	24,079	34,534	35,638	36,309	38,461
Contract construction and mining [1] .. [2]	720	1,006	1,875	1,848	1,788	1,929	1,991
Transportation & other public services [2]	2,468	3,276	4,237	5,309	5,907	6,111	6,020
Trade	4,728	5,989	8,340	10,217	10,675	11,110	11,811
Finance, insurance, real estate..........	3,896	5,730	9,977	14,267	14,833	15,927	16,391
Services..........................	3,015	4,724	6,603	7,965	8,277	8,572	8,867
Government	3,337	4,440	5,478	8,151	8,424	8,585	8,762
Commonwealth	2,884	3,793	4,601	7,032	7,204	7,281	7,351
Municipalities....................	453	647	877	1,118	1,220	1,304	1,412
Rest of the world...................	–8,985	–14,195	–20,283	–29,056	–29,425	–30,339	–32,476
Statistical discrepancy	–121	–703	585	141	221	-58	573
Net income...................	17,941	23,653	32,610	43,484	45,613	47,284	48,335
Agriculture	486	442	669	670	659	687	712
Manufacturing......................	11,277	16,685	22,348	32,443	33,479	34,101	36,180
Mining...........................	26	30	41	50	47	47	49
Contract construction	679	903	1,691	1,654	1,595	1,697	1,751
Transportation & other public services [2]	1,778	2,360	2,968	3,707	4,092	4,275	4,181
Trade	3,420	4,108	5,752	7,277	7,531	7,753	8,090
Finance, insurance, and real estate.......	3,280	4,735	8,264	11,750	12,153	13,150	13,499
Services..........................	2,643	4,146	5,682	6,840	7,058	7,327	7,587
Commonwealth government [3]	3,337	4,440	5,478	8,151	8,424	8,585	8,762
Rest of the world	–8,985	–14,195	–20,283	–29,056	–29,425	–30,339	–32,476

[1] Mining includes only quarries. [2] Includes other public utilities, and radio and television broadcasting. [3] Includes public enterprises not elsewhere classified.

Source: Puerto Rico Planning Board, San Juan, PR, *Economic Report of the Governor,* annual. See also <http://www.gobierno.pr/gprportal/inicio>.

Table 1288. **Puerto Rico—Transfer Payments: 1990 to 2008**

[In millions of dollars (4,871 represents $4,871,000,000). Data represent transfer payments between federal and state governments and other nonresidents. Data for 2008 are preliminary. Minus sign (-) indicates decrease]

Item	1990	1995	2000	2005	2006	2007	2008
Total receipts.................	4,871	6,236	8,659	10,551	11,210	11,827	13,563
Federal government	4,649	5,912	7,966	9,673	10,190	10,662	12,441
Transfers to individuals [1]	4,577	5,838	7,868	9,547	10,066	10,527	12,253
Veterans benefits...............	349	440	491	491	592	624	658
Medicare	368	661	1,196	1,825	2,056	2,016	2,114
Old age, disability, survivors (social security)...................	2,055	2,912	3,863	5,118	5,423	5,746	6,221
Nutritional assistance	880	1,063	1,193	1,306	1,352	1,472	1,513
Industry subsidies...............	72	74	98	127	124	135	188
U.S. state governments...........	18	18	15	15	18	23	23
Other nonresidents..............	205	307	679	863	1,003	1,142	1,099
Total payments................	1,801	2,301	2,763	3,583	3,742	3,677	3,639
Federal government	1,756	2,132	2,693	3,516	3,688	3,624	3,571
Transfers from individuals...........	817	1,052	1,326	1,792	1,869	1,805	1,827
Contribution to Medicare..........	97	162	191	303	340	362	373
Employee contribution for social security ..	720	888	1,133	1,483	1,524	1,435	1,446
Transfers from industries	16	49	51	74	115	98	101
Unemployment insurance...........	247	184	234	221	230	231	226
Employer contribution for social security	675	847	1,081	1,429	1,473	1,490	1,417
Other nonresidents [2]	45	164	70	67	54	54	68
Net balance	3,070	3,935	5,897	6,968	7,468	8,150	9,924
Federal government	2,893	3,780	5,273	6,157	6,502	7,038	8,870
U.S. state governments...........	16	13	10	10	15	20	20
Other nonresidents..............	162	143	614	801	952	1,092	1,034

[1] Includes other receipts and payments not shown separately. [2] Includes U.S. state governments.

Source: Puerto Rico Planning Board, San Juan, PR, *Economic Report of the Governor,* annual. See also <http://www.gobierno.pr/gprportal/inicio>.

Table 1289. **Puerto Rico—Merchandise Imports and Exports: 1980 to 2008**

[In millions of dollars (9,018 represents $9,018,000,000). Imports are imports for consumption; see text, Section 28]

Item	1980	1985	1990	1995	2000	2002	2003	2004	2005	2006	2007	2008
Imports.......	9,018	10,162	16,200	18,969	27,199	30,511	35,945	37,252	40,418	42,462	43,496	41,559
From U.S. ...	5,345	6,130	10,792	12,213	15,171	15,675	16,949	18,124	20,994	21,982	22,402	19,777
From other...	3,673	4,032	5,408	6,756	11,834	14,824	18,996	19,128	19,424	20,480	21,094	21,782
Exports	6,576	11,087	20,402	23,573	43,191	50,641	55,814	54,982	56,843	59,218	62,398	63,663
To U.S.	5,643	9,873	17,915	20,986	38,335	44,907	46,880	45,311	47,121	47,452	47,507	46,439
To other	933	1,214	2,487	2,587	4,856	5,734	8,934	9,671	9,722	11,766	14,891	17,224

Source: U.S. Census Bureau, *U.S. Trade with Puerto Rico and U.S. Possessions,* FT 895 and unpublished data. See also <http://www.census.gov/prod/www/abs/ftdpr895.html>.

U.S. Census Bureau, Statistical Abstract of the United States: 2010

Table 1290. Puerto Rico—Agricultural Summary: 2002 and 2007

[1 cuerda = .97 acre]

All farms	Unit	2002	2007	All farms	Unit	2002	2007
Farms............	Number...	17,659	15,745	Tenants	Number...	1,636	2,425
Farm land	Cuerdas ..	690,687	557,530	Farms by type of organization:			
Average size of farm .	Cuerdas ..	39.1	35.4	Individual or family...	Number...	15,843	13,958
Approximate land area..	Cuerdas ..	2,254,365	2,254,365	Partnership	Number...	162	49
Proportion in farms ..	Percent...	30.6	24.7	Corporation	Number...	595	575
Farms by size:				Other	Number...	1,059	1,163
Less than 10 cuerdas.	Number...	7,943	7,502				
10 to 19 cuerdas....	Number...	3,847	3,545	Farms by value of sales:			
20 to 49 cuerdas....	Number...	3,228	2,680	Less than $1,000 ...	Number...	3,977	4,442
50 to 99 cuerdas....	Number...	1,282	865	$1,000 to $2,499....	Number...	3,471	2,771
100 to 174 cuerdas ..	Number...	590	524	$2,500 to $4,499....	Number...	3,044	2,428
175 to 259 cuerdas ..	Number...	281	207	$5,000 to $7,499....	Number...	1,575	1,206
260 cuerdas or more .	Number...	488	422	$7,500 to $9,999....	Number...	1,087	882
Tenure of operator:				$10,000 to $19,999 ..	Number...	1,781	1,497
Operators	Number...	17,659	15,745	$20,000 to $39,999 ..	Number...	1,062	1,030
Full owners.....	Number...	13,693	11,402	$40,000 to $59,999 ..	Number...	375	281
Part owners	Number...	2,330	1,918	$60,000 or more	Number...	1,287	1,208

Source: U.S. Department of Agriculture, National Agricultural Statistics Service, *2007 Census of Agriculture-Geographic Area Series Part 52, Puerto Rico,* Volume 1. See also <http://www.agcensus.usda.gov/Publications/2007/Full_Report/index.asp>.

Table 1291. Puerto Rico—Farms and Market Value of Agricultural Products Sold: 2007

[515,686 represents $515,686,000]

Type of product	Number of farms	Market value ($1,000)	Average value per farm (dol.)	Type of product	Number of farms	Market value ($1,000)	Average value per farm (dol.)
Total..........	**15,745**	**515,686**	**32,752**	Horticultural specialties............	524	44,576	85,068
				Grasses and other crops	256	13,372	52,236
Crops, including horticultural specialties..	10,206	218,835	(NA)	Livestock, poultry, and their products........	5,662	296,850	52,428
Sugarcane.........	(NA)	(NA)	(NA)	Cattle and calves	3,568	33,005	9,250
Coffee...........	5,678	41,824	7,366	Poultry and poultry products ..	1,079	63,574	58,919
Pineapples	53	527	9,942	Dairy products	354	184,543	521,307
Plantains.........	3,756	44,875	11,947	Hogs and pigs	1,075	6,239	5,803
Bananas	1,980	10,082	5,092	Aquaculture........	40	833	20,818
Grains	969	1,553	1,603	Sheep and goats	(NA)	(NA)	(NA)
Root crops or tubers ..	1,691	6,683	3,952	Other	787	8,657	11,000
Fruits and coconuts...	2,350	19,904	8,470				
Vegetables and melons [1]........	1,007	35,440	35,194				

NA Not available.   [1] Includes hydroponic crops.

Source: U.S. Dept. of Agriculture, National Agricultural Statistics Service, *2007 Census of Agriculture-Geographic Area Series Part 52, Puerto Rico,* Volume 1. See also <http://www.agcensus.usda.gov/Publications/2007/Full_Report/index.asp>.

Table 1292. Guam, Virgin Islands, and Northern Mariana Islands—Economic Summary: 2007

[Sales and payroll in millions of dollars (6,244 represents $6,244,000,000). Based on the 2007 Economic Census; see Appendix III. Selected kinds of businesses displayed]

Selected kinds of business	Guam	Virgin Islands	Northern Mariana Islands	Selected kinds of business	Guam	Virgin Islands	Northern Mariana Islands
Total: Establishments: [1]	3,143	2,583	1,191	Paid employees [2]........	2,394	797	872
Sales................	6,244	19,479	1,284	Retail trade:			
Annual payroll.........	1,101	1,085	246	Establishments	660	641	255
Paid employees [2]........	52,394	35,300	22,622	Sales................	1,618	1,397	272
Construction:				Annual payroll.........	150	146	29
Establishments	317	195	50	Paid employees [2]........	8,219	6,773	2,770
Sales................	579	352	31	Professional, scientific, and technical services:			
Annual payroll.........	121	115	7	Establishments	227	257	87
Paid employees [2]........	6,011	3,388	528	Sales................	231	284	25
Manufacturing:				Annual payroll.........	77	60	9
Establishments	63	70	59	Paid employees [2]........	2,217	1,370	404
Sales................	167	(D)	190	Accommodation & Food Services			
Annual payroll.........	39	(D)	57	Establishments	429	255	140
Paid employees [2]........	1,495	([3])	7,094	Sales................	635	461	173
Wholesale trade:				Annual payroll.........	155	130	45
Establishments	191	58	72	Paid employees [2]........	11,477	6,146	4,772
Sales................	800	288	143				
Annual payroll.........	56	25	10				

D Withheld to avoid disclosing data for individual companies; data are included in higher level totals.   [1] Includes other kinds of businesses not shown separately.   [2] For pay period including March 12.   [3] 1,000 to 2,499 employees.

Source: U.S. Census Bureau, 2007 Economic Census of the Island Areas, "General Statistics for Island Areas: 2007"; using American FactFinder; <http://www.factfinder.census.gov> (accessed 27 May 2009).

804   Puerto Rico and the Island Areas

Section 30
International Statistics

This section presents statistics for the world as a whole and for many countries on a comparative basis with the United States. Data are shown for population, births and deaths, social and industrial indicators, finances, agriculture, communication, and military affairs.

Statistics of the individual nations may be found primarily in official national publications, generally in the form of yearbooks, issued by most of the nations at various intervals in their own national languages and expressed in their own or customary units of measure. (For a listing of selected publications, see Guide to Sources.) For handier reference, especially for international comparisons, the United Nations Statistics Division compiles data as submitted by member countries and issues a number of international summary publications, generally in English and French. Among these are the *Statistical Yearbook*; the *Demographic Yearbook; International Trade Statistics Yearbook; National Accounts Statistics: Main Aggregates and Detailed Tables; Population and Vital Statistics Reports* (quarterly); the *Monthly Bulletin of Statistics*; and the *Energy Statistics Yearbook*. Specialized agencies of the United Nations also issue international summary publications on agricultural, labor, health, and education statistics. Among these are the *Production Yearbook* and *Trade Yearbook* issued by the Food and Agriculture Organization, the *Yearbook of Labour Statistics* issued by the International Labour Office, *World Health Statistics* issued by the World Health Organization, and the *Statistical Yearbook* issued by the Educational, Scientific, and Cultural Organization.

The U.S. Census Bureau presents estimates and projections of basic demographic measures for countries and regions of the world in the *World Population Reports* (WP) series. The *International Population Reports* (Series IPC), and *International Briefs* (Series IB) also present population figures for many foreign countries. Detailed population statistics are also available from the Census Bureau's International Data Base (http://www.census.gov/ipc/www/idb/>.

The International Monetary Fund (IMF) and the Organization for Economic Cooperation and Development (OECD) also compile data on international statistics. The IMF publishes a series of reports relating to financial data. These include *International Financial Statistics, Direction of Trade,* and *Balance of Payments Yearbook,* published in English, French, and Spanish. The OECD publishes a vast number of statistical publications in various fields such as economics, health, and education. Among these are *OECD in Figures, Main Economic Indicators, Economic Outlook, National Accounts, Labour Force Statistics, OECD Health Data,* and *Education at a Glance.*

Statistical coverage, country names, and classifications—Problems of space and availability of data limit the number of countries and the extent of statistical coverage shown. The list of countries included and the spelling of country names are based almost entirely on the list of independent nations, dependencies, and areas of special sovereignty provided by the U.S. Department of State.

In recent years, several important changes took place in the status of the world's nations. In 1991, the Soviet Union broke up into 15 independent countries: Armenia, Azerbaijan, Belarus, Estonia, Georgia, Kazakhstan, Kyrgyzstan, Latvia, Lithuania, Moldova, Russia, Tajikistan, Turkmenistan, Ukraine, and Uzbekistan.

In the South Pacific, the Marshall Islands, Micronesia, and Palau gained full independence from the U.S. in 1991.

Following the breakup of the Socialist Federal Republic of Yugoslavia in 1992, the United States recognized Bosnia and Herzegovina, Croatia, Slovenia, and Macedonia as independent countries.

International Statistics   805

The Treaty of Maastricht created the European Union (EU) in 1992 with 12 member countries. The EU is not a state intended to replace existing states, but it is more than just an international organization. Its member states have set up common institutions to which they delegate some of their sovereignty so that decisions on specific matters of joint interest can be made democratically at a European level. This pooling of sovereignty is also called "European integration." The EU has grown in size with successive waves of accessions in 1995, 2004, and 2007. The 27 current members of the EU are: Austria, Belgium, Bulgaria, Cyprus, Czech Republic, Denmark, Estonia, Finland, France, Germany, Greece, Hungary, Ireland, Italy, Latvia, Lithuania, Luxembourg, Malta, the Netherlands, Poland, Portugal, Romania, Slovakia, Slovenia, Spain, Sweden, and the United Kingdom.

In 1992, the EU decided to establish economic and monetary union (EMU), with the introduction of a single European currency managed by a European Central Bank. The single currency—the euro—became a reality on January 1, 2002, when euro notes and coins replaced national currencies in 12 of the then 15 countries of the European Union (Belgium, Germany, Greece, Spain, France, Ireland, Italy, Luxembourg, the Netherlands, Austria, Portugal, and Finland). Since then, 12 countries have become members of the EU, but Slovakia, Slovenia, Malta, and Cyprus have been the only new members of the EU to adopt the euro as the national currency.

On January 1, 1993, Czechoslovakia was succeeded by two independent countries: the Czech Republic and Slovakia. Eritrea announced its independence from Ethiopia in April 1993 and was subsequently recognized as an independent nation by the United States. In May of 2002, Timor-Leste won independence from Indonesia.

Serbia and Montenegro, both former republics of Yugoslavia, became independent of one another on May 31, 2006. This separation is seen in the population estimates tables (Tables 1296, 1322, and 1367), but some tables still show both countries as combined. On February 17, 2008, Kosovo declared its independence from Serbia, making it the world's newest independent state.

The population estimates and projections used in Tables 1293–1296, 1298, and 1303 were prepared by the Census Bureau. For each country, the data on population, by age and sex, fertility, mortality, and international migration were evaluated and, where necessary, adjusted for inconsistencies and errors in the data. In most instances, comprehensive projections were made by the component method, resulting in distributions of the population by age and sex and requiring an assessment of probable future trends of fertility, mortality, and international migration.

Economic associations—The Organization for European Economic Co-Operation (OEEC), a regional grouping of Western European countries established in 1948 for the purpose of harmonizing national economic policies and conditions, was succeeded on September 30, 1961, by the Organization for Economic Cooperation and Development (OECD). The member nations of the OECD are Australia, Austria, Belgium, Canada, Czech Republic, Denmark, Finland, France, Germany, Greece, Hungary, Iceland, Ireland, Italy, Japan, Luxembourg, Mexico, the Netherlands, New Zealand, Norway, Poland, Portugal, Slovakia, South Korea, Spain, Sweden, Switzerland, Turkey, the United Kingdom, and the United States.

Quality and comparability of the data—The quality and comparability of the data presented here are affected by a number of factors:

(1) The year for which data are presented may not be the same for all subjects for a particular country or for a given subject for different countries, though the data shown are the most recent available. All such variations have been noted. The data shown are for calendar years except as otherwise specified.

(2) The bases, methods of estimating, methods of data collection, extent of coverage, precision of definition, scope of territory, and margins of error may vary

U.S. Census Bureau, Statistical Abstract of the United States: 2010

for different items within a particular country, and for like items for different countries. Footnotes and headnotes to the tables give a few of the major time-periods and coverage qualifications attached to the figures; considerably more detail is presented in the source publications. Many of the measures shown are, at best, merely rough indicators of magnitude.

(3) Figures shown in this section for the United States may not always agree with figures shown in the preceding sections. Disagreements may be attributable to the use of differing original sources, a difference in the definition of geographic limits (the 50 states, conterminous United States only, or the United States including certain outlying areas and possessions), or to possible adjustments made in the United States' figures by other sources in order to make them more comparable with figures from other countries.

International comparisons of national accounts data—In order to compare national accounts data for different countries, it is necessary to convert each country's data into a common unit of currency, usually the U.S. dollar. The market exchange rates, which are often used in converting national currencies, do not necessarily reflect the relative purchasing power in the various countries. It is necessary that the goods and services produced in different countries be valued consistently if the differences observed are meant to reflect real differences in the volumes of goods and services produced. The use of purchasing power parities (see Tables 1312, 1313, and 1356) instead of exchange rates is intended to achieve this objective.

The method used to present the data shown in Table 1313 is to construct volume measures directly by revaluing the goods and services sold in different countries at a common set of international prices. By dividing the ratio of the gross domestic products of two countries expressed in their own national currencies by the corresponding ratio calculated at constant international prices, it is possible to derive the implied purchasing power parity (PPP) between the two currencies concerned. PPPs show how many

units of currency are needed in one country to buy the same amount of goods and services that one unit of currency will buy in the other country. For further information, see *National Accounts, Main Aggregates, Volume I*, issued annually by the Organisation for Economic Cooperation and Development, Paris, France.

International Standard Industrial Classification—The original version of the International Standard Industrial Classification of All Economic Activities (ISIC) was adopted in 1948. Wide use has been made both nationally and internationally in classifying data according to kind of economic activity in the fields of production, employment, national income, and other economic statistics. A number of countries have utilized the ISIC as the basis for devising their industrial classification scheme.

Substantial comparability has been attained between the industrial classifications of many other countries, including the United States and the ISIC by ensuring, as far as practicable, that the categories at detailed levels of classification in national schemes fitted into only one category of the ISIC. The United Nations, the International Labour Organization, the Food and Agriculture Organization, and other international bodies have utilized the ISIC in publishing and analyzing statistical data. Revisions of the ISIC were issued in 1958, 1968, and 1989.

International maps—A series of regional world maps is provided on pages 808–816. References are included in Table 1296 for easy location of individual countries on the maps. The Robinson map projection is used for this series of maps. A map projection is used to portray all or part of the round Earth on a flat surface, but this cannot be done without some distortion. For the Robinson projection, distortion is very low along the Equator and within 45 degrees of the center but is greatest near the poles. For additional information on map projections and maps, please contact the Earth Science Information Center, U.S. Geological Survey, 507 National Center, Reston, VA 22092.

U.S. Census Bureau, Statistical Abstract of the United States: 2010

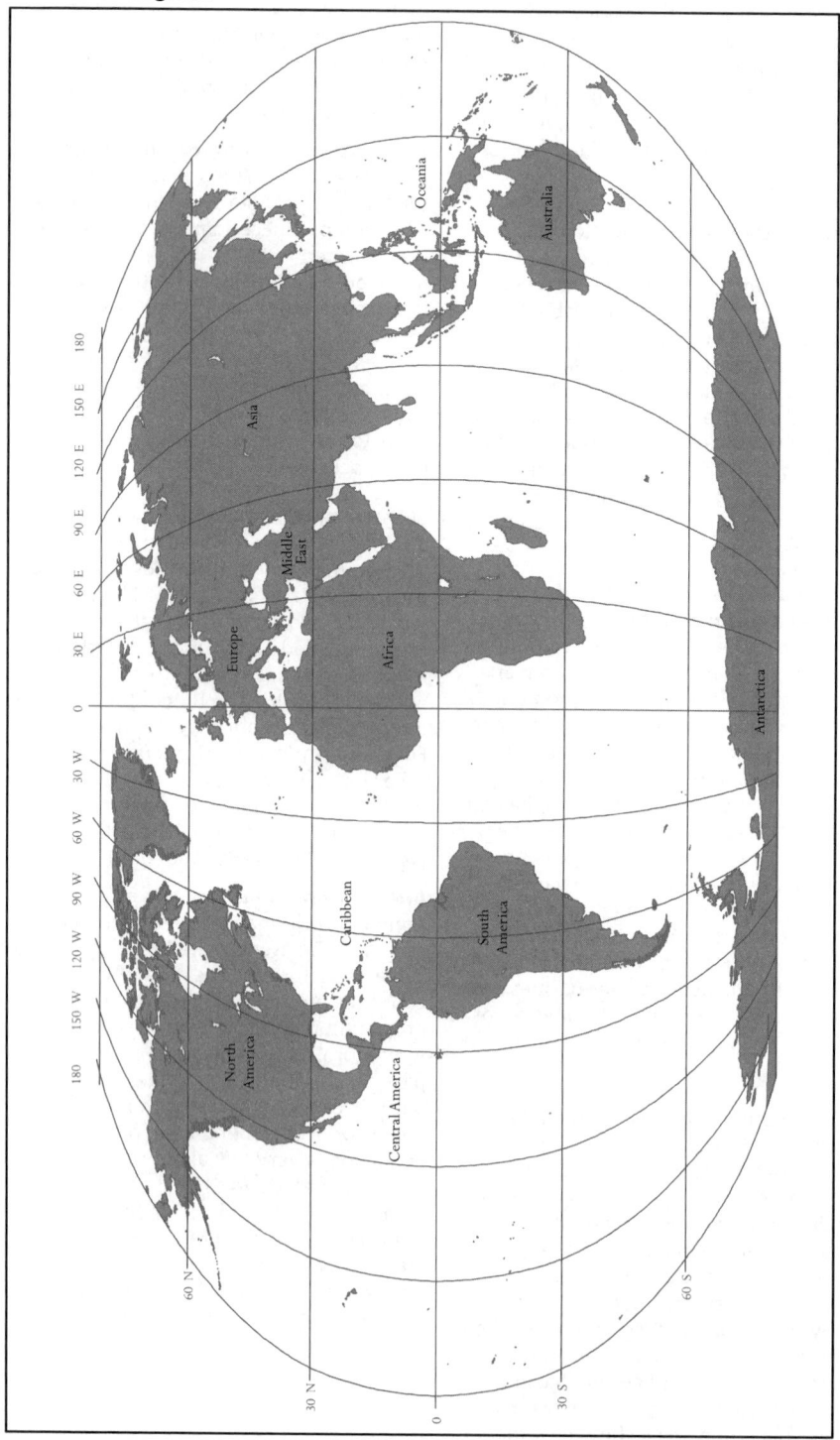

U.S. Census Bureau, Statistical Abstract of the United States: 2010

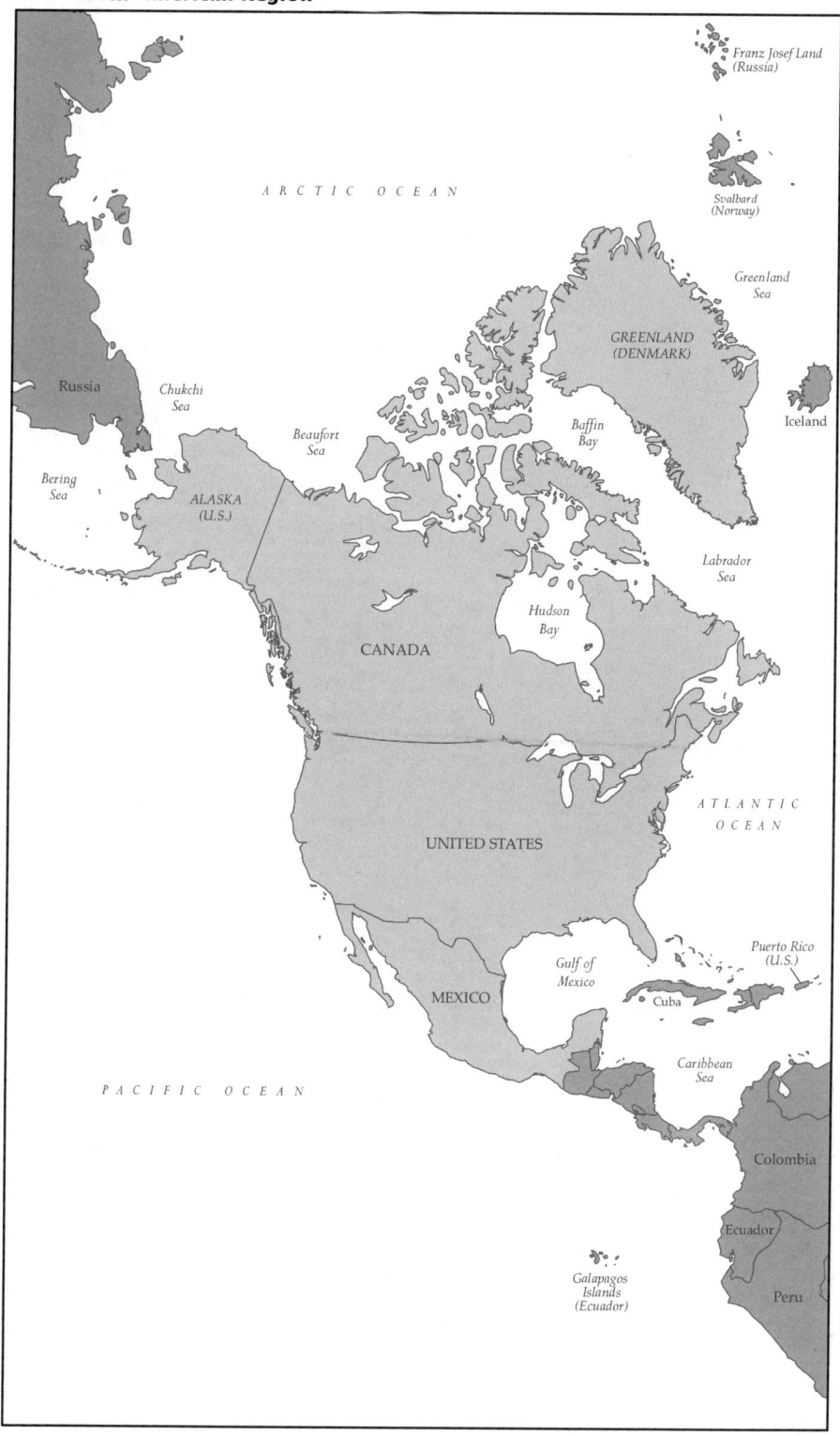

ARCTIC OCEAN

Franz Josef Land
(Russia)

Svalbard
(Norway)

Greenland
Sea

GREENLAND
(DENMARK)

Iceland

Russia

Chukchi
Sea

Beaufort
Sea

Baffin
Bay

Bering
Sea

ALASKA
(U.S.)

Labrador
Sea

Hudson
Bay

CANADA

ATLANTIC
OCEAN

UNITED STATES

PACIFIC OCEAN

Gulf of
Mexico

Puerto Rico
(U.S.)

MEXICO

Cuba

Caribbean
Sea

Colombia

Ecuador

Galapagos
Islands
(Ecuador)

Peru

U.S. Census Bureau, Statistical Abstract of the United States: 2010

U.S. Census Bureau, Statistical Abstract of the United States: 2010

Caribbean Sea

ATLANTIC OCEAN

VENEZUELA

SURINAME

GUYANA

FRENCH GUIANA (FR.)

COLOMBIA

ECUADOR

BRAZIL

PERU

BOLIVIA

CHILE

PARAGUAY

PACIFIC
OCEAN

ARGENTINA

URUGUAY

FALKLAND ISLANDS (U.K.)

SOUTH GEORGIA AND
SOUTH SANDWICH ISLANDS
(U.K.)

U.S. Census Bureau, Statistical Abstract of the United States: 2010

U.S. Census Bureau, Statistical Abstract of the United States: 2010

U.S. Census Bureau, Statistical Abstract of the United States: 2010

U.S. Census Bureau, *Statistical Abstract of the United States: 2010*

U.S. Census Bureau, Statistical Abstract of the United States: 2010

Table 1293. **Total World Population: 1980 to 2050**

[As of midyear (4,452 represents 4,452,000,000)]

Year	Population (mil.)	Average annual [1] Growth rate (percent)	Average annual [1] Population change (mil.)	Year	Population (mil.)	Average annual [1] Growth rate (percent)	Average annual [1] Population change (mil.)
1980......	4,452	1.7	76.2	2015......	7,229	1.0	75.7
1985......	4,852	1.7	83.7	2020......	7,600	0.9	71.6
1990......	5,282	1.6	83.3	2025......	7,947	0.8	66.1
1995......	5,694	1.4	80.5	2030......	8,268	0.7	61.2
2007......	6,615	1.2	76.6	2035......	8,565	0.7	56.7
2008......	6,691	1.1	76.8	2040......	8,840	0.6	52.1
2009......	6,768	1.1	77.0	2045......	9,091	0.5	47.2
2010......	6,845	1.1	77.2	2050......	9,317	(NA)	(NA)

NA Not available. [1] Represents change from year shown to immediate succeeding year.

Source: U.S. Census Bureau, "International Data Base" (published June 2009); <http://www.census.gov/ipc/www/idb/>.

Table 1294. **Population by Continent: 1980 to 2050**

[In millions, except percent (4,452 represents 4,452,000,000). As of midyear]

Year	World	Africa [1]	North America [1]	South America [1]	Asia	Europe [1]	Oceania
1980	4,452	478	371	242	2,644	695	23
1990	5,282	631	424	297	3,181	723	26
2000	6,086	804	485	348	3,688	731	31
2010	6,845	1,013	540	397	4,133	728	35
2020	7,600	1,254	597	442	4,549	719	40
2030	8,268	1,517	652	480	4,874	701	44
2040	8,840	1,804	702	508	5,101	677	47
2050	9,317	2,107	748	526	5,239	648	49
PERCENT DISTRIBUTION							
1980	100.0	10.7	8.3	5.4	59.4	15.6	0.5
2000	100.0	13.2	8.0	5.7	60.6	12.0	0.5
2050	100.0	22.6	8.0	5.6	56.2	7.0	0.5

[1] Estimates and projections for France now include the four overseas departments of French Guiana, Guadeloupe, Martinique, and Reunion in the national total. These areas will now be included in the same regions as France (Europe) and not in the regions where they were included in prior releases (French Guiana in South America, Guadeloupe and Martinique in North America, and Reunion in Africa). Saint Barthelemy and Saint Martin recently voted to become French overseas collectivities apart from Guadeloupe and are included in the totals for North America.

Source: U.S.Census Bureau, "International Data Base" (published June 2009); <http://www.census.gov/ipc/www/idb/>.

Table 1295. **Population and Population Change by Development Status: 1950 to 2050**

[(2,556 represents 2,556,000,000). As of midyear. Minus sign (–) indicates decrease. The "less developed" countries include all of Africa, all of Asia except Japan, the Transcaucasian and Central Asian republics of the New Independent States, all of Latin America and the Caribbean, and all of Oceania except Australia, New Zealand, and Hawaii. This category matches the "less developed country" classification employed by the United Nations]

Year	Number (mil.) World	Number (mil.) Less developed countries [1]	Number (mil.) More developed countries [1]	Percent of world Less developed countries [1]	Percent of world More developed countries [1]
POPULATION					
1950	2,556	1,749	807	68.4	31.6
1960	3,042	2,130	911	70.0	30.0
1970	3,712	2,707	1,005	72.9	27.1
1980	4,452	3,370	1,082	75.7	24.3
1990	5,282	4,137	1,145	78.3	21.7
2000	6,086	4,892	1,194	80.4	19.6
2010	6,845	5,621	1,224	82.1	17.9
2020	7,600	6,353	1,247	83.6	16.4
2030	8,268	7,010	1,258	84.8	15.2
2040	8,840	7,580	1,260	85.7	14.3
2050	9,317	8,061	1,256	86.5	13.5
POPULATION CHANGE					
1950–1960	486	382	104	78.6	21.4
1960–1970	670	577	93	86.1	13.9
1970–1980	740	663	78	89.5	10.5
1980–1990	830	767	63	92.5	7.5
1990–2000	804	755	49	93.9	6.1
2000–2010	759	728	31	95.9	4.1
2010–2020	755	732	22	97.0	3.0
2020–2030	668	657	11	98.4	1.6
2030–2040	572	570	2	99.7	0.3
2040–2050	477	481	–4	100.8	–0.8

[1] See footnote 1, Table 1294.

Source: U.S. Census Bureau, "International Data Base" (published June 2009); <http://www.census.gov/ipc/www/idb/>.

International Statistics   817

Table 1296. Population by Country or Area: 1990 to 2010

[5,282,213 represents 5,282,213,000. Population data generally are de facto figures for the present territory. Population estimates were derived from information available as of spring 2009. See text of this section for general comments concerning the data. For details of methodology, coverage, and reliability, see source. Minus sign (−) indicates decrease]

Country or area	Map refer- ence [1]	Mid-year population (1,000) 1990	2000	2009	2010, proj.	Popu- lation rank, 2009	Annual rate of growth, [2] 2000- 2010 (percent)	Popula- tion per sq. mile, 2009	Area [3] (sq. mile)
World	S0	5,282,213	6,085,977	6,768,168	6,845,147	(X)	1.2	132	51,168,469
Afghanistan..........	S6	13,449	22,021	28,396	29,121	43	2.8	114	250,000
Albania.............	S4	3,251	3,474	3,639	3,660	129	0.5	344	10,578
Algeria.............	S5	25,089	30,429	34,178	34,586	35	1.3	37	919,591
Andorra............	S4	53	65	84	85	199	2.6	464	181
Angola.............	S5	8,297	10,377	12,799	13,068	70	2.3	27	481,351
Antigua and Barbuda ...	S2	64	75	86	87	198	1.4	501	171
Argentina	S3	33,036	37,336	40,914	41,343	31	1.0	39	1,056,637
Armenia............	S6	3,377	3,043	2,967	2,967	137	−0.3	270	10,986
Australia...........	S8	16,956	19,053	21,263	21,516	55	1.2	7	2,941,285
Austria.............	S4	7,723	8,113	8,210	8,214	92	0.1	258	31,832
Azerbaijan..........	S6	7,200	7,809	8,239	8,304	91	0.6	248	33,243
Bahamas, The........	S2	245	283	308	310	177	0.9	79	3,888
Bahrain	S6	501	635	729	738	162	1.5	2,838	257
Bangladesh..........	S7	111,437	136,681	156,051	158,066	7	1.5	3,018	51,703
Barbados	S2	262	274	285	286	180	0.4	1,710	166
Belarus.............	S4	10,201	10,034	9,649	9,613	86	−0.4	120	80,154
Belgium............	S4	9,969	10,264	10,414	10,423	78	0.2	891	11,690
Belize.............	S2	191	248	308	315	176	2.4	35	8,805
Benin	S5	4,705	6,619	8,792	9,056	90	3.1	206	42,710
Bhutan.............	S7	615	606	691	700	164	1.4	38	18,147
Bolivia	S3	6,574	8,195	9,775	9,947	84	1.9	23	418,683
Bosnia and Herzegovina .	S4	4,424	4,035	4,613	4,622	119	1.4	233	19,767
Botswana	S5	1,265	1,680	1,991	2,029	146	1.9	9	226,012
Brazil	S3	151,170	176,320	198,739	201,103	5	1.3	61	3,265,061
Brunei	S8	253	325	388	395	175	1.9	191	2,035
Bulgaria	S4	8,894	7,818	7,205	7,149	98	−0.9	169	42,683
Burkina Faso.........	S5	8,361	11,588	15,746	16,242	61	3.4	149	105,714
Burma	S7	39,243	44,301	48,138	48,511	26	0.9	190	253,954
Burundi	S5	5,536	6,823	9,511	9,863	87	3.7	960	9,903
Cambodia...........	S7	9,345	12,396	14,494	14,753	66	1.7	213	68,154
Cameroon...........	S5	11,884	15,343	18,879	19,294	58	2.3	104	181,251
Canada	S1	27,791	31,100	33,487	33,760	36	0.8	10	3,511,006
Cape Verde.........	S5	349	402	429	432	171	0.7	276	1,557
Central African Republic .	S5	3,085	3,940	4,511	4,579	120	1.5	19	240,534
Chad	S5	5,841	7,943	10,329	10,543	79	2.8	21	486,177
Chile	S3	13,129	15,156	16,602	16,746	60	1.0	57	289,112
China [4]...........	S7	1,148,364	1,268,853	1,338,613	1,347,563	1	0.6	372	3,600,930
Colombia	S3	33,147	38,910	43,677	44,205	28	1.3	109	401,042
Comoros............	S5	429	579	752	773	161	2.9	898	838
Congo (Brazzaville) [5] ...	S5	2,266	3,104	4,013	4,126	127	2.8	30	131,853
Congo (Kinshasa) [5]	S5	39,047	51,849	68,693	70,916	18	3.1	78	875,521
Costa Rica	S2	3,027	3,711	4,254	4,311	123	1.5	217	19,560
Cote d'Ivoire	S5	12,491	16,885	20,617	21,059	57	2.2	168	122,780
Croatia.............	S4	4,508	4,411	4,489	4,487	121	0.2	206	21,781
Cuba	S2	10,513	11,106	11,452	11,477	72	0.3	268	42,803
Cyprus	S6	745	920	1,085	1,103	157	1.8	304	3,568
Czech Republic	S4	10,310	10,270	10,212	10,202	80	−0.1	342	29,836
Denmark............	S4	5,141	5,337	5,501	5,516	109	0.3	336	16,368
Djibouti.	S5	499	669	725	741	163	1.0	82	8,873
Dominica	S2	70	71	73	73	201	0.3	25	2,928
Dominican Republic	S2	7,083	8,410	9,650	9,794	85	1.5	517	18,680
Ecuador	S3	10,318	12,446	14,573	14,791	65	1.7	136	106,888
Egypt..............	S5	54,907	65,159	78,867	80,472	16	2.1	205	384,344
El Salvador	S2	5,100	6,126	7,185	7,304	99	1.8	898	8,000
Equatorial Guinea	S5	371	491	633	651	166	2.8	58	10,830
Eritrea	S5	3,138	4,197	5,647	5,793	108	3.2	121	46,842
Estonia............	S4	1,569	1,380	1,299	1,291	153	−0.7	78	16,684
Ethiopia	S5	48,397	64,165	85,237	88,013	14	3.2	197	432,310
Fiji...............	S8	738	833	945	958	158	1.4	134	7,054
Finland............	S4	4,986	5,169	5,250	5,255	112	0.2	45	117,557
France.............	S4	58,168	61,137	64,420	64,768	21	0.6	261	247,125
Gabon	S5	938	1,236	1,515	1,545	151	2.2	15	99,485
Gambia, The........	S5	949	1,368	1,778	1,824	148	2.9	461	3,861
Georgia	S6	5,426	4,777	4,616	4,601	118	−0.4	172	26,911
Germany [6]	S4	79,380	82,188	82,330	82,283	15	(Z)	611	134,835
Ghana	S5	15,408	19,752	23,888	24,340	47	2.1	268	89,166
Greece............	S4	10,130	10,559	10,737	10,750	75	0.2	213	50,502
Grenada	S2	92	89	91	91	196	0.2	683	133
Guatemala	S2	8,966	11,085	13,277	13,550	69	2.0	317	41,865
Guinea	S5	6,118	8,350	10,058	10,324	81	2.1	106	94,925
Guinea-Bissau........	S5	996	1,279	1,534	1,565	150	2.0	142	10,811
Guyana	S3	772	786	753	748	160	−0.5	10	76,004
Haiti..............	S2	6,289	7,639	9,036	9,203	89	1.9	849	10,641
Honduras	S2	4,794	6,359	7,834	7,989	93	2.3	181	43,201
Hungary	S4	10,372	10,137	9,906	9,880	82	−0.3	278	35,653
Iceland............	S1	255	281	307	309	178	0.9	8	38,707
India	S7	838,159	1,006,300	1,156,898	1,173,108	2	1.5	1,008	1,147,950
Indonesia	S8	181,770	213,829	240,272	242,968	4	1.3	341	705,189
Iran	S6	56,669	63,273	66,429	67,038	19	0.6	105	631,660

See footnotes at end of table.

U.S. Census Bureau, Statistical Abstract of the United States: 2010

Table 1296. **Population by Country or Area: 1990 to 2010**—Con.

[See headnote, page 818]

Country or area	Map reference [1]	Mid-year population (1,000)				Population rank, 2009	Annual rate of growth, [2] 2000–2010 (percent)	Population per sq. mile, 2009	Area [3] (sq. mile)
		1990	2000	2009	2010, proj.				
Iraq	S6	18,140	22,679	28,946	29,672	40	2.7	173	166,858
Ireland	S4	3,508	3,792	4,203	4,250	125	1.1	158	26,598
Israel	S6	4,478	6,115	7,234	7,354	97	1.8	922	7,849
Italy	S4	56,743	57,719	58,126	58,091	23	0.1	512	113,521
Jamaica	S2	2,347	2,616	2,826	2,847	138	0.8	676	4,182
Japan	S7	123,537	126,729	127,079	126,804	10	(Z)	878	144,689
Jordan	S6	3,267	4,688	6,269	6,407	104	3.1	177	35,510
Kazakhstan	S7	16,398	15,032	15,399	15,460	62	0.3	15	1,030,811
Kenya	S5	23,354	30,508	39,003	40,047	33	2.7	177	219,788
Kiribati	S8	71	92	113	115	190	2.3	360	313
Korea, North	S7	20,019	21,263	22,665	22,757	50	0.7	488	46,490
Korea, South	S7	42,869	46,839	48,509	48,636	25	0.4	1,280	37,911
Kosovo	S4	1,862	1,700	1,805	1,815	147	0.7	429	4,203
Kuwait	S6	2,142	1,974	2,693	2,789	139	3.5	391	6,880
Kyrgyzstan	S6	4,382	4,851	5,432	5,509	111	1.3	74	73,861
Laos	S7	4,210	5,497	6,834	6,994	102	2.4	77	89,112
Latvia	S4	2,664	2,376	2,232	2,218	141	−0.7	91	24,552
Lebanon	S6	3,150	3,581	4,017	4,061	126	1.3	1,017	3,950
Lesotho	S5	1,721	2,068	2,131	2,133	142	0.3	182	11,720
Liberia	S5	2,117	2,695	3,442	3,534	132	2.7	93	37,189
Libya	S5	4,146	5,125	6,324	6,461	103	2.3	9	679,359
Liechtenstein	S4	29	32	35	35	211	0.8	563	62
Lithuania	S4	3,695	3,654	3,555	3,545	130	−0.3	141	25,212
Luxembourg	S4	383	439	492	498	169	1.3	493	998
Macedonia	S4	1,861	2,015	2,067	2,072	144	0.3	215	9,597
Madagascar	S5	11,633	15,742	20,654	21,282	56	3.0	92	224,533
Malawi	S5	9,546	11,802	15,029	15,448	64	2.7	414	36,324
Malaysia	S8	17,507	21,804	25,716	26,160	46	1.8	203	126,853
Maldives	S7	217	300	396	396	174	2.8	3,422	116
Mali	S5	8,327	10,621	13,443	13,796	68	2.6	29	471,042
Malta	S4	359	390	405	407	173	0.4	3,321	122
Marshall Islands	S8	46	53	65	66	205	2.2	923	70
Mauritania	S5	1,925	2,501	3,129	3,205	135	2.5	8	397,838
Mauritius	S5	1,062	1,186	1,284	1,294	154	0.9	1,639	784
Mexico	S1	84,914	99,927	111,212	112,469	11	1.2	150	742,486
Micronesia, Federated States of	S8	109	108	107	107	192	−0.1	396	271
Moldova	S4	4,394	4,391	4,321	4,317	122	−0.2	335	12,885
Monaco	S4	30	32	33	33	212	0.4	42,690	1
Mongolia	S7	2,218	2,664	3,041	3,087	136	1.5	5	600,282
Montenegro	S4	583	732	672	667	165	−0.9	126	5,333
Morocco	S5	24,000	28,113	31,285	31,627	38	1.2	182	172,317
Mozambique	S5	12,667	18,125	21,669	22,061	53	2.0	72	302,737
Namibia	S5	1,471	1,893	2,109	2,128	143	1.2	7	318,694
Nauru	S8	9	12	14	14	221	1.9	1,729	8
Nepal	S7	18,918	24,818	28,563	28,952	42	1.5	517	55,282
Netherlands	S4	14,952	15,908	16,716	16,783	59	0.5	1,278	13,082
New Zealand	S8	3,414	3,802	4,213	4,252	124	1.1	41	103,483
Nicaragua	S2	3,685	4,935	5,891	5,996	107	1.9	127	46,430
Niger	S5	7,842	10,951	15,306	15,878	63	3.7	31	489,073
Nigeria	S5	96,604	123,179	149,229	152,217	8	2.1	424	351,648
Norway	S4	4,242	4,492	4,661	4,676	116	0.4	39	118,703
Oman	S6	1,773	2,534	3,418	3,526	133	3.3	42	82,031
Pakistan	S6	115,458	147,559	174,579	177,277	6	1.8	581	300,664
Palau	S8	15	19	21	21	218	0.7	118	177
Panama	S2	2,393	2,900	3,360	3,411	134	1.6	115	29,340
Papua New Guinea	S8	3,683	4,813	5,941	6,065	106	2.3	34	174,849
Paraguay	S3	4,244	5,592	6,996	7,162	101	2.5	46	153,398
Peru	S3	21,600	26,087	29,547	29,907	39	1.4	60	494,208
Philippines	S7	65,088	81,222	97,977	99,900	12	2.1	851	115,124
Poland	S4	38,119	38,654	38,483	38,464	34	(Z)	327	117,552
Portugal	S4	9,923	10,336	10,708	10,736	76	0.4	302	35,502
Qatar	S6	446	627	833	841	159	2.9	189	4,416
Romania	S4	22,866	22,452	22,215	22,181	51	−0.1	250	88,934
Russia	S7	147,973	146,710	140,041	139,390	9	−0.5	21	6,562,083
Rwanda	S5	6,999	8,398	10,746	11,056	74	2.7	1,116	9,632
Saint Kitts and Nevis	S2	42	39	40	40	210	0.4	398	101
Saint Lucia	S2	138	153	160	161	188	0.5	685	234
Saint Vincent and the Grenadines	S2	107	108	105	104	193	−0.3	696	150
Samoa	S8	172	197	220	223	184	1.3	194	1,133
San Marino	S4	23	27	30	31	213	1.3	1,281	24
Sao Tome and Principe	S5	119	160	213	219	186	3.2	550	386
Saudi Arabia	S6	16,061	23,147	28,687	29,207	41	2.3	35	829,996
Senegal	S5	8,001	10,678	13,712	14,086	67	2.8	185	74,131
Serbia	S4	7,786	7,604	7,379	7,345	95	−0.3	247	29,913
Seychelles	S5	71	79	87	88	197	1.1	498	176
Sierra Leone	S5	4,228	3,809	5,132	5,246	113	3.2	186	27,653
Singapore	S8	3,047	4,037	4,658	4,701	117	1.5	17,662	264
Slovakia	S4	5,263	5,400	5,463	5,470	110	0.1	290	18,842
Slovenia	S4	1,991	2,011	2,006	2,003	145	(Z)	258	7,780
Solomon Islands	S8	335	466	596	610	167	2.7	56	10,633
Somalia	S5	6,692	7,386	9,832	10,112	83	3.1	41	242,215

See footnotes at end of table.

U.S. Census Bureau, Statistical Abstract of the United States: 2010

Table 1296. **Population by Country or Area: 1990 to 2010**—Con.

[See headnote, page 818]

Country or area	Map refer- ence [1]	Mid-year population (1,000) 1990	Mid-year population (1,000) 2000	Mid-year population (1,000) 2009	Mid-year population (1,000) 2010, proj.	Popu- lation rank, 2009	Annual rate of growth, [2] 2000– 2010 (percent)	Popula- tion per sq. mile, 2009	Area [3] (sq. mile)
South Africa	S5	38,476	45,064	49,052	49,109	24	0.9	104	471,008
Spain	S4	39,351	40,016	40,525	40,549	32	0.1	210	192,873
Sri Lanka	S7	17,365	19,436	21,325	21,514	54	1.0	853	24,996
Sudan	S5	26,050	34,194	41,088	41,980	29	2.1	45	917,374
Suriname	S3	395	432	481	487	170	1.2	8	62,344
Swaziland	S5	882	1,144	1,337	1,354	152	1.7	201	6,642
Sweden	S4	8,601	8,924	9,060	9,074	88	0.2	57	158,662
Switzerland	S4	6,837	7,267	7,604	7,623	94	0.5	495	15,355
Syria	S6	12,500	16,471	21,763	22,198	52	3.0	306	71,062
Tajikistan	S6	5,272	6,230	7,349	7,487	96	1.8	133	55,097
Tanzania	S5	25,214	33,712	41,049	41,893	30	2.2	120	342,099
Thailand	S7	55,197	61,904	65,998	66,405	20	0.7	334	197,595
Timor-Leste	S8	746	847	1,132	1,155	156	3.1	195	5,794
Togo	S5	3,510	4,714	6,032	6,200	105	2.7	287	20,998
Tonga	S8	92	102	121	123	189	1.8	436	277
Trinidad and Tobago	S2	1,255	1,252	1,230	1,229	155	−0.2	621	1,980
Tunisia	S5	8,211	9,568	10,486	10,589	77	1.0	175	59,985
Turkey	S6	56,561	67,329	76,806	77,804	17	1.4	258	297,591
Turkmenistan	S6	3,658	4,385	4,885	4,941	114	1.2	26	188,456
Tuvalu	S8	9	11	12	13	222	1.5	1,233	10
Uganda	S5	17,456	23,956	32,370	33,399	37	3.3	420	77,108
Ukraine	S4	51,622	49,005	45,700	45,416	27	−0.8	196	233,089
United Arab Emirates	S6	1,826	3,219	4,798	4,976	115	4.4	149	32,278
United Kingdom	S4	57,493	59,522	61,113	61,285	22	0.3	655	93,278
United States	S1	250,132	282,172	307,212	310,233	3	0.9	87	3,537,421
Uruguay	S3	3,110	3,328	3,494	3,510	131	0.5	52	67,035
Uzbekistan	S6	20,530	25,042	27,606	27,866	44	1.1	168	164,247
Vanuatu	S8	154	190	219	222	185	1.5	46	4,710
Venezuela	S3	19,325	23,493	26,815	27,223	45	1.5	79	340,560
Vietnam	S7	67,258	79,178	88,577	89,571	13	1.2	705	125,622
Yemen	S6	12,416	17,407	22,858	23,495	49	3.0	112	203,849
Zambia	S5	7,978	10,205	11,863	12,057	71	1.7	41	285,994
Zimbabwe	S5	10,156	11,820	11,393	11,652	73	−0.1	76	149,293
OTHER									
Taiwan [4]	S7	20,278	22,183	22,974	23,025	48	0.4	1,845	12,456
AREAS OF SPECIAL SOVEREIGNTY AND DEPENDENCIES									
American Samoa	S8	47	58	66	66	203	1.4	854	77
Anguilla	S1	8	11	14	15	220	2.6	367	39
Aruba	S1	63	90	103	105	194	1.5	1,383	75
Bermuda	S1	58	63	68	68	202	0.8	3,296	21
Cayman Islands	S1	26	38	49	50	208	2.7	485	101
Cook Islands	S8	18	16	12	11	223	−3.5	130	92
Faroe Islands	S4	47	46	49	49	209	0.7	90	540
French Polynesia	S8	202	249	287	291	179	1.6	203	1,413
Gaza Strip [7]	S6	646	1,130	1,552	1,604	149	3.5	11,165	139
Gibraltar	S4	29	27	29	29	215	0.6	10,655	3
Greenland	S1	56	57	58	58	206	0.1	(Z)	160,075
Guam	S8	134	155	178	181	187	1.5	854	209
Guernsey	S4	63	64	65	66	204	0.3	2,174	30
Hong Kong	S7	5,688	6,659	7,055	7,090	100	0.6	17,536	402
Isle of Man	S4	69	73	77	77	200	0.5	346	221
Jersey	S4	84	89	92	92	195	0.3	2,046	45
Macau	S7	352	432	560	568	168	2.7	51,786	11
Mayotte	S5	90	156	224	231	183	3.9	1,550	144
Montserrat	S2	11	4	5	5	227	2.6	129	39
Netherlands Antilles	S2	189	210	227	229	182	0.8	613	371
New Caledonia	S8	168	202	227	230	181	1.3	32	7,172
Northern Mariana Islands	S8	44	70	51	48	207	−3.7	280	184
Puerto Rico	S2	3,537	3,814	3,966	3,978	128	0.4	1,158	3,425
Saint Barthelemy	S2	5	7	7	7	225	0.4	919	8
Saint Helena	S5	7	7	8	8	224	0.6	48	159
Saint Martin	S2	30	28	30	30	214	0.6	1,430	21
Saint Pierre and Miquelon	S1	6	7	7	7	226	0.2	76	93
Turks and Caicos Islands	S2	12	18	23	24	217	3.0	138	166
Virgin Islands	S2	104	109	110	110	191	0.1	822	134
Virgin Islands, British	S2	16	20	24	25	216	2.0	415	59
Wallis and Futuna	S8	13	15	15	15	219	0.5	145	106
West Bank [7]	S6	1,253	1,980	2,461	2,515	140	2.4	1,130	2,178
Western Sahara	S5	221	309	405	417	172	3.0	4	102,703

X Not applicable.   Z Less than 0.05 percent or less than one person per square mile.   [1] See maps on pp. 808–816 for geographic locations.   [2] Computed by the exponential method. For explanation of average annual percent change, see Guide to Tabular Presentation.   [3] Source: Central Intelligence Agency, "CIA World Factbook"; <https://www.cia.gov/library/publications/the-world-factbook/index.html#> (accessed 24 August 2009). (Data converted from square kilometers to square miles).   [4] With the establishment of diplomatic relations with China on January 1, 1979, the U.S. government recognized the People's Republic of China as the sole legal government of China and acknowledged the Chinese position that there is only one China and that Taiwan is part of China.   [5] "Congo" is the official short-form name for both the Republic of Congo and the Democratic Republic of the Congo. To distinguish one from the other the U.S. Dept. of State adds the capital in parentheses. This practice is unofficial and provisional.   [6] Data for 1990 are for former West Germany and East Germany combined.   [7] The Gaza Strip and West Bank are Israeli occupied with interim status subject to Israeli/Palestinian negotiations. The final status is yet to be determined.

Source: Except as noted, U.S. Census Bureau, "International Data Base" (published June 2009); <http://www.census.gov/ipc/www/idb/>.

Table 1297. **Foreign or Foreign-Born Population, Labor Force, and Net Migration in Selected OECD Countries: 2000 and 2006**

[31,108 represents 31,108,000. In Australia and the United States the data refer to people present in the country who are foreign born. In the European countries and Japan they generally refer to foreigners and represent the nationalities of residents]

Country	Foreign population [1]				Foreign labor force [2]				Average net migration 1990-2006 [3] (per 1,000 population)
	Number (1,000)		Percent of total population		Number (1,000)		Percent of total labor force		
	2000	2006	2000	2006	2000	2006	2000	2006	
United States	31,108	39,055	11.0	13.0	18,028.5	23,342.9	12.9	15.6	4.2
Australia.	4,412	4,957	23.0	24.1	2,372.8	2,670.1	24.7	24.9	5.3
Austria	702	818	8.8	9.9	345.6	432.9	10.5	11.9	3.9
Belgium	862	932	8.4	8.8	387.9	446.2	8.6	9.2	3.2
Denmark.	259	278	4.8	5.1	96.8	115.0	3.4	4.2	2.1
France	(NA)	(NA)	(NA)	(NA)	1,577.6	(NA)	6.0	(NA)	1.2
Germany	7,297	6,756	8.9	8.2	3,546.0	3,528.0	8.8	8.5	4.0
Italy [4]	1,380	2,939	2.4	5.0	837.9	1,463.1	3.9	5.9	3.8
Japan [5]	1,686	2,083	1.3	1.6	154.7	178.8	0.2	0.3	-0.1
Luxembourg	165	191	37.3	41.6	152.7	207.1	57.3	65.0	9.7
Netherlands	668	682	4.2	4.2	300.1	283.8	3.9	3.3	3.0
Spain [6]	1,371	4,520	3.4	10.3	454.6	1,824.0	2.5	8.5	6.4
Sweden	477	492	5.4	5.4	222.0	177.0	5.0	4.3	2.8
Switzerland [7]	1,384	1,524	19.3	20.3	717.3	849.9	20.1	21.0	4.0
United Kingdom [8]	2,342	3,392	4.0	5.8	1,107.0	1,773.0	4.0	6.3	1.4

NA Not available. [1] Data are from population registers of foreigners except for France, Greece, Mexico, and Poland (census), Ireland and the United Kingdom (Labour Force Survey), Portugal (residence permits), Australia (inter- and post-censal estimates), and the United States (Current Population Survey). [2] Includes unemployed except for Belgium, Greece, Norway, Luxembourg, Netherlands, and the United Kingdom. Germany, Luxembourg, and Netherlands include cross-border workers. Belgium and Italy include the self-employed. Data for Austria, Germany, and Luxembourg are from social security registers, and for Denmark, from the register of population. Data for Italy, Spain, and Switzerland are from residence or work permits. Figures for Japan and Netherlands are estimates. Data for other countries are from labor force surveys. [3] Or latest period available. [4] Children under 18 who are registered on their parents' permit are not counted. [5] Data are based on registered foreign nationals which include foreigners staying in Japan for more than 90 days. [6] Number of foreigners with a residence permit. Permits of short duration (less than 6 months) as well as students are excluded. [7] Number of foreigners with an annual residence permit or with a settlement permit (permanent permit). Seasonal and frontier workers are excluded. [8] Estimated from the annual labour force survey. Fluctuations from year to year may be due to sampling error.

Source: Organization for Economic Cooperation and Development, Paris, France, *International Migration Outlook* (2008 edition) (copyright). See also <http://www.oecd.org>.

Table 1298. **Age Distribution by Country or Area: 2009 and 2010**

[In percent. Covers countries with 13 million or more population in 2009]

Country or area	2009		2010, proj.		Country or area	2009		2010, proj.	
	Under 15 years old	65 years old and over	Under 15 years old	65 years old and over		Under 15 years old	65 years old and over	Under 15 years old	65 years old and over
World	27.0	7.6	26.8	7.7	Malawi.	45.4	2.7	45.3	2.7
					Malaysia	31.4	5.0	31.0	5.1
Afghanistan	43.6	2.4	42.9	2.4	Mali.	47.6	3.0	47.5	3.0
Algeria.	25.4	5.1	24.7	5.1	Mexico.	29.1	6.2	28.7	6.4
Argentina.	25.6	10.8	25.5	10.9	Morocco.	28.7	6.0	28.2	6.0
Australia.	18.6	13.5	18.4	13.7	Mozambique.	44.3	2.9	44.1	2.9
Bangladesh	34.6	4.0	34.1	4.1	Nepal	36.6	4.2	35.6	4.3
Brazil.	26.7	6.4	26.5	6.6	Netherlands	17.4	14.9	17.2	15.2
Burkina Faso	46.2	2.5	46.0	2.5	Niger.	49.6	2.3	49.7	2.3
Burma	25.3	5.4	24.9	5.5	Nigeria.	41.5	3.1	41.2	3.1
Cambodia.	32.6	3.6	32.2	3.7	Pakistan.	36.7	4.2	36.0	4.2
Cameroon	40.9	3.3	40.7	3.3	Peru	29.1	5.7	28.5	5.8
Canada	16.1	15.2	15.9	15.5	Philippines	35.2	4.1	34.9	4.2
Chile	23.2	9.1	22.7	9.3	Poland.	15.0	13.4	14.8	13.5
China [1]	19.8	8.1	19.6	8.3	Romania	15.5	14.7	15.5	14.7
Colombia	27.7	5.8	27.2	6.0	Russia.	14.8	13.7	15.0	13.3
Congo (Kinshasa) [2] . .	46.9	2.5	46.7	2.5	Saudi Arabia.	38.0	2.5	38.0	2.5
Cote d'Ivoire	40.6	2.9	40.2	2.9	Senegal	42.2	3.0	42.0	3.0
Ecuador	31.1	6.2	30.6	6.3	South Africa	28.9	5.4	28.6	5.5
Egypt	33.0	4.3	32.8	4.4	Spain	14.5	18.1	14.5	18.4
Ethiopia.	46.1	2.7	46.2	2.7	Sri Lanka	23.9	8.1	23.6	8.3
France.	18.6	16.4	18.6	16.5	Sudan	40.7	2.5	40.2	2.5
Germany	13.7	20.3	13.5	20.4	Syria	36.4	3.7	35.8	3.7
Ghana	37.2	3.5	36.8	3.6	Taiwan [1]	16.7	10.7	16.2	10.8
Guatemala	39.4	3.8	38.7	3.8	Tanzania	43.0	2.9	42.5	2.9
India	30.5	5.2	30.1	5.3	Thailand.	20.8	8.7	20.3	9.0
Indonesia.	28.1	6.0	27.7	6.1	Turkey.	27.2	6.1	26.9	6.2
Iran.	21.7	5.4	21.3	5.4	Uganda	50.0	2.1	50.0	2.1
Iraq.	38.8	3.0	38.4	3.1	Ukraine	13.8	15.9	13.7	15.5
Italy	13.5	20.2	13.4	20.3	United Kingdom.	16.7	16.2	16.5	16.4
Japan	13.5	22.2	13.3	22.6	United States.	20.2	12.8	20.1	13.0
Kazakhstan	21.8	7.9	21.6	7.6	Uzbekistan	28.1	4.9	27.3	4.7
Kenya	42.3	2.6	42.3	2.7	Venezuela	30.5	5.2	30.0	5.3
Korea, North.	21.3	9.4	20.9	9.6	Vietnam	26.1	5.6	25.6	5.5
Korea, South	16.8	10.8	16.2	11.1	Yemen.	43.9	2.6	43.5	2.6
Madagascar	43.5	3.0	43.3	3.0					

[1] See footnote 4, Table 1296. [2] See footnote 5, Table 1296.

Source: U.S. Census Bureau, "International Data Base" (published June 2009); <http://www.census.gov/ipc/www/idb/>.

International Statistics 821

Table 1299. Births to Unmarried Women by Country: 1980 to 2007

[Percent of all live births]

Country	1980	1990	2000	2004	2005	2006	2007
United States [1]	18.4	28.0	33.2	35.8	36.9	38.5	39.7
Canada	12.8	24.4	28.3	25.6	25.6	27.1	(NA)
Japan	0.8	1.1	1.6	2.0	2.0	2.1	(NA)
Denmark.	33.2	46.4	44.6	45.4	45.7	46.4	46.1
France	11.4	30.1	43.6	47.4	48.4	50.5	51.7
Germany [2]	(NA)	15.1	23.4	27.9	29.2	30.0	30.8
Ireland	5.9	14.6	31.5	31.9	32.0	33.2	(NA)
Italy	4.3	6.5	9.7	(NA)	15.2	16.2	(NA)
Netherlands	4.1	11.4	24.9	32.5	34.9	37.1	39.5
Spain	3.9	9.6	17.7	25.1	26.6	28.4	(NA)
Sweden	39.7	47.0	55.3	55.4	55.4	55.5	54.8
United Kingdom . . .	11.5	27.9	39.5	42.3	42.9	43.7	(NA)

NA Not available. [1] Marital status is inferred from a comparison of the child's and parents' surnames on the birth certificate for those states that do not report on marital status. No estimates are included for misstatements on birth records or failures to register births. [2] Data are for 1991 instead of 1990.
Source: U.S. Bureau of Labor Statistics, updated and revised from "Families and Work Transition in 12 Countries 1980–2001," *Monthly Labor Review*, September 2003, with national sources, some of which may be unpublished.

Table 1300. Marriage and Divorce Rates by Country: 1980 to 2007

[Per 1,000 population aged 15–64 years]

Country	Marriage rate				Divorce rate			
	1980	1990	2000	2007	1980	1990	2000	2007
United States [1]	15.9	14.9	12.5	10.9	7.9	7.2	6.2	5.4
Canada.	11.5	10.0	7.5	6.6	3.7	4.2	3.4	(NA)
Japan.	9.8	8.4	9.3	(NA)	1.8	1.8	3.1	(NA)
Denmark.	8.0	9.1	10.8	10.2	4.1	4.0	4.0	3.9
France	9.7	7.7	7.9	6.6	2.4	2.8	3.0	(NA)
Germany [2]	(NA)	8.2	7.6	6.8	(NA)	2.5	3.5	(NA)
Ireland [3]	10.9	8.3	7.6	(NA)	(NA)	(NA)	1.0	(NA)
Italy	8.7	8.2	7.3	6.4	0.3	0.7	1.0	1.3
Netherlands.	9.6	9.3	8.2	6.7	2.7	2.8	3.2	2.9
Spain	9.4	8.6	7.9	6.5	(NA)	0.9	1.4	(NA)
Sweden	7.1	7.4	7.0	8.0	3.7	3.5	3.8	3.4
United Kingdom	11.6	10.0	8.0	(NA)	4.1	4.1	4.0	(NA)

NA Not available. [1] Divorce rates exclude data for California, Georgia, Hawaii, Indiana, Louisiana, and Minnesota in 2007. [2] Data are for 1991 instead of 1990. [3] Divorce not allowed by law prior to 1997.
Source: U.S. Bureau of Labor Statistics, updated and revised from "Families and Work in Transition in 13 Countries, 1980–2001," *Monthly Labor Review*, September 2003, with national sources, some of which may be unpublished.

Table 1301. Single-Parent Households: 1980 to 2008

[In thousands (6,061 represents 6,061,000), except for percent. For the United Kingdom in 1981, children are defined as those under 15 and those who are 15, 16, or 17 and attended school full-time; for later years, children are defined as those under 16 and those who are 16 or 17 and attend school full-time. For Ireland, children are defined as those under 15. For France, children are defined as those under 25. For Canada for 2001 onward and for Germany for 1995 onward, children are of all ages. For Germany in 1991 and for all other countries, except Denmark in 2008, children are defined as children living at home, or away at school, under 18. In Denmark in 2008, children are defined as those under 25. Data are generally for the entire year, but in some instances they are only for a particular month within the year]

Country and year	Number (1,000)	Percent of all households with children	Country and year	Number (1,000)	Percent of all households with children
United States:			**Germany:**		
1980	6,061	19.5	1991	1,429	15.2
1990	7,752	24.0	1995 [1]	2,496	18.8
2000	9,357	27.0	2000 [1]	2,274	17.6
2007	10,600	28.8	2007	2,579	21.1
Canada:			**Ireland:** [2]		
1981	437	12.7	1981	30	7.2
1991 [1]	572	16.2	1991	44	10.7
2001 [1]	1,184	23.5	2002	50	17.4
2006	1,276	24.6	2006	78	22.6
Japan:			**Netherlands:**		
1980	796	4.9	1988	179	9.6
1990	934	6.5	2000	240	13.0
2000	996	8.3	2008	305	15.7
2005	1,163	10.2	**Sweden:**		
Denmark: [2]			1985	117	11.2
1980	99	13.4	1995 [1]	189	17.4
1990	117	17.8	2000	233	21.4
2001 [1]	120	18.4	2006	225	20.7
2008 [1]	161	21.3	**United Kingdom:** [3]		
France:			1981	1,010	13.9
1982	887	10.2	1991	1,344	19.4
1990	1,175	13.2	2000	1,434	20.7
1999	1,494	17.4	2008	1,750	25.0
2005 [1]	1,725	19.8			

[1] Break in series. [2] Data are from family-based, rather than household-based, statistics. [3] Great Britain only (excludes Northern Ireland).
Source: U.S. Bureau of Labor Statistics, updated and revised from "Families and Work in Transition in 12 Countries, 1980–2001," *Monthly Labor Review*, September 2003, with national sources, some of which may be unpublished.

Table 1302. **Percent Distribution of Households by Type and Country: 1980 to 2008**

[Data are generally for the entire year, but in some instances they are only for a particular month within the year]

Year	Total	Married-couple households [1]			Single parent [2]	One person	Other [3]
		Total	With children [2]	Without children [2]			
United States:							
1980	100.0	60.8	30.9	29.9	7.5	22.7	9.0
1990	100.0	56.0	26.3	29.8	8.3	24.6	11.0
1995	100.0	54.4	25.5	28.9	9.1	25.0	11.5
2000	100.0	52.8	24.1	28.7	8.9	25.5	12.7
2007	100.0	50.8	22.5	28.3	9.1	26.8	13.2
Canada:							
1981	100.0	66.8	36.3	30.5	5.3	20.3	7.6
1991	100.0	62.8	29.6	33.2	5.7	22.9	8.6
2001 [4]	100.0	58.5	33.4	25.2	10.2	25.7	5.5
2006	100.0	57.4	31.4	26.1	10.3	26.8	5.5
Japan:							
1980	100.0	68.4	42.9	25.6	2.2	19.8	9.5
1990	100.0	65.2	33.1	32.1	2.3	23.1	9.4
1995	100.0	62.8	27.4	35.4	2.0	25.6	9.6
2000	100.0	60.3	23.6	36.7	2.1	27.6	10.0
2005	100.0	57.6	20.8	36.8	2.4	29.5	10.5
Denmark: [5]							
1980	100.0	50.3	25.0	25.3	3.9	44.9	1.0
1990	100.0	45.6	19.5	26.1	4.2	49.6	0.6
1995	100.0	44.9	18.2	26.6	4.2	50.4	0.5
2001	100.0	45.7	18.5	27.2	4.2	49.6	0.6
2008 [4]	100.0	47.7	21.4	26.4	5.8	45.9	0.6
France:							
1982	100.0	67.5	39.8	27.7	4.5	24.6	3.4
1990	100.0	64.0	35.9	28.1	5.5	27.1	3.4
1999	100.0	59.3	29.9	29.4	6.3	31.0	3.4
2005 [4]	100.0	56.4	27.2	29.2	6.7	32.8	4.1
Germany:							
1991	100.0	55.3	31.6	23.7	7.1	33.6	4.0
1995	100.0	53.3	29.2	24.0	6.8	34.9	5.1
2000 [4]	100.0	56.8	28.0	28.8	6.0	36.1	1.2
2005	100.0	54.7	25.5	29.1	6.4	37.5	1.4
2007	100.0	53.4	24.3	29.1	6.5	38.7	1.4
Ireland:							
1981	100.0	(NA)	(NA)	(NA)	(NA)	16.9	(NA)
1991	100.0	61.6	47.9	13.7	10.6	20.2	7.6
1996	100.0	59.6	44.5	15.1	11.2	21.5	7.7
2002	100.0	59.2	41.4	17.7	11.7	21.6	7.6
2006	100.0	57.3	37.4	20.0	11.6	22.4	8.7
Netherlands:							
1988	100.0	64.7	37.3	27.4	5.4	28.7	1.2
1993	100.0	63.1	33.3	29.9	5.0	30.9	1.0
2000	100.0	60.2	30.6	29.6	5.6	33.4	0.7
2005	100.0	58.5	29.4	29.1	6.3	34.5	0.7
2007	100.0	57.7	28.7	28.9	6.4	35.3	0.7
2008	100.0	57.4	28.4	29.0	6.4	35.5	0.7
Sweden:							
1985	100.0	54.8	23.8	31.0	3.2	36.1	5.9
1990	100.0	52.1	21.9	30.2	3.9	39.6	4.4
1995 [4]	100.0	50.7	21.2	29.4	4.6	42.3	2.4
2000	100.0	45.8	19.1	26.7	5.3	46.5	2.3
2006	100.0	45.6	18.8	26.9	5.0	46.5	2.9
United Kingdom: [6]							
1981	100.0	65.0	31.0	34.0	5.0	22.0	8.0
1991	100.0	61.0	25.0	36.0	6.0	27.0	6.0
1994–95	100.0	58.0	25.0	33.0	7.0	27.0	8.0
2000	100.0	58.0	23.0	35.0	6.0	29.0	7.0
2008	100.0	56.0	21.0	35.0	7.0	30.0	7.0

NA Not available. [1] May include unmarried cohabiting couples. Such couples are explicitly included under married couples in Canada, Denmark, Ireland, France, the Netherlands, Sweden, and the United Kingdom. In Germany, cohabitants are grouped with married couples beginning in 2000. In other countries, some unmarried cohabitants are included as married couples, while some are classified under "other households." [2] Children are defined as unmarried children living at home according to the following age limits: under 18 years old in the United States, Canada (1981–96), Japan, Denmark (1980–2007), Sweden, and the United Kingdom, except that the United Kingdom includes 15-, 16-, and 17-year-olds in 1981 and 16- and 17-year-olds thereafter only if they are attending school full-time; under 25 years old in France and in Denmark in 2008; and children of all ages in Canada (2001 onward), Germany, Ireland, and the Netherlands. [3] Includes both family and nonfamily households not elsewhere classified. These households comprise, for example, siblings residing together, where households composed of relatives, and households made up of roommates. Some unmarried cohabiting couples may also be included in the "other" group. See footnote 1. [4] Break in series. [5] From family-based statistics. However, one person living alone constitutes a family in Denmark. In this respect, the Danish data are closer to household statistics. [6] Great Britain only (excludes Northern Ireland).

Source: U.S. Bureau of Labor Statistics, updated and revised from "Families and Work in Transition in 12 Countries, 1980–2001," *Monthly Labor Review*, September 2003, with national sources, some of which may be unpublished.

Table 1303. **Births, Deaths, and Life Expectancy by Country or Area: 2009 and 2010**

[Covers countries with 12 million or more population in 2009]

Country or area	Crude birth rate [1]		Crude death rate [2]		Expectation of life at birth (years)		Infant mortality rate [3]		Total fertility rate per woman [4]	
	2009	2010, proj.	2009	2010, proj.	2009	2010, proj.	2009	2010, proj.	2009	2010, proj.
United States......	13.8	13.8	8.4	8.4	78.1	78.2	6.2	6.1	2.05	2.06
Afghanistan	38.4	38.1	17.8	17.7	44.4	44.7	153.1	151.5	5.60	5.50
Algeria..........	16.9	16.7	4.6	4.7	74.0	74.3	27.7	26.8	1.79	1.76
Angola..........	43.7	43.3	24.1	23.7	38.2	38.5	180.2	178.1	6.12	6.05
Argentina........	17.9	17.8	7.4	7.4	76.6	76.8	11.4	11.1	2.35	2.33
Australia.........	12.5	12.4	6.7	6.8	81.6	81.7	4.8	4.7	1.78	1.78
Bangladesh	24.7	23.8	9.2	9.1	60.3	60.6	59.0	57.8	2.74	2.65
Brazil...........	18.4	18.1	6.4	6.4	72.0	72.3	22.6	21.9	2.21	2.19
Burkina Faso	44.3	44.0	13.3	13.0	53.0	53.3	84.5	83.0	6.28	6.21
Burma..........	17.0	16.7	9.1	9.1	63.4	63.8	47.6	46.2	1.89	1.86
Cambodia........	25.7	25.8	8.1	8.0	62.1	62.5	54.8	53.0	3.04	3.00
Cameroon	34.1	33.6	12.2	12.0	53.7	54.0	63.3	62.2	4.33	4.25
Canada	10.3	10.3	7.7	7.9	81.2	81.3	5.0	5.0	1.58	1.58
Chile	14.6	14.5	5.8	5.9	77.3	77.5	7.7	7.5	1.92	1.90
China [5]	14.0	14.3	7.1	7.1	73.5	73.8	20.3	19.4	1.79	1.80
Colombia........	18.1	17.8	5.2	5.2	74.1	74.3	17.4	16.9	2.22	2.18
Congo (Kinshasa) [6]..	42.6	42.3	11.6	11.4	54.4	54.7	81.2	79.4	6.20	6.11
Cote d'Ivoire......	32.1	31.5	10.8	10.4	55.5	56.2	68.1	66.4	4.12	4.01
Ecuador.........	20.8	20.3	5.0	5.0	75.3	75.5	20.9	20.3	2.51	2.46
Egypt	25.4	25.0	4.9	4.9	72.1	72.4	27.3	26.2	3.05	3.01
Ethiopia.........	43.7	43.3	11.6	11.3	55.4	55.8	80.8	79.0	6.12	6.07
France..........	12.6	12.4	8.6	8.7	81.0	81.1	3.3	3.3	1.98	1.97
Germany	8.2	8.2	10.9	11.0	79.3	79.4	4.0	4.0	1.41	1.42
Ghana..........	28.7	28.1	9.1	8.9	60.1	60.6	51.2	49.9	3.68	3.57
Guatemala	28.0	27.4	5.1	5.0	70.3	70.6	27.8	26.9	3.47	3.36
India...........	21.7	21.3	7.6	7.5	66.1	66.5	50.8	49.1	2.68	2.65
Indonesia........	18.8	18.5	6.3	6.3	70.8	71.1	30.0	28.9	2.31	2.28
Iran............	17.2	17.3	5.7	5.8	71.1	71.4	35.8	34.7	1.71	1.70
Iraq............	30.1	29.4	5.0	4.9	70.0	70.3	44.7	43.2	3.86	3.76
Italy...........	8.2	8.0	10.7	10.8	80.2	80.3	5.5	5.4	1.31	1.32
Japan	7.6	7.4	9.5	9.8	82.1	82.2	2.8	2.8	1.21	1.20
Kazakhstan	16.6	16.7	9.4	9.4	67.9	68.2	25.7	24.9	1.88	1.87
Kenya..........	36.6	35.1	9.7	9.3	57.9	58.8	54.7	53.5	4.56	4.38
Korea, North......	14.8	14.6	10.5	10.6	63.8	64.1	51.3	50.2	1.96	1.94
Korea, South	8.9	8.7	5.9	6.2	78.7	78.8	4.3	4.2	1.21	1.22
Madagascar	38.1	37.9	8.1	8.0	62.9	63.3	54.2	52.8	5.14	5.09
Malawi..........	41.7	41.3	14.2	13.7	50.0	50.9	86.0	83.5	5.59	5.51
Malaysia	22.2	22.1	5.0	5.0	73.3	73.6	15.9	15.4	2.95	2.92
Mali............	46.4	46.1	15.0	14.6	51.8	52.2	115.9	113.7	6.62	6.54
Mexico..........	19.7	19.4	4.8	4.8	76.1	76.3	18.4	17.8	2.34	2.31
Morocco.........	19.7	19.4	4.7	4.7	75.5	75.7	29.8	28.6	2.27	2.23
Mozambique......	38.0	37.8	20.1	19.8	41.2	41.4	105.8	103.8	5.18	5.13
Nepal	23.2	22.4	7.0	6.9	65.5	65.8	47.5	46.0	2.64	2.53
Netherlands	10.4	10.3	8.7	8.8	79.4	79.6	4.7	4.7	1.66	1.66
Niger...........	51.6	51.1	14.8	14.5	52.6	53.0	116.7	114.5	7.75	7.68
Nigeria..........	36.7	36.1	16.6	16.3	46.9	47.2	94.4	93.0	4.91	4.82
Pakistan.........	25.9	25.1	7.2	7.1	65.3	65.6	67.4	65.3	3.43	3.28
Peru	19.4	19.0	6.1	6.1	70.7	71.0	28.6	27.7	2.37	2.32
Philippines	26.0	25.7	5.1	5.1	71.1	71.4	20.6	19.9	3.27	3.23
Poland..........	10.0	10.0	10.1	10.1	75.6	75.9	6.8	6.7	1.28	1.29
Romania	10.5	10.4	11.9	11.9	72.5	72.7	22.9	22.1	1.39	1.40
Russia..........	11.1	11.1	16.1	16.0	66.0	66.2	10.6	10.3	1.41	1.41
Saudi Arabia......	28.6	28.2	2.5	2.5	76.3	76.5	11.6	11.2	3.83	3.77
Senegal.........	36.8	36.4	9.8	9.6	59.0	59.4	58.9	57.7	4.95	4.86
South Africa	19.9	19.6	17.0	17.0	49.0	49.2	44.4	43.8	2.38	2.33
Spain	9.7	9.5	10.0	10.1	80.1	80.2	4.2	4.2	1.31	1.32
Sri Lanka	16.3	15.9	6.1	6.2	75.1	75.3	18.6	18.1	1.99	1.96
Sudan	33.7	33.3	12.9	12.3	51.4	52.5	82.4	78.1	4.48	4.37
Syria	25.0	24.4	3.7	3.7	74.2	74.5	16.7	16.1	3.12	3.02
Taiwan [5]........	9.0	9.0	6.8	6.9	78.0	78.2	5.4	5.3	1.14	1.15
Tanzania	34.3	33.4	12.6	12.3	52.0	52.5	69.3	68.1	4.46	4.31
Thailand.........	13.4	13.2	7.1	7.2	73.1	73.4	17.5	16.9	1.65	1.65
Turkey..........	18.7	18.3	6.1	6.1	72.0	72.2	25.8	24.8	2.21	2.18
Uganda	47.8	47.6	12.1	11.9	52.7	53.0	64.8	63.7	6.77	6.73
Ukraine.........	9.6	9.6	15.8	15.7	68.3	68.5	9.0	8.7	1.26	1.27
United Kingdom.....	10.7	10.7	10.0	10.0	79.0	79.2	4.9	4.8	1.66	1.66
Uzbekistan	17.6	17.5	5.3	5.3	72.0	72.2	23.4	22.7	1.95	1.92
Venezuela	20.6	20.3	5.1	5.1	73.6	73.8	21.5	21.1	2.48	2.45
Vietnam.........	17.7	17.3	6.0	6.0	71.7	71.9	22.3	21.6	1.98	1.93
Yemen..........	35.3	34.4	7.5	7.2	63.0	63.4	58.4	56.8	5.00	4.81

[1] Number of births during 1 year per 1,000 persons (based on midyear population).   [2] Number of deaths during 1 year per 1,000 persons (based on midyear population).   [3] Number of deaths of children under 1 year of age per 1,000 live births in a calendar year.   [4] Average number of children that would be born if all women lived to the end of their childbearing years and, at each year of age, they experienced the birth rates occurring in the specified year.   [5] See footnote 4, Table 1296.   [6] See footnote 5, Table 1296.

Source: U.S. Census Bureau, "International Data Base" (published June 2009); <http://www.census.gov/ipc/www/idb/>.

Table 1304. **Life Expectancy at Birth and at Age 65 by Sex—Selected Countries: 1990 and 2006**

Country	Life expectancy at birth				Life expectancy at age 65			
	Females		Males		Females		Males	
	1990	2006	1990	2006	1990	2006	1990	2006
United States [1]	78.8	80.2	71.8	75.1	18.9	19.7	15.1	17.0
Australia.	80.1	83.5	73.9	78.7	19.0	21.5	15.2	18.3
Austria	78.8	82.7	72.2	77.1	17.8	20.6	14.3	17.2
Belgium	79.5	82.3	72.7	76.6	18.8	20.6	14.3	17.0
Canada	80.8	(NA)	74.4	(NA)	19.9	(NA)	15.7	(NA)
Czech Republic	75.5	79.9	67.6	73.5	15.3	18.3	11.7	14.8
Denmark.	77.8	80.7	72.0	76.1	17.9	19.2	14.0	16.2
Finland.	79.0	83.1	71.0	75.9	17.8	21.2	13.8	16.9
France	80.9	84.4	72.8	77.3	19.8	22.6	15.5	18.2
Germany	78.5	82.4	72.0	77.2	17.7	20.5	14.0	17.2
Greece.	79.5	82.0	74.6	77.1	18.0	19.6	15.7	17.4
Hungary	73.7	77.4	65.1	69.0	15.3	17.2	12.0	13.4
Iceland.	80.5	83.0	75.4	79.4	19.5	20.6	16.2	18.3
Ireland	77.7	82.1	72.1	77.3	17.0	20.2	13.3	16.8
Italy	80.4	(NA)	73.9	(NA)	18.9	(NA)	15.1	(NA)
Japan	81.9	85.8	75.9	79.0	20.0	23.4	16.2	18.5
Korea, South.	75.5	82.4	67.3	75.7	16.3	20.1	12.4	16.1
Mexico	74.1	78.1	68.3	73.2	18.0	18.8	16.2	17.2
Netherlands	80.1	81.9	73.8	77.6	18.9	20.1	14.4	16.7
New Zealand.	78.4	82.2	72.5	78.1	18.3	20.7	14.6	18.1
Norway.	79.9	82.9	73.4	78.2	18.7	20.9	14.6	17.7
Poland	75.2	79.6	66.2	70.9	16.1	18.8	12.4	14.5
Portugal	77.5	82.3	70.6	75.5	17.1	20.2	14.0	16.6
Slovakia	75.4	78.2	66.6	70.4	15.7	17.1	12.2	13.3
Spain.	80.6	84.4	73.4	77.7	19.3	22.0	15.5	17.9
Sweden	80.4	82.9	74.8	78.7	19.0	20.8	15.3	17.6
Switzerland.	80.9	84.2	74.0	79.2	19.7	22.1	15.3	18.5
Turkey	68.3	74.0	63.8	69.1	13.9	15.1	12.4	13.1
United Kingdom	78.5	(NA)	72.9	(NA)	17.9	(NA)	14.0	(NA)

NA Not available. [1] Source of 2006 life expectancy data: U.S. National Center for Health Statistics, *National Vital Statistics Reports, Deaths: Final Data for 2006*, Vol. 57, No. 14, 17 April 2009 and unpublished data.
Source: Organization for Economic Cooperation and Development, Paris, France, *OECD Health Data 2008* (copyright). See also <http://www.oecd.org/health/healthdata>.

Table 1305. **People Infected With HIV and AIDS-Related Deaths by Region: 2001 and 2007**

[In thousands (29,000 represents 29,000,000). Estimates are based on ranges, called 'plausibility bounds,' which reflect the certainty associated with each estimate and define the boundaries within which the actual numbers lie]

Region	Adults and children living with HIV		Adults and children newly infected with HIV		Adult prevalence (percent)		Adult and child deaths due to AIDS	
	2001	2007	2001	2007	2001	2007	2001	2007
Total.	29,000	33,200	3,200	2,500	0.8	0.8	1,700	2,100
Sub-Saharan Africa	20,900	22,500	2,200	1,700	5.8	5.0	1,400	1,600
North Africa and Middle East	300	380	41	35	0.3	0.3	22	25
South and South-East Asia	3,500	4,000	450	340	0.3	0.3	170	270
East Asia	420	800	77	92	(Z)	0.1	12	32
Oceania	26	75	4	14	0.2	0.4	(Z)	1,200
Latin America	1,300	1,600	130	100	0.4	0.5	51	58
Caribbean.	190	230	20	17	1.0	1.0	14	11
Eastern Europe and Central Asia .	630	1,600	230	150	0.4	0.9	8	55
Western and Central Europe	620	760	32	31	0.2	0.3	10	12
North America	1,100	1,300	44	46	0.6	0.6	21	21

Z Less than 0.1 percent or 500 deaths.
Source: Joint United Nations Programme on HIV/AIDS (UNAIDS) and World Health Organization (WHO), *AIDS Epidemic Update: December 2007* (copyright). See also <http://data.unaids.org/pub/EPISlides/2007/2007_epiupdate_en.pdf>.

Table 1306. **Percentage of the Adult Population Considered to Be Obese: 2006**

[Obesity rates are defined as the percentage of the population with a Body Mass Index (BMI) over 30 kg/m^2. The BMI is a single number that evaluates an individual's weight status in relation to height (weight/height^2, with weight in kilograms and height in meters). For Australia, the United Kingdom, and the United States, figures are based on health examinations, rather than self-reported information. Obesity estimates derived from health examinations are generally higher and more reliable than those coming from self-reports because they preclude any misreporting of people's height and weight. However, health examinations are only conducted regularly in a few countries. For more information on methods by country, see <http://www.irdes.fr/EspaceAnglais/home.html>]

Country	2006	Country	2006	Country	2006
United States	34.3	France	10.5	Luxembourg	[3]18.6
Australia	[1]21.7	Germany.	[3]13.6	Mexico	30.0
Austria	12.4	Greece	[4]21.9	New Zealand	[4]25.0
Belgium	[2]12.7	Hungary	[4]18.8	Norway.	[3]9.0
Canada	[3]18.0	Ireland	[5]13.0	Spain	14.9
Czech Republic	[3]17.0	Italy	10.2	Sweden	[3]10.7
Denmark.	[3]11.4	Japan.	[2]3.9	Switzerland	[5]7.7
Finland.	14.3	Korea, South	[3]3.5	United Kingdom	24.0

[1] 1999 data. [2] 2004 data. [3] 2005 data. [4] 2003 data. [5] 2002 data.
Source: Organization for Economic Cooperation and Development, Paris, France, *OECD Factbook*, 2009 (copyright). See also <http://www.oecd.org>.

International Statistics   825

Table 1307. **Daily Tobacco Consumption by Country and Sex: 1990 and 2006**

[**Smokers as percent of population**. Includes tobacco forms consumed by smoking only]

Country	Total		Females		Males	
	1990	2006	1990	2006	1990	2006
United States	25.5	16.7	22.8	14.5	28.4	19.0
Australia.	(NA)	(NA)	(NA)	(NA)	(NA)	(NA)
Canada	28.2	(NA)	26.7	(NA)	29.8	(NA)
Denmark.	44.5	(NA)	42.0	(NA)	47.0	(NA)
Finland.	25.9	21.4	20.0	18.9	32.4	24.4
France	30.0	25.0	20.0	21.0	38.0	30.0
Greece.	38.5	(NA)	26.0	(NA)	51.0	(NA)
Iceland.	30.3	19.3	29.9	17.4	30.8	21.3
Ireland	30.0	(NA)	29.0	(NA)	31.0	(NA)
Italy	27.8	23.0	17.8	17.2	37.8	29.2
Japan	37.4	26.3	14.3	12.4	60.5	41.3
Luxembourg	(NA)	21.0	(NA)	18.0	(NA)	24.0
Netherlands	37.0	31.0	32.0	26.0	43.0	36.0
New Zealand.	28.0	20.7	27.0	19.5	28.0	21.9
Norway.	35.0	24.0	33.0	24.0	36.0	24.0
Poland	(NA)	(NA)	(NA)	(NA)	(NA)	(NA)
Sweden	25.8	(NA)	25.9	(NA)	25.8	(NA)
United Kingdom	30.0	22.0	30.0	21.0	31.0	23.0

NA Not available.

Source: Organization for Economic Cooperation and Development, Paris, France, *OECD Health Data 2008* (copyright). See also <http://www.oecd.org>.

Table 1308. **Road Fatalities by Country: 1990 to 2007**

[Per million inhabitants]

Country	1990	2000	2005	2006	2007	Country	1990	2000	2005	2006	2007
EU-27 [1]	(NA)	117	91	87	(NA)	Italy	123	115	94	89	86
United States [2]	188	149	147	143	136	Japan	90	93	70	65	52
Australia	137	95	81	78	77	Korea, South	(NA)	218	132	(NA)	127
Austria	179	122	94	89	83	Luxembourg	188	172	101	78	90
Belgium	199	143	104	102	100	Mexico	66	53	46	47	51
Canada.	150	95	91	(NA)	83	Netherlands	92	73	50	50	48
Chile	120	110	100	101	99	New Zealand	217	121	99	95	100
Czech Republic	125	145	126	104	118	Norway	79	76	49	52	49
Denmark [3].	123	93	61	56	74	Poland	192	163	143	138	147
Estonia	(NA)	169	126	126	146	Portugal	267	186	118	104	81
Finland	130	76	72	64	72	Russia	238	203	237	230	235
France [4]	182	129	88	77	75	Slovakia	137	120	111	113	122
Germany.	126	91	65	62	60	Slovenia	259	157	129	130	145
Greece	171	193	150	149	141	Spain	179	143	89	94	85
Hungary	235	118	127	130	123	Sweden	90	67	49	49	51
Iceland	96	113	64	104	48	Switzerland	141	82	55	50	51
India.	50	77	87	92	(NA)	Turkey	124	58	62	62	68
Ireland	139	110	84	87	77	United Kingdom	97	62	55	55	50
Israel [5]	92	73	65	59	55						

NA Not available. [1] See footnote 2, Table 1336. [2] As of July 1. [3] As of January 1. [4] Data on January 1 of the following year. [5] For technical reasons, data include the Golan Heights, East Jerusalem, and Israeli settlements in the West Bank.

Source: Organization for Economic Cooperation and Development, Paris, France, *OECD Factbook 2009* (copyright). See also <http://www.oecd.org/>.

Table 1309. **Suicide Rates by Sex and Country: 2004**

[Per 100,000 persons. Data are for 2004 or latest available year]

Country	Total	Men	Women	Country	Total	Men	Women
OECD average . . .	11.9	19.0	5.4	Italy	5.6	9.3	2.4
United States	10.2	17.0	3.9	Japan.	20.3	30.5	10.4
Australia	11.1	17.6	4.7	Korea, South	18.7	28.1	11.1
Austria	14.5	24.0	6.4	Luxembourg	12.5	20.2	5.5
Belgium	18.4	28.0	9.8	Mexico	3.8	7.0	1.0
Canada.	10.6	16.7	4.6	Netherlands	7.9	11.1	4.9
Czech Republic	13.0	22.6	4.4	New Zealand	12.0	20.2	4.2
Denmark.	11.3	16.8	6.3	Norway	10.5	15.8	5.3
Finland	18.4	28.9	8.5	Poland	13.6	24.2	3.9
France	15.1	23.4	7.8	Portugal	8.7	14.6	3.8
Germany.	10.3	16.3	4.8	Slovakia	11.9	22.0	3.1
Greece	2.9	4.7	1.1	Spain	6.7	10.7	3.1
Hungary	22.6	39.0	8.9	Sweden	11.4	17.0	6.0
Iceland	8.7	13.2	4.2	Switzerland	16.3	23.9	9.6
Ireland	11.1	18.2	4.0	United Kingdom	6.3	10.0	2.8

Source: Organization for Economic Cooperation and Development, Paris, France, *OECD Factbook 2009* (copyright). See also <http://www.oecd.org/>.

Table 1310. **Health Expenditures as Percent of GDP by Country: 1980 to 2006**

[In percent. GDP = gross domestic product; for explanation, see text, Section 13]

Country	Total health expenditures					Public health expenditures				
	1980	1990	2000	2005	2006	1980	1990	2000	2005	2006
United States	8.7	11.9	13.2	15.2	15.3	3.7	4.7	5.9	7.0	7.0
Australia	6.3	6.9	8.3	8.8	8.7	3.9	4.6	5.5	5.9	5.9
Austria	7.5	8.4	9.9	10.3	10.1	5.1	5.3	6.5	6.8	7.7
Belgium	6.3	7.2	8.6	10.6	10.3	5.2	6.4	6.6	7.3	7.2
Canada	7.0	8.9	8.8	9.9	10.0	5.1	6.6	6.2	6.8	7.0
Czech Republic	(NA)	4.7	6.5	7.1	6.8	(NA)	4.6	5.9	6.3	6.0
Denmark	8.9	8.3	8.3	9.5	9.5	5.5	4.7	5.1	5.9	8.0
Finland	6.3	7.7	7.0	8.3	8.2	5.0	6.2	5.1	6.2	6.2
France . . , ...	7.0	8.4	10.1	11.1	11.0	5.6	6.4	7.3	7.8	8.8
Germany [1]	8.4	8.3	10.3	10.7	10.6	6.8	6.5	7.7	7.7	8.1
Greece	5.9	6.6	7.8	9.0	9.1	3.3	3.5	4.7	5.6	5.6
Hungary	(NA)	(NA)	6.9	8.5	8.3	(NA)	(NA)	4.9	6.0	5.9
Iceland	6.3	7.8	9.5	9.4	9.1	(NA)	5.8	6.5	6.3	7.5
Ireland	8.3	6.1	6.3	8.2	7.5	6.8	4.4	4.6	6.5	5.9
Italy	(NA)	7.7	8.1	8.9	9.0	5.5	6.1	5.8	6.8	6.9
Japan	6.5	6.0	7.7	8.2	8.1	4.6	4.6	5.9	6.3	6.5
Korea, South	3.4	4.0	4.5	5.9	6.4	(NA)	1.6	2.2	3.2	3.5
Luxembourg	5.2	5.4	5.8	7.8	7.3	4.8	5.0	5.2	7.0	6.6
Mexico	(NA)	4.8	5.6	6.4	6.6	(NA)	2.0	2.6	2.9	2.9
Netherlands	7.4	8.0	8.0	(NA)	(NA)	5.1	5.4	5.0	6.0	7.6
New Zealand	5.9	6.9	7.7	(NA)	(NA)	5.2	5.7	6.0	6.9	7.3
Norway	7.0	7.6	8.4	9.1	8.7	4.9	4.3	4.9	5.8	7.3
Poland	(NA)	4.8	5.5	6.2	6.2	(NA)	4.4	3.9	4.3	4.3
Portugal	5.3	5.9	8.8	10.2	10.2	3.4	3.8	6.4	(NA)	7.2
Slovakia	(NA)	(NA)	5.5	7.1	7.4	(NA)	(NA)	4.9	5.3	5.1
Spain	5.3	6.5	7.2	8.3	8.4	4.2	5.1	5.2	5.8	6.0
Sweden	8.9	8.2	8.2	9.2	9.2	8.2	7.4	6.3	6.8	7.5
Switzerland	7.3	8.2	10.3	11.4	11.3	3.5	3.9	5.1	6.1	6.8
Turkey	3.3	3.6	4.9	5.7	(NA)	0.9	2.2	(NA)	5.4	(NA)
United Kingdom	5.6	6.0	7.2	8.2	8.4	4.9	4.9	5.8	7.0	7.3

NA Not available.   [1] Data prior to 1991 are for former West Germany.

Source: Organization for Economic Cooperation and Development, Paris, France, *OECD Health Data 2008* (copyright). See also <http://www.oecd.org>.

Table 1311. **Medical Doctors and Inpatient Care—Selected Countries: 2000 to 2006**

Country	Medical doctors per 1,000 population			Acute inpatient care					
				Beds per 1,000 population			Average length of stay (days)		
	2000	2005	2006	2000	2005	2006	2000	2005	2006
United States	2.3	2.4	2.4	2.9	2.7	2.7	5.8	5.6	5.6
Australia	2.5	2.8	[1]2.8	3.6	3.5	[1]3.5	6.1	6.0	[1]6.0
Austria	3.1	3.5	3.6	6.3	6.1	6.1	6.9	5.9	5.8
Belgium	3.9	4.0	4.0	4.7	4.4	4.3	7.7	7.7	[1]7.7
Canada	2.1	2.1	2.1	3.2	2.8	[1]2.8	7.2	7.2	[1]7.2
Czech Republic	3.4	3.6	3.6	5.9	5.5	5.4	8.7	8.0	7.8
Denmark	2.9	3.3	[1]3.3	3.5	3.1	3.0	3.8	3.5	[1]3.5
Finland	2.8	2.7	2.7	3.4	3.1	3.1	5.0	4.8	[1]4.8
France	3.3	3.4	3.4	4.1	3.7	3.7	5.6	5.4	5.4
Germany	3.3	3.4	3.5	6.8	6.4	6.2	9.7	8.7	8.5
Greece	4.3	5.0	[1]5.0	3.8	3.9	[1]3.9	6.2	[2]5.7	[2]5.7
Hungary	3.1	2.8	3.0	5.8	5.5	5.5	7.1	6.3	6.1
Iceland	3.4	3.7	3.7	(NA)	(NA)	(NA)	6.1	5.4	5.5
Ireland	2.2	2.8	2.9	2.8	2.8	[1]2.8	6.4	6.6	[1]6.6
Italy	4.1	3.8	3.7	4.1	3.3	3.3	7.0	6.7	[1]6.7
Japan	1.9	(NA)	2.1	9.6	8.2	8.2	24.8	19.8	19.2
Korea, South	1.3	1.6	1.7	5.2	6.6	6.8	11.0	(NA)	(NA)
Luxembourg	2.1	2.5	2.8	(NA)	4.6	4.6	7.5	7.3	7.4
Mexico	1.6	1.8	1.9	1.0	1.0	1.0	4.0	4.0	3.9
Netherlands	3.2	3.7	3.8	3.1	3.1	3.0	7.7	6.8	6.6
New Zealand	2.2	2.1	2.3	(NA)	(NA)	(NA)	(NA)	(NA)	(NA)
Norway	2.9	3.7	3.7	3.1	3.0	3.0	6.0	5.2	5.0
Poland	2.2	2.1	2.2	5.2	4.7	4.7	8.9	6.5	6.1
Portugal	3.1	3.4	[1]3.4	3.2	3.0	[1]3.0	7.7	7.1	[1]7.1
Slovakia	3.1	(NA)	[2]3.1	5.8	5.0	4.9	8.5	7.3	7.2
Spain	3.2	3.8	3.6	2.8	2.5	[1]2.5	7.1	6.7	[1]6.7
Sweden	3.1	3.5	[1]3.5	2.4	2.2	2.2	5.0	4.6	4.6
Switzerland	3.5	3.8	3.8	4.1	3.6	3.5	9.3	8.5	8.2
Turkey	1.3	1.5	1.6	2.2	2.5	2.5	5.4	(NA)	(NA)
United Kingdom	1.9	2.4	2.5	2.4	2.3	2.2	8.2	7.8	7.5

NA Not available.   [1] 2005 data. [2] 2004 data.

Source: Organization for Economic Cooperation and Development, Paris, France, *OECD Health Data 2008* (copyright). See also <http://www.oecd.org>.

U.S. Census Bureau, Statistical Abstract of the United States: 2010

Table 1312. Gross National Income (GNI) by Country: 2000 and 2007

[49 represents $49,000,000,000. GNI measures the total domestic and foreign value added claimed by residents. GNI comprises GDP plus net receipts of primary income (compensation of employees and property income) from nonresident sources]

Country	Gross national income [1]				GNI on purchasing power parity basis [2]			
	Total (bil. dol.)		Per capita (dol.)		Total (bil. dol.)		Per capita (dol.)	
	2000	2007	2000	2007	2000	2007	2000	2007
Algeria	49	122	1,610	3,620	156	259	5,120	7,640
Argentina	276	239	7,470	6,040	327	512	8,860	12,970
Australia	397	751	20,710	35,760	477	702	24,920	33,400
Bangladesh	50	75	360	470	115	211	830	1,330
Belarus	14	41	1,380	4,220	51	104	5,120	10,750
Belgium	260	437	25,360	41,110	289	375	28,150	35,320
Brazil	674	1,122	3,870	5,860	1,187	1,776	6,810	9,270
Bulgaria	13	35	1,600	4,580	48	85	6,000	11,100
Burkina Faso	3	6	240	430	9	16	790	1,120
Cambodia	4	8	300	550	11	25	860	1,720
Cameroon	10	19	620	1,050	24	39	1,520	2,120
Canada	681	1,307	22,130	39,650	850	1,171	27,630	35,500
Chile [3]	75	136	4,840	8,190	137	205	8,910	12,330
China [3]	1,169	3,126	930	2,370	2,940	7,151	2,330	5,420
Colombia	91	180	2,280	4,100	221	363	5,550	8,260
Congo (Kinshasa) [4]	4	9	80	140	10	18	210	290
Cote d'Ivoire	11	18	630	920	25	31	1,450	1,620
Czech Republic	60	151	5,800	14,580	150	235	14,640	22,690
Ecuador	16	42	1,340	3,110	54	95	4,430	7,110
Egypt	97	119	1,460	1,580	250	405	3,760	5,370
Ethiopia	8	18	130	220	30	62	460	780
France	1,482	[5]2,467	24,450	[5]38,810	1,554	2,089	26,380	33,860
Germany	2,097	3,207	25,510	38,990	2,110	2,858	25,670	34,740
Ghana	6	14	320	590	18	31	870	1,320
Greece	137	288	12,560	25,740	201	312	18,440	27,830
Guatemala	19	33	1,730	2,450	39	60	3,470	4,520
Hong Kong	177	219	26,570	31,560	177	304	26,530	43,940
Hungary	48	117	4,660	11,680	120	176	11,730	17,470
India	458	1,071	450	950	1,528	3,083	1,500	2,740
Indonesia	122	373	590	1,650	462	804	2,240	3,570
Iran	107	251	1,670	3,540	434	770	6,790	10,840
Italy	1,190	1,988	20,890	33,490	1,445	1,793	25,370	30,190
Japan	4,393	4,829	34,620	37,790	3,288	4,440	25,910	34,750
Kazakhstan	19	78	1,270	5,020	67	149	4,480	9,600
Kenya	13	24	420	640	35	58	1,130	1,550
Korea, South	461	956	9,800	19,730	769	1,204	16,370	24,840
Madagascar	4	6	240	320	12	18	750	930
Malawi	2	4	150	250	7	11	610	760
Malaysia	80	170	3,450	6,420	194	351	8,350	13,230
Mexico	501	989	5,110	9,400	877	1,464	8,950	13,910
Montenegro	(NA)	3	(NA)	5,270	4	7	6,230	11,780
Morocco	38	71	1,340	2,290	73	125	2,570	4,050
Mozambique	4	7	230	330	8	16	420	730
Nepal	5	10	220	350	20	30	800	1,060
Netherlands	423	748	26,580	45,650	478	647	30,000	39,470
Niger	2	4	170	280	6	9	500	630
Nigeria	33	136	270	920	141	261	1,130	1,760
Pakistan	68	140	490	860	233	413	1,690	2,540
Peru	53	95	2,080	3,410	123	201	4,810	7,200
Philippines	80	142	1,050	1,620	189	326	2,480	3,710
Poland	176	375	4,570	9,850	400	591	10,410	15,500
Portugal	119	201	11,590	18,950	170	231	16,650	21,790
Romania	38	138	1,690	6,390	126	266	5,610	12,350
Russia	250	1,070	1,710	7,530	1,086	2,036	7,430	14,330
Saudi Arabia	168	374	8,140	15,470	361	554	17,490	22,950
Senegal	5	10	490	830	13	21	1,220	1,650
Serbia [6]	11	33	1,470	4,540	45	73	6,000	9,830
Singapore	93	148	22,970	32,340	132	220	32,740	47,950
South Africa	134	274	3,050	5,720	284	452	6,460	9,450
Spain	621	1,314	15,420	29,290	850	1,380	21,120	30,750
Sri Lanka	16	31	880	1,540	50	84	2,660	4,200
Sudan	11	37	330	950	37	73	1,120	1,880
Sweden	260	438	29,280	47,870	244	343	27,500	37,490
Switzerland	289	459	40,280	60,820	244	335	34,020	44,410
Syria	16	35	960	1,780	52	88	3,150	4,430
Tanzania	9	16	260	410	26	49	750	1,200
Thailand	122	217	2,010	3,400	303	503	4,990	7,880
Turkey	265	593	3,930	8,030	580	947	8,600	12,810
Uganda	6	11	260	370	17	32	670	1,040
Ukraine	34	119	700	2,560	156	317	3,170	6,810
United Kingdom	1,501	(NA)	25,480	(NA)	1,507	(NA)	25,590	(NA)
United States	**9,709**	**13,886**	**34,410**	**46,040**	**9,931**	**13,827**	**35,190**	**45,840**
Uzbekistan	15	20	630	730	35	65	1,420	2,430
Venezuela	100	208	4,100	7,550	203	338	8,360	12,290
Vietnam	30	65	390	770	108	215	1,390	2,530
Yemen	7	19	400	870	31	49	1,710	2,200
Zimbabwe	6	(NA)	450	(NA)	(NA)	(NA)	(NA)	(NA)

NA Not available. [1] Gross national income calculated using the World Bank Atlas method; for details, see source. [2] For explanation of Purchasing Power Parity, see headnote, Table 1313. [3] See footnote 4, Table 1296. [4] See footnote 5, Table 1296. [5] Include the French overseas departments of French Guiana, Guadeloupe, Martinique, and Reunion. [6] See footnote 4, Table 1367.

Source: The World Bank, Washington, DC, *World Development Indicators,* annual (copyright).

Table 1313. **Real GDP per Capita and per Employed Persons by Country:**
1990 to 2007

[U.S. figures based on the System of National Income and Product Accounts (NIPA) from the Bureau of Economic Analysis. All other countries, based on the 1993 United Nations System of National Accounts. Per capita data based on total resident population. Real GDP is a macroeconomic measure of the size of an economy adjusted for price changes and inflation. Employment data include people serving in the armed forces for some countries. Real dollars are calculated based on 2005 Purchasing Power Parities (PPPs). PPPs are currency conversion rates used to convert GDPs expressed in different currencies to a common value (U.S. dollars in this case). A PPP for a given country is the number of national currency units needed to buy the specific basket of goods and services that one dollar will buy in the United States. See text, this section]

Country	Real GDP per capita (2005 U.S. dollars)				Real GDP per employed person (2005 U.S. dollars)			
	1990	2000	2006	2007	1990	2000	2006	2007
United States	32,125	39,277	42,751	43,267	66,445	80,198	87,601	88,540
Canada	27,056	32,562	35,660	36,243	56,929	67,417	70,356	70,589
Australia	23,995	30,022	33,391	34,154	51,541	63,612	67,521	68,228
Japan	25,936	28,600	31,046	31,696	49,961	55,630	61,789	62,788
Korea, South	10,628	17,489	22,364	23,399	25,194	38,860	46,655	48,386
Austria	26,456	32,618	35,027	36,065	52,473	63,394	68,604	69,419
Belgium	22,336	30,296	32,759	33,607	57,528	75,877	81,036	81,092
Denmark	25,708	31,987	34,739	35,213	50,653	62,953	68,258	68,231
France	24,348	28,357	30,250	30,724	61,951	70,800	75,392	76,012
Germany	(NA)	29,738	31,407	32,228	(NA)	62,440	66,181	66,718
Italy	23,553	27,458	28,205	28,434	59,087	68,187	66,815	67,026
Netherlands	26,132	33,503	35,715	36,783	61,617	67,954	70,828	71,532
Norway	32,322	43,921	48,420	49,606	66,588	85,037	92,761	92,494
Spain	19,535	24,696	27,342	28,079	50,919	58,661	58,790	59,279
Sweden	24,916	29,364	33,798	34,457	46,539	60,649	69,639	69,973
United Kingdom	23,141	28,604	32,306	33,191	49,002	61,061	67,215	68,783

NA Not available.

Source: U.S. Bureau of Labor Statistics, "Comparative Real Gross Domestic Product per Capita and per Employed Person, Sixteen Countries, 1960–2007," published 7 July 2008; <http://www.bls.gov/fls/flsgdp.pdf>.

Table 1314. **Average Annual Percent Changes in International Economic**
Composite Indexes by Country: 1990 to 2008

[**Change from previous year**; derived from indexes with base 2000 = 100. The coincident index changes are for calendar years and the leading index changes are for years ending June 30 because they lead the coincident indexes by about 6 months, on average. The G-7 countries are United States, Canada, France, Germany, Italy, United Kingdom, and Japan. Minus sign (−) indicates decrease]

Country	Leading index						Coincident index					
	1990	2000	2005	2006	2007	2008	1990	2000	2005	2006	2007	2008
Total, 13 countries	2.1	6.3	4.6	4.8	3.3	0.3	4.5	5.0	2.4	4.0	3.3	−1.6
12 countries, excluding U.S.	3.8	7.7	5.7	5.1	4.4	0.7	6.8	5.4	2.1	4.6	4.7	0.3
G-7 countries	2.0	6.0	4.6	4.7	3.2	−0.2	4.5	4.8	2.2	3.9	3.2	−1.8
North America	−0.9	4.1	2.8	4.3	1.5	−0.3	−0.2	4.8	2.7	3.0	1.1	−4.4
United States	−1.0	3.9	2.8	4.2	1.4	0.5	−0.1	4.4	2.7	3.0	0.7	−4.9
Canada	−1.1	7.1	3.1	5.1	3.9	3.2	−1.7	9.7	3.5	3.7	5.2	−0.1
Four European countries	1.8	4.4	5.0	4.8	4.2	0.9	5.9	9.8	1.4	5.9	7.1	1.8
France	1.5	1.5	6.8	5.9	2.4	−0.6	5.7	14.4	2.0	4.4	6.1	−0.4
Germany	4.5	6.2	6.7	6.7	6.5	1.8	7.2	7.9	−1.3	5.8	8.4	4.9
Italy	0.2	7.2	2.7	4.4	5.0	−2.0	9.3	16.2	4.2	10.8	8.6	−1.2
United Kingdom	−0.3	2.5	1.8	0.4	1.6	4.3	0.9	4.0	3.3	3.7	4.8	2.0
Seven Pacific region countries . .	6.1	11.2	6.5	5.4	4.6	0.3	8.1	1.2	2.7	3.4	2.4	−1.2
Australia	−1.4	8.2	3.1	2.8	1.2	4.7	−0.4	5.1	4.7	4.6	6.5	2.2
Taiwan [1]	4.9	8.5	6.7	5.2	4.9	2.7	5.1	4.9	4.3	3.4	3.0	−1.0
Thailand	12.1	9.5	5.7	5.8	3.8	6.7	11.6	9.4	6.5	2.7	2.5	3.1
Japan	6.6	11.3	7.0	5.1	4.6	−1.3	8.6	−0.5	2.3	3.1	1.8	−1.9
Korea, South	6.5	15.9	7.1	11.9	7.5	9.9	9.9	13.7	4.3	5.8	5.6	3.1
Malaysia	5.0	19.8	9.0	7.9	8.2	12.7	9.1	11.1	2.9	4.6	3.3	0.3
New Zealand	0.8	4.6	2.7	2.1	3.1	1.1	−1.2	2.7	5.1	1.8	4.3	−1.9

[1] See footnote 4, Table 1296.

Source: Foundation for International Business and Economic Research, New York, NY, *International Economic Indicators*, monthly.

U.S. Census Bureau, Statistical Abstract of the United States: 2010

Table 1315. **Sectoral Contributions to Gross Value Added: 1996 and 2006**

[In percent. According to the 1993 System of National Accounts (SNA) and the International Standard Industrial Classification (ISIC), Revision 3. Value added is estimated at basic prices and includes financial intermediation services indirectly measured (FISIM). It represents an industry's contribution to national GDP and is calculated as the difference between production and intermediate inputs. Value added comprises labor costs, consumption of fixed capital, indirect taxes less subsidies, and net operating surplus and mixed income]

| Country | Agriculture | | Industry | | | | | | Services | |
| | | | Total | | Manufacturing | | | | | |
	1996	2006	1996	2006	1996	2006			1996	2006
United States [1]	1.8	1.1	25.9	22.4	[2]16.2	12.2			72.2	76.5
Australia	3.7	2.3	27.6	28.7	14.2	11.2			68.8	69.0
Austria	2.4	1.7	30.8	30.2	19.5	20.1			66.8	68.2
Belgium	1.6	0.9	28.0	[2]24.2	20.0	16.9			70.4	74.9
Canada	3.0	[3]2.2	30.9	[3]31.7	18.0	[3]16.2			66.1	[3]66.1
Czech Republic	4.7	2.6	41.8	38.2	26.3	26.3			53.5	59.2
Denmark	3.4	1.6	25.4	26.0	16.5	[4]14.2			71.2	72.5
Finland	4.0	2.5	32.0	32.4	24.3	23.7			64.0	65.1
France	3.3	2.1	24.1	20.7	16.0	12.6			73.1	77.3
Germany	1.3	0.9	31.2	29.4	22.2	22.7			67.4	69.8
Greece	8.2	3.7	21.3	24.3	[5]11.1	13.2			70.2	72.0
Hungary [1]	8.3	[4]4.1	29.8	[5]30.1	[5]23.5	22.5			62.5	65.8
Iceland [1]	10.8	[4]5.8	27.8	[4]23.7	[6]16.4	[4]10.1			61.3	[4]70.5
Ireland	6.4	1.7	36.9	34.9	29.3	23.3			56.7	63.4
Italy	3.3	2.1	29.7	26.8	21.8	18.3			67.0	71.1
Japan [7]	1.9	1.4	33.0	29.1	22.4	20.7			65.2	69.5
Korea	6.0	3.3	41.3	39.6	26.7	28.0			52.8	57.1
Luxembourg	0.9	0.4	20.2	14.6	12.5	7.9			78.9	85.1
Mexico	5.9	[3]3.8	27.7	[3]26.0	21.0	[3]17.9			66.3	[3]70.2
Netherlands	3.3	2.2	26.9	[3]24.1	16.8	13.3			69.8	73.7
New Zealand [8]	7.2	[9]6.5	25.8	[9]24.0	17.3	[9]15.2			67.0	[9]69.5
Norway	2.6	1.5	36.6	45.0	12.3	9.7			60.7	53.5
Poland	7.6	4.3	33.6	31.2	19.9	18.9			58.9	64.5
Portugal	5.5	2.9	28.9	24.3	19.0	[4]14.7			65.6	72.8
Slovakia	5.5	4.0	39.1	35.0	26.0	21.9			55.4	61.1
Spain	5.1	2.9	29.1	30.4	18.6	16.1			65.8	66.7
Sweden	2.6	1.4	29.3	28.5	21.7	20.0			68.1	70.1
Switzerland	1.9	1.2	29.1	27.7	20.0	19.9			69.1	71.2
Turkey	12.6	9.4	36.7	28.2	27.2	19.5			50.6	62.4
United Kingdom	1.7	0.9	30.6	22.9	20.5	12.6			67.7	76.2

[1] Value added is estimated at factor cost.   [2] 1998.   [3] 2004.   [4] 2005.   [5] 2000.   [6] 1997.   [7] Value added is estimated approximately at market prices.   [8] Value added is estimated at producer's prices.   [9] 2003.

Source: Organization for Economic Cooperation and Development, Paris, France, *OECD in Figures*, 2008 (copyright). See also <http://www.oecd.org/>.

Table 1316. **Index of Industrial Production by Country: 1980 to 2008**

[Annual averages of monthly data. Industrial production index measures output in the manufacturing, mining, electric, gas, and water utilities industries. Minus sign (–) indicates decrease]

| Country | Index (2005 = 100) | | | | | | | | Annual percent change | | | | |
	1990	1995	2000	2004	2005	2006	2007	2008	2000–2001	2004–2005	2005–2006	2006–2007	2007–2008
OECD, total	73.3	78.7	95.3	97.7	100.0	103.7	106.8	104.9	-2.3	2.3	3.7	3.0	-1.8
Australia	75.6	82.2	95.5	98.3	100.0	100.4	103.8	106.5	0.3	1.7	0.4	3.3	2.6
Austria	59.6	64.4	85.3	95.9	100.0	107.8	113.8	114.9	3.0	4.3	7.8	5.6	1.0
Belgium [1]	82.7	83.2	96.2	100.3	100.0	105.1	107.9	107.3	-1.0	-0.3	5.1	2.6	-0.5
Canada	68.4	77.9	99.1	98.3	100.0	99.8	99.7	95.1	-4.0	1.8	-0.2	-0.1	-4.6
Czech Republic [1]	89.9	67.9	74.9	96.2	100.0	108.3	119.8	117.7	10.0	3.9	8.3	10.6	-1.8
Denmark	71.9	82.0	96.5	96.7	100.0	103.2	102.2	101.7	1.2	3.4	3.2	-0.9	-0.5
Finland	55.3	63.5	91.2	99.9	100.0	109.6	114.4	113.5	0.7	0.1	9.6	4.4	-0.7
France	88.5	88.5	99.9	99.8	100.0	100.9	102.4	100.1	0.9	0.2	0.9	1.5	-2.2
Germany [2]	85.7	82.5	93.9	96.3	100.0	106.2	113.5	113.8	0.4	3.8	6.2	6.9	0.2
Greece	83.7	82.1	100.6	100.8	100.0	100.6	102.6	100.9	-1.8	-0.8	0.6	2.0	-1.7
Hungary [1]	51.9	45.6	76.0	93.6	100.0	109.9	118.5	118.5	3.5	6.8	9.9	7.9	(Z)
Ireland	24.2	38.9	78.4	97.1	100.0	105.1	112.7	111.6	10.0	3.0	5.1	7.2	-1.0
Italy	90.2	96.9	104.2	100.8	100.0	103.6	105.8	102.3	-1.1	-0.8	3.6	2.1	-3.3
Japan [1]	96.9	94.0	98.4	98.6	100.0	104.3	107.2	103.8	-6.3	1.4	4.3	2.8	-3.2
Korea, South [1]	31.7	47.9	74.3	94.0	100.0	108.4	115.9	119.5	0.6	6.3	8.4	6.9	3.1
Luxembourg	66.5	68.1	83.7	98.6	100.0	102.1	101.9	96.3	3.1	1.4	2.1	-0.3	-5.5
Mexico [3]	67.2	70.2	99.8	97.2	100.0	105.7	108.3	107.6	-3.5	2.8	5.7	2.5	-0.7
Netherlands	77.9	84.4	95.2	99.6	100.0	101.5	103.8	105.3	0.5	0.4	1.5	2.2	1.5
New Zealand	74.4	85.0	89.7	102.3	100.0	98.6	100.7	99.7	-0.2	-2.3	-1.4	2.2	-1.0
Norway	74.2	93.7	104.5	100.0	100.0	97.8	96.7	97.1	-0.7	(Z)	-2.2	-1.2	0.5
Poland	47.3	53.6	77.0	96.1	100.0	112.0	122.5	125.8	0.4	4.1	12.0	9.3	2.7
Portugal	93.3	90.7	107.1	103.6	100.0	103.1	103.0	98.6	3.1	-3.5	3.1	(-Z)	-4.2
Spain	79.1	82.0	97.8	99.3	100.0	103.9	106.0	98.4	-1.5	0.7	3.9	2.1	-7.3
Sweden [4,5]	64.3	77.0	92.4	97.8	100.0	103.6	107.7	104.5	-0.4	2.2	3.6	3.9	-2.9
Switzerland	78.3	81.4	99.0	97.4	100.0	107.7	118.1	119.6	-0.7	2.7	7.7	9.7	1.3
Turkey	57.1	66.8	81.0	96.6	100.0	107.8	115.3	114.3	-8.7	3.5	7.8	6.9	-0.9
United Kingdom	91.4	96.6	104.4	101.7	100.0	100.1	100.5	97.5	-1.4	-1.7	0.1	0.4	-3.0
United States	65.0	75.0	96.7	96.8	100.0	102.3	103.8	101.5	-3.4	3.3	2.3	1.5	-2.2

Z Less than .05 percent.   [1] Not adjusted for unequal number of working days in the month.   [2] Data prior to 1991 are for former West Germany.   [3] Including construction.   [4] Mining and manufacturing.   [5] Annual figures correspond to official annual figures and differ from the average of the monthly figures.

Source: Organization for Economic Cooperation and Development, Paris, France, *Main Economic Indicators*, monthly (copyright). See also <http://www.oecd.org>.

830   International Statistics

Table 1317. **Selected Indexes of Manufacturing Activity by Country: 1990 to 2007**

[**1996 = 100**. Data relate to employees (wage and salary earners) in Belgium, and to all employed persons (employees, self-employed workers, and unpaid family workers) in the other countries. Minus sign (−) indicates decrease. For explanation of average annual percent change, see Guide to Tabular Presentation]

Index	United States	Can- ada	Japan	Bel- gium	France	Ger- many [1]	Italy	Nether- lands	Nor- way	Swe- den	United King- dom
Output per hour:											
1990	80.1	85.2	81.3	84.7	84.2	86.1	82.5	81.4	96.8	73.9	87.8
1995	96.2	100.5	95.6	98.6	99.7	97.3	99.5	97.9	97.1	96.8	101.0
2000	126.1	121.1	113.0	110.9	124.5	116.5	106.7	115.2	104.2	134.8	115.4
2005	162.2	126.6	139.6	127.0	148.7	137.1	106.4	135.8	131.2	184.7	141.9
2006	169.9	129.3	141.0	131.8	154.6	148.6	105.9	140.2	128.5	202.0	149.1
2007	177.8	132.8	145.8	137.6	158.5	155.9	105.4	144.0	128.2	203.0	153.0
Average annual percent change:											
1995–2000	5.6	3.8	3.4	2.4	4.6	3.7	1.4	3.3	1.4	6.8	2.7
2005–2006	4.7	2.2	1.0	3.7	4.0	8.4	−0.4	3.2	−2.0	9.4	5.1
2006–2007	4.7	2.7	3.5	4.4	2.6	4.9	−0.5	2.8	−0.2	0.5	2.6
Compensation per hour, national currency basis: [2]											
1990	82.7	82.4	83.0	81.4	78.9	72.3	70.5	78.8	81.2	77.4	82.8
1995	98.1	98.5	99.2	98.2	98.1	95.5	94.9	98.1	96.0	92.8	100.3
2000	123.2	113.6	105.1	108.5	112.8	111.3	108.1	115.9	123.5	117.2	126.2
2005	150.5	135.5	106.8	129.0	134.4	122.4	127.4	140.3	156.2	143.6	163.2
2006	156.7	139.7	105.6	133.7	140.9	127.4	129.9	144.2	165.8	147.8	173.7
2007	162.2	144.6	105.4	140.7	145.0	129.5	132.7	148.5	173.7	154.8	174.9
Average annual percent change:											
1995–2000	4.7	2.9	1.2	2.0	2.8	3.1	2.7	3.4	5.2	4.8	4.7
2005–2006	4.1	3.1	−1.1	3.6	4.9	4.1	2.0	2.8	6.1	2.9	6.4
2006–2007	3.5	3.6	−0.2	5.3	2.9	1.6	2.1	2.9	4.8	4.8	0.7
Real hourly compensation: [3]											
1990	96.7	93.5	88.9	93.8	90.6	85.3	94.0	92.0	92.4	94.9	100.3
1995	100.7	100.0	99.3	100.3	100.2	96.8	98.7	100.1	97.1	93.9	102.8
2000	112.7	105.5	103.7	102.0	108.3	106.0	99.7	106.4	111.6	113.7	113.2
2005	121.4	112.2	107.6	109.2	117.0	108.1	104.2	113.9	124.4	129.2	129.8
2006	122.4	113.3	106.2	111.2	121.0	110.7	104.1	115.7	134.2	130.2	133.9
2007	123.3	114.7	105.9	115.0	122.4	110.1	104.4	117.2	139.6	133.9	129.3
Average annual percent change:											
1995–2000	2.3	1.1	0.9	0.3	1.6	1.8	0.2	1.2	2.8	3.9	1.9
2005–2006	0.8	1.0	−1.3	1.8	3.4	2.4	−0.1	1.6	3.7	0.8	3.2
2006–2007	0.7	1.2	−0.3	3.4	1.2	−0.5	0.3	1.3	4.0	2.8	−3.4
Unit labor costs, national currency: [2]											
1990	103.3	96.7	102.1	96.1	93.7	84.0	85.4	96.8	83.9	104.8	94.3
1995	102.0	98.0	103.8	99.6	98.5	98.2	95.3	100.3	98.9	95.8	99.4
2000	97.7	93.8	93.0	97.9	90.0	95.5	101.4	100.6	118.5	86.9	109.4
2005	92.8	107.1	76.5	101.5	90.4	89.3	119.8	103.3	119.1	77.8	115.1
2006	92.2	108.0	74.9	101.4	91.2	85.8	122.6	102.9	129.0	73.2	116.6
2007	91.2	108.9	72.3	102.3	91.5	83.1	125.8	103.1	135.5	76.3	114.3
Average annual percent change:											
1995–2000	−0.8	−0.9	−2.2	−0.4	−1.7	−0.5	1.2	0.1	3.7	−1.9	1.9
2005–2006	−0.6	0.9	−2.0	−0.1	0.9	−4.0	2.4	−0.4	8.3	−5.9	1.3
2006–2007	−1.1	0.8	−3.6	0.8	0.3	−3.1	2.6	0.2	5.0	4.2	−1.9
Unit labor costs, U.S. dollar basis: [2, 4]											
1990	103.3	113.1	76.6	89.1	88.0	78.2	110.0	89.6	86.6	118.7	107.8
1995	102.0	97.4	120.2	104.7	101.0	103.2	90.2	105.4	100.8	90.0	100.5
2000	97.7	86.1	93.9	69.4	65.2	67.8	74.6	71.1	86.9	63.6	106.3
2005	92.8	120.5	75.6	97.0	87.8	85.5	118.8	98.4	119.4	69.8	134.2
2006	92.2	129.9	70.1	97.8	89.3	82.9	122.7	98.9	130.0	66.6	137.7
2007	91.2	138.4	66.7	107.6	97.8	87.6	137.5	108.1	149.4	75.7	146.7
Average annual percent change:											
1995–2000	−0.8	−2.4	−4.8	−7.9	−8.4	−8.0	−3.7	−7.6	−2.9	−6.7	1.1
2005–2006	−0.6	7.8	−7.3	0.8	1.8	−3.1	3.3	0.5	8.9	−4.7	2.6
2006–2007	−1.1	6.5	−4.8	10.1	9.5	5.7	12.0	9.3	15.0	13.8	6.5
Employment:											
1990	102.6	105.9	109.2	113.2	114.6	118.7	111.5	109.9	96.7	119.7	113.5
1995	100.1	98.3	100.9	101.5	101.0	102.8	101.2	101.2	98.5	100.2	98.9
2000	99.9	109.6	91.2	98.5	99.4	98.7	100.0	101.6	99.3	101.1	92.9
2005	82.6	105.6	80.1	90.1	90.5	91.4	99.7	90.1	87.6	91.5	73.5
2006	82.2	102.8	81.4	89.0	88.7	90.7	100.6	89.6	92.0	90.8	71.5
2007	80.8	99.3	81.8	88.2	87.6	91.8	101.5	89.7	96.6	91.3	69.9
Average annual percent change:											
1995–2000	0.0	2.2	−2.0	−0.6	−0.3	−0.8	−0.2	0.1	0.2	0.2	−1.2
2005–2006	−0.6	−2.7	1.5	−1.1	−1.9	−0.8	0.9	−0.6	5.0	−0.8	−2.7
2006–2007	−1.7	−3.4	0.5	−0.9	−1.3	1.2	0.9	0.2	5.0	0.6	−2.2
Aggregate hours:											
1990	100.7	104.1	115.9	114.1	115.8	124.6	112.2	109.6	96.0	108.8	110.4
1995	100.2	98.3	100.4	101.0	100.6	105.0	100.9	100.7	99.0	100.0	98.3
2000	99.6	109.9	90.1	100.7	95.3	97.7	99.9	100.7	98.8	102.4	91.8
2005	80.9	105.0	79.6	89.0	84.7	89.2	96.4	89.0	88.4	93.0	73.3
2006	81.5	102.3	81.5	88.2	82.3	88.3	97.9	88.5	92.9	91.7	71.0
2007	80.1	98.7	81.6	86.7	81.2	89.3	99.4	88.9	98.0	93.4	69.6
Average annual percent change:											
1995–2000	−0.1	2.3	−2.1	−0.1	−1.1	−1.4	−0.2	–	–	0.5	−1.4
2005–2006	0.7	−2.5	2.4	−0.9	−2.8	−1.1	1.6	−0.5	5.1	−1.4	−3.1
2006–2007	−1.7	−3.5	0.2	−1.7	−1.3	1.2	1.5	0.4	5.5	1.8	−1.9

− Represents or rounds to zero.   [1] Data prior to 1991 are for the former West Germany.   [2] In Canada, France, Sweden, and the United Kingdom, compensation adjusted for employment taxes and government subsidies to estimate the actual labor cost to employers.   [3] 1996 = 100.Index of hourly compensation divided by the index of consumer prices to adjust for changes in purchasing power.   [4] Indexes in national currency adjusted for changes in prevailing exchange rates.

Source: U.S. Bureau of Labor Statistics, *International Comparisons of Manufacturing Productivity and Unit Labor Cost Trends 2007, Supplementary Tables 1950–2007* (published 3 March 2009). See also <http://www.bls.gov/ilc>.

International Statistics   831

Table 1318. **Indexes of Hourly Compensation Costs for All Employees in Manufacturing by Country: 2000 to 2007**

[United States = 100. Compensation costs include pay for time worked, other direct pay (including holiday and vacation pay, bonuses, other direct payments, and the cost of pay in kind), employer expenditures for legally required insurance programs and contractual and private benefit plans, and for some countries, other labor taxes. Data adjusted for exchange rates. Area averages are trade-weighted to account for difference in countries' relative importance to U.S. trade in manufactured goods. The trade weights used to compute the average compensation cost measures for selected economic groups are based on the relative dollar value of U.S. trade in manufactured commodities (exports plus imports) with each country or area in 2007; see source for detail]

Area or country	2000	2004	2005	2006	2007	Area or country	2000	2004	2005	2006	2007
United States	100	100	100	100	100						
Total [1]	68	79	80	82	88	Austria	100	123	124	128	141
OECD [2]	70	81	82	85	91	Belgium	89	114	113	116	127
Europe . . [3]	88	115	114	118	129	Czech Republic	14	23	24	27	32
Euro Area [3]	91	119	117	122	133	Denmark.	98	130	132	137	156
East Asia [4]	34	34	37	40	43	Finland	81	112	113	118	130
						France	88	109	108	112	123
Argentina	33	15	18	22	26	Germany.	119	152	147	154	166
Brazil	17	13	17	20	23	Hungary	14	26	27	28	34
Canada.	76	84	90	98	104	Ireland	66	98	99	103	117
Mexico	12	12	12	12	13	Italy	67	93	93	96	105
Australia	70	95	99	102	114	Netherlands.	85	118	117	118	129
Israel	52	47	47	48	52	Norway	106	145	150	157	180
Japan.	103	88	86	81	78	Poland	14	17	19	21	25
Korea, South	38	42	48	55	60	Portugal	22	31	31	31	34
New Zealand	38	52	56	54	63	Slovakia	11	18	20	22	28
Philippines.	4	3	4	4	4	Spain	50	69	69	72	80
Singapore	47	45	44	46	50	Sweden	89	113	110	114	127
Taiwan [5]	30	25	26	27	27	Switzerland	100	123	121	121	125
						United Kingdom	82	104	105	108	120

[1] Trade-weighted measure includes all 33 foreign economies. [2] Organization for Economic Cooperation and Development; see text of this section. [3] Euro area refers to European Union member countries that have adopted the Euro as the common currency as of 1 January 2009 (Austria, Belgium, Cyprus, Finland, France, Germany, Greece, Ireland, Italy, Luxembourg, Malta, Netherlands, Portugal, Slovakia, Slovenia, and Spain). [4] South Korea, the Philippines, Singapore, and Taiwan. [5] See footnote 4, Table 1296.

Source: U.S. Bureau of Labor Statistics, *International Comparisons of Hourly Compensation Costs in Manufacturing, 2007* (published 26 March 2009). See also <http://bls.gov/fls/>.

Table 1319. **Annual Percent Change in Labor Productivity and Hours Worked by Country: 1995 to 2008**

[Change for period shown. For OECD countries and Eastern Europe, labor productivity growth refers to the growth in gross domestic product per hour worked. Data are derived from an annual database maintained by the University of Groningen Growth and Development Centre at the University of Groningen, Netherlands, in association with The Conference Board. Growth for regional aggregates is calculated based on the sum of gross domestic product divided by the sum of total hours worked. Gross domestic product for each country was converted based on the 2005 OECD benchmark for purchasing power parities and updated to 2008 using the aggregate inflation rate for each country relative to U.S. inflation. Minus sign (−) indicates decrease]

Country	Labor productivity 1995–2000	Labor productivity 2000–2008	Total hours worked 1995–2000	Total hours worked 2000–2008	Country	Labor productivity 1995–2000	Labor productivity 2000–2008	Total hours worked 1995–2000	Total hours worked 2000–2008
All OECD.	2.0	1.7	1.3	0.5	European Union (EU-12, new) [3]	3.4	4.1	−0.2	0.6
All OECD, excl. United States	1.8	1.5	1.1	0.7	Bulgaria	1.0	3.1	0.1	2.4
United States	2.1	2.1	1.9	0.1	Cyprus	1.9	1.1	1.9	2.4
					Czech Republic	1.9	4.2	−0.4	0.1
European Union (EU-27, enlarged) [1] . .	2.1	1.5	0.8	0.6	Estonia.	7.8	5.0	−1.7	1.4
					Hungary	2.4	2.0	1.6	1.3
European Union (EU-15, old) [2]	1.7	1.2	1.1	0.6	Latvia.	5.9	5.6	−0.4	1.6
Austria	3.7	0.9	−0.7	1.2	Lithuania	4.6	5.8	0.1	1.5
Belgium	2.0	0.8	0.5	1.1	Malta	1.8	−0.3	1.0	2.3
Denmark.	1.1	0.3	1.7	1.0	Poland	5.5	3.0	−0.1	1.1
Finland	2.8	1.7	2.0	1.1	Romania	−0.6	7.5	−1.5	−1.2
France	2.1	1.0	0.7	0.6	Slovakia	4.9	5.2	−0.3	0.9
Germany.	2.0	1.2	(Z)	(Z)	Slovenia	4.8	3.3	−0.7	1.0
Greece	1.4	2.9	2.1	1.2	Other OECD members. .	1.5	1.7	1.2	0.6
Ireland	5.4	2.2	4.0	2.4	Japan.	1.7	1.7	−0.7	−0.4
Italy	1.1	(Z)	0.8	0.9	Australia	2.3	1.4	1.6	1.8
Luxembourg	2.6	0.7	3.4	2.8	Canada.	1.7	0.9	2.4	1.4
Netherlands.	1.8	1.3	2.3	0.6	Iceland	2.3	2.9	2.5	0.8
Portugal	1.5	1.2	0.4	−0.2	Mexico	0.8	0.7	4.6	1.6
Spain	−0.6	0.9	4.5	2.2	New Zealand	1.5	0.9	1.1	1.8
Sweden	2.5	1.8	0.8	0.6	Norway.	2.3	1.1	1.4	1.2
U.K.	2.4	2.2	1.0	0.2	South Korea	4.7	4.1	−0.4	0.3
					Switzerland	1.3	1.0	0.7	0.8
					Turkey	2.2	3.7	1.9	0.7

Z Less than .05 percent. [1] Referring to all members of the European Union as of 1 May 2004, and including Bulgaria and Romania, who joined on 1 January 2007. See footnote 2, Table 1336 for list of EU-27 countries. [2] Referring to membership of the European Union until 30 April 2004. See footnote 2, Table 1336 for list of EU-15 countries. [3] Referring to new membership of the European Union as of 1 May 2004, and including Bulgaria and Romania, who joined on 1 January 2007.

Source: The Conference Board, New York, NY, Total Economy Database. See <http://www.conference-board.org/economics /research.cfm> (June 2009). Reproduced with permission from The Conference Board, Inc. 2009, The Conference Board, Inc.

Table 1320. **Annual Percent Changes in Consumer Prices by Country: 2000 to 2008**

[**Change from previous year**. See text of this section for general comments concerning the data. For additional qualifications of the data for individual countries, see source. Minus sign (−) indicates decrease]

Country	2000	2005	2006	2007	2008	Country	2000	2005	2006	2007	2008
United States	3.4	3.4	3.2	2.9	3.8						
						Japan	−0.7	−0.3	0.2	0.1	1.4
Argentina.	−0.9	9.6	10.9	8.8	8.6	Kenya	10.0	10.3	14.5	9.8	26.2
Australia	4.5	2.7	3.5	2.3	4.4	Korea, South	2.2	2.8	2.3	2.5	4.7
Austria	2.4	2.3	1.4	2.2	3.2	Malaysia	1.5	3.0	3.6	2.0	5.4
Bangladesh	2.4	7.0	6.8	9.1	8.9	Mexico	9.5	4.0	3.6	4.0	5.1
Belgium.	2.5	2.8	1.8	1.8	4.5	Netherlands	2.5	1.7	1.2	1.6	2.5
Bolivia.	4.6	5.4	4.3	8.7	14.0	Nigeria	14.5	17.9	8.2	5.4	11.6
Brazil	7.0	6.9	4.2	3.6	5.7	Norway	3.1	1.5	2.3	0.7	3.8
Canada.	2.7	2.2	2.0	2.1	2.4	Pakistan	4.4	9.1	7.9	7.6	20.3
Chile.	3.8	3.1	3.4	4.4	8.7	Peru	3.8	1.6	2.0	1.8	6.6
Colombia.	9.2	5.0	4.3	5.5	7.0	Philippines	4.4	7.6	6.2	2.8	9.3
Ecuador	96.1	2.4	3.0	2.3	8.4	Portugal	2.8	2.3	2.7	2.8	2.6
Egypt	2.7	4.9	7.6	9.3	18.3	Romania	45.7	9.0	6.6	4.8	7.8
France	1.7	1.8	1.6	1.5	2.8	Russia.	20.8	12.7	9.7	9.0	14.1
Germany	1.5	1.6	1.6	2.3	2.6	South Africa	5.4	2.1	3.2	6.1	9.8
Ghana.	25.2	15.1	10.9	10.7	16.5	Spain	3.4	3.4	3.5	2.8	4.1
Greece	3.1	3.6	3.2	2.9	4.2	Sri Lanka.	6.2	11.6	10.0	15.8	(NA)
Guatemala.	6.0	8.6	5.8	8.7	6.7	Sweden.	0.9	0.5	1.4	2.2	3.5
India	4.0	4.2	5.8	6.4	8.3	Switzerland	1.5	1.2	1.1	0.7	2.4
Indonesia.	4.5	10.5	13.1	6.4	10.3	Thailand	1.6	4.5	4.6	2.2	5.4
Iran	14.5	13.4	11.9	17.2	25.5	Turkey.	54.9	10.1	10.5	8.8	10.4
Israel	1.1	1.3	2.1	0.5	4.6	United Kingdom	2.9	2.8	3.2	4.3	4.0
Italy	2.5	2.0	2.1	1.8	3.3	Venezuela	16.2	16.0	13.7	18.7	30.6

NA Not available.

Source: International Monetary Fund, Washington, DC, *International Financial Statistics*, monthly (copyright).

Table 1321. **Comparative Price Levels—Selected OECD Countries: 2009**

[Purchasing power parities (PPPs) are the rates of currency conversion that eliminate the differences in price levels between countries. Comparative price levels are defined as the ratios of PPPs to exchange rates. The PPPs are given in national currency units per U.S. dollar. The table is to be read vertically. Each column shows the number of specified monetary units needed in each of the countries listed to buy the same representative basket of consumer goods and services. In each case the representative basket costs a hundred units in the country whose currency is specified. Example of data: An item that costs $1.00 in the United States would cost $1.36 (U.S. dollars) in Japan]

Country	United States (U.S. dollar)	Canada (Canadian dollar)	Mexico (Mexican peso)	Japan (yen)	France (euro)	Germany (euro)	Italy (euro)	United Kingdom (pound)
United States	100	93	159	74	80	84	81	98
Australia [1]	115	107	183	84	92	96	93	113
Austria	119	111	190	88	96	100	97	117
Belgium	125	116	199	92	100	105	102	123
Canada.	107	100	171	79	86	90	87	105
Czech Republic	80	75	127	59	64	67	65	79
Denmark.	166	154	264	122	133	139	135	163
Finland	145	135	231	107	117	122	118	143
France	125	116	198	92	100	104	101	123
Germany.	119	111	190	88	96	100	97	117
Greece	107	100	171	79	86	90	87	106
Hungary	75	70	120	55	60	63	61	74
Iceland	105	98	167	77	84	88	85	103
Ireland	145	136	231	107	117	122	118	143
Italy	123	115	196	90	99	103	100	121
Japan.	136	127	217	100	109	114	111	134
Korea, South	72	67	115	53	58	60	59	71
Luxembourg	132	123	210	97	106	110	107	129
Mexico	63	59	100	46	50	53	51	62
Netherlands.	122	114	194	90	98	102	99	120
New Zealand [1]	98	92	157	72	79	82	80	97
Norway.	152	141	241	111	122	127	123	149
Poland	68	64	108	50	55	57	55	67
Portugal	99	93	158	73	80	83	81	98
Slovakia	88	82	140	65	70	74	71	86
Spain	109	102	174	80	88	91	89	107
Sweden	121	113	193	89	97	101	98	119
Switzerland	159	148	253	117	128	133	129	156
Turkey	79	74	127	58	64	67	65	78
United Kingdom	102	95	162	75	82	85	83	100

[1] Estimates based on quarterly consumer prices.

Source: Organization for Economic Cooperation and Development, Paris, France, *Main Economic Indicators*, May 2009 (copyright). See also <http://www.oecd.org/>.

U.S. Census Bureau, *Statistical Abstract of the United States: 2010*

Table 1322. Indexes of Living Costs Abroad: 2009

[As of January 2009. Washington, DC=100. Indexes compare the costs in dollars of representative goods and services (excluding housing and education) purchased at the foreign location and the cost of comparable goods and services in the Washington, DC area. The indexes are computed for private American employees and exclude special advantages that may be available only to U.S. Government employees. The indexes are place-to-place comparisons at specific times and currency exchange rates. They cannot be used for measuring cost changes over time at a foreign location. Since the indexes reflect only the expenditure pattern and living costs of American families, they should not be used to compare living costs of Americans in the United States with the living costs of foreign nationals living in their own country]

Country	City	Survey date	Living cost index [1]	Country	City	Survey date	Living cost index [1]
Algeria	Algiers	5/1/2007	115	Kenya	Nairobi	5/19/2008	143
Angola	Luanda	5/21/2008	190	Korea	Seoul	12/4/2007	176
Argentina	Buenos Aires	6/19/2008	95	Kuwait	Kuwait City	11/18/2007	132
Armenia	Yerevan	1/30/2007	138	Laos	Vientiane	12/30/2005	107
Australia	Canberra	5/23/2008	139	Latvia	Riga	05/302007	139
Austria	Vienna	3/11/2008	186	Lebanon	Beirut	4/23/2008	123
Azerbaijan	Baku	6/14/2007	145	Liberia	Monrovia	12/1/2007	135
Bahamas	Nassau	6/16/2008	144	Lithuania	Vilnius	9/25/2008	131
Bahrain	Bahrain	8/26/2007	123	Luxembourg		10/25/2007	160
Bangladesh	Dhaka	3/6/2006	88	Macedonia	Skopje	4/23/2007	135
Belarus	Minsk	3/15/2007	136	Madagascar	Antananarivo	1/23/2008	128
Belgium	Brussels	11/30/2007	191	Malaysia	Kuala Lumpur	8/24/2008	121
Belize	Belmopan	4/6/2008	132	Mexico	Mexico City	3/7/2007	123
Bolivia	La Paz	3/5/2007	84	Moldova	Chisinau	5/1/2008	115
Bosnia-Herzegovina	Sarajevo	1/3/2008	131	Mongolia	Ulaanbaatar	4/15/2008	114
Botswana	Gaborone	5/1/2006	111	Morocco	Rabat	3/13/2008	137
Brazil	Rio de Janeiro	12/22/2007	139	Mozambique	Maputo	1/2/2008	130
Bulgaria	Sofia	4/17/2008	135	Namibia	Windhoek	4/20/2006	122
Burma	Rangoon	3/4/2006	128	Nepal	Kathmandu	6/22/2007	103
Burundi	Bujumbura	1/15/2008	136	Netherlands	The Hague	4/27/2008	176
Cambodia	Phnom Penh	5/26/2008	118	New Zealand	Wellington	10/15/2007	157
Cameroon	Yaounde	3/27/2006	154	Nicaragua	Managua	4/15/2008	113
Canada	Montreal	1/12/2007	134	Niger	Niamey	3/25/2008	152
Central African Republic	Bangui	8/13/2008	189	Nigeria	Abuja	3/10/2008	148
Chad	Ndjamena	8/1/2006	152	Norway	Oslo	2/12/2007	187
Chile [2]	Santiago	3/31/2008	142	Oman	Muscat	1/13/2008	132
China [2]	Beijing	7/27/2007	130	Pakistan	Islamabad	12/10/2004	102
Colombia	Bogota	1/4/2008	109	Panama	Panama City	7/31/2008	119
Congo [3]	Brazzaville	(NA)	(NA)	Paraguay	Asuncion	1/16/2008	114
Costa Rica	San Jose	8/15/2006	108	Peru	Lima	12/7/2007	124
Cote d'Ivoire	Abidjan	12/10/2006	160	Philippines	Manila	4/16/2007	97
Croatia	Zagreb	3/22/2007	141	Poland	Warsaw	4/23/2008	140
Cuba	Havana	2/13/2008	145	Portugal	Lisbon	2/28/2008	148
Cyprus	Nicosia	2/26/2008	164	Qatar	Doha	8/15/2007	129
Czech Republic	Prague	9/15/2005	130	Romania	Bucharest	11/27/2006	125
Denmark	Copenhagen	6/28/2006	166	Russia	Moscow	12/20/2006	164
Djibouti	Djibouti City	4/10/2004	161	Rwanda	Kigali	2/25/2007	130
Ecuador	Quito	1/17/2005	126	Saudi Arabia	Riyadh	5/6/2008	120
Egypt	Cairo	3/13/2006	96	Serbia	Belgrade	4/21/2008	126
El Salvador	San Salvador	1/25/2007	108	Sierra Leone	Freetown	3/6/2008	141
Estonia	Tallinn	4/16/2008	141	Singapore		4/9/2007	140
Ethiopia	Addis Ababa	3/12/2008	120	Slovakia	Bratislava	5/31/2007	132
Finland	Helsinki	3/21/2007	179	South Africa	Johannesburg	10/23/2008	135
France	Paris	4/19/2007	190	Spain	Madrid	3/15/2008	169
Gabon	Libreville	5/2/2007	184	Sri Lanka	Colombo	4/9/2008	98
Georgia	Tbilisi	11/15/2007	143	Sudan	Khartoum	11/28/2007	139
Germany	Berlin	3/12/2008	179	Sweden	Stockholm	4/30/2008	204
Ghana	Accra	8/3/2008	134	Switzerland	Geneva	5/21/2008	235
Greece	Athens	7/20/2005	154	Syria [2,4]	Damascus	3/26/2008	96
Guatemala	Guatemala City	4/23/2007	116	Taiwan [2,4]	Taipei	3/6/2007	136
Guinea	Conakry	5/7/2007	151	Tajikistan	Dushanbe	3/19/2008	100
Guyana	Georgetown	3/12/2008	130	Tanzania	Dar es Salaam	11/15/2007	133
Haiti	Port-au-Prince	10/15/2007	120	Thailand	Bangkok	2/26/2008	126
Honduras	Tegucigalpa	6/10/2007	84	Timor Leste	Timor Leste	7/11/2007	128
Hong Kong		7/13/2007	154	Turkey	Istanbul	11/1/2007	156
Hungary	Budapest	6/30/2005	130	Turkmenistan	Ashgabat	10/31/2007	105
Iceland	Reykjavik	4/15/2008	182	Uganda	Kampala	3/1/2007	124
India	New Delhi	10/16/2006	97	Ukraine	Kyiv	10/13/2006	130
Indonesia	Jakarta	3/25/2008	112	United Arab Emirates	Dubai	4/15/2007	126
Ireland	Dublin	1/31/2008	175	United Kingdom	London	10/18/2006	183
Israel	Tel Aviv	4/6/2008	163	Uruguay	Montevideo	6/30/2005	117
Italy	Rome	2/27/2007	186	Uzbekistan	Tashkent	6/17/2008	93
Jamaica	Kingston	6/17/2008	117	Venezuela	Caracas	7/22/2008	147
Japan	Okinawa	5/24/2002	141	Vietnam	Hanoi	5/5/2008	113
Jordan	Amman	4/14/2008	130	Yemen	Sanaa	12/10/2005	129
Kazakhstan	Almaty	(NA)	(NA)	Zambia	Lusaka	3/16/2007	131
				Zimbabwe	Harare	1/14/2008	243

NA Not available.   [1] Also called the "local index," the living cost index measures living costs for private American citizens. The local index is a comparison of prices at the foreign post and in Washington, DC, with the price ratios weight the expenditure pattern of American employees living at the foreign post. It is, thereby, a measure of the cost of living for Americans at the foreign post compared with the cost of living in Washington, DC. This is the index most appropriate for use by business firms and other private organizations to establish cost-of-living allowances for their American employees stationed abroad.   [2] See footnote 4, Table 1296.   [3] See footnote 5, Table 1296.   [4] There are no U.S. Government employees in Taiwan. The figures listed in this column represent a living cost comparison for American employees of the American Institute in Taiwan, who have some duty-free and other special benefits that may not be available to other Americans in Taiwan.

Source: U.S. Department of State, Bureau of Administration, "Indexes of Living Costs Abroad, Quarters Allowances, and Hardship Differentials," January 2009; <http://aoprals.state.gov/content.asp?content_id=186&menu_id=81>.

Table 1323. Percent of Household Final Consumption Expenditures Spent on Food, Alcohol, and Tobacco Consumed at Home by Selected Countries: 2007

Country/Territory	Food [1]	Alcoholic beverages and tobacco	Country/Territory	Food [1]	Alcoholic beverages and tobacco
United States	6.9	2.1	Lithuania	23.8	6.1
Algeria	43.9	2.0	Malaysia	14.6	1.2
Australia	10.7	4.0	Mexico	24.2	2.5
Austria	10.3	2.5	Morocco	40.2	1.3
Azerbaijan	50.4	2.3	Netherlands	10.3	2.9
Belarus	44.6	5.9	New Zealand	12.1	4.3
Belgium	13.3	3.7	Nigeria	40.3	2.5
Bolivia	28.6	2.2	Norway	13.3	4.4
Brazil	24.6	1.9	Pakistan	45.7	2.5
Bulgaria	20.0	3.9	Peru	29.1	2.0
Canada	9.2	3.8	Philippines	37.3	1.6
Chile	23.4	0.8	Poland	20.6	6.6
China [2]	34.9	2.7	Portugal	17.3	3.9
Colombia	27.8	4.7	Romania	34.3	5.0
Croatia	26.3	2.9	Russia	28.7	2.3
Czech Republic	16.2	7.6	Saudi Arabia	23.8	1.3
Ecuador	20.9	1.7	Singapore	8.3	2.1
Egypt	38.8	2.3	Slovakia	17.9	4.5
Estonia	16.1	8.1	Slovenia	14.9	4.1
Finland	12.2	4.9	South Africa	20.6	4.6
France	13.7	3.0	Spain	13.6	3.1
Germany	11.4	3.6	Sweden	11.7	3.5
Hong Kong	12.5	0.7	Switzerland	10.3	3.6
Hungary	17.1	8.0	Taiwan [2]	24.2	2.1
Indonesia	45.7	5.9	Thailand	24.9	5.4
Ireland	8.2	5.2	Tunisia	35.8	1.0
Israel	17.8	1.7	Turkey	24.8	4.1
Italy	14.5	2.8	Turkmenistan	30.4	2.5
Japan	14.6	3.2	Ukraine	42.3	6.3
Jordan	40.9	4.9	United Arab Emirates . . .	9.4	0.4
Kazakhstan	35.9	3.5	United Kingdom	8.6	3.6
Korea, South	15.4	2.6	Venezuela	29.5	3.1
Kuwait	14.6	1.6	Vietnam	38.8	2.7
Latvia	19.2	6.3			

[1] Includes nonalcoholic beverages.   [2] See footnote 4, Table 1296.

Source: U.S. Department of Agriculture, Economic Research Service; "Food, CPI, Prices and Expenditures: Food Expenditure Tables"; <http://www.ers.usda.gov/Briefing/CPIFoodAndExpenditures/Data/>.

Table 1324. Gross Public Debt, Expenditures, and Receipts by Country: 1990 to 2008

[Percent of nominal gross domestic product. Gross debt includes one-off revenues from the sale of the mobile telephone licenses. Expenditures and receipts refer to the general government sector, which is a consolidation of accounts for the central, state, and local governments plus social security. Expenditures, or total outlays, are defined as current outlays plus capital outlays. Receipts cover current receipts, but exclude capital receipts. Nontax receipts consist of property income (including dividends and other transfers from public enterprises), fees, charges, sales, fines, capital transfers received by the general government, etc. Minus sign (−) indicates deficit]

Country	Gross debt			Expenditures			Receipts		
	1990	2000	2008	1990	2000	2008	1990	2000	2008
United States [1]	−4.2	1.6	−5.3	37.1	34.2	38.6	32.8	35.8	33.3
Australia	−2.0	[2] 0.9	1.8	35.7	[2] 35.2	33.7	33.7	36.1	35.5
Austria	−2.5	[2] −1.9	−1.0	51.9	[2] 52.1	48.4	49.4	50.3	47.4
Belgium	−6.8	(Z)	−0.7	52.2	49.2	48.9	45.5	49.1	48.2
Canada	−5.8	2.9	0.3	48.8	41.1	39.6	43.0	44.1	39.9
Czech Republic	(X)	−3.7	−1.6	(X)	41.7	41.5	(X)	37.9	39.9
Denmark	−1.3	2.3	2.4	55.9	53.3	50.4	54.6	55.5	52.9
Finland	5.4	6.9	4.6	47.9	48.4	47.3	53.3	55.3	51.9
France	−2.4	−1.5	−2.9	49.4	51.6	52.5	47.0	50.1	49.6
Germany	(X)	[2] 1.3	(Z)	(X)	[2] 45.1	43.4	(X)	46.4	43.4
Greece	−14.0	−3.7	−2.8	44.9	46.7	43.2	30.9	43.0	40.4
Hungary	(NA)	−2.9	−3.4	(NA)	46.5	48.6	(NA)	43.6	45.2
Iceland	−3.3	1.7	3.2	41.5	41.9	43.9	38.3	43.6	47.1
Ireland	−2.8	4.7	−5.6	42.9	31.5	39.6	40.1	36.2	34.0
Italy	−11.4	[2] −0.9	−2.5	52.9	[2] 46.1	48.4	41.5	45.3	45.9
Japan [3]	2.1	−7.6	−1.4	32.0	39.0	36.4	34.0	31.4	35.0
Korea, South	3.1	5.4	4.8	20.0	23.9	30.9	23.1	29.3	35.7
Netherlands	−5.3	[2] 2.0	1.0	54.9	[2] 44.2	45.1	49.6	46.1	46.0
New Zealand	−4.6	[2] 1.6	2.5	53.2	[2] 39.6	42.6	48.7	41.2	45.1
Norway	2.2	15.4	20.0	53.3	42.3	40.5	55.5	57.7	60.5
Portugal	−6.1	[2] −3.0	−2.2	40.5	[2] 43.1	46.3	34.5	40.2	44.1
Spain	−4.1	[2] −1.0	−1.5	42.8	[2] 39.1	39.7	38.7	38.1	38.2
Sweden	3.3	3.7	2.8	59.7	57.0	51.2	63.1	60.7	54.0
United Kingdom	−2.0	[2] 3.7	−3.6	41.5	[2] 36.6	45.4	39.4	40.3	41.9

NA Not available.   X Not applicable.   Z Less than 0.05 percent.   [1] Receipts exclude the operating surpluses of public enterprises, while expenditures include them.   [2] Includes substantial one-off revenues from the sale of the mobil telephone licenses.   [3] The 2000 expenditures include capital transfers to the Deposit Insurance Company. Receipts include deferred tax payments on postal savings accounts in 2000.

Source: Organization for Economic Cooperation and Development, Paris, France, *OECD Economic Outlook*, June 2009 (copyright). See also <http://www.oecd.org>.

International Statistics   835

Table 1325. Percent Distribution of Tax Receipts by Country: 1990 to 2007

Country	Total [1]	Income and profits taxes [2]			Social security contributions			Taxes on goods and services [3, 5]		
		Total [3]	Indi-vidual	Corpo-rate	Total [4]	Employ-ees	Employ-ers	Total [3]	General con-sump-tion taxes [6]	Taxes on specific goods and ser-vices [7]
United States:										
1990.........	100.0	46.0	37.1	8.9	25.1	11.0	12.9	17.4	8.0	7.0
2000.........	100.0	50.7	41.9	8.7	23.2	10.4	11.6	16.1	7.6	6.3
2007.........	100.0	49.1	37.7	11.4	23.6	10.3	12.0	16.4	7.6	5.9
Canada:										
1990.........	100.0	48.6	40.8	7.0	12.1	4.4	7.6	25.8	14.1	10.3
2000.........	100.0	50.1	36.8	12.2	13.6	5.5	7.8	24.2	14.3	8.5
2007.........	100.0	50.1	37.6	11.2	14.1	5.6	8.1	23.5	13.6	8.4
France:										
1990.........	100.0	16.1	10.7	5.3	44.1	13.2	27.2	28.4	18.8	8.7
2000.........	100.0	24.9	18.0	6.9	36.0	8.9	24.8	25.7	16.9	8.2
2007.........	100.0	23.9	17.3	6.6	37.1	9.2	25.2	24.7	17.0	7.1
Germany:										
1990.........	100.0	32.4	27.6	4.8	37.5	16.2	19.1	26.7	16.6	9.2
2000.........	100.0	30.1	25.3	4.8	39.0	17.2	19.2	28.1	18.4	8.8
2007.........	100.0	31.3	25.5	5.9	36.6	16.1	17.4	29.3	19.4	8.8
Italy:										
1990.........	100.0	36.5	26.3	10.0	32.9	6.3	23.6	28.0	14.7	10.6
2000.........	100.0	33.1	24.8	6.9	28.6	5.4	19.9	27.9	15.4	9.6
2007.........	100.0	34.2	25.9	8.7	30.2	5.3	20.8	24.5	14.4	8.5
Japan:										
1990.........	100.0	50.2	27.8	22.4	26.4	10.6	12.7	13.7	4.4	7.5
2000.........	100.0	34.8	21.1	13.8	35.2	14.7	16.4	19.3	9.1	8.0
2007.........	100.0	(NA)	(NA)	(NA)	(NA)	(NA)	(NA)	(NA)	(NA)	(NA)
United Kingdom:										
1990.........	100.0	39.3	29.4	9.9	17.0	6.6	9.9	31.1	16.9	12.6
2000.........	100.0	39.1	29.3	9.8	17.0	6.8	9.6	31.9	18.4	12.4
2007.........	100.0	39.3	29.8	9.4	18.6	7.7	10.4	29.1	18.2	9.7

NA Not available.   [1] Includes property taxes, employer payroll taxes other than social security contributions, and miscellaneous taxes not shown separately.   [2] Includes taxes on capital gains.   [3] Includes other taxes not shown separately.   [4] Includes contributions of self-employed not shown separately.   [5] Taxes on the production, sales, transfer, leasing, and delivery of goods and services and rendering of services.   [6] Primary value-added and sales taxes.   [7] For example, excise taxes on alcohol, tobacco, and gasoline.

Source: Organization for Economic Cooperation and Development, Paris, France, *Revenue Statistics*, annual (copyright). See also <htp:www.oecd.og>.

Table 1326. Household Tax Burden by Country: 2008

[**Percent of gross wage earnings of the average production worker**. The tax burden reflects income tax plus employee social security contributions less cash benefits. Minus sign (−) indicates tax credit]

Country	Single person without children	One earner family with two children	Country	Single person without children	One earner family with two children
Australia...........	22.6	9.8	Korea, South........	12.5	10.0
Austria............	33.9	20.5	Luxembourg........	27.2	1.0
Belgium...........	42.5	22.6	Mexico............	5.1	5.1
Canada............	23.4	11.0	Netherlands........	36.1	28.1
Czech Republic......	23.6	−7.1	New Zealand........	21.2	3.5
Denmark...........	40.9	29.1	Norway............	29.7	22.1
Finland............	30.0	23.1	Poland............	28.6	21.5
France............	27.8	17.6	Portugal...........	22.8	9.9
Germany...........	42.7	24.1	Slovakia...........	22.8	5.8
Greece............	26.3	26.6	Spain.............	19.0	11.2
Hungary...........	38.3	24.6	Sweden...........	26.7	19.1
Iceland............	24.5	5.6	Switzerland.........	21.7	7.5
Ireland............	14.6	−4.7	Turkey............	27.5	26.0
Italy..............	29.3	15.5	United Kingdom......	25.6	19.1
Japan.............	20.3	14.1	**United States**.......	24.7	11.3

Source: Organization for Economic Cooperation and Development, Paris, France, *Taxing Wages, 2007–2008*, (copyright). See also <http:www.oecd.org>.

Table 1327. **Civilian Labor Force, Employment, and Unemployment by Country: 1990 to 2007**

[125,840 represents 125,840,000. Data based on U.S. labor force definitions (see source) except that minimum age for population base varies as follows: United States, Canada, France, Sweden, and United Kingdom, 16 years; Australia, Japan, Netherlands, Germany, and Italy (beginning 1993), 15 years; and Italy (prior to 1993) 14 years]

Year	United States	Canada	Aus- tralia	Japan	France	Ger- many[1]	Italy	Nether- lands	Swe- den	United King- dom
Civilian labor force (1,000):										
1990	125,840	14,047	8,440	63,050	24,159	29,410	22,670	6,767	4,594	28,766
2000	[2]142,583	15,637	9,590	66,990	26,099	39,302	23,361	[2]8,052	4,482	28,962
2005	149,320	17,108	10,506	65,850	27,092	[2]40,760	24,179	8,459	[2]4,694	30,138
2006	151,428	17,351	10,699	65,960	27,322	41,250	24,395	8,541	4,748	30,600
2007	153,124	17,696	10,949	66,080	27,535	41,416	24,459	8,686	4,823	30,790
Labor force participation rate: [3]										
1990	66.5	67.4	64.7	62.6	55.7	55.3	47.2	57.0	67.3	64.3
2000	67.1	66.0	64.4	62.0	56.6	56.7	48.1	[2]63.4	63.7	62.8
2005	66.0	67.4	65.3	60.0	56.5	[2]57.6	48.7	64.7	[2]64.8	63.1
2006	66.2	67.4	65.6	60.0	56.6	58.2	48.9	65.1	64.9	63.5
2007	66.0	67.7	66.0	60.0	56.7	58.4	48.6	65.9	65.3	63.4
Civilian employment (1,000):										
1990	118,793	12,964	7,877	61,700	22,075	27,950	21,080	6,251	4,513	26,713
2000	[2]136,891	14,681	8,989	63,790	23,714	36,236	20,973	[2]7,813	4,222	27,375
2005	141,730	16,080	9,975	62,910	24,493	[2]36,185	22,290	8,056	[2]4,334	28,674
2006	144,427	16,393	10,186	63,210	24,717	36,978	22,721	8,205	4,416	28,930
2007	146,047	16,767	10,470	63,510	25,162	37,815	22,953	8,408	4,530	29,138
Employment-population ratio: [4]										
1990	62.8	62.2	60.4	61.3	50.9	52.6	43.9	52.7	66.1	59.8
2000	64.4	62.0	60.3	59.0	51.4	52.2	43.2	[2]61.5	60.0	59.4
2005	62.7	63.4	62.0	57.3	51.1	[2]51.2	44.9	61.6	[2]59.9	60.0
2006	63.1	63.6	62.5	57.5	51.2	52.2	45.5	62.5	60.4	60.1
2007	63.0	64.2	63.1	57.6	51.8	53.3	45.6	63.8	61.3	60.0
Unemployment rate:										
1990	5.6	7.7	6.7	2.1	8.6	5.0	7.0	7.6	1.8	7.1
2000	4.0	6.1	6.3	4.8	9.1	7.8	10.2	[2]3.0	5.8	5.5
2005	5.1	6.0	5.1	4.5	9.6	[2]11.2	7.8	4.8	[2]7.7	4.9
2006	4.6	5.5	4.8	4.2	9.5	10.4	6.9	3.9	7.0	5.5
2007	4.6	5.3	4.4	3.9	8.6	8.7	6.2	3.2	6.1	5.4
Under 25 years old	10.5	10.1	9.3	7.8	20.2	11.9	11.9	6.0	19.1	14.4
Teenagers [5]	15.7	13.6	13.7	8.9	27.3	12.9	31.7	8.7	29.7	21.2
20 to 24 years old	8.2	8.0	6.3	7.6	18.2	11.5	18.2	3.9	13.8	10.4
25 years old and over	3.6	4.3	3.2	3.5	7.3	8.3	5.0	2.7	4.3	3.7

[1] Unified Germany for 1991 onward. Prior to 1991, data relate to the former West Germany.   [2] Break in series. Data not comparable with prior years.   [3] Civilian labor force as a percent of the civilian working-age population. Germany and Japan include the institutionalized population as part of the working-age population.   [4] Civilian employment as a percent of the civilian working-age population. Germany and Japan include the institutionalized population as part of the working-age population.   [5] 16 to 19-year-olds in the United States, Canada, France, Sweden, and the United Kingdom; 15 to 19-year-olds in Australia, Japan, Germany, Italy, and the Netherlands.

Source: U.S. Bureau of Labor Statistics, *International Comparisons of Annual Labor Force Statistics, 10 Countries, 1960–2007* (published 21 October 2008). See also <http://www.bls.gov/fls/flscomparelf.htm>.

Table 1328. **Unemployment Rates by Country: 2000 to 2008**

[**Annual averages.** The standardized unemployment rates shown here are calculated as the number of unemployed persons as a percentage of the civilian labor force. The unemployed are persons of working age who, in the reference period, are without work, available for work, and have taken specific steps to find work]

Country	2000	2005	2007	2008	Country	2000	2005	2007	2008
OECD, total	6.2	6.8	5.7	6.0	Ireland	4.3	4.4	4.6	6.3
Euro area [1]	8.5	9.0	7.5	7.6	Italy	10.1	7.7	6.1	6.8
					Japan	4.7	4.4	3.9	4.0
United States	4.0	5.1	4.6	5.8	Korea, South	4.4	3.7	3.2	3.2
Australia	6.3	5.0	4.4	4.2	Luxembourg	2.2	4.6	4.2	4.9
Austria	3.6	5.2	4.4	3.9	Netherlands	2.8	4.7	3.2	2.8
Belgium	6.9	8.5	7.5	7.0	New Zealand	6.1	3.8	3.7	4.2
Canada	6.8	6.8	6.0	6.1	Norway	3.2	4.5	2.6	2.5
Czech Republic	8.7	7.9	5.3	4.4	Poland	16.2	17.8	9.6	7.2
Denmark	4.3	4.8	3.8	3.4	Portugal	4.0	7.7	8.1	7.8
Finland	9.6	8.3	6.8	6.4	Spain	11.1	9.2	8.3	11.4
France	9.0	9.3	8.3	7.8	Sweden	5.6	7.3	6.2	6.1
Germany	7.5	10.6	8.4	7.3	Switzerland	2.6	4.4	3.6	3.5
Hungary	6.4	7.2	7.4	7.8	United Kingdom	5.4	4.8	5.3	5.6

[1] See footnote 3, Table 1318.

Source: Organization for Economic Cooperation and Development, Paris, France, *Main Economic Indicators*, April 2008 and earlier releases (copyright). See also <http://www.oecd.org>.

Table 1329. **Percent of Persons Not in Education or at Work: 2006**

[Represents those persons not in education and either unemployed or not in the labor force]

Country	15 to 19 years old			20 to 24 years old		
	Total	Unemployed	Not in the labor force	Total	Unemployed	Not in the labor force
Australia	7.1	3.7	3.4	11.4	4.2	7.2
Belgium	7.1	2.4	4.7	16.9	9.9	7.0
Canada.	7.4	2.9	4.5	13.0	5.9	7.1
Czech Republic	4.5	3.1	1.4	14.1	7.9	6.2
Denmark.	4.4	1.9	2.5	5.8	2.4	3.4
Finland	3.6	1.7	1.9	13.3	6.9	6.4
France	6.4	3.8	2.6	16.5	11.0	5.5
Germany.	4.2	2.2	2.0	16.7	9.9	6.8
Greece	8.8	2.8	6.0	17.5	10.7	6.8
Hungary	6.0	1.8	4.2	18.5	6.8	11.7
Israel	24.2	1.6	22.6	40.6	6.9	33.7
Italy	11.8	3.5	8.3	22.8	10.1	12.7
Mexico	17.1	2.2	14.9	27.4	3.2	24.2
Netherlands.	3.1	1.2	1.9	7.3	2.1	5.2
Poland	3.8	2.2	1.6	20.6	13.8	6.8
Portugal	7.8	3.8	4.0	13.4	7.7	5.7
Spain	10.1	4.6	5.5	16.9	8.9	8.0
Sweden	5.3	2.0	3.3	15.2	8.2	7.0
Switzerland	7.6	2.8	4.8	10.8	5.3	5.5
United States	6.3	2.1	4.2	15.6	5.2	10.4

Source: Organization for Economic Cooperation and Development, Paris, France, *Education at a Glance 2008* (copyright). See also <http://www.oecd.org>.

Table 1330. **Female Labor Force Participation Rates by Country: 1980 to 2008**

[**In percent**. Female labor force of all ages divided by female population 15–64 years old]

Country	1980	1990	2000	2008	Country	1980	1990	2000	2008
Australia	52.0	61.8	65.4	69.9	Korea, South	46.3	49.9	52.0	54.7
Austria	(NA)	(NA)	61.8	68.6	Luxembourg	(NA)	42.4	51.7	59.4
Belgium	(NA)	46.1	56.6	59.7	Mexico	(NA)	(NA)	41.0	43.3
Canada.	57.4	68.4	70.4	74.4	Netherlands.	36.1	[1]53.1	65.2	72.6
Czech Republic	(X)	(X)	63.7	61.0	New Zealand	(NA)	[1]63.2	67.5	72.0
Denmark.	(NA)	77.6	75.9	77.3	Norway.	62.2	70.7	76.5	77.4
Finland	69.4	73.4	72.1	74.0	Poland	(NA)	(NA)	59.9	57.0
France . . [2].	55.1	57.2	61.7	65.2	Portugal	52.4	59.6	63.8	68.9
Germany [2].	51.9	55.5	63.3	69.7	Slovakia	(X)	(X)	63.2	61.4
Greece	(NA)	42.6	49.7	55.1	Spain	32.9	42.2	52.9	64.1
Hungary	(NA)	(NA)	52.6	55.0	Sweden	75.3	[1]82.5	76.4	78.2
Iceland	(NA)	(NA)	83.3	82.5	Switzerland	(NA)	(NA)	71.7	76.6
Ireland	(NA)	42.6	55.7	63.0	Turkey	(NA)	36.0	28.0	26.7
Italy	38.4	44.0	46.3	51.6	United Kingdom	(NA)	67.3	68.9	70.2
Japan.	52.5	57.1	59.6	62.2	**United States . . . .**	59.9	[1]67.8	70.7	69.3

NA Not available.   X Not applicable.   [1] Break in series. Data not comparable with prior years.   [2] Prior to 1991, data are for former West Germany.

Source: Organization for Economic Cooperation and Development, Paris, France, *OECD in Figures*, 2008 (copyright). See also <http://www.oecd.org>.

Table 1331. **Civilian Employment-Population Ratio: 1990 to 2007**

[Civilian employment as a percent of the civilian working-age population. See headnote, Table 1327]

Country	Women					Men				
	1990	1995	2000	2006	2007	1990	1995	2000	2006	2007
United States [1]. . .	54.3	55.6	57.5	56.6	56.6	72.0	70.8	71.9	70.1	69.8
Canada	54.1	52.7	56.0	58.9	59.7	70.6	66.1	68.2	68.6	68.8
Australia.	49.5	50.5	52.5	55.5	56.2	71.4	68.2	68.4	69.6	70.2
Japan	48.0	47.7	46.4	46.0	46.1	75.4	75.0	72.5	69.8	70.1
France. . [1].	41.5	41.9	44.5	45.8	46.8	61.4	57.4	59.0	57.1	57.4
Germany [1, 2, 3, 4] . .	40.9	42.7	44.4	46.0	47.1	65.6	63.1	60.6	58.8	59.9
Italy [1]	29.2	29.1	31.6	34.7	34.9	60.0	56.2	55.8	57.3	57.3
Netherlands [1, 3, 4] .	39.4	44.4	52.0	55.2	56.8	66.5	66.7	71.4	70.0	71.0
Sweden	[4]61.8	54.7	56.1	56.4	57.4	70.6	62.0	64.1	64.5	65.5
United Kingdom. . .	50.3	49.8	52.5	53.8	53.6	70.0	64.7	66.9	66.7	66.7

[1] Break in series between 1990 and 1995.   [2] Unified Germany for 1991 onward. Prior to 1991, data relate to the former West Germany.   [3] Break in series between 1995 and 2000.   [4] Break in series between 2000 and 2005.

Source: U.S. Bureau of Labor Statistics, *International Comparisons of Annual Labor Force Statistics, 10 Countries, 1960–2007* (published 21 October 2008). See also <http://www.bls.gov/fls/flscomparelf.htm>.

Table 1332. Civilian Employment by Industry and Country: 2000 and 2007

[**136,891 represents 136,891,000**. Civilian employment approximating U.S. concepts. See headnote, Table 1327]

Industry	United States [1,2]	Canada [1]	Aus-tralia	Japan	France	Ger-many [2]	Italy	Sweden [2]	United Kingdom
TOTAL EMPLOYMENT (1,000)									
2000, total	136,891	14,681	8,989	63,790	23,714	36,238	20,973	4,222	27,375
Agriculture, forestry, fishing [3]	2,464	481	446	3,070	922	952	1,120	122	419
Industry [4]	30,050	3,216	1,901	19,710	5,506	11,898	6,634	1,000	6,660
Manufacturing	19,644	2,247	1,129	13,180	4,087	8,647	4,944	762	4,617
Services [5]	104,377	10,984	6,642	41,010	17,286	23,388	13,219	3,100	20,296
2007, total	146,047	16,767	10,470	63,510	(NA)	37,815	22,953	4,530	29,138
Agriculture, forestry, fishing [3]	2,095	416	359	2,580	(NA)	853	920	101	402
Industry [4]	28,894	3,430	2,165	17,140	(NA)	11,023	6,860	956	6,260
Manufacturing	16,302	2,043	1,080	11,620	(NA)	8,391	4,867	660	3,728
Services [5]	115,058	12,921	7,946	43,790	(NA)	25,939	15,173	3,473	22,476
PERCENT DISTRIBUTION [6]									
2000, total	100.0	100.0	100.0	100.0	100.0	100.0	100.0	100.0	100.0
Agriculture, forestry, fishing [3]	1.8	3.3	5.0	4.8	3.9	2.6	5.3	2.9	1.5
Industry [4]	22.0	21.9	21.1	30.9	23.2	32.8	31.6	23.7	24.3
Manufacturing	14.4	15.3	12.6	20.7	17.2	23.9	23.6	18.0	16.9
Services [5]	76.2	74.8	73.9	64.3	72.9	64.5	63.0	73.4	74.1
2007, total	100.0	100.0	100.0	100.0	(NA)	(NA)	100.0	100.0	(NA)
Agriculture, forestry, fishing [3]	1.4	2.5	3.4	4.1	(NA)	2.3	4.0	2.2	1.4
Industry [4]	19.8	20.5	20.7	27.0	(NA)	29.1	29.9	21.1	21.5
Manufacturing	11.2	12.2	10.3	18.3	(NA)	22.2	21.2	14.6	12.8
Services [5]	78.8	77.1	75.9	68.9	(NA)	68.6	66.1	76.7	77.1

NA Not available. [1] Data for the United States and Canada are based on the 2002 North American Industry Classification System (NAICS). [2] Break in series between 2000 and 2007. [3] Includes hunting. [4] Includes manufacturing, mining, and construction. [5] Transportation, communication, public utilities, trade, finance, public administration, private household services, and miscellaneous services. [6] Civilian employment as a percent of the civilian working-age population.

Source: U.S. Bureau of Labor Statistics, *International Comparisons of Annual Labor Force Statistics, 10 Countries, 1960–2007* (published 21 October 2008). See also <http://www.bls.gov/fls/flscomparelf.htm>.

Table 1333. Educational Performance: 2006

[Tertiary-type A includes education leading to a Bachelor's, Master's, or equivalent degree, and advanced research programs. Performance figures were gathered from the Program for International Student Assessment (PISA), an internationally standardized assessment jointly developed by participating countries, which takes place in 3-year cycles. To implement PISA, each of the participating countries selects a nationally representative sample of 15-year-olds, regardless of grade level. Tests are typically administered to between 4,500 and 10,000 students in each country]

Country	Student performance on the combined reading, scientific, and mathematical literacy scales			Educational attainment of adult population and current graduation rates (percent)	
	Mean score on the combined reading literacy scale [1]	Mean score on the mathematical literacy scale [2]	Mean score on the scientific literacy scale [3]	Upper secondary or higher attainment (25 to 64 years old) [4]	Tertiary-type A attainment (25 to 64 years old) [5]
Australia	513	520	527	67	24
Austria	490	505	511	80	10
Canada	527	527	534	86	24
Czech Republic	483	510	513	90	14
Finland	547	548	563	80	19
France	488	496	495	67	16
Germany	495	504	516	83	15
Greece	460	459	473	59	15
Italy	469	462	475	51	12
Japan	498	523	531	(NA)	23
Korea	556	547	522	77	23
Luxembourg	479	490	486	66	16
Mexico	410	406	410	32	14
Poland	508	495	498	53	18
Spain	461	480	488	50	20
Sweden	507	502	503	84	22
Switzerland	499	530	512	85	20
United Kingdom	495	495	515	69	22
United States	(NA)	474	489	88	30
OECD mean	492	498	500	68	19

NA Not available. [1] Reading literacy is understanding, using, and reflecting on written texts in order to achieve one's goals, to develop one's knowledge and potential, and to participate in society. [2] Mathematical literacy is an individual's capacity to identify and understand the role that mathematics plays in the world, to make well-founded judgements, and to use and engage with mathematics in ways that meet the needs of that individual's life. [3] Scientific literacy is the capacity to use scientific knowledge to identify questions and to draw evidencebased conclusions in order to understand and help make decisions about the natural world and the changes made to it through human activity. [4] Excluding ISCED 3C short programs. [5] Includes advanced research programs.

Source: Organization for Economic Cooperation and Development, Paris, France, *OECD Factbook*, 2009 and *Education at a Glance*, 2008 (copyright). See also <http://www.oecd.org>.

U.S. Census Bureau, Statistical Abstract of the United States: 2010

Table 1334. **World Supply and Utilization of Major Crops, Livestock, and Products: 1995 to 2008**

[In millions of units (214.3 represents 214,300,000). For major crops, data ending in year shown. For meat and dairy, calendar year data, selected countries]

Commodity	1995	2000	2002	2003	2004	2005	2006	2007	2008 [1]
Wheat:									
Area (hectares)	214.3	215.4	215.2	215.2	210.2	217.6	218.8	213.0	218.2
Production (metric tons)	523.1	585.8	583.1	568.7	553.9	625.7	620.0	596.1	610.2
Exports (metric tons) [2]	101.5	113.4	105.7	105.7	108.6	111.2	116.8	111.2	115.4
Consumption (metric tons) [3]	545.0	585.1	587.2	605.1	588.8	606.6	623.4	616.7	617.8
Ending stocks (metric tons) [4]	160.2	208.5	203.2	166.8	131.9	151.0	147.6	127.0	119.4
Coarse grains:									
Area (hectares)	323.6	299.7	301.0	293.0	307.0	300.3	302.0	306.2	319.4
Production (metric tons)	869.7	877.7	895.1	875.8	916.6	1,016.4	980.2	988.6	1,077.6
Exports (metric tons) [2]	98.6	104.9	102.0	102.1	103.2	100.9	107.1	117.4	123.8
Consumption (metric tons) [3]	858.8	882.3	907.4	903.9	945.5	979.4	993.5	1,015.2	1,060.1
Ending stocks (metric tons) [4]	190.8	232.8	198.6	170.5	141.6	178.6	165.3	138.7	156.2
Rice, milled:									
Area (hectares)	147.4	155.3	150.8	146.2	148.6	151.0	153.1	153.9	154.3
Production (metric tons)	363.6	408.9	399.9	378.6	392.2	401.4	418.5	420.6	431.3
Exports (metric tons) [2]	20.7	22.8	26.9	28.7	27.4	28.5	30.4	31.3	30.4
Consumption (metric tons) [3]	365.2	399.7	413.6	408.3	414.3	409.4	416.0	420.9	428.0
Ending stocks (metric tons) [4]	118.3	143.5	133.0	103.3	81.1	73.2	75.7	75.4	78.7
Total grains: [5]									
Area (hectares)	685.3	670.4	666.9	654.5	665.8	668.9	673.9	673.0	691.9
Production (metric tons)	1,756.4	1,872.4	1,878.1	1,823.1	1,862.7	2,043.6	2,018.8	2,005.3	2,119.1
Exports (metric tons) [2]	220.8	241.1	234.6	236.4	239.2	240.6	254.2	260.0	269.6
Consumption (metric tons) [3]	1,769.0	1,867.2	1,908.3	1,917.4	1,948.6	1,995.5	2,032.9	2,052.8	2,105.9
Ending stocks (metric tons) [4]	469.3	584.9	534.8	440.6	354.6	402.7	388.6	341.1	354.2
Oilseeds:									
Crush (metric tons)	238.3	246.3	264.5	269.9	279.3	302.8	318.7	329.0	338.3
Production (metric tons)	299.5	304.3	324.8	331.7	335.9	381.5	391.3	404.5	391.3
Exports (metric tons)	47.5	59.2	62.3	69.7	67.0	74.4	75.8	83.6	92.6
Ending stocks (metric tons)	28.1	38.2	42.5	49.0	45.2	57.6	64.7	72.7	61.5
Meals: [6]									
Production (metric tons)	166.2	167.9	182.7	186.1	190.6	207.0	216.4	224.7	230.9
Exports (metric tons)	61.5	46.7	52.8	53.7	58.7	61.0	65.9	68.3	71.4
Oils: [7]									
Production (metric tons)	73.4	86.0	92.7	95.9	102.5	111.5	118.5	121.4	128.0
Exports (metric tons)	27.3	28.7	33.0	35.8	38.8	42.5	47.2	48.5	52.1
Cotton:									
Area (hectares)	32.2	32.3	33.7	30.8	32.3	35.7	34.7	34.7	33.2
Production (bales) [8]	85.9	87.9	98.7	91.0	96.8	121.4	116.6	122.0	120.5
Exports (bales) [8]	28.4	27.2	29.1	30.5	33.2	35.0	44.6	37.1	38.4
Consumption (bales) [8]	84.4	90.5	93.7	97.6	97.1	107.5	114.7	121.7	120.6
Ending stocks (bales) [8]	29.9	51.1	54.5	47.6	48.1	60.4	62.2	62.8	62.3
Beef and Pork:									
Production (metric tons)	124.2	138.8	143.3	145.0	147.6	151.2	154.3	153.7	156.0
Consumption (metric tons)	123.2	138.5	143.3	145.0	147.1	150.4	153.3	152.9	154.7
Exports (metric tons) [2]	7.6	9.0	10.2	10.7	11.4	12.3	12.7	12.9	13.9
Broilers and Turkeys:									
Production (metric tons)	43.6	57.9	62.3	63.1	64.6	68.0	69.2	73.3	77.0
Consumption (metric tons)	43.1	57.4	61.7	62.6	63.8	67.2	68.9	72.9	76.5
Exports (metric tons) [2]	5.0	5.3	6.2	6.5	6.6	7.4	7.1	7.9	8.8
Dairy:									
Milk production (metric tons)	(NA)	389.4	405.3	409.6	415.7	421.4	427.7	436.8	437.6

NA Not available. [1] Forecast for crops, preliminary for meat and dairy. [2] Excludes intra-EU (European Union) trade but includes intra-FSU (Former Soviet Union) trade. [3] Where stocks data are not available, consumption includes stock changes. [4] Stocks data are based on differing marketing years and do not represent levels at a given date. Data not available for all countries. [5] Wheat, coarse grains, and rice. [6] Includes the following types of meals: copra, cottonseed, fishmeal, palm kernel, rapeseed, sunflower, soybean, and peanut. [7] Includes the following types of oils: coconut, cottonseed, olive, palm, palm kernel, peanut, sunflower, rapeseed, and soybean. [8] 480-pound bales.

Source: U.S. Department of Agriculture, Economic Research Service, "Agricultural Outlook: Statistical Indicators" (published January 2009); <http://www.ers.usda.gov/publications/agoutlook/aotables/>.

Table 1335. **World Crop Production Summary: 2007 to 2009**

[In millions of metric tons, (611.0 represents 611,000,000), except as indicated]

Country	Wheat 2007–2008	Wheat 2008–2009, prel.	Coarse Grains 2007–2008	Coarse Grains 2008–2009, prel.	Rice (milled) 2007–2008	Rice (milled) 2008–2009, prel.	Oilseeds[1] 2007–2008	Oilseeds[1] 2008–2009, prel.	Cotton[2] 2007–2008	Cotton[2] 2008–2009, prel.
World	611.0	682.4	1,077.5	1,100.1	433.4	444.9	391.6	394.3	120.5	106.9
United States ...	55.8	68.0	349.9	326.1	6.3	6.5	82.5	89.0	19.2	12.8
Canada.	20.1	28.6	27.8	27.2	(³)	(³)	12.4	16.0	(³)	(³)
Mexico	3.6	4.0	30.8	32.3	0.2	0.2	36.0	0.7	0.6	0.6
EU-27 [4]	120.2	151.6	136.2	161.1	1.8	1.7	24.5	27.0	1.7	1.2
Russia	49.4	63.7	29.3	40.7	0.5	0.5	6.9	8.8	(³)	(³)
Ukraine.	13.9	25.9	14.6	26.2	0.1	0.1	6.0	10.2	(³)	(³)
China	109.3	112.5	159.1	173.2	129.9	134.3	53.4	57.9	37.0	35.8
India.	75.8	78.6	40.6	39.0	96.7	99.2	34.0	33.7	24.6	22.5
Indonesia	(³)	(³)	8.5	8.7	37.0	38.3	8.2	9.0	–	–
Pakistan	23.3	21.5	3.6	3.6	5.7	6.3	4.7	5.0	8.9	9.0
Thailand	(³)	(³)	3.9	4.3	19.3	19.4	0.6	0.6	–	–
Argentina	18.0	8.4	27.0	16.8	0.8	0.8	51.7	35.7	0.7	0.6
Brazil	3.8	6.0	61.3	52.6	8.2	8.6	64.2	59.5	7.4	5.5
Australia	13.8	21.5	11.5	11.1	–	0.1	1.4	2.5	0.6	1.5
South Africa.	1.9	2.1	13.7	12.5	(³)	(³)	1.3	1.4	–	–
Turkey	15.5	16.8	9.5	10.3	0.4	0.4	1.8	1.7	3.1	2.1
All others.	86.5	73.1	150.2	154.5	126.6	128.6	37.5	35.7	16.5	15.2

– Represents zero.   [1] Includes soybean, cottonseed, peanut (in shell), sunflower seed, rapeseed for individual countries. Copra and palm kernel are added to world totals.   [2] In millions of 480 pound bales.   [3] Indicates no reported or insignificant production.   [4] See footnote 2, Table 1336.

Source: U.S. Department of Agriculture, Foreign Agricultural Service, *World Agricultural Production*, August 2009. See also <http://www.fas.usda.gov/wap/circular/2009/09-08/productionfull08-09.pdf>.

Table 1336. **Wheat, Rice, and Corn—Exports and Imports of Leading Countries: 2000 to 2008**

[In thousands of metric tons (28,027 represents 28,027,000). Wheat data are for trade year beginning in July of year shown; rice data are for calendar year; corn data are for trade year beginning in October of year shown. Countries listed are the ten leading exporters or importers in 2008]

Leading exporters	Exports 2000	Exports 2005	Exports 2008 [1]	Leading importers	Imports 2000	Imports 2005	Imports 2008 [1]
WHEAT				**WHEAT**			
United States	28,027	27,424	26,500	Egypt	6,050	7,771	7,800
EU [2]	15,675	15,694	19,500	Iran	6,245	1,105	7,000
Canada.	17,351	15,631	19,000	Brazil	7,453	5,823	6,000
Russia	696	10,664	16,000	EU [2]	3,536	6,758	6,000
Australia	16,682	15,213	13,500	Algeria	5,600	5,469	5,600
Ukraine.	78	6,461	10,000	Japan	5,885	5,469	5,500
Argentina	11,396	8,301	5,800	Indonesia.	4,069	4,981	5,300
Kazakhstan	3,972	3,817	5,200	South Korea.	3,127	3,884	4,100
Pakistan	253	600	2,400	Iraq	3,200	4,878	3,700
Turkey	1,601	2,900	1,800	Mexico	3,066	3,549	3,600
RICE				**RICE**			
Thailand	7,521	7,376	9,000	Philippines	1,175	1,791	2,000
Vietnam	3,528	4,705	5,200	Nigeria	1,906	1,600	1,700
Pakistan	2,417	3,579	4,000	Iran	765	1,251	1,400
United States	2,541	3,307	3,100	Saudi Arabia	1,053	958	1,370
India.	1,936	4,537	2,500	EU [2]	1,295	1,083	1,200
China [3]	1,847	1,216	1,300	Bangladesh	401	531	1,000
Egypt	705	958	800	Iraq	959	1,306	1,000
Uruguay	806	812	800	Malaysia	633	886	830
Argentina	368	487	500	Cote d'Ivoire.	654	750	800
Burma	670	47	500	Indonesia.	1,500	539	800
CORN				**CORN**			
United States	48,329	56,084	44,000	Japan	16,340	16,617	16,500
Brazil	3,741	2,826	10,000	Mexico	6,017	6,787	7,500
Argentina	12,229	10,707	7,000	South Korea.	8,728	8,488	6,500
Ukraine.	397	2,464	4,000	Egypt	5,268	4,397	4,000
South Africa.	1,415	1,406	2,500	Taiwan [3]	4,924	4,533	3,500
EU [2]	585	449	2,000	Colombia	1,857	3,151	2,800
Paraguay	386	1,314	1,000	Iran	1,265	2,300	2,500
Serbia and Montenegro [4] . .	6	1,274	1,000	EU [2]	3,689	2,634	2,000
Russia	1	53	600	Malaysia	2,588	2,517	2,000
Canada.	127	239	500	Algeria	1,500	2,061	1,900

[1] Estimates.   [2] European Union (EU) has been updated to EU-27 for 1999–2008, but 1995–98 remains EU-15 data. EU15: Austria, Belgium, Denmark, Finland, France, Germany, Greece, Ireland, Italy, Luxembourg, Netherlands, Portugal, Spain, Sweden, and United Kingdom. EU-25 added: Poland, Czech Republic, Hungary, Slovakia, Slovenia, Latvia, Lithuania, Estonia, Cyprus, and Malta. EU-27 added: Romania, Bulgaria.   [3] See footnote 4, Table 1296.   [4] As of June 2006, Serbia and Montenegro are separate countries.

Source: U.S. Department of Agriculture, Economic Research Service, unpublished data from the PS&D (Production, Supply, and Distribution) database.

International Statistics   841

Table 1337. Fisheries—Commercial Catch by Country: 1990 to 2006

[In thousands of metric tons, live weight (97,852 represents 97,852,000). Catch of fish, crustaceans, mollusks. Includes aquaculture (the farming of aquatic organisms), but not marine mammals and aquatic plants]

Country	1990	2000	2005	2006	Country	1990	2000	2005	2006
World [1]	97,852	130,957	142,691	143,648	Norway	1,754	3,191	3,055	2,964
China [2]	31,136	41,568	49,469	51,521	Philippines	2,209	2,291	2,803	2,942
Peru	6,874	10,665	9,415	7,046	Burma	743	1,169	2,217	2,582
India	3,800	5,609	6,653	6,979	Bangladesh	846	1,661	2,216	2,329
Indonesia	3,022	4,909	5,893	6,052	Korea, South	2,843	2,118	2,076	2,263
United States [3]	5,871	5,174	5,385	5,325	Malaysia	1,005	1,441	1,390	1,465
Chile	5,195	4,692	5,027	4,971	Mexico	1,383	1,369	1,438	1,459
Japan	10,361	5,751	4,836	4,921	Iceland	1,508	1,986	1,673	1,335
Thailand	2,790	3,736	4,118	4,162	Taiwan [2]	1,444	1,338	1,322	1,278
Vietnam	939	1,949	3,367	3,618	Spain	(NA)	(NA)	1,066	1,243
Russia	7,604	4,048	3,312	3,390	Canada	1,685	1,125	1,235	(NA)

NA Not available. [1] Includes other countries not shown separately. [2] See footnote 4, Table 1296. [3] The weight of clams, oysters, scallops, and other mollusks includes the shell weight.

Source: U.S. National Oceanic and Atmospheric Administration, National Marine Fisheries Service, *Fisheries of the United States,* annual. Data from Food and Agriculture Organization of the United Nations, Rome, Italy.

Table 1338. Meat Production by Type and Country: 2007 and 2008

[In thousands of metric tons (58,898 represents 58,898,000). Carcass weight basis for beef, veal, and pork. Broiler (chicken, 16-week-old) weight based on ready-to-cook equivalent]

Country	Beef and veal [1]		Country	Pork		Country	Broiler meat [2]	
	2007	2008, prel.		2007	2008, prel.		2007	2008, prel.
World [3]	58,898	58,538	World [3]	94,700	98,441	World [3]	68,187	71,249
United States	12,096	12,163	China [4]	42,878	46,150	United States	16,225	16,561
Brazil	9,303	9,024	European Union [5]	22,858	22,530	China [4]	11,291	11,895
European Union [5]	8,188	8,100	United States	9,962	10,599	Brazil	10,305	11,033
China [4]	6,134	6,100	Brazil	2,990	3,015	European Union [5]	8,320	8,560
Argentina	3,300	3,150	Canada	1,894	1,920	Mexico	2,683	2,804
India	2,413	2,470	Russia	1,910	2,060	India	2,240	2,490
Mexico	2,207	2,225	Vietnam	1,832	1,850	Japan	1,250	1,267
Australia	2,172	2,159	Japan	1,250	1,249	Argentina	1,320	1,420
Russia	1,370	1,315	Mexico	1,152	1,160	Russia	1,350	1,600
Canada	1,279	1,285	Philippines	1,245	1,190	Iran	1423	1,425

[1] May include meat of other bovines. [2] Excludes chicken paws. [3] Includes other countries not shown separately. [4] See footnote 4, Table 1296. [5] See footnote 5, Table 1339.

Source: U.S. Department of Agriculture, Foreign Agricultural Service, *Livestock and Poultry: World Markets and Trade,* annual. See also <http://www.fas.usda.gov/dlp/circular/2009/livestock_poultry0409.pdf>.

Table 1339. Meat Consumption by Type and Country: 2007 to 2008

[In thousands of metric tons (58,308 represents 58,308,000). Carcass weight basis for beef, veal, and pork. Broiler (chicken, 16-week-old) weight based on ready-to-cook equivalent]

Country	Beef and veal [1]		Country	Pork		Country	Broiler meat [2]	
	2007	2008 [3]		2007	2008 [3]		2007	2008 [3]
World	58,308	57,769	World	94,549	98,269	World	67,917	70,518
United States	12,829	12,452	China [4]	42,726	46,357	United States	13,581	13,426
European Union [5]	8,691	8,362	European Union [5]	21,507	20,970	China [4]	11,415	12,009
Brazil	7,144	7,252	United States	8,966	8,811	European Union [5]	8,358	8,497
China [4]	6,065	6,062	Russia	2,803	3,112	Brazil	7,384	7,792
Argentina	2,771	2,733	Japan	2,473	2,486	Mexico	3,067	3,240
Mexico	2,568	2,591	Brazil	2,260	2,390	Russia	2,578	2,744
Russia	2,392	2,441	Vietnam	1,855	1,880	India	2,239	2,489
India [6]	1,735	1,845	Mexico	1,523	1,604	Japan	1,945	1,938
Japan	1,182	1,174	Korea, South	1,502	1,519	Iran	1,464	1,435
Pakistan	1,108	1,128	Philippines	1,270	1,235	Argentina	1,200	1,260
Canada	1,069	1,031	Canada	1,023	993	South Africa	1,239	1,258
Other countries	10,754	10,698	Other countries	6,641	6,912	Other countries	13,447	14,430

[1] May include meat of other bovines. [2] Excludes chicken paws. [3] Preliminary data. [4] See footnote 4, Table 1296. [5] European Union-27: Austria, Belgium, Bulgaria, Cyprus, Czech Republic, Denmark, Estonia, Finland, France, Germany, Greece, Hungary, Ireland, Italy, Latvia, Lithuania, Luxembourg, Malta, Netherlands, Poland, Portugal, Romania, Slovakia, Slovenia, Spain, Sweden, and United Kingdom. [6] Includes buffalo.

Source: U.S. Department of Agriculture, Foreign Agricultural Service, *Livestock and Poultry: World Markets and Trade,* annual. See also <http://www.fas.usda.gov/dlp/circular/2009/livestock_poultry0409.pdf>.

Table 1340. EU and U.S. Organic Land, Farm Sector, and Sales: 2006 and 2007

[EU numbers for land and farms include those certified organic and in-conversion; U.S. numbers include only certified organic farms and land. "Certified organic" means that agricultural products have been grown and processed according to USDA's national organic standards and certified by USDA-accredited state and private certification organizations. 1 hectare = 2.47 acres]

Country	2006			2007		
	Total organic land (hectares)	Organic farms (number)	Farmland under organic production (percent)	Total organic land (hectares)	Organic farms (number)	Farmland under organic production (percent)
Austria	361,817	20,162	13.3	372,026	19,997	13.4
Belgium	29,308	803	2.1	32,628	821	2.4
Denmark	138,079	2,794	5.3	145,393	2,835	5.5
Finland	144,667	3,966	6.5	148,760	4,406	6.5
France	552,824	11,640	2.1	557,133	11,978	1.9
Germany	825,539	17,557	4.9	865,336	18,703	5.1
Greece	302,256	23,900	3.8	278,397	23,769	3.3
Ireland	39,947	1,104	1.0	41,122	1,134	1.0
Italy	1,148,162	45,115	10.6	1,150,253	45,231	9.1
Luxembourg	3,630	72	2.8	3,380	81	2.6
Netherlands	48,425	1,448	2.5	47,019	1,374	2.5
Portugal	269,374	1,696	8.7	233,475	1,949	6.4
Spain	926,390	17,214	3.9	988,323	18,226	3.9
Sweden	225,385	2,380	7.1	248,104	3,028	8.0
United Kingdom	604,571	4,485	3.8	660,200	5,506	4.2
European Union [1]	5,620,374	154,336	4.4	5,771,549	159,038	(NA)
United States	(NA)	9,243	(NA)	(NA)	10,159	(NA)

NA Not available.   [1] See footnote 5, Table 1339.

Source: U.S. Department of Agriculture, Economic Research Service, "Market-Led Versus Government-Facilitated Growth: Development of the U.S. and EU Organic Agricultural Sectors," August 2005 and unpublished data. See also <http://www.ers.usda.gov/Publications/WRS0505/>.

Table 1341. World Production of Major Mineral Commodities: 1990 to 2007

[5,354 represents 5,354,000,000]

Commodity	Unit	1990	2000	2006	2007	Leading producers, 2006
MINERAL FUELS						
Coal	Mil. short tons	5,354	4,951	6,807	(NA)	China, [3] United States, India
Dry natural gas	Tril. cu. ft.	73.7	88.4	104.0	(NA)	Russia, United States, Canada
Natural gas plant liquids [1] . . .	Mil. barrels [2]	4,640	6,466	7,795	(NA)	United States, Saudi Arabia, Canada
Petroleum, crude	Mil. barrels [2]	22,079	25,001	26,813	(NA)	Russia, Saudi Arabia, United States
NONMETALLIC MINERALS						
Cement, hydraulic	Mil. metric tons . . .	1,160	1,600	2,600	2,770	China, [3] India, United States
Diamond, gem and industrial .	Mil. carats	111	(NA)	174	169	Australia, Russia, Botswana
Nitrogen in ammonia	Mil. metric tons . . .	97.5	109.0	126.0	131.0	China, [3] India, Russia
						China, [3] United States, Morocco
Phosphate rock, marketable . .	Mil. metric tons . . .	162	133	142	156	and Western Sahara
Potash, marketable	Mil. metric tons . . .	28.0	25.3	29.0	35.0	Canada, Russia, Belarus
Salt	Mil. metric tons . . .	183	214	251	257	United States, China, [3] Germany
Sulfur, elemental basis	Mil. metric tons . . .	58.0	57.2	66.0	68.0	Canada, United States, China [3]
METALS						
Aluminum [4]	Mil. metric tons . . .	19.3	24.0	34.0	38.0	China, [3] Russia, Canada
Bauxite, gross weight	Mil. metric tons . . .	113	135	190	199	Australia, China, [3] Brazil
Chromite, gross weight	1,000 metric tons . .	13,200	14,400	19,000	21,500	South Africa, Kazakhstan, India
Copper, metal content [5]	1,000 metric tons . .	8,950	13,200	15,100	15,400	Chile, United States, Peru
Gold, metal content [6]	Metric tons	2,180	2,550	2,460	2,380	South Africa, United States, Australia
Iron ore, gross weight [6]	Mil. metric tons . . .	983	1,060	1,800	2,000	China, [3] Brazil, Australia
Lead, metal content [5]	1,000 metric tons . .	3,370	3,100	3,650	3,770	China, [3] Australia, United States
Nickel, metal content [5]	1,000 metric tons . .	974	1,250	1,560	1,660	Russia, Canada, Australia
Tin, metal content [5]	1,000 metric tons . .	220	238	302	320	China, [3] Indonesia, Peru

NA Not available.   [1] Excludes China.   [2] 42-gallon barrels.   [3] See footnote 4, Table 1296.   [4] Unalloyed ingot metal.   [5] Mine output.   [6] Includes iron ore concentrates and iron ore agglomerates.

Source: Mineral fuels, U.S. Energy Information Administration, *International Energy Annual, 2006* (accessed 9 July 2008); nonmetallic minerals and metals, 1990, U.S. Bureau of Mines, thereafter, U.S. Geological Survey, *Minerals Yearbook; Annual Reports;* and *Mineral Commodity Summaries, 2008.*

International Statistics   843

Table 1342. **World Primary Energy Production by Region and Type: 1980 to 2006**

[In quadrillion Btu (287.6 represents 287,600,000,000,000,000). Btu = British thermal unit. For Btu conversion factors, see source]

Region and type	1980	1990	1995	2000	2001	2002	2003	2004	2005	2006 [1]
World total [2]	287.6	350.0	364.1	395.7	402.8	406.5	422.0	443.7	459.3	469.4
North America	83.2	92.0	96.2	99.0	99.4	100.1	98.6	99.3	98.9	100.6
United States	67.2	70.9	71.3	71.5	71.9	70.9	70.3	70.4	69.6	71.0
Central and South America	12.1	16.7	21.1	26.0	26.0	25.3	25.7	27.1	28.3	29.0
Europe	40.3	47.0	49.1	50.9	51.5	51.3	50.7	50.5	48.9	47.7
Eurasia [3]	56.5	72.1	52.3	55.7	57.6	59.3	63.1	66.3	68.3	70.1
Middle East	42.3	41.0	48.3	57.5	56.2	54.2	57.6	62.1	65.2	65.3
Africa	17.4	21.6	24.1	27.8	28.1	28.0	30.2	32.0	34.6	35.3
Asia and Oceania	35.8	59.6	73.0	78.9	84.1	88.3	96.1	106.3	115.2	121.5
Petroleum	133.1	136.2	141.8	156.5	155.7	153.8	159.1	166.5	169.1	168.7
Dry natural gas	54.7	76.1	80.4	91.0	93.3	96.3	98.5	101.5	104.8	107.2
Coal	71.3	91.0	88.5	90.4	95.7	97.7	105.3	114.1	122.1	128.5
Hydroelectric power	17.9	22.4	25.3	26.8	26.6	26.5	26.8	27.9	29.0	29.7
Nuclear electric power . . .	7.6	20.4	23.3	25.7	26.4	26.7	26.4	27.3	27.5	27.8
Geothermal, solar, wind, wood, and waste	0.5	1.7	2.2	3.0	3.1	3.4	3.7	4.0	4.3	4.7

[1] Preliminary.   [2] Includes geothermal, solar, and wood and waste energy produced in the United States and not used for generating electricity, not shown separately by type.   [3] Prior to 1992, data were for the former U.S.S.R. only.

Source: U.S. Energy Information Administration, "International Energy Annual, 2006"; <http://www.eia.doe.gov/emeu/iea/contents.html> (accessed 2 January 2009).

Table 1343. **World Primary Energy Consumption by Region and Type: 1980 to 2006**

[In quadrillion Btu (283.2 represents 283,200,000,000,000,000). Btu = British thermal unit. For Btu conversion factors, see source]

Region and type	1980	1990	1995	2000	2001	2002	2003	2004	2005	2006 [1]
World total [2]	283.2	347.7	365.6	397.9	402.2	410.6	426.0	447.1	462.1	472.3
North America	91.6	100.7	108.8	118.3	115.4	117.2	118.2	120.7	121.6	121.2
United States	78.1	84.7	91.2	99.0	96.3	97.9	98.2	100.4	100.5	99.9
Central and South America	11.5	14.5	17.6	20.8	21.2	21.1	21.6	22.4	23.4	24.2
Europe	71.9	76.4	76.9	81.5	82.8	82.5	84.2	85.7	86.2	86.4
Eurasia [3]	46.7	61.0	42.6	40.6	40.9	41.6	43.4	44.7	45.8	45.9
Middle East	5.8	11.2	13.8	17.3	17.9	19.0	19.8	20.9	22.7	23.8
Africa	6.8	9.5	10.6	12.0	12.6	12.7	13.4	14.0	14.5	14.5
Asia and Oceania	48.9	74.4	95.3	107.3	111.3	116.4	125.5	138.7	147.8	156.3
Petroleum	131.0	136.4	142.6	155.4	156.7	157.9	161.1	166.7	169.9	171.7
Dry natural gas	53.8	75.3	81.2	91.0	92.4	95.7	99.1	103.3	107.0	108.0
Coal	70.0	89.2	88.5	93.6	94.9	98.2	106.7	115.6	121.7	127.5
Hydroelectric power	17.9	22.4	25.3	26.8	26.6	26.5	26.8	27.9	29.0	29.7
Nuclear electric power . . .	7.6	20.4	23.3	25.7	26.4	26.7	26.4	27.3	27.5	27.8
Geothermal, solar, wind, wood, and waste	0.5	1.7	2.2	3.0	3.1	3.4	3.7	4.0	4.3	4.7

[1] Preliminary.   [2] See footnote 2, Table 1342.   [3] Prior to 1992, data were for the former U.S.S.R. only.

Source: U.S. Energy Information Administration, "International Energy Annual, 2006"; <http://www.eia.doe.gov/emeu/iea/contents.html> (accessed 2 January 2009).

Table 1344. **World Energy Consumption by Region and Energy Source, 1990 to 2005, and Projections, 2010 to 2025**

[In quadrillion Btu (347.3 represents 347,300,000,000,000,000). Btu = British thermal units. For Btu conversion factors, see source. Energy totals include net imports of coal coke and electricity generated from biomass in the United States. Totals may not equal sum of components due to independent rounding. The electricity portion of the national consumption values consists of generation for domestic use plus an adjustment for electricity trade based on a fuel's share of total generation in the exporting country]

Region and energy source	1990	2004	2005	Projections			
				2010	2015	2020	2025
World, total	347.4	447.3	462.2	512.5	563.0	608.4	651.8
North America	100.7	120.6	121.3	126.4	132.3	137.8	143.4
United States [1]	84.7	100.1	100.1	103.3	107.3	110.8	114.5
Western Europe	70.0	81.0	81.4	83.9	86.8	88.5	90.4
Industrialized Asia	26.8	37.8	38.2	39.3	41.4	42.7	43.7
Eastern Europe and former Soviet Union . . .	67.3	49.5	50.7	55.1	59.5	63.3	66.0
Developing Asia	47.4	101.0	109.9	137.1	164.2	189.4	215.3
Middle East	11.2	20.9	22.9	26.4	29.5	32.6	34.7
Africa	9.5	14.0	14.4	16.5	18.9	20.9	22.5
Central and South America	14.5	22.5	23.4	27.7	30.5	33.2	35.7
Oil	136.4	166.6	169.4	181.1	194.4	206.1	216.9
Natural gas	75.2	103.3	107.4	120.3	134.4	146.9	155.8
Coal	89.2	116.1	122.5	140.2	157.8	171.7	186.7
Nuclear	20.4	27.4	27.5	28.8	31.4	34.5	37.7
Other	26.2	33.8	35.5	42.0	45.0	49.3	54.7

[1] Includes the 50 states and the District of Columbia.

Source: U.S. Energy Information Administration (EIA), *International Energy Outlook 2008* (published June 2008). See also <http://www.eia.doe.gov/oiaf/ieo/ieorefcase.html>.

Table 1345. **Energy Consumption by Country: 2000 and 2006**

[**397.9 represents** 397,900,000,000,000,000. See text of this section for general comments about the data. For data qualifications for countries and Btu conversion factors, see source]

Country	Total (quad. Btu) 2000	Total (quad. Btu) 2006, prel.	Per capita (mil. Btu) 2000	Per capita (mil. Btu) 2006, prel.	Country	Total (quad. Btu) 2000	Total (quad. Btu) 2006, prel.	Per capita (mil. Btu) 2000	Per capita (mil. Btu) 2006, prel.
World total	397.9	472.3	65.6	72.4	Japan	22.4	22.8	177.0	178.7
United States	99.0	99.9	350.6	334.6	Korea, North	0.9	0.9	39.7	41.1
Algeria	1.2	1.5	40.7	46.6	Korea, South	7.9	9.4	166.6	193.4
Argentina	2.7	3.2	71.2	79.0	Kuwait	0.9	1.1	460.9	469.8
Australia	4.9	5.6	253.2	276.9	Libya	0.6	0.8	123.1	132.0
Austria	1.4	1.5	171.4	187.2	Malaysia	1.9	2.6	85.9	104.8
Bahrain	0.4	0.5	575.2	695.4	Mexico	6.3	7.4	63.3	68.5
Bangladesh	0.5	0.7	3.9	5.0	Morocco	0.4	0.5	14.8	15.2
Belarus	1.1	1.1	104.9	117.0	Netherlands	3.8	4.1	238.5	250.9
Belgium	2.7	2.8	266.3	265.1	New Zealand	0.8	0.9	223.3	211.2
Brazil	8.6	9.6	48.7	51.2	Nigeria	0.8	1.0	7.1	7.8
Bulgaria	0.9	0.9	111.3	121.5	Norway	2.0	1.9	436.2	410.8
Burma	0.2	0.2	3.5	5.0	Pakistan	1.9	2.3	12.9	14.2
Canada	12.9	14.0	416.4	427.2	Peru	0.5	0.6	20.3	21.6
Chile .	1.0	1.3	67.0	77.6	Philippines	1.3	1.3	15.7	14.2
China [1]	37.2	73.8	29.3	56.2	Poland	3.6	3.9	93.8	100.1
Colombia	1.2	1.3	29.4	29.8	Portugal	1.1	1.1	103.6	102.2
Congo (Kinshasa) [2]	0.1	0.1	1.8	1.6	Romania	1.6	1.7	70.6	75.2
Cuba	0.5	0.4	41.2	35.1	Russia	27.5	30.4	187.2	213.9
Czech Republic	1.6	1.8	156.7	176.6	Saudi Arabia	4.9	6.9	209.6	255.0
Denmark	0.9	0.9	163.8	161.3	Serbia and Montenegro [3] .	0.6	0.7	57.8	68.4
Ecuador	0.3	0.4	27.6	31.0	South Africa	4.6	5.2	104.2	117.2
Egypt	2.0	2.5	28.3	32.2	Spain	5.6	6.5	140.4	161.2
Finland	1.2	1.3	234.1	252.7	Sweden	2.3	2.2	254.2	245.8
France	10.8	11.4	177.4	180.7	Switzerland	1.3	1.3	178.1	170.7
Germany	14.3	14.6	173.5	177.5	Syria	0.8	0.8	48.0	42.9
Greece	1.3	1.5	126.7	139.1	Taiwan [1]	3.8	4.6	170.1	200.6
Hong Kong	0.8	1.2	121.0	167.7	Thailand	2.6	3.7	41.7	57.9
Hungary	1.0	1.1	101.3	114.7	Trinidad and Tobago	0.4	0.8	376.1	769.9
India	13.5	17.7	13.4	15.9	Tunisia	0.3	0.3	31.5	32.9
Indonesia	4.1	4.1	18.9	17.9	Turkey	3.2	3.9	48.2	55.5
Iran	5.0	7.7	79.2	118.2	Ukraine	5.8	5.9	117.4	125.9
Iraq	1.1	1.2	47.8	46.6	United Arab Emirates	1.9	2.5	579.7	577.6
Ireland	0.6	0.7	158.2	173.4	United Kingdom	9.7	9.8	163.2	161.7
Israel	0.8	0.8	132.7	123.5	Venezuela	2.8	3.2	117.9	124.4
Italy	7.6	8.1	132.2	138.7	Vietnam	0.8	1.4	9.6	16.6

[1] See footnote 4, Table 1296.   [2] See footnote 5, Table 1296.   [3] See footnote 4, Table 1336.

Source: U.S. Energy Information Administration, "International Energy Annual, 2006"; <http://www.eia.doe.gov/emeu/iea /contents.html> (accessed 9 July 2009).

Table 1346. **World Daily Crude Oil Production by Major Producing Country: 1980 to 2006**

[In thousands of barrels per day (59,558 barrels represents 59,558,000 barrels)]

Country	1980	1990	1995	2000	2002	2003	2004	2005	2006
World, total [1]	59,558	60,492	62,385	68,495	67,162	69,434	72,493	73,737	73,461
Algeria	1,106	1,175	1,202	1,254	1,306	1,611	1,677	1,797	1,814
Angola	150	475	646	746	896	903	1,052	1,250	1,413
Argentina	491	483	715	761	799	783	733	704	696
Australia	380	575	562	722	626	512	436	446	429
Brazil	182	631	695	1,269	1,455	1,496	1,477	1,634	1,723
Canada	1,435	1,553	1,805	1,977	2,171	2,306	2,398	2,369	2,525
China [2]	2,114	2,774	2,990	3,249	3,390	3,409	3,485	3,609	3,673
Colombia	126	440	585	691	577	541	529	526	531
Ecuador	204	285	392	395	393	411	528	532	536
Egypt	595	873	920	768	715	713	673	658	639
India	182	660	703	646	665	660	683	665	689
Indonesia	1,577	1,462	1,503	1,428	1,249	1,155	1,096	1,067	1,019
Iran	1,662	3,088	3,643	3,696	3,444	3,743	4,001	4,139	4,028
Iraq	2,514	2,040	560	2,571	2,023	1,308	2,011	1,878	1,996
Kazakhstan	(X)	(X)	414	718	939	1,027	1,203	1,288	1,313
Kuwait	1,656	1,175	2,057	2,079	1,894	2,136	2,376	2,529	2,535
Libya	1,787	1,375	1,390	1,410	1,319	1,421	1,515	1,633	1,681
Malaysia	283	619	682	690	698	738	755	631	613
Mexico	1,936	2,553	2,618	3,012	3,177	3,371	3,383	3,334	3,256
Nigeria	2,055	1,810	1,993	2,165	2,118	2,275	2,329	2,627	2,440
Norway	486	1,630	2,766	3,222	3,131	3,042	2,954	2,698	2,491
Oman	282	685	851	970	897	819	751	774	738
Qatar	472	406	442	737	679	715	783	835	850
Russia	(X)	(X)	5,995	6,479	7,408	8,132	8,805	9,043	9,247
Saudi Arabia	9,900	6,410	8,231	8,404	7,634	8,775	9,101	9,550	9,152
United Arab Emirates	1,709	2,117	2,233	2,368	2,082	2,348	2,478	2,535	2,636
United Kingdom	1,622	1,820	2,489	2,275	2,292	2,093	1,845	1,649	1,490
United States	8,597	7,355	6,560	5,822	5,746	5,681	5,419	5,178	5,102
Venezuela	2,168	2,137	2,750	3,155	2,604	2,335	2,557	2,565	2,511
Yemen	–	193	345	438	439	429	404	400	375

– Represents zero.   X Not applicable.   [1] Includes countries not shown separately.   [2] See footnote 4, Table 1296.

Source: U.S. Energy Information Administration, "International Energy Annual, 2006"; <http://www.eia.doe.gov/pub/international /iealf/table22.xls> (accessed 9 July 2009).

International Statistics   845

Table 1347. **World Dry Natural Gas Production by Major Producing Country: 1980 to 2006**

[In trillion cubic feet (53.35 represents 53,350,000,000,000)]

Country	1980	1990	2000	2001	2002	2003	2004	2005	2006
World total [1]	53.35	73.71	88.42	90.56	92.33	95.52	98.53	101.52	103.98
Russia	(X)	(X)	20.63	20.51	21.03	21.77	22.39	22.62	23.17
United States	**19.40**	**17.81**	**19.18**	**19.62**	**18.93**	**19.10**	**18.59**	**18.05**	**18.48**
Canada	2.76	3.85	6.47	6.60	6.63	6.45	6.48	6.56	6.55
Iran	0.25	0.84	2.13	2.33	2.65	2.86	2.96	3.56	3.84
Norway.	0.92	0.98	1.87	1.95	2.41	2.70	2.95	3.07	3.20
Algeria	0.41	1.79	2.94	2.79	2.80	2.85	2.83	3.11	3.08
United Kingdom	1.32	1.75	3.83	3.69	3.66	3.63	3.39	3.10	2.82
Netherlands	3.40	2.69	2.56	2.75	2.68	2.57	3.04	2.78	2.73
Saudi Arabia	0.33	1.08	1.76	1.90	2.00	2.12	2.32	2.52	2.59
Turkmenistan.	(X)	(X)	1.64	1.70	1.89	2.09	2.07	2.22	2.23
Uzbekistan	(X)	(X)	1.99	2.23	2.04	2.03	2.11	2.11	2.22
Malaysia.	0.06	0.65	1.50	1.66	1.71	2.01	2.20	2.24	2.19
China [2]	0.51	0.51	0.96	1.07	1.15	1.21	1.44	1.76	2.07
Indonesia	0.63	1.53	2.36	2.34	2.48	2.61	2.66	2.61	2.02
Qatar	0.18	0.28	1.03	0.95	1.04	1.11	1.38	1.62	1.79
Mexico	0.90	0.90	1.31	1.30	1.33	1.40	1.46	1.52	1.74
United Arab Emirates	0.20	0.78	1.36	1.39	1.53	1.58	1.63	1.66	1.72
Argentina	0.28	0.63	1.32	1.31	1.28	1.45	1.58	1.61	1.63
Egypt	0.03	0.29	0.65	0.87	0.88	1.06	1.15	1.50	1.60
Australia	0.31	0.72	1.16	1.19	1.23	1.27	1.31	1.44	1.51
Trinidad and Tobago	0.08	0.18	0.49	0.54	0.61	0.87	0.99	1.07	1.29
Pakistan	0.29	0.48	0.86	0.77	0.81	0.89	0.97	1.09	1.11
India	0.05	0.40	0.79	0.85	0.93	0.96	1.00	1.06	1.10
Nigeria	0.04	0.13	0.44	0.53	0.50	0.72	0.77	0.79	1.01
Venezuela.	0.52	0.76	0.96	1.12	1.00	0.86	0.96	1.01	0.92
Kazakhstan.	(X)	(X)	0.31	0.36	0.46	0.49	0.72	0.93	0.91
Thailand	–	0.21	0.66	0.66	0.71	0.77	0.79	0.84	0.86
Oman	0.03	0.10	0.32	0.49	0.53	0.56	0.61	0.70	0.84
Germany	(X)	(X)	0.78	0.79	0.79	0.78	0.73	0.70	0.69
Ukraine	(X)	(X)	0.64	0.64	0.65	0.69	0.68	0.69	0.69

– Represents or rounds to zero.   X Not applicable.   [1] Includes countries not shown separately.   [2] See footnote 4, Table 1296.

Source: U. S. Energy Information Administration, "International Energy Annual, 2006"; <http://www.eia.doe.gov/pub/international/iealf/table24.xls> (accessed 2 January 2009).

Table 1348. **World Coal Production by Major Producing Country: 1980 to 2006**

[In millions of short tons (4,186.4 represents 4,186,400,000)]

Country	1980	1990	2000	2001	2002	2003	2004	2005	2006
World, total [1]	4,186.4	5,353.8	4,950.5	5,244.1	5,271.5	5,659.5	6,092.9	6,490.9	6,807.0
China [2]	683.6	1,190.4	1,314.4	1,458.7	1,521.2	1,837.6	2,156.4	2,430.3	2,620.5
United States	**829.7**	**1,029.1**	**1,073.6**	**1,127.7**	**1,094.3**	**1,071.8**	**1,112.1**	**1,131.5**	**1,162.7**
India	125.8	247.6	370.0	388.7	401.1	425.9	455.3	471.7	498.9
Australia	116.1	225.8	338.1	362.9	376.8	377.2	390.7	414.0	419.6
Russia	(X)	(X)	276.4	285.4	273.2	294.7	295.6	321.0	322.8
South Africa	131.9	193.2	248.9	250.8	245.8	263.8	267.7	270.1	269.4
Germany	(X)	(X)	226.0	227.1	232.6	229.1	232.7	227.0	220.6
Indonesia	0.6	11.6	84.5	102.1	114.0	127.1	145.9	168.0	213.2
Poland	253.5	237.1	179.2	180.0	178.2	180.3	178.3	175.0	171.1
Kazakhstan.	(X)	(X)	81.7	87.2	81.3	93.6	95.8	95.4	106.2
Canada	40.4	75.3	76.2	77.6	73.4	68.5	73.1	74.5	72.8
Greece.	25.6	57.2	70.4	73.1	77.7	75.3	77.2	76.5	72.4
Turkey	20.8	52.3	69.7	68.5	59.5	53.5	51.1	64.3	71.5
Colombia	4.5	22.6	42.0	47.9	43.6	55.1	59.2	65.1	70.2
Czech Republic	(X)	(X)	71.8	72.9	70.4	71.0	68.6	68.9	69.7
Ukraine	(X)	(X)	68.8	68.0	67.9	70.8	65.7	66.5	68.0
Vietnam	5.7	5.3	13.9	15.8	19.9	21.1	31.7	38.4	45.1
Korea, North	48.6	51.0	32.8	33.7	32.4	33.3	35.0	38.2	39.1
Romania.	38.8	42.1	32.3	36.7	33.5	36.4	35.0	34.3	38.6
Bulgaria	33.3	34.9	29.2	29.4	28.7	30.1	29.2	27.2	28.1
Thailand	1.6	13.7	19.6	21.6	21.6	20.8	22.1	23.6	21.0
Spain	35.3	46.4	30.8	29.7	28.9	27.0	22.6	21.5	20.3
United Kingdom	143.8	104.1	33.7	34.7	32.6	30.6	27.0	22.1	19.9
Estonia.	(X)	(X)	12.9	13.0	13.7	16.4	15.4	16.1	15.6
Mexico	4.0	8.6	12.5	12.5	12.1	10.6	10.9	11.9	12.7
Hungary	28.7	19.7	15.5	15.3	14.4	14.7	12.4	10.5	11.0
Bosnia and Herzegovina . . .	(X)	(X)	8.9	8.2	9.5	9.0	9.5	10.0	10.1
Mongolia.	5.3	7.9	5.5	5.8	6.2	6.2	7.5	8.6	8.7
Venezuela	(Z)	2.4	8.7	8.4	8.1	7.3	7.4	7.9	8.2
Brazil	5.1	5.1	7.4	6.2	5.7	5.1	6.0	6.9	7.0

X Not applicable.   Z Less than 50,000 short tons.   [1] Includes countries not shown separately.   [2] See footnote 4, Table 1296.

Source: U.S. Energy Information Administration, "International Energy Annual, 2006"; <http://www.eia.doe.gov/pub/international/iealf/table25.xls> (accessed 2 January 2009).

Table 1349. Net Electricity Generation by Type and Country: 2005

[17,363.9 represents 17,363,900,000,000. kWh = kilowatt hours]

Country	Total [1] (bil. kWh)	Thermal [2]	Hydro	Nuclear	Country	Total [1] (bil. kWh)	Thermal [2]	Hydro	Nuclear
World, total [3]	17,363.9	66.0	16.7	15.2	Indonesia	120.3	85.9	8.9	–
					Egypt	102.8	87.3	12.2	–
United States	4,062.0	71.6	6.7	19.3	Argentina	100.3	59.3	33.1	6.4
China [4]	2,369.9	81.1	16.6	2.1	Venezuela	99.2	25.1	74.9	0.0
Japan	1,030.2	62.3	7.3	28.1	Netherlands	94.3	86.7	0.1	4.0
Russia	904.4	65.1	19.1	15.5	Pakistan	92.3	64.3	33.1	2.6
India.	661.8	81.2	15.2	2.4	Malaysia	82.9	93.1	6.9	0.0
Canada.	607.5	24.7	59.3	14.4	Belgium	80.8	40.8	0.4	55.9
Germany.	579.7	62.5	3.3	26.7	Czech Republic	77.4	65.7	3.0	30.4
France	544.4	10.6	9.4	78.8	Finland	67.1	32.8	20.3	32.9
Brazil	395.7	8.9	84.4	2.5	Kazakhstan	64.2	87.9	12.1	–
United Kingdom	373.0	74.2	1.3	20.8	Austria	61.0	35.7	58.2	–
Korea, South	366.2	60.8	1.0	38.1	United Arab Emirates. .	57.1	100.0	–	–
Italy	281.0	82.2	12.7	–	Romania	56.9	55.6	35.1	9.3
Spain	273.3	64.6	6.5	20.0	Greece	56.1	88.6	8.8	–
Australia	231.2	92.2	6.6	–	Switzerland	56.1	1.8	55.1	39.5
Mexico	229.1	79.3	12.0	4.5	Philippines.	53.7	67.0	15.5	–
South Africa.	228.3	94.1	0.4	5.4	Vietnam	51.3	58.6	41.4	–
Taiwan [4]	210.4	78.2	3.7	18.0	Paraguay	50.7	(Z)	100.0	–
Ukraine.	175.4	45.4	7.1	47.5	Colombia.	50.5	20.9	78.0	–
Iran	170.4	90.7	9.3	–	Chile	50.2	46.8	51.5	–
Saudi Arabia	164.5	100.0	–	–	Israel	46.8	99.9	0.1	–
Turkey	154.2	74.4	25.4	–	Uzbekistan	45.2	86.6	13.4	–
Sweden	153.3	2.4	47.0	44.8	Portugal	43.7	80.9	10.7	–
Poland	146.3	97.2	1.5	–	Bulgaria	41.8	47.2	11.2	41.5
Norway.	135.7	0.4	99.0	–					
Thailand	124.6	92.9	4.6	–					

– Represents zero. Z Less than 0.05 percent. [1] Includes thermal, hydro, nuclear, and geothermal, solar, wind, and wood and waste generation. [2] Electricity generated from coal, oil, and gas. [3] Includes countries not shown separately. [4] See footnote 4, Table 1296.

Source: U.S. Energy Information Administration, "International Energy Annual 2006"; <http://www.eia.doe.gov/pub/international/iea2006/table63.xls> (accessed 2 January 2009).

Table 1350. Commercial Nuclear Power Generation by Country: 1990 to 2008

[Generation for calendar years; other data as of December (1,743.9 represents 1,743,900,000,000). kWh = kilowatt-hours. kW = kilowatts]

Country	Reactors				Gross electricity generated (bil. kWh)				Gross capacity (1,000 kW)			
	1990	2000	2007	2008	1990	2000	2007	2008	1990	2000	2007	2008
Total.	368	433	439	439	1,743.9	2,540.5	2,666.9	2,690.2	301,745	373,804	395,644	396,361
United States . .	112	104	104	104	606.4	789.1	843.0	842.4	105,998	103,129	106,476	106,977
Argentina	2	2	2	2	7.0	6.2	7.2	7.4	1,005	1,005	1,005	1,005
Armenia	(NA)	1	1	1	(NA)	(NA)	2.5	2.5	(NA)	408	408	408
Belgium	7	7	7	7	42.7	48.2	48.2	45.8	5,740	5,995	6,101	6,101
Brazil.	1	2	2	2	2.0	6.1	12.4	14	657	1,966	2,007	2,007
Bulgaria	(NA)	6	2	2	(NA)	(NA)	14.2	15.8	(NA)	3,760	2,000	2,000
Canada	19	21	21	21	74.0	73.8	94.0	94.1	13,855	15,795	15,367	15,367
China [1]	(NA)	2	9	9	(NA)	14.7	62.9	42.6	(NA)	1,968	9,014	9,014
Czech Republic .	(NA)	4	6	6	(NA)	13.6	26.1	26.5	(NA)	1,760	3,760	3,834
Finland.	4	4	4	4	18.9	22.5	23.4	22.9	2,400	2,760	2,800	2,800
France	58	57	58	58	314.1	395.7	439.1	438.6	58,862	62,920	65,880	65,880
Germany	22	19	17	17	147.2	169.7	140.5	148.7	23,973	22,234	21,457	21,497
Great Britain . .	42	33	19	19	68.8	83.6	(NA)	(NA)	15,274	15,272	12,540	12,540
Hungary	4	4	4	4	13.6	14.1	14.7	14.8	1,760	1,851	1,910	1,940
India	6	13	17	17	6.0	15.5	17.8	15.5	1,330	2,960	4,120	4,120
Italy	2	(NA)	(NA)	(NA)	–	(NA)	(NA)	(NA)	1,132	(NA)	(NA)	(NA)
Japan	40	52	55	55	191.9	319.8	278.7	251.7	31,645	45,082	49,580	49,580
Korea, South . .	9	16	20	20	52.8	108.9	142.9	150.9	7,616	13,768	18,393	18,393
Lithuania	(NA)	2	1	1	(NA)	7.8	9.8	9.9	(NA)	3,000	1,500	1,300
Mexico	1	2	2	2	2.1	8.2	10.4	9.8	675	1,350	1,350	1,364
Netherlands . . .	2	1	1	1	3.4	3.9	4.2	4.2	540	480	512	515
Pakistan	1	1	2	2	0.4	0.4	2.5	1.9	137	137	462	462
Romania.	(NA)	1	2	2	(NA)	5.5	7.0	11.2	(NA)	706	1,412	1,412
Russia	(NA)	29	31	31	(NA)	128.9	158.3	162.3	(NA)	21,266	23,266	23,266
Slovakia	(NA)	6	5	5	(NA)	16.5	15.3	16.7	(NA)	2,640	2,200	2,200
Slovenia	1	1	1	1	4.6	4.8	5.7	6.3	664	664	727	727
South Africa . . .	2	2	2	2	8.9	13.6	13.2	13.3	1,930	1,930	1,930	1,930
Spain.	10	9	8	8	54.3	62.2	55.0	59	7,984	7,808	7,735	7,735
Sweden	12	11	10	10	68.2	57.3	66.9	63.9	10,344	9,844	9,356	9,611
Switzerland . . .	5	5	5	5	23.6	26.3	27.7	27.5	3,079	3,322	3,352	3,352
Taiwan [1]	6	6	6	6	32.9	38.5	40.6	40.8	5,146	5,144	5,144	5,144
Ukraine	(NA)	14	15	15	(NA)	77.3	92.4	89.8	(NA)	12,880	13,880	13,880

– Represents zero. NA Not available. [1] See footnote 4, Table 1296.

Source: Platts Energy, A Division of The McGraw-Hill Companies Inc., New York, NY, Nucleonics Week, February issue (copyright).

Table 1351. **Carbon Dioxide Emissions From Consumption of Fossil Fuels by Country: 1990 to 2006**

[In million metric tons of carbon dioxide (21,683.2 represents 21,683,200,000). Includes carbon dioxide emissions from the consumption of petroleum, natural gas, and coal, and the flaring of natural gas]

Country	1990	1995	2000	2002	2003	2004	2005	2006
World, total [1]	21,683.2	22,284.0	24,010.7	24,823.3	26,064.0	27,453.3	28,485.0	29,195.4
Australia	269.9	291.0	359.8	382.7	380.7	391.0	416.9	417.1
Brazil	237.7	289.5	344.9	347.2	346.4	356.3	370.6	377.2
Canada	474.8	510.8	565.2	573.3	602.5	614.7	632.0	614.3
China [2]	2,293.4	2,903.4	2,966.5	3,440.6	4,061.6	4,847.3	5,429.3	6,017.7
France	368.6	373.2	402.3	402.3	408.8	416.3	414.4	417.8
Germany	(X)	885.7	856.9	857.4	874.0	871.9	852.6	857.6
India	583.2	878.4	1,012.3	1,033.5	1,048.1	1,151.3	1,194.0	1,293.2
Indonesia	151.4	215.2	273.9	314.9	305.4	323.3	323.5	280.4
Iran	202.1	262.3	320.7	365.1	386.9	406.6	445.8	471.5
Italy	416.1	432.1	448.4	452.6	475.1	469.8	472.8	468.2
Japan	1,053.8	1,119.6	1,203.7	1,203.3	1,253.3	1,257.9	1,249.6	1,246.8
Korea, South	243.4	382.8	445.8	468.4	477.7	488.7	496.6	514.5
Mexico	302.4	321.6	383.4	383.8	389.1	384.7	406.5	435.6
Netherlands	212.1	223.7	251.7	259.1	261.4	270.6	272.7	260.5
Poland	336.4	310.7	295.0	276.4	289.2	294.5	289.8	303.4
Russia	(X)	1,638.4	1,582.4	1,571.8	1,626.9	1,663.4	1,698.6	1,704.4
Saudi Arabia	208.0	235.3	290.5	311.6	347.3	388.8	405.5	424.1
South Africa	301.0	351.4	391.7	385.2	418.2	447.7	437.8	443.6
Spain	236.8	251.2	326.9	349.0	357.3	370.9	384.0	372.6
Taiwan [2]	118.8	183.4	252.2	273.8	290.3	286.6	290.4	300.4
Thailand	83.9	145.1	161.9	187.2	205.9	225.7	242.7	245.0
Turkey	129.4	153.3	202.4	194.9	206.6	211.1	231.2	235.7
Ukraine	(X)	424.0	326.8	326.6	357.4	346.6	349.8	328.7
United Kingdom	605.0	562.5	561.2	563.9	575.2	582.3	584.7	585.7
United States	**5,028.5**	**5,324.0**	**5,860.4**	**5,823.8**	**5,877.7**	**5,969.3**	**5,994.3**	**5,902.7**

X Not applicable.   [1] Includes other countries not shown separately.   [2] See footnote 4, Table 1296.

Source: U.S. Energy Information Administration, "International Energy Annual, 2006" (published 2 January 2009); <http://www.eia.doe.gov /pub/international/iealf/tableh1co2.xls>.

Table 1352. **Average Temperatures and Precipitation—Selected International Cities**

[In degrees Fahrenheit, except as noted. Data are generally based on a standard 30-year period; for details, see source. For data on U.S. cities, see Tables 377–384. Minus sign (–) indicates degrees below zero]

City	January Average high	January Average low	January Warm-est	January Coldest	January Average precipi-tation (inches)	July Average high	July Average low	July Warm-est	July Coldest	July Average precipi-tation (inches)
Amsterdam, Netherlands . . .	41	34	57	3	3.1	69	55	90	39	2.9
Athens, Greece	55	44	70	28	1.9	89	73	108	61	0.2
Baghdad, Iraq	58	38	75	25	1.1	110	78	122	61	–
Bangkok, Thailand	89	71	95	54	0.4	90	78	99	72	6.2
Beijing, China	34	17	54	1	0.2	86	72	104	63	8.8
Berlin, Germany	35	26	58	–11	(NA)	73	56	95	41	(NA)
Bogota, Colombia	66	43	84	27	1.9	64	47	82	32	1.8
Brasilia, Brazil	81	64	95	54	(NA)	79	52	97	37	(NA)
Buenos Aires, Argentina . . .	85	64	104	44	4.2	58	41	88	23	2.3
Cairo, Egypt	65	49	86	32	0.2	93	72	108	63	–
Frankfurt, Germany	38	30	56	–4	1.8	75	57	97	38	2.4
Geneva, Switzerland	39	29	57	–2	2.2	77	56	96	41	2.8
Hong Kong, China	67	58	79	43	1.1	89	81	97	70	14.3
Istanbul, Turkey	46	37	64	16	3.7	82	66	100	50	0.7
Jakarta, Indonesia	83	75	92	72	(NA)	88	74	92	67	(NA)
Karachi, Pakistan	76	55	93	39	0.3	89	83	109	68	3.5
Lagos, Nigeria	82	79	93	64	(NA)	79	76	88	70	(NA)
London, England	45	36	61	15	2.4	72	56	93	45	1.8
Madrid, Spain	51	32	68	14	1.8	90	61	104	46	0.4
Manila, Philippines	86	71	95	61	0.8	88	76	99	70	15.9
Mexico City, Mexico	70	45	86	26	0.3	74	56	86	37	5.1
Montreal, Canada	21	7	52	–31	2.8	79	61	93	43	3.4
Moscow, Russia	21	11	46	–33	1.4	71	55	95	41	3.2
Nairobi, Kenya	77	58	88	45	1.8	71	54	85	43	0.5
New Delhi, India	68	48	85	32	0.9	93	81	111	70	7.9
Paris, France	43	34	59	1	(NA)	75	58	95	41	(NA)
Rio De Janeiro, Brazil	91	74	109	64	5.3	81	64	102	52	1.8
Rome, Italy	55	39	64	19	3.2	83	66	100	55	0.6
Seoul, Korea	33	21	55	–1	(NA)	82	71	97	55	(NA)
Singapore, Singapore	85	73	100	66	9.4	86	76	99	70	5.9
Sydney, Australia	79	65	109	49	4.0	62	44	80	32	2.5
Tel Aviv, Israel	62	46	84	32	(NA)	87	69	100	50	(NA)
Tokyo, Japan	48	35	66	25	2.0	82	71	95	55	5.3
Toronto, Canada	28	15	59	–24	1.9	79	60	99	45	2.8

– Represents zero.   NA Not available.

Source: U.S. National Oceanic and Atmospheric Administration, *Climates of the World*. See also <http://www.ncdc.noaa.gov/oa /oldpubs/>.

848   International Statistics

Table 1353. **Key Global Telecom Indicators for the World Telecommunication Service Sector: 1995 to 2008**

[In billions U.S. dollars **(779 represents $779,000,000,000), except as indicated**. All data were converted by annual average exchange rates. Country fiscal year data was aggregated to obtain calendar year estimates]

Indicators	1995	2000	2004	2005	2006	2007	2008
Telecom market total revenue (bil. dol.)	779	1,210	(NA)	(NA)	(NA)	(NA)	(NA)
Telecom telephone services revenue [1] (bil. dol.). . .	428	477	552	(NA)	(NA)	(NA)	(NA)
Other statistics:							
Main telephone lines [2] (mil.).	689	975	1,204	1,262	1,263	1,278	1,267
Mobile cellular subscribers (mil.)	91	738	1,763	2,219	2,757	3,305	4,100
International telephone traffic minutes [3] (bil.)	63	114	166	179	183	(NA)	(NA)
Personal computers (mil.).	235	500	775	808	(NA)	(NA)	(NA)
Internet users (mil.).	40	390	867	989	1,168	1,344	1,542

NA Not available.   [1] Revenue from installation, subscription and local, trunk and international call charges for fixed telephone service.   [2] See footnote 1, Table 1354.   [3] Including traffic between countries of former Soviet Union.

Source: International Telecommunication Union, Geneva Switzerland, 2008; <http://www.itu.int/ITU-D/ict/statistics/at_glance /KeyTelecom99.html>. Reproduced with the kind permission of ITU.

Table 1354. **Telephones, Cellular Phones, and Computers by Country: 2007**

[Rates per 100 persons. For data qualifications for countries, see source]

Country	Telephone main lines [1]	Cellular phone sub-scribers	Personal computers [2]	Country	Telephone main lines [1]	Cellular phone sub-scribers	Personal computers [2]
Afghanistan	0.30	17.20	(NA)	Italy.	42.61	152.52	(NA)
Australia.	47.05	102.49	(NA)	Japan	40.04	83.88	(NA)
Azerbaijan	14.80	53.37	2.43	Korea, South	46.44	90.20	57.83
Belize	11.78	41.12	15.64	Macedonia	22.74	95.50	36.78
Brazil.	20.54	63.08	(NA)	Mali.	0.65	20.51	0.81
Bulgaria	30.11	129.57	8.91	Mexico.	18.54	62.48	(NA)
Cambodia.	0.26	17.88	0.36	Morocco.	7.67	64.15	3.52
Canada	55.48	61.68	(NA)	Namibia	6.66	38.58	24.11
China [3]	27.52	41.19	(NA)	Pakistan	2.93	38.41	(NA)
Colombia	17.19	73.54	7.61	Portugal	39.49	126.62	17.22
Cuba	9.26	1.76	(NA)	Romania	19.86	95.24	19.33
Denmark	51.91	114.48	55.13	Russia	31.02	114.60	(NA)
Dominican Republic . .	9.29	56.49	3.51	Saudi Arabia	16.16	114.74	(NA)
Egypt	15.09	39.82	4.87	Serbia	30.36	85.74	18.26
Estonia	37.11	148.42	52.42	Singapore	41.97	133.54	76.87
Ethiopia	1.06	1.45	0.64	Slovak Republic.	21.35	112.58	51.50
France.	56.45	89.80	(NA)	Slovenia	42.83	96.35	42.87
Gambia	2.85	46.84	3.34	Spain	45.60	109.36	39.84
Georgia	12.65	59.15	5.41	Sweden	60.38	113.73	(NA)
Germany	64.65	117.62	(NA)	Switzerland.	65.84	109.69	92.60
Greece	53.92	110.30	(NA)	Syria	17.32	31.29	9.03
Haiti	1.13	26.05	5.21	Taiwan [3]	62.28	106.11	76.02
Honduras	11.56	58.89	2.00	Turkey	24.31	82.77	(NA)
Hong Kong, China . . .	57.24	149.20	65.91	United Kingdom	55.43	118.47	(NA)
Hungary	32.41	109.97	25.64	**United States. . . . . .**	**51.81**	**86.00**	**(NA)**
India	3.37	19.98	3.17	Venezuela	18.78	86.13	(NA)
Indonesia	7.70	35.33	(NA)				
Iran	33.47	41.81	(NA)				

NA Not available.   [1] Fixed telephone lines refer to telephone lines connecting a customers terminal equipment (e.g. telephone set, facsimile machine) to the public switched telephone network (PSTN) and which have a dedicated port on a telephone exchange. Fixed telephone lines per 100 inhabitants is calculated by dividing the number of fixed telephone lines by the population and multiplying by 100.   [2] In many countries mainframe computers are used extensively, and thousands of users can be connected to a single mainframe computer; thus the number of PCs understates the total use of computers.   [3] See footnote 4, Table 1296.

Source: International Telecommunications Union, Geneva, Switzerland, *World Telecommunication Indicators*, (copyright). See also <http://www.itu.int/itu-d/icteye/Indicators/Indicators.aspx>. Reproduced with the kind permission of ITU.

Table 1355. **Patents by Country: 2008**

[Includes only U.S. patents granted to residents of areas outside of the United States and its territories. See also Table 754]

Country	Total [1]	Inventions	Designs	Country	Total [1]	Inventions	Designs
Total.	**93,244**	**80,271**	**11,852**	Netherlands.	1,724	1,329	127
				Australia	1,614	1,292	253
Japan.	36,679	33,682	2,767	Switzerland	1,403	1,112	285
Germany	10,086	8,915	976	Israel	1,312	1,166	119
Korea, South	8,731	7,549	1,159	Sweden	1,260	1,060	190
Taiwan [2]	7,779	6,339	1,423	Finland	908	824	82
Canada.	4,125	3,393	705	Belgium	605	510	85
United Kingdom	3,843	3,094	687	Austria	574	463	107
France	3,813	3,163	600	Denmark	566	391	126
Italy	1,916	1,357	544	Other countries	6,306	4,632	1,617

[1] Includes patents for botanical plants and reissues, not shown separately.   [2] See footnote 4, Table 1296.

Source: U.S. Patent and Trademark Office, Technology Assessment and Forecast Database.

U.S. Census Bureau, *Statistical Abstract of the United States: 2010*

Table 1356. Research and Development (R&D) Expenditures by Country

[Figures are for 2006 or latest year available. GDP = gross domestic product; for explanation, see text, Section 13]

Country	GERD — Percent of GDP	GERD — financed by Government	GERD — financed by Industry	GERD — Per capita at current U.S. dollars, PPPs[1]	Gov. budget — Percent of GDP	Gov. budget — Percent defense R&D	Business — Percent of GERD	Business — financed by Government	Business — financed by Industry	BERD — High-tech indus[2]	BERD — Medium high-tech indus[3]	BERD — Medium low-tech and low-tech indus[4]	BERD — Service industries	HERD — Percent of GERD	HERD — Percent of GDP
OECD total	2.26	29.46	62.71	694	0.81	32.7	68.8	6.8	89.6	(NA)	(NA)	(NA)	(NA)	17.1	0.4
EU-15[5]	1.88	33.96	54.77	557	0.78	13.4	63.8	7.1	82.2	38.7	34.9	9.2	15.0	22.1	0.4
Australia[6]	1.78	40.51	52.97	578	0.52	6.5	54.1	4.3	93.4	10.0	11.7	16.9	39.7	26.8	0.5
Austria[6]	2.45	36.58	46.35	875	0.68	(Z)	67.8	6.4	67.2	31.0	27.8	12.9	27.4	26.7	0.7
Belgium	1.83	24.65	59.68	614	0.61	0.3	67.9	6.5	82.5	41.2	23.7	15.7	17.0	22.3	0.7
Brazil	1.02	57.88	39.38	92	0.53	1.2	47.9	0.8	99.2	(NA)	(NA)	(NA)	(NA)	38.4	0.3
Canada[6]	1.94	32.68	47.97	714	0.57	3.6	54.7	2.7	81.6	32.4	9.1	11.0	41.9	35.5	0.7
China[7,8]	1.42	24.71	69.05	66	(NA)	(NA)	71.1	4.5	91.2	(NA)	(NA)	(NA)	(NA)	9.2	0.1
Czech Republic	1.54	38.97	56.91	340	0.61	2.8	66.2	13.6	83.7	22.3	35.6	8.7	31.8	15.9	0.3
Denmark	2.43	27.58	59.53	856	0.79	2.4	66.6	2.4	86.0	39.4	16.2	8.5	35.0	26.1	0.6
Finland	3.45	25.11	66.56	1,129	0.98	2.4	71.3	3.7	89.9	63.8	13.5	12.1	8.2	18.7	0.7
France	2.11	38.39	52.24	656	0.77	22.4	63.3	10.1	80.8	44.6	29.9	11.5	8.4	18.2	0.4
Germany	2.53	28.38	67.57	810	0.76	6.4	69.9	4.5	92.0	29.6	52.2	8.3	9.4	16.3	0.4
Greece	0.57	46.82	31.06	156	0.29	0.5	30.0	5.6	85.7	21.8	13.8	17.2	44.9	47.8	0.3
Hungary	1.00	44.77	43.30	182	0.37	0.1	48.3	8.4	75.6	53.7	16.0	6.6	21.4	24.4	0.2
Ireland	1.32	30.13	59.26	539	0.61	—	67.5	3.9	86.5	48.0	9.0	9.3	33.6	26.0	0.3
Italy[6]	1.09	50.68	39.66	304	0.61	1.4	50.4	9.7	79.2	33.1	29.1	8.0	26.8	30.2	0.3
Japan[6]	3.39	16.18	77.07	1,086	0.68	5.1	77.2	1.0	98.5	44.7	40.4	2.9	10.4	12.7	0.4
Korea, South	3.23	23.07	75.45	743	0.91	16.6	77.3	4.7	94.8	53.8	27.9	8.3	7.1	10.0	0.3
Mexico	0.50	45.34	46.49	57	0.21	—	49.5	5.7	92.6	9.7	21.8	35.1	32.6	27.4	0.1
Netherlands	1.67	36.23	51.06	609	0.71	2.0	57.6	3.4	81.6	40.9	27.8	12.6	17.4	28.1	0.5
Norway	1.52	43.99	46.41	791	0.70	5.6	54.2	10.5	80.7	12.6	16.3	8.5	50.3	30.2	0.5
Poland	0.56	57.45	33.05	82	0.32	0.9	31.5	12.3	80.9	13.9	23.7	9.1	50.6	31.0	0.2
Portugal	0.83	55.20	36.27	174	0.76	0.7	41.7	4.2	91.4	17.6	17.6	10.9	44.0	35.4	0.3
Russia	1.08	61.10	28.81	141	0.36	52.1	66.7	52.0	35.7	7.7	5.1	3.4	78.6	6.1	0.1
South Africa	0.92	38.19	43.87	78	(NA)	(NA)	58.3	16.2	68.3	(NA)	(NA)	(NA)	36.4	19.3	0.2
Spain	1.20	42.49	47.07	354	1.00	16.6	55.5	14.4	79.0	20.5	18.8	15.1	41.8	27.6	0.3
Sweden	3.73	23.50	65.70	1,301	0.85	16.6	74.9	4.2	87.1	38.7	29.8	5.2	24.8	20.4	0.8
Switzerland	2.90	22.71	69.73	1,003	0.69	0.6	73.7	1.5	90.9	(NA)	(NA)	(NA)	19.6	22.9	0.7
Turkey	0.76	48.63	46.05	67	(NA)	(NA)	37.0	8.7	90.0	16.3	42.0	14.5	25.8	51.3	0.4
United Kingdom[6,9,10]	1.78	31.87	45.20	588	0.74	28.3	61.7	7.6	90.0	49.0	18.8	7.6	23.2	26.1	0.5
United States[6,9,10]	2.62	29.34	64.89	1,146	1.02	58.3	70.3	9.3	90.7	40.3	16.6	6.4	36.1	14.3	0.4

– Represents zero. NA Not available or not applicable. Z Less than 0.05 percent. [1] Purchasing power parities. See headnote, Table 1313. [2] Aerospace; office and computing equipment; pharmaceuticals; radio, TV, and communication equipment; medical, precision and optical instruments. [3] Motor vehicles; chemicals; electrical machinery; other transport; machinery and equipment. [4] Rubber and plastics; nonmetallic mineral products; shipbuilding; ferrous and nonferrous metals; metal products; petroleum; other manufacturing industries. [5] See footnote 2, Table 1336. [6] Government budget appropriations for R&D; federal government only. [7] See footnote 4, Table 1296. [8] Percent of GERD/BERD financed by government or industry; the sum of the breakdown does not add to the total. [9] GERD, BERD: Excluding most or all capital expenditures. [10] HERD: Excluding most or all capital expenditures.

Source: Organization for Economic Cooperation and Development, Paris, France, OECD in Figures, 2008 (copyright). See also <http://www.oecd.org>.

Table 1357. **Dow-Jones World Stock Index by Country and Industry: 2000 to 2008**

[Index figures shown are as of December 31. 1991 = 100. Based on share prices denominated in U.S. dollars. Stocks in countries that impose significant restrictions on foreign ownership are included in the world index in the same proportion that shares are available to foreign investors]

Country and industry	2000	2005	2007	2008	Country and industry	2000	2005	2007	2008
World, ...	210.9	234.1	300.9	171.9	Asia/Pacific	93.0	132.0	158.1	93.6
Americas.	299.1	307.3	376.9	226.1	Australia	156.0	312.5	500.1	228.9
United States.	306.9	302.4	357.5	219.7	Hong Kong.	245.6	273.6	546.5	253.3
Canada	225.3	365.4	541.7	278.6	Indonesia.	31.2	79.0	179.4	66.3
Mexico	132.2	360.1	555.8	334.6	Japan	88.3	113.5	108.9	77.6
Europe	241.2	264.8	385.7	198.7	Malaysia	88.5	119.5	229.7	127.3
Austria	86.2	335.5	469.5	160.6	New Zealand	96.7	227.3	261.9	124.7
Belgium	196.9	321.2	449.5	213.0	Singapore	135.2	176.3	319.0	154.1
Denmark	220.1	375.1	607.5	307.8	Thailand	27.2	76.7	112.9	56.6
Finland	1,537.8	948.5	1,691.7	732.9					
France	252.9	273.3	406.9	222.9	Basic materials.	117.6	213.8	372.8	176.8
Germany	219.1	224.3	398.2	214.2	Consumer goods	183.8	241.9	325.1	207.1
Ireland.	312.3	470.4	532.0	167.1	Consumer services	192.8	214.4	240.9	156.0
Italy	192.2	213.8	286.2	135.3	Oil and Gas	230.7	383.3	590.3	346.6
Netherlands	335.7	309.6	448.9	198.9	Financial	207.1	259.8	287.7	131.8
Norway	151.8	276.1	521.3	175.5	Healthcare.	329.9	310.6	353.4	272.0
Spain	193.5	288.6	497.0	282.0	Industrial	167.1	192.4	258.0	141.4
Sweden	339.0	378.3	526.7	250.8	Technology	552.7	375.1	459.2	251.4
Switzerland	388.8	452.5	606.3	416.9	Telecommunications . . .	273.3	201.6	313.4	199.8
United Kingdom	199.8	217.6	290.1	142.4	Utilities	156.0	176.9	276.0	188.0

Source: Dow Jones & Company, Inc., New York, NY, *Dow Jones Indexes*, (copyright).

Table 1358. **Foreign Stock Market Activity—Morgan Stanley Capital International Indexes: 2000 to 2008**

[Index figures shown are as of December 31. January 1, 1970 = 100, except as noted. Minus sign (–) indicates decrease. Based on share prices denominated in U.S. dollars. EM = Emerging Markets]

Index and country	Index			Percent change [1]		Index and country	Index			Percent change [1]	
	2000	2007	2008	2007	2008		2000	2007	2008	2007	2008
ALL COUNTRY (AC) INDEXES						Sweden.	4,240	6,746	3,276	–1.4	–51.4
						Switzerland	2,695	4,237	2,900	3.9	–31.6
AC World index [2]	290.1	403.3	227.7	9.6	–43.5	United Kingdom	1,146	1,593	788	4.7	–50.6
AC World index except USA [2]	193.5	333.9	176.7	14.1	–47.1	Hong Kong	5,475	9,967	4,697	37.5	–52.9
AC Asia Pacific [2]	89.6	157.8	89.6	12.3	–43.2	Japan	2,552	3,034	2,108	–5.4	–30.5
AC Europe [2]	376.5	594.0	301.0	11.8	–49.3	Singapore	2,081	4,213	2,125	23.9	–49.5
European Union [2]	361.5	551.7	276.8	11.7	–49.8						
						EMERGING MARKETS					
DEVELOPED MARKETS						EM Far East index [4] . .	127.9	437.1	209.8	33.6	–52.0
						India [6].	114.5	668.9	233.6	71.2	–65.1
World index [3]	1,221	1,589	920	7.1	–42.1	Indonesia.	77.8	677.6	287.5	50.8	–57.6
EAFE index [3]	1,492	2,253	1,237	8.6	–45.1	Korea, South	78.7	437.5	193.1	30.0	–55.9
Europe index	1,378	2,121	1,099	11.0	–48.2	Malaysia [6]	160.7	408.6	231.3	41.5	–43.4
Pacific index.	1,832	2,668	1,656	3.5	–37.9	Pakistan [6]	44.6	187.1	46.1	32.5	–75.4
Far East index	2,583	3,246	2,150	–1.2	–33.8	Philippines.	146.7	363.4	167.9	38.0	–53.8
						Sri Lanka [6].	36.3	154.0	58.9	–15.1	–62.1
United States	1,250	1,391	854	4.1	–38.6	Taiwan [7]	191.7	294.0	150.8	5.4	–48.7
Canada	832.5	1,930	1,031	27.6	–46.6	Thailand	58.9	267.4	132.8	40.9	–50.3
Australia	317.7	998.8	476.4	25.0	–52.3	EM Latin America. . . .	916	4,400	2,078	46.9	–52.8
New Zealand [4]	56.4	153.9	67.4	4.0	–56.2	Argentina.	1,233	2,919	1,304	–5.4	–55.3
Austria	708.3	3,273	1,016	0.7	–69.0	Brazil	763	3,867	1,638	75.3	–57.6
Belgium	1,222	2,142	697	–5.3	–67.5	Chile	605	1,803	1,131	20.8	–37.3
Denmark	2,201	6,037	3,130	24.2	–48.2	Colombia [6].	42.1	619.3	447.9	12.6	–27.7
Finland [4]	921.8	985.1	429.2	45.0	–56.4	Mexico [6]	1,465	5,992	3,357	9.3	–44.0
France	1,509	2,275	1,253	10.9	–44.9	Peru [6]	125.0	1,249	719	86.0	–42.4
Germany	1,436	2,521	1,330	32.5	–47.2	Venezuela [6]	106.1	163.4	(NA)	–6.2	(NA)
Greece [4]	475.8	1,036	341	29.2	–67.1						
Ireland [4]	308.4	441.8	120.4	–21.9	–72.7	Czech Republic [8]	79.9	828.9	455.5	51.7	–45.1
Italy	447.2	653.0	312.8	2.7	–52.1	Hungary [8]	233.6	1,137	427	13.4	–62.4
Luxembourg [5].	491.9	(NA)	(NA)	(NA)	(NA)	Jordan	55.1	252.9	162.5	20.9	–35.8
Netherlands	2,177	2,923	1,459	17.5	–50.1	Poland [6]	499.0	1,501	657	22.7	–56.2
Norway	1,181	4,349	1,513	28.4	–65.2	Russia [8]	155.2	1,536	397	22.9	–74.2
Portugal [4]	127.8	234.0	108.5	21.0	–53.6	South Africa [6].	157.6	508.3	305.1	14.7	–40.0
Spain	347.1	864.0	492.7	20.7	–43.0	Turkey.	247.7	751.1	275.0	70.0	–63.4

NA Not available. [1] Percent change during calendar year (e.g. December 31, 2007 through December 31, 2008). Adjusted for foreign exchange fluctuations relative to U.S. dollar. [2] January 1, 1988 = 100. [3] Europe, Australasia, Far East Index. Comprises all European and Far East countries listed under developed markets plus Australia and New Zealand. [4] January 1, 1988 = 100. [5] MSCI Luxembourg Index discontinued as of March 29, 2002. [6] January 1, 1993 = 100. [7] See footnote 4, Table 1296. [8] January 1, 1995 = 100.

Table 1359. Foreign Stock Market Indices: 1980 to 2008

[**As of year end**. The DAX-30 index is a total return index which includes dividends, whereas the other foreign indices are price indices which exclude dividends]

Year	London FTSE 100	Tokyo Nikkei 225	Hong Kong Hang Seng	Germany DAX-30	Paris CAC-40	Dow Jones Europe STOXX 50
1980	647	7,116	1,477	481	(X)	(X)
1985	1,413	13,113	1,752	1,366	(X)	(X)
1990	2,144	23,849	3,025	1,398	1,518	835
1994	3,066	19,723	8,191	2,107	1,881	1,299
1995	3,689	19,868	10,073	2,254	1,872	1,538
1996	4,119	19,361	13,452	2,889	2,316	1,850
1997	5,136	15,259	10,723	4,250	2,999	2,634
1998	5,883	13,842	9,507	5,002	3,943	3,320
1999	6,930	18,934	16,962	6,958	5,958	4,742
2000	6,223	13,786	15,096	6,434	5,926	4,557
2001	5,217	10,543	11,397	5,160	4,625	3,707
2002	3,940	8,579	9,321	2,893	3,064	2,408
2003	4,477	10,677	12,576	3,965	3,558	2,660
2004	4,814	11,489	14,230	4,256	3,821	2,775
2005	5,619	16,111	14,876	5,408	4,715	3,349
2006	6,221	17,226	19,965	6,597	5,542	3,697
2007	6,457	15,308	27,813	8,067	5,614	3,684
2008	4,434	8,860	14,388	4,810	3,218	2,065

X Not applicable.

Source: Global Financial Data, Los Angeles, CA, <http://www.globalfinancialdata.com>, unpublished data (copyright).

Table 1360. U.S. and Foreign Stock Markets—Market Capitalization and Value of Shares Traded: 2000 to 2008

[**In billions of U.S. dollars (15,104.0 represents $15,104,000,000,000)**. Market capitalization is the market value of all domestic listed companies at the end of the year. The market value of a company is the share price times the number of shares outstanding. Value of shares traded is the annual total turnover of listed company shares]

Country	Market capitalization				Value of shares traded			
	2000	2005	2007	2008	2000	2005	2007	2008
United States	15,104.0	16,970.9	19,947.3	11,737.6	31,862.5	21,510.0	42,613.2	36,467.4
Argentina	166.1	61.5	86.7	52.3	6.0	16.4	8.3	13.4
Australia	372.8	804.1	1,298.4	675.6	226.3	616.1	1,322.8	1,013.9
Austria	29.9	124.4	228.7	72.3	9.4	45.9	121.4	104.5
Belgium	182.5	288.5	386.4	167.4	38.0	125.7	255.7	211.3
Brazil	226.2	474.6	1,370.4	589.4	101.3	154.2	585.0	727.8
Canada	841.4	1,480.9	2,186.6	1,002.2	634.7	845.0	1,645.5	1,761.0
Chile	60.4	136.4	212.9	132.4	6.1	18.9	44.5	36.6
China [1]	581.0	780.8	6,226.3	2,793.6	721.5	586.3	7,791.7	5,470.5
Denmark	107.7	178.0	277.7	131.5	91.6	152.0	242.2	211.9
Egypt	28.7	79.7	139.3	85.9	11.1	25.4	53.1	69.6
Finland	293.6	209.5	369.2	154.4	206.6	273.5	543.3	390.4
France	1,446.6	1,758.7	2,771.2	1,492.3	1,083.3	1,526.1	3,418.9	3,257.7
Germany	1,270.2	1,221.3	2,105.5	1,108.0	1,069.1	1,763.2	3,363.1	3,093.8
Greece	110.8	145.0	264.9	90.4	95.1	65.3	151.5	105.6
Hong Kong	623.4	1,055.0	1,162.6	468.6	377.9	460.1	916.9	621.6
India	148.1	553.1	1,819.1	645.5	509.8	433.9	1,107.6	1,049.7
Indonesia	26.8	81.4	211.7	98.8	14.3	41.9	112.9	110.7
Iran	34.0	38.7	45.6	49.0	5.0	8.2	8.2	15.4
Ireland	81.9	114.1	144.0	49.4	14.4	64.7	136.6	82.5
Israel	64.1	120.1	236.4	134.5	23.4	59.9	113.5	109.2
Italy	768.4	798.2	1,072.7	520.9	778.4	1,115.2	2,313.5	1,478.8
Japan	3,157.2	4,736.5	4,453.5	3,220.5	2,693.9	4,997.4	6,497.2	5,866.4
Korea, South	171.6	718.2	1,123.6	494.6	1,067.7	1,203.0	1,974.0	1,466.0
Luxembourg	34.0	51.3	166.1	66.5	1.2	0.2	0.2	1.7
Malaysia	116.9	181.2	325.7	187.1	58.5	50.0	150.0	85.2
Mexico	125.2	239.1	397.7	232.6	45.3	52.7	115.6	108.2
Morocco	10.9	27.2	75.5	65.7	1.1	4.1	26.3	21.9
Netherlands	640.5	592.9	956.5	387.9	677.2	835.8	1,803.4	1,140.3
New Zealand	18.6	43.4	47.5	24.2	10.8	17.4	21.7	16.5
Norway	65.0	191.0	357.4	125.9	60.1	194.8	471.9	367.6
Philippines	51.6	40.2	103.2	52.1	8.2	7.0	29.3	17.2
Poland	31.3	93.9	207.3	90.2	14.6	30.0	84.6	68.0
Portugal	60.7	67.0	132.3	68.7	54.4	41.6	144.5	82.6
Russia	38.9	548.6	1,503.0	1,321.8	20.3	159.3	754.5	562.2
Saudi Arabia	67.2	646.1	515.1	246.3	17.3	1,103.5	679.8	524.7
Singapore	152.8	316.7	353.5	180.0	91.5	119.8	384.2	270.9
Sweden	328.3	403.9	612.5	252.5	390.0	464.0	968.8	638.8
Switzerland	792.3	938.6	1,274.5	862.7	609.1	883.3	1,777.8	1,511.0
Taiwan [1]	247.6	516.0	723.7	380.9	983.5	716.5	1,272.4	944.0
Thailand	29.5	124.9	196.0	102.6	23.3	89.3	108.2	116.8
Turkey	69.7	161.5	286.6	117.9	179.2	201.3	302.4	239.7
United Kingdom	2,580.0	3,058.2	3,858.5	1,852.0	1,835.3	4,167.0	10,324.5	6,484.3

[1] See footnote 4, Table 1296.

Source: Standard and Poor's, New York, NY, *Standard & Poor's Global Stock Markets Factbook 2009* (copyright).

Table 1361. **Foreign Exchange Rates: 2008**

[**Foreign currency units per U.S. dollar**. Rates shown include market, official, principal, and secondary rates]

Country	Currency	2008	Country	Currency	2008
Afghanistan [1]	Afghanis	(NA)	Laos	Kip	8,760.69
Albania	Leks	79.55	Latvia	Lats	0.47
Algeria	Algerian dinars	63.25	Lebanon	Lebanese pounds	1,507.50
Antigua and Barbuda	E. Caribbean dollars	(NA)	Lesotho	Maloti	7.75
Argentina	Argentine pesos	3.16	Liberia	Liberian dollars	(NA)
Armenia	Drams	303.93	Libya [1]	Libyan dinars	1.21
Aruba	Aruban guilders	(NA)	Lithuania	Litai	2.33
Australia	Australian dollars	1.21	Luxembourg	Euro	0.68
Austria	Euro	0.68	Macedonia	Denars	41.41
Bahamas, The	Bahamian dollars	1.00	Madagascar	Malagasy ariary	1,654.78
Bahrain	Bahrain dinars	0.38	Malaysia	Ringgit	3.33
Bangladesh	Taka	68.55	Mali	CFA francs	447.81
Barbados	Barbadian dollars	(NA)	Malta [5]	Euro	0.68
Belarus	Belarusian rubel	2,130.00	Mauritania	Ouguiyas	(NA)
Belgium	Euro	0.68	Mauritius	Mauritian rupees	27.97
Belize	Belizean dollars	2.00	Mexico	Mexican pesos	11.02
Benin	CFA francs	447.81	Moldova	Lei	10.33
Bolivia	Bolivianos	7.25	Mongolia	Togrogs	1,267.51
Botswana	Pula	6.80	Morocco	Dirhams	7.53
Brazil	Reals	1.86	Mozambique	Meticais	24.13
Bulgaria	Leva	1.32	Namibia	Namibia dollars	7.75
Burkina Faso	CFA francs	447.81	Nepal	Nepalese rupees	65.21
Burma [1]	Kyats	1,205.00	Netherlands	Euro	0.68
Cambodia	Riel	4,070.94	Netherlands Antilles	Guilders	(NA)
Cameroon	CFA francs	447.81	New Zealand	New Zealand dollars	1.42
Canada	Canadian dollars	1.04	Nicaragua	Cordobas	19.37
Central African Republic	CFA francs	447.81	Niger	CFA francs	447.81
Chad	CFA francs	447.81	Nigeria	Naira	117.80
Chile	Chilean pesos	509.02	Norway	Norwegian kroner	5.64
China [2]	Yuan	6.94	Oman	Rials omani	0.38
Colombia	Colombian pesos	2,243.60	Pakistan	Pakistan rupees	70.64
Comoros	Comorian francs	(NA)	Panama	Balboas	1.00
Congo (Brazzaville) [3]	CFA francs	447.81	Papua New Guinea	Kina	2.70
Costa Rica	Colones	530.41	Paraguay	Guaranies	4,337.70
Cote d'Ivoire	CFA francs	447.81	Peru	Nuevos soles	2.91
Croatia	Kunas	4.98	Philippines	Philippine pesos	44.44
Cyprus [4]	Euro	0.68	Poland	Zlotys	2.30
Czech Republic	Koruny	17.06	Portugal	Euro	0.68
Denmark	Kroner	5.24	Qatar	Qatar riyals	3.64
Djibouti	Djibouti francs	(NA)	Romania	Lei	2.50
Dominica	E. Caribbean dollars	(NA)	Russia	Russian rubles	24.30
Dominican Republic	Dominican pesos	34.78	Rwanda	Rwanda francs	550.00
Ecuador	U.S. dollars	1.00	Saint Kitts and Nevis	E. Caribbean dollars	2.70
Egypt	Egyptian pounds	5.40	Saint Lucia	E. Caribbean dollars	2.70
El Salvador	U.S. dollars	1.00	Saint Vincent and the		
Equatorial Guinea	CFA francs	447.81	Grenadines	E. Caribbean dollars	2.70
Estonia	Krooni	10.70	Saudi Arabia	Saudi A. riyals	3.75
Ethiopia [1]	Birr	9.57	Senegal	CFA francs	447.81
Fiji	Fiji dollars	(NA)	Sierra Leone	Leones	(NA)
Finland	Euro	0.68	Singapore	Singapore dollar	1.42
France	Euro	0.68	Slovakia [6]	Koruny	21.05
Gabon	CFA francs	447.81	Slovenia	Euro	0.68
Georgia	Lari	1.47	South Africa	Rand	7.96
Germany	Euro	0.68	Spain	Euro	0.68
Greece	Euro	0.68	Sri Lanka	Sri Lanka rupees	108.33
Guatemala	Quetzales	7.59	Sudan	Sudanese dinars	2.10
Guyana	Guyana dollars	203.86	Suriname [1]	Suriname dollar	(NA)
Haiti	Gourdes	39.22	Swaziland	Emalangeni	7.75
Honduras	Lempiras	18.98	Sweden	Swedish kronor	6.41
Hong Kong	Hong Kong dollars	7.75	Switzerland	Swiss francs	1.08
Hungary	Forint	171.80	Syria	Syrian pounds	46.53
Iceland	Kronur	85.62	Tanzania	Tanzania shillings	1,178.10
India	Indian rupees	43.32	Thailand	Baht	33.37
Indonesia	Rupiah	9,698.90	Togo	CFA francs	447.81
Iran	Rials	9,142.80	Trinidad and Tobago	Tt dollars	6.29
Iraq	Dinars	1,176.00	Tunisia	Tunisian dinars	1.21
Ireland	Euro	0.68	Turkey	Liras	1.32
Israel	New sheqalim	3.56	Uganda	Uganda shillings	1,658.10
Italy	Euro	0.68	Ukraine	Hryvnias	4.95
Jamaica	Jamaica dollars	72.24	United Arab Emirates	Dirhams	3.67
Japan	Yen	103.58	United Kingdom	Pounds sterling	0.53
Jordan	Jordinian dinars	0.71	Uruguay	Uruguayan pesos	20.94
Kazakhstan	Tenge	120.25	Vanuatu	Vatu	(NA)
Kenya	Kenya shillings	68.36	Venezuela [7]	Bolivares	2,147.00
Korea, South	Won	1,101.70	Yemen	Yemeni rials	199.76
Kuwait	Kuwaiti dinars	0.27	Zambia	Zambian kwacha	3,512.90
Kyrgyzstan	Soms	36.11	Zimbabwe	Zimbabwe dollar	(NA)

NA Not available.   [1] End-of-year values were used if annual averages were unavailable. Some values were estimated using partial year data.   [2] See footnote 4, Table 1296.   [3] See footnote 5, Table 1296.   [4] Starting 2008, the euro replaced the Cypriot pound as the official currency.   [5] Starting 2008, the euro replaced the Maltese liri as the official currency.   [6] Data are for the koruny, but on 1 January 2009, Slovakia adopted the euro as the official currency.   [7] Country's monetary unit was revalued at the beginning of the year.

Source: Central Intelligence Agency, *The World Factbook, 2009*. See also <https://www.cia.gov/library/publications/the-world-factbook/index.html/> (accessed 12 August 2009).

Table 1362. Reserve Assets and International Transaction Balances by Country: 2000 to 2008

[In millions of U.S. dollars (56,600 represents $56,600,000,000). Assets include holdings of convertible foreign currencies, special drawing rights, and reserve position in International Monetary Fund and exclude gold holdings. Minus sign (–) indicates debits]

Country	Total reserve assets 2000	Total reserve assets 2007	2008 Total	2008 Currency holdings [1]	Current account balance 2000	Current account balance 2007	Current account balance 2008	Merchandise trade balance 2000	Merchandise trade balance 2007	Merchandise trade balance 2008
United States	56,600	59,520	66,610	49,580	–415,150	–731,210	(NA)	–449,780	–815,300	(NA)
Algeria	12,024	110,318	143,243	143,102	(NA)	(NA)	(NA)	(NA)	(NA)	(NA)
Argentina	25,147	44,682	44,855	44,360	–8,981	7,122	(NA)	2,452	13,255	(NA)
Australia	18,118	24,768	30,691	29,867	–14,763	–57,682	(NA)	–4,862	–17,770	(NA)
Austria	14,319	10,689	8,912	8,244	–4,864	12,031	(NA)	–2,737	1,846	(NA)
Bangladesh	1,486	5,183	5,689	5,687	–306	857	(NA)	–1,654	–4,195	(NA)
Belgium [2]	9,994	10,384	9,318	7,767	11,381	7,216	(NA)	2,591	1,685	(NA)
Brazil	32,488	179,433	192,844	192,843	–24,225	1,550	–28,300	–698	40,031	24,746
Burma	223	(NA)	(NA)	(NA)	–212	(NA)	(NA)	–504	(NA)	(NA)
Cameroon	212	2,907	3,086	3,081	–249	–547	(NA)	502	295	(NA)
Canada	32,102	40,991	43,778	41,537	19,622	12,639	11,298	45,047	44,363	45,875
Chile	15,035	16,837	23,072	22,849	–898	7,200	(NA)	2,119	23,653	(NA)
China [3]	168,278	1,530,282	(NA)	(NA)	20,518	371,833	(NA)	34,474	315,381	(NA)
Colombia	8,916	20,767	23,479	22,810	764	–5,866	(NA)	2,633	-596	(NA)
Congo (Brazzaville) [4]	222	2,174	3,872	3,871	648	–2,181	(NA)	2,037	2,950	(NA)
Cote d'Ivoire	668	2,519	(NA)	(NA)	–241	–146	(NA)	1,486	2,544	(NA)
Denmark	15,108	[5]32,534	40,466	39,823	2,262	2,379	(NA)	6,641	-386	(NA)
Ecuador	947	2,816	3,738	3,686	921	1,598	(NA)	1,395	1,797	(NA)
Egypt	13,118	30,188	32,216	32,108	–971	412	(NA)	–8,321	–14,900	(NA)
Finland	7,977	7,063	6,979	6,398	10,526	10,121	(NA)	13,684	11,979	(NA)
France	37,039	45,710	33,617	30,382	18,580	–31,250	(NA)	–3,620	–54,880	(NA)
Germany	56,890	44,327	43,137	38,557	–31,960	252,930	(NA)	55,460	278,690	(NA)
Ghana	232	(NA)	(NA)	(NA)	–387	–2,152	(NA)	–830	–3,894	(NA)
Greece	13,424	631	344	159	–9,820	–44,587	(NA)	–20,239	–57,050	(NA)
Hungary	11,190	23,970	33,788	33,620	–4,004	–8,635	(NA)	-2,913	452	(NA)
India	37,902	266,988	247,419	246,603	–4,601	(NA)	(NA)	–10,640	(NA)	(NA)
Indonesia	28,502	54,976	49,597	49,339	7,992	10,492	606	25,042	32,754	23,309
Ireland	5,360	779	871	609	–516	–12,695	(NA)	25,010	31,292	(NA)
Israel	23,281	28,519	42,513	42,324	–854	4,523	(NA)	–3,540	–6,010	(NA)
Italy	25,567	28,385	37,085	35,303	–5,781	–51,032	(NA)	9,549	4,242	(NA)
Japan	354,902	952,784	1,009,365	1,003,674	119,660	210,490	(NA)	116,720	104,750	(NA)
Kenya	898	3,355	2,879	2,856	–199	–1,102	(NA)	–1,262	–4,258	(NA)
Korea, South	96,131	262,150	201,145	200,479	12,251	5,954	–6,350	16,954	29,409	6,051
Kuwait	7,082	16,660	17,046	16,544	14,679	47,471	(NA)	13,027	43,056	(NA)
Malaysia	28,330	101,019	91,149	90,605	8,488	28,931	(NA)	20,827	37,328	(NA)
Mexico	35,509	87,109	95,126	93,994	–18,707	–8,115	(NA)	–8,337	–10,074	(NA)
Morocco	4,823	24,123	22,104	21,976	–501	–224	(NA)	–3,235	–14,170	(NA)
Nepal	945	(NA)	(NA)	(NA)	–299	–130	(NA)	–814	–2,008	(NA)
Netherlands	9,643	10,270	11,476	9,369	7,264	59,586	(NA)	17,800	54,909	(NA)
Nigeria	9,911	51,334	(NA)	(NA)	7,429	21,972	(NA)	10,415	33,138	(NA)
Norway	27,597	60,840	50,950	50,214	25,851	60,459	(NA)	25,975	60,271	(NA)
Pakistan	1,513	14,044	7,194	7,011	–85	–8,295	(NA)	–1,157	–10,640	(NA)
Peru	8,374	26,857	30,272	30,263	–1,526	1,505	(NA)	–11	8,356	(NA)
Philippines	13,090	30,211	33,193	33,047	–2,225	6,301	(NA)	–5,971	-8,211	(NA)
Poland	26,562	62,967	59,306	58,931	–9,981	–18,595	(NA)	–12,307	–15,553	(NA)
Portugal	8,909	1,258	1,309	1,022	–11,748	–21,418	(NA)	–14,532	–24,108	(NA)
Romania	2,470	37,194	36,868	36,747	–1,355	–23,032	(NA)	–1,684	–24,566	(NA)
Saudi Arabia	19,585	33,760	30,342	28,223	14,317	95,080	(NA)	49,777	151,547	(NA)
Singapore	80,132	162,957	174,193	173,649	10,728	39,106	(NA)	13,956	49,099	(NA)
South Africa	6,083	29,589	30,584	30,238	–191	–20,780	(NA)	4,698	–5,741	(NA)
Spain	30,989	11,480	12,414	11,540	–23,185	–145,355	(NA)	–37,087	–123,515	(NA)
Sri Lanka	1,039	3,515	(NA)	(NA)	–1,044	–1,465	(NA)	–1,044	–2,430	(NA)
Sudan	138	1,378	(NA)	(NA)	–557	–3,447	(NA)	440	1,157	(NA)
Sweden	14,863	27,044	25,896	25,127	6,617	38,416	(NA)	15,215	18,232	(NA)
Switzerland	32,272	44,474	45,061	44,151	33,562	43,946	(NA)	2,071	12,750	(NA)
Syria	(NA)	(NA)	(NA)	(NA)	1,061	(NA)	(NA)	1,423	(NA)	(NA)
Thailand	32,016	85,221	108,661	108,317	9,313	15,755	(NA)	11,701	25,547	(NA)
Trinidad and Tobago .	1,386	6,694	9,443	9,380	544	5,364	(NA)	969	5,721	(NA)
Turkey	22,488	73,384	70,428	70,231	–9,822	–37,697	(NA)	–21,959	–46,669	(NA)
United Kingdom	38,770	48,960	44,350	41,550	–37,360	–78,760	(NA)	–49,850	–178,740	(NA)
Venezuela	13,088	24,196	33,098	32,581	11,853	20,001	39,202	16,664	23,702	45,447

NA Not available. [1] Holdings of convertible foreign currencies. [2] Balance of payments current account and trade balance data for 2000 are for Belgium-Luxembourg. Thereafter, data is for Belgium only. [3] See footnote 4, Table 1296. [4] See footnote 5, Table 1296. [5] Break in series. Data not comparable to earlier years.

Source: International Monetary Fund, Washington, DC, *International Financial Statistics*, monthly, (copyright).

Table 1363. International Tourism Arrivals, Expenditures, and Receipts—Leading Countries: 2000 to 2007

[Arrivals in thousands of nonresident tourists at national borders, except as noted (77,190 represents 77,190,000); expenditures and receipts in millions of dollars. Receipts are dollars spent by foreign tourists on travel inside the country shown. Expenditures are dollars visitors (same-day visitors and tourists) from a given country of origin spend on travel outside their country of residence. Excludes international transport receipts]

Country	Arrivals (1,000)					Expenditures (mil. dol.)				Receipts (mil. dol.)				
	2000	2004	2005	2006	2007	2000	2005	2006	2007	2000	2004	2005	2006	2007
France	77,190	75,121	75,908	78,853	81,940	17,715	30,458	31,264	36,743	30,641	44,895	43,942	46,512	54,165
Spain	46,403	52,430	55,914	58,004	58,666	5,922	15,046	16,697	19,724	29,802	45,067	47,789	51,297	57,883
United States	**51,238**	**46,086**	**49,206**	**50,978**	**55,986**	**67,043**	**73,320**	**76,946**	**81,092**	**97,943**	**94,107**	**102,070**	**106,836**	**119,223**
China	31,229	41,761	46,809	49,913	54,720	13,114	21,759	24,322	29,786	16,231	25,739	29,296	33,949	37,233
Italy	41,181	37,071	36,513	41,058	43,654	15,685	22,370	23,152	27,329	27,493	35,378	35,319	38,257	42,660
United Kingdom [2]	25,209	27,755	29,970	32,713	32,778	38,262	59,532	63,319	72,436	21,769	28,202	30,573	33,888	37,690
Germany [3]	18,983	20,137	21,500	23,569	24,421	52,824	74,189	74,123	82,966	18,611	27,613	29,121	32,888	36,092
Ukraine	6,431	15,629	17,631	18,936	23,122	470	2,805	2,834	3,293	394	2,560	3,125	3,485	4,597
Russia	21,169	22,064	22,201	22,486	22,909	6,848	17,434	18,235	22,258	3,429	5,530	5,870	7,628	9,607
Turkey	9,586	16,826	20,273	18,916	22,248	1,713	2,872	2,743	3,260	7,636	15,888	18,152	16,853	18,487
Mexico	20,641	20,618	21,915	21,353	21,424	5,499	7,600	8,108	8,378	8,294	10,796	11,803	12,177	12,901
Malaysia	10,222	15,703	16,431	17,547	20,973	2,075	3,711	4,020	5,252	5,011	8,203	8,846	10,427	12,905
Austria [3]	17,982	19,373	19,952	20,261	20,766	8,463	10,994	9,626	10,566	9,998	15,290	15,589	16,510	18,754
Canada	19,627	19,145	18,771	18,265	17,931	12,438	18,017	20,620	24,882	10,778	13,029	13,768	14,689	15,614
Greece	13,096	13,313	14,765	16,039	17,518	4,558	3,039	2,997	3,423	9,219	12,715	13,334	14,402	15,550
Hong Kong	8,814	13,655	14,773	15,821	17,154	12,502	13,305	14,044	15,086	5,868	8,918	10,179	11,461	13,566
Poland	17,400	14,290	15,200	15,670	14,975	5,315	5,548	7,224	7,753	5,677	5,833	6,274	7,239	10,599
Thailand	9,579	11,737	11,567	13,822	14,434	2,772	3,800	4,598	5,143	7,483	10,043	9,577	13,393	16,667
Macao [4]	5,197	8,324	9,014	10,683	12,942	(NA)	358	378	456	3,205	7,704	8,236	10,135	13,939
Portugal	12,097	10,639	10,612	11,282	12,321	2,228	3,050	3,340	3,922	5,243	7,672	7,676	8,416	10,162
Saudi Arabia [5]	6,585	8,599	8,037	8,620	11,531	(NA)	3,975	1,804	4,880	(NA)	3,916	5,626	5,391	6,020
Netherlands [3]	10,003	9,646	10,012	10,739	11,008	12,191	16,140	17,087	19,110	7,197	10,308	10,450	11,382	13,339
Egypt	5,116	7,795	8,244	8,646	10,610	1,072	1,629	1,784	2,446	4,345	6,125	6,851	7,591	9,303
Croatia [3]	5,831	7,912	8,467	8,659	9,307	568	754	737	985	2,758	6,727	7,370	7,990	9,233
South Africa	5,872	6,678	7,369	8,396	9,091	2,085	3,373	3,384	3,927	2,677	6,322	7,335	7,876	8,443
Hungary	(NA)	12,212	9,979	9,259	8,638	1,651	2,382	2,126	2,949	3,733	4,034	4,120	4,254	4,739
Switzerland [6]	7,821	(NA)	7,229	7,863	8,448	5,419	8,782	9,252	10,265	6,652	9,595	10,041	10,808	12,185
Japan	4,757	6,138	6,728	7,334	8,347	31,884	37,565	26,876	26,511	3,373	11,265	12,430	8,470	9,345
Ireland	6,646	6,953	7,333	8,001	8,332	2,525	6,074	6,862	8,682	2,615	4,375	4,782	5,369	6,140
Singapore [2]	6,062	6,553	7,079	7,588	7,957	4,535	10,011	10,989	11,844	5,142	5,229	5,909	7,204	8,680
Romania [2]	5,264	6,600	5,839	6,037	7,722	425	925	1,310	1,535	359	503	1,052	1,308	1,467
Morocco [3]	4,278	5,477	5,843	6,558	7,408	426	612	693	880	2,039	3,922	4,610	5,984	7,181
Belgium	6,457	6,710	6,747	6,995	7,045	9,429	14,948	15,574	17,268	6,592	9,208	9,845	10,311	10,898
Tunisia	5,058	5,998	6,378	6,550	6,762	263	374	410	437	1,682	1,970	2,143	2,275	2,575
Czech Republic [3]	4,666	6,061	6,336	6,435	6,680	1,276	2,405	2,765	3,647	2,973	4,187	4,676	5,541	6,637
Korea, South [2]	5,322	5,818	6,023	6,155	6,448	7,132	15,406	18,851	20,890	6,834	6,069	5,806	5,788	5,797
Indonesia	5,064	5,321	5,002	4,871	5,506	3,197	3,584	4,030	4,446	4,975	4,798	4,522	4,448	5,346
Bulgaria	2,785	4,630	4,837	5,158	5,151	538	1,309	1,474	1,829	1,074	2,202	2,412	2,612	3,130
Australia	4,530	4,774	5,020	5,064	(NA)	6,387	11,253	11,690	14,244	9,289	15,214	16,868	17,854	22,405
India	2,649	3,457	3,919	4,447	5,082	2,690	6,013	7,352	(NA)	3,460	6,170	7,493	8,634	10,729

NA Not available. [1] See footnote 4, Table 1296. [2] Arrivals are of nonresident visitors at national borders. [3] Arrivals are of nonresident tourists in all types of accommodation establishments. [4] Expenditures and receipts include both travel and passenger transport. [5] Receipts include both travel and passenger transport. [6] Arrivals of nonresident tourists in hotels and similar establishments.

Source: World Tourism Organization, Madrid, Spain, World Tourism Barometer, April 2009 (copyright).

Table 1364. **Household Expenditure on Recreation and Culture as a Percentage of GDP: 1980 to 2007**

[Household expenditure on recreation and culture includes purchases of audio-visual, photographic, and computer equipment; CDs and DVDs; musical instruments; camper vans; caravans; sports equipment; toys; domestic pets and related products; gardening tools and plants; newspapers; tickets to sporting matches, cinemas, and theatres; and spending on gambling (including lottery tickets) less any winnings. It excludes expenditures on restaurants, hotels, and travel and holiday homes but includes package holidays]

Country	1980	1990	2000	2001	2002	2003	2004	2005	2006	2007
Australia	5.8	6.1	7.3	7.1	7.2	7.1	7.0	6.8	6.6	(NA)
Austria	5.0	6.5	7.0	7.1	6.9	6.9	6.8	6.7	6.5	(NA)
Belgium	(NA)	(NA)	5.2	5.2	4.8	4.8	4.7	4.7	4.6	4.7
Canada	4.4	5.1	5.7	5.7	5.8	5.7	5.6	5.5	5.5	5.4
Czech Republic	(NA)	(NA)	6.1	6.2	6.0	6.2	6.0	5.9	5.7	5.6
Denmark.	4.8	4.9	5.2	5.1	5.1	5.3	5.5	5.5	5.6	5.6
Finland.	5.2	5.4	5.4	5.3	5.3	5.5	5.5	5.6	5.8	5.7
France	4.8	4.8	5.1	5.1	5.2	5.2	5.2	5.2	5.2	5.1
Germany	(NA)	(NA)	5.6	5.6	5.4	5.3	5.3	5.2	5.2	5.1
Greece.	(NA)	(NA)	5.1	5.8	5.8	5.4	5.5	5.6	6.6	6.3
Hungary	(NA)	(NA)	4.1	4.2	4.2	4.2	4.2	4.3	4.2	(NA)
Iceland.	(NA)	6.1	7.1	6.9	6.8	6.7	6.5	6.4	6.1	(NA)
Ireland	(NA)	(NA)	3.4	3.5	3.2	3.1	3.2	3.2	3.1	3.1
Italy	4.1	4.4	4.5	4.4	4.3	4.2	4.3	4.1	4.1	4.0
Japan	(NA)	(NA)	6.1	6.2	6.2	6.2	6.2	6.0	6.1	(NA)
Korea.	2.2	3.9	4.1	4.2	4.4	4.0	3.6	3.7	3.7	3.7
Luxembourg	(NA)	(NA)	3.6	3.8	3.9	3.5	3.5	3.2	2.9	2.8
Mexico	(NA)	2.2	2.0	2.0	1.9	1.9	2.0	(NA)	(NA)	(NA)
Netherlands	5.9	5.6	5.5	5.4	5.3	5.1	5.0	4.8	4.8	4.8
New Zealand.	(NA)	5.3	7.2	7.1	(NA)	(NA)	(NA)	(NA)	(NA)	(NA)
Norway.	(NA)	(NA)	5.2	5.3	5.5	5.6	5.5	5.1	(NA)	(NA)
Poland	(NA)	(NA)	5.6	4.9	4.8	5.0	5.0	4.7	4.5	(NA)
Portugal	(NA)	(NA)	4.2	4.1	4.1	4.1	4.2	4.3	4.5	(NA)
Slovakia	(NA)	(NA)	4.7	5.2	5.0	4.7	4.8	4.9	4.8	5.0
Spain.	(NA)	(NA)	5.7	5.7	5.6	5.5	5.5	5.5	5.3	(NA)
Sweden	(NA)	(NA)	5.6	5.6	5.5	5.5	5.4	5.3	(NA)	(NA)
Switzerland	(NA)	5.2	5.1	5.1	5.1	5.1	5.0	4.9	4.6	(NA)
Turkey	(NA)	(NA)	3.8	3.4	3.5	3.4	3.8	3.7	3.5	3.2
United Kingdom	5.5	6.3	7.3	7.3	7.5	7.5	7.7	7.7	(NA)	(NA)
United States	4.5	5.4	6.4	6.4	6.4	6.4	6.4	6.3	6.4	6.5
Israel	(NA)	(NA)	4.4	4.3	4.0	4.0	4.3	4.4	4.4	4.5
Slovenia	(NA)	(NA)	6.0	6.0	6.0	6.1	6.1	6.1	5.9	5.6

NA Not available.

Source: Organization for Economic Cooperation and Development, Paris, France, *OECD Factbook, 2009* (copyright). See also <http://www.oecd.org/>.

Table 1365. **Development Assistance by Country: 2006 and 2007**

[2,471 represents $2,471,000,000]

Country	Official development aid (ODA), 2007 [1]			2006	
	Million U.S. dollars	Percent of GNI [2]	Percent of total DAC ODA [3]	Multilateral aid (Percent of ODA)	Grants by NGOs [4] (Percent of GNI)
Australia	2,471	0.30	2.4	15.4	0.09
Austria	1,798	0.49	1.7	27.1	0.04
Belgium	1,953	0.43	1.9	31.4	0.06
Canada	3,922	0.28	3.8	31.3	0.09
Denmark.	2,563	0.81	2.5	34.5	0.03
Finland.	973	0.40	0.9	45.5	0.01
France	9,940	0.39	9.6	25.3	(NA)
Germany	12,291	0.37	11.8	32.6	0.05
Greece.	501	0.16	0.5	55.4	(Z)
Ireland	1,190	0.54	1.1	38.1	0.18
Italy	3,929	0.19	3.8	45.0	0.01
Japan	7,691	0.17	7.4	34.6	0.01
Luxembourg	365	0.90	0.4	29.5	0.02
Netherlands	6,215	0.81	6.0	21.5	0.04
New Zealand.	315	0.27	0.3	21.6	0.05
Norway.	3,727	0.95	3.6	25.6	(NA)
Portugal	471	0.22	0.5	46.7	(Z)
Spain.	5,134	0.37	5.0	45.1	(NA)
Sweden	4,334	0.93	4.2	27.9	(Z)
Switzerland	1,680	0.37	1.6	23.8	0.10
United Kingdom	9,921	0.36	9.6	30.0	0.02
United States	21,753	0.16	21.0	10.1	0.07
EU-15 [5]	61,577	0.40	59.7	31.4	0.02
DAC [3] total	103,136	0.28	100.0	26.3	0.04

NA Not available. Z Less than 0.05 percent. [1] Preliminary. [2] Gross national income. See headnote, Table 1312. [3] DAC: OECD Development Assistance Committee. [4] NGO: Non-governmental organizations. [5] See footnote 2, Table 1336.

Source: Organization for Economic Cooperation and Development, Paris, France, OECD in Figures, 2008 (copyright). See also <http://www.oecd.org>.

Table 1366. **Net Flow of Financial Resources to Developing Countries and Multilateral Organizations: 1995 to 2007**

[165,234 represents $165,234,000,000. Net flow covers loans, grants, and grant-like flows minus amortization on loans. Military flows are excluded. The Development Assistance Committee (DAC) determines those countries that are to be considered "developing." GNI = gross national income. For explanation of GNI, see headnote, Table 1312. Minus sign (–) indicates net inflow]

Type of aid and country	Amount (mil. dol.)					Percent of GNI		
	1995	2000	2005	2006	2007	1995	2000	2007
DAC countries, total	165,234	134,195	302,779	303,050	440,912	0.75	0.56	(NA)
United States	46,984	25,252	113,526	90,897	129,862	0.65	0.25	0.93
Australia	2,536	1,961	5,366	9,120	10,307	0.73	0.53	1.25
Austria	958	1,135	4,837	3,455	20,553	0.41	0.61	5.66
Belgium	–234	2,281	3,142	5,309	3,820	–0.09	1.00	0.83
Canada	5,724	6,483	13,373	14,233	17,161	1.04	0.95	1.22
Denmark	1,799	2,176	2,215	2,686	4,807	1.07	1.39	1.51
Finland	604	1,087	1,642	1,413	2,149	0.48	0.91	0.86
France	12,477	5,557	15,744	22,329	43,126	0.81	0.41	1.66
Germany	21,197	12,331	30,683	25,992	39,339	0.87	0.66	1.17
Greece	(NA)	229	709	2,896	3,391	(NA)	0.20	1.10
Ireland	247	740	5,298	5,237	5,840	0.46	0.93	2.70
Italy	2,800	10,846	4,103	5,512	4,422	0.26	1.01	0.21
Japan	42,295	11,423	23,238	26,179	30,315	0.79	0.24	0.67
Luxembourg	72	129	265	299	384	0.40	0.75	0.93
Netherlands	6,795	6,947	22,781	28,616	18,142	1.71	1.85	2.35
New Zealand	166	142	401	338	404	0.31	0.32	0.34
Norway	1,670	1,437	4,630	4,304	5,221	1.15	0.87	1.33
Portugal	395	4,622	1,109	666	2,215	0.38	4.45	1.03
Spain	2,025	23,471	6,801	11,146	21,662	0.37	4.25	1.55
Sweden	2,224	3,952	3,545	4,175	6,911	1.00	1.76	1.49
Switzerland	1,118	1,765	8,103	11,306	12,561	0.35	0.68	2.76
United Kingdom	13,382	10,230	31,269	26,941	58,319	1.19	0.72	2.05
Czech Republic	(NA)	(NA)	135	161	179	(NA)	(NA)	0.11
Korea	1,973	44	4,834	6,514	11,582	(NA)	0.01	1.19
Turkey	(NA)	141	1,052	1,663	1,337	(NA)	0.07	0.20

NA Not available.

Source: Organization for Economic Cooperation and Development, Paris, France, *Annual Reports of the Development Assistance Committee* (copyright).

Table 1367. **External Debt by Country: 1990 to 2007**

[In billions of dollars (28.1 represents $28,100,000,000). Total external debt is debt owed to nonresidents repayable in foreign currency, goods, or services. Total external debt is the sum of public, publicly guaranteed, and private nonguaranteed long-term debt, use of IMF credit, and short-term debt. Short-term debt includes all debt having an original maturity of one year or less and interest in arrears on long-term debt]

Country	1990	2000	2006	2007	Country	1990	2000	2006	2007
Algeria	28.1	25.4	5.7	5.5	Mexico	104.4	150.9	160.5	178.1
Angola	8.6	9.4	10.4	12.7	Montenegro	(NA)	(NA)	1.2	1.2
Argentina	62.2	140.9	115.9	127.8	Morocco	25.0	20.7	17.9	20.3
Bangladesh	12.4	15.7	20.5	22.0	Nepal	1.6	2.9	3.4	3.6
Brazil	119.7	241.6	193.5	237.5	Nigeria	33.4	31.4	7.8	8.9
Bulgaria	10.9	11.2	21.0	33.0	Pakistan	20.7	32.8	35.9	40.7
Cameroon	6.4	10.2	3.4	3.2	Panama	6.5	7.0	10.0	9.9
Chile	19.2	37.3	48.0	58.6	Peru	20.0	28.6	28.5	32.2
China [1]	55.3	145.7	325.1	373.6	Philippines	30.6	58.3	60.3	65.8
Colombia	17.2	33.9	38.9	45.0	Poland	49.4	64.8	139.0	195.4
Congo (Kinshasa) [2] .	10.3	11.7	11.2	12.3	Romania	1.1	11.2	54.0	85.4
Cote d'Ivoire	17.3	12.1	12.8	13.9	Russia [3]	(NA)	160.0	250.5	370.2
Croatia	(NA)	12.4	38.4	48.6	Serbia [4]	17.8	11.5	19.5	26.3
Ecuador	12.1	13.6	17.1	17.5	Sierra Leone	1.2	1.2	1.3	0.3
Egypt	33.0	29.0	28.8	30.4	South Africa	(NA)	24.9	35.5	43.4
Ethiopia	8.6	5.5	2.3	2.6	Sri Lanka	5.9	9.2	11.6	14.0
Ghana	3.7	6.1	3.2	4.5	Sudan	14.8	16.0	18.2	19.1
Guatemala	2.8	3.9	5.5	6.3	Tanzania	6.5	6.9	4.2	5.1
India	83.6	99.1	175.5	221.0	Thailand	28.1	79.7	55.0	63.1
Indonesia	69.9	144.3	130.8	140.8	Tunisia	7.7	11.3	18.8	20.2
Iran	9.0	8.0	20.1	20.6	Turkey	49.4	116.8	207.8	251.5
Jamaica	4.8	4.7	8.0	10.1	Ukraine	(NA)	12.2	49.9	73.6
Jordan	8.3	7.4	8.0	8.4	Uruguay	4.4	8.1	11.2	12.4
Kazakhstan	(NA)	12.4	74.1	96.1	Venezuela	33.2	42.0	44.6	43.1
Lebanon	1.8	9.9	24.0	24.6	Vietnam	23.3	12.8	20.2	24.2
Malaysia	15.3	41.9	56.5	53.7	Zimbabwe	3.3	3.8	4.7	5.3

NA Not available. [1] See footnote 4, Table 1296. [2] See footnote 5, Table 1296. [3] The debt of the former Soviet Union is included in Russia's data after 1990 on the assumption that 100 percent of all outstanding external debt as of December 1991 has become a liability of Russia. Beginning in 2000, the data for Russia has also been revised to include obligations to members of the former Council for Mutual Economic Assistance and other countries in the form of trade-related credits amounting to $15.4 billion as of the end of 1996. [4] In June 2006, Serbia and Montenegro became separate countries (formerly Yugoslavia). Data for 2000 are for Serbia and Montenegro. Starting 2006, data excludes Montenegro. External debt obligations, excluding IBRD, IMF, and short-term, of Bosnia and Herzegovina before 2000 are included under Serbia and Montenegro. Data from 2000 onwards are estimates and also reflect borrowing by the former Yugoslavia that are not yet allocated to the successor republics.

Source: The World Bank, Washington, DC, *2009 World Development Indicators* (copyright).

U.S. Census Bureau, *Statistical Abstract of the United States: 2010*

Table 1368. **Foreign Direct Investment Flows in OECD Countries: 2000 to 2007**

[In billions of dollars (1,073.9 represents $1,073,900,000,000). Data are converted to U.S. dollars using the yearly average exchange rate]

Country	Inflows				Outflows			
	2000	2006	2007 [1]	Cumulative, 1990–2007	2000	2006	2007 [1]	Cumulative, 1990–2007
OECD, total. .	1,073.9	1,059.5	1,597.9	9,319.8	1,017.1	1,230.2	1,911.5	12,687.0
Australia.	6.8	27.1	34.2	165.7	1.1	23.9	17.8	84.2
Austria	8.8	7.9	29.8	95.7	5.7	13.7	34.1	113.8
Belgium	(NA)	58.9	70.0	257.2	(NA)	50.7	52.5	220.5
Canada	66.8	69.0	108.6	443.6	44.7	45.2	53.8	478.4
Czech Republic .	5.0	5.5	9.1	69.3	(Z)	1.5	1.3	5.1
Denmark.	33.0	2.7	11.9	107.0	25.0	8.4	20.5	141.3
Finland.	8.8	5.6	11.4	73.3	24.0	3.2	7.1	119.5
France	42.9	78.2	158.0	768.4	175.6	121.4	224.7	1,453.4
Germany	198.3	55.2	51.8	639.7	56.6	94.8	169.9	1,270.8
Greece.	(NA)	5.4	1.9	18.4	(NA)	4.2	5.3	13.3
Hungary	2.8	20.0	47.2	109.8	0.6	18.8	42.7	69.1
Iceland.	0.2	4.0	3.1	12.1	0.4	5.3	12.9	29.8
Ireland	26.5	-5.5	30.6	123.5	4.6	15.3	20.8	107.0
Italy	13.4	39.3	40.2	215.2	12.4	42.1	90.8	340.4
Japan	29.0	-6.5	22.5	205.0	49.8	50.2	73.5	879.6
Korea, South. . .	8.6	5.0	(NA)	62.6	3.5	9.9	(NA)	50.0
Luxembourg . . .	(NA)	125.3	185.6	709.4	(NA)	110.8	247.0	789.6
Mexico	17.8	19.1	27.2	265.8	(NA)	(NA)	(NA)	2.7
Netherlands . . .	63.9	7.5	118.4	491.9	75.7	65.2	28.5	776.9
New Zealand. . .	1.4	8.0	2.5	42.7	0.6	0.4	3.2	9.7
Norway.	6.0	6.8	4.9	53.7	8.3	18.5	12.5	107.2
Poland	9.3	19.6	22.6	120.7	(Z)	8.9	4.7	19.1
Portugal	6.6	11.3	5.6	62.4	8.1	7.0	6.2	64.2
Spain	39.6	26.9	57.8	376.1	58.2	100.3	125.6	642.3
Sweden	23.2	23.1	12.5	224.7	40.6	20.6	29.1	296.4
Switzerland	19.3	30.9	49.3	175.5	44.7	75.9	49.7	471.0
Turkey	1.0	20.2	22.3	71.1	0.9	0.9	2.1	8.5
United Kingdom .	118.8	147.7	222.8	1,136.0	233.5	90.9	260.8	1,731.6
United States . .	**314.0**	**236.7**	**232.8**	**2,201.8**	**142.6**	**221.7**	**313.8**	**2,390.6**

NA Not available.   Z Less than $50 million.   [1] Preliminary.
Source: Organization for Economic Cooperation and Development, Paris, France, *OECD Factbook, 2009*. See also <http://oecd.org>.

Table 1369. **Military Expenditures, 2006, and Manpower, 2009, by Country**

[8,444 represents 8,444,000. Manpower covers males and females deemed fit for military service, ages 15–49]

Country	Expenditures (percent of GDP [1])	Manpower (1,000)	Country	Expenditures (percent of GDP [1])	Manpower (1,000)
Afghanistan	1.9	8,444	Israel	7.3	2,880
Albania	[2]1.5	1,569	Italy	[2]1.8	21,772
Algeria	3.3	16,684	Japan	0.8	44,678
Argentina.	[2]1.3	16,533	Kazakhstan	[6]0.9	6,439
Australia	2.4	8,521	Korea, North.	(NA)	8,597
Austria	[2]0.9	3,184	Korea, South	2.7	21,348
Bahrain	4.5	316	Kuwait.	5.3	1,455
Belarus	[2]1.4	3,790	Laos	0.5	2,108
Belgium.	[2]1.3	3,868	Lebanon	[2]3.1	1,903
Bolivia.	1.9	3,573	Libya	[2]3.9	2,876
Bosnia and Herzegovina. .	[2]4.5	1,951	Malaysia	[2]2.0	10,903
Brazil	2.6	82,311	Mexico	0.5	47,691
Bulgaria.	[2]2.6	2,732	Morocco	[5]5.0	15,661
Burma.	[2]2.1	18,667	Netherlands	[2]1.6	6,368
Cambodia	[2]3.0	5,437	New Zealand	[2]1.0	1,664
Canada	[2]1.1	13,061	Nicaragua	0.6	2,617
Chile	2.7	7,097	Nigeria	1.5	38,614
China [3]	4.3	611,222	Norway	[2]1.9	1,751
Colombia.	[2]3.4	18,258	Oman	[2]11.4	1,239
Congo (Brazzaville) [4]	3.1	1,066	Pakistan	[5]3.0	66,293
Cote d'Ivoire.	[2]1.6	6,058	Peru	1.5	12,281
Croatia	[2]2.4	1,621	Philippines	[2]0.9	39,806
Cuba	3.8	5,001	Poland	[2]1.7	15,787
Czech Republic.	[5]1.3	4,107	Russia.	[2]3.9	49,067
Denmark	[5]1.3	2,012	Saudi Arabia	[2]10.0	13,139
Ecuador	2.8	5,874	Singapore	[2]4.9	2,139
Egypt	[2]3.4	36,210	South Africa	1.7	14,160
El Salvador	5.0	2,749	Spain	[2]1.2	16,038
Ethiopia.	3.0	23,096	Sudan.	[2]3.0	11,779
Finland.	[2]2.0	1,883	Sweden.	[2]1.5	3,351
France	[2]2.6	23,899	Switzerland	[2]1.0	2,986
Germany	[2]1.5	30,647	Syria	[2]5.9	8,706
Greece	[2]4.3	4,118	Thailand	[2]1.8	27,213
Honduras.	0.6	2,800	Turkey.	[5]5.3	34,219
Hungary	[2]1.8	3,822	Ukraine	[2]1.4	16,291
India	2.5	480,319	United Arab Emirates. . . .	[2]3.1	2,870
Indonesia.	[2]3.0	105,501	United Kingdom	[2]2.4	23,741
Iran	2.5	34,807	**United States . . . .**	**[2]4.1**	**119,202**
Iraq	8.6	12,268	Venezuela	[2]1.2	11,265
Ireland	[2]0.9	1,712	Vietnam.	[2]2.5	39,959

NA Not available.   [1] GDP calculated on an exchange rate basis.   [2] 2005 data.   [3] See footnote 4, Table 1296.   [4] See footnote 5, Table 1296.   [5] 2007 data.   [6] 2002 data.   [7] 2003 data.
Source: Central Intelligence Agency, *The World Factbook, 2009*. See also <https://www.cia.gov/library/publications/the-world-factbook/index.html> (accessed 12 August 2009).

Guide to Sources of Statistics, State Statistical Abstracts, and Foreign Statistical Abstracts

Alphabetically arranged, this guide contains references to important primary sources of statistical information for the United States and other countries. Secondary sources have been included if the information contained in them is presented in a particularly convenient form or if primary sources are not readily available. Nonrecurrent publications presenting compilations or estimates for years later than 2000, or types of data not available in regular series, are also included. Data are also available in press releases.

Valuable information may also be found in state reports, foreign statistical abstracts, which are included at the end of this appendix, and in reports for particular commodities, industries, or similar segments of our economic and social structures, many of which are not included here.

Publications listed under each subject are divided into two main groups: "U.S. Government" and "Nongovernment." The location of the publisher of each report is given except for federal agencies located in Washington, DC. Most federal publications may be purchased from the Superintendent of Documents, U.S. Government Printing Office, Washington, DC, tel. 202-512-1800, (Web site <http://bookstore.gpo.gov>). In some cases, federal publications may be obtained from the issuing agency.

Title	Frequency	Paper	PDF	Other formats
U.S. GOVERNMENT				
Administrative Office of the United States Courts <http://www.uscourts.gov>				
Calendar Year Reports on Authorized Wiretaps (state and federal)	Annual	X	X	X
Federal Court Management Statistics.	Annual	X		X
Federal Judicial Caseload Statistics.	Annual	X		
Judicial Business of the United States Courts	Annual	X	X	
Statistical Tables for the Federal Judiciary.	Semiannual	X		X
Agency for International Development <http://www.usaid.gov>				
U.S. Overseas Loans and Grants: Obligations and Loan Authorizations	Annual		X	X
Army Corps of Engineers <http://www.usace.army.mil>				
Waterborne Commerce of the United States (in five parts).	Annual	X		X
Board of Governors of the Federal Reserve System <http://www.federalreserve.gov>				
Assets and Liabilities of Commercial Banks in the United States H.8	Weekly	X	X	X
Consumer Credit G.19	Monthly	X	X	X
Federal Reserve Bulletin	Annual	X	X	X
Foreign Exchange Rates H.10	Weekly			X
Flow of Funds Accounts of the United States Z.1.	Quarterly	X	X	X
Industrial Production and Capacity Utilization G.17.	Monthly	X	X	X
Money Stock and Debt Measures H.6	Weekly	X	X	X
Statistical Supplement to the Federal Reserve Bulletin	Monthly	X	X	X
Bureau of Economic Analysis <http://www.bea.gov>				
Survey of Current Business	Monthly	X	X	X
Bureau of Justice Statistics <http://www.ojp.usdoj.gov/bjs>				
American Indians and Crime: A BJS Statistical Profile, December 2004	Periodic	X	X	X
Background Checks for Firearm Transfers	Annual	X	X	X
Capital Punishment, 2006, December 2007.	Annual		X	X
Carjacking, 1993-2002, July 2004	Periodic		X	X
Census of Publicly Funded Forensic Crime Laboratories, February 2005	Periodic	X	X	X
Census of State and Federal Correctional Facilities, 2000, August 2003.	Periodic	X	X	X
Civil Rights Complaints in U.S. District Courts, July 2002.	Periodic	X	X	X
Civil Trial Cases and Verdicts in Large Counties, 2001, April 2004.	Periodic	X	X	X
Compendium of Federal Justice Statistics, 2004, December 2006.	Annual	X	X	X
Contacts Between Police and Public: Findings from the 2005 National Survey, April 2007	Periodic	X	X	X

Title	Frequency	Paper	Internet PDF	Internet Other formats
Bureau of Justice Statistics—Con.				
Contract Trials and Verdicts in Large Counties, 2001, February 2005	Periodic	X	X	X
Crime and the Nation's Households, 2005, April 2007	Annual	X	X	X
Crimes Against Persons Age 65 or Older, 1993–2002, January 2005	Periodic	X	X	X
Criminal Victimization in the United States, 2006, December 2007	Annual	X	X	X
Cross-National Studies in Crime and Justice, September 2004	Periodic	X	X	X
Defense Counsel in Criminal Cases, November 2000	Periodic	X	X	X
Education and Correctional Populations, January 2003	Periodic	X	X	X
Family Violence Statistics	Periodic	X	X	X
Federal Criminal Case Processing, 2002, January 2005	Periodic	X	X	X
Federal Law Enforcement Officers, 2004, August 2006	Biennial	X	X	X
Felony Defendants in Large Urban Counties, 2004, April 2008	Biennial		X	X
Felony Sentences in State Courts, 2004, July 2007	Biennial		X	X
Firearm Use by Offenders, November 2001	Periodic	X	X	X
Hepatitis Testing and Treatment in State Prisons, April 2004	Periodic	X	X	X
Hispanic Victims of Violent Crime, 1993–2000, April 2002	Periodic	X	X	X
HIV in Prisons 2006	Annual		X	X
Homicide Trends in the United States	Annual		X	X
Identity Theft, 2005, November 2007	Periodic	X	X	X
Immigration Offenders in the Federal Criminal Justice System, August 2002	Periodic		X	X
Incarcerated Parents and Their Children, August 2000	Periodic		X	X
Indicators of School Crime and Safety	Annual	X	X	X
Intimate Partner Violence, 1993 to 2001, February 2003	Periodic	X	X	X
Jails in Indian Country, 2004, November 2006	Annual	X	X	X
Justice Expenditure and Employment Extract Series, 2005, August 2007	Annual			X
Juvenile Offenders and Victims	Periodic	X	X	X
Juvenile Victimization and Offending, 1993–2003	Periodic	X	X	X
Law Enforcement Management and Administrative Statistics 2000: Data for Individual State and Local Agencies with 100 or More Officers	Periodic	X	X	X
Local Police Departments, 2003, May 2006	Periodic	X	X	X
Medical Malpractice Trials and Verdicts in Large Counties, April 2004	Periodic	X	X	X
Money Laundering Offenders, 1994–2001, July 2003	Periodic	X	X	X
Prevalence of Imprisonment in the U.S. Population, 1974–2001, August 2003	Periodic	X	X	X
Prison and Jail Inmates at Midyear, 2006, June 2007	Annual	X	X	X
Prisoners in 2006, December 2007	Annual	X	X	X
Probation and Parole in the United States	Annual	X	X	X
Profile of Jail Inmates, 2002, July 2004	Periodic	X	X	X
Prosecutors in State Courts, 2001, May 2002	Biennial	X	X	X
Rape and Sexual Assault: Reporting to Police and Medical Attention, August 2002	Periodic	X	X	X
Reentry Trends in the United States Current Data Electronic	Periodic		X	X
Sheriff's Offices, 2003, April 2006	Periodic	X	X	X
Sourcebook of Criminal Justice Statistics	Annual	X	X	X
State Court Prosecutors in Large Districts, December 2001	Periodic	X	X	X
State Court Prosecutors in Small Districts, 2001, January 2003	Periodic	X	X	X
State Court Sentencing of Convicted Felons, 2004, July 2007	Biennial		X	X
State Prison Expenditures, 2001, June 2004	Periodic	X	X	X
Summary of State Sex Offender Registries, 2001, March 2002	Periodic	X	X	X
Survey of DNA Crime Laboratories, 2001, January 2002	Periodic	X	X	X
Survey of State Criminal History Information Systems, September 2003	Biennial	X	X	X
Survey of State Procedures Related to Firearm Sales, 2005, November 2006	Periodic	X	X	X
Tort Trials and Verdicts in Large Counties, November 2004	Periodic	X	X	X
Traffic Stop Data Collection Policies for State Police, 2004, June 2005	Periodic	X	X	X
Violent Victimization of College Students, 1995–2002, January 2005	Periodic	X	X	X
Weapon Use and Violent Crime, 1993–2001, September 2003	Periodic	X	X	X
Bureau of Labor Statistics				
<http://www.bls.gov>				
100 Years of U.S. Consumer Spending: Data for the Nation, New York City, and Boston, Report 991	Periodic	X	X	
College Enrollment and Work Activity of High School Graduates	Annual	X	X	
Comparative Labor Force Statistics, Ten Countries	Semiannual	X	X	X
Compensation and Working Conditions	Quarterly		X	X
Consumer Expenditure Survey, Integrated Diary and Interview Survey Data	Annual	X	X	X
Consumer Prices: Energy and Food	Monthly	X	X	X
CPI Detailed Report	Monthly		X	X
Employer Costs for Employee Compensation	Annual	X	X	X
Employment and Earnings	Monthly		X	X
Employment and Wages	Annual	X	X	X
Employment Characteristics of Families	Annual	X	X	X
Employment Cost Index	Quarterly	X	X	X
Employment Cost Indexes and Levels	Annual	X	X	X
The Employment Situation	Monthly	X	X	X
Geographic Profile of Employment and Unemployment	Annual	X	X	X
International Comparisons of Hourly Compensation Costs for Production Workers in Manufacturing	Annual	X	X	X
International Comparisons of Manufacturing Productivity and Unit Labor Cost Trends	Annual	X	X	X
Metropolitan Area Employment and Unemployment	Monthly	X	X	X
Monthly Labor Review	Monthly		X	X
National Compensation Survey	Annual	X	X	X
Occupational Injuries and Illnesses in the United States by Industry	Annual	X	X	X
Occupational Projections and Training Data	Biennial	X	X	X
Producer Price Indexes Detailed Report	Monthly		X	X
Productivity and Costs by Industry	Periodic		X	X
Selected Service-Providing and Mining Industries, 2005	Annual	X	X	X
Manufacturing, 2005	Annual	X	X	X
Wholesale Trade, Retail Trade, and Food Services and Drinking Places, 2005	Annual	X	X	X
Real Earnings	Monthly	X	X	X

860   Appendix I

Title	Frequency	Paper	PDF	Other formats
Bureau of Labor Statistics—Con.				
Regional and State Employment and Unemployment	Monthly	X	X	X
Relative Importance of Components in the Consumer Price Indexes	Annual	X	X	X
Union Members	Annual	X	X	X
U.S. Import and Export Price Indexes	Monthly	X	X	X
Usual Weekly Earnings of Wage and Salary Workers	Quarterly	X	X	X
Work Experience of the Population	Annual	X	X	X
Bureau of Land Management				
<http://www.blm.gov/wo/st/en.html>				
Public Land Statistics	Annual	X	X	
Census Bureau				
<http://www.census.gov>				
2002 Economic Census				
Comparative Statistics.	Quinquennial	X	X	X
Bridge Between NAICS and SIC	Quinquennial	X	X	X
Business Expenses.	Quinquennial	X	X	X
Industry/Geography.	Quinquennial		X	X
2002 Economic Census, Company Statistics Series, Survey of Business Owners . .	Quinquennial	X	X	X
American Indian- and Alaska Native-Owned Firms.	Quinquennial	X	X	X
Asian-Owned Firms.	Quinquennial	X	X	X
Black-Owned Firms.	Quinquennial	X	X	X
Hispanic-Owned Firms.	Quinquennial	X	X	X
Native Hawaiian- and Other Pacific Islander-Owned Firms	Quinquennial	X	X	X
American Community Survey Annual Earnings and Poverty Report, 2006.	Annual	X	X	
Annual Revision of Monthly Retail and Food Services: Sales and Inventories	Annual		X	
Annual Revision of Monthly Wholesale Distributors: Sales and Inventories	Annual		X	X
Census of Governments	Quinquennial		X	X
Census of Housing Decennial (2000, most recent)	Decennial	X	X	X
Census of Population Decennial (2000, most recent)	Decennial	X	X	X
County Business Patterns	Annual		X	X
Current Construction Reports:				
New Residential Construction and New Residential Sales	Annual		X	
Value of Construction Put in Place, C30.	Monthly		X	
Residential Improvements and Repairs, C50.	Monthly		X	
Current Housing Reports:				
Housing Vacancies, H111	Quarterly		X	X
Who Could Afford to Buy a Home in 2002, H121	Occasional	X	X	X
Survey of Market Absorption of Apartments (SOMA)	Quarterly		X	X
Characteristics of Apartments Completed, H131.	Annual	X	X	X
American Housing Survey for the United States, H150	Biennial	X	X	X
American Housing Survey for Selected Metropolitan Areas, H170	Biennial	X	X	X
Current Industrial Reports			X	
Current Population Reports (Series P20 and P23)		X	X	X
Consumer Income and Poverty, P60, and Household Economic Studies, P70		X	X	
Alternative Poverty Estimates in the United States: 2003	Periodic	X	X	
Alternative Income Estimates in the United States: 2003	Periodic	X	X	
Income, Poverty, and Health Insurance Coverage in the United States, 2007	Annual	X	X	X
Economic Census of Outlying Areas	Quinquennial	X	X	
Global Population Profile: 2002 (Series WP)		X	X	X
International Briefs (Series IB)		X	X	
International Data Base				X
International Population Reports (Series P95)		X	X	
Manufacturer's Shipments, Inventories, and Orders	Monthly		X	
Manufacturer's Shipments, Inventories, and Orders: 1992–2005	Annual		X	
New York City Housing and Vacancy Survey, 2005.	Every 3 years		X	X
Nonemployer Statistics	Annual		X	X
Population Estimates and Projections.				X
Quarterly Financial Report for Manufacturing, Mining, and Trade Corporations.	Quarterly		X	
Residential Finance Survey, 2001	Every 10 years	X	X	X
Service Annual Survey Report	Annual		X	
Survey of Plant Capacity Utilization (Current Industrial Reports MQ-C1)	Annual		X	
U.S. International Trade in Goods and Services: includes cumulative data	Annual		X	X
U.S. Trade With Puerto Rico and U.S. Possessions (FT 895)	Monthly		X	
Vehicle Inventory and Use Survey (discontinued)	Quinquennial	X	X	
Centers for Disease Control and Prevention, Atlanta, GA				
<http://www.cdc.gov>				
CDC Injury Fact Book		X	X	X
Morbidity and Mortality Weekly Report	Annual	X	X	X
Centers for Medicare and Medicaid Services (CMS)				
<http://www.cms.hhs.gov>				
CMS Statistics	Annual	X	X	
Data Compendium	Annual	X	X	
Health Care Financing Review Medicare and Medicaid Statistical Supplement.	Annual	X	X	
Health Care Financing Review	Quarterly	X	X	
Trustees' Report	Annual	X	X	
Wallet Card	Annual	X	X	
Central Intelligence Agency				
<http://www.cia.gov>				
World Factbook	Annual	X	X	X
Coast Guard (See Department of Homeland Security)				
Comptroller of the Currency				
<http://www.occ.treas.gov>				
Quarterly Journal	Quarterly		X	X

Appendix I 861

Title	Frequency	Paper	Internet PDF	Internet Other formats
Office of the Clerk U.S. House of Representatives <http://clerk.house.gov>				
Statistics of the Presidential and Congressional Election	Biennial		X	X
Council of Economic Advisers <http://www.whitehouse.gov>				
Economic Indicators	Monthly	X	X	X
Economic Report of the President	Annual	X	X	
Department of Agriculture, Economic Research Service <http://www.ers.usda.gov>				
Agricultural Income and Finance (Situation and Outlook Report)	Annual		X	
Amber Waves	Periodic	X	X	X
America's Diverse Family Farms: Structure and Finances	Annual	X	X	
Cotton and Wool Yearbook	Annual		X	X
Dairy Yearbook	Periodic			X
Feedgrains Yearbook	Annual		X	X
Food Spending in American Households (Statistical Bulletin No. 824)	Periodic	X	X	
Food Marketing Review, (Agricultural Economic Report No. 743)	Periodic	X	X	
Fruit and Tree Nut Yearbook	Annual			X
Oil Crops Yearbook	Annual		X	X
Poultry Yearbook	Annual			X
Red Meat Yearbook	Annual			X
Rice Yearbook	Annual		X	X
Sugar and Sweeteners Yearbook	Periodic			X
Situation and Outlook Reports Issued for agricultural exports, cotton and wool, feed, fruit and tree nuts, livestock and poultry, oil crops, rice, sugar and sweeteners, vegetables, wheat, and world agriculture	Periodic	X	X	
Structure and Finances of U.S. Farms: Family Farm Report	Annual	X	X	
Vegetable and Melons Yearbook	Annual			X
World Agricultural Supply and Demand Estimates	Monthly	X	X	X
Department of Agriculture, Food and Nutrition Service <http://www.fns.usda.gov/fns/default.htm>				
Characteristics of Food Stamp Households Food and Consumer Service Programs				
Department of Agriculture, Foreign Agricultural Service <http://www.fas.usda.gov>				
Livestock and Poultry World Markets and Trade	Biannual	X	X	
Department of Agriculture, National Agricultural Statistics Service <http://www.nass.usda.gov>				
Agricultural Chemical Usage	Periodic	X	X	X
Agricultural Statistics	Annual	X	X	
Catfish Production	Annual	X	X	X
Cattle	Biennial	X	X	X
Census of Agriculture	Quinquennial	X	X	
Cherry Production	Annual	X	X	X
Chickens and Eggs	Annual	X	X	X
Citrus Fruits	Annual	X	X	X
Cranberries	Annual	X	X	X
Crop Production Reports	Monthly	X	X	X
Crop Values Report	Annual	X	X	X
Dairy Products	Annual	X	X	X
Farm Labor	Quarterly	X	X	X
Farms, Land in Farms, and Livestock Operations	Annual	X	X	X
Floriculture Crops	Annual	X	X	X
Land Values and Cash Rents	Annual	X	X	X
Livestock Slaughter	Annual	X	X	X
Meat Animals: Production, Disposition, and Income	Annual	X	X	X
Milk Production	Annual	X	X	X
Noncitrus Fruits and Nuts	Biennial	X	X	X
Poultry: Production and Value Summary	Annual	X	X	X
Stock Reports. Stocks of grain, peanuts, potatoes, and rice	Periodic	X	X	X
Trout Production	Annual	X	X	X
Turkeys: Hatchery and Raised	Annual	X	X	X
Usual Planting and Harvesting Dates	Periodic	X	X	X
Vegetable Reports	Periodic	X	X	X
Weekly Weather and Crop Bulletin Report	Weekly	X	X	
Winter Wheat Seedlings	Monthly	X	X	X
Department of Agriculture, Natural Resources and Conservation Service <http://www.nrcs.usda.gov>				
National Resources Inventory	Periodic	X		X
Department of Defense <http://www.defenselink.mil/pubs>				
Foreign Military Sales and Military Assistance Facts	Annual			X
Personnel Statistics	Annual		X	
Department of Education <http://www.ed.gov/index.jhtml>				
Department of Education, Rehabilitation Services Administration				
Caseload Statistics of State Vocational Rehabilitation Agencies in Fiscal Year	Annual	X	X	X
Department of Health and Human Services <http://www.os.hhs.gov>				
Annual Report	Annual	X		
Department of Homeland Security (DHS) <http://www.dhs.gov/index.shtm>				
Budget in Brief	Annual	X	X	

Title	Frequency	Paper	Internet PDF	Internet Other formats
Department of Homeland Security, Coast Guard <http://www.uscg.mil/default.asp>				
Fact File		X	X	X
Department of Homeland Security, Office of Immigration Statistics <http://www.dhs.gov/ximgtn/statistics/>				
Yearbook of Immigration Statistics	Annual	X	X	
Department of Housing and Urban Development <http://www.hud.gov>				
Survey of Mortgage Lending Activity	Monthly	X		X
Department of Labor <http://www.dol.gov>				
Annual Report of the Secretary	Annual	X	X	X
Department of State <http://www.state.gov>				
United States Contribution to International Organizations	Annual			X
Department of Transportation <http://www.dot.gov>				
Air Travel Consumer Report	Monthly	X	X	X
Airport Activity Statistics of Certified Route Air Carriers	Annual	X		X
Transportation Safety Information Report	Quarterly	X		X
U.S. International Air Travel Statistics	Quarterly	X	X	X
Wage Statistics of Class I Railroads in the United States	Annual	X	X	
Department of the Treasury, Alcohol and Tobacco Tax and Trade Bureau <http://www.atf.treas.gov>				
Alcohol and Tobacco Summary Statistics	Annual	X		
Tobacco Products Monthly Statistical Releases		X		
Department of the Treasury, Bureau of Public Debt <http://www.publicdebt.treas.gov>				
Monthly Statement of the Public Debt of the United States	Monthly	X	X	X
Department of the Treasury, Financial Management Services <http://www.fms.treas.gov>				
Active Foreign Credits of the United States Government	Quarterly	X		
Combined Statement of Receipts, Outlays, and Balances	Annual	X	X	X
Monthly Treasury Statement of Receipts and Outlays of the United States Government	Monthly	X	X	X
Treasury Bulletin	Quarterly	X	X	X
Financial Report of the United States Government	Annual	X	X	
Department of Veterans Affairs <http://www.va.gov>				
Disability Compensation, Pension, and Death Pension Data	Annual			X
Government Life Insurance Programs for Veterans and Members of the Service	Annual			X
Selected Compensation and Pension Data by State of Residence	Annual			X
Veterans Affairs Annual Accountability Report	Annual	X	X	X
Drug Enforcement Administration <http://www.whitehousedrugpolicy.gov>				
Drug Abuse and Law Enforcement Statistics	Irregular	X	X	X
Employment and Training Administration <http://www.doleta.gov>				
Unemployment Insurance Claims	Weekly			X
Energy Information Administration <http://www.eia.doe.gov>				
Annual Energy Outlook	Annual	X	X	X
Annual Energy Review	Annual	X	X	X
Annual Coal Report	Annual		X	X
Electric Power Annual	Annual		X	X
Electric Power Monthly	Monthly		X	X
Electric Sales, Revenue and Retail Price	Annual			X
Emissions of Greenhouse Gases in the United States	Annual		X	X
International Energy Annual	Annual			X
International Energy Outlook	Annual	X	X	X
Monthly Energy Review	Monthly		X	X
Performance Profiles of Major Energy Producers	Annual		X	X
Petroleum Marketing Annual	Monthly		X	X
Petroleum Marketing Monthly	Monthly		X	X
Petroleum Supply Annual, Volume 1	Annual		X	X
Petroleum Supply Annual, Volume 2	Annual		X	X
Petroleum Supply Monthly	Monthly		X	X
Quarterly Coal Report	Quarterly		X	X
Renewable Energy Annual	Annual		X	
Residential Energy Consumption Survey	Quadrennial		X	X
State Electricity Profiles	Annual		X	X
State Energy Data Report	Annual		X	X
State Energy Price and Expenditure Report	Annual		X	X
U.S. Crude Oil, Natural Gas, and Natural Gas Liquids Reserves	Annual		X	X
Weekly Coal Production	Weekly		X	X
Environmental Protection Agency <http://www.epa.gov/>				
Air Quality Data	Annual			X
Drinking Water Infrastructure Needs Survey	Periodic	X	X	
Needs Survey, Conveyance and Treatment of Municipal Wastewater Summaries of Technical Data	Biennial		X	
Toxics Release Inventory	Annual		X	X
National Water Quality Inventory: 2000 Report (EPA-841-T-01-001)	Biennial	X	X	

Appendix I 863

Title	Frequency	Paper	PDF	Other formats
Export-Import Bank of the United States <http://www.exim.gov/>				
Annual Report	Annual	X	X	
Report to the U.S. Congress on Export Credit Competition and the Export-Import Bank of the United States	Annual	X	X	
Farm Credit Administration <http://www.fca.gov/FCA-HomePage.htm>				
Annual Report on the Farm Credit System	Annual	X	X	
Federal Bureau of Investigation <http://www.fbi.gov/ucr/ucr.htm>				
Crime in the United States.	Annual		X	X
Hate Crime Statistics	Annual		X	X
Law Enforcement Officers Killed and Assaulted	Annual		X	X
Federal Communications Commission <http://www.fcc.gov/>				
Annual Report	Annual	X	X	
Statistics of Communications Common Carriers.	Annual	X	X	
Telecommunications Industry Revenue.	Annual	X	X	
Trends in Telephone Service	Annual	X	X	
Trends in the International Telecommunications Industry	Annual	X	X	
High-Speed Services for Internet Access	Annual	X	X	
Annual Assessment of the Status of Competition in the Market for the Delivery of Video Programming	Annual	X	X	
Federal Deposit Insurance Corporation <http://www.fdic.gov/>				
Annual Report	Annual	X	X	X
FDIC Quarterly	Quarterly	X	X	X
Historical Statistics on Banking	Annual			X
Quarterly Banking Profile	Quarterly	X	X	X
Statistics on Banking.	Quarterly			X
Summary of Deposits	Annual			X
Federal Highway Administration <http://www.fhwa.dot.gov/>				
Highway Statistics	Annual	X	X	
Federal Railroad Administration <http://www.fra.dot.gov> <http://safetydata.fra.dot.gov/officeofsafety>				
Railroad Safety Statistics	Annual	X	X	X
Fish and Wildlife Service <http://www.fws.gov/>				
Federal Aid in Fish and Wildlife Restoration	Annual	X	X	
National Survey of Fishing, Hunting, and Wildlife Associated Recreation.	Quinquennial	X	X	
Forest Service <http://www.fs.fed.us/>				
An Analysis of the Timber Situation in the United States 1996–2050	Periodic			X
Land Areas of the National Forest System	Annual	X		X
U.S. Timber Production, Trade, Consumption, and Price Statistics 2001	Biennial	X	X	
RPA Assessment Tables	Periodic			X
General Services Administration, Federal Real Property Council <http://www.gsa.gov/Portal/gsa/ep/home.do?tabId=5>				
Federal Real Property Profile	Annual		X	X
Geological Survey <http://ask.usgs.gov>				
A Statistical Summary of Data from the U.S. Geological Survey's National Water Quality Networks (Open-File Report 83-533).		X		
Estimated Use of Water in the United States in 2000	Quinquennial	X	X	X
Mineral Commodity Summaries.	Annual	X	X	
Mineral Industry Surveys	Monthly		X	X
Minerals Yearbook	Annual	X	X	X
Internal Revenue Service <http://www.irs.gov>				
Corporation Income Tax Returns	Annual	X	X	X
Individual Income Tax Returns	Annual	X	X	X
IRS Data Book.	Annual	X	X	X
Statistics of Income Bulletin	Quarterly	X	X	X
International Trade Administration, Office of Travel and Tourism Industries <http://www.tinet.ita.doc.gov>				
Travel Data reports.		X		
International Trade Commission <http://www.usitc.gov>				
Recent Trends in U.S. Services	Periodic	X	X	
Synthetic Organic Chemicals, U.S. Production and Sales	Annual	X	X	
Library of Congress <http://www.loc.gov/index.html>				
Annual Report	Annual	X	X	
Maritime Administration <http://www.marad.dot.gov>				
Annual Report	Annual	X	X	
Cargo-Carrying U.S. Flag Fleet by Area of Operation	Semiannual	X	X	X
Merchant Fleet Ocean-Going Vessels 1,000 Gross Tons and Over	Quarterly	X	X	X
Seafaring Wage Rates	Biennial	X	X	
Mine Safety and Health Administration <http://www.msha.gov>				

			Internet	
Title				
	Frequency	Paper	PDF	Other formats

Title	Frequency	Paper	PDF	Other formats
Mine Safety and Health Administration—Con.				
Informational Reports by Mining Industry: Coal; Metallic Minerals; Nonmetallic Minerals (except stone and coal); Stone, Sand, and Gravel	Annual			X
Mine Injuries and Worktime (Some preliminary data).	Quarterly	X		X
National Aeronautics and Space Administration <http://ifmp.nasa.gov>				
Annual Procurement Report	Annual	X	X	
The Civil Service Work Force		X	X	
National Center for Education Statistics <http://nces.ed.gov>				
Characteristics of the 100 Largest Public Elementary and Secondary School Districts in the United States.	Annual	X	X	X
Characteristics of Private Schools in the United States, 2005–2006.		X	X	X
College and University Library Survey				X
Computer and Internet Use by Students.	Biennial	X	X	
The Condition of Education	Annual	X	X	
Digest of Education Statistics	Annual	X	X	
Enrollment in Postsecondary Institutions, Graduation Rates, and Fianancial Statistics.	Annual		X	
Indicators of School Crime and Safety	Annual	X	X	
National Education Statistics Quarterly (last edition 4th quarter 2005)	Quarterly			X
The Nation's Report Card: Mathematics 2007	Periodic	X	X	
The Nation's Report Card: Reading 2007	Periodic	X	X	
The Nation's Report Card: Science 2005	Periodic	X	X	
The Nation's Report Card: History 2006	Periodic	X	X	
The Nation's Report Card: Writing 2007	Periodic	X	X	
Projections of Education Statistics.	Annual	X	X	X
School and Staffing Survey:	Quadrennial			X
Characteristics of Schools, Districts, Teachers, Principals, and School Libraries in the United States.	Annual	X	X	
Status and Trends in the Education of racial and ethnic minorities.		X	X	
National Center for Health Statistics <http://www.cdc.gov/nchs/>				
Ambulatory Care Visits to Physician Offices, Hospital Outpatient Departments, and Emergency Departments	Annual	X	X	
Health: United States	Annual	X	X	
Health Characteristics of Adults 55 Years of Age and Over	Periodic	X	X	
Fertility, Family Planning, and Reproductive Health of U.S. Women:				
Data from the 2002 National Survey of Family Growth.	Periodic		X	X
National Hospital Discharge Survey: Annual Summary	Annual		X	
National Vital Statistics Reports (NVSR)	Monthly		X	
Vital and Health Statistics				
Series 10: Health Interview Survey Statistics	Annual	X	X	
Series 11: Health and Nutrition Examination Survey Statistics.	Irregular	X	X	
Series 13: Data from National Health Care Survey	Irregular	X	X	
Series 14: Data on Health Resources: Manpower and Facilities	Irregular	X	X	
Series 20: Mortality Data	Irregular	X	X	
Series 21: Natality, Marriage, and Divorce Data	Irregular	X	X	
Series 23: Data from the National Survey of Family Growth	Irregular	X	X	
National Credit Union Administration <http://www.ncua.gov>				
Annual Report	Annual	X	X	
Yearend Statistics.	Annual	X	X	
National Endowment for the Arts <http://www.nea.gov>				
National Endowment for the Arts, Annual Report	Annual			X
The Performing Arts in the GDP, 2002	Periodic	X	X	
Artist Labor Force by State, 2000	Periodic	X	X	
Artist Employment, 2000–2002	Periodic	X	X	
The Arts in the GDP	Periodic	X	X	
Demographic Characteristics of Art Attendance, 2002	Periodic	X	X	
2002 Survey of Public Participation in the Arts.	Periodic	X	X	
National Endowment for the Humanities <ttp://www.neh.gov>				
Budget Request.	Annual	X		X
National Guard Bureau <http://www.ngb.army.mil/default.aspx>				
Annual Review of the Chief	Annual	X	X	
National Highway Traffic Safety Administration <http://www.nhtsa.dot.gov>				
Traffic Safety Facts.	Annual	X	X	
National Oceanic and Atmospheric Administration <http://www.lib.noaa.gov>				
Climates of the World, HCS 6-4	Monthly			X
Comparative Climatic Data.	Annual		X	X
Daily Normals of Temp, Precip, HDD, & CDD/Clim 84	Periodic			X
Fisheries of the United States.	Annual	X	X	
General Summary of Tornadoes	Annual			X
Hourly Precipitation Data Monthly with annual summary; for each state	Monthly			X
Local Climatological Data Monthly with annual summary; for major cities	Monthly			X
Monthly Climatic Data for the World.	Monthly			X
Monthly Normals of Temp, Precip, HDD, & CDD/Clim 84	Periodic		X	X
Our Living Oceans	Periodic	X	X	
Storm Data	Monthly			X

Title	Frequency	Paper	Internet PDF	Internet Other formats
National Oceanic and Atmospheric Administration—Con.				
U.S. Climate Normals.	Daily	X	X	X
Weekly Weather and Crop Bulletin National Summary	Weekly	X	X	
National Park Service				
<http://www.nps.gov/>				
Federal Recreation Fee Report.	Annual	X		
National Park Statistical Abstract.	Annual	X	X	
National Science Foundation				
<http://www.nsf.gov/statistics/				
Academic Institutional Profiles	Annual		X	X
Academic Research and Development Expenditures	Annual		X	X
Characteristics of Doctoral Scientists and Engineers in the United States	Biennial		X	X
Characteristics of Recent Science/Engineering Graduates	Biennial		X	X
Federal Funds for Research and Development	Annual		X	X
Federal Research and Development Funding by Budget Function	Annual		X	X
Federal Science and Engineering Support to Universities, Colleges, and Nonprofit Institutions	Annual		X	X
Graduate Students and Postdoctorates in Science and Engineering	Annual		X	X
National Patterns of Research & Development Resources	Annual		X	X
Research and Development in Industry	Annual		X	X
Science and Engineering Degrees.	Annual		X	X
Science and Engineering Degrees, by Race/Ethnicity of Recipients	Annual		X	X
Science and Engineering Doctorate Awards	Annual		X	X
Science and Engineering Indicators.	Biennial	X	X	X
Science and Engineering State Profiles	Annual		X	X
Science Resources Statistics Info Briefs (various topics)	Frequent	X	X	X
Scientific and Engineering Research Facilities at Universities and Colleges.	Biennial		X	X
Women, Minorities, and Persons with Disabilities in Science and Engineering	Biennial		X	X
National Transportation Safety Board				
<http://www.ntsb.gov>				
Annual Review of Aircraft Accident Data: U.S. Air Carrier Operations	Annual		X	
Annual Review of Aircraft Accident Data: US General Aviation	Annual		X	
Office of Juvenile Justice and Delinquency Prevention				
<http://ojjdp.ncjrs.org/>				
Highlights of the 2006 National Youth Gang Survey (FS-200805)	Annual		X	X
Juvenile Arrests 2004 (Bulletin, NCJ 214563)	Annual	X	X	X
Victims of Violent Juvenile Crime (Bulletin, NCJ 201628)	Periodic	X	X	X
Office of Management and Budget				
<http://www.whitehouse.gov/omb>				
The Budget of the United States Government	Annual	X	X	
Office of Personnel Management				
<http://www.opm.gov>				
Demographic Profile of the Federal Workforce.	Biennial		X	X
Employment and Trends	Bimonthly		X	X
The Fact Book.	Annual		X	X
Statistical Abstract for the Federal Employee Benefit Programs.	Annual			X
Work Years and Personnel Costs	Annual		X	X
Patent and Trademark Office				
<http://www.uspto.gov>				
Technology Assessment and Forecast Reports		X	X	X
All Technologies (Utility Patents)	Annual	X	X	X
Patent Counts by Country/State and Year, Utility Patents Report.	Annual	X	X	
Patenting Trends in the United States	Annual	X		
Railroad Retirement Board, Chicago, IL				
<http://www.rrb.gov/default.asp>				
Annual Report.	Annual		X	
Quarterly Benefit Statistics.	Quarterly	X		X
Securities and Exchange Commission				
<http://www.sec.gov/about.shtml>				
Select SEC and Market Data	Annual		X	
Small Business Administration				
<http://www.sba.gov>				
Annual Report.	Annual	X		X
Handbook of Small Business Data.		X	X	
Quarterly Indicators	Annual	X	X	X
Small Business and Micro Business Lending.	Annual	X	X	X
State and Territory Small Business Profiles.	Annual	X	X	X
The Small Business Economy	Annual	X	X	X
The State of Small Business	Annual	X	X	
Social Security Administration				
<http://www.ssa.gov>				
Annual Statistical Report on the Social Security Disability Insurance Program	Annual	X	X	X
Annual Statistical Supplement to the Social Security Bulletin	Annual	X	X	X
Children Receiving SSI.	Annual	X	X	X
Congressional Statistics.	Annual	X	X	X
Fast Facts & Figures about Social Security.	Annual	X	X	X
Income of the Population 55 and over	Biennially	X	X	X
State Assistance Programs for SSI Recipients.	Annual	X	X	X
SSI Annual Statistical Report	Annual	X	X	X
SSI Disabled Recipients Who Work.	Annual	X	X	X
SSI Recipients by State and County	Annual	X	X	X
OASDI Beneficiaries by State and County.	Annual	X	X	X
Social Security Bulletin	Quarterly	X	X	X

Title	Frequency	Paper	Internet PDF	Internet Other formats
Substance Abuse and Mental Health Services Administration <http://www.samhsa.gov/>				
National Survey on Drug Use and Health	Annual	X	X	X
National Survey on Substance Abuse Treatment Services (N-SSATS)	Annual	X	X	X
NONGOVERNMENT				
Aerospace Industries Association, Washington, DC <http://www.aia-aerospace.org>				
Aerospace Facts and Figures	Annual	X	X	X
Aerospace Industry Year-End Review and Forecast	Annual		X	
Commercial Helicopter Shipments	Annual		X	
Employment in the Aerospace Industry	Quarterly		X	
Exports of Aerospace Products	Quarterly		X	
Imports of Aerospace Products	Quarterly		X	
Manufacturing Production, Capacity, and Utilization in Aerospace and Aircraft and Parts	Quarterly		X	
Orders, Shipments, Backlog, and Inventories for Aircraft, Missiles, and Parts	Quarterly		X	
Air Transport Association of America, Inc., Washington, DC <http://www.airlines.org>				
Air Transport Association, Annual Report	Annual		X	
The Alan Guttmacher Institute, New York, NY <http://www.guttmacher.org>				
Perspectives on Sexual and Reproductive Health	Quarterly	X	X	X
American Bureau of Metal Statistics, Inc., Secaucus, NJ <http://www.abms.com>				
Non-Ferrous Metal Yearbook	Annual	X		X
American Council of Life Insurers, Washington, DC <http://www.acli.com/ACLI/DefaultNotLoggedIn.htm>				
Life Insurers Fact Book	Annual	X	X	
American Dental Association, Chicago, IL <http://www.ada.org>				
Dental Students Register	Annual	X		
Distribution of Dentists in the United States by Region and State	Triennial	X		
Survey of Dental Practice	Annual	X		
American Forest & Paper Association, Washington, DC <http://www.afandpa.org>				
Annual Statistical Summary of Recovered Paper Utilization	Annual	X	X	
Statistics of Paper, Paperboard, and Wood Pulp	Monthly	X	X	
American Gas Association, Washington, DC <http://www.aga.org>				
Gas Facts	Annual	X	X	
American Iron and Steel Institute, Washington, DC <http://www.steel.org/AM/Template.cfm?Section=Home>				
Annual Statistical Report	Annual	X		
American Jewish Committee, New York, NY <http://www.ajc.org/site/c.ijITI2PHKoG/b.685761/k.CB97/Home.htm>				
American Jewish Year Book	Annual	X	X	
American Medical Association, Chicago, IL <http://www.ama-assn.org>				
Physician Characteristics and Distribution in the United States	Annual	X		
State Medical Licensure Statistics, and License Requirements	Annual	X		
American Osteopathic Association, Chicago, IL <http://www.osteopathic.org/index.cfm>				
American Osteopathic Association Fact Sheet	Biennial	X	X	
American Petroleum Institute, Washington, DC <http://www.api.org>				
The Basic Petroleum Data Book (online subscription)	Annual	X		
Joint Association Survey on Drilling Costs (JA5)	Annual	X		
Petroleum Industry Environmental Report	Annual	X		X
Quarterly Well Completion Report (online subscription)	Quarterly	X	X	
American Public Transportation Association, Washington, DC <http://www.apta.com>				
Public Transportation Fact Book	Annual	X	X	
Association for Manufacturing Technology, McLean, VA <http://www.amtonline.org>				
Economic Handbook of the Machine Tool Industry 2003–2004 (online version by subscription only)	Annual		X	
Association of American Railroads, Washington, DC <http://www.aar.org>				
Analysis of Class I Railroads	Annual	X	X	X
Cars of Revenue Freight Loaded	Weekly		X	X
Freight Commodity Statistics, Class I Railroads in the United States	Annual	X	X	X
Yearbook of Railroad Facts	Annual	X	X	
Association of Racing Commissioners International, Inc., Lexington, KY <http://www.arci.com>				
Statistical Reports on Greyhound Racing in the United States	Annual	X		
Statistical Reports on Horse Racing in the United States	Annual	X		
Statistical Reports on Jai Alai in the United States	Annual	X		
Book Industry Study Group, Inc., New York, NY <http://www.bisg.org>				
Book Industry Trends	Annual	X		
Used-Book Sales	Periodic	X		

Title	Frequency	Paper	PDF	Other formats
Boy Scouts of America, Irving, TX <http://www.scouting.org>				
Annual Report	Annual	X		X
The Bureau of National Affairs, Inc., Washington, DC <http://www.bna.com>				
Basic Patterns in Union Contracts	Annual	X		
BNA's Employment Outlook	Quarterly	X		
BNA's Job Absence and Turnover	Quarterly	X		
Directory of U.S. Labor Organizations	Annual	X		
National Labor Relations Board Election Statistics	Annual	X		
Union Membership & Earnings Data Book	Annual	X		
Source Book on Collective Bargaining	Annual	X		
Carl H. Pforzheimer & Co, New York, NY				
Comparative Oil Company Statistics Annual	Annual	X		
Chronicle of Higher Education, Inc., Washington, DC <http://chronicle.com>				
Almanac	Annual	X		X
College Board, New York, NY <http://www.collegeboard.com>				
2007 College-Bound Seniors Total Group Profile Report	Annual	X	X	
Commodity Research Bureau, Logical Systems, Inc., Chicago, IL <http://www.crbtrader.com>				
Commodity Year Book Update CD	Quarterly			
CRB Commodity Index Report	Weekly	X		
CRB Commodity Year Book	Annual	X		
CRB Futures Perspective	Weekly	X	X	
Electronic Futures Trend Analyzer	Daily			X
Final Markets-End-of-Day Data	Daily			X
Futures Market Service	Weekly		X	
The Conference Board, New York, NY <http://www.conference-board.org> <http://www.conference-board.org/economics> <http://www.conference-board.org/economics/bci>				
Business Cycle Indicators	Monthly	X	X	
Corporate Contributions	Annual	X	X	
Productivity, Employment, and Income in the World's Economies	Annual	X	X	
CQ Press, Washington, DC <http://www.cqpress.com/gethome.asp>				
America Votes	Biennial	X		
Consumer Electronics Association (Electronic Industries Alliance), Arlington, VA <http://www.ce.org>				
Consumer Electronics Association (CEA) Sales and Forecasts	Semiannual	X	X	
The Council of State Governments, Lexington, KY <http://www.csg.org>				
The Book of the States	Annual	X	X	
State Administrative Officials Classified by Function	Annual	X		
State Elective Officials and the Legislatures	Annual	X		
State Legislative Leadership, Committees, and Staff	Annual	X		
Credit Union National Association, Inc., Madison, WI <http://www.cuna.org>				
The Credit Union Ranking Report	Annual	X		
Credit Union Services Profile	Annual	X		
Operating Ratios and Spreads	Semiannual	X		
Dow Jones & Co., New York, NY. <http://online.wsj.com/public/us?>				
Wall Street Journal	Daily	X		X
Edison Electric Institute, Washington, DC <http://www.eei.org>				
Statistical Yearbook of the Electric Power Industry	Annual	X	X	X
Editor & Publisher Co., New York, NY <http://www.editorandpublisher.com/eandp/index.jsp>				
Editor & Publisher	Monthly	X		
International Year Book	Annual	X		X
Market Guide	Annual	X		
Euromonitor International, London, England <http://www.euromonitor.com>				
Consumer Asia	Annual	X		
Consumer China	Annual	X		
Consumer Eastern Europe	Annual	X		
Consumer Europe	Annual	X		
Consumer International	Annual	X		
Consumer Latin America	Annual	X		
European Marketing Data and Statistics	Annual	X		
International Marketing Data and Statistics	Annual	X		
Latin America Marketing Data and Statistics	Annual	X		
World Consumer Expenditure Patterns	Annual	X		
World Consumer Income Patterns	Annual	X		
World Economic Factbook	Annual	X		
World Retail Data and Statistics	Annual	X		
Federal National Mortgage Association, Washington, DC <http://www.fanniemae.com>				
Annual Report	Annual	X	X	

868   Appendix I

Title	Frequency	Internet Paper	Internet PDF	Internet Other formats
Food and Agriculture Organization of the United Nations, Rome, Italy <http://www.fao.org>				
Fertilizer Yearbook	Annual	X		
Production Yearbook.	Annual	X		
Trade Yearbook	Annual	X		
Yearbook of Fishery Statistics.	Annual	X		
Yearbook of Forest Products	Annual	X		
The Foundation Center, New York, NY <http://www.foundationcenter.org>				
Foundation Yearbook	Annual	X		
FC Stats.	Annual			X
General Aviation Manufacturers Association, Washington, DC <http://www.gama.aero/home.php>				
Shipment Report	Quarterly	X		X
Statistical Databook	Annual	X	X	
Girl Scouts of the USA, New York, NY <http://www.girlscouts.org>				
Annual Report	Annual	X	X	
Giving Institute (previously AAFRC), Indianapolis, IN <http://www.aafrc.org>				
Giving USA	Annual	X		X
Health Forum, an American Hospital Association Company, Chicago, IL <http://www.ahadata.com>				
Annual Report	Annual	X		
AHA Hospital Statistics	Annual	X		X
Independent Petroleum Association of America, Washington, DC <http://www.ipaa.org>				
Domestic Oil and Gas Trends.	Monthly	X		
Oil & Natural Gas Production in Your State	Annual	X	X	X
U.S. Petroleum Statistics	Annual	X	X	X
Information Today, Inc., Medford, NJ <http://www.infotoday.com>				
American Library Directory.	Annual	X		
Bowker Annual Library and Book Trade Almanac	Annual	X		
Institute for Criminal Justice Ethics, New York, NY <http://www.lib.jjay.cuny.edu/cje>				
Criminal Justice Ethics	Semiannual	X		
Insurance Information Institute, New York, NY <http://www.iii.org>				
The I.I.I. Insurance Fact Book.	Annual	X	X	X
The Financial Services Fact Book (published jointly with the Financial Services Roundtable)	Annual	X		X
Inter-American Development Bank, Washington, DC <http://www.iadb.org>				
Annual Report	Annual	X	X	
Economic and Social Progress in Latin America.	Annual	X		
International Air Transport Association <http://www.iata.org/index.htm>				
World Air Transport Statistics	Annual	X	X	X
International City Management Association, Washington, DC <http://www.icma.org>				
Compensation: An Annual Report on Local Government Executive Salaries and Fringe Benefits.	Annual			X
Municipal Year Book	Annual	X		
International Labour Organization, Geneva, Switzerland <http://www.ilo.org/global/lang—en/index.htm>				
Yearbook of Labour Statistics	Annual	X		X
International Monetary Fund, Washington, DC <http://www.imf.org>				
Annual Report	Annual	X	X	X
Balance of Payments Statistics	Monthly	X		
Direction of Trade Statistics	Monthly	X		
Government Finance Statistics Yearbook	Annual	X		
International Financial Statistics	Monthly	X		
International Telecommunication Union, Geneva, Switzerland <http://www.itu.int/home/index.html>				
ITU Yearbook of Statistics	Annual	X		
World Telecommunication Indicators	Annual	X		
Investment Company Institute, Washington, DC <http://www.ici.org>				
Mutual Fund Fact Book	Annual	X	X	
Jane's Information Group, Coulsdon, UK, and Alexandria, VA <http://www.janes.com>				
Jane's Air-Launched Weapons	Monthly	X		X
Jane's All the World's Aircraft	Annual	X		X
Jane's Armour and Artillery.	Annual	X		X
Jane's Avionics	Annual	X		X
Jane's Fighting Ships	Annual	X		X
Jane's Infantry Weapons	Annual	X		X
Jane's Merchant Ships	Annual	X		X
Jane's Military Communications	Annual	X		X
Jane's Military Logistics.	Annual	X		X
Jane's Military Training Systems	Annual	X		X

Appendix I   869

Title	Frequency	Paper	Internet PDF	Internet Other formats
Jane's Information Group, Coulsdon, UK, and Alexandria, VA—Con.				
Jane's NATO Handbook	Annual	X		X
Jane's Spaceflight Directory	Annual	X		X
Joint Center for Housing Studies of Harvard University, Cambridge, MA <http://www.jchs.harvard.edu/>				
The State of the Nation's Housing	Annual	X	X	X
Joint Center for Political and Economic Studies, Washington, DC <http://www.jointcenter.org>				
Black Elected Officials: A Statistical Summary	Annual	X	X	
McGraw-Hill Construction Dodge, a Division of the McGraw-Hill Companies, New York, NY <http://www.construction.com> <http://www.dodge.construction.com/Analytics/>				
Dodge Construction Potential (online subscription)	Monthly	X	X	X
National Academy of Sciences, Washington, DC <http://www.pnas.org>				
Summary Report Doctorate Recipients From United States' Universities	Annual	X		
National Academy of Social Insurance, Washington, DC <http://www.nasi.org>				
Workers' Compensation, Benefits, Coverage, and Costs	Annual	X	X	
National Association of Home Builders, Washington, DC <http://www.nahb.org>				
Home Builders Forecast (online subscription)	Monthly			X
Housing Economics (online subscription)	Monthly			X
Housing Market Statistics (online subscription)	Monthly			X
National Association of Latino Elected and Appointed Officials, Washington, DC <http://www.naleo.org>				
National Directory of Latino Elected Officials	Annual		X	X
National Association of Realtors, Washington, DC <http://www.realtor.org>				
Real Estate Outlook: Market Trends & Insights (discontinued)	Monthly	X		X
Real Estate Insights	Monthly		X	X
Research Update				
Economist's Commentary	Daily			X
Profile of Home Buyer and Sellers	Annual	X		
Investment and Vacation Home Buyers Survey	Annual		X	
NAR Member Survey	Annual	X		
National Association of State Budget Officers, Washington, DC <http://www.nasbo.org>				
State Expenditure Report	Annual	X	X	
Fiscal Survey of the States	Semiannual	X	X	
National Association of State Park Directors, Raleigh, NC <http://www.naspd.org>				
Annual Information Exchange	Annual		X	X
National Catholic Educational Association, Washington, DC <http://www.ncea.org>				
Catholic Schools in America	Annual		X	X
United States Catholic Elementary and Secondary Schools Staffing and Enrollment	Annual	X		X
U.S. Catholic Elementary Schools and Their Finances	Biennial			
U.S. Catholic Secondary Schools and Their Finances	Biennial	X		
National Council of Churches USA, New York, NY <http://www.ncccusa.org>				
Yearbook of American and Canadian Churches	Annual	X		X
National Education Association, Washington, DC <http://www.nea.org/index.html>				
Rankings of the States and Estimates of School Statistics	Annual	X	X	
Status of the American Public School Teacher, 2000–2001	Quinquennial	X	X	
National Fire Protection Association, Quincy, MA <http://www.nfpa.org>				
NFPA Journal	Bimonthly			X
National Golf Foundation, Jupiter, FL <http://www.ngf.org/cgi/home.asp>				
Golf Consumer Profile	Annual		X	
Golf Facilities in the United States	Annual	X	X	
National Marine Manufacturers Association, Chicago, IL <http://www.nmma.org>				
Boating (A Statistical Report on America's Top Family Sport)	Annual	X	X	X
U.S. Recreational Boat Registration Statistics	Annual	X	X	
National Restaurant Association, Washington, DC <http://www.restaurant.org>				
Quick-Service Restaurant Trends	Annual	X		
Restaurant Economic Trends (online subscriptions)	Monthly			X
Restaurant Industry Forecast	Annual	X	X	
Restaurant Industry in Review	Annual	X	X	X
Restaurant Industry Operations Report	Annual	X		
Restaurant Industry Pocket Factbook	Annual			
Restaurant Industry 2015, 2005	Annual	X		
Restaurant Performance Index	Monthly	X		X
Restaurant Spending	Annual	X		
State of the Restaurant Industry Work Force	Annual	X		
Tableservice Restaurant Trends	Annual	X		

|---|---|---|---|---|
| | | | Internet | |

Title	Frequency	Paper	PDF	Other formats
National Restaurant Association, Washington, DC—Con.				
The Economic Impact of the Nation's Eating and Drinking Places.	Annual	X		
Hourly Wages for Food Service Occupations.	Annual	X		
Research News and Numbers	Monthy	X		
National Safety Council, Itasca, IL				
<http://www.nsc.org>				
Injury Facts	Annual	X		
National Sporting Goods Association, Mt. Prospect, IL				
<http://www.nsga.org/>				
The Sporting Goods Market in 2008	Annual	X	X	
Sports Participation in 2007	Annual	X	X	
New York Stock Exchange, Inc., New York, NY				
<http://www.nyse.com>				
Fact Book (online subscription)	Annual	X	X	
The New York Times Almanac, 2008	Annual	X		
Organisation for Economic Cooperation and Development, Paris, France				
<http://caliban.sourceoecd.org/vl=2166835/cl=28/nw=1/rpsv/home.htm>				
OECD-FAO Agricultural Outlook	Annual	X		X
Bank Profitability: Financial Statements of Banks, 1924–2003	Biannual	X		X
Central Government Debt: Statistical Yearbook, 1996–2005	Annual	X		X
Coal Information.	Annual	X		X
CO_2 Emissions From Fuel Combustion, 1971–2004	Annual	X		X
Communications Outlook.	Biannual	X		X
DAC Journal	Quarterly	X	X	
Education at a Glance: OECD Indicators	Annual	X		X
Electricity Information	Annual	X		X
Energy Balances of Non-OECD Countries	Annual	X		X
Energy Balances of OECD Countries.	Annual	X		X
Energy Prices and Taxes.	Quarterly	X	X	
Energy Statistics of Non-OECD Countries.	Annual	X	X	X
Energy Statistics of OECD Countries	Annual	X	X	X
Environmental Data Compendium	Annual	X		X
Environmental Outlook	Sporadic	X	X	
Financial Market Trends	Triennial	X	X	
Geographical Distribution of Financial Flows to Aid Recipients	Annual	X		
Historical Statistics, 1970–2000, 2001 Edition (discontinued as of 2001).		X	X	X
Information Technology Outlook, 2002 Edition	Biennial	X	X	X
Insurance Statistics Yearbook.	Annual	X	X	X
International Development Statistics.	Annual			X
Internal Migration Outlook	Annual	X	X	
International Trade by Commodity Statistics	Annual	X	X	
Iron and Steel Industry in 2002, 2004 Edition	Annual			
Labor Force Statistics	Annual	X	X	
Main Economic Indicators	Monthly	X	X	
Main Science and Technology Indicators, Vol. 2003	Biennial	X	X	
Measuring Globalisation: The Role of Multinationals in OECD Countries.	One time			
Monthly Statistics of International Trade	Monthly	X	X	
National Accounts of OECD Countries	Annual			
Volume I: Main Aggregates.		X	X	X
Volume II: Detailed Tables		X	X	X
Volume IIIa: Financial Accounts.	Annual		X	X
Volume IIIb: Financial Balance Sheets	Annual		X	X
Volume IV: Summary of General Aggregates and Balances			X	X
Natural Gas Information.	Annual	X	X	X
Nuclear Energy Data.	Annual	X		
OECD Economic Outlook.	Biennial	X		X
OECD Economic Studies.	Annual	X		X
OECD Economic Surveys	Annual	X		X
OECD Employment Outlook.	Annual	X		X
OECD Factbook.	Annual	X	X	X
OECD Health Data	Annual	X	X	X
OECD Science, Technology, and Industry Outlook	Biennial	X	X	X
OECD Territorial Reviews	Quarterly	X	X	
Organisation for Economic Cooperation and Development (OECD) in Figures.	Bimonthly	X		X
Oil Information 2003 Edition	Annual	X	X	
Oil, Gas, Coal, and Electricity Quarterly Statistics.	Quarterly	X	X	
Quarterly Labour Force Statistics (discontinued as of 4th quarter 2004)	Quarterly	X	X	
Quarterly National Accounts	Quarterly	X	X	
Research and Development Statistics	Annual	X	X	X
Revenue Statistics 1965–2005, 2006 Edition	Annual	X	X	
Review of Fisheries in OECD Member Countries	Annual	X	X	
Structural Statistics for Industry and Services	Annual	X	X	
Taxing Wages	Annual	X	X	
Trends in International Migration 2004 Edition	Annual	X	X	
Trends in the Transport Sector	Annual	X	X	
Uranium Resources Production and Demand, 2001	Biennial	X	X	
World Energy Outlook.	Annual	X	X	
PennWell Corporation, Tulsa, OK				
<http://www.pennwell.com>				
Offshore (online subscription)	Monthly	X	X	
Oil and Gas Journal (online subscription)	Weekly	X	X	
Population Association of America, Washington, DC				
<http://www.popassoc.org>				
Demography	Quarterly	X	X	X
Puerto Rico Planning Board, San Juan, PR				
<http://www.jp.gobierno.pr>				

Title	Frequency	Paper	Internet PDF	Internet Other formats
Puerto Rico Planning Board, San Juan, PR—Con.				
Activity Index	Monthly	X		X
Balance of Payments Puerto Rico	Annual	X		
Economic Report to the Governor	Annual	X		
External Trade Statistics 2007	Annual	X		X
Income and Product	Annual	X		
Projections	Annual	X		
Selected Statistics on Construction Industry	Annual	X		
Statistical Appendix-Economic Report to the Governor	Annual	X		X
Radio Advertising Bureau, New York, NY				
<http://www.rab.com>				
Media Facts	Annual		X	
Radio Marketing Guide and Fact Book	Quarterly		X	
Reed Business Information, New York, NY				
<http://www.reedbusiness.com/index.html>				
Library Journal	Semimonthly	X		X
Publishers Weekly	Weekly	X		X
School Library Journal	Monthly	X		X
Regional Airline Association, Washington, DC				
<http://www.raa.org>				
Statistical Report	Annual	X	X	X
Securities Industry Association, New York, NY				
<http://www.sia.com>				
Foreign Activity Report	Quarterly	X		
Securities Industry Trends	Periodic	X		
Securities Industry Yearbook	Annual	X		X
Standard and Poor's Corporation, New York, NY				
<http://www.standardandpoors.com>				
Analysts' Handbook	Monthly	X		
Corporation Records	Daily	X		
Daily Stock Price Records	Quarterly	X		
Standard and Poor's Global Stock Market Factbook	Annual	X		
United Nations Statistics Division, New York, NY				
<http://unstats.un.org/unsd/default.htm>				
Compendium of Human Settlements Statistics (Series N)	Annual	X		
Demographic Yearbook (Series R)	Annual	X	X	X
Energy Balances and Electricity Profiles (Series W)	Annual	X	X	
Energy Statistics Yearbook (Series J)	Annual	X	X	
Industrial Statistics Yearbook (Series P)				
Commodity Production Statistics	Annual	X		
International Trade Statistics Yearbook (Series G)	Annual	X		
Monthly Bulletin of Statistics (Series Q)	Monthly	X		
National Accounts Statistics (Series X)				
Main Aggregates and Detailed Tables	Annual	X		
Analysis of Main Aggregates	Annual	X		
Population and Vital Statistics Report (Series A)	Quarterly	X		
Social Statistics and Indicators (Series K)	Occasional	X		X
The World's Women: Progress in Statistics, 2005		X	X	X
Statistical Yearbook (Series; also available in CD-ROM, Series S/CD)	Annual	X		X
World Statistics Pocketbook (Series V)	Annual	X		
United Nations Conference on Trade and Development, Geneva, Switzerland				
<http://www.unctad.org/Templates/StartPage.asp?intItemID=2068&lang=1>				
Development and Globalization: Facts and Figures	Annual	X	X	X
Handbook of Statistics	Annual	X	X	X
United States Telecom Association, Washington, DC				
<http://www.usta.org>				
Statistics of the Local Exchange Carriers	Annual		X	X
University of Michigan, Center for Political Studies, Institute for Social Research, Ann Arbor, MI				
<http://www.umich.edu>				
National Election Studies Cumulative Datafile	Biennial	X		X
Warren Communications News, Washington, DC				
<http://www.warren-news.com>				
Cable and Station Coverage Atlas	Annual			X
Television and Cable Factbook	Annual	X		X
World Almanac, New York, NY				
<http://www.worldalmanac.com>				
The World Almanac and Book of Facts	Annual	X		X
The World Bank Group, Washington, DC				
<http://www.worldbank.org>				
Global Development Finance, 2008	Annual	X	X	
The Little Data Book, 2008	Annual	X	X	
Atlas of Global Development	Annual	X	X	
World Development Indicators, 2008	Annual	X		X
World Health Organization, Geneva, Switzerland				
<http://www.who.int/en/>				
Aid Epidemic Update	Annual	X	X	
World Health Statistics Report	Annual	X	X	
World Trade Organization				
<http://www.wto.org>				
International Trade Statistics	Annual	X	X	X

Guide to State Statistical Abstracts

This bibliography includes the most recent statistical abstracts for states published since 2000, plus those that will be issued in late 2009. For some states, a near equivalent has been listed in substitution for, or in addition to, a statistical abstract. All sources contain statistical tables on a variety of subjects for the state as a whole, its component parts, or both. Internet sites also contain statistical data.

Alabama

University of Alabama, Center for Business and Economic Research, Box 870221, Tuscaloosa, AL 35487-0221. 205-348-6191. Fax: 205-348-2951. Internet site <http://cber.cba.ua.edu/>.

Alabama Economic Outlook, 2009. Revised annually.

Alaska

Department of Commerce, Community, and Economic Development, State of Alaska, 550 West 7th Avenue, Suite 1770, Anchorage, AK 99501. 907-269-8100. Fax: 907-269-8125. Internet site <http://www.dced.state.ak.us/dca/misc_resources.htm>.

The Alaska Economic Performance Report, 2006. Online.

Arizona

University of Arizona Economic and Business Research Center, 1130 East Helen Street, McClelland Hall, Rm. 103, P.O. Box 210108, Tucson, AZ 85721-0108. 520-621-2155. Fax: 520-621-2150. Internet site <http://www.ebr.eller.arizona.edu/>.

Arizona Statistical Abstract, 2003.

Arizona's Economy. Quarterly online, Summer 2009.

Arizona Economic Indicators Databook, Fall 2008. Semiannual. Online.

Arkansas

University of Arkansas at Little Rock, Institute for Economic Advancement, College of Business, 2801 South University Avenue, Little Rock, AR 72204-1099. 501-569-8519. Fax: 501-569-8538. Internet site <http://www.aiea.ualr.edu/default.html>.

Arkansas State and County Economic Data, 2008. Annual.

Arkansas Personal Income Handbook, 2008.

Arkansas Statistical Abstract, 2008. Revised biennially.

California

California Department of Finance, 915 L Street, Sacramento, CA 95814. 916-445-3878. Internet site <http://www.dof.ca.gov/default.asp>.

California Statistical Abstract, 2009. Annual. Online only.

Colorado

University of Colorado at Boulder, Government Publications Libary, University Libraries, 184 UCB, 1720 Pleasant Street, Boulder, CO 80309-0184. 303-492-8705. Internet site <http://www.colorado.edu/libraries/govpubs/online.htm>.

Colorado by the Numbers. Online only.

Colorado Office of Economic Development and International Trade, 1625 Broadway, Suite 2700, Denver, CO 80202. 303-892-3840. Fax: 303-892-3848. Internet site <http://www.state.co.us/oed/>.

Colorado Data Book 2008–09. Online only.

Connecticut

Connecticut Department of Economic and Community Development, 505 Hudson Street, Hartford, CT 06106-7106. 860-270-8000. Internet site <http://www.ct.gov/ecd/site/default.asp>.

Connecticut Town Profiles, 2009.

Delaware

Delaware Economic Development Office, 99 Kings Highway, Dover, DE 19901. 302-739-4271. Fax: 302-739-5749. Internet site <http://dedo.delaware.gov>.

Delaware Statistical Overview, 2008. Online only.

District of Columbia

Business Resource Center, John A. Wilson Building, 64 New York Avenue, Suite 3149, Washington, DC 20002. 202-671-1552. Internet site <http://brc.dc.gov/resources/facts.asp>.

Market Facts and Statistics. Online only.

Florida

University of Florida, Bureau of Economic and Business Research, P.O. Box 117145, Gainesville, FL 32611-7145. 352-392-0171, ext. 219. Fax: 352-392-4739. Internet site <http://www.bebr.ufl.edu/>.

Florida Statistical Abstract, 2008. Annual. Also available on CD-ROM.

Florida County Perspective, 2008. One profile for each county. Annual. Also available on CD-ROM.

Florida County Rankings, 2008. Annual. Also available on CD-ROM.

U.S. Census Bureau, Statistical Abstract of the United States: 2010

Georgia

University of Georgia, Terry College of Business, Selig Center for Economic Growth, Athens, GA 30602-6269. 706-542-8100. Fax: 706-542-3858. Internet site <http://www.selig.uga.edu/>.
Georgia Statistical Abstract, 2008–09.

University of Georgia, Center for Agribusiness and Economic Development, 301 Lumpkin House, Athens, GA 30602-7509. 706-542-2434. Fax: 706-542-0770. Internet site <http://www.georgiastats.uga.edu/>.
The Georgia County Guide, 2009. Annual.

Hawaii

Sate of Hawaii Department of Business, and Economic Development and Tourism, P.O. Box 2359, Honolulu, HI 96804. 808-586-2423. Fax: 808-587-2790. Internet site <http://www.hawaii.gov/dbedt/>.
The State of Hawaii Data Book 2008. Annual. Periodically updated.

Idaho

Idaho Department of Commerce, P.O. Box 83720, Boise, ID 83720-0093. 208-334-2470. Fax: 208-334-6430. Internet site <http://labor.idaho.gov/dnn/default.aspx?alias=labor.idaho.gov/dnn/idl/>.
County Profiles Idaho. Online.
Idaho Community Profiles. Online.

Illinois

Institute of Government and Public Affairs, 1007 W. Nevada Street, Urbana, IL 61801 MC-037. 217-333-3340. Fax: 217-244-4817. Internet site <http://www.igpa.uiuc.edu/>.

Indiana

Indiana University, Kelley School of Business, Indiana Business Research Center, 100 South Avenue, Suite 240, Bloomington, IN 47404. Internet site <http://www.stats.indiana.edu/>.
STATS Indiana. Online only.

Iowa

Iowa State University, 17 East Hall, Ames, IA 50011. 515-294-9903. Fax: 515-294-0592. Internet site <http://www.seta.iastate.edu/>.

State Library of Iowa, State Data Center, Ola Babcock Miller Building, 1112 East Grand, Des Moines, IA 50319-0233. 800-248-4483. Fax: 515-242-6543. Internet site <http://www.iowadatacenter.org>.

Kansas

University of Kansas, Institute for Policy and Social Research, 1541 Lilac Lane, 607 Blake Hall, Lawrence, KS 66045-3129. 785-864-3701. Fax: 785-864-3683. Internet site <http://www.ipsr.ku.edu/>.
Kansas Statistical Abstract, 2008. 43rd ed. Online only.

Kentucky

Kentucky Cabinet for Economic Development, Old Capital Annex, 300 West Broadway, Frankfort, KY 40601-1975. 800-626-2930. Fax: 502-564-3256. Internet site <http://www.thinkkentucky.com/>.
Kentucky Deskbook of Economic Statistics. Online only.

Louisiana

Louisiana State Census Data Center, Division of Administration, Office of Information Technoloy, P.O. Box 94095, Baton Rouge, LA 70804. 225-219-9470. Fax: 225-219-4027. Internet site <http://www.louisiana.gov/>.

Maine

Maine State Planning Office, 38 State House Station, Augusta, ME 04333-0038. 800-662-4545. Fax: 207-287-6489. Internet site <http://www.maine.gov/spo/>.

Maryland

Towson University, Division of Economic and Community Outreach RESI, 7400 York Road, Towson, MD 21252-0001. 410-704-7374. Fax: 410-704-4115. Internet site <http://wwwnew.towson.edu/>.
Maryland Statistical Abstract, 2006.

Massachusetts

MassCHIP, Massachusetts Department of Public Health, 600 Washington Street, Boston, MA 02108. 617-624-6000. Internet site <http://masschip.state.ma.us/>.
Instant Topics. Online only.

Michigan

Michigan Economic Development Corporation, 300 North Washington Square, Lansing, MI 48913. 1-888-522-0103. Internet site <http://www.michigan.org/medc/miinfo>.

Minnesota

Minnesota Department of Employment and Economic Development (DEED), First National Bank Building, 332 Minnesota Street, Suite E200, Saint Paul, MN 55101-1351. 800-657-3858. Internet site <http://www.deed.state.mn.us/facts/index.htm>.
Compare Minnesota: Profiles of Minnesota's Economy & Population. Online only.

Minnesota State Demographic Center, 658 Cedar Street, Room 300, Saint Paul, MN 55155. 651-296-2557. Internet site <http://www.demography.state.mn.us/>.

Mississippi

Mississippi State University, College of Business and Industry, Office of Business—Research and Services, P.O. Box 5288, Mississippi State, MS 39762. 662-325-3817. Fax: 662-325-2410. Internet site <http://www.cbi.msstate.edu/dept/bizserv/abstract/>.
Mississippi Statistical Abstract, 2007. 39th ed. Also available on CD-ROM.

Missouri

University of Missouri, Columbia Economic and Policy Analysis Research Center, 10 Professional Building, Columbia, MO 65211. 573-882-4805. Fax: 573-882-5563. Internet site <http://econ.missouri.edu/eparc/>.

Statistical Abstract for Missouri, 2003. 13th ed. Online only.

Montana

Montana Department of Commerce, Census and Economic Information Center, 301 S. Park Avenue, P.O. Box 200500, Helena, MT 59620-0505. 406-841-2740. Fax: 406-841-2731. Internet site <http://ceic.mt.gov/>

Nebraska

Nebraska Department of Economic Development, Centennial Mall South, P. O. Box 94666, 301 Lincoln, NE 68509-4666. 800-426-6505. Fax: 402-471-3778. Internet site <http://info.neded.org/>.

Nevada

Department of Administration, Division of Budget and Planning, 209 East Musser Street, Room 200, Carson City, NV 89701. 775-684-0222. Fax: 775-684-0260. Internet site <http://www.budget.state.nv.us/>.

Nevada Statistical Abstract. Online only.

New Hampshire

New Hampshire Office of Energy and Planning, 4 Chenell Drive, Concord, NH 03301-8501. 603-271-2155. Fax: 603 271 2615. Internet site <http://www.nh.gov/oep/index.htm>.

New Jersey

State of New Jersey Department of Labor and Workforce Development, 1 John Fitch Plaza, P.O. Box 110 Trenton, NJ 08625-0110. 609-984-2595. Fax: 609-984-6833. Internet site <http://www.state.nj.us/labor/lra/>.

Labor Market Information. Online only.

New Mexico

University of New Mexico, Bureau of Business and Economic Research, MSC06 3510, 1 University of New Mexico, Albuquerque, NM 87131-0001. 505-277-6626. Fax: 505-277-7066. Internet site <http://www.unm.edu/~bber/>.

New Mexico Business, Current Economic Report Monthly.

FOR-UNM Bulletin. Quarterly.

New York

Nelson A. Rockefeller Institute of Government, 411 State Street, Albany, NY 12203-1003. 518-443-5522. Fax: 518-443-5788. Internet site <http://www.rockinst.org/>.

New York State Statistical Yearbook, 2008. 33rd ed.

North Carolina

North Carolina Office of State Budget and Management, 116 West Jones Street, Raleigh, NC 27603-8005. 919-807-4700. Fax 919-733-0640. Internet site <http://www.osbm.state.nc.us/osbm/>.

How North Carolina Ranks, 2009. Online only.

North Dakota

University of North Dakota, Bureau of Business and Economic Research, P.O. Box 8369, Grand Forks, ND 58202. 800-225-5863. Fax: 701-777-3365. Internet site <http://business.und.edu/bber/>.

North Dakota Statistical Abstract. Online only.

Ohio

Ohio Department of Development, Office of Policy, Strategic Research, and Strategic Planning, 77 Sartin High Street, P.O. Box 1001, Columbus, OH 43216-1001. 614-466-5017. Internet site <http://www.odod.state.oh.us/research>.

Research products and services. Updated continuously.

Ohio County Profiles, 2008.

Ohio County Indicators. Updated periodically.

Oklahoma

University of Oklahoma, Michael F. Price College of Business, Center for Economic and Management Research, 307 West Brooks, Room 3, Norman OK 73019-4004. 405-325-2931, Fax: 405-325-7688. Internet sites <http://cemr.ou.edu/academics> and <http://price.ou.edu/cemr_publications.aspx/cntremrcontact.aspx>.

Statistical Abstract of Oklahoma, 2005.

Oregon

Oregon State of Archives, 800 Summer Street, NE, Salem, OR 97310. 503-373-0701. Fax: 503-373-4118. Internet site <http://www.sos.state.or.us/bbook>.

Oregon Blue Book. 2009–2010. Biennial.

Pennsylvania

Penn State Harrisburg, Pennsylvania State Data Center, Institute of State and Regional Affairs, 777 West Harrisburg Pike, Middletown, PA 17057-4898. 717-948-6336. Fax: 717-948-6754. Internet site <http://pasdc.hbg.psu.edu>.

Pennsylvania Statistical Abstract, 2008. Also available on CD-Rom.

Rhode Island

Rhode Island Economic Development Corporation, 315 Iron Horse Way, Suite 101, Providence, RI 02908. 401-278-9100. Fax: 401-273-8270. Internet site <http://www.riedc.com/r/index.html>.

RI Databank. Online only.

South Carolina

Budget and Control Board, Office of Research and Statistics, 1919 Blanding Street, Columbia, SC 29201. 803-898-9960. Internet site <http://www.ors2.state.sc.us/abstract/index.asp>.

South Carolina Statistical Abstract, 2008. Also available on CD-Rom.

South Dakota

South Dakota State Data Center, Business Research Bureau, The University of South Dakota, 414 E. Clark Street,132 Patterson Hall, Vermillion, SD 57069. 605-677-5287. Fax: 605-677-5427. Internet site <http://www.usd.edu/>.

2006 South Dakota Community Abstracts.

Tennessee

University of Tennessee, Center for Business and Economic Research, College of Business Administration, 916 Volunteer Boulevard, Knoxville, TN 37996-0570. 865-974-5441. Fax: 865-974-3100. Internet site <http://cber.bus.utk.edu/Default.htm>.

Tennessee Statistical Abstract, 2003. Last printed edition.

Texas

Texas Almanac, University of North Texas, History Department 1155 Union Circle #310650, Denton, TX 76203-5017, 940-369-5200. Internet site <http://www.texasalmanac.com/>.

Texas Almanac, 2008–2009.

Texas State Data Center and Office of the State Demographer, Institute for Demographic and Socioeconomic Research, University of Texas at San Antonio, One UTSA Circle, San Antonio, TX 78249-0704. 210-458-6543. Fax: 210-458-6541. Internet site <http://txsdc.utsa.edu/>.

Utah

Governor's Office of Planning and Budget, Demographic and Economic Analysis, P.O. Box 132210, Salt Lake City, UT 84114-2210. 801-538-1027. Fax: 801-538-1547. Internet site <http://www.governor.utah.gov/dea/>.

Economic Report to the Governor, 2009. Annual.

Utah Data Guide Newsletter, 2008.

Vermont

Department of Labor, Labor Market Information, P.O. Box 488, Montpelier, VT 05601-0488. 802-828-4202. Fax: 802-828-4050. Internet site <http://www.vtlmi.info/>.

Vermont Economic-Demographic Profile, 2008. Annual.

Virginia

Weldon Cooper Center for Public Service, P.O. Box 400206, Charlottesville, VA 22904-4206. 434-982-5522. Fax: 434-982-5524. Internet site <http://www.coopercenter.org/>.

VaStat. Online only.

Washington

Washington State Office of Financial Management, P.O. Box 43113, Olympia, WA 98504-3113. 360-902-0555. Internet site <http://www.ofm.wa.gov/>.

Washington State Data Book. Online only.

West Virginia

West Virginia University, College of Business and Economics, Bureau of Business and Economic Research, Box 6025, Morgantown, WV 26506. 304-293-7831. Internet site <http://www.be.wvu.edu/bber/index.htm>.

2008 West Virginia County Data Profiles.

West Virginia Economic Outlook, 2008. Annual.

Wisconsin

Wisconsin Legislative Reference Bureau, One East Main Street, Suite 200, Madison, WI 53703. 608-266-3561. Fax: 608-266-5648. Internet site <http://www.legis.state.wi.us/lrb/pubs/bluebook.htm/>.

2007–2008 Wisconsin Blue Book. Biennial.

Wyoming

Department of Administration and Information, Economic Analysis Division, 2800 Central Avenue, Cheyenne, WY 82002-0060. 307-777-7504. Fax: 307-632-1819. Internet site <http://eadiv.state.wy.us/>.

The Equality State Almanac, 2008.

Guide to Foreign Statistical Abstracts

This bibliography presents recent statistical abstracts for member nations of the Organization for Economic Cooperation and Development and Russia. All sources contain statistical tables on a variety of subjects for the individual countries. Many of the following publications provide text in English as well as in the national language(s). For further information on these publications, contact the named statistical agency which is responsible for editing the publication.

Australia
Australian Bureau of Statistics, Canberra.
<http://www.abs.gov.au>.
Year Book Australia. Annual. 2008.
(In English.)

Austria
Statistik Austria, 1110 Wien.
<http://www.statistik.at/index.shtml>.
Statistisches Jahrbuch Osterreichs.
Annual. 2009. With CD-ROM.
(In German.) With English translations of table headings.

Belgium
L'Institut National de Statistique, Rue de Louvain; 44-1000 Bruxelles.
<http://statbel.fgov.be/info/links_en.asp>.
Annuaire statistique de la Belgique.
Annual. 1995. (In French.)

Canada
Statistics Canada, Ottawa, Ontario, KIA OT6. <http://www.statcan.ca/start.html>.
Canada Yearbook. 2001. (In English.)

Czech Republic
Czech Statistical Office, Na padesatem 81, Praha 10. <http://www.czso.cz/>.
Statisticka Rocenka Ceske Republiky
2007. (In English and Czech.)

Denmark
Danmarks Statistik, Sejrogade 11, 2100 Kobenhavn O. <http://www.dst.dk>.
Statistisk ARBOG. 2009. Annual. English version available only on Internet and is free of charge at:
<www.dst.dk/yearbook>.
(Printed version—In Danish only.)

Finland
Statistics Finland, Helsinki.
<http://www.stat.fi/comment>.
Statistical Yearbook of Finland, Annual.
2008. With CD-ROM. (In English, Finnish, and Swedish.)

France
Institut National de la Statistique et des Etudes Economiques, Paris 18, Bld. Adolphe Pinard, 75675 Paris (Cedex 14).
<http://www.insee.fr/fr/home/home_page.asp>.
Annuaire Statistique de la France.
Annual. 2003. (In French.) 2005.
CD-ROM only.

Germany
Statistische Bundesamt, D-65180 Wiesbaden. <http://www.destatis.de>.
Statistisches Jahrbuch fur die Bundesrepublic Deutschland. Annual. 2008.
(In German.)
Statistisches Jahrbuch fur das Ausland.
2006. Statistisches Jahrbuch 2005 Fur die Bundesreublik Deutschland und fur das Ausland CDROM.

Greece
National Statistical Service of Greece, Athens. <http:// www.statistics.gr/>.
Concise Statistical Yearbook 2008.
(In English and Greek.)
Statistical Yearbook of Greece. Annual.
2007. (In English and Greek.)

Hungary
Hungarian Central Statistical Office, 1024 Budapest. <http://www.ksh.hu>.
Statistical Yearbook of Hungary, 2007.
With CD-ROM.
(In English and Hungarian.)

Iceland
Hagstofa Islands/Statistics Iceland.
<http://www.hagstofa.is/>.
Statistical Yearbook of Iceland. 2008
(In English and Icelandic.)

Ireland
Central Statistics Office, Skehard Road, Cork. <http://www.cso.ie>.
Statistical Yearbook of Ireland. Annual.
2008. (In English.)

Italy
Istituto Nazionale Statistica.
<http://www.istat.it>. Via Cesare Balbo, 16 Roma.
Annuario Statistico Italiano. Annual.
2008. With CD-ROM. (In Italian.)

Japan

Statistics Bureau, Ministry of Internal Affairs and Communications, Statistical Research and Training Institute, Ministry of Internal Affairs and Communications, Japan. <http://www.stat.go.jp/english/data/index.htm>.

Japan Statistical Yearbook. Annual. 2009. (In English and Japanese.)

Korea, South

National Statistical Office, Government Complex, #920 Dunsan-dong Seo-gu Daejeon 302-701. <http://www.nso.go.kr/>.

Korea Statistical Yearbook. Annual. 2008. (In Korean and English.)

Luxembourg

Statec Centre Administratif Pierre Werner, 13 rue Erasme, B.P. 304, L-2013, Luxembourg. <www.statec.lu/>.

Annuaire Statistique du Luxembourg. 2008. (In French.) (Alphabetical numbering system).

Mexico

Instituto Nacional de Estadistica Geografia e Informatica, Av. Heroe Nacozari Num. 2301 Sur Fracc. Jardines del Parque, CP 20270 Aguascalientes, Ags. <http://www.inegi.gob.mx/difusion/ingles/fiest.html>.

Anuario estadistico de los Estados Unidos Mexicanos. Annual. 1998. Also on disc. (In Spanish.) *Agenda Estadistica 1999.*

Netherlands

Statistics Netherlands, Henri Faasdreef 312, 2492 JP The Hague. <http://www.cbs.nl/en/>. *Statistical Yearbook 2009 of the Netherlands.* (In English.)

Statistisch Jaarboek 2009.

New Zealand

Statistics, New Zealand, Wellington. <http://www.stats.govt.nz/>.

New Zealand Official Yearbook. Annual. 2006. (In English.)

Norway

Statistics Norway, Oslo/Kongsvinger. <http://www.ssb.no/english/subjects/>.

Statistical Yearbook. Annual. 2008. (In English.)

Poland

Central Statistical Office al. Niepodleglosci 208, 00-925 Warsaw. <http://www.stat.gov.pl/english/index.htm>. *Concise Statistical Yearbook 2005.* CD-ROM only. (In Polish and English.) *Statistical Yearbook of the Republic of Poland 2007.* CD-ROM only. (In Polish and English.)

Portugal

INE (Instituto Nacional de Estatistica.) <http://www.ine.pt/index_eng.htm>. Av. Antonio Jose de Almeida P-1000-043 Lisboa.

Anuario Estatistico de Portugal. 2001. (In Portuguese and English.)

Russia

State Committee of Statistics of Russia, Moscow. <http://www.gks.ru/eng/>.

Statistical Yearbook. 2008. (In Russian.)

Slovakia

Statistical Office of the Slovak Republic, Postovy Priecinok 2, 845 02 Bratislava 45. <http://www.statistics.sk/webdata/english/index2_a.htm>.

Statisticka Rocenka Slovenskej Republiky. 2008. (In English and Slovak.) With CD-ROM.

Spain

INE (Instituto Nacional de Estadistica); Paseo de la Castellana, 183, Madrid 16. <http://www.ine.es/welcoing.htm>.

Anuario Estadistico de Espana. 2009. CD-ROM only. (In Spanish.)

Sweden

Statistics Sweden, SE-104 51 Stockholm. <http://www.scb.se/indexeng.asp>.

Statistisk Arsbok for Sverige. Annual. 2009. (In English and Swedish.)

Switzerland

Bundesamt fur Statistik, Hallwylstrasse 15, CH-3003, Bern.

Statistisches Jahrbuch der Schweiz. Annual. 2009. With CD-ROM. (In French and German.)

Turkey

State Institute of Statistics, Prime Ministry, Necatibey Cad/Ankara. No. 114 06100.

Statistical Yearbook of Turkey. 2004. With CD-ROM. (In English and Turkish.)

Turkey in Statistics. 1999. (In English only.)

United Kingdom

The Stationary Office; P.O. Box 29, Norwich, NR3 1GN. <http://www.statistics.gov.uk/>.

Annual Abstract of Statistics. Annual. 2002. (In English.)

Metropolitan and Micropolitan Statistical Areas: Concepts, Components, and Population

The United States Office of Management and Budget (OMB) defines metropolitan and micropolitan statistical areas according to published standards that are applied to U.S. Census Bureau data. The general concept of a metropolitan or micropolitan statistical area is that of a core area containing a substantial population nucleus, together with adjacent communities having a high degree of economic and social integration with that core. Currently defined metropolitan and micropolitan statistical areas are based on application of 2000 standards (which appeared in the Federal Register on December 27, 2000) to 2000 decennial census data. Current metropolitan and micropolitan statistical area definitions were announced by OMB effective June 6, 2003, and subsequently updated as of December 2003, November 2004, December 2005, December 2006, November 2007, and November 2008.

Standard definitions of metropolitan areas were first issued in 1949 by the then Bureau of the Budget (predecessor of OMB), under the designation "standard metropolitan area" (SMA). The term was changed to "standard metropolitan statistical area" (SMSA) in 1959 and to "metropolitan statistical area" (MSA) in 1983. The term "metropolitan area" (MA) was adopted in 1990 and referred collectively to metropolitan statistical areas (MSAs), consolidated metropolitan statistical areas (CMSAs), and primary metropolitan statistical areas (PMSAs). The term "core-based statistical area" (CBSA) became effective in 2000 and refers collectively to metropolitan and micropolitan statistical areas.

OMB has been responsible for the official metropolitan areas since they were first defined, except for the period 1977 to 1981, when they were the responsibility of the Office of Federal Statistical Policy and Standards, U.S. Department of Commerce. The standards for defining metropolitan areas were modified in 1958, 1971, 1975, 1980, 1990, and 2000.

Defining Metropolitan and Micropolitan Statistical Areas—The 2000 standards provide that each CBSA must contain at least one urban area of 10,000 or more population. Each metropolitan statistical area must have at least one urbanized area of 50,000 or more inhabitants. Each micropolitan statistical area must have at least one urban cluster of at least 10,000 but less than 50,000 population.

Under the standards, the county (or counties) in which at least 50 percent of the population resides within urban areas of 10,000 or more population, or that contain at least 5,000 people residing within a single urban area of 10,000 or more population, is identified as a "central county" (counties). Additional "outlying counties" are included in the CBSA if they meet specified requirements of commuting to or from the central counties. Counties or equivalent entities form the geographic "building blocks" for metropolitan and micropolitan statistical areas throughout the United States and Puerto Rico.

If specified criteria are met, a metropolitan statistical area containing a single core with a population of 2.5 million or more may be subdivided to form smaller groupings of counties referred to as "metropolitan divisions."

As of November 2008, there are 366 metropolitan statistical areas and 574 micropolitan statistical areas in the United States. In addition, there are eight metropolitan statistical areas and five micropolitan statistical areas in Puerto Rico.

Principal Cities and Metropolitan and Micropolitan Statistical Area Titles— The largest city in each metropolitan or micropolitan statistical area is designated a "principal city." Additional cities qualify if specified requirements are met concerning population size and employment. The title of each metropolitan or micropolitan statistical area consists of the names of up to three of its principal cities and the name of each state into which the metropolitan or micropolitan statistical area extends. Titles of metropolitan divisions also typically are based on principal city names, but in certain cases consist of county names.

Defining New England City and Town Areas—In view of the importance of cities and towns in New England, the 2000 standards also provide for a set of geographic areas that are defined using cities and towns in the six New England states. The New England city and town areas (NECTAs) are defined using the same criteria as metropolitan and micropolitan statistical areas and are identified as either metropolitan or micropolitan, based, respectively, on the presence of either an urbanized area of 50,000 or more population or an urban cluster of at least 10,000 but less than 50,000 population. If the specified criteria are met, a NECTA containing a single core with a population of at least 2.5 million may be subdivided to form smaller groupings of cities and towns referred to as New England city and town area divisions.

Changes in Definitions Over Time—Changes in the definitions of these statistical areas since the 1950 census have consisted chiefly of (1) the recognition of new areas as they reached the minimum required city or urbanized area population and (2) the addition of counties (or cities and towns in New England) to existing areas as new decennial census data showed them to qualify.

In some instances, formerly separate areas have been merged, components of an area have been transferred from one area to another, or components have been dropped from an area. The large majority of changes have taken place on the basis of decennial census data. However, Census Bureau data serve as the basis for intercensal updates in specified circumstances.

Because of these historical changes in geographic definitions, users must be cautious in comparing data for these statistical areas from different dates. For some purposes, comparisons of data for areas as defined at given dates may be appropriate; for other purposes, it may be preferable to maintain consistent area definitions. Historical metropolitan area definitions are available for 1999, 1993, 1990, 1983, 1981, 1973, 1970, 1963, 1960, and 1950.

Excluding Tables 20 through 24 in the Population section; Table 581 in the Labor Force section; Table 667 in the Income section, and the tables that follow in this appendix, the tables presenting data for metropolitan areas in this edition of the *Statistical Abstract* are based on the 1999 or earlier metropolitan area definitions. For a list of component counties according to the 1999 definition, see Appendix II in the 2002 edition of the *Statistical Abstract* or <http://www.census.gov /population /www/estimates/pastmetro .html>.

Figure A1
Metropolitan and Micropolitan Statistical Areas of the United States
As defined by the U.S. Office of Management and Budget, November 2007

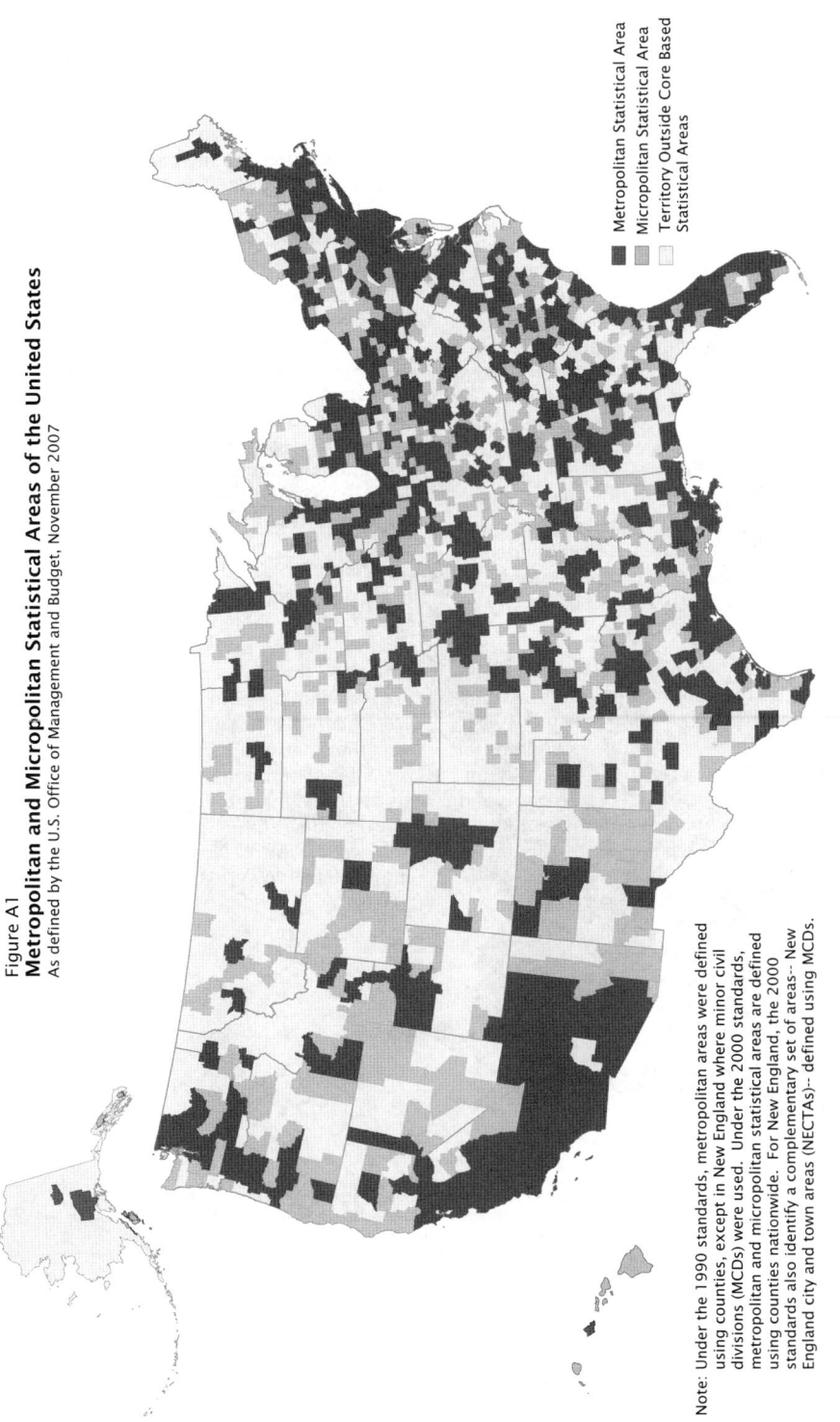

Metropolitan Statistical Area
Micropolitan Statistical Area
Territory Outside Core Based
Statistical Areas

Note: Under the 1990 standards, metropolitan areas were defined using counties, except in New England where minor civil divisions (MCDs) were used. Under the 2000 standards, metropolitan and micropolitan statistical areas are defined using counties nationwide. For New England, the 2000 standards also identify a complementary set of areas-- New England city and town areas (NECTAs)-- defined using MCDs.

U.S. Census Bureau, Statistical Abstract of the United States: 2010

Figure A2
Metropolitan and Micropolitan New England City and Town Areas (NECTAs)
As defined by the U.S. Office of Management and Budget, November 2007

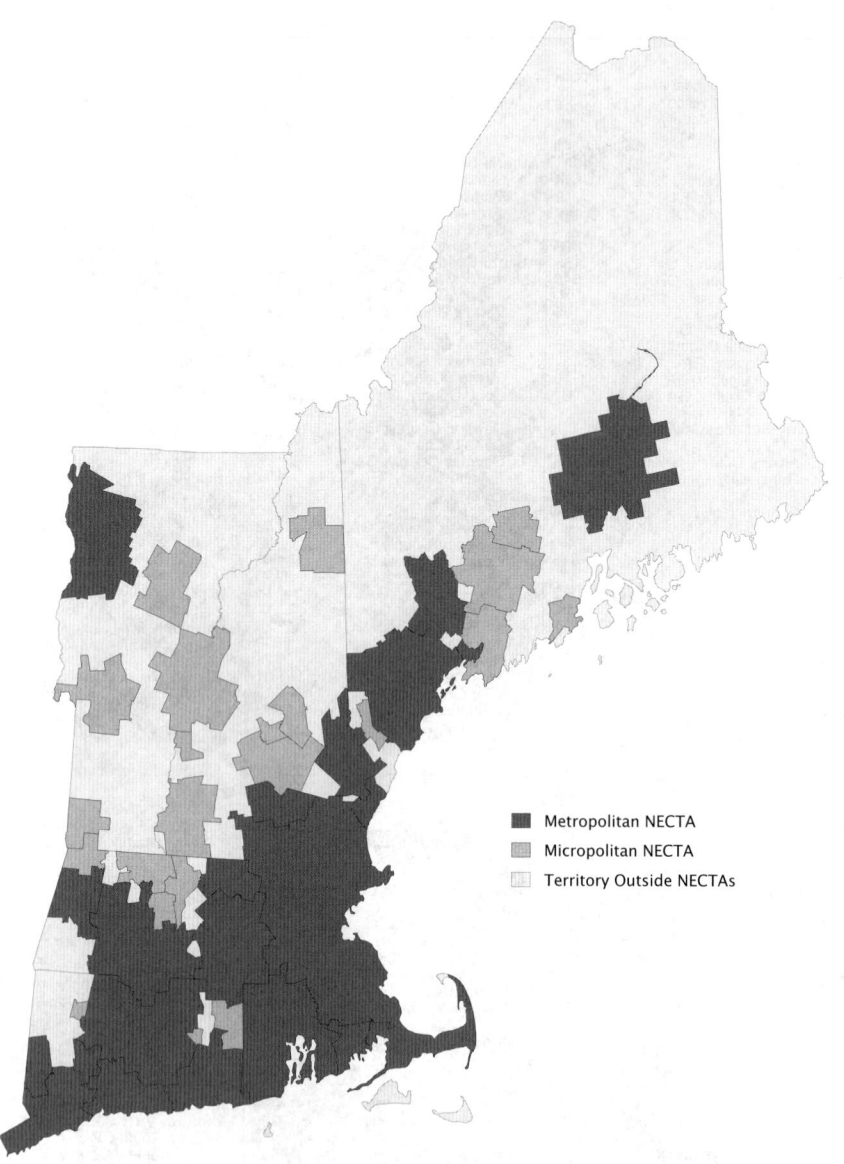

Metropolitan NECTA
Micropolitan NECTA
Territory Outside NECTAs

Note: Under the 2000 standards, metropolitan and micropolitan statistical areas are defined using counties nationwide. For New England, the 2000 standards also identify a complementary set of areas-- New England city and town areas (NECTAs) -- defined using MCDs.

U.S. Census Bureau, Statistical Abstract of the United States: 2010

Table A. Metropolitan Statistical Areas and Components—Population: 2008

[Population as of **July 2008. (160 represents 160,000)**. Metropolitan statistical areas as defined by the U.S. Office of Management and Budget as of November 2007. All geographic boundaries for 2008 population estimates are defined as of January 1, 2008. All metropolitan areas are arranged alphabetically]

Metropolitan statistical area / Metropolitan division / Component county	Population, 2008 (1,000)
Abilene, TX	160"
Callahan County, TX....	14
Jones County, TX......	19
Taylor County, TX......	127
Akron, OH	699
Portage County, OH....	156
Summit County, OH....	543
Albany, GA............	165
Baker County, GA	4
Dougherty County, GA ..	96
Lee County, GA........	34
Terrell County, GA	10
Worth County, GA	21
Albany-Schenectady-Troy, NY	854
Albany County, NY.....	298
Rensselaer County, NY..	155
Saratoga County, NY ...	217
Schenectady County, NY.	151
Schoharie County, NY...	32
Albuquerque, NM	846
Bernalillo County, NM...	635
Sandoval County, NM...	122
Torrance County, NM ...	16
Valencia County, NM ...	72
Alexandria, LA	153
Grant Parish, LA	20
Rapides Parish, LA.....	133
Allentown-Bethlehem-Easton, PA-NJ	808
Warren County, NJ.....	110
Carbon County, PA.....	64
Lehigh County, PA	340
Northampton County, PA.	295
Altoona, PA	125
Blair County, PA.......	125
Amarillo, TX	244
Armstrong County, TX...	2
Carson County, TX.....	6
Potter County, TX......	121
Randall County, TX	115
Ames, IA	87
Story County, IA.......	87
Anchorage, AK	365
Anchorage Municipality, AK............	279
Matanuska-Susitna Borough, AK............	85
Anderson, IN	132
Madison County, IN	132
Anderson, SC...........	183
Anderson County, SC...	183
Ann Arbor, MI..........	347
Washtenaw County, MI..	347
Anniston-Oxford, AL......	113
Calhoun County, AL	113
Appleton, WI............	220
Calumet County, WI....	45
Outagamie County, WI ..	175
Asheville, NC	408
Buncombe County, NC..	229
Haywood County, NC...	57
Henderson County, NC..	102
Madison County, NC....	20
Athens-Clarke County, GA .	189
Clarke County, GA	115
Madison County, GA....	28
Oconee County, GA	32
Oglethorpe County, GA..	14
Atlanta-Sandy Springs-Marietta, GA	5,376
Barrow County, GA.....	70
Bartow County, GA.....	95
Butts County, GA......	24
Carroll County, GA	114
Cherokee County, GA ...	211
Clayton County, GA	274
Cobb County, GA......	698
Coweta County, GA	123
Dawson County, GA	22
DeKalb County, GA	740
Douglas County, GA....	128
Fayette County, GA	106
Forsyth County, GA	168
Fulton County, GA	1,015
Gwinnett County, GA ...	789
Haralson County, GA ...	29
Heard County, GA	11
Henry County, GA	192
Jasper County, GA	14
Lamar County, GA	17
Meriwether County, GA..	23
Newton County, GA	99
Paulding County, GA ...	133
Pickens County, GA	31
Pike County, GA.......	18
Rockdale County, GA ...	83
Spalding County, GA ...	64
Walton County, GA.....	86
Atlantic City-Hammonton, NJ	271
Atlantic County, NJ.....	271
Auburn-Opelika, AL	133
Lee County, AL........	133
Augusta-Richmond County, GA-SC	534
Burke County, GA	23
Columbia County, GA...	111
McDuffie County, GA ...	22
Richmond County, GA ..	199
Aiken County, SC......	154
Edgefield County, SC ...	26
Austin-Round Rock, TX....	1,653
Bastrop County, TX	73
Caldwell County, TX	37
Hays County, TX......	149
Travis County, TX......	999
Williamson County, TX ..	394
Bakersfield, CA..........	800
Kern County, CA	800
Baltimore-Towson, MD	2,667
Anne Arundel County, MD................	513
Baltimore County, MD...	786
Carroll County, MD.....	169
Harford County, MD	240
Howard County, MD....	275
Queen Anne's County, MD................	47
Baltimore city, MD	637
Bangor, ME.............	149
Penobscot County, ME ..	149
Barnstable Town, MA	221
Barnstable County, MA..	221
Baton Rouge, LA	774
Ascension Parish, LA ...	102
East Baton Rouge Parish, LA	428
East Feliciana Parish, LA	21
Iberville Parish, LA.....	33
Livingston Parish, LA ...	120
Pointe Coupee Parish, LA	22
St. Helena Parish, LA...	11
West Baton Rouge Parish, LA	23
West Feliciana Parish, LA	15
Battle Creek, MI	136
Calhoun County, MI	136
Bay City, MI	107
Bay County, MI	107
Beaumont-Port Arthur, TX..	378
Hardin County, TX	52
Jefferson County, TX ...	243
Orange County, TX.....	83
Bellingham, WA	197
Whatcom County, WA...	197
Bend, OR	158
Deschutes County, OR ..	158
Billings, MT	152
Carbon County, MT	10
Yellowstone County, MT .	142
Binghamton, NY	245
Broome County, NY	195
Tioga County, NY......	50
Birmingham-Hoover, AL ...	1,118
Bibb County, AL	22
Blount County, AL	57
Chilton County, AL	42
Jefferson County, AL....	660
St. Clair County, AL.....	80
Shelby County, AL	188
Walker County, AL	69
Bismarck, ND	105
Burleigh County, ND....	79
Morton County, ND.....	26
Blacksburg-Christiansburg-Radford, VA	158
Giles County, VA	17
Montgomery County, VA .	90
Pulaski County, VA.....	35
Radford city, VA.......	16
Bloomington, IN	184
Greene County, IN	33
Monroe County, IN	129
Owen County, IN	22
Bloomington-Normal, IL ...	165
McLean County, IL.....	165
Boise City-Nampa, ID	600
Ada County, ID	381
Boise County, ID	8
Canyon County, ID.....	184
Gem County, ID.......	17
Owyhee County, ID	11

Metropolitan statistical area Metropolitan division Component county	Popu- lation, 2008 (1,000)
Boston-Cambridge-Quincy,	
MA-NH	**4,523**
Boston-Quincy, MA. . . .	**1,885**
Norfolk County, MA . . .	660
Plymouth County, MA . . .	492
Suffolk County, MA.	733
Cambridge-Newton-	
Framingham, MA	**1,482**
Middlesex County, MA . .	1,482
Peabody, MA	**736**
Essex County, MA	736
Rockingham County-	
Strafford County, NH. . .	**419**
Rockingham County, NH.	297
Strafford County, NH. . . .	122
Boulder, CO	**293**
Boulder County, CO	293
Bowling Green, KY	**118**
Edmonson County, KY . .	12
Warren County, KY.	106
Bradenton-Sarasota-Venice,	
FL.	**688**
Manatee County, FL. . . .	316
Sarasota County, FL. . . .	372
Bremerton-Silverdale, WA . .	**240**
Kitsap County, WA	240
Bridgeport-Stamford-	
Norwalk, CT	**895**
Fairfield County, CT	895
Brownsville-Harlingen, TX. .	**393**
Cameron County, TX . . .	393
Brunswick, GA	**103**
Brantley County, GA. . . .	16
Glynn County, GA	76
McIntosh County, GA . . .	11
Buffalo-Niagara Falls, NY . .	**1,124**
Erie County, NY	910
Niagara County, NY	214
Burlington, NC	**148**
Alamance County, NC. . .	148
Burlington-South Burling-	
ton, VT	**208**
Chittenden County, VT . .	153
Franklin County, VT	48
Grand Isle County, VT . .	8
Canton-Massillon, OH	**408**
Carroll County, OH.	28
Stark County, OH.	379
Cape Coral-Fort Myers, FL .	**593**
Lee County, FL	593
Carson City, NV	**55**
Carson City, NV	55
Casper, WY.	**73**
Natrona County, WY. . . .	73
Cedar Rapids, IA.	**255**
Benton County, IA	27
Jones County, IA	20
Linn County, IA	209
Champaign-Urbana, IL	**224**
Champaign County, IL . .	194
Ford County, IL	14
Piatt County, IL	17
Charleston, WV.	**304**
Boone County, WV.	25
Clay County, WV	10
Kanawha County, WV. . .	191
Lincoln County, WV	22
Putnam County, WV. . . .	55

Metropolitan statistical area Metropolitan division Component county	Popu- lation, 2008 (1,000)
Charleston-North	
Charleston-Summerville,	
SC	**645**
Berkeley County, SC . . .	169
Charleston County, SC . .	348
Dorchester County, SC . .	127
Charlotte-Gastonia-	
Concord, NC-SC	**1,702**
Anson County, NC	25
Cabarrus County, NC . . .	169
Gaston County, NC	207
Mecklenburg County, NC.	891
Union County, NC	193
York County, SC.	217
Charlottesville, VA	**194**
Albemarle County, VA. . .	94
Fluvanna County, VA . . .	26
Greene County, VA.	18
Nelson County, VA	15
Charlottesville city, VA. . .	41
Chattanooga, TN-GA.	**518**
Catoosa County, GA. . . .	63
Dade County, GA	16
Walker County, GA.	65
Hamilton County, TN. . . .	333
Marion County, TN	28
Sequatchie County, TN . .	14
Cheyenne, WY	**88**
Laramie County, WY. . . .	88
Chicago-Naperville-Joliet,	
IL	**9,570**
Chicago-Naperville-Joliet,	
IL	**7,990**
Cook County, IL	5,295
DeKalb County, IL	106
DuPage County, IL	931
Grundy County, IL	48
Kane County, IL	508
Kendall County, IL	103
McHenry County, IL	319
Will County, IL	681
Gary, IN	**702**
Jasper County, IN.	33
Lake County, IN	494
Newton County, IN	14
Porter County, IN	162
Lake County-Kenosha	
County, IL-WI	**877**
Lake County, IL	712
Kenosha County, WI. . . .	164
Chico, CA.	**220**
Butte County, CA	220
Cincinnati-Middletown,	
OH-KY-IN	**2,155**
Dearborn County, IN. . . .	50
Franklin County, IN .	23
Ohio County, IN	6
Boone County, KY	115
Bracken County, KY	9
Campbell County, KY . . .	87
Gallatin County, KY	8
Grant County, KY	26
Kenton County, KY.	158
Pendleton County, KY. . .	15
Brown County, OH	44
Butler County, OH	361
Clermont County, OH . . .	195
Hamilton County, OH . . .	851
Warren County, OH	207
Clarksville, TN-KY.	**261**
Christian County, KY . . .	80
Trigg County, KY	13
Montgomery County, TN .	155
Stewart County, TN	13

Metropolitan statistical area Metropolitan division Component county	Popu- lation, 2008 (1,000)
Cleveland, TN.	**112**
Bradley County, TN	96
Polk County, TN.	16
Cleveland-Elyria-Mentor,	
OH	**2,088**
Cuyahoga County, OH . .	1,284
Geauga County, OH	95
Lake County, OH	234
Lorain County, OH	304
Medina County, OH	171
Coeur d'Alene, ID	**137**
Kootenai County, ID	137
College Station-Bryan, TX. .	**207**
Brazos County, TX	175
Burleson County, TX. . . .	17
Robertson County, TX. . .	16
Colorado Springs, CO.	**618**
El Paso County, CO	596
Teller County, CO.	22
Columbia, MO.	**164**
Boone County, MO.	154
Howard County, MO. . . .	10
Columbia, SC	**728**
Calhoun County, SC. . . .	15
Fairfield County, SC	23
Kershaw County, SC . . .	59
Lexington County, SC. . .	249
Richland County, SC . . .	364
Saluda County, SC.	19
Columbus, GA-AL.	**288**
Russell County, AL.	51
Chattahoochee County,	
GA	14
Harris County, GA	29
Marion County, GA.	7
Muscogee County, GA . .	187
Columbus, IN	**75**
Bartholomew County, IN .	75
Columbus, OH	**1,773**
Delaware County, OH . . .	165
Fairfield County, OH	142
Franklin County, OH	1,129
Licking County, OH.	158
Madison County, OH . . .	42
Morrow County, OH	34
Pickaway County, OH. . .	55
Union County, OH	48
Corpus Christi, TX	**415**
Aransas County, TX	25
Nueces County, TX	322
San Patricio County, TX .	68
Corvallis, OR	**82**
Benton County, OR	82
Cumberland, MD-WV.	**99**
Allegany County, MD . . .	72
Mineral County, WV	27
Dallas-Fort Worth-Arlington,	
TX	**6,300**
Dallas-Plano-Irving, TX . .	**4,226**
Collin County, TX	762
Dallas County, TX.	2,413
Delta County, TX.	5
Denton County, TX	637
Ellis County, TX	148
Hunt County, TX	83
Kaufman County, TX . . .	101
Rockwall County, TX . . .	78
Fort Worth-Arlington,	
TX	**2,074**
Johnson County, TX . .	154
Parker County, TX.	112
Tarrant County, TX	1,750
Wise County, TX.	59

Metropolitan statistical area / Metropolitan division / Component county	Population, 2008 (1,000)
Dalton, GA	134
Murray County, GA	40
Whitfield County, GA	94
Danville, IL	81
Vermilion County, IL	81
Danville, VA	106
Pittsylvania County, VA	61
Danville city, VA	45
Davenport-Moline-Rock Island, IA-IL	378
Henry County, IL	50
Mercer County, IL	16
Rock Island County, IL	147
Scott County, IA	165
Dayton, OH	837
Greene County, OH	159
Miami County, OH	101
Montgomery County, OH	535
Preble County, OH	42
Decatur, AL	150
Lawrence County, AL	34
Morgan County, AL	116
Decatur, IL	108
Macon County, IL	108
Deltona-Daytona Beach-Ormond Beach, FL	498
Volusia County, FL	498
Denver-Aurora, CO	2,507
Adams County, CO	431
Arapahoe County, CO	554
Broomfield County, CO	55
Clear Creek County, CO	9
Denver County, CO	599
Douglas County, CO	281
Elbert County, CO	23
Gilpin County, CO	5
Jefferson County, CO	533
Park County, CO	17
Des Moines-West Des Moines, IA	556
Dallas County, IA	60
Guthrie County, IA	11
Madison County, IA	16
Polk County, IA	425
Warren County, IA	45
Detroit-Warren-Livonia, MI.	4,425
Detroit-Livonia-Dearborn, MI.	1,950
Wayne County, MI	1,950
Warren-Troy-Farmington Hills, MI	2,475
Lapeer County, MI	91
Livingston County, MI	183
Macomb County, MI	831
Oakland County, MI	1,202
St. Clair County, MI	169
Dothan, AL	141
Geneva County, AL	26
Henry County, AL	17
Houston County, AL	98
Dover, DE	155
Kent County, DE	155
Dubuque, IA	93
Dubuque County, IA	93
Duluth, MN-WI	275
Carlton County, MN	34
St. Louis County, MN	197
Douglas County, WI	44
Durham, NC	490
Chatham County, NC	63
Durham County, NC	263
Orange County, NC	127
Person County, NC	37
Eau Claire, WI	159
Chippewa County, WI	60
Eau Claire County, WI	98
El Centro, CA	164
Imperial County, CA	164
Elizabethtown, KY	112
Hardin County, KY	99
Larue County, KY	14
Elkhart-Goshen, IN	199
Elkhart County, IN	199
Elmira, NY	88
Chemung County, NY	88
El Paso, TX	742
El Paso County, TX	742
Erie, PA	279
Erie County, PA	279
Eugene-Springfield, OR	347
Lane County, OR	347
Evansville, IN-KY	350
Gibson County, IN	33
Posey County, IN	26
Vanderburgh County, IN	175
Warrick County, IN	58
Henderson County, KY	45
Webster County, KY	14
Fairbanks, AK	98
Fairbanks North Star Borough, AK	98
Fargo, ND-MN	196
Clay County, MN	56
Cass County, ND	140
Farmington, NM	123
San Juan County, NM	123
Fayetteville, NC	356
Cumberland County, NC	313
Hoke County, NC	43
Fayetteville-Springdale-Rogers, AR-MO	444
Benton County, AR	210
Madison County, AR	16
Washington County, AR	196
McDonald County, MO	23
Flagstaff, AZ	129
Coconino County, AZ	129
Flint, MI	429
Genesee County, MI	429
Florence, SC	200
Darlington County, SC	67
Florence County, SC	133
Florence-Muscle Shoals, AL	144
Colbert County, AL	55
Lauderdale County, AL	89
Fond du Lac, WI	99
Fond du Lac County, WI	99
Fort Collins-Loveland, CO	293
Larimer County, CO	293
Fort Smith, AR-OK	291
Crawford County, AR	60
Franklin County, AR	18
Sebastian County, AR	122
Le Flore County, OK	50
Sequoyah County, OK	41
Fort Walton Beach-Crestview-Destin, FL	180
Okaloosa County, FL	180
Fort Wayne, IN	411
Allen County, IN	351
Wells County, IN	28
Whitley County, IN	33
Fresno, CA	909
Fresno County, CA	909
Gadsden, AL	103
Etowah County, AL	103
Gainesville, FL	259
Alachua County, FL	241
Gilchrist County, FL	17
Gainesville, GA	185
Hall County, GA	185
Glens Falls, NY	129
Warren County, NY	66
Washington County, NY	63
Goldsboro, NC	114
Wayne County, NC	114
Grand Forks, ND-MN	97
Polk County, MN	31
Grand Forks County, ND	67
Grand Junction, CO	143
Mesa County, CO	143
Grand Rapids-Wyoming, MI.	777
Barry County, MI	59
Ionia County, MI	64
Kent County, MI	605
Newaygo County, MI	49
Great Falls, MT	82
Cascade County, MT	82
Greeley, CO	250
Weld County, CO	250
Green Bay, WI	303"
Brown County, WI	245
Kewaunee County, WI	20
Oconto County, WI	38
Greensboro-High Point, NC	706
Guilford County, NC	472
Randolph County, NC	141
Rockingham County, NC	92
Greenville, NC	177
Greene County, NC	21
Pitt County, NC	156
Greenville-Mauldin-Easley, SC	625
Greenville County, SC	438
Laurens County, SC	70
Pickens County, SC	117
Gulfport-Biloxi, MS	235
Hancock County, MS	40
Harrison County, MS	178
Stone County, MS	16
Hagerstown-Martinsburg, MD-WV	264
Washington County, MD	145
Berkeley County, WV	102
Morgan County, WV	16
Hanford-Corcoran, CA.	150
Kings County, CA	150
Harrisburg-Carlisle, PA	531
Cumberland County, PA	229
Dauphin County, PA	257
Perry County, PA	45
Harrisonburg, VA	118
Rockingham County, VA	74
Harrisonburg city, VA	44

Metropolitan statistical area / Metropolitan division / Component county	Population, 2008 (1,000)	Metropolitan statistical area / Metropolitan division / Component county	Population, 2008 (1,000)	Metropolitan statistical area / Metropolitan division / Component county	Population, 2008 (1,000)
Hartford-West Hartford-East Hartford, CT	1,191	**Jackson, MS**.	537	**Kingston, NY**	182
Hartford County, CT	877	Copiah County, MS	29	Ulster County, NY.	182
Middlesex County, CT. .	165	Hinds County, MS	248		
Tolland County, CT.	148	Madison County, MS . . .	91	**Knoxville, TN**	691
		Rankin County, MS. . . .	141	Anderson County, TN . . .	74
Hattiesburg, MS	141	Simpson County, MS . . .	28	Blount County, TN	122
Forrest County, MS	79			Knox County, TN	430
Lamar County, MS	49	**Jackson, TN**	113	Loudon County, TN	46
Perry County, MS.	12	Chester County, TN	16	Union County, TN.	19
		Madison County, TN	96		
Hickory-Lenoir-Morganton, NC	363			**Kokomo, IN**	99
Alexander County, NC . .	37	**Jacksonville, FL**	1,313	Howard County, IN.	83
Burke County, NC	89	Baker County, FL.	26	Tipton County, IN	16
Caldwell County, NC. . . .	80	Clay County, FL.	185		
Catawba County, NC . . .	157	Duval County, FL.	851	**La Crosse, WI-MN**.	132
		Nassau County, FL.	70	Houston County, MN . . .	19
Hinesville-Fort Stewart, GA .	70	St. Johns County, FL . . .	182	La Crosse County, WI. . .	11
Liberty County, GA.	58				
Long County, GA	11	**Jacksonville, NC**.	166	**Lafayette, IN**	193
		Onslow County, NC . . .	166	Benton County, IN	9
Holland-Grand Haven, MI . .	260			Carroll County, IN.	20
Ottawa County, MI	260	**Janesville, WI**	160	Tippecanoe County, IN . .	164
		Rock County, WI	160		
Honolulu, HI	905			**Lafayette, LA**	259
Honolulu County, HI	905	**Jefferson City, MO**	146	Lafayette Parish, LA	207
		Callaway County, MO . . .	43	St. Martin Parish, LA . . .	52
Hot Springs, AR	97	Cole County, MO	74		
Garland County, AR	97	Moniteau County, MO. . .	15	**Lake Charles, LA**	193
		Osage County, MO. . . .	13	Calcasieu Parish, LA . . .	186
Houma-Bayou Cane-Thibodaux, LA	201			Cameron Parish, LA	7
Lafourche Parish, LA . . .	93	**Johnson City, TN**	196		
Terrebonne Parish, LA . .	109	Carter County, TN	59	**Lake Havasu City-Kingman, AZ**	196
		Unicoi County, TN	18	Mohave County, AZ	196
Houston-Sugar Land-Baytown, TX	5,728	Washington County, TN .	119		
Austin County, TX	27			**Lakeland-Winter Haven, FL** .	581
Brazoria County, TX	301	**Johnstown, PA**	144	Polk County, FL.	581
Chambers County, TX. . .	29	Cambria County, PA. . . .	144		
Fort Bend County, TX. . .	532			**Lancaster, PA**	502
Galveston County, TX. . .	288	**Jonesboro, AR**	117	Lancaster County, PA . . .	502
Harris County, TX.	3,984	Craighead County, AR . .	93		
Liberty County, TX	75	Poinsett County, AR	25	**Lansing-East Lansing, MI** . .	454
Montgomery County, TX .	430			Clinton County, MI	70
San Jacinto County, TX. .	25	**Joplin, MO**	173	Eaton County, MI	107
Waller County, TX	36	Jasper County, MO.	117	Ingham County, MI.	278
		Newton County, MO	56		
Huntington-Ashland, WV-KY-OH	284			**Laredo, TX**	237
Boyd County, KY	49	**Kalamazoo-Portage, MI**	324	Webb County, TX.	237
Greenup County, KY. . . .	37	Kalamazoo County, MI . .	246		
Lawrence County, OH. . .	63	Van Buren County, MI. . .	78	**Las Cruces, NM**	202
Cabell County, WV	95			Dona Ana County, NM . .	202
Wayne County, WV	41	**Kankakee-Bradley, IL**	113		
		Kankakee County, IL . . .	113	**Las Vegas-Paradise, NV** . . .	1,866
Huntsville, AL.	396			Clark County, NV	1,866
Limestone County, AL. . .	76	**Kansas City, MO-KS**	2,002		
Madison County, AL	320	Franklin County, KS	27	**Lawrence, KS**	115
		Johnson County, KS. . . .	534	Douglas County, KS	115
Idaho Falls, ID	123	Leavenworth County, KS.	74		
Bonneville County, ID . . .	99	Linn County, KS.	10	**Lawton, OK**	112
Jefferson County, ID. . . .	24	Miami County, KS.	31	Comanche County, OK. .	112
		Wyandotte County, KS . .	154		
Indianapolis-Carmel, IN. . . .	1,715	Bates County, MO	17	**Lebanon, PA**.	129
Boone County, IN.	55	Caldwell County, MO . . .	9	Lebanon County, PA. . . .	129
Brown County, IN.	15	Cass County, MO.	98		
Hamilton County, IN	270	Clay County, MO	216	**Lewiston, ID-WA**	60
Hancock County, IN	67	Clinton County, MO	21	Nez Perce County, ID. . .	39
Hendricks County, IN . . .	137	Jackson County, MO. . . .	668	Asotin County, WA	21
Johnson County, IN	139	Lafayette County, MO. . .	33		
Marion County, IN	880	Platte County, MO	86	**Lewiston-Auburn, ME**	107
Morgan County, IN.	71	Ray County, MO	23	Androscoggin County, ME	107
Putnam County, IN.	37				
Shelby County, IN	44	**Kennewick-Pasco-Richland, WA**	236	**Lexington-Fayette, KY**.	453
		Benton County, WA	163	Bourbon County, KY. . . .	20
Iowa City, IA	149	Franklin County, WA. . . .	73	Clark County, KY	36
Johnson County, IA	128			Fayette County, KY	282
Washington County, IA . .	21	**Killeen-Temple-Fort Hood, TX**	379	Jessamine County, KY . .	47
		Bell County, TX	285	Scott County, KY	45
Ithaca, NY.	101	Coryell County, TX	73	Woodford County, KY . . .	25
Tompkins County, NY . . .	101	Lampasas County, TX. . .	21		
				Lima, OH	105
Jackson, MI	160	**Kingsport-Bristol-Bristol, TN-VA**.	305	Allen County, OH	105
Jackson County, MI	160	Hawkins County, TN	57		
		Sullivan County, TN	154	**Lincoln, NE**.	295
		Scott County, VA	23	Lancaster County, NE. . .	279
		Washington County, VA. .	53	Seward County, NE	17
		Bristol city, VA	17		

Little Rock-North Little Rock-Conway, AR	**675**
Faulkner County, AR. . . .	107
Grant County, AR.	18
Lonoke County, AR.	65
Perry County, AR	10
Pulaski County, AR.	377
Saline County, AR	98
Logan, UT-ID.	**125**
Franklin County, ID.	12
Cache County, UT	113
Longview, TX	**205**
Gregg County, TX	118
Rusk County, TX	49
Upshur County, TX.	38
Longview, WA.	**101**
Cowlitz County, WA	101
Los Angeles-Long Beach-Santa Ana, CA	**12,873**
Los Angeles-Long Beach-Glendale, CA.	**9,862**
Los Angeles County, CA .	9,862
Santa Ana-Anaheim-Irvine, CA.	**3,011**
Orange County, CA	3,011
Louisville/Jefferson County, KY-IN	**1,245**
Clark County, IN.	107
Floyd County, IN	74
Harrison County, IN	37
Washington County, IN . .	28
Bullitt County, KY.	75
Henry County, KY.	16
Jefferson County, KY . . .	714
Meade County, KY	27
Nelson County, KY	43
Oldham County, KY	57
Shelby County, KY.	41
Spencer County, KY	17
Trimble County, KY.	9
Lubbock, TX.	**271**
Crosby County, TX.	6
Lubbock County, TX. . . .	264
Lynchburg, VA	**246**
Amherst County, VA	33
Appomattox County, VA .	15
Bedford County, VA	67
Campbell County, VA . . .	53
Bedford city, VA	6
Lynchburg city, VA	73
Macon, GA	**231**
Bibb County, GA	155
Crawford County, GA . . .	13
Jones County, GA	28
Monroe County, GA	25
Twiggs County, GA.	10
Madera, CA.	**148**
Madera County, CA	148
Madison, WI	**562**
Columbia County, WI . . .	55
Dane County, WI	483
Iowa County, WI.	24
Manchester-Nashua, NH . . .	**402**
Hillsborough County, NH.	402
Mansfield, OH.	**125**
Richland County, OH . . .	125
McAllen-Edinburg-Mission, TX	**727**
Hidalgo County, TX	727
Medford, OR.	**201**
Jackson County, OR. . . .	201

Memphis, TN-MS-AR	**1,286**
Crittenden County, AR . .	53
DeSoto County, MS	155
Marshall County, MS . . .	37
Tate County, MS	27
Tunica County, MS.	10
Fayette County, TN	38
Shelby County, TN	907
Tipton County, TN	59
Merced, CA.	**246**
Merced County, CA	246
Miami-Fort Lauderdale-Pompano Beach, FL	**5,415**
Fort Lauderdale-Pompano Beach-Deerfield Beach, FL . . .	1,751
Broward County, FL	1,751
Miami-Miami Beach-Kendall, FL.	2,398
Miami-Dade County, FL .	2,398
West Palm Beach-Boca Raton-Boynton Beach, FL	1,265
Palm Beach County, FL .	1,265
Michigan City-La Porte, IN. .	**111**
LaPorte County, IN.	111
Midland, TX	**129**
Midland County, TX	129
Milwaukee-Waukesha-West Allis, WI	**1,549**
Milwaukee County, WI . .	953
Ozaukee County, WI. . . .	86
Washington County, WI. .	129
Waukesha County, WI . .	381
Minneapolis-St. Paul-Bloomington, MN-WI	**3,230**
Anoka County, MN	327
Carver County, MN.	90
Chisago County, MN. . . .	50
Dakota County, MN	393
Hennepin County, MN. . .	1,141
Isanti County, MN.	39
Ramsey County, MN	501
Scott County, MN	129
Sherburne County, MN . .	88
Washington County, MN .	229
Wright County, MN.	120
Pierce County, WI	40
St. Croix County, WI. . . .	82
Missoula, MT	**107**
Missoula County, MT . . .	107
Mobile, AL	**406**
Mobile County, AL	406
Modesto, CA.	**511**
Stanislaus County, CA . .	511
Monroe, LA.	**173**
Ouachita Parish, LA	150
Union Parish, LA	23
Monroe, MI	**153**
Monroe County, MI.	153
Montgomery, AL	**366**
Autauga County, AL	50
Elmore County, AL	78
Lowndes County, AL. . . .	13
Montgomery County, AL .	225
Morgantown, WV	**119**
Monongalia County, WV .	88
Preston County, WV	30
Morristown, TN.	**136**
Grainger County, TN. . . .	23
Hamblen County, TN . . .	62
Jefferson County, TN . . .	51

Mount Vernon-Anacortes, WA	**118**
Skagit County, WA	118
Muncie, IN	**115**
Delaware County, IN. . . .	115
Muskegon-Norton Shores, MI	**174**
Muskegon County, MI. . .	174
Myrtle Beach-North Myrtle Beach-Conway, SC	**257**
Horry County, SC.	257
Napa, CA	**133**
Napa County, CA.	133
Naples-Marco Island, FL . . .	**315**
Collier County, FL.	315
Nashville-Davidson—Murfreesboro—Franklin, TN	**1,551**
Cannon County, TN	14
Cheatham County, TN . .	39
Davidson County, TN . . .	626
Dickson County, TN	48
Hickman County, TN. . . .	24
Macon County, TN	22
Robertson County, TN . .	65
Rutherford County, TN . .	249
Smith County, TN.	19
Sumner County, TN	155
Trousdale County, TN . . .	8
Williamson County, TN . .	171
Wilson County, TN	110
New Haven-Milford, CT	**846**
New Haven County, CT .	846
New Orleans-Metairie-Kenner, LA	**1,134**
Jefferson Parish, LA. . . .	436
Orleans Parish, LA.	312
Plaquemines Parish, LA .	21
St. Bernard Parish, LA . .	38
St. Charles Parish, LA . .	52
St. John the Baptist Parish, LA	47
St. Tammany Parish, LA .	228
New York-Northern New Jersey-Long Island, NY-NJ-PA	**19,007**
Edison-New Brunswick, NJ.	2,325
Middlesex County, NJ. . .	789
Monmouth County, NJ . .	642
Ocean County, NJ	569
Somerset County, NJ . . .	325
Nassau-Suffolk, NY.	**2,864**
Nassau County, NY	1,352
Suffolk County, NY	1,512
Newark-Union, NJ-PA . .	**2,121**
Essex County, NJ.	771
Hunterdon County, NJ. . .	129
Morris County, NJ.	488
Sussex County, NJ.	151
Union County, NJ.	523
Pike County, PA.	60
New York-White Plains-Wayne, NY-NJ	**11,697**
Bergen County, NJ.	895
Hudson County, NJ	595
Passaic County, NJ	491
Bronx County, NY.	1,392
Kings County, NY.	2,557
New York County, NY. . .	1,635
Putnam County, NY	99
Queens County, NY	2,293
Richmond County, NY. . .	487
Rockland County, NY . . .	299
Westchester County, NY .	954
Niles-Benton Harbor, MI . . .	**159**
Berrien County, MI	159

U.S. Census Bureau, Statistical Abstract of the United States: 2010

Metropolitan statistical area Metropolitan division Component county	Population, 2008 (1,000)	Metropolitan statistical area Metropolitan division Component county	Population, 2008 (1,000)	Metropolitan statistical area Metropolitan division Component county	Population, 2008 (1,000)
Norwich-New London, CT . .	265	**Peoria, IL . . . .**	372	**Provo-Orem, UT . . . .**	541
New London County, CT .	265	Marshall County, IL.	13	Juab County, UT	10
Ocala, FL	330	Peoria County, IL	184	Utah County, UT	531
Marion County, FL	330	Stark County, IL.	6	**Pueblo, CO . . . .**	157
Ocean City, NJ	96	Tazewell County, IL	132	Pueblo County, CO. . . .	157
Cape May County, NJ. . .	96	Woodford County, IL. . . .	39	**Punta Gorda, FL . . . .**	150
Odessa, TX.	132	**Philadelphia-Camden-**		Charlotte County, FL. . . .	150
Ector County, TX	132	**Wilmington, PA-NJ-DE-MD.**	5,838	**Racine, WI . . . .**	200
Ogden-Clearfield, UT.	531	**Camden, NJ . . . .**	1,251	Racine County, WI	200
Davis County, UT.	295	Burlington County, NJ . . .	445	**Raleigh-Cary, NC . . . .**	1,089
Morgan County, UT	9	Camden County, NJ	517	Franklin County, NC	59
Weber County, UT	227	Gloucester County, NJ . .	288	Johnston County, NC . . .	163
Oklahoma City, OK	1,206	**Philadelphia, PA . . . . . .**	3,892	Wake County, NC.	866
Canadian County, OK. . .	106	Bucks County, PA.	622	**Rapid City, SD . . . .**	123
Cleveland County, OK. . .	240	Chester County, PA	491	Meade County, SD.	24
Grady County, OK	51	Delaware County, PA . . .	554	Pennington County, SD. .	99
Lincoln County, OK.	32	Montgomery County, PA .	778	**Reading, PA . . . .**	404
Logan County, OK	38	Philadelphia County, PA .	1,447	Berks County, PA.	404
McClain County, OK	32	**Wilmington, DE-MD-NJ .**	696	**Redding, CA. . . . .**	180
Oklahoma County, OK . .	707	New Castle County, DE .	530	Shasta County, CA.	180
Olympia, WA.	245	Cecil County, MD	100	**Reno-Sparks, NV . . . .**	415
Thurston County, WA . . .	245	Salem County, NJ	66	Storey County, NV	4
Omaha-Council Bluffs,		**Phoenix-Mesa-Scottsdale,**		Washoe County, NV	410
NE-IA	838	**AZ . . . .**	4,282	**Richmond, VA. . . . .**	1,226
Harrison County, IA	15	Maricopa County, AZ . . .	3,955	Amelia County, VA	13
Mills County, IA	15	Pinal County, AZ	327	Caroline County, VA	28
Pottawattamie County,		**Pine Bluff, AR. . . . .**	101	Charles City County, VA .	7
IA	90	Cleveland County, AR. . .	9	Chesterfield County, VA .	303
Cass County, NE	26	Jefferson County, AR . . .	78	Cumberland County, VA .	10
Douglas County, NE. . . .	502	Lincoln County, AR.	14	Dinwiddie County, VA . . .	26
Sarpy County, NE.	150	**Pittsburgh, PA . . . .**	2,351	Goochland County, VA . .	21
Saunders County, NE . . .	20	Allegheny County, PA . . .	1,215	Hanover County, VA	100
Washington County, NE .	20	Armstrong County, PA. . .	69	Henrico County, VA	293
Orlando-Kissimmee, FL. . . .	2,055	Beaver County, PA.	172	King and Queen County,	
Lake County, FL.	307	Butler County, PA	183	VA	7
Orange County, FL.	1,073	Fayette County, PA.	144	King William County, VA .	16
Osceola County, FL	264	Washington County, PA. .	206	Louisa County, VA	33
Seminole County, FL . . .	411	Westmoreland County,		New Kent County, VA . . .	18
Oshkosh-Neenah, WI	162	PA	362	Powhatan County, VA . . .	28
Winnebago County, WI . .	162	**Pittsfield, MA . . . .**	129	Prince George County,	
Owensboro, KY.	113	Berkshire County, MA. . .	129	VA	36
Daviess County, KY	94	**Pocatello, ID . . . .**	88	Sussex County, VA	12
Hancock County, KY. . . .	9	Bannock County, ID	81	Colonial Heights city, VA .	18
McLean County, KY	10	Power County, ID	8	Hopewell city, VA	23
Oxnard-Thousand Oaks-		**Portland-South Portland-**		Petersburg city, VA	33
Ventura, CA	798	**Biddeford, ME. . . . .**	514	Richmond city, VA	202
Ventura County, CA	798	Cumberland County, ME .	276	**Riverside-San Bernardino-**	
Palm Bay-Melbourne-		Sagadahoc County, ME .	36	**Ontario, CA. . . . .**	4,116
Titusville, FL.	537	York County, ME	202	Riverside County, CA . . .	2,101
Brevard County, FL	537	**Portland-Vancouver-**		San Bernardino County,	
Palm Coast, FL.	91	**Beaverton, OR-WA . . . . . .**	2,207	CA	2,015
Flagler County, FL	91	Clackamas County, OR. .	381	**Roanoke, VA. . . . .**	298
Panama City-Lynn Haven,		Columbia County, OR . . .	49	Botetourt County, VA	32
FL.	164	Multnomah County, OR. .	715	Craig County, VA	5
Bay County, FL	164	Washington County, OR. .	529	Franklin County, VA	51
Parkersburg-Marietta-		Yamhill County, OR	98	Roanoke County, VA	91
Vienna, WV-OH	161	Clark County, WA.	425	Roanoke city, VA	93
Washington County, OH .	62	Skamania County, WA . .	11	Salem city, VA	25
Pleasants County,		**Port St. Lucie, FL . . . .**	404	**Rochester, MN . . . .**	183
WV.	7	Martin County, FL.	139	Dodge County, MN.	20
Wirt County, WV	6	St. Lucie County, FL. . . .	265	Olmsted County, MN . . .	141"
Wood County, WV	86	**Poughkeepsie-Newburgh-**		Wabasha County, MN. . .	22
Pascagoula, MS	153	**Middletown, NY. . . . .**	673	**Rochester, NY. . . . .**	1,034
George County, MS	22	Dutchess County, NY . . .	293	Livingston County, NY. . .	63
Jackson County, MS. . . .	131	Orange County, NY	380	Monroe County, NY	733
Pensacola-Ferry Pass-		**Prescott, AZ . . . .**	216	Ontario County, NY	104
Brent, FL	453	Yavapai County, AZ	216	Orleans County, NY	42
Escambia County, FL . . .	303	**Providence-New Bedford-**		Wayne County, NY.	92
Santa Rosa County, FL. .	150	**Fall River, RI-MA . . . .**	1,597	**Rockford, IL . . . .**	354
		Bristol County, MA	546	Boone County, IL	54
		Bristol County, RI	50	Winnebago County, IL. . .	300
		Kent County, RI	168		
		Newport County, RI	80		
		Providence County, RI . .	626		
		Washington County, RI . .	126		

888   Appendix II

Metropolitan statistical area Metropolitan division Component county	Population, 2008 (1,000)
Rocky Mount, NC	146
Edgecombe County, NC .	53
Nash County, NC	94
Rome, GA	96
Floyd County, GA	96
Sacramento—Arden-Arcade—Roseville, CA . . .	2,110
El Dorado County, CA. . .	176
Placer County, CA	342
Sacramento County, CA .	1,394
Yolo County, CA.	198
Saginaw-Saginaw Township North, MI.	201
Saginaw County, MI	201
St. Cloud, MN.	187
Benton County, MN	40
Stearns County, MN	147
St. George, UT	138
Washington County, UT .	138
St. Joseph, MO-KS	126
Doniphan County, KS . . .	8
Andrew County, MO	17
Buchanan County, MO . .	89
DeKalb County, MO	12
St. Louis, MO-IL [1]	2,817
Bond County, IL.	18
Calhoun County, IL.	5
Clinton County, IL.	37
Jersey County, IL	23
Macoupin County, IL. . . .	48
Madison County, IL.	268
Monroe County, IL	33
St. Clair County, IL.	262
Franklin County, MO. . . .	101
Jefferson County, MO . . .	218
Lincoln County, MO	53
St. Charles County, MO .	349
St. Louis County, MO . . .	992
Warren County, MO	31
Washington County, MO .	25
St. Louis city, MO.	354
Salem, OR	392
Marion County, OR.	315
Polk County, OR	77
Salinas, CA.	408
Monterey County, CA . . .	408
Salisbury, MD	120
Somerset County, MD. . .	26
Wicomico County, MD. . .	94
Salt Lake City, UT	1,116
Salt Lake County, UT . . .	1,023
Summit County, UT	36
Tooele County, UT	57
San Angelo, TX.	110
Irion County, TX.	2
Tom Green County, TX . .	108
San Antonio, TX	2,031
Atascosa County, TX . . .	44
Bandera County, TX	20
Bexar County, TX.	1,623
Comal County, TX	110
Guadalupe County, TX . .	117
Kendall County, TX.	33
Medina County, TX.	44
Wilson County, TX	40
San Diego-Carlsbad-San Marcos, CA.	3,001
San Diego County, CA . .	3,001
Sandusky, OH.	77
Erie County, OH.	77

Metropolitan statistical area Metropolitan division Component county	Population, 2008 (1,000)
San Francisco-Oakland-Fremont, CA	4,275
Oakland-Fremont-Hayward, CA	2,504
Alameda County, CA . . .	1,474
Contra Costa County, CA	1,030
San Francisco-San Mateo-Redwood City, CA.	1,770
Marin County, CA.	249
San Francisco County, CA	809
San Mateo County, CA . .	713
San Jose-Sunnyvale-Santa Clara, CA	1,819"
San Benito County, CA. .	55
Santa Clara County, CA .	1,764
San Luis Obispo-Paso Robles, CA	265
San Luis Obispo County, CA	265
Santa Barbara-Santa Maria-Goleta, CA	405
Santa Barbara County, CA	405
Santa Cruz-Watsonville, CA.	253
Santa Cruz County, CA. .	253
Santa Fe, NM	144
Santa Fe County, NM . . .	144
Santa Rosa-Petaluma, CA . .	467
Sonoma County, CA. . . .	467
Savannah, GA.	334
Bryan County, GA	31
Chatham County, GA . . .	251
Effingham County, GA . .	52
Scranton—Wilkes-Barre, PA	549
Lackawanna County, PA .	209
Luzerne County, PA	312
Wyoming County, PA . . .	28
Seattle-Tacoma-Bellevue, WA	3,345
Seattle-Bellevue-Everett, WA	2,559
King County, WA	1,876
Snohomish County, WA . .	684
Tacoma, WA	786
Pierce County, WA.	786
Sebastian-Vero Beach, FL. .	132
Indian River County, FL .	132
Sheboygan, WI	115
Sheboygan County, WI . .	11
Sherman-Denison, TX	119
Grayson County, TX	119
Shreveport-Bossier City, LA	390
Bossier Parish, LA	110
Caddo Parish, LA.	253
De Soto Parish, LA.	26
Sioux City, IA-NE-SD.	143
Woodbury County, IA . . .	103
Dakota County, NE.	20
Dixon County, NE.	6
Union County, SD.	14
Sioux Falls, SD.	233
Lincoln County, SD.	40
McCook County, SD. . . .	6
Minnehaha County, SD . .	179
Turner County, SD	8

Metropolitan statistical area Metropolitan division Component county	Population, 2008 (1,000)
South Bend-Mishawaka, IN-MI.	317
St. Joseph County, IN. . .	267
Cass County, MI	50
Spartanburg, SC.	281
Spartanburg County, SC .	281
Spokane, WA	463
Spokane County, WA . . .	463
Springfield, IL.	207
Menard County, IL	12
Sangamon County, IL. . .	195
Springfield, MA.	688
Franklin County, MA. . . .	72
Hampden County, MA. . .	461
Hampshire County, MA. .	155
Springfield, MO.	426
Christian County, MO . . .	75
Dallas County, MO	17
Greene County, MO	267
Polk County, MO	30
Webster County, MO . . .	36
Springfield, OH.	140
Clark County, OH.	140
State College, PA	145
Centre County, PA	145
Stockton, CA	672
San Joaquin County, CA .	672
Sumter, SC	104
Sumter County, SC.	104
Syracuse, NY	644
Madison County, NY. . . .	70
Onondaga County, NY . . .	453
Oswego County, NY	121
Tallahassee, FL.	357
Gadsden County, FL. . . .	48
Jefferson County, FL. . . .	15
Leon County, FL	264
Wakulla County, FL	31
Tampa-St. Petersburg-Clearwater, FL.	2,734
Hernando County, FL . . .	172
Hillsborough County, FL .	1,181
Pasco County, FL.	471
Pinellas County, FL	910
Terre Haute, IN	170
Clay County, IN	27
Sullivan County, IN.	21
Vermillion County, IN . . .	16
Vigo County, IN	106
Texarkana, TX-Texarkana, AR	136
Miller County, AR	43
Bowie County, TX.	92"
Toledo, OH	649
Fulton County, OH	42
Lucas County, OH	440
Ottawa County, OH	41
Wood County, OH	125
Topeka, KS.	230
Jackson County, KS	13
Jefferson County, KS . . .	18
Osage County, KS	16
Shawnee County, KS . . .	175
Wabaunsee County, KS .	7

U.S. Census Bureau, Statistical Abstract of the United States: 2010

Metropolitan statistical area Metropolitan division Component county	Popu-lation, 2008 (1,000)	Metropolitan statistical area Metropolitan division Component county	Popu-lation, 2008 (1,000)	Metropolitan statistical area Metropolitan division Component county	Popu-lation, 2008 (1,000)
Trenton-Ewing, NJ	365	**Virginia Beach-Norfolk-**		**Wenatchee, WA.**	108
Mercer County, NJ	365	**Newport News,**		Chelan County, WA	72
Tucson, AZ	1,012	**VA-NC—Con.**		Douglas County, WA. . . .	37
Pima County, AZ	1,012	Virginia Beach city, VA . .	434		
		Williamsburg city, VA . . .	12	**Wheeling, WV-OH**	145
Tulsa, OK	916			Belmont County, OH. . . .	68
Creek County, OK	70	**Visalia-Porterville, CA**	426	Marshall County, WV . . .	33
Okmulgee County, OK . .	39	Tulare County, CA	426	Ohio County, WV	44
Osage County, OK	45				
Pawnee County, OK	16	**Waco, TX**	230	**Wichita, KS.**	604
Rogers County, OK	84	McLennan County, TX . . .	230	Butler County, KS.	64
Tulsa County, OK.	592			Harvey County, KS.	34
Wagoner County, OK . . .	69	**Warner Robins, GA**	133	Sedgwick County, KS . . .	483
		Houston County, GA. . . .	133	Sumner County, KS	24
Tuscaloosa, AL.	207				
Greene County, AL.	9"	**Washington-Arlington-**		**Wichita Falls, TX.**	147
Hale County, AL.	18	**Alexandria, DC-VA-MD-WV.**	5,358	Archer County, TX	9
Tuscaloosa County, AL	179	**Bethesda-Frederick-**		Clay County, TX.	11
		Gaithersburg, MD	1,176	Wichita County, TX.	127
Tyler, TX.	201	Frederick County, MD. . .	226		
Smith County, TX.	201	Montgomery County, MD.	951	**Williamsport, PA**	117
		Washington-Arlington-		Lycoming County, PA . . .	117
Utica-Rome, NY	294	**Alexandria, DC-VA-MD-WV.**	4,182		
Herkimer County, NY . . .	62	District of Columbia, DC .	592	**Wilmington, NC.**	347
Oneida County, NY.	232	Calvert County, MD	89	Brunswick County, NC . .	103
		Charles County, MD	141	New Hanover County,	
Valdosta, GA.	133	Prince George's County,		NC	193
Brooks County, GA.	16	MD	821	Pender County, NC	51
Echols County, GA.	4	Arlington County, VA	210		
Lanier County, GA	8	Clarke County, VA	14	**Winchester, VA-WV**	122
Lowndes County, GA . . .	105	Fairfax County, VA	1,015	Frederick County, VA	74
		Fauquier County, VA. . . .	67	Winchester city, VA.	26
Vallejo-Fairfield, CA	408	Loudoun County, VA. . . .	290	Hampshire County, WV. .	23
Solano County, CA.	408	Prince William			
		County, VA	365	**Winston-Salem, NC.**	468
Victoria, TX.	114	Spotsylvania County, VA .	120	Davie County, NC.	41
Calhoun County, TX	20	Stafford County, VA	122	Forsyth County, NC	343
Goliad County, TX	7	Warren County, VA.	37	Stokes County, NC.	46
Victoria County, TX.	87	Alexandria city, VA	144	Yadkin County, NC.	38
		Fairfax city, VA.	24		
Vineland-Millville-Bridgeton,		Falls Church city, VA. . . .	11	**Worcester, MA**	784
NJ	157	Fredericksburg city, VA . .	23	Worcester County, MA . .	784
Cumberland County, NJ .	157	Manassas city, VA	35		
		Manassas Park city, VA. .	11	**Yakima, WA**	235
Virginia Beach-Norfolk-		Jefferson County, WV . . .	52	Yakima County, WA	235
Newport News, VA-NC.	1,658				
Currituck County, NC . . .	24	**Waterloo-Cedar Falls, IA** . . .	164	**York-Hanover, PA**	425
Gloucester County, VA . .	39	Black Hawk County, IA . .	128	York County, PA.	425
Isle of Wight County, VA .	35	Bremer County, IA	24		
James City County, VA . .	62	Grundy County, IA	12	**Youngstown-Warren-**	
Mathews County, VA. . . .	9			**Boardman, OH-PA.**	566
Surry County, VA	7	**Wausau, WI**	131	Mahoning County, OH. . .	238
York County, VA.	61	Marathon County, WI . . .	131	Trumbull County, OH . . .	211
Chesapeake city, VA. . . .	220			Mercer County, PA	117
Hampton city, VA	145	**Weirton-Steubenville,**			
Newport News city, VA . .	180	**WV-OH**	122	**Yuba City, CA**	165
Norfolk city, VA	234	Jefferson County, OH . . .	69	Sutter County, CA	92
Poquoson city, VA	12	Brooke County, WV	24	Yuba County, CA	73
Portsmouth city, VA	101	Hancock County, WV . . .	30		
Suffolk city, VA.	82			**Yuma, AZ**	194
				Yuma County, AZ.	194

[1] The portion of Sullivan city in Crawford County, Missouri, is legally part of the St. Louis, MO-IL Metropolitan Statistical Area. The estimate shown here for the St. Louis, MO-IL Metropolitan Statistical Area does not include this area.

Source: U.S. Census Bureau, "CBSA-EST2008-alldata: Population Estimates and Estimated Components of Change for Metropolitan and Micropolitan Statistical Areas and Their Geographic Components: April 1, 2000 to July 1, 2008"; <http://www.census.gov/popest/metro/files/2008/CBSA-EST2008-alldata.csv>.

Table B. **Micropolitan Statistical Areas and Components—Population: 2008**

[Population as of July 2008. 56 represents 56,000. Micropolitan statistical areas as defined by the U.S. Office of Management and Budget as of November 2007. All geographic boundaries for 2008 population estimates are defined as of January 1, 2008. All micropolitan areas are arranged alphabetically]

Micropolitan statistical area / Component county	Population, 2008 (1,000)	Micropolitan statistical area / Component county	Population, 2008 (1,000)	Micropolitan statistical area / Component county	Population, 2008 (1,000)
Abbeville, LA	56	**Ashtabula, OH**	101	**Bennington, VT**.	36
Vermilion Parish, LA	56	Ashtabula County, OH.	101	Bennington County, VT	36
Aberdeen, SD	39	**Astoria, OR**.	37	**Berlin, NH-VT**	38
Brown County, SD	35	Clatsop County, OR	37	Coos County, NH	32
Edmunds County, SD	4			Essex County, VT	7
Aberdeen, WA.	71	**Atchison, KS**	16	**Big Rapids, MI**	42
Grays Harbor County, WA . .	71	Atchison County, KS	16	Mecosta County, MI	42
Ada, OK	37	**Athens, OH**.	63	**Big Spring, TX**	33
Pontotoc County, OK.	37	Athens County, OH.	63	Howard County, TX.	33
Adrian, MI.	101	**Athens, TN**.	53	**Bishop, CA**.	17
Lenawee County, MI	101	McMinn County, TN	53	Inyo County, CA	17
Alamogordo, NM.	63	**Athens, TX**	79	**Blackfoot, ID**.	44
Otero County, NM	63	Henderson County, TX	79	Bingham County, ID	44
Albany-Lebanon, OR.	115	**Auburn, IN**	42	**Bloomsburg-Berwick, PA** . .	83
Linn County, OR.	115	DeKalb County, IN	42	Columbia County, PA	65
Albemarle, NC	60	**Auburn, NY**.	80	Montour County, PA	18
Stanly County, NC	60	Cayuga County, NY	80	**Bluefield, WV-VA**.	105
Albert Lea, MN	31	**Augusta-Waterville, ME**. . . .	121	Tazewell County, VA	44
Freeborn County, MN	31	Kennebec County, ME.	121	Mercer County, WV.	62
Albertville, AL.	88	**Austin, MN**	38	**Blytheville, AR**	47
Marshall County, AL	88	Mower County, MN	38	Mississippi County, AR	47
Alexander City, AL	52	**Bainbridge, GA**.	29	**Bogalusa, LA**	45
Coosa County, AL.	11	Decatur County, GA	29	Washington Parish, LA	45
Tallapoosa County, AL.	41	**Baraboo, WI**	59	**Bonham, TX**	33
Alexandria, MN	36	Sauk County, WI.	59	Fannin County, TX	33
Douglas County, MN	36	**Barre, VT**	59	**Boone, IA**	26
Alice, TX.	41	Washington County, VT. . . .	59	Boone County, IA	26
Jim Wells County, TX	41	**Bartlesville, OK**.	50	**Boone, NC**	45
Allegan, MI.	113	Washington County, OK. . . .	50	Watauga County, NC.	45
Allegan County, MI	113	**Bastrop, LA**	29	**Borger, TX**	22
Alma, MI.	42	Morehouse Parish, LA.	29	Hutchinson County, TX	22
Gratiot County, MI.	42	**Batavia, NY**.	58	**Bozeman, MT**	90
Alpena, MI	30	Genesee County, NY	58	Gallatin County, MT	90
Alpena County, MI	30	**Batesville, AR**.	35	**Bradford, PA**.	44
Altus, OK	25	Independence County, AR . .	35	McKean County, PA	44
Jackson County, OK	25	**Bay City, TX**	37	**Brainerd, MN**	91
Americus, GA	37	Matagorda County, TX.	37	Cass County, MN	29
Schley County, GA	4	**Beatrice, NE**	23	Crow Wing County, MN	62
Sumter County, GA	32	Gage County, NE	23	**Branson, MO**	79
Amsterdam, NY.	49	**Beaver Dam, WI**	88	Stone County, MO	32
Montgomery County, NY . . .	49	Dodge County, WI.	88	Taney County, MO	47
Andrews, TX.	14	**Beckley, WV**	79	**Brenham, TX**.	32
Andrews County, TX	14	Raleigh County, WV	79	Washington County, TX. . . .	32
Angola, IN	33	**Bedford, IN**.	46	**Brevard, NC**	30
Steuben County, IN.	33	Lawrence County, IN.	46	Transylvania County, NC . . .	30
Arcadia, FL.	34	**Beeville, TX**	33	**Brigham City, UT**	49
DeSoto County, FL	34	Bee County, TX	33	Box Elder County, UT	49
Ardmore, OK	57	**Bellefontaine, OH**	46	**Brookhaven, MS**	35
Carter County, OK	48	Logan County, OH	46	Lincoln County, MS.	35
Love County, OK	9	**Bemidji, MN**	44	**Brookings, OR**	22
Arkadelphia, AR	24	Beltrami County, MN	44	Curry County, OR.	22
Clark County, AR	24	**Bennettsville, SC**	29	**Brookings, SD**	30
Ashland, OH.	55	Marlboro County, SC.	29	Brookings County, SD	30
Ashland County, OH	55			**Brownsville, TN**	19
				Haywood County, TN	19

U.S. Census Bureau, Statistical Abstract of the United States: 2010

Micropolitan statistical area Component county	Popu- lation, 2008 (1,000)	Micropolitan statistical area Component county	Popu- lation, 2008 (1,000)	Micropolitan statistical area Component county	Popu- lation, 2008 (1,000)
Brownwood, TX	**38**	**City of The Dalles, OR.**	**24**	**Crossville, TN.**	**54**
Brown County, TX.	38	Wasco County, OR	24	Cumberland County, TN . . .	54
Bucyrus, OH.	**44**	**Claremont, NH**	**43**	**Crowley, LA**	**60**
Crawford County, OH	44	Sullivan County, NH	43	Acadia Parish, LA.	60
Burley, ID	**40**	**Clarksburg, WV.**	**92**	**Cullman, AL**	**81**
Cassia County, ID.	21	Doddridge County, WV	7	Cullman County, AL	81
Minidoka County, ID	19	Harrison County, WV.	69	
Burlington, IA-IL	**48**	Taylor County, WV	16	**Culpeper, VA.**	**46**
Henderson County, IL	7	**Clarksdale, MS**	**27**	Culpeper County, VA.	46
Des Moines County, IA	41	Coahoma County, MS	27	**Danville, KY**	**54**
Butte-Silver Bow, MT	**33**	**Clearlake, CA**	**65**	Boyle County, KY	29
Silver Bow County, MT	33	Lake County, CA	65	Lincoln County, KY	25
Cadillac, MI.	**47**	**Cleveland, MS.**	**37**	**Daphne-Fairhope-Foley, AL.**	**174**
Missaukee County, MI.	15	Bolivar County, MS	37	Baldwin County, AL.	174
Wexford County, MI	32	**Clewiston, FL**	**39**	**Decatur, IN**	**34**
Calhoun, GA.	**53**	Hendry County, FL	39	Adams County, IN.	34
Gordon County, GA.	53	**Clinton, IA**	**49**	**Defiance, OH**	**39**
Cambridge, MD.	**32**	Clinton County, IA.	49	Defiance County, OH.	39
Dorchester County, MD	32	**Clovis, NM**	**44**	**Del Rio, TX.**	**48**
Cambridge, OH.	**40**	Curry County, NM	44	Val Verde County, TX	48
Guernsey County, OH	40	**Coffeyville, KS**	**34**	**Deming, NM**	**27**
Camden, AR	**31**	Montgomery County, KS . . .	34	Luna County, NM	27
Calhoun County, AR	5	**Coldwater, MI**	**46**	**De Ridder, LA.**	**35**
Ouachita County, AR.	26	Branch County, MI	46	Beauregard Parish, LA	35
Campbellsville, KY	**24**	**Columbia, TN**	**82**	**Dickinson, ND.**	**23**
Taylor County, KY.	24	Maury County, TN.	82	Billings County, ND	1
Canon City, CO.	**47**	**Columbus, MS**	**59**	Stark County, ND	23
Fremont County, CO	47	Lowndes County, MS	59	**Dillon, SC.**	**31**
Canton, IL.	**37**	**Columbus, NE**	**32**	Dillon County, SC	31
Fulton County, IL	37	Platte County, NE	32	**Dixon, IL.**	**35**
Cape Girardeau-Jackson,		**Concord, NH.**	**148**	Lee County, IL	35
MO-IL.	**93**	Merrimack County, NH	148	**Dodge City, KS.**	**33**
Alexander County, IL.	8	**Connersville, IN**	**24**	Ford County, KS.	33
Bollinger County, MO	12	Fayette County, IN	24	**Douglas, GA.**	**49**
Cape Girardeau County, MO.	73	**Cookeville, TN**	**103**	Atkinson County, GA.	8
Carbondale, IL	**58**	Jackson County, TN	11	Coffee County, GA	41
Jackson County, IL	58	Overton County, TN	21	**Dublin, GA**	**57**
Carlsbad-Artesia, NM	**51**	Putnam County, TN.	71	Johnson County, GA.	10
Eddy County, NM	51	**Coos Bay, OR.**	**63**	Laurens County, GA	48
Cedar City, UT	**45**	Coos County, OR	63	**DuBois, PA.**	**83**
Iron County, UT	45	**Corbin, KY**	**39**	Clearfield County, PA	83
Cedartown, GA.	**42**	Whitley County, KY	39	**Dumas, TX**	**20**
Polk County, GA.	42	**Cordele, GA**	**22**	Moore County, TX.	20
Celina, OH	**41**	Crisp County, GA	22	**Duncan, OK**	**43**
Mercer County, OH.	41	**Corinth, MS**	**36**	Stephens County, OK	43
Central City, KY	**31**	Alcorn County, MS	36	**Dunn, NC**	**112**
Muhlenberg County, KY. . . .	31	**Cornelia, GA.**	**43**	Harnett County, NC.	112
Centralia, IL	**40**	Habersham County, GA. . . .	43	**Durango, CO.**	**50**
Marion County, IL.	40	**Corning, NY**	**97**	La Plata County, CO	50
Centralia, WA	**74**	Steuben County, NY	97	**Durant, OK.**	**40**
Lewis County, WA.	74	**Corsicana, TX.**	**49**	Bryan County, OK.	40
Chambersburg, PA	**143**	Navarro County, TX	49	**Dyersburg, TN**	**38**
Franklin County, PA	143	**Cortland, NY.**	**48**	Dyer County, TN.	38
Charleston-Mattoon, IL	**63**	Cortland County, NY	48	**Eagle Pass, TX**	**52**
Coles County, IL.	52	**Coshocton, OH.**	**36**	Maverick County, TX.	52
Cumberland County, IL	11	Coshocton County, OH	36	**East Liverpool-Salem, OH** . .	**108**
Chester, SC	**33**	**Crawfordsville, IN**	**38**	Columbiana County, OH . . .	108
Chester County, SC	33	Montgomery County, IN. . . .	38	**Easton, MD.**	**36**
Chillicothe, OH	**76**	**Crescent City, CA**	**29**	Talbot County, MD	36
Ross County, OH	76	Del Norte County, CA	29	**East Stroudsburg, PA**	**165**
				Monroe County, PA.	165

892   Appendix II

Micropolitan statistical area / Component county	Popu-lation, 2008 (1,000)
Edwards, CO	60
Eagle County, CO	52
Lake County, CO	8
Effingham, IL	34
Effingham County, IL	34
El Campo, TX	41
Wharton County, TX	41
El Dorado, AR	43
Union County, AR	43
Elizabeth City, NC	64
Camden County, NC	10
Pasquotank County, NC	41
Perquimans County, NC	13
Elk City, OK	21
Beckham County, OK	21
Elko, NV	49
Elko County, NV	47
Eureka County, NV	2
Ellensburg, WA	39
Kittitas County, WA	39
Emporia, KS	38
Chase County, KS	3
Lyon County, KS	36
Enid, OK	58
Garfield County, OK	58
Enterprise-Ozark, AL	96
Coffee County, AL	48
Dale County, AL	48
Escanaba, MI	37
Delta County, MI	37
Espanola, NM	41
Rio Arriba County, NM	41
Eufaula, AL-GA	32
Barbour County, AL	29
Quitman County, GA	3
Eureka-Arcata-Fortuna, CA	129
Humboldt County, CA	129
Evanston, WY	21
Uinta County, WY	21
Fairmont, MN	20
Martin County, MN	20
Fairmont, WV	56
Marion County, WV	56
Fallon, NV	25
Churchill County, NV	25
Faribault-Northfield, MN	62
Rice County, MN	62
Farmington, MO	63
St. Francois County, MO	63
Fergus Falls, MN	57
Otter Tail County, MN	57
Fernley, NV	53
Lyon County, NV	53
Findlay, OH	74
Hancock County, OH	74
Fitzgerald, GA	28
Ben Hill County, GA	18
Irwin County, GA	10
Forest City, NC	63
Rutherford County, NC	63
Forrest City, AR	26
St. Francis County, AR	26
Fort Dodge, IA	39
Webster County, IA	39
Fort Leonard Wood, MO	45
Pulaski County, MO	45
Fort Madison-Keokuk, IA-MO	43
Lee County, IA	35
Clark County, MO	7
Fort Morgan, CO	28
Morgan County, CO	28
Fort Payne, AL	69
DeKalb County, AL	69
Fort Polk South, LA	46
Vernon Parish, LA	46
Fort Valley, GA	27
Peach County, GA	27
Frankfort, IN	34
Clinton County, IN	34
Frankfort, KY	70
Anderson County, KY	21
Franklin County, KY	49
Fredericksburg, TX	24
Gillespie County, TX	24
Freeport, IL	46
Stephenson County, IL	46
Fremont, NE	36
Dodge County, NE	36
Fremont, OH	61
Sandusky County, OH	61
Gaffney, SC	54
Cherokee County, SC	54
Gainesville, TX	38
Cooke County, TX	38
Galesburg, IL	69
Knox County, IL	52
Warren County, IL	18
Gallup, NM	71
McKinley County, NM	71
Garden City, KS	41
Finney County, KS	41
Gardnerville Ranchos, NV	45
Douglas County, NV	45
Georgetown, SC	61
Georgetown County, SC	61
Gettysburg, PA	101
Adams County, PA	101
Gillette, WY	41
Campbell County, WY	41
Glasgow, KY	52
Barren County, KY	42
Metcalfe County, KY	10
Gloversville, NY	55
Fulton County, NY	55
Granbury, TX	59
Hood County, TX	51
Somervell County, TX	8
Grand Island, NE	71
Hall County, NE	56
Howard County, NE	7
Merrick County, NE	8
Grants, NM	27
Cibola County, NM	27
Grants Pass, OR	82
Josephine County, OR	82
Great Bend, KS	28
Barton County, KS	28
Greeneville, TN	66
Greene County, TN	66
Greensburg, IN	25
Decatur County, IN	25
Greenville, MS	55
Washington County, MS	55
Greenville, OH	52
Darke County, OH	52
Greenwood, MS	46
Carroll County, MS	10
Leflore County, MS	35
Greenwood, SC	69
Greenwood County, SC	69
Grenada, MS	23
Grenada County, MS	23
Guymon, OK	20
Texas County, OK	20
Hammond, LA	117
Tangipahoa Parish, LA	117
Hannibal, MO	38
Marion County, MO	28
Ralls County, MO	10
Harriman, TN	53
Roane County, TN	53
Harrisburg, IL	26
Saline County, IL	26
Harrison, AR	45
Boone County, AR	37
Newton County, AR	8
Hastings, NE	40
Adams County, NE	33
Clay County, NE	6
Havre, MT	16
Hill County, MT	16
Hays, KS	28
Ellis County, KS	28
Heber, UT	21
Wasatch County, UT	21
Helena, MT	72
Jefferson County, MT	11
Lewis and Clark County, MT	61
Helena-West Helena, AR	22
Phillips County, AR	22
Henderson, NC	43
Vance County, NC	43
Hereford, TX	19
Deaf Smith County, TX	19
Hilo, HI	176
Hawaii County, HI	176
Hilton Head Island-Beaufort, SC	173
Beaufort County, SC	150
Jasper County, SC	22

U.S. Census Bureau, Statistical Abstract of the United States: 2010

Micropolitan statistical area Component county	Popu- lation, 2008 (1,000)	Micropolitan statistical area Component county	Popu- lation, 2008 (1,000)	Micropolitan statistical area Component county	Popu- lation, 2008 (1,000)
Hobbs, NM	59	**Kalispell, MT**	88	**Lebanon, NH-VT**	171
Lea County, NM	59	Flathead County, MT.	88	Grafton County, NH.	86
Homosassa Springs, FL . . .	141	**Kapaa, HI**	64	Orange County, VT	29
Citrus County, FL	141	Kauai County, HI	64	Windsor County, VT	57
Hood River, OR.	22	**Kearney, NE.**	52	**Levelland, TX**	22
Hood River County, OR. . . .	22	Buffalo County, NE	45	Hockley County, TX	22
Hope, AR	32	Kearney County, NE	6	**Lewisburg, PA**	44
Hempstead County, AR	23	**Keene, NH**	77	Union County, PA	44
Nevada County, AR.	9	Cheshire County, NH.	77	**Lewisburg, TN**	30
Houghton, MI	37	**Kendallville, IN**	48	Marshall County, TN	30
Houghton County, MI.	35	Noble County, IN	48	**Lewistown, PA**	46
Keweenaw County, MI.	2	**Kennett, MO**	31	Mifflin County, PA	46
Hudson, NY	62	Dunklin County, MO	31	**Lexington, NE.**	27
Columbia County, NY	62	**Kerrville, TX**	48	Dawson County, NE.	25
Humboldt, TN	49	Kerr County, TX	48	Gosper County, NE.	2
Gibson County, TN	49	**Ketchikan, AK.**	13	**Lexington Park, MD**	102
Huntingdon, PA	46	Ketchikan Gateway Bor- ough, AK	13	St. Mary's County, MD.	102
Huntingdon County, PA	46	**Key West, FL**	72	**Liberal, KS**	23
Huntington, IN	38	Monroe County, FL.	72	Seward County, KS.	23
Huntington County, IN	38	**Kill Devil Hills, NC**	34	**Lincoln, IL**	30
Huntsville, TX.	64	Dare County, NC	34	Logan County, IL	30
Walker County, TX	64	**Kingsville, TX**	31	**Lincolnton, NC**	75
Huron, SD.	16	Kenedy County, TX	(Z)	Lincoln County, NC.	75
Beadle County, SD	16	Kleberg County, TX.	31	**Lock Haven, PA**	37
Hutchinson, KS.	63	**Kinston, NC**	57	Clinton County, PA	37
Reno County, KS	63	Lenoir County, NC	57	**Logansport, IN**	39
Hutchinson, MN	37	**Kirksville, MO.**	29	Cass County, IN	39
McLeod County, MN	37	Adair County, MO	25	**London, KY**	58
Indiana, PA.	87	Schuyler County, MO	4	Laurel County, KY.	58
Indiana County, PA.	87	**Klamath Falls, OR.**	66	**Los Alamos, NM**	18
Indianola, MS	31	Klamath County, OR	66	Los Alamos County, NM . . .	18
Sunflower County, MS.	31	**Kodiak, AK**	13	**Lufkin, TX.**	83
Iron Mountain, MI-WI.	31	Kodiak Island Borough, AK .	13	Angelina County, TX	83
Dickinson County, MI.	27	**Laconia, NH**	61	**Lumberton, NC.**	129
Florence County, WI	5	Belknap County, NH	61	Robeson County, NC.	129
Jackson, WY-ID	29	**La Follette, TN**	41	**Macomb, IL.**	33
Teton County, ID.	9	Campbell County, TN	41	McDonough County, IL	33
Teton County, WY.	20	**La Grande, OR**	25	**Madison, IN**	33
Jacksonville, IL.	40	Union County, OR.	25	Jefferson County, IN	33
Morgan County, IL	35	**LaGrange, GA.**	64	**Madisonville, KY.**	46
Scott County, IL	5	Troup County, GA	64	Hopkins County, KY	46
Jacksonville, TX	48	**Lake City, FL**	69	**Magnolia, AR**	24
Cherokee County, TX	48	Columbia County, FL.	69	Columbia County, AR	24
Jamestown, ND.	20	**Lamesa, TX**	14	**Malone, NY.**	51
Stutsman County, ND	20	Dawson County, TX	14	Franklin County, NY	51
Jamestown-Dunkirk- **Fredonia, NY.**	134	**Lancaster, SC.**	76	**Manhattan, KS**	122
Chautauqua County, NY . . .	134	Lancaster County, SC	76	Geary County, KS.	31
Jasper, IN	54	**Laramie, WY**	33	Pottawatomie County, KS . .	20
Dubois County, IN.	41	Albany County, WY.	33	Riley County, KS	71
Pike County, IN	13	**Las Vegas, NM**	29	**Manitowoc, WI**	81
Jennings, LA	31	San Miguel County, NM. . . .	29	Manitowoc County, WI.	81
Jefferson Davis Parish, LA. .	31	**Laurel, MS**	85	**Mankato-North Mankato,** **MN .**	92
Jesup, GA	30	Jasper County, MS	18	Blue Earth County, MN	60
Wayne County, GA	30	Jones County, MS.	67	Nicollet County, MN	32
Juneau, AK.	31	**Laurinburg, NC.**	37	**Marinette, WI-MI**	66
Juneau City and Borough, AK	31	Scotland County, NC.	37	Menominee County, MI	24
Kahului-Wailuku, HI	144	**Lawrenceburg, TN**	41	Marinette County, WI.	42
Maui County, HI	144	Lawrence County, TN	41	**Marion, IN.**	69
		Lebanon, MO	36	Grant County, IN.	69
		Laclede County, MO	36	**Marion, OH.**	66
				Marion County, OH	66

894   Appendix II

Micropolitan statistical area / Component county	Popu- lation, 2008 (1,000)	Micropolitan statistical area / Component county	Popu- lation, 2008 (1,000)	Micropolitan statistical area / Component county	Popu- lation, 2008 (1,000)
Marion-Herrin, IL.	65	**Mineral Wells, TX**	27	**Newberry, SC**	38
Williamson County, IL	65	Palo Pinto County, TX	27	Newberry County, SC	38
Marquette, MI.	65	**Minot, ND.**	63	**New Castle, IN**	47
Marquette County, MI	65	McHenry County, ND.	5	Henry County, IN	47
		Renville County, ND	2		
Marshall, MN.	25	Ward County, ND	56	**New Castle, PA.**	90
Lyon County, MN	25			Lawrence County, PA	90
		Mitchell, SD	23		
Marshall, MO	23	Davison County, SD	19	**New Iberia, LA**	75
Saline County, MO	23	Hanson County, SD	4	Iberia Parish, LA.	75
Marshall, TX.	64	**Moberly, MO.**	26	**New Philadelphia-Dover,**	
Harrison County, TX	64	Randolph County, MO.	26	**OH.**	91
				Tuscarawas County, OH	91
Marshalltown, IA.	40	**Monroe, WI.**	36		
Marshall County, IA.	40	Green County, WI	36	**Newport, TN.**	36
				Cocke County, TN.	36
Marshfield-Wisconsin Rap-		**Montrose, CO.**	41		
ids, WI	74	Montrose County, CO	41	**Newton, IA**	37
Wood County, WI	74			Jasper County, IA	37
		Morehead City, NC	63		
Martin, TN.	33	Carteret County, NC	63	**New Ulm, MN**	26
Weakley County, TN	33			Brown County, MN	26
		Morgan City, LA	51		
Martinsville, VA.	70	St. Mary Parish, LA.	51	**Nogales, AZ**	43
Henry County, VA	55			Santa Cruz County, AZ	43
Martinsville city, VA	15	**Moscow, ID.**	36		
		Latah County, ID.	36	**Norfolk, NE.**	48
Maryville, MO	22			Madison County, NE	34
Nodaway County, MO	22	**Moses Lake, WA.**	85	Pierce County, NE	7
		Grant County, WA.	85	Stanton County, NE	6
Mason City, IA.	51				
Cerro Gordo County, IA.	44	**Moultrie, GA.**	45	**North Platte, NE**	37
Worth County, IA	8	Colquitt County, GA	45	Lincoln County, NE	36
				Logan County, NE.	1
Mayfield, KY.	37	**Mountain Home, AR**	42	McPherson County, NE	1
Graves County, KY	37	Baxter County, AR	42		
				North Vernon, IN.	28
Maysville, KY.	31	**Mountain Home, ID.**	29	Jennings County, IN	28
Lewis County, KY	14	Elmore County, ID.	29		
Mason County, KY	17			**North Wilkesboro, NC**	67
		Mount Airy, NC	72	Wilkes County, NC	67
McAlester, OK.	45	Surry County, NC	72		
Pittsburg County, OK.	45			**Norwalk, OH.**	60
		Mount Pleasant, MI.	67	Huron County, OH	60
McComb, MS	53	Isabella County, MI.	67		
Amite County, MS.	13			**Oak Harbor, WA.**	81
Pike County, MS.	40	**Mount Pleasant, TX.**	30	Island County, WA	81
		Titus County, TX.	30		
McMinnville, TN	40			**Oak Hill, WV.**	46
Warren County, TN	40	**Mount Sterling, KY**	44	Fayette County, WV	46
		Bath County, KY	12		
McPherson, KS.	29	Menifee County, KY	7	**Ocean Pines, MD**	49
McPherson County, KS	29	Montgomery County, KY	26	Worcester County, MD	49
Meadville, PA	88	**Mount Vernon, IL**	48	**Ogdensburg-Massena, NY.**	110
Crawford County, PA.	88	Hamilton County, IL.	8	St. Lawrence County, NY.	110
		Jefferson County, IL	40		
Menomonie, WI.	43			**Oil City, PA.**	54
Dunn County, WI	43	**Mount Vernon, OH**	59	Venango County, PA.	54
		Knox County, OH	59		
Meridian, MS.	106			**Okeechobee, FL.**	40
Clarke County, MS	17	**Murray, KY**	36	Okeechobee County, FL	40
Kemper County, MS	10	Calloway County, KY.	36		
Lauderdale County, MS.	78			**Olean, NY.**	80
		Muscatine, IA	54	Cattaraugus County, NY	80
Merrill, WI.	29	Louisa County, IA	12		
Lincoln County, WI	29	Muscatine County, IA	43	**Oneonta, NY.**	62
				Otsego County, NY.	62
Mexico, MO	26	**Muskogee, OK**	71		
Audrain County, MO	26	Muskogee County, OK.	71	**Ontario, OR-ID**	54
				Payette County, ID	23
Miami, OK.	32	**Nacogdoches, TX.**	63	Malheur County, OR	31
Ottawa County, OK.	32	Nacogdoches County, TX	63		
				Opelousas-Eunice, LA.	92
Middlesborough, KY	29	**Natchez, MS-LA**	50	St. Landry Parish, LA	92
Bell County, KY	29	Concordia Parish, LA	19		
		Adams County, MS.	31	**Orangeburg, SC**	90
Midland, MI.	83			Orangeburg County, SC	90
Midland County, MI.	83	**Natchitoches, LA**	40		
		Natchitoches Parish, LA	40	**Oskaloosa, IA**	22
Milledgeville, GA.	56			Mahaska County, IA	22
Baldwin County, GA	47	**New Bern, NC**	120		
Hancock County, GA.	9	Craven County, NC.	97	**Ottawa-Streator, IL**	153
		Jones County, NC.	10	Bureau County, IL.	35
Minden, LA.	41	Pamlico County, NC	13	LaSalle County, IL.	112
Webster Parish, LA.	41			Putnam County, IL	6

U.S. Census Bureau, Statistical Abstract of the United States: 2010

Micropolitan statistical area Component county	Popu- lation, 2008 (1,000)	Micropolitan statistical area Component county	Popu- lation, 2008 (1,000)	Micropolitan statistical area Component county	Popu- lation, 2008 (1,000)
Ottumwa, IA	36	**Point Pleasant, WV-OH**	57	**Roswell, NM**	63
Wapello County, IA	36	Gallia County, OH.	31	Chaves County, NM	63
		Mason County, WV	26		
Owatonna, MN	37			**Ruidoso, NM.**	21
Steele County, MN	37	**Ponca City, OK**	46	Lincoln County, NM.	21
		Kay County, OK	46		
Owosso, MI	71			**Russellville, AR**	82
Shiawassee County, MI. . . .	71	**Pontiac, IL**	38	Pope County, AR	60
		Livingston County, IL.	38	Yell County, AR	22
Oxford, MS.	44				
Lafayette County, MS	44	**Poplar Bluff, MO.**	41	**Ruston, LA.**	58
		Butler County, MO	41	Jackson Parish, LA.	15
Paducah, KY-IL.	98			Lincoln Parish, LA.	43
Massac County, IL.	15	**Portales, NM.**	19		
Ballard County, KY	8	Roosevelt County, NM.	19	**Rutland, VT**	63
Livingston County, KY	10			Rutland County, VT.	63
McCracken County, KY	65	**Port Angeles, WA**	71		
		Clallam County, WA	71	**Safford, AZ.**	44
Pahrump, NV	44			Graham County, AZ	36
Nye County, NV	44	**Portsmouth, OH**	77	Greenlee County, AZ.	8
		Scioto County, OH	77		
Palatka, FL.	73			**St. Marys, GA**	48
Putnam County, FL.	73	**Pottsville, PA**	147	Camden County, GA.	48
		Schuylkill County, PA.	147		
Palestine, TX	57			**St. Marys, PA**	32
Anderson County, TX	57	**Price, UT**	20	Elk County, PA	32
		Carbon County, UT.	20		
Pampa, TX	23			**Salina, KS.**	61
Gray County, TX.	22	**Prineville, OR**	23	Ottawa County, KS	6
Roberts County, TX.	1	Crook County, OR.	23	Saline County, KS.	55
Paragould, AR	41	**Pullman, WA.**	42	**Salisbury, NC**	139
Greene County, AR.	41	Whitman County, WA	42	Rowan County, NC.	139
Paris, TN	32	**Quincy, IL-MO.**	77	**Sanford, NC**	59
Henry County, TN.	32	Adams County, IL.	67	Lee County, NC	59
		Lewis County, MO.	10		
Paris, TX	49			**Sault Ste. Marie, MI.**	39
Lamar County, TX.	49	**Raymondville, TX**	21	Chippewa County, MI	39
		Willacy County, TX	21		
Parsons, KS	22			**Sayre, PA**	61
Labette County, KS.	22	**Red Bluff, CA**	62	Bradford County, PA	61
		Tehama County, CA	62		
Payson, AZ.	52			**Scottsbluff, NE**	37
Gila County, AZ	52	**Red Wing, MN.**	46	Banner County, NE.	1
		Goodhue County, MN	46	Scotts Bluff County, NE	37
Pecos, TX.	11				
Reeves County, TX.	11	**Rexburg, ID**	50	**Scottsboro, AL.**	53
		Fremont County, ID.	13	Jackson County, AL	53
Pella, IA	33	Madison County, ID.	37		
Marion County, IA.	33			**Scottsburg, IN**	24
		Richmond, IN	68	Scott County, IN	24
Pendleton-Hermiston, OR . .	85	Wayne County, IN.	68		
Morrow County, OR	11			**Seaford, DE**	188
Umatilla County, OR	74	**Richmond-Berea, KY.**	99	Sussex County, DE.	188
		Madison County, KY	82		
Peru, IN	36	Rockcastle County, KY	17	**Searcy, AR**	75
Miami County, IN	36			White County, AR	75
		Rio Grande City-Roma, TX .	62		
Phoenix Lake-Cedar Ridge, **CA**	56	Starr County, TX.	62	**Sebring, FL.**	100
Tuolumne County, CA	56			Highlands County, FL	100
		Riverton, WY	38		
Picayune, MS	57	Fremont County, WY.	38	**Sedalia, MO**	41
Pearl River County, MS. . . .	57			Pettis County, MO.	41
		Roanoke Rapids, NC.	75		
Pierre, SD.	19	Halifax County, NC	55	**Selinsgrove, PA**	38
Hughes County, SD	17	Northampton County, NC. . .	20	Snyder County, PA	38
Stanley County, SD.	3				
		Rochelle, IL	55	**Selma, AL.**	43
Pierre Part, LA	23	Ogle County, IL	55	Dallas County, AL	43
Assumption Parish, LA	23				
		Rockingham, NC.	46	**Seneca, SC.**	71
Pittsburg, KS	39	Richmond County, NC.	46	Oconee County, SC	71
Crawford County, KS.	39				
		Rockland, ME	41	**Seneca Falls, NY.**	34
Plainview, TX	35	Knox County, ME	41	Seneca County, NY.	34
Hale County, TX.	35				
		Rock Springs, WY.	40	**Sevierville, TN**	85
Platteville, WI	49	Sweetwater County, WY . . .	40	Sevier County, TN.	85
Grant County, WI	49				
		Rolla, MO	42	**Seymour, IN**	42
Plattsburgh, NY	82	Phelps County, MO.	42	Jackson County, IN.	42
Clinton County, NY	82				
		Roseburg, OR.	104	**Shawnee, OK**	70
Plymouth, IN.	47	Douglas County, OR	104	Pottawatomie County, OK . .	70
Marshall County, IN.	47				

896 Appendix II

Micropolitan statistical area Component county	Popu- lation, 2008 (1,000)	Micropolitan statistical area Component county	Popu- lation, 2008 (1,000)	Micropolitan statistical area Component county	Popu- lation, 2008 (1,000)
Shelby, NC	99	**Sulphur Springs, TX**	34	**Union, SC**	28
Cleveland County, NC	99	Hopkins County, TX	34	Union County, SC	28
Shelbyville, TN	45	**Summerville, GA**	27	**Union City, TN-KY**	38
Bedford County, TN	45	Chattooga County, GA	27	Fulton County, KY	7
Shelton, WA	58	**Sunbury, PA**	91	Obion County, TN	31
Mason County, WA	58	Northumberland County, PA .	91	**Urbana, OH**	40
Sheridan, WY	29	**Susanville, CA**	35	Champaign County, OH	40
Sheridan County, WY	29	Lassen County, CA	35	**Uvalde, TX**	26
Show Low, AZ	113	**Sweetwater, TX**	15	Uvalde County, TX	26
Navajo County, AZ	113	Nolan County, TX	15	**Valley, AL**	34
Sidney, OH	49	**Tahlequah, OK**	46	Chambers County, AL	34
Shelby County, OH	49	Cherokee County, OK	46	**Van Wert, OH**	29
Sierra Vista-Douglas, AZ . . .	129	**Talladega-Sylacauga, AL** . . .	80	Van Wert County, OH	29
Cochise County, AZ	129	Talladega County, AL	80	**Vermillion, SD**	14
Sikeston, MO	41	**Tallulah, LA**	12	Clay County, SD	14
Scott County, MO	41	Madison Parish, LA	12	**Vernal, UT**	30
Silver City, NM	30	**Taos, NM**	32	Uintah County, UT	30
Grant County, NM	30	Taos County, NM	32	**Vernon, TX**	14
Silverthorne, CO	27	**Taylorville, IL**	35	Wilbarger County, TX	14
Summit County, CO	27	Christian County, IL	35	**Vicksburg, MS**	48
Snyder, TX	16	**The Villages, FL**	75	Warren County, MS	48
Scurry County, TX	16	Sumter County, FL	75	**Vidalia, GA**	37
Somerset, KY	61	**Thomaston, GA**	28	Montgomery County, GA . . .	9
Pulaski County, KY	61	Upson County, GA	28	Toombs County, GA	28
Somerset, PA	77	**Thomasville, GA**	46	**Vincennes, IN**	38
Somerset County, PA	77	Thomas County, GA	46	Knox County, IN	38
Southern Pines-Pinehurst,		**Thomasville-Lexington, NC** .	158	**Wabash, IN**	33
NC	86	Davidson County, NC	158	Wabash County, IN	33
Moore County, NC	86	**Tiffin, OH**	56	**Wahpeton, ND MN**	23
Spearfish, SD	24	Seneca County, OH	56	Wilkin County, MN	6
Lawrence County, SD	24	**Tifton, GA**	42	Richland County, ND	16
Spencer, IA	17	Tift County, GA	42	**Walla Walla, WA**	58
Clay County, IA	17	**Toccoa, GA**	25	Walla Walla County, WA . . .	58
Spirit Lake, IA	17	Stephens County, GA	25	**Walterboro, SC**	39
Dickinson County, IA	17	**Torrington, CT**	188	Colleton County, SC	39
Starkville, MS	44	Litchfield County, CT	188	**Wapakoneta, OH**	47
Oktibbeha County, MS	44	**Traverse City, MI**	142	Auglaize County, OH	47
Statesboro, GA	68	Benzie County, MI	17	**Warren, PA**	41
Bulloch County, GA	68	Grand Traverse County, MI .	86	Warren County, PA	41
Statesville-Mooresville, NC .	155	Kalkaska County, MI	17	**Warrensburg, MO**	52
Iredell County, NC	155	Leelanau County, MI	22	Johnson County, MO	52
Staunton-Waynesboro, VA . .	117	**Troy, AL**	30	**Warsaw, IN**	76
Augusta County, VA	71	Pike County, AL	30	Kosciusko County, IN	76
Staunton city, VA	24			**Washington, IN**	30
Waynesboro city, VA	22	**Truckee-Grass Valley, CA** . .	97	Daviess County, IN	30
Stephenville, TX	36	Nevada County, CA	97	**Washington, NC**	46
Erath County, TX	36	**Tullahoma, TN**	99	Beaufort County, NC	46
Sterling, CO	21	Coffee County, TN	52	**Washington Court House,**	
Logan County, CO	21	Franklin County, TN	41	**OH**	28
Sterling, IL	59	Moore County, TN	6	Fayette County, OH	28
Whiteside County, IL	59	**Tupelo, MS**	133	**Watertown, SD**	32
Stevens Point, WI	69	Itawamba County, MS	23	Codington County, SD	26
Portage County, WI	69	Lee County, MS	81	Hamlin County, SD	6
Stillwater, OK	78	Pontotoc County, MS	29	**Watertown-Fort Atkinson,**	
Payne County, OK	78	**Tuskegee, AL**	22	**WI**	81
Storm Lake, IA	20	Macon County, AL	22	Jefferson County, WI	81
Buena Vista County, IA	20	**Twin Falls, ID**	95	**Watertown-Fort Drum, NY** . .	118
Sturgis, MI	62	Jerome County, ID	20	Jefferson County, NY	118
St. Joseph County, MI	62	Twin Falls County, ID	74	**Wauchula, FL**	29
		Ukiah, CA	86	Hardee County, FL	29
		Mendocino County, CA	86		

Micropolitan statistical area Component county	Popu- lation, **2008** (1,000)	Micropolitan statistical area Component county	Popu- lation, **2008** (1,000)	Micropolitan statistical area Component county	Popu- lation, **2008** (1,000)
Waycross, GA.	54	**Williston, ND**.	20	**Woodward, OK**.	20
Pierce County, GA	18	Williams County, ND	20	Woodward County, OK	20
Ware County, GA	36				
		Willmar, MN	41	**Wooster, OH**.	114
West Plains, MO	39	Kandiyohi County, MN.	41	Wayne County, OH.	114
Howell County, MO.	39				
		Wilmington, OH	43	**Worthington, MN**.	20
West Point, MS	21	Clinton County, OH	43	Nobles County, MN.	20
Clay County, MS.	21				
		Wilson, NC	78	**Yankton, SD**	22
		Wilson County, NC	78	Yankton County, SD	22
Whitewater, WI	101				
Walworth County, WI.	101	**Winfield, KS**	34	**Yazoo City, MS**	28
		Cowley County, KS.	34	Yazoo County, MS	28
Willimantic, CT	117				
Windham County, CT	117	**Winona, MN**	50	**Zanesville, OH**	85
		Winona County, MN	50	Muskingum County, OH. . . .	85

Source: U.S. Census Bureau, "CBSA-EST2008-alldata: Population Estimates and Estimated Components of Change for Metropolitan and Micropolitan Statistical Areas and Their Geographic Components: April 1, 2000 to July 1, 2008" <http://www.census.gov/popest/metro/files/2008/CBSA-EST2008-alldata.csv>.

U.S. Census Bureau, Statistical Abstract of the United States: 2010

Appendix III
Limitations of the Data

Introduction- The data presented in this *Statistical Abstract* came from many sources. The sources include not only federal statistical bureaus and other organizations that collect and issue statistics as their principal activity, but also governmental administrative and regulatory agencies, private research bodies, trade associations, insurance companies, health associations, and private organizations such as the National Education Association and philanthropic foundations. Consequently, the data vary considerably as to reference periods, definitions of terms and, for ongoing series, the number and frequency of time periods for which data are available.

The statistics presented were obtained and tabulated by various means. Some statistics are based on complete enumerations or censuses while others are based on samples. Some information is extracted from records kept for administrative or regulatory purposes (school enrollment, hospital records, securities registration, financial accounts, social security records, income tax returns, etc.), while other information is obtained explicitly for statistical purposes through interviews or by mail. The estimation procedures used vary from highly sophisticated scientific techniques, to crude "informed guesses."

Each set of data relates to a group of individuals or units of interest referred to as the *target universe* or *target population*, or simply as the *universe* or *population*. Prior to data collection the target universe should be clearly defined. For example, if data are to be collected for the universe of households in the United States, it is necessary to define a "household." The target universe may not be completely tractable. Cost and other considerations may restrict data collection to a *survey universe* based on some available list, such list may be inaccurate or out of date. This list is called a *survey frame* or *sampling frame*.

The data in many tables are based on data obtained for all population units, *a census,* or on data obtained for only a portion, or *sample,* of the population units. When the data presented are based on a sample, the sample is usually a scientifically selected *probability sample.* This is a sample selected from a list or sampling frame in such a way that every possible sample has a known chance of selection and usually each unit selected can be assigned a number, greater than zero and less than or equal to one, representing its likelihood or probability of selection.

For large-scale sample surveys, the probability sample of units is often selected as a multistage sample. The first stage of a multistage sample is the selection of a probability sample of large groups of population members, referred to as primary sampling units (PSUs). For example, in a national multistage household sample, PSUs are often counties or groups of counties. The second stage of a multistage sample is the selection, within each PSU selected at the first stage, of smaller groups of population units, referred to as secondary sampling units. In subsequent stages of selection, smaller and smaller nested groups are chosen until the ultimate sample of population units is obtained. To qualify a multistage sample as a probability sample, all stages of sampling must be carried out using probability sampling methods.

Prior to selection at each stage of a multistage (or a single stage) sample, a list of the sampling units or sampling frame for that stage must be obtained. For example, for the first stage of selection of a national household sample, a list of the counties and county groups that form the PSUs must be obtained. For the final stage of selection, lists of households, and sometimes persons within the households, have to be compiled in the field. For surveys of economic entities and for

U.S. Census Bureau, Statistical Abstract of the United States: 2010

the economic censuses the Bureau generally uses a frame constructed from the Bureau's Business Register. The Business Register contains all establishments with payroll in the United States including small single establishment firms as well as large multi-establishment firms.

Wherever the quantities in a table refer to an entire universe, but are constructed from data collected in a sample survey, the table quantities are referred to as *sample estimates*. In constructing a sample estimate, an attempt is made to come as close as is feasible to the corresponding universe quantity that would be obtained from a complete census of the universe. Estimates based on a sample will, however, generally differ from the hypothetical census figures. Two classifications of errors are associated with estimates based on sample surveys: (1) *sampling error*-the error arising from the use of a sample, rather than a census, to estimate population quantities and (2) *nonsampling error*-those errors arising from nonsampling sources. As discussed below, the magnitude of the sampling error for an estimate can usually be estimated from the sample data. However, the magnitude of the nonsampling error for an estimate can rarely be estimated. Consequently, actual error in an estimate exceeds the error that can be estimated.

The particular sample used in a survey is only one of a large number of possible samples of the same size which could have been selected using the same sampling procedure. Estimates derived from the different samples would, in general, differ from each other. The *standard error* (SE) is a measure of the variation among the estimates derived from all possible samples. The standard error is the most commonly used measure of the sampling error of an estimate. Valid estimates of the standard errors of survey estimates can usually be calculated from the data collected in a probability sample. For convenience, the standard error is sometimes expressed as a percent of the estimate and is called the relative standard error or *coefficient of variation* (CV). For example, an estimate of 200 units with an estimated standard error of 10 units has an estimated CV of 5 percent.

A sample estimate and an estimate of its standard error or CV can be used to construct interval estimates that have a prescribed confidence that the interval includes the average of the estimates derived from all possible samples with a known probability. To illustrate, if all possible samples were selected under essentially the same general conditions, and using the same sample design, and if an estimate and its estimated standard error were calculated from each sample, then: 1) approximately 68 percent of the intervals from one standard error below the estimate to one standard error above the estimate would include the average estimate derived from all possible samples; 2) approximately 90 percent of the intervals from 1.6 standard errors below the estimate to 1.6 standard errors above the estimate would include the average estimate derived from all possible samples; and 3) approximately 95 percent of the intervals from two standard errors below the estimate to two standard errors above the estimate would include the average estimate derived from all possible samples.

Thus, for a particular sample, one can say with the appropriate level of confidence (e.g., 90 percent or 95 percent) that the average of all possible samples is included in the constructed interval. Example of a confidence interval: An estimate is 200 units with a standard error of 10 units. An approximately 90 percent confidence interval (plus or minus 1.6 standard errors) is from 184 to 216.

All surveys and censuses are subject to nonsampling errors. Nonsampling errors are of two kinds-*random* and *nonrandom*. Random nonsampling errors arise because of the varying interpretation of questions (by respondents or interviewers) and varying actions of coders, keyers, and other processors. Some randomness is also introduced when respondents must estimate. Nonrandom nonsampling errors result from total nonresponse (no usable data obtained for a sampled unit), partial or item nonresponse (only a portion of a response may be usable), inability or unwillingness on the part of respondents to provide correct information, difficulty interpreting questions, mistakes in recording or keying data, errors of collection or processing, and coverage problems (overcoverage and undercoverage of the target universe). Random nonresponse errors usually, but not always, result in an understatement of sampling errors and thus an overstatement of the precision of survey estimates. Estimating the magnitude of nonsampling errors would require special experiments or access to independent data and, consequently, the magnitudes are seldom available.

Nearly all types of nonsampling errors that affect surveys also occur in complete censuses. Since surveys can be conducted on a smaller scale than censuses, nonsampling errors can presumably be controlled more tightly. Relatively more funds and effort can perhaps be expended toward eliciting responses, detecting and correcting response error, and reducing processing errors. As a result, survey results can sometimes be more accurate than census results.

To compensate for suspected nonrandom errors, adjustments of the sample estimates are often made. For example, adjustments are frequently made for nonresponse, both total and partial. Adjustments made for either type of nonresponse are often referred to as *imputations*. Imputation for total nonresponse is usually made by substituting for the questionnaire responses of the nonrespondents the "average" questionnaire responses of the respondents. These imputations usually are made separately within various groups of sample members, formed by attempting to place respondents and nonrespondents together that have "similar" design or ancillary characteristics. Imputation for item nonresponse is usually made by substituting for a missing item the response to that item of a respondent having characteristics that are "similar" to those of the nonrespondent.

For an estimate calculated from a sample survey, the *total error* in the estimate is composed of the sampling error, which can usually be estimated from the sample, and the nonsampling error, which usually cannot be estimated from the sample. The total error present in a population quantity obtained from a complete census is composed of only nonsampling errors. Ideally, estimates of the total error associated with data given in the *Statistical Abstract* tables should be given. However, due to the unavailability of estimates of nonsampling errors, only estimates of the levels of sampling errors, in terms of estimated standard errors or coefficients of variation, are available. To obtain estimates of the estimated standard errors from the sample of interest, obtain a copy of the referenced report which appears at the end of each table.

Source of Additional Material: The Federal Committee on Statistical Methodology (FCSM) is an interagency committee dedicated to improving the quality of federal statistics <http://fcsm.ssd.census.gov>.

Principal data bases—Beginning below are brief descriptions of 35 of the sample surveys and censuses that provide a substantial portion of the data contained in this *Abstract*.

U.S. DEPARTMENT OF AGRICULTURE, National Agriculture Statistics Service

Census of Agriculture

Universes, Frequency, and Types of Data: Complete count of U.S. farms and ranches conducted once every 5 years with data at the national, state, and county level. Data published on farm numbers and related items/ characteristics.

Type of Data Collection Operation: Complete census for number of farms; land in farms; farm income; agriculture products sold; farms by type of organization; total cropland; irrigated land; farm operator characteristics; livestock and poultry inventory and sales; and selected crops harvested. Market value of land, buildings, and products sold, total farm production expenses, machinery and equipment, and fertilizer and chemicals.

Data Collection and Imputation Procedures: Data collection is by mailing questionnaires to all farmers and ranchers. Producers can return their forms by mail or online. Nonrespondents are contacted by telephone and correspondence follow-ups. Imputations were made for all nonresponse item/characteristics and coverage adjustments were made to account for missed farms and ranches. The response rate for the 2007 Census was 85.2 percent.

Estimates of Sampling Error: Weight adjustments were made to account for the undercoverage and whole-unit nonresponse of farms on the Census Mail List (CML). These were treated as sampling errors.

Other (nonsampling) Errors: Nonsampling errors are due to incompleteness of the census mailing list, duplications on the list, respondent reporting errors, errors in editing reported data, and in imputation for missing data. Evaluation studies are conducted to measure certain nonsampling errors such as list coverage and classification error. It is a reasonable assumption that the net effect of non measurable errors is zero (the positive errors cancel the negative errors).

Sources of Additional Material: U.S. Department of Agriculture (NASS), 2007 Census of Agriculture, Appendix A-1 Census of Agriculture Methodology, Appendix B-1 General Explanation and Census of Agriculture Report Form.

Basic Area Frame Sample

Universe, Frequency, and Types of Data: June agricultural survey collects data on planted acreage and livestock inventories on all land in the 48 contiguous states and Hawaii. The survey also serves to measure list incompleteness and is subsampled for multiple frame surveys.

Type of Data Collection Operation: Stratified probability sample of about 11,000 land area units of about 1 sq. mile (range from 0.1 sq. mile in cities to several sq. miles in open grazing areas). Sample includes 42,000 parcels of agricultural land. About 20 percent of the sample replaced annually.

Data Collection and Imputation Procedures: Data collection is by personal enumeration. Imputation is based on enumerator observation or data reported by respondents having similar agricultural characteristics.

Estimates of Sampling Error: Estimated CVs range from 1 percent to 2 percent for regional estimates to 3 percent to 6 percent for state estimates of major crop acres and livestock inventories.

Other (nonsampling) Errors: Minimized through rigid quality controls on the collection process and careful review of all reported data.

Sources of Additional Material: U.S. Department of Agriculture, National Agricultural Statistics Service, USDA's National Agricultural Statistics Service: The Fact Finders of Agriculture, March 2007.

Multiple Frame Surveys

Universe, Frequency, and Types of Data: Surveys of U.S. farm operators to obtain data on major livestock inventories, selected crop acreage and production, grain stocks, and farm labor characteristics, farm economic data, and chemical use data. Estimates are made quarterly, semi-annually, or annually depending on the data series.

Type of Data Collection Operation: Primary frame is obtained from general or special purpose lists, supplemented by a probability sample of land areas used to estimate for list incompleteness.

Data Collection and Imputation Procedures: Mail, telephone, or personal interviews used for initial data collection. Mail nonrespondent follow-up by phone and personal interviews. Imputation based on average of respondents.

Estimates of Sampling Error: Estimated CVs range from 1 percent to 2 percent at the U.S. level for crop and livestock data series and 3 to 5 percent for economic data. Regional CVs range from 3 to 6 percent, while state estimate CVs run 5 to 10 percent.

Other (nonsampling) Errors: In addition to above, replicated sampling procedures used to monitor effects of changes in survey procedures.

Sources of Additional Material: U.S. Department of Agriculture, National Agricultural Statistics Service, USDA's National Agricultural Statistics Service: The Fact Finders of Agriculture, March 2007.

Objective Yield Surveys

Universe, Frequency, and Types of Data: Monthly surveys during the growing season of corn, cotton, potatoes, soybeans, and winter wheat fields in top producing states for forecasting and estimating yield per acre.

Type of Data Collection Operation: Random location of plots in probability sample. Corn, cotton, and soybeans, are selected in June from Basic Area Frame Sample (see above). Winter wheat and potatoes are selected from March and June multiple frame surveys, respectively.

Data Collection and Imputation Procedures: Enumerators count and measure plant characteristics in sample fields. Production is measured from plots at harvest. Harvest loss is measured from post harvest gleanings.

Estimates of Sampling Error: CVs for national estimates of production are about 2 to 3 percent.

Other (nonsampling) Errors: In addition to above, replicated sampling procedures are used to monitor effects of changes in survey procedures.

Sources of Additional Material: U.S. Department of Agriculture, National Agricultural Statistics Service), USDA's National Agricultural Statistics Service: The Fact Finders of Agriculture, March 2007.

U.S. BUREAU OF JUSTICE STATISTICS (BJS)

National Crime Victimization Survey

Universe, Frequency, and Types of Data: Monthly survey of individuals and households in the United States to obtain data on criminal victimization of those units for compilation of annual estimates.

Type of Data Collection Operation: National probability sample survey of about 40,000 interviewed households in 203 PSUs selected from a list of addresses from the 2000 census, supplemented by new construction permits and an area sample where permits are not required.

Data Collection and Imputation Procedures: Interviews are conducted every 6 months for 3 years for each household in the sample; 6,600 households are interviewed monthly. Personal interviews are used in the first interview; the intervening interviews are conducted by telephone whenever possible.

Estimates of Sampling Error: CVs for 2007 estimates are: 3.9 percent for personal crimes (includes all crimes of violence plus purse snatching crimes), 4.0 percent for crimes of violence; 13.2 percent for estimate of rape/sexual assault counts; 9.2 percent for robbery counts; 4.3 percent for assault counts; 14.5 percent for purse snatching/pocket picking; 2.0 percent for property crimes; 4.0 percent for burglary counts; 2.0 percent for theft (of property); and 6.5 percent for motor vehicle theft counts.

Other (nonsampling) Errors: Respondent recall errors which may include reporting incidents for other than the reference period; interviewer coding and processing errors; and possible mistaken reporting or classifying of events. Adjustment is made for a household noninterview rate of about 8 percent and for a within-household noninterview rate of 14 percent.

Sources of Additional Material: U.S. Bureau of Justice Statistics, *Criminal Victimization in the United States,* annual.

U.S. BUREAU OF LABOR STATISTICS

Consumer Expenditure Survey (CE)

Universe, Frequency and Types of Data: Consists of two continuous components: a quarterly interview survey and a weekly diary or recordkeeping survey. They are nationwide surveys that collect data on consumer expenditures, income, characteristics, and assets and liabilities. Samples are national probability samples of households that are representative of the civilian noninstitutional population. The surveys have been ongoing since 1980.

Type of Data Collection Operation: The Interview Survey is a panel rotation survey. Each panel is interviewed for five quarters and then dropped from the survey. About 7,000 consumer units are interviewed each quarter. The Diary Survey sample is new each year and consists of about 7,000 consumer units. Data are collected on an ongoing basis in 91 areas of the country.

Data Collection and Imputation Procedures: For the Interview Survey, data are collected by personal interview with each consumer unit interviewed once per quarter for five consecutive quarters. Designed to collect information that respondents can recall for 3 months or longer, such as large or recurring expenditures. For the Diary Survey, respondents record all their expenditures in a self-reporting diary for two consecutive one-week periods. Designed to pick up items difficult to recall over a long period, such as detailed food expenditures. Missing or invalid attributes, expenditures, or incomes are imputed. Assets and liabilities are not imputed. The U.S. Census Bureau collects the data for the Bureau of Labor Statistics.

Estimates of Sampling Error: Standard error tables are available since 2000.

Other (nonsampling) Errors: Includes incorrect information given by respondents, data processing errors, interviewer errors, and so on. They occur regardless of whether data are collected from a sample or from the entire population.

Sources of Additional Material: Bureau of Labor Statistics, see Internet site <http://www.bls.gov/cex>.

Consumer Price Index (CPI)

Universe, Frequency, and Types of Data: A monthly survey of price changes of all types of consumer goods and services purchased by urban wage earners and clerical workers prior to 1978, and urban consumers thereafter. Both indexes continue to be published.

Type of Data Collection Operation: Prior to 1978, and since 1998, sample of various consumer items in 87 urban areas; from 1978 - 1997, in 85 PSUs, except from January 1987 through March 1988, when 91 areas were sampled.

Data Collection and Imputation Procedures: Prices of consumer items are obtained each month from about 25,500 retail outlets and from about 4,000 housing units in 87 areas. Prices of

food, fuel, and a few other items are obtained monthly; prices of most other commodities and services are collected every month in the three largest geographic areas and every other month in others.

Estimates of Sampling Error: Estimates of standard errors are available.

Other (nonsampling) Errors: Errors result from inaccurate reporting, difficulties in defining concepts and their operational implementation, and introduction of product quality changes and new products.

Sources of Additional Material: U.S. Bureau of Labor Statistics, Internet site <http://www.bls.gov/cpi/home.htm> and *BLS Handbook of Methods*, Chapter 17, see Internet site <http://www.bls.gov/opub/hom/pdf/homch17.pdf>.

Current Employment Statistics (CES) Program

Universe, Frequency, and Types of Data: Monthly survey drawn from a sampling frame of over 8 million unemployment insurance tax accounts in order to obtain data by industry on employment, hours, and earnings.

Type of Data Collection Operation: In 2006, the CES sample included about 150,000 businesses and government agencies, which represent approximately 390,000 individual worksites.

Data Collection and Imputation Procedures: Each month, the state agencies cooperating with BLS, as well as BLS Data Collection Centers, collect data through various automated collection modes and mail. BLS Washington staff prepares national estimates of employment, hours, and earnings while states use the data to develop state and area estimates.

Estimates of Sampling Errors: The relative standard error for total nonfarm employment is 0.1 percent. From April 2002 to March 2003, the cumulative net birth/death model added 469,000.

Other (nonsampling) Errors: Estimates of employment adjusted annually to reflect complete universe. Average adjustment is 0.2 percent over the last decade, with an absolute range from less than 0.1 percent to 0.6 percent.

Sources of Additional Material: U.S. Bureau of Labor Statistics, Employment and Earnings, monthly, Explanatory Notes and Estimates of Errors, Tables 2-A through 2-F. See <http:// www.bls.gov/web/cestntab.htm>.

National Compensation Survey (NCS)

Universe, Frequency, and Types of Data: NCS collects data from establishments of all employment-size classes in private industries as well as state and local governments. The survey stratifies its data by geographic area and industry. NCS collects data on work schedules, wages, salaries, and employer costs for employee benefits. For approximately 80 metropolitan areas and the nation, NCS produces information on workers' earnings and benefits in a variety of occupations at different work levels. NCS is also responsible for two quarterly releases: the Employment Cost Index (ECI), which measures percent changes in the cost of employment, and the Employer Costs for Employee Compensation (ECEC), which measures costs per hour worked for individual benefits. The survey provides data by industry sector, industry division, occupational group, bargaining status, metropolitan area status, census region, and census division. ECEC also provides data by establishment-size class.

Type of Data Collection Operation: Establishments are selected for the survey based on a probability-proportionate-to-employment technique. NCS replaces its sample on a continual basis. Private industry establishments are in the survey for approximately 5 years.

Data Collection and Imputation Procedures: A personal visit to the establishment is the initial source for collecting data. Communication via mail, fax, and telephone provide quarterly updates. Imputation is done for individual benefits.

Estimates of Sampling Error: NCS uses standard errors to evaluate published series. These standard errors are available at <http://www.bls.gov/ncs/ect /home.htm>.

Other (nonsampling) Errors: Nonsampling errors have a number of potential sources. The primary sources are (1) survey nonresponse and (2) data collection and processing errors. Nonsampling errors are not measured. The use of quality assurance programs reduces the potential for nonsampling errors. These programs include the use of reinterviews, interview observations, and the systematic professional review of reports. The programs also serve as a training device that provides feedback on errors for field economists (or data collectors). Quality assurance programs also provide information on sources of error. This information is used to improve procedures that result in fewer errors. NCS also conducts extensive training of field economists to maintain high standards in data collection.

Sources of Additional Material: Bureau of Labor Statistics, *BLS Handbook of Methods*, Chapter 8 <http://www.bls.gov /opub/hom/pdf/homch8.pdf>.

Producer Price Index (PPI)

Universe, Frequency, and Types of Data: Monthly survey of producing companies to determine price changes of all commodities and services produced in the United States for sale in commercial transactions. Data on agriculture, forestry, fishing, manufacturing, mining, gas, electricity, construction, public utilities, wholesale trade, retail trade, transportation, healthcare, and other services.

Type of Data Collection Operation: Probability sample of approximately 30,000 establishments that result in about 120,000 price quotations per month.

Data Collection and Imputation Procedures: Data are collected by mail and facsimile. Missing prices are estimated by those received for similar products or services. Some prices are obtained from trade publications, organized exchanges, and government agencies. To calculate index, price changes are multiplied by their relative weights taken from the Census Bureau's 2002 shipment values from their Census of Industries.

Estimates of Sampling Error: Not applicable.

Other (nonsampling) Errors: Not available at present.

Sources of Additional Material: U.S. Bureau of Labor Statistics, *BLS Handbook of Methods*, Chapter 14, Bulletin 2490. U.S. Bureau of Labor Statistics Internet site <http://stats.bls.gov/ppi>.

BOARD OF GOVERNORS OF THE FEDERAL RESERVE SYSTEM

Survey of Consumer Finances

Universe, Frequency, and Types of Data: Periodic sample survey of families. In this survey a given household is divided into a primary economic unit and other economic units. The primary economic unit, which may be a single individual, is generally chosen as the person or couple who either holds the title to the home or is listed on the lease, along with all other people in the household who are financially interdependent with that person or couple. The primary economic unit is used as the reference family. The survey collects detailed data on the composition of family balance sheets, the terms of loans, and relationships with financial institutions. It also gathers information on the employment history and pension rights of the survey respondent and the spouse or partner of the respondent.

Type of Data Collection Operation: The survey employs a two-part strategy for sampling families. Some families are selected by standard multistage area probability sampling methods applied to all 50 states. The remaining families in the survey are selected using statistical records derived from tax returns, under the strict rules governing confidentiality and the rights of potential respondents to refuse participation.

Data Collection and Imputation Procedures: National Opinion Research Center (NORC) at the University of Chicago has collected data for the survey since 1992. Since 1995, the survey has used computer-assisted personal interviewing. Adjustments for nonresponse are made through multiple imputation of unanswered questions and through weighting adjustments based on data used in the sample design for families that refused participation.

Estimates of Sampling Error: Because of the complex design of the survey, the estimation of potential sampling errors is not straightforward. A replicate-based procedure is available.

Other (nonsampling) Errors: The survey aims to complete 4,500 interviews, with about two thirds of that number deriving from the area-probability sample. The response rate is typically about 70 percent for the area-probability sample and about 35 percent over all strata in the tax-data sample. Proper training and monitoring of interviewers, careful design of questionnaires, and systematic editing of the resulting data were used to control inaccurate survey responses.

Sources of Additional Material: Board of Governors of the Federal Reserve System, "Recent Changes in U.S. Family Finances: Evidence from the Survey of Consumer Finances," *Federal Reserve Bulletin*, 2009, <http://www.federalreserve.gov /Pubs/Bulletin>.

U.S. CENSUS BUREAU

2007 Economic Census
(Industry Series, Geographic Area Series and Subject Series Reports) (for NAICS sectors 21 to 81).

Universe, Frequency, and Types of Data: Conducted every 5 years to obtain data on number of establishments, number of employees, payroll, total sales/ receipts/revenue, and other industry-specific statistics. The universe is all establishments with paid employees excluding agriculture, forestry, fishing and hunting, and government. (Nonemployer Statistics, discussed separately, covers those establishments without paid employees.)

Type of Data Collection Operation: All large employer firms were surveyed (i.e., all employer firms above payroll-size cutoffs established to separate large from small employers) plus, in most sectors, a sample of the small employer firms.

Data Collection and Imputation Procedures: Mail questionnaires were used with both mail and telephone follow-ups for nonrespondents. Businesses also had the option to respond electronically. Data for nonrespondents and for small employer firms not mailed a questionnaire were obtained from administrative records of other federal agencies or imputed.

Estimates of Sampling Error: Not applicable for basic data such as sales, revenue, receipts, payroll, etc. for sectors other than Construction (NAICS 23). Estimates of sampling error for construction industries are included with the data as published on the Census Bureau web site. Other (nonsampling) errors: establishment response rates by NAICS sector in 2002 ranged from 80 percent to 89 percent. Nonsampling errors may occur during the collection, reporting, keying, and classification of the data.

Sources of Additional Material:
U.S. Census Bureau, see
<http://www.census.gov/econ/census07/census07/www/methodology>.

American Community Survey (ACS)

Universe, Frequency, and Types of Data: Nationwide survey to obtain annual data about demographic, social, economic, and housing characteristics of housing units and the people residing in them. It covers the household population and, beginning in 2006, also includes the group quarter population living in prisons, nursing homes and college dormitories, and other group quarters.

Type of Data Collection Operation: Housing unit address sampling is performed twice a year in both August and January. First-phase of sampling defines the universe for the second stage of sampling through two steps. First, all addresses that were eligible for the second-phase sampling within the past four years are excluded from eligibility. This ensures that no address is in sample more than once in any 5-year period. The second step is to select a 20 percent systematic sample of "new" units, i.e. those units that have never appeared on a previous Master Address File (MAF) extract. All new addresses are systematically assigned to either the current year or to one of four back-samples. This procedure maintains five equal partitions of the universe. The second-phase sampling is done on the current year's partition and results in approximately 3,000,000 housing unit addresses in the

U.S. and 36,000 in Puerto Rico (PR). Group quarter sampling is performed separately from the housing unit sampling. The sampling begins with separating the small (15 persons or fewer) and the large (more than 15 persons) group quarters. The target sampling rate for both groups is a 2.5% sample of the group quarters population. It results in approximately 200,000 group quarter residents being selected in the U.S., and an additional 1,000 in Puerto Rico.

Data Collection and Imputation Procedures: The American Community Survey is conducted every month on independent samples. Each housing unit in the independent monthly samples is mailed a prenotice letter announcing the selection of the address to participate, a survey questionnaire package, and a reminder postcard. These sample units addresses receive a second (replacement) questionnaire package if the initial questionnaire has not been returned by mid-month. Sample addresses for which a questionnaire is not returned in the mail and a telephone number is available is forwarded to telephone centers is available, is forwarded to telephone centers for follow-up. Interviewers attempt to contact and interview these mail nonresponse cases by telephone. Sample addresses that are still unresponsive after two months of attempts are forwarded for a possible personal visit. Unresponsive addresses are subsampled at rates between 1 in 3 and 2 in 3. Those addresses selected through this process are assigned to Field Representatives (FRs), who visit the addresses, verify their existence, determine their occupancy status, and conduct interviews. Collection of group quarters data is conducted by FR's only. Their methods include completing the questionnaire while speaking to the resident in person or over the telephone, or leaving paper questionnaires for residents to complete for themselves and then pick them up later. This last option is used for data collection in federal prisons. If needed, a personal interview can be conducted with a proxy, such as a relative or guardian. After data collection is completed, any remaining incomplete or inconsistent information on the questionnaire are imputed during the final automated edit of the collected data.

Estimates of Sampling Error: The data in the ACS products are estimates and can vary from the actual values that would have been obtained by conducting a census of the entire population. The estimates from the chosen sample addresses can also vary from those that would have been obtained from a different set of addresses. This variation causes uncertainty, which can be measured using statistics such as standard error, margin of error, and confidence interval. All ACS estimates are accompanied by margin of errors to assist users.

Other (nonsampling) Errors: Nonsampling Error — In addition to sampling error, data users should realize that other types of errors may be introduced during any of the various complex operations used to select, collect and process survey data. An important goal of the ACS is to minimize the amount of nonsampling error introduced through coverage issues in the sample list, nonresponse from sample housing units, and transcribing or editing data. One way of accomplishing this is by finding additional sources of addresses, following up on nonrespondents and maintaining quality control systems.

Sources of Additional Material:
U.S. Census Bureau, American Community Survey Web site <http://www .census.gov/acs/www/index.html>. U.S. Census Bureau, American Community Survey Accuracy of the Data documents at <http://www.census.gov/acs/www /UseData/Accuracy/Accuracy1.htm>.

American Housing Survey

Universe, Frequency, and Types of Data:
Conducted nationally in odd numbered years to obtain data on the approximately 124 million occupied or vacant housing units in the United States (group quarters are excluded). Data include characteristics of occupied housing units, vacant units, new housing and mobile home units, financial characteristics, recent mover households, housing and neighborhood quality indicators, and energy characteristics.

Type of Data Collection Operation: The national sample was a multistage probability sample with about 57,000 units

eligible for interview in 2005. Sample units, selected within 394 PSUs, were surveyed over a 4-month period.

Data Collection and Imputation Procedures: For 2005, the survey was conducted by personal interviews. The interviewers obtained the information from the occupants or, if the unit was vacant, from informed persons such as landlords, rental agents, or knowledgeable neighbors.

Estimates of Sampling Error: For the national sample, illustrations of the Standard Error (SE) of the estimates are provided in the Appendix D of the 2005 report.

Other (nonsampling) Errors: Response rate was about 90 percent. Nonsampling errors may result from incorrect or incomplete responses, errors in coding and recording, and processing errors. Appendix D of the 2005 report has a complete discussion of the errors.

Sources of Additional Material:
U.S. Census Bureau, *Current Housing Reports*, Series H-150 and H-170, *American Housing Survey* see <http://www .census.gov/hhes/www/ahs.html>.

Annual Survey of Government Employment and Payroll

Universe, Frequency, and Types of Data:
The survey measures the number of state, local and federal civilian government employees and their gross payrolls for the pay period including March 12. The survey is conducted annually except in years ending in '2' and '7', when a census of all state and local governments is done. The survey provides data on full-time and part-time employment, part-time hours worked, full-time equivalent employment, and payroll statistics by governmental function (elementary and secondary education, higher education, police protection, fire protection, financial administration, central staff services, judicial and legal, highways, public welfare, solid waste management, sewerage, parks and recreation, health, hospitals, water supply, electric power, gas supply, transit, natural resources, correction, libraries, air transportation, water transport and terminals, other education, state liquor stores, social insurance administration, and housing and community development).

Type of Data Collection Operations: The survey sample was taken from the 2002 Census of Governments and contains approximately 11,000 local government units. These units were sampled from a sampling frame that contained 83,767 local governments (county, city, township, special district, school districts) in addition to 50 state governments and the District of Columbia. This frame was slightly different from the Annual Finance Survey sampling frame. Forty-two of the state governments provided data from central payroll records for all or most of their agencies/institutions. Data for agencies and institutions for the remaining state governments were obtained by mail canvass questionnaires. Local governments were also canvassed using a mail questionnaire. However, elementary and secondary school system data in Florida, North Dakota, and Washington were supplied by special arrangements with the state education agency in each of these states. All respondents receiving the mail questionnaire had the option of responding using the Employment Web site developed for reporting data. Approximately 26% of the state agency and local government respondents chose to respond on the Web.

Editing and Imputation Procedures: Editing is a process that ensures survey data are accurate, complete, and consistent. Efforts are made at all phases of collection, processing, and tabulation to minimize errors. Although some edits are built into the Internet data collection instrument and the data entry programs, the majority of the edits are performed after the case has been loaded into the Census Bureau's database. Edits consist primarily of two types: consistency and a ratio of the current year's reported value to the prior year's value. The consistency edits check the logical relationships of data items reported on the form. For example, if a value exists for employees for a function then a value must exist for payroll also. If part-time employees and payroll are reported then part-time hours must be reported and vice versa. The current year/prior year edits compare data for the number of employees, the function reported for the employees, and the average salary

between reporting years. If data fall outside of acceptable tolerance levels, the item is flagged for review. Some additional checks are made comparing data from the Annual Finance Survey to data reported on the Annual Survey of Government Employment and Payroll to verify that employees reported on the Annual Survey of Government Employment and Payroll at a particular function have a corresponding expenditure on the Finance Survey. For both types of edits, the edit results are reviewed by analysts and adjusted when needed. When the analyst is unable to resolve or accept the edit failure, contact is made with the respondent to verify or correct the reported data.

Imputation: Not all respondents answer every item on the questionnaire. There are also questionnaires that are not returned despite efforts to gain a response. Imputation is the process of filling in missing or invalid data with reasonable values in order to have a complete data set. For general purpose governments and for schools, the imputations were based on recent historical data from either a prior year annual survey or the most recent Census of Governments, if it was available. These data were adjusted by a growth rate that was determined by the growth of units that were similar (in size, geography, and type of government) to the nonrespondent. If there was no recent historical data available, the imputations were based on the data from a randomly selected donor that was similar to the nonrespondent. This donor's data were adjusted by dividing each data item by the population (or enrollment) of the donor and multiplying the result by the nonrespondent's population (or enrollment). For special districts, if prior year data are available, the data are brought forward with a national level growth rate applied. Otherwise, the data are imputed to be zero. In cases where good secondary data sources exist, the data from those sources were used.

Estimates of Sampling Error: For intercensal surveys, estimated coefficients of variation for all variables are given in tabulations on the Website. For U.S. and

U.S. Census Bureau, Statistical Abstract of the United States: 2010

state-and-local government-level estimates of total full-time equivalents and total payroll, most relative standard errors are generally less than one percent, but vary considerably for detailed characteristics.

Other (nonsampling) Errors: Although every effort is made in all phases of collection, processing, and tabulation to minimize errors, the sample data are subject to nonsampling errors such as inability to obtain data for every variable from all units in the sample, inaccuracies in classification, response errors, misinterpretation of questions, mistakes in keying and coding, and coverage errors. These same errors may be evident in census collections and may affect the Census of Governments data used to adjust the sample during the estimation phase and used in the imputation process.

Sources of Additional Material:
<http://www.census.gov/govs/www/apes/index.html> and
<http://www.census.gov/govs/www/apestl06.html>.

Annual Survey of Government Finances

Universe, Frequency, and Types of Data: The United States Census Bureau conducts an Annual Survey of Government Finances, as authorized by law under Title 13, United States Code, Section 182. Alternatively, every 5 years, in years ending in a '2' or '7', a Census of Governments, including a Finance portion, is conducted under Title 13, Section 161. The survey coverage includes all state and local governments in the United States. For both the Census and annual survey, the finance detail data is equivalent, encompassing the entire range of government finance activities—revenue, expenditure, debt, and assets.

Type of Data Collection Operations: The data collection phase for the annual survey made use of three methods to obtain data: mail canvass, internet collection, and central collection from State sources. In 28 states, all or part of the general purpose finance data for local governments was obtained from cooperative arrangements between the Census Bureau and a state government

agency. These usually involved a data collection effort carried out to meet the needs of both agencies—the state agency for purposes of audit, oversight, or information, and the Census Bureau for statistical purposes. Data for the balance of local governments in this annual survey were obtained via mail questionnaires sent directly to county, municipal, township, special district, and school district governments. School district data were collected via cooperative arrangements with state education agencies. Data for state governments were compiled by analysts of the Census Bureau, usually with the cooperation and assistance of state officials. The data were compiled from state government audits, budgets, and other financial reports, either in printed or electronic format. The compilation generally involved recasting the state financial records into the classification categories used for reporting by the Census Bureau.

Data Collection and Imputation Procedures: Survey is conducted by mail with mail follow-ups of nonrespondents. Imputation for all nonresponse items is based on previous year reports or, for new governments, on data from similar donors.

Estimates of Sampling Error: The local government statistics in the intercensal survey years are developed from a sample survey. Therefore, the local totals, as well as aggregates of state and local government data, are considered estimated amounts subject to sampling error. State government finance data are not subject to sampling. Consequently, State-local aggregates shown here have a relative standard error less than or equal to the local government estimates they include. Estimates of major United States totals for local governments are subject to a computed sampling variability of less than one-half of 1 percent. State and local government totals are generally subject to sampling variability of less than 3 percent.

Other (nonsampling) Errors: The estimates are also subject to inaccuracies in classification, response, and processing. Efforts were made at all phases of collection, processing, and tabulation to minimize errors. However, the data are still subject to errors from imputations for missing data, errors from misreported data, errors from miscoding, and difficulties in identifying every unit that should be included in the report. Every effort was made to keep such errors to a minimum through care in examining, editing, and tabulating the data reported by government officials.

Sources of Additional Material:
<http://www.census.gov/govs/index.html> and <http://www.census.gov/govs/state/index.html>.

Annual Survey of Manufactures (ASM)

Universe, Frequency, and Types of Data: The Annual Survey of Manufactures is conducted annually, except for years ending in '2' and '7' for all manufacturing establishments having one or more paid employees. The purpose of the ASM is to provide key intercensal measures of manufacturing activity, products, and location for the public and private sectors. The ASM provides statistics on employment, payroll, worker hours, payroll supplements, cost of materials, value added by manufacturing, capital expenditures, inventories, and energy consumption. It also provides estimates of value of shipments for 1,800 classes of manufactured products.

Type of Data Collection Operation: The ASM includes approximately 50,000 establishments selected from the census universe of 346,000 manufacturing establishments. Approximately 24,000 large establishments are selected with certainty, and the remaining 26,000 other establishments are selected with probability proportional to a composite measure of establishment size. The survey is updated from two sources: Internal Revenue Service administrative records are used to include new single-unit manufacturers and the Company Organization Survey identifies new establishments of multiunit forms.

Data Collection and Imputation Procedures: Survey is conducted by mail with phone and mail follow-ups of nonrespondents. Imputation (for all nonresponse items) is based on previous year reports, or for new establishments in survey, on industry averages.

Estimates of Sampling Error: Estimated relative standard errors for number of employees, new expenditures, and for value added totals are given in annual publications. For U.S. level industry statistics, most estimated relative standard errors are 2 percent or less, but vary considerably for detailed characteristics.

Other (nonsampling) Errors: The unit response rate is about 85 percent. Nonsampling errors include those due to collection, reporting, and transcription errors, many of which are corrected through computer and clerical checks.

Sources of Additional Material: U.S. Census Bureau, *Annual Survey of Manufactures*, and Technical Paper 24.

Census of Population

Universe, Frequency, and Types of Data: Complete count of U.S. population conducted every 10 years since 1790. Data obtained on number and characteristics of people in the U.S.

Type of Data Collection Operation: In the 1990, and 2000 censuses the 100 percent items included: age, date of birth, sex, race, Hispanic origin, and relationship to householder. In 1980, approximately 19 percent of the housing units were included in the sample; in 1990 and 2000, approximately 17 percent.

Data Collection and Imputation Procedures: In 1980, 1990, and 2000, mail questionnaires were used extensively with personal interviews in the remainder. Extensive telephone and personal follow-up for nonrespondents was done in the censuses. Imputations were made for missing characteristics.

Estimates of Sampling Error: Sampling errors for data are estimated for all items collected by sample and vary by characteristic and geographic area. The coefficients of variation (CVs) for national and state estimates are generally very small.

Other (nonsampling) Errors: Since 1950, evaluation programs have been conducted to provide information on the magnitude of some sources of nonsampling errors such as response bias and undercoverage in each census. Results from the evaluation program for the 1990 census indicated that the estimated net undercoverage amounted to about 1.5 percent of the total resident population. For Census 2000, the evaluation program indicated a net overcount of 0.5 percent of the resident population.

Sources of Additional Material:
U.S. Census Bureau, *The Coverage of Population in the 1980 Census*, PHC80-E4; *Content Reinterview Study: Accuracy of Data for Selected Population and Housing Characteristics as Measured by Reinterview*, PHC80-E2; *1980 Census of Population*, Vol. 1, (PC80-1), Appendixes B, C, and D. *Content Reinterview Survey: Accuracy of Data for Selected Population and Housing Characteristics as Measured by Reinterview*, 1990, CPH-E-1; *Effectiveness of Quality Assurance*, CPH-E-2; *Programs to Improve Coverage in the 1990 Census*, 1990, CPH-E-3. For Census 2000 evaluations, see <http://www.census.gov/pred/www>.

County Business Patterns

Universe, Frequency, and Types of Data:
County Business Patterns is an annual tabulation of basic data items extracted from the Business Register, a file of all known single- and multilocation employer companies maintained and updated by the U.S. Census Bureau. Data include number of establishments, number of employees, first quarter and annual payrolls, and number of establishments by employment size class. Data are excluded for self-employed individuals, private households, railroad employees, agricultural production workers, and most government employees.

Type of Data Collection Operation: The annual Company Organization Survey provides individual establishment data for multilocation companies. Data for single establishment companies are obtained from various Census Bureau programs, such as the Annual Survey of Manufactures and Current Business Surveys, as well as from administrative records of the Internal Revenue Service, the Social Security Administration, and the Bureau of Labor Statistics.

Estimates of Sampling Error: Not applicable.

Other (nonsampling) Errors: The data are subject to nonsampling errors, such as inability to identify all cases in the universe; definition and classification difficulties; differences in interpretation of questions; errors in recording or coding the data obtained; and estimation of employers who reported too late to be included in the tabulations and for records with missing or misreported data.

Sources of Additional Materials:
U.S. Census Bureau, County Business Patterns <http://www.census.gov/econ/cbp/view/cbpview.html>.

Current Population Survey (CPS)

Universe, Frequency, and Types of Data:
Nationwide monthly sample designed primarily to produce national and state estimates of labor force characteristics of the civilian noninstitutionalized population 16 years of age and older.

Type of Data Collection Operation: Multistage probability sample that currently includes 72,000 households from 824 sample areas. Sample size increased in some states to improve data reliability for those areas on an annual average basis. A continual sample rotation system is used. Households are in sample 4 months, out for 8 months, and in for 4 more. Month-to-month overlap is 75 percent; year-to-year overlap is 50 percent.

Data Collection and Imputation Procedures: For first and fifth months that a household is in sample, personal interviews; other months, approximately 85 percent of the data collected by phone. Imputation is done for item nonresponse. Adjustment for total nonresponse is done by a predefined cluster of units, by state, metropolitan status and CBSA size; for item nonresponse imputation varies by subject matter.

Estimates of Sampling Error: The national total estimates of the civilian labor force and of employment have monthly CVs of about .2 percent and annual average CVs of about .1 percent. Unemployment is a much smaller characteristic and consequently has substantially larger CVs than the civilian labor force or employment. The national unemployment rate, the most important CPS statistic, has a monthly CV of about 2 percent and an annual average CV of about 1 percent.

Assuming a 6 percent unemployment rate, states have annual average CVs of about 8 percent. The estimated CVs for family income and poverty rate for all persons in 2005 are 0.4 percent and 1.2 percent, respectively. CVs for subnational areas, such as states, tend to be larger and vary by area.

Other (nonsampling) Errors: Estimates of response bias on unemployment are available. Estimates of unemployment rate from reinterviews range from –2.4 percent to 1.0 percent of the basic CPS unemployment rate (over a 30-month span from January 2004 through June 2006). Eligible CPS households are approximately 82 percent of the assigned households, with a corresponding response rate of 92 percent.

Sources of Additional Material: U.S. Census Bureau and Bureau of Labor Statistics, Current Population Survey: Design and Methodology, (Technical Paper 66), available on the Internet <http://www.census.gov/prod/2006pubs/tp-66.pdf> and the Bureau of Labor Statistics, <http://www.bls.gov/cps/> and the *BLS Handbook of Methods*, Chapter 1, available at <http://www.bls.gov/opub/hom/homch1a.htm>.

Foreign Trade—Export Statistics

Universe, Frequency, and Types of Data: As of October 1, 2008, the Shipper's Export Declaration (SED) Form 7525-V became obsolete. Electronic Export Information (EEI) replaced the SED and all export information must be filed through the Automated Export System (AES) by either a United States Principal Party in Interest (USPPI) or an Authorized U.S. agent. The EEI filings are processed each month to obtain data on the movement of U.S. merchandise exports to foreign countries. Data obtained include value, quantity, and shipping weight of exports by commodity, country of destination, district of exportation, and mode of transportation.

Type of Data Collection Operation: USPPIs or Authorized U.S. Agents are required to submit EEI for exportation of merchandise valued over $2,500. Data for shipments valued under $2,501 are estimated, based on established percentages of individual country totals.

Data Collection and Imputation Procedures: The EEI filings are received on a daily basis from ports throughout the country and subjected to a monthly processing cycle. They are fully processed to the extent they reflect items valued over $2,500. Estimates for shipments valued at $2,500 or less are made, based on established percentages of individual country totals.

Estimates of Sampling Error: Not applicable.

Other (nonsampling) Errors: The goods data are a complete enumeration of EEI reported in AES and are not subject to sampling errors; but they are subject to several types of nonsampling errors. Quality assurance procedures are performed at every stage of collection, processing and tabulation; however the data are still subject to several types of nonsampling errors. The most significant of these include reporting errors, undocumented shipments, timeliness, data capture errors, and errors in the estimation of low-valued transactions. The number of data errors and the overall data quality are expected to improve due to the elimination of paper SEDs and the mandatory filing of export data through the AES. Additional information on errors affecting export data can be found at <http://www.census.gov/foreign-trade/Press-Release/currentpressrelease/explain.pdf>.

Sources of Additional Material: Effect of Mandatory Electronic Filing on Export data, <http://www.census.gov/foreign-trade/aip/mandatoryelectronicfiling.html>. U.S. Census Bureau, FT 900 U.S. International Trade in Goods and Services, FT 925 (discounted after 1996), U.S. Merchandise Trade, FT 895 U.S. Trade with Puerto Rico and U.S. Possessions, FT 920 U.S. Merchandise trade: selected highlights, and Information Section on Goods and Services at <http://www.census.gov/ft900>.

Foreign Trade—Import Statistics

Universe, Frequency, and Types of Data: The import entry documents collected by U.S. Customs and Border Protection are processed each month to obtain data on the movement of merchandise imported into the United States. Data obtained include value, quantity, and shipping weight by commodity, country of origin, district of entry, and mode of transportation.

Type of Data Collection Operation: Import entry documents, either paper or electronic, are required to be filed for the importation of goods into the United States valued over $2,000 or for articles which must be reported on formal entries. U.S. Bureau of Customs and Border Protection officials collect and transmit statistical copies of the documents to the Census Bureau on a flow basis for data compilation. Estimates for shipments valued under $2,001 and not reported on formal entries are based on estimated established percentages for individual country totals.

Data Collection and Imputation Procedures: Statistical copies of import entry documents, received on a daily basis from ports of entry throughout the country, are subjected to a monthly processing cycle. They are fully processed to the extent they reflect items valued at $2,001 and over or items which must be reported on formal entries.

Estimates of Sampling Error: Not applicable.

Other (nonsampling) Errors: The goods data are a complete enumeration of documents collected by the U.S. Customs and Border Protection and are not subject to sampling errors; but they are subject to several types of nonsampling errors. Quality assurance procedures are performed at every stage of collection, processing, and tabulation; however the data are still subject to several types of nonsampling errors. Quality assurance procedures are performed at every stage of collection, processing, and tabulation; however the data are still subject to several types of nonsampling errors. The most significant of these include reporting errors, undocumented shipments, timeliness, data capture errors, and errors in the estimation of low-valued transactions. Additional information on errors affecting import data can be found at <http://www.census.gov /foreign-trade/Press-Release /currentpressrelease/explain.pdf>.

Sources of Additional Material: U.S. Census Bureau, FT 900 U.S. International Trade in Goods and Services, FT 925 (discounted after 1996), U.S. Merchandise Trade, FT 895 U.S. Trade with Puerto Rico and U.S. Possessions, FT920 U.S. Merchandise Trade: selected highlights, and Information Section on Goods and Services at <http://www .census.gov/ft900>.

Monthly Retail Trade and Food Service Survey

Universe, Frequency, and Types of Data: Provides monthly estimates of retail and food service sales by kind of business and end of month inventories of retail stores.

Type of Data Collection Operation: Probability sample of all firms from a list frame. The list frame is the Bureau's Business Register updated quarterly for recent birth Employer Identification (EI) Numbers issued by the Internal Revenue Service and assigned a kind of business code by the Social Security Administration. The largest firms are included monthly; a sample of others is included every month also.

Data Collection and Imputation Procedures: Data are collected by mail questionnaire with telephone follow-ups and fax reminders for nonrespondents. Imputation is made for each nonresponse item and each item failing edit checks.

Estimates of Sampling Error: For the 2006 monthly surveys, CVs are about 0.4 percent for estimated total retail sales and 0.7 percent for estimated total retail inventories. Sampling errors are shown in monthly publications.

Other (nonsampling) Errors: Imputation rates are about 22 percent for monthly retail and food service sales, and 29 percent for monthly retail inventories.

Sources of Additional Material: U.S. Census Bureau, Current Business Reports, Annual Revision of Monthly Retail and Food Services: Sales and Inventories.

Monthly Survey of Construction

Universe, Frequency, and Types of Data: Survey conducted monthly of newly constructed housing units (excluding mobile homes). Data are collected on the start, completion, and sale of housing. (Annual figures are aggregates of monthly estimates.)

Type of Data Collection Operation: A multistage probability sample of approximately 900 of the 20,000 permit-issuing jurisdictions in the U.S. was selected. Each month in each of these permit offices, field representatives list and select a sample of permits for which to collect data. To obtain data in areas where building permits are not required, a multistage probability sample of 80 land areas (census tracts or subsections of census tracts) was selected. All roads in these areas are canvassed and data are collected on all new residential construction found. Sampled buildings are followed up until they are completed (and sold, if for sale).

Data Collection and Imputation Procedures: Data are obtained by telephone inquiry and/or field visit. Nonresponse/undercoverage adjustment factors are used to account for late reported data.

Estimates of Sampling Error: Estimated CV of 5 percent to 6 percent for estimates of national totals of units started, but may be higher than 20 percent for estimated totals of more detailed characteristics, such as housing units in multiunit structures.

Other (nonsampling) Errors: Response rate is over 90 percent for most items. Nonsampling errors are attributed to definitional problems, differences in interpretation of questions, incorrect reporting, inability to obtain information about all cases in the sample, and processing errors.

Sources of Additional Material: All data are available on the Internet at <http://www.census.gov/starts>, <http://www.census.gov/newhomesales>, or <http://www.census.gov/const/www/newsresconstindex.html>. Further documentation of the survey is also available at those Web sites.

Nonemployer Statistics

Universe, Frequency, and Types of Data: Nonemployer statistics are an annual tabulation of economic data by industry for active businesses without paid employees that are subject to federal income tax. Data showing the number of firms and receipts by industry are available for the U.S., states, counties, and metropolitan areas. Most types of businesses covered by the Census Bureau's economic statistics programs are included in the nonemployer statistics. Tax-exempt and agricultural-production businesses are excluded from nonemployer statistics.

Type of Data Collection Operation: The universe of nonemployer firms is created annually as a byproduct of the Census Bureau's Business Register processing for employer establishments. If a business is active but without paid employees, then it becomes part of the potential nonemployer universe. Industry classification and receipts are available for each potential nonemployer business. These data are obtained primarily from the annual business income tax returns of the Internal Revenue Service (IRS). The potential nonemployer universe undergoes a series of complex processing, editing, and analytical review procedures at the Census Bureau to distinguish nonemployers from employers, and to correct and complete data items used in creating the data tables.

Estimates of Sampling Error: Not applicable.

Other (nonsampling) Errors: The data are subject to nonsampling errors, such as industry misclassification as well as errors of response, keying, nonreporting, and coverage.

Sources of Additional Material: U.S. Census Bureau, Nonemployer Statistics.

Service Annual Survey

Universe, Frequency, and Types of Data: The U.S. Census Bureau conducts the Service Annual Survey to provide nationwide estimates of revenues and expenses for selected service industries. Estimates are summarized by industry classification based on the 2002 North

American Industry Classification System (NAICS). Selected service industries covered by the Service Annual Survey include all or part of the following NAICS sectors: Transportation and Warehousing (NAICS 48-49); Information (NAICS 51); Finance and Insurance (NAICS 52); Real Estate and Rental and Leasing (NAICS 53); Professional, Scientific, and Technical Services (NAICS 54); Administrative and Support and Waste Management and Remediation Services (NAICS 56); Health Care and Social Assistance (NAICS 62); Arts, Entertainment, and Recreation (NAICS 71); and Other Services, except Public Administration (NAICS 81). Data collected include total revenue, total expenses, detailed expenses, revenue from e-commerce transactions; and for selected industries, revenue from detailed service products, revenue from exported services, and inventories. For industries with a significant nonprofit component, separate estimates are developed for taxable firms and firms and organizations exempt from federal income taxes. Questionnaires are mailed in January and request annual data for the prior year. Estimates are published approximately 12 months after the initial survey mailing.

Type of Data Collection Operation:
The Service Annual Survey estimates are developed from a probability sample of employer firms and administrative records for nonemployers. Service Annual Survey questionnaires are mailed to a probability sample that is periodically reselected from a universe of firms located in the United States and having paid employees. The sample includes firms of all sizes and covers both taxable firms and firms exempt from federal income taxes. Updates to the sample are made on a quarterly basis to account for new businesses. Firms without paid employees, or nonemployers, are included in the estimates through imputation and/or administrative records data provided by other federal agencies. Links to additional information about confidentiality protection, sampling error, nonsampling error, sample design, definitions, and copies of the questionnaires may be found on the Internet at <http://www.census.gov/services/index.html>.

Estimates of Sampling Error: Coefficients of variation (CVs) for the 2007 Service Annual Survey estimates range from 0.7 percent to 2.3 percent for total revenue estimates computed at the NAICS sector (2-digit NAICS code) level. The full 2007 Service Annual Survey results, including coefficients of variations (CVs), can be found at <http://www.census.gov/services/index.html>. Links to additional information regarding sampling error may be found at <http://www.census.gov/services/sas/cv.html>.

Other (Nonsampling) Errors: Data are imputed for unit nonresponse, item nonresponse, and for reported data that fails edits. The percent of imputed data for total revenue for the 2007 Service Annual Survey estimates range from 6.4 percent to 14.2 percent for total revenue estimates computed at the NAICS sector (2-digit NAICS code) level.

Sources of Additional Material:
U.S. Census Bureau, Current Business Reports, *Service Annual Survey* at <http://www.census.gov/services/index.html>.

U.S. DEPARTMENT OF EDUCATION
National Center for Education Statistics

Integrated Postsecondary Education Data Survey (IPEDS), Completions

Universe, Frequency, and Types of Data: Annual survey of all Title IV (federal financial aid) eligible postsecondary institutions to obtain data on earned degrees and other formal awards, conferred by field of study, level of degree, sex, and by racial/ethnic characteristics (every other year prior to 1989, then annually).

Type of Data Collection Operation: Complete census.

Data Collection and Imputation Procedures: Data are collected through a Web-based survey in the fall of every year. Missing data are imputed by using data of similar institutions.

Estimates of Sampling Error: Not applicable.

Other (nonsampling) Errors: For 2005–06, the response rate for degree-granting institutions was 100.0 percent.

916   Appendix III

Sources of Additional Material:
U.S. Department of Education, National
Center for Education Statistics, *Post-
secondary Institutions in the United
States: Fall 2007 and Degrees and
Other Awards Conferred: 2006–07
and 12-month enrollment, 2006–07.*
See <http://www.nces.ed.gov/ipeds/>.

National Household Education Surveys (NHES) Program

Universe, Frequency, and Types of Data:
The National Household Education
Surveys Program is a system of telephone surveys of the noninstitutionalized civilian population of the United
States. Surveys in NHES have varying
universes of interest depending on the
particular survey. Specific topics covered by each survey are at the NHES
Web site <http://nces.ed.gov/nhes>.
A list of the surveys fielded as part of
NHES, each universe, and the years they
were fielded is provided below: 1) Adult
Education—Interviews were conducted
with a representative sample of civilian,
noninstitutionalized persons aged 16
years and older who were not enrolled
in grade 12 or below (1991, 1995,
1999, 2001, 2003, 2005); 2) After-
School Programs and Activities—
Interviews were conducted with parents
of a representative sample of students
in grades K through 8 (1999, 2001,
2005); 3) Civic Involvement—Interviews
were conducted with representative
samples of parents, youth, and adults
(1996, 1999); 4) Early Childhood
Program Participation—Interviews were
conducted with parents of a representative sample of children from birth
through grade 3, with the specific age
groups varying by survey year (1991,
1995, 1999, 2001, 2005); 5) Household
and Library Use—Interviews were conducted with a representative sample of
U.S. households (1996); 6) Parent and
Family Involvement in Education—
Interviews were conducted with parents
of a representative sample of children
aged 3 years through grade 12 or in
grades K through 12 depending on the
survey year (1996, 1999, 2003, and
2007 forthcoming); 7) School Readiness
—Interviews were conducted with parents of a representative sample of 3-to-
7-year-old children (1993 and 1999) and
of 3-to-5-year-old children, not yet in

kindergarten (2007 forthcoming);
8) School Safety and Discipline—
Interviews were conducted with a
representative sample of students in
grades 6 through 12, their parents, and
the parents of a representative sample
of students in grades 3 through 12
(1993).

Type of Data Collection Operation: NHES
uses telephone interviews to collect
data.

*Data Collection and Imputation Proce-
dures:* Telephone numbers are selected
using random digit dialing (RDD) techniques. Approximately 45,000 to
64,000 households are contacted in
order to identify persons eligible for the
surveys. Data are collected using
computer-assisted telephone interviewing (CATI) procedures. Missing data are
imputed using hot-deck imputation procedures.

Estimates of Sampling Error: Unweighted
sample sizes range between 2,250 and
55,708. The average root design effects
of the surveys in NHES range from 1.1
to 1.5, except for the Adult Education
survey of 1991. In 1991, average root
design effects for the Adult Education
survey ranged from 2.3 to 4.5.

Other (nonsampling) Errors: Because of
unit nonresponse and because the
samples are drawn from households
with telephone instead of all households, nonresponse and/or coverage
bias may exist for some estimates.
However, both sources of potential bias
are adjusted for in the weighting process. Analyses of both potential sources
of bias in the NHES collections have
been studied and no significant bias has
been detected.

Sources of Additional Material: Please see
the NHES Web site at <http://nces.ed
.gov/nhes>.

Schools and Staffing Survey (SASS)

Universe, Frequency and Types of Data:
NCES designed the SASS survey system
to emphasize teacher demand and
shortage, teacher and administrator
characteristics, school programs, and
general conditions in schools. SASS also
collects data on many other topics,
including principals' and teachers' per-
ceptions of school climate and problems

U.S. Census Bureau, Statistical Abstract of the United States: 2010

in their schools; teacher compensation; district hiring practices and basic characteristics of the student population. The SASS has had four core components: the School Questionnaire, the Teacher Questionnaire, the Principal Questionnaire, and the School District Questionnaire. For the 2003–04 SASS, a sample of public charter schools is included in the sample as part of the public school questionnaire. Since 1987–88, the SASS is the largest, most extensive survey of K through 12 school districts, schools, teachers, and administrators in the U.S. Surveys have been conducted every 3 to 4 years depending on budgetary constraints. The SASS includes data from public, private, and Bureau of Indian Education (BIE) school sectors. Therefore, the SASS provides a multitude of opportunities for analysis and reporting on elementary and secondary educational issues

Type of Data Collection Operation: The U.S. Census Bureau performs the data collection and begins by sending advance letters to the sampled Local Education Agencies (LEAs) and schools in August and September of collection years. Beginning in October, questionnaires are delivered by U.S. Census Bureau field representatives. The sampling frame for the public school sample is the most recent Common Core of Data (CCD) school file. CCD is a universe file that includes all elementary and secondary schools in the United States. Schools operated by the Department of Defense or those that offered only kindergarten or pre-kindergarten or adult education were excluded from the SASS sample. The list frame used for the private school sample is the most recent Private School Universe Survey (PSS) list, updated with association lists. An area frame supplement is based on the canvassing of private schools within specific geographical areas. A separate universe of schools funded by the Bureau of Indian Education (BIE) is drawn from the Program Education Directory maintained by the BIE. To avoid duplicates in the BIE files, BIE schools in the CCD school file are treated as public schools.

Estimates of Sampling Error: Sample errors can be calculated using replicate weights and Balanced Repeated Replication complex survey design methodology. Errors depend on cell sizes and range from less than 1 percent to over 5 percent (for reasonable cell sizes).

Other (nonsampling) Errors: Because of unit nonresponse, bias may exist in some sample cells. However, bias has been adjusted for in the weighting process. Analysis of bias has been studied and no significant bias has been detected.

Sources of Additional Material: Please see the SASS Web site at <http://nces.ed .gov/surveys/sass/>.

U.S. DEPARTMENT OF JUSTICE, FEDERAL BUREAU OF INVESTIGATION

Uniform Crime Reporting (UCR) Program

Universe, Frequency, and Types of Data: Monthly reports on the number of criminal offenses that become known to law enforcement agencies. Data are also collected on crimes cleared by arrest or exceptional means; age, sex, and race of arrestees and for victims and offenders for homicides, number of law enforcement employees, on fatal and nonfatal assaults against law enforcement officers, and on hate crimes reported.

Type of Data Collection Operation: Crime statistics are based on reports of crime data submitted either directly to the FBI by contributing law enforcement agencies or through cooperating state UCR Programs.

Data Collection and Imputation Procedures: States with UCR programs collect data directly from individual law enforcement agencies and forward reports, prepared in accordance with UCR standards, to the FBI. Accuracy and consistency edits are performed by the FBI.

Estimates of Sampling Error: Not applicable.

Other (nonsampling) Errors: During 2007, law enforcement agencies active in the UCR Program represented 94.6 percent of the total population. The coverage amounted to 95.7 percent of the United States population in Metropolitan

Statistical Areas, 88.0 percent of the population in cities outside metropolitan areas, and 90.0 percent in nonmetropolitan counties.

Sources of Additional Material:
U.S. Department of Justice, Federal Bureau of Investigation, *Crime in the United States, annual, Hate Crime Statistics,* annual, *Law Enforcement Officers Killed and Assaulted,* annual, <http://www.fbi.gov/ucr/ucr.htm>.

U.S. INTERNAL REVENUE SERVICE

Corporation Income Tax Returns

Universe, Frequency, and Types of Data:
Annual study of unaudited corporation income tax returns, Forms 1120, 1120-A, 1120-F, 1120-L, 1120-PC, 1120-REIT, 1120-RIC, and 1120S, filed by corporations or businesses legally defined as corporations. Data provided on various financial characteristics by industry and size of total assets, and business receipts.

Type of Data Collection Operation: Stratified probability sample of approximately 112,000 returns for Tax Year 2006, allocated to sample classes which are based on type of return, size of total assets, size of net income or deficit, and selected business activity. Sampling rates for sample classes varied from .25 percent to 100 percent.

Data Collection and Imputation Procedures: Computer selection of sample of tax return records. Data adjusted during editing for incorrect, missing, or inconsistent entries to ensure consistency with other entries on return and to comply with statistical definitions.

Estimates of Sampling Error: Estimated CVs for Tax Year 2006: Coefficients of variation are published in the 2006 Statistics of Income Corporation Income Tax Returns, Table 1, by industry group. Sampling rates are contained in Section 3 of the same report.

Other (nonsampling) Errors: Nonsampling errors include coverage errors, processing errors, and response errors.

Sources of Additional Material:
U.S. Internal Revenue Service, *Statistics of Income, Corporation Income Tax Returns,* annual.

Individual Income Tax Returns

Universe, Frequency, and Types of Data:
Annual study of unaudited individual income tax returns, Forms 1040, 1040A, and 1040EZ, filed by U.S. citizens and residents. Data provided on various financial characteristics by size of adjusted gross income, marital status, and by taxable and nontaxable returns. Data by state, based on the population of returns filed, also include returns from 1040NR, filed by nonresident aliens plus certain self employment tax returns.

Type of Data Collection Operation: Stratified probability sample of 321,006 returns for tax year 2006. The sample is classified into sample strata based on the larger of total income or total loss amounts, the size of business plus farm receipts, and other criteria such as the potential usefulness of the return for tax policy modeling. Sampling rates for sample strata varied from 0.01 percent to 100 percent.

Data Collection and Imputation Procedures: Computer selection of sample of tax return records. Data adjusted during editing for incorrect, missing, or inconsistent entries to ensure consistency with other entries on return.

Estimates of Sampling Error: Estimated CVs for tax year 2006: Adjusted gross income less deficit 0.09 percent; salaries and wages 0.16 percent; and tax exempt interest received 1.17 percent. (State data not subject to sampling error.)

Other (nonsampling) Errors: Processing errors and errors arising from the use of tolerance checks for the data.

Sources of Additional Material:
U.S. Internal Revenue Service, *Statistics of Income, Individual Income Tax Returns,* annual, (Publication 1304).

Partnership Income Tax Returns

Universe, Frequency, and Types of Data:
Annual study of preaudited income tax returns of partnerships related to financial and tax-related activity during calendar years 2003 to 2006 and reported on

Forms 1065 and 1065B to the IRS in calendar year 2007. Data are provided by industry, based on the NAICS industry coding used by IRS.

Type of Data Collection Operation: Stratified probability sample of approximately 45,000 partnership returns from a population of 3.2 million filed during calendar year 2007. The sample is classified based on combinations of industry code, gross receipts, net income or loss, and total assets. Sampling rates vary from 0.07 percent to 100 percent.

Data Collection and Imputation Procedures: The sample of tax return records are selected via computer after data are transcribed by IRS and placed on an administrative file. Data are manually adjusted during editing for incorrect, missing, or inconsistent entries to ensure consistency with other entries on return. Data not available due to regulations are handled with weighting adjustments.

Estimates of Sampling Error: Some of the estimated Coefficients of Variation (the estimated standard error of the total divided by the estimated total) for tax year 2006: For number of partnerships, 0.36 percent; business receipts, 0.18 percent; net income, 0.73 percent; and ordinary business income; 0.53 percent.

Other (nonsampling) Errors: The potential exists for coverage error due to unavailable returns; processing errors; and taxpayer reporting errors, since data are preaudit.

Sources of Additional Material: U.S. Internal Revenue Service, *Statistics of Income, Partnership Returns and Statistics of Income Bulletin*, Vol. 27, No. 2 (Fall 2007).

Sole Proprietorship Income Tax Returns

Universe, Frequency, and Types of Data: Annual study of unaudited income tax returns of nonfarm sole proprietorships, Form 1040 with business schedules. Data provided on various financial characteristics by industry.

Type of Data Collection Operation: Stratified probability sample of 88,619 sole proprietorships for tax year 2006. The sample is classified based on presence or absence of certain business schedules; the larger of total income or loss; size of business plus farm receipts, and other criteria such as the potential usefulness of the return for tax policy modeling. Sampling rates vary from 0.1 percent to 100 percent.

Data Collection and Imputation Procedures: Computer selection of sample of tax return records. Data adjusted during editing for incorrect, missing, or inconsistent entries to ensure consistency with other entries on return.

Estimates of Sampling Error: Estimated CVs for tax year 2006 are available. For sole proprietorships, total business receipts, 0.54 percent; depreciation 1.25 percent.

Other (nonsampling) Errors: Processing errors and errors arising from the use of tolerance checks for the data.

Sources of Additional Material: U.S. Internal Revenue Service, *Statistics of Income, Sole Proprietorship Returns* (for years 1980 through 1983) and *Statistics of Income Bulletin*, Vol. 28, No. 2 (Fall 2008, as well as bulletins for earlier years).

U.S. NATIONAL CENTER FOR HEALTH STATISTICS (NCHS)

National Health Interview Survey (NHIS)

Universe, Frequency, and Types of Data: Continuous data collection covering the civilian noninstitutional population to obtain information on demographic characteristics, conditions, injuries, impairments, use of health services, health behaviors, and other health topics.

Type of Data Collection Operation: Multistage probability sample of 49,000 households (in 198 PSUs) from 1985 to 1994; 36–40,000 households (358 design PSUs or 449 effective PSUs when divided by state boundaries) from 1995 to 2005; an estimated completed 35,000 households (428 effective PSUs) beginning in 2006.

Data Collection and Imputation Procedures: Some missing data items (e.g., race, ethnicity) are imputed using a hot deck imputation value. Sequential regression models are used to create

920   Appendix III

multiple imputation files for family income. Unit nonresponse is compensated for by an adjustment to the survey weights.

Estimates of Sampling Error: For 2006 medically attended injury episodes rates in the past 12 months by falling for: females 49.93 (4.44), and males 38.83 (4.59) per 1,000 population; for 2006 injury episodes rates during the past 12 months inside the home—34.89 (2.81) per 1,000 population.

Other (nonsampling) Errors: The response rate was 93.8 percent in 1996; in 2006, the total household response rate was 87.3 percent, with the final family response rate of 87.0 percent, and the final sample adult response rate of 70.8 percent. (Note: the NHIS questionnaire was redesigned in 1997, and a new sample design was instituted in 2006).

Sources of Additional Material: National Center for Health Statistics, Summary Health Statistics for the U.S. Population: National Health Interview Survey, 2006, Vital and Health Statistics, Series 10 #236; National Center for Health Statistics, Summary Health Statistics for U.S. Children: National Health Interview Survey, 2006, Vital and Health Statistics, Series 10 #234; National Center for Health Statistics, Summary Health Statistics for U.S. Adults: National Health Interview Survey, 2006, Vital and Health Statistics, Series 10 #235; U.S. National Center for Health Statistics, Design and Estimation for the National Health Interview Survey, 1995-2004, Vital and Health Statistics, Series 2 #130.

National Survey of Family Growth (NSFG)

Universe, Frequency, and Types of Data: Periodic survey of men and women 15–44 years of age in the household population of the United States. Interviews were conducted in 2002 in person by trained female interviewers. Interview topics covered include births and pregnancies, marriage, divorce, and cohabitation, sexual activity, contraceptive use, and medical care. For men, data on father involvement with children were collected. The most sensitive data—on sexual behavior related to HIV

and Sexually Transmitted Disease risk—were collected in a self-administered form in which the data are entered into a computer.

Type of Data Collection Operation: In the 2002 (Cycle 6) NSFG, the sample was a multistage area probability sample of men and women 15–44 years of age in the household population of the United States. Only one person 15–44 was selected from households with one or more persons 15–44. Data were collected and entered into laptop (notebook) computers. In the self-administered portion, the respondent entered his or her own answers into the computer. Sample included 12,571 interviews. The response rate was 79 percent. Hispanic and Black persons, as well as those 15–19 years of age, were sampled at higher rates than White adults. All percentages and other statistics shown for the NSFG are weighted to make national estimates. The weights adjust for the different rates of sampling for each group, and for nonresponse.

Data Collection and Imputation Procedures: When interviews are received, they are reviewed for consistency and quality, and analysis variables (recodes) are created. Missing data on these recodes were imputed using multiple regression techniques and checked again for consistency. Variables indicating whether a value has been imputed ("imputation flags") are included on the data file.

Estimates of Sampling Error: Sampling error codes are included on the data file so that users can estimate sampling errors for their own analyses. Sampling error estimates for nine illustrative analyses are shown on the NSFG Web site at <http://www.cdc.gov/nchs /nsfg.htm>. Sampling error estimates are also shown in most NCHS reports.

Other (nonsampling) Errors: In any survey, errors can occur because the respondent (the person being interviewed) does not recall the specific fact or event being asked about. The NSFG questionnaire in 2002 was programmed to check the consistency of many variables during the interview, so that the interviewer and respondent had a chance to correct any inconsistent information. Further checking occurred after the interview and during recoding and imputation. Typically, less than 1 percent of cases need imputation because of missing data.

Sources of Additional Material: The following references can be found at <http://www.cdc.gov/nchs/nsfg.htm>. "National Survey of Family Growth, Cycle 6: Sample Design, Weighting, and Variance Estimation." Vital and Health Statistics, Series 2, Number 142, July 2006. "Plan and Operation of Cycle 6 of the National Survey of Family Growth." Vital and Health Statistics, Series 1, No. 42. August 2005. "Sexual Behavior and Selected Health Measures: Men and Women 15–44 Years of Age, United States, 2002." *Advance Data from Vital and Health Statistics*, No. 362, Sept 15, 2005.

National Vital Statistics System

Universe, Frequency, and Types of Data: Annual data on births and deaths in the United States.

Type of Data Collection Operation: Mortality data based on complete file of death records, except 1972, based on 50 percent sample. Natality statistics 1951–1971, based on 50 percent sample of birth certificates, except a 20 percent to 50 percent sample in 1967, received by NCHS.

Data Collection and Imputation Procedures: Reports based on records from registration offices of all states, District of Columbia, New York City, Puerto Rico, Virgin Islands, Guam, American Samoa, and Northern Marianas.

Estimates of Sampling Error: For recent years, there is no sampling for these files; the files are based on 100 percent of events registered.

Other (nonsampling) Errors: It is believed that more than 99 percent of the births and deaths occurring in this country are registered.

Sources of Additional Material:
U.S. National Center for Health Statistics, *Vital Statistics of the United States*, Vol. I

and Vol. II, annual, and the *National Vital Statistics Reports.* See the NCHS Web site at <http://www.cdc.gov/nchs/nvss.htm>.

National Highway Traffic Safety Administration (NHTSA)

Fatality Analysis Reporting System (FARS)

Universe, Frequency, and Types of Data: FARS is a census of all fatal motor vehicle traffic crashes that occur throughout the United States including the District of Columbia and Puerto Rico on roadways customarily open to the public. The crash must be reported to the state/jurisdiction and at least one directly related fatality must occur within thirty days of the crash.

Type of Data Collection Operation: One or more analysts, in each state, extract data from the official documents and enter the data into a standardized electronic database.

Data Collection and Imputation Procedures: Detailed data describing the characteristics of the fatal crash, the vehicles and persons involved are obtained from police crash reports, driver and vehicle registration records, autopsy reports, highway department, etc. Computerized edit checks monitor the accuracy and completeness of the data. The FARS incorporates a sophisticated mathematical multiple imputation procedure to develop a probability distribution of missing blood alcohol concentration (BAC) levels in the database for drivers, pedestrians, and cyclists.

Estimates of Sampling Error: Since this is census data, there are no sampling errors.

Other (nonsampling) Errors: FARS represents a census of all police-reported crashes and captures all data reported at the state level. FARS data undergo a rigorous quality control process to prevent inaccurate reporting. However, these data are highly dependent on the accuracy of the police accident reports. Errors or omissions within police accident reports may not be detected.

Sources of Additional Material: The FARS Coding and Validation Manual, ANSI D16.1 Manual on Classification of Motor Vehicle Traffic Accidents (Sixth Edition).

Appendix IV
Weights and Measures

For assistance on metric usage, call or write:

Elizabeth J. Gentry
National Institute of Standards and Technology (NIST)
Weights and Measures Division
100 Bureau Drive – Mail Stop 2600
Gaithersburg, MD 20899-2600

Telephone: 301-975-3690 or 4004   FAX: 301-975-8091

E-mail: TheSI@nist.gov

Internet site: <http://ts.nist.gov/WeightsAndMeasures/Metric/mpo_home.cfm>

[Conversions provided in table are approximate]

Symbol	When you know conventional	Multiply by	To find metric	Symbol
in	inches	2.54	centimeters	cm
ft	feet	30.48	centimeters	cm
yd	yards	0.91	meters	m
mi	miles	1.61	kilometers	km
in^2	square inches	6.45	square centimeters	cm^2
ft^2	square feet	0.09	square meters	m^2
yd^2	square yards	0.84	square meters	m^2
mi^2	square miles	2.59	square kilometers	km^2
	acre	0.41	hectare	ha
oz	ounces [1]	28.35	grams	g
lb	pounds [1]	0.45	kilograms	kg
oz (troy)	ounces [2]	31.10	grams	g
	short tons (2,000 lb)	0.91	metric tons	t
	long tons (2,240 lb)	1.02	metric tons	t
fl oz	fluid ounces	29.57	milliliters	mL
c	cups	0.24	liters	L
pt	pints	0.47	liters	L
qt	quarts	0.95	liters	L
gal	gallons	3.78	liters	L
ft^3	cubic feet	0.03	cubic meters	m^3
yd^3	cubic yards	0.76	cubic meters	m^3
°F	degrees Fahrenheit (subtract 32)	0.55	degrees Celsius	°C

Symbol	When you know metric	Multiply by	To find conventional	Symbol
cm	centimeters	0.39	inches	in
cm	centimeters	0.03	feet	ft
m	meters	1.09	yards	yd
km	kilometers	0.62	miles	mi
cm^2	square centimeters	0.15	square inches	in^2
m^2	square meters	10.76	square feet	ft^2
m^2	square meters	1.20	square yards	yd^2
km^2	square kilometers	0.39	square miles	mi^2
ha	hectares	2.47	acre	
g	grams	0.04	ounces [1]	oz
kg	kilograms	2.21	pounds	lb
g	grams	0.04	ounces [2]	oz (troy)
t	metric tons	1.10	short tons (2,000 lb)	
t	metric tons	0.98	long tons (2,240 lb)	
mL	milliliters	0.03	fluid ounces	fl oz
L	liter	4.23	cups	c
L	liters	2.13	pints (liquid)	pt
L	liters	1.05	quarts (liquid)	qt
L	liters	0.26	gallons	gal
m^3	cubic meters	35.32	cubic feet	ft^3
m^3	cubic meters	1.32	cubic yards	yd^3
°C	degrees Celsius (after multiplying, add 32)	1.80	degrees Fahrenheit	°F

[1] For weighing ordinary commodities.   [2] For weighing precious metals, jewels, etc.

U.S. Census Bureau, Statistical Abstract of the United States: 2010

Tables Deleted From the
2009 Edition of the Statistical Abstract

U.S. Census Bureau, Statistical Abstract of the United States: 2010

926   Appendix V

Index

NOTE: Index citations refer to **table** numbers, not page numbers.

U.S. Census Bureau, Statistical Abstract of the United States: 2010

NOTE: Index citations refer to **table** numbers, not page numbers.

NOTE: Index citations refer to **table** numbers, not page numbers.

U.S. Census Bureau, Statistical Abstract of the United States: 2010

NOTE: Index citations refer to **table** numbers, not page numbers.

U.S. Census Bureau, Statistical Abstract of the United States: 2010

NOTE: Index citations refer to **table** numbers, not page numbers.

U.S. Census Bureau, Statistical Abstract of the United States: 2010

NOTE: Index citations refer to **table** numbers, not page numbers.

NOTE: Index citations refer to **table** numbers, not page numbers.

NOTE: Index citations refer to **table** numbers, not page numbers.

NOTE: Index citations refer to **table** numbers, not page numbers.

U.S. Census Bureau, Statistical Abstract of the United States: 2010

NOTE: Index citations refer to **table** numbers, not page numbers.

NOTE: Index citations refer to **table** numbers, not page numbers.

U.S. Census Bureau, Statistical Abstract of the United States: 2010

NOTE: Index citations refer to **table** numbers, not page numbers.

NOTE: Index citations refer to **table** numbers, not page numbers.

U.S. Census Bureau, Statistical Abstract of the United States: 2010

NOTE: Index citations refer to **table** numbers, not page numbers.

NOTE: Index citations refer to **table** numbers, not page numbers.

U.S. Census Bureau, Statistical Abstract of the United States: 2010

NOTE: Index citations refer to **table** numbers, not page numbers.

U.S. Census Bureau, Statistical Abstract of the United States: 2010

NOTE: Index citations refer to **table** numbers, not page numbers.

U.S. Census Bureau, Statistical Abstract of the United States: 2010

NOTE: Index citations refer to **table** numbers, not page numbers.

NOTE: Index citations refer to **table** numbers, not page numbers.

U.S. Census Bureau, Statistical Abstract of the United States: 2010

NOTE: Index citations refer to **table** numbers, not page numbers.

NOTE: Index citations refer to **table** numbers, not page numbers.

U.S. Census Bureau, Statistical Abstract of the United States: 2010

NOTE: Index citations refer to **table** numbers, not page numbers.

NOTE: Index citations refer to **table** numbers, not page numbers.

NOTE: Index citations refer to **table** numbers, not page numbers.

NOTE: Index citations refer to **table** numbers, not page numbers.

U.S. Census Bureau, Statistical Abstract of the United States: 2010

NOTE: Index citations refer to **table** numbers, not page numbers.

NOTE: Index citations refer to **table** numbers, not page numbers.

U.S. Census Bureau, Statistical Abstract of the United States: 2010

NOTE: Index citations refer to **table** numbers, not page numbers.

NOTE: Index citations refer to **table** numbers, not page numbers.

NOTE: Index citations refer to **table** numbers, not page numbers.

NOTE: Index citations refer to **table** numbers, not page numbers.

NOTE: Index citations refer to **table** numbers, not page numbers.

NOTE: Index citations refer to **table** numbers, not page numbers.

U.S. Census Bureau, Statistical Abstract of the United States: 2010

NOTE: Index citations refer to **table** numbers, not page numbers.

NOTE: Index citations refer to **table** numbers, not page numbers.

U.S. Census Bureau, Statistical Abstract of the United States: 2010

NOTE: Index citations refer to **table** numbers, not page numbers.

NOTE: Index citations refer to **table** numbers, not page numbers.

U.S. Census Bureau, Statistical Abstract of the United States: 2010

NOTE: Index citations refer to **table** numbers, not page numbers.

NOTE: Index citations refer to **table** numbers, not page numbers.

NOTE: Index citations refer to **table** numbers, not page numbers.

NOTE: Index citations refer to **table** numbers, not page numbers.

U.S. Census Bureau, Statistical Abstract of the United States: 2010

NOTE: Index citations refer to **table** numbers, not page numbers.

NOTE: Index citations refer to **table** numbers, not page numbers.

U.S. Census Bureau, Statistical Abstract of the United States: 2010

NOTE: Index citations refer to **table** numbers, not page numbers.

NOTE: Index citations refer to **table** numbers, not page numbers.

U.S. Census Bureau, Statistical Abstract of the United States: 2010

NOTE: Index citations refer to **table** numbers, not page numbers.

NOTE: Index citations refer to **table** numbers, not page numbers.

U.S. Census Bureau, Statistical Abstract of the United States: 2010

NOTE: Index citations refer to **table** numbers, not page numbers.

NOTE: Index citations refer to **table** numbers, not page numbers.

U.S. Census Bureau, Statistical Abstract of the United States: 2010

NOTE: Index citations refer to **table** numbers, not page numbers.

U.S. Census Bureau, Statistical Abstract of the United States: 2010

NOTE: Index citations refer to **table** numbers, not page numbers.

U.S. Census Bureau, Statistical Abstract of the United States: 2010

NOTE: Index citations refer to **table** numbers, not page numbers.

NOTE: Index citations refer to **table** numbers, not page numbers.

U.S. Census Bureau, Statistical Abstract of the United States: 2010

NOTE: Index citations refer to **table** numbers, not page numbers.

NOTE: Index citations refer to **table** numbers, not page numbers.

U.S. Census Bureau, Statistical Abstract of the United States: 2010

NOTE: Index citations refer to **table** numbers, not page numbers.

U.S. Census Bureau, Statistical Abstract of the United States: 2010

NOTE: Index citations refer to **table** numbers, not page numbers.

U.S. Census Bureau, Statistical Abstract of the United States: 2010

NOTE: Index citations refer to **table** numbers, not page numbers.

NOTE: Index citations refer to **table** numbers, not page numbers.

U.S. Census Bureau, Statistical Abstract of the United States: 2010